# Child Health Care

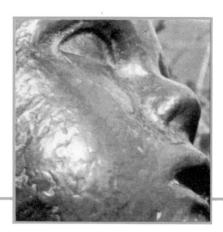

## Patricia Thorson Castiglia, Ph.D., R.N.-C., P.N.P.

*Dean, School of Nursing and Allied Health*
*University of Texas*
*El Paso, Texas*


## Richard E. Harbin, M.S.N., M.Ed., R.N., C.P.N.P.

*Adjunct Faculty, San Diego State University*
*San Diego, California*
*Private Practice, Escondido, California*

## With 28 contributors

*J.B. Lippincott Company*
*Philadelphia*

# Child Health Care
## *Process and Practice*

*Photograph by David Finn*

Sponsoring Editor: Barbara Cullen
Coordinating Editorial Assistant: Jennifer Brogan
Project Editor: Tom Gibbons
Indexer: Ellen Murray
Design Coordinator: Susan Hermansen
Interior Designer: Anne O'Donnell
Cover Designer: Susan Hermansen
Cover Illustration: Leslie Roesler
Production Manager: Helen Ewan
Production Coordinator: Nannette Winski
Compositor: Circle Graphics
Printer/Binder: Courier Book Company/Westford
Cover Printer: Lehigh Press

6  5  4  3  2  1

**Library of Congress Cataloging-in-Publication Data**

Child health care: process and practice / [edited by] Patricia T.
  Castiglia, Richard E. Harbin; with 28 contributors.
      p.      cm.
    Includes bibliographical references and index.
    ISBN 0-397-54728-5
    1. Pediatric nursing.   I. Castiglia, Patricia Thorson, 1935–
II. Harbin, Richard E.
    [DNLM: 1. Child Development—nurses' instruction.   2. Nursing
Process.   3. Pediatric Nursing.   WY 159 C5363]
RJ245.C474   1992
610.73'62—dc20
DNLM/DLC
for Library of Congress                                                        91-46703
                                                                                    CIP

Any procedure or practice described in this book should be applied by the healthcare practitioner under appropriate supervision in accordance with professional standards of care used
with regard to the unique circumstances that apply in each practice situation. Care has been
taken to confirm the accuracy of information presented and to describe generally accepted
practices. However, the authors, editors, and publisher cannot accept any responsibility for errors or omissions or for any consequences from application of the information in this book
and make no warranty express or implied, with respect to the contents of the book.

Every effort has been made to ensure drug selections and dosages are in accordance with
current recommendations and practice. Because of ongoing research, changes in government
regulations and the constant flow of information on drug therapy, reactions and interactions,
the reader is cautioned to check the package insert for each drug for indications, dosages,
warnings and precautions, particularly if the drug is new or infrequently used.

*This book is dedicated to my parents' memory, Theodore and Isabelle Thorson, for always making me feel that I could do anything; to my children, Karen, Tricia, and Joe, who are my joy and who always have supported my efforts; to my grandsons Dennis and Alex, who, I hope, will have the opportunities to accomplish their dreams; and to David, Bea and Tom, Rosie and Carl, Clara and Tom, and Marlene and Peter for their continued support and encouragement.*

*Pat .*

*To my loving wife, Rebecca, as proof that this book is not an eternal project.*

*Rick*

*To Nan, Steve, Brian, Meg, and Annie, with love and thanks.*

*Dave*

# Reviewers

Joan Devilbiss, R.N., M.A., M.Ed.
Assistant Professor
Texas Women's University
College of Nursing
Houston, Texas

Faith T. Edwards, R.N., M.S.
Director of Nursing Programs
Luna Vocational Technical Institute
Las Vegas, New Mexico

Julie LaMothe, R.N., M.S.N., C.P.N.P.
Adjunct Lecturer
Indianapolis University School of Nursing
Pediatric Nurse Practitioner, Developmental Pediatrics
Riley Hospital
Indianapolis, Indiana

Marlene McClure, R.N., M.S.N.
Professor
Pittsburgh State University
Department of Nursing
Pittsburgh, Pennsylvania

Michelle Mendes, M.S., R.N.
Adjunct Instructor
Boston College
School of Nursing
Chestnut Hill, Massachusetts

Adele D.S. Mitchell, Ph.D., R.N.
Professor of Nursing
Hawaii Loa College
Kaneohe, Hawaii

Janetta Tradup, R.N.C., M.S.N.
Assistant Professor of Nursing
Texas Tech University Health Science Center
School of Nursing
Lubbock, Texas

Betty J. Witt, R.N., M.A.
Professor of Nursing Education
San Diego City College
San Diego, California

# Contributors

Suzanne Aquilina, B.S., M.S.
Clinical Assistant Professor of Nursing
Tonawanda Pediatrics and State University of New York
   at Buffalo
Buffalo, New York

Thomas R. Beam, Jr., M.D.
Associate Chief of Staff for Education
Associate Professor of Medicine and Microbiology
State University of New York at Buffalo
Buffalo, New York

Marian J. Brook, R.N., M.S., C.P.N.P.
Doctoral Student
School of Nursing
State University of New York at Buffalo
Buffalo, New York

Mary Burke, R.N., D.N.Sc.
Associate Professor
Rhode Island College
Department of Nursing
Providence, Rhode Island

Marianne Buzby, R.N., M.S.N., C.P.N.P.
Pediatric Nurse Practitioner
Division of Gastroenterology and Nutrition
Children's Hospital of Philadelphia
Part-time Lecturer
Primary Care Program
School of Nursing
University of Pennsylvania
Philadelphia, Pennsylvania

Joan T. Duer, R.N., M.A., C.N.A.
Adjunct Faculty
College of Mount St. Vincent
Riverdale, New York

Carolyn M. Fong, Ph.D., R.N.
Professor
San Francisco State University
San Francisco, California

Mary Jo Gorney-Lucero, R.N., Ph.D.
Professor
San Jose State University
San Jose, California

Janice S. Hayes, R.N., Ph.D.
Research Coordinator
Miami Children's Hospital
Miami, Florida

Patricia Iacovitti, M.S.N., P.N.P.
PNP Same Day Surgery Unit
Children's Hospital of Buffalo
Buffalo, New York

Mary Ann Jezewski, R.N., Ph.D.
Assistant Professor, Nursing
State University of New York at Buffalo
Buffalo, New York

Sherry E. Johnson, R.N., Ph.D.
Private Practice
South Shore Counseling Center
Hingham, Massachusetts

Deborah Kramer, Ed.D., C.P.N.P., R.N.
Associate Professor
College of Mount St. Vincent
Bronx, New York

Terri H. Lipman, R.N., Ph.D.
Lecturer
University of Pennsylvania
School of Nursing
Clinical Nurse Specialist
Diabetes/Endocrinology
St. Christopher's Hospital for Children
Philadelphia, Pennsylvania

Mary Ann Ludwig, P.N.P., Ph.D.
Clinical Associate Professor
State University of New York at Buffalo
Buffalo, New York

Donna C. Maheady, M.S., C.P.N.P., R.N.
Adjunct Faculty, School of Nursing
Barry University
Miami Shores, Florida
Visiting Nurse Association of Palm Beach County
West Palm Beach, Florida

Darlene A. Martin, Ph.D., R.N.
Associate Professor of Health Care Ethics, Law, and
    Policy
Department of Community Health and Gerontology
University of Texas Medical Branch
School of Nursing
Galveston, Texas

Linda Heim McCausland, R.N., Ed.D.
Clinical Associate Professor
State University of New York at Buffalo
Buffalo, New York

Mary Ann McClellan, R.N., M.N., P.N.P.
Assistant Professor
University of Oklahoma College of Nursing
Oklahoma City, Oklahoma

Susan J. Smith Millet, R.N., Ph.D.
Associate Professor of Nursing
University of New Mexico
Albuquerque, New Mexico

Maribeth L. Moran, M.S.N., R.N.
Assistant Professor
University of Oklahoma College of Nursing
Oklahoma City, Oklahoma

Michael W. Neft, R.N., B.S.N., C.C.R.N.
Captain, U.S. Army Nursing Corps
Student, U.S. Army/Baylor University Graduate Program
    in Health Care Administration
Ft. Sam Houston, Texas

Carolyn M. Orlowski, M.S., R.N.
Vice President, Nursing
Valley Children's Hospital
Fresno, California

Sallie Page-Goertz, R.N., M.N.
Instructor, Department of Pediatrics
Pediatric Clinical Specialist, Ambulatory Care and
    Rheumatology
University of Kansas
Schools of Medicine and Nursing
Kansas City, Kansas

Susan N. Peck, R.N., M.S.N., C.P.N.P.
Clinical Nurse Specialist/Gastroenterology and Nutrition
Children's Hospital of Philadelphia
Philadelphia, Pennsylvania

Pamela L. Pitts-Wilhelm, R.N., M.N., C.C.R.N.
Nurse Manager of Cardiothoracic ICU
University of Washington Medical Center
Seattle, Washington

Mary Theresa Urbano, R.N., A.R.N.P., Ph.D.
Associate Professor of Pediatrics
University of Miami School of Medicine
Mailman Center for Child Development
Miami, Florida

M. Angie Wieser, R.N., B.S.N., M.S.N.
Director of Nursing Research and Development
Childrens Hospital of Buffalo
Adjunct Clinical Faculty
State University of New York at Buffalo
Buffalo, New York

# Foreword

The arrival of *Child Health Care: Process and Practice* is a timely and welcome addition to the pediatric nursing literature. This textbook is uniquely designed to assist faculty in teaching essential pediatric content within increasingly limited time constraints. More importantly, it offers nursing students the potential to master the process and practice of child health care, given the explosion of knowledge and pressures of time.

This book fills a need not met by standard pediatric nursing texts. From a single volume, nursing students will be able to learn the essentials of child health care from conception through adolescence using a growth, development, and health framework and the nursing process. In addition, the textbook discusses the health problems of children and adolescents using nursing diagnosis and provides chapters on special considerations, including the care of children with disabling conditions and the care of children in the home.

The authors have organized the textbook by fully outlining and explaining each step of the nursing process, using a case study approach to the development of care plans, and have continued this framework throughout the text. The application of content to nursing's problem-solving process is therefore consistently reinforced.

The value of this textbook comes from its comprehensive, integrated physiological and psychosocial approach to the care of pediatric patients and their families using the nursing process. For example, the chapter on the effects of substance abuse on children and families provides content on the physiological effects of substance abuse and addiction, as well as a discussion on the coping strategies of children and adolescents.

The contemporary discussions of family, culture, ethics, and legal issues are invaluable in viewing the child and the family within a larger, increasingly diverse social framework. This textbook successfully incorporates this content. It is gratifying to see that the definition of family is broadly framed and includes a discussion of existing non-traditional family structures. These structures are not static; they are changing and evolving to suit the needs of individuals in contemporary American society. The recognition of cultural variations in the care of children and their families is also important. As America becomes increasingly more ethnically diverse, it is essential that students are sensitive to ethnic and cultural variations in the delivery of health care.

Of special merit is the inclusion of federal legislative initiatives and their impact on the delivery of child health care. Future practitioners of nursing must understand the relationship between politics and the delivery of health care. The ability of nurses to render health care is shaped within the political arena.

The authors and contributors are to be congratulated for combining a wealth of knowledge and information in a format that promises to assist nursing students in mastering both the content and the process of child health care.

*Marilyn P. Chow, D.N.Sc., R.N., F.A.A.N.*
*Director of Nursing Practice*
*California Nurses Association*
*San Francisco*

# Preface

Children are the visible sign of the continuation of one generation to the next. Beliefs, values, and traditions are perpetuated, altered, or discarded as generations of children survive by adapting to changes in society. Since the beginning of time the fundamental needs of children have changed very little; in order to survive, they need nourishment, physical care, safety, nurturing, and cognitive stimulation. Without these essential ingredients, optimal growth is not possible.

As we approach the 21st century, many aspects of life remain the same as they were long before the 1st century. Technology has provided ways to improve our quality of life, but not without risks. The discovery of fire was quickly followed by the first burn injury; paint that beautifies homes can cause lead poisoning; asbestos that conserves heat causes cancer; the effect on health of high-voltage electrical wires is not completely understood. Yet, through advances in technology and health care, children who would not have survived infancy—much less childhood and adolescence—now lead full, normal lives. Many congenital defects and common childhood illnesses that were once sentences of death, or of a life of possible ridicule and disability, have been eliminated or their effects minimized through advances in science and technology.

Nursing care, in the generic sense of the term, has not changed since the first birth took place. However, the role of nurses has evolved from that of handmaidens and custodians of the ill into that of professional members of the health care team, with distinct duties and responsibilities for promoting health as well as caring for those who are ill. Nurses no longer simply care for sick children; rather, they take an active role in promoting health and in providing anticipatory guidance to children and their families.

Advances in technology, as well as the increased responsibilities of nurses, require that nurses master a far greater amount of technical information than ever before. This expansion in the required knowledge base has also led to changes in textbooks and other learning materials. Many well-intentioned authors have attempted to address this "information explosion" by writing texts that include not only essential information but additional material that, although useful for its reference value, presents far more information than students need or can be used. This "information overload" makes the necessary content less accessible and overwhelms students.

## Philosophy of Child Health Care

From the first discussions about this text among the authors and editors, the intent of *Child Health Care: Process and Practice* has been to provide pediatric nursing students with sufficient information to enable them to provide children and their families with safe, competent, compassionate nursing care. With the understanding that students have a limited amount of time, every attempt has been made to provide information in as succinct and accessible a manner as possible. Content from courses that nursing students have taken before this course has not been repeated, except for information that pertains specifically to the care of children and their families.

In planning this text, a variety of structures were considered for use as the organizational framework. Since the nursing process is familiar to all nursing students, this systematic, logical format was selected as the primary organizational structure. To the greatest extent possible, information is structured around the five steps of the nursing process. In addition, the content of the text proceeds from general considerations that affect all of child health care to nursing care for specific health problems and disorders.

## Organization of Child Health Care

Part I, *Essential Concepts and Influences in Child Health Care,* explains key concepts that pertain specifically to child health care and provides a foundation for material presented in the remaining chapters of the text. Chapter 1, "Contemporary Concepts in Child Health Care," explores such topics as historical and current perspectives of children and health care, influences on child health care, and the role of nurses in providing child health care. Chapter 2, "Family and Cultural Concepts Affecting Pediatric Nursing," discusses the influences of family structure and culture on child rearing, in addition to the concepts of parenting and discipline. Chapter 3, "Ethical and Legal Issues in Child Health Care," defines and explains the rights of children to receive health care and the responsibilities of nurses to help ensure these rights. Topics such as withholding or withdrawing medical treatment, treatment of children with disabilities, and protecting children in research are discussed in detail. Chapter 4, "Developing a Theoretical Framework for Growth and Development," introduces the major theories of growth and development that have influenced child health care and applies them to today's practice of pediatric nursing.

Part II, *The Child Health Nursing Process,* establishes the structure for the information that is provided in the rest of the text. Five chapters discuss each step of the nursing process: nursing assessment, nursing diagnosis, planning nursing care, health care interventions, and evaluating nursing care. The information that is presented is not intended to duplicate coverage of the nursing process from other courses but, rather, to demonstrate how the nursing process is specifically applied to health care of children and families. To illustrate how the nursing process applies to child health care practice, each chapter in this unit concludes with a nursing care plan that shows how the individual step of the nursing process discussed in that chapter is documented in the plan of care. For example, at the end of Chapter 5, "Assessment of Children and Families," the assessment portion of a care plan for a child with croup is introduced. Each remaining chapter in this unit adds the appropriate information to the same care plan, so that by the end of Chapter 9 the care plan is completed. This provides students with a thorough understanding of the steps of the nursing process as they apply to child health care and helps illustrate the rationale for including each step.

Part III contains seven chapters that explore the concepts of growth and development from conception through adolescence. Each chapter includes a description of normal physical growth along with a discussion of cognitive and psychosocial development. Nursing assessment and health promotion, including common health problems specific to each age group, are discussed in detail. Common concerns and parenting development are included in each chapter to provide students with guidelines for understanding normal growth, development, and behavior, so that they can assist parents in anticipating problems and providing solutions.

In Part IV, *Special Considerations in Child Health Nursing,* topics covered include the effects of hospitalization on children and families; nursing care of children in the home; caring for children with infectious diseases or disabling conditions; the effects of substance abuse on children and families; and dying, death, and bereavement.

In Part V, *Health Problems of Children and Adolescents,* each chapter begins with a brief overview of the anatomy and physiology of the body system, including embryology when appropriate. In keeping with the philosophy of the text, this discussion serves as a review of material that was presented in other courses and is specifically applied here to child health care. The organization of each chapter consistently follows the nursing process. Assessment guidelines are provided; these include taking a nursing history, performing a physical examination, and the nurse's role in diagnostic procedures. Nursing diagnoses specific to health problems discussed in the chapter are listed.

Since a variety of factors must be taken into account when caring for children with illnesses, the next section of each chapter discusses developmental, acute, chronic, and home care considerations that affect the planning of nursing care. Appropriate nursing interventions that are frequently used for problems affecting the specific body system are then presented, followed by general guidelines for evaluating the effectiveness of nursing care.

Specific health problems are then discussed, organized by the developmental period in which they are *most likely* to occur. It is hoped that this organizational structure will reinforce students' understanding of the developmental nature of child health care. In most chapters, health problems that are usually considered either acute or chronic, and that affect several age groups, are presented after the age-specific problems. Within the discussion of each health problem, every attempt has been made to follow the same organizational structure. The pathophysiological basis of the health problem is described, followed by a discussion of the medical diagnosis and management. Each step of the nursing process is then detailed to provide easy access to information in a consistent, familiar organization. Several chapters conclude with nursing care plans that demonstrate the application and documentation of nursing care in the same format that was shown in Part III. Current references and bibliographies provide sources for further information.

## Features That Enhance the Teaching and Learning Process

In addition to textual material, careful consideration has gone into developing additional pedagogical devices that will facilitate student learning. Drawings and photographs, most of which were created specifically for *Child Health Care,* enhance student learning by graphically depicting essential concepts. Numerous tables, charts, and displays summarize important information.

The text consistently uses nursing diagnoses that are currently approved and accepted by the North American Nursing Diagnosis Association (NANDA). By doing so, it is hoped that students will become familiar with standardized nursing terminology. In keeping with NANDA's continuing refinement of nursing diagnoses, the term "high risk for" has been substituted for the previously used term "potential for" to identify possible complications. In addition, the diagnosis "knowledge deficit" is seldom used, since it is felt that health care education of children and their families is implicit in each step of the nursing process.

Twenty-four full-color plates are included to help students identify dermatological and infectious disease conditions. In addition, six appendixes contain useful assessment tools, physical growth and development standards, normal laboratory values, guidelines for calculating pediatric drug dosages, and temperature and weight conversion tables, as well as the most recent recommended immunization schedule. The appendixes provide a convenient reference for students and practicing nurses.

A complete teaching and learning package is provided with *Child Health Care: Process and Practice*. The package includes a *student study guide* to reinforce concepts and principles presented in the text. In addition, *50 acetate overhead transparencies* are available to instructors who adopt the text for classroom use. The transparencies can be used to demonstrate important concepts depicted in illustrations from the text. The *instructor's manual* contains a variety of useful classroom and clinical teaching strategies, as well as additional resources to help instructors facilitate student learning. A *computerized testing program* is also available.

It is our hope that *Child Health Care: Process and Practice* will help students master the application of the nursing process in the practice of child health care, and that by doing so they will enjoy the challenges and rewards of providing nursing care for children and their families.

*Patricia T. Castiglia*

*Richard E. Harbin*

# Acknowledgments

The evolutionary process of taking a book from an idea to a reality requires the concerted effort of many professionals. Without the combined efforts of those listed below this book would not have been. We wish to acknowledge the support and assistance of the following individuals:

The contributors to *Child Health Care* have willingly shared their expertise and understanding of the special needs of children and families, and the ways in which nurses can promote optimal growth and development as well as assist in the restoration of health. Often under demanding deadlines, they have made every effort to ensure that the content of this book is accurate and up to date.

The reviewers, who remained anonymous to us throughout this process, labored hard to critique each chapter and provided us and the contributors with many useful suggestions, insights, and perspectives.

The use of sculpture to illustrate a book about children and families may appear anomalous at first, since children are sources of activity and virtually constant motion whereas sculpture is fixed and frozen in time. Yet, just as no two children are alike, no two pieces of sculpture are the same. Children and families have been the objects of sculptors' labors since the beginning of time, and thanks to the generosity of world-renowed photographer David Finn and sculptor Charles Parks, many classic and contemporary sculptures of children and families are shown throughout this text. Their creative geniuses, as well as those of the other sculptors whose work is portrayed here, demonstrate the enduring qualities of children and families.

We also gratefully acknowledge the assistance of Jennifer Smith, who provided original illustrations, and photographer Chad Puerling of the University of Texas–El Paso. Jennifer and Chad both worked under virtually impossible deadlines to achieve what we hope you will agree are outstanding results. Evonne Taylor, Associate Adminis-trator for Nursing Services, and Jennifer Gapner, Assistant Director of Nursing at Thomason Hospital, El Paso, Texas, provided invaluable assistance in arranging and supervising photographing sessions to ensure accuracy.

Handling an "electronic manuscript" was a learning experience for us, particularly when the computer "ate" a chapter! Thanks to Mark Jacobson and Bob Martin for being there to bail us out.

Even an electronic manuscript requires human intervention. Mary Boldt, Elsa Diaz, and Donna Throop labored long and hard through many revisions to turn our scribblings into something even a computer could read, and Ivy Whelpdale efficiently coordinated a myraid of details; we thank them.

No book like this can come to be without the skill and expertise provided by the publisher. We have been most fortunate to work with an outstanding group at Lippincott, and we wish to thank:

Diana Intenzo, Vice President and Publisher, for her support;

Helen Ewan, Production Manager, for helping us find ways to make this book a reality;

Tom Gibbons, Senior Project Editor, for his careful attention to detail and his sense of calm amid the storm;

Nannette Winski, Production Coordinator, for making sure that all of the pieces fell together at the right times;

Susan Hermansen, Art Director, for coordinating the endless details that go into the creation of an art program;

Leslie Roesler, Artist, for showing the uniqueness of children and sculpture with the painting on the cover;

Patty Shear and Amy Stonehouse, Editorial Assistants, for attending to many of the details and easing the burden;

Jennifer Brogan, Editorial Assistant, for calmly and efficiently coordinating what appeared to be *almost everything;*

And finally, Barbara Nelson Cullen, Nursing Editor. Barbara's guidance, support, and assistance went far beyond the call of duty. Somehow she always knew when to simply listen, when and what suggestions to make, the right type of encouragement to provide, or when to just "go ahead and do it."

Throughout the process of putting this book together our families have provided us with a constant source of support and encouragement (perhaps with the hope that it would soon be done). Without them, it would not have been possible.

# Contents

## Part I
### Essential Concepts and Influences in Child Health Care    2

### 1  Contemporary Concepts in Child Health Care    5
*Patricia T. Castiglia*

The Challenges and Rewards of Child Health Nursing    6

Contemporary Concepts in Child Health Nursing    7

Historical Concepts of Children    8
   The Perspective of the Family    9
   Mortality Trends—Children in the United States    9
   The Meaning of Health and Illness    11
   Children's Rights    12
   The Significance of State and Federal Legislation    14
   Current Problems and Future Directions    16

Changes in the Health Care System Affecting Pediatric Nursing    17
   Technological Advances    17
   Public Awareness    17
   Increased Costs of Health Care    17
   Cost Containment    18

Concepts Related to Pediatric Nursing    18
   Nursing Process as Tool for Practice    18
   Nursing Theory as a Basis for Practice    18
   Nursing Theories Related to Pediatric Nursing Practice    19
   Integrating Knowledge in Child Health Nursing    21
   Expanded Roles, Professional Organizations, and Publications    21

Summary    22

### 2  Family and Cultural Concepts Affecting Pediatric Nursing    23
*Richard E. Harbin*

Historical Concept of the Family in the United States    25

Today's Families    25

Varieties of Family Structure    25
   The Nuclear Family    26
   The Extended Family    26
   The Single-Parent Family    26
   The Gay/Lesbian Family    27
   The Adolescent-Parent Family    27
   The Stepfamily or Blended Family    27
   The One-Child Family    28
   The Older-Parent Family    28
   Alternative Family Structures    28
   The Homeless Family    28

Family Developmental Stages and Tasks    28

Family Function Assessment    30

Culture, Ethnicity, and Environment    31
   Heritage Consistency    33

Ethnic Family Organization    33
   Acculturation and Assimilation    33

Heritage-Consistent Family Concepts    34
   Collecting Data    34
   The Interview    34
   The Hot/Cold Health Model    34

The Asian Family    34

The Hispanic Family    36

The Black-African Family    37

The Native American Family    37

Parenting    37

Discipline    38
   Corporal Punishment    38
   Psychological Intervention    39
   Behavior Modification    39

Summary    39

*3* **Ethical and Legal Issues in Child Health Care** 41

*Darlene A. Martin*

Rights of Children   43

Nurse Advocacy   43

Ethical Decision Making   43

Legal Responsibilities in Nursing   44
  Elements of a Malpractice Claim   44
  Professional Standards of Care   44
  Abandonment   45
  Doctrine of Respondeat Superior   45
  Doctrines of Contributory and Comparative
  Negligence   46
  Doctine of Res Ipsa Loquitur   46

Informed Consent   46
  Elements of Informed Consent   46
  Informed Consent for Adolescents   47

Withholding or Withdrawing Medical Treatment
from Children   47
  Withholding Treatment from Newborns with
  Severe Disabilities   48
  Baby Doe Regulations   49
  Baby Jane Doe   49
  Child Abuse Amendments   50

Treatment of Children with Disabilities   50
  Children with Mental Illness   51
  Sterilization of Minors with Mental
  Retardation   52
  Nursing Care of Disabled Children in Schools
  52

Protection of Children in Research   54
  Institutional Review Board   54

Summary   55

*4* **Developing a Theoretical Framework for Growth and Development** 57

*Patricia T. Castiglia*

The Concepts of Growth and Development   59

Principles of Growth and Development   59

Maslow's Hierarchy of Needs Applied to Growth and
Development   60

Stage Theories of Development   60
  Freud's Theory   61
  Erikson's Theory   62
  Piaget's Theory   63
  Kohlberg's Theory   65

Learning Theories   66
  Social Learning Theory   67
  Developmental Task Theory   67

Maturation Theory   68

Play Theories   68

Theories of Language Development   69

Attachment Theories   69
  Maternal Attachment   69
  Paternal Attachment   71

Growth and Development of Parents   72

Nursing Implications of Growth and Development
Concepts   72

Summary   73

**Part II**
**The Child Health Nursing Process** 76

*5* **Assessment of Children and Families** 79

*Joan T. Duer*

The Interview   81
  Components of the Communication Process   81
  Communicating With Parents   82
  Communicating With Pediatric Clients   82
  Setting the Stage for Successful Interviews   83
  Communication Techniques   84

Family Assessment   85
  Family History   85
  Family and Home Assessment Tools   87

Developmental Assessment   87
  Developmental Assessment Tools   87

Health History   88
  Medical History   88

Review of Systems   90

Physical Assessment Skills   90
  Inspection   90
  Auscultation   90
  Percussion   91
  Palpation   92

Physical Examination   92
  Developmental Approaches to Physical
  Examination   92
  Growth Measurements   93
  Vital Signs   95
  General Survey   97
  Skin   97
  Head and Neck   98
  Eyes   99
  Ears   101
  Nose   101

Mouth and Throat    102
Thorax and Lungs    102
Heart    102
Abdomen    104
Genitalia    104
Musculoskeletal    105
Neurological    105
Sensory Function    106
Summary    107
Nursing Care Plan    107

## 6  Nursing Diagnosis in Child Health Care    111

*Joan T. Duer*

The Evolution of Diagnostic Reasoning
in Nursing    112
Nursing Diagnosis    112
    Definition of Nursing Diagnosis    113
    Types of Nursing Diagnoses    113
    Components of Nursing Diagnosis    114
The Diagnostic Process in Nursing    114
    Data Collection and Interpretation    114
    Hypothesis Generation and Testing    114
    Validation of Findings    115
    The Diagnostic Statement    115
Nursing Diagnosis in the Pediatric Setting    115
The North American Nursing Diagnosis Association
(NANDA)    115
NANDA Nursing Diagnosis Taxonomy I    115
Summary    116
Nursing Care Plan    118

## 7  Planning Child Health Nursing Care    121

*Joan T. Duer*

Planning as an Integral Part of Nursing Practice    122
Setting Priorities    123
Nursing Care Planning    123
    Individualized Care Planning    123
    Standardized Care Planning    123
Clients' and Families' Roles in Planning Nursing
Care    123
    Developing Goals    123
    Deciding on Interventions for Children and
    Families    123
Discharge Planning    126
DRGs and Child Health Care    126
Nursing Care Plan    127
Summary    128

## 8  Implementing Child Health Nursing Interventions    131

*Joan T. Duer*

Developmental Considerations in Nursing
Implementation    132
    Medications    133
    Procedures    137
    Nutrition    139
Health Teaching    139
    Settings    139
    Determination of Health Teaching Needs    140
    Teaching Methods    140
    Teaching Tools    142
Comprehensive Child Health Care    143
    Consultation    143
    Referrals    143
    Continuity of Care    143
Nursing Care Plan    144
Summary    147

## 9  Evaluating Child Health Nursing Care    149

*Joan T. Duer*

Evaluation Methods    150
Documentation and Communication of Client Health
Care Evaluation    151
Evaluation of Nursing Practice    151
Self-Evaluation    152
Summary    152
Nursing Care Plan    152

## *Part III*
## Growth, Development, and Health: Conception Through Adolescence    156

## 10  Prenatal Growth, Development, and Health    159

*M. Angie Wieser*

Stages in Fetal Development    161
    Embryonic Development    161
    Physiological Process: Placenta and Umbilical
    Cord    161
Genetic Influences on Development    164
    Chromosomal Abnormalities    165
    Single Gene or Mendelian Disorders    165
    Polygenic and Multifactorial Disorders    166

Teratogenic Disorders from Extracellular
Factors    166
Environmental Influences on Development    167
Psychosocial Impact of the Prenatal Period on Parents
and Families    168
  Preparation for Pregnancy and Parenthood    168
  Preparation of Siblings    169
  Nutrition Requirements: Mother and Fetus    170
Assessment of Fetal Growth and Development    170
  Prenatal Assessment and Diagnosis of Genetic
  Disorders    171
  Assessment of Fetal Development    172
  Assessment During Labor    174
Summary    175

## 11   Neonatal Growth, Development, and Health    177

*Patricia T. Castiglia*
Neonatal Adaptations to the Environment    178
  Physiological Adaptations During the Transitional
  Period    179
  Parenting and Sibling Relationships in Promoting
  Adaptation    184
Assessment of the Newborn    185
  Apgar Scoring    185
  Body Measurement and Vital Signs    186
  The Neonatal Behavioral Assessment Scale    187
  Assessment of Infant State    187
  Assessment of Premature Infants Behavior    187
  Assessment of the Head    187
  Assessment of the Eyes, Nose, Ears, Mouth, and
  Cry    188
  Assessment of the Integument    189
  Assessment of the Back and Extremities    189
  Assessment of Reflexes    191
  Assessment of the Genitalia and Anus    191
  Gestational Age Assessment    191
  Assessment of Parent–Child Interactions    194
Health Promotion    194
  Maintaining a Patent Airway    194
  Prevention of Infection or Injury    194
  Nutritional Needs    200
Neonatal Risk Factors    202
  Prenatal Assessment    203
  Identifying Infants at Risk During Labor and
  Delivery: Postnatal Assessment    207
  Risk Associated with Maturity    210
  Postmaturity    210
Parenting Development    211
Summary    211

## 12   Infant Growth, Development, and Health    215

*Suzanne Aquilina*
Goals of Nursing Care During Infancy    216
Physical Growth and Development    217
  General Growth Characteristics    217
  Brain Growth    217
  Motor Development    218
  Sensory Development    220
  Body System Development    221
  Nutrition    224
  Sleep    226
  Dentition    227
Cognitive Development    228
  Piaget    228
  Play    230
Psychosocial Development    231
  Erikson    231
  Freud    233
  Attachment    233
  Communication    234
  Cultural Influences    235
Assessment    235
  Body Measurements    235
  Developmental Assessment    236
  Assessment of Home and Family    238
Health Promotion    239
  Health Maintenance    239
  Procedures    241
  Routine Care    243
  Common Concerns    248
Parenting Development    250
Summary    251

## 13   Toddler Growth, Development, and Health    255

*Mary L. Burke*
Physical Growth and Development    256
  General Growth Characteristics    256
  Motor Development    258
  Sensory Development    259
  Nutrition Needs    260
  Sleep    261
Cognitive Development    261
  Piaget    261
  Play    262
Psychosocial Development    262
  Erikson    262
  Freud    262
  Mastering Separation    263

Language Development    264
Sex Role Identification    264

Assessment    265
Body Measurements    265
Denver Developmental Screening Test    265
Washington Guide to Promoting Development
in the Young Child    265
Assessment of Home and Family    266

Health Promotion    266
Health Maintenance Visits and
Immunizations    266
Dental Care    266
Recognizing Developmental Tasks    267
Common Concerns    269

Parenting Development    273

Summary    273

14    **Preschool Growth, Development, and
Health    275**
*Marian J. Brook*

Physical Growth and Development    278
General Growth Characteristics    278
Motor Development    278
Sensory Development    280
Nutrition Needs    280
Sleep    283

Cognitive Development    284
Piaget    284
Play    285
Moral Development    286

Psychosocial Development    287
Freud    287
Erikson    287
Language Development    287
Sex-Role Identification    288
Day Care and Nursery School    288

Assessment    290
Body Measurements    290
Denver Developmental Screening Test    290
Washington Guide to Promoting Development
in the Young Child    290
Assessment of Home and Family    290

Health Promotion    291
Health Maintenance Visits and
Immunizations    291
Dental Care    293
Recognizing Developmental Tasks    293
Common Concerns    294

Parenting Development    302

Summary    303

15    **School-Age Growth, Development, and
Health    307**
*Janice S. Hayes*

Physical Growth and Development    309
General Growth Characteristics    309
Motor Development    309
Sensory Development    309
Nutrition Needs    309
Sleep    310

Cognitive Development    311
Piaget    311
Play    312
School    313

Psychosocial Development    313
Freud    313
Erikson    313
Peer Significance    314
Sex Role Identification    315

Moral Development    315
Piaget    315
Kohlberg    316

Assessment    316
Body Measurements    316
Assessment of Home and Family    317
School Adjustment    317

Health Promotion    318
Health Maintenance Visits and
Immunizations    318
Dental Care    320
Recognizing Developmental Tasks    320
Common Concerns    320

Parenting Development    324

Summary    325

16    **Adolescent Growth, Development, and
Health    329**
*Richard E. Harbin*

Stages of Adolescence    332
Early Adolescence    332
Middle Adolescence    332
Late Adolescence    333

Morbidity and Mortality    333

Physical Growth and Development    334
The Tanner Scales    335
Puberty    337
Nutrition Needs    338
Sleep    339
Physical Appearance    339

Psychosexual Development    340
Freud    340

Cognitive Development    340
Piaget    340

Egocentrism    340
Idealism    340
Moral Development    340
Psychosocial Development    341
Erikson: The Sense of Identity    341
Interpersonal Relationships    341
Sex Role Identification    341
Emotional Concerns    342
Peer Relationships    342
Assessment    343
Communicating With Adolescents    343
The Interview    343
The History    344
Physical Examination    345
Nutrition Assessment    345
Health Promotion    346
Recognizing Developmental Tasks    346
Health Care for Adolescents    346
Medical Rights    346
Dental Health    346
Accident Prevention    347
Common Health Concerns    347
Menstruation    347
Breast Size and Shape    348
Penis Size    348
Testicular Self-Examination    348
Stature    348
Acne    349
Muscle Development    349
Gynecomastia    349
Masturbation    349
Sexual Behavior    349
Contraception    350
Adolescent Pregnancy    352
Eating Disorders    353
Substance Abuse    355
Androgenic-Anabolic Steroids    357
Depression    358
Suicide    358
Summary    360
Eating Disorders—National Organizations    360

*Part IV*
Special Considerations in Child Health
Nursing    364

*17*  **Effects of Hospitalization on Children
and Families    367**
*Patricia A. Iacovitti*
Hospitalization    369
Factors Affecting Hospitalization    369

Hospitalization and Developmental Stages    369
Infants    369
Toddlers    371
Preschoolers    373
School-Aged Children    374
Adolescents    376
Preparing Children for Hospitalization    377
Children's Responses to Hospitalization    377
Methods of Preparing Children
for Hospitalization    377
Timing of Preparation    377
Special Preparation Needs    378
Parental Responses to Hospitalization    378
Minimizing the Effects of Hospitalization    378
Preparation for Hospitalization    379
Atraumatic Care    379
Stress Immunization    379
Play    380
Hospital Admission    382
Types of Admissions    382
Children's and Families' Responses
to Admission    384
The Admission Interview    385
Orientation to the Hospital    385
Teaching Parents of Hospitalized Children    385
Discharge Planning    386
Summary    386

*18*  **Nursing Care of Children
in the Home    389**
*Mary Theresa Urbano*
Historical Background of Home Care    391
Factors Contributing to the Development of Home
Care    391
Cost Containment Initiatives    391
Changing Health Care Needs of Children    391
Changing Health Care Delivery    391
Changing View of the Family    392
Case Management    392
The Multidisciplinary Health Care Team    393
Assessment    393
Child and Family Readiness for Home Care    394
Nursing Diagnoses    396
Planning    397
Educating the Client and Family    397
Identifying Home Care Providers    398
Selecting an Equipment Vendor    398
Establishing a Community Support Network
399
Identifying the Family and Respite Support

Network    400
Completing the Discharge    400
Implementation    401
The Art of Home Care Nursing: Interpersonal
Processes    401
The Science of Home Care Nursing: Technological
Competence    405
Evaluation    410
Legal and Ethical Issues    410
Summary    411

**19    Caring for Children With Infectious
Diseases    415**
*Patricia T. Castiglia*
Public Health Concepts    416
Immunizations    417
Legal Aspects of Immunizations    418
Immunizations for Foreign Travel    420
Future Viral Vaccines    420
Isolation Precautions    421
Infectious Diseases Characterized by Rashes    421
Fifth Disease (Erythema Infectiosum)    422
Kawasaki Disease    422
Lyme Disease    423
Rubeola (Measles)    424
Rocky Mountain Spotted Fever    425
Roseola (Exanthem Subitum, Sixth Disease)    426
Rubella (German Measles)    426
Scarlet Fever (Scarlatina)    427
Varicella (Chickenpox)    427
Infectious Diseases Without Rashes    428
Diphtheria    428
Mumps    429
Pertussis (Whooping Cough)    429
Poliomyelitis    430
Tetanus (Lockjaw)    430
Hepatitis Infections    431
Hepatitis A    431
Hepatitis B    431
Non-A, Non-B Hepatitis    432
Gastrointestinal Diseases    432
Ascariasis (Roundworm Infestations)    432
Enterobiasis (Pinworm Infestations)    432
Giardiasis    433
Shigella    433
Other Infectious Diseases    434
Infectious Mononucleosis    434
Influenza (Grippe, Flu)    434
Rabies    435
Tuberculosis    436
Summary    437

**20    Nursing Care of Children With Disabling
Conditions    439**
*Donna C. Maheady*
Handicapped or Disabled?    441
Legislation    441
Educational Programs    441
Early Intervention/Stimulation Programs    441
Mainstreaming Versus Selective Educational
Settings    442
Case Managed Coordinated Care    442
Health Care    442
Family-Centered Models of Care    442
Role of the Nurse    442
Ethical Considerations    443
Selected Disabling Conditions and Nursing
Interventions    443
Cerebral Palsy    443
Incidence and Etiology    443
Classification    443
Clinical Manifestations of Types of Cerebral
Palsy    444
Diagnosis    445
Treatment    446
Nutrition    446
Physical Therapy    447
Positioning and Handling    447
Education    450
Play Materials and Activities    450
Nursing Care    450
Mental Retardation    451
Incidence and Etiology    451
Prevention    451
Classification of Mental Retardation    451
Types of Mental Retardation    452
Early Identification    453
Markers for Developmental Dysfunction    453
Treatment    453
Exercise    453
Nursing Care    454
Down Syndrome    455
Incidence and Etiology    455
Associated Conditions    456
Development    456
Early Intervention    456
Treatment    457
Sexual Development    457
Nursing Care    457
Autism    458
Incidence and Etiology    458
Characteristics    458
Diagnosis    458
Treatment    460
Nursing Care    460

Common Needs of Children With Disabling
Conditions    461
 Family Support and Recognition of Individual
 Coping Methods    461
 Siblings and Other Family Members    461
 Recreation and Play Needs    462
 Discipline    463
 Advocacy    463
 Record Keeping    464
 Long-Term Planning    464
 Sex Education    464
 Dental Care    465
 Respite Care    465
Summary    465

## 21  Effects of Substance Abuse on Children and Families    471

*Mary Jo Gorney-Lucero*

Definition of Terms    473
Scope of the Problem    473
Causes of Substance Abuse    474
A Developmental Approach to the Effects of Substance
Abuse    475
 The Effects of Substance Abuse
 on Neonates    475
 The Effects of Substance Abuse
 on Children    476
 The Effects of Substance Abuse
 on Adolescents    478
The Nursing Process in Substance Abuse    478
 Assessment    478
 Nursing Diagnoses    479
 Planning and Implementation    480
 Evaluation    480
Treatment Options    481
Prevention Strategies    481
 Early Prenatal Instruction    482
 Early Classroom Intervention    482
Sources of Information    482
Support Groups    485
Summary    486

## 22  Children's Experiences With Dying, Death, and Bereavement    489

*Sherry E. Johnson*

Dying    491
Types of Death    491
Bereavement, Grief, and Mourning    491
Development of a Concept of Death    491
 Infancy to Two Years    491
 Two to Seven Years    491
 Seven to Eleven Years    492
 Adolescence    492
The Nursing Process in Dying, Death, and
Bereavement    492
 Assessment    492
 Nursing Diagnoses    500
 Planning Nursing Care    502
 Nursing Interventions    503
 Evaluating Nursing Care    506
Effects of Dying, Death, and Bereavement on Parents
and Families    507
Effects of Dying, Death, and Bereavement
on Nurses    507
Summary    508

## Part V
## Health Problems of Children and Adolescents    512

## 23  Alterations in Respiratory Function    515

*Susan J. Smith Millet*

Embryology    517
Anatomy    517
 Upper Airways    517
 Lower Airways    518
Physiology    519
 Respiratory Mechanics    519
 Pulmonary Gas Exchange    520
Assessment    520
 History    520
 Physical Examination    521
 Diagnostic Procedures    525
Nursing Diagnosis    527
Planning Nursing Care    527
 Developmental Considerations    527
 Acute Care Considerations    527
 Chronic Care Considerations    527
 Home Care Considerations    528
Nursing Interventions    528
 Inhalation Therapy    528
 Postural Drainage and Chest Physiotherapy    530
 Drug Therapy    530
 Artificial Ventilation    534
 Nutrition    535

Evaluating Nursing Care    535
Congenital Respiratory Problems    536
    Laryngeal Stridor    536
    Choanal Atresia    536
Respiratory Problems of Neonates    537
    Meconium Aspiration Syndrome    537
    Asphyxia Neonatorum    538
    Bronchopulmonary Dysplasia    539
    Respiratory Distress Syndrome    540
    Pneumothorax    541
    Apnea of Prematurity    542
Respiratory Problems of Infants    542
    Otitis Media    542
    Croup    542
    Sudden Infant Death Syndrome    543
    Bronchiolitis    544
    Pertussis    545
    Retropharyngeal Abscess    545
Respiratory Problems of Toddlers and Preschool-Aged
Children    546
    Foreign-Body Aspiration    546
    Pharyngitis    547
    Acute Pharyngitis    547
    Epiglottitis    547
Respiratory Problems of School-Aged Children
   548
    Tonsillitis    548
Acute Respiratory Problems    549
    Streptococcal Pharyngitis    549
    Pneumonia    549
    Bacterial Pneumonia    549
    Viral Pneumonia    550
    Aspiration of Hydrocarbons    551
    Lipoid Pneumonia    551
    Diphtheria    552
Chronic Respiratory Problems    552
    Cystic Fibrosis    552
    Asthma    555
    Tuberculosis    558
Summary    558
Nursing Care Plan    559

## *24* Alterations in Cardiovascular Function    565

*Pamela L. Pitts-Wilhelm*

Embryology    567
    Fetal Circulation    567
    Circulatory Changes at Birth    567
Anatomy    568
    The Heart    568

    Blood Flow    568
    Conduction System    568
Physiology    570
    Hemodynamic Considerations    570
    Oxygen Delivery    571
Assessment    571
    History    571
    Physical Examination    572
    Diagnostic Procedures    576
Nursing Diagnosis    577
Planning Nursing Care    578
    Developmental Considerations    578
    Acute Care Considerations    578
    Chronic Care Considerations    578
    Home Care Considerations    579
Nursing Interventions for Cardiovascular
Problems    579
    Cardiopulmonary Resuscitation    579
    Nursing Interventions Related to Cardiac
    Surgery    580
    Drug Therapy    582
    Nutrition    582
Evaluating Nursing Care    583
Congenital Heart Defects    583
Acyanotic Heart Defects    583
    Atrial Septal Defects    583
    Ventricular Septal Defects    584
    Endocardial Cushion Defects    585
    Patent Ductus Arteriosus    586
    Coarctation of the Aorta    587
Acyanotic Heart Defects With Normal or Decreased
Pulmonary Blood Flow    588
    Aortic Stenosis    588
    Pulmonic Stenosis    589
Cyanotic Heart Defects With Increased Pulmonary
Blood Flow    590
    Transposition of the Great Arteries    590
    Truncus Arteriosus    591
Cyanotic Heart Defects With Decreased Pulmonary
Blood Flow    592
    Tetralogy of Fallot    592
    Tricuspid Atresia    593
    Nursing Care for Children With Congenital Heart
    Defects    594
Acquired Cardiovascular Diseases    595
    Bacterial Endocarditis    595
    Pericarditis    596
    Rheumatic Fever    597
    Kawasaki Disease    598
    Congestive Heart Failure    598
    Hypertension    600
Summary    601
Nursing Care Plan    601

**25 Alterations in Hematological Function 605**

*Joan T. Duer*

Embryology 606

Physiology 607
 Erythrocytes 607
 Leukocytes 608
 Thrombocytes 608
 Plasma 609

Assessment 609
 History 609
 Physical Examination 609
 Diagnostic Procedures 609

Nursing Diagnosis 610

Planning Nursing Care 611
 Developmental Considerations 611
 Acute Care Considerations 611
 Chronic Care Considerations 611
 Home Care Considerations 611

Nursing Interventions 612
 Nutrition 612
 Hydration 612
 Drug Therapy 612
 Blood Product Administration 612
 Bone Marrow Transplants 613

Evaluating Nursing Care 613

Hematological Problems of Neonates 614
 Hyperbilirubinemia 614
 Hemolytic Disease of the Newborn 615
 Rh Incompatibility (Isoimmunization) 616
 ABO Incompatibility 616
 Hemorrhagic Disorders 617
 Polycythemia 617
 Glucose 6-Phosphate Dehydrogenase Deficiency 618
 Anemia 618

Hematological Problems of Infants 619
 Anemia 619
 Iron Deficiency Anemia 620
 Thalassemia (Cooley Anemia) 621

Hematological Problems of Toddlers 622
 Hemophilia 622
 Sickle Cell Disease 624

Hematological Problems of Preschool- and School-Aged Children 626
 Aplastic Anemia 626
 Idiopathic Thrombocytopenic Purpura 627
 Acute Leukemia 628

Hematological Problems of Adolescents 629
 Hodgkin Disease 629

Summary 631

**26 Alterations in Neurological Function 633**

*Mary Ann Jezewski*

Embryology 634

Anatomy and Physiology 635
 The Central Nervous System 635
 The Peripheral Nervous System 636

Assessment 637
 History 637
 Physical Examination 638
 Diagnostic Procedures 638

Nursing Diagnosis 638

Planning and Implementing Nursing Care 642

Nursing Interventions 642

Evaluating Nursing Care 643
 Intracranial Hypertension 643

Neurological Problems in Infants 647
 Congenital Febrile Seizures 647
 Neural Tube Defects 649
 Hydrocephalus 654
 Microencephaly 656
 Neonatal Meningitis 656

Neurological Problems of Toddlers 657
 Lead Poisoning (Plumbism) 657
 Neurocutaneous Syndromes 659

Neurological Problems of Preschool Children 660
 Meningitis 660
 Encephalitis 661

Neurological Problems of School-Age Children 662
 Reye Syndrome 662
 Guillain-Barré Syndrome 663
 Headaches 664
 Attention Deficit Disorder 665
 Brain Tumors 666
 Seizure Disorders (Epilepsy) 668

Neurological Problems of Adolescents 674
 Head Injuries 674
 Spinal Cord Injury 676

Summary 681

**27 Alterations in Immune System Function 685**

*Mary Ann Ludwig and Thomas Beam*

Anatomy 686
 Cells 686
 Vessels 689
 Development of Lymphoid Organs 689

Physiology 690
 Basic Pathology 690

Functional Physiology    691
Aberrant Immune Responses    692
Assessment    693
History    693
Physical Examination    693
Diagnostic Procedures    694
Nursing Diagnosis    694
Planning Nursing Care    694
Developmental Considerations    694
Acute Care Considerations    695
Home Care Considerations    696
Nursing Interventions    696
Desensitization    696
Environmental Control    697
Drug Therapy    697
Nutrition    698
Evaluating Nursing Care    698
Immune Health Problems of Children    698
Acquired Immunodeficiency Syndrome    698
X-Linked Agammaglobulinemia    703
DiGeorge Syndrome    705
Wiskott-Aldrich Syndrome    706
General Allergic Reactions    707
Anaphylaxis    707
Hypersensitivity Pneumonitis    709
Allergic Rhinitis    710
Food Allergies    712
Local Allergic Reactions    715
Asthma    715
Autoimmune Disorders    716
Juvenile Rheumatoid Arthritis    716
Systemic Lupus Erythematosus    719
Summary    723
Nursing Care Plan    723

**28  Alterations in Fluid and Electrolyte Balance    729**
*Carolyn M. Orlowski and Richard E. Harbin*
Fluid Compartments    730
Fluid Balance    731
Factors Affecting Water Movement and Balance    731
Water Transport Mechanisms    731
Regulatory Mechanisms    732
Electrolytes    732
Acid–Base Balance    733
Regulation of Acid–Base Balance    734
Fluid and Electrolyte Requirements    734
Metabolic Rate    734
Body Surface Area    735
Body Weight    735

Assessment    736
History    736
Physical Examination    736
Diagnostic Procedures    738
Nursing Diagnosis    739
Planning Nursing Care    739
Nursing Interventions    741
Oral Fluid and Electrolyte Replacement Therapy    741
Gastric Feeding    742
Parenteral Administration of Fluids and Electrolytes    743
Evaluating Nursing Care    743
Alterations in Acid–Base Balance    744
Metabolic Acidosis    744
Metabolic Alkalosis    744
Respiratory Acidosis    745
Respiratory Alkalosis    746
Alterations in Electrolyte Balance    747
Hypercalcemia    747
Hypocalcemia    748
Hypermagnesemia    749
Hypomagnesemia    750
Hyperkalemia    750
Hypokalemia    751
Hypernatremia    752
Hyponatremia    752
Alterations in Fluid Volume    753
Fluid Volume Excess    753
Fluid Volume Deficit    754
Summary    755

**29  Alterations in Gastrointestinal Function    757**
*Susan N. Peck and Marianne Buzby*
Embryology    759
Anatomy    759
Digestive Physiology    760
Ingestion    760
Digestion    761
Absorption    761
Excretion    761
Assessment    761
History    761
Physical Examination    762
Diagnostic Procedures    762
Nursing Diagnosis    764
Planning Nursing Care    765
Developmental Considerations    765
Acute Care Considerations    765

Chronic Care Considerations    765
Home Care Considerations    765
Nursing Interventions    765
Nutrition    766
Decompression    766
Elimination    766
Drug Therapy    767
Preoperative and Postoperative Nursing
Care    767
Evaluating Nursing Care    767
Common Gastrointestinal Disorders    767
Acute and Infectious Diarrhea    767
Constipation    769
Encopresis    770
Acute Vomiting    771
Congenital Problems of Ingestion    772
Cleft Lip and Palate    772
Tracheoesophageal Fistula and Esophageal
Atresia    774
Diaphragmatic Hernia    776
Ingestion Problems of Infants and Children    777
Gastroesophageal Reflux    777
Herpes Stomatitis    778
Ingestion of Foreign Bodies    779
Ingestion of Corrosive Substances    780
Acetaminophen Ingestion    781
Congenital Problems of Digestion    782
Biliary Atresia    782
Neonatal Liver Disease    782
Wilson Disease    783
Intestinal Atresia    785
Digestion Problems of Infants and Children    786
Colic    786
Pyloric Stenosis    787
Congenital Disorders of Absorption    788
Gastroschisis and Omphalocele    788
Absorption Problems of Infants and Children    789
Necrotizing Enterocolitis    789
Malabsorption    790
Celiac Disease    792
Meckel Diverticulum    793
Inflammatory Bowel Disease    793
Congenital Problems of Elimination    794
Hirschsprung Disease    794
Anorectal Malformations    795
Malrotation    796
Meconium Ileus    796
Excretion and Elimination Problems of Infants and
Children    796
Intussusception    796
Umbilical Hernias    798
Inguinal Hernia    799
Anal Fissures    800
Intestinal Polyps    800

Other Gastrointestinal Problems    800
Omphalitis    800
Appendicitis    801
Hepatitis    802
Cholecystitis    803
Pancreatitis    803
Peptic Ulcer Disease    803
Summary    804
Nursing Care Plan    804

**30  Alterations in Renal Function    809**
*Richard E. Harbin and Michael W. Neft*
Embryology    811
The Kidney and Ureter    811
The Bladder and Urethra    811
The Adrenal Glands    811
Anatomy and Physiology    811
Renal Function    811
Assessment    812
History    813
Physical Examination    814
Diagnostic Procedures    814
Nursing Diagnosis    816
Planning and Implementing Nursing Care    816
Nursing Interventions    817
Catheterization    817
Intake and Output    818
Maintaining Hydration    818
Drug Therapy    818
Evaluating Nursing Care    818
Congenital Renal Problems    818
Exstrophy of the Bladder    818
Hypospadias    819
Epispadias    820
Renal Problems of Neonates    821
Wilms' Tumor    821
Renal Problems of Infants    822
Hemolytic-Uremic Syndrome    822
Renal Problems of Toddlers and Preschoolers    823
Acute Glomerulonephritis
(Poststreptococcal)    823
Alport Syndrome    824
Nephrotic Syndrome (Nephrosis)    825
Urinary Tract Infections    826
Vesicoureteral Reflux (VUR)    827
Acute Renal Problems    829
Acute Renal Failure    829
Renal Trauma    831
Chronic Renal Problems    831
Chronic Glomerulonephritis    831
Chronic Renal Failure    832

Dialysis   833
   Hemodialysis   833
   Peritoneal Dialysis   835
Renal Transplantation   836
Summary   837
Nursing Care Plan   **838**

## 31  Alterations in Reproductive Function   841

*Richard E. Harbin*

Embryology   842
Anatomy and Physiology   843
   Female   843
   Male   843
Female Reproductive Development   843
   The Menstrual Cycle   844
Male Reproductive Development   845
Assessment of Reproductive Function   845
   History   845
   Physical Examination   846
Nursing Diagnoses   847
Planning and Implementing Nursing Care for Reproductive Disorders   847
Evaluating Nursing Care   848
Reproductive Problems of Neonates and Infants   848
   Ambiguous Genitalia   848
   Hydrocele   848
   Phimosis   849
   Testicular Torsion   849
Reproductive Problems of Toddlers and Preschoolers   850
   Cryptorchism   850
Reproductive Problems of School-Aged Children   851
   Precocious Puberty   851
Reproductive Problems of Adolescents   852
   Delayed Maturation   852
Menstrual Problems of Adolescents   853
   Amenorrhea   853
   Dysmenorrhea   854
   Premenstrual Syndrome   854
   Dysfunctional Uterine Bleeding   855
   Endometriosis   856
Vulvovaginitis   856
   Candidiasis   856
   Trichomoniasis   857
   Bacterial Vaginosis   857
   Foreign Bodies   857
Breast Problems   858
   Polythelia   858
   Idiopathic Breast Hypertrophy   858
   Benign Breast Disease   858
   Traumatic Breast Lesions   858

Reproductive Problems of Male Adolescents   859
   Gynecomastia   859
Sexual Abuse   859
   Incest   861
   Rape   861
Sexually Transmitted Diseases   862
   Pelvic Inflammatory Disease   862
   Chlamydia Trachomatis   863
   Gonorrhea   864
   Syphilis   864
   Human Papillomavirus   865
   Genital Herpes   866
   Acquired Immune Deficiency Syndrome   867
Summary   867
Nursing Care Plan   868

## 32  Alterations in Endocrine Function   871

*Patricia T. Castiglia, Deborah Kramer, Carolyn Fong, and Terri H. Lipman*

Embryology   872
Anatomy and Physiology   873
   The Pituitary Gland   873
   The Thyroid   876
   The Parathyroids   876
   The Thymus   876
   The Islets of Langerhans   876
   The Adrenal Glands   878
   The Gonads   880
Assessment   880
   History   880
   Physical Examination   881
   Diagnostic Procedures   881
Nursing Diagnosis   881
Planning Nursing Care   882
   Developmental Considerations   882
   Acute Care Considerations   883
   Chronic Care Considerations   883
   Home Care Considerations   883
Nursing Interventions   883
   Client and Parent Education   883
   Drug Therapy   884
   Nutrition   884
Endocrine Problems of Infancy and Early Childhood   884
   Hypopituitarism   884
   Hypothyroidism   885
   Congenital Hypothyroidism   885
   Acquired Hypothyroidism   887
   Hypoparathyroidism   888
   Diabetes Insipidus   889
   Hypoglycemia   890
   Adrenal Crisis (Acute Adrenocortical Insufficiency)   891

Congenital Adrenal Hyperplasia    892
Cushing Syndrome (Hypercortisolism)    892
Endocrine Problems of School-Aged Children and
Adolescents    893
Anterior Pituitary Dysfunction    893
Hyperthyroidism (Graves Disease,
Thyrotoxicosis)    894
Thyroiditis (Hashimoto Disease)    896
Hyperparathyroidism    897
Chronic or Primary Adrenocortical Insufficiency
(Addison Disease)    899
Pheochromocytomas    900
Chronic Endocrine Disorders    900
Diabetes Mellitus    900
Summary    908
Nursing Care Plan    908

## 33 Alterations in Musculoskeletal Function    915

*Sallie S. Page-Goertz*

Embryology    916
Anatomy    917
Bones    917
Bone Growth and Ossification    917
Joints    918
Skeletal Muscles    918
Physiology    919
Functions of Bones, Joints, and Muscles    919
Hematopoiesis    919
Bone Healing and Remodeling    919
Assessment    920
History    920
Physical Examination    920
Diagnostic Procedures    921
Nursing Diagnosis    922
Planning Nursing Care    923
Developmental Considerations    923
Acute Care Considerations    923
Chronic Care Considerations    923
Home Care Considerations    923
Nursing Interventions    924
Pre- and Postoperative Care    924
Care of a Child in a Cast    924
Care of a Child in Traction    926
Care of a Child with an Ilizarov External
Fixator    928
Drug Therapy    930
Nutrition    930
Child/Parent Education    930
Evaluating Nursing Care    930
Common Musculoskeletal Problems in Children    932
Sprains, Strains, Avulsions, and Contusions    932

Dislocations    933
Fractures    933
Congenital Musculoskeletal Problems    935
Congenital Hip Dysplasias    935
Talipes Equinovarus (Clubfoot)    938
Metatarsus Adductus    938
Congenital Torticollis    939
Osteogenesis Imperfecta    939
Musculoskeletal Problems of Infants, Toddlers, and
Preschoolers    940
Torsional Deformities    940
Genu Varum and Genu Valgum    941
Septic Arthritis    941
Musculoskeletal Problems of School-Age Children and
Adolescents    942
Osteomyelitis    942
Abnormal Spinal Curves    943
Idiopathic Scoliosis    943
Osteosarcoma    946
Ewing Sarcoma    947
Slipped Capital Femoral Epiphysis    947
Legg-Calvé-Perthes Disease    948
Duchenne Muscular Dystrophy    949
Patellofemoral Stress Syndrome    950
Osgood-Schlatter Disease    950
Sports-Related Injuries    951
Summary    951
Nursing Care Plan    952

## 34 Alterations in Integumentary Function    955

*Mary Ann McClellan and Maribeth L. Moran*

Anatomy and Physiology    956
Skin    957
Hair    958
Nails    958
Assessment    958
History    958
Physical Examination    958
Diagnostic Tests    960
Nursing Diagnosis    968
Planning Nursing Care    968
Developmental, Racial, and Ethnic
Considerations    968
Acute Care Considerations    968
Chronic Care Considerations    969
Home Care Considerations    969
Evaluating Nursing Care    970
Integumentary Problems of Infants    970
Hemangiomas    970
Diaper Dermatitis    971
Atopic Dermatitis (Eczema)    971

Integumentary Problems of Children    972
    Psoriasis    972
    Poison Ivy, Oak, and Sumac Dermatitis    973
    Impetigo    974
    Seborrheic Dermatitis    975
Integumentary Problems of Adolescents    975
    Acne Vulgaris    975
Infestations    976
    Pediculosis    976
    Scabies    977
    Insect Bites and Stings    978
Viral Infections    979
    Warts (Verruca)    979
Fungal Infections    979
    Candidiasis    979
    Tinea    980
Bacterial Infections    981
Drug Reactions    982
Acute Integumentary Disorders    983
    Burns    983
Summary    989


*35*  **Alterations in Sensory Function    991**
*Patricia T. Castiglia*
Embryology    992
Anatomy and Physiology    993
    The Eye    993
    The Ear    994
    The Nose    995
    The Taste Buds    995
Assessment    996
    History    996
    Physical Examination    996
Nursing Diagnosis    1000
Planning Nursing Care    1001
Nursing Interventions    1001
    Eye Medications    1001
    Ear Medications    1001
    Interventions for Epistaxis (Nosebleeds)    1002
Evaluating Nursing Care    1002
Congenital Vision Disorders    1002
    Congenital Cataracts    1002
    Congenital and Juvenile Glaucoma    1003
    Dacryostenosis    1003
Vision Problems of Infants and Toddlers    1004
    Retinopathy of Prematurity    1004
    Ophthalmia Neonatorum    1005
    Trachoma    1005
    Inclusion Conjunctivitis (Blennorrhea)    1006
    Strabismus (Squint)    1006

    Retinoblastoma    1007
    Rhabdomyosarcoma    1008
Vision Problems of Preschool- and School-Aged
Children    1009
    Refractive Errors    1009
    Myopia    1009
    Hyperopia    1009
    Astigmatism    1010
Vision Problems of Adolescents    1010
    External Hordeolum (Stye)    1010
    Retinal Detachment    1010
Acute Vision Problems    1011
    Eye Trauma    1011
Chronic Vision Problems    1011
    Impaired Vision    1011
Hearing Problems of Infants and Toddlers    1012
    Acute Otitis Media    1012
    Chronic Middle-Ear Effusion    1013
    Mastoiditis    1014
    Otitis Externa (Swimmer's Ear)    1015
Hearing Problems of Children and Adolescents    1015
    Hearing Loss Induced by Noise    1015
Nasal Problems of Infants, Toddlers, and
Adolescents    1016
    Acute Nasopharyngitis (Common Cold)    1016
    Acute Pharyngitis    1016
    Chronic Tonsillitis    1017
    Sinusitis    1017
    Allergic Rhinitis    1017
Summary    1018
Nursing Care Plan    1019

*Appendixes*

**Appendix A: Assessment Tools    1027**
**Appendix B: Physiological**
**Measurements    1036**
**Appendix C: Normal Laboratory**
**Values    1044**
**Appendix D: Calculating Pediatric Drug**
**Dosages (Age, Weight, Body Surface**
**Area)    1050**
**Appendix E: Temperature and Weight**
**Conversion    1053**
**Appendix F: Vaccines Commonly Used in the**
**United States    1055**

**Index**

# Essential Concepts and Influences in Child Health Care

*Contemporary Concepts in Child Health Care*

*Family and Cultural Concepts Affecting Pediatric Nursing*

*Ethical and Legal Issues in Child Health Care*

*Developing a Theoretical Framework for Growth and Development*

*I*

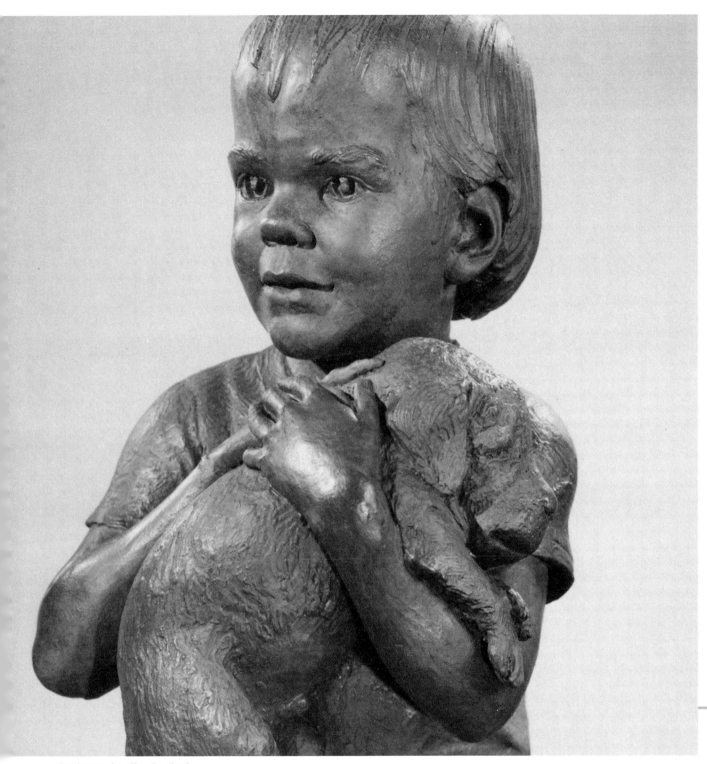

*Sculpture by Charles Parks*

# Contemporary Concepts in Child Health Care

Patricia T. Castiglia

*1*

*The Challenges and Rewards of Child Health Nursing*

*Contemporary Concepts in Child Health Nursing*
   *Historical Concepts of Children*
   *The Perspective of the Family*
   *Mortality Trends—Children in the United States*
   *The Meaning of Health and Illness*
   *Children's Rights*
   *The Significance of State and Federal Legislation*
   *Current Problems and Future Directions*

*Changes in the Health Care System Affecting Pediatric Nursing*
   *Technological Advances*
   *Public Awareness*
   *Increased Costs of Health Care*
   *Cost Containment*

*Concepts Related to Pediatric Nursing*
   *Nursing Process as a Tool for Practice*
   *Nursing Theory as a Basis for Practice*
   *Nursing Theories Related to Pediatric Nursing Practice*
   *Integrating Knowledge in Child Health Nursing*
   *Expanded Roles, Professional Organizations, and Publications*

*Summary*

*Photograph by David Finn*

### Learning Objectives

*Upon completion of this chapter the reader will be able to:*

1. *Describe, in general terms, how children have been viewed from a historical perspective.*

2. *Relate the significance of mortality rates for children.*

3. *Analyze the concept of children's rights.*

4. *Discuss the general types of legislation that currently have an impact on children.*

5. *Discuss the effects that technological advances, public awareness, increased costs of health care, and cost containment efforts have had on pediatric nursing practice.*

6. *Explain the relationship of the nursing process and nursing theory to caring for children.*

7. *Recall organizations and publications that are concerned with child health.*

### Key Terms

*evaluation*

*health assessment*

*informed consumerism*

*intervention*

*morbidity*

*mortality*

*nursing diagnosis*

*nursing process*

*nursing theory*

*planning*

*right*

*theory*

## The Challenges and Rewards of Child Health Nursing

. . . A newborn baby's first cry . . . Observing the reactions of siblings and other family members to a new baby . . . Seeing an infant and family "survive" colic . . . Just "being there" when a child needs you most . . . Waving goodbye to a child and family as they depart from the hospital after a serious illness . . . The look of relief from a troubled adolescent.

From first experiences as a student nurse through the many years spent dealing with children and families, child health nursing provides vast opportunities for professional and personal growth and satisfaction. Child health nursing offers unique challenges to those willing to accept them. Nurses must be educated and prepared to function in a variety of roles, including the following:

- *Guide.* Nurses can influence parents and children as they relate to each other and as they relate to society.
- *Teacher.* Nurses teach preventive health practices, strategies for maintaining optimal health, and appropriate health intervention measures.
- *Communicator.* Nurses use communication to share perceptions, ideas, goals, and aspirations. Nurses communicate by listening as well as by verbal and nonverbal techniques.
- *Facilitator.* Nurses serve as a "bridge" between client(s) and other members of the health care team by interpreting or ensuring the child and parents' understanding of the situation, by making appropriate referrals, and by serving as the child's advocate.
- *Case manager.* In the current complex health care delivery system, nurses serve as coordinators or directors of care. They refer or assign the responsibility for certain aspects of care to others, but they oversee and direct the administration of all care.

- *Advocate.* Children and parents are often in vulnerable positions when they assert themselves to obtain medical, social, and financial resources. Nurses must be prepared to recognize the needs of children and parents, to speak for them when necessary, and to educate them about their rights.
- *Counselor.* Nurses serve as advisers for children and their families and offer them knowledge and caring related to their concerns.
- *Comforter.* When problems arise nurses can provide consolation, encouragement, strength, and hope to clients in need of emotional and physical support.
- *Friend.* Nurses need to be able to show kindly interest and demonstrate esteem for children and their families.

Each nursing role is equally important. The relationships among them are continually evolving, and any one might dominate the dynamics of the child–family–nurse interaction at any given time. Many nurses derive a great deal of pleasure and satisfaction from these demanding roles (Fig. 1-1).

Professional child health nurses must develop specialized knowledge and skills in order to effectively implement the nursing process. Working with children is different from working with other populations because changes in child health status occur more rapidly, children are often unable to communicate verbally, and children cannot be viewed in isolation from their families.

## Contemporary Concepts in Child Health Nursing

The concepts of the child and the child's relationship within the family and society have evolved through time to accommodate social, political, economic, and environmental factors. By the turn of the 20th century, training schools for nursing preparation were well established in hospitals. With this labor supply, hospitals expanded. Nurses worked long hours, and nursing care of children was structured to adhere to hospital policy rather than to the needs of children and their families.

The contemporary concept of the child incorporates individuality, discernible developmental sequences, and a recognition of the interaction that occurs among biolog-

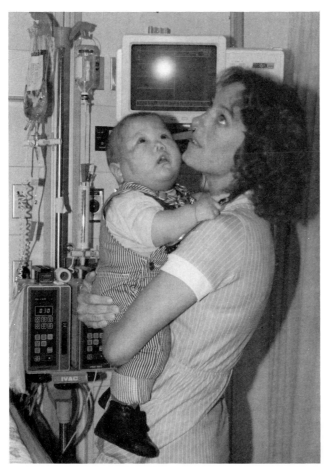

*Figure 1–1. Nursing roles.*

*Center for the Study of the History of Nursing, School of Nursing, University of Pennsylvania*

ical, cultural, social, and environmental forces (Cherry and Carty, 1986). Caregivers should understand that this view of childhood has not always existed, and that these same forces may alter the currently accepted view.

## Historical Concepts of Children

Before World War I, children were viewed as miniature adults. They were considered "barbarians," who needed to be civilized under pressure. Parents were "in charge" of the child until the child achieved economic independence. Children were considered assets of the family. Especially during the 16th, 17th, and 18th centuries, children were necessary contributors to the economic welfare, and the future, of the family. They often worked in the family trade. Marriages were arranged to benefit the family. Parents had large families for economic survival. Because the infant mortality rates were so high, each family needed enough children to ensure family survival.

In 1909, the first White House Conference was held to address concerns about cruel and inhumane treatment in orphanages and foundling homes, as well as the exploitation of children in work settings. This conference resulted in the development of the Children's Bureau in 1912. Since 1930, a White House Conference on Children has been held at the beginning of each decade.

After World War I, the recognition of the importance

of hygiene, based on the "germ theory," resulted in a significant decrease in infant mortality. People became very optimistic about the ability of "science" to control all facets of the environment. It is not surprising that this confidence in a scientific approach extended to child rearing. The emphasis in child rearing was on a rigid approach to scheduling infants' and children's activities. The behaviorists believed that controlling children's environments would shape their development.

In the early 1940s, Spitz pioneered research investigating the effects of separation on children. He found that children over 6 months of age exhibited behaviors such as loud, demanding crying when separated from their mothers. After the first month of this behavior, he observed that the children withdrew from approaches by others and might scream. They lost weight and their physical development slowed. In the third month of separation they also developed insomnia, and they seemed prone to minor ailments and infections. These children tested lower on IQ tests after separation than before. Spitz (1945) also studied the reversibility of the effects of separation, and found that when children were returned to their mothers after three months or less of separation, they were usually able to regain their relationships with their mothers. The effects of longer separations were not easily reversed. After more than six months of separation, irreversible changes, such as silence, occurred.

Robertson (1958) studied separation effects of hospitalized children. He named the stages that Spitz had observed *protest, despair,* and *denial.* Bowlby (1963) reported that children who were separated from their parents in order to remove them from the bombing of London during World War II demonstrated flat, affectless facial expressions and had a tendency to steal.

Toward the middle of the 20th century, a change occurred in the concept of the child's interaction with the environment. Parents were admonished not to interfere with the child's natural developmental progression. Emphasis shifted now to the biological or maturation factors as typified by Gesell's developmental sequences. Gesell's advice to parents was to be patient, that all stages would pass, and that parental interference in the process would not be beneficial and, in fact, might be harmful. A famous cartoon during this period depicts a child asking "Do I have to do what I want to do today?" Developmental theorists and their work are discussed in more detail in Chapter 4.

About the time of World War II, and during the next 20 years, the psychoanalytic approach to child rearing became popular. The needs of children, and how best to meet those needs, became the theme. It was postulated that if parents did a better job in child rearing, then it would be possible to avoid most problems in adulthood. Parents were advised to avoid frustrating their children, and discipline became a major topic of discussion. There was great uncertainty regarding discipline, and new interpretations of parenting developed the concept of parents as "pals" or friends of the child.

In the 1960s and 1970s families were smaller and more isolated than before. The "high-tech" age began to mushroom—more mothers began working outside the home, and more opportunities became available to women in previously male-dominated jobs, thus increasing the use of day care facilities by families in which both parents worked. These factors contributed to the idea that the child was a prized possession, to be groomed with care and offered the best advantages possible. Many couples postponed having children until their careers were established and they were financially secure.

By the 1980s there were more older first-time mothers. New advances in genetic engineering offered infertile couples the opportunity to have children. Whereas in vitro fertilization and surrogate motherhood proved to be an answer for some couples, at the same time these issues raised broad legal and moral issues. Financially secure parents developed a renewed interest in employing nannies. New "nanny schools" opened and offered a career option that had formerly been available only in other countries, especially England. Fathers began to assume increasing responsibility for the daily care of children. Some fathers obtained paternity leaves from their jobs. Other fathers elected to become "house husbands," assuming the major responsibility for home management, including child care. However, in most dual-career families mothers continue to assume the primary responsibility for child care.

## The Perspective of the Family

The term "family" has had two major interpretations—that of the *nuclear family* (mother, father, and children) and that of the *extended family* (the nuclear family plus others such as grandparents, aunts, uncles, and cousins). One family structure that has grown more in our society is the *single parent family.* Single parent families result from divorce, death, choice, or other circumstances affecting the parents. Other family forms include the *blended family,* in which each partner brings their own children to form a combined family. *Adoptive families* may fit into any of the family forms mentioned. Today the term "family" no longer has one specific meaning. Variables influencing the concept and functioning of the family include financial resources, emotional support resources, and physical support resources. A reflection of the change of interpretation of "the family" was evidenced in the last U.S. census, when all persons living together could be classified as a family.

The recognition of variations of the concept of *the family* is important for nurses. Communication, assessment, and interventions are influenced by the nurse's sensitivity to family dynamics. The family is discussed in more detail in Chapter 2.

## Mortality Trends—Children in the United States

Despite all medical advances, mortality and morbidity rates for infants and children are still high. *Mortality,* in this case, refers to the number of deaths of infants and children per unit of population (usually expressed as deaths per 1000, 10,000, or 100,000). *Morbidity* is defined as the rate at which an illness occurs in a specific population (e.g., children). Nurses need to be aware of current mortality and morbidity rates because these statistics can assist them in assessing clients and in planning health promotion interventions. In addition, mortality and morbidity statistics influence federal, state, and local allocations of money as well as preventive and health education programs offered in communities and in schools. Nursing research can also make a valuable contribution to the body of knowledge concerning mortality and morbidity.

In 1984, the infant mortality rate was 10.8 per 1000 live births and 34.1 per 1000 for children between 1 and 14 years old (Congress of the United States, Office of Technology Assessment, 1988). The high infant mortality rate among blacks, approximately double that of whites, continues to be a major concern (Miller, et al., 1985). Table 1-1 shows infant mortality rates for a variety of countries.

*Table 1–1. Comparison of Infant Mortality Rates in the United States and Other Countries (1985)*

| Country | Infant Mortality Rate* |
|---------|------------------------|
| 1. Japan | 5.5 |
| 2. Finland | 6.3 |
| 3. Sweden | 6.7 |
| 4. Switzerland | 6.9 |
| 5. Denmark | 7.9 |
| 6. Canada | 7.9 |
| 7. Netherlands | 8.0 |
| 8. France | 8.1 |
| 9. Norway | 8.3 |
| 10. Ireland | 8.9 |
| 11. United Kingdom | 9.4 |
| 12. Belgium | 9.4 |
| 13. West Germany | 9.5 |
| 14. East Germany | 9.9 |
| 15. Australia | 9.9 |
| 16. Spain | 10.5† |
| 17. United States | 10.6 |
| 18. Italy | 10.9 |
| 19. New Zealand | 11.0 |
| 20. Austria | 11.0 |
| 21. Israel | 11.9 |
| 22. Brunei | 12.0 |
| 23. Malta | 13.6 |
| 24. Greece | 14.0 |
| 25. Czechoslovakia | 15.3†† |
| 26. Bulgaria | 15.8 |
| 27. Cuba | 16.5 |
| 28. Poland | 18.5 |
| 29. Hungary | 20.4 |
| 30. Romania | 23.4†† |

* The infant mortality rate is defined as the number of infants who die in the first year of life per 1,000 live births.
† This is Spain's infant mortality rate in 1983.
†† These infant mortality rates are for 1984.
(Von Cube, A. (1987). Population Reference Bureau. Washington, D.C.: personal communication.)

Almost 1% of all babies born in the United States die in the first year of life and, of those who succumb, two thirds of the deaths occur in the neonatal period. The United States ranks 17th among industrialized countries in infant mortality (Congress of the United States, Office of Technology Assessment, 1988). This low ranking may be explained by our high-technology efforts in neonatology, which sustain life in infants who might, in other countries, be born dead or die shortly after birth. Fetal death rates might reflect or confirm this suspicion, although fetal deaths are not reported in some countries.

Poverty conditions have always been linked to infant mortality. It must be noted that whereas the poverty rate for infants and children has risen, financial aid has declined (Fig. 1-2). There has been a rise in the number of infants born to poor families—from 18% in 1978 to 24% in 1984. During the same period there was a 13% decline in Medicaid expenditures per child (Congress of the United States, Office of Technology Assessment, 1988).

Another situation that has had an impact on infant mortality is adolescent pregnancy. The number of births to teenage mothers in 1984 was about 470,000 (National Academy of Sciences, 1987). Teenagers are among the high-risk group for low-birth-weight infants and for infant mortality. There are several strategies for addressing the issue of adolescent motherhood with an eye to prevention, including Planned Parenthood, sex education, family preparation courses, and comprehensive school-based clinics.

The burden of illness in children in the United States is detailed in Table 1-2. For both blacks and whites, mortality rates decline each year from age 1 to age 15 and then increase greatly from 15 to 19 years of age. Leading causes of death are shown in Table 1-3.

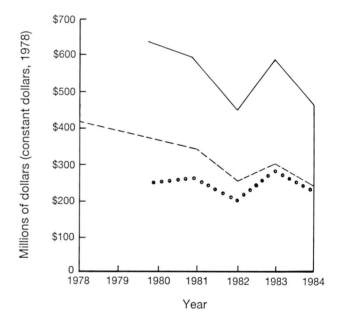

———— Total (State and Federal)
— — — Federal
∘ ∘ ∘ ∘ ∘ State

*Figure 1–2. Estimates state and federal funding for maternal and child health services, 1978–1984. (State funding data comparable to federal funding data for the years 1978 and 1979 are not available. Estimates are unavailable for 1979; value for 1979 is based on a linear interpretation between 1978 and 1980.) (Office of Technology Assessment, 1988, based on actual federal funding and reported data by state health agencies to the Public Health Foundation, Washington, DC).*

*Table 1–2. Burden of Illness in U.S. Children*

| Problem | Burden of Illness or Cost |
|---|---|
| Infant mortality and low birthweight | Almost 40,000 babies (1% of all U.S. births) die in the first year of life each year. The United States ranks 17th among industrialized countries in infant mortality. 6.7% of all U.S. newborns are low birthweight babies (under 2500 grams; about 5 lbs, 8oz). 16% of all very low birthweight (i.e, those weighing under 1500 grams; about 3 lbs, 5oz) are moderately or severely handicapped. |
| Congenital disorders detectable by newborn screening | About 4500 cases of detectable disorders or diseases causing death or mental retardation occur each year. |
| Conditions preventable through well-child care | 37% of U.S. infants were fully immunized against diphtheria, tetanus, and pertussis (whooping cough) in 1983.<br>78% of white children and 62% of nonwhite children from 1 to 4 years old were immunized against polio in 1985.<br>Almost 8000 cases of measles occurred in the United States in 1986. |
| Accidental childhood injuries | 7,850 deaths were caused by accidental injuries in children under 15 years old in 1984.<br>1 in every 9 children is hospitalized for accidental or other injuries before age 15. 10 million emergency room visits per year are made for accidental or other injuries. |
| Child mistreatment | At least 1200 deaths of children in 1986 occurred as a result of child abuse.<br>24,000 children sustained serious physical injury due to child abuse in 1983.<br>1.9 million cases of suspected child abuse and neglect were reported in 1985.<br>150,000 to 200,000 cases of sexual abuse occur in the United States each year. |

(U.S. Congress, Office of Technology Assessment (1988). *Healthy children: Investing in the future* [OTA-H-345], p. 5. Washington, D.C.: U.S. Government Printing Office.)

White males aged 15 to 24 have the highest suicide rate. In 1981, the suicide rate was 11.1 per 100,000, compared with females in the same age group, who had a suicide rate of 4.9 per 100,000 (Miller et al., 1985).

## The Meaning of Health and Illness

How health and illness are defined is largely determined by self-perceptions, the perceptions of others, and classifications established by insurance companies and federal agencies. How individuals perceive their own health is usually the most important consideration. When nurses ask "How are you?" they usually expect an answer that reflects the person's self-perception of how they are. Sometimes self-perception and the perception of others are disparate. When inquiring about young children nurses often ask the parent or caregiver how the child is. This is done based on the assumption that that person knows the child well and would be able to identify signs of illness or wellness that might escape the more casual or infrequent observer.

It is possible to conceptualize health and illness on the same continuum or on two different but parallel continuums (Figs. 1-3 and 1-4). The concept of two simultaneously occurring continuums allows for the interpretation of a person with a chronic illness (e.g., diabetes) being considered well when controlled. It also allows for the conceptualization of a well person, that is, a person with no overt signs and symptoms of illness, having a degree of illness (e.g., asthma). Movement along these continuums is fluid and is influenced by physiological and environmental factors.

The interpretation of health/illness as one continuum is frequently used in secondary and tertiary care settings. This occurs because of the focus on illness and the attempts to remedy or rectify acute episodes in order to make the child "well."

Single Continuum of Health and Illness

HEALTH <————————————————————> ILLNESS

*Figure 1–3. Single continuum of health and illness.*

The intent of this book is to focus on the child, recognizing that wellness coexists with illness. The parallel focus allows for an assessment of relative health, which dictates the formulation of nursing diagnoses and the planning, implementation, and evaluation of nursing care.

## Children's Rights

The Constitution of the United States guarantees equal rights. However, not all individuals have enjoyed those rights at all times. Among those who have had to fight for recognition of their rights are minorities and children. Of these, the most defenseless are children. Because children are evolving in physical size and mental ability, they are generally unable to advocate for themselves and must rely on others (e.g., parents, teachers, nurses, physicians, social workers, etc.) to fight for their rights.

What are these rights? In order to have a right, a person must claim it. A right may be defined as "that which is due to anyone." Rights may be claimed as moral or legal on the basis of principles or laws. Rights form the underlying foundation for truth, justice, and morality. Children's rights have been stated by the Geneva Declaration of the Rights of the Child (1924) and the United Nations Declara-

Parallel Continuum of Health and Illness

*Figure 1–4. Parallel continuum of health and illness.*

tion of the Rights of the Child (General Assembly of the United Nations, November 20, 1959). In the latter, the United Nations recognizes that children need special safeguards and care because of their physical and mental immaturity, and that they require this protection before birth as well as after birth. The declaration calls upon men and women to recognize these rights and to work toward observance of these rights by legislation and other measures. The best interest of the child is of paramount importance. There is no distinction on the basis of race, sex, language, religion, etc., and the child is entitled from birth to a name and nationality. Each child has the right to special care and protection and the right to adequate medical services, housing, nutrition, and recreation. Handicapped children are to be given special consideration. All children are entitled to free and compulsory education (at least at the elementary level), to a home atmosphere of caring, and to protection from neglect and abuse. It is

*Table 1–3. Leading Causes of Death Among U.S. Infants and Children (1984)*

| Cause of Death† | Mortality Rate by Age* | | | | |
|---|---|---|---|---|---|
| | <1 yr | 1–4 yrs | 5–9 yrs | 10–14 yrs | 15–19 yrs |
| All causes | 1086.6 | 51.9 | 25.1 | 28.2 | 81.9 |
| Malignant neoplasms (140–208) | 3.1 | 4.0 | 3.6 | 3.5 | 4.8 |
| Major cardiovascular disease (390–448) | 29.7 | 2.9 | 1.4 | 1.4 | 2.7 |
| Pneumonia (480–486) | 18.7 | 1.4 | 0.5 | 0.4 | 0.5 |
| Congenital anomalies (740–759) | 234.4 | 6.7 | 1.5 | 1.4 | 1.3 |
| Certain conditions originating in the perinatal period (760–779) | 512.4 | 1.4 | 0.1 | 0.0 | 0.0 |
| Symptoms, signs, and ill-defined conditions (780–799) | 161.1 | 1.8 | 0.3 | 0.3 | 1.3 |
| All other diseases (residual) | 49.3 | 6.6 | 3.1 | 3.2 | 4.6 |
| Motor vehicle accidents (E810–E825) | 4.4 | 6.9 | 6.2 | 7.1 | 34.6 |
| All other accidents and adverse effects (E800–E807/ E826–E949) | 18.6 | 12.9 | 5.5 | 5.9 | 10.5 |
| Suicide (950–E959) | — | — | 0.0 | 1.3 | 9.0 |
| Homicide and legal intervention (E960–E978) | 6.5 | 2.4 | 0.9 | 1.6 | 8.3 |
| All other external causes (980–E999) | 1.6 | 0.4 | 0.2 | 0.3 | 0.8 |

*The mortality rate is defined here as the number of deaths per 100,000 population in each specified group.
† International Classification of Diseases code number is in parentheses.
(Office of Technology Assessment (1988). Calculated from unpublished data from the U.S. Vital Statistics, provided by the National Center for Health Statistics, Public Health Service, U.S. Department of Health and Human Services, Hyattsville, MD, 1986)

## United Nations Declaration of the Rights of the Child

*Whereas* the peoples of the United Nations have, in the Charter, reaffirmed their faith in fundamental human rights, and in the dignity and worth of the human person, and have determined to promote social progress and better standards of life in larger freedom,

*Whereas* the United Nations has, in the Universal Declaration of Human Rights, proclaimed that everyone is entitled to all the rights and freedoms set forth therein, without distinction of any kind, such as race, colour, sex, language, religion, political or other opinion, national or social origin, property, birth, or other status,

*Whereas* the child, by reason of his physical and mental immaturity, needs special safeguards and care, including appropriate legal protection, before as well as after birth,

*Whereas* the need for such special safeguards has been stated in the Geneva Declaration of the Rights of the Child of 1924, and recognized in the Universal Declaration of Human Rights and in the statutes of specialized agencies and international organizations concerned with the welfare of children,

*Whereas* mankind owes to the child the best it has to give,

*Now therefore the general assembly proclaims this Declaration of the Rights of the Child* to the end that he may have a happy childhood and enjoy for his own good and for the good of society the rights and freedoms herein set forth, and calls upon parents, upon men and women as individuals and upon voluntary organizations, local authorities and national governments to recognize and strive for the observance of these rights by legislative and other measures progressively taken in accordance with the following principles:

### Principle 1

The child shall enjoy all the rights set forth in this Declaration. All children, without any exception whatsoever, shall be entitled to these rights, without distinction or discrimination on account of race, colour, sex, language, religion, political or other opinion, national or social origin, property, birth or other status, whether of himself or of his family.

### Principle 2

The child shall enjoy special protection, and shall be given opportunities and facilities, by law and by other means, to enable him to develop physically, mentally, morally, spiritually and socially in a healthy and normal manner and in conditions of freedom and dignity. In the enactment of laws for this purpose the best interests of the child shall be the paramount consideration.

### Principle 3

The child shall be entitled from his birth to a name and a nationality.

### Principle 4

The child shall enjoy the benefits of social security. He shall be entitled to grow and develop in health; to this end special care and protection shall be provided both to him and to his mother, including adequate prenatal and postnatal care. The child shall have the right to adequate nutrition, housing, recreation and medical services.

### Principle 5

The child who is physically, mentally, or socially handicapped shall be given the special treatment, education and care required by his particular condition.

### Principle 6

The child, for the full and harmonious development of his personality, needs love and understanding. He shall, wherever possible, grow up in the care and under the responsibility of his parents, and in any case in an atmosphere of affection and of moral and material security; a child of tender years shall not, save in exceptional circumstances, be separated from his mother. Society and the public authorities shall have the duty to extend particular care to children without a family and those without adequate means of support. Payment of state and other assistance towards the maintenance of children of large families is desirable.

### Principle 7

The child is entitled to receive education, which shall be free and compulsory at least in the elementary stages. He shall be given an education which will promote his general culture, and enable him on a basis of equal opportunity to develop his abilities, his individual judgment and his sense of moral and social responsibility, and to become a useful member of society.

The best interests of the child shall be the guiding principle of those responsible for his education and upbringing; that responsibility lies in the first place with his parents.

The child shall have full opportunity for play and recreation, which should be directed to the same purposes as education; society and the public authorities shall endeavour to promote the enjoyment of this right.

*(continued)*

energy and talents should be devoted to the service of
his fellow men.

(United Nations. *Declaration of the Rights of the Child,* 1959.)

further stated that children should not be employed before they reach an acceptable minimum age.

Advocates for children's rights must be vigilant about the need for social policies to help children develop to their utmost capability. Advocates need to remember, and need to remind society, of the vulnerability of children. Nurses must not only render safe and effective nursing care but must also serve as leaders in recognizing and supporting the rights of children. Children are not able to compete for tax dollar allocations—adults must do it for them. Children's rights advocates would point out that limitations or programs for children reflect a decline in society's responsibility for succeeding generations. Actions to protect children are a heritage of each generation.

## The Significance of State and Federal Legislation

The government's role in child welfare has expanded. This has been made evident by an increasing number and variety of federal initiatives for children and families. There are more than 260 programs administered by 20 agencies in the federal government that affect children and their care givers (Hayes, 1982). These programs include "tax benefits and income supplements for families with dependent children; health, education and specialized services for needy children, regulations governing the delivery of aid and services; personnel training, technical assistance and institutional support for agencies serving children and a wide variety of research on the problems facing children and families" (Hayes, 1982, p. 3).

Early legislation that had an impact on children included the Social Security Act of 1935, which provided for child welfare services, aid to dependent children, and maternal and child health services. This legislation is known as the Aid to Families with Dependent Children (AFDC). The Fair Labor Standards Act of 1938 prohibited the shipment of goods produced by oppressive child labor. Investigations and inspections of child labor were done by the Chief of the Children's Bureau in the Department of Labor.

More recent legislation is attempting to expand governmental support for the development of children. The Omnibus Reconciliation Act of 1986 (Public Law 99-509) gave states the authority to expand Medicaid eligibility to include a new group of previously ineligible pregnant women. These women have incomes above the state's standards for Aid to Families with Dependent Children (AFDC) but below the Federal poverty level. States can select any standard for the extension as long as the standard is below the federal poverty level. By January 1988, 26 states had expanded Medicaid eligibility.

The Omnibus Reconciliation Act of 1987 (Public Law 100-203) permitted states to offer Medicaid to infants whose family incomes are below 185% of the Federal poverty level, and to children up to age 8 whose family incomes are below the poverty level. One of the problems with Medicaid-affiliated programs is the limited participation by physicians because of low Medicaid reimbursement fees. Insurance coverage continues to be a problem. In 1986, 14% to 19% of all American children under the age of 13 had no health insurance eligibility (U.S. Congress, Office of Technology Assessment, 1988). There is a direct relationship between family income and the use of health care services for children; it has been found that very poor children who have access to Medicaid are more similar to middle-income children in the use of medical care than are other poor or low-income children (U.S. Congress, Office of Technology Assessment, 1988). There has been a decline in the number of children receiving

Medicaid—from 95% in the 1970s to 75% in 1982. Even though there have been increased allocations to health financing and social support programs, fewer children receive aid because of eligibility restrictions and benefit declines (Miller et al., 1985).

Each state receives funding under the Preventive Health and Health Services Block Grant. The state determines how the funds are spent in the following categories:

Health education and risk reduction

Comprehensive public health services

Emergency medical services

Home health services

Rodent control

Community and school-based fluoridation

Detection and prevention of hypertension

Rape crisis and prevention services (U.S. Congress, Office of Technology Assessment, 1988)

The Head Start Program, which began in 1965, provides educational, social, nutritional, and medical services to low-income preschool children. It is administered locally, and there are 1305 programs today (U.S. Congress, Office of Technology Assessment, 1988). Medical services are also provided. These services include complete physical examinations with vision and hearing screening, the identification of handicapping conditions, immunizations, a dental examination, and mental health and nutritional services. Treatment is provided for conditions identified through the program.

Under Section 330 of the Public Health Services Act, community health centers are made available. The goal of these centers is to provide primary care to medically underserved areas. Services are provided on a sliding fee scale based on family income and size. Families under the federal poverty level get free care.

The same bureau that administers community health centers, the Bureau of Health Care Delivery and Assistance, also administers migrant health centers. The Indian Health Service, part of the Public Health Services, offers free health care services to Native American and children who are natives of Alaska.

States enact other laws to protect children, such as seat belt laws and screening for genetic birth defects. Further protection is provided by the Consumer Product Safety Commission, created in 1972 (Public Law 92-573). This commission has the authority to mandate safety standards for any consumer product that may pose an "unreasonable risk" of injury or illness (U.S. Congress, Office of Technology Assessment, 1988). The Product Safety Commission regulates bicycles, toys, childproof caps on drugs and household products, all-terrain vehicles (ATVs), hot water heaters, and other products attractive to children. There is also a Poison Prevention Packaging Act passed in 1970 (Public Law 91-601), which requires that all potentially hazardous household chemicals and drugs be sold in child-resistant packaging.

## Nutrition

In the mid 1930s the Agricultural Adjustment Act gave millions of dollars and surplus food to the U.S. Department of Agriculture (USDA). Schools and relief programs became the beneficiaries of the surplus food. In 1947 the School Lunch Program was made permanent, and in 1965 the Special Milk Program provided for milk distribution in schools, summer camps, and other institutions. In 1966, nutrition efforts were directed toward the poor and disadvantaged by the Child Nutrition Act. This was followed in 1967–68 by the Supplemental Food Program, which supplied special nutritionally sound food packages to babies and pregnant women (Hayes, 1982). Unfortunately, the nutrition of this group did not improve significantly, probably because the food was shared with other family members. As a result the program was phased out in 1971–72.

However, the 1967–68 legislation provided a valuable foundation for the Special Supplemental Food Program for Women, Infants, and Children (WIC), which has continued since 1972. It is an amendment to the Child Nutrition Act and has a medical requirement for eligibility. A public interest law firm, the Food Research and Action Coalition (FRAC), brought a suit in 1973 to initiate the spending of WIC funds. An evaluation of infants in the WIC program in 1978 found that these infants displayed increases in weight, height, head circumference, and mean hemoglobin concentrations. Evaluation also found that anemia had decreased (Hayes, 1982). In addition to legislation for nutrition, there has also been legislation dealing with child abuse, day care, and children with disabilities.

## Child Abuse and Neglect

Laws requiring mandatory reporting of suspected cases of child abuse and neglect began in earnest in the 1960s. In 1974, the Federal Child Abuse Prevention and Treatment Act was passed. All 50 states and the District of Columbia have laws defining child maltreatment and mandating that professionals working with children report suspected cases.

Most state laws require that the agency that receives a report of abuse or neglect initiate an investigation within 48 hours, and that appropriate action be taken to protect the child. Reportable cases are suspected cases of abuse or neglect in which the children are younger than 18 years of age. Nurses and other professionals must report suspected cases. Some states authorize the immediate removal of the child from the environment.

## Day Care

Legislation regulating child day care resulted from an awareness that children who are placed for temporary or time-limited care must have some protection. The National Institute of Child Health and Human Development was established in 1960. Basically, the day care legislation (the Welfare Reform Act of 1962, the Work Incentive Program of 1967, and the Family Assistance Plan of 1969) recognizes a need to break a poverty cycle by providing care for children in order to enable the parents to seek employment or to enhance the child's physical, emotional, and cognitive development. The Head Start Program of 1964 is an example of this type of legislation (Hayes, 1982). The Federal Interagency Day Care Requirements (1980) mandated strict staff-to-child ratios.

Legislation was also needed to make working, rather than public assistance, attractive to families with marginal incomes. An early attempt was the Child Care Deduction (1954). A Presidential Commission on the Status of Women was created by President Kennedy in 1961. This commission suggested changing the allowable child care deductions. The Equal Pay Act of 1963, and revisions to it, have further raised the allowable deductions. In 1967, an amendment to the Social Security Act provided aid to families with dependent children.

As more and more women have entered the work force, society has had to respond to their needs. In 1976, Child Care Credit, which appeared to give more tax relief to low- and middle-income groups than that received through itemized deductions, was enacted.

### Handicapped Children

Child health policy for handicapped and poor children is reflected in two programs: the Maternal and Child Health Program (Title V) and Medicaid (Title XIX) provisions of the Social Security Act (Goggin, 1987). An earlier program, the Early and Periodic Screening and Treatment Program of 1968 (EPSDT), an amendment to Title XIX of the Social Security Act, never really lived up to its potential. States were allowed unrestricted time to implement the program; however, four years after its initiation none of the nine states audited were in compliance. The program was redesigned, resulting in the 1977 Child Health Assessment Program (CHAP). It should be noted that none of the CHAP bills were ever enacted into law (Goggin, 1987). Further reform attempts were made in 1981 but were unsuccessful.

The Education for All Handicapped Act (Public Law 94-142) guarantees all children the right to free, appropriate education. Every child with a handicap must have an Individualized Education Plan (IEP): a written plan developed by the teacher, a special education teacher, and an expert in the evaluation of handicapped children and their parents. An amendment to this legislation mandates that states provide comprehensive programs for children from birth to age three. (This legislation is described further in Chapter 20.)

Advocates for children are vigilant and are consis-

tently proposing legislation to protect children and to promote their welfare. Legislation that has had an impact on child welfare is summarized in Table 1-4.

## Current Problems and Future Directions

Whereas many childhood diseases have been either eradicated or controlled by immunizations, many problems still remain. New diseases, such as AIDS, and new strains of illness continue to present public health challenges. Although neonatology has become a major subspecialty, and the survival rate for preterm infants has dramatically increased, some of these children have associated cognitive and motor disabilities. Care is costly; can the cost be minimized? What about the long-term costs? Can disabled persons finally be recognized as important contributors to society? What can be done to reverse the high black infant mortality rate?

Accidental injuries continue to be the leading cause of death in children after the first few months of life. Restraints have helped, but more can be done to ensure compliance and to better protect car drivers and passengers. Table 1-5 lists actions that can be taken to reduce the number of deaths of children from accidental injuries.

With changes in family structure the need for quality day care for all is being pursued. A question that must follow relates to the extent of governmental involvement in the care of children and the transmission of values.

There has been a rise in the number of immigrants from impoverished countries. Many of their health beliefs and customs are different from those of Americans. However, as with all new immigrants to this country, they must be assimilated, and their special health care needs must be taken into consideration. The needs of immigrants include nutritional counseling, health promotion, and treatment of illnesses endemic to their homelands.

*Table 1–4.  Legislation Affecting Child Welfare*

| Year | Legislation |
|------|-------------|
| 1935 | Social Security Act |
| 1938 | Fair Labor Standards Act |
| 1947 | School Lunch Program |
| 1965 | Special Milk Program |
| 1966 | Child Nutrition Act |
| 1967–68 | Supplemental Food Program |
| 1972 | Special Supplemental Food Program for Women, Infants, and Children (WIC); Education for All Handicapped Act (Public Law 94-142) |
| 1986 | Omnibus Reconciliation Act (Public Law 99-509) |
| 1987 | Omnibus Reconciliation Act (Public Law 100-203) |

Helmets for bicyclists
Barriers around swimming pools
Universal use of smoke detectors
Window bars in windows above the first floor
Hot water heater temperatures of no more than 120°F
Stringent limits on the sales and use of ATVs
No right-turn-on-red laws

(Congress of the United States, Office of Technology Assessment. (1988). *Healthy children: Investing in the future* [OTA-H-345], p. 16. Washington, D.C.: U.S. Government Printing Office)

Related to this is a world-wide perspective. Millions of children continue to starve to death each year or succumb to diseases that have known cures. International and private organizations are working to try to maximize health care for all children.

The future also holds questions about health care in different atmospheric pressures. What might be the implications or special concerns if a child is born in space? What will be the health concerns for families living in space stations?

## Changes in the Health Care System Affecting Pediatric Nursing

### Technological Advances

Technology within the health care system has advanced more in the past several decades than at any other time in the history of modern medicine. Sophisticated equipment and modern technology now give the health care profession a far greater variety of options and abilities to prevent, diagnose, and treat illnesses. For example, sophisticated screening devices and laboratory tests now enable doctors and nurses to detect congenital problems in utero; countless cases of sudden infant death syndrome (SIDS) are now prevented with the use of apnea monitors; and magnetic resonance imaging (MRI) provides far clearer images of abnormalities than x-rays. In addition, many procedures that were once limited to use in hospitals, such as tracheostomy care and chemotherapy, are now performed routinely in the home.

The implications of technological advances for pediatric nursing practice are very evident. Nurses have a tremendous responsibility to keep abreast of the latest advances in all aspects of nursing care. Equipment and drug therapies change almost daily, thus increasing the need for patient and family teaching and discharge planning. Nursing research continues to refine the ways in which pediatric nurses promote health, assess, diagnose, intervene, and evaluate.

### Public Awareness

As technological advances have taken place, so has public awareness of the health care system, signs and symptoms of illness, and treatment alternatives. Patients' "blind faith" in the health care professions has been replaced by "informed consumerism." Patients and families are far more aware of their rights and are becoming increasingly vocal in exercising their rights. Whereas it was once almost unheard of to question the advice or opinion of a physician, it is now becoming standard procedure to request a second opinion before a major treatment regimen is begun. In fact, most insurance carriers require that patients obtain a second opinion. An increase in public awareness of health issues has also been demonstrated by the dramatic increase in the number of medical malpractice cases that are initiated each year.

Nurses, in their roles as child and family teachers and advocates, have a responsiblity to be certain that parents and children are informed regarding health promotion, health problems, and treatment alternatives. Because of their close contact with children and families, nurses are in an excellent position to help them become informed consumers and active participants in health promotion and health care delivery.

### Increased Costs of Health Care

Increased costs have come along with advances in health care technology. In 1987, the total cost of health care accounted for 11.1% of the gross national product. In 1988, the only items for which Americans spent more money than medical care ($433 billion) were food and tobacco ($596.6 billion) and housing ($501.3 billion)(Statistical Abstract of the United States, 1990).

Although normal inflation has taken its toll on health care costs, a variety of other factors have also increased the cost. Research and development, a necessary part of technological advancement, is expensive. The continuing development and testing of new drugs used to prevent and treat illnesses is extremely costly. Many routine procedures that were once performed by health care professionals are now done with sophisticated equipment, but not without a high cost.

As noted above, as public awareness of health care has increased, so has the number of malpractice suits, some of which are justified, while others are frivolous. The increased cost of malpractice insurance is, for the most part, reflected in higher costs to the consumers of health care services. In order to avoid expensive litigation, additional diagnostic tests are frequently ordered, thus raising the cost to consumers and insurance companies.

Additionally, much of the increased cost associated with health care can be attributed to unnecessary or questionable spending. Ordering additional diagnostic or lab studies "just to be safe" certainly raises the cost of health care. Improper use of equipment and unnecessary use of supplies also increases costs.

## Cost Containment

Many steps have been taken in recent years to attempt to curtail the rising cost of health care. One fundamental change is the increasing emphasis on health promotion and health maintenance. Nurses continue to play an important role in the prevention of illness and the promotion of wellness. Child health nurses are in an excellent position to be able to provide parents and children with guidance directed toward optimization of health.

Other changes have taken place within the health care delivery system. Health maintenance organizations (HMOs) offer subscribers prepaid health care services, generally provided within group practices. By providing comprehensive care to individuals and families, HMOs are able to reduce costs by eliminating duplication of services. In general, HMOs have proved to be a cost-effective method of health care delivery.

Another method of cost containment has been to limit the length of hospitalizations in all but critical cases. Many surgical procedures that formerly required one or more days of hospitalization are now being done in ambulatory surgical settings, with patients being admitted and discharged the same day.

Although the impact on the care of children is not yet completely known, diagnostic related groups (DRGs) have had a definite effect on much of the health care industry. DRGs are used to establish fixed payments for Medicare reimbursement of hospital care of patients with similar problems. If the hospital is able to provide adequate care for less than the predetermined payment, it makes a profit. However, if the cost of providing care exceeds the payment, the hospital loses the difference. Thus, hospitals have a strong financial incentive to release patients as early as possible, often while they are still in need of acute care. There is still controversy over early discharges, and the reality is that much of the burden for discharge planning and for providing home health care falls on nursing. Pediatric nurses are often faced with having to teach apprehensive parents or care givers how to perform procedures on sick children.

## Concepts Related to Pediatric Nursing

### Nursing Process as a Tool for Practice

A systematic method of resolving problems is the mark of scientific inquiry. Although the nursing profession has long used the scientific method, the *nursing process* was formally identified by Yura and Walsh in 1967. The steps of the process are sequential yet interrelated (Fig. 1-5).

*Health assessment* involves collecting objective and subjective data in order to form a data base. The complete nursing assessment includes the health history, a health examination, and the review of laboratory and diagnostic test results. Data may be collected from parents, or from children when they are old enough to participate, and supplemented by parents or caregivers.

Analysis of the data gathered during the assessment stage leads to the next step of the nursing process, the formulation of a *nursing diagnosis*. The diagnosis presents directions for interventions. Diagnostic groupings of the nursing diagnoses accepted by the North American Nursing Diagnosis Association (NANDA) are listed in Chapter 6. A nursing diagnosis is the statement of a health need that can be influenced by nursing interventions. It reflects client behaviors that maintain and promote health. Also, it may lead to an actual health need or problem, or the diagnosis may indicate the presence of a health need or problem. The nursing diagnoses listed are being evaluated and are subject to change.

The *planning* phase involves setting priorities, stating goals and objectives, and selecting nursing actions. Life-threatening problems are followed by actual and potential problems. Most goals are mutually derived by the nurse and the client or the nurse and the caregiver. Care is given during the *intervention* phase, and information is gathered to be used for the *evaluation*. The efficiency and effectiveness of the nursing actions are measured. A comparison is made to the stated outcome criteria and goals. It may be necessary to reassess and repeat the steps in the nursing process.

Using the nursing process in caring for children requires that nurses understand growth and development and family interactions. Nurses must also understand health promotion and health problems. Using the nursing process encourages a holistic approach to child care and, by its systematic nature, provides for incorporation of principles in a logical manner.

Because the nursing process is a systematic and logical method for the care of chidren and their families, it has been adopted as the organizational framework for this text. Although the nursing process is applicable to all clients and patients and their families, there are some variations in its application in child health nursing. Therefore, Chapters 5 through 9 are devoted to each step of the nursing process. Special care has been take to ensure that specific adaptations of the nursing process that apply to children and their families have been incorporated.

The American Nurses Association has developed *Standards of Maternal–Child Health Nursing Practice*, which are based on the nursing process. These standards identify essential characteristics of quality nursing care.

### Nursing Theory as a Basis for Practice

Theories attempt to depict or explain events in the real world so that predictions can be made and appropriate interventions can be planned. What distinguishes nursing theory from other theories is the specific consideration of

The Nursing Process in Child Health Care

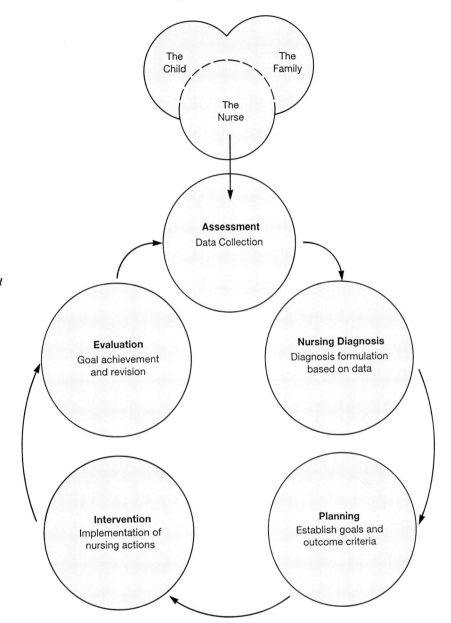

*Figure 1–5.    The nursing process in child health care.*

the relationship(s) among four major concepts: the nurse, the client, health, and the environment.

Nurses who study a variety of theories usually select one that makes the most sense for them in their practice (i.e., that which explains and directs the practice actions to be taken). The identification and use of a theory base for practice distinguishes professionals from nonprofessionals.

A theory base for nursing practice influences the specific data obtained during history taking, the analysis of data in terms of the theory, the implementation of activities based on a scientific/theoretical base, and the evaluation design. Theory, research, and practice must be linked conceptually. Trying to make an ex post facto fit of theory and research with existing practice seldom works.

## Nursing Theories Related to Pediatric Nursing Practice

No nursing theories have yet been developed that are specific to pediatric nursing practice, but many of the existing theories can be adapted for use with children and their families. A brief synopsis of five nursing theories is presented as a means of stimulating further interest in analyzing theories and incorporating theory into practice.

*Nightingale* (1860) clearly emphasized that nursing should be concerned with the environment. She felt that nature would heal but that it needed assistance from nurses in manipulating the environment in ways that would restore or preserve health, or prevent or cure

## American Nurses' Association Standards of Maternal–Child Health Nursing Practice

### Standard I

Maternal and child health nursing practice is characterized by the continual questioning of the assumptions upon which practice is based, retaining those which are valid and searching for and using new knowledge.

### Standard II

Maternal and child health nursing practice is based upon knowledge of the biophysical and psychosocial development of individuals from conception through the childrearing phase of development and upon knowledge of the basic needs for optimum development.

### Standard III

The collection of data about the health status of the client/patient is systematic and continuous. The data are accessible, communicated and recorded.

### Standard IV

Nursing diagnoses are derived from data about the health status of the patient.

### Standard V

Maternal and child health nursing practice recognizes deviations from expected patterns of physiologic activity and anatomic and psychosocial development.

### Standard VI

The plan of nursing care includes goals derived from the nursing diagnoses.

### Standard VII

The plan of nursing care includes priorities and the prescribed nursing approaches or measures to achieve the goals derived from the nursing diagnoses.

### Standard VIII

Nursing actions provide for client/patient participation in health promotion, maintenance and restoration.

### Standard IX

Maternal and child health nursing practice provides for the use and coordination of all services that assist individuals to prepare for responsible sex roles.

### Standard X

Nursing actions assist the client/patient to maximize his health capabilities.

### Standard XI

The client's/patient's progress or lack of progress toward goal achievement is determined by the client/patient and the nurse.

### Standard XII

The client's/patient's progress or lack of progress toward goal achievement directs reassessment, reordering of priorities, new goal setting and revision of the plan of nursing care.

### Standard XIII

Maternal and child health nursing practice evidences active participation with others in evaluating the availability, accessibility and acceptability of services for parents and children and cooperating and/or taking leadership in extending and developing needed services in the community.

(From American Nurses Association. [1983]. *Standards of maternal-child health nursing practice.* Kansas City: American Nurses Association. Used with permission)

disease and injury. This manipulation included keeping the air as pure as possible and keeping utensils and equipment used for and by the patient clean. To control the environment, Nightingale stressed elimination of odors and reduction of noises and emphasized serving appropriate portions of food. When caring for children it is easy to understand how the environment is, can, or should be controlled.

*Orem's self-care theory* focuses primarily on nursing. Orem describes her self-care deficit theory of nursing as a general theory composed of three related theories: self-

care, self-care deficit, and nursing systems. Most of Orem's early theory development dealt with the nursing care of adults. She states that nursing care of young children may involve direct care or providing assistance to parents/caregivers in order to help them care for their children. Caring for, acting for, or doing for, and providing an environment that promotes development are valid ways for providing nursing care for infants and young children (Orem, 1985). It is essential for nurses to know developmental progressions and to communicate in ways that foster trust. Nursing based on this theory is related to the child's therapeutic self-care demands, self-care agency (specialized abilities), and the relationships between them. There are three types of nursing care: wholly compensatory, partially compensatory, and self-care. This theory allows children to assume care for themselves as they are prepared to do so. The goal is optimal wellness.

*Roy's adaptation theory* emphasizes interactions as stimulated by an individual's attempts at adapting. Adaptability is the capacity for behavior that is in accord with the attainment of goals and with maintenance of a valued state. A positive response to environmental stimuli necessitates adaptation. Stimuli evoking these responses may be focal, background, or residual. Parents and family members may be conceptualized as stimuli. The function of nursing is to support and promote client adaptation. The client—the child and family—is assessed for adaptation abilities, and interventions are planned, as necessary, to promote adaptation. Adaptations are made in four modes: basic physiological needs, self-concept, role mastery, and interdependence. Nurses using this framework differentiate and manipulate the stimuli so that they fall within the client's zone of positive coping (Roy, 1981). Goals are mutually decided by the client, the child and parents, and nurse. The nurse provides intervention options.

*King's theory of goal attainment* (1981) is usually considered an interpersonal theory. King identifies relationships about fundamental concepts for the practice of nursing. The major concepts of the theory are interaction, perception, communication, transaction, role, stress, growth and development, and time and space. King identifies a dynamic interacting system with three distinct levels of operations: individuals, groups, and society. King has indicated that this framework is appropriate for use with children when one expands the definition of communication to include nonverbal communication. Perceptions of the client and the nurse must be assessed. It is important in implementing this theory to set mutual goals, to develop plans with alternate means to achieve goals, and to evaluate goal attainment. Human interactions are classified as reactions, interactions, and transactions with transactions being the desired purposeful interaction.

*Neuman's health care system model* can be useful for the analysis of individuals or groups. The design of the model reflects the complexity of the health care delivery system today (Neuman, 1982). The model presents a total person approach as a means for understanding individuals and their environments. Stressors impinge on people and may reach the basic structure energy resources if they can penetrate flexible and normal lines of defense and resistance that serve to protect the basic structure. Early intervention is recommended when stressors are suspected. The model also includes three levels of prevention: primary, secondary, and tertiary. Because perception influences nursing care, the client's and the nurse's perceptions must be assessed. Neuman cites the use of the model for assessment of two child day care centers (Neuman, 1982).

A number of nursing theorists have developed frameworks for nursing care. Some of these are applicable to the care of children. It is impossible to list all of these nursing theorists; the reader is advised to consult a book on nursing theories for more theorists and for more in-depth information on the theorists presented here.

## Integrating Knowledge in Child Health Nursing

Child health care nurses (pediatric nurses) have an important role to play in advancing health care for children. In order to provide direct care to children and families, child health care nurses must possess and integrate into their practices knowledge from supportive disciplines such as anatomy, physiology, pharmacology, nutrition, growth and development, and communication. They must also be advocates for children and must lead the fight for social policies to reduce mortality and morbidity.

The systems approach to child health care requires that nurses understand how the various interactions that occur affect the child. Some of the systems that could have an impact on the child include interactions among the child, the parents, nurses, and other health professionals; changes in the environment, such as family moves or financial losses; and cultural variables such as dietary restrictions. Nurses need to be aware that changes within one of the child's systems can cause multiple changes within other systems. Working with parents and children in setting goals and implementing and evaluating care helps to maximize progress.

## Expanded Roles, Professional Organizations, and Publications

Nurses who are involved in caring for children usually join either general professional organizations or specialized groups such as Pediatric Intensive Care Nurses or Neonatal Nurses. Within the American Nurses Association (ANA) there is a Maternal-Child Council. The nurse with advanced preparation can become certified by the ANA as a pediatric nurse practitioner/pediatric or child health specialist, school nurse practitioner/school health specialist, or pediatric nurse (child and adolescent nurse).

Nurses who have successfully completed the certification examination are entitled to use the letters RNC (Registered Nurse, Certified) after their names. It is also possible to be certified by the ANA as a Clinical Specialist in Child and Adolescent Psychiatric and Mental Health Nursing. These graduates use the initials RN, CS (Registered Nurse, Certified Specialist). Pediatric Nurse Practitioners can join NAPNAP, the National Association for Pediatric Nurse Associate/Practitioners. Pediatric Nurse Practitioners can be certified by NAPNAP or by the ANA. Nurses certified by NAPNAP use the letters CPNP (Certified Pediatric Nurse Practitioner).

There are many journals available for child health nurses. Nursing journals focusing on pediatric topics of interest to nursing include *Pediatric Nursing, Journal of Pediatric Health Care, Maternal Child Nursing,* and *Issues in Comprehensive Pediatric Nursing.* There are also medical journals and journals from other disciplines, including *Pediatrics, American Journal of Diseases of Children, Archive of Diseases in Childhood, Clinical Pediatrics, Pediatric Clinics of North America, Child and Family,* and *Child Development,* among others. A variety of newsletters are also available through drug and baby formula companies.

## Summary

Caring for children in a professional manner requires knowledge concerning how children are viewed and how families function. Nurses must be aware of current legislation pertaining to children and must be proactive advocates for children in order to obtain needed legislation.

The mark of a profession relates to theory development and use. Family theories are discussed in Chapter 2, and Growth and Development theories are discussed in Chapter 4. Nursing theories and models have been developing at a more accelerated pace over the last twenty years. Designing nursing care from a theoretical base influences the application of the nursing process. Sometimes agencies (hospitals, schools of nursing, etc.) adopt one nursing theory to be used within that agency. It is more common, however, for individual nurses to identify and use the theory with which they feel most comfortable for administering care and for research.

Child health is a subspecialty in nursing, and neophytes in the field need to become aware of the publications and organizations that facilitate the sharing of ideas and current research in the field. Involvement in these types of activities also differentiates professional nurses from others interested in caring for children.

## References

Bowlby, J. (1963). *Child care and the growth of love.* Baltimore: Penguin Books.

Cherry, B. S., & Carty, R.M. (1986). Changing concepts of childhood in society. *Pediatric Nursing, 12,* 421–424.

Fair Labor Standards Act of 1938. (1938). *United States Statutes at Large,* 25 June 1938, pp. 75–718, 52, p. 1067.

Goggin, M. L. (1987). *Policy design and the politics of implementation.* Knoxville: University of Tennessee Press.

Hayes, C. D. (1982). *Making policies for children: A study of the federal process.* Washington, D.C.: National Academy Press.

King, I. M. (1981). *A theory for nursing.* New York: John Wiley & Sons.

Miller, C. A., Coulter, E. J., Fine, A., Adams-Taylor, S., & Schorr, L. B. (1985). 1984 update on the world economic crisis and the children: A United States case study. *International Journal of Health Services, 15,* 431–450.

National Academy of Sciences. (1987). *Risking the future: Adolescent sexuality, pregnancy and childbearing.* Washington, DC: National Academy Press.

Neuman, B. (1982). *The Neuman systems model.* Norwalk, CT: Appleton-Century-Crofts.

Nightingale, F. (1969). *Notes on nursing.* New York: Dover Publications. (Original work published 1860)

Orem, D. M. (1985). *Nursing: Concepts of practice.* New York: McGraw-Hill.

Robertson, J. (1958). *Young children in hospitals.* New York: Basic Books.

Roy, Sr. C., & Roberts, S. L. (1981). *Theory construction in nursing: An adaptation model.* Englewood Cliffs, NJ: Prentice-Hall.

Spitz, R.A. (1945). Hospitalism: An inquiry into the genesis of psychiatric conditioning in early childhood. *Psychoanalytic Studies of the Child, 1,* 53–74.

*Statistical abstract of the United States, 1990.* (1990). Washington, D.C.: U.S. Government Printing Office.

U. S. Congress, Office of Technology Assessment. (1988). *Healthy children: Investing in the future.* (OTA-H-345) Washington, D.C.: U.S. Government Printing Office.

Yura, H., & Walsh, M. (1967). *Nursing process.* New York: Appleton-Century-Crofts.

## Bibliography

Pollack, L.A. (1983). *Forgotten children: Parent–child relations from 1500–1900.* Cambridge: Cambridge University Press.

U. S. Department of Health and Human Services. (1980). *Learning together: A guide for families with genetic disorders.* (DHHS Publication No. HSA 80-5131) Rockville, MD: Health Services Administration.

# Family and Cultural Concepts Affecting Pediatric Nursing

Richard E. Harbin

*Sculpture by Charles Parks*

*Historical Concept of the Family in the United States*

*Today's Families*

*Varieties of Family Structure*
    *The Nuclear Family*
    *The Extended Family*
    *The Single-Parent Family*
    *The Gay/Lesbian Family*
    *The Adolescent-Parent Family*
    *The Stepfamily or Blended Family*
    *The One-Child Family*
    *The Older-Parent Family*
    *Alternative Family Structures*
    *The Homeless Family*

*Family Developmental Stages and Tasks*

*Family Function Assessment*

*Culture, Ethnicity, and Environment*
    *Heritage Consistency*

*Ethnic Family Organization*
    *Acculturation and Assimilation*

*Heritage-Consistent Family Concepts*
    *Collecting Data*
    *The Interview*
    *The Hot/Cold Health Model*

*The Asian Family*

*The Hispanic Family*

*The Black-African Family*

*The Native American Family*

*Parenting*

*Discipline*
    *Corporal Punishment*
    *Psychological Intervention*
    *Behavior Modification*

*Summary*

The past 150 years have seen a dramatic change in the health care of children. Children were historically viewed as miniature adults and considered the property of their parents. The value of children to the community was measured in economic terms. That view is in marked contrast to the current status afforded children as our country's future and one of its most precious resources. The evolution of family and cultural influences involving child rearing brings us to the present recognition and appreciation of children as unique individuals with their own qualities and specific needs.

The evolution of this attitude toward children has also shifted the focus of child health care from an acute illness model to a holistic approach that encompasses the physical, emotional, social, and environmental aspects of health. An important factor in this change is the emphasis on disease prevention and health promotion.

These changes have had an impact on the role of nurses and have created changes in the health care delivery system. The nurse's role has changed to incorporate not only caretaking but also child advocacy. Contemporary child health nurses are members of the health care team, providing total care to children and families.

## Historical Concept of the Family in the United States

The family in colonial America was a highly structured and organized unit, traditionally headed by the male. The general health and survival of children were at great risk. Uncontrolled epidemics were common and specific treatments were unknown. Epidemic diseases included smallpox, measles, mumps, cholera, whooping cough, diphtheria, and others. It is interesting to note that despite such epidemic diseases, dysentery was the principal cause of childhood death in colonial times.

The typical colonial family lived and farmed in a rural area, and all family members were expected to work at the difficult task of farming. There were few physicians, and most of those lacked formal medical training. Child care information in printed form was scarce and usually of little value because of the high illiteracy rate. Medical care was available only to those who could pay and was limited to the more populated areas. Childhood was only beginning to be considered as a recognized stage of life, and children's names and birth dates had just begun to be recorded.

In the decades before the Civil War, there was an increased recognition and interest in children and the process of child rearing. Parents believed that rigid schedules molded children to the parents' desire. Mothers assumed the role as children's disciplinarians and were responsible for their character development; fathers played a very minimal role in child rearing.

The major health issues for children at the turn of the 20th century were sanitation and infection control. Communicable diseases were prevalent, and contaminated milk was a major health hazard. Rigid child rearing practices and schedules were still advocated by experts. It was not until after World War II that a more relaxed approach toward child rearing became accepted.

## Today's Families

Changing and adapting a set of beliefs about health and child-rearing practices involves looking at the manner in which individuals arrange themselves in groups to fulfill their needs. The family is among the most important of these groups.

The family has been defined in many ways. The traditional definition specifies that a family is composed of individuals related by blood or marriage. This definition is commonly expanded to include other people such as aunts and uncles. Household membership may also be considered as a functional definition of family membership (Karpel, 1983). Many traditional views of the family have changed as societal roles and relationships have changed. The family unit may require a more fluid defini-

tion, but the basic family functions, as described in Table 2-1, remain unchanged. The family is characterized by mutual availability of its members to one another, responsiveness to socially accepted norms for behavior and symbolic meanings, an identity as a family, a common living territory, and a shared history.

Nurses need to understand and support the basic functions of the family. A fundamental nursing goal is to provide family-centered nursing care. Viewing the family as a unit means that no single family member can receive effective care unless every member of the family is considered. Nurses must remember that other members of the family affect and are affected by the care provided. Nurses should recognize families' primary responsibility for children and their role in child development.

Families are children's principal nurturing and socializing force. Functional families provide optimal nurturing environments for children. One role of nurses working with children and families is to identify primary caretakers and those who provide support. Family units must be accurately understood and described in order to gain a clear view of children's total environment. One nursing goal is to observe child and family behavior. This assessment usually involves observation over a period of time and in a variety of settings. Nursing assessment should focus on the children's interaction within the family unit, with an awareness that observed behavior may not accurately represent the child's actual daily experiences.

## Varieties of Family Structure

The family's ability to function effectively depends on structure: the organization of relationships among members. Structural requirements of the family depend on the functions it has to perform and what these tasks demand of the family.

There is no fixed pattern of family structure across cultures. It is culture, not biology, that determines the rules of organization within the family. Most primitive societies were organized along matrilineal lines. Women were the heads of families and controlled all major decisions regarding the family. Eventually men assumed control of the family, and patrilineal organization emerged with the development of agriculture and the concept of property ownership, which made the transfer from father

### Table 2-1. Basic Functions of the Family

Ensure survival of the unit
Raise and develop its members
Provide physical needs
Give love, recognition, and security
Strengthen self-esteem

to son an important socioeconomic factor. Family structure affects the family's ability to meet its health care responsibilities. Today's family structures are varied and changing. A child may belong to, and experience, numerous family units during childhood.

Significant changes have occurred in the role structure of the American family and the patterns of child rearing. There is increased concern about the changing American family (Table 2-2). Many questions center on the family's ability to provide for and meet the needs of the next generation. The following trends have significantly altered more traditional family patterns:

1. An increased divorce rate
2. A rising number of mothers employed outside the home
3. Delayed marriage and childbearing
4. A decreasing birth rate
5. An increase in the number of single adults

These social trends all have an impact on the family.

## The Nuclear Family

The nuclear family consists of a man, a woman, and their offspring (natural or adopted) living in a common household. The marital tie, either legal or common, is the principal binding force in this unit. The household in the nuclear family may also include additional persons such as friends, foster children, or relatives.

## The Extended Family

This family unit includes the nuclear family plus relatives. The unit may include two or more nuclear families affiliated across generations to include grandparents, aunts, uncles, or cousins. Extended families are usually headed by a resident family member who provides leadership. Interdependency among members for emotional, social, and material support also characterizes this type of family unit. The decline of the extended family means that few children have the experience of growing up in a household of related adults. Geographic distances have further disintegrated this unit. Although there has been a change in extended families, grandparents still play an important role in relation to children in our society, especially in some cultures (Fig. 2-1).

Friendship and emotional support are reasons for maintaining family ties. The increase in the number of mothers working outside the home has affected dependency on relatives to provide child care. The extended family has endured among low-income and poverty-level families owing to economic necessity. The extended family structure is also prevalent among families that are poorly assimilated culturally or those that resist assimilation. Mutual support among members and shared languages and cultures provide comfort from within the family unit.

## The Single-Parent Family

This type of family unit accounts for an increasing proportion of families, owing to an increasing divorce rate and a more liberal atmosphere that allows single persons of either sex to adopt children. Nearly 26% of all children live in single-parent homes (U.S. Bureau of Census, 1985), and

*Table 2–2.  White, Black, and Hispanic Family Households, 1970–1988*

|  | 1970 (%) | 1980 (%) | 1985 (%) | 1988 (%) |
|---|---|---|---|---|
| **Married Couples** | | | | |
| White | 72.5 | 63.2 | 60.6 | 59.4 |
| Black | 53.3 | 40.0 | 36.6 | 36.1 |
| Hispanic | 70.1 | 61.9 | 57.8 | 56.2 |
| **Male Householder** | | | | |
| White | 1.8 | 8.6 | 9.2 | 9.2 |
| Black | 2.9 | 3.0 | 3.6 | 4.1 |
| Hispanic | 3.6 | 3.7 | 4.3 | 5.5 |
| **Female Householder** | | | | |
| White | 7.2 | 8.6 | 9.2 | 9.2 |
| Black | 2.9 | 3.0 | 3.6 | 4.1 |
| Hispanic | 13.3 | 16.6 | 18.5 | 18.8 |

(Source: U.S. Department of Commerce, Bureau of the Census. (1990). *Statistical abstract of the United States 1990:* Washington, DC: U.S. Government Printing Office, p. 46)

*Figure 2–1.  Grandparents continue to play an important role in the extended family.*

the great majority (89%) of these 6.7 million children live with their mothers (Norton, 1986) (Fig. 2-2).

The pattern of single-parent families is changing in two important aspects. The largest growing segment among single-parent households is "never married" mothers, who account for 28% of mother-headed families. There has also been a decline in the maternal age of single-parent families because of the increased number of younger, never-married mothers and the higher divorce rate among women who marry at very young ages (Norton, 1986).

There are also significant racial differences among single-parent families, with 59% of black children living in single-parent households compared with 20% of white children (U.S. Bureau of Census, 1985).

The economic disadvantage faced by women following divorce holds important implications for children in single-parent families. In 1980, the median income for mother-headed families was $11,789, compared with father-headed families' median income of $21,845. Fifty-five percent of the mother-headed single-parent families made less than $10,000 per year (U.S. Bureau of Census, Current Population Reports, 1985).

There are few conclusions about child health or functional consequences of living in a single-parent family. Studies indicate that when socioeconomic factors are accounted for, there are no significant differences in health status or psychological outcomes between children from single-parent homes and those from two-parent homes (Jennings, 1985; Blechman, 1982). However, single-parent family status is often associated with lower educational and economic status later in life (Mueller, 1986; Krein, 1986).

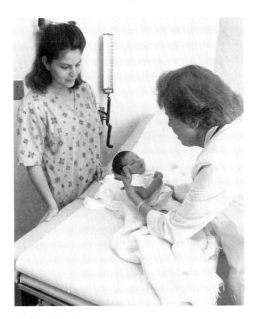

*Figure 2–2. Single-parent families continue to increase in the United States. (Courtesy Texas Tech University Health Sciences Center)*

## The Gay/Lesbian Family

Two same-sex adults living together, with or without children present, are regarded as a family. The developmental, social, and cultural implications for children within these family units are receiving increased attention and study. These family members usually deal with complex issues, including prejudice and discrimination. In addition, there are questions concerning sex role orientation and enactment. Nurses must accept the sexual orientation of these individuals in order to help gay and lesbian families deal with the problems of child rearing and health maintenance. Many communities have organizations or support groups to help these families, and nurses should be aware of them as possible referral sources.

## The Adolescent-Parent Family

There are nearly 500,000 births to adolescents in the United States every year (Congressional Budget Office, 1985). Adolescent parenthood is defined as fathering or giving birth to a child before the age of 18. Approximately half of these adolescents are married at the time of delivery, but the divorce rate for this group is four times greater than the national average for all marriages ending in divorce. Although adolescent parents may have the energy to deal with infants and toddlers, they usually lack the maturity and experience to administer effective solutions to child rearing problems. Adolescent parents may lack knowledge regarding health maintenance, safety, and immunization requirements. These parents also often lack knowledge of normal growth and development.

## The Stepfamily or Blended Family

The creation of a new family unit that blends families disrupted by divorce is common. The *stepfamily* is a family in which at least one adult is a stepparent; the most common form involves stepfathers. This family form, also called a *reconstituted* or *blended family,* is rapidly increasing owing to the rising divorce and remarriage rates in the last 10 to 15 years. More than 35 million adults are stepparents (Rubin, 1986), and one of every six children is a stepchild (Prosen, 1982). Whereas previously the non-biological parent was referred to as stepfather or stepmother, today the new parent in this unit is often addressed by first name or an endearing term.

Perhaps due to their increasing numbers, the stigma once attached to stepfamilies is disappearing. There are few differences between children and stepchildren in nuclear or single-parent households (Ganong, 1984). Children in these families do face unique challenges, most of them regarding new relationships. Although these challenges present pressures, they also allow children the opportunity to develop new skills and become more flexible and adaptable.

## The One-Child Family

The delay of pregnancy and the decision to limit family size has created an increase in the number of *one-child* families. The growth of this unit has created an interest in the "only" child and the possible advantages and disadvantages of being an only child.

## The Older-Parent Family

The current trend of delaying pregnancy has resulted in an increase in the birth rate for women aged 35–39 years. Older mothers are often career-oriented, and many resume employment following childbirth. This family unit is often more established and economically affluent. Older parents often find the demands of child rearing physically taxing because physical stamina usually decreases with age. However, the advantage of increased maturity levels may augment child rearing techniques and abilities.

## Alternative Family Structures

The *communal family* shares some of the attributes of an extended family structure. The number of communal families peaked in the United States during the 1960s and 1970s. These families are usually established because their members are dissatisfied with existing social systems. The members share beliefs, ideologies, and life goals.

Structure and roles in this unit vary widely from formal and defined patterns to informal groups with diffuse roles and relationships. Communal families often hold children's potential and freedom of creativity among their highest values. Children are encouraged to develop family relationships with other adults as well as with their own parents. There are so many forms of family structures within such an environment that it is difficult to make generalizations regarding child development characteristics or specific influences.

## The Homeless Family

The number of homeless families in America continues to increase (Committee on Government Operations, 1986). These families typically include single mothers with two or three children, usually of preschool age (Bassuk, 1987). The stress placed on these children is enormous and often results in health, psychological, and academic problems.

Shelters often provide optimal conditions for transmission of infectious and communicable diseases (Gross, 1987). Homeless children usually have an incomplete immunization status and face the possibility of physical and sexual abuse. Homeless adolescents have markedly in-

creased rates of pregnancy, sexually transmitted diseases, and alcohol and drug abuse (Wright, 1990). General morbidity among homeless children appears to be greater than among children in general. The plight of the homeless family—a complex problem created by recent trends in the United States' political economy—is a crisis for which we have instituted programs of amelioration rather than solutions.

## Family Developmental Stages and Tasks

The family is a dynamic system, growing and changing as it proceeds through the life cycle. The major functions of the family have been outlined, but many of these functions have been assumed by social institutions, e.g., schools and day care centers. Today's families face the challenge of providing for the relational needs of their members. Among these needs are love, nurturing, caring, support in adversity, intimacy, and self-acceptance. As nurses consider the trends affecting family structure and function, they must also be aware of the characteristics of families of today that address these relational and affective needs. It is important that nurses recognize, and be able to identify, the various family traits and patterns that are essential in childhood to provide for successful adulthood. This knowledge allows nurses to further examine family interactional patterns and the impact of social, cultural, and environmental influences.

It is clearly recognized that children must accomplish specific developmental tasks in order to succeed in growth and development. All children progress through these various stages at their own rate, and the parents' ability to understand this process and apply this knowledge to parenting can either enhance or retard a child's development. The child's developmental needs and progress are also affected by the parents' developmental needs as they deal with adult life cycle issues. These factors are further complicated by the married couple and the family as a whole progressing through their own developmental stages, which involves issues requiring adaptation at each stage.

The family life cycle is similar to that of individuals: it involves a series of periods characterized by states of change and stability. The family structure experiences instability during these periods of change. The family also experiences normative events, such as births, deaths, and school entry. Paranormative events, such as illness, conflict, and external factors, may also affect the family unit.

The stages of family life-cycle development described by Duvall (1977) are the foundation for developmental theories about the family. Duvall identified eight successive stages of development and related developmental tasks for the family, as shown in Table 2-3. As with individual development, the family can experience difficulty in

*Table 2–3.  Developmental Stages and Developmental Tasks of Families*

| Stage of Development | Developmental Tasks |
| --- | --- |
| 1. Newly married couple | Redirecting primary gratification from parents and friends into the marriage<br>Fitting into a new kin network<br>Planning for establishment of a family<br>Establishing and maintaining first home<br>Establishing mutually satisfactory ways of economic and emotional support<br>Attempting role negotiation<br>Beginning to establish identity as a family in the community |
| 2. Childbearing | Solidifying marriage<br>Having, adjusting to, and encouraging the development of infants<br>Negotiating and establishing parental roles<br>Establishing family as a stable unit<br>Reconciling conflicting developmental tasks of individual family members<br>Providing mutual support and growth<br>Establishing constructive patterns of family interaction |
| 3. Parents of preschool-age child(ren) | Continuing modification and adjudication of family roles<br>Encouraging individualization of each member over time<br>Adapting to the critical needs and interests of preschool children in stimulating, growth-promoting ways.<br>Maintaining constructive patterns of family interaction<br>Supplying adequate space, facilities, and equipment for the maturing family<br>Establishing economic stability<br>Interacting with the community<br>Beginning to establish family values and to make plans for the future |
| 4. Parents of school-age child(ren) | Fitting into the community in constructive ways<br>Encouraging children's educational achievement<br>Providing for privacy of family members<br>Keeping financially solvent<br>Planning for the future<br>Furthering socialization and growth of family members |
| 5. Parents of teenage child(ren) | Maintaining family integrity as some members seek to identify with others outside the family<br>Beginning to establish postparental interests and careers as growing parents<br>Providing facilities for widely divergent needs within the family<br>Keeping the marriage relationship in focus<br>Continuing kinship relationship<br>Supporting and tolerating family members |
| 6. Launching center | Reworking of parental roles to becoming parents of adult children<br>Releasing young adults into work, military |

*(continued)*

*Table 2–3.  Developmental Stages and Developmental Tasks of Families (Continued)*

| Stage of Development | Developmental Tasks |
| --- | --- |
| | service, college, marriage, and so forth with appropriate rituals and assistance<br>Maintaining a supportive home base<br>Rearranging physical facilities and resources<br>Meeting economic obligations<br>Continuing to build and modify the marriage relationship<br>Accepting new members into the family |
| 7. Middle-aged parents | Integrating and maintaining ties with both older and younger generations<br>Assuming role of children of aging parents<br>Planning for retirement<br>Resolving the empty-nest syndrome<br>Accepting illness, disability, and death of first-generation family members (parents' parents)<br>Assuming role of grandparents |
| 8. Aging family members | Accepting social, economic, and physical changes that occur with old age<br>Adjusting to retirement<br>Deciding on living arrangements of older family members<br>Accepting a new family generation<br>Adapting to loss and death |

(Lamberton, M. (1980). Alterations in family dynamics. In L.M. Shortridge & E.J. Lee (Eds.). *Introduction to nursing practice* (pp. 487–488). New York: McGraw-Hill. Adapted from Duvall, E.M. (1977). *Marriage and family development* (5th ed.). Philadelphia: J.B. Lippincott)

addressing the tasks of the next stage if it fails to accomplish the tasks associated with each preceding stage. A variety of frameworks for analyzing family development are based on Duvall's work.

Many factors influence the ability of families to meet developmental tasks. Changes in roles (particularly for men and women in dual-income households), added social and economic pressures, geographic isolation from support systems, and lack of governmental support for families can have an impact on a family's ability to accomplish developmental objectives. Nurses should assess a family's level of development by exploring roles, relationships, and activities within the family system. Nurses must have a clear understanding of the various family developmental stages and the tasks associated with each stage when assessing families.

## Family Function Assessment

In order to assess a child's health and to provide adequate health care, nurses need to understand the family's cultural environment. The social-cultural environment includes ethnic family and child rearing practices, economic status, educational levels, status in the community, reli-

gious beliefs, and availability of support systems. An initial family assessment is critical in order to initiate family-centered care. The information obtained can influence nursing interventions. Assessment of families with children or adolescents is important because implementation of the nursing care plan depends on the family's ability to consistently implement the plan.

The *family function assessment* is more accurate if it is conducted entirely or partially in the home environment. Accuracy is also increased if all family members participate. Specific interviewing techniques are helpful in making a family assessment. Conducting a portion of the interview with only the adult member(s) or with only the child or children present is an important technique. When the parent or child is alone with the nurse, he or she is more likely to develop a rapport with the nurse and provide more candid or truthful responses to questions. The assessment should include not only actual responses but also the nurse's observations of behavioral and emotional interactions. Nurses should use instruments that gather clinically relevant information. The instrument should measure specific nursing concerns for which nursing interventions may be planned.

Several objective data collection tools are available for assessing family function. Each instrument has strengths, as well as limitations, and may be used for specific purposes. The *Feetham Family Functioning Survey (FFFS)* (Feetham, 1982) is used to gather data about family functioning under stress. The tool takes about 10 minutes to complete and measures three major areas of family relationships:

- Between the family and broader social units such as school
- Between the family and its subsystems
- Between the family and individuals within the family

It is important to have both parents complete the tool to help identify discrepancies in their views of family life. The FFFS is useful for the assessment of traditional middle-class families with children.

The *Family Adaptability, Partnership, Growth, Affection, and Resolve (APGAR) Test* can be used to assess a family member's satisfaction with the family's functional state (Smilkstein, 1978). This questionnaire takes about five minutes to complete and can be used in a wide variety of family forms. This tool's utility is limited, however, because it does not help nurses identify specific intervention strategies.

The *Family Functioning Index (FFI)* was designed to identify families at risk (Pless, 1973). However, it does not measure the *level* of risk or distress. This tool is inappropriate for families with no children. Nurses might find the FFI helpful in assessing traditional families that include two parents and at least one child. The instrument cannot detect short- or long-term changes in family dynamics.

Table 2-4 presents a summary of nine family assessment tools. Each instrument has some value, although no one tool alone accomplishes a complete family assessment.

## Culture, Ethnicity, and Environment

Society, culture, and environment form the framework within which families exist. *Culture* is defined as a learned system of beliefs that includes values, attitudes, customs, and behaviors. Culture is shared by members of a particular social group; it is transmitted to new generations through a process called *enculturation.* Culture can be viewed as the human-made component of the environment. As members of specific ethnic groups, all children share a common background and culture with other members of the group. This shared culture often stems from a distinct geographic area as well as a common language, history, and religion.

Culture also influences how individuals view health and illness, health care systems, and health care providers. Culture determines the family's decision-making structure and also influences what type of health care is sought, as well as a wide variety of behaviors related to disease and illness.

Several basic principles of nursing care may need to be adjusted to make allowances for variations in culture. Touch is an important nursing concept, and generally nurses are encouraged to touch clients. Nurses should be aware, however, that some cultures view touch as an invasion of privacy or even as aggression. Culture may also influence the concept of time. This may have an impact on a client's perception concerning punctuality for medical appointments. Nurses must also realize that culture determines how individuals interact. This has important implications for nurses involved in the education and instruction of clients. In some cultures, for instance, individuals do not express feelings or question authority figures. Asian

*Table 2–4. Summary Characteristics of Nine Family Assessment Tools*

| Tool | Dimensions Measured | Understandable | Ease of Administration and Scoring | Appropriate for All Types of Families | Clinical Relevance |
|---|---|---|---|---|---|
| FFI[a] | Communication Togetherness Closeness Decision making Child orientation | Yes | 15 items Quickly administered Complicated scoring | Not for families without children or those with adult children | Not sensitive to short-term change |
| FAD[b] | Problem solving Communication Roles Affective responsiveness Affective involvement Behavior control General functioning | Yes | 53 items Easy to administer | Requires individual to "speak for family" | Measures areas that nurses could change through care plans |

*(continued)*

*Table 2–4. Summary Characteristics of Nine Family Assessment Tools (Continued)*

| Tool | Dimensions Measured | Understandable | Ease of Administration and Scoring | Appropriate for All Types of Families | Clinical Relevance |
|---|---|---|---|---|---|
| FES[c] | Relationships Personal growth System maintenance and change | Yes | 90 items, true/false Lengthy for clinical use (short form available) Scoring is complex. Standardized scores, two categories. | Universally appropriate | Useful to measure change after interventions |
| SFIS[d] | Enmeshment/disengagement Neglect/overprotection Rigidity/flexibility Conflict/avoidance Patient management Triangulation of parent/child coalition Detouring | Easier to understand for those familiar with Minuchin's family functioning theory | 85 items on 4-point agreement scale Easy to administer | Unknown at this time | Further testing required Useful for family counseling assessment |
| FFFS[e] | Parent's perception of relationship and family functions | Somewhat difficult | Somewhat complicated scoring | Useful with middle-class families | Measures factors that nurses could help change through care plans |
| CICI:PQ[f] | Perceptions of stressors Coping strategies | Yes | 48 items Scoring unknown | Only for families with chronically ill children | Identifies nursing intervention areas for families with chronically ill children |
| Family APGAR[g] | Adaptability Partnership Growth Affection Resolve | Requires global assessment of five areas | Five items Quick to administer | No data reported | Measures relevant factors |
| IFF[h] | Positive/negative feelings toward each member | Yes Complicated for large families | 38 items, 3-point Likert-like scale Easily scored | Unknown at this time | Limited clinical usefulness because of unidimensionality |
| FACES II[i] | Cohesion Adaptability Social desirability | Easily understood | 30 items on 4-point Likert-like scale Easy to administer | Universally useful Family members may be unwilling to assess themselves | Measures relevant factors for nursing Can use as real and ideal |

[a] Family Functioning Index
[b] The Family Assessment Device
[c] Family Environment Scale
[d] Structural Family Interaction Scale
[e] Feetham Family Functioning Survey
[f] Chronicity Impact and Coping Instrument: Parent Questionnaire
[g] Family Adaptability, Partnership, Growth, Affection, and Resolve Test
[h] The Inventory of Family Feelings
[i] Family Adaptability and Cohesion Evaluation Scale
(Speer, J. J., & Sachs, B. (1985). Selecting the appropriate family assessment tool. *Pediatric Nursing, 11,* 349–355)

patients may indicate understanding rather than acknowledge confusion or misunderstanding. In other cultures, family structure may be different from what the nurse expects—for example, in the Cambodian culture, it is the child's grandmother, not the parents, who makes the final decision regarding care.

Nurses need to become aware of the methods of communication that individual families use. One of the most significant barriers to effective interaction with clients is the confusion and misunderstanding that may result from the communication process. Nurses need to be sensitive to personal space, the use of voice tones, hand and arm movements, and body language, and must evaluate how they might affect communication.

In situations where clients or families speak a language with which nurses are not familiar, it may be necessary to find alternative methods of communication. These may include the use of foreign language patient information booklets, drawings or photographs, or the assistance of an interpreter.

Nurses can often facilitate the communication process by determining which family member has decision-making authority. Nurses should also be aware of how disagreement is expressed and what methods for expressing feelings are accepted among family members.

The term *ethnicity* is often equated with the term race, but its meaning is different. Ethnicity involves belonging to a group identified by distinctive patterns of family life, language, and customs (Henderson, 1981). Groups whose members share a common social and cultural heritage that is transmitted from generation to generation are known as ethnic groups. These group members share a sense of identity and common values.

*Environment* helps to shape culture and, in turn, culture influences the family's approach to child rearing, health orientation, illness prevention beliefs, and disease treatment. The child's development is influenced by numerous factors in this framework, and this also becomes a significant concern for nurses working with children.

## Heritage Consistency

It is important for nurses to understand ethnic variations in relation to families, child rearing, and health care beliefs. Nurses should use the *heritage consistency theory* (Spector, 1989) to determine family identification with the dominant culture and the extent of identification with a traditional culture. This theory considers *acculturation* on a continuum, and an individual may possess characteristics of both a traditional and an acculturated nature. The three main components of heritage consistency are ethnicity, culture, and religion.

Ethnicity plays an important role in how children are viewed. Ethnic factors define child health and who assumes child care responsibilities within the family. Additionally, knowledge of the range of ethnic variations, including physical growth rate, body structure, susceptibility to disease, and behavioral and psychological characteristics (such as self-concept), is necessary to accurately assess clients and families.

Western scientific concepts of health and illness are not accepted by all people. Other ethnic groups may subscribe to beliefs and practices based on their culture that have a powerful impact on their concept of illness and what constitutes appropriate treatment. The concept of heritage consistency provides nurses with a way to understand families' backgrounds and how their backgrounds affect their viewpoint. Nurses need to learn as much as possible about ethnic beliefs and practices of the children and families in their care. This knowledge assists in establishing a relationship of trust and mutual respect. Showing respect for the family's culture may provide an opportunity to turn a client's skepticism of Western medicine into receptiveness and may help in providing effective health care. However, families may still supplement the scientific methods of health care with native treatments to show their love for the ill family member.

*Religion* is the third key component of heritage consistency. In some instances religion so dominates the members of a culture that the religion and the culture must be considered together. Religion can dictate the entire cultural behavior of a group. Nurses must be aware of client's religious beliefs as they relate to health care, as well as to specific interventions. For example, certain religious groups prohibit blood transfusions; others place dietary restrictions on their members. Nurses need to show concern for the religious and spiritual practices of clients and families, even when the beliefs differ from their own.

## Ethnic Family Organization

American society is composed of people from diverse ethnic and racial backgrounds. Ethnic groups are defined by race, religion, country of origin, or some combination of these categories. Generally, our society has ignored the reality of these different cultures, thus creating an overall lack of understanding about ethnic groups. This lack of understanding is particularly apparent in relation to ethnic groups of color. In order to understand family organization in society, it is critical to consider the diversity among cultural groups. Through the processes of assimilation and acculturation, ethnic families have adapted in order to survive.

## Acculturation and Assimilation

*Acculturation* is the process of smaller groups within a society being obligated to assume the various cultural elements of the dominant group or society. Acculturation usually occurs when one society or group has power over another group in a relationship. *Assimilation* is based on the concept of acculturation and occurs when the weaker group acquires numerous characteristics of the dominant group.

Ethnic groups experience three different patterns involving the dominant white majority: forced immigration (African slaves), voluntary immigration (Asians, Mexicans, Cubans, and West Indians), and overpowered groups (Native Americans). The motivation to "be American" often helps voluntary immigrants adjust more easily to American culture. Ethnic groups in America are pressured to adjust and perhaps even replace their own cultural traditions with Western cultural forms.

## Heritage-Consistent Family Concepts

Although this section describes "typical" members of specific cultures and their responses to the health care system, it is important to avoid stereotypes. All ethnic communities share certain ideological and behavioral characteristics, but nurses must also recognize the range of health related beliefs, attitudes, and behaviors—particularly those that reflect socioeconomic status—that also exist within these ethnic communities. It is important to realize that great differences may exist between the elite and lower classes of an ethnic community. A Chinese fisherman and a Chinese schoolteacher may share many cultural features, but their adjustments to this country will be influenced by many factors such as educational level, English-language skills, and degree of comfort and experience in dealing with Western institutions. Nurses should approach clients as individuals, while retaining an awareness of ethnicity.

## Collecting Data

There are certain general areas of belief and behavior that may represent barriers to health care delivery for some ethnic clients. Useful social and demographic characteristics of clients can be assessed by eliciting the client's concept of disease and personal condition. It may be helpful to determine the following characteristics in initial discussions with clients:

- Level of education, literacy, and skills in English
- Number of generations in this country
- Household composition/family members in vicinity
- Proximity of others with the same ethnic background
- Previous experiences with scientific medical systems
- Age at immigration
- Contact with country of origin after immigration
- Residence—rural or urban—in home country (Harwood, 1981)

This information can help in predicting an individual's level of acculturation and in making a judgment about the client's ability and likelihood to comply with advice and treatment.

## The Interview

Specific interview questions may also be used to determine how the health–illness models of nurses and clients differ. These questions can be deleted or adapted to fit various health care settings:

- What do you think caused your illness?
- Why do you think you became ill when you did?
- What do you think your illness does to you? How?
- How severe is your illness?
- What problems has your illness caused you?
- What do you fear most about your illness?
- How do you care for your illness at home?
- How has your illness changed your family life?
- What kind of treatment do you expect to receive?
- Could someone or something besides the hospital and the doctors help you get better?
- Who would best help you get better: a doctor, a nurse, a priest, a faith healer, or someone with supernatural powers? (Harwood, 1981)

These questions can help reveal the differences between common views and expectations held by nurses and clients that might interfere with providing health care.

## The Hot/Cold Health Model

One prominent view held by some Hispanics, Haitians, and Southeast Asians is the *hot/cold theory* of health and illness. This concept involves foods possessing qualities of heat and cold unrelated to their measurable temperatures. These temperatures must be balanced to achieve good health. Depending on the cultural setting or the individual, the same food can be considered either hot or cold. Health and well-being are perceived as requiring a balance of heat and cold; the need for medication, therapy, and food may be shaped by this belief system. Nurses may also encounter clients who believe that their conditions are caused by events or agents that are not acknowledged by modern Western medicine. Noncompliance may occur when treatments violate clients' perceptions of the nature of their condition and its culturally appropriate treatment.

## The Asian Family

There is broad diversity among the Asian populations in the United States. Asian-American families base their various cultural and social attitudes and values on thousands of years of history and strong religious traditions. As increasing numbers of generations of Asians are reared in the United States, there are subsequent changes in family roles, patterns of interaction, and child rearing practices. Traditionally, parents hold authoritarian positions and children are expected to display great respect. Even with gradual assimilation, the family unit frequently retains importance, for example, and respect for parents and older relatives is expected in Asian-American families. Decisions to seek medical care, and which kind of medical care, are usually made by the oldest member of the family (Hoang, 1985) (Fig. 2-3).

Families from Vietnam, Cambodia, and Laos share similar health views and practices with the Chinese. Family roles are clear-cut, with men playing the dominant role as breadwinners and women assuming responsibility for running the household. The family holds the highest position, and respect for males and elders is critical.

An individual or family may appear very westernized while still clinging to traditional cultural beliefs. Many Southeast Asians believe in the spiritual nature of health. The advice of a *shaman,* who Cambodians believe can communicate with ancestral spirits, is often sought regarding health issues. Traditional healers, who are also fortune tellers, are often consulted. Common folk treatments include burning alcohol spots dabbed on the body, which is believed to improve circulation, and burning lime powder on a leaf and sprinkling the mist over the client. Fearing chastisement, Southeast Asian families may hesitate to disclose that they are employing traditional treatment methods.

The Chinese have great respect for their bodies. They believe that a significant part of health involves a harmony between the spirit and the body in concert with nature. This harmony is centered on the principle of yin and yang. *Yin* represents the female, the negative force producing cold, darkness, and emptiness. *Yang* represents the male and is the positive force producing warmth, light, and fullness. Chinese people view their bodies as trusts to be honored and requiring proper care. Body organs have intricate relationships and are responsible for maintaining physical harmony. Chinese people believe that the weather influences the body. Nurses should also be aware that early toilet training is valued in the traditional Chinese family.

Within Asian cultures, there are important beliefs that are crucial to effective nursing care. Religious beliefs urge people to be shy and modest. Women are extremely modest, and unmarried women may refuse routine pelvic examination (Hoang, 1985). Nurses need to remember that proper form and appearance are very important to Asians. The head is the most sacred part of the body; therefore, it is taboo to touch a child on the top of the head without asking permission. It is believed that it will "startle the soul out of the body" (Leyn, 1978). When examining the ears or palpating the neck, care should be taken to move the head

gently. The feet are considered the lowliest part of the body, and it is considered very offensive to point one's feet at the client (Hoang, 1985). It is also believed that looking another person directly in the eye is disrespectful and that asking questions is impolite. Nurses must remember that Asian clients seldom question, complain, or demand.

Vietnamese people believe that the universe and all human relationships are controlled by natural forces. As with the Chinese theory of balance, Vietnamese believe in *am,* the equivalent of yin, and *duong,* the equivalent of yang (Calhoun, 1986). Health is considered the perfect equilibrium of these two elements.

Vietnamese mothers equate a fat infant with health and may need nutrition counseling. Vietnamese newborns are often dressed in old clothes, and a child's hair or nails will usually not be cut for fear that this causes illness.

Folk medicine is widely practiced throughout Asian cultures. Nurses should be familiar with the more common folk remedies. One of the most commonly used techniques is *cao gio,* which involves vigorously rubbing the skin with either a coin or spoon. This rubbing is usually preceded by the application of wintergreen or other oils. *Giac,* another common cure, involves applying a hot cup to the forehead or an exposed area for a prolonged time (Hoang, 1985). The scars and marks from these practices should not be mistaken for signs of physical abuse.

The Japanese people believe that health is achieved through harmony and balance between the individual and society, and that disease results from disharmony. Energy may be restored by acupuncture, acupressure, and massage. The Japanese take pride in the good health of children.

*Figure 2–3. In the Asian family, the grandmother is usually the person who makes medical decisions.*

## The Hispanic Family

*Hispanic* is a term that refers to several unique groups who share a common language and Spanish heritage. Mexican-American (Chicanos) and Puerto Rican-Americans are the predominant Hispanic groups in the United States. The Hispanic family is highly patriarchal. The husband and father is the head of the household and the ultimate authority in the family. Children are highly valued, but the Hispanic father's involvement in the day-to-day activities of child rearing is minimal; daily care is the responsibility of the mother (Fig. 2-4).

Hispanics view health from several seemingly simultaneous approaches. Many believe that health is controlled by external forces. Health may also be viewed as a gift or reward from God, whereas illness may be considered a punishment for sin. Evil spirits are viewed as threats to health, and religious relics or medals are often used to guard against these spirits. Nurses may see a medal taped to a newborn's umbilicus to prevent an umbilical hernia. Puerto Ricans may pin a *mano negro* (an amulet of a black hand shaped in a fist with a coral bead on top) to the baby's shirt for protection from evil. Hispanic folk beliefs about illness and its treatment are practiced in addition to seeking traditional medical care. Nurses may see a client with an apparently neglected illness. The client may have delayed seeking medical care because of earlier use of folk remedies to cure the illness.

Nurses working with Hispanics may find that they do not distinguish between natural and supernatural or between scientific and superstitious. Their folk beliefs are a part of their daily living. If a folk remedy works, there is no surprise; if it fails, reasons are found and another cure is attempted. Nurses should also be aware of individuals in the Hispanic culture who function as healers. The most frequent healer encountered is the *curandero* (male) or *curandera* (female). These healers usually practice in their own home where an altar has been installed. Curanderas do not deal with the supernatural or with diseases involving spells or hexes but will treat such things as *susto* (fright) or *susto pasado* (passed fright) and *mal ojo* (evil eye). Herbs are most often used as cures, in the form of teas, poultices, and baths. Healers do not usually charge fees but ask for donations. Respectable curanderas do not become involved with critically ill people but usually advise the family to seek professional medical care. In the barrios, *espiritistas* (spiritualists) are found. Their function is mainly to communicate with the dead, particularly relatives who have suffered a sudden death.

Several folk ailments are prevalent in the Hispanic culture. These ailments usually involve specific remedies. One of the most prevalent diseases is mal ojo or evil eye. The belief involves a person, especially a woman, admiring and looking at a child without touching him or her. In this way, the child may later become ill due to the "evil eye." Nurses who work with Hispanic families should know about this belief. If a nurse admires an infant or child, the nurse should also touch the child's head or face; this touch breaks the evil bond. Symptoms of evil eye may include fretful sleep, vomiting, fever, diarrhea, and excessive crying.

A traumatic or frightening experience can cause susto (fright). The symptoms involve excessive nervousness, loss of appetite, and loss of sleep. If it is not resolved promptly, susto pasado (passed fright) can occur with the same symptoms. This ailment usually requires treatment by a folk healer.

*Sereno* (dew or draft) causes another common illness. It is believed that evil spirits that live in the night air create sereno; thus, a young child is always covered before being taken outside in the evening.

*Resfriado* (a cold or chill) is usually treated by rubbing the patient with mentholatum and covering with warm blankets. *Empacho* (blocked intestine) may occur at any age and is attributed to a bolus of undigested food sticking to the stomach lining. The folk treatment involves rubbing and pinching the back or rubbing the stomach. Herbal tea is often given after the rubbing process (Reinert, 1986).

There are some beliefs involving infants that are im-

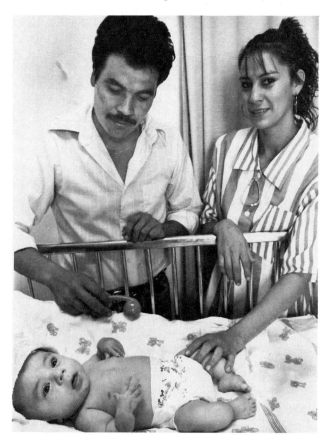

*Figure 2–4.   Children are highly valued in Hispanic culture. (Courtesy of Nursing Department, Thomason Hospital, El Paso, Texas)*

portant for nurses to know. It is believed that cutting a baby's fingernails or toenails with a metal instrument causes near-sightedness; therefore, nurses may see mittens placed on the infant's hands to prevent scratching the face.

It is important for nurses working with Hispanic families to understand their culture and these numerous beliefs, customs, and remedies. The male head of the family should be included in counseling sessions. Important decisions may require consultation of the entire family (Reinert, 1986). In working with a family that uses a combination of folk practices and Western health resources, nurses should consider the folk health care practices in the teaching and care. Nurses must access the family structure to identify the authority for family decisions. This person must be present when care instructions and explanations are made. The Hispanic family has a strong sense of family privacy and traditionally does not reveal problems to outsiders. Nurses must respect this privacy. Intrusive questions may cause resentment and may not be answered. This may create problems in collecting data during the assessment phase of the nursing process and necessitate more than one session to collect data.

## The Black-African Family

The health practices, as well as values, of many black American families reflect those of the general population. Family patterns closely resemble those of white families; differences are due to geographic, economic, social, and educational experiences (Greathouse, 1981). The nuclear family structure with two parents exists in as many as 61% of black families (U.S. Bureau of Census, Household and Family Characteristics, 1985). The extended family has an important impact on child rearing in black families. Patterns of discipline in the black family vary widely and, as in the Anglo culture, are related to the social, educational, and economic level of the parents.

In African heritage–consistent families, health may be viewed as a state of harmony of body, mind, and spirit with nature (Jacques, 1976). The power of both good and evil spirits is a prevalent theme. Illness may be attributed to evil spirits or may be seen as a punishment from God.

There are many traditional folk medicine beliefs and practices among black Americans. One of the more frequent preventive measures seen is the use of a belly band to prevent or treat an infant's umbilical hernia. Spector (1985) notes common home remedies seen in the black community:

1. Numerous types of poultices to fight infection and inflammation
2. Herbal teas to treat pain and colds and to reduce fevers

3. Hot drinks concocted with alcoholic beverages to treat colds and congestion
4. Garlic placed on the ill person or in the room to remove the "evil spirits" that have caused an illness. West Indians and Haitians often wear bangles (bracelets) for protection from evil spirits. These bracelets should not be removed from children.

## The Native American Family

There are more than 350 different Native American tribes in the United States. These individuals usually reside in rural reservation communities or in urban areas. The way in which the essence of a Native American family is expressed in our pluralistic society is related to the demographic, economic, and social setting experienced by that family.

Relatives are highly valued in the Native American culture, and the two most important groups in the family are grandparents and children (Backup, 1979). Children are viewed as assets to the family and are often raised by grandparents in the rural reservation communities because their parents have migrated to urban areas. In their socialization, Native American children are encouraged to be independent (there are no rigid eating or sleeping schedules) and patient and to behave in an unassuming manner (Backup, 1979). Grandmothers are very important, and the aged are looked to for wisdom and counsel.

The concept of health is based on the concept of living in total harmony with nature. Native Americans believe that humans have an intimate spiritual relationship with nature and the earth, and that in order to stay healthy a positive relationship must be maintained with nature. The key to this relationship involves a state of equilibrium with the earth. Health involves a harmony of two equal forces, a positive and negative energy pole, within the body. Illness results from disharmony between these two energy poles.

Effective health care is often enhanced when the care provider works in conjunction with a traditional Native American medicine man. Nurses can be more effective if they carefully pay attention to their approach, which should reflect a belief that the client is both an organism reacting to inner and outer environments and a creature endowed with dignity. Nurses should attempt to demonstrate tradition and dignity in providing nursing care. Care to Native Americans is also often enhanced by involving the family.

## Parenting

The family is the major nurturing and socializing force for children. One of the strongest human relationships is the attachment between parents and their children. This unique relationship allows parents and children to love each other; parents also provide the nurturing and caring that is essential for the development of the child's self-concept.

The relationship between parents and children creates a partnership involving the coordination of giving and receiving. Parents influence their children and are also influenced by them. Such an interrelationship strengthens the concept of the family as a system in which each part affects the others. This creates what Erikson (1963) called the "cogwheeling" of life cycles, involving the mutual development of strengths in parents and children. Parents experience anxieties and doubts as their children progress through various developmental stages and deal with each stage's developmental tasks. In this way parents reexamine and rework previous experiences and behavioral patterns as their children experience new developmental tasks.

Parenting is not instinctive, and it may be stressful. For some it may seem intuitive, but parenting patterns are established through role model observation and exploration of viable alternative patterns. Parenting is a skill that can be learned. There are voluntary groups that teach parenting skills, such as Effective Parenting Information (EPIC) and Parent Effectiveness Training (PET). A combination of experience, knowledge, and skills is the foundation of parenting. A framework for parenting is developed from the parents' experiences as children and the interpersonal relationship skills they have developed. The varied demands of parenthood also require external personal and material support for positive parenting. Parents need a basic understanding of child growth and development. An individual's experiences in his or her own family help to shape attitudes toward parenting. Cultural experiences also play a significant role in shaping parenting decisions.

Through parenting, a child learns to function in the micro-society of the family and then in society at large. The most important result of good parenting is providing the child with a sense of belonging to a particular family group (Brink, 1982).

Patterns of parenting can be viewed on a continuum from authority and control to freedom and autonomy. This continuum involves four major parental types:

1. *Autocratic,* in which parents make decisions and children have no input
2. *Democratic,* in which parents and children both have input, although not necessarily on an equal basis
3. *Permissive,* in which children decide whether or not to accept parental wishes
4. *Ignoring,* in which parents do not involve themselves in directing the children's behavior

These varied patterns play a critical role in personality development. Parenting styles are often mixed and may create confusion as children receive both autocratic and permissive messages. Nurses need to recognize and understand the various parenting styles and be able to offer suggestions to parents. Many styles of parenting can be effective as long as expectations are consistent and appropriate for the child's age.

Nursing intervention is based on understanding how parents view their role as parents in general and their relationship to their children in particular. Other factors that should be considered include the child's birth order, gender, and temperament. Parenting style is composed of how the parent responds to these various attributes, interaction with the child, and methods of discipline.

Nurses should be aware of the various community resources available to help parents with parenting skills. These resources should also include help for parents who lose control. Many communities have instituted telephone hot lines for parents who need help.

## Discipline

Discipline has been defined as training in proper conduct and action. It can also be viewed as mental and moral training. The skill of discipline is involved in every aspect of emotional correction, whether it is the control of anger or worry, overcoming unacceptable habits such as laziness, or the teaching of correct behavior. Parents may have concerns about the appropriate exercise and use of discipline. Parents often have wrong notions of how to accomplish effective discipline. Yelling, nagging, inconsistent punishment, and physical force are too frequently used as tools of discipline.

## Corporal Punishment

The traditional management approach by many American families has been corporal, or physical, punishment. Corporal punishment is nonbrutal physical punishment. Spanking is the primary punishment method. Most parents resort to physical punishment at some time, and many parents believe that such discipline is the most effective means of control. Occasional spankings are probably not harmful, but the harmful aspects involve hostile and aggressive parental attitudes. Numerous experts have disapproved of physical punishment. The use of physical punishment effectively removes the opportunity to instruct, and children responding to fear might fail to solve problems or resolve conflicts without resorting to physical aggression.

It also seems reasonable that a child would avoid the parent who administers corporal punishment, thus affecting the parent–child relationship. The practice of delaying punishment until one parent returns home makes the punishment less effective and may create more psychological problems than a prompt spanking. It is also problematic that corporal punishment begins to require increasing severity to produce the same results. Corporal punishment alone fails to provide any insight or teach self-control, and the modeling of aggressive behavior is undesirable (Hammer and Drabman, 1981).

## Psychological Intervention

Psychological intervention includes such punishments as withholding desired privileges and activities, expressing shame and disapproval, and withdrawing love or respect. Another method involves cognitive processes such as labeling, reviewing, correcting, rehearsing, and reasoning. A third psychological method is *modeling,* a technique in which the parents' actions—how they react to various circumstances—teach the child. Modeling can be a very effective tool. It can also become contradictory if, for example, a parent loses control while correcting a child for a temper tantrum. As the child matures, various models are presented through contact with others and through television viewing. The child may be confused about which model to accept.

## Behavior Modification

This method of discipline is based on the principles of behaviorism and encourages positive behavior. The parent generally ignores undesirable behavior and reinforces the desired behavior, focusing only on the observable, current behaviors, without consideration of their motivations. Nursing interventions should include encouraging parents to respond positively to the child's desirable behaviors. Parents also need to be aware that children's behavior usually becomes worse when the undesirable behavior is ignored. This worsening of behavior, or "response burst," occurs when children realize that the current behavior no longer receives the previous attention. The children then increase the intensity or frequency of behavior to regain the lost attention. If the parents continue to ignore the behavior during this period, the behavior will diminish and eventually disappear. The nurse's role is to help parents understand what causes this negative response burst and to explore the appropriate actions to continue affecting behavior change.

Parents need to be secure and explicit in their attitudes and values regarding discipline of their children. Behavior problems or difficulties in adaptive socialization often stem from parental inconsistencies and contradictions regarding expectations, rewards, and punishments related to discipline.

Nurses should also be aware of temperamental differences in children that may affect management approaches. The "difficult" child, as described by Chess and Thomas (1985), displays temperamental characteristics involving a high level of intensity, some degree of impulsiveness, a low tolerance for frustration, negative mood, and a tendency to recoil from new experiences. These children are usually described as disciplinary problems.

Nurses should always be aware and attempt to guide and counsel parents in developing and maintaining consistent disciplinary techniques. It is important to point out that consistency is a relative term, and that no one person, much less two parents, can be totally consistent in every aspect of childrearing. The critical factor is that parents establish a general consistency of style in relation to what, when, how, and to what degree punishment is appropriate for each particular transgression. Nurses can help parents by encouraging patience and persistence. Parents may expect immediate results in the child after only a few trials at a changed pattern of discipline, and they may need to be reminded that patterns of behavior take months or even years to develop and that it is unrealistic to expect immediate change.

## Summary

Many factors affect how families functions, view health and child rearing, and react to nursing care. Despite the increasing changes facing the family, the family continues to endure and fulfill a primary role in meeting the intimate needs of its members and imparting the culture to the next generation. Culture plays a critical role in the health care system and has an impact on each aspect, from the decision of who provides care to the concept of health maintenance. Nurses must be familiar with a variety of subjects and concepts that affect care delivery. A family's feelings and attitudes regarding health, children, and the health care delivery system are influenced by cultural values, family structure, and past health care experiences.

In order to become culturally sensitive and meet clients' health needs, nurses must be aware of their own culture and values and how these values influence their thoughts and actions. Developing such an awareness should allow nurses to explore the uniqueness of clients and their cultures and obtain insight about the motivating factors that influence the understanding and participation in health care.

## References

Backup, R. (1979). Implementing quality care for the American Indian patient. *Washington State Journal of Nursing* (Special Supplement), 20–24.

Bassuk, E. & Rubin, L. (1987). Homeless children: A neglected population. *American Journal of Orthopsychiatry, 57,* 279–286.

Blechman, E. A. (1982). Are children with one parent at psychological risk? A methodological review. *Journal of Marriage and Family, 44,* 179.

Brink, P. J. (1982). An anthropological perspective on parenting. In Horowitz, J.A., Hughes, C.B., & Perdue, B.J. (Eds.).

*Parenting reassessed: A nursing perspective.* Englewood Cliffs, NJ: Prentice-Hall.

Calhoun, M. A. (1986). Providing health care to Vietnamese in America: What practitioners need to know. *Home Healthcare Nurse, 4*(5), 14–22.

Chess, S., & Thomas, A. (1985). Temperamental differences: A critical concept in child health care. *Pediatric Nursing, 11,* 176–171.

Committee on Government Operations. U.S. House of Representatives. (1986). *Homeless families: A neglected crisis.* Washington, D.C.: U. S. Government Printing Office.

Congress of the United States Congressional Budget Office. (1985). *Reducing poverty among children.* Washington, D.C.: Congressional Budget Office.

Duvall, E. R. (1977). *Family development* (5th ed.). Philadelphia: J.B. Lippincott.

Erikson, E. (1963). *Childhood and society.* New York: W. W. Norton.

Feetham, S., & Humenick, S. (1982). Feetham Family Functioning Survey. In S. Humenick (Ed.). *Analysis of current assessment strategies in the health care of young children and childbearing families.* Norwalk, CT: Appleton-Century-Crofts.

Ganong, L. H., & Coleman, M. (1984). The effects of remarriage on children: A review of the empirical literature. *Family Relations, 33,* 389–406.

Greathouse, B., & Miller, V. (1981). The black American. In Clark, A. (Ed.). *Culture and childrearing.* Philadelphia: F. A. Davis.

Gross, T. P., & Rosenberg, M. L. (1987). Shelters for battered women and their children: Under-recognized source of communicable disease transmission. *American Journal of Public Health, 77,* 1198–1201.

Hammer, D., & Drabman, R. S. (1981). Child discipline: What we know and what we can recommend. *Pediatric Nursing, 7* (May/June), 31–35.

Harwood, A. (1981). Guidelines for culturally appropriate health care. In A. Harwood (Ed). *Ethnicity and medical care.* Cambridge, MA: Harvard University Press, 482–507.

Henderson, G., & Premeaux, M. (Eds.). (1981). *Transcultural health care.* Reading, MA: Addison-Wesley.

Hoang, G. N., & Erickson, R. V. (1985). Cultural barriers to effective medical care among Indochinese patients. *Annual Review of Medicine, 36,* 229–239.

Jacques, G. (1976). Cultural health traditions: A black perspective. In M. F. Branch & P. P. Paxton (Eds.). *Providing safe nursing care for ethnic people of color.* Norwalk, CT: Appleton-Century-Crofts.

Jennings, A. J. & Sheldon, M. G. (1985). Review of the health of children in one-parent families. *Journal of the Royal College of General Practitioners, 35,* 478.

Karpel, M. A., & Strauss, E. S. (1983). *Family evaluation.* New York: Gardner Press.

Krein, S. F. (1986). Growing up in a single-parent family: The effect on education and earnings of young men. *Family Relations, 35,* 161.

Leyn, R. B. (1978). The challenge of caring for child refugees from Southeast Asia. *American Journal of Maternal Child Nursing, 3,* 178–182.

Mueller, D. P., & Cooper, P. W. (1986). Children of single parent families: How they fare as young adults. *Family Relations, 35,* 169.

Norton, A. J. & Glick, B. C. (1986). One-parent families: A social and economic profile. *Family Relations, 35,* 9.

Pless, I. & Satterwhite, B. (1973). A measure of family functioning and its application. *Social Science and Medicine, 7,* 613–621.

Prosen, S., & Farmer, J. (1982). Understanding stepfamilies: Issues and implications for counselors. *The Personnel and Guidance Journal, 60,* 393–397.

Reinert, B. R. (1986). The health care beliefs and values of Mexican-Americans. *Home Healthcare Nurse, 4*(5), 23–31.

Rubin, S. (1986, August 26). The stepparent's guide to life. *San Francisco Chronicle,* p. 15.

Smilkstein, G. (1978). The family APGAR: A proposal for a family function test and its use by physicians. *Journal of Family Practice, 6*(6), 1231–1239.

Spector, R. (1985). *Cultural diversity in health and illness* (2nd ed.). Norwalk, CT: Appleton-Century-Crofts.

Spector, R. (1989). Heritage consistency: A predictor of health beliefs and practices. *Recent Advances in Nursing, 23,* 23–35.

U. S. Bureau of the Census. (1985). *Household and family characteristics.* (Current Population Reports, Series P-20, No. 398) Washington, D.C.: U. S. Government Printing Office.

Wright, J. D. (1990). Homelessness is not healthy for children and other living things. *Child and Youth Services, 14,* 65–88.

## Bibliography

Barnard, K. E. (1984). The family as a unit of measurement. *MCN, 9* (January/February), 21.

Bloch, B. (1983). Bloch's assessment guide for ethnic/cultural variations. In Orque, M.S., Bloch, B., & Monrroy, L.S.A. (Eds.). *Ethnic nursing care: A multicultural approach.* St. Louis: C. V. Mosby.

Clark, A. L. (1981). *Culture and childrearing.* Philadelphia: F. A. Davis.

daSilva, G. C. (1984). Awareness of Hispanic cultural issues in the health care setting. *Association for the Care of Children's Health, 13*(1), 4–10.

Dung, T. N. (1984). Understanding Asian families: A Vietnamese perspective, *Child Today, 13* (March/April), 10.

Fong, C. M. (1985). Ethnicity and nursing practice. *Topics in Clinical Nursing, 7*(3), 1–10.

Leininger, M. N. (1985). Transcultural care diversity and universality: A theory of nursing. *Nursing Health Care, 6,* 208.

Niederhauser, V. P. (1989). Health care of immigrant children: Incorporating culture into practice. *Pediatric Nursing, 15*(6), 569–577.

Pennington, S. B. (1987). Children of lesbian mothers. In Bozett, F.W. (Ed.). *Gay and lesbian parents.* New York: Praeger.

Pruett, K. D. (1985). Fathers as "mothers": How are their children doing? *Consultant, 25,* 152.

Queen, S. A., Haberstein, R. W., & Quadagno, J. S. (1985). *The family in various cultures.* New York: Harper and Row.

Speer, J. J., & Sachs, B. (1985). Selecting the appropriate family assessment tool. *Pediatric Nursing, 11,* 349–355.

# Ethical and Legal Issues in Child Health Care

Darlene A. Martin

*3*

*Sculpture by Charles Parks*

*Rights of Children*

*Nurse Advocacy*

*Ethical Decision Making*

*Legal Responsibilities in Nursing*
    *Elements of a Malpractice Claim*
    *Professional Standards of Care*
    *Abandonment*
    *Doctrine of Respondeat Superior*
    *Doctrines of Contributory and*
      *Comparative Negligence*
    *Doctrine of Res Ipsa Loquitur*

*Informed Consent*
    *Elements of Informed Consent*
    *Informed Consent for Adolescents*

*Withholding or Withdrawing Medical*
    *Treatment from Children*
    *Withholding Treatment from*
      *Newborns with Severe*
      *Disabilities*
    *Baby Doe Regulations*
    *Baby Jane Doe*
    *Child Abuse Amendments*

*Treatment of Children with*
    *Disabilities*
    *Children with Mental Illness*
    *Sterilization of Minors with*
      *Mental Retardation*
    *Nursing Care of Disabled*
      *Children in Schools*

*Protection of Children in Research*
    *Institutional Review Board*

*Summary*

*Upon completion of this chapter the reader will be able to:*

1. *Analyze selected ethical and legal dilemmas that may confront professional nurses in a variety of pediatric health care settings.*

2. *Discuss the application of ethical principles to nursing care of children and adolescents.*

3. *Analyze the basis for nurses' ethical and legal responsibilities toward their child patients.*

4. *Examine the interrelationship between law and ethics.*

5. *Analyze the impact of current case law and developing judicial trends on professional clinical practice.*

6. *Discuss the elements of ethical and legal decision-making models.*

7. *Examine the role of nurses in helping to resolve ethical and legal dilemmas in pediatrics.*

8. *Explore strategies for increasing children's participation in the informed consent process regarding their medical treatment.*

## Key Terms

*abandonment*

*assent*

*Baby Doe regulations*

*comparative negligence*

*contributory negligence*

*due process*

*emancipated minors*

*ethical dilemma*

*informed consent*

*Institutional Review Board*

*malpractice*

*negligence*

*res ipsa loquitur*

*respondeat superior*

*standard*

*sterilization*

*tort*

*withholding medical treatment*

Nurses in pediatric settings are frequently confronted with some of the most complex and agonizing ethical and legal dilemmas in health care. Many of these dilemmas arise as families and health professionals attempt to make hard choices about the use of advanced medical technologies—for example, whether or not to continue life-support systems for a child who is in an irreversible coma. The dilemmas are made more difficult because the patients are children who may be unable to voice their needs and wishes or to protect themselves from harm. Decisions about their treatment are usually made by surrogates, such as parents, other relatives, or court-appointed guardians.

Since pediatric nurses frequently have extended contact with children and their families, they are in a unique position to serve as patient advocates and to help ensure that treatment decisions are in the best interests of these children. It is important that nurses clearly understand and fulfill their ethical and legal responsibilities to their child clients and their families. Ethical and legal obligations are, in some respects, more stringent and more subject to scrutiny because the clients are children.

This chapter examines some of the substantial ethical and legal issues that may arise in nursing care of children and adolescents and the scope of nurses' ethical and legal obligations to their pediatric patients and families. It specifically addresses issues related to professional negligence, malpractice, informed consent, treatment of children with life-threatening illnesses and severe disabilities, children who have been abused, children with acquired immunodeficiency syndrome (AIDS), and children as research subjects, as well as the emerging area of adolescent rights. In addition, the chapter focuses on the process of ethical decision making and the pivotal role of nurses in helping to resolve ethical and legal dilemmas.

## Rights of Children

The concept of "children's rights" within society, and specifically in health care, is a relatively new phenomenon in the United States. Before the last several decades, children were not considered to have rights separate from their parents (Sher, 1983). The children's rights movement of the 1970s, however, focused unprecedented attention on children's issues and problems as well as on the need to extend to children the same rights and protection guaranteed to adults. Those specific legal rights have gradually evolved through the enactment of federal and state statutes and the development of case law.

Many of the legal rights now accorded to children were derived from decisions rendered by the U.S. Supreme Court in a series of significant cases in which the constitutional rights of children were under consideration. In the first of these cases, *In re Gault* (1967), the Court found that the Fourteenth Amendment and the Bill of Rights should apply to minors in the protection of their rights to *due process* (procedural requirements that help assure fairness). The Court also identified a minor's right to freedom of speech and expression under the First Amendment in *Tinker v. Des Moines School District* (1969). The procedural safeguards against self-incrimination that are established in the Fifth Amendment were extended to minors in *In re Winship* (1971). The Supreme Court also held that parents do not have absolute power to veto a minor child's decision regarding abortion in *Planned Parenthood of Missouri v. Danforth* (1976). These important decisions rendered by the country's highest court have clearly established that children in the United States have constitutionally protected rights.

Although not all the cases noted above directly involved health care issues, the precedents they established can be applied to many situations that involve health care of children. The extension of these civil rights to children is explored through discussion of actual legal cases in various sections of this chapter. It is important that nurses understand the impact of these laws on their practices with children, adolescents, and families. They must also remain aware that the law is dynamic and constantly changing.

The importance of children's ethical and legal rights has been underscored by the United Nations Declaration of the Rights of the Child. Although not legally binding, the precepts expressed in this exceptional document provide an international standard for treatment of children. Chapter 1 contains a complete copy of the United Nations Declaration of the Rights of the Child.

## Nurse Advocacy

It is clear from evolving case law, as well as from developing concepts of nurse advocacy, that nurses have both ethical and legal obligations to help promote and protect the best interests and welfare of their child patients. Although nurses' legal responsibilities to patients are substantial and frequently command the most attention because of growing concerns about malpractice, their ethical obligations are equally significant and may, at times, transcend legal considerations.

The duty to practice ethically and to serve as an "ethical agent" on behalf of patients is an integral part of nurses' professional ethics. Those obligations are unequivocally stated in the Code for Nurses with Interpretive Statements, which was adopted by the American Nurses Association (ANA) in 1976 and revised in 1985 (see display, p. 44).

## Ethical Decision Making

As reflected in the ANA Code of Ethics, one of the primary responsibilities of a professional nurse is to help ensure that the basic rights of patients are protected. This obligation requires that nurses learn to recognize ethical dilemmas that may interfere with patients' rights and participate in the resolution of those dilemmas.

An *ethical dilemma* can be characterized as an inherently difficult problem or situation in which there are conflicting moral claims about the "right" thing to do (Davis & Aroskar, 1985). An example of an ethical dilemma in pediatric nursing involves the question of whether to inform all nurses on a unit that a newly admitted child has been diagnosed with AIDS. The conflicting claims that have to be evaluated are the child's rights to privacy and confidentiality versus the care-givers' rights to know or have information that may have an impact on their safety or ability to give effective care.

The resolution of this type of complex dilemma requires a thoughtful and systematic analysis that can help lead to a decision that is in the best interest of the child. A morally justifiable decision may be facilitated by using a structured decision-making process (Fig. 3-1) that includes all relevant medical information, knowledge of the patient's and family's ethical beliefs and preferences about treatment, and pertinent legal facts. Based on a thorough assessment of the data, the child, family, and health team evaluate various options and their possible consequences and then select the best option. The process also involves developing a plan for implementation of the decision and for both short-term and long-term evaluation of the action. Evaluation allows for meaningful revisions in and reflections about the plan or action. The final step in the process involves analyzing the overall process and outcomes and deriving generalizations about the resolution of similar dilemmas in the future.

## The American Nurses Association Code of Ethics

1. The nurse provides services with respect for human dignity and the uniqueness of the client, unrestricted by considerations of social or economic status, personal attributes, or the nature of health problems.

2. The nurse safeguards the client's right to privacy by judiciously protecting information of a confidential nature.

3. The nurse acts to safeguard the client and the public when health care and safety are affected by the incompetent, unethical, or illegal practices of any person.

4. The nurse assumes responsibility and accountability for individual nursing judgments and actions.

5. The nurse maintains competence in nursing.

6. The nurse exercises informed judgment and uses individual competence and qualifications as criteria in seeking consultation, accepting responsibilities, and delegating nursing activities to others.

7. The nurse participates in activities that contribute to the ongoing development of the profession's body of knowledge.

8. The nurse participates in the profession's efforts to implement and improve standards of nursing.

9. The nurse participates in the profession's efforts to establish and maintain conditions of employment conducive to high-quality nursing care.

10. The nurse participates in the profession's effort to protect the public from misinformation and misrepresentation and to maintain the integrity of nursing.

11. The nurse collaborates with members of the health professions and other citizens in promoting community and national efforts to meet the health needs of the public.

(Copyright, the American Nurses Association. Used with permission)

## Legal Responsibilities in Nursing

In addition to the ethical obligations that nurses have to pediatric patients, they also have specific legal responsibilities. Those responsibilities have expanded dramatically during the past two decades as nurses have assumed more complex clinical roles in hospitals, community clinics, schools, and other health facilities. This expansion of nursing practice has been accompanied by a parallel increase in nurses' direct legal accountability for the care they provide.

No longer legally "invisible," nurses have been increasingly named as defendants in legal suits alleging negligence and have been held to a steadily escalating standard of care in state courts across the United States, such as in *Darling v. Charleston Community Hospital* (1965), *Sanchez v. Bay General Hospital* (1981), *Lunsford v. Board of Nurse Examiners* (1983), and *Baylis v. Wilmington Medical Center, Inc.* (1984).

This section of the chapter briefly explores theories of nursing negligence and malpractice as well as other legal doctrines that are relevant to clinical practice. When nurses understand the nature of law and legal liability, they can protect their patients and avoid allegations of malpractice.

Negligence is a category of tort law. A *tort* is a legal wrong committed against the person or property of another. The law provides that the person who is injured may bring a civil suit against the person who caused the harm to recover monetary or other forms of compensation.

*Negligence* is the failure of a person to act in a reasonable and prudent manner and is considered to be an unintentional tort or harm. If the person's actions cause harm to another, that person may be held legally liable for the actions that caused the harm. When negligent actions are committed by a professional during the discharge of professional duties, the professional may be liable for *malpractice*. Negligence may include acts of *commission* (e.g., giving a wrong medication dosage to a child) or acts of *omission* (e.g., failing to raise the side rails on the bed of a child who is sedated). The professional nurse's conduct is measured against a standard of care, or what other reasonably prudent nurses would have done or not done in the same or similar circumstances.

## Elements of a Malpractice Claim

In a medical malpractice case, the *plaintiff* (the person bringing the suit) has the burden of proving that the *defendant* (the person being sued) is liable by a preponderance of the evidence. In order for the malpractice claim to be found in favor of the plaintiff, the plaintiff must establish proof of the following elements: (1) duty to the patient; (2) a breach or failure to carry out the duty to the patient; (3) proximate cause or evidence that the injury was actually caused by the breach of duty; (4) foreseeability, or the defendant's knowledge that the breach of duty could cause the injury; and (5) damages or harm to the patient resulting from the negligent action.

## Professional Standards of Care

One of the most crucial aspects of malpractice cases in which nurses are defendants is determining what standards of care should be used to measure or evaluate the conduct of professional nurses. From a legal perspective, a *standard* is defined as the general recognition of, and conformity to, established practice. In order for plaintiffs to win suits against nurses, they must usually introduce evidence of

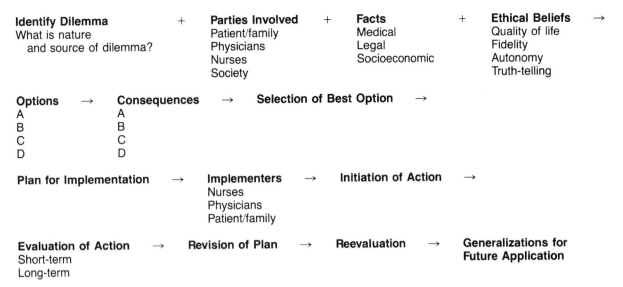

*Figure 3–1. The process of ethical decision making. (Model developed by Darlene A. Martin, Ph.D., University of Texas Medical Branch School of Nursing, Galveston, and Angela Clark, Ph.D., University of Texas School of Nursing at Austin)*

the existing standard during the trial and establish proof of the nurse's failure to meet the accepted standard.

Standards of professional nursing practice are derived from a variety of external sources, including expert nurse testimony, state nurse practice acts, the American Nurses Association Standards of Practice, accreditation standards and regulations, authoritative publications, and internal institutional policies and protocols. In addition, courts may review nursing job descriptions and nursing care plans as a means of establishing the standard of care. Important resources for nurses who practice in pediatrics are the ANA's Maternal and Child Nursing Practice Standards (shown on p. 20) and the Standards of Practice for Perinatal Nurse Specialists shown in the display on page 46.

## Abandonment

*Abandonment* has been defined as the severance of a professional relationship with a patient who is still in need of medical care and attention without providing adequate notice. Although malpractice cases based on the legal theory of patient abandonment have primarily involved physicians, case law exists that indicates that nurses may be increasingly vulnerable to allegations of abandonment. This may be especially true for nurses in expanded practitioner roles and those in independent practice who provide primary care to patients in clinic and home settings.

Nurses working in pediatric settings have a particularly important duty to help ensure that their child clients are provided with safe and continuous care and that they are not abandoned by nurses or other health professionals. A common theme in reported cases of nurse abandonment is an apparent disregard for the welfare of the patient as well as unreasonable and incompetent nursing practice.

One example of abandonment and disregard for the welfare of a child by nurses occurred in *Duling v. Bluefield Sanitarium* (1965). In this case, nurses failed to monitor and attend to a 13-year-old child who had been admitted to the hospital with a diagnosis of acute rheumatic fever. Over the course of the evening, the mother repeatedly sought nurses and reported signs and symptoms that were indicative of heart failure and pulmonary edema. In spite of the mother's pleading, the nursing staff failed to assess the child, and her condition continued to deteriorate. The mother finally insisted that a resident physician be called, but by the time he arrived the child was in critical condition and did not respond to emergency treatment. She died the next day. At trial, the court held that the nurses had clearly violated the acceptable standard of care in failing to monitor the child and take appropriate action. Expert testimony established that the child's death could have been prevented if the nurses had performed their duties appropriately.

## Doctrine of Respondeat Superior

The *doctrine of respondeat superior* is a legal concept that holds an employer liable for the negligent acts of an employee when carrying out the employer's orders or otherwise serving the employer's interests. This doctrine applies only when there is an employee–employer relationship and only when the negligent act committed is within the scope of employment. This doctrine does not relieve the negligent employee of liability, but it does provide the injured person another party to sue. Thus, an employer, even if blameless except for the negligence of the employee, can be found liable because of this doctrine. The employer can, in turn, sue the negligent employee to recover whatever loss the employer sustained.

## Doctrines of Contributory and Comparative Negligence

If a patient fails to exercise reasonable care and thus contributes to an injury initially caused by the practitioner's negligence, the patient's action is referred to as *contributory negligence,* and the patient is not permitted to recover damages. Since this is a rather harsh doctrine, there is a trend for courts to weigh degrees of negligence and apportion recovery accordingly. This doctrine is referred to as *comparative negligence.*

## Doctrine of Res Ipsa Loquitur

The *doctrine of res ipsa loquitur* (literally, "the thing speaks for itself") can be used when plaintiffs sustain injuries under circumstances that make it difficult or impossible for them to prove how the injury was sustained or who was liable. In a case such as this, the jury is permitted to infer that the defendant was negligent without the need for any expert testimony. This doctrine can only be applied when (1) the injury is of a type that ordinarily does not occur unless someone has been negligent, and (2) the conduct causing the injury was under the exclusive control of the defendant.

## Informed Consent

One of the most complex aspects of providing medical treatment to children and adolescents is obtaining *informed consent.* The doctrine of informed consent is based on the principle that competent adults have the right to make decisions regarding their acceptance of proposed medical treatment or procedures. This process is complicated by the fact that pediatric patients, in most instances, are legally considered minors, and consent must be obtained from their parents or legal guardians.

## Elements of Informed Consent

Three primary elements must be present for a consent to be considered effective and legally valid: capacity, voluntariness, and information (Rozovsky, 1984).

*Capacity* refers to the ability to understand and comprehend information, a critical prerequisite to a person's participation in the medical decision-making process. Generally, minors have been considered to have diminished capacity for making decisions for themselves, and the authority to do so has been given to their parents or legal guardians. Although parents are, legally, the key decision makers in the informed consent process, there has been a growing recognition that many older children and adolescents do have the ability to comprehend some aspects of proposed treatments and should be given the opportunity to participate in a meaningful way in decisions that affect them (Gaylin & Macklin, 1982; Erlen, 1987; Holder, 1988). Most states provide that mature and emancipated minors may make medical decisions without parental consent. These exceptions are discussed at length in the following section on adolescent decision making.

The second element necessary for an informed consent is *voluntariness*. This aspect requires that the consent be freely given without coercion or under conditions of fraud or extreme duress. There have been some abuses in this area, including the Willowbrook School case, in which parents were required to subject their children to an experimental hepatitis study in order for them to be admitted to a state institution for the mentally retarded (Davis & Aroskar, 1985).

The third aspect of consent involves *information*. Parents who are making decisions on behalf of their minor children must be given adequate information on which to base their decisions. Basic information generally considered to be necessary for patient decision making includes the following:

- A diagnosis of the specific health problem or condition that the patient is experiencing
- The nature and purpose of the proposed treatment or procedure, including the duration of the treatment
- The probable outcome of any medical or surgical intervention
- The likely benefits from any medical or surgical intervention
- Any potential risks or hazards that may be involved in the treatment
- Any alternative treatment methodologies and indications of their feasibility
- The patient's prognosis (both short-term and long-term) if the proposed treatment is not provided (Rozovsky, 1984; Northrop & Kelly, 1987)

A lack of adequate and truthful information was the basis for a case in Oklahoma (*Johnson v. Gross*, 1987). Parents of 24 infants with myelomeningocele alleged that their children died because the parents were denied accurate information about therapies, which led them to forgo treatment for their infants. The Federal Court held that the infants' constitutional rights had been violated.

## Informed Consent for Adolescents

Adolescents are considered to be minors up to the age of 18 in most states, and consent for medical treatment must be obtained from their parents or legal guardians. There are, however, several specific exceptions to the requirement of parental consent for treatment of minors, including emergency care, medical care of emancipated minors, and the minor treatment statutes.

### Emergency Treatment

Virtually all states have statutes that provide for the emergency treatment of minors when there is a life-threatening condition and parents are unavailable to provide consent. Once the emergency has passed, however, consent to continue the medical treatment must be obtained from parents.

### Emancipated Minors

The second exception to parental consent involves *emancipated minors*. Although the exact definition of emancipation varies from state to state, it generally includes adolescents who no longer live at home with their parents, economically support themselves, are married, or are in the military service. The presumption is that these minors are no longer subject to the control or regulations of their parents and can, therefore, make their own independent decisions about medical treatment.

### Minor Treatment Statutes

A third exception to the parental consent requirement is the statutory provision that allows unemancipated minors to consent to certain specific types of medical care without parental notification. These minor treatment statutes were largely enacted in an attempt to encourage adolescents to seek treatment for sexually transmitted diseases but have been expanded to provide for treatment of substance abuse, rape, and emotional disorders (Holder, 1988).

### Contraceptive Use and Abortion

Two other significant areas in which minors have been granted rights to seek medical treatment independent of their parents' consent include the procurement of contraceptives and, in some instances, the right to obtain an abortion. In 1977, the U.S. Supreme Court struck down a New York law that stated that the selling or distribution of nonprescription contraceptives to minors under the age of 16 was a criminal act (*Carey v. Population Services International*, 1977). The Court said that minors had a right of access to contraceptives based on a constitutional right of privacy. The right to privacy was construed to apply to procreation decisions that are made by both minors and adults.

The courts have also addressed the issue of whether parents must be notified before minors are counseled about or receive contraceptive devices or medicine. In *Doe v. Irwin* (1980), the court found that minors had a constitutional right to privacy that allowed them to seek contraceptive counseling without their parents being informed. Although the court acknowledged that parents have the right to care for and counsel their minor children, it noted that the minor's right to privacy in regard to contraceptive counseling supersedes the parents' rights to be notified (Cushing, 1988).

## Withholding or Withdrawing Medical Treatment from Children

Although the courts have generally given great deference to parents' decisions regarding most aspects of child rearing, including medical decision making, they have intervened under the state's *parens patriae* power (i.e., legal duty of the state to protect its citizens) when it has been determined that the parents' decisions could cause harm to the child or potentially lead to the child's death.

One of the most publicized cases that illustrates the tendency of the courts to intervene in parents' decision making was that of Chad Green (*Custody of a Minor*, 1978). Chad was diagnosed with acute lymphocytic leukemia when he was 22 months old. The child was treated with antileukemia drugs for 1 month and went into remission. His physician then initiated a program of maintenance therapy that included monthly injections of vincristine and oral medication. After several months, Chad's parents stopped giving him the oral antileukemia drugs, and he suffered a relapse. His physician obtained a court order for the appointment of a temporary guardian who consented to the reinstatement of Chad's chemotherapy. His parents appealed the appointment of a guardian, but this appeal was denied by the Massachusetts Supreme Judicial Court on the grounds that the parents' refusal to continue Chad's medical treatment constituted a threat to his life. The Court's reasoning is reflected in the following statement:

> *The evidence supported the judge's finding that the parents' refusal to continue with chemotherapy amounted to an unwillingness to provide the type of medical care which was necessary and proper for their child's well-being. Where, as here, the child's very life was at stake, such a finding is sufficient to support an order removing legal custody from the parents, even though the parents are loving and devoted in all other respects (Custody of a Minor, 1978, p. 1053).*

Several months after their appeal was denied, Chad's parents asked the court for permission to supplement their son's court-ordered chemotherapy with a metabolic regimen that included megadoses of vitamins, enzymes, and Laetrile. After lengthy deliberations, the court denied the parents' request for metabolic treatments on the grounds that such treatment had not been found to be effective in treating leukemia and, in fact, could cause further deterioration in Chad's condition. Before the court issued its final ruling, however, Chad's parents left Massachusetts and took him to Mexico for treatment. Physicians at the Mexican clinic prescribed a regimen of Laetrile, enzyme enemas, large vitamin doses, and a low-protein diet. The physicians also prescribed oral chemotherapy for Chad, but his parents only gave him the antileukemia medications for a short period of time and then discontinued them. Three months after his chemotherapy was stopped, Chad died.

It is clear from the extensive legal proceedings that, while the court acknowledged the strong precedent of parental rights, it did not hold those rights to be absolute, especially when parental decisions threatened the life of the child.

The largest group of cases involving parents' legal rights to withhold or withdraw children from therapy is based on parents' religious beliefs. Many of these cases involve parents whose religious beliefs have led them to object to their children receiving blood transfusions or other medical interventions. In one of these cases, *Morrison v. State* (1952), parents refused to allow their 12-year-old daughter, who was diagnosed with erythroblastic anemia, to have blood transfusions. In a strongly worded opinion, the court overrode the parents' decision and ordered that the child be given the transfusion:

> *The right to practice religion freely does not include the liberty to expose . . . a child . . . to ill health or death. Parents may be free to become martyrs themselves. But it does not follow that they are free, in identical circumstances, to make martyrs of their children before they have reached the age of full and legal discretion when they can make that choice for themselves (Morrison v. State, 1952, p. 97).*

In a growing number of cases in the United States involving deaths of children due to parents' refusal to seek medical care on religious grounds, courts have tended to find parents guilty of manslaughter. Although the specific punishment of parents has varied, it is clear that courts are willing to set harsh penalties for parental medical neglect when it results in death. For example, a California court held that parents were guilty of involuntary manslaughter for not seeking appropriate treatment for their child. The child died of acute bacterial meningitis after the parents' attempts to heal his illness through prayer sessions with their Christian Scientist colleagues (Cushing, 1988).

In a somewhat similar case, parents who refused to seek medical treatment for their 2-year-old son, who became ill and later died of Wilms' tumor, were found guilty of involuntary manslaughter by a Pennsylvania court. The parents were members of a fundamentalist religion and believed that prayer and faith were the primary means of healing. It was noted by the prosecution, however, that both parents had sought regular dental treatment for themselves during the child's illness (Cushing, 1988).

## Withholding Treatment from Newborns with Severe Disabilities

The issue of withholding life-sustaining treatment from severely handicapped newborns is one of the most complex and controversial dilemmas in modern medicine. The treatment issue has raised profound questions about the constitutional rights of handicapped newborns to receive life-sustaining treatment, the rights of parents to make decisions on behalf of their infants, the rights and responsibilities of health professionals to initiate or continue medical care, and the rights of the state to intervene in treatment decisions (Martin, 1987).

The cases of Baby Doe in Indiana (*Doe v. Bloomington Hospital,* 1983) and Baby Jane Doe in New York (*Weber v. Stony Brook Hospital,* 1983) thrust the issue into the public arena and generated significant judicial and legislative responses at both state and federal levels. Those actions culminated in 1984 in the passage of legislation that incorporated the withholding of medically indicated treatment into the existing Federal Child Abuse Prevention and Treatment Act of 1974 (Public Law 98-457, 98 Stat 1749-55 [1984]). Accompanying regulations mandated that child protective agencies in each state monitor the treatment of handicapped newborns and initiate legal action, when necessary, against physicians, nurses, parents, and others who are deemed to have participated in nontreatment decisions that are considered unjustified according to the regulations.

The dilemma of treatment for severely handicapped newborns is not a new issue. What is new, however, is the growing magnitude and complexity of the treatment dilemma and the degree to which it has come under public scrutiny. In many respects, the dilemma is a by-product of the technological revolution in medicine. Rapidly advancing medical technology has provided the means for treating and sustaining life in many premature and severely handicapped infants who would have died only one decade ago. About 4% of the 3.3 million children born in the United States are infants who have multiple congenital anomalies. An additional 7%, or 230,000 infants, weigh 2500 grams or less at birth and are at high risk for developing significant anomalies as well as for premature death (President's Commission, 1983).

Although it is clear that many of these infants have benefited substantially from new and aggressive medical therapies, troubling questions remain about the appropriateness of aggressive treatment for infants who are severely premature or irreversibly dying, those for whom treatment outcomes may be unknown or deleterious, and for certain infants with severe, permanent mental and physiological impairments. These questions are intrinsically tied to a larger societal inquiry into the appropriate uses and limits of life-saving technology. A decade of prolonged debate, punctuated by the cases of Karen Ann Quinlan (*In re Quinlan,* 1976) and Nancy Cruzan (*Cruzan v. Director, Missouri Dept. of Health,* 1990), has focused unprecedented attention on ethical and legal issues surrounding the care of terminally ill or irreversibly comatose patients.

Although public sentiment and judicial opinions generally support the decisions of competent, adult patients and families of incompetent adults to forgo life-sustaining treatment, there remains sharp controversy about withholding such treatment from severely handicapped newborns. At the heart of the dilemma are conflicting beliefs about whether it is ever morally and legally justifiable to allow multihandicapped infants to die by withholding treatment or food.

## Baby Doe Regulations

The Indiana case, discussed earlier as "Baby Doe," generated a massive public response as well as a personal response from President Reagan. In May, 1982, President Reagan instructed the Secretary of the Department of Health and Human Services (DHHS) to issue a directive to hospitals across the country informing them of the potential loss of federal funds if they withheld nutritional sustenance or medical or surgical treatment from handicapped infants. The authority for the threatened withholding was the Reagan Administration's interpretation of Section 504 of the Rehabilitation Act of 1973, which forbids a recipient of federal financial assistance from denying a person the benefits of a program solely on the basis of handicap (Martin, 1987).

In March 1983, DHHS proposed a formal regulation specifying that hospitals receiving federal financial assistance must display a poster detailing the illegality of denying customary medical care or nutrition to handicapped infants. In addition, the poster carried the requirement that any person who was aware of violations of the regulation should contact a newly established National Handicapped Infant Hotline, which would initiate an on-site investigation. The regulation further provided that DHHS had authority to act to protect a reported infant. The regulation was intended to take effect immediately, ignoring the required minimum 30-day notice and comment period specified in the Federal Administrative Procedures Act.

Negative response from the medical community resulted in a suit being filed against DHHS by the American Academy of Pediatrics, the National Association of Children's Hospitals, and the Children's Hospital National Medical Center. On April 14, 1983, U.S. District judge Gerhard Gesell issued a ruling that the regulation was illegal because of DHHS's failure to follow proper procedures in putting forth the regulation. Judge Gesell further commented on the potentially disruptive effects that could occur with the use of Baby Doe hot lines and investigative teams. DHHS revised the regulations and resubmitted them for public comment. These regulations were later struck down in a series of judicial opinions discussed later.

## Baby Jane Doe

Following closely behind the case of Baby Doe was a third and perhaps more graphically publicized case involving a baby girl who came to be known as "Baby Jane Doe." Born on October 11, 1983, on Long Island, New York, Baby Jane had multiple congenital handicaps, including myelomeningocele at L3 to L4, hydrocephalus, and microcephaly. In addition, she had spasticity in her upper extremities and a prolapsed rectum.

Initial medical evaluations indicated that the infant would probably have significant paralysis of the lower limbs and severe mental retardation. After consultation with physicians, clergy, and family members, the parents requested that physicians forgo surgical repair of the baby's myelomeningocele and proceed with a conservative course of medical intervention including antibiotics and nutritional support. The infant's physicians at Stony Brook Hospital concurred with the parents' decision and initiated a medical regimen. Within a few days, however, an anonymous member of the hospital staff alerted Lawrence Washburn, an attorney who was involved in the right to life movement in a neighboring state. Washburn initiated legal action to force surgical treatment of the infant.

After an evidentiary hearing of the case, Justice Melvyn Tanenbaum ruled that the infant must have corrective surgery. The parents' attorney filed an immediate appeal, and 1 day later an appellate panel of the New York Supreme Court reversed the earlier ruling and allowed a course of conservative therapy to be initiated. The court stated that "concerned and loving parents have made an informed, intelligent, and reasonable determination based upon and supported by responsible medical authority" (*Weber v. Stony Brook Hospital,* 1983, p. 685). The New York Court of Appeals upheld the decision by the appellate court on the grounds that Mr. Washburn did not have standing to bring the suit and had not appropriately contacted state welfare authorities to initiate action.

During the ensuing legal action, the federal government also became involved by way of a Justice Department suit requesting that Stony Brook Hospital turn over Baby Jane Doe's medical records. Access was denied by the U.S. Court of Appeals, which raised questions about whether, under Section 504, the neonatal unit was a "recipient" of federal financial assistance; whether corrective surgery was a "program"; and whether there was discrimination, that is, whether the surgery would have been performed if the infant were not handicapped. The U.S. Supreme Court, in *Bowen v. American Hospital Association* (1985), affirmed the lower court's denial of governmental access to records and invalidated the basis on which the Reagan administration had promulgated the "Baby Doe" regulations.

Although there has been some misperception that the Supreme Court ruling struck down the only law governing decision making about newborns, the new child abuse amendments shift responsibility of protecting handicapped infants to the states.

In the midst of the litigation and regulation, the parents of Baby Jane made a decision to allow physicians to establish a shunt to decrease the baby's hydrocephaly. Following surgery, Baby Jane was taken home by her parents.

## Child Abuse Amendments

Following in the wake of the Baby Jane Doe controversy, there was increased activity by some members of Con-

gress in pushing for further protection for handicapped infants. In the summer of 1984, the House and Senate drafted legislation that incorporated the withholding of medically indicated treatment from handicapped infants into the existing Federal Child Abuse Prevention and Treatment Act of 1974. The legislation mandated that child protective agencies in each state monitor the treatment of handicapped newborns and initiate legal action when necessary. The proposed legislation was signed into law as PL 98-457 by President Reagan on October 9, 1984, and accompanying regulations were promulgated in 1985.

Although the legislation specifies that medical treatment that would ameliorate or correct a life-threatening condition must be given, it provides that such treatment may be withheld under the following circumstances:

- If the infant is chronically and irreversibly comatose
- If the the treatment will merely prolong dying
- If the treatment would be futile in terms of the infant's survival and, under such circumstances, would be inhumane

An additional important feature of this law is the emphasis on the establishment of Infant Care Review Committees (ICRCs) within hospitals, particularly those with tertiary level neonatal care units. The purpose of the ICRCs is to establish guidelines and policies regarding withholding of treatment from handicapped newborns and to provide counsel and review of cases in which withholding treatment is being considered. The Department of Health and Human Services has published model ICRC guidelines that describe the composition of the committee (which should include a practicing professional nurse) and the role of the committee in developing policy, reviewing cases, and serving as an educational resource for staff and families of handicapped infants.

Although the full weight of the new regulations and judicial opinions on treatment decisions cannot yet be accurately evaluated, it may be substantial. There will undoubtedly be closer scrutiny of all nontreatment decisions by child protective agencies and others to determine if withholding treatment meets new federal definitions of child abuse. If child abuse as defined by the regulations is found to exist, parents, physicians, nurses, and others who participated in nontreatment decisions or in implementing those decisions may be subject to prosecution.

## Treatment of Children with Disabilities

In many respects, children with disabilities represent a special population within pediatrics who may be especially vulnerable to infringement of their legal and ethical rights within the health care system. For that reason, nurses who provide care for children with long-term disabilities have unique ethical and legal obligations to be advocates for health care that serves their special needs but also protects their basic human and civil rights.

Historically, children with mental and physical impairments were often institutionalized or segregated from the rest of society due to public misconceptions about the disabled and the lack of effective treatment within the community. During the past two decades, however, there have been dramatic changes in the public's attitudes about the ethical and legal rights of the disabled and in the development of community-based treatment programs. These shifts in public perceptions have been reflected in both legislative enactments and judicial rulings that underscore the rights of disabled children and adults to participate fully in our society.

## Children with Mental Illness

Some of the most potentially troubling ethical and legal dilemmas arise in the care of children and adolescents with mental illness because treatment often involves commitment of the child to a mental health facility with significant restrictions on the child's individual liberty. It is important for nurses who practice in mental health settings to be knowledgeable about the rights of minors in commitment proceedings and during various phases of treatment. Nurses have both ethical and legal responsibilities to help plan and implement treatment regimes that are appropriate and safe for children, but they also have a responsibility to monitor the effectiveness of treatment.

Although, in general, minors may be admitted to a mental health facility by their parents or guardians, procedural safeguards exist that protect minors from capricious or unwarranted hospitalization. Each state has specific statutes that govern the conditions for the admission and release of minors. The use of criteria or standards for the admission of children is, however, a fairly recent development in the law. Before the late 1960s, parents could voluntarily commit their children to mental institutions with little or no review from the state. During the latter part of the 1960s, however, the courts began to recognize that children who were accused of crimes should receive the same procedural protection that is guaranteed to adults. In a far-reaching opinion, the U.S. Supreme Court (*In re Gault*, 1967) found that criminal defendants who were minors do have the right to receive notice about impending criminal charges, the right to have an attorney, and the right to receive a record of the proceedings in a delinquency hearing.

Further procedural guidelines for the admission of minors to mental health facilities were established by the U.S. Supreme Court in *Parham v. J. L.* (1979). In this case, two minor residents of a Georgia psychiatric facility challenged the Georgia statute that permitted their parents to voluntarily commit them without a hearing. The Supreme Court held that, although children do have a constitutional right to due process, parents could place their children in institutions without a hearing. The Court's rationale for the decision was that the child's rights are adequately safeguarded by a staff physician who examines and reviews the child's history and makes a determination about whether the child meets the state's statutory requirements for commitment. If, in the physician's judgment, the child does not meet the criteria, the parent may not admit the child to the hospital.

Three of the justices dissented from the majority opinion, stating that they believed the evidence suggested that children needed more procedural safeguards than adults since they are more vulnerable and may be traumatized by being labeled "mentally ill." The Parham decision also generated tremendous controversy among legal professionals and child advocacy groups who felt it did not adequately protect the rights of children. In spite of the limitations of the decision, many states have enacted statutes that require a hearing before a minor is admitted as well as other mechanisms for assuring that the rights of minors are not overridden.

In addition to the procedural safeguards that must be afforded to minors during the admission process, several other important rights must be protected during a minor's course of treatment within a mental health facility. These include the right to treatment in the *least restrictive setting* and the rights to privacy and confidentiality. These rights have evolved during the past two decades in a series of significant cases that addressed the constitutional rights of individuals within institutions for the mentally impaired. Although these cases involved adult patients, the important precedents that they established are applicable to minors in similar situations.

### Right to Treatment

One of the most important concepts to emerge in mental health law was the right of patients in a mental health facility to receive adequate therapeutic treatment. Both the U.S. Supreme Court (*O'Connor v. Donaldson*, 1975) and a federal district court (*Wyatt v. Stickney*, 1971) found that the failure of an institution to provide adequate treatment for patients who have been involuntarily committed is a violation of their constitutional rights prohibiting cruel and unusual punishment and of their constitutional rights to due process and equal protection.

In noting the deplorable conditions and lack of adequate staffing in Alabama state institutions for the mentally ill, the court stated, "To deprive any citizen of his or her liberty upon the altruistic theory that the confinement is for humane therapeutic reasons and then fail to provide adequate treatment violates the very fundamentals of due process" (*Wyatt v. Stickney*, 1971, p. 781).

Both these cases forced important changes in the treatment of those with mental illness. Institutions could no longer merely provide custodial care but rather had to develop detailed treatment plans that would be periodically reviewed by competent professionals and modified according to the patient's progress. In addition to these changes, the judicial rulings mandated that care for those with mental illness be offered in the least restrictive alternative or in a setting in which there are the least number of restrictions possible on the person's freedom.

### Rights to Privacy and Confidentiality

Two other important rights of individuals receiving treatment for mental illness are the rights to privacy and confidentiality. The *right to privacy* implies that individuals have the right to conduct their personal affairs without unreasonable interference from others. The *Wyatt v. Stickney* (1971) decision, noted above, spoke directly to the issue of privacy; subsequently, many states have enacted legislation that specifically provides that individuals who are hospitalized for mental illness should be afforded as much privacy as possible in sleeping accommodations, telephone calls, visitors, and personal possessions.

Patients also have the *right to confidentiality* and should be able to expect that information they share with nursing and medical staff will be kept confidential. Most states have statutes that provide that mental health records and patient communications cannot be disclosed without consent of the patient or, in the case of children, consent of the parents or legal guardians. Some state laws allow minors who are considered to be mature to give informed consent to the release of records to appropriate parties.

There are some instances when the right of patient confidentiality may be overridden. These exceptions to patient confidentiality are generally specified in state statutes or case law but may include situations in which a minor is under investigation for a homicide or when it appears that the minor's behavior may be a threat to the minor or to others. The duty of a mental health professional to disclose confidential information when a patient poses serious danger to someone was identified in *Tarasoff v. Regents of the University of California* (1976).

### Sterilization of Minors with Mental Retardation

One of the most controversial issues in pediatrics has been the sterilization of minors who have mental retardation. Although sterilization of those with mental retardation was once commonplace in the United States as a primary means of birth control, relatively stringent laws now govern its use among people who have mental impairment. The change in the law reflects a growing societal recognition of the civil rights of those with mental retardation, including the right to bear children.

Since nurses may provide health care to adolescents and young adults who have mental retardation, it is important that they be aware of specific laws that apply to sterilization within their own states. Although several states have legislation that specifically addresses whether incompetent minors may be sterilized and, if so, under what conditions, many states do not provide such authorization. In the absence of statutory guidelines, any request for sterilization of a minor must be addressed through the courts.

Several state supreme courts have established procedural guidelines that must be followed in determining whether or not sterilization is in the "best interest" of a minor with mental retardation (*In the Matter of Grady*, 1981). These guidelines have generally included provisions that (1) a guardian be appointed to protect the interest of the individual with mental retardation; (2) an independent evaluation of the individual's medical, social, and psychological status be conducted for the court; and (3) the court determines that the individual is not currently capable of making an informed decision about sterilization and would probably not be able to do so in the future. In addition, the court must evaluate the likelihood of the individual engaging in sexual activity and conceiving a child and whether there are less drastic means of birth control that could be used.

## Nursing Care of Disabled Children in Schools

One of the clinical areas in which pediatric nurses may have the greatest opportunity to function as patient advocates is in the care of children with disabilities in the school setting. An estimated 4.8 million disabled children in the United States are attending school or receiving educational services in home-bound or residential programs (U.S. Office of Special Education Programs, 1990). The integration of children with disabilities into regular public and private school programs has dramatically altered the role of school nurses. They not only have to develop more expertise in caring for children with a wide range of chronic and potentially life-threatening disabilities but also must be more knowledgeable about the ethical and legal rights of these children within the educational system.

The inclusion of children with disabilities in classrooms across the country is mandated by Public Law 94-142, the Education for All Handicapped Children Act of 1975. The intent of this law was to assure that all children with disabilities, from the ages of 3 to 21, receive a free public education that is appropriate to their unique needs. Before this act, many thousands of children with disabilities were excluded from public schools and were either educated at home by parents or segregated in institutions for the disabled that often had little or no special education programs. This lack of access to education forced many disabled children to remain isolated and dependent on their families or the state for support. It also prevented them from achieving their individual potentials.

One of the primary provisions of this act is particularly relevant to school nurses working with disabled children. Each child is to receive an Individualized Educational Program (IEP). The IEP specifies the unique educational needs of the child and specific goals to meet those needs. An important feature of the plan is that it should include related services such as nursing care, occupational therapy, and speech therapy that the disabled child may need to remain in school and participate fully in the educational process.

The law requires that the educational plan be developed, evaluated, and revised by a team of relevant school professionals and the child's parents or guardian. Although school nurses were not specifically mentioned in the legislation as part of the IEP team, they should be an integral part of the planning process, specifically as it relates to health care needs of the child. School nurses are in a unique position to contribute relevant information about the child's health status and the effect that health-related problems may have on the child's educational progress. They may also play an invaluable role in consulting with the child's family and health professionals in the community as the IEP is being developed, implemented, and evaluated. The need for nursing involvement in the planning process is especially crucial when the child has severe medical problems or needs frequent nursing or health-related intervention and monitoring of health status.

Nurses' legal responsibilities for providing health care services that enable the child to remain in school have been addressed in several significant legal cases. The leading case on school health services is *Irving Independent School District v. Tatro* (1984). Amber Tatro was born with spina bifida and, as a result, had a neurogenic bladder. At the time she started school, she needed to have clean intermittent catheterization performed (requiring the insertion of a catheter into her urethra to empty her bladder) every 3 or 4 hours. The school district refused to provide that service during the school day, claiming that clean intermittent catheterization could only be performed by a physician or by a nurse with a physician in attendance. The school argued that this type of health service was beyond its responsibility under The Education of the Handicapped Act and refused to perform the procedure. As a result, Amber was effectively barred from attending school. The U.S. Supreme Court ordered the school to provide catheterization for Amber because the Education for All Children Act specifically requires that children receive health services that can be carried out by a nurse or other qualified individual. Only services that would require a licensed physician to perform them are excluded under the Tatro decision.

In *Department of Education v. Dorr* (1982), the parents of a child with cystic fibrosis and tracheomalacia wanted the child to be placed in a regular classroom in a public school. They requested that the teacher be given special training to suction a tracheostomy tube and to reinsert the cuff if it dislodged from the windpipe. They also requested that the school nurse be available to assist with these procedures. The child's doctor trained the school staff in these procedures. During the course of the training, the staff expressed reservations about providing the service; they also filed grievances to clarify whether their contract required them to perform these types of health services. The federal court noted that when a plan (IEP) was developed to deliver these services, the school personnel "responded to the plan with fear and trepidation," and that "the attitude of the school personnel toward the plan made it completely unworkable and ineffectual" (p. 529). The case was resolved when the student was placed in a regular private school that would meet her needs, at public expense.

In *Detsel v. Board of Education* (1987), involving a child with multiple cardiac disabilities who needed continuous monitoring, and in *Clovis Unified School District v. California Office of Administrative Hearings* (1990), involving the provision of psychiatric services to a school-aged child, the courts held that extensive health services that are unduly expensive and beyond the competence of school personnel are not required under the Education of the Handicapped Act. At this writing, it is unclear to what extent schools will be required to hire nurses to perform certain procedures or use nurses to supervise other personnel performing procedures. With regard to the obvious question of liability, the U.S. Supreme Court in Tatro stated that this was the kind of child that Congress intended to be in school, and if this increased the school's liability, then the school should increase its liability policy.

Even if children are not entitled to services under the Individuals with Disabilities Education Act (1990), their school health needs may entitle them to services under the Rehabilitation Act of 1973, Section 504. In *Elizabeth S. v. Gilhool* (1987), the state admitted its duty under Section 504 to provide services in regular education classes to an insulin-dependent diabetic student whose blood sugar level had to be monitored. Provisions had to be made for insulin injections and providing snacks during the school day, and there had to be a plan to manage any medical emergency that might arise. Section 504 has been held to apply to children with problems such as chronic asthma, severe allergies, arthritis, and epilepsy.

Another category of children in public schools who are eligible to receive health care services under Section 504 are children with infectious diseases. The leading case is *Martinez v. School Board of Hillsborough County* (1988), which involved a student with AIDS. That court established the following five-step process for evaluating whether a child could be safely admitted into a regular classroom:

1. What is the appropriate educational setting for the student, without regard to the disease?
2. Is there a significant risk of transmission of the disease to others? If not, can the child be served in the regular educational setting?
3. If there is a significant risk of transmission, is there a reasonable accommodation that would enable the student to be in the regular school setting?
4. What is the probable effect of the accommodation on the child's psychological and educational development?
5. Would the accommodation pose such an undue financial or administrative burden on the school that it would not be a "reasonable" accommodation?

In this case, the court found that, even with a diagnosis of AIDS, the child's presence in school did not pose a significant risk of transmission to other children; the school was ordered to place the child in the regular school classroom rather than to segregate her.

## Protection of Children in Research

Federal regulations govern the involvement of children in research that is conducted in any institution receiving federal funding within the United States. These regulations are related to the definition of children, the age of majority, and other aspects of children in research and are specifically enumerated in a document referred to as the Code of Federal Regulations (CFR; 1985).

Although the regulations provide for the participation of children in research, there are relatively stringent requirements regarding the evaluation of risks to the child versus benefits to the participating child and other children. The regulations cite four different categories or levels of research in which children may participate with the consent of parents or guardians and approval by the appropriate Institutional Review Board:

1. The first category includes research that poses only minimal risk to the child. The research has no direct benefit to the child (CFR, Section 46.404 [1985]).
2. The second category provides for research that may pose more than a minimal risk to the child but can potentially provide a direct benefit to the participating child (CFR, Section 46.405 [1985]).
3. The third category allows for certain types of research that may pose more than a minimal risk to the child and, potentially, have no direct benefit to the child if it can be shown that the research

could produce generalizable knowledge about the child's illness or condition (CFR, Section 46.406 [1985]). Important requirements are that the risk to the child not be great and that the research procedures are similar to others that the child might encounter in a regular course of therapy (CFR, Section 46.406 [B] [1985]).
4. The fourth category permits, under restrictive conditions, research with children that may carry a higher degree of risk than other types of research and that may have no direct benefit to the child. In this category, there must be a strong possibility that the research results can lead to the prevention, alleviation, or improved understanding of a serious illness or health problem affecting children. This type of research requires review and approval by the Secretary of the United States Department of Health and Human Services (CFR, Section 46.407 [1985]).

One important aspect of the regulations is the emphasis on obtaining, when possible, the *assent* of the child to be involved in the research study. The inclusion of assent in the regulations reflects a growing societal awareness of the rights of children to participate in decisions affecting their own bodies and medical care whenever they are capable of doing so. If a child is unable to assent because of diminished mental capacity, age, or maturity, the Institutional Review Board (discussed later) may waive this requirement (CFR, Section 46.402 [B] [1985]).

Only a few types of research that involve children are excluded from the federal regulations. These include: (1) research conducted in established or commonly accepted educational settings that involves normal educational practice, (2) research in which the investigator observes public behavior but does not manipulate it in any way, (3) research that involves the use of educational testing, and (4) research that involves the collection or study of existing data, documents, records, or specimens (CFR, Section 46.401 [b] [1985]).

## Institutional Review Board

The *Institutional Review Board* (IRB) is the primary mechanism used by hospitals and other health care institutions to review and monitor research and to ensure the protection of human subjects, including children. Federal regulations mandate that all institutions that conduct federally funded research establish an IRB. The regulations also specify that IRBs must have at least five members with diverse backgrounds, including one member who does not have a medical background (e.g., an attorney or ethicist) and one from the community.

Although federal regulations do not require that a nurse be appointed to the IRB, they do note that nurses can be effective members of those groups. There has been a growing trend among health care institutions to appoint nurses to IRBs. Northrop notes that because of the crucial role that nurses play in health care delivery and the various phases of research, "it is almost undefensible and unjustifiable that an IRB would not have a nurse member" (Northrop & Kelly, 1987, p. 338).

## Summary

The ethical and legal responsibilities of nurses who work in pediatric settings have increased dramatically during the past decade. As nurses have developed greater autonomy and have assumed more complex expanded roles in clinical practice, they have also assumed more responsibility and accountability for their practice.

It is clear from evolving case law, as well as from state nurse practice acts, that nurses are being held to a higher standard of care and that they are also being held directly accountable for their individual nursing actions. This increase in professional standards is also reflected in the revised code of ethics recently adopted by the American Nurses Association. In response to the changes in standards, nurses must maintain and continually update their knowledge base and clinical competencies. Failure to do so could not only potentially cause harm to patients but also could put nurses and their employers at risk for allegations of negligence.

One of the primary obligations of pediatric nurses is to help ensure that the care given to their child patients is safe, appropriate, and ultimately in the child's best interest. Nurses must be cognizant of the evolving legal rights of children and adolescents within the health care system. Those rights have been expanded substantially in recent years by a series of U.S. Supreme Court decisions. Nurses have a professional duty to act when there are potential or actual violations of the child's civil or human rights. Although the rights of all children receiving health care must be protected, there is an especially strong need to safeguard the rights of children who may be more vulnerable to abuses, such as those with mental retardation, mental illness, or other serious developmental disabilities.

Because of their close and extended interactions with families and children, nurses are in a unique position to serve as advocates on behalf of their child patients. The role of advocate requires that nurses examine their own ethical and legal obligations to children and that they participate as fully as possible in the process of developing fair and humane health policies for children.

## References

American Nurses Association, Division of Maternal and Child Health Nursing Practice. (1983). *Standards of maternal and child health nursing practice*. Kansas City, MO: American Nurses Association.

American Nurses Association. (1976, 1985). *Code for nurses with interpretive statements*. Kansas City, MO: American Nurses Association.

*Baylis v. Wilmington Medical Center, Inc.,* 477 A.2d 1051 (Del. Sup. 1984).

*Bowen v. American Hospital Association,* 106 S. Ct. 2101 (1985).

*Carey v. Population Services International,* 97 S. Ct. 2010 (1977).

*Clovis Unified School District v. California Office of Administrative Hearings,* F. 2d 9th Cir. (1990).

*Code of federal regulations.* (1985). Washington, D.C.: U.S. Government Printing Office.

*Cruzan v. Director, Missouri Dept of Health,* 58USLW 4916 (US, June 25, 1990).

Cushing, M. (1988). *Nursing jurisprudence.* Norwalk, CT: Appleton & Lange.

*Custody of a Minor,* 379 N.E. 2nd 1053 (MA, 1978).

*Darling v. Charleston Community Hospital,* 211 N.E. 2d 253 (Ill. 1965), cert. denied, 383 US 946 (1966).

Davis, A. J., & Aroskar, M. A. (1985). *Ethical dilemmas and nursing practice.* Norwalk, CT: Appleton & Lange.

*Department of Education v. Dorr.* (D. Hi, 1982). *Education for the handicapped law report, 553,* 529.

*Detsel v. Board of Education,* 820 F. 2d 587 (2nd Cir. 1987).

*Doe v. Bloomington Hospital,* 464 U.S. 961 (1983).

*Doe v. Irwin,* 615 F. 2nd 1162 (1980).

*Duling v. Bluefield Sanitarium,* 142 S.E. 2nd 754 (WV, 1965).

*Elizabeth S. v. Gilhool,* F. Supp. (M.D. Pa 1987).

Erlen, J. A. (1987). The child's choice: An essential component in treatment decisions. *Children's Health Care, 15*(3), 156–160.

Federal Child Abuse Prevention and Treatment Act of 1974, Amendments of 1984, Pub. L. No. 98-457, 98 Stat. 1749-55 (1984).

Gaylin, W., & Macklin, R. (1982). *Who speaks for the child: The problems of proxy consent.* New York: Plenum Press.

Holder, A. R. (Winter, 1988). Disclosure and consent problems in pediatrics. *Law, Medicine, and Health Care, 16,* 219–228.

*In re Gault,* 387 U.S. 1 (1967).

*In re Quinlan,* 70 NJ 10, 355 A 2d 647 (1976).

*In re Winship,* 406 U.S. 243 (1971).

*In the Matter of Grady,* 426 A. 2nd 467 (NJ, 1981).

Individuals with Disabilities Education Act of 1990, 20 U.S.C. 1400 *et. seg.,* 34 C.F.R. 300.1 *et. seg.*

*Irving Independent School District v. Tatro,* 468 U.S. 883 (1984).

*Johnson v. Gross* (W.D. Okla., 1987).

*Lunsford v. Board of Nurse Examiners,* 648 S.W. 2nd 391 (Tex. App. 1983).

Martin, D. A. (1987). The legacy of Baby Doe: Nurses' ethical-legal responsibilities to handicapped newborns. In Humber, J. N., & Almeder, R. F. (Eds.). *Biomedical ethics reviews 1987.* Clifton, NJ: Humana Press, 15–30.

*Martinez v. School Board of Hillsborough Co.,* 861 F 2d 1502. (11th Cir. 1988).

*Morrison v. State,* 252 S.W. 2d 97 (1952).

Northrop, C. E., & Kelly, M. E. (1987). *Legal issues in nursing.* St. Louis: Mosby-Year Book.

*O'Connor v. Donaldson,* 422 U.S. 563 (1975).

*Parham v. J. L.,* 442 U.S. 584 (1979).

*Planned Parenthood of Missouri v. Danforth,* 96 S.C. 2831 (1976).

President's Commission for the Study of Ethical Problems in Medicine and Biomedical Research. (1983). *Deciding to forego life-sustaining treatment.* Washington, DC: Author, pp. 197–229.

Rehabilitation Act of 1973, 29 U.S.C. 794, 34 C.F.R. 104.1 *et. seg.*

Rozovsky, F.A. (1984). *Consent to treatment—A practical guide.* Boston: Little, Brown & Co.

*Sanchez v. Bay General Hospital,* 172 Cal. Rptr. 342 (Cal. App. 1981).

Sher, E. J. (1983). Choosing for children: Adjudicating medical care disputes between parents and the state. *New York University Law Review, 58,* 157–203.

*Tarasoff v. Regents of University of California,* 551 P. 2nd 334 (CA, 1976).

*Tinker v. Des Moines School District,* 393 U.S. 503 (1969).

U.S. Office of Special Education Programs. (1990). *Annual report.* Washington, DC: Department of Health and Human Services.

*Weber v. Stony Brook Hospital,* 456 N.E. 2d 1186 N.Y. 1983, cert. denied, 464 U.S. 1026 (1983).

*Wyatt v. Stickney,* 344 F. Supp. 373 (M.D. Ala 1971).

## Bibliography

Black, H. C. (1983). *Black's law dictionary* (5th ed.). St. Paul, MN: West Publishing Co.

Callahan, D. (1989). Mercy, murder and morality: Perspectives on euthanasia. *The Hastings Center Report, 19*(1), special supplement.

Ethics and Social Impact Committee. (1988). Anencephalic infants as sources of transplantable organs. *The Hastings Center Report, 18*(5), 28–29.

Lyon, J. (1985). *Playing god in the nursery.* New York: W. W. Norton & Co.

Murphy, C. P. (1984). The changing role of nurses in making ethical decisions. *Nursing Law and Ethics,* September, 173–184.

Phillips, D. E. (1989). The Linares case. *Hospital Ethics, 5*(4), 11–14.

Robertson, J. A. (1983). *The rights of the critically ill.* New York: Bantam Books

Robertson, J. A. (1988). Rights, symbolism, and public policy in fetal tissue transplants. *The Hastings Center Report, 18*(6), 5–12.

# Developing a Theoretical Framework for Growth and Development

Patricia T. Castiglia

4

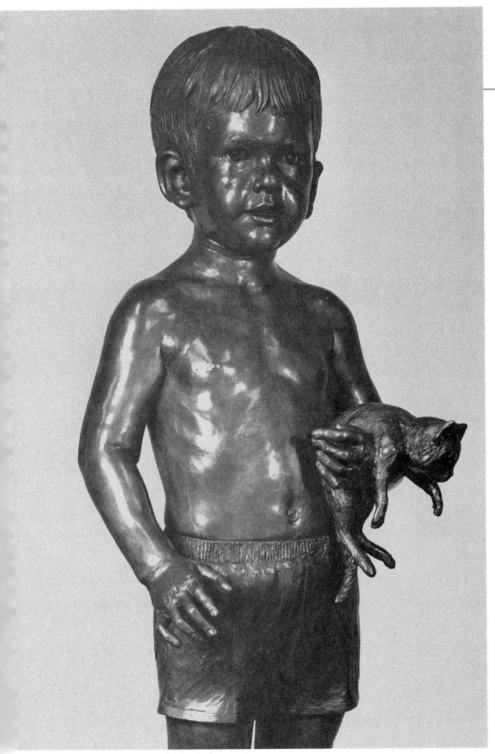

*Sculpture by Charles Parks*

*The Concepts of Growth and Development*

*Principles of Growth and Development*

*Maslow's Hierarchy of Needs Applied to Growth and Development*

*Stage Theories of Development*
    *Freud's Theory*
    *Erikson's Theory*
    *Piaget's Theory*
    *Kohlberg's Theory*

*Learning Theories*
    *Social Learning Theory*
    *Developmental Task Theory*

*Maturation Theory*

*Play Theories*

*Theories of Language Development*

*Attachment Theories*
    *Maternal Attachment*
    *Paternal Attachment*

*Growth and Development of Parents*

*Nursing Implications of Growth and Development Concepts*

*Summary*

## Learning Objectives

*Upon completion of this chapter the reader will be able to:*

1. *Describe and differentiate between the concepts of growth and development.*

2. *Name the principles of growth.*

3. *Recognize environmental and genetic factors influencing growth and development.*

4. *Compare and contrast the basic tenets of the stage theorists: Freud, Erikson, Piaget, and Kohlberg.*

5. *Interpret Maslow's Hierarchy of Needs as a developmental framework.*

6. *Discuss the major impact of the learning theorists for the care of children.*

7. *Compare Havighurst's approach to development with other learning theorists, Gesell's maturation theory, and the stage theorists.*

8. *Discuss various play theories.*

9. *Trace language development in children.*

10. *Appraise parental and family growth and development as it affects child growth and development.*

11. *Select growth and development concepts that can be used to formulate a personal framework of growth and development.*

## Key Terms

*adaptation*

*assimilation*

*attachment*

*behavior modification*

*bonding*

*cephalocaudal development*

*critical period*

*defense mechanism*

*development*

*developmental milestones*

*developmental task*

*ego*

*engrossment*

*equilibration*

*extinction*

*growth*

*id*

*magical thinking*

*maturation*

*moral realism*

*operant conditioning*

*organization*

*play therapy*

*proximal-distal development*

*sensitive period*

*stimulus discrimination*

*stimulus generalization*

*superego*

*therapeutic play*

Theories are useful in describing and explaining events in the real world. Acceptable theories must offer logical descriptions, must be in accord with available scientific knowledge from the biological and psychosocial disciplines, and must allow predictions, based on the theory, to be made. When theories are used to describe what occurs during childhood, two concepts emerge: growth and development. Both of these concepts are characterized by periods of rapid change.

## The Concepts of Growth and Development

*Growth* is generally defined as an increase in the physical size of the body (or body part). Growth involves an increase in the number of cells (hyperplasia), an increase in the size of cells (hypertrophy), and the differentiation of cells. Assessment of growth is routinely done during well-child visits to a private physician's office or clinic, and includes the measurement and charting of height, weight, and head circumference. The accurate measurement and recording of growth are important components of the nursing assessment. In certain growth concern situations it is also important to measure leg length, arm length, and torso length.

*Development* involves gradual changes in function. These changes result in increasingly more complex skills and abilities. These qualitative changes (increased complexity) can be assessed in terms of physical, mental, personal, or social skills. A variety of developmental assessment tools are presented in Chapter 5 and are also incorporated in Part III. *Developmental milestones* are specific activities that usually appear at certain ages. *Maturation* refers to a genetic endowment in development that unfolds naturally.

## Principles of Growth and Development

Growth and development are continuous processes. Although both proceed in an *orderly sequence,* they are often *asynchronous* and there are also *individual rates and styles.* This means that children will pass through the same sequence but not necessarily at the same time. All body systems do not develop at the same rate—perhaps the most obvious example is the reproductive system.

Areas of growth and development are *interrelated* and are influenced by both *genetic* and *environmental factors.* Two principles of physical development are generally accepted. The first principle states that physical development proceeds from head to toe (*cephalocaudal*) and from the

center of the body to the extremities (*proximal–distal*). For example, children learn to control their heads before their legs (cephalocaudal) and to move their arms before grasping (proximal–distal) (Fig. 4-1). The second principle is the *increasing refinement* of movement during development. Gross movements of the body parts become increasingly more refined. Neonatal reflexes must be lost before motor development can proceed. A baby, for example, must lose the step-and-place reflex before standing and walking.

A number of factors have been studied and found to influence both growth and development. Sex differences, race and nationality, general health status, and environmental factors such as nutrition and socioeconomic level have been shown to have an effect on various aspects of growth and development. The effects of other factors such as parent–child relationships and ordinal position in the family have also been studied.

Parents tend to treat their firstborn child differently from subsequent children. This may be due to inexperience, anxiety, and their feeling that everything needs to be done "right." Parenting is different when there are more children, because parents have less time for individual parent–child interactions. Therefore, children spend more time playing, communicating, and learning from one another. Parents also react differently to children at various stages of development. Infants, toddlers, school-age, and adolescents all require different parenting techniques. For example, independence is different for toddlers and adolescents. Whereas parents might be able to accept a toddler who says "no," they would probably have more difficulty accepting an adolescent who rebels against rules.

*Figure 4–1. Cephalocaudal development: control of the head precedes control of the legs.*

## *Maslow's Hierarchy of Needs Applied to Growth and Development*

Maslow's Hierarchy of Needs theory (1968, 1970) is widely used as a basis for the interpretation and subsequent care of adults and children. These needs are considered basic to human growth and development. Maslow theorized that these needs emerge in the following order: physiological drives, safety, love, esteem, and self-actualization (Fig. 4-2). Once one need is satisfied another need becomes dominant. A need may never be completely satisfied but may be satisfied enough to allow the person to move on developmentally.

*Physiological needs* include the needs for oxygen, food and fluids, sleep, shelter, sex, rest, and activity. Sometimes these are referred to as "survival needs." Unless these needs are fulfilled the person will not be able to move to the next level. The succeeding levels are generally categorized as secondary or social levels. They are secondary not in importance but rather in terms of the requirement that physiological needs have to be met first. For example, an infant must be nourished before being able to bond or attach (see Failure to Thrive Infants).

The next need is for *safety and security.* Safety means the absence of danger or the threat of danger. The danger may be in the internal or external environment. An example of a threat to safety from an internal cause might be the uncertainty and fear that a child feels concerning a particular illness. An external threat might be a family move to a new community or the child's placement in a foster home.

Needs for *love, affection,* and *belongingness* emerge next. The child needs to know the quality of the affection of those around him (Fig. 4-3) and be able both to give and to receive love. The need for affection frequently coincides with increasing interactions with the peer group. For example, children shunned by their peer group may engage in behaviors to try to win love and affection such as "buying" friends with gifts or including them in trips and outings.

When a person is able to love and be loved, it is possible to discover the self and to develop *self-esteem.* When an evaluation of self is positive, the person feels self-confident and capable. That person is worthy of praise and acclaim by others. If self-esteem needs are unmet, the person feels weak, ineffective, and helpless. For example, if the adolescent who has been the star of the high school team suffers a leg amputation for osteocarcinoma, he will probably have difficulty adjusting to a new image of himself if his self-esteem has been tied to his success at football.

Maslow states that most of us are too busy meeting prior needs to be able to reach the last level of *self-actualization.* Self-actualization is the attainment of self-fulfillment. Only about 1% of people are said to be self-actualized; this generally occurs in the later years of life.

Occurring concurrently with these needs are the *need to know* and to *understand.* Although it is important to know which need is most urgent at a particular point in time, the clear implication is that each person must be actively involved in the process of developing. Therefore it is important to listen to the child to ascertain his or her understanding and to clarify (teach) appropriately.

## *Stage Theories of Development*

All stage theories share core concepts: all stages are *invariant,* that is, they occur in the same sequence; each stage is typified by a *predominant behavior*; and each stage *builds*

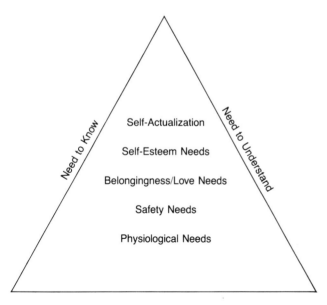

Figure 4–2.  *Maslow's Needs Theory. All needs are present throughout the life span. The needs most crucial for survival are closer to the base of the hierarchy. (Adapted from Maslow, A.H. (1954).* Motivation and personality. *New York: Harper)*

Figure 4–3.  *Love and security from grandparents.*

*upon the previous stage.* A *transition phase* can be identified when one stage merges with another.

Progression from one stage to another occurs when a developmental task(s) has been successfully mastered. A *developmental task* is a skill or ability that is best learned at a particular period in development. Most children learn specific skills at about the same age. The notion of a developmental task implies that there is a *critical period* when learning best occurs. If learning does not occur at this time, the child may be seriously handicapped in terms of mastery of that behavior. This sensitive period occurs for both physiological and psychological development.

Developmental psychologists use the term *sensitive period* more often than "critical period" because it is difficult to ascertain precise critical periods in human development. Sensitive periods occur for both physiological and psychological development. For example, some theorists believe that the brain is ready (sensitive) for language acquisition between 18 months and puberty. This appears to be verified by the relative ease of prepubertal children in learning new languages compared with adults, who generally have considerable difficulty (Mussen et al., 1984).

The most general classification of developmental stages has seven stages:

*1.* Prenatal (conception to birth)
*2.* Neonatal (birth to 28 days)
*3.* Infant (1 month to 1 year)
*4.* Toddler (1 year to 3 years)
*5.* Preschool (3 years to 6 years)
*6.* School-age (6 years to 12 years)
*7.* Adolescent (12 years to 18 years)

The stage theories presented are the Freudian Theory (psychoanalytic theory), the Eriksonian Theory (psychosocial theory), the Piagetian Theory (cognitive theory) and Kohlberg's Theory (moral reasoning theory).

## Freud's Theory

Sigmund Freud (1856–1939) was an Austrian physician who became interested in physical (somatic) illnesses with psychological origins. He studied people who had problems and decided that the causes of these problems were conflicts hidden in the unconscious portion of the mind. Freud maintained that increased anxiety threatened self image and that all behavior has meaning. He further believed that the origin of all emotions and thoughts was the unconscious. He helped patients to recognize these traumatic events through the processes of word association and hypnosis. Both of these methods were used to attempt to free the conscious mind of its vigilance in pushing back (repressing) what is painful. The mind uses various means for allowing the person to "get on" with life. Such *defense mechanisms* include repression, denial, re-

gression, sublimation, displacement, and reaction formation. The reader is referred to psychology texts for further discussion of defense mechanisms.

Freud's theory is unique because it is concerned with both structure and function of the personality. The structure of the personality comprises the *id,* the *ego,* and the *superego.* Function is concerned with predominant needs at a particular period in development. The focus of the functions is on inner psychic conflict. Anxiety that results from conflict is viewed as a major motivator of behavior.

Freud did not study children, but he identified childhood events as the precursors of later conflict. The major conflict, he believed, was sexual. Sexual energy was said to be the major life force. Therefore, a particular body region (erogenous zone) was identified as the main source of pleasure and satisfaction for each stage.

### Structure of the Mind

Freud postulated that the mind was composed of three parts: the id, the ego, and the superego. The id (the unconscious) operates on the pleasure principle, seeking gratification of needs. The ego (the conscious mind) operates on the reality principle. It contains memory, intelligence, cognition, and problem-solving abilities. The ego acts to mediate between the pleasure drives of the id and reality; it strives overall to help the person function in the real world. The superego is composed of two parts: the ego ideal, which is concerned with how one measures up to the ideal person, and the conscience, which regulates right and wrong behavior.

### Function

The functional stages in Freudian theory are the oral, anal, phallic, latency, and genital periods of development. The *oral period* constitutes the first year of life. All pleasure is derived from the mouth, both from sucking and from the satisfaction of hunger. The eyes and hands are used to obtain oral satisfaction; the eyes identify objects of pleasure (such as a bottle), and the hands bring objects to the mouth to satisfy sucking needs. Early oral experiences are said to be the foundation for personality development. In older people, unfavorable oral experiences are manifested by such things as eating problems, dependency, and passivity.

As children learn to control oral needs, they transfer the expression of sexual pleasure (libido) from the mouth to the anal area. The successful completion of this stage is related to whether the parents allow the child sufficient anal exploration and pleasure. For many parents and children, the crucial conflict in this stage centers on toilet training. Eventually the child must relinquish the (libidinal) enjoyment of the bowel function to the external controls (societal expectations) exerted. Characteristics associated with adults who have not successfully passed through this stage include aggressiveness, extremes of tidiness or messiness, punctuality, possessiveness, and shame.

The next shift of focus for the child is to the genital area (*phallic stage*). This occurs at about 4 years of age. Both sexes are said to put emphasis on the penis. Boys are fearful of injury to it (castration anxiety), and girls wish they had one (penis envy). Curiosity, questioning, self-stimulation, and self-comfort develop at this time. Parental relationships also are affected. Boys unconsciously wish to have sexual possession of their mothers and exhibit protectiveness, gift-giving, and fantasizing about a life with her. This is called the *Oedipus conflict*. The boy must resolve the jealousy and competitiveness he feels toward his father because he also fears that his father may punish him for these thoughts, perhaps by castration. Similarly, at this stage girls unconsciously develop sexual fantasies about the father. The girl employs seductive (coy) behaviors with him and is very jealous, yet fearful, of her mother. This is called the *Electra complex*. At about six years of age boys and girls recognize the futility of these wishes and solve the dilemma by identifying with the parent of the same sex. Personality is essentially formed, Freud believed, by the end of the phallic stage.

During the *latency period* (5–12 years) the child learns and practices the skills and role of the same-sex parent. This is a relatively tranquil period.

Adolescence ushers in another period of turmoil, the *genital phase*. A resurgence of earlier libidinal interests is manifested in (nonincestuous) heterosexual relationships. Some psychoanalysts refer to adolescence as a state of normal psychosis because of the disturbance in ego function that occurs.

Freud's basic assumptions, his techniques, and his data collection methods have stood the test of time and have, in fact, served as foundations for other theorists. Jung proposed that there is a deeper level of consciousness than exists in Freud's unconscious. He also proposed that there is a collective unconscious—an inherited knowledge from generation to generation. The collective unconscious consists of archetypes, which are unconscious figures seen in dreams and fantasies. Jung also defined the libido as a general life energy behind all human action. Basically, he believed that there were two major developmental phases. The first occurs up to about age 40, with people striving to achieve and to meet society's expectations. After age 40, people begin to try to fulfill their own personal goals and aspirations.

## Erikson's Theory

Erik Erikson (1902–1982) was a psychoanalyst who worked with children. He developed eight stages to explain conflicts arising from birth to old age (1963). The resolution of the crisis at each stage is necessary in order to prepare a firm foundation for success in succeeding stages.

If a conflict is not mastered, anxiety will result and subsequent developmental resolutions might be difficult.

Although the theories of Freud and Erikson have some elements in common, there are basic differences between the two theorists. Erikson believed that the ego, rather than the id, is the main motivating force in human development. Freud focused on the unhealthy personality, whereas Erikson focused on the healthy personality. Erikson introduced the social component by focusing on the child's relationship with parents and family within their culture. All of Erikson's stages are stated as conflicts (Fig. 4-4).

Stage 1, *trust versus mistrust,* occurs in infancy (birth to 1 year). If a child's basic needs for food and comfort are satisfactorily met, the child acquires a sense of trust because the world is safe and predictable.

*Autonomy versus shame and doubt* occurs during the toddler period (2 to 3 years). Children who have developed the ego quality of trust, but whose efforts at independence are thwarted, may develop shame and doubt instead of self-control and self-worth (Fig. 4-5). If they find that their assertiveness is ineffectual, they develop doubt; if the assertiveness is unacceptable, they develop shame. At this stage children need to develop confidence that they can control their behavior. Toddlers who come to this stage with mistrust rather than trust are vulnerable to shame and doubt. Erikson believes that unsuccessful completion of any stage will result in decreased ability for success at the next stage.

Preschool age children (4 to 5 years) strive to develop a sense of *initiative rather than a sense of guilt.* Typical preschool children are questioning, inquisitive, noisy, and involved in physical and mental explorations (Fig. 4-6). They are likely to develop guilt if their wishes cannot be permitted or when they fail to receive praise for their endeavors. At this time the superego has also appeared and inflicts personal disapproval of actions on the child. The superego acts as the conscience; if children believe that something is wrong, they feel disapproval and guilt that originates from their own beliefs.

During the school-age years (6 to 12), the conflict is one of *industry versus inferiority.* Children now focus on learning what they need to know for success in the adult world. They focus on reality. If children find themselves lacking in these endeavors, they develop a sense of inferiority.

During adolescence (13 to 18 years) the struggle is for *identity versus role confusion.* The adolescent is involved in establishing a sexual and an occupational identity. During adolescence a number of individuals serve as role models: parents, relatives, friends, teachers, movie stars, etc. Adolescents study these people and try to decide who they are. They must find a consistency in their view of themselves and the view that others have of them. At the completion of this stage, adolescents should have developed a sense of self, a sexual orientation, and a sense of

*Figure 4–4. Erikson's stages of development. (Reprinted with permission from Erikson, E.H. [1968].* Childhood and society. *New York: W.W. Norton)*

what they want to be and do. Role confusion can result from the inability of adolescents to identify themselves; this may be due to a series of rapid life changes. Sometimes adolescents select "negative" self-images rather than remain in a confused role.

Erikson's theory is not empirically testable because it is not possible to test the conflicts at the stages proposed. Despite this drawback, the theory has served as a conceptual model or framework for many persons involved in caring for children.

## Piaget's Theory

Jean Piaget (1896–1980) was a French zoologist and epistemologist. He was interested in intellectual development and felt that each child has a biological blueprint for his or her intellectual potential. A basic premise of his theory is that experiences rather than maturation are the foundations for cognitive development. He further believed that children's thoughts are derivatives of motor actions in utero.

Piaget was a stage theorist: all the principles related to stage theories apply to his theory. He further developed some concepts particular to his theory. The major function for cognition is the processing of interactions occurring between the child and the environment. The ultimate goal is the attainment of *equilibration,* which is a state of relative equilibrium. Equilibration is achieved through *adaptation* and *organization.* Organization is the biological way in which the infant is organized. Adaptation is the means by which a relatively balanced organization is achieved. Adaptation consists of two complementary pro-

*Figure 4–5.   Toddler drinking by himself. The child exhibits self-control, adequacy, and confidence by this ability.*

cesses: *assimilation* and *accommodation*. These processes are interrelated and operate simultaneously. Assimilation is analogous to "taking in." This process is most prominent in infancy. Once the "taking in" of information occurs, *a schema* or map of that information is made in the brain. Subsequent exposures to related information and experiences may alter or reinforce the schema. Accommodation is the process involved in adjusting new content to an existing schema.

Piaget's first stage is the *sensorimotor stage*. During this stage (birth to 2 years) the infant develops a rudimen-

*Figure 4–6.   Noisy, physical behavior of preschooler with younger child.*

tary grasp of cause and effect. Particular objects exist only as the child may see, touch, or hear them. The child is able to complete small goal-directed tasks. The sensorimotor stage is composed of six sub-stages:

1. Birth to 1 month: reflexive responses
2. 1 to 4 months: primary circular reactions—the modification of reflexes, e.g., accidental thumb sucking
3. 4 to 8 months: secondary circular reactions—repetition of earlier actions, intentionality, and means-to-an-end
4. 8 to 12 months: coordination of secondary schema—more purposeful manipulation of the environment; causality
5. 12 to 18 months: tertiary circular reactions—the generalization of knowledge learned from one situation to another
6. 18 to 24 months: invention of new means through mental combinations. Problem-solving and imitation are manifested.

Piaget's second stage is the *preoperational stage,* which occurs between 2 and 7 years of age. Representational thought begins and is evidenced by the use of symbols. Centration, the focusing on single characteristics of objects, is predominant. Toward the latter part of this stage, the child is able to think and talk about the characteristics of an object and to make simple classifications. The child has difficulty differentiating between what is real and what is unreal. Magical thinking, such as the idea that reality can be modified by thoughts or actions, is present. Toward the end of this stage the child acquires the notion of invariance, that is, that physical properties of an object remain the same even though the shape or form of the object may change.

*Concrete operations,* the third stage, occurs between the ages of 7 and 11 years. Logical reasoning emerges, but it is concrete and action-oriented. Symbols are increasingly used to represent reality. The child begins to group objects and concepts. During this time the child is involved in increased conservation tasks, for example, knowing when volume remains the same in two differently shaped containers. They are also able to reverse mental operations, that is, to return changed objects to the original state. Table 4-1 identifies conservation tasks and provides evaluation criteria.

Piaget's final stage is that of *formal operations,* from ages 11 to 15. Truly logical thinking emerges and the capacity for abstract thought occurs. The child is able to predict and to formulate hypotheses.

Because Piaget observed and studied his own three children to formulate his theory, it originally met with skepticism. However, a number of research studies have tended to support his theory. A comparison of Piaget's and Erikson's stages is found in Figure 4-7.

*Table 4–1. Evaluating Conservation Activities*

| Approximate Chronologic Age | Conservation Task | Evaluation* |
|---|---|---|
| 6–7 years | Conservation of number. (The number of items in a group remains the same, even if rearranged.) | Make two rows of checker pieces† of 10 each. Now take one row and place in a pile. Ask the child which group has the greater number of checkers. |
| 6–8 years | Conservation of length. (Length will remain the same if configuration is changed.) | Arrange two pipe cleaners† of equal length, side by side. Then twist one pipe cleaner. Ask the child which is longer. |
| 7–8 years | Conservation of substance. (The amount of material in an object remains the same even if altered.) | Align two equal, rectangular pieces of clay† side by side. Flatten one piece. Ask the child which piece has more clay. |
| 7–8 years | Conservation of area. (The amount of surface covered remains the same even if figures are rearranged.) | Arrange 20 playing cards† into rectangles of 10 each. Rearrange one rectangle so that the cards are randomly distributed. Ask the child which group of cards covers more of the table top. |
| 9–10 years | Conservation of weight. (Items weigh the same, although their appearance may change.) | Show the child a small bag of potato chips.† Ask the child to hold it, then crush the bag and ask the child to hold it again. Ask the child which weighs more. |
| 10–12 years | Conservation of volume. (The volume of a given amount of liquid remains the same if displaced.) | Present a glass partially filled with water. Next place an object such as an eraser in the glass. Ask the child which glass has more water. |

*After each evaluation activity, the child is also to be asked, "How do you know this?" This is done to identify whether or not the child has attained the ability to return physical operations he or she has altered to the original state—*reversibility.*
† Any other suitable objects may be used.

## Kohlberg's Theory

Lawrence Kohlberg (1927–1987) expanded the work of the stage developmental theorists to include moral development. Moral development means the development of a person's concept of justice. It is the framework that guides a person's ideas about what is right.

Piaget dealt with moral reasoning in a general classification. He thought that young children (those under the age of 10) base their moral judgments on consequences of the action, whereas older children have a more realistic view. Children from 3 to 9 years of age reason by a literal interpretation of rules. This is called *moral realism* and is characterized by the child's inability to think about more than one thing at a time or to imagine consequences of actions or alternatives to action. Older children (10 years

and older) realize that rules are not unbreakable but are actually examples of mutual agreement. Piaget called this *moral relativism.* Children can now consider others and can see alternative paths and several solutions.

Kohlberg expanded and validated Piaget's moral development framework by developing three levels of development, each of which has two stages. Kohlberg, like Piaget, emphasized that in cognitive operations, the sequence of the stages is invariant and that the stages do not result from cultural teaching but rather from the spontaneous activities of the child. It is also important to understand that Kohlberg's stages are concerned with moral thinking, not with moral action.

In the first level, the *preconventional stage,* the child responds to cultural influences in terms of either the physical or the hedonistic consequences of action (reward,

Piaget's Stages of Intellectual Development

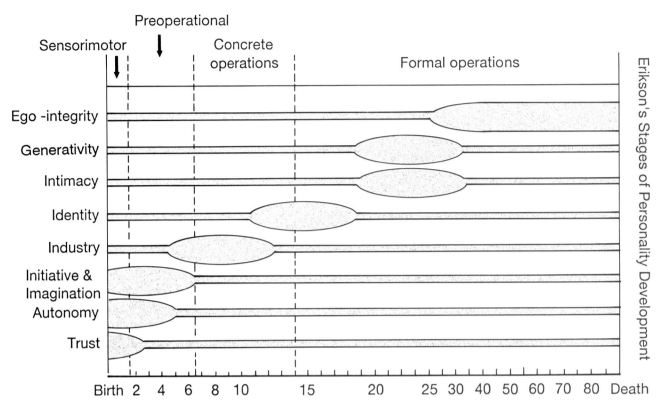

*Figure 4–7.    Comparison of Piaget's and Erikson's stages of life span development. (Craig, G.J. [1976].* Human development. *Englewood Cliffs, N.J.: Prentice-Hall, p. 35)*

punishment, exchange of favors) or the physical powers of those who make the rules and labels. The first level (5 to 8 years) has *stage 1, the orientation toward punishment* and the unquestioning deference to power figures, and *stage 2,* in which the right action first satisfies one's own needs and occasionally the needs of others (ages 7 to 10). Children in stage two seek their own pleasure as the basis of reasoning.

Level 2 is the *conventional level* (ages 10 to 13). In this stage children feel that maintaining the expectations of the individual's family or societal group (conformity) is important, and that these expectations are valuable in their own right (loyalty). There are two stages in the conventional level. *Stage 3* is termed the *interpersonal concordance of "good boy, nice girl" orientation.* Behavior that pleases or helps others is good behavior, and behavior is often judged by intent (e.g., meaning well). *Stage 4* is the *law and order orientation* in which behavior is governed by a sense of doing one's duty, maintaining the social order, and respecting authority.

The last level is the *postconventional, autonomous, or principled level.* It may occur after about age 13 and throughout young adulthood, or it may never occur. There is a clear effort to define moral values and principles as separate from other persons or groups. *Stage 5 is the*

*social-contract legalistic orientation,* in which right action is defined in terms of general individual rights that have been examined and accepted by society. *Stage 6* is the *universal ethical principle orientation.* At this stage the person has chosen ethical principles (abstract) that are judged to be logical, universal, and consistent. Kohlberg believed that few people reach moral maturity, defined as the capacity for principled reasoning.

In addition to Piaget and Kohlberg, three other theorists have contributed to cognitive development analyses. Vygotsky (1934–1962) stated that language without thinking was impossible because thinking and reasoning are based on internalized language or inner speech. Luria (1976) believed that language development is essential for cognition and for psychosocial development. Loevinger (1966), expanding on Piaget and Kohlberg, proposed that cognitive development continues into adulthood rather than ceasing after the formal operations stage.

## Learning Theories

The learning theorists (behaviorists, environmentalists) believe that the environment influences development in a more pronounced manner than do inborn qualities of individuals. Typically, in a behaviorist view, an unconditioned stimulus that elicits a desired response is paired with a conditioned stimulus so that either stimulus will elicit the same response. Pavlov's classical conditioning experiment, which involved inducing salivation in dogs when a buzzer was sounded, is an example.

During the 1920s Watson stated his view that all behavior is learned and that no behavior is hereditary. He and his followers sought to produce evidence that anxieties and phobias could be created and cured by (1) *stimulus generalization* (the transfer of learning from one situation to the next), (2) *stimulus discrimination* (the reaction to differences in stimuli), and (3) *extinction* (the process by which a conditioned response diminishes).

Early behaviorists were not concerned with the causes of behavior, but they were concerned with producing evidence that anxieties and phobias could be cured by behavioral means. B. F. Skinner (1953) introduced *operant conditioning,* thus popularizing stimulus–response (S–R) learning. According to Skinner, reinforcement means that the response to any stimulus is likely to recur when the same stimulus is reintroduced. Reinforcers can be either positive or negative, with positive reinforcers occurring in response to pleasant stimuli and negative reinforcers occurring in response to aversive stimuli. In continuous reinforcement, every desired response is rewarded. In partial or intermittent reinforcement, responses are sometimes rewarded.

The nursing implications of the behavioral theories include the notion that behaviors can be changed or modified. If an undesirable behavior exists (such as overeating), regardless of the cause, behavioral techniques can be used to change that behavior to a more desired behavior.

## Social Learning Theory

*Social learning theory* has added yet another dimension to the effect of learning on development. Social learning takes place when responses do not occur naturally. Miller and Dollard (1941) suggested that imitation is an explanation of how some behaviors are acquired. Bandura (1973) proposed that new behaviors may be acquired by watching other people, that is, by observation. He also emphasized that when children are punished for aggressive acts, the aggression increases rather than decreases. He proposed that the observation of aggression by children leads to an increase in aggressive behavior. This is the theoretical orientation used by groups attempting to control media programs viewed by children.

## Developmental Task Theory

Another learning theory is the *developmental task theory.* Havighurst (1972) proposed that effective learning brings satisfaction and reward whereas poor learning brings un-

### Table 4–2. Havighurst's Developmental Tasks of Infancy and Early Childhood

1. Learning to walk (9–15 months)
2. Learning to take solid foods
3. Learning to talk (2–3 years)
4. Learning to control the elimination of body wastes
5. Learning sex differences and sexual modesty
6. Forming concepts and learning language to describe social and physical reality
7. Getting ready to read (6 years)
8. Learning to distinguish right and wrong and beginning to develop a conscience.

(Havighurst, R. J. [1951]. *Developmental tasks and education.* New York: Longman's, Green)

happiness and social disapproval. Individuals have tasks to learn during their lifetimes that may arise from societal expectations, personal values and aspirations, or physical maturation. Mastery of these tasks helps the individual toward a healthy and satisfactory growth in society.

Havighurst describes the "teachable moment," that is, the time when a task should be learned. This theoretical approach is in concert with the work of Piaget, Spitz, and Lorenz, who described the *critical period.* The critical period concept holds that there is a finite period of time during which certain experiences must occur if they are to be in the child's repertoire. At a given point in time the child is endowed with an increased ability or readiness to learn a specific task. Developmental tasks for infancy and early childhood (Table 4-2), middle childhood (6 to 12 years) (Table 4-3), adolescence (13 to 18 years) (Table 4-4), early adulthood (18 to 30 years), middle age (30 to 60 years), and later maturity have been identified. The pattern of expectations (tasks) appears as a function of biological changes and cultural expectations.

### Table 4–3. Havighurst's Developmental Tasks of Middle Childhood

1. Learning physical skills necessary for ordinary games
2. Building wholesome attitudes toward oneself as a growing organism
3. Learning to get along with age-mates
4. Learning an appropriate masculine or feminine social role
5. Developing fundamental skills in reading, writing, and calculating
6. Developing concepts necessary for everyday living
7. Developing conscience, morality, and a scale of values
8. Achieving personal independence
9. Developing attitudes toward social groups and institutions

(Havighurst, R. J. [1951]. *Developmental tasks and education.* New York: Longman's, Green)

## Table 4–4. *Havighurst's Developmental Tasks of Adolescence*

1. Achieving new and more mature relations with age-mates of both sexes
2. Achieving a masculine or feminine social role
3. Accepting one's physique and using the body effectively
4. Achieving emotional independence of parents and other adults
5. Achieving assurance of economic independence
6. Selecting and preparing for an occupation
7. Preparing for marriage and family life
8. Developing intellectual skills and concepts necessary for civic competence

(Havighurst, R. J. [1951]. *Development tasks and education.* New York: Longman's, Green)

Some of Havighurst's tasks, especially those of adolescence, have been criticized because of an interpreted sexist orientation as evidenced in the emphasis on masculine and feminine roles. Additionally, many adolescent care givers would extend the time frame for adolescence or move some of the tasks in this period to early adulthood. This is a result of the interpretation of an extended adolescent period in American society today.

Learning theories underlie the *behavior modification* approach to development. The goal of behavior modification is to eliminate reinforcers that contribute to maladaptive behaviors and to provide positive reinforcement for new, adaptive behaviors. This approach has been widely used in a number of situations and is popular in the treatment of anorexia nervosa.

## Maturation Theory

Gesell's theory of *maturation*, developed in 1925, emphasizes that behavior has both pattern and shape, and also grows (Gesell and Amatruda, 1947). Gesell's emphasis was on the role of internal programming. The pattern and shape of behavior is related to this genetic or biological endowment. Behavior, such as talking or walking, grows (develops) over time. The stages in this growth are largely predictable. Environmental factors may support or modify the development, but the regulatory mechanisms are internal. Parental expectations and demands are unnecessary and may exert a negative influence. As children mature there will be periods of both calm and turmoil. The "terrible twos" reflect the description of the child during the latter. Gesell's advice was that these stages eventually pass and that parents need to be patient with children during these stages.

## Play Theories

Ethologists have pointed out that the more complex the nervous system, the more playful the species. Children's play activities coordinate with increased motor and speech ability as well as with the increased ability for abstract thought. Play is universal and is associated with the health or well-being of the child (Fig. 4-8). It is known that very ill or very disturbed children do not play. Play is voluntary and should give pleasure and satisfaction. In addition, children must be active participants and must be able to stop playing when they wish to do so.

Early or classical play theories cannot be universally applied, but parents and professionals still use them. Among the classical theories are the surplus energy theory, the relaxation theory, the pre-exercise theory, and the recapitulation theory. In the surplus energy theory, children are said to play because they have not used up all of their available energy in work, and, therefore, must expend it in play activities. The relaxation theory presents an opposite view; play is seen as a way to replenish energy that has been "used up" in work. The pre-exercise theory maintains that children play in order to rehearse for a mature role that they will assume. The recapitulation theory states that through play, children are able to rid themselves of primitive and unnecessary instinctual skills so that they may progress to more complex activities.

The more popular theories of play today are the *dynamic theories. Psychoanalytic play* theory views play as a catharsis. Play is an activity that allows children to express and master difficult situations. This is the basis for *therapeutic play,* which nurses and other professionals use, and for *play therapy,* which is used by professionals with special preparation. In therapeutic play, nurses use play activ-

*Figure 4–8.  Children playing: school-aged child pushing toddler; active, voluntary participation in play.*

ities normal to all children to express concerns in a non-threatening environment. Nurses observe the play and use the data when planning care, because play reveals the real or fantasized concerns of children. Play therapy is a more guided experience. Selected play activities are employed as a way for trained therapists to allow children to express fears, concerns, and anxieties so that therapists can plan interventions designed to alleviate children's concerns. Children whose behavior is disruptive or unusual may be referred for play therapy. Play therapists help these children recognize and confront their concerns so that the children can proceed with normal life activities.

Piaget viewed play as a tool for children to assimilate the outside world and manipulate (accommodate) that reality to an existing schema. Play is conceptualized as an intellectual activity. Piaget identified three stages of play: the sensorimotor stage, the symbolic play stage, and the "games with rules" stage. Children are believed to work through play to acquire knowledge.

A contemporary approach to play is the *arousal-seeking* theory. This theory maintains that children need the intellectual stimulation of play and seek materials and activities to help them develop competence and the satisfaction that results from competence. Children will create exciting environments for themselves.

Trends in play can be identified from a developmental perspective. Biological maturation is evidenced by increasing skill and competence. Aspects and activities of play become more complex and elaborate as children develop. New experiences become incorporated into play, and play becomes increasingly controlled by mental activity. Play in infancy involves sensations (feeling various textures), manipulation (shaking rattles, picking up objects), and motion (cradling, rocking). Infants under 12 months usually play either alone or with adults. They are encouraged to play by visual, auditory, and tactile stimulation.

## Theories of Language Development

Chomsky (1959) maintains that language is acquired through innate knowledge. That is, individuals are born with an intrinsic mental structure for acquiring language. This is the language acquisition device (LAD), which makes the processing of language from the environment possible. From listening, rules are identified. This process is said to follow a developmental progression.

Bloom (1970) identified a relationship between language development and cognition. Basically, he stated that a regular speech pattern will not develop until the child understands the concept behind it. Children are able to express only concepts they have mastered.

Most parents and care givers use imitation and reinforcement as ways of encouraging the development of language abilities in children. Imitation usually involves simple labels for objects. Reinforcement usually occurs when parents respond with smiles, attention, or praise. The developmental milestones of motor development, language acquisition, self-help skills, and play are summarized in Table 4-5.

## Attachment Theories

### Maternal Attachment

Theoretical approaches to the attachment between parents and children have been based on many animal studies. *Attachment* may be defined as a specific, enduring relationship involving mutual trust, responsivity, and caring or affection. Although there is a distinction between the terms "bonding" and "attachment," they are frequently used interchangeably. Bonding is a precursor to attachment. It is a unilateral relationship in which a parent forms a tie with the infant. Parents must reconcile their self-concept and their image of the expected child with the child who is born in order to develop the child's "belonging" or fit into the family.

The theory of *bonding* was presented by Klaus and Kennell (1976). They stated that there is a sensitive period occurring after birth when it is essential for mother–infant contact to occur. If contact does not occur during this period, there is no attachment. This theory is based on the work of Lorenz (1957), who studied *imprinting*—the critical period of time when a relatively permanent bond with the parent must be formed. Lorenz's most famous experiment found that orphaned goslings, whom he nurtured during the first 24 hours after birth, followed him rather than another goose. More recently, the idea of the sensitive period has been disputed, and research is being conducted related to the validity of this construct.

Harlow (1963) studied attachment behavior in monkeys and the effects of separation on mother and infant monkeys. He focused on social interaction, substitute mothers, and tactile stimulation. Social interaction was found to be required for the healthy emotional development of the baby monkeys. Baby monkeys with surrogate mothers were less afraid of strange environments. However, even the babies raised by surrogate mothers did not demonstrate completely normal behavior in adulthood. This ethological research tends to support yet another theoretical approach to attachment. This position postulates that the ability of a woman to "mother" is influenced by her own experience of being mothered.

Rubin (1967), a nurse-researcher, has advanced the theory of a claiming process. Attachment is said to be

*Table 4–5.  Development Milestones of Motor Development, Language, and Self-Help and Play (2 Months to 48 Months)*

| Age in Months | Gross Motor Development | Fine Motor Development | Language | Self-Help and Play |
|---|---|---|---|---|
| 2 | Holds head in same plane as the rest of the body; raises head and maintains position; some head lag when pulled to a sitting position | Able to hold rattle for short periods of time | Differential cry, e.g., hunger; smiles reflexively | Watches people |
| 4 | Able to lift chest from surface; looks around actively; turns head from side to side; rolls over; no head lag when pulled to a sitting position | | | |
| 6 | Able to rest weight on hands with extended arms when on abdomen; sits momentarily without support; reaches to be picked up | Able to hold objects for longer periods, e.g., teething rings | Babbles, makes imitative sounds, e.g., cough | Enjoys bathtub toys, mobiles |
| 9 | Sits steadily; able to lean forward and regain balance; creeps (with abdomen off floor); moves one hand and leg, then the other; stands while holding onto an object or person | Pincer grasp used to explore small objects | Continues to babble; first words are usually "Dada" and "Mama" | Enjoys nesting toys and stacking rings |
| 12 | Stands alone briefly; takes a few steps; walks when led by one hand | Drinks from small cup; uses a spoon with some success; imitates scribbling | Indicates wants by gestures or holophrases (one word sentences); says "no" and responds to "no"; vocabulary of 3 to 6 words, mostly names | Enjoys putting objects in and out of containers or boxes; looks at books |
| 15 | Walks upstairs with one hand held; walks alone; climbs into adult chair; can stoop to recover objects without falling | Scribbles spontaneously; uses hands to reach and grasp | More understandable words, e.g., dog, yes; understands simple directions; names a few pictures | Pulls toys; hugs dolls or stuffed animals; feeds self with some spilling |
| 18 | Walks fast, runs stiffly, throws ball underhanded; seats self in small chair; squats in play | Transfers objects to hand at will; turns 2–3 pages at a time; strokes imitatively (imitates examiner's motion) | Uses two-word combinations, e.g., drink juice; vocabulary of about 200 words; understands simple verbal directions | Enjoys push and pull toys; imitates household chores, e.g., sweeping; builds tower of 3–4 blocks |
| 21 | Walks upstairs, holding rail; walks downstairs with one hand held | Handles cup well | Combines 2–3 words spontaneously | Builds tower of 5–6 blocks |
| 24 | Walks up and down stairs alone; jumps from low objects; runs without falling; throws ball overhand | Turns pages of a book one at a time; imitates vertical and circular strokes with crayon and paper when demonstrated | Uses 3-word sentences; refers to self by name; verbalizes immediate experiences; vocabulary of 300–400 words | Explores drawers and cupboards; plays alongside other children; builds tower of 6–7 blocks |

*(continued)*

*Table 4–5. Development Milestones of Motor Development, Language, and Self-Help and Play (2 Months to 48 Months) (Continued)*

| Age in Months | Gross Motor Development | Fine Motor Development | Language | Self-Help and Play |
|---|---|---|---|---|
| 30 | Walks on tiptoe (after demonstration) | Holds crayon with fingers; imitates vertical and horizontal strokes | Refers to self by pronoun; gives full name | Can help put things away; builds tower of 8 blocks |
| 36 | Alternates feet going upstairs; pedals tricycle | Imitates a cross with paper and crayon after demonstration; unbuttons clothes; copies a circle; prefers to use one hand or the other | Tells sex; uses plurals; names 6–8 objects in a picture book; vocabulary of 1000+ words; understands 2 prepositions; repeats 3 numbers | Feeds self without spilling; washes hands; plays catch; understand taking turns; enjoys imitation games |
| 42 | Balances on 1 foot briefly | | Understands 4 prepositions (on, under, behind, beside) | Plays with other children (real social interchange); washes hands and face; brushes teeth |
| 48 | Skips clumsily with 1 foot; throws ball well overhand; alternates feet going down stairs | Draws simple faces; draws a "man" with 2 parts; buttons and unbuttons clothes; colors with crayons and tries to stay within lines | Longer and more complex conversations; asks many questions; can describe in detail; vocabulary of about 1500 words | Laces shoes; dresses self; enjoys rough and imitative play; has imaginary friends |

fostered by the ability to ascribe certain characteristics of the child to family members, for example, "grandma's eyes." Rubin identified a progression of physical activities by the mother that can be interpreted as stages in claiming. She described the progression of maternal touch from fingertip touching, to the use of the palms, to use of the whole arm and body encirclement (Rubin, 1963). This progression was validated by Klaus, Kennell, Plumb, and Zuehlke (1970), who found that although the progression identified by Rubin remained the same, the time span for the sequence was much shorter at the time of their investigation. They found that the progression took from 4 to 8 minutes, in contrast to the 3 to 5 days observed by Rubin.

Brazelton (1974, 1979) proposes that attachment is influenced by the infant's ability to shape the environment (responses of care givers). He asserts that the infant has the ability to tune into or shut out the environment. This ability affects the mother's response to the child (Fig. 4-9).

Ainsworth (1973) identified the following stages in the development of the concept of attachment. Social responsiveness occurs in the first 2 to 3 months of life when the child seeks to establish contact with others by crying, smiling, etc. At about 7 months the child seeks to gain control over attachment by actively seeking proximity or contact. The child at this stage resists separation from the familiar caregiver. Around 3 years of age, children become aware of themselves and their caregiver as separate persons and attempt to find out what that person wants and how to manipulate their own behavior.

The effect of hospitalization in relation to separation from an attached caregiver was studied by Bowlby (1969). He proposed that the child who has formed a full attachment reacts differently from the child who has never formulated this relationship. The stages he found included protest, despair, and detachment. The effects of hospitalization on children are discussed in Chapter 17.

## Paternal Attachment

Research by Parke (1974) fosters a theoretical orientation of learning attachment for fathers. He found that prenatal and immediate post partum paternal involvement had a

*Figure 4–9. Attachment process: neonate focusing on mother.*

positive impact on the father–infant relationship (Klaus and Kennell, 1976). Greenburg and Morris (1974) identified aspects of the father's bonding including his attraction to the infant, his perception of the newborn as perfect, elation, and an increased sense of self-esteem. They used the term *engrossment* to describe the powerful impact of the newborn on the father (Fig. 4-10).

A more recent study by May (1982) sought to identify a pattern of development of fathering that might begin during pregnancy. She identified three phases of development: an announcement phase (a few hours to a few weeks), a moratorium phase (the 12th to the 25th week), and a focusing phase (the 25th to the 30th week). The findings of the study suggest that there may be a relationship between role preparation in the last trimester of pregnancy and the man's subsequent effectiveness and satisfaction in the birth process and subsequent fathering.

## Growth and Development of Parents

It is obvious that the child does not grow and develop in a vacuum. Major interactions occur with parents, siblings, and other family members (Fig. 4-11).

The function of all families is to provide physical care and emotional nurturance for the child. The child must develop a sense of belonging. The extended family involves the larger society. For a detailed discussion of the family, its role, and its impact on the child, see Chapter 2.

Friedman (1957) identified stages of parent development that seem to have universal applicability. The first

*Figure 4–11.   Paternal attachment: father and child interact in reading a book.*

stage is *learning the cues.* This occurs during infancy and is evidenced by the need of parents to recognize the meanings of various infant cries. The second stage is *learning to accept growth and development,* which occurs during the toddler stage with its associated turmoil related to the child's beginning strivings for independence and control. During the preschool stage, parents must *learn to separate* as the child expands the environment to school and neighborhood activities. *Learning to accept rejection without deserting* is the stage coinciding with the school-age period. The child is moving increasingly away from the parents and seeks increasing independence. The last stage, *learning to build a new life having been thoroughly discredited by one's teenager,* speaks for itself.

Although these stages have not been empirically tested, they present a viewpoint that is shared by many parents and professionals as representative of parental stages of development. The interaction of parents and children is not static; it changes as changes in the individuals and the family dynamics occur.

## Nursing Implications of Growth and Development Concepts

Professional nurses must formulate a framework for practice. The framework provides the unifying theme for nursing approaches to caring for children and families. By incorporating concepts of growth and development into a nursing framework, nurses are better able to understand why children behave as they do and the most appropriate nursing strategies and interventions for each developmental stage.

Another important role for pediatric nurses is parent education. Having a thorough understanding of the principles of growth and development enables nurses to better

*Figure 4–10.   Engrossment: father's preoccupation with newborn.*

educate parents in normal growth and developmental patterns and teach them what to expect at each developmental level. It also allows them to teach parents to be alert for deviations from normal patterns, thereby allowing for earlier intervention if problems arise. Nurses must be able to listen and observe parent–child interactions, to assist parents in developing appropriate parenting strategies, or to refer parents to support groups such as Parent Effectiveness Training (PET), a self-help program for parents. Effective parenting approaches that are appropriate to the developmental stages of childhood can reduce the potential for physical and emotional abuse of children. In addition, effective parenting can alleviate many of the frustrations and emotional stresses that can arise in parent–child interactions and the long-term effects of these problems.

## Summary

The growth and development of children, from conception through adolescence, is a fascinating topic that has been the primary interest of many philosophers, researchers, theorists, and parents. Physical, intellectual, personality, and social development all take place at the same time, and are separate but interdependent processes. In addition to physical growth, it is essential to understand children's cognitive, moral, and psychosocial development. Knowledge of basic human needs and the stage theories helps nurses provide anticipatory guidance and gives them a basis for reassuring parents that children are developing appropriately. The developmental, learning, and play theories have been presented in an attempt to emphasize the importance of recognizing the theoretical bases for child health care. Theories of parental attachment and parental growth and development have also been presented since these can have a major impact on the growth and development of children.

## References

Ainsworth, M. D. S. (1973). The development of infant-mother attachment. In B.M. Caldwell & H.N. Ricciuti (Eds.). *Review of child development research* (Vol. 3). Chicago: University of Chicago Press.

Bandura, A. (1973). *Aggression: A social learning analysis.* Englewood Cliffs, NJ: Prentice-Hall.

Bloom, L. (1970). *Language development: Form and function in emerging grammars.* Cambridge: MIT Press.

Bowlby, J. (1969). *Attachment and loss. Vol. 1: Attachment.* New York: Basic Books.

Brazelton, T. B. (1974). Does the neonate shape his environment? In D. Bergsman (Ed.). *The infant at risk.* White Plains, NY: National Foundation–March of Dimes.

Brazelton, T. B. (1979). Behavioral competence of the newborn infant. *Seminars in Perinatology, 3,* 35–44.

Chomsky, N. G. (1959). Review of *Verbal behavior* by B. F. Skinner. *Language, 35,* 26–58.

Erikson, E. (1963). *Childhood and society* (2nd ed.). New York: W.W. Norton Co.

Friedman, D. B. (1957). Parent development. *California Medicine, 86,* 25–28.

Gesell, A., & Amatruda, C. (1947). *Developmental diagnosis* (2nd ed.). New York: Paul B. Hoeber, Inc.

Greenburg, M., & Morris, N. (1974). Engrossment: The newborn's impact upon the father. *American Journal of Orthopsychiatry, 44,* 520–531.

Harlow, H. F., Harlow, M. K., & Hanson, E. W. (1963). The maternal affectional system of Rhesus monkeys. In H. R. Rheingold (Ed.). *Maternal behavior in mammals* (pp. 252–281). New York: John Wiley & Sons.

Havighurst, R. J. (1972). *Developmental tasks and education.* New York: David McKay.

Klaus, M. H., Kennell, J. H., Plumb, N., & Zuehlke, S. (1970). Human maternal behavior at the first contact with her young. *Pediatrics, 46,* 187–192.

Klaus, M. H., & Kennell, J. H. (1976). *Maternal-infant bonding.* St. Louis: C.V. Mosby.

Loevinger, J. (1966). The meaning and measurement of ego development. *American Psychologist, 21,* 195–206.

Lorenz, K. (1957). Comparative study of behavior. In C. H. Shiller (Ed.). *Instinctive behavior.* New York: International Press.

Luria, A. (1976). *Cognitive development: Its cultural and social foundations.* Cambridge, MA: Harvard University Press.

Maslow, A. (1968). *Toward a psychology of being* (2nd ed.). New York: Van Nostrand.

Maslow, A. H. (1970). *Motivation and personality* (2nd ed.). New York: Harper & Row.

May, K. A. (1982). Three phases of father involvement in pregnancy. *Nursing Research, 31,* 337–342.

Miller, N., & Dollard, J. (1941). *Social learning and imitation.* New Haven: Yale University Press.

Mussen, P. H., Conger, J. J., Kagan, J., & Huston, A. C. (1984). *Child development and personality* (6th ed.). New York: Harper & Row.

Parke, R. (1974). Father–infant interaction. In M. H. Klaus, T. Leger, & M. A. Trause (Eds.). *Maternal attachment and mothering disorders: A roundtable.* Sausalito, CA: Johnson and Johnson Co.

Rubin, R. (1963). Maternal touch. *Nursing Outlook, 11,* 828.

Rubin, R. (1967). Attainment of the maternal role, part 1: processes. *Nursing Research, 16,* 237–245.

Skinner, R. F. (1953). *Science and human behavior.* New York: Macmillan.

Vygotsky, L. S. (1962). *Thought and language.* Cambridge, MA: MIT Press.

## Bibliography

Ainsworth, M. D. S. (1969). Object relations, dependency and attachment: A theoretical review of the infant-mother relationship. *Child Development, 40,* 969–1025.

Bandura, A. (1969). *Principles of behavior modification.* New York: Holt, Rinehart, & Winston.

Bowlby, J. (1963). *Child care and the growth of love.* New York: Penguin.

Caldwell, B. M., & Richmond, J. B. (1970). The impact of theories of child development. In F. Rebelskiy & L. Dorman (Eds.). *Child development and behavior.* New York: Alfred A. Knopf.

Caplan, F., & Caplan, T. (1962). *The power of play.* New York: Anchor Press.

Duska, R., & Whelan, M. (1975). *Moral development: A guide to Piaget and Kohlberg.* New York: Paulist Press.

Elkind, D. (1974). *Children and adolescents: Interpretive essays on Jean Piaget.* London, Oxford University Press.

Flavell, J. H. (1963). *The developmental psychology of Jean Piaget.* New York: Van Nostrand Company.

Freud, S. (1946). *The ego and the mechanisms of defense.* New York: International Universities Press.

Freud, S. (1962). *Three essays on the theory of sexuality.* New York: Hearst Corporation.

Ilg, F. L., & Ames, L. B. (1955). *The Gesell Institute's child behavior.* New York: Harper and Row.

Illingworth, R. S. (1987). *The development of the infant and young child.* Edinburgh: Churchill Livingstone.

Kagan, J. (1984). *The nature of the child.* New York: Basic Books.

Klaus, M. H., & Kennell, J. H. (1982). *Parent–infant bonding* (2nd ed.). St. Louis: C. V. Mosby.

Knobloch, H., & Pasamanick, B. (Eds.). (1974). *Gesell and Amatruda's developmental diagnoses* (3rd ed.). New York: Harper & Row.

Kohlberg, L., & Hersh, R. (1977). Moral development: a review of theory. *Theory Into Practice, XVI*(2), 53–59.

Langer, J. (1968). *Theories of development.* New York: Holt, Rinehart & Winston.

Musick, J. S., & Householder, J. (1986). *Infant development: From theory to practice.* Belmont, CA: Wadsworth.

Nelms, B. C., & Mullins, R. C. (1982). *Growth and development: A primary health care approach.* Englewood Cliffs, NJ: Prentice-Hall.

Papalia, D. E., Olds, S. W. (1989). *Human development* (4th ed.). New York: McGraw-Hill.

Piaget, J. (1961). *The growth of logical thinking from childhood to adolescence.* New York: Basic Books.

Piaget, J. (1962). *Play, dreams and imitation in childhood.* New York: W. W. Norton.

Piaget, J. (1963). *The origins of intelligence in children.* New York: W. W. Norton.

Piaget, J., & Inhelder, B. (1969). *The psychology of the child.* New York: Basic Books.

Piaget, J. (1973). *Psychology of intelligence.* Totowa, NJ: Littlefield, Adams and Co.

Sears, R. (1957). Identification as a form of behavioral development. In D. B. Harris (Ed.). *The concept of development* (pp. 149–161). Minneapolis: University of Minnesota Press.

Storr, A. (1973). *C. G. Jung.* New York: Viking Press.

Winnicott, D. W. *Babies and their mothers.* Reading, MA: Addison-Wesley.

# The Child Health Nursing Process

*Assessment of Children and Families*

*Nursing Diagnosis in Child Health Care*

*Planning Child Health Nursing Care*

*Implementing Child Health Nursing Interventions*

*Evaluating Child Health Nursing Care*

*Sculpture by Charles Parks*

# Assessment of Children and Families

Joan T. Duer

Photograph by David Finn

5

*The Interview*
   *Components of the*
     *Communication Process*
   *Communicating With Parents*
   *Communicating With Pediatric*
     *Clients*
   *Setting the Stage for Successful*
     *Interviews*
   *Communication Techniques*

*Family Assessment*
   *Family History*
   *Family and Home Assessment*

*Developmental Assessment*

*Health History*

*Review of Systems*

*Physical Assessment Skills*

*Physical Examination*
   *Developmental Approaches to*
     *Physical Examination*
   *Growth Measurements*
   *Vital Signs*
   *General Survey*
   *Skin*
   *Head and Neck*
   *Eyes*
   *Ears*
   *Nose*
   *Mouth and Throat*
   *Thorax and Lungs*
   *Heart*
   *Abdomen*
   *Genitalia*
   *Musculoskeletal*
   *Neurological*
   *Sensory Function*
   *Summary*

*Upon completion of this chapter the reader will be able to:*

1. *Identify components of the communication process and their application to the assessment of children and families.*

2. *Describe the necessary elements for a successful interview of children and families.*

3. *Describe communication techniques appropriate for the developmental needs of pediatric clients and their families.*

4. *Summarize the principal elements of a family history.*

5. *Explain the purpose of family assessment tools in assessing family functioning of childrearing families.*

6. *Explain the purpose of developmental assessment tools and their applicability to child health assessment.*

7. *Identify the components of the medical history and questions necessary to elicit assessment data.*

8. *Describe the purpose and components of the review of systems in assessing the health status of pediatric clients.*

9. *Describe observational and manual approaches to the pediatric physical examination.*

10. *Identify physical assessment techniques and findings that are unique to pediatric clients.*

*graphesthesia*

*hypospadias*

*kyphosis*

*lordosis*

*nonverbal communication*

*nystagmus*

*open-ended questions*

*paraphrasing*

*pectus carinatum*

*pectus excavatum*

*phimosis*

*ptosis*

*reflecting*

*scoliosis*

*silence*

*stereogenesis*

*strabismus*

*summarizing*

*superficial reflexes*

*verbal communication*

**Key Terms**

*aniscoria*

*Brushfield's spots*

*closed questions*

*deep tendon reflexes*

*epicanthal folds*

*epispadias*

Nursing assessment is the first and most fundamental step of the nursing process. During the assessment phase nurses collect data on all aspects of children and their families' health history, physical systems, and psychosocial and environmental well-being. Although this nursing function may appear routine, the implications and findings of the nursing assessment affect every other aspect of the nursing process.

Based on the results of the nursing assessment, nursing diagnoses are established, care is planned and implemented, and outcomes are evaluated. Virtually every nursing action is derived from the assessment process.

Nursing assessment requires considerable skill and practice. Nurses must understand the principles of verbal and nonverbal communication with both adults and children (who are often unable to verbally communicate their thoughts or how they feel). Pediatric nurses must also have a through understanding of growth and development, as well as anatomy, physiology, and pathophysiology, in order to determine which findings are normal and which require further evaluation or referral. Thus, the assessment of children and their families forms the basis for all nursing care.

## The Interview

"The major purpose of the interview before the physical examination is to obtain a health history and to elicit symptoms and the time course of their development" (Malasanos et al., 1990, p. 3). In a pediatric setting, children may present with symptoms of acute illnesses or for initial or continued assessments of normal growth and developmental processes. When performing an assessment of either well or ill children, the goal of the interview is to obtain complete and accurate data bases. To elicit meaningful data from pediatric clients and their families, nurses must first establish relationships with the primary caregivers (usually the parents and particularly the mother), with the children, and perhaps with siblings or extended family members. As with all therapeutic relationships, trust between clients and nurses provides the foundation for the nurse–client relationship and nursing care activities. The interview is an excellent opportunity to establish a bond of trust between caregivers and clients. Table 5-1 provides a checklist of important items to help ensure a successful interview.

## Components of the Communication Process

The interview is usually the first encounter between nurses and clients and serves as the foundation for the nurse–client relationship. The interview process in pediatrics is particularly complex and challenging. As interviewers, nurses' objectives are twofold: first, the establishment of a trusting relationship with children and adult caregivers; and second, the attainment of complete and accurate assessment data. Communication approaches and responses to the interview are influenced by many factors. These include culture, environment, developmental age of children, previous experiences of the clients and families with the health care system, and nurses' experiences as interviewers. Some of these factors can be addressed with knowledge and skillful use of various communication techniques.

Communication is an active process whereby information is transmitted to or among individuals through the use of symbols. These symbols (for example, words, behavior, sign language) must hold the same meaning for each of the individuals involved in the interaction in order for information to be transmitted effectively.

*Table 5–1. A Checklist for Nurse-Interviewers*

| | |
|---|---|
| Environment: | Has a quiet area free from noise and interruptions been arranged for performance of the interview? Is the interview area comfortable? Is there adequate space, lighting, seating? |
| Confidentiality: | Has confidentiality of the spoken and written word been ensured by the nurse? |
| Development of format: | Have past medical records (if available) been received? Is the reason for the client's visit (if possible) known? Have questions to elicit necessary data been developed? Have the assessment questions been organized in an orderly, logical manner? |
| Time frame: | Has the amount of time necessary for the interview been estimated? Have other commitments been postponed so as not to be interrupted? |
| Documentation: | Are materials necessary for documentation of assessment data available? |

The interview process requires the use of verbal and nonverbal communication techniques by nurses. *Verbal communication* includes words that are either written or spoken. The exchange of words is always accompanied by nonverbal communication. *Nonverbal communication* is composed of facial expressions, body language, gestures, and physical appearance. Because both verbal and nonverbal communication take place at the same time, they must be viewed together. Nurses must be acutely aware of the nonverbal communication that accompanies the exchange of words between themselves and clients. Nonverbal communication provides extremely useful information about the validity of verbal interchanges.

For example, Tommy A. is a 9-year-old boy who comes to the emergency room with a 1-day history of nausea, vomiting, and fever of 38.8°C (102°F). During the interview, Tommy denies any physical pain. However, the nurse observes that Tommy avoids eye contact in answering questions about pain. The nurse also notices that he is shifting in his seat, holding his arm across his abdomen, and is unable to stand fully erect. These nonverbal cues clearly conflict with Tommy's verbal denial of pain. The nurse can now make inferences and judgments about the existence of pain based on complete and valid assessment data. Nonverbal communication may support, strengthen, or contradict clients' verbal exchanges. Additionally "nonverbal behavior may add emotional color to verbal messages" (Haber & Leach, 1987, p. 242).

For example, Christine B. is a 17-year-old sexually active college student. She arrives at the gynecological clinic for a routine examination. During the interview, the nurse asks Christine about her preferred form of birth control. Christine (who has never used birth control) tells the nurse that she is on "the pill." Christine avoids eye contact when answering the question. As the nurse continues to question her about the incidence of side effects, Christine continues to avoid eye contact, speaks softly and rapidly, turns away from the nurse, and begins tapping her foot on the floor. Based on these nonverbal behaviors, the nurse correctly infers that Christine provided what she thought was the expected, rather than true, response.

Nonverbal messages may be expressed in a variety of ways. Facial expressions (frown, raised eyebrows), body position (leaning forward or away, crossed arms or legs), gestures (shrugs, nods), eye contact, and touch are all means of nonverbal communication. Characteristics of spoken words, such as tone of voice, inflection, emphasis, pauses, rate of speech, and vocalizations such as sobbing, laughing, and grunting are also significant forms of nonverbal communication. Nonverbal messages can also be communicated by physical appearance (grooming, hygiene, dress) and the proximity or amount of "personal space" an individual requires. For example, if parents or children move away from the nurse during the beginning of the interview, the nurse might infer that the child or

parents need more personal space and should continue the interview accordingly.

Communication may be influenced by cultural or religious beliefs and values, gender, occupational role, social status, and the extent of the relationship between nurses and clients. Awareness of these influences, and attention to both verbal and nonverbal messages, assist nurses in obtaining the most accurate and meaningful data possible from the interview process.

## Communicating With Parents

The interview process in pediatrics is usually enhanced by the mutually shared goal of nurses and primary caregivers; children's well-being. It is important, however, that nurses do not assume that the caregivers know of the nurses' concerns for children's well-being. For example, if clients are inexperienced with the health care system or have had a previous negative experience, they may be uncertain of nurses' objectives and unclear about the purpose of the interview. If both parents are present, they may be uncertain about the role each should play in the interview process. Nurses must share their purposes for and expectations of the interview with the clients from the outset of the interaction. These objectives can be accomplished as nurses introduce themselves to children and caregivers, and they help to allay the anxiety associated with new experiences for both clients and nurses.

The sharing of information, thoughts, concerns, and feelings is greatly facilitated when clients perceive that nurses want to contribute to their well-being. This realization is of particular importance in interactions with pediatric clients and their families because parents often need support and information to cope with developmental issues. The interview process provides excellent opportunities for nurses to assess parental concerns related to growth and development and parental willingness to participate in health-promoting activities.

## Communicating With Pediatric Clients

The question is frequently asked: "At what age should nurses include children in the interview process?" Pediatric clients should *always* be included in the interview process, beginning with newborns. The role of children throughout the interview process depends directly on the child's levels of cognitive, social, and emotional development. A sound knowledge of growth and development provides nurses with a range of realistic expectations concerning children's ability to participate in the interview. Ways in which nurses can establish the importance of infants as unique individuals and as central figures in the interview process are by referring to children by names or nicknames (instead of as "he," "she," or "the baby"); attempting to elicit eye contact or a smile; and touching, holding, and speaking to them when interviewing.

When nurses introduce themselves to toddlers *and* the parents, the significance of these children to the interview process is further validated. Activities such as toys, books, and videotapes should be available to occasionally distract children so that caregivers have time to focus on the interview. Preschool children readily communicate through play; nurses can use dolls, puppets, or other toys to ask questions and make observations. School-aged children are generally anxious to learn about their bodies and their health. They should be encouraged to make comments or ask questions during the interview. When questioning school-aged children, nurses should use clear, concrete terms and avoid lengthy, excessive, or obvious questions.

Adolescents require validation of their developing independence; nurses should address them directly and allow parents secondary roles or opportunities to "fill in the gaps." Although this approach is a less efficient means of interviewing, it supports the developmental stage of adolescents and acknowledges the timely need for a shift in accountability for personal health from parents to adolescents. Approaching adolescents as the primary source of information is particularly helpful in early adolescence when they have yet to fully exert their independence and parents may be resisting such efforts. Nurse-interviewers should also provide time for adolescents to express thoughts or concerns without having parents present. Additionally, this "private time" provides an opportunity to address important issues such as sexuality and recreational drug use that adolescents are characteristically reluctant to discuss in the presence of their parents. Occasionally parents object to an unsupervised interview with adolescents. In such instances, nurses should attempt to provide for confidential discussion with adolescents before or after the interview, for example, during the physical examination. Table 5-2 provides developmentally appropriate suggestions for including pediatric clients in the interview process.

## Setting the Stage for Successful Interviews

The success of the interview depends greatly on nurses' interviewing skills. Preparation of themselves and the environment, particularly for inexperienced interviewers, is essential. Beginning interviewers should develop or use written guidelines that contain pertinent assessment questions to facilitate the collection of relevant data. These guidelines assist nurses in directing the course of interviews by allowing them to focus on communication skills while obtaining necessary data in a smooth, timely fashion.

Nurses must be careful, however, not to merely read lists of successive questions, because this approach is counterproductive to the goals of the interview. Such an approach severely limits data collection, reflects minimal personal interest in clients (in fact, it supports the "you're just a number" notion), and inhibits the formation of therapeutic nurse–client relationships. Focusing on written guidelines instead of clients also prevents nurses from receiving valuable nonverbal feedback in response to interview questions.

In order for nurses to meet their need for organization and clients' needs for personal interaction, nurses should address these issues at the initiation of the interview so as to clarify the nurses' concerns, and reassure the clients of their concerns for their unique and individual characteristics and concerns. For example, nurses can tell clients: "You may notice that I'll be referring to a sheet of questions at times throughout the interview. This is to help ensure that I have asked all the important questions about the health of your child and family." Although an apparently simple statement, this explanation can be very reassuring to both nurses and clients. Nurses should follow the same procedures when taking notes during the interview. They should inform clients of the intended action and rationale and assure confidentiality before the interview begins. If the interview is to be tape recorded, nurses should first receive permission from clients. Although permission may be given at the beginning of the interview, clients may withdraw permission at any time during the interview, and this should be made clear. Nurses should give clients an approximation as to the probable length of the interview without giving a sense of being rushed. If the interviews must be time-limited, offer clients the option of additional meetings to address their remaining concerns. Clearly stating the purpose of the interviews and being aware of clients' expectations at the beginning of the interactions serve to decrease anxiety and facilitate the interview process.

Another technique that nurses can use is to conduct the interview in segments, leaving the room for brief periods. This process makes the interview less structured and often gives parents and children time to reflect on what has taken place so far and recall additional details.

Ideally, interviews should take place in environments suitable for interpersonal interaction. Nurses should try to select areas that are comfortable for both parents and children, without distractions or the likelihood of interruption. If these environments are not possible, nurses should create an unhurried atmosphere. Confidentiality *must* be ensured; clients are usually not comfortable discussing personal concerns when other clients are behind curtains or uninvolved health care professionals are nearby. Clients' privacy is of the utmost importance.

Nurse-interviewers must demonstrate verbal and nonverbal support of clients throughout the interview pro-

*Table 5–2. Including Pediatric Clients in the Interview Process*

| Age Group | Suggestions |
|---|---|
| Infants | Address by given name rather than "baby," "honey," or other endearing terms.<br>Address by nickname.<br>Hold, touch, or rock infants before or occasionally during interview.<br>Speak softly to infants occasionally during interview.<br>Direct eye contact toward infants. |
| Toddlers | Introduce yourself to toddlers.<br>Allow toddlers to remain close to parents, but continue to direct eye contact and occasional verbalizations toward children.<br>Address children by names or nicknames.<br>Acknowledge some favorite toy or unique characteristic about children. |
| Preschoolers | Introduce yourself to children.<br>Address children by names or nicknames.<br>Direct eye contact and simple questions (likes, dislikes) toward children.<br>Allow children opportunities to touch and manipulate examination equipment.<br>Provide simple explanations before performing activities.<br>Use play, puppets, or toys to demonstrate and communicate. |
| School-aged children | Introduce yourself to children.<br>Address children by names or nicknames.<br>Address questions to children: habits, likes, dislikes, activities, awareness of health.<br>Provide explanations before performing activities.<br>Provide health teaching information directly to children.<br>Use play to demonstrate and communicate. |
| Adolescents | Introduce yourself to adolescents.<br>Address adolescents by name.<br>Advise adolescents and parents that health care at this stage requires some degree of confidentiality.<br>After obtaining necessary information from parents ask to speak to adolescents alone.<br>Encourage open and honest communication.<br>Listen and respond in a nonjudgmental manner.<br>Use open-ended questions to elicit information (e.g., "Tell me about your sexual activity"). |

cess. Eye contact, gestures, proximity, and statements such as "go on, tell me more . . ." and so on can be used by nurses to reflect genuine interest in, and support of, children. Affirmation of support throughout the interview process contributes to clients' senses of acceptance by nurses and fosters the growth of the nurse—client relationship. In pediatrics, it is essential that nurses inform parents or primary care givers that the information they possess about their children is valuable and that this information will be included in care decisions. Validating parental information fosters continued openness. Significant details are often not shared with interviewers because parents do not believe health care professionals would view them as important.

## Communication Techniques

There are several communication techniques that nurses can use during the interview to obtain necessary data. These techniques are composed of open-ended and closed questions, paraphrasing information, reflection, summarizing, and silence.

*Open-ended questions* are general questions that encourage a variety of responses. Nurses use open-ended questions to provide parents with the opportunity to speak freely and contribute valuable data not directly addressed by *closed questions. Closed questions* require no more than a simple one- or two-word answer, often "yes" or "no." For example, to assess the dietary intake of a toddler, nurses can pose an open-ended question in the following manner: "Tell me what Billy usually eats on a typical day" rather than "Is Billy a good eater?" (a closed question). The use of biased or leading questions should also be avoided. To use the above example, the question: "What does Billy eat for breakfast, lunch, and dinner?" implies that Billy should be eating three meals per day when, in fact, toddlers rarely eat three full meals but tend to take small feedings.

Paraphrasing is restatement of messages in a different form than originally communicated. *Paraphrasing* or *restating* the content of clients' messages serves to validate that nurses have accurately understood data provided by caregivers and indicates attentiveness on the part of nurse-interviewers.

*Reflecting* is a technique that is used to repeat clients' feelings, ideas, or questions. This technique helps to further elaborate or clarify clients' facts or feelings. *Summarizing* the highlights of the interview provides additional opportunities for clarification or elaboration of accumulated data. It can also be used during the interview process to refocus attention on the objectives of the interaction. This technique is particularly useful if clients tend to digress from the topic. Summarizing is most commonly used upon completion of the interview and usually signals impending termination of the interaction.

*Silence,* when skillfully used, provides an opportunity for both nurse-interviewers and clients to collect their thoughts and reflect on what has been said. Silence on the part of clients may exhibit anxiety, boredom, lack of comprehension, or introspection. Most interviewers (especially inexperienced ones) are uncomfortable with silence and tend to rush questions one after the other. A silent, slow count of ten (one, one thousand, two, one thousand . . . ) may help interviewers gain greater ease with the use of silence as a communication technique. When terminating the interview, a period of silence following the summary of the interaction allows clients a final opportunity to reflect on the content of the interview and any additional information or feelings they may wish to share.

The importance of supportive remarks and gestures throughout the interview process cannot be emphasized enough. Warm, genuine interest and openness, as well as empathy and respect for clients' knowledge and feelings, are essential to a successful interview process and the development of therapeutic nurse—client relationships. Table 5-3 presents a summary of therapeutic and non-therapeutic communication techniques.

## Family Assessment

Families are the basic units of physical and emotional support for children. They are the primary influences on children's development, because they shape who one is

*Table 5–3. Therapeutic and Non-Therapeutic Communication Techniques*

| Therapeutic Communication Techniques | Non-Therapeutic Communication Techniques |
| --- | --- |
| Open-ended questions | Biased, leading questions |
| | Closed questions |
| Reflection | Assumption |
| Silence | Successive questions |
| Supportive gestures | Judgmental tone |
| Eye contact | Avoidance of eye contact |
| Openness | Preconceived ideas |
| Honesty | Evasion |
| Proximity | Distance |

and who one becomes. The interconnectedness of individuals and families is very apparent in pediatric settings. Nurses cannot provide care to children that is exclusive of their families. Nurses must understand the family system and the relationships and functioning behaviors among members. In effect, child health nursing care is family nursing care.

Today's complex and rapidly changing society does not allow for a single, all-inclusive definition of the family. For physical health assessment purposes, it is essential to receive information about children's biological parents, siblings, aunts, uncles, and grandparents (maternal and paternal). It is also important to inquire about individuals who live with the children (whether or not they are a biological relation, i.e., stepchildren, cousins), because children's health is directly affected by the health status of those in the immediate environment. In assessing social and emotional health, the term "family" may represent a social network composed of relatives, friends, or neighbors. Nurses should be aware that although "family" may represent a variety of relationships and living arrangements, the concept of family is central to the care of pediatric clients. The variety of family configurations is discussed in Chapter 2.

## Family History

According to Malasanos (1990), "the purpose of the family history is to learn about the general health of the client's blood relatives . . . and to identify any illnesses of environmental, genetic, or familial nature that might have implications for the client's current or future health problems and needs or to their solution or resolution" (p. 117). To record family history data, nurses may use a genogram or family tree. This symbolic, graphic representation of family relationships provides a clear and concise means of tabulating assessment data (Fig. 5-1).

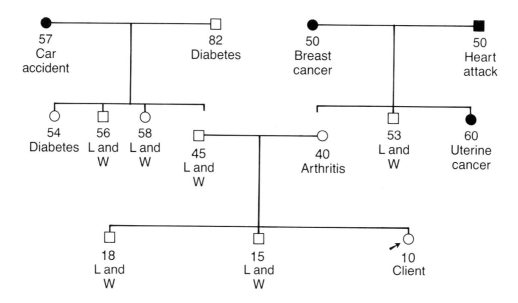

*Figure 5–1.  This genogram illustrates the client's family history in a clear and concise manner.*

As previously stated, a family health history should include the children's parents, siblings, aunts, uncles, and both maternal and paternal grandparents. Interviewers should inquire about the age, general health, and current health status as well as the incidence of chronic or acute illnesses in each family member. For deceased family members, it is important to ascertain the age at death and cause of death. For siblings, it is necessary to obtain a history of immunizations and childhood illnesses, as well as grades in school, activities, and other indicators of development. Family history should include an inquiry into the incidence of genetic and familial illnesses as well as the incidence of common diseases. In order to obtain the family history, questions should include, but not be limited to, the incidence of the following:

Alcoholism
Allergies
Asthma
Birth defects
Cancer
Cystic fibrosis
Diabetes
Emotional illnesses
Endocrine diseases
Genetically transmitted diseases
Heart disease/heart problems

Hypertension
Infant deaths
Kidney diseases
Learning problems
Mental retardation
Obesity
Pulmonary diseases
Sickle cell anemia and other hematological disorders
Seizure disorders
Stroke
Tuberculosis

Assessment of family health practices is also part of the family history. These data provide valuable insights into the health-promoting behaviors of the family and have implications for probable compliance with present medical regimens and predictability of future health problems. Nurse-interviewers should obtain data regarding family nutrition, sleep and exercise habits, the use of prescription or illicit drugs, smoking and alcohol use, and patterns of health maintenance and promotion, i.e., frequency of medical and dental care. While obtaining assessment data regarding family health practices, nurses should also attempt to gain insight into the rationale behind these practices or lack thereof. For example, has the family neglected dental care because of finances, geographic accessibility, or a knowledge deficit regarding the need for frequent dental exams? These examples require very different nursing plans and interventions to assist children and families in attaining and maintaining dental health. Thus, obtaining the family history not only provides data but reflects attitudes, beliefs, and values about health, all of which are essential to the provision of nursing care for pediatric clients and families.

In order to assess the roles and relationships among pediatric clients and their families, it is essential for nurses to understand the factors that have an impact on children and families. Some of these factors include families' developmental stages, the interaction among family members, the support systems available to families and how they avail themselves of these supports, and families' cultural backgrounds. These concepts are discussed in detail in Chapter 2.

## Family and Home Assessment Tools

Several objective data collection tools are available to assist nurses in assessing family functioning. The Feetham Family Functioning Scale (Roberts & Feetham, 1982) gathers data about the family's functioning under stress. This tool assesses parents' perceptions of family relationships and relationships among the family and other social systems. Another tool that assesses family functioning is the Family APGAR Test (Smilkstein, 1978). This tool facilitates assessment of family adaptability, relationships, and growth. Family assessment tools provide nurses with additional mechanisms for the collection of objective data.

Although assessment usually takes place in a clinical setting, it is also important for nurses to observe the interactions of children and their families in the home environment. The Home Observation for Measurement of the Environment (HOME) was developed by Caldwell and Bradley (1984) to provide an inventory to evaluate the cognitive, social, and emotional environment of children within the home. Two separate scales (birth to 3 years and 3 to 6 years) provide nurses with a tool to measure the impact of the home environment on children's growth and development. The Feetham Family Function Scale, the Family APGAR, the Family Environment Scale, and the HOME are discussed in more detail in Chapter 2.

Before using any standard assessment tool, nurses should investigate the reliability and validity of the tool and its ease of use and appropriateness in the family assessment.

## Developmental Assessment

Children are unique individuals who develop physical, cognitive, social, and emotional capabilities throughout childhood and into adulthood. Although each child is a unique being, certain expected patterns of behavior may be anticipated during the course of development. Developmental screening tests assess child development in relation to an expected norm. Assessment findings that fall outside the norm (particularly those below the norm) require an examination of the possible influences on children's development. Developmental screening or assessment is a routine part of the well or ill child's health care.

## Developmental Assessment Tools

Developmental assessment tools are standardized formats for assessing children's growth and development as compared with the norm. The most common type of assessment tool is the growth chart (included in Appendix B). This graphic representation of average weight and height according to age allows for continued assessment of physical growth and development. The section on physical examination describes the techniques for measuring weight and height.

The Brazelton Neonatal Behavioral Assessment Scale (BNBAS) (1973) assesses neurological reflexes, temperament, and social interaction of neonates. Twenty-seven behaviors (such as responses to light, alertness, and irritability) and 20 reflexes (such as plantar grasp, Moro, and sucking intensity) are assessed when newborns are 3 days old. Parents participate in performing this assessment by observing for the stated behaviors. The BNBAS has been shown to be a reliable predictor of infant developmental problems; it also provides fascinating insight into the varied capabilities of newborns.

The Denver Developmental Screening Test (DDST) (included in Appendix A) is a systematic means of assessing children from birth to 6 years. Skills in gross motor, language, fine-motor-adaptive, and personal/social areas are assessed and compared with a range of normal findings. The DDST was revised in 1978 (DDST-R) to reflect concerns that the assessment was culturally biased, lengthy to administer, of limited value in assessing children less than 30 months of age, and of questionable predictive value (Lynn, 1987). Nurses using the DDST-R should be trained in eliciting the desired skills from children. They must be extremely familiar with the tool so that they are able to follow children's cues and obtain accurate data. The DDST is useful in providing nonthreatening interactive opportunities for children and nurses. It can also be used to demonstrate children's developing skills to parents and provides an excellent opportunity for health teaching. However, it should be remembered that the DDST is a screening tool and, as such, does not provide diagnoses of problems; rather, it should be used to determine whether further evaluation is necessary.

Another test that is useful as a prescreening device is the Denver Prescreening Developmental Questionnaire (PDQ). A total of 97 questions are included, but only 10 questions are applicable for any specific age group, from 3 months to 6 years. The major advantage of the PDQ is that parents can answer the 10 questions in a very short period of time. Children who show delays in two or more areas are usually referred for complete developmental testing with the DDST-R.

# Health History

On completion of the family assessment, nurses should focus on the specific needs of pediatric clients. Information about children's present health and medical history is elicited. A review of systems, followed by growth and physiological measurements and physical examinations, complete the child health assessment process.

The pediatric health history provides specific information about children's health, development, relationships with others, and care. The pediatric health history addresses all areas included in an adult health history with the addition of information that is significant to the health concerns of children.

The informant for the health history is usually a parent (often the mother) but may also be a primary care giver, another relative, or even the child. After receiving biographical data from the informants (name, address, date of birth), the nurse-interviewer elicits clients' chief complaints or reasons for seeking care. In pediatrics, children may present with acute or chronic problems or with normal growth and development. If possible, it is best to record the chief complaint in children's own words. For example, a child's statement that "my ear hurts" is assessment data, whereas the parent's statement that "he has an earache" is a judgment. Both types of information are considered *subjective* data.

Nurses should then inquire about the history of the present illnesses. Interview questions should obtain data about children's normal state of health and the onset and duration of symptoms. Current medications and treatment of the problem should be recorded. The purpose of this component of the health history is to obtain a clear and accurate sequence of the events that have led clients and families to seek assistance. The therapeutic communication techniques that were previously discussed should be used, and judgmental statements should be avoided. For example, if while recounting the history of the present illness, the mother states that the child had a fever for three days before seeking care, the nurse must be cautious not to appear shocked, angered, or judgmental. Although this parent obviously needs health teaching, this is not the time to address that need. Doing so could potentially damage the nurse–client relationship and hamper continued data collection.

When the visit is for a regularly scheduled check-up and there is no present illness, nurses have an ideal opportunity to answer parental questions and concerns, as well as time to provide additional information on health promotion and normal growth and development.

# Medical History

## Past History

A child's past medical history begins with the mother's prenatal history, continues through birth and perinatal history, and incorporates all aspects of the child's development to the present.

## Prenatal History

The following information should be included in assessing the health and health practices of the mother during the prenatal period:

1. General state of health throughout pregnancy. Was the mother fatigued, uncomfortable, energetic?
2. Feelings about the pregnancy. Was it planned or unexpected; was the mother anxious, happy, or depressed?
3. Extent of prenatal care. When did prenatal care begin and how frequently was prenatal care obtained?
4. Health habits. Did the mother smoke or use alcohol or recreational, prescription, or over-the-counter drugs? Did she exercise, maintain proper nutrition, and rest?
5. Complications. Any incidence of bleeding, hypertension, toxemia, or exposure to communicable diseases or infection?

## Birth History

The following information should be included in assessing the mother's labor and delivery:

1. The child's date of birth
2. Birth weight and length
3. Hospital, home, or birthing center where child was born
4. Duration of pregnancy
5. Parity of mother (number of live births)
6. Duration of labor
7. Incidence of complications during labor—hypertension, fetal distress, arrested labor (dystocia)
8. Type of delivery—vaginal or cesarean. Note use of forceps, or vacuum extractor.
9. Use of anesthesia, sedation
10. Postpartum complications—hypertension, hemorrhage, infection
11. Newborn complications—respiratory, physiological jaundice (Adapted from Malasanos et al., 1990, p. 598)

## Perinatal History

The nurse should then gather information about the child in the newborn period. Difficulties with sleeping, feeding, weight gain, infection, skin color, or rashes are documented. Determine if a male child was circumcised and if there were any complications. Note the age and weight of the child when discharged from the hospital and the incidence of the above problems during the newborn period.

## Feeding History and Nutritional Assessment

In assessing the child's nutritional status, the nurse should inquire about the feeding history. Determine if the child was breast- or bottle-fed, for what period of time, and the age at which solid foods were introduced. Note the development of food preferences and food allergies. The nurse should ask parents to describe what their child eats in a typical day rather than report that the child is a "good" or "picky" eater. The nurse should include the child in the discussion when possible. Inquire how many times per week (if at all) the child eats fruit, cereals, juice, and eggs. What type of snacks does the child eat, and how often? Who feeds the child, and does he or she enjoy mealtime? Note the administration of vitamin or fluoride supplements. The nurse should be alert to emotional problems that are manifested in eating disorders, particularly among female adolescents.

## Previous Illnesses, Injuries, and Hospitalizations

The nurse should record incidences of recurrent childhood illnesses and communicable diseases. Date of onset, duration of illness, and treatment received should be included. Injuries such as fractures, sprains, and cuts should be noted and the onset, duration, and treatment of these should be documented.

If the child has been previously hospitalized, note the hospital name, date of admission, reason for admission, treatment received (including surgical treatment), response to treatment, discharge date, and follow-up care received. Record the names of the physicians or health care professionals involved in the child's care.

## Allergies

Allergies to food, medications, or environmental allergens (dust, pollen, fur) are recorded in a *prominent* place on children's health records. Nurses should obtain full descriptions of symptoms that signal allergic reactions.

## Immunization Status

Nurses should ask parents to show evidence of the child's immunization status. In the United States it is mandatory for children to be immunized before they start school. The suggested schedule for immunizations is listed in Appendix A. Note reactions to previously administered immunizations, such as convulsions, fever, rashes, or swelling.

## Growth and Development

Nurses should assess physical growth and development through the use of a growth chart (included in Appendix B). Parents should be asked how they perceive their child's growth and development. Parents should compare the child's development to that of siblings, if applicable. Nurses should obtain data about the "developmental milestones," the age at which children attained the following skills:

Held head erect
Rolled over
Sat alone
Crawled
Walked alone
Eruption of the first tooth
Said words
Used sentences
Attained bladder and bowel control

Attainment of developmental milestones can also be assessed through use of a screening tool such as the DDST.

Further assessment is indicated if developmental delays are noted among developmental milestones items or if the parent perceives a developmental delay compared with siblings or peers.

## Activity Patterns

Nurses should note children's usual patterns of sleep, play time, and heightened activity. Participation in athletic, dance, musical, or artistic activities provides clues to children's areas of interest and enjoyment.

## School Performance

School performance is a major part of school-aged and adolescent development. Although academic achievement provides some information about children's cognitive development, nurses must be alert to problems of inattentiveness or short attention span, disinterest, reading and comprehension, and peer relations.

## Behavior and Personality

Nurses should assess the patterns of behavior that children exhibit in the home, school, and social settings, and determine whether children display tendencies such as aggressiveness, passivity, or assertiveness. Nurses should ask parents to describe the child: for example, is the child shy, outgoing, serious, light-hearted? Ask children to describe themselves. Assess how the child reacts to stress, disappointment, failure, and limit setting. This information provides data that summarize children as unique individuals. Together with the previous assessment data, a comprehensive picture of the child's past development and present abilities is being created.

## Review of Systems

The review of systems is generally organized from head to toe and seeks to identify strengths or problems not mentioned in the health history. Table 5-4 provides a problem-oriented format to guide nurses in performing a review of systems.

## Physical Assessment Skills

Performing a physical assessment requires both an extensive knowledge base and command of manual and observational skills.

### Inspection

The physical assessment process always begins with inspection. *Inspection* is detailed observation of clients and includes attention to sounds and odors that emanate from clients. Good lighting is essential to the inspection process.

## Auscultation

*Auscultation,* or listening to the body, often follows inspection. Auscultation can be used for assessment of the cardiovascular system (the sounds of the heart and movement of blood) and the thoracic and abdominal viscera. *Direct* or *immediate* auscultation is the use of the unaided ear to listen to sounds. Most auscultation, however, is performed with a stethoscope that is used to augment sounds. Three types of stethoscopes are commonly used today: acoustic, magnetic, and electronic.

Auscultation skills are a key component of the pediatric physical examination. Nurses should auscultate the thorax (heart and lung sounds) before any other assessment (except observation) because infants and younger children tend to cry as the physical exam becomes more invasive.

Auscultation should be performed in an area free from extraneous noises, and clients should be requested not to speak (unless asked) during this part of the physical examination.

The diaphragm and bell of the stethoscope should be

### Table 5—4.  Review of Systems

**Physical Systems**

| | |
|---|---|
| **General** | Complaints of pain over sinuses |
| Usual state of health | Allergies |
| Frequency of colds, infections, illnesses, fevers, or sweats | Change in olfactory ability |
| Activity patterns: note extremes | Incidence of sore throats, chewing, swallowing difficulties |
| Recent weight loss or failure to gain weight | Presence of tonsils |
| Regular health habits such as use of drugs, alcohol, or tobacco | **Chest** |
| **Integumentary** | Breasts (if applicable): swelling, nipple discharge, lumps, pain, tenderness |
| Skin: frequent rashes, bruises, itching, dryness, bleeding, presence of lesions, growths, or acne. | Knowledge of breast self-exam |
| Hair: changes in amount, texture, presence of infections, lice. | **Respiratory** |
| Nails: changes in appearance, texture, color. | Incidence of coughing, croup, wheezing, stridor, noisy breathing |
| Oral mucosa: presence of lesions, color | Rapid breathing |
| **Head and Neck** | Shortness of breath |
| History of trauma, dizziness, syncope, headaches (frequency, location, duration, treatment) | **Cardiovascular** |
| Tenderness, stiffness or limitation of neck movement. | History of murmur, defect, palpitations, hypertension, cool extremities |
| Swollen glands | Cyanosis, dyspnea on exertion, fatigue |
| **Eyes** | **Gastrointestinal** |
| Change in visual acuity: diplopia, blurring, myopia, hyperopia, excessive blinking, difficulty reading or watching TV | Incidence of vomiting, diarrhea, constipation, abdominal pain, rectal bleeding, change in stool color |
| Strabismus | **Urinary** |
| Incidence of infection, discharge, pruritus, tearing, swelling | History of infection, frequency, urgency (assess use of bubble baths) |
| **Ears, Nose, and Throat** | Dysuria, nocturia, incontinence |
| Incidence of infection, earaches, discharge, tinnitus | Polyuria, oliguria, hematuria |
| Change in auditory acuity | |
| Incidence of nasal discharge, stuffiness, discharge, epistaxis | |

*(continued)*

*Table 5—4. Review of Systems (Continued)*

**Physical Systems**

**Genital**

Presence of discharge, rash, odor
Knowledge of sexuality
Frequency of sexual activity
Use of birth control, barrier methods (if applicable)
Females
   Menstruation (if applicable): age at onset, frequency, duration, intensity, discomfort
Males
   Knowledge of testicular self-exam

**Musculoskeletal**

Muscle twitching, cramping, weakness, pain
Joint swelling, stiffness, pain
Coordination and strength

Curvature of spine
History of fractures or dislocation

**Neurological**

History of birth injury, central nervous system (CNS) disease, seizures
Speech delays, impediments
Motor coordination, balance
Altered sensorium
Learning difficulties

**Endocrine**

Incidence of precocious puberty, exophthalmos
Changes in weight, skin texture, hair distribution, and pigmentation
Heat/cold intolerance
Polydypsia, polyuria, polyphagia

**Psychosocial Systems**

**Feelings About Self**

Child's perception
Parents' perception

**Family**

Ordinal position, number of family members, number of siblings, and living arrangements

**School**

Grade, performance, behavior, attendance, attitude

**Coping Ability**

Responses to daily stress, crisis, disappointment, failure, uncertainty, new situations

**Activities**

Sleep/activity pattern
Preferred play activities
Hobbies, interests, enjoyment

**Safety**

Knowledge of personal safety precautions (strangers, sexual abuse), auto, bike, swim, and fire safety

**Health Maintenance**

Frequency of medical, dental, ophthalmic care
Exercise
Diet
Self-care activities

(Adapted from Bowers, A., & Thompson, J. [1988]. *Clinical manual of health assessment* [3rd ed.]. St. Louis: C.V. Mosby)

warmed in the hands. A systematic assessment pattern should be followed for both heart sounds and breath sounds: heart sounds should be auscultated apex to base, anterior to posterior. Breath sounds should be auscultated in the following progression: anterior, upper right lobe, upper left lobe, lower right lobe, lower left lobe. Posterior auscultation should follow the same progression. The bell of the stethoscope should be used to auscultate breath sounds in pediatric clients because the chest walls are very thin and breath sounds are naturally magnified. Nurses should enlist the parents' participation by requesting that they hold children during this part of the physical exam. Older children should be allowed to participate in the examination by listening to their own heart and breath sounds. Nurses should provide age-appropriate explanations of heart and lung functioning to enhance this health education opportunity.

There is no one correct way to approach auscultation of the thorax or abdomen. What is most important is that the examiner use a systematic approach to ensure that no area is overlooked.

## Percussion

The technique of *percussion* consists of two distinct actions. Nurses first tap body surfaces such as the posterior chest, then listen and interpret the sound produced as a result of this action. In tapping the body, one hand should be placed on the body surface ensuring that the distal portion of the middle finger is held firmly against the body. This finger should then be tapped at or distal to the distal interphalangeal joint of the stationary finger. The tap is delivered in a crisp, sharp, and smooth manner by the middle finger of the striking hand. The speed and force of the blow can be manipulated by action of the wrist (Fig. 5-2).

The sound produced as a result of this striking action may be either *tympanic, hyperresonant, resonant, dull,* or *flat.* These sounds are characterized by differences in intensity, pitch, duration, and quality (Table 5-5).

Percussion is useful for assessment of the thorax and abdomen. Percussion of the thorax proceeds systematically (Fig. 5-3) from posterior to lateral, then anterior, chest. In pediatric clients, percussion findings of the thorax are usually of a hyper-resonant nature throughout all chest fields. Decreased hyper-resonance is an abnormal finding and may indicate fluid collection or solid tissue presence.

Percussion of the abdomen includes all four abdominal quadrants, with special attention paid to the liver and spleen. Borders of the liver and splenic dullness are identified and compared with standard measurements. Enlargement of the liver or spleen is an abnormal finding and requires immediate follow-up. Additionally, nurses may detect a greater amount of air in the abdomens of infants and young children due to the swallowing of air when they are feeding or crying.

## Palpation

*Palpation* is the use of the sense of touch through the hands to gather assessment data. Palpation encompasses a broad array of assessment techniques: use of the dorsal surface of the hand to assess temperature, the use of the palm of the hand to assess vibration, and use of the pads of the fingers to assess individual structures such as lymph nodes, abdominal organs, and circulation.

In pediatric clients, palpation of peripheral pulses provides valuable information about cardiovascular structure and function. For example, absence of a femoral pulse may indicate a congenital heart defect such as coarctation of the aorta. Palpation of the abdomen assesses muscle tone, tenderness, liver and spleen size, and the presence of hernias or superficial masses. Light (gentle pressure) and deep palpation is performed in all four abdominal quadrants. Palpation of lymph nodes is performed in the same manner as for adults.

## Physical Examination

### Developmental Approaches to Physical Examination

Although it is customary to follow a head-to-toe assessment pattern when performing physical examinations of adults, this approach is not as effective with pediatric clients.

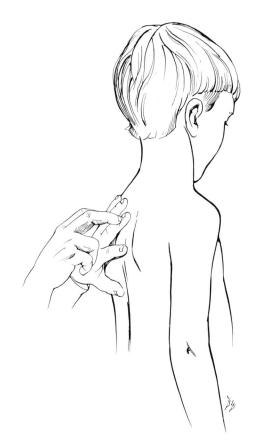

*Figure 5–2. Position of the hands for percussion.*

Nurses should understand children's developmental needs and approach the examination in a developmentally appropriate and supportive manner.

Infants characteristically become agitated and cry as the physical examination progresses. Techniques that need to be conducted when children are calm and quiet, such as auscultation of heart and lung sounds, should be performed first; those that are likely to upset children, such as otoscopic exams, should be performed last. Newborns dislike having their clothes removed, whereas older infants often like being without clothes. The best time to examine infants is 1 to 2 hours after they have eaten. They should not be examined when they are hungry or immediately after their feedings. The examination environment should be warm and without drafts. The parents should be included in as much of the examination as possible to enhance children's sense of security and performance of the exam.

Toddlers can rarely be examined without the assistance of the parents since they are usually more anxious. Nurses should become familiar with both toddlers and preschoolers before the physical exam. The physical exam should start with inspection of nonthreatening areas such as the hands. Children should be allowed to

*Table 5–5. Percussion Sounds*

| Note | Characteristics | Structures Percussed |
|---|---|---|
| Tympany | Loud, high-pitched note of drumlike quality and moderate duration | Produced by percussion of a closed, air-filled structure that vibrates along with surrounding tissue. Examples: stomach, intestines |
| Hyper-resonance | Extremely loud and very low note of booming quality and long duration | Produced by percussion of air-filled lungs. Examples: emphysema, chronic obstructive pulmonary disease (COPD) |
| Resonance | Moderate to loud, low note of hollow quality and long duration | Produced by percussion of normal lung |
| Dullness | Soft to moderate, high note of thudlike quality and moderate duration | Produced by percussion of liver |
| Flatness | Soft, high note of flat quality and short duration | Produced by percussion of muscle |

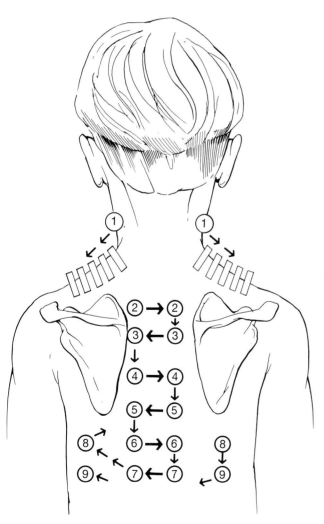

*Figure 5–3. Procedure sites for percussion of the chest.*

manipulate exam equipment, play with favorite toys, and have parents nearby. Play is extremely valuable in developing rapport with children and decreasing anxiety. Performing an exam on a toy doll or animal often reassures fearful children.

School-aged children are very interested in the "hows and whys" of body function. Involving these children in the examination process allows them to master the experience. School-aged children benefit from brief explanations of procedures before they are performed. They also prefer to undress alone and do not like to remove their underwear. School-aged children should be given privacy to undress and should be provided with examination gowns, if desired.

Physical examination of the adolescent proceeds in the same manner as for the adult, with added attention to the adolescent's need for privacy. Physical examination of the adolescent is discussed further in Chapter 16.

## Growth Measurements

Measurements of growth (length, height, weight, and head and chest circumference) are routine components of pediatric examinations. These measurements are calibrated at each contact with pediatric clients, beginning in infancy. The successive measurements are plotted against average measurements for each age on standard growth charts (see Appendix B). The pattern of growth is assessed; alterations may or may not indicate developmental problems. Growth measurements are screening rather than diagnostic tools. Alterations in growth patterns require follow-up.

## Length and Height

For children under 3 years of age, recumbent body length is measured by use of a tape measure or measuring board (Fig. 5-4). Paper or metal measuring tapes rather than of cloth tapes should be used, because cloth tapes stretch and provide inaccurate measurements. The parents hold their child's head steady while the nurse holds the feet, and the measurement is noted. If a measuring board is available, the child's head is held against the stationary headboard while the nurse fully extends the legs and rests the moving footboard against the child's heels. In the absence of a tape measure or measuring board, the child should be placed on a paper-covered surface that is marked at the top of the child's head and the bottom of the heels. The distance between the markings is measured after the child is removed.

Children aged 3 years and older can be measured standing (Fig. 5-5). Height can also be measured against a wall hanging or wall surface. Height measurement on a weight scale is difficult and usually not as accurate. Children should stand erect with heels, buttocks, shoulders, and head against the wall. A mark is made at the top of the head (usually by holding a ruler or other flat object perpendicular to the wall) while distance from the floor is measured.

Children generally enjoy having their height measured. They take pride in "how big" they have grown. Nurses should enlist children's participation in measuring their height and should support their excitement with their growth. Nurses should also be aware that patterns of height are familial and should recognize that it is the pattern of growth, rather than the actual measurement, that is most significant.

## Weight

Infants are weighed nude on a balance beam or electronic scale. A barrier (cloth or paper) should be placed between the baby and the scale. The scale should be balanced to zero with the barrier in place. The nurse should place the child on the scale and obtain the weight measurement.

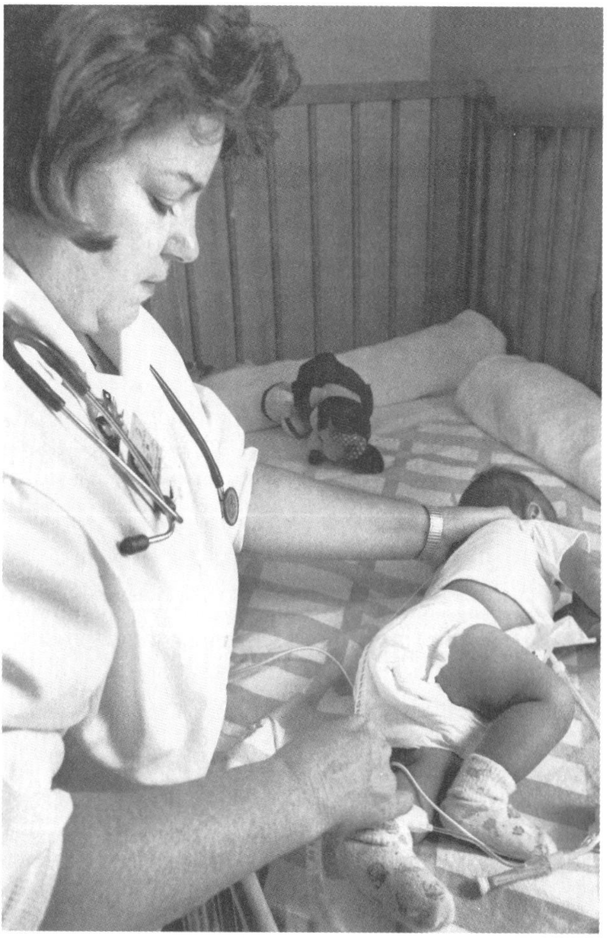

*Figure 5–4.    Measurement of body length. (Courtesy of Nursing Department, Thomason Hospital, El Paso, Texas)*

*Figure 5–5.    Measurement of standing height. (Courtesy of Texas Tech University Health Sciences Center)*

Children should never be left unattended. One hand should hover over (but not rest on) the child to ensure safety.

Older children are weighed on an adult scale while wearing only their underpants. Adolescents may prefer to wear a light gown as well. Techniques for balancing the scale and obtaining the weight are the same as for adults.

Again, the pattern of weight gain, rather than an individual measurement, is most indicative of potential growth problems. Weight losses are of concern, particularly in infancy, and require further assessment. Even small weight losses in infants who have had fevers, diarrhea, or vomiting are potentially serious because they may indicate dehydration and subsequent electrolyte imbalances.

### Head and Chest Circumference

Head circumference is measured at every visit during the first 2 to 3 years of life. The measurement is obtained by placing a paper measuring tape around the child's head while he or she is supine. The tape should cross the forehead and occiput but should not cross the ears (Fig. 5-6). Measurements are recorded in centimeters and plotted on standard growth charts (see Appendix B).

Chest circumference is measured with a measuring tape placed around the chest at the level of the nipples, midway between inspiration and expiration. Chest circumference is usually measured only within the first year of life, because it loses its screening significance in the normal child following this period. Chest circumference is measured in centimeters and is usually equal to or slightly less than head circumference. Variations in chest circumference may indicate cardiac or respiratory defects.

## Vital Signs

Measurement of temperature, pulse, respirations, and blood pressure provide information about the status of

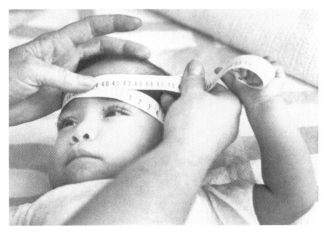

*Figure 5–6. Measurement of head circumference. (Courtesy of Nursing Department, Thomason Hospital, El Paso, Texas)*

physiological systems. Vital sign measurements are compared against baseline and average measurements for age.

### Temperature

Temperature may be measured in Celsius or Fahrenheit scales using a mercury or electronic thermometer. Temperature measurements are obtained in rectal, oral, and axillary body areas. There is no single recommendation regarding the amount of time required to obtain an accurate temperature in each of the body areas. Times given are based on current research and practice and the type of thermometer used. Electronic thermometers record temperature in less time and with minimal hazard when compared to mercury thermometers. Some electronic thermometers signal when proper contact is not being maintained. Nurses should use thermometers that are appropriate to children's developmental stages. Tympanic membrane sensors are also being used more commonly because of their high degree of accuracy and the short length of time needed for accurate measurement.

Rectal temperatures are commonly taken in infants and young children. Since the insertion of the thermometer into the rectum stimulates the central nervous system, a bowel movement often results in normal children. Rectal temperatures should not be performed on newborns, children with diarrhea, and children with CNS, bleeding, or immune disorders.

To assess rectal temperature, children should be placed either prone or supine on a flat surface area or on the parent's lap. Parents should place their hands across the child's hips to prevent raising of the buttocks. Nurses should separate the buttocks with one hand while gently inserting the lubricated thermometer with the other hand (Fig. 5-7). Resistance to the thermometer (pushing out) is a normal response to stimulation of the rectal sphincter. The thermometer should be inserted no more than one half inch or on observation of the rise of the mercury upon insertion, to avoid tissue injury and assure adequate placement. Mercury thermometers are held in place for a minimum of 3 to 5 minutes; electronic thermometers are withdrawn when they signal completion of the measurement.

Rectal temperatures were formerly thought to be more accurate than oral or axillary temperatures. Research shows, however, that oral and axillary temperatures are equally accurate when taken properly (Eoff and Joyce, 1981). These findings are an important consideration for nurses because rectal temperatures are an invasive procedure and may be upsetting to children.

Oral temperatures can be taken as soon as children are able to cooperate with the placement of the thermometer in their mouths. This type of temperature measurement had been recommended for children aged 5 and above. Proper placement of the thermometer for an oral temperature is under the tongue in the right or left posterior sublingual pocket (Fig. 5-8). Contrary to former be-

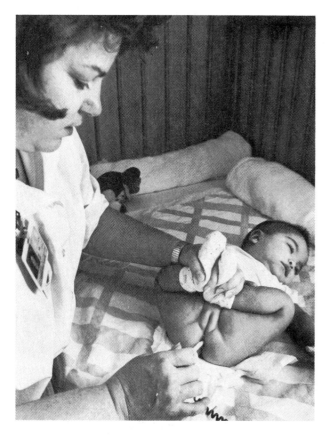

*Figure 5–7. Measurement of rectal temperature. (Courtesy of Nursing Department, Thomason Hospital, El Paso, Texas)*

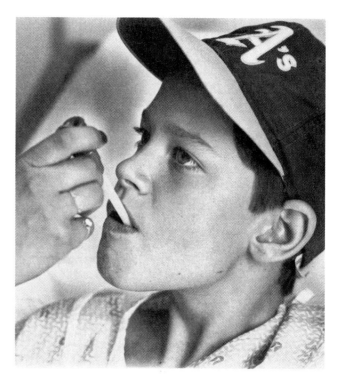

*Figure 5–8.    Placement of thermometer for oral temperature. (Courtesy of Nursing Department, Thomason Hospital, El Paso, Texas)*

liefs and practices, this—not the front of the tongue—is the most accurate area for temperature assessment. The posterior sublingual pockets have a rich blood supply derived from the carotid arteries, which are near the thermoregulating center in the brain and the central circulation of the heart (Erickson, 1980).

Axillary temperatures are taken by placing the mercury or electronic thermometer in the axilla and holding the arm against the body. The optimal length of time for an axillary temperature with a mercury thermometer is 11 minutes. Electronic thermometers indicate that a temperature has been recorded with a "beep" signal. With this method, children can either sit on the parents' laps and "be hugged" or parents can hold them over their shoulders, maintaining a hold on their arms. The axillary temperature is noninvasive and is useful for children who are anxious and fearful, as well as for those for whom other methods of temperature measurement are not appropriate.

### Pulse

Auscultation of the apical pulse while children are calm or sleeping is the most appropriate means of measuring pediatric clients' heartbeats. Nurses should listen for one

full minute because young children are more likely to exhibit cardiac rhythm irregularities.

Children's pulse rates vary with age (see Appendix B). The normal pulse rate of a newborn can be as high as 140–160 beats per minute. It is difficult for inexperienced examiners to monitor both rapid beats and the 60-second clock. Nurses should monitor the number of heart beats, and the parent or another health care practitioner should note the passage of 60 seconds.

Nurses should also assess peripheral pulses, particularly the brachial and femoral pulses. Weak, bounding, or absent pulses indicate cardiac abnormalities and require follow-up.

### Respiration

The respiratory rate of children can be obtained by observation or auscultation. In young children, observation of diaphragmatic excursions for assessment of respiratory rate is performed by placing the hands on the child's abdomen and counting respirations for one full minute (breathing rhythms are often irregular in young children). Auscultation of respiratory rate is commonly used with older children and follows the same procedure as for adults.

### Blood Pressure

The blood pressure readings of children vary widely (see Appendix B). Blood pressure, when consistently monitored from the neonatal period on, can provide important information about cardiac status. It is recommended that all children aged 3 and over receive blood pressure monitoring as part of their routine medical care.

The actual technique of assessing blood pressure is the same as for adults. A variety of pediatric blood pressure cuff sizes are available, depending on children's sizes and weights. Standard pediatric sizes are 2.5 inches, 5 inches, 8 inches, and 12 inches. The nurse determines appropriate cuff size by ensuring that the cuff size is neither more than two thirds nor less than one half the length of the upper arm (Alexander & Brown, 1979). The cuff should completely encircle the upper arm or leg, with or without overlap, and should be wide enough to cover 75% of the arm or leg. A wider cuff can provide a lower reading, whereas a cuff that is too narrow can give an abnormally high reading (Hoekelman, 1991) (Fig. 5-9).

Five sounds can be detected in a blood pressure reading, but for most examiners, these sounds are difficult to hear accurately. Three of the five sounds should be recorded as the measurement of blood pressure: the point at which sounds first appear, the point at which sounds become muffled, and the point at which sounds disappear. The appearance of the sound represents systolic blood pressure; the muffling of sounds represents diastolic blood pressure. Since crying, pain, vigorous activity, and anxiety affect blood pressure, the measurement is best taken when children are calm and sitting with their arms at heart level.

## General Survey

The general survey is an overall observation of a child's physical appearances and behaviors. It includes the nurse's impressions of the child's physical health status based on facial expressions, gait, coordination, movement and activity, cleanliness, appropriateness of dress, and apparent nutritional status. Nurses should also observe manifestations of emotional and developmental health such as verbal and nonverbal communication, parent–child interaction, interaction with the environment, and personality attributes. The summary of the nurse's overall impressions of the child should be recorded before the physical examination begins.

## Skin

Color, pigmentation, moisture, texture, turgor, and temperature of the skin should be observed. Skin color is genetically determined, and the extent of pigmentation varies among racial and ethnic groups. Children's skin color and pigmentation that is markedly different from the parents' deserves further inquiry. Pallor is usually associated with anemia, yellow tones are usually associated with jaundice, and reddish pigmentation (flushed) is usually associated with fever. Cyanosis of the nails of the hands or feet is seen in hypothermia and severe cardiac and respiratory conditions. Nurses should observe for the presence of ecchymotic areas and inquire about multiple bruises or

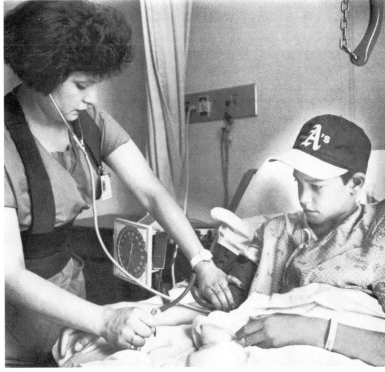

*Figure 5–9.  Placement of pediatric blood pressure cuff. (Courtesy of Nursing Department, Thomason Hospital, El Paso, Texas)*

bruises in unlikely areas. Nurses should also note the presence of birthmarks and other congenital integumentary problems, which are discussed in more detail in Chapters 11 and 34.

Skin should feel warm, smooth, and moist and demonstrate good turgor. Generalized dry skin may indicate poor nutrition, excessive bathing, or sun exposure. Localized dry skin may indicate dermatitis or eczema. Coolness of the skin, particularly the extremities, may indicate hypothermia or a cardiovascular problem.

Assessment of hydration (skin turgor) can be performed by pinching the skin between the fingers and immediately releasing it. In well-hydrated children, skin will return to normal. In dehydrated children, the creases made will not immediately disappear and will remain peaked for a few seconds. Assessment of skin turgor on infants and young children is best performed using the skin of the abdomen. Poor skin turgor usually indicates dehydration and electrolyte imbalances but is also seen with malnutrition and chronic disease states.

Hair should be smooth, soft, and evenly distributed. Sparse, brittle hair is seen with nutritional deficiencies.

Nails should be clean and smooth without clubbing or curving. Clubbing of the nails is often seen in cardiac and respiratory disorders, and convex or concave curving is associated with malnourishment.

## Head and Neck

The head is examined for shape, size, contour, and movement. Newborns often have asymmetrical heads due to molding during the birth process. The location of the anterior and posterior fontanels is shown in Figure 5-10. In infants the anterior fontanel may remain open for up to 2 years, but the posterior fontanel closes by 2 months of age. Assess the anterior fontanel for bulging (increased intracranial pressure manifested by meningitis, hydrocephaly) or depression (dehydration). The presence of a visible pulsation while resting is also an abnormal finding. Early closure of the fontanels may indicate microcephaly, and delayed closure may indicate increased intracranial pressure. Head size is monitored by obtaining head circumference measurements. Increased head circumference may indicate hydrocephaly, which is discussed in more detail in Chapters 11 and 26. Problems with movement of the head may indicate nervous system disorders. Most infants gain control of the head when pulled to a sitting position by 3 months of age. Delayed head control is often the first sign of cerebral palsy (Alexander & Brown, 1979).

Observe the face for symmetry and placement of features. Eyes should neither be widely spaced nor appear too close together. The nose should be at the midline, with symmetrical nares. The mouth and lips should also be symmetrical and intact. (Cleft lip is a congenital anomaly

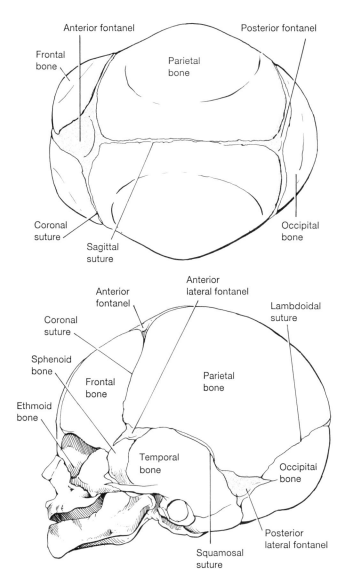

*Figure 5–10.   Location of anterior and posterior fontanels.*

detectable at birth.) Ears should be symmetrical with each other, and the top of the pinna should be on line with the lateral corner of the eye (Fig. 5-11). Low-set ears are associated with mental retardation and Down syndrome.

In examining the neck in children, limited range of motion may indicate injury to neck muscles or meningeal irritability. Nurses should observe children as they turn their heads to the right, left, up, and down to assess range of neck motion. Nurses should move infants' heads through those positions while supine. Younger children should follow the path of a bright object or toy. Strength of the muscles may be tested in older children by attempting to pull the face forward as children are looking over their shoulders.

Assess swelling of the parotid gland as children are sitting with their necks slightly extended. Bilateral or unilateral swelling under the jaw usually indicates mumps.

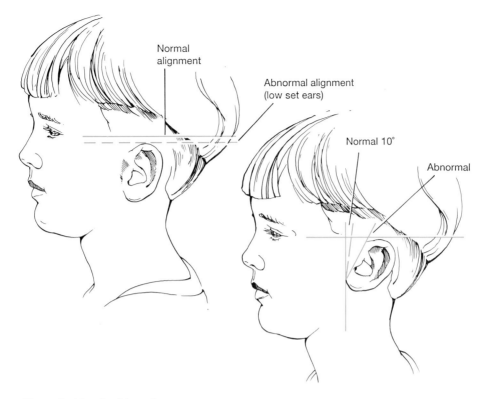

Normal alignment

Abnormal alignment (low set ears)

Normal 10°

Abnormal

*Figure 5–11. Position of ears.*

Lymph nodes are normally not palpable in adults and older children but are often palpable in infants and young children. Palpation is carefully performed to determine the significance of findings. Warm, enlarged, and tender lymph nodes signal a current infection, whereas small, firm "shotty" nodes (similar to small pellets or buckshot) indicate previous respiratory infections. All chains of lymph nodes (Fig. 5-12) should be palpated, preferably while examining the body area where they are located.

## Eyes

Placement of the eyes is assessed during observation of the face. The external structures of the eye are examined first. The eyelids are examined for *ptosis* (drooping), which may indicate oculomotor nerve damage. Ptosis may also result from edema of the eyelids secondary to infections such as nephritis, sinusitis, and infectious mononucleosis.

The presence of epicanthal folds is also assessed. *Epicanthal folds* are vertical folds of skin covering the inner canthus of the eye (Fig. 5-13). Epicanthal folds are a normal finding in Asian infants and are also observed in 20% of Caucasian children. In 97% of these cases, the folds disappear by 10 years of age. Epicanthal folds may indicate Down syndrome, renal agenesis, or glycogen storage disease (Alexander & Brown, 1974).

The presence of eyelashes and tears is also noted. Tears are present after 3 months of age. Absence of tears after 3 months may indicate a blocked tear duct. Tears prior to 3 months of age may also indicate a blocked lacrimal duct, because lacrimal fluid overflows as tears in the presence of a blocked tear duct.

The bulbar and palpebral conjunctiva are examined for color, hemorrhage, and inflammation. The bulbar conjunctiva is normally transparent; redness indicates hemorrhage due to eye strain. The palpebral conjunctiva is observed by gently pulling the lower eyelid down and by gently everting the upper eyelid, if feasible. Normal color is pink and shiny. Redness and discharge may indicate infection, and a cobblestone appearance is seen in children with chronic allergies. The pallor of anemia can also be seen in the palpebral conjunctiva.

The iris is observed for color. In most children, permanent eye color is observed between 6 months and 1 year of age. *Brushfield's spots* (a light or white speckling of the outer two thirds of the iris) may occur in normal children but is usually associated with Down syndrome and mental retardation. An irregular iris may be due to inflammation; follow-up with an ophthalmologist is indicated.

The pupils are observed for size, roundness, equality, and reaction to light. Difference in pupil size (*aniscoria*) is normal in 5% of the population. It usually indicates central nervous system damage. Dilated or constricted pupils are abnormal and may be related to central nervous system damage or drug or toxin poisoning. Direct and consensual reactions to light are assessed. Nurses should instruct

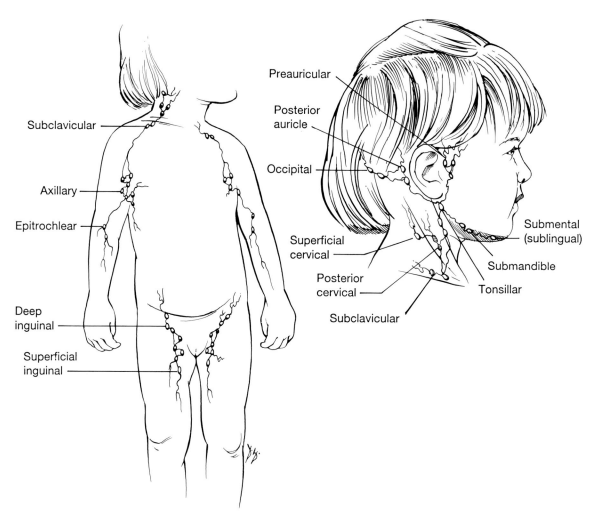

*Figure 5–12.  Location of lymph nodes.*

children to observe favorite toys or interesting objects on the other side of the room. Children should have to look beyond the nurse to facilitate this assessment. Since children may become upset if the lights are turned off suddenly, gradually dimming the lights or darkening the room may allay their fears. If such a tactic is not possible, distracting children with the light from a flashlight may achieve the same objective.

The sclera should be clear, but they often have a bluish tint in infants due to the thinness of the tissue. The cornea and lens should also be clear and without cataracts. Shining a light into the eye at an oblique angle highlights opacities of the lens.

Eye movements are assessed by observing for nystagmus and strabismus. *Nystagmus,* or jerky eye movements, may be due to vestibular, ocular, or neurologic causes. Although eye movement in infants may not be symmetrical, this usually resolves by about 6 months. The presence of *strabismus* (crossed eyes or squint) should be assessed in children 6 months of age and older. Inward or convergent rotation of the eye(s) is called *esophoria,* and

outward or divergent rotation is called *exophoria.* To test for strabismus, the nurse should darken the room and shine a penlight into the child's eyes. The reflection of the light should be in exactly the same place on each pupil. A slight difference in the reflection indicates strabismus. Another screening test for strabismus is the cover test. The child should focus on objects one foot away. While the child keeps both eyes open, the nurse should quickly cover, then uncover one eye and observe for any inward or outward movement of the previously covered eye.

Examination of the internal structures of the eye requires an ophthalmoscope. Parental assistance is required to assess these structures in infants and young children. Older children are asked to focus on an object in the room, and nurses should challenge them to maintain their focus on the object even if nurses step in front of them. Nurses should elicit the red reflex and examine the optic disc, macula, fundus, vessels, and the vitreous and aqueous humors.

Newborns are capable of visual fixation at 2 weeks of age. Assessment of visual acuity should begin at 2 weeks

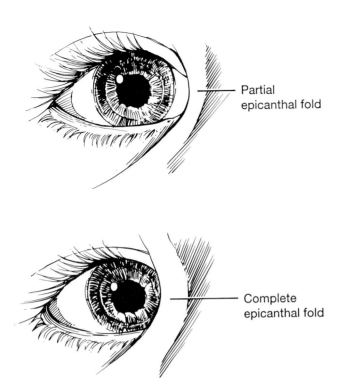

*Figure 5–13.  Epicanthal folds.*

and continue throughout childhood. Infants are most interested in faces, and their visual acuity can be assessed by observing their eye contact with parents and nurses. Toddlers are interested in pictures and can identify simple forms. At age 3 visual acuity can be assessed with the "E-Test." Children are asked to identify the direction that the letter "E" is facing from 20 feet away. This test is useful for preschoolers and for older children who may not know the alphabet letters of the Snellen Chart. Because preschoolers do not always follow directions well, nurses should validate poor results before referring clients for additional testing. Older children have their visual acuity tested with the Snellen Chart and follow similar techniques used in adult vision screening. Additional discussion of vision assessment and screening can be found in Chapter 35.

## Ears

This component of the physical examination should be performed at the end of the examination because most children find it distressing. The external ears are examined for position, symmetry, shape, size, and the presence of lesions. The external ear canal is examined for the presence of edema, exudate, and redness (abnormal findings) and the amount and texture of cerumen. Hard cerumen can be softened with a variety of products, including a few drops of mineral oil, and removed with cloth or cotton.

The middle ear is examined with an otoscope. Although this examination is not usually painful (unless an

infection is present), most children are fearful and distressed during otoscopic examination. The nurse should enlist the help of parents or other health care practitioners to hold the child's head while he or she is supine. Older children can be examined either while sitting or supine. The pinnas of infants' and young children's ears are pulled down and outward for visibility of internal structures (Fig. 5-14). The pinnae of the ears of older children are pulled in the same direction as adults' (up and backward). The tympanic membrane and its landmarks are assessed. A red or pink tympanic membrane may indicate infection, but it may also result from crying. A bulging, nonfluctuating membrane is a better indicator of infection.

Assessment of auditory functioning can begin in the neonatal period. Newborns startle in response to noise. At 3 months of age, infants turn their heads toward noises. In preschoolers, auditory acuity can be assessed with the same procedures used for adults. These procedures are considered screening tests and are not used for diagnostic purposes. Nurses can make assessment of auditory acuity an enjoyable game for children. Toddlers can sit in their parents' laps with the nurses behind them making noises with bells, keys, or their voices to the right or left of the children. School-aged children may want to name the object as well as locate the direction of the sound. Assessment of auditory function provides an opportunity for nurses to become familiar with clients and prepare them for the otoscopic exam. Additional information on assessment of the ear can be found in Chapter 35.

## Nose

The nose is examined for size, shape, symmetry, patency of the nares, condition of the mucous membranes, and evidence of nasal discharge. Patency of the nares is assessed

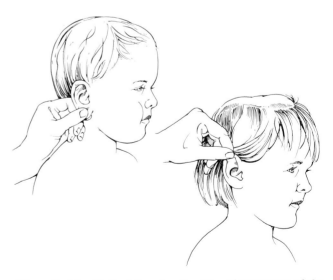

*Figure 5–14.  Method for visualization of structures of the inner ear.*

by observing air emanating from each nostril. Nurses can place a small mirror, the diaphragm of a stethoscope, or a finger in front of one nostril and observe the presence of air exiting from this nostril while occluding the other with a finger. This assessment is performed for each nostril. The condition of the mucous membranes is examined with a flashlight or nasal speculum. In children with chronic allergies, the mucous membranes are gray, pale, and swollen rather than pink. Watery nasal discharge may also indicate allergies. Palpation of the maxillary and ethmoid sinuses and frontal sinuses after age 8 for tenderness or pain may indicate sinusitis, because the sinuses are not normally palpable. Purulent nasal discharge may also indicate sinus infection.

## Mouth and Throat

Examination of the mouth and throat often provokes fear in children. These assessments are perceived by children as invasive and should also be performed at the end of the physical examination. External structures of the mouth are assessed as part of the observation of the face. Lips should be symmetrical and pink. Circumoral pallor may reflect cardiac or respiratory distress. Nurses should be attuned to any odors that emanate from the mouth, because these may reflect poor hygiene, nasal obstruction, or metabolic disorders.

The buccal mucosa should be moist, pink, and without lesions. *Milk curd* patches that do not wash away in newborns or immunocompromised clients indicate thrush (*Candida albicans*). Sticky (tacky) mucous membranes may indicate dehydration. The salivary glands, such as Stentsen's duct (opposite the upper second molar) and Wharton's duct (located at the base of the tongue), are assessed for patency. Saliva is not present until 3 months of age in normal children. Swelling of these ducts indicates obstruction. The gums should be pink without bleeding or puffiness. Such symptoms indicate gingival disease. The tongue is assessed for color and texture. The normal tongue is pink. A "geographic tongue" is gray with exaggerated grooves and may be a normal finding for children or may be related to allergies, fever, or medications. Although infants may have a reflexive tongue thrust, a protruding tongue is often seen with mental retardation.

The hard and soft palate and the pharynx are assessed for color, integrity, and the presence and condition of tonsils. Cleft palate is a congenital defect that is present at birth and is correctable by surgery. Tonsils are assessed for size, color, symmetry, and the presence of exudate or tonsillar crypts (scars). The posterior pharynx is also assessed for the presence of exudate. White patches in the throat are characteristic of streptococcal infections. The presence of the gag reflex is also assessed using a tongue depressor.

The presence of teeth will depend on children's ages.

The pattern of tooth development is shown in Figure 5-15. When present, teeth should be white, without discoloration or dental caries. Children should begin a program of dental hygiene with the appearance of the first tooth. The first appointment with a dentist should be made between the ages of 2 and 3. Parents should be advised *never* to put children to bed with bottles because of the risk of aspiration, as well as the pooling of milk or other fluids that can cause dental caries.

## Thorax and Lungs

Physical examination of the thorax begins with inspection. In infancy, the chest is almost round with the anterior–posterior diameter equaling the transverse diameter. At age 6, the anterior–posterior diameter equals the lateral diameter, and a rounded chest is associated with obstructive respiratory diseases. Asymmetrical abnormalities of the thorax may be present at birth (*pectus excavatum*—abnormal depression of the sternum) or develop in early childhood (*pectus carinatum*—abnormal prominence of the sternum, also known as pigeon chest).

Respirations are abdominal until about 7 years of age. Infants and young children demonstrate little intercostal muscle use; in fact, observation of intercostal muscle use in infants and young children may indicate respiratory disease. Labored breathing in children is evident by the use of accessory muscles, nasal flaring, fatigue, cyanosis, restlessness, and apprehension. Rate of breathing varies greatly with age; extremely rapid or extremely slow rates are of concern. (See Appendix B for the range of normal breathing rates for children from infancy to 15 years of age.) Breath sounds in children are primarily bronchovesicular. Diminished or absent sounds, wheezes, and rales are abnormal. Auscultation of breath sounds should take place when children and the environment are quiet. The bell of the stethoscope is most useful for assessing breath sounds.

Percussion of the thorax proceeds in systematic fashion, as previously described (see the discussion of percussion earlier in this chapter). Increased resonance is a normal finding in pediatric clients, whereas decreased resonance may indicate fluid or tissue accumulation.

A vibration (*tactile fremitus*) may be felt if the hand is held against the infant's chest while he or she is crying. In older children, the thorax and lungs are assessed in the same manner as they are in adults.

## Heart

Landmarks of the heart are slightly different in pediatric clients than in adults (Fig. 5-16). The apex of the heart is one to two intercostal spaces above what is normal for adults. The point of maximal impulse (PMI) is located at the fourth intercostal space, slightly to the left of the mid-

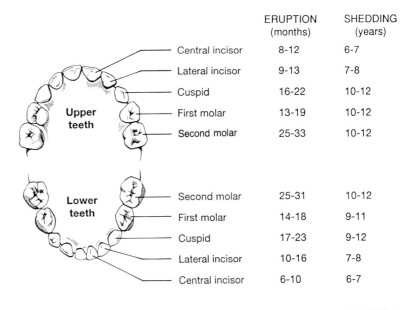

| | ERUPTION (months) | SHEDDING (years) |
|---|---|---|
| Central incisor | 8-12 | 6-7 |
| Lateral incisor | 9-13 | 7-8 |
| Cuspid | 16-22 | 10-12 |
| First molar | 13-19 | 10-12 |
| Second molar | 25-33 | 10-12 |
| Second molar | 25-31 | 10-12 |
| First molar | 14-18 | 9-11 |
| Cuspid | 17-23 | 9-12 |
| Lateral incisor | 10-16 | 7-8 |
| Central incisor | 6-10 | 6-7 |

*Figure 5–15. Pattern of tooth eruption.*

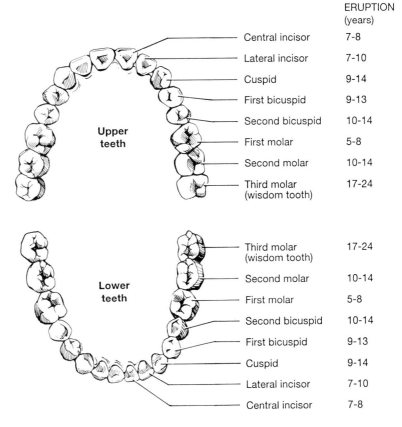

| | ERUPTION (years) |
|---|---|
| Central incisor | 7-8 |
| Lateral incisor | 7-10 |
| Cuspid | 9-14 |
| First bicuspid | 9-13 |
| Second bicuspid | 10-14 |
| First molar | 5-8 |
| Second molar | 10-14 |
| Third molar (wisdom tooth) | 17-24 |
| Third molar (wisdom tooth) | 17-24 |
| Second molar | 10-14 |
| First molar | 5-8 |
| Second bicuspid | 10-14 |
| First bicuspid | 9-13 |
| Cuspid | 9-14 |
| Lateral incisor | 7-10 |
| Central incisor | 7-8 |

clavicular line. Assessment of cardiovascular status includes measurement of the apical pulse, peripheral circulation, and blood pressure. Auscultation of the apical pulse should be assessed for 1 full minute because sinus arrhythmias are common in children. Many children also have functional (or innocent) heart murmurs. Functional murmurs can be heard with the normal turbulence of blood flowing through the heart; they are common in children and usually resolve spontaneously by late adolescence.

Electrocardiograms and x-rays should be used to rule out heart defects.

Heart sounds in the pediatric client are louder (owing to thin chest walls), of higher pitch, and of shorter duration than adult heart sounds. Assessment of blood pressure, temperature, color, pulse, and capillary refill of extremities also provides significant data regarding cardiac status. Cardiac assessment is discussed in more detail in Chapter 24.

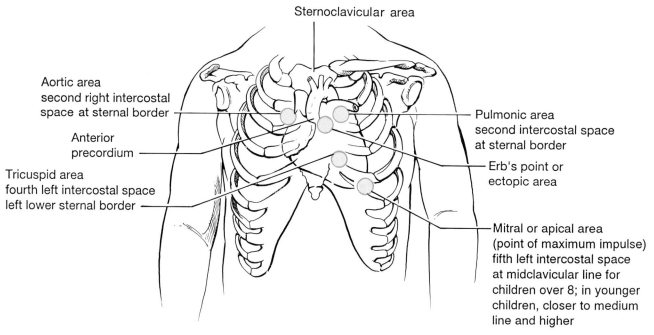

Sternoclavicular area

Aortic area
second right intercostal
space at sternal border

Anterior
precordium

Tricuspid area
fourth left intercostal space
left lower sternal border

Pulmonic area
second intercostal space
at sternal border

Erb's point or
ectopic area

Mitral or apical area
(point of maximum impulse)
fifth left intercostal space
at midclavicular line for
children over 8; in younger
children, closer to medium
line and higher

*Figure 5–16.    Anatomical landmarks of the heart.*

## Abdomen

Examination of the abdomen is best performed when children are relaxed. Nurses should enlist the assistance of the parents, as needed, to facilitate the examination.

In children under 4, inspection of the abdomen reveals a protuberant "pot belly" musculature while standing, sitting, and supine. This protuberance is seen in older children while they are standing until about age 13. This appearance is due to the immature development of the abdominal musculature and, as a normal finding, must be distinguished from abdominal distention. Hernias are also a common finding in white children younger than 2 years and in black children younger than 7 years. *Inguinal hernias* occur when the intestine protrudes through the inguinal ring due to a weakness or failure to close. *Umbilical hernias* occur at the navel and are more common in females. The abdomen is observed for peristaltic waves and dilated veins. These abnormal findings may indicate pyloric stenosis or other types of abdominal obstructions.

Auscultation of all four abdominal quadrants is performed. If bowel sounds are not immediately heard, nurses should listen for 1 full minute in each quadrant before concluding that bowel sounds are absent. Absent bowel sounds are a serious assessment finding and require immediate follow-up with physicians. A consistent bruit (even in light movement) is also an abnormal finding that requires follow-up.

Percussion of the abdomen assists in identifying the location of the liver, spleen, and kidneys. The nurse should percuss down the midaxillary line and right side of the client. Notes are tympanic except in areas of body organs. Shifting areas of dullness may indicate fluid collection.

During palpation infants may suck on a pacifier, and nurses should request parental assistance to help children maintain composure. Nurses' hands should be warm before touching children's skin, and nurses should look for nonverbal manifestations of discomfort. Palpation of the abdomen assists in identification of liver and splenic borders as well as a generalized assessment of abdominal tenderness. Children's livers are usually palpable 1 to 2 cm below the right costal margin during the first year, and 1 to 3 cm below the right costal margin thereafter. A liver extending below 3 cm is considered abnormally enlarged. Liver enlargement requires immediate follow-up with physicians because it may indicate a severe infectious process. The spleen may be palpated by asking the child to lie on the right side. The nurse should push up gently with one hand from behind the child's left costal vertebral area while simultaneously gently pushing under the left anterior costal margin with the other hand. The child should take deep breaths, and the tip of the spleen should strike the nurses' fingers. Nothing more than the tip should be felt. An enlarged spleen requires further assessment since it may indicate a blood disorder or infectious process.

## Genitalia

Examination of the genitalia should be performed in a relaxed manner by use of inspection and palpation. As children become older, they are more modest and self-conscious, so they may prefer that examination of the genitalia be performed by a health care practitioner of the same sex. If this is not possible, an efficient exam alleviates children's sense of discomfort.

In male children, the *penis* and *scrotum* are examined. Males may be circumcised or uncircumcised, depending on religious and cultural beliefs. It is no longer thought that a circumcision is necessary for hygienic purposes, yet it remains a common procedure for American males. In uncircumcised newborns, the foreskin of the penis is tight and difficult to retract. Difficulty retracting the foreskin persisting beyond 3 months of age is called *phimosis,* and the nurse must determine if it causes any interference with urination. The meatus should be located at the tip of the shaft. *Hypospadias* is the presence of the meatus on the ventral surface of the penis; *epispadias* is the presence of the meatus on the dorsal side. Children with these problems should be referred, because both defects are surgically correctable.

The scrotum is assessed for signs of swelling that may indicate a hernia or hydrocele. Nurses should palpate the scrotum for the presence of descended testicles. The inguinal canal should be blocked with the index finger before palpating the scrotum to prevent the testes from being pushed back up out of the scrotum. Nurses should be aware of the procedure for testicular self-exam and provide client teaching beginning in early adolescence.

In female children, the *labia majora, labia minora, urethral meatus,* and *vaginal orifice* are examined. Owing to the presence of maternal hormones, neonates may have enlarged labia minora, bloody discharge, or an enlarged clitoris. Purulent or mucoid discharge from the urethra or vagina indicates infection. Assessment of lesions associated with sexually transmitted diseases is performed. Sexually active adolescents should have internal pelvic examinations despite their characteristic reluctance about these procedures. Adolescent females who have experienced breast development should have a complete examination of the nipples, breast tissue, and lymph nodes. The nurse should instruct clients in the purpose and techniques of breast self-examination (BSE).

The presence of secondary sex characteristics in pubescent adolescents should be documented. Nurses should also assess the adolescents' knowledge of sexuality and sexual activity so that supportive counseling can be given. Adolescent sexuality is discussed in more detail in Chapter 16.

## Musculoskeletal

Assessment of the musculoskeletal system begins with observation of clients' movements such as sitting, crawling, walking, and coordination, and fine and gross motor movements. Range of motion should be observed by watching young children at play.

Upper and lower extremity joints are palpated for tenderness, warmth, pain, or swelling. Muscles are inspected and palpated bilaterally for strength, symmetry, tone, and development. Nurses should ask children to see "how hard they can push" with their feet or hands against the nurses' hands. Children should be asked to demonstrate "great strength." Encouraging children to push up

with their shoulders (while the nurse resists) is part of the same game.

Extremities are assessed according to size, symmetry, and range of motion. Young children often demonstrate a "bowing" of their legs (genu varum) until they are about 3 years of age. This position is often related to the wide stance children use when they begin to walk. Persistence of bowed legs beyond 3 years of age may indicate weakening of the bone and requires further assessment. Young children's feet are characteristically flat owing to the presence of additional fat pads. Complaints of foot discomfort and the presence of high arches or flat feet should always be followed. Deformities of the foot are documented and referred for orthopedic treatment.

Assessment of the hips begins in infancy with observation of a "hip click" and continues through childhood. The hips should be examined for congenital dislocation or subluxation at every health care visit during the first year of life. Asymmetry of gluteal or leg folds and unequal leg length indicate a hip abnormality. Nurses should be able to abduct the infant's legs with hips and knees flexed to almost 90 degrees. Any resistance to this movement or production of a "clicking" sound indicates a dislocated hip. Further assessment techniques for dislocated hips, including the Ortolani and Barlow tests, are discussed in Chapter 33.

To assess the presence of a flexion deformity in older children, the hips are flexed intentionally on one side. If a flexion deformity exists, the opposite side will unintentionally flex.

Examination of the spine is a routine part of the pediatric physical exam. Children's spines are palpated while prone and also while standing for areas of tenderness and stiffness. Symmetry of movement is observed, and the presence of exaggerated curves is documented. Children should be carefully observed for any unusual lateral anterior or posterior curvature of the spine. Abnormal curvatures of the spine, including *scoliosis, kyphosis,* and *lordosis,* are discussed in detail in Chapter 33.

Assessment of fine motor coordination is also part of the examination of the musculoskeletal system. The nurse should select activities that are within the child's expected levels of mastery and ask him or her to demonstrate the activities. This strategy enforces the child's self-esteem and encourages cooperation as the nurse attempts to assess higher level skills.

## Neurological

### Cerebral Function

The neurological exam can be divided into several distinct areas. Assessment of cerebral function is based upon inferences made throughout the interview and physical examination processes. According to Alexander and Brown (1979), "Generalized cerebral function is manifested in general behavior; level of consciousness, orientation, intellectual performance (including knowledge, judgment, calculation, memory, and thought content); and mood and behavior" (p. 329). Knowledge of developmentally appropriate behaviors and children's past activities provides important clues to their level of cerebral functioning. For example, even infants possess the ability to be oriented to person. Orientation to time, however, is a less significant indicator of neurological function in children than it is in adults owing to developmental processes.

Memory may be assessed in children as young as 4 years of age. Immediate recall is assessed by asking children to repeat three digits, letters, or sounds after nurses state them. This ability increases to four digits at 5 years and five digits at 6 years. Lack of immediate recall in the absence of anxiety or fear can indicate generalized cerebral disease. Recent memory is tested by showing children an object early in the examination and asking children to remember what it was 5 minutes later. Remote memory is tested by asking children about an activity or event in the past (for example, summer vacation). Assessment of memory is feasible within developmentally appropriate expectations.

Nurses may wish to elicit responses to specific tests of cerebral function, including cortical sensory interpretation, cortical motor integration, and language. *"Cortical sensory interpretation* is the ability to recognize objects through the different senses" (Alexander & Brown, 1979, p. 330). Pediatric clients find many of these tests interesting, and little resistance is offered to participating in them. *Stereogenesis* (recognition through feel) can be tested with objects such as jacks, coins, paper clips, and keys. Nurses should challenge children to close their eyes and identify the objects in their hands. *Graphesthesia* is the ability to identify shapes traced on clients' backs or hands. Younger children more readily detect geometric shapes, while school-aged children detect certain numbers (0, 7, 3, 8, 1) (Alexander & Brown, 1979). Auditory evaluation can be performed by asking children to close their eyes and identify a familiar sound. Visual evaluation can be performed by showing children several objects and asking them to identify a specific object out of that group.

*"Cortical motor integration* is tested by having the child perform a semicomplex skill, such as folding a piece of paper and sealing it in an envelope" (Alexander & Brown, 1979, p. 331). Most developmental screening tests assess these abilities.

Speech and articulation are evaluated throughout the assessment process. In preverbal children, characteristics of crying (such as a high pitch) can indicate neurological dysfunction.

### Cranial Nerve Assessment

Assessment of cranial nerve function in children is performed in the same manner as it is for adults, with adjustments for developmental age. Ideally, examination of the cranial nerves is incorporated into body area and systems assessment.

### Cerebellar Function

Cerebellar function is usually assessed by using a developmental screening test such as the Denver Developmental Screening Test. Manifestations of cerebellar function are observed in children's gait, and inferences about this aspect are based on developmental expectations. Motor skills necessary for dressing, undressing, writing, kicking a ball, and putting a raisin in a bottle can all be readily observed during the physical examination. Another way to assess cerebellar function is to ask children to touch their noses with a finger of one hand, then the other, and finally both in succession, while their eyes are closed. Children can also be asked to pat their knees first with their palms, then with the backs of their hands, with increasing speed. Cerebellar function is difficult to assess in infants: Coordination of sucking/swallowing and gagging (reflex) activities provides some clue as to cerebellar function in infants. Normal and abnormal findings are discussed in Chapter 11.

### Motor Function

Motor function is primarily assessed during examination of the musculoskeletal system. Muscle tone, development, strength, and movement are components of motor function assessment.

### Sensory Function

Assessment of sensory function is composed of evaluation of superficial sensation (pain, temperature, touch) and deep sensation (vibration, deep pain, and discrimination). Sensory function is assessed symmetrically.

Superficial pain is assessed by alternating light sticks with sharp and blunt ends of a pin and asking the child to distinguish between them. Temperature is assessed using warm and cold water (never hot water, for safety purposes). Sensitivity to touch varies with the body part used to elicit a response.

In assessing deep sensation, vibration is tested by placing a vibrating tuning fork on the client's sternum, knees, toes, or iliac crest. Children are instructed to respond when the vibration ceases. Nurses check for continued vibration of the tuning fork by self-testing. Both sides of children's bodies are tested in this way. These assessments of sensory function are not applicable to infants and young children but can be used to assess older children. Sensory function in infants and young children can be tested to some degree by their response to tactile stimulation, pain, and temperature.

## Reflexes

*Reflexes* are automatic muscular responses to specific stimuli. They are classified as *deep tendon reflexes,* belonging to large muscle groups, or *superficial reflexes* caused by irritation of the skin. Reflex activity is measured on a scale from 0 to 4, where 0 indicates the absence of a reflex, 2 indicates an average response, and 4 indicates a hyperactive response. Reflexes present at birth include the Moro, palmar grasp, and rooting reflexes. Absence of these reflexes indicates severe neurological problems. Newborn reflexes disappear by 4 months of age. Another newborn reflex is the *Babinski reflex,* which is elicited by stroking the lateral aspect of the sole of the foot with a sharp object and observing hyperextension of the toes and dorsiflexion of big toe. This reflex disappears by 2 years of age. A positive Babinski is frequently seen in older children with neurological injuries.

Deep tendon reflexes include the *biceps, triceps, brachioradialis, patellar,* and *Achilles* reflexes. Deep tendon reflexes are elicited by stretching the tendon slightly and briskly tapping with a reflex hammer. The superficial reflexes include the *abdominal, cremasteric, plantar,* and *superficial anal* reflexes. Assessment of these reflexes should be included in examination of body areas and systems.

## Summary

The child health assessment process is a long and comprehensive examination of patterns of physical, cognitive, social, and emotional growth and development. Pediatric nurses are challenged to use their clinical knowledge and interpersonal skills to meet the health needs of clients and their families.

Nurses begin the assessment process with the establishment of trusting, open nurse–client relationships among pediatric clients, adult caregivers, and themselves. Nurses should approach the interview process with a sound knowledge of communication techniques, patterns of child and family development, and personal, environmental, and professional preparation for the task at hand. By respecting the clients' and families' values, cultures, and beliefs, nurses provide supportive care that addresses individual and unique care needs.

Physical assessment techniques are performed within a framework of developmental understanding. Upon completion of the assessment and data collection phase, nurses can formulate and prioritize nursing diagnoses. Once nursing diagnoses are established, nurses work with clients and families to formulate care plans.

# Nursing Care Plan

Beginning with this chapter and continuing throughout each of the remaining chapters in this unit, a nursing care plan will be developed. Because this chapter has addressed the topic of nursing assessment, only this part of the care plan will be included in this chapter. At the end of Chapter 6, which discusses nursing diagnosis, nursing diagnosis will be added to the same care plan. The remaining stages of the care plan will subsequently be added at the ends of the planning, implementation, and evaluation chapters so that the complete plan will be shown in Chapter 9. The objective is to demonstrate how each step of the nursing process has a place in nursing care plans, and how each step builds on the previous steps.

### Assessment

Meghan Caldwell is a two-year-old girl brought to the emergency room at 3:30 AM by her parents.

### Chief Complaint

Meghan's mother reports a harsh, barky cough with apparent increasing difficulty in breathing.

### Subjective Assessment

*Past History:* Seen regularly since birth by a pediatrician for routine well-child care. No prior illnesses or hospitalizations; immunizations up-to-date.

*Present History:* Symptoms of upper respiratory infection for 48 hours; increasing respiratory distress for the past 6 hours.

*Family History:* Mother is 31; father is 34; both are well; no siblings. Maternal and paternal grandparents are alive and well. No family history of asthma, allergies, or chronic respiratory conditions.

*(continued)*

# Nursing Care Plan *(Continued)*

## Objective Assessment

***Physical Examination:*** T. 102°F (rectal); P. 162 (apical); R. 46; B P 90/48 (R. arm); weight 11 kg (22%); height 89 cm (75%).

| | |
|---|---|
| Integument: | Clear, warm, moist, good turgor |
| Head: | Normal |
| Eyes: | PERRLA, EOM's intact, funduscopic exam normal |
| Ears: | Otoscopic exam normal |
| Nose: | Increased viscous secretions; nasal flaring |
| Mouth: | Lips dry, circumoral cyanosis |
| Throat: | Erythema, tonsils normal, no exudate, voice hoarse, barky cough |
| Neck: | Nodes non-palpable |
| Thorax and Lungs: | Tachypnea, inspiratory dyspnea, substernal and suprasternal retractions, decreased breath sounds, bilaterally scattered rales and rhonchi |
| Heart: | Tachycardiac, normal rhythm, no murmur |
| Abdomen: | Active bowel sounds in all quadrants; no pain, tenderness, or masses |
| Genitalia: | Normal |
| Musculoskeletal: | Full ROM |
| Neurological: | Reflexes normal and symmetrical; anxious, irritable, restless |

## Medical Diagnosis:

Laryngotracheobronchitis (croup)

## Medical Plan:

Admit to hospital; mist tent with 30% $O_2$; antibiotics

## Nursing Care Plan for a Child With Croup

| Goals | Nursing Interventions | Evaluation Criteria |
|---|---|---|

**NURSING DIAGNOSIS #1**

## References

Alexander, M., & Brown, M. (1979). *Pediatric history taking and physical diagnosis for nurses* (2nd ed.). New York: McGraw-Hill.

Brazelton, T. B. (1973). *The neonatal behavior assessment scale.* Philadelphia: J. B. Lippincott.

Caldwell, B.M., & Bradley, R. (1984). *Home observation for measurement of the environment* (rev. ed.). Little Rock, AR: Bureau of Educational Research, University of Arkansas.

Eoff, M. J., & Joyce, B. (1981). Temperature measurements in children. *American Journal of Nursing, 81,* 1010.

Erickson, R. (1980). Oral temperature differences in relation to thermometer and technique. *Nursing Research, 29,* 157.

Haber, J., & Leach, A. (1987). Family theory and application. In J. Haber, P. Hoskins, A. Leach, & B. Sideleau (Eds.). *Comprehensive psychiatric nursing* (3rd ed.). St. Louis: C. V. Mosby.

Hoekelman, R. (1991). The physical examination of infants and children. In B. Bates (Ed.). *A guide to physical examination* (5th ed.). Philadelphia: J. B. Lippincott.

Lynn, M. (1987). Update: Denver Developmental Screening Test. *Journal of Pediatric Nursing, 2,* 348.

Malasanos, L., Barkauskas, V., Stoltenberg-Allen, K., & Moss, M. (1990). *Health assessment* (4th ed.). St. Louis: C. V. Mosby.

Roberts, C., & Feetham, S. (1982). Assessing family functioning across three areas of relationships. *Nursing Research, 31,* 231.

Smilkstein, G. (1978). The family APGAR: A proposal for a family function test and its use by physicians. *Journal of Family Practice, 6,* 1231.

# Bibliography

Ackerhalt, J. (1987). Nurse–client relationship. In J. Haber, P. Hoskins, A. Leach, & B. Sideleau (Eds.). *Comprehensive psychiatric nursing.* St. Louis: C. V. Mosby.

Baker, N. C. (1984). The effect of type of thermometer and length of time inserted on oral temperature measurement of afebrile subjects. *Nursing Research, 33,* 109–111.

Barus, D. H. (1983). A comparison of rectal and axillary temperatures by electronic thermometer measurement in preschool children. *Pediatric Nursing, 9,* 424.

Bates, B. (1991). *A guide to physical examination* (5th ed.). Philadelphia: J. B. Lippincott.

Blumenthal, S., et al. (1977). Report of the task force on blood pressure control in children. *Pediatrics, 59* (supplement), 797.

Bowers, A., & Thompson, J. (1988). *Clinical manual of health assessment* (3rd ed.). St. Louis: C. V. Mosby.

Brazelton, T. B. (1984). The neonatal assessment scale and its significance. In M. E. Avery, & H. Tauesch (Eds.). *Schaffer's diseases of the newborn.* Philadelphia: W. B. Saunders.

Britton, C. N. (1985). Blood pressure measurement and hypertension in children. *Pediatric Nursing, 11,* 8.

Brown, M., & Murphy, M. (1981). *Ambulatory pediatrics for nurses* (2nd ed.). New York: McGraw-Hill.

Chow, M., Durand, B., Feldman, M., & Mills, M. (1986). *Handbook of pediatric primary care.* New York: John Wiley & Sons.

Church, J. L., & Baer, K. (1987). Examination of the adolescent, a practical guide. *Journal of Pediatric Health Care, 1,* 65.

Frankenberg, W. K., & Camp, B. W. (Eds.). (1975). *Pediatric screening tests.* Springfield, IL: Charles C Thomas.

Giuffra, M. Sociocultural issues. In J. Haber, Hoskins, P, Leach, A, & Sideleau B. (1987). *Comprehensive psychiatric nursing* (3rd ed.). St. Louis: C.V. Mosby.

Koniak-Griffin, D. (1987). Developmental assessment with Denver Developmental Screening Test: An effective approach for clinical instruction and performance evaluation. *Journal of Pediatric Nursing, 2,* 102.

Lenninger, M. (1978). *Transcultural nursing: Concepts, theories and practices.* New York: John Wiley and Sons.

Maheady, D. C. (1986). Cultural assessment of children. *American Journal of Maternal–Child Nursing, 11,* 128.

Mitchell, J. R. (1980). Male adolescents' concern about a physical examination by a female. *Nursing Research, 29,* 165–169.

Moss, J. R. (1981). Helping young children cope with physical examination. *Pediatric Nursing, 7,* 17–20.

Orque, M. S., Bloch, B., & Mourroy, L. S. A. (1983). *Ethnic nursing care: A multicultural approach.* St. Louis: C. V. Mosby.

Powell, M. L. (1981). *Assessment and management of developmental changes in children.* St. Louis: C. V. Mosby.

Sturner, R. A., Green, J. A., & Funk, S. G. (1985). Preschool Denver Developmental Screening Test as a predictor of later school problems. *Journal of Pediatrics, 107,* 615–621.

Yoos, L. (1981). A developmental approach to physical assessment. *American Journal of Maternal–Child Nursing, 6,* 168.

# Nursing Diagnosis in Child Health Care

Joan T. Duer

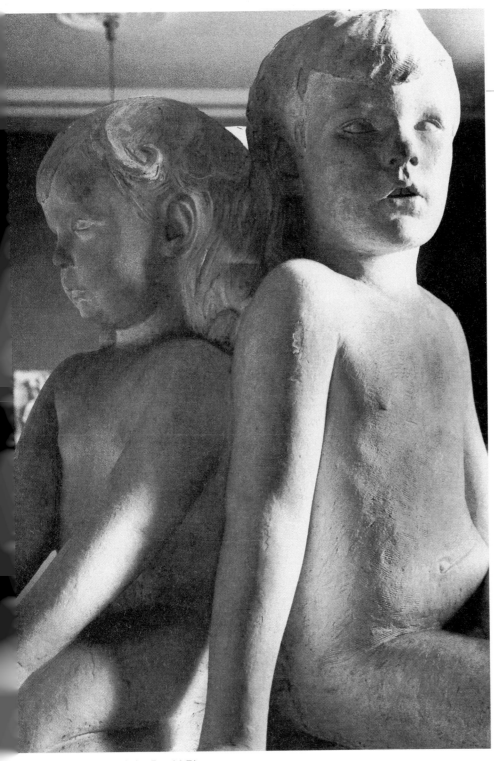

Photograph by David Finn

6

*The Evolution of Diagnostic*
*    Reasoning in Nursing*

*Nursing Diagnosis*
*        Definition of Nursing Diagnosis*
*        Types of Nursing Diagnoses*
*        Components of Nursing Diagnosis*

*The Diagnostic Process in Nursing*
*        Data Collection and*
*            Interpretation*
*        Hypothesis Generation and*
*            Testing*
*        Validation of Findings*
*        The Diagnostic Statement*

*Nursing Diagnosis in the Pediatric*
*    Setting*

*The North American Nursing*
*    Diagnosis Association (NANDA)*

*NANDA Nursing Diagnosis Taxonomy*
*    I*

*Summary*

*Nursing Care Plan*

### Learning Objectives

*Upon completion of this chapter the reader will be able to:*

1. *Define nursing diagnosis.*
2. *Identify components of a nursing diagnosis.*
3. *Describe the evolution of diagnostic reasoning in nursing.*
4. *Demonstrate the applicability and differences in the use of nursing diagnosis in the pediatric setting.*
5. *Describe the diagnostic process in nursing.*
6. *Explain the role of the nurse in the diagnostic process.*
7. *Identify appropriate NANDA-approved nursing diagnoses based on assessment data.*

### Key Terms

*actual nursing diagnoses*

*data analysis*

*defining characteristics*

*diagnostic statement*

*high risk nursing diagnoses*

*hypothesis*

*nursing diagnosis*

*PES*

*taxonomy*

*wellness nursing diagnoses*

## The Evolution of Diagnostic Reasoning in Nursing

The concept of nursing diagnosis is not new to the nursing profession. The actions of accumulating and analyzing data, making clinical judgments, and acting to alleviate identified health problems can be traced to Florence Nightingale. Nursing clinical judgments were first labeled as nursing diagnoses in the 1950s. In 1960, a classification system identified 21 clinical problems. This system was adopted by many nursing schools to assist students in identifying client health problems (Iyer, Taptich, & Bernocchi-Losey, 1986).

It was not until the 1970s that attempts were made to develop consistent terminology to describe health problems that are diagnosed and treated by nurses. In 1973, a list of 34 diagnoses was developed at the First National Conference on the Classification of Nursing Diagnoses (Gebbie & Lavin, 1975). The American Nurses Association began to include nursing diagnoses in their published standards of nursing practice. Many states followed with the inclusion of nursing diagnoses in Nurse Practice Acts or legal descriptions of nursing practice (Iyer et al., 1986).

Seven additional conferences have been conducted since 1973 to identify and develop nursing diagnoses. As of 1990, 99 diagnoses have been identified and organized into 9 human response patterns approved for use by the North American Nursing Diagnosis Association (NANDA).

## Nursing Diagnosis

The assessment process yields a wealth of data that provide clues about clients' physical, developmental, emotional, and social health status. The diagnostic process in nursing begins with the analysis of accumulated data. Nurses classify and organize collected data to identify significant patterns or trends. Inferences about the data, based on theoretical knowledge and experience, are developed through inductive or deductive reasoning. The accuracy of findings may be validated directly with clients or indirectly through consultation with colleagues or comparison with authoritative references. Nurses are then able to formulate care plans that begin with the generation of a nursing diagnosis.

## Definition of Nursing Diagnosis

A *nursing diagnosis* is a summary statement of actual or potential alterations in health related to actual or perceived threats to the integrity of physical, social, or emotional systems. Nursing diagnoses describe "actual or potential health problems which nurses by virtue of their education and experience are capable and licensed to treat"(Gordon, 1976, p. 1299). Nursing diagnoses are derived from the assessment process, and support the notion that nurses are independently accountable for the assessment, planning, implementation, and evaluation of nursing care.

Although nursing diagnoses may coexist with disease processes, they are not medical diagnoses. Nursing diagnoses do not include health problems for which treatments or interventions are strictly within the legal power of physicians, such as ordering drugs or performing surgery (Gordon, 1987). For example, "fractured tibia" is a medical diagnosis, whereas "impaired physical mobility" is a nursing diagnosis. Characteristics of medical and nursing diagnoses are listed in Table 6-1. Several nursing diagnoses are often formulated in response to an identified medical problem (Table 6-2).

## Types of Nursing Diagnoses

There are three types of nursing diagnoses: actual nursing diagnoses, high risk nursing diagnoses, and wellness nursing diagnoses. All three types of diagnoses will be discussed in this chapter.

### Table 6–2. Example of Medical Diagnosis and Formulation of Possible Nursing Diagnoses

| Medical Diagnosis | Possible Nursing Diagnoses |
| --- | --- |
| Gastroenteritis | Alteration in bowel elimination: diarrhea<br>High risk for fluid volume deficit related to diarrhea and vomiting<br>Alteration in nutrition: less than body requirements related to anorexia and vomiting<br>High risk for impairment of skin integrity related to diarrhea<br>High risk alteration in body temperature related to gastrointestinal infection |

### Actual Nursing Diagnoses

*Actual nursing diagnoses* are used to identify existing health problems. Diagnoses, or diagnostic labels, are identified by NANDA in *Taxonomy I* (NANDA, 1990). Diagnoses are brief statements that identify the existence of a pattern of signs and symptoms. "Related factors are conditions or circumstances that can cause or contribute to the development of a diagnosis" (NANDA, 1990, p. 115). These include factors that are manifested by the diagnosis, etiologies, or risk factors. "Defining characteristics are the clinical criteria that validate the presence of a diagnostic category" (Carpenito, 1989, p. 14), and are divided into *major characteristics* (which must be present to identify the diagnosis) and *minor characteristics* (which might be present). An example of an actual nursing diagnosis might be: *Anxiety related to lack of knowledge of postoperative care of an infant with hydrocephalus as manifested by*

### Table 6–1. Characteristics of Medical and Nursing Diagnoses

| Medical Diagnosis | Nursing Diagnosis |
| --- | --- |
| Describes a specific disease or process | Describes an individual's response to a disease process, condition, or situation |
| Is oriented to pathology | Is oriented to the individual |
| Remains constant throughout the duration of illness | Changes as the patient's responses change |
| Guides medical management, some of which may be carried out by the nurse | Guides independent nursing care, that is, nursing orders (therapies) and evaluation. |
| Is complementary to nursing diagnosis | Is complementary to the medical diagnosis |
| Has a well-developed classification system accepted by the medical profession | Has no universally accepted classification system; such systems are currently being developed and promoted |

(Kozier, B., & Erb, G. [1991]. *Fundamentals of nursing* [4th ed.]. Redwood, City, CA: Addison-Wesley, p. 191.)

*inability to retain information and perform return demonstrations.*

### High Risk Nursing Diagnoses

The category *High risk nursing diagnoses* became effective in 1992, when NANDA changed the diagnostic labels that were formerly "potential for" to "high risk for." This change better identifies individuals who are more susceptible to developing problems. For example, all individuals have a "Potential for Infection," but premature infants with immature immune systems are at "High Risk for Infection."

### Wellness Nursing Diagnoses

*Wellness nursing diagnoses* identify the potential of an "individual, family, or community in transition from a specific level of wellness to a higher level of wellness" (NANDA, 1990, p. 117). Rather than focusing on actual or high risk problems, wellness diagnoses are intended to demonstrate the ability of individuals (and nurses working with them) to maintain or increase health. For example, as a family adjusts to the illness of a child and learns home care, the diagnosis could be: "Family Coping: Potential for Growth."

## Components of Nursing Diagnosis

The nursing diagnosis consists of three components, known as PES (Gordon, 1976):

*P*: the health problem

*E*: etiological or related factors

*S*: signs and symptoms or the defining characteristics

The health problem (*P*) is a brief, concise statement of an actual or potential individual, family, or community health issue. The health problem is derived from the assessment and diagnostic process—for example, a child with otitis media experiences ear pain. The health problem, therefore, is *pain.*

The etiology or related factors (*E*) refer to probable causes of, or influences upon, the health problem. These factors may involve physical, cognitive, social, emotional, spiritual, or environmental items. Continuing the example from above, the etiology of the problem is added to the problem statement and is expressed as *pain related to middle ear infection.*

Signs and symptoms (*S*) and critical defining characteristics are the primary criteria for diagnostic judgment. Supporting characteristics are observations that further validate and add to the critical defining characteristics. These observations are frequently documented in the assessment data base. Continuing with the same example, signs and symptoms that support the diagnosis are added to the problem and etiology and are expressed as *pain related to middle ear infection as manifested by fever, red tympanic membrane, and child tugging at the ear.*

Certain guidelines in writing nursing diagnoses are helpful. The diagnosis is stated in terms of the health response rather than the needed intervention. The diagnosis is written without implied value judgments and should not contain the medical diagnosis. Nurses should keep the diagnosis concise, avoiding multiple problems and etiologies in the diagnostic statement. The diagnosis should be clear, logical, and in legally advisable terms. Before documentation, nurses should review the following questions to verify accuracy of the diagnosis:

- Is the data base sufficient and accurate?
- Does a pattern exist?
- Are the signs and symptoms characteristic of the identified pattern?
- Is the nursing diagnosis based on nursing knowledge?
- Can the nursing diagnosis be altered by independent nursing actions?
- Would other nurses formulate the same nursing diagnosis based on the data? (Price, 1980)

## The Diagnostic Process in Nursing

The diagnostic phase of the nursing process consists of data collection and processing, verification of findings, and the formulation and documentation of the nursing diagnosis (Iyer et al., 1986). The diagnostic process serves to determine clients' health status and evaluate the factors influencing that state.

## Data Collection and Interpretation

Collection of data is the goal of the assessment phase of the nursing process. The importance of the nurse–client relationship in collecting meaningful data is presented in Chapter 5. Gordon (1987) states: "the quality of the nurse–client interaction directly affects information obtained and subsequently, what diagnostic judgment is made."

Once data have been collected they must be organized, interpreted, and validated. Data classification is assisted by using an organized approach to the assessment process. Data are sorted and classified by system, theme, or recurrent pattern. Interpreting data includes the selection of important data, comparing this selected data with accepted standards (for example, lab test results) and identifying significant patterns (Iyer et al., 1986). Nurses use clinical and theoretical knowledge, past experience, and perceptions to make inferences about the data collected.

## Hypothesis Generation and Testing

Nurses generate diagnostic hypotheses based on data interpretation. Diagnostic hypotheses are generated from selective attention to diagnostic cues and development of likely diagnoses to explain their meaning. Nurses should not be limited to one interpretation of data. Multiple interpretations require an analysis of diagnostic cues within a physical, psychological, and sociological framework (Gordon, 1987). Nurses attempt to determine the likelihood of each hypothesis and prioritize them in order of probability. The most likely diagnosis provides a focus for reviewing data, consulting with the client, and attempting to validate the diagnostic hypotheses.

## Validation of Findings

Nurses need to validate the accuracy of data interpretation and the diagnostic hypothesis. Ideally, nurses should validate findings directly with clients. In the case of pediatric clients it is often necessary or helpful to verify or validate findings with family members or care givers. The use of reflective statements facilitates this action. Data interpretation may also be validated with other professionals or references. Errors in data interpretation may result in the false exaggeration or underestimation of the existence or extent of a health problem.

## The Diagnostic Statement

Validation of data leads to an accurate judgment about the client's actual and potential health problems. The diagnostic statement is documented in standard form using an approved nursing diagnosis. Validation and documentation of the nursing diagnosis provides direction for development of the care plan.

## Nursing Diagnosis in the Pediatric Setting

The NANDA-approved nursing diagnoses are valuable in describing the actual and potential health problems of pediatric clients and their families. Approved nursing diagnoses can be applied to the physical, emotional, and developmental problems commonly encountered in the care of children and families. Nursing diagnosis provides a succinct statement of the identified health problem and the direction for planning and implementing nursing care.

As previously discussed, the health care needs of children and their families are not usually confined to a single physical ailment. The use of nursing diagnoses to document health care needs related to growth and developmental processes is valuable in ensuring that these needs are addressed as effectively as physical concerns. Nursing diagnoses such as "Family coping: potential for growth" can document positive strengths of the child and family. Providing continued support to the family that is effectively coping may prevent problems associated with ineffective coping.

The NANDA-approved nursing diagnoses have been criticized for being limited in addressing client/family strengths. It is also felt that they are often too broad for application in specialties such as pediatrics and community health. Fortunately, nursing diagnoses continue to evolve. Pediatric nurses can make valuable contributions to this process by identifying and researching nursing diagnoses that are specific to the care of children and their families.

## The North American Nursing Diagnosis Association (NANDA)

The North American Nursing Diagnosis Association (NANDA) was formed in 1982 from a task force appointed at the First National Conference on Classification of Nursing Diagnosis. NANDA's responsibilities include the following:

1. Review of diagnosis and taxonomy (classification system)
2. Promotion of the use of nursing diagnosis and taxonomy
3. Promotion of research and development activities
4. Communication of information at state, regional, and national levels through programs, conferences, newsletters, and books

Membership in the organization is open to registered nurses. Associate membership is available for nursing students and non-nurses (Gordon, 1987). NANDA's focus is the promotion of a universally accepted classification system. Development efforts are concentrated on identifying and refining nursing diagnoses, as well as measuring their reliability and validity. Since 1982, amendments in the classification system can be made only when based on research (Gordon, 1987). This provides stability to the classification system and supports the reliability of nursing diagnosis as a clinical tool.

## NANDA Nursing Diagnosis Taxonomy I

A taxonomy is a classification system. NANDA's *Taxonomy I* is a formal classification of nursing diagnoses according to nine human response patterns: exchanging, communicating, relating, valuing, choosing, moving, perceiving, knowing, and feeling. These response patterns are briefly defined in Table 6-3. Subcategory levels describe response pattern alterations. Alterations refer to differences or evolutions that occur without changing into something else (Gordon, 1987). This change is viewed not as positive or negative, but as neutral. These alterations represent increasing degrees of clinical specificity. Table 6–4 presents the NANDA-approved nursing diagnoses, arranged by diagnostic category.

*Table 6–3.  Definitions and Examples of Human Response Patterns*

| Pattern | Definition | Examples |
|---|---|---|
| Exchanging | Mutual giving and receiving | Nutrition<br>Infection<br>Thermoregulation<br>Elimination<br>Tissue perfusion<br>Gas exchange<br>Injury |
| Communicating | Sending messages | Verbal communication |
| Relating | Establishing bonds | Social interaction<br>Role performance<br>Sexuality |
| Valuing | Assigning relative worth | Spirituality |
| Choosing | Selecting alternatives | Coping, adjustment<br>Noncompliance<br>Decisional conflict<br>Health-seeking behaviors |
| Moving | Activity | Mobility<br>Sleep patterns<br>Diversional activity<br>Home maintenance management<br>Self-care |
| Perceiving | Receiving information | Body image<br>Sensory/perceptual alterations<br>Hopelessness |
| Knowing | The meaning associated with information | Knowledge deficit<br>Thought processes |
| Feeling | The subjective awareness of information | Pain<br>Grieving<br>Anxiety |

## Summary

The process of diagnosing has always been a part of nursing care. Nurses make clinical judgments based on their interpretation of accumulated data. Validation of inferences contributes to the accuracy of clinical decision making.

Nursing diagnosis provides a formal mechanism for documentation of identified actual and potential health needs of pediatric clients and their families. The statement of the nursing diagnosis includes the identified problem and its etiology. Nursing diagnoses differ from medical diagnoses by describing the individual's response to a disease process, condition, or situation, rather than merely identifying the disease process. Nursing diagnoses are categorized within a classification system developed and regulated by the North American Nursing Diagnosis Association.

The nursing diagnosis provides direction for the planning, intervention, and evaluation phases of the nursing process. It documents accountability for nursing actions throughout the nursing process. Pediatric nurses contribute to the promotion of client and family well-being through the use of the diagnostic process in nursing.

## References

Carpenito, L. J. (1989). *Nursing diagnosis: Application to clinical practice* (3rd ed.). Philadelphia: J. B. Lippincott.

Gebbie, K. M., & Lavin, M. A. (1975). *Classification of nursing diagnosis: Proceedings of the first national conference.* St. Louis: C. V. Mosby.

Gordon, M. (1976). Nursing diagnosis and the diagnostic process. *American Journal of Nursing, 76,* 1298–1300.

Gordon, M. (1987). *Nursing diagnosis: Process and application* (2nd ed.). New York: McGraw-Hill.

Iyer, P., Taptich, B. J. & Bernocchi-Losey, D. (1986). *Nursing process and nursing diagnosis.* Philadelphia: W. B. Saunders.

North American Nursing Diagnosis Association (NANDA). (1990). *Taxonomy One: Revised 1990.* St. Louis: NANDA.

Price, M. (1980). Nursing diagnosis: Making a concept come alive. *American Journal of Nursing, 80,* 666.

*Table 6–4. 1990 Nursing Diagnoses*

**Pattern 1: Exchanging**

Altered Nutrition: More than body requirements
Altered Nutrition: Less than body requirements
Altered Nutrition: High risk for more than body requirements
High Risk for Infection
High Risk for Altered Body Temperature
Hypothermia
Hyperthermia
Ineffective Thermoregulation
Dysreflexia
Constipation
Perceived Constipation
Colonic Constipation
Diarrhea
Bowel Incontinence
Altered Urinary Elimination
Stress Incontinence
Reflex Incontinence
Urge Incontinence
Functional Incontinence
Total Incontinence
Urinary Retention
Altered (Specify Type) Tissue Perfusion
(Renal, cerebral, cardiopulmonary, gastrointestinal, peripheral)
Fluid Volume Excess
Fluid Volume Deficit
High Risk for Fluid Volume Deficit
Decreased Cardiac Output
Impaired Gas Exchange
Ineffective Airway Clearance
Ineffective Breathing Pattern
High Risk for Injury
High Risk for Suffocation
High Risk for Poisoning
High Risk for Trauma
High Risk for Aspiration
High Risk for Disuse Syndrome
Altered Protection
Impaired Tissue Integrity
Altered Oral Mucous Membrane
Impaired Skin Integrity
High Risk for Impaired Skin Integrity

**Pattern 2: Communicating**

Impaired Verbal Communication

**Pattern 3: Relating**

Impaired Social Interaction
Social Isolation
Altered Role Performance
Altered Parenting
High Risk for Altered Parenting
Sexual Dysfunction
Altered Family Processes
Parental Role Conflict
Altered Sexuality Patterns

**Pattern 4: Valuing**

Spiritual Distress (distress of the human spirit)

**Pattern 5: Choosing**

Ineffective Individual Coping
Impaired Adjustment
Defensive Coping
Ineffective Denial
Ineffective Family Coping: Disabling
Ineffective Family Coping: Compromised
Family Coping: Potential for Growth
Noncompliance (Specify)
Decisional Conflict (Specify)
Health Seeking Behaviors (Specify)

**Pattern 6: Moving**

Impaired Physical Mobility
Activity Intolerance
Fatigue
High Risk for Activity Intolerance
Sleep Pattern Disturbance
Diversional Activity Deficit
Impaired Home Maintenance Management
Altered Health Maintenance
Feeding Self-Care Deficit
Impaired Swallowing
Ineffective Breastfeeding
Effective Breastfeeding
Bathing/Hygiene Self-Care Deficit
Dressing/Grooming Self-Care Deficit
Toileting Self-Care Deficit
Altered Growth and Development

**Pattern 7: Perceiving**

Body Image Disturbance
Self-Esteem Disturbance
Chronic Low Self-Esteem
Situational Low Self-Esteem
Personal Identity Disturbance
Sensory/Perceptual Alterations (Specify)
(Visual, auditory, kinesthetic, gustatory, tactile, olfactory)
Unilateral Neglect
Hopelessness
Powerlessness

**Pattern 8: Knowing**

Knowledge Deficit (Specify)
Altered Thought Processes

**Pattern 9: Feeling**

Pain
Chronic Pain
Dysfunctional Grieving
Anticipatory Grieving
High Risk for Violence: Self-directed or directed at others
Post-Trauma Response
Rape-Trauma Syndrome
Rape-Trauma Syndrome: Compound Reaction
Rape-Trauma Syndrome: Silent Reaction
Anxiety
Fear

North American Nursing Diagnosis Association. (1990). *Taxonomy I.* St. Louis: North American Nursing Diagnosis Association.

# Nursing Care Plan

In the nursing care plan that follows, the nursing diagnosis component of the nursing process has been added. The diagnoses are based on the assessment findings and are arranged in priority order. There are many other diagnoses that could be listed (depending on the individual child), but those included below represent commonly identified diagnoses for children with croup. Subsequent chapters will add further details regarding care planning, implementation, and evaluation.

## Assessment

Meghan Caldwell is a two-year-old girl brought to the emergency room at 3:30 AM by her parents.

### Chief Complaint

Meghan's mother reports a harsh, barky cough with apparent increasing difficulty in breathing.

### Subjective Assessment

*Past History.* Seen regularly since birth by a pediatrician for routine well-child care. No prior illnesses or hospitalizations; immunizations up-to-date.

*Present History.* Symptoms of upper respiratory infection for 48 hours; increasing respiratory distress for the past 6 hours.

*Family History.* Mother is 31; father is 34; both are well; no siblings. Maternal and paternal grandparents are alive and well. No family history of asthma, allergies, or chronic respiratory conditions.

### Objective Assessment

*Physical Examination.* T. 102° (rectal); p. 162 (apical); R. 46; B.P. 90/48 (R. arm); weight 11 kg (22%); height 89 cm (75%).

| | |
|---|---|
| Integument: | Clear, warm, moist, good turgor |
| Head: | Normal |
| Eyes: | PERRLA, EOMs intact, funduscopic exam normal |
| Ears: | Otoscopic exam normal |
| Nose: | Increased viscous secretions; nasal flaring |
| Mouth: | Lips dry; circumoral cyanosis |
| Throat: | Erythema, tonsils normal, no exudate, voice hoarse, barky cough |
| Neck: | Nodes nonpalpable |
| Thorax and Lungs: | Tachypnea, inspiratory dyspnea, substernal and suprasternal retractions, decreased breath sounds, bilaterally scattered rales and rhonchi |
| Heart: | Tachycardiac, normal rhythm, no murmur |
| Abdomen: | Active bowel sounds in all quadrants; no pain, tenderness, or masses |
| Genitalia: | Normal |
| Musculoskeletal: | Full ROM |
| Neurological: | Reflexes normal and symmetrical; anxious, irritable, restless |

*Medical Diagnosis:* Laryngotracheobronchitis (croup)

*Medical Plan:* Admit to hospital; mist tent with 30% $O_2$; antibiotics

## Nursing Care Plan for a Child With Croup

| Goals | Nursing Interventions | Evaluation Criteria |
|---|---|---|

*NURSING DIAGNOSIS #1: Activity Intolerance related to insufficient oxygenation as manifested by dyspnea, substernal and suprasternal retractions, rales, and rhonchi*

*continued*

## Nursing Care Plan *(Continued)*

| Goals | Nursing Interventions | Evaluation Criteria |
|---|---|---|

*NURSING DIAGNOSIS #2: High Risk for Fluid Volume Deficit related to decreased oral intake as manifested by the child's refusal to drink.*

*NURSING DIAGNOSIS #3: Hyperthermia related to the infectious process*

*NURSING DIAGNOSIS #4: Anxiety (child) related to respiratory distress and hospitalization as manifested by irritability and restlessness*

*NURSING DIAGNOSIS #5: Anxiety (parental) related to apprehension concerning child's welfare as manifested by nervous speech and obvious concern*

## Bibliography

Carpenito, L. J. (1992). *Handbook of nursing diagnosis* (4th ed.). Philadelphia: J. B. Lippincott.

Carroll-Johnson, R. (1989). *Classification of nursing diagnoses: Proceedings of the seventh national conference.* Philadelphia: J. B. Lippincott.

Davidson, S. (1984). Nursing diagnosis: Its application in the acute care setting. *Topics in Clinical Nursing, 5,* 50.

Gordon, M., Sweeney, M. A., & McKeehan, K. (1980). Nursing diagnosis: Look at its use in the clinical area. *American Journal of Nursing, 80,* 672.

Kim, M. J., McFarland, G., & McLain, A. (1989). *A pocket guide to nursing diagnosis.* St. Louis: C. V. Mosby.

Kim, M. J., & Moritz, D. A. (Eds.). (1982). *Classification of nursing diagnoses: Proceedings of the third and fourth national conferences.* New York: McGraw-Hill.

Long Island Jewish–Hillside Medical Center. (1985). *Computerized nursing care planning utilizing nursing diagnosis.* Washington, D.C.: Oryn Publications.

Lunney, M. (1982). Nursing diagnosis: Refining the system. *American Journal of Nursing, 82,* 456.

Maas, M. (1986). Nursing diagnoses in a professional model of nursing: Keystone for effective nursing administration. *Journal of Nursing Administration, 16,* 39.

Martens, K. (1986). Let's diagnose strengths, not just problems. *American Journal of Nursing, 86,* 192.

McLane, A., et al. (eds.). (1984). *Classification of nursing diagnoses: Proceedings of the fifth national conference.* St. Louis: C. V. Mosby.

North American Nursing Diagnosis Association. (1986). 21 new diagnoses and a taxonomy. *American Journal of Nursing, 86,* 1414.

Westfall, U. E. (1984). Nursing diagnosis: Its use in quality assurance. *Topics in Clinical Nursing, 5,* 78.

# Planning Child Health Nursing Care

Joan T. Duer

7

*Planning as an Integral Part of*
 *Nursing Practice*

*Setting Priorities*

*Nursing Care Planning*
  *Individualized Care Planning*
  *Standardized Care Planning*

*Clients' and Families' Roles in*
 *Planning Nursing Care*
  *Developing Goals*
  *Deciding on Interventions to Use*
   *With the Patient and Family*

*Discharge Planning*

*DRGs and Child Health Care*

*Summary*

*Nursing Care Plan*

*Photograph by David Finn*

*Upon completion of this chapter the reader will be able to:*

1. *Describe the role of planning in the care of pediatric clients and their families.*

2. *Differentiate the types of planning needs common to the care of pediatric clients and their families.*

3. *Describe the nurse's role in developing goals of care with pediatric clients and their families.*

4. *Describe theoretical foundations of nursing care used in planning for pediatric clients and their families.*

5. *Explain the role of standardized care plans, addressing the actual and potential health problems of children and families.*

6. *Describe the role of the nurse in discharge planning for hospitalized pediatric clients.*

7. *Explain the significance of DRGs to child health nursing.*

## Key Terms

*discharge planning*

*DRG*

*individualized care plan*

*planning*

*standardized care plan*

## Planning as an Integral Part of Nursing Practice

A plan is a way or method of proceeding that is determined in advance. Planning nursing care can be described as a jointly prepared (by nurse, client, and family), coherent approach to addressing a client's identified health care needs. Without these elements, a plan may actually obstruct achievement of health care goals. Nursing care planning is an active process that requires the following:

1. Previous data interpretation and analysis
2. Identification of nursing diagnoses
3. Determination of realistic health care goals (by both client and nurse)
4. The proposal of standard and creative nursing actions to resolve those needs

Data interpretation and analysis and the identification of nursing diagnoses are accomplished in the diagnostic process. Formulating nursing diagnoses serves as the foundation for nursing care planning. Nurses, clients, and families determine the goals of nursing actions, designing them to address the health problem outlined by the nursing diagnosis. Realistic, attainable nursing care goals should reflect both short- and long-term improvements in client well-being. These goals provide clear direction for nurses in developing interventions designed to facilitate achievement of expected results. Nurses use both standard actions and creative strategies to address the individual developmental and health needs of the clients.

The diagnostic process is meaningless unless a specific care plan can be developed to address the identified health problem. Thus, pediatric nurses must carefully and systematically develop specific, individualized plans of care in consultation with both children and families to promote optimal health and well-being of pediatric clients and families. Care plans need to reflect both needs and problems. For example, in spite of illness children still need to eat and drink in order to regain their health. A problem exists when children have difficulty swallowing or fear that eating or drinking will cause them to vomit. A true nursing challenge is to find ways to maintain nutrition and hydration when children are resistant to acting to improve their own health.

Children's ages, physical development, developmental levels, personalities, and acuity levels must all be taken into consideration when planning nursing care. In addition, since children live and grow within family units, it is essential that families be involved in the process of planning nursing care. Although these characteristics are not unique to children, planning nursing care for pediatric clients differs from planning nursing care for adults. Adults can usually make decisions for themselves; children usually cannot (although they may try). In addition, because of their smaller physical size children tend to react more quickly to therapeutic measures (e.g., drug treatments). Therefore, more careful assessment and monitoring is necessary, and frequent revisions of nursing care plans are often required.

## Setting Priorities

The diagnostic process may result in the identification of a large number of actual and potential nursing diagnoses. Nurses must systematically review all nursing diagnoses, identify those that need immediate attention, and rank them in priority order. Nursing care plans are developed to address the most urgent problems first (Iyer, Taptich, & Bernocchi-Losey, 1986). For example, a hospitalized toddler with croup becomes stridorous and is suffering from respiratory distress. The need for air (easing the child's breathing) must be met before the nurse can address the child's needs for activity and security. The care plan is directed toward promoting improved air exchange, with the expected outcome of a decrease in respiratory distress. Although a hospitalized toddler needs diversional activity and security, the physical needs are clearly the first priority in this example.

Nurses rely on a variety of resources to assist in identifying the priorities of nursing care. Nursing judgment is based on a scientific rationale for nursing actions, experience, and collaboration with clients, families, and other professionals. Additionally, nurses uses theoretical frameworks to provide a background from which to view the client and clarify priority nursing diagnoses. Theoretical frameworks that can provide useful guidelines for identifying nursing care priorities are identified in Chapter 4.

## Nursing Care Planning

### Individualized Care Planning

The concept of the client as an individual is central to all nursing activities. Regardless of the conceptual framework that directs the course of nursing care, recognition of the individuality of clients is paramount to a successful care plan.

Nursing care plans must clearly reflect the nurse's belief that clients are individuals with unique needs and capabilities. In pediatric nursing each child must be recognized as the focus of nursing care within the context of family environments. Nurses will observe a wide range of adaptive behaviors and self-care practices in pediatric clients and their families. Nursing interventions are developed in light of the unique needs, abilities, attitudes, and value systems of the child and family. Individualized care plans facilitate documentation of information specific to the client.

### Standardized Care Planning

According to Mayers (1983, p. 121) "a standard care plan is a specific protocol of care that is appropriate for patients who are experiencing the usual or predictable problems associated with a given diagnosis or disease process." Standardized care plans present actual, potential, or possible nursing diagnoses, goals, and suggested interventions in a preprinted format. Standard care plans are often developed from an institution's standards of care, usually by committees of clinical experts.

Standardized care plans may be used as a resource in writing individualized care plans or may serve as the actual models. Standardized care plans are clinically current and time efficient. However, they are intended to serve only as prototypes and must be individualized to reflect the unique needs and concerns of clients and families. Modified standardized care plans (blank spaces allow for individualization) are more appropriate in pediatrics since they allow for variations in diagnostic etiology, mutuality in goal setting, and developmentally appropriate interventions (Nodhturft and MacMullen, 1982).

Standardized care plans are gaining popularity as nursing documentation systems are becoming computerized. Computer-based care plans provide opportunities for adaptation in light of client differences. Computer systems include nursing care plans in a client's medical records for future reference and evaluation. Figure 7-1 shows a computerized nursing care plan for a child with diabetes.

## Clients' and Families' Roles in Planning Nursing Care

### Developing Goals

Pediatric nurses consult with both children and their families to determine or validate priority nursing diagnoses that provide the direction for development of nursing care goals. Depending on their developmental age, children may experience fear, anxiety, powerlessness, frustration, or lack of motivation. Involving them in the goal-setting

```
************************************************************************
                   PATIENT CARE ACTIVITY REPORT
                     07/27/1999  07:01AM

   GALE, ANTHONY    15Y C¹ M² CAT³ HT:5FT 8 IN      ADM:07/12/1989
   30000205                       WT:130 LB 0OZ          SCV:MED
   ADM DR:BATAGLIA, SUZANNE       DX:DIAB INSULIN DEPEND TYPE I
   ATT DR:SILVERMAN, IRVING       DX:


   PCH3⁴      :5.42              INFEC IND:  ALG:PCN, CODEINE
   CARE PTS⁵  :41                ISOL IND⁷:W ALG:SEA FOOD-IODINE?
   PT COND⁶   :FR                AMBUL STS:  DIET:2400 CAL ADA DIET

   *******************PATIENT CLASSIFICATION ASSESSMENT*******************

   ACTIVITY          P⁸   A5¹⁰     AMBULATION/EXERCISE ASSIST
   TEACHING          C⁹   T3¹¹     MAXIMUM REQUIREMENT
                     C    T5       DIET
                     C    T7       SPECIAL INSTUCTION
   VITAL STATS       P¹²  V3       BP-P

   *****************************PATIENT CARE PLANS***************************
   -----------------------------------------------------------------------
   1 KNOWLEDGE DEFICIT:USE/ACTION INSULIN;DIET  NRS  ASG  7/15/99¹³    JMF
                                                     1402¹⁴
       call attn if blood sugar > 260
       1 EXPLAINS ACTION/USE OF INSULIN & SELF ADMIN INSULIN  7/15¹⁵  7/20¹⁶
       very hesitant about self administration of insulin     7/15
       1 BEGIN DIABETIC TEACHING        reinforce q shift      7/15
       2 TEACH ACTION & USE OF INSULIN  provided instruc-¹⁷   7/15
         tion sheet for self admin of insulin:mother present


   2 COMPLIES WITH DIET PRESCRIBED                            7/15     7/28
     maintain 2400 ADA diet                                   7/15
       1 EXPLAIN EFFECTS OF DIET          stressed import.    7/15
         of regular meal times and reason
       2 REINFORCE DIET WITH FAMILY     mother supportive &   7/15
         involved in pt teaching
       3 schedule pt for diet consult    -                    7/15
   -----------------------------------------------------------------------
   2 POTENTIAL FOR COMPLICATIONS-DIABETES      NRS  ASG   7/15/99    JMF
                                                    1405
     developing r foot ulcer from tennis shoes
       1  VERBALIZES COMMON COMLICATIONS OF DIABETES          7/15    7/30
          verbalizes common complications and sequelae        7/15
          1 TEACH PROPER FOOT CARE         -r ankle ulcer is  7/15
            2cm diam, red & flakey. teach drsg chngs, need
            to wear cotton stockings-                          7/15
          2 STRESS VISITS TO DENTIST - last visit 2 years      7/15
          3 EXPL S&S HYPO/HYPERGLYCEMIA                         7/15    7/30

   -----------------------------------------------------------------------
```

*Figure 7–1.  Computerized nursing care plan.*

process affirms their identity and importance and provides greater opportunities for their participation and subsequent compliance with the nursing care plan. Parents often fear a loss of control in decision making concerning their children. Mutually set goals can confirm the important role parents have in promoting the health of their children. Isolated development of a nursing care plan is appropriate only in emergency situations when immediate action is required.

Nursing care goals must reflect a specific time frame for achievement. For example, in the case of a newly diagnosed, hospitalized adolescent diabetic, a long-term goal might be "The client will demonstrate the ability to regularly and correctly administer insulin within one week," whereas a short-term goal might be "The client will verbally demonstrate knowledge of insulin action and side effects within three days." Both goals clearly describe the desired goals in terms of client behaviors, as well as the time expected for achievement.

Goals are written in terms of the observable client behaviors expected in response to nursing interventions. Goals should be measurable, as well as observable, realistic, and achievable. Client/family readiness to actively participate in the achievement of nursing care goals, the need and availability of resources, and other limitations must be considered. The evaluation of goals will be discussed in Chapter 9.

## Deciding on Interventions for Children and Families

Once the goals of care have been mutually determined by nurses, children, and families, attention can be given to the suggested interventions. Nurses may propose interventions based on clinical experience, knowledge of the health care problem, or use of other resources such as their own creativity or that of colleagues, standards of care,

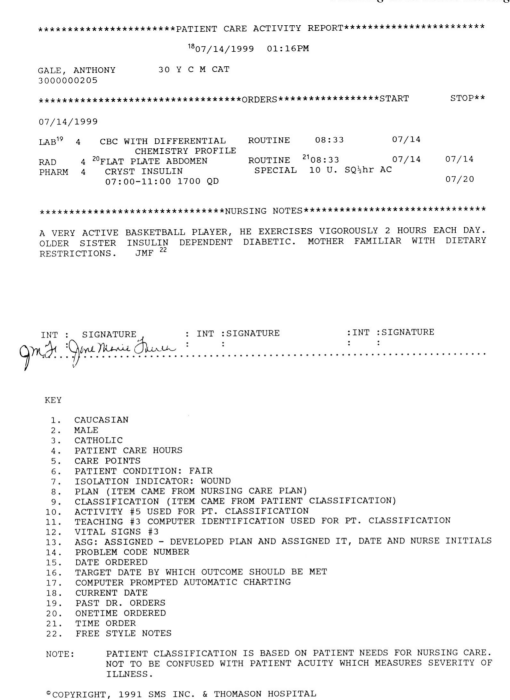

Figure 7–1. *Continued*

nursing research, standard care plans, or other resources. Proposed interventions are discussed with pediatric clients and parents for feasibility. For example, home administration of total parenteral nutrition, antibiotics, or respiratory treatments may be possible if parental interest and abilities, as well as necessary physical resources, are deemed appropriate.

Interventions are adapted as much as possible to make them more acceptable to children and families. For example, dietary modifications made necessary by physi-

ical illness should always reflect consideration of cultural foods and values, when possible. Nurses must have a clear understanding of families' cultures and values to prevent suggesting potentially unacceptable interventions. It is equally important that nursing interventions reflect an awareness of children's individual developmental capabilities. The lack of consideration of developmental aspects may be the greatest cause of failure to carry out nursing interventions successfully in pediatric settings.

## *Discharge Planning*

Preparation for discharge begins when children are admitted to the hospital. Nursing assessments focus on the ability of children and parents to provide for necessary health needs. Learning needs, skills, tasks, or behavior modifications that are necessary for the child's health maintenance and health promotion are documented, and interventions are planned. The willingness and ability of children and families to provide care are constantly evaluated. Home environments are assessed for modifications that might be necessary to accommodate children's health status. Home care or visiting nurses are consulted to assist in the discharge process and to evaluate home environments, and social workers coordinate the acquisition of supplies and financial resources. Home care is discussed in more detail in Chapter 18.

Families' perceptions of their needs and capabilities must be assessed. Families who are anxious about accepting responsibility for children's care at home must receive educational and emotional support. Consultations with community support groups and volunteer agencies before the child's discharge can provide a great deal of reassurance for parents and families. Knowledge of community services such as transportation for children with physically disabling conditions, respite care, and local support groups reassures the parents that they are not alone in providing care for their children outside the hospital. Arranging for in-home therapy and tutoring is an integral part of the recovery period and helps children maintain adequate school performance. Many parents are eager to perform tasks at home that were previously considered the domain of the hospital staff. Nurses must be advocates for these families, because many services (IV therapy, pain management, respiratory support) are now available to support the care of ill children in the home environment. Making recommendations to physicians, initiating social

service involvement, and providing opportunities for learning are means of supporting the desire of families to care for their ill children at home.

The key to successful discharge planning lies in understanding the needs, capabilities, and resources of children, parents, and families. The primary nurse, acting as a case manager, is most effective in coordinating members of the multidisciplinary team (Fig. 7-2). Together the team addresses the stated and anticipated needs of children and families as they strive toward goals for each identified nursing diagnosis.

## *DRGs and Child Health Care*

In 1983, the system of reimbursement for hospital care underwent a dramatic change. Medicaid and Medicare costs for patient care were no longer paid upon the client's discharge from the hospital but were paid *prospectively* based on the medical diagnosis and the average length of hospitalization for clients with that diagnosis. A classification system known as *diagnostic related groups* (DRGs) was developed for purposes of prospective payment.

A DRG represents the combination of a medical diagnosis, surgical procedures needed, potential complications, and the client's age. There are dozens of major categories and hundreds of numerically coded DRGs. When a client is admitted to the hospital, the medical diagnosis is identified within a major diagnostic category. Thus, the expected length of stay (for which the hospital receives reimbursement) is established. If the client's condition worsens, the DRG is changed to reflect the need for additional hospitalization and subsequent payment. For example, a child with a cold enters the hospital as a result of an accident and is placed in traction. If, because of the resulting immobility, the child develops pneumonia, it would be necessary to change the child's DRG code. Review boards monitor the validity of code changes and

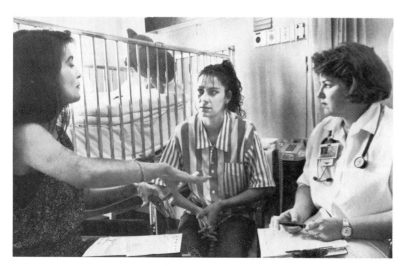

*Figure 7–2. Nurse coordinating discharge planning activities. (Courtesy of Nursing Department, Thomason Hospital, El Paso, Texas)*

# Nursing Care Plan

The next step of the nursing process, *planning,* is now applied to the following nursing care plan. In the previous two chapters, assessment and diagnosis have been documented in the plan. Based on these two elements, *goals* are now set and added to the care plan. For the purposes of this care plan, as was discussed in this chapter, goals have been identified as either short-term (S) or long-term (L).

## Assessment

Meghan Caldwell is a two-year-old girl brought to the emergency room at 3:30 AM by her parents.

### Chief Complaint:

Meghan's mother reports a harsh barky cough with apparent increasing difficulty breathing.

### Subjective Assessment:

*Past History:* Seen regularly since birth by a pediatrician for routine well-child care. No prior illnesses or hospitalizations; immunizations up-to-date.

*Present History:* Symptoms of upper respiratory infection for 48 hours; increasing respiratory distress for the past 6 hours.

*Family History:* Mother is 31; father is 34; both are well; no siblings. Maternal and paternal grandparents are alive and well. No family history of asthma, allergies, or chronic respiratory conditions.

### Objective Assessment

*Physical Examination:* T. 102° (rectal); P. 162 (apical); R. 48; B.P. 90/48 (R. arm); weight 11 kg (22%); height 89 cm (75%).

Integument:
   Clear, warm, moist, good turgor

| | |
|---|---|
| Head: | Normal |
| Eyes: | PERRLA, EOMs intact, fundu-scopic exam normal |
| Ears: | Otoscopic exam normal |
| Nose: | Increased viscous secretions; nasal flaring |
| Mouth: | Lips dry, circumoral cyanosis |
| Throat: | Erythema, tonsils normal, no exudate, voice hoarse, barky cough |
| Neck: | Nodes nonpalpable |
| Thorax and Lungs: | Tachypnea, inspiratory dyspnea, substernal and suprasternal retractions, decreased breath sounds, bilaterally scattered rales and rhonchi |
| Heart: | Tachycardiac, normal rhythm, no murmur |
| Abdomen: | Active bowel sounds in all quadrants; no pain, tenderness, or masses |
| Genitalia: | Normal |
| Musculoskeletal: | Full ROM |
| Neurological: | Reflexes normal and symmetrical; anxious, irritable, restless |

*Medical Diagnosis:* Laryngotracheobronchitis (croup)

*Medical Plan:* Admit to hospital; mist tent with 30% O$_2$; antibiotics

## Nursing Care Plan for a Child With Croup

| Goals | Nursing Interventions | Evaluation Criteria |
|---|---|---|

NURSING DIAGNOSIS #1: Activity Intolerance related to insufficient oxygenation as manifested by dyspnea, substernal and suprasternal retractions, rales, and rhonchi

(S) Child's breathing will be facilitated

*continued*

# Nursing Care Plan *(Continued)*

| Goals | Nursing Interventions | Evaluation Criteria |
|---|---|---|
| (L) Child will resume normal respiratory function | | |

*NURSING DIAGNOSIS #2: High Risk for Fluid Volume Deficit related to decreased oral intake as manifested by the child's refusal to drink*

| | | |
|---|---|---|
| (S) Child's hydration status will be maintained and improved | | |

*NURSING DIAGNOSIS #3: Hyperthermia related to the infectious process*

| | | |
|---|---|---|
| (S) Child's temperature will return to normal (98.6°F) | | |

*NURSING DIAGNOSIS #4: Anxiety (child) related to respiratory distress and hospitalization as manifested by irritability and restlessness*

| | | |
|---|---|---|
| (S) Child's anxiety will be reduced | | |
| (L) Child will comply with treatment plan | | |

*NURSING DIAGNOSIS #5: Anxiety (parental) related to apprehension concerning child's welfare as manifested by nervous speech and obvious concern*

| | | |
|---|---|---|
| (S) Parents' anxiety will be reduced | | |
| (L) Parents will comply with treatment plan | | |
| (L) Parents will demonstrate knowledge of etiology, treatment, and home care for croup | | |

compliance with DRG regulations (McKibbin, Brimmer, & Galliher, 1985).

Pediatric health care has not been immune to the effects of DRGs. Even in states where pediatric clients are exempt from DRG coding, the provision of high-quality, efficient, and cost-conscious care remains a priority. Nurses must be aware of their client's DRG coding (or expected length of hospital stay) and must develop realistic care plans within the time allotted. Excellent communication networks with community health nurses and services must be established. Nurses must be advocates for the needs of individual children and families within the realistic constraints of the larger system.

## Summary

Planning is an integral part of the nursing process. In consultation with pediatric clients and their parents and families, nurses identify priority nursing diagnoses and develop goals of nursing care. These measurable short- and long-term goals provide direction for nursing care activities. Interventions to achieve health goals that are developmentally appropriate and acceptable to the client and family are selected by nurses, the child, and the family.

Theoretical frameworks provide a means of examining the planning process, establishing priorities, and selecting interventions to facilitate achievement of health goals. Care plans can be documented by creating individual nursing care plans or by amending standardized care plans to reflect the unique needs of the client and family.

Discharge planning for hospitalized clients is a comprehensive progress that is initiated on admission. Discharge planning involves assessment, diagnosis, teaching interventions, evaluation, coordination among disciplines, and establishment of community-based supports for clients and their families. DRGs have influenced pediatric nursing by necessitating comprehensive, efficient, and rapid discharge planning as a means of containing hospital costs.

## References

Iyer, P., Taptich, B. J., & Bernocchi-Losey, D. (1986). *Nursing process and nursing diagnosis* Philadelphia: W. B. Saunders.

Mayers, M. (1983). *A systemic approach to the nursing care plan* (3rd ed.). Norwalk, CT: Appleton & Lange.

McKibbin, R., Brimmer, B. F., & Galliher, J. M. (1985). Nursing costs and DRG payments. *American Journal of Nursing, 85,* 1353.

Nodhturft, V., & MacMullen, J. (1982). Standard nursing care plans. *Nursing Management, 15,* 33.

## Bibliography

Blount, M., & Sanborn, C. (1984). Standard plan for care and discharge. *American Journal of Nursing, 84,* 1394.

Bower, F. (1982). *The process of planning nursing care* (3rd ed.). St. Louis: C. V. Mosby.

Glesy, J. (1987). Teaching discharge management. *Journal of Pediatric Nursing, 2,* 353.

Gordon, M. (1987). *Nursing diagnosis: Process and application* (2nd ed.). New York: McGraw-Hill.

Kalish, R. (1983). *The psychology of human behavior* (5th ed.). Monterey, CA: Brooks/Cole.

Smith, C. (1985). DRGs—making them work for you. *Nursing 85, 15,* 34.

Wesseling, E. (1988). Automating the nursing history and care plan. In R. Zielstorff (Ed.). *Computers in nursing.* Rockville, MD: Aspen, pp. 73–80.

# Implementing Child Health Nursing Interventions

Joan T. Duer

*Photograph by David Finn*

8

*Developmental Considerations in*
  *Nursing Implementation*
    *Medications*
    *Procedures*
    *Nutrition*

*Health Teaching*
    *Settings*
    *Determination of Health Teaching*
      *Needs*
    *Teaching Methods*
    *Teaching Tools*

*Comprehensive Child Health Care*
    *Consultation*
    *Referrals*
    *Continuity of Care*

*Summary*

*Nursing Care Plan*

*Upon completion of this chapter the reader will be able to:*

1. *Describe the role of nurses in the implementation phase of the child health nursing process.*

2. *Discuss developmentally appropriate nursing interventions for pediatric medication administration.*

3. *Describe developmentally appropriate strategies to prepare children and families for medical and nursing procedures.*

4. *Identify developmental considerations of pediatric nutritional health.*

5. *Describe the roles of nurses in schools, clinics, private practice settings, and hospitals in providing child health care teaching.*

6. *Explain the diagnostic processes used in identifying child and family health teaching methods.*

7. *Describe teaching methods that can be used to address the health needs of children and families.*

8. *Describe teaching tools that can be used to address the health needs of children and families.*

9. *Identify resources for consultation in planning, implementing, and evaluating child health care interventions.*

10. *Describe the use of referrals by nurses in implementing child health nursing interventions.*

11. *Explain the need for continuity in the care of pediatric clients and their families.*

*Key Terms*

*consultation*

*continuity of care*

*implementation*

*referral*

*Implementation* is the initiation of the nursing care plan. During the implementation phase of the nursing process, nurses take specific actions or perform interventions that are dictated by the nursing diagnoses established following the nursing assessment. The implementation process requires independent, dependent, or interdependent actions designed to meet the physical and emotional needs of children and families. *Independent* nursing interventions are actions taken by nurses based on their own clinical judgment (e.g., sponge baths to reduce fever or range-of-motion exercises, unless contraindicated). *Dependent* nursing interventions consist of nursing actions that are taken as a result of orders by physicians (e.g., the administration of prescribed medications). *Interdependent* nursing interventions are actions that nurses take in conjunction with other members of the health care team (e.g., discharge planning in collaboration with nutritionists, respiratory therapists, physical therapists, etc.). These nursing actions must be appropriate to children's and families' developmental stages, cultures, and value systems (Iyer, Taptich, & Bernocchi-Losey, 1986).

Preparation is essential for successful nursing interventions. Nurses must review the suggested actions of the plan and determine the knowledge, skills, and resources that are necessary for performing the specified interventions, while also being aware of potential barriers or complications that may arise during this process (Bulechek and McCloskey, 1987).

In pediatric health care settings the needs of children and families are rarely simple. In addition to performing interventions designed to address specific nursing diagnoses, nurses should also support their clients' developmental processes.

## Developmental Considerations in Nursing Implementation

Children respond to nursing interventions in both predictable and unpredictable ways. Nursing interventions should reflect an understanding of children's unique developmental capabilities, needs, and concerns. Three major areas of nursing interventions that involve specific age-related developmental concerns are medications, nutrition, and procedures. This chapter includes a general discussion of developmental considerations used in implementing various pediatric procedures. Specific pediatric adaptations of nursing procedures are included, where appropriate, in Part V.

## Medications

The proper administration of medications to children and adolescents is even more critical than in adults because of their smaller body mass, and also because of the unpredictability of drug reactions in children whose body systems are not fully developed. Although in most cases physicians prescribe medications, nurses are responsible for their administration and can be held legally liable for medication errors. Therefore, it is imperative that nurses have a thorough knowledge of medications that are commonly used in pediatrics (and reliable sources of information such as physicians, pharmacists, and drug handbooks when administering drugs that are used less frequently). Nurses must be familiar with standard dosages, routes of administration, timing, and available forms of medications and should question medication orders that they do not understand *before* administering the medications.

### Dosage Calculation

Because unit dose packaging often does not include pediatric dosages, nurses are usually responsible for calculating correct dosages. Various formulas are used to calculate pediatric dosages, but the most reliable are the body surface area method and the weight methods.

***Body Surface Area (BSA).*** The West nomogram (Fig. 8-1), which is generally used to calculate body surface area, is available in most pediatric health care settings. A straight line is drawn from the child's height (in the left column) to the child's weight (in the right column). Body surface area is determined by the intersection of this straight line with the column labeled SA (surface area), which is calculated in square meters ($m^2$). Because the average adult has 1.7 $m^2$ of body surface area, the following formula is applied:

$$\text{Estimated child's dose} = \frac{\text{BSA of child (in m}^2)}{1.7 \text{ m}^2 \text{ (BSA of adult)}} \times \text{Adult dose}$$

***Weight Method.*** This method assumes that the average adult weighs 150 pounds and that the dosage-to-weight ratio is the same for children as it is for adults. Using this method, the following formula is applied:

$$\text{Estimated child's dose} = \frac{\text{Child's weight (lb)}}{150 \text{ lb (avg. adult weight)}} \times \text{Adult dose}$$

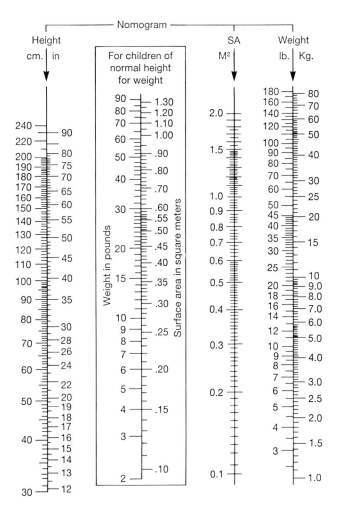

*Figure 8–1. West nomogram for calculation of body surface area. (Behrman, R.E., & Vaughan, V.C. [1987]. Nelson textbook of pediatrics [13th ed.] Philadelphia: W.B. Saunders)*

## Oral Administration

The preferred method for administering medications to children is by the oral route, because children usually prefer noninvasive techniques and prefer eating or drinking to such painful methods of medication administration as IM, IV, or rectal administration. Although oral medications are easier to administer, nurses must be aware that children can aspirate oral medications. This danger is greatly increased if medications are administered while the child is not fully conscious or is crying, or if the child resists taking medications.

Most oral medications for children are available in liquid form. Pharmaceutical manufacturers produce many pediatric medications that are both colorful and pleasant-tasting. These medications are readily swallowed by most children. However, nurses may want to offer children sips of water or juice following the administration of medications that have a strong or unpleasant taste in order to help eliminate unpleasant aftertastes. Care givers can provide nurses with advice about which administration techniques work best at home or, if children are old enough, they can be asked about their preferences for administration of medications.

Nurses can make unpleasant-tasting medications more palatable by mixing them with small amounts of food, fluid, or syrup. Applesauce and ice cream are two food products usually available in pediatric settings that are effective in masking the taste of medications. Nurses must be certain to separate the food products containing the medications from other foods to ensure that the entire prescribed dose is administered. Children should be informed that the food products contain their medications and that this should help to improve the taste of the medications. Honest communication is necessary to maintain trust between nurses and children and to prevent children from developing negative associations with the foods being used. Essential foods (e.g., milk) should not be used in order to keep children from forming negative associations between these foods and medications. Nurses should either explain the mixture of medications with food products or confirm that children will briefly experience an unpleasant aftertaste, and not lie about the means of administration.

Pediatric oral medications are measured according to the identified dose strength. Most liquid oral medications are concentrated and require only small amounts of fluid to deliver the prescribed dose. The most accurate means of measuring small amounts of liquid oral medications is the disposable syringe calibrated at 1-cc, 3-cc, 5-cc, and 10-cc measurements. These syringes are specifically intended for the oral administration of medications and are useful and accurate vehicles for measuring, transporting, and administering liquid oral medications. Toddlers, pre-schoolers, and school-aged children enjoy "pushing" the syringe plunger in their mouths, which eases medication administration. Young children are usually cooperative if medications are given to them in calibrated tube-like dispensers with a spoon at the end. After the correct dosage has been measured, an eye dropper can be a very effective tool for administering liquid medications to infants. Figure 8-2 shows one of the more common devices used for administration of liquid medications.

Standard plastic medicine cups are used to administer more than one teaspoon (4 to 5 mL) of liquid oral medications. Paper medicine cups are never used to measure or contain oral liquids because they are easily misshaped by fluid volume and often "leak" liquid contents. Household teaspoons are inappropriate for administering oral medications as well because they vary greatly in size, which makes it difficult to measure the dose accurately. Droppers are appropriate for administering oral medications only if the correct dose has been measured in advance.

Tablets are crushed with a mortar and pestle and mixed with a small amount of food, fluid, or syrup. The amount of food or other medium for administering the medicine is determined by the child's age. It is best if the

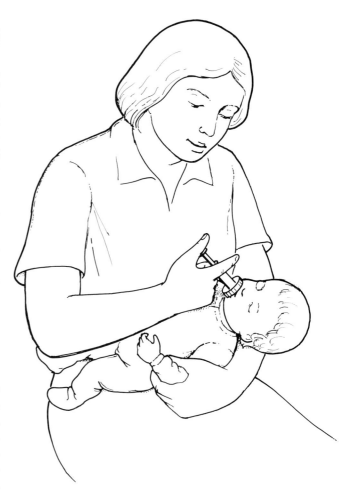

*Figure 8–2. Common device used to administer pediatric oral medications.*

amount of food is no larger than a normal mouthful; that way, if the child decides not to eat more than one mouthful, the medication will have been administered. School-aged children are usually able to chew tablets and will do so if the taste is somewhat palatable. Nurses should assess whether the child has previously had experience chewing tablets like vitamins. Capsules are generally considered inappropriate for pediatric medications because they are difficult to swallow and should not be chewed because of the necessity for timed release of the contents. The notable exception is enteric-coated capsules and tablets. These medications must be swallowed whole since their coating prevents breakdown in the stomach. Substitution for other forms of medication must be discussed with physicians if children are unable to swallow such tablets or capsules.

Infants and children who are crying risk aspiration of oral medications. Infants should be held in a semireclining position. Oral medications can be administered slowly via syringes placed on the side of the mouth against the buccal mucosa. Nurses should encourage infants to suck and swallow the medications intermittently with use of pacifiers or by gently squeezing their cheeks. Medications should not be mixed with formula and given in bottles because the complete dose may not be administered if the infant does not finish the bottle. Infants should be closely observed during and after the administration of oral medications for signs of choking or respiratory distress. Infants should be placed prone with their heads to the side following medication administration in case of regurgitation.

Uncooperative children provide challenges to administration of oral medications. Nurses should use developmentally appropriate strategies to enlist children's cooperation (Table 8-1). Children may take medications more easily if they give them to themselves or receive them from their parents rather than from nurses. Providing honest and clear explanations is more effective than demanding that children "must" take the medications. Nurses should always approach children in a calm, reinforcing manner and should never threaten or bribe children into submission. Uncooperative children should never be held down and forced to take oral medications. In these situations, the nurse should allow a period of time to pass and then reapproach the child using different strategies. As in all interactions with children, negative behavior should be ignored and positive behavior should be reinforced. With younger children, nurses can explain that the medication will help make them feel better; reasoning with older children can be very effective if they are told that the medication will help them get rid of an infection or a fever. If children begin to cry, it is best to wait until they have calmed down before attempting to get them to take medications. Parents may also be able to provide tips that are uniquely effective with their children.

### Rectal Administration

Rectal administration is used when children are unable to tolerate oral medications owing to gastrointestinal illness, vomiting, or surgery. The tapered end of the suppository is gently inserted into the rectum with a gloved finger. The buttocks are held together until the urge to expel the suppository passes. Because rectal administration is seen as highly invasive and threatening by children, developmentally appropriate explanations of the procedures and feelings associated with them are essential to decrease children's anxieties and fantasies.

### Intramuscular Administration

Decreasing associated trauma and fear should be the goal during the administration of intramuscular medications in children. Preparation of children and families through developmentally appropriate explanations and play helps children cope with the experience. Involving children in preparing for injections may help reduce active resistance. Nurses may ask older children to help feel for the muscles in which the injections are to be given and have them rub the muscles to "get ready." Appropriate sites for intramuscular injections are shown in Figure 8-3. Children can

clean the site with alcohol and hold the bandages. Nurses can also provide children with toys or hands to squeeze when the injections are being administered.

Although older children are usually able to hold still during an injection, younger children are seldom able to do so. If children are not able to hold still, it is important for their own safety to restrain them. There is some controversy over whether parents should help restrain their children during injections or other procedures. Some feel that children should view their parents as sources of comfort, and that when parents assist in restraining their children this parental role is altered and children are not as trusting of their parents. Others, however, feel that parents are better able than anyone else to comfort their children while they are restraining them.

Nurses should communicate honestly with children and encourage them to express pain or fear if necessary. Creative strategies can promote positive perceptions of the experiences. Nurses should comfort children, offer words of praise, and encourage parents to do the same. Opportunities for play should be allowed after injections so that children can ventilate their feelings.

### Intravenous Administration

Intravenous (IV) medications may be administered in homes or hospitals. Intravenous access is established with central venous catheters through peripheral veins of the hand, foot, wrist, arm, or scalp. Nurses must be knowledgeable and attentive regarding compatibility of drugs and IV solutions, amount of diluents, and rates of infusion because of the rapid effects of drugs administered by this method (Zenk, 1986). These factors are essential to safe and effective administration of IV medications. A variety of infusion pumps with specific adaptations for pediatric use are currently available. Nurses must be familiar with the equipment used in their practice settings and should constantly be alert for indications of equipment malfunction and complications such as infiltration or phlebitis. Policies for IV drug administration are clearly outlined in hospital procedures manuals; pharmacists and resources such as the *Physician's Desk Reference* and nursing drug handbooks provide information about the action, administration, and side effects of IV medications in children. See Chapter 28 for a further discussion of administration of IV medications.

During IV administration of medications it is frequently necessary to restrain infants or children to prevent them from removing the equipment or hurting themselves. The need for restraints should be clearly explained to children and their parents. Restraints should be removed at periodic intervals, usually every 2 to 3 hours, to allow children to move the restrained limbs. Parents can often assist in providing exercise while restraints are removed and in replacing the restraints. Restraints that are commonly used in pediatrics are shown in Figure 8-4.

*Table 8—1. Developmental Guidelines for Medication Administration**

| Developmental Level | Developmental Characteristics | Nursing Considerations |
| --- | --- | --- |
| Infants 1–12 months Trust versus mistrust | Strong sucking reflex | Oral medications are more easily administered using a syringe placed toward the back of the mouth along the inside of the cheek. |
| | Ability to spit out food or medication With increasing age, gross motor skills (arm and leg movements) become more developed | Medications should be as pleasant-tasting as possible. Increasing need for gentle restraint to prevent spilling medications or injury during injections. |
| Toddlers 12–36 months Autonomy versus shame and doubt | Begin standing with support and continue to advance to walking alone | Allow children to select position for taking medication or gently hold them for control; allow as much freedom as is safely possible. |
| | Can deliberately spit out foods and medicines with disagreeable tastes | It may be necessary to disguise medications in *small* amounts of familiar foods; may be necessary to re-feed medications. |
| | Independent and self-assertive | Permit children to assert themselves by choosing a drink to wash down medications; use a consistent, firm approach. |
| | Increasingly proficient at feeding self | Allow children to drink medications from a cup or to push plunger on a syringe. |
| Preschool 3–6 years Initiative versus guilt | Increased strength and motor skills; children may become more physically resistive | Behavior is influenced by others' reactions; abrupt or terse responses usually elicit the same from children; allow as much freedom as safely possible; restrain only when absolutely necessary. |
| | Able to understand simple explanations and concrete terms | Use concrete terms; use a calm, consistent, positive approach with explanations at cognitively appropriate levels of detail. |
| | Able to make decisions and choices | Allow children to make a choice if the situation warrants it; if no choice is possible, do not offer one. |
| School-age 6–12 years Industry versus inferiority | Having mastered a variety of skills, children now look for new tasks and skills to accomplish | Encourage children to take responsibility for administration of their own medications. |
| | Increasing cognitive growth | Explanations can be more advanced and can include cause-and-effect relationships. |
| | Increasing self-esteem | Encourage active participation and decision making when possible. |
| Adolescence 12–18 years Identity versus role confusion | Rapid emotional growth and periods of rebellion | Encourage compliance with medication regimens while supporting adolescents during periods of noncompliance. |
| | Seeking independence | Using a positive approach, show adolescents how they can assume responsibility for their own medication administration. |
| | Developing self-esteem | If applicable, encourage adolescents to assist in self-help groups with peers (e.g., adolescent diabetic groups or chemotherapy administration). |
| | Increasing cognitive ability | Explain side effects and encourage adolescents to monitor their own progress. |

*These are general guidelines and obviously must be tailored to the behavioral and developmental level of each child or adolescent.

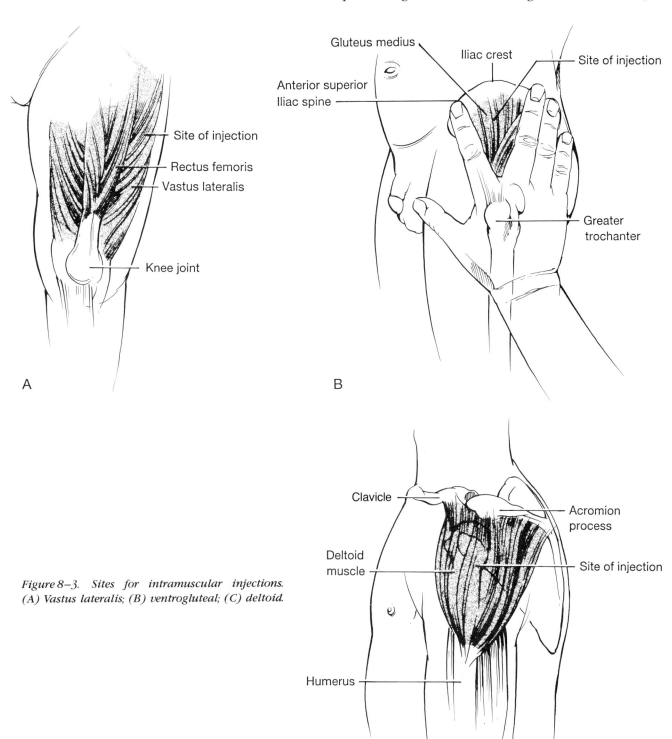

*Figure 8–3. Sites for intramuscular injections. (A) Vastus lateralis; (B) ventrogluteal; (C) deltoid.*

## Procedures

Children in hospitals, outpatient clinics, or home care settings may be exposed to a variety of invasive (e.g., injections or enemas) and noninvasive (e.g., x-rays or height and weight measurements) assessment and diag-

nostic procedures. Children may experience many fears and fantasies that are related to their developmental stages about these procedures. All children require developmentally appropriate explanations for any procedure or activity to which they are subjected (Pass & Pass, 1987). For example, telling young children that medications will help

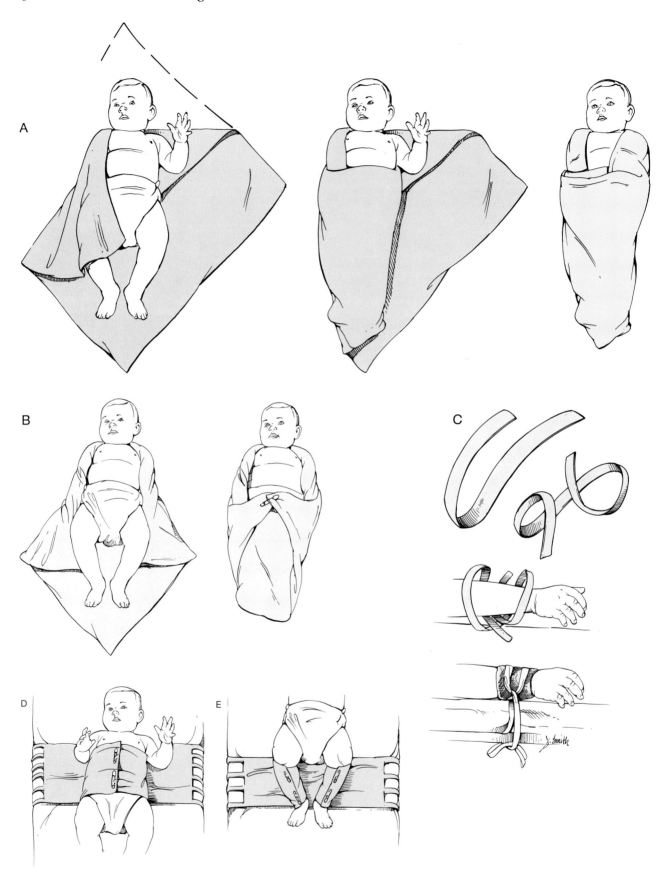

*Figure 8–4.   Pediatric restraints.*

make them feel better is usually sufficient explanation. With older children it might be appropriate to tell them that the medication will reduce their fever or help eliminate muscle spasms.

Play can help prepare and educate children and families before invasive and noninvasive procedures. Nurses must be aware of children's perceptions of the procedures in order to dispel any misconceptions about them. The child's preparation for procedures is most effective when parents are actively involved in all phases of preparation. Providing clear and honest explanations helps decrease the parents' anxiety as well as the child's. When possible, children and families should visit areas where procedures are actually performed (such as operating rooms, x-ray departments, and catheterization laboratories) in preparation for their experiences. Introductions to the nurses and physicians who will be caring for them during and after the procedure are also excellent preparation strategies. Minimizing parental anxieties about procedures helps minimize children's fears.

In many hospitals, parents are able to remain with their children during entire procedures. Some institutions allow parents in the operating room until anesthesia is induced; others allow parents to wait in the recovery areas for their children to awaken from the anesthesia. Research has shown that these are extremely supportive policies for both children and families. In the event that parents and children must be separated, nurses should address these concerns honestly. The time when parents and children can expect to be reunited should be emphasized rather than the duration of the separation. Opportunities for children to express their feelings after the procedures through art, play, and verbalization contribute to the child's sense of mastery over the experiences and provide increased confidence for coping with future stressors (Pridham, 1987).

## *Nutrition*

Knowledge of proper nutritional practices is essential in caring for pediatric clients and their families. Because the nutritional practices of children usually reflect the practices of their parents, nutritional counseling for both may be required.

Performing a complete nutritional assessment of pediatric clients (and often their families) is necessary to determine children's and families' knowledge bases and diagnose actual and potential nutritional problems. Height and weight measurements plotted on standard growth charts provide a means of comparing children to other children of the same age. These procedures are particularly useful in diagnosing problems such as failure to thrive or childhood obesity. However, for most children greater significance is placed on reviewing typical daily and weekly intake of food and fluids. This review provides information

for nurses in assessing the nutritional knowledge and practices of children and families. Nurses should focus on the nutritional balance of the diet, the variety of foods, the adequacy of calories and fluids, and the use of vitamins as nutritional supplements. Recommended amounts of foods and fluids for each age group are discussed in Chapters 11 to 16.

Many parents have preconceived ideas, based on their own childhood experiences, of which foods constitute a healthy diet. Cultural and extended family influences regarding the type and amount of foods given to children are also very significant. Nurses must provide nutritional counseling in a nonjudgmental, culturally acceptable manner to effectively change children's and families' knowledge and behavior. Nurses should also assess parental expectations of their children's nutritional intake and compare these behaviors to the developmental norms. Parents need information on patterns of physical growth and caloric demands and how these patterns change throughout childhood. For example, as infants begin to eat solid foods, their fluid intake usually decreases. This is often a source of concern for parents. The unpredictable and "finicky" eating patterns characteristic of toddlers are often a great source of stress for parents. Preschoolers and school-aged children are exposed to a wide variety of foods through peer interactions. Adolescents, who are also often influenced by peers and who have a greater degree of independence and financial resources, tend to eat foods that they like regardless of nutritional considerations. After infancy, snacks are usually more appealing than meals. The timing and nutritional quality of snacks should be carefully monitored by parents. Parents should also be reminded that their eating patterns may be scrutinized by children.

When parents are given information on nutritionally sound foods and diets, as well as the developmental needs of their children, most of them are able to make effective changes to foster nutritional health of their children and families. Behavior is difficult to change, however, particularly as it relates to nutritional practices. The sociocultural value of food and mealtime rituals may be deeply ingrained in both children and families. Nutritional counseling requires careful follow-up and evaluation to accurately measure the effectiveness of nursing interventions.

## *Health Teaching*

### *Settings*

Nurses use clinical expertise, knowledge of growth and developmental processes, and principles of teaching to provide information and influence behavior in a variety of settings. In pediatrician's practices and clinics, nurses are active in health teaching. The goal of health teaching is to provide information and guidance concerning children's patterns and stages of development and the implications for family life. Parenting issues such as discipline, sibling rivalry, the development of self-esteem, communication strategies, and safety serve as the focus of discussions.

School health nurses provide additional health teaching to children and families. Although most of the attention in this setting is focused directly on children, school health nurses also assess signs of family disruption, make referrals to other health care professionals, and provide follow-up care. In addition, formal programs that address family health issues such as sex education and safety practices are also provided by school nurses (Green & Bird, 1986).

Health teaching in hospitals begins with an orientation to the hospital setting, provides information and establishes interventions for pathology, medications, procedures, nutrition, and behavior, and ends with preparation for discharge. Health teaching focuses on practices for health restoration, rehabilitation, and maintenance.

Nurses must anticipate common health education needs in pediatric age groups based on their knowledge of growth and developmental processes. These anticipated needs are the result of the formulation of possible and potential nursing diagnoses and should be documented in the nursing care plan.

## Determination of Health Teaching Needs

The steps of the nursing process are applied to the health teaching process as a means of guiding nursing interventions (Rankin & Duffy-Stallings, 1990). Throughout assessment, nurses accumulate data and make judgments about the significance of that data. Inferences developed from pertinent assessment data result in diagnoses of health teaching needs. Nurses may also recognize evidence of health teaching needs through nonverbal cues that provide insight into requirements for information and support. Nurses should never assume that if children or parents do not verbalize specific problems, health teaching needs have been completely met. When planning for health teaching needs nurses must take into consideration the results of the assessment phase, as well as the identified nursing diagnoses. The child's age, developmental abilities, and family-related factors must be taken into consideration when planning nursing care. Anticipatory guidance must be a part of any pediatric care plan. Health teaching interventions specific to either a developmental age or illness, crisis, or family change should *always* be planned. Evaluation of the nursing care plan should identify the effectiveness of interventions in meeting the stated goals, and alternate strategies for achieving goals that were not fully met should be developed.

Health teaching is directed toward attaining and main-

taining wellness. Nurses must be aware of the family's cultural, social, and belief systems and the impact of these factors on the success of health teaching interventions. Noncompliant behaviors are often related to a lack of understanding about the significance of health practices or interventions or the possibility that they are inappropriate for the child's and family's belief system (Ranking & Duffy-Stallings, 1990). Noncompliance can be decreased if health teaching interventions are derived from a comprehensive client and family assessment. Although many standard interventions for common pediatric health problems are documented, the unique and specific health teaching needs required for each child and family should be assessed and specific interventions should be planned.

## Teaching Methods

Before adopting any of the variety of methods available for health teaching, nurses must assess the willingness of the child and family to receive information and their desire to change their behavior. Several informational sessions may be needed before behavioral change occurs. In order to prepare appropriate teaching plans, nurses must recognize the value families place on health promotion.

Goals of the teaching session are established with the child and the family. Documentation of these goals is stated in terms of desired client behaviors, conditions under which they will be demonstrated, and the criteria for evaluation. Goals must be client-specific, measurable, realistic, and attainable.

In developing teaching plans, previous learning should be evaluated, learning needs should be reassessed, and goals should be reviewed with the child and family. Teaching plans should reflect presentation of small amounts of information at several sessions. Time should be allowed for questions to clarify that the child and family understand.

Depending on the goals of the plan, nurses can schedule either individual or group teaching sessions. For example, in the ambulatory setting, presenting health teaching classes on the safety needs of toddlers may be an effective strategy that provides the added benefits of socialization and support for young families. Skills such as dressing changes are best taught individually to allow supervised practice and to reduce anxiety.

Children's developmental needs are paramount in selecting education strategies. Health teaching strategies according to age group and developmental abilities are presented in Table 8-2.

In all age groups nurses should approach health teaching interventions with an organized, concise format. Visual aids such as models, photos, samples, posters, and video demonstrations add to the appeal of the presentation for both adults and children. Teaching psychomotor skills such as dressing changes and medication administra-

*Table 8–2.  Health Teaching Strategies by Age*

| Age Group | Developmental Ability | Strategy |
|---|---|---|
| Infant | Visual, motor, cognitive, and social skill development | Parent-directed use of role modeling very effective. Stimulation of infants through visual, auditory, and kinesthetic means. |
| Toddler | Negativistic Ritualistic Short attention span Understands simple directions Able to identify needs Magical thinking Transductive reasoning Solitary play | Brief teaching sessions with frequent repetition are most effective. Brief visual stimulation: videos, photos, books. Puppets, dolls, stuffed animals (particularly ones belonging to child) are useful vehicles for explanations. |
| Preschool | Increased attention span Improved fine motor skills Gains an orientation to time Parallel and associative play | Can expand length of teaching sessions and variety of materials used: drawing, painting, manipulating, music. Responds well to immediate, concrete rewards. Puppets, dolls, stuffed animals (particularly ones belonging to child) are useful vehicles for explanations. Enjoys interactive games. |
| School-age | Achievement oriented Good verbal, comprehension, and fine motor skills Concrete operational thought | "Project" development: drawings, puzzles, models, paintings are useful teaching methods. Use of demonstration models, manipulation. Contracts and rewards are effective tools. Books, audio, and videotapes as well as games are useful teaching tools. |
| Adolescent | Formal operational thought Peer significance | Provide adolescents with role models and meet learning needs. Peer group presenters/counselors/educators. Allow time following the teaching session for questions and concerns. Contracts are very effective with this age group. |

tion should be accompanied by the opportunity for children and parents to practice the skills. It is helpful to use learning contracts with noncompliant or adolescent clients. Contracts are statements of agreement between nurses and clients about the health teaching interventions and the participant's role in the process. An example of a learning contract for an adolescent client with diabetes is shown in Table 8-3. Goals are established gradually in a step-by-step manner, with reassessment of the goals throughout the teaching process. This attention and commitment to the teaching/learning process benefits attainment of goals (Rankin & Duffy-Stallings, 1990).

Selection of appropriate teaching methods depends primarily on the specific needs of pediatric clients and their families. Attention to developmentally appropriate strategies ensures a more productive educational interaction, and providing comfortable, distraction-free environments allows for total concentration.

*Table 8–3.  Sample Learning Contract*

| Objectives | Nursing Actions | Learner Actions | Evaluation |
|---|---|---|---|
| Assist Brian in understanding the nature of diabetes and its management, including: | Provide Brian with pamphlets and videos that explain diabetes and its management. | Brian will have read the pamphlets and will have watched the video before his next appointment (2 weeks). | Brian will be able to discuss the signs and symptoms of diabetes, and begin to formulate his own care plan. |
| 1. Dietary management | Schedule appointment with a dietitian to answer Brian's questions. | Brian will meet with dietitian. | Kept appointment |
| | Provide Brian with a sample diet and exchange lists (including "junk" foods). | Brian will adhere to the diet and will record all foods eaten in his notebook. | Brian's record in his notebook |
| 2. Medication administration | In one-on-one discussion the nurse will explain the need for Brian's medication, how it is mixed, and how it is administered. | Brian will actively participate with the nurse. | Brian's understanding of the need for, mixing, and administration of insulin; return demonstration |
| 3. Self-monitoring | Provide Brian with instructions on the necessary urine and glucose monitoring as well as techniques and use of forms to record results. | Brian will monitor his own urine and glucose levels and will bring completed forms to each appointment (every 2 weeks). | Return demonstration of monitoring techniques and use of forms. Completed forms will be included in Brian's notebook |
| 4. Activity and exercise | Help Brian establish a plan for activity and exercise. Explain doctor's instructions about the need to adjust diet and medications to activity levels. | Work with the nurse to help develop an activity and exercise routine. | Record in notebook showing activity/exercise and diet/medication adjustment, as needed |
| 5. Adjustment to the diagnosis | Provide Brian with names and telephone numbers of local adolescent diabetic support groups or individuals. | By his next visit (2 weeks) Brian will contact at least one of the individuals or groups. | Contact made |
| | | Brian will bring a list of any specific problems to each visit for the next 8 weeks. | Notebook record |
| **Length of Contract:** | 8 weeks | | |
| **Bonus Clause:** | One "junk" food meal permitted each week provided Brian follows the contract | | |
| **Signatures:** | _____ | _____ | |
| | Nurse | Brian | |
| **Date:** | _____ | | |

## Teaching Tools

Imaginative approaches to teaching interventions add appeal and effectiveness to nursing actions. Nurses can use many common items in innovative ways to stimulate interest in learning. A vinyl or latex glove can become a puppet with the help of a marking pen. A tongue depressor can be decorated with crayons and gauze or topped with a plastic cup to become a puppet. Involving children in creating teaching tools (puppets, drawings, or charts) stimulates their interest in the health teaching intervention. A variety of videotapes, films, books, cassettes, and coloring books are available on topics such as safety, physical and dental health, hospitalization, and surgery. These can be given or loaned to children and their families before health care interventions. Child life departments at hospitals, public health departments, schools, and other agencies often provide such resources.

Teaching plans are usually part of the nursing care standard for particular illnesses or health issues. Standard teaching plans that have been created to address the common health problems of pediatric clients and families are valuable resources in planning health teaching interventions. Nurses should modify standard teaching plans to reflect each client's individual goals, developmental levels, and specific concerns. Modifications to intervention activities must also reflect the unique needs and abilities of children and families.

Standard teaching plans are also useful when children are discharged from the hospital. Community health, clinic, school, or private practice nurses can evaluate the effectiveness of the teaching interventions in meeting the health goals at the time of discharge. Effective teaching intervention strategies require follow-up and ongoing evaluation.

## Comprehensive Child Health Care

### Consultation

*Consultation,* applied to the health care setting, is the act of seeking advice or information from other health professionals. In the implementation process nurses consult with many people, depending on the identified nursing diagnoses and the interventions planned. Children and families consult with nurses in order to share information about the specific actions that are to be implemented and to review the resources that are available to them. Health care professionals such as pediatric nurse practitioners, clinical nurse specialists, social workers, physicians, psychiatrists, psychologists, dietitians, physical, occupational, and recreational therapists, and specialists in client education and discharge planning contribute valuable input during the implementation process. Institutions and community agencies also participate in the consultation process. Nurses may also use textbooks, research articles, standards of practice, and nursing care in developing and enacting the care plan.

Nurses interact with identified resources and elicit feedback and input concerning the effectiveness of the nursing interventions. Nursing actions should be congruent with those of other disciplines and should be modified continually as feedback is obtained. Evaluation of nursing interventions is an essential part of the nursing process and helps nurses determine which interventions are most successful and which need to be modified. An open, collegial approach to child health care by all members of the health care team provides highly individualized and effective health care for pediatric clients and their families.

### Referrals

*Referral* is the act of sending or directing people to other sources for information or treatment. Nurses refer pediatric clients to other health care professionals, institutions,

or community agencies for care that is beyond the domain of the identified nursing diagnoses. Clinics, private physician practices, health maintenance organizations, extended and rehabilitation care centers, and community agencies and support groups provide resources for child and family health care.

Ill children may be discharged to home environments with community support for their health care needs. Nurses coordinating their discharge must be sure that appropriate referrals for physical, cognitive, emotional, and social care needs of the children and their families are made by members of the health care team. Successful management of ill children in home settings depends on smooth coordination of necessary referrals.

Follow-up care referrals should be made in an organized and efficient manner. Written referrals should always accompany telephone contacts, and should include:

1. A summary of the child's past and present health status
2. Significant family data
3. Current nursing diagnoses
4. Plans of care (highlighting effective interventions)
5. Nurses' evaluations of current attainment of health goals

Based on these evaluations, projected needs and anticipation of potential problems are also discussed. Clear, concise communication expedites the referral process and provides for continuity of care.

### Continuity of Care

Continuity or consistency of care is essential to the successful implementation of the nursing care plan. *Continuity of care* ensures that the same care givers who are involved in care planning are also responsible for delivering and evaluating the effectiveness of nursing actions.

Continuity of care is enhanced by the *primary nursing* model. The primary nursing model places 24-hour accountability for client care on designated nurses. Although primary nurses are not the only nurses who care for children and families, they are responsible for directing and evaluating the care plan. The plan is documented in the Kardex, the computerized care plan, or in progress notes. This documentation allows other nurses caring for the children and families to continue the prescribed nursing actions, identify new nursing diagnoses, continue effective interventions or determine possible other nursing actions, and contribute feedback concerning the attainment of goals.

Primary nursing is a highly desirable practice mode in pediatric settings. Consistency and continuity are priority needs of children and families, and children's heightened responsiveness to care is an added benefit of care continuity. Children's fears of interventions performed by health

(*text continues on page 146*)

# Nursing Care Plan

Implementation of nursing care follows assessment, diagnosis, and planning. In this phase, specific nursing interventions are implemented and documented. Nursing interventions for the child with croup, as well as the parents, are shown in the following additions to the nursing care plan that has been developed in the previous chapters in this unit. It is important to remember that all nursing care must take into consideration the child's and family's cultural background, as well as the fact that nursing interventions very often can be frightening to children and their parents. Because discharge planning begins with admission to the hospital, it is important to remember that the parents will assume responsibility for care of the child upon discharge. Each nursing intervention provides an opportunity to provide children and parents with important information regarding health promotion and restoration.

## Assessment

Meghan Caldwell is a two-year-old girl brought to the emergency room at 3:30 AM by her parents.

### Chief Complaint

Meghan's mother reports a harsh, barky cough with apparent increasing difficulty in breathing.

### Subjective Assessment

*Past History:* Seen regularly since birth by a pediatrician for routine well-child care. No prior illnesses or hospitalizations; immunizations up-to-date.

*Present History:* Symptoms of upper respiratory infection for 48 hours; increasing respiratory distress for the past 6 hours.

*Family History:* Mother is 31; father is 34; both are well; no siblings. Maternal and paternal grandparents are alive and well. No family history of asthma, allergies, or chronic respiratory conditions.

### Objective Assessment

*Physical Examination:* T. 102° (rectal); p. 162 (apical); R. 46; B.P. 90/48 (R. arm); weight 11 kg (22%); height 89 cm (75%).

| | |
|---|---|
| Integument: | Clear, warm, moist, good turgor |
| Head: | Normal |
| Eyes: | PERRLA, EOMs intact, fundu-scopic exam normal |
| Ears: | Otoscopic exam normal |
| Nose: | Increased viscous secretions; nasal flaring |
| Mouth: | Lips dry; circumoral cyanosis |
| Throat: | Erythema, tonsils normal, no exudate, voice hoarse, barky cough |
| Neck: | Nodes nonpalpable |
| Thorax and Lungs: | Tachypnea, inspiratory dyspnea, substernal and suprasternal retractions, decreased breath sounds, bilaterally scattered rales and rhonchi |
| Heart: | Tachycardiac, normal rhythm, no murmur |
| Abdomen: | Active bowel sounds in all quadrants; no pain, tenderness, or masses |
| Genitalia: | Normal |
| Musculoskeletal: | Full ROM |
| Neurological: | Reflexes normal and symmetrical; anxious, irritable, restless |

*Medical Diagnosis:* Laryngotracheobronchitis (croup)

*Medical Plan:* Admit to hospital; mist tent with 30% O$_2$; antibiotics

## Nursing Care Plan for a Child With Croup

| Goals | Nursing Interventions | Evaluation Criteria |
|---|---|---|

*NURSING DIAGNOSIS #1: Activity Intolerance related to insufficient oxygenation as manifested by dyspnea, substernal and suprasternal retractions, rales, and rhonchi*

| Goals | Nursing Interventions | Evaluation Criteria |
|---|---|---|
| (S) Child's breathing will be facilitated | Provide cool humidified mist tent, as ordered | |

*(continued)*

# Nursing Care Plan *(Continued)*

| Goals | Nursing Interventions | Evaluation Criteria |
|---|---|---|
| (L) Child will resume normal respiratory function | Administer O$_2$ as ordered; assess for proper O$_2$ concentration every 8 hours | |
| | Administered aerosol treatments as ordered | |
| | Position child for maximum inspiration (high Fowler's) | |
| | Monitor respiratory status every 30 min | |
| | Limit treatment to those that are absolutely essential to allow for rest and calm | |
| | Assess for signs and symptoms or hypoxia—increased cyanosis, restlessness, sudden fatigue, confusion | |
| | Assess child's clothing, bed linens, and possessions within mist tent for excess moisture collection, and change as needed | |

*NURSING DIAGNOSIS #2: High Risk for Fluid Volume Deficit related to decreased oral intake as manifested by the child's refusal to drink*

| Goals | Nursing Interventions | Evaluation Criteria |
|---|---|---|
| (S) Child's hydration status will be maintained and improved | Assess child's ability for intake | |
| | Encourage small amount of fluid (60 mL every hour, as tolerated) | |
| | Provide maintenance IV fluids if NPO | |
| | Carefully monitor intake and output | |
| | Assess hydration status—crying with tears, moist mucous membranes, skin turgor, sunken eyes | |

*NURSING DIAGNOSIS #3: Hyperthermia related to the infectious process*

| Goals | Nursing Interventions | Evaluation Criteria |
|---|---|---|
| (S) Child's temperature will return to normal (98.6°F) | Monitor temperature every 2 hours | |
| | Administer antipyretics, as ordered | |
| | Apply tepid water sponges to axilla, groin, head, and abdomen | |

*(continued)*

# Nursing Care Plan *(Continued)*

| *Goals* | *Nursing Interventions* | *Evaluation Criteria* |
|---|---|---|
| | Encourage fluids as tolerated | |
| | Use hyperthermia blanket when indicated | |

*NURSING DIAGNOSIS #4: Anxiety (child) related to respiratory distress and hospitalization as manifested by irritability and restlessness*

| *Goals* | *Nursing Interventions* | *Evaluation Criteria* |
|---|---|---|
| (S) Child's anxiety will be reduced | Limit procedures to those that are absolutely essential | |
| (L) Child will comply with treatment plan | Explain all procedures before initiation | |
| | Encourage parents to stay with the child throughout the hospitalization | |
| | Provide age-appropriate diversional activities | |
| | Encourage use of child's favorite possession—toy, blanket, etc. | |
| | Provide a consistent nursing care giver | |

*NURSING DIAGNOSIS #5: Anxiety (parental) related to apprehension concerning child's welfare as manifested by nervous speech and obvious concern*

| *Goals* | *Nursing Interventions* | *Evaluation Criteria* |
|---|---|---|
| (S) Parents' anxiety will be reduced | Provide parents with information regarding the illness and the planned treatment | |
| (L) Parents will comply with treatment plan | Involve parents in decision making | |
| (L) Parents will demonstrate knowledge of etiology, treatment, and home care for croup | Allow parents to provide direct care for their child | |
| | Facilitate parent's staying with the child during the hospitalization | |
| | Allow parents an opportunity to ventilate fears and feelings | |

care professionals may be allayed by their perception that "their" nurses are exercising responsibility over the delivery of care. In addition, the opportunity to establish working relationships between nurses and clients contributes to the accuracy of assessment, data evaluation, and the effectiveness of the nursing care.

Many hospitals and community settings have adopted the primary nursing model. In clinical settings where other models of nursing practice are followed, however, excellent documentation of nursing care plans provides continuity and consistency of actions.

In order to provide comprehensive health care, pediatric nurses and members of the multidisciplinary team can work together in implementing the nursing care plan through the process of consultation, referrals, and continuity of care.

## Summary

Implementation of the nursing process is the initiation of the delivery of nursing care. Implementing pediatric nursing interventions, including administration of medications, nutritional counseling, health education, and procedures, occurs within a developmental framework.

Health teaching is a major intervention employed by pediatric nurses who evaluate health teaching needs related to illnesses and developmental stages. Teaching methods and tools are adapted to clients' individual needs. Creative learning approaches benefit children and their families. Teaching tools provide reinforcement and follow-up of health teaching interventions.

Nurses may consult with colleagues, clinical experts, health care professionals, clients, and families in order to provide effective and comprehensive health care. Nurses make referrals for additional or follow-up care, assume responsibility for managing the health care plan, and provide consistency among all members of the health care team.

## References

Bulechek, G., & McClosky, J. (1987). Nursing interventions: What they are and how to choose them. *Holistic Nursing Practice, 1*(3), 36.

Green, K., & Bird, J. E. (1986). The structures of children's beliefs about health and illness. *Journal of School Health, 56,* 325.

Iyer, P., Taptich, B. J., and Bernocchi-Losey, D. (1986). *Nursing process and nursing diagnosis.* Philadelphia: W. B. Saunders.

Pass, M. D., & Pass, C. M. (1987). Anticipatory guidance for parents of hospitalized children. *Journal of Pediatric Nursing, 2,* 250.

Pridham, K., Adelson, F., & Hansen, M. F. (1987). Helping children deal with procedures in a clinic setting: A developmental approach. *Journal of Pediatric Nursing, 2,* 13.

Rankin, S., & Duffy-Stallings, K. (1990). *Patient education: Issues, principles, and practices* (2nd ed.). Philadelphia: J. B. Lippincott.

Zenk, K. E. (1986). Administering IV antibiotics to children. *Nursing '86, 16*(12), 50.

## Bibliography

Bates, T., & Broome, M. (1986). Preparation of children for hospitalization and surgery: A review of the literature. *Journal of Pediatric Nursing, 1,* 230.

Broome, M. (1986). The relationship between children's fears and behavior during a painful event. *Child Health Care, 14*(3), 142.

Burrows, C. (1984). IV needle selections. *Nursing '84, 14*(12), 32.

Evans, M. L., & Hansen, B. (1981). Administering injections to different aged children. *American Journal of Maternal–Child Nursing, 6,* 194.

Funk, M., et al. (1984). Teaching children to swallow pills: A case study. *Child Health Care, 1*(1), 20.

Garot, P. (1986). Therapeutic play: Work of both child and nurse. *Journal of Pediatric Nursing, 2,* 111.

Powell, M. L. (1981). *Assessment and management of developmental changes in children.* St. Louis: C. V. Mosby.

Roberts, S. (1987). Food first: Educating our children. *Health Education, 18*(2), 17.

Ryan, N. (1988). The stress-coping process in school age children: Gaps in the knowledge needed for health promotion. *Advances in Nursing Science, 11,* 1–12.

Siaw, S., et al. (1986). Knowledge about medical instruments and reported anxiety in pediatric surgery patients. *Child Health Care, 14*(3), 134.

Steele, N., & Harrison, B. (1986). Technology-assisted children; Assessing discharge preparation. *Journal of Pediatric Nursing, 1,* 150.

Vernon, D., et al. (1965). *The psychological responses of children to hospitalization and illness.* Chicago: Charles C Thomas.

Zweig, D. (1986). Reducing stress when a child is admitted to the hospital. *American Journal of Maternal–Child Nursing, 11,* 24.

# Evaluating Child Health Nursing Care

Joan T. Duer

Photograph by David Finn

9

Evaluation Methods

Documentation and Communication
of Client Health Care Evaluation

Evaluation of Nursing Practice

Self-Evaluation

Summary

Nursing Care Plan

## Learning Objectives

*Upon completion of this chapter the reader will be able to:*

1. *Identify the role of evaluation in the child health care nursing process.*

2. *Describe methods of evaluating the effectiveness of nursing care.*

3. *Discuss the importance of documenting and communicating evaluation of the client health care plan.*

4. *Identify the significance of the evaluation process to nursing practice.*

5. *Describe the need for frequent self-evaluation by professional nurses.*

## Key Terms

*documentation*

*evaluation*

*intershift report*

*quality assurance*

*self-evaluation*

Evaluation is an integral component of the child health nursing process. Judging the effectiveness of nursing interventions used to promote child and family health or restoration to wellness is a major component of the pediatric nursing role. It is difficult, yet essential, to critique ourselves and our actions. Without critical appraisal of the effectiveness of nursing interactions, quality care cannot be assured. One of the hallmarks of a profession is the responsibility for self-regulation. Evaluation of nursing care and quality assurance are not only the responsibility of every nurse but are obligatory components of nurses' professional roles.

## Evaluation Methods

Nurses use a variety of strategies to evaluate the effectiveness of nursing interventions. Accomplishment of goals, and the establishment of goals that are not beyond the ability of children and families to achieve them, is one strategy. Well-written goals provide time lines and criteria for evaluating the effectiveness of interventions and the achievement of health goals. Because nursing interventions in pediatric settings often require behavioral changes on the part of children or families, changes often demonstrate child or family learning in response to effective nursing interventions or teaching. Nurses measure, either directly or indirectly (objectively or subjectively), the extent to which clients meet health care goals.

When measurement criteria indicate that goals have not been achieved, nurses, in consultation with clients and families, must critique the effectiveness of the interventions, as well as the appropriateness of the time frame, and make necessary adjustments or develop alternative interventions (Iyer, Taptich, & Bernocchi-Losey, 1986).

Nurses observe clients directly for evidence of achievement of health care goals. General survey and physical assessment techniques provide valuable data about the child's health status. Often this data helps to indicate health status changes related to nursing interventions.

Observation of children and parents while they perform specific skills or participate in interactions is another useful evaluation technique. Nurses can make *objective* judgments about clients' abilities to perform skills or participate in interactions and can provide immediate reinforcement for learned behavior. They can also provide immediate feedback if procedures are not being conducted correctly. Examination of medical records may also provide useful information in evaluating the effectiveness of the nursing care plan.

Feedback (subjective data) from clients and families is a valuable source of evaluation data. Clients' experiences and perceptions contribute to an accurate evaluation of the nursing plan. To assess client knowledge, nurses may ask clients to recall facts or discuss their understanding of facts. Knowledge can be formally validated through a written test or questionnaire. Younger pediatric clients may reflect their knowledge through drawings, stories, or play. Even when parents believe the care plan is progressing well, nurses must consider the child's perception as well. It is the combined evaluation by the nurse, the child, and the family that best indicates the success of the nursing care plan.

## Documentation and Communication of Client Health Care Evaluation

Nurses must continually evaluate the effectiveness of interventions in achieving health care goals. The plan of care may be altered based on the nurse's evaluation and consultation with the child and family. Goals may be modified to reflect different time lines and evaluation criteria, and alternate interventions may be proposed. For example, a hospitalized adolescent whose insulin-dependent diabetes had recently been diagnosed refused to handle an insulin syringe, denying that insulin administration would be a continuing need. The goal of "self-administration of insulin prior to hospital discharge" may not have been realistic. Instead, the care plan should have been amended to shift responsibility for insulin administration to another care giver while developing interventions to promote the adolescent's intellectual and emotional acceptance of the illness and its implications. New health care needs and, subsequently, new nursing diagnoses may arise and provide direction for future nursing care plans.

Nurses must communicate the evaluation to other members of the health care team. Documentation on the nursing care plan or progress notes is essential. This documentation provides for continuity of care, particularly when clients are referred to other institutions, health care providers, or community resources. Evaluation information regarding a hospitalized child must be communicated on a daily basis. Nurses are responsible for updating the care plan and documenting a current evaluation of client health status. Patient care conferences and other presentations allow for comprehensive evaluation of the client's progress in meeting health goals and provide an opportunity for professional interchange of ideas (Table 9-1). This multidisciplinary dialogue is useful not only for evaluating the current status of the care plan but also for identifying possible impediments to the stated interventions, and it provides a forum for developing alternatives with a greater likelihood of goal achievement.

## Evaluation of Nursing Practice

Evaluation of nursing care is a daily responsibility for all nurses. Each nursing action should be evaluated by the individual practitioner as an integral component of their nursing care. For example, evaluating the effectiveness of a routine such as taking vital signs every 4 hours may indicate that professional nursing time should be redirected by abolishing such routines or by delegating these tasks to auxiliary personnel so that the nurse can attend to more complex patient care needs.

Formal methods of evaluating nursing practice are

*Table 9–1. Nursing Guidelines for Intershift Report*

1. Provide basic client information: Name, age, room number, medical diagnosis, reason for admission.
2. Highlight any pertinent family issues: Brief description of family issues that may have an impact on nursing care. Give factual details only, not interpretations of observed behaviors.
3. Highlight physical assessment data abnormalities: Focus on systems related to the diagnosis and pertinent (past 24 hours) data. *Discuss only variations. Do not spend time on temperature, pulse, or neuro assessments if they are normal.*
4. Medical treatments and procedures: Current/scheduled. Include related patient and family teaching needs.
5. Summarize how the child and family are coping with the illness/hospitalization. Avoid vague terms; describe specific, observed behaviors.
6. Identify three top priority nursing diagnoses.
7. Describe objectives and interventions to address priority health needs.
8. Share evaluation of above data.
9. Give specific instructions to be continued, if they are not clearly documented.
10. Allow for questions.

(Adapted from Graham, N. [1982]. *Quality assurance in hospitals: Strategies for assessment and implementation.* Rockville, MD: Aspen Publications)

part of quality assurance monitoring. Every discipline within the hospital and community health care setting is obligated to formally evaluate its practice against the standards of care outlined for that discipline and/or institution. Quality assurance activities in nursing are often directed by an individual or a department, although they rely on the accountability of individual nurses. In more progressive settings quality assurance activities are directed and implemented by staff nurses who focus not only on general standards of care but also on issues that are specific to the delivery of care on their units. Quality assurance activities are reported for the nursing unit to multidisciplinary institutional committees and are overseen by regulatory agencies such as the state department of health and the Joint Commission for the Accreditation of Hospital Organizations.

Retrospective or current chart audits, nurse and client interviews, questionnaires, or observations provide data to evaluate the effectiveness of nursing care against documented standards. The same approaches are used to evaluate the effectiveness of new or innovative client care strategies. Evaluation contributes to the development of new standards of care as well as the maintenance of existing standards of care.

## Self-Evaluation

*Self-evaluation* is an important part of the formal evaluation process in most clinical settings because it provides for personal and professional growth. It gives insight about individual strengths and weaknesses and promotes self-confidence. This self-knowledge enhances effectiveness in the nursing role. For the nurse to remain positive about the process, self-evaluation should focus on what nurses do

well, not only on areas where improvement is needed (Ellis & Hartley, 1992).

The steps in the self-evaluation process include validation of identified strengths as well as areas for further professional growth. Both areas should be formally discussed by nurses and their managers at least once each year. The performance appraisal process should serve to validate and reinforce individual nurses' perceptions regarding their performance as well as providing direction and support for continued development. Evaluation in the form of "feedback" from peers is extremely useful for modeling desired behaviors and enhancing professional collegiality.

## Summary

Evaluation is an integral component of the child health nursing process. Nurses use a variety of direct and indirect evaluation methods to measure clients' and families' progress in meeting health goals. The nursing care plan is continually modified based on the evaluation data.

Nurses share observations with peers and other members of the health care team through written documentation, verbal interchanges, and formal presentations. Intershift reports among nurses should focus on clients' health status in relation to nursing, rather than medical, care plans.

Evaluation of nursing practices through quality assurance monitoring is an important part of professional self-evaluation. Quality assurance monitoring validates the significance of nursing actions and provides for development of nursing care standards. Self-evaluation of nursing practices provides validation of abilities and direction for future growth, as well as meeting nurses' ultimate objective: better care for children and their families.

# Nursing Care Plan

*Evaluation* of nursing care is the last step of the nursing process. Based on the assessment, diagnoses, plans, and interventions, the resolution of the problem is measured against the goals that were set. At this point it is essential to measure the effectiveness of the care plan. Goals that were not achieved within the expected time frames may need to be reevaluated, requiring new or modified interventions.

## Assessment

Meghan Caldwell is a two-year-old girl brought to the emergency room at 3:30 AM by her parents.

### Chief Complaint

Meghan's mother reports a harsh, barky cough with apparent increasing difficulty in breathing.

*(continued)*

# Nursing Care Plan *(Continued)*

## Subjective Assessment

***Past History:*** Seen regularly since birth by a pediatrician for routine well-child care. No prior illnesses or hospitalizations; immunizations up-to-date.

***Present History:*** Symptoms of upper respiratory infection for 48 hours; increasing respiratory distress for the past 6 hours.

***Family History:*** Mother is 31; father is 34; both are well; no siblings. Maternal and paternal grandparents are alive and well. No family history of asthma, allergies, or chronic respiratory conditions.

## Objective Assessment

***Physical Examination:*** T. 102° (rectal); P. 162 (apical); R. 46; B.P. 90/48 (R. arm); weight 11 kg (22%); height 89 cm (75%).

| | |
|---|---|
| Integument: | Clear, warm, moist, good turgor |
| Head: | Normal |
| Eyes: | PERRLA, EOMs intact, funduscopic exam normal |
| Ears: | Otoscopic exam normal |

| | |
|---|---|
| Nose: | Increased viscous secretions; nasal flaring |
| Mouth: | Lips dry; circumoral cyanosis |
| Throat: | Erythema, tonsils normal, no exudate, voice hoarse, barky cough |
| Neck: | Nodes non-palpable |
| Thorax and Lungs: | Tachypnea, inspiratory dyspnea, substernal and suprasternal retractions, decreased breath sounds, bilaterally scattered rales and rhonchi |
| Heart: | Tachycardiac, normal rhythm, no murmur |
| Abdomen: | Active bowel sounds in all quadrants; no pain, tenderness, or masses |
| Genitalia: | Normal |
| Musculoskeletal: | Full ROM |
| Neurological: | Reflexes normal and symmetrical; anxious, irritable, restless |

***Medical Diagnosis:*** Laryngotracheobronchitis (croup)

***Medical Plan:*** Admit to hospital; mist tent with 30% $O_2$; antibiotics

## Nursing Care Plan for a Child With Croup

| Goals | Nursing Interventions | Evaluation Criteria |
|---|---|---|
| *NURSING DIAGNOSIS #1: Activity Intolerance related to insufficient oxygenation as manifested by dyspnea, substernal and suprasternal retractions, rales, and rhonchi* | | |
| (S) Child's breathing will be facilitated | Provide cool humidified mist tent, as ordered | Child's respiratory effort is decreased |
| (L) Child will resume normal respiratory function | Administer $O_2$ as ordered; assess for proper $O_2$ concentration every 8 hours | Child's air exchange is improved—no signs of hypoxia |
| | Administer aerosol treatments as ordered | |
| | Position child for maximum inspiration (high Fowler's) | |

*(continued)*

# Nursing Care Plan *(Continued)*

| Goals | Nursing Interventions | Evaluation Criteria |
|-------|----------------------|---------------------|
| | Monitor respiratory status every 30 min | |
| | Limit treatments to those that are absolutely essential to allow for rest and calm | |
| | Assess for signs and symptoms of hypoxia—increased cyanosis, restlessness, sudden fatigue, confusion | |
| | Assess child's clothing, bed linens, and possessions within mist tent for excess moisture collection, and change as needed | |

*NURSING DIAGNOSIS #2: High Risk for Fluid Volume Deficit related to decreased oral intake as manifested by the child's refusal to drink*

| Goals | Nursing Interventions | Evaluation Criteria |
|-------|----------------------|---------------------|
| (S) Child's hydration status will be maintained and improved | Assess child's ability for intake | Child's fluid intake is within the normal range for weight |
| | Encourage small amounts of fluid (60 mL every hour, as tolerated) | |
| | Provide maintenance IV fluids if NPO | |
| | Carefully monitor intake and output | |
| | Assess hydration status—crying with tears, moist mucous membranes, skin turgor, sunken eyes | |

*NURSING DIAGNOSIS #3: Hyperthermia related to the infectious process*

| Goals | Nursing Interventions | Evaluation Criteria |
|-------|----------------------|---------------------|
| (S) Child's temperature will return to normal (98.6°F) | Monitor temperature every 2 hours | Child's temperature is normal (98.6°F) |
| | Administer antipyretics, as ordered | |
| | Apply tepid-water sponges to axilla, groin, head, and abdomen | |
| | Encourage fluids as tolerated | |
| | Use hyperthermia blanket when indicated | |

*(continued)*

# Nursing Care Plan *(Continued)*

| Goals | Nursing Interventions | Evaluation Criteria |
|---|---|---|
| *NURSING DIAGNOSIS #4: Anxiety (child) related to respiratory distress and hospitalization as manifested by irritability and restlessness* | | |
| (S) Child's anxiety will be reduced | Limit procedures to those that are absolutely essential | Child displays decreased anxiety with routine hospital procedures |
| (L) Child will comply with treatment plan | Explain all procedures before initiation | Child interacts with hospital care givers |
| | Encourage parents to stay with the child throughout the hospitalization | |
| | Provide age-appropriate diversional activities | |
| | Encourage use of child's favorite possession—toy, blanket, etc. | |
| | Provide a consistent nursing care giver | |
| *NURSING DIAGNOSIS #5: Anxiety (parental) related to apprehension concerning child's welfare as manifested by nervous speech and obvious concern* | | |
| (S) Parents' anxiety will be reduced | Provide parents with information regarding the illness and the planned treatment | Parents demonstrate confidence in care givers and planned course of treatment |
| (L) Parents will comply with treatment plan | Involve parents in decision making | Parents remain involved in their child's care throughout the course of the illness |
| (L) Parents will demonstrate knowledge of etiology, treatment, and home care for croup | Allow parents to provide direct care for their child | |
| | Facilitate parents' staying with the child during the hospitalization | |
| | Allow parents an opportunity to ventilate fears and feelings | |

## References

Ellis, J., & Hartley, C. L. (1992). *Nursing in today's world* (4th ed.). Philadelphia: J. B. Lippincott.

Iyer, P., Taptich, B. J., & Bernocchi-Losey, D. (1986). *Nursing process and nursing diagnosis.* Philadelphia: W. B. Saunders.

## Bibliography

Lederer, J. R., et al. (1986). *Case planning pocket guide.* Menlo Park, CA: Addison-Wesley.

Rankin, S., & Duffy-Stallings, K. (1990). *Patient education: Issues, principles, and practices* (2nd ed.). Philadelphia: J. B. Lippincott.

Richard, J. (1988). Congruence between intershift reports and patient's actual conditions. *Image: Journal of Nursing Scholarship, 20,* 4.

# Growth, Development, and Health: Conception Through Adolescence

*Prenatal Growth, Development, and Health*

*Neonatal Growth, Development, and Health*

*Infant Growth, Development, and Health*

*Toddler Growth, Development, and Health*

*Preschool Growth, Development, and Health*

*School-Age Growth, Development, and Health*

*Adolescent Growth, Development, and Health*

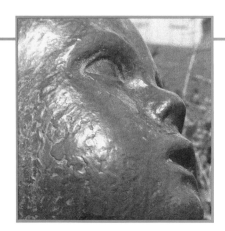

*Photograph by David Finn*

# Prenatal Growth, Development, and Health

M. Angie Wieser

*Photograph by David Finn*

10

*Stages in Fetal Development*
  *Embryonic Development*
  *Physiological Process: Placenta
    and Umbilical Cord*

*Genetic Influences on Development*
  *Chromosomal Abnormalities*
  *Single Gene or Mendelian
    Disorders*
  *Polygenic and Multifactorial
    Disorders*
  *Teratogenic Disorders from
    Extracellular Factors*

*Environmental Influences on
  Development*

*Psychosocial Impact of the Prenatal
  Period on Parents and Families*
  *Preparation for Pregnancy and
    Parenthood*
  *Preparation of Siblings*
  *Nutritional Requirements: Mother
    and Fetus*

*Assessment of Fetal Growth and
  Development*
  *Prenatal Assessment and
    Diagnosis of Genetic Disorders*
  *Assessment of Fetal Development*
  *Assessment During Labor*

*Summary*

### Learning Objectives

*Upon completion of this chapter the reader will be able to:*

1. *Identify the function and relationship of the placenta and umbilical cord to fetal development.*

2. *Briefly describe and give examples of the four categories of genetic disorders: chromosomal, single gene, polygenic and multifunctional, and teratogenetic.*

3. *Identify the factors that indicate that a prenatal cytogenic study should be performed.*

4. *Discuss the psychosocial impact of pregnancy on parents and siblings.*

5. *Discuss the basic nutritional requirements of mothers and fetuses.*

6. *Identify invasive and noninvasive procedures for prenatal assessment of genetic disorders.*

7. *Discuss the nurse's role in the assessment and monitoring of fetal well-being and the identification of fetal distress.*

### Key Terms

*amniocentesis*

*amnion*

*blastocyst*

*chorion*

*chorionic villi sampling*

*chromosome*

*couvade syndrome*

*dizygotic*

*ectoderm*

*embryo*

*endoderm*

*fetal distress*

*fetography*

*fetoscopy*

*fetus*

*gestation*

*mesoderm*

*monozygotic*

*multiple fetuses*

*percutaneous umbilical blood sampling*

*teratogen*

*translocation*

*trisomy*

*ultrasound*

*umbilical cord*

*zygote*

The prenatal period is usually a time of parental expectations about what the child will look like, how the child will behave, and how the parents will function in the parental role. It is a time to prepare for the new child and to share those expectations with family and friends.

Health promotion is a major focus for parents and caregivers as they try to provide an environment that will result in an optimal health state for the child. Supportive health care alternatives that the family may select during this critical period are explored. Parental preparation includes information related to nutrition, diagnostic and assessment procedures, labor and delivery, and care of the newborn.

## Stages in Fetal Development

Prenatal development begins at fertilization or conception when the male sperm and female ovum meet and their cell nuclei fuse. The fertilized ovum is initially called a *zygote*; during the first estimated 2 weeks of its growth, primary villi appear and the process of implantation into the mother's uterus is completed. At the end of the ovum stage, the organism becomes an *embryo*. This period is the most critical time in development of the organism because of the rapid cell growth and early development of all major organ systems. The embryonic period continues from 2 to 8 weeks of gestation. At the end of the embryonic stage, the embryo is called a *fetus*; it continues its growth and development until the pregnancy ends and the infant is born, usually at 40 weeks of gestation.

## Embryonic Development

When the developing ovum passes through the maternal fallopian tube into the uterus, it is surrounded by uterine fluid and is free-floating. Between the 5th and 7th days after conception, implantation occurs. A cellular structure called a *blastocyst* "implants" itself into the endometrium of the maternal uterus, where it is nourished with blood and tissue secretions. The blastocyst is composed of an outer cell mass that becomes the fetal part of the placenta and an inner cell mass that divides into three germ layers or groups of cells called the *ectoderm, mesoderm,* and *endoderm.* Each layer forms into specific body organs or parts, as shown in Table 10-1. Finger-like chorionic villi develop from the outer layer of cells, called the *trophoblast.* The cells of the villi begin to secrete human chorionic gonadotropin, a hormone that maintains progesterone production. Progesterone stimulates endometrial growth that prepares the uterus for the reception of the fertilized ovum and provides the environment for continued embryonic development.

The thickening of the maternal endometrium forms a structure divided into three portions: the *decidua basales,* which lies under the embedded ovum; the *decidua cap-sularis,* which is pushed out and expands over the growing embryo; and the *decidua vera,* the portion that is not in immediate contact with the ovum. The placenta is formed by the union of the decidua basalis with the chorionic villi.

Two separate membranes that develop from the zygote also surround the developing embryo: an inner membrane, the *amnion,* which covers the inner side of the placenta; and an outer membrane, the *chorion,* which forms about 2 weeks after fertilization. These translucent, stringy membranes contain the fetus and amniotic fluid. The amniotic fluid provides protection for the embryo against possible injury, maintains a more even temperature control, allows ease in fetal movements, and is a medium for active chemical exchange.

## Physiological Process: Placenta and Umbilical Cord

In addition to connecting the fetus to the uterine wall, the placenta performs a number of critical functions to support the fetus. It is the organ of nutrition, excretion, and respiration for the fetus. It secretes progesterone and estrogen and acts as a limited protective barrier by preventing some harmful drugs and organisms from entering the fetal circulation.

The placenta is not simply the organ for transport between mother and fetus; it is an active site for synthesis of steroids and all other hormones, except adrenocorticotropic hormone and thyroid-stimulating hormone, which are large and do not cross the placental membrane. Fetal oxygen and nutrients may be influenced to a significant extent by placental metabolism as well as by their concentrations in maternal blood and by the transport mechanism of the placenta. It is estimated that about half the oxygen and as much as 70% of the glucose that leaves the mother to nourish the uterus and the fetus may be used by the placenta (Bissonette, 1986). Placental functioning depends to a great extent on maternal circulation. The structures of the placenta are shown in Figure 10-1.

The *umbilical cord* links the fetus to the placenta. The cord normally consists of one large vein and two small arteries. The vein carries oxygenated blood and nutrients to the fetus while the arteries return unoxygenated blood to the chorionic villi. The umbilical cord is 45 to 55 cm long (slightly longer than the fetus) and about 1.5 to 2 cm in diameter; it usually leaves the placenta near the center and enters the abdominal wall of the fetus at the umbilicus. The blood vessels are supported by the loose connective tissue of the cord and Wharton's jelly, a protective mucous coating. This mucoid substance prevents kinking off or collapsing of the cord and interference with fetal circulation.

Growth and development of the human embryo continues to take place in an orderly and predictable pattern

*Table 10–1. The Three Germ Layers*

| Germ Layer | Developmental Source for |
|---|---|
| Ectoderm (outer layer) | Nails<br>Hair<br>Skin<br>Sweat and sebaceous glands<br>Tooth enamel<br>Central nervous system |
| Mesoderm (middle layer) | Muscles<br>Bone<br>Ligaments and tendons<br>Kidneys<br>Ovaries and testes<br>Heart and blood vessels |
| Endoderm (inner layer) | Pancreas<br>Liver<br>Digestive system<br>Respiratory system |

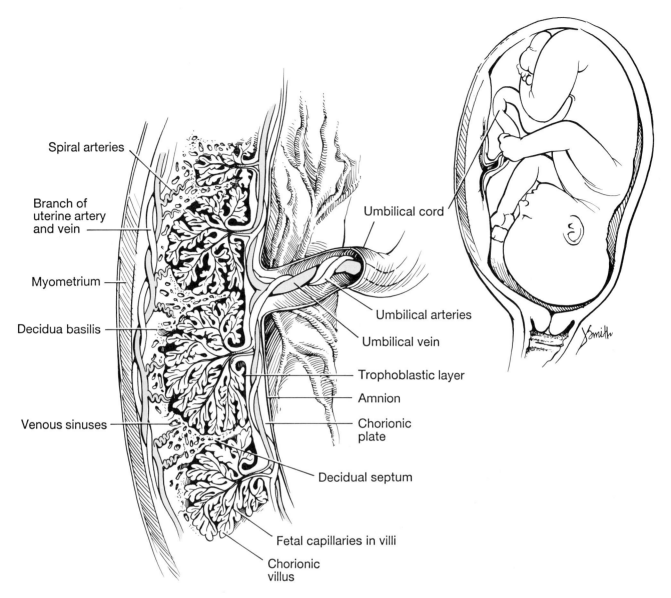

*Figure 10–1.  Structures of the placenta.*

(Fig 10-2). An example of this principle is the embryo's *cephalocaudal* (head to tail) development that continues through the growing infant's motor development, enabling an infant to manipulate the hands long before walking. All major organ systems—the heart, spine, digestive tract, eyes, ears, nose, arm and leg buds—begin to form and are highly vulnerable to developmental interference by viruses, drugs, infection, and radiation. At the end of the embryonic period, about 8 weeks after conception, the embryo measures about 2.6 cm from head to buttocks, weighs about 1/39 of an ounce, and has a prominent head, rudimentary human facial features, and the beginnings of all main systems.

Whereas pregnancy is usually calculated according to lunar months (4 weeks per month), fetal growth and development is estimated according to gestational age (Fig. 10-3). *Gestation* is the period of intrauterine fetal development from conception to birth and is measured by weeks. Growth and developmental changes that take place from the 12th to the 40th weeks are shown in Table 10-2.

## Genetic Influences on Development

Genetic disorders account for about 20% of pediatric hospital admissions, with an even higher percentage for children who require long-term hospital stays (Gabbe, Niebyl, & Simpson, 1986). For this reason, it is important for nurses involved in the care of children to understand genetic factors that influence development.

## Fetal Development

### 1st Lunar Month

The fetus is 0.75 cm to 1 cm in length.

Trophoblasts embed in decidua.

Chorionic villi form.

Foundations for nervous system, genitourinary system, skin, bones, and lungs are formed.

Buds of arms and legs begin to form.

Rudiments of eyes, ears, and nose appear.

4 weeks

### 2nd Lunar Month

The fetus is 2.5 cm in length and weighs 4 g.

Fetus is markedly bent.

Head is disproportionately large, owing to brain development.

Sex differentiation begins.

Centers of bone begin to ossify.

8 weeks

### 3rd Lunar Month

The fetus is 7 cm to 9 cm in length and weighs 28 g.

Fingers and toes are distinct.

Placenta is complete

Fetal circulation is complete.

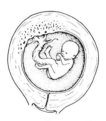

3   months

### 4th Lunar Month

The fetus is 10 cm to 17 cm in length and weighs 55 g to 120 g.

Sex is differentiated.

Rudimentary kidneys secrete urine.

Heartbeat is present.

Nasal septum and palate close.

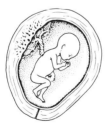

4   months

### 5th Lunar Month

The fetus is 25 cm in length and weighs 223 g.

Lanugo covers entire body.

Fetal movements are felt by mother.

Heart sounds are perceptible by auscultation.

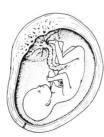

5   months

### 6th Lunar Month

The fetus is 28 cm to 36 cm in length and weighs 680 g.

Skin appears wrinkled.

Vernix caseosa appears.

Eyebrows and fingernails develop.

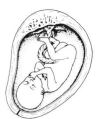

6   months

### 7th Lunar Month

The fetus is 35 cm to 38 cm in length and weighs 1200 g.

Skin is red.

Pupillary membrane disappears from eyes.

The fetus has an excellent chance of survival.

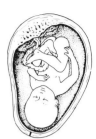

7   months

### 8th Lunar Month

The fetus is 38 cm to 43 cm in length and weighs 2.7 kg.

Fetus is viable.

Eyelids open.

Fingerprints are set.

Vigorous fetal movement occurs.

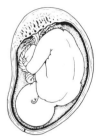

8   months

### 9th Lunar Month

The fetus is 42 cm to 49 cm in length and weighs 1900 g to 2700 g.

Face and body have a loose wrinkled appearance because of subcutaneous fat deposit.

Lanugo disappears

Amniotic fluid decreases.

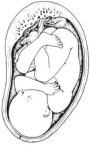

9 months

### 10th Lunar Month

The fetus is 48 cm to 52 cm in length and weighs 3000 g.

Skin is smooth.

Eyes are uniformly slate colored.

Bones of skull are ossified and nearly together at sutures.

*Figure 10–2.* **Fetal growth and development.** *(Reeder, S.J., & Martin, L.L. (1987).* **Maternity nursing** (16th ed.). Philadelphia: J.B. Lippincott, p. 159)

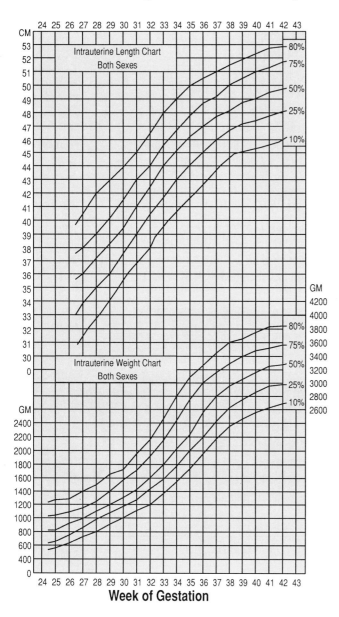

*Figure 10–3. Fetal growth and development estimated by gestational age. (Lubchenko, L.O., et al. [1966] Pediatrics, 37; 403)*

**Table 10–2.  Fetal Development: 12 to 40 Weeks**

| Gestation | Development |
|---|---|
| 12 weeks | Fetal circulation is complete<br>Fingers and toes are present<br>Ears and eyelids are formed<br>Length 8 cm<br>Weight 28 g |
| 16 weeks | Heartbeat<br>Kidneys secrete urine<br>Sexually differentiated<br>Nasal septum and palate close<br>Length 15 cm<br>Weight 114 g (about 4 oz) |
| 20 weeks | Fetal movements can be felt<br>Heart sounds can be auscultated<br>Lanugo covers fetal body<br>Length 25 cm<br>Weight 227 g (about ½ lb) |
| 24 weeks | Eyebrows<br>Fingernails<br>Skin appears wrinkled<br>Vernix caseosa develops<br>Length 30 cm (12 inches)<br>Weight 680 g (1 lb 8 oz) |
| 28 weeks | Eyes open occasionally<br>Skin is red<br>Length 38 cm<br>Weight 1200 g<br>Fetus has excellent chance of survival |
| 32 weeks | Vigorous fetal movement<br>Footprints set<br>Length 38–43 cm<br>Weight 2000 g |
| 36 weeks | Face and body appear increasingly less wrinkled because of subcutaneous fat deposit<br>Lanugo disappears<br>Length 42–49 cm<br>Weight 1900–2700 g |
| 40 weeks | Smooth skin<br>Skull bones ossified and nearly joined at sutures<br>Length 48–52 cm<br>Weight 3000 g |

A human cell normally contains 23 pairs of chromosomes, for a total of 46; 22 pairs are called *autosomes* and one pair is known as the *sex* (X and Y) *chromosomes* (Fig. 10-4). Chromosomes contain *genes*—ultramicroscopic particles that are the basic units of heredity. During the earliest stages of fetal development, abnormalities may occur during cell division. Chromosomal defects may occur because of too much or too little chromosomal material in an autosome or sex chromosome pair. A translocation or crossover of chromosomes can also produce a defect. About 3% of all newborns have a major congenital anomaly or defect. Although about half of the anomalies are evident at birth, the remainder may not become

known until later in childhood or, less often, in adulthood (Gabbe, Niebyl, & Simpson, 1986).

Genetic disorders that affect a child's development and ability to live are classified in four categories: chromosomal abnormalities, single gene or mendelian disorders, polygenetic and multifactorial disorders, and teratogenic disorders.

## Chromosomal Abnormalities

A *numerical chromosome error* occurs when an abnormal number of chromosomes during conception results in a major physical and mental defect. For example, if an

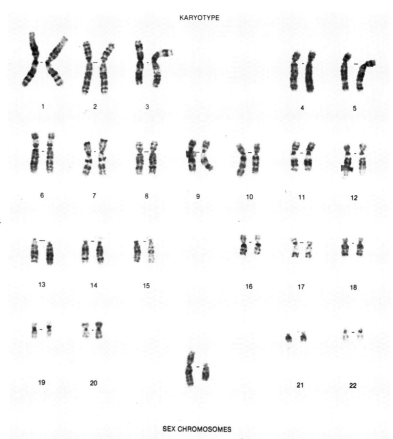

KARYOTYPE

SEX CHROMOSOMES

*Figure 10–4. Karyotype depicting 23 pairs of chromosomes.*

extra chromosome develops in each cell, the defect is called a *trisomy*. When there is a missing chromosome in each cell, the defect is called a *monosomy*. A variety of numerical chromosome errors can take place at conception or after fertilization of the ovum. During germ cell formation in the mother, *nondisjunction,* the separation and migration of chromosomes during cell division, may occur. Following fertilization, nondisjunction can also occur and results in mixed cell lines. Cells with mixed chromosomal counts are called *mosaics.* Variations in chromosomal counts may be discretely identified and are called trisomies, for example, trisomy 21 (Down syndrome) and XXY (Klinefelter's syndrome).

A *structural chromosome error* occurs when chromosomes break and reunite. As a result of this action, some chromosome parts are exchanged between chromosomes in a process known as *translocation.* As a result of the translocation, chromosomes may (1) contain a normal makeup, (2) be balanced or rearranged chromosomes, or (3) combine with missing or duplicated chromosome segments. The child may have an appropriate number of chromosomes (46) but with a different structure. Infants born with missing or extra chromosome segments are likely to have severe mental and physical handicaps. The

presence of 45 chromosomes is not compatible with life, and the embryo or fetus is usually spontaneously aborted. A child who has an extra chromosome (for a total of 47) can live but will have a trisomy, such as trisomy 21.

## Single Gene or Mendelian Disorders

Genetic disorders that follow the inheritance patterns described by Mendel are identified according to the following principles:

**The law of segregation** states that the pair or partner genes (*alleles*) that determine a particular trait are transmitted separately, with rare exceptions; therefore, no pair of alleles is normally transmitted from one generation to another. This accounts for contrasting traits in successive generations since some characteristics of each parent will not combine or change each other in the child.

**The law of independent combination** states that various environmental factors can affect genes, and these genes determine some traits by combination according to change.

**The law of dominance** states that a recessive trait may appear in a child only if both pairs of genes are recessive. A significant number of genetic disorders that appear to occur according to the inheritance patterns described by Mendel are recognized as *dominant gene, recessive gene,* and *X-linked* gene disorders. These disorders are listed in Table 11-14 in Chapter 11.

## Polygenic and Multifactorial Disorders

The cumulative effect of interaction of several genes predisposes the fetus to an abnormality. Many of the common birth defects, such as cleft palate, pyloric stenosis, congenital heart disease, and neural tube defects, are considered to belong in this category. Environmental factors can also contribute to developmental disorders. Parents who have children with conditions such as spina bifida have an estimated equal risk for subsequent children having either spina bifida or anencephaly. Prenatal diagnosis of such problems can be done by 20 to 24 weeks' gestation so that fetal surgery or preterm delivery, followed by neonatal surgery, can be planned if parents elect not to terminate the pregnancy.

## Teratogenic Disorders from Extracellular Factors

A *teratogenic disorder* is a genetic disorder caused by exposure to external factors that harmfully affect an embryo that otherwise would have developed normally. This is discussed in more detail in the section on environmental influences.

A number of methods of genetic screening can be used to routinely monitor apparently healthy fetuses for the presence or absence of disorders (Fig. 10-5). Extensive genetic testing, however, is usually performed only if an abnormal finding would change the plan for clinical management of the fetus. Although most chromosomal disor-

*Figure 10–5. Family discussing implications of genetic testing.*

ders can be detected before birth, the risks associated with performing the tests often outweigh the diagnostic benefits.

There are several indications when prenatal cytogenetic study should be performed, including:

**Advanced maternal age.** It is a general medical recommendation to offer prenatal diagnosis to women who will be 35 or older when their infants are born. Although no biological explanation has yet been found, there is a relationship between older mothers and trisomy 21 (Down syndrome) as well as other trisomy genetic disorders. Advanced age of the father has also been associated with trisomy 21, but to a much lesser degree than maternal age.

**Exposure to chemotherapeutic agents or irradiation.** Women who have received massive therapeutic dosages of x-rays or chemotherapy before pregnancy should also have chromosome studies performed before they become pregnant. Chemotherapeutic agents and x-rays can produce chromosome damage and mutations in vitro.

**Previous sibling with a chromosomal abnormality.** Although the risk factor is not greatly increased, a couple who has previously had a child with a chromosomal abnormality is considered at greater risk for having another child with the same or a different chromosomal abnormality, even when the parents' chromosomal studies are normal. Also at risk is the mother who has had a stillborn infant or natural abortion who did not have a chromosomal analysis. Research has shown that 50% to 60% of first trimester abortions result from chromosomal disorders (Gabbe, Niebyl, & Simpson, 1986).

**Previous sibling with a metabolic disorder.** Although prenatal studies for metabolic disorders are performed less often than chromosomal studies, it is possible to diagnose at least 80 inborn errors of metabolism in the fetus. Galactosemia is an example of an inborn error of metabolism.

**Exposure to intrauterine infection.** Intrauterine infection may cause abnormal embryonic or fetal development. Although German measles (rubella) is usually a mild viral disease in children, a fetal infection can have devastating consequences. After a rubella infection, malformations have been diagnosed in half of fetuses infected in the 1st month, in 20% in the 2nd month, and in 6% in the 3rd month of gestation (Gabbe, Niebyl, & Simpson, 1986). Problems affecting a severely infected infant may include cataracts, cardiac defects, intrauterine growth retardation, deafness, and purpura.

The cytomegalovirus is considered the most common cause of intrauterine infection. Infants who acquire this infection in utero may have severe health problems, including microcephaly, deafness, jaundice, growth retardation, and mental retardation.

The role of the nurse in fetal assessment, history taking, and procedures associated with genetic screening is presented later in this chapter. It is important to maintain an up-to-date knowledge of genetic screening and testing procedures that are available in order to provide health teaching and supportive interventions for patients and family members.

## Environmental Influences on Development

In addition to genetic influences on fetal development, it is also important to recognize the role of the environment. *Teratogens* are agents, such as drugs and pollution, that affect the developing fetus and can result in abnormalities and increase the incidence of infant morbidity and mortality. Knowledge of environmental factors can help nurses assess the health of clients through early identification of exposure, anticipatory care planning, health teaching that includes measures to avoid or reduce exposure, and coping strategies used to deal with the consequences of negative environmental exposure. A variety of common teratogens are listed in Table 10-3.

Environmental causes of developmental defects in humans have been attributed to four major sources: (1) drugs and environmental chemicals (including pollution), (2) infections, (3) maternal metabolic imbalances, and (4) ionizing radiation, such as x-rays (Gabbe, Niebyl, & Simpson, 1986). Environmental factors are either *exogenous*

## Table 10–3. Examples of Suspected Human Teratogens

**Infectious Agents**

Cytomegalovirus
Rubella virus
Varicella virus
Herpes (hominis type II) virus

**Chemicals/Drugs**

Alcohol
Nicotine
Lead
Organic mercury compounds
Polychlorinated biphenyls
Tetracyclines
Coumarin anticoagulants
Thalidomide

**Physical Agents**

Hyperthermia
Ionizing radiation

(taking place outside the mother's body) or *intrinsic* (related to the mother or "maternal environment"). One example of an exogenous factor known to cause human birth defects is the chemical pollutant methylmercury. Maternal thyroid disease is an intrinsic factor in which the physical condition of the mother can adversely affect intrauterine development.

For a harmful effect to occur, the teratogen must reach the infant by being transmitted either *directly* from the mother's body or *indirectly* through maternal tissues. Excessive radiation and intense heat are direct effects that adversely affect the fetus. Indirect effects could result from the passage of a chemical through maternal tissues to the fetus.

Before birth, the developing infant's susceptibility to the teratogen depends on (1) the genetic makeup of the fetus (*genotype*), (2) the interaction of the genotype with the environmental factor, and (3) the developmental age of the fetus at the time of exposure. Consideration of the critical stages of fetal development is especially important in understanding the sites of defects resulting from environmental assault.

A teratogen can have one effect if exposure occurs during the embryonic stage of development and another effect if the exposure occurs later during fetal development. The variety of adverse effects to the developing infant in utero can range from death to congenital malformations, developmental disabilities, and some childhood cancers. Females exposed to diethylstilbestrol have an increased risk of cervical or vaginal cancer.

Generally, exposure to a teratogen during the embryonic stage of development is likely to result in a *structural defect* or embryonic death. A *functional defect* or growth retardation is found with teratogenic exposure later in the fetal period. Additional factors that affect an adverse environmental influence include the dosage or degree of exposure, the duration of exposure, the mother's metabolism, and placental function.

Most structural defects occur between the 2nd to 8th weeks of development—the embryonic period. It is believed that if the fetus develops past this period without exposure to a teratogen, certain structural abnormalities will not occur. For example, the limb buds are most susceptible to injury by teratogens during the 5th week. Spina bifida results from the failure of the neural tube to close between about 22 and 28 days of development. Any exogenous effect of a teratogen on development must occur at or before this critical period. Teratogenic exposure after this period usually does not cause structural defects.

Environmental issues are of particular concern for nurses. Fetal exposure to known harmful agents can be prevented. For example, alcohol abuse is cited as the most preventable health problem in the United States. Several of the U.S. Department of Health and Human Services' 1990 Objectives for the Nation relate to reducing risk factors for alcohol. An important issue of this campaign is public education related to the dangers of alcohol consumption during pregnancy and its irreversible effects on the fetus (Robbins, 1988).

The Food and Drug Administration guidelines that regulate premarket testing of drugs have been incorporated into the Environmental Protection Agency guidelines. These guidelines are used for almost all drugs and chemical tests done by manufacturers. Health care professionals can refer to these agencies for information about risks from prenatal exposure to specific drugs and chemicals. The Centers for Disease Control established a Birth Defect Monitoring System to provide national monitoring of infants born with congenital malformations to detect changes in incidence or unusual patterns that might suggest environmental influences (Gabbe, Niebyl, & Simpson, 1986).

It is difficult to answer questions about environmental or occupational exposure that may adversely affect fetal development. If risk data are available, nurses should provide the information for pregnant women and their partners in understandable language. Realistically, living and working in today's society is not risk free, but efforts can be made to reduce fetal exposure to potentially harmful agents. Nurses should be familiar with available information resources and try to keep up with environmental influences that may have an impact on child and family health. Prevention of environmental disease is a major pediatric challenge since pediatric nurses must deal with the physical and psychosocial effects of teratogens on children and their families.

## Psychosocial Impact of the Prenatal Period on Parents and Families

Pregnancy involves changes in established relationships among a couple, prior siblings, grandparents, and other family members. It also frequently involves changes in lifestyles. The period before a child is born is filled with anticipatory planning and psychological adjustments, in addition to the physiological changes taking place in the mother. The prenatal period is referred to as a period of crisis for those involved because of the variety of personal changes experienced. Nurses can assist families to adjust in the prenatal period through supportive interventions, such as counseling for effective parenting and assisting the parents in recognizing lifestyle changes that occur with the addition of a new baby to the family. Nurses need to recognize that these include the perceptions of the couple, their coping mechanisms, and the support systems that are available to them.

During the 9 months of pregnancy, certain psycho-logical tasks are accomplished by the parents. In the first 3 months, the mother needs to adjust to the idea of being pregnant and must accept the reality that a growing infant is being nourished through her body. The father and other family members must deal with the fact that a baby is actually present in the mother's body. It is not unusual for nurses to hear fathers complain of their own morning sickness or to have other physical symptoms in sympathy with their wives. This is called the *couvade syndrome.*

Women who are not prepared to accept a pregnancy may postpone seeking medical care and may continue some daily activities, such as taking drugs or smoking, that will be harmful to the developing fetus. Nurses in all settings who encounter pregnant women should encourage them to seek prenatal care as soon as pregnancy is suspected.

Premature labor occurs in about 10% of all deliveries in the United States. Premature labor is yet another psychological stress with which the family must deal. The mother may experience sudden physical complications, such as bleeding, that heighten concern for the infant's survival. The couple may feel guilt that physical activity may have caused complications of pregnancy. When premature labor and delivery occur, parents must cope with the loss of some of the expected events in pregnancy and delivery—the total length of time to prepare for the child's arrival, the characteristics of a full-term infant (size and maturation), being able to have a "normal delivery," perhaps using Lamaze techniques for the delivery, and preparing the nursery. Additionally, they must deal with the stress of having the infant in an intensive care unit, which might even be located in another hospital. The well-intended sense of urgency and tension focused on caring for the preterm infant by health care personnel provides limited time for attention to psychological support of the mother, father, and other family members. Parental reactions and their expressed needs should be an integral part of the nursing care plan throughout the labor process, particularly in the event of premature labor.

## Preparation for Pregnancy and Parenthood

It is a challenge for nurses to become knowledgeable about, and sensitive to, the impact of pregnancy and parenthood. The beliefs, values, and practices that pregnant women, their partners, and family members have developed about childbearing and parenting have a significant effect on the way they interpret their experiences as well as on their behavior during the pregnancy, childbirth, and early interactions with their infants.

The importance of children and their impact on the family lifestyle is well described by sociologists for many cultures and is included as part of the Western health care culture. For example, almost all cultures stress the importance of a harmonious environment for the mother and baby. Although parent education may provide accurate scientific and practical information about conception, pregnancy, childbirth, and family life, nurses should be aware of clients' health beliefs and adapt this knowledge for appropriate nursing care. Similarly, Western culture encourages women to seek prenatal care early in pregnancy. Individual cultural beliefs or other factors, however, such as lack of transportation, may prevent mothers from seeking prenatal care. It is important for nurses to learn about and identify these issues so they do not misinterpret behaviors as laziness, ignorance, or lack of concern for the infant.

Another decision facing parents during the prenatal period is determining where the baby will be born. Although most babies are born in hospitals, alternate birthing arrangements are becoming increasingly common in response to consumer demand.

Alternative birthing centers, located either in or outside a hospital, offer another choice for childbirth. A birthing center is designed to have homelike accommodations with emergency equipment and drugs stored discreetly (Fig. 10-6). Ideally, this setting allows the opportunity for the birth experience to be normal, natural, and private. When the birthing center is located in a hospital, the family also has immediate access to the medical management and technical resources needed to cope with any complication that could threaten the safety of the mother or baby. If the birth center is freestanding or outside the hospital, it is generally located close to a major hospital so that quick transport to the hospital can be arranged in the event of an emergency. Some factors related to the fetus that exclude participation in an alternate birth center include (1) gestational age of less than 37 weeks or greater than 42 weeks, (2) multiple fetuses, (3) abnormal presentation, (4) evidence of intrauterine growth retardation, and (5) any other chronic or acute condition that would increase risk to the infant.

Home delivery is another childbirth alternative that is gaining in popularity. Over the past 10 years, an estimated 3% of births have been reported as home deliveries (Baldwin, 1991). Home delivery enables the entire family to share in the birthing experience and promotes early bonding. In the event of a crisis, however, it may be more difficult to quickly obtain medical assistance.

The decision regarding where the birth should take place depends on the outcome of an assessment of the mother and fetus. Criteria for determination of a possible high-risk labor or delivery can be found in most maternity nursing textbooks.

## Preparation of Siblings

Siblings respond to pregnancy in a variety of ways. All children's dependency needs have an impact on their personal adjustment and coping behaviors in relation to the pregnancy itself and then to the newborn sibling.

Even toddlers notice the physical changes in their mother's appearance. Preschool-aged children also express interest in the developing infant. Listening to the unborn "new baby's" heartbeat can be an enjoyable activity (Fig. 10-7). Children need a stable environment, so they react to changes, including their mother's physical condition. They may express anger when there is an inter-

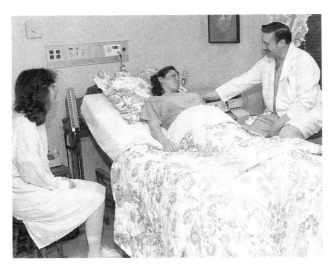
*Figure 10–6. Birth center environment reflects a more homelike atmosphere.*

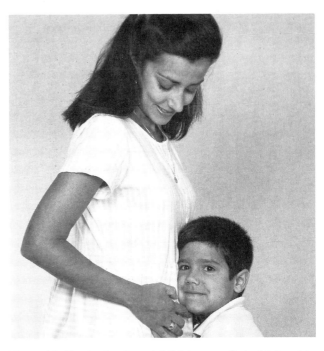
*Figure 10–7. A school-aged child shows a clinical interest in his mother's pregnancy.*

ference in an established routine, such as no longer being able to sit on the mother's lap. Generally, school-aged children have a more intense interest in pregnant women. They ask questions about pregnancy and childbirth. They enjoy the period of "active nesting" in preparation for the baby, look forward to the baby's arrival, and may act the role of parent during play activities. Adolescents may be critical of the mother's pregnancy because of the sexuality associated with conception. This may occur because adolescents are involved with the establishment of their own sexual identity. Older adolescents are usually not unduly disturbed by the mother's pregnancy and act more like adults than children in their coping behaviors.

Nurses can help parents understand the needs and behaviors of siblings during pregnancy, the childbirth experience, and early contact with the newborn. Parents should include siblings in preparatory behaviors such as setting up the nursery. A number of books about anticipating a new baby are designed to be read with young children. After the birth, special time with siblings with each parent alone or activities with both parents without the new baby often help in adjusting to the arrival of a newborn. A good way to prepare children for their own future parenting role is through participation in caring for siblings as well as in the events related to the addition of a new family member (Bobak, Jensen, & Zalar, 1989).

## Nutritional Requirements: Mother and Fetus

Although many factors interact to affect the outcome of pregnancy, women can make a major contribution to the good health of their developing fetuses through proper nutrition. Nurses who understand the importance of good nutrition during pregnancy can promote the well-being of both mothers and infants through dietary assessment, health education, and other supportive measures.

Physiological, biochemical, and hormonal changes of pregnancy affect nutritional requirements that promote fetal growth and regulate maternal metabolism. For example, an infant of a malnourished woman might be small for gestational age since the maternal placenta often has a reduced ability to synthesize substances needed by the fetus for growth.

Weight and weight gain during pregnancy is one component of the physical assessment of nutritional status. Weight gain in normal pregnancy varies among women, but a gain of 22 to 32 pounds is generally acceptable (Naeye, 1979). Weight gain is primarily due to growth in maternal tissues during the first and second trimesters and in fetal tissues during the third trimester. Failure to gain weight during pregnancy is a sign of nutritional difficulties. Although deviations from usual weight values are common, it is important for nurses to recognize the need to assess weight gain throughout pregnancy because of its strong influence on the infant's birth weight, which in turn is significantly related to infant mortality and morbidity.

The recommended daily allowances (RDAs) for pregnant women vary according to the individual woman's weight, health status, and activity level. Nurses involved in prenatal care should refer to current RDAs when providing nutritional assessment, education, and counseling. Nurses also need to evaluate whether clients have the appropriate knowledge, motivation, and income to follow nutritional guidance. Nurses may need to adapt the nursing care plan accordingly for individual clients. Current nutritional references should be readily available for nurses, in addition to patient education materials for clients.

Individual assessment of nutritional status, including ethnic and cultural beliefs and practices, should be made at the beginning of prenatal care and monitored throughout pregnancy. Methods of maternal assessment are based on clinical observation, including a complete history and physical examination, biochemical tests, and a dietary assessment. A more direct assessment of the infant throughout pregnancy is reflected in the intrauterine fetal growth, which should remain appropriate for gestational age.

A major goal of nursing is to involve pregnant women as participants in their care by helping them understand both the maternal and fetal demands on their nutritional body stores and daily intake. Nursing goals during the prenatal period should also include anticipatory planning and preparation for feeding newborns either by breast or bottle. Referral to physicians, nutritionists, or community agencies may be necessary to assist clients in obtaining necessary foods, food preparation, and food storage both during pregnancy and after the birth of infants. A federal food supplement program, the Special Supplemental Food Program for Women, Infants, and Children (WIC), provides coupons for nutritious foods such as milk, cheese, eggs, fruit juices, and iron-fortified cereals and also provides nutrition education programs. This assistance is available throughout pregnancy, lactation, and the child's first 5 years of life.

## Assessment of Fetal Growth and Development

A variety of techniques are used to evaluate the health of the embryo and fetus. Advances in prenatal diagnosis now make it possible to identify the presence or absence of physical abnormalities and functional problems in children before birth. In some instances, surgical as well as medical treatment can be provided before delivery while the fetus continues to grow and develop. Many prenatal surgical procedures are still experimental, but progress is being made, and surgical interventions have been employed for conditions such as obstructive hydrocephalus.

## Prenatal Assessment and Diagnosis of Genetic Disorders

Genetic assessment of the fetus is done by both noninvasive and invasive procedures.

### Noninvasive Assessment Procedures

*Ultrasound* is a noninvasive assessment procedure that is commonly used during pregnancy. Ultrasonography uses high-frequency sound waves—over 20,000 vibrations per second. Ultrasound is used to monitor the growing fetus in a variety of ways, including:

- Early identification of the intrauterine pregnancy
- Identification of multiple fetuses
- Measurement of fetal anatomy—particularly head, abdominal circumference, and femur length—to help in identifying the gestational age of a normal fetus. When several fetal measurements are taken over a period of time, ultrasound can identify a growth-retarded fetus.
- Comparison of fetal head and chest or abdominal circumference to identify serious health problems, such as hydrocephaly or microcephaly, in the fetus
- Early detection of fetal problems, including intestinal obstruction, polycystic kidney, and meningomyelocele as well as limb defects and other deviations in fetal growth

Ultrasound provides the opportunity for observation of fetal breathing, cardiac action, fetal movement, and the presence of normal amounts of amniotic fluid. Ultrasound testing is widely used in prenatal studies and is routinely performed before amniocentesis (Fig. 10-8).

*Alpha-fetoprotein* (AFP) screening is another noninvasive procedure that is commonly used during pregnancy. *Fetoprotein* is a glycoprotein produced by the fetal liver. It is secreted in the fetus's urine, the amniotic fluid, and in maternal serum. If there is a break in the fetal skin—for example, an open neural defect—the AFP level rises. AFP levels also rise in multiple gestations; therefore, a second AFP screening should be done, followed by ultrasound. If these are all abnormal, an amniocentesis is ordered.

*Echocardiography* can be used to detect a variety of cardiac abnormalities in the fetus (Pritchard, MacDonald, & Gant, 1985). In addition, special radiographic studies called *fetography* can be used to detect bone abnormalities in the fetus. A contrast medium injected into the amniotic fluid produces a fetal outline on x-ray film. The diameter of the head and circumference of the trunk can be measured.

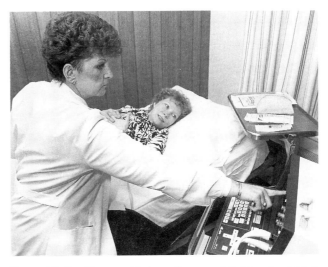

*Figure 10–8. Nurse explains ultrasound "picture" of fetal movement.*

Another means of assessment of the fetus is nuclear *magnetic resonance imaging* (MRI). MRI is being used experimentally at present; however, it is expected to make great advances in the prenatal assessment of fetal structure and functions. Early research suggests the value of MRI in evaluating fetal anomalies and intrauterine growth retardation, especially in cases in which ultrasound has not been satisfactory because of fetal position (Pernoll & Benson, 1989).

### Invasive Assessment Procedures

*Amniocentesis* is an invasive intrauterine technique for prenatal diagnosis in which the physician removes some of the amniotic fluid from the mother's uterus by careful insertion of a needle through the abdomen into the amniotic sac. Some disorders that can be diagnosed by analysis of amniotic fluid include chromosomal abnormalities, skeletal disorders, fetal infections, central nervous system defects, hematological disorders (e.g., sickle cell anemia), and inborn errors of metabolism. The risks involved in performing the procedure include trauma to the fetus or placenta, infection, and premature labor. Injury to the fetus is more common when amniotic fluid volume is small compared with the size of the fetus or when the amniotic fluid is thick. After the amniocentesis the fetal heart rate should be closely monitored, especially if the procedure was thought to be traumatic.

Amniocentesis was initially used to identify hemolytic disease in the fetus by measuring the concentration of bilirubin in the amniotic fluid. Currently, it is also used to identify the fetus at risk of developing respiratory distress at delivery. Analysis of the amniotic fluid determines the concentration of surfactant-active phospholipids that are essential for the infant's maintenance of effective respiration immediately after birth. The evaluation of other properties of amniotic fluid has been suggested to try to identify fetal maturity (Pritchard, MacDonald, & Gant, 1985). The test is most often performed when the fetus is at 16 to 18 weeks of gestation and when a sufficient number of fetal cells are likely to be present in the amniotic fluid.

Amniocentesis is most often indicated in the following circumstances:

- Pregnant women 35 years of age or older
- Previous pregnancy that resulted in birth of a sibling with a known or suspected chromosomal disorder
- Chromosomal disorder in either parent or close family members, including identification of one parent as a balanced translocation carrier
- Pregnancy after three or more spontaneous abortions
- Fetal sex determination when the fetus is at risk due to a serious X-linked hereditary disorder, such as hemophilia. It should be noted that even if a biochemical diagnosis cannot be made, the sex of the fetus can be determined.
- Fetal risk due to a serious autosomal disorder such as cystic fibrosis, an X-linked recessive disorder such as fragile X syndrome, or inborn errors of metabolism such as Tay-Sachs disease
- Previous sibling or parent with a neural tube defect or on routine screening of the maternal serum

*Fetoscopy* is of considerable interest for prenatal evaluation because it provides for direct visualization of the fetus through a small telescope-like instrument, a fiberoptic scope about the size of a hypodermic needle. The physician must first make a 4-mm incision in the abdomen into the amniotic sac. Just as in amniocentesis, ultrasonography is first used to locate the placenta and fetus. Antibiotics may be prescribed for the mother as a prophylaxis against infection. Fetoscopy allows the visualization of anatomic defects as well as the sampling of placental and fetal cord blood, the liver, and the skin. This procedure aids in the diagnosis of infection and blood and enzyme defects. Risks of fetoscopy include infection, hemorrhage, and rupture of the membranes. Spontaneous abortion rates after this procedure have been reported to be between 5% and 10%. A premature delivery reaction rate of about 10% has also been reported.

*Chorionic villi sampling* (CVS) is a prenatal test originally designed to predict the sex of the child. Today, applications of this test are used to examine the genetic makeup of the fetus in the 3rd month of pregnancy. In this surgical procedure, a piece of chorion—the outer tissue of the sac surrounding the embryo—is removed. A major advantage of CVS is the earlier diagnosis of conditions such as Down syndrome, Tay-Sachs disease, and cystic fibrosis; however, CVS cannot identify neural tube disorders such as spina bifida.

*Percutaneous umbilical blood sampling* is a procedure in which a needle is introduced into the umbilical blood vessels to take a sample of fetal blood for genetic analysis. It is currently being done only in special circumstances. It can also be used for intrauterine blood transfusions and to administer medications.

## Assessment of Fetal Development

### Routine Procedures: Intrauterine Growth Patterns

Assessment of fetal well-being is measured by recording the fetus's weight, length, and head circumference on an intrauterine growth chart. Growth patterns and relationships are used to determine unusual intrauterine growth if problems are suspected. Since growth measurements of fetuses in utero cannot be precisely obtained, a chart of intrauterine growth is an approximation of a group pattern of fetal growth with gestational age (see Fig. 10-3). Growth should be appropriate for gestational age (Fig. 10-9).

Some interesting fetal growth patterns include the following:

1. Fetuses' weight/length ratio increases as gestation progresses; that is, infants become heavier for their length as they grow to full term.
2. Weight gain appears to spurt faster than length between 30 and 31 weeks' gestation and between 34 and 38 weeks' gestation. Afterward, the relationship between length and weight is fairly constant.

Measurements may indicate that the fetus is within the usual boundaries of growth for gestational age, is near or outside the extremes for normal growth, or has a disproportion in weight, length, or head circumference. For example, infants of diabetic mothers are heavy for gestational age and are also long, with large head circumferences. *Intrauterine growth failure* may be due to several problems, including intrauterine infection, undernutrition, and congenital malformations.

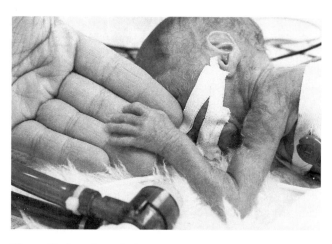

*Figure 10–9.    Growth should be appropriate for gestational age.*

As previously described, ultrasound is frequently used to establish fetal gestational age according to head size. For example, a term pregnancy and fetal maturity may be diagnosed by measurement of biparietal cephalometry by ultrasound. Ultrasound can demonstrate the general rate of growth and can compare fetal head and chest size to identify hydrocephalus, among other fetal anomalies.

Measurement of the maternal fundal height is a simpler but less reliable method of assessing fetal growth. Fundal height may help in the identification of such high-risk factors as intrauterine growth retardation of the infant or the presence of multiple fetuses.

### Multiple Fetuses

*Multiple fetuses* refers to the gestation of two, three, or more fetuses during the same pregnancy. Researchers are interested in studying the uniqueness of multiple births for many reasons, including understanding the influence of genetic and environmental factors on fetal development (Fig. 10-10). Pregnancies with multiple fetuses are considered to be at higher risk than those with one fetus.

The incidence of twins is about 12 per 1000 births in the United States (Gabbe, Niebyl, & Simpson, 1986). Twins are either *monozygotic* (from a single, fertilized ovum) or *dizygotic* (if two separate ova are fertilized). Monozygotic twins are usually genetically identical and therefore of the same sex; dizygotic twins are as genetically distinct as any other children that the couple may have. Whereas monozygotic twins occur randomly at a fairly constant rate in all populations, the frequency of dizygotic twins varies among races and cultures. The rate of dizygotic twins seems to be affected by maternal age and parity. More than 15% of infant twins weigh less than 2500 g at birth, and they are often born prematurely. The clinical diagnosis of multiple fetuses or a multiple pregnancy is accurate in only about 75% of cases. The recognition of multiple fetuses during the pregnancy is often missed, not so much because of difficulty in the diagnosis but because the examiner fails to consider the possibility. Other reasons for the inability to detect twins may be because one twin overlies the other, because of maternal obesity, or because hydramnios is present (Cunningham, MacDonald, & Grant, 1989). Some of the problems associated with a multiple pregnancy that are related to fetal development include the following:

1. **Maternal anemia** results from an increased demand for iron by the fetuses.
2. **Placenta previa** occurs because of the large size and placement of the placenta and fetuses. Premature separation of the placenta is also a risk before delivery of the second and subsequent fetuses.
3. **Breech presentation** occurs in one infant of a twin pregnancy in about one third of all deliveries.
4. **Premature deliveries** a serious problem for any neonate because of potential complications from immature development (e.g., respiratory distress).
5. **Birth weight** is usually less for each infant in a multiple birth.
6. **Congenital malformations** occur twice as often in monozygotic twins than in infants from a single pregnancy (Cunningham, MacDonald, & Grant, 1989).
7. **Twin-to-twin transfusion**—the shunting of blood between placentas (an artery-to-vein anastomosis)—occurs, with the result that the recipient twin may develop congenital heart failure during the first 24 hours after birth. The donor twin may be small, malnourished, dehydrated, and hypovolemic because blood has been chronically shunted away from one twin, which results in growth retardation. In addition, the donor twin develops anemia, and the receiving twin develops polycythemia. The anemic twin may also be hypoglycemic from the lack of glucose stores. A transfusion may be indicated. The polycythemic twin manifests jaundice from the breakdown of excessive bilirubin in the serum (hyperbilirubinemia). An exchange transfusion may be necessary. Hemoglobin analysis should be done on all twins at birth; if there is a difference of more than 5 g per 100 mL, an in utero transfusion has probably occurred.

When a diagnosis of multiple fetuses is established, parents may find their coping mechanisms overwhelmed by the thought of caring for two or more infants. A multiple birth may be socially perceived as a positive and exciting experience; however, parent–infant attachment, synchronization of the infants' care schedules, and care-giver rest periods are some issues that may need to be explored when a multiple birth is anticipated.

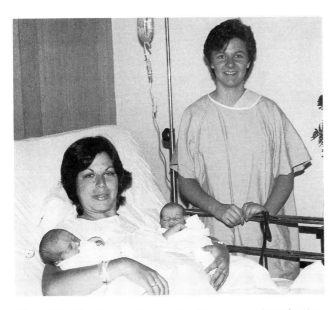

*Figure 10–10. Nurse offers support to new mother of twins.*

## Assessment During Labor

### Fetal Monitoring

Throughout the mother's labor, fetal well-being is preserved by the early detection and relief of fetal distress. During labor, there is a temporary variable reduction in the flow of oxygenated maternal blood through the placenta with each contraction. Normally, the fetus can compensate for this stress. However, a decrease in blood perfusion because of contractions (such as when the maternal uterus becomes hypertonic) can result in fetal distress.

*Fetal distress* is associated with a potential or actual threat to the infant's well-being that is usually assessed by the variability in fetal heart rate. The average fetal heart rate for a full-term fetus is 140 beats per minute, with a normal range of 120 to 160 beats per minute. The heart rate may show frequent periodic variations for several reasons, including uterine contractions or compression of the umbilical cord.

Initial nursing interventions upon assessment of *deceleration* (a decrease in the fetal heart rate) should include ascertaining that the mother is resting comfortably on her side and checking the monitor for proper functioning (Pritchard, MacDonald, & Gant, 1985). Placing the mother in the left lateral recumbent position can decrease contraction frequency and increase intensity if uterine hypertonia is the probable cause of fetal hypoxia with prolonged decelerations (Murray, 1989). When variable decelerations are associated with fetal distress due to cord compression, the compression of the umbilical cord can be relieved by turning the mother from one side to the other (Pernoll & Benson, 1989). It should also be noted that during labor, the mother's uterus impinges on her aorta and inferior vena cava, causing additional physiological stress (Gabbe, Niebyl, & Simpson, 1986).

Fetal monitoring methods are usually described as either *external* or *internal.* The fetal heart rate may be monitored in several external ways through the mother's abdominal wall (Fig. 10-11). Ultrasound or sonograms may be used during the antepartum and early intrapartum period. A detector is placed on the mother's abdomen at a site where fetal heart action is best detected. *Acoustic stimulation* is another method used to assess fetal status. When there is a question of fetal well-being during electronic fetal monitoring, an acoustic stimulator is used to arouse the fetus with audible sound. The test is considered reactive (positive) when there is an increase in fetal heart rate accelerations. *Phonocardiographic recording* and an *abdominal fetal electrocardiogram* are additional methods of external fetal monitoring.

An electrode may be attached directly to the fetus for internal monitoring of the fetal heart rate. The insertion of the electrode may be performed by a trained registered nurse under aseptic conditions. The mother's membranes must have already been ruptured either spontaneously or

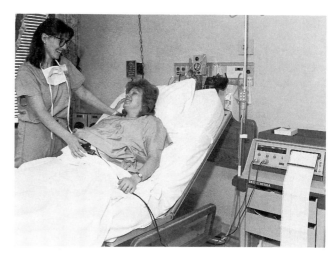

*Figure 10–11. Nurse adjusts fetal monitor for woman in active labor.*

artificially before insertion of the spiral electrode. The spiral electrode with a guide tube is passed through the mother's cervix and is attached to the infant's skin at a benign site (i.e., other than the infant's face, genitals, suture lines, or fontanels). Usually, the electrode is placed on the infant's scalp. Some contraindications to the insertion of an electrode include a face presentation of the fetus, placenta previa, insufficient dilatation, effacement or descent, and maternal genital tract infection (Murray, 1989). Proper electrode placement provides fetal electrocardiographic signals, which are recorded on a calibrated moving paper strip that continually monitors the fetal heart rate.

Whereas external monitoring does not provide precise measurements of the fetal heart rate, internal monitoring presents an increased risk of trauma and infection to the fetus. The techniques used for continuous monitoring of the fetal heart rate should not be relied on alone to effectively monitor the fetus. Knowledgeable nursing personnel must be immediately available to assess both the fetus and the mother, to review and interpret the monitoring data being recorded, and to respond with appropriate interventions.

### Fetal Blood Sampling

An important technique that is used to obtain accurate data about fetal well-being is the collection of small amounts of fetal blood. Capillary blood samples can be analyzed to determine the fetal acid–base balance. In this way, the physician and nurse can evaluate the fetus's pH and oxygenation levels during labor. A number of investigators have found that a pH of 7.25 or greater is normal for the fetus during labor. Whereas a pH range of 7.2 to 7.24 has been considered preacidotic, a fetal capillary pH value of 7.19 or less is recognized as potentially serious fetal acidosis (Gabbe, Niebyl, & Simpson, 1986). Also, it is important to realize that the pH of fetal capillary blood may not accurately reflect the degree of fetal hypoxia since fetal pH is influenced by maternal pH (Cunningham, MacDonald, & Grant, 1989).

Fetal blood sampling is used in high-risk situations when chronic fetal distress may be present from the beginning of labor (for example, with intrauterine growth-retarded infants). It is also useful when fetal heart rate patterns are unclear or difficult to interpret.

The fetal blood sample is usually collected from the infant's scalp. The chorion and amnion must first be ruptured, and the mother's cervix must be dilated to expose the infant's head or buttocks (if the infant is in a breech position). A skin area is cleansed and punctured to collect the fetal blood in a special capillary tube. Pressure is then applied at the puncture site.

## Summary

The nurse's role during the prenatal period is supportive and educative and also involves direct care. The health status of the fetus, the status of the family, and the quality of the health care given during the prenatal period affect the status of the neonate and may have long-term effects on both children and families. When nurses have the opportunity to provide nursing interventions, care and parent education should be focused on the following:

- A healthy lifestyle during pregnancy that includes proper nutrition, exercise, rest, health care, and psychological adjustment
- Positive coping with the stress of labor and delivery
- Constructive adaptation to early parenthood demands (NAACOG, 1978)

It is helpful for mothers, fathers, and involved family members to understand the basic process of fetal growth and development as well as expected maternal changes during pregnancy. Health education can have a positive influence on social behavior to promote prenatal care of the mother, emotional adjustment to the pregnancy experience and parenting, and knowledge of the prenatal development of infants and their special needs.

## References

Baldwin, R. Personal communication with nurse midwife and author. February 6, 1991. Ann Arbor, MI.

Bissonette, J. (1986). Placental and fetal physiology. In Gabbe, S. G., Niebyl, J. R., & Simpson, J. L. (Eds.). *Obstetrics: Normal and problem pregnancies*. New York: Churchill Livingstone.

Cunningham, F. G., MacDonald, P. C., & Gant, N. F. (1989). *Williams obstetrics* (18th ed.). Norwalk, CT: Appleton and Lange.

Bobak, I. M., Jensen, M. D., & Zalar, M. A. (1989). *Maternity and gynecologic care* (4th ed.). St. Louis: Mosby-Year Book Publishers.

Gabbe, S. G., Niebyl, J. R., & Simpson, J. L. (Eds.). (1986). *Obstetrics: Normal and problem pregnancies*. New York: Churchill Livingstone.

Murray, M. (1989). *Antepartal and intrapartal fetal monitoring*. Washington, DC: NAACOG.

NAACOG *Technical Bulletin*. (1978). Prepartion for parenthood. Washington, D.C.: NAACOG.

Naeye, R. L. (1979). Weight gain and the outcome of pregnancy. *American Journal of Obstetrics and Gynecology, 135*, 3.

Pernoll, M. L., & Benson R. C. (Eds.). (1989). *Current obstetric and gynecologic diagnosis and treatment* (6th ed.). Norwalk, CT: Appleton and Lange.

Pritchard, J. A., MacDonald, P. C., & Gant, N. F. (1985). *Williams obstetrics* (17th ed.). Norwalk, CT: Appleton and Lange.

Robbins, G. J. (Ed.). (1988). *MCH Letter, 1*(1). Bethesda, MD: Healthworks Co.

## Bibliography

Ahn, M. O., Phelan, J. P., Smith C. V., Jacobs, N., & Rutherford, S. E. (1987). Antepartum fetal surveillance in the patient with decreased fetal movement. *American Journal of Obstetrics and Gynecology, 157*, 4 (Part I).

Chicago Diabetes Association and South Surbarban Diabetes Association. (1988). *Manual of clinical diabetes*. Alexandria, VA: American Diabetes Association.

Brown, R. A. (1987). Midwifery and home birth: An alternative view. *Canadian Medical Association Journal, 137*, 10.

Catlin, E. A., Carpenter, M. W., Brann, B. S., Mayfield, S. R., Shaul, P. W., Goldstein, M., & Oh, W. (1986). The Apgar score revisited: Influence of gestational age. *Journal of Pediatrics, 109*, 5.

Davis, L. (1987). Daily fetal movement counting: A valuable assessment tool. *Journal of Nurse Midwifery, 32*, 1.

Gagnon, R., Campbell, K., Hunse, C., & Patrick, J. (1987). Patterns of human fetal heart rate accelerations from 26 weeks to term. *American Journal of Obstetrics and Gynecology, 157*, 3.

Griffith, S. (1982). Childbearing and the concept of culture. *Journal of Obstetric, Gynecologic, and Neonatal Nursing, 11*, 181.

Grabstein, C. (1988). *Science and the unborn*. New York: Basic Books.

Halpern, S. L. (1987). *Quick reference to clinical nutrition* (2nd ed.). Philadelphia: J. B. Lippincott.

Monsen, E. (Ed.). (1989). The 1980s: A look at a decade of growth in dietetics through the pages of the *Journal. Journal of the American Dietetic Association, 8*, 5.

Lockwood, C. J., & Weimer, S. (1986). Assessment of fetal growth. *Clinics in Perinatology, 13*, 1.

Lubchenco, L. O., Hansman, C., & Boyd, E. (1966). Intrauterine growth in length and head circumference as estimated from live births at gestational ages from 26 to 42 weeks. *Pediatrics, 37*, 3.

Mayer, J. L., & Balk, S. J. (1988). A pediatrician's guide to environmental toxins. *Contemporary Pediatrics, 6,* 63.

Mayer, J. L., & Balk, S. J. (1988). A tip-toe through the toxins. *Contemporary Pediatrics, 5,* 22.

Miller, S. J. (1986). Prenatal nursing assessment of the expectant family. *Nurse Practitioner, 11,* 5.

Moore, K. L. (1982). *The developing human: Clinically oriented embryology* (3rd ed.). Philadelphia: W. B. Saunders.

Newton, E. R. (1986). Antepartum care in multiple gestation. *Seminars in Perinatology, 10,* 1.

Olds, S. B., London, M. L., & Ladewig, P. A. (1988). *Maternal newborn nursing* (3rd ed.). Menlo Park, CA: Addison-Wesley.

Reeder, S., Martin, L., & Koniak, D. (1992). *Maternity nursing* (17th ed.). Philadelphia: J. B. Lippincott.

Sherwin, L. N., & Mele, N. C. (1986). Assessing and identifying the high risk pregnancy: A holistic approach. *Topics in Clinical Nursing, 8,* 1.

Spradley, B. W. (1990). *Community health nursing* (3rd ed.). Boston: Little, Brown & Co.

Wheeler, T., Roberts, K., Peters, J., & Murrills, A. (1987). Detection of fetal movement using Doppler ultrasound. *Obstetrics and Gynecology, 70,* 2.

# Neonatal Growth, Development, and Health

Patricia T. Castiglia

*Photograph by David Finn*

11

*Neonatal Adaptations*
*to the Environment*
 *Physiological Adaptations During*
  *the Transitional Period*
 *Parenting and Sibling Relationships*
  *in Promoting Adaptation*

*Assessment of the Newborn*
 *Apgar Scoring*
 *Body Measurement and Vital Signs*
 *The Neonatal Behavioral*
  *Assessment Scale*
 *Assessment of Infant State*
 *Assessment of Premature Infants*
  *Behavior*
 *Assessment of the Head*
 *Assessment of the Eyes, Nose, Ears,*
  *Mouth, and Cry*
 *Assessment of the Integument*
 *Assessment of the Back*
  *and Extremities*
 *Assessment of Reflexes*
 *Assessment of the Genitalia*
  *and Anus*
 *Gestational Age Assessment*
 *Assessment of Parent–Child*
  *Interactions*

*Health Promotion*
 *Maintaining a Patent Airway*
 *Prevention of Infection or Injury*
 *Nutritional Needs*

*Neonatal Risk Factors*
 *Prenatal Assessment*
 *Identifying Infants at Risk*
  *During Labor and Delivery*
 *Postnatal Assessment*
 *Risk Associated With Maturity*
 *Postmaturity*

*Parenting Development*

*Summary*

## Learning Objectives

*Upon completion of this chapter the reader will be able to:*

1. *Explain the physiological adaptations required by the neonate in adapting to the environment.*

2. *Discuss the sensory, cognitive, and psychosocial adaptations the neonate makes in adapting to the environment.*

3. *Examine parent/sibling relationships in promoting the neonate's adaptation.*

4. *Describe assessments that are useful in evaluating the neonate—Apgar scoring, behavior and state assessment, body measurements and vital signs, appearance, and gestational age.*

5. *Appraise the physical appearance of the neonate, including the head, eyes, ears, mouth, cry, skin, back and extremities, and genitalia.*

6. *Assess the reflexes of the newborn.*

7. *Describe the relevant aspects of: maintaining a patent airway and preventing infection or injury to the airway.*

8. *Discuss the problems that can be seen in the neonatal period: hemorrhage, thrush, and septicemia.*

9. *Compare breast- and bottle-feeding in terms of constituents, caloric composition, and feeding techniques.*

10. *Name prenatal, natal, and postnatal risk factors.*

11. *Describe the special care needs of the premature infant.*

## Key Terms

*adaptation*

*attachment*

*bonding*

*classification of newborns*

*critical periods*

*engrossment*

*fontanels*

*gestational age*

*postmaturity*

*prematurity*

*reactive periods*

*reflexes*

*thrush*

# Neonatal Adaptations to the Environment

The neonatal period lasts from birth through the first 28 days of life. The necessary adaptations are of such great magnitude that this period has the greatest number of infant deaths. In fact, the neonatal mortality rate is approximately twice that of the postneonatal period. The reason for this statistic will become apparent as the adaptations required of neonates are presented in this chapter.

The concept of adaptation has been developed in theoretical formulations by Helson (1964), a physiological psychologist, and Roy (1970, 1971, 1984), a nursing theorist. Both theorists use the concept of the person interacting with the environment in a manner that results in the person reacting positively to environmental changes. Positive adaptations allow the person to attend to other stimuli.

As neonates emerge into cold, bright, noisy, and possibly painful environments at birth, the necessity to adapt is immediate. The stimuli confronting children may be viewed from Roy's perspective as focal, basically physiological; contextual; environmentally negative in terms of being different from the uterine environment; and residual in terms of innate genetic endowment. The modes of adaptation used during the neonatal period involve meeting basic physiological needs and developing the rudimentary foundation for the development of self-concept.

The primary goal of nursing during the neonatal period is to foster positive adaptations by neonates. This is done by acquiring the necessary knowledge base, assessing neonatal growth and development by reliable methods, formulating appropriate nursing diagnoses, developing nursing interventions that are theoretically sound and in concert with medical interventions, and evaluating the effectiveness of the nursing plans developed and implemented.

Healthy infants are generally seen by a physician or nurse practitioner for their first health maintenance visit when they are between 1 and 2 months of age. If problems occur prior to the scheduled visit, the parents are instructed to seek appointments as needed.

## Physiological Adaptations During the Transitional Period

The first 24 hours after birth are the most critical period for neonates. Many adaptations must be made during this short period of time, including respiratory, circulatory, hematopoietic, thermoregulatory, and fluid and electrolyte adjustments.

While these physiological adaptations are occurring, the neonate's state of responsiveness varies. For the first hour the infant is alert and active (a *reactive period*). This is followed by 2 to 6 hours of sleep when the neonate is unresponsive and inactive. A more active period follows when the baby is alert and exhibits an increased heart rate, respiratory rate, and muscle tone. Transient tremors are frequently seen. The second reactive period (lasting about 6 hours) is the best time to initiate parental bonding with the newborn. Following this reactive stage, the neonate becomes quiet and unresponsive, and physiological processes once again slow down.

The mechanisms involved in establishing respiration and systemic circulation occur almost simultaneously. Because of this interdependence, adaptations in both systems are discussed together.

### Respiratory Adaptations

In the course of a normal vertex vaginal delivery, the thorax becomes compressed as the baby passes through the birth canal. In fetal life the lungs were filled with lung fluid. The mechanical compression of the thorax forces most of the fluid from the lungs, and the remaining fluid is absorbed by the blood vessels and the lymphatic system. At the moment of birth, the compression on the thorax is released. This action may help in causing the inspiration of air. The negative pressure exerted in taking the first breath is great. Compression of the umbilical cord also occurs during the birth process. These activities result in an increased $Pco_2$, a decreased pH, and a decreased $Po_2$.

Babies delivered in the breech position or by cesarean section do not have the mechanical assistance (chest compression) to facilitate respirations. These babies fre-

quently exhibit a transient tachypnea (rapid breathing) for several days.

A substance in the lungs called *surfactant* lines the alveoli and decreases tension at the first breath. Surfactant prevents the alveoli from collapsing completely. This means that the newborn's next few breaths require a decreased negative pressure.

It is thought that the respiratory center is located in the hypothalamus. A number of factors cause the respiratory center to begin to function at birth, e.g., gravity pressure during birth, the cold environment after birth, a decreased blood pH, and an increased $CO_2$. Table 11-1 presents the normal values for arterial blood gases.

### Circulatory Adaptations

As the neonate establishes breathing, pulmonary blood flow increases, which causes an increase in left atrial pressure. Recall that in fetal life there is an opening between the left and right atria called the *foramen ovale*. The foramen ovale allowed blood flow in one direction only, from right to left. It functionally closes when pressure gradients within the heart chambers change. Actual anatomic closure does not usually occur for several months or even a year.

The increase in systemic blood pressure causes the *ductus arteriosus* to close. The ductus arteriosus served as a shunting mechanism, providing for passage between the pulmonary artery and thoracic aorta in fetal life. It is thought that the constriction of the ductus arteriosus is influenced by the interaction of prostaglandins with the oxygen tension of the blood. Usually the ductus arteriosus is completely closed by 24 hours after birth.

### Hematopoietic Adaptations

At birth the bone marrow is actively involved in the production of red blood cells (RBC). These red blood cells are very large and are more rapidly eliminated than those of an adult. It is interesting, however, that this production virtually ceases after birth, resuming again at 2 months of age. Whenever blood values for the neonate are assessed, the gestational age of the neonate must be considered. For example, acute anemia of the immediate neonatal period

*Table 11–1. Normal Values for Arterial Blood Gases in Neonates*

| Age | pH | $Pao_2$ | $Paco_2$ |
|---|---|---|---|
| Newborn | 7.25–7.35 | 50–70 | 26–40 |
| 24 hours | 7.30–7.40 | 60–80 | 26–40 |
| 2 days–1 month | 7.32–7.43 | 85–95 | 30–40 |

(Adapted from Wilkins, R. L., Sheldon, R., & Krider, S. J. (1985). *Clinical assessment in respiratory care.* St. Louis: C. V. Mosby Company, p. 209)

is associated with low-birth-weight infants. Other factors that may also cause this anemia include infant sepsis, a difficult delivery, and obstetrical problems such as placenta previa.

As listed in Table 11-2, the hemoglobin range for preterm and term infants is 15 g to 19 g/100 mL and falls in the first weeks of life. The umbilical cord is usually not clamped until a full 2 minutes after birth (unless there are complications such as asphyxia) so that the baby can receive extra hemoglobin and iron as well as an increased blood volume. To facilitate the flow of blood from the placenta, the baby is held below the level of the placenta until the cord is clamped.

Capillary samples of blood (from the neonate's heel or toe) contain a greater number of WBCs than do venous samples. The WBC differential for neonates is found in Appendix C. This may be attributed to relatively poor circulation. Blood volume is frequently calculated as approximately 85 mL/kg, or 40 mL/lb, of body weight. Most infants cannot tolerate a loss of more than 10% of their blood volume.

Vitamin K–dependent coagulation factor is reduced in the neonate because the intestinal flora are not developed. The bacterial colonization in the intestine is necessary for the synthesis of vitamin K. For this reason most nurseries today usually administer vitamin K (0.5–1.0 mg) intramuscularly after birth. If vitamin K is not administered, bleeding, usually from the intestinal tract, can occur in the third to sixth day. Bleeding may require transfusion with whole blood to restore blood volume and to provide clotting ability.

The newborn is acidotic at birth, but this corrects itself in the first hour as respiratory exchanges are stabilized. The $Pao_2$ (arterial blood concentration) should be 85 to 95 from 2 days to 1 month of age. Arterial samples can be obtained from an umbilical artery catheter or the right radial artery. Capillary samples are of considerably less value in determining oxygenation because these levels measure approximately one half of arterial oxygen values. A non-invasive measure of oxygenation may be accomplished by monitoring the transcutaneous oxygen levels (tc $Po_2$). Transcutaneous measurement is usually done as an adjunct measure.

The concept that immunoglobulins are transported from mother to child has received strong support, because the newborn's level of gamma globulin has often been found to be higher than the mother's level, indicating that transfer has taken place. The gamma globulin level falls at about 3 months of age and then rises again. It should be noted that the infant receives antibodies at birth against viral, rather than bacterial, attack (Behrman & Vaughan, 1987).

Jaundice that appears within the first 24 hours after birth is usually a result of hemolytic disease of the newborn or sepsis (discussed later in this chapter). Figure 11-1 shows how physiological jaundice progresses. Jaundice that appears after 3 days is usually caused by sepsis. Jaundice occurs because of the large amount of bilirubin formed and can be detected by pressing a finger on the skin, releasing it, and observing the color after the release. Jaundiced skin is yellow or orange and does not blanch to white. Jaundice in yellow-skinned or dark-pigmented children appears as various shades of yellow or green. Jaundice is best determined by assessing the sclerae or mucous membranes in daylight (Chow, Durand, Feldman, & Mills, 1984). Jaundice spreads in a cephalocaudal fashion. The level of indirect bilirubin must be 5 mg/dL for visible detection. If the soles of the feet are jaundiced, the serum bilirubin level is usually above 13 mg/dL.

It is necessary, however, to rule out other conditions that might result in jaundice; therefore a complete blood

*Table 11–2.  Neonatal Hematologic Values*

| Component | Term Baby's Value | Pre-term Baby's Value (gestational adjustments needed) |
|---|---|---|
| Hemoglobin | 17–19 g/100 mL | 15–17 g/100 mL |
| Hematocrit | 57%–58 | 45%–55% |
| WBC | 15,000/mm³ | 10,000–20,000 |
| Platelets | 100,000–300,000/mm³ | 120,000–180,000/mm³ |
| Reticulocytes | 3%–7% | up to 10 |

(Adapted from Pierog, S. H., & Ferrara, A. [1976]. *Medical care of the sick newborn* [2nd ed.]. St. Louis: C. V. Mosby Company, p. 332)

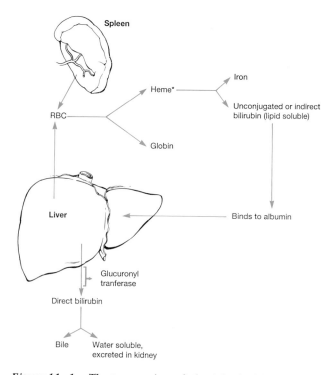

*Figure 11–1.  The progression of physiological jaundice.*

count (CBC), mother and infant blood typing, a Coomb's test, and liver function tests may be done. No therapy is indicated unless the bilirubin reaches (or is close to) 20 mg/dL. The treatment is phototherapy.

Infants receiving phototherapy must be carefully monitored. In phototherapy, the strength of the lights used is between 200 to 500 foot candles (three to six fluorescent light tubes). Blue light wares assist in breaking down unconjugated bilirubin into a non-toxic, excretable by-product. Patches must be placed over the infant's eyes for protection, but should be removed every 4 hours when the baby's eyes are checked for redness, swelling, or discharge; problems should be reported to the physician. Proper placement of the patches should be assessed on a continuous basis. Patches are placed over closed eyes and should be tight enough to block the light. Too much pressure or tightness could, however, cause corneal abrasions. Phototherapy lights should be discontinued when blood samples are drawn. This is an appropriate time to hold, feed, and visually stimulate the infant.

During phototherapy the infant is unclothed in order to expose as much of the skin surface as possible. The child should be repositioned every 1 or 2 hours in order to provide exposure to all parts of the body. Since the infant is unclothed, temperature control is very important; a temperature probe should be used, and the child may be placed in an incubator or under a radiant warming light. Because of the heat generated by phototherapy, hyperthermia can be a problem, and hydration must be assessed frequently. Skin turgor, as well as intake and output, must be monitored. Vital signs are taken at least every 4 hours, and hydration must be maintained. These babies frequently have loose stools, so crib linens and diapers must be kept clean. Stools are frequently bright green due to the presence of excreted bilirubin. Urine may be dark in color.

Even after removal from phototherapy, the child must be observed carefully because there can be a rebound increase in bilirubin.

Phototherapy is not usually indicated for normal physiological jaundice of the newborn, or for breast-feeding jaundice. In breast-feeding jaundice, hyperbilirubinemia is thought to be caused by the secretion of a substance in the mother's milk that acts as an inhibitor of bilirubin glucuronyl transferase. In this case breast-feeding is usually ceased for 12 hours to permit the enzyme to become active.

## Thermoregulation Adaptations

The newborn's temperature regulating mechanism is immature. The regulating center is located in the hypothalamus, and body heat is produced by oxygen metabolism. The two factors that have the greatest effect on neonatal temperature regulation (maintaining heat) are the proportionately large body surface area of the neonate relative to weight, and the small amount of subcutaneous fat present. The newborn is also relatively inactive after birth, which results in decreased metabolism. Prolonged hypothermia is serious and can result in neurological problems. Heat loss can occur through conduction, convection, evaporation, and radiation. Table 11-3 shows how heat is lost in the neonate and provides appropriate preventive measures.

Babies have some physiological mechanisms that help to conserve heat. For example, they usually assume a flexed position. They are also born with a substance called *brown fat* (brown adipose tissue or BAT). Because brown fat begins to accumulate about the fifth month of fetal life, premature infants obviously have a reduced supply and have less access to this heat conservation method. Brown

*Table 11–3. Neonatal Heat Loss*

| Method | Common Route of Heat Loss | Preventive Measures |
|---|---|---|
| Conduction | Placing infant on cold surface, e.g., cold mattress or scale | Warm bassinet, use warm blankets, use diaper or paper cover on scale |
| Convection | Placing newborn in a draft; administering unwarmed and non-humidified oxygen | Place bassinet away from draft; humidify oxygen |
| Evaporation | Bathing before temperature stabilizes; not using appropriate bathing technique, i.e., not covering infant except for part being washed | Delay bathing until temperature stabilizes; expose only areas to be cleansed at any one time |
| Radiation | Failure to clothe infant; failure to use cap or head covering; failure to keep crib away from external walls or drafts; temperature in room or incubator too low | Use shirt and diaper; wrap in receiving blanket; use cap until temperature stabilizes; maintain room temperature and keep crib away from walls and drafts |

fat is located between the scapulae at the base of the neck and around the kidneys, the adrenal glands, and the mediastinum. It is thought that the metabolism of brown fat is triggered by the release of norepinephrine, which is caused by cold stress. Brown fat is important because when oxygen intake is increased, as in stress situations, glucose is usually metabolized, and the newborn has very little glucose to be metabolized to generate heat. The infant does not shiver to produce heat; therefore, brown fat metabolism is important for thermoregulation.

Care-givers should strive to maintain a neutral thermal environment for the newborn. In this environment the baby is able to maintain a normal body temperature with a minimal metabolic rate by posture and by vasomotor and sudomotor control. If properly clothed, most newborns can adapt to average environmental temperatures (18°–20°C). The neutral thermal range varies because of the baby's weight, gestational age, and the relative humidity. Temperature is assessed by axillary or rectal thermometer readings, although rectal temperatures are not usually taken because of the risk of bowel perforation. Servocontrols or skin probes may also be used when neonates are in incubators or on radiant heaters (Fig. 11-2). The skin sensor is usually placed on the liver area or between the scapulae, and the temperature is set at 36.5°C (97°–98°F). Unfortunately, skin probes can be easily dislodged; it is necessary to check probe placement periodically.

Radiant warmers provide heat from above the baby in an effort to compensate for heat loss via the modes described. One major advantage of having the baby unclothed is the obvious ease of observation and facility of treatments. However, the range of temperatures tolerated by the baby is narrow. An alarm sounds when the temperature is outside the normal range (36°–37°C).

Incubators use the principle of heat convection by providing warm air to the infant's environment. Incubators are usually single-walled and thus are affected by room temperature. Radiant heat shields are often used to minimize heat loss. Oxygen hoods are also frequently used in incubators to maximize oxygen administration. Servocontrols for monitoring the temperature may be used in the incubator. It is important that both the baby's temperature and the incubator temperature be recorded at regular intervals. Figure 11-3 shows some of the more common heat-conserving equipment.

### Fluid and Electrolyte Adaptations

The volatile nature of maintaining fluid and electrolyte balance in the newborn results from each neonate's physiological development and size. Neonates have an increased metabolic rate that is approximately twice that of adults. Metabolism requires that their gastrointestinal enzymes digest protein and carbohydrates better than fat.

The determination of normal fluid requirements is based on estimates of how much water will be required by each individual infant. Estimates are usually obtained by either the surface area method or the caloric method (see Chapter 28). Usually newborns take 60 to 90 mL (2–3 oz) every 2 to 3 hours, and intake progresses as children grow. For example, by 4 or 5 months of age most infants take 200 to 240 mL (7–8 oz) per feeding, four or five times per day.

The increased body surface area of the neonate results in a considerable loss of fluids by evaporation. Neonates need a significant amount of fluid because their proportion of water to body mass is about 75%; adults have a 58% to 60% proportion of water to body mass.

Neonates also have a decreased ability to concentrate urine; therefore, water cannot be conserved. Urination usually occurs in the first 24 hours; frequently babies urinate in the delivery room. A pink-stained diaper, often observed during the first week of life, is due to protein and increased urates.

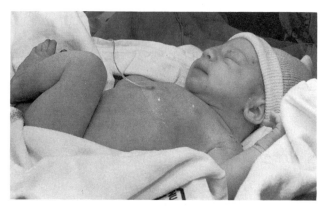

*Figure 11–2.    Newborn under radiant warmer with skin probe in place and stockinette cap to retain heat.*

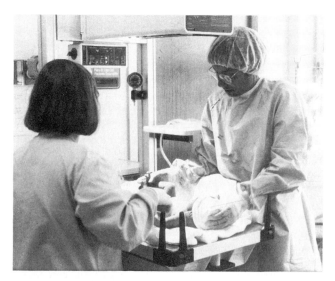

*Figure 11–3.    Heat-conserving equipment, including radiant warmer, incubator, radiant heat shield, and oxygen hood. (Courtesy of Texas Tech Health Science Center, El Paso, Texas)*

Any upset in water balance, of course, means a disruption of sodium and potassium levels. Neonates must be weighed every 24 hours. A weight loss might be due to insensible water loss. A weight loss over 10% to 15% is considered a sign of dehydration. Intake and output must be measured. Urine output can be determined by measuring the contents of a urine collection bag or by weighing the diaper when dry and then when wet. A disadvantage of urine collection bags is that they may cause skin irritation if they must be left in place for long periods of time. Signs of dehydration in the neonate include dry skin, sunken fontanels, loose abdominal skin turgor, oliguria, tachycardia, mottled skin, and dry mucous membranes. IV fluids are administered as indicated. See Chapter 28 for a discussion of intravenous calculations.

### Sensory, Cognitive, and Psychosocial Adaptations

All infants differ in their responses to environmental stimuli. Some of these differences may be attributed to heredity; however, the influence of environment in the development of cognition and psychosocial adaptations seems clear. Environmental effects on infant development have been explained by the concept of "critical periods." This viewpoint emphasizes that there are inherently programmed timetables in humans that control when certain developmental tasks usually occur (e.g., walking, talking). If environmental factors support this development, the child will accomplish these tasks at the same time most other children accomplish them.

Neonates require stimulation of all their senses in order to develop normally. Studies by Spitz (1949) and Bowlby (1956) document the deleterious effects of the lack of stimulation, particularly maternal stimulation. Their work supports the idea of a "critical period."

The birth process is often hypothesized as a traumatic event for the baby, which can affect the psychosocial relationship with the mother. One of the most famous proponents of this theory was LeBoyer (1975), who suggested that lights be dimmed during delivery, that infants be bathed in warm water after delivery (to simulate uterine fluid), and that the baby be placed on the mother's abdomen after birth. This approach to delivery has been controversial but clearly reflects the "traumatic" interpretation of birth. Other factors identified as having an impact on the delivery process and subsequent development of the infant include the age of the mother (especially adolescent mothers or older first-time mothers) and chronic health problems of the mother.

*Sensory Development.*  Newborns have well-developed senses of touch, taste, and smell. Touch is the most highly developed, as is evidenced by sensitivity in the areas of the mouth, lips, tongue, ears, and forehead. The *rooting reflex* is an example of the effect of touch. When an infant's cheek is stroked, the child turns the head in the direction of the touch. Infants are believed to be able to smell within 2 hours after birth. It is believed that they smell the mother's breast milk very early and that they will search for it. It is also believed that taste discrimination begins early and that many infants refuse water or different formulas on the basis of taste.

Infants are born with the ability to hear, although amniotic fluid in the ear canal may diminish hearing for the first few days. The baby should be able to hear loud, sharp noises and should react with a jerk or startle (the *Moro reflex*). Eliciting the Moro reflex verifies the hearing ability of the neonate. Further documentation of hearing by differentiating vocal patterns was demonstrated by De-Casper and Fifer (1980), who found that by the third day of life the neonate preferred the mother's voice. Movements of infants have also been shown to be coordinated with speech inflections.

Neonates are also born with the ability to see; however, it is believed that they have a restricted visual field. They appear to focus on objects that are about 18 to 20 inches away. They also tend to focus on faces and on black and white rather than colored objects. Neonates frequently cross their eyes because the eye muscles are not yet well-developed. Parents should be encouraged to make eye contact with neonates. They should understand that new babies like to look at faces and that this activity facilitates attachment. Parents tend to want to believe that neonates smile in response to visual stimulation. However, smiling is thought to be an innate response and is not caused by mental association with particular individuals or events. This is followed by non-selective smiling, when infants smile in response to any voices or faces. Vision becomes important at this stage of development. Social smiling begins at 5 to 6 months of age; infants usually smile only at their care-givers.

The overall state of the neonate is one of either comfort or distress, with crying serving to signal the latter. Distress cries include those of hunger, pain, and thirst. Parents must learn how to differentiate among various cries if they are to respond effectively to the infant.

Questions remain about the extent of pain felt by newborns. It is generally thought that a decrease in the pain threshold occurs about 4 to 5 days after birth. Proponents of the traumatic birth theory interpret the higher pain threshold at birth as nature's way of protecting the infant through this period. However, recent studies indicate that neonates do feel pain from procedures such as heel lancing and circumcision; this is demonstrated by increased heart rates, elevated blood pressure, and increased sweating (Anand & Hickey, 1987; Grunau & Craig, 1987; Stang, Snellman, Condon, & Kastenbaum, 1988; American Academy of Pediatrics, 1987). Anand, Sippell, and Green (1987) reported that complete myelination of the pain pathways to the brain stem and thalamus is achieved by 30 weeks' gestation.

*Cognitive Development.* Piaget's (1952, 1963) formulation of cognitive development places the neonate in sub-stage 1 (reflexive action) of stage 1, the sensorimotor period. During this stage, reflex activity occurs with no differentiation. Babies predominantly use assimilation functions (taking-in) and, as schemas are developed, begin to use more and more accommodation (fitting into their already formed image or map of the circumstance). Elicitation of the sucking reflex supports this notion. Sucking is present at birth, and the reflex lasts until 10 to 12 months of age.

*Psychosocial Development.* Freud (1933) proposed that the neonate operates using the pleasure principle in which the id is predominant. Infants are activated by biological needs that trigger reflex activity.

The psychosocial stages proposed by Erikson (1950, 1963) begin with the "trust versus mistrust" stage. The primary task is the development of security and love in the initial relationship (usually with the mother). If the neonate develops feelings of comfort, warmth, and security, the foundation for the development of trust is laid. It is anticipated that a favorable resolution of this conflict will emerge at the end of the first year.

## Parenting and Sibling Relationships in Promoting Adaptation

The mother–infant relationship is usually the first relationship formed. Research in bonding and attachment originally focused on this relationship but has extended to fathers and siblings over the past 15 years.

*Bonding* is defined as a relationship between two people that endures through time (Klaus & Kennell, 1982). *Attachment* is the strong emotional union of the infant to the parent. Attachment begins when the parent "falls in love" with the baby; this may take from hours, days, or weeks to months to occur and sometimes never occurs. Bonding is said to occur in a unilateral direction from the parent to the child (e.g., the mother bonds to the baby), whereas attachment progresses from the infant to the parent (e.g., the baby forms an attachment to the mother, which stimulates the parent to attach to the infant). Prenatal signs of bonding include selecting a name, excitement over fetal movement, and preparing accommodations for the baby.

Parenting relationships are influenced by a variety of factors. Most parents base their parenting activities on their personal experience, using their parents as role models. Different cultures place different expectations on parents. In some cultures babies are placed in the care of others so that parents may work; in others the child is kept totally with the mother for a number of years.

Parents have their own temperamental and psychological endowments that influence the interactions. They are also influenced by career and financial considerations.

In particular, mothers usually form a prenatal mental image of what the baby will look like. After birth an important task is the reconciliation of that image with the "real" baby.

Recognition of the infant's state can help parents to identify optimal periods for establishing the relationship with the baby. Nurses can help parents identify infant states and should encourage parents to center activities and interactions around these states.

### Effects of Mothering

Bowlby originated the term "monotrophy," which describes the ability of a mother to bond to only one child at a time (Klaus & Kennell, 1982). This proposition is important in a variety of situations, such as in the case of twins. If the mother can only bond to one of the twins at a time, every effort should be made to discharge the twins from the hospital at the same time in order to minimize a singular bonding. Bowlby (1963) also studied the effects of maternal separation on infants. His work is based on the concept of the critical period and reflects the stance of many ethologists who have found (for example) that baby birds mothered by humans later fail to attach to a mother bird. Bowlby found that the age of the child when separated from the mother is a major factor in determining the extent of harmful effects such as mental retardation or the inability to form relationships.

Eye movements are an important response for mothers during the bonding process. Mothers like to feel that the infant is making eye contact, and they may bring the baby to an *en face* position to accomplish this (Fig. 11-4). Other behaviors that seem to help mothers react positively include smiling and feeding (sucking) well. Inherited physical characteristics also seem to help mothers bond, e.g., the recognition of such features as "dad's nose" or "grandma's mouth." If a mother feels that she is failing in activities such as feeding, she may feel distressed and be unable to establish a warm feeling toward the infant.

The 24-hour period right after birth has been considered the critical period for bonding to occur. This time period is negatively affected if the mother receives anesthesia and is unable to actively participate. Rubin (1963) examined the activities of mothers after birth and identified a progression of touching that took 3 days to complete. The sequence usually indicates bonding stages. The progression moves from finger-tip touching to massaging, stroking and, finally, encompassing with the arm. Klaus, Kennell, Plumb, and Zuehlke (1970) confirmed Rubin's findings but found that the progression was much more rapid, taking only from 4 to 8 minutes.

### Effects of Fathering

The concept of fathering has not been defined nearly as well as mothering. Frequently the fathering relationship is viewed as less important; however, bonding is an impor-

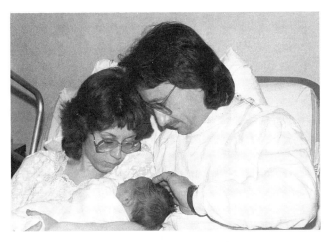

*Figure 11–4. Attachment: first visit after birth. Mother makes eye contact with neonate while father strokes infant's head.*

tant process for fathers also. *Engrossment* is the term, first used by Greenberg and Morris (1974), to describe the strong impact of the newborn on the father (Fig. 11-5). Fathers appear to have a separate and distinct role from mothers in terms of their interactions with infants. They tend to spend less time in caretaking and more time in play activities. Parke (1975, 1979) observed infants from 2 to 4 days old as they interacted with mothers alone, fathers alone, and with both parents. Fathers tended to hold (touch) and talk more with the infants but also tended to smile less.

The long-term effect of fathers' participation in Lamaze classes and/or labor and delivery has not been well documented. It is generally assumed that such participation fosters a positive relationship by making the father feel that he is an important person for both the mother and baby. Although an increasing number of fathers actively participate in providing infant care, some fathers choose not to be as involved. In view of the fact that successful parenting includes a number of variables, the individual father's decision regarding degree of involvement should be recognized and accepted.

### Effects of Sibling Interaction

In recent years, interest has increased in sibling/newborn bonding. Many hospitals have visiting hours for siblings; others conduct classes to prepare siblings for the new baby. However, the short- or long-term effectiveness of these interventions has not been well documented. Supporters accept the same premise as for fathers—that early, close interaction facilitates sibling/infant bonding.

The sibling(s) should be prepared for the arrival of the new baby before birth. It is generally thought that a good time to begin discussions is during pregnancy when the mother starts to "show." The sibling(s) can be involved

in making plans for the baby: shopping, getting equipment ready, discussing names, etc.

Marecki, Wooldridge, Dow, Thompson, and Lechner-Hyman (1985) videotaped siblings and parents with newborns prior to discharge from the hospital. Analysis of 30 videotapes indicated that sisters appear to bond better than brothers. The question of whether or not this is an innate ability has not been determined.

## Assessment of the Newborn

Comprehensive assessment during the neonatal period can be a major factor in determining the outcome, and the adaptations required, of the neonate. Observation and the use of reliable tools aid in the assessment process. Physiological, psychological, temperamental, and environmental assessments are important parameters. Assessments other than the Apgar should not be performed immediately after birth if the baby is distressed, or just before or after a feeding.

### Apgar Scoring

The Apgar scoring chart (Table 11-4) offers a rapid means of assessing the general condition of the infant at 1 and 5 minutes of age. It measures the neonate's ability to adapt to the environment by assigning points from 0 to 2 for five categories: heart rate, respiratory effort, muscle tone, reflex response, and color.

A score of 10 indicates the optimal condition. This is seldom achieved because most infants have some acrocyanosis. *Acrocyanosis* is characterized by cyanosis, coldness, and sweating of the extremities. A total score of 0 to 3 indicates a severely depressed baby, a score of 4 to 6

*Figure 11–5. Attachment: father and newborn communicating.*

*Table 11–4.  Apgar Scoring Chart*

| Sign | 0 | 1 | 2 | 1 minute | 5 minutes |
|---|---|---|---|---|---|
| Heart rate | Absent | Slow (<100) | Over 100 | | |
| Respiratory effort | Absent | Weak cry Hyperventilation | Strong cry | | |
| Muscle tone | Limp | Some flexion of extremities | Well-flexed | | |
| Reflex response | | | | | |
| 1. Response to catheter in nostril (tested after esophagus is clear) | No response | Grimace | Cough or sneeze | | |
| 2. Tangential foot slap | No response | Grimace | Cry with withdrawal of foot | | |
| Color | Blue, pale | Body pink; extremities blue | Completely pink | | |

signals a moderately depressed baby, and a score of 7 to 10 is considered very good.

In scoring, the heart rate is counted by using a stethoscope over the heart or by palpating the pulse in the umbilical cord. Muscle tone is assessed by extending the extremities and observing the tone when they return to the usual flexed position. Other signs are elicited as indicated in the tool.

## Body Measurement and Vital Signs

The neonate's measurements are significant when compared with standardized norms. They provide baseline data that are helpful in establishing the presence or absence of anomalies. Figure 11-6 shows how routine body measurements are taken in neonates.

Normal length varies from 45 cm to 52.5 cm (18–21

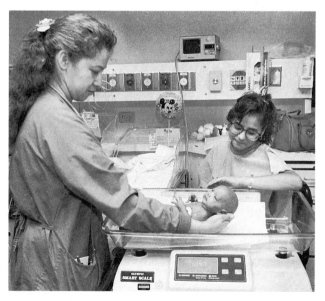

*Figure 11–6.  Newborn being weighed.*

inches). A head-to-heel measurement is obtained either by placing the baby on a measuring board, being careful to extend one leg, or by placing the baby on one side and, using a measuring tape, measuring from the crown, along the spine to the rump, and then down one extended leg to the heel. The normal crown-to-rump measurement is from 31 cm to 35 cm (121/2–14 inches). This measurement is approximately equal to the head circumference.

The chest usually measures 30.5 cm to 33 cm (12–13 inches), which is 2 cm to 3 cm (1 inch) less than the head circumference. If the head circumference is significantly smaller than the chest, microcephaly or craniostenosis is suspected. If the head is more than 4 cm (13/4 inches) larger than the chest, hydrocephalus is suspected.

Head circumference is usually 33 cm to 35.5 cm (13–14 inches). A measuring tape is placed across the forehead, encircling the head at its widest point. Occasionally the head circumference is less than the chest circumference after birth because of molding.

Body weight is measured soon after birth because weight loss occurs rapidly. Ten percent of the body weight is lost by 3 to 4 days because of the loss of excessive extracellular fluid, limited food intake, and the passage of meconium (the first stool of the newborn; it is thick, sticky, and greenish-black). This weight is usually regained by the tenth day of life. The average birth weight is between 2700 g and 4000 g (6–9 pounds); the mean weight is 3400 g (71/2 pounds). Males generally weigh more than females.

Temperature, pulse, and respirations are also recorded. They should be taken for 1 full minute when the baby is quiet. Axillary temperatures are taken because a rectal thermometer may cause perforation of the rectal mucosa. The core body temperature is 35.5° to 37.5°C (96° to 99.5°F). The normal apical pulse rate is from 120 to 160 beats per minute. Respirations are abdominal and range from 30 to 50 breaths per minute. Blood pressure is usually not taken, but the average systolic pressure is 70 mmHg at 2 days and 93 mmHg at 6 weeks.

## The Neonatal Behavioral Assessment Scale

The Neonatal Behavioral Assessment Scale, developed by Brazelton in 1955, measures 27 behavioral responses of the infant. It is used to determine how well the infant attunes to environmental stimuli, how the infant is able to shut out stimuli, and how the infant responds to stimuli. Each item is rated on a nine-point scale. All items are grouped into six categories: habituation, orientation, motor maturity, variation, self-quieting abilities, and social behaviors. During this assessment the sleep and awake states of the infant are an important consideration. This assessment is useful for early detection of infants at developmental risk and should be performed by trained examiners. The results are also useful when shared with parents as a means of making them aware of their infant's abilities.

## Assessment of Infant State

Infant states include the sleep states of deep sleep (NREM) and light sleep (REM) and the awake states of drowsiness, quiet alert, active alert, and crying. For 4 to 6 hours after birth the neonate is in the initial state of reactivity. For about one half hour after birth the infant appears alert and interested in the environment, cries vigorously, and may suck the fist. Because the newborn's eyes are open, this is a good time to begin establishing bonding and breast-feeding. Next, the neonate falls into a deep sleep that lasts from 2 to 4 hours, with all processes slowing down.

The second period of reactivity begins when the baby awakens from this deep sleep. All functions increase; for example, meconium is usually passed at this time.

Awareness of the reactivity periods during the transitional neonatal adjustment period has changed the timing of some procedures. Eye drops are now usually instilled after the parents and newborn have had the opportunity to make eye contact. The initial bath is postponed until after the infant's body temperature has stabilized. Breast- or bottle-feeding is begun during the appropriate alert phase.

## Assessment of Premature Infants Behavior

The Assessment of Premature Infants Behavior (APIB) is a tool developed to assess the adaptation of premature infants to the extrauterine environment. The tool builds on the earlier tool developed by Brazelton (Als, 1982; Als, Lawhon, Brown, Gibes, Duffy, McAnulty, & Blickman, 1986). Because this is a very time-consuming tool to administer, another tool, the Neonatal Individualized Developmental Care and Assessment Plan (NIDCAP), was devel-

oped (Als et al., 1986; Vandenberg, 1990). This tool organizes nursing care around the infant's behavioral cues in an effort to reduce environmental overload.

## Assessment of the Head

The head is assessed for symmetry, sutures, and fontanels. As the baby passes through the vagina, the cranial bones overlap to facilitate the birth; the ridges then relax. Six bones form the skull: the frontal, the occipital, two parietals, and two temporals. The connective tissues where the bones come together are called *sutures.* The sagittal sutures divide the head in half; the coronal suture crowns the head. About the second day after birth, small openings called "soft spots" or *fontanels* appear. These openings perform an important function for the first 12 to 18 months by providing room for the cranial vault to expand to accommodate the growing brain.

The two fontanels usually palpated are the anterior and posterior fontanels. The size and shape are ascertained; molding or abnormal closure is noted. The *anterior fontanel* is diamond-shaped and is found at the junction of the sagittal and coronal sutures. It may be as large as 5 cm (2 inches) at its widest part. The *posterior fontanel* is located at the junction of the sagittal and lambdoid sutures. It is triangular in shape, much smaller than the anterior fontanel (measuring about 1 cm), and usually closes by the second month (in contrast to the anterior fontanel, which closes much later, from 12–18 months). Both fontanels should be flat, and any tensing should be reported. Sometimes a *sagittal* or *parietal fontanel* is found, located at a point of the sagittal suture, along the midline from back to front of the skull. This should always be recorded because it may indicate other conditions, such as trisomy 21. The measurement of fontanels is always recorded with two dimensions, length and width, e.g., 3 cm × 2 cm. Figure 11-7 shows the skull and the location of the fontanels.

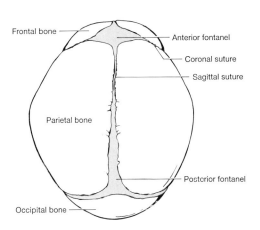

*Figure 11–7.  Anatomy of the infant's skull.*

Any unusual masses or swelling of the head should be recorded. Several types of swelling are considered normal. *Craniotabes* is a soft localized area of swelling. It is spongy and easily indented by the finger, resuming its shape when the finger is removed. The cause is unknown. There is no treatment, and the swelling recedes in a matter of months.

Edema found on the presenting portion of the scalp is called *caput succedaneum*. This swelling is poorly defined and involves superficial tissue. The swelling may cross the suture line and may persist for several months. Figure 11-8 shows caput succedaneum.

Swelling over one cranial bone is known as a *cephalhematoma*. Blood collects between the bone and the periosteum. The swelling takes several hours to develop and is bounded by the suture lines. The mass is soft and usually absorbs within a few weeks.

*Head lag,* the inability to hold the head up, should be evaluated. When pulled to a sitting position the infant should attempt to maintain the head in an erect position; once the infant is in a sitting position and the head falls forward, the infant should attempt to draw it erect. The baby should be able to lift the head slightly when placed on the abdomen.

If the head seems abnormally large or asymmetrical, the baby can be taken to a darkened room where transillumination can be performed. A rubber-cuffed flashlight is held tightly against the head and moved to various positions. Normally a faint halo of light, from 1 cm to 2 cm wide, is seen around the cuff. An abnormality is indicated if the halo is large or irregular or if the light is seen on the other side of the head. Possible problems include hydranencephaly, hydrocephalus, or a cyst.

## Assessment of the Eyes, Nose, Ears, Mouth, and Cry

The sclera of the newborn's eye should be white and clear. The iris of Caucasian babies is gray-blue, whereas darkly pigmented babies have dark eyes. Absence of color of the iris is indicative of albinism.

It is often difficult to examine the newborn's eyes because newborns tend to keep their eyes tightly closed and because the eyelids are usually edematous for the first few days. Funduscopy is not usually performed except to elicit the red reflex. A red or orange color is normally reflected from the fundus. The eyes should be examined for symmetry, discharge, hemorrhage, edema, and jaundice.

Most eye irritation is caused by the instillation of silver nitrate drops after birth. Any purulent discharge observed should be reported, because it might be due to ophthalmia neonatorum. *Ophthalmia neonatorum* results when the newborn passes through the birth canal of a mother infected with gonorrhea. The infection results in a purulent conjunctivitis and keratitis and inflammation of the cornea.

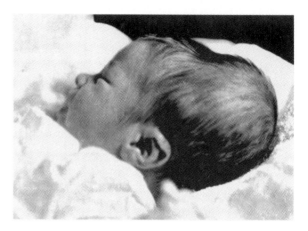

*Figure 11–8.    Caput succedaneum. (MacDonald House, University Hospitals of Cleveland)*

A lateral upward slope of the eyes with an inner epicanthal fold could be indicative of trisomy 21. *Strabismus* (malalignment of the eyes) and *nystagmus* (involuntary movement of the eyeball) are frequent findings. Tears usually do not appear until the baby is about 2 months old. For additional information on assessment of the eyes see Chapter 35.

Newborns' noses usually have a flattened appearance. Most newborns breathe through their noses rather than through their mouths. One test of nasal patency is to hold the newborn's mouth closed and observe whether the baby has difficulty in breathing; if so, the child might have congenital choanal atresia. A stuffy nose could be a sign of congenital syphilis.

The ears are observed for position on the head, shape, size, and auditory function. The upper part of the ears should be on the same plane as the angle of the eye. The position of the ears can be checked by imagining a line from the outer canthi of the eyes to the ears (see Fig. 5-11). Renal anomalies or chromosomal disorders should be suspected if the ears are low or if there is a malformation. Because the neonate's ear canals are usually filled with vernix caseosa and amniotic fluid, it is difficult to observe the tympanic membranes.

When examining the newborn's mouth, the gums should be pink and free of cysts or tumors. Teeth buds are visible but rarely are teeth present. The palate is normally narrow with a high arch. It should be palpated with a finger cot or a gloved finger to check for cleft palate, a fissure in the midline of the palate that results from incomplete fusion during embryonic development. Often the infant develops a sucking blister on the upper lip. The frenulum linguae should be checked. The baby should be able to extend the tongue to the lower lip. White nodules called *Epstein's pearls* frequently are found along the midline of both sides of the palate; these disappear spontaneously in a few weeks. The differentiation between Epstein's pearls and *thrush* (moniliasis), a yeast-like fungus, can be made on the basis of distribution and appearance.

Thrush is a patchy exudate appearing on the palate, tongue, and cheeks; if it is removed, the area bleeds.

The mouth is best checked when the baby opens it voluntarily. Two reflexes, the *sucking reflex* and the *rooting reflex,* are easily checked at this time. Placing a finger or nipple in the infant's mouth should elicit the sucking reflex; stroking the baby's cheek should result in turning the head toward that side (rooting reflex).

Cries should be assessed for intensity, frequency, and pitch. If crying requires an effort, this should also be noted. A weak cry is exhibited by ill babies. A shrill, high-pitched cry can be a sign of central nervous system damage. This shrill cry is also heard in babies of drug-addicted mothers. The cri-du-chat (cat's cry) syndrome is characterized by "mewing" crying. It signals a chromosomal disorder usually accompanied by severe mental retardation, microcephaly, heart disease, and small physical stature. Babies with cretinism have a hoarse, low-pitched cry. Crying is the infant's form of communication, and care-givers must learn to interpret various cries. When the baby cries and the care-givers can associate events with the crying, it helps them interpret the reasons for it.

## Assessment of the Integument

The skin is assessed for color, rashes, birthmarks, tone, and hydration. Most white babies have a bright red color on the second day of life because of their high hematocrit level. Ethnicity affects normal color: Hispanic infants may have an olive or yellowish skin tint, whereas black infants may appear pink or yellowish brown. Skin tone should evidence adequate hydration; the skin should be smooth and velvet-like, and it is usually puffy. Pallor should be reported. The hands and feet of the neonate are often blue owing to cooling (*acrocyanosis*). Generalized cyanosis is abnormal.

When low-birth-weight infants are placed on one side, the body sometimes appears to be bisected into a pale upper half and a red lower half. This is referred to as a *harlequin color change*; it usually resolves when the infant is placed in a supine position. Jaundice, occurring from 24 to 72 hours after birth and lasting for 3 to 7 days, is a normal physiological event. Jaundice occurring within the first 24 hours after birth is a sign of hemolytic disease, which can be life threatening (see Chapter 25). Infants should always be checked for jaundice in daylight. When a finger is pressed against the infant's nose and released, the skin appears yellow instead of white. A bilirubin test will confirm the existence of jaundice.

*Erythema toxicum* usually occurs within the first 2 days of life, with lesions that appear erythematous and blotchy; however, it may occur up to 2 weeks after birth. The rash is sometimes called "flea bite rash" and usually appears over the trunk and back; occasionally the lesions are pustular. It is transient and requires no treatment.

The normal newborn has a variety of skin markings.

*Milia* are yellow-white 1-mm cysts distributed over the cheeks, forehead, nose, and nasolabial folds and are due to clogged sebaceous glands; they disappear spontaneously in a few weeks. *Lanugo* is the fine, downy hair usually found on the forehead, ears, and shoulders. *Vernix caseosa* is the cheesy-like protective material covering the skin at birth. Remnants can still be seen in the skin folds (especially the labia) several days after birth.

*Nevi* or birthmarks are frequently found on newborns. *Hemangiomas* are vascular nevi. *Superficial telangiectasia* (stork bites, flammeus nevi) are flat, reddened, vascular areas found on the nape of the neck, the forehead between the eyes, and over the eyelids; they fade almost completely in the first year. *Port-wine stain birthmarks* are larger, elevated hemangiomas that are bright red or dark purple; they do not fade. *Strawberry nevi* usually become prominent in the first few weeks of life. They are red and nodular, with a rough surface; they feel rubbery and can become quite large as the child grows. Usually located on the head or neck, they disappear over a period of years with no treatment. *Cavernous hemangiomas* are not well demarcated and are bluish-red or skin colored; the visible portion represents only a portion of the whole hemangioma. They do not regress spontaneously.

Another pigmentation found in neonates is *Mongolian spots.* These are blue or blue-black spots commonly found on the genitalia and lower back in Oriental and black children and children of Mediterranean descent. Sometimes babies receiving phototherapy may have a bronze color of the skin or "flea bite" dermatitis; this disappears when the treatment is discontinued. Any signs of pustules should be carefully noted because they may indicate a staphylococcal infection.

Generalized edema is abnormal and may indicate *hydrops fetalis* or congestive heart failure. Hydrops fetalis is fatal unless exchange transfusions are done as rapidly as possible after delivery; it is associated with severe erythroblastosis fetalis, and the infant exhibits massive edema. Edema of the hands and feet is often present in Turner's syndrome (only one X chromosome with 44 autosomes).

## Assessment of the Back and Extremities

The infant's general body appearance is evaluated for symmetry, malformations, or signs of trauma. Both sides of the body should have the same general proportions. Signs of trauma might include abrasions, fractures, or dislocations. Inspection of the back should be done with the infant lying on the abdomen. Tufts of hair along the spinal column may indicate pathology (see Chapter 26).

All extremities are tested for range of motion and for polydactyly (extra digits). Hips are checked to determine if congenital hip dysplasia is present. *Dysplasia* refers to

*Table 11—5.  Neonatal Reflexes*

| Reflex | Method of Obtaining | Function |
| --- | --- | --- |
| Babinski | Stroke the lateral aspect of the plantar surface of the foot from heel to toes. Use a blunt object. Hyperextension or fanning of the toes occurs. | A sign that myelinization is not complete. When myelinization is completed the normal response becomes flexion of all toes. The positive (pathogenic sign) is hyperextension (dorsiflexion) of the great toe with or without fanning of the remaining toes. |
| Cough and sneeze | Observation | Helps to rid the respiratory system of amniotic fluid and protects from inhaling foreign substances |
| Dance | The infant is held upright with the feet touching a solid surface. The infant begins a dancing movement. | A sign of CNS integrity. It is present at birth but disappears soon. |
| Gagging and vomiting | Observation during and after feeding | Rejection of irritating or toxic substances. |
| Grasp | A finger is placed from the underside, in the palm of the infant's hand, and the infant curls his or her fingers around it in a grasp. | Beginning ability to hold, then release objects. |
| Landau | Suspend the infant carefully in the prone position by supporting the infant's abdomen with the examiner's hand. | Abnormal response is collapse of the neonate in a limp concave position. |
| Moro | When the infant is resting quietly, the crib is jostled or a loud noise is made. The infant responds by drawing up his legs and throwing his arms forward. | Neurological injury should be suspected if the movements are absent or if the movements are assymetrical. Sometimes the Moro reflex is absent for the first 24 hours and appears on the second day. This may be due to cerebral edema after birth. If the reflex is present at birth but disappears shortly after birth, increasing intracranial pressure may be present. A sign of CNS integrity, the Moro reflex is present until the 4th or 5th month. |
| Placing | Infant is held erect and one foot touches the undersurface of the table top. The infant will flex the hip and knee and place the stimulated foot on top of the table. | This reflex is present at birth and disappears at about 6 weeks old. It is absent in paralysis and in infants born breech. |
| Rooting | If the baby's cheek is stroked with a nipple or a finger, the baby will respond by opening the mouth and turning toward the stroked side. | Obtaining nourishment. |
| Wallowing | Observed during feeding. | Allows infant to ingest food. |
| Tonic neck | The infant may be observed when lying on the back to have his or her head turned either to the left or right and to have the arm and leg on the side to which he or she is facing extended. The position is similar to that of a fencer. | Well developed at birth, this reflex gradually disappears over several months as the CNS develops and the baby gradually gains control over his or her movements and assumes a symmetric position. |
| Yawning | Observation | Enables the newborn to draw in a supply of oxygen when respiration exchange is insufficient to meet his or her needs. |

abnormal development. There are three types: subluxation, dislocatable, and dislocated. Congenital hip dysplasia occurs frequently, especially in females. Frank breech delivery may also cause hip dislocation, as may the estrogen hormone relaxin. Congenital hip dislocation (displacement of the femoral head from the acetabulum) appears to be influenced by heredity since it may be seen in several children of the same family.

The mildest form of hip dysplasia, in which the femoral head remains in the acetabulum, is called *preluxa-* *tion* or *acetabular dysplasia*. Subluxation of the hip occurs when the head of the femur is partially displaced. When dislocated, the femoral head is displaced posteriorly and superiorly over the fibrocartilaginous rim.

The assessment of hip status is accomplished by two maneuvers: the *Ortolani* and *Barlow* tests. The infant is placed in a supine position with the examiner at the feet. The hips are flexed at a right angle. During the Ortolani test the thumbs are placed on the inner aspects of the thighs opposite the lesser trochanters, and the middle fingers are placed over the greater trochanter. The procedure is to flex the knees and abduct the hips up and out. If there is resistance in having the flexed legs abducted 175° or if a click is heard as the femur slips into the acetabulum, the hip is dislocated. A dislocated hip will return to the acetabulum; there is a sensation of movement or a "clunk" as this occurs. In the Barlow test, as the hips are adducted, the thumbs press backward and may displace the head of the femur from the acetabulum. Other signs of hip dislocation, although not as reliable, include restricted abduction on the affected side; Allis' sign, which is shortening of the limb on the affected side; and asymmetrical thigh and gluteal folds. Congenital hip dysplasia is discussed in more detail in Chapter 33.

Subluxable hips may be treated by triple diapering. Dislocated or dislocatable hips usually must be treated with a splint such as a Pavlik harness or the Frejka pillow splint. The former is an adjustable chest halter that extends to the lower legs; the latter looks like a huge diaper. Treatment started at birth usually results in success when the baby is about 3 months old.

Neonates usually appear bowlegged, and this persists until the child has been walking for about a year. The newborn's feet usually appear flat owing to fat pads. At birth the feet have a greater degree of dorsiflexion than is seen later in life. *Clubfoot* (talipes equinovarus) is evidenced by a heel that is medially turned (plantar flexion with inversion and adduction). Treatment for clubfoot consists of stretching exercises, taping, plaster casts, and shoe splints; sometimes surgery for heel-cord lengthening is required. Chapter 33 contains a complete discussion of clubfoot.

## Assessment of Reflexes

Reflexes are specific muscular responses to specific stimuli; the most common are shown in Table 11-5. They are elicited to assess neurological status. Several reflexes en-hance the infant's chances of survival. The universal reflex, recognized as the sign of discomfort, is the cry.

## Assessment of the Genitalia and Anus

In female neonates the urinary meatus is located behind the clitoris, and a hymenal tag may be visible, which disappears in a few weeks. The labia minora and the clitoris are usually edematous. Girls usually have a thick, white mucus discharge, which is occasionally blood-tinged; this ordinarily disappears within the first month of life.

In males the urinary meatus is normally at the tip of the penis. *Hypospadias* occurs when the urethra opens on the ventral surface of the penis. *Epispadias* occurs if the urethral opening is on the dorsal aspect of the penis. In either case these babies should not be circumcised since the foreskin may be used for repair when the child is about 2 years old. The foreskin completely covers the entire glans penis and usually cannot be retracted without trauma until about 3 years of age. *Circumcision* is the surgical removal of the foreskin, which is done for cultural or religious reasons. Swelling of the scrotum is common for the first few days. Peritoneal fluid in the scrotum is called a *hydrocele*. Usually the testicles are descended.

All unusual findings should be reported. Cases of ambiguous genitalia require a specialized team approach and good communication with the parents in planning interventions.

The anus is assessed for muscle tone and the presence of fissures. Failure of the neonate to pass meconium within 24 hours may indicate the presence of an *imperforate anus*. Stool patterns of neonates are shown in Table 11-6.

## Gestational Age Assessment

Assessment of gestational age (GA) is important in determining risk factors in the neonate. Gestational age refers to the age of a fetus (in weeks, since first day of the last

*Table 11–6. Neonatal Stool Patterns*

| Age (in days) | Name | Description |
| --- | --- | --- |
| 1 | Meconium | Blackish-green; sticky, odorless; tar-like. Contains mucous, vernix, lanugo, hormones, and carbohydrates |
| 2–3 | Transitional stool | Green; loose |
| 4 | Breast–fed stool | 3 or 4 light yellow stools per day; sweet-smelling |
| 4 | Formula–fed stool | 2 or 3 bright yellow stools per day; have an odor |
| | Jaundice stools | Bright green |
| | Bile duct obstruction | Clay-colored (gray) |
| | Anal fissure stools | Bloody |
| | Intestinal bleeding stools | Black or tarry |

menstrual period). The tool most frequently used to determine GA is the *Estimation of Gestational Age by Maturity Rating* by Ballard, Kazmaier, and Driver (1977), shown in Figure 11-9. A simplified version of the tool developed by Dubowitz, Dubowitz, and Goldberg (1970), it contains six neuromuscular signs and six physical maturity signs. Observation and scoring takes approximately 10 minutes and should be performed within 48 hours after birth. The scores from the neuromuscular and physical maturity signs are combined to determine the maturity rating in weeks.

Another frequently used tool is the *Classification of Newborns—Based on Maturity and Intrauterine Growth,* developed by Lubchenco, Hansman, and Boyd (1966), shown in Figure 11-10. The neonate's length, head circumference, and weight are plotted on a growth grid to determine maturity.

## ESTIMATION OF GESTATIONAL AGE BY MATURITY RATING          Side 1
### Symbols:    X - 1st Exam    O - 2nd Exam

### NEUROMUSCULAR MATURITY

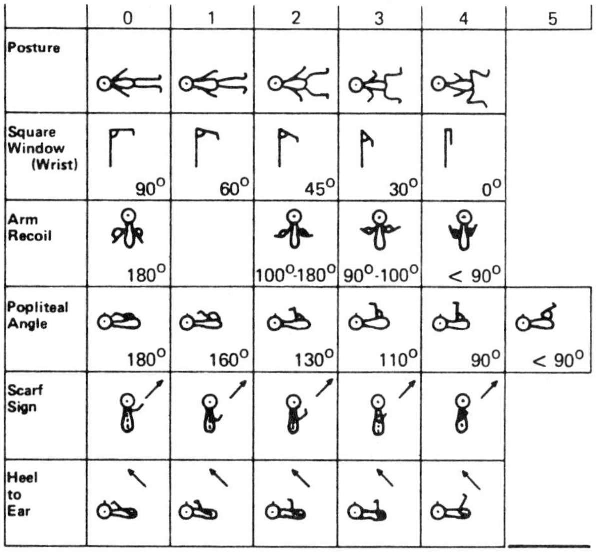

| | 0 | 1 | 2 | 3 | 4 | 5 |
|---|---|---|---|---|---|---|
| Posture | | | | | | |
| Square Window (Wrist) | 90° | 60° | 45° | 30° | 0° | |
| Arm Recoil | 180° | | 100°-180° | 90°-100° | < 90° | |
| Popliteal Angle | 180° | 160° | 130° | 110° | 90° | < 90° |
| Scarf Sign | | | | | | |
| Heel to Ear | | | | | | |

### PHYSICAL MATURITY

| | 0 | 1 | 2 | 3 | 4 | 5 |
|---|---|---|---|---|---|---|
| SKIN | gelatinous red, transparent | smooth pink, visible veins | superficial peeling &/or rash, few veins | cracking pale area, rare veins | parchment, deep cracking, no vessels | leathery, cracked, wrinkled |
| LANUGO | none | abundant | thinning | bald areas | mostly bald | |
| PLANTAR CREASES | no crease | faint red marks | anterior transverse crease only | creases ant. 2/3 | creases cover entire sole | |
| BREAST | barely percept. | flat areola, no bud | stippled areola, 1—2 mm bud | raised areola, 3—4 mm bud | full areola, 5—10 mm bud | |
| EAR | pinna flat, stays folded | sl. curved pinna, soft with slow recoil | well-curv. pinna, soft but ready recoil | formed & firm with instant recoil | thick cartilage, ear stiff | |
| GENITALS Male | scrotum empty, no rugae | | testes descending, few rugae | testes down, good rugae | testes pendulous, deep rugae | |
| GENITALS Female | prominent clitoris & labia minora | | majora & minora equally prominent | majora large, minora small | clitoris & minora completely covered | |

Gestation by Dates _____ wks

Birth Date _____ Hour _____ am / pm

APGAR _____ 1 min _____ 5 min

### MATURITY RATING

| Score | Wks |
|---|---|
| 5 | 26 |
| 10 | 28 |
| 15 | 30 |
| 20 | 32 |
| 25 | 34 |
| 30 | 36 |
| 35 | 38 |
| 40 | 40 |
| 45 | 42 |
| 50 | 44 |

### SCORING SECTION

| | 1st Exam=X | 2nd Exam=O |
|---|---|---|
| Estimating Gest Age by Maturity Rating | _____ Weeks | _____ Weeks |
| Time of Exam | Date _____ am Hour _____ pm | Date _____ am Hour _____ pm |
| Age at Exam | _____ Hours | _____ Hours |
| Signature of Examiner | _____ M.D. | _____ M.D. |

*Figure 11—9.    Estimation of gestational age by maturity rating. (Scoring system: Ballard, J.L., et al. [1977]. A simplified assessment of gestational age.* Pediatric Research, 11, 374. *Figures adapted from Sweet, A.Y. [1977]. Classification of the low-birth-weight infant. In M.H. Kalus & A.A. Fanaroff [Eds.].* Care of the high-risk infant. *Philadelphia: W.B. Saunders)*

## CLASSIFICATION OF NEWBORNS –
## BASED ON MATURITY AND INTRAUTERINE GROWTH
### Symbols:   X - 1st Exam   O - 2nd Exam

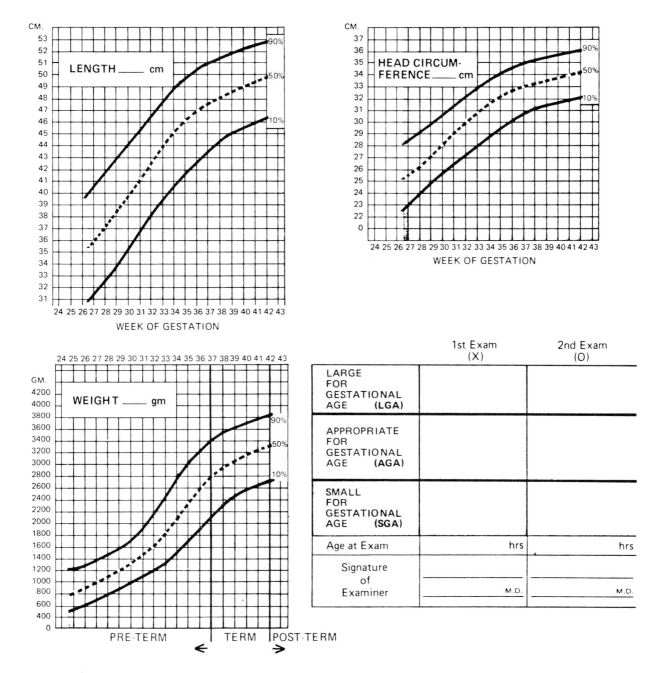

*Figure 11–10.   Classification of newborns based on maturity and intrauterine growth. (Adapted from Lubchenko, L.C., Hansman, C., & Boyd, E. [1966].* Pediatrics, 37,403; *Battaglia, F.C., & Lubchenko, L.C. [1967].* Journal of Pediatrics, 71, 159*)*

## Newborn Classifications

Newborns are usually classified according to gestational age (completed weeks of gestation, regardless of size) and according to size. Gestational age is divided into the following three classifications:

Term: 38 to 41 completed weeks of gestation

Premature: up to 37 completed weeks of gestation

Postmature: over 42 completed weeks of gestation

Newborns can also be classified by size at birth, according to the following criteria:

Low birth weight (LBW): less than 2500 grams

Small-for-gestational-age (SGA): below the 10th GA percentile

Appropriate-for-gestational-age (AGA): between the 10th and 90th GA percentiles

Large-for-gestational-age (LGA): above the 90th GA percentile

Newborn size may be combined with GA to classify the neonate (e.g., it is possible to have a term LBW infant or a postmature SGA infant).

## Assessment of Parent–Child Interactions

One of the most useful assessment tools for the neonatal period is the *Neonatal Perception Inventory* (NPI) developed by Broussard in 1978 (Fig. 11-11). The NPI is designed to measure the mother's perception of the average baby and her perception of her own baby in six areas: crying, spitting, feeding, elimination, sleeping, and predictability. The tool is administered on the second postpartum day and repeated at 1 month of age. The difference between the two scores (average baby and own baby) represents the NPI score. A positive score indicates a positive mother–infant relationship; a negative score may indicate the need for interventions designed to improve the mother's perception of the infant and to foster attachment. A third component of the tool is the Degree of Bother Inventory (Fig. 11-12), administered at 1 month of age. Fortunately, most mothers perceive their babies as being better than the average baby.

Research on father–infant interactions during the neonatal period is very limited. Wieser and Castiglia (1984) developed a 33-item tool that attempts to identify early attachment behaviors of fathers and infants. The tool assesses the infant's state, the father's activities (inspection, verbalization, tactile contact, and care-taking), and the impact of others on the interaction. Observations are made during the course of routine postpartum care. Trends are analyzed on an item-by-item basis. It is thought that data collected over a period of time will be most valuable.

## Health Promotion

Respiration must be established immediately before attention can be given to other aspects of health. Once established, attention can be directed toward maintaining a neutral thermal environment (as previously discussed), preventing illness and infection, and ensuring adequate nutrition.

## Maintaining a Patent Airway

In utero the fetal lungs are filled with lung fluid, which is mechanically expressed during the birth process. Once the head is delivered, a bulb syringe is used to clear fluid

from the nose and mouth. The baby is then placed on one side to facilitate further drainage. Usually the head is slightly inclined. Babies delivered by cesarean section usually have fluid in their lungs for several days because they do not experience the thoracic compression for fluid expulsion.

Deep suctioning is avoided because of the danger of laryngospasm, trauma with hemorrhage, and edema. If meconium is evident at birth, the baby is suctioned before the first breath by endotracheal suctioning; this is done because the first breath might force the meconium down the respiratory tract.

Three breathing problems may occur: the baby is breathing, but not regularly; the baby breathed but stopped; or the baby never breathed. For the first two problems, the cause must be determined quickly and ventilatory assistance initiated. All babies are entitled to expert resuscitation by competent, confident persons with appropriate skills (Bloom & Cropley, 1987). If the baby never breathed, efforts to stimulate ventilation should be made. If obstruction occurs, the location of the obstruction determines the treatment. If the baby requires mechanical ventilation, a face mask can be used for resuscitation when high pressure is not required. The face mask must fit tightly over the nose and throat to form a seal. The bag connected to the face mask is squeezed about 40 to 60 times per minute. The primary treatment of hypoxia is oxygenation, so the face mask can be connected to oxygen. It is important to listen for air entering and leaving the chest when trying to ventilate the infant. Usually artificial inflation of the lungs stimulates the reflexes and results in the initiation of respiration. Higher pressures than those created by bagging (compressing and releasing the bag attached to the face mask) are necessary for babies who have never breathed. Endotracheal and nasotracheal tubes are used most often for ventilation. Endotracheal intubation is always used if the larynx or upper trachea is obstructed. Higher obstruction is treated by using oropharyngeal airways; deep obstruction requires immediate surgery.

## Prevention of Infection or Injury

Care of the umbilicus, eyes, circumcision, and skin is directed toward preventing infection. Preventing impetigo, thrush, hemorrhage, septicemia, hemolytic disease, and ABO incompatibility requires an understanding of the physiological mechanisms operating and effective treatment.

### Umbilical Cord Care

Care of the umbilicus is geared to ensuring cleanliness, thereby preventing infection. At birth the cord is checked to ascertain that it contains three vessels—one vein and two arteries. The presence of only one umbilical artery should be recorded because this finding is associated with one or more congenital anomalies.

**NEONATAL PERCEPTION INVENTORY I**

AVERAGE BABY

How much crying do you think the average baby does?

| a great deal | a good bit | moderate amount | very little | none |

How much trouble do you think the average baby has in feeding?

| a great deal | a good bit | moderate amount | very little | none |

How much spitting up or vomiting do you think the average baby does?

| a great deal | a good bit | moderate amount | very little | none |

How much difficulty do you think the average baby has in sleeping?

| a great deal | a good bit | moderate amount | very little | none |

How much difficulty does the average baby have with bowel movements?

| a great deal | a good bit | moderate amount | very little | none |

How much trouble do you think the average baby has in settling down to a predictable pattern of eating and sleeping?

| a great deal | a good bit | moderate amount | very little | none |

**A**

**NEONATAL PERCEPTION INVENTORY I**

YOUR BABY

How much crying do you think your baby will do?

| a great deal | a good bit | moderate amount | very little | none |

How much trouble do you think your baby will have feeding?

| a great deal | a good bit | moderate amount | very little | none |

How much spitting up or vomiting do you think your baby will do?

| a great deal | a good bit | moderate amount | very little | none |

How much difficulty do you think your baby will have sleeping?

| a great deal | a good bit | moderate amount | very little | none |

How much difficulty do you expect your baby to have with bowel movements?

| a great deal | a good bit | moderate amount | very little | none |

How much trouble do you think that your baby will have settling down to a predictable pattern of eating and sleeping?

| a great deal | a good bit | moderate amount | very little | none |

**B**

*Figure 11–11. Neonatal Perception Inventory. (Broussard, E.R. [1978]. Psychosocial disorders in children: Early assessment of infants at risk.* Continuing Education for the Family Physician, 8, 44)

## DEGREE OF BOTHER INVENTORY

| | | | | |
|---|---|---|---|---|
| Crying | a great deal | somewhat | very little | none |
| Spitting up or vomiting | a great deal | somewhat | very little | none |
| Sleeping | a great deal | somewhat | very little | none |
| Feeding | a great deal | somewhat | very little | none |
| Elimination | a great deal | somewhat | very little | none |
| Lack of a predictable schedule | a great deal | somewhat | very little | none |
| Other (specify): | | | | |
| _____ | a great deal | somewhat | very little | none |
| _____ | a great deal | somewhat | very little | none |
| _____ | a great deal | somewhat | very little | none |
| _____ | a great deal | somewhat | very little | none |

*Figure 11–12.   Degree of Bother Inventory. (Broussard, E.R. [1978]. Psychosocial disorders in children: Early assessment of infants at risk.* Continuing Education for the Family Physician, 8, *44)*

Usually the cord is blue-white; any change in color should be noted. Yellow discoloration, for example, could indicate hemolytic disease. Bleeding around the cord could be due to either inadequate cord-tying or a bleeding disorder. A purulent and foul-smelling discharge or redness should be reported since this is a sign of infection, which is often due to *Staphylococcus aureus*. The infecting organisms enter the cut surface of the cord. Infection of the umbilicus is called *omphalitis.*

Since the umbilical cord may be a source for bacterial infection, parents should be instructed in how to care for the umbilicus and what to expect. Umbilical cord care varies. Parents may be instructed to use an antibiotic ointment two or three times a day; to use alcohol wipes once a day; or to give no special care at all until the cord falls off. However, the umbilicus should be kept dry until it is healed. The diaper is kept under the cord to prevent irritation from rubbing and dampness from urine (Fig. 11-13), and parents are usually advised not to place the baby in a bath until the cord falls off—normally 7 to 10 days after birth.

### Eye Care

There are three common types of neonatal conjunctivitis: chemical/allergic, chlamydial, and bacterial. Bacterial causes of conjunctivitis include staphylococci, streptococci, or pneumococci. These infections begin about the third day of life;

signs include inflamed conjunctivae, edematous lids, and purulent discharge. They usually disappear by themselves in about 10 days (Cugali & Moore, 1984).

It has been 100 years since Crede began preventing gonococcal ophthalmia by instillation of silver nitrate. This treatment resulted in a dramatic decrease in what had been the leading cause of blindness. Signs of a bacterial infection caused by *Neisseria gonorrhoeae* occur from 8 to 10 days after birth with edema and a purulent profuse exudate. The cornea can become scarred in a very short period of time—within 24 hours—so treatment must be initiated immediately.

The American Academy of Pediatrics currently recommends instillation of a 1% silver nitrate solution in single-dose ampules or single-use tubes, or an ophthalmic ointment containing 1% tetracycline or 0.5% erythromycin (American Academy of Pediatrics, 1988). A 1% solution of silver nitrate is administered, using a separate ampule for each eye. The drops are placed into the conjunctival sac. After 1 minute any excess is wiped away. Silver nitrate was originally administered shortly after birth, but research on the importance of eye contact in the bonding process has resulted in the recommendation that it be delayed until 1 hour after birth.

The Centers for Disease Control (CDC) has approved tetracycline and erythromycin ophthalmic preparations as

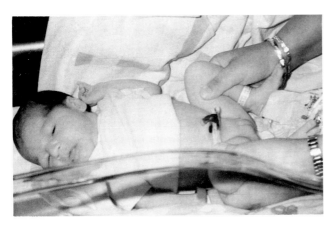

*Figure 11–13. Umbilical stump. (Courtesy of Early Discharge Planning, Texas Tech University Health Sciences Center, El Paso, Texas)*

alternatives to silver nitrate. Mooney, Green, Epstein, and Hashisaki (1984) conducted a study of ophthalmitis following the instillation of all three preparations. They found an unacceptably high rate of bacterial ophthalmitis in neonates receiving erythromicin ointment for prevention of gonococcal ophthalmia neonatorum. It was suggested that the increased rate of infection is related to the fact that erythromycin ophthalmic preparation is available only in the ointment form, which is difficult to apply to the neonate's eye. They also indicated that the incidental insertion of ungloved fingers into the eye during the instillation process provided an opportunity for contamination (Mooney, Green, Epstein, & Hashisaki, 1984). The use of a liquid tetracycline preparation resulted in a decrease in non-gonococcal ophthalmitis rates. Because ophthalmia neonatorum is caused by chlamydia as well as gonorrhea and erythromycin acts on both organisms with fewer side effects, erythromycin theoretically seems to be the drug of choice. However, the research of Mooney et al. (1984) indicates that further research must be conducted before silver nitrate is completely abandoned.

Silver nitrate can cause severe chemical conjunctivitis in a number of cases, and overdoses may cause blindness. In fact, some authorities think that if a chemical conjunctivitis does not result from the instillation, the prophylaxis is inadequate (Cugali & Moore, 1984). This irritation should disappear in 1 or 2 days.

Chlamydial infections are acquired as the infant passes through the birth canal. Signs of infection occur from 5 to 14 days after birth and include profuse purulent discharge and edema. The treatment consists of local applications of tetracycline or erythromycin; silver nitrate is ineffective.

An interesting treatment for eye infections is the use of human milk, especially *colostrum*—the thin yellowish fluid secreted from the breasts before birth and for the first few days after birth. It has been proposed that the mammary glands and the conjunctiva are part of a shared mucosal defense system. Therefore, the antibodies produced by the mammary glands could be passed to the neonate by human milk. Colostrum would be injected into the infant's eyes at birth and continued oral ingestion would assist in fighting pathogens (Cugali & Moore, 1984). It has been well over 10 years since early publication of this treatment; more research needs to be done before it would be widely accepted.

## Circumcision Care

Circumcision, the surgical removal of the prepuce or foreskin of the penis, is elected by various cultural and religious groups as well as many segments of the general population. It is not usually performed for medical reasons. However, parents frequently ask nurses for guidance regarding whether or not their son should be circumcised. Some proponents feel that circumcision reduces the risk of penile cancer; however, the relationship between circumcision and various types of cancer has not been conclusively established. Parents often express concern over whether the neonate experiences pain during the procedure. The American Academy of Pediatrics (1987) is currently investigating the possible use of anesthetics for circumcision. Nurses should be familiar with the factors involved in the decision about whether a child should be circumcised, but parents must ultimately make the decision.

The procedure is accomplished by restraining the child (Fig. 11-14) and using either a clamp device or a plastic bell. The clamp crushes the nerve endings and blood vessels. If the plastic bell is used, it is secured around the glans by a tight string. The parents should be instructed that the bell will remain in place until the foreskin atrophies and falls off, along with the bell (usually within 10 days). Postoperatively a petroleum dressing is applied loosely for a few hours to prevent adherence to the diaper. Dry dressings must be moistened with hydrogen peroxide for removal.

Because most mothers and babies are discharged between 1 and 3 days after delivery, nursing interventions should include checking the status of healing while the infant is in the hospital and educating the parents about signs of infection and hemorrhage. Urinary flow should be checked to be certain that no obstruction is present.

Parents should be told that the glans will form a white mucoid coating. They should not attempt to remove this protective coating. In order to prevent the diaper from adhering to the penis, petroleum jelly can be applied to the glans and covered with a clean gauze square. The parents should be instructed to cleanse the penis with clear water and to apply petroleum jelly and a fresh gauze square with each diaper change. Although some blood-tinged discharge may be seen during the first few days, there should not be obvious bleeding. Complications from circumcision are infrequent but can be serious and

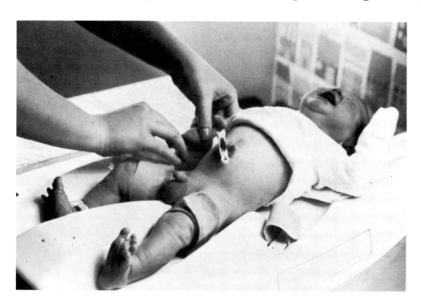

*Figure 11–14.   Infant in restraint for circumcision.*

include infection; hemorrhage; injury to the penis, scrotum, or glans (e.g., coronal fistula); or loss of penile skin. Bleeding, continuous oozing, or a foul-smelling discharge should be reported to the physician.

### Skin Care

Immediately after birth the baby has blood on the face and head that can be removed by washing. *Vernix caseosa* is found in varying amounts on the neonate; because it is thought to be both bacteriostatic and insulating, it is not immediately removed. The initial bath is done after the vital signs have stabilized. The baby is sponged with plain water, and the nurse uses this opportunity to carefully observe the infant.

Sometimes neonatal *impetigo* is identified. This is an infectious disease caused by *Staphylococcus aureus*. The lesions are pustular and the vesicles rupture, which results in moist yellow crusts. The crusts must be soaked off with warm water before topical antibiotics, such as bacitracin or neosporin, are applied. The disease can become epidemic if precautions are not taken. Skin and wound isolation techniques should be used, including isolating the infant from other babies and wearing overgowns and gloves. Many times the lesions are pruritic, necessitating covering the hands with the undershirt or using elbow restraints. Parents should be taught how to prevent the spread of infection by careful handwashing and disposal of used compresses. The infant's arms may need to be restrained, so parents must be taught to properly apply restraints and to provide periods of movement.

### Thrush

*Thrush* is an infection caused by the fungus *Candida albicans*. When examining the mouth, numerous small white and gray patches are visible on the tongue and mouth.

These patches cannot be scraped away as milk curds can. Neonates can become infected with thrush as they pass through the vagina, by poor handwashing techniques of care-givers, or by contaminated bottles, nipples, or pacifiers. Babies of diabetic mothers are at risk because the high glucose of the maternal urine provides a good medium for yeast to grow; it is then easy for the infection to spread to the vaginal canal, where the infant is exposed during delivery. Babies receiving antibiotic therapy and those with immunological deficiencies are particularly susceptible.

Treatment consists of the topical application of nystatin (Mycostatin) in a dosage of 100,000 to 200,000 units (1–2 mL), given slowly and gently over the entire oral cavity four times a day after feedings. The baby's mouth should be rinsed with water after feedings and before the medication is applied. Bottles and nipples should be carefully washed and boiled. Treatment usually lasts for 1 week. Sometimes a 1% solution of aqueous gentian violet is used on the lesions. After application the baby is placed on the abdomen so that the saliva will drain out. Gentian violet will stain clothing purple (sodium bicarbonate is helpful in removing these stains). Sometimes a bright red monilial rash occurs in the diaper area along with the oral infection. The rash associated with thrush is smooth, shiny, bright red, papular, and nummular (coin shaped). It has well-circumscribed borders and occasionally has satellite lesions in the inguinal creases. The diaper area must be kept as dry as possible. The physician may order nystatin cream or lotion, which is applied two or three times a day for 7 to 10 days.

### Hemorrhage

*Hemorrhage* in the newborn is due to a deficiency of vitamin K. The fetus receives vitamin K in utero, but colonization of the intestinal flora must occur before it is synthesized. Therefore, all infants' supply of vitamin K is inadequate for the first few days of life. Vitamin K is essential for the synthesis of prothrombin and other coagulation factors in the liver. Vitamin K deficiency may result in a generalized tendency toward bleeding, with the gut as the most frequent site. Bleeding usually occurs on the second or third day postpartum. Signs to observe for include epistaxis, hematuria, bloody/black stools, ecchymosis of the skin or scalp, or blood oozing from the umbilicus or circumcision. If active bleeding occurs, it may be treated with 1 mg to 2 mg of vitamin K intravenously. Fresh whole blood transfusions may be required for severe bleeding.

Most hospitals follow a preventive procedure of an IM injection of vitamin K (0.5–1.0 mg) after birth. The vastus lateralis muscle is used for the injection. In addition, breast-fed infants must receive vitamin K supplementation because of the initial period of relative starvation before milk is established and the low vitamin K content of human milk.

## Neonatal Septicemia

*Neonatal septicemia* is a generalized bacterial infection occurring during the first month of life. It affects one in 250 premature infants and one in 1500 term infants (Aronoff & Speck, 1983). The mortality rate is high, usually between 30% and 50%. Males, premature infants, and bottle-fed babies appear to have increased susceptibility.

It is generally believed that all neonatal infections are opportunistic and that any bacterial species is capable of causing neonatal septicemia. The group B streptococcus is considered the predominant cause, but *E. coli,* group A streptococcus, and *Streptococcus viridans* have also been found (Aronoff & Speck, 1983). Infections acquired perinatally present with non-specific signs during the first 4 days of life: poor feeding, weak suck, weak cry, lethargy, and irritability. The signs and symptoms of dehydration, such as sunken fontanels, dry skin, and decreased skin turgor, are treated with intravenous therapy. Temperature instability is also evident. Gastrointestinal disturbances; neurological disturbances such as seizures, hypotonia, or tremors; and a full fontanel or respiratory and cardiac symptoms of distress may also be present. Late onset septicemia may occur at any time up to 4 months of age. The most common presentation for late onset septicemia is meningitis.

The direct technique for the diagnosis of septicemia is a blood culture; a positive blood culture confirms the diagnosis. Cerebrospinal fluid cultures are obtained in all infants with suspected neonatal sepsis because nervous system involvement occurs in approximately 30% of all cases. Urine cultures are necessary because the genitourinary tract may serve as a portal of entry as well as a deposit site for bacteria disseminated by the blood stream. Surface cultures—that is, cultures from the skin, external auditory canal, and umbilicus—and gastric aspirate are of little or no value in the diagnosis and treatment (Aronoff & Speck, 1983).

Indirect diagnostic tests include a white blood count and, more importantly, the differentiated white blood count. In the differentiated WBC there may be an increase in the number of immature neutrophils, or the absolute neutrophil count may be decreased. The erythrocyte sedimentation rate (ESR) is elevated in infants with bacterial infection, and abnormal values for the C-reactive protein are evident in 85% of these cases (Aronoff & Speck, 1983).

Treatment of septicemia includes a combination of antimicrobial agents consisting of a broad-spectrum semisynthetic penicillin (such as ampicillin) and an aminoglycoside antibiotic (such as gentamicin or tobramicin). Treatment for early onset neonatal septicemia should begin within the first 72 hours of life. When the infant is over 1 week of age, treatment for septicemia must include additional coverage for staphylococcus and hospital-acquired, gram-negative enteric microorganisms. Drug therapy is continued for a minimum of 10 days and is often administered via intravenous infusion. Important aspects of care include minimizing physiological and environmental stressors, maintaining a neutral thermal environment, isolation, and proper handwashing. Nursing observations should be directed toward measuring of the anterior fontanel, watching for signs of bulging, and observing for pyarthrosis (pus in joint cavities), which may present with limited joint movement and signs of shock.

## Hemolytic Disease of the Newborn

*Hemolytic disease of the newborn* (erythroblastosis fetalis) results when an Rh-negative mother receives Rh-positive blood that contains the D antigen, e.g., from a blood transfusion or from fetal blood. The mother forms antibodies against the D antigen. Ordinarily the firstborn child is not affected. If untreated, however, subsequent Rh-positive children will develop hemolytic disease and anemia. In this disease, the liver is unable to handle the large amounts of bilirubin, which results in hyperbilirubinemia and jaundice. Milder types of the disease are associated with ABO incompatibilities.

Identification is done by history of the mother's blood type and by analysis of cord blood for direct and indirect bilirubin, fetal blood type, and hemoglobin concentration. A reticulocyte count and a Coomb's test to identify antibodies in the infant's red blood cells are also frequently done.

Prevention of maternal sensitization is a primary goal. RhoGAM-R, an immune globulin against the D antigen, should be given to Rh-negative mothers in the seventh month of pregnancy and within 72 hours after the delivery or abortion. This is done to prevent the mother from forming antibodies that would be harmful to her next child. When compensation by the liver and spleen is not sufficient, the infant can develop *hydrops fetalis,* which is characterized by edema, ascites, and cardiac decompensation.

## ABO Incompatibility

*ABO incompatibility* occurs when a mother having type A blood, with A antigen and antibodies to type B blood, carries a baby with B antigen or type B blood, or when a mother with B antigen and antibodies to type A blood carries a baby having type A blood. A mother with O blood has no antigens but does have antibodies to A and B blood types. In ABO incompatibility, the mother's antibodies attack the antigens or the infant's red blood cells. Red blood cell destruction results in anemia. The red blood cell destruction increases the amount of bilirubin transported to the liver. The liver is unable to accommodate the hemolysis of the large amount of bilirubin; this results in hyperbilirubinemia and jaundice.

When a diagnosis of hydrops fetalis is made, an intrauterine exchange transfusion can be done or an early delivery may be indicated. Amniocentesis is done, and if the fetus is beyond 33 weeks' gestation it is delivered. The exchange transfusion is done as quickly as possible to prevent *kernicterus.* In kernicterus, unconjugated bilirubin is deposited in the basal ganglia and cerebellum, and irreversible brain damage results.

At birth the child appears free from jaundice but within the first few hours rapidly develops hyperbilirubinemia. Lethargy, decreased reflexes, and poor feeding are additional signs of severe hyperbilirubinemia. Neurological signs might include irritability, a high-pitched cry, and arching of the back. Infants who are severely affected should have an exchange transfusion as soon as possible. In this procedure, one catheter is inserted into the umbilical vein and another into the umbilical artery. The latter is used to monitor blood pressure and blood gases and to administer fluids. A two-times blood volume exchange is done for a total volume of 150 mL to 170 mL/kg. The blood used is the baby's blood type and must also be Rh-negative. The baby's blood is removed and replaced in quantities of 10 mL at a time until the procedure is completed. Calcium is administered during the exchange to combat hypocalcemia. Complications might include shock, hypotension, and electrolyte imbalance. The nurse must carefully assess the child during the procedure for untoward signs and must record accurately the "in and out" amounts of blood removed and transfused and the total transfusion volume. The infant is then given phototherapy. Bilirubin, electrolytes, hematocrit, and hemoglobin levels are monitored. A second exchange may be done if needed.

Throughout these procedures, parents must be kept informed and encouraged to participate in the care of their infant whenever possible.

## Nutritional Needs

The decision whether the baby is to be breast- or bottle-fed is made by the parents, usually before birth. A prime consideration once feeding has begun is whether the infant is getting enough nourishment. It is important to ensure that the mother is in a comfortable position for feeding, that there is enough time to feed the baby (about 30 minutes), and that the atmosphere is as private and relaxed as possible to facilitate bonding.

### Breast-Feeding

Success at breast-feeding is related to maternal desire to breast-feed, the mother's intake of sufficient fluids, and the mother's ability to obtain sufficient rest (Fig. 11-15). Success is also related to the infant's ability to suck and swallow. Sucking and swallowing improve with maturity of the orofacial muscles; conditions such as cleft palate and cerebral palsy may make these motions difficult. Beginning breast-feeding in the delivery room has two major advantages: colostrum is drained rapidly, which aids in the peristalsis of meconium, and lactation is stimulated. If the first breast-feeding is delayed, the baby should not be fed for the first few hours. Sometimes a small amount of plain water is offered to the baby about an hour before the first breast-feeding in order to observe for signs of excessive mucus. Milk begins to replace colostrum in the second to fourth day, and the baby will probably need to nurse every 3 hours because breast milk is more readily assimilated than cow's milk. Infants should be fed on demand; a baby who sleeps well between feedings and gains weight is being adequately fed.

If the child cannot suck, the mother should be taught to pump her breasts. An electric or hand pump can be used. For premature or ill babies, milk can be pumped at home, frozen, and brought to the hospital for feedings. Breast milk provides adequate nutrition for all babies (Table 11-7). There is no need for vitamin D supplementation if the baby is routinely exposed to sunlight. Fluoride

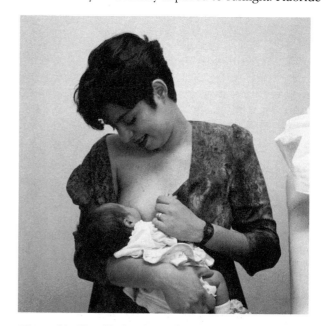

*Figure 11–15.   Mother breastfeeding.*

*Table 11–7. Composition of Milk*

| Component | Human Milk | Cow's Milk |
|---|---|---|
| Water (mL/100 mL) | 87.1 | 87.2 |
| Energy (cal/100 mL) | 60–75 | 66 |
| Total solids (g/100 mL) | 12.9 | 12.8 |
| Protein (%) | 0.8–0.9 | 3.5 |
| Fat (%) | 3–5 | 3.7 |
| Lactose (%) | 6.9–7.2 | 4.9 |
| Ash (minerals) (%) | 0.2 | 0.7 |
| Protein (% of total protein) | | |
|   Casein | 40 | 82 |
|   Whey | 60 | 18 |
| Ash, major components per liter | | |
|   Calcium (mg) | 340 | 1170 |
|   Phosphorus (mg) | 140 | 920 |
|   Sodium (mEq) | 7 | 22 |
| Vitamins per liter | | |
|   Vitamin A (IU) | 1898 | 1025 |
|   Thiamin (mg) | 160 | 440 |
|   Riboflavin (mg) | 360 | 1750 |
|   Niacin (mg) | 1470 | 940 |
|   Vitamin C (mg) | 43 | 11 |

(From Lauwers, J., Woessner, C., & CEA of Greater Philadelphia. [1983]. *Counseling the nursing mother.* Wayne, NJ: Avery Publishing Company)

supplementation is recommended until the infant is able to take a sufficient amount of water.

Breast milk contains macrophages that phagocytose microorganisms and kill bacteria. The highest concentration of immunoglobulins is found in colostrum, and they continue to be found in smaller amounts in milk. Lactoferrin, an iron-binding glycoprotein, is found in breast milk also. Physiologically the intestines of breast-fed infants are colonized by *Lactobacillus bifidus,* which is gram-positive and is thought to contain the antiviral substance interferon (Chow et al., 1984).

There are only a few cases in which mothers should not breast-feed. Infants with galactosemia should not breast-feed because they lack the ability to metabolize lactose. Mothers who have hepatitis B or who are asymptomatic carriers of hepatitis B should not breast-feed because of the possibility of infecting the infant. Infants diagnosed as having phenylketonuria (PKU), an inborn error of metabolism, must receive a special formula. In this condition there is an absence of the liver enzyme phenylalanine hydrolase, which is essential for the breakdown of tyrosine, an amino acid. Without this breakdown, mental retardation occurs. Lofenalac is the most commonly used formula. It is a casein hydrolysate, with 95% of phenylalanine removed. Parents should be informed of the required long-term dietary restrictions. In older children, Phenyl-free, a formula completely free of phenylalanine,

may be used. These formulas must be supplemented with evaporated milk or other formulas because phenylalanine is necessary for growth. This means that mothers who wish to breast-feed may do so on a limited basis.

Problems mothers may encounter in breast-feeding include sore nipples, breast engorgement, and mastitis. If any of these conditions persist, mothers should be advised to consult with their physician, nurse midwife, or nurse practitioner.

## Bottle Feeding

The manufacture and sale of all formulas is governed by the Infant Formula Act of 1980. Infant formulas have protein, carbohydrates, fats, vitamins, and minerals. Approximately 40% to 50% of all newborns in the United States are bottle-fed, despite the increased rate of breast-feeding.

Infants need 50 calories per pound of body weight per day. Formulas are standardized at 20 calories per ounce. A seven-pound infant would need 350 calories, or 17.5 ounces, per day. The clean technique for formula preparation has been found to be as effective as sterilization. The bottle can be left at room temperature for about 1 hour before feeding. Frequently parents cannot wait an hour before feeding the baby, so the bottle can be placed in a pan of hot water. The temperature of the formula must be checked by shaking several drops of the warmed formula on the inside of the wrist to be certain that the formula is neither too cold nor too warm.

The various techniques for preparing bottle formula are shown in Table 11-8; these include the aseptic, terminal sterilization, and single bottle methods. Depending on the method selected, nurses should instruct parents in the proper techniques.

The baby should always be held for bottle feeding, and the bottle should be tilted so that the formula fills the neck of the bottle (Fig. 11-16). This prevents the baby from swallowing too much air. The infant should be burped frequently, at least once midway through the feeding and again after the feeding. Babies may be burped while being held over the shoulder or when held on the lap in a sitting position. If the baby is seated on the lap, the chest is supported with one hand while the back is gently rubbed or patted with the other hand. The support of the chin and trunk allows for the clear passage of air from the stomach. After either bottle- or breast-feeding, the infant should be placed on the right side to facilitate the rising of air (Fig. 11-17).

The infant's size has a direct bearing on the amount of formula needed. After the first week, and for the first month, about 2 to 2¼ ounces of formula per pound of body weight is the general rule for feeding. The intervals between feedings may vary. Within one 24-hour period there may be one period of time when closer feedings are necessary. Parents need to learn to distinguish their baby's hunger cries from other cries.

*Table 11-8.  Formula Preparation Methods*

**Aseptic Formula Preparation**

1. Wash all equipment that will be used (including measuring cups, spoons, mixing bowls, and bottles) in warm, soapy water, and rinse thoroughly.
2. Place all equipment, except nipples, in a large pan, cover with water, cover pan, and boil for 10 minutes.
3. Place nipples in a small pan and boil for 3 minutes.
4. Boil water needed for formula for 5 minutes.
5. Drain water from equipment pan and let stand for several minutes. Do not touch any surface that will come into contact with the formula, such as the insides of containers or measuring cups.
6. Pour the specified amount of boiled water into the measuring cup or bowl.
7. Measure and mix the prescribed amount of formula or evaporated milk into the boiled water.
8. Stir with a long-handled spoon that has been boiled.
9. Pour into sterile bottles.
10. Put nipples and caps on bottles, being certain to touch only the edges.
11. Refrigerate the formula until it is needed.

**Terminal Sterilization**

1. Wash bottles, nipples, and caps in warm soapy water and rinse thoroughly.
2. Prepare formula using clean equipment.
3. Put formula in bottles and put nipples and caps in place, being careful not to screw caps on too tightly.
4. Place filled bottles in sterilizer rack (or a large pan with a pie pan that has been pierced with holes placed in the bottom).
5. Fill sterilizer with water up to the level of the shoulders of the bottles, cover, and bring to a boil. Boil for 25 minutes.
6. Remove sterilizer from heat. Do not lift the lid until the sides are cool to the touch. Cooling takes about 2 hours.
7. Remove the bottles, tighten the caps, and refrigerate until needed.

**Single Bottle Formula Preparation**

1. Wash bottles, nipples, and caps in warm soapy water, rinse thoroughly, and let dry.
2. Pour the desired amount of (ready-to-pour) formula into the bottle. If condensed formula is used, the formula and water are added.
3. Put the nipples and caps in place and feed infant.

## Neonatal Risk Factors

The neonatal period is the highest risk period for survival among all childhood age groups. "At risk" babies have life-threatening problems or problems that may have serious consequences affecting their subsequent quality of life. Male neonates continue to have the highest mortality rates.

The United States ranked twenty-first in infant mortality in 1988, with 10.0 deaths per 1000 live births (Wegman, 1990). As birth weight increases up to 4000 g, neonatal mortality decreases. Two-thirds of infant deaths occur in the neonatal period, and over half of these neonates have birth weights under 2500 g (Hogue, Strauss, Buehler, &

*Figure 11-16.  Proud grandmother bottle-feeding infant. Note position of bottle.*

Smith, 1989). These statistics may reflect advanced technology in instituting and maintaining pregnancies in cases requiring extensive medical support that may not be available in other areas of the world. In 1980, the neonatal mortality (NNM) statistics ranged from 647.6 per 1000 liveborn infants weighing 500 g to 999 g, to 1.4 per 1000 liveborn infants weighing 3500 g to 3999 g (Hogue et al., 1989). In 1988, 5.6% of white babies, 4.7% of Chinese babies, and 13.0% of black babies weighed less than 2500 g. The rate for black babies is twice as high as for other groups (Wegman, 1990). The goal for the United States is an infant mortality rate of no more than 9 deaths per 1000 live births, as stated in the 1990 Objectives for the Nation (Hogue et al., 1989).

To assist in caring for babies at risk, regionalization for providing neonatal care has been developed. Table 11-9 shows the levels of care and characteristics of these levels.

*Figure 11-17.  Infant lying on right side after feeding.*

### Table 11–9. Regionalization of Neonatal Care and Facility Characteristics

| Level of Care | Characteristics |
|---|---|
| Level I | Small, usually rural community hospitals providing primary obstetric and neonatal care to "normal" patients |
| Level II (Intermediate Care) | Larger hospitals with the ability to care for moderate risk pregnant women and moderately ill infants in addition to "normal" mothers and babies |
| Level III | Large teaching hospitals serving a large geographic area that accept referrals from all Level I and II hospitals in their area. They treat neonates with serious problems and, when located in a children's hospital, can perform surgery. Frequently they have associated high risk obstetrical units. |

Factors associated with neonatal risk can be identified by careful prenatal history-taking and monitoring, assessment and intervention during labor and delivery, and careful postnatal assessment.

## Prenatal Assessment

### Prenatal History and Risk Factors

An extensive, accurate prenatal history is essential for the anticipation and preparation for babies who may be at risk. The history should be obtained by asking for information using terms the client can readily understand, e.g., "Did you have any problems with your other pregnancies? Did you have to stay in the hospital longer than expected? Did the baby come home with you?" A history that suggests problems may be further investigated by evaluative tests such as sonograms or amniocentesis.

Prenatal risk factors are identified in Table 11-10. Four

### Table 11–10. Prenatal Risk Factors

Inadequate education in health maintenance
Financial deficits (e.g., no transportation, no insurance)
Maternal malnutrition
Emotional unreadiness (one or both parents)
Inherited conditions
Age of parents (other younger than 16 years or older than 35 years; father older than 40 years)
Size of mother: Height less than 5 ft; more than 20% over or under height and weight standards
Member of a ethnic minority
Substance use/abuse; use of certain medications
Multipara
Bleeding in the third trimester

major risk factors are genetic factors, intrauterine growth retardation, infections, and drug use.

*Genetic Factors.* A variety of genetic disorders can be detected during the prenatal period by the use of amniocentesis. Amniocentesis is usually performed between the fourteenth and sixteenth week from the first day of the last menstrual period. It is designed to detect chromosomal disorders such as trisomy-21 (Down syndrome), trisomy-13, trisomy-18, and abnormalities of the sex chromosomes, including Klinefelter syndrome and fragile X syndrome. Chromosomal disorders are changes in the structure or number of any of the chromosomes; see Table 11-11 for a list of the incidence of selected chromosomal abnormalities. Selected autosomal dominant and recessive, as well as X-linked dominant and recessive disorders, are shown in Table 11-12.

There are 23 pairs of chromosomes in humans that are responsible for transmitting genetic traits and conditions. Twenty-two of these pairs of chromosomes are autosomes—chromosomes that are not sex chromosomes. Trisomy-21 is an autosomal trisomy. In addition to sex-

### Table 11–11. The Incidence of Selected Chromosome Abnormalities in Liveborn Infants*

| Abnormality | Incidence |
|---|---|
| **Autosomal Trisomies** | |
| Down syndrome | 1:650–1:1000 live births |
| Trisomy 13 (Patau syndrome) | 1:4000–1:10,000 live births |
| Trisomy 18 (Edwards syndrome) | 1:3500–1:7500 live births |
| **Sex Chromosome Disorders** | |
| 45, X (Turner syndrome) | 1:2500–1:8000 live female births |
| 47, XXX (triple X) | 1:850–1:1250 live female births |
| 47, XXY (Klinefelter syndrome) | 1:500–1:1000 live male births |
| 47, XYY | 1:840–1:1000 live male births |
| Other sex chromosome abnormalities (males) | ~1:1300 live male births |
| Other sex chromosome abnormalities (females) | ~1:3000 live female births |
| **Structural Rearrangements (e.g., translocations, deletions, etc.)** | ~1:440 live births |

*Based on statistics from surveys in different populations and not age-adjusted.
(From Cohen, F. L. [1984]. *Clinical genetics in nursing practice.* Philadelphia: J. B. Lippincott Company, p. 34)

*Table 11–12.  Selected Genetic Disorders*

| Disorder | Occurrence | Brief Description |
|---|---|---|
| **Autosomal Dominant Inheritance** | | |
| Achondroplasia | 1:10,000–1:12,000 | Short-limbed dwarfism, large head, narrowing of spinal canal |
| Familial hypercholesterolemia (Type II) | 1:200–1:500 | Deficiency in cell receptors regulating degradation of low-density lipoproteins and cholesterol synthesis; xanthomas, coronary disease |
| Huntington's disease | 1:18,000–1:25,000  (United States) 1:333,000 (Japan) | Progressive neurologic disease; involuntary muscle movements with jerkiness, gait changes, lack of coordination; mental deterioration with memory loss, speech problems, personality changes, confusion, and decreased mental capacity |
| Neurofibromatosis (von Recklighausen's disease) | 1:3000–1:3300 | Disorder of neural-crest derived cells with skin, central and peripheral nervous system manifestations; café-au-lait spots, neurofibromas, and malignant progression are common; variable expression |
| Nail–patella  syndrome | ? | Nail abnormalities, hypoplasia or absent patella, iliac horns, elbow dysplasia, renal lesions, iris abnormalities |
| Polydactyly | 1:100–1:300  (blacks) 1:630–1:3300  (Caucasians) | Extra (supernumerary) digit on hands or feet |
| Polycystic renal disease (adult) | 1:250–1:1250 | Enlarged kidneys, hematuria, proteinuria, abdominal mass; may be associated with hypertension, hepatic cysts; see cystic kidneys on x-ray films. |
| Osteogenesis imperfecta | 1:25,000 | Blue sclera, fragile bones with multiple fractures, dental anomalies |
| Heriditary spherocytosis | 1:4500–1:5000 | Red cell membrane defect leading to abnormal shape, impaired survival and hemolytic anemia |
| Tuberous sclerosis (epiloia) | ~1:100,000 | White leaf-shaped macules, seizures, mental retardation, erythemic nodular rash in butterfly pattern on face; may develop retinal pathology and rhabdomyosarcoma of the heart |
| von Willebrand's disease | 1:100,000 | Deficiency or defect in plasma protein called von Willebrand factor, leading to prolonged bleeding time, bleeding from mucous membranes |
| **Autosomal Recessive Inheritance** | | |
| Albinism (tyrosinase negative) | 1:15000–1:40,000 1:85–1:650 (Native Americans) | Melanin lacking in skin, hair and eyes; nystagmus; photophobia; susceptible to neoplasia |
| Cystic fibrosis | 1:2,000–1:2500 (Caucasians) 1:16,000 (American blacks) | Pancreatic insufficiency and malabsorption; abnormal exocrine glands; chronic pulmonary disease; basic defect unknown |
| Argininosuccinic-aciduria | 1:60,000–1:70,000 | Hyperammonemia, mental retardation, vomiting, seizures, coma, abnormal hair shaft; urea cycle disorder in which argininosuccinase is deficient |
| Familial dysautonomia (Riley-Day syndrome) | 1:10,000–1:20,000 (Ashkenazi Jews) | Dysfunction of autonomic nervous system, sensory abnormalities, small stature, poor coordination, scoliosis, lack of tears leading to corneal ulcers. |
| Hurler syndrome | 1–2:100,000 | α-L-iduronidase deficiency leading to storage of dermatan and heparan sulfate; psychomotor retardation, corneal clouding, skeletal and connective tissue abnormalities, coarse facies |
| Sickle cell disease | 1:400–1:600 (American blacks) | Hemoglobinopathy with chronic hemolytic anemia, growth retardation, susceptibility to infection, painful crises, leg ulcers, dactylitis |
| Tay-Sachs disease | 1:3600 (Ashkenazi Jews) 1:360,000 (others) | Progressive mental and motor retardation with onset at about 6 months, poor muscle tone, deafness, blindness, convulsions, decerebrate rigidity and death by 3 to 4 years of age |

*(continued)*

*Table 11—12.  Selected Genetic Disorders (Continued)*

| Disorder | Occurrence | Brief Description |
| --- | --- | --- |
| Xeroderma pigmentosa | 1:60,000–1:100,000 | Defective DNA repair; sun sensitivity, freckling, skin atrophic lesions, skin cancer develops; photophobia and keratitis; death usually by adulthood |
| Metachromatic leukodystrophy | 1:40,000 | Arylsulfatase A deficiency leading to disintegration of myelin and accumulation of lipids in white matter of brain; psychomotor degeneration |
| **X-Linked Dominant Inheritance** | | |
| Orofaciodigital syndrome | 1:50,000 | Cleft palate, tongue or lip; facial hypoplasia; clinodactyly, short digits, possible impaired intelligence |
| Pseudohypoparathyroidism (Albright's hereditary osteodystrophy) | Rare | Short stature, delayed dentition, hypocalcemia, hyperphosphatemia, mineralization of skeleton, round facies |
| Vitamin D–resistant rickets (familial hypophosphatemia) | 1:25,000 | Disorder of renal tubular phosphate transport; low serum phosphate, rickets, bowed legs, growth deficiency with ultimate short stature |
| **X-Linked Recessive Inheritance** | | |
| Color blindness (red green deutan) | 8:100 Caucasian males 4:100–5:100 Caucasian females 2:100–4:100 black males | Normal visual acuity, defective color vision with red–green confusion |
| Duchenne muscular dystrophy | 1:3000–1:5000 males | Muscle weakness, atrophy contractures with progression; eventual respiratory insufficiency and death |
| Fabry disease | 1:40,000 males | Inborn error of sphingolipid metabolism with deficient lysosomal enzyme, $\alpha$-galactosidase A; skin lesions, corneal opacities, episodic pain; renal and cardiac dysfunction and brain lesions |
| G6PD deficiency | 1:10 black American males 1:50 black American females | Enzyme deficiency with subtypes, showing effects in RBC; usually asymptomatic unless under stress or exposed to certain drugs or infection (see Chap. 15) |
| Hemophilia A | 1:2500–1:4000 male births | Coagulation disorder due to deficiency of Factor VIII |
| Hemophilia B (Christmas disease) | 1:4000–1:7000 male births | Coagulation disorder caused by deficiency of Factor IX |
| Hunter syndrome | 1:100,000 male births | Mucopolysaccharide storage disorder with iduronate sulfatase deficiency; mental retardation, dwarfing, stiff joints, deafness; mild and severe forms |
| Lesch-Nyhan syndrome | 1:300,000 male births | Deficiency of purine metabolism enzyme HGPRT; hyperuricemia, mental retardation, spasticity, athetosis, self-mutilation |
| Menkes disease | 1:35,000 male births | Copper deficiency due to defective transport; psychomotor retardation, seizures, spasticity, hypothermia, kinky, sparse hair (pili torti) |
| X-linked ichthyosis | 1:5000–1:6000 males | May be born with sheets of scales (collodion babies); dry scaling skin; corneal opacities; steroid sulfatase deficiency |

(From Cohen, F. L. [1984]. *Clinical genetics in nursing practice*. Philadelphia: J. B. Lippincott Company, p. 81)

chromosome abnormalities, there are a number of autosomal inherited conditions.

In *autosomal dominant inheritance,* the traits are found in both sexes in equal proportions; there is no sex difference in clinical manifestations. Later age of onset is frequent, and male-to-male transmission is possible. There is no carrier status. Disorders caused by autosomal dominant inheritance are listed in Table 11-12.

*Autosomal recessive conditions* can affect either sex, since the mutant gene is located on an autosome rather than a chromosome. Both parents carry the mutant gene but do not manifest the disease. With each pregnancy there is a 25% chance that the child of carriers will receive the gene from each parent and consequently manifest the disease. Children born without the trait have approximately a 65% chance of receiving the gene from one parent and, consequently, being a carrier. See Table 11-12 for a list of autosomal recessive disorders.

*X-linked dominant disorders* are seen less frequently than X-linked recessive disorders. They are carried on the X chromosome, a sex chromosome, and, therefore, are not autosomal inherited disorders. Males always inherit these disorders from the mother; they cannot inherit them from the father. There is a 50% chance for each pregnancy that the offspring will be affected (Cohen, 1984). A list of X-linked dominant disorders is shown in Table 11-12.

*X-linked recessive conditions* occur most frequently in males, who pass the gene to their daughters; they become carriers and then pass it on to their sons. The risk for male children is 50%. The risk for females is much lower because the probability of two X chromosomes having a problem gene is less than that for a male who may have an affected X and Y chromosome. A list of X-linked recessive disorders is found in Table 11-12.

Factors other than genetic inheritance may also place a baby at risk. Sometimes there is a tendency for certain conditions to occur in families, yet they do not fit into the mendelian pattern, e.g., hip dislocation. A number of conditions may be caused by a combination of genetic and environmental factors (*multifactorial causation*). A list of congenital anomalies of multifactorial origin is found in Table 11-13.

***Intrauterine Growth Retardation.*** Babies with *intrauterine growth retardation* (IUGR) receive

***Table 11–13. Common Congenital Anomalies of Multifactorial Origin***

| Congenital Anomaly | Incidence* | Sex Most Frequently Affected |
|---|---|---|
| Anencephaly | 1:1000 | Female |
| Spina bifida | 1:1000 | Female |
| Cleft lip with/without cleft palate | 1:1000-Caucasian 1.7:1000-Japanese 0.7:1000-Blacks | Male |
| Cleft palate alone | 1:2000–1:2500 | Female |
| Congenital heart defect | 6–8:1000 | Equal |
| Congenital dislocation of the hip | 1:1000–1:100 | Female |
| Pyloric stenosis | 5:1000-males 1:1000-females | Male |
| Clubfoot | 1:1000 | Male |
| Hirschsprung disease | 1:5000 | Male |
| Hypospadias | 6:1000-Caucasian 2:1000-Blacks | Males only |

* Frequency in U.S. unless stated otherwise.
(From Cohen, F. L. [1984]. *Clinical genetics in nursing practice.* Philadelphia: J. B. Lippincott Company, p. 101)

enough oxygen and nutrients during pregnancy to maintain life, but not enough to grow normally. They are dehydrated and look old at birth; the skin on their hands and feet is dry and cracked and often meconium-stained. The cord is thin and the infant has "high color" due to polycythemia. Causes include placental dysfunction, multiple pregnancy, intrauterine infections, socioeconomic factors, major malformations, and racial/genetic factors (Greer, 1985).

***Infections.*** Other problems that place a baby at risk are TORCH infections. These are maternal infections during early pregnancy that cause serious problems at birth and include:

**T**oxoplasmosis
**O**ther (e.g., Type B hepatitis virus, coxsackievirus B, mumps, poliovirus, rubeola, varicella, listeria, gonorrhea, streptococcus, syphilis)
**R**ubella
**C**ytomegalic inclusion disease
**H**erpes simplex type II

Infants affected by toxoplasmosis have a poor prognosis: 10% to 15% die, 85% of the survivors have severe psychomotor retardation, and 50% develop visual problems (DeVore, 1983). Infants are treated with pyrimethamine (Daraprim) and sulfadiazine, which are used to prevent progression of the disease. Before birth, mothers may be treated with spiramycin.

Hepatitis B offers the greatest danger of the "other" infections. It is most contagious for the infant if the mother contracts it shortly before delivery. Prematurity and stillbirths are sequelae. If the baby survives, the child frequently does not have an acute form of the disease but becomes a carrier. About 12 hours after birth, or when the neonate is stable, hepatitis B immune globulin (HBIG) and Heptavax are administered IM. Heptavax may be given up to 7 days after birth (Withers & Bradshaw, 1986).

Rubella may damage the fetus's eyes (cataracts), ears (deafness), and heart and may cause IUGR and mental retardation. Prevention is the only treatment.

Cytomegalic inclusion disease affects many body systems and may involve the liver. There may also be neurological problems resulting in mental retardation and cerebral palsy. Cytomegalovirus is the most common cause of perinatal infection. Treatment with antimetabolites or antiviral agents may decrease CNS destruction.

Approximately 30% to 50% of infants delivered vaginally of mothers with herpes virus are infected; about half of these die or are severely damaged. Prevention is essential since there is no known cure. Cesarean section is performed unless the mother has two consecutive negative cultures in the week prior to labor. There is no proven effective treatment yet.

Mothers afflicted with *sexually transmitted diseases*

(STDs) also present threats to their neonates. Neonates with congenital syphilis are often asymptomatic at birth but then present with sniffles and skin eruptions. Almost all organs are involved in syphilis. Swallowing and breathing may be difficult because of the swelling of the mucous membranes, and the baby's cry may sound hoarse from infection of the nasopharynx. Penicillin is the pharmacological treatment; babies are isolated for the first 24 hours of treatment.

Gonorrhea does not cause congenital abnormalities but may cause premature labor. It also places the baby at risk for acquiring gonococcal ophthalmia as he or she passes through the vagina. Immediate prevention after birth consists of instilling either 1% silver nitrate, 0.5% erythromycin ointment, or 1% tetracycline ointment into each eye. Infants born to mothers diagnosed with gonorrhea should receive penicillin intramuscularly.

Another sexually transmitted disease is chlamydia trachomatis. Babies are infected as they pass through the birth canal and may develop inclusion conjunctivitis of the newborn (ICN) or pneumonia. If the eyes of the newborn are untreated, the infection can last from 3 to 12 months and can result in scarring and corneal vascularization. The infant must be treated with sulfonamide drops, topical 1% tetracycline ointment, or 0.5% erythromycin ointment for 2 to 3 weeks. Silver nitrate is not effective for ophthalmia neonatorum caused by chlamydia.

*Drug Use.* It is important to document drug or alcohol use or abuse during the prenatal history. (For a detailed discussion of drug and other substance abuse, see Chapter 21.) Prescription drugs can have teratogenic effects on fetuses; for example, it is believed that phenytoin (Dilantin) taken by a pregnant woman may cause mental retardation in her baby. It is also important to identify nonprescription drug use. Street drugs such as heroin, cocaine, or crack can cause severe withdrawal symptoms for the neonate. Symptoms of drug withdrawal include hyperactivity, a shrill cry, irritability, coarse tremors, excessive mucus, seizures, excessive yawning, hyperthermia, tachypnea, hyperactive reflexes, and diaphoresis. After 24 hours, vomiting and diarrhea may occur. Infants are given supportive care, including drug therapy, to decrease the withdrawal symptoms. They are placed in a quiet environment, and their heart rate, temperature, respiration, color, activity, and skin turgor are monitored to prevent complications.

Alcohol ingestion during pregnancy can result in *fetal alcohol syndrome,* which is evidenced by mental retardation, delayed growth, and developmental delay. These babies have a characteristic facies with long upper lips, small palpebral fissures, and small heads (Fig. 11-18). Cardiovascular defects are also common (see Chapter 24). Nurses involved in prenatal care must use interviewing, communication, and physical assessment skills to identify mothers who are consuming alcoholic beverages. New-

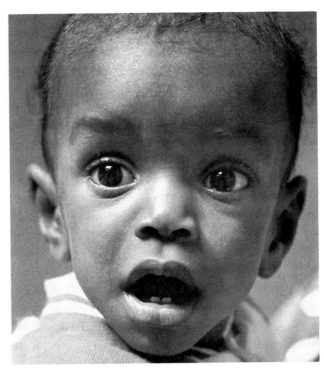

*Figure 11–18. A 15-month-old child with fetal alcohol syndrome. (Source: Kathy Sloane)*

borns must be carefully assessed for signs of fetal alcohol syndrome since they may experience withdrawal symptoms. The severity of these symptoms is related to the amount of the mother's alcohol consumption and how long before the birth the mother consumed alcohol.

## Identifying Infants at Risk During Labor and Delivery: Postnatal Assessment

A history of the labor and delivery is also helpful in identifying risk factors during the natal period. Common risk factors in the present or past obstetrical history are listed in Table 11-14. Bradycardia and meconium in the amniotic fluid are signs of fetal distress. Analgesics, such as barbiturates and meperidine hydrochloride (Demerol), depress the newborn. The position of the neonate at delivery may cause problems, e.g., babies born in the breech position frequently have fractures.

A prolapsed umbilical cord, knots in the umbilical cord, or a tight umbilical cord (as occurs when the cord is wrapped around the neck) may cause fetal distress. A prolonged or a premature labor may also adversely affect fetal status. Fetal distress signs include tachycardia (fetal heart rate [FHR] over 180), bradycardia (FHR under 120), an irregular heart rate, and/or a scalp vein pH of 7.2 or less (vertex presenting). If the fetus is being electronically

*Table 11–14. Risk Factors in the Present or Past Obstetrical History*

Previous stillbirths or premature births
Previous neonatal deaths
Previous multiple births
Previous miscarriages or abortions
History of cesarean sections
Tumors or reproductive problems
History of tuberculosis or sexually transmitted diseases (STDs)
Other medical problems (e.g., hypertension, diabetes)
Toxemia, present or past
Premature rupture of membranes, present or past
Premature labor, present or past
Labor over 20 hours, present or past
History of placenta previa or placenta abruptio
Fetal distress
  Tachycardia, 180 beats/min
  Bradycardia, 120 beats/min
  Meconium-stained amniotic fluid
  Abnormal deceleration curve
Intrauterine growth retardation (IUGR), present or past
Acute surgical procedures for mother
Polyhydramnios or oligohydramnios
Breech delivery or forceps delivery
Prolapsed umbilical cord

monitored, an abnormal deceleration curve also indicates fetal distress.

Assessment of the infant at the time of delivery is essential for rapid diagnosis and care. The Apgar tool assesses color, respiration, heart rate, muscle tone, and reflex irritability at 1 and 5 minutes. The nurse also assesses for petechiae (thrombocytopenia), abnormalities, cyanosis, and seizures. The infant is further monitored in the nursery for jaundice, vomiting, difficulty in swallowing, failure to urinate or pass meconium in the first 24 hours, and weight status. In the first 3 to 5 days the neonate loses up to 10% of the birth weight; this weight is usually regained from the tenth to the twelfth day.

## Prematurity

The most common postnatal risk factors are shown in Table 11-15. Prematurity is the leading cause of infant mortality. Prematurity is defined as any birth that takes place prior to 37 weeks' gestation, regardless of birth weight.

Premature infants have little subcutaneous fat and thin, transparent skin. Their increased body surface area in relation to their weight means that they lose heat at a faster rate. Thermoregulation is a major concern.

The lungs of premature infants are often not sufficiently developed for the exchange of air (see Chapter 23). They have limited defenses against infections and also have an immature digestive system. Premature babies are fre-

quently "jittery," which may be due to hypoglycemia. Hypoglycemia is a condition in which there is a low blood serum glucose. Symptoms are seen in the first few hours or days after birth. Although the brain needs glucose for growth, it can neither make nor store it, and immature infants do not have an adequate supply of glucose in the liver to use for glycogenesis. In addition, infants with respiratory distress may not be able to suck well enough to take in sufficient glucose, which is further depleted if they are cold or in a hypoxic state and use their glucose supply to maintain body temperature.

The average level of glucose in cord blood is 60 mg to 80 mg per 100 mL of blood. Levels below 30 mg per 100 mL in the first 3 days of life, or below 40 mg per 100 mL after 3 days of life, indicate hypoglycemia. Infants should have at least one blood test for glucose in the first few hours of life, before being fed. Heel pricks (Dextrostix) can be used.

Hypoglycemia in newborns may be attributed to immaturity, small size for gestational age, a poorly controlled diabetic mother, respiratory difficulty, failure to suck well, postmaturity, twinning, a mother with pregnancy-induced hypertension, either intra- or extrauterine stress, or hemolytic disease. In these cases, either the infant is unable to take in enough glucose, the liver is unable to store sufficient glucose, or the infant uses more than the available glucose.

Nursing interventions are based on the assessment. If infants have difficulty sucking, feedings may be given by gavage or intravenous therapy may be indicated. A bolus of glucose may be given IV, followed by a slow infusion of glucose. Blood glucose levels should be closely monitored.

The amount of pain premature infants feel has not been well established. It seems reasonable to assume that they do experience some discomfort while undergoing procedures, but the age when pain discrimination occurs is not documented.

*Table 11–15. Postnatal Risk Factors*

Low birth weight (LBW): 2500 g (5½ lbs)
Small for date, small for gestational age (SGA)
Intrauterine growth retardation (IUGR): Birthweight less than the 10th percentile for the period of gestation
Large for gestational age (LGA): birthweight is 90th percentile or above on intrauterine growth curves
Jaundice
Abnormal respirations
Pallor, cyanosis
Apnea
Difficulty in swallowing
Vomiting
No voiding by end of first 24 hours
No meconium passed by end of first 24 hours
Limpness
Failure to regain birth weight by 10 days of age
Thermal instability

Besides looking thin and small, the premature infant has abundant lanugo and few creases on the hands and feet. The infant usually extends the extremities, which does not help conserve body heat. In females the labia are prominent; males often have undescended testicles. Reflexes, including sucking, are usually weak.

The prognosis for premature infants is related to birth weight and the degree of immaturity of various organs. Complications frequently include pneumothorax, jaundice, anemia, retrolental fibroplasia, and bonding disruptions. Premature infants weighing from 400 g to 1000 g have a poor prognosis for survival; those weighing 2000 g and over have a very good prognosis. Survival is related to the degree of immaturity and the availability of specialized neonatal care.

## Special Care Needs of Premature Infants

*Thermoregulation.* Conservation of body heat by neonates is crucial. Whenever an infant's core temperature falls below 36.5°C (97.7°F), the infant is losing heat more rapidly than it is being produced (Daze & Scanlon, 1985). As the central nervous system develops, metabolic processes mature, the baby feeds more effectively, and the risk of cold stress is reduced.

Heat loss by evaporation can be minimized by using a stockinette cap, which eliminates heat loss from the head. When possible, a diaper and shirt help prevent heat loss through evaporation. A radiant heated table also helps conserve heat. A heat-sensing probe is placed on the skin, and heat is produced when the infant's skin temperature drops below a pre-set temperature (thermo-controlled). The skin probe must always be in place when the infant is on the table since the infant is unclothed and even more vulnerable to heat loss.

Isolettes may also be used to provide a neutral thermal environment through the convection principle. Air is warmed, filtered, and circulated over the baby. However, heat loss must be continuously monitored; even when there are cuffs around the portholes, heat is lost when the portholes are opened. Neonates can also lose heat to an unheated mattress.

High-risk newborns, premature infants, or those with physiological problems are placed in a heated environment after birth. They remain in this environment until their temperature is stabilized. This is important because an infant whose metabolism increases in an effort to generate heat requires more oxygen and may develop hypoxia, hypoglycemia, or acidosis.

*Nutrition.* Several factors impinge on the premature infant's ability to obtain adequate nourishment. The sucking reflex is not well developed, and the swallowing reflex is not coordinated with sucking. Pacifiers are useful for stimulating sucking if they do not overly tire the baby.

The premature infant's stomach is small, and there are decreased digestive enzymes and decreased gastric acidity. Additionally, the premature infant has a decreased supply of glycogen, calcium, and iron.

The nutritional plan includes reducing stressors that deplete caloric supplies. Assessment of nutrition is done by daily weight measurements and weekly length and head circumference measurements.

For small or ill babies, the method of obtaining nutrition usually progresses from parenteral to continuous tube feedings, to gavage feedings, and finally to oral feedings. Usually 10% dextrose in water is given parenterally immediately after birth, when the infant cannot be fed orally, to prevent dehydration and hypoglycemia. Hyperalimentation may subsequently be used for feeding. The superior vena cava is the site for hyperalimentation, using a cutdown of the internal or jugular vein. The umbilical catheter is never used because of the risk of infection. If the infusion rate is too rapid, hyperglycemia can occur. Infusion pumps help to prevent this.

With either oral or tube feedings there is always the danger of formula aspiration. Positioning the infant on the right side or on the abdomen after feeding is thought to decrease this risk. Dangers associated with tube feedings include perforation of the gastrointestinal tract, including the esophagus, or necrotizing enterocolitis. Gastrointestinal problems of neonates are discussed in Chapter 29.

Few mothers of pre-term infants elect to breast-feed, for a variety of reasons. Sometimes the mother is physically separated from the child. She may have had a difficult or prolonged labor. Many mothers return to work and find it difficult to pump their breasts. Other mothers have psychological barriers related to self-image. Milk from a breast milk bank may be used. Although this breast milk provides adequate nutrition, it cannot protect the infant from infection since the milk must be pasteurized to destroy pathogenic bacteria.

## Problems of Prematurity

*Hemorrhage. Intracranial hemorrhage* may occur at delivery due to the baby's soft, pliable skull bones and the wide sutures and fontanels. An early episiotomy, which helps prevent a prolonged second stage, may alleviate this problem. Hypoxia can also cause intracranial hemorrhage. In premature infants intracranial hemorrhage is usually of intraventricular or subarachnoid origin.

Another type of intracranial hemorrhage, *subdural,* is seldom seen today. In the past, subdural hematomas were caused by the use of forceps during delivery. Alternative approaches to delivery, such as cesarean sections, have decreased the use of forceps. In intracranial hemorrhage, blood collects in the subdural space owing to stretching and tearing of the large veins in the tentorium cerebelli and, occasionally, the tearing of the veins in the subdural space over the brain's surface. Aspiration of subdural hematomas is difficult.

*Intraventricular hemorrhage* occurs in approximately 40% to 60% of small pre-term infants. Usually this is attributed to hypoxia, with resultant rupture in the region of the ventricles. Hydrocephalus may result. A tense, bulging anterior fontanel, separated sutures, and neurological signs such as twitching, convulsions, and stupor may be present. Assessment techniques include repeated head measurements, lumbar punctures (sometimes daily to reduce pressure), and computed tomography (CT) scans. Treatment for hydrocephalus is the ventriculo-peritoneal (VP) shunt, which directs the cerebrospinal fluid from the ventricles to the peritoneal cavity. Most VP shunts are placed on the right side—the usual non-dominant side. There are other shunting locations, such as the jugular vein, atrium, pleura, and spinal epidural space, but these have higher failure rates. Care of children with shunts is discussed in Chapter 26.

*Anemia.* The most common blood loss anemia of premature infants is *iatrogenic anemia,* caused by the excessive removal of blood for diagnostic procedures. It occurs between the third and seventh day and is produced by removal of more than 20% of the baby's blood volume in 24 to 48 hours.

Anemia can also result from occult hemorrhage before birth or during the birth process. *Hemolytic anemia* of the newborn is characterized by shortened red blood cell life and a drop in the production of fetal hemoglobin. Blood volume increases at the same time hemoglobin concentration decreases. *Physiological anemia* is a normal condition that occurs in infants between 2 and 3 months of age. At birth, infants have high hematocrit and hemoglobin levels. These levels gradually decline between 2 and 3 months of age, then rise when the bone marrow begins active erythropoiesis (Chow et al., 1984). Physiological anemia is self-correcting in all babies. The physiological decrease occurs earlier in premature infants and ultimately reaches a lower level. Minimum values are achieved by 4 to 7 weeks, and hemoglobin concentrations of 7 to 8 mg/dL may occur in apparently healthy infants (Gross, Shurin, & Gordon, 1983).

Symptoms of neonatal anemia include pallor of lips and nail beds, poor weight gain, tachypnea or tachycardia, unexplained acidosis, lethargy, increased oxygen requirement, apnea, or heart failure (Daze & Scanlon, 1985). The hemoglobin (Hgb) and hematocrit (Hct) levels are usually low (Hgb under 14.8 g/100mL; Hct under 45). Hemolytic anemias are discussed further in Chapter 25.

*Retinopathy of Prematurity and Retrolental Fibroplasia (RLF).* *Retinopathy of prematurity* (ROP) refers to all retinal changes in premature infants. Retrolental fibroplasia refers to the scar tissue formation behind the lens, which is the end point of the retinopathy process. It was originally associated with high levels of oxygen concentration administered to premature infants, but other factors are now being considered as causes. Since the late 1950s, maintaining an oxygen concentration below 40% has resulted in a decrease in retinopathies. With the advent of the ability to monitor blood gases, the amount of oxygen to be administered became more individualized. The goal is to maintain a $Pao_2$ between 50 and 80 mm Hg; the amount of oxygen administered depends on the oxygen level in the blood (Korones, 1986).

In recent years the incidence of ROP has increased. It is thought that this partially reflects the increasing survival rate of very small neonates (under 1000 grams), as well as other factors. Although the exact reason is not known, it is clear that smaller neonates are at greater risk. One current treatment (also popular in the 1940s) includes vitamin E supplementation. Hittner, Kretzer, and Rudolph (1984), reported evidence from several clinical trials that supports the administration of vitamin E at birth and continuing until vascularization is complete.

*Environmental Factors.* Continuous noise and light are two of the major environmental pollutants that affect premature infants. Incubator noise can reach 90 db to 100 db, with each additional piece of equipment adding to that total. Babies are kept in bright lights for observation purposes. It has been suggested that periodic eye covering may help simulate night and day for premature infants.

The effect of tactile stimulation has also been examined in numerous studies. Nelson, Heitman, and Jennings (1986) studied the effect of substituting human touch with an "other than human" tactile stimulator, a pile decubitus pad. No statistical difference in weight gain was found. The investigators suggested that the use of such pads be coupled with other types of sensory stimulation.

Other environmental factors, such as socioeconomic status, maternal anxiety, and level of parental education have also been studied. A number of animal studies have linked maternal stress to fetal and newborn problems, but human longitudinal studies are limited and more research needs to be done in this area (Lederman, 1986).

## Risk Associated with Maturity

Although prematurity is the most common risk associated with gestational age, there are other problems related to maturity, even in term infants. Large-for-gestational-age (LGA) newborns are frequently seen with diabetic mothers or in families with genetic predispositions. Small-for-gestational-age (SGA) newborns are frequently seen with mothers with a history of alcohol, drug, or tobacco abuse.

## Postmaturity

Babies born after 42 weeks' gestation are said to be postmature. Sometimes the extended gestation causes a deterioration of maternal–fetal support, and the infant may be small for gestational age (SGA).

Postmature neonates often have dry, cracking skin. Vernix caseosa and lanugo are absent. The nails are long and hard; frequently the nails and skin are meconium stained (green to golden yellow). Their bodies are long and thin, and the skull often looks large. These babies may appear alert and wide-eyed, but this may indicate chronic intrauterine hypoxia (Korones, 1986). When a baby is significantly overdue, either induction of labor or cesarean section is indicated, because the greatest risk for the baby occurs during labor. In fact, postmaturity is said to account for morbidity in 12% of all births (Ouimette, 1986).

Problems seen in postmature infants include asphyxia, meconium aspiration syndrome, hypoxia with subsequent CNS damage, and hypoglycemia. Many postmature infants are delivered by cesarean section, which may cause problems in establishing respiration. Postmature infants may have aspiration meconium and may have to be intubated and suctioned. Oxygen is not administered under pressure until intubation and suctioning has been completed in order to prevent additional blockage further down the respiratory tract in the lungs. Nursing interventions include monitoring respirations and assisting in respiratory efforts, as ordered. Temperature regulation may also be affected; nurses should institute measures to be sure that infants do not become chilled. Fluid balance must be monitored and maintained. The dry, cracked skin that results from a lack of amniotic fluid and vernix must be cleansed carefully with clear water to avoid further drying.

## Parenting Development

During the neonatal period, infants and their parents are establishing the bonding and attachment process. Parenting of neonates focuses on meeting physiological and safety needs (Maslow), establishing trust (Erikson), responding to the child's instinctual needs, and id development (Freud). The infant's responses are focused on oral satisfaction (Freud) while they respond to external stimuli in a sensorimotor (reflexive) manner.

These considerations are the foundation for parental activities that facilitate the child's progression through this stage. The needs of neonates must be met. Crying should be recognized as the child's way of communicating hunger or discomfort; thus, parents should respond to cries promptly. This assists in the development of trust rather than mistrust. In addition, feeding or sucking activities (such as pacifier use) help satisfy oral needs. Holding the infant close to the parent's body, talking, and smiling are activities that can be soothing or stimulating for the child. Parents of "fussy" neonates need to be reminded to try to get as much rest as possible and to provide some time alone for themselves, especially if they feel tired or frustrated in caring for their child.

Parents have to learn how to meet every need of their neonate—how to hold, change, feed, and bathe a very small person. Most parents feel some anxiety at first about their ability to do this. They need to have positive feedback that they are successful as parents. Nurses working in hospitals, physicians' offices, and clinics have frequent contact with neonates and their parents and, thus, are in an excellent position to provide information, parent teaching, and encouragement. Individual and group parenting classes, books, and videos are also useful tools that can facilitate the development of parenting skills.

## Summary

Although each neonate is unique, all newborns share many similarities in adapting to the environment. These similarities can be used for comparison. Effective assessment of all facets of neonatal development depends on the knowledge and skill of the examiner. Astute observation is essential, because changes often take place rapidly. Promotion of optimal health is a responsibility shared by all.

Improvements in neonatal care have resulted in the survival of many babies who were previously at risk for death or serious complications. The survival of these infants requires intensive care and treatment.

## References

Als, H. (1982). Toward a synactive theory of development: Promise for the assessment and support of infant individuality. *Infant Mental Health Journal, 3*(4), 229–243.

Als, H., Lawhon, G., Brown, E., Gibes, R., Duffy, F. H., McAnulty, G., & Blickman, J. G. (1986). Individualized behavioral and environmental care for the very low birth weight preterm infant at high risk for bronchopulmonary dysplasia: Neonatal intensive care unit and developmental outcome. *Pediatrics, 78*(6), 1123–1132.

American Academy of Pediatrics Committee on Infectious Diseases. (1988). *Report of the Committee on Infectious Diseases* (21st ed.). Elk Grove Village, IL.: American Academy of Pediatrics.

American Academy of Pediatrics Committee on Fetus and Newborn. (1987). Neonatal anesthesia. *Pediatrics, 80*(3), 446.

Anand, K., Sippell, W., & Green, A. (1987). Randomized trial of fentanyl anesthesia in preterm babies undergoing surgery: Effects on the stress response. *Lancet, 1,* 243–248.

Anand, K. J. S., & Hickey, P. R. (1987). Pain and its effect in the human neonate and fetus. *New England Journal of Medicine, 317*(21), 1321–1329.

Aronoff, S. A., & Speck, W. T. (1983). Neonatal septicemia. In R. A. Polin & E. D. Bury (Eds.). *Workbook in practical neonatology* (pp. 57–71). Philadelphia: W. B. Saunders.

Ballard, J. L., Kazmaier, K., & Driver, M. (1977). A simplified assessment of gestational age. *Pediatric Research, 11,* 374.

Behrman, R. E., & Vaughan, V. C. (1987). *Nelson textbook of pediatrics* (13th ed.). Philadelphia: W. B. Saunders.

Bloom, R. S., & Cropley, C. (1987). *Textbook of neonatal resuscitation*. Los Angeles: American Heart Association.

Bowlby, J., Ainsworth, M., Bostoo, M., & Rosenbluth, D. (1956). The effects of mother–child separation: A follow-up study. *British Journal of Medical Psychology, 29*(2), 211–247.

Bowlby, J. (1963). *Child care and the growth of love*. Baltimore: Penguin Books.

Broussard, E. (1978). Psychosocial disorders in children: Early assessment of infants at risk. *Continuing Education, 44,* 57.

Chow, M. P., Durand, B. A., Feldman, M. M., & Mills, M. A. (1984). *Handbook of pediatric primary care* (2nd ed.). New York: John Wiley & Sons.

Cohen, F. L. (1984). *Clinical genetics in nursing practice*. Philadelphia: J. B. Lippincott.

Cugali, N., & Moore, D. S. (1984). Current considerations in neonatal conjunctivitis. *Journal of Nurse-Midwifery, 29*(3), 197–204.

Daze, A. M., & Scanlon, J. W. (1985). *Neonatal nursing*. Baltimore: University Park Press.

DeCasper, A. J., & Fifer, W. P. (1980). The fetal sound environment of sheep. *Science, 208,* 1173–1176.

DeVore, N. E. (1983). TORCH infections. *American Journal of Nursing, 113*(12), 1660–1665.

Dubowitz, L. M. S., Dubowitz, V., & Goldberg, C. (1970). Clinical assessment of gestational age in the newborn infant. *Journal of Pediatrics, 77*(1), 1–10.

Erikson, E. (1950). *Children and society*. New York: W. W. Norton.

Erikson, E. (1963). *Youth; change; challenge*. New York: Basic Books.

Freud, S. (1933). *New introductory lectures on psychoanalysis*. New York: W. W. Norton.

Greenberg, M., & Morris, N. (1974). Engrossment: The newborn's impact upon the father. *American Journal of Orthopsychiatry, 44,* 520–531.

Greer, I. (1985). Intrauterine growth retardation. *The Lamp, 41*(9), 38–40.

Gross, S., Shurin, S. B., & Gordon, E. M. (1983). The blood: Hematopoietic system. In A. A. Fanaroff & R. J. Martin (Eds.). *Behrman's neonatal-perinatal medicine: Diseases of the fetus and infant* (pp.708–752). St. Louis: C. V. Mosby.

Grunau, R., & Craig, K. (1987). Pain expression in neonates: Facial action and cry. *Pain, 28,* 395–410.

Helson, H. (1964). *Adaptation-level theory*. New York: Harper and Row.

Hittner, H. M., Kretzer, F. L., & Rudolph, A. S. (1984). Prevention and management of retrolental fibroplasia. *Hospital Practice, 19*(2), 85–99.

Hogue, C. J. R., Strauss, L. T., Buehler, J. W., & Smith, J. C. (1989). National infant mortality surveillance (NIMS) 1980. *Morbidity and Mortality Weekly Report, 38*(SS-3), 1–46.

Klaus, M. H., Kennell, J. H., Plumb, N., & Zuehlke, S. (1970). Human maternal behavior at first contact with her young. *Pediatrics, 46,* 187–192.

Klaus, M. H., & Kennell, J. H. (1982). *Parent–infant bonding*. St. Louis: C. V. Mosby.

Korones, S. B. (1986). *High-risk newborn infants* (4th ed.). St. Louis: C. V. Mosby.

LeBoyer, F. (1975). *Birth without violence*. New York: Random House.

Lederman, R. P. (1986). Maternal anxiety in pregnancy: Relationship to fetal and newborn health status. *Annual Review of Nursing, 4,* 3–19.

Lubchenco, L. O., Hansman, C., & Boyd, E. (1966). Intrauterine growth in length and head circumference as estimated from live births at gestational ages from 26–42 weeks. *Pediatrics, 37,* 403.

Marecki, M., Wooldridge, P., Dow, A., Thompson, J., & Lechner-Hyman, C. (1985). Early sibling attachment: What happens when sibling and baby first meet and do sibling preparation classes for pre-school children make a difference? *Journal of Obstetric, Gynecologic and Neonatal Nursing, 14*(5), 418–423.

Mooney, B. R., Green, J. A., Epstein, B. J., & Hashisaki, P. A. (1984). Non-gonococcal ophthalmitis associated with erythromycin ointment prophylaxis of gonococcal ophthalmia neonatorum. *Infection Control, 5*(3), 138–140.

Nelson, D., Heitman, R., & Jennings, C. (1986). Effects of tactile stimulation on premature infant weight gain. *Journal of Obstetric and Gynecologic Nursing, 15*(3), 262–267.

Ouimette, J. (1986). *Perinatal nursing: Care of the high-risk mother and infant*. Boston: Jones and Bartlett.

Parke, R. D. (1975). In M. H. Klaus, T. Leber, & M. A. Trause (Eds.). *Father-infant interaction in maternal attachment and mothering disorders: A roundtable* (pp. 61–70). New Brunswick, NJ: Johnson & Johnson Baby Products Company.

Parke, R. D., Power, T. G., Tinsley, B. R., & Hymel, S. (1979). The father's role in the family system. *Seminars in Perinatology, 3,* 25–34.

Piaget, J. (1952). *The origins of intelligence in children*. New York: International Universities.

Piaget, J. (1963). *The psychology of intelligence*. Paterson, NJ: Littlefield, Adams.

Roy, S. C. (1970). Adaptation: A conceptual framework for nursing. *Nursing Outlook, 18*(3), 42–45.

Roy, S. C. (1971). Adaptation: A basis for nursing practice. *Nursing Outlook, 19*(4), 254–257.

Roy, S. C. (1984). *Introduction to nursing: An adaptation model* (2nd ed.). Norwalk, CT: Appleton-Century-Crofts.

Rubin, R. (1963). Maternal touch. *Nursing Outlook, 11,* 823–831.

Spitz, R. A. (1949). The role of ecological factors in the emotional development of infancy. *Child Development, 20,* 145–156.

Stang, H. J., Snellman, L., Condon, L. M., & Kastenbaum, R. (1988). Local anesthesia for neonatal circumcision. *Journal of the American Medical Association, 259*(10), 1507–1511.

Vandenberg, K. A. (1990). Behvaiorally supportive care for the extremely premature infant. In Gunderson, L. P., & Kenner, C. (Eds.). *Care of the 24–25 week gestational age infant (small baby protocol)* (pp. 129–157). Petaluma, CA: Neonatal Network.

Wegman, M. E. (1990). Annual summary of vital statistics, 1989. *Pediatrics, 86*(6), 835–847.

Wieser, M. A., & Castiglia, P. T. (1984). Assessing early father–infant attachment. *Maternal-Child Nursing, 9,* 104–106.

Withers, J., & Bradshaw, E. (1986). Preventing neonatal hepatitis-B infection. *Journal of Maternal-Child Nursing, 11,* 270–272.

## Bibliography

Apgar, V. (1966). The newborn (Apgar) scoring system. *Pediatric Clinics of North America, 13,* 645–659.

Brazelton, T. B. (1979). Behavioral competence of the newborn infant. *Seminars in Perinatology, 3*(1), 35–44.

Broussard, E. R., & Hartner, M. S. S. (1970). Maternal perceptions of the neonate as related to development. *Child Psychiatry and Human Development, 1,* 16–25.

Broussard, E. (1979). Assessment of the adaptive potential of the mother-infant system: The neonatal perception inventories. *Seminars in Perinatology, 3,* 91–100.

Dick, H. M. (1983). Orthopedic problems. In A. A. Fanaroff & R. J. Martin (Eds.). *Behrman's neonatal-perinatal medicine: Diseases of the fetus and infant* (pp. 1004–1012). St. Louis: C. V. Mosby.

Fanaroff, A. A., & Martin, R. H. (1983). *Behrman's neonatal-perinatal medicine: Diseases of the fetus and infant.* St. Louis: C. V. Mosby.

Gromada, K. (1986). Maternal-infants attachment: The first step toward individualizing twins. *American Journal of Maternal-Child Nursing, 6*(2), 129–134.

Merenstein, G. B., & Gardner, S. L. (1989). *Handbook of neonatal intensive care* (2nd ed.). St. Louis: Mosby-Year Book, Inc.

Pierog, S., & Ferrara, A. (1976). *Medical care of the sick newborn* (2nd ed.). St. Louis: C. V. Mosby.

Wilkins, R. L., Sheldon, R. L., & Krider, S. J. (1985). *Clinical assessment in respiratory care.* St. Louis: C. V. Mosby.

# Infant Growth, Development, and Health

Suzanne Aquilina

*Photograph by David Finn*

**12**

*Goals of Nursing Care During Infancy*

*Physical Growth and Development*
    *General Growth Characteristics*
    *Brain Growth*
    *Motor Development*
    *Sensory Development*
    *Body System Development*
    *Nutrition*
    *Sleep*
    *Dentition*

*Cognitive Development*
    *Piaget*
    *Play*

*Psychosocial Development*
    *Erikson*
    *Freud*
    *Attachment*
    *Communication*
    *Cultural Influences*

*Assessment*
    *Body Measurements*
    *Developmental Assessment*
    *Assessment of Home and Family*

*Health Promotion*
    *Health Maintenance*
    *Procedures*
    *Routine Care*
    *Common Concerns*

*Parenting Development*

*Summary*

*Upon completion of this chapter the reader will be able to:*

1. *Analyze the genetic and environmental factors influencing the physical growth and development of infants.*

2. *Describe how the various body systems mature, and discuss the influence of nutrition on this maturation process during the first year of life.*

3. *Describe how cognitive skills develop during infancy.*

4. *Explore the psychosocial aspect of infant development using the interaction of various theories and extrinsic factors.*

5. *Describe nursing assessments that help evaluate infants' body measurements, development, temperament, and home and family environment.*

6. *Describe the purpose, schedule, and content of health maintenance visits.*

7. *Discuss the role of daily routine care (bathing, clothing, nutrition, safety) in promoting health for infants.*

8. *Discuss various approaches to common concerns during infancy, such as weaning, crying, sleep problems, and thumb sucking.*

9. *Integrate cultural, environmental, and hereditary factors into the assessment of the development of parenting behaviors.*

*Key Terms*

*attachment*

*causality*

*mutual regulation*

*object permanence*

*oral-aggressive*

*oral-dependent*

*separation anxiety*

*symbolic play*

*trust versus mistrust*

*weaning*

For 9 months the anticipation and excitement mounts, culminating in the birth of a small but powerful human being. After the parents' initial joy and exhilaration subside, childbirth brings with it the realization that this new human being is totally dependent on others for survival yet has the potential for magnificent accomplishments during his or her first year of life. Infancy, the period from 1 to 12 months of age, is the period in which newborns mature faster, both physically and emotionally, than in any other stage of life. This chapter focuses on the normal parameters of growth and development, including both the genetic potential of individuals and the environment.

## Goals of Nursing Care During Infancy

Professional nurses have an opportunity and a responsibility to assist in the development of parenting knowledge and skills. No other "job" in our universe carries as much responsibility, yet encompasses so little formal preparation, as parenting. Parents are often expected to "know" intuitively how to parent. Nursing goals for parenting development include educating parents about normal growth and development (e.g., nutrition, temperament); helping parents to integrate infants into the new family structure (dyad to triad or sibling adjustment); promoting health and preventing illness; helping parents to develop the ability to carry out physical and emotional tasks; and acting as positive parental role models, so that parents' interactions with their infants enhance growth and development.

## Physical Growth and Development

### General Growth Characteristics

The first year of life represents the body's fastest growth period. By the end of the first year, infants triple their birth weights and increase birth lengths by 50%. Growth follows a predictable sequence. Infants develop in a *cepholocaudal* (from the head downward) direction. As newborns, infants' heads are unsteady, but by the end of the first month of life, they strive to hold their heads erect for 15 to 20 seconds. By 1 year of age infants often not only have full control of their heads but also have learned to use their lower extremities, advancing from crawling to walking.

In *proximodistal* development, infants' growth proceeds from the middle to the periphery. In early infancy, infants can flail their arms. Purposeful movement appears toward the third month of life when they begin to grasp objects intentionally (grasp is no longer a reflex). The ability to grasp continues to be refined. Infants usually can hold a bottle at 6 months, and they can use their fingers and thumbs to pick up raisins at about 10 months.

Another pattern of growth is *mass to specific,* in which physical, emotional, and social growth occurs from the simple to the more complex. Infants mature from random muscle movements to specific, purposeful crawling, to walking, to games or sports. Speech develops from coos to babbling to specific words. Emotionally, infants' initial responses are positive toward any caregiver who meets their daily needs. As they mature infants prefer their predominant caregiver (usually either the mother or father) to others.

Three factors contribute to infant growth: genetic endowment, intrauterine environment, and extrauterine environment. Although growth is predictable, it varies with each individual. Stature in particular is related to the inherited genes. During the first year of life an infant grows in a manner similar to that of his or her family members. Weight in the first year is not always predictive of adult weight status, although this too is strongly influenced by genetic factors. The expected weight gain in the first year is approximately triple the birth weight. A study by Charney, Goodman, McBride, Lyon, and Pratt (1976) found that only 14% of infants who surpassed the 90th percentile during the first 6 months of life were obese in adulthood. This finding tends to support the proposition that, although a relation exists, adult height and weight cannot be predicted by measurements in infancy. Aberrations in the genetic makeup that affect growth, such as achondroplasia, can be noted at birth.

The intrauterine environment also augments or inhibits an infant's growth potential. Maternal malnutrition, alcohol consumption, and smoking or drug intake (legal or illicit) during pregnancy are just some of the elements that can affect an infant's growth. As mentioned in Chapter 11, problems at birth may be readily apparent, for instance, low birth weight, fetal alcohol syndrome, or polydactyly.

By 1 month of age low birth weight infants often have growth spurts and catch up with other infants their age. This is in contrast to infants with fetal alcohol syndrome or intrauterine growth retardation, who may always be smaller than normal.

The extrauterine factors that affect growth and development include nutrition, nurturing, and environment. These are discussed in more detail later in the chapter.

Some growth problems are not apparent until later in the first year, such as cerebral palsy and cystic fibrosis. Nurses need to continually assess physical and developmental progression to verify normal patterns and to identify areas that are lagging.

### Brain Growth

Infants' heads constitute one quarter of their bodies. The total number of adult brain cells is formed by 15 months of age. Therefore, the need to maximize brain growth during the first year is apparent.

The parts of the brain mature at different times during the prenatal and postnatal period. The cerebellum undergoes its most rapid growth during infancy. Growth peaks at 8 months of age when the glial cells in the cerebellum expand. The forebrain and brain stem also have a growth spurt during the first 12 months, with a slower but steady increase during the second year (Levine, Carey, Crocker, & Gross, 1983).

Because of the cell migration and differentiation of neurons, much of the biochemical maturation of the brain takes place during the fetal period. The brain demands good nutrition for proper functioning both before and after birth. For example, the brain uses 20% of all the body's available oxygen, and neurons depend on glucose for proper metabolism and as a source of energy. The function of neurons is complicated, but basically glucose and proteins are essential to their proper functioning (Levine et al., 1983). Fat intake during the first year of life is believed to be critical for the completion of the mylenization process (Mahoney, 1987).

Many studies have supported the theory that iron in the diet also is essential for optimal brain growth. Although the exact mechanism has not been identified, proper central nervous system function depends on this mineral (Levine et al., 1983).

### Variations in Head Growth

Growth of the brain can be best ascertained in two ways. First, infants' head circumferences should be carefully measured at birth and during the next 2 years of life, by which time maximum brain growth is usually achieved. During the first year of life the head circumference increases by 10 cm (4 inches). The head circumference reaches about 47 cm (18.5 inches) by 1 year of age. Between 1 and 7 years of age, head circumference increases by 5 cm (2 inches). In conjunction with this raw measurement, nurses need to assess and verify normal brain function. An aberration in either size or function does not necessarily denote an abnormality, but further investigation is critical.

*Microcephaly* is defined as an abnormally small head—below the 5th percentile on standard growth charts (see Appendix B). Microcephaly noted at birth is discussed in Chapter 11. Some of the possible causes of microcephaly include trauma, infection (meningitis), metabolic disorders (hypothyroidism), and, more rarely, malnutrition.

*Macrocephaly* is defined as an abnormally large head—above the 95th percentile on standard growth charts. When head growth occurs at an unusually fast rate during the first year of life, it may be caused by hydrocephalus (fluid accumulation due to a defect in the ventricles of the brain), metabolic disorders, or a brain mass.

The skull should be transilluminated with a flashlight to examine its contents (see Chap. 11 for a further discussion). Transparency often indicates an increase in fluid in the brain; a delineated opaqueness may define a mass. With the sophistication of radiological techniques, precise diagnoses can be made using computed tomographic scans. Both microcephaly and macrocephaly usually warrant radiological evaluation.

Making judgments based strictly on the information on the growth charts may be premature. Infants' nutritional, developmental, and environmental data need to be assessed in conjunction with the findings on the growth chart. Genetic factors play a role in growth; sometimes all members of a family may have large or small heads without physiological dysfunction. Physiological causes must be ruled out, however.

Another variant in brain growth during the first year is *craniostosis,* or premature closing of the sutures. Although often diagnosed at birth, this condition may manifest itself only after the first few months of life. Unlike microcephaly, in which brain growth is retarded, craniostosis involves only the skull but can eventually affect brain growth. A decrease in head circumference may not be the initial indicator of a problem; the nurse's assessment may identify premature closure of the fontanelles, a peculiar head shape, or developmental lags. Further medical evaluation is warranted to rule out other underlying disorders (aberrant brain growth or hyperthyroidism) before a craniectomy is performed.

Brain growth has normal parameters, and most infants fall within these ranges. It is important to evaluate growth over time and to take into consideration the infant's genetic endowment as well as his or her environment.

## Motor Development

The central nervous system is immature at birth, so motor functions of newborns are regulated at the subcortical levels of the brain. Many of these motor activities are called *reflexes* and persist into early infancy (see Chapter 11 for a discussion of newborn reflexes). Cortical functioning starts to develop later in the first month of life. The specific reflex patterns eventually disappear and some become purposeful voluntary movements. Gross and fine motor movements should develop symmetrically.

### Gross Motor Development

Parents eagerly await any change in an infant's development, especially gross motor changes that are readily visible to all. The most notable change after 1 month of age is the ability to hold the head erect. This ability is strengthened throughout the first 4 months of life. Sitting, crawling, and standing are some of the other milestones anxiously awaited and encouraged by most parents (Figs. 12-1 and 12-2). To perform these activities, infants must develop three qualities:

1. Extension—Infants' muscle tone progresses from the neonatal state of predominant flexion to a balance in the tones of flexor and extensor muscles. As this balance develops, the flexed newborn posture gradually unfolds until, by 6 months, babies can extend their legs so far that they can put their toes in their mouths.
2. Flexibility—The decline of obligatory primary reflexes permits infants more flexible movement. A 1-month-old infant cannot look to one side or the

*Figure 12–1. Four-month-old infant lifting his head and chest with arm support.*

*Figure 12–2.  Six-month-old girl sitting, leaning forward on her hands.*

Table 12–1.  Gross Motor Skills in Infancy

| Age | Skill |
|---|---|
| 4 wk | Turns head; lifts head momentarily when in prone position. Moderate head lag when pulled to sitting position |
| 12 wk | Lifts head 90°; mild head lag. Moro relex disappearing; withdrawal reactions purposeful |
| 16 wk | Lifts head and chest with arm support. No head lag; holds head steady in sitting position. May roll front to back; adds back-to-front motion by 20 wk |
| 28 wk | Sits, leaning forward on hands. Bears weight on legs |
| 40 wk | Sits with back straight. Pulls to standing position. Creeps or crawls |
| 52 wk | Walks holding onto hand or furniture |

other without assuming the fencing posture of the asymmetrical tonic neck reflex. Until this reflex dissolves, the child's arm position is determined by the head's orientation. As this reflex disappears, infants develop the ability to bring their hands toward the midline.

3. Equilibrium and protective responses—These responses are the automatic changes in trunk and extremity positions that babies use to balance and keep from falling when sitting and walking. An example of such protective reactions is the familiar "parachute" response of 9-month-old infants who extend arms or legs to catch themselves when dropped toward the ground (Levine et al., 1983).

It takes months of waiting and hours of practice for infants to walk with their arms outstretched to hug their parents—a wonderful reward for a year's work well done! Other gross motor skills are presented in Table 12-1.

### Fine Motor Development

The gross, sporadic movements of infants' arms in the first month slowly progress to more definitive gestures by 1 to 2 months of age, demonstrating the proximodistal pattern of development. By 1 month most infants can involuntarily clasp their hands together. This is followed by grasping objects, which by 3 or 4 months of age is a voluntary gesture instead of the infantile automatism of newborns. When a mobile or any colorful hanging object attracts an infant's attention, he or she first reaches for it, then bangs

the object with the hands, and finally is able to open the hands and grasp the object. Because infants' visual abilities mature by 4 or 5 months of age, they are able to reach for objects and pull them close to themselves. By 9 months of age infants try to form their hands in preparation for holding onto a particular object. By 1 year of age they purposefully reach for objects with a direct motion rather than a flailing motion as seen earlier (Levine et al., 1983).

The grasping gesture evolves from using the whole hand to using the fingers in a more articulate manner (Fig. 12-3). By 5 months of age infants start using their thumbs in conjunction with the fingers and palm. At 6 or 7 months of age they use the thumb and fingers to grasp objects; this "raking" motion is used to pick up rattles, food, and even dry cereal. The task of eating and holding toys is facilitated

*Figure 12–3.  Six-month-old girl reaching and grasping for a rattle.*

at 9 months of age by the "pincer grasp," in which objects are handled with the thumbs and forefingers (Fig. 12-4). Infants at this age start to hold a cup for drinking, and by the end of their first year they can use their hands proficiently to feed themselves. Table 12-2 summarizes fine motor development for the first year of life.

### Normal Variations

Timing of various gross and fine motor achievements is subject to wide variations among all infants. Most parents have an inherent urge to compare their children with other children. Whether it is parental pride or parental anxiety over the achievement of developmental tasks, comparing the accomplishments of children is usually neither a positive nor productive endeavor. Nurses can educate parents about the variables that affect how and when infants perform certain tasks. Temperament, socioeconomic status, and position in the family (number of siblings) all influence how infants develop. Parents need to be cautioned that although encouragement to master tasks is positive, frequent repetition of tasks is not a good practice. For example, grasping a cup is accomplished as children gain motor control; repeatedly trying to have children do this when they are not ready may result in their withdrawing from this task.

## Sensory Development

### Hearing

Assessing infants' ability to hear is subjective unless sophisticated evaluations are done by an audiologist. The sense of hearing is critical to language development, and failure to discover hearing loss within the first 3 years of life can be

*Figure 12–4. An 11-month-old using a neat pincer grasp.*

*Table 12–2. Fine Motor Skills in Infancy*

| Age | Skill |
| --- | --- |
| 4 wk | Follows to midline, hands fisted |
| 12 wk | Follows 180°, grasps rattle |
| 16 wk | Hands open, reaches for object |
| 28 wk | Reaches and grasps large objects, transfers objects from hand to hand. Palmer (raking) grasp |
| 40 wk | Pincer grasp. Uncovers hidden toy |
| 52 wk | Neat pincer grasp. Releases object on request or demonstration |

permanently detrimental to a child's ability to communicate. Infants' hearing acuity is similar to that of adults. The maturation of the hearing center in the cortex allows infants to localize sounds progressively over the first year.

At birth infants' inner, middle, and external ears are essentially developed; some structural changes occur with maturation. The tympanic membrane is more horizontal than vertical, as is the eustachian tube. Changes to the vertical position occur gradually, reaching adult angles by the age of 5 years. The mastoid cells of infants increase over the first few years of life. This increase, plus the horizontal position of the tympanic membrane and eustachian tube, contributes to a high incidence of otitis media in infancy.

Infants can distinguish both high- and low-frequency sounds, and they prefer multifrequency tones. They readily respond to the human voice by 1 month of age.

Hearing screening should be done at every well-child visit; this is especially critical in the first year of life. Parents are often the best evaluators of hearing problems. Newborns initially respond to sound by the startle reflex. As they grow, however, they are able to turn toward sounds, stop crying in response to music or a soft voice, and eventually make verbal noises in response to sounds made to them.

Because 1 in 1000 children is born deaf and an additional 2 in 1000 more are affected during childhood, evaluation of hearing is critical to normal speech and development (Coplan, 1987). The ability to hear facilitates infant–parent bonding; it is critical for optimal communication between infants and parents; and it is essential for normal language, emotional, social, and intellectual development. When hearing and the other senses are intact, infants have strong potential for developing into productive adults.

### Vision

Vision, the least developed sense in newborns, grows at an astounding rate during the first year of life. At birth visual acuity is thought to be at least 20/670; by 12 months of age, it improves to 20/40 to 20/60 (Rudolph & Hoffman, 1987). This improvement can be seen by the actions of infants. In the first month of life they gaze at large objects; by 2 months of age more specific detail of an object is noted. At this point parents and infants can enjoy looking back and forth at each other because it is such a purposeful reciprocal behavior. At 3 months of age the eyes begin to converge, with an increase in eye–hand coordination; infants learn to reach for objects and bring them close to themselves. By 6 to 7 months of age infants can distinguish different faces, resulting in the beginning of stranger anxiety (see Cognitive Development).

Blindness due to cataracts should be discovered in the newborn period, but evaluation of the red reflex should be performed at every well-child visit in the rare event that cataracts develop later. When a light is shined directly into the pupil, a circular red reflex should appear, indicating that the choroid and retina are intact. Searching nystagmus, absent blinking to a threat, or lack of horizontal and vertical following by 2 months of age requires further evaluation.

### Taste, Smell, and Touch

The senses of taste and smell are often interdependent. Infants can discriminate the smell of their mothers from other nursing mothers even during the first weeks of life. In the first months of life infants can differentiate between various types of formulas. Early in their first year sweet and salty taste buds are developed enough to allow taste preferences. Solid foods are introduced into the diet of a 5- or 6-month-old infant not to benefit the infant's nutritional status but to expose him or her to textures other than liquids (Barness, 1985).

Infants readily respond to touch in the early minutes after birth. Usually they are highly sensitive to being held, caressed, and stroked throughout the first months of life. In turn they initiate touching very early in life. Although the grasp reflex is present for the first few months, it is the sensation of touching another object that helps this develop into a purposeful gesture. Infants learn much about their environment by manipulating the objects around themselves.

## Body System Development

### Gastrointestinal Tract

Although the gastrointestinal tract is not primitive at birth, during the first year of life this system matures almost to adult capacity. The sucking reflex, seen in the fetus in the first trimester, enables infants to be nurtured. Infants can coordinate sucking, swallowing, and respiration until 6 months of age, at which point breathing and swallowing occur separately (Godfrey & Baum, 1979). Tongue thrust is present until 3 months of age, when infants are finally able to move food to the back of their mouths; this is one of many reasons why the introduction of solid food before 4 months of age is not recommended. By 3 months of age

salivation increases to the extent that swallowing large quantities of saliva is difficult, and drooling begins. Carbohydrate digestion is aided by ptyalin in the saliva, which increases steadily during the first 6 months of life.

Gastric motility varies depending on volume and type of feeding and even the emotional environment in which infants are fed. Emptying time of the stomach varies. Although each infant's feeding period differs, an important fact to remember is that breast milk has less fat content than formula. Diets that are high in fat (which deters motility) stay in the stomach longer. Therefore, bottle-fed infants may have longer intervals between feedings.

Digestion is aided by the enzyme rennin, in conjunction with hydrochloric acid. These secretions change the casein in the milk to a curd that remains in the stomach longer and allows further digestion. Digestion is further facilitated in the small intestine (duodenum) by the pancreatic juices and bile. Amylase helps to break down complex carbohydrates, lipase helps reduce fats, and trypsin enhances protein digestion.

Gastroesophageal reflux is normal in infants, although severe reflux requires intervention (see Chap. 29). Gastroesophageal reflux is regurgitation of stomach contents into the esophagus caused by immaturity of the sphincter mechanism at the junction of the esophagus and stomach (Aquilina, 1987). Spitting up is common in infancy and usually abates by 5 or 6 months of age. Overfeeding, the need for an increase in burping, and reflux are all frequent causes of spitting up. Because of the immaturity of the cardiac sphincter, frequent burping is often necessary to release swallowed air, relieving some of the spitting up. If infants regurgitate after every feeding, are extremely irritable, and are losing weight, other pathological causes of spitting up need to be investigated.

***Stools.*** The gastrointestinal tract is usually sterile at birth; within hours bacteria enter through the mouth and anus. Bacteria play an important role in the gut by enhancing the formation of nutrients, natural antibiotics, and B vitamins, and by being a source of vitamin K. The amount and type of bacteria are affected by diet. Lactobacilli colonize the gut of breast-fed infants, whereas the sugar and protein content of formula determines the flora in bottle-fed infants (Godfrey & Baum, 1979).

Stools vary in consistency, color, and frequency depending on infants' nutrition. They often are a good indication of the functioning of infants' digestive processes. During the first month of life, the stools of breast-fed infants are yellow, are often loose with some solid particles, and vary from one stool every 3 or 4 days to five to seven stools per day, the latter pattern being more common. The stools change occasionally from yellow to green and vice versa as a result of the less efficient intestinal reducing power of infants. Stools of formula-fed infants are generally much firmer, yellow, and less frequent. These infants usually have one or two bowel movements per day.

When solid foods are added to infants' diets, stool color and consistency change. The stools become firmer and often take on the color of the food eaten (spinach, green; beets, red). The odor also changes and reflects the foods that are eaten. When table foods are eaten later in the first year of life, the immaturity of the digestive system is revealed as food particles such as corn, carrots, and raisins come out in the stool undigested.

## The Liver

The liver accounts for 5% of body weight during infancy. This relatively large organ has four lobes and is usually situated 1 or 2 cm below the right costal border. The liver's enzymatic mechanisms necessary for glucose homeostasis, bile acid synthesis, bilirubin and bile acid conjugation and secretion, and detoxification of drugs all develop throughout gestation and during the first year of life (Behrman & Vaughan, 1987).

## Respiratory System

The primary purpose of the lungs is to deliver oxygen to the body and transport carbon dioxide from the body. Gas exchange occurs at the alveolar level. The alveolar system is present at birth but continues to grow throughout childhood; 70 million alveoli at birth multiply to about 400 million by adolescence (Behrman & Vaughn, 1987). The main bronchi and trachea are small and easily obstructed in infancy. Airway resistance is higher than in adults.

Breathing is probably regulated by the brain stem. Breathing patterns in early infancy are irregular (primary apnea), but a regular breathing rhythm develops with maturity. A normal respiratory rate for the first year is 20 to 40 breaths/min with predominately the same abdominal breathing of the newborn. This abdominal pattern persists at least through early school age when the adult thoracic pattern is established.

## Cardiovascular System

The circulatory system of the newborn changes drastically with the first breath; gas exchange is transferred from the placenta to the lung (see Chap. 11). The cardiovascular system continues to mature throughout infancy. The foramen ovale closes at or shortly after birth (the first few hours to days of life) and is usually closed by about 3 months of age, whereas the ductus arteriosus closes much more quickly, by 2 or 3 days of age. Because mild openings persist in these fetal shunts, functional murmurs are commonly heard during early infancy.

The heart rate drops slowly throughout the first year of life to an average 120 beats/min, with a normal range of 80 to 160 beats/min. Blood pressure also changes during this period; the average blood pressure is 90/60 with variations due to activity level and weight. Average heart rates and blood pressures can be found in Appendix B. As the fetal circulation ceases, an increase occurs in volume and pressure loads to the left ventricle. The myocardium is able to perform better because of maturation of the sympathetic nervous system and contractility of the muscle. All these factors contribute to a rapid rise in blood pressure after birth. The heart itself is situated slightly higher in infants (fourth intercostal space) than in the adult (fifth intercostal space). By the end of the first year its weight is about double what it was at birth.

Hematopoiesis occurs primarily in the bone marrow. High infant metabolism requires a continuous supply of oxygen; the hemoglobin component of the red blood cell is the oxygen-carrying protein of the body. Hemoglobin contains two pairs of globin chains. The different chains and their ratio within the hemoglobin molecule give the hemoglobin a specific name. Although there are six varieties of hemoglobin, the ratio of the predominant types change after birth. Hemoglobins F, A, and $A_2$ are the predominant hemoglobin molecules after birth. The production of hemoglobin F decreases after birth, and this hemoglobin is only slightly present in the blood of a 6-month-old. Hemoglobin A accounts for 30% of blood at birth, increasing to adult levels by 6 months of age. Hemoglobin $A_2$ attains adult levels by 12 months of age but makes up only 2% to 3% of the total blood hemoglobin.

After birth, fetal hemoglobin levels decrease until 6 to 8 weeks of age; adult hemoglobin levels form at about 13 weeks of age. A sudden cessation of erythropoiesis occurs at birth, when there is an increase in oxygen saturation. Concurrently, fetal erythropoietin drops, and red cell survival length is only 90 days, compared with 120 days in adults (Behrman & Vaughan, 1987). The physiologic anemia that occurs by 3 months of age is reversible. The bone marrow senses a decrease in hemoglobin, and erythropoietin production in the kidney then increases. Dietary iron is necessary at this time for normal hematopoiesis to continue.

## Endocrine System

Although the endocrine system is adequately developed at birth, its functions are immature. The master gland of the endocrine system is the pituitary gland. Homeostasis is attained by the appropriate functioning of this gland and the interrelations between the nervous system and the hormonal system. Although the pituitary gland is well formed at birth, maturation continues throughout the first year of life. The anterior pituitary is regulated by the hypothalamus. This lobe has six types of secretory cells. Growth hormone, mediated by peptides called *somatomedins*, stimulates growth. Other functions include lipolysis of adipose tissue, a decrease in carbohydrate metabolism, and protein synthesis in the liver.

Prolactin is stored in the pituitary in much larger amounts than is growth hormone. It is required for lactation. Unlike the other hormones, which are influenced by releasing factors, prolactin is controlled by a prolactin-inhibiting factor.

Thyrotropin secretion stimulates the thyroid gland. Thyrotropin (thyroid-stimulating hormone) and thyroxine are necessary for normal metabolism. The hormone levels continue to rise throughout infancy.

Adrenocorticotropin stimulates the adrenal gland to produce glucocorticoids and aldosterone, which influence fluid and electrolyte balance and the metabolism of carbohydrates, fats, and proteins. A feedback system exists between adrenocorticotropin and the cortisols: as one rises, the other decreases. These levels reach their peak in early morning (4 : 00 A.M.) and fall to their lowest level in the evening. This diurnal variation becomes established by about 6 months of age (Rudolph & Hoffman, 1987). The posterior lobe of the pituitary gland is the source of anti-diuretic hormone, which is important for maintaining body water homeostasis.

### Immune System

The immune system begins its development early in fetal life; without this complex protective mechanism, infants cannot survive and thrive outside the uterus. The immune system has four components:

1. Bone marrow–derived lymphocytes (B cells) generate antibodies in plasma, secretions, and interstitial space. B-lymphocytes differentiate into memory cells and plasma cells when exposed to antigens. Plasma cells secrete antibodies capable of destroying specific antigens. Memory cells retain the ability to produce specific immunoglobulins.
2. T cells from the thymus are in the blood and peripheral lymphoid tissue. There are three types of T cells: killer cells, helper cells, and suppressor cells. Killer cells bind to the surface of antigens and, by destroying the cell membrane, destroy the cell. They secrete lymphokines, which prevent the spread of antigens. An example of a lymphokine is interferon. Helper cells stimulate T-lymphocytes to divide and mature into plasma cells. Suppressor cells diminish the production of immunoglobulins against a specific antigen. This mechanism may be responsible for immunodeficiency diseases.
3. The phagocytic system destroys microorganisms and is composed of macrophages, monocytes, and polymorphonuclear leukocytes (neutrophils). Macrophages are the phagocytes of the tissue, monocytes come from bone marrow, and neutrophils are in the circulatory system. Phagocytosis, the ingestion of replicating and nonreplicating organisms, begins by the phagocyte moving toward the bacteria that is emitting chemotactic factors. After the phagocyte and foreign antigen intersect, the bacteria is engulfed and neutrophils destroy it (Rudolph & Hoffman, 1987).

4. A complement system consisting of 20 native proteins works with the other three components to increase antimicrobial resistance (Rudolph & Hoffman, 1987).

An important part of this protective mechanism is the development of immunoglobulins. It is the function of the B cells, with the assistance of the T cells, to initiate the production of these antibody molecules by the eighth week of gestation. Although all are formed in fetal life, the maturation of this system occurs up through adult life. Table 12-3 displays the normal values for the three main immunoglobulins. One can see that IgG is high at birth because it is the only immunoglobulin that crosses the placenta to the developing fetus. Its primary function is the protection of infants from viruses, bacteria, and fungi for the first 3 or 4 months of life. After this time, the other immunoglobulins begin to rise rapidly as a primary defense mechanism for the body.

### Renal System

The human kidney has many diverse functions. The important roles of toxic waste removal and conservation of essential electrolytes are present at birth but immature. This immaturity results in a decreased ability of the kidney to concentrate urine and to cope with fluid and electrolyte stresses such as dehydration. The glomerular filtration rate increases from 10 to 15 mL/min/m$^2$ to 50 mL/min/m$^2$ in the first 12 months, with this function increasing especially after 8 months of age (Behrman & Vaughan, 1987). Thus, breast milk and infant formula are prepared not only for easy digestion but also for easy filtration through the

*Table 12–3. Normal Values for Immunoglobulins at Various Ages*

| Age* | IgG (mg/dL) | IgA (mg/dL) | IgM (mg/dL) |
|---|---|---|---|
| Newborn | 600–1670 | 0–5 | 6–15 |
| 1–3  mo | 218–610 | 20–53 | 11–51 |
| 4–6  mo | 228–636 | 27–72 | 25–60 |
| 7–9  mo | 292–816 | 27–73 | 12–124 |
| 10–18  mo | 383–1070 | 27–169 | 28–113 |
| 2 y | 423–1184 | 35–222 | 32–131 |
| 3 y | 477–1334 | 40–251 | 28–113 |
| 4–5  y | 540–1500 | 48–336 | 20–106 |
| 6–8  y | 571–1700 | 52–535 | 28–112 |
| 14 y | 570–1570 | 86–544 | 33–135 |
| Adult | 635–1775 | 106–668 | 37–154 |

* Difference in immunoglobulin levels as reported by several authors based on the use of different reference antigens.
(Buckley, R., Dees, S., & O'Fallon, W. M. [1968]. Serum immunoglobulin levels in normal children and in uncomplicated childhood. *Pediatrics, 41,* 600)

kidney. Skim milk, for example, has a high solute load that infant kidneys are unable to handle.

## Musculoskeletal System

Bone size increases by a process called *ossification.* Long bones grow in circumference by intramembranous ossification, that is, mesenchymal cells in the periosteal surface differentiate and accumulate to form bone. For long bones to grow in length, proliferation and hypertrophy of cells must occur (enchondral ossification). In long bones, growth occurs in the growth cartilage called the *physis* or *growth plate* (Rudolph & Hoffman, 1987). The long bones grow very rapidly in the first year, with much of the growth occurring at the following ossification centers:

- Distal end of the femur
- Proximal end of the tibia
- Talus (forms ankle joint)
- Calcaneus (forms heel)
- Cuboid (between calcaneus and fourth and fifth metatarsals)

Endocrine, mechanical, nutritional, or vascular factors can alter ossification (Rudolph & Hoffman, 1987). An adequate supply of vitamin D and calcium in the diet is especially important, as are ample supplies of growth and sex hormones. By 5 or 6 months of age, ossification in the wrist begins. The number of ossification centers in the wrist is a good indicator of bone age, especially before the age of 6 years.

Muscles and connective tissue are an important part of this system. The adult number of muscle fibers is present at birth, but elongation and hypertrophy of these fibers persist throughout childhood. Tendons continue to increase in number during this time. Thus, by the end of the first year most infants learn to walk, in part due to the maturation of the musculoskeletal system.

## Nutrition

Feeding infants involves much more than just supplying adequate calories for growth. As infants' hunger is abated by feeding, they feel the pleasure of fullness as well as the comfort of being held and cuddled. Mutual eye contact, verbal communication, and tactile stimulation during feeding aid the development of a reciprocal relationship between infants and their caretakers. Most theories agree that a positive feeding experience has a beneficial effect on development (Pencharz, 1985). As infants mature from total dependency to increasing independence by 1 year of age, feeding concerns arise. Parents need to be educated about the exact nutritional needs during the first year of life and how personality and developmental tasks influence children's eating habits. Table 12-4 details the nutrient content of mature human milk and the recommended standards for formula. Table 12-5 compares the nutrient

*Table 12–4.   Nutrient Content of Mature Human Milk and Recommended Standards for Formula*

| Nutrient (U/100 mL) | Mature Human Milk | Formula Standards |
|---|---|---|
| Protein (g) | 1.1 | 1.2–2.9 |
| Fat (g) | 4.5 | 2.1–3.9 |
| Carbohydrates (g) | 6.8 | (40%–50% of Energy) |
| Energy (kcal) | 75 | 65 |
| Thiamin ($B_1$)($\mu$g) | 16 | 26 |
| Riboflavin ($B_2$)($\mu$g) | 36 | 39 |
| Niacin ($\mu$g) | 147 | 162 |
| Pyridoxine ($\mu$g) | 10 | 23 |
| Folacin ($\mu$g) | 5.2 | 2.6 |
| Vitamin C (mg) | 4.3 | 5.2 |
| Vitamin $B_{12}$ ($\mu$g) | 0.03 | 0.1 |
| Vitamin A (IU) | 189 | 162–487 |
| Calcium (mg) | 34 | 32.5 |
| Iron (mg) | 0.05 | 0.1–1.6 |
| Magnesium (mg) | 4 | 3.9 |
| Zinc (mg) | 0.4 | 0.3 |

(Anderson, G. H. [1985]. Human milk feeding. *Pediatric Clinics of North America, 32,* 345)

content of human milk and formula with recommended nutrient intakes of infants.

### Essential Nutrients

Specific nutrients are essential for optimal growth and development. A full-term infant requires 115 to 130 kcal/kg/day for the first 3 months of life. This can easily be obtained from breast milk or formula, which supplies 20 kcal/oz and results in a weight gain of about 1 oz/day. By 3 to 6 months of age an infant's caloric requirement decreases to 100 to 110 kcal/kg/day.

Nutrients essential for growth include lipids, protein, carbohydrate, water, salt, minerals, and vitamins. A discussion of the nutritional content of breast milk follows. Because formulas are manufactured to simulate breast milk as much as possible, they are not discussed in detail.

*Lipids.* Most calories are provided by milk lipids. Although the exact fat content of breast milk varies depending on the timing of the feeding and the nutritional status of the mother, in general, the fat supply is adequate. Breast milk is high in linoleic acid, an essential unsaturated fat. Mothers who are malnourished respond to increasing the calories and fat content of their diets. The importance of a low-fat diet in the prevention of heart disease remains unclear, but most studies support this theory as well as the beneficial effects of low-fat diets on

*Table 12–5. Comparison of Nutrient Content of Mature Human Milk and Formula with Recommended Nutrient Intakes of Infants*

| Nutrients | Recommended Intake* | | | | Content | |
| --- | --- | --- | --- | --- | --- | --- |
| | 0–2.9 Months | | 3–5.9 Months | | | |
| | 97.5% | 50% | 97.5% | 50% | Milk† | Formula |
| U/1000 kcal | | | | | | |
| Protein (g) | 25 | 16 | 22 | 15 | 15 | 18 |
| Thiamin (mg) | 0.4 | 0.3 | 0.4 | 0.3 | 0.2 | 0.4 |
| Riboflavin (mg) | 0.5 | 0.4 | 0.5 | 0.38 | 0.48 | 0.6 |
| Niacin (equivalents) | 7.1 | 5.5 | 7.1 | 5.5 | 2 | 2.5 |
| Folacin (μg) | 64 | 42 | 73 | 47 | 69 | 40 |
| Vitamin $B_{12}$ (μg) | 0.85 | 0.46 | 0.61 | 0.33 | 0.4 | 1.54 |
| Ascorbic acid (mg) | 56 | 30 | 40 | 21 | 57 | 80 |
| Vitamin A (retinol equivalent, μg) | 1150 | 600 | 800 | 450 | 2530 | 2492 |
| Vitamin E (mg) | 8.5 | 4.6 | 6.1 | 3.3 | 8 | 7 |
| Calcium (mg) | 990 | 540 | 710 | 380 | 453 | 500 |
| Iron (mg) | 1.1 | 0.6 | 10 | 5.4 | 0.67 | 1.54 |
| Magnesium (mg) | 76 | 49 | 73 | 47 | 53 | 60 |
| Zinc (mg) | 5.6 | 3 | 6.1 | 3.3 | 5.3 | 4.6 |
| U/g protein | | | | | | |
| Vitamin $B_6$ (μg) | 15 | 11.5 | 15 | 11.5 | 8.9 | 19.7 |

*Indicates the nutrient density of diets recommended to meet the needs of 97.5% or 50% of infants.
† Mature human milk.
(Anderson, G. H. [1985]. Human milk feeding. *Pediatric Clinics of North America, 32,* 345)

weight control. Up through the age of 2 years children need at least 30% to 40% of their calories from fat for completion of the myelination process (American Academy of Pediatrics, Committee on Nutrition, 1986a).

*Protein.* During the first month of life, the protein content of breast milk undergoes changes until whey makes up the largest portion of the proteins. Casein, another protein, gives the milk its white appearance (American Academy of Pediatrics, Committee on Nutrition, 1981). Whether the amount of breast milk protein depends on the mother's dietary protein is still unclear (Anderson, 1985).

*Carbohydrate.* Lactose is the main sugar in human milk. Its production creates an electrochemical reaction that aids the transportation of sodium and potassium into the milk. The amount of sodium declines in the first months of lactation. Water constitutes 85% to 95% of milk and is essential for adequate milk production (American Academy of Pediatrics, Committee on Nutrition, 1981).

*Minerals.* Calcium and phosphorus are essential for bone development. In general, mothers' diets supply most of the nutrients needed for infants to grow. Studies have shown though, that breast-fed infants need supple-

ments of 400 IU of vitamin D and 0.25 mg of fluoride daily. Because absorption of vitamin D depends on sunlight, the amount infants receive may vary. To prevent rickets, a supplement is necessary. The fluoride content of breast milk is low, and because unerupted teeth are mineralized during infancy, an additional source is needed (American Academy of Pediatrics, Committee on Nutrition, 1986b).

By the time infants are 3 months old, their mothers' iron stores from pregnancy are depleted, necessitating an additional source of iron. Iron passes through the breast milk, with only a small fraction bound to lactoferrin; the unbound portion is readily absorbed by infants.

Formula has all the vitamins added to it, but not all formulas are fortified with iron. The American Academy of Pediatrics recommends that formula be supplemented with iron in a bioavailable form (Miller & Chopra, 1984). Ideally infants should have iron-fortified formula until 1 year of age, after which table food that contains iron should be sufficient. A fluoride supplement is needed only if the formula is not being prepared with fluoridated water.

Solid foods may be introduced between 4 and 6 months of age (see section on feeding). Baby food is manufactured only for the convenience of the caretakers; unseasoned table food in a pureed form may be given to infants as their first solid food. Table 12-6 describes the

*Table 12–6.  Energy Value of Strained Foods for Infants*

| Type of Food | Average Energy (kcal/100 g) | Average kcal from Carbohydrate (%) |
|---|---|---|
| Juices | 65 | 96 |
| Fruits | 85 | 96 |
| Vegetables | | |
|   Plain | 45 | 80 |
|   Creamed | 63 | 74 |
| Meats | 106 | 1 |
| Egg yolk | 192 | 3 |
| High meat dinners (meat and vegetable) | 58 | 56 |
| Desserts | 96 | 89 |
| Cereals | | |
|   With milk | 105 | — |
|   With water | 52 | — |
|   Dry | 360 | — |
| Formula and cow's milk | 67 (/100 mL) | — |
| Human milk | 70 (/100 mL) | — |

(Adapted from Anderson, T. A., & Foman, S. J. [1974]. In S. J. Foman [Ed.]. *Infant nutrition* [3rd ed.]. Philadelphia: W. B. Saunders)

calories available in prepared infant food (Anderson & Foman, 1974; Levine et al., 1983). For the second half of the first year infants need 80 to 100 kcal/kg/d for optimal growth. Infants may be given whole milk from cows at 6 months of age if they have a variety of solid foods and a supplemental source of iron. Because the amount and variety of solid foods vary greatly among infants, a multivitamin with iron is necessary. Therefore, breast milk or formula is still recommended, but 24 to 30 oz/d is adequate. Ideally whole milk should be started around the first birthday; skim milk is not recommended because of its high solute load and low fat content (Barness, 1985). Desserts are never recommended, nor is the addition of salt to infants' meals ever necessary.

## Vegetarian Diets

In the past 20 years vegetarian diets have become more popular in the United States. These diets have long been the mainstay of life in many parts of the world. Many health professionals unfamiliar with the various types of vegetarian diets are concerned about whether infants eating only vegetarian foods receive a well-balanced diet during this fast growing period.

The five types of vegetarian diets are shown in Table 12-7. Parents need to understand the balance of nutrients required for growth. The eight amino acids essential for growth are not generally found in one protein source, so a

variety of foods should be eaten at each meal. Fruits, vegetables, and cereal provide fiber that is necessary for proper digestion. Adequate fat intake is necessary for myelination of the brain as well as for the absorption of the fat-soluble vitamins (A, D, E, and K). Iron, found in legumes and dark green leafy vegetables, is necessary for adequate growth. Ideally infants should be breast-fed or formula-fed for at least 6 months. Vegetarian mothers need to monitor their diets carefully so that they can provide adequate nutrition through the breast milk. Infants need vitamin D and fluoride supplements for proper bone and teeth development. Soy formulas can be used instead of cow's milk–based formula for bottle-fed infants. Solid foods should be introduced in the same manner as for other infants, and a variety of foods should be combined to provide all the essential nutrients.

Total vegetarian and Zen macrobiotic diets do not provide growing infants with essential nutrients. Health professionals need to seriously discuss with the parents the role proper nutrition plays in child development.

Some parents have diets that are nontraditional for religious or medical reasons. It is important to respect these preferences while planning appropriate ways to provide balanced diets in the first year of life.

## Sleep

By 1 month of age infants sleep, on the average, 15½ hours per day. Sleep time decreases about 15 to 30 minutes every 3 months thereafter. By 1 year of age, most infants sleep 13¾ hours per day (Ferber, 1985). Many variables influence both the quantity and the quality of sleep. Temperament is one of these variables. Passive, easygoing infants may initially sleep 18 hours per day, whereas active infants may thrive on 14 hours per day.

Infants have different sleep patterns that affect their bodily movements during sleep. The two types of sleep are rapid eye movement (REM) sleep, which develops in the

*Table 12–7.  Types of Vegetarian Diets*

| Diet | Included Foods |
|---|---|
| Lacto-ovovegetarian | Plant foods, eggs, and dairy products |
| Lactovegetarian | Plant foods and dairy products |
| Total vegetarian | Plant foods |
| Ovovegetarian | Plant foods and eggs |
| Zen macrobiotic | Ten diets: lowest (−3)—10% cereals, 30% vegetables, 10% soup, 30% animal products, 15% salad and fruit, and 5% dessert; highest (7)—100% cereals, fluids avoided as much as possible |

(Rudy, C. [1984]. Vegetarian diets for children. *Pediatric Nursing, 10,* 329–333)

seventh month of gestation, and non-REM sleep, which develops in the seventh or eighth month of gestation (Ferber, 1985). Non-REM sleep is the state in which the body is quiet and has a regular heart and respiratory rate. Whereas REM sleep has only one stage of electro-encephalographic (EEG) activity, non-REM sleep has four stages:

*Stage 1*—low voltage, fast pattern

*Stage 2*—sleep spindles with low voltage background

*Stages 3 and 4*—slow, high voltage waves called slow-wave sleep

REM sleep is considered active sleep in which there is a fast-frequency EEG pattern and diminished muscle tone. Sleep patterns consist of two non-REM phases followed by one REM sleep phase. This 2 : 1 pattern recurs throughout the sleep period and continues throughout life. Infants may partially wake or cry out when moving from one stage to another.

By 3 months of age the initial stage of sleep changes from REM to non-REM sleep. Frequently parents report that infants develop regular patterns of nighttime sleep and napping. These different sleep patterns should be defined here because some common sleep problems are often directly related to a particular pattern.

Newborns often are very sleepy from the birthing process, and it may be a week before they arouse more readily. Most infants do not have a regular sleep pattern until they are 2 or 3 months of age. By 1 month of age infants often sleep between feedings with a few hours of wakefulness during the day and evening. By 3 or 4 months of age some infants sleep 5 to 9 hours at night with three or four naps during the day (Ferber, 1985). By 6 months of age most infants take two naps a day, which eventually abbreviates to one long daily nap.

These are averages; some infants may sleep 12 hours at night, and others might take numerous 20-minute catnaps during the day. Although this variation is normal, parents can help shape infants' sleep patterns to best accommodate both infants and their families.

When a pattern develops in which 5- to 6-month-old infants continue to awake during the night, it is termed *trained night crying*. It is to infants' best advantage if parents do not respond with attention and affection, which, in essence, reward negative behavior (McIntosh, 1989).

Ferber (1985) states that helping infants learn how to fall asleep on their own is essential for developing good sleep patterns. Although infants enjoy cuddling and rocking to relax, this should be done before falling asleep. It is difficult to break any habit (like nursing, taking a bottle, or rocking) after months of mutual enjoyment. Allowing infants to fall asleep on their own sets the stage for easier bedtime rituals as infants mature (Fig. 12-5).

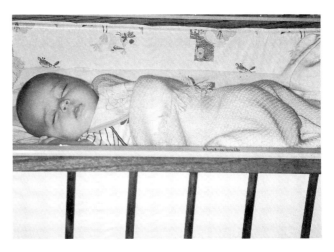

*Figure 12–5. Child sleeping in a crib.*

## Dentition

In normal dentition there are 20 primary teeth: one central and one lateral incisor, one canine, and two molars in each quadrant of the mouth. The development of the primary tooth buds begins during the 12th week of fetal life. Permanent teeth form in two groups: the incisors, cuspids, and premolars develop from about the fifth month of gestation to 10 months of age. The three permanent molars form at 4 months' gestation, 1 year, and 4 years, respectively.

Each tooth is made up of a crown and a root. Enamel covers the crown and cementum covers the root. The main portion of the tooth is composed of dentin and pulp. Table 12-8 shows the average tooth eruption during infancy. Mandibular teeth usually erupt first, followed by the maxillary teeth; teeth often erupt earlier in girls than boys. Most children have at least one tooth by 14 months of age.

Primary teeth are just as important as permanent teeth; they are necessary for chewing, speaking, and appearance. More important is the fact that primary teeth create the space in the jaw for permanent teeth. Thus, caution during development and eruption is necessary to ensure proper dental growth.

Normal development of teeth can be interrupted by (1) disturbances in formation of the matrix, (2) a lack of one or more of the necessary minerals, or (3) ingestion of toxic substances. Alterations in tooth formation can change the color, texture, and thickness of the tooth surface

*Table 12–8. Average Tooth Eruption During Infancy*

|  | Mandibular | Maxillary |
| --- | --- | --- |
| Central incisors | 5–7 mo | 6–8 mo |
| Lateral incisors | 7–10 mo | 8–11 mo |

(Behrman & Vaughan, 1987). For example, tetracycline taken by a pregnant mother can permanently damage the color of the developing teeth. Therefore, caution should be exercised when giving medication to pregnant women or children up to 13 years of age. Enamel hypoplasia is characterized by pits or fissures on the enamel surface and can occur as a result of high fevers, chemical ingestion (i.e., excessive amounts of fluoride) at the time of enamel development, or deficiency of vitamins A, C, or D (Shafer, Hine, & Levine, 1974).

Prevention is the key to good oral hygiene. After teeth have erupted, parents should clean them with a washcloth until children can brush their own teeth (Fig. 12-6). Fluoride is another essential element in good oral hygiene. Fluoride affects the chemistry and structure of teeth during tooth development (birth through 13 years of age). After the tooth crown develops and before eruption, the tooth absorbs more fluoride. This continues during tooth eruption (Kula & Tianoff, 1982) The daily requirement of fluoride for prevention of tooth decay is 0.25 mg. If the drinking water is fluoridated and infants' formula is prepared with water, supplemental fluoride is not necessary during the first year of life. Infants who are solely breast-fed need 0.25 mg of fluoride supplement daily. Fluoride may be supplemented either by itself or in combination with vitamins. Drinking water is prepared for the infant by adding either tablets or drops of fluoride to achieve the proper concentration of 1 part per million. For example, one 2.2-mg tablet of sodium fluoride dissolved in 1 quart of water provides the proper concentration. Parents must be cautioned that exceeding the recommended dosage can cause mottling of the teeth.

### Teething

The gums may be tender while teeth are erupting. Infants may experience a feeling of pressure before a parent can

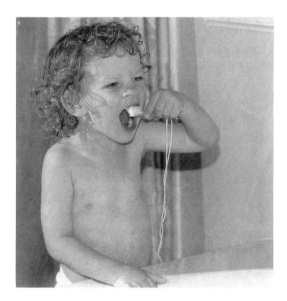

*Figure 12–6.   Child cleaning teeth.*

actually feel or see a tooth. The presence of saliva and drooling does not necessarily indicate teething.

If infants are slightly irritable, it is often soothing to rub the gums with fingers, apply a topical anesthetic such as a teething lotion that contains benzocaine, or have the child bite on a teething ring. By 6 or 7 months of age infants can suck on ice wrapped in a washcloth. This numbs the gums while providing minimal fluid. Teething biscuits are messy and can be dangerous if infants bite off a piece. Occasionally infants bite on the bottle nipple or even refuse the bottle for a day or two. Parents should try using a cup or offer other foods until infants can suck again. Refusing a bottle is usually temporary, lasting only 1 or 2 days. Infants should not get high fevers while teething; temperatures of 101°F (38.4°C) or higher warrant further investigation, as does extreme fussiness.

## Cognitive Development

From the moment of their first breath infants have the potential for great intellectual accomplishments. This very first opportunity to interact with their environment sets the stage for future learning experiences.

Physical, emotional, and cognitive development progresses at an astounding rate during the first year. Much of the learning occurs as a result of maturation of the five senses. For example, during the second month of life infants learn to blink at objects that come close to them. Their eyes work synchronously, enabling them to see one object, and the lenses accommodate for distance, so that by $3\frac{1}{2}$ months of age infants can see objects clearly. This allows the senses of vision and touch to work together. The eyes can now see the hands, which leads to swiping at objects with a closed fists, to reaching for objects, and eventually, after much trial and error, to grasping objects and bringing them to their mouths. Parents need to know very early in their infants' lives that this is true learning and, indeed, a great accomplishment. It is apparent how much infants have learned about their environments long before the end of their first year, when they respond negatively if told not to touch a forbidden object.

### Piaget

Piaget's developmental theory provides a clinical framework for infants' cognitive growth. More detail on Piaget's theory can be found in Chapter 4.

There are three cognitive goals of infancy:

*Object permanence*—learning that objects still exist even when they are not in sight

*Causality*—learning that there is a relation between objects and events

*Symbolic play*—representation of one object by another

Piaget (1952) identified six stages of cognitive development; three of the six sensorimotor stages occur during infancy (Table 12-9).

### Stage Two (1–4 Months)

In stage two, infants accidentally produce an action that is pleasurable and gradually learn how to produce the event over and over again. Examples of this include thumb sucking or waving their hands in front of themselves and then putting the hands in their mouths (Fig. 12-7). After many repetitions during the first 3 or 4 months, they might discover that their hands meet each other and can feel a different sensation. They become aware that their hands and feet are extensions of themselves. Toward the end of this stage, parents realize that infants can pay attention longer; they might be fascinated by clasping and unclasping their hands or by watching a mobile. They might smile and wave their hands when they see a bottle; they now anticipate that the bottle means nourishment, which means pleasure. Although they are assimilating a lot from their surroundings, they still do not perceive that there is an environment outside their own bodies.

### Stage Three (4–8 Months)

In stage three, infants learn that objects in the environment, which are separate from their bodies, can make events happen. For example, when infants look at themselves in a mirror, this self-exploration facilitates their

*Table 12–9.  Cognition, Play, and Language Development: Sensorimotor Stages*

| Piagetian Stage | Age | Object Permanence | Causality | Play | Receptive Language | Expressive Language |
|---|---|---|---|---|---|---|
| I | <1 mo | Shifting images | Generalization of reflexes | | Turns to voice | Range of cries (hunger, pain) |
| II | 1–4 mo | Stares at spot where object disappeared (looks at hand after yarn drops) | Primary circular reactions (thumb sucking) | | Searches for speaker with eyes | Cooing Vocal contagion |
| III | 4–8 mo | Visually follows dropped object through vertical trajectory (tracks dropped yarn to floor) | Secondary circular reactions (recreates accidentally discovered environmental effects, e.g., kicks mattress to shake mobile) | Same behavioral repertoire for all objects (bangs, shakes, puts in mouth, drops) | Responds to own name and to tones of voice | Babbling Four distinct syllables |
| IV | 9–12 mo | Finds an object after watching it hidden | Coordination of secondary circular reactions | Visual motor inspection of objects Peak-a-boo | Listens selectively to familiar words Responds to "no" and other verbal requests | First real word Jargoning Symbolic gestures (shakes head no) |
| V | 12–18 mo | Recovers hidden object after multiple visible changes of position | Tertiary circular reactions (deliberately varies behavior to create novel effects) | Awareness of social function of objects Symbolic play centered on own body (drinks from toy cup) | Can bring familiar object from another room Points to parts of body | Many single words—uses words to express needs Acquires 10 words by 18 mo |
| VI | 18–24 mo | Recovers hidden object after invisible changes in position | Spontaneously uses nondirect causal mechanisms (uses key to move wind-up toy) | Symbolic play directed toward doll (gives doll a drink) | Follows series of two or three commands Points to pictures when named | Telegraphic two-word sentences |

(Levine, M., Carey, W., Crocker, A., & Gross, R. [1983]. *Developmental–behavioral pediatrics.* Phialdelpiha: W. B. Saunders, p. 91)

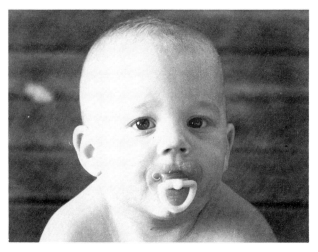

*Figure 12–7.   Infant with pacifier in mouth.*

learning that they are separate from their environments. They alternately handle toys and fingers and put them into their mouths until they realize the toys are separate from their bodies. During this phase infants realize that their bodies and those of their caretakers are separate. Another name for this phenomenon is *stranger anxiety.* Infants' love for their primary caretakers, usually their mothers, becomes exclusive; they now realize that their mothers have met most of their needs and that they are important. No longer are they satisfied by anyone who feeds or changes them, they want their mothers. Their mother makes them feel good and satisfied. This becomes evident when the mother leaves the room or when an infant awakens during the night and is not able to see her. Infants now have a memory and a mental image of what their mothers look like; when they do not see them, they are anxious and unhappy.

During play an infant in stage three looks for a ball that rolls away from him or her. No longer is the phrase "out of sight, out of mind" applicable to infants. Their mental capacities are growing and incorporating the world around them. The interaction game of peek-a-boo is the beginning of object permanence. Infants continue to search for the parent even if the parent's face is hidden by hands or a blanket. They realize that an object can be hidden from sight but still exist. This leads infants into the fourth stage.

### Stage Four (9–12 Months)

In stage four, the object permanence concept advances. Infants now know to uncover objects that are hidden. They also learn through imitation. Hands, eyes, and voices are used in games such as pat-a-cake, so-big, and bye-bye; they learn that these gestures have meanings. Thus, by the end of the first year infants imitate more by making the sounds and gestures of others around them. Their increasing motor skills allow more exploration and repetition and,

therefore, more play. Learning through play increases over the entire first year.

### Play

Rosenblatt (1977) describes play as the "external evidence of the internal processes of cognitive development" (Levine et al., 1983, p. 91). Play provides infants with the opportunity to explore their environments and develop a sense of reality. It is voluntary and unstructured. Early theorists proposed that play served the following purposes: Aristotle, catharsis; Lord Kames, recreation; Schiller-Spencer, surplus energy; Groos, instinctive practice; G. Stanley Hall, recapitulation; and Solomon, symbolism (Hott, 1970). Beverly (1947) discussed play in relation to infants' motor development; that is, play allows children to eventually increase their skills, release emotional energy, and increase their imagination. More recently, Erikson (1963) identified play as an attempt to strengthen the ego. Healthy play development begins early by allowing infants to investigate their environments by themselves. Thus, play provides infants with the opportunity to learn, discover, and cope with the world, spontaneously and with repetition. Learning is and should be fun.

Usually by the third month infants' visual and motor maturation enables them to explore visually. With rudimentary manipulation they can also explore much of their immediate surrounding environment. They watch all shapes and colors and benefit greatly from bright mobiles, posters, and toys. The initial swiping at a mobile eventually becomes purposeful, with vigorous movement of all body parts, and results in hitting the object to make it move. Infants also play with their hands a lot, studying them in detail, then mouthing them to feel their pleasurable sensation (Fig. 12-8). By 5 or 6 months of age an infant can hold a toy, put it in the mouth, wave it, and then transfer it to the other hand to repeat the process (Brazelton, 1969). Imitation, by moving an object from one hand to the other, is a form of play. At this age infants begin to grasp paper, crinkle it, rip it, and chew on it, all to their delight and their mothers' surprise. They will try this with any toy or object. Nine-month-old infants become more observing and manipulate their toys in more detail. This, along with the increase in finger dexterity (pincer grasp), allows infants to pick up blocks, look at them, throw them, bang them together, and repeat this process over and over again. This process *integrates* their sense of vision, tactile sensation, and auditory ability and *reinforces* itself. Repetition actually becomes a game in itself. Throwing a toy and seeing how many times the mother retrieves it becomes fun. Eating finger foods, mashing them, and making silly faces are all games, especially if others laugh and reinforce this behavior.

Infants' urge to explore their toys carries over to exploration of body parts. Toes, navels, penises, ears—

*Figure 12–8. Infant playing with hands.*

everything is touched. "This little piggy," sung while counting infants' toes, is a fun game that infants enjoy.

By 1 year of age infants understand the function of some objects (Levine et al., 1983). They might point to the sky when the word *airplane* is said, or they understand that a toy truck with wheels can be pushed. They now enjoy toys that move, either self-propelled or propelled by the infants.

Toys, or "tools of play," can be categorized into four types: (1) language toys, (2) muscular activity toys, (3) imaginative projection toys, and (4) props (Davidson, 1949).

Verbal expressions are one of infants' first avenues of play and joyful satisfaction. Babbling and repeating sounds is pleasurable and is reinforced if the parents respond with the same sound. Nursery rhymes and songs (e.g., pat-a-cake) usually help infants to relax or to get excited, depending on the content. Once infants can participate with hand motions and sound, the playful experience becomes even more rewarding. Both gross and fine motor activities can offer infants chances to expend energy (kicking, crawling, running) and learn relations (banging blocks together, putting dry cereal in a bowl).

Imaginative projection is used more after the first year of life, but its roots start as early as 9 months of age. Brazelton (1969) states that play at this early age can symbolize a child's fears or wishes, bringing them to consciousness where the infant can control them better. For example, Brazelton discusses a 9-month-old who began to show some fears of the large bathtub and heights. He played out some of his anxieties by dropping a toy dog from a chair to the floor repeatedly and then sitting next to him to comfort him. Props that are creative play materials (i.e., blocks, wind-up toys, clay for older children) are the only objects necessarily provided by an adult.

Some general guidelines for using toys include the following:

1. Toys should be appropriate for the child's age.
2. Toys should be safe for infants to handle, without sharp edges or loose parts.
3. Toys should be easy to clean whenever possible.

Table 12-10 gives examples of the types of play materials for infants that are usually enjoyable while stimulating a specific area of development. Once again, the temperament of children is seen in how they play. Some infants are aggressive, some are more passive, and some are more patient. Active infants may become impatient and begin to cry as they try to grasp their twirling mobiles. Should mothers interpret this as boredom, frustration, or some other need? Conversely, quiet infants may swat at the mobile for literally an hour, watching it closely, repeating their gestures to see what type of response they can elicit. All of this is play, but certainly each infant approaches play differently and learns differently from the results.

## Psychosocial Development

The necessity of interdependence becomes evident moments after infants are born. They have basic needs for survival that include food, shelter, and clothing. For positive growth and development, these survival needs must be met by a warm, loving caretaker in secure surroundings. In addition to the basic requirements, infants grow by accomplishing specific developmental tasks. The interaction of infants and their environments determines the success they have in accomplishing these tasks. Psychosocial development has been studied by many theorists. The tasks that each theorist has proposed is discussed in relation to how infants accomplish these tasks in their first year of life.

### Erikson

The underlying premise of Erikson's theory (1963) is that an interplay exists between heredity and environment, internal and external forces, and infants and their caretakers. It is this interaction that shapes infants' development. Erikson's theory defines development as the ego development of autonomy and the personality, both of which develop through interactions with the environment.

Erikson's theory is based on *mutual regulation*— family members grow and develop together, and each one affects the development of the other individuals. Erikson's first of eight stages, *trust versus mistrust,* is relevant to infancy (discussed in more detail in Chap. 4). Trust develops when infants feel confident that their needs are met and they feel physically safe. When these needs are met consistently, anticipation of satisfaction happens. Both the

*Table 12–10.   Creative Play Materials*

| Age (mo) | Play Material | Value |
|---|---|---|
| 1–3 | Hang colorful pictures on wall next to crib and changing table | Visual development |
|  | Show infant bold, patterned, noisy objects from around the house—boxes, shiny spoons | Auditory stimulation |
|  | Make a rattle filling a plastic container with large spools |  |
|  | Allow baby to be in infant seat or swing in an upright position to watch family in their daily activities | Visual and auditory stimulation; interpersonal relationship development |
|  | Talk and sing to infant; play music; repeat baby's noises | Language and personal–social development |
| 1–6 | Allow infant to be on stomach on a blanket; surround with colorful objects | Motor development; visual stimulation |
| 3–6 | While infant is upright—in an infant seat or swing—make a noise (shake a box, ring a bell, rustle papers) on one side of him or her, then change sides; continue alternating | Auditory stimulation |
|  | Encourage baby to swipe at mobile or hanging toy | Motor development; knowledge that he or she can change the environment |
| 3–12 | Sit infant on your knee, bouncing gently up and down or sideways; sing a rhyme while doing this | Increased posture control; personal–social interaction, language development |
|  | Tickle infant while reciting "Itsy, Bitsy Spider" | Language development, tactile stimulation |
| 6–12 | Tell baby what you're doing—"Now we're going to take a bath"; "These are the dishes"; etc. | Language development; personal–social interaction |
|  | Point to objects and people and repeat their name | Language development |
|  | Allow infant to watch self in the mirror, talking, moving | Personal–social development; encourages baby to see self separate from the mother |
| 9–12 | Make soft cuddly toys (stuff old socks); use a variety of textures—sponges, velvet | Tactile development |
|  | Allow exploration and encourage manipulating—pots, pans, rubber bowls, lids, rolling pin | Tactile and motor development |
|  | Fill large coffee can or oatmeal box with measuring spoons, clothes pins, etc; can be shaken with lid on or lid can be removed and toys dumped out to be replaced | Motor development; personal–social interaction; object permanence |

quality and quantity of the mother–infant relationship helps determine infants' sense of trust. This is seen when infants depend on their mothers to meet their nutritional needs. Studies have shown that for optimal growth to occur, infants need to be fed in a warm, secure position. Meeting their caloric needs without nurturing their emotional needs results in mistrust of their environment. With repetition and consistency, trust develops and infants begin to explore unknown situations with less fear. For example, stranger anxiety is alleviated when, through repetition, infants learn to trust that the mother will return.

Erikson's oral stages are similar to those of Freud. His first social modality is called *oral.* Infants' hunger is satisfied only by food or vigorous sucking. This is definitely a pleasurable sensation. By 5 to 6 months of age the ego begins to develop. Infants learn to delay their immediate oral gratification by interacting with their environment—visually, tactilely, and vocally. Frustration and mistrust develop when there is a prolonged delay of gratification.

The second stage, *grasping and biting,* occurs in the second half of the first year when infants are more active. They can control their environment by purposefully grasping and biting. The mother–infant relationship is tested when infants bite (whether to control the breast or to relieve teething pressure). Infants become anxious if the breast is suddenly pulled away. Resolution of this conflict is important if infants are to develop trust in their mothers. In conclusion, meeting the oral needs of infants through feeding, thumb sucking, or using a pacifier helps them feel more secure as they begin to have control over their actions and as they begin to trust themselves and others around them.

## Freud

According to Freud, personality development is based on the region of the body (erogenous zone) that is responsible for libidinal pleasure and gratification. The mouth or oral area is the predominant socialization zone in the first 18 months of life; thus, pleasure comes from sucking and eating. The two substages are the *oral-dependent* phase, characterized by incorporating or taking in food, and the *oral-agressive* phase, characterized by biting. During the first few months of life the id processes are apparent: infants' oral needs demand immediate gratification (Giovachini, 1982). Thus, within the first 6 months of life, tension decreases when mothers satisfy infants' oral needs. With good mothering infants decrease attention toward themselves and direct it toward their mothers. Primary anxiety develops in the latter half of the first year when the threat of losing the mother produces tension. This tension resolves with coping mechanisms such as imitation, avoidance, and denial.

## Attachment

"*Attachment* is an active, affectionate reciprocal relationship specifically between two individuals, as distinguished from all other persons" (Papalia & Olds, 1989, p. 164). Attachment usually begins in utero as mothers feel their infants move. Once infants are born, this process continues for the mother and probably truly begins for the father, who is now able to hold, see, and talk to a real baby. The bonding that occurs between parent and child strengthens over time. Parents usually feel they are just beginning to know their infant when he or she is 1 or 2 months old. It is from infants' daily activities of sleeping, feeding, and crying that parents learn how to respond in a positive, loving manner. Attachment necessitates the interaction of both infant and parent; it is not unilateral. Klaus, Kennell, Plumb, and Zuehlke (1970) believe that there is a critical period, minutes after delivery, in which a mother and child need closeness and contact to bond. It is obvious that there are instances when immediate close contact is not possible, yet a positive relationship develops. The critical postnatal period is discussed in Chapter 11.

Nurses have an important role in facilitating this early bonding process, both in the immediate newborn period and throughout infants' first year. Parent education must include normal growth and development, personality development, and the effects of these on the attachment process. By 1 month of age infants usually respond differently to faces and voices than to inanimate stimuli. This response is often the mother's first positive reinforcement for all the loving caretaking that has taken place over the first few weeks. The acknowledgment of a significant caregiver can take the form of watching the parent intently or even responding with a smile. This small act rewards the mother immensely and she in turn increases her behavior to elicit the response again. It is the repetition and reinforcement of each other's behaviors that increases parent–infant attachment over time. Other evidence of attachment can be seen in increased vocalization and generalized motor activity. Infants respond to their mothers' soothing attempts more quickly than to those of strangers. Beginning around the sixth month, infants' strong attachment to their mothers surfaces in the response termed *stranger anxiety.* By this time infants have a mental image of the important caretaker and feel secure when that person is present and fearful when absent. Children enjoy playing with their mothers and being held by them. If the mother leaves the room or the infant is held by someone else, the response may be extreme crying or clinging to the mother. This separation protest usually peaks at 9 or 10 months of age and decreases throughout the remainder of the first year. Remnants of this security base are seen as infants' independence increases. As they crawl, climb, or even walk to explore new places, they often gaze at their mother or return to her momentarily for a security hug or encouragement.

Although the predominant caretaker is often the mother, infants in today's world grow up with a variety of caretakers. If both parents work, infants often also become attached to the babysitter. Infants are capable of attaching to a few significant persons, especially if the interaction time of parents and infants is very positive.

In the past decade the role of the father has changed significantly in the caretaking process. Although some attachment begins when he feels the fetus move or hears the fetal heartbeat, strong bonding is often enhanced when the father can participate in the birthing process. It has been shown that within the first few days of life fathers develop a preoccupation with and interest in their babies. Although many of mothers' interactions with infants are for caretaking, eventually fathers hold infants in a more playful manner. Within the first year infants often eagerly await special times with their fathers because these interactions are usually different from those with the mother. If the father is the primary daily caretaker, these roles are usually reversed.

One important factor in the attachment process is infant temperament. From early in the newborn period, parents develop an awareness of their child as easygoing, active, or aggressive. The response parents receive from infants can either increase or decrease the parents' behavior toward infants. Nurses can help the parents of a quiet, easy baby learn how to stimulate the child and how to get rewards from little responses the child may give back. Infants, in turn, benefit from the increased interest in their responses. When nurses discuss normal developmental milestones and how they are influenced by infants, parents' expectations of their infants should be more realistic. The individuality of each infant needs to be stressed. Attachment can also be influenced by other events affecting the family. Whether there has been a recent death in the family, an unwanted pregnancy, disappointment over the sex of the baby, or the realization that the infant differs from their preconceived ideas, nurses can help parents deal with reality and stress the positive.

## Communication

Communication involves both verbal and nonverbal interactions. Within weeks after birth infants' responses to their environment change. By the time an infant is 1 month old, mothers can often distinguish cries of hunger, discomfort, and pain. The reciprocal relationship between infants and parents fosters language development. Infants cry to communicate their hunger, and parents respond by feeding them. Cognitively, infants learn that vocalizations bring rewards (or at least attention). Along with meeting their nutritional needs, parents hold and touch infants, speak to them, and look lovingly at them. All of these gestures encourage verbal and nonverbal interactions.

Theorists differ on how language develops. Piagetian theory proposes that infants are born with the ability to learn language but do not have specific language skills (Castiglia, 1987). Chomsky (1969) believes that language acquisition is facilitated by an innate linguistic structure. Another speculation is that there is a critical period for speech development, between birth and 2 years of age (Ruben, 1986).

Language can be either receptive (auditory) or expressive (Fig. 12-9). *Receptive milestones* begin with responding to a bell with a cry or a start. By 4 months of age, infants can turn toward the source of a stimulus. This listening response is refined during the next few months until at 9 months infants can respond directly to the source of a sound. Other milestones in the receptive area include, in order of achievement, social smile, understanding the word *no*, gesture games (peek-a-boo, pat-a-cake), and following a single command with a gesture (Capute, Shapiro, & Palmer, 1987). Acquisition of gestures is an important indicator of language development because both gestures and language are formed from the same part of the brain.

*Expressive milestones* start at 2 to 3 months of age when infants begin making cooing sounds. Squeals and babbling often surprise infants themselves when they first hear their shouts of joy. "Dada" and "mama" are phrases that excite all parents when they are used around 8 months of age. Usage is initially indiscriminate, but it becomes more specific by about the first birthday. Many social milestones combine both language (auditory) and problem-solving (visual/motor) abilities (Capute et al., 1987). These are good predictors of cognition.

An infant's approach to language often depends on his or her temperament. Early babblers may be early talkers. They may be active infants who attack every developmental milestone with vim and vigor. Quiet infants may listen carefully and wait cautiously before responding. There are normal variants of language acquisition; assessment should be included in every well-child visit to detect infants with unusual delays.

Parents must foster language development since it depends on a reciprocal relationship. The early bonds between infants and parents are strengthened when each responds to the other verbally and through visual cues. Parents need to constantly make eye contact and verbal sounds to infants. Often young mothers wonder why they should talk to infants when infants cannot respond verbally. Nurses can explain to parents that infants are capable of responses—first by eye contact and eventually with verbal responses (not necessarily words). Parents should repeat sounds, "raspberries," and words along with ges-

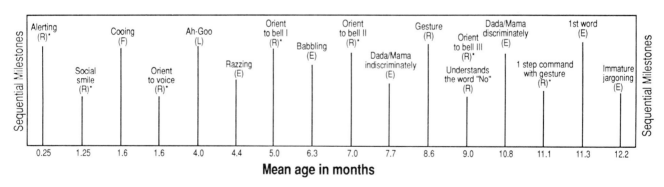

*Figure 12–9.    The Clinical Linguistic and Auditory Milestone Scale. E = expressive; R = receptive. (Capute, A., et al. [1987]. Marking the milestones of language development.* Contemporary Pediatrics, 4, 26–27)

tures (pointing and naming objects). Speech develops more readily if parents encourage sounds and gestures during feeding, bathing, dressing, or playing.

## Cultural Influences

Developmental theorists have long given up the notion that behavior depends strictly on either genetic endowment or the environment. Rather, it is the interaction of these two factors, and all the variables inherent in each, that produce an individual human being.

Whether psychosocial development is viewed from a Freudian perspective or from the perspective of a combination of many theorists, the effects of the cultural environment in which infants are reared must be taken into account. Nurses can truly individualize the care they give patients if they assess all the patient's assets (age, sex, family structure), including the cultural milieu in which children live. Communication among nurses, patients, and families is essential to develop a meaningful relationship. Levine et al. (1983) discuss ethnicity as belonging to a group that shares cultural traditions, belief systems, genetic history, and language. Thus, infants' cultural backgrounds influence what they eat, perhaps how they work, how they relax, how they perceive pain, and even how they feel about living and dying. Even at this early age, parents' ethnic habits influence infants' development.

Nurses, as well as parents, bring to the interview their own thoughts and ideas about how infants should grow. When obtaining a social history, cultural influences become obvious. It is extremely important to know with whom infants are living and who is primarily responsible for their care. Then, when issues such as feeding, sleep, and discipline arise, the guidance can be individualized to fit into a particular family's lifestyle. For example, if the grandmother is the primary caretaker of the infant, and she fed her children solid food at 2 months of age, it might be wise for the nurse to discuss the child's nutrition with the mother and the grandmother and come to an understanding with both of them that will benefit the child. Ethnic table foods may be fed earlier than the nurse would normally think appropriate and this too should be discussed.

Discipline is another area that is strongly influenced by cultural mores. For example, the Asian culture uses shame as a primary method of discipline. When infants start crawling and exploring, they begin to learn right from wrong by being made to feel remorseful for what they have done wrong. Nurses should not attempt to change this type of parenting, as long as they believe that it is not physically or emotionally harmful. Asian cultures also respect males more than females; the male is the leader and provider. Both parents might accompany the child to well-child visits or to the hospital, but it is often the father who speaks and makes the decisions. The mother is the primary nur-

turant, but she listens rather than participates in the decision making. If the parents feel comfortable with this and the child is adjusting well, it is not appropriate for nurses to change this lifestyle. Efforts should be made to include both parents in all discussions.

Socioeconomic status also influences the environment in which infants are reared. The effects of socioeconomic status on children, families, and child-rearing practices are discussed in detail in Chapter 2. Nurses should not assume, however, that they understand a particular family's socioeconomic status based on the family's cultural or ethnic background.

Thus, from the day they are born infants are exposed to a cultural environment from which they cannot escape. The way they are fed, what stimuli they are exposed to, and even how their rites of passage are celebrated (baptism, circumcision) are all affected by the cultural traditions of those involved in shaping their behavior.

## Assessment

Assessment of infants' physical and emotional growth is a key nursing function. Prevention, by means of education, can alleviate problems before they exist. By monitoring infants' growth and development, nurses can determine if there are any problems and how they can best be treated (Fig. 12-10). Assessment tools are used to determine both physical and behavioral growth as well as to provide guidelines for nurses to assist in differentiating normal from abnormal. These should only be used in conjunction with all other data about infants, including genetic endowment, environment, nutrition, and other factors.

## Body Measurements

Physical growth measurements are extremely important in assessing the health status of infants. Measuring weight, height, and head circumference should be routine parts of every physical examination. These parameters are essential for judging the nutritional status of infants. Additional measurements of skinfold thickness, body segments (e.g., arm and leg length), or bone age might be necessary if further growth information is needed.

Standardized growth charts have been developed to depict the wide variety of normal growth patterns (see Appendix B). There are separate growth charts for the two sexes. Growth charts provide nurses with an indication of how individual infants compare with the general population. They do not necessarily adequately display the growth variability of individuals. Infant growth measurements through the second year may span many percentiles; this indicates the physiologic change from intrauterine environment to infants' genetic potential (Mahoney, 1987).

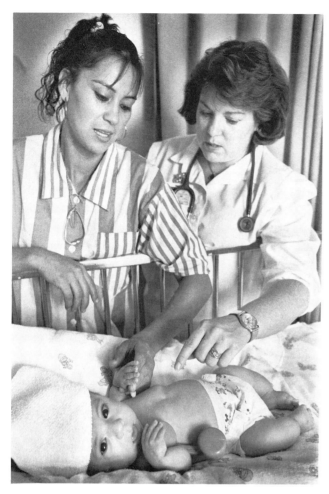

*Figure 12–10. Nurse with parent and child. (Courtesy of Nursing Department, Thomason Hospital, El Paso, Texas)*

## Measurement Techniques

Accuracy of measurements and monitoring growth over time are essential elements in assessing the true health status of infants. Depending on which growth chart is used, the normal percentiles for the charts are either the 5th to 95th or 10th to 90th. Children whose growth falls above or below these percentiles need to be evaluated on an individual basis. However, a single measurement above or below a normal percentile does not indicate an abnormal growth pattern. An infant's growth should be measured several times at varying intervals. In early infancy, height, weight, and head circumference might need to be monitored monthly if there is concern about alterations in normal growth patterns.

Some generalizations can be made about growth during infancy. By about 5 or 6 months of age infants usually double their birth weight. By about 12 months the birth weight is usually tripled. Male infants generally grow at a faster rate during the first 3 to 6 months of life; after that there are usually no sex differences in growth rate (Levine et al., 1983). Racial differences are rare in well-nourished populations.

Growth patterns differ slightly for premature infants. Their head circumferences catch up to term infants by 18 months of age, weight by 24 months, and height by 40 months of age. Small for gestational age (SGA) infants have less predictable growth patterns, depending on the cause and severity of the intrauterine problem (Levine et al., 1983). Prenatal growth retardation may be caused by maternal smoking, drug or alcohol use, or infection. Usually SGA infants who grow rapidly in the first 6 months of life have a better prognosis for normal growth.

Other explanations for deviations in the normal growth pattern include illness, inadequate nutrition, poor parenting, and genetic peculiarities. For example, an infant with low height but normal weight might have had nutritional or growth failure in the past. If both parameters are low, however, long-term nutritional deprivation should be suspected. Weight is the body's most labile parameter. Height and head circumference change only after a lengthy problem.

Constitutional growth delay (where birth size is normal but height and weight eventually fall below the 5th percentile) may be seen by the end of infancy. "Growth velocity remains normal for bone age" (Mahoney, 1987, p. 828). A family history of delayed puberty but normal size in adulthood usually accounts for the small size in the first year of life. Growth variations are normal in infancy, as long as there is a steady increase in growth (see growth charts in Appendix B). Infants occasionally develop their own growth curve. If the growth curve becomes horizontal, however, aggressive investigation of the cause is warranted. Growth charts, an integral part of every infant's record, can be enlightening for parents. Using this concrete, visual tool to explain physical growth to parents may allay their fears by showing them that their child is within normal growth ranges, even though the child might be smaller or heavier than other children.

## Developmental Assessment

Developmental screening is important for early detection and treatment of developmental delays. Developmental evaluation should be an integral part of a child's health assessment. Developmental testing can be performed through screening or diagnostic procedures. The ideal screening tool is quick, simple, cost-effective, appropriate for the population, reliable, and accurate (Levine et al., 1983), but it is often difficult to find a tool that meets all of these criteria. It is essential to have such tools to detect and record developmental delays for children who would benefit from further specific diagnostic tests. Many diagnostic tests are performed by individuals who specialize in one particular area, but nurses can play a key role in screening children for a variety of problems, including developmental delays.

Infancy is a period of rapid changes—both physical and behavioral. A specific tool is needed to assess infants' development objectively. Although in many areas, such as gross motor and personal–social, changes seem to occur daily. The area of language does not have as many objective items for testing until later in the first year.

### Denver Developmental Screening Test

The Denver Developmental Screening Test (DDST) (see Appendix A) was devised to aid in the early detection of developmental delays from infancy through the preschool years. Premature infants' ages are calculated by subtracting the number of weeks of prematurity from the present age to arrive at an adjusted age. The line is then drawn from the adjusted age. The DDST should be administered at least once before the infant's first birthday. For example, at 9 months of age a fine motor assessment would determine whether an infant can bang two cubes together and use the finger and thumb to grasp an object. If an infant is at high risk for developmental delays because of a poor social environment, prematurity, or other physical abnormalities, more frequent administration of the DDST and close observation are recommended. The DDST is only one part of the total assessment of the child, so nurses need to use these data in conjunction with the health history and physical examination to plan nursing care for infants and families.

### Temperament Assessment

Infants' development and behavior depend on many variables: genetic endowment, environment, and parenting, among others. Infants' personalities—whether they are labeled happy, sad, or easygoing—make all infants individuals. Infants' temperaments affect how they eat, sleep, relax, and behave and consequently affect the infant–parent interaction. Studies conducted by Brazelton (1969) and Thomas and Chess (1977) have categorized infants broadly into easygoing, difficult, or average—slow to warm up. Assessing infants' temperament affords nurses the opportunity to teach parents about normal developmental milestones while incorporating their own infant's temperament into the anticipatory guidance.

Within the first months, nurses can subjectively assess infants' temperaments by asking the parents about infants' daily routines. A more accurate, objective assessment tool has been developed by Thomas and Chess (1977). This 95-item questionnaire can be used for infants 4 to 8 months of age. From these answers, nine categories of temperament can be established (Table 12-11). From these nine categories, the temperament constellation of easy, difficult, and easygoing were derived. Assessment of temperament is critical for helping to foster positive infant–parent relationships. Infants' daily activities—sleeping, eating, voiding—activity level, and the achievement of developmental milestones are influenced by genetic makeup, culture, and temperament. For example, an easygoing 3-month-old

**Table 12–11. Categories for Assessment of Infant Temperament**

*Activity level*—the amount of motor activity

*Rhythmicity (regularity)*—the predictability or unpredictability of the infant's cycles (awake–asleep, feeding, elimination)

*Approach or withdrawal*—whether child responds to new situations (persons, toys) either positively or negatively

*Adaptibility*—how long it takes child to adapt to a given situation

*Threshold of responsiveness*—how intense a stimulus needs to be to evoke a response

*Intensity of reaction*—the force of the response not its direction (positive or negative)

*Quality of mood*—(in general) happy versus fussy

*Distractibility*—the ease with which an infant's behavior is changed by stimuli within the environment

*Attention span and persistence*—relates to the time a child stays with one activity and whether he or she continues or returns to this same activity after being distracted

(Carey, W., & McDevitt, S. [1978]. Revision of the infant temperament questionnaire. *Pediatrics, 61,* 735)

may sit contentedly in a swing for hours. Because the child is not vocally protesting, a parent might think that the infant is content. Yet for infants to reach the developmental milestones of reaching for objects, rolling over, and babbling, they need stimulation and opportunities that encourage these behaviors. Parents who understand their infant's temperament also understand the importance of anticipating activities to foster development (Fig. 12-11). Usually a positive response by an infant reinforces the mother's behavior. Introducing solid foods may be wearisome with a "difficult" child if parents are not prepared for the child's response. If parents understand that the infant might not want to sit long enough for a feeding or might

*Figure 12–11. Parent playing with an infant.*

push foods away (initially because it is a change from the usual bottle), they can adapt the routine and approach appropriately. It is extremely important that parents not wholly interpret their child's behavior as a reflection of their parenting.

If the Brazelton Temperament Assessment Tool was used in the nursery (see Chap. 11), the nurse can counsel the parents about their infant's adaptability to the rapidly changing environment. These generalizations do not always carry over into the first few months of life, however, and another tool should then be used. Administering the Carey Temperament Questionnaire (1978) between 4 and 8 months of age can help nurses individualize anticipatory guidance and parenting recommendations. Nurses can emphasize that each infant is an individual, that each temperament constellation is normal, and that there are many variations of normal within each constellation. By classifying infants' temperament, nurses can objectively discuss each child's uniqueness and its impact on the family.

## Assessment of Home and Family

### Environmental Data

Knowing the physical attributes of childrens' homes helps nurses educate parents about infants' needs. Do they live in an apartment or a single family dwelling? Is there running water? Are there a lot of stairs? What type of heat is used? Answers to these questions yield information that helps nurses realistically explain preparing formula, safety factors about falls and burns, and a variety of other anticipatory guidelines that affect a particular family. In addition, it is helpful to know the type of neighborhood in which they live and what community resources are available.

### Family Structure

The structure of the family is just as important as the physical properties of the home. The varieties of family structures are discussed in detail in Chapter 2.

### Single-Parent Families

Numerous studies of adolescent parents have determined that they are at high risk for unsuccessful fulfillment of their own development needs, as well as those of their infants. McArnarney, Laurence, Ricciuti, Polley, and Szilagyi (1986) studied 9- to 12-month-old infants of adolescent mothers. They found that younger mothers were less accepting, less cooperative, less sensitive, and less apt to reinforce infant vocalizations. An 11-month-old infant who is striving for independence is in direct conflict with the adolescent mother who is striving for the same. Thus, with adolescent mothers nurses need to explore financial situations, support systems, educational goals, and motivation levels, so that they can help them feel better as individuals and better prepare them to parent their children.

Single-parent families are also prevalent today as a result of divorce and because some women are electing to have children without being married. Single-parenting has the added stress of one person's being responsible for parenting and maintaining a family. Infancy is a period of change, excitement, fatigue, uncertainty, and vacillation. Performing the physical tasks of caring for an infant (feeding, changing, rocking) often leaves little time for nurturing or extra stimulation. Nurses should understand the tiring demands of infancy and should help single parents explore support systems or outlets where they can periodically feel re-energized as parents.

Family assessment tools have been developed to investigate the functioning levels of families and to identify families at risk for discord. Any change in the functioning ability of families ultimately affects infants. A good history from the family usually yields adequate information to understand the environment in which infants live. If there are many uncertainties, family assessment tools can be used, depending on the type of data needed to complete the care plan for infants and their families. Family assessment is discussed in Chapter 2.

### Sexuality

Sexuality is more than the assignment of gender that takes place at birth. Infants are socialized into male or female roles early in life. Physiologic studies have reported some differences between the sexes, although most are minimal. Jacklin, Snow, and Maccoby (1981) found newborn boy's grips to be stronger than those of girls. Korner, Hutchinson, Koperski, Kraemer, and Schneider (1981) studied activity level and could not find a significant difference between the sexes. The belief that girls mature faster verbally or are advanced in the sensory motor area has not been substantiated during the first year of life (Bayley, 1956).

Although objective differences are not striking, there are both subtle and blatant differences in how boys and girls are reared in today's society. Most people either consciously or subconsciously think differently about and behave differently toward boys and girls. Parents often handle, dress, and play with boys in ways other than they do with girls, although nurturing itself is fairly consistent. This complex subject is also influenced by whether the parents preferred the birth of one sex over the other or if their culture has certain customs that dictate sex role differentiation.

Sexuality is determined by a combination of hormones and parental influences, as well as by society's preconceived sex role differentiation. An infant's self-image begins in the first months of life and depends on the quality of interaction with others.

The first time parents see their infant touching his penis or her vagina may be the first time they have viewed the infant as a sexual being. At about 5 or 6 months of age infants explore all of their body parts, not truly differentiating one from another. Because the genital area is usually covered, opportunities for exploration are limited. The genital area provides infants with a pleasurable sensation and, therefore, repeated tactile stimulation is often seen (Brazelton, 1969). Sexuality increases and changes after the first year of life, but how these early encounters are handled by the parents sets the stage for infants' viewing themselves sexually in a positive or negative manner.

## Health Promotion

### Health Maintenance

The area of child health is unique because most children are born healthy. Major congenital anomalies in the first year of life are seen in only 4% to 7% of infants (Cohen, 1984). Professional nurses help to maintain health by preventing illness and by health promotion. Even children with chronic illnesses need health maintenance visits to help them develop at their own optimal level. Health promotion and illness prevention need to be incorporated into all levels of care. Both the physical and emotional well-being of children are the focus of health maintenance visits.

Because growth and change are so rapid in this first year of life, frequent health evaluations are warranted. The basic components of health supervision should include:

- Evaluation of the child's health and nutritional status, which includes a health history and physical examination
- Parent counseling, including anticipatory guidance
- Immunization against infectious disease
- Screening procedures

In addition, any other topics that are pertinent to the individual child should be included. The American Academy of Pediatrics' schedule for preventive pediatric health care is shown in the display. Six visits are recommended during the first year of life, but additional visits should be scheduled if the individual warrants further supervision.

### History

Eliciting a history from the parent or caretaker of an infant provides much useful information. The general categories of information to be obtained during a history are included in Table 12-12. The history also includes any concerns the parent has, health status since the last visit, nutritional status, elimination and sleep patterns, developmental parameters, and temperament. Only when these subjective findings are evaluated in conjunction with the objective data can comprehensive nursing care be provided for infants and their families.

### Height, Weight, and Head Circumference

All visits should include measurement of infants' height, weight, and head circumference. As discussed earlier, these parameters are measured at every visit because they are a good indication of infants' overall growth.

### Vision

Vision assessment is based on subjective evaluation during infancy. The progression of visual acuity to 20/40 by 1 year of age can be evaluated by asking parents if babies follow with their eyes and watch the parents' faces. Acquisition of other developmental milestones depends on good vision, for example, grasping an object, looking at a moving object, and mimicking facial expressions. Objective assessment of these developmental tasks may alert nurses to visual problems.

### Recommendations for Preventive Pediatric Health Care, Committee on Practice and Ambulatory Medicine[1]

Each child and family is unique; therefore these recommendations are designed for the care of children who are receiving competent parenting, have no manifestations of any important health problems, and are growing and developing in satisfactory fashion. Additional visits may become necessary if circumstances suggest variations from normal. These guidelines represent a consensus by the Committee on Practice and Ambulatory Medicine in consultation with the membership of the American Academy of Pediatrics through the Chapter Presidents. The Committee emphasizes the great importance of continuity of care in comprehensive health supervision and the need to avoid fragmentation of care.

A prenatal visit by the parents for anticipatory guidance and pertinent medical history is strongly recommended.

Health supervision should begin with medical care of the newborn in the hospital.

*(continued)*

| | Infancy | | | | | | Early Childhood | | | | | Late Childhood | | | | | Adolescence[2] | | | |
|---|---|---|---|---|---|---|---|---|---|---|---|---|---|---|---|---|---|---|---|---|
| | By 1 mo | 2 mo | 4 mo | 6 mo | 9 mo | 12 mo | 15 mo | 18 mo | 24 mo | 3 y | 4 y | 5 y | 6 y | 8 y | 10 y | 12 y | 14 y | 16 y | 18 y | 20+ y |
| History (initial/interval) | • | • | • | • | • | • | • | • | • | • | • | • | • | • | • | • | • | • | • | • |
| **Measurements** | | | | | | | | | | | | | | | | | | | | |
| Height and weight | • | • | • | • | • | • | • | • | • | • | • | • | • | • | • | • | • | • | • | • |
| Head circumference | • | • | • | • | • | • | • | • | | | | | | | | | | | | |
| Blood pressure | | | | | | | | | | • | • | • | • | • | • | • | • | • | • | • |
| **Sensory screening** | | | | | | | | | | | | | | | | | | | | |
| Vision | S | S | S | S | S | S | S | S | S | S | O | O | O | O | S | O | O | S | O | O |
| Hearing | S | S | S | S | S | S | S | S | S | S | O | O | S3 | S3 | S3 | O | S | S | O | S |
| Development/behavior assessment[4] | • | • | • | • | • | • | • | • | • | • | • | • | • | • | • | • | • | • | • | • |
| Physical examination[5] | • | • | • | • | • | • | • | • | • | • | • | • | • | • | • | • | • | • | • | • |
| **Procedures[6]** | | | | | | | | | | | | | | | | | | | | |
| Hereditary/metabolic screening[7] | • | | | | | | | | | | | | | | | | | | | |
| Immunization[8] | | • | • | • | | | • | • | • | | • | | | | | | • | | | |
| Tuberculin test[9] | ←——————————————————→ • | | | | | | ←————→ • | | | ←→ | | | | | | | ←——————————————→ • | | | |
| Hematocrit or hemoglobin[10] | ←————————————→ • | | | | | | ←—————————→ • | | | | | ←————→ • | | | | | ←——————————→ • | | | |
| Urinalysis[11] | ←————————————→ • | | | | | | ←—————————→ • | | | | | ←————→ • | | | | | ←——————————→ • | | | |
| Anticipatory guidance[12] | • | • | • | • | • | • | • | • | • | • | • | • | • | • | • | • | • | • | • | • |
| Initial dental referral[13] | | | | | | | | | | • | | | | | | | | | | |

1. If a child comes under care for the first time at any point on the schedule, or if any items are not accomplished at the suggested age, the schedule should be brought up to date at the earliest possible time.
2. Adolescent-related issues (e.g., psychosocial, emotional, substance usage, and reproductive health) may necessitate more frequent health supervision.
3. At these points, history may suffice: If a problem is suggested, a standard testing method should be used.
4. By history and appropriate physical examination: If suspicious, by specific objective developmental testing.
5. At each visit, a complete physical examination is essential, with infant totally unclothed, older child undressed and suitably draped.
6. These may be modified, depending upon entry point into schedule and individual need.
7. Metabolic screening (e.g., thyroid, PKU, galactosemia) should be done according to state law.
8. Schedules per Report of Committee on Infectious Disease, 1986 Red Book.

9. For low-risk groups, the Committee on Infectious Diseases recommends the following options: (1) no routine testing or (2) testing at three times—infancy, preschool, and adolescence. For high-risk groups annual TB skin testing is recommended.
10. Present medical evidence suggests the need for reevaluation of the frequency and timing of hemoglobin or hematocrit tests. One determination is therefore suggested during each time period. Performance of additional tests is left to the individual practice experience.
11. Present medical evidence suggests the need for reevaluation of the frequency and timing of urinalyses. One determination is therefore suggested during each period. Performance of additional tests is left to the individual practice experience.
12. Appropriate discussion and counselling should be an integral part of each visit for care.
13. Subsequent examinations as prescribed by dentist.
N.B.: Special chemical, immunological, and endocrine tests are usually carried out on specific indications. Testing other than for newborns (e.g., inborn errors of metabolism, sickle disease, lead) is discretionary with the physician.

Key: •, to be performed; S, subjective, by history; O, objective, by a standard testing method.

(*Pediatrics, 81,* 466, 1988)

240

*Table 12–12. Child History Profile*

| Medical History | Review of Systems |
|---|---|
| Gestation | Head |
| Birth history | Skin |
| Neonatal period | Ears, nose, throat |
| Immunizations | Dentition |
| Laboratory tests | Heart |
| Infectious diseases | Lungs |
| Operations | Blood |
| Hospitalizations | Gastrointestinal |
| Accidents | Genitourinary |
| Safety measures | Skeletal |
| Allergies | Neuromuscular |
| Current medications | |

## Hearing

Hearing evaluation is very subjective during the first year of life unless sophisticated equipment is used. During the first month of life, infants should have an auditory alerting response, that is, startling or crying in response to a bell rung 6 inches behind them (Capute et al., 1987). At about 4 months of age infants respond to their mothers' voices by turning their heads *toward* the mothers. By 9 months of age infants can turn *directly* to the source of a sound. Other receptive milestones include smiling, understanding *no* by about 9 months of age, and playing pat-a-cake or peek-a-boo (Capute et al., 1987).

## Developmental and Behavioral Assessment

As discussed, a variety of tools can be used to assess infants' cognitive growth. Evaluation of cognitive development is necessary at each visit. The DDST and the Bayley Scales of Infant Development are two valuable tools that can be used with infants. The entire tools may be administered only once or twice within the first year, but parts of each may be used at each visit.

## Procedures

### Immunizations

Preventable diseases, once dreaded for their debilitating and often deadly outcomes, have dramatically declined as the result of immunizations. Immunizations are an essential component of many well-child visits and are given at three of the six routine visits during the first year. Although immunizations are essential to protect infants and the community, they should not be the only reason that parents seek health care. Protection from infectious disease is just one important component of comprehensive care delivered to children and families. "The ultimate goal of immunizations is eradication of disease; the immediate goal is prevention of disease in individuals or groups"

(American Academy of Pediatrics, Committee on Infectious Diseases, 1988, p. 5). Recent studies have shown a decrease in the number of children being immunized. This may be due to lack of access to health care, religious beliefs, parental fear about the safety of vaccines, or lack of knowledge about the importance of this preventive measure. Failure to obtain immunizations puts infants as well as other members of the community at risk. Thus, educating the public is critical for eliminating many communicable diseases.

Primary immunizations should begin at 2 months of age. Some vaccines may be given later, but the primary series is recommended during the first year. A complete immunization schedule is shown in Appendix F.

***Site and Route of Immunization.*** All vaccines except oral polio vaccine are administered by injection. Because of this, nurses need to understand the anatomy of infants to choose the safest sites for injections. The anterolateral aspect of the upper thigh is usually used for intramuscular injections in this age group. This site allows for the best absorption (because of larger muscle mass) and safety (fewer vascular and neural structures). A new needle and syringe should be used for each injection and then disposed of properly. The package insert should be read carefully for information about storage, dilution, injection route, and special precautions of administration.

Contraindications to routine immunization include any acute febrile illness; immunodeficiency diseases, malignancies, or leukemia; and immunosuppressive therapy. These are in addition to the contraindications for each vaccine. Common adverse reactions, contraindications, and nursing implications for most immunizations are shown in Table 12-13.

## Special Considerations

***Preterm Infants.*** Because there has been uncertainty about the safety and effectiveness of immunizations given to premature infants, the American Academy of Pediatrics has developed guidelines for this group. It states that immunizations should begin at 2 months of chronological age and should then follow the normal immunization schedule. If the infant is still hospitalized at 2 months of age, oral polio vaccine should be delayed until discharge (American Academy of Pediatrics, Committee on Infectious Diseases, 1986).

***Travel.*** Many communicable diseases that are not found in the United States are common in other countries. Before traveling, parents need to consult the Health Information for International Travel for current recommendations for prophylaxis. Infants under 6 months of age are not required to receive all vaccines, but this must be evaluated on an individual basis (American Academy of Pediatrics, Committee on Infectious Diseases, 1988).

*Table 12–13.* Immunizations

| Immunization | Adverse Reactions | Contraindications | Nursing Implications |
|---|---|---|---|
| Diphtheria | Local swelling, redness, soreness Temperature within 24–48 h | | Initiate appropriate local treatment (i.e., ice); use acetaminophen to reduce fever and discomfort; notify physician immediately if unusual side effects occur (as discussed under pertussis) |
| Tetanus | Local swelling, redness | | |
| Pertussis | Local swelling, redness, temperature within 24–48 h Rare adverse effects include loss of consciousness, convulsions | Encephalopathy within 7 d; convulsion within 3 d; unconsolable crying >3 h within 48 h; temperature of 40.5°C within 48 h; neurologic disorder—progressive developmental delay; history of convulsions | |
| Polio | Usually none; rare temporary polio-like paralysis | Not to be given to patient if he or immediate family member is immunodeficient, or undergoing chemotherapy | |
| Measles | Minimal fever Macular rash 10–14 d after immunizations | Anaphylactic symptoms to egg Immunosuppressed patient | |
| Mumps | | Same as measles Immunosuppressed patient | |
| Rubella | | Immunosuppressed patient | |
| Hib. | Minimal fever | | |

*Record Keeping.* Nurses who administer immunizations must document this in the patient's chart as well as in a convenient record book for the parents. Documentation of proper immunizations is especially important for school attendance.

*Tuberculin Test.* The value of routinely testing all children for tuberculosis has recently become a controversial issue involving the Centers for Disease Control, The American Thoracic Society, and the American College of Chest Physicians. False-positive tests have caused a number of children to be unnecessarily treated with isoniazid. Therefore, the American Academy of Pediatrics recommends that low-risk groups undergo skin tests at three intervals during routine health appraisals (12–15 months of age; before entering school, 4–6 years; and in adolescence, 14–16 years). Annual testing is recommended for children at greater risk, such as American Indian children and children of parents from Asia, Africa, the Middle East, Latin America, or the Caribbean (American Academy of Pediatrics, Committee on Infectious Diseases, 1988).

Tuberculin skin testing should be given before or on the same day as the measles vaccine; otherwise, the vaccine may suppress tuberculin reactivity. The tuberculin test may be administered 4 to 6 weeks after the measles vaccine for an accurate screening.

There are two types of tuberculin testing: purified protein derivative (PPD), which is intracutaneous, and Old tuberculin (tine and Mono-Vac tests), which has dried or liquid tuberculin on multiple puncture prongs. The positive reaction (hardness or swelling) is measured. An area less than 2 mm is negative; 2 to 4 mm is a doubtful reaction; 5 mm or more is a positive reaction. The PPD (Mantoux) test should be used if the tine or mono-vacc test is positive, as well as in high-risk populations. A positive reaction to the Mantoux is manifested by erythema (redness), swelling, and induration (hard swelling), which is measured against a scale. A reactions of less than 5 mm is negative; 5 to 9 mm is doubtful, and the test should be repeated; 10 mm or more is positive, and the test is not repeated.

### Other Screening Procedures

*Hemoglobin.* Another important screening procedure is testing an infant's hemoglobin between 9 and 12 months of age. Infants' iron sources from their mothers are depleted by 3 months of age; additional iron is received through breast milk or iron-fortified formula. After 6 months of age, the amount of milk intake may decrease. Infants are at risk for iron-deficiency anemia if foods containing iron are not abundant in the diet. Iron is essential for tissue and brain growth.

*Urinalysis.* Urinalysis is not performed routinely on children under 1 year of age. Because occult bacteriuria can be a source of infection in infancy, failure to thrive or any persistent fever without apparent cause warrants investigation.

## Routine Care

### Bathing

Babies may be bathed in a tub after the stump of their umbilical cord falls off (usually 2–4 weeks of age). Bathing every other day with plain water or a mild soap is sufficient. Bathing is usually an enjoyable event for both infants and parents.

### Clothing

Initially, when the subcutaneous fat is thin and infants' ability to retain heat is limited, more clothing is required. This begins to change within the first months of life. Infants should be dressed in clothing similar to adults, perhaps with one more layer in cooler weather. Clothing should be used as protection from the cold and the sun.

Clothing should be appropriate for the season and climate in which infants live. Infants are comfortable with socks on their feet during cold weather, but there is no need for shoes or sneakers until infants start to walk. Four- to 5-month-old infants especially enjoy playing with their feet and putting them in their mouths. Leaving socks off allow infants freedom to explore and enjoy their body parts. Toward 8 to 9 months of age infants usually enjoy standing and possibly even walking by holding on to furniture. Walking is much easier in bare feet. Shoes or sneakers are not necessary for good ambulation; their only true function is to protect the feet.

### Skin Care

Each infant's skin is different, and because the skin is very sensitive, infants are prone to rashes and other skin problems. Even with careful bathing and drying the skin can become dry. Lotions may be used if the skin is dry or cracked, but heavy oils and creams are not recommended because they can clog the sebaceous ducts.

Because their skin is thin and fragile, infants are particularly susceptible to sunburn. A sunscreen should be used whenever covering the skin is not possible. Sunscreens with higher sun protection factors (SPFs) are recommended for infants 6 months of age and older (DeSimone, 1986).

Often the first rash an infant gets is *infantile acne*. The sebaceous glands on the face and neck become clogged, and small papules form about the third week of life. The rash usually disappears by the second month. Washing with water is the best form of treatment. *Cradle cap* can also develop around this same time. Because of a lack of oil in the skin, yellow flakes form on the scalp. This can happen any time within the first 6 months and is best treated by applying baby oil to the scalp for 30 minutes, then shampooing, rinsing well, vigorously towel drying the scalp, and combing with a fine-toothed comb.

As long as a child is in diapers, the potential for *diaper dermatitis* exists. The contact of feces and urine with an infant's skin often results in irritation. Weston, Lane, and Weston (1980) define four types of diaper dermatitis: (1) chafing—mild redness and scaliness in diaper area; (2) sharply demarcated confluent erythema; (3) discrete shallow ulcerations throughout diaper area; and (4) confluent erythema over entire diaper area with satellite oval lesions on the periphery.

The best treatment for a diaper rash is cleansing the area with water and exposing the skin to the air. It is also important to change the diaper frequently to decrease the contact time between the skin and the irritant. Rigorous use of cleansing products or alcohol can decrease the skin's natural barriers and make it more susceptible to dermatitis. It is unclear whether the use of lubricating ointments (A & D, zinc oxide) or talc reduces skin irritation. If the diaper dermatitis has been present for 72 hours, overgrowth of *Candida albicans* is likely, and an antifungal agent may be prescribed. Steroid cream should only be prescribed for severe inflammation; 1% hydrocortisone is safe if used sparingly over the diaper area for no longer than 1 week.

Frequently, the diaper itself can be implicated in irritating the skin. Detergents, softeners, or bleaches added to the wash of cloth diapers can be irritating to infants' sensitive skin. Prerinsing diapers, using mild soap, rinsing diapers two or three times, and avoiding fabric softeners may help prevent dermatitis. Using disposable diapers, especially when the plastic lining rubs against the skin, can exacerbate redness.

## Feeding

Feeding should always be a pleasant time. What begins as a passive interaction between parent and infant is, by the end of the first year, a purposeful, often self-initiated activity. Early in infancy, whether the baby is bottle- or breast-fed, feeding time allows the mother an opportunity to hold the infant closely, talk to him or her, and reinforce the developing bond.

*Breast-Feeding.* Breast milk is an ideal source of nutrition for infants. In the nineteenth and early twentieth centuries, most infants were breast-fed. With the production of infant formula, mothers had to decide which form of feeding would be best for their infants. Over the years financial considerations, as well as societal pressures, have influenced women's decisions on how to feed their children. When formula first became available, it was a symbol of status and wealth to be able to purchase formula and feed an infant from a bottle. Although manufacturing a variety of formulas similar to breast milk has become a sophisticated, lucrative business, the 1970s saw the "rebirth" of breast-feeding as the preferred method of feeding infants. Professionals once again realized that breast milk provided a perfectly balanced diet for fast-growing infants. During the prenatal period mothers should decide how they will feed their infants. This allows time for reading, discussion, and breast preparation.

Mothers who choose to breast-feed may continue this form of feeding as long as they desire. It takes at least the first 3 or 4 weeks of breast-feeding for both the mother and infant to feel comfortable with this process. At about 1 month of age infants nurse every 3 or 4 hours, 15 minutes or so on each breast. This pattern changes by between 3 and 4 months of age, when infants feed four or five times in a 24-hour period. Growth spurts at 6 weeks and 3 months of age necessitate more frequent feedings for a few days to satisfy infants' increased caloric need. It is important to prepare mothers for this change because they often interpret this as a decrease in their milk supply and may terminate breast-feeding.

The advantages of breast-feeding are numerous. The transfer of immunoglobulin IgA through the breast milk appears to help prevent infections. Breast milk is readily available, no preparation or refrigeration is necessary, and it is less expensive than formula. Some believe that breast-feeding can be difficult because it keeps the mother "confined" to the baby, although use of an occasional bottle is both practical and nutritionally sound. Mothers need to eat three nutritionally balanced meals daily and drink 1 to 2 quarts of fluids to produce adequate milk for their infants.

*Bottle-Feeding.* Infants who are fed commercially prepared formula can grow and develop just as well as breast-fed infants; the important point is that the mother feels comfortable with the method of feeding she chooses and that she cuddles and nurtures her infant while providing the necessary calories for growth. The only major advantage of bottle-feeding is that the father can become an active participant in the feeding process, thereby permitting him to have time with the infant and giving the mother a break (Fig. 12-12).

Numerous infant formulas are available; pediatricians usually suggest the one they think is best for each infant. By the time the baby is 1 month old, mother and infant have usually adapted to the type of bottle and nipple the infant enjoys, the position he or she prefers for feeding, and the position in which the baby burps best. Also, although infants vary, most drink about 3 or 4 oz every 3 or 4 hours by 2 months of age. Formula with iron provides infants with all the nutrients they need for their first 6 months. Infants do not need more than 32 oz of formula daily. Nurses should caution parents not to put infants to bed with bottles because of the possibility of aspiration, as well as the fact that formula that pools in the mouth can cause tooth decay.

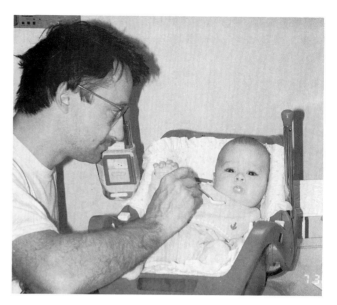

*Figure 12–12.    Father feeding an infant.*

*Introduction of Solid Foods.* The appropriate age for introducing solid foods remains controversial. Nutritionally, breast milk or prepared formula provides all the necessary calories and nutrients for optimal growth for the first 6 months of life. By 6 months of age infants have attained other developmental capabilities that make the introduction of supplemental foods easier. For example, the extrusion tongue reflex is gone, sitting up is a possibility, esophageal motility is normal, and intestinal permeability (sensitization) is reduced. However, these concepts are difficult for many people to understand. Many parents believe that infants cannot grow well on "milk" alone but need solid foods to make a diet complete. Nurses may need to explain to parents that breast milk and prepared formulas are not cow's milk but rather nutritionally sound diets in liquid form.

Nurses need to explain to parents within the first month that introduction of solids should be delayed until the baby is 4 to 6 months old. This suggestion might be altered, however, in some circumstances. The physician or nurse practitioner should be notified if there is a problem. If a 3- to 4-month-old infant is feeding every 2 or 3 hours, is fussy and not pacified by other sucking measures, or is drinking more than 32 oz of formula daily (without spitting up a lot during feeding), solid foods may be introduced.

To ensure good nutrition, parents must encourage older infants to have a well-balanced, diversified diet that will help them establish good habits and eating patterns. Mealtime should be pleasant; this is a new experience for infants, and patience is required.

The first foods should be low in allergy potential—for example, cereals made with rice and barley are easier to digest than oats, corn, and wheat. Parents can add vegetables, then fruits, and then meats. Certain guidelines help when foods are added to infants' diets. Start with small servings, 1 or 2 teaspoons, gradually increasing to 3 or 4 tablespoons. Single foods should be given for 4 or 5 days before introducing another food. This procedure helps detect food sensitivities and may avert developing food intolerances. If diarrhea, urticaria, or severe nasal congestion occur, eliminate the food introduced most recently and reintroduce it in 1 to 3 months.

Prepared baby foods are made for the convenience of adults. There is no nutritional reason why infants should not have table food as long as it is pure (without added salt or seasonings) and pureed for easy intake. The use of a food blender or baby food grinder is helpful. Rather than adding solid food to a bottle, infants should always be fed with a spoon so they can experience different textures in their mouth.

Prepared baby food may contain added salts or preservatives that may not be good for infants. If prepared foods are purchased, single meats or vegetables should be obtained. Meat dinners are misleading; they consist predominantly of vegetables and starch, with meat constituting only some 10% of the contents. Reading the labels on baby food jars is imperative to know what ingredients infants are receiving.

For older infants (8–9 months of age), three meals a day plus a snack are suggested. The "basic four" food groups (milk, meat, bread/cereal, and fruits and vegetables) should be included. The texture of the food given to infants should be compatible with their ability to chew and swallow. Also, once solid foods are integrated into the diet, daily formula intake should decrease to about 20 to 24 oz. This allows infants the opportunity to take their calories from an array of foods providing them with the necessary minerals and vitamins needed for growth. Although an iron-fortified formula is recommended for the first year of life, infants about 10 months old are able to digest cow's milk. This means they must obtain iron from other sources —meats, vegetables, and cereals. Once solid foods are introduced, infants' iron absorption ability from breast milk decreases. Therefore, they need solid foods that are high in iron content. At this age use of a cup helps infants experience independence.

Another interesting phenomenon may occur within the first 4 months after solid foods are introduced. *Carotenemia,* the yellow discoloration of the skin from carotene (a yellow pigment found in many vegetables), affects many infants. They experience an increase in yellow pigment, especially on the face and palms of the hands. The sclera are white, however, and the liver is normal in size. Although the possibility of jaundice is of concern, this diagnosis can be eliminated by obtaining a serum bilirubin level and a carotene level. Carotenemia is not harmful and is easily treated by reducing the intake of foods that contain carotene.

With an increase in mobility toward the end of the first year, infants increasingly want to feed themselves. Ten-month-old infants may suddenly push away their mothers' spoonful of food and splatter it all over the floor. They are saying that they want to feed themselves. Although finger foods—soft, small bits of food—may be messy, they afford infants the opportunity to be people in their own right. This is often the first time parents have experienced "defiance" from their once totally dependent infants. Parents can enjoy this developmental milestone if they realize that this is normal; messiness can be controlled with large bibs and plastic rugs under the high chair. Table manners can be nurtured more in the second and third years of life.

## Safety

Beginning with the first moments of life, infants depend on caregivers for protection from harm. In 1985, accidents accounted for 900 deaths in children under 1 year of age; many of these accidents were preventable (Department of Commerce, Bureau of the Census, 1988). In the beginning of the first year of life, most accidents are caused by falls, suffocation, or motor vehicle accidents, but as infants become more mobile and learn how to explore their environment, a wealth of temptations becomes accessible. The most common accidents include motor vehicle accidents, falls, suffocation, drowning, poisoning, burns, and choking.

*Motor Vehicle Accidents.* Deaths of infants due to motor vehicle accidents are tragedies that, for the most part, can be prevented. Automobile safety begins prenatally. Parents-to-be need to be informed about different types of safety seats that are manufactured to meet the Federal Motor Vehicle Safety Standards. There are many sizes and shapes (for use during different ages and stages), as well as a variety of price ranges. The safety seat needs to be purchased before the infant is born because a baby's ride home from the hospital should be in a safety seat *not* in the mother's arms. Beginning life in a safety-conscious environment can help foster positive safety habits that should continue throughout life. This form of safety needs to be emphasized so that parents realize their important role in teaching safety to their children. Parents also need to wear safety belts as positive models for their children. Although there is car safety legislation in all 50 states, only parents can enforce proper, consistent use of car seats.

The safest position for any car seat is in the middle of the back seat. A variety of car seats are available. Convertible car seats can be used from birth until a child weighs about 40 pounds. The car seat should face the rear of the car until an infant is 7 to 9 months old and weighs 17 to 20 pounds (Fig. 12-13). The seat is usually in the reclined position when it faces the rear of the car but is changed to an upright position when it faces forward. Harness straps also need to be moved as the child grows. Positioning the

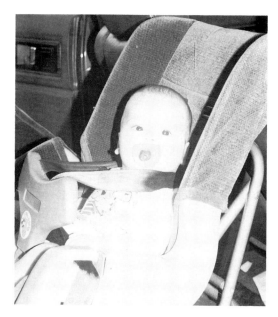

*Figure 12–13.    Infant in rear-facing car seat.*

seat belt through the car seat depends on the type of seat purchased but is necessary for proper stability. A tether strap (a strap hooked to a bracket behind the seat) is essential for proper anchoring of most car seats. Placement of this device varies depending on the type of car (van, station wagon, etc.). All car seats should be installed according to manufacturers' instructions. Parents should be cautioned about the differences between car seats and infant carriers. Infant carriers are not to be used in the car.

*Falls.*    Falls can occur at any time but are more frequent after infants learn how to roll over at about 4 months of age. Before this, infants may still fall because of a sudden startle or scooting movement. Infants should never be left unattended in a high place. A hand should be placed on infants at all times when they are being changed. Even when parents are in a hurry, putting infants on a blanket on the floor is much safer than on a couch or a chair.

During infants' second 6 months, their mobility increases, as does their desire to explore their environment. Dressing infants becomes a challenge; if parents are concerned that children could fall off a changing table or couch, it is much safer to change them on a blanket on the floor.

The use of infant seats is desirable because it allows infants to be elevated enough to see their surroundings and at the same time allows the mother a free hand to do other things. Infant seats are safe only if they are placed in the middle of a counter, table, or bed and the infants are strapped in securely. Even then, infants should never be left alone in these seats. Infants enjoy walkers because they allow increased mobility and a view of their environment in an upright position. It also gives parents a break from carrying them. Unfortunately, there are risks to using

some of these devices. First and foremost is the opportunity for falling. Serious injuries have occurred when walkers topple over or, worse yet, fall down a flight of stairs. As infants grow, the use of high chairs, swings, buggies, and strollers requires appropriate restraining devices. Cribs and playpens should always have the railings locked securely in place. Cribs should have the mattress in its lowest slot to prevent the child from climbing out of the crib.

Gates are another safety device and are needed at the bottom and top of stairs. By 9 months of age, many infants start to walk while holding onto objects or even alone. Falling on coffee tables or edges of toys is common; parents need to make the home as childproof as possible to ensure that early walking and exploration are safe and exciting. Parents should keep ice readily available to apply to bumps and bruises on the head, and popsicles should be handy for infants to suck on to reduce swelling or bleeding on cut lips.

*Suffocation.*    Another devastating accident is suffocation. Infants are usually strong enough to turn their heads from side to side, but they may be unable to wiggle free of blankets that are tucked in too tightly, restricting their movements. Suffocation from plastic bags is more common in this age group. Plastic bags should *never* be allowed around infants, whether for play or to wrap a mattress.

Cribs must be manufactured according to federal safety standards that require that slats be no more than $2^3/8$ inches apart. Wider openings allow the potential risk of infants getting their head caught and suffocating. The mattress should also fit closely to the top, bottom, and sides of the crib, to prevent infants from getting caught in between. Once infants can pull themselves up, any mobiles or toys strung across the crib should be removed to prevent strangulation.

Other potential threats of strangulation are caused by pacifiers tied on strings around the neck and long bib strings. Parents should be cautioned to tie pacifiers to infants' shirts, not around their necks, and to take bibs off after use.

*Drowning.*    An adult should *always* be present when children are around water. This rule should never be altered. Infants should never be left alone in the tub. Even though many can sit alone by 6 or 7 months, bathwater facilitates slipping under the water and drowning. Pools and ponds are additional risks for crawling or walking infants. Yearning for adventure, infants are eager to explore them without knowing the danger involved. Infants need constant protection, and parents must be made acutely aware of the potential risks in their childrens' immediate surroundings. Infants should be checked frequently in their cribs to make sure they have not gotten out; tubs, large pails, and wading pools should be emptied immediately after use. In recent years, parents have begun early swimming instruction with the hope of decreasing drowning accidents. Although this is a positive habit, infants cannot save themselves and should never be alone in the water.

*Poisoning.* Children are naturally curious. As mobility increases (usually around 7 months), exploring the environment becomes a goal of every infant. Touching, smelling, and tasting are all parts of learning. Inherent in each of these senses is the risk of danger. Because infants are still in the oral stage of development, their natural tendency is to put everything into their mouths. As their world expands from a crib to virtually every part of the house, so does their exposure to potentially toxic products. The variety of drugs and household chemicals increases daily in our homes. Therefore, parents must be aware of infants' whereabouts at all times to prevent accidental poisoning. The parents' responsibility is to remove any potentially harmful substance from infants' environment by safely locking these substances away and to watch infants closely as their mobility increases from a creep to a run.

Most ingestions of poisonous substances by children under 5 years of age are attributed to plants, soaps and detergents, cold medications, perfumes, vitamins, and aspirin. Certain conditions can create an environment that increases the risk of poisoning:

*Mealtimes*—Adults are usually very busy and, therefore, children are not watched as closely as usual.

*Child care*—Babysitters and grandparents are often not accustomed to the quickness of infants and the environment may not be childproof.

*Stress*—Any illness or change in the daily routine (even holidays or vacations) disrupts the normal vigilance of a family.

*Guests*—Suitcases or purses may contain medications or cosmetics that are enticing for inquisitive children.

Lack of education plays a large role in the frequency and severity of poisonings. Parents often store or leave substances within easy reach of children and do not lock household products or medications away. They also fail to realize that a bitter taste or bad odor (as in lye or kerosene) often does not deter children from experimentation. Changing a substance from its original container can be dangerous; even with proper labeling children may mistake a substance for food because it is in an attractive container. Vitamins must be placed out of reach of children because the color, shape, and taste may make children think they are candy. Although plants are attractive, many are potentially lethal if eaten. Children cannot discern which plants are edible and which are not. Plants should be kept out of reach of infants.

Prevention is the primary intervention for poisonings. Parents should have the telephone number of the nearest poison control center. These centers have developed across the country as a life-saving service to the public. With the increase in technology, poison control centers can easily access a list of ingredients and quickly ascertain the risk to the patient.

Syrup of ipecac helps to induce vomiting. This can be purchased at a pharmacy and should be kept out of reach of a child. If an ingestion occurs, the poison control center should be called and syrup of ipecac may be ordered. Infants under 1 year of age are given 10 mL; children are given 15 mL. Administration is followed by 4 to 8 oz of fluid. Vomiting results in 90% of cases. If vomiting does not occur in 20 to 30 minutes, a second dose may be given. Precious minutes are saved when vomiting can be induced at home. Certain volatile substances should not be vomited back up (e.g., kerosene, lye); therefore, syrup of ipecac should be used only on instruction from a poison control center or physician.

Hazardous substances in the home should be labeled with stickers that the children are taught mean *bad.* Medicine should never be referred to as candy or "yummy"; childproof caps should be placed on medicine bottles, and childproof safety locks and latches should be installed on cupboard doors.

Although lead poisoning is not as prevalent in this age group, all infants should be screened for lead in their blood by 1 year of age. Sources of lead include inhaled contaminated air, dust particles, and lead in food and water. Ingestion of lead-contaminated paint chips is no longer the primary source of lead poisoning. Since 1977, the use of more than 0.06% lead in household paint had been prohibited (Mahaffey, Gartside, & Gluek, 1986). Paint in older homes may contain lead, however, so parents should be cautioned about the potential danger. Lead can cause severe neurotoxicity; therefore, childrens' exposure to lead must be carefully monitored. Lead poisoning is discussed further in Chapter 26.

*Burns.* A variety of hazardous situations put infants at risk for burns: scalding from hot substances, touching hot objects like radiators or stoves, playing with electrical sockets, biting electrical wires, and even sunburn. Once again, mobility exposes infants to situations in which burns can occur quickly.

Bathwater should always be checked for a safe temperature. Infants seated at a table move their hands and bodies quickly and can easily spill hot liquids on themselves; mothers should not hold infants while cooking near a stove or drinking hot beverages.

As mentioned previously, infants' skin is very sensitive and lacks the fat layers that insulate the body. These protective layers develop as infants grow; therefore, burns at this age are more serious because of the increased permeability of the skin and lack of ability to fight off infection. Protective clothing and sunscreen should always be used.

Crawling infants are on the same level as electrical cords and sockets. Exploring infants can easily place their small fingers in electrical sockets, or they might try to meet their oral needs by biting on an electrical cord; both of these can lead to serious injury. Protective coverings are made for electrical outlets, and cords from any electrical appliances should be kept away from infants' reach.

Touching radiators, portable heaters, and fireplaces can result in serious burns. If these are necessary to heat the home, protective gates need to surround these devices to prohibit infants from getting within their reach.

Legislation passed in 1971 mandated that children's sleepwear (size 0–6x) be flame-retardant. What this actually means is that the fabric will smolder but will not burst into flames; thus burns are still possible. Frequent washings reduce this protection. Although it is important to buy sleepwear with this protection, burns can be prevented only by constant vigilance and education.

Cigarette smoking not only harms infants' lungs but also puts them at risk for burns. Infants can touch or walk into cigarettes or can play with matches and lighters. These must be kept out of the reach of children.

Oral burns have been sustained by infants drinking bottles heated in microwave ovens. Even if mothers test the liquid's temperature, parts of the formula may be hotter because of the uneven distribution of heat throughout the bottle. Caution should be exercised when eating liquids or foods heated in a microwave oven.

*Choking.* In early infancy, the most common cause of choking is from makeshift or unapproved pacifiers. Pacifiers should be one piece and should be large enough so that they cannot be swallowed. As infants begin to crawl, they may choke on anything they find that is small enough to pick up and put into their mouths. Paper clips, hairpins, small parts of toys, balloons, and buttons can all potentially obstruct an infant's airway.

Once table food is introduced, the risk of choking increases. Parents should always be certain that food is of the appropriate size and texture for children. Prohibited foods include peanuts, raisins, hot dogs, carrots, and popcorn.

*Accident Prevention.* Many deaths due to illnesses, malignancies, and birth defects are not preventable, but deaths due to accidents *are* preventable. Nurses have a responsibility to parents and children to help prevent accidents through protection, legislation, and education. Parents may be exposed to education through the media, but one-to-one relationships with nurses allow individual anticipatory guidance.

Accident prevention must be a priority and should be woven throughout all other areas of infants' lives. Safety needs depend on the various ages and stages of development and should be discussed by nurses and parents before children reach a particular stage. Parents can participate with nurses and can decide how to best protect infants in their own homes. It is often a challenge to allow children the freedom to explore and experience different sensations while maintaining safety. Removing potential dangers allows infants the opportunity to explore within a safe environment. When it is not possible to remove environmental hazards (e.g., furniture or stairs), firm, consistent discipline can teach children right from wrong at an early age. As infants strive for independence they often repeat potentially dangerous acts. Parents need to discipline consistently but lovingly and need to offer children more positive alternatives.

## Common Concerns

### Weaning

The age when infants relinquish the bottle or breast for a cup varies. Most sucking needs are fulfilled within the first year. Sucking the breast or bottle after 12 months has no detrimental effects on dentition as long as it is done for nutrition and is not used as a day-long pacifier. Weaning from the bottle can be accomplished easiest if one bottle (usually at midday) is eliminated for 3 or 4 days; gradually, all bottles can be eliminated. Substituting a cup or other manipulative toy often makes this transition easier. Some children have greater sucking needs than others. If the caloric and fluid intake is sufficient, a pacifier can be used.

Weaning from the breast depends on the age of infants. Before 6 to 7 months, infants still need to suck, so they should be weaned from the breast to a bottle. If infants are weaned from the breast after 10 months of age, the use of a cup is usually sufficient to meet their nutritional needs.

Gradual weaning from the breast is beneficial for both mothers and infants. First, the mother should eliminate the feeding least interesting to infants, usually the midday feeding. Substituting a bottle or cup or extra playtime often distracts infants through this period. Mothers need to eliminate each feeding over a period of 4 or 5 days. Mothers should manually express their milk for only 2 or 3 minutes to decrease engorgement but should not stimulate further milk production. Nurses need to assist mothers during the weaning process because it often signifies the end of a special time between mothers and their infants. If breast weaning is premature, the mother may feel a sense of failure or loss. Nurses can help mothers through the weaning process, whether it is planned or sudden.

### Crying

Crying is a means of communication. From the first moments after birth, infants make their needs and desires known by crying. Initially adults may have difficulty interpreting the meaning of infants' cries. By 1 month of age, many parents are able to discern differences in their infants' vocalizations. Crying may mean "I'm hungry," "I'm tired," "My diaper is wet," or even "I just need to blow off steam." The actual time infants spend crying varies from 2 to 4 hours every 24 hours. Duration and intensity of crying varies with the temperament of infants. Easygoing infants may cry for a few minutes to express hunger or fatigue and then be easily calmed. Strong-willed infants may cry with such vigor and strength that parents find it difficult to calm them.

Crying in the first months does have a pattern. Often infants have a "fussy period," starting as early as 2 weeks of age, peaking around 6 weeks of age, and often ending by 3 months of age. This fussy period is usually about the same time each day and is not relieved by milk, sleep, or diaper changing. It is proposed that from a neurological development perspective, infants need this time to verbally express their energy. Nurses should reassure parents that this is a normal developmental phase. Rocking, cuddling, nursing, and use of pacifiers all help to relieve infants' anxiety.

### Sleep Problems

Once infants develop a sleep pattern, many parents believe that life is slowly becoming more predictable, then suddenly their infants start waking at night or skip a nap, and once again the questions of "why?" and "what should we do?" arise. Night wakings can occur at 4 to 5 months of age when an infant learns to roll over; initially they only roll from front to back and awake crying because they cannot voluntarily return to their prior position. Parents need to quietly (without much verbal interaction) assist in turning them onto their stomachs again. This type of awakening may occur again when infants begin to stand in their cribs but do not know how to get down into a sitting or lying position (Fig. 12-14).

Six to 8 months of age is a common time for night waking in infants who have previously slept well. Three common developmental milestones occur around this age: teething, stranger anxiety, and the beginning of infants' ability to form habits. Although the timing of teething is unpredictable, by this age teeth often begin to protrude through the gums or at least are moving in that direction. Teething is usually accompanied by some discomfort. Also, stranger anxiety may begin at this age. In essence, infants know their parents' faces, feel comfortable and secure with them, and are unsure of others that they see infrequently. Therefore, when they awake during the night and look around for their parents (they now have a memory), the parents' absence usually creates mild anxiety and crying. Anytime during the first year infants may become ill with colds, ear infections, rashes, and so forth. Discomfort may awaken them, and only cuddling, rocking, and perhaps a feeding will settle them. Habits begin early in

*Figure 12–14. Older infants standing in cribs.*

life; infants are smart enough to know that cuddling feels good, even if it is late at night. Thus, one or all of the above may initiate night arousal. It is important for parents to know that these habits should not be encouraged. They need to know that during this stage of night waking, the least amount of interaction is best and helps infants gain control over learning how to put themselves back to sleep.

Studies have shown that infant temperament definitely affects the management of night waking. A study by Keene, Zeanah, and Anders (1988) found that most infants awoke during the night, but two distinct groups emerged. Self-soothing infants calmed themselves back to sleep without complete arousal by means of a pacifier, toy, or blanket. Signaling infants expressed themselves by crying and demanding attention. Thus, sleep problems before 1 year of age are usually self-limiting and easy to change if nurses help parents realize that they are in control and help them understand normal infant sleep patterns.

### Thumb Sucking

The need to suck is a natural phenomenon in infants. In utero photographs depict 28-week fetuses sucking their thumbs. Sucking is essential for life; it provides infants with a sense of security and therefore should not be discouraged. Because this is such a strong reflex, trying to interpret infants' needs early helps to comfort them and relieves parental anxiety. The sucking urge can be satisfied by feeding, using a pacifier, or finger or thumb sucking. Feeding does not always satisfy infants' need to suck, so nurses should caution parents not to misinterpret the sucking sensation for hunger and therefore overfeed infants. Using a pacifier helps infants meet their oral needs. The tongue has a natural tendency to protrude until the age of 4 months; caretakers might need to assist by holding the pacifier in the infant's mouth. The advantage of this method is that parents can remove the pacifier when they feel the infant no longer needs it. Dental abnormalities occur when the use of a pacifier or thumb sucking continues past the age of 4 years. Discarding the pacifier between 12 and 18 months discourages this sucking pleasure from becoming a habit.

Sucking the thumb or fingers provides the same secure feeling as a pacifier; the disadvantage is that it may be difficult to break the child of this habit because the thumb is so readily available. During the first year of life though, thumb sucking is usually pacifying and will not harm mouth structure.

## Parenting Development

What makes a person a "parent"? Is there a magical spell that transforms people into parents when they see their newborn infants? Does one learn how to be a parent from a parenting course? All these questions go through the minds of expectant parents. The answer is not simple: parenting is not simple. Parenting is a complex experience that brings with it joy, sorrow, anger, rewards, satisfaction, and, most of the time, love.

Parenting actually begins when the parents themselves are born. Early in life they learn from their parents how to relate to other humans and to their environment. This cyclical pattern continues when their own infant is born. Both parents bring to a relationship what they have learned in the past. Often they are not conscious of why they behave as they do. Most parents claim that they do not *feel* like parents when they first come home with their new infant, and those feelings are probably very sincere. It is the daily interaction of infants with parents that helps their relationship grow. The bonding that takes place within the first days of life and the attachment that strengthens within the first months of life grows only after infants' and parents' relationships have had many trials and tribulations. Is it difficult to cuddle an infant who has been screaming for 5 hours at night? Certainly, but a hug or the words *mama, mama* often relieve all the tension because parents have learned to love their infants even though some of their behavior is occasionally almost intolerable.

Levine et al. (1983) discuss five propositions that help to explain the complexity of the parenthood process. Proposition 1 considers the fact that a dyad evolves into a triad, and all the persons involved have to learn how to respond to one another in an interactional pattern. A parental relationship can be severed only through death, and even then the remaining person would argue that parental feelings never die.

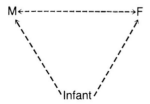

Proposition 2 reminds us to include the developmental stages of parents when discussing the developmental tasks of infancy. The tasks of an adolescent mother differ greatly from those of a 35-year-old corporate executive mother, yet the tasks their infants strive to accomplish during their first year of life are the same. These parents approach their children's development differently because of where they are in their own life cycle.

Proposition 3 holds that parents bring to a relationship all that has previously taken place in their own lives. Life has good and bad moments; humans often try to repress the negative experiences of their past only to have them surface when they see their own child in a similar situation. Their interpretation of their child's behavior may be egocentric and far from objective.

Proposition 4 notes that in this fast-changing society, the desires and unfulfilled dreams of the parents are often subconsciously forced on their children. Although this is not always evident during infancy, verbal preparation takes place when a father discusses a future football career as his 12-month-old son throws a ball or a mother discusses piano lessons as her daughter delicately manipulates a toy.

Proposition 5 reminds us that several generations interact at the same time in today's society. Sometimes the birth of an infant renews a relationship for the new grandparents because they may previously have been "put on hold" while the young adults were striving for independence and career stability. Suddenly parents must interact with their parents and infants simultaneously. Feeling secure in their role as parents facilitates a positive, balanced relationship with the grandparents and infant. Yet, as stated earlier, feeling secure in a parental role takes months to develop; even then, this stability is challenged with each new developmental task or crisis.

Another complex variable involved in parenting is the relationship of the parent to the family. Is the parent a teenage adolescent, a single parent, a married couple, or an adoptive family? Other variables that affect parenting are the cultural and ethnic backgrounds of the parents, their socioeconomic status, their own temperaments and their infant's, and even the changing mores in today's society. All of these variables interact to shape how parents interpret infants' behavior and how they respond.

Parents have an important role as teachers of their infants, just as nurses have a critical role in teaching parents about their infants. Even though parents have a wealth of information, habits, and expectations, nurses must teach them how their infant will develop and how they can facilitate the infant's growth and development. Anticipatory guidance, or preparing parents for what is to come, helps them realize the normalcy of their infant's behavior and gives them preparation time to make necessary changes that will foster growth. Beginning at birth, parents "teach" their infants by verbal and tactile stimulation, trust develops as they consistently meet infants' basic needs, and gross motor accomplishments are enhanced by parents' provocations. Parents are teachers and role models as long as the relationship exists.

Nurses need to prepare parents for rapid changes that occur within the first year. The physical changes are great, but even more phenomenal is the personality development of infants. By their first birthday, there is no question that they are individuals in their own right. Parents need to allow infants opportunities to grow in all areas, and nurses can help them do this within the family's own social and cultural context.

Nurses need to help parents love and nurture their children without fear of "spoiling" them. McIntosh (1989) discusses a variety of behaviors that could be interpreted as negative because of spoiling. In reality, however, it is the parents' insecurity and misinterpretation of these behaviors that lead them to reinforce these negative behaviors. For instance, an infant needs to cry for certain periods during the day. Although crying may be stimulated by hunger, sleepiness, or being wet, it also might allow infants time to release built-up energy. If parents feel unable to comfort their infants because of the fear that carrying out their natural tendency to hold and cuddle the babies will spoil them, a vicious circle arises when parents feel that they have lost control of the situation. These parental feelings can continue in this first year when infants persist past 4 months of age to wake for a feeding or wake nightly for a good cry. Parents often are overwhelmed and unable to console their crying infants. Again, nurses can teach parents that there is no physical need for feeding or crying in the middle of the night for infants older than 4 to 5 months, and it is the parents' responsibility to take control of the situation. This is an early form of discipline or truly using the principles of behavior modification to shape the infant's behavior (McIntosh, 1989). During the early months of life, both parents need to agree on a management plan and carry it out consistently. McIntosh reminds us that infants' early needs seem insatiable, and parents are responsible for helping their children to realize that all their needs do not warrant immediate gratification.

There are many other areas in which parents feel challenged during this first year. Although children adjust differently to the arrival of a new brother or sister, once the infant begins to respond, older children often share warm times with the infant (Fig. 12-15). However, sibling rivalry occurs sooner or later in almost all cases and tries any parent's patience. The birth of an infant into a triad family requires all family members to readjust their roles and relationships within the family. Parents often feel they are giving a lot of themselves to everyone but themselves. Nurses can review certain tasks each family member can perform to facilitate the transition of this new family member into the restructured family unit. Support from extended family members or friends can help parents deal with this new phase of parenting.

During the past few decades, the changing roles of mothers have often necessitated using additional care-takers for children. Infants no longer are necessarily bathed, diapered, and fed by their mothers. These needs might be met by a relative or caretaker in the home or in a day-care setting. Parenthood is at times more difficult because of the changing schedules of both parents working outside the home and the need for flexibility for infants. Parenthood is sometimes put off because of the fear of being burdened with the task of finding caretakers who will share in rearing and nurturing their infant. Parents have to deal with their own feelings of leaving their infant. In the latter part of the first year, when stranger anxiety appears, their guilt often intensifies as they leave a sobbing 9-month-old with outstretched arms. Parenthood is not easy, but it is very rewarding. Nurses can help parents anticipate these "crises" and deal with them so both infant and parent feel comfortable.

## Summary

Infancy, the period from 1 to 12 months of age, is filled with wondrous changes for children and their families. During this time infants triple their birth weight, begin the formation of personalities, and evolve from relying totally on their parents to actively seeking independence.

Physical growth includes rapid increases in height and weight, as well as the maturation of virtually every body system. Gross motor development progresses as infants learn to hold their heads erect, turn over, sit, crawl, stand, and eventually walk. Fine motor development progresses from purely reflexive responses, through many trials and errors, to purposeful actions.

Infants' cognitive development during this period is just as rapid as their physical growth. The maturation of the senses enables infants to initiate activities that lead to cognitive growth. Complex concepts such as object permanence are developed and mastered as infants explore their environments and their bodies. Psychosocial development takes place as infants learn to trust that their needs will be met and as they interact with their families. Communication progresses from cries of need, to smiles, to coos and babbling, and on to the beginning of language development.

To accomplish the "tasks" of infancy, children need proper nutrition, adequate sleep, and an environment that provides for optimal growth. By working with parents, nurses can help promote healthy behaviors in both parents and infants.

Because the groundwork for all later growth and development is laid during infancy, health maintenance and health promotion are essential. Nurses have a critical role in working with parents to be certain that infants progress at normal but individual rates, that developmental or physical problems are discovered early and corrective measures are initiated, and that parents are provided with anticipatory guidance about accident prevention, com-

*Figure 12–15.   Sibling interactions.*

mon concerns, and parenting. Nurses provide a crucial source of support for infants and parents during the first year.

## References

American Academy of Pediatrics, Committee on Infectious Diseases. (1988). *Report of the Committee on Infectious Diseases* (21st ed.). Elk Grove Village, IL: American Academy of Pediatrics.

American Academy of Pediatrics, Committee on Nutrition. (1981). Nutrition and lactation. *Pediatrics, 68,* 435–445.

American Academy of Pediatrics, Committee on Nutrition. (1986a). Prudent life-style for children: Dietary fat and cholesterol. *Pediatrics, 78,* 521–528.

American Academy of Pediatrics, Committee on Nutrition. (1986b). Fluoride supplementation. *Pediatrics, 77,* 758–761.

Anderson, H. G. (1985). Human milk feeding. *Pediatric Clinics of North America, 32,* 335–353.

Anderson, T. A., & Foman, S. J. (1974). Vitamins. In S. J. Foman (Ed.). *Infant nutrition* (3rd ed.). Philadelphia: W. B. Saunders.

Aquilina, S. (1987). Gastroesophageal reflux: Problem or nuisance? *Journal of Pediatric Health Care, 1,* 233–239.

Barness, L. (1985). Infant feeding: Formula, solids. *Pediatric Clinics of North America, 32,* 355–362.

Bayley, N. (1956). Individual patterns of development. *Child Development, 27,* 45.

Behrman, R. E., & Vaughan, V. C. (1987). *Nelson textbook of pediatrics* (13th ed.). Philadelphia: W. B. Saunders.

Beverly, B. (1947). *A psychology of growth.* New York: McGraw-Hill.

Brazelton, T. B. (1969). *Infants and mothers.* New York: Dell Publishing.

Capute, A., Shapiro, B., & Palmer, F. (1987). Marking the milestones of language development. *Contemporary Pediatrics, 4,* 24–41.

Carey, W., & McDevitt, S. (1978). Revision of the infant temperament questionnaire. *Pediatrics, 61,* 735–739.

Castiglia, P. (1987). Speech language development. *Journal of Pediatric Health Care, 1,* 165–167.

Charney, E., Goodman, H., McBride, M., Lyon, B., & Pratt, R. (1976). Childhood antecedents of adult obesity. *New England Journal of Medicine, 295,* 6–9.

Chomsky, N. (1969). Language and the mind. *Psychology Today, 4,* 1–8.

Cohen, F. L. (1984). *Clinical genetics in nursing practice.* Philadelphia: J. B. Lippincott.

Coplan, J. (1987). Deafness: Ever heard of it? Delayed recognition of permanent hearing loss. *Pediatrics, 79,* 206–213.

Davidson, E. R. (1949). Play for the hospitalized child. *The American Journal of Nursing, 49,* 138–141.

Department of Commerce, Bureau of the Census. (1988). *National data book and guide to census: Statistical abstract of the United States, 1988* (108th ed.). Washington, D. C.: U.S. Government Printing Office.

DeSimone, E. M. (1986). Sunscreen and suntan products. In *Handbook of nonprescription drugs* (8th ed.). Washington, D. C.: American Pharmaceutical Association.

Erikson, E. (1963). *Childhood and society* (2nd ed.). New York: W. W. Norton.

Ferber, R. (1985). *Solve your child's sleep problems.* New York: Simon & Schuster.

Giovachini, P. (1982). *A clinician's guide to reading Freud.* New York: Aronson.

Godfrey, S., & Baum, F. D. (1979). *Clinical pediatric physiology.* Oxford: Blackwell Scientific Publications.

Hott, J. (1970). Play PRN in pediatric nursing. *Nursing Forum, 9,* 288–308.

Jacklin, C. N., Snow, M. E., & Maccoby, E. E. (1981). Tactile sensitivity and strength in newborn boys and girls. *Infant Behavior Development 4,* 285.

Keene, M., Zeanah, C., & Anders, T. (1988). Infant temperament, sleep organization, and nighttime parental interventions. *Pediatrics, 81,* 762–771.

Klaus, M. H., Kennell, J. H., Plumb, N., & Zuehlke, S. (1970). Human maternal behavior at first contact with her young. *Pediatrics, 46,* 187–192.

Korner, A. F., Hutchinson, C. A., Koperski, J. A., Kraemer, H. C., & Schneider, P. A. (1981). Stability of individual differences of neonatal motor and crying patterns. *Child Development, 52,* 83.

Kula, K., & Tianoff, N. (1982). Fluoride therapy for the pediatric patient. *Pediatric Clinics of North America, 29,* 665–680.

Levine, M., Carey, W., Crocker, A., & Gross, R. (1983). *Developmental–behavioral pediatrics.* Philadelphia: W. B. Saunders.

Mahaffey, K., Gartside, P., & Glueck, C. (1986). Blood lead levels and dietary calcium intake in 1 to 11 year old children. *Pediatrics, 78,* 257–262.

Mahoney, C. P. (1987). Evaluating the child with short stature. *Pediatric Clinics of North America, 34,* 825–849.

McArnarney, E., Laurence, R., Ricciuti, H., Polley, J., & Szilagyi, M. (1986). Interventions of adolescent mothers and their 1 year old children. *Pediatrics, 78,* 585–590.

McIntosh, B. (1989). Spoiled child syndrome. *Pediatrics, 83,* 108–115.

Miller, S., & Chopra, J. (1984). Problems with human milk and infant formulas. *Pediatrics, 74*(Suppl 2), 639–649.

Papalia, D. E., & Olds, S. W. (1989). *Human development* (4th ed.). New York: McGraw-Hill.

Pencharz, P. (1985). Foreword. *Pediatric Clinics of North America, 32,* 273–274.

Piaget, J. (1952). *The origins of intelligence in children.* New York: International University Press.

Rosenblatt, D. (1977). Developmental trends in infant play. In B. Tizard & D. Harvey. *Biology of play.* Philadelphia: J. B. Lippincott.

Ruben, R. J. (1986). Unsolved desires around critical periods with emphasis on clinical application. *Acta Otolaryngology, 429*(Suppl), 61–64.

Rudolph, A., & Hoffman, J. (1987). *Pediatrics.* East Norwalk, CT: Appleton & Lange.

Shafer, W., Hine, M., & Levy, B. (1974). *A textbook of oral pathology.* Philadelphia: W. B. Saunders.

Thomas, A., & Chess, S. (1977). *Temperament and development.* New York: Brunner-Mazel.

Weston, W., Lane, A., & Weston, J. (1980). Diaper dermatitis: Current concepts. *Pediatrics, 66,* 532–536.

## Bibliography

American Academy of Pediatrics, Committee on Nutrition. (1980). Vitamin and mineral supplement needs in normal children in the United States. *Pediatrics, 66,* 1015–1020.

Buckley, R., Dees, R., & O'Fallon, W. M. (1968). Serum immunoglobulin levels in normal children and in uncomplicated childhood. *Pediatrics, 41,* 600.

Dworkin, P., Allen, D., Geertsma, A., Solkoske, L., & Cullina, J. (1987). Does developmental content influence the effectiveness of anticipatory guidance? *Pediatrics, 80,* 196–202.

Einon, D. (1985). *Play with a purpose.* New York: Duncan Petersen.

Elliott, R (1986). *Vegetarian mother baby book.* New York: Random House.

Frank, D., Zuchermen, B., Amaro, H., Aboagye, K., Bauchner, H., Cabral, H., Fried, L., Hingson, R., Kayne, H., Levenson, S., Parker, S., Reece, H., Vinci, R. (1988). Cocaine use during pregnancy: Prevalence and correlates. *Pediatrics, 82,* 888–895.

Frankenburg, W., & Dodds, J. (1967). The Denver Developmental Screening Test. *The Journal of Pediatrics, 71,* 181–191.

Frankenburg, W., Dodds, J., & Fandol, A. (1970). *Denver Developmental Screening Test manual.* Denver, CO: University of Colorado Medical Center.

Gaffney, K. F. (1988). New directions in maternal attachment research. *Journal of Pediatric Health Care, 2,* 181–188.

Gain, S. (1985). Continuities and changes in fatness from infancy through adulthood. *Current Problems in Pediatrics, 15,* 4–47.

Gunnip, A., Roberson, C., Meredith, J., Bull, M., Stroup, K., & Branson, M. (1987). Car seats: Helping parents do it right. *Journal of Pediatric Health Care, 1,* 190–195.

Hermann, H., & Roberts, M. (1987). Preventive dental care: The role of the pediatrician. *Pediatrics, 80,* 107–110.

Hoekelman, R. A. (1991). The physical examination of infants and children. In B. Bates. *A guide to physical examination and history taking* (5th ed.). Philadelphia: J. B. Lippincott.

Neifert, M., & Seacat, J. (1986). Medical management of successful breast-feeding. *Pediatric Clinics of North America, 34,* 743–761.

Roche, A., Mukherjee, D., Guo, S., & Moore, W. (1987). Head circumference reference data: Birth to 18 years. *Pediatrics, 79,* 706–712.

Rudy, C. (1984). Vegetarian diets for children. *Pediatric Nursing, 10,* 329–333.

# Toddler Growth, Development, and Health

Mary L. Burke

13

*Physical Growth and Development*
  *General Growth Characteristics*
  *Motor Development*
  *Sensory Development*
  *Nutrition Needs*
  *Sleep*

*Cognitive Development*
  *Piaget*
  *Play*

*Psychosocial Development*
  *Erikson*
  *Freud*
  *Mastering Separation*
  *Language Development*
  *Sex Role Identification*

*Assessment*
  *Body Measurements*
  *Denver Developmental Screening Test*
  *Washington Guide to Promoting Development in the Young Child*
  *Assessment of Home and Family*

*Health Promotion*
  *Health Maintenance Visits and Immunizations*
  *Dental Care*
  *Recognizing Developmental Tasks*
  *Common Concerns*

*Parenting Development*

*Summary*

*Photograph by David Finn*

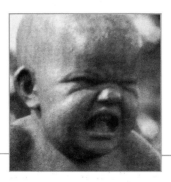

*Upon completion of this chapter the reader will be able to:*

1. *Identify the characteristics of normal physical growth and development in toddlers.*

2. *Describe toddlers' usual pattern of cognitive development.*

3. *Discuss the normal psychosocial development of toddlers.*

4. *Describe at least three methods of assessing toddlers' development and environment.*

5. *Discuss the role of nurses in health promotion for toddlers and their families.*

*Key Terms*

*discipline*

*food jags*

*parallel play*

*punishment regression*

*separation anxiety*

*sex role*

*sex role stereotype*

*symbolic play*

The toddler period of child development spans the 24 months between the child's first and third birthdays. During this time children's rate of physical growth slows, and toddlers acquire numerous motor, cognitive, and psychosocial skills in moving toward independence. This period is frequently a difficult one for parents because of toddlers' rapid development and struggle for autonomy. During the toddler period, nurses are likely to interact with children and families during several health maintenance visits. Nursing goals for this period are (1) to promote the child's physical health, (2) to support the accomplishment of age-appropriate developmental tasks, (3) to promote the child's safety, and (4) to provide guidance to promote normal parenting skills.

## Physical Growth and Development

### General Growth Characteristics

By the beginning of the toddler period, the child's birth weight has usually tripled. Weight gain from 1 to 2 years, however, usually equals only the amount gained between 6 and 12 months of age. A further slowing of the overall growth rate occurs from 2 to 3 years. Increases in the child's weight and height taper off in this period. The average toddler grows only as much in length between ages 2 and 3 years as in the first 3 months of life. The normal growth pattern includes short periods of rapid growth that alternate with periods of little or no growth that are characteristic of this age group. The average weights and heights of boys and girls at 1, 1½, 2, and 3 years of age are listed in Table 13-1. A child attains about half of the ultimate adult height at age 2. This measure is often used to project the height when fully grown.

Toddlers also assume characteristic body proportions that indicate changes in the rate at which different parts of the body are growing. The head, which grew rapidly

*Table 13–1. Average Weights and Heights During the Toddler Years*

| Age | Boys | Girls |
|---|---|---|
| 1 y | | |
| Weight | 22.2 lb (10.06 kg) | 21.5 lb (9.75 kg) |
| Height | 29.6 in (75.2 cm) | 29.2 in (74.1 cm) |
| 18 mo | | |
| Weight | 25.2 lb (11.43 kg) | 24.5 lb (11.11 kg) |
| Height | 32.2 in (81.8 cm) | 31.8 in (80.8 cm) |
| 2 y | | |
| Weight | 27.7 lb (12.56 kg) | 27.1 lb (12.29 kg) |
| Height | 34.4 in (87.4 cm) | 34.1 in (86.6 cm) |
| 3 y | | |
| Weight | 32.2 lb (14.61 kg) | 31.8 lb (14.43 kg) |
| Height | 37.9 in (96.3 cm) | 37.7 in (95.8 cm) |

(Adapted from The Diagram Corp. [1980]. *The human body*. New York: Facts on File, Inc.)

during the prenatal period, reaches 19 inches in circumference between the ages of 1½ and 2 years and grows only ⅛ inch more by age 3. By 1½ years, the anterior fontanelle has closed. During the second year of life, the head and chest circumferences become equal. The chest circumference continues to increase and exceeds the head circumference by the end of the toddler period. Beginning at 1 year of age, the legs become the fastest growing part of the child's body. Toddlers are typically short-necked, high-shouldered, pot-bellied, slightly bow-legged, and sway-backed, with a wide-stance gait. This appearance reflects the gradual development and strengthening of the muscles to accommodate the increases in weight, height, and upright posture. Figure 13-1 illustrates the changing proportions of the toddler's body during this developmental period. Standard growth charts are included in Appendix B.

Various internal body structures and systems grow and change remarkably during the toddler years. By 1 year of age the immune system is fully functional, and the child's ability to produce antibodies is mature. The thymus gland, thought to produce the cell precursors of lymphocytes and plasma cells, grows in size throughout the period. The number of circulating red blood cells reaches the normal adult level (4.7 million/μL) by age 2.

Unlike that of the older child, the heart of the toddler is relatively larger than the rest of the chest. Heart sounds are of higher pitch and greater intensity than in the adult because of the thinness of the chest wall. The heart rate gradually slows, and the systolic blood increases slightly from later infancy. Table 13-2 lists the average values for pulse, blood pressure, respirations, and temperature during the toddler period.

The larynx grows rapidly in both width and length until age 3. The alveoli of the lungs increase in both size and number. The supporting structures grow proportionately. The airways continue to be small in diameter, making the respiratory system especially vulnerable to narrowing during inflammation. Respirations are diaphragmatic or abdominal, as opposed to the thoracic respirations of later childhood, and slowly decrease in rate throughout this period.

By the age of 2 the gastrointestinal system is mature enough to handle any foods that are usually included in a well-balanced adult diet. The salivary glands are functioning in an adult manner, although saliva production may increase in response to teething. The stomach capacity increases to about 500 mL. The gastric emptying time remains faster than in the adult. Bowel movements become more regular in character and timing.

Teeth erupt throughout the toddler period. Between ages 1 and 2 the lower incisors, the first molars, and the canine teeth emerge. During the third year the second

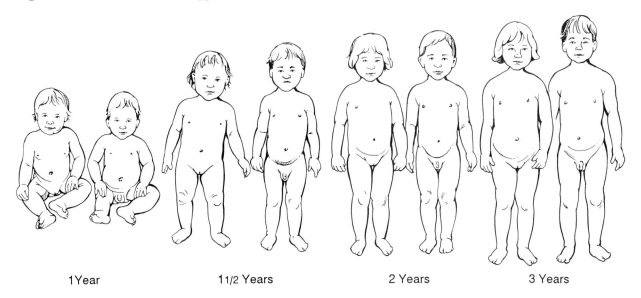

| 1Year | 1 1/2 Years | 2 Years | 3 Years |

*Figure 13–1. The changing appearance of the toddler.*

*Table 13–2.  Average Vital Sign Measures of Toddlers*

| Age (y) | Temperature (°C) | Average Pulse (beats/min) | Blood Pressure | Respirations (breaths/min) |
|---|---|---|---|---|
| 1 | 37.6 | 120 | 92/60 | 30 |
| 2 | 37.4 | 110 | 97/60 | 28 |
| 3 | 37.2 | 100 | 99/60 | 26 |

molars erupt. All 20 primary teeth should be present by the child's third birthday.

The kidneys continue to develop functionally during the toddler years. By age 3 kidney function is considered mature. Urinary output is about 500 to 600 mL in 24 hours, divided into 8 to 10 voidings.

The ossification of the skeleton continues during the toddler period, with marked male–female differences in development. Toeing-in due to metatarsus adductus usually corrects itself as the toddler's locomotion skills increase. Some tibial torsion is usually present as part of the normal growth pattern. The longitudinal arch becomes apparent as the fat pad on the foot is worn away by walking.

By 2 years, the brain size reaches about 90% of its future adult size. *Myelination,* the process in which a white lipid sheath forms around cranial and spinal nerve fibers, is complete by 2 years of age. The formation of myelin is associated with increased speed of impulse transmission and with the development of functional capacities, including bowel and bladder control.

Physical growth and development during the toddler period allows for mature functioning in many areas. This provides the basis for children's ability to accomplish the developmental milestones of this age group.

## Motor Development

Both gross and fine motor development in the toddler demonstrate three general trends of motor development: (1) central body areas function before outer areas, (2) control progresses from head to foot, and (3) large muscles are controlled before small muscles. In general, there is an orderly progression from the simple to the complex.

### Gross Motor Development

The ability to walk unaided is often described as the single most important task of motor development in the toddler period. Locomotion affects toddlers' physical, cognitive, and social development because it permits children to explore the environment, satisfy curiosity, experience new sensations, and develop new skills of manipulation.

By the beginning of the toddler period (12–15 months), children crawl with agility, crawl upstairs, pull themselves upright and lower themselves using furniture, briefly stand unaided, walk forward with adult assistance or unaided, and cruise sideways while holding onto furniture (Fig. 13-2). True mobility is now a reality.

By 18 months, toddlers kneel upright unsupported, squat to reach objects and stand up again by using hand support, crawl up and down stairs, walk easily with controlled starting and stopping, run clumsily with eyes on the ground, and carry or pull objects while walking. Children at this age are immensely active and try out newly acquired skills.

Two-year-olds squat steadily and stand without the assistance of hand support; run easily with controlled stops, starts, and dodges; climb on furniture and get down unaided; walk up and down steps while holding onto a handrail, placing both feet on each step; throw small balls forward while standing; and push tricycles with both feet. No longer unsteady, children of 2 years love to romp, chase, and be pursued.

By the third birthday, children stand briefly on one foot, stand and walk on tiptoe, place one foot on each step when walking upstairs but both feet on each step when walking down, jump off one step, catch large balls between outstretched arms, and pedal tricycles. At the end of the toddler period, the child's erect posture and arm-swinging, as well as closed gait, provide a glimpse of the adult of the future. None of these milestones are absolute, however, because children may progress at individual rates that fall within the accepted norms.

### Fine Motor Development

The pincer grasp, manipulation, and hand preference are the major fine motor abilities that mature during the toddler period. The development and refinement of these skills allow for the purposeful activity that is the hallmark of the toddler years.

At 1 year of age, toddlers can lift small objects between the thumb and tip of the index finger (pincer grasp), may begin to favor the use of one hand, begin to notice pictures, can clap two cubes together, and deliberately drop and throw toys. This last activity may lead to a favorite game of the 1-year-old, repeatedly letting objects fall one by one to be retrieved by another person.

Children of 18 months transfer objects hand to hand at

*Figure 13–2. Toddler pushing himself to standing position. (Courtesy Child Care Center, University of Texas at El Paso)*

will, can swiftly pick up small objects using a pincer grasp, successfully imitate the building of a three-cube tower, turn groups of pages in books when looking at pictures, grip pencils with the palm of the hand to scribble, and become noticeably right- or left-handed. Lacking precise control, toddlers at 18 months often throw most of their bodies into every activity.

By 2 years of age, toddlers have a refined pincer ability, use four or five cubes to build a tower, turn the pages of a book one at a time, grip pencils near the point between the first two fingers and thumb, make circular scribbles and dots, and imitate the drawing of a vertical line. The hand movements of 2-year-olds are more varied and assured, allowing for testing and exploring objects by touch and manipulation.

Children of 3 years can use one hand to cut with scissors, build a tower of six to eight cubes, build a three-cube bridge, put large beads on a string, control a pencil well between the thumb and first two fingers, draw a person that has at least two body parts, and copy a circle. By the end of the toddler period, 3-year-olds have sufficient hand–eye coordination and fine motor skill to allow the imitation of many adult activities.

## Sensory Development

The eyeball is small and short throughout the toddler period, causing light rays to focus behind the retina. As a consequence, toddlers are hyperopic (farsighted). At 2 years of age, children's visual acuity is estimated at between 20/50 and 20/30. Coupled with toddlers' soft lens, which accommodate and focus readily, this results in normal vision for children's needs. Vision provides a window

for learning. Depth perception results from cerebral rather than visual development and is poor until near the end of the toddler period. At age 2, children misjudge distances and bump into many objects. By 3 years of age, however, depth perception allows the accurate judgment of the location and size of objects.

During the toddler years, the external ear canal slowly ossifies and assumes a slightly more vertical position than during infancy. The tympanic membrane remains shorter and more oblique than in older children. The eustachian tube between the middle ear and pharynx remains short and broad. This allows for the transport of infectious material to the middle ear, as well as closure during sleep. When the eustachian tube closes, air pressure in the middle ear is not equalized, and hearing may be affected. Because of the crucial role of hearing in the development of speech, a hearing evaluation is indicated if the child's speech is delayed.

The toddler's nasal structures are fully mature, but the nose still has a short, pug appearance. Whereas the receptors for the sense of smell are fully developed at birth, the sense of smell develops in relation to learned associations with pleasant and unpleasant odors throughout the toddler period.

Toddlers' abilities to chew and swallow secretions are mature. Taste discrimination continues to develop as connections between the cortex and taste buds allow for the association of agreeable and disagreeable tastes.

The sense of touch is well developed by the beginning of the toddler period. Tactile stimulation through touching and being touched allows toddlers to explore and interact with the environment.

In general, neurosensory development progresses

rapidly between the ages of 1 and 3 years. Therefore, normal sensory development approaches a mature level by the end of the toddler period.

## Nutrition Needs

Nutritional requirements decline somewhat during the toddler years as the result of the lower basal metabolic demand and the decreased rate of growth. Toddlers eat in response to (1) the unpleasant sensation of hunger and (2) the appetite—pleasant associations of food with past experiences. In exerting independence, however, toddlers may refuse or play with food. One or several meals may go uneaten. It is important to be aware of the changing eating patterns of toddlers to avoid the long-lasting effects of battles over food. Table 13-3 summarizes the recommended daily intakes of selected nutrients for children between their first and third birthdays.

These nutrients are provided in adequate amounts by a daily menu that corresponds to the following pattern:

*Breakfast*

1 serving high-protein food: egg, cheese, meat, or cereal

1 serving bread group: slice of whole grain or enriched white

1 serving milk: 6–8 oz to drink or on cereal

1 serving fruit: citrus fruit or 4 oz juice

*Lunch*

1 serving high-protein food: thick soup, stew, or casserole

1 serving vegetables: 2 tablespoons raw or cooked

1 serving bread group: whole grain crackers

1 serving milk: 6–8 oz to drink or in food

Dessert: fruit or pudding

*Dinner*

1 serving high-protein food: meat, cheese, egg, or casserole

1 serving vegetables: 2 tablespoons raw or cooked

1 serving bread group: slice of whole grain or enriched white

1 serving milk: 6–8 oz to drink

Dessert: fruit or dairy dessert

If food is refused or ignored at mealtimes, it should be removed without comment. Often, children become hungry before the next scheduled meal and a snack is eagerly accepted. Between-meal snacks should be selected from the following list to replace foods missed previously or to supplement those eaten:

Dry cereal, fruit juice, or skim milk

Raw fruit or vegetable, bread or toast

Crackers, cheese wedges

Toddlers have sporadic appetites. Consequently, they may refuse previously accepted foods or stage "hunger strikes" for one or several meals. They may have food "jags" where only certain foods are acceptable for extended periods. Usually, an adequate diet can be provided by working within the child's preferences. What is eaten over a long period is more important than meal-to-meal intake.

Foods should be offered in a variety of forms so that toddlers can both eat with their fingers and use utensils. An appropriate serving size for a toddler is 1 tablespoon for each year of age. Child-sized eating utensils are helpful. Messy eating is to be expected, but the practice gained by self-feeding results in some proficiency by age 2 (Fig. 13-3). The use of a bib, high chair, and a layer of newspapers on the floor helps to minimize the effects of spills as the child learns. Table manners should not be emphasized. Food and utensils should be removed and toddlers should be allowed to leave the table as soon as eating is obviously completed. Young children have little tolerance for prolonged family mealtimes.

Concerned parents should be reassured that when children get hungry enough, they will eat. This can be exploited by offering small helpings of nutritious foods at intervals when children seem hungry. By being flexible in their expectations of the type and quantity of food that

## Table 13–3. Recommended Daily Intakes for Toddlers

| Nutrient | Measure |
| --- | --- |
| Calories | 1300 kcal (range 900–1800) |
| Protein | 1.8 g/kg body weight |
| Fat | 30%–50% of total calories |
| Water | 120–125 mL/kg body weight |
| Calcium | 800 mg |
| Phosphorus | 800 mg |
| Iodine | 70 μg |
| Iron | 15 mg |
| Fluoride | 0.5–1.5 mg |
| Sodium | 325–975 mg |
| Potassium | 550–1650 mg |
| Chloride | 500–1500 mg |
| Vitamin A | 400 μg |
| Vitamin D | 10 μg |
| Thiamine | 0.7 mg |
| Riboflavin | 0.8 mg |
| Niacin | 9 mg |
| Ascorbic acid | 45 mg |

(Adapted from Pipes. P. L. [1989]. *Nutrition in infancy and childhood* [4th ed.]. St. Louis: Mosby-Year Book)

*Figure 13–3. Toddler eating.*

*Figure 13–4. Toddler exploring the environment.*

children consume, parents of toddlers can avoid many potential feeding problems.

## Sleep

The amount of time spent sleeping decreases throughout the toddler period. Until age 1, most children require at least 12 hours of sleep at night and two naps each day. By 18 months of age, 12 hours of nighttime sleep and one daytime nap have become the normal pattern. By the end of the toddler period, children may sleep 12 hours at night and begin to give up naps altogether on some days.

## Cognitive Development

Piaget's description of the development of intelligence in infants and young children provides a useful framework for assessing the cognitive development of toddlers. This theory also explains how play during the toddler period facilitates the process of learning.

## Piaget

During the second year of life, toddlers remain in Piaget's sensorimotor phase of cognitive development. The period from 1 year to 18 months constitutes stage five of this phase, tertiary circular reactions. In this stage, toddlers begin purposeful trial-and-error activity, making accidental discoveries of actions while exploring the environment and repeating these actions. They also begin to discover new ways of attaining certain goals, making experimentation the hallmark of this phase (Fig. 13-4). In addition, the concept of *object permanence* has become complete. When an object disappears from view, toddlers know that

it still exists and will search for it in places where it could logically be found.

Between 18 months and 2 years, toddlers progress through stage six, invention of new means through mental combinations. In this stage children display a fairly good understanding of the nature of objects and the results of actions. Trial-and-error actions are no longer necessary, for children can picture events mentally to solve new problems. Learning to think is the primary activity of this phase, as words become attached to the mental pictures. This use of symbols allows children to remember, plan, imitate, and imagine. All of these cognitive processes are based in true thought: the ability to conceptualize. The purposeful use of language begins, and the concepts of object permanence and causality are completely established. The tasks of the sensorimotor phase have been completed.

At about age 2, toddlers advance to Piaget's *preoperational phase* of cognition. For the remainder of the toddler period, children progress through stage one of this phase, the *preconceptual stage. Egocentrism,* the ability to see the world only from one's own point of view, is characteristic of this stage. The use of words to represent objects and actions within the environment greatly increases. Because of egocentrism, however, objects are described only in terms of how they appear to the child. The concept of *conservation* remains undeveloped; that is, children are not yet able to understand that changing the shape or position of a substance does not increase or decrease its quantity. During the third year of life, toddlers may begin fundamental classification according to one characteristic of an object. The concept of temporal relations is beginning to develop. By the end of the toddler period, it is possible for children to associate events with times of the day and to understand such concepts as first, next, and after.

## Play

Throughout the toddler period, children learn by means of activities that are the essential components of play. Play is often described as the work of the toddler period. True play differs from work in one important aspect—it is not goal-directed. It is enjoyable, spontaneous, and voluntary. Despite these attributes, play makes the following contributions to the total development of toddlers: (1) physically, it helps to develop healthy bodies and refine muscle control; (2) socially, it allows children to experience companionship and begin to cope with others; (3) cognitively, it provides opportunities for learning, understanding, and intellectual success; (4) emotionally, it allows for appropriate relief of pent-up feelings; and (5) creatively, it provides for expression of original thought.

Early in the toddler period, children begin to move from solitary play to *parallel play,* where they play individually but close to other children (Fig. 13-5). During this introductory experience of companionship, there is no interaction with the other children, though the toys and activities may be similar.

The content of play between the ages of 1 and 2 is largely sensorimotor. It includes such activities as sucking, mouthing, making sounds, listening, visually following objects, grasping and handling objects, crawling, walking, running, and exploring the body. Play materials are used primarily for sensory pleasure and exploration. By the age of 2, children expand play activities to include the use of simple play materials to reproduce things previously ex-

perienced. This use of objects to integrate environmental experiences into children's lives is known as *symbolic play.*

Safety should be the first consideration in selecting toys and other play materials for toddlers. Because of mouthing and sucking activities, all toys should be too large to be placed completely in the mouth. Toys should preferably be constructed in one piece, or small parts of toys should be securely attached. Because of toddlers' lack of gross and fine motor refinement and depth perception, toys with sharp edges and points should be avoided. Toys that are durable and washable are the most practical. All paint and materials should be nontoxic. The display lists appropriate toys for promoting development of toddlers.

## Psychosocial Development

The toddler's psychosocial development parallels the physical and cognitive development of this period. Table 13-4 displays the relation of the stages of the three major child development theorists—Piaget's phases of cognitive development, Erikson's stages of psychosocial development, and Freud's stages of psychosexual development—during the toddler years.

### Erikson

Children begin the toddler period in Erikson's (1963) psychosocial stage of *basic trust versus basic mistrust.* Until around 18 months of age, the developmental task of children is to resolve this crisis by developing considerable trust in others. The quality of care in meeting children's needs largely determines the positive or negative resolution of this developmental crisis.

For the remainder of the toddler period, children are working through Erikson's second crisis of *autonomy versus shame and doubt.* In an attempt to master personal behavior, children typically become less compliant with parental requests. It is the age of negativism, in which children respond to most suggestions with an emphatic "no!" as a means of self-assertion. This crisis is consistent with toddlers' developing motor and mental capabilities that allow for increasing independence. Parents often find this period particularly frustrating as once compliant infants suddenly demand to be in control without adequate judgment of the consequences of actions. Autonomy is the outcome of this crisis if parents patiently provide protection from excesses while allowing children choices in simple matters.

### Freud

Corresponding with these psychosocial stages of development are Freud's stages of psychosexual development. Until 18 months of age, children are usually considered to

*Figure 13–5.   Parallel play.*

---

### Play Materials for Toddlers

| | |
|---|---|
| Soft dolls and stuffed animals | Hats and dress-up clothing |
| Simple cloth or plastic books | Nesting toys |
| Large balls | Toy telephone |
| Building blocks | Transportation toys |
| Plastic pail and shovel | Small wagon |
| Musical toys | Hand puppet |
| Straddle toys for riding | Jack-in-the-box |
| Small tricycle | Push–pull toys |
| Water toys | Sandbox |
| Large box or cardboard playhouse | Toy dishes and pans |
| Art supplies: paper, large crayons, blunt scissors, clay | |

---

be in Freud's first stage of psychosexual development, the oral stage. During this period, children gains satisfaction chiefly from feeding, sucking, and exploring objects through mouthing them. This is consistent with Piaget's stage of tertiary circular reactions in which the mouth is a means of exploration and experimentation. It also suggests that satisfying children's oral needs is helpful in their developing a basic sense of trust.

Around 18 months of age, toddlers enter Freud's *anal stage*. This psychosexual stage continues for the rest of the toddler period. During this time, children derive pleasure from holding onto and letting go of bowel movements. It coincides with the myelination of the nervous system so that children are able to control the anal sphincter. It also corresponds with toddlers' need for autonomy over behavior and the increasing knowledge of cause and effect described by the theories of Erikson and Piaget.

## Mastering Separation

Mastery of the concepts of object permanence and of differentiation of self from others helps toddlers begin to deal with separation anxiety. In mastering object perma-

nence, children realize that the parents still exist when they are out of sight and that they can be expected to reappear. Although separation anxiety occurs in this period, children have begun to understand that parents are separate individuals. There is also a realization that the disappearance of parents is only a temporary matter and that they will return. Periods of long separation, however, are likely to evoke the stages of separation anxiety identified in infancy: protest, despair, and detachment.

In the protest stage children actively and aggressively react to separation by crying, screaming, attacking strangers physically or verbally, and searching for the parents (Fig. 13-6). If this separation continues, children may enter the stage of despair. The aggressive behavior gives way to withdrawal, sadness, and regression. Prolonged separation may cause toddlers to progress to the stage of detachment. In this stage children become resigned to separation but are not truly content. The first two stages are easily reversed when the period of separation ends. Detachment reflects a longer period of unmet needs and is less readily reversible.

In the early toddler period, children's locomotion skills are becoming established. Children begin to sponta-

*Table 13–4. Stages of Child Development Theorists in the Toddler Period*

| Age (mo) | Erikson's Stage | Freud's Stage | Piaget's Phase and Stage |
|---|---|---|---|
| 13–18 | Trust versus mistrust | Oral | Sensorimotor phase<br>5. Tertiary circular reactions |
| 19–24 | Autonomy versus shame and doubt | Anal | Sensorimotor phase<br>6. Invention of new means through mental combinations |
| 25–36 | Autonomy versus shame and doubt | Anal | Preoperational phase<br>1. Preconceptual stage |

*Figure 13–6.  Child holding security blanket as parents leave.*

neously practice the start of separation behaviors. The parents are used as a base from which to explore the environment. Children return for contact with the parents to reinforce feelings of security. Gradually, these explorations increase in range and require fewer reassuring trips to the parents.

Separation anxiety is thought to peak at about 1 year of age and again just before the age of 2, gradually tapering off as children get older. Providing some separation from the parents as a normal occurrence is beneficial in helping children to master separation. During short separations, children may protest the parents' leaving and may reject the substitute caregiver. However, if the separations are dealt with firmly and honestly and the parents return as promised, children begin to accept them. Periodic separation under normal circumstances helps prepare children for separation that may occur in more stressful situations, such as hospitalization.

## Language Development

The increasing ability to understand and use language for communication is a crucial aspect of toddlers' psychosocial development. The toddler's expressive vocabulary grows from about 3 words at 1 year to more than 900 words at 3 years of age. Sentence structure remains incomplete during the toddler period. The toddler says, "Go potty," "Mommy come," or "Cookie *now!*" This typically condensed, telegraphic speech pattern (so called because it is clipped, essential content and resembles a telegram) effectively conveys children's meaning to others. It is children's ability to comprehend a large number of words in combination that is the most significant language gain of the period, however. Increasingly, spoken words become children's means of interacting with others.

The acquisition of speech is a complex process that involves making and monitoring sounds. Sensory nerves

relay signals to the brain from the speech muscles and from the ears. The brain monitors these messages and allows children to modify the sounds produced to match the speech of others. Therefore, the rate of vocabulary growth in toddlers is affected by several factors: (1) children's physical and cognitive aptitude, (2) the vocal activity of the parents or primary caregivers, (3) the presence or absence of siblings, and (4) general living patterns (Papalia & Olds, 1989). Although overall milestones are predictable, there may be considerable variation with the individual child. Table 13-5 summarizes language development during the toddler years.

## Sex Role Identification

The term *sex role* generally refers to the social, psychological, and behavioral implications of male or female gender. Children are exposed to gender-related social feedback from birth onward that, in turn, influences their social behavior along gender lines.

By the age of 2, toddlers can assign correct gender labels to pictures of males and females and accurately use gender nouns. At the end of the toddler period, children also show an awareness of sex role stereotypes. That is, the 3-year-old knows that certain objects and activities are associated with one sex or the other.

The internalization of sex role stereotypes depends on an interplay of modeling, imitation, and cognitive development that allows for recognition of norms. Thus, toddlers' behavior tends to become increasingly sex-typed (Fig. 13-7). Before the age of 2, children are usually aware of their own sex and begin to recognize the expected set of

*Table 13–5.  Language Development in the Toddler*

| Age | Language Skill |
| --- | --- |
| 1 y | Has spoken vocabulary of 3–4 simple words<br>Uses 1-word sentences (holophrases)<br>Relies on pointing to convey needs<br>Understands simple commands<br>25% of speech is understandable |
| 18 mo | Has spoken vocabulary of 50 words<br>Says "no" frequently<br>Uses telegraphic speech to convey needs<br>Understands most commands<br>50% of speech is understandable |
| 2 y | Has spoken vocabulary of 300 words<br>Uses sentences of 2 words or more<br>Talks frequently during play<br>Comprehends most daily conversation<br>66% of speech is understandable |
| 3 y | Has spoken vocabulary of 900 words<br>Uses sentences of 3 words or more<br>Adds adjectives and adverbs to sentences<br>>80% of speech is understandable |

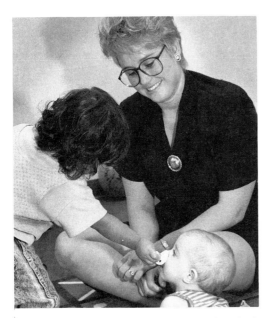 

*Figure 13–7. Girl imitating mother; boy imitating father.*

behaviors associated with it. The rate at which these are assimilated is affected by the degree of identification with the parent of the same sex, family practices, and the expectations of caregivers. The process of sex role identification continues into the preschool years as children's cognitive skills and social exposure increase.

## Assessment

Total assessment of the toddler involves the comparison of physical, cognitive, and psychosocial development to the established norms for the age. Standardized instruments are commonly used to obtain objective data in each of these areas. Some of these assessment tools include physical growth percentile charts, the Denver Developmental Screening Test, and the Home Observation and Measurement of the Environment. These assessment tools are shown in Appendix A.

## Body Measurements

The body measurements used to evaluate the physical growth and development of toddlers are primarily height and weight graphs that are standardized for age and sex. These permit the plotting of children's height and weight to determine the percentile rank for age. A commonly used graph for children up to 3 years of age is the Physical Growth Percentiles distributed by Ross Laboratories (National Center for Health Statistics, 1982). One of these graphs also incorporates standardized head circumferences, another measure of importance until the age of 24 months. Recorded over time, these measurements provide a visual representation of toddlers' overall growth patterns.

## Denver Developmental Screening Test

In the United States, the most widely used developmental screening test for the toddler age group is the Denver Developmental Screening Test (DDST). This instrument provides monthly age divisions for testing through 18 months of age, as well as 6-month age marks for the remainder of the toddler period. It tests four areas of toddler development: personal–social, fine motor–adaptive, language, and gross motor. Approaching the administration of the DDST as a game may help to elicit toddlers' cooperation (Fig. 13-8). Two advantages of this test are the appeal of its required activities to young children and its relatively short testing time (15–20 minutes). One disadvantage of the DDST is its limited predictive value in lower socioeconomic groups and children of different cultures (Frankenburg, Dick, & Carland, 1975; Miller, Onotera, & Deinard, 1984). A toddler from one of these groups requires additional screening before being labeled developmentally delayed. The newly available DDST II, a major revision and restandardization of the DDST, allows for evaluation of whether delays are due to sociocultural or environmental factors.

## Washington Guide to Promoting Development in the Young Child

Another developmental screening test appropriate for toddlers is the Washington Guide. This instrument allows for assessment of toddlers by direct observation of behaviors in eight areas: feeding, sleep, play, language, motor activities, discipline, toilet training, and dressing. This tool has the unique advantage of including a list of specific activities for parents to use in providing developmental stimulation in each area (Powell, 1981).

*Figure 13–8. Child stacking blocks during administration of DDST.*

## Assessment of Home and Family

A thorough assessment extends beyond the child to include the family and environment. The Home Observation and Measurement of the Environment (HOME) tool provides for the assessment of children's development and interaction with caregivers in the context of the home environment. The HOME inventory for families of infants and toddlers is used for children up to 3 years of age. It combines observation and questioning to obtain information in six categories: responsivity, acceptance, organization, play materials, involvement, and variety (Caldwell & Bradley, 1984). Although this tool may yield rich information, it has the disadvantage of requiring both a home visit and the presence of the child and the primary caregiver.

A second instrument for assessing toddlers' family environment is the Home Screening Questionnaire. This tool, based on the HOME, also has a form for children up to 3 years of age. It includes 34 questions and a checklist of toys in the child's home (Frankenburg & Coons, 1986). This screening inventory may be completed by parents in 15 to 20 minutes in any setting, but it eliminates the advantage of direct observation by a professional. It is sometimes used as a preliminary screening of the home and family and followed up by the HOME if its results are questionable.

## Health Promotion

Nurses promote toddlers' health in three ways: (1) by assessing children's physical and developmental status at regular intervals, (2) by supporting the attainment of age-appropriate developmental tasks, and (3) by providing anticipatory guidance for the parents in areas of special concern. These health promotion activities are often carried out during children's periodic health maintenance visits.

## Health Maintenance Visits and Immunizations

Health maintenance visits during the toddler period are usually scheduled annually around children's birthdays and at additional times to coincide with recommended schedules (Fig. 13-9). Table 13-6 shows a typical health maintenance schedule for toddlers.

This schedule may be altered to allow for administering missed immunizations. The recommended schedules for children not immunized during the first year of life are available from the Committee on Infectious Diseases of the American Academy of Pediatrics. Some health care providers routinely see children only once between the first and second birthdays, giving the diphtheria-pertussis-tetanus, oral polio vaccine, *Haemophilus influenzae* type b vaccine, and measles-mumps-rubella simultaneously between the ages of 15 and 18 months. This simultaneous administration of these immunizations is also consistent with the guidelines of the American Academy of Pediatrics (1986).

## Dental Care

Dental care of toddlers involves dental hygiene, fluoride supplements, good dietary habits, and visits to the dentist. The use of a toothbrush for dental hygiene is recommended by 18 months of age. A soft toothbrush, a small amount of fluoride toothpaste, and a gentle up-and-down stroke should be used by the parents in brushing toddlers'

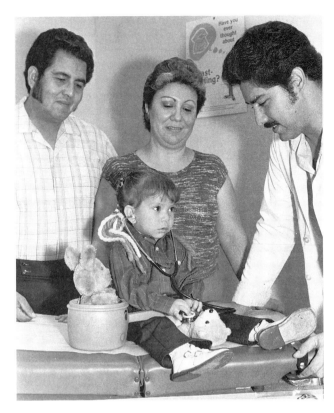

*Figure 13–9. Toddler being examined uses a stethoscope to listen to her bear. (Courtesy of Texas Tech University Health Sciences Center, El Paso, Texas)*

### Table 13–6. Recommended Schedule of Visits and Immunizations for Toddlers

| Age | Health Maintenance Activity |
| --- | --- |
| 1 y | Physical examination, developmental screening, tuberculin skin test |
| 15 mo | Physical examination, developmental screening, measles-mumps-rubella immunization, Hib booster |
| 18 mo | Physical examination, developmental screening DPT, OPV boosters |
| 2 y | Physical examination, developmental screening |
| 3 y | Physical examination, developmental screening, tuberculin skin test |

teeth. This should be done twice a day. In communities where drinking water is not fluoridated, a daily supplement of fluoride should be given. A diet that is low in sweets should be provided. Snacks should consist of natural foods rather than sticky treats that are high in carbohydrate content.

A visit to the dentist by 2 years of age is recommended. At this visit toddlers should be allowed to sit in the dental chair and become familiar with the surroundings. Dentists should limit the care at the first visit to a brief inspection of children's teeth to identify problems and initiate preventive measures.

## Recognizing Developmental Tasks

Eight specific tasks have been identified as the essential work of the toddler period of development: (1) to acquire beginning socialization skills, (2) to continue to develop cognitive abilities, (3) to continue to develop perceptual abilities, (4) to develop a sense of autonomy, (5) to further develop a sense of self, (6) to master beginning bladder and bowel control, (7) to master beginning self-help skills in feeding and dressing, and (8) to master motor and locomotion skills (Nelms & Mullins, 1982). Many behaviors of toddlers that are troublesome for parents reflect progress toward achieving these tasks.

## Independence

The toddler's increasing independence demonstrates the struggle to achieve autonomy in all aspects of daily life. Failure to develop autonomy results in feelings of shame and doubt (Erikson, 1963). Although autonomy is the desirable outcome, it causes mixed emotions in both parents and children.

Toddlers typically alternate between independence and dependence, running away from the parents at times but often returning for reassurance or security. A toddler who darts away from the mother to explore a crowded store may dissolve in tears if the mother cannot be readily found moments later. Tasks undertaken aggressively often are quickly abandoned when children become tired or insecure. For example, children may insist on pushing their own strollers one minute, only to beg to be carried or pushed a short time later. New activities may require parental support. While displaying bravado in going down a playroom slide, children may need to cling to the parent's hand.

On one hand, the parents may feel pride in children's grown-up behavior and accomplishments. On the other hand, they may long for the simpler times when children relied on them and things were done more quickly and efficiently. They are often uncertain about how much they can trust toddlers' new competence.

Nurses should encourage parents to allow children opportunities for independent activity while setting limits that ensure safety. Play should be spontaneous while adequately supervised in a safe environment. This provides an appropriate outlet for experiencing outcomes of behaviors and testing the environment in a controlled setting. Children should be allowed to make simple choices about daily activities when possible. Allowing increasing independence in self-care activities provides for mastery in this area. Exploration and independence should be fostered, with the parents standing by to encourage, assist, or rescue children when limits are overreached.

## Separation

Toddlers are better able to withstand periods of separation from the parents because of the developing sense of self (Bowlby, 1969, 1973). Because some separation is necessary for children to further develop this sense of self and autonomy, parents should be counseled to leave children with other caretakers at times. This is also helpful for providing the parents with much-needed relief from their constant responsibilities, and they return to children refreshed and relaxed. Parents should tell children that they are leaving, say goodbye cheerfully but firmly, be sure that the caretaker is aware of rituals and supplied with favorite toys, tell children when they will return (relative to some daily ritual), and return when they have promised. Although children may protest separation initially, these periods are usually increasingly tolerated if these guidelines are followed.

## Routines

Established routines are a source of security to toddlers. Routines allow children to know what to expect and when to expect it. Often routines evolve into elaborate rituals that toddlers set up around such daily activities as eating and sleeping. These provide a sense of control over the situation and are a part of the developing senses of autonomy and self. Parents should be advised that following simple rituals is helpful in smoothly accomplishing such daily activities as meals, bathing, and bedtime. Necessary changes in daily activities should be planned so that they do not interfere with these key routines, thereby reducing any stress imposed by the changes.

## Sibling Rivalry and Regression

The arrival of a new baby in the household requires considerable adjustment on the part of toddlers. Parents should be advised to begin preparing toddlers for this event about 1 or 2 months before the anticipated birth. Children's interest will not be sustained if preparation is begun earlier. If the new sibling will be taking over the toddler's crib, the toddler should be moved to a new bed well in advance of the baby's arrival. Parents should explain what babies are like and the things that will have to be done for the new baby. Showing children their own baby pictures and talking about that period may be helpful. If possible, toddlers should be introduced to a young infant and allowed to observe the caregiving it receives. The new baby should not be described as a playmate for the toddler, or the child may develop unrealistic expectations.

Because of the security offered by familiar rituals, toddlers should be reassured about the specific routines that will remain the same. Above all, parents should let children know that their love for the toddler is special and will not decrease or be taken away by the baby.

Actively involving toddlers in preparing a room and clothing for the baby is beneficial. Pointing out how help-ful children are being makes children feel important and a part of the event. Discussing ways in which children may continue to help when the baby arrives provides a blueprint for future routines.

Preparation for the coming separation from the mother is essential. The substitute caregiver should be introduced in advance. If possible, children should be cared for in the home while the mother is hospitalized to provide continuity. Talking to the mother on the telephone may be helpful, particularly for older toddlers. Increased attention from the father may be comforting.

Some hospitals sponsor preparation classes for siblings as part of their prenatal education program. In these classes siblings are allowed to tour the maternity unit and watch nurses caring for newborns through the nursery window. The children are encouraged to ask questions, which are answered simply and honestly. When the family's own baby is born, the sibling is allowed to visit the mother and baby.

Some hospitals allow sibling visitation without participation in special preparatory programs. Parents should determine the policy in advance to avoid disappointment. Being able to visit their mother and new sibling in the hospital may be a positive and exciting experience for toddlers.

Despite thorough preparation, many toddlers regress in several areas of behavior after the arrival of a sibling. Their behavior may be clingy, jealous, or aggressive. Trying to climb into the mother's lap while she is feeding the new infant is common. There may be lapses in toilet training, table manners, or self-care skills. Nurses should inform parents that these problems are attempts to gain their attention and are usually temporary. By behaving like babies, children hope to receive the kind of attention given to the baby. Returning to the behavior of an earlier age provides comfort and removes many of the demands of developmental mastery.

Paying undue attention to these episodes or scolding children should be avoided. Children should be given help with some activities without comment. Praise should be given when children's behavior is age-appropriate. Rituals that are important to toddlers should be maintained. New expectations, such as toilet training, should be avoided in the period surrounding the arrival of the new sibling. Setting aside special times to be spent alone with toddlers is essential. Children should be allowed to help with the infant and play with it, but these interactions should be closely supervised and clear limits set on behavior (Fig. 13-10). Most reassuring of all are consistent interest in and affection for toddlers, for these convey his or her continuing importance in the lives of the parents.

## Mobility

The ability to walk independently is the major accomplishment of motor development during the toddler period. This new mobility requires additional space for play and

*Figure 13–10. Toddler with new infant.*

of the home environment are particularly likely to influence toddlers' accidental injury (Matheny, 1986). Therefore, assessment of the family and home environment and planning appropriate preventive strategies are crucial in preventing accidents during the toddler period.

The Injury Prevention Program developed by the American Academy of Pediatrics recommends that health providers should advise parents to (1) use federally approved toddler car seats, (2) install smoke detectors in the sleeping area of the home, (3) set hot tap water temperatures at a safe level, (4) use window and stairway guards, and (5) acquire a 1-oz bottle of syrup of ipecac (Krassner, 1984). Table 13-7 lists additional preventive strategies for the common accidents of the toddler period that should be components of parental guidance. Simple safety teaching for children is included.

Many motor vehicle accident injuries and deaths in the toddler period result from failure to use restraint systems or using them incorrectly. When children weigh 17 to 20 pounds and can sit unaided, a toddler restraint system is needed. Federally approved restraints for toddlers are either convertible models or models specifically designed to be installed in the backseat of the car. The convertible models are designed for both infants and toddlers, but when used for toddlers they must be reinstalled in the forward-facing position, similar to models that are designed strictly for toddlers. Both are anchored by lap belts

exploration. It also poses a variety of potential hazards to children's safety.

Nurses serve as important resources for parents by providing information that allows them to promote toddlers' mastery of motor skills and provide adequate protection. A teaching plan for parents includes education about (1) the nature and rapid pace of development of toddlers' motor skills, (2) the need for an area set aside specifically for children's play and made completely childproof, (3) potential home safety hazards, (4) a plan for childproofing or providing continuous close supervision throughout the home, (5) periodic re-evaluation of the plan in relation to children's progressive motor skills, (6) consistency in enforcing limits, and (7) the communication of limits to all family members and substitute caregivers.

## Common Concerns

Several concerns about child rearing are consistently raised by parents of toddlers. These include accidents, poisoning, sleep problems, toilet training, discipline, and temper tantrums.

### Accidents

Accidents are the leading cause of death and the second leading cause of morbidity in children after 1 year of age. The leading causes of accidental death during the toddler period are motor vehicle accidents (including passengers, pedestrians, and bicycles), drowning, fires and burns, falls, and ingestion or aspiration of food or other objects (National Safety Council, 1986).

There appears to be an increased incidence of accidents associated with family stress, lack of parental supervision, and single parenting. Attributes of the parents and

*Table 13–7. Accident Prevention Strategies*

| Accident | Prevention Strategy |
|---|---|
| Motor vehicle | Restrain in safety seat for *all* trips in car<br>Closely supervise when out of doors<br>Provide fenced-in play area<br>Teach child never to ride or run into street |
| Drowning | Supervise child near water, including tub<br>Empty wading pools after use; fence in pools<br>Teach child not to run near bodies of water |
| Fire or burns | Turn handles of pans toward center of stove<br>Keep child away from stoves, fires, matches<br>Set hot water temperature at 120°–130°F<br>Test water temperature before immersion<br>Use safety covers on electrical outlets<br>Teach child not to touch matches, stove, electrical cords, wall sockets, etc |
| Falls | Gate stairways; teach child to hold railing<br>Open windows from top; use window guards<br>Move furniture away from upstairs windows |
| Ingestion or aspiration | Avoid nuts, grapes, hot dots, popcorn, raisins, hard candy, lollipops<br>Childproof home for coins, pins, balloons<br>Teach child not to run with objects in mouth |

and a tether strap that must be installed according to the system's instructions. In addition, the restraint system's harness or shoulder belt must be correctly and securely fastened to hold toddlers in place. Figure 13-11 gives examples of approved toddler restraints.

The "rule of fours" dictates that a toddler restraint is necessary throughout the toddler period. According to this guide, children are to be restrained in a toddler system up to the age of 4, 40 pounds, and 40 inches in height. Parents should require that toddlers use the restraint whenever riding in the car. Parents should be advised to set an example for toddlers by fastening their own restraints before starting the car.

Water can be a hazard for toddlers since it can cause drowning and burns. Toddlers need constant supervision when in or near bathtubs, swimming pools, or other bodies of water. To prevent burns from hot water, the household water temperature should be set at 120° to 130°F. Water temperature should always be checked before immersing toddlers.

When toddlers are placed in a crib or playpen, the sides should be up and locked in place. Federal regulations require that slats should be no more than 2³/₈ inches apart, and the mattress or pad should fit snugly against the sides and ends. Cribs and playpens should be positioned away from windows, electrical cords and outlets, and large pieces of furniture. Plastic bags should be kept away from cribs and playpens to reduce the risk of suffocation.

## Poisoning

Another hazard of the toddler period is accidental poisoning. Toddlers' increased mobility and fine motor ability make it possible to venture into new areas of the home, reaching and manipulating drawers, cupboard doors, and

*Figure 13–11. Appropriate car safety seat system for toddlers.*

*Figure 13–12. Toddler opening a cupboard. (Courtesy Child Care Center, University of Texas at El Paso)*

container lids (Fig. 13-12). The toddler's urge to investigate new objects by tasting and mouthing is accompanied by an inability to recognize dangerous substances.

As a result, close supervision and childproofing of the home must be stressed as the first line of prevention. Parents need to be provided with a list of the common sources of poisons in the home (Table 13-8). Parental guidance also includes education about safe storage or removal of these agents.

Improper storage of poisonous substances is the chief cause of accidental poisoning in the toddler period. Parents should request and use child-resistant lids for all prescription medications. The 1970 Poison Prevention Packaging Act requires child-resistant packaging of potentially hazardous drugs and household chemicals. Although these containers and cupboard-locking devices may slow children's efforts, they are not infallible. It should be stressed that such devices do not take the place of adequate supervision and the removal of poisonous agents to places that toddlers cannot enter.

Nurses should give parents instructions about what to do if accidental poisoning occurs. Parents should be given the number of the local Poison Control Center to be posted with other emergency numbers near the telephone. If poisoning is suspected, parents should contact the Poison Control Center immediately for expert advice before beginning any emergency treatment. The only action to be taken prior to this call should be removing any remaining poison from the child's mouth. When calling the center, they should be prepared to give essential information regarding (1) the age of the child; (2) the name and

*Table 13–8. Common Sources of Poisons in the Home*

| Poisonous Agent | Examples |
| --- | --- |
| Plants and flowers | Rhododendron, laurel, ivy, azalea, foxglove, mistletoe, chrysanthemum |
| Cleaning products | Dishwater detergent, cleansers, drain cleaners, ammonia, oven cleaners |
| Cosmetics/personal care products | Nail polish, nail polish remover, cuticle remover, hair sprays, waving lotion, alcohol, hair removers |
| Hydrocarbons | Gasoline, kerosene, turpentine, paint thinner, lighter fluid, furniture polish |
| Medicines | Aspirin, acetaminophen, vitamins, iron, prescription drugs, topical ointments |

amount of the poison taken, if known, or any evidence of the suspected poison, such as containers, plant leaves, or pills; (3) the time that has elapsed since the poison was ingested; (4) whether the child has vomited; and (5) the child's apparent status.

Expert advice should be obtained before any treatment of poisoning is attempted so that emergency actions do not cause complications. Treatment is directed toward removing the poison or preventing its absorption. This is accomplished by diluting the poison, evacuating gastric contents, or hastening elimination.

Dilution is recommended if the poison is an irritant or corrosive. It is usually done before inducing emesis so that the poisonous substance is weakened and less harmful to the digestive tract during vomiting.

Evacuation of the gastric contents is accomplished by inducing vomiting or by gastric lavage. Syrup of ipecac is the agent most commonly used to induce vomiting.

Parents should obtain a 30-mL bottle of syrup of ipecac, but it should only be used on the advice of the Poison Control Center or a physician. The dosage for toddlers is 15 mL (1 tablespoon), followed by 4 to 8 oz of water. Another dose of ipecac and water should be repeated once if vomiting has not occurred in 30 minutes.

Vomiting should not be induced in any of the following circumstances: (1) alteration in consciousness, (2) absence of the gag reflex, (3) occurrence of seizures, or (4) ingestion of a petroleum distillate. Children should be transported to an emergency department immediately if any of these conditions exist. An unconscious child should be placed in a side-lying position to prevent aspiration.

Vomiting should never be induced by using fingers or a spoon to cause gagging. If vomiting does not occur when indicated, gastric lavage is the next method used. A nasogastric tube is inserted, the gastric contents are removed, and normal saline is inserted. If it is necessary to hasten elimination of gastric contents, the nasogastric tube can also be used to administer saline cathartics, such as sodium sulfate and magnesium citrate.

## Sleep

Toddlers are very likely to exert newfound powers of independence and resist settling down for sleep, which can be troublesome for parents. Nurses should advise parents that the observance of a few general rules can help to make bedtime easier for both toddlers and parents. The period before bedtime should be as quiet and calm as possible. Physical and emotional stimuli should be kept to a minimum. Reading a favorite story is an excellent way of helping toddlers to wind down. A simple bedtime routine should be established and followed, providing toddlers with a sense of structure and security. Children should be encouraged to take an active part in bedtime preparations and offered simple choices within the established routine to allow for some autonomy. The use of security blankets, favorite soft toys, and nightlights as bedtime accompaniments is helpful throughout this period. Parents should be loving but firm and consistent, behaving as if they expect children to settle down.

Crying or refusing to lie down is usually testing behavior on the part of toddlers. If parents say goodnight cheerfully when the bedtime ritual is completed, leave firmly, and resist returning, children usually cry for only a short period before drifting off to sleep. Persistent refusal to go to bed may indicate the need to adjust the timing of daytime naps or the usual bedtime. Nurses may suggest eliminating naps to allow toddlers to be adequately tired to fall asleep quickly at night.

## Toilet Training

The mastery of beginning bladder and bowel control is a major developmental task of the toddler period. Toddlers are usually both physically and psychologically ready for toilet training shortly after the second birthday. However, complete naptime and nighttime bladder control is often not achieved until well after the third birthday. Some preparatory activities, such as introducing children to the potty chair, may begin as early as 18 months of age (Brazelton, 1962). In general, bowel training is usually accomplished first because of the more regular pattern and stronger urge associated with defecation.

In determining readiness for toilet training, the following should be assessed in children: (1) regularity in patterns of elimination; (2) the ability to walk, sit still, and remove clothing; (3) the ability to recognize urges to defecate and urinate and communicate these needs verbally; and (4) the desire to please the caregiver by cooperating in holding on and letting go. In addition, the parents should be assessed for (1) their recognition of children's levels of readiness, (2) their ability and desire to invest the necessary time and energy, and (3) the absence of other stressors. When all of these factors are present, toilet training can usually be accomplished with relative ease if the task is approached calmly and positively.

Children should be provided with a comfortable potty chair, introduced to it gradually, and then placed on it before the time of day when a bowel movement usually occurs (Fig. 13-13). Punishment for lack of success or noncompliance should be avoided. Children should not be forced to sit on the potty chair or kept sitting on it for more than 10 to 15 minutes at a time. Praise and affection should be used to reinforce positive results. Training pants can be introduced when children have had several successes on the potty chair and are remaining clean and dry for predictable periods.

Nurses should counsel parents to temporarily abandon efforts at toilet training if children become overly negative and resistant or make no progress in learning. New stressors in the family may also dictate the need to temporarily terminate efforts. Persistence in attempting to continue toilet training under these circumstances usually results in frustration and failure. Training is more likely to be successful if it is resumed when children again indicate readiness and other conflicts have been resolved.

*Figure 13–13.   Toddler on a potty chair.*

## Discipline

Providing toddlers with direct, well-planned discipline fosters healthy growth and development. It is often difficult, however, for parents to discipline toddlers effectively. They may be concerned that discipline will undermine children's sense of trust. This concern is usually accompanied by the realization that it is increasingly necessary to place limits on children's behavior. These conflicting concerns may result in parents giving inconsistent messages to children regarding acceptable behaviors.

Parents may equate discipline with punishment, so it may be necessary for nurses to help them distinguish between the two. *Discipline* involves shaping toddlers' behavior to provide protection and to teach socially acceptable conduct. *Punishment* refers to applying unpleasant or painful measures in response to wrongdoing. At least one study suggests that physical punishment does not teach toddlers compliance and impulse control (Power & Chapieski, 1986).

Discipline may take many forms. However, certain characteristics are essential for discipline to be effective. Table 13-9 pairs these principles with specific strategies that may be particularly appropriate for toddler discipline.

Toddlers are struggling to achieve independence. When rules of conduct are planned and lovingly administered to achieve safety and social acceptance, children gain security from knowing that limits and protection have been provided. Appropriate limit-setting during the toddler period provides a basis for enhanced trust and future family cooperation.

## Temper Tantrums

Toddlers typically respond to frustrated efforts at independence by uncontrolled outbursts of anger known as temper tantrums. These outbursts may include crying, throwing objects, striking out at others, breath holding, and head banging. Temper tantrums are most common between the ages of 18 months and 3 years. Because children of this age have not yet learned how to control or express anger, these outbursts serve to release built-up tension.

Although temper tantrums are normal occurrences during the toddler period, their severity and frequency can be reduced. Because parents frequently seek guidance from nurses in handling temper tantrums, the following suggestions should be provided:

1. Ignore the behavior so that the tantrum accomplishes nothing—avoid giving in or responding in kind.
2. Separate the child from the immediate situation.
3. Calmly restrain the child on the floor away from other people, furniture, or objects that may cause injury to the child or may be damaged.
4. Provide distraction and comfort when the tantrum is waning.

*Table 13–9. Characteristics of Effective Discipline for Toddlers*

| Operating Principle | Strategy |
| --- | --- |
| Firmness | State expected behavior in a manner that does not imply a choice |
| Consistency | Enforce rules in the same manner from day to day and from person to person |
| Timing | Disciplinary action should immediately follow misbehavior and be linked to it |
| Appropriateness of response to behavior | Provide attention when child is behaving<br>Praise child for following the rules<br>Plan in advance how to handle misbehavior<br>Verbal disapproval and time-outs (moving the child to a quiet location for a brief period—5–10 min) are effective |

5. Look for the causes of recurring tantrums—fatigue, inappropriate or inconsistent discipline, lack of attention, excessive demands.
6. Avoid the identified precipitating factors.

Parents may need ongoing encouragement and support in addition to these suggestions. In the case of frequent, intense tantrums, they may require assistance in identifying and avoiding the precipitating causes. In counseling these parents, nurses must recognize that it is easier to offer advice than it is to deal with this problem on a daily basis. Providing parents with the opportunity to express their feelings and frustrations about the situation may be the most valuable form of support.

## Parenting Development

During the toddler period, parents must continue to develop their parenting abilities to provide stability in the face of changing family needs. Goals of parenting in this period are (1) to adapt the household to allow for the additional demands of an active, growing child; (2) to refine the marital relationship to include the developing child without sacrificing its essential intimacy; and (3) to derive satisfaction from meeting the needs of all family members. How these goals are met varies with the individual family and depends on a variety of factors, including the age and experience of the parents, the number of children, and available resources.

To support parental development, nurses need to prepare parents for the changes that will occur in toddlers' abilities and behavior. Guidance should begin with an assessment of what the parents need and want to know. Nurses should provide specific advice directed toward promoting children's development and addressing parental concerns. In planning interventions, each family member should be considered. Providing opportunities for questions and expressing feelings and concerns related to all aspects of family life should be considered an essential component of supporting parental development.

## Summary

The toddler period is one of slowing physical growth but rapid motor, psychosocial, and cognitive development. During this time, children master the basic skills of locomotion, manipulation, socialization, and language. In the process of seeking autonomy and independence, toddlers learn personal and environmental limits. However, the typical behaviors that accompany this learning may compromise children's safety and raise many parental concerns. Nursing activities during this period focus on maintaining children's health, supporting the development of children and families, promoting safety, and supplying appropriate parental guidance.

## References

American Academy of Pediatrics. (1986). *Report of the Committee on Infectious Diseases* (20th ed.). Elk Grove, IL: American Academy of Pediatrics.

Bowlby, J. (1969). *Attachment and loss: Vol. 1, Attachment.* New York: Basic Books, Inc.

Bowlby, J. (1973). *Attachment and loss: Vol. 2, Separation, anxiety and anger.* New York: Basic Books.

Brazelton, T. B. (1962). A child-oriented approach to toilet training. *Pediatrics, 29,* 121–128.

Caldwell, B. M., & Bradley, R. H. (1984). *Home observation for measurement of the environment* (rev. ed.). Little Rock, AK: University of Arkansas.

Erikson, E. (1963). *Childhood and society* (2nd ed.). New York: W. W. Norton.

Frankenburg, W. K., & Coons, C. (1986). Home Screening Questionnaire: Its validity in assessing home environment. *Journal of Pediatrics, 108,* 624–626.

Frankenburg, W. K., Dick, N. P., & Carland, J. (1975). Development of preschool-aged children of different social and ethnic groups: Implications for developmental screening. *Journal of Pediatrics, 87,* 125–132.

Krassner, L. (1984). TIPP usage. *Pediatrics, 74*(Suppl.), 976–980.

Matheny, A. P. (1986). Injuries among toddlers: Contributions from child, mother, and family. *Journal of Pediatric Psychology, 11,* 163–176.

Miller, V., Onotera, R., & Deinard, A. (1984). Denver Developmental Screening Test: Cultural variations in Southeast Asian children. *Journal of Pediatrics, 104,* 481–482.

National Center for Health Statistics. (1982). *NCHS growth charts.* Columbus, OH: Ross Laboratories.

National Safety Council. (1986). *Accident facts.* Chicago: National Safety Council.

Nelms, B. C., & Mullins, R. G. (1982). *Growth and development: A primary health care approach.* Englewood Cliffs, NJ: Prentice-Hall.

Papalia, D. E., & Olds, S. W. (1989). *Human development* (4th ed.). New York: McGraw-Hill.

Powell, M. L. (1981). *Assessment and management of developmental changes and problems in children* (2nd ed.). St. Louis: C. V. Mosby.

Power, T. G., & Chapieski, M. L. (1986). Childrearing and impulse control in toddlers: A naturalistic investigation. *Developmental Psychology, 22,* 271–275.

## Bibliography

Behrman, R. E., & Vaughan, V. C. (eds.). (1987). *Nelson textbook of pediatrics* (13th ed.). Philadelphia: W. B. Saunders.

Brazelton, T. B. (1976). *Toddlers and parents.* New York: Dell.

Castiglia, P. T., & Petrini, M. A. (1985). Selecting a developmental screening tool. *Pediatric Nursing, 11,* 8–17.

Diagram Group. (1980). *The human body.* New York: Facts on File.

Flavell, J. H. (1963). *The developmental psychology of Jean Piaget.* Princeton, N.J.: D. Van Nostrand.

Fraiberg, S. H. (1981). *The magic years: Understanding and handling the problems of early childhood.* New York: Macmillan.

Ginsburg, H., & Opper, S. (1969). *Piaget's theory of intellectual development: An introduction.* Englewood Cliffs, NJ: Prentice-Hall.

Illingworth, R. S. (1987). *The development of the infant and young child: Normal and abnormal* (9th ed.). New York: Churchill Livingstone.

Mussen, P. H., Conger, J. J., & Kagan, J. (1990). *Child development and personality* (7th ed.). New York: Harper & Row.

Pipes, P.L. (1989). *Nutrition in infancy and childhood* (4th ed.). St. Louis: Mosby-Year Book.

Smart, M. S., & Smart, R. C. (1982). *Children: Development and relationships* (4th ed.). New York: Macmillan.

Stephens, K. S. (1973). A toddler's separation anxiety. *American Journal of Nursing, 73,* 1553–1554.

White, B. L. (1985). *The first three years of life* (rev. ed.). New York: Prentice-Hall.

# Preschool Growth, Development, and Health

Marian Brook

Sculpture by Charles Parks

14

*Physical Growth and Development*
  *General Growth Characteristics*
  *Motor Development*
  *Sensory Development*
  *Nutrition Needs*
  *Sleep*

*Cognitive Development*
  *Piaget*
  *Play*
  *Moral Development*

*Psychosocial Development*
  *Freud*
  *Erikson*
  *Language Development*
  *Sex-Role Identification*
  *Day Care and Nursery School*

*Assessment*
  *Body Measurements*
  *Denver Developmental Screening Test*
  *Washington Guide to Promoting Development in the Young Child*
  *Assessment of Home and Family*

*Health Promotion*
  *Health Maintenance Visits and Immunizations*
  *Dental Care*
  *Recognizing Developmental Tasks*
  *Common Concerns*

*Parenting Development*

*Summary*

## Learning Objectives

*Upon completion of this chapter the reader will be able to:*

1. *Identify the characteristics of normal physical growth and development in preschool-aged children.*

2. *Describe the usual pattern of cognitive development in preschool-aged children.*

3. *Discuss the normal psychosocial and moral development of preschool-aged children.*

4. *Explain assessment strategies used to evaluate preschoolers' development and environment.*

5. *Discuss the role of nurses in health promotion for preschoolers and their families.*

6. *Identify appropriate parenting development strategies for common concerns about preschool-aged children.*

## Key Terms

*centration*

*chelation*

*collective monologue*

*individual monologue*

*mental symbols*

*night terror*

*nocturnal enuresis*

*pica*

*primary enuresis*

*secondary enuresis*

*semiotic function*

*symbolic play*

*transductive reasoning*

The period of child development from age 3 to 5 is sometimes termed "the age of socialization." Socialization begins with the child's learning of toilet habits and proceeds through many dimensions: impulse control, control of aggression, sex-role learning, and cooperation with others.

Maturation of the brain enables the child to think symbolically, to learn from past experience, and to replace sensorimotor functioning with mental symbols. As this new ability emerges, children exercise mental and symbolic power just as they previously exercised physical power. Children strive to get their needs met, to make sense of their own mental and social world, to influence others, and to define their identities and roles in the family and the peer group.

Three-, 4-, and 5-year-olds are generally active, vigorous, curious, imaginative, talkative, and outgoing. Typical characteristics of this age group are summarized in Table 14-1.

The goals of nursing care in the preschool period are to support the child's development; to maintain maximum sensory and motor functioning; to detect deviations from normal physical and psychological growth, development, and function; to initiate corrective interventions when appropriate; and to support parents' abilities and development. When caring for preschool-aged children, nurses must consider the qualitatively different way that children understand illness and bodily functions.

Children's responses have more to do with their cognitive style than with their chronological age. Children of 3 or 4 may connect illness with a concrete external phenomenon that has no temporal or spatial proximity. "How do people get colds?... From the sun... From trees... From God" (Bibace & Walsh, 1981, p. 36). According to Bibace and Walsh,

> *Comments children make regarding health-related issues that appear on the surface to be cute, silly or haphazard, actually are part of an orderly sequence of knowledge. This means first, that a par-*

*Table 14—1. Typical Characteristics of Preschool Children*

| 3 Years | 4 Years | 5 Years |
|---|---|---|
| **Physical Abilities** | | |
| Jumps in place; kicks a ball<br>Balances; stands briefly on one foot<br>Pedals a tricycle<br>Alternates feet ascending stairs<br>Can open doors<br>Feeds self, using utensils correctly<br>Dresses with supervision<br>Copies a circle<br>Builds a tower of 9 small blocks<br>Imitates a bridge made of 3 blocks | Can walk on tiptoes<br>Hops or jumps forward<br>Alternates feet descending stairs<br>Can climb a ladder<br>Builds a tower of 10 blocks<br>Holds a pencil with control<br>Draws a person with a face, arms, and legs; copies a circle, a cross, and possibly a square<br>Can cut and paste<br>Dresses self except for tying laces and doing back buttons<br>Brushes own teeth, combs hair | Skips, broad jumps<br>Throws overhand with some accuracy<br>Can catch a bounced ball<br>Handles scissors and pastes skillfully<br>Dresses, washes, combs hair unaided |
| **Language** | | |
| Vocabulary of up to 900 words; understands up to 2400 words*<br>May give full name; knows age, sex<br>May comprehend "cold," "hungry," and some prepositions<br>Can convey use of simple objects<br>Mild speech dysfluency (stuttering) may occur between 2 and 4½ years, transiently<br>Does not comprehend jokes | Initiates conversation, asks how, when, and why questions—up to 500 questions a day*<br>Vocabulary of 1500 words; uses average of 5-word sentences*<br>Asks meaning of words<br>Enjoys jokes; can sing a song<br>Names and matches three or four colors<br>Uses language to manipulate people, situations | Vocabulary of over 1800 words; uses sentences averaging 5½ to 6 words*<br>Names 5 or 6 colors<br>Can tell a simple story<br>Defines at least one word (e.g., "ball," "chair," or "shoe"); can name material of which objects are made<br>Can repeat several nursery rhymes |
| **Social** | | |
| May discontinue daytime nap<br>Increased curiosity about bodies, differences between boys and girls, where babies come from<br>Begins domestic role play and symbolic play<br>Increased interest in, and interaction with, other children<br>Can accept limits<br>Begins to express feelings using words together with, or in place of, actions<br>Likes to make simple choices (e.g., clothing to wear, food to eat)<br>Begins to share | Prefers to play with same-sex playmates<br>Activity becomes more purposeful<br>Engages in imaginative "let's pretend" play; assumes fantasy roles (queen, Batman, astronaut, etc.)<br>Plays cooperatively<br>Shows interest in other children's bodies | Enjoys the companionship of other children; plays cooperatively<br>Begins to understand right and wrong, fair and unfair<br>Takes pleasure in using new skills |

*Data from Chow, Durand, Feldman & Mills, 1984.
(American Academy of Pediatrics. [1985]. *Guidelines for health supervision.* Evanston, IL.: American Academy of Pediatrics)

*ticular type of response will predominate within a certain age group and, more importantly, that the formal aspects of the responses correspond to the mental structures that determine how the world in general is conceived. In such responses, the cardinal dimension for assessing development is the degree of differentiation between self and other (1981, p. 1).*

In the next category of thinking, children may have a notion of contagion from people or objects in their environments. Such thinking can create anxiety for young hospital patients who may fear that they will "catch" whatever their roommate has.

Children who employ preoperational thinking do not conceptualize the interior of their bodies but are aware only of those parts that they can see or touch. The stomach is often the first or only internal organ known because it is the repository of something (food) that they have put into their bodies (Crider, 1981). When explaining procedures or surgery to young children, it is best to focus on those aspects that they directly sense, such as the lights, the garb

## Nursing Interventions to Support Preschool Growth and Development

| | |
|---|---|
| Support the child's growth and development | Encourage curiosity, answer questions, offer explanations of new routines and procedures at the child's level of understanding |
| | Respect the child's need for body integrity; prepare for and give support during intrusive procedures |
| | Provide opportunities for motor activity, free play, and interaction with peers as condition permits |
| | Use words carefully; be aware that the child may confuse the meaning of homonyms (e.g., dye and die) and misinterpret adult and medical conversations |
| | Offer nutritious food in a form and setting that encourages the child to eat adequate amounts; appetite may decline during illness or stress |
| | Give emotional support in stressful situations |
| | Offer acceptable ways (play, drawing, story telling) for the child to release and express feelings |
| Maintain maximum sensory and motor functioning | Create an environment that is pleasant to the child's senses (colorful, free of noise and air pollution) and that allows for some free movement with clear boundaries |
| | Monitor and structure the environment for safety to prevent injury |
| Detect deviations from normal in physical and psychological growth and development | Assess the child's physical, mental, and developmental status and sensory abilities using observation techniques or standardized screening instruments |
| Initiate corrective interventions | Refer the child for follow-up care, institute changes in the child's diet, routine, or interactions |
| Support parents' abilities and developmemt | Give emotional support to parents in stressful situations so that they may be emotionally available to the child |
| | Offer information and anticipatory guidance to parents relative to medical procedures or expected developmental or other events |
| | Teach and model restorative and preventive health practices |

of the doctors and nurses, or the sting of a hypodermic needle. The display presents a summary of interventions that support the goal of developmentally appropriate nursing care for 3-, 4-, and 5-year-old children.

## Physical Growth and Development

### General Growth Characteristics

After their second birthdays, children's metabolic needs decrease and their growth rates slow considerably. Weight gain is about 2.25 kg (5 lb) a year; height gain averages 6.4 to 9 cm (2½–3½ in) a year. Linear growth continues at a faster rate than weight gain, leading to a taller, slimmer appearance than in the toddler period. Head circumference also continues to increase, but careful measurements are needed to detect the change. The child's body proportions become more like those of an adult. This change is marked by the child's legs growing faster than the trunk, improved posture, and increased abdominal muscles. At the same time, the child's genetically deter-

mined body build becomes apparent. In general, boys tend to be slightly taller and heavier than girls, but the differences are not as marked as they will be at maturity, and there is a wide range of differences between individual boys and girls. Whether the child is taller or shorter than average in the preschool years does not necessarily predict the relative adult height, since some children's growth accelerates while others' decelerates before mature height is reached.

## Motor Development

### Gross Motor Development

Motor development between the ages of 3 and 6 is rapid and is characterized by two tendencies: (1) the child's movements become more smooth and regular (e.g., the child's gait is more regular when both walking and running), and (2) the young child seeks variations within a given set of movement skills, such as moving sideways and backward, jumping, hopping, and skipping (Cratty, 1986).

The ability to balance, which underlies physical competency, continues to mature during these years. Balance requires that children use vision to stabilize their visual-perceptual field and the motor system to bring about precise correction and integration of visual and motor information in the balance organ of the inner ear. The ability to balance or lack of it affects the child's ability to perform a large variety of motor skills, such as jumping, hopping, galloping, skipping, throwing, and catching (Cratty, 1986).

By the age of 3, children have usually acquired a wide range of fine motor skills such as those involved in self-care activities. Buttoning skill is perfected between the third and fourth years when it has been demonstrated and the child is given time to practice. Many clothes for children do not have buttons, so a doll or buttoning book or toy with well-anchored buttons may assist the child in practicing this skill.

### Fine Motor Development

By age 3, the preschooler can draw a circle with a single circumference as a result of learning to control the circular movement of the hand. About the same time, the child begins to draw other geometrical shapes using visual models as cues. By age 4, children's drawings contain more angles, and they may be able to reproduce several letters of the alphabet. By age 5, children have refined their ability to draw straighter lines and sharper angles. Five-year-old children also draw things they see in their environment (Figs. 14-1 and 14-2).

*Figure 14–1. This drawing was made by a three-year-old when asked to "draw a picture of a person." The body or clothing is sometimes added by filling in the space between the stick legs (Goodnow, 1977).*

*Figure 14–2. A four-and-a-half-year-old drew a person on request but was more interested in completing the building with its many geometric elements.*

Four-year-old children may be able to print some letters and numerals. These are typically scattered on a page with no base line. Letters with horizontal and vertical lines (e.g., T, I, H) are easier for young children to reproduce than are letters with slanting lines or those that combine straight and curved elements. Young children first print the upper case letters and may not reproduce lower case letters accurately until the third grade (Cratty, 1986).

*Handedness,* the dominant use of either the right or left hand, which may have shown variability at younger ages, tends to become fixed between the ages of 3 and 6. Eighty-five percent of the population is right-handed (Coren, 1991). "Overall, the data indicate that when a large undifferentiated group of left handers are compared to right handers little or no differences are seen in their abilities to perform physical skills" (Cratty, 1986, pp. 244–245). Some recent studies have linked left-handedness with increased incidence of alcohol and tobacco use, increased risk of accidental injury, and decreased life expectancy (Coren, 1991). Genetic factors in handedness are significant, but environmental and social pressures undoubtedly influence the final decision on which hand dominates.

Parents should be advised to let the child's handedness emerge naturally. If both parents are right-handed, they give more right-handed cues to the young child, thus encouraging right-handedness. If the child shows a strong preference for using the left hand at age 3 or after, it is best for the parents to allow this tendency without pressure to change.

## Sensory Development

Children involved in motor tasks at this age exhibit decreased sensory awareness to their environment and a certain mechanical persistence at some tasks (Fig. 14-3). Adults often complain that children act as though they do not hear when called from a task in which they are engrossed. Parents should not mistake this total engrossment for disobedience or for impaired hearing.

By the age of 3, children's senses (taste, touch, vision, hearing, and smell) are well developed and continue to be used to gather information to form the basis for the child to accommodate to the environment. The ability of children to integrate sensory and motor tasks matures, allowing activities such as following a short series of verbal directions or catching a ball that is thrown to them (Fig. 14-4). Children are interested in learning the language of the senses (i.e., words that describe color, shape, texture, or odor), and by doing so, they increase their self-awareness and ability to communicate with others. It is essential for preschoolers to have complete use of their sensory systems in order for their perceptual development to take place.

*Figure 14–3.    A three-year-old may be so engrossed in a task that all sensory experience is shut out.*

## Nutrition Needs

Several characteristics of 3- to 6-year-old children influence eating behavior and the ability to meet nutritional needs. These include decelerated growth rate, size, a short attention span, the child's sociable nature, and the quest for independence.

*Figure 14–4.    Imitating what he has seen older children do on equipment designed for his size enables this three-year-old to practice a motor skill and increase his self-confidence.*

Caloric requirements are decreased owing to the slower growth rate. The preschool child needs an average of 100 kcal/kg. These calories need to be of a high quality. Preschoolers need four daily servings from the milk, fruit and vegetable, and cereal and bread groups and two or more daily servings from the meat group. Calcium intake is important in this age group for developing bones and teeth. The daily requirement of 800 mg of calcium can be met by the child drinking two to three glasses (8 oz) of milk or from other sources, such as yogurt, ice cream, or cheese. Preschoolers need 1.5 to 1.8 g/kg of protein. This requirement can be met through two 8-oz glasses of milk and a 2-oz serving of meat.

A variety of foods from the basic four food groups can supply an adequate amount of nutrients for healthy growth between the ages of 3 and 6. If all foods from any one group are rejected for an extended period of time, a nutritional problem may result. Children who eat an adequately balanced diet do not need additional vitamin supplements; however, many parents and health care providers favor giving children a standard multivitamin with iron supplement in the early years of life when appetites are small and healthful dietary habits are not yet established. Families who follow one of the forms of vegetarian diet should ensure that the child receives an adequate supply of complete protein, iron, and calcium (Johnson, 1984). It is almost impossible for a child to obtain all nutritional needs from a "strict" vegetarian diet. If a registered dietitian is available, the nurse should request a consultation for these cases.

The consistency of food is an important consideration for younger children. They prefer meat that is cooked enough to be tender and served in pieces cut small enough to be easily chewed. Moist pieces of meat are more easily chewed and more palatable than dry ones. Pieces of meat that can be easily chewed also pose less of a choking hazard at any age. The serving size for food offered should be about 1 tbsp per year of age (McWilliams, 1986).

To improve the acceptance of foods prepared for preschool children, the following factors should be taken into consideration:

1. Room temperature foods and beverages are generally preferred.
2. Spicy, highly seasoned foods are generally disliked. This includes the excessive use of onion, ginger, garlic, and pepper.
3. Although children may refuse cooked vegetables or canned fruits, they may accept raw vegetables and fresh fruit.
4. Easily identified foods are generally preferred to casseroles and mixed dishes.

It is difficult to ensure an adequate iron intake for preschoolers because their small appetites do not encour-

age them to eat a sufficient amount of iron-rich foods. The most iron-rich foods are in the meat group and, as mentioned, meat is the most difficult food for young children to chew and swallow. Meat is also the most costly food group; this may pose a problem for low-income families. Daily servings of iron-fortified hot cereals, eggs, and green leafy vegetables can boost the preschooler's iron intake to acceptable levels. Since vitamin C increases iron absorption, a small glass of orange juice or another source of vitamin C at mealtime also promotes adequate iron intake.

Growing bones and teeth require a good daily source of calcium and phosphorus; the dairy group provides these nutrients best. A preschooler should have at least 16 oz of milk daily, and 24 oz is even better. Too much milk consumption may interfere with eating a variety of foods from the other three groups. In this case, the lower limit of milk intake per day (16 oz) should be encouraged. Some children are unwilling or unable to drink even the lower limit of milk. When this happens, parents should be encouraged to use creative ways to supplement the diet by adding milk to cereal or by serving cream soups, pudding, or ice cream desserts. If preschoolers do not drink enough milk, parents should be instructed to "fortify" whole milk by adding 1⅓ cup of nonfat dry milk to every quart of liquid milk. Dried (powdered) milk can also be used to supplement meat loaf, mashed potatoes, macaroni and cheese, and even hamburgers.

The preschooler's relatively small stomach size, small appetite, and high energy expenditure means that a meal pattern of six small meals or three meals and three nutritious snacks is more likely to meet the child's energy and nutritional needs than three large meals. In this case, the snacks should supply part of the necessary nutrients rather than empty calories (Fig. 14-5). Small snacks (e.g., fresh vegetables, fruit, or part of the day's milk requirement) should be eaten at least 2 hours before a regular meal. Mid-morning or mid-afternoon snacks give children a rest from active play and an energy lift so that they are not overly hungry or too tired to eat well at lunch or supper.

Fried or salted snacks (e.g., potato or other "chips") should not be given since they provide too much fat and an unnecessary amount of sodium. The data on the exact role of childhood intake of sodium and excessive fats on the subsequent development of arteriosclerosis and hypertension are not yet conclusive (American Academy of Pediatrics, 1986). A habit of increased intake of these foods in early childhood, however, may be difficult to modify in later years.

High-calorie, low-nutrient baked goods such as doughnuts or cupcakes also predispose children to obesity and dental caries from their high sugar and fat contents. Raisins, although an acceptable source of iron for most children, can cause dental caries. Raisins and other dried fruits should be avoided as snacks, or children

*Figure 14–5. Healthful snacks enjoyed as a family help to ensure adequate intake of nutrients for growth and good health.*

should clean their teeth after the snack. Similarly, pure fruit juice fortified with vitamin C (with no sugar added) is preferable to juice "drinks," which, although they contain added vitamin C, also have added sugar and water and have little nutritional value.

In general, nurses should advise parents to avoid C.A.N.D.Y.—*C*ontinuously *A*dvertised, *N*utritionally *D*eficient *Y*ummies (Lansky, 1978). During the preschool years, children are so eager to imitate and please others that important nutritional habits are being formed. If extra sugar and salt are avoided, children learn to appreciate the natural taste of foods and not acquire a taste for an excess of these seasonings.

Other aspects of mealtime can encourage or detract from the preschooler's adequate nutrition. Eating with other children or adults provides preschoolers with a pleasurable social experience and an opportunity to learn by imitating others. Children should be seated comfortably in chairs that fit them. A small table and low chairs are ideal for groups of preschoolers. At home, children can use a high chair with a foot rest placed at the family table. Either arrangement gives children stability and allows them to focus on eating. In a hospital setting, group eating for noninfectious preschoolers often enhances appetite.

Food should be prepared and offered attractively, in small portions so that the child's small appetite is not overwhelmed. To overcome some preschoolers' reluctance to try new foods, "no thank you" portions can be served. A "no thank you" portion is a teaspoonful of the food, offered matter-of-factly with the stated expectation that the child will eat that amount and decide if more is desired. If this rule is followed consistently (for all family members) and individual preferences are honored, the child usually learns to eat a wide variety of foods with few active dislikes.

Parents should also realize that a child's refusal to eat specific foods may simply be another means of demonstrating the continuing need for independence. This should not be a cause for alarm. Once parents understand that this is a normal part of development, other strategies can be used.

Preschool children generally discriminate against vegetables. Nurses can help reduce parents' apprehension about children's refusal to eat vegetables by offering the following advice:

1. Most children who refuse to eat cooked vegetables will eat them raw. Also, raw vegetables generally provide more nutrients.
2. Encourage children to eat vegetables by offering them at times when they are most hungry, such as at snack time or at the beginning of meals.
3. Serve a new or unusual vegetable with a familiar, well-liked food to increase acceptance.
4. Cook rice or macaroni in, or make soups from, pot liquor (the water vegetables were cooked in).
5. Parents serve as role models and should be encouraged to prepare, serve, and eat a variety of vegetables.

The social atmosphere of mealtime is important to the preschooler's appetite, and the adults in charge should take care to keep it relaxed. A positive social atmosphere can be promoted by involving preschoolers in meal preparation activities. Some of these activities might include input into menu planning, setting the table, peeling vegetables, mixing various ingredients, or growing a small herb or vegetable garden.

Mealtime conversation should be light, and everyone, even the preschooler, should be invited to tell a positive aspect of the day. Discussions of stressful subjects between adults or between an adult and a child should not be held at mealtime. Excessive concern with "manners" creates stress for both adults and preschoolers and interferes with the children's appetites. Social graces are better taught by modeling than by demanding. Since preschoolers have short attention spans, parents can matter-of-factly remove utensils when children signify that they are finished by "playing" with food. Young children can be allowed to leave the table after 10 to 15 minutes rather than being required to sit and wait until all others are finished eating. Activities such as clearing their own utensils can be welcome to preschoolers tired of sitting still.

## Sleep

Three- to 5-year-old children require 10 to 12 hours of sleep every 24 hours, including a 1½- to 2-hour afternoon nap for the younger child. Most children give up the afternoon nap by age 3½ to 4. The length of nighttime sleep required decreases by ½ hour per year from ages 3 to 5 and by ¼ hour per year during the remainder of childhood (Ferber, 1985a). The need to eliminate the nap is signaled by the child's increasing resistance to going to bed and falling asleep at the usual nap time or by resistance to going to bed at night until much later than the usual bedtime. When one or both of these signs appear, it is useful to continue to provide the child with a "quiet time" at the usual nap time, during which the child plays alone, perhaps resting on the bed with some favorite books or toys. This continues to give the adult caretaker some time free from the demands of the youngster and allows the child some self-directed, low-stimulation time. Dinner time and bedtime may have to be adjusted to an earlier hour for a period until the child becomes accustomed to the new schedule.

Nighttime sleep is characterized by alternating periods of rapid eye movement (REM) and non-REM sleep, with brief periods of waking occurring at the transition time between the two stages. During these brief wakings, children may scan and check the environment. If they find that conditions are the same as when they went to sleep, they will be able to return to sleep (Ferber, 1985b). When children are in a strange environment or have been dreaming, they may call out at this time. They may expect to find objects, people, or animals from the dream present in the room until they learn to differentiate dream images (a mental process) from reality.

Common sleep disturbances of this age group include "night terrors" and sleepwalking, which generally occur when children partially awaken from deep non-REM sleep 2 to 3 hours after falling asleep. Characteristics of a night terror include moaning, crying out, or screaming, sometimes accompanied by intense motor activity, such as rolling, thrashing, or banging into walls. The child's eyes may be open and staring blankly, giving no evidence of seeing the parent who responds or of being aware of being spoken to. The child may become more agitated, though still not awake, if physically restrained in any way. These episodes usually last for 15 to 30 minutes, although sometimes they may last longer. An adult should stay nearby and protect the child from injury if he or she is physically active. Little other intervention is necessary. Persistent night terrors after age 5 may indicate that the child is under psychological tension (Ferber, 1985a).

Sleepwalking is thought to be a different form of night terror since it occurs in the same time period—early in the child's sleep time—and has many of the same features. Sleepwalking is more common after age 6. Again, management is directed toward the safety of the child. An adult should stay with the child to prevent falls down stairs or wandering out of doors. The adult should guide the child back to bed without waking the child. In the morning, the child will have only a vague memory of the episode or none at all.

Nightmares occur in REM sleep, and the child fully awakens and is very fearful. The child may or may not be able to relate in some detail the fearful content of the dream, but the remaining feeling of fear is real. An adult should stay with the child in the child's own room and offer reassurance that the cause of the fear (the dream) is gone. The adult should talk quietly to the child in the dark and ask the child to identify familiar objects in the room, especially the things the child relies on for comfort at bedtime. Turning on lights and making a search to be sure the frightening figure is gone only reinforces the child's belief that there was something frightening, making it more difficult for the child to separate the world of objects from the fantasy or mental world of dreams (Clarke, 1978).

Nightmares represent a relatively benign way of expressing fears during sleep. Occasional nightmares are normal ways for children to process psychologically disturbing experiences. Children who experience frequent nightmares may be exposed to too many fearful stimuli, such as adult television programs showing violence, family arguments or violence, or other stress.

For active preschoolers, bedtime signifies separation from the pleasurable activities of the day as well as separation from the parents and being left alone. These factors, as well as children's active imaginations and their inability to clearly differentiate their own mental activity from the objective world, may make children very reluctant to go to bed. Parents who are experiencing sleep-onset problems with a preschooler can be helped to set appropriate expectations and routines and should be supported for making changes in accordance with their child's and their own needs.

The following advice will assist parents in managing the preschoolers' bedtime:

1. Be aware of the usual sleep requirements of children of this age and of the child's individual needs and signals.

2. Keep bedtime consistent and part of a predictable routine. Be sure the child gets enough exercise, some outdoors, during the day.

3. Set the bedtime to accommodate your own need for privacy and rest as well as the child's need for sleep. The least fatigued or stressed adult should be in charge, participating with the child in a relaxed, unhurried, but purposeful manner. The last interactions of the day should be loving and peaceful.

4. Keep activity unstimulating for an hour or so before bedtime. Quiet play with gentle physical contact, a story, or singing is appropriate. Violent or overstimulating television programs may leave the child unable to relax for sleep.

5. Start the going-to-bed process 30 minutes or more before bedtime to allow for a slow pace, pleasurable interactions with the parents, and gradual removal from the family's presence. A regular ritual, such as a snack, brushing teeth, bath, story, and lights out, helps the child to move from a social setting to the solitude of bed in a predictable sequence that strengthens the child's growing temporal awareness and helps the child feel a measure of control.

6. Finally, tuck the child into the bed, turn out the light (or leave a night light on), and leave the room. Children should fall asleep on their own in their own beds.

For some families, having preschoolers share the parents' bed may be a problem. This practice often begins at a young age and may have been started to meet the child's need for comfort and reassurance when ill, the parents' need for undisturbed rest, or, inappropriately, a parent's need for close contact. In some cultures across the world and in the United States, this is an accepted practice. The current thinking of developmental theorists, however, is that learning to sleep alone represents an important step in the young child's autonomy and should be encouraged. If either parent considers it a problem for the child to share the parents' bed or if the child shows signs of tension about sleeping with the parents (children around 4 or 5 may be ready to sleep alone even if they have not done so before), the parents can be helped to set up a program for teaching the child to sleep alone (Brazelton, 1984).

## Cognitive Development

### Piaget

According to the observations and theory of Jean Piaget, preschool children are in the *preoperational stage* of cognitive development. They begin this stage after the sensorimotor period (at about age 2) and complete it at about age 7, when they enter the concrete-operations stage. Between the ages of 2 and 4, children's cognitive functioning takes on the characteristics of *semiotic* (or *symbolic*) *function,* and they are able to make a mental image (a word or an object) stand for something else that is not present. This is observed in children's use of mental symbols, symbolic play, and words.

Mental symbols are inferred when children demonstrate (by word or action) the ability to remember something that has occurred in the past (Ginsburg & Opper, 1979). Piaget cited the example of his own daughter Jacqueline imitating behavior she had observed in a playmate the day before. Another example can be seen in the case of the mother of a 3-year-old being startled to have the child identify "John's house," where the mother had taken the child only once, several weeks before. Piaget conceptualized mental symbolism as "internal imitation," an extension of the imitative behavior that was part of the accommodation process in the sensorimotor period.

Symbolic play involves using an object as though it were something else. For example, a child might hold an elongated object to the ear and talk into it as though it were a telephone. This activity requires that the child have a mental image of a real telephone.

Using words in a representational way is the third manifestation of semiotic function. At about age 2, children can use words to tell about an event that has occurred. Elaboration of the semiotic function characterizes much of the cognitive activity of children between the ages of 2 and 4.

During this period, children exhibit three different styles of reasoning. In the first type of reasoning, *deduction,* they apply past experience directly to new situations, reasoning very concretely. For example, Jacqueline Piaget, observing her father getting hot water, concluded that "Daddy's getting hot water, so he's going to shave" (Piaget, 1962, p. 231).

In a second way of reasoning, *induction,* the child may distort thinking in accordance with desire. For example, Jacqueline wanted to eat oranges. Her parents explained that this was not possible because the oranges were still green and not yet ripe. A moment later, as she was drinking her camomile tea, she said "Camomile isn't green it's yellow already . . . Give me some oranges!" (Piaget, 1962, p. 232).

Piaget called the third type of reasoning *transductive* reasoning. "The child does not go from the general to the particular (deduction) or from the particular to the general (induction) but rather from the particular to the particular without touching on the general . . . [A child may say] 'I haven't had my nap so it isn't afternoon!' " (Ginsburg & Opper, 1979, p. 81).

During this period, *egocentrism* dominates. Because of egocentric thinking, the child is unable to deal with more than one aspect of a situation at a time or to recognize the point of view of another person. Egocentrism is evident in certain noncommunicative verbalizations used by the young child: repetition, the individual monologue, and the collective monologue. *Repetition* of others' verbalizations involves direct mimicking of something the child has heard another say. For example, a child observing a playmate hopping up and down and exclaiming "Ouch, my foot hurts!" might immediately cry, "Ouch, my foot hurts!" while hopping up and down. The *individual monologue* is observed when children are alone and talk aloud, often about the activity in which they are engaged (Fig. 14-6). Another type of language use is the *collective monologue,* where children in a group engage in soliloquies in which the others do not participate. This is reminiscent of the parallel play of the younger child. Piaget saw these noncommunicative verbalizations being used for the pure pleasure of playing with words. Such verbalizations are similar to the assimilative repetition of motor schemata seen in infancy.

When children intend to communicate, they use pronouns without clear referents, put events in incorrect order, omit important features (although these can be related if questioned), and fail to express causality (Ginsburg & Opper, 1979).

Children between the ages of 4 and 7 use preoperational thought. Preoperational thought is characterized by

centration, that is, focusing on a limited aspect of the information available. In the conservation of number demonstration, for example, the child concentrates on the length of the line of objects, ignoring the number of elements in each (Fig. 14-7). Even after establishing equivalence of objects, as in part A, the child believes there are more circles than squares when the line of squares is compressed, as in part B. Similarly, the child fails to conserve volume and substance. Preoperational thought is *static* since it focuses on states and ignores transformations. For example, a child may believe that a ball of plasticene contains a different amount of substance when it is shaped into a sausage. Preoperational thought lacks *reversibility*—it does not recognize the relationship between pouring from container A to container B and then from B to A (Ginsburg & Opper, 1979).

## Play

Piaget identified *play*—defined broadly as the variety of activities that occupy the child's waking hours—as a vehicle of adaptation. Through play, which is a self-directed activity, children practice fine motor, gross motor, or social routines. Activities such as climbing, riding tricycles, running, and jumping lead to mastery of large muscle coordination. In play, preschoolers practice dressing and undressing, going to sleep, and eating. Around age 3, children begin to play at acting like adult models and imitating adult activities such as going to work, getting supper, or taking care of the baby (Fig. 14-8). Initially, both boys and girls play in a domestic scene that is familiar to both sexes, but the boys, failing to find well-defined male roles, soon leave to play with each other and create imaginary male roles to imitate (Pitcher & Schultz, 1983; Fig. 14-9).

Play is crucial for preschool children because their experience grows through direct encounters with the environment. Children may play at one activity repetitiously, with each encounter assisting them in accommodating to that event. As children learn more from each interaction, knowledge increases about more aspects of a situation,

*Figure 14–6. This four-year-old is playing at combining known routines in new and sometimes symbolic ways. An individual monologue may accompany this kind of activity.*

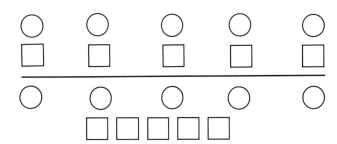

*Figure 14–7. Conservation of number. (From Ginsburg, H. & Opper, S. [1979]. Piaget's theory of intellectual development [2d ed.]. Englewood Cliffs, NJ: Prentice-Hall)*

*Figure 14–8.    Three-year-old girls imitate domestic roles and tasks.*

and they lose some egocentricity. Piaget conceptualized these contacts with the environment as a spiral, with each encounter bringing the child closer to a shared reality with others. The display lists appropriate toys, play materials, and activities for preschool children.

Play and language serve to draw children from the autistic world of the sensorimotor period, in which secondary circular reactions dominate, to the egocentric position, in which children are aware of the environment but only from a limited perspective. As play becomes more truly social, with exchange of ideas and information be-

*Figure 14–9.    These four-and-a-half-year-old boys are practicing the tasks, language, and roles of baseball.*

### Appropriate Toys, Play Materials, and Activities for Preschool Children

Friends
Props for "let's pretend"
   Hats, shoes, clean clothing
   Accessories (jewelry, badges, etc.)
Music makers
   Songs to sing
   Instruments
   Records, tapes
Art supplies
   Paper and pencils, markers, crayons, paints
   Safe scissors and old cloth, wallpaper, pictures
   from magazines to cut and paste
   Clay, playdough
Books and stories
Age-appropriate puzzles
Safe outdoor play space
   Riding toys
   Climbers, swings, slides
   Sand
   Safe water
Field trips
   Libraries, stores, fire stations, parks, banks, doctors' offices

tween two or more individuals, children learn to "decenter." As children move into the next stage of cognitive development, they take into account more than one aspect of an event and begin to appreciate others' points of view.

## Moral Development

Piaget also explored the moral behavior and reasoning of children, identifying two stages of development: the stage of *moral realism* and the stage of *moral relativism*. He stated that young children, aged 3 to 9, subscribe to a literal interpretation of the rules they believe to be unalterable. This is coupled with a belief that the criterion of guilt is not intention but the amount of damage resulting from an act. Piaget termed this "moral realism." Since older children are able to appreciate another's point of view, they attend more to motivation or intention. Piaget named this "moral relativism."

Kohlberg (1984) proposed three levels of moral development: the *preconventional, conventional,* and *postconventional.* Preschool children are at the preoperational thinking stage and are limited to the *preconventional level* of moral development. This level is characterized by egocentricity or self-interest, which initially arises out of fear of punishment. Children at this level make decisions based on consequences to themselves. Preschoolers learn not to repeat behaviors that result in parental disapproval or punishment.

## Psychosocial Development

### Freud

In the psychoanalytic theory of psychosexual development, Freud described the ages of 3 to 5 or 6 as the *phallic stage.* In this stage, the energy of the id becomes focused on the genital organs, particularly on the male organ, the penis. This causes (or coincides with) the recognition of the anatomical differences between boys and girls around the age of 4 or 5. In order to explain to himself a little girl's lack of a penis, the boy imagines that she must have had one but that it was cut off. Such a formulation leads the boy to experience "castration anxiety"—the fear that his penis might be removed in retaliation for some misdeed. Freud theorized that the "misdeed" was the attachment the little boy felt for his mother, which, for the first time, he associated with pleasurable sensations in his genitals. This erotic love was believed by the boy to arouse envy in his father who would retaliate by castrating him. Girls, realizing their lack of a penis, develop "penis envy," which Freud theorized was resolved by bearing male children.

This "Oedipal situation," the erotic love of the child for the parent of the opposite sex, creates anxiety for both boys and girls. This anxiety is resolved when the child identifies with the parent of the same sex. For the boy, this means switching from a dependence on the mother (usually the principal caretaker) to an identification with his father. By thus allying himself with his father, the boy defends himself against the anxiety of having the father as a powerful rival. Similarly, girls ultimately realize that they do not need to compete with the mother for the father's affection.

This process is accomplished at an unconscious level. The resolution of the Oedipal situation was considered by Freud to be a crucial event in the development of the personality. Freud believed that unsuccessful resolution of this situation by the ego caused most of the psychopathology observed in his adult patients. Freud proposed that the superego, the part of the personality that consists of the moral standards of society, arises at the time of resolution of the Oedipal situation, around age 5.

### Erikson

Erikson began as a student of Freud, but in his early work he departed from Freud's emphasis on the id in favor of exploring the development of the ego's importance in determining human personality. He believed that the sequence of development of the ego proceeds according to a plan, the *epigenetic principle,* which is present at birth.

Through an orderly sequence of interactions (*crises*) with the environment, the ego reaches full maturity, leading, at the end of life, to a sense of integrity or wholeness for the person.

At around age 3, the developing child, having passed through the crises of trust versus mistrust and autonomy versus shame and doubt, confronts the problem of initiative versus guilt.

> *Initiative adds to autonomy the quality of undertaking, planning, and "attacking" a task for the sake of being active and on the move, where before, self-will, more often than not, inspired acts of defiance or, at any rate, protested independence . . . The danger of this stage is a sense of guilt over the goals contemplated and the acts initiated in one's exuberant enjoyment of new locomotor and mental power . . . (Erikson, 1963, p. 255)*

Further, Erikson states that "initiative brings with it 'anticipatory rivalry' with those who have been there first" (p. 256). Children may express the quest for power in fantasies of being superheroes, tigers, or giants and then experience fear at these imaginings. Erikson acknowledges "castration anxiety" as a result of fantasies attached to the erotic feelings now localized in the genitals. He identifies conscience (the superego) as a set of instinct fragments that take on "self-observation, self-guidance and self-punishment" and notes that the superego of a child of this age can be "primitive, cruel and uncompromising" and of an all-or-nothing, black-or-white variety. When the superego is activated to curb initiative that has gone too far, overinhibition may result. Psychosomatic diseases arise as a "way out" when initiative leads children too far beyond their capabilities.

Erikson also believes that play is crucial to development. He notes that growing implies two parts moving at different rates and that "play, then, is a function of the ego, an attempt to synchronize the bodily and the social processes within the self . . . To hallucinate ego mastery and yet also to practice it in an intermediate reality between fantasy and actuality is the purpose of play" (pp. 211–212). Play allows children to indulge in initiative in situations in which they are master.

## Language Development

Language also serves as play for the 3- to 5-year-old child. "His language not only repeats sensorimotor history, it replaces it. The more a child verbally expresses desire, experience or thought without having to act it out, the more it is indicated that he accepts speech as a conveyer of meaning" (Maier, 1969, p. 120). Hence, children imitate words, voice tone, and gestures that accompany the roles being played.

## Sex-Role Identification

During the preschool years, children move from the simple gender identity, "I am a girl" or "I am a boy," to the acquisition of complex sex-role behavior. The recent emphasis in the United States on reducing stereotyped sex-role behavior has led developmentalists and parents to look carefully at the issue of what is "masculine" or "feminine" behavior, how much is determined by physical factors (i.e., hormones, genetic makeup), and to what extent masculinity or femininity is defined and shaped by culture.

In no other area of child development are the roles of genetic factors and learning (nature versus nurture) as often debated as in the area of gender identification. Many cross-cultural studies have found that boys are judged significantly "more aggressive" than girls. Yet groups seeking to promote equality between the sexes reject Freud's assertion that "biology is destiny." Recent studies of girls who received higher than normal levels of prenatal androgens (when their mothers were treated with hormones to prevent spontaneous abortions) revealed that " . . . the androgenized girls were much more likely to engage in activities involving energy expenditure and competitiveness; they preferred clothes that were utilitarian and functional (and avoided fashionable dresses); they were indifferent to dolls and later to human infants; but they were attracted to toy cars, trucks and guns" (Biehler, 1976, p. 253).

Children begin to identify sex differences and, through play with both boys and girls, receive gender stimuli from both sexes that, responding egocentrically, they code as positive (like me) or negative (not like me). The first gender awareness is a cognitive act, "probably based on a limited set of features—gender label, hair style, dress, name and organized rules that they have observed or that have been dictated by adults" (Pitcher & Schultz, 1983, p. 153).

Pitcher and Schultz observed nursery school children at free play and identified a sequence of stages of peer interactions that lead to development of sex-role behavior. Three-year-olds of both sexes initially play in the domestic setting, in which girls, identifying with their mothers, readily fill the mother role. Boys, finding the father role not so clearly defined and unwilling to accept for long the baby role, soon leave the domestic scene to engage in fantasy and power play with other boys. Because of the egocentric cognitive style, concepts of masculinity and femininity tend to be stereotyped, rigid, and overlearned, leading to exclusive same-sex play groups among 4- and 5-year-olds. This process has been observed in 3- to 5-year-old children from families in which male and female roles are reversed or blended as well as in children from families maintaining the traditional male and female roles. Pitcher and Schultz conclude that only when children's cognitive development proceeds past the "5-to-7 cognitive shift" can they assimilate more sophisticated variations in the male or female roles. Despite this early polarization, adults should present non–sex-stereotyped messages and experiences for children of both sexes during these years, and should continue to confront and discourage sex-stereotyping throughout childhood.

## Day Care and Nursery School

The need for and desirability of preschool education has long been debated by developmentalists, educators, and parents. Although gains in I.Q. scores have been demonstrated following a preschool education program, other research shows that the gap between I.Q. scores of children who have attended preschools and those who have not largely disappears by the end of first grade—the so-called *fade factor* (Biehler, 1976).

Head Start is a federally funded program for 3- to 5-year-old children. It was established in 1965 to assist children in overcoming the effects of developmental delays due to their environment (Kotelchuck & Richmond, 1987). Recent evaluations have focused on cognitive results that reflect the fade factor; however, evaluation of Head Start's success in meeting its objectives in the broad areas of health, nutrition, cognitive development, parent education, and involvement "reveal[s] successes across a wide range of domains" (Kotelchuck & Richmond, 1987, p. 442).

Deciding to enroll a child in day care or nursery school represents a major step for many parents. It involves selecting an adult or adults to assume a prominent role in their child's life. Choosing day care usually reflects the need of the parent to have time away from child care for work, study, or individual pursuits. Day care placement may occur before the child is 3 years old. The decision whether to enroll a child in a day care facility and the choice of a facility is often highly emotional since parents must give up some of their exclusive relationship with the child and allow others to play a significant role in their child's development and nurturance.

Day care refers to any group child care facility licensed by a state to provide such services. In general, there are two types of day care: center-based or family day care. Center-based facilities usually care for a large number of children, perhaps up to 100, divided into smaller groups or classes. These centers are staffed by a mixture of professional child care workers (who have had postsecondary education for child care or early childhood education) and aides who have been trained on the job. Each state has staff training requirements in licensed day care facilities and mandates certain staff/child and space/child ratios for each age group. A center may enroll only children in the age group for which it is licensed. Food preparation and sanitary facilities in the center are inspected and monitored by the state health department. Center-based facilities may be run for profit, as part of an employee benefit package, or not for profit, as in churches, community centers, or university settings.

Group family day care centers are licensed facilities operated in homes. State requirements regulate the number of children that may be cared for. The care-giver may or may not have formal training in early childhood care or education. Either type of center may care for the child for up to 10 hours each day or may have a provision for short-term drop-in care.

When choosing a day care center, parents should evaluate the center's license, program, cost, and location. The parents and child should visit a center when children are present and observe the physical plant and the staff/child interactions and form an overall impression of the center. The child's reaction is important because the child's first group experiences should be positive. The parents should also consider how well they can communi-

cate with the day care staff and whether the values and objectives of the program are compatible with their own. The major considerations in selecting a day care center or nursery school are summarized in the display.

Parents usually see enrolling the child in nursery school as a positive move to meet the needs of the child for social, cognitive, and emotional growth. Most nursery school programs are designed for children 3 and 4 years old. Nursery schools may differ from day care programs in the goals of the program and the length of time a child may attend (usually 2–3 hours per session, from 2 to 3 sessions per week). One nursery school may emphasize emotional and social development through structured and free play, with little or no effort to teach the child reading or writing skills. Other nursery schools may be cognitively oriented toward "school readiness," teaching young children to make and recognize letters and to read simple words. Parents should determine the goal of the nursery school and decide whether it matches their own objectives for their child.

## Important Considerations in Selecting a Day Care Facility or Nursery School

### Licensing and Accreditation Status

Is the facility currently licensed and accredited by the appropriate state or local authority?

### Qualifications and Personal Attributes of Staff

Do the staff members meet state requirements for education and training for the type of facility?
Are the interactions between the staff and the children positive?
Is there an adequate staff/child ratio?
How are staff absences filled? By qualified substitutes? By volunteers?
How, and by whom, are staff supervised?
How do staff handle shy or aggressive children?

### Physical Environment

Are indoor and outdoor spaces large enough for the number of children?
Is the space clean, free from hazards, and attractive?
Is there personal storage space for each child?

### Program

What is the philosophy of the center?
What kinds of activities are available to the children?

Is there an opportunity for children to choose from a variety of planned activities?
How is television used in the center?
Is children's independence in personal care and daily living skills encouraged?

### Health and Safety

What is the center's policy on recieving ill children?
How does the center care for children who become ill during the day?
How are emergencies handled?
Who is trained in first aid, cardiopulmonary resuscitation, and care of simple illness?
How clean are the food preparation and toilet facilities?
What are the center's food preparation arrangements?

### Communication

How accessible is the staff for parents' questions?
Do staff communicate regularly to parents about the child's activities and adjustment?
Can parents visit the center unannounced?
Are there parent meetings, newsletters, or other notices?

## Assessment

### Body Measurements

Regular assessment of the child's height and weight and comparison of these with the child's previous measurements as well as with standardized norms will alert health care professionals early to possible growth problems. The child's height and weight are measured at least annually, at which time they are plotted on an appropriate growth chart (see Appendix B). At age 2 or 3, the child can cooperate in the assessment by standing barefoot on a scale for height and weight measurement. Weight should be measured when the child is nude or in underclothing.

Comparisons of measurements taken over a time span show an uneven pattern of rate of growth (the child grows faster in some time periods than in others); however, a steady overall gain in both height and weight is expected. Weight is more sensitive to environmental factors; thus, a weight loss or marked slowing may reflect illness, stress, poor nutrition, or temporary "developmental" reduction in appetite. Prolonged slowing of increase in height is usually indicative of constitutional factors (Lippe, 1988).

Measurements should be plotted on a graph for comparison with norms and to establish the child's individual growth curve. The child whose measurements have been at or near the tenth percentile since infancy can be considered to be growing according to potential, whereas the child whose growth "falls off" the established curve and does not level off can be considered at risk; possible underlying factors should be sought.

Assessment of development continues to be important as a basis for advising parents about common problems as well as for entry into preschool. Developmental assessment is also essential to plan interventions for any identified problems or developmental delays.

### Denver Developmental Screening Test

The administration and scoring of the Denver Developmental Screening Test is discussed in Chapter 5 and is shown in Appendix A. For the 3- to 5-year-old child, the personal-social items are reported by the mother, since these involve dressing, washing, and interactive skills that may not be readily observed in a testing situation.

Fine motor skills are assessed by asking the child to copy or draw certain figures. This also reveals the child's ability to follow simple directions. Language comprehension is assessed by asking the child to respond verbally to questions such as "What do you do when you are hungry?" or "What is a ball?" Children show their comprehension of prepositions by placing a block "under," "beside," or "in front of" a chair. Observable gross motor skills include elaborations of balancing: hopping, heel-to-toe walking (forward and backward), and catching.

As with younger children, it is important to start the screening test with some items that the child can easily complete, since this establishes an atmosphere of play rather than examination. The child should be praised for all efforts as well as for accomplishments. The nurse should ask parents to avoid prompting or assisting the child and should reassure the parents that children do not accomplish all tasks at the same time. It is usually better to assess gross motor skills last, since it is frequently difficult to return the child to a quieter task after a period of movement. The child's own responses should dictate the order and pace of presentation of tasks.

### Washington Guide to Promoting Development in the Young Child

The Washington Guide to Promoting Development in the Young Child includes groups of items for children up to 52 months of age. Expected tasks from 36 to 52 months of age are characterized by increased gross and fine motor coordination, increased independence in self-care activities, increased willingness to conform to parental requests, and increased imitation of behavior observed in parents, peers, or other models. Language development is characterized by longer sentences; spontaneous story telling; understanding of concepts such as hungry, cold, and tired; asking of questions; identification of colors and coins; and some simple counting of objects. Suggested activities support independence and encourage creative expression through music, pretending, painting, drawing, and story telling. Parents are encouraged to expand the child's experiences by reading stories, taking the child to parks, zoos, shopping, and so forth, and talking about the experiences with the child. Group play with other children is recommended. The excerpt from the Washington Guide included in Table 14-2 illustrates its form.

### Assessment of Home and Family

The Home Observation and Measurement of the Environment (HOME) is discussed in Chapter 5 and is presented in Appendix A. In assessing preschool children using HOME, the categories for consideration focus on availability of toys, equipment, and experiences to stimulate manipulation, free expression, music skills, and verbal skills. The interviewer observes opportunities for the child to acquire skill in color and shape identification and telling time as well as to learn numbers and letters. The interviewer also observes social skills such as following simple rules, recognizing the rights of others, simple manners, and the delay of food gratification. Assessment of the physical environment includes building safety, interior brightness, noise, space, and clutter. The language environment provided by the parents is observed; assessment includes

*Table 14–2. Preschool Language Development*

| Expected Tasks | Suggested Activities |
|---|---|
| **37 to 48 Months** | |
| 1. Expresses appropriate responses when asked what child does when tired, cold, or hungry | 1. Provide visual stimuli while reading stories |
| 2. Tells stories | 2. Have child repeat story |
| 3. Common expression: "I don't know" | 3. Arrange trips to zoo, farms, seashore, stores, and movies and discuss with child |
| 4. Repeats sentence composed of twelve to thirteen syllables, e.g., "I am going when daddy and I are finished playing" | 4. Give simple explanations in answering questions |
| 5. Has mastered phonetic sounds of p, k, g, v, tf, d, z, lr, hw, j, kw, l, e, w, qe, and o | |
| **49 to 52 Months** | |
| *Receptive Abilities* | 1. Play games in which child names colors |
| 1. Points to penny, nickel or dime on request | 2. Encourage use of "please" and "thank you" |
| 2. Carries out in, order, command containing three parts, e.g., "Pick up the block, put it on the table, and bring the book to me" | 3. Encourage social–verbal interactions with other children |
| | 4. Encourage correct usage of words |
| *Expressive Abilities* | 5. Provide puppets or toys with movable parts that child can converse about |
| 1. Names penny, nickel, or dime on request | 6. Provide group activity for child; children may stimulate each other by taking turns naming pictures |
| 2. Replies appropriately to questions such as, "What do you do when you are asleep?" | 7. Allow child to make choices about games, stories, and activities |
| 3. Counts three objects, pointing to each in turn | 8. Have child dramatize simple stories |
| 4. Defines simple words, e.g., "hat." "ball" | 9. Provide child with piggy bank and encourage naming coins as they are handled or dropped into bank. |
| 5. Asks questions | |
| 6. Can identify or name four colors | |

(Barnard, K. E., & Erickson, M. L. [1976]. *Teaching children with developmental problems* [2nd ed.]. St. Louis: C. V. Mosby, p. 87)

the complexity of words and sentences used, the grammatical correctness, the audibility, and the intelligibility of speech. The presence and use of television, magazines, newspapers, and books should be noted.

The emotional climate of the home is also noted. This includes the avoidance of punishment and unnecessary restriction of the child's activities, parental expression of positive regard for the child, and encouragement of independence from parental control. The presence and amount of masculine interaction are noted.

As with younger children, the emphasis of the HOME inventory is to make accurate observations of the child's home environment. This assessment should complement other evaluations of the child for developmental delays, growth failure, or possible child abuse (Bradley & Caldwell, 1988).

## Health Promotion

### Health Maintenance Visits and Immunizations

Health maintenance visits for preschoolers are directed toward preventing disease, early detection and treatment of disease, and counseling parents in various aspects of child rearing. The American Academy of Pediatrics recommends an annual visit, with more frequent visits scheduled if closer surveillance of the child's growth and development or treatment of some condition is necessary.

If the child's immunizations are up to date, none are scheduled until the prekindergarten booster of diphtheria-pertussis-tetanus and polio vaccine. Usually the trivalent oral polio vaccine is given, except to children who are immunocompromised or who live with an immunocompromised person; in these cases, the injectable polio vaccine may be given. Tuberculosis screening tests may be repeated if a recent test is required by a day care program or nursery school. If the child has been exposed to tuberculosis, purified protein derivative rather than a tine test is performed. Other immunizations, such as hepatitis B immune globulin and serotype-specific vaccine for *Neisseria meningococcus,* are available for children who have had home or day care contacts with these infections. A vaccine for varicella (chickenpox) has been developed and tested, but guidelines for its use are being established.

Disease prevention also includes making parents aware of the relationship between nutrition and health and of accident prevention. Discussion of and instruction in dental and personal hygiene contributes to prevention of caries, common colds, and gastrointestinal infections as well as their complications. Anticipatory guidance regarding expected behaviors helps to prevent behavioral maladjustments and poor interactive patterns from developing. Discussion of these behaviors and some possible ways of handling them before they arise can encourage parents to plan positive strategies for responding.

Periodic blood and urine screening detects iron deficiency, lead poisoning, blood abnormalities, and urinary tract infections.

Currently, the American Academy of Pediatrics does not recommend universal testing of blood cholesterol in children because of technical problems in obtaining precise measurements. Testing for elevated cholesterol is recommended for children over age 2 when there is a family history of hyperlipidemia or early myocardial infarction. If elevated or borderline values are obtained, several serial fasting total cholesterol, triglyceride, and high-density lipoprotein measurements should be taken before interventions are implemented. Unwarranted severe dietary restrictions or pharmacological control could adversely affect growth and development. Long-term effects have not yet been evaluated in children (American Academy of Pediatrics, Committee on Nutrition, 1989).

At 3 years of age, blood pressure screening begins. This measurement is taken and recorded at each visit. It is important that the correct size blood pressure cuff is used to ensure accurate measurement (see Appendix B for normal blood pressure values).

Vision screening can be carried out by objective means after age 3. There are standardized picture or "illiterate E" charts that many 3-year-olds and most 4- and 5-year-olds can use when tested by a person familiar to the child or skilled at working with young children.

Hearing screening is most successfully assessed by parental report or by Inferred Impedance Tympanometry until the child is at least 4 years old. Many 3-year-olds are anxious about the earphones of an audiometer and cannot follow directions reliably enough to complete an audi-

ological screening. With specially trained personnel, it is possible to perform audiological testing with young children if a hearing deficit is suspected. Older children may enjoy wearing the earphones and can attend well enough to complete an audiological screening in a short period of time. Routine screening for hearing and vision, using standardized eye charts and an audiometer, familiarizes children with these instruments at an early age, thus increasing the accuracy of the screening (Sullivan, 1988).

It is crucial to assess the integrity of the child's sensory system. This is done by parental report or by direct screening, when possible. Children depend on their senses for information necessary for the formation of self-concept, their view of the world, and their role in it. Thus, it is essential that children have full use of their senses.

Other than "shots," the physical examination is the most stressful part of the health maintenance visit to children. Children's anxiety can be decreased if examiners explain what is being done during the procedure. Children can be actively included by telling them how they can help (e.g., "Lie still on your back," or "Turn your head to look at Mommy"). If part of the examination seems to have been uncomfortable for the child, it is important to ask the child about the experience and to allow the child to express feelings about it. Providing an opportunity for the expression of feelings avoids labeling behavior as "uncooperative" or making false assumptions about the degree of discomfort. A skilled examiner can complete a physical examination in a brief time by pacing the examination to the child's tolerance level.

It is important to prepare children between the ages of 3 and 5 in advance for health maintenance visits or for any other procedure. When young children know what to expect, they find it easier to cooperate. Many fearful 3-year-olds cope with health maintenance visits effectively when parents give simple explanations before the visit, encourage them to play with toy stethoscopes, or read to them one of the many picture books that explain "visits to the clinic."

The preschool immunization creates a great deal of anxiety for the 4- or 5-year-old, which may be expressed by the child actively and loudly protesting and resisting the procedure. Usually, the child has been made aware of the impending injection before coming to the office, and the anxiety may build to a peak, making the child uncharacteristically uncooperative for the visit. When it is time to give an injection to a 5-year-old (or any preschooler), nurses must be sure that the child is gently but firmly *immobilized* during the procedure for the child's own safety and comfort (Fig. 14-10). The health care professional who is administering the injection should assess the willingness or ability of the parent to assist by holding the child. If the parent does not wish to do this, another helper should be enlisted. The helper should be instructed to hold the child close on a lap or on the examination table

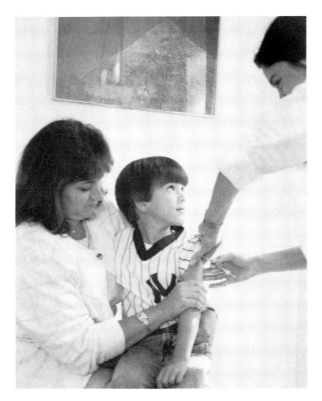

*Figure 14–10. The preschool shot is made easier when accompanied by a firm, gentle hug to help the child hold still.*

"in a big bear hug." The arm to be injected should be held firmly at the elbow so the child cannot move it. The child can be told, "I'm going to give you a shot in your arm. Mommy is going to give you a big bear hug because it's always nice to have a hug when something may hurt a bit."

After the injection has been given, ask the child "Did it hurt? Did it hurt as much as you thought it would?" This gives the child a chance to express feelings about the experience and to be aware of the reality of the shot relative to how it was imagined. The child should never be made to feel shame for the fear, noise, or resistance and should be complimented for any degree of cooperation exhibited. "Hero" stickers are appropriate rewards for a preschooler after any examination, screening, or other medical procedure.

Making up stories, a typical behavior for 4- to 5-year-old children, often leads parents to worry that children may be lying. Making up stories represents children's egocentric thought processes and their interest in "pretend." Parents can help by making sure that children understand what is fact and what is fiction and by not overreacting to "stories."

Preschool children show an increased interest in sexuality, and parents may need help to define what they believe are appropriate and inappropriate expressions of this interest. Parents should be ready to discuss bodies and anatomical differences and provide books or anatomically correct dolls for children to explore at home, while setting limits on public exploration or sex play with other children.

Aggression or shyness may become concerns to parents as children begin to socialize with other children. Nurses can help parents identify children's behavioral styles and prepare them to set appropriate limits on aggression or give encouragement to shy children as they move into new situations at their own pace.

Finally, the health maintenance visit provides an opportunity for parents to ask questions about child-rearing concerns. Health care professionals offer anticipatory guidance at each age by addressing issues that may arise in the coming months. Preparation of the child for a new sibling, consideration of day care or preschool, safety awareness, and readiness for kindergarten are all topics that may be raised by nurses. These questions should direct parents' attention to events that are developmentally expected and stimulate their thinking and information-seeking.

The health maintenance visit, therefore, is an information exchange among the child and parents and the nurse or doctor caring for the child. The health care professional obtains information for the child's data base and identifies any current health or developmental problems. Preventive and treatment measures are instituted as needed. Parents are reassured about the growth and health of their child, given an opportunity to have specific concerns addressed, and made aware of developmental or behavioral issues that may arise in the immediate future. For children, the health maintenance visit is an opportunity to learn about the body, to learn health-promoting practices, and to experience positive feelings of mastery over a situation that is initially somewhat anxiety-producing.

## Dental Care

Preschool children should be taught about preventing dental caries through proper nutrition. Candy, gum, and other foods that cause cavities should be discouraged, whereas nutritious snacks should be encouraged. Dental care, including correct brushing techniques, should be emphasized. Parents should be reminded about the importance of regular dental examinations.

## Recognizing Developmental Tasks

Children are motivated to undertake developmental tasks both from within themselves and from a conscious awareness of the environment. Development is change, and change always creates stress until individuals adjust to the new set of circumstances. Adults caring for children must know the tasks for each age so that they can have realistic expectations and provide experiences and interactions that allow children to master the necessary tasks. Unrealistic expectations or experiences add stress and interfere with mastery. Clarke (1978) describes the tasks of the 3- to 6-year-old as follows:

> *The job of the three to six year old is learning who he is. [He] is focusing on himself in relationship to other people and to his world.*
> *A. He needs to establish his identity in relationship to other people.*
> *B. He needs to expand his imagination and differentiate between reality and fantasy.*
> *C. He needs to acquire information about the world, himself, his body, his sex role.*
> *D. He needs to start to practice socially appropriate behavior.*
>    *The job of the adults caring for the three to six year old is to provide a support system that will continue to nurture him while it allows him to explore his expanding world of people, things, ideas and feelings. (p. 136)*

Developmental affirmations give verbal support to children for accomplishing developmental tasks (Clarke, 1988). Using them helps parents to identify the developmental task their child is engaged with and to focus on the positive aspect of each developmental crisis. When children hear affirmations from adults, they incorporate the positive messages into their self-concept, thereby raising their self-esteem. According to Clarke (1988), the developmental affirmations for ages 3 to 6 are as follows:

> You can explore who you are and find out who other people are.
> You can be powerful and ask for help at the same time.
> You can try out different roles and ways of being powerful.
> You can find out the results of your behavior.
> All of your feelings are OK with me.
> You can learn what is pretend and what is real.
> I love who you are (p. 37).

## Common Concerns

Often, parents come to nurses with concerns about common problems they are experiencing with their children. Nurses can help by listening to the parents' description of the problem, accepting the parents' feelings of frustration or anger, and affirming the positive steps the parents have taken toward solving the problem. Nurses should offer authoritative information about children's developmental stages and needs and can often suggest alternative approaches that parents might use. Reading material recommended by nurses may be welcomed by parents as a source of further information.

## Child Abuse and Neglect

In the United States, an estimated 1.4 million children are physically abused annually (Whitehead, Elvik, Hicks, & Pecoraro, 1987). Types of abuse include physical, sexual, and failure to thrive resulting from neglect. Child abuse exists at all socioeconomic levels, but exact figures are difficult to obtain because of unevenness in reporting: clinics and public agencies report disproportionately more cases than private health care providers (Chow, Durand, Feldman, & Mills, 1984). Two thirds of all physically abused children are under the age of 3. The abuser is usually a caretaker related to the child but may be a male friend of the mother, an unrelated caretaker, or a sibling.

Child abuse and neglect may take many forms, and the causes are complex and deeply rooted in our society as well as in the dynamics of individual families (Hoekelman, Blatman, Friedman, Nelson, & Seigel, 1987). Physical abuse usually happens in a moment of anger when the abuser is under economic, personal, or marital stress. A history of drug or alcohol abuse is often present in the family.

When the parent–child interaction is observed, nurses may note that (1) the parent treats and responds to the child as an object, with no recognition of the child's feelings; (2) the parent shows little knowledge or appreciation of the child's needs; and (3) the child may be more sensitive to the parent's needs than the parent is to the child's. "The behavior of both children and parents reflects a particular form of poverty—that is, a very limited repertoire of responses which does not address their needs adequately and a low estimate of their personal worth" (Bridges, 1978, p. 69). Continuing observation and assessment of children and communication with parents can help prevent child abuse since nurses may be able to identify atypical interaction patterns and provide parents with counseling and support before abuse occurs.

Sometimes characteristics of children predispose them to abuse. Children who have "difficult" temperaments or who are perceived as different (chronically ill, disabled, hyperactive, premature, or smarter than the parents) are often the target of abuse (Chow, Durand, Feldman, & Mills, 1984).

Misunderstanding children's normal developmental needs often contributes to abuse or neglect; there are certain developmental characteristics of preschool children that make them vulnerable (Clarke, 1987). Preschool children are learning to separate fantasy from reality and often tell "stories." Adults who overreact and label this behavior "lying" may psychologically or physically abuse children as a form of punishment.

The child's growing sense of independence and increased verbal ability may lead to "power struggles" with parents. Parents who need to "win" these struggles may lose control and verbally or physically abuse the child.

Unrealistic expectations based on ignorance of child development or on the seeming maturity of children as they imitate words and actions of older children or adults may lead to frustration for parents and abuse for children when these expectations are not met.

As children learn about sexuality, they may engage in sexual play. Parents who overreact to this may be physically or psychologically abusive. Play with sexual overtones may lead to sexual abuse by older children or adults who respond inappropriately to the flirtatious or coquettish behaviors of preschoolers exploring their sexual identity. Adults or older children may expose their genitals or require that preschoolers touch them, or they may touch or fondle the child's genitals. This activity may have some initial pleasurable aspects for the preschooler, especially since the abuser is often someone the child knows and trusts, and the abuser often characterizes the activity as "our game" or "our secret." Sometimes, children are threatened with punishment if they do not keep the secret. Young children are *never* responsible for the inappropriate sexual activity of adults or older children.

Parents may worry about their child's safety when the child begins to spend more time away from them, whether in day care, preschool, or playing away from home. Nurses can help by listening to parents' concerns, teaching them about developmentally appropriate behavior, and helping them teach their preschoolers appropriate measures for protecting themselves. Parents should know who is in charge when their children are in day care, nursery school, or another home and should never leave them unsupervised. Baby-sitters should be chosen with care, and parents should be sensitive to any reports by children that suggest physical, psychological, or sexual abuse. Parents should note and follow up on any unexplained injuries.

Nurses in any setting may be the first individuals to suspect child abuse. Nurses may observe atypical parent–child interaction patterns or overly submissive behavior from children during health maintenance examinations or treatments. When a child who was developing normally deviates from expected developmental norms, he or she should be assessed for abuse. Other clinical signs that suggest child abuse include any injury that cannot be explained, a history of unexplained injuries, multiple bruises on the thighs or upper arms, slap marks, straight-line bruises (as from a belt or ruler), and round burns (as from a cigarette) (Clarke, 1987). Sometimes, behavior changes are a clue that children may be encountering abuse (Elvik, Berkowitz, & Greenberg, 1986; Elvik, 1987). Table 14-3 lists some of the behavioral clues that children might exhibit.

When nurses have supportive relationships with parents, the parents may reveal that they or someone they know may be abusing the child. When nurses become

*Table 14–3. Behavioral Clues of Possible Child Abuse*

Sudden change in eating, sleeping, or bowel habits
Secondary enuresis
Increased separation anxiety
Refusal to attend day care or to go to someone's house
Avoidance of a particular person
Personality changes: withdrawal, hyperactivity, aggressiveness
Excessive masturbation or sexually explicit acts

aware or suspicious of abuse, they have a dual responsibility: to protect the child (see the discussion of legal issues in Chapter 3) and to help the parents learn the skills they need to stop abusing the child and to protect the child from abuse by others. Maintaining a therapeutic, supportive relationship with abusive parents can be crucial in encouraging and assisting them to seek further help (Bridges, 1978). Nurses should offer support and acceptance of the parents as individuals without condoning the abusive behavior. Abusive parents may be referred by their health care provider or mandated by the court to an agency such as Parents Anonymous, which works with parents to help them stop abusing their children. Some local chapters provide a 24-hour hotline that parents may call when they feel that they may hurt their child. The national office of Parents Anonymous is located in Los Angeles and can be reached at (800) 421-0353 for information about the location and services of local chapters. Crisis services, telephone numbers, and locations of agencies concerned with treatment and protection of abused children are also available from Child Help, U.S.A. National Abuse Hotline, (800) 422-4453. Nurses working with families should learn about the local resources for abused children and abusive parents.

Learning how to parent has only recently moved out of the extended family and into the community. In the absence of community programs, nurses who care for children and parents may find themselves in the role of surrogate parents to parents by providing them with information and support for effective parenting and by setting limits on unacceptable actions. If programs do exist, nurses need to motivate and encourage parents to participate in parent education and give emotional support to them as they continue to change their behavior. If no programs exist, nurses may become advocates and may help establish parent help and education groups in the community.

### Sibling Rivalry

During the preschool years, children may experience the arrival of a new sibling. Any change, such as the addition or subtraction of a person from the family unit, creates a temporary imbalance and a realignment of roles to which each family member must adjust. For the young child, the birth of a sibling has elements both of separation and inclusion. Separation from the mother when she is in the hospital may be a major issue for the younger preschooler, who may not have completely resolved separation anxiety.

For siblings, the process of bonding with the new baby is similar to the parental experience. New babies are uniquely attractive (at times) to the preschooler, and most 3- to 5-year-olds readily imitate the loving behavior that they themselves have experienced and that they observe in others. Parents can be encouraged to make firm safety rules about handling the baby, to guide the preschooler in recognizing the kinds of interactions that elicit a positive response from the baby, and to continue to give individual attention to the older child as well as to the new baby. The preschooler should be allowed to express both positive and negative feelings about the new sibling. There are numerous books written for preschoolers about a new baby in the family to help parents help their children make this initial adjustment.

Sibling relationships with stepbrothers and stepsisters in a newly blended family have some unique features. The preschooler who was oldest or youngest in the family may suddenly become a "middle child." This status change may lead to intense sibling rivalry until the new roles are established and accepted.

Some degree of sibling rivalry is always present between siblings as they struggle to express their own identities and to have their own needs met (Fig. 14-11). This rivalry can be positive insofar as the struggle strengthens both children and does not become an "I win, you lose"

*Figure 14–11.    Sibling rivalry is always present to some degree as children struggle to express their identities and have their needs met.*

situation. The degree to which parents allow children to work out their differences, while enforcing rules controlling physical and psychological aggression, is a determining factor in the amount and effects of sibling rivalry.

Some basic recommendations that nurses might give to parents include the following:

1. Know each child as an individual. Be sure you are sincere in valuing each child equally.
2. Communicate this to each child in ways appropriate to the child's age. All young children need body contact, hugging, and cuddling. Affirm all children for being themselves, and affirm their individual and developmental characteristics; do not compare one child's performance or characteristics with those of another.
3. Set family rules about how anger may and may not be expressed. Enforce and model these rules.
4. Plan activities in which all family members can participate together.
5. Allow each child some privacy from the other: the child's own room, toy shelf, or some "unsharable" toys. Children must feel the sense of possession before they can learn to share.
6. Provide a daily period of one-to-one time for parent and child. "Quality time" is when the adult's attention is focused on the child in a positive way, sharing an activity of the child's choice and communicating the adult's enjoyment of this special time (Clarke, 1987).

### Fears

Fears arise from real encounters with threatening events or from children's own mental images. Fears are also learned by imitation of another child or of an adult model. As preschool children venture more on their own, encounters with elements in the environment may frighten them. For example, dogs, especially large ones, are very threatening to a 3-year-old who can be knocked over easily by a friendly or exuberant dog. Even the loud, rough-and-tumble play of older children may be threatening to a small child venturing too close or unsupported by the presence of a parent. Fear can be triggered by the emotional reactions of adults, especially if they are loud and have physical components, such as fist-shaking or hitting, even if these actions are not directed at the child. Fear can be learned from parents, siblings, or other models. For example, Amy was unconcerned during thunderstorms until she was 5. Her 2-year-old brother began to wake and cry whenever a storm occurred; soon Amy, too, began to cry and say that she was afraid of the storm. Similarly, fears of animals or situations can be learned when a child observes fearful reactions or verbalizations by others.

Usually, young children express fear by some degree of avoidance behavior. Later, angry or aggressive behavior may emerge to substitute for fear. In particular, boys often are not allowed or encouraged to express fear. When a child indicates fear, it is helpful to accept this feeling by using words that may be imitated, such as "You are scared by the loud noise the thunder makes." If the child's feeling is discounted or belittled by having a parent say, "Big boys aren't afraid of dogs [or needles or the like]," the child may develop the habit of denying real feelings and substituting an aggressive front as a cover-up. A feeling that is denied is never mastered.

If a fear has developed as a result of some experience, an adult can help by accepting the child's feeling and gradually reintroducing the child to the feared object. This can be done by reading stories or looking at pictures that encourage the child to talk about the experience and to begin to develop a sense of mastery. When the child is ready, the adult can provide support while bringing the child into contact with the feared object or experience in a carefully controlled situation. The effect of modeling cannot be overemphasized. If the adult displays a calm, realistic attitude toward fearful stimuli, the child will imitate this and draw confidence from this demeanor.

Children of 4 or 5 are prone to fears generated by their own imaginings. Mental images of objects or events may exaggerate the child's fears and powerlessness. The adult may respond by telling the child, "You have really imagined a scary thing. What do you imagine you could do?" This encourages the child to arrive at a solution while making it clear that it is "make believe."

The adult may choose to reinforce reality by stating calmly, "There is no monster [animal, storm, fire, or whatever] here." The adult, then, should not reinforce the fantasy by searching in closets or under the bed to disprove the presence of ghosts or monsters. Encouraging the child to relate the dream or fantasy will give the adult a clue to any underlying concern, which can then be addressed directly. This allows the child to experience mental image as words and thus to gain a sense of control.

Adults caring for children should be aware of the special vulnerability of preschool children to fear because of their size, their exposure to the world beyond the home, and their new ability to form mental symbols that carry great power for them.

Nurses can help parents to identify the origin of the child's fear and to decide what interventions are appropriate. In particular, nurses should stress the reassuring effect on the child when the parent or another child models confidence in facing a feared situation or object. Nurses should show parents how to avoid shaming or belittling the child for being afraid while, at the same time, not reinforcing the fear by overreacting to it.

## Temper Tantrums

Three-year-old children still have temper tantrums, but as they grow and begin to use and master language skills, they begin to use words rather than actions to express their frustrations or anger. For example, 3-year-olds, when frustrated, may throw themselves to the floor and cover their heads in an abbreviated form of the temper displays exhibited at the age of 2. The child may repeat strongly, "I want it, I want it," seeming to have lost track of what had been originally denied. By the age of 3, children occasionally tell their mother that they are "cross" about something. Frequent temper tantrums after the age of 3 may indicate too much stress and frustration in the child's life.

Nurses can show parents how to manage temper tantrums and encourage appropriate expression of anger in preschool children. Temper displays often occur in public places as the child becomes frustrated with having to conform to expectations of "appropriate" behavior. In these situations, it is usually best for the parent to take the child out of the situation temporarily or permanently if the child cannot regain control. For example, shopping expeditions are often prime times for temper tantrums since children become bored or frustrated by restrictions on their activity and explorations. The nurse can suggest to parents that they plan in advance any expedition such as shopping and keep the activity brief when young children must go along. Parents should be encouraged to clearly tell the child what behavior is expected during the expedition and to praise and talk to the child when the expected behavior is demonstrated. Parents can encourage the child to participate by putting nonbreakable items in the cart or by pointing to familiar items from the shopping list. The parent should tell the child in advance whether or not a toy or treat will be allowed. If the child loses control and cannot regain it in 1 or 2 minutes, it is advisable to remove the child from the situation.

Management of temper displays in the preschooler is directed toward helping the child substitute words for actions. The temper behavior should not be rewarded by attention. The child should be protected from injury and prevented from hurting others or damaging property. Adults should take care to protect themselves from being kicked or butted. The child should be taken onto the adult's lap with an explanation such as, "I understand that you are angry and I won't let you hurt yourself or someone else, so I will hold you until you can calm down."

An acceptable activity such as hitting a pillow or a "spanking stool" with a ruler can be offered to the child who needs a physical discharge for feelings. At the same time, adults should begin to supply words for children to imitate as they learn to express their feelings in words. For example, the adult might say, "I can see that you are mad because I won't let you play outside right now."

If frequent temper tantrums continue past age 3, the nurse should help the parent review the child's routine to determine possible sources of stress. If stress might be a cause of the continued temper tantrums, corrections should be made to the environment if possible. An effective stress reliever for young children is quality time with the parent each day (Fig. 14-12). This should be 15 to 20 minutes of time when the child is the focus of the adult's positive attention and the activity is something they both enjoy.

### Bed-Wetting

*Nocturnal enuresis,* or bed-wetting, is a problem for many families of preschoolers. Occasional lapses in control can be attributed to too much fluid intake, illness, or environmental stress. *Primary enuresis* refers to a child who has never attained consistent dryness. About 15% of 5-year-olds have nocturnal enuresis. *Secondary enuresis* occurs in children who have previously been bladder-trained for at least 6 months and who then lose control. A family history may reveal that one or both parents of an enuretic child may have experienced delayed bladder control, possibly as late as into adolescence.

Parents and children should be helped to understand that the child is not aware of the bed-wetting and is not doing it to misbehave or to upset the parents (Ferber, 1985b). If the boy or girl is under 5, a "wait and see" attitude is appropriate in the absence of signs of urinary tract infection or obstruction, diabetes mellitus, or neuromuscular abnormality.

To minimize disruption to the family's sleep, the parents may restrict fluids after dinner, have the child void before going to sleep, or wake the child to void before the parents' bedtime. The child's mattress should be well protected by a waterproof cover, and the bedclothing and the child's sleepwear should be easy to change and launder. These measures have not been shown to hasten re-

mission, but the parents' sense of efficacy may be enhanced if they can "do something." It is important, however, that the parents' need to "do something" does not contribute to conflict or to a lowering of the child's self-esteem.

The nurse can offer reassurance about the probability of a resolution to the problem as the child grows older. It is usually encouraging to parents that each year after age 5, 15% of children who are enuretic experience a spontaneous cure. The nurse should help parents find the most efficient solution for the problem of frequent bed changes and should acknowledge the difficulty in managing this problem.

Bed-wetting after the age of 5 or 6 becomes more of a problem for the child's self-esteem even when the parents are supportive and nonblaming. Behavioral and pharmacological approaches can be used by the older child's primary care provider to help achieve control.

School-aged children with decreased bladder capacity have been helped by participating in a program of bladder-training. This program takes 6 months and requires the motivation and cooperation of the child. At a set time during the day, the child consciously refrains from voiding for as long as possible, while drinking a large amount of fluid during the same period. Positive reinforcement is given after every night that the child remains dry. With continued participation, functional bladder capacity increases.

Conditioning or waking devices have a 50% to 75% success rate among older children who agree to use them. The device consists of a pad that is placed on the bed under the child. When the pad becomes wet with urine, an

*Figure 14–12.   "Quality time" is a potent stress reliever for both parent and child.*

electrical circuit is completed, triggering a loud alarm that wakes the child. When this device is used, children learn to waken to the cue of a full bladder. The average time needed to achieve control is 16 weeks (Novello & Novello, 1987). This method requires that the child sleeps alone and is willing to cooperate. Skin rashes and ulceration have been reported, so it is essential to inspect the child's skin. No complications related to the electrical nature of the device have been reported (Novello & Novello, 1987).

Pharmacological management in the past frequently included the use of the antidepressant imipramine hydrochloride. A highly successful new treatment regimen is the use of desmopressin acetate nasal spray, a synthetic analog of antidiuretic hormone (ADH), which provides physiological control of night-time production of urine in children 6 years of age and older. The spray is administered at bedtime. Treatment studies show 70% of patients are completely dry after 4 weeks of therapy. After the desired level of response is reached, the dosage is titrated down and discontinued.

## Accident Prevention

According to the National Safety Council, the leading causes of death in children under the age of 4 are motor vehicles, drowning, fire, suffocation, poisoning, and ingestion (National Safety Council, 1988). As with the younger age group, the responsibility for prevention rests primarily with adult structuring and supervision of the environment to remove or reduce hazards. However, since preschool children spend more time moving about on their own in places other than home, it is necessary to begin teaching them to care for their own safety.

Tricycle riding is a major activity beginning at age 3, and this brings the child into contact with traffic. Traffic and pedestrian safety is taught by modeling and instruction. The 3-year-old should be walked across streets and taught to stop and look before crossing a driveway on a tricycle. The play area should be carefully circumscribed to avoid driveways, parking lots, and streets except when directly supervised by an adult. Simple rules, such as "hold my hand when walking through a parking lot," "walk, don't run at street crossings," "no crossing streets without a grown-up," and "stop and look both ways before crossing," should be modeled and verbalized until the child has incorporated them. By age 5, the actual physical control (hand holding) may not be necessary in ordinary circumstances, and the child should be reliable in respecting play boundaries.

All states now have automobile restraint laws for children under 10 years of age. Adults should model responsible behavior by wearing seat belts and by being sure that children wear the appropriate restraining device properly.

In 1984, 568 children under the age of 4 and 532 between the ages of 5 and 14 drowned (National Safety Council, 1988). Adults must be aware of the water hazards in their home and neighborhood and provide supervision at all times when children are in or near water, whether it is a bathtub, wading pool, or larger body of water. Adults can teach children to respect, but not fear, the water by entering into water activities with them and teaching basic water safety by example. All participants in water sports or boating activities should wear approved life jackets.

Fire prevention is adults' responsibility. Matches, lighters, and open flames should be carefully supervised and restricted from children's use and exploration. Smoke detectors save lives by giving early warning of a fire in the home. Parents should be sure that a sufficient number of smoke detectors are properly installed and checked routinely to be certain that they function properly. Each family should have a fire evacuation plan for their home and should conduct routine fire drills to teach each member what to do in case a fire breaks out. Some community fire companies offer stickers to place on children's bedroom windows to help firefighters identify where to go first to assist young children. Children need to be taught how to handle hot liquids, to stay away from open flames, and how to "drop and roll" if their clothing catches fire.

Toys and play activities constitute several kinds of hazard that might lead to suffocation. Plastic bags (especially the thin, cleaner-bag variety) are never appropriate playthings and should not be used to waterproof a child's bed. Parents should immediately knot and discard any bag large enough to go over a child's head. Toys should be routinely inspected for parts small enough to be aspirated, and the child should be taught not to put small objects into the mouth. Ropes and cords are not safe playthings for young children. Drapery or blind cords should be secured out of the child's reach; the child should be taught never to loop a cord around his or another child's neck. Young children should eat while sitting still and should be taught to chew food thoroughly. "Don't talk with your mouth full" has as much to do with preventing aspiration as it does with politeness! The doors of discarded refrigerators and freezers should be removed to prevent trapping a child who might crawl inside.

Because of their tendency to imitate observed adult behavior and to engage in "let's pretend" activities, preschoolers are vulnerable to poisoning. Most poisonings occur in children under 5 years of age, with a peak incidence at age 2. Poisoning occurs when children ingest, inhale, or have external contact with toxic substances. The poison is often out of its usual place, not in its original container, or not stored securely when the child comes in contact with it.

To prevent accidental poisoning, all medications, cleaning products, and other chemicals should be stored out of children's reach, and children should be instructed that these items are not to be eaten. Adults need to take special care in how they model medication use and to be sure that children understand that they should not take any medication unless given to them by the parents or regular care-giver. Medications should *never* be described as "candy." Certain garden plants can be toxic to small children, so they should be taught never to use plant parts as "pretend" food.

Cough and cold mixtures, acetaminophen, and iron preparations are among the most common prescription or nonprescription medications ingested by children (American Academy of Pediatrics, Committee on Accident and Poison Prevention, 1983). Any medication kept in the household is a potential toxin if taken by a young child. All such preparations should be stored with childproof caps in a secure location out of the reach of children.

If children ingest nonfood substances, nurses or parents need to assess the potential toxicity. Local or regional Poison Control Centers can supply information about the toxicity of specific substances or classes of products as well as immediate measures to be taken. Parents should keep the telephone number of the nearest Poison Control Center easily accessible with other emergency numbers. First aid measures for poisoning can be life-saving. If the substance has been inhaled, the child should immediately be moved to fresh air; if the substance has come into contact with the eye or skin, the area should immediately be rinsed with water, and medical follow-up is advisable. Ingestion of a toxin requires medical advice, management, and follow-up.

When children drink potential poisons, nurses should ascertain the substance ingested, the estimated amount, the time since ingestion, the age and weight of the child, and the child's immediate condition. Children who are unconscious or who are in respiratory distress should be transported immediately to an emergency facility.

If the child's general condition is satisfactory, measures may be instituted to dilute the toxin before going to an emergency facility. If a strong acid or alkali has been swallowed, milk or water should be given immediately to dilute the substance. Gastric lavage, performed in an emergency room, is preferable to emesis in order to prevent further damage to the upper gastrointestinal tract.

For other ingested substances, emesis is desirable. Syrup of ipecac should be available in the home, day care location, and any other location where children are present. Syrup of ipecac is supplied in 15-mL or 30-mL vials. The usual dose for a child under age 10 is 15 mL, followed by 6 to 8 oz of water. A larger quantity of water may cause the pylorus to open, resulting in wider distribution of the toxin (American Academy of Pediatrics, Committee on Accident and Poison Prevention, 1983). Milk is not recommended. After administration of syrup of ipecac, emesis usually takes place within 15 to 20 minutes. The dose of ipecac may be repeated once if emesis does not occur within 30 minutes. Syrup of ipecac should be stored carefully, as with all medications, to prevent its accidental use. During this period, the child's state of consciousness and respiratory status should be monitored constantly. When emesis occurs, the child should be supported in a position that protects against aspiration. Vomited material should be saved for laboratory examination if the child's condition is serious or if the substance is unknown or highly toxic.

If the situation requires, emergency room treatment includes airway maintenance, gastric lavage and catharsis to remove the toxin, or measures to neutralize the action of the toxin. A specific antidote is administered if the toxin is known, or activated charcoal may be used if the antidote is not known. Activated charcoal adsorbs and inactivates many poisons but should not be used for strong acids or alkalis.

Management of poisoned children requires careful assessment of the child's condition as well as specific knowledge of the toxins and antidotes. Acetaminophen, commonly present in preschoolers' homes, is often the cause of accidental poisoning of young children. An overdose of acetaminophen may lead to liver damage. During the first 24 hours after the overdose, only a general malaise, drowsiness, or vomiting may appear. Other symptoms may not appear for up to 5 days after ingestion. Emesis or gastric lavage, followed by the specific antidote (N-acetylcysteine) for blood levels of acetaminophen greater than 200 $\mu$g/mL, at 4-hour intervals after ingestion, is the recommended treatment (American Academy of Pediatrics, Committee on Accident and Poison Prevention, 1983).

Salicylates (aspirin and aspirin-containing compounds, methyl salicylate, oil of wintergreen) cause acute symptoms of deep rapid respirations that lead first to respiratory alkalosis, then to metabolic acidosis, and then to vomiting, which causes dehydration. Treatment includes removal of ingested material by early emesis or gastric lavage, followed by careful monitoring and supportive treatment for acid–base imbalance.

Iron is highly toxic to children, yet it is available in many homes in children's vitamin preparations or in preparations intended for adults. As few as 10 ferrous sulfate tablets (300 mg) may provide the minimum lethal dose for a child (600 mg of elemental iron; American Academy of Pediatrics, Committee on Accident and Poison Prevention, 1983). Severe symptoms may follow ingestion of 200 to 400 mg of elemental iron. Immediate symptoms (30–60 min after ingestion) may include epigastric pain, hematemesis, and shock; later (after 12–24 h) symptoms may include delayed shock, liver damage, metabolic acidosis, fever, leukocytosis, and coma. Children can be given milk and observed at home if it is certain that they took less than half the minimal toxic dose and are asymptomatic. If it is uncertain how large a dose the child took or if symptoms are present, emesis or gastric lavage and close medical observation are indicated.

### Lead Poisoning

Acute or chronic lead poisoning (*plumbism*) is another concern for preschool-aged children. Since lead has no biological value, the ideal blood level is 0 μg/dL. In a study conducted between 1976 and 1980, the mean blood lead level in preschool children in the United States was about 16 μg/dL. Behavioral and learning difficulties have been associated with blood levels under 35 μg/dL (American Academy of Pediatrics, Committee on Environmental Hazards & Committee on Accident and Poison Prevention, 1987). The highest blood levels were associated with low family income and were found in densely populated urban areas. Black children had higher mean blood lead levels than others (Mahaffey, Annest, Roberts, & Murphy, 1982).

Urban areas contain more sources for lead: old homes with lead-based paint and old lead plumbing, airborne lead from automobile exhaust, and perhaps a concentration of industrial sources. Improperly disposed of lead batteries or industrial waste containing lead may leach lead into the soil of play areas. *Any* environment that contains one or more of these sources is unsafe, whether in urban or rural areas. Nutritional deficiency, especially iron deficiency, increases children's risk of plumbism. *Pica* (the ingestion of materials not fit for consumption, including dirt, clay, ashes, plaster, or paint) or age-related oral behaviors increase children's vulnerability. Even children who do not ingest foreign substances but who live in areas with high concentrations of lead are at high risk.

Some sources of lead are unique to certain groups or cultures that use food containers or cooking utensils glazed with lead or cosmetics or folk remedies containing lead salts (Centers for Disease Control, 1985). Children of workers in lead-based industries are exposed to lead particles in their parents' clothing, shoes, or automobiles.

The manufacture and use of lead-based paint for interiors has declined since the 1950s, but lead-based exterior paint was available until the mid-1970s, and lead-based paint for maritime, outdoor equipment, and machinery continues to be available (American Academy of Pediatrics, Committee on Environmental Hazards & Committee on Accident and Poison Prevention, 1987). The process of removing old lead-based paint can release a considerable amount of dust or particles that contain lead. Young children and pregnant women should stay out of homes where lead is being removed until all loose paint is removed and the area is thoroughly vacuumed and wet-mopped.

Lead poisoning is preventable. The average blood levels of children in the United States decreased between 1976 and 1980 (Annest, Pirkle, Makuc, Neese, Bayse, & Kovar, 1983), largely due to the replacement of leaded gasoline with unleaded fuel. The American Academy of Pediatrics recommends mandatory reporting of lead poisoning in every state and, for primary prevention, encourages the inspection for and removal of lead from old housing. The Academy deplores the use of children as biological markers of unsafe housing (American Academy of Pediatrics, Committee on Environmental Hazards & Committee on Accident and Poisoning Prevention, 1987).

The American Academy of Pediatrics recommends annual or semiannual screening of children (through the age of 6) who have significant predisposing factors or who live in high-risk environments. Ideally, all children should be screened between 9 and 12 months of age. All children's blood lead levels are higher between May and October, so screening should be done during those months (Centers for Disease Control, 1985).

Lead affects several body systems. "Lead lines" can be found on the gums and in the metaphyseal plates of long bones, where lead interferes with the deposit of calcium during bone growth. Lead affects the gastrointestinal system and hemoglobin synthesis and can damage the kidneys. Central nervous system damage is seen in symptoms that range from restlessness and irritability to irreversible learning impairment and seizures, even at relatively low levels of exposure (American Academy of Pediatrics, Committee on Environmental Hazards & Committee on Accident and Poison Prevention, 1987).

Early symptoms appear in the first 3 to 6 weeks of exposure, are of insidious onset, and include anorexia, apathy, anemia, hyperirritability, and loss of newly learned skills. As blood lead levels rise, acute encephalopathy follows. Gross ataxia, persistent vomiting, lethargy, and stupor may progress to convulsions and coma. With prolonged exposure children may exhibit hyperkinesis, seizure disorders, and mental retardation.

The erythrocyte porphyrin level is a useful screening test to determine both iron deficiency and the presence of lead. Children found to have an elevated erythrocyte porphyrin level (greater than 50 μg/dL) should be further evaluated, including environmental assessment, a lead level from venous blood, a complete blood count, radiographic studies to detect lead deposits in the skeleton or particles in the gastrointestinal tract, and a lead mobilization test to determine if the child will respond to chelation therapy (Chow, Durand, Feldman, & Mills, 1984).

*Chelation* is the process of binding lead to other molecules that can be excreted in the urine. Calcium disodium edetate is the chelating agent of choice for lead removal. The calcium in the salt is replaced by the lead circulating in the body. This therapy is parenteral and is given over several days. If necessary, a second course may be given after an interim period of 4 or more days. Chelation therapy is potentially damaging to the kidneys; kidney function tests (blood urea nitrogen or serum creatinine) should be done to rule out occult kidney damage before therapy is started. Children should be removed from the lead-containing environment until the lead has been removed, and siblings should be screened.

Nurses play a role at all stages of prevention and treatment of lead poisoning. Interviews with parents, observation of children, and knowledge of the environment can alert health care professionals to the need for screening or further evaluation. Nurses should teach parents about the hazards of lead and should enlist their assistance in monitoring their homes and neighborhoods. Nurses play an important role in chelation therapy by supporting the child and family through painful injections, possible separation from home during hospitalization, and disruption of home life. Nurses should be advocates for better housing and safe disposal of lead waste.

### Discipline

Discipline for preschoolers is directed at teaching acceptable behavior rather than at punishment for misbehavior. Adults should communicate their expectations to preschoolers in simple rules such as "no hitting another child." They should then offer two acceptable alternatives, such as "you may tell the person that you feel angry or you may punch this pillow instead." It is important that the child learn that there are consequences for not following a rule and that they will be carried through by the adult. For example, if a child continues an activity, having been warned by the adult that it is unacceptable, the adult might suggest a "timeout." "Timeout" is a calming device, not a punishment (Clarke, 1987). Timeout for a child under age 5 is generally 5 minutes; 10-minute timeouts are appropriate for older children. Consequences should be immediate for the young child; they should also be appropriate to the situation and in proportion to the infraction.

Both parents should agree on the rules they will enforce and should agree to back up the other when a consequence has been invoked. Parents should talk together about how they wish to discipline their children and think ahead of "things to do instead of hitting" to help them handle their own anger at children's misbehavior (Clarke, 1978).

### Sex Education

Many parents are concerned about the exploratory sexual behavior of young children aged 3, 4, and 5. Exploration and manipulation of their own sexual organs is normal and expected behavior for young children. When children become aware of differences in anatomy between boys and girls, it is normal for this curiosity to extend to their playmates of either sex. Playing "doctor," peeking at other children in bathrooms, or undressing with other children is often a manifestation of this interest. It is desirable that children be taught culturally approved behavior in the area of sex exploration, both to help them channel their curiosity in acceptable ways and to protect them against sexual exploitation by others.

In families, young children of both sexes often bathe or undress together and so have a chance to have their curiosity about bodies satisfied in a routine way. Children should be taught that all parts of their bodies are important and that some parts of the body—the parts covered by their bathing suits—are personal and private and that these parts should not be shared with other children or adults. Children who do not have routine opportunities to observe anatomical differences in others can be shown "anatomically correct" dolls or picture books written to help them learn.

Preschool children also imitate and experiment with sexual language they may hear. Teaching children the correct anatomical terms, asking that they use the correct terms instead of slang, and setting limits on when and with whom such topics are appropriate help children learn socially approved behavior.

Children of 3 or 4 may be curious about "where babies come from" but are limited by their preoperational thinking to a spatial explanation ("from a store" or "from tummies") or a manufactured explanation ("You just make the baby first. You put some eyes on it. You put the head on, and hair, some hair, all curls. You make it with head stuff . . .") (Bibace & Walsh, 1981, p. 14). Their inability to interpret the world except as they have experienced it (egocentrism) leads them into the "digestive fallacy," and they "believe that babies are conceived by swallowing and born by elimination" (Bernstein & Cowan, 1981, p. 14).

Local libraries and bookstores contain a variety of educational materials designed to assist parents in educating their children about sex. Parents should be advised to carefully select material that is appropriate to the child's developmental stage.

## Parenting Development

Parenting development is part of the ongoing development of the adult (Cataldo, 1987). Erikson (1963) identified two stages of adult development that may coincide with the childbearing and rearing years. Parents of preschoolers may be encountering their own crises of intimacy versus isolation and generation versus stagnation. Further, Levin (1985) proposes "If we (adults) have failed to integrate or resolve a childhood trauma or meet a need in the past, our (the adult's) current reality may become charged and contaminated affecting our actions and experiences" (p. 12). Levin states, however, that childhood stages of development are reexperienced (recycled) by the adult as part of a "normal, natural process, part of the unfolding of life itself" (p. 13). Clarke (1978), a parent educator, says that "Parents are triggered to re-experience their own early stages of growth as they watch their children go through each growing stage. Each recycling is a new opportunity to resolve any developmental tasks unsuccessfully completed earlier" (p. 272). Parents, then, continue to develop as individuals at the same time that they must learn new skills to meet the needs of their preschoolers.

Tasks for parents of preschoolers include the following:

- To assist the child in acquiring the ability to use words to make needs known and to express thoughts and feelings

- To assist the child in moving into peer relationships
- To assist the child in learning to separate fantasy from reality
- To be aware of the model parents present and the fact that children will imitate the parents
- To set realistic expectations and limits for the child and communicate these to the child
- To assist the child to realize and enjoy his or her own gender identity
- To assist the child in learning about cause and effect in the object world and in relationships
- To convey positive regard and delight for the child in words and actions

Just as preschool children need peer relationships, parents also need peer groups. Whether formal or informal, parental peer groups help them learn about the developmental characteristics of the 3- to 5-year-old, share solutions to problems, and gain support for their own personal growth.

Parents of preschoolers become aware of the new skills required of them. Many need to improve their ability to interact verbally with their children and to use words to express their own feelings and expectations to the child. They seek information about effective ways of discipline and examine their own beliefs about spanking and the role of punishment in shaping their children's behavior. Parents are concerned about society's changing sex roles and how this will affect their children's gender identification. They are concerned about explaining birth, death, and divorce and offering emotional support to their children during these and other life events.

As 3- and 4-year-olds begin to be responsible for more self-care activities and to relate to their peers, the quality of the relationship with the parents (particularly the mother) changes, and parents may experience a sense of separation and loss. Entrance of the child into formal school or preschool may be perceived by the parents as a new opportunity to expand their own horizons or may be experienced as a threat or loss.

In some segments of our society, parents, wishing to give their child "the best," hurry preschoolers into formal instructional programs to learn verbal or motor skills. Parents often begin these programs when the children are 3 or 4 or even younger. The parents' intent to provide enriched experiences for the preschooler instead becomes detrimental since they are offering instruction beyond the child's cognitive level (Howes, 1989).

Parents need to be aware of the characteristics of the mental and emotional processes of the 3- to 6-year-old so that they may value the unique way in which preschoolers think, feel, and learn. Parents need to appreciate that the curiosity and love of learning fostered at this age are an important foundation for the formal learning that is appropriate to the next cognitive and psychosocial stage.

## Summary

In the years from ages 3 to 6, children undergo significant changes. The most profound of these are not visible but must be observed by talking with the children and eliciting what they think and feel. Continuing maturation of the brain lays down new pathways, freeing children from purely sensorimotor ways of exploring and understanding the world. Instead, they become capable of using mental symbols. They learn language at an astonishing rate by imitation and by initiating information-seeking in the many "why?" questions they ask. Their verbal ability often misleads adults into believing that children are more cognitively and emotionally mature than is the case.

Cognitively, children use preoperational modes of thought that are characterized by egocentricity, centration, attention to states rather than processes, and irreversibility.

Preschoolers conceptualize various body functions and illness in ways that reflect their preoperational mode of thinking. Adults caring for young children need to understand these ways so that they may address concerns and offer information in ways that can be assimilated.

Play is central to the life of preschoolers. Through this self-directed activity, children practice complex social and motor routines and experience the joy that initiating and mastering activities can bring. Illness or hospitalization often interrupt the child's play and add to stress by denying an outlet for feelings. Participating with a child in play helps to create rapport between the nurse and the child; it also may help the nurse to assess inner concerns that the child may not be able to verbalize but that may become apparent directly or symbolically through play activities.

The child learns by direct experience, by imitation, and by experiencing consequences of self-initiated behavior. Adults are important to preschoolers as sources of nurturance and protection, as models for behavior, and as sources of information.

## References

American Academy of Pediatrics. (1985). *Guidelines for health supervision.* Evanston, IL: American Academy of Pediatrics.

American Academy of Pediatrics, Committee on Nutrition. (1986). Prudent life-style for children: Dietary fat and cholesterol. *Pediatrics, 78,* 521–525.

American Academy of Pediatrics, Committee on Accident and Poison Prevention. (1983). *Handbook of common poisonings in children.* Evanston, IL: American Academy of Pediatrics.

American Academy of Pediatrics, Committee on Environmental Hazards and Committee on Accident and Poison Prevention. (1987). Statement on childhood lead poisoning. *Pediatrics, 79,* 457–465.

American Academy of Pediatrics, Committee on Nutrition. (1989). Indications for cholesterol testing in children. *Pediatrics, 78,* 141–142.

Annest, J. L., Pirkle, J. L., Makuc, D., Neese, J. W., Bayse, D. D., & Kovar, M. G. (1983) Chronological trend in blood lead levels between 1976 and 1980. *New England Journal of Medicine, 308,* 1373–1377.

Barnard, K. E., & Erickson, M. L. (1976). *Teaching children with developmental problems* (2nd ed.). St. Louis: C. V. Mosby.

Bernstein, A. C., & Cowan, P. A. (1981). Children's conceptions of birth and sexuality. In R. Bibace & M. E. Walsh (Eds.). *Children's conceptions of health, illness, and bodily functions.* San Francisco: Jossey-Bass.

Bibace, R., & Walsh, M. E. (Eds.). (1981). *Children's conceptions of health, illness, and bodily functions.* San Francisco: Jossey-Bass.

Biehler, R. F. (1976). *Child development: An introduction.* Boston: Houghton Mifflin.

Bradley, R. H., & Caldwell, B. M. (1988). Using the HOME inventory to assess the family environment. *Pediatric Nursing, 14,* 97–102.

Brazelton, T. B. (1984). *To listen to a child.* Reading, MA: Addison-Wesley.

Bridges, C. L. (1978). The nurse's evaluation. In B. D. Schmitt (Ed.). *The child protection team handbook.* New York: Garland STPM Press.

Cataldo, C. Z. (1987). *Parent education for early childhood.* New York: Teacher's College Press.

Centers for Disease Control. (1985). *Preventing lead poisoning in young children.* Atlanta, GA: U.S. Department of Health and Human Services.

Chow, M. P., Durand, B. A., Feldman, M. N., & Mills, M. A. (1984). *Handbook of pediatric primary care* (2nd ed.). New York: John Wiley & Sons.

Clarke, J. (1978). *Self esteem: A family affair.* Minneapolis: Winston Press.

Clarke, J. (Ed.) (1987). *Help! For parents of children 3 to 6 years old.* San Francisco: Harper & Row.

Clarke, J. (1988). *Affirmation ovals: 139 ways to give and get affirmations.* Plymouth, MN: Daisy Press.

Coren, S., & Halpern, D. F. (1991). Left-handedness: A marker for decreased survival fitness. *Psychological Bulletin, 109,* 90–106.

Cratty, B. J. (1986). *Perceptual and motor development in infants and children* (3rd ed.). Englewood Cliffs, NJ: Prentice-Hall.

Crider, C. (1981). Children's conception of the body interior. In R. Bibace & M. E. Walsh (Eds.). *Children's conceptions of health, illness and bodily functions.* San Francisco: Jossey-Bass.

Elvik, S. L. (1987). From disclosure to court: The facets of sexual abuse. *Journal of Pediatric Health Care, 1,* 136–140.

Elvik, S. L., Berkowitz, C. D., & Greenberg, C. S. (1986). Child sexual abuse: The role of the PNP. *Nurse Practitioner— The American Journal of Primary Health Care, 11,* 15–22.

Erikson, E. (1963). *Childhood and society* (2nd ed.). New York: W. W. Norton.

Ferber, R. (1985a). Sleep, sleeplessness, and sleep disruptions in infants and young children. *Annals of Clinical Research, 17,* 227–234.

Ferber, R. (1985b). *Solve your child's sleep problem.* New York: Simon & Schuster.

Ginsburg, H. A., & Opper, S. (1979). *Piaget's theory of intellectual development.* Englewood Cliffs, NJ: Prentice-Hall.

Hoekelman, R. A., Blatman, S., Friedman, S. B., Nelson, N. M., & Seigel, H. M. (Eds.). (1987). *Primary pediatric care.* St. Louis: C. V. Mosby.

Howes, C. (1989). Pressuring children to learn versus developmentally appropriate education. *Journal of Pediatric Health Care, 3,* 181–186.

Johnson, P. (1984). Getting enough to grow on. *American Journal of Nursing, 84,* 336–339.

Kohlberg, L. (1984). *Essays on moral development: Vol. 2, The psychology of moral development.* San Francisco: Harper & Row.

Kotelchuck, M., & Richmond, J. B. (1987). Head start: Evolution of a successful comprehensive child development program. *Pediatrics, 79,* 441–444.

Lansky, V. (1978). *The taming of the C.A.N.D.Y. monster.* Wayzata, MN: Meadowbrook Press.

Levin, P. (1985). *Becoming the way we are.* Wenatchee, WA: Directed Media.

Lippe, B. M. (1988). Short stature in children: Evaluation and management. *Journal of Pediatric Health Care, 1,* 313–322.

Mahaffey, K. R., Annest, J. L., Roberts, J., & Murphy, R. S. (1982). National estimates of blood lead levels: United States 1976–1980: Associated with selected demographic and socioeconomic factors. *New England Journal of Medicine, 307,* 573–579.

Maier, H. W. (1969). *Three theories of child development* (rev. ed.). New York: Harper & Row.

McWilliams, M. (1986). *Nutrition for the growing years* (4th ed.). New York: John Wiley & Sons.

National Safety Council. (1988). *Accident facts.* Chicago: National Safety Council.

Novello, A. C., & Novello, J. R. (1987). Enuresis. *Pediatric Clinics of North America, 34,* 719–733.

Piaget, J. (1962). *Play, dreams and imitation in childhood.* New York: W. W. Norton.

Pitcher, E. G., & Schultz, L. H. (1983). *Boys and girls at play.* South Hadley, MA: Beigin & Garvey.

Sullivan, L. (1988). How effective is preschool vision, hearing, and developmental screening? *Pediatric Nursing, 14,* 181–183.

Whitehead, P., Elvik, S., Hicks, M., & Pecoraro, N. (1987). NAP-NAP policy statement on child abuse and neglect. *Journal of Pediatric Health Care, 1,* 42.

## Bibliography

American Academy of Pediatrics, Committee on Accident and Poison Prevention. (1987). *Injury control for children and youth.* Evanston, IL: American Academy of Pediatrics.

Bee, H. (1989). *The developing child* (5th ed.). New York: Harper & Row.

Calderone, M. S., & Johnson, E. W. (1981). *The family book about sexuality.* New York: Harper & Row.

Castiglia, P. (1987). Growth and development. *Journal of Pediatric Health Care, 1,* 48–49.

Castiglia, P. (1987). Speech-language development. *Journal of Pediatric Health Care, 1,* 165–167.

Castiglia, P. T., & Petrini, M. A. (1985). Selecting a developmental screening tool. *Pediatric Nursing, 11,* 8–17.

Cohen, L. J. (1987). Bibliotherapy. *Journal of Psychosocial Nursing, 25,* 20–24.

Elkind, D. (1987). *Miseducation: Preschoolers at risk.* New York: Alfred A. Knopf.

Erickson, M. L. (1976). *Assessment and management of developmental changes in children.* St. Louis: C. V. Mosby.

Goodnow, J. (1977). *Children drawing.* Cambridge, MA: Harvard University Press.

Hurley, A., & Whelan, E. G. (1988). Cognitive development and children's perception of pain. *Pediatric Nursing, 14,* 21–24.

Lee, E. J., & Fowler, M. D. (1986). Merely child's play? Developmental work and playthings. *Journal of Pediatric Nursing, 1,* 260–270.

McCowan, D. E. (1984). Moral development in children. *Pediatric Nursing, 10,* 42–44.

Smith, D. P. (1986). Common day-care diseases: Patterns and prevention. *Pediatric Nursing, 12,* 175–179.

Steele, S. M. (1988). Assessing developmental delays in preschool children. *Journal of Pediatric Health Care, 2,* 141–145.

# School-Age Growth, Development, and Health

Janice S. Hayes

Physical Growth and Development
    General Growth Characteristics
    Motor Development
    Sensory Development
    Nutrition Needs
    Sleep

Cognitive Development
    Piaget
    Play
    School

Psychosocial Development
    Freud
    Erikson
    Peer Significance
    Sex Role Determination

Moral Development
    Piaget
    Kohlberg

Assessment
    Body Measurements
    Assessment of Home and Family
    School Adjustment

Health Promotion
    Health Maintenance Visits and
        Immunizations
    Dental Care
    Recognizing Developmental Tasks
    Common Concerns

Parenting Development

Summary

Sculpture by Charles Parks

## Learning Objectives

*Upon completion of this chapter the reader will be able to:*

1. *Describe the usual physical development of the school-aged child.*

2. *Describe the usual cognitive development of the school-aged child.*

3. *Explain the psychosocial and moral development of school-aged children.*

4. *Explain assessment strategies to be used for evaluating the status of school-aged children.*

5. *Employ health promotion strategies for school-aged children.*

6. *Discuss common concerns of school-aged children.*

7. *Select appropriate parenting development strategies.*


## Key Terms

*conservation*

*cooperative play*

*decentering*

*field dependence/field independence*

*latchkey children*

*morality of constraint*

*morality of cooperation*

*multiple classification*

*reflection/impulsivity*

*school phobia*

*seriation*

During the school-age years children's social circles widen to include peers and more of the greater community. This period is often referred to as the "gang age." The increased influence of people outside the home, such as teachers, peers, and neighbors, contributes to self-image and self-esteem.

Physical growth is slower than during developmental stages. Fine motor development and coordination continue to progress.

Piaget (1969) describes cognitive development as the stage of *concrete operations*. Psychosocial development centers around Erikson's conflict of *industry versus inferiority*. Moral development is linked to cognitive development but also depends on the child's experience in considering choices of right and wrong.

The school-age period is one of the healthiest. Good immunity to common infections has been built, and there is an increase in organ maturity. Body growth is such that there is now less surface-to-mass ratio and, consequently, less susceptibility to dehydration with fluid losses. The resiliency of this age allows quick recovery when an illness does occur.

The goals of nursing care during this age relate to keeping the child healthy. The nurse continues to offer anticipatory guidance to parents during office or clinic visits. However, as the school-age child grows and gains competencies, the nurse can begin to discuss in greater detail the child's own role and responsibilities in keeping healthy. The school nurse now plays a role with the child and the family; follow-up with families and coordination with pediatricians, hospitals, and community health nurses may be necessary in providing health care for the child. All nurses working with this age group, whether in the hospital, the community, physicians' offices, or schools, are concerned with educating the child and family. Supporting nutritional needs and maintaining safety are two major concerns. Sex education and education on substance abuse are also important.

## Physical Growth and Development

### General Growth Characteristics

The school-age years constitute the period from age 6 to approximately age 12. This period begins with the broadening of children's social circles to include peers and more of the community as a whole. During this period children generally reach a plateau in physical growth; this is a period of refinement. However, individual patterns of development may deviate from this generalization. Each child's pattern is influenced by heredity and environment, and deviations from average are often normal. However, general relationships to the average do not vary appreciably after the age of 6 years—that is, a child whose height is at the 25th percentile will likely remain near the 25th percentile in the future.

Body organs continue to mature. The central nervous system has improved transmission due to continuing myelinization (the acquisition of the myelin coating on the nerve). Cardiac growth results in a more vertical position of the heart within the chest cavity. The diaphragm descends, giving more room within the chest cavity. Lung capacity becomes proportional to body size, and the tidal volume doubles between 5 and 10 years of age. The immune system becomes better able to localize infections and has better antibody production with faster response to antigens (Green & Haggerty, 1990).

Body proportions change during this period. The child appears to "thin out" owing to growth of the extremities. By age 6, the child is usually able to put one arm over the head and touch the opposite ear. The 7-year-old often appears gangly and awkward. Growth during middle childhood is steady (about 3–3.5 kg/yr and 5–6 cm/yr) and ends in a preadolescent growth spurt. This growth spurt occurs at about 10 years of age in girls and at about 12 years of age in boys. There is also an increase in subcutaneous fat (Vaughan & Litt, 1990).

The most rapid growth of the school-age child is in the long bones of the extremities and the facial bones. Consequently, the muscles and ligaments may be stretched. These stretched muscles have a tendency to respond with jerky movements. "Growing pains" frequently begin between 8 and 12 years; the reported incidence varies from 4.2% to 33.5%, with girls being more frequently affected. The exact cause is unknown, but they are encountered in healthy children. Other than ruling out serious bone or joint disorders, interventions are symptomatic (Szer, 1989).

Posture changes are apparent as the center of gravity moves downward and muscle strength increases. The posture appears straighter and a convex curvature appears in the thoracic spine area. Poor posture can reflect fatigue or skeletal defects. However, the suppleness of the child's body allows the assumption of postures that may disturb parents and teachers. The child needs appropriate exercise to help develop and maintain muscle development and flexibility. This should be a time of vigorous physical activity. The motor activities of the earlier years become more directed toward specialized activities and games with particular physical and motor skills.

### Motor Development

Maturation of the central nervous system allows refinement of gross and fine motor control that continues through this age. Brain growth is about 95% complete by 9 years of age. Head circumference correlates well with DNA content of the brain: the larger the head circumference, the greater the DNA content (Cooke, 1968).

Increased myelinization allows more rapid conduction of nerve impulses and improves reaction time and coordination. Increasing levels of motor skills depend on this maturation. Participation in sports becomes popular with school-age children, and the particular skills that are developed depend on the sports and activities they select.

### Sensory Development

Visual development is closely related to improved coordination, which usually matures by age 6 or 7. Most children have 20/20 vision by age 5. Depth perception, which is necessary for some sports and eye–hand skills, requires the coordinated use of both eyes. Therefore, strabismus may be a cause for delay in these skills. Corrective lenses or eye exercises may be indicated, and a referral should be made for appropriate intervention.

### Nutrition Needs

A well-balanced diet, selected from the four basic food groups, provides all the necessary nutrients. Vitamin and iron supplements are usually not needed. The diet should derive 15% of calories from protein, 35% from fat, and 50% from carbohydrates (Behrman & Vaughan, 1987). Recommended foods for school-age children are shown in Table 15-1.

Breakfast is an important meal. A number of studies have linked breakfast consumption with school performance (Tuttle, 1974; Pollitt, Leibel, & Greenfield, 1981; Morgan, Zabik, & Leville, 1981). Lunches are also a concern. Children who do not participate in the school lunch program may consume fewer nutrients than those who do participate (Fig. 15-1). Lack of refrigeration limits the variety of food that can be used. Lunches provided by The National School Lunch Program must meet established nutritional guidelines (Pipes, 1989).

Children now participate in sports at earlier ages. This requires a greater caloric intake than is required for sedentary activities. Different activities determine different calorie needs; however, higher calorie expenditures auto-

Table 15–1. *Foods to Meet the Nutritional Needs of the Elementary School Child*

| Food | 6 to 10 Years | 10 to 12 Years |
|---|---|---|
| Milk, vitamin-D fortified | 2–3 cups | 3–4 cups |
| Eggs | 3–4 per week | 3–4 week |
| Meat, poultry, fish | 2–3 ounces (small serving) | 3–4 ounces (average serving) |
| Dried beans, peas, or peanut butter | 2 servings each week. If used as an alternative for meat, allow ½ cup cook beans or peas or 2 tablespoons peanut butter for 1 ounce meat | |
| Potatoes, white or sweet (occasionally spaghetti, macaroni, rice, noodles, etc.) | 1 small or ⅓ cup | 1 medium or ½ cup |
| Other cooked vegetable (green leafy or deep yellow 3 to 4 times a week) | ¼ cup | ⅓ cup |
| Raw vegetable (salad greens, cabbage, celery, carrots, etc.) | ¼ cup | ⅓ cup |
| Vitamin C food (citrus fruit, tomato, cantaloupe, etc.) | 1 medium orange or equivalent | 1 medium orange or equivalent |
| Other fruit | 1 portion or more as: 1 apple, 1 banana, 1 peach, 1 pear, ½ cup cooked fruit | |
| Bread, enriched or whole grain | 3 slices or more | 3 slices or more |
| Cereal, enriched or whole gain | ½ cup | ¾ cup |
| Additional foods | Butter or margarine, desserts, etc., to satisfy energy needs. | |

(Robinson, C.H., Lawler, M.R., Chenoweth, W.L., & Garwick, A.E. [1986]. *Normal and therapeutic nutrition* [17th ed.]. New York: Macmillan.)

matically increase appetite. Food intake should be increased without changing the proportions of nutrients (DeAngelis, 1984). Fluids and electrolytes lost during sports activities should be replaced. Eating before competition should be scheduled so that food has been digested prior to the activity; foods should be selected that are easily digested, for example, complex carbohydrates such as pasta (Pipes, 1989). Special food supplements such as vitamin and protein preparations are unnecessary. Water intake should be scheduled before, during, and after athletic events (Behrman & Vaughan, 1987) because thirst is not necessarily a good guide to necessary fluid intake.

Obesity affects about 30% of boys ages 6 to 11 and about 25% of girls ages 6 to 11 (Dietz, 1986). *Obesity* is defined as an excessive deposit of adipose tissue. Weight greater than 20% over normal for height has been used as one criterion; however, such a standard is based on population trends and may not be applicable to an individual child. Triceps fatfold measurement with calipers can also be used. Standards are available for all age groups (Pipes, 1989).

Much of obesity is due to the consumption of high-carbohydrate foods or "empty calories." However, there may also be a genetic basis or organic malfunction (Neu-

man, 1977). A precipitating event or situation can often be identified when obesity starts during mid-childhood; these events can include loss of friends, a school change, or surgery. Decreased physical activity and increased television viewing may also be associated with childhood obesity.

Intervention for childhood obesity should be directed toward increasing the child's physical activity and reducing dietary fat intake to 35% of total calories. Parent education and cooperation are needed. Community-based action may help to influence advertising directed at children; these commercials often advertise foods that are full of empty calories, and they make the child want these foods.

## Sleep

The amount of sleep needed decreases throughout this period. Six- or 7-year-old children generally require 11 or 12 hours per night, whereas a 12-year-old may require only 8 or 9 hours. Each child's pattern is individual, but a minimum of 8 hours of sleep per night is recommended even for older school-age children.

Sleep problems at this age often relate to delaying strategies on the part of the child who does not want to go

*Figure 15—1.  School lunch programs help children to eat nutritional meals.*

to bed. Parents may need to be taught the importance of adequate sleep so that they can enforce limits and ensure that the child gets enough sleep.

Other potential sleep problems may be related to overexcitement at bedtime or to anxieties and fears. The possible causes of these anxieties and fears need to be investigated. Potential causes may include school performance, peer impressions, anxiety about new situations, or conflicts with family members. Assistance may be needed in establishing a bedtime routine that allows the child to "wind down" before trying to sleep.

## Cognitive Development

### Piaget

*Concrete operational thought* is the stage that is most representative of the school-age period. Although Piaget does not apply age norms, the ages of 7 through 11 are most often considered to constitute this stage.

Several transitions in thinking occur. Children move from *intuitive thought* to *objective thought,* from *egocentrism* to *relativism,* and from dependence on *reproductive imagery* to *anticipatory imagery. Intuitive thought* allows the child to begin to understand the rationale behind actions. The logic is based on any phenomenon and the child's own point of view. During the concrete operations stage the child can realize that there are other ways of thinking than his or her own. This less egocentric thought process is *objective thought.* Logic is still bound by immediate physical realities (the here and now), but the child becomes more adept at processing information.

The progression from *egocentrism* to *relativism* is part of the transition. It allows the child to visualize something from another's perspective. For instance, a younger child would assume that a person seated across a table would see an object (such as a teddy bear placed on the table) from the same perspective. That is, if the child is facing the bear, the child assumes that the person across the table sees the bear's front as well. As thought develops relativism, the child realizes that the person seated across the table sees the bear's back.

*Anticipatory imagery* can be compared to a mental movie camera that is capable of reverse, forward, and stop action. An activity such as throwing a ball can be imagined, and the action can be anticipated at various points in the trajectory. This can be done without actually seeing it happen. The previous ability to use reproductive images allowed the imagination only of what had actually been seen.

The hallmarks of this stage are decentering, seriation, multiple classification, and conservation. *Decentering* is a shift from egocentrism and allows the child to see things as more relative to the self. This is a step toward seeing the world as others see it and is important to moral development. *Seriation* is the placement of objects as they relate to each other in terms of specific characteristics, i.e., such features as size, color, and gradations, in serial order. Children also learn that what is small in one situation is big in another and vice versa. *Multiple classification* allows the placement of something in more than one conceptual group, i.e., a figure can be large and round and red. *Conservation* is the ability to understand that the mass or amount of something is not changed when its shape changes. This is illustrated by the task of pouring equal amounts of water into a wide glass and a narrow glass. If the child has not mastered the concept of conservation, he or she will believe that the glass with the highest water level holds more water. Conservation of quantity is usually achieved by age 9; conservation of volume is usually achieved by age 11 (Vander Zanden, 1978). Figure 15-2 lists the sequence in which conservation skills are achieved and the approximate ages at which they are achieved. An explanation of each ability is also given.

| Conservation Skill | Basic Principle | Test for Conservation Skills | |
| --- | --- | --- | --- |
| | | Step 1 | Step 2 |
| Number (Ages 5 to 7) | The number of units in a collection remains unchanged even though they are rearranged in space. |  Two rows of pennies arranged in one-to-one correspondence |  One of the rows elongated or contracted |
| Substance (Ages 7 to 8) | The amount of a malleable, plastic-like material remains unchanged regardless of the shape it assumes. | 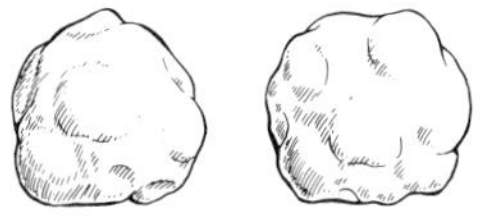 Modeling clay in two balls of the same size |  One of the balls rolled into a long, narrow shape |
| Length (Ages 7 to 8) | The length of a line or object from one end to the other end remains unchanged regardless of how it is rearranged in space or changed in shape. | 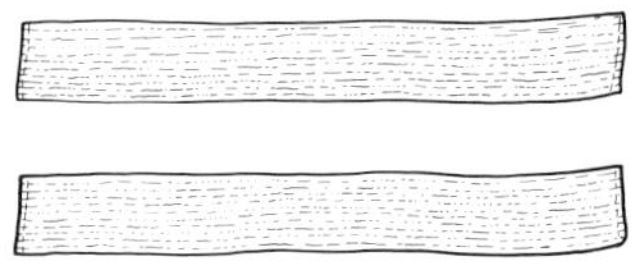 Strips of cloth placed in a straight line | 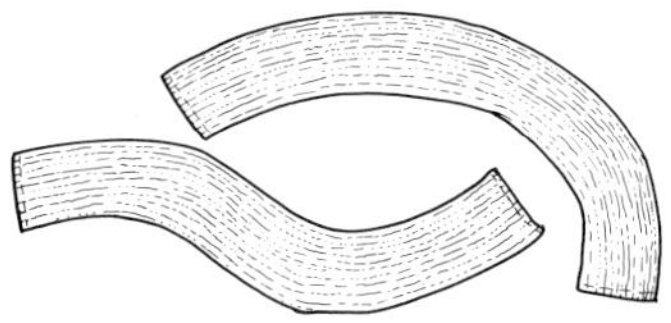 Strips of cloth placed in altered shapes |
| Area (Ages 8 to 9) | The total amount of surface covered by a set of plane figures remains unchanged regardless of the position of the figures. | 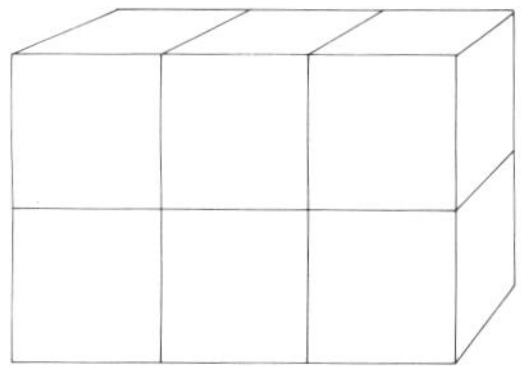 Square units arranged in a rectangle | 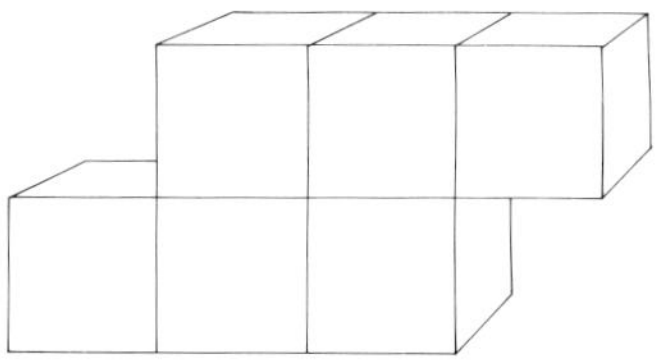 Square units rearranged |
| Weight (Ages 9 to 10) | The heaviness of an object remains unchanged regardless of the shape that it assumes. | 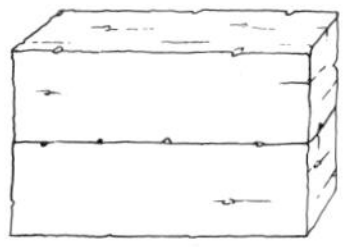 Units placed on top of each other | 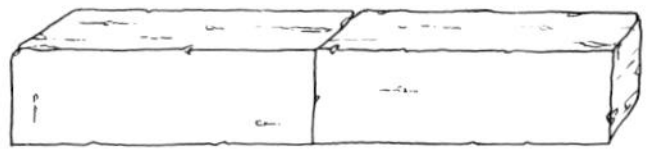 Units placed side by side |
| Volume (Ages 12 to 14) | The space occupied by an object remains unchanged regardless of a change in its shape. | 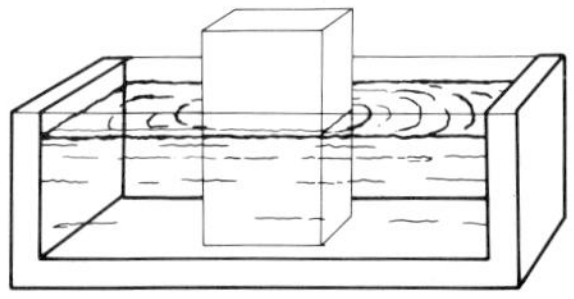 Displacement of water by object placed vertically in the water | 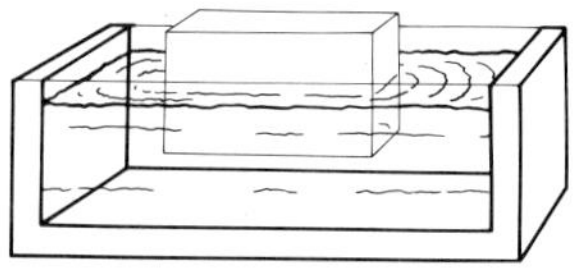 Displacement of water by object placed horizontally in the water |

Figure 15–2.   Sequential acquisition of conservation skills. (Vander Zanden, J.W. [1978]. Human development. New York: Alfred A. Knopf)

## Play

For the school-age child play involves group interaction (Fig. 15-3). These groups may be organized or unorganized, but even solitary activities such as video games are usually done with friends. The activities chosen by children change as their development progresses.

The 6-year-old is very energetic. Rough-and-tumble play predominates; athletic abilities are beginning. Gross motor activities provide the major outlet. Egocentrism is still apparent in peer interactions. Conflicts and show-off behavior occur as the child tries to dominate the situation.

By age 7, the child is more cautious in group interac-

tions and is consequently easier to deal with. Gross motor skill continue to improve; fine motor skills are beginning to develop as well. Team sports become a favorite as cooperation and skills improve.

Muscle coordination is even better in the 8-year-old. Activities such as soccer, baseball, and skateboarding are favorites. Fine muscle control allows the child to begin cursive handwriting.

During the rest of the school-age years, skills learned at the younger ages continue to be perfected. Strength and endurance increase. Differences in athletic ability in those who have practiced the skills become apparent.

Cooperative play replaces parallel and associative

*Figure 15–3. Group interaction is an important part of play for school-age children.*

*Figure 15–4. The classroom offers many new challenges and experiences for the school-age child.*

play, and sharing takes place among more than two children at a time. The new ability to cognitively separate themselves from the environment allows them to understand another person's point of view. They are less egocentric and better able to see other individuals as separate from themselves. Group members and team members can learn to work together. Games with rules can be understood and are enjoyed.

## School

Entry into school brings to the child new ways of being evaluated and judged (Fig. 15-4). Teacher and peer expectations are new and different, which may place children in situations in which expectations are less individualized. Children's success depends to some extent on the match between their unique styles and the expectations of others. All children possess learning styles that may or may not match with their environments. Research on cognitive style demonstrates better performance when the child and teacher have compatible styles. Several cognitive styles have been identified. The two most commonly applied to research with children are field dependence/field independence and reflection/impulsivity. The *field dependence/field independence* dimension refers to the child's ability to separate the parts of a scene from the background. Some children approach a problem by looking at the parts and then at the whole; others look at the whole and then break it into parts. *Reflection/impulsivity* takes into account the child's ability to respond quickly. Some children respond quickly without regard for error, whereas others respond more slowly and make fewer errors. When the teaching style and the learning style do not match, the difficulty is apparent. Recognition of the disparity that may exist between teaching/learning styles may serve to alleviate some school problems.

## Psychosocial Development

With the onset of school attendance, children's social horizons widen. Development now proceeds to balance home, peers, and school. The child's success in this balancing act depends, to a large extent, upon affectional ties at home. School experiences can lead to feelings of inadequacy and inferiority or to success and self-esteem. An important way to assist children to maintain a favorable balance between home and school and to be successful in school is through parent education.

### Freud

Freud's *psychosexual theory* places the school-age child in the *latency stage*. During this phase sexual drives are said to be dormant. The child expands same-sex peer relationships. Freud believed that the child's personality was well formed by the end of the phallic stage, which precedes this stage. He was less interested in this period. With the resolution of the Electra and Oedipal conflicts, the child is able to identify with the same-sex parent and accept parental values. There is rigid adherence to parental and societal rules at this time, which is reflected in the discussion of moral development. The interest in sexual matters conforms to social standards.

### Erikson

Freud's theory provided the foundation for the work of Erikson (1963), who called this the stage of *industry versus inferiority*. The emphasis of this stage is on children's meaningful efforts or desires to accomplish something of consequence. Having established a repertoire of skills and abilities in previous stages, children are eager for new tasks and skills. Success in these leads to a desire for more new tasks and skills. These successes win recognition for children and increase their self-esteem.

Lack of success in accomplishing new skills leads children to feelings of inferiority. At this age, children need to be helped to feel that their accomplishments are adequate. The competitive atmosphere that is often perpetuated in school, organized sports, and possibly home life may affect children's abilities to feel successful in comparison with others. Assistance may be needed in order to see accomplishments as meaningful.

For the sense of industry to be achieved, children must perceive themselves as separate from their families and capable of accomplishing the tasks that are given to them. Prolonged dependency on the family contributes to feelings of inferiority. Table 15-2 shows Erikson's descriptions of conflict, followed by a list of behaviors that foster the development of industry or inferiority.

## Peer Significance

Central to the concepts of Erikson and Freud is the increasing influence of peer groups on the continued development of children. Peers are important socializing agents and compete with the influence of parents, family members, teachers, and others.

The child's identity develops as interaction with peers proceeds. Early in the school years this identity is influenced by same-sex peers (Fig. 15-5). Before the age of 8 or 9, the opposite sex may be deliberately avoided or disliked. The closer the child gets to pubescence and the adolescent years, the more likely there is to be a shift away from this attitude.

Children test the values and rules they have learned at home with their peers. The more democratic nature of the peer group allows children to question ideas. Consequently, values and rules from the family may be reinforced or challenged, depending on interaction in the peer group. For example, if acceptance by a peer group is contingent upon performing an act in opposition to the parental values, the child may elect to abandon parental values in order to gain acceptance.

Certain children in some groups may be more powerful and influential than others, which may encourage some less powerful children to engage in behaviors they would not ordinarily undertake. The peer group's influence may create conflict at home, particularly if the importance of peer acceptance appears stronger to the child.

Friendships become more stable. Children who interact with the peer group in situations requiring teamwork build both respect for and the ability to work with others. These group settings may include organized activities such as scouting or sports, as well as school.

Peer acceptance is important during the school-age years. A lack of acceptance by peers can have a detrimental effect on self-esteem. Consequently, the effects of prejudice are powerful and may be exhibited in a variety of settings, from peer groups to the community level.

Deprivation or loss of a peer group represents a threat to developing self-esteem and identity. Socialization is disrupted or stunted if such a loss occurs. Imposed isolation resulting from chronic illness and hospitalization requires special consideration so that the child's develop-

*Table 15—2.  Erikson's Fourth Nuclear Conflict: Industry Versus Inferiority*

| Eriksonian Descriptions | Fostering Adult Behaviors |
|---|---|
| Application of self to given skills and tasks | Give systematic instruction in skills and tasks |
| Effort to bring productive situation to completion | Give recognition of things produced |
| Attention and perseverance at work with pleasure obtained from effort | Specialized adults and older children outside family also instruct and recognize progress |
| Work beside and with others brings sense of need to divide labor | |
| Disappointment in own tool use and skills | Family failed to prepare child for life in school and with other adults and unrelated children |
| Sense of inadequacy among tool partners | School failed to sustain promises of earlier stages |
| Lost hope of association in industrial society | Adult makes child feel that external factors determine worth rather than wish and will to learn |
| Sense of being mediocre | |

(Frieberg, K. [1987]. *Human development: A life-span approach* [3rd ed.]. Boston: Jones and Bartlett, p. 305.)

*Figure 15–5. During the school years, identity is influenced by the peer group. (Copyright 1990, Kathy Sloane)*

ment suffers minimal setback. Of great concern, as well, is the child who engages in solitary activities to the exclusion of interacting with a peer group. Assistance in changing this pattern may be needed. There are a variety of ways parents can encourage participation in group activities such as Scouts, organized sports, and clubs. In addition, nurses can suggest that parents develop an atmosphere in the home that encourages children to invite their friends there.

## Sex Role Identification

School-age children identify with the same-sex parent and associate with same-sex peers (Fig. 15-6). This reinforces sex role identity and is an important step before moving into adolescence and heterosexual relationships.

Children learn sex role identity in the peer group and in the home. For some children there may be conflict

*Figure 15–6. School-age child with parent of same sex.*

between the behaviors expressed in each group. For example, a peer group may express very traditional gender role orientation for boys and girls, whereas a parent may have feminist values. Where there is conflict, the child will assume the values of the group perceived to be most nurturant.

Freud explained the sex role identity in this age through his conceptualization of the *latency period.* By age 6 boys are said to have renounced their Oedipal complexes and girls their Electra complexes. Therefore, they are free to identify with the same-sex parent. Social learning theorists believe that this is due to the rewards and attention given to children when they display these behaviors. Cognitive theorists believe that this is caused by children seeing the similarity between themselves and the same-sex parent and wanting to imitate the person whom they most closely resemble.

Although most of the child's peer group activities are with same-sex peers, curiosity about gender differences may be intensified. Many children explore their own bodies as well as peers'. This is usually attributed to curiosity rather than sexual urges.

## Moral Development

### Piaget

Piaget believed that the passage from preoperational thought to concrete operational thought changed the child's moral judgments. He identified two levels of morality: *morality of constraint* and *morality of cooperation.* Morality of constraint emphasizes submission to authority; morality of cooperation establishes rules by mutual agreement. During the school-age years, as the child begins to see the world as others see it and gains an appreciation for rules, morality of cooperation begins to develop (Piaget, 1965).

## Kohlberg

Kohlberg (1968) focused on moral judgments rather than actions. *Moral development* occurs as children actively interact with the world. He identified six stages that are grouped into three levels. Most school-age children fall into the first level, the *preconventional level,* in which rules and expectations are imposed on the child by others. There are two stages in this level: the *obedience–punishment orientation* and the *naive hedonistic–instrumental orientation.* For example, in the obedience–punishment orientation stage, the child obeys the parent's request to pick up toys in order to avoid punishment. In the naive hedonistic–instrumental orientation second, the child's desire to have a neat bedroom is the motivation for picking up toys.

Older school-age children (10 years and above) may begin to exemplify the second or *conventional* level. At this time rules and expectations are internalized. The third stage is the *good boy* or *good girl orientation.* Rules are extremely important at this stage, and the motivation is to win approval and avoid disapproval, especially by the peer group. A very mature school-age child may reach stage four, the *law and order orientation.* This is characterized by the literal acceptance of society's conventions and rules.

According to Kohlberg, these stages are invariable in order and are cross-cultural. Individuals differ only in how quickly they pass through the stages and how far they advance. The validity of Kohlberg's work has been questioned because it is thought to reflect sex bias. Some authors believe that sex differences exist in reasoning and valuing. However, research following this criticism has shown that sex differences in moral reasoning are not significant (Walker, 1984).

## Assessment

### Body Measurements

The individuality of children, which is due to their genetic makeup and environment, becomes more apparent in the school-age years. Individual differences make comparison to a norm more difficult.

Gross and fine motor development generally progress according to particular milestones. Deviations from these developmental patterns may reflect "soft signs" that are often associated with learning disabilities. Tasks that can be used to assess gross motor function are shown in Table 15-3. Fine motor milestones include:

7 years—consistent hand preference

8 years—finger-thumb apposition; identification of own right and left

*Table 15–3. Tasks for the Assessment of Gross Motor Function*

| Age | Gross Motor Function |
| --- | --- |
| 5–6 years | Skip<br>Walk on heels<br>Tandem gait forward<br>Hop in place |
| 6–7 years | Tandem gait backward<br>Stand on one foot, eyes open (10 sec) |
| 7–8 years | Crouch on tiptoes, eyes closed (10 sec)<br>Hop twice in place on each foot in succession (3 cycles)<br>Stand in tandem gait position (heel-toe), eyes closed (10 sec) |
| 9–10 years | Tandem gait sideways<br>Catch tennis ball in air, one hand<br>Throw tennis ball at target |
| 10–12 years | Balance on tiptoes, eyes closed (15 sec)<br>Jump in air, clap heels together<br>Jump in air, clap hands three times |

(From Levine, M.D. [1987]. The elements of development function. In R.E. Behrman & V.C. Vaughan III [Eds.]: *Nelson textbook of pediatrics* [13th ed.]. Philadelphia: W.B. Saunders Company, p. 89)

9 years—crossed lateral commands on self ("touch your right eye with your left thumb")

10 years—synkinesis (mirror movements)

11–12 years—finger localization ("with your eyes closed tell me which of your fingers I'm touching") (Vaughan & Litt, 1990)

Growth patterns established in the earlier years can guide judgments, and these patterns are more significant than individual measurements. A child's normal growth pattern is usually established by 6 years of age and does not usually differ significantly after that (Schuster & Ashburn, 1986). By 6 years of age, adult body proportions are becoming evident. Variations from the child's pattern of growth can herald the onset of disorders such as endocrine problems. Therefore, the child's height and weight should be measured and recorded regularly.

A weight gain of 3 to 3.5 kg per year is about average during the school years. The height gain is about 5 to 6 cm per year. These figures should be used as an approximation until the child's own pattern can be discerned. Growth in head circumference is slower. It increases from 51 cm to 53–54 cm between 5 and 12 years of age. The brain has reached very nearly adult size by this time (Behrman & Vaughan, 1987). Growth standards can be found in Appendix B.

The first permanent teeth, often called 6-year molars, usually erupt during the seventh year, and the loss of the deciduous or "baby teeth" begins at about the same time.

Teeth are lost and replaced at the rate of about four per year for the next 5 years.

## Assessment of Home and Family

Assessment of the home and family has two purposes. One is the assessment of family functioning and the supporting role it provides the child. The other is the assessment for actual or potential child abuse or neglect.

The Home Observation for Measurement of the Environment (HOME) Inventory can be applied to the measurement of quality and quantity of cognitive, social, and emotional development provided for the child at home (see Appendix A). (Copies of the HOME and the Administration Manual may be obtained from Bettye M. Caldwell, University of Arkansas at Little Rock, Little Rock, Arkansas.) There are three versions of the instrument, one of which is designed for children ages 6 to 10 years. This version is relatively new and, consequently, has not been used as extensively as the versions for younger children. However, there have been modest correlations to Science Research Associates (SRA) academic achievement tests (Bradley & Caldwell, 1988). There are 59 items within the following subscales:

1. Emotional and verbal responsivity of parent
2. Encouragement and maturity
3. Emotional climate
4. Growth-fostering materials and experiences
5. Provision for active stimulation
6. Family participation in developmentally stimulating experiences
7. Paternal involvement
8. Aspects of physical environment

Information is gathered through observation and interview in the child's home with the primary care giver. This inventory is not diagnostic but is designed to complement other information about children and families. It is useful where information about environment helps one understand the dynamics of the child's environment.

Several studies have attempted to identify characteristics that differentiate abusing/neglecting from nonabusing/non-neglecting parents and families. One instrument that may be used for screening is the Parenting Profile Assessment (Anderson, 1987), which assesses risk for child abuse. A combination of five variables identified 90.6% of abusive parents in a matched sample of 32 abusive and 30 nonabusive mothers. These variables included:

1. Annual income under $20,000
2. High-school education or less
3. Frequent police involvement
4. High incidence of perceived harsh discipline to children

5. Moderate to high scores on scales that measure important life changes

Neglecting families have been reported to show some common characteristics. These include:

1. Eighth-grade education or less
2. Depression
3. High unemployment rates
4. Parents who were neglected as children
5. Impoverished support system
6. Withdrawal in response to difficult tasks (Crittenden, 1988)

Developmental delay or deviation may be found in abused school-age children. This may be evidenced by school failure or underachievement or as peer relationship problems. Siblings of abused children have also been found to be at risk academically. It should be noted that a wide range of behavioral outcomes have been reported for abused children. This suggests that each situation should be carefully assessed on an individual basis (Wolf, 1988).

Profiles of abusing/neglecting families and parents are useful as indices of risk. They are not diagnostic tools and should not be regarded as such. Rather, they should serve to alert the observer that intervention and further assessment may be needed.

## School Adjustment

Children's adjustment to school depends largely on school readiness. The increasing use of child day care, nursery schools, and preschool has changed the level of skill with which children now enter school. These children have learned some social skills with teachers and other children, as well as some beginning academic skills. Children should have learned that they can be comfortable away from home.

Many schools now have mandatory screening procedures to determine school readiness. These include screening of language skills, social skills, and peer interaction; general school readiness; knowledge; and pre-reading skills. Children may not be allowed to enter first grade until school readiness is demonstrated at a level judged to be sufficient by the school. This has led to some innovative approaches, such as pre–first grade classes for children who have completed a year of kindergarten but have not demonstrated readiness for first grade work. The current trend is to push back the entry birthdate and allow the child to be more mature when entering school. Many parents and educators agree that a delayed school entrance, based on the child's maturity level, enhances the likelihood of the child's future academic and social success.

In a recent study of the use of school health services,

stressful life events were found to be related to both absenteeism and use of the nurse's office or health room (Grey, 1988). One hundred twenty four parents of 124 6- to 11-year-old children were questioned. Undesirable stressful life events, baseline health status, family structure, and family routines were measured. In addition, data on absentee days and number and reason for visits to the school health room were collected. The study found that children who experienced a stressful event and had unstable family characteristics were more likely to be absent than those who had either alone. Most of the visits to the health room by the high users were for recurrent complaints such as headaches, abdominal pain, and obesity. The survey results indicated that the school health services need to include services for stress management as well as for acute, infectious illnesses.

School adjustment problems may be reflected in school avoidance or *school phobia*. In this condition the child develops physical symptoms (headaches, stomachache, vomiting, diarrhea) when left at school. School phobia is generally caused by anxiety over separation from the mother, or it may be associated with a traumatic event at school. Both possibilities need to be investigated. Parents may need to help the child become more independent. Teachers and parents should recognize the need to work together in addressing and seeking a solution to the problem. Difficulties with peers at school and fears of teasing or rejection may require intervention by the teacher. When physical symptoms are present, the school nurse should evaluate the symptoms and refer the child for medical evaluation, as necessary. A physical exam is essential in order to rule out organic problems.

Scholastic underachievement is another school adjustment problem. Children who do not achieve well in school are at great risk for diminished self-esteem. When a sense of industry cannot be achieved, a sense of inferiority develops. These children may be labeled by teachers and peers as "lazy" or "stupid." Behavioral and psychological problems that compound the existing disabilities can result. Such problems often come to the attention of the nurse. A thorough physical exam is needed to rule out other problems, and a referral for psychological evaluation is needed. Early detection and intervention with special educational techniques and programs are necessary to ameliorate the escalating problems and to set the child on the road to more effective school performance.

## Health Promotion

### Health Maintenance Visits and Immunizations

The school-age child should have one complete physical examination each year to assess growth and development and to detect signs of illness. Many schools require a physical exam and a dental exam, in addition to proof of immunization, before entrance into kindergarten or first grade.

Although individual states mandate health programs, school health nurses are responsible for screening for health problems as well as for monitoring the health status of school-age children. These programs include periodic physical exams; vision and hearing tests; evaluation of dental, psychosocial, and immunization status; and health education.

Immunizations need to be completed or updated with boosters before entry into kindergarten. Once a series of immunizations has been started, regardless of the lapse of time between administrations, it is necessary to restart the entire regimen. Immunization schedules are included in Appendix F. The immunization schedule for children over 6 who have never been immunized is included in Table 15-4.

In 1989, approximately 17,000 cases of rubeola were reported in the United States. This was a clear departure from the usual pattern. There were two groups identified in that outbreak: preschoolers who were mostly not immunized and 15–19-year-olds who predominantly were immunized (Brunell, 1990). In response to this outbreak, the Advisory Committee on Immunization Practices (ACIP) and the American Academy of Pediatrics (AAP)(1988) both recommended that a second vaccine be administered. The first would be administered at 15 months of age; the second would be administered at entrance to kindergarten or first grade (ACIP) or at entrance to middle school or junior high school (AAP). The combined MMR vaccine is recommended for both vaccinations, although there is no evidence for waning immunity to Rubella or mumps (Lepow, 1990).

*Vision and hearing screening* should be done before school entry and at periodic intervals (Fig. 15-7). Accom-

*Table 15—4.   Recommended Schedules of Active Immunization for Children Not Immunized Until 7 Years of Age and Older But Less Than 18 Years of Age*

| Initial | Td and OPV |
| --- | --- |
| 1 month later | Measles, mumps, rubella |
| 2 months later | Td and OPV |
| 6–12 months later | Td and OPV |
| 14–16 years of age | Td |
| Every 10 years thereafter | Td |

TD, Diphtheria–tetanus vaccine, adult preparation; OPV, Live polioviruses types 1, 2, and 3 in liquid form for oral administration; measles, mumps, rubella: All are live vaccines administered subcutaneously. Live measles vaccine may be administered alone or in commercially prepared combinations. (Adapted from American Academy of Pediatrics. [1988]. *Report of the Committee on Infectious Diseases* [21st ed.], pp. 15–16.)

*Figure 15–7. School-age child undergoing hearing screening assessment.*

modation problems, strabismus, and astigmatism are common in school-age children and should be corrected immediately. Children should also be screened for color blindness. Significant hearing loss is frequently overlooked and results in the belief that the child is not paying attention or does not understand. Recurrent or chronic otitis media can lead to a decrease in auditory acuity. Uncorrected vision and hearing problems can lead to early frustration with academic tasks, labeling of the child, lower academic achievement, and lower self-esteem. See Chapter 35 for a detailed discussion of vision and hearing screening.

*Urinalysis and blood counts or hematocrits* should be done prior to school entry and at periodic intervals. Urinary tract infections are common, especially in girls. Routine urine screening is useful for detection. Iron deficiency anemia can be detected and corrected by iron-rich diets or iron supplementation. Uncorrected anemia can lead to susceptibility to infections, fatigue, and shorter attention spans. The mean hemoglobin (Hb), hematocrit (Hct), and mean corpuscular volume (MCV) values for this age are presented in Table 15-5.

*Tuberculosis screening* is required by many schools. The *tine test* is most commonly used. Yearly tests are advised in communities where the rate of new positive results is 1% or higher or for children who have household members with tuberculosis (Wasserman, 1990). Otherwise, testing at 12–15 months of age, prior to school entrance, and at adolescence is adequate. The tine, Heaf, SchavoTest, Aplitest, and Mono-Vacc are multiple puncture skin tests applied to the skin on the palm side of the forearm. The largest diameter of induration is measured at 48–72 hours; a measurement of 10 mm or more is considered positive. This test is made to over-identify, so a positive result should be followed with one of the more definitive intradermal skin tests such as the Mantoux (Newton, 1989). Children who react positively should be followed by the health department. Children who have had a previous positive reaction to a skin test should not receive another. Instead, they may be screened by chest x-ray.

*Blood pressure screening* has received more attention recently. Elevated blood pressure may be detected and treated in childhood to prevent further problems in adulthood. High-risk groups of children are being identified; they include obese children and prematurely born or low-birth-weight children who received nephrotoxic drugs during the neonatal period, as well as children whose parents are hypertensive (Feld & Springate, 1988). The Pediatric Task Force Classification of Hypertension (1987) suggested the following criteria for significant hypertension):

Children aged 6–9: systolic BP, 122; diastolic BP, 78
Children aged 10–12: systolic BP, 126; diastolic BP, 82

*Scoliosis screening* should be done during primary grade visits. The condition is aggravated by the adolescent growth spurt and should be detected early. During screening the child stands with the feet together while the back is observed for differences in level of hips and shoulders and

*Table 15–5. Mean Hemoglobin, Hematocrit, and Corpuscular Volume Values*

| Age | Hb | (−2sd) | Hct | (−2sd) | MCV | (−2sd) |
|---|---|---|---|---|---|---|
| 5–7 years | 13.0 | (11.5) | 39 | (35) | 81 | (75) |
| 8–11 years | 13.5 | (12.0) | 40 | (36) | 83 | (76) |

The figures in parentheses represent values that are 2 standard deviations below the norm.
(From Ritchey, A.K. [1990]. Anemia. In M. Green & R. Haggerty [Eds.]. *Ambulatory pediatrics,* p. 377. Philadelphia: W. B. Saunders)

symmetry of scapulae. The child is then asked to bend forward and backward while the spine is observed for lateral curvature. (See Chapter 33 for a further discussion of scoliosis screening.) Mass screening is often done in schools. Children with suspected abnormalities should be referred for further evaluation.

## Dental Care

Dental checkups are recommended every 6 months. The child's face and permanent teeth are developing rapidly. Dental caries are common among children and should receive prompt attention. Fluoridation of water or fluoride supplementation can significantly reduce the incidence of caries. Good dental hygiene can also have a beneficial effect. Children who have been introduced to the responsibility of brushing their own teeth (with reminders) should be able to assume full responsibility for brushing and flossing by age 6 or 7.

Half of the children in the United States have dental caries, and many need operative dental services (USDHHS, 1989). The school-aged child should be under the care of a dentist for supervision. A significant number of children are without regular dental care. Minority status and the lack of dental insurance have been found to be factors in this (Waldman, 1990). Legislators, funding agencies, and the general public need to be aware of the need for services.

Children begin to loose their baby teeth at about 6 years of age. Although this is often a status symbol, it can be frightening to some children, especially when bleeding accompanies the loss. The emergence of the permanent teeth changes the children's appearance because the new teeth are larger and appear out of proportion to the rest of the face.

## Recognizing Developmental Tasks

Developmental screening should be performed in order to detect developmental delays by comparing the child's progress to the averages for the major developmental milestones. Some of these may be found in Table 15-6. Deviations from the milestones should be followed up with further developmental screening or testing.

## Common Concerns

### Safety

The most common cause of death and physical handicap during the school-age years is motor vehicle accidents (Frieberg, 1987). Other causes include bicycle accidents, water-related accidents, sports injuries, and poisoning. Children of this age are less closely supervised by responsible adults than they have been previously. It is important for parents to emphasize the necessity of using protective gear for activities such as skateboarding. When skateboarding, children should wear approved helmets, knee pads, and elbow pads. They need to be taught about accident hazards and safety. Parents need to be educated about the possible and actual hazards of many recreational activities (i.e., all-terrain vehicles, lawn darts, trampolines, etc.).

The use of seat belts in automobiles is now legislated in most states, but often their use becomes more lax once children have outgrown car seats. The importance of wearing seat belts may need periodic reinforcement. The child needs to weigh at least 45 kg and be 104 cm tall to be adequately protected by passive shoulder harnesses (Behrman & Vaughan, 1987). Children who are too small for the proper positioning of the shoulder harness should use specially designed booster seats (Fig. 15-8). The best predictor of whether the child uses safety restraints is whether the parents wear them. Being restrained in a motor vehicle should be a condition for any travel (Wilson, 1989).

Water safety and swimming lessons should be taught to all school-age children. Drowning is the second leading cause of accidental death at this age; the most likely site is a lake or pool. Parents should be cautioned that safe behavior cannot be assumed just because the child knows how to swim. Situations may arise where children do not always exercise good judgment. Equipment for rescue and resuscitation should be available where swimming is allowed. All persons in a boat should wear Coast Guard–approved life vests. Diving should be attempted only from official diving boards (Wilson, 1989).

Families may need counseling on the use of smoke detectors, and a family fire escape plan should be developed and practiced. School systems have been integrating content and approaches on "stranger danger." Local police often visit classrooms to discuss the necessity of refusing to accept things from, speak to, or ride with strangers. Parents need to discuss this with children at home as well. Nurses may need to assist parents in identifying ways to discuss this with their children and help them locate resources within the community. Nurses can also reinforce this information during office visits. School and community health nurses should be active in planning and implementing such programs.

Participation in competitive sports has become increasingly common during the elementary years. Many league activities begin as early as 5 or 6 years of age. The Committee on Sports Medicine of the American Academy of Pediatrics (1988) has developed a classification of sports based on type of contact involved (Table 15-7). It should be used as a guideline for practitioners when advising children on participation in athletic events.

Not all states require an annual physical examination and a physician's approval in order to participate in school athletics. Nevertheless, an examination should be con-

*Table 15—6. Developmental Milestones for the School-Age Child*

| Age | Physical | Motor | Social | Language | Perceptual | Cognitive |
|---|---|---|---|---|---|---|
| 6 years | Average height 116 cm Average weight 21 kg Loses first tooth Six-year molar | Ties shoes Can use scissors Runs, jumps, climbs, skips Constant activity | Increased need to socialize with same sex Egocentric | Uses every form of sentence structure Vocabulary of 2500 words Sentence length about 5 words | Knows right from left May reverse letters Can discriminate vertical, horizontal, and oblique Perceives pictures in parts or in wholes but not both | Recognizes simple words Conservation of number Defines objects by use Can group according to an attribute to form subclasses |
| 7 years | Weight is 7 times birth weight Gains 2–3 kg/yr Grows 5–6 cm/yr | More cautious Swims Rides a bicycle Printing is smaller than 6-year-old's Activity level lower than 6-year-olds | More cooperative Same-sex play group and friend Less egocentric | Can name day, month, season Produces all language sounds | b, p, d, q confusion resolved Can copy a diamond shape | Begins to use simple logic Can group in ascending order Grasps basic idea of addition and subtraction Conservation of substance Can tell time |
| 8 years | Average height 127 cm Average weight 25 kg | Movements more graceful Writes in cursive Can throw and hit a baseball Has symmetrical balance and can hop | Adheres to simple rules Hero worship begins Same-sex peer group | Gives precise definitions Articulation is near adult level | Can catch a ball Visual acuity is 20/20 Perceives pictures in parts and whole | Increasing memory span Interest in causal relationships Conservation of length Seriation |
| 9–10 years | Average height 132–137 cm Average weight 27–35 kg | Good coordination Can achieve the strength and speed needed for most sports | Enjoys team competition Moves from group to best friend Hero worship intensifies | Can use language to convey thoughts and look at other's point of view | Eye–hand coordination almost perfected | Classifies objects Understands explanations Conservation of area and weight Describes characteristics of objects Can group in descending order |
| 11–12 years | Average height 144–150 cm Average weight 35–40 kg Pubescence may begin Girls may surpass boys in height Remaining permanent teeth erupt | Refines gross and fine motor skills Can do crafts Uses tools increasingly well | Attends school primarily for peer association Peer acceptance is very important | Vocabulary of 50,000 words for reading Oral vocabulary of 7200 words | Can catch or intercept ball thrown from a distance Possible growth spurts may cause myopia | Begins abstract thinking Conservation of volume Understands relationship among time, speed, and distance |

*Figure 15–8.   School-age child in passive shoulder harness.*

ducted at least 1 month prior to the start of competition in order to correct minor problems without delaying participation. Although no standard format exists, the focus should be on the musculoskeletal and cardiovascular systems. The time frame of 1 month allows for further evaluation or intervention, if needed, that might disqualify the child. Although none currently exist, national standards are needed for sports participation (Tanji, 1990).

## Latchkey Children

One of the largest unmet child care needs in this country is for children over the age of 6 years. This unmet need contributes to the phenomenon of the *latchkey child.* Reported estimates say that there are 2 to 5 million latchkey children between 6 and 13 years of age (Lewis & Volkmar, 1990). These children are left alone to care for themselves after school and during vacations while parents are at work. Such children are at risk for accidents, injuries, and delinquent behavior when they are unsupervised; they also report being afraid and lonely (McClellan, 1984). Nursing intervention for this problem must be a two-faceted approach. First, parent education is needed to ensure that the issues are clear. Parents may erroneously believe that their children will learn more responsible behavior as a result of being left alone; they may not realize the risks. The second approach is community action to encourage the creative development of affordable care for children after school. Some school systems and community centers provide extended day or after-school care at nominal cost. "Telephone friends" have also been established in areas where after-school care does not exist. Some of these programs work by having adults available to answer telephone calls from children; others periodically phone the child at home. Survival skill classes can also be offered to children so that they know the appropriate action to take in various situations. Nurses can suggest some of these approaches to parents and community groups.

*Table 15–7.   Classification of Sports*

| | | Noncontact | | |
| Contact/Collision | Limited Contact/Impact | Strenuous | Moderately Strenuous | Nonstrenuous |
| --- | --- | --- | --- | --- |
| Boxing | Baseball | Aerobic dancing | Badminton | Archery |
| Field hockey | Basketball | Crew | Curling | Golf |
| Football | Bicycling | Fencing | Table tennis | Riflery |
| Ice hockey | Diving | Field | | |
| Lacrosse | Field |   Discus | | |
| Martial arts |   High jump |   Javelin | | |
| Rodeo |   Pole vault |   Shot put | | |
| Soccer | Gymnastics | Running | | |
| Wrestling | Horseback riding | Swimming | | |
| | Skating | Tennis | | |
| |   Ice | Track | | |
| |   Roller | Weight lifting | | |
| | Skiing | | | |
| |   Cross-country | | | |
| |   Downhill | | | |
| |   Water | | | |
| | Softball | | | |
| | Squash, handball | | | |
| | Volleyball | | | |

(From Committee on Sports Medicine. [1988]. Recommendations for participation in competitive sports. *Pediatrics, 81* [5], 737–738)

## Substance Abuse

A complete discussion of substance abuse can be found in Chapter 21. The use and abuse of any substance is potentially a problem at this age. However, the use of inhaled solvents occurs more frequently at this age than at later ages. The major psychoactive agents abused in this age group are alcohol and organic solvents such as airplane glue and paint thinner. Children who seek the euphoria and intoxication of solvents tend to come from economically disadvantaged communities where the children are attempting to model street behaviors observed in the neighborhood (Cohen, 1979). Factors that can contribute to the use of either of these substances include poor academic performance in school, anxiety, depression, and family disorganization.

During the time of intoxication, the child is at greater risk for accidents and injury. Continued use can lead to chronic brain deficit. Solvent use is usually replaced by the use of other substances as the child grows older.

Alcohol is often a "gateway drug" (one of the first used), and its use may begin in childhood. Alcohol is also more readily available to school-age children because it may be found in the home, and its use may not be regarded as serious by adults since it is not a "hard" or illicit drug. However, alcohol diminishes children's ability to master developmental tasks, and physical or psychological dependency can develop insidiously (Bailey, 1989).

The focus of nursing management is prevention. Creative educational approaches are needed—the "just say no" campaign is one example. This program presents drug and alcohol refusal as a peer-accepted behavior and models that behavior.

When prevention is not accomplished, early detection is essential. Parents need to be taught the signs and symptoms of use of these substances, and they need to be encouraged to discuss drug use with their school-age children. Table 15-8 lists the signs of alcohol and organic solvent intoxication.

## Child Abuse and Neglect

Maltreatment of children is a major social problem. Even though children of school age are more verbal, nurses must continue to be alert for signs of child abuse or neglect. This topic is discussed in detail in Chapter 14.

## Sex Education

With curiosity at a peak and sexual urges dormant, this is a comfortable time to begin children's sex education. Children can be taught about differences in bodies and about what will happen to them when they begin to approach puberty. This advance preparation makes later adjustment easier. General information about reproduction can be presented in an age-appropriate manner before the child becomes self-conscious about his or her emerging sexuality.

Nurses should discuss with parents the child's need for information and assist them in selecting resource material. The child's questions can be answered in a matter-of-fact way, giving only the information requested in the question. However, the person providing the information needs to feel comfortable about the discussion. It may help some parents if nurses role-play common questions with them and assist them in formulating responses.

Parents may need assistance in the ongoing sex education of the child. Many schools are now discussing AIDS at the elementary school level. The Centers for Disease Control recommends that school-age children be taught about AIDS and how it is spread (Palfrey, Rappaport, & DeGraw, 1989). Other sexually transmitted diseases, "safe sex," birth control, and sexual behaviors are topics parents need to discuss and clarify with their children. School-age children will gather a great deal of misinformation from peers which parents should be prepared to correct.

## Mainstreaming Handicapped Children

The Education for All Handicapped Children Act of 1975 (PL 94-142) guarantees appropriate educational placement for all handicapped children. Handicapped children are to be placed in the least restrictive environment. This means that these children are not to be segregated unnecessarily and that barriers to their educational needs are to be removed. This "mainstreaming" may result in classroom placements where special needs are less understood. Architectural barriers need to be removed. This may mean widening doorways for wheelchairs and building wheelchair ramps, as well as having appropriate bathroom facilities. Other barriers to education might include the need for certain procedures such as clean intermittent catheterization. The provision of these services removes barriers to the child's education. The nurse may need to act as child and family advocate (Palfrey, Rappaport, & DeGraw, 1989).

Children who need remedial help must be screened and tested by the school. Individual educational plans (IEP) must be developed that delineate specific educational adaptations needed by the child. The plan must be evaluated and refined periodically (Landman, 1986).

## Television Viewing

The average American school-age child spends a significant amount of time in front of a television screen. Nielsen Ratings report that children aged 6 to 11 years watch about 26 hours of television per week (1985). This time was spent viewing programs and does not include the time spent playing video games and watching VCR tapes.

Although there are educational programs that are beneficial to children, problems may result from spending less time with other activities such as reading and exercise. An additional concern is the amount of violence on televi-

*Table 15–8.   Characteristics of Abuse of Alcohol and Organic Solvents*

|  | Signs/Symptoms of Abuse | General Comments |
| --- | --- | --- |
| Alcohol | Euphoria, loss of inhibition, emotional lability, impaired judgment, hostility, aggressiveness, incoordination, lethargy, stupor, blackouts | Alcohol dependence is a progressive disease. Psychological dependence precedes physical dependence. Tolerance develops at varying rates. High tolerance is suggestive of alcoholism. *Withdrawal:* anxiety, tremors, hallucinations, hyperreflexia convulsions, and death. Brain damage subtle to pronounced. Liver damage. |
| Inhalants and organic solvents | Some degree of short-term intoxication, euphoria, impaired perception and coordination, loss of consciousness | Some degree of psychological dependence in the broad sense (abuser becomes dependent on the euphoric state). Most often seen with younger substance abusers. Users have an increased probability of alcohol or other substance abuse. *Medical complications:* asphyxia from plastic bags used to inhale fumes; ventricular fibrillation; arrhythmias; lead poisoning; possible irreversible damage to CNS, liver, kidneys, and bone marrow. Psychosis similar to that evoked by hallucinogenic drugs may occur. |

Adapted from Rode, S. [1987]. Management of substance abuse. In J. Servansky & S. Opas [Eds.]. *Nursing management of children.* Boston: Jones and Bartlett, pp. 456, 459)

sion and videotapes, as well as in video games. There is increasing concern that aggressive behavior, intellectual passivity, and inhibited creativity may result from excessive television viewing.

A significant amount of television advertising targets children. Merchandise modeled on television characters and programs is promoted heavily. Most of the best-selling toys today are based on television programs, and most of them have a violent theme (American Academy of Pediatrics, 1988). This commercial effect also extends to food items. Much food advertised during children's programs is of limited nutritional value and may be high-calorie junk food. The promotion of empty calories along with the physical passivity of television viewing can contribute to obesity.

Parents need to be encouraged to become involved in the selection of video activities. Discussion of television programs between parents and children may enhance communication and create an opportunity to think about and critique programming, rather than viewing it passively. Video games may be used as family games, thereby providing more social interactive time. The Committee on Communications of the American Academy of Pediatrics has issued recommendations to parents and concerned adults about television viewing (American Academy of Pediatrics, 1988). These are found in Table 15-9.

## Parenting Development

As children grow and develop, parenting roles change. The child's entry into school brings new challenges to parents. Children's acceptance of peer groups may appear in some respects to represent rejection of the parents. It is essential for parents to understand that this behavior is normal and does not represent outright rejection. Realistic parental expectations of children are important at all times but particularly during the industry versus inferiority

*Table 15–9.  Recommendations from the American Academy of Pediatrics Committee on Communications*

1. Parents should be educated concerning the hazards of prolonged television viewing and should, therefore, limit the amount of time their children spend watching television and monitor the programs they are viewing.
2. Parents and pediatricians should actively oppose television-activated toys, as well as the the growing commercialization of children's television that these toys represent. They should register their disapproval by writing to legislators and the television networks.
3. Congress should continue to hold hearings on the effect that televised violence and toys that glorify war have on children.
4. Research on the impact of children of televised violence and toys that glorify violence should be encouraged and supported.
5. Legislation that mandates daily broadcasts of educational and instructional programs and provides alternatives to programs that promote toys should be introduced and supported.

(From Committee on Communications. [1988]. Commercialization of children's television and its effect on imaginative play. *Pediatrics, 81*[6], 900–901)

stage. The importance of children's self-esteem needs special emphasis. Unrealistic expectations may make children feel that they do not measure up to parental standards that lead to parental approval.

In order for parents to accept their children's loosened parental ties and promote high self-esteem in their children, they need to have a healthy level of self-esteem themselves. It is important to help parents recognize when they are doing a good job and understand that they are still important to their children.

Children's temperaments and matches with parental expectations are important throughout childhood, but there are special considerations during the school-age years. The child who does not persevere but whose parents expect behavior that reflects high motivation to achieve may be in jeopardy. The child's temperament must fit with the teacher's expectations as well; otherwise, this provides a situation whereby the child may experience new conflicts.

At numerous points in this chapter, the need to teach parents has been mentioned. School-age children can also begin to understand their roles as future parents. Creative programs have been adopted by a variety of groups that place responsibility on the child for the care of an object, such as an egg, that represents a baby. Care of the "baby" must be maintained 24 hours a day. Similarly, sex education programs can prepare children for responsible behavior. Many of these programs have as their major goal the prevention of teenage pregnancy but, in fact, they may serve a dual role.

## Summary

Growth during the school-age years is at a plateau. Development is characterized by refinement; motor development progresses from gross to fine motor control. Nutritional needs can be met with a balanced diet. Cognitively, the child is entering Piaget's stage of concrete operations. The ability to apply rules and classify is required. Decentering, seriation, and conservation are also achieved. The child's new ability to reason allows the beginning of moral judgments.

Entry into school marks a transition away from home and parents. The peer group and teachers become influential. Sex role identity is also affected by peer interaction. Play usually involves groups, and cooperative play begins.

Psychosocial development is exemplified by Erikson's stage of industry versus inferiority. Success in accomplishing tasks and the resulting self-esteem are important to the school-age child. The school-age period represents a relatively healthy phase in the child's life. Annual health assessments are recommended to detect signs of illness or developmental problems. Dental checkups are recommended every 6 months. Vision and hearing screening should be done before the child begins school and at regular intervals thereafter.

Common concerns of this period include safety issues. Motor vehicle and bicycle accidents and sports injuries are frequent sources of injury. The latchkey child is a fairly recently recognized phenomenon that is widespread in this country. Substance abuse may begin at this age; early detection and preventive programs are needed.

Parents also need education. Parenting education is often directed to the parents of infants and young children, leaving the parents of older children without needed help. Nurses should remember that anticipatory guidance is still needed during the school years. School nurses can help provide parenting classes through the school and other community agencies.

## References

American Academy of Pediatrics Committee on Communications. (1988). Commercialization of children's television and its effect on imaginative play. *Pediatrics, 81*(6), 900–901.

American Academy of Pediatrics. (1988). *Report of the Committee on Infectious Diseases* (21st ed.). Elk Grove Village, IL: American Academy of Pediatrics.

American Academy of Pediatrics Committee on Sports Medicine. (1988). Recommendations for participation in competitive sports. *Pediatrics, 81*(5), 737–739.

Anderson, C. L. (1987). Assessing parenting potential for child abuse risk. *Pediatric Nursing, 13*(5), 323–327.

Bailey, G. W. (1989). Current perspectives on substance abuse in youth. *Journal of American Academy of Child and Adolescent Psychiatry, 28*(2), 151–162.

Behrman, R.E., & Vaughan, V.C. (Eds.). (1987). *Nelson textbook of pediatrics* (13th ed.). Philadelphia: W. B. Saunders.

Bradley, R. H., & Caldwell, B. M. (1988). Using the home inventory to assess the family environment. *Pediatric Nursing, 14*(2), 97–102.

Brunell, P. A. (1990). Measles one more time. *Pediatrics, 86*(3), 474–476.

Cohen, S. (1979). Inhalants. In R. Dupont, O. Golstein, & J. O'Donnel (Eds.). *Handbook of drug abuse.* Washington, D.C.: National Institute on Drug Abuse.

Cooke, R.E. (Ed.). (1968). *The biological basis of pediatric practice.* New York: McGraw-Hill.

Crittenden, P. (1988). Family and dyadic patterns. In K. Browne, C. Davies, & P. Stratton (Eds.). *Early prediction and prevention of child abuse.* New York: John Wiley & Sons.

DeAngelis, C. (1984). *Pediatric primary care* (3rd ed.). Boston: Little, Brown.

Dietz, W. H. (1986). Prevention of childhood obesity. *Pediatric Clinics of North America, 33*(4), 823–833.

Erikson, E. H. (1963). *Childhood and society* (2nd ed.). New York: W. W. Norton.

Feld, L. G., Springate, J. E. (1988). Hypertension in children. *Current Problems in Pediatrics, 28*(6), 323–367.

Forbes, G. B. (1968). Obesity. In M. Green & E. Haggarty (Eds.). *Ambulatory pediatrics.* Philadelphia: W.B. Saunders.

Green, M., & Haggerty, R. J. (1990). *Ambulatory pediatrics* (4th ed.). Philadelphia: W. B. Saunders.

Grey, M. (1988). Stressful life events, absenteeism, and the use of school health services. *Journal of Pediatric Health Care, 2*(3), 121–127.

Kohlberg, L. (1968). The child as a moral philosopher. *Psychology Today, 2*(4), 25–30.

Landman, G. B. (1986). Preventing school failure: The physician as child advocate. *Pediatric Clinics of North America, 33*(4), 935–953.

Lepow, M. L. (1990). Measles vaccine and measles control. *Pediatric Annals, 19*(9), 542–550.

Lewis, M., & Volkmar, F. (1990). *Clinical aspects of child and adolescent development.* Philadelphia: Lea and Febiger.

McClellan, M. A. (1984). On their own: Latchkey children. *Pediatric Nursing,* May-June, 198–201.

Morgan, K. J., Zabik, M. Z., & Leville, G. A. (1981). The role of nutrient intake of 5–12 year old children. *American Journal of Clinical Nutrition, 34,* 1418.

Newton, J. (1989). *The new school health handbook.* Englewood Cliffs, NJ: Prentice-Hall.

Nielsen Company. (1985). *1985 Nielsen report on television.* Chicago: A.C. Nielsen.

Palfrey, J. S., Rappaport, L., & DeGraw, C. (1989). The school-age child: Putting it all together. *Current Problems in Pediatrics, 18*(6), 380–387.

Piaget, J. (1965). *The moral judgment of the child* (M. Gabain, Trans.). New York: Free Press.

Piaget, J., & Inhelder, B. (1969). *The psychology of the child.* New York: Basic Books.

Pipes, P. L. (1989). *Nutrition in infancy and childhood* (4th ed.). St. Louis: C. V. Mosby.

Pollitt, E., Leibel, R. L., & Greenfield, D. (1981). Brief fasting, stress, and cognition in children. *American Journal of Clinical Nutrition, 34,* 1526–1533.

Schuster, C. S., & Ashburn, S. S. (1986). *The process of human development: A holistic life-span approach* (2nd ed.). Boston: Little, Brown.

Szer, I. S. (1989). Are those limb pains "growing" pains? *Contemporary Pediatrics, 6,* 143–148.

Tanji, J. L. (1990). The preparticipation physical examination for sports. *American Family Physician,* August 1990, 397–402.

Tuttle, W. W. (1974). Effect on school boys of omitting breakfast. *Journal of the American Dietetic Association, 39,* 674.

Vander Zanden, J. W. (1978). *Human development.* New York: Knopf.

Vaughan, V. C., & Litt, F. L. (1990). *Child and adolescent development: Clinical implications.* Philadelphia: W. B. Saunders.

Walker, L. J. (1984). Sex differences in development of moral reasoning: A critical review. *Child Development, 55,* 677–691.

Wolf, D. A. (1988). Child abuse and neglect. In E. Marsh & L. G. Terdal (Eds.). *Behavioral assessment of childhood disorders* (2nd ed.). New York: Guilford Press.

Waldman, H. B. (1990). Are minority children getting their fair share of dental services? *Journal of Dentistry for Children,* Sept-Oct, 380–384.

Wasserman, R. C. (1990). Screening tests in general pediatric practice. In M. Green & R. Haggerty (Eds.). *Ambulatory pediatrics* (pp. 83–87). Philadelphia: W. B. Saunders.

Wilson, M. H. (1989). Preventing injury in the "middle years." *Contemporary Pediatrics, 6,* 20–54.

## Bibliography

Dietz, W. H., & Gortmaker, S. L. (1985). Do we fatten our children at the TV set? Television viewing and obesity in children and adolescents. *Pediatrics, 75,* 807–812.

Dworkin, P. H. (1989). Behavior during middle childhood: developmental themes and clinical issues. *Pediatric Annals, 18*(6), 347–355.

Freiberg, K. L. (1987). *Human development: A life-span approach* (3rd ed.). Boston: Jones & Bartlett.

Hayes, J. S. (1987). Theories of child development. In J. Servansky & S. Opas (Eds.). *Nursing management of children.* Boston: Jones & Bartlett.

Kempe, C. H., Silver, H. K., & O'Brien, D. (1987). *Current pediatric diagnosis and treatment* (9th ed.). Los Altos, CA: Appleton-Lange.

McHugh, M. J. (1987). The abuse of volatile substances. *Pediatric Clinics of North America, 34*(2), 333–340.

Neumann, C. G. (1977). Obesity in pediatric practice: Obesity in preschool and school-age children. *Pediatric Clinics of North America, 24*(1), 117–122.

O'Brien, D., & Hambridge, K. M. (1987). Normal childhood nutrition and its disorders. In C. H. Kempe, H. K. Silver, & D. O'Brien (Eds.). *Current pediatric diagnosis and treatment* (9th ed.). Los Altos, CA: Appleton-Lange.

Report of the Second Task Force on Blood Pressure Control in Children. (1987). *Pediatrics, 79,* 7.

Ritchey, A. K. (1990). Anemia. In M. Green & R. Haggerty (Eds.). *Ambulatory Pediatrics* (pp. 376–383). Philadelphia: W. B. Saunders.

Sandler, A. (1989). Social development in middle childhood. *Pediatric Annals, 18*(6), 380–387.

Snell, M. E., & Fisher, M. M. (1988). The school. In Matson, J. L., & Marchetti, A. (Eds.) *Developmental disabilities: A lifespan perspective.* Orlando, FL: Grune & Stratton.

U. S. Department of Health and Human Services (1989). National Institute of Dental Research. Oral health of U.S. children: National and regional findings, 1986–1987 (NIH Publication #89-2247). Washington, D.C.: U. S. Government Printing Office.

Winklestein, M. L. (1989). Fostering positive self-concept in the school-age child. *Pediatric Nursing, 15*(3), 229–233.

Zigler, E. & Hall, N. W. (1988). Day care and its effect on children: An overview for pediatric health professionals. *Developmental and Behavioral Pediatrics, 9*(1), 38–46.

# Adolescent Growth, Development, and Health

Richard E. Harbin

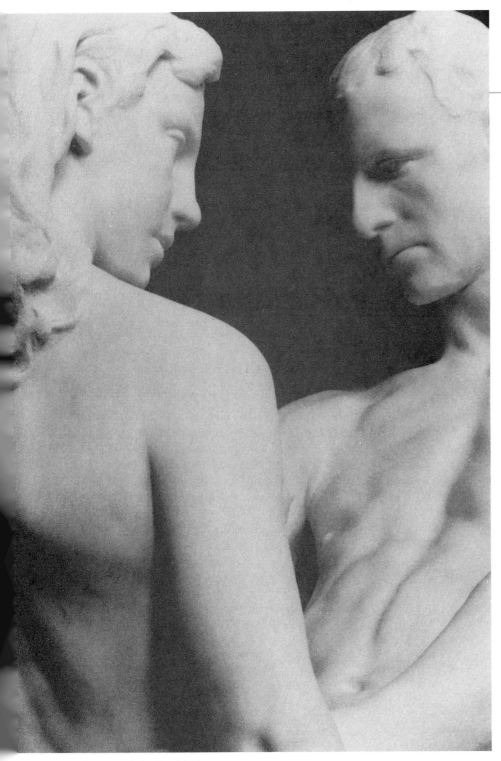

16

*Stages of Adolescence*

*Morbidity and Mortality*

*Physical Growth and Development*
  *The Tanner Scales*
  *Puberty*

*Psychosexual Development*
  *Freud*

*Cognitive Development*
  *Piaget*
  *Moral Development*

*Psychosocial Development*
  *Erikson: The Sense of Identity*
  *Interpersonal Relationships*
  *Sex-Role Identification*

*Assessment*

*Health Promotion*

*Common Health Concerns*
  *Menstruation*
  *Breast Size and Shape*
  *Penis Size*
  *Stature*
  *Gynecomastia*
  *Masturbation*
  *Sexual Behavior*
  *Contraception*
  *Adolescent Pregnancy*
  *Eating Disorders*
  *Substance Abuse*
  *Androgenic-Anabolic Steroids*
  *Depression*
  *Suicide*

*Summary*

*Photograph by David Finn*

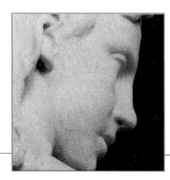

## Learning Objectives

*Upon completion of this chapter the reader will be able to:*

1. *Identify the three stages of adolescence and discuss the developmental tasks of each stage.*

2. *Relate the significance of mortality rates for adolescents.*

3. *Discuss the cognitive development of the adolescent.*

4. *Explain the importance of peer relationships in adolescence.*

5. *Discuss the important components of the adolescent health history and identify appropriate communication techniques.*

6. *Analyze the current sexual behavior code of adolescents.*

7. *Discuss the factors affecting adolescent contraceptive use and nonuse.*

8. *Discuss the etiology and medical management of eating disorders, depression, and suicide and formulate appropriate nursing interventions for adolescents with these problems.*

9. *Develop nursing interventions for accident prevention.*

## Key Terms

*chumship*

*egocentrism*

*emancipated minor*

*formal operations*

*growth spurt*

*homosexual identity development*

*idealism*

*identity versus identity diffusion*

*menarche*

*peer group*

*pubescence*

*risk-taking behavior*

*self-image*

*sense of identity*

*sex maturity rating*

*sex role identity*

*thelarche*

The term adolescence defies a precise definition. It is a long developmental stage and can be defined in chronological, biological, cognitive, or social terms. Biological changes take place in all body systems in a predictable order, but it is difficult to assign age markers to the adolescent period. There is no typical 15- or 16-year-old, because each individual follows her or his own biological timetable. Cognitive development in adolescence focuses on the transition from concrete thinking to the ability to think in increasing levels of abstraction. Adolescent psychosocial development is influenced by cultural, familial, religious, and educational factors that shape the adolescent's adjustment in society.

Although adolescence has been defined in various ways, it is generally considered to be a 10- to 12-year period that begins with the onset of puberty. This event radically changes the pattern of childhood growth, which, to this point, has been characterized by relatively constant annual increments in height and weight. Adolescent growth varies in each individual as well as in the length of time it takes to occur. Growth in the adolescent stage eventually reaches a peak and then decreases until adult size is attained.

Because adolescence is a unique developmental period, the health care needs of adolescents are specific, and it is critical that services be adapted in accordance with these needs. Nearly every aspect of providing care—the setting, interviews and obtaining histories, physical examination, and the actual care providers—must reflect the needs of the adolescent.

Nurses must be familiar with the developmental stages of adolescence in order to understand adolescent health issues. Expected behaviors, priorities, concerns, and strategies for working with adolescents vary with each stage of development. The stages of psychosocial development and their implications for adolescent health care providers are summarized in Table 16-1.

It is important for the nurse to remember that adolescence is a period during which many lifelong health practices are established. Nursing care goals include preventing and treating problems that occur during adolescence and providing young people with the knowledge, skills, and behaviors that will promote positive health throughout their lifetime.

*Table 16–1. Adolescent Psychosocial Development*

| | Early Adolescence (Females 11–14 years, males 13–15) | Middle Adolescence (Females 15–17 years, males 16–19) | Late Adolescence (Females 18–25 years, males 20–26) |
|---|---|---|---|
| **Cognitive Thinking** | *Concrete Thinking:* Here and now. Appreciate immediate reactions to behavior but no sense of later consequences. | *Early Abstract Thinking:* Inductive/deductive reasoning. Able to connect separate events, understand later consequences. Very self-absorbed, introspective, lots of daydreaming and rich fantasies. | *Abstract Thinking:* Adult ability to think abstractly. Philosophical. Intense idealism about love, religion, social problems. |
| **Task Areas** | | | |
| Family–Independence | Transition from obedient to rebellious. Rejection of parental guidelines. Ambivalence about wishes (dependence/independence). Underlying need to please adults. Hero worship ("crushes") | Insistence on independence, privacy. May have overt rebellion or sulky withdrawal. Much testing of limits. Role-playing of adult roles (but not felt to be "real"—easily abandoned) | Emancipation (leave home). Re-establishment of family ties. Assume true adult roles with commitment. |
| Peers–Social/Sexual | Same-sex "best friend". "Am I normal?" concerns. Giggling boy–girl fantasies. Sexual experimentation (intercourse) *not* normal at this age: Done to counteract fears of worthlessness, obtain "friends," humiliate parents | Dating, intense interest in opposite sex. Sexual experimentation begins. Risk-taking common. Unrealistic concept of partner's role. Need to please significant peers (of either sex). For females, boyfriend alone may be the "significant peer" | Partner selection. Realistic concept of partner's role. Mature friendships. True intimacy possible only after own identity is established. Need to please self too ("enlightened self-interest") |
| School–Vocation | Still need structured school setting. Goals unrealistic, changing. Want to copy favorite role models. Grades often drop due to priority set on socializing with friends | More class choices in school setting. Beginning to identify skills, interests. Start part-time jobs. Begin to react to system's expectations: may decide to beat the establishment at its own game (super achievers) or to reject the game (drop-outs) | Full-time work or college. Identify realistic career goals. Watch for apathy (no future plans) or alienation, since lack of goal-orientation is correlated with unplanned pregnancy, juvenile crime, etc. |
| Self-Perception Identity Social responsibility | Incapable of true self-awareness while still concrete thinkers. Losing child's role but do not have adult role, hence *low self-esteem*. Tend to use denial (it can't happen to me) | Confusion/flux about self-image. Seek *Group identity*. Vary narcissistic. Impulsive, impatient | Realistic, positive self-image. Able to consider others' needs, less narcissistic. Able to reject group pressure if not in self-interest |

*(continued)*

*Table 16–1.  Adolescent Psychosocial Development (Continued)*

| | Early Adolescence (Females 11–14 years, males 13–15) | Middle Adolescence (Females 15–17 years, males 16–19) | Late Adolescence (Females 18–25 years, males 20–26) |
|---|---|---|---|
| Values | Stage II Values (Backscratching) (Good behavior in exchange for rewards) | Stage III Values (Conformity) (Behavior that peer group values) | Stage IV Values (Social Responsibility) (Behavior consistent with laws and duty) |
| Chief Health Issues (Other Than Acute Illness) | Psychosomatic symptoms Fatigue and "growing pains" Concerns about normalcy Screening for growth and development problems | Outcomes of sexual experimentation (pregnancy, STD) Health-risk behaviors (drugs, alcohol, driving) Crisis counseling (runaways, acting out, family, etc.) | Health promotion/Healthy lifestyles Contraception Self-responsibility for health and health care |
| **Professional Approach** | | | |
| To retain sanity, staff should:   Like teenagers   Understand development   Be flexible   Be patient   Keep a sense of humor | Firm, direct support Convey limits—simple, concrete choices Do *not* align with parents, but do be an objective, caring *adult* Encourage transference (hero-worship) Sexual Decisions—directly encourage to wait, to say "No" Encourage parental presence in clinic, but interview teen alone | Be an objective sounding board (but let them solve own problems) Negotiate choices Be a role model Don't get *too* much history ("grandiose stories") *Confront* (gently) about consequences, responsibilities Consider: what will give them status in eyes of peers? Use peer group sessions Adapt system to crises, walk-ins, impulsiveness, "testing" Ensure confidentiality Allow teens to seek care independently | Allow mature participation in decisions Act as a resource Idealistic stage, so convey "professional" image Can expect patient to examine underlying wishes, motives (e.g., pregnancy wish if poor compliance with contraception) Older adolescents able to adapt to policies/needs of clinic system |

(Source: Roberta K. Beach, M.D. [adapted in part from L. Fine and G. Zackus])

## Stages of Adolescence

Adolescence is commonly divided into three stages: early (12–14 years), middle (15–16 years), and late (17 to adulthood).

### Early Adolescence

In early adolescence adolescents are focused initially on the task of becoming comfortable with their own bodies. They are experiencing a significant growth spurt and are trying to cope with the rapid changes in hormone levels, body mass, distribution of fat, muscles, and growth of pubic and axillary hair. They are very concerned with their own growth and development and how it compares with their peers. Very early or very late development can cause great concern. Loss of role identity (no longer a child, but not yet an adult) may cause low self-esteem and acute self-consciousness.

Struggles with dependence/independence emerge as adolescents seek emancipation from parents and other adults. The adolescent in this phase often vacillates between adult and childish behavior, creating turmoil in the adolescent–parent relationship. Abrupt expressions of independence alternate with continued dependence upon parents and others. Friends become increasingly important during the attempt at separation from parents. The peer group in early adolescence usually consists of friends of the same sex, and group activities are the norm (Fig. 16-1).

### Middle Adolescence

Membership in a peer group assumes prime importance in middle adolescence. This membership is marked by participation in current fads, music, and often a unique language. This is a time of continued absorption with physical image and of evaluating cultural expectations. Middle adolescence is also marked by experimentation as teens explore adult-like behavior. Experimentation can be positive, allowing adolescents to explore their own potentials. However, it is often viewed negatively because of the

Figure 16–1. *In early adolescence, the peer group is a major influence.*

Figure 16–2. *Risk-taking behavior often marks middle adolescence.*

behavior that occurs when adolescents attempt to prove themselves to peers. Common behaviors include drinking, drug use, and reckless driving.

As they move through this middle phase, adolescents focus on the next developmental task of building new and meaningful relationships with members of the same and opposite sexes. Middle adolescents experiment with different styles of interaction with peers and adults. Changing relationships, social exploration, and general inquisitiveness often lead to sexual experimentation and risk-taking behavior (Fig. 16-2). This is the period when cognitive function progresses from concrete thinking to formal operational thought. The adolescent begins to move from thoughts about only the here and now to abstract thoughts. This cognitive growth continues into adulthood.

The middle adolescent phase is often viewed as the most difficult period in terms of family relationships. The many changes occurring with the adolescent and the accompanying anxieties created by each change cause a great deal of stress in the adolescent–parent relationship.

## Late Adolescence

During late adolescence, adolescents continue to develop their own value system. Cognitive abilities also continue to develop, and adolescents begin to verbalize conceptually. The development of a workable value system often leads to the idealism that is characteristic of this phase.

The peer group loses its primary importance as late adolescents seek to form more intimate and intense sexual relationships with other individuals (Fig. 16-3). Some

teens may establish their independence from parents by moving away from home, but many choose to continue their education, which may prevent the economic freedom they seek. This delay can be a source of personal or familial conflict for many young people.

Various ethnic groups may exhibit differences in the manner in which these developmental tasks are approached, as well as in their criteria for successful completion. It is important that nurses view the performance and progress of adolescents in each of these task areas in the context of the client's particular cultural norms and expectations.

## Morbidity and Mortality

Although the adolescent period is often viewed as a healthy developmental period, there are significant health care problems that have an impact on this population. Ironically, owing to their overall good health, adolescents are often neglected by the health care system. Adolescents and young adults receive the least attention from health care providers. Data suggest that they receive a minimal amount of health counseling from health care providers (Joffe, 1988). This failure to deliver health care to adolescents may account for the fact that they are the only age group with increasing morbidity and mortality statistics.

The adolescent period evokes a variety of images. The prevalence of youth-oriented advertising leads many

*Figure 16–3.   Establishing heterosexual relationships is a vital part of adolescence.*

adults to view adolescents as attractive, energetic, free, idealistic, highly advantaged, and carefree. Adolescents may also be perceived as rebellious, insensitive, unappreciative, self-centered, and perhaps irresponsible. These conflicting views combine with the various images adolescents have of themselves to make this a stressful and often difficult period for them.

Adolescents differ from adults in their perceptions and assessment of risk. They tend to believe that the benefits of risky actions outweigh their costs. This approach makes young people highly vulnerable to injuries resulting from risk-taking behavior. Adolescents may also have feelings of immortality, which, combined with the need for experimentation and peer group pressure, can also lead to risk-taking behavior. The high death and injury rates from motor vehicle accidents involving adolescents are related to a combination of this behavior and lack of driving experience.

One of the most striking problems among adolescents involves violent behaviors. The leading causes of death for young people 15 to 24 years of age are accidents, homicide, and suicide. Accidents, including those involving motor vehicles, are the leading cause of death for the 10- to 19-year age group. In 1989 the fatality rate for drivers under 20 years of age was 79 per 100,000 (National Safety Council, 1990). One of every 1600 10- to 19-year-olds will die from accidents.

Suicide rates continue to rise in the adolescent population, particularly in 15- to 19 year-old males, resulting in a death rate of 16.4 per 100,000 population (Centers for Disease Control, 1988). This dramatic increase makes suicide the second leading cause of death in this age group.

Actual figures are difficult to ascertain because all attempts may not be reported. Suicides are also included in other reportable categories, such as accidental injuries. It is thought that 10% to 15% of all single-car crashes are actually suicides (Imajo, 1983).

Interpersonal violence and homicides account for a large number of deaths and disabilities among adolescents. Homicide is the leading cause of death among young African-Americans. It should be noted that poverty, not race, is a major risk factor for homicide (Prothrow-Stith, 1986). Violent deaths are often associated with substance abuse. Nearly two thirds of all American adolescents have used an illicit drug by the time they complete high school (Johnston, 1987). Alcohol is a factor in more than half the injuries resulting from interpersonal violence (Baker, 1979).

Other problems, often identified as the "new morbidities," also involve adolescents and have a major impact on our society. One out of every 30 adolescents runs away from home; over 1 million drop out of school every year. Additional problems include learning disabilities, behavioral disturbances, emotional disorders, cigarette smoking, and child abuse.

The United States continues to record the highest teenage pregnancy rate of any developed country. Childbearing and childrearing by adolescents is linked to adverse outcomes for both mother and child. Mothers younger than 16 years of age, both black and white, have a higher incidence of low-birth-weight babies. This statistic continues to increase, an apparent failure of existing programs to decrease this rate.

## Physical Growth and Development

Adolescence is characterized by growth. Except for infancy, there is no period of significant growth velocity like that of the adolescent period. The majority of this growth happens during a "growth spurt" period that typically lasts about 2 years. Adolescents of both sexes achieve approximately 15% of their ultimate adult height and as much as 48% of their maximum skeletal mass during and after this growth spurt. Girls experience this growth spurt before boys, usually at age 8 to 10 years, and reach their maximum velocity in linear growth around 12 years of age. Boys usually start the growth spurt at about 12 years of age, with the maximal velocity in linear growth occurring around age 14. The growth rate of various organ systems differs, with the result that different body parts grow at different rates. The majority of growth occurs in the trunk, but growth begins in the extremities, which results in the awkward, gangling appearance displayed by adolescents. Poor posture may result because the skeletal system is growing faster than its supporting muscles, and the rapid growth of hands and feet often causes coordination problems. The large muscles grow faster than small muscles, creating additional coordination problems. There may also be racial factors that affect the growth rate. Finkelstein (1980) noted that black females mature physically at an earlier chronological age than white females.

Body composition also changes, marked by a doubling of skeletal mass, which accounts for the pubertal weight gain. Muscle mass also dramatically increases and is greater in males than in females. Nonlean body mass, mainly fat, also increases during adolescence but occurs within a less orderly growth pattern. Females eventually end up with twice as much body fat as males.

During adolescence the heart grows larger and lung capacity increases. This growth may occur more slowly than the growth of the rest of the body, causing an inadequate oxygen supply and resulting in the adolescent's feeling tired. The adolescent's pulse rate decreases as the heart grows, and blood pressure increases. Systolic blood pressure is usually slightly higher in adolescent males, with no difference in diastolic pressure noted between the sexes. As the number and size of alveoli in the respiratory system increase, oxygen exchange becomes more efficient, and respiratory rate decreases to 15 to 20 respirations/minute. The lymphatic system decreases during adolescence.

Adolescent hormonal influences at puberty cause significant changes in the integumentary system. The *sebaceous* glands of the face, neck, upper back, and chest become active during adolescence and play an important role in the appearance of acne. The *eccrine* sweat glands also become fully functional, resulting in increased perspiration.

In addition to the increases in height and weight there are marked changes in body proportion. Female hips become wider, with a narrowing of the shoulders. The shoulders become broader in males, with a narrowing of the hips. Facial structure also changes as the facial profile straightens owing to growth of the maxilla and mandible.

## The Tanner Scales

A useful tool for estimating the stage of physical development during adolescence, detecting growth abnormalities, and estimating further changes was developed by Tanner (1962). These sequential developments in sexual maturity are often referred to as "Tanner Stages," and the rating scale is called the *sex maturity rating (SMR)*. These ratings allow a comparison of adolescents at different chronological ages and make clinical observations much more meaningful, because growth in adolescence is so variable that chronological age is a poor reference standard for evaluating change.

The sex maturity ratings identify adolescent development, from Stage 1 to Stage 5, based on the development of secondary sexual characteristics. In males the development of pubic hair, the testes, and the penis are evaluated (Figs. 16-4 and 16-5). Figures 16-6 and 16-7 demonstrate the evaluation of pubic hair and breast development in females. Stage 1 is a prepubertal state; Stage 5 indicates that breasts, genitalia, and/or pubic hair have attained adult size and shape. The progression from Stage 1 to Stage 5 typically takes from 3 to 4 years. The characteristics of each stage are outlined in Table 16-2 (boys) and Table 16-3 (girls).

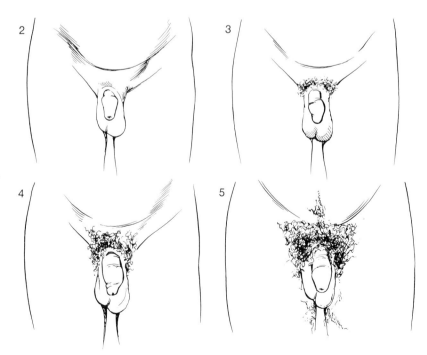

*Figure 16–4.  Standards for pubic hair ratings in boys.*

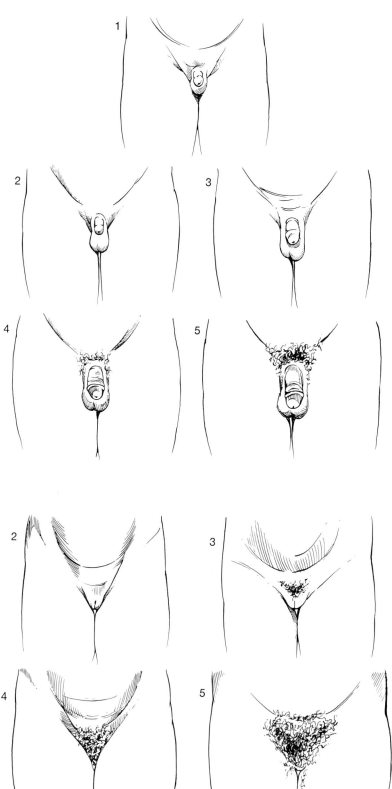

Figure 16–5.    Standards for genital maturity in boys.

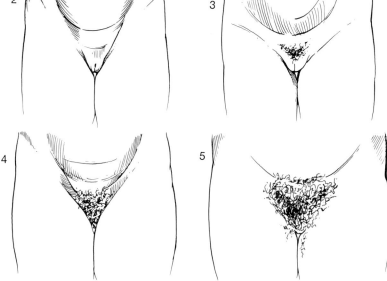

Figure 16–6.    Standards for pubic hair ratings in girls.

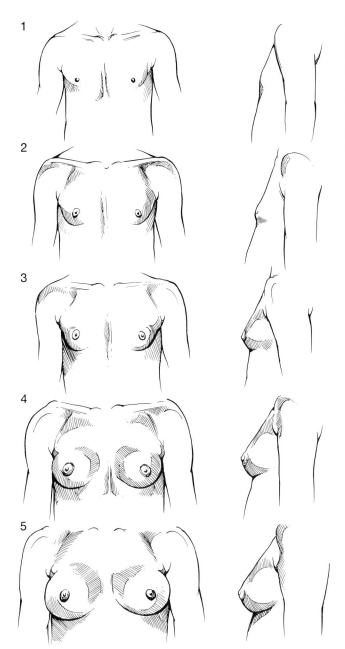

*Figure 16–7.* **Standards for breast development ratings.**

## Puberty

### Onset of Puberty

Puberty signifies the beginning of maturation of the physical manifestations of sex. *Pubescence* refers to development of sex organs and the growth of hair in the pubic and other areas. Pubertal development is initiated by a series of endocrinological events. There are numerous hypotheses concerning the triggering mechanism of puberty; current thought postulates that the initiation and control of puberty depend on a complex interaction among the hypothalamus, anterior pituitary, gonads, and body tissue. The

hypothalamus plays a central role in this process. Before puberty, the rate at which gonadotropic-releasing hormones are secreted and luteinizing (LH) and follicle-stimulating (FSH) hormones are released is kept low by circulating steroid hormones. The extreme sensitivity of hypothalamic receptor sites causes this low level. With increased maturation, these receptor sites become less sensitive. This causes an increase in serum gonadotropins, LH, and FSH. Gonadal hormone output subsequently exceeds the level necessary to affect peripheral tissue, and the changes involving puberty are initiated. Other hypotheses concerning puberty are related to genetics, nutrition, and environment.

### Pubertal Development in Girls

The initial sign of puberty in girls is the appearance of the breast bud. This event is termed *thelarche.* The breast buds commonly appear first and are followed by sparse hair along the medial borders of the labia. In about 16% of girls, pubic hair appearance precedes thelarche (Marshall, 1969). Initially pubic hair is typically straight and light in color. The amount of hair then increases, spreads over the labia, and becomes pigmented and more curly. The adult pattern occurs with further growth, ending with distribution to the medial surface of the thighs.

Girls reach peak growth velocity in height soon after thelarche. The onset of menstruation, *menarche,* typically occurs during Stage 4, but many girls begin menstruating during Stage 3. Menstruation begins about 2 years after the appearance of the breast buds and approximately 1 year after attainment of peak height velocity. The average age at menarche for North American girls is 12.9 years, with an age range of 10 to 16.5 years. This event usually occurs during early or middle adolescence. Menstrual periods are initially scanty and irregular, and although ovulation does not normally begin for 12 to 24 months after menarche, it is apparent that a significant number of girls ovulate earlier, some even at menarche.

Following Stage 2 development, breasts enlarge, and at Stage 4 the areola and nipple form a second mound. This breast stage is often difficult to discern. During the final stage the breast assumes the adult contour, in which only the nipple projects.

### Pubertal Development in Boys

Enlargement of the testes is the first sign of pubertal change. This change is very subtle and is difficult to detect in its earliest stage; using testicular size alone to ascertain if puberty has begun is not practical. At the same time as testicular enlargement occurs, the scrotum becomes larger and (in Caucasian males) changes to a pinker color. The texture of the surface of the scrotum changes from smooth to wrinkled *(rugae)* as the color darkens. The penis increases in length, and long, straight, slightly pigmented hair appears

*Table 16–2.  Classification of Genitalia Maturity Stages in Boys*

| Stage | Pubic Hair | Penis | Testes |
|---|---|---|---|
| 1 | None | Preadolescent | Preadolescent |
| 2 | Sparse growth, long, slightly pigmented | Slight enlargement | Scrotal reddening; coarse texture |
| 3 | Darker, more curled, small amount | Longer | Further increase |
| 4 | Resembles adult type, but less in quantity, no spread to medial thigh | Increase in width | Larger, scrotum dark |
| 5 | Adult quality and distribution | Adult size | Adult size |

(Adapted from Tanner, J. M. [1962]. *Growth at adolescence* [2nd ed.]. Oxford: Blackwell Scientific Publications; Daniel, W. A., Jr. [1985]. Growth of adolescence. *Seminars in Adolescent Medicine, 1*(1):15–24)

laterally at the base of the penis. This hair growth is usually the first visible sign that puberty has begun. According to Marshall and Tanner (1970), genital growth generally precedes further change in pubic hair pattern. Boys experience peak height velocity during genital Stage 4 and pubic hair during Stages 3 and 4. Genital Stages 3 and 4 mark the usual appearance of axillary hair.

Stage 4 is characterized by the growth of the testes and scrotum and by penile enlargement. The scrotal skin becomes darker in color as the penis becomes longer and broader, with the glans enlarging to adult size. Pubic hair darkens, becomes coarse and curlier, and extends toward the midline of the pubis. Pubic hair is similar to that of the adult but not as wide in distribution. In Stage 5 pubic hair growth spreads to the medial thigh areas. This final pubic hair growth marks the end of pubertal development, although some continued growth in height usually occurs.

## Nutrition Needs

Adolescents are at risk for nutritional problems. Adolescents often have a low dietary intake of certain vitamins and minerals (Driskell, 1987). These nutritional problems are present particularly among teens of low socioeconomic status, certain ethnic groups, and females. Numerous factors affect what adolescents eat, including peer pressure, a desire to make independent choices, media promotion of fast and junk foods, stress and anxiety surrounding self-image and body changes, the desire to be attractive, and eating "on the run." Cultural and familial

*Table 16–3.  Classification of Sex Maturity Stages in Girls*

| Stage | Pubic Hair | Breasts |
|---|---|---|
| 1 | None | Elevation of papilla only |
| 2 | Sparse growth, long, slightly pigmented downy hair along the labia | Breast bud: elevation of breast and papilla as small mound; areolar diameter increased |
| 3 | Increased amount, darker and coarser; spread over junction of pubes | Enlargement of breast and areola; no contour separation |
| 4 | Resembles adult type, but less area covered | Separation of contour; areola and papilla form secondary mound |
| 5 | Adult quality and distribution | Mature breast contour. Projection of papilla only |

(Adapted from Tanner, J. M. [1962]. *Growth at Adolescence* [2nd ed.]. Oxford: Blackwell Scientific Publications; Daniel, W. A., Jr. [1985]. Growth of adolescence. *Seminars in Adolescent Medicine, 1*(1):15–24)

importance placed on food also plays an important role in adolescent eating behaviors. Food may also be used as part of adolescent rebellion, as when teens refuse to eat the well-balanced meals advocated by their parents and instead chose junk foods.

Determining nutritional needs during adolescence is difficult because individual growth rates vary widely. Caloric needs depend primarily on the rate of growth and physical activity. The nutritional requirements of adolescent males are greater than those of adolescent females owing to their larger body size and prolonged growth period. Typical recommended daily requirements for calorie and protein intake in the average adolescent are listed in Table 16-4. Both adolescent females and males need 18 mg of iron daily. Girls frequently lack adequate iron and calcium intake. Vitamin C intake for both sexes is also low. Fast foods are low in iron and Vitamin C.

Nurses can play a role in nutrition counseling for adolescents by suggesting "healthier" fast foods such as pizza, salads, and baked or stuffed potatoes. Over one quarter of teen calories are typically derived from snacks. Nurses can help educate adolescents about empty calories. Good snack ideas include popcorn, yogurt, nuts, whole wheat crackers, fresh fruit, and cheese.

## Sleep

Proper sleep and rest are important to health during adolescence. This period is typically marked by increased sleep; parents may complain that their adolescent sleeps too much. Rapid physical growth and increased physical activity create fatigue in adolescents. Most adolescents are aware of their body needs and find sleep pleasurable. They sleep late whenever possible and often have problems getting up in the morning.

## Physical Appearance

Adolescents spend a great deal of time in front of the mirror. They study their reflection and attempt to decipher who they are and how others see them. They posture, practice various facial expressions, alter hairstyles, agon-

ize over pimples, and search for the best way to present themselves. Physical appearance is of critical importance, because it can significantly affect the quality and quantity of relationships with peers. Physical appearance or attractiveness often has a direct relation to popularity in high school.

Adolescents continually compare themselves with their peers and measure their own normalcy by such comparisons. Typical adolescents want to act and look just like their friends. Any changes or deviations from this standard image are threatening. Problems such as acne or the delay of maturity often create major concerns.

Nurses must be aware of the various implications these differing rates of maturation can have for adolescents. Self-image, personality, and behavior can be affected by the rate and timing of maturation. Adults may expect teens who mature early physically to act in a more mature manner, even though cognitive ability and social skills are not yet fully developed. Unreasonable expectations can affect later emotional adjustment. Teens who mature late also face potential emotional implications. These teens can be shy and insecure, experiencing a lowered self-esteem because their bodies are less developed than those of their friends.

Boys who mature late may experience teasing from peers, which can result in a poor self-image. They also may be excluded from heterosexual social situations, struggle with athletic skills, and be given less responsibility in the home. Girls who mature late may also feel isolated from peers and be excluded from social experiences. Adolescents who mature early may face problems in feeling "out of synch" with peers. Early physical maturation may lead to sexual relationships beyond maturity level. Lowered self-esteem can result from unwanted sexual activities or pregnancy.

Educating adolescents and showing an appreciation for their concerns are important nursing functions. Nurses must be aware of various, often subtle, signs that indicate adolescent concerns. Noting these signs and using them in discussion with adolescents may help to lessen anxieties. Often, the use of visual materials such as Tanner stage photos help the adolescent to better understand growth and maturation.

It is common for adolescents to fear that they will not be taken seriously. Thus they may be vague when discussing symptoms and evade the real reason for seeking health care. An example of this is the adolescent female who seeks health care because she started her menstrual period several months ago and now has missed two periods. Although she has never been sexually active, she fears that no one will believe her. Nurses must attempt to identify adolescents' concerns and intervene in appropriate ways designed to develop adolescents' self-image in a positive manner. This understanding and appreciation, combined with the knowledge that no pathology exists, normally results in alleviating the anxiety.

*Table 16–4. Typical Adolescent RDAs of Calories and Protein*

|  | Age | Calories/Kg | Protein (gm)/Kg |
|---|---|---|---|
| **Boys** | 11–14 | 60 | 1.0 |
|  | 15–18 | 42 | .9 |
|  | 19–22 | 41 | .8 |
| **Girls** | 11–14 | 48 | 1.0 |
|  | 15–18 | 38 | .8 |
|  | 19–22 | 38 | .8 |

## Psychosexual Development

Adolescence is described by Freud as the genital stage of psychosocial development. In this stage, full sexual potency is achieved, and libidinal impulses are aimed toward sexual involvements. If the adolescent has resolved the conflicts of earlier stages, there is a strong motivation to establish meaningful relationships with the opposite sex. Adolescents generally reach genital maturity and are capable of reproduction long before they are psychologically ready for sexual relationships. This discrepancy in maturity is the basis for a great deal of conflict for adolescents and, of course, their parents. Adolescents are bombarded with a virtually unending series of sexual messages in advertising, movies, and nearly every aspect of daily life. They also face another message involving social disapproval and conflicts involving their own moral standards. Stress occurs when these strong sexual desires are denied.

### Freud

Freud's psychodynamic theory presents the adolescent period as a time when a level of harmony is achieved between the unconscious drives of the id, the conscious ego, and the unconscious superego. Freud views the adolescent as internalizing the concepts of right and wrong and thus understanding how to function in society. In addition to refocusing the sexual drive to a member of the opposite sex, the adolescent must sublimate the second major drive, aggression, into productive work.

## Cognitive Development

Changes in mental development occur over time and follow similar patterns. Nurses must assess the adolescent's stage of cognitive growth. This knowledge will aid in the nurse's interactions with the adolescent client by focusing on cognitively appropriate strategies.

### Piaget

Piaget's first three stages of cognitive development have been discussed in the previous chapters of this unit. The fourth and final of Piaget's stages, the period of *formal operations,* usually begins around 12 years of age. Piaget studied a limited number of adolescents, but Elkind (1968) validated Piaget's thinking. During this stage cognitive ability progresses from concrete to formal operations. This means the child is no longer restricted to the here and now, as in the concrete thought stage, but can think about the abstract—from sequence of events, to various possibilities, to consequences of actions. This stage provides an entirely new way of thinking about the world and is characterized by orientation toward abstract thought.

Formal operations allow adolescents to make use of assumptions while thinking, formulating hypotheses, and constructing theories. The adolescent begins to think in classes, relations, and dimensions. Formal thought allows the individual to vary a single factor while keeping others constant and to think mathematically. Formal thought does not occur in all areas of cognition at the same time, which often presents a challenge for parents and teachers as well as health care providers. It is important to note that some adolescents never progress to this formal operational stage and, even as adults, fail to reach this level of cognition.

### Egocentrism

Young adolescents often think that the world revolves around them. They are intensely concerned about themselves, their thoughts and feelings, and how they appear to others. These young adolescents can be quite self-conscious and introspective. They believe that they are "on stage" and that everyone is observing their actions. Elkind (1967) describes this phase as egocentrism and proposes that adolescents create an imaginary audience to which they react.

### Idealism

As the egocentric phase fades, adolescents pass through a stage of *idealism* in attempting to grasp an understanding of life and its purpose. Adolescents use new cognitive abilities to evaluate the world and visualize various unrealistic possibilities for change. They view the world as less than ideal and often feel a desire to make reforms. Because they are experiencing so much uncertainty, adolescents seek something with lasting value. They place great importance on certain ideals, such as honesty and genuineness, and are very intolerant of anything viewed as hypocritical or deceitful. Adolescents often become involved with broad idealistic causes and movements; conflict and confusion can occur when others do not share their ideals. They usually experience periods of helplessness and depression as they face reality, but begin learning to relate their ideals to appropriate social action and to be more tolerant. This period of idealism paves the way for the development of adult values (Erikson, 1963).

## Moral Development

Before adolescence, moral judgments are made on the basis of right and wrong. Kohlberg (1976) proposes that preadolescents and young adolescents then reach the *conventional level* of morality in which judgments are based on expectations or behavior that gains or maintains approval of others. At this level attention is paid to obeying rules and respecting authority.

Increasing cognitive skills allow the older adolescent

to proceed from the conventional level to Kohlberg's last stage of moral development, the *postconventional level.* As adolescents question existing moral values, they begin to realize the irrationality of various moral codes. Cognitive development, which allows for understanding of concepts such as justice, human rights, and obligation, leads to moral judgment founded on conscience and principles of universal understanding. In the postconventional level, the adolescent develops an individual conscience and a defined set of moral values.

Nurses should realize that, as with cognitive formal operations, some adolescents never attain the ability to make postconventional moral judgments. Most adolescents continue to formulate moral codes as they move toward adulthood.

## Psychosocial Development

The transition from childhood to adulthood is usually turbulent. Adolescents seek to learn who they are while questioning many of their beliefs and modifying their conscience. This is a stressful time for both adolescents and parents. Added to the intellectual and emotional confusion is the rapid growth of their bodies and the further cultural pressures and uncertainties of today's world.

### Erikson: The Sense of Identity

Erikson (1963) refers to the central task of the early adolescent period as the establishment of a sense of identity. Erikson modified the psychosexual developmental theory of Freud to include social and cultural influences. Adolescents are in Stage 5 of Erikson's eight developmental stages in which the psychosocial task is *identity versus identity diffusion.* The adolescent must overcome the numerous sources of confusion during this period to develop a stable identity. This is the formation of *ego identity,* which Erikson defines as one's self-perceived, consistent individuality.

The establishment of *ego identity* is viewed as part of a continuum that begins in infancy and lasts until old age and death. Erikson states that each stage-specific task must be mastered and integrated into the personality before further psychosocial development can take place. *Ego diffusion* results when adolescents fail to establish a sense of identity. This can lead to numerous problems, such as a sense of futility, neuroses, and in some cases, psychotic disorders.

Childhood personality development is an important factor in ego identity formation. Social and cultural influences also play major roles. Adolescents must work through these factors to find a meaning to life and a role for themselves as individuals.

The development of identity leads to Erikson's sixth stage, a *sense of intimacy.* This involves the capacity for commitment in the face of difficulty. A weak ego or self-doubt interferes with establishing close relationships with other people.

### Interpersonal Relationships

Sullivan (1953) viewed development according to interpersonal relationships. Two of his concepts, "chumship" and the psychodynamics of the integration of lust, help in further understanding the adolescent's psychosocial development. *Chumship* is a special relationship with one same-sex friend, which is seen as a prerequisite for later heterosexual intimacy and mature sexuality. Chumship allows adolescents to look at themselves through the friend's eyes and to learn about another person by observing and analyzing experiences.

Sullivan further identified lust and the need for intimacy as interwoven, but not identical, drives. His integration of the lust concept involved three factors: (1) sexual unity based on genital urges, (2) construction of a motive system directed toward involvement with or the avoidance of others, and (3) construction of a chosen heterosexual interpersonal situation.

### Sex-Role Identification

During adolescence the sex-role identity is unified with the search for identity and self-esteem. Children learn typical female and male role expectations early in life. By the age of 6 years, they have a clear idea of their own gender and have adopted gender-specific behaviors and attitudes. In adolescence, sex roles become clearer as adolescents face expectations regarding sex-role behavior from peers and adults and learn to express themselves sexually. This expression is *sexuality*—a vital component of an individual's personality.

Sexual identity is a critical aspect of self-concept. Society has a strong influence on appropriate sex-role behavior. The causes determining sexual preference, either heterosexual or homosexual, are unknown. Various factors involving sexual identity, such as genetic influence, prenatal hormone levels, and environment, have all been postulated. A certain amount of homosexual experimental behavior is common for many adolescents and is usually part of the developmental process leading to a heterosexual identity. Some normally heterosexual adolescents may also engage in homosexual behavior under certain restrictive circumstances, such as boarding schools or prison settings.

The homosexual adolescent typically reports that he or she began to feel different or estranged from peers sometime during childhood. In studies of male homosexuality, the mean age at the time of awareness of same-sex attraction is approximately 13 years (American Academy of

Pediatrics, 1983; Suicide, 1988). Troiden (1988) has outlined a four-stage process involving homosexual identity development: *sensitization, identity confusion, identity assumption,* and *commitment.* This process begins with the child's profound sense of feeling "different" from peers, then developing a same-sex crush without awareness of a homosexual orientation, and finally assuming and sharing a homosexual identity with others. This ultimately leads to *commitment,* in which a self-identity as gay or lesbian is validated and the individual finds satisfaction with that identity.

Approximately 5% of males and 2% of females are exclusively homosexual; this percentage is doubled to include those who have a predominantly homosexual orientation. Despite this rather significant number of individuals, the issue of adolescent homosexuality is largely ignored. Remafedi (1987) describes how the issue of adolescent homosexuality brings into conflict two fundamental sociocultural beliefs: "One upholds the innate innocence and goodness of children, and the other decries homosexuals as 'assertive, destructive and deviant.' " Denial of the existence of adolescent homosexuality results in numerous problems. These adolescents are denied any role models and are consequently prevented from developing a positive homosexual identity. Suicide is a significant problem among gay and lesbian adolescents. Homosexual adolescents have strong feelings of self-hatred and self-destructiveness. These adolescents are also in increased danger of acquiring AIDS and other sexually transmitted diseases.

## Emotional Concerns

The adolescent period is a time of turmoil created by the many physical and psychological changes that occur. Adolescents try to deal with many new feelings and stimuli they do not understand; consequently, mood swings, behavioral extremes, and exaggerated responses are common. Such behavior is often confusing to others, as well as to the adolescent. It is important for nurses to remember, and to point out to parents, that this age-specific behavior is caused by the adolescent's inadequate ability to face these new and stressful situations.

Early adolescence is often marked by restlessness. Sitting quietly and concentrating are difficult tasks. Adolescents of this age also display aimless worry and anxiety about appearance and friends.

Difficulty involving feelings characterizes middle and late adolescence. Frustration often evokes outbursts of anger, ranging from slamming doors and shouting to insults and profanity. Adolescents may also respond to feelings of anger with impulsive or risk-taking behavior such as truancy from school or reckless driving, or they may react by indirect behavior such as being passive, withdrawn, or depressed.

This behavior may be disturbing, but most adolescents return to a more acceptable behavior within a short time. Nurses should give adolescents an opportunity to express thoughts and feelings, because they need encouragement and acceptance. Nurses need to be open to allow their adolescent clients to experiment with new behaviors and various modes of expression, and must also be aware of the adolescent's need for privacy.

## Peer Relationships

Peers play a critical role in the adolescent's *sense of identity.* The adolescent peer group can serve to enforce individual capabilities, but the adolescent must be careful not to exceed group limits in expressing individuality. Belonging to a peer group and gaining acceptance from peers are important as adolescents attempt to separate from their families. The various fads and values of peer groups add a sense of security for adolescents when family values are questioned.

Adolescent fads are important because they reflect the efforts of each group as it strives for identity. Perhaps most notable are changes in vocabulary, clothes, and music. Within these peer groups are numerous subcultures, each attempting to define itself and be recognized as the most desirable group.

The composition of peer groups varies according to the adolescent's developmental level. In early adolescence, groups are usually small and members are of the same sex; this is the solitary friendship or chumship period. These peer relationships provide support and mutual understanding when parents are still viewed as authority figures. Influence from the peer group usually centers on dress and interests.

Middle adolescence peer groups are larger and involve expansion to members of the opposite sex. Dating is often the key to membership in an older adolescent group. Usually group dating evolves to double dating and then to solo dating. Dating can be a difficult experience for both sexes as adolescents strive for acceptance. As middle adolescence progresses, adolescents usually gain greater self-confidence and feel more comfortable in forming heterosexual relationships. "Going steady" can provide a measure of security and help the adolescent gain acceptance. The dating relationship can also be harmful if the adolescent falls prey to sexual expectations and other group pressures, which may lead to unwanted sexual activity and pregnancy.

During middle adolescence the peer group influences gain priority and begin to replace parental standards and views. This usually leads to conflict with parents and results in stress for both parties. This is a difficult period marked by trial and error and experimentation. It is a time when adolescents attempt to define their sexual identity.

Toward late adolescence, heterosexual relationships

usually become more important than peer group associations. As the peer group influence lessens, adolescents begin to choose partners based on mutual enjoyment and understanding. The peer group continues to lose its importance in late adolescence, and the need for conformity to the group diminishes. Vocational training or college enrollment frequently brings separation from friends and broadens the circle of acquaintances.

## Assessment

### Communicating With Adolescents

Adolescents may be seen in an ambulatory setting or in the hospital, accompanied by a parent or alone. There are several approaches to interviewing an adolescent who is accompanied by parents. A common method is first to see the adolescent alone and then to interview or summarize findings with the parent. Many professionals believe that this approach is the best way to deliver the message that the adolescent is the client and is the focus of the visit. Other approaches involve seeing the parents initially or seeing the family together for all or a portion of the visit. It is important to recognize the need for varying approaches based on individual cases. The key factor is that the adolescent is identified as the client. Parents often need preparation for making this shift. Questions and attention should be focused on and directed to the adolescent rather than the parent. Time to see the adolescent alone should always be allowed so that sensitive topics such as sexuality or family relationships can be openly discussed. Some time must be spent with parents as well, to identify their concerns and to allow them to assist in completing the overview of the adolescent's level of functioning.

Establishing rapport with the adolescent is a critical factor in the delivery of health care to this population. Adolescents are usually fearful of health care visits, uncomfortable talking to an unfamiliar adult, and anxious about being examined and about any procedures that might be performed. Adolescents do not want care providers who imitate them in dress and speech. It is best to be friendly and concerned, while maintaining a professional manner; projecting a capable and competent attitude is important in making the adolescent more at ease.

Establishing confidentiality with the adolescent is important and should be accomplished during the initial visit. Nurses need to explain that no information will be discussed with the parents without the adolescent's permission. The limits of this confidentiality should be established; possible exceptions include problems that may be harmful to the client or others, such as attempted suicide, threats to run away, or pregnancy. Setting these ground rules of confidentiality seldom discourages open exchange of information and typically helps establish a feeling of trust.

## The Interview

There is no single method of interviewing an adolescent. One interview rarely provides all the information required. Interviewing is more comprehensive than history taking. In addition to a chronological description of events, the nurse should attempt to gain an appreciation of the client's feelings, beliefs, suspicions, actions, and reactions. Underlying any interaction is the critical factor involving the consideration of developmental aspects of adolescence. These aspects cannot be ignored if the nurse is to help the adolescent.

Establishment of trust is the necessary foundation for the development of a professional relationship between the nurse and the adolescent. Adolescents need to feel that the nurse has a sincere interest in them as individuals and views their concerns and feelings seriously. Establishing this degree of trust requires honesty and a genuine interest in adolescents.

Privacy must be provided for the adolescent during the interview. The nurse needs to be attentive to the adolescent and to respond nonjudgmentally. Verbal and nonverbal cues need to be identified. Nonverbal clues might include shaking of the head, avoidance of eye contact, or body posture. The length of the interview should be flexible, although the adolescent should understand that only a certain amount of time has been allotted. Setting time limits helps to prevent the adolescent from thinking that there is unlimited time to avoid discussing the problem. If the interview is rushed or there are distractions, the adolescent typically withdraws.

As the interview progresses and additional data are gathered, the nurse needs to use language appropriate to the adolescent's developmental and cultural background. Avoid using adolescent jargon or mannerisms—most adolescents view this as insincerity. Familiarity with current adolescent vocabulary helps more effective communication, however, because it helps the nurse to understand what the adolescent says. Allow time for the adolescent to ask questions and engage in discussion. Discussion and information sharing leads to goal setting. Goal setting should be done by the adolescent; discussion can help formulate acceptable strategies for accomplishment of these goals. Nurses should not set these goals, because this takes control away from the adolescent and he or she is not invested in the process.

The adolescent's presenting or chief complaint, like the tip of an iceberg, is often just the "way in" during the search for health care. The stated complaint may not be what is actually bothering the adolescent. When the interview is conducted in an environment that is comfortable, confidential, and accepting, the adolescent may reveal more serious concerns. Many adolescents want to avoid discussing the reason for seeking care and divulge this reason only when asked directly. Some adolescents are determined to say nothing and remain silent for most of the interview. In such a circumstance, the nurse should communicate acceptance of the client's behavior and explain that the interview will be attempted at a more acceptable time.

Ending an interview is a skill that requires practice. The adolescent usually resents a quick end to the interview and may interpret this to mean that something or someone else is more important. Information should be summarized and important aspects of the problem reviewed. Expectations can be clarified, and if goal setting is not completed, the nurse can ask the adolescent to think about various questions before the next interview. If follow-up is needed, an appointment should be made.

## The History

The adolescent medical and social history is dramatically different from the pediatric history. This difference is marked by questions dealing with sexual activity and drug, alcohol, and cigarette use. These are vital health questions that must be asked of every adolescent. The way in which this information is obtained and the timing of these questions are very important. The nurse needs to establish rapport with the client before approaching these areas. Asking the adolescent, "Do you have any questions about sex?" is totally useless and will usually draw a headshake. The nurse must ask specific questions: "Are you having sex with anyone? Do you use any kind of contraception? What kind and how often? (or Why not?) Do your parents know you are having sex? If they found out, what would they say?"

"Are you having sex with anyone?" is probably the easiest way to ask about sexual activity and the best understood. Inquiring "Are you sexually active?" can lead to a variety of interpretations. Questioning males about intercourse with a "girlfriend" will block communication with the homosexual adolescent.

The nurse should be aware of supporting the adolescent who is *not* sexually active. At age 17, perhaps 40% of teenagers have not had sexual intercourse. Most adolescents are prone to think that "everyone is doing 'it' except me." Masturbation is also a frequent concern, yet this is one topic adolescents are extremely embarrassed to discuss. The fear and guilt once associated with masturbation are much less today, but uninformed adolescents will be relieved to learn that it is not physically or mentally harmful. Nurses play an important role by helping relieve any guilt adolescents may feel regarding masturbation. Nurses may be able to encourage adolescents to discuss their feelings about masturbation.

Questions related to drugs must also be concrete and specific. Asking "Do you use any drugs?" is easily answered in the negative, even if that is not the case. Asking about specific drugs and circumstances acknowledges that the

adolescent has possibly experimented with drugs and that the nurse will discuss this. The nurse should use questions such as "Do you drink? What, how much, and how often? How many times have you been drunk?" Specific amounts need to be clarified—two six-packs, half a quart, etc. Other specific questions should include "Do you smoke cigarettes? How many? Have you ever used amphetamines, depressants, cocaine, crack, marijuana, or any hallucinatory drugs?" There are other important areas that require specific history-taking. These topics are summarized in Table 16-5.

In questioning about family and school, just as with sex and drug usage, specific, concrete questions are necessary. The nurse should avoid yes/no questions. Despite a warlike atmosphere at home, the answer may be "Fine" if the adolescent is asked "How are things going at home?" Direct questions such as "Tell me about your relationship with your father [mother]?" and "What were your grades for the last report?" usually gain more specific answers and open the way for improved insight. Showing a specific interest in the adolescent often helps the nurse to establish rapport.

Evaluation of immunization status is often neglected, but this is an important component of every adolescent health screening. It is important to ascertain as precisely as possible the dates of childhood immunizations and previous episodes of significant infectious disease. Client or parent recall of immunization status or infection is very inaccurate; immunization records and data should be obtained from physicians, clinics, or schools. Serologic test-

*Table 16–5.  Important Areas of the Adolescent History*

**Family**

1. Marital status of parents. If parents have remarried, relationships with stepparent. Relationship/contact with noncustodial parent
2. Relationship with siblings—natural and step-related
3. Home environment conflicts—curfews, dress, school performance, peers, dating, driving, responsibilities

**School**

1. Grade level
2. Grades
3. Involvement in sports/school activities
4. Behavior problems

**Social**

1. Friends/peer group
2. Interests—recreation, sports, hobbies
3. Television—viewing hours per day: favorite programs
4. Drugs—alcohol, cigarettes, marijuana, cocaine, crack, hallucinogens, stimulants, depressants
5. Sex—sexual intercourse, contraception, history of previous sexually transmitted disease, masturbation

ing for antibody levels may be necessary in some situations to ensure optimal immune status throughout adolescence and into adulthood. Adolescents should receive a diphtheria-tetanus booster if it has been more than 10 years since the last one. Periodic tuberculin skin testing (usually every 2 years) is also recommended. Clients with no history of mumps, rubeola, or rubella or with no evidence of serologic immunity should be immunized. Reimmunization for measles is recommended by the Centers for Disease Control (see discussion in Chapter 19). Girls receiving live rubella vaccine must understand that they must not be pregnant and that pregnancy must be prevented for 3 months following immunization.

## Physical Examination

The physical examination provides an excellent opportunity to teach adolescents about their own bodies and to provide assurance regarding the normalcy of their development. The nurse should attempt to make the adolescent feel comfortable since the exam can create anxiety. The exam should not be hurried, and the nurse should explain procedures and comment about the results. The adolescent may be concerned that a long period of time is spent listening to the heart; the nurse can help relieve anxiety by explaining that auscultation takes a long time. Adolescents are usually very modest; often an extra drape helps with this concern. If paper gowns are used, it is helpful to have the adolescent put it on with the split down the front. This facilitates auscultation and palpation of the chest and abdomen, as well as the breast exam in females. The gown can easily be held together during the rest of the exam with another drape placed over the legs. This method creates a minimal "undressed" feeling.

The adolescent physical exam should include the usual procedure to assess health status. Height and weight should be carefully obtained and plotted on a growth chart. Visual acuity should be checked. Blood pressure is taken with the correct-size cuff. It is important to assess dental health status in the adolescent, checking for caries, gum disease, and orthodontic problems. Examination of the back for scoliosis is another important aspect of the adolescent exam (see Chapter 33).

As stated previously, chronological age of the adolescent is often a poor indicator of biological maturity. Thus, each adolescent should be rated according to Tanner stage. Physical examination of the adolescent female includes breast exam and instruction regarding self-examination. A pelvic examination can be very stressful, particularly if it is the first. The nurse should attempt to help the adolescent relax as much as possible. Indications for pelvic examination include:

1. Sexual activity
2. Gynecological complaints
3. Exposure to sexually transmitted disease
4. Plans for initiating a contraceptive method

Generally, the nonsexually active adolescent female with normal menstrual function does not require a pelvic examination. Examination of the external genitalia should be included in a routine physical examination.

Physical examination of the male adolescent includes palpation of the testes and instruction on self-examination. Rectal examination of the adolescent is not performed unless there are specific indications or complaints.

Adolescents usually do not verbalize physical concerns; the nurse can play an important role in informing the client and discussing various aspects of normal body changes. Adolescent boys may be concerned about short stature, muscle development, and level of sexual development, whereas girls worry about height, weight, breast size, and onset of menstruation.

## Nutrition Assessment

Nutritional assessment is an essential factor of any complete health appraisal. Nurses can play a major role in teaching adolescents about nutrition, because problems related to nutrition are common. Nurses should not overlook the valuable resource of the registered dietitian. Dietitians or nutritionists usually coordinate a comprehensive nutritional assessment for adolescents. The purpose is to evaluate nutritional status, which is the balance between nutrient intake and nutrient requirements. Assessment of nutritional status includes:

1. Anthropometric and biochemical measures
2. Clinical examination
3. Dietary intake
4. Evaluation of eating behavior

Anthropometric measurements include height, weight, skinfold thickness, and arm circumference. Skinfold thickness helps determine the percentage of body fat. Arm circumference is applied to a mathematical formula that indicates total muscle mass. Biochemical measures include analysis of blood, urine, and even hair and fingernails. A typical assessment of nutritional status usually includes a complete blood count, urinalysis, cholesterol levels, and amino acid screen.

The key part of nutritional assessment is the dietary intake. The first step involves a dietary history, which may give the nurse a general overview that is helpful in understanding the client's eating pattern. Factors involving the family, such as culture, socioeconomic status, educational levels, food supplementation program, food preparation, vitamin and mineral supplements, and various likes and dislikes, can affect the accuracy of a dietary assessment. A dietary history is necessary to evaluate daily food intake; a 24-hour recall or a 3-day record may be used. The 24-hour recall may be the easiest to obtain, but a particular day may not be representative of a typical daily intake. Portion size can also be misstated, so food models are helpful in obtaining accuracy. A 3-day record should include two weekdays and one weekend day. The nurse should also ask the adolescent about eating responses to stress, anxiety, or boredom. Adolescents seldom admit to bingeing, purging, or vomiting; this area must be carefully approached by the nurse. Usually such information is obtained only after a strong rapport has been established.

The assessment should also involve questions concerning the adolescent's amount of exercise. The amount of aerobic exercise during a period of a week should be established, as well as the amount and type of daily activities.

## Health Promotion

### Recognizing Developmental Tasks

Each stage of adolescence involves specific developmental tasks. Certain psychological tasks must be accomplished at each stage in order for the individual to move successfully into the next developmental stage. Nurses must be familiar with this normative behavior because many adolescent needs evolve from developmental tasks. These tasks include

1. Becoming comfortable with their own bodies
2. Striving for independence
3. Building relationships with the same and opposite sexes
4. Seeking economic and social stability
5. Developing a value system
6. Learning to verbalize and think conceptually (Havighurst, 1979)

### Health Care for Adolescents

Adolescents are often viewed as being in a limbo of health care. Despite the fact that they account for 17% of the U.S. population and have recognized special health needs, they have been ignored by the health care sector (American Medical Association, 1987). Only recently has adolescence been recognized as a separate period in human growth and development. Adolescent medicine as a medical specialty traces its origin to the early 1950s with the first adolescent clinic at Boston Children's Hospital. Adolescent medicine was designated as a specialty within the field of pediatrics in 1977. The Society for Adolescent Medicine was founded in 1968.

Unlike the elderly or the very young, adolescents do not exhibit a clear pattern of disease. Many adolescents receive little or no medical care, except in emergencies, between their last visit to the pediatrician (around age 12)

and adulthood. Services for adolescents tend to be fragmented because there is no consensus regarding the status of adolescents as patients. Many adolescents feel that the current health care system is not responsive to their needs. Adolescents see themselves as too old for pediatricians and not old enough—or sick enough—to have a private internist or gynecologist. Many teens seek health care and counseling from alternative systems—family planning centers, mental health agencies, social agencies, and public health clinics. Ideally, adolescents can seek care in specialized adolescent centers and clinics, but such facilities are scarce.

The adolescent population is an ideal patient population for preventive health services. Owing to their relative good health, they are able to direct their attentions to health maintenance rather than disease treatment. As they mature, adolescents assume responsibility for their own physical and health care. During the process of seeking independence from parents and other authorities, adolescents are also developing personal health habits and acquiring skills as health care consumers. The habits and knowledge they acquire during adolescence are important for their future good health. Additionally, for those adolescents who ultimately become parents, these skills are transferred to their children and help ensure proper childhood health care.

### Medical Rights

Most states have legislation addressing the issue of consent for health care. The laws differ according to state, and the legal aspects of providing care without parental consent may be vague. Many states employ the concept of the *mature minor doctrine,* which states that a minor of a specific age possesses sufficient maturity to decide if health care is needed and is, therefore, able to give consent. This is somewhat different from the *emancipated minor provision,* in which a minor may give consent if he or she is financially independent. This status usually includes those who are married or in the armed forces. Several states also have legislation permitting a minor to seek care for specific conditions—usually pregnancy, contraception, sexually transmitted disease, drug and alcohol dependency, mental health, and reportable diseases. The various terms and interpretations continue to change; the nurse should know the law and its interpretation.

### Dental Health

Adolescents should be reminded about the importance of regular dental care. Dental caries often increase in adolescence owing to poor nutrition and inadequate tooth cleaning. Adolescents should be encouraged to brush their teeth 2 to 3 times daily and to floss daily. Orthodontic devices are usually applied during early adolescence, and nurses should reinforce correct use and care of the appliances, as well as the need for toothbrushing.

## Accident Prevention

### Automobiles

Nearly half of all deaths of driving-age adolescents are due to motor vehicle accidents. Adolescent drivers are responsible for five times as many crash deaths per license holder as drivers over 35, and 75% of passengers killed in cars driven by teenagers are teenagers themselves (National Safety Council, 1990). Two thirds of all males 19 or under own or have regular use of a car. One third of these drivers confess to exceeding 70 miles per hour at least once a week; one fourth of them drink and drive once a week or more (Abrahamson, 1988).

Adolescents' lack of driving experience, judgment, and skills places them at special risk. The safety factor in operating an automobile results from experience. Adolescents not only lack such experience but are subject to several other factors that also contribute to the high automotive accident rate. In the struggle to be independent and come to terms with various childhood fears and feelings, adolescents often react in dangerous and defiant ways, such as reckless and daredevil driving. Social experimentation as adolescents attempt to define their self-identity and sexual identity may involve speeding, overcrowding vehicles, drinking or drug use while driving, and refusing to wear seat belts.

Driver education does not seem to be the solution to motor vehicle accidents involving adolescents. Any benefit that may be attributed to driver education appears to be short-lived. One proven approach is conditional or probationary licensing for teens, which uses licensing as a reward mechanism. The state of Maryland uses a provisional license for all 16- and 17-year-olds. These adolescents cannot drive between midnight and 5 AM unless accompanied by a licensed driver over 21 years of age; a regular license is issued after 1 year of conviction-free driving. If the adolescent commits a traffic offense, he or she must attend a driver improvement program and may be punished by having the 1-year probation period reinstated. Numerous states are enacting legislation to prohibit teens with poor school attendance records from obtaining drivers' licenses. Students may have their license revoked for missing a specified number of school days; dropouts face license suspension until age 18.

Nurses can teach parents that they must be more involved in the adolescent's early driving experiences. Many parents see the driver's license as the end of their years as a taxi service, but their involvement actually becomes even more crucial when adolescents start driving. The nurse can help parents remember that some things have to be earned and that part, if not all, of the car's cost can be the responsibility of the teen.

The nurse can become involved within the community as an educator to promote safe driving. Important points to emphasize are family use of seat belts and the role parents serve as models for their teens. Students Against Drunk Driving (SADD) is an active safety program in many high schools that uses peer pressure to encourage safe driving behavior. The nurse can actively support and recognize these programs. The nurse can emphasize the problems of risk-taking behavior, the influence of peers, and the risk inherent in combining intoxicants with driving.

### Skateboarding

This increasingly popular sport can result in a variety of injuries. The nurse can question the adolescent regarding skateboarding activities and encourage the use of helmets, knee and elbow pads, and gloves. Adolescents who jump from ramps on skateboards must be made aware of the possibility of head injuries and the necessity of proper headgear.

## Common Health Concerns

The basic question behind the health concerns of adolescents is whether they are growing and developing normally. This overriding concern must be recognized by nurses dealing with adolescents. Nurses should remember that complaints by adolescents are often related to all of the various physiological and emotional changes that are taking place.

## Menstruation

Menarche is usually seen by the adolescent girl as part of normal development. It can create a concern when a girl has not yet begun menstruating after the other girls in her peer group have reached menarche. It is helpful to obtain a family menstrual history. Most girls begin menses spontaneously. The nurse can offer support and reassurance.

A variety of chromosomal, endocrinological, and structural defects may cause primary and secondary amenorrhea. (Amenorrhea is discussed in detail in Chapter 31.) It is important for the nurse to explain that menstrual flow and occurrence will be irregular during the first year or more after menarche. The young adolescent may skip several months between periods. This occurs because initial menstruation in most females is anovulatory, meaning that it occurs without ovulation. Stress and emotional changes can also delay menstruation.

The nurse should discuss the use of tampons and sanitary napkins with the adolescent girl to determine and encourage correct usage. Superabsorbent tampons should be avoided (see Toxic Shock Syndrome, Chapter 31). Nurses can also teach the adolescent (of both sexes) why menstruation occurs. Any myths about avoiding baths and physical exercise during menstruation should be clarified. Discomfort during menstruation, or dysmenorrhea, is discussed in detail in Chapter 31. The nurse should encourage adolescent girls to keep a record of their menstrual cycles. Such a record can allow the teen to see how various factors (illness, crisis, travel) affect her cycle. Such awareness also helps the adolescent to be more aware of and comfortable with her body and can strengthen body image.

## Breast Size and Shape

Because of our society's focus on women's breasts, the adolescent female may express anxiety about breast size and shape. Breasts play an important part in body image, and perception of one's own breasts can create a great deal of concern. It is helpful for the adolescent to understand that breasts, like the rest of the body, are not symmetrical and that one breast will differ slightly from the other. Explanations of changes in breast size and tenderness during the menstrual cycle and breast self-examination are important teaching points. Pamphlets on breast self-examination are useful reinforcement and teaching tools. It is important that the habit of regular breast self-examination be established in adolescence. The procedure advised by the National Cancer Institute is depicted in Figure 16-7.

## Penis Size

The size of the penis may create a great deal of concern for adolescent boys. Males often believe that penis size is related to virility, and much teasing is directed toward boys with small penises. Anxiety may be somewhat relieved by the knowledge that erect penis size cannot be judged by the flaccid size. Males should also be aware that penis size has nothing to do with sexual performance or satisfaction of one's partner.

Erections and nocturnal emissions can also be anxiety-producing for the adolescent. These are signs of normal development. The nurse may also assure the boy that erections often occur for no particular reason and that there is nothing wrong if this happens. Adolescent males are often extremely fearful of having an erection during a physical examination. The frequency of these chance erections decreases as the adolescent grows older.

## Testicular Self-Examination

Adolescent males should be instructed to seek medical care if testicular pain occurs. Testicular torsion, tumors, and other disorders can occur in the adolescent (see Chapter 31). Cancer of the testicles can be detected early if young men are taught to perform testicular self-examination each month. Examination is best done during or after

a warm bath or shower. Warmth relaxes the scrotal skin, making palpation easier. Any swelling should be noted. Each testicle should be palpated with both hands, with the index and middle fingers placed beneath the testicle and the thumbs on top. Each testicle should be rotated gently between the thumbs and fingers. The adolescent should be informed that one testicle (usually the left) is larger than the other and that he will feel the epididymis, a cord-like structure, on the top and back of the testicle.

The normal testicle will feel smooth and firm. Any lump on the front or side of the testicle is abnormal. These lumps are usually painless. Lumps should be reported to a physician immediately. Educational materials about testicular self-examination are available from the Office of Cancer Communications, National Cancer Institute, Bethesda, MD 20892 or by calling the Cancer Information Service (1-800-4-CANCER) to order NIH Publication No. 86-2636, *Testicular Self-Examination*. This pamphlet should be given to all adolescent males.

## Stature

Adolescents can be very concerned about height, in particular about being too tall or too short in comparison with peers. Extremes of stature may leave adolescents with emotional scars that can affect their entire lives.

Short stature is more stressful to boys and is often the only sign indicating the need for an endocrine evaluation. Genetic (or familial) short stature is the most common cause. A history will reveal that parents, siblings, and grandparents are or were short. There is no medical treatment, but counseling is very important. Parental attitudes play a critical role, and the adolescent needs support and love from parents. Nurses can help with education about general health and nutrition and should provide these adolescents with detailed explanations and reassurance.

Delayed growth (puberty) can also be familial. This type of growth delay is related to retarded sexual development and treatment is psychologic. Growth will occur in a normal sequence and manner, but at a later date than expected.

Other infrequent causes of short stature include growth hormone deficiency and genetic aberrations such as Turner's syndrome, both of which are discussed in Chapter 31. Tallness in girls is usually related to genetic influence, and often presents a stressful problem. Girls who are destined to be very tall usually display this as children. If treatment is desired, the diagnosis must be made prior to puberty. Treatment with hormones may be used if this is desired by the parents and the girl. The teen should be involved in the treatment decision, in spite of her immaturity, because the therapy is lengthy, exacting, and prone to undesired side effects. As might be expected, such treatment for tall stature is very controversial.

## Acne

Acne is the most common skin disorder in adolescents and has a great impact on the affected adolescent. It is caused by androgen stimulation in the skin structures, and occurs in both sexes, although it is more frequent in males. A detailed discussion of this condition is found in Chapter 34.

## Muscle Development

Concern with body image creates male anxiety about muscular development. The adolescent male needs to understand that muscle mass is related to puberty and maturity. Weightlifting is not recommended for prepubescent children, and the nurse should understand the differences between weightlifting and strength training. Strength training is a noncompetitive method of increasing muscle strength that also contributes to musculoskeletal development. Weightlifting is a competitive sport based on lifting a maximum weight at one time. Single-repetition maximum lifts by adolescents are dangerous and can result in skeletal trauma and growth plate damage. Nurses should make adolescents aware of the dangers involved in such lifts. Adolescents need to understand the benefits and purpose of strength training and that such activities require the supervision of a trainer (Kennedy, 1988). Desire for muscle mass and strength also leads to adolescent use of steroids.

## Gynecomastia

Up to 40% of adolescent males may have gynecomastia, enlargement of breast tissue. Enlargement and tenderness of the breasts is usually bilateral, but may be unilateral. In the majority of cases the breast tissue regresses within 2 years, but in the meantime the adolescent needs reassurance that his hormones have not betrayed him.

Gynecomastia may occur with Klinefelter syndrome or endocrine dysfunction. Klinefelter syndrome is a sex chromosome disorder in which an extra X chromosome is present. Affected males share certain physical characteristics, one of which is gynecomastia (see Chapter 32). In some cases plastic surgery is employed to prevent emotional problems.

## Masturbation

Masturbation is one of the biggest concerns of young people. Adolescents should learn that masturbation is a normal expression of sexuality. The answer to the strong sexual urges of adolescence is not "Go take a cold shower." Masturbation is a much more effective solution to relieving tension and sexual urges. The nurse can assure the adolescent that masturbation is common and normal for both sexes. Psychological problems can occur if the adolescent feels guilt after experiencing pleasure from masturbation. Conflict occurs when the adolescent attempts to enforce self-control and then feels increased guilt with masturbation.

## Sexual Behavior

Reports from the Alan Guttmacher Institute (1981) show that approximately 12 million individuals between the ages of 13 and 19 are sexually active. Other reports have confirmed these findings. Although the rate of adolescent premarital sexual intercourse has leveled off in the past decade, the incidence of sexual activity remains higher than at any time in 3 decades (Hofferth, 1987). Hayes (1987) revealed that 53% of black females and 40% of white females aged 15 to 19 years have experienced sexual intercourse. An increasing rate of adolescents under the age of 15 are engaging in sexual intercourse, with 5% of females and 17% of males reporting sexual intercourse. Harris (1986) reported similar findings and found that 57% of all 17-year-olds had been sexually active.

Heterosexual attitudes among adolescents have shown significant changes in recent years, particularly in relation to the "double standard," which allowed boys but not girls to experience premarital intercourse. Adolescent girls are permitted an increased degree of sexual behavior today without censure from their peers.

Numerous factors influence the age at which a girl becomes sexually active. There is a connection between delayed sexual activity and girls who are successful in school and have higher intelligence scores and academic motivational scales (Atrash, 1987). Sexual intercourse at an early age is often related to risk-taking and problem behaviors. Early sexual activity is also related to female-headed households (Hayes, 1987) and is more common among daughters of women who themselves initiated sexual intercourse at a young age and experienced adolescent pregnancy (Newcomer, 1983).

Many adolescents are beginning to view sexuality as a personal choice rather than a behavior decided by adults. Despite this liberalized attitude, there is still a degree of conservatism. Casual sexual intercourse is generally not seen as acceptable, and a relationship based on commitment and monogamy is viewed as necessary prior to sexual intimacy. The presence of a loving relationship is the single most important determinant of adolescents' attitudes regarding the permissibility of sexual intercourse (Coles, 1985).

Traditionally the first steps in the sequence of adolescent heterosexual behavior have been kissing and petting. Oral sex precedes intercourse for many adolescents and may serve as a substitute. Sixteen percent of teens who had engaged in oral sex had never experienced intercourse

(Coles, 1985). Haas (1979) reported that among 17- to 18-year-olds, 59% of girls and 56% of boys had engaged in oral sex.

Despite the data showing a high proportion of adolescents with sexual experience, data also show infrequent intercourse and a limited number of premarital sex partners. Zelnick (1980) found that 50% of sexually active girls had only one partner, and only 16% reported four or more partners. It is apparent that the vast majority of today's sexually active adolescents are not promiscuous.

Contrary to adolescents' confidence about their sexual awareness, they are frequently misinformed about basic reproductive anatomy and physiology. They are even more ignorant regarding the issues of contraception and normal sexual response. Coles (1985) conducted a thorough study of adolescent sexuality that revealed significant misinformation about even the most basic reproductive facts. Table 16-6 outlines adolescents' sources of sexual information in Coles's study. Although most adolescents learn about puberty and reproductive physiology from schools and parents, they are seldom educated about human sexual behavior from these sources.

The United States has the highest rate of teenage pregnancy in the industrialized world. One of every ten adolescent females becomes pregnant each year, resulting in more than 400,000 abortions and 500,000 live births (Hayes, 1987). Five out of every six of these adolescent pregnancies are unintended (Trussell, 1988). Current birth rates show a small increase for women younger than 15 years of age, accounting for over 10,000 births. In 1985 birth rates for teenagers between 15 and 19 years of age decreased to the lowest level since the 1930s, with this group accounting for 12.6% of all births (National Center for Health Statistics, 1987). This decline is due in part to the decline in the number of adolescents.

Adolescents state that sexual pressure is the main reason for having sexual intercourse (Coles, 1985). Both sexes report they are pressured by peers to have sex before they are really ready. These new attitudes may result in girls having more sexual partners and more frequent intercourse, and starting at younger ages. The changes in teen sexual behavior and attitudes are increasingly reflected in popular culture, from television specials and weekly series to movies and magazines.

Nurses can also help adolescents by being aware of the myths and misconceptions regarding sexual experiences. Misinformation is often the source of physical and emotional problems for the adolescent. Adolescents often believe that sexual intercourse is the ultimate expression of love, and that it will therefore be totally pleasurable. In reality, this is not always the case, and the unknowing adolescent may be overcome with fear and guilt which, combined with unfulfilled expectations, leads to frustration, anxiety, and self-doubt. Many adolescent females have no idea of what orgasm is or should be, and may begin to doubt their own sexual ability and adequacy. They may worry that if they let their partner know that intercourse is unfulfilling, the relationship will end. Adolescent males may feel pressure to perform and believe that intercourse affirms their sexuality. Often the sexual concerns of the individual partners are not openly communicated. Nurses can help adolescents understand more about sexual relationships and help them to communicate their feelings, concerns, and needs.

## Contraception

Contraceptive use among adolescents is notoriously haphazard. Very few adolescents consistently use a contraceptive method, saying that stopping to insert foam or put on a condom interferes with sexual spontaneity and implies that the sex was planned. For most adolescents, planned sex is not "right"; sex must be spontaneous and to plan for it seems wrong or "dirty." Failing to anticipate intercourse and believing that the risk of pregnancy is small are the two most common reasons for adolescents not utilizing contraceptives.

While occasional contraceptive use in sexually active teens between the ages of 15 and 19 has increased, 40% of these adolescents reported inconsistent use, with black adolescents the least likely to use contraceptives (Hayes, 1987). The Harris Report (1986) indicated that fear of a

*Table 16-6. Adolescents' Sources of Sexual Information*

| | Sources of Information (%) | | | | | | |
|---|---|---|---|---|---|---|---|
| Subject | School | Parents | Sex Partner | Friends | Books/Media | Clinic/Doctor | Sibling |
| Reproduction | 50 | 23 | | 15 | 9 | | 2 |
| Birth control | 37 | 17 | 1 | 17 | 20 | 4 | 4 |
| Masturbation | 21 | 12 | 1 | 32 | 30 | 1 | 3 |
| Homosexuality | 22 | 14 | 1 | 26 | 35 | | 2 |
| Sexual techniques | 14 | 9 | 17 | 26 | 32 | | 2 |

(From Coles, R., & Stokes, G. [1985]. *Sex and the American teenager.* New York: Harper & Row)

pelvic exam was one of the greatest obstacles to contraceptive use. Sixty-nine percent of adolescent females listed this fear as a factor in not seeking contraception. Other factors affecting contraceptive use include geographic and monetary restrictions, and fear of parents finding out. Some adolescents just do not know where or how to obtain contraceptives. Even when contraceptive information is available, adolescents display irrational thinking about contraceptive use. Contraception is often used with minimal instruction and even less understanding of how it works. Few teenagers understand the relationship between the menstrual cycle and the risk of pregnancy.

Surveys regarding the type of contraception used at last intercourse by adolescents who use contraception indicate that 62% of teens use oral contraceptives, 22% use condoms, and 6% use a diaphragm (Hayes, 1987). Adolescents are still greatly misinformed regarding contraception and harbor many misconceptions. Many adolescents believe the pill is ineffective, that withdrawal is effective, and that oral contraceptives cause cancer and infertility (Harris, 1986). Despite the prevalence of sex education, adolescents are misinformed and ignorant regarding reproductive anatomy and physiology.

The availability of contraception does not encourage adolescents to initiate sexual intercourse, nor does the initiation of intercourse seem to lead to the immediate use of contraception. The average delay between initiation of intercourse and use of a prescribed method is 16.6 months (Zabin, 1981). Fifty percent of all first premarital pregnancies occur in the first 6 months after initiation of intercourse, with 20% of all pregnancies occurring in the first month alone (Zabin, 1979). Inconsistent use of contraceptives results in 15% of adolescent women using a medical method becoming pregnant (Hayes, 1987). Age is a strong determinant of effective adolescent contraceptive use. Adolescents in the early stage of adolescence seldom use any contraceptive method other than withdrawal. They may later use methods such as foam or condoms that have been recommended by peers, but they still use them inconsistently. The establishment of more prolonged monogamous relationships in late adolescence brings more consistency in contraceptive use.

Some girls want to become pregnant, viewing pregnancy as a sign of adulthood or proof of their femininity. Other adolescent females may risk pregnancy as an act of hostility or self-assertion. In some cultures, fertility is a highly valued indicator of a man's virility, and the girl may want to satisfy her partner's desire to prove his manliness. Some adolescents want a baby as someone to love and love them, thinking a child will fill a missing part of their life.

Table 16-7 reviews the contraceptive options available to the adolescent. The nurse can help the adolescent choose a method that suits him or her. Each client must be considered on an individual basis. The nurse may be

## Table 16–7. Contraceptive Comparison

| Method | Actual Effectiveness | Advantages | Disadvantages | Contraindications |
|---|---|---|---|---|
| Abstinence | — | 100% effective if truly practiced | Numerous factors lead to high failure rate | |
| Condom | 85% | Nonprescription; easy to use; protects against STDs | High motivation needed; must be removed carefully; dulls penile sensation | |
| Foam and condom | 95% | Nonprescription; protects against STDs | High motivation needed; expensive if intercourse frequent | |
| Spermicides | 70% | Nonprescription; no side effects | Use indicates intent to have coitus; messy; unpleasant odor; must be deposited at cervical onset | Allergy to solution |
| Diaphragm | 85% | May be inserted several hours prior to coitus; no side effects | Needs fitting and prescription; cream must be applied within 1 hour prior to coitus; must be left in 6–8 hours after coitus | Severely displaced uterus; cystocele |
| Oral contraceptives | 99% | Regulate menstrual cycle; minimize dysmenorrhea; easy to take | Must be taken daily; requires prescription | Sickle cell anemia; hepatitis; over age 40; diabetes; epilepsy; severe renal disease |

involved in assessing the number of sex partners, frequency of sexual intercourse, cognitive maturity, and the client's level of comfort with handling the genitals to determine the appropriate method. An important nursing role is that of instructor in the correct use of contraceptive methods. Nurses should be knowledgeable concerning contraception and be aware that adolescents may be misinformed. An attitude to the sexually active adolescent that is open and accepting is critical to the nurse's success.

## Adolescent Pregnancy

Adolescent pregnancy is a complex medical, social, and economic problem. Early childbearing is associated with serious health consequences for both the mother and the child. The mortality and morbidity rates for mother and child are higher for younger mothers. Those under the age of 16 are more likely to suffer complications, particularly anemia, toxemia, and pregnancy-induced hypertension (PIH), and are more likely to deliver low birth weight infants.

Fetal, neonatal, and infant mortality are higher when the mother is an adolescent. Babies of teenaged mothers are two to three times more likely to die during the first year than are infants born to mothers 20 years or older (Ventura, 1984). Low birth weight infants are subject to high risks of respiratory problems, neurological impairment, and mental retardation.

### Adolescent Fathers

Very little research on adolescent fathers has been done. Many young men believe that the female should take the responsibility and initiative regarding contraception. Most of these adolescent fathers are as ignorant about sex as the young woman. They seldom consider the possibility of pregnancy when engaging in intercourse. Often their initial reaction to learning that their girlfriend is pregnant is denial, disinterest, and abandonment of the girl.

In the past, these adolescent fathers were ignored and left out of any decisions involving the pregnancy. Today, they are increasingly included in the management of adolescent pregnancy. Many boys are concerned about the pregnant girl, and want to accept their responsibility for the situation. Others may become involved because of guilt feelings or as a way to prove virility. The father may exert a strong influence on whether the pregnancy is terminated or carried to term. Despite a move by some states to enact stronger laws regarding financial support to the child, such financial assistance is seldom the reality.

### Prenatal Care

Inadequate or no prenatal care is an important factor related to adolescent pregnancy. Adolescents often deny that they are pregnant and delay initiation of prenatal care. They may also delay seeking care because of fear that their parents will find out, belief that they cannot pay for the care, or because they don't know where to go for care. This delay also limits their available options. As with all pregnancies, a favorable outcome is directly related to the adolescent obtaining appropriate prenatal care.

### Psychological Considerations

Pregnancy only adds to the psychological stress for the adolescent, as well as the family. The pregnant adolescent is more vulnerable to the dysfunctional consequences of stress due to her immaturity. The pregnant adolescent may face three crises concurrently—adolescence, marriage, and pregnancy—each of which creates characteristic adjustment tasks. Adolescents rarely have developed the skills to handle any of these factors, much less all three at once.

### Social and Economic Considerations

The issues involving teen pregnancy are intertwined with the rapidly changing social context. There are many negative consequences for everyone involved in an unplanned adolescent pregnancy. Pregnancy is one of the primary reasons for dropping out of school. Many girls never resume their education, particularly if they have additional children. Adolescents who intend to return to school after delivery face two major obstacles: a lack of day-care facilities and the need to earn a living. Adolescent pregnancy often leads to the vicious cycle of unemployment, poverty, and welfare dependency.

Marriage, which some young couples consider, seldom offers an improved situation. The economic burden and outlook is unchanged if the male drops out of school to work. This results in low-income employment with little opportunity for advancement or higher wages. Adolescent marriages are 2 to 3 times more likely to end in divorce than those occurring after age 20 (Hayes, 1987). An even sadder part of this cycle is the problem of repeated pregnancies, each of which further limits options and outlook for the mother and children.

Children of adolescent pregnancies are at risk for abuse, neglect, delayed development, school failure, and behavior problems. Because many adolescent mothers have a poor understanding of child development, they have unrealistic expectations, use inappropriate punishments, and cannot handle the parental role. Factors directly related to the ease of transition to parenthood include socioeconomic status, age, timing of parenthood, marital adjustment, parental support, availability of an extended family, and a commitment to the parental role.

### Nursing Implications Involving Adolescent Pregnancy

When the pregnancy has been confirmed, the adolescent should be informed and counseled regarding her various options. Her parents should be involved to provide appropriate support, and, if possible, the father should be included. Options include continuing the pregnancy to term and keeping the baby, placing the baby for adoption, or abortion. The nurse is often the first health care provider these adolescents encounter, and plays an important role in providing support and guidance to the girl. Often the girl will be unable to verbalize her concern, and may relate vague symptoms or complaints. These girls are usually very reluctant to seek medical care, and nurses play a key role in establishing trust and a foundation for good prenatal care.

Nurses should be involved in providing prenatal care to adolescents who decide to carry their pregnancies to term. Education regarding pregnancy, nutrition, self-care, childbirth, infant care, and parenting is a vital component of health care goals. Nurses can also help to involve the young father if he is available. Adolescent fathers should be encouraged to participate in prenatal care visits and attend educational programs such as childbirth preparation or parenting classes. Instruction in parenting techniques and child development norms is critical in helping adolescents establish an effective parenting style based on a realistic understanding of their child's capabilities.

Nurses can also help involve the family. This is not always an easy task. The feelings aroused by these pregnancies often create numerous problems and need to be expressed and resolved before family members can help in providing needed support and in solving problems regarding the pregnancy.

The responsibility of nurses to the well-being of the adolescent mother and her infant does not end with birth. Adolescent girls should be informed of available community services to facilitate the transition to their new roles. Family members should be encouraged to be supportive. At delivery, early bonding and breast-feeding should be promoted. Infant stimulation programs and quality day care may alter the differences in cognitive development seen in children of young mothers. Nurses should advocate strongly for postnatal return to school or vocational training.

## Eating Disorders

Obesity, anorexia nervosa, and bulimia are the three major classifications of eating disorders. The misuse of food to hide or disguise a problem regarded as unresolvable to the individual is termed an eating disorder. These conditions can be life-threatening and have a significantly negative effect on health and function.

### Obesity

Obesity may be termed an epidemic disease. It is of special concern for adolescents. There is a significant risk involving adolescent obesity that persists into adulthood. Unlike younger children, obese adolescents are likely to remain obese as adults. There is a significant cardiovascular risk

factor for obese adolescents. Abnormal glucose tolerance, hypertension, and abnormal lipoprotein metabolism are the principal complications. Obesity is the chief cause of hypertension in adolescents.

Even lean adolescents may perceive themselves as fat. The truly obese adolescent usually faces immense and often devastating peer pressures. Obese adolescents may be motivated to lose weight because they want to wear more attractive clothes, or because they believe that weight loss will help them excel in sports or become more popular. Such adolescents are often attracted to crash diets and gimmicks. They are impatient for results and fare poorly in weight reduction programs. The desired and more effective approach is one that combines diet, structured physical activity, and behavior techniques. Psychological support is very important and group therapy is often helpful with these adolescents.

Although many diseases are associated with obesity, they are rarely the cause. It may also be difficult to determine what constitutes obesity. Diagnosis by appearance may be all that is needed with some children, but more discriminating measures are required for most children. This is particularly true in attempting to identify those in the process of becoming obese.

Growth charts for adolescents should be used. Weight-for-height above the 95th percentile or weight greater than 20% more than normal is often regarded as diagnostic. Measures based only on weight and height can be misleading, however, especially during the rapid growth changes in adolescence. A more precise method of identifying obesity is skin-fold measurements (triceps, subscapular, pectoral, umbilical, iliac or thigh skin-fold). Triceps measurements, the most common caliper measurement, produce a high correlation with the percentage of body weight that is fat. A measurement of tricep skin-fold at or above the 85th percentile is the level usually accepted for the diagnosis of obesity (Castiglia, 1989a).

An analysis of data from four national surveys has identified significant increases in adolescent obesity (Gortmaker, 1987). The greatest increase in obesity during adolescence occurred in girls. The prevalence of superobesity, defined by tricep skin-fold measurements equal to or greater than the 95th percentile, increased by 87% in adolescent girls. There is a continuing debate regarding genetic predisposition versus environmental factors as the cause of obesity. Proponents of genetic predisposition acknowledge an environmental factor, but argue that genes influence metabolism and adipose tissue formation.

Treatment involves a reduction of calorie intake combined with behavior modification techniques and physical activity programs. Weight loss programs require active involvement by the adolescent. Nurses should attempt to determine the adolescent's motivation before planning care, because strategies to be implemented are more successful if they are related to personal motivators (Castiglia, 1989a). The adolescent should be involved in all activity decisions as well as food intake decisions. Maintaining a diary sometimes is beneficial because it presents an objective evaluation measure. The program needs to be planned to minimize family disruption. The family's sedentary lifestyle and poor eating habits are often major obstacles to the adolescent's successful weight loss. Everyone involved must understand that weight loss is a long, slow process.

The longer the duration of obesity, the more pessimistic one must be about the outcome of treatment. Follow-up statistics of adolescents are generally discouraging. The nurse's recognition of the difficulty in modifying obesity points to the importance of prevention. Nurses can help promote an active lifestyle for children of all ages.

### Anorexia Nervosa

Anorexia is an eating disorder seen with increasing frequency among adolescents. It is usually associated with adolescent girls, but there have been documented cases in children as young as 7 years old. Despite the low fatality rate, this disease has serious long-term consequences for developing adolescents. Females are affected by anorexia nine times more than males, with one of every 200 adolescent girls displaying anorexic symptoms. The disorder involves a set of abnormal behaviors associated with food and weight control. A major symptom involves a significant disturbance in body image that causes these adolescents to believe that they are overweight. Anorexia is characterized by an obsessive pursuit of thinness that leads to emaciation and possibly even death. Food is viewed phobically; any intake is seen as a loss of control with resultant weight gain (Harding, 1985). The term "anorexia" (loss of appetite) is a misnomer, since anorexics do not lack hunger but, rather, deny its existence. They also deny their thinness and fatigue.

The etiology of anorexia nervosa is unknown. Certainly the disorder is influenced by various biological and experiential factors. Many factors may contribute to the disorder, including adolescent desires for personal autonomy, control, and physical attractiveness, combined with current cultural pressures to be thin.

Psychological disturbances in the disorder are similar to the characteristics of starvation—depression, irritability, poor memory, diminished concentration, and diminished physical energy. Other factors may involve inability to deal with stress or separate from parents.

Three areas of disordered psychological functions mark this disease:

1. Disturbance, of delusional proportions, in body image. Anorexics claim that their cachexic appearance is normal.
2. Inaccurate perceptions or interpretations of internal stimuli. The anorexic fails to recognize hunger or nutritional needs. These individuals are often defensive and uncommunicative about this problem.
3. A paralyzing sense of ineffectiveness. This characteristic, more difficult to identify, involves a feeling of helplessness that makes anorexics feel they are always responding to demands from others, rather than doing as they choose (Brunch, 1978).

It is perplexing for both parents and nurses when they are confronted with an adolescent girl diagnosed as having anorexia nervosa. Typically she has been so clever in hiding her weight loss and altered eating behavior that by the time her disorder is finally detected she must be hospitalized. These adolescents usually come from middle- and upper-income families, do well in school, and have average intelligence. They also tend to be perfectionists, and to have low self-esteem (Castiglia, 1989b). Control is also a critical issue to these individuals. They interpret thinness as an indicator of self-control, and their weight loss is an attempt to control their body and environment (Hsu, 1986).

A multidisciplinary approach is needed in treating anorexia nervosa. Psychological, nutritional, health, and social factors all interact. Treatment goals focus on restoring optimal nutritional status and preventing recurrence. The nurse should be aware that goal achievement includes nutritional therapy, psychotherapy, and family therapy. Treatment is often difficult and lengthy. Unfortunately, anorexia nervosa is marked by relapse, and many individuals require repeated hospitalization.

A wide variety of treatment programs exist. Treatment usually involves separating the patient from the family. Another popular treatment modality involves behavior modification techniques, including contracts with patients that involve increasing privileges as desired weight levels are reached. This desired weight gain in usually one-quarter to one-half pound per day or 1 kilogram per week. The focus of psychotherapy has been studied. Russell (1987) found that family therapy was more effective than individual therapy in patients under age 19 and whose illness began at an early age, but had not become chronic.

Some research has been done to identify the condition in its early stages. Garner and Garfinkel (1979) developed an Eating Attitudes Test that is useful in older adolescents as an index of the symptoms of the condition. Vacc and Rhyne (1987) developed an adapted version of the test for use with elementary school children.

Nurses should remember that anorexia nervosa can be a fatal disorder, and some of these adolescents die of complications from self-induced starvation.

### Bulimia

There is often confusion regarding this disorder because of its association with anorexia nervosa. Approximately half of all anorexics also suffer from bulimia, which makes it difficult to clearly isolate bulimia from anorexia nervosa. The anorexic's goal is to lose weight, whereas the bulimic wants to eat without weight gain. Anorexia may produce bulimia, but rarely does the bulimic become anorexic (Muuss, 1986).

The term *bulimia* means "ox hunger." Bulimia is characterized by overeating and then purging. The food binges involve overeating with excessive calorie consumption over a short period of time, usually less than 2 hours. Because of associated shame, this bingeing is usually done secretly. Purging may involve self-induced vomiting, laxative abuse, and excessive exercise. The actual incidence is unknown, but it has been found to be most prevalent among females in late adolescence and early adulthood. Zuckerman (1986) studied 907 college freshman and seniors for the prevalence of bulimia and bulimic symptoms. Four percent (4%) of the women and 0.4% of the men were classified as bulimic. Limited investigation involving bulimia in younger adolescents suggests that the disorder may be present in a significant number of these individuals (Killen, 1986; Van Thorre, 1985). This disorder is seldom seen in lower socioeconomic groups because of the cost of food. Diagnosis is often not made until a patient is 30 or even 40 years old because of the secretive nature of most bulimics (Farley, 1986).

Bulimia begins as an attempt to control weight and ends with a loss of self-control. The individual initiates dieting, which leads to intense hunger and consequent binge eating. Binges usually involve carbohydrates, with caloric intake up to 20,000 calories (Castiglia, 1989c). Many bulimics maintain a normal weight range, but weight variations of 5 to 25 pounds each week are possible. Binge eating creates feelings of guilt and re-establishment of strict dieting, but the individual soon realizes the self-induced vomiting works faster. This vomiting behavior is interpreted as permission to engage in more binge eating, satisfying hunger and relieving anxiety. Bulimics also engage in other impulse activities, including shoplifting (especially of food), excessive alcohol ingestion, and other self-destructive behaviors (Casper, 1986).

These individuals are aware of the disorder and are distressed by their behavior. They feel that the symptoms are out of their control, are ashamed, and will not admit that they are bulimic. Bulimics engage in self-destructive thoughts and often feel depressed about the repetitive pattern of binge–purge.

Following elimination of organic causes for vomiting, diagnosis is based on criteria provided by the American Psychiatric Association (1987):

1. Recurrent episodes of binge eating (rapid consumption of a large amount of food in a discrete period of time)
2. A feeling of a lack of control over eating behavior during the eating binges
3. The person regularly engages in self-induced vomiting, use of laxatives or diuretics, strict dieting or fasting, or vigorous exercise in order to prevent weight gain.

4. A minimum average of two binge eating episodes a week for at least 3 months
5. Persistent overconcern with body shape and weight (American Psychiatric Association, 1987, p. 68–69).

In addition to these symptoms, distinctive hand lesions are associated with bulimia. The backs of hands are often scarred and the fingers cut from rubbing against the front teeth while self-inducing vomiting (Williams, Friedman and Steinder, 1986).

Bulimics may suffer from a variety of complications: epigastric distress caused by chronic esophagitis, gastrointestinal bleeding due to excessive vomiting, potassium depletion, spastic colitis, tooth enamel erosion, hypertension, and dehydration resulting from laxative abuse. Chronic vomiting may lead to hypokalemic alkalosis.

Treatment is similar to that for anorexia nervosa, and includes physiologic regulation, behavioral therapy, psychotherapy, and family counseling. As with anorexia, treatment methods are varied and often controversial. There are some data that indicate the possibility that the pathogenesis of bulimia may involve specific disturbances in brain or hypothalmic neurochemical functions (Bond, 1986). Antidepressant drugs have been used as an effective treatment.

Food journals can help in assessing eating patterns. Bulimic diet plans involve strict control of carbohydrate intake. Distracting activities and removal from surroundings which emphasize food may also help. It is important for bulimics to be aware of support groups. Nurses can refer clients to the organizations listed at the end of this chapter which provide assistance and information about eating disorders.

## Substance Abuse

### Smoking

Despite a decline in cigarette smoking by adolescents in the past decade, it remains the second most common drug problem in adolescents (Johnston, 1987). Most smokers begin the habit in adolescence. Adolescent use of cigarettes increases fivefold between junior and senior high school (Killen, 1985). Despite increased warnings and education concerning the health hazards and consequences of smoking, few adolescents take the threat personally. Typically, they believe they can stop smoking whenever they wish. Of teenagers who smoke two or more cigarettes completely, 85% become regular smokers (Silvis, 1987).

### Smokeless Tobacco

There has been a tremendous increase in the number of adolescents using and becoming habituated to smokeless tobacco (snuff and chewing tobacco). Smokeless tobacco has been proved to be carcinogenic, in addition to causing serious dental problems. Current estimates indicate that these products are used by 3 million American adolescents, the majority (98%) male (Silvis, 1987).

Interventions to prevent and stop tobacco use vary according to the extent of the patient's use. The following strategies are recommended:

### Children

Give information about the health consequences of smoking.

Correct mistaken notions that smoking is prevalent in adults and that they enjoy their habit.

Emphasize that not starting is the best way to avoid becoming a regular smoker.

Analyze smoking advertisements in magazines.

Provide a nonsmoking environment in the hospital and office waiting room.

### Nonsmoking Adolescents

Deemphasize the long-term risks of smoking.

Describe the immediate negative physiological effects of smoking (accelerated heart rate, elevated blood pressure, tremor).

Point out negative social consequences (bad breath, malodorous clothing, finger stains).

Offer techniques for resisting peer pressure.

Reinforce current nonsmoking and encourage commitment to future nonsmoking.

### Habituated Adolescents

Obtain a history of tobacco use.

Motivate the adolescent to make an attempt to quit, and provide follow-up.

Request quit date, ideally one with special meaning (birthday, end of school, New Year's Day).

When smoking-cessation behavior begins, offer reinforcement (Silvis, 1987).

Education regarding smoking should be emphasized in early adolescence. It is important to note that adolescents often pay little attention to negative messages regarding the health risks of smoking, and that such negative messages may encourage smoking as an expression of risk taking (Clarke, 1986).

## Chemical Dependency

A majority of today's adolescents have tried some illicit drug. The use of drugs to alter the state of consciousness seems to be a common rite of passage among American adolescents. The use of legal drugs by adolescents is even greater: 66% use alcohol and 20% smoke cigarettes regularly. There are an estimated 3.3 million problem drinkers in the 14- to 17-year age range (American Medical Association, 1986).

Although the period from 1979–1985 marked a decline in drug use, the 5 years from 1985–1990 reflected a leveling off of usage or, in some cases, an increase. Cocaine use continues to increase among adolescents, marked by the advent of "crack," which is a solid form of cocaine. Crack is very potent, and its solid form makes it easy to market. Reported use in adolescents has increased dramatically. This fact has critical implications for the long-term health of this generation. A significant proportion of today's adolescents are placing themselves at risk for the harmful effects of this dangerous drug. Follow-up studies show a dramatic increase in cocaine use after high school (O'Malley, 1985).

There are many theories involving substance abuse; however, the parent–child relationship is a critical factor. Drug abuse can be traced to many causes, but a significant factor in adolescents involves rebellion against parents and society, a need to escape the "boredom" of daily life, a desire to create pleasurable feelings, and the always present need to conform to a chosen peer group. Lack of a satisfactory emotional environment may also be a factor in adolescent substance abuse.

Rebellious adolescents gain a feeling of satisfaction through disobedient behavior, which combats feelings of helplessness. By using drugs, they obtain momentary feelings of independence and power. The rebellious satisfaction they experience gives them a reinforcing motive to continue abuse (Pallikkathayil, 1983).

Nurses should be aware that the pattern of substance abuse among adolescents is continually evolving, as shown in Table 16-8. Adolescent drug abuse of the 1990s is different from the drug abuse of the 1960s. New drugs, with their associated slang terms, are an invariable feature of substance abuse. Alcohol and marijuana are the main drugs of abuse among today's adolescents. Examination for cocaine erosion of the nasal septum or needle tracks in the arm are important, but of low yield. Adolescent substance abuse may be the most commonly missed major pediatric diagnosis. Today's abused substances are not associated with frequent illness, and the teens using these agents are usually seen only when they seek routine health maintenance, such as an annual school or sports-participation physical. This highlights the importance of asking very specific questions regarding substance use.

The early stages of substance abuse are often subtle and are missed because they are confused with the normal maturation process of adolescence. The danger is that the early stages, which begin as a normal adolescent quest for identity, may lead to entrapment in a web of easily available drugs. The nurse should be alert for signs of the early stages of substance abuse. It is important to acknowledge and carefully consider parental instincts about their children. If parents express concern it should arouse suspicion. Many parents are often advised by physicians or counselors to regard pathologic change as an adolescent "phase."

The nurse can play a leading role in helping to identify adolescents at risk for substance abuse as well as those who demonstrate the signs and symptoms of abuse. The

*Table 16–8. Stages of Drug Abuse*

| Stage | Mood Alteration | Feelings | Drugs | Sources | Behavior | Frequency |
|---|---|---|---|---|---|---|
| 1: Learning the mood swing | Euphoria Normal Pain | Feel good Few consequences | Tobacco Marijuana Alcohol | "Friends" | Little detectable change Moderate "after the fact" lying | Progresses to weekend usage |
| 2: Seeking the mood swing | Euphoria Normal Pain | Excitement Early guilt | All of the above plus: Inhalants Hash oil, hashish "Ups" "Downs" Prescriptions Cocaine/"crack" | Buying | Dropping extracurricular activities and hobbies Mixed friends (straight and druggie) Dress changing Erratic school perform- ance and "skipping" Unpredictable mood and attitude swings "Conning" behavior | Weekend use progressing to 4–5 times per week Some solo use |
| 3: Preoccupation with the mood swing | Euphoria Normal Pain | Euphoric highs Doubts, including: Severe shame and guilt Depression Suicidal thoughts | All of the above plus: Mushrooms PCP LSD | Selling | "Cool" appearance Straight friends dropped Family fights (verbal and physical) Stealing—police incidents Pathologic lying School failure, skipping, expulsion, jobs lost | Daily Frequent solo use |
| 4: Using drugs to feel normal | Euphoria Normal Pain | Chronic Guilt Shame Remorse Depression | Whatever is available | Any way possible | Physical deterioration (weight loss, chronic cough) Severe mental deteriora- tion (memory loss and flashbacks) Paranoia, volcanic anger, and aggression School dropout Frequent overdosing | All day every day |

(From Wilford, B. B. [1981]. *Drug abuse: A guide for the primary care physician.* Chicago: American Medical Association)

nurse may use the following specific criteria to identify existing or potential substance abuse:

1. Poor school adjustment and deteriorating perfor- mance
2. Deterioration in family relationships
3. Negative personality changes—rapid mood swings, depression, irritability
4. Physical changes—frequent sore throat, cough, red eyes
5. Changes in hygiene and dress style
6. Legal problems, disappearance of money or valu- ables at home, shoplifting, traffic offenses
7. Change in peer group (MacDonald, 1989).

The nurse must realize that adolescent drug use, abuse, and dependency are parts of a continuum, the course of which is preventable. As with most disease proc- esses, the earlier that intervention occurs the better the results. Nurses need to be familiar with the nature of chemical dependency and acknowledge it as a primary disease that is chronic, contagious, and progressive. Drug

dependency creates major problems for the adolescent, family, and society.

Accurate assessment is an important priority involving the treatment and rehabilitation of adolescent substance abusers. The nurse must know the manifestations of the various forms of substance abuse. The nurse can play an important role in helping adolescents identify the factors that led them to substance use and recognize self-destruc- tive behavior. The nurse can assist adolescents to stop denying that there is a problem and become willing to work toward a change. Initiating active family involvement is often frustrating due to parental denial. The nurse should be aware that family therapy is often a critical component of adolescent treatment. Helping to educate family members and referral to community resources are important roles for nursing management.

## Androgenic-Anabolic Steroids

Androgenic-anabolic steroids are derivatives of the natural hormone testosterone. They were developed to maximize testosterone's anabolic effects and minimize its androgenic effects. Therapeutically, they are used in the treatment of certain anemias and to stimulate sexual development in hypogonadal males. The increased and widespread abuse of steroids by adolescents has only recently been recognized. The use of steroids by high school athletes is spreading across the country faster than experts can track the usage. It is estimated that 5%–10% of all high school students currently use steroids (Buckley, 1988). They are used principally to increase lean body mass and strength, but may also be used to prevent or treat injuries. Athletes are not the only users. Many boys resort to steroids for the same effects to promote social acceptance and popularity. Adolescents term it "getting big," connoting bypassing adolescence and jumping straight to manhood. The current proliferation of muscle magazines reflects this belief. Advertisements and features in these publications usually push "sexier living through bodybuilding." The magazines sell a wide variety of bodybuilding supplements and protein powders. Adolescent boys view muscles as a way to attract girls. Many adolescents view muscles as synonymous with power and confidence.

Steroid use among adolescents can be directly related to the medical profession's continued denial that steroids can enhance performance and improve muscular strength: such statements were clearly and forever refuted by Ben Johnson's 100-meter performance at the 1988 Olympic Games. Despite the risks, many adolescents feel either that steroids cause no harm or that the results are worth the risk. The problem is compounded by the fact that in many states, the possession and use of steroids is legal, although selling them is punishable by a prison term of up to 6 years and/or a fine. Recent deaths related to adolescent steroid use may bring a rapid change in current laws.

There are numerous risks and negative side effects involving the use of androgenic-anabolic steroids. High blood pressure and decreased levels of high-density lipoprotein cholesterol are cardiovascular risks. Liver disease, including hepatic tumors, is a possible side effect. Irreversible changes include masculinization in women and gynecomastia and alopecia in men. Adolescent use of these steroids also results in early closure of the epiphyses (American Academy of Pediatrics Committee on Sports Medicine, 1989). Androgenic-anabolic steroids may also result in marked psychologic changes. These typically involve increased aggressiveness ('Roid Rage), wide mood swings, and changes in libido.

Nurses can play an important role in counseling adolescents and families about the use of these steroids. Factual information should be provided, and the negative side effects should not be exaggerated, nor should the advantages of their use be denied. Educating athletes and coaches is a major focus of intervention. Coaches should be taught how to recognize that an athlete is using steroids. Information regarding the use of steroids should be included in all drug education and prevention programs.

## Depression

During the last decade, researchers and clinicians have come to agree that children and adolescents, like many adults, suffer from severe depressive disorders. They also agree that the symptoms of depression are the same for all age groups, and that behavior problems such as truancy and delinquency are not masks for depression, but evidence of other psychiatric disorders (Puig-Antich, 1980). This knowledge allows for early identification of depressive disorders and appropriate intervention to avert problems, including suicide.

Depression is generally defined as an overall feeling of sadness, unhappy mood, or hopelessness. It has been only in the past decade that the existence of depression in children and adolescents has been formally recognized. Table 16-9 outlines a proposed diagnostic system for use in children and adolescents. Due to the diverse criteria currently in use, there are varying estimates as to the prevalence of adolescent depression.

Most adolescents experience mood swings, and the nurse needs to distinguish these normal "ups and downs" from profound depression. The nurse must be familiar with adolescent biologic and psychosocial development. It is important to note that depression may present in numerous forms, from withdrawal to extreme behavioral changes.

When depression has been identified, the nurse needs to assist in seeking appropriate referrals to establish a treatment plan. Treatment plans should involve a mental health professional. The nurse can also play a critical role by establishing a relationship with the depressed adolescent. Such a relationship can offer a sense of hope. The nurse can also help support the adolescent's family by assisting in the identification of available resources. The nurse may also help the family vocalize treatment expectations and help them realize that treatment may involve a long period of time. Interventions focused on the learning and development of parenting skills are essential.

The nurse's role in prevention involves the promotion of good mental health habits. Nurses working with adolescents can help them recognize stress and learn problem solving skills to reduce stress.

## Suicide

Suicide is the third leading cause of death among adolescents in the United States. In the larger group of 15- to 24-year-olds it is now the second leading cause of death (Alcohol, Drug Abuse, and Mental Health Administration, 1989). Statistics reveal that preadolescent children are also increasingly at risk (Valente, 1987). It is believed that because of under-reporting, the actual suicide death rate is even higher. Many suicidal deaths, such as single car crashes, some poisonings, and homicides, are reported as "accidental." Many single car fatalities involve self-destruc-

*Table 16–9. Proposed Developmentally Specific Criteria for Depression\**

| Dysphoric Mood (Must Be Present) | Dysfunctional Behavior (At Least 4 Must Be Present) |
|---|---|
| | 13–18 yr (Postpubertal) |
| Appearance of sadness, apathy, helplessness, or irritability | 1. Somatic disorders (anorexia nervosa, ulcerative colitis, abdominal pain, conversion reactions) |
| | 2. Loss of pleasure in usual activities |
| | 3. Restlessness or lethargy |
| | 4. Phobic behavior and/or separation problems |
| | 5. Antisocial behavior |
| | 6. Recurrent thoughts of death or suicide |
| | 7. Appetite or weight changes |
| | 8. Sleeping difficulties |
| | 9. Decreased ability to concentrate |
| | 10. Excessive guilt, self-deprecation |

\* Symptoms have to be present for at least two weeks. The system is clinically derived, empirically based, and modeled after the *DSM-III-R* format. It strives to portray a developmentally accurate symptom picture of depression from its unique manifestation in infancy through its adult-like manifestation in late adolescence. The diagnostic system described is currently under study in child populations at risk for depression.
(From Herzog, D. B., & Rathburn, J. M. [1982]. Childhood depression: Developmental considerations. *American Journal of Diseases of Children, 136,* 115)

tive behavior, especially in boys. Numerous medical examiners and coroners believe that the reported number of suicides may be less than one half the true number. Another problem is the lack of statistics on unsuccessful attempts, which greatly outnumber successful suicides.

While more than 80% of suicide attempts are by females, three fourths of completions are by white males. Black suicide rates are nearly half of those of whites, for both men and women. Suicide methods differ between the sexes, with females more likely to use passive methods such as poisoning with a drug overdose and males preferring more violent methods, usually firearms. There is an increase in use of firearms for both sexes. The western states have the highest adolescent suicide rates, and the northeastern states have the lowest rates (Alcohol, Drug Abuse, and Mental Health Administration, 1989). Several signs that can alert observers who are assessing suicide risk are presented in Table 16-10.

Family dynamics play an important role in predicting suicide. Most adolescents clearly communicate suicidal intent before they act out. Nurses must take any suicide threat as serious and alert parents to this fact.

Suicidal acts can be related to family conflict, separation, or divorce, and the loss of a close friend or relative can lead to suicidal acts. Suicidal behavior by a parent and suicide by another adolescent can serve as models for suicidal behavior. It is important for the nurse to realize that most suicidal adolescents exhibit the alerting signs for at least a month before the suicide or suicide attempt.

Because it is difficult to detect suicidal intentions, the nurse should approach the adolescent in a direct manner.

Through concern and caring, the nurse may be viewed as a confidant. The nurse must pose direct and detailed questions:

1. Is suicidal behavior a possibility?
   a. Is there an expression of intent?
   b. Is there any evidence of lack of control? (Is the adolescent rageful, violent, manic-depressive)
   c. Is there evidence of a mismatch between the youth and the environment?
   d. Is there evidence of a dramatic unexplainable change in affect?

*Table 16–10. Alerting Signs of Suicide Risk*

**Background**

Family history of suicide or depression
Exposure to suicide
Prior attempt
Significant anticipated or real changes
Parental conflict
Parental pathology

**Current**

Depression/withdrawal
Acting-out behavior
Hopelessness
Drug/alcohol abuse
Rigid perfectionism
Friend of someone who is currently suicidal

*2.* Might a suicidal urge be acted upon?
   a. Does the adolescent have a plan?
*3.* If so, how imminent is that possibility?
   a. Is there a compulsion to act? ("command" hallucinations)
   b. Is there a readily available method?

Following a suicide attempt, hospitalization is recommended (American Academy of Pediatrics, 1988). Evaluation is done and intervention is initiated. All adolescents with a suicide attempt need careful follow-up.

The nurse's role is critical, and involves showing the adolescent that someone cares. Communicating a positive feeling involving options and resources helps the adolescent recognize this caring. The nurse can also play a role in prevention by recognizing signs of emotional distress and knowing the resources available in the community. Local mental health centers are an important resource. Many communities have a telephone suicide prevention hotline. Many schools have instituted suicide prevention programs, and counseling adolescents after a suicide is a new feature of such programs. Information on suicide prevention programs can be obtained from the American Association of Suicidology, 2459 South Ash, Denver, CO 80222, (303) 692-0985.

## Summary

Adolescence is a difficult time for everyone involved. Changes occur in the body, emotions, and social context of the young person. They are as rapid, varied, and confusing to the adolescent as they are to the adolescent's family. The nurse plays an important role in helping to explain these changes and in helping all parties understand each other and function in a reasonable manner. Despite behavior that is often contrary, parents must provide the adolescent with clear and reasonable limits. They also must allow the adolescent to suffer the consequences of his or her choices. Communication is aided if parents can listen and accept the adolescent's views, even when they clash with their own. The nurse can often help relieve parental frustration by reminding them that wisdom is seldom imparted at this stage—adolescents learn by doing. Parents should avoid lectures and will be better heard if they stick to answering questions and providing information.

## Eating Disorders— National Organizations

National Association for Anorexia Nervosa and Related
   Disorders
Box 271
Highland Park, IL 60035

National Anorexic Aid Society
550 S. Cleveland Avenue, Suite F
Westerville, OH 43081

American Anorexia/Bulimia Association
133 Cedar Lane
Teaneck, NJ 07666

Anorexia Nervosa and Bulimia Resource Center
2699 S. Bayshore Dr., Suite 800F
Coconut Grove, FL 33133

## References

Abrahamson, D. (1988). Teens and cars: A lethal mix. *Autoweek, 38,* 17-23.

Alan Guttmacher Institute. (1981). *Teenage pregnancy: The problem that hasn't gone away.* New York: Alan Guttmacher Institute.

Alcohol, Drug Abuse, and Mental Health Administration. (1989). *Report of the Secretary's Task Force on Youth Suicide. Volume 1: Overview and recommendations.* (DHHS Publication No. ADM 89-1621). Washington, DC: U.S. Government Printing Office.

American Academy of Pediatrics Committee on Adolescence. (1983). Homosexuality and adolescence. *Pediatrics, 72,* 249-250.

American Academy of Pediatrics Committee on Adolescence. (1988). Suicide and suicide attempts in young adolescents and young adults. *Pediatrics, 81,* 322-324.

American Academy of Pediatrics Committee on Sports Medicine. (1989). Anabolic steroids and the adolescent athlete. *Pediatrics, 83,* 127-128.

American Medical Association. (1987). *AMA white paper on adolescent health.* Chicago: American Medical Association.

American Psychiatric Association. (1987). *Diagnostic and statistical manual of mental disorders—revised (DSM III-R).* Washington, DC: Author.

Atrash, H., Rhodenhiserr, E., & Hogue, C. (1987). Abortion surveillance: preliminary analysis—United States, 1982-1983. *Morbidity and Mortality Weekly Report Surveillance Summary, 35,* 2SS.

Baker, S. P., & Dietz, P. E. (1979). Injury prevention. In *Healthy people: The Surgeon General's report on health promotion and disease prevention.* U. S. Department of Health, Education and Welfare Publication No. (PHS) 79-55071A.

Bond, W. S., Crabe, S., & Sanders, M. C. (1986). Pharmocotherapy of eating disorders: A critical review. *Drug Intelligence and Clinical Pharmacy, 20,* 659-665.

Brunch, H. (1978). Anorexia nervosa. *Nutrition Today, 13*(5), 14-18.

Buckley, W. E., Yesalis, C. E. III, Friedl, K. E., Anderton, W. A., Streit, A. L., & Wright, J. E. (1988). Estimated prevalence of anabolic steroid use among male high school seniors. *Journal of the American Medical Association 260,* 3441-3445.

Casper, R. C. (1986). The pathophysiology of anorexia nervosa and bulimia nervosa. *Annual Reviews of Nutrition, 6,* 299-316.

Castiglia, P. T. (1989). Anorexia nervosa. *Journal of Pediatric Healthcare, 3*(2), 105-107.

Castiglia, P. T. (1989). Obesity in adolescence. *Journal of Pediatric Healthcare, 3*(4):221–223.

Castiglia, P. T. (1989). Bulimia. *Journal of Pediatric Health Care, 3,* 167-169.

Centers for Disease Control. (1988). Progress toward achieving the national 1990 objectives for injury prevention and control. *Morbidity and Mortality Weekly Report, 37,* 2069-2077.

Clarke, J. H., MacPherson, B., & Holmes, D. R. (1986). Reducing adolescent smoking: A comparison of peer-led, teacher-led, and expert interventions. *Journal of School Health, 56,* 102-106.

Coles, R., & Stokes, G. (1985). *Sex and the American teenager.* New York: Harper and Row.

Driskell, J. A., Clark, A. J., & Moak, S. E. (1987). Longitudinal assessment of vitamin B-6 status in Southern adolescent girls. *Journal of the American Dietetic Association, 87,* 307.

Elkind, D. (1968). Cognitive development in adolescence. In Adams, J. F. (Ed.). *Understanding adolescence.* Boston: Allyn and Bacon.

Elkind, D. (1967). Egocentrism in adolescence. *Child Development, 38,* 1025-1034.

Erikson, E. H. (1963). *Childhood and society* (2nd ed.). New York: W. W. Norton.

Farley, D. (1986). *Eating disorders—when thinness becomes an obsession.* (DHSS Publication No. FDA 86-2211). Washington, DC: U. S. Government Printing Office.

Finkelstein, J. W. (1980). The endocrinology of adolescence. *Pediatric Clinics of North America, 27*(1), 53-69.

Garner, D. M., & Garfinkel, P. E. (1979). The Eating Attitudes Test: an index of the symptoms of anorexia nervosa. *Psychological Medicine, 9,* 273-279.

Gortmaker, S. L., Dietz, W. H., Sobol, A. M., & Wehler, C. A. (1987). Increasing pediatric obesity in the United States. *American Journal of Disease of Children, 141,* 535-540.

Haas, A. (1979). *Teenage sexuality—a survey of teenage sexual behavior.* New York: Macmillan.

Harding, S. E. (1985). Anorexia nervosa. *Pediatric Nursing, 11,* 275.

Harris, L. (1986). *American teens speak: Sex, myths, TV, and birth control.* New York: Lewis Harris and Associates.

Havighurst, R. J. (1979). *Developmental tasks and education* (3rd ed.) New York: David McKay.

Hayes, C. D. (1987). *Risking the future: Adolescent sexuality, pregnancy, and childbearing* (Vol. 1). Washington, DC: National Academy Press.

Hofferth, S. L., Kahn, J. R., & Baldwin, W. (1987). Premarital sexual activity among U.S. teenage women over the past three decades. *Family Planning Perspectives, 19,* 46.

Hsu, L. K. (1986). The treatment of anorexia nervosa. *American Journal of Psychiatry, 143,* 573-581.

Imajo, T. (1983). Suicide by motor vehicle. *Journal of Forensic Sciences, 28*(1): 83-89.

Joffe, A., Radius, S., & Gall, M. (1988). Health counseling for adolescents: What they want, what they get, and who gives it. *Pediatrics, 82,* 481-485.

Johnston, L. D., O'Malley, P. M., & Bachman, J. G. (1987). Psychotherapeutic, licit and illicit use of drugs among adolescents. *Journal of Adolescent Health Care, 8,* 36-51.

Kennedy, P. M. (1988). Adolescent strength training. *Sports Medicine Digest, 10*(12):1-2.

Killen, J. D. (1985). Prevention of adolescent tobacco smoking: The social pressure resistance training approach. *Journal of Child Psychology and Psychiatry, 26,* 7-15.

Killen, J. D., Taylor, C. B., Telch, M. J., Saylor, K. E., Maron, D. J., & Robinson, T. N. (1986). Self-induced vomiting and laxative and diuretic use among teenagers. *Journal of the American Medical Association, 255,* 1447-1449.

Kohlberg, L. (1976). Moral stages and moralization: the cognitive-developmental approach. In Lickona, T. (Ed.). *Moral development and behavior: Theory, research and social issues.* New York: Holt, Rinehart & Winston.

Macdonald, D. I. (1989). Diagnosis and treatment of adolescent substance abuse. *Current Problems in Pediatrics, 19*(8).

Marshall, W. A., & Tanner, J. M. (1969). Variations in pattern of pubertal changes in females. *Archives of Diseases of Children, 44,* 291-303.

Marshall, W. A., & Tanner, J. M. (1970). Variations in the pattern of pubertal changes in boys. *Archives of Diseases of Children, 45*(13), 13-23.

Muuss, R. E. (1986). Adolescent eating disorder: Bulimia. *Adolescence, 21,* 257-267.

National Center for Health Statistics. (1987). Advance report of final natality statistics, 1985. *Monthly Vital Statistics Report, 36*(4).

National Safety Council. (1990). *Accident facts.* Chicago: National Safety Council.

Newcomer, S., & Udry, J. (1983). Adolescent sexual behavior and popularity. *Adolescence, 18,* 515

O'Malley, P. M., & Johnston, L. D. (1985). *Cocaine use among American adolescents and young adults.* Rockville, MD: National Institute on Drug Abuse.

Pallikkathayil, L., & Tweed, S. (1983). Substance abuse: Alcohol and drugs during adolescence. *Nursing Clinics of North America, 18,* 313-321.

Prothrow-Stith, D. (1986). *Interdisciplinary interventions applicable to prevention of interpersonal violence and homicide in black youths.* U. S. Department of Health and Human Services, Publication No. (PHS) HRS-D-MC 86-1.

Puig-Antich, J. (1980). Affective disorders in childhood: A review and perspective. *Psychiatric Clinics of North America, 3,* 403-424.

Remafedi, G. (1987). Homosexual youth: A challenge to contemporary society. *Journal of the American Medical Association, 258,* 222-225.

Russell, G. F. M., Szmukler, G. I., Dare, G., & Eisler, I. (1987). An evaluation of family therapy in anorexia nervosa and bulimia nervosa. *Archives of General Psychiatry, 44,* 1047-1056.

Silvis, G. L., & Perry, C. L. (1987). Understanding and deterring tobacco use among adolescents. *Pediatric Clinics of North America, 34,* 363-379.

Sullivan, H. S. (1953). *The interpersonal theory of psychiatry.* New York: W. W. Norton.

Tanner, J. M. (1962). *Growth of adolescence* (2nd ed.). Oxford: Blackwell Scientific Publications.

Troiden, R. R. (1988). Homosexual identity development. *Journal of Adolescent Health Care, 9,* 105-113.

Trussell, J. (1988). Teenage pregnancy in the United States. *Family Planning Perspectives, 20,* 262-272.

Vacc, N. A., & Rhyne, M. (1987). The Eating Attitudes Test: Development of an adapted language form for children. *Perceptual and Motor Skills, 65,* 335-336.

Valente, S. M. (1987). Assessing suicide rate in the school-age child. *Journal of Pediatric Health Care, 1*(1), 14-20.

Van Thorre, M. D., & Vogel, F. X. (1985). The presence of bulimia in high school females. *Adolescence, 20,* 45-51.

Ventura, S. J., & Hendershot, G. E. (1984). Infant health consequences of childbearing by teenagers and older mothers. *Public Health Reports, 99,* 138.

Williams, J. F., Friedman, J. M., & Steiner, H. (1986). Hand lesions characteristic of bulimia. *American Journal of Diseases of Children, 140,* 28-29.

Zabin, L., & Clark, S. (1981). Why they delay: A study of teenage family planning clinic patients. *Family Planning Perspectives, 13,* 205.

Zabin, L. S., Kantner, J. F., & Zeknik, M. (1979). The risk of adolescent pregnancy in the first months of intercourse. *Family Planning Perspectives, 11,* 215-222.

Zelnick, M., & Kantner, J. F. (1980). Sexual activity, contraception use and pregnancy among metropolitan area teenagers: 1971-1979. *Family Planning Perspectives, 12,* 2.

Zuckerman, D. M., Colby, A., Ware, N. C., & Lazerson, J. S. (1986). The prevalence of bulimia among college students. *American Journal of Public Health, 76,* 1135-1137.

## Bibliography

Alan Guttmacher Institute. (1989). *Teenage pregnancy in the United States.* New York: Author.

Brown, R. C., Sanders, J. M., Jr., & Schonberg, S. K. (1986). Driving safety and adolescent behavior. *Pediatrics, 77,* 603-607.

Fleming, D. (1989). *How to stop the battle with your teenager.* Englewood Cliffs, N.J.: Prentice-Hall.

Martin, S. (1988). Self-esteem of adolescent girls as related to weight. *Perceptual and Motor Skills, 67,* 879-884.

Muscari, M. E. (1988). Effective nursing strategies for adolescents with anorexia nervosa and bulimia nervosa. *Pediatric Nursing, 14,* 475-481.

Nelson, M. (1989). Androgenic-anabolic steroid use in adolescents. *Journal of Pediatric Health Care, 3,* 175-180.

Suicide—United States, 1979-1980: Leads from the MMWR. (1985). *Journal of the American Medical Association, 254,* 479-480.

Thornton, L. P., & DeBlassie, R. R. (1989). Treating bulimia. *Adolescence, 24,* 631-637.

Wilson, D., & Molloy-Martinez, T. (1989). Promoting driving safety for teens and adults. *Nurse Practitioner, 14*(10), 28-39.

# Special Considerations in Child Health Nursing

*Effects of Hospitalization on Children and Families*

*Nursing Care of Children in the Home*

*Caring for Children With Infectious Diseases*

*Nursing Care of Children With Disabling Conditions*

*Effects of Substance Abuse on Children and Families*

*Children's Experiences With Dying, Death, and Bereavement*

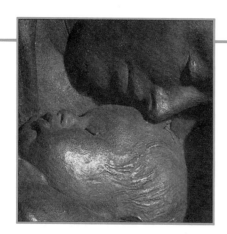

*Photograph by David Finn*

# Effects of Hospitalization on Children and Families

Patricia A. Iacovitti

*Sculpture by Charles Parks*

17

*Hospitalization*
  *Factors Affecting Hospitalization*

*Hospitalization and Developmental
  Stages*
    *Infants*
    *Toddlers*
    *Preschoolers*
    *School-Aged Children*
    *Adolescents*

*Preparing Children for
  Hospitalization*
    *Children's Responses
      to Hospitalization*
    *Methods of Preparing Children
      for Hospitalization*
    *Timing of Preparation*
    *Special Preparation Needs*

*Parental Responses to Hospitalization*

*Minimizing the Effects
  of Hospitalization*
    *Preparation for Hospitalization*
    *Atraumatic Care*
    *Stress Immunization*
    *Play*

*Hospital Admission*
    *Types of Admissions*
    *Children's and Families'
      Responses to Admission*
    *The Admission Interview*
    *Orientation to the Hospital*

*Teaching Parents of Hospitalized
  Children*

*Discharge Planning*

*Summary*

## Learning Objectives

*Upon completion of this chapter the reader will be able to:*

1. *Describe children's responses to illness as they relate to cognitive development, past experiences, and levels of knowledge.*

2. *Discuss the impact of hospitalization, based on developmental stages, from infancy through adolescence.*

3. *Present principles of nursing management to alleviate deleterious effects of hospitalization on children and families as well as to promote optimal growth and development during hospitalization.*

4. *Relate the effects of hospitalization during infancy, including parent–child relationships, feeding, sleeping, crying, and sensory overload.*

5. *Identify toddlers' responses to hospitalization by discussing separation anxiety, loss of control, and regression.*

6. *Describe effects of hospitalization on preschoolers by incorporating major developmental milestones related to separation anxiety, fear, and behavior.*

7. *Recognize the impact of industry versus inferiority when school-aged children are hospitalized and discuss their fears and perceptions of illness.*

8. *Explain the loss of independence and identify what occurs when adolescents are hospitalized, including the impact of peers, change in body image, and emotions.*

9. *Explain methods used by pediatric nurses to minimize the effects of hospitalization.*

10. *Discuss parental responses to hospitalization of children.*

11. *Describe hospital admission and discharge of pediatric patients.*

12. *Identify key elements of discharge planning for infants, children, and adolescents.*

## Key Terms

*atraumatic care*

*behavioral control*

*behavioral rehearsal*

*cognitive control*

*cognitive rehearsal*

*magical thinking*

*modeling*

*relaxation training*

*sensory deprivation*

*sensory overload*

*separation anxiety*

*stress immunization*

*systematic desensitization*

All children's responses to illness are influenced by a number of variables, including age, developmental level, seriousness of the problem, coping patterns, previous experiences with hospitalization, whether the hospitalization was planned or an emergency, cultural and religious beliefs, and parental reactions. All these factors must be incorporated into the child's care plan.

Nursing care of hospitalized children, from infancy through adolescence, requires an understanding of the effects hospitalization has on children in various age groups as well as on their families. This information assists nurses in assessing, diagnosing, planning, implementing, and evaluating comprehensive nursing care and helps minimize the negative effects.

Adequate preparation for hospitalization can also assist children and families in coping with the event. Specific preparation methods, timing of the preparation, and response to children with special needs can alleviate some of the stress associated with hospitalization.

Nursing care of pediatric patients must also include consideration of the parents' needs and responses to hospitalization. The trend toward short hospital stays often necessitates teaching parents various procedures in a shorter period of time.

## Hospitalization

Hospitalization can be a threatening and stressful experience for children and families. Despite efforts to avoid hospitalization of children, 4.5 million children are hospitalized each year in the United States. Two percent of children in the United States suffer from a serious, major childhood illness, such as cystic fibrosis, asthma, sickle cell anemia, or leukemia. With recent advances in pediatric medical technology, newborns who are barely viable at birth are surviving, and children with chronic conditions are living longer. As a result, the number of technology dependent-children is rising (Feeg, 1989). Hospital admissions of children for acute conditions, such as trauma, account for a large number of pediatric hospitalizations.

### Factors Affecting Hospitalization

Cognitive development, previous experiences with hospitalization, level of knowledge, and parental involvement affect children's responses to illness and hospitalization.

Children pass through various stages of cognitive development. Children progress through four stages of development by incorporating new information into established categories (Piaget, 1962). In view of this theory, it should be determined how much children understand before attempting to provide explanations of medical conditions or procedures. This knowledge is acquired through careful questioning. Then, when explanations are given, further inquiries are needed to determine that children understand the explanations (Piaget, 1962).

As children's cognitive abilities increase, they can understand the causes of illness and understand the related treatments for it. This knowledge allows them control over an illness. With increased understanding, they are able to take measures to prevent some illnesses from occurring, such as avoiding people with communicable diseases.

Knowledge of children's previous experiences with hospitalization and health care personnel contributes to understanding their responses to current hospitalizations. Children who have experienced positive outcomes from health care probably perceive hospitalization more accurately and demonstrate more positive coping strategies than those who perceive hospitalization as a source of pain and punishment. Knowledge of children's fears of hospitalization must be determined, since fears may be exaggerated with illness.

Recent changes or stresses, such as moving, starting school, weaning from the bottle, or divorce, may negatively affect a child's ability to cope with illness.

Age and developmental levels influence children's perceptions of experiences. Level of development is an important consideration in the nursing care of children. Nurses must understand concepts of growth and development to meet the needs of pediatric patients. Piaget demonstrated that in space, time, cause, and number, children adhere to a logic that follows a developmental sequence. Bibace and Walsh (1980) found that children's personal control increases with development. They also reported that health professionals are more reassuring in the pediatric setting when they take into account psychological level of children's beliefs about illness. Nursing care must be planned and individualized according to developmental level. This practice helps nurses prepare children for procedures by using age-appropriate strategies and enables nurses to focus on fears or concerns that children have of hospitalization so they can implement coping strategies for these children and their parents.

## Hospitalization and Developmental Stages

### Infants

Infancy is a period of rapid growth and development. Piaget (1962) defines it as the sensorimotor period of development in which the major task is to coordinate sensory perceptions and motor activities.

Erikson (1964) describes infancy as a time when infants develop a sense of trust and must have their needs met promptly. Trust develops in a consistent environment. In the first few months of life, growth occurs through the senses of sight, hearing, and touch. Infants have few coping mechanisms; they respond to stress with reactions such as crying, behavioral changes, and irritability.

#### Assessment of Hospitalized Infants

The factors that influence infants' responses to hospitalization are attachment behaviors, nutritional patterns, sleep patterns, communication, and stimulation.

***Attachment Behaviors.*** When infants are hospitalized, they are taken away from their usual environments and primary care-givers. They experience additional stresses related to different care-givers, strange environments, and different sounds. Infants cannot communicate discomfort or uncertainty with words, nor do they understand.

During the first few months of life, infants develop attachments to primary care-givers, usually their mothers. Infants under 6 months of age respond better to care-givers other than primary ones as long as their basic needs are met. During the second 6 months of life, infants become very attached to their parents, begin to recognize their mothers and familiar sights, and become upset when they are not present. When infants become ill, the usual energies for meeting basic needs are redirected to focus on coping with the illness.

*Nutritional Patterns.* During infancy, feeding is a pleasurable experience for infants and parents because it fosters growth and attachment and sets the stage for positive eating habits in later life. During an illness, an increased caloric intake is necessary to cope with the demands on the body's metabolic and compensatory mechanisms. Adequate nutrition for infants, therefore, is important. Regular feeding schedules may be interrupted during hospitalization, and infants may have decreased appetites. This situation may be further exaggerated in a hospital setting by the use of alternate feeding methods, such as intravenous fluids or nasogastric tubes.

*Sleep Patterns.* During an illness, infants may require more sleep to conserve energy and promote healing. The fulfillment of this need may be impeded by an altered environment with different sounds, more or less light, and a different crib. Sleep patterns may also be disrupted by waking infants frequently for procedures such as assessment of vital signs or administration of medications. Regular routines for settling infants are likely to be disturbed, thus contributing to the stress of hospitalization. Lethargy needs to be distinguished from an increased need for sleep since it can be a sign of a serious neurological problem.

*Communication.* Crying is a means by which infants communicate needs since they are unable to communicate their basic needs or describe pain through speech. Infants express themselves with different types of cries, and parents quickly learn to identify them. Pain cries usually occur with painful stimulation, such as a pin or needle prick, but may also occur when infants are too hot or cold, have wet diapers, or are experiencing gas pains. Cries of hunger are usually rhythmic. Pleasure cries do not usually occur until 3 months of age.

*Stimulation.* Hospitalized infants are frequently kept in their cribs and left in sleepwear. Home routines are disrupted, parents respond differently to hospitalized infants, and diversions are often limited. These factors can cause either sensory deprivation or sensory overload and lead to impaired development.

Babies who do not normally cry excessively are at risk in the hospital for *sensory deprivation* because they do not demand as much attention as infants who cry frequently.

*Sensory overload* during hospitalization is stressful for infants. Stimulation such as beepers, pages, alarms, voices, equipment, and other children crying is almost continuous and does not allow infants to respond effectively. When infants receive too much stimulation, they

may regress to safer and more comfortable states. For example, infants may pull blankets over their heads, avoid eye contact, or sleep excessively. When infants are presented with too much stimulation at one time, they are unable to absorb it, and they become frightened.

## Nursing Management of Hospitalized Infants

Nurses must understand the stresses that hospitalized infants experience so they can minimize the infants' physiological and psychological distress. Nursing care is oriented to promoting trust among nurses, parents, and infants. Nurses should anticipate infants' needs, interview the parents to determine the infants' routine, and develop this knowledge into a workable nursing care plan. The primary nursing care model should be used, in which the same nurses care for the same infants whenever possible. Parents should be encouraged to participate in routine care of their infants and should be given the opportunity to room in with their children. In early infancy, this practice enhances the bonding between parents and infants, and in later infancy, it reduces the effects of stranger anxiety.

A safe environment must be provided for infants. Side rails of cribs must be up at all times when infants are unattended. Mattresses should fit securely in the crib frames to prevent infants from falling. Harmful objects should be kept out of reach. Cribs should not be placed near electrical outlets that infants can reach with their hands. Nurses should avoid leaving infants alone in cribs with bottles to prevent aspiration of the feedings. All toys left in the crib must be safe. Toys with small detachable pieces on which infants can choke should be avoided.

Infants must be restrained for procedures since they are unable to understand directions. Nurses should always allow time to comfort infants after painful procedures. While administering medications to infants, elevate their heads to prevent the possibility of aspiration. Procedures should be performed before feeding to prevent vomiting. Young infants have tongue thrust, so it may be necessary to place medications and food toward the backs of their mouths or refeed them, as necessary.

Nurses should observe infants for signs of stranger anxiety, which is frequently manifested by 8 months of age. Initial contacts with infants should be made in the mothers' presence, approaching infants slowly to allow them to feel safe. Nurses should maintain eye contact with infants, especially during feedings. Parents should be encouraged to maintain eye contact as well, to promote bonding.

Nurses should attempt to minimize sensory deprivation and sensory overload for infants. Infants need tactile and sensory stimulation, which can be provided by talking, singing, musical toys, mobiles, swings and strollers, rocking, and cuddling. Nurses should frequently change infants' positions and imitate infants' sounds to increase vocalization. Sensory stimulation to provide optimal development during hospitalization should be encouraged. Specific stimulation measures are outlined in Table 17-1.

To decrease sensory overload, nursing care should be organized so that the number of interruptions to infants is minimized. Examples include keeping doors to patients' rooms closed, keeping voices low, and limiting voice pages to emergencies.

Comfort measures promote trust in hospitalized infants. Infants should be held as much as possible. When nurses or parents are not available, allow volunteers to hold and cuddle infants. Rocking while being held provides a sense of comfort and security. When infants are distressed, allow them to suck on pacifiers or feed them on demand. This response satisfies the need to suck.

Older infants should be given the opportunity for movement, and safe spaces should be provided for crawling or walking at regular intervals (Fig. 17-1). If infants need to be restrained, nurses should release the restraints frequently and at regular intervals while supervising the infants. By incorporating these measures into the care of infants, nurses can minimize the potential trauma of hospitalization.

Infancy is a time of rapid physical growth and development. When normal infancy is interrupted with illness and hospitalization, it provides a threat to the infant and family; however, positive growth can occur if nurses understand principles of infant growth and development and implement nursing care individually to meet specific needs of infants.

## Toddlers

Toddlers are busy developing autonomy. The impact of hospitalization on toddlers is affected by the manner in which toddlers' needs have been met since birth, previous

---

*Table 17—1. Adding Stimulation to Hospital Encounters*

**While Measuring Vital Signs**

Talk soothingly and calmly. Explain what you are doing as you do it.

Blow on the stethoscope. Ask child to imitate. Name body parts and touch them. "Foot. Here is my foot." "Where are my eyes? There are my eyes!" Guide the child's hands to touch.

Use diversions—another toy, tickles (especially abdomen).

Play peek-a-boo: Cover your eyes, then baby's. Hide your head with blanket, then infant's head. When an older infant covers his own head, say, "Where's (name)?" Then delight in discovery.

**While Diapering**

Use body movement, exercising infant's legs rhythmically.
Sing a nonsense tune or talk animatedly.
Talk about sensations; wet/dry, warm/cold, soft/rough, as sensations are presented.
Name body position: up/down. Tickle.
Play "Gotcha"—especially delightful with crawlers.

**While Bathing**

Experiment with the properties of water in a small tub. Use items that float and sink—washcloth, plastic soap dish, paper cup, plastic lid, empty plastic cylinders, ping-pong balls. Talk about what happens.

Identify body parts as you wash them. Give simple directions ("Close your eyes." "Raise your arms." "Wash your hair."). Be sure to praise all help.

Demonstrate problem solving by hunting for hidden objects. Partially cover a familiar toy with the washcloth. Cover the entire toy while the child watches, then ask where the toy is. Add different covering material and move the toy in full view of the infant from under one to under the other. See if the child goes to the right one or the first one.

**While Feeding**

Place the child in high chair or walker once he can sit unsupported. Tie toy or utensil to high chair to facilitate retrieval.

Discuss the food: hot/cold, colors, textures, which utensils to use.*

Use an extra spoon and cup: one for you, one for baby.

Experiment with food: fingerpaint on tray, make lines.

**During Dressing Changes and Treatments**

Distract the child with empty dressing packages, encouraging crushing and listening to sounds.

Make the sounds and touch different parts of baby's body.

Talk about what you are doing.

**During Nap Times**

Turn off TV sets. Place favorite toy in crib.

Encourage slow-down routines—stories, rocking, quiet singing.

**Through Environmental Noises**

Say "Listen to that sound (name). That means the solution has gone in. I'll take care of that" or "Oh, look at that pretty red light. Let's see what that means."

Talk about telephones ringing, water running.

**Depending on Floor/Layout**

Place infants in the same room to encourage socialization.

Talk to other children in room while caring for one child.

Open curtains between rooms and hallways to encourage the child to look about.

---

*Talking during feeding may be too distracting for young bottle-fed infants. Instead, maintain eye contact and play after feeding or at another alert period.

(Verzemnieks, I. [1984]. Developmental stimulation for infants and toddlers. *American Journal of Nursing, 6,* 748–752)

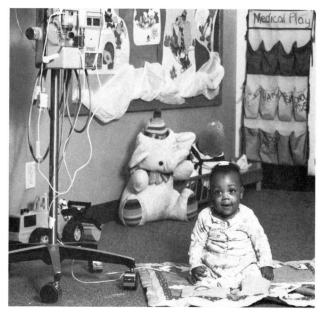

*Figure 17–1. Older infants should be given opportunities for movement.*

experiences with illnesses and separations, the length of the hospitalizations, and the relationships with parents.

Hospitalized toddlers are taken out of their homes and placed in different environments. Since toddlers' recently discovered energy must be directed toward the illness instead of to the performance of newly learned tasks, they frequently regress to earlier and safer forms of behavior. Regression can be accompanied by return to thumb-sucking, loss of bowel and bladder control, or the need for a bottle.

### Assessment of Hospitalized Toddlers

The factors that affect toddlers' responses to hospitalization are attachment behaviors and the need for autonomy and consistent routines.

*Attachment Behaviors.* The major stressor related to attachment is separation anxiety. *Separation anxiety* is the outward manifestation of children's displeasure at being separated from their parents or familiar surroundings. Separation anxiety occurs in three phases. During the initial phase of protest against the separation, children display uncontrollable crying and may be aggressive. The second phase is despair, in which children may be less active, withdrawn, and depressed but cry less. In the third phase of detachment, children appear to have adjusted to the surroundings. They begin to play and form new relationships. In this phase, toddlers detach themselves from parents to avoid emotional pain associated with the parents' departure. It is important to note that children may not go through all three phases in succession. Serious developmental damage or delays can be

expected, however, when children reach the stage of detachment. This response occurs more often with long-term hospitalization.

*Autonomy and Routines.* Toddlers are seriously threatened by the loss of control imposed by hospitalization. They have many routines and need consistency in their lives. These highly regulated activities are centered around eating, sleeping, playing, and toileting. Completion of age-specific tasks contributes to toddlers' autonomous and egocentric natures. Changes in these routines because of illness or hospitalization inhibit growth and development. Toddlers sense their lack of control and, because of limited coping mechanisms, protest vehemently. Their responses may be displayed as temper tantrums initially but, if their autonomy continues to be disrupted, they may become more passive and withdrawn. Fortunately, many potentially damaging situations related to hospitalization of toddlers can be minimized by good nursing care.

### Nursing Management of Hospitalized Toddlers

To maximize toddlers' development during hospitalization, nurses should incorporate age-specific measures into the care plan and encourage parent–child contact. Nurses should explain to parents the need for their presence during the interview process with children. The initial parental interview ascertains toddlers' schedules at home, and nurses can incorporate as much of it as possible into the care plan. The parents should also participate in the physical examination, and children should remain on parents' laps, when possible. By establishing effective relationships with parents, positive nurse–child relationships are developed.

It is best to prepare toddlers for diagnostic and laboratory procedures just before the procedures take place (Fig. 17-2). Nurses should either explain the procedures themselves or help the parents describe them to their children. Nurses should encourage parents to hold and cuddle toddlers after painful procedures.

Parents should be encouraged to spend as much time as possible with hospitalized toddlers. Having a parent room in with a hospitalized toddler can often be beneficial to both parents and children. If parents are unable to remain with toddlers, nurses should determine when they plan to return so that appropriate explanations can be provided to the children. Toddlers do not have a fully developed concept of time, but they may understand explanations such as "Mommy will return when it gets light outside, or after breakfast." It is often helpful to have parents leave personal items for toddlers to keep, since children associate these items with the parents and feel certain they will return for the items. The same nurses should be assigned to care for the toddlers whenever pos-

*Figure 17–2. Allowing toddlers to handle equipment relieves some of their fears.*

sible since this contributes to toddlers' senses of routine as well as assists in maintaining a therapeutic relationship with toddlers and families.

Parents should be allowed to perform care activities for their children, such as bathing and feeding. This interaction promotes parent–child bonding, reduces anxiety, and allows parents to continue their parental roles. Nurses should supervise these situations carefully since there may be occasions when parents are unable to cope with caring for toddlers; nurses must then intervene to support parents and help them overcome guilty feelings they may have about their responses.

Nurses and parents should be truthful with toddlers, since lying contributes to mistrust. Nurses or health care personnel should not attempt to frighten toddlers into submission by using punishment tactics. For example, statements such as "If you don't go to sleep, the nurse will give you a shot" must be avoided.

Toddlers should participate in self-care activities such as eating or bathing as much as possible to promote their need for autonomy and control. Since toddlers are active and mobile, restraints usually lead to fierce protest. This situation can be handled by providing opportunities for some freedom and movement. For example, toddlers who are immobilized by casts or traction can keep the rest of their bodies active by playing catch with soft balls or balloons or by blowing soap bubbles. Nurses, parents, child-life personnel, or volunteers must be present during play to prevent injuries.

Toddlers should be able to bring a few personal items

and toys from home. These items promote their sense of security and consistency. Toddlers should be allowed to wear their own clothes, when possible.

During hospitalization, toilet-trained toddlers often revert to the need for diapers. This can be upsetting to parents; nurses need to reassure parents that this situation is normal and usually temporary. Nurses should determine the words toddlers use to describe toileting so that communication between toddlers and nurses regarding this need is clear.

## Preschoolers

Preschoolers can exhibit the same needs as toddlers when hospitalized. Preschool-age development is characterized by a growing sense of initiative and is cognitively centered around the preoperational phase. Preschoolers shift from egocentricity to awareness of others. Actual physical growth and development is slower than during the infancy and toddler age periods.

### Assessment of Hospitalized Preschoolers

Factors that affect hospitalization of preschoolers are attachment behaviors, perception of reality, psychosexual beliefs, and sleep patterns.

***Attachment Behaviors.*** Separation anxiety is manifested less aggressively since preschoolers are able to tolerate separation for brief periods of time better than infants and toddlers. Preschoolers may refuse to eat or sleep and may continually ask when their parents will return. Preschoolers may seem more grown up, and they are more flexible than toddlers. Their sense of time allows them to understand more clearly when parents will return. They are beginning to enter play relationships with age-mates and possess expanded coping abilities.

***Perception of Reality.*** Preschoolers are not capable of abstract thought, so all their interpretations are based on reality. They are just beginning to differentiate themselves from their environment and use only past experiences as references for current situations. Preschoolers frequently misinterpret hospital events since the basis for their thoughts are past experiences. Hospitalization is often associated with pain; subsequently, this aspect remains foremost in preschoolers' thoughts. To understand concepts or situations that are not within their realm of knowledge, preschoolers use *magical thinking*—the desire to have their thoughts or wishes turn into reality. Their literal interpretations of words and expressions may lead them to feel that hospitalization is a punishment for misbehavior. The vivid imagination of preschoolers also leads to the development of fear of bodily mutilation.

*Psychosexual Beliefs.* Fantasies and magical thoughts are complicated by intense psychosexual preoccupations. Both sexes feel the need for close association with their fathers. Surgery or procedures that involve the genitals can be especially disturbing to preschoolers because of the fear of castration or mutilation.

Masturbation is a normal part of development, and there is heightened interest in it by preschoolers even though it may be noted earlier. Statistics regarding masturbation are frequently incorrect since many parents are reluctant to admit that their children masturbate. Preschoolers discover that genital stimulation produces pleasant sensations, which increases their interest in their genitals and those of others. Parents need to be reassured that this curiosity is normal and that masturbation does not cause either physiological or psychological injury. Children must learn socially acceptable behavior, however, and must understand that masturbation is a private act. Families' cultural and religious beliefs regarding this issue must be considered and respected as well. Genital stimulation is not always masturbation; it may be related to boredom or insecurity. A young boy who frequently touches his penis may, in fact, not be masturbating but reassuring himself that his penis is still there. When preschoolers are hospitalized for procedures involving their genitals, they may fear that they are being punished for touching their genitals.

*Sleep Patterns.* Preschoolers need a consistent bedtime pattern. The hospital environment causes changes in these patterns by its different sights and sounds and by prescribing different bedtimes and locations than usual. These factors can predispose preschoolers to sleep disturbances. Additionally, stress imposed by illness on both parents and preschoolers can result in sleep alterations that can be manifested by nightmares, frequent waking during the night, or night fears (these are often of a fantastic or magical nature, with monsters or "bogey men").

### Nursing Management of Hospitalized Preschoolers

Nursing measures for hospitalized preschoolers must center on their needs for initiative and the feelings of shame and guilt that they may be experiencing about hospitalization. Nurses and parents must be truthful since lying promotes mistrust, and children will feel out of control.

Rooming in should be encouraged. Preschoolers need to know that their parents love them and that they are not being punished. The same nurses should care for preschoolers, when possible, since this helps preschoolers and parents feel more comfortable. When parents need to leave children, even briefly, they should be told that the parents will return and when.

Nurses are responsible for preparing preschoolers for hospitalization. This activity is best accomplished shortly before procedures occur. Preparation too far in advance of the hospitalization fosters the development of fantasies and fears.

Play can be helpful in preparing preschoolers for hospitalization or procedures. By allowing preschoolers to manipulate hospital equipment in a nonthreatening area such as the playroom, stress is reduced, control and initiative are promoted, and the spirit of exploration is fostered. Hospital playrooms equipped with dolls in casts or with intravenous tubes help children to act out fears (Fig. 17-3). By playing doctor, nurse, or patient, preschoolers can work through stress and fears relating to hospitalization. This type of play can be a useful tool for nurses since it can help identify problems not manifested or expressed by children in other ways.

Quiet time must be allotted to answer children's questions with either age-appropriate explanations or by using dolls as demonstration models. If the doll gets a "shot," the nurse or playroom volunteer must hold and cuddle the doll, thereby reassuring children about procedures.

Preschoolers should be encouraged to feed and bathe themselves when possible, and parents should allow them to perform basic tasks on their own. Preschoolers should stay in rooms with children of their own age because at this age they are beginning to enter relationships with their peers.

## School-Aged Children

School age is the age of industry. Children leave the home and parents, and peers and school become essential activities. School-aged children must be successful in complet-

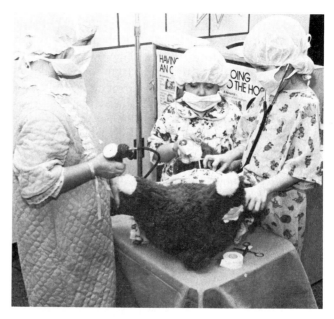

*Figure 17–3. Two preschoolers play-act an operation with an older child.*

ing age-appropriate tasks because failure leads to feelings of inferiority. They are entering the phase of concrete operational thought. Since thought processes are concrete, nurses must consider these fears in the care plan as well as in their approach to school-aged children.

### Assessment of Hospitalized School-Aged Children

Factors that affect hospitalization of school-aged children are attachment behaviors, body image, immobility and confinement, loss of control, and death.

*Attachment Behaviors.* Separation anxiety is still observed in school-aged children; however, the degree of separation varies. It is manifested more severely in younger school-aged children. They need to have their parents present but tolerate their absence with greater ease than infants, toddlers, or preschoolers. With hospitalization, school-aged children feel threatened because they are unable to be at school or with their peers. Hospitalization imposes greater dependence on parents. Separation anxiety presents mixed feelings for school-aged children. The stress of illness and hospitalization imposes physical and psychological dependency on them; conflict arises because they need to be independent and with their peers.

*Body Image.* Physical appearance that is altered by illness or surgery can be a major problem for school-aged children. During this phase of development, children have a need to look like their age mates. Being different from their peers is a threat to their ability to succeed. A fractured femur, for example, may render them incapable of playing on the soccer team or swimming.

*Loss of Control.* When school-aged children are hospitalized, their feelings of loss of control are directly related to being removed from their secure environments of friends, family, and school. Even minor restrictions on activities are a threat to their sense of industry and independence. They should be given as much control as possible during all activities and procedures. This is often difficult because hospital procedures do not routinely allow much freedom of choice.

### Nursing Management of Hospitalized School-Aged Children

Nursing implications to promote a positive hospital experience for school-aged children must focus on their sense of industry and productivity. Nurses must be honest in all interactions with children to promote a sense of security. The knowledge level of school-aged children regarding the reasons for hospitalization and procedures should be determined. They should be included in providing the health history since they are concerned about their well-being and can identify symptoms or relate changes in their

health. Interest in their credibility offers them some control.

Before hospitalization, nurses should orient school-aged children to the nursing unit, routine, and equipment and give them time to look around and ask questions. They should be reassured that it is natural to be afraid and not to know what questions to ask about hospitalization. Upon admission, nurses should take time to introduce the child to other patients of the same age, and children of similar ages should room together. This helps prevent boredom, minimizes some stress, and promotes normal development.

Depending on the children's ages, preparation for hospital procedures can be accomplished by using either dolls and simple diagrams or diagrams and anatomical models. Nurses should provide opportunities for children to manipulate hospital equipment since they are interested in how certain machinery works, such as cardiac monitors or intravenous pumps. With the development of rational thought, they have an understanding of cause and effect.

School-aged children should be allowed to make choices in daily routines and should be encouraged to assist with or complete their own self-care. Nurses should encourage children to express their feelings and ask questions.

Opportunity for play must be included in the plan for daily activities. Parents should be encouraged to spend time playing with their children (Fig. 17-4). As long as they are not under isolation orders, school-aged children who are able should be encouraged to go to the playroom and to interact with children of their own ages. School-aged children thrive on group play such as board or card games,

*Figure 17–4. Parents should try to play with their child as often as possible.*

craft projects, or puzzles. When they are confined to their rooms or immobilized by traction, play activities should be brought to them. Such activities often need creative thought. For example, a basketball hoop can be attached to the wall or a trashcan; arts and craft activities can be brought to the bedside.

Discipline, limit setting, and rules have an important place in the pediatric setting. Parents and children should be informed of limits upon admission. Too often, parents become overindulgent with their children when they are hospitalized, and children may expect this behavior to continue indefinitely. This response may occur because parents may feel guilty, thinking that they did something that led to hospitalization. Thoughts such as "If I had only taken him to the doctor sooner, this may have been prevented" are common. Often, parents need as much reassurance as the children.

## Adolescents

Hospitalization has been described as a more difficult event for adolescents than for all other age groups because of their reaction to the experience and their inability to effectively cope with it. Adolescence is subdivided into three phases: early, middle, and late.

Early adolescence begins with the onset of puberty and extends approximately from ages 13 to 14. This phase is noted for the initial growth spurt. For adolescents, body awareness is paramount. They are concerned about how they appear to others, especially those of the same sex. Gradual separation from parents occurs during this time.

Middle adolescence occurs from ages 14 to 16. Physical growth is generally complete. The focus of this phase is independence, sexual identity, and physical appearance. They are attempting to fit into society and take their places in the adult world; at the same time conflict remains, due to the security of dependence of childhood. Hospitalization is the greatest threat to this age group since physical appearance and place among peers are threatened.

Late adolescence, ages 16 to 21, focuses on the future, including partners, work, and lifestyle.

During adolescence, thought becomes abstract. Adolescents are able to think about thinking, and their thoughts extend beyond the present. When adolescents are hospitalized, their advanced cognitive state is an advantage since they can draw from previous experiences and have developed a variety of coping patterns.

### Assessment of Hospitalized Adolescents

Factors that affect hospitalization of adolescents are attachment behaviors, independence versus dependence, and body image.

*Attachment Behaviors.* Separation from parents no longer remains a major threat, but adolescents resent separation from their peer groups. As a result of hospitalization, they are removed from group activities such as school or social events.

*Independence Versus Dependence.* Hospitalization is a serious threat to adolescents' independence and identity. It places them in a dependent state with many restrictions and inhibits their sense of freedom and mobility. Although adolescents resent the loss of their independence, they revert to increased dependence on their parents when they are hospitalized; this contributes to a sense of conflict. As a result, they often feel bored, frustrated, and angry, and they manifest either aggressive, withdrawn, regressed, noncompliant, or depressed behaviors. They may be uncooperative and seek out opportunities to be disagreeable. These responses are attempts to maintain some sense of control and independence.

*Body Image.* Physical changes during adolescence are extensive, and much emphasis is placed on physical appearance. It is important for adolescents to be viewed as attractive and desirable. Hospitalization can result in minor or major physical changes; this possibility is extremely frightening to adolescents. Concerns about disfigurement, and the potential for peer rejection, can be devastating.

### Nursing Management of Hospitalized Adolescents

Nursing care of adolescents must be directed at maintaining a sense of independence and promoting positive self-esteem. This process should occur from the time of admission throughout hospitalization. Most adolescents are capable of describing their own health and health problems, so interviewing should be directed toward them (Fig. 17-5).

*Figure 17–5. It is important to involve adolescents in their own care whenever possible.*

It is important to address adolescents in a manner that does not belittle their intelligence; nurses should avoid using names such as "dear," which may be interpreted as talking down to them.

Nurses should protect adolescents' sense of privacy by closing doors and pulling drapes during procedures. Adolescents should be given adequate clothing to cover their bodies. Treatments or procedures should not be discussed in front of peers or other patients. Nurses should provide accurate information about procedures and acknowledge when they do not know answers to questions. Providing less than truthful answers to adolescents' questions serves to foster mistrust.

Adolescents should be oriented to surroundings and introduced to patients of the same ages, especially those with similar diagnoses, when this is therapeutically acceptable. Nurses should discuss rules and regulations of the hospital unit with adolescents at the time of admission, and limits should be enforced consistently. Adolescents should be allowed time for questions or expressions of concern. They should be encouraged to participate in self-care as much as their physical conditions permit. Adolescents should be allowed to wear their own clothing as much as possible, and girls should wear make-up and style their hair in the usual manner to enhance their sense of control.

Peers should be allowed to visit or telephone. Ideally, adolescent units should have a recreation center in which they can visit with peers and family or play games.

## Preparing Children for Hospitalization

The American Academy of Pediatrics recommends that children be psychologically prepared before admission to the hospital. This preparation helps reduce the anxiety that children experience during hospitalization and helps shorten recovery periods and postdischarge adjustment (Azarnoff & Woody, 1981). Preparing children for hospitalization is a complex task that is compounded by the changing cognitive and emotional responses of the specific levels of development. Factors such as reaction to stress stimuli, cultural and religious backgrounds, family environments, past experiences, coping patterns, and support offered by families influence this process (Prugh & Eckhardt, 1975).

## Children's Responses to Hospitalization

Infants, toddlers, and preschoolers are susceptible to the negative effects of hospitalization since they are vulnerable to separation anxiety and may feel as though they are not supported by parents. Children at these age levels lack the cognitive skills to understand hospitalization and are most likely to exhibit regression behaviors.

## Methods of Preparing Children for Hospitalization

In most pediatric hospitals, preparation for hospitalization is an organized event that involves physicians, nurses, parents, children, and volunteers or child-life specialists. The intent of preparation is to minimize potential trauma to children. Two basic assumptions about this process are that preparation benefits all children and that honesty must be the core of all preparation. A significant part of the preparation procedure involves assessing families to determine how the members deal with crises as well as how much children really know about the event. It should not be assumed that because children do not ask questions, they do not need to be prepared. The assessment process provides the opportunity to clear up misconceptions about hospitalization. If it is found that family members have previously had bad experiences with hospitalization, these situations must be discussed so that hospitalization of the children can be a positive experience.

Written information is often given to parents in advance of their children's hospitalization. This should contain information about hospital routines, visiting plans, rooming in, and explanations about personnel who can assist families in acquainting children with the hospital. Children can also be given storybooks or coloring books that depict children being hospitalized for similar conditions who have experienced favorable outcomes. Children can view these at their own pace and actively participate in their own learning.

Preadmission visits help prepare children for hospitalization, particularly when the hospitalization is for an elective or planned procedure, such as a tonsillectomy. These visits are usually conducted by child-life professionals or trained volunteers and are usually completed shortly before the hospitalization. Preadmission visits include brief explanations about hospitalization and can use slides, videos, or puppets. This preparation is often followed by a short tour of the facility that allows children and families to see hospital rooms, playrooms, nurses' stations, and operating and recovery rooms (if applicable). These visits are usually concluded with a question-and-answer period and opportunities for children to manipulate hospital equipment or role-play with equipment such as gowns, masks, gloves, or stethoscopes. It is advantageous if preadmission visits are viewed positively by the parents.

The methods used to prepare children before hospitalization can also be used when the hospitalization is not anticipated. Even for emergency or unplanned hospital stays, efforts must be made to facilitate children's adjustment to hospitalization. Preparations must be streamlined to help these children cope with events.

## Timing of Preparation

Timing is a major consideration in preparing children for hospitalization. It is not necessary to prepare infants and toddlers in the same manner as older children since they do not experience the same stresses to hospitalization. For these younger children, preparation is geared toward the family and emphasizes the importance of the parents' presence. Parents of preschoolers, school-aged children, and adolescents should be aware that children can sense an altered emotional climate as a result of the prospect of hospitalization. Preschoolers benefit most if preparation is completed less than a week before the hospitalization.

Preparation of school-aged children and adolescents can be accomplished a week or more before hospitalization. After assessment of the children's or adolescents' levels of understanding, preparation can be accomplished by a variety of methods, such as preadmission visits or small group discussions with peers. Professional or trained volunteer group leaders can also answer questions about hospitalization. The use of videos, slides, diagrams, anatomical models, or pamphlets can supplement this type of preparation.

## Special Preparation Needs

Children with chronic illnesses or those who require repeated hospitalizations also need to be prepared for those experiences. Children's understanding of both their illnesses and hospitalization for these conditions varies at different age levels. Therefore, it is important for children with chronic illnesses to have their needs related to hospitalizations reassessed as they progress through different levels of development. For example, a child diagnosed with cystic fibrosis at age 3 needs more advanced explanations about the disease and treatment at each admission as well as reinforcement of the information already learned during previous preparations.

Special preparation should be established in hospitals to meet the needs of children who have disabilities such as mental retardation or impairments in vision or hearing or who speak different languages.

## Parental Responses to Hospitalization

Nursing care of pediatric patients involves caring for children and their parents. Hospitalization is also a stressful time for parents. Observed parental reactions to hospitalization include overt anxiety and passive behaviors, such as withdrawal, denial, fear, and guilt about feelings toward the child and the cause of the illness (Eiser, 1984). Parents are an important part of the care plan; pediatric nurses must help parents continue to parent when their children are hospitalized.

Parenting hospitalized children is difficult. Since parents are trying to handle their own fears and anxieties about hospitalization, they often have difficulty helping their children cope with their fears. Parents must share the responsibility of caring for their children; this role may be difficult for them to manage. They feel that although they know what is best for their children, they have lost control. Pediatric nurses must understand that parents' views regarding hospitalization are different from their own.

Helping parents adapt to the pediatric hospital setting involves careful interviewing and assessment. When strategies are employed to meet special parental needs, they promote positive parent–child–nurse relationships. To help parents cope with hospitalization of their children, nurses should include parents in preadmission preparation programs. Nurses can begin caring for parents even before the time of admission. Parents need to learn about illnesses, treatments, medical terminology, hospital environments, and staff. Nurses should determine parents' perceptions of their children's illnesses and offer explanations. Nurses also should inquire about parents' previous experiences with hospitalization. If other family members have had bad experiences with hospitalization, this situation must be discussed so that the current hospitalization can be a more positive experience.

If parents are reluctant to prepare children for hospitalization, the reasons for this decision should be explored. If parents state that hospitalization for their children would be too overwhelming, they may be referring more to their own feelings about this event. This response is a cue to help parents work through their feelings by relating positive outcomes achieved by children who were prepared for their hospital stays.

Parents sometimes withhold explanations about their children's health because of insufficient knowledge. Occasionally, parents attempt to deceive their children about hospitalization. Parents need to be told that this action is detrimental to the child's sense of security and that children need to deal with their illnesses and come to terms with hospitalization. This process can only be accomplished by truthful explanations and parental support. When parents are taught how to explain hospitalization to their children, they frequently comply.

After children are admitted to the hospital, parents should be included in planning children's care. Parents should be encouraged to room in or visit (Fig. 17-6). Parents must be able to trust the nurses caring for their children and may also need other adults with whom they can discuss their situation. Many pediatric hospitals have coffee hours when parents can meet other parents or meet with child-life specialists who can help them share concerns about their children.

## Minimizing the Effects of Hospitalization

The goal of health care professionals is to minimize or prevent psychological and physical stress associated with the hospitalization of children. The previous sections have discussed age-specific nursing interventions to meet the

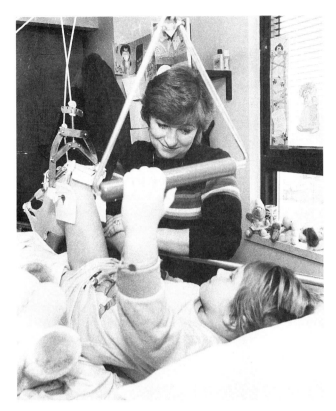

*Figure 17–6. The close proximity of a parent is reassuring to the ill child.*

needs of hospitalized children. General strategies to minimize the effects of hospitalization include preparing the child, providing atraumatic care, and using stress immunization and play.

## Preparation for Hospitalization

The American Academy of Pediatrics recommends psychological preparation for hospitalization. Azarnoff and Woody (1981) reported that preparation results in less anxious patients, a shortened recovery time, and less psychological trauma.

## Atraumatic Care

Providing *atraumatic care* prevents psychological and physical stress. "Do no harm" is a major principle of atraumatic care and is concerned with the complete welfare of children. (See Chapter 3 for a further discussion.)

It is important to maintain the parent–child relationship during hospitalization. The impact of separation has been studied throughout the various age groups. Nurses can facilitate continued parent–child relationships by encouraging rooming in or by using primary nursing.

Hospitalization deprives children of a sense of control. This loss can be especially deleterious to children who are just learning to gain control, such as school-aged children and adolescents. To minimize these problems, nurses should allow choices whenever possible, include free time in children's daily routines, encourage self-care, and offer age-appropriate explanations about procedures.

Another issue is the treatment of pain in children. Nurses must be advocates in preventing physical pain and in recognizing the need for appropriate analgesic medications. Nurses should teach patients comfort measures and relaxation techniques. Invasive devices, such as intravenous tubes, should be monitored closely to prevent dislodgment or infiltration.

## Stress Immunization

*Stress immunization* is a method of minimizing the effects of hospitalization. Children are vulnerable to the stresses of hospitalization because they have limited coping mechanisms. Through behavioral and cognitive controls, however, they can gain the ability to cope with stressful situations. *Behavioral controls* are the ways in which individuals interpret and mentally cope with situations to lessen their impact (Poster & Betz, 1983). *Cognitive controls* provide the means to understand and deal with stressful situations to decrease their impact; for example, an adolescent might imagine being in a favorite place with friends during a painful procedure.

Stress immunization introduces children to small doses of stress (which create low levels of anxiety) over a period of time. Children can manage these low levels of anxiety and eventually learn to master them. Stress immunization techniques that are useful for pediatric patients include systematic desensitization, behavioral and cognitive rehearsal, modeling, positive self-statements, and relaxation training.

### Systematic Desensitization

*Systematic desensitization* is the concept of gradually introducing stressful parts of a procedure. Real materials in play sessions are frequently used with this concept. For example, children may first read a story about a child who receives an injection. They see an actual syringe but do not receive an injection. They then see a stuffed toy receive an injection, are allowed to manipulate the syringe, give the toy an injection, and finally receive an injection themselves (Poster & Betz, 1983; Fig. 17-7).

Desensitization can also be accomplished by imagery. Nurses describe a pleasant scene to children, who are then asked to close their eyes and imagine the scene. Relaxation techniques and imagery are often successful when used in combination with systematic desensitization.

### Behavioral and Cognitive Rehearsal

*Behavioral and cognitive rehearsal* are mental practices that help children manage anxiety. Role-playing may be used for this procedure. Nurses first explain the procedure and describe exactly what children will see, hear,

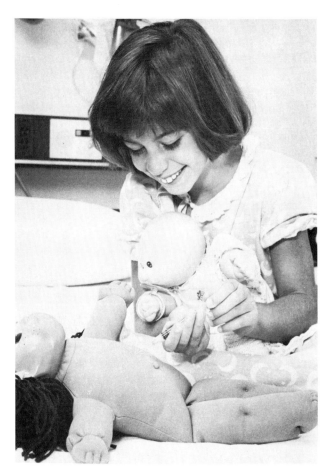

*Figure 17–7. Giving her doll an injection represents the last step of desensitization for this child.*

and feel. When measuring blood pressure, for example, nurses should explain, depending on children's ages, the purpose of taking blood pressure. Children should then be shown the stethoscope and sphygmomanometer. Nurses should encourage children to keep their arms and hands still and discuss the tight feeling they will experience as the cuff is inflated but emphasize that they will not experience pain. Children should watch the dial and see the indicator move slowly down. They should be allowed to manipulate the materials and practice the technique. Cognitive rehearsal can be applied to more complex procedures as well. Behavioral control works well with cognitive rehearsal. In the previous example of measuring blood pressure, children should visualize themselves sitting still, keeping their arms down, and watching the numbers on the dial of the cuff or holding a favorite toy. Older children can be asked to review in their mind the way the procedure was practiced.

### Modeling

*Modeling* is used to facilitate learning certain behaviors by observing the behaviors of others. Modeling in a hospital environment can decrease fears and anxiety in children by

allowing them to see how other children are able to deal with their fears and anxiety successfully. The use of films, television, or presentations are effective tools. An example of this method is having children view a child undergoing surgery. Allowing children to see how other people cope with stress may help them manage similar situations. It is helpful if the child in the presentation is of a similar age and race.

Other examples of stress immunization techniques include teaching children positive self-statements and *relaxation training*. It helps to use these techniques before procedures, to reinforce the techniques as they are used, and to include parents in the presentation.

## Play

Play is often referred to as the work of children and is a universal phenomenon. Childhood play begins soon after birth and continues through the adult years. Play occupies most of young children's waking time. Infants play in their cribs before they get up. Toddlers often play with the food on their plates at mealtime. Children who are not allowed to play demonstrate developmental deprivation. Play enables the child to explore and experiment with movement, relationships, and sensations.

### Theories

Theories of play have existed since the late 19th century. Many of the early theorists state that play is a diversion from boredom and is something for children to do when physiological needs are met. More recent theories suggest that play has more specific purposes. Anna Freud (1946) describes play as a coping mechanism that allows children to escape to a "fantasy world" to act out anxieties, stress, and emotional problems that may interfere with learning. Erikson (1964) concurs with Freud but adds that play is a positive and constructive form of human behavior and helps children to act out their identities and appropriate sexual roles. Piaget (1962) sees play as a tool to assimilate and accommodate the world and links it to intellectual growth and cognitive development.

The use of play as a means of communication is significant for children. When children are unable to express their thoughts or feelings in words, play may be the vehicle to allow them to express themselves. Play is especially helpful when children are hospitalized. During this experience, they are bombarded with new and unknown stimuli, some of which may be painful and most of which are threatening. Depending on children's abilities to cope, play may be the most beneficial means they have to deal with the anxieties of hospitalization.

Azarnoff (1974) believes that children who can express fears and anxieties through play need fewer medications or physical restraints during painful procedures and are better able to conserve energy that is needed for healing. It is important to incorporate play into children's nursing care plans, with particular attention paid to selecting developmentally appropriate activities.

### Types of Play

Deciding on the appropriate type of play for hospitalized children is important. Children's ages must be considered because age is a starting point for developmental observations. Determining the specific developmental level helps in toy or game selection since this knowledge indicates the ability of children's skills. Safety must always be considered; play activities should never put children in potentially dangerous situations. For example, sharp or very small objects should not be used as playthings for young children.

Individual preferences, activity levels, interests, and attention spans should also be considered when planning play activities. Ill children may have less energy than healthier age mates. To help these children conserve energy, quiet types of play or diversions, such as listening to music or reading, should be encouraged.

### Purposes of Play

Play in the hospital can serve a variety of purposes, including helping to prepare children for procedures or surgery. Demonstrations with puppets or role-playing with dolls can assist children to understand what to expect during these events and can help them to allay fears or work through their anxieties. Play can also help in managing children who are very upset. Some forms of play give children the opportunity for self-expression and limited control over strange and threatening environments.

On the lighter side, play can provide opportunities for recreation. Children are often bored in the hospital, especially if they feel well. Organized play can give children chances to interact with age mates and have fun as well as pass the time (Fig. 17-8).

The importance of play for infants involves promoting or maintaining normal growth and development through stimulation. Stimulation is achieved through the senses by holding infants, talking to them during bathing or procedures, and providing a variety of sights and sounds, such as musical mobiles.

Older children or adolescents have special play needs. They need the opportunity to interact with their peers and to discuss concerns in group sessions. They need a place away from their hospital room where they can meet with friends and play board games, video games, or just sit and listen to music.

Nurses should recognize children's need for play since it is an effective strategy to help children learn about themselves and master stress. Because of their many responsibilities, nurses may not be able to spend as much time playing with children as they would like. When nurses are unable to play with their patients, they must recruit the help of parents, volunteers, or child-life workers.

Many pediatric hospitals have a Child Life Department, the major function of which is to coordinate therapeutic play opportunities throughout the hospital. The department comprises trained professionals, assisted by

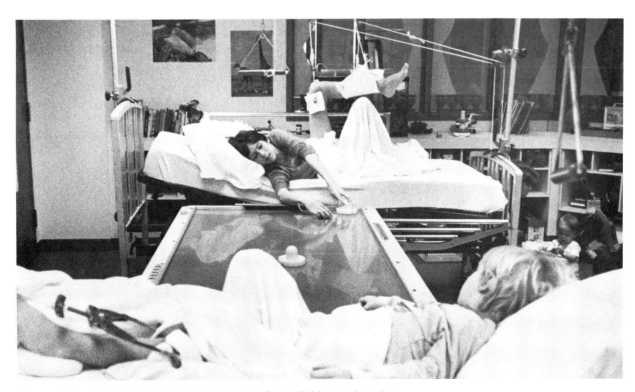

*Figure 17–8.  Creative solutions help these confined children enjoy play.*

volunteers, to help meet the special needs of hospitalized children.

## Hospital Admission

### Types of Admissions

#### Day Hospital Stays

The trend toward shortened hospital stays is growing, primarily due to the rising cost of inpatient care. A number of medical and surgical procedures for pediatric patients, primarily elective surgery, can be performed and still enable children to return home within 24 hours. Day hospital stays for children are becoming increasingly popular. They benefit children, families, and the health care delivery system since treatment is provided efficiently and children can return to their homes quickly, thereby alleviating the stress related to surgery. Success largely depends on timing, cooperation, and organization of care, with pediatric nurses playing significant roles in the process.

Surgery is a risk no matter how long patients are in the hospital, and measures to ensure patients' safety must be implemented. Examples of procedures that can be performed on children within 24 hours include endoscopies, transfusions for patients with chronic blood dyscrasias, circumcisions, herniorrhaphies, and bilateral tympanoplasties.

The severity of the threat of surgery is minimized by the planned ability to go home within 24 hours. If a procedure is elective, successful preparation of children and families for the event is essential. These patients should undergo preoperative blood tests and radiographs several days before the surgery, and they should be given a preoperative tour of the facility and a presentation about the procedure to be performed.

Day hospital stays vastly limit the amount of time allowed for admission and orientation to the unit since both children and parents must be admitted quickly, oriented to the unit, and placed at ease. Nurses play essential roles in this process. Even though these stays are abbreviated, thorough nursing care is important. Nurses are responsible for recording health histories and performing physical assessments to ensure that children are physically and psychologically stable. Children should be allowed to ask questions, and nurses should assess patients' and families' levels of knowledge concerning the situation. A baseline set of vital signs must be documented, and many hospitals use preoperative checklists to facilitate obtaining vital information. Nurses are responsible for ensuring that children and families completely understand the procedures to be performed, and they must ensure that consents for procedures are signed and witnessed.

Nurses should give children and parents a tour of the nursing units, provide information about who will be caring for the child, describe the order in which events of the procedure or surgery are to take place, and explain where the parents can wait while the procedure is being performed.

In the process of settling children in their rooms, nurses should discuss safety procedures such as the use of side rails or the need to remain in bed, especially if preoperative sedation is given. Orientation to the room includes location of bathrooms, telephones, and operation of call lights (Fig. 17-9). This information may have been included in the preoperative visit, but it needs to be reviewed again with children and parents. This phase can include a visit from the anesthesiologist and the surgeon.

In the postoperative phase, nurses must monitor patients' vital signs, levels of consciousness, and operative sites. Deterioration in any of these areas may indicate that children need to remain overnight. If subtle changes are not recognized by nurses, patients may be discharged prematurely, and these problems may result in major complications such as hemorrhaging or respiratory distress.

If children are stable, the discharge process can be initiated. Discharge instructions include identification of complications and steps to take if they occur, limits on physical activity, diet, prescriptions for medications, scheduled follow-up visits, and restrictions for school. Nurses should give families telephone numbers of the discharge planning offices so that they can call if they have any

*Figure 17–9.  The nurse plays a key role in familiarizing children with the hospital environment.*

questions once they are home. Nurses must make sure discharge instructions are understood by children and their parents; written information should be included when necessary.

## Emergencies

Admission of children through emergency rooms presents special challenges. Nurses must use careful assessment skills and knowledge of acute interventions to minimize potentially devastating results while keeping in mind the unique considerations of children, such as the level of physical and psychosocial development.

Children are not small adults, and their bodies' responses to trauma or injury vary greatly. Subtle changes can be life-threatening. Children are more susceptible to shock and electrolyte imbalances. Dosages of fluids and medications are based on weight, and equipment must be scaled down to appropriate sizes for children.

Since emergency room visits are not planned, formal preparation for the event is not possible, but explanations should be provided while procedures are performed. Emergency room nurses must gain the cooperation of patients quickly; when this is not possible, restraints must be used. Children need to be comforted and reassured after frightening or painful procedures.

Nurses can determine children's abilities to cope with emergency treatment by determining their cognitive abilities as well as how they communicate their previous experiences with hospitalization. For children admitted to emergency settings, the immediate goals are to prevent separation anxiety from parents, decrease fears of bodily injury, minimize pain, reduce loss of control, and promote positive coping (Joy, 1989).

To accurately identify the needs of children brought to the emergency room, parents or families must be included in the assessment process. The nature of the accident or illness must be determined as well as any treatment provided before arrival at the emergency room. Nurses should also determine how the family responds to crisis and the support systems that are available to them.

Emergency room nurses must consider how the parents are affected by this event. Parents frequently feel guilty when children need emergency care, even if they are not at fault. They may feel that they were not monitoring their children's activities closely enough to prevent the injuries or that they should have sought treatment sooner.

Accidents or injuries can result from purposeful abuse or neglect. Emergency room nurses must identify these volatile situations, intercede as children's advocates, and report the situation to the proper authorities. Nurses must also recognize that parents of abused or neglected children are troubled and need assistance.

Emergency room admissions of children are stressful for parents. Nurses can minimize stress by providing timely and accurate information about the children's status to the parents. Physicians frequently may be too busy treating children to speak with parents initially, so nurses should offer explanations about treatment during this time. Emergency room nurses should consider the manner and the environment in which information is given. They should assure the parents that the physicians will speak with them as soon as possible. A quiet room, away from the activity of the waiting or treatment rooms, should be used to speak with the parents.

During traumatic events parents want to be close to their children, but this need cannot always be met in an emergency room. Nurses can respond to this need by using this time to interview the parents and obtain a thorough history. It is helpful to explain to parents how useful this information will be in the care of their children. They must be reassured that they will be able to be with their children as soon as possible. Given the fact that parents in this situation are distracted and anxious, nurses should repeat and reinforce pertinent information.

## Pediatric Intensive Care Units

The critical care environment is highly stressful and may be devastating for parents and children. Humanistic care must be provided for children and families, with special attention to emotional and developmental needs. These needs can easily be slighted in critical care units when demands of physical care are overwhelming.

For children and their parents, the Pediatric Intensive Care Unit (PICU) is an atmosphere of bright lights, unfamiliar sounds, and complex machines (Fig. 17-10). The environment of the PICU is crisis-oriented, with more activity and personnel than are found on hospital floors that parents or children may have seen before. Health care personnel are occupied with monitors and technical procedures. The PICU is foreign, with many stimuli that inhibit a child's ability to process stressors (Stevens, 1981). Visiting is often restricted, and children's contact with parents is limited.

To help children cope with these events, critical care nurses must be aware of developmental factors when determining children's understanding of what is happening to them. Knowledge of specific developmental levels can help nurses interact with children and offer explanations for procedures. Added stresses can include perceptual distortions that can occur with physiological and metabolic disorders, such as acidosis or increased intracranial pressure.

In assessing children who are admitted to PICUs, nurses should consider whether the admission was planned or is an emergency and determine the level of preparation. Even if children are prepared for admission, information and explanations must be reinforced. Children's perceptions of events, rather than what they have been told, should be explored.

When assessing pediatric patients, nurses should elicit

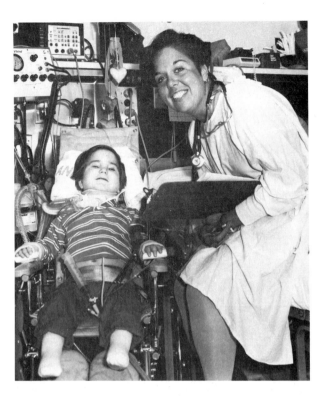

*Figure 17–10. The pediatric intensive care unit can be intimidating to children, and nurses need to reassure them.*

information about how children communicate, including special words for various activities. The same nurses should care for these patients whenever possible, and familiar routines should be restored as soon as possible. Young children should have a favorite object with them, such as a toy or blanket. Special fears, such as loud noises, should be explored, and nurses should attempt to minimize them. If the admission to the PICU is planned before major surgery, nurses should obtain histories and baseline assessments before admission. Parents are likely to be stressed when their children are actually in the PICU and therefore less able to provide the necessary information.

On admission to PICUs, comfort measures, such as appropriate administration of pain medications, frequent position changes, back rubs, or holding children when possible, should be used to minimize stress. These interventions should be scheduled to allow rest periods. Monitors or equipment should be placed in full view of children, with explanations about their uses.

Parents' participation in the care of critically ill children remains important. Their presence provides security, and parents should be encouraged to participate in children's care by regular visits and talking to, holding, or touching their children. These actions decrease the parents' feelings of helplessness. Nurses in PICUs should acknowledge the needs of the parents in this situation and provide support in maintaining the parent–child relationship.

## Isolation

General pediatric nursing measures focus on integrating hospitalized children with age mates, facilitating group activities in playrooms, and placing patients with similar diagnoses and ages in rooms together. Placing pediatric patients in isolation can limit these practices and inhibit normal growth and development.

Physical conditions that may warrant isolation include certain infectious diseases, such as chicken pox, early pretested stages of bacterial meningitis, or bacterial or viral gastroenteritis. Other children who may require isolation include burn patients or seriously immunosuppressed children.

Stress related to hospitalization is intensified when children are isolated. Feelings of separation, loss of control, and loneliness are magnified by isolation. Stimulation tends to be limited by the various measures prescribed by isolation care. Voices cannot be heard clearly through closed doors. Nurses tend to organize care to limit the number of times they need to enter the room. Isolation clothing can inhibit touch and vocalization that is especially necessary for infants or very young children. School-aged children and adolescents feel more separated from their peers.

To minimize the hazards of isolation, nurses should explain the reasons for isolation to patients and families. Parents should be instructed on appropriate use of isolation techniques. Age-appropriate stimulation should be provided, such as music or musical mobiles for infants and toys or television for older children. For example, a tic-tac-toe game for an isolated child and another child who is not isolated can be devised by making the board game from tape applied to the glass window between rooms. The game pieces of X's and O's can be made of tape or plastic that adhere to glass. This game provides a unique diversion and an excellent means for isolated children to communicate with other children through play. If possible, children with the same contagious disease should room together. Nurses should plan to spend time in the children's rooms; parents should be encouraged to visit and participate in care. If appropriate, nurses should allow for supervised mobility within the isolation space. Young children should be encouraged to role-play using masks, gowns, and gloves.

## Children's and Families' Responses to Admission

Admission to the hospital is a stressful time for both children and families. Even if children and families participated in preadmission programs or were prepared for hospitalization, it remains a frightening experience.

Families who have been prepared for hospitalization may still have unanswered questions and anxieties about the event. Under such stressful conditions, they may forget some or much of what they have learned and need additional teaching. Fears are heightened with hospitalization for acute illnesses or emergency admissions. In these situations, the health care team focuses on stabilizing patients physiologically. During an emergency, however, efforts must be made to comfort children and to help them feel as secure as possible. Once the immediacy of these threats has passed, interventions must be directed at helping children and families cope with admission to the hospital.

The initial contact between children and families, hospital personnel, and the hospital environment is important. This contact may have a significant impact on the outcome of hospitalization, since it frequently sets the tone for children's and families' responses to hospitalization. The initial greeting and interview must be strongly positive, reassuring to both children and parents, honest, and nonthreatening. Pediatric nurses have a major role in this endeavor.

## The Admission Interview

The admission interview should be conducted in a quiet and private place, such as the child's room or in a treatment room where noise and stimulation are kept to a minimum. Nurses should allow adequate time for the admission interview so that patients and families do not feel rushed or unimportant.

During the interview, nurses should establish therapeutic relationships with families since interaction is viewed positively by children. Parents' and children's perceptions of the reasons for hospitalization should be explored. Nurses should be sensitive to underlying fears about hospitalization; these fears should be disclosed through the use of effective interviewing techniques. Nurses should assess children's degree of magical thinking or fantasies regarding hospitalization and explain the event in realistic terms with examples. Young children may be certain they are being hospitalized for arguing with siblings or disobeying their parents. Conversely, parents may believe (for example) that their children's heart anomalies are related to something the mother ate during pregnancy. Such misconceptions must be resolved with basic explanations that are developmentally appropriate for both parents and children.

The admission interview should involve both parents and child if the child is able to understand the process. The child should be included as health historian to promote a sense of control. The interview should be comprehensive and include medical and social history, history of present illness, and physical and developmental assessment.

The patient history should be personal and individualized since it will be the framework on which the the nursing care plan is developed. It should contain pertinent information about nutritional habits, sleep patterns, toilet-

ing, favorite toys, and habits. For older children or adolescents, private interviews away from the parents should be conducted to elicit sexual histories or histories of substance abuse. Older children or adolescents must be assured of confidentiality if they disclose any personal information.

The admission interview can be lengthy, and since similar information is necessary for both the medical and nursing histories, it is advantageous for nurses to work with physicians to avoid duplication. Information obtained during this interview should be documented in the medical record and incorporated into a nursing care plan.

## Orientation to the Hospital

Once the admission interview is completed, children and families should be given tours of the pediatric units, including introductions to children with similar diagnoses. Regulations and standards of the nursing unit should be explained to patients during this process. Children should be informed of meal, rest, and play times. Daily routines should be reviewed to give children opportunities for involvement in these events or to suggest changes in them.

Children should be oriented to their rooms through a discussion of safety measures such as side rails, call lights, and location of bathroom facilities. They also need to be reassured that nurses are available to help them. Nurses should introduce themselves at the beginning of each shift. Rooming in policies and telephone and television use should be reviewed; written information concerning these policies should be provided to patients and families.

Admission of children to the hospital must be expedited efficiently and comprehensively. This initial contact between children and nurses facilitates positive hospital experiences. Nurses must be alert to cues from patients and families so they can prevent problems.

## Teaching Parents of Hospitalized Children

Owing to the trends toward shortened hospital stays and the number of children who have either chronic health problems or who are technology-dependent, parents need formal instruction regarding their children's care. Some of the techniques that parents may need to learn are wound care, cast care, insertion of a nasogastric tube, enteral feeding, suctioning, administration of medications, and anticipatory guidance strategies for growth and developmental norms.

Parents' learning needs should be identified at the time of their children's admission to the hospital. This assessment involves determining parents' developmental levels, including their cognitive abilities. Once learning needs have been identified, nurses can develop teaching plans that are individually based on the learners' needs.

Teaching plans should include objectives or goals based on the material the parents need to learn, and the methods of instruction should be identified. These methods can be composed of pictures, diagrams, textbooks, models, and return demonstrations. The quantities and kinds of materials depend on the nature and complexity of the subject matter.

Once the teaching plan is formulated, the content of the instruction needs to be outlined. Either preprinted instructional content guidelines or blank forms to document specific teaching content can be used. Copies of these outlines should be part of the permanent medical record. Outlines should be kept in the chart or placed at the children's bedside since more than one nurse is usually responsible for the parents' teaching. As each of the items in the outline is taught, the objectives should be checked off or initialed so that other nurses can continue with the teaching plans at the point at which the last instruction was given. Primary nurses should ultimately be responsible for coordinating parents' education.

It is imperative that parents be able to redemonstrate procedures and verbalize understanding of care that needs to be carried out at home. Nurses must evaluate parental competence in performing procedures before children can be discharged. Guidelines or booklets are often given to children and their families for reference at home. If parents are unable to learn or do not feel competent in performing specific techniques, home health care services may be needed.

When teaching parents of hospitalized children, nurses should consider the "reachable teachable moment." In other words, parents must be willing and ready to learn. Parents who are grieving over their child's diagnosis of chronic illness are not ready for formal instructions until they have worked through their feelings. Parents often need reinforcement in the material they learn, which can be frustrating or misunderstood by nurses. Teaching remains a significant aspect of nursing care; nurses should develop their skills as educators to help children and their families effectively manage their health problems.

## Discharge Planning

The discharge process begins when children enter the hospital. The primary goal of nursing care is to help children return to their homes, families, and friends in optimal health.

There are many factors to consider when preparing children for discharge. Children's physical status should be stable. These conditions should be determined by complete head-to-toe assessments; nurses should report any unexpected deviations to physicians. The psychosocial statuses of children and families should also be assessed. Children should feel ready and comfortable to be discharged, and questions and concerns about health care should be answered. In most situations, children are receptive to the prospect of discharge and look forward to going home. Nurses should be suspicious when children prefer the hospital to home and investigate and rule out potential neglect or abuse.

Discharge orders should be given to children and families. Nutritional considerations, hygiene, and activity levels should be discussed as well as when children can return to school. Previous teaching should be reviewed. Nurses should ask children and parents to verbalize understanding of the material. Adequacy of special supplies in the home, such as dressings or suction catheters, should be assessed. Pediatric hospitals usually provide sufficient medical supplies until families can make arrangements to purchase their own.

The medications that children are required to take should be reviewed, and patients and families should understand instructions for taking medications. Nurses should note if patients are given any prescriptions. Follow-up care is recommended; appointments are often made before discharge. Parents should be given copies of discharge instructions as well as emergency phone numbers to call if questions or complications arise. Children who are not in optimal health but who are discharged need continued care that is provided either by their families or by home health care agencies. In these situations, patients and families need to feel confident that their care needs will be met and be aware of the options available to them after discharge.

Once children are discharged, nurses should bid farewell to them and their families. It is helpful to telephone patients and families shortly after they get home to ask how they are adjusting and to determine if they have any questions that were forgotten or unanswered at the time of discharge.

## Summary

The effects of hospitalization on children and families need not be deleterious; hospitalization can be a positive growth experience. The key to understanding the effect hospitalization has on children and families is to recognize their level of growth and development and to consider past experiences. Assessment of this information provides a base on which to build nursing care.

Advocacy for the child and family is a primary nursing consideration. During infancy, nurses must intervene to promote a sense of security by meeting infants' most basic needs while also supporting parents as they continue to bond with and care for their infants. Nurses must recognize the serious threat that separation poses when toddlers are hospitalized; nursing actions must echo the importance of autonomy in a toddler's world.

Fears are rampant when preschoolers are hospitalized. Knowledge of these fears assists nurses in helping preschoolers and their families cope with them. The thrust of a school-aged child is out of the home and into a world of peers and school, with a focus on industry versus inferiority. Nurses can minimize the impact of hospitalization on these children by letting them have some control and recognizing their perception of illness and fear of pain.

Nursing care of adolescents requires promotion of independence and identity—not an easy task with the restrictions imposed by a hospital stay. Nurses caring for adolescents must recognize that peers are extremely important and that an altered body image or peer rejection can be devastating.

In dealing with pediatric patients and their families during hospitalization, nurses' energies must remain focused through all aspects of hospitalization, from preparing for hospitalization to admission, length of stay, discharge, and follow-up or home care.

Children continue to be children when they are hospitalized. Nurses must provide opportunities for their optimal growth and development, protect them from harm, and minimize or alleviate their pain.

## References

Azarnoff, P. (1974). Mediating the trauma of serious illness and hospitalization. *Children Today, 3,* 12–17.

Azarnoff, P., & Woody, P. D. (1981). Preparation of children for hospitalization in acute care hospitals in the U.S. *Pediatrics, 68*(3), 361–368.

Bibace, R., & Walsh, M. (1980). Development of children's concepts of illness. *Pediatrics, 66,* 912.

Eiser, C. (1984). Communicating with sick and hospitalized children. *Journal of Child Psychology and Psychiatry, 25*(2), 181–189.

Erikson, E. H. (1964). *Childhood and society* (2nd ed.). New York: W. W. Norton.

Feeg, V. D. (1989). *Pediatric nursing forum on the future: Looking toward the 21st century.* Pitman, NJ: Anthony J. Jannetti, Inc.

Freud, A. (1946). *The ego and mechanisms of defense.* New York: International Universities Press.

Joy, C. (1989). *Pediatric trauma nursing.* Rockville, MD: Aspen Publishers, Inc.

Piaget, J. (1962). *Play, dreams and imitation in childhood.* New York: W. W. Norton.

Poster, E. C., & Betz, C. L. (1983). Allaying the anxiety of hospitalized children using stress immunization techniques. *Issues in Comprehensive Pediatric Nursing, 6,* 227.

Prugh, D., & Eckhardt, L. (1975). Psychiatric rounds on a pediatric intensive care unit. *Critical Care Medicine, 1,* 269–273.

## Bibliography

Alexander, D., Powell, G. M., Williams, P., White, M., & Conlon, M. (1988). Anxiety levels of rooming-in and non rooming-in in parents of young hospitalized children. *Maternal Child Nursing Journal, 17*(2), 29–99.

Bishop, J. (1988). Spotlight on children. Sharing the caring. *Nursing Times, 84*(30), 601.

Bosworth, T. L. (1985). Human response to high technology. Inside the bedrails: One child's view. *American Journal of Maternal Child Nursing, 10,* 243.

Broome, M. E. (1985). Working with the family of a critically ill child. *Heart and Lung, 14*(4), 368–372.

Byers, M. L. (1987). Same day surgery. A preschooler's experience. *Maternal Child Nursing Journal, 16*(6), 277–282.

Carter, J. H., & Hancock, J. (1988). Caring for children. How to ease them through surgery. *Nursing 88, 18*(10), 46–50.

Coulson, D. (1988). A proper place for parents. *Nursing Times, 84*(19), 26–28.

Day, A. (1987). Spotlight on children. Can mummy come too? *Nursing Times, 83*(51), 51–52.

Glasper, A., & Dewar, A. (1987). Spotlight on children. Help or hazard. *Nursing Times, 83*(51), 53–54.

Hobbie, C. (1989). Relaxation techniques for children and young people. *Journal of Pediatric Health Care, 3,* 83–87.

Kidder, C. (1989). Reestablishing health factors influencing the child's recovery in pediatric intensive care. Jounal of Pediatric Nursing: *4*(2), 96–103.

Knafl, K., Cavallari, K. A., & Dixon, D. M. (1988). *Pediatric hospitalization: Family and nurse perspectives.* Glenview, IL: Scott, Foresman & Co.

Licamele, W., & Goldberg, R. (1987). Childhood reactions to illness and hospitalization. *American Family Physician, 36*(3), 227.

Marriner, J. (1988). A children's tour. *Nursing Times, 84*(40), 38–40.

Patterson, K. L., Ware, L. L. (1988). Coping skills for children undergoing painful medical procedures. *Issues in Comprehensive Pediatric Nursing, 11*(2–3), 113–143.

Pigeon, C. (1985). Children's concepts of illness. *Maternal Child Nursing Journal, 14,* 23.

Reynolds, E. A., & Ramenofsky, M. L. (1988). The emotional impact of trauma on toddlers. *Maternal Child Nursing Journal, 13*(2), 106–109.

Saddler, C. (1988). Being there. *Nursing Times, 84*(34), 19.

Saddler, C. (1988). Those little extras. *Nursing Times, 84*(31), 18.

Zurlinden, J. K. (1985). Minimizing the impact of hospitalization for children and their families. *Maternal Child Nursing Journal, 10,* 178.

Zweig, C. D. (1986). Reducing stress when a child is admitted to the hospital. *Maternal Child Nursing Journal, 11,* 29.

Stevens, K. R. (1981). Symposium on pediatric critical care: Humanistic nursing care for critically ill children. *Nursing Clinics of North America, 16,* 611–622.

# Nursing Care of Children in the Home

Mary Theresa Urbano

*Sculpture by Charles Parks*

*18*

*Historical Background of Home Care*

*Factors Contributing to the*
*    Development of Home Care*
*        Cost Containment Initiatives*
*        Changing Health Care Needs*
*            of Children*
*        Changing Health Care Delivery*
*        Changing View of the Family*

*Case Management*
*        The Multidisciplinary Health*
*            Care Team*

*Assessment*
*        Child and Family Readiness*
*            for Home Care*

*Nursing Diagnoses*

*Planning*
*        Educating the Client and Family*
*        Identifying Home Care Providers*
*        Selecting an Equipment Vendor*
*        Establishing a Community*
*            Support Network*
*        Identifying the Family and*
*            Respite Support Network*
*        Completing the Discharge*

*Implementation*
*        The Art of Home Care Nursing:*
*            Interpersonal Processes*
*        The Science of Home Care*
*            Nursing: Technological*
*            Competency*

*Evaluation*

*Legal and Ethical Issues*

*Summary*

*Nursing Care Plan*

*Learning Objectives*

*Upon completion of this chapter the reader will be able to:*

1. *Describe the factors that influenced the evolution of home health care.*

2. *Interpret the concept of case management as it affects family-centered coordinated care.*

3. *Discuss the concept of the interdisciplinary team approach to home health care.*

4. *Assess the factors influencing family and child readiness for home care.*

5. *Examine the factors that need to be considered in discharge planning for home care.*

6. *Describe the three phases that nurses and families experience in adapting to children's acute and chronic illnesses.*

7. *Analyze the relationship between the concept of family empowerment and home health care.*

8. *Discuss a few of the specific nursing interventions for high technology techniques delivered in the home, such as apnea monitoring, tracheostomy management, administration of oxygen, tube feedings, and home parenteral nutrition.*

9. *Select appropriate variables for evaluating the effectiveness of home health care.*

10. *Discuss the legal and ethical implications of pediatric home care.*

*Key Terms*

*adversary phase*

*alliance phase*

*care contract*

*case management*

*coordinator phase*

*discharge planning*

*empowerment*

*home care*

*interdisciplinary health care team*

*respite care*

The field of pediatric home care is one of the most rapidly changing areas in nursing today. Factors such as technological innovations in health care, cost containment pressures, and the growing involvement of the family in its own care are a few reasons for these changes. The role of family-centered, coordinated home care in reducing psychosocial and behavioral sequelae of pediatric acute and chronic illness has also contributed to the renewed interest in pediatric home health care. As a result, community-based pediatric nursing has expanded from the traditional model of maternal/child health care and illness prevention to new roles that combine components of both hospital-based pediatric nursing and public health nursing.

In defining home care, Stein (1984) states

> *the term* home care *has been used for services which range from mothers treating children's minor illnesses to programs in which home visitors offer social support geared to increasing maternal-bonding or to prevent child abuse. It includes programs to avoid hospitalization for acute illness in otherwise healthy children, monitoring infants at risk for sudden infant death, and supplying visiting nurse services or physical therapy for stable patients as well as organized hospices for chronically and terminally ill children (p. 2).*

Thus, *home care* refers to the processes of assessment, diagnosis, planning, intervention, and evaluation that are conducted by a variety of health care providers within the home setting. This chapter discusses historical influences on the provision of home care services, the current emphasis on case management, interdisciplinary teams, assessment of child and family readiness for home care, nursing diagnoses, discharge planning, nursing interventions, and the evaluation of home health care.

## Historical Background of Home Care

Community-based nursing services began in the early 1900s. The emphasis of these early programs was on communicable disease control and maternal/child health. In the 1930s and 1940s, public health nurses provided general health supervision and parent education on a wide variety of issues related to infant and well-child care. In the early 1970s, nursing joined other public health fields in examining population aggregates, and the community-based focus shifted to that of system-wide health needs.

## Factors Contributing to the Development of Home Care

Cost containment initiatives, changing health care needs of children, evolving health care and service delivery, and interest in family-centered care influenced the development of current home care practice.

### Cost Containment Initiatives

Since the mid-1960s, economic strategies to reduce the cost of hospitalization have greatly influenced the evolution of home care. In an effort to control escalating hospital costs, third-party payers developed prospective payment arrangements that effectively limit reimbursements to predetermined levels. Hospital utilization reviews have also been developed to control the length of hospital stays to reduce costs of inpatient services. As a result, health care providers are forced to look for alternatives to hospital-based care. Home care has proved to be one viable option.

Studies have documented that managed home care is more cost-effective than maintaining the child in the hospital (Kaufman & Hardy-Ribakow, 1987). As a result, there has been increasing pressure to discharge children into the care of their families in the home, thus avoiding costly hospital expenses. Funding of pediatric home care, however, continues to be a significant barrier to achieving this goal (Mitchell, 1986; Richardson, 1983). Private insurance companies, federal funds (Medicaid waivers), and state crippled children's programs currently provide most of the funding (Kaufman & Hardy-Ribakow, 1987). There are currently many federal and state proposals to improve funding of community-based home care services and to expand training and technical assistance programs. Even with these resources, many families are confronted with insurance and governmental agency regulations that hinder or limit expenses incurred in pediatric home care, especially for technologically dependent children.

## Changing Health Care Needs of Children

The decade between 1970 and 1980 brought several major changes in the health care needs of children. The emphasis in pediatric health care shifted from treatment of acute illnesses to that of chronic illnesses as a result of the development of new vaccines and improved antibiotic therapies that have reduced the incidence of acute diseases (Stein & Jessop, 1984). Correspondingly, advances in computerized imaging techniques, life-support interventions, laboratory testing, and knowledge have altered the prognosis of many chronically ill children (Kaufman & Hardy-Ribakow, 1987). Improved prenatal and perinatal care, and the development of regionalized tertiary centers providing specialized perinatal services, have led to increased survival rates for very-low-birth-weight infants and children with complex medical problems. Prompt identification of, and intervention for, children with serious medical problems, as well as advances in medical technology, have resulted in an increased population of chronically ill children (Newacheck, Budetti, & McManus, 1984).

Improved technology and advances in the management of chronic childhood illness have led to increased longevity of children with chronic conditions and a reduction in the relative proportion of acute pediatric conditions (Stein & Jessop, 1984). An estimated 10 million children in the United States suffer from chronic illnesses (Perrin, 1985; Andrews & Nielson, 1988). Children with severe chronic illnesses constitute between 1% and 2% of America's pediatric population (Perrin, 1985; Andrews & Nielson, 1988). Between 2% and 5% of ill children are candidates for home care services (Cabin, 1985).

## Changing Health Care Delivery

As a result of cost containment initiatives and the changing health care needs of children, the number of acutely and chronically ill children cared for in home settings has dramatically increased. As a result, community facilities such as home care agencies received requests for improved technical support. Although these agencies had anticipated the need for these services, appropriate technology and trained personnel were not always available, owing to budgetary constraints.

In response to these requests for services and an improved financial reimbursement system, a rapid growth in ambulatory care services occurred. Home care expanded at a phenomenal pace in the 1980s (Morris & Fonseca, 1984); home-based high-technology care services also proliferated (Raulin & Shannon, 1986; Taylor,

1985). Early home health care services to children focused on health maintenance and management of acute common childhood diseases. With the development of safer and more efficient technological advances, home-based high technology care became possible (Haddad, 1987; Morris & Fonseca, 1984). With this type of home care, the range of services for acutely and chronically ill children has been expanded to include the care of children who are developmentally disabled, at risk for developmental disabilities, or in need of more complex medical and nursing care.

Children who are dependent on technology for health maintenance or activities of daily living are one of the newest populations of pediatric clients (Raulin & Shannon, 1986). Many children who require medical interventions such as tracheostomies, ventilators, parenteral and enteral nutritional support, IV antibiotics, and apnea monitors are now being cared for in the home. These children compose only 1% of the pediatric population but use between 25% and 40% of the health care resources (Hobbs, Perrin, & Ireys, 1985; Mitchell, 1986). Before the increased use of home care services, these children had to live in hospital intensive care units or specialized pediatric extended care units (Mitchell, 1986; Raulin & Shannon, 1986).

The 1982 Report of the Surgeon General's Workshop on Children with Handicaps and Their Families focused on ventilator-dependent children, and its recommendations served as a catalyst for increased awareness of children needing home care. The Workshop's recommendations served as the basis for developing regionalized systems of care, improved financing, and principles of care for a variety of home-based pediatric care (Kaufman & Hardy-Ribakow, 1987).

The evolution of the delivery of health care services from hospital settings to home settings offers both advantages and disadvantages to nurses, children, and families. The advantages include reduced incidence of nosocomial infections (McCarthy, 1986); reduced cost (Raulin & Shannon, 1986); improved physical and psychosocial growth and development for acutely and chronically ill children due to care in a familiar, family environment; increased family support and decreased family strain due to separation; and increased family satisfaction (Stein & Jessop, 1984). The disadvantages include increased family responsibility for care and corresponding increase in family anxiety, often complicated by limited preparation and inadequate community professional backup; invasion of family privacy by health care professionals; difficulties in paying for expenses that are not covered by insurance or other third party payers; and lack of social support and respite for care givers.

## Changing View of the Family

Owing to the complexity of medical and nursing interventions that can be delivered in homes, health care providers need to communicate more directly than before with fam-

ily members. The increased interaction among families and health care team members led to the professional realization that traditional child health care practice needed to be modified. As a result, child health services that have been expanded beyond biomedical therapies for specific disease conditions include interventions to enhance the total life experience of children and their families (Stein & Jessop, 1984). There is a growing awareness of the need for partnership between parents and health care professionals in the development of comprehensive family-centered, coordinated care at the family and community levels (Fig. 18-1). This reinforces the fact that because the family is the consistent influence in the life of a acutely or chronically ill child, it is advantageous for it to assume a central role in coordinating the child's care (Freedman, 1986).

In home care delivery, the child and family become the center of the health care system. This concept, however, has been difficult to translate into practice. Health care professionals who are experienced in identifying problems and providing expert advice need to modify traditional approaches to client care when this care is provided in home settings (Barnard, 1985). The traditional roles of health care providers have dictated assumption of responsibility for total client care; the transition to family control of health care in the home may cause conflict. Health care professionals and families are challenged to form collaborative partnerships for the best interests of the child (Healey & Lewis-Beck, 1987). The process of case management is an effective conceptual framework for examining family-centered coordinated care.

## Case Management

Case management is the critical process that underlies family assessment, family/professional interactions, and nursing interventions in home care for acutely and chronically ill children. Case management has evolved from its original focus on coordination and resource procurement on behalf of clients to the current conceptualization of a family-centered, helping relationship leading to family empowerment (Dunst, 1988).

The philosophy behind this approach to case management recognizes that multiple, dynamic, and interdependent forces influence the life and well-being of ill children and their families. There is a critical need to consider the interrelationships among social, educational, health, and community factors as they nurture children and their families. The family should provide the essential means for enhancing children's strengths and assisting them to achieve their maximum degree of independence, integration into the community, personal productivity, and achievement of potential and actual life satisfaction. Members working on an interdisciplinary health care team must have knowledge and skills in assessment, intervention, and evaluation in order to assist children and their families in meeting these goals. They must also recognize

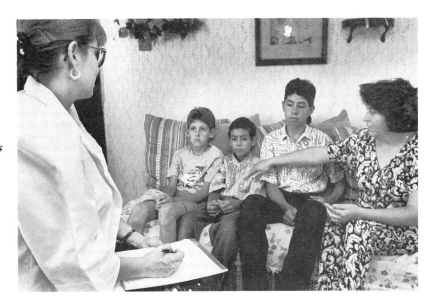

*Figure 18–1. Nurse and family members in home setting providing care.*

family strengths and diversity, accept individual differences, and encourage and facilitate family collaboration in all endeavors.

Case management must involve the community as well as the family. On the community level, case management serves as a problem-solving approach to ensure responsive service coordination and continuity of care from hospital to home and back. Health care professionals teach families to identify appropriate community resources, use these services effectively, and effect changes in the system. This approach facilitates family involvement in the child's care and reduces service fragmentation and inaccessibility.

The philosophy of case management considers the family a critical part of the team. The family, not the team of health care professionals, should be the key decision maker and should assume control of decisions regarding its daily functioning and future endeavors to the extent that it is willing and able.

## The Multidisciplinary Health Care Team

The composition of a *multidisciplinary health care team* that coordinates home care activities varies. Such a team consists of representatives of professions such as nursing, pediatric medicine, nutrition, occupational therapy, physical therapy, psychology, speech therapy, social work, and education, as well as home care vendors and third-party payers. The child and family should be an integral part of the team and the nucleus around which all activities revolve.

In contrast to medically directed teams, the multidisciplinary health care team participates in collaborative decision making. Each profession has a core of knowledge and skills and respects the unique contributions of the other disciplines. Each member is responsible for role

definition, collaboration with others on the team, mutual respect, and joint decision making (Haddad, 1987). The family, traditionally omitted from hospital-based teams, is a critical component. The goals of this team are to assess child and family readiness for home care, to prepare the family and community to provide a safe standard of home care, and to provide ongoing support and assistance to families providing care at home through long-term coordination and follow-up. In most multidisciplinary teams, the nurse functions as a generalist, client advocate, and case manager. During the assessment process, the nurse collects data regarding child and family history, level of development, physical and psychosocial needs, and family concerns in need of intervention.

The multidisciplinary team process begins at the time a child is first considered as a potential home care client. At that time a comprehensive family assessment, which includes identification of general child and family characteristics as well as specific factors that reflect the child and family's readiness for home care, is conducted.

## Assessment

"The goal of home care ... is the provision of comprehensive, cost effective health care within a nurturing home environment that maximizes the capabilities of the individual and minimizes the effects of the disabilities." Early and comprehensive planning " ... minimizes emotional risk to the patient, adverse effects on the family members, or unforeseen financial burdens" (American Academy of Pediatrics, 1984, p. 434). The critical first step in instituting home care is a comprehensive assessment of personal, familial, physical, psychosocial, developmental, cultural, behavioral, and environmental factors that may influence the child/family's health status. (See Chapter 5 for a complete discussion of child and family assessment.) Each of these areas should be reviewed as extensively or as briefly as warranted by the individual child and family situation.

Assessment is based on the concept that the child is an integral part of the family system. In this system, the family functions as a series of interwoven, dynamic parts. The child's needs affect all other members of the family, just as their needs affect the child's general well-being and care.

## Child and Family Readiness for Home Care

The general child and family assessment provides valuable baseline data for nursing practice in the home. As integral members of the interdisciplinary health care team, nurses are actively involved in all aspects of home care, including assessing a family's ability and readiness to care for a child in the home.

The American Academy of Pediatrics Task Force on Home Care (1984) identified the following four factors to be considered in determining child and family readiness for home care:

- Client
- Family
- Environment
- Community

### Client Factors

Client factors reflect the child's condition. The child's medical condition should be predictable and manageable without immediate physician involvement and additional diagnostic and treatment regimens. This stability may be based either on the child's physiological status or on the assistance of technological equipment such as ventilatory support, tracheostomies, or parenteral nutrition. The child's status should be evaluated in terms of medical stability versus the capacity to provide backup and emergency care (American Academy of Pediatrics, 1984). It should include the availability of required levels of support and intervention within the home setting. Risks of infection or deterioration of current status within the home setting, as opposed to the potential benefits of home care for the child, should also be examined.

### Family Factors

Family factors must first include the family's interest in providing home care. It should be recognized that not all families are interested in or capable of providing home care. Family variations in coping abilities should be respected and considered when determining the child's candidacy for home care.

Family interest in bringing the child home is not the only criterion, however. If the family is interested in providing home care, the current coping abilities demonstrated by family members should be considered. Family members need time to work through the grieving process

about their child's condition and learn how to deal with a child's acute or chronic illness. It is often helpful for the nurse to introduce the family to parents of other children with similar problems so that they can see that home care can be managed successfully (McCarthy, 1986).

Once the family has worked through the initial stages of the grieving process and is beginning to cope effectively, their cognitive and psychological resources must be examined. The nurse should ask questions regarding the family's perceived need for home care; their expectations, goals, and anticipated level of participation; the interface that will be possible between home care and pre-established educational or work activities; and the type of program (supportive, custodial, or aggressive) that will be required for the care of the child (Haddad, 1987).

The family's psychomotor ability to learn and safely perform necessary procedures and treatment regimens must also be assessed. This assessment includes the ability to make informed and clear decisions regarding courses of action, ability to work collaboratively with other members of the health care team, knowledge and experience base, and additional instruction needed prior to discharge and on initiation of home care.

When families are still unsure or are reluctant to participate in home care, a *care contract* may be useful (McCarthy, 1986). This contract outlines a goal and the learning objectives and responsibilities of the nurse and family. Thus, a written contract obligates the staff to teach the parents aspects of the child's care and commits the parents to demonstrate an acceptable level of knowledge and skills (McCarthy, 1986). Following completion of the contract requirements by both parties, a decision regarding home discharge can be made (McCarthy, 1986). Figure 18-2 shows a sample care contract.

The family's ability to care for a child in the home must consider family responsibilities, the complexity of and time requirements for care, and the number of individuals available to participate in the child's care. It is essential to have two trained adults in each home setting to ensure adequate routine and emergency coverage of health care needs. Consideration should also be given to training other family members who do not live in the home. These individuals can provide necessary respite and serve as a backup in the event the primary care-giver becomes ill or injured.

### Environmental Factors

In addition to the suitability of the child's and family's status, the nurse should assess *environmental factors* in the home. This assessment should include the following:

Type of residence (house, trailer, apartment)

Location of residence (urban or rural)

Availability of electricity, running water, and other basic necessities including heating and cooling

**Goal:** Mrs. Jones will successfully demonstrate safe tracheostomy suctioning.

| Skill | RN Demonstration Init. & Date | RN and family jointly Date | Family independent demonstration Date |
|---|---|---|---|
| By the end of the training, the learner will be able to: | | | |
| 1. State 5 indicators for tracheostomy suctioning. | | | |
| 2. Demonstrate appropriate handwashing technique. | | | |
| 3. Assemble/set up equipment. | | | |
| 4. Correctly position the child. | | | |
| 5. Pre-oxygenate or perform chest physiotherapy (per physician's order). | | | |
| 6. Put on gloves and attach catheter to suctioning machine. | | | |
| 7. Suction child appropriately. | | | |
| 8. Hyperoxygenate child. | | | |
| 9. Observe child's status. | | | |
| 10. Observe and describe secretions. | | | |
| 11. Clean work area (using universal precautions). | | | |
| 12. Operate all equipment in a safe manner. | | | |
| 13. Perform comfort measures. | | | |
| 14. Document actions and observations appropriately. | | | |
| 15. List signs of hypoxia. | | | |
| 16. List signs of cannula obstruction. | | | |

*Figure 18–2. Sample learning contract (tracheostomy suctioning).*

Adequate sleeping space for the child and space in other rooms in which the child will be spending time

Necessary equipment

Distance from emergency backup and the presence of a telephone for emergency contacts

The general level of cleanliness and health promotion activities within the home environment, as well as risk factors such as cigarette smoking, should be assessed. However, the health care team should consider the environmental norms of the client and not those of the home care provider unless those norms jeopardize client safety or create a sanitation hazard (Haddad, 1987).

Physical modifications or alternate living arrangements often must be made to the house to permit wheelchair access, an additional electrical load, or other adaptive equipment.

Transportation resources for routine health follow-up and emergency care must be considered. If the home is in a rural area or is far from the hospital, physician, pharmacy, or equipment vendor, arrangements must be made for provision of these services.

### Community Factors

The fourth area of consideration recommended by the American Academy of Pediatrics is the *community*. "The establishment of an individualized, multi-tiered, coordinated service delivery system must begin at the time of determination of the child as a potential home candidate" (Kaufman & Hardy-Ribakow, 1987, p. 245). The medical, social, and educational resources of the child's community play a critical role in successful home care. The presence and suitability of community support personnel and agencies must be assessed in light of the child's and family's strengths and needs.

The availability of community resources is particularly important if the child needs special equipment or supplies. The interdisciplinary health care team should identify any necessary supplies and equipment that need to be accessible within the home. These materials should meet the child's and family's needs and be attainable within the community. Community resources also include the telephone company and public utilities, which must be notified in order to provide continuous service in the event of an emergency.

Community support may also include supportive care provided by registered nurses, respiratory therapists, home health aides, social workers and other professionals. These professionals may be employed by equipment vendors, state agencies, or local organizations. The interdisciplinary health care team must make provisions for hiring independent or agency staff and arrange for scheduling, supervision, monitoring, and coordination of information and services.

### Economic Factors

Cost considerations must be added to the four assessment areas recommended by the American Academy of Pediatrics. Equipment and services can be very expensive, and many insurance companies will pay for only a portion of the costs of home care (Burr, Guyer, Todres, Abrahams, & Chiodo, 1983). Expenses for items that are not covered, such as insurance deductibles, traveling expenses during hospitalizations, home renovations, expensive medications, physician fees, home care equipment, and increased utility bills can cause serious financial stress for a family (Kahn, 1984; McCarthy, 1986).

The multidisciplinary health care team can help the family identify safe cost-cutting approaches and seek and apply for supplemental funding. A major area of cost containment is in the selection of a community equipment vendor. Vendor choices should be evaluated for financial policies, fair billing procedures, and competitive fees. Rental and purchase options on equipment should be available as well as free replacement or loaner equipment in the event purchased equipment fails. Ideally, the vendor should be an authorized Medicaid vendor that bills insurance companies directly so that the family is billed only for the unpaid portion of the cost rather than paying for all services initially and being reimbursed later. Vendors who are willing to be paid on an installment basis assist families in budgeting for expenses (Hartsell & Ward, 1985).

The team can also refer the family to state crippled children's agencies, health maintenance organizations, private insurance, and public medical assistance (Medicaid) for eligibility determination and application services.

After the interdisciplinary health care team has completed its assessment of general child and family characteristics and the specific assessment of the child, family, environmental, community, and cost considerations, a final determination of the child's suitability for home care can be made. For those clients who are found to be not appropriate for home care, this process can facilitate referral to other programs and services that will meet their needs (Haddad, 1987).

## Nursing Diagnoses

Based on the data collected during the nursing assessment, a nursing diagnosis is identified. The nursing diagnosis will acknowledge and describe an actual problem, a potential problem, an unmet need, or an unrealized expectation. Specific diagnoses vary as a result of the child's condition, health status, and personal/family characteristics. Some examples of nursing diagnoses that are applicable to the child with a chronic health problem in the home setting are ineffective airway clearance; high risk for infection; self-esteem disturbance; and ineffective family coping: compromised. Other examples of common nursing diagnoses and related nursing actions are as follows:

| Nursing Diagnosis | Nursing Action |
|---|---|
| Knowledge Deficit related to procedures and equipment | Assessment of family knowledge and skill base; teach as appropriate. |
| Altered Family Processes related to situational crisis | Assessment of family, friends, and community supports. Referral to community agencies, as indicated. |
| Ineffective Coping: Family compromised, related to situational crises; temporary family disorganization | Assessment of family, friends, and community supports. Referral to community agencies, as indicated. |
| High Risk for Infection related to increased susceptibility and increased chance of infection spread due to required home procedures | Assessment of family knowledge and skill base re infection control procedures and universal precautions; teach as appropriate. |
| Self-Esteem Disturbance related to chronic condition | Refer for counseling as indicated. Identify and encourage activities that offer a high potential for success. |
| Fear related to uncertainty about parental role in home care | Explore family feelings, reinforce appropriate behaviors. |
| Altered Growth and Development related to inability to reach appropriate developmental milestones | Stimulate normal growth and development activities. |

| Nursing Diagnosis | Nursing Action |
|---|---|
| Pain related to chemotherapy treatments | Assess comfort status. Initiate comfort supportive activities; teach child relaxation, visual imagery. |

## Planning

The comprehensive child and family assessment elicits much disjointed information. The interdisciplinary health care team (including the family) sifts through the available information, organizes relevant data, and identifies primary and secondary needs. In collaboration with the family, priority goals and objectives are determined. Both long- and short-term goals and objectives should be stated in realistic, measurable behavioral terms. Based on these objectives, alternative action plans can be explored with the family to determine feasibility and acceptability, and a priority action plan can be established. *Discharge planning* is the process of establishing short- and long-term goals, identifying necessary client/family teaching and other needs, and preparing for discharge to the home. It is an integral part of the planning process, and begins during the child's hospitalization. Discharge planning is used to determine what information is relevant to the child's symptoms, the family's perception of the condition, and treatment goals (Haddad, 1987).

The next step is the development of an *Individual Family Service Plan* (IFSP). The IFSP, basically an extension of the nursing care plan, is based on Public Law 99-457, passed in 1986, which provides for interdisciplinary assessment and evaluation of infants and children from birth to 3 years of age who either are at risk for or have developmental delays. The intent of the legislation is to aid children who have acute or chronic illnesses that can place them at risk. The broad influence of this legislation and national efforts to develop coordinated, community-level service delivery for acutely and chronically ill children escalated the acceptance of the IFSP as an integral part of interdisciplinary health care team function for children of all ages.

Although the IFSP may change in format, the basic components include the following:

1. Statement of the infant's or child's present level of physical, cognitive, language, speech, and psychological development, and self-help skills
2. Statement of the family's strengths and needs related to enhancing the growth and development of the child
3. Statement of the major outcomes expected to be achieved for the child and family, with criteria, procedures, and timelines to be used
4. Statement of specific intervention services neces-

sary to meet the needs of the child and family, including the frequency, intensity, and method of delivering services, as well as projected dates for initiation and anticipated duration of services. When caring for a developmentally delayed child, it is especially important to promote activities that encourage normalization of growth and development, independence, and integration into the community. Children with medically complex problems need to have defined back-up plans for medical emergencies and family access to a telephone.
5. The name of the case manager from the profession most relevant to the child's and family's needs
6. A plan for periodic review with parents and re-evaluation, as indicated. Frequently, this is done in conjunction with pre-established follow-up appointments.

In addition to an individualized family service plan, discharge planning typically includes client/family education, identification of home care providers, selection of an equipment vendor, establishment of a community support network (including emergency protocols), and the identification of family and respite support groups.

## Educating the Client and Family

Frequently, a family wants very much to bring an acutely or chronically ill child home but fears they will not be able to provide safe, comprehensive care. This anxiety is heightened when the child needs complex treatment regimens or requires high-technology equipment. In response to these concerns, the nurse should assess the family's understanding in order to develop an effective teaching plan. Education in the hospital setting, prior to discharge, can improve the family's readiness and ability to participate in home care. Areas of client/family instruction should include treatment modalities, signs of complications or distress, emergency and consultation procedures (including pediatric cardiopulmonary resuscitation), common problems and their solutions, special precautions, and long-term follow-up arrangements. Anticipatory guidance regarding normal growth and development patterns, establishment of realistic treatment schedules, and methods of incorporating treatment regimens into the family lifestyle reduce anxiety and facilitate adaptation.

Educational activities should include opportunities for the child to assume responsibility for self-care, if he or she is able. If the child is too young or is unable to manage self-care, the family should be given an opportunity to actually provide complete care for the child in the hospital setting, with the backup of the hospital staff nearby. Practice sessions help the family overcome fear, provide an opportunity for feedback, and increase family competence and self-confidence. These feelings of self-confidence are particularly important if the child is going to be discharged to a rural area with limited availability of properly trained professionals.

Frequently, the hospital staff also teaches community-based nurses, school personnel, or others directly involved with the child how to provide for a child's special needs. These professionals may also benefit from a hospital trial prior to the child's discharge.

Educational programs should allow time for the family and other care-givers to discuss their fears, frustrations, and feelings about taking responsibility for care of children in the home. Parents should be reassured that their feelings are normal and should be encouraged to take time for themselves. Emotional support and preparation is also important for the child, if the child is able to understand. If possible, friends of older sick children may make trips to the hospital to learn about their friend's condition prior to discharge (McCarthy, 1986). This approach eases peer concern and facilitates re-entry into the home environment and community.

## Identifying Home Care Providers

Whether the child is acutely or chronically ill, the family often needs additional help, support, and community-based supervision of treatment regimens. In these cases, the discharge team should also help the family identify a community-based home care provider prior to discharge. In the past, most home care providers provided services only to adults. Recently, however, a growing number of home care agencies have initiated pediatric programs. The role, scope, and quality of these programs vary considerably; for that reason, it is important to investigate potential programs carefully. Briggs (1987) offers a list of relevant questions that families can use when interviewing administrators of home care agencies to obtain information related to program development, supervision and quality assurance, and reimbursement (Table 18-1).

## Selecting an Equipment Vendor

Identification of vendors in the community who provide equipment and supplies, as well as store and service equipment, is an important component of discharge planning, especially if the child is dependent on complex equipment. Vendors contract with families and home care agencies for provision and maintenance of equipment, delivery of supplies, and routine and emergency service of equipment in home settings. Equipment and supplies include respiration and heart rate monitors, ventilators, oxygen-therapy and suction machines, and catheter equipment.

Before selecting an equipment vendor, it is important to determine whether the vendor has had experience with the special needs of acutely and critically ill children and their equipment requirements. Emergency maintenance and replacement of equipment should also be ensured (American Academy of Pediatrics, 1984). The family must

*Table 18–1. Guidelines for Selecting a Pediatric Home Care Program*

**Program Development Issues**

What is the history of the pediatric program?

How long has the program been operational?

Are any of the following therapies provided: speech, respiratory, physical, and occupational?

Are social work services provided?

Is the program affiliated with a Durable Medical Equipment (DME) company?

Is the program affiliated with a home parenteral company?

What professional guidelines or standards are utilized in program development?

Does the program conduct client satisfaction surveys?

Does the program have a Board of Directors?

What is the program experience with high technology pediatric cases?

Request a profile sheet of pediatric cases arranged by diagnosis, age of child, acuity, length of service, and staffing patterns.

**Supervision and Quality Assurance Issues**

Is there a pediatric program director?

What are the credentials of the director?

Is the program available 24 hours a day, 7 days a week?

Do all staff have at least 1 year of recent pediatric hospital experience?

Are recruitment and interview policies for potential employees explained?

Are written references required on potential employees?

Are employees bonded and insured?

What is the attrition rate of employees?

Who performs the initial patient assessment?

Who designs and updates the care plans?

Does each patient have a case manager?

Does the program director periodically evaluate each case?

**Reimbursement Issues**

Does the program have a reimbursement specialist to profile each patient's health insurance?

Are all health insurance benefits determined prior to beginning service?

Does the program accept Medicaid patients?

What are the costs for each service?

How are patients billed?

(From Briggs, N. J. [1987]. Selecting a pediatric home care program. *Pediatric Nursing, 13,* 191)

have immediate access to emergency backup and information. "If a parent is frantic about a problem, it is not enough to say someone will call in an hour" (Hartsell & Ward, 1985, p. 27). Prompt answering services, quick return calls, and prompt delivery of equipment are imperative.

Some equipment vendors also provide professional

services such as home visits by respiratory therapists. Although these specialized services are frequently provided at an additional cost, they are often valuable (Hartsell & Ward, 1985). Arrangements should be made for the professional staff members employed by the equipment vendor to conduct a home visit within the first 24 hours after a child's discharge to the home. Even though the family has effectively demonstrated the use of procedures and equipment in the hospital, they usually experience a high degree of anxiety when they must finally put procedures into operation in the home setting. Equipment vendors should provide emotional support, reinforce hospital discharge instructions, and assist the family in adapting protocols to the home setting. They can often provide written materials about the care, maintenance, and operation of the equipment. Staff also play a critical role in early identification of potential problems and can facilitate communication between the family and the hospital (Hartsell & Ward, 1985).

When identifying potential vendors, the interdisciplinary health care team should be aware that requirements for home care equipment are not currently standardized. Safety of equipment should be assessed when evaluating vendors' qualifications, and the team or family should ask the equipment vendor to provide service or maintenance records on equipment to ensure that it is in good working order (Hartsell & Ward, 1985). It is important to remember that failure to provide ongoing maintenance is a major contributor to equipment failures. Figure 18-3 provides a checklist for selecting and evaluating home care equipment vendors.

## Establishing a Community Support Network

When the child has complex medical needs and is dependent on technology, it is especially important to establish a community support network before the child is discharged. This support network includes the child's community physician, who is responsible for routine management of the child's medical condition and primary care needs, visiting nurse and social work services, the school, equipment vendors, and specialized technical support such as respiratory therapists.

---

## CHECKLIST FOR SELECTING AND EVALUATING HOME-CARE EQUIPMENT VENDORS

| | Yes | No | | Yes | No |
|---|---|---|---|---|---|
| 1. Does the vendor provide professional services? | ☐ | ☐ | 13. Are the vendor's fees competitive? | ☐ | ☐ |
| 2. Does the vendor provide 24-hour service? | ☐ | ☐ | 14. Does the vendor offer rental and purchase options on equipment? | ☐ | ☐ |
| 3. Does the vendor quickly return telephone calls when clients have problems? | ☐ | ☐ | 15. Does the vendor provide free replacement or loaner equipment in case of equipment failure? | ☐ | ☐ |
| 4. Does the vendor make home visits? | ☐ | ☐ | 16. Does the vendor accept returned equipment that is unused and unopened? | ☐ | ☐ |
| 5. Does the vendor have a large enough staff to provide all necessary services expediently and adequately? | ☐ | ☐ | 17. Does the vendor retrieve rental equipment promptly and report to the hospital that it has been returned? | ☐ | ☐ |
| 6. Are the vendor's employees committed and professional, and do they have pediatric experience? | ☐ | ☐ | 18. Does the vendor do preventive maintenance on rental equipment and keep service records? | ☐ | ☐ |
| 7. Are the vendor's employees willing to collaborate with the hospital team? | ☐ | ☐ | 19. Is the vendor an authorized Medicaid provider? | ☐ | ☐ |
| 8. Does the vendor provide a record of after-hours and weekend calls? | ☐ | ☐ | 20. Does the vendor have experience in dealing with insurance companies? | ☐ | ☐ |
| 9. Is the vendor an authorized dealer? | ☐ | ☐ | 21. Does the vendor bill third-party payers directly? | ☐ | ☐ |
| 10. Does the vendor provide written materials on the care, maintenance, and operation of equipment? | ☐ | ☐ | 22. Does the vendor bill parents for their portion of payments on a monthly basis? | ☐ | ☐ |
| 11. Does the vendor stock an appropriate range of equipment and supplies for children of all ages? | ☐ | ☐ | 23. Does the vendor accept some charity cases and provide assistance to families in finding sources of reimbursement? | ☐ | ☐ |
| 12. Are the vendor's employees knowledgeable about differences between pediatric and adult equipment? | ☐ | ☐ | | | |

*Figure 18–3. Checklist for selecting and evaluating home-care equipment vendors. (Hartsell, M.B., & Ward, J.H. [1985]. Selecting equipment vendors for children on home care.* MCN, 10, *27)*

However, the network does not end there. A comprehensive emergency action plan must also be established. The family and other care-givers must be competent in pediatric cardiopulmonary resuscitation as well as appropriate actions for rescue breathing and choking. Community resources that are helpful in an emergency should be contacted. The community's emergency rescue system should be notified that a child who is dependent on technology resides in the area, and emergency provisions for the child's care should be established. If the child lives in a rural area or in an area that is not easy to find on maps or through road signs, the emergency rescue system should be given detailed directions. Area electrical and water companies should also be notified so interrupted service can be returned on a priority basis.

## Identifying the Family and Respite Support Network

Parenting any child is a time-consuming, energy-draining activity. Providing home care for a child who is acutely or chronically ill presents special challenges at a time when emotional supports may be limited. When parents first learn of a handicapping condition or serious illness, they frequently withdraw from their family and friends. This withdrawal can be related to either the family's stage of grieving or their discomfort in telling other family members or friends the unpleasant news. Whereas parents of well newborns frequently spend a great amount of time on the telephone or with their friends comparing their infant's latest accomplishments with those of the baby book, parents of an ill or handicapped child are often consumed with "trying to make it through the day." They often dread the questions of an idle passerby and prefer to stay isolated in the safety of their homes.

As parents work through their own feelings regarding their situations, they may become frustrated by professional advice and long to talk with others who have been through the same experiences. Parent support groups are valuable resources through which these needs can be met. There are often local, state, or national organizations and parent support networks related to the child's specific diagnosis for families of children with chronic problems. Examples include the Muscular Dystrophy Association and the National Hemophilia Foundation. In many instances, families of children with various health problems band together. Sick Kids (Need) Involved People (SKIP) is one such group. This organization is especially concerned with improving specialized pediatric home care, particularly for children dependent on technology, and in matching community resources to family needs. A list of additional resources can be found in the display.

Participation in support groups is an effective form of therapeutic support in that parents' participation is a strong predictor of future adaptation. The discharge team can facilitate this process by supplying parents with the names and phone numbers of active local members of parent support groups. With the family's permission, the team may also contact the parent group representative and let them know that the family lives or is moving into the area.

Emotional support through parents' groups is only one type of support needed by parents providing home care. The physical energy expenditure involved in 24-hour-a-day care, even when additional help is available, is exhausting. Without provision of respite, family care-givers will experience burnout. In the case of home care, *respite care* is defined as the provision of care for an ill child in the home by someone other than parents or the usual care-givers. Respite care enables the primary care-givers to "take a break," giving them temporary diversion from the demands of caring for an ill child. Respite care is limited in many areas, and care-givers who are willing and able to care for ill children are scarce. If competent help cannot be hired, parents sometimes exchange services. This approach provides qualified care in exchange for valuable free time.

Ideally, families should not carry the full burden of locating respite care. A growing number of parents' organizations, church groups, and professional associations offer total family respite or sponsored weekend family outings at camps or hotels. These outings are family-oriented, but professional volunteers provide child care for children with complex medical problems and their well siblings. This arrangement provides free time for adult care-givers to participate in recreational activities or solitary pursuits, or to renew relationships with their spouses. At a recent conference, one father commented, "I haven't really had much time alone with my wife since our child was born. We really needed this time as husband and wife, for I feel I am losing my identity as a spouse. I should be a husband as well as a father."

## Completing the Discharge

At the completion of discharge planning, the family actually takes the child home. Transportation may be made by car or ambulance, depending on the child's condition and the distance to the child's home. If the child is on ventilatory equipment, arrangements must be made for a portable ventilator, suction machine, and emergency equipment (McCarthy, 1986). Depending on the policies and procedures of the discharging hospital, hospital staff may accompany the family on their trip home and meet with community professionals to formally transfer the responsibility for care, or a nurse from a home care agency may meet the child and family at the hospital and accompany them home.

Many tertiary facilities also help the family ease the transition from hospital to home through follow-up telephone calls. These calls may be to reinforce teaching, answer questions, or provide emotional support through the early

## Selected Parent Support Groups

Association for the Care of Children's Health
7910 Woodmont Ave
Suite 300
Bethesda, MD 20814
(301) 654-6549

Association for Retarded Citizens
2501 Avenue J.
P.O. Box 6109
Arlington, TX 76005
(817) 244-1807

Council for Exceptional Children
1920 Association Drive
Reston, VA 22019
(703) 620-3660

Epilepsy Foundation of America (EFA)
44351 Garden City Drive
Landover, MD 20785
(800) EFA-1000

March of Dimes Birth Defects Foundation
1275 Mamaroneck Ave
White Plains, NY 10605
(914) 428-7100

National Association for Minorities with Disabilities
3508 West North Avenue
Milwaukee, WI 53208
(414) 442-0522

National Easter Seal Society
70 East Lake Street
Chicago, IL 60601
(800) 221-6827

Autism Society of America
8601 Georgia Avenue
Silver Spring, MD 20910
(301) 565-0433

Parents of Chronically Ill Children
1527 Maryland Street
Springfield, IL 62702
(217) 522-6801

SKIP (Sick Kids Need Involved People) of New York
990 2nd Ave
New York, NY 10022
(212) 421-9161

Spina Bifida Association of America
1700 Rockville Pike, Suite 250
Rockville, MD 20852-1654
(800) 621-3141

United Cerebral Palsy Association
7 Penn Plaza, Suite 804
New York, NY 10001

days of home care. Once the family returns home, the focus of health care delivery changes drastically. Even if the child has complex medical problems or is dependent on equipment, the home is not just an extension of the hospital. The family controls the home and faces the daily joys and sorrows of routine domestic life. It must deal with the long-term consequences of daily decisions regarding care and cost. Thus, the family should have the final decision regarding its own destiny. In clients' homes, nurses must be sensitive to their positions as visitors. Although nurses continue to have professional responsibilities and obligations, the family, consciously or unconsciously, decides whether nursing recommendations should be accepted or ignored. Nurses must accept the reality of this position and alter their nursing approaches accordingly. These modified approaches exemplify the need to combine "high touch with high tech." In other words, nursing interventions must address both the art and the science of home care nursing.

## Implementation

Nursing activities in the delivery of home care, having formerly focused on assessment, nursing diagnosis, and planning, now are concerned with the implementation of these plans in the home/community setting. This phase can be divided into interventions based on interpersonal processes (the art of home care nursing) and those based in technological expertise (the science of home care nursing).

## The Art of Home Care Nursing: Interpersonal Processes

The *art* of home care nursing combines the human aspects of caring with technological advances. Although technological competence is frequently essential to maintain life, the human factor is critical in improving families' quality of life. "The selling point of high tech home care is not the technology but the healing potential of the home environment" (Haddad, 1987, p. 91).

## Phases in Interpersonal Relationships

The art of nursing rests in the development of interpersonal relationships between the nurse and family that are based on an individualized assessment of the child and family. This assessment provides an analysis of the child and family's current level of functioning and serves as a guide to the most appropriate nursing role to be used in each situation. Thus, when the family needs guidance in performing its roles, the nurse's interventions are directive. When the family acts independently, the nurse assumes a collaborative role.

Observations of family/nurse relationships over time indicate the development of certain behavioral patterns as the family proceeds through its adaptation to the child's illness. Monsen (1986) classified these patterns of family behavior interactions into three phases: adversary, alliance, and coordinator.

### Adversary Phase.
In the hospital, when the family experiences the initial shock and denial process relating to the awareness of the child's illness, hospital staff necessarily assume a more authoritative role. Monsen (1986) classifies this response as the *adversary phase* of the evolving nurse/family relationship. This phase is characterized by the relinquishment of responsibility for management decisions by family members and dependence on the nurse to provide direct care, support the family, and provide liaisons to other members of the health care team. During this phase, the nurse perceives " . . . that the family does not seem to be working smoothly with the health care team in meeting the needs of the child." At that time, family members may have a limited ability to understand technical information or participate in care (Monsen, 1986, p. 316). "The parent's presence without interference is often the expectation" (Raulin & Shannon, 1986, p. 340). During this phase, family members benefit from emotional support and information regarding their child's condition, patterns of health care delivery, team composition and functioning, and community resources (Monsen, 1986).

### Alliance Phase.
As the family proceeds through the grieving process, it begins to accept the child as an individual with strengths as well as needs. The *alliance phase* is characterized by the family showing an increased ability to understand diagnostic and treatment information as well as demonstrating independence in providing for the child's care needs. This phase may occur in either the hospital or the home setting.

In the alliance phase, the family begins to develop

individualized approaches to the care of their child. They become equal and involved members of the health care team and assume increased responsibility for case management and care planning activities. "Anticipatory counseling at this point involves explaining expected health care needs and goals as well as developmental behaviors in the child" (Monsen, 1986).

This phase requires the nurse to make a critical role change from expert care-giver to teacher and equal partner. It is very difficult for many nurses to give up the technological "doer" role that proves its worth due to clinical competence. Many nurses in this phase state that they are uncomfortable in the new setting since they feel as though they do not do anything for the child and family except talk. The ability of nurses, therefore, to relinquish their power of technical competence and transfer it to the family is an even greater test of nursing art.

### Coordinator Phase.
In the *coordinator phase,* the roles of the nurse and family are reversed—parents become the teachers and the nurse becomes the student. Parents learn the newest information, techniques, and methods for providing care for their child and share it with nurses. A collaborative relationship between families and nurses develops in which alternatives are explored and decisions are made for the good of the child and family. The family assumes the major case management responsibilities. Family members may also become actively involved in leadership activities with parent support groups or serve as advocates for ill or handicapped children on a community level (Monsen, 1986).

When the family is in the coordinator phase, the nurse assumes the role of consultant/advisor, assisting the family to assume responsibility for problem identification, exploration of intervention alternatives, and decision making regarding an action plan. The nurse may ask thought-provoking questions, explore potential issues, and offer additional information or seek clarification, but the family assumes responsibility for case management in its broadest sense. Table 18-2 summarizes the three phases in the nurse–family relationship.

## Family Empowerment

As the concept of case management has evolved to the acceptance of the family as the primary case-manager in children's care and professionals have begun to acknowledge the need to relinquish control to the family, the concept of empowerment has gained increasing acceptance. *Empowerment* is defined as "participatory competence" (Kahn, 1970). "People who can participate with competence in the decisions that affect their lives 'feel more powerful.' A feeling of power increases morale, productivity, and compliance" (Miner, 1988). Thus, empowerment permits the family to have greater self-esteem and a stronger sense of control.

*Table 18–2. Stages in the Nurse/Family Relationship*

| Family Roles | Nursing Goals | Nursing Actions |
|---|---|---|
| **Adversary** | | |
| Undergo grief process<br>  Shock<br>  Denial<br>  Anger<br>  Bargaining | Establish therapeutic relationships with family<br>Promote family use of health care and other services<br>Encourage family acceptance of/adjustment to child's disability | Assess health care needs of child and family coping patterns, culture, and resources<br>Orient family to health care and other services<br>Refer family to other support services/SCAN team, if indicated |
| **Ally** | | |
| Accept/adjust to child's disability<br>Implement care recommendations<br>Devise and adapt care techniques for home setting<br>Teach individualized care techniques to health team<br>Form partnership with health care team<br>Begin to participate in coordination of health care and other support services | Encourage family to anticipate and meet child's needs<br>Encourage family and child to cooperate with health care team<br>Encourage family and child to participate in self-help and support groups | Act as role model/teacher for health care<br>Act as liaison with health care team and other support services<br>Accept family's regression to adversary phase if it occurs |
| **Coordinator** | | |
| Continue partnership with health care team<br>Coordinate health care and other support services<br>Become advocates for needs of child and other family members<br>Become advocates for handicapped persons on the local, regional, and national levels | Promote family commitment to meeting child's needs<br>Encourage child's responsibility, self-sufficiency, and self-advocacy<br>Promote participation in community efforts to assist the handicapped | Act as adviser and consultant to family and child<br>Locate new health care resources and support services for family<br>Accept family's regression to adversary or ally phase if it occurs |

(From Monsen, R. [1986]. Phases in the caring relationship: From adversary to ally to coordinator. *Maternal Child Nursing, 11,* 316. Copyright 1986 American Journal of Nursing Company. Used with permission. All rights reserved)

The need for family empowerment is documented by observations of families with children who are chronically ill or handicapped. Many of these parents have been found to lack self-esteem, especially if the family has been overwhelmed by the child's illness or handicapping condition. Poor parental self-esteem is aggravated by the diagnosis of a genetic disorder, because parents perceive that the child's condition is a result of their genetic defects. Children with chronic illnesses or handicapping conditions often demonstrate reduced self-esteem as well. Children who experience frequent hospitalizations due to their conditions show increased levels of guilt, anxiety, fantasies regarding body parts, and, often, psychosocial maladjustment.

Family empowerment contributes to increased abilities in meeting the responsibilities associated with case management and home care, and thus increases self-esteem and decreases anxiety. Nurses can enhance family empowerment by increasing parents' confidence in child care through information and skill building. If the child is developmentally and functionally able to participate in his or her own care, empowerment can also be achieved through the development of self-help activities. This competence-building contributes to increased independence of family members and children and provides the necessary abilities for being case-managers (Raulin & Shannon, 1986). Practicing the art of nursing uses many techniques designed to enhance family empowerment, as described below.

*Listening.* Empowerment necessitates that the nurse listen more than talk. Families frequently complain that health care professionals do not listen but prescribe therapies without really considering the family's status, needs, and concerns. Such unjustified prescriptions frequently result in lack of compliance, as families fail to follow through on suggestions that they consider inappropriate or unfeasible. Instead, nurses should listen nonjudgmentally to the child and family, supplement listening with touch and humor, and plan nursing interventions according to what they learn from and of the family.

***Teaching Cognitive Information.*** Parent teaching should be based on the information gathered by listening. The nurse should be aware that the family has probably forgotten much of the information they learned in the hospital and may need review or validation of information that was previously presented. The nurse should not rely strictly on parents' affirmations of understanding but should test their knowledge by asking questions in a non-threatening manner. In addition to information regarding treatment routines and procedures, family members frequently benefit from information in the following related areas:

1. The child's disease or disorder (cause, course, outcome, limitations, treatment regimens, the impact of the illness on the child's education and general family life, the probability of recurrence in siblings). If the condition is of genetic origin, the family generally wants further information about inheritance patterns and assistance in coping with feelings of resentment or guilt.
2. Ways to explain the condition to others
3. Management of the child's needs on a day-to-day basis
4. Incorporating care regimens into daily family life style routines
5. Anticipatory guidance regarding potential problems. A knowledge of problems in home care commonly experienced by other parents provides the family with anticipatory guidance and an opportunity to participate in contingency planning. Potential areas of concern include trouble-shooting problems with equipment and coping with the multiple stressors involved in managing an acute or chronically ill child at home; funding; school placement; sibling interference in the form of equipment tampering; and disruption of sleep (Andrews & Nielson, 1988).
6. Techniques for coordinating community agencies. Parents benefit from knowledge and tools that empower them to handle case management responsibilities. These might include survey forms, checklists, lists of minimum equipment, solutions to frequently experienced problems, and skill checklists. Knowledge and skill increase family independence as case managers (Kaufman & Hardy-Ribakow, 1987).
7. Normal growth and development patterns. Many families do not understand normal growth and development patterns. They may view behavioral changes associated with different developmental levels as indicative of the child's disorder. The nurse can assist parents by providing anticipatory guidance and by teaching parents activities to promote their child's growth and development. Parents also benefit from knowing that even if the child is demonstrating delayed development, even on a temporary basis, the sequence of developmental milestones is unchanged. Developmental tasks for all family members can be addressed and ways to facilitate their attainment can be explored. Care planning should include periodic reassessment of growth and development.
8. Normalization refers to the concept of "treating the child as normally as possible." Nurses should assist in the development and demonstration of parenting behaviors that permit the ill child to participate in as many peer activities as possible. Normalization includes the use of discipline as a vehicle for teaching the child about behavioral limits and establishing self-control. Methods to increase the child's independence should also be developed in conjunction with the family so as to prevent overprotection and unnecessary restrictions.
9. Primary health care. An awareness of primary health care needs is particularly important. This care includes immunizations, care of routine childhood illnesses, promotion of dental health, and proper nutrition and fluid intake. Many nurses and families become so involved in high-tech needs that they fail to observe common pediatric illnesses. The nurse should consult with the child's physician regarding contraindications before teaching plans are implemented.
10. Recreation resources for the child and family. Since the child's job is play, it is very therapeutic to involve him or her in a variety of play activities, taking energy and interest levels into consideration (Fig. 18-4). Relaxation and health promotion activities reduce stress for all family members.
11. Siblings. Whether the child is acutely or chronically ill, the family should be encouraged to explain the situation to the child's siblings. Early research about the effects of acute or chronic illnesses on families was not encouraging in terms of the emotional health of siblings of chronically ill or handicapped children; recent research, however, indicates that siblings adapt better than originally thought (Brett, 1988; Thibodeau, 1988). Adaptation by siblings is also facilitated when they are given knowledge about and skills to use in these situations. Siblings are interested in learning more about the child's condition and want to be involved to some extent in the ill child's care and decisions about health. Parents frequently need assistance from nurses in learning how to explain conditions to siblings at an age-appropriate level.

*Figure 18–4. Child receiving care at home involved in play activity.*

*Teaching Problem-solving Skills.* Empowerment comes from recognizing the problem, trying a solution, accepting the resolution, receiving acknowledgment, and being willing to try again (Kahn, 1970). The nurse can assist the family in developing skills in this process through positive feedback and rewarding progress toward achieving the desired goal. As the family members begin to feel more confident in problem recognition and resolution, they feel more competent and self-assured of their abilities, and improved client care and family adaptation follow.

*Assisting the Family in Developing Intra-family and Community Networks.* This process is begun in the hospital during discharge planning. Initially, the nurse continues the process by including other members in the child's care, helping the family evaluate the effectiveness of home care providers and treatment regimens, serving as liaison to other providers (such as the tertiary center or school), and assisting the family to identify and obtain community resources. As the family gains competence in these areas, the nurse can assist the family in developing effective advocacy skills and strategies for obtaining assistance.

## The Science of Home Care Nursing: Technological Competence

The science of nursing challenges the nurse to assist the family in adapting and providing safe, comprehensive, high-technology care in the home setting. The technical aspects of home care are fairly similar, regardless of the specific support system (i.e., mechanical ventilation, dialysis, parenteral nutrition). In addition, the process and principles underlying hospital procedures remain intact, even though implementation may vary in the home setting.

Modifications that must be made in the home setting generally relate more directly to normalization activities than to actual differences in procedures. For example, the child's bed and equipment may be located in the living room so the child can readily participate in family activities. A child's wagon may be used to carry portable ventilators and oxygen on family outings or trips to the doctor. The child may receive therapeutic physical therapy during play activities.

Record keeping is necessary in the home just as it is in the hospital. If most of the care is being provided by health care professionals, formal charting is usually done for quality assurance and funding purposes. If the child is less severely ill or the family provides most of the care without reimbursement, charting may be simple, consisting primarily of flow sheets. At times, the nurse may assist the family in developing simple charts that are color-coded or use stars and checks. Medication records may also be color-coded to facilitate administration recall.

The technological aspects of home care primarily involve appropriate implementation and individualization of the discharge plan. However, a few particular areas of home care create anxiety in families and children—interventions such as apnea monitoring, tracheostomies, oxygen administration, tube feedings, and parenteral nutrition.

### *Apnea Monitoring*

In recent years, there has been increasing interest in sudden infant death syndrome (SIDS) and episodes of infant apnea (absence of breathing for more than 20 seconds). There is also a growing association being made between SIDS and episodes in which sleep apnea in children is accompanied by changes in color and muscle tone, requiring stimulation of the torso or cardiopulmonary resuscitation to restore breathing. Concern regarding these conditions contributed to the development and refinement of home apnea monitoring equipment. This equipment monitors the infant for apnea and bradycardia and sounds an alarm when the baby stops breathing for an abnormally long time or the heart rate drops too low (Fig. 18-5). Monitors are used when an infant is at risk for a life-threatening event such as sleep apnea but does not have a condition that can be treated medically or surgically. Monitoring generally continues for 4 to 6 months and is terminated when the infant has had no episodes of apnea for 2 to 3 months and has no abnormal results on diagnostic tests (Valdes-Dapena & Steinschneider, 1983).

Home apnea monitoring generally reduces the fear that an episode will occur undetected; however, parents of infants on apnea monitors demonstrate high levels of anxiety. Parents' concerns usually relate to the changes in their lifestyles that occur with this situation and their abilities to use the monitor, respond to alarms, and provide cardiopulmonary resuscitation (CPR) appropriately (Dimaggio & Sheetz, 1983; Graber & Balas-Stevens, 1984). "False alarms are frequent and tend to increase the parents' anxiety, confirming their fears about the risk of death" (Mark & Zahr, 1986, p. 224). Parents of infants on apnea monitors also commonly voice concerns regarding infant care and postpartum recovery, concerns that are shared by all new parents. The nurse can respond to parental anxiety through teaching, family practice sessions on pediatric CPR, and anticipatory guidance.

Nursing interventions for children and families dependent on apnea monitors include education and family support. Families should be educated on possible causes of apnea; proper positioning to prevent gastroesophageal reflux and to accommodate any anatomical abnormalities; medication use, dosages, administration, and side effects; skin care; proper use of the apnea monitor; methods of monitoring equipment function (including proper maintenance and checks for malfunction); responses to the alarms (ranging from tactile stimulation to pediatric cardiopulmonary resuscitation); and emergency response measures.

Anticipatory guidance should be given regarding the following frequently observed problems:

Parental inability to distinguish between real and false alarms

Over-stimulation of the infant

Improper placement of electrodes (see Fig. 18-6 for proper placement)

Failure to recognize malfunctioning equipment

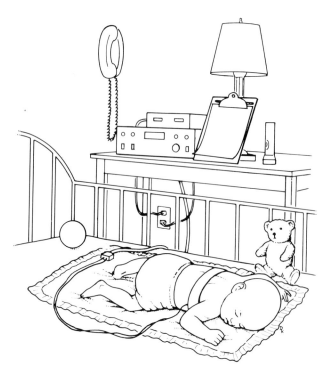

*Figure 18–5.  Apnea monitor.*

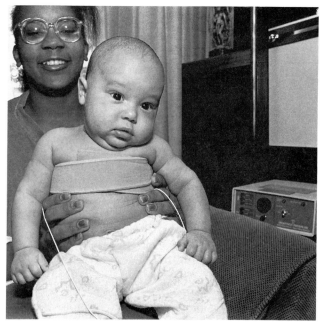

*Figure 18–6.  Placement of apnea monitor electrodes on infant. (Copyright 1991 by Kathy Sloane)*

Difficulty coping with increased alarms during illness

Skin irritation where the monitor's leads are attached to the infant

Family's difficulty adapting to a normal lifestyle

Safety precautions

Parental anxiety when the apnea monitor is discontinued

Many families find it helpful to record the date and time of alarms, whether they are real or false, and what interventions are taken. Such records provide valuable information about alarm patterns to both the family and the physician. Forms are generally available from the vendor responsible for the apnea monitor, or they may be developed by the nurse.

Finally, nurses can personally offer support, as well as fostering the development of appropriate behaviors of friends, family and community resources.

## Home Tracheostomy Management

An increasing number of children are being sent home with tracheostomies in place (Fig. 18-7). Tracheostomies are established in response to one or more of the following indications:

Upper airway obstruction

Laryngeal or subglottic stenosis

Central nervous system trauma

Neuromuscular disease

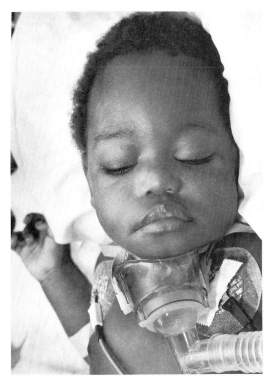

*Figure 18–7. Infant with a tracheostomy.*

Specific family education for home care of children with tracheostomies should include the following topics:

Altered physiology that necessitated the tracheostomy

Tracheostomy equipment and procedures for cleaning, changing, and emergency responses

Suctioning equipment, procedures, and emergency responses and indications for need of suctioning

Sterilization and storage of equipment

Use of universal infection precautions such as handwashing, gloves, disposal of contaminated materials, and cleansing of working solutions

Pediatric cardiopulmonary resuscitation and rescue breathing

Medication administration (as indicated)

Moisture control and related administration of mist and aerosols (as indicated)

Monitoring pulse, temperature, and respirations

Stoma skin care

Observations to note and what to report to the nurse and/or physician

Loss of voice and alternative communication strategies

Feeding and bathing precautions to prevent food or water from entering the tube

Clothing and bedding precautions (avoiding turtlenecks, fuzzy toys or blankets, and small toys that can enter the tube)

Eliminating fumes and avoiding the use of powders around the child

Stimulation of normal growth and development

Traveling with the child

Obtaining appropriate school placements

Sibling adjustment

Tracheostomy care is discussed in detail in Chapter 23.

## Home Administration of Oxygen

An increasing number of children with pulmonary or cardiac disorders are sent home on oxygen therapy. Although home oxygen administration is complex and often anxiety-producing for the family and the nurse, a comprehensive knowledge of oxygen usage and equipment can ensure safe compliance with treatment protocols.

As in the hospital, the physician decides whether the child needs oxygen in the home. If oxygen therapy is required, the physician determines whether this treatment should be administered by cannula, nasal tube, or mechanical ventilation (ventilator). In making this decision, the physician considers the following factors: prescribed liter flow or concentration, degree of portability of equipment and the length of time portable oxygen is necessary, whether the oxygen will be used continuously or intermittently, and the amount of humidity needed by the child (Ahmann, 1986).

Once the decision regarding the appropriate type of oxygen therapy has been made, the most suitable types of equipment can be determined. In general, equipment for home oxygen therapy can be put into three categories: oxygen source, method of oxygenation humidification, and equipment to deliver the oxygen from the source to client.

*Oxygen Source.* Several types of oxygen sources can be used in the home setting. The most frequently used are oxygen concentrators, liquid oxygen, and cylinder oxygen.

Oxygen concentrators take the oxygen already present in the child's room air and concentrate it into a usable form. This approach is more cost effective than purchasing individual oxygen tanks. However, oxygen concentrators pose several disadvantages. First, most are bulky and take up a lot of space in the home. As a result, discharge planning must include an assessment of available space in the home to accommodate the equipment (Groeneveld, 1986). Second, some types of medication nebulizers and oxygen masks cannot be used with the concentrators. Third, it is necessary to have oxygen stored in cylinders as a backup for times when portable oxygen is needed or when power failure or equipment malfunction occurs.

Liquid oxygen is used when a small amount of oxygen flow is needed or as a base for refilling lightweight portable units (Ahmann, 1986). Liquid oxygen generally re-

quires an additional humidity source to ensure that the child's airways remain moist.

Cylinder oxygen is generally used when portable oxygen is necessary. Small tanks of oxygen can be purchased so the child can be taken on outings easily. Cylinder oxygen is also advised as a backup for electrically controlled oxygen sources.

*Oxygen Humidification.* Humidification devices provide molecular water to the air the child breathes. Humidification is necessary to prevent excessive drying of the airways and subsequent predisposition to infection. A frequently used humidification device is a nebulizer, which delivers a visible mist to clients who need endotracheal tubes or tracheostomies.

*Equipment.* A variety of delivery systems may be used to deliver the oxygen. Some of the most common are mask, nasal cannula, intermittent positive breathing machines, and oxygen tents (Fig. 18-8). The choice of delivery method depends on the child's oxygen needs, age and corresponding developmental level, and visual and mobility levels.

Generally, home oxygenation is the responsibility of a respiratory therapist, who is frequently a staff member with the equipment vendor. The therapist sets up and monitors the equipment and is often available for emergencies on a 24-hour basis. The vendor assumes responsibility for correcting equipment difficulties and for coordinating therapeutic oxygenation regimens with the child's physician.

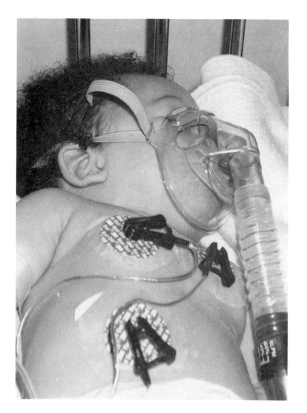

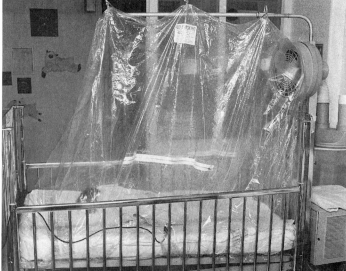

*Figure 18–8.  Child with an oxygen delivery system.*

The nurse has the overall responsibility for case management and coordination of oxygenation services with the other needs of the child and family. This responsibility includes general assessment, care planning activities, and specific interventions for children and families. Examples of these interventions are:

Coordination with respiratory therapists and other professionals regarding treatment protocols (such as methods of oxygen delivery) as they relate to the child's developmental and functional needs

Modifying environmental suitability for oxygen administration in the home. This process includes providing space for equipment; providing electricity, if needed, for oxygen equipment; removing heat sources that are a potential source of combustion and fire; and preventing cigarette and pipe smoking in the home.

Monitoring respiratory and circulatory status appropriately and teaching the family proper monitoring techniques and indications for referral to the physician or other care giver

Teaching family members safe equipment usage, accident prevention, emergency procedures and problem solving techniques

Teaching family members the prevention and management of infection

Demonstrating feeding and communication modifications, as indicated by the special needs of the child

Referring the family for social and financial support and respite

*Tube Feedings.* Children receiving home care often need special assistance in meeting nutritional needs or receiving medications. Conditions such as underdeveloped or absent sucking or swallowing reflexes; neurological, cardiac or respiratory disorders that interfere with eating; or the need to increase calories prior to surgery or during an acute illness indicate the need for supplemental nutrition therapy. Nutritional management of these conditions often involves the insertion of a plastic nasogastric tube or a gastrostomy tube in children in order to deliver the appropriate nutrients when oral intake is not possible.

The nasogastric tube is generally used for short-term delivery of food or specialized feedings directly into the stomach, where digestion can begin. The tube comes in various sizes and lengths. Before insertion, the nurse must determine the correct length of the tube. Procedures for tube feedings are discussed in more detail in Chapter 29.

Correct placement of the nasogastric tube in the stomach (rather than in the respiratory tract) should always be verified by one of the following techniques. The nurse can insert 3 to 5 mL of air into the tube, then place a stethoscope over the stomach; proper placement is verified if the nurse hears a popping sound through the stethoscope. A second method of tube placement verification is accomplished by attaching a syringe to the end of the tube to withdraw stomach contents. This material should be replaced prior to feeding.

The nasogastric tube may be left in place for up to 5 days or inserted prior to a feeding and then removed. Because the tube is not aesthetically appealing and is very irritating to the nose and throat, it is used only as a temporary measure. When feeding tubes are needed for periods longer than 5 days, a gastrostomy is often performed.

A gastrostomy is a surgical opening through the abdominal wall into the stomach. A plastic gastrostomy tube is then inserted into that opening for purposes of long-term feeding. The end of the catheter generally has a basket-type end or a balloon tip to ensure maintenance of proper position. This technique allows food to bypass the mouth and esophagus and enter the stomach directly. It eliminates the need for repeated insertions of the tube and appears to be less irritating to the child than a nasogastric tube.

The actual feeding procedure with the gastrostomy tube is the same in the home as it is in the hospital. All necessary materials for the procedure and the actual feeding are gathered first. The feeding may consist of either home-prepared mixtures of normal food or a commercial formula. Regardless of actual composition, the mixture is known as a feeding. It should be warmed to room temperature to avoid reactions such as cramping. As in the hospital, care must be taken to ensure proper positioning of the child and the tube, and the appropriate feeding technique must be used.

With both nasogastric and gastrostomy tube feedings, the child may require either periodic large bolus feedings or fewer, smaller feedings over time. In bolus feedings, the material is warmed to room temperature and placed in a container that is connected directly to the nasogastric or gastrostomy tube. The nurse or parent can then use gravity to control the rate of infusion of the feeding by raising or lowering the height of the feeding container in relation to the child's position.

In children who cannot tolerate large volumes of feedings at one time, a continuous infusion may be given using an automatic feeding pump. These devices, which are similar to an intravenous pump, deliver feedings at predetermined rates. For small children, the nurse may have difficulty locating a feeding pump that provides the precision volume control necessary to prevent fluid overload; in some cases, an IV pump may be useful. As with any other type of equipment, familiarization with the machinery, problem-solving skills, and emergency procedures is necessary when using feeding pumps.

The use of feeding tubes in the home requires extensive client education and continuous assessment. Nursing interventions include teaching the family the following:

1. Appropriate use of tubing and equipment
2. Appropriate tube placement (in the case of a nasogastric tube) or checks for placement (nasogastric and gastrostomy)

3. Appropriate positioning of the child before, during, and after feedings
4. Preparation, storage, and administration of feedings
5. Appropriate feeding procedure
6. Observation for possible side effects
7. Emergency and problem solving approaches
8. Procedures for monitoring growth
9. Procedures for monitoring intake and output

Comprehensive client education and monitoring can help to prevent common tube feeding problems. Frequently, inadequate monitoring of feeding volume and administration rate can contribute to diarrhea, cramping, constipation, stomach upset, and vomiting. Improper tube placement can result in aspiration. Incorrect tube positioning and feeding procedures can contribute to tube blockage. Inadequate skin care can lead to breakdown and infections.

Special care should be taken to promote normal growth and developmental patterns. Infants should be given a pacifier to suck during feedings (Paarlberg & Balint, 1985). Children on restricted diets should be given the opportunity to experiment with different food tastes and textures. Care should be taken to make socialization and interactions during feeding times as nearly normal as possible.

### Home Parenteral Nutrition

Although most tube feedings in the home include the use of nasogastric or gastrostomy tubes, an increasing number of children are being discharged on home parenteral nutrition. This therapy is given on either a continuous or periodic basis (Berry & Jorgensen, 1988a). In home parenteral nutrition a highly concentrated solution, usually consisting of glucose, electrolytes, amino acids, and vitamins, is administered. The physician orders each component of the solution individually so as to meet the child's unique needs. The properties of the solution require that it be diluted quickly, so it needs to be infused directly into the circulatory system.

In short-term situations the solution is administered through the peripheral blood supply. For long-term administration, modifications are made in the solution and it is administered through a catheter that is threaded directly into the child's heart. This special tube is known as a central line and generally uses a Hickman or Broviac catheter. The parenteral nutrition (hyperalimentation) solution is then pumped into the circulatory system by an infusion pump.

The use of home parenteral nutrition requires careful monitoring by the nurse. Specific nursing interventions include the following:

1. If the solution is administered peripherally, the nurse will use infection and circulatory precautions similar to those for intravenous solutions. It is par-

ticularly important to maintain a slow and consistent rate of administration to avoid untoward physiological responses.
2. If the solution is being administered through the use of a central line, special precautions must be taken. Because of the direct line into the child's heart, infection of the line is a major potential complication. Aseptic techniques, sterile dressing changes, and heparinization are necessary.
3. The nurse will teach and monitor technique, intake and output, and skin care.
4. Frequent laboratory tests, such as complete blood counts and electrolytes, are used to guide the physician in modifying solutions.
5. Careful observation for signs of potential complications is critical. These complications may include sepsis, hyperglycemia, acidosis, thrombus formation, air embolism, and serious infections (Berry & Jorgensen, 1988b).

## Evaluation

Evaluation of the child's health status and the family's adaptation to caring for the child at home should be conducted at the time of discharge as well as throughout and at the end of a home care program. The evaluation should be done by the family, the discharge team, and the health care professionals who are collaborating with the child and family.

The evaluation should consist of a review of the child's current status; the original goals, objectives, and the initial time lines; the effectiveness of planned interventions (including the adequacy of home health agencies, equipment companies, parental care, and services provided by community agencies); the child's need for subsequent rehospitalizations; the child's developmental progress; and the problems the family has experienced. It is more helpful if data are obtained from a variety of sources, such as equipment vendors, physicians, parents, and schools. Follow-up plans can be made based on the results of these evaluations.

## Legal and Ethical Issues

There are many legal and ethical issues in the field of pediatric home care. Client confidentiality must be maintained, since the nurse has access to non-medical information that might not normally be available to health care professionals. Other legal issues relate to nursing responsibilities for client education; standards of conduct or moral behavior in the family's home setting; liability when the family provides care in the absence of a health care professional; the nurse's responsibilities when family members fail to follow through on client teaching or refuse to give required care; informed consent for treatment; and quality assurance issues.

Ethical issues revolve around several questions:

- Is it ethical to transfer the burden of care from the hospital to the family in the home setting?
- What is the extent of parental responsibility for care of the child in the home?
- What are the safe limits of pediatric home care?
- How should scarce resources such as expensive high-technology equipment and/or surgical procedures be allocated?
- For what services should local, state, and federal governments provide funding?
- Who should determine the standards for home care personnel and equipment?
- What should be included in standards for home care personnel and equipment?

## Summary

Pediatric home care is an exciting and rapidly developing area of nursing. As an increasing number of children with complex medical problems are transferred to their homes, community-based nursing is expanding in order to integrate elements of pediatric nursing. Nursing and related personnel are facing new interpersonal and technical challenges. Comprehensive pre-discharge family assessment; multidisciplinary team-oriented discharge planning; family-centered, coordinated care; and adaptation of complex nursing interventions to the home setting are just a few of the components of this new area of nursing. The rewards to the nurse, to the child, and to the family are great because home care provides the opportunity for children to receive care for their physical, emotional, and social needs within the normal home environment.

## References

Ahmann, E. (1986). *Home care for the high risk infant: A holistic guide to using technology.* Rockville, MD: Aspen.

American Academy of Pediatrics, Ad Hoc Task Force on Home Care of Chronically Ill Infants and Children. (1984). Guidelines for home care of infants, children and adolescents with chronic disease. *Pediatrics, 74*(3), 434–436.

Andrews, M., & Nielson, D. (1988). Technology dependent children in the home. *Pediatric Nursing, 14*(2), 111–151.

Barnard, K. (1985). *Towards an era of family partnership: Parents of disabled and at risk infants and toddlers speak to professionals.* Washington, DC: National Center for Clinical Infant Programs.

Berry, R., & Jorgensen, S. (1988a). Growing with home parenteral nutrition: Adjusting to family life and child development (Part 1). *Pediatric Nursing, 14*(1), 43–45.

Berry, R., & Jorgensen, S. (1988b). Growing with home par-

enteral nutrition: Maintaining a safe environment (Part 2). *Pediatric Nursing, 14*(2), 155–157.

Brett, K. (1988). Sibling response to chronic childhood disorders: Research Perspectives and Practical Implications. *Issues in Comprehensive Pediatric Nursing, 11*(1), 43–57.

Briggs, N. (1987). Selecting a home care program. *Pediatric Nursing, 13*(3), 191.

Burr, B., Guyer, B., Todres, I., Abrahams, B., & Chiodo, T. (1983). Home care for children on respirators. *The New England Journal of Medicine, 309*(21), 1319–1323.

Cabin, B. (1985). Cost effectiveness of pediatric home care. *Caring, (4),* 48–51.

Dimaggio, G., & Sheetz, A. (1983). The concerns of mothers caring for an infant on an apnea monitor. *Maternal Child Nursing, 8,* 294–297.

Dunst, C. (1988, June). *Case management practices and the Individual Service Plan.* Presented at the Third Annual Gulf Coast Conference on Early Intervention, Pt. Cleare, Ala.

Freedman, L. (1986, June). *Perspectives from states.* Presented at the Association for the Care of Children's Health's Family Centered Panel, Washington, DC.

Graber, H., & Balas-Stevens, S. (1984). A discharge tool for teaching parents to monitor. *Maternal Child Nursing, 9,* 178–180.

Groeneveld, M. (1986, May/June). Sending infants home on low-flow oxygen. *Journal of Obstetrical and Gynecological Nursing,* 237–241.

Haddad, A. (1987). *High tech home care: A practical guide.* Rockville, MD: Aspen.

Hartsell, M., & Ward, J. (1985). Selecting equipment vendors for children on home care. *Maternal Child Nursing, 10,* 26–28.

Healey, A., & Lewis-Beck, J. (1987). *Guidelines for therapists: Improving health care for children with chronic conditions.* Iowa City, Iowa: University of Iowa.

Hobbs, N., Perrin, J., & Ireys, H. (1985). *Chronically ill children and their families.* San Francisco, Ca.: Jossey-Bass.

Kahn, L. (1984). Ventilator dependent children heading home. *Hospitals, 58,* 54–55.

Kahn, S. (1970). *How people get power.* New York: McGraw-Hill.

Kaufman, J., & Hardy-Ribakow, D. (1987). Home care: A model of a comprehensive approach for technology assisted chronically ill children. *Journal of Pediatric Nursing, 2*(4), 244–249.

Mark, K., & Zahr, L. (1986). Parental anxiety related to the care of a child with apnea. *Issues in Comprehensive Pediatric Nursing, 9,* 223–228.

McCarthy, M. (1986). A home discharge program for ventilator assisted children. *Pediatric Nursing, 12*(5), 331–335, 380.

Miner, K. (1988, August). *The role of the health consultant.* Presented at the Headstart Conference for Consultants. Atlanta, Georgia.

Mitchell, K. (1986). Taking children home where they belong. *Pediatric Nursing, 12*(4), 256.

Monsen, R. (1986). Phases in the caring relationship: From adversary to ally to coordinator. *Maternal Child Nursing, 11,* 316–318.

Morris, E., & Fonseca, J. (1984). Home care today. *American Journal of Nursing, 84,* 1342.

Newacheck, P., Budetti, P., & McManus, P. (1984). Trends in childhood disability. *American Journal of Public Health, 74*(3), 232–236.

Paarlberg, J., & Balint, J. (1985). Gastrostomy tubes: Practical guidelines for home care. *Pediatric Nursing, 11*(2), 99–102.

Perrin, J. (1985). Chronically ill children in America. *Caring, 4,* 17.

Raulin, A., & Shannon, K. (1986). PNPs: Case managers for technologically dependent children. *Pediatric Nursing, 12*(5), 338–340.

Richardson, D. (1983). Parents' time is worth money. *Pediatrics, 71*(3), 466–467.

Stein, R. (1984). Home care: A challenging opportunity. *Home care for children with serious handicapping conditions: Proceedings of Association for the Care of Children's Health Conference,* Houston, 2-8.

Stein, R., & Jessop, D. (1984). Does pediatric home care make a difference for children with chronic illness? Findings from a pediatric ambulatory care study. *Pediatrics, 73*(6), 845–852.

Taylor, M. (1985). The effect of DRGs on home health care. *Nursing Outlook, 33*(6), 288–289.

Thibodeau, S. (1988). Sibling response to chronic illness: The role of the clinical nurse specialist. *Issues in Comprehensive Pediatric Nursing, 11*(1), 17–28.

Valdes-Dapena, M., & Steinschneider, A. (1983). Sudden Infant Death Syndrome (SIDS), apnea and near miss for SIDS. *Emergency Medicine Clinics of North America, 1*(1), 27–43.

## Bibliography

Abman, S. H., Accurso, F. J., & Koops, B. L. (1984). Experience with home oxygen in the management of infants with bronchopulmonary dysplasia. *Clinical Pediatrics, 23*(9), 471–476.

Association for the Care of Children's Health. (1984). *Home care for children with serious handicapping conditions.* Washington, DC: Author.

Banagale, R. C., Roloff, D. W., & Howatt, W. F. (1984). Apnea in newborn infants: Approach to management. *Resuscitation, 11*(1-2), 9–20.

Bender, J. H., & Faubion, W. C. (1985). Parenteral nutrition for the pediatric patient. *Home Healthcare Nurse, 3,* 32–39.

Bock, R. H., Lierman, C., Ahmann, E., Weinstock, N., Alweis, M., Mitchell, R., & Oritz, M. (1093). There's no place like home. *Children's Health Care, 12*(2), 93–96.

Brault, G. L. (1986). 1980's reorientation to home health care. *Journal of Pediatric Health Care, 1*(1), 8–13.

Cacioppo, B. (1979). Respite care for parents of handicapped children. *Social Work and Health Care, 5,* 97–101.

Cohen, S. (1986). Home care—high tech and high touch. *The Journal of the New York State Nurses Association, 17*(4), 35–42.

Combs-Orme, T., Reis, J., & War, L. D. (1985). Effectiveness of home visits by public health nurses in maternal and child health: An empirical review. *Public Health Reports, 100*(5), 490–499.

Fischer, D. A. (1985). Long-term management of the ventilator patient in the home. *Cleveland Clinic Quarterly, 52*(3), 303–306.

Foster, S., & Hoskins, D. (1981) Home care of the child with a tracheotomy tube. *Pediatric Clinics of North America, 28*(4), 855–857.

Giovanni, R. M., Goldberg, A. I., Keens, T. G., Make, B. J., O'Donahue, W. J., Jr., Plummer, A. L., & Prentice, W. S. (1986, July). Long-term mechanical ventilation. Guidelines for management in the home and at alternate community sites. Report of the Ad Hoc Committee, Respiratory Care Section, American College of Chest Physicians. *Chest, 90*(Suppl.), 15–375.

Givan, D. C., & Wylie, P. W. (1986). Home oxygen therapy for infants and children. *Indiana Medicine, 79,* 849–853.

Glassanos, M. R. (1980). Infants who are oxygen dependent—sending them home. *Maternal Child Nursing, 5*(1), 42–45.

Goldberg, A. I., Faure, E. A., Vaughn, C. J., Snarski, R., & Seleny, F. L. (1984). Home care for life-supported persons: An approach to program development. *Journal of Pediatrics, 104*(5), 785–795.

Gray, S. W., & Wandersman, L. P. (1980). The methodology of home-based intervention studies: Problems and promising strategies. *Child Development, 51*(4), 993–1009.

Joyce, K., Singer, M., & Isralowitz, R. (1983). Impact of respite care on parents' perceptions of quality of life. *Mental Retardation, 21,* 153–156.

Kaufman, J., & Lichensteing, K. (1984). *The family as care manager: Home care coordination for medically fragile children.* Washington, DC: Georgetown University Child Development Center.

Light, M. J., & Sheridan, M. S. (1985). The home apnea monitoring program for newborns: The first 300 patients. *Hawaii Medical Journal, 44*(11), 423–424.

Maguire, M., Miller, T. V., & Young, P. (1982). Teaching patient's families to provide ventilator care at home. *Dimensions of Critical Care Nursing, 1,* 244–255.

McCarthy, S. (1986). Discharge planning for medically fragile children. *Caring, 5*(11) 38–39, 41.

Mitchell, K. (Ed.). (1986). Pediatric home tracheostomy care alternatives. *Pediatric Nursing, 12*(3), 223–225.

Mueller, M., & Leviton, A. (1986). In-home versus clinic-based services for the developmentally disabled child: Who is the primary client—parent or child? *Social Work Health Care, 12*(1), 51–65.

Odnoha, C. (1986). Respite programs for families of chronically ill children. *Caring, 5*(12), 20–24.

Rathlev, M. C., & McNamara, M. A. (1982). Teaching families to give trach care at home. *Nursing 82, 12*(6), 70–71.

Robinovitch, A. (1981). Home total parenteral nutrition: A psychosocial viewpoint. *Journal of Parenteral and Enteral Nutrition, 5*(6), 522–525.

Rosen, C. L., Glaze, D. G., & Frost, J. D., Jr. (1986). Home monitor follow-up of persistent apnea and bradycardia in preterm infants. *American Journal of Disabled Children, 140*(6), 547–550.

Rowland, T. W., Donnelly, J. H., Landi, J. N., Lemoine, M. E., Ruben, R. J., Newton, L., Jornsay, D., Stein, R., Chambers, H., Liquori, J., & Lawrence, C. (1982). Home care of the pediatric patient with a tracheotomy. *Annals of Otology, Rhinology and Laryngology, 91,* 633–640.

Sartucci, J. A., & Christoffers, C. A. (1986, April). *How do families spell relief? R-E-S-P-I-T-E.* ANA Publication, 77–80.

Schreiner, M. S., Donar, M. E., & Kettrick, R. G. (1987). Pediatric home mechanical ventilation. *Pediatric Clinics of North America, 34*(1), 47–60.

Sigelman, D. R., & Tanella, C. J. (1987). Infant home apnea monitoring. A five-year assessment. *Clinical Pediatrics, 26*(8), 383–387.

Spitzer, A. R. & Fox, W. W., (1986). Infant apnea. *Pediatric Clinics of North America, 33*(3), 561–581.

Thilo, E. H., Comito, J., & McCulliss, D. (1987). Home oxygen therapy in the newborn. *American Journal of Diseases of Children, 141*(7), 766–768.

Trofino, J. (1989). JCAHO nursing standards, nursing care hours and LOS per DRG. Part l. *Nursing Management, 20*(1), 29–32.

Wills, J. M. (1983) Concerns and needs of mothers providing home care for children with tracheostomies. *Maternal Child Nursing, 12*(2), 89–107.

Young L., Creighton, D., & Suave, P. (1988). The needs of families of infants discharged home with continuous oxygen therapy. *Journal of Obstetric, Gynecologic and Neonatal Nursing, 17*(3).

# Caring for Children
# With Infectious Diseases

Patricia T. Castiglia

*19*

*Photograph by David Finn*

*Public Health Concepts*

*Infectious Diseases Characterized by
Rashes*
    *Fifth Disease*
    *Kawasaki Disease*
    *Lyme Disease*
    *Rubeola*
    *Rocky Mountain Spotted Fever*
    *Roseola*
    *Rubella*
    *Scarlet Fever*
    *Varicella*

*Infectious Diseases Without Rashes*
    *Diphtheria*
    *Mumps*
    *Pertussis*
    *Poliomyelitis*
    *Tetanus*

*Hepatitis Infections*
    *Hepatitis A*
    *Hepatitis B*
    *Non-A, Non-B Hepatitis*

*Gastrointestinal Diseases*
    *Ascariasis*
    *Enterobiasis*
    *Giardiasis*
    *Shigella*

*Other Infectious Diseases*
    *Infectious Mononucleosis*
    *Influenza*
    *Rabies*
    *Tuberculosis*

*Summary*

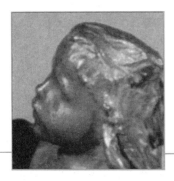

### Learning Objectives

*Upon completion of this chapter, the reader will be able to:*

1. *Describe the concepts related to the transmission of infectious diseases, including prevention.*

2. *Explain routine immunization schedules.*

3. *Demonstrate an understanding of the legal aspects of immunization.*

4. *Differentiate the types of isolation precautions.*

5. *Categorize selected infectious diseases into those characterized by rashes, those without rashes, gastrointestinal, and other.*

6. *Assess a child with an infectious disease.*

7. *Formulate nursing diagnoses related to specific infectious diseases.*

8. *Plan and implement appropriate nursing care measures for specific infectious diseases.*

9. *Analyze the effectiveness of nursing interventions including prevention, education, therapeutic, and supportive measures.*

10. *Synthesize knowledge about infectious diseases with aspects of total care of the child, the family, and the community.*

### Key Terms

*anaphylactic reactions*

*desquamation*

*endemic disease*

*enteric precautions*

*epidemic*

*epidemiology*

*hydrophobia*

*hyperendemic disease*

*Koplik's spots*

*monovalent vaccine*

*nosocomial infections*

*outbreak*

*strawberry tongue*

*vaccines*

*vector*

*vehicle*

## Public Health Concepts

The morbidity and mortality rates for most children in the United States have declined since early in the nineteenth century for most diseases. Unfortunately, these declines have not yet been evidenced in many third world countries. Conditions of poverty exist with concurrent poor hygiene, overcrowding, and poor nutrition. Frequently there is a lack of adequate immunization.

All children encounter infectious (communicable) diseases of one type or another. It is important to know the status of disease occurrence; therefore, most states require the reporting of certain diseases to local public health authorities. The list of reportable diseases varies in each state but usually includes hepatitis A and B, diphtheria, gonorrhea, syphilis, acquired immune deficiency syndrome (AIDS), mumps, pertussis, polio, psittacosis, rubella, smallpox, tuberculosis, tetanus, and typhoid fever, among others. Some states may require the reporting of endemic diseases such as Rocky Mountain spotted fever.

Hospitals are also required to report nosocomial infections, which are those that are acquired during hospitalization. Most of these infections are caused by group A *Streptococcus pyogenes, Staphylococcus aureus, Escherichia coli, Klebsiella, Proteus, Pseudomonas, Haemophilus influenza,* hepatitis viruses, and *Candida albicans.*

It is important to understand terms related to the transmission of diseases from one person to another, ei-

*Table 19–1. Terms Related to the Transmission of Infectious Diseases*

| Term | Definition |
|------|------------|
| Epidemic | A disease occurring at a level that is higher than normal |
| Outbreak | The sudden appearance of a disease that is frequently seen in a small sample of the population (sometimes this is regional) |
| Epidemiology | The study of factors related to the occurrence, frequency, and distribution of disease in a given population |
| Endemic disease | A disease that remains present in a given geographic area |
| Hyperendemic disease | A disease that is persistent with a high incidence |
| Vector | The source of transmission, which may be an arthropod (e.g., mosquito) or a person, who is called a *carrier* |
| Vehicle | The means of transmission (e.g., contaminated water) |

ther directly or indirectly (communicable diseases). A brief definition of relevant terms is found in Table 19-1. Microorganisms responsible for infectious diseases include viruses, bacteria, chlamydias, spirochetes, protozoa, and fungi. Brief descriptions of causative agents are found in Table 19-2. In addition, larger parasites such as roundworms or flatworms may also cause disease. Table 19-3 presents the four most common modes of disease transmission.

## Immunizations

*Vaccines* provide one of the most cost-effective means of preventing infection. Mass immunization efforts and the routine immunization of infants and children has almost eliminated such diseases as smallpox, tetanus, diphtheria, and paralytic poliomyelitis. Effective vaccines significantly reduce the occurrence of disease in individuals receiving immunization.

There are two types of immunization: active and passive. In *active immunization,* all or part of a microorganism is administered to evoke a mild immunologic response. These vaccines may be live (usually attenuated or weakened) or killed (inactivated). Some active vaccines offer immunity for life, e.g., smallpox vaccine, whereas others offer protection for periods of time but must be readministered, e.g., the measles vaccine. *Passive immunity* results from antibodies that are naturally transferred through the placenta to the fetus, through colostrum to the infant, or by injection of antiserum for treatment or prophylaxis. Passive immunity is not permanent and does not last as long as active immunity.

Almost all antibodies produced in defense of the body are gamma globulin molecules that are derived from blood serum. *Gamma globulins* are specific protein molecules that react chemically with the invading agent and are capable of preventing, modifying, and treating various infectious diseases. Gamma globulin provides passive immunity for about 6 weeks. Certain specific types of gamma globulin may be used to develop the body's resistance to measles, mumps, and poliomyelitis. It is administered intramuscularly, and peak antibody levels are achieved in 48 to 72 hours. The serum half-life is 3 to 4 weeks. Systemic reactions are rare. It is usually administered to close personal contacts of persons with hepatitis A. It does not

*Table 19–2. Agents Responsible for Many Infectious Diseases*

| Agent | Description |
|-------|-------------|
| Viruses | The smallest known organisms. They are made up of an RNA or DNA nucleus covered with proteins. |
| Bacteria | These are single-cell microorganisms and can be classified according to shape: cocci (spherical), bacilli (rod-shaped), and spirilla (spiral-shaped). They may also be classified according to their response to staining (gram-positive, gram-negative, or acid-fast). They may also be encapsulated or motile or nonmotile. |
| Chlamydiae | These agents are larger than viruses but smaller than bacteria. |
| Rickettsiae | These are gram-negative and similar to bacteria. They are relatively uncommon in the United States. |
| Spirochetes | These agents are anaerobic, and there are three pathogenic forms in humans: *Treponema, Leptospira,* and *Borrelia.* |
| Protozoa | These are the simplest cell organisms and have a nucleus surrounded by ceil membranes. |
| Fungi | These agents occur as yeasts or molds or both yeasts and molds. In humans, fungal diseases are called *mycoses.* |

*Table 19–3. The Four Most Common Modes of Disease Transmission*

| | |
|---|---|
| Contact transmission | Direct contact, as in sexually transmitted disease. Indirect contact, as in touching a contaminated inanimate object or exposure to droplets, as from a sneeze or cough |
| Airborne transmission | Inhalation of contaminated evaporated droplets that may be suspended in airborne dust particles |
| Enteric transmission | Feces are the source of the organism. The organism is ingested through fecally contaminated food or the lack of handwashing by food preparers. |
| Vectorborne transmission | A vector such as a mosquito transfers the organism to the victim. |

appear to afford protection against hepatitis B, but hepatitis B immune globulin is effective if administered in a large dose within 10 days of exposure. Gamma globulin should not be given to persons with coagulation disorders.

Sometimes *anaphylactic* (hypersensitivity) reactions to immunizations occur. Anaphylactic reactions include difficulty breathing, hives, swelling of the mouth and throat, hypotension, and shock. Reaction time is related to the intensity of the reaction; a severe reaction, for example, may occur within minutes after exposure. Reactions may occur anywhere from 15 to 20 minutes to 24 hours after the immunization. Many physicians and clinics request that patients remain in the office for 15 to 20 minutes after the immunization. Because of the possibility of an anaphylactic reaction, medications and equipment to maintain a patent airway and to manage cardiovascular support should always be available when immunizations are given. Epinephrine is the primary drug used in the treatment of anaphylaxis (Table 19-4).

There have been a number of changes in immunization practices over the past 25 years. Immunizations for three infectious diseases have been implemented: mumps, rubella, and Haemophilus influenza type B (HIB). Smallpox has been curtailed to the extent that immunization in the United States is no longer required. Other changes that have occurred include the following:

An increased interval for the three primary doses of diphtheria/pertussis/tetanus (DPT)

Withdrawal of the requirement that gamma globulin be given with the measles vaccine

The combination of types 1, 2, and 3 poliovirus into the trivalent live oral poliovirus vaccine (TOPV)

The elimination of some doses of tetanus/diphtheria (Td) for adequate immunization

The addition of a booster dose of measles/mumps/rubella vaccine (MMR) (Frenkel, 1990)

Vaccines commonly administered in the United States, along with their routes of administration, schedules, contraindications, and side effects, are found in Table 19-5.

*Table 19–4. Epinephrine (Adrenaline) Use in the Treatment of Anaphylaxis\* (Subcutaneous or Intramuscular Administration)*

Epinephrine 1:1,000 (aqueous): 0.01 mL/kg per dose repeated every 15 to 30 minutes. Usual dose:
   Infants: 0.05 to 0.1 mL
   Children: 0.01 to 0.03 mL
Long-acting epinephrine suspension (Sus-Phrine): 0.005 mL/kg per dose as a single dose. The usual dose in infants and children is one half that of epinephrine 1:1,000.

\* In addition to epinephrine administration, maintenance of an airway is critical.
(Adapted from American Academy of Pediatrics. [1988]. *Report of The Committee on Infectious Diseases* [21st ed.]. Elk Grove Village, IL: Author, p. 40)

## Legal Aspects of Immunizations

States generally use their "police power" rights when it is found necessary to make health care decisions for a child that are not in accord with the parents' wishes. This is done on the premise that the state can enact coercive legislation when it is in the best interest of the health and safety of the general public.

Courts have ruled that immunization requirements such as compulsory immunizations before attending school do not violate education laws, personal rights, or religious freedom. Some states do allow exemptions from immunizations on religious grounds but do not extend that right to include personal objection to immunizations.

Informed consent must always be obtained for immunizations. Informed consent means that the risks, benefits, and alternatives must be presented to the parents in a way that allows them to make an informed decision. Usually documentation is required to verify that the parent(s) has been informed about the immunization, i.e., parents must sign a statement affirming that they know about, and consent to, the immunization.

*Table 19–5. Vaccines Commonly Used in the United States*

| Name of Vaccine | Route of Administration | Primary Immunization Schedule | Booster Schedule | Contraindications | Side Effects |
|---|---|---|---|---|---|
| DPT* Diphtheria/Pertussis/Tetanus | IM | 2 months, 4 months, 6 months | 15–18 months, 4–6 years | CNS disease, history of screaming, high fever or seizures after previous DPT | Tenderness at injection site, redness at sites, or swelling |
| TD (Tetanus/Diphtheria) | IM | | Every 10 years after age 15 | | Urticaria, anaphylactic reactions |
| TOPV* Trivalent Oral Polio Virus Vaccine (Sabine Vaccine) | PO | 2 months, 4 months | 18 months and 4–5 years | Pregnancy/immunodeficiency | Rarely, paralytic disease in recipients or contacts |
| IPV Inactivated Polio Virus Vaccine (Salk Vaccine) | PO | 2 months, 4 months, 16–18 months | Every 5 years | Pregnancy | Local irritation at injection site |
| MMR* Measles/Mumps/Rubella | SC | 15 months | Either at school entry (4–6 yrs) as recommended by the Advisory Committee on Immunization Practices (ACIP) or at junior high school (11–12 yrs) as recommended by the American Association of Pediatrics (AAP)† | Pregnancy, febrile illness, recently received immune serum globulin (ISG) Immunodeficiency disease | Irritation at injection site; generalized rash 10–14 days after injection. Fever after 5–12 days |
| *Haemophilus influenzae* (HIB) | SC | 2 months, 4 months, 6 months | 15 months or older | Pregnancy | Local irritation at injection site; fever |
| Hepatitis B Plasma Derived (HBIG) or Recombinant DNA | IM | Babies born to HBsAg-positive mothers should receive HBIG at birth | Series of 3 doses protection for 5 years 1 month and 6 months after first injection | Only plasma-derived vaccine should be used for immunosuppressed patients | Arthralgia, neurological reactions |

\* DPT, TOPV, and MMR may be administered simultaneously.
† In high risk areas, children can receive the first dose at 12 months. In epidemics, children 6 months and older should be immunized. In these cases, the school doses are given as described.

Manufacturers of vaccines have been sued under the theory of product liability, of which there are three types: breach of warranty, negligence, and strict liability (Landwirth, 1990). In a breach of warranty, manufacturers are sued on the premise that they failed to deliver what was promised. Negligence suits claim that the manufacturer did not adhere to acceptable standards. Strict liability is used most often. Even if the manufacturer has used all possible care in the manufacture, sale, and distribution of the vaccine, it is sued on the premise that a product was placed on the market that was defective and more dangerous than the ordinary consumer would expect.

Because profits from the sale of vaccines constitute a minor portion of revenue for most manufacturers, many have given up the manufacture of DPT. This action resulted in shortages in 1984, and the National Childhood Vaccine Injury Act of 1986 was enacted as a no-fault compensation system for injuries from vaccines. Parents of children who have documented complications as a result of vaccine administration receive compensation from a fund established through this act. The manufacturer and the person who administers the vaccine are no longer individually liable. This act also requires that the person who administers the vaccine must record the date, dose, lot number, and manufacturer, as well as his or her own name, address, and title.

## Immunizations for Foreign Travel

An increasing number of families are traveling to or living in countries that are underdeveloped. Children in these families are at a high risk for contracting either exotic diseases or diseases that, in developed countries, are quite well controlled.

Children traveling to foreign countries may need adjustments to the routine immunization schedules. For example, the risk of diphtheria, tetanus, and pertussis is higher in developing countries than in the United States because of variations in required immunizations. American children need to be as well immunized as possible before they leave the United States. The Centers for Disease Control (CDC) publishes a book of information for foreign travel. The basic immunizations for children traveling overseas are found in Table 19-6. Requirements are based on the traveler's destination. In 1988, the World Health Organization (WHO) eliminated the requirement for vaccination for cholera. Because of the danger of hepatitis A in developing countries, immune globulin is currently recommended for infants and children.

## Future Viral Vaccines

*Herpes simplex* is an infection caused by a herpes simplex virus (HSV) that produces small, sometimes painful, fluid-filled blisters on the skin and mucous membranes. Infec-

**Table 19–6. Basic Immunizations for All Children Traveling Overseas***

1. Diphtheria, tetanus, pertussis (DPT) under age 7; tetanus-diphtheria (Td), age 7 and older
2. *Haemophilus influenzae* (Type B)
3. Hepatitis B
4. Immune globulin (gamma globulin)
5. Measles, mumps, and rubella (MMR)
6. Poliomyelitis (OPV or IPV)
7. Rabies
8. Typhoid
9. Yellow fever

*Requirements depend on destination
(From Wolfe, M. S. [1990]. Vaccines for foreign travel. *Pediatric Clinics of North America, 37*[3], 757)

ted areas around the mouth and nose are HSV-1 infections, whereas those appearing on the genitalia are HSV-2 infections. *Herpes zoster* is an acute infection caused by the varicella-zoster virus (VZV). Also called shingles, it is manifested primarily in adults by the development of painful vesicular skin eruptions that follow the route of inflamed cranial or spinal nerves. *Herpes zoster virus* (HZV) is the cause of *chickenpox* (varicella) discussed later in this chapter. It has been found that VZV remains latent in the body of a person who has been infected. Herpes zoster is produced by reactivation of latent varicella virus. Thus, varicella is the primary infection and zoster is a secondary infection that results from reactivation of the skin (Gershaw, 1990). Some studies suggest that VZV is shed from the skin and that the skin may be the source of transmissible viruses. However, it may also be possible that transmission occurs via the respiratory route (Gershaw, 1990). It is anticipated that live attenuated varicella vaccine will be licensed in the 1990s.

Another vaccine still in the developmental stage is the cytomegalovirus (CMV) vaccine. A live attenuated vaccine is being tested; it has been found to induce antibody and cell-mediated immunity. CMV infections affect approximately 5000 infants each year and cause mental retardation and hearing loss. CMV vaccination of girls or young women might offer protection against intragestational primary infection (Gershaw, 1990).

Other vaccines being developed include vaccines for hepatitis A and herpes simplex. Hepatitis A has become a relatively common infection among children in day care centers and their parents, as well as among people living in poverty and unsanitary conditions.

Herpes simplex virus (HSV) in neonates is most often acquired during passage through the birth canal. Older children contract HSV-1 from direct contact with infected secretions (usually oral) or HSV-2 from sexual activity. The HSV vaccine being developed is directed toward the prevention of neonatal or genital cases; therefore, it would need to be administered prior to the beginning of sexual activity (Gershaw, 1990).

Immunization against HIV infection (AIDS) is also being investigated. At present, it is not clear whether it is possible to develop immunity or whether antibodies are helpful or harmful.

## Isolation Precautions

Isolation techniques and procedures are usually stressed in nursing fundamentals courses where gowning, handwashing, gloving, masking, and equipment care are emphasized. When discussing infectious diseases, the isolation precautions necessary are determined by the mode of transmission of the disease. Handwashing is an important element in all of the precautions.

The CDC has classified the types of isolation as strict, respiratory, enteric, wound and skin, discharge precautions, and protective isolation. Table 19-7 specifies isolation precautions for hospitalized patients. The CDC recommended in 1987 that blood and body fluid precautions be used for all patients, especially those seen in emergency rooms, where the risk of exposure to blood is greater and where the patient's history is unknown.

## Infectious Diseases Characterized by Rashes

A *rash* is a skin eruption. Childhood rashes caused by a systemic disease (usually accompanied by fever) are called *exanthems*. "Exanthem" is a term used to describe an eruption on the skin.

Rashes can be classified by appearance (maculopapular, petechial, pustular) or by the total illness pattern (e.g., rubella-like) (Moffett, 1989). *Erythematous* rashes are red areas that blanch when pressed. They are generalized and extensive but may involve only a part of the body. *Papular* rashes are like fine sandpaper. *Macular* rashes are flat. *Urticaria*, also known as hives, is characterized by pale red, elevated, intradermal edematous plaques.

### Table 19–7. Isolation Precautions for Hospitalized Patients

| Type of Precaution | Examples of Diseases Where Recommended | Gown | Gloves | Mask | Private Room | Precautions |
|---|---|---|---|---|---|---|
| Strict | Smallpox Rabies | X | X | X | X | Dishes, linens, secretions |
| Respiratory | Mumps Rubella Pertussis | 0 | 0 | X | X | Secretions |
| Enteric | Ascariasis Shigella Giardiasis Salmonellosis | X | X | 0 | Poor hygiene patients | Fecal matter, linens, and bed |
| Wound and skin | Impetigo Infected burns | X | X | X For dressing changes | 0 | Instruments used in dressing changes |
| Discharge | Scarlet fever AIDS | X If soiling is likely | X For touching infectious material | 0 | 0 | Dressing (double bag), excretions |
| Protective (reverse) | Leukemia (children) | X | X | X and cap | X Germ-free plastic tents | 0 |
| Universal | All patients because of inability to identify all HIV- or hepatitis B-infected people | X If soiling is likely | X For touching blood or body fluids | 0 | 0 | Needle sticks |

X, must be used; 0, not necessary

## Fifth Disease (Erythema Infectiosum)

| | |
|---|---|
| Incubation period | 2 to 14 days |
| Contagion period | Before the onset and a few days after the onset |
| Causative agent | Parvovirus B19 |
| Mode of transmission | Respiratory tract, blood transfusions, and across the placenta from mother to fetus |

*Fifth disease* is so named because it is the fifth most common childhood exanthem. Usually considered a mild disease, it begins with an erythematous rash on the cheeks that looks like "slapped cheeks." This is followed by a reticulated (netlike pattern), maculopapular rash that usually lasts 2 to 5 days but may come and go for up to a month. The rash appears on the arms but moves to the trunk, the buttocks, and thighs. Arthralgia and arthritis may occur. The child does not feel sick, but medical diagnosis is sought because of the appearance of the rash. The spread of this infection is unknown, and humans are the only known host. Outbreaks are usually associated with students in elementary or junior high schools and occur most often in the spring.

Medical diagnosis usually is based on the clinical presentation. Laboratory diagnosis is done by B19 IgM antibody assay. No control measures have been identified.

Nursing assessment is based on the current history and physical findings. The nurse should assess and document the nature and location of the rash and ascertain if there are complaints of pain in any joints.

Nursing diagnoses include:

- Altered Body Image related to the appearance of the rash
- Social isolation related to the communicable stage of the disease

Nursing care planning and interventions are directed toward reassuring the child and family that this is a mild transient disease and that the child should not be allowed to go to school or socialize during the contagious period. Evaluation is related to stemming the spread of the disease during localized epidemics. Those affected may see a reappearance of the rash after sun exposure, friction, or temperature change, and they should be evaluated after any reappearance of the rash.

## Kawasaki Disease

*Kawasaki disease* (formerly mucocutaneous lymph node syndrome) occurs primarily in children under 5 years of age, with a peak incidence between 6 months and 2 years. It is an acute systemic vasculitis with no known cause (McEnhill & Vitale, 1989). Children of Asian ancestry are at greatest risk, followed by black children (Wood, Fosarelli, Hudak, Lake, & Modlen, 1989). The etiology, incubation period, contagion period, and mode of transmission have not been established.

Medical diagnosis is made by the clinical criteria (Table 19-8). For the diagnosis to be made, children must have a fever and four of the five features listed in the table. There are three stages of the disease: febrile (up to 14 days), subacute (15 to 25 days), and convalescent (26 to 60 days). The first symptom is a high fever with intermittent spiking; this must be present for 5 days for Kawasaki disease to be considered. The other signs in Table 19-8 then appear, including irritability and loss of appetite. The rash is erythematous and is found on the face and trunk; it may have irregular plaques (flat, often raised patches on the skin). It is never vesicular, does not crust, and is not bulbous. Arthritis-like symptoms occur in the subacute phase and last for several weeks. Myocarditis and coronary aneurysms are major complications. Left ventricular dysfunction is commonly found, and these children are also at risk for coronary thrombosis because of sluggish blood flow (McEnhill & Vitale, 1989). Coronary artery aneurysms occur in approximately 20% of all cases (Wood et al., 1989).

In the convalescent stage, children become less irritable and their appetites improve. The possibility of coronary aneurysms persists, and one third of affected children with coronary artery aneurysms still have them 1 year later.

Usually aspirin therapy is recommended. It is commonly given in a high dose initially for its anti-inflamma-

*Table 19–8. Principal Diagnostic Criteria for Kawasaki Disease (Mucocutaneous Lymph Node Syndrome)*

Fever, persisting for more than 5 days

Conjunctival infection

Changes in the mouth consisting of:
  Erythema, fissuring and crusting of the lips
  Diffuse oropharyngeal erythema
  Strawberry tongue

Changes in the peripheral extremities consisting of:
  Induration of hands and feet
  Erythema of palms and soles
  Desquamation of finger and toetips approximately 2 weeks after onset
  Transverse grooves across fingernails 2 to 3 months after onset

Erythematous rash

Enlarged lymph node mass measuring more than 1.5 cm in diameter

(From Melish, M. (1980). Kawasaki syndrome (mucocutaneous lymph node syndrome). *Pediatrics Review, 2*(4), 107–114)

tory effect, then in low doses for its antiplatelet aggregation action. Low to moderate doses of aspirin seem to reduce the risk of coronary artery thrombosis. If no coronary artery abnormalities develop, low-dose aspirin therapy should be continued until the sedimentation rate returns to normal (about 2 months). High doses of gamma globulin are currently given with aspirin; this combination has been found to reduce the incidence of aneurysms. This therapy is given for 4 days. If coronary artery abnormalities develop, salicylate therapy is continued indefinitely. Steroids are not used because they may be associated with increased aneurysm formation. Echocardiography to detect aneurysms is recommended at the third and fourth weeks. Close monitoring of these patients is necessary for months to years following the acute phase.

Nursing assessment includes physical examination and assessment of stress and anxiety levels for parents and child. Nursing assessment of all systems should be done every 8 hours to prevent complications (e.g., cardiac). The assessment should include observation of the conjunctiva, mucosa, the rash, hydration, and peripheral circulation, as well as for edema. Accurate intake and output, weight, and levels of consciousness must be recorded. Intravenous administration must be carefully monitored for clotting in the intravenous cannula and for possible gamma globulin infiltration. The site should be observed for edema, and pain should be evaluated. Signs of congestive heart failure, such as decreased urinary output, increased respiratory rate and effort, and tachycardia with a gallop rhythm, should be assessed. Cardiac monitoring should be used (1) for children under 1 year of age, (2) if a single large infusion of gamma globulin is given, or (3) if the child shows symptoms of cardiac problems (McEnhill & Vitale, 1989).

Nursing diagnoses include:

- High risk for complication of myocarditis and coronary aneurysms
- Decreased cardiac output related to left ventricular involvement
- Hyperthermia related to the infectious process
- Alteration in nutrition related to sensitive oral mucous membranes
- Pain related to stiff joints, eye irritation, hyperthermia
- High risk for alteration in bowel elimination related to diarrhea
- High risk for altered skin integrity related to dehydration/immobility
- Alteration in family processes related to an ill child
- Anxiety related to possible coronary artery aneurysms

Nursing care is directed toward providing comfort measures to reduce the fever, preventing complications, ensuring adequate nutrition, promoting skin integrity, and decreasing irritability. The child may wear sunglasses, or the room may be darkened to relieve eye irritation. Cool sponge baths can be given to assist in reducing the fever and for comfort. Sheepskin can be used on the bed to promote skin integrity. Intravenous fluids may be ordered to promote hydration. Children should be allowed to choose food and fluids that they like. Intake and output records should be carefully kept. Oral hygiene might include the use of a soft toothbrush or gentle swabbing of the inside of the mouth with mouthwash or dilute hydrogen peroxide (1 part hydrogen peroxide to 4 parts of saline).

The child, the parents, and the family will experience stress and anxiety. Clear explanations of the disease process, treatment, and discharge planning must be given. Parents need to be included in the care plan. Instruction regarding the need for follow-up medical supervision and instructions on signs of cardiac complications should be included. Children with coronary artery involvement are followed by echocardiograms at intervals determined by the extent of the involvement. The medication regimen to be followed should be explained, as well as the necessity to follow the physician's orders related to the physical activity allowed. Parents should be instructed about the signs of aspirin toxicity—vomiting, hyperpnea, and fever. They should also be informed that, in general, measles, mumps, and rubella vaccines should not be given within 3 months of the time that the child received gamma globulin because the desired immune response may be inhibited. Data suggest that the immune globulins do not significantly affect the responses of infants to DPT (American Academy of Pediatrics, 1988). Parents should be advised to check with their physician before any immunizations are given. Without causing too much alarm, parents should be instructed in cardiopulmonary resuscitation (CPR) and should be alerted to call 911 in an emergency.

Evaluation of nursing measures may be immediate, such as increasing the fluid intake, or long-term, as in parent education.

## Lyme Disease

| | |
|---|---|
| Incubation period | 3–32 days |
| Contagion period | None |
| Causative agent | *Borrelia burgdorferi* (spirochete) |
| Mode of transmission | Tick bite; rarely, by blood transfusion |

*Lyme disease* (LD or erythema chronicum migrans) is a tick-borne spirochetal infection. The national surveillance of the disease began in 1982. Lyme disease accounted for 50% of all vector-borne infections from 1983–1987 (Centers for Disease Control, 1989). Lyme disease is transmitted by bites from ticks and is, therefore, more prevalent in the summer months. It occurs most frequently in the Northeast, the Midwest, and the West.

Deer ticks are very small (about the size of a pin head) and have a life cycle of about two years. Tick eggs are deposited in the spring and are not infected when they hatch. Young ticks attach themselves to small animals, where they may become infected with spirochetes when sucking the animal's blood. White-footed mice appear to be the infective agent. The ticks are dormant in the winter, but the larvae become nymphs in the spring. In the second fall, the nymphs mature into adults and mate, and the female deposits her eggs the following spring (Kamper, 1991), laying 2000 to 3000 eggs in clusters. Adult ticks prefer large animals as hosts; since deer are commonly found in these areas they often become the hosts. Wherever female deer ticks appear, Lyme disease is found. The ticks are commonly found in humid brush, and approximately 70% of all individuals who acquire Lyme disease are infected in their own back yards.

After the tick infects the host, *B. burgdorferi,* the infecting agent, makes its way to the bloodstream and moves throughout the body. In stage I, the rash is initially a red macule or papule; however, the lesion expands and becomes annular with partial clearing. The lesion may reach 70 cm in diameter; multiple lesions may also occur (Friedman, 1987). Stage II occurs in the untreated patient weeks or months later. The central nervous system may be involved, and symptoms of meningitis may appear. Other manifestations may include carditis and neuropathies. Stage III occurs months to years after the initial infection, when arthritis or late neurological disease occurs. There have been reports of bone and joint destruction.

The medical diagnosis is made by the clinical manifestations: the lesion(s), fever, neck stiffness, malaise, fatigue, headache, arthralgias, and lymphadenopathy. The lesions must be over 5 cm in diameter, round or oval, and must increase in size over a period of time. The lesions have ill-defined borders and may be warm to the touch. Multiple lesions may occur if the spirochete disseminates in the body.

Weeks after the appearance of the lesion, cardiac, arthritic, or neurological sequelae may appear. Cardiac complications might include myocarditis and conduction defects. Arthritis usually involves the large joints. Neurological complications include Bell's palsy, peripheral neuritis, and meningoencephalitis (Friedman, 1987). Thirty to forty percent of those who have have the infection have seventh nerve involvement.

Tetracycline is prescribed for children over 9 years of age who have the lesion. Children under 9 years receive penicillin V. Penicillin-sensitive children receive erythromycin. The antimicrobial therapy is prescribed for 10–20 days. It is believed that early treatment decreases the potential for later complications (American Academy of Pediatrics, 1988). Despite the apparent effectiveness of antibiotic therapy, small numbers of spirochetes remain and produce a continued immune response.

The medical diagnosis of Lyme disease can be difficult to establish in some cases. The general symptoms in Stage I are nonspecific, and diagnosis is difficult if the rash is not present. There is no reliable test for Lyme disease, especially in the early stages. In addition, many people are not aware that they have been bitten by a tick. The detection of antibodies to the *B. burgdorferi* spirochete is determined by fluorescence microscopy or colorimetry. The indirect immunofluorescent antibody (IFA) and enzyme-linked immunosorbent assays (ELISA) are currently used (Kamper, 1991). All cases should be reported to the Centers for Disease Control.

Nursing assessment includes an accurate history (to determine the possibility of exposure to ticks), the review of systems to elicit all symptoms, and physical examination.

Nursing diagnoses include:

- High risk for infection related to the tick bite
- Altered skin integrity related to the lesion(s)
- Noncompliance related to the treatment regimen and follow-up care
- Fatigue related to the disease
- High risk for impaired physical mobility related to arthralgia
- Decreased cardiac output related to cardiac involvement

Nursing care involves supportive care for the presenting symptoms; the administration of medications; and teaching parents and the child about the disease, the treatment modalities, and the need for follow-up. A major public health effort must address public awareness of the disease. Areas known to have ticks should be avoided. Protective clothing must be worn, e.g., pant legs must be placed inside socks when walking in suspect areas such as woods. Insect repellants are not generally useful and, if overused, can cause seizures; if they are used, they should be applied to clothing. Ticks attached to the skin should be removed as quickly as possible with forceps after application of alcohol. Care must be used not to crush the tick, since incomplete removal can lead to formation of a nodule that may need to be surgically incised (Chow, Durand, Feldman, & Mills, 1984). If the tick is removed within 24 hours of attachment, the disease will not be transmitted.

## *Rubeola (Measles)*

| | |
|---|---|
| Incubation period | 10–12 days |
| Contagion period | From 4 days before to 4 days after the rash |
| Causative agent | Measles virus |

| Mode of transmission | Airborne droplet, spread of oropharyngeal secretions (direct contact) |

*Rubeola (measles)* is an acute epidemic disease caused by a relatively large virus (see Color Plate 19-1). Worldwide, it is the most common vaccine-preventable cause of death in children. In 1989, the Expanded Programme on Immunization (EPI) of the World Health Organization (WHO) estimated that about a million and a half children died from measles and its complications each year (Markowitz & Orenstein, 1990). Measles occurs most frequently in temperate climates in the winter and spring months.

The prodromal symptoms include fever (103°–105°F [39.4°–40.6°C]) and malaise followed by cough, coryza, and conjunctivitis. Small bluish-white spots on a red background, called *Koplik's spots* (see Color Plate 19-2), are observed on the buccal mucosa (an *enanthem*) from 2 days before to 2 days after the appearance of the rash. The rash appears 2 to 4 days after the prodromal symptoms. The rash is maculopapular (confluent on the face) and spreads from the face to the trunk and then to the extremities. The rash lasts 5 to 7 days and fades in the order of the appearance on the body. Complications include otitis media and pneumonia, which is the most frequent cause of death from this disease.

Medical diagnosis is usually made on the basis of presenting symptoms and the physical examination, which verifies the rash and Koplik's spots. Measles can be diagnosed by viral isolation in tissue culture, but this technique is not generally available. The presence of specific IgM antibody can be detected in serum. IgM antibody is not detectable, however, for the first day or two after the onset of the rash, and cannot usually be detected 60 days after rash occurs.

The usual immunization schedule for measles is given in Table 19-5. If the measles vaccine is given within 72 hours after exposure, it will be effective. The measles vaccine is a live, attenuated vaccine. It is available alone (monovalent), but more often it is given in combination as the *measles-mumps-rubella (MMR)* vaccine. Side effects are usually mild and include fever and rash between the 5th and 12th days after vaccination. The rash lasts 1 to 2 days. Children with a history of anaphylactic reactions after egg ingestion should be vaccinated only with extreme caution. Children who have had anaphylactic reactions to neomycin should not be vaccinated. If a child has received whole blood, immune globulin, or other antibody-containing blood products, vaccination should be deferred for 3 months because of the possible passive immunity states offered by these measures.

Nursing assessment involves assessment by history and physical examination. High fever associated with cold symptoms are signs that usually are documented. If the rash is present, its character and distribution should be noted and the buccal mucosa should be checked for Koplik's spots.

Nursing diagnoses include:

- Altered nutrition: Less than body requirements related to general malaise
- High risk for hyperthermia related to the infectious process
- Ineffective airway clearance related to secretions
- Altered skin integrity related to the rash
- Impaired social interaction related to the isolation period

Nursing care includes providing for adequate fluid and food intake, instructing parents about respiratory isolation requirements, liquefying secretions by encouraging fluid intake and humidity control, and observing for complications such as pneumonia. Patients are contagious from 1 to 2 days before the onset of symptoms and up to 4 days after the appearance of the rash (American Academy of Pediatrics, 1988). Parents and the child need to be taught about the disease and prevention measures. Evaluations should establish that there was minimal spread of the disease and that preventive immunization measures are understood.

## Rocky Mountain Spotted Fever

| Incubation period | Usually 1 week, range of 1–14 days |
| Contagion period | None |
| Causative agent | *Rickettsia rickettsii* |
| Mode of transmission | Transmitted by the bite of ticks |

*Rocky Mountain spotted fever* is widespread in the United States, with most cases occurring in the South Atlantic, Southeastern, and South Central states. It is caused by *Rickettsia rickettsii*, which is found in many hosts, including ground squirrels, chipmunks, weasels, and wood rats. Transmission from animal to animal, and from animals to humans, is usually achieved through the wood tick. Dogs are frequent hosts for ticks and, thus, are responsible for most of the transmission to humans. The disease occurs most often in the summer (American Academy of Pediatrics, 1988).

Rocky Mountain spotted fever is a systemic febrile illness with a characteristic rash that occurs before the sixth day following a tick bite. The rash is initially erythematous and macular; later it becomes maculopapular and may become petechial. The palms and soles of the feet are involved. The rash first appears on the wrists and ankles and quickly spreads to the trunk (see Color Plate 19-3). Before the rash appears the child may complain of nonspecific symptoms such as headache, nausea and vomiting, fever, or myalgia (diffuse muscle pain). Severe cases may include the following: myocarditis; pneumonitis; central nervous system symptoms; pulmonary, renal, or gastrointestinal system symptoms; splenomegaly; or peripheral vascular collapse. Medical diagnosis is made on the basis of the rash. Chloramphenicol or a tetracycline is then prescribed for 5 to 7 days. Tetracycline is not given to children under 9 years of age (American Academy of Pediatrics, 1988).

Nursing assessment includes careful recording and reporting of the characteristics of the rash and the history of the illness. Careful documentation of the type of rash and its progression is important. A detailed review of systems should be done to elicit other symptoms. It should be ascertained if the child has a dog or has been in contact with a dog in the week prior to the appearance of the rash since dogs frequently carry ticks.

Nursing diagnoses include:

- Impaired skin integrity related to the rash
- Fatigue related to headache, nausea, and vomiting
- Pain related to headache or myalgia
- Anxiety related to parental and child concerns

Nursing interventions include administration of medications, teaching the child and parents about the disease, and teaching about clothing to be worn in the woods—e.g., pants tucked into socks and long-sleeved shirts—to prevent future episodes. Evaluation includes the successful resolution of the illness and incorporation of preventive techniques by the child and family.

## Roseola (Exanthem Subitum, Sixth Disease)

| | |
|---|---|
| Incubation period | 5–15 days |
| Contagion period | Unknown |
| Causative agent | Herpesvirus 6 |
| Mode of transmission | Unknown |

*Roseola* is a common, acute, febrile illness of young children usually seen between 6 months and 2 years of age, but it can be found in children up to 4 years of age. The child has a high fever (to 105°F [40.6°C]) for 2 to 5 days and does not appear to be seriously ill but may exhibit irritability. Sometimes "droopy" eyelids (periorbital edema) are noted on the days when the fever is present. Periorbital edema is also seen with other conditions such as scarlet fever and sinusitis. About the time that the temperature returns to normal, a faint, sparse pink macular rash is noted (see Color Plate 19-4). Complications include febrile convulsions and, occasionally, encephalitis and thrombocytopenia. Febrile seizures are related to a familial history or a

sudden temperature elevation. The period of communicability is unknown, and cases occur sporadically. In temperate climates, roseola is most often seen in the spring and summer. Medical diagnosis is made on the clinical evidence.

Nursing assessment includes identification of the rash and obtaining a history that includes a high fever preceding the rash. The history confirms that the rash appeared after the temperature returned to normal.

Nursing diagnoses include:

- Hyperthermia related to the infectious process
- Altered skin integrity related to the rash
- Fatigue related to the disease process

Nursing care is supportive, and includes measures to decrease the temperature (administration of acetaminophen, cool water sponging, and encouraging fluid intake), and encouraging rest periods to decrease irritability.

There is no immunization available against roseola. Evaluation of nursing care includes documentation of an uneventful recovery period.

## Rubella (German Measles)

| | |
|---|---|
| Incubation period | 2–3 weeks |
| Contagion period | From 1 week before to 1 week after the rash |
| Causative agent | Rubella virus |
| Mode of transmission | Direct or indirect contact with droplets, blood, secretions, urine, or stools |

There are two types of *rubella*: congenital rubella and postnatal rubella. The cause of rubella is an RNA virus. Humans are the sole source of infection. Rubella is shown in Color Plate 19-5.

*Congenital rubella* is a serious disease. The most common sequelae are ophthalmological (cataracts, glaucoma, microphthalmia, and salt and pepper retinopathy), cardiac (patent ductus arteriosus, pulmonary artery stenosis, and myocarditis), auditory (sensorineural deafness), neurological (mental retardation, microcephaly, and meningoencephalitis), and liver involvement (hepatosplenomegaly and cholestasis). Infants with congenital rubella are considered contagious until they are 1 year old unless nasopharyngeal and urine cultures are negative. Parents should be aware of the potential danger of exposing pregnant women to the infected child. Pregnant women should have an antibody test performed to determine immunity.

A presumptive medical diagnosis is made if there is a maternal history of exposure to rubella during pregnancy or if maternal seroconversion occurred during pregnancy. The rubella virus can be isolated from the nose. Throat swabs, blood, urine, and cerebrospinal fluid also may verify the presence of the virus. There is no current therapy for rubella. Prevention is the only way to decrease the incidence of congenital rubella.

*Postnatal rubella* is transmitted through direct or droplet contact from nasopharyngeal secretions. It usually occurs in late winter and early spring. It is characterized by an erythematous maculopapular discrete rash, postauricular and suboccipital lymphadenopathy, and a slight fever (American Academy of Pediatrics, 1988). Children should be excluded from school for 7 days after the rash appears.

The rubella vaccine immunization schedule is found in Table 19-5. Immunization should be performed unless documented evidence of rubella immunization or serologic evidence of naturally acquired immunity is provided.

Nursing assessment of postnatal rubella is based on the physical findings of slight fever, mild rhinitis, a diffuse macular rash lasting for three days, occipital and post-auricular node enlargement, and occasionally headaches, conjunctivitis, and arthralgia.

Nursing diagnoses include:

- High risk for altered body temperature related to the disease process
- Altered skin integrity related to the rash
- Pain related to headaches

Nursing care is supportive; acetaminophen can be administered for discomfort and fever. Adequate hydration and nutrition should be maintained. Isolation must be maintained during the communicable period, and caution should be exercised to avoid contact with pregnant women. Evaluation involves containing the spread of infection and preventing complications.

## Scarlet Fever (Scarlatina)

| | |
|---|---|
| Incubation period | 2–5 days |
| Contagion period | 10–20 days |
| Causative agent | Group A streptococci |
| Mode of transmission | Direct contact with an infected person or carrier droplet spread by oral–nasal secretions |

*Scarlet fever* is an acute disease that can occur more than once. Typical symptoms include fever, headache, abdominal pain, vomiting, malaise, irritability, and a sore throat. The rash is characterized by very small, frequently confluent, fine red papules that occur on the trunk and extremities. The rash is increasingly red in the folds of the skin (inguinal or antecubital creases). The face appears flushed with circumoral pallor. The tongue is rough and red, giving it the appearance of a "strawberry tongue" (see Color Plate 19-6). Sometimes the tongue has a white coat-

ing. The skin feels rough to the touch. After 7 to 10 days desquamation (peeling) of the superficial layers of the skin on the hands and feet occurs (see Color Plate 19-7).

The infection is confirmed by throat culture. Penicillin V is the preferred medication for treatment. Erythromycin can be used for penicillin-sensitive children. Intramuscular benzathine penicillin can also be used. Penicillin prevents rheumatic fever, which is a possible complication, as are glomerulonephritis and pneumonia. Children should not return to school until at least 24 hours after beginning antimicrobial therapy and until they are afebrile (American Academy of Pediatrics, 1988).

Nursing assessment includes observation of the rash and a history of other symptoms. The distribution of the rash and subsequent peeling of the hands and feet is characteristic. The tongue should be examined for a strawberry-like appearance. The history will reveal that the child has been ill and usually has had a sore throat prior to the appearance of the rash.

Nursing diagnoses include:

- Hyperthermia related to the infectious process
- Altered nutrition: Less than body requirements related to impaired swallowing
- Impaired skin integrity related to the rash
- High risk for altered cardiac function
- Alteration in fluid and electrolyte balance related to vomiting or refusal to eat or drink

Nursing care interventions include keeping the child in bed during the febrile period, encouraging fluid and soft food intake, maintaining isolation during the communicable stage, and administering antibiotics and acetaminophen as prescribed. Since most children are not hospitalized, parents, the child, and family members must understand the illness, its communicability, treatment, and possible complications. Evaluation includes the prevention of complications and the control of the spread of the disease.

## Varicella (Chickenpox)

| | |
|---|---|
| Incubation period | 14–16 days |
| Contagion period | 5 days after the rash and for the duration of the vesicular eruptions |
| Causative agent | Varicella zoster virus (VZV) |
| Mode of transmission | Direct contact with droplets or indirect contact with skin lesions, discharges, or nasal–pharyngeal secretions |

The primary infection by the varicella-zoster virus (VZV), a herpes virus, results in *chickenpox*. The virus remains latent after the primary infection and, when reactivated, results in zoster or shingles, a secondary infection.

Varicella is a highly contagious disease. Children with

uncomplicated chickenpox can return to school on the sixth day after the onset of the rash (American Academy of Pediatrics, 1988).

Symptoms include a pruritic (itchy) vesicular rash, mild fever, malaise, headache, and fatigue. The rash progresses from an erythematous rash to a macular rash, then a papular, and finally a vesicular rash. Eventually the vesicles scab and crust. The rash can be at different stages at different places on the body, and generally begins on the head and spreads to the rest of the body (see Color Plate 19-8). Most cases occur in children between 5 and 10 years of age, most often in the winter and early spring. Complications are rare but may include secondary bacterial skin infections, impetigo, erysipelas, cellulitis, or conjunctivitis. Immunosuppressed children may develop encephalitis, pneumonia, or disseminated varicella (American Academy of Pediatrics, 1988).

Medical diagnosis is made by assessing the rash. Infection can be confirmed by staining smears with VZV-specific antibody. If necessary, viral cultures of pustular lesions can be done.

Children with varicella should not receive salicylates because of the association between salicylates given for chickenpox and Reye's syndrome. Acetaminophen should be used for fever and discomfort. Lotions, such as calamine, can be used to relieve pruritus. Oral antihistamines, such as Benadryl, should be used for severe itching.

Nursing assessment includes observation of the rash and the identification of accompanying symptoms.

Nursing diagnoses include:

- High risk for infection related to pruritic rash
- Altered nutrition: Less than body requirements related to general malaise
- Altered skin integrity related to the rash
- Fatigue related to general malaise

Nursing care includes measures to relieve itching; maintaining isolation during the communicable stage; encouraging fluid intake for hydration; and preventing secondary skin infection by keeping fingernails cut, by keeping the skin clean and dry, and by keeping bedclothes and linen clean and dry. Children should be provided with activities to keep them occupied and distracted from scratching. Evaluation includes a diminished spread of the disease and no complications. A vaccine is expected to be approved for use in the next few years.

## Infectious Diseases Without Rashes

### Diphtheria

| | |
|---|---|
| Incubation period | 2–5 days |
| Contagion period | Usually 2 weeks or less, but may persist for months with antibiotic treatment less than 4 days |
| Causative agent | *Corynebacterium diphtheria* |
| Mode of transmission | Discharges from nose, throat, skin, eye, and lesions of infected persons |

*Diphtheria* is an infectious disease characterized by a gray coating on any mucous membrane. Although it is rare today, diphtheria still occurs in non-immunized populations. Humans are the only known source of the disease. Unimmunized, immunized, and partially immunized persons may contract the disease. The incidence is greater in the fall and winter. Cultures of specimens from the nose, throat, or lesions confirm the medical diagnosis. Immunization for diphtheria (DPT) is required before admission to schools in this country. However, some parents are fearful of possible side effects of the immunization and, therefore, delay having their children immunized until they begin school. Children with diphtheria usually have a low-grade fever and gradual symptoms for 1 to 2 days, including nasopharyngitis (membranous) or obstructive laryngotracheitis. Strict isolation must be maintained for pharyngeal diphtheria. The most serious complications include neuritis and myocarditis, which may result in congestive heart failure. Universal diphtheria toxoid immunization is the effective control mechanism (see Table 19-5).

Nursing assessment includes the physical examination finding of a gray membrane (exudate) on the tonsils and uvula (see Color Plate 19-9). The membrane bleeds easily. The history may be negative for immunization against diphtheria, or there may be a history of exposure to unimmunized persons, or a history of crowded living conditions.

Nursing diagnoses include:

- Altered nutrition: Less than body requirements related to difficulty in swallowing
- Ineffective airway clearance related to palatal paralysis
- Altered oral mucous membrane related to membranous covering of tonsils, pharynx, soft palate, or uvula
- High risk for decreased cardiac output related to development of congestive heart failure
- Impaired social interaction related to required isolation
- Altered parenting related to required isolation
- Fatigue related to the systemic disease process
- Pain related to throat discomfort

Nursing interventions include maintaining strict isolation during the period of communicability, maintaining fluid and electrolyte balance and nutritional status, administering antibiotics as ordered, encouraging bed rest, and providing appropriate sedatives during the convalescent period. Evaluation measures include limiting the spread of the disease (isolation for the ill child and immunization for unimmunized contacts) and preventing complications.

## Mumps

| | |
|---|---|
| Incubation period | 16–18 days |
| Contagion period | As long as 7 days prior to parotid swelling and 5 to 9 days after the onset of parotid swelling |
| Causative agent | *Paramyxovirus* |
| Mode of transmission | Direct contact via respiratory route (droplet spread) or indirect contact with respiratory secretions |

Swelling of the salivary glands is the usual sign of *mumps* (see Color Plate 19-10). Parotitis (swelling of the parotid glands) is painful and is accompanied by fever, headache, and vomiting, which may be severe. The infection occurs most often in late winter or early spring. Patients should be isolated until the swelling has subsided. The mumps virus can be isolated in tissue cultures of throat washing, and in urine and spinal fluid. Complications in adolescent males may include orchitis, which is usually unilateral and develops within 2 weeks of the infection. Meningoencephalitis may follow parotitis by 3 to 10 days. Signs and symptoms include fever, nausea, vomiting, headache, nuchal rigidity (involuntary neck stiffness), Brodzinski's sign, and Kernig's sign.

Nursing assessment includes findings on physical examination of enlarged, tender, parotid glands, general malaise (with headache and fever), and a history of nonimmunization or exposure to mumps.

Nursing diagnoses include:

- Altered nutrition: Less than body requirements related to difficulty in chewing and inability to tolerate spicy foods
- Impaired social interaction related to required isolation
- High risk for altered parenting related to isolation
- Fatigue related to general malaise
- Pain related to enlarged parotid glands
- Anxiety in male adolescents related to the potential for infection of the testes

Nursing care includes strict respiratory isolation during the communicable period; immunization of unprotected, exposed contacts (see Table 19-5); provision of adequate rest until the swelling subsides; attention to nutrition and fluid and electrolyte balance by providing fluids and a soft bland diet; administration of mouth care several times a day; and administration of acetaminophen to relieve pain. When orchitis occurs, treatment includes bed rest and support of the testicles. Corticosteroids may be prescribed to relieve the pain. Parents should be taught the signs and symptoms of complications so that they can seek medical treatment should complications arise. Evaluation consists of containment of the disease, maximizing the patient's comfort, and minimizing complications.

## Pertussis (Whooping Cough)

| | |
|---|---|
| Incubation period | 7–10 days |
| Contagion period | 4 weeks |
| Causative agent | *Bordetella pertussis* |
| Mode of transmission | Droplet exposure—direct contact; exposure to contaminated articles—indirect contact |

*Pertussis* is a highly contagious infection, but widespread pertussis vaccination has resulted in low morbidity and mortality rates. Pertussis occurs most commonly in infants under 6 months of age because they have not yet completed their immunization regimen.

There are two stages of the disease: the catarrhal stage and the paroxysmal stage. The *catarrhal stage* occurs at the beginning of the illness, and consists of mild upper respiratory tract symptoms with a cough. The cough gets worse rather than improving during the second week. The *paroxysmal stage* is evidenced by severe paroxysms of cough with an inspiratory whoop. The paroxysms can occur from 4 to 40 or more times per day and persist from 4 to 6 weeks. Vomiting follows. There is little or no fever. The illness lasts from 6 to 10 weeks. Young infants require hospitalization, and respiratory isolation should be initiated for 5 days after the introduction of erythromycin therapy (American Academy of Pediatrics, 1988). The medical diagnosis of pertussis can be verified by the culture of nasopharyngeal secretions. Complications include pneumonia, hemorrhages (e.g., epistaxis), hernia, trauma to the tongue, and rectal prolapse. Pertussis immunoglobulin is recommended for children under 2 years of age or for children with severe cases. Antibiotic therapy is not effective in lessening the severity of the disease but can eliminate the organism and the spread of the disease (Chow et al., 1984).

Nursing assessment includes a history of exposure or non-immunization and a finding of the typical cough on examination. The cough is distinctive because of the paroxysmal nature and the inspiratory whoop. Assessment should also include ascertaining the existence of cyanosis, tachycardia, and hydration.

Nursing diagnoses include:

- Altered nutrition: Less than body requirements related to paroxysmal coughing
- Ineffective breathing pattern related to paroxysmal coughing
- Impaired social interaction related to isolation

- Fatigue related to coughing
- Sleep pattern disturbance related to coughing
- Anxiety related to inability to control coughing episodes

Nursing interventions include maintaining strict respiratory isolation, encouraging bed rest and a quiet environment, maintaining adequate fluid and nutritional intake, and administering antibiotics for bacterial infections and sedation to relieve coughing paroxysms. Evaluation includes minimizing the child's discomfort, ensuring a non-eventful recovery, and stemming the spread of the infection.

## Poliomyelitis

| | |
|---|---|
| Incubation period | 7–14 days for paralytic polio |
| Contagion period | Greatest shortly before and after the onset of clinical illness. Virus persists for about 1 week after onset of the illness and is excreted in the feces for several weeks or months |
| Causative agent | Poliovirus, types 1, 2, or 3 |
| Mode of transmission | Fecal–oral or possibly oral–oral routes |

Poliomyelitis is caused by three types of enteroviruses: 1, 2, and 3. Most poliovirus infections are asymptomatic. Chronic disease manifestations, in order of frequency, are *abortive poliomyelitis* (nonspecific febrile illness), *nonparalytic poliomyelitis* (aseptic meningitis without paralysis), and *paralytic poliomyelitis* (paralytic disease involving the lower motor neurons). Paralytic poliomyelitis is characterized by destruction of the anterior horn cells of the spinal cord, which results in flaccid paralysis (American Academy of Pediatrics, 1988). Poliomyelitis is rare in the United States today because of widespread immunization, but it is still prevalent in many underdeveloped countries.

Symptoms may include fever, headaches, diarrhea, nausea and vomiting, stiff neck, and pain and tenderness in the lower extremities that progresses to paralysis. The respiratory muscles can be involved, which necessitates mechanical ventilation.

Medical diagnosis is confirmed by culture of specimens from the feces or throat. Because wild strains of poliomyelitis can occur, the Centers for Disease Control (CDC) must establish vaccine strains from wild strains of the disease.

Nursing assessment includes any documentation of the clinical symptoms and a history of non-immunization, travel to geographic areas where the polio virus is endemic, a history of recent polio immunization, or contact with others diagnosed with polio. Physical findings include tenderness or pain in the lower extremities that progresses to paralysis. Fever and associated malaise can be documented when reviewing systems.

Nursing diagnoses include:

- Altered nutrition: Less than body requirements related to nausea and vomiting and/or fatigue
- High risk for impaired skin integrity related to immobility
- Impaired social interaction related to strict isolation with enteric precautions
- High risk for ineffective breathing pattern related to involvement of respiratory muscles
- Impaired physical mobility related to flaccid paralysis of muscles
- Fatigue related to the systemic illness
- Body image disturbance related to paralysis
- Anxiety related to long-term outcomes of the illness

Nursing interventions include maintaining strict isolation with enteric precautions, maintaining strict bed rest during the febrile illness, frequent turning and positioning, assisted ventilation, range-of-motion exercises, and providing opportunities to discuss fears and anxieties. Evaluation includes the successful immunization of contacts, minimal spread of the disease, decreasing complications, and the resumption of normal activities to the greatest extent possible.

## Tetanus (Lockjaw)

| | |
|---|---|
| Incubation period | 3 days to 3 weeks |
| Contagion period | None |
| Causative agent | *Clostridium tetani* (a spore-forming anaerobic gram-positive bacillus) |
| Mode of transmission | Not transmitted person to person; inhabits soil and animal and human intestines; transmitted by wound contamination |

The toxin produced by *Clostridium tetani* has an affinity for the nervous system. The onset of tetanus is gradual (1 to 7 days) and progresses to severe, generalized muscle spasms. Stiffness of the jaw is often the first symptom. Medical diagnosis is made by excluding other possibilities. Antitoxins are given to neutralize the toxin, and antibiotics are given for the wound infection. Sedatives or muscle relaxants are prescribed to prevent convulsions and to reduce muscle contractions. A tetanus toxoid booster is not required if a clean minor wound has occurred and tetanus toxoid has been received within 10 years. For more serious wounds (e.g., wounds contaminated with dirt or feces), a dose of tetanus toxoid should be given as soon as possible after the injury (American Academy of Pediatrics, 1988). Individuals with serious wounds who have incomplete tetanus immunization should receive tetanus immune globulin, human (TIG). Sedatives or muscle relaxants should be given as ordered and should relieve muscle spasms. Neonatal tetanus, which is usually seen in underdeveloped countries, is caused by contamination of the umbilical stump.

Nursing assessment includes identifying the site of the wound, ascertaining how the wound occurred, and whether it is a clean wound. Treatment should be instituted immediately. All wounds should be properly cleaned and debrided, if necessary. All dead tissue and foreign material should be removed. Documentation of the current status of immunization is important.

Nursing diagnoses include:

- High risk for injury related to possible seizures
- High risk for ineffective breathing pattern related to muscle stiffness of the jaw
- Altered tissue integrity related to the wound
- Activity intolerance related to neurological involvement
- Anxiety related to possible outcomes of the infection

Nursing interventions include cleansing the wound; administering medications; preventing overstimulation by controlling environmental stimuli, such as keeping the room quiet and darkened; observing for convulsions; and maintaining a patent airway. Evaluation includes the noneventful, uncomplicated recovery.

## Hepatitis Infections

### Hepatitis A

| | |
|---|---|
| Incubation period | 1–2 months |
| Contagion period | 1–3 weeks, 2 weeks preceding jaundice |
| Causative agent | Hepatitis A virus (HAV) |
| Mode of transmission | Fecal–oral route |

*Hepatitis A* (HAV) is an acute, febrile illness characterized by jaundice, anorexia, nausea, malaise, abdominal pain, headache, and fever. Preschool children and infants are asymptomatic or have mild cases without jaundice (American Academy of Pediatrics, 1988). The liver may be tender (right upper quadrant of the abdomen), the urine may be dark, and stools may be clay colored. Hepatitis A is endemic in many developing countries. It can be a major health problem in day care centers (American Academy of

Pediatrics, 1988). Enteric precautions must be taken to prevent spreading the disease for 1 week after the onset of jaundice. All household contacts should receive immune globulin (IG) as soon as possible after the diagnosis is made. Diagnosis is confirmed by serologic tests for total anti-HAV and IgM anti-HAV antibodies. The presence of IgM anti-HAV antibodies usually indicates recent infection. The presence of IgG anti-HAV antibodies is indicative of past infection (American Academy of Pediatrics, 1988).

Nursing assessment includes obtaining a history of the illness and handwashing habits; physical assessment to ascertain jaundice and abdominal tenderness; and urine and stool observation and laboratory analysis. A history of the family's daily living environment is important: Does the family use well water? Is a septic tank used? Where are these located in relation to each other? Is there a family history of hepatitis A? Have any contacts had the same symptoms?

Nursing diagnoses include:

- Altered nutrition: Less than body requirements related to nausea and anorexia
- Noncompliance related to enteric precautions
- Fatigue related to malaise

Nursing interventions focus on supportive care to relieve the symptoms and to prevent the spread of the infection. Adequate rest and a balanced, high-calorie diet are essential. Fat intake should be restricted, and vitamin supplements are helpful. Proper handwashing techniques should be taught. Evaluation includes attempts to prevent the spread of the infection and recovery of those affected. Public health environmental measures must be instituted and supported, including handwashing requirements for food handlers and appropriate disposal measures for feces.

### Hepatitis B

| | |
|---|---|
| Incubation period | 50–180 days, average of 120 days |
| Contagion period | 10% become chronic carriers |
| Causative agent | Hepatitis B virus |
| Mode of transmission | Saliva, serum, blood, vaginal secretions, breast milk, associated with sexually transmitted diseases |

Many cases of *hepatitis B* are undetected because those affected are asymptomatic. Acute active infection is confirmed by the presence of hepatitis B surface antigen (HBsAg) with or without antibodies. A variety of symptoms occur, including fever, anorexia, nausea and vomiting, diarrhea, fatigue and malaise, abdominal discomfort, and pain. The liver area may be tender to the touch. Because a number of people may be chronic carriers, there is a constant source of infection. Chronic carriers have an increased risk for liver cirrhosis and primary hepatocellular carcinoma. Hepatitis B vaccine is available for active immunizations (see Table 19-5). Regular immune globulin (IG) and hepatitis B immune globulin are available for passive immunization. The diagnosis is established by laboratory tests that indicate an abnormal SGOT and SGPT, and the presence of IgM anti-HBC antibody. Complications include the possibility of developing chronic and acute hepatic failure in severe cases. Chronic infection can lead to cirrhosis.

Nursing assessment documents the symptoms and the possible cause of the infection—for example, a needle prick. It is also important to document if anyone else in the family or any close contacts have had hepatitis B. A tender liver area and elicitation of associated symptoms may be obtained.

Nursing diagnoses include:

- Potential activity intolerance related to fatigue and malaise
- Diarrhea related to the infectious process
- Altered nutrition: Less than body requirements related to nausea and vomiting
- Anxiety related to consequences of the illness

Nursing interventions are primarily supportive care measures to alleviate the symptoms. Blood and body fluid precautions must be maintained as long as the patients are HBsAG positive.

Evaluation of nursing interventions includes the success of patient comfort measures, prevention of further spread of the disease, and patient/family education.

## Non-A, Non-B Hepatitis

| Incubation period | 2–12 weeks |
|---|---|
| Contagion period | Unknown |
| Causative agent | Non-A, non-B hepatitis virus |
| Mode of transmission | Parenteral administration of blood or blood products (transfusion-associated); fecal–oral (enteric) is acquired from contaminated drinking water or person-to-person contact |

Symptoms of *non-A, non-B hepatitis* are usually mild, with an insidious onset of jaundice and malaise. Severe hepatitis can occur. Most of the cases caused by transfusions have recurrent episodes. Although the illness is more prevalent in adults than in children, it can occur in children and may be chronic for several years. The medical diagnosis is made on the exclusion of A and B hepatitis.

Nursing assessment includes documenting symptoms and possible exposures. It should be ascertained whether

the child has received a blood transfusion. The extent of the jaundice should be noted.

Nursing diagnoses include:

- Fatigue related to general malaise
- Altered nutrition: Less than body requirements related to loss of appetite
- Anxiety—parental related to consequences of the disease

Nursing interventions are supportive, and blood/body fluid precautions should be employed. Evaluation includes relief of physical symptoms and anxiety.

## Gastrointestinal Diseases

### Ascariasis (Roundworm Infestations)

| Incubation period | Mature in 8 weeks |
|---|---|
| Contagion period | While ova are excreted |
| Causative agent | *Ascariasis lumbricoides* (roundworm) |
| Mode of transmission | Ingestion of embryonated eggs |

*Ascariasis (roundworm)* is the most common worm infection in the world, occurring in temperate as well as tropical climates. The adult worm can live in the small intestine for up to 2 years. Early symptoms can resemble pneumonitis, whereas heavy infestation may be associated with intestinal obstruction. In underdeveloped countries, ascariasis is associated with malnutrition. Stool examination revealing ova confirms the medical diagnosis.

Nursing assessment includes stool collection and examination, and the observation of ova or worms. Nursing assessment should include taking weight measurements to identify weight loss and obtaining a history of defecation patterns.

Nursing diagnoses include:

- Constipation related to infestation
- Anxiety related to vague symptoms

Nursing interventions include the administration of medications (pyrantel pamoate, one dose) and instruction regarding the sanitary disposal of feces. Handwashing techniques should be taught. Clothes and linens should be washed in very hot or boiling water. Evaluation involves the successful expulsion of the roundworm infestation.

### Enterobiasis (Pinworm Infestations)

| Incubation period | Unknown |
|---|---|
| Contagion period | Presence of eggs |
| Causative agent | *Enterobius vermicularis* |
| Mode of transmission | Ingestion of pinworm eggs |

*Enterobiasis* is an infestation of the nematode (parasite) *Enterobius vermicularis,* commonly known as pinworms. Pinworms can be found in animals and their excrement; after entering humans, they hatch in the duodenum and migrate to the area of the appendix. The female pinworm goes outside the anus, lays thousands of eggs in the perianal area, and then dies. The perianal area becomes very itchy, and if the child scratches the area and does not properly wash the hands, the eggs are reingested. Sometimes girls develop a vaginitis also. The diagnosis is confirmed by placing a strip of transparent tape over the perianal area at night or early in the morning. Microscopic examination discloses the presence of the eggs. One dose of pyrvinium pamoate (Povan), 5 mg/kg of body weight, is the drug of choice. A repeat dose is given after 2 weeks to prevent reinfection. Other family members are also treated with this medication. Parents and the child must be warned that the stools, urine, and vomitus will turn bright red from the medication and that this is not blood.

Nursing assessment includes a finding of thready, white, wiggly strands in the stool and a history of perianal itching. The history should elicit whether other family members have or have had pinworm infestations or if the family has a dog, cat, or sandbox (where children might come in contact with animal feces). Other children in the same family are likely to be infected, especially if they sleep in the same bed.

Nursing diagnoses include:

- High risk for impaired skin integrity related to pruritus
- High risk for infection related to secondary bacterial infections

Nursing interventions include instructing parents regarding the special handling of bed linens and night clothing (e.g., never shake these items, as the eggs can become airborne; never remove clothing over the child's head). Instruct parents regarding keeping the child's fingernails short so that contaminated feces are not harbored under the fingernails if the child scratches; frequent handwashing, especially after touching the perianal region; washing linens and underwear in hot water; and changing the child's underwear each day. Sometimes it is recommended that linens and underwear be boiled. Retreatment may be necessary after 2 weeks to 1 month to eliminate the possibility of eggs that might have hatched after the original treatment. Evaluation should reveal the successful elimination of the pinworm.

## Giardiasis

| | |
|---|---|
| Incubation period | 1–4 weeks |
| Contagion period | Communicable while cysts are being excreted |
| Causative agent | *Giardia lamblia* |
| Mode of transmission | Hand-to-mouth transfer of cysts from feces of infected people or contaminated food or water |

Children in day care centers and children with immunodeficiency disease are very susceptible to giardiasis, a protozoal infection that inflames the intestines. Many times those infected are asymptomatic. Giardiasis can be a debilitating disease characterized by foul-smelling diarrhea or soft stools accompanied by flatulence, abdominal distention, and anorexia. Significant weight loss, failure to thrive, and anemia can result. Stool analysis confirms the infection. Symptomatic infections are treated. Quinacrine hydrochloride is the most effective drug, but young children have difficulty taking quinacrine because of its bitter taste. Furazolidone is less effective but more acceptable to children.

Nursing assessment includes the description of stooling patterns and the identification of other symptoms, such as anorexia and weight loss. It is important to ascertain if the child attends a day care center and if other children in the facility have been affected.

Nursing diagnoses include:

- Diarrhea related to the infectious process
- Fatigue related to the loss of body fluids and electrolytes
- Altered nutrition: Less than body requirements related to diarrhea

Nursing interventions include supportive care, the administration of medications, enteric precautions, exclusion from day care until asymptomatic, advocacy for adequate sanitation measures, and instruction regarding the necessity to avoid drinking from streams. Evaluation assesses the resolution of the disease and the success of preventive measures.

## Shigella

| | |
|---|---|
| Incubation period | 1–7 days |
| Contagion period | Within 4 weeks of the onset |
| Causative agent | *Shigella* gram-negative rods |
| Mode of transmission | Feces of infected humans |

*Shigella* is a bacterial infection that causes acute diarrhea. Most common in children 1 to 4 years of age, it is an important problem for day care centers. Symptoms in mild cases consist of watery or loose stools for several days. In more severe cases, headaches, abrupt onset of fever, systemic toxicity, and possible convulsions may occur; dehydration, abdominal cramps, and mucoid stools may also be present. Crowded living conditions, substandard sanitation, and travel to countries with poor sanitation are among the agents of transmission. Stool cultures should be performed.

Ampicillin and tetracycline (child must be over 9 years of age for tetracycline) are effective antimicrobial agents for shortening the duration of diarrhea and eliminating the organism from the feces. Enteric isolation techniques should be employed until three consecutive stool specimens (24 hours apart) are negative after the cessation of antimicrobial therapy (American Academy of Pediatrics, 1988).

Nursing assessment includes documentation of the physical symptoms and living or day care arrangements. The child should be assessed for signs of dehydration, irritability, and stooling patterns.

Nursing diagnoses include:

- Diarrhea related to the infectious process
- Fatigue related to electrolyte disturbances
- Hyperthermia related to the infectious process
- High risk for fluid and electrolyte imbalance related to anorexia and abdominal cramps

Nursing interventions include enteric precautions, administration of antimicrobial therapy, and establishing fluid and electrolyte balance. Evaluation measures include the success of patient comfort measures and the prevention of the spread of the disease.

## Other Infectious Diseases

### Infectious Mononucleosis

| Incubation period | 30–50 days |
|---|---|
| Contagion period | Indeterminate |
| Causative agent | Epstein-Barr virus (EBV) |
| Mode of transmission | Saliva—direct contact; occasionally by blood transfusions |

*Infectious mononucleosis* is an infectious disease that primarily affects lymphoid tissue and is commonly found in adolescents. It has frequently been called the "kissing disease" because of the mode of transmission. The most common clinical signs are fever; fatigue; exudative pharyngitis; enlarged lymph nodes, especially cervical nodes; malaise; enlarged liver and spleen; maculopapular rash; and periorbital edema (see Color Plate 19-11). The disease symptoms can range from asymptomatic to fatal infections. The central nervous system can be affected and, in rare cases, splenic rupture, thrombocytopenia, hemolytic anemia, or cardiac involvement occur. Acetaminophen is prescribed for general discomfort. Steroids are sometimes used for tonsillar swelling and other lymphadenopathy.

Rest is the primary treatment. Serological tests can confirm the presence of the Epstein-Barr virus (EBV).

Nursing assessment involves ascertaining the physical symptoms by a thorough history, review of systems, and physical examination. Findings of fatigue, sore throat, enlarged lymph nodes, or enlarged liver and spleen in adolescents suggest mononucleosis.

Nursing diagnoses may include:

- Hyperthermia related to the infectious process
- Altered nutrition: Less than body requirements related to loss of appetite
- High risk for secondary infections related to the severity of the primary infection
- Ineffective individual coping related to required convalescent period
- Fatigue related to the disease process
- Self-esteem disturbance related to inability to continue normal activities

Nursing interventions focus on maintaining adequate rest and preventing fatigue; convalescence may take several weeks. Analgesics are given as necessary. Fluids and soft, bland foods are recommended because of the sore throat. Persons with a history of this disease should not donate blood. The prognosis is usually good, and evaluation includes a successful resolution of the disease process.

### Influenza (Grippe, Flu)

| Incubation period | 1–3 days |
|---|---|
| Contagion period | 24 hours before symptoms through approximately 7 days after onset of symptoms |
| Causative agent | 3 types of myxovirus influenzae: type A, type B, type C |
| Mode of transmission | Inhalation of a respiratory droplet from an infected person or by indirect means such as a contaminated glass |

*Type A influenza* is the most lethal form of influenza. It occurs every 2 to 3 years, and a new strain appears every 10 to 15 years. *Type B influenza* causes epidemics and occurs every 4 to 6 years. *Type C influenza* causes sporadic cases. Cultures of nasopharyngeal secretions confirm the diagnosis. The symptoms include fever (101°–104°F [38.5°–40°C]), a sudden onset of chills, malaise, headache, myalgia, a non-productive cough, conjunctivitis, laryngitis, and rhinitis. The major symptoms may subside in about 5 days, but a cough and weakness may persist. Treatment is supportive—bed rest, fluids, analgesic-antipyretics, and expectorants. Amantadine (an antiviral agent) may diminish the severity of Type A influenza.

*Haemophilus influenza Type B (HIB)* remains a major health problem. It is still the most common cause of bacterial infection in children between 3 months and 3 years of age (Shapiro, 1990). HIB not only causes a large number of deaths (about 1000 per year in the United States) but also is responsible for high morbidity rates such as those caused by neurological sequelae to meningitis. In 1985, Haemophilus B polysaccharide was licensed in the United States and appears to be decreasing the incidence of this type of influenza (see Table 19-5). Nose and throat cultures and increased serum antibody titer confirm the medical diagnosis. Treatment is supportive. For all types of influenza, children should be given acetaminophen for fever. Contact isolation with an emphasis on handwashing should also be employed.

Nursing assessment includes a review of the symptoms, the history of the illness, and physical examination. Cold symptoms, followed by weakness and a cough, are major findings in this disease. Frequently other members of the family or close contacts are also affected.

Nursing diagnoses may include:

- Altered nutrition: Less than body requirements related to general malaise
- High risk for hyperthermia related to the infectious process
- Altered family processes related to illness of family member(s)
- Fatigue related to the disease process
- High risk for infection related to the severity of the infection

Hospitalization is not usually required unless there are complications. Nursing interventions must include teaching care givers how to provide comfort measures such as increasing fluid intake, the use of mouthwashes, and keeping visitors away; proper handwashing technique; proper disposal of tissues; and education about influenza immunizations for adults as well as children. Evaluation of nursing interventions is difficult during epidemics, but an uncomplicated recovery for the affected child, immunization for adults and children, and consumer knowledge of the disease may be indicators. Aspirin should not be given to children with flulike symptoms because of the relationship between the ingestion of salicylates and Reye's syndrome, an acute and sometimes fatal illness in children.

## Rabies

| | |
|---|---|
| Incubation period | 2–6 weeks in humans but may be as long as 2 years |
| Contagion period | 3–5 days before onset of symptoms through the course of the disease |
| Causative agent | Neurotropic virus |
| Mode of transmission | Transmitted to humans in the saliva of infected wild animals (bats, skunks, squirrels) or by infected domestic animals (dogs, cats) |

*Rabies* is an acute infectious disease usually transmitted to humans by bites from infected animals. The rabies virus travels from the site of the bite to the central nervous system. Cranial nerve and spinal cord nuclei become affected, and the disease is almost always fatal if untreated. Rabies has three stages: the prodromal stage, the excitement or furious stage, and the paralytic or terminal stage.

The *prodromal stage* lasts from 2 to 4 days and is characterized by a sensation at the site of the bite that may be described as itching, burning, or tingling. Accompanying symptoms include headache, fever, sore throat, irritability or restlessness, diaphoresis, increased salivation, and sensitivity to loud noises or bright lights.

In the *excitement stage* (1 to 3 days), the child becomes increasingly apprehensive and excitable. Muscle twitching and generalized convulsions may occur, as well as *hydrophobia*—an extreme fear of water such that throat spasms occur when the child tries to eat or drink or when the sound of running water is heard. Swallowing is very painful so the child drools. The respiratory muscles may also have spasms, and sometimes the child experiences continuous convulsions. Most children affected die during this stage. Those who survive this stage progress to the *paralytic stage,* which consists of paralysis, coma, and eventually death.

Most communities have regulations that require rabies immunization for all pets. Other preventive enforcement policies include leash laws and regulations pertaining to stray animals.

If a child is bitten by any animal, the area should be washed well with soap and water and 70% alcohol or povidone-iodine should be applied. Animal bites should be reported to the local public health department. If the owner of the animal is unknown, the animal should be described as carefully as possible, and an effort should be made by the agency to find the animal. The immunization status of the animal must be obtained, and the animal must be confined for 10 days to observe for signs of rabies. If the animal is found dead, its head should be packed in ice and sent to the Department of Health for testing. If the animal is not identified or found, rabies prophylaxis may be prescribed. This decision is influenced by the geographic area and the incidence of rabies.

Medical diagnosis is confirmed by positive culture from saliva, blood, lymph, urine, and the central nervous system of an infected animal. Postmortem examination documents Negri bodies (cytoplasmic inclusion bodies) in brain cells; this is a definitive finding.

Treatment consists of establishing active immunity with rabies vaccine, which is used in conjunction with a rabies serum (passive immunity). The vaccine is the human diploid cell vaccine (HDCV). It is given intramuscularly for five consecutive doses, beginning with the day of the bite, and at days 3, 7, 14, and 28. Human rabies immune globulin (HRIG) should be used with the first dose of the vaccine for postexposure prophylaxis.

Nursing assessment must include a thorough history to confirm an animal bite. The history will also reveal the prodromal symptoms. The site of the bite should be examined. Numbness at the site of the bite or along the involved nerves may occur. Since attacks by rabid animals tend to be unprovoked, children should be asked what they were doing at the time of the bite. The bite area should be cleansed, but the wound should not be sutured because closing the wound may cause the virus to spread.

Nursing diagnoses include:

- Pain related to the traumatic skin and tissue damage
- High risk for secondary infection related to the animal bite
- Altered nutrition: Less than body requirements related to difficulty in swallowing in the excitement phase
- High risk for altered central nervous system function
- High risk for fluid and electrolyte imbalance related to difficulty in swallowing

Nursing interventions in the immediate phase are directed toward providing wound care, identifying the biting animal, and reporting the case to the public health department, and may also include administering the vaccine and serum intramuscularly. As symptoms occur, they are treated supportively. Strict isolation is maintained for the duration of the illness. Care givers should be informed that the patient's saliva could contaminate an open wound or mucous membrane. Parents and the child usually become very anxious over the bite, the possible diagnosis of rabies, and the treatment; they require a great deal of support and preparation to cope with the situation.

Evaluation of nursing care must include treatment prophylaxis for a successful recovery, preventive measures in the community (an active rabies awareness program), and minimal physical and emotional complications for the child.

## Tuberculosis

| | |
|---|---|
| Incubation period | 2–10 weeks |
| Contagion period | Primary—None if on chemotherapy. Infectious pulmonary tuberculosis—sputum smears show decreasing numbers of organisms and cough has abated |
| Causative agent | *Mycobacterium tuberculosis* |
| Mode of transmission | Inhalation of droplets from coughs or sneezes of infected persons |

*Tuberculosis* is an infectious disease caused by the tubercle bacillus *Mycobacterium tuberculosis*. Infants and pubertal females are at the greatest risk for developing tuberculosis in the United States (American Academy of Pediatrics, 1988). The highest incidence rates are among minority groups and the homeless. The child may be asymptomatic or may be very ill with respiratory distress. The inhaled droplets go to the alveoli and are disseminated via the lymph system throughout the body. The primary site of infection is the lungs, but other parts of the body, such as the kidneys and lymph nodes, may be involved. Symptoms may include fatigue, anorexia, night sweats, weight loss, and low-grade fever. Medical diagnosis is confirmed by chest x-ray and tubercular skin tests. Sputum may also be obtained by gastric lavage because the tuberculosis bacteria are acid-fast and are not destroyed by gastric secretions.

Nursing assessment should include auscultation, which may reveal crepitant rales, bronchial breath sounds, and wheezes. Chest percussion reveals dullness over the affected area due to consolidation or the presence of pleural fluid as the tuberculosis advances. A detailed family and contact history is important to identify the source of the infection. Public health nurses frequently assess the status of persons in relation to established cases of tuberculosis. The contacts may be found to (1) have no exposure and no evidence of infection, (2) have been exposed to tuberculosis infection but do not have the disease, or (3) be infected with the disease.

Two types of skin tests are used for screening and diagnosis: intradermal (Mantoux) and multiple puncture (tine). The *Mantoux test* (0.1 mL of 5 TV-PPD) is the standard tubercular test. The test is given on the inner forearm and circled so that it can be read within 48 to 72 hours. Multiple puncture tests (*tine test*) are also administered on the inner forearm. A positive reaction is evidenced by a vesicle in 48 to 72 hours. Reactions of 10 mm or more are considered positive.

Two antituberculosis drugs are usually employed for treatment: isoniazid and rifampin. They are given for at least 1 year in children under 2 years of age and for a minimum of 9 months for children over 2 years of age. Other drugs that are used include ethambutol, para-aminosalicylic acid, and streptomycin. A combination of two drugs is given.

Nursing diagnoses that may be applicable include:

- Ineffective airway clearance related to excessive mucus
- Alteration in nutrition: Less than body requirements related to anorexia

- Ineffective individual coping related to interference with normal activities
- Ineffective family coping related to the communicability of the disease
- Fatigue related to respiratory discomfort
- Non-compliance related to inability to link the treatment with the disease
- Anxiety related to the effects of the illness

Nursing interventions are supportive and educative. The patient should be isolated until there is no longer any danger of contagion. If the sputum is negative on acid-fast smear and the cough is gone, the person is no longer considered infectious. This usually occurs 2 to 4 weeks after treatment is started. The patient should be taught to use tissues while coughing, sneezing, blowing the nose, or expectorating, and to dispose of them properly. Rest and adequate nutrition are very important. Observation of the patient for reactions to medications, such as peripheral neuritis, is required. Teaching should emphasize the importance of medical follow-up examinations for the child and family members. Children who are receiving chemotherapy may attend school or day care once it has been determined that they are no longer contagious. Exposed persons should have tubercular skin testing and chest x-rays and should be given isoniazid as a preventive measure even if the skin test is negative.

BCG vaccine (bacille Calmette-Guérin) has not yet proved its efficacy. It should be considered for infants who test negative but who live in a household with untreated or ineffectively treated sputum-positive persons, and for groups without a source of regular health care (American Academy of Pediatrics, 1988). Vaccination with BCG usually induces a positive tubercular skin test. All cases of positive tuberculosis must be reported to the public health authorities. Evaluation of nursing interventions must assess containment of the disease and effective care of the patient.

## *Summary*

The care of children with infectious diseases is determined by the nature of the disease, its severity, the mode of transmission, the short- and long-term sequelae, and the public health regulations and implications. Complacency is not permitted, and vigilance through preventive education and immunization must be persistent. Research to increase available immunizations and to identify new strains of diseases is ongoing.

## References

American Academy of Pediatrics. (1988). *Report of the Committee on Infectious Diseases* (21st ed.). Elk Grove Village, IL: Author.

Centers for Disease Control. (1989). Lyme disease United States 1989 and 1988. *Morbidity and Mortality Weekly Reports, 38*, 668–672.

Chow, M. P., Durand, B. A., Feldman, M. N., & Mills, M. A. (1984). *Handbook of pediatric primary care.* New York: John Wiley & Sons.

Frenkel, L. D. (1990). Routine immunizations for American children in the 1990s. *Pediatric Clinics of North America, 37*, 531–548.

Friedman, A. D. (1987). *Handbook of pediatric diseases.* St. Louis: Ishiyaku Euro America, Inc.

Gershaw, A. A. (1990). Viral vaccines of the future. *Pediatric Clinics of North America, 37*, 689–708.

Kamper, C. (1991). Treatment of Lyme disease. *Journal of Pediatric Health Care, 3*(2), 99–105.

Landwirth, J. (1990). Medical-legal aspects of immunization. *Pediatric Clinics of North America, 37*, 771–778.

Markowitz, L. E., & Orenstein, W. A. (1990). Measles vaccine. *Pediatric Clinics of North America, 37*, 603–625.

McEnhill, M., & Vitale, K. (1989). Kawasaki disease: New challenges in care. *Maternal-Child Nursing, 14*, 406–410.

Moffet, H. L. (1989). *Pediatric infectious diseases: A problem-oriented approach* (3rd ed.). Philadelphia: J. B Lippincott Company.

Shapiro, E. D. (1990). New vaccines against hemophilus influenzae type B. *Pediatric Clinics of North America, 37*, 567–583.

Wood, R. A., Fosarelli, P., Hudak, M., Lake, A., & Modlen, J. (1989). *Pediatrics.* Philadelphia: J. B. Lippincott Company.

## Bibliography

Bellanti, J. A. (1990). Basic immunologic principles underlying vaccination procedures. *Pediatric Clinics of North America, 37*, 513–530.

Edwards, K. M., & Karzon, D. T. (1990). Pertussis vaccines. *Pediatric Clinics of North America, 37*, 549–566.

Feigin, R. D., & Cherry, J. D. (1987). *Textbook of pediatric infectious diseases* (2nd ed.). Volumes I and II. Philadelphia: W. B. Saunders Company.

Krugman, S., Katz, S. L., Gersham, A. A., & Wilfert, C. (1985). *Infectious diseases of children* (8th ed.). St. Louis: Mosby-Year Book.

Wolfe, M. S. (1990). Vaccines for foreign travel. *Pediatric Clinics of North America, 37*, 757–769.

# Nursing Care of Children
# With Disabling Conditions

Donna C. Maheady

## 20

*Handicapped or Disabled?*

*Legislation*

*Educational Programs*
   *Early Intervention/Stimulation*
    *Programs*
   *Mainstreaming Versus Selective*
    *Educational Settings*
   *Case Managed Coordinated Care*

*Health Care*
   *Family-Centered Models of Care*
   *Role of the Nurse*
   *Ethical Considerations*
   *Selected Disabling Conditions and*
    *Nursing Interventions*

*Cerebral Palsy*

*Mental Retardation*

*Down Syndrome*

*Autism*

*Common Needs of Children With*
  *Disabling Conditions*
   *Family Support and Recognition*
    *of Individual Coping Methods*
   *Siblings and Other Family*
    *Members*
   *Recreation and Play Needs*
   *Discipline*
   *Advocacy*
   *Record Keeping*
   *Long-term Planning*
   *Sex Education*
   *Dental Care*
   *Respite Care*

*Summary*

*Photograph by David Finn*

## Learning Objectives

*Upon completion of this chapter the reader will be able to:*

1. *Identify factors that predispose children to disabling conditions.*

2. *Discuss legislation that provides rights for children with disabling conditions.*

3. *Compare educational programs that are available for children with disabling conditions.*

4. *Summarize the incidence, etiology, and medical treatment for children with cerebral palsy, mental retardation, Down syndrome, and autism.*

5. *Differentiate among the clinical manifestations of cerebral palsy, mental retardation, Down syndrome, and autism.*

6. *Identify nursing interventions that are appropriate when caring for children with disabling conditions and their families.*

7. *Discuss eight common needs of children with disabling conditions and their families.*


## Key Terms

*adaptive behavior*

*ataxia*

*athetosis*

*autism*

*case management*

*developmental delay*

*diplegia*

*disability*

*handicappism*

*mainstreaming*

*mental retardation*

*mixed-type cerebral palsy*

*monoplegia*

*mosaicism*

*paraplegia*

*quadriplegia*

*sociocultural retardation*

*spasticity*

*translocation*

Some ancient societies had a quick solution to the problems caused by a child born with a disability—they threw the infant off a cliff. Other societies simply abandoned infants with disabilities in the wilderness or found other ways to ensure that the child died and did not become a burden.

In the United States, as recently as 20 to 30 years ago, doctors recommended institutionalization of all children with Down syndrome. Parents were told to place their child in a special school or institution when a diagnosis of mental retardation was confirmed. Many children with disabilities have lived out their lives in institutions, denied the opportunity to experience life to their fullest potential.

Fortunately, government legislation and a general change in the attitudes of health care providers and society at large have done much to improve the quality of life for people with disabilities. The public now supports the need to make conditions of general society available as much as possible to citizens with disabilities. Change in public sentiment is reflected in national trends such as deinstitutionalization; mainstreaming in education; competitive employment opportunities; and the involvement of persons with disabilities in programs, services, and activities enjoyed by the general public (Gleeson, 1987). Much has been accomplished in providing humane, dignified care for children with disabilities, but much remains to be done. Attitudes continue to need improvement, and implementation of government legislation is an ongoing challenge for those who provide services to children with disabilities.

## Handicapped or Disabled?

Consensus is lacking regarding how we should label, categorize, or describe children with disabilities. Are they disabled or handicapped? The term *handicappism* has been proposed to refer to the prejudicial treatment given to certain minority groups based on labeled stereotypes of behavior, given certain descriptive characteristics of individuals (Martin, Holt, & Hicks, 1981). A handicap can also refer to environmental barriers such as curbs or steps for a person in a wheelchair. *Disability* is a term that refers to the loss of function or limiting effect of a chronic condition on an individual's role performance. Many people are offended by what is implied by the term "handicapped," and prefer the term "disabled" or "differently abled." Nurses should be aware that these terms are used interchangeably by professionals in a variety of settings and may offend the client. For purposes of this chapter, emphasis will be placed on children with a disability or disabling condition.

## Legislation

The civil rights movement of the 1960s and early 1970s forced our nation to examine its treatment of minorities and to institute legislation to correct identified inequities. An outgrowth of this movement was the passage of The Education of All Handicapped Children Act (1975), Public Law 94-142, which stipulates that each state must do the following:

1. Develop a plan for a systematic search (identification, location, and evaluation) for all children who are handicapped
2. Provide a free, appropriate education and related services to these children
3. Prepare an individualized education plan (IEP) that requires parental approval for each child
4. Ensure for handicapped children an education in the least restrictive environment, with children who are not handicapped whenever possible
5. Provide parents with the procedural safeguards of due process, which include the right to notification in writing of a change in their child's program, the right to examine all records related to the individualized education plan (IEP), and the right to request a reevaluation

Congress abolished the definition of a developmental disability based on categories of disabilities such as cerebral palsy, epilepsy, or autism in favor of a functional approach by enacting PL 95-602, the Rehabilitation, Comprehensive Services, and Developmental Disabilities Amendments of 1978. Developmental disability is defined as a severe, chronic disability that is attributable to a mental or physical impairment or combination of mental and physical impairments. This impairment must be manifested before the person is 22 years old and be likely to continue indefinitely. The disability also must result in substantial functional limitations in three or more of the following areas of major life activity:

1. Self-care
2. Receptive and expressive language
3. Learning
4. Mobility
5. Self-direction
6. Capacity for independent living
7. Economic self-sufficiency

In 1986, Congress enacted PL 99-457, which provided additional amendments to the Education of the Handicapped Act. Two major portions of these amendments are critical to the expansion and improvement of services to infants, toddlers and preschoolers. A discretionary program, to be phased in over a 5-year period, assists states to plan, develop, and implement comprehensive programs for all young children with disabilities from birth to three years of age. In addition, enhanced incentives have been created so that all states will provide a free and appropriate education to all eligible three- to five-year-old children with disabilities by the school year 1991–92 (Trohanis, 1989).

The U.S. Department of Education (1985) reported that just over 4 million children were served under P.L. 94-142 during the school year 1983–1984. This figure includes children who are learning disabled, speech impaired, mentally retarded, emotionally disturbed, hearing impaired, multihandicapped, orthopedically impaired, health impaired in other ways, visually handicapped, and deaf–blind.

On July 26, 1990, President George Bush signed the Americans With Disabilities Act of 1990 into law. This legislation is considered the world's strongest civil rights protection for the disabled. It prohibits discrimination against individuals with disabilities in employment, public accommodations, transportation, and telecommunications.

## Educational Programs

### Early Intervention/ Stimulation Programs

In order to minimize the effects of disabling conditions, early intervention programs have been initiated for children with disabilities. They facilitate growth and development, as well as acquisition of new skills, independent functioning, and prevention of secondary problems (Bailey & Wolery, 1984). A diversity of programs that can be matched to the individual needs of children with disabilities and their families are offered by various community agencies and services. Interventions depend on the needs of the child and family but generally include the developmental areas of cognition, socialization, language development, motor training, and self-help skills (feeding, toileting, and dressing). Although the merits of some early intervention programs have not been proved, it is generally accepted that early intervention is essential and should begin as soon as possible after the diagnosis of a disability. The programs can be beneficial for both children and their families.

The setting for the early intervention program may be home-based, agency/center-based, or a combination of both. Home-based programs are located in the children's own home, where services are delivered on an individual basis by child development specialists. The goal of most programs is to train the mother or primary caregiver to work with the child. Home-based programs have several advantages:

> They lend themselves well to rural communities or areas that have a low incidence population of children with disabilities.
>
> They are useful for infants who are too young to benefit from the social setting of a center.
>
> They are helpful for parents who are uncomfortable about sending their young child away from home to participate in a program.

Center/agency-based programs are practical in more densely populated areas and may be located in churches, schools, clinics, or in facilities on college or university campuses. Center/agency-based programs have these advantages: they offer access to staff members (e.g., physical, occupational, and speech therapists) and their expertise if the child needs it; the staff is able to give the child intensive and consistent training; the program enables the child to have social contact with other children; and there is greater availability of special equipment and materials (Peterson, 1987).

## Mainstreaming Versus Selective Educational Settings

Many school-age children with disabilities are *mainstreamed,* or placed in a classroom with children who do not have disabilities for part of the day or the entire day. Public Law 94-142 does not mandate mainstreaming for all children with disabilities, nor does it abolish special or residential settings. It does require that the child be educated in the "least restrictive" environment possible. This means that to the maximum extent appropriate, each child with a disability is to be educated with children without disabilities. Much controversy exists over the interpretation of "least restrictive" environment. Mainstreaming may

not be the best educational setting for every child with a disability.

## Case Managed Coordinated Care

Systematic approaches have evolved to coordinate the diverse needs of children with disabilities. In most cases, central orchestration of services results in the child receiving more comprehensive services. *Case management* is defined as a process of supporting individuals and their significant others to integrate services within the constraints of health deviations, insurance coverage, personal resources, and available technology and services. The goal is to provide the individual family the least costly combination of services that are efficient and effective in meeting their child's needs (Dienemann, 1989). In an effort to avoid communication problems and fragmentation of care, each individual case is managed by a professional who is usually not directly involved in providing services, which affords the case manager the perspective to evaluate all of the child's areas of need. The case manager provides intake and screening, assessment of the child and community, treatment planning, referrals, coordination, collaboration, monitoring, and evaluation, and serves as a supportive liaison between the family and service providers. Case managed care is implemented in different ways by various agencies, school boards, hospitals, health maintenance organizations (HMOs), and insurance companies throughout the country.

## Health Care

### Family-Centered Models of Care

Family-centered models of care have evolved from the general change in attitudes among health care professionals who provide care to children with disabilities. This new philosophy has progressed from an institution/agency approach to a child-centered approach to a family-centered approach. There is growing recognition that the best approach to health care of children with disabilities must be family-centered and community-based.

### Role of the Nurse

Today, countless parents elect to keep their children with disabilities at home where they can provide as near normal a life as possible. Many of these children require a broad spectrum of services to meet their physical, emotional, and educational needs. This deinstitutionalization movement has increased nursing involvement in the care of children with disabilities in a variety of settings. Nurses now care for these children in homes, alternative living arrangements, and schools, in addition to facilities for well, acute, and chronic care. Further nursing involvement is needed in case finding, case management, advocacy, administration, policy making, and research involving children with disabilities. There continues to be a great need for innovative nursing care in respite, infant, preschool, and afterschool programs. Nurses must also be active forces of change to instill positive attitudes in non-disabled children, adults, and professionals toward children with disabilities. Puppet educational programs and the book series *The Kids on the Block* (Aiello & Shulman, 1988) have done much to influence attitudes among children and adults. This change in attitudes will ultimately benefit all.

## Ethical Considerations

Nurses who work with children with disabilities and their families are increasingly confronted with ethical dilemmas regarding their care. Some ethical questions that arise are the following:

What are the rights of the child, the parents, the state, and the nurse?

What are the duties and responsibilities of each of these?

How should medical treatments and nursing care be allocated?

What will be the quality of the child's future life?

Should every child with a disability be mainstreamed?

When should a child be placed in an institution?

Do the rights of children with disabilities differ from those who are not disabled?

Analyzing nursing interventions from an ethical standpoint is a necessary part of responsible nursing care for children with disabilities. Many feel that justice requires giving additional attention to disabled individuals. This becomes especially important as nurses clarify their own values about the care of children with disabilities. The reader is referred to Chapter 3 for further discussion of ethical issues in child health care.

## Selected Disabling Conditions and Nursing Interventions

The balance of this chapter focuses on a discussion of four disabilities that are identified during childhood—cerebral palsy, mental retardation, Down syndrome, and autism. The disabilities selected are representative of the group of disabling conditions and the order in which they are presented is not related to prognosis or degree of disability. Nurses will care for children with each of these disabilities who are affected to lesser and greater extents. Nurses should remember that all children with disabilities are no more alike than all children without disabilities.

Some of the common needs and concerns that relate to most children with disabilities and their families are presented at the end of the chapter. Other conditions that are also considered disabilities are presented elsewhere in this text.

## Cerebral Palsy

*Cerebral palsy* (CP) is the term used to describe a group of disabilities caused by injury or insult to the brain either before or during birth or in early infancy. These disabilities usually result from injury to the cerebellum, the basal ganglia, or the motor cortex. CP causes the greatest amount of irreversible physical disability in children. The disability is nonprogressive but may become more obvious as affected infants grow older and secondary complications, such as contractures and deformities, develop.

## Incidence and Etiology

It is estimated that cerebral palsy occurs in between 1 and 5 per 1000 live births each year. High risk factors in the development of cerebral palsy include prematurity, asphyxia, and ischemia, as well as perinatal trauma. Other causes include congenital and perinatal infections, congenital brain anomalies, and perinatal metabolic conditions such as hyperbilirubinemia and hypoglycemia (Paneth, 1986). Infection, trauma, and brain tumors may cause CP during infancy. Some cases of CP remain unexplained (Nelson & Ellenberg, 1986).

Other disorders associated with CP may include mental retardation, hyperactivity, emotional problems, and seizures. Additional sensorineural problems include speech and articulation problems, and hearing loss, as well as vision problems such as nystagmus and strabismus. Approximately 40% of those affected by CP have normal intelligence (Shapiro & Caputo, 1990).

## Classification

Cerebral palsy can be classified by the limbs involved (e.g., monoplegia, diplegia, paraplegia) (Table 20-1) or by the type of motor dysfunction that resulted from the injury to

*Table 20–1. Limb (Extremity) Involvement in Cerebral Palsy*

| Type | Extremity Involved |
|---|---|
| Diplegia | Paralysis of the same limb on both sides of the body, usually with mild upper extremity involvement |
| Hemiplegia | Paralysis of the arm and leg on the same side of the body |
| Monoplegia | Paralysis of one limb |
| Paraplegia | Paralysis of both legs |
| Quadriplegia | Paralysis of both arms and both legs |

the brain (e.g., spasticity, dyskinesia, or ataxia). The severity of CP can also be classified as minimal, mild, moderate, or severe. See Table 20-2 for an expanded classification.

## Clinical Manifestations of Types of Cerebral Palsy

Children in whom all four limbs are involved are called *spastic quadriplegics.* Their speech is invariably impaired (pseudobulbar palsy). Swallowing saliva may be difficult, because these children either swallow improperly or swallow at a rate that is inadequate to keep the oral cavity free of saliva (Koheil, Sochaniwskyj, Bablich, Kenny, & Milner, 1987). Respiratory infections, seizures, and mental retardation are common.

*Diplegia* affects the same limb on both sides of the body but is much more severe in the lower extremities. Involvement of the hands may be minimal, expressed only as clumsiness in grasping. This form tends to occur most frequently in children with low birth weights.

*Spasticity* is the most common type of motor dysfunction. The child has increased muscle tone, exaggerated deep tendon reflexes, and abnormal clonus. In some cases, early clinical manifestations include hypotonicity (floppy infant) with the gradual appearance of hypertonicity in the affected extremities. Neonatal reflexes, such as the tonic neck reflex, persist past the age when they would usually disappear. After 4 to 5 months of age, hyperactivity of the grasp reflex leads to the hands being held in a tight-fisted position. A positive Babinski sign after the age of 2 years aids in the diagnosis. When an infant is held in a ventral suspension, the back arches and the arms and legs extend abnormally. The infant is unable to demonstrate a parachute reflex. If the infant's hip abductors are spastic, the legs rebound into a scissored position after being pulled apart while changing diapers. If elbow extensors are spastic, the infant's arms stiffen when put into the sleeves of a shirt. Spasticity and rigidity become more evident as the child matures. Abnormal postures and contractures may develop. Tightening of the heel cords usually is so severe that these children walk on their toes with a scissors gait, crossing one foot in front of the other. Some children are never able to walk due to contractures, severe gait disturbances, balance problems, or extreme spastic movements.

The child who has *dyskinetic cerebral palsy* has slow,

## Table 20–2.    Expanded Classification of Cerebral Palsy

| Rate of Motor Development | Motor Signs | Associated Dysfunction |
|---|---|---|
| Minimal: Normal<br>  Qualitative abnormalities only | Subtle, transient abnormalities of tone<br>Persistence, exaggeration of some primitive reflexes to a mild degree<br>Deviant postural development<br>Soft signs reflected as clumsy or awkward motor performance | Communicative disorder<br>Specific learning disability<br>Strauss syndrome* |
| Mild: Two thirds normal<br>  Walks by 24 months | Transient abnormalities of tone<br>Occasional "hard" signs; more persistent, exaggerated primitive reflex development<br>Delayed postural responses<br>Exaggeration, persistence in soft signs; some may have functional importance (e.g., tremor, poor coordination) | Communicative disorder<br>Specific learning disability<br>Mental retardation<br>Strauss syndrome* |
| Moderate: Half normal<br>  Assisted ambulation<br>  May need bracing<br>  Usually does not require assistive devices or surgery | Traditional neurologic findings<br>Exaggeration, persistence of primitive reflexes<br>Postural responses delayed or absent | Mental retardation<br>Communicative disorder<br>Specific learning disability<br>Seizures<br>Expanded Strauss syndrome† |
| Severe, profound: less than half normal<br>  Wheelchair ambulation<br>  Usually needs bracing, assistive devices, and orthopedic surgery | Traditional neurologic signs predominate<br>Obligatory primitive reflexes<br>Postural reactions absent | Mental retardation<br>Seizures<br>Expanded Strauss syndrome†<br>Nutritional disorders and others |

*Strauss syndrome: hyperkinesis, attentional peculiarities (short attention span to perseveration), distractibility, easily frustrated, temper tantrums.
†Expanded Strauss syndrome: components of Strauss to a greater degree and include repetitive stereotypic activities, such as rocking, head banging, flapping or spinning, and self-injurious behavior.
(Shapiro, B. K., Palmer, F. B., & Capute, A. J. [1987]. Cerebral palsy: History and state of the art. In Gottlieb, M., & Wilhams, J. [Eds]. *Textbook of developmental pediatrics.* New York: Plenum)

involuntary, irregular, writhing movements (*athetosis*) that occur both randomly and when purposeful movements are attempted. The athetoid movements usually present after the child is 18 months old. The child may also have sudden, involuntary movements of the limbs (*chorea*) or facial grimacing. These movements disappear when the child is sleeping and are aggravated by anxiety and stress. The child may also have problems with swallowing, drooling, and speaking.

The rarest form of cerebral palsy, *ataxia,* is cerebellar rather than cerebral. Clinical manifestations include disturbed balance, irregular muscle action, hypoactive reflexes, muscle weakness, tremor, lack of leg movement during infancy, and a wide gait as the child begins to walk. It is difficult for these children to accomplish tests of cerebellar function, including repetitive movements in quick succession. They are unable to perform the finger-to-nose test. With age most children outgrow many of the symptoms of ataxic CP.

Children with *mixed-type cerebral palsy* have symptoms of ataxia and athetosis or of spasticity and athetosis, which results in severe impairment.

## Diagnosis

Severe cases of cerebral palsy may be detected at birth. Mild and moderate forms can remain undiagnosed until the child is 1 or 2 years old. Failure to achieve age-appropriate developmental milestones may be the first clue to the diagnosis. There is no specific test to establish the diagnosis of CP. Diagnosis is based on the prenatal, birth, and postnatal history; neurological examination; and assessments of muscle tone, behavior, and abilities. Metabolic disorders, degenerative disorders of the central nervous system, and spinocerebellar degenerations need to be considered in the differential diagnosis.

All infants and children should receive periodic developmental screening tests (Castiglia & Petrini, 1985). Infants who are known to be at high risk of developing CP include those who were small for gestational age or premature, suffered perinatal trauma, or suffered from postnatal anoxia, infection, or trauma.

The first clinical manifestations of CP include weak sucking and swallowing, feeble cry, seizures, tremors, and *hypotonia* (floppy baby). Muscle tone may change from hypotonic to hypertonic as the child grows. CP should be suspected when any of the following are observed:

The infant seldom moves voluntarily.

The infant crosses his or her legs when lifted up from behind rather than pulling the legs up and "bicycling" (Fig. 20-1*A*).

The infant prefers the extensor posture rather than the prone-flexion posture (arms flexed beside chest, knees drawn under the abdomen).

The infant's legs are difficult to separate when changing diapers.

The infant turns from prone to supine at an unusually early age. If spinal extensors are extremely tense, the ability to roll over may be purely accidental.

The infant is a "good baby" who takes long naps and seldom cries.

The infant or toddler has early hand preference—before 18 months to 2 years of age. This may be due to a motor deficit of the opposite hand.

The infant has poor head control.

The infant or toddler does not achieve age-appropriate motor development milestones, such as rolling over, sitting, crawling, or walking.

The infant's hands are held in a fisted position after 4 to 5 months of age.

The infant or toddler has abnormal posturing or weakness of one side of the body.

The infant fails to transfer objects from one hand to the other by 7 months of age.

The infant has feeding difficulties such as poor suck, poor lip closure, regurgitation, frequent thrusting of the tongue, impaired swallowing, and gag reflex.

The infant has a tonic neck, Moro, or palmar grasp reflex that remains after 6 months of age.

The infant has ankle clonus.

The infant's or toddler's tongue moves continuously in and out of the mouth.

The infant's head circumference is smaller than normal for age.

The infant or toddler uses hands well, but not legs.

The infant lifts his or her head higher than normal due to arching of the back.

The infant exhibits "scissoring" when picked up and held with legs dangling (Fig. 20-1*B*).

The infant or toddler has grimacing, drooling, or writhing movements.

The infant has a delay in appearance of Landau, parachute, or protective extension reflexes.

The infant or toddler has uncoordinated, uncontrolled movements that occur spontaneously or when he or she attempts to reach for an object.

The infant sits in the air when lifted, with the hips flexed and knees extended (Fig. 20-1*C*).

The infant or toddler walks by placing the toes down first.

A screening test that can be used with the 6-month-old infant consists of placing a blanket or diaper over the baby's face. The infant who is developing normally pulls the blanket or diaper off with both hands. An infant with CP uses only one hand or will not be able to pull the cover off at all (Fig. 20-2).

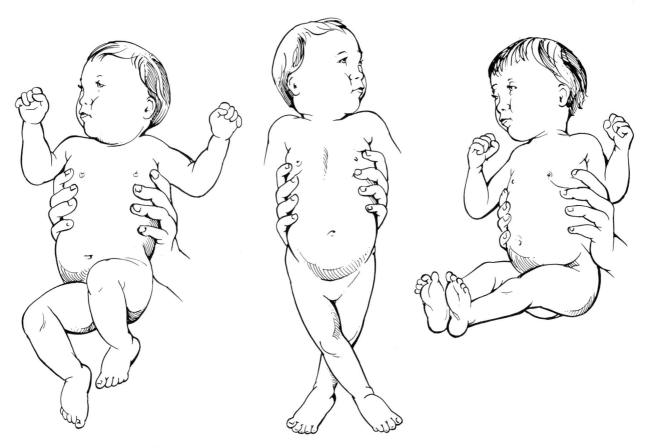

*Figure 20–1.    Clinical manifestations that suggest cerebral palsy. (A) A normal baby, when lifted under the arms, pulls the legs up or bicycles. (B) A spastic baby goes into the extensor thrust or scissors. (C) An ataxic baby sits in the air with the hips flexed and knees extended. (Redrawn from Brown, M.S. [1979]. How to tell if a baby has cerebral palsy . . . and what to tell his parents when he does.* Nursing 79 *(May), 88–91).*

## Treatment

There is no cure for cerebral palsy, but these children can be assisted to reach their highest potential. The efforts of a multidisciplinary team that includes nursing, medicine, education, social work, and speech as well as occupational and physical therapy, are necessary for effective, positive developmental outcomes. The parents should be integral members of the team, and should be encouraged to participate to whatever extent they are able.

Medical and surgical treatments may be indicated in order to improve the child's ability to function. These may include corrective devices such as casts or braces, or surgery to decrease spasticity or to correct a variety of other deformities. The objective of medical and surgical interventions is to prevent contractures and to facilitate normal movement. Drooling has been treated with surgery, behavior modification, oral-motor therapy, and biofeedback (Koheil et al., 1987). Medications such as phenytoin and phenobarbital can be prescribed to control seizures. Occasionally, medications are used to decrease spasticity. These include diazepam (Valium), dantrolene (Dantrium), and baclofen (Leoresal).

Early intervention is essential. The parents are taught techniques for handling and feeding the child (Fig. 20-3), methods of stimulation that facilitate sensorimotor development, range of motion exercises (Fig. 20-4), positioning, and appropriate play activities.

## Nutrition

Feeding children with CP can be especially challenging. The initial step is to assist the child into an appropriate position. For example, the child who is hypotonic may be most comfortable in a chair with a high back. A jacket, or restraint, can be used to keep the child's trunk stabilized and support the child in an upright position. A wheelchair with foot supports is adequate for most hypertonic children. Beanbag chairs are inexpensive and can be molded to any desired shape. The utensils that are used should promote normalcy, efficiency, and safety. Figure 20-5 shows common adaptations of eating utensils. The child should be allowed adequate time to eat without feeling hurried. High calorie diets should be provided to children with constant motion and poor growth. Nasogastric feeding has led to highly significant increases in weight in

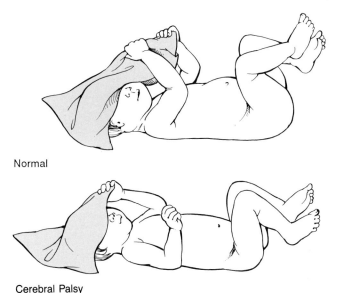

Normal

Cerebral Palsy

*Figure 20–2.    Screening test for cerebral palsy. When a blanket or diaper is placed over the infant's face, an infant who is developing normally will use both hands to pull the blanket off, whereas the infant with CP uses one hand or cannot remove the blanket at all. (Redrawn from Brown, M.S. [1979]. How to tell if a baby has cerebral palsy . . . and what to tell his parents when he does.* Nursing 79 *(May), 88–91).*

children with severe CP (Patrick, Boland, Stoski, & Murray, 1986). Gastrostomy tube feedings have also helped some severely affected children achieve better nutritional status (Shapiro, Green, Krick, Allen, & Capute, 1986) (see Chapter 29). If the child has reduced physical motion, it may be

necessary to reduce caloric intake to prevent obesity. Foods with a high sugar content increase salivation, which can be a problem for children who have difficulty with drooling, controlling secretions, and swallowing. Children should be given biscuits rather than cookies, and fruit juice rather than soft drinks (Kosowski & Sopczyk, 1985). Pureed foods are often easier for children to swallow than juices. Speech and occupational therapists should be consulted in designing a feeding program for children with CP. Control of the jaw (see Fig. 20-3), lip closure, tongue thrust, and a hyperactive gag reflex are common feeding problems.

## Physical Therapy

Physical therapy is an important part of the child's long-term management. Treatment approaches may vary, but the usual goals include inhibiting abnormal and facilitating normal reflex patterns, strengthening equilibrium, facilitating normal muscle tone to maintain normal postural and movement patterns, and preventing contractures through active and passive exercises.

## Positioning and Handling

Positioning and handling children with CP can also be challenging. The family is taught techniques that promote normal movement, balance, and posture. Positioning interventions are designed to keep the child's body in alignment and promote symmetry, comfort, and safety. Methods of handling and positioning recommended by Steele (1985) will be discussed in the following sections.

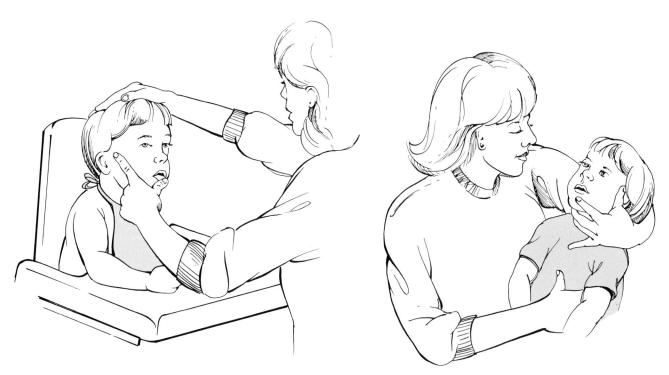

*Figure 20–3.    Feeding techniques to promote jaw control. (Redrawn from Kosowski, M.M., & Sopczyk, D.L. [1985]. Feeding hospitalized children with developmental disabilities.* American Journal of Maternal Child Nursing, 10, *193).*

*Figure 20–4.    Range-of-motion exercises for the baby with cerebral palsy. (Redrawn from Brown, M.S. [1979]. How to tell if a baby has cerebral palsy... and what to tell his parents when he does. Nursing 79 (May), 88–91).*

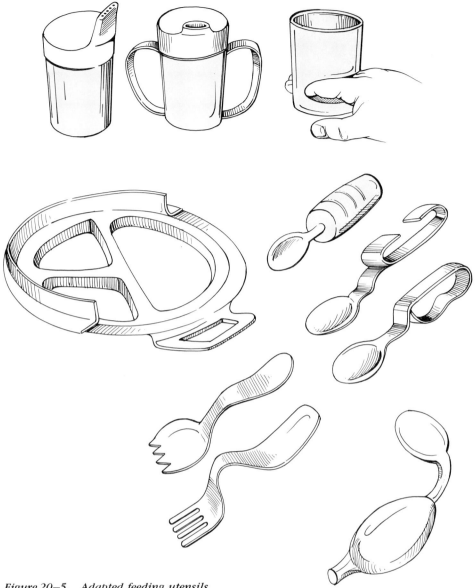

*Figure 20–5.  Adapted feeding utensils.*

### Positioning

Mild to severe:

Corner sitting can be used for the child who is unable to sit.

Discourage the child with hypotonia from assuming the W-shaped seating position (Fig. 20-6). Side sitting and Indian sitting are preferred positions.

Moderate to severe:

Position the child over a wedge or bolster in such a way that the arms are brought forward. The prone position encourages head righting, stimulates head control, and encourages extension of the back, neck, and hips.

Position the hypertonic or dyskinetic child in a side-lying position. Put a small pillow under the head and flex the knees and hips.

Use the supine position infrequently. When used, keep the child's head midline and flex the hips, knees, and shoulders. Place a pillow under the head and thighs.

### Handling

Moderate to severe:

Carry the child in a prone position to strengthen head control.

Carry the child with dyskinesia (athetosis) in a sitting position while controlling arm and leg movements.

Carry the child who has tight adductors with an arm between the child's legs.

Bend the child with spasticity forward at the hips and sit the child up before lifting.

*Figure 20–6.   The W-shaped sitting position should be discouraged.*

## Education

The educational program is an integral part of the child's management. The program should integrate all of the goals for the child into an individualized program. Speech, occupational, and physical therapy are included with self-help skills such as feeding, toileting, dressing, and hygiene, depending on the child's needs and abilities. Adapted equipment can aid the child in play and socialization. Computers have done much to facilitate communication and learning for children with CP. Pre-computer skills are included in many preschool programs. Computers can increase the options for children with disabilities and can provide them with future occupations, as well as education and control of their environment (Johnson, 1986).

## Play Materials and Activities

Play materials and activities are an important part of the therapeutic program, as well as being fun for the child. Battery-operated toys may be adapted with different kinds of on/off switches for the child with severe cerebral palsy. Less severely impaired children may respond to electronic toys and technological devices such as toys that speak, respond to touch, light up, or move, along with academic learning toys and computers (Anderson, Hinojosa, & Strauch, 1987).

## Nursing Care

Children with cerebral palsy need much support throughout life, depending on the level of severity of their cerebral palsy. Temperament will influence the child's develop-

ment by exacerbating or reducing the stresses he or she faces (Chess & Thomas, 1986). Adolescence, when the physical self becomes a central concern in influencing self-esteem, is a particularly difficult time. Adolescents should be encouraged to participate in group activities with other adolescents with CP whenever possible. Aquatics may be a useful group activity to improve self-image (Magill & Hurlbut, 1986).

Some children with CP who also have seizure disorders represent a nursing challenge. Nursing care of children with seizures is discussed in Chapter 26.

Families of children with CP need much support during the initial diagnosis, subsequent well-child visits, hospitalizations, and long-term care. Nursing assessment and formulation of nursing diagnoses, as well as planning, interventions, and evaluation should be done in collaboration with children and their families.

Nursing diagnoses that may apply to children with CP and their families include the following:

- Grieving or Ineffective Family Coping related to having a child with a disability
- Altered Nutrition: less or more than body requirements related to chewing and swallowing difficulties or reduced or constant physical motion
- Altered Growth and Development related to the disability
- High Risk for Impaired Skin Integrity related to immobility
- High Risk for Injury related to uncoordinated movements
- Impaired Verbal Communication related to neurological impairment
- Self-Care Deficit: bathing/hygiene, dressing/grooming, feeding, toileting related to neuromuscular impairment or cognitive deficit
- Social Isolation related to disability
- Self-concept Disturbance related to body image, self-esteem, role performance, personal identity

Mutually defined, realistic goals are essential. Nurses must assess what families view as problems and what goals they are willing to set. The responsibilities of caring for children with cerebral palsy are great. Parents often feel anger, guilt, grief, fear, concern for the future, and overwhelming fatigue. Nurses should refer parents to support groups such as Parent-to-Parent and the United Cerebral Palsy Association. Siblings should also be referred to support groups and the Sibling Information Network. Grandparents can be referred to Especially Grandparents. Professional counseling and spiritual support should be recommended if indicated. Parents should be referred to social services for financial assistance and to organizations such as the Shriners if orthopedic treatment is needed. Reports have shown a relationship between child abuse and childhood disability. Nurses should be involved in initiatives to prevent, recognize and report suspected cases of abuse or neglect. Common concerns of children with disabilities are presented at the end of this chapter.

Evaluation of nursing care is determined by the nurse in collaboration with the child and parents. All aspects of growth and development should be evaluated to determine that the child and family are developing as normally as possible. The child should be able to engage in developmentally appropriate self-care, educational, and recreational activities, and the family should be able to demonstrate that they are comfortable with care routines and are positively adjusting to the emotional aspects of caring for a child with cerebral palsy. The family should be aware of community support groups and services.

## Mental Retardation

The term "retarded" is usually defined as slowed or delayed in achieving developmental milestones. Nurses may encounter health and education professionals who use the terms developmental delay, developmental disability, and mental retardation interchangeably. *Developmental delay* is defined as functioning below the expected level for chronological age. *Mental retardation* is considered to be a part of the broad category of developmental disability and is defined by the American Association of Mental Deficiency (AAMD) as "significantly subaverage, general intellectual functioning existing concurrently with deficits in adaptive behavior and manifested during the developmental period. The developmental period extends to approximately 18 years of age" (Grossman, 1983, p. 1).

It is important to note that a diagnosis of mental retardation cannot be made on the basis of intellectual ability alone. A child is classified as retarded only if both intellectual functioning and adaptive behavior are impaired. Commonly used intelligence tests include the Stanford-Binet Intelligence Scale, Weschler Intelligence Scale for Children—Revised (WISC-R), and the Bayley Scales of Infant Development. *Adaptive behavior* refers to how well a person meets the standards of personal independence and social responsibility expected for age and cultural group. Adaptive behavior is measured by tests such as the Vineland Social Maturity Scale and the AAMD Adaptive Behavior Domains. Adaptive behavior is more difficult to measure than intelligence because many assessments involve subjective findings. It is generally recognized that testing is only as reliable as the tester and the informant.

It is generally agreed that children with mental retardation develop in the same way as other children, but they develop more slowly and reach a lower overall level of functioning. Some suggest that children with mental retardation have problems in specific areas such as attention, memory, or perception. Children with mental retardation have the capacity to learn, develop, and grow; most can

become productive, full participants in society, as well as important, loving members of their families. The maximum potential for many children with mental retardation remains unknown. Factors that enhance the child's potential include early intervention, special education programs, therapy, and loving, supportive family members.

## Incidence and Etiology

It is estimated that between 2% and 2.5% of the population of the United States, or 4.6 to 5.75 million people, are mentally retarded (Zigler & Hodapp, 1986). Although there are more than 200 known causes of mental retardation (some of which are listed in Table 20-3), the majority of cases nurses encounter have no known etiology.

## Prevention

Many cases of mental retardation could be prevented through intervention strategies such as the following:

* Improved prenatal care
* Proper nutrition during pregnancy
* Improved support of the small, premature, or high-risk newborn
* Rubella immunization
* Genetic counseling and prenatal diagnosis
* Education regarding the danger of use of drugs and alcohol during pregnancy
* Education regarding the danger of ingesting lead during childhood and programs to remove the lead paint in old buildings
* Control and early treatment of disease
* Screening for treatable inborn errors of metabolism such as congenital hypothyroidism, phenylketonuria, and galactosemia
* Prevention of childhood accidents and injuries
* Prevention of child abuse
* Early identification and treatment of learning problems

## Classification of Mental Retardation

A classification system of mental retardation has been developed by the American Association on Mental Deficiency (Grossman, 1983). The categories and their corresponding IQ ranges are:

| Category | IQ Range |
| --- | --- |
| Mild mental retardation | 50–55 up to approximately 70 |
| Moderate mental retardation | 35–40 to 50–55 |
| Severe mental retardation | 20–25 to 35–40 |
| Profound mental retardation | Below 20–25 |

### Table 20–3. Prenatal, Perinatal, and Postnatal Causes of Mental Retardation

**Prematurity, low birth weight, and postmaturity**

**Infection and intoxication**

Rubella
Syphilis
Toxoplasmosis
Maternal drug or alcohol consumption
Exposure to industrial chemicals
Increased blood levels of lead
Rh incompatibility that results in kernicterus

**Trauma or physical injury**

Brain injury
Lack of oxygen
Exposure to radiation during the prenatal, perinatal or postnatal period

**Metabolism or nutrition**

Nutritional deficits
Imbalances in fat, carbohydrates or amino acids
Metabolic disorders such as phenylketonuria or congenital hypothyroidism

**Gross postnatal brain disease**

Neurofibromatosis
Tuberous sclerosis

**Chromosomal abnormalities**

Caused by:
  Radiation
  Viruses
  Chemicals
  Parental age and genetic mutations (e.g., Down and fragile X syndromes)

**Cerebral, spinal, and craniofacial malformations**

Microcephaly
Hydrocephaly
Myelomeningocele
Craniostenosis

**Psychiatric disorders**

Autism

**Environment**

Deprived environment
Abuse
Neglect
Family history of mental retardation

## Mild Mental Retardation

Children who are mildly mentally retarded usually learn to walk, talk, and perform other activities of daily living, but at a slower pace than normal children. They may be termed "educable" by the educational system and can learn to read, write, and perform basic mathematical skills up to about a sixth-grade level. As adults, they are usually able to live independently and are able to provide for themselves with assistance during crisis periods. Approximately 80% of children with mental retardation fall into this category.

## Moderate Mental Retardation

Children who are moderately mentally retarded have marked developmental delays. They are termed "trainable" by the educational system, usually do not progress beyond second-grade-level subjects, and attain a mental age of up to 7 years. They can communicate in simple sentences and learn routine tasks. As adults, they can function in well-supervised work situations and may be able to live in group homes.

## Severe Mental Retardation

Severely mentally retarded children can often be diagnosed at birth due to obvious physical disabilities. As preschoolers, they develop only minimal speech and usually have poor motor development. During the school years, they may learn to talk and perform basic hygiene and dressing skills. Children with severe mental retardation usually have cognitive abilities up to a preschool level. As adults, they may be able to perform simple work tasks under close supervision.

## Profound Mental Retardation

Less than 1% of children with mental retardation fall into the category of profound mental retardation. They usually have a functional age of less than 18 months and show severe developmental delays. Some children with profound mental retardation may walk and talk, whereas others will never learn to speak and may never be toilet trained. As adults they may be institutionalized, or, in some cases, they may be able to live in group homes.

# Types of Mental Retardation

Two basic types of mental retardation were identified by Edgerton (1979): clinical retardation and sociocultural retardation. *Clinical retardation* is usually diagnosed at birth or during the first few years of life. The cause may be clearly determined. Clinical retardation occurs in all socioeconomic classes. Intellectual impairment ranges from moderate to profound. These children may have other disabling conditions, such as visual or hearing impairment, in addition to mental retardation. Typically, parents of children with clinical retardation seek professional help early.

Children with *sociocultural retardation* often come from socially and economically disadvantaged groups. The degree of intellectual impairment is usually mild or borderline. The child with sociocultural retardation may not be identified until the school years, when poor school performance occurs. Parents often react with anger, and refuse to accept the diagnosis. The exact causes of sociocultural retardation remain controversial. Influential factors include heredity, poverty, lack of prenatal care, close spacing of pregnancies, home environment, poor attachment between child and parent, understimulation, low parental aspirations regarding education, and the school system.

## Early Identification

Early identification of children who are at risk for mental retardation is essential in order to maximize the child's potential. Infants may be identified in the newborn nursery or not until later when developmental milestones such as sitting, crawling, walking, and talking are delayed. The importance of routine screenings with tools such as the Denver Developmental Screening Test (DDST) cannot be overemphasized. Parents may state that the child "seems slow," "is not keeping up with children of the same age," "does not seem normal," or is "doing poorly in school." Statements such as these should be taken very seriously. Montgomery (1988) surveyed the charts of children with mental retardation and found that speech delay, developmental delay, and school failure were the three most common parental concerns initially brought to the attention of the pediatrician. Often well-meaning friends and family can discourage parents from proceeding with further tests and delay the identification process. Statements such as "Einstein didn't talk until he was three," "he's just a little slow, he'll grow out of it," and "she's so cute, she can't be retarded" are common. It should be stressed that not all children with mental retardation look "retarded" and when children begin to walk is not indicative of intelligence (Hreidarsson, Shapiro, & Capute, 1983).

## Markers for Developmental Dysfunction

Neurological signs are often associated with mental retardation. Rare, but highly related, signs include depressed consciousness/coma and neonatal seizures. Other signs are more common and less specific, such as abnormality of muscle tone, feeding dysfunction, seizures, and gross motor delay. Muscle tone is not considered to be directly related to cognitive ability, but abnormality in the evolution of muscle tone suggests that other aspects of brain function should be assessed. Gross motor delay is a common presenting symptom of mental retardation. Delay in motor development does not represent cognitive delay, but it does represent aberrant neural development and can be considered a marker of risk (Shapiro, Palmer, & Capute, 1987).

## Treatment

Children who demonstrate developmental delays should be referred to a professional who is trained in administering formal assessment tools. There is no cure for mental retardation, but much can be done to enhance the child's potential. When indicated, the child should be referred to an infant stimulation, preschool, or special education program. Physical, occupational, and speech therapy, along with self-help skills such as feeding, toileting, dressing, and hygiene should be included in an individualized program. The benefits of early intervention should be stressed to the parents.

## Exercise

Recreation and exercise are especially important for children who are mentally retarded. Efforts should be made to encourage integration of children with mental retardation with children who have normal intelligence in athletic activities and play groups. There may be greater success in individual and dual sports rather than team sports. Specific physical problems need to be considered (e.g., atlantoaxial instability in a child with Down syndrome) along with the child's size, coordination, degree of physical fitness, physical maturity, developmental age, health, and motivation when recommending athletic activities (American Academy of Pediatrics, 1987).

Children usually perform best with children of the same developmental age. There are mutual benefits when children who are mentally retarded participate in sports and play activities with children who have normal intelligence. "Normal" children get to know and learn about children with disabilities. Children with mental retardation can achieve weight control, development of physical coordination, maintenance of cardiopulmonary fitness, and decreased social isolation, along with improved social skills and self-esteem. Further discussions of the need for play and recreation are located at the end of this chapter.

### Special Olympics

Nurses should recommend the Special Olympics program to parents of children with mental retardation. The program provides year-round, nation-wide training and athletic competition. The program was started in 1968 by the Joseph P. Kennedy, Jr. Foundation. Its purpose is to contribute to the physical, social, and psychological development of children and adults with mental retardation. All activities have been tested and adapted so that they can be performed by people of all ages and degree of disability. Special Olympians are grouped according to age, ability, and skill. Official sports of the Special Olympics include basketball, bowling, hockey, gymnastics, soccer, softball, swimming, track and field, volleyball, wheelchair events, snow skiing, and ice skating.

## Nursing Care

Families of children with mental retardation need strong support as they meet the ongoing challenges of raising their children. Nursing assessments, diagnoses, planning, interventions, and evaluations should be formulated in collaboration with the family. Mutually defined, realistic goals are essential. Nurses must assess the goals that families are willing to set.

It is more difficult for parents and health professionals to detect illness in children with mental retardation. The child may not be able to describe pain or localize an area of discomfort. Parents must be encouraged to observe their child closely for symptoms such as fever, pulling at an ear, refusing to swallow food, rapid breathing, limping, or a change in usual temperament. Nurses should advise parents to have their child wear a Medic Alert bracelet or necklace.

When formulating a nursing care plan for children with mental retardation and their families, the following nursing diagnoses should be considered:

- Self-Care Deficit: bathing/hygiene, dressing/grooming, feeding, toileting related to neuromuscular impairment or cognitive deficit
- Altered Nutrition: more than body requirements related to diet and inactivity
- Impaired Verbal Communication related to neurologic impairment or inability to articulate spoken words due to developmental disability
- Ineffective Family Coping related to having a child with a disability
- Altered growth and development related to developmental disability
- High Risk for Injury related to uncoordinated movements
- Social Isolation related to developmental disability
- Sexual Dysfunction related to cognitive deficit or lack of knowledge

Because needs and goals change as the child and parents grow older, planning nursing care is very important. Completion of the school years can be a particularly stressful period for adolescents and their families because of the lack of programs that assist with the transition from school to employment. Supported work programs, workshops, and group homes are desperately needed in most communities. When planning nursing care, nurses should be aware of community resources that are available to meet the needs of children and families throughout the lifespan.

A primary nursing intervention for mental retardation is prevention. Prevention strategies (listed on p. 451) include early prenatal care, such as ensuring that mothers have received immunizations against rubella and ascertaining that they are aware of the harmful effects of alcohol and substance abuse. Nurses may refer mothers who are at risk for having infants with mental retardation for amniocentesis or genetic counseling.

Early detection and screening can also help prevent some of the more serious consequences of mental retardation. Referral to infant stimulation programs, special education programs, and other therapies can help support the child and family while reducing the long-term effects of mental retardation.

Nursing interventions should focus on providing parents with current, factual information regarding what is known not only about the child's disabilities but also about his or her strengths and abilities. The benefits of early intervention and home care should be stressed. Families should be referred to support groups such as Parent-to-Parent, respite care programs, and the Association for Retarded Citizens. Siblings should be referred to the Sibling Information Network, and grandparents should be referred to Especially Grandparents. (Addresses for these organizations appear at the end of the chapter.) Nurses can recommend appropriate literature and genetic counseling. Spiritual support and professional counseling should be suggested if indicated. Family members should be encouraged to express their feelings and should be supported in their decision, whether it is to keep the child at home or to place the child in residential or adoptive care. Nurses should be alert to signs of ineffective coping, such as abuse or neglect, throughout the child's life.

Parents should be referred to an appropriate infant stimulation, preschool, or special education program. They should also be aware of their child's educational rights under PL 94-142. Community programs, adapted sports activities, and Special Olympics should be recommended.

Parents should be encouraged to have their child's vision tested, because children with mental retardation are more likely to suffer from visual problems than are other children. Adapted vision tests that use acuity cards have been used successfully (Hertz, 1987). The child's optimum development will be enhanced with corrected vision.

When a child with mental retardation is hospitalized, nurses should follow the child's normal routine and established program as much as possible. Collaboration with the parents regarding the best approach to care is essential. Nurses should promote the child's independence in self-care activities such as feeding, toileting, dressing, and hygiene. Normalizing experiences such as eating, playing, and socializing with other children should be encouraged.

Non-verbal children should be encouraged to communicate using a communication/picture board or sign language. Nurses should anticipate problems with long- and short-term memory. When teaching the child a new skill, motivation for learning, such as generous praise, should be used. Instructions should be presented in small, sequential steps. The child should receive prompt and consistent feedback, with emphasis on successes. Nurses should prepare children for procedures according to their developmental age rather than their chronological age. Concrete explanation and materials should be used.

The hospitalized child with mental retardation should be checked frequently. The side rails of the bed should be kept up. The nurse should remain with the child until food or medications have been swallowed safely; meal trays and utensils should be removed from the room as soon as the meal is completed. A family member should be encouraged to stay with the child, if possible.

## Down Syndrome

*Down syndrome* (DS) is the most frequently observed chromosomal alteration in humans, resulting in over 50 different characteristics (some of which are listed in the display). Children with DS typically have epicanthal folds, short stature, a flattened nose (Fig. 20-7), Brushfield's spots (gray or yellow spots around the edges of the iris), a single crease in the palm (simian crease) (Fig. 20-8), a protruding tongue, and low-set ears. Virtually all children with DS are mentally retarded to varying degrees.

## Incidence and Etiology

The incidence of Down syndrome is approximately 1 in every 700 to 1000 live births and is related to advanced maternal age. Mothers who are under 30 years of age have a 1 : 1000 chance; at 35 years old, mothers have a 1 : 400

*Figure 20–7. Typical facial features of Down syndrome.*

chance; and at 40 years old, the chances increase to 1 : 105. Research studies have disputed the accepted beliefs regarding maternal causation by indicating that in some cases the father may contribute to the extra abnormal chromosome (de la Cruz & Muller, 1983; Cohen, 1984).

Prebirth detection of DS is possible early in pregnancy by chromosome study of amniotic fluid obtained through amniocentesis. The maternal serum alpha fetoprotein (MSAFP), a less invasive method, can also screen for Down syndrome. These tests are recommended for women who are at increased risk of having a child with DS.

---

### Characteristics Associated With Down Syndrome

Muscle hypotonia
Hyperextensible and lax joints
Broad, flat nose
Eyes that slant up and out with internal epicanthal
   folds
Small mouth
Large, protruding tongue
Small, underdeveloped ears
Short, thick fingers
Short neck with loose folds
Nystagmus
Brushfield's spots
Enlarged liver and spleen
Dry, cracked skin
Broad, short hands
Single palmar crease, a simian line (see
   Figure 20-8)
Incurved little finger
Wide gap between first and second toes

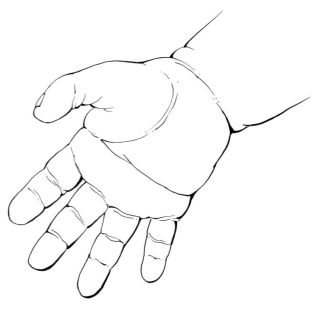

*Figure 20–8. Single palmar crease (simian line) in a child with Down syndrome.*

There is no known etiology of DS. It occurs equally across all races and socioeconomic groups. The genetic defect associated with DS is the presence of extra material on the chromosome pair that is designated 21. The forms in which the extra material can appear are classified as trisomy 21, translocation, and mosacism.

### Trisomy 21

Trisomy 21 is the presence of three rather than the normal pair of chromosomes designated as 21. This form, which is not inherited, is associated with 95% of all cases of DS. It results from an error in cell division or an error in the sperm or ovum that causes the zygote to receive an extra chromosome.

### Translocation

Translocation is an interchange of chromosomes or parts of chromosomes that may result in a mismatched pair. This type occurs in about 4% of all cases and is known to be hereditary. Children with translocation have an extra number 21 chromosome that has broken and become attached to another chromosome. An arm of one chromosome abnormally attaches itself to the arm of another. It is possible for a person to carry a broken chromosome 21 without showing any DS characteristics because the correct amount of genetic material is there, even though some of it is out of place (de la Cruz & Muller, 1983). It is important to karyotype each of the parents to determine if either is a balanced translocation carrier. If one of them is a carrier, there is a risk of having another child with DS and they should be counseled accordingly. The risk that future offspring will be affected is much greater than in DS caused by trisomy 21.

### Mosaicism

Mosaicism is a rare form of Down syndrome, appearing in about 1% of children with DS. It results when some cells have a normal chromosome count and some cells show trisomy 21. Depending on the ratio of normal cells to trisomic cells, these children may or may not exhibit as many of the clinical signs of DS. This type of DS is not known to be carried in the parents' chromosomes; it is accidental, resulting from an error in cell division of the fertilized egg.

## Associated Conditions

Congenital heart defects, especially atrioventricular septal defects, are common in children with Down syndrome. Other problems often seen in children with DS include duodenal atresia, tracheoesophageal fistulas, and Hirschsprung disease. They are prone to chronic respiratory infections, recurrent pneumonia, tonsillitis, and otitis media. Studies suggest that children with DS have fewer and less responsive cells needed for a normal immunological response to infection. Hypothyroidism is common. Vertebral instability and gait problems occur due to hypotonia and flexible joints. Atlanto-axial subluxation of C1-C2 is a musculoskeletal problem with an unknown etiology. Children with DS are prone to strabismus, cataracts, refractive errors, and speech and hearing problems. Down syndrome has been linked to increased risk of Alzheimer's disease and leukemia.

Obesity is common in children with DS and is often related to physical inactivity combined with a high caloric intake. Hypothyroidism can also contribute to obesity. Obesity is complicated by linear growth abnormalities and delayed skeletal maturity. People with DS are usually shorter than the general population. Life expectancy is improving due to surgical treatment of congenital heart defects, the use of antibiotics to treat infections, and the avoidance of early institutionalization.

## Development

The cognitive functioning of children with Down syndrome ranges from mild to severe mental retardation. Most children fall into the mildly to moderately retarded range. Evidence of developmental delays occurs during the early months of life. Infants with DS are slow to turn over, sit, stand, walk, and speak. The delay in speech and language is usually more noticeable than the delay in postural-motor development. Weak motor development reduces self-initiated activities such as rolling over or reaching for a toy in these infants. This may be complicated by parents or caregivers who do not interact with them— smiling, talking, and singing while feeding or changing diapers is as important for children with DS as it is with normally developing infants.

## Early Intervention

For many years, it was standard procedure to institutionalize children with DS. They were considered uneducable and unable to live a meaningful, productive life. Currently more and more families raise their children with DS at home. With early intervention, great progress has been made with children with DS. Effective early intervention can alter the subsequent educational progress of a child with DS. A child who is classified as educable, rather than trainable, is qualified for different educational opportunities. It is unclear exactly how much these children can achieve when provided appropriate and early intervention (Miola, 1987). Many children with DS can learn self-care, reading, and vocational skills. Some live semi-independently in group homes and hold jobs in workshops and private businesses. Most importantly, many are loving, contributing, positive members of their families.

## Treatment

There is no cure for Down syndrome. However, surgery can correct cardiac and other congenital defects such as duodenal atresia. In addition, cosmetic approaches have attempted to "normalize" the characteristic stigmatizing features of children with DS in the belief that if these children look more "normal," teachers, peers, and society may expect them to be more normal and encourage them to achieve more. Another advantage of surgery may be to reduce macroglossia and thereby facilitate nose breathing, speech, and eating, and alleviate the characteristic constant drooling. It can also provide improvement in aesthetic appearance for those children who are more severely affected. Oral motor treatment, behavior modification, and overcorrection have also been used to reduce tongue protrusion and drooling (Purdy, Deitz, & Harris, 1987; Trott & Maechtlen, 1986).

## Sexual Development

The sexual development of adolescents with DS usually takes place later than normal. Secondary sex characteristics may or may not become evident. Females may menstruate and can be fertile. Males are infertile and have low testosterone levels. Teaching sex education and socially acceptable behavior is especially important to avoid sexual exploitation or abuse of individuals with DS. Some children with DS can be overly affectionate and may be unwittingly seductive (Williams, 1983). Parents of daughters with DS must be educated regarding their daughters' reproductive potential. Further discussion regarding sexual emergence of children with disabilities is included later in this chapter.

## Nursing Care

Nursing assessments, formulation of nursing diagnoses, planning, interventions, and evaluations should be done in collaboration with the parents and child when possible. Realistic, mutually defined goals are essential. Nurses must assess what the parents see as problems, and what goals they are willing to set for their child.

Special attention must be directed toward watchfulness for the development of otitis media, tonsillitis, and pneumonia. Common anatomical abnormalities in children with Down syndrome, including small nose with depression of nasal bridge, antiverted nares and narrow nostrils, deviated septum, small ears, and narrow ear canals (Pueschel, Sassaman, Scola, Thuline, Stark, & Horrobin, 1982), may contribute to an increased incidence of upper respiratory infections. Parents should be taught to

use a vaporizer, postural drainage, or suctioning of the nares when indicated. The importance of completing a full course of antibiotic therapy when prescribed should be stressed. Weight, vision, hearing, and thyroid function must be carefully monitored and appropriate interventions provided when indicated. Interventions might include diet changes, glasses, hearing aids, or thyroid hormone replacement.

Pueschel (1983) recommends regular cervical x-rays to rule out atlanto-axial subluxation in children over 2 years old. Parents need to be taught the neurological signs and symptoms of the problems that require prompt attention, e.g., neck discomfort, weakness, and torticollis. The child should be evaluated for atlanto-axial subluxation before participating in sports activities such as gymnastics, diving, or soccer.

Nursing diagnoses that should be considered when caring for a child with DS include:

- Grieving, parental related to loss of their perceived image of a perfect child
- Altered Parenting related to the birth of a child with a congenital defect
- Altered Growth and Development related to developmental disability
- Self-care Deficit: bathing/hygiene, dressing/grooming, feeding, toileting related to neuromuscular impairment and/or cognitive deficit
- Altered Nutrition: more than body requirements related to diet and physical inactivity
- Potential for Infection related to congenital anatomical anomalies
- Sexual Dysfunction related to lack of information or cognitive deficit
- Self-concept Disturbance related to body image, self-esteem, role performance, personal identity
- Social Isolation related to developmentally disability

During the initial diagnosis, well child visits, or hospitalizations, nurses should focus on what the child can do, rather than what he or she cannot do. The parents should be provided with current, factual information regarding Down syndrome. Nurses should recommend appropriate literature and genetic counseling. The benefits of early intervention and home care should be stressed. Resources such as a DS support group, Parent-to-Parent, and the Association for Retarded Citizens should be recommended. The parents will need support both at the time of the initial diagnosis and in the future. The parents' decision either to keep the child at home or to place the child in foster or adoptive care should be supported. Nurses should encourage the parents to express their feelings. Professional counseling and spiritual support should be recommended if indicated. Throughout the child's life, nurses should be alert to such signs of ineffective coping as child abuse or neglect.

Bonding is promoted by including the parents in caregiving. Nurses should model and reinforce acceptance behaviors such as maintaining eye contact with the infant, as well as talking, singing, and giving tactile stimulation. The nurse should stress that children with DS have the same needs for love, affection, play, social interaction, and discipline as other children.

Nurses should refer parents to an infant stimulation program if one is available. If a program is not available, nurses should collaborate with physical, occupational, and speech therapists to devise a developmentally appropriate stimulation program. The parents should be informed of their child's educational rights under PL 94-142.

Parents should be cautioned not to overfeed their child, because obesity can impede gross motor skills. Exercise and sound nutrition should be encouraged. The parents need to be made aware of adapted sports activities, Special Olympics, scouting, and community park and recreation department activities. Nurses should recommend that a child with DS wear a Medic Alert bracelet or necklace.

When the child with DS is hospitalized, nurses should follow the child's normal daily routine as much as possible. The nonverbal child can be encouraged to communicate using gestures, sign language, or a communication/picture board. If able, the child should be encouraged to perform self-care activities such as eating, toileting, and toothbrushing. Normalizing experiences such as eating meals, playing, and socially interacting with other children should be promoted. The child should be provided with appropriate toys, games, and educational activities that promote development of cognitive, motor, and social skills. Nurses should explain procedures to the child in small, sequential steps, review each step frequently, and use concrete terms and examples.

## Autism

Autism is a lifelong developmental disability manifested by cognitive, social, and language deficits. It is one of the most serious psychiatric disorders of childhood. The American Psychiatric Association's *Diagnostic and Statistical Manual of Mental Disorders, Third Edition-Revised* (DSM-III-R, 1987) identifies the following criteria for autism:

- Qualitative impairment in reciprocal social interaction
- Qualitative impairment in verbal and nonverbal communication and in imaginative activity
- Markedly restricted repertoire of activities and interests
- Onset during infancy or childhood

The DSM-III-R includes specific criteria within each of these categories.

## Incidence and Etiology

It is estimated that autism occurs in 2 to 4 of every 10,000 children. Although boys are more frequently affected, the disorder is more severe in girls. The etiology of autism is not known. Several possible causes have been investigated, including prenatal and perinatal complications, genetic transmission, biochemical problems, and parental personalities. Parents who have one child with autism have a greater risk of having another child with autism. The fragile X chromosomal aberration has been found in some males with autism. Levels of serotonin may be above or below normal. Children with congenital rubella have an increased incidence of autism. Children with untreated phenylketonuria (PKU) may be autistic. Epilepsy is frequently associated with autism (Olsson, Steffenburg, & Gillberg, 1988). For many years, cold, unaffectionate, stiff parents were believed to cause autism, but there is currently no evidence that parents cause autism in their children. Researchers are still not clear whether children with autism have a common unidentified medical problem or whether a number of insults have resulted in brain damage and autistic behavior.

## Characteristics

The most common characteristic of children with autism is their failure to respond to social stimuli. Children with autism generally prefer to be alone and are unable to relate to others, including parents, with even simple eye contact. Some of the characteristics typical of children with autism include remaining mute, parrot-like repetition (echolalia), ignoring signs and sounds, aversion to body contact, motor control problems, rocking, head banging, sleep disturbances, insensitivity to pain, hyperactivity, and tantrums. Some children manifest signs of autism early in infancy; others develop normally and then regress or experience delayed development. Possible autistic behaviors can be identified for each developmental stage (Table 20-4).

Although some children with autism have normal intelligence, most are mentally retarded (Harris, 1990). Placement in school depends upon the results of testing and on options available within the community. Occasionally, a child with autism may have an isolated, remarkable talent in an area such as music or mathematics, and be referred to as having splinter skills or be called an "autistic savant." Most adults with autism are incapable of caring for themselves and require close supervision.

## Diagnosis

The diagnosis of autism is made by a multidisciplinary team. Mental retardation, schizophrenia, and speech or hearing impairments need to be ruled out in order to differentiate autism from other disorders of childhood

*Table 20–4.  Developmental Stages and Possible Autistic Behaviors*

| Stage | Response to Environment | Social/Interactive Patterns | Language/ Communication Patterns | Feeding/Eating Patterns | Motor Development |
|---|---|---|---|---|---|
| Infancy | Quiet and placid, seldom cries *or* Very irritable, screams, and may be comforted only by rocking or car rides. Difficult to feed, bathe, or dress. Stiff, hard to cuddle, doesn't mold into parent's arms when being held. Body rocks, head bangs. | Unresponsive to parent's presence Little eye contact No interest in toys May enjoy rough play No social smile Does not reach to be picked up | Ignores speech and loud sounds (deafness may be suspected) Decreased verbalizations May be fascinated with soft sounds | Poor suck Does not cry when hungry Refuses to eat lumpy foods | May be normal or delayed May bypass a motor stage such as creeping |
| Toddler | Self-stimulating behaviors such as rocking, head banging, flapping of arms Irregular sleep patterns Does not respond to painful stimuli May be fascinated by light patterns, music, or different textures Resists changes in routine Ignores objects of usual childhood interest | Inappropriate use of and attachment to objects Stereotypic, repetitive play May be passive or destructive, aggressive and self-injurious Frequent temper tantrums | Unresponsive to voice, or being called by name Echolalia (parrotlike repetition of words spoken by others), may be immediate or delayed Screams May lead parent by the arm May respond to simple commands | Likes pureed foods Will eat only a limited variety of foods Unable to recognize a food in another form, such as a banana without the peel | May be normal Prolonged cruiser May tiptoe walk May be hyperactive |
| Preschool | Responses of toddler stage continue | May be aloof and expressionless May be more affectionate Socially embarrassing behaviors Tantrums continue Stereotypic, repetitive play continues Passivity may continue | Echolalia may develop Meaningful speech is produced with effort—poor pronunciation and voice control Unable to understand most speech Can understand short, concrete sentences Confusion with pronouns, similar sounding words, and word order. Pronomial reversal—tendency to use "you" for "I" Uses and understands limited gestures | Food idiosyncracies, such as holding food in the mouth, preferring some foods over others, refusing solid foods and insisting on soft foods, smelling foods before eating | May be normal May jump, spin, flap arms or hands May be graceful or clumsy Fine motor ability may differ from gross Difficulty with copying movements May walk with elbows bent, hands together, and wrists dropped Hyperactivity may continue |

*(continued)*

*Table 20—4.  Developmental Stages and Possible Autistic Behaviors (Continued)*

| Stage | Response to Environment | Social/Interactive Patterns | Language/ Communication Patterns | Feeding/Eating Patterns | Motor Development |
|---|---|---|---|---|---|
| School years | Tantrums may decrease<br>Sleep irregularities may continue<br>Continues to have disturbances in response to stimuli | Increased affection<br>Improved social skills<br>May help with simple household chores | Language skills may increase<br>Problems of the preschool years may continue | Food idiosyncracies continue.<br>May begin to try new foods | Increased motor skills<br>Unusual walk<br>Splinter skill may develop<br>May pace, jump, spin |

This table represents a compilation of many behaviors seen in autistic children. The behaviors are not always related to a developmental stage, and no child exhibits all of the behaviors.
(Adapted from Zoltak, B. B. [1986]. Autism: Recognition and management. *Pediatric Nursing, 12,* 90. Reprinted with permission)

(Lee-Dukes, 1986). Developmental assessment and intelligence and language testing assist in the diagnosis.

## Treatment

A variety of treatments have been used with autistic children, but success has been quite limited. Behavior modification techniques have been the most successful. Tranquilizers have been used to control destructive, self-mutilating behaviors, and low doses of antipsychotic drugs may bring improvement in stereotypic behavior, withdrawal, and ability to learn. Amphetamines may be used to decrease hyperactivity. Fenfluramine has been useful in decreasing autistic behaviors in some children. Motor activity, distractibility, and inattention have decreased and affect has improved (August, Raz, Papanicolaou, Baird, Hirsh, & Hsu, 1984).

## Nursing Care

Nurses may care for children with autism in well, acute, or chronic care settings; schools; or residential programs. When assessing children with autism it is important for nurses to note a variety of factors, including the child's developmental level, coping skills, communication abilities, and interaction skills. Nurses should also assess the parents' and families' level of understanding of autism, their coping abilities, and their access to support groups or services, as well as their willingness to avail themselves of these services.

Nursing diagnoses that may apply to the child with autism include:

- Impaired Verbal Communication related to disability or language deficit
- Altered growth and development related to the disability
- High Risk for Injury related to uncoordinated movements

- Altered Nutrition: less or more than body requirements related to diet or activity level
- Altered Parenting related to the stress of having a child with autism
- Grieving or Ineffective Family Coping related to having a child with autism
- Self-care Deficit: bathing/hygiene, dressing/grooming, feeding, toileting related to cognitive deficit or disability
- Sensory Perceptual Alteration related to excess stimuli

The parents and family of a child with autism need a tremendous amount of support. Feelings of grief, anger, guilt, frustration, and overwhelming fatigue are common. Family members should be encouraged to express their feelings. The nurse should refer the family to the Autism Society of America, Sibling Information Network, respite care programs, Parent-to-Parent, and counseling, if indicated. Nurses should offer praise and encouragement regarding the parent's caregiving abilities. The family should be assisted to locate educational programs that incorporate consistency, structure, behavior modification, communication skills, and family involvement. The family may need additional support if it becomes necessary to institutionalize the child.

When planning care for a child with autism in an acute care setting, nurses should collaborate with the parents or program staff regarding the ongoing treatment plan and integrate similar interventions into the nursing care plan. Because children with autism depend on their own rituals and resist change, hospitalization can be very traumatic for them. Parents can advise nurses on the child's daily routine and preferences. Care should be provided in short, frequent blocks of time, and environmental stimui should be kept to a minimum. Nurses should encourage the child to perform self-care activities such as eating, dressing, toileting, and toothbrushing as much as possible.

Communication with a child with autism can be facilitated by observing the child's body language and speaking to the child in short sentences using concrete terms. Nonverbal children may be encouraged to communicate by using gestures, sign language, or a communication/picture board.

The safety of the child should be promoted by keeping the side rails of the bed up, and the child should be checked often. Meals should be supervised, with trays and utensils removed as soon as the meal is completed. Equipment should be kept out of the child's reach.

Evaluation of nursing care of children with autism, whether at home or while the child is hospitalized, centers on determining that the child and family are functioning at their optimum levels. To the greatest extent possible, the child and family should demonstrate the ability to cope with the disability in order to foster normal growth and development.

## Common Needs of Children With Disabling Conditions

### Family Support and Recognition of Individual Coping Methods

The diagnosis that a child has a disabling condition or special needs is a major stressor on family life. The diagnosis affects the entire family as a group and also affects each person individually—mother, father, brother, sister, or grandparent. The situation can provide an opportunity either for growth or for destruction. Many families can become "disabled" families whose adaptation results in dysfunction.

The additional stress of raising a child with a disability can also cause disintegration of the family through parental abandonment or divorce. Finding meaning in the situation is an important coping mechanism for some family members. Many become advocates for the disabled, change to professions that help the disabled, or write about important related issues.

Most stage theories oversimplify a complex process. Some parents pass through predictable time-bound stages—denial, anger, bargaining, depression, and acceptance; others may move in less predictable directions; some may remain in a state of chronic sorrow with feelings of ongoing sadness (Olshansky, 1962; Wikler, Wasow, & Hatfield, 1981). It is important for nurses to recognize and assess each parent's individual method of coping. Responses will be influenced by many factors, including family and community support, the parent's developmental stage, cultural group, religion, socioeconomic resources, and experience with stress. Nurses should be alert to life-cycle crises that have been identified (Olshansky, 1962; Wikler, Wasow, & Hatfield, 1981) as

particularly difficult times for parents. These include the following:

• Time of diagnosis
• Time that children without disabilities begin to walk
• Time that children without disabilities begin to talk
• Time that younger siblings surpass the child
• Time that alternative placement becomes necessary
• Time of entry into school
• Onset of puberty
• Twenty-first birthday
• Time of naming a guardian for after the parents die or are unable to care for their child

How successfully a family responds to and copes with the situation may depend on the resources available outside the family. Many families have discovered that they can receive more help and support from strangers who share a similar type of problem than they can from those closer to them. There are countless organizations throughout the United States that offer a variety of services to families with special needs (Table 20-5).

Nurses must carefully assess the family's strengths and weaknesses, coping methods, and degree of acceptance before recommending an organization. The timing of the suggestion and approach is important. Just after the initial diagnosis is made the family may not be open to considering involvement with an organization, whereas later the same family may be eager to participate. Some families are private and would not enjoy active participation in an organization. They may appreciate receiving a newsletter, recommendations regarding books and magazines, or the name and address of a contact person for future reference. Nurses should write down the information or give the parents a brochure about the organizations that they can contact when they are ready (Steele, 1988). Other families may receive the support they need from their family members, friends, or religious group. For most, participation in an organization may be one of the most significant and inexpensive resources available to parents of a child with a disability. Membership provides the person with a common bond that helps to reduce feelings of social isolation. Abbott and Meredith (1986) studied the strengths of parents with retarded children and found that families who adapted best were those who participated in a support group and had a strong personal faith with a religious affiliation.

### Siblings and Other Family Members

Siblings of children with disabilities need special consideration. Often, they are "invisible" family members during clinic visits or hospitalizations and are overlooked. Because the parents are overtaxed and distracted by the child with a disability, the siblings suffer a loss of attention. Often

## Table 20–5. Services and Activities Provided by Organizations

**Self-Help**

Group sharing sessions
Visitation programs (e.g., Parent-to-Parent)
Phone networks
Sibling/grandparent groups

**Information**

Newsletters
Libraries
Handbooks
Clearinghouses
Educational meetings

**Community Outreach Programs**

Speakers' bureau
Professional inservice programs
Health fairs
Workshops/seminars

**Membership Services**

Needs assessment
Financial assistance, equipment
Transportation
Social/recreational activities
Respite care

**Political Action**

Lobbying
Meeting with legislators
Keeping members apprised of upcoming child health issues

**Fund-Raising**

Groups such as the Sibling Information Network assist in locating siblings of children with similar disabilities through a newsletter. A group called Especially Grandparents was developed to meet the needs of grandparents of children with disabilities. They also publish a newsletter.

## Recreation and Play Needs

Play and recreation activities are an essential part of development for all children. Activities can be included in an infant stimulation program or as part of physical or occupational therapy. Many children with disabilities, as well as their parents, need assistance in learning how to use toys appropriately. Parents need to be encouraged to play with their child regardless of the child's age, size, temperament, or disability (Steele, 1988). Switches can be placed on toys so they can be easily operated by children with various disabilities. In some areas, there are toy libraries that provide toys on a loan basis. Computers offer children with disabilities the opportunity to learn new skills, communicate, and play. When a child is hospitalized, nurses should question the parents regarding favorite toys, preferred type of play (solitary, parallel, or group), and usual pastimes. This information should be included in the child's nursing care plan.

School systems, organizations, and community parks and recreation programs provide adapted sports activities (Fig. 20-9), including swimming, table tennis, bowling, horseback riding, marathon racing, skiing, and Special Olympics. Scouting provides many opportunities for growth for children with disabilities (Fig. 20-10). In some

older siblings must assume caregiving responsibilities for the child with a disability. Anger, jealousy, sibling rivalry, and resentment are common reactions among siblings (Futcher, 1988). They may also become isolated from their peer group and be at higher risk for academic failure.

Nurses can assist parents in recognizing the impact that the care of a child with a disability has on the normal child. It puts a strain on a child who is less equipped to understand and cope (Scheiber, 1989). As siblings struggle with their own developmental issues, they are also struggling with their sibling's disability and its implications for their own lives (Rothery, 1987). Nurses should recommend that parents spend quality time with their children without disabilities. Reading a bedtime story, with parent and child alone, or using bedtime to catch up on the news of the child's day can be beneficial. Taking the child on a special "date" or activity each week can be a major event (Scheiber, 1989). Many organizations provide support groups for siblings. For those children who are unable to attend a support group, a "pen pal" who is the sibling of a child with a similar disability may provide support.

*Figure 20–9. Children with disabilities engaged in an adapted sports activity.*

*Figure 20–10. Special Needs Girl Scout Troop #425, co-sponsored by the Association for Retarded Citizens, Palm Beach County, and the Palm Glades Girl Scout Council, Florida.*

areas, facilities and nature trails have been adapted to meet the needs of special Scouts.

Camp programs and facilities that do not further handicap the child with a disability through physical or attitudinal barriers can be a therapeutic tool and a rewarding experience. Therapeutic recreation helps many children with disabilities find the courage to test their abilities and to attempt new experiences (Kawasaki, 1981). Camp experiences can promote independence, self-care, and improved interpersonal relationships. Pediatric nurses are in a position to suggest a camp experience to a child's parents. Coordinating the child's home school program with the camp's program may help to keep the child from losing the accomplishments of the school year, which often happens during a summer of inactivity (Kawasaki, 1981).

Pediatric nurses should consult with instructors of adapted physical education, therapeutic recreation specialists, child life specialists, and occupational and physical therapists to devise appropriate play and recreation activities for children with disabilities in various health care settings. Efforts should be made to include children without disabilities in these play or recreation activities whenever possible.

## Discipline

Children with disabilities have the same need for discipline as children without disabilities. They live in an organized society and must be prepared to accept restrictions on their behavior. Like all children, they need to learn acceptable behavior that permits them to live enjoyably with themselves and others. There are rules that govern behavior at home, in school, and within the neighborhood and community. Appropriate discipline provides children with protection from danger, relieves them of the burden of decisions that they are not prepared to make, and allows them to develop independence within a secure framework. Discipline is one of the most challenging aspects of parenting a child with a disability. Parents of children with

disabilities often tend to overlook the need for discipline. The poorer the prognosis, the more lenient parents tend to be. For a child who has shown little activity, any behavior (kicking, screaming, biting) can be viewed as positive. "Some" behavior is better than none.

Consistent discipline helps to show children acceptable limits of behavior, and helps them learn self-control. By reinforcing acceptable behavior and correcting unacceptable behavior, parents can help children with disabilities to interact better with their peers and siblings. Discipline also helps children learn. Children with poor discipline have a difficult time learning, because without adequate self-control they cannot pay the attention that is required in order to learn and grow.

Pediatric nurses should encourage parents to begin discipline early in the child's life. Discipline should be appropriate for the child's developmental level, memory, and sense of time. Correction should occur at the time of the behavior, not "when Dad gets home." Children should be given real choices in order to learn independence. Choices might include: "Do you want to wear the red shirt or the green one?" or "Do you want to drink your milk before or after dinner?" Positive phrasing is important also. Instead of saying "Don't stand on the chair," parents might say "Put your feet on the floor." Discipline should include logical consequences. If a toddler deliberately drops a cup of milk, the consequence is no milk. If older children spill their milk, they should help clean it up to the extent they are able. Other methods of discipline include behavior modification, time out (placing the child in a quiet environment for a specified period of time), ignoring (often any response from the parent is very encouraging), generous rewards for positive behaviors, and praise and affection, including hugging. Vibrators can be used as positive rewards for visually impaired children and glow sticks for those who are hearing impaired.

## Advocacy

Advocacy is defined as "pleading another's cause or speaking or writing in support of something; to be in favor of." Nurses who work with children with disabilities must be strong advocates in order to facilitate the child's receiving needed services. They need advocacy as the nurse collaborates and coordinates care with other disciplines such as occupational therapy, physical therapy, speech therapy, psychology, and education. Nurses must be aware of how the system works and of the legal rights of parents to due process, so they can help the family obtain services from government and social service agencies. Sometimes it is necessary to "label" a child in order for that child to obtain needed services, but labeling can influence the expectations of people working with the child and may compromise insurance benefits. It becomes a "catch-22."

Nurses must also teach parents how to be advocates

for themselves and their children. Advocacy is a total commitment. Many parents find it difficult to be an advocate for their children. They back off quickly when they are told "no" to a request. Health care providers and government agencies can be very intimidating. Knowledge can be power for parents of children with disabilities. The more parents know about their rights and what their children are entitled to, the more effective advocates they can be. Parents tend to ask too few questions during conferences with teachers and health care providers, assume a passive role, and, consequently, do not obtain all of the information they need in order to make decisions. Nurses need to invite and encourage parents and children to ask questions and become active participants in the decision-making process.

## Record Keeping

Nurses should encourage parents of children with disabilities to keep accurate records of their child's growth, developmental milestones, diagnostic tests, physician's names and addresses, dates of office visits, procedures, and medications. A scrapbook, file folder, or notebook can help to keep everything in one place. Parents should ask for copies of all test results, assessments, and reports. This will help the parents inform other members of the health care team and community agencies about their child. Parents should be encouraged to keep their photo album in chronological order. This will aid in identifying achievement of developmental milestones and describing the child's behavior. When available, a periodic videotape of the child serves as an excellent aid in recalling milestones and visualizing progress in a particular area.

## Long-Term Planning

As former Senator Lowell P. Weicker, Jr., said in a message to parents, regarding his son and other children who have Down syndrome, "Don't look back. Rather, prepare for your child's future—a future that one day will have to be lived without you. So start today" (1986, p. iii). It is not easy for parents to plan for the future of a child who has a disabling condition. Doing so means admitting that there will come a time when the child will be virtually alone in a world that is not always compassionate and caring. Nurses should advise parents to seek legal counsel early in their child's life from an attorney who is sensitive to the needs of children with disabilities and is familiar with state and federal entitlement programs upon which the child may depend for lifetime care. In an effort to protect their children from losing government benefits, families of children with disabilities must plan their estates carefully. Most families want to ensure that their children remain qualified for federal and state entitlement programs, while protecting the family's assets and the children's inheri-

tance from seizure by the state or federal government (Varnet, 1988). Wills, trusts, and guardianship are three important areas for families to consider in planning for the future.

As the parents of children with disabilities age and become physically or emotionally unable to care for their children, nurses can help parents explore available alternatives. Options may include group homes, foster care, nursing homes, and institutions. The decision to place children with disabilities outside the home is difficult for many parents. The decision should be made by the parents and accepted and supported by nurses. Every effort should be made to facilitate contact between these children and their families.

## Sex Education

Sexual emergence is a difficult developmental process for all adolescents. The difficulties of this rite of passage are compounded when the adolescent is disabled (Taylor, 1989). Parents often are not prepared for their child's sexual maturation and may tend to deny their child's developing sexuality, attempting to keep the child asexual. Most children with disabilities experience similar physical, sexual, social, and emotional developmental processes to those of their peers without disabilities. Sex education must begin early in the child's life and should be presented in simple language with audiovisual materials. Resources are available from organizations such as Planned Parenthood or the Association for Retarded Citizens. It is essential to explain to adolescents with disabilities what sexual developments will occur and how they can assume responsibility for their own self-care needs, e.g., during menstruation. School and home sex education should include information on acquired immune deficiency syndrome (AIDS). Parents need to know that children with disabilities are more frequently the victims of sexual exploitation, abuse, and rape. Children need to be taught about "good touch" and "bad touch" and told never to go anywhere with someone they don't know. Parents need to carefully monitor their child's activities and friends. Nurses need to encourage parents to discuss appropriate activities, birth control, normal physiological responses, and locations for engaging in private matters, such as masturbation. Children with disabilities can be just as surreptitious about meeting their sexual needs as their unimpaired peers (Taylor, 1989).

Contraceptive alternatives include condoms, diaphragms, intrauterine devices (IUDs), birth control pills, and subdermal implants. The benefits and risks of each method must be evaluated based upon the individual's needs and ability to assume responsibility. Sterilization is a difficult moral and ethical question. The sterilization of minors and incompetent adults is almost exclusively a matter of individual state laws.

## Dental Care

Dental irregularities are common among children with disabilities. Teeth may be slow to erupt, maloccluded, or misshapen. Nurses should encourage parents to begin dental hygiene as soon as the first tooth erupts. Parents should brush the child's teeth, especially at bedtime, and refrain from giving the child a bottle of milk or juice at bedtime. This helps prevent dental caries. Soft toothbrushes, fluoride, and flossing are also recommended. A new toothbrush should be used every 3 to 4 months or after an infection (Steele, 1988). Tablets that show where children have failed to brush are often a useful and fun way to promote oral hygiene. Children who are on seizure medications such as Dilantin need special dental care due to the development of gingival hyperplasia.

Nurses should recommend dentists who are sensitive and experienced in meeting the special needs of children with disabilities. Some major hospitals and medical centers have dental specialty clinics for the physically and mentally disabled. Parents may also contact The National Foundation of Dentistry for the Handicapped or their local dental society for a referral to a facility or dentists who may specialize in working with children with disabilities.

## Respite Care

Respite is essential for families of a child with a disability. The physical and emotional demands of raising a child with special needs can be overwhelming and place a tremendous burden on the parents in all aspects of their lives. The opportunity to have time alone or together, while participating in recreational activities or personal interests, can enable the parent to return refreshed and better able to meet the ongoing challenge. In addition, because of the special needs of children with disabilities, it is often more difficult to obtain child care providers who are willing to accept the child and capable of providing adequate care. Access to respite care can be very difficult for parents of children with disabilities. Nurses should be aware of respite programs in the community and should make appropriate referrals.

The constant role of nurse, teacher, and physical, occupational, and speech therapist can detract from a normal parent–child relationship. Parents and children need to take time out, or "respite," from the parent-therapist role and make time to hug, laugh, and play. Children with disabilities need real parents, too.

## Summary

Whether they have physical, cognitive, or emotional impairments, children with disabilities and their families have special needs. Nurses can do a great deal to enhance the potential for growth and development, and to help these children and their families achieve as normal a life as possible. By using the nursing process, nurses can continually assess growth and development to identify problems early and can formulate diagnoses to help overcome the problems. Through planning and intervention nurses can work with parents and families to determine goals and strategies to help disabled children reach their highest level of potential.

## References

Abbott, D. A., & Meredith, W. H. (1986). Strengths of parents with retarded children. *Family Relations, 35,* 371.

Aiello, B., & Shulman, J. (1988). *The kids on the block* book series. Frederick, MD: Twenty-First Century Books.

American Academy of Pediatrics. (1987). Exercise for children who are mentally retarded. *Pediatrics, 80,* 447.

American Psychiatric Association (APA). (1987). *Diagnostic and statistical manual of mental disorders* (3rd ed., revised) (DSM-III-R). Washington, DC: Author.

Anderson, J., Hinojosa, J., & Strauch, C. (1987). Integrating play in neurodevelopmental treatment. *The American Journal of Occupational Therapy, 41,* 421.

August, G. J., Raz, N., Papanicolaou, A. C., Baird, T. D., Hirsh, S. L., & Hsu, L. L. (1984). Fenfluramine treatment in infantile autism. *The Journal of Nervous and Mental Disease, 172*:604.

Bailey, D. B., & Wolery, M. (1984). *Teaching infants and preschoolers with handicaps.* Columbus, OH: Charles Merrill.

Castiglia, P. T., & Petrini, M. A. (1985). Selecting a developmental screening tool. *Pediatric Nursing, 11,* 8.

Chess, S., & Thomas, A. (1986). *Temperament in clinical practice.* New York: The Guilford Press.

Cohen, F. L. (1984). *Clinical genetics in nursing practice.* Philadelphia: J. B. Lippincott Company.

de la Cruz, F. F., & Muller, J. Z. (1983). Facts about Down syndrome. *Children Today, 12,* 2.

Dienemann, J. A. (1989). Case managed/coordinated care. Pediatric Nursing Forum on the Future: Looking Toward the 21st Century. *Proceedings and report from an invitational conference.* Pitman, NJ: Anthony Jannetti, Inc., 51.

Edgerton, R. E. (1979). *Mental retardation.* Cambridge, MA: Harvard University Press.

Futcher, J. A. (1988). Chronic illness and family dynamics. *Pediatric Nursing, 14,* 381.

Gleeson, S. V. (1987). Public sector perspective: Potential nursing services in mental retardation. *Pediatric Nursing, 13,* 81.

Grossman, H. J. (1983). *Classification in mental retardation.* Washington, DC: American Association on Mental Deficiency.

Harris, J. C. (1990). The biopsychosocial approach to pediatrics. In F. A. Oski, C. D. DeAngelis, R. D. Feigin, & J. B. Warshaw (Eds.). *Principles and practice of pediatrics.* Philadelphia: J. B. Lippincott, pp. 636–678.

Hertz, B. G. (1987). Acuity card testing of retarded children. *Behavioral Brain Research, 24,* 85.

Hreidarsson, S. J., Shapiro, B. K., & Capute, A. J. (1983). Age of walking in the cognitively impaired. *Clinical Pediatrics, 22,* 248.

Johnson, E. L. (1986). Keyboards for the handicapped. *Journal of Medical Systems, 10,* 277.

Kawasaki, M. A. (1981). Summer camp and the disabled child. *Pediatric Nursing, 7,* 9.

Koheil, R., Sochaniwskyj, A. E., Bablich, K., Kenny, D. J., & Milner, M. (1987). Biofeedback techniques and behavior modification in the conservative remediation of drooling by children with cerebral palsy. *Developmental Medicine and Child Neurology, 29,* 19.

Kosowski, M. M., & Sopczyk, D. L. (1985). Feeding hospitalized children with developmental disabilities. *The American Journal of Maternal Child Nursing, 10,* 190.

Lee-Dukes, G. (1986). Infantile autism. *Academy of Family Physicians,* 33:149, 1986.

Magill, J., & Hurlbut, N. (1986). The self-esteem of adolescents with cerebral palsy. *The American Journal of Occupational Therapy, 40,* 402.

Martin, N., Holt, N. B., & Hicks, D. (1981). *Comprehensive rehabilitation nursing.* New York: McGraw-Hill.

Miola, E. S. (1987). Down syndrome: Update for practitioners. *Pediatric Nursing, 13,* 233.

Montgomery, T. R. (1988). Clinical aspects of mental retardation. *Clinical Pediatrics, 27,* 529.

Nelson, K. B., & Ellenberg, J. H. (1986). Antecedents of cerebral palsy. *The New England Journal of Medicine, 315,* 81.

Olshansky, S. (1962). Chronic sorrow: A response to having a mentally defective child. *Social Casework, 43,* 190.

Olsson, I., Steffenburg, S., & Gillberg, C. (1988). Epilepsy in autism and autisticlike conditions. *Archives of Neurology, 45,* 666.

Paneth, N. (1986). Etiological factors in cerebral palsy. *Pediatric Annals, 15,* 191.

Patrick, J., Boland, M., Stoski, D., & Murray, G. E. (1986). Rapid correction of wasting in children with cerebral palsy. *Developmental Medicine & Child Neurology, 28,* 734.

Peterson, N. L. (1987). *Early intervention for handicapped and at-risk children.* Denver: Love Publishing.

Pueschel, S. M. (1983). Altanto-axial subluxation in Down syndrome. *Lancet, 1,* 980.

Pueschel, S. M., Sassaman, E. A., Scola, P. S., Thuline, H. C., Stark, A. M., & Horrobin, M. (1982). Biomedical aspects in Down syndrome. In S.M. Pueschel & J.E. Rynders (Eds.). *Down syndrome.* Cambridge, MA: Ware Press.

Purdy, A. H., Deitz, J. C., & Harris, S. R. (1987). Efficacy of two treatment approaches to reduce tongue protrusion of children with Down syndrome. *Developmental Medicine and Child Neurology, 29,* 469.

Rothery, S. A. (1987). Understanding and supporting special siblings. *Journal of Pediatric Health Care, 1,* 21.

Scheiber, K. K. (1989). Developmentally delayed children: Effects on the normal sibling. *Pediatric Nursing, 15,* 42.

Shapiro, B. K., & Capute, A. J. (1990). Cerebral palsy. In F. A. Oski, C. D. DeAngelis, R. D. Feigin, & J. B. Warshaw (Eds.). *Principles and practice of pediatrics.* Philadelphia: J. B. Lippincott, pp. 616–622.

Shapiro, B. K., Green, P., Krick, J., Allen, D., & Capute, A. J. (1986). Growth of severely impaired children: Neurological versus nutritional factors. *Developmental Medicine & Child Neurology, 28,* 729.

Shapiro, B. K., Palmer, F. B., & Capute, A. J. (1987). The early detection of mental retardation. *Clinical Pediatrics, 26,* 215.

Steele, S. (1985). Young children with cerebral palsy: Practical guidelines for care. *Pediatric Nursing, 11,* 259.

Steele, S. M. (1988). Preschool children with developmental delays: Nursing intervention. *Journal of Pediatric Health Care, 2,* 245.

Taylor, M. O. (1989). Teaching parents about their impaired adolescent's sexuality. *MCN: American Journal of Maternal Child Nursing, 14,* 109.

The Education of All Handicapped Children Act of 1975, P.L. 94-142, U.S.C. *Federal Register, 42,* 42473 (August 23), 1977.

Trohanis, P. (1989). An overview to P.L. 99-457. *Exceptional Parent, 19,* 46.

Trott, M. C., & Maechtlen, A. D. (1986). The use of overcorrection as a means to control drooling. *The American Journal of Occupational Therapy, 40,* 701.

U.S. Department of Education. (1985). Seventh Annual Report to Congress on the Implementation of the Education of the Handicapped Act, 1.32:199.

Varnet, T. M. (1988). Future financial planning. *Exceptional Parent, 18,* 32.

Weicker, L. P. (1986). Foreword. In Stray-Gundersen, K. (Ed.). *Babies with Down syndrome. A new parents' guide.* Kensington, MD: Woodbine House.

Wikler, L., Wasow, M., & Hatfield, E. (1981). Chronic sorrow revisited: Parent vs. professional depiction of the adjustment of parents of mentally retarded children. *American Journal of Orthopsychiatry, 51.*

Williams, J. K. (1983). Reproductive decisions: Adolescents with Down syndrome. *Pediatric Nursing, 9,* 43.

Zigler, E., & Hodapp, R. (1986). *Understanding mental retardation.* New York: Cambridge University Press.

# Bibliography

## Children With Disabilities

Adams, R. C., Daniel, A. N., McCubbin, J. A., & Rullman, L. (1982). *Games, sports and exercises for the physically handicapped.* Philadelphia: Lea & Febiger.

Bailey, C. F. (1986). Withholding or withdrawing treatment on handicapped newborns. *Pediatric Nursing, 12,* 413.

Barnard, K. E., & Erickson, M. L. (1976). *Teaching children with developmental problems* (2nd ed.). St. Louis: C. V. Mosby.

Davis, B. O., & Steele, S. (1991). Case management for young children with special health care needs. *Pediatric Nursing, 17,* 15.

Greenberg, C. S. (Ed.). (1988). *Nursing care planning guides for children.* Baltimore: Williams & Wilkins.

Guralnick, M. J., & Groom, J. M. (1987). The peer relations of mildly delayed and nonhandicapped preschool children in mainstreamed playgroups. *Child Development, 58,* 1556.

Phillips, M., & Brostoff, M. Working collaboratively with parents of disabled children. *Pediatric Nursing, 15,* 180.

Shelton, T. L., Jeppson, E., & Johnson, B. H. (1987). *Family centered care for children with special health care needs* (2nd ed.). Washington, DC: Association for the Care of Children's Health.

Steele, S. M. (1988). Assessing developmental delays in preschool children. *Journal of Pediatric Health Care, 2,* 141.

Strauss, S. S., & Munton, M. (1985). Common concerns of parents with disabled children. *Pediatric Nursing, 11,* 371.

Tabeek, E. S., & Conroy, M. G. (1981). Teaching sexual awareness to the significantly disabled school-age child. *Pediatric Nursing, 7,* 21.

Thompson, J. E., & Thompson, H. O. (1988). Living with ethical decisions with which you disagree. *Journal of Maternal/Child Nursing, 13,* 245.

Williams, J. K. (1986). Genetic counseling in pediatric nursing care. *Pediatric Nursing, 12,* 287.

## Cerebral Palsy

Bertoti, D. (1986). Effect of short leg casting on ambulation in children with cerebral palsy. *Physical Therapy, 66,* 1522.

Coffman, S. P. (1983). Parents' perceptions of needs for themselves and their children in a cerebral palsy clinic. *Issues in Comprehensive Pediatric Nursing, 6,* 67.

Cohen, S., & Warren, R. D. (1987). Preliminary survey of family abuse of children served by United Cerebral Palsy Centers. *Developmental Medicine and Child Neurology, 29,* 12.

Davis, G. T., & Hill, P. M. (1980). Cerebral palsy. *Nursing Clinics of North America, 15,* 35.

Hinderer, K. A., Harris, S. R., Purdy, A. H., Chew, D. E., Staheli, L. T., McLaughlin, J. F., & Jaffe, K. M. (1988). Effects of "tone-reducing" vs. standard plaster casts on gait improvement of children with cerebral palsy. *Developmental Medicine and Child Neurology, 30,* 370.

Watt, J., Sims, D., Harckham, F., Schmidt, L., McMillan, A., & Hamilton, J. (1986). A prospective study of inhibitive casting as an adjunct to physiotherapy for cerebral-palsied children. *Developmental Medicine and Child Neurology, 28,* 480.

## Mental Retardation

Beitchman, J. H., & Peterson, M. (1986). Disorders of language, communication, and behavior in mentally retarded children. *Psychiatric Clinics of North America, 9,* 689.

Gleeson, S. V. (1987). Public sector perspective: Potential nursing services in mental retardation. *Pediatric Nursing, 13,* 81.

Grossman, H. (Ed.). (1983). *Manual on terminology and classification in mental retardation* (2nd ed.). Washington, DC: American Association on Mental Deficiency.

Seligman, M. (1987). Adaptation of children to a chronically ill or mentally handicapped sibling. *Canadian Medical Association Journal, 136,* 1249.

Williams, D. N. (1987). The girl who is mentally retarded. *Pediatric Nursing, 13,* 89.

## Down Syndrome

Baird, P. A., & Sadovnick, A. D. (1988). Causes of death to age 30 in Down syndrome. *Journal of Human Genetics, 43,* 239.

Cronk, C. E., Chumblea, W. M., & Roche, A. F. (1985). Assessment of overweight children with trisomy 21. *American Journal of Mental Deficiency, 89,* 433.

Davis, W. (1986). Assessing children with Down syndrome. *Physical Therapy, 66,* 1779.

Margar-Bacal, F., Witzel, M. A., & Munro, I. (1987). Speech intelligibility after partial glossectomy in children with Down's syndrome. *Plastic and Reconstructive Surgery, 79,* 44.

Pipes, P. L., & Holm, V. A. (1980). Feeding children with Down's syndrome. *American Dietetic Association Journal, 77,* 277.

Steele, S., Russell, F., Hansen, B., & Mills, B. (1989). Home management of URI in children with Down syndrome. *Pediatric Nursing, 15,* 484.

Stray-Gundersen, K. (Ed.). (1986). *Babies with Down syndrome. A new parents' guide.* Kensington, MD: Woodbine House.

Thome, R. (1986). Stimulating Daniel. *Nursing Times, 82,* 44.

## Autism

Gualtieri, C. (1986). Fenfluramine and autism: Careful reappraisal is in order. *Journal of Pediatrics, 108,* 417.

Morgan, S. B. (1984). Helping parents understand the diagnosis of autism. *Journal of Developmental and Behavioral Pediatrics, 5,* 78.

Sigman, M., Mundy, P., Sherman, T., & Ungerer, J. (1986). Social interactions of autistic, mentally retarded and normal children and their caregivers. *Journal of Child Psychology and Psychiatry, 27,* 647.

Simons, J., & Oishi, S. (1985). *The hidden child. The Linwood method for reaching the autistic child.* Kensington, MD: Woodbine House.

Zoltak, B. B. (1986). Autism: Recognition and management. *Pediatric Nursing, 12,* 90.

## Organizations

Academy of Dentistry for the Handicapped
211 E. Chicago Avenue
Suite 1616
Chicago, IL 60611

American Association on Mental Deficiency
  (AAMD)
1719 Kalorama Road, NW
Washington, DC 20008

Autism Society of America
8601 Georgia Avenue, Suite 503
Silver Spring, MD 20910

The Epilepsy Foundation of America
4351 Garden City Drive
Landover, MD 20785

The ERIC Clearinghouse on Handicapped and
  Gifted Children
The Council for Exceptional Children
1920 Association Drive
Reston, VA 22091

Especially Grandparents
(for grandparents of children with developmental
  disabilities)
King County ARC
2230 8th Avenue
Seattle, WA 98121

International Shriners Headquarters
2900 Rocky Point
Tampa, FL 33607

March of Dimes Birth Defects Foundation
1275 Mamaroneck Avenue
White Plains, NY 10605

National Association of Mothers of Special Children
9079 Arrowhead Court
Cincinnati, OH 45321

National Association of Retarded Citizens
2709 Avenue E East
P.O. Box 6109
Arlington, TX 76011

National Down Syndrome Congress
1800 Dempster Road
Park Ridge, IL 60068-1146

National Down Syndrome Society
141 Fifth Avenue
New York, NY 10010

National Easter Seal Society for Crippled Children
2023 W. Ogden Avenue
Chicago, IL 60612

National Foundation of Dentistry for the Handicapped
1600 Stout Street, Suite 1420
Denver, CO 80202-3132

Sibling Information Network
"Network Newsletter"
Connecticut's University Affiliated Program on
  Developmental Disabilities
991 Main Street
East Hartford, CT 06108

United Cerebral Palsy Association
66 East 34th Street
New York, NY 10016

## Clothing and Equipment

Clothing for the Handicapped
Sister Kenny Institute
2727 Chicago Avenue
Minneapolis, MN 55407

Columbia Orthopedic Positioning Car Seat
Columbia Medical Manufacturing Corp.
P.O. Box 633
Pacific Palisades, CA 90272

E-Z-On Safety Vest (Car Seat)
E-Z-On Products, Inc.
500 Commerce Way West
Jupiter, FL 33458

Levi's: Custom jeans for people with special needs
Levi's E.P.P. Dept. 888, 6621 Geyser Springs Road
Little Rock, AK 77209

Medic Alert Foundation International
Turlock, CA 95381-1008

Rifton Equipment for the Handicapped
Route 213
Rifton, NY 12471

Special Clothes for Special Children
P.O. Box 4220
Alexandria, VA 22303

## Recreation and Adapted Sports

Adapted Sports Association
Allen Hayes
P.O. Box 299
Miller Place, NY 11764

Boy Scouts of America
Scouting for the Handicapped
1325 Walnut Hill Lane
P.O. Box 152079
Irving, TX 75015

Camps for Children with Special Needs and Their
  Families
1987 Parents' Guide to Accredited Camps
American Camping Association
100 Bradford Woods
Martinsville, IN 46151

Girl Scouts of the USA
830 Third Ave. & 51st St.
New York, NY 10022

International Council on Therapeutic Ice Skating
P.O. Box 4541
Winter Park, FL 32793

National Association of Sports for Cerebral Palsy
United Cerebral Palsy Association
66 East 34 Street
New York, NY 10016

National Easter Seals Society
Directory of Camps for the Handicapped
2023 West Ogden Avenue
Chicago, IL 60612

National Wheelchair Athletic Association
Nassau Community College
Garden City, NJ 11530

North American Riding for the Handicapped
  Association
Box 100
Ashburn, VA 22011

Special Olympics
Suite 203
1701 K St., NW
Washington, DC 20006

U.S.A. Toy Library Association
2719 Broadway Avenue
Evanston, IL 60201

## Recommended Reading for Families

Association for the Care of Children's Health. *Let's play with our children*. New Directions for Exceptional Parenting. Booklets available from the Association, 3615 Wisconsin Avenue, N.W., Washington, DC 20016.

Christopher, W., & Christopher, B. (1989). *Mixed blessings*. New York: Avon Books.

Exceptional Parent Magazine, P.O. Box 3000, Dept. EP, Denville, NJ 07834-9919

Featherstone, H. (1982). *A difference in the family: Living with a disabled child*. New York: Penguin Books.

Fink, D. (1988). *School age children with special needs: What do they do when school is out?* Boston: Exceptional Parent Press.

Finnie, N. (1975). *Handing the young cerebral Palsied child at home* (2nd ed.). New York: E. P. Dutton.

Gerver, J.M. (1983). A grandparent's view. *Children Today, 12,* 12.

Goldfarb, L., Brotherson, M. J., Summers, J. A., & Turnbull, A. P. (1986). *Meeting the challenge of disability or chronic illness—a family guide*. Baltimore, MD: Paul H. Brookes.

Kaufman, S. Z. (1988). *Retarded isn't stupid, mom!* Baltimore, MD: Paul H. Brookes.

Kushner, H. S. (1981). *When bad things happen to good people*. New York: Avon.

Simons, R. (1985). *After the tears*. New York: Harcourt Brace Jovanovich.

Sinker, M. (1986). *Toys for growing*. Chicago: Year Book Medical Publishers.

Stray-Gundersen, K. (1986). *Babies with Down syndrome. A new parent's guide*. Washington, DC: Woodbine House.

Turnbull, H. R., Turnbull, A. P., Bronick, G. J., Summers, J. A., & Roeder-Gordon, C. (1989). *Disability and the family. A guide to decisions for adulthood*. Baltimore, MD: Paul H. Brookes.

# Effects of Substance Abuse on Children and Families

Mary Jo Gorney-Lucero

21

*Definition of Terms*

*Scope of the Problem*

*Causes of Substance Abuse*

*A Developmental Approach to the*
*Effects of Substance Abuse*
   *The Effects of Substance Abuse on*
   *Neonates*
   *The Effects of Substance Abuse on*
   *Children*
   *The Effects of Substance Abuse on*
   *Adolescents*

*The Nursing Process in Substance*
*Abuse*
   *Assessment*
   *Nursing Diagnoses*
   *Planning and Implementation*
   *Evaluation*

*Treatment Options*

*Prevention Strategies*
   *Early Prenatal Instruction*
   *Early Classroom Intervention*

*Sources of Information*

*Support Groups*

*Summary*

*Photograph by David Finn*

## Learning Objectives

*Upon completion of this chapter the reader will be able to:*

1. *Analyze precipitating factors that contribute to the development of substance abuse and addiction.*

2. *Cite the possible effects of maternal substance abuse on neonates.*

3. *Differentiate among the coping strategies of children and adolescents who live in homes where substance abuse is prevalent.*

4. *Describe the nurse's role in assessing substance abusers.*

5. *Identify treatment and recovery issues and resources for substance abusers and their families.*

6. *Cite substance abuse prevention strategies for early prenatal and early classroom intervention.*

7. *Develop a nursing care plan for an adolescent substance abuser.*

## Key Terms

*addiction*

*alcoholism*

*codependency*

*delirium tremens*

*detoxification*

*fetal alcohol effects*

*fetal alcohol syndrome*

*multiple addiction*

*neonatal withdrawal syndrome*

The extent of the substance abuse problem in the United States is overwhelming. National statistics indicate that 28 million Americans have at least one addicted parent. Black (1981) estimates that between 12 and 15 million children under the age of 16 are now being raised in homes with at least one alcoholic parent. Many of these children suffer from a variety of problems related to parental drug abuse, including school phobias, learning disabilities, attention disorders, depression, anxiety, and mood disturbances (Brown, 1988).

Only within the last 10 years have the problems of children of alcoholics and adult children of alcoholics been acknowledged by the health care community. Therapists now specialize in the treatment of these populations. Furthermore, self-help support groups are available solely to work on issues related to children of alcoholics.

Substance abuse is a family disease. Everyone living within a family system with an addicted person is affected since the addicted person's behavior is characterized by both repeated drug and alcohol abuse and the inevitable personality changes, such as procuring behaviors and guilt and remorse after using. Black (1981) maintains that for children in an alcoholic family, "the combination of alcoholism and co-alcoholism results in neither parent being responsive or available on a consistent predictable basis" (p. 4). As a consequence, children are affected by what cartoonist Al Capp (creator of Lil' Abner) might call a "triple whammy"—the interaction of one or more of the following factors: the alcoholic parent, the nonalcoholic or codependent parent, and the abnormal family dynamics of a home distorted by addiction-related behavior.

Woititz (1983) contends that children of alcoholic families spend their time trying to figure out what is normal, then try very hard to act normally. This occurs because the parents' responses to the children's behavior are not based strictly on the child's behavior itself; instead, they are based on the parent's degree of intoxication, guilt over being intoxicated again, or, in the codependent's case, fear that the addict will drink or use drugs again. It is difficult for children to predict correct or normal responses to their behavior if they only rarely experience appropriate responses.

## Definition of Terms

According to Schaef (1986):

> [W]ithin the chemical dependency field, an addiction *is broadly considered to be the compulsive need for any substance or process outside the person that becomes more important than sobriety—the state of functioning in a way that is clear, healthy, and normal for the human organism . . . an addiction to food and/or chemicals is often called an ingestive addiction.*
>
> *A process addiction is an addiction (by an individual, groups or even societies) to a way (or process) of acquiring addictive substances. The function of an addiction is to keep us out of touch with ourselves (our feelings, morality, awareness—our living process) (p. 24).*

Since alcohol is just one of the many drugs to which individuals can become addicted, an *alcoholic* is considered to have the same problem as a person addicted to other substances, such as morphine or heroin. Psychological treatment is not based on the drug being abused; rather, treatment focuses on the addictive process.

Another frequent problem is *multiple addiction* or *polysubstance abuse,* where individuals become dependent on more than one substance at the same time or in patterns over a period of time. Multiple addiction is the simultaneous abuse of various mood-altering drugs or drug abuse in combination with alcohol. Many who work in the alcoholism field have come to believe that addiction is addiction, regardless of the substance being abused. For these people, basic principles of treatment for drug abuse vary little from alcoholism treatment. This can be illustrated by the well-known case of child actress Drew Barrymore, granddaughter of John Barrymore, who died of alcoholism at the age of 60. Drew was a star of the movie *E.T.* at age 7; she started drinking at age 9; she added using marijuana at age 10; and she began using cocaine at the age of 12. In 1989, by the age of 13, she had twice undergone extensive drug rehabilitation treatment. She told her story in the hope of helping other kids.

Drew's case in not atypical. Many people who are addicted to chemicals switch to other substances or another process when they stop the first one. In terms of cross-addictions, they frequently become addicted to food, sex, work, or exercise; however, this is not recovery. The aim of recovery is freedom from addictive behaviors, leading the individual to a self-directed, fulfilling life.

An early definition of individuals who were *codependent* or *co-alcoholic* included those whose lives became unmanageable as a result of living in a committed relationship with an alcoholic. As a result of intensified interest, research, and discussion of the topic, a much broader definition emerged: "A codependent is one who has let another person's behavior affect him or her, and who is obsessed with controlling that person's behavior" (Beattie, 1987, p. 31). Some of the caretaking behaviors codependents exhibit include feeling responsible for substance abusers' feelings, thoughts, actions, or well-being. The codependent person can be a child or an adult. Assuming responsibility for an addictive parent's behavior and well-being is an enormous burden for a child to undertake. Children caught in this process never have a chance to experience what it is like to be cared for and to be children; rather, they are the care-givers, assuming roles only appropriate for mature adults.

## Scope of the Problem

Alcohol and drug abuse are major problems facing American society today. It is estimated that 10% of the population is chemically dependent.

Suicide, along with homicide and accidental death, is one of the three leading causes of death among males 15 to 34 years of age (Abel & Zeidenberg, 1985). In an analysis of 3400 violence-related deaths in which blood alcohol concentration was measured, 21% percent of the deaths were suicides. In 35% of the suicides the victim had been drinking, and 23% of victims were legally intoxicated at the time of death.

Traffic crashes cause more deaths in the United States for people 1 to 34 years of age (National Center for Health Statistics, 1988). Nearly half of all traffic fatalities are alcohol-related; an estimated 40% of all people in the United States are involved in an alcohol-related traffic crash at some time during their lives. This report summarized data from the National Highway Traffic Safety Administration's Fatal Accident Reporting System on trends in alcohol-related traffic fatalities in the United States during 1982 through 1989 (Centers for Disease Control, 1990b).

The focus of the Centers for Disease Control's (1990a) *Morbidity and Mortality Weekly Report* for March 23, 1990 was the impact of alcohol-related disease in the state of Wisconsin in 1988. Based on the Center's Behavioral Risk Factor Surveillance System, Wisconsin is among the leading states nationally in estimates of alcohol-related risk factors. During 1988, in Wisconsin alone, "the direct costs of fetal alcohol syndrome (FAS) were estimated at $34 million; 80% of these costs were for residential care and support services for mentally retarded adults over 21 years of age whose impairment was considered to be caused by FAS. Indirect costs (i.e., potential goods and services not produced because of lost or diminished productivity) were estimated at $1.13 billion. In 1988, the alcohol-related economic cost per resident in Wisconsin was $305" (p. 185).

## Causes of Substance Abuse

The etiological bases of alcoholism and drug addiction are still much studied and debated issues, with both environmental and genetic factors posed as potential causes. Recent research findings (Blum et al., 1990), such as family, twin, and adoption studies, support the hypothesis that genetic factors are significant contributors to alcoholism. This information can be helpful to nurses trying to predict those at risk for alcoholism based on the patient history.

Fewer studies appear, however, on the etiological basis of drug abuse; instead, studies focus on the incidence of abuse. Studies dealing with drug abuse focus on factors that promote or facilitate the initiation of substance use (Blum & Richards, 1979). These studies suggest that people from families in which one or more members (generally parents or older siblings) smoke, drink, or use drugs are more likely to become substance abusers themselves.

Another category of studies attempts to demonstrate a relationship between which family influences contribute to drug abuse (Brook, Lettieri, & Brook, 1985). Available information, however, is inconclusive and has unclear clinical value. Although Denoff (1988) attempted to show a relationship between contributions made by irrational beliefs and parental interactions to adolescent drug abuse, the study was hampered by a small sample size (78) and its use of only cross-sectional data from adolescents and was restricted to middle- and upper-class white adolescents. Questions still remain about the ethnic and cultural relevance of the data gathered thus far.

Concern is frequently raised about the possible consequences of glamorization of alcohol and drug use in the media and advertising as causative factors in drug use and abuse. The validity of these concerns is demonstrated in the report of a survey of 180 children (ages 8–12) conducted by the Center for Science in the Public Interest in Washington, D.C. This study showed that young children can name more alcoholic drinks than U.S. presidents (MADD, 1990). One 10-year-old girl could correctly spell Michelob, Jack Daniel, and Heineken but could only spell our first president's name "George Wash." Michael Jacobson, executive director for the Center for Science in the Public Interest, states that this survey indicates the extent to which alcohol is part of the daily lives of children who cannot drink legally for another 10 years.

Another study (Christiansen, Smith, Roehling, & Goldman, 1989) measured the *expectancy effect*—how beliefs about alcohol's effects influence drinking behavior. For example, people who think that drinking increases sexual drive expect sexual advances from those who are drinking. This study looked at alcohol expectancies in seventh- and eighth-grade children and compared these expectations with the children's self-reported drinking onset and drinking behavior 1 year later. The researchers found that five of the expectancy scores strongly predicted initiation, quantity, frequency of drinking, and associated problems in adolescence. Furthermore, they found that children at highest risk were most likely to expect social enhancement as a result of drinking and to believe that alcohol improves both cognitive and motor functioning. Activists concerned with the environmental prevention of addictions, including groups such as Doctors Ought to Care (DOC) and Mothers Against Drunk Driving (MADD), are working to change this image of alcohol, tobacco, and drug use in the media. DOC is a coalition of health professionals and other concerned people who help educate the public, especially young people, about the major preventable causes of poor health and high medical costs. Their focus is the "killer habits," with particular emphasis on counteracting the promotion of tobacco and alcohol. DOC is solely concerned with health promotion and has pioneered the concept of paid advertising aimed at reducing lethal lifestyles. (For information write to DOC, 5510 Greenbriar, Suite 235, Houston, TX 77005. An example of a poster that it has published and distributed is shown in Figure 21-1.)

In summary, there is a great deal of evidence that one of the greatest risk factors for becoming an alcoholic is to be the child or sibling of one. Research studies indicate that

*Figure 21–1.  Example of a poster distributed by Doctors Ought to Care (DOC).*

both genetics and environment are involved in the development of addiction and abuse. Social and psychological factors influence drug and alcohol use behaviors. Research continues on the interaction of genetics and environment on the development of addiction.

## A Developmental Approach to the Effects of Substance Abuse

### The Effects of Substance Abuse on Neonates

The effects on neonates of maternal substance abuse depend on the specific drug used as well as on the patterns of abuse. Nurses should discourage the use of any drugs during pregnancy without prior consultation with a health professional. Each substance abused, as well as the amounts used, results in a different variety of symptoms in newborns. Commonly identified syndromes exist for alcohol, cocaine, heroin, and marijuana. The discussion that follows summarizes the research on the effects on newborns of maternal drug use.

Recent studies estimate that 10% to 25% of all neonates are exposed to drugs before birth (Dixon, 1989; Petitti & Coleman, 1990). Effects on the child depend on the mother's choice of drug. Heroin, methadone, and heavy alcohol consumption during pregnancy are associated with lower birth weight and central nervous system dysfunction (Zuckerman, 1985). Many questions remain, however, because of the unreliability of self-reported drug abuse and polysubstance abuse. The association between low birth weight and certain substances, such as cigarettes, cocaine (Dixon, 1989; Smith, 1988), heroin, phencyclidine hydrochloride (PCP; Howard, Kropenske, & Tyler, 1986), and methadone, is fairly consistent across studies.

### Alcohol

*Fetal alcohol syndrome* (FAS) is a pattern of physical and behavioral anomalies in children of alcoholic women who drink heavily during pregnancy. It is suggested that the effects of alcohol and smoking may be dose-related (Mills, Graubard, Harley, Rhoads, & Heinz, 1984). FAS represents a major public health problem, with treatment costs for FAS in the United States estimated at nearly a third of a billion dollars per year (Abel & Sokol, 1987).

The diagnostic criteria for FAS comprise both prenatal and postnatal growth retardation, a characteristic group of craniofacial anomalies, central nervous system dysfunction, and major organ malformation such as congenital heart defects (U.S. Department of Health and Human Services, 1990). If a child has one or two of these characteristics, the condition is called *fetal alcohol effects* (FAE). The harmful effects of prenatal exposure to alcohol are known to exist on a continuum that ranges from gross structural and functional defects at the more severe extreme to more subtle cognitive and behavioral dysfunctions at the other.

### Marijuana

Marijuana use is also considered harmful during pregnancy because of its ability to impair DNA and RNA formation. Although not certain, it is thought that marijuana may decrease maternal oxygenation, making less oxygen available to the fetus.

### Cocaine

*Cocaine* is a crystalline powder that is either manufactured synthetically or made from cocoa leaves. The white powdery substance is often inhaled through the nose, causing damage to the nasal membranes. *Crack*, which first appeared in the United States in 1983, is a highly concentrated form of cocaine that causes almost immediate addiction. It derives its name from the crackling sound that is heard when it is heated. Crack is known as the "equal opportunity drug" since it is relatively inexpensive and readily available.

Cocaine use during pregnancy can cause extreme problems. For women who use cocaine during pregnancy, the rate of spontaneous abortion is even higher than among pregnant women who use heroin. In a review of the literature by Cregler and Mark (1986), six occurrences of abruptio placentae were reported in mothers with a mean maternal age of 22 years in association with cocaine use. Five patients had onset of labor and vaginal bleeding immediately after administration of intravenous cocaine; the sixth had contractions and vaginal bleeding within a few hours after intranasal ingestion. Other factors, such as coagulation problems, were ruled out as causative in these cases. Current information suggests that infants exposed to cocaine are at risk for higher rates of congenital malformations, perinatal mortality, and neurobehavioral impairments.

"Snorting" cocaine may also have a negative effect on the mother. Cocaine is a strong vasoconstrictor that can cause pregnant women to develop seizures, hypertension, cardiac arrhythmia, and, in rare cases, cardiac failure. Premature labor is an acknowledged complication of substance abuse in pregnancy. Recent reports indicate that some mothers use cocaine in an attempt to hasten labor and delivery. Ney, Dooley, Keith, Chasnoff, and Socol (1990) recommend that patients admitted in possible preterm labor be encouraged to submit to screening for substance abuse so that appropriate counseling, as well as prenatal and neonatal care, is provided for these high-risk groups.

Newborns who have been exposed to cocaine in utero go through an extremely difficult period during the days and weeks after birth. Some have birth defects (such as deformed hearts, lungs, and digestive systems) that can be attributed to cocaine use in utero (Rist, 1990). Many are small, underweight, and hypersensitive. Picking the child up can cause uncontrollable tremors and crying. These children cry when awake and do not sleep well. Furthermore, crack babies typically exhibit "gaze aversion," avoiding eye contact. They have a significantly higher rate of sudden infant death syndrome than infants who were not exposed to crack.

One psychologist describes children exposed to crack cocaine as children who are wired for 110 volts living in a 220-volt world. This graphically describes what is now happening to these children in the school system. The initial wave of crack babies, born after crack cocaine became available in the mid-1980s, is now in school. In the typical classroom environment, where noises, voices, instructions, and directions all occur simultaneously, these children tend to react in one of two ways—they either withdraw completely or they become wild and difficult to control. Like fuses when a burst of current pulses through and overloads them, these children are liable to short-circuit or burn out with too much stimulation (Rist, 1990). This behavior requires special intensive programs in schools that provides highly structured and supportive learning environments because these children typically lack the skills and characteristics for self-organization, initiative, and follow-through without adult guidance.

### Opiates and Heroin

Opiate-dependent women are at grave risk for serious obstetrical complications. The infants of these women have a death rate four times higher than that of other newborns. Children of opiate-dependent women are known to be at risk of undergoing an opiate-abstinence syndrome in the neonatal period (Szeto & Umans, 1985). Common manifestations of this withdrawal syndrome include irritability, hyperactivity, increased eye movements, diarrhea, tachypnea, tremors, exaggerated reflexes, and occasionally generalized seizures and abnormal sleep patterns (Dinges, Davis, & Glass, 1980). Existing studies on the effects of alcohol and drug abuse on the developing fetus begin to suggest an understanding of the process and the effects it causes during the neonatal period (Hayes, Dreher, & Nugent, 1988; Petitti & Coleman, 1990; Weston, Ivins, Zuckerman, Jones, & Lopez, 1989).

Zagon (1985) reports that the best-recognized sign of fetal exposure to opioids is the *neonatal withdrawal syndrome,* with 60% to 90% of opioid-exposed infants manifesting some degree of symptoms. Withdrawal symptoms include irritability, tremors, high-pitched cry, hyperactivity, wakefulness, diarrhea, disorganized sucking reflex, respiratory alkalosis, and lacrimation as well as hiccups, sneezing, twitching, myoclonic jerks, or seizures.

The Brazelton Neonatal Behavioral Assessment Scale, discussed in Chapter 11, is the most commonly used tool to assess neurobehavioral functioning. Some of the specific behavioral characteristics of opiate-addicted newborns identified by this scale include numerous state changes, tremors, motor immaturity, decreased alertness, decreased ability to habituate to stimuli, and decreased auditory and visual orientation (Zuckerman, 1985).

Many heroin addicts are put on a methadone maintenance program to help them withdraw from heroin. Methadone relieves the craving for heroin in most addicts and allows them to function effectively in the community while leading law-abiding lives. Babies born of mothers who are in methadone maintenance programs are at a higher risk of being affected by the heroin than those of nonaddicted mothers; however, they are at a much lower risk than those of mothers still using heroin.

## The Effects of Substance Abuse on Children

### The Effects of Parental Substance Abuse on Children

One out of every eight Americans comes from an alcoholic home. Seven million of these youngsters face the daily fear, uncertainty, and problems that result from their parents' alcohol abuse (Woodside, 1986). It has been shown that children of chemically dependent parents have an increased vulnerability for substance abuse themselves; in fact, children of alcoholics are four times more likely than others to become alcoholics.

*The Alcoholic Family Environment.* The alcoholic family environment consists of chaos, inconsistency, unpredictability, unclear roles, arbitrariness, changing limits, arguments, repetitious and illogical thinking (denial), secrets, and perhaps violence and neglect (Black, 1981; Brown, 1988; Seixas & Youcha, 1985). Experts on physical abuse estimate that 60% of such abuse is related to the use of drugs or alcohol by parents. Tolerance for normal (often noisy) childlike behavior is lessened by the use of drugs. Patterns of abuse affecting children of alcoholics tend to be sex-related. "Alcoholic fathers are more likely to physically or sexually abuse their children, whereas mothers more often abuse through neglect" (Brown, 1988, p. 15). Evidence indicates that these children are at both physical and psychological risk for developing health problems resulting from emotional neglect, physical abuse, and inconsistent parenting (Moos & Billings, 1982). In addition, "adults find many of these youngsters are prone to reality distortion, and have difficulty in separating the real from the unreal. Their confusion stems from the implied family conspiracy to deny, overlook, or ignore the bizarre events at home" (Woodside, 1986, p. 448). These children have difficulty trying to understand what is predictable in life and how to get a consistent response from parents. Unfortunately, they are doomed in this quest and, therefore, remain very confused.

Life is confusing and frustrating for children of addicts and alcoholics. They usually do not have good peer relationships, partially because of low self-esteem and because they are afraid to bring friends home owing to the unpredictability of the addicted parent's behavior. The parent may regularly pass out on the sofa or the floor after a "liquid dinner" or may have drug paraphernalia lying around the house. Even more frustrating, however, is the fact that these secrets are kept hidden. The child usually does not mention parental intoxication or physical or sexual abuse to the other parent or siblings. The child of the addict or alcoholic is afraid to tell anyone about what happens at home for fear of being blamed for the parental behavior, of not being believed, or of being deemed weird or different from classmates. They may be so immersed in denial that they do not consciously acknowledge the addicted parent's behavior.

Many children from alcoholic homes have ongoing problems with chronic depression and addictive behaviors, such as substance abuse and eating disorders, as they become adults (Black, 1981). Thus, it is important that nurses understand the long-term effects of parental alcoholism and addiction. Student nurses usually see such problems during their mental health rotation, particularly if they spend time on a substance abuse unit. Patients with problems related to drug or alcohol abuse exist in all settings, however, so students may encounter them in medical-surgical, pediatric, and maternity settings. It is important for student nurses to learn how to identify clients with these problems and to know referral resources for children of alcoholics and addicts (see Support Groups).

Brown (1988) focuses on the serious developmental problems of these children. She maintains that, both as children and adults, children of alcoholics have difficulty with the cognitive process of identity formation. This results in clients who enter treatment with a variety of problems related to failure to differentiate and separate from the chemically dependent family whose organizing "glue" was alcohol and denial.

## *Behavioral Models of Coping*

Four behavioral paradigms have been drawn of the patterns followed by children of alcoholic parents in their attempts to cope with the confusing, rejecting, inconsistent behavior demonstrated by addicted parents (Black, 1981). Although these patterns have been described as behavioral responses of children of alcoholics, again it seems appropriate to expect to see these behaviors in children regardless of the parents' drug of choice. Nurses should remember that these behaviors are responses not only to the addicted parent's behavior but also to the codependent behaviors of the nonaddicted parent.

According to Black (1981), the four behavioral models are (1) the responsible child, (2) the adjuster, (3) the placater, and (4) the acting-out child. The *responsible child* is 9 years old going on 40—taking care of the house, doing the shopping, cooking, and cleaning and caring for younger siblings. The *adjuster* is always in the middle. He or she appears slightly more flexible than the responsible one and is available to adjust and handle whatever changes take place. The *placater* assumes responsibility for the family's feelings. Placaters listen to a sibling's embarrassment, or a parent's sadness, or a sister's fear of an enraged father who is now passed out on the floor. Although these first three behavioral patterns are seen by society as positive manners of adaptation, they are not desirable for young children who need the time to grow and learn with support. The fourth pattern, the *acting-out child,* exhibits the disturbed, delinquent type of behavior that is expected in such a dysfunctional family. This child is the most likely to be identified by the traditional helping agencies and may receive help. The other children, who assume the quieter roles, also need help yet are rarely diagnosed as needing help. Frequently, they do not receive help with their issues until they are mature and find an Adult Children of Alcoholics group.

## *The Effects of Substance Use and Abuse by Children*

In the 1990 Office for Substance Abuse Prevention publication, *Youth and Drugs: Society's Mixed Messages,* many hypotheses are proposed about why children in our society use drugs and alcohol. Some of the factors that influence drug use among the young include the availability and relatively low cost of some drugs, the values associated with drug use (particularly those in the media that promise a "quick fix"), the desire to belong to a social group, the dangers associated with drug use (thrill-seeking behavior), and the premium placed on achieving personal satisfaction by chemical means. Among all these factors, excitement, easy pleasure, and fast relief from the stresses of life are primary reasons for drug use.

The use of alcohol and drugs in America's children is not limited to any one socioeconomic or racial group. It is not a problem relegated to the ghetto; affluence can engender problems of equal or greater magnitude. Substance abuse is pervasive. Tobacco's toll is higher than that of all other addictive drugs combined—about 57 million Americans are hooked on cigarettes. About 1000 people die of illnesses related to smoking each day. There are about 18 million alcoholics. More than 10 million people abuse tranquilizers and other psychotherapeutic drugs. More than 1 million people are hooked on each of the following: crack, heroin, and hallucinogens such as LSD and PCP (Office for Substance Abuse Prevention, 1990). There are constant horror stories about children showing up in school drunk or high. School nurses must effectively use their assessment and communication skills to work with these children and their families to direct them to the help they need. Nurses must start by being familiar with the signs and symptoms of drug use, support students during the "coming down" period, and notify their parents to come and take them home while they remain under the influence. The nurse, ideally with the school counselor, will then explain the situation to the parents and may be included in a caring confrontation with the student once he or she is no longer under the influence. School nurses are in an ideal position to provide children and their families with additional information and sources for referrals (see Sources of Information and Support Groups).

## The Effects of Substance Abuse on Adolescents

### The Effects of Parental Substance Abuse on Adolescents

Adolescence can be a troubled time under the best of circumstances. Parental substance abuse puts additional psychological and emotional burdens on adolescents along with the potential for physical abuse. Parents who are substance abusers are unable to provide appropriate role models for adolescents. In addition, because of their abuse, they are often unavailable to help adolescents progress and develop through this period. Adolescents with substance abusing parents often need to work to help support parent's habits or to simply make ends meet at home. Often, because the parents are unable to function in a parenting role, adolescents or even younger children need to care for siblings. Frequently, these adolescents are unable to participate in peer activities because of embarrassment that their peers may find out that their parents are abusers or out of fear that their friends may be subjected to hostile or inappropriate outbursts from the parents.

### The Effects of Substance Abuse by Adolescents

According to Kinney and Leaton (1991), there is a growing number of reliable statistics on the incidence of teen-age alcohol and drug problems. A few of the statistics that are particularly informative include the following:

- *In the 13 to 17 year age group, it is estimated that there are 3 million problem drinkers, and over 300,000 teen-agers who are alcohol dependent.*
- *97% of drug-abusing adolescents also use alcohol.*
- *Over the last 20 years, life expectancy has increased for all age groups except ages 15 to 24. The three leading causes of death in this age group are accidents, suicide, and homicide, all closely linked to alcohol and drug use.*
- *The leading cause of death between the ages 16 and 24 is driving while alcohol impaired.*
- *Drivers age 16 to 24 years constitute 17% of the population; they are involved in 48% of fatal accidents (p. 320).*

In spite of these overall alarming statistics, some promising information was recently released by the University of Michigan in their annual survey of about 16,000 high school seniors at 137 public and private schools, financed by the National Institute on Drug Abuse. This annual nationwide survey found that in 1990, about 47.9% of the high school seniors had used an illegal drug at least once. This is a decline from a high of about 66% in the early 1980s and of about 55% in 1975 (Kolberg, 1991).

Marijuana remained the most widely used illegal drug among high school seniors, but use declined from 29.6% in 1989 to 27% of 1990 seniors. Furthermore, annual cocaine use among seniors fell from 6.5% in 1989 to 5.3% in 1990—the lowest level since the survey began in 1975. Also, annual use of crack fell about two fifths, from 3.1% in 1989 to 1.9% in 1990 (Kolberg, 1991). It is too early to tell if this signals a positive trend toward the goal of becoming a drug-free society.

Some of the reasons that adolescents use drugs are problems with self-esteem, peer pressure, parental role models, the need to escape from abusive homes, boredom, thrill-seeking behavior, or simply availability. The child's development is fixated at the point at which drug abuse begins. Typical symptoms include a decline in school performance, frequent absences from school, behavioral problems, scrapes with the law, drunken driving, and accidents.

## The Nursing Process in Substance Abuse

### Assessment

The nurse's role in working with substance abusers begins with assessment, when it is important to ask specific questions about past alcohol and drug use. Nurses in all clinical settings need to ask screening questions to determine whether clients are at risk for alcoholism or addiction. If the answers to these initial questions in the history lead the nurse to believe that there may be a problem, further screening tools should be used to determine whether the client is addicted. The quickest and easiest tool to use is the four-item CAGE questionnaire shown in Table 21-1.

Kinney and Leaton (1991) developed a list of some of the most common signs of adolescent alcohol or substance abuse. This list can be used by nurses to evaluate the possibility of substance abuse and includes the following:

- Unexplained drop in grades
- Irregular school attendance
- Inability to account for personal time
- Increased money or poor justification of how money was spent
- New group of friends
- Change in health or grooming
- Failure to provide specific answers to questions about activities

*Table 21–1.  Alcoholism Screening Test (CAGE)*

| | | |
|---|---|---|
| 1. **C** | Have you ever felt you ought to **C**ut down on your drinking? |
| 2. **A** | Have people **A**nnoyed you by criticizing your drinking? |
| 3. **G** | Have you ever felt bad or **G**uilty about your drinking? |
| 4. **E** | Have you ever had a drink first thing in the morning to steady your nerves or get rid of a hangover (**E**ye-opener)? |

(Ewing, J. A. [1984]. Detecting alcoholism: The CAGE questionnaire. *JAMA, 252*[14], 1905–1906)

- Possession of drug paraphernalia (such as syringes or tobacco rolling paper)
- Desire to be secretive or isolated
- Unexplained disappearance of possessions in the home (p. 322)

These signs are of particular value to school nurses because they often are the first professionals to be alerted. It is important to remember, when assessing clients, that the criteria for diagnosing an alcohol or drug problem in children or adolescents include a *pattern* of pathological use as well as an impairment in social or occupational functioning. Nurses should be particularly alert to any of these signs and symptoms in children of alcohol and drug users because of the genetic predisposition and the additional burdens placed on adolescents during this difficult developmental time by the presence of a chemically dependent parent.

Nurses must also observe for signs and symptoms of alcohol and drug withdrawal during hospitalization. Typical groups of symptoms are shown in Table 21-2.

## Nursing Diagnoses

During the assessment process, nurses obtain information on all aspects of suspected or actual substance abuse. A thorough assessment enables nurses to identify diagnoses and establish plans and interventions to overcome the abuser's problem as well as to decrease the effects of the substance abuse on family members. Nursing diagnoses for clients or families in which substance abuse is a problem include the following:

- Alteration in neurological function related to maternal drug and alcohol abuse during pregnancy, as manifested by newborn's frantic sucking, irritability, hyperactivity, high-pitched cry, sneezing, tremors, vomiting, feeding problems, diaphoresis, seizures, respiratory distress (grunting, nasal flaring), diarrhea with rectal irritation, and hyperthermia
- Real or high risk for altered parenting related to possible maternal substance abuse during pregnancy, as manifested by a lack of prenatal care, reported IV drug use during pregnancy, and a symptomatic infant
- Ineffective individual coping related to under-developed ego, dysfunctional family system, and negative role modeling, as manifested by under-age substance abuse, unexplained decrease in school performance, and irregular school attendance
- Self-esteem disturbance related to dysfunctional family system and lack of positive feedback from addicted parents, as manifested by self-destructive behavior (substance abuse), social isolation (truancy from school), behavior that is highly critical and judgmental of self and others
- Ineffective denial related to fixation in early level of development and low self-esteem, as manifested

*Table 21–2.  Withdrawal Symptoms*

| Alcohol | Opioids | Stimulants (Cocaine, Crack, Amphetamines) |
|---|---|---|
| Anxiety | Runny nose | Disturbed sleep |
| Hand tremors | Tearing | Fatigue |
| Nausea and lack of appetite | Diarrhea | Emaciation |
| Tachycardia | Abdominal cramps | Cravings |
| Sweating | Sweating | Depression |
| Depression and irritability | Hot flashes | Restlessness |
| Grand mal seizures or delirium tremens (an acute psychotic state usually accompanied by hallucinations) | Insomnia | Hallucinations |
| | Irritability | Paranoia |
| | Loss of appetite | |
| | Muscle and joint pain | |

(Gorney-Fadiman, M. J. [1989, November 27]. The faces of recovery: An addictions update. *The Nurse's Newspaper*, pp. 14–15)

by denial that substance abuse creates problems such as poor grades in school, only friends being drug users and school drop-outs, rationalization and projection to explain poor grades, constant need for more money and poor excuses about how money was spent
- Altered nutrition, less than body requirements, related to cocaine or crack use resulting in anorexia, or drinking rather than eating nutritious foods, as manifested by weight loss, pale conjunctiva, and irritated mucous membranes
- Altered parenting related to intoxication, as manifested by the inability of the parent to provide consistent parental support
- High risk for violence directed at self or others related to substance-induced altered mental state, as manifested by threats or initiation of acts of violence
- Fear related to altered behavior patterns of substance abusing parent or guardian, as manifested by either withdrawn or acting-out behaviors

## Planning and Implementation

After establishing nursing diagnoses for the problem, the nurse's primary responsibility is to make appropriate referrals for substance abusers and their families. Many programs have been successful in helping addicts or alcoholics, such as the 12-step programs of Alcoholics Anonymous, Narcotics Anonymous, Adult Children of Alcoholics, and other groups (see Support Groups).

There are many resources, such as workbooks, that nurses can use to help children get in touch with the problem of addicted parents. One of the most popular is Claudia Black's (1979) *My Dad Loves Me, My Dad Has a Disease*. In the foreword Black explains that she grew up in an alcoholic home, where she lived by the rule that it was unacceptable to discuss alcoholism in the family. By the age of 6, however, she shared her frustrations as well as the feelings of fear and loneliness of living in an alcoholic family. Her workbook, which is intended for children between the ages of 6 and 14 who live in alcoholic families, gives them the opportunity to work through their loneliness, fear, and frustration by expressing feelings. It helps them to share their thoughts and feelings and to better understand the disease of alcoholism. Children are instructed to draw pictures such as the following, which is designed to elicit denial: "Draw a picture about something you want to forget, something you want to pretend never really happened" (p. 22). It is an excellent resource for children of alcoholics to help them get in touch with their own feelings and to teach them the concepts of alcoholism and recovery.

It is important to caution children not to try to tell their parents how they feel about the alcohol or drug use when the parents are high. Children must be told that it is impossible to try to communicate with people who are in an altered state of consciousness due to alcohol or drugs.

Nurses who work in schools, doctors' offices, and emergency rooms where they meet children of addicts need to be knowledgeable about referral sources for children.

### Reporting to Child Protective Services

The decision regarding whether nurses should report pregnant substance abusers to Child Protective Services is based on local legal and hospital protocols. In some communities, it is mandatory to report all women in whom drug and alcohol dependency is suspected (even those in treatment), whereas in others it is required that all mothers with positive toxicology screens be reported.

A report to Child Protective Services may result in the child not being released to the mother upon discharge. The infant may then be sent to a foster care home or other placement while the legal system proceeds with action. In the ideal scenario described by Jessup and Roth (1988), the pregnant mother begins a treatment program and complies with it until delivery. Then, with compliance and recovery after delivery, the service provider advocates for the parent to retain custody with public health nurse home follow-up. This plan provides a positive approach because the patient (1) receives assistance in recovery from the dependency, (2) delivers a healthier infant, and (3) retains custody of the child rather than temporarily having the child placed in foster care.

Wilson and Kneisl (1988) note that "alcohol is involved in 90 percent of child abuse [and] in 60 percent of sex crimes against children" (p. 349). According to one expert on school nursing, Dr. Virginia Young (San Jose State University), school nurses need to be alert to signs and symptoms of abuse in students. These symptoms include multiple bruises or injuries, injuries that do not heal, and incidents in which the child's explanation does not fit the injury. Young also states that students frequently disclose abuse problems after school programs on appropriate and inappropriate touching, such as "Red Light, Green Light." Therefore, all nurses who work in settings where there are children of substance-abusing parents need to assess the children for the possibility of physical or substance abuse and report these cases to the appropriate authorities.

### Evaluation

Evaluation of nursing care is based on determining whether the specific behavioral criteria defined in the objectives and expected outcomes of the planning stage were met within a reasonable period of time. Usually, the first goal when working with children and adolescent substance abusers is total abstinence from all mood-altering chemicals. Success is evaluated in terms of the number of days of abstinence. Other goals to be evaluated are attendance at 12-step support groups (discussed later), obtaining a sponsor in a support group, and use of alternative coping mechanisms such as physical exercise, talking to a friend in the program, using relaxation tapes, and others.

## Treatment Options

Stephanie Brown (1985) has proposed a useful conceptualization for treating alcoholism by viewing it as a developmental process with four central phases: (1) drinking, (2) transition, (3) early recovery, and (4) ongoing recovery. Treatment of alcoholism and drug addiction consists of a comprehensive system of services, including, but not limited to, *detoxification, inpatient rehabilitation, outpatient services, aftercare, residential treatment, pharmacotherapies,* and *self-help groups.* Research on treatment options is not definitive in predicting which form of treatment is most appropriate for a particular alcoholic or addict. It is important for nurses in all settings to be aware of the variety of treatment options available and the research regarding evaluation of these programs so that they can make appropriate referrals.

A variety of treatment options are available for chemically dependent children and adults. Inpatient programs usually last from 21 days to 6 months. Outpatient programs frequently begin with an intensive 6-week, 5-day-a-week program, followed by 6 months to 1 year of aftercare. Residential programs are available in which mothers and children can live in a clean and sober environment, attend meetings, and begin to return to school and work. Other treatment programs have been developed specifically for children, usually teen-agers, with alcohol and drug problems. Information about these treatment centers is available from organizations listed in the telephone book, including local chapters of the National Council on Alcoholism.

Trained counselors and support groups work specifically with the children of addicts. An example, offered through the National Council of Alcoholism in Saginaw, Michigan, is a children's support group that consists of eight sessions specially designed to help children aged 5 to 12 years. The goals are to increase feelings of self-worth, maintain better personal relationships, develop healthier personal outlooks, and find alternative ways of responding to life in alcoholic-dependent families. The topics of the sessions include: (1) intake and goal setting, (2) feelings, (3) defenses, (4) substance abuse, (5) risks and choices, (6) families, (7) specialness, and (8) parent–child communication. The sessions are directed by elementary school teachers certified in substance abuse treatment.

Most programs have a family treatment component in which a meeting is held one night a week for the family of the addict. The meeting frequently consists of educational elements, the family is introduced to the disease concept of addiction and codependency, and families are acquainted with the 12-step support groups available (e.g., Al-Anon, Alateen, Ala-Kid, Nar-Anon). The meeting usually includes a socialization period with the person in treatment. With inpatient programs, families frequently are required to attend family night and learn about their own, as well as the addict's, disease before they are allowed to visit with the addict.

## Prevention Strategies

Although prevention of substance abuse is difficult, like most other major problems, it is easier to prevent than cure. Prevention begins before birth with early prenatal education about the dangers to the fetus of drug and alcohol use; it proceeds from early childhood, through adolescence, and into adulthood. Various prevention strategies are discussed for each of these groups.

Three major prevention strategies are (1) dissemination of information; (2) effective education aimed at enhancing young people's self-esteem, interpersonal skills, and techniques for decision-making and problem-solving; and (3) advocacy for societal and environmental change to prevent the disastrous results of substance abuse.

One organization that has been particularly successful in bringing about an awareness of the effects of one form of substance abuse is Students Against Driving Drunk (SADD). SADD is an international youth activist organization that was founded by Robert Anastas after the loss of two students in highway accidents in 1981. The goals of SADD are the following:

- To encourage students to use positive peer pressure and adopt a no-use lifestyle in their efforts to end underage drinking, drug abuse, and death due to drinking and driving
- To promote a frank dialogue between teen-agers and their parents through the "contract for life," which serves as a means to develop both a no-use lifestyle for the student and a safety net for parents and children
- To empower students to conduct student, parent, and community awareness programs in alcohol and drug education that promote the care-giving triangle of the home, the school, and the community
- To deal with all these issues in an affirmative fashion and to stress the concept of celebrating life

Students Against Driving Drunk has chapters in over 17,000 high schools, 8000 middle schools, and 1500 colleges. Several examples of SADD logos are shown in Figure 21-2. More information about SADD is available from SADD, P.O. Box 800, Marlboro, MA 01752, 508-481-3568.

*Figure 21–2.  Examples of logos used by Students Against Driving Drunk (SADD).*

## Early Prenatal Instruction

The "new prevention approach" focuses on changing the *environment* through education and legislation so that people become more aware of the hazards of using drugs and alcohol, particularly during pregnancy. Signs posted prominently in settings that sell alcoholic beverages frequently say: "Warning: Drinking distilled spirits, beer, coolers, wine, and other alcoholic beverages during pregnancy can cause birth defects." There is a national movement for legislation requiring that all alcoholic beverages be labeled with a hazardous beverage warning similar to that found on cigarette packages.

## Early Classroom Intervention

School nurses may be the first health care professionals to have the opportunity to see and assess children of substance-abusing parents. These children often complain of abdominal pain, headaches, tics, and nausea for which no physical causes can be found (Woodside, 1986). It is important for children of chemically dependent parents to find help from caring adults to support them through their parents' addiction. That person might be a relative, someone at their church or synagogue, a counselor at school, a teacher, or the school nurse.

> *It is important that the helping professional/caring adult be willing to listen to the child in a non-judgmental supportive manner. It is critical to let children of alcoholics know it is all right to disclose the family secret; to find out they are not alone; to learn they cannot cause, control, or cure their parents' disease; to know chemically dependent adults can and do recover, and above all, that youngsters deserve and warrant help for themselves (Woodside, 1986, p. 449).*

*Teachers Looking Carefully* (TLC) is an excellent example of an assessment tool that can be used by teachers in any classroom setting to determine potential substance abuse problems by students. Developed by Dr. Jerry Stamper, it is intended to assess students' behavioral changes over a period of time that may indicate whether a problem with substance abuse exists or is developing. As a result of

the TLC score, students with potential substance abuse problems can be systematically assessed and guided to assistance, when indicated.

A group of students, in many ways, represents society as a whole, with additional factors that may place them at higher risk. These risk factors include the following:

- Peer pressure
- An experimentation mentality
- Lack of familial constraints
- Developmental level stressors
- Relative affluence and the availability of substances with the potential for abuse

The basic assumptions behind the TLC program include the following:

> Substance abuse is a progressive illness with identifiable stages; intervention is possible at any stage.
>
> Teachers have an extended period of time with students and can observe change.
>
> Substance abuse *will* affect academic performance.
>
> A systematic assessment is more reliable than recognition of isolated behaviors.
>
> Negative behaviors that are progressive are more problematic than are isolated incidents.

The TLC Student Assessment Instrument, Interpretation of Scores, and Action Groups are shown in the display.

## Sources of Information

Many organizations have been formed to help with the problem of alcohol and drug use. In 1980, Mothers Against Drunk Driving (MADD) was founded in California. This group was originally composed of people who had been victimized both by the loss of a loved one due to drunk driving and by the criminal justice system they had relied on for justice and support. Members put together an aggressive campaign to pass the toughest drunk driving laws in the country (at the time) in California. Within 10 years, MADD has grown to an international, nonprofit organization with more than 1 million members, becoming America's leading victim assistance organization. Since 1980, MADD has assisted in the passage of more than 1000 drunk driving laws nationwide. In addition, MADD is credited with pressuring Congress to enact several key bills to establish a uniform minimum drinking age of 21 and to provide federal incentive grants to assist states in their efforts to better enforce laws against drunk driving. Through the efforts of MADD, the rights of victims and survivors of alcohol-related crashes are now viewed more equitably by the criminal justice system. Youth programs affiliated with MADD have sprung up in nearly every state, educating children and teen-agers about the dangers of alcohol and drug abuse. Two of MADD's goals for the 1990s

## Teachers Looking Carefully (TLC)

Idea: A student assessment scale to identify potential substance abuse problems

Use: By teachers in any discipline classroom

Purpose: 1. To asses students when behaviors change over a period of time that *may* indicate a problem is or has developed with substance abuse
2. To guide the individual to assistance

Rationale: A college population in many ways represents general society, with some special factors that may place this population at risk, including:
1. Peer pressure
2. Experimentation mentality
3. Lack of familial constraints
4. Developmental level stressors
5. Relative affluence and availability of money/substances

Assumptions: 1. Substance abuse is a progressive illness with identifiable stages; intervention is possible at any stage.
2. Teachers have an extended period of time with students and can observe change.
3. Substance abuse *will* affect academic performance.
4. A systematic assessment is more reliable than recognition of isolated behaviors.
5. Negative behaviors that are progressive are more problematic than are isolated incidents.

### A Student Assessment Instrument

DIRECTION: Choose one score from each category listed below.

1. Grades
   a. Inconsistent = 1
   b. Dropping = 2
   c. Failing = 3
   Subtotal _____

2. Attendance
   a. Tardiness = 1
   b. Inconsistent = 2
   c. Poor = 3
   Subtotal _____

3. Assignments
   a. Quality dropping = 1
   b. Poor quality = 2
   c. Not completed = 3
   Subtotal _____

4. Appearance
   a. Inconsistent = 1
   b. Unkept = 2
   c. Deteriorated = 3
   Subtotal _____

5. Attitude
   a. Labile = 1
   b. Disinterested = 2
   c. Disruptive = 3
   Subtotal _____

6. Interpersonal Relations
   a. Withdrawing = 1
   b. Antisocial = 2
   c. Isolated = 3
   Subtotal _____

7. Alertness
   a. Poor attention = 1
   b. Sleeping = 2
   c. Disoriented = 3
   Subtotal _____

TOTAL SCORE = _____

*(continued)*

## *Teachers Looking Carefully (TLC)* *(Continued)*

### *Interpretation of Scores*

SCORE

| | |
|---|---|
| 19–21 | Serious impairment is present. Many factors point to substance abuse. *Refer to action group 1.* |
| 16–18 | Strongly suspect that substance abuse is impairing the student. *Refer to action group 2.* |
| 13–15 | A problem is present; may be related to substance abuse. *Refer to action group 3.* |
| 10–12 | Assessments indicate definite problems are present on a continuing basis. *Refer to action group 4.* |
| 7–9 | A potential problem related to substance abuse may be present. *Refer to action group 5.* |
| 4–6 | Inadequate data to substantiate problem with substance abuse. Problems are episodic. *Refer to action group 6.* |
| 1–3 | No basis for problem identification related to substance abuse. *Refer to action group 6.* |

### *Action Groups*

DIRECTIONS: Choose one or more options from the action groups.

Action Group 1
1. Offer to take the student to health or counseling service.
2. Notify appropriate security of the situation.
3. Notify counseling center of the situation.
4. Assume a directive role with the student.

Action Group 2
1. Assess student each class period.
2. Confer with counseling center.
3. Recommend that student seek counseling.
4. Confer with student to discuss progress in course.

Action Group 3
1. Assess student each class period.
2. Distribute materials in class regarding counseling services.
3. Confer with student to discuss course progress.

Action Group 4
1. Assess student weekly.
2. Confer with student to discuss course progress.

Action Group 5
1. Assess student weekly.

Action Group 6
1. Assess student only if behavior changes.

(Used with permission of Gerald Stamper, Ph.D., San Jose State University, San Jose, CA.)

are related to children—reducing the risk of crash involvement among our youth and passing child endangerment laws in all 50 states. More information about MADD is available from the MADD National Office, P.O. Box 1217, Hurst, TX 76053.

Another resource that exists in most hospitals, major corporations, and school systems is an Employee Assistance Program (EAP). This person, or group of counselors, can provide advice about available treatment options as well as insurance benefits for chemically dependent adults and children in their community. Their primary function is to assist employers, usually through supervisors, in the early identification of employees whose problems impair job performance. Frequently, this impairment is due to the use of alcohol or drugs. EAPs work with the employees to identify the problem, provide them with treatment options, and follow-up when they return to work. In many instances, EAPs are also available to assist the dependents of chemically dependent employees.

## Support Groups

A wide variety of self-help support groups are available for addicts and their friends and families. They started with a single group, *Alcoholics Anonymous* (AA), which began in 1935—before health care professionals even admitted that there was a disease called "alcoholism." It was the only source of help for alcoholics for many years.

Alcoholics Anonymous is a program of recovery for alcoholics, although it is open to anyone with a substance abuse problem. It is a spiritually oriented program based on the concept that the addict must work through 12 steps to progress toward recovery from disease. Addiction is viewed as a lifelong, progressive disease that requires work "one day at a time" for the rest of the addict's life. It is generally believed that successful recovery requires total abstinence from all mood-altering chemicals for the rest of the person's life. There are no age restrictions for attendance, only an honest and sincere desire to stop drinking or using. It is not unusual to have people from the ages of 15 to 90 in the same room working together.

In the last 10 years, there has been a continuing proliferation of 12-step programs. Some are related to the use of a specific substance, such as Narcotics Anonymous (NA), Cocaine Anonymous (CA), Pills Anonymous (PA), and Overeaters Anonymous (OA). Others are client related, such as Al-Anon (families of alcoholics), CoDependents Anonymous (CODA), Nar-Anon (families of addicts), Adult Children of Alcoholics (ACA), Alateen (for teen-agers of alcoholics), and Alatot (for young children of alcoholics).

*Al-Anon* is for children, spouses, parents, and friends of alcoholics. It is a mutual-help group for family members of chemically dependent people and codependents. Al-Anon literature points out that the well-being of anyone living with an alcoholic is affected emotionally, physically, and spiritually. This group focuses on the behavior of the people involved with the chemically dependent person and helps them to learn that they can only control their own behavior, not anyone else's. This can be a freeing concept as these people realize that they are no longer responsible for the drinking or substance-using behavior of a friend or family member. The introduction to the *AA Guide for the Family of the Alcoholic* describes Al-Anon Family Groups as a fellowship of relatives and friends of alcoholics who share their experience, strength, and hope to solve common problems. It is their belief that alcoholism is a family illness and that changed attitudes can aid recovery.

*CoDependents Anonymous* (CODA) is a 12-step program of recovery from codependency. Codependents attempt to use others (i.e., their mates, their friends, and even their children) as their sole source of identity, value, and well-being and as a way of trying to restore the emotional losses from their childhoods. Many codependent people have experienced the painful trauma of emptiness in their childhood, which persists in their relationships with others throughout their lives. Codependents have learned to survive life, but in CODA they learn to live and enjoy life. By applying the 12 steps and principles found in CODA to their daily lives and relationships, both present and past, they learn to experience a new freedom from past self-defeating lifestyles. It is an individual growth process. Many theorists now recommend CODA groups for members of helping professions, such as nurses, social workers, psychologists, and so on. Codependency is seen as an occupational hazard for individuals in health care careers because many come from dysfunctional families and because of the nature of the work, which requires so much giving.

*Nar-Anon* is the family group for members of Narcotics Anonymous or for people who have a family member with a narcotic problem. There are even Alatot groups in some locations for very young children. All groups are open to any significant other of an addict; most people find one or two groups with which they feel comfortable and call these their "home groups." Information about all the self-help groups is available through Alcoholics Anonymous and Narcotics Anonymous.

*Alateen* is a fellowship of young people whose lives have been affected by alcoholism in family members or close friends. Members of these groups, 12 years and older, help one another by sharing their experiences, strength, and hope. Alateen believes that alcoholism affects all members of a family emotionally and, occasionally, physically. Alateen's approach is to teach children that they can detach themselves from their parents' problems while still continuing to love them. Members find out how other young people handle the problems of an addicted parent and how others feel when they have parents who are addicted. Meetings are open to all teens; there is no charge for attending. Times and dates of meetings can be found by calling the local Alcoholics Anonymous chapter.

In recent years, a trend has begun to offer therapy and support groups for adult children of alcoholics. Brown (1988) found that there is a residual effect on the personality of adults who grew up with one or both parents being chemically dependent. Al-Anon literature describes a phenomenon in which adult children of chemically dependent parents become aware that the scars of alcoholism have left them with a lingering pain that continues to affect their relationships, their self-esteem, and their sense of family life. It is desired that through Al-Anon, children of alcoholics find the tools that enable them to put the past to rest, forgive, and go on to meaningful adult lives.

## Summary

Entering life with a physical and emotional legacy due to a parent's drug and alcohol use can result in lifelong consequences. It is important for nurses to assess and intervene to prevent the consequences of parental drug and alcohol abuse from the prenatal period through adolescence. Children and adolescents need nurses to act as advocates for them when parents may be too impaired or guilty to be able to acknowledge the problems. Nurses can also identify children and adolescents at risk for developing substance abuse problems and assist in prevention of addiction in both childhood and adolescence.

Adolescence is a period characterized by dramatic changes and growth in physical, social, mental, emotional, and spiritual domains. The effects of parental substance abuse or adolescents' own dependence on drugs or alcohol during this tremendously dynamic phase of life can have implications for the rest of their lives.

Once addiction has occurred, a variety of treatment options are available, ranging from self-help groups to programs requiring hospitalization. Many sources of information also are available on a wide variety of addictions. In addition, support groups are available to substance abusers as well as to their children and other family members.

## References

Abel, E. L., & Sokol, R. J. (1987). Incidence of fetal alcohol syndrome and economic impact of FAS-related anomalies. *Drug and Alcohol Dependence, 19*(1), 51–70.

Abel, E. L., & Zeidenberg, P. (1985). Age, alcohol and violent death: A postmortem study. *Journal of Studies on Alcohol, 46,* 228–231.

Beattie, M. (1987). *Codependent no more.* New York: Harper/Hazelden.

Black, C. (1979). *My dad loves me, my dad has a disease: A workbook for children of alcoholics.* Denver: MAC.

Black, C. (1981). *It will never happen to me.* New York: Ballantine Books.

Blum, K., Noble, E., Sheridan, P., Montgomery, A., Ritchie, T., Jagadeeswaran, P., Nogami, H., Briggs, A., & Cohn, J. (1990). Allelic association of human dopamine D2 receptor gene in alcoholism. *JAMA, 263*(15), 2055–2059.

Blum, R., & Richards, L. (1979). Youthful drug use. In Dupont, R., Goldstein, A., & O'Donnell, J. (eds.). *Handbook on drug abuse. NIDA Research Monograph Series.* Washington, DC: Superintendent of Documents, 257–267.

Brook, J., Lettieri, D., & Brook, D. (1985). *Alcohol and substance abuse in adolescence.* New York: Haworth Press.

Brown, S. (1985). *Treating the alcoholic: A developmental model of recovery.* New York: John Wiley & Sons.

Brown, S. (1988). *Treating adult children of alcoholics: A developmental perspective.* New York: John Wiley & Sons.

Centers for Disease Control. (1990a). Alcohol-related disease impact—Wisconsin, 1988. *Morbidity and Mortality Weekly Report, 39*(11), 178–188.

Centers for Disease Control. (1990b). Alcohol-related traffic fatalities—United States, 1982–1989. *Morbidity and Mortality Weekly Report, 39*(49), 889–891.

Christiansen, B., Smith, G., Roehling, P., & Goldman, M. (1989). Using alcohol experience to predict adolescent drinking behavior after one year. *Journal of Consulting and Clinical Psychology, 57,* 93–99.

Cregler, L., & Mark, H. (1986). Special report: Medical complications of cocaine abuse. *The New England Journal of Medicine, 315*(23), 1495–1499.

Denoff, M. (1988). An integrated analysis of the contribution made by irrational beliefs and parental interaction to adolescent drug abuse. *The International Journal of the Addictions, 23*(7), 655–669.

Dinges, D. F., Davis, M., & Glass, P. (1980). Fetal exposure to narcotics: Neonatal sleep as a measure of nervous system disturbance. *Science, 209,* 619–621.

Dixon, S. (1989). Effects of transplacental exposure to cocaine and methamphetamine on the neonate. *Western Journal of Medicine, 150*(4), 436–442.

Ewing, J. A. (1984). Detecting alcoholism: The CAGE questionnaire. *JAMA, 252*(14), 1905–1906.

Hayes, J., Dreher, M., & Nugent, J. (1988). Newborn outcomes with maternal marijuana use in Jamaican women. *Pediatric Nursing, 14*(2), 107–110.

Howard, J., Kropenske, V., & Tyler, R. (1986). The long term effects on neurodevelopment in infants exposed prenatally to PCP. *National Institute of Drug Abuse Monograph Series, 64,* 237–251.

Jessup, M., & Roth, R. (1988). Clinical and legal perspectives on prenatal drug and alcohol use: Guidelines for individual and community response. *Medicine and Law, 7,* 1–12.

Kinney, J., & Leaton, G. (1991). *Loosening the grip: A handbook of alcohol information* (4th ed.). St. Louis: Mosby-Year Book.

Kolberg, R. (1991, January 25). Drug use among high school seniors drops. *San Francisco Examiner,* p. D-16.

MADD. (1990). MADD—The first ten years. *MADD Student Library.* Hurst, TX: MADD National Office, 1–16.

Mills, J., Graubard, B., Harley, E., Rhoads, G., & Heinz, W. B. (1984). Maternal alcohol consumption and birth weight. *JAMA, 252*(14), 1875–1879.

Moos, R., & Billings, A. (1982). Children of alcoholics during the recovery process: Alcoholic and matched control families. *Addictive Behavior, 7*, 155–163.

National Center for Health Statistics. (1988). *Health, United States*. Washington DC: U.S. Department of Health and Human Services, Public Health Service, CDC, 1989; DHHS publication no. (PHS) 89–1232.

Ney, J., Dooley, S., Keith, L., Chasnoff, I., & Socol, M. (1990). The prevalence of substance abuse in patients with suspected preterm labor. *American Journal of Obstetrics and Gynecology, 162*(5), 1562–1567.

Office for Substance Abuse Prevention. (1990). *Youth and drugs: Society's mixed messages*. OSAP Prevention Monograph 6. Rockville, MD: U.S. Department of Health and Human Services.

Petitti, D., & Coleman, M. (1990). Cocaine and the risk of low birth weight. *American Journal of Public Health, 80*(1), 25–28.

Rist, M. (1990, July 9). The shadow children: Preparing for the arrival of crack babies in schools. *Research Bulletin*, Phi Delta Kappa, Center on Evaluation Development and Research.

Schaef, A. (1986). *Co-dependence: Misunderstood—mistreated*. San Francisco: Harper & Row.

Seixas, J., & Youcha, G. (1985). *Children of alcoholism: A survivor's manual*. New York: Harper & Row.

Smith, J. (1988). The dangers of prenatal cocaine use. *MCN, 13*, 174–179.

Szeto, H., & Umans, J. (1985). Pharmacodynamics of fetal exposure to narcotics. *NIDA Research Monograph Series*. Washington, DC: Superintendent of Documents, 60, 78–87.

U.S. Department of Health and Human Services. (1990). *Seventh special report to the U.S. Congress on alcohol and health*. Rockville, MD: National Institute on Alcohol Abuse and Alcoholism.

Weston, D. R., Ivins, B., Zuckerman, B., Jones, C., & Lopez, R. (1989). Drug exposed babies: Research and clinical issues. *National Center for Clinical Infant Programs Bulletin, IX*(5).

Wilson, H. S., & Kneisl C. R. (1988). *Psychiatric nursing* (3rd ed.). Menlo Park, CA: Addison-Wesley.

Woititz, J. G. (1983). *Adult children of alcoholics*. Hollywood, FL: Health Communications.

Woodside, M. (1986). Children of alcoholics: Breaking the cycle. *Journal of School Health, 56*(10), 448–449.

Zagon, I. (1985). Opioids and development: New lessons from old problems. *Prenatal Drug Exposure: Kinetics and Dynamics. NIDA Research Monograph Series*. Washington, DC: Superintendent of Documents, Monograph 60, 58–77.

Zuckerman, B. (1985). Developmental consequences of maternal drug use during pregnancy. *NIDA Research Monograph Series*. Washington, DC: Superintendent of Documents.

## Bibliography

Ackerman, R. J. (1987). *Children of alcoholics: A bibliography and resource guide*. Pompano Beach, FL: Health Communications.

American Nurses Association, Drug and Alcohol Nursing Association, & National Nurses Society on Addictions. (1987). *The care of clients with addictions: Dimensions of nursing practice*. Kansas City, MO: American Nurses Association (PMH-9).

Arneson, S., Schultz, M., & Triplett, J. (1987). Nurses' knowledge of the impact of parental alcoholism on children. *Archives of Psychiatric Nursing, 1*(4), 251–257.

Bartek, J., Lindeman, M., Newton, M., Fitzgerald, A., & Hawks, J. (1988). Nurse-identified problems in the management of alcoholic patients. *Journal of Studies on Alcohol, 49*(1), 62–69.

Bingham, A., & Bargar, M. A. (1985). Children of alcoholic families. *Journal of Psychosocial Nursing, 23*(12), 13–15.

Bluhm, J. (1987). *When you face the chemically dependent patient: A practical guide for nurses*. St. Louis: Ishiyaku EuroAmerica.

Chasnoff, I., Burns, W., Schnoll, s., & Burns, K. (1985). Cocaine use in pregnancy. *New England Journal of Medicine, 313*(11), 666–669.

Chasnoff, I., Griffith, D., Macgregor, S., Dirkes, K., & Burns, K. (1989). Temporal patterns of cocaine use in pregnancy: Perinatal outcome. *Journal of the American Medical Association, 261*, 1741–1744.

Free, T., Russell, F., & Mills, B. (1989). NCAST scales used to assess children of prenatal substance abuse. *Nursing Child Assessment Satellite Training National News, V*(3), 3–7.

Halebsky, M. A. (1987). Adolescent alcohol and substance abuse: Parent and peer effects. *Adolescence, XXII*(88), 961–967.

Jaffe, S. (1990). *The step workbook for adolescent chemical dependency recovery: A guide to the first five steps*. Washington, DC: American Psychiatric Press.

Neerhof, M., MacGregor, S., Retzky, S., & Sullivan, T. (1989). Cocaine abuse during pregnancy: Peripartum prevalence and perinatal outcome. *American Journal of Obstetrics and Gynecology, 161*(3), 633–638.

Nubel, A., & Solomon, L. Z. (1988). Addicted adolescent girls. *Journal of Psychosocial Nursing, 26*(1), 32–35.

Robinson, D., & Greene, J. (1988). The adolescent alcohol and drug problem: A practical approach. *Pediatric Nursing, 14*(4), 305–309.

Secretary of Health and Human Services. (1987). *Sixth special report to the U.S. Congress on alcohol and health*. Rockville, MD: U.S. Department of Health and Human Services, Public Health Service, Alcohol, Drug Abuse, and Mental Health Administration, National Institute on Alcohol Abuse and Alcoholism.

Sweeney, L. B. (1989). Cocaine babies: The latest management dilemma. *Nursing Child Assessment Satellite Training National News, V*(3), 1–2.

# Children's Experiences With Dying, Death, and Bereavement

Sherry E. Johnson

*Photograph by David Finn*

22

*Dying*

*Types of Death*

*Bereavement, Grief, and Mourning*

*Development of a Concept of Death*
    *Infancy to Two Years*
    *Two to Seven Years*
    *Seven to Eleven Years*
    *Adolescence*

*The Nursing Process in Dying, Death,*
    *and Bereavement*
    *Assessment*
    *Nursing Diagnoses*
    *Planning Nursing Care*
    *Nursing Interventions*
    *Evaluating Nursing Care*

*Effects of Dying, Death, and*
    *Bereavement on Parents and*
    *Families*

*Effects of Dying, Death, and*
    *Bereavement on Nurses*

*Summary*

*Upon completion of this chapter the reader will be able to:*

1. *Understand the historical importance of Elisabeth Kübler-Ross's work.*

2. *Differentiate between short and long preparation time for death, and describe the impact of each.*

3. *Distinguish among the terms "bereavement," "grief," and "mourning."*

4. *Explain how a child develops a concept of death.*

5. *Use the nursing process when working with a dying child and his or her family.*

6. *Begin to communicate with well and sick children about dying and death.*

7. *Describe the impact that a dying child can have on a family.*

8. *Relate the role of nurses when working with dying children and their families.*

9. *Explain ways that nurses can take care of themselves when working with dying children.*

*Key Terms*

*bereavement*

*care goals*

*conspiracy of silence*

*cure goals*

*detachment*

*displacement*

*family themes*

*grief*

*guilt*

*guilt movie*

*mourning*

*object and person permanence*

*projection*

*scapegoating*

*thanatology*

Grief over the loss of a loved one is a powerful experience. It makes no difference whether the one who has died is a child or a person important to a child; the individual or the family is never the same. Unresolved or complicated grief can be a destructive process physically, emotionally, financially, or spiritually (Johnson, 1983, 1986, 1987; Parkes, 1965; Worden, 1982). This destructive process can affect children, adults, and the entire family or family system. The effect may have such far-reaching implications that it becomes a generational issue. However, in working with children and families who face death, nurses can and do help families thorough the process of dying, death, and bereavement.

When dealing with children in grief, as with others, appropriate nursing interventions are to assist them in expressions of grief healthy for both their age and their cognitive and emotional developmental stages; prevent complications of grief; help them heal complications that may have developed from the grief; assist them in moving toward a healthy detachment from the person who is dying or has died, and assist them in reattaching to others; and help them develop healthy goals in life. This chapter discusses types of death and bereavement, grief, and mourning; the development of children's concepts and perceptions of death; the nursing process in dying, death, and bereavement; and effects of dying, death, and bereavement on parents, families, and nurses.

Throughout this chapter dying children, as well as children who survive the death of other loved ones, will be discussed. Because the concepts of dying, death, and bereavement cross all ages, problems that face dying children and their families, as well as children and families who are exposed to the death of others, will be discussed under each appropriate heading.

## Dying

Elisabeth Kübler-Ross opened the area of *thanatology* (the study of death) in the late 1960s (Kübler-Ross, 1969). In her book *On Death and Dying,* she categorized five stages that people experience when they are dying. The first stage, *shock,* occurs when individuals hear painful information; they deny what they hear or, often, cannot believe it. In the second stage they become *angry.* The third stage is *depression.* In the fourth stage the person attempts to *bargain,* often with God, for more time or for some "last wish." The fifth and final stage is *acceptance,* which tends to be very peaceful; however, acceptance does not mean resignation.

It is assumed that people experience these stages in an orderly fashion, but in reality the process is not so simple. People often become disappointed that the five-stage "recipe" did not work for them or that they did not experience a certain stage—for example, those who are not angry in life will probably not be angry dying. Ultimately, grief is far too complicated to reduce it to five stages. However, shock does tend to be an almost universal reaction (Johnson, 1987).

## Types of Death

Johnson (1987) divides preparation for death into two categories: short preparation time and long preparation time. People with a *short preparation time* for death have 14 days or less warning that death is imminent. These types of death include accidents, homicides, suicides, or sudden infant death syndrome (SIDS). A *long preparation time* for death may include such diagnoses as cancer or AIDS.

With a short preparation time, there may be little or no time for the survivors to say goodbye or to accomplish other aspects of their "grief work." This can complicate and prolong the bereavement. When there is a long preparation time, the dying person and the family have an opportunity to do much of the grief work during the anticipatory period. The length of preparation time, and what is accomplished in that period, is important because it often affects the type, duration, and potency of survivor bereavements.

## Bereavement, Grief, and Mourning

The terms to describe grief are frequently used interchangeably. However, their meanings are different. *Bereavement* includes the physical, emotional, social, spiritual, and cultural responses to the pain of loss. *Grief* is the physical and emotional reaction and feeling that accompanies a loss. *Mourning* is the process of readjustment to living life with the loss (Johnson, 1987).

## Development of a Concept of Death

The development of a child's concept of death is a complicated and lengthy process. It results in the understanding that death is irreversible, permanent, and universal (happens to everyone). The process of developing a concept of death from infancy to 2 years, 2 to 7 years, 7 to 12 years, and during adolescence will be presented in this chapter.

## Infancy to Two Years

Healthy newborns react to any life situation with a stimulus-and-response behavior, according to their level of development. This also seems to be true when a life-threatening situation is at hand. How, then, does an infant learn to understand the emotional and intellectual aspects of the concept of death?

As early as 3 months of age, the infant begins to experiment with issues of presence and absence via games like peek-a-boo and, later, hide-and-seek. These games, as well as other play, help the child develop the concept of *object and person permanence:* "things" and people exist even though the infant cannot see them. Up to about 6 months of age, if the object or person cannot be experienced (seen, heard, smelled, etc.), it does not exist. Understanding that people and things exist even if they are not in the immediate environment is a difficult concept to master.

Also during this time, *separation anxiety* begins to develop and is displayed through a series of protest responses that occur when children are removed from the sight of their parents (Schaffer & Emerson, 1964). Separation anxiety begins at about 5 weeks, peaks at about 7 to 10 months, and then levels off at about 18 months.

Once children grasp the concepts of object and person permanence and separation anxiety, they can distinguish between presence and absence. Children in this age group probably do not comprehend the difference between absence and death. However, these concepts are precursors to the understanding and fear of death.

The question of whether children experience separation anxiety or grief and mourning is controversial. It appears that until object and person permanence has developed and separation anxiety has decreased, the child experiences separation anxiety, not grief. However, the symptoms of both are similar: crying, sadness, or anger (Bowlby, 1960; Deutsch, 1959).

## Two to Seven Years

Two- to seven-year-old children develop skills to interact with the environment, like speaking and walking. This is known as the *preoperational stage* (Piaget, 1965). In addition, Anthony (1940), Steiner (1965), and Koocher (1974) suggest that 3- to 6-year-olds tend to mix magic or fantasy with reality. Children often believe that things are either temporary or reversible, even death. For example, death is viewed like flowers dying in the fall but blooming again in the spring.

Not only do children not have a clear distinction between fantasy and reality, they also relate all external events to their inner world of thought and fantasy (egocentric thinking). Children believe in the omnipotence of their fantasy world since they think it can cause external events. Therefore, children often believe that they have caused a death if it is related to an event in their fantasy world. For example, a 5-year-old boy was referred for evaluation by the school nurse. The child had always been a discipline problem until his mother was killed in a car accident. Soon after her death he become a very compliant child. Although his teacher and father were pleased with his new behavior, the school nurse was very perceptive in noticing that something was wrong. It was discovered in therapy that the boy believed he caused his mother's death by telling her that he hated her. He told her that he was going to run away from home after they had an argument (an example of mixing fantasy and reality). Later that day the mother was killed. The boy hoped that his mother would come back (death being reversible) and find the apple he left for her to say he was sorry.

Cognitive and language skills are needed to understand the concept of death. Therefore, it is not necessarily the child's age, but life experiences and cognitive growth, that enable him or her to develop a concept of death. Situational and environmental factors, such as an accident or illness, the death of a grandparent, parent, pet, or friend, or a disaster, can make the child confront the reality of death at an early age. For example, one of the first memories of a patient was of being 3 years old and watching "John John" Kennedy saluting his father's casket as it passed by him. She identified with him because he was also 3. She understood very quickly, and at a young age, the meaning of death.

Many researchers have studied whether or not children are aware of the serious nature of their illness. Waechter (1971), using eight picture completions, found that fatally ill children, 6 to 10 years of age, could express death themes and fear of body intrusion more overtly than they could explain mutilation or separation. Her study suggests that terminally ill children may be aware that they are dying and be able to express it verbally.

Spinetta, Rigler, and Karon (1973) tested Waechter's findings and found that fatally ill children who were not aware that their illnesses were fatal were more fearful of threats and intrusions into their bodies than they were of death itself. They also concluded that fatally ill children are aware of the seriousness of their illnesses.

## Seven to Eleven Years

Between the ages of 7 and 11 children become aware that death is irreversible, permanent, and universal. They have learned the words relating to death and can give specific examples of death; they are also able to give abstract causes of death and express logical thoughts and fears about death (Johnson, 1987). In developing fears they also develop ways to cope with the fears. For example, during Halloween children dress up as feared objects such as ghosts and skeletons, thereby identifying with them and with their powers to cause fear. Children may practice superstitions such as holding their breath as they pass by a graveyard.

## Adolescence

There is little published research on adolescents' concepts of death. Normal adolescents respond with appropriate grief feelings and reactions. However, they often do not have the ability to prioritize their losses; therefore, the loss of a friend may be as debilitating as the loss of a mother.

The adolescent's primary developmental task is searching for and defining a sense of self. In accomplishing such an overwhelming task, death seems remote: How can one think of one's death when one is trying to define one's life? With this need to define self, adolescents often test the boundaries between life and death.

In addition to the developmental concepts that have been outlined, nurses must also take into account children's socialization regarding death, both in the home and in the wider environment. There are many personal, cultural, media, socioeconomic, and religious influences that can affect the development of a concept of death and hasten it for the normal child. For example, even a young child who experiences the death of someone with whom there was a strong attachment learns quickly that death is not reversible and happens to all of us.

## The Nursing Process in Dying, Death, and Bereavement

### Assessment

Nurses have an important role to play in helping the child and family understand death and dying and begin and maintain a healthy grieving process. A thorough grief assessment is imperative, including the following fundamental areas, each of which will be discussed in detail:

- Developmental level of the child
- Cultural implications
- Spiritual issues
- Socioeconomic issues
- Social support network of the family
- Family themes
- Grief symptoms
- Unfinished business among the child and family

Table 22-1 identifies areas for assessment, possible nursing diagnoses, plans, interventions, and evaluation criteria.

*(text continues on page 497)*

*Table 22–1. Nursing Actions for Children and Families Experiencing Dying and Death*

| Areas of Assessment | Assess | Possible Diagnoses | Possible Nursing Plan | Possible Interventions | Possible Evaluations |
|---|---|---|---|---|---|
| Developmental level of child | a. Child's understanding of dying and death.<br><br>b. Child's past experience with dying and death<br>c. Child's awareness that he/she has a terminal illness.<br><br>d. Child's feelings: scared, suspicious, abandoned, etc. | Anxiety<br>Defensive coping<br>Ineffective coping individual<br>Fear<br>Powerlessness<br>Growth and development, altered<br>Knowledge deficit | a. Discuss with parents/family child's experience with dying and death.<br>b. Explore with parents/family how child exhibits fear.<br>c. Determine comforting and security objects and people.<br>d. Develop ways to diminish anxiety, fear, and powerlessness. | a. Talk with parents about child's experiences with dying and death.<br>b, c. Use comfort devices to decrease fear (teddy bear, blanket, tape of mom or dad singing).<br>d. Child understands death and needs to work out feelings more directly—talked to child, read book about a cat that died, drew pictures of what was happening in her body from her cancer. | a. Poor—parents need more work in order to talk about this<br>b, c. Fear decreased in child<br><br>d. Child slept through the night for the first time after interventions completed. |
| Cultural implications for the family | a. Based upon their culture, explore how long grief should last.<br>b. Superstitions<br><br>c. Customs<br>d. Foods<br>e. Rituals<br>f. Taboos and norms | Anxiety<br>Fear<br>Powerlessness<br>Knowledge deficit<br>Decisional conflict<br>Ineffective denial | a. Help parents/family prepare for dying and death.<br>b. Utilize customs, foods, rituals, whenever possible.<br>c. Be respectful of the taboos, norms and mores of culture. | a, b, c. Child wanted a last taste of favorite ethnic food, mother and father able to bring; parents, child, and nurse went through old pictures together and cried and laughed. | a, b, c. Accomplished—with a big smile; parents more peaceful. Difficult process, but closeness, tears, and peace achieved for the moment. |

*(continued)*

*Table 22–1.  Nursing Actions for Children and Families Experiencing Dying and Death (Continued)*

| Areas of Assessment | Assess | Possible Diagnoses | Possible Nursing Plan | Possible Interventions | Possible Evaluations |
|---|---|---|---|---|---|
| Spiritual needs | a. Rituals<br>b. Practices<br><br><br>c. Beliefs about death and life after death<br><br>d. Hopes | Anxiety<br>Altered family process<br>Parental role conflict<br>Noncompliance (e.g., spiritual beliefs)<br>Impaired adjustment<br>Spiritual distress<br>Decisional conflict<br>Fear<br>Altered family processes<br>Anticipatory grieving | a, b. Support rituals, specific religious practices.<br><br>c. Support hopes and be aware of changing hopes in the child.<br>d. Refer family to clergy person if needed.<br>e. Allow family to express feelings (e.g., anger) about religious dissonance. | a. Called priest to have last rites performed for child; nurse supported.<br>b, c. Hopes have changed for a peaceful death rather than a cure<br>Morphine increased to p.r.n.<br>Cots and pillows now in room for parents<br>Visitors restricted only to *helpful* and close people<br>Signs of death explained to parents<br>Bible readings done by nurse<br>Clergy called | a. Parents felt relieved<br>b. Child died peacefully; parents doing as well as possible; all unfinished business complete and grief therapy in place for parents and grandparents.<br>c. Clergy was guilt-instilling; nurse helped parents ask him to leave; need to discuss with parents another possible clergyperson to visit. |
| Socioeconomic issues | a. Explore how socioeconomic differences affect concept of death.<br>b. Because of socioeconomic level, how does family respond to child's illness and impending death?<br>c. Questions family asks<br>d. Involvement in care | Anxiety<br>Self-esteem, disturbance<br>Powerlessness<br>Ineffective denial<br>Parental role conflict<br>Altered family processes | a. Determine need for socioeconomic assistance.<br><br>b. Assist parents/family to deal with socioeconomic issues.<br><br>c. Help parents/family to learn how to assist in child's care. | a, b. Called social worker who is working on funds for family.<br><br>c. Parents need to be at work because of financial problems; nurse and parents set up schedule for other helpful people to be with child. | a, b. In process<br><br><br>c. In process; working well; significant others are taping observations and conversations so parents can hear. |

| | | | | | |
|---|---|---|---|---|---|
| Social support network of the family | a. People in the support network<br>b. Who are the helpful people and why?<br>c. Who are the hindering people and why?<br>d. Who are the guilt-instilling people and why? | Anxiety<br>Defensive coping<br>Ineffective individual adjustment<br>Ineffective denial<br>Altered family processes<br>Social isolation<br>Impaired social interaction | a, b. Mobilize help from support system<br><br>c, d. Assist parents/family to set boundaries and limits on hindering people. | a. Support system in place; they know who they are and have access to the room—others to report to desk; sign on door.<br>b. Working with parents to set limits on hindering grandfather. | a. Accomplished—child feels protected.<br><br>b. Continue to support parents. |
| Family themes | a. Scapegoating<br><br>b. Conspiracy of silence<br><br>c. Detachment<br><br>d. Guilt | Coping, defensive<br>Coping, ineffective individual and for family<br>Grieving, dysfunctional<br>Anxiety<br>Powerlessness<br>Self-esteem<br>—chronic low<br>—disturbance<br>—situational low<br>Spiritual distress<br>Decisional conflict<br>Parental role conflict | a. Help parents/family to understand scapegoating process and attempt to stop and express feelings directly.<br>b. Assist parents/family to be able to talk about and feel their trauma.<br>c. Determine if detachment needs to be discouraged or allowed for a time.<br>d. Assist parents/family to express and work through their guilt: create a safe environment for these things to be worked through. It is important for the nurse not to be judgmental, distancing, rejecting, or discounting—refer to grief therapist if needed. | a. Dealing with parents on<br>• Scapegoating<br>• Conspiracy of silence<br>b. Talked to child alone and privately; drew feelings, played with clay, read stories.<br>c. Parents detaching<br>• Parents to go to dinner—*ALONE*<br>• Assured parents nurse would stay until they got back<br>• Ground rules set with parents for dinner: no discussion of "hot" topics, go someplace peaceful and comforting. | a. In process<br>Referral to grief therapist<br>Closer in acceptance.<br>b. Child cried and verbalized own sadness and fear for first time.<br>c. Parents felt somewhat reconnected—decided to get grief therapy. |

*(continued)*

*Table 22–1.  Nursing Actions for Children and Families Experiencing Dying and Death (Continued)*

| Areas of Assessment | Assess | Possible Diagnoses | Possible Nursing Plan | Possible Interventions | Possible Evaluations |
|---|---|---|---|---|---|
| Grief symptoms | a. Symptoms | Anticipatory grieving Dysfunctional grieving Hopelessness Post-trauma response Powerlessness Self-esteem —disturbance —chronic low —situational low Spiritual distress | a. Identify child, parents, and —family symptoms —behaviors —reactions —feelings | a. List was made of child's and family's grief symptoms, behaviors, reactions, and feelings—discussed with parents and child. | a. All felt more normal and assured they were not "going crazy." No relief at present—but also not expected because child is getting worse; there is more understanding and acceptance for all. |
|  | b. Behaviors c. Reactions d. Feelings |  | b. Assist them in working through their symptoms, behaviors, reactions, and feelings. | b. Working on talking and playing (coloring, clay, hammer pounding) are all symptoms. |  |
| Unfinished business among the child and family | a. Areas of unfinished business— Symptoms related to unfinished business | Guilt and shame Anxiety Powerlessness Spiritual distress Grieving, dysfunctional Ineffective coping Fear Social isolation | a. Assist individual/family to define unfinished business. | a. Child wants to go home —To ride bike one last time —See the cat (hospital refused entrance to cat) | a. Child went home with hospice care —Got to ride her bike —Died peacefully with family, friends, and cat around her the next day |
|  |  |  | b. Assist them directly or indirectly in meeting the unfinished business (e.g., saying what needs to be said to another); indirectly develop a ritual with the person/family. | b. Discussion with parents about taking child home to die —Hospice called —Social worker called —Nurse discharge planner called |  |
|  |  |  | c. Refer for grief therapy if needed. |  |  |

## Developmental Level of the Child

Nurses need to understand how children develop a concept of death in order to assess their level of understanding. However, children do not live in isolation and can gain a better or more sophisticated understanding of death by the introduction of external variables: the media, the socioeconomic background, religion, environment, and other experiences with death (e.g., a grandparent or other family member or a pet). Nurses need to explore children's past experiences with death, as well as how they reacted to the death.

Once children are aware that they have a terminal illness, they may quickly understand the concept of death because they are experiencing it internally as well as externally. Waechter (1971) suggested that terminally ill children may be aware that they are dying and be able to express it verbally.

Very young children often know that their illnesses are serious and may be fatal. In spite of this knowledge, they are still upset when their bodies are invaded, poked, and prodded. Developmental levels and painful clinical procedures are two separate issues that should not be confused.

Fears associated with death and the dying child tend to coincide with the age and developmental level of the child. Children under the age of 3 are usually more afraid of parental abandonment than of death itself; 3- to 5-year-old children are afraid of bodily mutilation; 5- to 7-year-old children view death as a personification of something inhuman, such as the "boogie man." Children in this age group may not see death as permanent but may realize that it is different from the dead individual merely departing for a period of time. Their fears may be expressed in dreams, separation anxiety, or direct or symbolic verbalizations (Johnson, 1987). From 7 years of age to adolescence, children may express fears about not being liked or may fear rejection by peers. These fears tend to be verbalized with a threatened or actual change of physical appearance, e.g., loss of hair due to chemotherapy. Table 22-2 identifies the fears of each age group.

Although children may not understand death cognitively, they do realize, and often verbalize, that something is seriously wrong. Therefore, they may express their feelings or thoughts, although it may not be clear what is troubling the child. For example, during the Persian Gulf crisis a child became very anxious and refused to go to sleep. As the therapist explored this with her parents, they were finally able to help her articulate her fear: she was frightened that they were going to be bombed and did not have gas masks. She did not understand the difference between the city of Jerusalem and Jerusalem Road (her address).

Other children may make vague statements indicating that they are "scared of something" or that "something terrible might happen." Nurses should record these statements and consider them as they assess children's under-

*Table 22-2. Dying Children's Fears Associated With Death (Categorized by Age and Developmental Level)*

| Age | Fear |
|---|---|
| Under 3 years | Parental abandonment |
| 3–5 years | Mutilation |
| 5–7 years | Personification of something inhuman |
| 7 years–adolescence | Rejection |

standing of death. Even if children are unaware of the seriousness of their illnesses, they may be suspicious. Each of these feelings must be assessed by the nurse.

It is also important in the bereavement process to assess the understanding of the death of one member of the family by the other children in the family. Their grief will also parallel their understanding. For example, a 3-year-old whose sister had died was very fearful of the cemetery. A therapist discovered that the sprinkler system was operating the first time the girl and her parents went to the cemetery, and she secretly feared that her sister would drown. Although she had not yet developed the concept of the permanence of death, this experience was very traumatic for her.

## Cultural Implications

Most cultures tend to deny death. Individuals may look at death and grieving for a short time but, as with the sun, look away because it hurts too much. In some cultures there are also subtle but powerful messages that when a death occurs grieving should not last "too long." Those who have not experienced a loss of a family member or have not allowed themselves to grieve properly often think that grief should last no longer than 48 hours to 2 weeks (Johnson, 1987). In reality, there is no set period for grieving; it varies widely from individual to individual.

People often avoid families with a dying child because they are uncomfortable with the situation. Not only is it a reversal of the "natural order" to have children die before their parents, but individuals frequently do not know what to say or do. Some even suspect that if they become involved they may bring "the curse" to themselves or their family.

It is important to be aware of any superstitions, cultural customs, foods, or rituals that may help the family during the time before and after the death. These measures can be comforting to the family when all else may seem meaningless.

## Spiritual Issues

Although there has not been much research on the religious influences on the development of a child's concept of death, a socialization and philosophical process occurs. As the child is confronted with death or the concept of death, religious rites, practices, or beliefs are taught. Regardless of the religious framework, it becomes a means to make feelings and reactions expressible and acceptable. Religious rituals instill hope and become a means of working through thoughts and feelings. They also provide a framework for personal growth as individuals struggle through difficult questions that may not have answers.

In a religious framework, a sense of hope is always needed and should never be taken away from the family. Nurses need to assess the hope(s) of families and be aware of how the hope may change over a period of time, e.g., from "I hope he gets better and never has leukemia again" to "I hope he has a peaceful death."

It is important to assess the family's religious framework, participation in meaningful rituals, the extent of the involvement and participation of the community in religious practices, and specific religious ceremonies. As with all assessments, nurses should not assume information without clarification from the family.

During a terminal illness or after a death, many people find that their faith is their strength and sustenance, whereas others lose their faith. It is very difficult to understand why a child must die. Therefore, there can be much anger and resentment toward God. Nurses should allow the family to show their anger; they should not try to take it away, rationalize it, or give simple and quick answers, e.g., "God needed a little angel in heaven." These types of answers often only enrage the parents and hinder and complicate their grieving. It is better to empathize by saying, "It must be so hard to have a child die." Nurses should make a point of talking about the child by name in order to help the parents feel that their child was a distinct individual.

## Socioeconomic Issues

McIntire, Angle, and Strumpler (1972) found that socioeconomic status is an influencing factor in a child's development of a concept of death. Children from urban environments were more likely to cite violence as the primary cause of death. Middle-class children and older children are more likely to cite disease and old age as general causes of death. These conclusions were based on the assumption that children in the low socioeconomic group have early and repeated exposure to death due to long-term illness, violence, and exploitation, whereas middle-class children were already familiar with the tactics of denying death since they often are not exposed to death until they are older (Johnson, 1987).

Socioeconomic factors may also influence how the family responds to the terminal illness and death, how they ask questions, their involvement in the child's care, or how strong or articulate an advocate they are for their child. These factors may also affect their bereavement. Because

of socioeconomic pressures, some families are unable to take the necessary time to grieve; this can complicate bereavement, particularly if they are not aware of the need to grieve.

Nurses may find that they are in conflict with families over socioeconomic issues, so it is essential to clarify issues rather than be judgmental. For example, it was very difficult for nurses to understand why a mother never visited her dying daughter. When the nurse clarified the situation with the mother, she discovered that the mother was a single parent, had five other children, needed to work to support the children, and that her mother was also dying. Once the nurse had this information, it was easier to work out a plan so that the child did not feel so abandoned.

## Social Support Network of the Family

Nurses also need to assess the social support network available to the family during a child's terminal illness. Even though family and friends are available, it does not mean that they are necessarily helpful or supportive. Most parents of a dying child find that they are avoided and not cared for as needed during anticipatory or survivor bereavement.

Families often find that they are abandoned by family and friends after being supported by them for the first several weeks after the diagnosis or death. Close family and friends may allow individuals to grieve for 6 months to a year, then pressure them to "get on with their lives." The second and third years of bereavement can be more difficult than the first, since the protective mechanism of shock fades and reality becomes painful (Johnson, 1987).

It is also important to assess whether the parents and child know how to ask for what they need from others. There may be a support network, but if the family members do not know how or what to ask, or are fearful to do so, their needs may not be met. Many individuals find it easier to be the "helper" rather than the "helped."

It is essential for nurses to assess the composition of the support network and determine which individuals *help* and which *hinder* children and families during the stages of dying and bereavement. Bereaved individuals usually are aware of those who are helpful and those who hinder and why they behave as they do.

Helpful people are trustworthy, reliable, and supportive and allow others to express their feelings. They give empathetic responses and are protective and understanding. Helpful people are important in the process of healing and in preventing complications in the grieving child and family.

Characteristics of people who hinder are that they are critical and rejecting, attempt to control and take over, instill guilt and shame, do not follow through on promises, render others powerless, break boundaries, or are verbally wounding. Nurses need to help families deal with hindering individuals.

## Family Themes

*Family themes* are recurring subjects or motifs that appear (and sometimes reappear) throughout the family's history without apparent resolution. These themes often describe family behavior during crisis situations including terminal illness and bereavement. The most common family themes are scapegoating, conspiracy of silence, detachment, and guilt.

*Scapegoating.* "A scapegoat is a race, person, institution, or sex that bears the blame, prejudice, displaced aggression, irrational hostility, or projected feelings of others" (Johnson, 1987, p. 16). Scapegoating is a process of singling out one or more persons to bear the brunt of the family's or group's dissatisfaction.

When a family's history is assessed, nurses will sometimes find that the family has used scapegoats in the past as a means of coping with a difficult situation. Two primary defense mechanisms are used: projection and displacement. *Projection* occurs when an attitude or feeling is emotionally unacceptable in oneself and, therefore, is unconsciously rejected and then attributed to another. *Displacement* permits emotions or reactions (e.g., anger, resentment, anxiety) to be transferred from the self to the scapegoat. Often health care providers become scapegoats for unresolved anger about the child's impending death.

The Leek family had a 6-year-old son, Oliver, who died in a tragic farm accident. No one was really sure how the accident occurred. At the time there were three other children, one of whom was an infant. After the accident, the two older children became scapegoats for the parents. The children, along with the father, had been in the farmyard when the accident occurred. After the accident, the children constantly received messages of "Why are you alive while your brother is dead?" and "You are bad, awful kids."

As they became adolescents, the children began to act out the "bad behavior." This masochistic behavior continued the scapegoating process, but now they were doing it to themselves. They abused drugs and alcohol and were sexually promiscuous.

Eighteen years after the accident, the daughter underwent psychiatric treatment because of her destructive relationships with men. She began to realize that she and her brother had been used as scapegoats for all those years. She secretly believed that she had caused her brother's death, although she could not remember what had happened. The nurse may help the person begin to recognize his or her behaviors and problems, but usually therapy is required.

*Conspiracy of Silence.* The *conspiracy of silence* occurs when families either consciously or unconsciously refuse to discuss a painful topic. The object and the behaviors in the conspiracy of silence are to avoid the topic of death and dying and to survive at all costs. This is done verbally and nonverbally. For example, a couple whose child died from Reye's syndrome were out for dinner for the first time since the child's death. One woman asked how they were doing, but before the couple could respond, a diversion was introduced by another guest who said, "My, I like your new carpeting." This type of behavior can occur within families as well as in interactions with individuals outside the family.

There are several reasons for the conspiracy of silence. Death is still a culturally taboo topic, and in social situations individuals try to prevent others from talking about difficult topics; people are often uncomfortable with their own and others' feelings. The conspiracy of silence leaves people feeling alone, lonely, and guilty.

*Detachment.* *Detachment* is the process whereby people pull away from each other because of their own bereavement pain. The primary reason for the detachment is that the individuals are in such pain that they cannot minister to, or support, others. If this process is not "lengthy," it tends to be normal. Although 2 to 3 years may be a "typical" period of detachment, the longer it lasts, the less chance there is for reattachment. Other reasons for detachment include protection of the self or others, testing behavior, the precipitation of withdrawal by the initial shock, the fact that individuals grieve in different ways at different times, and the possibility that the marriage or relationship may have been unstable or detached before the crisis (Johnson, 1987).

One couple became progressively more detached from each other as they watched their daughter dying after an automobile accident and through their first year of bereavement. The father became very angry and aggressive, whereas the mother became depressed. They were not communicating in any way until she said that she was going to get help and that he was welcome to come along. He did, and their therapy became the beginning of a long reuniting process.

*Guilt.* Guilt, probably the most powerful factor in a terminal or death situation, holds the key to the survivor's mental and physical health. *Guilt* is a feeling of culpability for offenses of commission (actions that are regretted) or omission (inactions that are regretted).

Individuals tend to express at least two reasons for the guilt they feel. One is the legitimate reason for what happened: "My child got hit by a car. If I had only held his hand tighter he couldn't have darted into the street. I feel so guilty for that." The other reason is usually of a secretive nature and often deals with past "sins" or "wrongdoings" that have been kept from others. The most potent reason for the feelings of guilt is usually unrelated to the legitimate reason. A statement such as "My child died because I had an affair, and now I am being punished" is an example of a secret guilt.

Johnson (1982, 1987) found that women expressed significantly more guilt than men; although men may feel guilt, they may not be as verbal about it. Also, parents with a short preparation time for the death of their child (2 weeks' or less warning that death was imminent) expressed more guilt than parents with a long preparation time (15 days or more). Finally, guilt seems to generate a contagious effect in that if the mother feels very guilty, so does the father.

In addition to the existing guilt experienced by survivors, other individuals also instill guilt in the survivor, whether in fantasy or reality. This situation only reinforces the person's guilt feelings. Close family members or significant others are usually more direct in their guilt-instilling statements: "Why didn't you know something was wrong with Ruth? You should have been a better mother and insisted that she be taken to the doctor."

A *guilt movie* is a repetitive, compulsive, and often secret "movie" or flashback of the person's most intense guilty feeling. These flashbacks, for the most part, are in color and occur sometimes hundreds or thousands of times a day (Johnson, 1982, 1987).

Guilt movies are often sacrificial in nature. For example, one mother felt as though she had sacrificed her child when she handed the baby over to the nurse for the surgery during which the baby died. Other flashbacks deal with the guilt surrounding either the scene of death or experiences just prior to the death. Families whose children were struck by cars saw either the accident itself or the scene of the accident in their flashbacks and were thereby connected to their most potent guilt feelings.

Guilt movies are usually kept a secret because the individuals are frightened that others will think they are "crazy." Nurses should prepare bereaved individuals for the fact that these experiences may occur and that it is a normal way of working through guilty feelings.

### Unfinished Business Among the Child and Family

As the child approaches death, it is important for nurses to assess whether there is any unfinished business for the child and family. Such unfinished business usually relates to healing an old emotional wound, fulfilling a last wish, or saying goodbye. One little girl who was dying of leukemia wanted to go home and ride her bike "one more time." She was able to do this and died peacefully the next day.

Unfinished business needs to be assessed because it must be completed before the death, if at all possible. Nurses should be alert for verbal or nonverbal clues that there is unfinished business, because it is easier to resolve unfinished business before death than it is to undo guilt after the death.

### Grief Symptoms

*Anticipatory grief* occurs before the time of death and includes the signs, symptoms, feelings, behaviors, and re-

actions of the dying person, loved ones, and significant others. *Survivor grief* includes the signs, symptoms, feelings, behaviors, and reactions of the dead person's loved ones and significant others. All of these are normal and necessary: the only way to grieve is to grieve. However, if these symptoms continue over extended periods of time, without apparent resolution, there may be reason for concern that grief has become pathological.

It is difficult to be specific about the time frame of normal versus pathological grief, because every person is different. However, some grief work needs to be accomplished during the first year of bereavement or pathological grief may begin. Although the grief work may be minimal, it tends to relate to accepting the reality that death has occurred and beginning to experience the pain of death. If grief is avoided, repressed, or diminished, the ground is fertile for the development of pathological grief.

Many people in grief keep their symptoms secret, for a variety of reasons. Some believe that people become tired of hearing about their grief and choose not to share with others. Society can be intolerant of grief, and people hide their feelings because it is more socially acceptable. In addition, some symptoms of grief are kept secret because individuals fear that they will be considered disturbed if they tell others about them (e.g., hallucinations or smelling the dying or dead person's clothes).

Symptoms occur in both anticipatory and survivor bereavement. It is important for nurses to assess for the symptoms, understand their meaning, help people work through them, and assist in preventing other symptoms such as guilt. It may be necessary to refer some individuals to grief specialists. Table 22-3 provides a list of common grief symptoms.

## Nursing Diagnoses

As a result of the nursing observation and assessment, diagnoses must be established before an appropriate care plan can be implemented. When arriving at nursing diagnoses it is essential for nurses to consider the child, the parents, the siblings, the family as a whole, and significant others. Although this may seem overwhelming, a good treatment plan needs to include all members, since a child rarely exists in isolation from others.

Many diagnoses may be possible, based on the family themes and symptoms outlined above as well as physical symptoms. The following nursing diagnoses may apply:

- Impaired Social Interaction
- Social Isolation
- Altered Family Processes
- Parental Role Conflict
- Spiritual Distress (distress of the human spirit)
- Ineffective Individual Coping

*Table 22–3.   Common Grief Symptoms*

| Feelings | Physical Responses | Reactions and Behaviors |
|---|---|---|
| Shock<br>  Hysterical<br>  Tranquil<br>Anger—often inappropriate<br>Guilt<br>Sadness<br>Powerlessness<br>Helplessness<br>Hopelessness<br>Relief<br>Emancipation<br>Pining<br>Anxiety and fear<br>Fatigue<br>Loneliness<br>Depression<br>Self-hatred | Vacant or hollow feeling inside<br>Backaches<br>Aching arms<br>Anorexia or weight gain<br>Xerostomia<br>Dyspnea<br>Hyperventilation<br>Sighing<br>Lump in one's throat<br>Headaches<br>Sleep disturbances<br>Nightmares<br>Crying or total inability to cry<br>General malaise<br>Nasal congestion<br>Scratchy eyes<br>Food does not taste right, if at all<br>Uncontrollable shaking<br>Overactivity<br>Oversensitivity to stimuli<br>Muscle weakness<br>Weight pulling from back of neck, down arms and shoulders<br>Lack of strength<br>Multiple somatic symptoms<br>Exhaustion | Depersonalization<br>Time confusion<br>Difficulty concentrating<br>Suicidal ideation and/or plans<br>Increased accidents<br>Social withdrawal<br>Preoccupation with dead person<br>Storytelling<br>Secret behaviors and/or thoughts<br>Hallucinations<br>Guilt movies<br>Phobias<br>Obsessions<br>Compulsions<br>Flight behaviors<br>  Alcohol abuse<br>  Drug abuse<br>  Affairs<br>  Running away |

(Adapted from Johnson, S. [1983]. Guiding adults through bereavement. *Nursing Life,* January/February, 34–39)

- Impaired Adjustment
- Defensive Coping
- Ineffective Denial
- Ineffective Family Coping: Disabling
- Ineffective Family Coping: Compromised
- Non-compliance
- Decisional Conflict
- Self-Esteem Disturbance
- Chronic Low Self-Esteem
- Situational Low Self-Esteem
- Altered Growth and Development
- Hopelessness
- Powerlessness
- Knowledge Deficit
- Dysfunctional Grieving
- Anticipatory Grieving
- Post-Trauma Response
- Anxiety
- Fear

The connection between identification of a nursing diagnosis and planning and implementation can be seen in the following example. A little girl dying of cystic fibrosis was socially isolated. Because of the need to guard against infection, she could not have friends visit her in the hospital. Her school friends and teachers felt helpless and isolated from her as well. They planned a walkathon "for Julie" to show her their support and caring and that they missed her. Julie was very excited and wanted to be there the day the march was scheduled; however, she died that day. Her courageous parents took part in the walkathon.

Although Julie could not participate in school or in the planning of the walkathon, she felt connected and less socially isolated. Connections do not always need to occur in person; a card, pictures on the bedside table, a phone call, or other reminders from home, family, or friends can all help alleviate feelings of isolation.

Helplessness and powerlessness may be connected. During a child's illness parents often feel out of control of everything, particularly their child's condition. Because a major role of parents is to protect and nourish their children, when a catastrophic illness or accident occurs they are confronted with major and overwhelming feelings of helplessness and powerlessness.

Nurses must realize that children who are terminally ill, as well as their families, are dealing with difficult issues and problems. Therefore, there may be many complicated nursing diagnoses. However, nurses should be realistic about what can be accomplished and understand that it is not possible to achieve a positive outcome for all nursing diagnoses.

## Planning Nursing Care

Although nurses work with many diagnoses, plans, and interventions, certain basic principles, which include all assessment and diagnostic areas, must be considered when planning care for dying children and their families:

- Explain procedures to children and their families in terms that they can understand.
- Answer questions about medical diagnoses and what can be expected during the course of the illness (progression). Nurses may need to refer children and parents to the physician to answer specific questions about treatment or prognosis.
- Prepare children for painful, lengthy, or difficult procedures.
- If possible, schedule activities that are enjoyable, comforting, or playful immediately after the unpleasant procedure.
- Provide time for children to discuss feelings, thoughts, and reactions before and after painful procedures.
- Anticipate and help prepare children and their families for feelings of abandonment. If parents cannot be with the child constantly, which is usually the case, other connections must be available, such as a favorite blanket, a teddy bear, a tape of the mother and/or father singing favorite songs, or the presence of the nurse.
- Provide children with the opportunity to make choices, thereby providing a sense of control, e.g., "Would you rather have a bath now, or eat your breakfast first?"
- Provide as consistent a routine and staff as possible.
- Include well-rounded activities each day that encourage fun, play, and laughter.
- Provide symbolic play material for children to work out their feelings. Giving children art supplies, puppets, or blocks can help them describe or vent their frustrations. Dolls can help children overcome their fears of needles, stethoscopes, blood pressure cuffs, and other equipment. A

sandbox is a wonderful tool that children can use to cover up things that are too painful. Attempt to incorporate the child's own talents such as music, art, or humor.
- Always consider the child's emotional and physical safety.

### Cure Versus Care

In planning nursing care for dying children and their families, it is important to differentiate between *cure* goals and *care* goals. Care and cure goals are not mutually exclusive. As long as there is hope for a cure, care goals exist at the same time. However, when there is no more hope for a cure it is necessary to begin implementing strictly care goals. Cure versus care goals are identified in Table 22-4.

When planning care goals prior to death, nurses must remember that families have certain needs. They must be kept informed of the child's status; they need to participate in the child's care; and they must retain a sense of power. They will have to make decisions regarding organ donation and autopsy as well as funeral arrangements. As discussed earlier, it is also important that any unfinished business between the child and parents be completed in order to prevent later parental feelings of guilt.

### Settings

Dying children may be exposed to a variety of settings, including hospitals, hospices, or their own homes. In addition to the setting, it is important for nurses to understand the child's developmental level, the child's possible fears of abandonment or mutilation, and the child's and family's understanding of the illness. Each of these is important in planning nursing care. Nursing care planning varies ac-

*Table 22–4.  Cure Versus Care Goals*

| Hope | Expectations |
|---|---|
| **Cure** | |
| "She will get better." | Improvement |
| "She has a 90% chance of recovery." | Possibly realistic<br>Possibly denial |
| **Care** | |
| "There is little hope now." | Care, comfort, safety, as the child dies |
| "I hope she has no pain." | |
| "I hope death comes quickly." | Watch for signs of death:<br>• Extremities become cold.<br>• Breathing changes.<br>• Urine output decreases or stops.<br>• Blood pressure and pulse decrease.<br>• Child loses consciousness. |

cording to the setting because of the need to arrange for nursing staff or equipment outside the hospital, as well as the need to modify the home or hospice environment to best meet the requirements of the child and family.

Different settings have a variety of assets and liabilities. In a hospital setting, children are cared for by health professionals and are able to benefit from the available resources and technology that hospitals provide. Parents, though, often feel powerless and like "outsiders" in hospital settings since they have very little control over the environment. Therefore, they may need encouragement and even "permission" to participate in their child's care (Fig. 22-1).

It is also helpful to dying children and their families if there can be a consistent, competent, and caring nursing staff. The nursing staff can provide a sense of consistency and reliability when there is chaos in their lives. Parents need breaks from hospital routines, so it is important for them to know that the staff will be there and can be trusted to care for the child in their absence. Nurses can help provide trust, consistency, power, and reliability for dying children and their families.

Home and hospice care provides dying children and their families with the safety and security of a familiar environment (Fig. 22-2). However, both types of care necessitate intervention by others (e.g., hospice nurses, volunteers, equipment suppliers), and this can be disruptive to the family. Nurses need to explain the purposes of home and hospice care and describe the options that are available to children and parents in both types of care.

### Resources

When planning nursing care for dying children and their families, nurses should always consider the variety of resources that are available. Grief therapy may be necessary for the family's healing. Support groups can be helpful because they affirm that the families are not alone and that others have experienced similar tragedies. Groups like Compassionate Friends, Candlelighters, Sunshine Kids, and SIDs can help. Each community has its own support groups; a list of national support groups is provided at the end of this chapter. Nurses should advise parents to check the front of the telephone book for community agencies. Many communities have a resource book that identifies support groups and community agencies (often published by a private company or the United Way). In addition, organizations like Ronald McDonald House provide housing and support for parents who must travel to obtain health care for their dying children.

### Nursing Interventions

Nursing interventions are based on the nursing assessment, the nursing diagnoses, and the care plan. However, with dying children and their families it is also important to determine whether the interventions are based on cure goals, care goals, or both (Johnson, 1987).

#### Hope

When discussing the concept of death with a child, it is helpful to introduce the idea of hope. Hope is the process whereby the person finds something "to live for." It reflects religious beliefs, values, thoughts, or one's own experiences. Although the process of dying and death can be very frightening to children as well as adults, hope allows one to see some light in an otherwise dark and sad subject (Johnson, 1987).

Hope may be reflected in many ways: "I hope I see my grandmother again someday in heaven" or "We hope the doctors and nurses do their very best." This is not false

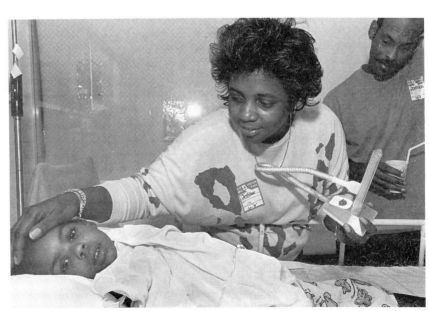

*Figure 22–1. Child in hospital room with parents.*

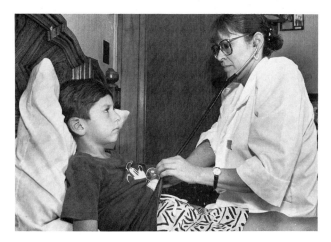

*Figure 22–2. Child being cared for in a home setting.*

hope, which would present an impossible dream and can be harmful to children. Realistic and supportive hope deals with truth and trust.

Immediately after a child dies, it is often helpful to allow the parents to spend as much time as they need with the child. They may want to participate in preparing the child to be transported to the funeral home. Parents may wish to care for the dead child in the hospital, or they may find it meaningful to dress the child at the funeral home. In such a powerless time, parents may feel that this process is something they can do "for the child." The nurse is often the one who can give permission for these actions and help the family do what is meaningful for them.

The nurse may also encourage the hospital or funeral home staff to take pictures of the body so that if the family later needs to see evidence of that person's death, there is a record of it. This situation occurs if the death was sudden and the body was not seen by the family at the time of death. There is often disbelief, possibly years later, that the person is in fact dead.

### Communicating With Children About Dying, Death, or Survivor Bereavement

Children cannot be protected from the reality of death. It is healthier if children are helped to express, in their own ways, their feelings and thoughts regarding death. Many clinicians have found that children, even very young children, know their illnesses are serious and perhaps fatal. In spite of this, they are still upset when their bodies are invaded, poked, or prodded. Fatal illness and bodily intrusions are separate issues and should not be confused. Children may know that they are dying but may protest having their bodies invaded.

As with sex education, nurses should answer questions that children ask on the level of the children's understanding and give only the information they seek. Although

it should be obvious that all children are unique and that their questions will differ depending on their age and level of understanding, the questions and *possible* responses are shown in Table 22-5. These are simply guidelines and should be adapted to individual situations. Often too much information is provided, which may relate to adult anxiety about the topic of death. If children need more information, they will usually ask for it, particularly if they have verbal and nonverbal permission from adults to ask questions. It is very important to remember, in discussing death with children, that the conversation must be short but hugs and closeness must be "long."

Children's needs, concerns, and fears are very real. They need attention from loving and caring adults. Often adults are so uncomfortable with their own grief that they try to avoid their feelings or develop the conspiracy of silence. This process often arrests children's mourning processes. It is helpful if adults can model for children what they are feeling, e.g., "I am very sad because Amy is very sick right now with her leukemia, and that is why I am crying."

Parents and nurses should also avoid using words that might confuse the child when referring to death. For example, adults often compare death with sleep or state that death is "God's will" or that "God just takes the very best." These rationalizations can cause needless and secret fears in children. Instead, nurses and parents should use specific and true reasons for the death, e.g., "She died of cancer." If the reason is not known, share that with the child; it is not wrong for parents or nurses to admit that they do not know everything.

### Alternative Forms of Communication

In addition to hope, dying children and their families also need to feel some form of power in what appears to be a

### Table 22–5. Children's Questions About Death and Possible Responses

| Question | Possible Response |
|---|---|
| Why did God let this happen? | I wish I knew. Right now it seems like we don't have an answer. |
| How could this happen to me? | I'm not sure, but I am very sorry that it is happening to you. |
| Why am I sick? | I'm wondering why you think you are sick. |
| Am I dying? | What do you think? |
| Will Mommy and Daddy be OK without me? | They will be very sad, and will miss you more than words can ever say, but if they have a lot of trouble there is help for them. |

powerless situation. People often "give up," not necessarily because of the severity of the situation but because they feel unable to change the situation. If one is not able to change death, one may be able to exercise control over other aspects, such as prayer, rituals, actions, meditation, relaxing, and decision making.

For example, the mother in a family was murdered, leaving the father and two daughters, one aged 4 years and the other 6 months. The 4-year-old had never experienced anyone's death before her mother's. Contrary to the research indicating that young children do not understand the permanence, irreversibility, or universality of death, these were never questions for her. In therapy, the 4-year-old attempted to work out two major issues. The first was trying to "fix Raggedy Ann" (her mother) by bandaging the doll, taking her blood pressure, checking her heart, giving her "get better" pills, and just holding her. Although she knew that her mother could not come back "in real life," she needed to work through what had happened and needed the assurance that she did all that could be done to "help Mom." The second issue was rearranging the puppets (her family) from four members to three. She worked with these concepts for almost a year.

Almost 2 years to the day from the murder, the trial was set to begin. The district attorney wanted the daughters (now 6 and 2) to appear in the court room. The 6-year-old was frightened at the thought of having to confront the man who might have killed her mother. During a therapy session when her fears were being discussed, she drew a picture (Fig. 22-3). She drew three stars at the top of the page (one each for her father, her sister, and herself), a rainbow with lots of red (blood was an issue that was reflected in trying to "fix Raggedy Ann"), and a path with a star heading to the rainbow ("Mom going to heaven"). She felt very powerless and unprotected if she had to go to court, "even though daddy and police would be there."

It was decided that the star would be used as a symbol of power. She drew a big star, colored it, and cut it out. The nurse therapist gave her some beautiful silver metal thread for the chain. The child first decided that she would put the star in her pocket for safety. Then she thought it should be worn on her wrist. Finally, she decided it needed to be hung around her neck so that everyone could see that she was protected by "her mommy's star" if she had to go to court. In this way, power developed even in a powerless and frightening situation such as this.

In communicating about dying, death, and bereavement with children, it is important and necessary to use a variety of media because they may not have learned yet to use talk as a coping skill. Children often express their thoughts and ideas easier and better through games, drawing, and puppets or reading and talking about a book. A list of appropriate children's books is provided at the end of this chapter.

It may take a long time for parents to give children

*Figure 22–3. Picture drawn by a 6-year-old girl during a therapy session.*

permission to talk about or experience sadness. Many young children learn not to show their feelings because expressions of feelings "make Mom and Dad sad." Unfortunately, many children are still told not to cry, e.g., "Big boys don't cry." Thus, they are prevented from expressing feelings. However, this response only complicates the situation for all involved. If feelings cannot be directly expressed, they are often expressed in fears, phobias, or physical symptoms. It seems ironic that as children develop a concept of death and the wide range of feelings that accompany grief, they are taught not to experience their feelings.

One 6-year-old girl tried hard to be a "good girl" after her 3-year-old brother drowned in their family pool. She continued to do well in school, looked happy, didn't cry, and always tidied up her room (a new behavior, which her parents liked). After several months she finally admitted that she had found her brother in the pool, panicked, and run across the street while pretending not to know what happened. She was trying to be "good" in order to defend against what she thought was "bad"—for example, thinking "Maybe if I had stayed I could have saved him." It also hurt her very much to see her mother and father cry, which was connected to her own secret guilt. She had to work very hard to deal with her pain, sadness, and guilt.

With sick or well children, an honest and caring response is needed when questions are asked regarding dying, death, or bereavement. They need to know that they can talk and play and that they can share what they are thinking and feeling. When children can respond openly, trust and security are increased.

### Communicating With Parents and Families About Dying, Death, and Bereavement

How do nurses help parents cope with the realization that their child is dying? Parents and families of dying children can often be more resilient than nurses might expect, if these difficult messages are communicated with care and hope. Nurses should always impart a sense of hope to the parents and family. As goals change ("cure versus care"), hope may change over a period of time. "She will get better" may change to "We will not let her suffer any pain."

It is often helpful for nurses to ask the parents what the physician has told them, what they think the news is, or how sick they think their child is before sharing information. This gives nurses the opportunity to assess the parents' thoughts and feelings. Usually parents know intuitively what is happening.

When sharing sad news with parents—whether the results of a lab test or, with the physician's consent, the prognosis—it is best to talk to the parents in a quiet environment, away from the child. The news should be given as compassionately and succinctly as possible. Consider the two following scenarios and decide which is most appropriate.

1. "Your daughter's kidneys are failing. She will be dead in 24 to 48 hours."
2. "I have seen how much loving support and comfort you have given your daughter, so I understand her determination and will to live. In spite of her will to live, and everything that can and has been done for her, her kidneys cannot withstand much more and are failing. The nurses and doctors will do everything they can to be certain that she is comfortable in her last hours. Try to spend as much time as you can with her. Having her family around her will help her a great deal."

Nurses should allow the parents time to be alone together in order to process the information, and should ask if there are helpful people that they need with them. However, nurses should not assume that the most helpful people will come from inside the family unit; often they prove to be the most hindering.

Another important nursing intervention is the referral of children and families for grief therapy, when appropriate. Based on the nursing assessment and nursing diagnoses, those who are at risk for developing complicated grieving patterns should be advised to seek the services of

grief therapists. Individuals who should be referred are identified in Table 22-6.

It is never easy to discuss difficult topics with families. To communicate successfully, different approaches that depend on age and developmental levels, as well as the family's needs and requests, are required. For example, the family may want the nurse to call a distant friend or relative but may wish to tell their own children. They may need assistance and support to accomplish such a difficult and painful task. Caring, hope, trust, a safe environment, and honesty are the most helpful approaches.

## Evaluating Nursing Care

Evaluation of nursing care must be based on the entire nursing process. Nurses should evaluate the results of the care as well as their observations, assessments, diagnoses, plans, and interventions. It is important to be realistic and to realize that nursing cannot work miracles. In spite of the best implementation of the nursing process, the child may still die or experience the death of a loved one.

If nurses have done all they can, based on the nursing process, the cure goals will have been separated from the care goals, complications of grief will have been prevented, and unfinished business will have been com-

### Table 22–6. Appropriate Individuals to Refer for Grief Therapy

Anyone who has sustained a "significant loss" from death, a move, surgery, or divorce

Individuals whose relationship with the dead person was extremely attached or ambivalent

Those who have had a short preparation time for death (2 weeks or less warning that death was imminent)

Those who have had a long preparation time for death but did not use the anticipatory period for grief work

Individuals who feel that the death of a loved one could have been prevented

Those who feel an "extreme" amount of guilt regarding the death

Anyone involved with a death that was a suicide or homocide

Families or individuals who have had multiple losses or changes within the last 12 months or 2 years

Families of a dead child

Individuals involved in the death of a "socially significant" person, such as a mother of small children, or the early death of a spouse or child

Those who, by the end of the first year of bereavement or into the second and third years, have exaggerated physical or emotional symptoms or have not reorganized their lives

Individuals who have a history of depression or psychosomatic problems that may be related to death or losses

Those in whom a death stimulates a clinical depression

Individuals who have had multiple deaths or losses all of their lives

pleted. A safe, comfortable, and open environment must then be created so that the child may die in peace and love.

It is also essential for nurses to evaluate how they feel, think, and respond when working with dying children and their families. Nurses also need time to grieve.

## Effects of Dying, Death, and Bereavement on Parents and Families

The dying or death of a child is probably the worst pain parents can experience. Parents feel helpless and powerless. They cannot do what parents "should do"—protect their child from harm. It is also against the order of nature; parents should die before their children. As an old Chinese proverb states, "If our parents die we have lost our past, but if our children die we have lost our future."

Parents seem to have less guilt and fewer regrets if they feel that they have done all they possibly can do for their child; communicate with each other and the health care providers; know that their other children are cared for; are surrounded by helpful, rather than hindering, people; and share their feelings. When this is not possible, therapy is often needed, not only to heal the present situations but also to rework past problems that may not have been resolved.

Death, whether of a child or a significant other, has a great impact on a family. Major unresolved losses can be a basis for physical or emotional pathology. It is important for all to have an opportunity to work through their grief.

Parents react and behave in many different ways. It is important for nurses to realize that there is no one right way to grieve. Some parents may work hard and avoid the issue of dying or death; others may direct their anger toward anyone or everyone; still others may cry. Just because some parents or children may not grieve in the same way as others, it does not mean they are not grieving. It is important for nurses to understand the concept of grieving and to acknowledge that grief on the part of the survivors is natural and to be expected.

If grief is not worked through, far-reaching and generational effects can result. Divorce, alcoholism and drug addiction, depression, and physical conditions such as ulcers, headaches, ulcerative colitis, "heart aches," and backaches are reported frequently by parents whose children have died. There are often problems with relationships at home, at work, or in the community. If grief is not resolved, the issues may be passed down to the next generation. After a death, it is very difficult to develop trust and security in people or life in general, which often causes more withdrawal and depression (Johnson, 1987).

Parents may be so consumed by their grief that their other children are ignored, abandoned, and left alone to handle their own grief. They have lost not only their sibling

but, in many ways, their parents. In addition, they may be experiencing feelings, thoughts, reactions, and behaviors that they never had before, which can be extremely frightening to them. These children need a lot of support and reassurance, as well as connections with others. Otherwise, major scars that may have tragic effects during adolescence and into adulthood can be left.

For example, 6-year-old Susan's sister was hit and killed by a car the day before her fourth birthday. Her father abandoned his grief and his family by working very hard. Her mother was distraught with her grief about the loss of her "favorite blonde-haired, blue-eyed little girl." Susan was left all alone to suffer in silence.

Susan's grief over her sister's death was complicated by the fact that her mother made no secret that she wished Susan had died instead of her sister. Her mother disliked Susan because she was so much like her (the mother had a great deal of self-hatred). All the mother wanted was her "little Betsy" back. In the second year of bereavement the mother became pregnant. Amniocentesis indicated that the fetus was a girl and that the anticipated due date was Betsy's birthday. The mother truly believed that her prayers had been answered—that Betsy would be brought back to her because her death was a mistake.

After the baby's (Betty's) birth, Susan became more and more isolated, abandoned, and depressed. She was learning that she "should not exist." To comply with the message "don't be alive" that was given to her by her mother, she made a serious suicide attempt at the age of 13. However, the attempt acted as a "call for help" and resulted in the beginning of healing for Susan and her family.

Families should be encouraged to undergo grief therapy following the death of a child. They also need to know that the process of grieving may last for years. Most people who have not experienced grief think that grief lasts from 48 hours to about 2 weeks. Specific time frames for the grieving process can create problems, because many people are not willing to support and allow grief to last for long intervals, either in themselves or others. However, "time doesn't heal, hard grief work does" (Johnson, 1987).

## Effects of Dying, Death, and Bereavement on Nurses

It is also important to consider the impact of a death on nurses and other staff. In working with a family in which a member is dying, a relationship develops; when the person dies, nurses also experience losses. They lose not only the person who died but the whole family, whom they probably will not see again.

Nurses need time to grieve, to talk about their feelings and reactions, to debrief, and to work through unfinished business. It is important for nurses to know and understand grief, with its many symptoms and reactions, so that it may be identified not only in patients but also in themselves. Often a consultant is needed to help with this process. There exists a method of learning to take care of oneself so that "burnout" does not occur (Johnson, 1987).

Nurses need therapy and opportunities to share their feelings, thoughts, and reactions about these experiences because they may trigger issues and symptoms that they have held unconsciously for years. For example, a student nurse developed physical and psychological symptoms of illness when working with a child dying from leukemia. It was uncovered that the student nurse's sister had died of leukemia at the age of 12, the same age as her patient. There had been a conspiracy of silence in the family, and her sister's illness and death were never discussed. Through grief therapy the student nurse was better able to understand her own feelings and reactions.

When nurses are extremely involved with the family, it may be helpful for them to attend the wake or funeral. This ritual allows for closure. Some nursing units have found it helpful to develop their own rituals following the death of a patient. For example, staff members get pictures of the people for whom they cared and put the pictures up in the office during a moment of silence. This practice proves to be meaningful for the nurses and staff and gives them some power in this situation.

## Summary

This chapter provides an overview of the concepts of dying, death, grief, mourning, and bereavement. It outlines the development of a concept of death from infancy through adolescence and shows how nurses apply the nursing process while working with children, parents, and families facing death. The nursing process, as applied to dying, death, and bereavement, was discussed in depth. It focuses on communicating with children about dying, death, and bereavement, and explores the impact of dealing with death on children, families, and nurses.

Nurses are instrumental in helping families to work through grief and prevent complicated and pathological grief. Nurses are the health care professionals who are most involved in dealing with families and patients who are dying. They have the psychological and physical background to assist in this critical and potentially damaging process of loss. Nurses need to keep this vital role and not give it away to others.

## References

Anthony, S. (1940). *The child's discovery of death.* New York: Harcourt Brace.

Bowlby, J. (1960). Grief and mourning in infancy and early childhood. *Psychoanalytic Study of the Child, 15,* 9–52.

Deutsch, H. (1959). A two-year-old boy's first love comes to grief. In L. Jessner & E. Pavenstedt (Eds.). *Dynamics of psychopathology in childhood.* New York: Grune & Stratton.

Johnson-Soderberg, S. (1982). The ethos of parental bereavement and guilt. Doctoral dissertation, University of Michigan.

Johnson, S. (1983). Giving emotional support to families after a patient dies. *Nursing Life, 34–39.*

Johnson, S. (1986). The grieving patient. In J. D. Durham & S. B. Hardin (Eds.). *The nurse psychotherapist in private practice.* New York: Springer Publishing Co.

Johnson, S. (1987). *After a child dies: Counseling bereaved families.* New York: Springer Publishing Co.

Koocher, G. (1974). Talking with children about death. *American Journal of Ortho-Psychiatry, 44,* 404.

Kübler-Ross, E. (1969). *On death and dying.* New York: Macmillan.

McIntire, M., Angle, C., & Strumpler, L. (1972). The concept of death in midwestern children and youth. *American Journal of the Diseases of Children, 123,* 527–532.

Parkes, C. M. (1965). Bereavement and mental illnesses. Part 1: A clinical study of the grief of bereaved psychiatric patients. *British Journal of Medical Psychology, 38,* 1–12.

Piaget, J. (1965). *The moral judgment of the child.* New York: Free Press.

Schaffer, H. R., & Emerson, P. (1964). The development of social attachment in infancy. *Monographs of the Society for Research in Child Development, 29*(3, Serial No. 94).

Spinetta, J. J., Rigler, D., & Karon, M. (1973). Anxiety in the dying child. *Pediatrics, 52,* 841–845.

Steiner, G. L. (1965). Children's concepts of life and death: A developmental study. Doctoral dissertation, Columbia University.

Waechter, E. H. (1971). Children's awareness of fatal illness. *American Journal of Nursing, 71,* 1168–1172.

Worden, J. W. (1982). *Grief counseling and grief therapy.* New York: Springer Publishing Co.

## Bibliography

Demi, A. S., & Miles, M. S. (1987). Parameters of normal grief: A Delphi study. *Death Studies, 11,* 397–412.

Dubik-Unruh, S. (1989). Children in chaos: Planning for the emotional survival of dying children of dying families. *Journal of Palliative Care, 5*(2), 10–15, 1989.

Edelstein, L. (1984). *Maternal bereavement: Coping with the unexpected death of a child.* New York: Praeger.

Fish, W. C. (1986). Differences of grief intensity in bereaved parents. In T. S. Rando (Ed.). *Parental loss of a child* (pp. 415–428). Champaign, IL: Research Press.

Gray, E. (1989). The emotional and play needs of the dying child. *Issues in Comprehensive Pediatric Nursing, 12,* 207–224.

Klass, D. (1987). John Bowlby's model of grief and the problem of identification. *Omega: Journal of Death and Dying, 18*(1), 13–32.

Kovarsky, R. S. (1989). Loneliness and disturbed grief: A comparison of parents who lost a child to suicide or accidental death. *Archives of Psychiatric Nursing, 3*(2), 86–96.

Miles, M. S., & Demi, A. S. (1986). Guilt in bereaved parents. In T. S. Rando (Ed.). *Parental loss of a child* (pp. 97–118). Champaign, IL: Research Press.

McGoldrick, M., Pearce, J., & Giordano, J. E. (1982). *Ethnicity and family therapy.* New York: The Guilford Press.

National Center for Health Statistics. (1989). *Vital statistics of the United States: Vol. 2. Mortality. Part B.* Washington, D. C.: U.S. Government Printing Office.

While, A. E. (1989). The needs of dying children and their families. *Health Visit, 62*(6), 176–178.

## *Support Groups for Those Involved With Dying and Death*

Alan Foss Leukemia Memorial Fund
730 East 79th Street
Brooklyn, NY 11236

American Cancer Society
1599 Clifton Road, NE
Atlanta, GA 30329
(404) 329-7617

Candlelighters Foundation (for parents with children who have cancer or who have died from it)
1901 Pennsylvania Avenue, NW
Washington, DC 20006
(202) 659-5136

Centre for Living with Dying
1542 Los Padres Boulevard
Santa Clara, CA 95050
(408) 243-0700

Compassionate Friends (for parents and siblings of children who have died)
P.O. Box 3696
Oak Brook, IL 60522
(708) 990-0010

Grief Education Institute
6198 South Westview
Littleton, CO 80120

Kara: Volunteer Emotional Support Services (for individuals who are terminally ill or near death and their families)
457 Kingsley Avenue
Palo Alto, CA 94301

Leukemia Society of America
733 Third Avenue
New York, NY 10017
(212) 573-8484

National Mental Health Association
1021 Prince Street
Alexandria, VA 22314
(703) 684-7722

National Cancer Foundation
1 Park Avenue
New York, NY 10016
(212) 679-5700

Parents Without Partners
P.O. Box 8506
Silver Spring, MD 20907
(202) 638-1320

Shanti Project (grief counseling for patients and families)
980 Hayes Street
San Francisco, CA 94117
(415) 555-9644

Sudden Infant Death Syndrome Alliance
National Sudden Infant Death Syndrome Foundation
10500 Little Patuxent Parkway, Suite 420
Columbia, MD 21044
(301) 964-8000

## Children's Books for Nurses Caring for Dying Children and Their Families

Aliki. (1979). *The two of them.* New York: Greenwillow Books.

Brown, M. W. *The dead bird.* New York: Young Scott Books.

Carrick, C. (1976). *Accident.* New York: Seabury Press.

Cohen, M. (1974). *Jim's dog muffins.* New York: Greenwillow Books.

Hanson, J. *I'm going to run away.* New York: Platt & Munk.

Hoffman, A. (1988). *At risk.* New York: Berkley Books.

Kraus, R., & Aruego, J. (1971). *Leo the late bloomer.* New York: Simon & Schuster.

Lobel, A. (1980). *Fables.* New York: Harper & Row.

Paterson, D. (1976). *Smile for Auntie.* New York: The Dial Press.

Dr. Seuss. (1990). *Oh, the places you'll go!* New York: Random House.

Smith, D. B. (1973). *A taste of blackberries.* New York: Thomas Y. Crowell.

Viorst, J. (1972). *The tenth good thing about Barney.* New York: Atheneum Publishers.

Viorst, J. (1973). *Alexander and the terrible, horrible, no good, very bad day.* New York: Atheneum Publishers.

Viorst, J. (1973). *My mama says there aren't any zombies, ghosts, vampires, creatures, demons, monsters, fiends, goblins or things.* New York: Atheneum Publishers.

White, E. B. (1952). *Charlotte's web.* New York: Harper & Row.

# Health Problems of Children and Adolescents

*Alterations in Respiratory Function*

*Alterations in Cardiovascular Function*

*Alterations in Hematological Function*

*Alterations in Neurological Function*

*Alterations in Immune System Function*

*Alterations in Fluid and Electrolyte Balance*

*Alterations in Gastrointestinal Function*

*Alterations in Renal Function*

*Alterations in Reproductive Function*

*Alterations in Endocrine Function*

*Alterations in Musculoskeletal Function*

*Alterations in Integumentary Function*

*Alterations in Sensory Function*

V

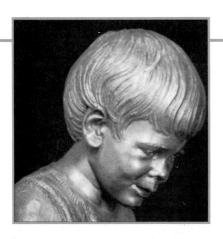

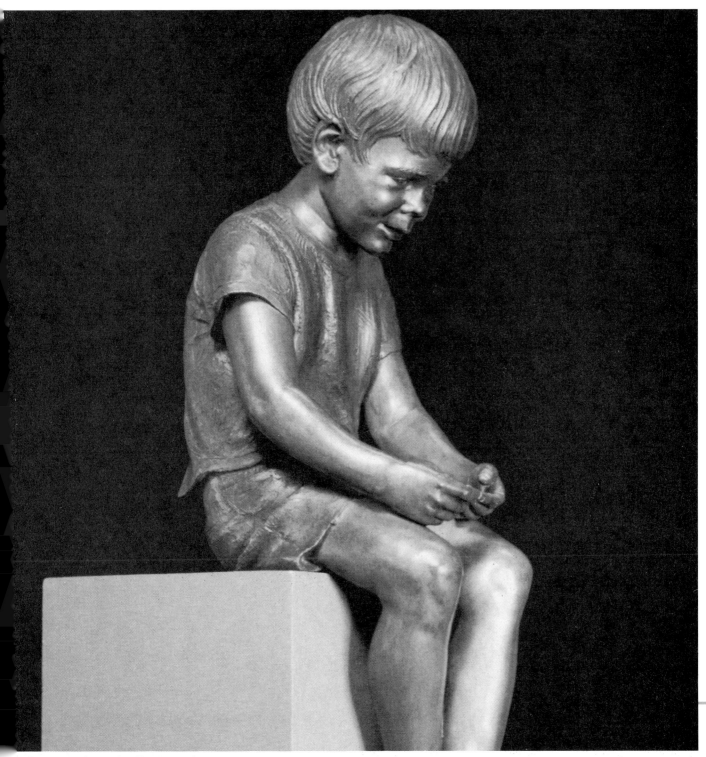

*Sculpture by Charles Parks*

# Alterations in Respiratory Function

Susan J. Smith Millet

Photograph by David Finn

23

*Embryology*

*Anatomy of the Respiratory System*

*Physiology*

*Assessment*

*Nursing Diagnosis*

*Planning Nursing Care*

*Nursing Interventions*

*Evaluating Nursing Care*

*Congenital Respiratory Problems*

*Respiratory Problems of Neonates*

*Respiratory Problems of Infants*

*Respiratory Problems of Toddlers and Preschool-Aged Children*

*Respiratory Problems of School-Aged Children*

*Acute Respiratory Problems*

*Chronic Respiratory Problems*

*Summary*

*Nursing Care Plan*

## Learning Objectives

*Upon completion of this chapter the reader will be able to:*

1. Describe the embryonic development of the respiratory system.

2. Discuss the anatomy and physiology of the respiratory system.

3. Assess respiratory function.

4. State nursing diagnoses for respiratory problems.

5. Identify nursing interventions for respiratory problems.

6. Develop a plan for evaluation of nursing interventions for respiratory problems.

7. Describe the following congenital respiratory problems: laryngeal stridor and choanal atresia.

8. Demonstrate an understanding of the following respiratory problems affecting neonates: meconium aspiration syndrome, asphyxia neonatorum, bronchopulmonary dysplasia, respiratory distress syndrome, pneumothorax, and apnea of prematurity.

9. Describe the following respiratory problems affecting infants: croup, sudden infant death syndrome, bronchiolitis, pertussis, and retropharyngeal abscess.

10. Discuss the following respiratory problems affecting toddlers, preschoolers, and school-aged children: foreign-body aspiration, pharyngitis, tonsillitis, and epiglottitis.

11. Describe the following acute and chronic respiratory problems: nasopharyngitis, streptococcal pharyngitis, pneumonia, diphtheria, cystic fibrosis, asthma, and tuberculosis.

## Key Terms

adenoids
alveoli
apnea
atopy
Biot's respirations
bradypnea
bronchi
bronchioles
Cheyne-Stokes respirations
cilia
crackles
crepitation
dyspnea
expiration
fremitus
hyperpnea
hyperventilation
hypoventilation
hypoxemia
inspiration
Kussmaul's respirations
laryngopharynx
larynx
nasopharynx
obstructive breathing
oropharynx
orthopnea
parietal pleura
periodic breathing
pharynx
pleura
rhonchi
stridor
sudden infant death syndrome
surfactant
tachypnea
trachea
tracheobronchial tree
visceral pleura
wheezes

Because oxygen is a requisite for the survival of all cells and tissues, disorders of the respiratory system can threaten life. The role of the nurse in caring for the child with respiratory problems is essential in minimizing this threat to life. Pediatric respiratory nursing can be both challenging and rewarding as nurses provide comprehensive care to children and their families.

## Embryology

Fetal lung development occurs in four periods or stages. The first stage, the embryonic stage, occurs about 24 days after fertilization of the ovum. During this stage, the lung begins to develop as an outpouching or bud on the embryonic gut, and the two major bronchi form from the bud.

The second period is called the pseudoglandular or glandular stage and occurs between the 5th and 16th weeks of gestation. During this period, the major airways or branches of the conducting system form, including the trachea and terminal bronchioles. About 20 generations of these irregular dichotomous branches form, after which they grow in size, and no new branches are added. In addition to the completed conducting airway system, the diaphragm and mesothelial lining, which later becomes the pleura, form.

The third period is called the canalicular stage and occurs between the 16th and 24th weeks of gestation. During this period, the number of bronchioles increases, and a rich vascular supply develops. The respiratory bronchioles are delineated into the acinus, which becomes the gas-exchange portion of the lung. The pulmonary circulation develops after the airways and terminal sacs. The capillaries come into close proximity to the airway surface so that at the end of this period, respiration becomes possible.

The last period is called the terminal sac or alveolar stage. It begins at about 24 weeks of gestation and continues until birth. During this stage, alveolilike structures called saccules appear and come in close contact with the pulmonary capillaries. Saccules differ from alveoli in shape and size, but they can function as gas-exchange units because the thickness of the saccule wall is about the same as that of an adult alveolar unit. As this stage progresses, the epithelial walls of the airways become thinner. By weeks 34 to 36, type II alveolar cells appear and begin to produce surfactant. By weeks 37 to 40, near-mature surfactant levels are present.

Gas exchange during gestation occurs through the placenta; the lungs have no function. In fact, the fetal lungs are filled with fluid that becomes part of the amniotic fluid. The fluid produced by the fetal lungs is thought to contribute to the size and volume of the peripheral lung units.

At birth, the lungs must be cleared of fluid so they can sustain respiration after delivery. About one third is squeezed out as the fetus passes through the birth canal. The other two thirds of the fluid is absorbed and removed by the pulmonary vascular and lymphatic circulation.

## Anatomy

### Upper Airways

The upper respiratory tract includes the nasal cavity, the pharynx, and the larynx. The upper airway conducts gas from the environment to the lower airways or lungs.

#### Nasal Cavity (Nose)

A complete discussion of the anatomy and functions of the nose can be found in Chapter 35.

#### Pharynx

The *pharynx,* or throat, conducts air to the trachea and serves as the passageway for food to the esophagus. It is divided into three sections: the nasopharynx, the oropharynx, and the laryngopharynx.

The *nasopharynx* is the uppermost section of the pharynx and connects the internal nares or choanae to the soft palate. The two eustachian tube orifices open into the nasopharynx, which allows equalization of pressure between the middle ears and pharynx during swallowing.

Located in the posterior of the nasopharynx are the pharyngeal tonsils or adenoids. *Adenoids* consist of an aggregate of lymphatic tissue and are thought to play a role in development of immunity in children.

The *oropharynx* is located behind the oral cavity and connects the soft palate to the entrance of the larynx. It serves as a common passage for food and air. When food is introduced into the mouth, a swallowing reflex propels food posteriorly. At the same time, the *epiglottis,* a thin structure located posterior to the root of the tongue, closes and prevents aspiration of food into the trachea. Lingual tonsils are located at the base of the tongue, and two palatine or faucial tonsils are located laterally, one on each side of the larynx. The tonsils play a role in humoral immunity through antibody production. They filter and protect the respiratory tract from invasion by microorganisms.

The *laryngopharynx* is the lowest segment of the pharynx and extends from the oropharynx to the esophagus posteriorly and larynx anteriorly. It serves as a passageway for both air and food.

#### Larynx

The *larynx* (voice box) connects the pharynx with the trachea and provides a passageway for airflow between the upper and lower airways, protects the lower airways from aspiration of food and foreign objects, and assists in the defensive cough mechanism and phonation. The opening of the larynx is called the glottis. The upper part of the laryngeal cavity contains a pair of laryngeal folds called vestibular or false vocal cords. The lower portion contains a pair of true vocal cords.

## Lower Airways

The lower respiratory tract extends from the trachea to the alveolar sacs and can be divided into two sections: the tracheobronchial tree and the lung parenchyma.

### Tracheobronchial Tree

The *tracheobronchial tree* provides heated and humidified air from the external environment to the lower airways and allows molecular gas exchange between blood and alveolar air distal to the terminal bronchioles.

*Trachea.* The *trachea,* or windpipe, provides an open passage for airflow from the atmosphere to the lungs.

*Bronchi.* The *bronchi* are the two principal branches leading from the trachea to the lungs. The lower portion of the trachea divides or bifurcates into two main-stem bronchi, the right and the left.

*Bronchioles. Bronchioles,* or transitional airways, are airways less than 1 mm in diameter that branch from the small bronchi.

### Lung Parenchyma

The lungs are cone-shaped and completely fill the thoracic cavity. They extend from the apex, which protrudes slightly above the clavicles, to the base, which lies on the diaphragm. At the bases, the lungs are concave along the dome-shaped diaphragm. They are also somewhat concave along the medial surfaces to allow for the myocardium and other mediastinal structures. The main-stem bronchi and pulmonary blood vessels are held together by connective tissue and enter each lung at the hilum, which is an opening on the medial lung surface. Grooves or fissures divide each lung into its lobes.

The right lung is divided into three separate lobes, known as the superior, middle, and inferior (upper, middle, and lower) lobes. The left lung is divided into two lobes, known as the superior and inferior lobes.

The lobes of each lung are divided into bronchopulmonary segments. The right lung contains ten segments; the left lung contains eight segments. Each segment is supplied by a tertiary bronchus with its branches and a branch of the pulmonary artery. Pulmonary veins are present to drain the various segments.

The last generation of the airways are the alveolar sacs. They have the same functions as the alveolar ducts. *Alveolar sacs* are grapelike clusters of alveoli, and they increase the surface area of the lung. They are responsible for about 65% of the alveolar gas exchange.

The alveolar epithelium is made up of type I, type II, and type III alveolar pneumonocytes. Type I alveolar pneumonocytes arise from type II cells. They are very thin and provide the surface area for diffusion of gases. Type II pneumonocytes secrete surfactant, which lines the alveoli. *Surfactant* is a phospholipid that decreases the surface tension of the alveoli, thus allowing the alveoli to remain open. Type III pneumonocytes are contained in the fluid lining of the alveoli. These cells are called macrophages and are responsible for phagocytosis within the pulmonary alveoli.

The space between the alveoli and capillary endothelium is made up of collagen, water, and electrolytes. The pulmonary lymphatic system also lies within the pulmonary interstitial space. The lymphatic system drains fluid that leaks from the pulmonary capillary system.

The *pleura* is a sac that surrounds each lung and consists of a double-walled serous membrane. The *parietal pleura* lines the thoracic cavity and adheres to the rib cage and superior surface of the diaphragm. The *visceral pleura* lies against the parietal pleura and surrounds each lung. The parietal and visceral pleura are separated by the pleural space, a thin space that contains a small amount of serous pleural fluid that acts as a lubricant. This allows the pleural layers to slide over one another as the lungs inflate and deflate.

### The Pulmonary Circulation

The pulmonary arteries supply unoxygenated blood from the right ventricle to the alveoli and pleura. The unoxygenated blood flows from the pulmonary arteries through the pulmonary capillaries, where oxygen diffuses from the alveoli to the blood. Oxygenated blood then flows through the bronchial arteries to the tracheobronchial tree, the pulmonary blood vessels, the peripheral visceral pleura, the pulmonary nerves, and lymphatic and connective tissue.

Most of the blood in the lungs drains to the pulmonary veins from the pulmonary capillaries and then to the left atrium. The rest of the blood supply drains into the right atrium. The pulmonary lymphatic system drains excess protein and water from the vascular and interstitial spaces and returns it to the general circulation.

## Physiology

### Respiratory Mechanics

Respiratory mechanics refers to the mechanical process of inspiration and expiration as well as to support of the lungs (Fig. 23-1). The mechanics of respiration includes the respiratory muscles, the elastic properties of the lungs and chest wall, and the pressures and resistances of breathing.

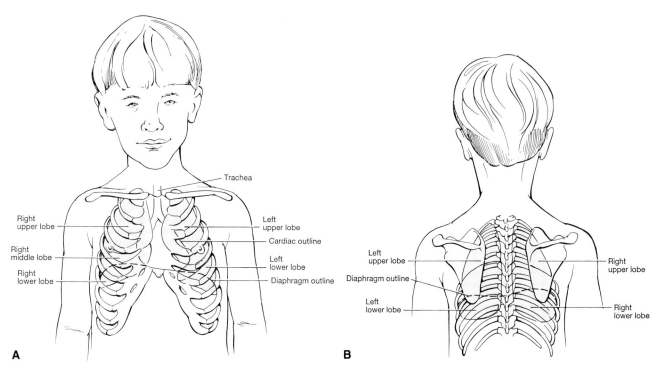

*Figure 23–1. Respiratory mechanics.*

The respiratory muscles act in a coordinated pattern to expand the thorax and to fill the lungs with air. Muscle groups used during respiration differ with active and passive breathing. *Inspiration* is the process of drawing air into the lungs. It is an active process. Eighty percent of the active work of inspiration is performed by the diaphragm. The other 20% is performed by the external intercostal muscles and the parasternal muscles located between the cartilaginous portions of the ribs. The scalene muscles and sternocleidomastoid muscles are used during active inspiration, which includes deep breathing, forced inspiratory movement, or dyspnea. During inspiration, the diaphragm flattens, which increases the dimensions of the thorax. When the diaphragm contracts, the lower rib cage is displaced outward. The lateral and anteroposterior dimensions increase as the ribs move upward.

The external intercostal muscles raise the ribs upward, which increases the anteroposterior diameter of the thorax. During contraction of the external intercostal muscles, the chest is stabilized, which prevents intercostal retractions during inspiration.

*Expiration* is the process of expelling air from the lungs. It is generally a passive process that results from the elastic recoil of the lungs. During increased work of breathing, as in respiratory obstruction, accessory muscles take an active role in expiration and inspiration. The abdominal muscles and the internal intercostal muscles become active during expiration. The abdominal muscles pull the ribs downward and inward. They also cause compression of the abdominal contents. This pushes the relaxed diaphragm upward

and causes it to lengthen. The internal intercostal muscles pull the lower ribs downward and inward. They assist the abdominal muscles in active expiration.

During inspiration, the inspiratory muscles contract, causing the lungs to fill the chest cavity. Intrapulmonary pressure becomes subatmospheric; that is, it falls below atmospheric pressure. The difference in alveolar pressure, which is less than the pressure at the mouth or airway opening, causes air to move into the lungs until the alveolar pressure equals atmospheric pressure. At this point, airflow into the lungs ceases. During inspiration, the lung and chest wall expand, largely as a result of the elastic properties of the tissues involved. The tissues are stretched up to twice their resting length.

During expiration, the elastic fibers recoil or contract, returning the airways and lung tissue to their resting state. The elastic fibers in the lung parenchyma and chest wall are similar to a rubber band. When the rubber band is stretched, it will automatically return to its resting state.

During expiration, the elastic recoil of the lung causes the alveolar pressure to exceed atmospheric pressure. This positive pressure produces a driving force or pressure that results in a flow of air from the alveoli to the mouth. This airflow continues until the alveolar pressure equals atmospheric pressure.

### Respiratory Control

The three methods by which respiration or breathing is controlled are neural or nervous control, mechanical control, and chemical control.

*Neural or Nervous Control.* The respiratory center for control of breathing is located in the brain stem. It consists of a group of interconnected neurons that are responsible for various aspects of respiration.

The medullary respiratory center regulates the inspiratory and expiratory phases of breathing. During inspiration, the expiratory phase of breathing is temporarily inhibited. During expiration, the inspiratory phase is temporarily inhibited.

The apneustic and pneumotaxic centers are located in the pons, which sits anterior to the medulla. The apneustic center can stimulate inspiration by transmitting signals to the medullary inspiratory center to prevent inspiratory inhibition.

The pneumotaxic center located in the pons transmits signals to the medullary inspiratory center to inhibit inspiration. This prevents the lungs from overfilling. The pneumotaxic center helps regulate respiratory rate by strength of its signal. A strong pneumotaxic signal shortens inspiration, thus increasing the respiratory rate. A weak pneumotaxic signal results in prolonged deep inspirations, thus decreasing the respiratory rate.

The cerebral cortex also controls respiration by overriding the medullary respiratory center in the brain stem. Through voluntary control, people can hyperventilate or hold their breath. Activity of the respiratory center in the medulla and pons is involuntary.

*Mechanical Control.* Several reflexes affect both depth and rate of respiration. These reflexes are triggered by mechanical stimuli.

The first mechanical reflex is called the Hering-Breuer reflex. Within the smooth muscle of the lung parenchyma are stretch receptors. When these receptors are stimulated by lung distention, impulses are sent to the respiratory center in the medulla to inhibit further inspiration, thus preventing overdistention of the lung. In neonates, the Hering-Breuer reflex shortens inspiration by inhibiting this phase of respiration.

Another mechanical reflex is initiated by inhaled irritants, such as dust, cigarette smoke, cold air, or narrowed or collapsed airways as seen in asthma. When airways are narrowed or collapsed, or when irritants are inhaled, receptors located in the trachea and the bronchioles are stimulated. This results in coughing and hyperventilation.

A third mechanical factor controlling respiration are the J receptors that consist of sensory nerve endings in the alveolar walls in juxtaposition to the capillaries. They are stimulated when the pulmonary capillaries become engorged or pulmonary edema is present. The J receptors, when stimulated, result in shallow, rapid respiration as well as the sensation of dyspnea.

*Chemical Control.* Chemical control of respiration is accomplished by chemical changes in the blood and body fluids and the response of chemoreceptors to these changes. Chemoreceptors are located both centrally and peripherally.

## Pulmonary Gas Exchange

Gas moves by means of the process of diffusion, which is movement by random molecular motion and mass airflow. The gases of concern in respiration are oxygen and $CO_2$. These gases diffuse across the alveolar capillary membrane based on their partial pressures.

The partial pressure of a gas is defined as the pressure exerted by a gas in a mixture of gases or in a liquid. The partial pressure of a gas is directly related to its concentration. Gas diffuses based on concentration gradients, moving from an area of higher concentration to an area of lower concentration. The gases continue to diffuse until the concentrations on either side of the membrane are equal. Each gas diffuses based on its own partial pressure and is not influenced by other gases and their partial pressures.

In the lung, oxygen in the inspired air moves by mass airflow from the atmosphere to the terminal respiratory units. From here to the alveoli, gas movement occurs through diffusion based on concentration gradients. The partial pressure of oxygen in the alveoli is 100 mmHg. The partial pressure of oxygen in the pulmonary capillaries equals 40 mmHg. Thus, oxygen diffuses from the alveoli into the blood in the pulmonary capillaries. Once in the pulmonary capillaries, most of the oxygen attaches to hemoglobin in the red blood cell, where it is transported to all body tissues.

Carbon dioxide also diffuses by means of pressure gradients. $CO_2$ diffuses out of the cells into the capillaries, in which it is then carried back to the lungs. Because the partial pressure of $CO_2$ in the blood is 46 mmHg, higher than in the alveoli (40 mmHg), $CO_2$ diffuses from the pulmonary capillary blood to the alveoli. Once in the alveoli, $CO_2$ is excreted into the atmosphere.

## Assessment

### History

Physical assessment is an important part of the total nursing assessment since it aids in planning comprehensive nursing care. The history is the first component of the physical assessment process.

Children differ from adults in several ways in terms of their health care and assessment of their needs. First, children are growing and developing, which results in physical, emotional, and developmental changes. Second, children are dependent on their family for care. It is essential for the nurse to form a supportive and trusting relationship with the child's family in order to give effective care.

A complete health history is important when assessing respiratory function, and as part of that history, the family's health history needs to be obtained because several respiratory problems are inherited or have a genetic cause. Cystic fibrosis, for example, is an inherited disease, and conditions such as asthma, bronchitis, and bronchiectasis may also have a genetic basis. If either or both parents have a history of *atopy,* the inherited tendency to produce antibodies to antigens from the environment, the child may also exhibit symptoms of asthma, hay fever, infantile eczema, localized skin rash, allergic rhinitis, and anaphylaxis.

The family history can be helpful in identifying pulmonary disease caused by environmental exposure to a microorganism or physical agent. For example, if either parent smokes, the child may develop respiratory problems at an early age as a result of the secondary smoke present in the environment. Also, if parents or older children in the home have gastrointestinal infections, the same organisms can result in upper or lower respiratory tract infections.

It is important to determine the child's neonatal history. For example, premature infants or infants with neonatal respiratory distress syndrome often develop bronchopulmonary dysplasia as a result of oxygen therapy, toxicity, barotrauma, or inflammation of immature lungs. They may also develop chronic bronchitis or asthma later in life. The child may develop recurrent upper or lower respiratory tract infections. A comprehensive history may include whether treatment for these infections was successful.

The history should include questions related to the present illness, and the following areas should be addressed:

### Cough

Information about onset, frequency, duration, recurrence, sound (harsh, barking, whooping), and productivity should be recorded. The parent or child may remember when the cough first started. The parent or child should be asked what precipitated the cough. Is there a particular time of day that the cough occurs? (Children with asthma or cystic fibrosis typically cough in the morning upon awakening because the secretions have pooled during sleep.) How long does the cough last? Is the cough intermittent or continuous? Is the cough productive or nonproductive?

### Sputum Production

The sputum produced as the result of coughing should be examined in terms of amount, color, odor, and consistency. Children with cystic fibrosis tend to produce sputum that is thick or viscous. Color of sputum varies from clear or white to yellow, green, brown, or blood-tinged. Yellow, green, or brown sputum suggests infection.

### Exposure to Infectious Agents or Irritants

The history of present illness should include questions related to exposure to infectious agents or irritants. If an infection is present, questions should be asked about exposure to other children or family members with a similar infection, such as influenza or tuberculosis. If the child lives in an area or has moved from an area where endemic microorganisms exist, the nurse should inquire whether the child has experienced symptoms related to these agents. If the child has asthma, exposure to environmental irritants should be questioned. Air quality in the home, pets, foods, the heating and cooling systems, and neighborhood air quality are important items to assess.

### Respiratory Pattern

Information about shortness of breath or dyspnea should be obtained. For example, answers to questions about play activities may reveal a child who is quiet, inactive, and lacking in enthusiasm for normal play due to difficulty in breathing. The nurse should also ask if the parents have noticed that the child is having difficulty in breathing and is expending more than the usual energy in inspiration and expiration.

### Pain

The child should be asked to describe the location, onset, duration, intensity, nature of pain, and events or positions that relieve the pain or intensify the pain. The reaction of the child to the pain varies with the age of the child. A neonate or infant reacts to pain by crying, withdrawal, irritability, disinterest in food or fluids, and changes in vital signs. A young child may only state, "it hurts," but may not be able to give any additional information.

### Alterations in Weight and Height

The nurse should inquire about unusual weight gain or failure to gain weight. Weight gain may indicate fluid retention from pulmonary edema or right ventricular failure. Failure to gain weight with failure to gain height may be a sign of chronic pulmonary disease.

## Physical Examination

### Chest

Physical examination of the chest includes inspection, palpation, percussion, and auscultation. When describing any abnormalities, landmarks are commonly used. These landmarks are seen in Figure 23-2.

Inspection of the chest for a change in shape is important. Children with chronic obstructive respiratory disease may have an increased anterior–posterior diameter, which gives the chest a barrel shape. This is also called pectus

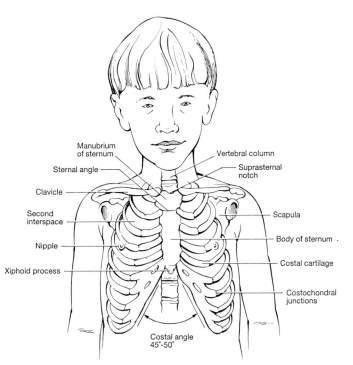

Manubrium
of sternum

Sternal angle

Clavicle

Second
interspace

Nipple

Xiphoid process

Vertebral column

Suprasternal
notch

Scapula

Body of sternum

Costal cartilage

Costochondral
junctions

Costal angle
45°-50°

*Figure 23–2.   Landmarks of the chest.*

profundum. Examples of chronic obstructive respiratory disease include asthma and cystic fibrosis.

Other abnormalities of the thorax include pectus excavatum, or funnel chest (Fig. 23-3*A*). In this deformity, the sternum is depressed and attached to the spine by fibrous bands. It is often seen in children with chronic active allergies. There is a genetic predisposition to this deformity, and it is also associated with Marfan syndrome.

The opposite of pectus excavatum is pectus carinatum, or pigeon chest (Fig. 23-3*B*), in which the sternum protrudes forward. This condition is associated with rickets, Marfan's syndrome, severe kyphoscoliosis, and atrial or ventricular septal defect. Some children with this deformity seem to be more susceptible to respiratory tract infections.

In addition to shape of the thorax, the nurse assesses chest expansion. Both sides should be symmetrical, expanding equally. The respiratory movements seen in children who are older than 6 or 7 years of age are costal or thoracic. Younger children normally breathe using abdominal movements. If one side lags behind the other or does not expand symmetrically, the child may be splinting one side. Splinting results most often from pain related to fractured ribs, surgery, or chest trauma. Unequal chest expansion may be due to pneumothorax or skeletal deformities.

## *Respiratory Rate and Pattern*

The respiratory rate, depth, rhythm, and quality should be assessed. In the child, it is important to count the respiratory rate for 1 full minute to observe any abnormalities in rate, depth, or rhythm. Respiratory rates vary with age. Normal rates are displayed in Table 23-1.

The respiratory pattern in neonates, especially premature infants, is irregular and uneven in depth. This is called *periodic breathing* and is defined as a change in respiratory rate, depth, or tidal volume that is occasionally interspaced with periods of *apnea,* or cessation of breathing. Periodic breathing occurs in the neonate, especially during sleep. After several weeks, a periodic breathing pattern occurs during sleep only and should not be the baseline respiratory pattern. In the adolescent, periodic breathing occurs during the light stages of sleep. Apneic periods in normal infants should not last more than 10 to 15 seconds.

Other abnormal breathing patterns that may be observed include the following:

*Tachypnea*: A respiratory rate that is rapid and elevated above normal.

*Bradypnea*: A respiratory rate slower than normal.

*Dyspnea*: Labored or difficult breathing. It is important to note if the dyspnea occurs at rest or upon exertion.

*Orthopnea*: Discomfort in breathing in all positions except erect sitting or standing postures.

*Apnea*: Total cessation of breathing or airflow to the lungs for more than 15 seconds.

*Hyperpnea*: Increased depth of respiration. It usually occurs with an increased rate of respiration.

*Hyperventilation*: Increase in both rate and depth of respiration. Hyperventilation is seen in fever and with low arterial oxygen tensions.

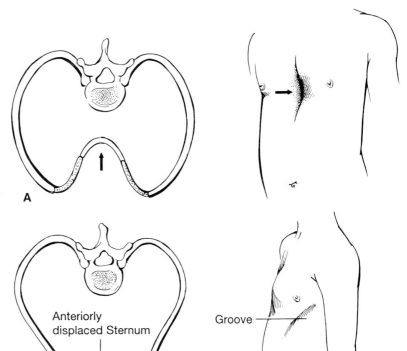

*Figure 23–3. Physical abnormalities of the chest.* (A) *Pectus excavatum.* (B) *Pectus carinatum.*

*Hypoventilation*: A slow and irregular respiratory pattern with shallow breaths. It is seen in children with drug overdoses or anesthesia and when children splint due to chest pain. If prolonged, it can lead to respiratory failure.

*Cheyne-Stokes respirations*: A cyclic pattern of progressively deeper respirations followed by progressively more shallow respirations with a period of apnea. It is seen in children with congestive heart failure or increased intracranial pressure.

*Biot respirations*: A rapid respiratory rate with irregular breaths of varying depths. This pattern is punctuated with periods of apnea. It is often seen in children with spinal meningitis and other neurological problems.

*Kussmaul respirations*: Deep, regular and rapid breaths.

*Table 23–1. Normal Respiratory Rate by Age*

| Age | Respiratory Rate |
| --- | --- |
| Premature | 40–90 |
| Neonate | 30–60 |
| Infant | 20–40 |
| Young child | 15–25 |
| Adolescent | 10–20 |

*Obstructive breathing*: This respiratory pattern is seen in children with obstructive problems such as retained secretions, cystic fibrosis, and asthma. Inspiratory retractions, where the complete exhalation of air is prevented, may be seen in several locations: intercostally (between ribs), substernally (below the sternum), suprasternally (above the sternum), or supraclavically (above the clavicles).

The nurse should observe the child for dyspnea and orthopnea when in a supine position. Children with asthma or pulmonary edema experience orthopnea and prop themselves up by resting their weight on their arms. Children with airway obstruction demonstrate intercostal and sternal retractions. Disorders in which retractions are seen include asthma, cystic fibrosis, bronchiolitis, and laryngotracheobronchitis. Grunting and nasal flaring are symptoms that must be assessed as part of the respiratory pattern. These symptoms are usually seen in neonates with respiratory distress syndrome or hyaline membrane disease. Grunting on expiration is usually associated with forcing air past a partially closed or obstructed glottis. Nasal flaring is seen on inspiration along with accessory muscle use and, since neonates are obligatory nose breathers, this symptom is a sign of respiratory distress.

Palpation is used to identify areas of tenderness, assess any abnormalities that are found on inspection, and measure chest expansion laterally.

To assess chest expansion, both hands are placed on the lower thorax with thumbs adjacent to each other on the anterior chest below the rib cage and the fingers over the lateral chest. As the child inhales and exhales, the nurse assesses symmetrical or asymmetrical chest expansion. The hands may be placed over the posterior chest with thumbs adjacent and fingers wrapped around the lateral chest.

Palpation of any lumps, cysts, or abnormal growths should be done. Note location, tenderness, movement, and quality of these abnormalities. Tracheal deviation should also be noted. Tracheal deviation may be present with intrathoracic growths; however, in the young infant, slight tracheal deviation to the left or right is normal.

Air conductance is assessed by the presence or absence of fremitus. *Fremitus* is a vibration felt through the chest wall and can be classified as being tactile or vocal. Tactile fremitus is assessed by feeling the voice by using the palmar surface of the hand over the anterior, lateral, or posterior chest walls. Ask the child to say "one, two, three" or "ninety-nine." The spoken word is transmitted from the airways to the chest wall and is felt somewhat like the purr of a cat. The intensity of the vibrations should be equal on each side of the thorax. If tactile fremitus is not well felt, ask the child to speak louder. Intensity of fremitus should be equal on both sides and varies with age of the child, thickness of the chest wall, pitch and quality of the voice, anatomical variations, and area palpated.

Pleural friction rubs are present when the pleura become inflamed. Pleural friction rubs can be felt as fine vibrations on the tips of the examiner's fingers. If the child is sitting, the vibrations will be felt over the lower anterolateral chest. *Crepitation,* a crackling or popping sound, can also be palpated and is caused when air leaks into subcutaneous tissue. When it is palpated, it feels like bubbles in plastic packing material. It occurs in subcutaneous emphysema, pneumothorax, or in children with fresh tracheostomies (the sound is heard around the newly made incision). It is usually harmless.

Percussion is used to assess amounts of gaseous, liquid, or solid material in underlying lung tissue and to determine diaphragmatic movement and resting levels. Percussion should be done in a systematic, organized manner, comparing the right and left sides (see Chap. 5).

Auscultation of the chest is performed using an appropriate bell and diaphragm. Because most sounds heard in the child's thorax are high-pitched, the diaphragm is used. Auscultation is used to assess airflow through the tracheobronchial tree, the presence or absence of fluid, mucus in the airways, obstruction of airflow, and the condition of lung tissue and the pleural space.

Auscultation should be performed in a systematic, organized manner. The anterior, lateral, and posterior chest should be auscultated, and each side should be compared with the other. The child should be asked to breathe through the mouth.

Breath sounds are described in terms of location, intensity, pitch, quality, and the inspiratory/expiratory ratio (I/E ratio). Breath sounds are of four types: normal or vesicular, bronchovesicular, bronchial, and tracheal.

Normal or vesicular sounds are heard throughout the lung fields, except over the larger central airways. They are low to moderate in intensity and have a low to medium pitch with a breezy, rustling quality. Inspiration is heard three times as long as expiration, yielding a 3 : 1 I/E ratio.

Bronchovesicular sounds are heard over the large central airways, over the upper third of the sternum and intracapsular area, and sometimes over the posterior right upper lobe. They are of moderate intensity and have a medium to high pitch with a hollow, blowing, muffled sound. Inspiration is equal to expiration, yielding a 1 : 1 I/E ratio. Bronchovesicular sounds are heard over consolidated lung tissue. When heard in areas where vesicular sounds should be present, they are abnormal.

Bronchial breath sounds are heard over the manubrium. They are loud, high-pitched, and hollow or tubular in quality. Expiration is twice as long as inspiration. The I/E ratio is 1 : 2 but may be as high as 2 : 3. When heard in the periphery of the lung, they are abnormal, as in conditions such as pneumonia or tuberculosis. Occasionally, bronchial breath sounds are heard above the level of a pleural effusion.

Tracheal breath sounds are heard over the trachea and are generally not auscultated over the lung periphery. They are loud, high-pitched, and have a harsh, hollow quality. The I/E ratio is usually 5 : 6.

Adventitious sounds are sounds not normally heard. They are produced from abnormal airflow and secretions within the airways. There are four major types of adventitious sounds: crackles (rales), rhonchi, wheezes, and pleural friction rubs.

*Crackles,* or rales, are discontinuous cracking or popping sounds usually heard during inspiration. They are thought to be caused by air bubbling through fluid or by the sudden explosive opening of the small airways that closed during the previous expiratory phase. The American Thoracic Society classifies crackles as either fine or coarse. Fine crackles are high-pitched, soft sounds of short duration. They are heard in children with areas of atelectasis, early pulmonary edema, and pneumonia. Coarse rales are low-pitched and loud, and they last longer than fine rales. They are heard in children with resolving pneumonia, pulmonary edema, and bronchitis.

*Rhonchi* are sonorous or snoring sounds that change location and quality depending on the location and quality of mucus or fluid. They are continuous sounds that usually occur during expiration when the airways are more narrow; however, if there are excessive secretions, rhonchi may appear during inspiration as well. Fremitus may be felt over the large airways. Rhonchi clear with coughing and are clearly heard upon deep breathing. If the child is dehydrated, however, rhonchi may not be heard until rehydration occurs.

*Wheezes* are described as musical, whistling, or sighing sounds that occur as air moves through narrowed airways. They are continuously high- or low-pitched squeaking sounds usually heard during expiration, but they may occur during both inspiration and expiration if the airway narrowing is severe. High-pitched wheezes are usually heard in the smaller peripheral airways, whereas low-pitched wheezes tend to occur in the larger airways. Wheezes may be heard in children with asthma, bronchiolitis, laryngeal edema, or foreign-body aspiration. They may also be heard in early pulmonary edema and cystic fibrosis.

*Stridor* is a loud musical sound with a constant pitch. It is classified as a wheeze. It is a sign of upper airway obstruction and is commonly heard without the aid of a stethoscope in children with croup (laryngotracheo-bronchitis). If children aspirate a foreign body that lodges in the upper airway, stridor may also be heard. When obstruction is severe, stridor is heard with gasping respirations and accessory muscle use.

The *pleural friction rub* produces a grating or creaking sound that results when inflamed pleural layers rub against each other. Friction rubs are usually heard during inspiration, but they may be heard during expiration with deep breathing. Pleural friction rubs range from high to low in pitch and from soft to loud in intensity. Diminished or absent breath sounds may occur in children with thick chest walls, pleural fluid or pleural thickening, hyperinflation of the chest, atelectasis, or pneumothorax.

## Diagnostic Procedures

### Pulmonary Function Tests

Pulmonary function tests are used to assess lung function in health and disease. They can help assess severity of disease, evaluate changes in lung function, and determine the effectiveness of therapy. They are not often performed on children under 6 or 7 years of age because they require cooperation of the child. Children with cystic fibrosis, asthma, or bronchopulmonary dysplasia or who are ventilator dependent require pulmonary function tests at an earlier age and at regular intervals. Normal or predicted values vary with the age, sex, height, and weight of the child.

The common indicators of pulmonary function include the following:

*Tidal volume* (TV): The amount of gas inhaled or exhaled during each respiration.

*Inspiratory reserve volume* (IRV): The maximum volume of gas that can be inhaled over and above a normal inspiration.

*Expiratory reserve volume* (ERV): The maximum amount of gas that can be forcefully exhaled after a normal expiration.

*Residual volume* (RV): The volume of gas remaining in the lungs after a maximal expiration.

*Functional residual capacity* (FRC): The volume of gas in the lungs after a normal expiration. FRC = ERV + RV.

*Inspiratory capacity* (IC): The maximum volume of gas that can be inhaled after a normal expiration. IC = TV + IRC.

*Total lung capacity* (TLC): The volume of gas in the lungs after a maximum inspiration. TLC = TV + ERV + IRV + RV.

*Forced vital capacity* (FVC): Vital capacity performed rapidly with a maximum effort.

*Forced expiratory volume in 1 second* ($FEV_1$): The volume of gas that can be forcefully exhaled during the first second of an FVC.

*Forced expiratory flow 25%–75%* ($FEF_{25\%-75\%}$): This is also called the forced midexpiratory flow because it is the mean rate of airflow over the middle half of the FVC.

The nurse's role in this procedure is to prepare the child for pulmonary function studies by having the child practice breathing with the mouth piece and practice mouth breathing with the nose clips and by demonstrating the appropriate breathing maneuvers. Parental involvement should be encouraged in these teaching efforts.

### Arterial Blood Gases

Arterial blood gas (ABG) levels are tested to assess oxygenation status and acid–base balance of the body. In infants and children older than 1 year, the radial artery is generally used to obtain arterial blood. Arterial blood is preferred to venous blood because it assesses how well the lungs are oxygenating the blood and is not affected by the metabolism of the particular extremity from where the sample is drawn. In premature infants, samples are drawn from an umbilical catheter. Using a heparinized syringe, only a small amount of blood is taken, and the amount is recorded on the intake and output record. In neonates and infants less than 1 year of age, capillary blood is used for blood gas determination. Capillary blood is obtained from the infant's heel or toe. Capillary oxygen is the only value that differs from the arterial blood values. Capillary oxygen values normally range from 40 to 50 mmHg. Normal ABG values are found in Table 23-2.

Two noninvasive methods of measuring arterial oxyhemoglobin saturation include pulse oximetry and transcutaneous oxygen monitoring. *Pulse oximetry* measures arterial oxygen saturation in pulsating blood vessels. Oxygenated and deoxygenated blood are differentiated through red and infrared light waves. The pulse oximeter sensor is placed on the child's ear, nose, toe, or finger or on the infant's foot, and light is shined through a vascular bed. Oxygen saturation is determined by calculating the ratio of infrared light absorbed to the red light absorbed. The greatest advantage of pulse oximetry is that it is nonin-

*Table 23–2.  Normal Arterial Blood Gas Values\**

| Gas | Normal Range |
|---|---|
| $P_aO_2$ | 80–100 mmHg |
| $S_aO_2$ | 95%–100% |
| pH | 7.35–7.45 |
| $P_aCO_2$ | 35–45 mmHg |
| $HCO_3$ | 22–26 mEq/L |

*Values at sea level and below 5000 feet.

vasive, and the data are quickly obtained and updated. The disadvantage is that it does not detect changes in acid–base balance.

*Transcutaneous oxygen monitoring* is most often used in children. An electrode is usually placed on the infant's chest, abdomen, or back and is heated to 44°C. The heat brings peripheral arterial blood to the surface so it can be read for oxygen content. The advantage of this method is that the electrode easily remains in place. The disadvantages are that the electrode must be moved every 2 to 4 hours to prevent blistering of the skin; the monitor must be recalibrated every 3 to 6 hours; and it does not correlate well if the infant's skin is thick or if the infant is anemic, severely acidotic, or hypothermic.

*Interpreting ABG Levels.* Interpretation of ABG levels is often difficult. The following guidelines can assist in interpreting the results of ABG tests:

First, assess the oxygenation parameters, $P_aO_2$, and $O_2$ saturation ($S_aO_2$). $P_aO_2$ and $O_2$ saturation are affected by age, altitude, disease, and supplemental oxygen administration. They are easily interpreted. If the $P_aO_2$ is increased above normal, it may indicate excessive or supplemental oxygen administration. When decreased below normal, the hypoxemia usually results from pulmonary or cardiac disease. $S_aO_2$ is the actual $O_2$ content of hemoglobin as compared with the maximal potential of $O_2$ carrying capacity. When $S_aO_2$ is increased, it usually results from excessive oxygen administration. When $S_aO_2$ is decreased, the hypoxemia results from cardiac or pulmonary disease.

The parameters used to assess acid–base balance are the pH, $P_aCO_2$, and $HCO_3^-$. The interpretation of acid–base status is done in three steps (Table 23-3). First assess the pH. If the pH is below 7.35 it is labeled acidosis; if the pH is above 7.45 it is labeled alkalosis. The pH identifies the primary acid–base imbalance that is occurring. In the example seen in Table 23-3, the pH is 7.30. Because the pH is acidotic, the primary disorder is acidosis.

The next step is to label the $P_aCO_2$. The $P_aCO_2$ is the respiratory parameter because it is controlled by the lungs. It reflects the chief acid in the blood ($H_2CO_3$). A $P_aCO_2$ level above 45 is labeled respiratory acidosis; a $P_aCO_2$ level below 35 is labeled respiratory alkalosis. In the example, the $P_aCO_2$ is 50 and therefore is labeled respiratory acidosis.

The third step is to label the metabolic parameter, the $HCO_3^-$, which is regulated in part by the kidneys. An $HCO_3^-$ level below 22 is labeled metabolic acidosis because there is a deficit of base. An $HCO_3^-$ level above 26 is labeled metabolic alkalosis. In the example, the $HCO_3^-$ is 33, so it is labeled metabolic alkalosis.

In the example, the pH is acidotic, so the primary problem is acidosis. The parameter that matches the pH is the respiratory parameter; that is, they are both acidotic. Therefore, the primary problem is respiratory acidosis. The metabolic parameter is alkalotic, indicating that the metabolic parameter is the compensatory buffer.

Remember that this method of ABG interpretation is to be used only as a guide. Observation and assessment of the child is as important as the laboratory results. At times, the laboratory results may not match the patient's history or appearance. Without a clinical history and assessment of the patient, laboratory results may be misleading.

## Other Diagnostic Procedures

*Bronchoscopy.* Bronchoscopy has several purposes. First, it is used to visualize the vocal cords, trachea, and large bronchi. Second, it can be used to determine the cause of airway obstruction and possibly the removal of an aspirated foreign body. Third, it can be used to remove thick tenacious secretions as are seen in atelectasis and other conditions. Fourth, it can be used to obtain bronchial washings for culture and pathology and small tissue samples for biopsy.

Bronchoscopy can be performed using either a flexible or rigid bronchoscope. The flexible fiberoptic bronchoscope can be used with local anesthesia while the child

*Table 23–3.  Interpretation of Acid–Base Status Using pH, $P_aCO_2$, and $HCO_3$ Levels*

**Step 1: Label pH**

If pH is <7.35, label pH acidosis
If pH is >7.45, label pH alkalosis

**Step 2: Label $P_aCO_2$ (Respiratory Parameter)**

If $P_aCO_2$ is >45, label $P_aCO_2$ as respiratory acidosis
If $P_aCO_2$ is <35, label $P_aCO_2$ as respiratory alkalosis

**Step 3: Label $HCO_3$ (Metabolic Parameter)**

If $HCO_3$ is <22, label $HCO_3$ as metabolic acidosis
If $HCO_3$ is >26, label $HCO_3$ as metabolic alkalosis

**Example:**

pH = 7.30, acidosis
$P_aCO_2$ = 50, respiratory acidosis
$HCO_3$ = 33, metabolic alkalosis

Interpretation: Respiratory acidosis with metabolic alkalosis as the compensatory buffer.

is awake or mildly sedated and can be used on an intubated patient who is manually ventilated. Also, the flexible bronchoscope can visualize bronchi that branch off at greater angles.

The nurse should explain the purpose of the test to the child in understandable terms. The child should be NPO for at least 4 to 8 hours before the bronchoscopy to avoid vomiting and aspiration during the procedure. After the procedure is completed, the nurse should observe for signs of laryngeal swelling due to insertion of the tube and respiratory distress (increasing stridor, increasing dyspnea, change in color, and hemoptysis if a biopsy was done). To reduce this complication, supplemental oxygen and mist should be given to the child through a face mask. The nurse should inform the child and the family that the child may have a sore throat because of manipulation of the bronchoscope. After the child is fully awake, the nurse should assess for the return of the gag reflex and patency of the airway before oral fluids are started.

*Radiological Evaluation.* Chest radiographs are ordered for several reasons. They are used to help diagnose pulmonary disease, assess changes in lung pathology, locate foreign bodies in the airways, and verify placement of endotracheal tubes, chest tubes, and monitoring lines.

The most common views are the posteroanterior view and the lateral view. The film is taken with the child either standing or sitting unsupported. If the child cannot sit or stand, both views are taken with the child in the recumbent position.

## Nursing Diagnosis

Common nursing diagnoses used for respiratory problems include the following:

*Pattern 1: Exchanging*
- High risk for aspiration
- High risk for infection
- Impaired gas exchange
- Ineffective airway clearance
- Ineffective breathing pattern

*Pattern 3: Relating*
- Altered family processes
- High risk for altered parenting
- Social isolation

*Pattern 5: Choosing*
- Health seeking behaviors (specify)
- Ineffective family coping: compromised
- Ineffective individual coping
- Noncompliance (specify)

*Pattern 6: Moving*
- Activity intolerance
- Altered growth and development
- Bathing/hygiene self-care deficit
- Fatigue
- Sleep pattern disturbance

*Pattern 7: Perceiving*
- Hopelessness
- Powerlessness

*Pattern 9: Feeling*
- Anxiety
- Fear

## Planning Nursing Care

Once the nursing assessment is completed and nursing diagnoses are formulated, planning nursing care begins. When planning nursing care for children with respiratory problems, it is essential to take into consideration the child's age and developmental level, the family's functional ability and coping mechanisms, the severity of the problem, and where the care will be provided.

### Developmental Considerations

Nurses must be sensitive to children's stages of development in terms of biophysical, emotional, cognitive, and social development. Chronological age must not be the sole consideration when evaluating the child. The nurse must be aware of the child's particular characteristics when establishing a therapeutic relationship. Nurses must use all resources available when assessing and establishing a plan of care. What are the child's abilities and developmental stage? What is the child's educational level? How does the child interact with family members? How is the family coping with the illness? The family must be included in the planning of care to ensure a positive outcome.

### Acute Care Considerations

Certain acute respiratory problems can present a challenge to health professionals in providing the best care possible to children and their families. The acutely ill child and the family will experience some degree of stress and anxiety related to the illness. Sensitivity to the child's and family's needs helps to reduce anxiety.

Children who are ill are frightened, fatigued, and often short of breath. They need their parents with them for support. This is especially true of younger children. In addition, the stress of hospitalization and painful procedures associated with the hospitalization require support from the nurse and family members.

### Chronic Care Considerations

The chronically ill child and family experience special needs and challenges. The child as well as family members can benefit from support systems such as parents' groups and home health care. Children with chronic respiratory problems pose special problems that are discussed later in this chapter.

## Home Care Considerations

Home care for the child and family with chronic respiratory problems involves helping the parents find and use appropriate equipment, correctly administer medications, implement effective treatments, obtain respite care, and receive emotional support. Home care may also involve working with the school to provide medications and treatments to the child during the school day.

## Nursing Interventions

### Inhalation Therapy

#### Oxygen Therapy

Oxygen is administered for *hypoxemia* (insufficient oxygenation of the blood). The signs and symptoms of hypoxemia include tachycardia, tachypnea, pallor, headache, and cyanosis. Mental confusion occurs when hypoxemia is severe. The degree of hypoxemia is determined with ABG levels, pulse oximetry, or transcutaneous monitoring.

Oxygen is administered through various oxygen delivery devices. These include nasal cannulas, Venturi masks, simple face masks, oxygen hoods, isolettes, and mist tents. The particular device used depends on the child's age and the concentration of supplemental oxygen required. For low concentrations of oxygen, nasal cannulas are used most often, even with neonates. To prevent skin breakdown, a skin protective agent such as transparent dressing or Duoderm should be placed on the child's cheeks. The cannula may then be taped to the dressing.

When high concentrations of oxygen are required, a hood or mask must be used. A hood can deliver between 22% and 100% oxygen. Venturi masks can deliver between 24% and 50% oxygen, whereas partial rebreathing masks deliver up to 80%, and nonrebreathing masks deliver 90% to 100%.

Venturi masks deliver a specific concentration of oxygen by providing a high-velocity jet of 100% oxygen through a small orifice. This jet entrains room air, which mixes with the oxygen to deliver a specific oxygen concentration. The size of the orifice determines the oxygen concentration. The child's ventilatory pattern does not affect the oxygen concentration delivered.

A partial rebreathing mask delivers between 60% and 80% oxygen. A bag is connected to the tight-fitting mask and serves as a reservoir for 100% oxygen. The flow rate is maintained at 5 to 6 L/min so that the bag does not collapse when the child inhales. As the child exhales, gas leaves through holes on the sides of the mask. Very little exhaled gas enters the reservoir bag.

A nonrebreathing mask delivers up to 100% oxygen. It is similar to a partial rebreathing mask in that it has an oxygen reservoir bag, but it contains one-way valves on the sides of the mask and between the mask and the bag. This allows exhaled air to leave the mask, and during inspiration, only oxygen is drawn from the reservoir. Various oxygen masks are shown in Figure 23-4.

Mist tents are generally used to provide cool, high-humidity environments, but they can be used to deliver up to 60% supplemental oxygen. The disadvantage is that the child must remain in a closed environment (Fig. 23-5). Also, a flow rate of at least 10 L/min must be maintained to ensure that exhaled $CO_2$ is eliminated.

Safety precautions must be taken when using tents. Since the air is cooler than environmental air, the child's temperature must be monitored to prevent hypothermia. The child should be kept warm by wearing clothes or pajamas while in the tent. If the humidity is high, moisture may accumulate on the inside of the tent, which may interfere with observation of the child. The nurse should either reduce the amount of mist or periodically wipe the inside of the tent.

When oxygen is used in combination with the mist, safety precautions must be observed. These include not smoking in the child's room and not using electrical devices in the tent. All electrical devices used in the child's room must be properly grounded. The child cannot have any toys that create sparks inside the tent.

The tent must be tightly tucked under the mattress to keep the plastic away from the child's face. In addition, side rails must be up for all children whenever they are left alone.

#### Aerosol Therapy

Aerosol therapy delivers medication or large amounts of liquid to help liquefy or mobilize secretions. Therapeutic doses of drugs commonly used to treat respiratory problems may also be delivered through aerosolization. Drugs typically used in aerosol form include bronchodilators, antibiotics, steroids, antihistamine release agents, and mucolytic agents.

Nebulizers are used to deliver aerosols, which are liquid or solid particles suspended in a gas (Fig 23-6). Nebulizers deliver various sizes of particles. Ultrasonic nebulizers deliver very small particles; other nebulizers deliver larger particles. The effectiveness of aerosol therapy depends on depth of deposition of the particles, which is influenced by many factors including particle size and density, gas viscosity, kinetic activity of molecules, the patient's breathing pattern, and patency of airways.

Hand-held nebulizers are most often used at home, although small, portable, compressor-driven nebulizers are available. Education of the parents and cooperation of the child are essential for successful aerosol therapy.

Teaching the child and parents how to safely use the nebulizer is important, especially in the home setting. The parents should be taught about the proper functioning of the equipment as well as the procedure for cleaning the

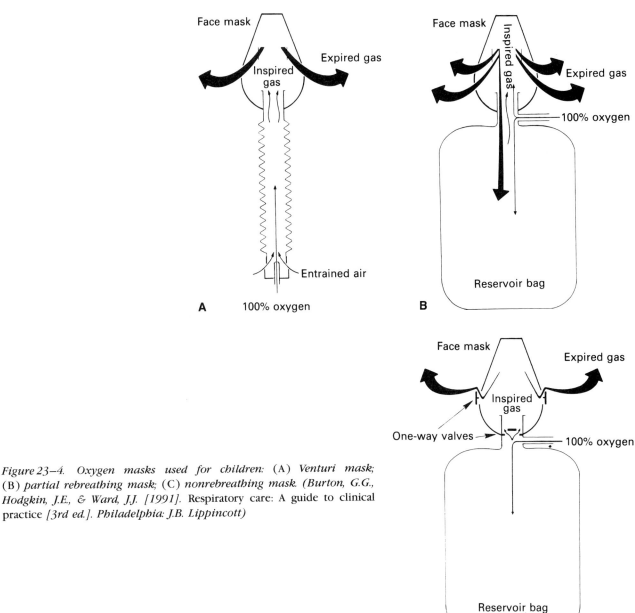

*Figure 23–4. Oxygen masks used for children:* (A) *Venturi mask;* (B) *partial rebreathing mask;* (C) *nonrebreathing mask. (Burton, G.G., Hodgkin, J.E., & Ward, J.J. [1991].* Respiratory care: A guide to clinical practice *[3rd ed.]. Philadelphia: J.B. Lippincott)*

nebulizer. This decreases bacterial growth and reduces the chance of transmission of organisms to the child. Return demonstrations should be required.

### Humidification

Humidification is often confused with aerosol therapy. Humidification produces water vapor with a relative humidity between 60% and 100%. Humidification is used to prevent the complications of breathing dry gases. These complications include decreased mucociliary movement, drying of the mucous membranes, and increased body heat loss (Shapiro, Kacmarek, Cane, Peruzzi, & Hauptman, 1991). Humidification is considered necessary and beneficial when the upper airway is bypassed, as in children with tracheostomies or endotracheal tubes. It may also benefit children receiving oxygen at a flow rate greater than 2 L/min or greater than 30% concentration (Ward, 1991).

Humidification may be beneficial for children with croup, bronchiolitis, or exercise-induced asthma. Cool-air humidification is recommended because warm-air humidifiers may be overturned, which can result in burns to the child.

Parents should be taught to keep the water reservoir clean and to use sterile water. Humidification is often associated with gram-negative bacteria, especially *Pseudomonas*. When humidification is used, the child should be dressed warmly. If the clothes or bed sheets become wet, they should be changed.

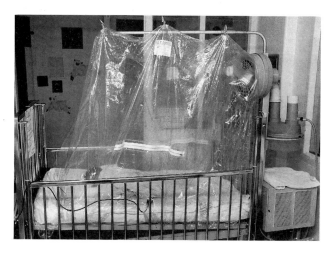

*Figure 23–5.   Mist tent. (Skale, N. [1992].* Manual of pediatric nursing procedures. *Philadelphia: J.B. Lippincott)*

## Postural Drainage and Chest Physiotherapy

*Postural drainage* involves positioning of the body so that gravity enhances mucous drainage. It is done with deep breathing and coughing or with chest percussion and vibration. The positions for postural drainage are illustrated in Figure 23-7.

The purpose of postural drainage is to drain peripheral pulmonary secretions into large airways using gravity. By accomplishing this, pulmonary mechanics and gas exchange improve. By removing peripheral secretions, the incidence of respiratory infections may decrease. Postural drainage is contraindicated in children who cannot tolerate the various positions.

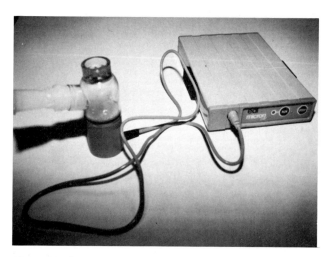

*Figure 23–6.   Small-volume medication nebulizer used in aerosol therapy. (Burton, G.G., Hodgkin, J.E., & Ward, J.J. [1991].* Respiratory care: A guide to clinical practice *[3rd ed.]. Philadelphia: J.B. Lippincott)*

Breathing exercises are used in conjunction with postural drainage to enhance the child's ability to remove pulmonary secretions. Deep breathing and coughing are used together to assist in mucus removal from large airways. Coughing alone in the absence of pulmonary secretions has no physiological benefit and may actually be detrimental to the child's pulmonary status since it may cause airway collapse (Breslin, 1981). If the cough is uncontrollable, huffing is instituted. *Huffing,* also known as the forced exhalation technique, assists in mucus clearance. It is used in children with asthma or cystic fibrosis. The technique of huffing consists of one to two forced expiratory efforts or huffs made with the glottis open and a middle to low lung volume. It is followed by a period of relaxation. The child is positioned sitting up and leaning slightly forward.

Deep breathing assists with maximal alveolar inflation and helps to maintain normal functional residual capacity. Use of incentive spirometry can assist in preventing atelectasis.

Specific breathing exercises may be prescribed, and their use strengthens respiratory muscles and increases lung capacity. There is no one best technique for coughing and deep breathing; the techniques are adapted to each child.

In *chest physiotherapy,* percussion and vibration are used to dislodge and mobilize peripheral secretions into larger airways where they can be more easily expectorated or removed with suctioning. Percussion in children is performed using a cupped hand clapped over the child's chest. For infants, commercially made percussors are available. Percussion should be avoided over the sternum, spine, stomach, and kidneys. It is generally not performed over bare skin; usually a towel is placed over the skin. Percussion is performed for 20 or 30 seconds and is followed by vibration, usually performed with a commercial vibrator. Vibration is done during expiration to facilitate and enhance the child's expectoration of secretions. Percussion and vibration are performed in each position for 1 to 2 minutes. Contraindications for chest physiotherapy are the same as for postural drainage. Research has shown that chest physiotherapy is of greatest benefit to patients who expectorate large amounts of sputum; it is less beneficial to patients who expectorate little sputum (Sutton, 1988; Klein, Kemper, Weissman, Rosenbaum, Askanazi, & Hyman, 1988).

## Drug Therapy

Several categories of medications are used for children with respiratory problems. For an in-depth discussion of these agents, refer to a pharmacology text.

There are several differences between neonates, infants, children, and adults with respect to drug therapy. Drugs given to the mother may be absorbed by the fetus through the placenta. Neonates have variable gastric pH, prolonged gastric transit time, no intestinal flora, and delayed development of intestinal enzymes. They also have a low concentration of plasma proteins, with a decreased plasma protein–binding capacity, which can result in adverse drug effects. Because of immature hepatic enzymes, neonates cannot metabolize drugs well, and they are at risk for toxic effects. Finally, neonates excrete drugs more slowly because of decreased renal function. Renal function approaches normal adult levels at about 1 year of age.

Gastric acidity approaches adult levels between 2 and 3 years of age. The lack of gastric acid causes increased absorption of some medications. Gastric emptying in children is slower than in adults until about 6 to 8 months of age (Benitz & Tetatro, 1988). Protein-binding capacity reaches adult levels by 1 year of age. Metabolic rates in infants are generally higher than in adults for the first 2 to 3 years. Thus, in some children, therapeutic doses may be higher relative to body weight than in adults. Renal and hepatic function does not reach maturity until the child is 6 to 12 months old. In view of these differences between children and adults, doses of medications must be given with caution to children.

The major groups of medications used for children with respiratory problems include bronchodilators, antibiotics, steroids, decongestants, antihistamines, antitussives, and mucokinetic agents. A brief discussion of each category is included in this chapter. Refer to a pharmacology text for information on specific drugs.

### Bronchodilators

Bronchodilators are used to relieve bronchoconstriction. The three major groups of bronchodilators are adrenergic sympathomimetics, anticholinergics, and methylxanthines.

*Adrenergic Sympathomimetics.* Adrenergic sympathomimetics mimic the sympathetic nervous system and stimulate three different types of receptors: $\alpha$-, $\beta_1$-, and $\beta_2$-receptors.

$\alpha$-Receptors are located in peripheral smooth muscle, bronchial smooth muscle, cardiac muscle, and mucosal blood vessels. Drugs with $\alpha$-receptor activity are used to reduce upper respiratory tract congestion. An example of an $\alpha$-stimulator agent is phenylephrine. These drugs are used with caution because repeated use results in rebound congestion. For example, overuse of over-the-counter nasal sprays is likely to cause worsening of the upper respiratory tract congestion.

$\beta_1$-Receptors are located primarily in cardiac muscle but are also found in mucosal blood vessels. Drugs with strong $\beta_1$-receptor activity are epinephrine and isoproterenol. Because the use of drugs that stimulate $\beta_1$-receptors results in unwanted cardiac dysrhythmia, including tachycardia, they are used with caution. Although

their use results in bronchodilation, they also may increase airway edema, which results in airway obstruction.

$\beta_2$-Receptors are found primarily in peripheral smooth muscle and skeletal muscle. Stimulation of these receptors produces bronchodilation. The optimal bronchodilator of the adrenergic sympathomimetic agents has maximal $\beta_2$-receptor activity and minimal $\beta_1$- and $\alpha$-receptor activity. Examples of drugs with $\beta_2$-receptor activity include terbutaline, albuterol, metaproterenol, fenoterol, and bitolterol. Stimulation of $\beta_2$-receptors causes some adverse effects, including tremor and peripheral vasodilation, which result from stimulation of $\beta_2$-receptors located in skeletal muscle and peripheral smooth muscle. Peripheral vasodilation results in venous pooling in the extremities, with a subsequent effect on cardiac output. Blood pressure may fall, causing a reflex tachycardia.

*Anticholinergics.* Anticholinergics act by blocking acetylcholine, which in turn blocks bronchoconstriction. An example of an anticholinergic agent is atropine. Anticholinergics have a wide variety of adverse effects on respiratory conditions, the most serious of which is mucus plugging due to drying.

*Methylxanthines.* Methylxanthines increase cyclic adenosine monophosphate (cAMP) levels, thus inhibiting breakdown of cAMP. An example of a methylxanthine agent is theophylline. Respiratory adverse effects of methylxanthines include increased respiratory rate.

### Antibiotics

Antibiotics are either bacteriostatic agents, which inhibit growth of bacteria, or bactericidal agents, which kill the microorganisms. Antibiotics may be aerosolized when microorganisms colonize along the respiratory mucosa. Children with cystic fibrosis who experience chronic respiratory tract infections often use aerosolized antibiotics. Since antibiotics have a wide variety of adverse effects that depend on the specific drug and the route of administration, nurses should be aware of the adverse effects for the specific drug being administered.

### Steroids

Corticosteroids are used to treat both acute and chronic respiratory problems. As anti-inflammatory agents, they are useful in relieving bronchospasm. Use of steroids requires careful monitoring because of the many side effects of these drugs, including immunosuppression, which increases the child's susceptibility to infections; cushingoid effects; emotional responses, such as mood swings; and gastrointestinal effects, such as gastric irritation and ulceration.

In children, long-term steroid use may cause growth retardation. This can sometimes be avoided with an alter-

(*text continues on page 534*)

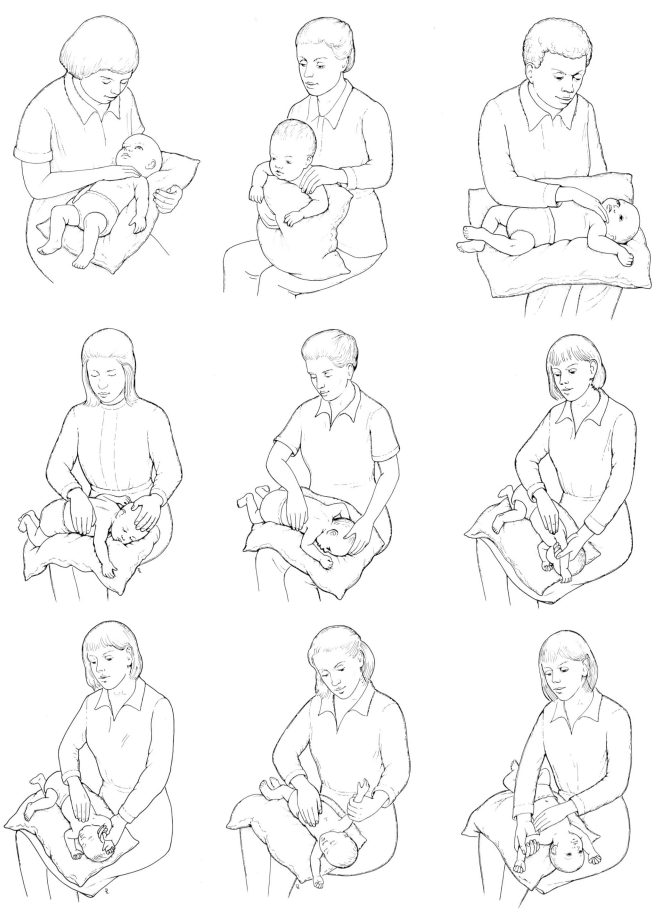

Figure 23–7. *Positions for postural drainage.* (Skale, N. [1992]. Manual of pediatric nursing procedures. *Philadelphia: J.B. Lippincott)*

532

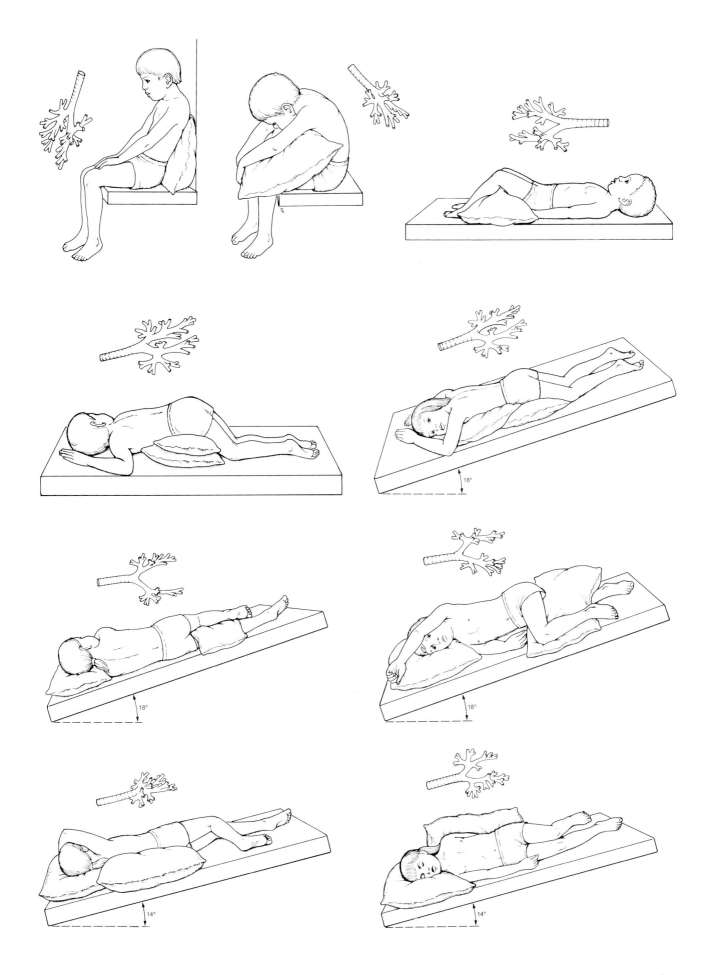

nate-day dosage schedule. The growth retardation involves slowing of skeletal maturation as well as slowing of linear growth. When steroids are stopped, a compensatory growth period may occur.

Steroid therapy may result in hyperglycemia. If hyperglycemia is already present, steroid therapy may aggravate the condition. Patients should have blood glucose levels monitored periodically.

Steroids may be taken orally or inhaled. Inhaled steroids are sometimes preferable because systemic absorption is minimal and there are fewer side effects. Inhaled steroids are particularly effective in children with labile asthma. Dosages are individualized based on age, history, frequency of asthma attacks, degree of severity of attacks, and pulmonary function tests.

## Decongestants and Antihistamines

Decongestants and antihistamines are used to treat symptoms of nasal congestion and hay fever. They are found in many over-the-counter cough and cold remedies. Parents should be taught to follow directions carefully and not to use multiple preparations because many medications contain similar drugs and overdosage may result. The primary respiratory side effects of antihistamines are dyspnea and wheezing. The primary respiratory side effect of decongestants is rebound congestion.

## Antitussives

Antitussives suppress coughs and are used for nonproductive cough. They are contraindicated in children with retained secretions. Over-the-counter preparations that contain dextromethorphan or benzonatate are effective for cough suppression. If the cough continues, the child should be examined by a physician. If an antitussive is needed, codeine or hydrocodone are often prescribed. These agents are effective cough suppressants, but they have side effects such as dry mouth, ciliary depression, drowsiness, and dizziness.

## Mucokinetic Agents

Mucokinetic agents are drugs that promote mobilization and removal of secretions. Their actions include humidification and lubrication of secretions, decreased viscosity of secretions, and mucolysis, which disrupts chemical bonds in secretions and thereby decreases viscosity of secretions. Specific types of mucokinetic agents include wetting agents, which consist of nebulized sterile water or saline; expectorants such as guaifenesin; and mucolytics such as N-acetyl-L-cysteine (Mucomyst). Adverse effects of mucokinetic agents vary depending on the agent used. Mucomyst irritates the respiratory tract and may result in bronchospasms.

Specific drug therapy is identified under each respiratory problem discussed in this chapter.

## Artificial Ventilation

### Intubation

Intubation is insertion of an endotracheal tube through the nose or mouth. Indications for intubation include upper-airway obstruction, clearance of retained secretions, protection of the airway against aspiration, and mechanical ventilation. Tubes are made of plastic or silicone and are available with or without cuffs. Endotracheal tubes used in neonates and children up to 8 years of age do not have cuffs because the use of cuffed tubes is associated with an increased incidence of subglottic stenosis. Complications of intubation include trauma during insertion, hypoxia, dysrhythmias, laryngospasm, gastric aspiration, bronchospasm, and right main-stem intubation.

The primary goal with the intubated child is to maintain a patent airway through stabilization of the tube so it cannot be displaced and so the airway can be suctioned. The frequency of suctioning depends on the individual child. If the child is placed on mechanical ventilation, suctioning is performed when peak airway pressures increase. Sterile technique is used during suctioning. Before suctioning, the child is hyperventilated with 100% oxygen to prevent hypoxemia during the procedure. If secretions are thick and difficult to remove, a few drops of sterile saline are injected into the endotracheal tube to help liquefy and remove the secretions.

When the child's airway problem has been resolved and the child is able to clear the airway alone, extubation or removal of the tube occurs. The nurse should prepare the child with an explanation that is appropriate and spoken in understandable terms. The child is then hyperventilated with 100% oxygen and suctioned to clear any secretions in the lung and oropharynx. The child takes a maximal inspiration, and the tube is pulled during expiration. After extubation, supplemental oxygen is often ordered. The equipment should be ready and placed on the child immediately after extubation.

### Tracheostomy

A tracheostomy is performed when there is a prolonged need for an artificial airway, when acute upper airway obstruction is present and endotracheal intubation is not possible, when there is retention of secretions, when cardiopulmonary failure occurs, or when neurological problems exist that interfere with adequate gas exchange.

Tracheostomy tubes used in infants and children are most often made of lightweight plastic or Silastic material instead of metal (Fig. 23-8). These tubes conform more readily to the shape of the trachea. (In infants, the trachea is short and the neck is flexible.) A new tracheostomy set should always be available at the bedside of any patient with a tracheostomy.

The most frightening aspect of having a tracheostomy is the inability to verbalize. This is especially difficult for

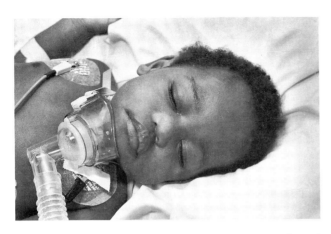

*Figure 23–8. Pediatric tracheostomy tube. (Skale, N. [1992]. Manual of pediatric nursing procedures. Philadelphia: J.B. Lippincott)*

the young child or infant. It is also stressful for the parents who sit by a silently crying child. The child and parents need to be reassured that the ability to speak will return.

Suctioning of the tracheostomy tube is performed as needed. Indications that suctioning is necessary include increased congestion in the lungs, coarse breath sounds, the presence of mucus or sputum in the airway, and decreased oxygen saturation. Suctioning through the tracheostomy tube is performed in a similar manner to endotracheal suctioning. Attention must be given to preventing complications such as hypoxemia and cardiac dysrhythmias. Because the upper airway is bypassed with a tracheostomy, the normal functions of air filtering, humidifying, and warming are absent and must be performed artificially. This is accomplished through the use of a T tube or tracheostomy collar. Warm, filtered, and moist air can be delivered, along with supplemental oxygen, through these devices.

Tracheostomy care is important to maintain airway patency, prevent infection, and observe the site for irritation, bleeding, or air leaks. A sterile gauze is used around fresh tracheostomy tubes to keep the site clean. When soiled, the dressing is changed and the stoma site cleaned with hydrogen peroxide and saline using aseptic technique. Suctioning is performed during tracheostomy care, and the inner cannula is cleaned or replaced with convenient disposable inner cannulas. A duplicate tracheostomy tube with inner cannula and stylet should be kept at the child's bedside.

The tracheostomy tube is held in place with soft cotton tape. The tape is applied loosely so as not to compress the stoma. If the tape is too loose, however, the tube may slide in and out with inspiration, expiration, and coughing. This may cause tracheal irritation and injury. The tape is sufficiently tight if one finger can be inserted between the tape and the child's neck. The tape is changed whenever soiled.

Tracheostomies may be temporary or permanent.

Children with permanent tracheostomies and their parents must be prepared for discharge and home care. Although tracheostomy care at home is similar to that in the hospital, several differences exist. The parents or the child, or all three, must be taught to perform the tracheostomy care. Clean technique is used instead of aseptic technique because cross-contamination is not a problem. Good handwashing must be emphasized. Gloves are an unnecessary expense, usually not required unless someone other than the parents or the child is cleaning the inner cannula. Tracheostomy dressings are not recommended because they encourage collection of secretions and moisture around the stoma. These conditions predispose the child to infection.

The parents must be taught to change the tracheostomy tube in case the child accidentally removes the tube or coughs it out. If the tracheostomy tube has been in place for some time and the stoma site is well healed, the tube is easily changed.

If the tracheostomy is temporary, once it is removed the stoma usually heals within a week. Until the stoma closes, the child must cover the stoma site when coughing.

The child must be observed for stridor, laryngospasm, or edema around the glottis. Stridor indicates severe airway narrowing and is usually treated with steroids. If stridor does not respond to treatment, reintubation may be necessary. Other complications that may occur are hoarseness, sore throat, and dysphagia.

## Nutrition

Infants and children with respiratory problems often have specific nutritional needs. When the infant or child expends extra energy to breathe, additional calories are required. The calories are usually given using Intralipid, medium-chain triglyceride oil added to formulas, or high-calorie infant formulas. Control of weight gain is desirable to prevent further respiratory distress and increased tissue oxygen requirements.

Infants and children who lack the ability to swallow, expend large amounts of energy during respiration, or are intubated are fed by tube. Tube feedings can be administered continuously as well as through bolus feedings given every 2 to 3 hours. The goal of feeding is accomplished when adequate calories are delivered for each 24-hour period. The amount of food given is individually determined and adjusted as the child gains weight. Other specific nutritional problems are discussed later under the individual problems.

## Evaluating Nursing Care

Specific nursing care of the child with respiratory problems depends on the disease process, its location, and its severity. Evaluation of nursing care includes observing the child's and parents' responses to nursing care, determining progress toward realistic goals, and revising and modifying the nursing care plan. The parents and the child are essential sources when evaluating the effectiveness of nursing care. Compliance with prescribed treatments is an indication that adaptation to the problem is occurring. Measurable outcomes include knowledge of the disease and its treatment; mastery of respiratory care treatments, such as tracheostomy care, postural drainage, and medication administration; and the child's continuing growth and development. Referrals to appropriate agencies, support groups, and educational programs for parents and children should be made. Home care by visiting nurses and other health care personnel may be appropriate to assist the parents and the child to achieve a better quality of life.

# Congenital Respiratory Problems

## Laryngeal Stridor

### Pathophysiology

*Laryngeal stridor,* also called laryngomalacia, is one of the most common congenital problems seen in infants. It results from the anterior and inferior displacement and vibration of the aryepiglottic folds during inspiration. At birth or shortly after birth, the neonate develops persistent, noisy inspirations. The sound changes as the neonate's position changes. When the child is in the supine position, the sound intensifies.

*Laryngeal webbing* is less common and results in airway obstruction at the glottis. Laryngeal webbing occurs when a membranous or tissue web either partially or completely obstructs the larynx. The web results in difficulty with the first inspiration.

### Medical Diagnosis and Management

Congenital laryngeal stridor requires no treatment and usually disappears by 18 months of age (Avery & First, 1989).

The laryngeal web is apparent on direct laryngoscopy. If the web is thin, it may be perforated and dilated; if thick, it may have to be surgically removed. When the web is membranous, it may be possible to intubate the neonate. If intubation is unsuccessful, a tracheostomy is performed. Treatment of laryngeal webbing requires immediate intervention in the delivery room.

### Nursing Assessment and Diagnosis

Nursing assessment begins at the time of delivery. The neonate is observed for signs of respiratory distress, including cyanosis, retractions, tachypnea, and periods of apnea. If stridor is present but the neonate appears to be ventilating normally, careful observation is necessary. If signs of respiratory distress are present with the first attempted inspiration, emergency intervention to establish a patent airway is necessary.

Nursing diagnoses for laryngeal stridor might include the following:

- Ineffective breathing pattern related to airway obstruction
- Impaired gas exchange related to decreased oxygen/carbon dioxide exchange
- Ineffective airway clearance related to anatomical deformity
- Ineffective family coping: compromised related to the medical diagnosis and treatment
- Altered growth and development related to illness
- High risk for infection related to tracheostomy care

### Planning and Implementing Nursing Care

Planning and implementation of nursing care involves continuous monitoring of the neonate for signs of respiratory distress and management of airway patency. If the child is intubated or if a tracheostomy is performed, airway management includes maintaining a patent airway by suctioning excess pulmonary secretions. Because the neonate's immune system is not mature, tracheostomy care must be performed using sterile technique. When releasing the child from the hospital, parents are taught to perform tracheostomy care and suctioning. They must be able to recognize the signs of infection and airway distress and take appropriate action. Parents should be taught that children with tracheostomies do not cry; therefore, they should be given information about communicating with a child who does not cry, and encouraged to express their concerns about caring for the infant with a tracheostomy. Home care referrals should be made if appropriate. The nurse should emphasize follow-up care for the child.

### Evaluating Nursing Care

Evaluation of care is accomplished by analyzing the neonate's and parents' progress toward nursing care goals and achieving expected outcomes. Parents should be able to return demonstrations of suctioning and tracheostomy care. The infant should maintain a patent airway and remain free from infection. Parents should demonstrate appropriate care, communication with the infant, and appropriate parenting techniques.

## Choanal Atresia

### Pathophysiology

*Choanal atresia* is a condition that results in either unilateral or bilateral obstruction of the posterior nares (choanae) caused by a membranous covering or thick bony plate. This congenital disorder is the most common form of nasal obstruction in the neonate. Seventy-five percent or more of neonates born with choanal atresia have at least one other anomaly, such as congenital heart disease or esophageal atresia. Choanal atresia occurs more commonly in girls than boys (Kaplan, 1985; Chernick & Kendig, 1990).

Because the neonate is primarily a nose-breather, this condition, if bilateral, is life-threatening. Neonates experience cyanosis, retractions, and periods of apnea that are relieved with crying. When the condition is unilateral, it may not be diagnosed during infancy and may result in only minimal problems.

### Medical Diagnosis and Management

Diagnosis of choanal atresia is suspected when a suction catheter cannot be passed through the nasal passages. A computed tomography scan confirms the presence and determines the extent of the lesion.

The treatment of choanal atresia consists of placement of an oral airway. If this is not successful, oral intubation is performed. The infant is fed by gavage. Surgical removal of the obstruction occurs shortly after the diagnosis is made. Nasal stents are placed during surgery and remain in place for several weeks.

### Nursing Assessment and Diagnosis

The nurse should assess the neonate with choanal atresia for signs and symptoms of respiratory distress, including cyanosis, retractions, tachypnea, and periods of apnea. In addition, the nurse should assess the child for problems with feeding, such as aspiration.

Nursing diagnoses for choanal atresia might include the following:

- Ineffective breathing pattern related to blockage of the nares
- Impaired gas exchange related to disturbed oxygen/carbon dioxide exchange
- Ineffective airway clearance related to blockage of the nares
- Altered nutrition: less than body requirements related to feeding difficulties
- Ineffective family coping: compromised, related to the child's illness
- Anxiety related to short- and long-term complications
- High risk for altered parenting related to a lack of knowledge about choanal atresia and alternate feeding methods
- Altered growth and development related to the child's illness

### Planning and Implementing Nursing Care

Planning and implementation of nursing care includes maintaining a patent airway with an oral airway or endotracheal tube before surgery and caring for the nasal stents

postoperatively. Patency of stints is maintained by irrigation with sterile saline and suctioning. Parents are taught to care for the stints at home. The stints are removed after 6 weeks. Instruction is provided on gavage feeding through gastrostomy tubes, and parents are taught the signs of respiratory distress, cardiopulmonary resuscitation (CPR), and other emergency interventions. Follow-up care should be emphasized. Parents should be encouraged to express their feelings and verbalize their concerns.

### Evaluating Nursing Care

Evaluation of care consists of determining parental mastery of care procedures through successful return demonstrations of stint care, gavage feedings, CPR, and other emergency interventions. The child should demonstrate appropriate growth and development milestones.

## Respiratory Problems of Neonates

### Meconium Aspiration Syndrome

#### Pathophysiology

Meconium aspiration occurs in 10% to 15% of all deliveries and can occur in both preterm and full-term neonates. While in utero, the fetus experiences an episode of asphyxia. This increases intestinal peristalsis, with relaxation of the anal sphincter. In *meconium aspiration syndrome,* meconium is released into the amniotic fluid and is aspirated by the fetus in variable amounts. After delivery, the neonate aspirates the major portion of meconium during the first breaths. Meconium that is aspirated into the airways causes obstruction by setting up a ball valve mechanism that allows air to enter during inspiration but prevents the exit of air during expiration. This causes air-trapping, with regional emphysema. In addition, atelectasis and pneumothorax may occur.

### Medical Diagnosis and Management

Before delivery, meconium aspiration is diagnosed if meconium-stained amniotic fluid is released from the vagina. After delivery, symptoms of meconium aspiration in the neonate include cyanosis, retractions, tachypnea, grunting, nasal flaring, increased secretions that are meconium-stained, and hypoxemia. Breath sounds over areas of atelectasis are decreased, with bronchial or tubular breath sounds present. Crackles (rales) are heard in areas where secretions are present.

Treatment involves suctioning, preferably before the first breath is taken or as soon as the neonate's head presents. Continued suctioning of the oropharynx and trachea is performed as the thorax presents. This removes a substantial quantity of meconium and reduces the amount of complications postnatally. If the quantity of aspirated meconium is large, endotracheal intubation may be necessary, with mechanical support. Suctioning should be frequent to remove the meconium-stained fluid.

### Nursing Assessment and Diagnosis

Nursing assessment for meconium aspiration begins during labor. The nurse watches for meconium-stained amniotic fluid from the vagina before delivery. Suction equipment should be available for use during the delivery. After delivery, the nurse should observe the neonate for signs of respiratory distress, airway obstruction, and pneumothorax.

Nursing diagnoses for meconium aspiration syndrome might include the following:

- Impaired gas exchange related to blockage of airway by meconium
- Ineffective breathing pattern related to expiratory difficulties
- Ineffective airway clearance related to presence of meconium
- Anxiety related to infant's breathing difficulty
- Ineffective family coping: compromised, related to newborn's illness

### Planning and Implementing Nursing Care

Planning and implementation of care includes clearing the airway of meconium-stained fluid and secretions through suctioning. Frequent position change helps drain fluid from the airways. Oxygen therapy is administered by means of cannula, hood, or ventilator. If mechanical ventilation is instituted, it requires careful monitoring. Recognition of a pneumothorax requires prompt treatment with chest tube insertion. Nursing care for pneumonia is discussed later in this chapter. Supportive reassurance and explanation of equipment and treatments is helpful in reducing anxiety of the parents.

### Evaluating Nursing Care

Evaluation of care is accomplished by assessing the resolution of nursing problems identified by nursing diagnosis. The neonate's pulmonary function should improve, and hypoxia should resolve. If present, atelectasis should resolve as evidenced by an improvement in breath sounds and decreased secretions.

## Asphyxia Neonatorum

### Pathophysiology

*Asphyxia neonatorum,* or neonatal hypoxic–ischemic encephalopathy, is respiratory failure in the neonate. It can result from intrauterine asphyxia, with cardiac or respiratory insufficiency before birth or at the time of birth; postnatal respiratory insufficiency due to hyaline mem-

brane disease; cardiac insufficiency due to severe congenital heart disease or recurrent apnea; or severe cyanotic heart defects (right-to-left shunts) or persistent fetal circulation (persistent pulmonary hypertension) (Chernick & Kendig, 1990). The manifestations of this condition result from decreased cerebral blood flow that follows the episode of asphyxia.

### Medical Diagnosis and Management

Apgar scores of less than 6 at 1 and 5 minutes are present after delivery. Signs of encephalopathy appear within hours of the hypoxic episode. The neonate with severe neurological problems is stuporous or comatose. In half the neonates with this condition, seizures begin within 6 to 12 hours and increase in frequency within 12 to 24 hours. Respiratory depression accompanies the seizures. Level of consciousness deteriorates, with brainstem abnormalities and intermittent decerebration. These neonates lose the Moro and sucking reflexes. They may become totally unresponsive as cerebral edema increases. Unless treated immediately and vigorously, these neonates will die. If they survive, the rate and degree of recovery vary.

Treatment consists of emergency CPR at birth. Mechanical ventilation is instituted. Seizure control is accomplished pharmacologically. Cerebral edema is treated pharmacologically to ensure cerebral perfusion.

### Nursing Assessment and Diagnosis

Nursing assessment of neonates with asphyxia neonatorum includes careful observation for signs of cerebral ischemia, seizures, and permanent neurological damage. Recognition of high-risk pregnancies allows the nurse to anticipate potential problems at birth.

Nursing diagnoses for asphyxia neonatorum might include the following:

- Ineffective breathing pattern related to asphyxia
- Impaired gas exchange related to cardiac or respiratory insufficiency
- Anticipatory grieving related to perceived loss of a "normal" neonate
- Ineffective family coping: compromised related to having a child with respiratory distress
- Altered growth and development related to infant's illness
- Altered parenting related to the severity of the child's illness
- Anxiety related to the child's illness

### Planning and Implementing Nursing Care

Planning and implementation of care includes emergency CPR with institution of mechanical ventilation. Monitoring ventilatory support and intravenous therapy with pharmacological intervention for cerebral edema and seizures is essential. Explanation of equipment and therapeutic procedures for the parents provides information. Supportive reassurance reduces parental anxiety. Assisting the parents in developing a realistic plan of care for the child in the future is essential for parental coping and adaptation as well as for the child's optimal growth and development. Referrals should be made to appropriate agencies that can assist the parents with future care of the child.

### Evaluating Nursing Care

Evaluation of nursing care depends on the degree of neurological impairment and neonatal survival. Although these children usually have developmental delays, they should be assisted in achieving age-appropriate developmental tasks to the degree that they are able. Parents should have a realistic outlook and plan for home care and the child's special needs.

## Bronchopulmonary Dysplasia

### Pathophysiology

*Bronchopulmonary dysplasia* (BPD) is a chronic lung disease that occurs after long periods of mechanical ventilation with increased inspired oxygen concentrations. It occurs most often in neonates born prematurely who require supplemental oxygenation. Chronic changes seen in the lungs include hyperinflation of air spaces, interstitial fibrosis, and thickening of the alveolar ducts and walls. These changes impair diffusion of oxygen from the alveoli to the pulmonary capillaries.

### Medical Diagnosis and Management

Symptoms of respiratory distress include cyanosis, tachypnea, retractions, grunting, and nasal flaring. As the disease progresses, retractions persist and rales are heard bilaterally. To maintain adequate tissue oxygenation, oxygen concentrations are increased. The lungs become hyperinflated, with an increased anteroposterior diameter that may produce pectus excavatum.

Mortality rate is high. Up to 25% of the neonates who develop BPD die within the first year of life (Behrman & Vaughan, 1987). Healing of the lungs may take up to 3 years. Because the healing process requires years, some children with this condition develop pulmonary hypertension and congestive heart failure.

Treatment of BPD includes life-support measures. Oxygen concentrations and peak inspiratory pressures are reduced as soon as possible to limit the extent of the disease process. High-frequency ventilatory techniques may be used to deliver oxygen at lower pressures. To decrease interstitial lung water, the neonate is not overhydrated. An increase in pulmonary interstitial fluid causes airway obstruction by compression of the small airways, which leads to necrosis of these airways. Drug therapy for infants with BPD varies with each child because of the complexity of the disease; often several drugs are given. Diuretics are used to reduce edema and improve pulmonary function. Bronchodilators are used to improve lung mechanics and gas exchange. Use of steroids is controversial, but a study by Cummings, D'Eugenio, and Gross (1989) suggests that they may be useful in reducing the duration of mechanical ventilation and oxygen dependence.

### Nursing Assessment and Diagnosis

Assessment of a neonate with BPD includes observation of the child's oxygenation status and signs of respiratory distress. Monitoring for signs of infection is important since neonates with BPD have impaired mucociliary function. Careful observation of hydration status is important during the acute stages of the disease because of the possibility of pulmonary edema. Assessment of temperature is important because hyperthermia can increase the oxygen requirements of an already compromised neonate. Assessment of nutritional status is important to determine caloric intake for energy and growth requirements, but care should be taken not to increase calories to a level where oxygen demand increases. Weight is measured daily, and caloric intake is determined by weight, hydration status, and oxygen status.

Nursing diagnoses of bronchopulmonary dysplasia might include the following:

- Ineffective breathing pattern related to hyperinflation of air spaces, interstitial fibrosis, or thickening of alveolar ducts
- Impaired gas exchange related to anatomical changes
- Ineffective airway clearance related to anatomical changes
- High risk for infection related to impaired mucociliary function
- Altered growth and development related to the child's illness
- Ineffective family coping: compromised, related to the need to care for an ill child
- Altered parenting related to difficulties in communicating with an ill infant
- Altered nutrition: less than body requirements related to the child's inability to eat
- Fatigue related to increased respiratory efforts
- Hyperthermia related to infection
- Anxiety (parental) related to the prognosis

### Planning and Implementing Nursing Care

Planning and implementation of care includes maintaining a patent airway by suctioning, postural drainage, chest physiotherapy, and elevation of the neonate's head and maintaining the endotracheal tube. Minimizing the risk for infection includes practicing good handwashing, using sterile suctioning techniques, obtaining cultures as appropriate, and administering antimicrobial agents as ordered. Maintaining hydration status is accomplished by careful regulation of fluids, daily weights, and accurate intake and output and continual assessment for signs of pulmonary edema. To maintain adequate nutritional status, caloric requirements are first met with hyperalimentation fluids and lipids. As the neonate gains weight, gavage or oral feedings are started. Energy expenditure in these children is minimized by reduced handling and by allowing for periods of rest and sleep. The family is kept informed of progress throughout the course of treatment. Explanation of procedures, equipment, and limited visiting and handling of the neonate reduces parental anxiety and fear. The nurse should encourage verbalization of fears or concerns. If the neonate's status improves to the degree that the child can be cared for at home, the nurse should teach the parents the appropriate procedures and refer them to health care agencies that can provide multidisciplinary care.

### Evaluating Nursing Care

Evaluation of care involves determining whether adequate oxygenation is maintained. The neonate's respiratory status should improve as measured by acceptable parameters of oxygenation, decreased secretions, and decreased signs of respiratory distress. The neonate should maintain a temperature within normal limits, and insertion sites of intravenous catheters should not be red or draining purulent material. Hydration status is evaluated using weight, urinary output, and absence of signs of pulmonary edema. Nutritional status is evaluated by weight gain, appropriate bone growth, and appearance of skin. Parents should verbalize their understanding of the disorder and should feel confident in their ability to manage care of the child at home.

## Respiratory Distress Syndrome

### Pathophysiology

*Respiratory distress syndrome* (RDS), also known as hyaline membrane disease, occurs in premature neonates who lack the ability to synthesize pulmonary surfactant. The lack of surfactant results in high alveolar surface tension, which leads to alveolar collapse with respiration. Widespread atelectasis (lung collapse) results, with decreased gas exchange leading to hypoxemia and hypercapnia.

### Medical Diagnosis and Management

Symptoms of RDS include cyanosis, grunting, nasal flaring, tachypnea, retractions, and decreased breath sounds with crackles heard throughout both lung fields. In neonates weighing 1500 g or more, RDS persists for 3 to 7 days and usually resolves within 7 to 10 days. Neonates who weigh less than 1500 g may have a more prolonged course. For neonates at risk, tests for lung maturity are performed on amniotic fluid. The test for lung maturity is the lecithin/sphingomyelin (L/S) ratio. This test is not always reliable if the amniotic fluid is stained with blood or meconium. Also, half of fetuses born with an immature L/S ratio do not develop hyaline membrane disease (Burton, Hodgkin, & Ward, 1991). The shake test is used to measure surfactant function. A positive test indicates negligible risk, but a negative test does not indicate a risk.

Treatment for neonates with RDS consists of early supportive care, including oxygen therapy, nutrition, thermal support, protection from infection, and phototherapy for hyperbilirubinemia. Complications of RDS include hypoxemia from endotracheal tube obstruction and cardiac arrest. Prolonged intubation can lead to subglottic stenosis, ulceration, and edema of the larynx with hoarseness and stridor.

### Nursing Assessment and Diagnosis

Nursing assessment includes monitoring oxygenation parameters, including ABG levels, breath sounds, and ventilatory support. $P_aO_2$ is usually maintained between 50 and 80 mmHg. In addition, the nurse should monitor cardiac status for dysrhythmia related to hypoxemia. Observation of chest movement and auscultation of breath sounds should be done with spontaneous or positive-pressure ventilation. Inspired oxygen concentration is recorded hourly. Pulse oximetry or transcutaneous oxygen monitoring is done continuously. If necessary, measures such as an oxygen hood, continuous positive air pressure (CPAP), or mechanical ventilation are instituted to improve oxygenation.

Assessment of nutrition is performed by weight, heart rate, respiratory rate and effort, color, blood glucose, urine output, and stools. Caloric requirements are determined systematically and are ordered by a physician.

Thermal regulation is assessed by measurement of neonate and environmental temperatures. The neonate is assessed for hyperthermia, hypothermia, and signs of infection. Temperature and results of laboratory values, such as blood counts and cultures, are helpful when assessing for the presence of infection. Hyperbilirubinemia is best assessed by serum bilirubin levels and the observation of jaundice.

Nursing diagnoses for respiratory distress syndrome might include the following:

- Impaired gas exchange related to the inability to synthesize surfactant
- Ineffective airway clearance related to atelectasis
- Ineffective breathing pattern related to alveolar collapse

- High risk for altered body temperature related to infection
- High risk for infection related to compromised respiratory status
- Altered tissue perfusion related to decreased oxygenation
- Ineffective family coping: compromised, related to having an ill baby
- High risk for fluid volume deficit related to hyperthermia or ductus arteriosis
- Altered nutrition: less than body requirements related to feeding difficulty
- Altered parenting related to care needs of the ill child
- Sleep pattern disturbance related to intensive care procedures

### Planning and Implementing Nursing Care

Planning and implementation of care includes care of the neonate requiring assisted ventilation with CPAP, mechanical ventilation, or high-frequency ventilation. Maintaining a patent airway is essential in preventing hypoxemia. When the ductus arteriosus (the channel between the main pulmonary artery and the aorta of the fetus) remains patent, signs of fluid overload are present. The nurse maintains a strict fluid restriction and administers indomethacin as ordered. Temperature regulation requires the nurse to maintain a thermal environment that reduces metabolism, caloric requirements, and demands for oxygen. Fluid administration is titrated to maintain adequate hydration and prevent fluid overload that would further impair gas exchange. Blood pressure must be maintained to ensure adequate tissue perfusion. Caloric intake must be adequate to meet minimal nutritional needs for growth during this period. With the presence of severe anemia, packed red blood cell transfusions are performed by the nurse. If metabolic acidosis develops or persists and is severe, sodium bicarbonate may be ordered. The nurse should carefully monitor acid–base status. The nurse administers antibiotics therapy as ordered and obtains cultures when appropriate. Adequate rest and sleep necessitate minimal handling of the child by the nurse. Parents should be given relevant information on all procedures performed.

### Evaluating Nursing Care

Evaluation consists of determining whether arterial oxygen tensions are maintained between 50 and 80 mmHg. The neonate should remain free of signs of fluid overload. The child's skin temperature should remain at 36.6°C (98°F) to prevent increases in metabolism and oxygen demand, and the neonate should remain free of infection. The child should gain weight and grow, but only to the degree that oxygenation is not compromised. Finally, the neonate's acid–base status should remain balanced without respiratory or metabolic acidosis.

## Pneumothorax

### Pathophysiology

*Pneumothorax,* a collection of air in the pleural cavity, may result from CPAP, mechanical ventilation, or meconium aspiration syndrome. Asymptomatic pneumothorax occurs in 1% to 2% of all neonates and most likely results from the high intrathoracic pressures that occur during the first few breaths. Pneumothorax occurs when alveoli rupture. The air then leaks into the mediastinum and pleural spaces.

### Medical Diagnosis and Management

Early manifestations of pneumothorax include tachypnea, retractions, grunting, and apnea. The apical impulse may shift from its normal position toward the unaffected side. Auscultation may not be helpful because breath sounds are widely referred and may be detected as normal over the affected area. Chest radiographs confirm the presence of pneumothorax.

Asymptomatic pneumothorax requires no specific treatment. If the pneumothorax is symptomatic, needle aspiration is performed or a chest tube is placed anteriorly to drain free air. The chest tube is connected to continuous water-seal suction (Fig. 23-9).

### Nursing Assessment and Diagnosis

Assessment of the neonate with a pneumothorax includes monitoring for signs of respiratory distress and decreased cardiac output.

Nursing diagnoses for pneumothorax might include the following:

- Ineffective breathing pattern related to air in the pleural cavity
- Impaired gas exchange related to air leakage into the mediastinum and pleural spaces

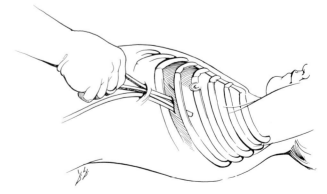

*Figure 23–9. Chest tube connected to water seal suction.*

- Decreased cardiac output related to pressure on the heart
- Anxiety related to parental concerns regarding the prognosis

### Planning and Implementing Nursing Care

Planning and implementation of nursing care includes measures to ensure integrity and patency of the chest drainage system. The nurse maintains water-seal and suction levels as ordered, maintains an occlusive dressing over the chest tube insertion site, maintains the chest drainage apparatus below the neonate's chest, and keeps the drainage tubing free of kinks. If oxygen therapy is ordered, the nurse implements and maintains the correct oxygen concentration. Explanation and reassurance for the parents helps relieve fear and anxiety.

### Evaluating Nursing Care

Evaluation of care consists of determining whether the child has a normal respiratory pattern, no respiratory distress, and normal oxygenation parameters. The neonate should experience normal cardiac output. The parents' anxiety about the neonate's condition should be decreased, and they should be informed about the child's care.

## Apnea of Prematurity

### Pathophysiology

*Apnea of prematurity* occurs in immature neonates in whom apneic episodes come about when breathing ceases for more than 20 seconds. Prolonged apneic periods can lead to hypoxemia, cyanosis, bradycardia, and respiratory acidosis.

Two possible mechanisms are thought to cause apnea in premature neonates. The first involves disruption of the neural control of respiration due to immaturity. The second mechanism is pharyngeal obstruction. During quiet sleep, a flaccid pharyngeal muscle allows collapse of the hypopharynx. Collapse occurs as a result of negative pressure during inspiration.

### Medical Diagnosis and Management

Treatment consists of tactile stimulation of the neonate to reestablish breathing during apneic episodes and CPAP. Most neonates respond to tactile stimulation and pulsating water beds. CPAP is particularly successful in reducing apneic episodes that persist, but the mechanism of action is not understood. Pharmacological intervention consists of administration of theophylline and caffeine, which increase central respiratory drive and improve $CO_2$ sensitivity. Another drug used is doxapram hydrochloride, which in low doses stimulates the peripheral chemosensor and in high doses stimulates respiratory neurons.

### Nursing Assessment and Diagnosis

Assessment of the neonate with apnea of prematurity consists of monitoring the neonate for episodes of apnea by means of apnea and cardiac monitors. Airway obstruction, cyanosis, and bradycardia should also be carefully assessed.

Nursing diagnoses for apnea of prematurity might include the following:

- Ineffective breathing pattern related to disruption of neural control of respiration
- Impaired gas exchange related to pharyngeal obstruction
- Anxiety (parental) related to the neonate's survival

### Planning and Implementing Nursing Care

Planning and implementation of care consists of tactile stimulation during periods of apnea. If unsuccessful, the neonate should be ventilated with an Ambu-bag. Another method of stimulation involves placing the neonate on a rocker bed. The nurse should avoid measures that result in apnea, such as suctioning or prolonged oral feedings. When oral feedings are given, frequent interruptions and supplemental oxygen are needed. Gavage feeding may be necessary. Reassurance and support should be provided for the parents because of typical high levels of anxiety.

### Evaluating Nursing Care

Evaluation includes analysis of the frequency of apneic episodes. The child is usually free of apneic episodes by 36 weeks' gestational age. Parents should know how to perform CPR, and their anxiety about preventing apnea episodes should be decreased.

## Respiratory Problems of Infants

### Otitis Media

For a complete discussion of otitis media and the nursing care of the infant with otitis media, refer to Chapter 35.

### Croup

#### Pathophysiology

*Croup* is the term commonly used to describe an inflammation and narrowing of the laryngeal and tracheal areas. Causes of croup include viral as well as other infections, genetic predisposition, allergic reactions, and emotional upset. Croup usually affects children under the age of 4 and is more common in boys than girls. It usually is seen in late fall or early winter.

## Medical Diagnosis and Management

Initially, croup begins suddenly in the form of a cold with a low-grade fever. The child awakens at night with a barking cough, hoarseness, inspiratory difficulty, laryngeal stridor (a high-pitched, crowing sound), and anxiety. Respiratory distress may become so severe that respiratory obstruction occurs, in which case endotracheal intubation or tracheostomy is required.

Treatment varies with severity of the disease. Cool-mist therapy is the most often recommended therapy. Since most croup is caused by viral infections, antibiotics are not prescribed unless there is a secondary bacterial infection present. The use of corticosteroids is controversial. Sedatives are contraindicated since restlessness is one of the cardinal signs of severity of the obstruction and the need for intubation or tracheostomy. Croup generally resolves in 1 week.

## Nursing Assessment and Diagnosis

Nursing assessment for croup includes observing the infant for signs and symptoms of respiratory distress and dehydration. Signs of severe respiratory distress may indicate a need for hospitalization and relief of airway obstruction.

Nursing diagnoses for croup might include the following:

- Ineffective breathing pattern related to inflammation of the larynx and trachea
- Ineffective airway clearance related to respiratory obstruction
- High risk for fluid volume deficit related to dehydration
- Anxiety (child) related to difficulty in breathing

## Planning and Implementing Nursing Care

Planning and implementation of care includes instructions for the parents. Parents should be able to recognize the symptoms of croup and respiratory distress and take steps to humidify the child's environment by either having the child sit in a steamy bathroom, using cool-air humidifiers, or exposing the infant to cool and humid night air. If a humidifier is used, the parents must clean the unit after each episode to prevent the spread of viral or bacterial organisms. Parents are taught to recognize the signs of dehydration, including sunken anterior fontanels; dry, sticky mucous membranes; decreased skin turgor; and decreased urination as evidenced by a decrease in wet diapers, which contain a concentrated urine. If the symptoms of croup intensify or laryngeal stridor occurs at rest, the child should be taken to the emergency room for immediate treatment.

## Evaluating Nursing Care

Evaluation of care includes close observation of the child. The child should maintain a patent airway and adequate hydration status. Urine specific-gravity values should range between 1.002 and 1.030.

# Sudden Infant Death Syndrome

## Pathophysiology

*Sudden infant death syndrome* (SIDS), or "crib death," refers to a sudden, unexpected death of an infant that cannot be explained by a postmortem examination. In the United States, SIDS is the leading cause of death of infants between the ages of 28 days and 1 year. The incidence of SIDS varies from 0.2 to 3.0 deaths per 1000 live births (Behrman & Vaughan, 1987). Black and Native American infants have significantly higher SIDS death rates: 2.90 per 1000 and 5.93 per 1000 deaths, respectively. Boys are affected more often than girls. Low-birth-weight infants are affected at a rate that is four times higher than normal-birth-weight infants. There is a higher rate of SIDS in infants of mothers who are addicted to narcotics and who are younger than 20 years of age (Kaplan, Bauman, & Kraus, 1984; McClain, 1985; Peterson, Sabotta, & Daling, 1986). SIDS occurs most often in infants between 2 and 8 months of age. Although it can occur at any age, it rarely is seen in infants over 18 months old (Bass, Kravath, & Glass, 1986).

## Medical Diagnosis and Treatment

Treatment is based on the presence of any underlying conditions that may predispose the infant to apneic episodes. If no underlying cause is identified, methylxanthines may be prescribed, along with careful monitoring of heart rate and drug levels. Home monitoring of cardiorespiratory status is helpful in alleviating anxiety of parents with infants who experience apneic episodes. Monitoring is usually continued until the infant reaches 9 months of age, at which time sudden unexpected death is unlikely.

## Nursing Assessment and Diagnosis

Nursing assessment of the infant at risk for SIDS includes observing the infant for apneic episodes. Usually, however, nursing assessment consists of observing for appropriate grief patterns in the parents and siblings.

Nursing diagnoses for sudden infant death syndrome might include the following:

- Spiritual distress related to coping with the possibility of death
- Ineffective family coping: compromised related to potential loss of an infant

- Anticipatory grieving related to the possibility of death
- Dysfunctional grieving related to the parents' inability to cope

## Planning and Implementing Nursing Care

Planning and implementation of care includes discussing the symptoms of grief with parents, referring families to appropriate health professionals for assistance in dealing with grief or to SIDS support groups, and referring siblings to age-appropriate counseling. Planning, implementing, and evaluating nursing care for families facing dying, death, and bereavement are discussed in detail in Chapter 22.

# Bronchiolitis

## Pathophysiology

*Bronchiolitis* is inflammation of the bronchioles. It is a common condition that is primarily seen in infants and children under the age of 2. The peak incidence occurs at 6 months of age, often during the winter and early spring. Bronchiolitis most often develops in infants who are exposed to older children and adults with upper respiratory infections or in children exposed to viral infections in day care situations. Respiratory syncytial virus (RSV) is associated with most cases of bronchiolitis, although parainfluenza and some adenoviruses have been identified. Mortality in infants with bronchiolitis caused by the RSV can be high. Some infants develop chronic inflammatory changes with bronchiolitis that result in a gradual obliteration of the smaller airways.

The respiratory viruses enter the lower respiratory tract, where they are deposited in the lower airways and alveoli, causing inflammation and mucosal necrosis. The walls of the small bronchi and bronchioles become inflamed and edematous. A tenacious exudate of leukocytes and debris may cause partial or complete obstruction of the small and medium airways. Partially obstructed bronchioles lead to air-trapping. Air is pulled into the airways on inspiration as intrapulmonary pressures fall below atmospheric pressure. On expiration, intrapulmonary pressures rise above atmospheric pressure and the airways collapse, trapping the air. This leads to hyperinflation. The exudate in the alveoli causes atelectasis and alveolar collapse. If a large number of alveoli are affected, hypoxemia, hypercapnia, and respiratory acidosis occur.

## Medical Diagnosis and Management

Symptoms of bronchiolitis include nasal flaring, a hyperinflated chest with retractions on inspiration, and rapid shallow respirations at a rate ranging between 60 and 80 breaths per minute. The infant's breathing is rapid and shallow to prevent paroxysms of coughing. As the work of breathing increases, cyanosis appears, especially during sleep. The infant becomes restless and develops a hacking cough. Crying and feeding may exaggerate the symptoms, so the infant often eats poorly. The infant may be hypothermic, afebrile, or hyperthermic. Diagnosis of acute bronchiolitis is determined by the clinical signs and symptoms, the age of the child, and the presence of an outbreak of RSV in the community.

Treatment of bronchiolitis includes administration of oxygen. It is best delivered by hood or tent since nasal prongs may cause a reflex bronchoconstriction (Behrman & Vaughan, 1987). Intravenous fluids are necessary to prevent dehydration. Fluids must be administered carefully and sparingly to prevent fluid overload and pulmonary edema. Bronchodilators are used to reverse bronchospasm. They are given intravenously or subcutaneously rather than by aerosol because the aerosol method may cause a reflex bronchoconstriction. Since the cause is usually viral, antibiotics are not given unless a secondary bacterial infection is present. Ribavirin, an antiviral agent that inhibits replication of RSV, is used to treat bronchiolitis in infants and children. Ribavirin is given over 12 to 18 hours per day for a minimum of 3 to a maximum of 7 days. It is delivered through a small-particle aerosol generator (SPAG-2) and is not mixed with other medications (Outwater, Meissner, & Peterson, 1988). Use of corticosteroids is controversial and generally not considered effective. One percent of infants with bronchiolitis develop respiratory failure because of disease severity and exhaustion from the increased work of breathing. If respiratory failure develops, intubation and ventilatory support are necessary.

## Nursing Assessment and Diagnosis

Assessment of the infant with bronchiolitis includes observation of signs of respiratory distress such as nasal flaring, retractions, tachypnea, dyspnea, cyanosis, and apnea. A complete respiratory history is important and includes onset and duration of symptoms, apneic episodes, activity level, feeding problems, and presence of fever.

Nursing diagnoses for bronchiolitis might include the following:

- Impaired gas exchange related to inflammation of the bronchioles
- Ineffective breathing pattern related to edema of the bronchioles
- Ineffective airway clearance related to exudate in the airway
- Hyperthermia related to infection
- High risk for fluid volume deficit related to inability to take fluids orally
- Anxiety (child) related to difficulty in breathing

- High risk for altered parenting related to the child's hospitalization

### Planning and Implementing Nursing Care

Planning and implementation of care includes stabilization and maintenance of a patent airway. Delivery of supplemental oxygen is accomplished by use of an oxygen hood or tent. The amount of oxygen delivered is based on ABG results and pulse oximetry values. Mist tents are generally not recommended because of reflex bronchoconstriction. Bronchodilators and Ribavirin are administered as ordered. Nursing interventions include monitoring the child for adverse reactions. The parents are taught how to prepare and administer the drug using a SPAG-2. The solution is discarded if it turns cloudy. Respiratory isolation may be instituted in the hospital to prevent the spread of the virus to other infants and children.

Positioning of the infant is done to optimize oxygenation as well as to facilitate drainage of pulmonary secretions. The child's position is changed frequently. Infant car seats are used to support the infant and elevate the head. Postural drainage may or may not be ordered, depending on the severity of the illness.

Hydration status is monitored. Fluid is administered sparingly to maintain adequate hydration but to prevent pulmonary edema. The specific-gravity value of the urine is measured with each urination, and accurate intake and output records are kept.

Support and reassurance for the parents is important since they are often anxious. Explanation of the disease process, equipment, and procedures helps reduce parental anxiety.

### Evaluating Nursing Care

Evaluation of care consists of determining whether a patent airway and oxygenation are maintained. Auscultation should reveal decreasing rales, rhonchi, and wheezes. The infant should have decreasing signs of respiratory distress and decreasing hypoxemia. The infant should be able to tolerate oral feedings without increasing hypoxemia. Urine output should be adequate, with specific-gravity values between 1.002 and 1.030. Skin turgor and fontanels should be evaluated at least once every shift. The child's temperature should be normal.

The parents should be taught about the disease process and should be able to verbalize signs of respiratory distress. They should demonstrate mastery of CPR skills. The parents should return the child for follow-up care.

### Pertussis

Pertussis is discussed in Chapter 19.

### Retropharyngeal Abscess

#### Pathophysiology

*Retropharyngeal abscess* is an abscess of the lymph nodes in the pharynx. Retropharyngeal abscess can result from an infection of the tonsils and surrounding tissues. Most children affected are under the age of 2 years. Retropharyngeal abscess may lead to rupture of the lesion and aspiration of purulent material, with resulting pneumonia, airway obstruction, aspiration, erosion of a large vessel with fatal hemorrhage, or septicemia. The infection may extend up to the cranial base or down into the mediastinum.

#### Medical Diagnosis and Management

Signs and symptoms include an acute sore throat with difficulty swallowing and difficulty breathing. The child salivates and lies on one side with the head drawn backward. The infant's cry is husky, and the cervical lymph nodes are enlarged.

Treatment consists of drainage of the abscess and intravenous antibiotics. Intravenous fluids are continued until the child can take oral fluids. Antipyretics may be prescribed for fever.

#### Nursing Assessment and Diagnosis

Assessment of the infant with retropharyngeal abscess includes observation for signs of airway obstruction, septicemia, and hemorrhage. The child is assessed for the presence of sore throat and dehydration because of difficulty swallowing. A careful history is taken regarding onset and severity of symptoms.

Nursing diagnoses for retropharyngeal abscess might include the following:

- Ineffective airway clearance related to abscess of lymph nodes in the pharynx
- Hyperthermia related to infection
- Pain related to inflammation of the throat
- Potential fluid volume deficit related to decreased fluid intake
- Anxiety (child) related to pain and difficulty in swallowing

#### Planning and Implementing Nursing Care

Planning and implementation of care includes maintenance of a patent airway, administration of antibiotics and antipyretics, and maintenance of hydration through intravenous and oral fluids. Education of parents about medication administration, follow-up care, and emergency measures for airway obstruction is important. Analgesics are administered for pain.

### *Evaluating Nursing Care*

Evaluation of care consists of assessing whether a patent airway has been achieved and whether the child is free of respiratory distress. The child should remain afebrile, with the infection clearing, and should be well hydrated.

## *Respiratory Problems of Toddlers and Preschool-Aged Children*

### *Foreign-Body Aspiration*

#### *Pathophysiology*

Infants and children between the ages of 6 months and 3 years are most likely to aspirate foreign objects and substances. Aspiration of small objects often occurs while children are running, jumping, or laughing. The severity of the problems associated with aspiration depend largely on the nature of the object aspirated, where it lodges, and the degree of obstruction.

Peanuts are the most common food aspirated. Other nuts, seeds, popcorn kernels, pieces of hot dogs and hamburgers, and other particles of food may be aspirated. The danger is that once aspirated, the piece of food enlarges and softens so that obstruction increases and removal is difficult. Other objects that are aspirated are small toys, beads, safety pins, paper clips, coins, buttons, and marbles. Small children also insert objects and food into nostrils and ears. In the nose, infection may result because of mucosal irritation and swelling.

#### *Medical Diagnosis and Management*

Manifestations of aspirated foreign objects depend on location and size of the object. The smaller the object, the more it advances in the airways. Foreign objects that lodge in the larynx or trachea result in acute, severe obstruction. Respiratory distress with hoarseness, cyanosis, apnea, stridor, wheezing, a croupy cough, and aphonia (inability to produce speech sounds) or dysphonia (difficulty in speaking) may occur. If opaque, the object can be detected on radiograph. Direct laryngoscopy allows visualization of the object and access for removal.

Symptoms of bronchial aspiration depend on the degree of obstruction and pathology created by the object. After aspiration, explosive coughing and dyspnea occur. Hemoptysis (release of blood from the bronchi) and signs of infection may result if the airway is lacerated. If the object is small and lodges in the small airways, a mild cough is the only symptom. If not removed, the cough continues and fever and production of purulent secretions occur. Inhaled organic matter produces inflammation and infection distal to the obstruction, with abscess formation. Treatment depends on the symptoms and location of

the aspirated material. If lodged in the larynx or trachea, direct laryngoscopy can provide access for removal. When access to an emergency room is not possible, the abdominal thrust is recommended to expel the object from the larynx or trachea (Grauer, Cavallro, & Gums, 1991; Fig. 23-10). If lodged in a large bronchus, bronchoscopy is used to remove the object. Infection is treated with antibiotics. Postural drainage may be helpful in removing the object.

#### *Nursing Assessment and Diagnosis*

Assessment of foreign-body aspiration includes monitoring the toddler for signs of partial or complete airway obstruction. With nasal aspiration, the nurse assesses for the presence and characteristics of any nasal discharge, sneezing, or coughing. After removal of the object, the child is monitored for laryngeal edema.

Nursing diagnoses might include the following:

- Ineffective airway clearance related to the presence of a foreign object
- Ineffective breathing pattern related to blockage of the airway
- High risk for infection related to presence of a foreign object
- Anxiety (child) related to difficulty in breathing

#### *Planning and Implementing Nursing Care*

Planning and implementation of care includes seeking immediate medical treatment for complete or partial airway obstruction that causes respiratory distress. Following removal of a foreign object, the toddler remains NPO until the gag reflex returns. When the gag reflex is present, fluids are encouraged. Hydration and mist therapy assists in liquefaction of secretions. If infection is present, antibiotics are administered. Parental education includes safety

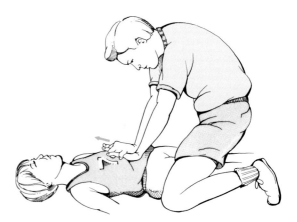

*Figure 23–10.   Abdominal thrust.*

precautions such as removal of toys with small parts, avoidance of foods that are likely to be aspirated, and not allowing children to put small objects in their mouths.

### Evaluating Nursing Care

Evaluation consists of determining whether parents are adequately educated about enhancing safety, aiding postural drainage for the toddler, taking appropriate emergency measures if aspiration occurs again, and scheduling follow-up visits. The child should be free from infection and should maintain a patent airway without signs of respiratory distress.

## Pharyngitis

### Pathophysiology

*Pharyngitis* consists of generalized erythema of the pharynx without tonsilar involvement. The most common cause of pharyngitis is viral, although β-hemolytic streptococcus may also cause pharyngitis.

### Medical Diagnosis and Management

When the cause is viral, symptoms include low-grade fever, mild headache, sore throat, mild nasal congestion, hoarseness, and productive cough. Upon inspection, small patches of yellow exudate appear on the pharynx. Viral pharyngitis usually lasts from 1 to 5 days. Symptoms associated with bacterial infection include sore throat, fever, headaches, muscle aches, difficulty swallowing, and difficulty breathing. Bacterial pharyngitis may last up to 2 weeks. Complications of streptococcal infections include rheumatic fever and glomerulonephritis.

Treatment for viral pharyngitis includes bed rest, fluids, acetaminophen, and warm saline gargles. Treatment for bacterial pharyngitis includes the above measures as well as throat cultures and administration of prescribed antibiotics, such as penicillin.

### Nursing Assessment and Diagnosis

Assessment of the toddler with pharyngitis includes inspection of the throat for exudate and erythema. The child is assessed for pain, signs of respiratory distress, and dehydration. A complete history includes onset, duration, and severity of symptoms.

Nursing diagnoses might include the following:

- Ineffective breathing pattern related to edema of the pharynx
- Pain related to inflammation of the pharynx
- High risk for fluid volume deficit related to difficulty in swallowing
- Altered nutrition: less than body requirements related to sore throat

### Planning and Implementing Nursing Care

Planning and implementation of care includes supportive care for viral pharyngitis since there is no specific therapy available. Care of the child with bacterial pharyngitis includes supportive care, cultures, administration of antibiotics, and administration of fluids to maintain hydration. If the sore throat persists, the child should be encouraged to eat soft foods to maintain nutrition.

### Evaluating Nursing Care

Evaluation of care consists of determining whether the child has achieved a normal respiratory pattern and is free of respiratory distress. The child should receive and respond to antibiotic therapy. Adequate hydration and nutritional status should be maintained.

## Acute Pharyngitis

Refer to Chapter 35 for a discussion of acute pharyngitis.

## Epiglottitis

### Pathophysiology

*Epiglottitis* is an acute and severe inflammation of the epiglottis caused primarily by *Haemophilus influenzae* type B infections. The soft tissue of the epiglottis becomes severely edematous, with the supraglottic structures and aryepiglottic folds obstructing the laryngeal outlet during inspiration. Expiration is usually not obstructed. It affects children of any age, but most cases are seen in children between the ages of 1 and 5 years.

### Medical Diagnosis and Management

The onset is acute and follows a mild respiratory infection. Fever and lethargy occur suddenly. Dyspnea occurs within 2 to 4 hours. The toddler becomes anxious due to difficult inspirations, hyperextends the neck, and protrudes the chin. Drooling occurs because of difficulty with swallowing. The sore throat is so severe that the child refuses to eat, drink, or lie down. Signs of respiratory distress and obstruction include restlessness, tachycardia with mouth breathing, rapid thready pulse, inspiratory stridor and snoring expirations, and hypoxia. On radiograph the hypopharynx is dilated, and the tissue thickens in the epiglottic area. Direct visualization of the epiglottitis is not recommended because it can lead to airway obstruction.

Treatment of epiglottitis includes emergency hospitalization. Endotracheal intubation or tracheostomy may be required. Humidified oxygen is given for hypoxia. Antibiotics such as ampicillin or chloramphenicol are administered. Corticosteroids may be used. The endotracheal tube is usually left in place 2 to 3 days or until the epiglottic edema subsides.

### Nursing Assessment and Diagnosis

Assessment of epiglottitis includes observing the toddler for fever, muffled voice, sore throat, dysphagia, drooling, refusal to eat or drink, and signs of respiratory distress and obstruction. Age and developmental level are assessed. Although an explanation of the condition should be given to the child at the appropriate level, time for explanation may be short.

Nursing diagnoses for epiglottitis might include the following:

- Ineffective breathing pattern related to edema of the epiglottis
- Ineffective airway clearance related to inflammation of the epiglottis
- Impaired gas exchange related to difficulty in inspiration
- Anxiety (child) related to difficulty in breathing
- Pain related to the inflammation
- High risk for fluid volume deficit related to the inability to swallow
- Hyperthermia related to the presence of infection

### Planning and Implementing Nursing Care

Planning and implementation of care includes maintaining a patent airway by observing for increasing respiratory distress. Emergency airway equipment should be readily available. Oxygen therapy, administration of medications, and maintenance of a calm and quiet environment are important nursing measures. Intravenous fluids are administered, with accurate intake and output, weight, and specific-gravity value measurements. Reassurance for both parents and child is necessary to reduce anxiety.

### Evaluating Nursing Care

Evaluation of care includes determining whether adequate ventilation is maintained as evidenced by normal respiratory rate and effort with no signs of distress. Auscultation of the chest should reveal clear breath sounds. Adequate hydration status should be maintained, with the child exhibiting normal urine output, normal specific-gravity values, and no signs of dehydration. Temperature should return to normal. Anxiety should be absent or mild.

## Respiratory Problems of School-Aged Children

### Tonsillitis

#### Pathophysiology

*Tonsillitis* is a local infection of the tonsils and occurs as a result of pharyngitis. The tonsils are involved in immunity and antibody production. Because of their location, tonsils are exposed to pathogens on a regular basis. This can lead to microabscesses with chronic or recurring infections.

Most cases of tonsillitis are caused by viruses. A small percentage of tonsillitis cases are caused by β-hemolytic streptococcus. As the palatine tonsils become inflamed and enlarged, they obstruct airflow and passage of food. If the adenoids become inflamed, they obstruct the posterior nares, and the child needs to breathe through the mouth. In addition, with inflamed adenoids, the eustachian tubes may become obstructed, resulting in otitis media.

### Medical Diagnosis and Management

Manifestations of tonsillitis include sore throat, dry and irritated oropharyngeal membranes, low-grade fever, mild headache, and loss of appetite. The child's voice is hoarse, and a productive cough may be present. With chronic infections, there is persistent anterior or posterior cervical adenopathy.

Treatment of viral tonsillitis consists of supportive care. Bacterial tonsillitis requires culture of the organism and appropriate antibiotic therapy. Tonsillectomies are performed when tonsillitis causes airway obstruction; they may also be helpful in reducing the number of recurrent throat infections.

### Nursing Assessment and Diagnosis

Assessment of tonsillitis includes inspection of the pharyngeal area for erythema and exudate. Palpation of lymph nodes may indicate chronic infection. The nurse assesses the child for severity of respiratory distress associated with airway obstruction. Hydration and nutritional status are closely monitored. A history should include questions related to onset of symptoms and number of episodes of tonsillitis.

Nursing diagnoses for tonsillitis might include the following:

- Ineffective airway clearance related to inflammation of the oropharyngeal membranes
- Ineffective breathing pattern related to blockage of the upper airways
- Hyperthermia related to the infection
- Pain related to inflammation
- Altered nutrition: less than body requirements related to sore throat and anorexia
- High risk for fluid volume deficit related to the inability to take fluids
- Anxiety (child) related to respiratory involvement and the infective process

### Planning and Implementing Nursing Care

Planning and implementation of nursing care includes supportive and comfort measures such as salt water gargles, throat sprays, and cold liquids. Acetaminophen is given for fever and pain. A soft diet should be provided; drinking fluids should be encouraged. Administration of antibiotics is appropriate for bacterial tonsillitis. Parents are instructed about medication administration, signs of respiratory distress, and follow-up visits.

### Evaluating Nursing Care

Evaluation of care is similar to evaluation of care for pharyngitis.

## Acute Respiratory Problems

A wide variety of acute respiratory problems are found in children. The problems discussed in this section include streptococcal pharyngitis and the pneumonias. Nasopharyngitis is discussed in Chapter 35.

## Streptococcal Pharyngitis

### Pathophysiology

*Streptococcal pharyngitis,* or strep throat, is an inflammation of the pharynx caused by β-hemolytic streptococcus. Fifteen percent of children have throat cultures that are positive for this organism but do not exhibit symptoms of streptococcal pharyngitis; therefore, a positive culture does not invariably indicate the presence of this condition.

### Medical Diagnosis and Management

Manifestations of streptococcal pharyngitis include mild to severe sore throat, fever, headache, abdominal pain, vomiting, and difficulty swallowing. In addition, the throat is erythematous, exudate may be present, and the tonsils may be enlarged. Cervical adenopathy may be present. Symptoms normally last from 1 to 5 days but may persist for up to 2 weeks. Complications of streptococcal pharyngitis include rheumatic fever and glomerulonephritis.

Treatment consists of antibiotic therapy. Oral penicillin is usually given for 10 days unless the child is allergic to this drug. Erythromycin is given when penicillin allergy occurs.

### Nursing Assessment and Diagnosis

Assessment of streptococcal pharyngitis includes inspection of the throat for the presence of redness, exudate, and swelling of the pharyngeal structures. The child is observed for signs of respiratory distress, such as tachypnea, retractions, stridor, cyanosis, and tachypnea. The child also is assessed for dehydration. After the onset of symptoms, the child is assessed for complications of streptococcal pharyngitis.

Nursing diagnoses for streptococcal pharyngitis might include the following:

- Ineffective breathing pattern related to inflammation of the pharynx

- Hyperthermia related to infection
- Pain related to inflammation of the pharynx
- Fatigue related to the infectious process
- High risk for fluid volume deficit related to difficulty in swallowing

### Planning and Implementing Nursing Care

Planning and implementation of care includes supportive therapy, rest, hydration, administration of antibiotics and antipyretics, and isolation from others until the risk of spread of the infection has passed. Parents are taught about medications, the importance of finishing the entire course of antibiotics, hydration, and symptoms of respiratory distress.

### Evaluating Nursing Care

Evaluation of care includes assessing whether symptoms of streptococcal pharyngitis are resolved. The child's fever should return to normal within a week. The child should not exhibit signs of dehydration, pain, or fatigue.

## Pneumonia

*Pneumonia* is an infection of the lung tissue caused by bacterial, viral, fungal, and mycoplasmal organisms. Of these infectious agents, only bacterial and viral causes are discussed in this chapter.

## Bacterial Pneumonia

### Pathophysiology

*Bacterial pneumonia* is an infection of the lungs caused by bacteria. Bacterial pneumonia occurs most frequently in infancy. The causative organisms are pneumococci, streptococci, staphylococci, and chlamydia. Pneumococcal pneumonia is the most common form of bacterial pneumonia seen in childhood. In this type of bacterial pneumonia, pneumococcal organisms are commonly aspirated from the nasopharynx. Streptococcal pneumonia is usually seen in children between the ages of 3 and 5 years; it rarely occurs in infants. Streptococcal pneumonia is often preceded by a viral infection. Staphylococcal pneumonia can progress rapidly unless diagnosed and treated early. The disease occurs most often between October and May, and usually affects children under the age of 1 year. Staphylococcal pneumonia is often preceded by a viral infection. Chlamydial infections occur in infants up to 4 months of age and are acquired at the time of vaginal delivery from an infected mother.

In bacterial pneumonia, the alveoli become inflamed, with increased capillary permeability. Fluid leaks into the interstitial space and fills the alveoli. The exudative fluid that fills the alveoli contains fibrin, bacteria, leukocytes, and erythrocytes. Streptococcal pneumonia may result in large serosanguineous or purulent pleural effusions. Staphylococcal pneumonia is often unilateral, with large areas of hemorrhagic necrosis that results in lung abscesses. All types of bacterial pneumonia may result in varying degrees of residual fibrosis.

### Medical Diagnosis and Management

Symptoms of bacterial pneumonia include a sudden onset of high fever, "bed-shaking" chills, cough, and signs of respiratory distress, including tachypnea, dyspnea, retractions, nasal flaring, grunting, cyanosis, hypoxia, and anxiety. White blood cell counts are elevated. Bronchial or tubular breath sounds are heard over consolidated lung tissue. Scattered rales and rhonchi are heard over the affected areas. If pleural effusion is present, breath sounds are decreased, and a pleural friction rub can be heard.

Treatment includes antibiotic therapy, drainage of purulent secretions, hydration, and oxygen therapy. If empyema (pus in the pleural cavity) occurs, drainage with a thoracotomy tube may be necessary.

### Nursing Assessment and Diagnosis

Assessment of the child with bacterial pneumonia includes observation of respiration, with particular attention to signs of respiratory distress. Breath sounds are auscultated for areas of consolidation. Cardiac status is monitored for decreased cardiac output. Temperature is measured for degree of elevation.

Nursing diagnoses for bacterial pneumonia might include the following:

- Ineffective airway clearance related to inflamed alveoli
- Ineffective breathing pattern related to exudate in the alveoli
- Impaired gas exchange related to decreased lung capacity
- Fluid volume deficit related to decreased cardiac output
- Hyperthermia related to the infectious process
- Fatigue related to the infection
- Anxiety (child) related to symptoms
- Pain related to lung consolidation

### Planning and Implementing Nursing Care

Planning and implementation of care is supportive and aimed at promoting rest. Oxygen is administered for hypoxemia by means of a mist tent or nasal cannula. To facilitate secretion removal, the child's position is changed every 1 to 2 hours, and postural drainage is performed if the child can tolerate the procedure. Intravenous fluids maintain hydration and provide a route for antibiotic administration. Specific-gravity value and accurate intake and output measurements are necessary. Antipyretics are given to reduce fever. Promotion of rest is accomplished by organizing care to allow for prolonged rest periods. Support and reassurance should be provided for parents to reduce anxiety. Isolation is instituted if the child is contagious. Play should consist of low-energy activities. Discharge planning includes instructing the parents about medication administration, increased fluid intake, humidified air, signs of respiratory distress, postural drainage techniques, and follow-up care.

### Evaluating Nursing Care

Evaluation of the child with bacterial pneumonia includes observing the child for absence of respiratory distress and fever. The child should exhibit improved breath sounds and maintenance of adequate hydration status. In addition, the child should participate in activities appropriate for age and developmental level.

## Viral Pneumonia

### Pathophysiology

*Viral pneumonia* is caused by a variety of viruses, the most common of which is RSV. Other viruses causing pneumonia include parainfluenza viruses, adenoviruses, enteroviruses, rhinoviruses, and herpes simplex virus.

### Medical Diagnosis and Management

Symptoms of viral pneumonia are similar to bacterial pneumonia. Usually, viral pneumonia occurs after several days of cough and rhinitis. Fever is present but generally is lower than with bacterial pneumonia. Cough may become productive as the disease progresses. Adventitious pulmonary sounds are absent or minimal, with scattered rales.

Viral pneumonia has no specific treatment. Antibiotics are given when secondary bacterial infections develop. Supportive measures include oxygen, fluids, and rest.

### Nursing Assessment and Diagnosis

Assessment and diagnosis of the child with viral pneumonia is the same as for bacterial pneumonia.

### Planning and Implementing Nursing Care

Planning and implementation of care for viral pneumonia is similar to that for bacterial pneumonia. In viral pneumonia, however, antibiotics are generally ineffective and are not prescribed. If a secondary infection develops, the nurse administers prescribed antibiotics as appropriate.

### Evaluating Nursing Care

Evaluation of care is the same as for bacterial pneumonia.

## Aspiration of Hydrocarbons

### Pathophysiology

Aspiration or inhalation of hydrocarbons in children under 6 years of age accounts for up to 10 percent of childhood poisonings. The hydrocarbons most often inhaled or aspirated are furniture polish, kerosene, airplane glue, paint removers, charcoal lighter fluid, and gasoline. Teenagers may aspirate gasoline when siphoning gasoline for their cars. These substances enter the lungs by aspiration during swallowing, vomiting, or gastric lavage. Once in the lungs, the interaction of the hydrocarbons with surfactant increases surface tension. Increased surface tension results in alveolar collapse, edema, and hemorrhage. Alveolar macrophages and lung epithelium are damaged. Bronchospasm occurs because of irritation to the airways. Impaired gas exchange results in hypoxemia.

### Medical Diagnosis and Management

Symptoms may not be seen for up to 12 to 24 hours after ingestion, depending on the substance. Symptoms include infiltrates bilaterally as seen on chest radiograph; fever; dyspnea; cough; and blood-tinged, watery secretions. Breath sounds are similar to those heard in other pneumonias. Signs of respiratory distress may be present and depend on the amount of hydrocarbons ingested. Complications of hydrocarbon ingestion include pneumothorax, pleural effusion, pneumatoceles (swelling of lung tissue), and subcutaneous emphysema. Secondary bacterial and viral infections may occur.

Treatment includes supportive measures. Children who remain asymptomatic for 6 hours are observed closely at home for signs of respiratory distress. When respiratory distress is present, the child is treated with oxygen. Depending on the substance ingested, aspiration of the substance through a nasogastric tube may be performed. Some clinicians insert an endotracheal tube before lavage to ensure that aspiration does not occur. The endotracheal tube also allows for oxygen delivery and removal of secretions. Vomiting is not induced because of the risk of aspiration. Chest physiotherapy may be instituted. Antibiotics are not prescribed unless secondary bacterial infections develop.

### Nursing Assessment and Diagnosis

Assessment of the child with hydrocarbon aspiration includes observing the child to be certain that the airway is patent and for signs of respiratory distress, including dyspnea, tachypnea, cyanosis, nasal flaring, retractions, and hypoxemia. A complete history is obtained, with careful attention given to the hydrocarbon ingested.

Nursing diagnoses for hydrocarbon aspiration might include the following:

- Impaired gas exchange related to increased surface tension in the lungs
- Ineffective breathing pattern related to damage to the alveoli and lung epithelium
- Ineffective airway clearance related to pneumothorax
- Altered tissue perfusion related to decreased oxygenation
- High risk for infection related to stasis
- High risk for fluid volume deficit related to inability to swallow
- Hyperthermia related to infection
- Anxiety (child) related to severity of symptoms
- Fear related to the possible outcome
- Ineffective family coping: compromised related to the child's acute condition and hospitalization

### Planning and Implementing Nursing Care

Planning and implementation of care includes intubation, mechanical ventilation, and oxygen therapy if the aspiration is severe. Nasogastric lavage may also be performed after intubation. ABG levels and pulse oximetry are monitored continuously for changes in oxygenation. Intravenous fluids are given to maintain hydration, and urine output is monitored. Since gastroenteritis may result from the ingested hydrocarbon, the child is observed for signs of infection. Antipyretics are administered for fever.

Support for the parents helps reduce guilt, fear, and anxiety. Parents often experience guilt for leaving harmful substances within reach of the child. They also experience fear and anxiety related to the degree of illness experienced by the child. Parents should be instructed about how to "childproof" their home. Harmful substances should be kept out of reach of children. Parents should be given the telephone number of the nearest poison control center in their area.

### Evaluating Nursing Care

Evaluation consists of observing the child for improvement of respiratory status. The child should maintain adequate hydration, tissue perfusion, and cardiac output. The child should remain afebrile and should show no signs of infection. The parents should understand the importance of making sure that hazardous substances in the home cannot be reached by children.

## Lipoid Pneumonia

### Pathophysiology

*Lipoid pneumonia* is an infection of the lungs that occurs after aspiration of material with a lipoid base, such as mineral or castor oil. It is a chronic, interstitial, proliferative, inflammatory process. It occurs most often in children who have difficulty swallowing, e.g., those with a cleft palate, debilitated children, or those who are fed and remain in a supine position, who are force-fed, or who are given oil-based products when crying. Also, aspiration of milk during the first year of life can result in lipoid pneumonia.

After aspiration of the lipoid substance, a proliferative, interstitial, inflammatory reaction occurs that may produce an exudative pneumonia, which then results in a bacterial or viral infection. Next, a diffuse, chronic, proliferative fibrosis occurs; finally, multiple pulmonary nodules form.

### Medical Diagnosis and Management

Symptoms of lipoid pneumonia include cough and dyspnea. Unless a secondary infection develops, the child remains afebrile. Changes detectable by chest radiograph depend on the type of oil aspirated and the degree of aspiration.

Treatment consists primarily of eliminating exposure to lipoid substances. If secondary bacterial infections occur, antibiotics are prescribed. Airway closure and collapse may result, causing hypoxemia. When airway closure and/or collapse occur, continuous distending airway pressure of the lungs is instituted and may result in decreased hypoxemia.

### Nursing Assessment and Diagnosis

Assessment of the child with lipoid pneumonia includes a complete history of ingested substances, feeding patterns, and sleeping positions. Sleeping patterns are assessed to determine if the child is at risk for aspiration. The nurse assesses airway patency and oxygenation status and observes for signs of respiratory distress.

Nursing diagnoses for lipoid pneumonia might include the following:

- Impaired gas exchange related to aspiration of lipoids into the lungs
- High risk for infection related to secondary bacterial infections
- Anxiety related to impaired respirations
- Ineffective family coping: compromised related to feelings of guilt and concern

### Planning and Implementing Nursing Care

Planning and implementation of care consists of maintaining a patent airway and adequate oxygenation. These measures include feeding the infant or child slowly and positioning the child with the head elevated. Water-based medications should be substituted when possible. Positioning the child on the abdomen or side, rather than on the back, during sleep lessens the possibility of aspiration.

Parental education includes feeding techniques, positioning, and administration of medications.

### Evaluating Nursing Care

Evaluation of the child with lipoid pneumonia includes observing the proper positioning of the child by the parents when feeding or during sleep. The child should not exhibit further signs of anxiety, respiratory distress, or worsening hypoxemia. The child should remain free of infection or be treated with antibiotics if fever develops.

## Diphtheria

Diphtheria, an infectious disease, is discussed in detail in Chapter 19.

# Chronic Respiratory Problems

## Cystic Fibrosis

### Pathophysiology

*Cystic fibrosis* is an autosomal recessive hereditary disorder of the exocrine glands that affects the pancreas, respiratory system, gastrointestinal tract, salivary glands, liver, nose, paranasal sinuses, sweat glands, and reproductive tract. In 1989, the specific gene responsible for cystic fibrosis was identified (Summitt, 1990). Cystic fibrosis affects whites most often and occurs at the rate of 1 in every 1600 to 1700 live births.

Several mechanisms result in the pathology associated with cystic fibrosis. First, exocrine gland ducts and passageways become obstructed with viscous, tenacious mucous secretions. Second, electrolyte concentrations in exocrine secretions are abnormal. The pathology related to the respiratory system includes excess secretion of viscous mucus that has increased calcium and potassium concentrations and decreased sodium and chloride levels. The ciliary lining in the respiratory tract moves five to ten times slower than normal, a condition identified as ciliary dyskinesia. As a result, secretions accumulate in the respiratory passages that predispose the child to respiratory infections. Third, secretions accumulate in the airways, which result in obstruction, air-trapping, and infection. Finally, infection initiates pathological changes.

The initial insult results from a combination of infection and excess secretions. As the infection develops, excess mucus is produced. The mucus is viscous and tenacious, resulting in thick mucous plugs that obstruct the bronchioles and bronchi. When airways are obstructed, further infection occurs, producing more secretions. Recurrent infections lead to bronchiectasis and fibrosis.

*Pseudomonas aeruginosa* is the organism that most commonly causes infection in cystic fibrosis, and it becomes resistant to medications. The child is susceptible to infections because the alveolar macrophages have decreased phagocytic ability. As the infections recur, they cause bronchial wall destruction and fibrosis.

When the bronchial walls are destroyed, the ciliary lining is affected, resulting in impaired secretion clearance. The thick, tenacious mucus collects in the lungs. The combination of bronchial wall destruction and secretion accumulation increases airway pressure. Increased intra-luminal pressure produces dilation of the airways. As the disease progresses due to recurrent infections and bron-chiectasis, the lung becomes increasingly hyperinflated (Kersten, 1989). Thus, cystic fibrosis is considered a self-perpetuating disease. The overall effect of cystic fibrosis is airway obstruction, impaired ventilation, and decreased oxygenation.

One complication for older children with cystic fibro-sis is pneumothorax. It may be unilateral and asymptoma-tic, requiring no treatment, or it may be bilateral and symptomatic, requiring placement of chest tubes and drainage. A second complication is hemoptysis (streaks of blood in the sputum), which occurs with severe bron-chiectasis. If the amount of blood in the sputum is small, the child is placed on antibiotic therapy and bed rest, and chest physiotherapy is stopped. If hemoptysis becomes severe and life threatening, bronchial artery embolization is performed.

### Medical Diagnosis and Management

Symptoms of cystic fibrosis depend on the severity of the disease and reflect exocrine gland abnormalities. The se-cretions from sweat glands contain elevated sodium and chloride levels. In the neonate, inspissated meconium may result in small bowel obstruction. As the child ages, growth failure, steatorrhea, abdominal cramps, flatus, constipa-tion, and increased appetite are common clinical features. The portal system is also affected. Portal hypertension with esophageal varices and hemorrhoids may occur. De-creased fertility in women and sterility in men are com-monly seen.

Pulmonary involvement begins with a dry, repetitive cough that becomes productive as the disease progresses. In the infant, wheezing is a predominant symptom be-cause of the infant's small airways. Also, the child has a persistent runny nose. Because of the chronicity of the disease, the child develops clubbing (curvature of the nails accompanied by soft tissue enlargement), a hyperinflated or barrel chest, hemoptysis, and pulmonary fibrosis.

Diagnosis of cystic fibrosis is suspected in infants who fail to gain adequate weight, have a persistent cough, and have multiple pulmonary infections. The sweat test is per-formed and considered positive when sweat chloride is greater than 60 mEq/L. Any level of chloride above 30 mEq/L is considered suspicious.

There are four major goals in the treatment of cystic fibrosis. The first goal is to maintain a patent airway through postural drainage and bronchodilator therapy.

The second goal is to control pulmonary infections with antibiotic therapy. Antibiotic therapy includes drugs that target destruction of *Pseudomonas aeruginosa* and *Staph-ylococcus aureus,* which are the most commonly identi-fied organisms in cystic fibrosis. These drugs include am-inoglycosides (gentamycin, tobramycin, amikacin) and semisynthetic penicillins (piperacillin, ticarcillin, meth-icillin, and nafcillin). The third goal is to maintain electro-lyte balance, especially of sodium and chloride. Extra salt-ing of food accomplishes this goal. In hot and humid weather, supplemental salt tablets may be required. The fourth goal is to maintain adequate nutritional status. Chil-dren with cystic fibrosis have pancreatic involvement, with pancreatic insufficiency. Due to this problem, infants are given predigested protein formulas, and increased calo-ries are supplied by medium-chain triglyceride oil. Pan-creatic enzymes, including lipase, amylase, and protease, are given with meals and snacks to help in the digestion of food. Because children with cystic fibrosis are unable to completely absorb fat-soluble vitamins, vitamins A, D, E, and K are supplemented. Vitamin K deficiency can result in prolonged prothrombin time. Iron supplements may also be required. If the child continues to lose weight, total parenteral nutrition becomes necessary. As of 1988, most agencies reported the median life expectancy for people with cystic fibrosis to be greater than 27 years (Summitt, 1990).

### Nursing Assessment and Diagnosis

Assessment of the child with cystic fibrosis includes mon-itoring parameters such as respiratory status, nutritional status, fluid and electrolyte balance, elimination, and cop-ing abilities.

Respiratory status is measured by pulmonary function studies. Oxygenation status can be quantified with pulse oximetry and ABG studies. The child is observed for signs of respiratory distress, including tachypnea, retractions, dyspnea, and cyanosis. Clubbing of fingers and toes occurs over time. Auscultation of the chest may reveal bilateral crackles and wheezes. Sputum is observed for signs of infection or hemoptysis.

Nutritional status is assessed by measuring the child's height and weight. These measurements are compared with the initial admission assessment of height and weight. The child is assessed for signs of pancreatitis, which in-clude epigastric pain, abnormal laboratory values, nausea, and vomiting. Hyperglycemia, polyuria, polydipsia, and polyphagia may be present if the child develops diabetes.

Stools are observed for color, consistency, frequency, and odor. Electrolytes are monitored, especially sodium, chloride, potassium, and calcium.

Coping abilities of the child and parents are assessed with respect to management of stress, the disease process, and medications. It is also important to assess the coping abilities of siblings.

Nursing diagnoses for cystic fibrosis might include the following:

- Ineffective gas exchange related to impaired respiratory effort
- Ineffective airway clearance related to increased mucus secretions
- High risk for infection related to accumulated secretions in the respiratory tract
- Altered nutrition: less than body requirements related to anorexia
- Self-esteem disturbance related to a chronic illness
- Body image disturbance related to physical appearance
- Ineffective individual coping related to the prognosis
- Ineffective family coping: compromised related to the chronicity of the disease
- Anticipatory grieving related to the prognosis
- Anxiety related to exacerbations of the disease process

## Planning and Implementing Nursing Care

Planning and implementation of nursing care includes assisting the child to maintain optimal functioning. Pulmonary infections are prevented and controlled by identification of infection with sputum cultures and compliance with antibiotic therapy. Maintenance of a patent airway includes postural drainage and breathing exercises. Bronchodilators are aerosolized several times per day. If oxygen is needed at home, appropriate home care referrals are made to provide this therapy, and the parents are instructed in its use. Emergency telephone numbers are listed and kept by the telephone.

Infants with cystic fibrosis require predigested formula. For older children, the parents should plan balanced meals that are high in protein and carbohydrates and contain variable amounts of fat, depending on the child's need for calories and tolerance of fat. Medium-chain triglycerides are used as dietary supplements. Pancreatic enzymes are given with meals and snacks. For younger children, these enzymes may be mixed with pureed fruit. Older children can swallow capsules whole. Fat-soluble vitamins (A,D,E, and K) are given in a water-soluble base. Children with liver disease or who are taking large doses of antibiotics may need additional B-complex, C, and K vitamins and folic acid. Children with diarrhea or who fail to thrive may need iron and other mineral supplements. In the summer or during exercise, sodium chloride supplements should be administered. Parents should be given instructions about enzyme administration, vitamin and mineral supplements, and electrolyte replacement. In addition, parents are instructed about signs of electrolyte imbalance and congestive heart failure.

Coping with a chronic debilitating disease is difficult for both parents and child. Parents may experience guilt for "causing" the disease. A genetic counselor can explain and clarify information about the hereditary aspect of the disease and provide information that needs to be considered before future pregnancies are attempted.

The family should be referred to all available support systems. Community agencies such as the Cystic Fibrosis Foundation and the American Lung Association can provide information about the disease. State agencies can provide financial support and home care support for families with children who have cystic fibrosis. Parents often are unable to cope with the demands of these children. They need respite care so they have time away from these demands. They need reassurance that they are not being bad parents when they enjoy time away from the child. Nurses should allow the family members to express and work through feelings of anger, guilt, and frustration. The parents are taught stress management techniques. Referrals for counseling are initiated when appropriate. The parents may need assistance with anticipatory grieving as the child becomes weaker and more seriously ill.

Children with cystic fibrosis appear wasted. They do not grow and thrive as do their peers. They develop barrel chests and have chronic coughs. During adolescence, they do not mature as quickly as normal children. Girls suffer amenorrhea and lack breast development. These factors contribute to impaired body image and low self-esteem.

Psychological support for the child with the disease is as important as it is for the parents. The child may experience many of the same emotions as the parents, including anger, frustration, hostility, and sadness. Through involvement in support groups for children with cystic fibrosis, the child can establish new friendships and peer support. Summer camps are available for these children that provide activities appropriate for age and developmental level; nurses are available at these camps to provide care for the child. Time away from home also allows a respite for the parents.

## Evaluating Nursing Care

Evaluation of nursing care is accomplished by determining the degree of success in achieving patient care goals. The child should maintain a patent airway with no signs of respiratory distress. Breath sounds should be clear over the entire chest. The child should be able to clear the airway of the thick secretions. The parents and child should be able to demonstrate pulmonary exercises, including postural drainage and breathing exercises. They should verbalize the importance of taking medications and performing breathing exercises. The child should demonstrate positive self-esteem and an appropriate perception of body image. The child and parents should be able to recognize the signs and symptoms of respiratory infections or deterioration. Follow-up care should be arranged.

Parents should be able to plan and follow the prescribed diet. They should recognize the importance of administration of the pancreatic enzymes and supplemental vitamins and minerals. The child's gastrointestinal function should remain adequate, without steatorrhea. Serum electrolytes should remain within normal limits.

The parents should demonstrate appropriate coping strategies. They should include all therapeutic measures in the child's daily care. They should facilitate normal growth and development of the child. The family should seek support as needed. The child should participate in age- and developmentally appropriate activities.

## Asthma

### Pathophysiology

*Asthma,* a condition in which labored breathing is accompanied by wheezing, is caused by a spasm of bronchial tubes or swelling of their mucous membranes. The most common chronic disease in children, it affects 5% to 10% of all children and accounts for 4000 deaths annually. Most children experience their first symptoms before the age of 5. Half of the new cases of asthma diagnosed in children occur before the age of 1 year (Traver & Martinez, 1988). About half of all children with asthma become asymptomatic as they reach adulthood. Before adolescence, boys are affected twice as often as girls; after adolescence, girls and boys are equally affected (Avery & First, 1989).

Asthma is a reversible form of airway obstruction. Three events contribute to the symptoms experienced in asthma: bronchial smooth muscle spasm, inflammation and edema of the bronchial mucosa, and production and retention of thick, tenacious pulmonary secretions. The result is an increased airway resistance, premature closure of the airways, hyperinflation, increased work of breathing, and impaired gas exchange. Normally, during inspiration, the negative pressure within the thorax pulls the airways open, allowing air to enter. On expiration, the lungs contract and air moves out of the lungs. In asthma, the airways are swollen and mucus filled. Air moves into the lungs and becomes trapped because of the obstruction. The lungs become hyperinflated. In addition, spasm of the bronchial smooth muscle contributes to this overinflation. The child expends increased energy to breathe and experiences hypoxemia and hypercapnia.

Asthma attacks may be triggered by extrinsic factors such as pollen, dust, mold, feathers, and animal dander. Foods that may trigger asthma attacks include eggs, milk, nuts, grains, and chocolate. Other extrinsic factors include viral agents, especially the respiratory syncytial virus, parainfluenza viruses, rhinoviruses, and influenza viruses. Psychogenic factors have also been found to be responsible for initiation of asthma attacks. Stress or emotionally charged or exciting events can stimulate an attack. Finally, air pollution, tobacco smoke, changes in climate, excessive exercise, and medications can all trigger an asthma attack. See Chapter 22 for the role of the immune system in asthma.

### Medical Diagnosis and Management

Clinical manifestations of asthma are similar to those of airway obstruction and include dyspnea, retractions, tachypnea with prolonged expiration, cyanosis, wheezing, use of accessory muscles, and a cough. At first, the cough is nonproductive, but as the intensity of the cough increases, the child coughs up thick, tenacious secretions. During extreme respiratory distress, wheezing may be absent because of the lack of air movement. The child assumes a "tripod" position, sitting and hunched over. This position makes breathing easier. Many children complain of abdominal pain because of strenuous use of the abdominal muscles and diaphragm. Diaphoresis is common.

When a child does not respond to drugs that are normally effective and the asthma becomes increasingly more severe, a diagnosis of status asthmaticus is made. The child with status asthmaticus is admitted to the hospital and monitored in the intensive care unit. Endotracheal intubation is often required.

Treatment of asthma consists of maintaining optimal function, a normal life-style, and normal developmental pattern; minimizing symptoms of asthma; preventing acute attacks; and avoiding the side effects of therapy (Traver & Martinez, 1988). The most commonly administered medications used for children with asthma are listed in Table 23-4. During an acute attack, bronchodilators are administered to relieve bronchospasm and control symptoms. In a mild attack, sympathomimetic bronchodilators are nebulized and then inhaled. If the child does not respond, epinephrine is given subcutaneously. During an acute attack, humidified oxygen is administered to maintain arterial oxygen levels between 70 and 80 mmHg. The humidified oxygen is not supersaturated or heavily misted because it may worsen the bronchospasm. If inhaled bronchodilators and subcutaneous epinephrine fail, aminophylline is administered intravenously. Steroids may also be given early in the course of treatment.

In children with asthma, preventing acute attacks is the desired goal. Removal of environmental pollutants such as dust and tobacco smoke is beneficial. Exposure of the child to known allergens is minimized or eliminated. If the child develops a bacterial superinfection, antibiotics are given. The child is placed in a humidified environment and encouraged to increase fluids to facilitate removal of secretions. When the child experiences seasonal asthma, hypersensitization (allergy "shots") may be effective in decreasing or eliminating attacks.

*Table 23–4. Medications Used for Asthmatic Children*

| Action | Dosage | Side Effects | Nursing Implications |
|---|---|---|---|
| **Bronchodilators** | | | |
| *Epinephrine (Adrenalin)*<br>Bronchial smooth muscle relaxant; decongestant | 0.01 mg/kg sub q, up to 0.5 mg maximum in children 12 years of age and under. May be repeated at 20 min intervals up to 3 times | Tachycardia, palpitations, headache, increased blood pressure, pallor, tremors, nausea, vomiting | Monitor child's response to drug, including vital signs and oxygenation status; double check dosage before injecting. |
| *Aminophylline (Theophylline)*<br>Relaxes bronchial smooth muscle | Varies with age, body weight, and form of drug administered; therapeutic serum levels are maintained between 10 and 20 g/mL. Administered IV for an attack; may be administered orally or rectally | Nausea, vomiting, abdominal cramps, diarrhea, sleeplessness, tachycardia, headache, hypotension, nervousness, seizures | Monitor heart rate and rhythm with cardiac monitor. Monitor serum theophylline levels for toxicity. Infuse slowly when giving intravenous bolus. Monitor blood pressure for hypotension. Infuse no faster than 25 mg/min. |
| *Albuterol sulfate (Proventil, Ventolin)*<br>Relaxes bronchial smooth muscle | Inhalation: Children older than 12 years of age, 1–2 inhalations q 4–6 h; not recommended for children under 12 years old.<br>Oral: 2–6 years old, 0.1 mg/kg tid, not to exceed 4 mg, 3 times daily; 6–14 years old, 2 mg tid or qid, not to exceed 24 mg in 24 h; >14 years old, 2–6 mg tid or qid, not to exceed 32 mg in 24 h. Tablets and extended tablets are not given to children under 12 years old. | Tachycardia, palpitations, nervousness, dizziness, hypertension, nausea | Teach child proper use of inhaler. Not to be taken with over-the-counter medications because many cold remedies contain sympathomimetics that may intensify albuterol's action. |
| *Isoetharine (Bronkosol, Bronkometer)*<br>Relaxes bronchial smooth muscle | < 12 years old, 1–2 inhalations q 3–4 h, prn; >12 years old, 2 inhalations q 4–6 h, prn | Tachycardia, palpitations, nervousness, agitation, tremors, sleeplessness | Teach child proper use of inhaler. |
| *Metaproterenol (Alupent, Metaprel)*<br>Relaxes bronchial smooth muscle | Inhalation: Children > 12 years old, 2–3 inhalations q 6–8 h; not recommended for children < 12 years old<br>Oral: Not recommended for children < 6 years old; children < 27 kg = 10 mg/kg q 6–8 h; children > 27 kg = 20 mg/kg q 6–8 h | Tachycardia, palpitations, nervousness, nausea, vomiting, headache, hypertension, bad taste in mouth | Child must be instructed in proper use of inhaler. Rapid onset of action; with inhalation, effect occurs within 1 min; oral dose effect occurs within 15 min. Shake liquid thoroughly before giving dose. Store in airtight container between 15–30°C; protect from light; discard solutions that have turned brown or contain precipitate. |

*(continued)*

*Table 23–4. Medications Used for Asthmatic Children (Continued)*

| Action | Dosage | Side Effects | Nursing Implications |
|---|---|---|---|
| *Terbutaline (Brethine, Bricanyl)*<br>Relaxes bronchial smooth muscle | Oral: Children 12–15 years old, 2.5 mg tid<br>Subcutaneous: Children 12–15 years old, 0.1 mg/kg to maximum dose of 0.25 mg/kg<br>Inhalation: Children > 12 years old, 2 inhalations q 4–6 h; not recommended for children < 12 years old | Tachycardia, headache, tremors, nausea | Do not give to children under 12 years of age. Note that subcutaneous and oral dosages are different. Do not exceed recommended dose. If no improvement, notify physician. |
| Steroids | | | |
| *Prednisone*<br>Anti-inflammatory, anti-allergy activity. Decreases histamine production, enhances response of bronchial smooth muscle to sympathomimetic drugs | Children, total of 0.1–0.15 mg/kg/day or 4–5 mg/m² body surface area/day q 12 h, administered orally | Hyperglycemia, cushingoid features, striae, poor wound healing, susceptibility to infection, weight gain, edema, disturbance in linear growth, bruises easily, mood swings, increased blood pressure | Do not stop drug abruptly. Monitor for hyperglycemia. Monitor blood pressure at each office visit. Avoid exposure to infection. Maintain dosage schedule. Medication should be taken with food. In general, vaccinations are not recommended for children on steroids. |
| Mast Cell Stabilizer | | | |
| *Cromolyn Sodium (Intal)*<br>Stabilizes mast cells, which prevent release of chemical substances that cause bronchoconstriction, local edema, and inflammation | Children > 5 years old, 1 capsule (20 mg) inhaled q 6 h | Coughing, reflex bronchospasm, nasal congestion, pharyngeal irritation | Must teach child how to use Spinhaler. Drug will not stop an existing asthma attack. Teach child to use inhaler 10–15 min before exposure to irritants that initiate an asthma attack (*e.g.*, cold air, tobacco smoke). |

## Nursing Assessment and Diagnosis

Assessment of the child with asthma includes a thorough history of symptoms when exposed to irritants such as environmental and dietary factors and activities. A family history of asthma and a history of respiratory problems should be taken. A careful and complete history of medications is important, especially those causing symptoms and respiratory-related drugs.

Assessment during an acute attack consists of monitoring signs of respiratory distress, ABG results, and level of consciousness. The chest is auscultated for adventitious sounds, especially rhonchi and wheezes. Breath sounds may also be diminished. Vital signs and hydration status are assessed for changes or signs of dehydration. Both parents and child are anxious, depending on the severity of the attack.

Nursing diagnoses for asthma might include the following:

- Ineffective breathing pattern related to airway obstruction
- Impaired gas exchange related to air trapped in the lungs
- Ineffective airway clearance related to edema of the airway
- Fatigue related to increased respiratory effort
- Anxiety related to difficulty in breathing
- High risk for infection related to bacterial superinfection
- High risk for fluid volume deficit related to difficulty in swallowing

- Ineffective family coping: compromised related to chronic illness

## Planning and Implementing Nursing Care

Planning and implementation of care consists of maintaining a patent airway and adequate oxygenation, decreasing fatigue and anxiety, enhancing verbal communication, preventing infection, maintaining hydration, and promoting optimal function and coping.

During an acute attack, the nurse assists in maintaining adequate oxygenation by administering humidified oxygen by means of nasal prongs or mask. A mask is more efficient than nasal prongs but is not tolerated as well by younger children. Positioning the child in a high Fowler's position or sitting forward over the bedside table facilitates lung expansion. If respiratory distress is severe, endotracheal intubation is necessary, and mechanical ventilation is instituted. In general, patients are extubated within 24 to 48 hours.

Bronchodilators are administered by the nurse and are given intravenously, subcutaneously, or by means of a hand-held nebulizer. The bronchodilators commonly used for children with asthma are listed in Table 23-4. When aminophylline is given intravenously, especially bolus doses, the child is usually placed on a cardiac monitor to observe for dysrhythmias. The child is placed on bed rest or on rest periods between activities to combat fatigue and promote rest. Quiet play activities appropriate to the child's age and developmental level are encouraged. Rest periods are provided while performing activities of daily living to lessen fatigue. Sleep periods are encouraged and are not interrupted unless necessary. The nurse should approach the child in a calm and supportive manner to reduce anxiety.

Intravenous fluids are given for two reasons: to provide access for medication administration, and to prevent dehydration. If the child is alert and cooperative, drinking fluids is encouraged to prevent dehydration and help liquefy secretions.

Antibiotics are started if there is evidence of bacterial infection. The parents are taught the importance of following the dosage schedule and completing the course of the medications.

After the attack subsides and the child is nearing discharge, the nurse discusses prevention and early interventions for an asthma attack. Avoidance or removal of irritants in the home is important. Skin-testing may be recommended to identify the specific allergens that affect the child. Stress-reduction techniques are taught to minimize stress-induced attacks. Appropriate activities are discussed if the attack is exercise-induced. The parents are also taught immediate interventions that minimize an attack or support the child until help arrives, such as removal of the allergen, administration of a bronchodilator or epinephrine, and emotional support.

Adaptive coping abilities should be strengthened. The child's and parents' perceptions and responses to breathing difficulties are determined. The child and the parents are assessed for their abilities to cooperate and participate in intervention strategies that promote wellness. Families are taught about the disease and the rationale for interventions. Families should be involved in the child's care and are encouraged to verbalize their feelings and concerns.

## Evaluating Nursing Care

Evaluation of care of the child with asthma begins with determining to what degree the goals are met. The child's pulmonary function should be optimal for his or her age and condition. The ABG values should be within normal limits. Auscultation of the chest should reveal clear breath sounds without rhonchi or wheezes. The child and family should be able to verbalize and demonstrate proper breathing techniques and exercises that enhance optimal ventilation. The child's hydration status should be normal. No evidence of secondary infection should be present. The parents and child should know about the medications prescribed and should comply with the prescribed regimen. They should be referred to support groups as necessary. The parents and child should return for follow-up care.

## Tuberculosis

See Chapter 19 for a discussion of tuberculosis.

## Summary

All cells and tissues of the body require oxygen for their existence. Any problem that interferes with oxygen delivery or $CO_2$ removal threatens life. The nurse's role in care of the child with respiratory problems is extremely important. The nurse plays an active role in assessment, diagnosis, planning, implementation, and evaluation of nursing care for the child with respiratory problems. The nurse must have an understanding of child development when designing nursing care. The nurse must help children grow and reach their optimal potential despite their respiratory problems. In addition, the nurse must provide care to the child's parents and family. The child learns health-related attitudes from the parents and family members. Parents usually make health care decisions for the child; therefore, the family must be involved in planning, implementing, and evaluating care of the child with respiratory problems.

# Nursing Care Plan

## Assessment

Mary Smith is a 3-month-old black female being discharged to her home with a tracheostomy secondary to bronchopulmonary dysplasia.

### Chief Complaint

Mary's family expresses concern over care of the infant at home.

### Subjective Assessment

*Past History:* Born at 36 weeks' gestation, secondary to spontaneous premature labor. Mary was found to have immature lungs and was placed on mechanical ventilation. As a result of long-term mechanical ventilation, Mary developed bronchopulmonary dysplasia.

*Present History:* Mary was discharged to her home with a tracheostomy at 3 months of age.

*Family History:* Mother is 24; father is 28; both are well; no siblings. Maternal and paternal grandparents are alive and well.

## Objective Assessment

*Physical Examination:* Temp. 37.5°C (99.4°F) (rectal); pulse 120, right arm; resp. 33; B.P. 89/51; weight 4.2 kg. (9.25 lb.); height 55 cm. (21.75 in.).

Integument: Clear, normal turgor

Head: Normocephalic; anterior fontanelle open and soft

Eyes: Red reflex × 2; follows well

Ears: Tympanic membranes normal; canals clear

Nose: Patent

Throat: Tracheostomy in place

Neck: Supple without lymphadenopathy

Thorax and Lungs: Symmetrical; crackles heard in upper lobes; no intercostal retractions

Heart: RRR without murmurs; equal pulses

Abdomen: Soft masses or organomegaly

Genitalia: Normal female

Musculoskeletal: Full range of motion; without deformities

Neurological: Grossly intact

## Medical Diagnosis

Bronchopulmonary dysplasia

## Medical Plan

Tracheostomy

## Nursing Care Plan for a Child with a Tracheostomy

| Goals | Nursing Interventions | Evaluation Criteria |
|---|---|---|

*NURSING DIAGNOSIS #1: Ineffective Airway Clearance related to altered anatomic structure*

| Goals | Nursing Interventions | Evaluation Criteria |
|---|---|---|
| (L) Maintain patent airway | Suction tracheostomy tube when needed to clear thick secretions or mucous plugs, or when indicated by signs of respiratory distress | Child will maintain a clear airway<br>Child will breathe without difficulty |

*(continued)*

# Nursing Care Plan *(Continued)*

| Goals | Nursing Interventions | Evaluation Criteria |
|---|---|---|
| | Position infant on side or in prone position to avoid aspiration of secretions | Child will be able to maintain respirations within normal limits for quantity and quality |
| | Position infant to avoid hyperextention of neck and subsequent possible occlusion of airway | The child's family will be able to independently identify signs and symptoms of possible airway obstruction (pallor, cyanosis, retractions), and initiate appropriate interventions (suctioning, repositioning) to reinstate clear airway |
| | Avoid getting water into the airway during bathing | |
| | Avoid the use of turtlenecks and other clothing that could block the airway | |
| | Avoid use of baby powders and heavy perfumes around the infant | |
| | Avoid fuzzy clothing that could be picked off and placed by the child into the airway | |
| | Avoid small toys that could be placed by the child into the airway | |

*NURSING DIAGNOSIS #2: High Risk for Infection related to compromised skin integrity around tracheostomy tube*

| Goals | Nursing Interventions | Evaluation Criteria |
|---|---|---|
| (L) No signs of respiratory infection | Utilize clean technique, including handwashing, when performing procedures related to care and maintenance of the tracheostomy | The child will have no episodes of respiratory infection |
| | Utilize universal precautions when dealing with blood and body fluids | Any deviations from normal (for the child) are identified and referred to the physician |
| | Keep infant away from other children and adults who demonstrate signs of respiratory infection | |
| | Provide continuous sources of humidified air to tube through use of an artificial nose | |
| | Maintain adequate levels of hydration, to minimize the development of thick, mucous secretions | |

*(continued)*

# Nursing Care Plan *(Continued)*

| Goals | Nursing Interventions | Evaluation Criteria |
|---|---|---|
| | Monitor respirations for rate, depth, pattern, evidence of difficulty breathing (retractions, nasal flaring) | |
| | Observe for signs of possible respiratory infection (elevated temperature, irritability, restlessness, respiratory distress, decreased breath sounds). Consult the physician appropriately. | |

*NURSING DIAGNOSIS #3: Impaired Skin Integrity related to tracheostomy stoma, secretions, and presence of tracheostomy ties*

| Goals | Nursing Interventions | Evaluation Criteria |
|---|---|---|
| (S) Intact skin integrity around stoma | Three times a day, check area around stoma for evidence of redness, pressure, or skin breakdown | The child will maintain intact skin around stoma |
| | Avoid mechanical irritation from pressure of tracheostomy tubing, ties, or equipment on skin areas | The child's family will be able to independently recognize signs of infection, skin rash, or skin breakdown and will contact physician appropriately |
| | Keep skin areas dry and clean | |
| | Change tracheostomy ties frequently, especially if ties are moist | |
| | Clean skin around stoma with half strength hydrogen peroxide and rinse with clear water at last twice a day, and more often if necessary | |
| | Contact physician if area shows signs of infection (redness, swelling, discharge), skin rash, or skin breakdown | |

*NURSING DIAGNOSIS #4: High Risk for Activity Intolerance related to the imbalance between oxygen supply and demand*

| Goals | Nursing Interventions | Evaluation Criteria |
|---|---|---|
| (S) Avoid unnecessary energy expenditure | Encourage rest by providing quiet activities like reading a story or rocking in chair | The child will rest quietly, thereby avoiding unnecessary energy expenditure |
| | Provide for a quiet place for naps, away from other active siblings | |
| | Organize care, so the child can get rest between care activities | |

## References

Avery, M. E., & First, L. R. (1989). *Pediatric medicine.* Baltimore: Williams & Wilkins.

Bass, M., Kravath, R. E., & Glass, L. (1986). Death scene investigation in sudden infant death. *New England Journal of Medicine, 315,* 100–105.

Behrman, R. E., & Vaughan, V. C. (1987). *Nelson textbook of pediatrics* (13th ed.). Philadelphia: W. B. Saunders.

Benitz, W., & Tetatro, D. (1988). *Pediatric drug handbook* (2nd ed.). St. Louis: Mosby-Year Book.

Breslin, E. (1981). Prevention and treatment of pulmonary complications in patients after surgery of the upper abdomen. *Heart and Lung, 10*(3), 511–519.

Burton, G., Hodgkin, J., & Ward, J. (1991). *Respiratory care* (3rd ed.). Philadelphia: J. B. Lippincott.

Chernick, V., & Kendig, E. (1990). *Disorders of the respiratory tract in children* (5th ed.). Philadelphia: W. B. Saunders.

Cummings, J., D'Eugenio, D., & Gross, W. (1989). A controlled trial of dexamethasone in preterm infants at high risk for bronchopulmonary dysplasia. *New England Journal of Medicine, 320,* 1505.

Fine, P., & Clarkson, J. (1987). Reflections on the efficacy of pertussis vaccines. *Review of Infectious Disease, 9,* 866.

Grauer, K., Cavallro, D., & Gums, J. (1991). New developments in cardiopulmonary resuscitation. *American Family Physician, 43*(3), 832–844.

Kaplan, D. W., Bauman, A. E., & Kraus, H. F. (1984). Epidemiology of sudden infant death syndrome in American Indians. *Pediatrics, 74,* 1041–1046.

Kaplan, L. C. (1985). Choanal atresia and its associated anomalies. Further support for the CHARGE syndrome. *International Journal of Pediatric Otorhinolaryngology, 8,* 237.

Kersten, L. D. (1989). *Comprehensive respiratory care: A decision making approach.* Philadelphia: W. B. Saunders.

Klein, P., Kemper, M., Weissman, G., Rosenbaum, S., Askanazi, J., & Hyman, A. (1988). Attenuation of the hemodynamic responses to chest physiotherapy. *Chest, 93,* 38–42.

McClain, M. (1985). Sudden infant death syndrome: An update. *Journal of Emergency Nursing, 11*(5), 227–230.

Outwater, K., Meissner, H., & Peterson, M. (1988). Ribavirin administration to infants receiving mechanical ventilation. *American Journal of Diseases of Children, 142,* 512.

Peterson, D. R., Sabotta, M. A., & Daling, J. R. (1986). Infant mortality among subsequent siblings of infants who died of sudden infant death syndrome. *Journal of Pediatrics, 108*(6), 911–914.

Shapiro, B., Kacmarek, R., Cane, R., Peruzzi, R., & Hauptman, D. (1991). *Clinical application of respiratory care* (4th ed.). St. Louis: Mosby-Year Book.

Summitt, R. L. (1990). *Comprehensive pediatrics.* St. Louis: Mosby-Year Book.

Sutton, P. (1988). Chest physiotherapy: Time for reappraisal. *British Journal of Diseases of the Chest, 82,* 127–137.

Traver, G. A., & Martinez, M. (1988). Asthma update, part II: Treatment. *Journal of Pediatric Health Care, 2,* 227–233.

Ward, J. (1991). Applied humidity and aerosol therapy. In Burton, G., Hodgkin, J., & Ward, J. (Eds.). *Respiratory care* (3rd ed.). Philadelphia: J. B. Lippincott.

## Bibliography

Anthony, C. P., & Thibodeau, G. A. (1987). *Textbook of anatomy and physiology* (12th ed.). St. Louis: Mosby-Yearbook.

Buckley, R. H. (1987). Allergy. In Rudolph, A. M., & Hoffman, J. I. E. (Eds.). *Pediatrics* (18th ed.). Norwalk, CT: Appleton-Lange.

Burgess, W. R., & Chernick, V. (1985). *Respiratory therapy in newborn infants and children.* New York: Thieme-Stratton.

Carlo, W. A., & Chatburn, R. L. (1988). *Neonatal respiratory care* (3rd ed.). Chicago: Year Book Medical Publishers.

Castiglia, P. T., & Aquilina, S. (1982). Streptococcal pharyngitis: A persistent challenge. *Pediatric Nursing, 8*(6), 377–382.

Cystic Fibrosis Foundation. (1989). *Guide to diagnosis and management of cystic fibrosis.* New York: National Cystic Fibrosis Foundation.

Donohue, J. F. (1986). Status asthmaticus. *Consultant, 26*(7), 43–48, 48, 50.

Engel, N. S. (1989). Multiple drug therapy for pediatric tuberculosis. *MCM: American Journal of Maternal-Child Nursing, 14,* 169.

Fanconi, S. (1988). Reliability of pulse oximetry in hypoxic infants. *Journal of Pediatrics, 112*(3), 424–427.

Greenberg, C. S. (1988). *Nursing care planning guides for children.* Baltimore: Williams & Wilkins.

Guyton, A. C. (1991). *Textbook of medical physiology* (8th ed.). Philadelphia: W. B. Saunders.

Hagedorn, M., Gardner, S., & Abman, S. (1989). Respiratory diseases. In Merenstein, G., & Gardner S. *Handbook of neonatal intensive care* (2nd ed.). St. Louis: Mosby-Year Book.

Idell, S. (1987). Management of pneumothorax. *Emergency Medicine, 19*(17), 39–49.

Koff, P., Eitzman, D., & Neu, J. (1988). *Neonatal and pediatric respiratory care.* St. Louis: Mosby-Year Book.

Krohmer, J. R. (1988). Asthma out of control. *Emergency Medicine, 20*(9), 96–100, 105, 109.

Mack, J. E. (1988). Ribavirin: An antiviral agent with promise. *Pediatric Nursing, 14*(3), 220–221.

Mauro, R. D., Poole, S. R., & Lockhart, C. H. (1988). Differentiation of epiglottitis from laryngotracheitis in children with stridor. *American Journal of Diseases of Children, 142,* 679–682.

McKenry, L. M., & Salerno, E. (1989). *Mosby's pharmacology in nursing* (17th ed.). St. Louis: Mosby-Year Book.

Meyers, P. (1988). Parental adaptation to cystic fibrosis. *Journal of Pediatric Health Care, 2*(1), 20–28.

Nunn, J. F. (1969). *Applied respiratory physiology: With special reference to anesthesia.* New York: Butterworth.

Ray, C. G. (1988). Ribavirin. *American Journal of Diseases of Children, 142*(5), 488–489.

Reed, C. E. (1988). Basic mechanisms of asthma: Role of inflammation. *Chest, 94*(1), 175–177.

Rudolph, A. M., & Hoffman, J. I. E. (1987). *Pediatrics* (18th ed.). Norwalk, CT: Appleton-Lange.

Schafer, P., Kelly, M. K., Lehr, K., & Saracco, J. (1988). *Nursing care plans for the child: A nursing diagnosis approach.* Norwalk, CT: Appleton-Lange.

Shlafer, M., & Marieb, E. N. (1989). *The nurse, pharmacology, and drug therapy.* Menlo Park, CA: Addison Wesley.

Simon, B. M., & McGowen, J. S. (1989). Tracheostomy in young children: Implications for assessment and treatment of communication and feeding disorders. *Infants and Young Children, 1*(3), 1–9.

Stratton, C. W. (1986). Bacterial pneumonias—An overview with emphasis on pathogenesis, diagnosis, and treatment. *Heart and Lung, 15*(3), 226–244.

Thompson, J. M., McFarland, G. K., Hirsch, J. E., Tucker, S. M., & Bower, A. C. (1989). *Mosby's manual of clinical nursing* (2nd ed.). St. Louis: Mosby-Year Book.

Ulrich, S. P., Canale, S. W., & Wendell, S. A. (1990). *Nursing care planning guides: A nursing diagnosis approach* (2nd ed.). Philadelphia: W. B. Saunders.

Weinberg, H. (1988). Long term management of asthma. *Physician Assistant, 12*(6), 30–31, 35–36, 41–42.

Zahr, L. K., Connolly, M., & Page, D. R. (1989). Assessment and management of the child with asthma. *Pediatric Nursing, 15*(2), 109–114.

# Alterations in Cardiovascular Function

Pamela L. Pitts-Wilhelm

*Photograph by David Finn*

24

*Embryology*

*Anatomy*

*Physiology*

*Assessment*

*Nursing Diagnosis*

*Planning Nursing Care*

*Nursing Interventions*

*Evaluating Nursing Care*

*Congenital Heart Defects*

*Acyanotic Heart Defects*

*Acyanotic Heart Defects With Normal
    or Decreased Pulmonary Blood
    Flow*

*Cyanotic Heart Defects With Increased
    Pulmonary Blood Flow*

*Cyanotic Heart Defects With
    Decreased Pulmonary Blood Flow*

*Acquired Cardiovascular Diseases*

*Summary*

*Nursing Care Plan*

## Learning Objectives

*Upon completion of this chapter the reader will be able to:*

1. *Describe the embryonic development of the cardio-vascular system.*

2. *Discuss the anatomy and physiology of the cardio-vascular system.*

3. *Identify important data that should be collected during assessment of cardiovascular function.*

4. *State nursing diagnoses that apply to most cardio-vascular problems.*

5. *Identify nursing interventions that are common to most cardiovascular problems.*

6. *Describe pre-, intra-, and postoperative care for children undergoing cardiac surgery.*

7. *Develop a plan for evaluating nursing interventions for cardiovascular problems.*

8. *Demonstrate an understanding of the acyanotic heart defects, including atrial septal defects, ventricular septal defects, endocardial cushion defects, patent ductus arteriosus, and coarctation of the aorta.*

9. *Demonstrate an understanding of the acyanotic heart defects with normal or increased pulmonary blood flow, including aortic stenosis and pulmonic stenosis.*

10. *Demonstrate an understanding of the cyanotic heart defects with decreased pulmonary blood flow, including tetralogy of Fallot and tricuspid atresia.*

11. *Demonstrate an understanding of the following acquired cardiovascular diseases: bacterial endocarditis, pericarditis, rheumatic fever, congestive heart failure, and hypertension.*

12. *Explain why bacterial endocarditis represents a constant threat for children with cardiovascular disorders.*

13. *Identify strategies for helping children and families adapt to cardiovascular problems.*

## Key Terms

*angiography*
*aortic valve*
*arteriosclerosis*
*atherosclerosis*
*atrioventricular valves*
*cardiac catheterization*
*cardiac output*
*cardiac tamponade*
*cardiogenic shock*
*clubbing*
*coarctation*
*conduction system*
*congestive heart failure*
*cyanosis*
*diastole*
*ductus arteriosus*
*ductus venosus*
*echocardiography*
*electrocardiogram*
*endocarditis*
*endocardium*
*epicardium*
*flow*
*foramen ovale*
*heart rate*
*hypertension*
*mediastinum*
*mitral valve*
*murmur*
*myocardium*
*pericardium*
*point of maximum impulse*
*pressure*
*pulmonary compromise*
*pulmonary valve*
*pulse oximetry*
*resistance*
*stroke volume*
*systole*
*thrills*
*tricuspid valve*

Alterations in cardiovascular function arise from either congenital or acquired cardiovascular anomalies. Advances in medical and nursing management during the past three decades now allow many infants with cardiovascular problems to survive into adolescence and adulthood.

A congenital heart defect results from abnormal development of the heart, great blood vessels, or both during embryonic life, and leads to altered organ function. Approximately 0.5% to 1.0% of infants have congenital heart defects (Boughman et al., 1987; Hoffman, 1990). Defects may be caused by genetic, environmental, or genetic–environmental factors.

Acquired cardiovascular diseases result from pre-existing defects, complications of acute disease, or unknown causes. Congestive heart failure, the most common form, is often related to congenital heart defects.

Children with cardiovascular alterations and their families have many needs. Nurses must understand embryology as well as normal and altered cardiac anatomy and physiology. They must be competent in nursing assessment, diagnosis, planning, implementation, and evaluation of care for children and families who are affected by cardiac disease. The nursing process plays a critical role in the management of these individuals and provides an effective framework for nursing action.

## Embryology

The heart and circulatory system components develop from mesoderm. Two separate cardiogenic areas are first identified around the 15th day of gestation. The paired tubes, each filled with a hypocellular material known as cardiac jelly, fuse from a cephalic to caudal direction to create a single endocardial tube. Initially located above the head, the heart is one of the first organs to develop; its first pulsations begin during the third week of gestation. By the fourth week it contracts powerfully and efficiently enough to move blood. Most fetal cardiac development takes place between the fourth and tenth weeks of fetal gestation. The entire process of cardiac septation occurs between the 26th and 37th days (Colvin, 1990). Congenital defects may occur if this partitioning process is disturbed. By the seventh week of gestation, all four chambers and valves have formed, yet the heart is only 3 mm in size.

## Fetal Circulation

There are two essential concepts to keep in mind when considering fetal circulation, changes occurring at birth, and various congenital heart defects. These are that blood flows from an area of high resistance to low resistance, and that movement of blood through the vascular system is regulated by pressure and resistance.

Three types of fetal circulation exist: a high resistance pulmonary arterial system, and low resistance systemic and placental systems. Fetal blood flow patterns depend on the interaction of the two concepts about blood flow mentioned above with the three circulatory systems.

Understanding the concepts of pressure, flow, and resistance is essential. Pressure is a compression or force exerted on the body and is determined by a variety of factors, including blood volume, hydrostatic and osmotic forces, and resistance. Equally exerted in all directions, pressure is primarily expressed in millimeters of mercury (mm Hg). The difference in pressure between two points determines flow. Flow is movement of blood, usually expressed in liters per minute. Resistance to flow is the ease or difficulty fluid has flowing from one region to another. The friction of blood against blood vessel walls creates resistance. In addition, blood vessel size and blood viscosity have special relationships with resistance: as blood vessel size increases, resistance decreases; as blood viscosity increases, so does resistance. All three terms are interrelated and can be expressed by the formula:

$$\text{Pressure} = \text{resistance} \times \text{flow} \ (P = r \times f)$$

Two major structural components redirect fetal circulation: the foramen ovale and the ductus arteriosus. The foramen ovale is an opening in the atrial septum that allows blood to move from the right to the left atrium, thus bypassing the lungs. The remaining blood follows the neonatal and adult pattern of circulation. The ductus arteriosus allows blood to flow between the pulmonary artery and the aorta. Approximately 92% of the blood in the pulmonary artery does not perfuse the lungs but is shunted through the ductus arteriosus into the descending aorta. This shunting occurs because the pulmonary vascular resistance in the fluid-filled lungs is greater than the systemic vascular resistance. Blood returns to the placenta via umbilical arteries. Fetal circulation is shown in Figure 24-1.

## Circulatory Changes at Birth

Two major events that cause changes in circulation occur at birth: (1) the infant takes a breath of air, and (2) the infant is separated from the placenta.

Pulmonary vascular resistance and pulmonary blood pressure decrease with breathing and lung inflation; pulmonary arterial blood flow increases due to expansion of the pulmonary parenchyma. Vasodilation occurs because of increased partial pressure of oxygen, elevated pH, and various endogenous enzymes. Increased pulmonary blood flow increases pulmonary venous return. Left atrial pressure becomes greater than right atrial pressure, causing the foramen ovale to close and stopping the flow of blood from the right to left atrium. Pressure on the left side of the heart also increases due to a sudden rise in systemic vascular resistance following placental separation. Left ventricular muscle mass rapidly increases as the ventricle becomes

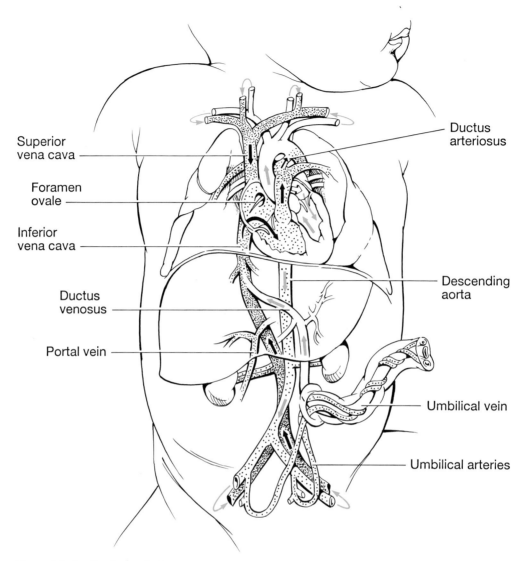

*Figure 24–1.  Fetal circulation.*

accustomed to pumping an increased volume and pressure load.

Aortic pressure is high enough to reverse blood flow through the ductus arteriosus for 15 to 20 hours after birth. Neurohormonal mediators and change in plasma oxygen tension (to approximately 50 mm Hg) cause the ductus arteriosus to constrict and close within a few days following birth.

Some of the above changes in circulation (Fig. 24-2) occur instantaneously at birth. Others are effected over hours or days. Failure of these alterations to take place may result in specific congenital heart defects.

## Anatomy

### The Heart

The heart is a muscular, four-chambered, blood-pumping organ that lies in the space between the two pleural cavities, which is called the mediastinum (Fig. 24-3). The heart

is located slightly to the left of the sternum, between the lungs, and above the diaphragm. The apex of the mature heart lies left of the midclavicular line and in the fifth intercostal space. Because an infant's heart is larger in relation to total body size, it is more horizontally positioned, with the apex at the third to fourth intercostal space and left of the midclavicular line.

The heart is enclosed by a double-walled, fibrous sac, the pericardium. This sac is filled with pericardial fluid, which lubricates the moving surfaces of the heart. The pericardium helps keep the heart in position, limits cardiac dilatation, and provides a protective barrier against infection and abnormal growth.

Three layers of tissue comprise the heart: the epicardium or outer layer; the myocardium, or middle layer and main muscle mass whose thickness varies with the amount of work required to pump blood; and the endocardium, or inner layer.

Four valves prevent backward flow of blood within the heart. Each valve is attached to the heart muscle by

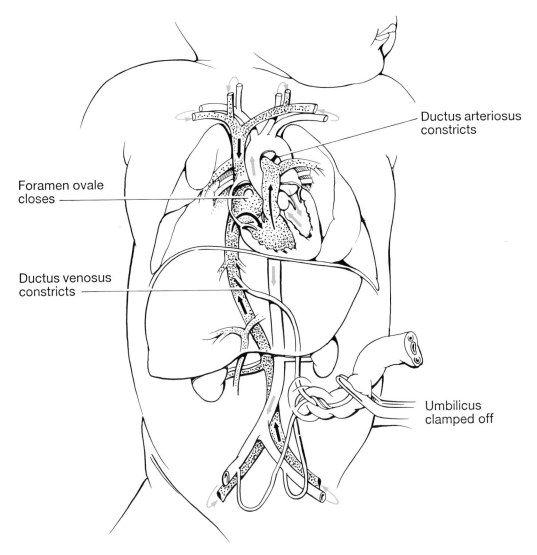

Ductus arteriosus
constricts

Foramen ovale
closes

Ductus venosus
constricts

Umbilicus
clamped off

*Figure 24–2.  Changes that occur in neonatal circulation.*

small tendinous cords called chordae tendineae. Two valves, the tricuspid and the mitral, are atrioventricular valves, meaning that they relate to both the atrium and the ventricle. The aortic and pulmonary valves are both known as semilunar valves. Mechanical sounds produced by valve closure create the familiar "lub-dub" of heart sounds, which result from the vibrations of valve closure.

## Blood Flow

The heart receives its blood supply via coronary arteries, which normally arise from the aorta, just above the aortic valve. Coronary veins collect desaturated myocardial blood and return it to the right atrium via the coronary sinus. Blood flow through the normal heart is shown in Figure 24-4. Systemic blood enters the right atrium from the inferior and superior vena cavae. It is pumped into the right ventricle and through the pulmonary artery into the lungs for oxygenation. After oxygenation, the blood returns to the left atrium through the pulmonary veins.

From there, it is pumped into the left ventricle and out the aorta into the systemic circulation.

## Conduction System

Most cardiac cells are working myocardial cells that generate the contractile force needed for coordinated muscular contraction. Special neuromuscular cells comprise what is referred to as the conduction system, the specialized nervous tissue in the heart that conducts electrical impulses through the heart. These cells are capable of *automaticity,* the spontaneous initiation of an organized and rhythmic electrical impulse. Tissue included in the conduction system includes the sinoatrial (SA) node (the cardiac pacemaker), three internodal atrial tracts (Bachmann, Wenckebach, and Thorel tracts), the atrioventricular (AV) node, the bundle of His, left and right bundle branches, and the Purkinje fibers. Impulses originate in the SA node and pass to the AV node. A fibrous ring between the atria and ventricles isolates each chamber anatomically and

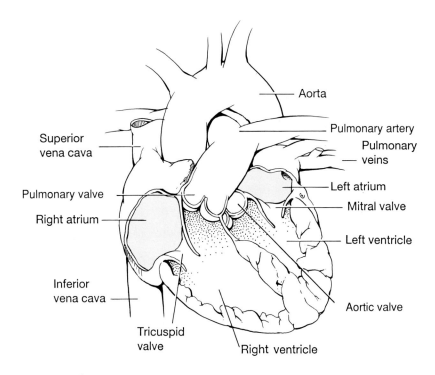

*Figure 24–3.   Anatomy of the heart.*

electrically. The conduction system passes through this ring. After a short delay of 0.08 to 0.12 second in the AV node, the wave of electrical excitation passes to the bundle of His, down the right and left bundle branches, and through the Purkinje fibers. These fibers transmit the electrical excitation rapidly through the inner surface of both ventricles, and contraction ensues. Electrical events always precede mechanical events. Sequential contraction

(systole) and relaxation (diastole) of both the atria and the ventricles is termed a cardiac cycle.

## Physiology

### Hemodynamic Considerations

Cardiac output, blood pressure, and resistance regulate blood flow to the tissues. Cardiac output (CO) is the amount of blood flow, in liters, pumped per minute by one ventricle. CO is determined by the formula

$$CO = SV \times HR$$

Stroke volume (SV) is the amount of blood pumped with each contraction, and heart rate (HR) is the number of cardiac contractions per minute. In young infants, regulation of cardiac output is largely dependent upon heart rate, as they have little ability to increase stroke volume and contractility. Stroke volume of the newborn is about 4 mL/beat (Adams, 1983), increasing to 60 to 120 mL/beat in adults.

Low cardiac output is a major cause of postoperative death in infants and children with heart disease. As cardiac output decreases, peripheral vasoconstriction shunts blood to vital internal organs. Early signs of decreasing CO include slight increases in HR, cool extremities, decreased urine output, and anxiety or irritability.

An easy, noninvasive, inexpensive method of monitoring CO is peripheral perfusion assessment. Close monitor-

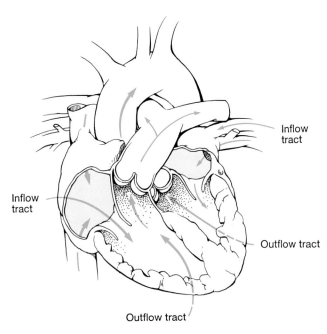

*Figure 24–4.   Blood flow through the heart.*

*Table 24–1. Peripheral Perfusion
Assessment*

| | Peripheral Pulses | Lower Extremity Warmth | Capillary Refill Time |
|---|---|---|---|
| 0 | Absent | Cool everywhere | >4 sec |
| 1 | Present only with Doppler | Warm from thigh to knee | >3 sec |
| 2 | Barely palpable | Warm from thigh to ankle | >2 sec |
| 3 | Normal | Warm from thigh to foot | >1 sec |
| 4 | Bounding | Warm from thigh to toe | <1 sec |

(Adapted from Fagan, M.J. [1988]. Relationship between nurses' assessments of perfusion in pediatric patients with cardiovascular disease. *Heart & Lung, 17*[2]:157–165)

ing of toe and foot temperature, capillary refill, and strength of pulses provides early, reliable indications of changes in CO. Assessment of peripheral perfusion is outlined in Table 24-1.

## Oxygen Delivery

The pulmonary system receives the same amount of cardiac output that the rest of the body receives. However, its holding capacity is only one tenth that of the systemic circulation. Of this blood, 30% is in the pulmonary arteries, 20% is in the capillaries, and the remaining 50% is in the pulmonary veins (Ilkiw, Miller-Hance, & Nihill, 1990). Thus, the pulmonary venous system also acts as a reserve for blood. The primary function of the pulmonary system is to take oxygen from the environment, transfer it into the body, and remove waste products from the blood. This activity can be partially assessed by measuring arterial blood gases (ABGs).

The heart requires a continuous oxygen supply. Electromechanical contraction work accounts for approximately 80% of myocardial oxygen consumption ($MVo_2$). If the oxygen supply is cut off, the oxygen present in the system will maintain the heart for only 2 to 6 beats (Patel, Jeroudi, & Bolli, 1990).

The complex protein in red blood cells (RBCs) that carries oxygen to the periphery and carbon dioxide to the lungs is known as *hemoglobin.* Each molecule consists of four heme molecules attached to four globin chains. When oxygen binds to all four heme or iron atoms, arterial blood takes on a bright red color. Blood with reduced hemoglobin has a dark red color.

Long-standing hypoxia causes kidney release of erythropoietin, which stimulates bone marrow to boost erythrocyte production. The ensuing polycythemia, or increased red blood cell mass, augments the body's oxy-

gen-carrying capacity. The increased RBC mass also increases blood viscosity and eventually impairs circulation to tissues. Other consequences of polycythemia include defective platelet aggregation, reduced clotting factors (V and VIII), and decreased fibrinogen levels.

Polycythemia is beneficial until the hematocrit reaches 60% to 65%, at which point a sharp increase in the viscosity of the blood occurs. Children over 2 years of age with polycythemia and severe cyanosis are at high risk for developing brain abscesses. When blood shunts from right to left, it bypasses the natural filtering action of phagocytes within the pulmonary capillary bed. Thus, blood-borne bacteria may colonize in the brain. Infants less than 2 years of age with iron deficiency anemia and cyanosis are prone to cerebrovascular accidents due to inadequate oxygen supply to the brain.

## Assessment

Cardiovascular assessment enables the health team to acquire and interpret data necessary to make diagnoses, provide appropriate management, and monitor the child's status. For a complete review of assessment procedures for infants and children, see Chapter 5.

## History

The interview portion of the assessment should be as relaxing and nonthreatening as possible for patient and family. Both child and family may be afraid of contact with health professionals because of their fear of painful procedures or what may be said regarding diagnosis, treatment, and prognosis. The interview process not only establishes rapport with the child and family but also provides one of the most valuable sources of information. Most health agencies use a standard health history form. However, each child is unique, so history taking must be individualized. Nurses are responsible for modifying the health history form according to the child's age and suspected or probable diagnosis. History taking assesses the child's life style and the impact of cardiac disease on performing activities of daily living. An individualized, holistic nursing care plan can then be established for the child.

Identifying the source of information in the health history is essential. Data should be collected from the child if possible, then supplemented with parental validation or additional information. Fears, concerns, or comments such as "He is such a good baby—he is quiet all of the time" or "She doesn't eat very well" may be clues to an alteration in cardiovascular function.

The assessment begins with identifying the chief complaint. Parents often seek medical treatment because their child has poor feeding habits, becomes fatigued during feedings, or does not gain weight as expected. Questions about symptoms, their onset, and their duration provide useful information. A detailed history of the antepartum period is essential for diagnosis of some cardiac anomalies. Past medical, family, personal, and social histories should be assessed as well. Available resources and support persons must be identified in order to plan effective nursing care.

## Physical Examination

Assessment of the child's cardiovascular status includes both qualitative and quantitative information. A complete physical examination provides essential data on the child's current status, as well as baseline information from which clinical trends will be observed and response to treatment evaluated. Assessment of cardiovascular status can also assist in in diagnosing problems resulting from alterations in other body systems.

### Vital Signs

**Heart Rate and Pulse.**    Table 24-2 gives the normal heart rates for infants and children. Infant heart *rates* are rapid and subject to wide fluctuations due to the continued development of the cardiac conduction system and sympathetic innervation of the heart. Heart *rhythm* should be regular. Any infant with a sustained heart rate of over 195 beats per minute, less than 70 beats per minute, or with irregular rhythm should undergo further evaluation immediately.

An apical heart rate is always taken in children with suspected heart disease. The apical impulse is normally auscultated near the apex of the heart. This area has the loudest heartbeat, and is referred to as the point of maximum impulse (PMI). PMI location is important for palpating thrills. *Thrills* are vibrations produced by blood flowing from one chamber to another through a narrow or abnormal opening, such as a stenosed valve or septal defect. They are best felt during expiration, and feel like a cat purring.

Auscultation is a difficult skill to acquire, and must be

### Table 24–2.    *Normal Heart Rates for Infants and Children*

| Age | Heart Rate (beats/min) | | |
| --- | --- | --- | --- |
| | Resting Awake | Resting (Sleeping) | Exercise (Fever) |
| Newborn | 100–180 | 80–160 | Up to 200 |
| 1 wk–3 mo | 100–220 | 80–200 | Up to 220 |
| 3 mo–2 yr | 80–150 | 70–120 | Up to 200 |
| 2 yr–10 yr | 70–110 | 60–90 | Up to 200 |
| 10 yr–adult | 55–90 | 50–90 | Up to 200 |

continuously and systematically practiced. Infants and young children may have difficulty remaining still and quiet during examination. If possible, it is best to examine infants and children while they are sleeping. To prevent disturbing the child, warm the stethoscope by holding the diaphragm against the palm of the hand.

Four valve areas should be auscultated, as shown in Figure 24-5. The primary aortic area is along the sternal edge and right second intercostal space. The pulmonic area is along the sternal edge and the left second intercostal space. The tricuspid and secondary aortic area are along the left lower sternal border and fourth intercostal space. The mitral area is along the left midclavicular line and fourth and fifth intercostal spaces, or at the heart apex if the heart is dilated. Nurses should also auscultate over the carotid arteries, intraclavicular areas, each axilla, and on the back, both below and medial to the scapula.

Murmurs may be heard while auscultating the heart. Murmurs are produced when blood flows back and forth within the heart chambers or major arteries and makes a swishing sound. The greater the turbulence of blood flow, the louder the murmur. For example, a small hole in the ventricular septum may have a louder murmur than a large hole. Blood is trying to flow through a narrower opening, so turbulence increases. Most murmurs in infants and children with a cardiovascular defect or physiologic abnormality are called organic murmurs. Other murmurs are classified as innocent or functional when no cardiac pathology exists. Nurses should be able to identify an abnormal sound and record location, time of occurrence during the cardiac cycle, intensity, radiation to other areas, and estimated loudness of the murmur. Quality of the murmur may be defined as musical, blowing, squeaking, rumbling, rough, or harsh. Murmurs are graded by intensity from Grade I to Grade VI (Table 24-3).

Changing the position of the child changes murmur intensity through variations in hemodynamics. Stroke volume immediately increases when the child is lying supine due to increased systemic venous return to the right atrium, followed by increased pulmonary venous return to the left atrium. As a result, intensity increases. Alternately, standing reduces systemic venous return, lowering ventricular diastolic filling volume, and murmur intensity decreases. Squatting may either increase or decrease murmurs, depending on what type of cardiac alteration is present. Lying on the left side increases murmur intensity because the heart moves closer to the lateral chest wall (McNamara, 1990). Many healthy children have innocent murmurs or physiologic variations in heart sounds. Unusual heart sounds and murmurs increase in intensity with fever, infection, or excitement.

**Blood Pressure.**    Blood pressure (BP) varies with age and is closely related to weight and height. Normal blood pressures for each age group are shown in Appendix B. The Second Task Force on Blood Pressure Control in

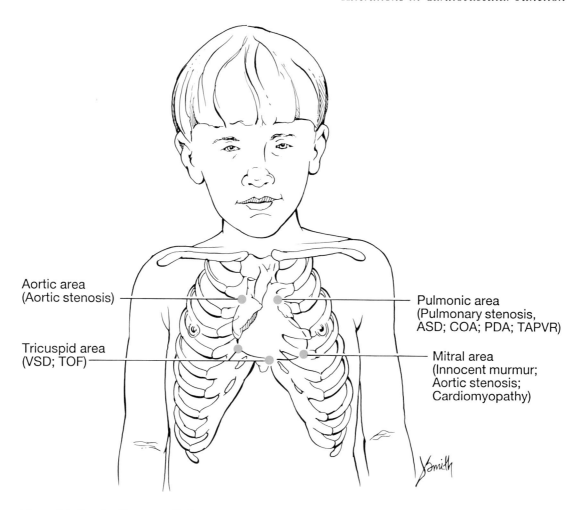

Aortic area
(Aortic stenosis)

Tricuspid area
(VSD; TOF)

Pulmonic area
(Pulmonary stenosis,
ASD; COA; PDA; TAPVR)

Mitral area
(Innocent murmur;
Aortic stenosis;
Cardiomyopathy)

*Figure 24–5. Cardiac auscultation areas.*

Children (1987) recommends that children over the age of 3 have their blood pressure measured annually.

Record the child's activity when taking blood pressure. Crying increases readings, whereas deep sleep lowers them. Sucking may increase BP. As a child's BP varies with the time of day, attempts should be made to take readings at one consistent time. Blood pressure can be measured by noninvasive or invasive means. Noninvasive techniques involve wrapping a cuff around a limb. Use of the correct size cuff is imperative (Table 24-4). Size refers to the internal bladder, not the size of the entire cuff. The inflatable cuff bladder should completely encircle the

arm or thigh. The cuff bladder width should be 40 to 50% of the circumference of the limb on which the measurement is being taken. For example, the appropriate cuff size for a child with an arm circumference of 15 cm (3 inches) is a cuff width of 6–8 cm (1.5 inches). A cuff that is too

*Table 24–3. Murmur Grading*

| I | Barely audible; often not discovered initially |
| II | Faint and soft but easily audible |
| III | Moderately loud; not accompanied by a thrill |
| IV | Loud; associated with palpable thrill |
| V | Audible with stethoscope partially lifted off chest |
| VI | Audible with stethoscope completely off chest |

*Table 24–4. Blood Pressure Cuff Sizes*

| Cuff Name* | Bladder Width (cm) | Bladder Length (cm) |
|---|---|---|
| Newborn | 2.5–4.0 | 5.0–9.0 |
| Infant | 4.0–6.0 | 11.5–18.0 |
| Child | 7.5–9.0 | 17.0–19.0 |
| Adult | 11.5–13.0 | 22.0–26.0 |
| Large arm | 14.0–15.0 | 30.5–33.0 |
| Thigh | 18.0–19.0 | 36.0–38.0 |

*Cuff name does not guarantee that the cuff will be appropriate size for a child within that age range.
(From Report of the Second Task Force on Blood Pressure Control in Children. [1987]. *Pediatrics*, 79[1], 3)

small will give falsely high readings while a large one will give falsely low readings.

In infants, blood pressure is obtained by auscultation or palpation. To palpate BP, the pulse is located and the cuff inflated. Systolic BP corresponds to the point at which the pulse is first felt with cuff deflation. This reading is often 5 to 10 mm Hg lower than the measurement obtained by auscultation. Auscultation of BP of infants and small children is often difficult. Therefore, devices that use ultrasound, such as Dopplers or oscillometers, are often used.

Invasive techniques are used during surgery and in the ICU after a child has undergone surgical repair of a heart defect. A catheter is placed in the femoral or radial artery. The monitoring line is then connected to a pressure line, a transducer, and a monitor that displays systolic, diastolic, and mean arterial pressures.

Physical examination of a child with alterations in cardiovascular function involves the skills of inspection, palpation, percussion, and auscultation. These skills enable the nurse to collect data for formulating nursing diagnoses, establishing goals, planning care, and evaluating nursing interventions.

## General Assessment

The general appearance of an infant or child should be observed throughout the exam. Many clues can be obtained to help gain an overall picture of the child. Facial expression and body positioning provide information about an infant or child who is in pain or experiencing dyspnea, or who may be afraid.

Nutritional assessment is also essential. A history of the feeding pattern from birth to the present should be summarized and recorded. Any identified problems should be documented in detail. An infant with altered cardiovascular function may consume less volume per feeding, may become dyspneic while sucking, and may perspire profusely. The baby with inadequate intake may fall into an exhausted sleep for a brief period, then waken for another feeding. This pattern results in a failure-to-thrive appearance characterized by poor weight gain. Poor nutritional status may also result from parental neglect, lack of information, lack of parenting skills, or poor living conditions. These possibilities must be carefully assessed.

Delayed growth and development may be related to inadequate nutrition. Several causative factors have been identified in infants and children with cardiovascular anomalies. Hypoxia and breathlessness create feeding problems. Anoxia or venous congestion of the bowel leads to malabsorption. Increased metabolic rate results in insufficient intake of energy for normal growth and development. Peripheral anoxia and acidosis lead to poor utilization of nutrients. Finally, high amounts of energy are lost through urine, stool, and vomit (Menon & Poskitt, 1985; Poskitt, 1987). Poor nutritional reserves lead to decreased ability to resist infections and stressors.

Accurate measurement and documentation of physical growth is a key element in the evaluation of health status of a child. Weight, height, and head circumference should be taken, recorded, and compared to standardized growth charts. The comparison of present measurements with previous ones to detect sudden changes in the infant or child's growth pattern is necessary. Many children with heart defects have a "normal" birth weight but eventually become underweight and small for their age. Sudden changes in growth patterns can signal a decreasing ability of the child to cope with altered cardiovascular function.

Developmental status should be carefully assessed. Observations should be detailed and documented by use of screening tests, such as the Denver Developmental Screening Test (DDST).

## Integument

All of the child's clothes should be removed before beginning the physical examination. Skin color assessment must be done in a well lighted room. Room temperature should be comfortable, because a warm or hot environment can cause flushing of the skin by blood vessel dilatation, and a cool or cold environment can cause cold-induced cyanosis through vasoconstriction.

*Cyanosis.* Cyanosis (derived from a Greek word meaning "dark blue") is the blue or gray coloring of mucous membranes, skin, or nailbeds that results from at least 5 g/dL deoxygenated hemoglobin (hemoglobin not bound to oxygen) in the blood. It is a frequent initial sign and important clinical manifestation of heart disease in children. In anemic infants, hemoglobin levels may be too low to produce a cyanotic color. Polycythemic patients may appear ruddy or cyanotic even with normal partial pressure of oxygen in arterial blood.

There are two types of cyanosis: peripheral and central. Peripheral cyanosis results from increased oxygen extraction from peripheral blood due to sluggish blood flow. Arterial oxygen saturation, however, is still normal. Peripheral cyanosis is seen with vasoconstriction due to cold temperature, congestive heart failure, circulatory shock, polycythemia, and hypovolemia. It is seen in the lips, fingernails, and earlobes. Central cyanosis is due to severe respiratory distress, and is best observed in the buccal mucosa. It is accompanied by peripheral cyanosis.

Cyanosis in the newborn may be produced by a number of factors, including cardiac, pulmonary, metabolic, and hematologic diseases. Cyanosis may be produced by any condition that causes cardiogenic shock (failure to maintain blood supply to the circulatory systems and tissues due to inadequate cardiac output). An easy way to differentiate between cardiac- and pulmonary-induced cyanosis is to observe the newborn crying. If cyanosis is caused by a cardiac problem, crying will worsen the cyanosis. Resistance to pulmonary blood flow increases during the expiratory phase of crying. More blood bypasses the pulmonary circuit through an increase in the right-to-left shunting of blood. If the problem is pulmonary, cyanosis will improve with crying. The concentration of oxygen in arterial blood ($Pao_2$) will increase with oxygen administration for children with lung disease, whereas $Pao_2$ usually remains low during oxygen administration in children with cardiac disease.

Slight or mild cyanosis may be too subtle for parents to notice in children and, thus, is often overlooked. Parents may exhibit an inability to recognize cyanosis, or they may deny their child's heart condition. Observant parents can notice cyanosis during feeding in infants or with exercise in the older child. The best areas to assess for cyanosis are the sclera, conjunctiva, nail beds, lips, tongue, buccal mucosa, palms, and soles of the feet.

*Clubbing.* One of the earliest signs of prolonged deoxygenated blood is reddened, shiny fingertips. The child appears to have been playing in Jello. Color change is usually obvious after more than six months of desaturation. Clubbing of the phalanges develops next. Clubbing is characterized by a widened and thickened phalange, convex nail beds, and loss of angle between nail and nailbed. The first noticeable change often occurs in the thumbs. A comparison of normal and clubbed fingers is shown in Figure 24-6.

### Hepatic Assessment

When the heart is malformed other organs may also be involved. Therefore, the liver may not always be located on the right side of the body. With heart failure the liver becomes enlarged and tender. The hepatic vein is the last large vein connecting with the inferior vena cava before caval blood drains into the right atrium. When the right heart fails, blood backs up in the systemic circulation, and the liver is one of the first organs to become congested.

It is important to note liver size and any extension below the costal margin. The edge should feel smooth and firm; palpation should not cause pain. In older children, there may not be a firm, discrete liver edge. The most consistent sign of systemic venous congestion is hepatomegaly.

Additionally, the livers of young infants and children do not have adequate glycogen stores to meet their increased metabolic demands, placing them at risk for developing hypoglycemia. Glucose is an important source of energy for the myocardium. One molecule of glucose converts to two molecules of ATP (adenosine triphosphate), which is essential for cardiac muscle activity to occur.

### Renal Assessment

The renal system is very sensitive to changes in cardiac output and blood flow. The kidney attempts to retain salt and water when it senses a decreased blood flow. This retention enhances venous return, ventricular end-diastolic volume, and cardiac output (CO). However, the compensatory mechanism aggravates a low CO state if the ventricles cannot effectively pump the blood they already contain. Ventricular workload increases, and the infant or child is at risk for volume overload. Eventually, decreased

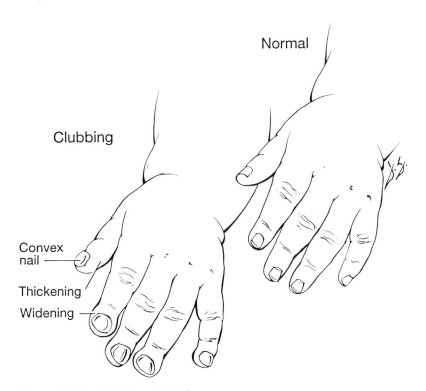

*Figure 24–6. Clubbing of the fingers.*

renal blood flow results in oliguria, increased urine specific gravity, hematuria, and albuminuria.

Nurses should carefully assess urine output, because decreased flow may indicate the development or presence of severe heart failure. Urine output should be 0.5 to 1 mL/kg/hour. Many children are placed on a combined therapy of digoxin and diuretics to limit or prevent congestive heart failure and promote removal of excess fluid volume.

## Diagnostic Procedures

Technologic advances now allow more accurate diagnosis and management, both medical and nursing, of children with alterations in cardiovascular function.

### Electrocardiography

The electrocardiogram (ECG) is a measurement of the heart's electrical activity. It is a recording of cardiac depolarization and repolarization. The ECGs of premature infants, full-term infants, and older children have many differences. Most variations are related to anatomical changes in the ratio of weight between the right and left ventricles during the first 6 months of life. For example, the right ventricle is thicker than the left during the first month of life. By 3 years of age, the ECG should be similar to that of an adult.

### Echocardiography

Echocardiography is the use of ultrasound, or high-frequency sound waves, in a noninvasive and painless procedure that provides information about cardiac anatomy, physiology, and function. Echocardiography may be used in diagnosis, in the operating room for postoperative repair evaluation, and postsurgically. Fetal cardiac defects may be identified with echocardiography performed between 16 and 32 weeks of gestation (Fyfe & Kline, 1990). Although diagnosis of mild forms of heart disease is possible, major malformations are detected more easily.

### Radiologic Studies

Radiographic and fluoroscopic tests may be used to aid in the diagnosis of heart defects. X-rays provide information on heart size, pulmonary blood flow, pulmonary parenchyma, location of the descending aorta in the thorax, specific chamber enlargement, and skeletal formation.

### Cardiac Catheterization

Cardiac catheterization is the passage of a small tube into the heart through a blood vessel. It is an invasive procedure, and is often the final, definitive cardiovascular test. Radiopaque catheters are placed, usually percutaneously, into a peripheral vessel, usually the femoral vein. Guide wires are passed through the vena cava into the right atrium for right-sided catheterizations, and into the descending aorta for left-sided catheterization or visualization of the coronary arteries.

Cardiac catheterization is usually combined with angiography, in which a radiopaque contrast media is injected through the catheter to observe the flow of blood through the heart. These procedures provide definitive information about cardiac chamber size and function, anatomy, patency of septal walls, valve functioning, and hemodynamic variables. Aortic, pulmonary, and coronary artery origins and patencies can be determined. Various pressures, blood flow calculations, and oxygen saturation throughout the heart can be measured. Palliative procedures for children with cardiac defects can also be accomplished with cardiac catheterization. For example, life-saving atrial septal defects can be created (discussed later in this chapter). Alternatively, cardiac repairs can also be done, such as closing a septal defect by umbrella patch or plugging a patent ductus arteriosus.

*Care of the Child Undergoing Cardiac Catheterization.* Nurses provide information to patients and families about pre-catheterization, catheterization, and post-catheterization procedures, care, and what physical, visual, and auditory perceptions are likely to be experienced. Children are given nothing by mouth for 4 to 6 hours before the procedure. A sedative is given before the catheterization, and the child is sleepy afterward. Contrast medium functions as an osmotic diuretic, so children should be encouraged to drink liquid, if possible, following the procedure–if they are fully awake and are not experiencing nausea or vomiting. The child should be assessed for signs of dehydration and hypovolemia. Potential complications of cardiac catheterization include dysrhythmias, bleeding, low cardiac output, infection, and adverse reaction to the contrast medium. Many catheterizations are now done on an outpatient basis so additional information on home and follow-up care is required.

### Hematologic Tests

Congenital heart defects can produce hematologic abnormalities. Certain hematologic tests are extremely important in evaluating, monitoring, and treating children with alterations in cardiovascular function. Different tests are required to monitor various diseases. Two of the more important tests related to the cardiovascular system are hemoglobin (Hgb) and arterial blood gases (ABGs).

Blood gas monitoring is used to assess the status of tissue oxygenation, carbon dioxide removal, and acid–base balance. The results of blood gas monitoring can provide information on which to base interventions when needed, and note response to treatment. Any change in the infant that increases oxygen demand and consumption will be reflected in ABGs. Electrolytes are often monitored with blood gases. ABGs must be drawn through an artery. The preferred vessel is the radial artery, although the femoral artery may be used, especially in infants. Normal values for ABGs are presented in Chapter 23.

Two noninvasive tests used to monitor oxygenation are transcutaneous oxygen saturation and pulse oximetry. Transcutaneous oxygenation saturation is measured by heated electrodes placed on the patient's skin. Heat vasodilates the vascular bed. Oxygen and carbon dioxide from the dermal capillary bed diffuse to the skin surface and are measured by these electrodes. Because of the risk of skin burn, electrode sites should be changed every 2 hours for premature babies, every 4 hours for infants, and every 6 hours for children (Brown & Vender, 1988).

Pulse oximetry uses the principle of spectrophotometric analysis to measure arterial oxygen saturation. A patch is placed on a highly vascularized area of skin, such as the patient's big toe, finger, or earlobe. Two wavelengths of light pass through the tissue, and changes in light absorption (based on how much oxygen the hemoglobin is carrying) are used to measure oxygen saturation of the blood.

### Intraaortic Balloon Pumps

The intraaortic balloon pump (IABP) is a circulatory assist device. In the pediatric population, the goal of therapy is to increase low cardiac output, a serious complication following open heart surgery. IABPs may also be used as a bridge to cardiac transplantation, to manage critically ill children preoperatively, and to support the child if the surgeon is unable to wean the patient off the cardiac bypass machine.

A special catheter with a long balloon at the tip is inserted (percutaneously or through a cut-down) through the femoral or iliac artery and threaded into the descending aorta below the left subclavian artery. The IABP works by counterpulsation, inflating during diastole and deflating during systole. Thus, it is "active" when the heart is resting and vice versa. Diastolic inflation increases blood pressure during diastole by providing an additional forward push to aortic blood. It improves coronary blood flow by pushing blood against the aortic valve and into the coronary ostia. Therefore, use of the IABP in children with aortic regurgitation (leakage of blood from the aorta through the aortic valve back into the left ventricle) is contraindicated because of the increased backward pressure of blood against the aortic valve. Balloon deflation, occuring just prior to systole, reduces afterload by creating a space in the aorta where the balloon had been. The left ventricle does not have to work as hard to overcome aortic pressure, stroke volume (SV) increases, and myocardial oxygen consumption decreases.

Nurses should be knowledgeable regarding the mechanics of intraaortic balloon pumps. Urine output must be monitored hourly. Decreased output may result from continuing or deteriorating physiologic changes or may result from the balloon obstructing the renal arteries. Vital signs and hemodynamic parameters (sure, right atrial pressure or central ve monary artery pressure), must be rec often more frequently. Bleeding fror hematoma development in the low thigh must be reported to the physic could indicate a femoral or iliac arterial tear and requ treatment.

Close attention must be paid to peripheral circulation, especially in the limb affected by the IABP. Circulation will be diminished in that leg, which could potentially lead to leg ischemia. A Doppler may be used to hear pulses that cannot be palpated. Wrapping the affected extremity in warm towels and keeping it covered may promote circulation through vasodilation. If the pulse cannot be felt, it is imperative to notify the physician immediately. The extremity must be immobilized by restraint or IV board. Flexing the limb will further decrease peripheral circulation. If hemodynamically stable, the child should be turned by logrolling. Frequent turning and use of devices such as sheepskin and egg-crate mattresses minimize skin breakdown. Particular care must be taken to protect the child from infection that can result from invasive lines, decreased immunologic status, and decreased nutritional status.

## Nursing Diagnosis

A common nursing language facilitates care planning, implementation, and evaluation among nurses. Certain NANDA-approved nursing diagnoses are particularly applicable to children with congenital or acquired cardiovascular disease. These diagnoses are appropriate at different times in the child's life, and with variations of disease among different children. Appropriate nursing diagnoses for children with impaired cardiovascular function may include the following:

*Pattern 1: Exchanging*
- Altered nutrition: Less than body requirements
- Altered tissue perfusion
- Decreased cardiac output
- Fluid volume excess
- High risk for altered body temperature
- High risk for infection
- Impaired gas exchange
- Impaired skin integrity
- Ineffective airway clearance
- Ineffective breathing pattern

*Pattern 3: Relating*
- Altered family processes
- Altered parenting
- High risk for altered parenting
- Impaired social interaction
- Social isolation

*Pattern 5: Choosing*
- Ineffective family coping: compromised
- Noncompliance

*Pattern 6: Moving*
- Activity intolerance
- Altered growth and development
- Bathing/hygiene self-care deficit
- Diversional activity deficit
- Dressing/grooming self-care deficit
- Fatigue

*Pattern 7: Perceiving*
- Body image disturbance
- Self-esteem disturbance
- Sensory/perceptual alterations

*Pattern 9: Feeling*
- Anxiety
- Dysfunctional grieving
- Fear
- Pain

## Planning Nursing Care

### Developmental Considerations

Nursing care of children with cardiovascular disease must be based in part on the developmental level of the child. The foundation of nursing assessment, diagnosis, and planning, implementing, and evaluating care is twofold: the child and the parents. The child born with a heart defect usually reaches normal milestones, but at a slower rate than a normal, healthy child. Through education, nurses can help parents understand normal child growth and development, including motor abilities, nutritional requirements, elimination patterns, and emotional and intellectual achievements. Parents then learn how their child deviates, if at all, from the norm so interventions may be applied as appropriate to maximize the child's potential.

Most children with cardiac anomalies who display poor growth were born within a normal weight range. Many of these children demonstrate improvement in growth after undergoing cardiac surgical repair. Catch-up growth of males, who are usually more growth-delayed than females, will be less than that seen in females (Poskitt, 1987).

In order for initial parent–infant bonding to occur, parents and infant need a sufficient amount of time with each other. When a newborn is diagnosed with a congenital heart defect, the child may be immediately separated from the parents. This separation puts an initial strain on the developing relationship. Parents may feel hesitant in attaching to their newborn for fear the child may die. Additional strains may develop from frequently occurring feeding difficulties, an often fussy infant, grief over loss of a perfect baby, and a host of other overwhelming, fatiguing emotions, including guilt, frustration, sense of failure, anxiety, fear, helplessness, and denial. Feelings of incompetence surface when parents feel unsure of how to perform everyday tasks as well as unexpected new, necessary tasks in caring for their child.

The complex attempt to treat an ill child in a normal fashion is called *normalization*. The goal of this active and accommodating process is to integrate the child into the family instead of centering the family around the child (Deatrick, Knafl, & Walsh, 1988). In managing the child's illness, parents attempt to minimize what they believe are important differences between the ill child and healthy peers, while maximizing the child's potential to lead as normal a life as possible. A great deal of energy is spent keeping family life as normal as possible, and attempting to convey this "normalness" to outsiders.

Normalization has been identified as the most common management style used by families raising a chronically ill child (Deatrick, Knafl, & Walsh, 1988; Knafl & Deatrick, 1986). When assessing and planning nursing care, it is essential to remember that what is "normal" for one family may be highly "abnormal" for another.

### Acute Care Considerations

Discrepancies may develop between families and health care workers over the importance of normalization versus medical care when a child with a heart defect is hospitalized. Parents are concerned with maintaining a normal routine during the child's hospitalization. Health care workers are likely to view interruptions of normalization as an unavoidable, integral part of being chronically ill. Effective communication between nurses and families is a key factor in overcoming this hurdle and making the hospital stay as positive as possible. Ways to accommodate parental wishes include keeping bathtime consistent with the usual time at home, extending visiting hours, and having parents bring in items (i.e., toys, blankets, pictures) from home to make the child feel more comfortable.

Planning nursing care for children hospitalized for surgical treatment of a cardiac abnormality is similar to that for any hospitalized child. These techniques are described in detail in Chapter 17. These plans include such things as explanations of what to expect when, involvement in the child's care, and how to care for the child when he or she is released from the hospital (i.e., care of the surgical incision, observation for signs of infection, medication administration, and return appointments).

### Chronic Care Considerations

Most children with cardiac disease are cared for in the home environment. Hospitalizations are related to respiratory illnesses, acute cardiac problems (i.e., congestive heart failure), or surgical repair. Children who have had devastating sequelae to brain abscesses or embolization may live in a rehabilitation center if the parents are unable to care for them at home.

## Home Care Considerations

Congenital heart defects may be apparent at birth or may not be detected until the child is several years old. Each parent responds differently to their child's diagnosis. Parents may more readily accept visible disorders because it is harder to use denial as a defense. Many parents of children with heart defects make statements such as "You would never know she has a heart defect by just looking at her" or "He doesn't ever look sick, and he is as active as a normal child."

Areas of parental concern for children with congenital cardiac defects include changes in respiratory rate, heart rate, or behavior patterns; sweating; change in skin color; feeding difficulties; and medication administration. Nurses can help parents learn how to recognize when their child's physical or behavioral changes call for professional intervention (Table 24-5).

To intervene successfully with children and families, the nurse should determine the extent of the family's understanding of the heart defect, their desire to participate in care, and the treatment plans and goals. Some parents cannot seem to get enough information. Others have a tremendous need not to know specific information, such as details of a surgical procedure. This "don't want to know" approach is often an attempt to control a situation in which parents feel they have little control. It may represent an attempt to maintain normalization by not drawing

## Table 24-5. When to Notify Medical Personnel

Call for medical evaluation if the child is/has:
  pale
  tachypneic (20–40 breaths/min above normal rate)
  bradycardic/tachycardic for the child's age, usual heart rate, and current activity level
  not eating as well as usual
  diaphoretic with feeding
  decrease in urination (e.g., trips to bathroom, number of diapers changed)
  listless
  sleeping much more than usual
  irritable
  cool, mottled extremities
  vomiting/diarrhea leading to dehydration or inability to take prescribed medications
  unexplained fever
  fever following any invasive procedures
  color change
  cyanosis of tongue, gums
  hypoxic spells

attention to the cardiac defect. Fear of bad news is probably a component of this approach. Assessing parents' needs and fears, then mutually determining what they need to know, is helpful in establishing a therapeutic relationship. Some parents respond best in the home environment, where they feel least threatened.

A discrepancy is often seen between parents' words and actions regarding normalization and their child with a cardiac defect. Although parents want to treat the child normally, they are often not consistent. Discipline is often problematic for these parents. They recognize the need for discipline, but have difficulty imposing it. Parents need to know that discipline provides a source of security for their child. The type of discipline selected depends on the individual child. Under most circumstances, it does not hurt to let the child with a heart defect cry occasionally.

Problems often occur in the parents' sleeping patterns when caring for a child with cardiovascular problems. The child's cardiac defect often results in parental lack of sleep at night since they may prefer to watch over their child rather than sleep. Lack of movement by the child between checks or quiet breathing may cause panic. Parents may sleep with their children to provide continuous observation, and this practice may continue well into childhood. Nurses should discourage this practice in the interest of normal child development. Parents are often afraid to leave the house after their child falls asleep, fearing the child may die while they are gone.

Finding babysitters is difficult, and thus normal social life is impaired. Family and friends are often afraid to stay with the child for fear of a cardiac emergency. Parents may be reluctant to leave the child due to the same fears. Nurses should refer parents to respite care.

Parents often find it difficult to manage the child's activity level. They often feel the child is too active, even when no activity restrictions have been prescribed. Parents may need reminding that normal childhood development is largely based on the child's experimentation with the environment. Most children self-limit their own activity, and nurses can help parents understand this.

A major, chronic fear of families raising a child with a congenital cardiac defect is the sudden, unexpected death of their child. This fear is a common denominator in the development of overprotection, a coping response that causes a child to become spoiled, manipulative, difficult to handle, and unhappy.

## Nursing Interventions for Cardiovascular Problems

### Cardiopulmonary Resuscitation

Families (parents, grandparents, siblings, and other significant others) who live with a child with a heart defect should learn cardiopulmonary resuscitation (CPR) as taught by the American Heart Association. Parents often feel this is a formidable task. Motivation to learn this procedure should come from the knowledge that CPR could save the life of the child. In addition, it can help parents increase their situational control by knowing how to cope with an emergency. Although the seriousness of learning CPR needs to be understood, families should not be frightened by it. Use of appropriate humor relaxes people adequately so their stress level decreases enough to allow learning to occur. Teaching only infant or child CPR minimizes confusion over technique and counting. Eventually, learners may also want to know adult CPR, as well as management of the choking victim.

Nurses should encourage parents to participate in formal classes in CPR and, in addition, should provide families with written and illustrated information on how to perform CPR. This information should be kept in an easily accessible and logical place, such as with 911 or other emergency telephone numbers. Some communities have emergency numbers answered by operators who coach people through steps in performing CPR until rescuers arrive.

## Nursing Interventions Related to Cardiac Surgery

### Preoperative Interventions

Many preoperative interventions for children undergoing heart surgery parallel those for any child and parents dealing with an impending surgical procedure. Interventions include monitoring laboratory values, vital signs, electrocardiograms, nutritional status, and coping mechanisms. Interventions are based on nursing assessment and diagnosis.

Teaching the child about the procedure should be based on the child's age, cognitive level, and what the child already understands. Using pictures and allowing the child to handle equipment enhances his or her understanding. The child can be taught techniques to aid in recovery after surgery, such as how to deep breathe, cough, splint the chest, and either blow bubbles or use the triflow or incentive spirometer. Chest physiotherapy can be demonstrated to the child. If intubation is planned following surgery, children are told they will wake up with a tube in their mouths and will not be able to talk until the tube is taken out when they are more awake. The nurse should briefly explain bandages and tubes, what they will feel like, and what they do. How much information is given varies with each child.

Children are not allowed anything by mouth for a specified time prior to surgery. Digoxin is usually not given the day of surgery. Other drugs may or may not be given.

Certain cardiovascular problems that are present pre-

operatively will still be present to some degree postoperatively, and may prolong the child's recovery. For example, a child with pulmonary hypertension or pulmonary venous congestion will probably require prolonged ventilatory support following surgery as the lungs adapt to a change in blood flow. A child with congestive heart failure (CHF) preoperatively will still have some degree of CHF postoperatively. Anticoagulants, coagulopathy, and previous surgeries may cause more postoperative bleeding than is normal.

### Intraoperative Interventions

Cardiovascular surgery is performed through either a closed-heart or an open-heart approach. In closed-heart surgery the heart is not opened to do the procedure. Closed-heart surgery is used for procedures such as closing a patent ductus arteriosus, pulmonary artery banding, and placement of systemic-to-pulmonary shunts.

During the course of the surgery, the family should be informed at regular intervals regarding the progress of the procedure. One person should be responsible for talking with the family. This individual is usually a member of the operating team, although a staff nurse from the ICU may assume this role. If the nurse assigned to the child has not yet met the parents, this is an appropriate time for introductions. Although brief, the meeting establishes a relationship between nurse and family. The nurse may then be more effective in interacting with the family on the first visit with the child.

### Postoperative Interventions

Parents of children with heart defects need a great deal of support when their child is hospitalized for cardiac surgery. The child typically enters the operating room appearing healthy, and returns to the intensive care unit looking critically ill. Even when the family has received excellent teaching about what to expect and is aware of what is happening, the child's appearance is still a shock. Nurses provide reassurance when explaining the child's status and what, why, and how things are being monitored. Informing the parents that each day (under normal circumstances) the child will look better may be helpful.

Children undergoing cardiac surgery return to the ICU with many monitoring devices. Before the child arrives, it is important to have the room set up with all needed or anticipated equipment. A list of emergency drug dosages based on the child's weight should be kept available to save time during emergencies.

The child's ECG must be monitored at all times. Atrial and ventricular pacemaker wires are usually inserted during surgery. If the child is not already hooked up to a pacemaker, nurses should do so and turn the pacemaker on a ventricular demand of about 60 beats per minute. The pacemaker senses the child's heart rate and fires only if the rate drops below 60 beats per minute. It simply functions as a backup to prevent a crisis from developing. An arterial line, inserted in either the femoral or radial artery, continuously monitors blood pressure. Continuous IV medications are ordered to keep the blood pressure at a certain level. Small tubes, protruding through the chest, monitor pressure in the right and left atrium. The surgeon places either a Swan-Ganz catheter or double or triple lumen central venous pressure catheter to monitor pressures and give fluids. One to four chest tubes (mediastinal and pleural) are inserted to restore negative intrathoracic pressure and allow fluid to drain from the chest. All children must be restrained to prevent pulling on tubes and lines. Restraints may be restricted to both arms or may need to include both feet. Young children have been known to extubate themselves using their feet.

A urine catheter or "tinkle bag" allows observation of urine output. Monitoring of urinary output can also be done by weighing diapers. Urine may be hematuric for a day or so following surgery as a result of hemolysis during cardiopulmonary bypass.

Electrolytes must be closely monitored and replaced as necessary. The most frequently encountered electrolyte abnormality is hypokalemia. Calcium, phosphorus, and magnesium may also be abnormal.

Nurses must be aware of complications that arise as a result of the cardiopulmonary bypass machine. Alterations in blood composition include destruction of both red and white blood cells, thrombocytopenia, denaturation of proteins, and altered fibrinolytic activity. Bleeding occurs if heparin has not been adequately reversed with protamine sulfate or if a site somewhere inside the chest is oozing blood. These sites most often include small vessels, vascular anastomoses (pathological connection of two tubular structures), and adhesions from previous surgeries.

Nurses must closely monitor bleeding. If the child is losing 4 mL of blood per kilogram each hour from chest tubes, the child is "wet" and requires close observation. If hourly blood drainage is 8 or more mL of blood per kilogram, the child may need to be returned to the operating room so the surgeon can locate and stop the source of bleeding. Laboratory coagulation studies to be monitored include hemoglobin, hematocrit, platelets, prothrombin time, partial thromboplastin time, and activated clotting time.

All children are at risk for decreased cardiac output following surgery. This may be due to hypovolemia, dysrhythmias, increased systemic vascular resistance, and cardiac tamponade.

*Cardiac tamponade* results when fluid accumulates in the pericardial sac, causing decreased pericardial compliance. Diastolic filling is impaired and is compounded by premature closing of the atrioventricular valves. Without early intervention, decreased cardiac output, hypotension, shock, and death ensue. Signs of tamponade include a sudden decrease in chest tube output, muffled heart sounds, tachycardia, pericardial friction rub, decreasing blood pressure, narrowing of the pulse pressure (difference between systolic and diastolic blood pressure), and increased central venous pressure. Emergency treatment consists of removing the fluid by pericardiocentesis; if tamponade is severe the child's chest may need to be opened, a procedure that may be initiated in the ICU and finished in the operating room.

Pulmonary compromise, manifested by atelectasis due to loss of surfactant, pulmonary edema, and hypoxia, may result from the bypass procedure. Severity varies according to the child's preoperative pulmonary status as well as length of time on the bypass machine. Nursing care is directed at maintaining a patent airway with adequate gas exchange. Many children arrive in the ICU intubated. Upon the patient's arrival, one of the first nursing tasks is to secure the endotracheal tube. (See Chapter 23 for information on respiratory care.) After extubation, children have difficulty clearing secretions due to thickness of secretions, pain, and weakness. Repositioning at least every two hours, chest physiotherapy (CPT) as often as every hour, and stimulation of deep breathing and coughing are important nursing interventions.

All children undergoing cardiac surgery have thoracic pain. Signs of discomfort include fussiness, anxiety, facial expressions, stiffness when turning, refusal to cough, anorexia, attempts not to cry, withdrawal from interaction, and increased heart and respiratory rates. Negative consequences of pain include inhibition of respiratory function and increasing myocardial oxygen demand and workload. Nurses must ensure that their patients have adequate pain relief, particularly before any procedures are done, such as CPT or removal of chest tubes. The only time the child must not be medicated is during the process of weaning from the ventilator, when the child should be as alert as possible so that independent respiratory function can be assessed adequately. Evaluation of pain relief measures is based on resolution of the signs indicating the child is in pain. If pain is still not under control, the plan of care needs to be revised.

*Pacemakers.* If a pacemaker is necessary after a surgical repair, nurses must provide the child and family with information regarding pacemaker implantation, function, and care. It is helpful to show them the type of pacemaker to be implanted, and allow the child to play with it. Following implantation, the child should avoid major contact sports. Microwave ovens no longer affect the pacemakers being implanted. The family needs to be told to seek medical attention if signs of infection occur. Nurses must be familiar with pacemaker therapy and different modes of pacing, such as fixed (the pacemaker fires at a set rate, regardless of the child's intrinsic rhythm), and demand (the pacemaker fires only when the child's intrinsic rate falls below a set point).

## Drug Therapy

Pharmacologic treatment of children with congenital or acquired heart defects varies according to the individual child and presenting physiological state. Many children may only take antibiotics prophylactically, whereas others require extensive therapy. During hospitalization, various medications are often used to improve cardiac and renal function.

Diuretics are used in children with expanded fluid volume states and to control blood pressure in children with hypertension. They are used to treat complications of congenital or acquired heart disease, such as heart failure, pulmonary edema, renal failure, and ascites. The most commonly used drugs are furosemide, ethacrynic acid, and spironolactone. Furosemide and ethacrynic acid are loop diuretics, working in the thick ascending limb of the loop of Henle. Mechanism of action inhibits absorption of sodium, potassium, and chloride. Spironolactone is known as a "potassium-sparing" diuretic. This drug blocks the effects of aldosterone so that sodium is excreted but potassium is retained. Spironolactone is often used when the child is also taking digoxin to reduce the chance of developing hypokalemia.

Cardiac drugs are often referred to as chronotropic (affecting heart rate) or inotropic (affecting force and velocity of contractility) agents. Many drug effects are based on stimulation of different adrenergic receptors (those releasing norepinephrine) in the heart and lungs.

Digoxin (Lanoxin) is a cardiac glycoside that enhances myocardial function. It is routinely prescribed in combination with diuretics. Effects of this positive inotropic drug include increasing ventricular contractility and cardiac output. The mechanism of action is through inhibition of the sodium-potassium pump across myocardial cell membranes. Hypokalemia potentiates the effects of digoxin. Digoxin is used in pediatrics because of its rapid onset, decreased risks of toxicity, and short half-life. Blood levels of digoxin must be carefully monitored. The normal therapeutic range is 1.1 to 2.2 ng/mL. *Any dysrhythmia seen in children taking digoxin should be considered a side effect of the drug until proven otherwise.* One frequent sign of impending digoxin toxicity is bradycardia (below 90 to 110 in infants; below 70 in children).

In children with failing hearts, digitalis results in better ventricular systolic emptying, less end-diastolic ventricular volume, decreased ventricular distention, and lower filling pressures. *Digitalization* is the term used for the initiation of digitalis therapy. Loading doses of digitalis must be given prior to maintenance doses. This loading dose is known as the total digitalizing dose (TDD). It is derived by taking the body surface area of the child, multiplying by a constant of 6, and dividing by 8. Half of that number is given for the first dose, and then a fourth of the TDD is given for each of the next two doses. The maintenance dose is one eighth of the TDD, given every 12 hours.

*Vasodilators* are used to increase cardiac outflow by decreasing respiratory rate and effort and increasing perfusion in systemic circulation. Sodium nitroprusside (Nipride), tolazine hydrochloride (Priscoline), and prazosin hydrochloride (Minipress) are commonly used vasodilators. These are potent drugs and may cause serious side effects, especially hypotension. Blood pressure must be monitored frequently after administration.

Morphine is a narcotic used for multiple purposes in children with cardiovascular disease. Pain control is accomplished by altering perception of the painful stimuli. The drug decreases anxiety and helps children relax by causing lethargy and drowsiness. Decreased peripheral resistance reduces venous return, easing cardiac workload and lowering oxygen consumption. With administration of this drug, children must be carefully monitored, especially following extubation after surgery, because morphine can cause respiratory depression. Following surgery, many children experience nausea and vomiting. If these symptoms occur, nurses should consider morphine as one possible cause.

Warfarin is used as an anticoagulant for children following surgery where thrombus formation is of concern (i.e., placement of Gore-tex grafts). It may also prevent extension of existing thrombi. Warfarin alters clotting factors II (prothrombin), VII, IX, and X by interfering with action of vitamin K in the liver. Therapeutic levels are 1.5 to 2.5 times greater than control values. Children receiving warfarin need consistent, frequent monitoring of prothrombin time (PT).

## Nutrition

The inability to tolerate feedings or have adequate intake of nutrients is problematic for many infants with congenital cardiac defects. These two factors, combined with the child's increased need for calories, combine to inhibit weight gain and normal growth. Feeding, which normally enhances bonding, becomes a time of frustration for both parent and infant. The infant eats a small amount, tires, and falls asleep. Hunger soon awakens the infant, however, and parents often feel unable to care for and satisfy their child. Breast milk does not supply the necessary caloric requirements of children with congenital cardiac defects. Powders to increase calorie intake, such as Portagen powder (13 calories per teaspoon), may be mixed with breast milk in a bottle. This supplementation lessens the mother's feelings of inadequacy and is beneficial for the infant. Other methods of feeding an infant include nasogastric or gastrostomy tube feedings. Nurses can teach parents how to insert nasogastric tubes and care for gastrostomy tubes. Teaching then focuses on how to feed the infant through these passages as well as how to nurture the child during this process (i.e., holding the infant, providing a pacifier to satisfy sucking needs).

If the infant or child has any difficulty breathing,

placing them in a sitting position during feeding will help minimize the likelihood of aspiration and increase their ability to take in food or formula. Children accustomed to gastrostomy feedings may have difficulty accepting oral foods. Infants and children with cyanotic heart disease require increased dietary iron, and supplements may be necessary.

## Evaluating Nursing Care

Nursing focuses on the human response to illness. By this definition, care must be individualized to client, family, and individual situations. Evaluating nursing care for a child with cardiovascular problems includes observing the child's physical response to care, as well as the child's and parent's adaptation to the illness. Compliance with the treatment plan is evidence that the child and family are adapting to the illness. Assessing goals in terms of measurable patient outcomes provides essential information for modifying nursing care plans, when necessary. Measurable outcome criteria include the ability of both child and family to demonstrate their understanding of the illness and its treatment, as well as their willingness to avail themselves of available resources.

## Congenital Heart Defects

The classification of congenital heart defects is based on two variations in each defect: the presence or absence of cyanosis, and the quantity of pulmonary blood flow (PBF) (Table 24-6). Understanding these variations helps to identify the defect and guides nurses in planning effective care for children.

Blood shunts from left to right (due to pressure gradients) in acyanotic cardiac defects. Oxygenated blood returns to the pulmonary system as well as flowing into the systemic system. Thus, PBF is increased. PBF may not be increased if incoming blood flow is obstructed in the presence of a left-to-right shunt.

A right-to-left shunt in the pulmonary or systemic systems results in mixing of unoxygenated with oxygenated blood. Cyanosis results when blood bypasses the lungs. Pulmonary blood flow is usually decreased. If the pulmonary and systemic systems fail to develop into two separate systems, blood mixing still occurs, but pulmonary blood flow tends to be increased.

## Acyanotic Heart Defects

### Atrial Septal Defects

If septal tissue does not fuse appropriately during embryonic development, an *atrial septal defect* (ASD) occurs. Between 5% and 10% of all congenital heart defects are

### Table 24-6. Classification of Congenital Heart Defects

| Classification | Pulmonary Blood Flow | Defect |
|---|---|---|
| Acyanotic | Increased | Atrial septal defect |
| | | Ventricular septal defect |
| | | Endocardial cushion defect |
| | | Patent ductus arteriosus |
| | Normal | Coarctation of the aorta |
| | | Aortic stenosis |
| | | Pulmonary stenosis |
| Cyanotic | Increased | Transposition of the great arteries |
| | | Total anomalous pulmonary venous return |
| | | Persistent truncus arteriosus |
| | Decreased | Tetralogy of Fallot |
| | | Tricuspid atresia |
| | | Ebstein's anomaly |

ASDs. Females are affected more often than males, and the defect may be hereditary. Three common forms of atrial septal defects occur. Ostium secundum defects are located at the foramen ovale; ostium primum defects are located low in the septum by the atrioventricular valves; and sinus venosus defects are located near the superior vena cava. Figure 24-7 shows the location of atrial septal defects. Most

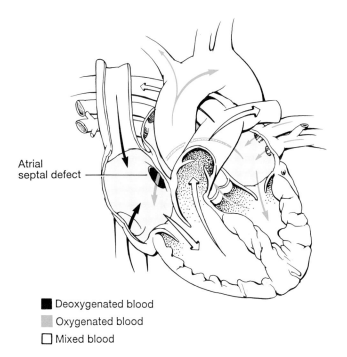

Atrial septal defect

■ Deoxygenated blood
■ Oxygenated blood
□ Mixed blood

*Figure 24-7. Atrial septal defects.*

ASDs are isolated defects. An ASD may be essential for survival in the presence of other more serious defects.

## Pathophysiology

In the presence of an ASD, pressure is higher in the left atrium than the right atrium, so blood shunts through the ASD from the left to the right side of the heart. Since the right atrial wall is more distendible than the left, it enlarges. The right ventricle and pulmonary artery enlarge because they handle three to four times the normal amount of blood (Feldt, Porter, Edwards, Puga, & Seward, 1989).

## Medical Diagnosis and Management

Most infants with ASDs tend to be asymptomatic until early childhood. Up to 40% of ASDs may spontaneously close in the first 5 years of life (Park, 1988). Symptoms vary depending on the size of the ASD. Fatigue and dyspnea are the most common complaints. Cardiac dysrhythmias may produce fatigue or palpitations. Congestive heart failure may develop if valve abnormalities occur in conjunction with an ASD. Although pulmonary blood flow is markedly increased, pulmonary hypertension does not usually develop until adulthood.

A systolic ejection murmur produced by increased blood flow across the pulmonary valve (not across the ASD) may be heard along the upper left sternal border. With large shunts, a low-pitched or rumbling diastolic murmur may be heard along the lower left sternal border because of increased blood flow across the tricuspid valve. The diagnosis is confirmed with echocardiography.

Because of the possibility of spontaneous closure, some physicians prefer to treat children medically until they are 5 or 6 years old. Treatment is usually limited to observation. Digoxin and diuretics may be prescribed if the child shows signs of congestive heart failure.

A few medical centers are occluding ASDs using the Lock Clamshell Septal Occluder. Two Dacron umbrellas open and close in opposite directions of each other. Via catheterization, the distal umbrella is placed on the distal side of the defect, and the proximal umbrella is placed on the near side of the defect, thus closing the opening.

Some physicians recommend surgical closure between the ages of 2 and 5 years or upon identification of the ASD. Through a sternotomy or right anterolateral thoracotomy, the ASD edges are sutured together or a Dacron patch is applied over the hole. Postoperative complications are rare, but may include cardiac dysrhythmias and transient pulmonary edema.

## Ventricular Septal Defects

If ventricular septal tissue fails to fuse, *ventricular septal defects* (VSDs) result. VSDs are the most common form of congenital cardiac defects, accounting for 20% to 25% of all cardiac malformations. VSDs are a component of many other types of congenital cardiac defects, such as tetralogy of Fallot or pulmonic stenosis. Both sexes are affected approximately equally.

## Pathophysiology

Four types of VSDs have been identified. Type I defects are located just below the pulmonary valve. Type II are membranous defects located in the right ventricular outflow tract. Type III defects are underneath the AV valves and are endocardial cushion defects. Type IV VSDs are located in the muscular portion of the septal wall. "Swiss cheese" defects occur when the interventricular septum is riddled with holes (Fig. 24-8).

Pulmonary vascular resistance (PVR) and VSD size determine the child's status. Immediately following birth, pulmonary arteries have narrow lumens and thick walls. With maturation, PVR gradually decreases as lumen size increases and wall thickness decreases. With large defects, this maturational process is delayed as a protection against flooding the lungs with excess volumes of blood.

Small defects limit the left-to-right shunt. There is little or no increase in PVR. More than 60% of small VSDs close spontaneously (Graham, Bender, & Spach, 1989). Moderate defects have variable PVR, and provide some resistance to blood flow across the VSD. Large VSDs, equal to or greater than the size of the aortic orifice, have mild to markedly elevated PVR, and blood flow across the VSD is unrestricted. Between 5% and 10% of large defects close spontaneously (Graham et al., 1989). If large defects are untreated, pulmonary vascular obstructive disease develops. Right-sided pressure becomes high enough to

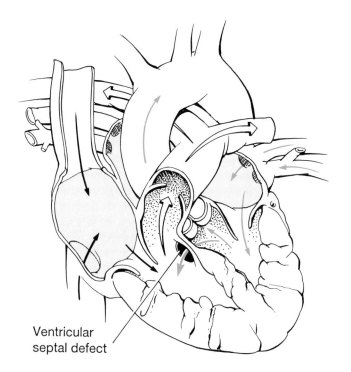

Ventricular
septal defect

*Figure 24-8.  Ventricular septal defects.*

reverse the direction blood is shunted, and the shunt becomes right-to-left. This development, known as Eisenmenger syndrome, is most common after the child is 2 years of age; however it may develop within the first 6 to 8 months of an infant's life (McNamara, 1990). Children affected by this syndrome display cyanosis and clubbing of the fingernails and toenails.

### Medical Diagnosis and Management

Many VSD murmurs are not heard until the infant returns for the initial well child check. Symptoms are related to the size of the defect, the child's age, and the pulmonary vascular resistance. Children with small VSDs are usually asymptomatic, and experience normal growth and development. Infants and children with moderate-sized defects may appear of normal size but are usually underweight. They are usually asymptomatic except for a predilection for respiratory infections and increased fatigability. Infants and children with large VSDs often have retarded growth. Infants sweat excessively, are tachypenic, and demonstrate markedly increased precordial activity. Respiratory infections are frequent and exercise tolerance is decreased.

VSDs produce a systolic murmur that ranges from Grade II to Grade IV. The murmur is best heard along the lower left sternal border. Large left-to-right shunts produce a diastolic flow rumble as the blood returns from the lungs across the mitral valve. Echocardiography and electrocardiograms are used to confirm the diagnosis, and show an enlarged heart.

Medical management consists of monitoring for and treating congestive heart failure, discussed later in this chapter. VSD closure during catheterization using umbrellas may be a treatment option. Two surgical options are available. Palliatively, a pulmonary artery band may be placed around the pulmonary artery to decrease pulmonary blood flow. VSD closure, done through the right atrium or ventricle, involves sewing the edges of the defect together or placing a Dacron patch over the hole. The PA band is then removed, and the pulmonary artery is repaired, if necessary.

Postoperative complications vary. The chest wall, ventriculotomy, or patch periphery may hemorrhage. Dysrhythmias may occur. If the child has pulmonary hypertension or increased PVR, complications may include decreased cardiac output, hypotension, and increased central venous pressure.

### Endocardial Cushion Defects

*Endocardial cushion defects* may also be called atrioventricular canal defect, atrioventricular septal defect, ostium primum ASD, or common AV orifice. In embryological development, the atrioventricular (AV) canal connects the common atria and the ventricle. Endocardial cushions appear at the edges of this canal, and fusion of these cushions creates a right and left AV canal. Further tissue growth results in valve leaflet development as well as septal tissue above and below the AV valves. Abnormal endocardial and septal tissue development results in many variations of endocardial cushion defects (Fig. 24-9). Endocardial cushion defects (ECDs) are divided into two categories: partial atrioventricular (AV) canal (1%–2% of all congenital heart defects) and complete AV canal (2% of

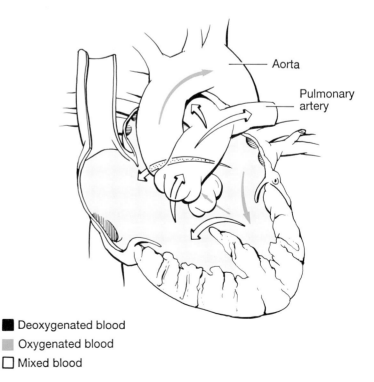

*Figure 24–9.   Endocardial cushion defects.*

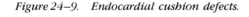

■ Deoxygenated blood

▨ Oxygenated blood

☐ Mixed blood

all heart defects). Males and females are equally affected. Thirty percent of all ECDs occur in children with Down syndrome (Park, 1988).

### Pathophysiology

The size of the septal defect and the degree of atrioventricular valve involvement determine blood flow in this defect. Children with a partial AV canal usually have an ostium primum ASD and mitral valve abnormalities. Most often, the mitral valve is cleft. It may be either competent or incompetent. If the valve functions normally, the child will present with the hemodynamics of an ASD; if the child has mitral valve insufficiency in the presence of a small ASD, the left side of the heart is overworked.

Children with complete AV canal have three major deformities: an ostium primum ASD, VSD in the upper ventricular septum, and a single, common AV valve which usually has five leaflets. Free communication exists among all four heart chambers. Pulmonary blood flow is markedly increased and eventually results in pulmonary hypertension.

### Medical Diagnosis and Management

Diagnosis of both partial and complete AV canals is made early in infancy. Infants with partial AV canal have prominent murmurs. A holosystolic murmur (from mitral insufficiency) may be heard at the apex, an ejection systolic murmur is heard over the left sternal border, and a low-pitched mid-diastolic murmur may be heard at either the apex or the lower left sternal border. These children often manifest heart failure, retarded growth, fatigue, dyspnea, and recurrent respiratory infections. Unless congestive heart failure is present, these children are treated as if they have an ASD.

Surgical repair is generally done electively when the child is between 2 and 4 years old. The ASD is closed with pericardial tissue or Teflon, and valves are repaired. Complications of this surgery include mitral regurgitation, endocarditis, and atrial and nodal dysrhythmias.

Infants with complete AV canal manifest severe cardiac failure, growth retardation, malnourishment, tachypnea, tachycardia, and recurrent respiratory infections. Congestive heart failure occurs frequently in these infants. Recurrent pneumonia is common. Significant pulmonary vascular obstructive disease is likely to occur after 2 years of age.

Without surgical intervention, most infants die within 2 or 3 years. Those who survive without surgery develop pulmonary vascular disease and die in late childhood or early adulthood. It is best to repair the heart in one surgery when the infant is between 6 and 12 months old, closing both the ASD and VSD. The single AV valve is divided, and the two resulting AV valves are repaired or replaced. Complications include mitral regurgitation, complete heart block, and dysrhythmias.

## Patent Ductus Arteriosus

### Pathophysiology

*Patent ductus arteriosus* (PDA) results from a failure of the ductus arteriosus to close. Although PDA may occur alone, it is an integral part of many complex cardiac defects. Premature infants frequently have PDA, and term infants with PDA account for 5% to 10% of all congenital cardiac defects. Females are three times as likely to be affected as males. German measles may cause PDA if contracted by the mother during the 5th to 10th week of gestation because the Rubella virus inhibits growth of elastic tissue within the ductus (Sadler, 1985).

The ductus remains open in PDA. Blood flows from the aorta through the PDA, and back to the pulmonary artery and lungs (Fig. 24-10). The left heart pumps increased volumes because blood shunted through the PDA returns to the left side. The amount of shunting depends on three factors: PDA diameter, pressure difference between the aortic and pulmonary artery, and systemic and pulmonary vascular resistances.

### Medical Diagnosis and Management

If the PDA is small, the infant is asymptomatic. Infants with large PDAs may experience frequent lower respiratory tract infections, endocarditis, and atelectasis. Congestive heart failure may occur, with hepatomegaly and splenomegaly. These infants feed poorly, gain weight slowly, and are tachypneic, easily fatigued, and irritable. If the PDA is

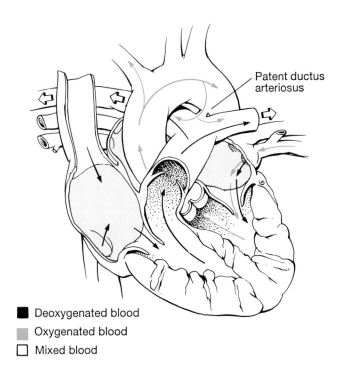

■ Deoxygenated blood
▨ Oxygenated blood
☐ Mixed blood

*Figure 24–10.  Patent ductus arteriosus.*

large and is left untreated, pulmonary hypertension develops into pulmonary vascular obstructive disease. A loud murmur, heard continuously throughout systole and diastole, is heard in the left infraclavicular area or along the upper left sternal border. The murmur is easily heard over the back. The diagnosis of PDA is confirmed by radiographic studies and an echocardiogram, which show left atrial and ventricular enlargement.

Placental prostaglandin has been identified as playing a role in keeping the ductus open. Indomethacin, a prostaglandin inhibitor, may be used to promote closure of the ductus, but is effective only in preterm infants.

A conical foam plastic plug (Ivalon foam plug) may be placed in the ductus during cardiac catheterization. The plug is placed in the aortic end of the ductus and is held in place by aortic pressure. It is eventually incorporated into a fibrous mass (Radtke & Lock, 1990). The PDA may also be closed by using a Double-Umbrella Rashkind Occluder, following a procedure similar to that discussed in the section on ASD.

If these procedures are unsuccessful, surgical treatment is indicated. Surgical closure is done through a left posterolateral thoracotomy. The PDA is tied off or a clamp is placed on the ductus, tissue is cut, and each divided end is sewn shut. Complications are rare.

## Coarctation of the Aorta
### Pathophysiology

Eight percent of all congenital cardiac defects are classified as *coarctation,* or constriction, of the aorta (COA) (Fig. 24-11). The heart must work harder because of the obstruction to blood flow. There are numerous associated anomalies, of which bicuspid aortic valve is the most common. Males are affected nearly twice as often as females. COA is present in 30% of infants with Turner syndrome (Park, 1988).

The narrowing, which may either be isolated to one small area or affect a long segment, is usually located below the origin of the left subclavian artery. The degree of narrowing is the major factor in coarctation. *Preductal* or *infantile* coarctation is located before the ductus, which remains open. Trunk blood flow is supplied predominantly by right ventricular outflow into the pulmonary artery and into the aorta through the PDA. Blood that shunts through the PDA is desaturated, but cyanosis is not usually observed. The right ventricle and pulmonary artery enlarge, and the descending aorta dilates. This defect is associated most often with severe cardiac abnormalities, and the COA is of long length (Gersony, 1989).

If the narrowing is located distal to the ductus, the

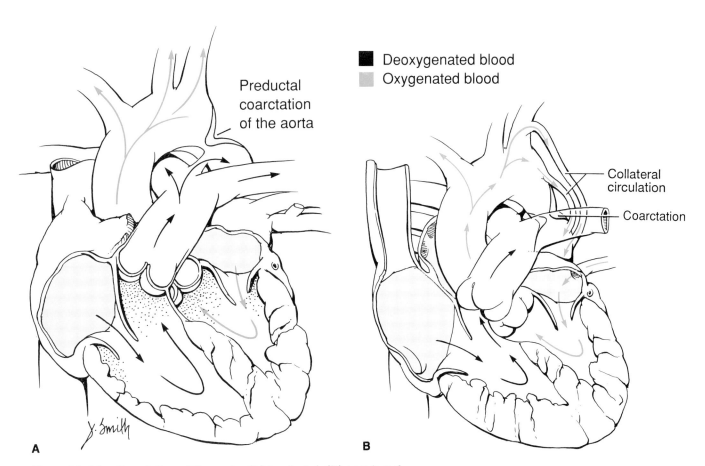

Preductal coarctation of the aorta

■ Deoxygenated blood
□ Oxygenated blood

Collateral circulation

Coarctation

A

B

*Figure 24–11. Coarctation of the aorta: (A) preductal; (B) postductal.*

defect is postductal or adult, and the ductus is closed. Trunk blood flow is supplied with left ventricular output through the aorta. Both left heart chambers enlarge. Blood flow follows a normal pattern, without extra communication between pulmonary and systemic circulations. Collateral circulation develops around the COA in order to adequately perfuse the lower body with blood.

A classic sign in many children with COA is a difference in BP and pulse quality between the upper and lower extremities. Femoral and pedal pulses are weak or absent. The arms tend to have much higher systolic BP and full pulses when compared to the legs. Other symptoms include epitaxis, headaches, fainting, and lower leg muscle cramps.

### Medical Diagnosis and Management

Asymptomatic infants are monitored until elective surgery is performed. Symptomatic infants tend to develop CHF within the first 2 to 4 weeks of life. CHF is evident by 3 months of age in more than 80% of children with preductal COA (Park, 1988). Infants with COA display poor feeding, poor weight gain, lethargy, dyspnea, and paleness, and may exhibit lower body cyanosis. CHF and renal failure are major causes of mortality. The clinical symptoms of COA aid in its diagnosis. Radiographic studies may show an enlarged heart, and the coarctation may be detected by echocardiography. Cardiac catheterization and angiography can be used to confirm the diagnosis and investigate for other defects.

Medical management depends on the child's status. If the child is unresponsive to medical treatment, urgent surgery is performed. In symptomatic infants surgery is usually performed as soon as possible, and the infant is stabilized. For asymptomatic children, elective surgery is done between 3 and 5 years of age, when the child's aorta approximates the size of an adult's.

Surgical correction of coarctation involves numerous options. Surgical procedures include resecting the constricted portion of the aorta and sewing the two ends together (an end-to-end anastomosis); excising the constriction and applying a patch (patch aortoplasty); replacing the coarcted segment with a Dacron tube; or creating a patch using a flap of the subclavian artery (Fig. 24-12). The most common postoperative complication is hypertension. Because the aorta is clamped during surgery, the child is at risk for spinal cord ischemia and paralysis.

## Acyanotic Heart Defects With Normal or Decreased Pulmonary Blood Flow

### Aortic Stenosis

#### Pathophysiology

*Aortic stenosis* (AS) is a narrowing of the aortic valve (Fig. 24-13). If valve cusps fail to form correctly, or if tissue above or below the valve develops abnormally, AS results.

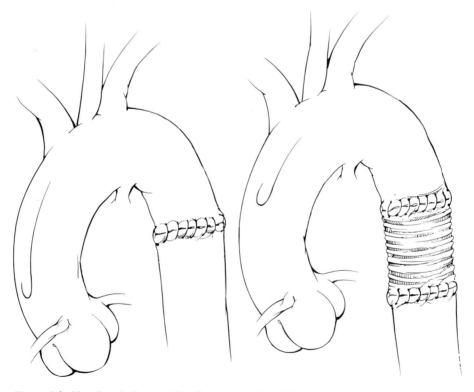

*Figure 24–12.  Surgical correction for coarctation of the aorta.*

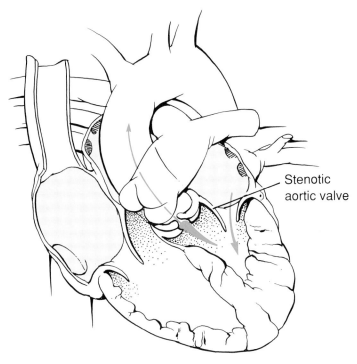

*Figure 24–13.  Aortic stenosis.*

There are three types of aortic stenosis: valvular, subvalvular, and supravalvular. Valvular aortic stenosis (narrowing) accounts for 5% of all congenital cardiac defects, and involves obstruction of blood flow from the left ventricle of the heart. Males are affected four times more frequently than females. PDA, COA, and bicuspid aortic valves often occur in the presence of aortic stenosis (Friedman, 1989).

In subvalvular AS, stenosis may result from a fibromuscular tunnel or a localized muscular ring below the valve. Supravalvular AS, which results from localized or diffuse aortic lumen narrowing, is rare.

Aortic stenosis produces obstruction to left ventricular output. The ventricle must pump harder to overcome this elevated pressure, resulting in left ventricular hypertrophy, which can cause compromised blood supply to the heart muscle (ischemia). Pulmonary edema can also result from increased pulmonary venous pressure.

### Medical Diagnosis and Management

Most children with mild aortic stenosis are asymptomatic. The defect is often discovered during routine physical examination, when a systolic aortic murmur is heard at the right upper sternal border. Symptoms in older children usually include complaints of angina, fatigue, and syncope. Fainting occurs when the left ventricle cannot keep a CO high enough to maintain cerebral blood flow. Infants with critical aortic stenosis may experience CHF early in life, and medical and surgical intervention is indicated.

Aortic stenosis is repaired by resecting and widening

areas of narrow tissue or repairing or replacing the aortic valve. Complications of this procedure include cardiac failure, aortic insufficiency, persistent stenosis or restenosis, and heart block. A permanent pacemaker may be required if the child is not in sinus rhythm following surgery.

## Pulmonic Stenosis

### Pathophysiology

*Pulmonic stenosis* (PS) is a narrowing of the opening through which blood is ejected from the right ventricle into the pulmonary artery (Fig. 24-14). It accounts for between 5% and 8% of all congenital cardiac defects, and is associated with many cardiac anomalies. The obstruction may be valvular, subvalvular (infundibular), or supravalvular.

Valvular pulmonic stenosis usually results from fusion of all three cusps of the pulmonic valve, which controls blood flow from the right ventricle into the pulmonary artery. Subvalvular PS develops from a ring of fibrous and muscular tissue that surrounds the right ventricular outflow tract. This ring is usually located between 1 cm and 3 cm below the pulmonary valve. Supravalvular PS may involve the main pulmonary artery, either of its branches, or both branches. The narrowing may be either localized or diffuse.

PS obstructs ventricular output. The right ventricle hypertrophies as it attempts to maintain a normal stroke volume against increased pressure. The ventricle eventually dilates and then fails. Pulmonary blood flow then decreases. For a time, the body compensates by increasing oxygen extraction at the tissue level, but cyanosis eventu-

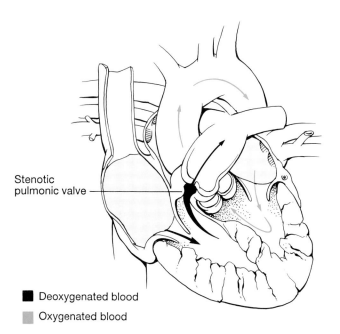

■ Deoxygenated blood
▨ Oxygenated blood

*Figure 24–14.  Pulmonic stenosis.*

ally develops. The tricuspid valve may thicken as a result of the stress placed on it, and the right atrium may dilate and hypertrophy. As pressure on the right side of the heart increases, a right-to-left shunt may develop at the atrial level through the foramen ovale. Infants with severe PS may suffer small myocardial infarcts due to subendocardial ischemia.

### Medical Diagnosis and Management

The degree of obstruction determines the child's symptoms. Most children with mild or moderate PS are asymptomatic, and the defect is discovered on routine examination. If PS is severe, symptoms may include fatigue, dyspnea, and signs of heart failure. Cardiac output is low and does not increase with exercise, so myocardial perfusion decreases. Exercise may precipitate chest pain, fainting, dysrhythmias, and sudden death.

A loud, systolic ejection murmur is heard best along the left upper sternal border, radiating to the back, the neck, and the rest of the precordium. A systolic thrill is easily felt along the second and third intercostal spaces along the left sternal border, radiating to the suprasternal notch. The diagnosis is confirmed by radiographic studies and echocardiogram.

Children with asymptomatic mild or moderate PS may not require surgery; however, they must be followed carefully. Treatment is primarily surgical if children are symptomatic or PS is severe. As with aortic stenosis, repair is done by resecting or widening areas of narrow tissue. If the stenosis is severe, a soft conduit may be placed to bypass blood around the stenosis. In other cases, surgical correction consists of repairing the valve. Balloon valvuloplasty may be successful in some children. Complications are rare but include hemorrhage, CHF, or pulmonary regurgitation.

## Cyanotic Heart Defects With Increased Pulmonary Blood Flow

All children with cyanotic defects are prone to a variety of complications, including growth retardation, brain abscess, cardiovascular accidents (CVA), infective endocarditis, polycythemia, hypochromic anemia, and coagulopathies after long-standing hypoxia and cyanosis.

### Transposition of the Great Arteries

#### Pathophysiology

During the fifth week of gestation, a ridge of tissue grows within the truncus arteriosus, dividing it into a pulmonary artery and aorta. Failure of this ridge to spiral results in *transposition of the great arteries* (TGA). The aorta arises from the right ventricle, and the pulmonary artery arises from the left ventricle. Another cardiac defect, such as PDA, ASD, or VSD, must be present to allow mixture of oxygenated and venous blood so the child can survive. TGA accounts for roughly 5% of all congenital cardiac defects. The anomaly affects males three times more frequently than females.

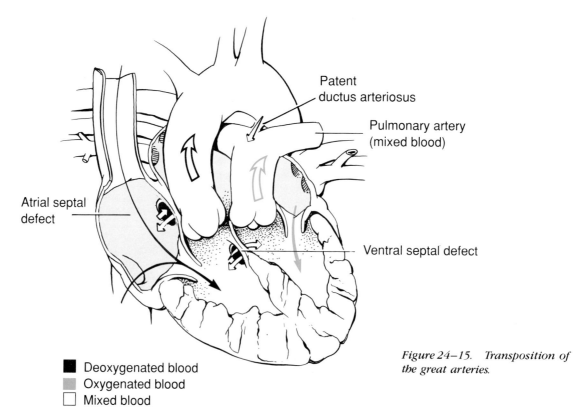

Patent
ductus arteriosus

Pulmonary artery
(mixed blood)

Atrial septal
defect

Ventral septal defect

■ Deoxygenated blood
▨ Oxygenated blood
☐ Mixed blood

*Figure 24–15.  Transposition of the great arteries.*

In TGA, blood flows from the right atrium to the right ventricle to the aorta and eventually back into the right atrium. On the other side, blood flows from the left atrium to the left ventricle to the pulmonary artery and lungs and then back into the left atrium. The two circuits function entirely separately from each other (Fig. 24-15). Thus, blood flowing to the body cannot be oxygenated unless a shunt occurs somewhere between the two systems. These infants must either shunt left to right through an ASD or from the aorta to the pulmonary artery through a PDA. If a neonate is born without a true ASD and an intact ventricular septum, immediate creation of a shunt (i.e., balloon atrial septostomy) is essential if the child is to survive.

In TGA, the right atrium, right ventricle, and pulmonary artery receive an increased volume of blood and become stressed. Pulmonary hypertension often results. A PA band may help decrease pulmonary blood flow. If the infant has pulmonary stenosis (PS), blood flow to the lungs is decreased, and the left side of the heart is stressed. A variety of shunts can be placed to increase pulmonary blood flow.

### Medical Diagnosis and Management

Without medical intervention, 90% of infants with TGA would die within 6 months of birth (Park, 1988). Most neonates with TGA experience cyanosis within the first hours or days of life. Congestive heart failure develops early in infants with a large VSD. Cyanosis, tachycardia, hepatomegaly, and feeding difficulties are noted. Eventually, polycythemia, clubbing, dyspnea, and poor exercise tolerance develop. There is no characteristic murmur, but if present, murmurs are variable and usually associated with other anomalies. Echocardiography is used to confirm the diagnosis, and cardiac catheterization is used to obtain additional data about the defect.

Oxygen therapy is of limited value, and aggressive management of hypoxemia and acidosis is important. Surgical repair is accomplished by the Mustard, Senning, Rastelli, or arterial switch (Jatene) procedures. The Mustard and Senning repair are similar, redirecting blood flow from the right atrium to the left ventricle and from the left atrium to the right ventricle. These procedures are usually done in infants between 6 and 12 months of age. The Rastelli procedure is performed by separating the pulmonary artery from the left ventricle and sewing the cardiac end of the pulmonary artery shut. The VSD is closed. Finally, a conduit is placed between the right ventricle and pulmonary artery. The Jatene switch must be done very early in the neonate's life, usually within the first three weeks, before pulmonary vascular resistance decreases and the left ventricle becomes accustomed to pumping under a low pressure system (Driscoll, 1990). The pulmonary artery and aorta are disected, the distal ends switched, and the coronary arteries moved from the aortic base to that of the pulmonary artery. Surgical complications may include pulmonary edema, atrial arrhythmias, hemorrhage, tunnel leaks, or conduit obstruction.

## Truncus Arteriosus

### Pathophysiology

*Truncus arteriosus* (TA) develops when the spiral ridge within the truncus arteriosus fails to develop or to fuse and descend to the ventricle. TA accounts for 1% to 4% of all congenital cardiac defects, and is characterized by one great artery arising from both ventricles, overriding a large VSD. This common artery has one valve, which is malformed, and gives rise to the pulmonary, coronary, and systemic arteries (Fig. 24-16).

The output of both ventricles is ejected into the common trunk. Unoxygenated blood from the right ventricle and oxygenated blood from the left ventricle are mixed incompletely in the trunk. Pulmonary blood flow is usually increased, causing CHF to develop in the first weeks of life. The degree of cyanosis is related to the amount of pulmonary blood flow.

Four types of PTA exist. Pulmonary blood flow is increased in type I, normal in II and III, and decreased in IV. The different types are classified according to the size and location of pulmonary arteries off the truncus.

### Medical Diagnosis and Management

Cyanosis is seen at birth or shortly thereafter due to elevated pulmonary vascular resistance. As resistance decreases and pulmonary blood flow increases, cyanosis may disappear. As excessive blood flow through the pulmonary system and, thus, increased volume load of the

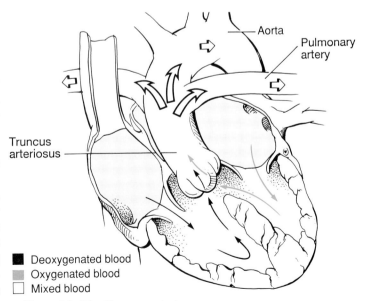

■ Deoxygenated blood
▨ Oxygenated blood
□ Mixed blood

*Figure 24–16.   Truncus arteriosus.*

heart develop, signs of CHF appear within the first weeks after birth. These children are dyspneic with feeding, fail to thrive, are irritable, tachycardic, and very diaphoretic, and experience frequent respiratory infections.

Stenosis at the pulmonary artery origins may produce a continuous murmur. A harsh, systolic, ejection murmur of valvular stenosis may be heard over the upper right intercostal spaces. A loud holosystolic murmur may be heard over the left sternal border. Without intervention, 50% of these infants die within the first month of life, and most die within 6 to 12 months.

Medical therapy consists of digitalis and diuretics to treat congestive heart failure. Surgery may be either palliative or a total repair. Palliative surgical procedures depend on the degree of pulmonary blood flow. If it is decreased, systemic-pulmonary shunts (such as the Blalock-Taussig) will improve PBF and, thus, oxygenation. Corrective surgery is preferred over placement of a pulmonary artery band because the PA band often distorts pulmonary arteries and increases the risk of future surgery. Corrective surgical procedures involve separation of the pulmonary artery or arteries from the common trunk, closure of the VSD, and insertion of a right ventricular-to-pulmonary artery valved conduit.

Long-term complications include valve calcification, pulmonary vascular disease, and residual VSDs. Subsequent conduit replacement is required to accommodate the infant's growth.

## Cyanotic Heart Defects With Decreased Pulmonary Blood Flow

### Tetralogy of Fallot

#### Pathophysiology

Tetralogy of Fallot (TOF) is one of the most common congenital heart defects, with an incidence rate of 10%. It is the most common cyanotic heart defect. Associated cardiac defects include PDA, ASD, and aortic regurgitation.

Four major anomalies constitute TOF:

1. A VSD
2. Right ventricular hypertrophy
3. Pulmonary stenosis that is usually infundibular
4. An aorta that overrides the VSD

Interference of ventricular septation and valve formation results in TOF. When septal tissue in the truncus develops anteriorly instead of midline, the right ventricular outflow tract is narrowed, and a VSD forms. Because the aorta is directly over the VSD, pressures in both the right and left ventricle equalize and the right ventricle hypertrophies (Fig. 24-17).

Pathophysiology varies according to the size of the VSD and the degree of pulmonary stenosis. Cyanotic TOF is referred to as "blue tet" whereas the acyanotic form is called "pink tet" (resulting from milder pulmonary stenosis with less right-to-left shunting). These children become cyanotic by the age of 1 to 3 years as pulmonary infundibular stenosis increases with physical growth. If an ASD is present, the defect is known as pentalogy of Fallot.

### Medical Diagnosis and Management

Many neonates with TOF are not hypoxemic. Hypoxemia increases after approximately 2 months because the infant sleeps less and is more active. Oxygen demands increase, but the infant may not have the ability to increase oxygenation. Symptomatic children display cyanosis, clubbing, exertional dyspnea, squatting, and hypoxic spells. A harsh systolic murmur may be heard at the middle and upper left sternal border. Although an echocardiogram and cardiac catheterization are performed to determine the extent of the malformation, diagnosis is usually made based on the history and physical examination.

A classic symptom of TOF is hypoxic or tet spells, which are characterized by increased cyanosis, tachypnea, and loss of consciousness. These spells may result from pulmonary infundibular spasm, causing increased right-to-left shunting across the VSD, and thus hypoxia. Severe tet spells may lead to seizures, cerebral vascular accidents, and death. Tet spells most often occur in the morning, following bowel movements, feeding, or hard crying. The child with this symptom displays rapid, deep breathing, deepening cyanosis, limpness or convulsions, and syncope, and the potential for death exists. Careful observation of hemoglobin and hematocrit levels is important to assess oxygen-carrying capacity and blood viscosity. Viscous blood decreases pulmonary blood flow velocity, increases the work of breathing, and predisposes the child to cerebral insult.

Morphine relaxes the child experiencing a tet spell, and depresses the respiratory center, thus decreasing hyperpnea. Propranolol, a beta-adrenergic blocker, may also be used to increase pulmonary blood flow and decrease infundibular spasm. The knee–chest or squatting position may help to relieve tet spells by increasing pressure on the left side of the heart and thus decreasing the amount of right to left shunting.

Several palliative surgical procedures are available to increase pulmonary blood flow. The preferred procedures are the Blalock-Taussig shunt for infants older than 3 months of age or placement of a Gore-tex shunt between subclavian and ipsilateral (same side) pulmonary artery in infants less than 3 months of age. The Waterston (connection between ascending aorta and right pulmonary artery) and Potts (connection between the descending aorta and left pulmonary artery) shunts are no longer recommended because of the severity of complications

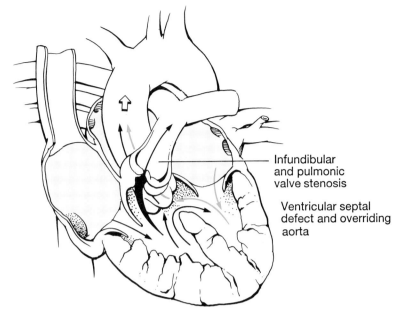

*Figure 24–17. Tetralogy of Fallot.*

Infundibular
and pulmonic
valve stenosis

Ventricular septal
defect and overriding
aorta

associated with them. However, they may be performed palliatively if total correction is impossible. Complications include heart failure and pulmonary hypertension from increased pulmonary blood flow.

Total repair is usually done between the ages of 6 and 18 months. The VSD is closed, and the right ventricular outflow tract is enlarged. Complications of this procedure include bleeding, transient congestive heart failure, persistent right ventricular failure, pulmonary valve regurgitation, heart block, and ventricular dysrhythmias.

## Tricuspid Atresia

The tricuspid valve forms at about the 34th day of gestation. If valve cusps fail to form or fuse together, *tricuspid atresia* (TA) results. TA accounts for 1% to 2% of all congenital cardiac defects, and is the third most common cyanotic anomaly. Other cardiac defects are associated with this lesion, including transposition of the great arteries, coarctation of the aorta, and PDA. This anomaly involves total occlusion of the tricuspid valve, with no communication between the right atrium and the right ventricle (Fig. 24-18). An ASD and VSD or PDA is essential for blood oxygenation and survival. The right ventricle is usually hypoplastic, receiving minimal blood flow through a VSD. The pulmonary artery is also hypoplastic.

### Pathophysiology

In tricuspid atresia, blood flow through the heart is altered. Venous blood flows into the right atrium, across an ASD to the left atrium, and into the left ventricle. Most of the blood is then pumped out the aorta. If a PDA is present,

some aortic flow perfuses the lungs. The rest of the left ventricular blood flows across a VSD, if present, into the right ventricle and into the pulmonary system. Therefore, the left ventricle pumps both the systemic and pulmonary venous return. Because of altered blood flow, the right atrium, left atrium, left ventricle, and aorta will be enlarged.

Brain abscesses are a concern in children with tricuspid atresia. The right-to-left shunt bypasses blood around the phagocytic filtering action of the pulmonary bed. Bacteria may colonize cerebral tissue already weakened by previous hypoperfusion or hypoxemia. Mortality is high, and many survivors suffer neurologic impairment.

### Medical Diagnosis and Management

Because of cyanosis or murmur, approximately 50% of neonates with TA are diagnosed within 24 hours of birth, and 85% within 2 months (Sade & Fyfe, 1990). Neonates usually present at birth with central cyanosis due to decreased pulmonary blood flow. They are tachypneic, dyspneic upon exertion, hypoxic, poor feeders, and often in metabolic acidosis. Hypoxic spells similar to tet spells are ominous and indicate the need for surgery. A narrowing VSD or PDA size reduces pulmonary blood flow and increases cyanosis. If the ASD is too small and blood is backed up into the right atrium, or if the child is in CHF, hepatomegaly will be present. A VSD murmur and the continuous murmur of PDA may be heard. Diagnosis is based on signs of acidosis and hypoxia, and is confirmed by cardiac catheterization.

A balloon or blade atrial septostomy may be done during cardiac catheterization to increase the right-to-left

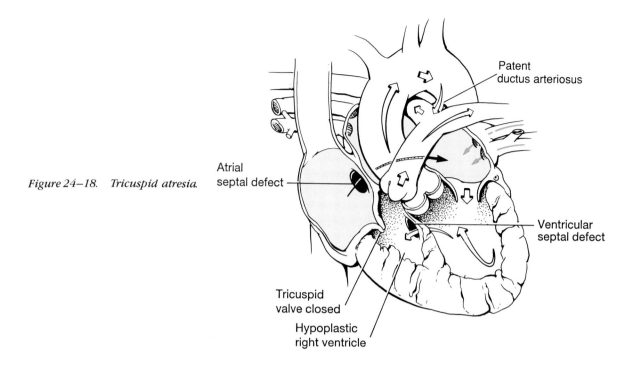

*Figure 24–18.  Tricuspid atresia.*

Labels: Patent ductus arteriosus; Atrial septal defect; Ventricular septal defect; Tricuspid valve closed; Hypoplastic right ventricle

atrial shunt. If PBF is low, a Gore-tex graft or Blalock-Taussig shunt may be done palliatively. The Blalock-Taussig shunt is preferred because the diameter of the subclavian artery limits pulmonary blood flow. Therefore, the incidence of CHF due to excessive pulmonary blood flow is rare. A Glenn procedure, anastomosing the superior vena cava to the right pulmonary artery, may be done if corrective surgery either is not feasible or did not work well.

Corrective repair is done by performing the Fontan procedure. This surgery, first performed in 1968, has several modifications. The right atrium may be directly anastomosed to the pulmonary artery. Another approach involves placing a conduit between the right atrium and pulmonary artery. A third modification is placing a conduit from the right atrium to the right ventricle, bypassing the atretic valve. Complications of this procedure include transient right heart failure, pleural effusions, protein-losing enteropathies, conduit obstruction or stenosis of conduit valve, ascites, transient superior vena cava syndrome, and dysrhythmias. Pleuroperitoneal shunts have been placed in some children after surgery in attempts to control pleural effusions.

## Nursing Care for Children With Congenital Heart Defects
### Nursing Assessment and Diagnosis

Assessment of children with congenital heart defects is a continuous process. Nursing assessment is used to screen infants for possible congenital defects, as well as to monitor their progress after surgery and during follow-up care.

The assessment process is also used to determine the child's and parents' developmental levels, the need for teaching, and their compliance with therapeutic measures.

By assessing these areas nurses will be better able to arrive at diagnoses, as well as more effectively plan and intervene.

The following nursing diagnoses may apply for children with congenital heart defects and their families:

*Pattern 1: Exchanging*
- Altered nutrition: Less than body requirements related to dyspnea, fatigue, vomiting, increased metabolic rate, or impaired absorption and transport of nutrients
- Decreased cardiac output related to dysrhythmias, altered contractility, altered preload or afterload
- Fluid volume excess related to cardiac failure, volume overload
- High risk for altered body temperature related to respiratory infection, dehydration
- High risk for infection related to malnutrition, disruption of normal skin barrier, immunosuppression
- Impaired gas exchange related to pulmonary congestion
- Impaired skin integrity related to immobility and inability to move self due to young age
- Ineffective airway clearance related to young age, inability to cough, and thick secretions and pain
- Ineffective breathing pattern related to bilateral lung congestion or postoperative pain

*Pattern 3: Relating*
- Altered family processes related to hospitalization and impending surgery
- Altered parenting related to birth of a critically ill infant necessitating immediate separation and hospitalization
- High risk for altered parenting related to lack of time for bonding with infant
- Impaired social interaction related to exercise limitations
- Social isolation related to visible medical abnormality

*Pattern 5: Choosing*
- Ineffective family coping: Compromised related to separation from child during hospitalization
- Noncompliance with bacterial endocarditis precautions related to feeling of well-being and need for a life-long regimen

*Pattern 6: Moving*
- Activity intolerance related to dysrhythmias, fatigue, or fear of injuring the heart
- Altered growth and development related to parental overprotection of the child

*Pattern 9: Feeling*
- Anxiety (child) related to parental separation
- Anxiety (parental) related to impending hospitalization and surgery
- Dysfunctional grieving related to loss of idealized perfect baby
- Fear related to potential death of the infant or child
- Pain related to illness or surgery

## Planning and Implementing Nursing Care

The first step in planning and implementing nursing care based on nursing diagnoses is to establish outcome criteria. Since many infants and children with congenital heart defects undergo surgery, nursing care is planned and implemented during the pre-, intra-, and postoperative periods, as was discussed earlier in the chapter. The goal of care during this period is to prepare the child and family for the surgery, and to facilitate recovery.

Following surgery, the nurse is responsible for considerable physical care that includes providing relief from pain; administering medications and evaluating their effectiveness and side effects; appraising the physical status of the child by continuous assessment; and monitoring for signs of complications. Common problems in children who have undergone cardiac surgery include dysrhythmias, fluid excess and deficit, infection, fever, pulmonary complications, and alterations in nutrition. Although many of the possible complications that arise are discussed under the medical management sections with each problem, the nurse, in fact, is primarily responsible for monitoring

for these complications. The primary nursing goal during this period is to be certain that the child remains free from complications, and, if problems are encountered, that corrective measures are instituted as quickly as possible.

Although child and parent education begins with admission and continues throughout the child's hospitalization, education is particularly important during the recovery period as the child and parents prepare for the child's discharge from the hospital. The parents need information about the nature of the problem, the treatment plan, the prognosis, home care, and long term care.

Another area where nurses intervene is in the child's and family's psychosocial development and adaptation to the illness. Because of the serious nature of most cardiac defects, parents and children often have difficulty expressing their feelings, emotions, and anxieties. By providing care that is sensitive to more than just physical needs, nurses can assist families in adapting to the illness and can promote growth within the family. Referrals for additional information or support are often very helpful. A primary goal of nursing care is to facilitate normal growth and development for the child and family.

## Evaluating Nursing Care

As noted above, planning and implementing care requires establishing clear outcome criteria for each goal. For children with cardiac defects, expert physical care is essential to ensure the child's maximal recovery from the illness. The child should remain free from complications, and should show signs of normal growth and development. The parents should demonstrate their understanding of the health problem, the prescribed treatment plan, and the care they will be required to provide for the child at home. Adaptation to the illness is demonstrated by the ability of the child (if appropriate) and parents to ask questions, express emotions, and avail themselves of resources and available support.

# Acquired Cardiovascular Diseases

Acquired cardiovascular disease arises from many factors and appears in a variety of forms. Causative or contributory factors include infectious processes, connective tissue disease (i.e., metabolic or degenerative disease), or complications from any of the above factors.

## Bacterial Endocarditis

### Pathophysiology

*Endocarditis* is an infection of the endocardium or valves of the heart caused by bacteria, rickettsia, or fungal agents. Two components are necessary for development of most forms of endocarditis: a congenital or acquired cardiac lesion, and an infective organism. The infectious agent is introduced in a variety of ways, including intravenous catheter insertion and maintenance, pacemakers, placement of foreign materials (i.e., conduits or mechanical valves) during surgery, and dental work with disruption of normal gum barriers. Many children with congenital heart defects have a predisposition for developing endocarditis.

Bacterial endocarditis is frequently caused by staphylococci or streptococci. The gram-negative organism *Haemophilus* also causes bacterial endocarditis. *Candida albicans* and *Aspergillis* organisms frequently cause fungal endocarditis. Mortality rates are high for patients with fungal endocarditis.

The mechanism behind endocarditis is turbulent blood flow or existence of a significant pressure gradient resulting from cardiac lesions. This turbulence eventually produces endocardial tissue damage. Platelets and fibrin adhere to the injured area, and a thrombus forms. Infective organisms get trapped in the forming meshwork, or adhere to tissue surfaces. Large colonies of bacteria, known as vegetation, become encased in a fibrin mass. This mass prevents phagocytic leukocytes and antimicrobial agents from attacking the vegetation.

## Medical Diagnosis and Management

Children with endocarditis have nonspecific symptoms, such as loss of appetite, general malaise, headaches, myalgias, and arthralgias. Anemia is a common finding, with hemoglobin levels often less than 12 mg/100 mL. Microemboli appear as petechiae on the skin, mucous membranes, or conjunctiva.

Treatment requires 4 to 6 weeks of intravenous antibiotic therapy. Treatment is extended because the fibrin mass in which the infectious agent grows is relatively protected from host defenses and antimicrobial matter. Surgery is performed if the child experiences difficulty with embolization or progressive cardiac failure. The procedure depends on the child and the underlying cardiac anomaly. Valves or conduits may need to be replaced.

## Nursing Assessment and Diagnosis

Because bacterial endocarditis most commonly occurs in children with a history of congenital or acquired heart disorders, nurses should assess these children carefully for signs of fever, loss of appetite, weight loss, and general malaise. Because of the long duration of antibiotic therapy, the traumatic effect of hospitalization on the child, and the cost of hospitalization, some institutions allow home antibiotic therapy. The nurse must assess the child's response to this treatment as well as parental coping.

Nursing diagnoses for bacterial endocarditis might include the following:

- Fear related to painful invasive procedures
- Diversional Activity Deficit related to long-term antibiotic therapy and fatigue
- Noncompliance with endocarditis precautions related to life-long need for prophylactic measures

## Planning and Implementing Nursing Care

Goals of nursing care for children with bacterial endocarditis include prevention of complications, child and family education, and support of the child and family through therapy. Nurses monitor the child for signs of adverse drug reactions, as well as other potential complications such as CHF. Cultures are taken to monitor the course of therapy, so nurses must use strict aseptic technique to prevent contamination of blood samples.

Because treatment for bacterial endocarditis is prolonged, prevention is a crucial nursing intervention. Parents should be instructed to be certain that the child maintains good oral hygiene, and that prophylactic antibiotics are administered before dental procedures. Parents should also be informed of signs and symptoms of potential infection, such as low-grade fever, anorexia, or general malaise, and should seek medical attention immediately.

Because treatment is prolonged, whether in the hospital or home setting, nurses should attempt to find diversional activities for the child. The use of a heparin lock facilitates ambulation and activity, which help to relieve the boredom that can accompany treatment.

## Evaluating Nursing Care

Evaluation is based on meeting goals established in the nursing care plan. The child should remain free from complications, and should show coping skills in adapting to the treatment regimen. The child and parents should demonstrate their understanding of the condition and its prevention.

# Pericarditis

## Pathophysiology

Inflammation of the parietal (outer) and visceral (inner) pericardial surfaces is known as *pericarditis*. This infection arises from multiple sources, including renal failure, infective organisms, connective tissue disease, drugs, cardiac surgery, and anticoagulant therapy. The cause is sometimes unknown. Pericardium involvement may either be dry or involve an effusion. Slowly-accumulating fluid in the pericardial space is generally well-tolerated, but acute pericarditis can be life-threatening. Increased fluid volume within the pericardial space increases intrapericardial pressure. The AV valves close prematurely, so diastolic filling time is decreased. Stroke volume, cardiac output, and systolic blood pressure all decrease. Three compensatory mechanisms evolve:

1. Venous constriction occurs in the systemic and pulmonic beds in order to improve diastolic filling of the heart by increasing venous return.
2. Systemic vascular resistance increases in an attempt to maintain adequate blood pressure.
3. Tachycardia occurs in an effort to maintain adequate cardiac output.

## Medical Diagnosis and Management

The cardinal physical sign of pericarditis is a scratchy, high-pitched friction rub. It is best heard along the middle-to-lower left sternal border, but is often heard over the entire precordium. The chief complaint is chest pain described as either sharp or dull, oppressive, or aching. The echocardiogram helps diagnose tamponade.

Treatment varies according to the type of pericarditis. Observation, rest, and nonsteroidal anti-inflammatory medication may be all that is required. Some forms of this condition require draining of the pericardial fluid, or pericardiocentesis. If pericarditis is recurrent, the pericardium can be surgically removed.

## Nursing Assessment and Diagnosis

A child with thoracic, neck, shoulder, or arm pain relieved by position change (i.e., sitting up or leaning forward) may have pericarditis. If the pericarditis is acute, children look and act ill, with signs and symptoms of decreased cardiac output. Nurses must carefully assess these children for signs of cardiac tamponade.

Nursing diagnoses for pericarditis might include the following:

- Decreased cardiac output related to decreased preload and tachycardia
- Fear related to rapidly deteriorating physical condition
- Anxiety related to recurrence of pericarditis
- Pain related to friction rub

## Planning and Implementing Nursing Care

If acute pericarditis is suspected and pericardiocentesis is necessary, nurses explain the procedure to the parents and child, answer questions, provide reassurance as appropriate, and obtain necessary supplies. Salicylates provide relief from discomfort as well as having anti-hyperthermic and anti-inflammatory properties.

## Evaluating Nursing Care

Goals established when nursing diagnoses were identified are evaluated for achievement, with revisions or resolutions as appropriate. Pain relief is evaluated by observation of the child, noting such things as decrease in restlessness, fussiness, and anxiety, lower respiratory and heart rates, and relaxed facial expressions. Effectiveness of communication can be evaluated following recovery from an acute attack of pericarditis.

## Rheumatic Fever

*Rheumatic fever* is a systemic inflammatory disease of childhood that may involve the heart, joints, skin, central nervous system, and connective tissue. The disease is common in underdeveloped countries, and an estimated 100,000 cases are still seen each year in the United States (Lockley & Bukantz, 1987). The disease tends to be associated with individuals living in low socioeconomic environments. A familial predisposition has been suggested, and the infection may recur. Rheumatic fever develops in between 0.3% and 3.0% of individuals with streptococcal infections, and is most common in children between the ages of 6 to 15 years (Park, 1988). Acute rheumatic fever (ARF) is the most common cause of acquired heart disease worldwide (Ayoub, 1989).

### Pathophysiology

Rheumatic fever is a delayed response (10 to 42 days post-infection) to group A hemolytic streptococcal infection of the pharynx. If a child's cold or sore throat is not treated or is inadequately treated, bacteria may be transported from tonsil to heart via lymph channels. Aschoff bodies are small nodules located in the interstitial tissue of the myocardium. These nodules, a form of granuloma, are characteristic lesions of rheumatic fever, and scar over as tissue heals. Valvular damage is a serious complication, and occurs as the valve leaflets become scarred. The mitral valve is most frequently involved, followed by the aortic valve. Carditis (inflammation of the heart muscles) occurs in 40% to 50% of patients with rheumatic fever, and results in valve scarring, with subsequent thickening and shortening of the chordae tendinae.

### Medical Diagnosis and Management

The modified Jones criteria are used to establish a diagnosis. Major manifestations include carditis, arthritis, chorea, and erythema marginatum. Minor manifestations include arthralgia, fever, previous ARF disease, leukocytosis, elevated erythrocyte sedimentation rate, positive C-reactive protein, and prolonged PR interval on ECG. Positive diagnosis of ARF is made on the presence of two major criteria or one major and one minor criteria, plus a history of recent Group A streptococcal infection.

ARF may present gradually or suddenly. Arthralgia is a common symptom in acute onset, usually occuring in one or more of the large joints (knees, elbows, and wrists). The pain is migratory, does not result in contractures, and generally lasts from 1 to 4 weeks. Subcutaneous nodules may be found on the flexor surfaces of the joints and bony prominences. These nodules occur during the febrile stage and are small, firm, and nontender; they are long lasting and eventually resolve. Sydenham's chorea, also known as St. Vitus' dance, appears late in the disease course and is characterized by involuntary, purposeless movement, muscle weakness, and emotional instability. Carditis is the most dangerous manifestation and is evidenced by murmurs, cardiomegaly, pericardial friction rub, and ECG changes. Erythema marginatum is uncommon and may appear at any time during the disease. Abdominal pain and pleurisy are less commonly seen manifestations.

Treatment is based on preventing cardiac complications. Aspirin is used to reduce inflammation and pain. Prednisone is prescribed if carditis is present. If the child has a streptococcal infection, penicillin is used; erythromycin may be used if the child is allergic to penicillin. Complete bedrest is prescribed. When Sydenham's chorea is severe, haloperidol, phenobarbital, diazepam, or chlorpromazine may be used to help control movement (Homer & Shulman, 1991). Full recovery may take 2 to 3 months.

Penicillin is usually used prophylactically to prevent recurrences. Prophylaxis may be an indefinite plan or may be discontinued at age 21 to 25 years if there is no evidence of vascular involvement. Penicillin should be taken when undergoing dental, gastrointestinal, or genitourinary procedures. Prevention is accomplished by antibiotic course, usually for 10 full days. ARF has a tendency to reoccur, often within 3 to 5 years of the first episode.

### Nursing Assessment and Diagnosis

Assessment inolves a detailed patient history. A throat culture is important in determining the presence of Group A beta-hemolytic streptococcus. Nurses should be aware that ARF may follow streptococcal infection at any site.

Nursing diagnoses for rheumatic fever might include the following:

- Activity intolerance related to joint pain, carditis
- Noncompliance with prophylactic measures related to emotional and financial burden of lifelong treatment
- High risk for impaired skin integrity related to prolonged bedrest
- Pain related to arthritis or arthralgia

### Planning and Implementing Nursing Care

Vital signs must be taken and carefully recorded. Record sleeping pulse rates in children without fevers, because tachycardia during sleep may indicate carditis. Anti-inflam-matory or suppressive drugs should not be given until a definite diagnosis is made, because the drugs could mask the infection and make identification impossible. Once the drugs have been given, parents can expect joint pain and fever to disappear within a few days. Nurses must be sensitive to arthritic pain. Initially, it may be so severe that the light weight of a sheet or blanket is painful. The parents should be reassured that polyarthritis will not be crippling. Warm baths and gentle range-of-motion exercises may help reduce discomfort and maintain maximal joint functioning.

### Evaluating Nursing Care

Evaluation of nursing care is based on meeting established goals. Ensuring adequate pain control and rest will improve the child's ability to cope with the disease. Early incorporation of the child as a responsible member of the health care team increases the chance of successful compliance with lifelong prophylaxis measures.

## Kawasaki Disease

### Pathophysiology

Also known as mucocutaneous lymph node syndrome, Kawasaki disease was first identified in Japan. It is a febrile, multisystem disorder, with an average age of onset of about 4 years. At least 30% of affected children have cardiac involvement (Hicks & Melish, 1986).

Cardiac diseases resulting from Kawasaki disease include pericarditis, myocarditis (inflammation of the myocardium), mitral insufficiency, valve dysfunction, myocardial infarction, and sudden death from coronary thrombosis. Congestive heart failure complicates these problems. Some children develop aseptic meningitis.

Kawasaki disease is discussed in further detail in Chapter 19.

## Congestive Heart Failure

Congestive heart failure (CHF) is characterized by the heart's inability to meet the metabolic demands of the body and/or its inability to pump the blood it contains. The most common cause of CHF in children is related to congenital anomalies.

### Pathophysiology

The mechanism behind CHF is volume or pressure overload due to congenital or acquired myocardial abnormalities. It may also be caused by electrolyte imbalances, bronchopulmonary dysplasia, acute hypertension, severe anemia, and certain dysrhythmias.

The end result of CHF is a decrease in cardiac output. Inability to pump contained blood results in increased end-diastolic ventricular pressure, and thus increased pressures in the atrial, pulmonary, and systemic venous systems.

In an attempt to compensate for these alterations, the sympathetic nervous system is stimulated. The resulting increase in heart rate and contractility improves stroke volume and cardiac output. The kidneys attempt to conserve water and sodium to increase cardiac output through increased blood volume. Peripheral vasoconstriction shunts blood to vital organs such as the heart and brain.

Theoretically, there are two classifications of heart failure. Left-sided failure results in pulmonary venous congestion as blood backs up from the left atrium into the pulmonary system. Normally, any increase in pulmonary interstitial fluid is matched by its removal through lymph flow. Disturbances of this balance lead to congestion. Fluid leaks into and remains in the interstitial space and eventually into the alveoli. Congestion reduces lung compliance and increases the work of breathing.

Right-sided failure results in systemic symptoms such as hepatomegaly and edema. (The latter symptom is manifested in puffy eyelids in infants and children.) Gastrointestinal complaints are common, probably resulting from increased intra-abdominal pressure and venous engorgement. Peripheral edema is uncommon in infants and small children, but manifests itself in older children. Most infants and children present with biventricular failure.

## Medical Diagnosis and Management

Children demonstrate adaptations to compensate for impaired cardiac function. They are tachycardic, with a pulse rate greater than 160 BPM in infants and over 100 BPM in older children. Pulses are thready and weak. Children display signs of sympathetic system overload (i.e., excessive diaphoresis, cold skin, and growth failure). Extremities may be mottled. Cyanosis is independent of left-to-right shunts. If normally cyanotic, the child will appear bluer than usual. If cardiomegaly is not seen on X-ray, congestive heart failure is doubtful. ABGs identify decreased levels of arterial oxygen and carbon dioxide. Decreased carbon dioxide is due to hyperventilation as the child attempts to improve oxygenation. Laboratory tests may reveal severe hypoglycemia from depletion of liver glycogen stores. Calcium levels may also be low.

Signs of pulmonary venous congestion include crackles, rales and wheezes, tachypnea, poor feeding in infants, dyspnea, orthopnea, coughing, and sometimes hemoptysis.

Standard pharmaceutical treatment involves digitalis and diuretics. Afterload reducing agents improve CO and decrease systemic vascular resistance. Venodilators (i.e., nitroglycerin, nitrates) reduce venous congestion and thus decrease pulmonary edema. Arteriolar vasodilators (i.e., captopril, hydralazine) decrease systemic vascular resistance by dilating arteriolar beds. Some drugs cause both venodilation and vasodilation (i.e., nitroprusside, prazosin). Intra-aortic balloon pumps may be used to support children through congestive heart failure crises.

If congestive heart failure cannot be controlled medically, surgery to correct the underlying problem should be performed. Surgical approaches vary according to the type of congenital cardiac defect. Additionally, some of these patients who are not surgical repair candidates may qualify for a cardiac transplant.

## Nursing Assessment and Diagnosis

Assessment of use of accessory muscles, head bobbing, grunting, tachypnea, skin coloring, and presence of mottled skin provides valuable information regarding the pulmonary status of children in CHF. A thorough assessment of medication administration should be done. Vital signs must be carefully assessed. The child's skin may be very cold to the touch due to vasoconstriction, yet the child may have an extremely high core temperature.

Subtle signs may signal impending CHF, such as irritability, increased feeding time with decreased total intake, infants falling asleep during feeding, vomiting after meals from air swallowed while trying to eat and breathe at the same time, and a decrease in diaper changes.

Nursing diagnoses for congestive heart failure might include the following:

- Decreased CO related to altered preload, afterload, and contractility
- Ineffective breathing pattern related to restricted lung expansion
- Ineffective airway clearance related to weakness and immobility
- Impaired gas exchange related to pulmonary venous congestion
- Fluid volume excess related to increased sodium and water retention
- High risk for altered body temperature related to hypoglycemia
- Altered nutrition: Less than body requirements related to decreased intake, fatigue with feeding, vomiting, and impaired nutrition absorption and transport
- Impaired skin integrity related to vasoconstriction, edema, and decreased activity
- Activity intolerance related to decreased tissue perfusion and gas exchange
- Bathing, hygiene, dressing, grooming self-care deficits related to fatigue and dyspnea

## Planning and Implementing Nursing Care

The goals of nursing care are to reduce oxygen demands and ease workload of the heart. Ensuring adequate rest and promoting anxiety reduction is essential, sometimes requiring the use of sedation. Respiratory distress is relieved by sitting the infant or child up in an infant seat or cardiac chair. Keeping the child in a semi-Fowler position pools fluid in the dependent areas of the lungs. Lung congestion is then decreased, breathing becomes easier, and less volume returns to the left atrium since less is reabsorbed from the lungs. An additional benefit of sitting is the use of gravity to keep the enlarged liver from pushing on the diaphragm and limiting thoracic expansion with breathing.

Oxygen must be humidified to loosen secretions, and is usually best tolerated when administered through a tent or hood. Hypothermia and hyperthermia place increased workload demands on a heart unable to meet those demands. Thus, it is important to keep the infant or child within a normal thermoregulatory range. Management of a balance in fluid and electrolytes is essential. Parents and the child, if appropriate, need to be instructed in a low sodium diet. Infants are not usually placed on severe salt and fluid restriction.

Feeding often exhausts infants in congestive heart failure. Use of a soft nipple helps conserve strength by decreasing the amount of energy the baby must use to suck. Formula or food should be high quality and given frequently in small feedings. High protein or highly concentrated formula should not be given, because the child fails to receive adequate fluid and the kidneys are overworked by the resulting increased osmotic load.

Nurses need to be aware of side effects of medication, such as hypokalemia with many diuretics. Parents must know how to use a calibrated dropper to dispense medication. Oral and parenteral digitalis doses differ in concentration, and cannot be used interchangeably. Parents should be taught to take the child's pulse for 1 minute before administering digitalis. The medication should be withheld and the physician called if the pulse rate is under 90 to 110 BPM in infants and 70 to 80 in older children. If the child vomits after digitalis is given, it is best to recommend skipping that dose because it is impossible to know how much drug the child has absorbed. If a dose is accidentally forgotten until 6 or 7 hours later, it is best to skip that dose. If both doses can still be scheduled for the day, parents may go ahead and give each dose at a delayed time. Parents should also be taught how to administer diuretics. Parents should be taught to watch for decreased amount or frequency of voiding. Decreased diaper changes may signal developing CHF.

### Evaluating Nursing Care

Assessment, intervention, and evaluation vary depending on the child's physiologic status. Because these children often experience repeated bouts of CHF, nurses and parents must be able to move within an established but flexible framework of care to maximize health for the child. In general, the child should exhibit normal vital signs, and unlabored respirations. Urine output should increase, and there should be less evidence of edema. The parents should demonstrate their understanding of the condition, its treatment, and home care.

## Hypertension

*Hypertension* is defined as the consistent elevation of systolic or diastolic pressure greater than the 95th percentile for the child's age and weight on three separate measurements. High blood pressure is a major risk factor for developing coronary heart disease, and is the single most important contributor to the development of cerebral vascular accidents. Since these diseases may have origins in childhood, it is important to target this population for prevention and control approaches.

Hypertension involves two major categories. A specific etiology cannot be identified for primary hypertension, but a causative factor is known for secondary hypertension. Cardiovascular causes of childhood hypertension include coarctation of the aorta, PDA, and aortic insufficiency. Other causes of hypertension include renal disease, endocrine disorders, neurogenic factors, and drugs.

Blood pressure varies with age and is closely related to weight and height. Normal blood pressures for each age group are shown in Appendix B. The Second Task Force on Blood Pressure Control in Children (1987) recommends that children over the age of 3 have their blood pressure measured annually. In addition, children who have experienced trauma or who are hypertensive should have their blood pressure monitored routinely. Measurements need to be taken in both arms as well as both legs, and must be carefully recorded. Systolic blood pressure in the thigh is approximately 10% to 20% higher than in the arm due to lack of a well-designed thigh cuff (Park, 1988).

Many children are asymptomatic; however, some children complain of headaches, dizziness, nausea, vomiting, anxiety, and personality changes. The first approach for treatment is nonpharmacologic. Counseling for weight loss, low sodium diets, activity promotion, and cessation of both smoking and use of oral contraceptives should be undertaken. Drug therapy is next instituted, although long-term effects of these drugs in children is unknown.

### Nursing Care for Children With Hypertension

An important nursing function is obtaining an accurate blood pressure. As discussed earlier, blood pressure should be measured at routine intervals and carefully monitored. Nurses must be aware of how the environment is affecting the child. Developmental assessment provides clues as to how involved and responsible the child can be in participating in self care. Parental assessment provides information on how well they may be able to establish a positive, healthy, and supportive environment for a child with hypertension.

Planning and implementing nursing care should focus on developing a good working relationship with child and family. Therapeutic interventions for the child may necessitate family participation in lifestyle changes, so their cooperation and support are essential. In addition to medication administration, education about weight control, diet, exercise, and smoking is important. The nurse can assist the child and family in establishing a weight control program using the proper diet, and can provide suggestions for an exercise regimen that is tailored to the child's needs. The child should be involved in self-care (including medication administration and diet control) if possible, thus increasing the child's sense of accomplishment and compliance. Accurate BP recordings help identify continuing or new client needs.

## Summary

Although the body can adapt to malfunction in many organs, it cannot survive in the presence of major cardiovascular problems. As the central pumping organ of the body, the heart moves blood that is rich in oxygen and nutrients to all parts of the body, enabling them to function. At the same time, it receives blood from all parts of the body and moves it to the pulmonary system, where the depleted oxygen is replaced. Any malfunction of the heart, whether structural, obstructive, or resulting from infection or inflammation, places every other body system at risk. Because of the serious nature of cardiovascular problems, nurses working with children who have cardiovascular problems and their families are challenged to provide optimal care. Nurses are active participants in assessing, diagnosing, planning, implementing, and evaluating care for children with cardiovascular problems. Not only are nurses responsible for physical care, but they must also meet the needs of the child and family as individuals. By providing physical care, as well as education and support, nurses help children and families adapt to cardiovascular problems and their treatment.

# Nursing Care Plan

## Assessment

Tanya is a 6-month-old infant being admitted to the hospital for evaluation of congestive heart failure.

### Chief Complaint

Tanya has gained only 3 ounces in the last 6 weeks. When feeding she is short of breath and diaphoretic.

### Subjective Assessment

*Past History:* Tanya was diagnosed at her 4 week well child examination with a ventricular septal defect and mild congestive heart failure.

*Present History:* She has done well at home until 3 weeks ago, when a cough and upper respiratory congestion developed. She is on formula and was taking a 6-oz. bottle 5 times a day and eating cereal and strained vegetables. Since becoming ill she is taking only 3–4 oz. in each bottle every 3–4 hours and shows little interest in solids.

*Family History:* Tanya is the fifth and youngest child in the family. Her mother is 33 years old, and her father is 34 years old. Both are in good health. Her siblings include two sisters, ages 5 and 11, and two brothers, ages 10 and 14. These children are in good health with no cardiac problems.

### Objective Assessment

*Physical Examination:* T. 37.5°C (99.5°F); P. 140; R. 31; B.P. 91/53; weight: 5.8 kg (12¾ lb) (5% [NCHS percentile]); height 61.8 cm (24¼ in) (5% [NCHS percentile]).

| | |
|---|---|
| Integument: | Mottled |
| Head: | Normocephalic; anterior fontanel open and soft 2.5 cm × 2 cm |
| Eyes: | PERRLA, slight periorbital edema |
| Ears: | Otoscopic exam normal |
| Nose: | Clear nasal drainage |
| Throat: | Mildly inflamed but without exudates |
| Neck: | Supple, without lymphadenopathy |
| Thorax and Lungs: | Symmetrical shape, clear lung fields, very slight subcostal retractions |

*(continued)*

# Nursing Care Plan *(Continued)*

| | | |
|---|---|---|
| Heart: | Grade III/VI murmur heard throughout systole, loudest at the fourth interspace of the left sternal border | |
| Abdomen: | Liver is palpated 1 cm below the costal margin | |
| Genitalia: | Normal | |
| Musculoskeletal: | FROM, without deformities | |
| Neurological: | Grossly intact | |

**Medical Diagnosis**

Ventricular septal defect and mild congestive heart failure

**Medical Plan**

Admission to hospital for evaluation of CHF

## *Nursing Care Plan for a Child with Ventricular Septal Defect*

| Goals | Nursing Interventions | Evaluation Criteria |
|---|---|---|
| **NURSING DIAGNOSIS #1: Decreased cardiac output, related to structural defect, edema, easy fatigability** | | |
| (S) Child will obtain sufficient rest | Plan nursing care to provide optimum amount of uninterrupted rest | Child is sleeping comfortably for sustained periods |
| (S) Child will have fewer episodes of crying/frustration | Reduce child's crying/frustration by meeting needs as quickly as possible | Child's crying is kept to a minimum |
| **NURSING DIAGNOSIS #2: Ineffective airway clearance, related to immobility, weakness, dyspnea, and inability to cooperate in respiratory care** | | |
| (S) A patent airway will be maintained | Observe for early detection of ineffective airway clearance | Airway remains clear |
| **NURSING DIAGNOSIS #3: Fluid volume excess related to ineffective regulatory mechanisms** | | |
| (S) A normal fluid level will be maintained | Monitor intake and output<br><br>Observe for signs of fluid retention | Fluid volume is normal |

## References

Adams, F. H. (1983). Fetal and neonatal circulations. In F. H. Adams & G. C. Emmanouilides (Eds.). *Moss' heart disease in infants, children, and adolescents* (3rd ed.) (pp. 11–12). Baltimore: Williams & Wilkins.

Ayoub, E. M. (1989). Acute rheumatic fever. In F. H. Adams, G. C. Emmanouilides, & T. A. Riemenschneider (Eds.). *Moss' heart disease in infants, children, and adolescents* (4th ed.) (pp. 692–704). Baltimore: Williams & Wilkins.

Boughman, J. A., Berg, K. A., Astemborski, J. A., Clark, E. B., McCarter, R. J., Rubin, J. D., & Ferencz, C. (1987). Familial risks of congenital heart defect assessed in a population-based epidemiologic study. *American Journal of Medical Genetics, 26*(4): 839–849.

Brown, M., & Vender, J. S. (1988). Noninvasive oxygen monitoring. *Critical Care Clinics, 4*(3), 493–509.

Colvin, E. V. (1990). Cardiac embryology. In A. Garson, J. T. Bricker, & D. G. McNamara (Eds.). *The science and practice of pediatric cardiology* (Vol. 1) (pp. 71–108). Philadelphia: Lea & Febiger.

Deatrick, J. A., Knafl, K. A., & Walsh, M. (1988). The process of parenting a child with a disability: Normalization through accommodations. *Journal of Advanced Nursing, 13*(1), 15–21.

Feldt, R. H., Porter, C. J., Edwards, W. D., Puga, F. J., & Seward, J. B. (1989). Defects of the atrial septum and the atrioventricular canal. In F. H. Adams, G. C. Emmanouilides, & T. A. Reimenschneider (Eds.). *Moss' heart disease in infants, children, and adolescents* (4th ed.) (pp. 170–189). Baltimore: Williams & Wilkins.

Friedman, W. F. (1989). Aortic stenosis. In F. H. Adams, G. C. Emmanouilides, & T. A. Reimenschneider (Eds.). *Moss' heart disease in infants, children, and adolescents* (4th ed.) (pp. 224–243). Baltimore: Williams & Wilkins.

Fyfe, D. A., & Kline, C. H. (1990). Fetal echocardiographic diagnosis of congenital heart disease. *Pediatric Clinics of North America, 37*(1), 45–67.

Gersony, W. M. (1989). Coarctation of the aorta. In F. H. Adams, G. C. Emmanouilides, & T. A. Reimenschneider (Eds.). *Moss' heart disease in infants, children, and adolescents* (4th ed.) (243–255). Baltimore: Williams & Wilkins.

Graham, T. P., Bender, H. W., & Spach, M. S. (1989). Ventricular septal defect. In F. H. Adams, G. C. Emmanouilides, & T. A. Reimenschneider (Eds.). *Moss' heart disease in infants, children, and adolescents* (4th ed.) (189–209). Baltimore: Williams & Wilkins.

Hicks, R. V., & Melish, M. E. (1986). Kawasaki syndrome. *Pediatric Clinics of North America, 33*(5), 1151–1175.

Hoffman, J. I. E. (1990). Congenital heart disease. *Pediatric Clinics of North America, 37*(1), 25–43.

Homer, G., & Shulman, S. T. (1991). Clinical aspects of acute rheumatic fever. *Journal of Rheumatology, Suppl. 29*(18), 2–13.

Ilkiw, R. L., Miller-Hance, W. C., & Nihill, M. R. (1990). The pulmonary circulation. In A. Garson, J. T. Bricker, & D. G. McNamara (Eds.). *The science and practice of pediatric cardiology* (Vol. 1) (360–385). Philadelphia: Lea & Febiger.

Knafl, K. A., & Deatrick, J. A. (1986). How families manage chronic conditions: An analysis of the concept of normalization. *Research in Nursing and Health, 9*(3), 215–222.

Lockley, R. F., & Bukantz, S. C. (1987). *Principles of immunology and allergy.* Philadelphia: W. B. Saunders.

McNamara, D. G. (1990). Value and limitation of auscultation in the management of congenital heart disease. *Pediatric Clinics of North America, 37*(1), 93–113.

Melish, J. E. (1987). Kawasaki syndrome: A 1986 perspective. *Rheumatic Disease Clinics of North America, 13,* 7–17.

Menon, G., & Poskitt, E. M. (1985). Why does congenital heart disease cause failure to thrive? *Archives of Diseases in Childhood, 60*(12), 1134–1139.

Park, M. K. (1988). *Pediatric cardiology for practitioners* (2nd ed.). Chicago: Year Book Medical Publishers.

Patel, B., Jeroudi, M. D., & Bolli, R. (1990). Pathogenesis of ischemic myocardial injury and methods for myocardial protection. In T. J. Bricker, D. G. McNamara (Eds.). *The science and practice of pediatric cardiology*, Vol. 1. Philadelphia: Lea & Febiger.

Poskitt, E. M. (1987). Food, growth and congenital heart disease. *Nutrition and Health, 5*(3/4), 153–161.

Report of the second task force on blood pressure control in children. (1987). *Pediatrics, 79*(1), 1–25.

Sade, R. M., & Fyfe, D. A. (1990). Tricuspid atresia: Current concepts in diagnosis and treatment. *Pediatric Clinics of North America, 37*(1), 151–169.

Sadler, T. W. (1985). *Langman's medical embryology* (5th ed.). Baltimore: Williams & Wilkins.

## Bibliography

Donner, R. M., & Goldman, B. I. (1990). Monitoring and treatment of rejection. In J. M. Dunn & R. M. Donner (Eds.). *Heart transplantation in children* (pp. 161–180). Mount Kisco, NY: Futura Publishing.

Altman, G. (1989). Development of the cardiovascular system. In S. L. Underhill, S. L. Woods, E. S. Sivarajan Froelicher, & C. J. Halpenny (Eds.). *Cardiac nursing* (2nd ed). Philadelphia: J. B. Lippincott.

Anella, J., McCloskey, A., & Vieweg, C. (1990). Nursing dynamics of pediatric intraaortic balloon pumping. *Critical Care Nurse, 10*(4), 24–36.

Clare, M. D. (1985). Home care of infants and children with cardiac disease. *Heart & Lung, 14*(3), 218–222.

Driscoll, D. J. (1990). Evaluation of the cyanotic newborn. *Pediatric Clinics of North America, 37*(1), 1–23.

Elixson, E. M. (1989). Hemodynamic monitoring modalities in pediatric cardiac surgical patients. *Critical Care Nursing Clinics of North America, 1*(2), 263–273.

Fagan, M. J. (1988). Relationship between nurses' assessments of perfusion and toe temperature in pediatric patients with cardiovascular disease. *Heart & Lung, 17*(2), 157–165.

Foldy, S. M., & Gorman, J. B. (1989). Perioperative nursing care for congenital cardiac defects. *Critical Care Nursing Clinics of North America, 1*(2), 289–295.

Fukuda, N. (1990). Outcome standards for the client with chronic congestive heart failure. *Journal of Cardiovascular Nursing, 4*(3), 59–70.

Gardner, P., & Woods, S. (1989). Hemodynamic monitoring. In S. L. Underhill, S. L. Woods, E. S. Sivarajan Froelicher, & C. J. Halpenny (Eds.). *Cardiac nursing* (2nd ed.). Philadelphia: J. B. Lippincott.

Gerraughty, A. B. (1989). Caring for patients with lesions obstructing systemic blood flow. *Critical Care Nursing Clinics of North America, 1*(2), 231–243.

Hazinski, M. F. (1990). Shock in the pediatric patient. *Critical Care Nursing Clinics of North America, 2*(2), 309–324.

Higgins, S. S., & Kashani, I. A. (1986). The cyanotic child: Heart defects and parental learning needs. *Maternal Child Nursing, 11*(14), 259–262.

Hutchings, S. M., & Monett, Z. J. (1989). Caring for the cardiac transplant patient. *Critical Care Nursing Clinics of North America, 1*(2), 245–261.

Joffe, M. (1987). Pediatric digoxin administration. *Dimensions of Critical Care Nursing, 6*(3), 136–145.

Kulik, L. A. (1989). Caring for patients with lesions decreasing pulmonary blood flow. *Critical Care Nursing Clinics of North America, 1*(2), 215–229.

Loeffel, M. (1985). Developmental considerations of infants and children with congenital heart disease. *Heart & Lung, 14*(3), 214–217.

Maron, B. (1989). Cardiomyopathies. In F. H. Adams, G. C. Emmanouilides, & T. A. Reimenschneider (Eds.). *Moss' heart disease in infants, children, and adolescents* (4th ed.) (pp. 189–209). Baltimore: Williams & Wilkins.

Medicus, L. (1987). Kawasaki disease: What is this puzzling childhood illness? *Heart & Lung, 16*(1), 55–60.

O'Brien, P., & Boisvert, J. T. (1989). Discharge planning for children with heart disease. *Critical Care Nursing Clinics of North America, 1*(2), 297–305.

Pinsky, W. W., & Arciniegas, E. (1990). Tetralogy of Fallot. *Pediatric Clinics of North America, 37*(1), 179–192.

Radtke, W., & Lock, J. Balloon dilation. *Pediatric Clinics of North America, 37*(1), 193–213.

Roberts, P. J. (1989). Caring for patients undergoing therapeutic cardiac catheterization. *Critical Care Nursing Clinics of North America, 1*(2), 275–288.

Tucker, S. C. (1987, October). Dopamine use in neonates. *Neonatal Network,* 21–24.

Van Mierop, L. H. S., Kutsche, L. M., & Victorica, B, E. (1989). Ebstein anomaly. In F. H. Adams, G. C. Emmanouilides, & T. A. Reimenschneider (Eds.). *Moss' heart disease in infants, children, and adolescents* (4th ed.) (pp. 361–371). Baltimore: Williams & Wilkins.

Wiles, H. B. (1990). Imaging congenital heart disease. *Pediatric Clinics of North America, 37*(1), 115–136.

Wiles, H. B. (1989). Increasing pulmonary blood flow. *Critical Care Nursing Clinics of North America, 1*(2), 195–213.

# Alterations in Hematological Function

Joan T. Duer

*Sculpture by Charles Parks*

25

*Embryology*

*Physiology*

*Assessment*

*Nursing Diagnosis*

*Planning Nursing Care*

*Nursing Interventions*

*Evaluating Nursing Care*

*Hematological Problems of Neonates*

*Hematological Problems of Infants*

*Hematological Problems of Toddlers*

*Hematological Problems of Preschool- and School-Aged Children*

*Hematological Problems of Adolescents*

*Summary*

Since ancient times, blood has been equated with life. The hematological system, composed of blood and blood-forming organs, regulates complex and crucial physiological interactions necessary for the continuance of human life. Disruptions in the normal functioning of the hematological system may be minor and easily corrected, or they may be serious, possibly resulting in death. To gain a more complete understanding of alterations in hematological functions, the components of the hematological system and their functions should be reviewed.

## Embryology

"Among all of the body's tissues, blood is unique: It is the only fluid tissue" (Marieb, 1989, p. 569). *Blood* is living cells (formed elements) suspended in a fluid matrix (plasma). Plasma is composed of 90% water and 10% solutes. Proteins such as albumins, globulins, and fibrinogen are the principal solutes in plasma. The formed elements are erythrocytes (red blood cells), leukocytes (white blood cells), and thrombocytes (platelets).

In utero, there are many sites of blood cell formation, including the fetal yolk sac, liver, spleen, and thymus. The predominant blood-forming, or hemopoietic, organ during extrauterine life is the myeloid tissue, or red bone marrow. In infants and young children, all of the bone is composed of red bone marrow. With the cessation of bone growth in late adolescence, sites of red bone marrow are limited to the ribs, sternum, vertebrae, and pelvis. The remaining bone marrow is inactive yellow bone marrow in which fatty tissue is deposited. In cases of severe hemolysis, the body can increase the production of blood cells by stimulating the conversion of inactive yellow bone marrow to red bone marrow. The liver, spleen, and lymph nodes may also be stimulated to resume their blood-forming functions.

The reticuloendothelial system also plays a role in blood cell production and is described as a widely dispersed network of cells of mesodermal origin lining vascular and lymph channels. These cells are capable of *phagocytosis,* the formation of immune bodies, and differentiation into hemocytoblasts (premature reticuloendothelial cells), lymphoblasts (immature lymphoblasts), or myeloblasts (immature bone marrow cells).

Most of the formed elements have a definitive life span, which necessitates replacement of lost cells. The origin of cells that develop into mature, formed elements has been the source of much scientific inquiry. The stem cell theory is useful in explaining the differentiation of cells within the bone marrow that results in erythrocyte, leukocyte, and thrombocyte formation. Incompletely differentiated cells, called *stem cells,* transform and mature into precursors of the formed elements. Stem cells may be described as *pluripotent,* from which any type of blood cell may form, or *unipotent,* from which only one type of blood cell develops.

## *Physiology*

### *Erythrocytes*

*Erythrocytes* are small, nonnucleated cells shaped like biconcave disks (Fig. 25-1). Their primary function is to facilitate the transportation of oxygen to the tissues. They originate from stem cells, called hemocytoblasts, in the red bone marrow. These cells follow a sequential pattern of increasing differentiation, the most noteworthy steps of which are the synthesis of hemoglobin and the loss of cell nucleus, which contributes to their disk-like shape. The shape allows erythrocytes to transverse very small capillaries and enables them to facilitate gaseous exchange. The hemoglobin contained within the erythrocyte binds loosely with oxygen and carbon dioxide to carry essential gases to and from the tissues. In the lungs, about 95% of hemoglobin becomes saturated with oxygen. It is the high density of hemoglobin in each erythrocyte that allows such a large amount of oxygen to be transported by a single red blood cell.

The average life span of a mature erythrocyte is 120 days. Old erythrocytes are continuously destroyed, and

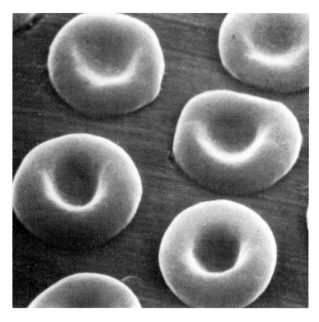

*Figure 25–1. Scanning micrograph of normal red blood cells (×5000). (Courtesy of STEM Laboratories and Fischer Scientific Company)*

new ones are regenerated daily for replacement. It is thought that as the erythrocyte ages, its cell membrane weakens and eventually ruptures, thereby releasing the contents of the cell into the bloodstream. These contents are phagocytized (ingested) by the reticuloendothelial cells in the spleen, liver, and bone marrow. Hemoglobin is broken down into its constituent parts: the iron-containing pigment (hemosiderin) and the bile pigments (biliverdin and bilirubin). The iron is conserved for immediate use in the bone marrow or stored in the liver or other tissues for future use in red blood cell production. The bile pigments are excreted by the liver in the form of bile.

There is normally little variation in the rate of erythrocyte destruction and production. *Erythropoiesis,* or erythrocyte production, is primarily regulated by the adequacy of tissue oxygenation. In cases of acute or chronic tissue hypoxia, erythropoietin (also known as hemopoietin), a hormone that stimulates red blood cell production, is released from the kidneys and acts to stimulate erythropoiesis by accelerating both mitosis and maturation of red blood cells. Thus, a feedback system exists that regulates the rate of red blood cell production based on satisfaction of tissue oxygen requirements.

It is important to remember that for normal erythropoiesis to occur, adequate amounts of iron and B-complex vitamins, such as vitamin $B_{12}$ and folic acid, must be available. Assessment of dietary intake of iron and B-complex vitamins is an important part of a pediatric nutritional evaluation as related to the hematological system.

## Antigenic Properties of Erythrocytes

Antigenic properties of red blood cells are genetically determined. "The antigens in the blood of one person may react with plasma or cells of another, especially during or after a blood transfusion. The antibody to the RBC antigen attaches to the antigenic sites and may cause hemolysis or agglutination of the RBCs" (Bullock & Rosendahl, 1988, pp. 219–220).

Classification of blood groups and types is determined by the presence or absence of commonly found antigens on the red blood cell. The most commonly found antigens are A, B, and Rh. A person may inherit one of these antigens (type A or B blood), both of these antigens (type AB blood), or neither of these antigens (type O blood). Type O blood is considered the universal donor since there are neither A nor B antigens present. Type AB blood is considered the universal recipient since there are neither anti-A nor anti-B antibodies contained within it. Type O blood is the most common, followed by type A. It is estimated that type B blood is seen in less than 10% of the population and that type AB blood is seen in less than 3% of the population.

*Rh typing* indicates the presence or absence of particular antigens on the erythrocytes. Rh positive typing indicates the presence of these antigens, and Rh negative typing indicates the absence of these antigens on the red blood cell. In the United States, 85% of white people and 95% of blacks are Rh positive.

## Leukocytes

*Leukocytes,* or white blood cells, are far less numerous than erythrocytes, yet they play a critical role in the body's ability to fight infection. Leukocytes are divided into two major classifications based on structural and chemical characteristics: granulocytes and agranulocytes.

### Granulocytes

*Granulocytes* are granular leukocytes. The cytoplasmic granules of granulocytes exhibit a specific response to staining, thereby enabling identification of three cell types: neutrophils, basophils, and eosinophils. *Neutrophils* are the most numerous of white blood cells and demonstrate a neutral or pale pink response to staining. Neutrophil nuclei are multilobular, contributing to the name *polymorphonuclear leukocytes* or *polys.* Neutrophils are rapidly attracted to sites of inflammation and are active phagocytes. They are most effective against bacteria and fungi, which they can ingest and destroy. The numbers of neutrophils increases dramatically in the presence of acute infections.

*Basophils* are the least numerous of white blood cells. They demonstrate a purple response to staining. Basophils prevent clotting and mediate allergic reactions in the microcirculation. Basophils are present predominantly in the connective tissue and pericapillary areas, and they contain histamine and heparin.

*Eosinophils* demonstrate a red response to staining. Their exact function is unknown, but it is speculated that eosinophils assist in the detoxification of foreign proteins; they are also present in large numbers in people with allergies. Eosinophils are present primarily in the mucosa of the intestinal tract and lungs.

Granulocytes are produced in the bone marrow, and their production is responsive to hormonal and chemical stimulation. Tissue damage from bacterial, viral, or physical agents promotes leukocyte production and circulation. The exact life span of the granulocyte is unknown. The bone marrow stores mature granulocytes in quantities 10 to 20 times greater than are found in the blood (Marieb, 1989). Granulocytes spend about 12 hours in the bloodstream and 2 to 3 days in the tissues before they are destroyed.

### Agranulocytes

*Agranulocytes* are white blood cells that lack apparent granules. Agranulocytes migrate from the bone marrow to the lymphatic tissue to continue reproduction. The two types of agranulocytes are lymphocytes and monocytes.

*Lymphocytes* are second in quantity to neutrophils. Only a few lymphocytes are found in the bloodstream, however, since most are located in the lymphoid tissue. Lymphocytes play an active role in regulating and maintaining immune function.

*Monocytes* are large macrophages, or cells of the reticuloendothelial system, that demonstrate increased production and phagocytic action in the presence of chronic infections, viruses, and parasites. They also contribute to the immune response by activating lymphocytes.

Lymphocyte production begins in the bone marrow and is completed in lymphoid tissue. The average life span of a lymphocyte varies greatly; they may live from 2 days to 2 years. Monocytes are produced in the bone marrow and usually live for several months.

## Thrombocytes

*Thrombocytes,* or platelets, are not actual cells but are fragments of multinucleated bone marrow cells called megakaryocytes. Megakaryocytes, arising from the hemocytoblast and myeloid stem cell, follow unique patterns of differentiation that include mitosis without cytoplasmic reproduction. The cytoplasm becomes compartmentalized by membranes that eventually fragment and release round or oval disk-shaped thrombocytes.

The function of thrombocytes is the clotting process. When tissue injury occurs, thrombocytes change in shape to expanded spheres that adhere at the site of bleeding.

The initial platelets attract other thrombocytes and form a seal that prevents further leakage.

The formation of a platelet plug and the process of coagulation are influenced by more than 30 different substances in the body. Blood coagulation factors (factors I–XIII), or procoagulants, play a significant role in determining the effectiveness of the coagulation response. Deficiencies in factor VIII (antihemophilic factor) or factor IX (Christmas factor) are seen in types of hemophilia.

Platelet concentration in the body remains relatively constant and is thought to be regulated by the hormone thrombopoietin, although its exact mechanism of function is unknown. Thrombocytes do not have a long life span—they exist for about 10 days before they are removed by the liver and spleen.

## Plasma

*Plasma* is the fluid within which the formed elements of blood are suspended. Plasma is a sticky, straw-colored liquid that comprises 55% of blood volume. "The composition of plasma varies continuously as cells remove or add substances to the blood" (Marieb, 1989, p. 582). Homeostatic mechanisms act to keep the composition of plasma relatively stable. Not only does plasma transport substances throughout the body, but plasma helps to distribute heat across the body.

## Assessment

Comprehensive physical and diagnostic assessments are necessary to ascertain hematological function. General guidelines for history-taking, physical examination, and commonly used diagnostic tests are discussed next. Variations in normal findings, as well as more specific diagnostic measures, are discussed in relation to hematological problems in each age group later in this chapter.

## History

To assess for indications of problems in hematological function, the nurse obtains information from the client (if the child is old enough) and family regarding any observable changes in health status. The nurse's goal in obtaining the health history is to identify any significant changes in behavior or physical condition that may be related to an alteration in hematological function. In particular, evidence of fatigue, bruising, or bleeding are of great significance. Symptoms such as fever, poor wound healing, persistent infections (particularly upper respiratory infections), weight loss, and complaints of dizziness or malaise may indicate alterations in hematological function and require additional follow-up examination.

The health history should also include a review of the child's overall growth and development; nutrition and dietary habits; immunization history and current status; and incidence of accidents, hospitalizations, surgeries, and infectious diseases. The nurse should also determine whether there is any family history of hematological problems or bleeding disorders.

## Physical Examination

A complete physical assessment is a routine component of any pediatric health care visit. The objective of the physical assessment is to identify variations from normal findings that may indicate alterations in hematological function. In particular, evaluation of hematological system function requires careful attention to assessments of the skin, lymphatic, cardiovascular, and respiratory systems. Pallor, icteric sclera or skin color, petechiae, purpura, and increased incidence of ecchymosis are abnormal physical assessment findings that usually indicate an alteration in hematological function. Increased heart rate, decreased blood pressure, and enlarged liver, spleen, or lymph nodes are also abnormal physical assessment findings that may reflect an alteration in hematological function and warrant additional follow-up examination.

## Diagnostic Procedures

Diagnostic tests and procedures are used to confirm and differentiate among hematological disorders. Diagnostic assessment of hematological system function may begin during intrauterine life. In cases of suspected or confirmed Rh incompatibility, a delta optical density analysis of the amniotic fluid may be performed at 26 weeks' gestation. Amniotic fluid, obtained by transabdominal amniocentesis, is separated from its cellular components. The quantity of pigment present (from the hemolysis of red blood cells) and the results of spectrographic analysis of the fluid provide valuable indications of the severity of the hemolytic process and likely fetal prognosis. Transabdominal and vaginal ultrasonography provide for diagnostic assessment of increased fetal heart size, the presence of ascites, and subcutaneous edema often seen in fetal hemolytic disease.

During the newborn period, diagnostic assessment of hematological system function is performed through measurement of newborn serum bilirubin. Unconjugated (indirect) bilirubin is a by-product of hemolysis derived from hemoglobin and is a potentially toxic substance. Unconjugated bilirubin is not in excretable form. Activity of the enzyme glucuronyl transferase results in the conversion of unconjugated bilirubin to conjugated (direct) bilirubin. The conjugated bilirubin is then excreted as the yellow-brown pigment in stools. The fetus does not conjugate bilirubin so that it can cross the placenta. During the first few days of life, the newborn begins to conjugate bilirubin in the liver. This adaptation often results in a temporary increase in serum bilirubin levels during the first few days of life. Peak bilirubin levels are reached between 3 and 5 days in full-term newborns and between 5 and 6 days in premature newborns. Bilirubin levels are monitored through measurement of both direct and indirect bilirubin, which comprises the serum bilirubin level. High serum bilirubin levels for the child's age or prolonged elevation of bilirubin levels may indicate hematological system dysfunction. Serum bilirubin values are shown in Appendix C.

The complete blood count is the most common diagnostic test of hematological system function. It provides data about the number of red blood cells present and the hematocrit, which is the volume of packed red blood cells in a whole blood sample. The amount of hemoglobin in the blood can also be determined. Normal values for these measurements depend on the age and sex of the child (see Appendix C). Other indices of red blood cell structure and function are the mean corpuscular volume and the mean corpuscular hemoglobin concentration. These measurements provide assessment of the average size of a red blood cell and the average weight and average concentration of hemoglobin in a single red blood cell, respectively. The reticulocyte count provides an assessment of the production of mature red blood cells.

The complete blood count also provides diagnostic assessment data about the number and types of white blood cells present in the blood. White blood cell counts may vary greatly and are of less clinical significance than the white blood cell differential counts. The number of neutrophils, bands (immature neutrophils), eosinophils, basophils, lymphocytes, and monocytes are determined in a white blood cell differential count. This measurement provides important information about the presence of infection; immunosuppression, inflammatory, and allergic processes; and particular metabolic disorders.

The platelet count is also a component of the complete blood count, providing insight into the body's ability to clot blood in the presence of injury. Normal values depend on the age of the child. More specific diagnostic assessments of platelet activity may be performed in the presence of an abnormal platelet count or active bleeding. Bleeding times, measures of capillary fragility, platelet aggregation tests, and coagulation studies also provide valuable information about hematological function. The activated partial thromboplastin time screens for clotting factor deficiencies, and the prothrombin time is useful in evaluating the extrinsic coagulation system. Plasma thrombin time provides an estimation of plasma fibrinogen levels. Direct measurement of plasma fibrinogen is also possible.

Detailed diagnostic studies of the structure and function of hemoglobin are also widely available. Hemoglobin electrophoresis, hemoglobin S test (sickle cell test), serum iron, total iron-binding capacity, and serum ferritin assessments provide valuable diagnostic information. These tests usually are not performed without clinical manifestations of a possible hematological disorder.

Bone marrow aspiration and bone marrow biopsy are two highly invasive yet extremely valuable diagnostic assessment tests. These are only administered in light of previous abnormal blood work and clinical manifestations of hematological dysfunction. The retrieval of bone marrow and analysis of its components are essential for the differential diagnosis of leukemia, malignancy, or bone marrow failure. Patient preparation and follow-up nursing care are more involved and of greater significance than for the previously discussed diagnostic tests. Clients receive sedation or anesthesia before the procedure. Bone marrow is removed during a sterile procedure by means of a large bore needle from the iliac crest or sternum in older children or from the tibia in children less than 1 year of age (Fig. 25-2). The client experiences intense pressure and some pain at the site. A pressure dressing is placed on the site, and a primary nursing responsibility is to monitor for signs and symptoms of bleeding. The nurse also provides comfort and routine postanesthesia care as indicated.

Arterial blood gases, serum electrolyte measurements, serum enzyme levels, and urinalysis may also be used to provide diagnostic information about the function of the hematological system.

## Nursing Diagnosis

*Pattern 1: Exchanging*
- Altered nutrition: less than body requirements
- Altered oral mucous membrane
- Altered peripheral tissue perfusion
- Decreased cardiac output
- Fluid volume deficit
- High risk for altered body temperature
- High risk for fluid volume deficit
- High risk for impaired skin integrity
- High risk for infection
- High risk for injury
- Impaired gas exchange

*Pattern 3: Relating*
- Altered family processes

*Pattern 5: Choosing*
- Ineffective individual/family coping

*Pattern 6: Moving*
- Activity intolerance
- Altered growth and development
- Altered health maintenance
- Diversional activity deficit
- Impaired physical mobility

*Pattern 7: Perceiving*
- Body image disturbance

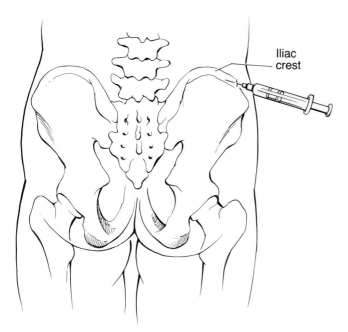

Iliac
crest

*Figure 25–2. Site for bone marrow aspiration.*

*Pattern 9: Feeling*
- Anticipatory grieving
- Anxiety
- Fear
- Pain

## Planning Nursing Care

When planning nursing care for children with hematological problems and their families, nurses must recognize that hematological problems may range from those that are viewed as common, manageable, and self-limiting, such as hyperbilirubinemia of the newborn, to those that are chronic, genetically transmissible, acutely life-threatening, or terminal, such as leukemia or aplastic anemia. Thus, it is extremely important for the nurse to have an excellent understanding of the pathophysiology, diagnosis, treatment, and prognosis of the hematological disorder. With such an expanded knowledge base, the nurse can provide teaching and support to the client and family throughout the diagnostic, treatment, recovery, or terminal phases of a hematological disorder.

## Developmental Considerations

As with all nursing care, before intervening, the nurse should assess the developmental level of both the child and the family and plan nursing actions accordingly. Level of cognitive, social, and emotional development may be assessed during the interview and orientation phases of

the nurse–client–family relationship. Attention to developmental concerns expressed by children and families are of great importance for care of both acute and chronic hematological problems. It is imperative to assess the significance of the hematological problem to the client and family in light of their developmental stages and needs. For example, an elevated bilirubin in a 3-day-old neonate may be viewed as normal by the nurse, but to a new mother this condition may seem life-threatening. By assessing the significance of invasive procedures to children and recognizing their developmental capabilities and concerns, nurses can plan effective and supportive nursing interventions that contribute to maintenance or enhancement of coping skills.

## Acute Care Considerations

Many hematological problems experienced by children are, or have the potential to be, life-threatening. Assessment, diagnosis, and treatment of an acute disorder may be invasive, uncomfortable, frightening, and anxiety-producing for both the child and parents. Competent and emphatic delivery of nursing care actions, together with appropriate cognitive and emotional support, assists pediatric clients and their families in managing the multiple crises associated with acute hematological disorders. Nursing care in acute situations focuses on interventions designed to communicate knowledge about the disorder, allay client and parental anxiety, address immediate physiological concerns related to the disorder, prevent or limit complications, and promote return to maximum well-being.

## Chronic Care Considerations

Ideally, the nurse working with the pediatric client experiencing a chronic hematological disorder has previously established a positive working relationship with both the client and the family. It is extremely important when working with these clients and their families that the nurse recognize their knowledge, experience, and emotional concerns. They are likely to be knowledgeable about the hematological disorder and its treatment, but this can never be assumed without validation. They may be angry and hostile toward health professionals, or they may be accepting and cooperative. Often, the behaviors manifested by such clients and families relate directly to the amount of social and emotional support the child and family experience, the extent of changes in activities of daily living, and the degree of discomfort experienced by the child. Nursing interventions for pediatric clients with chronic illness are directed at promoting the maximum level possible of physical, social, and emotional health. Nurses should support normal developmental processes while enhancing client well-being and family function.

## Home Care Considerations

In most instances, home care is provided for children with chronic or terminal, rather than acute, hematological disorders. With the delivery of care in the home setting, greater attention to the need for educational and emotional support for the child is necessary. Coordination of additional resources to facilitate care of the child at home is a responsibility shared by the primary nurse, discharge planner, home care or community health nurse, physician, and social worker (see Chap. 18 for further discussion of nursing considerations for caring for children in the home).

In some cases, home care can be successfully managed for self-limiting hematological disorders (e.g., elevated bilirubin in the neonate). Coordination of care, educational and emotional support, and excellent communication between clients and health care professionals can provide a positive experience for clients and families.

## Nursing Interventions

Although specific medical and nursing interventions appropriate for the treatment of individual hematological disorders are discussed later in this chapter, general guidelines for common interventions are described next.

### Nutrition

A well-balanced diet contributes greatly to optimal hematological function. A careful nursing analysis of dietary intake provides a baseline assessment from which nursing interventions can be planned. Diets should provide sufficient protein, iron, and nutrients to maximize hematological function. The nurse should be aware of developmentally and culturally appropriate foods that support the hematological functioning of pediatric clients. Such knowledge may be shared with clients and families in informal and formal teaching sessions. Anorexia related to hematological dysfunction or its treatments presents a nursing challenge. Offering small, appealing, nutritious meals at frequent intervals is usually a more effective intervention than the traditional three-meal-per-day diet. In some cases, the use of oral or intramuscular vitamin and iron supplements or hyperalimentation may be necessary to maintain nutritional well-being.

### Hydration

Adequate hydration is necessary for normal hematological function and essential for treatment of volume-depleting or obstructive hematological disorders. The nurse can enlist the client and family in monitoring fluid intake and output. Challenging pediatric clients to drink one glass of fluid per hour can be an enjoyable, nonstressful way to facilitate maintenance of adequate hydration. Additional fluid needs are often met through the intravenous administration of intravenous fluids. Close hourly monitoring of the intravenous tube insertion site, intake and output, and electrolyte status are important nursing responsibilities during this treatment.

### Drug Therapy

A wide variety of pharmacological agents are available for the management of hematological disorders in pediatric clients. They range from supplemental iron preparations for anemic children to potent chemotherapeutic agents used in the treatment of leukemia. As with the administration of any drug, nursing responsibilities involve knowledge of the action, rationale for use, proper dose and route, contraindications, and immediate and long-term side effects of the specific agent. Educating the client and family about the drug and monitoring for local and systemic responses to drug administration aid in assuring safe, effective pharmacological treatment of hematological disorders.

### Blood Product Administration

The administration of blood products for the treatment of hematological disorders requires many nursing interventions. For instance, parents and children may be concerned about the possibility of disease transmission from donated blood products. It is extremely important for nurses to communicate to clients and families that *all* blood products undergo strict screening procedures to detect the presence of illnesses such as cytomegalovirus, hepatitis, and human immunodeficiency virus. The nurse should be aware of the institution's policy and availability of direct blood donation (donor–recipient specified) and facilities for general blood bank donation.

Procedures for the administration of blood products are usually well documented in the institution's policy and procedure manual. In general, before administering a blood product to a client, two people are required to validate that the blood product is correct and specific for the client. ABO incompatibility is the most common cause of death from blood transfusions, and human error is usually responsible (Kasprisin, 1986). This hemolytic reaction is the most serious and immediate type of transfusion reaction. Although these reactions are uncommon, the nurse must take frequent periodic assessments (i.e., every 15 minutes for the first hour, then every 30 minutes for the second hour, etc.) throughout the transfusion process. Shaking, chills, fever, headache, tightness in the chest, and signs of shock or renal failure are associated with hemolytic reactions. The priority in this situation is to stop the transfusion and obtain immediate medical attention.

Febrile reactions to transfusions are manifested by fever and chills and are often treated supportively with acetaminophen. Allergic reactions are often clinically manifested with flushing, urticaria, and wheezing. They may be treated with antihistamines or epinephrine. In both instances, the nurse should stop the transfusion immediately upon clinical presentation of symptoms, and immediate medical assessment should follow.

Transfusion of blood products to pediatric clients carries the additional concern of circulatory overload. Careful regulation of fluids, slowed rate of transfusion, and frequent assessments of cardiopulmonary status are indicated.

Some hematological disorders may necessitate frequent blood product transfusions. In these instances, the blood products may be irradiated to decrease likelihood of sensitivity reactions. Some hematological disorders may require exchange transfusions in which blood is removed from the client and immediately replaced with compatible red blood cells or plasma. This is a sterile procedure often done with the use of central venous access lines, such as an umbilical vein catheter in newborns or a jugular venous catheter in older children. Attention to fluid and electrolyte balance, particularly signs of hypocalcemia, are primary nursing goals.

## Bone Marrow Transplants

"Bone marrow transplantation offers a therapeutic option for children with hematological and oncological disorders involving the bone marrow when these diseases are refractory to conventional therapy" (Kelleher, 1986, p. 347). There are three types of bone marrow transplants classified according to donor. *Autologous transplants* involve the reinfusion of the client's own bone marrow; *syngeneic transplants* involve the donation of bone marrow from an identical twin; and *allogenic transplants* involve the donation of bone marrow from a human lymphocytic antigen–matched donor (usually a sibling or relative). Experiments are being conducted using a technique that purifies donor blood marrow, eliminating the need for a matched donor.

Bone marrow transplantation is an extremely rigorous process for both the child and the family. Preparation involves complete immunosuppression and possibly total body irradiation. Clients are hospitalized in single isolation rooms, and strict reverse isolation precautions are maintained throughout the long transplantation process. All health care professionals involved in the child's care and parents who room-in must wear gowns, gloves, and masks. This procedure can be extremely distressing to both the child and parents. High-risk clients often receive bone marrow transplants in a completely sterile environment specific for these procedures. Because of the high

level of care and specialized equipment needed for bone marrow transplantation, not all medical facilities offer this treatment option.

Complications of bone marrow transplantation can be numerous. Complications related to immunosuppression are most acute in the first 2 to 4 weeks, during the period of profound bone marrow aplasia. The major cause of morbidity and mortality after transplant is related to infection (Kelleher, 1986). Nutritional complications (nausea, vomiting, diarrhea, mucositis), fluid and electrolyte imbalances, hemorrhage, venoocclusive disease, and graft-versus-host disease are other serious complications of bone marrow transplantation.

Nurses caring for children undergoing bone marrow transplantation must demonstrate a high level of knowledge and clinical competence while providing crucial emotional support to the pediatric client and family. Ideally, preparation for a bone marrow transplant includes a physical orientation to the hospital setting, explanation of anticipated procedures, and an opportunity to establish a relationship with health care personnel who will be involved in the transplant process. A great deal of information about anticipated physical care needs, necessary nursing and medical interventions, and potential complications must be communicated to the child and family. Validation of their understanding of the information provided is essential. Identifying and helping the family establish support networks and resources before transplantation is also an important component of the preparation process.

The nurse caring for a child undergoing a bone marrow transplant must have a broad knowledge base and a wide variety of technical skills. Some of the nursing interventions for these patients include administering chemotherapeutic and antiinfective agents, blood products, hyperalimentation, and fluids and electrolytes. In addition, nurses help to manage pain, immunosuppression, immobility, isolation, and anxiety, and they provide emotional support for the child and family.

## Evaluating Nursing Care

Evaluation of hematological nursing care is based on the premise that the goal of nursing care should be to facilitate the pediatric client's maximum health potential. Depending on the type and extent of the hematological disorder, maximum health may be defined as return to normal hematological functioning, decreasing the incidence of systemic complications, or providing for an emotionally supportive and comfortable death. Evaluation of hematological nursing care involves not only the health care team but the pediatric client and family. A holistic approach to care from assessment through evaluation assures the provision of quality nursing care to both the pediatric client and the family.

## Hematological Problems of Neonates

### Hyperbilirubinemia

#### Pathophysiology

At birth, normal fetal serum bilirubin levels usually measure less than 3 mg/dL. During the first few days of life, the neonate begins to conjugate bilirubin in the liver. The rate and amount of conjugation is influenced by the maturity of the liver, the availability of albumin-binding sites, and the rate of erythrocyte hemolysis. This adaptation often results in a temporary increase in serum bilirubin levels during the first few days of life. In normal neonates, peak bilirubin levels usually do not exceed 10 to 12 mg/dL. Obvious evidence of jaundice depends on the level of severity; in severe cases, it usually becomes apparent within 24 hours.

Certain physiological conditions may affect the liver, the availability of serum albumin-binding sites, or the rate of erythrocyte hemolysis and result in an elevation of the serum bilirubin known as *hyperbilirubinemia.* Pathophysiological conditions associated with hyperbilirubinemia are maternal diabetes, intrauterine infections, maternal drug ingestion (sulfur, salicylates, oxytocin, diazepam), hemolytic disease, sepsis, enclosed hemorrhage, polycythemia, neonatal asphyxia, hypothermia, hypoglycemia, pyloric stenosis, and biliary duct obstruction or atresia.

The exact mechanism of bilirubin-related neonatal injury is unclear; however, it is widely accepted that high concentrations of unconjugated bilirubin can be neurotoxic to the neonate (Avery & Taeusch, 1984). Unconjugated bilirubin has an affinity for extravascular tissue. Cells of the central nervous system are particularly vulnerable since unconjugated bilirubin readily crosses the blood–brain barrier. *Kernicterus* results from the deposition of levels of unconjugated bilirubin in the basal ganglia of the brain greater than 20 mg/dL in full-term neonates and greater than 10 mg/dL in preterm or acutely ill neonates. Long-term neurological effects associated with kernicterus include mental retardation, auditory impairment, learning disabilities, and motor impairment.

### Medical Diagnosis and Management

Prompt diagnosis and treatment of neonates at risk for hyperbilirubinemia is essential to limit the effects of elevated serum bilirubin levels. Laboratory evaluations may be indicated for diagnosis of hyperbilirubinemia and determination of its pathological origin. These evaluations may include a Coombs' test; direct, indirect, and total bilirubin levels; hemoglobin; reticulocyte; and white blood cell counts. Hyperbilirubinemia may be considered pathological (regardless of origin) if any of the following clinical manifestations are observed:

- Jaundice within the first 24 hours of life and persisting beyond 7 days in full-term neonates and beyond 14 days in preterm neonates
- Abnormal bilirubin concentrations such that serum bilirubin increases by 5 mg/dL/day, levels exceed 12.9 mg/dL in full-term neonates or 15 mg/dL in preterm neonates, or conjugated bilirubin levels are above 2 mg/dL

Prompt medical management is aimed at minimizing the consequences of hyperbilirubinemia and preventing kernicterus. Therapeutic treatments may include phototherapy, exchange transfusion, administration of albumin, and pharmacological therapy. Selection of a single or combined-method treatment plan is usually determined by the neonate's gestational age, weight, and serum bilirubin level.

### Nursing Assessment and Diagnosis

By performing a thorough maternal health history and highlighting any prenatal risk factors (Rh status, blood type, drug use, illnesses), the nurse has a sound knowledge base from which to physically assess the neonate. Assessments of skin color, hepatosplenomegaly, signs of bleeding, edema, and respiratory and neurological status provide a baseline and monitor changes in neonates suspected to be at risk for hyperbilirubinemia. Assessment of the skin is best done near a source of natural daylight. Blanching the skin over a bony prominence such as the nose or sternum and observing a yellow hue before the return of normal color is indicative of jaundice. In dark-skinned infants, assessment of the oral mucosa and hard palate may indicate jaundice. In all neonates, the sclera of the eyes should be assessed for the yellow pigmentation characteristic of jaundice.

Relevant nursing diagnoses for neonates with hyperbilirubinemia relate to manifestations of physiological processes and ramifications of therapies. Nursing diagnoses for hyperbilirubinemia might include the following:

- High risk for fluid volume deficit related to phototherapy or insensible fluid loss
- High risk for altered body temperature related to being unclothed during exposure to fluorescent light
- Altered family process related to impediments to attachment and bonding
- Anxiety related to necessary treatments

### Planning and Implementing Nursing Care

Nursing care of the neonate with hyperbilirubinemia is aimed at minimizing the consequences of an elevated serum bilirubin level, administering medically prescribed therapy, assessing response to therapy, and preventing complications of therapy. Additional nursing responsibilities include maintaining adequate hydration and warmth, protecting the eyes, and facilitating infant–parent bonding.

*Phototherapy.* *Phototherapy* is the application of intense fluorescent light on the exposed skin of the neonate. An additional discussion of phototherapy can be found in Chapter 11. Phototherapy is an effective treatment for hyperbilirubinemia since light in the blue range of the spectrum enhances bilirubin excretion. *Photoisomerization* is the process whereby a structural change in bilirubin to a more soluble form results from exposure to light in the blue range of the spectrum. Administration of phototherapy requires maximum exposure of the neonate's skin to the light source. Neonates are usually placed in an incubator or radiant warmer to assist thermoregulation. A Plexiglas shield must be placed between the neonate and the light source to filter potentially damaging ultraviolet rays. Frequent temperature and vital sign monitoring are essential. The neonate's eyes must be shielded from potentially damaging effects of the lights. Eye shields or bands are fashioned by the nurse, and their integrity should be checked frequently. The neonate's fluid needs may increase by as much as 25% because of phototherapy administration. Therefore, fluid intake and output and hydration status must be assessed regularly. Assessment of the skin and sclera for jaundice should also be performed regularly. A bronze discoloration of the skin may occur in neonates with an elevated direct serum bilirubin or in neonates with liver disease. This is usually a transient phenomenon but one that indicates careful follow-up examination and attention to direct serum bilirubin levels.

Careful documentation of these nursing assessments provides a sound knowledge base from which to monitor the neonate's response to phototherapy and progress.

*Exchange Transfusions.* Exchange transfusions involve the removal of blood from the neonate and its immediate replacement with compatible red blood cells or plasma. Exchange transfusions are usually performed when indirect serum bilirubin levels reach 20 mg/dL in full-term neonates, 15 mg/dL in high-risk neonates weighing 1500 g, and about 10 mg/dL in neonates weighing 1000 g or less (Cashore & Stern, 1982). An exchange transfusion removes sensitized erythrocytes, decreases serum bilirubin levels, and prevents associated anemia and cardiac failure.

An exchange transfusion is a sterile procedure that usually involves the placement of an umbilical vein catheter and an umbilical artery catheter. Up to twice the neonate's estimated blood volume is exchanged in 5- to 10-mL increments as the neonate's blood is removed through the umbilical artery catheter and new blood is administered through the umbilical vein catheter. Just before the exchange transfusion, 25% normal serum albumin may be administered. This greatly enhances (up to 50%) the amount of bilirubin removed by drawing bilirubin from the extravascular tissues into circulation.

During the exchange transfusion, the nurse may be required to assist in the placement of the umbilical catheters. The nurse also may be required to monitor administration and withdrawal of blood volumes, vital signs, thermoregulation needs, signs of electrolyte imbalances, and transfusion reactions. Continued critical assessment of circulatory, respiratory, and neurological function; of bilirubin, hematocrit, hemoglobin, and electrolyte levels; and of fluid balance is required after completion of the exchange transfusion.

*Administration of Albumin.* Albumin is administered with the same caution used during the administration of other blood products. Vital sign monitoring and fluid management are nursing priorities for the administration of albumin.

*Family Support.* A nursing priority in delivering care to neonates with hyperbilirubinemia and their families is the provision of emotional support. Parents are usually extremely stressed and anxious about this condition, especially since it occurs during a time when they should be bonding to the neonate. Providing information in repeated small, manageable pieces helps facilitate the parents' coping. Involving the parents in the neonate's care and feeding while providing tactile and auditory stimulation support the emotional needs of both parents and neonates. In some institutions, once a neonate has shown a positive response to phototherapy, these treatments may be administered in the mother's room. Nurses must be advocates for the physical and emotional needs of the parents and neonates during this stressful period.

### Evaluating Nursing Care

Evaluation of nursing care focuses on assessment of decreasing serum bilirubin levels, minimal or no incidence of complications related to treatment, and observation of normal developmental bonding processes between neonate and parents. Maintenance of fluid balance and warmth, protecting the eyes, and facilitating infant–parent bonding are the desired outcomes for the neonate with hyperbilirubinemia.

## Hemolytic Disease of the Newborn

*Hemolytic disease* of the newborn is the most common cause of hyperbilirubinemia and results from transmission of maternal antibody through the placenta to the fetus. It can be classified according to the incompatibility that exists—either Rh incompatibility or ABO incompatibility.

## Rh Incompatibility (Isoimmunization)

### Pathophysiology

The Rh group consists of several antigens. The D antigen is the dominant, most common, and most likely antigen to be involved in Rh incompatibility. The recessive antigen, d antigen, represents complete absence of D antigen. Eighty-five percent of whites and 95% of the black population are Rh positive (DD or Dd).

Rh incompatibility arises when a mother is Rh negative and a fetus is Rh positive. Although maternal and fetal circulations are separate and distinct, fetal erythrocytes that carry antigens foreign to the mother may enter maternal circulation, particularly during separation of the placenta at delivery, and stimulate antibody production. Thus, sensitization rarely takes place with a first pregnancy but occurs in subsequent pregnancies. Women can become sensitized unrelated to pregnancy, however, if they receive a blood transfusion of Rh-positive blood.

In a sensitized woman, maternal antibodies enter the fetal circulation and cause destruction of fetal erythrocytes. The fetus attempts to compensate for this hemolysis by increasing red blood cell production. Immature erythrocytes (erythroblasts) are released into the fetal circulation and *erythroblastosis fetalis* results.

A wide variability in consequences to the fetus may be observed with erythroblastosis fetalis. Its most severe complication is *hydrops fetalis,* in which, as a result of progressive hemolysis, the fetus experiences hypoxia, cardiac failure, generalized edema, pericardial, pleural, and peritoneal effusions, and severe respiratory distress at birth or is stillborn. Hydrops fetalis has a poor prognosis even with immediate exchange transfusions at birth.

### Medical Diagnosis and Management

In women with a history or risk of Rh incompatibility, careful prenatal monitoring of fetal status is essential. Assessment of bilirubin levels in amniotic fluid, rising anti-D antibody titers in maternal circulation (indirect Coombs test), and ultrasonography provide valuable insight into severity of the disease and fetal development. Postnatal assessment of the antibodies attached to the circulating erythrocytes of the neonate (direct Coombs test) are also measured.

Comprehensive physical assessment focusing on clinical manifestations of hyperbilirubinemia and cardiac, respiratory, and hemopoietic status are crucial to diagnosis and treatment of the neonate. Use of phototherapy or exchange transfusions to treat hyperbilirubinemia and associated anemia may be indicated.

The incidence of Rh incompatibility has greatly decreased in recent years since the development of an Rh immunoglobulin vaccine called RhoGAM. RhoGAM is administered within 72 hours after the birth or abortion of an Rh-positive infant to an Rh-negative mother. The injected Rh antibodies destroy fetal erythrocytes that have entered maternal circulation before their stimulation of antibodies. RhoGAM must be administered at the first sensitization and for all subsequent births and abortions to be effective. Perinatal use of RhoGAM for initial sensitizations is a relatively new practice in the United States but is rapidly gaining acceptance.

## ABO Incompatibility

### Pathophysiology

The incidence of a particular blood group varies depending on race and location of the population. ABO antibodies occur naturally and do not require a previous sensitization as with Rh antibodies. Antibodies in the plasma of one blood group (except type AB) produce agglutination when mixed with antigens of a different blood group. These agglutinated cells become trapped in peripheral blood vessels, resulting in hemolysis, elevation of serum bilirubin, and in its most severe form, renal failure. These clinical manifestations are the same as those of a transfusion reaction.

The most common form of maternal–fetal ABO incompatibility is that in which the mother is type O and the fetus type A or B. Maternal antibodies cross the placenta and attack fetal erythrocytes, resulting in hemolysis. The hemolytic reaction observed with ABO incompatibility is less severe than that seen with Rh incompatibility.

### Medical Diagnosis and Management

As previously stated, the hemolytic reaction observed with ABO incompatibility is rarely severe. The hemolysis of erythrocytes may result in clinical manifestations of mild to moderate anemia. Hyperbilirubinemia may become evident with the presentation of jaundice during the first 24 hours of life. Hepatosplenomegaly is found only in severe cases.

Medical management varies depending on the severity of clinical manifestations and is aimed at preventing complications of hyperbilirubinemia and reversing the hemolytic process. Phototherapy or exchange transfusion may be indicated depending on the infant's clinical status.

### Nursing Assessment and Diagnosis

The nursing assessments for Rh and ABO incompatibilities are similar to those described for neonates with hyperbilirubinemia. A complete maternal history and comprehensive physical examination focusing on manifestations of hyperbilirubinemia, anemia, and cardiac or respiratory failure provide a sound baseline from which to assess newborn progress.

Nursing diagnoses for hemolytic disease of the newborn might include the following:

- High risk for fluid volume deficit related to phototherapy
- High risk for altered body temperature related to exposure of body surface during phototherapy
- Altered family process related to impediments to bonding necessitated by phototherapy

Additional nursing diagnoses may be generated to address specific care needs emanating from treatment modalities selected.

### Planning and Implementing Nursing Care

Nursing care goals for the management of hemolytic disease of the newborn are similar to those previously described for implementation of treatments of hyperbilirubinemia. These goals include maintaining adequate hydration and warmth, protecting the neonate's eyes, and facilitating infant–parent bonding. It is important to recognize that care of the Rh-sensitized mother is imperative since RhoGAM must be administered within 72 hours to eligible mothers in order to be effective.

Often, the diagnosis of hemolytic disease of the newborn gives parents a sense of guilt because of the incompatibility of Rh factor or blood type. It is important to support the parents in expressing these feelings and to emphasize that they should not feel guilty for the incompatibility. Focusing on the prenatal and postnatal health care provided for the newborn and encouraging bonding activities assists parents in resolving guilt-related issues.

### Evaluating Nursing Care

Evaluation of nursing care focuses on assessment of decreasing serum bilirubin levels; return to normal cardiovascular, respiratory, and hemopoietic function; minimal or no complications related to hemolytic disease or its treatment; and observation of normal developmental bonding processes between newborn and parents.

## Hemorrhagic Disorders

### Pathophysiology

*Neonatal hemorrhagic disorders* are bleeding disorders that are manifested within the first 5 days of life and are related to a deficiency of vitamin K. In neonatal hemorrhagic disorders, vitamin K stores are essentially absent in the newborn, thereby impeding the action of vitamin K–dependent coagulation factors II, VII, IX, and X.

### Medical Diagnosis and Management

Medical manifestations of a hemorrhagic disorder usually present during the second or third day of life. Oozing from the umbilicus or circumcision site, bloody or tarry stools, hematuria, ecchymosis, petechiae, or epistaxis may indicate a hemorrhagic disorder. Diagnosis is confirmed through laboratory findings of abnormal clotting times when a normal platelet count and fibrinogen levels are found.

Management of hemorrhagic disorders in newborns is aimed at prevention. Vitamin K is administered intramuscularly into the vastus lateralis muscle to all newborns in the United States within the first 24 hours of life. In the presence of clinical manifestations of bleeding related to vitamin K deficiency, an intravenous dose of vitamin K (which prevents a hematoma at the muscle site) may be administered.

### Nursing Assessment and Diagnosis

Nursing assessment of hemorrhagic disorders in newborns focuses on identifying clinical manifestations of internal and external bleeding. Ecchymoses, petechiae, oozing from the umbilicus or circumcision site, tarry stools, epistaxis, or heme-positive urine or stools may be observed. The nurse should be cognizant of the feeding method selected for the newborn since breast milk is low in vitamin K.

The primary nursing diagnosis for the newborn with a hemorrhagic disorder is high risk for injury related to hemorrhage.

### Planning and Implementing Nursing Care

The goal of nursing care for hemorrhagic disorders in neonates is prevention. Prompt administration of intramuscular vitamin K and clear documentation of administration provides preventive care for hemorrhagic disorders in neonates. When hemorrhagic disease exists, interventions are designed to prevent bleeding by avoiding taking temperatures rectally, giving injections, or drawing blood. The infant is handled gently to avoid exacerbation of the condition. Cardiovascular status, the skin, and vital signs are closely monitored for for signs of bleeding.

### Evaluating Nursing Care

Evaluation of nursing care for neonates with hemorrhagic disorders focuses on the absence of further clinical manifestations of internal or external bleeding.

## Polycythemia

### Pathophysiology

*Polycythemia* is an elevation of blood volume and hematocrit count. A newborn is considered polycythemic when the central venous hematocrit is greater than 65% to 70%

or the venous hemoglobin level is greater than 22 mg/dL during the first week of life (Avery, 1987). Polycythemia may be a result of physiological adaptation to advancing gestational age, small size for gestational age, maternal diabetes, high altitudes, or in utero twin-to-twin transfusion. Polycythemia is also associated with chromosomal abnormalities and endocrine disorders, such as hypocalcemia and hypoglycemia.

## Medical Diagnosis and Management

Many neonates are asymptomatic of polycythemia, and diagnosis evolves from routine hematocrit screening. Newborns with this condition have a characteristic ruddy appearance but may have discoloration of the extremities and decreased peripheral pulses. Clinical manifestations of polycythemia result from the effects of increased blood volume and viscosity, and impaired tissue perfusion and may lead to congestive heart failure, respiratory distress, hyperbilirubinemia, and neurological impairment. Complete laboratory assessment is indicated after an abnormal screening hematocrit or with any of the above symptoms. Normal laboratory values are included in Appendix C. Detailed review of the prenatal and perinatal history for contributing or related factors is also essential to diagnosis.

The aim of medical management is to decrease the central venous hematocrit through a partial exchange transfusion in which blood is removed and replaced with plasma in symptomatic newborns. Treatment of asymptomatic newborns remains debatable.

## Nursing Assessment and Diagnosis

Nursing assessment for the neonate with confirmed or suspected polycythemia focuses on clinical manifestations of impaired tissue perfusion and increasing cardiorespiratory distress. A careful history of prenatal and perinatal associated factors provides a valuable baseline. Physical assessment focusing on skin, cardiac, respiratory, hepatic, and neurological status provides a valuable baseline from which to monitor the neonate's course. Clinical manifestations of polycythemia include ruddy color, jaundice, tachycardia, tachypnea, peripheral pulses, hepatosplenomegaly, lethargy, and poor feeding.

Nursing diagnoses for polycythemia might include the following:

- Altered peripheral tissue perfusion related to increased hematocrit and increased viscosity of blood
- Impaired gas exchange related to increased volume and viscosity of blood
- Decreased cardiac output related to increased workload of heart and increased viscosity of blood

## Planning, Implementing, and Evaluating Nursing Care

Planning, delivery, and evaluation of nursing care for neonates receiving an exchange transfusion and their families was discussed previously.

## Glucose-6-Phosphate Dehydrogenase Deficiency

*Glucose-6-phosphate dehydrogenase (G6PD) deficiency* is an extremely rare, genetically transmitted enzyme abnormality in which the ingestion of certain foods or drugs, such as fava beans, aspirin, sulfonamides, or antimalarials, or exposure to naphthalene mothballs, may result in the development of an acute hemolytic anemia. G6PD deficiency is most prevalent in those of Mediterranean, African, and Asian descent. Nursing care for G6PD is the same as for hemolytic anemia.

## Anemia

### Pathophysiology

*Anemia* is the condition in which either the number of circulating red blood cells, amount of hemoglobin, or volume of packed red blood cells is reduced. Full-term neonates with hemoglobin values less than 14 g/dL and preterm neonates with values less than 13 g/dL are classified as anemic. Blood loss, impaired red blood cell production, and hemolysis are the most common causes of neonatal anemia.

Hypovolemia, or decreased blood volume or blood loss, in the newborn is most often related to placental bleeding in utero, umbilical cord bleeding, or birth trauma to abdominal organs or the cranium. Hemolysis is usually related to blood incompatibilities or sepsis. Impaired red blood cell production is most commonly caused by G6PD deficiency.

### Medical Diagnosis and Management

Diagnosis of anemia is based on laboratory values and clinical manifestations such as pallor, tachypnea, tachycardia, and hypotension. In cases of acute bleeding, signs and symptoms of shock may be evident. Medical management is aimed at prompt identification and correction of anemia. Treatment varies with the severity and etiology of the anemia. Use of iron supplements, iron-fortified formulas, or transfusions may be indicated.

### Nursing Assessment and Diagnosis

Nursing assessment of the newborn focuses on the clinical manifestations of anemia, such as pallor, tachycardia, tachypnea, and hypotension. Poor weight gain and fatigue at feedings may also be noted. Monitoring for signs and symptoms of shock is essential until blood loss can be ruled out as the cause of the anemia.

Nursing diagnoses for anemia might include the following:

- Activity intolerance related to insufficient oxygen
- High risk for infection related to decreased resistance
- Decreased cardiac output related to increased workload of the heart
- Altered nutrition: less than body requirements related to fatigue during feeding
- Altered family processes related to need for hospitalization

### Planning and Implementing Nursing Care

Nursing care is aimed at facilitating correction of the anemia. Use of iron supplements or iron-fortified formula may be indicated. Careful intake records and weights are necessary to monitor growth. Transfusions may be administered for severe anemia. Frequent monitoring of the neonate's cardiorespiratory status is essential to determine the response to therapy. Nursing care should focus on preserving the infant's energy by limiting procedures to those that are essential and by offering small, high-calorie, frequent feedings. Parent–infant bonding should be facilitated.

### Evaluating Nursing Care

Evaluation is based on resolution of the anemia and observable clinical manifestations. The infant's activity level should return to normal, with no signs of fatigue, and feeding should return to normal.

## Hematological Problems of Infants

### Anemia

#### Pathophysiology

Anemia is the most common hematological problem of infancy and childhood. Actual laboratory values depend on the age of the infant (see Appendix C for normal laboratory values). Although anemia is not a disease, it reflects an underlying alteration in normal hematological processes.

The three major causes of anemia in infants are blood loss, decreased or impaired red blood cell production, and increased red blood cell destruction. Acute blood losses seen in trauma situations usually result in limited periods of anemia since replacement of red blood cells usually occurs within 3 to 4 weeks. In instances of chronic blood loss, however, there may be an insufficient amount of iron available for hemoglobin formation and body demands, thereby prolonging the anemia. Decreased or impaired red blood cell production occurs when the bone marrow fails to produce red blood cells or when there is a deprivation of essential vitamins and nutrients. Increased destruction of red blood cells may be due to a defect within the cell that contributes to hemolysis, as seen in sickle cell disease; or it may occur outside the red blood cell, as seen in blood incompatibility reactions.

Anemia affects the body's oxygen-carrying capacity. Clinical manifestations are related to the degree of tissue hypoxia experienced. In infants, anemia often develops slowly. Physiological adaptation, such as the production of additional red blood cells, and compensatory mechanisms, such as tachycardia, often delay the manifestation of clinical symptoms.

### Medical Diagnosis and Management

Anemia may be suspected in an infant who presents with pallor, tachycardia, muscle weakness, fatigue, and in severe cases, signs of increased cardiac workload. A detailed history must be obtained, with particular attention given to dietary intake; eating habits, such as pica; exposure to lead-based paints; incidence of black, tarry stools or other bleeding; and family history of genetically transmissible diseases, such as thalassemia or sickle cell anemia. Stools may be tested for the presence of occult blood. Diagnosis is confirmed through laboratory analysis of the complete blood count, which shows decreased red blood cells, hemoglobin, and hematocrit.

Management of anemia is aimed at treating the underlying cause and may include nutritional support, vitamin and mineral supplements, rest, and transfusions.

### Nursing Assessment and Diagnosis

Complete examination of the hemopoietic organs (heart, liver, and spleen) is essential. Tachycardia and hepatosplenomegaly are commonly seen in cases of anemia. The infant with anemia may be underweight and appear poorly nourished; however, it is common for infants with iron deficiency anemia to be overweight or chubby-looking. A detailed history of dietary intake is a primary nursing assessment since vitamin and mineral deficiencies are a common cause of anemia. Nurses should be nonjudgmental when interviewing and use developmentally appropriate questions. Exposure to lead-based paints, incidence of tarry stools, or other bleeding and family history of hematological disorders are also significant assessment data for the nurse. Nursing diagnoses for anemia are the same as those discussed under neonatal anemia.

## *Planning and Implementing Nursing Care*

Nursing care for the infant with anemia and family varies depending on the etiology of the anemia. In instances of nutritional deficiency, the nurse can instruct parents regarding dietary management. The use of iron-fortified formula (not cow's milk) and cereal is recommended for children less than 1 year of age. Iron supplements are best absorbed when given with citrus products, and they are not absorbed well when given with milk. Administration of medications and family teaching regarding medications may also be indicated. Oral iron supplements may temporarily stain the teeth, so they should be given through a straw or a dropper. The child should get sufficient rest and should limit strenuous activities. Providing clear client teaching to parents in advance of treatments is an essential part of the nursing role.

### *Evaluating Nursing Care*

Evaluation of nursing care is based on resolution of the underlying cause of the infant's anemia and the observable clinical manifestations. The infant's activity level should return to normal, with no signs of fatigue. The parents should demonstrate an understanding of the cause of the anemia and interventions to overcome it.

## Iron Deficiency Anemia

### *Pathophysiology*

*Iron deficiency anemia* is the most prevalent nutritional disorder in the United States, most frequently affecting children 3 to 36 months of age, with peak incidence between 10 and 15 months of age (Lanzkowsky, 1985). *Iron deficiency anemia* results from decreased iron stores at birth in light of excessive demands (premature infants) or decreased dietary intake. Since iron is essential for hemoglobin formation, iron deficiency results in decreased hemoglobin concentration and decreased oxygen-carrying capacity.

### *Medical Diagnosis and Management*

Medical diagnosis is based on physical assessment findings consistent with anemia (particularly in light of the infant's age) and laboratory analysis. A complete blood count, serum iron concentration, and total iron-binding capacity are likely diagnostic tests.

Treatment is aimed at prevention. Prescribing the use of iron-containing vitamin supplements, particularly during the third trimester of pregnancy, while breast-feeding, and for infants after 6 months of age, is common medical practice. Encouraging dietary intake of iron-fortified formulas, cereals, and foods and providing developmentally appropriate nutritional counseling are significant in reducing the incidence of iron deficiency anemia.

### *Nursing Assessment and Diagnosis*

Nursing assessment of the infant with iron deficiency anemia parallels the guidelines outlined in the previous section on the assessment of the child with anemia. Careful attention to dietary intake and indicators of parental nutritional knowledge should be emphasized. It is not uncommon to observe an overweight child with iron deficiency anemia. Excessive milk consumption, milk being a poor source of iron, at the expense of solid food intake often results in the "milk baby" appearance seen in iron deficiency anemia.

Nursing diagnoses for iron deficiency anemia are the same as for the anemias previously discussed, with the addition of high risk for injury related to weakness and fatigue.

### *Planning and Implementing Nursing Care*

Nursing care focuses on the prevention of iron deficiency anemia during infancy. Providing parents with nutritional education is essential, including highlighting sources of iron-fortified foods and recommending delaying the introduction of cow's milk until 1 year of age. Educational efforts should begin prenatally and continue through infancy. Correcting common misconceptions about iron deficiency anemia and other nutritional education deficits can facilitate the health of both the infant and family. The use of teaching aids, such as pamphlets and diagrams, are helpful for reinforcement. Knowledge of culturally acceptable iron-rich foods may also help to enhance compliance.

Oral iron supplements are often prescribed for the treatment of iron deficiency anemia. Iron should be given in divided doses between meals and with a source of citrus (fruit or juice) for maximum absorption. Oral forms of iron should not be given with antacids or milk. Parents should be advised that oral iron supplements usually turn stools black. Parenteral administration of iron necessitates a Z-track injection; the injection site should not be massaged. When iron deficiency anemia is severe, the infant may need to be hospitalized and may require oxygen for tissue hypoxia. Children with iron deficiency anemia are prone to infection, so parents should be instructed in infection control measures, such as avoiding exposure to infections and practicing proper hand-washing techniques. Because these children often exhibit weakness or fatigue, they are at increased risk for injury. Parents should be advised to institute precautions, such as bed rails, and to monitor the child's activities carefully.

### *Evaluating Nursing Care*

Evaluation of nursing care focuses on the rapid resolution of the iron deficiency anemia (usually in 3–4 weeks) and prevention of recurrences. This condition is generally viewed as self-limiting and highly responsive to treatment. The child should remain free from infection and injury, and parents should demonstrate an understanding of the disorder and comply with the prescribed treatment regimen.

## Thalassemia (Cooley Anemia)

### Pathophysiology

*Thalassemia* is a genetically transmitted hematological disease characterized by a defect in the production of specific globin chains in hemoglobin. It is an autosomal recessive disorder with clinical manifestations of varying severity. The most severe form of the disease, *thalassemia major* or β-*thalassemia*, refers to the homozygous genetic representation of the disease. The incidence of thalassemia is predominantly confined to those of Mediterranean ancestry.

A defect in one chain of the hemoglobin molecule (most commonly β) results in compensatory increases in hemoglobin production among other hemoglobin chains. These chains become unbalanced, disintegrate, and destroy red blood cells. Compensatory increases in erythropoiesis cannot address the underlying physiological disorder, and severe anemia results.

### Medical Diagnosis and Management

Infants with thalassemia present with clinical manifestations of anemia, fever, poor feeding and weight gain histories, and splenomegaly. In severe instances, clinical manifestations of chronic hypoxia, such as headache, precordial and bone pain, diminished exercise tolerance, epistaxis (cause unknown) and hyperuricemia, are also present. Evidence of hemochromatosis, or damage to the tissues of the spleen, liver, lymph, pancreas, or heart related to the storage of excess iron, may be present. Family history of thalassemia may or may not be previously documented but is likely in clients of Mediterranean descent. Physical characteristics are distinctive and include slight jaundice or a bronze skin tone, thickened cranial bones, prominent cheekbones, and a flat nose (Fig. 25-3). Older children with thalassemia exhibit delayed sexual maturation. Diagnosis is confirmed through laboratory analysis of hemoglobin (hemoglobin electrophoresis studies), complete blood count, and assessment of structural changes in erythrocytes.

Medical management of thalassemia is aimed at maintaining normal levels of red blood cells. Transfusions of packed red blood cells are frequently administered along with chelating agents that help rid the body of excess iron that results from multiple transfusions. A splenectomy is indicated if the spleen destroys the transfused red blood cells.

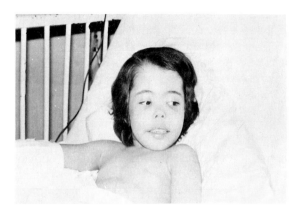

*Figure 25–3. Child with thalassemia. (Mauer, A.M. [1969]. Pediatric hematology. New York: McGraw-Hill)*

### Nursing Assessment and Diagnosis

Infants with thalassemia present a complex physical assessment picture. The previously mentioned clinical manifestations of anemia and tissue hypoxia may vary widely in severity. A detailed physical examination focusing on the hemopoietic system and a comprehensive family and health history are integral to planning quality nursing care for the child and family.

Nursing diagnoses for thalassemia might include the following:

- Activity intolerance related to insufficient oxygen
- High risk for infection related to decreased resistance
- Decreased cardiac output related to increased workload of the heart
- Altered family processes related to need to care for the child with a chronic illness
- Altered growth and development related to delayed maturation

It should be emphasized that thalassemia is a chronic and life-threatening illness. Thus, nursing diagnoses may need to focus on the complex physical and emotional needs of the child and family, particularly in later or severe stages of the illness.

### Planning and Implementing Nursing Care

Nursing care for infants with thalassemia is aimed at providing physical and emotional support. Physical care needs often necessitate frequent transfusions of blood. Deferoxamine (Desferal), an iron-chelating agent, is prescribed to diminish excess iron stores. This drug can be given intravenously or subcutaneously and is often given in the home setting by means of a subcutaneous infusion pump for 8 to 10 hours daily. Intravenous deferoxamine is administered at the time of blood transfusions (Festa, 1985). Children who have had a splenectomy are usually placed on antibiotic prophylaxis because of their increased risk of infection. They should not be exposed to people with active infections.

Other nursing interventions may be indicated in light of manifestations of worsening tissue hypoxia. Provision for rest, adequate nutrition, and cardiovascular monitoring are essential. An important nursing intervention is emotional support of the child and family during the numerous invasive blood tests and treatments. Supporting the growth and developmental needs of both the infant and family are of great significance in the management of a chronic illness such as thalassemia. Nurses may also provide referrals for genetic counseling and to the Cooley Anemia Foundation (105 E. 22nd St., New York, NY 10010) for support and information.

### Evaluating Nursing Care

Evaluation of nursing care focuses on the prevention of complications and infections related to the disease process and its treatment. The child should remain as active as possible and should demonstrate normal growth and development. The child and family should demonstrate their ability to cope throughout the course of this life-threatening illness.

# Hematological Problems of Toddlers

## Hemophilia

### Pathophysiology

*Hemophilia* is a sex-linked congenital bleeding disorder characterized by a disturbance of blood clotting factors, most notably factor VIII (known as *classical hemophilia* or *hemophilia A*) and factor IX (known as *Christmas disease* or *hemophilia B*). A deficit in either of these clotting factors interferes with the production of thrombin, which is necessary for blood clotting, and can result in uncontrolled bleeding. "Hemophilia occurs in approximately 1 : 10,000 newborn males. Hemophilia A is five times more common than Hemophilia B" (Warren & McMillan, 1986 p. 252). Hemophilia is almost always seen in males, since females transmit the defective gene in a sex-linked pattern. Hemophiliac males pass the gene along to their daughters (who become carriers), but male offspring are unaffected. The male offspring of the female carrier has a 50% chance of having hemophilia (Miller, 1982).

The severity of hemophilia is dependent on the extent to which normal levels of the involved clotting factor are present. Normal clotting factor activity levels range from 60% to 150%. Hemophilia may be classified as mild with factor levels greater than 5% of normal. These people rarely bleed, except with trauma or invasive procedures. In moderate hemophilia, factor levels are 1% to 5% of normal, and spontaneous bleeding, particularly into the joints and muscles, may occur (Miller, 1982).

### Medical Diagnosis and Management

Diagnosis of hemophilia may often be made after a traumatic episode in which excessive bleeding is noted. In most toddlers, a history of easy bruising and bleeding, increasing as the child becomes more physically active, is highly significant for the disease. Sites where bleeding commonly occurs in hemophilia are shown. Skin is assessed for ecchymosis and petechiae. *Hemarthrosis,* or swelling, tenderness, pain, and limited joint range of motion, may result from spontaneous bleeding into the joint. The most commonly affected joints are the knees, elbows, ankles, hips, and shoulders (Warren & McMillan, 1986). A history of spontaneous hematuria may also be present. Auditory, visual, and neurological deficits may also be clinical manifestations of internal bleeding, necessitating a comprehensive physical and developmental assessment.

Family history of the severity of hemophilia is an important assessment finding since family members often follow the same pattern of bleeding severity.

Laboratory diagnosis of hemophilia is made by analyzing prothrombin time, activated partial thromboplastin time, thrombin clotting time, bleeding time, and a specific factor VIII or IX assay. In hemophilia A and B, the activated partial thromboplastin time is prolonged, the prothrombin time, thrombin clotting time, and bleeding time are normal, and the level of either factor VIII or factor IX is low (Warren & McMillan, 1986).

Medical management of hemophilia is primarily aimed at controlling bleeding episodes. Minor, superficial bleeding responds well to the rapid application of pressure and cold. Hematuria usually resolves spontaneously, and renal workups are indicated only in light of flank pain and persistent bleeding. Gastrointestinal bleeding is commonly seen in adult hemophiliacs but not in children.

Severe bleeding requires the replacement of the missing clotting factor. Factor VIII and factor IX concentrates are pharmacologically prepared for infusion, as is a cryoprecipitate of factor VIII derived from fresh frozen plasma. Fresh frozen plasma may itself be administered promptly after thawing to preserve the function of factor VIII. Donated fresh frozen plasma should be ABO compatible with the recipient, although cross matching is not necessary. Factor replacement may be given prophylactically as well as in acute bleeding episodes.

Acute hemarthrosis is managed with factor replacement, immobilization of the joint, application of ice, and possibly joint aspiration or synovectomy. With chronic hemarthrosis, management is aimed toward preservation of joint function. Intramuscular bleeding most commonly occurs in the calves, forearms, thighs, and iliopsoas muscles (Warren & McMillan, 1986). Management consists of factor replacement and assessment for secondary nerve and blood vessel damage. Clients are at risk for the development of contractures, and medical management is aimed at prevention.

Pain management consists of application of ice, splinting the affected joint, and application of elastic bandages. Nonsteroidal anti-inflammatory drugs should not be administered since they alter platelet function.

Major bleeding episodes may occur spontaneously and are considered life-threatening. These include intracranial bleeding and bleeding into the neck and pharynx. Such complex client care situations require the replacement of the deficient factor, immediate and extensive follow-up assessments, and interventions.

Because hemophilia is a lifelong disease, there are many opportunities for complications to occur. Some hemophiliacs develop an antibody to factor activity that inhibits factor function. This inhibitor serves to greatly complicate the medical management of the disease. Hepatitis and acquired immune deficiency syndrome are blood-borne diseases for which the hemophiliac is at risk. Thrombosis secondary to factor IX infusion and hemolysis secondary to factor VIII infusion are additional potential complications that require ongoing assessment and intervention.

### Nursing Assessment and Diagnosis

Assessment findings for children with hemophilia are likely to be clinical manifestations of acute or chronic bleeding. Examination of the skin, joints, and musculature are assessment priorities. Physical assessment should include visual, auditory, and neurological examination as well as a developmental assessment. Detailed, objective data concerning cases of hematuria or bleeding from the lips, gums, mouth, or other body parts should be obtained from the parents. Information concerning family history of hemophilia, as well as severity of the bleeding pattern, is also a key component of the nursing data base.

Since the prevention of injury is a primary goal in the care of children with hemophilia, assessment of the home setting for safety concerns should be included in the nursing data base. Nonjudgmental questions about the type of objects the child is most likely to "bump into" provides valuable information about potential safety hazards. It is virtually impossible to create an environment that is completely safe all of the time. Toddlers must have their developmental tendencies toward exploration supported for normal growth and development. Identifying recurring obstacles or hazards may provide a focus for client education and intervention.

Nursing diagnoses for hemophilia might include the following:

- High risk for injury related to hemorrhage
- Pain related to joint swelling

- Impaired physical mobility related to joint swelling
- Altered health maintenance related to insufficient knowledge of the condition, treatments, and hazards
- Altered family processes related to having a chronically ill child
- Diversional activity deficit related to need to protect the child from injury

### Planning and Implementing Nursing Care

Care of children with hemophilia requires collaboration among nurses, physicians, clients, and families. Children with hemophilia are managed primarily at home except during major bleeding episodes. Therefore, nursing care is aimed at providing families with the necessary skills and knowledge to effectively and safely manage these children at home.

Parents or other care-givers need to learn about the storage and reconstitution of the factor product and develop the skills necessary to prepare and administer the factor intravenously. It is extremely frightening for parents to think of "sticking" their child. Opportunity for practice and emotional support must be provided, particularly if the child does not comprehend the rationale for factor administration. Superficial injuries are treated with ice packs and pressure, signs of hemarthrosis are observed for, and parents are instructed to immobilize the joint, apply ice packs, and administer the factor. Involving children and parents in the prevention of joint deformity is another important nursing intervention.

Parents must learn the signs and symptoms of a major bleed. Reviewing the likely changes in neurological status observed with a central nervous system bleed, such as headache, vomiting, seizures, lethargy, confusion, and blurred vision, helps to ensure rapid medical attention. Complaints of bleeding in the throat must be carefully monitored to assess for hematoma development that impinges on the airway and results in respiratory distress. Major bleeding episodes are intensively managed in a hospital setting and require factor replacement, cardiovascular and neurological monitoring, assessment and intervention for sequelae, and emotional support for the child and family.

Education and support regarding balancing safety concerns and developmental needs (present and future) is a major area of intervention for the nurse. Use of carpeting in the home and knee and elbow pads when toddlers are learning to walk are just two examples of safety implementations that do not impede a child's normal growth and development. Exercise is recommended, but contact sports and activities such as tennis and skiing are not advised because of high stress on joints. Since hemophilia is a lifelong illness, the emotional, physical, and financial needs of the family do not abate. Parents, particularly mothers, often feel guilty about transmitting the disease to their sons. Maintaining the emotional and developmental integrity of the family is a primary nursing goal. Additional psychosocial and informational support are available through local and national chapters of the National Hemophilia Foundation (110 Greene Street, New York, NY 10012).

### Evaluating Nursing Care

Evaluation of nursing care focuses on the ability of the child and family to manage the hemophilia at home and to decrease the likelihood of major bleeding episodes and bleeding complications. The child should demonstrate normal growth and developmental milestones while preventing excessive bleeding. The child and family should demonstrate knowledge of the condition, the treatment regimen, and strategies for prevention of complications.

## Sickle Cell Disease

### Pathophysiology

*Sickle cell disease* is a disease of genetic origin characterized by the production of an abnormal hemoglobin, hemoglobin S. Hemoglobin S has an altered amino acid structure that causes normally round erythrocytes to sickle or become crescent-shaped when oxygenation of the blood is decreased (Fig. 25-4). Hemoglobin SS (the homozygous form) is the most common form of the disease and is known as *sickle cell anemia*. This disease is transmitted by autosomal recessive inheritance. *Sickle cell trait* is transmitted by autosomal dominant inheritance, and symptoms are not usually evident. This disorder is found predominantly in blacks, and about 1 in 10 African

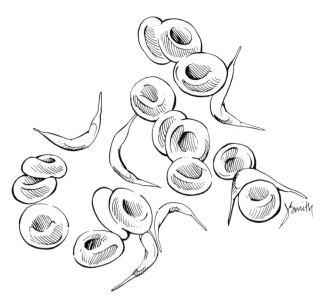

*Figure 25–4. Abnormal shape of cells seen in sickle cell disease.*

Americans has sickle cell disease or trait (Jenkins, 1983). Wide variability in severity of the disease exists among those with sickle cell disorders, even among those with the same form of the disease.

In the infant with sickle cell disease, hemoglobin S is present from conception, but fetal hemoglobin tends to inhibit sickling and anemia until 6 months of age. After 6 months of age, erythrocytes with hemoglobin S overtake cells with normal hemoglobin, and clinical manifestations of a progressive, lifelong anemia develop (Johnson, 1985).

### Medical Diagnosis and Management

Laboratory diagnosis of sickle cell disease includes a complete blood count, hemoglobin electrophoresis, and the *Sickledex,* which is a screening test for the presence of hemoglobin S. When oxygen is removed from the erythrocytes, normal erythrocytes retain their shape, while erythrocytes with hemoglobin S form the classical sickle shape. Since both sickle cell trait and sickle cell anemia may result in a positive test, hemoglobin electrophoresis is used to confirm the diagnosis of sickle cell anemia. Clinical manifestations of sickle cell disease include profound and chronic anemia. A history of poor feeding, poor weight gain, irritability, and fatigue may be present. Pallor, scleral icterus, and splenomegaly may be observable on physical examination. Evidence of delayed physical and sexual maturation, hepatomegaly, and manifestations of cardiomegaly may be present in older children.

*Dactylitis,* or hand and foot syndrome, may be the first indication of sickle cell anemia in children 6 months to 4 years of age. Dactylitis is characterized by symmetric swelling of the soft tissues of the hands and feet. Pain and warmth in the area are often noted. The cause is unknown, and treatment is symptomatic, including administration of fluids and analgesics and application of moist heat.

Children with sickle cell disease are likely to present with recurrent severe infections, leg ulcers, priapism (abnormal, painful erection of the penis), hematuria, bone weakness, and enuresis. They often manifest higher susceptibility to pneumococcal and *Salmonella* infections. They may experience periods when their only complaint is their chronic anemia; however, even a common childhood illness, such as an upper respiratory infection, may trigger an acute illness reaction, known as a crisis. *Sickle cell crisis* occurs when physiological stresses reduce hydration or deprive the hemoglobin S of oxygen. The sickle cells clump, occlude small blood vessels, and are rapidly destroyed. The net effect on the body is anemia, decreased oxygen transport, decreased tissue perfusion, subsequent tissue necrosis of body organs, and tissue death (infarcts) in the kidneys, spleen, and bone. Pain is a visible clinical manifestation of altered tissue perfusion, tissue necrosis, and cell death.

There are three types of sickle cell crises. A *splenic*

*sequestration crisis* results when sickling causes the pooling of blood in the spleen and liver. This is a life-threatening crisis that requires immediate attention. It is more common in children aged 6 months to 4 years. Clinical manifestations include a history of an acute illness of less than 24 hours duration, progressive pallor, irritability, abdominal distention, and pain. The child may be hypotensive and tachycardiac. Immediate therapy is aimed at restoring blood volume by transfusions or a double-volume exchange transfusion. If the child is unresponsive to treatment, a splenectomy is performed. Since risk of recurrence is high, implementation of a chronic transfusion program or elective splenectomy is recommended.

*Aplastic crises* are infrequent complications of sickle cell disease characterized by bone marrow failure lasting 10 to 14 days. Clinical manifestations may be pallor, tachycardia, fever, or signs of congestive heart failure. Treatment is symptomatic.

Vasoocclusive crises or *thrombocytic crises* are the most common complication of sickle cell disease. The clumping of erythrocytes in small blood vessels leads to tissue death. These crises can last from 4 to 7 days and are characterized by severe pain in the bones, joints, and abdomen; fever; swelling; and in some instances, respiratory distress and stroke, depending on the area of tissue infarct. Treatment consists of hydration (usually one and one-half times maintenance fluid) to provide hemodilution and prevent sickling, pain, and thrombosis. Electrolyte supplementation aids in correcting the metabolic acidosis of tissue hypoxia. Bed rest conserves energy, while transfusion of red blood cells helps correct severe anemia. Exchange transfusions are only used in life-threatening instances. Broad-spectrum antibiotics are often initiated during a vasoocclusive crisis. Oxygen therapy is only used for children with severe hypoxemia. Treatment for priapism includes hypotonic fluids and warm baths. It is important that the erection be relieved within a few hours to prevent ischemia of the penile tissue.

Treatment of the pain associated with sickle cell crisis is a major management concern. During acute periods, the preferred route of narcotic administration is intravenous. Administering pain medications on a standing basis, rather than p.r.n., is more effective. The use of aspirin or products containing aspirin is contraindicated for children with sickle cell disease.

### Nursing Assessment and Diagnosis

Nursing assessment of children with sickle cell disease focuses on clinical manifestations of chronic anemia and acute crisis episodes. Assessment of intake and output and weight gain patterns, activity, incidence of infection and family history of sickle cell disease are important components of the nursing history. Physical assessment focusing on the cerebrum, skin, sclera, spleen, liver, kidneys, chest, heart, abdomen, and extremities provides valuable data

about the severity of the child's disease. Observing for clinical manifestations of an impending crisis and assessing the parents' knowledge of the disease and associated crises is imperative. Recognition of stresses that appear to precipitate a crisis are highly significant for nursing care planning and intervention.

Nursing diagnoses for sickle cell disease might include the following:

- Altered peripheral tissue perfusion related to increased viscosity of blood
- Pain related to tissue hypoxia
- Fluid volume deficit related to failure of the kidneys to concentrate urine
- High risk for infection related to decreased tissue oxygenation
- Impaired physical mobility related to pain
- High risk for altered health maintenance related to lack of knowledge of condition, fluid requirements, and signs and symptoms of complications
- Altered family processes related to having a child with a chronic illness

### Planning and Implementing Nursing Care

Care of the child with sickle cell disease focuses on minimizing the effects of the anemia, preventing systemic complications, and minimizing the incidence of crises.

A nutritionally balanced diet, additional fluid intake, rest, nonstrenuous exercise, avoidance of known sources of infection and areas with low oxygen concentrations, and enhanced management of physical and emotional stresses supports the child with sickle cell disease in maintaining optimal health. Nurses should monitor intake and output, urine specific-gravity values, weight patterns, and other values to assess hydration status. Parents should recognize the early signs of infection and crisis and seek appropriate medical attention. Some children require pain medication or moist heat compresses at home for pain management. Anxiety heightens the perception of pain; therefore, information should be shared with the child to alleviate anxiety.

Crises are usually managed in the hospital during their initial phases and require careful monitoring of fluids and electrolytes as well as of cardiac, abdominal, and neurological status. Complications of sickle cell disease, such as strokes, cardiomyopathy, and sepsis, may require intensive nursing management. Nursing care is directed toward maintaining hemodynamic balance and minimizing long-term sequelae.

Pain management, particularly during the acute phase of a crisis, is a primary nursing goal. Unfortunately, many physicians and nurses are unfamiliar with the severity of sickle cell pain and the waxing and waning pattern it may present. A sound knowledge of pharmacology assists nurses in advocating effective pain management. Even young children may require narcotic administration during the acute phases of a crisis. Most children have an established intravenous route for hydration and should receive their initial narcotics by this route. Older children may be able to regulate their own pain medication administration by using a patient controlled analgesia pump. This pump provides a basal rate of narcotic (usually morphine sulfate) and allows the patient to administer additional small doses of medication. The pump is programmed to prevent overdosage of medication. Research has shown that patients who use these pumps use less narcotics than patients who receive narcotics p.r.n.

Sickle cell disease is a chronic, lifelong disease. Families require emotional, educational, and physical support to adjust to the wide variations in health experienced by children with this disease.

### Evaluating Nursing Care

Evaluation of nursing care for children with sickle cell disease focuses on observing minimal effects of the anemia, absence of systemic complications, and minimal crises. Observing normal growth and developmental patterns in the child and family further supports the effectiveness of the nursing interventions.

# Hematological Problems of Preschool- and School-Aged Children

## Aplastic Anemia

### Pathophysiology

*Aplastic anemia* is a rare disorder in which the formation of erythrocytes, granulocytes, and platelets is severely depressed. This results in profound anemia, granulocytopenia, and thrombocytopenia. It may be caused by injury or by destruction of or a low population of stem cells in the bone marrow. About half of all aplastic anemias have an acquired or secondary cause. Exposure to radiation, toxic agents (benzene), drugs (chloramphenicol), severe disease (viral hepatitis), and immunological deficiencies (leukemia) have been cited as causes of aplasia. Half of aplastic anemia cases are considered idiopathic; that is, they have no readily identifiable cause. The mortality rate for aplastic anemia is extremely high, with 50% to 60% of deaths occurring in the first 6 months after diagnosis (Hutchinson, 1983). Less than 10% of all cases recover spontaneously.

### Medical Diagnosis and Management

Clinical manifestations of aplastic anemia reflect the absence of erythrocytes, granulocytes, and platelets. Depression of erythrocytes results in severe anemia, manifested by pallor, tachycardia, and possibly heart failure. Leukopenia may be clinically manifested, with increased incidence of fever and bacterial infection. Petechiae, ecchy-mosis, and hemorrhage may be observed with thrombocytopenia.

Laboratory analysis of the complete blood count reveals depression of all formed elements. The diagnosis is confirmed by obtaining a hypoplastic marrow specimen through bone marrow aspiration and biopsy.

Bone marrow transplantation is the treatment of choice for children with severe aplastic anemia. It is recommended that bone marrow transplantation be done before administration of blood transfusions or that only irradiated blood products are administered. This has been shown to diminish likelihood of rejection. Androgenic steroids (e.g., testosterone), often supplemented by corticosteroids, are administered in instances in which bone marrow transplantation is not feasible. Recent clinical trials with globulins designed to suppress the autoimmune process show some promise in treating aplastic anemia. Transfusion of blood products and aggressive antibiotic therapy provide continued medical support for the child with aplastic anemia throughout the course of the illness.

### Nursing Assessment and Diagnosis

Nursing assessment focuses on clinical manifestations of bone marrow depression. Symptoms of anemia, such as pallor, tachycardia, and tachypnea, may be present as may symptoms of heart failure. The skin is assessed for petechiae, ecchymoses, edema, and infection. The eyes are assessed for retinal hemorrhage. A history of hematuria, tarry stools, and spontaneous bleeding is highly significant. Signs of localized and systemic infection must be assessed on a frequent basis.

Exploration of the past health and environmental history may provide some indication as to the cause of the aplastic anemia, but it is imperative to remember that in half of cases the cause is unknown. Since treatment options are limited, and decisions may be urgently needed, it is essential to assess the child's and parent's understanding of the disease. Bleeding is extremely frightening to both parent and child, and the family's ability to cope with such monumental stresses cannot be taken for granted.

Nursing diagnoses for aplastic anemia might include the following:

- High risk for injury related to bleeding tendencies
- High risk for infection related to increased susceptibility
- Activity intolerance related to insufficient oxygen
- Altered family processes related to caring for a child with a chronic illness

### Planning and Implementing Nursing Care

Nursing care for the child with aplastic anemia is focused on preventing complications of bleeding and infection, administering treatments, and providing educational and emotional support to children and parents.

Prevention of injury focuses on creating a safe environment, avoiding invasive treatments, such as taking rectal temperatures and giving intramuscular injections, and continuing assessment of skin, urine, and stool for bleeding. Prevention of infection may involve implementation of reverse isolation precautions or strict isolation precautions. Asepsis is a priority. Children may be bathed twice daily with antibacterial soap to prevent sepsis from body flora. It is essential to assess for toxic side effects of antibiotic use as well as for transfusion reactions.

Bleeding is an extremely frightening experience for parents and children. Knowledge concerning frequency of bleeding and blood product administration helps the child and family to see the crisis as manageable. It may also help to allay the child's natural fear of death.

Bone marrow transplantation is an extremely rigorous process. Educational and emotional preparation must begin as soon as this treatment modality has been decided on. Care of children undergoing bone marrow transplantation is discussed earlier in this chapter.

Aplastic anemia is a life-threatening illness that generates severe emotional upset for children and families. Calm, competent, empathic nurses can attend to both the demanding physical care needs and emotional care needs of the children and their families. Although the prognosis is poor, nurses must continually frame their actions within a developmental perspective, attempting to enhance coping and growth in both the children and their families. This same principle is instrumental in caring for children and families during the terminal stages of the illness.

### Evaluating Nursing Care

Evaluation of nursing care aims to observe resolution of the aplastic anemia with minimal, if any, sequelae. Resolution of bleeding or infectious crises, preparation for and successful participation in bone marrow transplantation, and enhancement of family developmental growth are possible outcomes, in spite of the prognosis of this disease. In some instances, acute care nursing may rapidly become terminal care nursing. The goals of providing comfort and emotional support for children and families remain relevant and important for evaluation.

## Idiopathic Thrombocytopenic Purpura

### Pathophysiology

*Idiopathic thrombocytopenic purpura* (ITP) is a condition in which the number of circulating platelets is reduced as a result of the action of an antiplatelet antibody produced in the spleen. This autoimmune thrombocytopenia results in bleeding into the tissues or purpura.

### Medical Diagnosis and Management

Medical diagnosis of ITP is founded on a platelet count of less than 50,000/mm$^3$ and clinical manifestations of pe-

techiae, ecchymosis, bleeding from mucous membranes, hematuria, and bloody stools. Diagnosis is confirmed by bone marrow examination that reveals normal erythrocyte and granulocyte counts and a decreased platelet count.

Treatment for ITP varies. The use of steroids is controversial; some physicians use steroids only for children with platelet counts less than 30,000 (Dubansky & Oski, 1986), whereas others administer steroids only for platelet counts less than 10,000. Platelet administration is generally not recommended since the antiplatelet antibody destroys the new platelets. ITP generally resolves spontaneously within 6 months. The primary management goal is the provision of safety until the platelet count has returned to normal. In instances of chronic ITP, splenectomy is performed to remove the source of antiplatelet antibody.

### Nursing Assessment and Diagnosis

Nursing assessment focuses on clinical manifestations of bleeding. Observation of the head, skin, eyes, stool, and urine provide valuable information for the nursing data base. Nurses should assess for signs of change in central nervous system function, including headaches, vision changes, lethargy, or vomiting.

Nursing diagnoses for ITP might include the following:

- High risk for injury related to hemorrhage
- Altered peripheral tissue perfusion related to decreased platelet count
- Anxiety related to change in health status

### Planning and Implementing Nursing Care

Nursing care is directed toward providing safety for the child until the platelet count returns to normal. The child's activity is restricted, protective helmets are used, and contact sports are avoided. Parents should be taught to avoid substances that may enhance bleeding, such as aspirin. Invasive treatments, such as taking rectal temperatures and giving intramuscular injections, are also avoided. Children on steroid therapy are at increased risk for infection and should not be exposed to people with active infections. Parents should be taught the common gastrointestinal side effects of steroid therapy. If a splenectomy is to be performed, nurses intervene with the child and family as discussed earlier in this chapter. The child and family should be encouraged to express their fears and concerns.

### Evaluating Nursing Care

Evaluation of nursing care focuses on successful prevention of injury during resolution of the illness and maintenance of normal growth and developmental processes. The child and parents should demonstrate their understanding of the disorder, the necessary safety precautions, and the side effects of treatment.

## Acute Leukemia

### Pathophysiology

Leukemia is the most common form of childhood cancer, comprising 34% of all childhood malignancies. Incidence of leukemia ranges from 9.4 to 12.1 cases per 100,000 (Castoria & Harris, 1986). *Leukemia* is characterized by unrestricted proliferation of immature white blood cells in the bone marrow and certain blood-forming tissues. These cells then infiltrate other tissues (particularly the liver, spleen, and lymph glands) and replace functional cells with leukemic cells. Large numbers of immature and nonfunctional white blood cells create a great potential for infection.

Leukemia may be classified as acute or chronic. Ninety percent of childhood leukemia is acute, meaning that excess immature or blastic cells are produced. *Acute lymphocytic leukemia* involves lymphoid tissue or the lymphatic system and is the most common form of leukemia in children. The three subtypes of acute lymphocytic leukemia are T-lymphocyte, B-lymphocyte, and null cell (having neither T-cell nor B-cell characteristics). The null cell type is the most common and carries the best prognosis. Other positive prognostic indicators at diagnosis are absence of lymphadenopathy, hepatosplenomegaly, or central nervous system involvement; white blood cell count less than 50,000; and age between 2 and 10 years (Poplack, 1989). With good prognostic indicators, the survival rate of acute lymphocytic leukemia can reach 70% (Simone & Rivers, 1984). *Acute nonlymphocytic leukemia* may be divided into six subgroups, the most notable of which is *acute myelocytic leukemia*. This type of leukemia is less common, is seen more frequently in adolescence, and carries a much graver prognosis.

### Medical Diagnosis and Management

The presenting symptoms of acute leukemia reflect the physiological changes occurring in the bone marrow. Leukemic cells crowd out normal cells, resulting in impaired production of erythrocytes, platelets, and normal granulocytes. Clinical manifestations of anemia (fatigue, pallor, tachycardia), bleeding (petechiae), purpura, hematuria (tarry stools, epistaxis), hyperuricemia, and immunosuppression (fever, infection) are usually present at diagnosis. If leukemic cells have migrated outside the bone marrow, hepatosplenomegaly, lymphadenopathy, or a mediastinal mass may also be present at diagnosis. Complaints of bone or joint pain and symptoms of meningeal irritation (headache, vomiting, papilledema) may reflect infiltration of leukemic cells into the bone and central nervous system. The history may reveal recent weight loss, anorexia, fatigue, easy bleeding or bruising, and an apparently minor infection that did not resolve.

Leukemia is strongly suspected in light of positive physical assessment findings and a high proportion of blastic cells in the white blood cell differential count. The actual number of white blood cells can range from near-normal values to over 300,000/mm$^3$. Confirmation of diagnosis is made by bone marrow aspiration. A lumbar puncture is performed to assess the presence of leukemic cells in the central nervous system.

Treatment of leukemia is divided into three phases. The initial phase of *remission induction* aims to reduce the number of leukemic cells so that there is no evidence of leukemia. Combination chemotherapeutic agent therapy is used and may include vincristine, prednisone, and L-asparaginase for treatment of acute lymphocytic leukemia. The selection of chemotherapeutic agents may vary according to the child's projected risk, based on prognostic factors at diagnosis. About 95% of children with acute lymphocytic leukemia achieve remission 2 to 4 weeks after treatment is initiated (Simone & Rivers, 1984).

The next phase of treatment is called *sanctuary*, or treatment of the body areas that are not reached by the systemic effects of chemotherapy. This involves treatment of the central nervous system with intrathecal methotrexate, possible cranial radiation, or radiation to the testes in males.

The third phase of treatment is called *maintenance therapy*. Maintenance is aimed at reducing the possibility of growth of leukemic cells so that a relapse does not occur. Although a variety of drug combinations are administered, the most widely used are 6-mercaptopurine and methotrexate. Treatment for leukemia may last 24 to 36 months.

A second, reinduction protocol is initiated for children with acute lymphocytic leukemia experiencing a bone marrow relapse. While remission is achievable, it is usually shorter than the first remission. Thus, bone marrow transplantation after the second remission is recommended when possible. Relapse in the extramedullary sites is usually followed by bone marrow relapse. In these cases, aggressive treatment to the site of relapse and initiation of systemic therapy to head off a bone marrow relapse is begun.

Treatment of acute nonlymphocytic leukemia is more difficult and requires more intensive chemotherapeutic agents to achieve remission. Cytosine arabinoside, vincristine, and daunorubicin are the chemotherapeutic agents commonly used for induction. Only 60% to 70% percent of children with acute nonlymphocytic leukemia achieve a first remission (Castoria & Harris, 1986). Because of the poor prognosis, bone marrow transplantation is recommended when possible after achieving a first remission.

Additional medical management of the child with leukemia focuses on monitoring for side effects of the chemotherapy, evidence of infection (local or systemic), and signs of anemia or bleeding; assessing nutritional status; and providing ongoing information and emotional support to the child and family.

## Nursing Assessment and Diagnosis

Assessment of the child with leukemia focuses on the clinical manifestations of the underlying disease process. Symptoms of anemia and thrombocytopenia were reviewed previously in this chapter. Clinical manifestations of localized infection are redness, edema, warmth, and possibly exudate at the site. Symptoms of systemic infection are more insidious and require ongoing monitoring of vital signs. A detailed history of prior infections, bleeding and bruising episodes, weight loss, anorexia, behavior changes, or complaints of pain must be thoroughly investigated.

Although the physical care needs of the child with leukemia are the apparent assessment priority, it must be remembered that the diagnosis of leukemia is an extremely traumatic and often devastating event for the child and family. Anxiety and fear are often incapacitating. It is imperative to assess child and family coping and communication problems. Assessment of the educational needs and abilities of the child and family and community resources may provide additional support for the child and family throughout the course of the illness.

Nursing diagnoses for leukemia might include the following:

- High risk for infection related to altered immune system
- High risk for injury related to bleeding tendencies
- Pain related to effects of chemotherapy and the disease process
- Altered nutrition: less than body requirements related to anorexia
- Altered oral mucous membranes related to effects of chemotherapy
- High risk for impaired skin integrity related to decreased hydration and effects of chemotherapy
- Activity intolerance related to fatigue
- Altered health maintenance related to lack of knowledge about the condition and its treatment
- Body image disturbance related to alopecia and weight loss
- Altered family processes related to the treatment regimen
- Anxiety related to the treatment regimen
- Ineffective individual/family coping related to the diagnosis and prognosis
- Anticipatory grieving related to the prognosis

## Planning and Implementing Nursing Care

Nursing care for the child with leukemia focuses on prevention of anemia, bleeding, and infection; safe administration of the therapeutic regimen; minimization of side effects of therapy; and enhancement of family coping through provision of educational and emotional support.

Ongoing assessments, administration of blood products, provisions for safety, meticulous hand washing, and use of aseptic technique are just a few of the nursing interventions commonly employed in the care of the child with leukemia. In addition, invasive procedures that can cause bleeding (e.g., giving injections, taking rectal temperatures, and vigorous tooth brushing) should be avoided. Hyperalimentation may be necessary to provide adequate nutrition if the child has recurrent nausea and vomiting.

The most common side effects of chemotherapy are nausea and vomiting; however, the nurse must be aware of the common potential side effects of all the chemotherapeutic agents and treatment modalities as well as pharmacological and nonpharmacological means of support.

Children with leukemia and their families must cope with the demands of a life-threatening illness that they hope is of limited duration. The educational and emotional needs of children and families must be incorporated into every nursing interaction. Peak stresses are reported by families at the time of diagnosis, relapse, transplant, or death. Families can be referred to the local chapters of the American Cancer Society and Leukemia Society support groups for information and counseling about this disorder. Nurses collaborate with clients and families to offer highly skilled yet empathic care supportive of the family's individual emotional and developmental needs.

## Evaluating Nursing Care

Evaluation of nursing care focuses on preventing and minimizing complications related to the disease process and its treatment. Maintenance or enhancement of child and family coping abilities, particularly through crisis periods, attests to the comprehensive support child and family receive from the health care team. The child should remain free from infection and should experience minimal episodes of bleeding. The child should receive adequate nutrition and rest and should demonstrate positive coping strategies and body image (Fig. 25-5). Disruptions in family processes should be kept to a minimum, and the family should demonstrate decreased anxiety and anticipatory grieving. Goals of care may need to be reevaluated in light of relapse, terminal illness, or bone marrow transplantation.

# Hematological Problems of Adolescents

## Hodgkin Disease

### Pathophysiology

*Hodgkin disease* is a malignant disorder of the lymph nodes in which abnormal proliferation of lymphocytes, eosinophils, histiocytes, or collagen and fibrous tissue may

*Figure 25–5. Special summer camps provide opportunities for normal activities that help improve self-image. (Courtesy of Camp Can-Do, Pennsylvania Division, American Cancer Society)*

occur. Hodgkin disease is considered to have only one primary site but subsequently spreads to nearby lymph nodes.

Hodgkin disease accounts for 6.5% of childhood cancer. Its incidence is higher in males and increases throughout childhood, most dramatically at adolescence (Boren & Sullivan, 1986).

## Medical Diagnosis and Management

Adolescents diagnosed with Hodgkin disease most commonly present with a painless, swollen lymph node usually (in 60%–90% of cases) in the cervical chain. Other clinical manifestations may include a history of anorexia, weight loss, malaise, fever, night sweats, and possibly respiratory distress.

The histological type and the extent of the disease must be determined before treatment. *Staging* is the assessment of the extent of lymph node and extra nodal (spleen, liver, lung, mediastinum, central nervous system, bone) disease involvement and may involve local or generalized surgical procedures. A most favorable prognosis is associated with disease confined to the lymph nodes and presenting on only one side of the diaphragm (stages I and II). Absence of systemic symptoms, such as fever, weight loss, and night sweats, also adds favorably to the prognosis. Stage III disease is characterized by lymph node involvement on both sides of the diaphragm, with extra nodal involvement commonly occurring in the spleen. Stage IV disease is characterized by involvement of more than one extranodal organ or tissue. The stages are further categorized as either A (absence of systemic symptoms) or B (presence of systemic symptoms).

Before staging procedures, a complete workup is per-

formed, including chest radiography, abdominal computed tomography scans, lymphangiography, gallium scan, liver and spleen scans, skeletal survey, and bone marrow aspiration. A lymph node biopsy is performed to obtain a definitive diagnosis. The presence of Reed-Sternberg cells (abnormally large cells containing one or more nuclei and covered with a stained nuclear membrane) is indicative of Hodgkin disease.

Treatment is based on staging and histology findings. Treatment for stages I, II, and IIIA is radiation therapy. For stages IIIB and IV disease, a combination of radiation and chemotherapy is used. Chemotherapeutic agents most likely to be employed are nitrogen mustard, Oncovin, procarbazine, and prednisone. The overall prognosis is good, reaching 90% in children with early-stage disease (Boren & Sullivan, 1986).

## Nursing Assessment and Diagnosis

Nursing assessment of the adolescent with Hodgkin disease focuses on the clinical manifestations of the underlying disease process. A detailed history of presenting symptoms, such as anorexia, weight loss, fever, and night sweats, are crucial to determination of the prognosis and treatment plan. Assessment of potential side effects of radiation and chemotherapy must be ongoing.

The diagnosis of Hodgkin disease is traumatic for both adolescent and parents. Wide variations in adolescents' behavior may be observed depending on their level of cognitive and emotional development. It is imperative to accurately assess the level of cognitive and emotional development of clients and the communication and support patterns exhibited in interactions with their families.

Nursing diagnoses for Hodgkin disease might include the following:

- High risk for infection related to altered immune system
- High risk for injury related to bleeding tendencies
- Pain related to effects of chemotherapy, disease process
- Altered nutrition: less than body requirements related to anorexia
- Altered oral mucous membranes related to effects of chemotherapy
- High risk for impaired skin integrity related to decreased hydration and effects of chemotherapy
- Activity intolerance related to fatigue
- Altered health maintenance related to lack of knowledge about the condition and its treatment
- Body image disturbance related to alopecia and weight loss
- Altered family processes related to the treatment regimen
- Anxiety related to the treatment regimen
- Ineffective individual/family coping related to the diagnosis and prognosis
- Anticipatory grieving related to the prognosis

## *Planning and Implementing Nursing Care*

Nursing care for the adolescent with Hodgkin disease is similar to that provided for children with leukemia and focuses on prevention of complications related to the disease process and therapeutic regimen. Ongoing assessments, administration of blood products, meticulous hand washing, and use of aseptic technique are just a few of the nursing interventions employed in the care of the adolescent with Hodgkin disease.

Side effects of radiation therapy may require specific nursing interventions. Keeping skin dry, avoiding perfumes, lotions, and soap, and encouraging the client to wear loose cotton clothing and to avoid sun exposure are considered supportive actions. Attention to nutritional needs and body image concerns (e.g., alopecia) are paramount during adolescence. Knowledge of the chemotherapeutic regimen side effects and appropriate interventions are also included in care planning and implementation.

Hodgkin disease is a potentially life-threatening illness. Attention to the educational and emotional needs of the adolescent and family must be an integral part of every nursing interaction. Nurses must be available to provide safe, competent, holistic, and empathic care to the adolescent with Hodgkin disease and the family.

## *Evaluating Nursing Care*

Evaluation of nursing care focuses on preventing and minimizing complications related to the disease process and its treatment. Maintenance or enhancement of the adolescent and family's coping abilities, particularly through crisis periods, should be evident. The adolescent should remain free from infection and should experience minimal episodes of bleeding. The adolescent should receive adequate nutrition and rest and should demonstrate positive coping strategies and body image. Disruptions in family processes should be kept to a minimum, and the family should demonstrate decreased anxiety and anticipatory grieving. Goals of care may need to be reevaluated in light of relapse or terminal illness.

## *Summary*

Caring for children and adolescents with alterations in hematological function present complex challenges for nurses. A sound knowledge of pathophysiology, pharmacology, growth and development, and a multitude of treatment modalities is essential in assessing, diagnosing, planning, implementing, and evaluating nursing care for these clients and their families. Skills in nursing assessment, intervention, client teaching, and counseling serve to make the pediatric hematology nurse a valuable member of the health care team.

## References

Avery, G. B. (1987). *Neonatology: Pathophysiology and management of the newborn.* Philadelphia: J. B. Lippincott.

Avery, M. E., & Taeusch, H. W. (Eds.). (1984). *Schaffer's diseases of the newborn.* Philadelphia: W. B. Saunders.

Boren, H., & Sullivan, M. (1986). Hodgkin's disease. In Hockenberry, M., & Coody, D. (Eds.). *Pediatric oncology and hematology.* St. Louis: C. V. Mosby.

Bullock, B., & Rosendahl, P. P. (1988). *Pathophysiology.* Glenview, IL: Scott, Foresman.

Cashore, W. J., & Stern, L. (1982). Neonatal hyperbilirubinemia. *Pediatric Clinics of North America, 29*(5), 1191–1203.

Castoria, H., & Harris, M. (1986). Childhood leukemias. In Hockenberry, M., & Coody, D. (Eds.). *Pediatric oncology and hematology.* St. Louis: C. V. Mosby.

Dubansky, A. S., & Oski, F. A. (1986). Controversies in the management of acute ITP: A survey of specialists. *Pediatrics, 77*(1), 49–52.

Festa, R. S. (1985). Modern management of thalassemia. *Pediatric Annals, 14*(9), 597–606.

Hutchinson, M. (1983). Aplastic anemia. *Nursing Clinics of North America, 18*(3), 543.

Jenkins, J. (1983). *Human genetics.* Redwood City, CA: Benjamin/Cummings.

Johnson, C. S. (1985). Sickle cell anemia. *Journal of the American Medical Association, 254*(14), 1958–1963.

Kasprisin, C. A. (1986). Recipient considerations. In Reynolds A.W., & Steckler, D. (Eds.). *Practical aspects of blood administration.* Arlington, VA: American Association of Blood Banks.

Kelleher, J. (1986). Bone marrow transplantation. In Hockenberry, M., & Coody, D. (Eds.). *Pediatric oncology and hematology.* St. Louis: C. V. Mosby.

Lanzkowsky, P. (1985). Problems in diagnosis of iron deficiency anemia. *Pediatric Annals, 14*(9), 618–636.

Marieb, E. N. (1989). *Human anatomy and physiology.* Redwood City, CA: Benjamin/Cummings.

Miller, C. (1982). Genetics of hemophilia and van Willebrand's disease. In Hilgartner, M. W. (Ed.). *Hemophilia in the child and adult.* New York: Masson Publishing.

Poplack, D. G. (1989). Acute lymphoblastic leukemia. In Pizzo, P. A., & Poplack, D. G. *Principles and practice of pediatric oncology.* Philadelphia: J. B. Lippincott.

Simone, J. V., & Rivers, G. (1984). Management of acute leukemia. In Sutow, W. W., Fernbach, D. J., & Vietti, T. J. (Eds.). *Clinical pediatric oncology.* St. Louis: C. V. Mosby.

Warren, M., & McMillan, C. (1986). Hemophilia. In Hockenberry, M., & Coody, D. (Eds.). *Pediatric oncology and hematology.* St. Louis: C. V. Mosby.

## Bibliography

Battista, E. (1986). Educational needs of the adolescent with cancer and his family. *Seminars in Oncology Nursing, 2*(2), 123–125.

Bianchi, D. W., Beyer, E., Stark, A., Saffan, D., Sachs, B., & Wolfe, L. (1986). Normal long-term survival with beta thalassemia. *Journal of Pediatrics, 108*(5), 716–718.

Blotcky, A. (1986). Helping adolescents with cancer cope with their disease. *Seminars in Oncology Nursing, 2*(2), 117–122.

Braune, K. W., & Lacey, L. (1983). Common hematologic problems of the immediate newborn period. *Journal of Obstetric, Gynecologic, and Neonatal Nursing, 12*(Suppl), 195.

Deinard, A. S., List, A., Lindgren, B., Hunt, J., & Chang, P. (1986). Cognitive deficits in iron deficient and iron deficient anemic children. *Journal of Pediatrics, 108*(1), 681–689.

Dortch, E., & Spottiswoode, P. (1986, February). New light on phototherapy: Home use. *Neonatal Network, 4,* 30.

Dunne, C. (1989). Safe handling of anti-neoplastic agents. *Cancer Nursing, 12*(2), 120–127.

Edwardson, S. (1983). The choice between hospital and home care for terminally ill children. *Nursing Research, 32*(1), 29–34.

Fergusson, J., Ruccione, K., & Waskerwitz, M. (1987). Time required to assess children for the late effects of treatment: A report from the Children's Cancer Study Group. *Cancer Nursing, 10*(6), 300–310.

Hockenberry, M., & Hoots, W. (1986). Childhood anemias. In Hockenberry, M., & Coody, D. (Eds.). *Pediatric oncology and hematology.* St. Louis: C. V. Mosby.

Klaus, M. H., & Fanaroff, A. A. (1986). *Care of the high risk neonate.* Philadelphia: W. B. Saunders.

McClowry, S. (1987). Research and treatment: Ethical distinctions related to the care of children. *Journal of Pediatric Nursing, 2*(1), 23–29

Nierenberg, A., & Bridgewater, C. (1986). Malignancies in adolescents. *Seminars in Oncology Nursing, 2*(2), 75–83.

Pack, B., & Kenney, T. (1986). Sickle cell disease. In Hockenberry, M., & Coody, D. (Eds.). *Pediatric oncology and hematology.* St. Louis: C. V. Mosby.

Porth, C. M. (1990). *Pathophysiology.* Philadelphia: J. B. Lippincott.

Sanders, J. E. et al. (1986). Bone marrow transplant experience for children with aplastic anemia. *Pediatrics, 77*(2), 179–186.

van der Wal, R., Nims, J., & Davies, B. (1988). Bone marrow transplantation in children: Nursing management of late effects. *Cancer Nursing, 11*(3), 132–143.

Waskerwitz, M. (1984). Special nursing care for children receiving chemotherapy. *Journal of the Association of Pediatric Oncology Nurses, 1*(1), 16–25.

# Alterations in Neurological Function

Mary Ann Jezewski

*Photograph by David Finn*

26

*Embryology*

*Anatomy and Physiology*

*Assessment*

*Nursing Diagnosis*

*Planning and Implementing Nursing Care*

*Nursing Interventions*

*Evaluating Nursing Care*

*Intracranial Hypertension*

*Neurological Problems of Infants*

*Neurological Problems of Toddlers*

*Neurological Problems of Pre-school Children*

*Neurological Problems of School-Age Children*

*Neurological Problems of Adolescents*

*Summary*

## Learning Objectives

*Upon completion of this chapter the reader will be able to:*

1. *Describe the anatomy and physiology of the nervous system.*

2. *Assess the neurological status of infants and children.*

3. *Prepare a child for procedures and diagnostic tests common in neurological dysfunction.*

4. *Select appropriate nursing diagnoses for pediatric patients with neurological dysfunction.*

5. *Describe the nursing management of a child with increased intracranial pressure.*

6. *Plan the nursing care for the child with various neurological and neuromuscular problems.*

## Key Terms

*aura*

*blood–brain barrier*

*cerebral spinal fluid*

*clonic*

*contrecoup*

*coup*

*decerebrate posturing*

*decorticate posturing*

*Glasgow Coma Scale*

*level of consciousness*

*Macewen's sign*

*myelinization*

*shunt*

*tonic*

Neurological problems in children may be acquired or congenital. These problems can be frustrating to both health care professionals and the family, because neural tissue does not have the regenerative capabilities of other body tissues. Therefore, acute neurological problems can evolve into long-term chronic conditions that must be managed throughout the life cycle.

Neurological disorders in children may result in severe and permanent disabilities, but many of these disabilities can be prevented or minimized by effective medical and nursing management. Children with neurological problems require complex nursing management to achieve optimal function. The nurse must integrate knowledge of the pathophysiologic processes, normal neuroanatomy and physiology, and the growth and development of the child into a sound understanding of the child's problems. An important component of nursing care is the assessment of the family and provision of support and counseling to the entire family system.

## Embryology

The central nervous system is one of the first systems to develop in utero. By the end of the first month of gestation the neural tube closes and widens at the uppermost area to form the brain. The posterior end forms the spinal cord. In the second and third month the cerebral hemispheres form and cerebellar development occurs. Neurological development continues in utero and in the postnatal period, especially in the first year of life. The myelin sheath (conductive coat on nerve fibers) is incomplete at birth and continues to form postnatally. Because of this, the newborn has limited functions. As myelinization progresses, the infant and young child are able to perform more complex tasks (increased coordination, walking, talking).

## Anatomy and Physiology

### The Central Nervous System

The nervous system consists of two systems—the central nervous system and the peripheral nervous system. The central nervous system consists of the brain and the spinal cord. The system is bathed in cerebrospinal fluid and covered with membranes (meninges). These serve, in part, as a cushion to minimize normal neurological trauma. The central nervous system is also protected by the skull and vertebral column. The spinal cord, which is encased in the spinal vertebrae, conducts nerve impulses between the brain stem and the peripheral nervous system.

The brain consists of the brain stem, cerebellum, diencephalon, and cerebrum (Fig. 26-1). The brain stem, which controls involuntary activity such as respirations and heart rate, is situated between the spinal column and the cerebrum. Many of the cranial nerves originate in the brain stem.

The cerebellum is located at the base of the brain. It coordinates muscle movement. It also receives sensory information (hearing, vision, and touch), which assists in balance and body positioning as well as coordination.

The diencephalon consists of the thalamus and hypo-thalamus. The thalamus aids in relaying sensory stimuli from the cerebellum to the cerebral cortex. The hypo-thalamus controls homeostatic mechanisms of the body by influencing the autonomic and endocrine systems, which, in turn, control body temperature regulation, the stress response, thirst, and appetite.

The cerebrum, consisting of two hemispheres, accounts for the largest portion of the brain tissue. It controls the higher functions of the body. Each hemisphere contains four furrowed lobes and an outer layer called the cerebral cortex. Each lobe controls specific body functions. The cerebral hemispheres are connected centrally by the corpus callosum, a large bundle of nerve fibers. The corpus callosum connects the cortical areas of the left and right hemispheres. The basal ganglia are situated deep within each hemisphere. The cerebrum is the center of consciousness, memory, thought processes, sensory input, and some motor activity.

The brain is composed of two types of cells: neuronal (impulse-conducting) and glial (support structure). Three meninges (membranes) surround the brain. The dura mater, the outermost covering, consists of fibrous connective tissue. The arachnoid layer is a delicate middle layer that forms a watertight membrane, and the pia mater is the third, highly vascular layer.

The cerebrospinal fluid (CSF) is an important component of the central nervous system. In addition to protecting the brain and spinal column, it also functions to nourish the brain. Cerebrospinal fluid is formed in the choroid plexes and flows around and through a series of

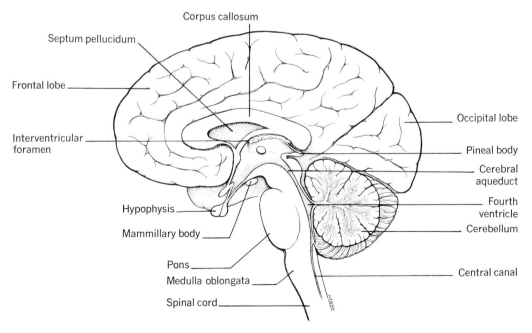

*Figure 26–1. Anatomy of the brain. (Chaffee, E.E., & Lytle, I.M. [1980]. Basic physiology and anatomy. Philadelphia: J.B. Lippincott, p. 214)*

ventricles (collecting cavities in the brain), ducts, and the length of the spinal column, as shown in Figure 26-2. The CSF is colorless and clear. Its pH is alkaline, with a specific gravity from 1.004 to 1.008. It contains glucose (60% to 80% of blood serum value), traces of protein, lymphocytes, and body electrolytes.

## The Peripheral Nervous System

The peripheral nervous system comprises the autonomic nervous system, the spinal nerves (31 pairs), and the cranial nerves (12 pairs). Each of the spinal and cranial nerves contains a motor and sensory component.

The autonomic nervous system comprises two subsystems: the sympathetic and the parasympathetic systems. These control involuntary responses and are under the control of the hypothalamus. The parasympathetic and sympathetic systems function to maintain body system homeostasis. The systems act to stimulate (sympathetic) or relax (parasympathetic) body organs (complementary or antagonistic). The sympathetic system reacts in time of physiological and psychological stress to mobilize the flight-or-fight responses in the body.

## Intracranial Pressure

It is necessary to understand the physiology of intracranial pressure (ICP) in order to be able to understand the pathophysiological process occurring with many neurological problems. Intracranial pressure is determined by the volumes and pressures exerted by brain, blood, and cerebrospinal fluid (CSF). Normal ICP measures between 0 mm Hg and 15 mm Hg. Any measurement over 15 mm Hg is considered increased ICP. Normally ICP is a continually fluctuating parameter that changes minimally in response to body movements such as standing (which causes it to decrease) or coughing, sneezing, and actions that precipitate the Valsalva movement (which cause it to increase).

The Monro-Kellie hypothesis is an essential concept in understanding the pathophysiological process of increased ICP. The hypothesis states that because the skull is a rigid, nondistendible container filled to capacity with essentially noncompressible contents (blood, brain, and CSF) whose volume remains unchanged, an increase in one component or the addition of another component (i.e., tumor) must be accompanied by a decrease in one of the other components. If not, ICP will rise. (This hypoth-

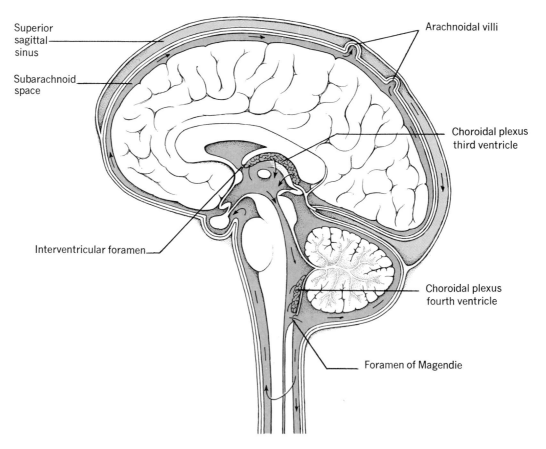

Superior sagittal sinus

Subarachnoid space

Interventricular foramen

Arachnoidal villi

Choroidal plexus third ventricle

Choroidal plexus fourth ventricle

Foramen of Magendie

*Figure 26–2.    Flow of cerebrospinal fluid. (Chaffee, E.E., & Lytle, I.M. [1980].* **Basic physiology and anatomy.** *Philadelphia: J.B. Lippincott, p. 221)*

esis excludes infants and young children whose cranial sutures have not fused and whose heads increase in size in response to increased intracranial pressure.)

The compensating mechanisms put forth by the hypothesis involve several processes to equalize ICP: a decrease in CSF production, cerebral vasoconstriction to decrease cerebral blood flow, and increased absorption of CSF. These compensating mechanisms have limited capabilities in controlling increasing ICP. They can accommodate small increases in pressure or increases that occur over long periods of time. When they reach their compensating limits, decompensation occurs. At this time, because these mechanisms no longer maintain homeostasis, a small increase in cranial vault contents produces a large rise in pressure.

### Cerebral Blood Flow

The brain uses approximately 20% of the body's oxygen. A constant supply of blood and oxygen to the brain, which is essential, depends on cerebral perfusion pressure (CPP), cerebral vascular resistance (CVR), and the autoregulatory mechanism. Blood flows to the brain via the internal carotid artery. Under normal conditions the cerebral blood flow (CBF) is maintained at a fairly constant rate, independent of physical activity or alteration in blood pressure. Increased cerebral metabolism increases the brain's need for oxygen. With the increased metabolism, cerebral vasodilation occurs, increasing CBF and cerebral blood volume.

### Cerebral Perfusion Pressure

The cerebral perfusion pressure (CPP), which is the amount of pressure needed to maintain a flow of blood into the brain, is the difference between the mean systemic arterial pressure and the mean ICP. The normal CPP is between 80 mm Hg and 100 mm Hg, with a range of 60 mm Hg to 150 mm Hg. A CPP below 60 mm Hg results in ischemia to brain tissue because of a decrease in blood flow to the brain. A CPP below 30 mm Hg is incompatible with life and results in cerebral anoxia and brain death. As ICP rises, CPP decreases despite the body's attempt to increase CPP by increasing systemic arterial pressure.

### Cerebral Vascular Resistance

Cerebral vascular resistance (CVR) is the resistance created by the constriction and dilation of cerebral vessels and is controlled by the autoregulatory mechanism. CVR varies inversely with cerebral blood volume and increases with vasoconstriction.

### Autoregulation

Autoregulation is an important mechanism in the control of CBF. Autoregulation controls the diameter of cerebral vessels in response to fluctuations in CPP. Cerebral vessels maintain a constant flow of blood to the brain tissues despite normal changes in blood pressure, body postures, increased ICP, carotid narrowing, and decreased cardiac output.

Metabolic as well as pressure mechanism work to control autoregulation. Changes in $Pao_2$ and $Paco_2$ have a profound effect on autoregulation. Carbon dioxide in the blood (hypercapnia) causes vasodilation, which increases the blood supply to the brain in an attempt to remove metabolic wastes and maintain an oxygen level that meets the metabolic demands of brain cells. This also increases cerebral blood volume, which can aggravate already increasing ICP.

Autoregulation can fail when other mechanisms cause it to reach a critical point. Factors that can cause the failure include injury to cerebral tissue, CPP outside the normal range of 60 mm Hg to 150 mm Hg, and increased ICP greater than 30 mm Hg. With a loss of autoregulators, cerebral blood flow is dependent on systemic blood pressure and CPP.

### The Blood–Brain Barrier

The capillaries of the brain are distinctly different from other capillaries in the body. Brain capillaries provide a protective mechanism that prevents toxic or other harmful substances from passing into the brain. The intact, mature blood–brain barrier allows oxygen, carbon dioxide, glucose, and the passive diffusion of water to cross freely, but prevents most proteins and most other substances from crossing the barrier. The blood–brain barrier of the newborn and young infant is not fully mature, and substances that do not ordinarily permeate the blood–brain barrier indiscriminately cross this barrier in the newborn and infant. This increases the danger of cerebral edema and increased ICP.

## Assessment

### History

Eliciting a patient health history is an important part of any nursing assessment (see Chapter 5 for discussion of routine health history). A comprehensive family, parental, and child medical history is a necessary aspect of caring for patients with suspected or diagnosed neurological or neuromuscular problems. The history of any family members with neurological problems—including hearing, visual, and learning deficits as well as a history of seizures, mental illness, or congenital or degenerative problems—should be carefully documented.

Parental history is important to determine developmental and growth patterns of the parents (ages walked and talked, and history while in school). Parental history should also include age of the parents at the child's conception and their current state of health.

Maternal history should include a history of previous pregnancies (including number of stillbirths and spontaneous abortions) and the prenatal and birth data of the child (patient), including information on prenatal care received by the mother; duration of labor; type of delivery and complications at delivery; and any drugs, medications, alcohol, or tobacco consumed by the mother prior to conception or during her pregnancy. Nurses should also ask about any accidents or illnesses during the prenatal period.

A comprehensive history of the child is also important. This includes route of delivery, Apgar scores, any health problems diagnosed immediately after birth (e.g., increased bilirubin, respiratory distress, birth defects). The growth and development history of the child is elicited (ages at which walking, talking, and toileting milestones were reached). Sleeping, eating, and socialization patterns are also obtained. A history of childhood illnesses, accidents, immunizations, use of medications, and behavioral characteristics is also important.

A description of events leading up to the present symptoms or concerns of the parents should be carefully elicited. Parental concerns about the child's present illness, including their perception of the problem, should be seriously considered by the professional care giver.

Each area of the family history elicits important data that aid the health care providers in diagnosis and treatment. (Chapter 5 gives detailed information on assessing the child and the family.)

## Physical Examination

The influence of the brain and nervous system is varied and can affect other body systems either directly or indirectly. Pathophysiological processes in other body systems can also affect neurological function. Therefore, it is important to complete a neurological assessment on any children who are ill, regardless of their specific diagnosis. An extensive neurological examination is not necessary for every child who requires medical and nursing care, but an abbreviated assessment should be completed as part of routine health assessment. After this abbreviated examination the nurse can then decide if more extensive neurological assessment is necessary. The neurological examination involves six major areas: cerebral function, cerebellar function, cranial nerves, sensory functions, motor functions, and reflexes. Children with neurological problems or pathophysiological processes in body systems that frequently affect the neurosystem (such as the hepatic and renal systems) should have a complete neurological assessment and frequent monitoring of neurological function throughout their altered state of health.

There are two levels of neurological assessment. The first is the complete neurological physical examination, usually completed by the physician or clinical nurse specialist. The focus of this level of neurological assessment is to determine whether pathology exists in the child and to attempt to pinpoint the location of the problem.

The second level of neurological assessment is an examination that allows the nurse to quickly and competently assess the neurologically compromised child. This level of assessment focuses on trends of deterioration or improvement of the child, paying particular attention to signs and symptoms of increasing intracranial pressure. This abbreviated assessment allows the nurse to assess the child's neurological status frequently.

It is important to consider the child's developmental level while attempting to elicit normal neurological responses. The nurse must have a sound knowledge of normal growth and development in order to detect abnormalities and initiate appropriate methods of assessment. This knowledge also enables the nurse to evaluate the child's ability to perform activities of daily living within what are considered normal developmental parameters.

The Denver Developmental Screening Test (DDST) can be a useful tool in evaluating the development of a child under 6 years of age. The results of the DDST in the hospitalized child should be used with caution when planning nursing care, because the child may regress during hospitalization, which will alter results.

## Diagnostic Procedures

A child with neurological deficits may have cognitive, motor, or sensory functioning below normal age-specific levels. The nurse must assess each of these areas to prepare the child adequately for diagnostic tests. This also ensures that the safety of the child will be considered and that compensation for motor or sensory deficits will be incorporated in the preparation of the child for diagnostic testing. Table 26-1 reviews the diagnostic studies most commonly used in determining neurological problems. Included in the table are guidelines for preparation of the child as well as nursing management considerations.

## Nursing Diagnosis

The diagnoses approved by the North American Nursing Diagnosis Association are used when neurological system problems are discussed. The most common diagnoses used for neurological problems include the following:

*Pattern 1: Exchanging*
- Altered nutrition: Less than body requirements
- High risk for infection
- Altered patterns of urinary elimination
- Altered cerebral tissue perfusion

(*text continues on page 642*)

*Table 26–1. Neurological Diagnostic Tests*

| Study | Procedure | Outcomes | Nursing Management |
|---|---|---|---|
| Lumbar puncture | The child is placed in a side-lying position with the head flexed and back bowed by drawing the knees up to the chest. Most children need to be held in this position during the procedure. Continual verbal and tactile support is important throughout the procedure. Preparation prior to the procedure should be appropriate for the child's age. Parents should be fully informed about the procedure.<br><br>A small amount of CSF is removed from the spinal column at the level of L3–L4 by introducing a spinal needle with stylet into the subarachnoid space. A local anesthetic is injected into the dermis. CSF pressure readings may also be obtained by use of a 3-way stopcock and a manometer. | Lumbar puncture aids in diagnosis of meningitis, encephalitis, and hemorrhage by obtaining CSF cultures and microscopic studies. Pressure readings can also detect low-grade elevations in intracranial pressure. Lumbar punctures should never be done if the presence of acutely increased intracranial pressure is suspected. This could cause brain herniation, a life-threatening complication of increased intracranial pressure. | Holding, supporting, and comforting the child during the procedure. Preparing the child in a developmentally appropriate manner will increase cooperation of the child and help to allay fears. *Post-procedure*: To prevent headaches, the child should lie flat (horizontal) for 4 to 8 hours. Turning from side to side is permitted. Fluids are encouraged to prevent or relieve headaches.<br><br>Observe the child for changes in neurological status: altered level of consciousness, increased blood pressure, elevated temperature, irritability, or motor or sensory changes in lower extremities. |
| Cerebral angiography | A method of studying vascular structures of the cerebral vascular system using x-ray examination. A catheter is inserted into a major artery (femoral or carotid) using fluoroscopy for visualization. A contrast medium is injected into the artery and a series of x-rays are obtained. A blocking agent (potassium or Lugol solution) may be given prior to the contrast to prevent uptake of the medium into other organs. A pressure dressing is applied over the insertion site after the catheter is removed. Children require sedation or general anesthesia. | Detects abnormal cerebral blood flows, vascular tumors, and vessel abnormalities. | Explanation of the procedure to parents and patient. Obtain signed consents. Administer sedation. *Post-test*: The child should remain on bed rest for 6 to 8 hours. Immobilize catheter insertion site and observe for bleeding. If child's extremity is used for catheter insertion, monitor circulatory status (color, temperature, capillary return, pulses distal to the insertion site). Monitor vital signs and neurologic status. |
| Computed tomographic brain scan (CT) | Radionuclide imaging is used to allow visualization of the brain and regions within the brain that cannot be visualized with x-rays. A radioactive isotope is injected intravenously. The isotope concentrates in or around intracerebral lesions, which allows visualization with scanning. Lesions appear as an area of high radioactivity. An oral blocking agent is given to reduce uptake of the isotope in other organs (salivary glands, choroid plexus, thyroid). Children are most often sedated for the procedure. | Used to detect hematomas, brain tumors, aneurysms, metastatic and benign brain tumors, vascular malformations. The results are nonspecific in that the scan does not reveal types of lesions, i.e., tumor types. | Correct age and weight must be charted. CT is used to calculate the dosage of the isotope. Administer sedation. Prepare the child by explaining the procedure. The child must remain still during the scan. Movement will distort the scan pictures. *Post-test*: Monitor the patient for any allergic reactions to the isotope. |

*(continued)*

*Table 26–1.  Neurological Diagnostic Tests (Continued)*

| Study | Procedure | Outcomes | Nursing Management |
|---|---|---|---|
| Electroencephalography, electroencephalogram (EEG) | Nineteen to 25 electrodes in the form of disks are placed on the scalp over the cranial vault to record the brain's electrical activity. A paste is used to adhere the disks to the skin and to promote electrical conduction. The child should be relaxed, generally with his eyes closed. Recordings may be taken during sleep, while awake, or during light stimulation and hyperventilation. Sleep deprivation EEG study may also be done. The exam takes about 1–1½ hours. | EEG records the electrical activity of the cerebral cortex. The test is used to diagnose seizures, brain tumors, inflammation, and intracranial hemorrhages. EEG may be used to validate cerebral death. | Administer sedation if ordered. Sedatives may affect EEG patterns. Explain that the procedure does not hurt. May help the child to have a parent for company and comfort during the test. Body movements can affect wave patterns. *Post-test*: shampoo hair to remove residue of electrode paste. |
| Electromyoneurogram (EMG) (electromyography/electroneurography) | Combination of electromyography and electroneurography. Two-part test. First part (electroneurography) is done to determine nerve conduction. An electrode is placed over a specific nerve and a mild electrical current is passed through the patient and recorded on an oscilloscope, to measure the rapidity with which the nerve transmits the signal.<br><br>The second part (electromyography) is done to measure muscle potential by inserting fine needle electrodes into the muscle. This measures electrical activity of the muscle on an oscilloscope and over a sound system. Test time—45 to 60 minutes. | Abnormal results are indicative of nerve or muscle disorders such as tumors, juvenile muscular dystrophy, Gillain-Barré syndrome, trauma, toxic ingestions, or complications from treatments such as chemotherapy, some antibiotics. | Prepare child. The myography may cause pain as the needle is inserted, and the sight of needles may make the child fearful and anxious. Pain and random muscle movement will distort the result of the test. The neurography is essentially painless, but there will be some tingling sensation from the electric current. Administer sedation as ordered. *Post-test*: If pain is experienced, provide analgesic relief. In rare instances hematomas may form at needle insertion sites. |
| Magnetic resonance imaging (MRI); nuclear magnetic resonance (NMR) | Noninvasive technique that produces cross-sectional images of the soft tissue of the body by placing patients in a strong magnetic field and bombarding them with specific radio wave frequencies. The effect of this on hydrogen atoms is measured and converted to computer-enhanced images. The patient is prone and passes in and out of a large circular magnet as radiowaves are passed through the patient. No radiation is involved. Test time—60 minutes. | Abnormalities are manifested in waveforms, signal intensity, and spectral peaks and may indicate tumors, infections, ischemia. | Explain the purpose of the test. Explain that it is noninvasive and does not cause pain. All metal objects should be removed from the patient's body (medals, pins, hair clips, clothing with metal fasteners). Patient history should be elicited regarding implantation of metal prostheses (plates, screws, clips). Patients must remain completely still throughout the procedure. Children may require sedation. *Post-test*: No special care. |

*(continued)*

*Table 26–1. Neurological Diagnostic Tests (Continued)*

| Study | Procedure | Outcomes | Nursing Management |
|---|---|---|---|
| Myelography; myelogram | Iodine contrast medium and/or air is introduced into the spinal subarachnoid space, followed by fluoroscopic x-rays. The puncture is done either in the lumbar or cervical region, depending on the area of suspected pathology. The patient is tilted during the procedure. Test time—45–90 minutes. Patients with suspected acutely elevated intracranial pressure should not undergo puncture of this type as it could cause brain herniation, a life-threatening condition. | There is distortion of the subarachnoid space and dura matter with abnormalities. The test is performed when compression of the spinal cord, obstruction of the spinal canal, or intravertebral tumors are suspected. | Patient preparation and after-care is basically the same as for a lumbar puncture. A legal consent form is usually required. *Post-test*: Bedrest is necessary for several hours after the myelogram. Patient position depends on the type of contrast medium used for visualization. The nurse should observe for headaches, fever, nausea, seizures, paralysis, and change in level of consciousness. |
| Air encephalography; pneumonencephalography; ventriculography | Permits visualization of the intracranial CSF-containing spaces by withdrawing CSF, introducing air or oxygen, and obtaining x-rays of the cranium for the purpose of examining the CSF pathways. Pneumoencephalogram—air or oxygen is introduced into the subarachnoid space at a lumbar site. With the child sitting, the air rises and fills the ventricles and subarachnoid space. Ventriculogram—Air or oxygen is introduced into the lateral ventricle after removal of CSF. This allows determination of any displacement of the ventricles due to space-occupying lesions. | Aids in the diagnosis of brain tumors, obstructive hydrocephalus. Noninvasive procedures such as CT scans and MRI are replacing air encephalography as a diagnostic test. | Child is usually NPO for 6 to 8 hours. General anesthesia or heavy sedation is usually administered. *Post-test*: The child is on bedrest for 24 hours. The child's position depends on the type of procedure performed and the outcome. Child is observed for neurologic changes (pupillary reaction, level of consciousness, meningeal irritation). Fluids are offered to minimize the potential headaches. |
| Brain stem evoked potentials: Brain stem auditory evoked responses (BAER); visual evoked potentials (VEP) Somatosensory evoked potentials | A noninvasive procedure that tests neural activity of the central and peripheral nervous system. Small voltage changes that occur as a result of specific stimuli are recorded and evaluated via a small scalp electrode and a computer. | These evoked potentials that result from sensory stimuli can be evaluated for the presence of neurological dysfunction or disease. Visual evoked potentials are used in diagnosing optic nerve tumors or neuropathies. The brain stem auditory evoked responses are useful in diagnosing acoustic neuromas, some cerebellar tumors, conductive hearing loss, or demyelinating diseases. Somatosensory evoked potentials are used to evaluate spinal cord function. | Preparation and support of the child are similar to preparation for an electroencephalogram (EEG). BAER can be performed on a comatose patient as well as one who is alert and oriented. In VEP testing the child must be alert and able to follow directions. Somatosensory evoked potentials testing may be uncomfortable, as electrical or mechanical stimuli are repeatedly applied to peripheral nerves. |

- Hyperthermia
- Impaired gas exchange
- Ineffective breathing pattern
- High risk for injury
- Impaired skin integrity

*Pattern 3: Relating*
- Impaired social interaction
- Social isolation
- Altered parenting
- Altered family processes

*Pattern 5: Choosing*
- Ineffective individual coping
- Ineffective family coping
- Noncompliance

*Pattern 6: Moving*
- Impaired physical mobility
- Impaired swallowing

*Pattern 7: Perceiving*
- Body image disturbance
- Self esteem disturbance
- Sensory/perceptual alterations
- Powerlessness

*Pattern 9: Feeling*
- Pain
- Anxiety
- Fear

## Planning and Implementing Nursing Care

Planning and implementing nursing care for a child with alteration in neurological function is discussed in relation to each problem presented in this chapter. The care of the child who is neurologically compromised is often complex and requires expert nursing care and advanced skills. The plan of care should always include the family unit.

Careful assessment of the child's development is important in planning care that is appropriate. The assessment should evaluate the child's present abilities, and nurses should not rely on the child's chronological age. Assessment also involves the child's overall state of neurological maturation and function. The child very often must undergo numerous diagnostic and treatment procedures. These tests and procedures should be carefully explained, using words the child can understand. Therapeutic play in which the child can relate to dolls or puppets is helpful in the young child. Most children benefit from handling equipment and "using" the equipment with dolls. Children also should be involved whenever possible in their care and be permitted to assist in procedures. This gives the child a sense of control in an unfamiliar environment where they have limited control. Planning for active participation by the child should be a vital component of planning the child's care.

## Nursing Interventions

The nurse caring for a child with a neurological impairment is responsible for performing interventions that include careful monitoring of neurological status and assisting with activities of daily living. Nurses should encourage the child with a sensory or motor impairment to participate in his or her care. Nurses must remember that nursing care should take into account age-related differences in structure and function. These differences must also be considered when interpreting diagnostic tests. Nurses must have a working understanding of the principles of neurological function and how various alterations can affect the brain differently at different stages of development.

Nurses may be involved in teaching these children how to maximize their sensory or motor potential in order to compensate for their impairment. Adaptation to a disability requires a multidisciplinary team, but it is often the nurse who spends the most time with the child and is best suited for planning and coordinating care. It is important that nursing interventions include a family support component.

Nursing care may also involve complex procedures for the acutely ill child. These procedures may include mechanical ventilation, total parenteral nutrition or intravenous fluid therapy, enteral nutrition, urinary catheterization, and total physical care.

***Family Support.*** The level of understanding of family members must be carefully assessed. Nurses should carefully explain the child's condition and the treatments that may be employed. Explanations may have to be repeated several times, and the nurse should correct any misinformation the family might have in relation to the child's condition. The family should be encouraged to ask questions and to participate in the child's physical and psychosocial care. Nurses should direct the family to additional resources as needed. These resources might include religious leaders, support groups, social service, and home care agencies. Family members are under a great deal of stress if the child is acutely or critically ill. The family may also be anxious regarding home care once the child is discharged.

Nursing interventions should include keeping family members informed of the child's status, explaining all procedures, and using a nonjudgmental approach, especially when an accident has caused the injury and parents feel guilty. Nurses should encourage the parents to remain with the child as much as possible.

***Increased Intracranial Pressure.*** The child with an acute neurological disorder is at risk for developing increased ICP, and much of the nursing care for an acutely ill child is concerned with assessment for, prevention of, and treatment of this. The nursing care of a child with increased ICP is discussed in detail later in the chapter.

***Seizures.*** The child with a neurological impairment is at risk for physical injury and may develop seizures. Nursing interventions should include keeping the child's bed locked in the low position to allow easy access in and out of bed and keeping the siderails up when the child is in bed. If the child is at risk for seizures, the siderails and bed should be padded. The child should wear a helmet when he or she is out of bed. It is important to maintain the child's safety during a seizure and to monitor and carefully record any seizure activity.

***Impaired Mobility.*** The child with mobility problems needs to be protected from injury. Care should also include interventions that promote function. This should include performing passive and active range of motion exercises, encouraging mobility according to the child's ability, positioning the child to prevent contractures, and minimizing spasticity by using splints and braces. Interventions that prevent accidental falls should be instituted, including assistance with toileting and ambulating until the child is proficient in assuming these activities.

***Impaired Sensory Perception.*** The plan of care for a child with impaired sensory perception should include regular assessment and evaluation of the impairment. The child also needs auditory, tactile, visual and kinesthetic stimulation that is developmentally appropriate, but he or she should not be overstimulated. The nurse should assess the child for restlessness, hyperactivity, and irritability, all of which may indicate overstimulation.

## Evaluating Nursing Care

Evaluation of nursing care involves the careful documentation of changes in neurological status, including level of consciousness and sensory, motor, and psychological status. It is important for measurable, patient-centered, short-term goals to be established as part of the nursing care plan so that the nurse can evaluate the attainment of these goals. These goals should be established with the assistance of the family, and the child, when appropriate. Patient-centered long-term goals will guide nursing care through discharge planning and home care for the child.

## Intracranial Hypertension

Cranial hypertension is defined as a sustained elevated ICP of 15 mm Hg or above (Hickey, 1986). A level above 15 mm Hg can cause cerebral ischemia and neuronal damage. A child who develops increased ICP is at risk for developing serious permanent neurological disability or death if it is not diagnosed early and treated vigorously. The nurse plays an important role in detecting increasing ICP and managing the threat of increased ICP.

### Pathophysiology

Intracranial hypertension is a symptom, not a disease. There are many diseases and pathological conditions that can cause an increase in intracranial pressure. It is important also to remember that any condition that causes cerebral edema (kidney failure, lead poisoning, Reye syndrome) may result in intracranial hypertension.

According to the Monro-Kellie hypothesis (discussed earlier), when brain tissue becomes edematous the homeostatic mechanism of compensation (cerebral vasoconstriction resulting in decreased blood flow to the brain, decreased CSF production, increased CSF absorption) maintains the ICP within normal limits. When these homeostatic mechanisms reach their limit, decompensation occurs and ICP rises, causing damage to brain tissue and decreased cerebral perfusion. As cerebral perfusion decreases, autoregulation fails and cell hypoxia (an increase in $Paco_2$ and a decrease in pH) occurs, causing further brain cell destruction. This then causes vasodilation, an increase in cerebral edema and intracranial pressure. If this cycle of events is left untreated the cell destruction will continue and result in brain herniation, coma, and death.

Infants and young children are able to tolerate significant increases in ICP without brain damage because their CNS is less mature and their skulls are expandable. In these children head size will increase in response to rising ICP. The open fontanel functions much like a burr hole (an opening in the cranium that is created surgically to relieve pressure) in the adult.

Cerebral edema is defined as an increase in fluid accumulation in the extracellular or intracellular spaces of brain tissue that increases cerebral tissue volume and frequently results in increased ICP. There are two principal types of cerebral edema: cytotoxic and vasogenic.

Cytotoxic edema is an increase in intracellular fluid volume in the brain tissue, occurring principally in gray matter. Sodium and water accumulate in the brain cells as a result of a disturbance in cell metabolism. The development of cytotoxic edema is most likely to occur when patients experience hypoxia/anoxia resulting from respiratory or cardiac compromise.

Vasogenic edema is the most common type of cerebral edema. It can result from a head injury (contusions, lacerations), subdural hematomas, space-occupying masses (tumors), neurosurgical interventions, and abscesses. As a result of rupture or increased permeability of the cerebral vascular system, plasma proteins enter the extracellular spaces of the white matter. Vasogenic edema spreads primarily in the white matter of the brain because the extracellular spaces offer less resistance than the gray matter does.

## Clinical Manifestations

Clinical manifestations of increased ICP depend on the child's age, the efficacy of the function of the compensating mechanisms, and the degree of fluctuation in ICP. The signs and symptoms of increased ICP include:

Deterioration in level of consciousness

Changes in pupillary functions

Changes in vital signs

Motor dysfunction (weakness, hemiplegia, decerebrate and decorticate posturing)

Headache

Vomiting

Bulging fontanels and increasing head size greater than chest circumference in children younger than 18 months to 2 years

Children with neurological problems that may precipitate increased ICP should be carefully assessed for the above symptoms. The nurse should keep in mind that these symptoms may not be present if compensating mechanisms are equalizing the ICP. Symptoms can appear rapidly once the compensating mechanisms reach their limit if the underlying pathological process continues to increase ICP.

Older children with increased ICP may experience headache, vomiting, blurred vision, or dizziness. Headaches may range from mild and transient to severe, especially upon rising in the morning. Vomiting may be projectile (forceful) without nausea or accompanied by nausea and gastrointestinal discomfort.

It is also important to keep in mind that ICP continually fluctuates. Serial assessments are important to determine trends (changes) in vital signs, pupillary function, motor function, and fontanel size. Flow charts are most helpful for recording the frequent assessments necessary in children with actual, suspected, or anticipated increases in ICP.

The most reliable source for evaluating increasing ICP is continuous ICP monitoring. There are three ways to monitor ICP, all of which are invasive procedures: inserting a catheter into the brain's ventricles, using a subarachnoid bolt, or using epidural sensors. The monitoring device is attached to a transducer and recording apparatus that facilitate interpretation of the intracranial pressure. Several studies confirm that intraventricular pressure monitoring is the most accurate method of monitoring increased ICP (Mendelow, Rowan, & Murray, 1983; Barlow, Mendelow, & Lawrence, 1985).

Infection is a major risk with ICP monitoring, and a protocol must be instituted that will minimize this risk. This protocol should include careful and regular assessment for signs of infection, meticulous aspectic technique, and prophylactic use of local and systemic antibiotics. Studies have found that patients with a diagnosis of intracranial hemorrhage and those requiring neurologically invasive procedures are at higher risk for infection (Aucain, 1986; Franges & Beideman, 1988). Upon completion of their initial study, Franges and Beideman (1988) recommended that important aspects of nursing policy in the care of patients with ICP monitoring devices include the following:

- The use of sterile gloves when manipulating the device
- A sterile procedure for redressing the insertion site
- Maintenance of a closed monitoring system

Monitoring devices are not used with every patient with a disease process that could lead to increased ICP, but they are useful for patients at high risk for developing increased ICP. For those patients with intracranial hypertension, ICP monitoring aids in evaluating stimuli that can produce life threatening ICP spikes. Monitoring has been especially helpful in detecting changes in ICP while performing nursing care, because routine nursing care activities may cause a rise in ICP. Several clinical research studies have demonstrated that nursing care (positioning, turning, suctioning) can cause ICP spikes (Bruya, 1981; Mitchell & Mauss, 1978; Parsons, Pearce, & Page, 1985; Snyder, 1983). These studies guide the nurse in planning care for patients with intracranial hypertension. ICP monitoring is useful in evaluating the effectiveness of the various treatment modalities that can be used to control intracranial hypertension.

*Level of Consciousness (LOC).* One of the first and most sensitive signs of increasing ICP is deterioration in the child's level of consciousness. The cerebral cortex, which controls the higher levels of body function, is very sensitive to decreases in oxygen that result from increasing ICP.

The earliest signs of increasing ICP may be drowsiness, confusion, and restlessness, which can progress to coma as ICP continues to rise. Initial alterations may be subtle but significant indicators of changes in ICP. Again, frequent assessment will demonstrate trends that indicate rising ICP.

Evaluating and recording the child's LOC has at times been based on subjective criteria, using subjective terms such as "stuporous," "semi-comatose," "lethargic," and "comatose." More frequently, LOC is evaluated by using the Glasgow coma scale (GCS), a simple standardized scale developed in the mid-1970s and first described by Teasdale and Jennett (1979). The GCS is an objective measure of a patient's LOC using three modes of behavior: eye opening, verbal response, and motor response. Each response is independently assessed and assigned a number of points depending on the method needed to elicit each response. The responses are recorded on a flow sheet. Table 26-2 summarizes the methods of eliciting and scoring responses from the patient. Scores are based on the patient's best response and range from 3 to 15, with the best response receiving the highest score. Scores in each mode of behavior should be evaluated individually, as well as the total score. Changes in LOC can be quickly evaluated using the GCS.

The principal advantage of using the GCS is its simplicity and effectiveness in communicating a patient's LOC quickly and concisely. A disadvantage is that it has limited use in assessing LOC in certain patients, e.g., patients with spinal cord injuries, aphasia, or hemiplegia. For instance, a patient who is intubated on a ventilator cannot speak and, therefore, cannot respond appropriately to the verbal por-

tion of the GCS. A score of 1 would be inappropriate for this patient. In this case, it should be noted in the nurse's notes and/or flow sheet that the patient is intubated. The nurse should attempt to assess the patient's ability to communicate and whether or not the patient is oriented by other means, such as writing.

Drugs used to control increased ICP can also affect the usefulness of the GCS. These drugs may include barbiturates, neuromuscular blocking agents (e.g., Pavulon), and anticonvulsants. Each of these drugs alters the child's LOC or physical mobility and would prevent appropriate evaluation with the GCS.

The GCS has been modified to meet the needs of particular patients in specific nursing care situations (Ingersoll & Leyden, 1986; Morray, Tyler, Jones, Stuntz, & Lemire, 1984; Zeidelman, 1980). Nurse researchers have

## Table 26–2.  Glascow Coma Scale

### Objective

To quantitatively designate the severity of head injury and predict outcome by measuring the patient's degree of consciousness. This scale relates "consciousness" to motor responses, verbal responses, and eye opening. In each category the examiner determines the best response the patient can make to a set of standardized stimuli.

### Best Motor Response

Obeys commands (6 points): i.e., once aroused, the patient raises an arm on request.
Localizes noxious stimuli (5 points): Patient fails to obey commands, but moves either arm toward a noxious cutaneous stimulus and finds it with hands.
Flexion withdrawal (4 points): Patient flexes either arm in response to a noxious stimulus but does not manually localize the irritant.
Abnormal flexion (3 points): Patient slowly adducts shoulder, flexes and pronates arm to a noxious stimulus (decordicate).
Abnormal extension (2 points): Patient adducts and internally rotates at shoulder, extends forearm, flexes wrist, and makes a fist (decerbrate).
No motor response (1 point): Stimulus must be sufficiently noxious.

### Best Verbal Response

Oriented (5 points): Patient carries on a conversation and can correctly relate to time and place.
Confused (4 points): Patient conversant but not fully oriented.
Verbalizes (3 points): Patient utters intelligible words in disorganized manner.
Vocalizes (2 points): Patient makes sounds (moaning or groaning), but not recognizable words.
No vocalization (1 point): No sound in response to noxious stimuli.

### Eye Opening

Eyes open spontaneously (4 points).
Eyes open to speech (3 points): calling patient's name.
Eyes open to noxious stimuli (2 points): stimuli applied similar to that used for motor response.
No eye opening (1 point).

Scores from each category are added to determine the total Glasgow Coma Scale score. Scores can range from 15 to 3 if all three categories can be used for evaluation. All scores of 7 or less but no scores of 9 or more constitute coma.

(Teasdale, G. & Jennett, B. [1979]. Assessment of coma and impaired consciousness: A practical scale. *Lancet, 1,* 81–84)

also used the scale in their studies (Jones, 1979; Martin, 1987; Neatherlin & Brillhart, 1988; Snyder, 1983).

*Changes in Pupillary Function.* Assessment of pupils is useful in determining neurological status. Pupils are examined for size, shape, symmetry, and reaction to light (cranial nerves II and III). Normally round, equal, and reactive, pupils can change as a result of neurological insults (anoxia), rising ICP, and drugs. Drugs such as atropine produce dilated and poorly reactive pupils. Barbiturate therapy and hypothermia produce fixed pupils.

As ICP rises, due to supratentorial masses or edema, pressure on the oculomotor nerve (cranial nerve III) occurs ipsilaterally (on the same side). Pressure on the oculomotor nerve is manifested by changes in pupil size, shape, and reaction to light. As pressure rises, the pupil reacts slowly to light and gradually dilates. In the later stages of intracranial hypertension, the pupil becomes dilated and fixed (nonreactive to light). If the increased ICP is left untreated, pupils are affected bilaterally. The dilated and fixed pupil is a manifestation of uncontrolled intracranial hypertension and is indicative of brain herniation. Subtle changes in pupillary function, including sluggish reaction to light, should be documented and reported immediately, as should any change in pupillary size and function. With vigorous and effective treatment of increased ICP, the patient should not experience dilated and fixed pupils. Papilledema (edema of the optic disc) is considered a late-stage symptom in intracranial hypertension and is not evident in all patients with increased ICP.

The nurse should also remember that not all changes or abnormalities in pupillary response are due to increasing ICP. In the young child strabismus (weak ocular muscles) is common. Anisocoria (normal unequal pupil size), although rare, does occur. A blow to the eye can cause damage to the eye muscle and result in abnormal findings. In the older child and teenager whose neurological problems stem from accidents, the added variables of drugs and alcohol may be involved. Certain drugs and alcohol can affect pupillary reaction. The many variables that can cause changes in pupillary response point out the need for comprehensive histories along with complete assessments.

Changes in pupillary response can indicate serious and life-threatening elevated ICP, but are only one aspect of the assessment process. It is necessary to integrate this finding into the total assessment of the patient.

*Changes in Vital Signs (TPR, Blood Pressure).* In the early stages of increased ICP the vital signs may remain relatively stable. As the ICP increases, the blood pressure rises as a compensating response to preserve CPP. Cushing's response occurs and includes a rising systolic pressure, a widening pulse pressure, and bradycardia. In early stages the heart rate is full and bounding, but as decompensation occurs the pulse becomes rapid, thready, and irregular. Respirations become slow and irregular.

*Motor Dysfunction.* Deterioration in motor function occurs contralaterally (opposite) to the side of the brain affected by increased pressure. Early dysfunction depends on the area of the brain affected and may be manifested by hemiplegia or monoplegia. Varying degrees of muscle weakness may be present. If the intracranial hypertension is uncontrolled, motor dysfunction progresses to include decortication and decerebration. Decortication and decerebration are abnormal responses to interruption of the motor tracts (Fig. 26-3). Decortication is caused by lesions of the cerebral hemisphere or internal capsule interrupting corticospinal pathways. Decerebrate posturing occurs as a result of lesions that cause damage to the midbrain and pons as a result of expanding cerebral lesions. Decerebration indicates more serious cerebral dysfunction. Patients may experience both posturings separately, consecutively, or intermittently.

*Figure 26–3.  Decortication and decerebration.*

Sustained, prolonged, or increasing ICP can result in herniation of the brain (the displacement of a part of the brain through other brain structures, which results in pressure on an adjacent portion of the brain). Herniation results in severe circulatory compromise of the affected brain tissue. Herniation usually involves the tentorium, a tentlike structure that separates and supports the various parts of the brain. Herniation can occur either above or below the tentorium, but most commonly occurs above, causing compression of the cerebral and brain stem structures. This leads to decreasing vital signs and a life-threatening situation. Brain herniation should be anticipated in patients with increased ICP and prevented by vigorous treatment of the intracranial hypertension.

### Medical Therapy

Vigorous treatment is most important in controlling ICP. The medical management is often complex and involves the use of pharmacotherapeutic agents that need continual monitoring by the nursing and medical team. These medical therapies are outlined in Table 26-3. One or more of these treatment modalities may be used to control the child's ICP. Many of the therapies discussed in Table 26-3 (barbiturate therapy, pancuronium therapy, seizure control) make physical assessment of neurological function difficult or impossible. Mechanical ICP monitoring is necessary to evaluate the effectiveness of these therapies in normalizing the child's ICP.

### Nursing Management

The nursing plan of care for actual or potential increased ICP in children presents a complex configuration that makes demands on the nurse's assessment and organizational skills. The goal of nursing management is to control ICP and to minimize or prevent changes in ICP wave form patterns that compromise cerebral perfusion. Frequent assessment of the child's neurological status—every 15 minutes to 1 to 2 hours, depending on the severity of the child's condition—is important. Monitoring trends in neurological status and vital signs is an important factor. A slowing pulse and respiratory rate and an increasing blood pressure are indications of increasing ICP. This trend should be reported to the physician for immediate evaluation.

Maintaining a patent airway is vital in minimizing increasing ICP in the early stages. The placement of an endotracheal tube or a tracheostomy tube may be necessary. Nurses must monitor respiratory rhythm, rate, and depth and auscultate breath sounds every hour during the acute illness phase. Nursing care includes suctioning of the airway, which can can cause an increase in ICP. Before, during, and after suctioning, the lungs should be hyperventilated with 100% oxygen. Suctioning should be gentle and should be limited to 15 seconds during each catheter insertion. If suctioning causes increased wave forms (spikes) on the ICP monitor, muscle relaxants may be used. If the child is on mechanical ventilation, the machine's functioning must be checked on a regular basis.

Nurses may also be responsible for administering oxygen and monitoring blood gases. Nurses should discourage any activity that precipitates the Valsalva movement, as this increases intrathoracic and intra-abdominal pressure, which increases ICP. Activities such as hip flexion equal to or greater than 90 degrees, straining with bowel movement, breath holding, coughing, sneezing, nose blowing, and isometric exercises should be discouraged. Nurses should also attempt to minimize the child's crying, as this also may increase ICP.

Nursing care also includes interventions to promote cerebral venous drainage. Spinal injuries should be ruled out before carrying out these interventions, which include elevating the head of the bed 15 to 30 degrees, and maintaining the child's head in a midline position. If the child is heavily sedated, nurses must observe and record ICP monitor readings at frequent intervals. Nurse should watch for signs of infection, such as elevated temperature, redness or inflammation at insertion site, and changes in the color or consistency of CSF. Nurses should observe for sharp increases (spikes) in ICP wave form and record factors such as stimuli, turning, or suctioning that cause the increases. Observation for any additional signs of increased ICP, such as headaches, high-pitched cry in the infant, irritability, or vomiting, is important.

Nurses may also be involved in caring for the child being treated with cooling blankets. Hypothermia decreases CNS oxygen requirements and cerebral blood flow, which decreases ICP. The child's skin must be assessed for signs of frostbite. A rectal probe is used for continuous temperature monitoring. Nurses should not allow the child's temperature to fall below the prescribed limit. Children being treated by hypothermia should not receive IM or subcutaneous injections, as these may cause abscesses due to decreased absorption of the medication caused by vasoconstriction and decreased circulation.

## Neurological Problems of Infants

### Congenital Febrile Seizures

Infants and young children may suffer from convulsions associated with an acute, benign febrile illness. A febrile convulsion is most often grand mal and manifested by an active tonic–clonic pattern, usually lasting less than a minute. Seizure disorders are discussed in depth later in this chapter.

### Pathophysiology

Febrile convulsions are considered a benign condition if underlying neurological and physiologic problems have been ruled out. Electroencephalogram (EEG) tracings are

*Table 26–3.  Medical Therapies for the Control of Acute Increased Intracranial Pressure (ICP)*

| Treatment | Physiological Mechanism |
| --- | --- |
| The goal of each of these treatment modalities is to decrease ICP. | |
| Controlled hyperventilation | Raising the $Po_2$ (100 mm Hg) level of the blood and reducing the $Pco_2$ (maintaining in a range of 25–30 mm Hg) results in vasoconstriction of cerebral arteries, reduction of cerebral blood flow, and increased venous return. $Po_2$ and $Pco_2$ levels are best maintained by placing the patient on a ventilator. Levels may also be maintained by ambu bag and oxygen. |
| Surgery | Surgical removal of brain tumors, abscesses, or hematomas is indicated when possible, to eliminate the cause of increased intracranial pressure. |
| Osmotic diuretics | Hyperosmolar agents whose high osmotic concentration causes water to be extracted from edematous tissue of the brain into the vascular system. |
| Mannitol | Is administered IV with rapid diuresis and rapid reduction of ICP. It is used primarily with cytotoxic cerebral edema. <br><br> Renal function and fluid and electrolyte balance must be monitored closely. The use of mannitol can sometimes cause a secondary increase in ICP (rebound). |
| Loop diuretics <br> Furosemide (Lasix) <br> Acetazolamide | Lasix has greater selectivity for dehydration of injured cerebral tissue than does mannitol. Diuretics such as furosemide can produce significant potassium depletion and must be monitored. |
| Corticosteroids | Steroid use is controversial (Harper, 1989). The drug of choice, when used, is Decadron. The drug is used most commonly with vasogenic edema. <br><br> It is given intravenously in relatively high doses. Administration of corticosteroids produces an intracellular sodium/potassium exchange and reduces intracellular water volume by activation of the sodium pump. It is also hypothesized that corticosteroids help to stabilize cell membranes, stabilizing the blood–brain barrier. |
| Fluid restriction | Restriction of fluids reduces total blood volume, decreasing ICP. The child is watched closely for hypovolemic shock (increased pulse, decreasing blood pressure, pallor, and change in LOC). |
| Maintenance normothermia | Hyperthermia can increase intracranial pressure by vasodilation, increasing cerebral blood flow and increasing the body's metabolic rate and need for oxygen. Antipyretics, tepid baths, and/or hypothermia blankets may be ordered to reduce the child's elevated temperature. |
| Hypothermia | The use of hypothermia to decrease ICP is still very controversial. Rendering the child hypothermic reduces the cerebral metabolic rate and cerebral oxygen requirements. Shivering must be avoided to prevent sharp increases in ICP (spikes). Muscle relaxants are used to prevent shivering during hypothermia therapy. |
| Barbiturate therapy <br> Thiopental sodium <br> Pentabarbital sodium | The use of barbiturates to control increased ICP reduces the cerebral metabolic rate and oxygen consumption. The full extent of the effects of barbiturates on ICP is not known. It is theorized that they also induce vasoconstriction in undamaged areas of the brain, thereby shunting blood to ischemic areas. Seizure activity is often prevented by barbiturate therapy. |
| Pancuronium therapy <br> Pavulon | Neuromuscular blocking agents paralyze voluntary skeletal muscles, reducing oxygen consumption, intrathoracic pressure, and CVP. Inducing paralysis in the child also reduces or eliminates the response to noxious stimuli that can cause life-threatening spikes in ICP. Because Pavulon paralyzes the child, intubation and mechanical ventilation are necessary. |
| Prevention or control of seizures <br> Diazepam (Valium) <br> Phenobarbitol <br> Phenytoin (Dilantin) | Convulsions can increase ICP and cerebral metabolic rates. Cerebral activity must be reduced. Phenytoin is used prophylactically to prevent seizures or long-term to control seizure activity. |

usually normal. There may be a family history of febrile convulsions.

## Medical Diagnosis and Management

Febrile seizures are most commonly associated with illness causing high fever of 102° to 104° F, such as upper respiratory tract infections, otitis media, and tonsillitis. The seizure typically results from the rapid rise in temperature with the initial presentation of fever. Laboratory and diagnostic evaluation is done to rule out neurological and metabolic abnormalities. Lumbar puncture is often done to rule out meningitis.

Treatment is aimed at reducing the fever and the underlying causes of the seizure. There is controversy regarding the use of prophylactic anticonvulsant therapy, of which phenobarbital is the most common. Prophylactic therapy does not reduce the risk of subsequent epilepsy.

The outcome for most young children with a febrile convulsion is good, because the majority of these seizures are benign and cause no neurological impairment.

### Nursing Assessment and Diagnosis

A thorough history is a critical component of assessment. Causative factors such as illness, trauma, or drugs must be investigated. Nursing diagnoses related to the child with febrile convulsions may include:

- Hyperthermia, related to underlying infection
- Potential for injury, related to convulsive activity
- Potential altered parenting, related to uncertainty of diagnosis

### Planning and Implementing Nursing Care

Parents need to be taught how to prevent febrile convulsion by administering acetaminophen regularly in appropriate dosages at the first sign of infection. Administration of antipyretics (acetaminophen) as well as measures to cool the body (tepid sponge or tub baths) can reduce the fever. Nurses should also educate parents regarding the importance of keeping the child well hydrated. Parents should be instructed to consult the child's physician if an infection is suspected or fever occurs.

If anticonvulsant prophylaxis therapy is started, nurses should teach parents the need for consistent drug administration and any possible medication side effects. Parents must understand that seizures can occur if the medication is stopped suddenly. An important nursing function is helping parents deal with their anxieties and fears regarding subsequent seizures. Parents should be instructed in how to care for the child if another seizure occurs.

### Evaluating Nursing Care

Evaluation is based on reduction of the fever without neurological impairment. Parents should understand the cause of the seizure and how to prevent further occurrences.

## Neural Tube Defects

Neural tube malformations (myelodysplasia) encompass a group of related defects of the central nervous system. These defects involve the cranium or spinal column and vary from mildly to severely disabling. These disorders result from malformations of the neural tube during embryonic development. During the third to fourth week of gestation the neural plate closes to form the neural tube, which eventually forms the spinal cord and the brain. The vertebral column develops along with the spinal cord. Abnormal closure (Fig. 26-4A) of the neural tube can result in a variety of defects.

Anencephaly is a severe defect involving absence of the entire brain or cerebral hemispheres. The brain stem and cerebellum may be intact. Total anencephaly is incompatible with life. Most of these fetuses are aborted or stillborn; the living infant with anencephaly usually survives for only a few hours after birth.

Encephalocele is a neural tube malformation that occurs when meningeal and cerebral tissue protrudes in a sac through a defect in the skull. The most common site is the occipital region (Fig. 26-4B). When possible, the sac is surgically replaced within the skull. Hydrocephalus is a frequent postoperative occurrence and requires a shunt procedure. Less severe forms of encephalocele result in minimal or no residual neurological impairment.

Spina bifida, or myelodysplasia, refers to a congenital malformation involving defective closure of the vertebral column. It is the most common defect of the central nervous system, occurring in about 1 to 2 of every 1000 live births. It may occur anywhere along the spine, but the most common site is the lumbosacral area. There are three principal types of spinal bifida: spina bifida occulta, meningocele, and myelomeningocele (Fig. 26-4C, D, and E).

### Pathophysiology

Spina bifida occulta results from failure of the spinous process of the vertebrae to fuse posteriorly. The etiology of these defects is unknown. The spinal cord is not usually affected. External signs may include a dimpling of the skin, nevi, lipomas, or tufts of dark hairs over the dermal sinus tract (pilonidal sinus). The condition may go undetected, and most children with the defect do not display any abnormal sensory or motor signs. If neurological symptoms do occur, they consist of motor or sensory disturbance in the lower extremities. Urinary and bowel sphincter function may also be involved. The symptoms may be more pronounced during late childhood or late adolescence.

Meningocele is a sac containing meninges and cerebrospinal fluid that protrudes outside the vertebrae. The most common location is the lumbosacral area. The sac may be covered with skin or a thin membrane. The spinal cord is not contained within the sac and, therefore, there is usually little or no impairment or neurological function in the lower extremities or sphincter muscles.

Myelomeningocele is a saclike cyst, similar to meningocele but including a portion of the spinal cord and accompanying nerve roots. It is the most severe and most common of the CNS anomalies. The lumbosacral area is the most common site of myelomeningoceles.

### Medical Diagnosis and Management

The cystic forms of this defect are easily identified. Computed tomography (CT) scans, ultrasonography, and magnetic resonance imaging (MRI) may be used to determine the contents of the sac and associated CNS involvement.

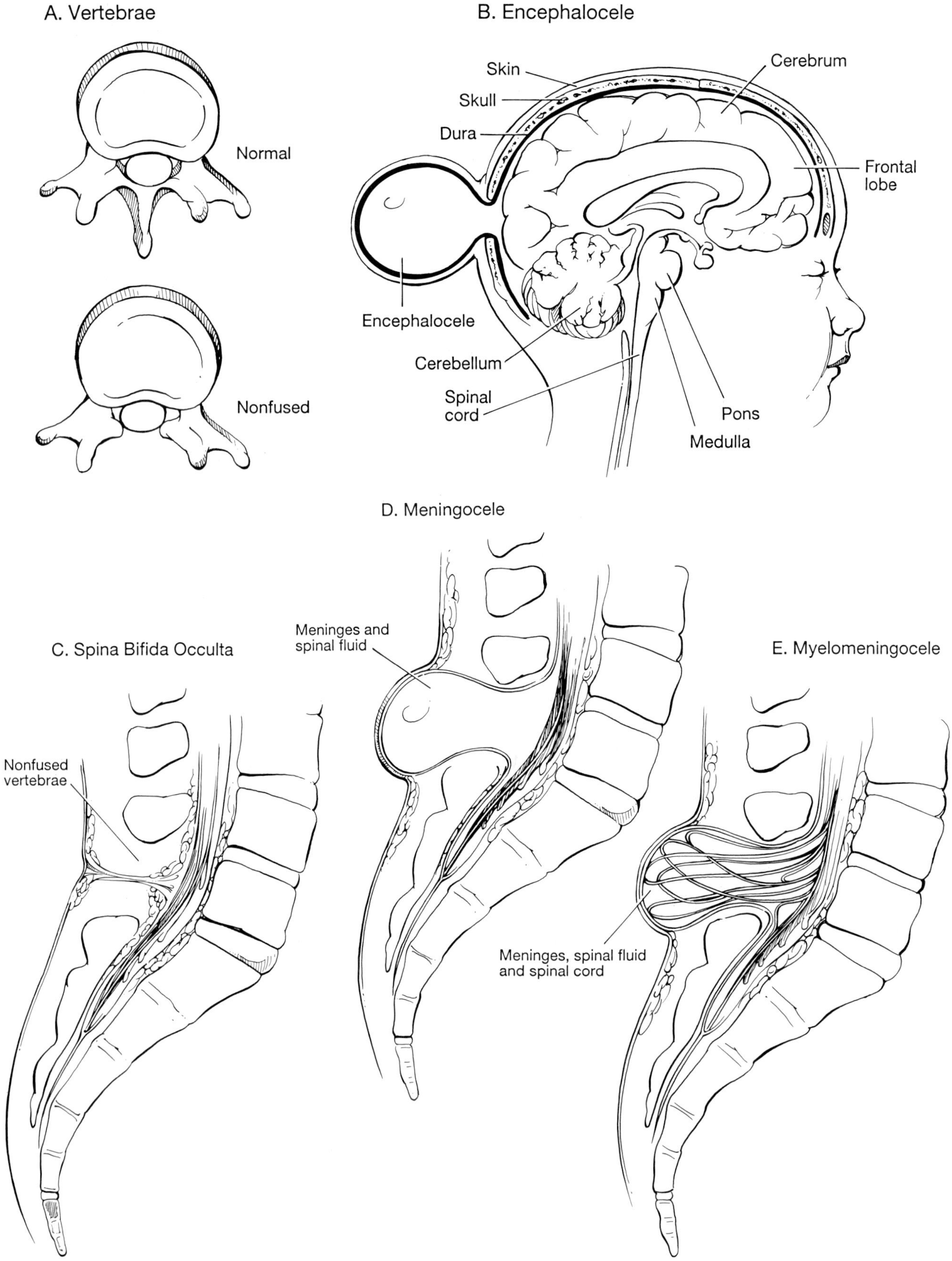

## A. Vertebrae

Normal

Nonfused

## B. Encephalocele

Skin

Skull

Dura

Cerebrum

Frontal lobe

Encephalocele

Cerebellum

Spinal cord

Pons

Medulla

## D. Meningocele

Meninges and spinal fluid

## C. Spina Bifida Occulta

Nonfused vertebrae

Meninges, spinal fluid and spinal cord

## E. Myelomeningocele

*Figure 26–4.   Neural tube defects. (A) Normal and nonfused vertebrae; (B) encephalocele; (C) spina bifida occulta; (D) meningocele; (E) myelomeningocele.*

The renal system is also evaluated to determine urinary tract dysfunction.

Intrauterine diagnosis of these defects is indicated by the presence of elevated alpha-fetoprotein (AFP) levels in maternal serum or amniotic fluid. Levels may be obtained between the 14th and 16th week of gestation. Accurate estimation of gestational age is imperative in interpreting results. Evaluation of AFP levels is recommended for pregnant women with a family or paternal history of neural tube defects or women who have previously had a child with this defect, because there is an increased chance of these women having another child with a neural tube defect. Therapeutic abortions can be considered if a defect is detected through amniocentesis.

No treatment of spina bifida occulta is indicated unless there is neurological impairment. If a dermal sinus tract is present, surgical intervention may be necessary to close the tract and prevent future infection.

Treatment of meningocele is surgical closure of the sac as soon as possible after birth. The infant should be monitored postoperatively for signs of hydrocephalus, meningitis, and spinal cord dysfunction. Surgical shunting is usually necessary if hydrocephalus is diagnosed.

A long-term multidisciplinary approach is needed to care for children with myelomeningocele. There is no cure. Surgical closure of the defect is usually performed early (within 24 hours) to minimize the incidence of CNS infection and prevent further damage to the cord and nerve roots. Surgical closure also allows easier handling of the infant, which facilitates infant bonding. If the lesion was covered only by a membrane, skin grafting may be necessary. If hydrocephalus is present, a shunting procedure will be performed to relieve the increased ICP. Antibiotics are initiated soon after diagnosis and continue throughout the surgical and postsurgical phase of treatment.

Sensory and motor defects are present in varying degrees. Nerves of the cauda equina are involved when the defect is below the second lumbar vertebrate. This results in flaccid paralysis of the lower extremities, with sensory deficits as well as functional bowel and bladder sphincter deficits. Because of this flaccid paralysis, which begins in utero, these infants most often have bilateral clubbed feet (talipes varus) and bilateral dislocated hips (dysplasia).

Approximately 75% of infants born with myelomeningocele also have the accompanying complication of hydrocephalus. Suspected hydrocephalus is diagnosed by CT or MRI.

Later in life urinary tract infections, which can result in kidney failure, as well as respiratory problems resulting from scoliosis or kyphosis, can cause serious complications and, in some instances, may be the cause of death. As the child grows older, fecal continence can be maintained by dietary control and regular toileting habits. Some children require glycerin suppositories and stool softeners to prevent constipation and fecal impaction.

Orthopedic anomalies are evaluated and managed soon after birth if the infant's condition permits. Early intervention with casting, bracing, or traction to correct hip dysplasia or talipes varus allows for optimal locomotion later in life (see Chapter 33 for specific treatment and care modalities). The degree of locomotion in later life depends on the level of the lesion along the vertebrae. Children are encouraged to ambulate as much as possible. The child with a lesion in the lumbosacral area is often able to ambulate with braces, a walker, or crutches. Children with higher-level lesions may have to use a wheelchair. To prevent contractions and osteoporosis, these children are encouraged to exercise and bear weight as often as possible.

Urologic management focuses on preventing infection, reflux, and renal damage. A major goal is to promote urinary continence. The child's urologic status is monitored through a wide variety of tests and lab studies. Prophylactic drugs or agents may be used to increase urine acidity and prevent infection. Medication to assist complete emptying of the bladder and improve bladder tone may also be used.

The prognosis for children born with myelomeningocele has greatly improved over the last 20 years. Improved surgical techniques and advances in long-term care have contributed to the quality of life for these children. The best prognosis occurs in children with a low lumbar or lumbosacral defect without hydrocephalus. Many children with myelomeningocele, although they may have serious sensory and motor deficits, have normal intelligence and mature into productive members of society. In recent years there has been serious debate about whether children with myelomeningocele should be treated if they have other serious congenital defects or severe hydrocephalus. Although criteria have been proposed that would exclude children with multiple defects from treatment, the debate over these ethical issues is unresolved.

### Nursing Assessment and Diagnosis

Nursing assessment of these malformations involves several body systems. The area of the defect must be closely monitored for signs of infection. The infant's head circumference and anterior fontanel are checked at regular intervals for developing hydrocephalus. Vital signs and neurological status are also assessed. Nursing assessment also involves bladder and bowel function as well as sensory and motor function. Assessment of the family to determine their understanding of the multiple problems and their ability to cope with the stress being placed on them is a critical nursing role.

Nursing diagnoses related to the child with a neural tube defect might include the following:

- Potential for infection: meningitis, related to the open sac; possible CSF leak
- Potential for injury: neurological trauma, related to possible sac rupture

- Altered skin integrity, related to decreased mobility, sensitive neonatal skin
- Altered tissue perfusion: cerebral, related to hydrocele
- Impaired physical mobility, related to neuromuscular and sensory deficits
- Alteration in patterns of urinary elimination, related to decreased or absent motor or sensory innervation
- Alteration in family process, related to the child with a congenital anomaly; lengthy hospitalization
- Potential for ineffective coping: individual, related to physical dysfunction, chronic illness

### Planning and Implementing Nursing Care

**Preoperative Nursing Management.** Particular attention must be paid to meticulous care of the protruding sac. Proper positioning of the infant in the sidelying or prone position, with the hips elevated using a sponge roll, prevents urine and feces from contaminating the sac. This position also allows for the best positioning of the hips to minimize the dysplasia. The child is usually placed in an isolette to maintain normal body temperature. The use of a shield or barrier between the anus and the sac may be used to minimize the chance of stool contaminating the sac. A piece of plastic draped over the sac, taped below the sac, and brought down over the buttocks and taped to each thigh prevents fecal contamination of the sac. This should be changed if feces contaminate the tape between the sac and the anus. Diapers or clothing should not be placed over the lesion. If the sac is covered only with a membrane, sterile saline dressings should be placed over the sac to keep it moist. These are usually changed every 2 to 4 hours—more frequently if the heat from the isolette or heat lamp tends to dry the dressing sooner. Careful assessment of the lesion includes checking for signs of infection (purulent discharge, redness, irritability, decreased appetite, change in level of consciousness, fever, or increased white blood cell count). The lesion should also be assessed for leakage of CSF (any nonpurulent drainage).

The child's head circumference is checked daily, with the same measuring tape at the same points on the cranium. The anterior fontanel is also assessed for bulging and tension. An increase in head circumference and a bulging fontanel indicate hydrocephalus.

Skin care over pressure areas is also important. Since the child is in a prone position most of the time, pressure areas occur on the knees, ankles, and toes. The infant can be placed on soft fleece to minimize abrasion. The area can be rubbed gently with a mild lotion to stimulate circulation. Areas affected by sensory and motor deficits are more prone to skin breakdown.

Feeding the infant with myelomeningocele presents a challenge to the nurse. Small frequent feedings with a soft nipple and gentle stroking of the cheek will stimulate the sucking reflex and minimize fatigue. If the baby is to be fed in the prone position it is helpful to raise the baby's head, neck, and chest with one hand. In a sidelying position the head, neck, and shoulders of the infant can be slightly elevated. In some instances it may be possible to remove the child from the isolette and cradle the head, neck, and shoulder area with one hand while resting the buttocks on the parent's or nurse's lap.

A challenging aspect of nursing care of these newborns is promoting parent–infant bonding. Parents suffer the stress and grief associated with having a child with a serious anomaly. They should be encouraged and supported to stroke and talk to the baby. Participation in basic care should also be encouraged. Family teaching should be started immediately after birth, especially when informed surgical consent must be obtained within 24 hours of birth. The nurse should provide information and answer parents' questions, and may act as a liaison/advocate between the surgical team and the parents.

**Postoperative Nursing Management.** Postoperative care focuses on neurological status, sphincter control, and movement in the lower extremities. Care involves monitoring vital signs, intake and output, and the specific gravity of urine, as well as watching for signs of infection. The infant is placed in a prone position to prevent pressure on the operative site. The operative site is protected from contamination of urine and feces in the same manner as in preoperative management. Diapers may be used, and the child may be held and placed in a supine position after the incision is healed. Head circumference is assessed daily for signs of hydrocephalus, which develops in the majority of neural tube closures. Careful monitoring for signs of increasing ICP is imperative. Comparison of neurological function pre- and postoperatively is important. There may be decreased function of the lower extremities postoperatively.

Stimulation of the infant is necessary to promote development. Visual (bright colored objects), auditory (verbal and musical), and tactile stimulations (stroking, holding, cuddling) are essential. Support for the parents must continue through this period. Nurses should involve the parents in holding, feeding, and caring for their child. Nursing should include activities designed to help the parents cope. This may include introducing parents to support groups or other organizations or to another family with a child with myelomeningocele.

**Chronic Care Management of Children with Neural Tube Defects.** In order for the habilitation of these children to be successful, the interdisciplinary team must evaluate the parents' abilities to care for their child. The learning needs of the parents must be carefully assessed and documented before a teaching plan is developed.

Each activity of daily living presents problems that need to be resolved by individual adaptation. The motor deficit experienced by these children is more evident to parents than the sensory deficits. Parents must be taught that the decrease or absence of sensation on the skin surfaces means that the child is not alert to painful sensations that result from pressure, cuts, or extremes of cold or heat. Therefore, as parents, they must protect the child and carefully assess the child's skin to minimize or prevent the effects of trauma. The older child can also be taught to routinely inspect areas most likely to be affected. Safety precautions can also be taught to parents and children. Precautions include prevention of breakdown through meticulous skin care, and promoting circulation through exercise, weight bearing, and massage. Children in wheelchairs should be taught the hazards of carrying hot liquids or foods in their laps while transferring such items from one place to another, because this type of activity can lead to severe burns of the thighs and abdomen.

Mobility can be achieved in the young child through the use of a scooter board and low-sitting caster carts. These devices, in addition to providing mobility and a degree of independence, also increase the child's upper body strength. In the older child ambulation is encouraged when possible. There are a variety of assistive devices that can be used during ambulation, including braces, splints, and crutches. Mobility training consists of exercises, gait training, and instruction in the proper techniques for sitting, standing, and climbing stairs.

Bladder and bowel control is maintained primarily through intermittent straight urinary catheterization using a clean technique. This procedure completely empties the bladder and minimizes the incidence of urinary tract infections. Catheterization is performed every 3 to 4 hours, although time intervals can vary. Older children may be able to sleep through the night without the need for catheterization.

Other methods of bladder control are controversial and have been proved to be less effective. The Credé method is a method of manually expressing urine by increasing intra-abdominal pressure. This method does not always empty the bladder, and the remaining urine acts as a possible source for infection. It has also been demonstrated that manual expression can force urine back into the ureters, creating vesicoureteral reflux; this can result in permanent kidney damage. Indwelling catheters and internal urinary diversion (ileal loop) are used less frequently today because intermittent urinary catheterization has proved to be a less invasive and more effective means of controlling bladder elimination.

A bowel control program is initiated when the child is about 2 years old. The parents are instructed to put the child on the toilet at the same times each day. Back, side, and foot supports are important to give the young child the feeling of stability during bowel elimination. In order to establish a regular elimination program, a combination of enemas, suppositories, diet, and stool softeners may be needed. Usually a regular pattern has developed by the time the child is between 8 and 10 years old, and bowel elimination can be controlled with diet and suppositories. The regular elimination of feces not only permits emptying of the colon but minimizes soiling that can occur because of the inadequate functioning of the external anal sphincter. Dribbling of stool is not only an embarrassment to the child but can cause skin irritation and breakdown. The amount of sphincter control possessed by the child depends on the severity of the defect.

Diet is important not only for maintaining regular bowel functioning but also to maintain an ideal weight. Obesity in children with myelomeningocele makes it difficult for them to reach optimal mobility, and can create a cycle of increased immobility. Additional orthopedic problems may develop as the child grows; most commonly these involve scoliosis or kyphosis. These conditions, if they develop, need to be carefully evaluated, followed, and treated on an individual basis. Surgical correction of scoliosis may be needed in adolescence because of decreased pulmonary function.

At discharge, all of this information may seem overwhelming to the parents. The primary nursing goal is to provide support to parents through effective discharge planning and teaching. This includes referrals (community health) to aid the parents in home care. Extended family members, when available, should also be encouraged to participate in the child's care and thereby be able to relieve parents.

Although parent teaching is initiated soon after the baby's birth and parents are encouraged to participate in their newborn's care, the impending discharge of the infant becomes a time of increased anxiety for the parents. This is a time when they may question their ability to care for this child outside the structured hospital environment. The final discharge teaching should be given to parents over an extended period of time to allow them to practice the psychomotor skills necessary for home care under the guidance of the nurse. This time also gives them an opportunity to assimilate the information presented during discharge teaching and gives the primary nurse time to review the information with the parents.

### Evaluating Nursing Care

Close follow-up of these families is important. Frequent physical psychological and coping evaluations are necessary to maintain optimal habilitation. Parents and children should be encouraged to participate in support groups. The child with a myelomeningocele must be viewed as a member of a functioning family unit. Each family member has their own needs for personal growth, and these needs (parental and sibling) must be met in order for the family to remain intact and functioning.

## Hydrocephalus

Hydrocephalus is a condition caused by abnormalities in the production, absorption, or flow of CSF within the intracranial cavity. The increased volume raises ICP and enlarges the cerebral ventricles.

### Pathophysiology

Hydrocephalus has numerous causes. It can occur as a result of meningitis, a genetic defect, or trauma during or after birth, or as a complication of other congenital anomalies, e.g., myelomeningocele. Hydrocephalus is usually classified as communicating or noncommunicating, depending on the underlying cause of the accumulation of excess CSF in the central nervous system. Communicating hydrocephalus results from inadequate circulation of CSF or a disruption of the reabsorption mechanism in the subarachnoid space. Noncommunicating hydrocephalus, the most common type, results from an obstruction of CSF flow from the ventricles to the subarachnoid space.

*Aqueduct of Sylvius stenosis* is the most common cause of obstructive hydrocephalus and results from a stenosis of the Sylvian aqueduct between the third and fourth ventricles. This condition can result from neural tube defects or following an inflammatory process in the CNS. CNS tumors (e.g., medulloblastoma) also account for a small percentage of noncommunicating hydrocephalus.

*Arnold-Chiari malformation* includes several variations of herniation of CNS tissue that results in obstruction of CSF, most commonly as a result of myelomeningocele. For example, Type II involves downward displacement of the brain stem, fourth ventricle, and a portion of the cerebellum through the foramina magnum as a result of the spinal cord being attached to the vertebrae at the site of the myelomeningocele.

*Dandy-Walker syndrome* is caused by an obstruction of the foramina of Luschka and Magendie. This results in a large, dilated fourth ventricle and resultant hydrocephalus. This defect occurs most often as a result of neural tube defects.

The obstruction of the CNS pathway, the overproduction of CSF, or the malabsorption of CSF causes a distension of the CSF-filled ventricles that results in the compression of brain tissue. If left untreated this condition can result in continually increasing head size, destruction of brain tissue, mental retardation, convulsions, and death.

### Medical Diagnosis and Management

Symptoms that accompany hydrocephalus depend on the age of onset and severity of the accumulation of CSF. As the head of the young child (before the age of 18 months to 2 years) enlarges, there is a separation of the cranial sutures, an increase in the size of the posterior and anterior fontanels, a thinning of the bones of the cranium, and an increase in head circumference. Percussion of the skull with these separated sutures produces a high-pitched, "cracked pot" sound (Macewen's sign).

In addition to increasing head circumference, nystagmus (rapid movement of the eyeball) or strabismus (weak eye muscles) may be present. The scalp veins may be dilated; the skin over the cranium may become thin and translucent. As the child's head size increases and the skin becomes taut, the sclera of the eyes becomes visible above the iris ("setting sun sign"). The fontanels bulge and become tense. Other symptoms include poor feeding, irritability, vomiting, lethargy, a high-pitched cry, and developmental delays. The onset of hydrocephalus, after the age of 2, when the fontanels have closed and the sutures have fused, results in classic signs of increased ICP. Complaints of headache and vomiting are typically present.

CT scanning is used to determine the size and position of the ventricles. Dye may be injected into the lumbar subarachnoid space during the scan to determine CSF circulation and identify obstructions in the CSF pathways. The use of CT greatly reduces the need for more invasive procedures such as pneumoencephalograms.

Hydrocephalus is most often treated surgically. The goal in management is to maintain cerebrospinal fluid pressures within normal limits by removal of the underlying cause of obstruction, the diversion of excess CSF away from the central nervous system, or reduction of CSF produced by the CNS.

Extracranial shunting is the procedure most frequently used to relieve hydrocephalus. The surgical procedure consists of inserting a small catheter into the lateral ventricle through a burr hole in the skull and attaching the catheter to a one-way pressure valve placed just under the scalp. Another catheter is attached to the valve and threaded subcutaneously along the chest wall. The distal end of this catheter is most commonly placed in the peritoneum, to form a ventriculoperitoneal (VP) shunt. A ventriculoatrial (VA) shunt may also be used, in which the catheter is threaded through the jugular vein into the right atrium of the heart. These shunting procedures are performed on children with acute, rapidly progressing hydrocephalus (Fig. 26-5).

The external shunting procedures may require periodic revisions as the child grows or if obstruction of the shunt occurs. During the initial surgery an extra length of catheter may be coiled and left in the peritoneal cavity to allow for growth. Shunt complications include infections, obstructions, and disconnection of the tubing. These complications can cause sudden or gradual symptoms of recurring hydrocephalus and increased ICP.

Control of hydrocephalus through medications has proved ineffective in most cases of rapidly progressive hydrocephalus. Furosemide, isosorbide, and acetazola-

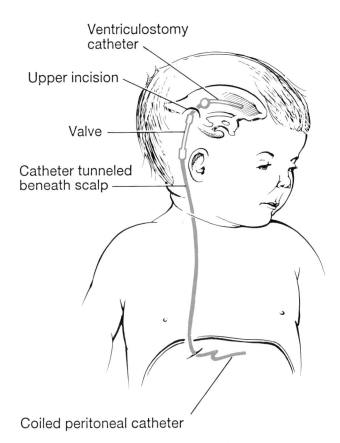

Ventriculostomy catheter

Upper incision

Valve

Catheter tunneled beneath scalp

Coiled peritoneal catheter

*Figure 26–5. Ventriculoperitoneal (VP) shunt.*

mide administration, in conjunction with lumbar punctures to remove CSF, have been successful in selected children whose hydrocephalus is caused by pathology known to spontaneously resolve (e.g., intracranial hemorrhage, subdural hematomas).

## Nursing Assessment and Diagnosis

Postoperative assessment of the child's neurological status is focused on watching for signs of increasing ICP. The head circumference is measured daily, and the anterior fontanel is checked for size and fullness. Nurses also assess for changes in the child's behavior. Checking for proper function of the shunt is an important nursing function. Nursing assessment also includes evaluation of the parent's understanding of the signs of shunt malfunction and signs of infection. Nursing diagnoses related to the child with hydrocephalus might include the following:

- Altered tissue perfusion; cerebral, related to increased ICP
- Altered nutrition: less than body requirements, related to poor appetite, nausea and vomiting caused by ICP
- Impaired physical mobility, related to enlarged head
- Potential for injury: neurological compromise, related to seizure activity, pressure on brain stem

- Altered skin integrity, related to postsurgical immobility
- Anxiety: parental, related to the diagnosis
- Ineffective family coping, related to life-threatening disease
- Pain, related to surgical incision
- Potential for infection, related to insertion of foreign body; poor skin integrity
- Body image disturbance, related to hair loss, restrictions on activities

## Planning and Implementing Nursing Care

***Preoperative Nursing Management.*** The child's neurological status is evaluated at frequent and regular intervals. In the infant, head circumference is measured, preferably by the same person and with the same tape measure each time. The occipital/frontal circumference of the head is measured. The fontanels are evaluated for tenseness and bulging, and cranial sutures are palpated to determine any separation. Level of consciousness, feeding habits, and the presence of irritability, restlessness, and high-pitched cry are also evaluated.

General nursing care may present special problems. If the child's head is markedly enlarged, the child may not be able to move or control the head. Holding the child is difficult, and the head and neck must be firmly supported. A pillow under the child's head and shoulders helps to maintain a comfortable position while holding. The skin over the cranium may be thin and prone to pressure areas and breakdown. Sheepskin under the child's head, along with frequent position changes, helps prevent skin breakdown.

Nutrition is maintained by small, frequent feedings in a relaxed atmosphere that increases toleration of feedings and reduces the incidence of vomiting. Holding the child during feedings is recommended. These children are very often difficult to feed and nurses must allow sufficient time to administer the feedings slowly, with frequent burping.

Parents are encouraged to hold the child and participate in his or her care. This helps them to bond with their infant and increases their self-confidence in caring for the child.

***Postoperative Nursing Management.*** In addition to routine postoperative care, the nursing assessment carried out preoperatively continues in the postsurgery phase. Postoperatively, previously tense and bulging fontanels should be soft and flat, indicating that the shunt is functioning properly. If the fontanels again become tense or bulging, or the child shows signs of increased ICP, the physician should be notified. There may be postoperative orders to test the shunt for patency when these symptoms appear. This is accomplished by depressing the shunt valve with the forefinger firmly and quickly. If the valve is difficult to depress, the shunt may be blocked and immediate medical intervention is needed.

Some valves used in shunt procedures require regular pumping. Medical orders are written instructing the nurse on the frequencies and the number of times to pump the shunt valve. The child is positioned on the side opposite the shunt. Dressings are observed for any drainage (bloody or clear). Drainage should be checked (using Dextrostix) for the presence of glucose, which is indicative of CSF. In ventriculoperitoneal shunt, the abdomen is observed for distention, redness, or tenderness.

Usually the child is kept flat in bed for the first 24 hours, although in some cases there may be orders to elevate the head of the bed. Elevation of the head and pumping of the shunt valve can sometimes cause too rapid CSF drainage, which is manifested by sunken fontanels and can cause a rapid decrease in ventricle size. This results in the cerebral cortex being pulled away from the meninges, causing breaks in small veins and capillaries, which may result in subdural hematomas.

Intake and output are carefully monitored. Fluids may be restricted initially, and intravenous therapy is closely monitored to prevent fluid overload. Normal feedings are resumed based on the child's tolerance and the presence of bowel sounds, especially in children with VP shunts. Children with VP shunts may have a tendency toward constipation, which is usually regulated through diet. Antibiotics are routinely administered postoperatively. Intravenous and intraventricular administration are the most frequently used routes. Infection is the most serious complication following shunting.

Discharge planning includes teaching the parents to look for signs of infection and shunt malfunction. Parents should also be prepared for the possibility of the child's readmission to the hospital. The majority of these children remain dependent on a shunt. Infections and shunt malfunction usually require hospitalization.

### Evaluating Nursing Care

Regular follow-up evaluations help measure the child's development and plan for necessary rehabilitation. Children with well functioning shunts should resume normal activities with few restrictions, except competitive contact sports.

## Microencephaly

Microencephaly is an abnormally small head, caused by a malformed or incomplete brain. Maternal infections such as toxoplasmosis, as well as numerous genetic or environmental factors, may cause this condition. Microencephaly may be diagnosed in newborns whose chest circumference exceeds head circumference. The sutures may be open at birth, but close prematurely. The child is mentally retarded with accompanying motor, sensory, and growth disorders. There is no known corrective treatment. Prog-

nosis depends on the severity of the brain abnormality. This defect involving arrested brain growth contrasts with *craniosynostosis,* in which the brain is of normal size but the fontanels and sutures are closed at birth or close in early infancy. Craniosynostosis can be corrected by surgery.

## Neonatal Meningitis

Neonatal meningitis is an acute inflammatory process of the meninges that occurs during the first month of life. Meningitis is the most common complication of sepsis in the neonate.

### Pathophysiology

The major causative organisms of neonatal meningitis are *Escherichia coli* and group B streptococci. Neonatal meningitis results from an introduction of the pathogen into the bloodstream and invasion of the central nervous system. This results in an inflammatory response in meningeal tissue. Transmission of organisms to the neonate may occur prenatally, due to premature or prolonged rupture of the membranes, and maternal infection. Postnatally, transmission occurs most often through the contaminated hands of care givers. The mortality rate for neonatal meningitis is high (40%–80%)(Gaddy, 1980). The outcome depends on the age of onset, severity of symptoms, and response to treatment. Treatment within 24 to 48 hours results in a more favorable prognosis.

### Medical Diagnosis and Management

Neonates with meningitis display variable clinical signs, including disturbances in temperature regulation (hypothermia, hyperthermia), feeding difficulties, vomiting, diarrhea, and abdominal distention. Other clinical manifestations include lethargy, irritability, convulsions, fever, irregular respiratory patterns, tachycardia, or bradycardia. A tense or bulging anterior fontanel may or may not be present.

Diagnosis is confirmed by staining cell counts and cultures of blood and CSF. CSF cell counts are high, particularly the neutrophil count. CSF protein concentrations are elevated and glucose levels are decreased in meningitis. Identification of infecting organisms is important in determining appropriate antibiotic therapy. New and more sophisticated lab tests continue to be developed to aid in the diagnosis of neonatal meningitis. These tests include the litmus lystate test, latex particle agglutination test (LPA), and counterimmunoelectrophoresis (CIE).

Treatment is antibiotic therapy begun after CSF cultures are obtained. The initial antibiotic therapy may consist of penicillin and chloramphenicol administered intravenously in dosages sufficiently large to cross the blood–brain barrier. Dosages depend on the infant's weight. Antibiotic therapy is adjusted once the strain of meningitis is identified. Antibiotic therapy is continued for

10 to 14 days, with frequent cultures of blood and CSF to monitor the course of the disease. If the infant experiences seizures, anticonvulsants may be ordered.

### Nursing Assessment and Diagnosis

Neurologic assessment is a critical nursing function that is often complicated by the child's young age. Nurses must pay attention to parental observations and comments, particularly concerning poor feeding, vomiting, or diarrhea. The neonate's cry is also helpful in assessment. A weak cry is an early sign of meningitis. Nursing diagnoses related to the child with neonatal meningitis may include the following:

- Potential for injury: cerebral, related to infective process, increased ICP
- Potential for injury: physiologic, related to disease complications
- Pain, related to headache, joint pain
- Hyperthermia, related to infective process
- Anxiety: child and family, related to diagnosis and hospitalization

### Planning and Implementing Nursing Care

Nurses must focus on any changes in behavior or vital signs. Attention must be paid to whether these changes continue or return to normal. Changes in neurological function may indicate serious complication of cerebral edema or obstructive hydrocephalus. Observation includes monitoring the tension of the fontanel, any increase in head circumference, level of consciousness, and the presence of irritability.

Vital signs are closely monitored, and intake and output are noted. To decrease neurological irritation it is important to maintain a quiet environment and provide frequent rest periods.

### Evaluating Nursing Care

Once antibiotics are started, the child should be free of hyperthermia. Neurological symptoms should decrease and resolve within a week. Continuation of neurological abnormalities may indicate permanent CNS damage. The neonate should have no recurrence of illness after antibiotic therapy is completed.

## Neurological Problems of Toddlers

### Lead Poisoning (Plumbism)

Lead poisoning, or plumbism, is a relatively common pediatric problem that results from the ingestion or inhalation of lead-containing substances. Health care authorities are beginning to realize not only the prevalence of lead poisoning but also the tragic consequences of this hazard. The highest incidence of lead poisoning occurs in late infancy and toddlerhood as the mobility of the child increases. Sources of lead include paint chips or powder of lead paint, soil contamination, and inhaled lead from automobile exhausts. Although lead-based paint has been banned for many years, chipping paint in structures built before the 1960s may contain several layers, and the older layers may consist of lead-based paints. Although it banned these paints in 1978, the federal government has done nothing to deal with the 3 million tons of old lead that line the walls and fixtures of 57 million private American homes. Children may ingest this paint from interior or exterior sources. Just a few chips of paint may contain several hundred times the safe daily level of lead ingestion. Lead dust from the friction of opening and closing windows can be an even greater source of lead. Sources of lead paint contamination may not be in the child's own home but in buildings the child may frequent, e.g., day care centers and the homes of relatives, friends, or caretakers. Lead poisoning can also result from pica, a compulsive, habitual ingestion of nonfood substances.

Young children are at risk for lead poisoning because of their high level of oral activity. Putting objects in their mouths is one way infants and toddlers learn about their environment. This oral activity plus increased mobility puts the child at greater risk for ingestion of toxic substances. The risk of lead poisoning is increased because lead is more readily absorbed in children than in adults. This absorption is accelerated when the child also exhibits deficiencies in iron and calcium. It takes only minimal amounts of lead to cause lead poisoning. A child can become severely lead poisoned by ingesting 1 mg of lead-paint dust—equivalent in size to about 3 granules of sugar—each day during childhood.

Certain parenting behaviors also contribute to increased ingestion of lead. Young children left unsupervised to explore their environment are more likely to ingest lead substances. Lack of proper stimulation with appropriate toys, poor personal and environmental hygiene, and a diet low in iron and calcium can contribute to lead toxicity. However, lead poisoning is not exclusively a problem of ghettos or lower-income families. Many children from upper-income families are exposed to lead during renovation of an old house.

### Pathophysiology

Lead is absorbed through the GI or respiratory tract and excreted slowly through the gastrointestinal tract and kidneys. When the rate of absorption exceeds the rate of excretion, the excess lead is deposited in the soft tissue of the body and bone and attaches itself to blood erythrocytes. Lead interferes with heme production and the formation of hemoglobin. The resultant affect on the body is microcytic hypochromic anemia. Lead affects the kidneys by altering the permeability of the proximal tubules, resulting in increased elimination of glucose and proteins in the urine. Lead salt deposits increase CNS vascular permeability, which results in fluid shifts causing encephalopathy (brain swelling) and increased ICP. Lead may also be distributed to soft tissue and deposited in the metaphyses of long bones.

## Medical Diagnosis and Management

The symptoms and effects of lead poisoning can affect many body systems. Table 26-4 outlines affected body systems and accompanying symptoms based on the degree of severity. Diagnosis is based on measuring blood lead levels and erythrocyte-to-protoporphyrin (EP) ratios. Blood lead levels reflect recent absorption of lead, and EP levels represent adverse effect of lead on erythrocyte formation. The CDC is calling for a lowering of the definition of lead poisoning from a blood level of 25 μg/dL to 10 μg/dL. Case management should begin for children with levels of 15 μg/dL. It is recommended that medical management begin for children with lead levels of 20 μg/dL or greater. Numerous studies have shown multiple problems related to increased blood levels, including reading disabilities, decreased intelligence scores, hyperactivity, aggressive behavior, and developmental delays. When levels reach 30 μg/dL, problems such as anemia, irritability, abdominal complaints, vomiting, and ataxia appear.

Additional diagnostic testing includes x-rays to evaluate the presence of lead in long bones or lead deposits in the abdomen. Serial urine tests for elevated levels of coproporphyrin (greater than 150 μg/24 hours) aids in diagnosis.

The goal of treatment is to remove the lead from the blood and soft tissue. Chelation therapy involves the removal of a substance from the body by binding it to another substance and subsequent excretion of the bound substances. Calcium disodium edetate (CaEDTA) and British anti-lewisite (BAL) are the most common chelating agents. CaEDTA is usually given intravenously; BAL is given via deep intramuscular injection. Chelation therapy is continued for 3 to 5 days and may need to be repeated if urinary coproporphyrin levels remain elevated. Several oral preparations are being tested clinically, but they tend to be less effective. Long-term prognosis depends on the amount of lead ingested and the length of time the lead is allowed to remain in the child. Chronic lead ingestion in children leads to many long-term and chronic disabilities.

## Nursing Assessment and Diagnosis

Careful physical, developmental, and social assessment is important in formulating the diagnosis of lead poisoning and preventing its long-term effects. A careful history during well-child visits assists nurses in identifying children at risk for lead poisoning. Nurses should ask about any history of pica. The history should also include information about recent changes of residence or exposure to lead fumes. Nurses should also ask about where children play to determine the possibility of exposure.

The following nursing diagnoses may be appropriate for the child with lead poisoning:

- Pain, related to administration of BAL and CaEDTA
- Altered patterns of urinary elimination, related to renal injury from CaEDTA administration
- Potential for injury: poisoning, related to exposure to lead in environment
- Altered tissue perfusion: cerebral, related to lead toxicity

### Planning and Implementing Nursing Care

The nurse must prepare the child and the family before chelation therapy begins. IV therapy is becoming the most acceptable route of administration for chelation therapy. If

## Table 26-4. Body Organ Involvement in Lead Poisoning

| System | Severity | Manifestations |
|---|---|---|
| Hematological | Mild to severe | Varying degrees of anemia—characterized by pallor and listlessness |
| Renal | Mild to severe | Increasing degrees of glycosuria, proteinuria, ketonuria, and hyperphosphaturia |
| Gastrointestinal | Chronic ingestion | Acute crampy abdominal pain, vomiting, constipation, anorexia most frequently caused by chronic inhalation |
| Orthopedic | Mild asymptomatic | May be short stature due to impaired growth without additional symptoms |
| | Severe | Bone marrow involvement with lead lines as evidenced in x-rays of the long bones; increased density of long bones |
| Central nervous system (CNS) | Mild | Behavioral changes—irritability, hyperactivity, aggressive behavior, lethargy, learning difficulties, delays in developmental milestones, short attention span, clumsiness, and deficits in sensory perception |
| | Severe and/or chronic | Convulsions, mental retardation, encephalopathy with resultant increased ICP, paralysis, sensory loss, coma, and death |

IM injections are to be the route of administration, therapeutic play with a needle and syringe is helpful to allow the child to work through fears and anxiety. Because many injections will need to be given during therapy, a site rotation schedule for injections should be planned. Careful assessment of injection sites is important because fibrosis can occur. CaEDTA is usually given with procaine 0.5% (a local anesthetic) to lessen discomfort of the injection. The CaEDTA is drawn up first, followed by the procaine. A bubble of air is then introduced into the syringe. At the time of the injection, the procaine enters first and is slowly injected, followed by the CaEDTA. Finally, the bubble of air pushes the last bit of CaEDTA out of the needle and prevents tracking of the medications through the dermal layers as the needle is withdrawn from the patient.

During chelation therapy adequate fluid intake must be maintained, because the lead is excreted primarily by the kidneys. Careful recording of intake and output with regular monitoring of kidney function is important. Serial urine collections are obtained during chelation therapy and tested to determine the rate and amount of lead excretion. Blood lead and EP levels are also collected routinely during therapy to determine the effectiveness of therapy. Urine protein, BUN, and serum creatine levels are monitored. Increases in these parameters indicate drug toxicity and impending renal complications. Nurses must also monitor the child for signs of encephalopathy resulting from chelating agents. Nurses must be familiar with the side effects of these drugs. Seizure precautions should also be instituted.

Parents must be educated regarding factors that put a child at risk for lead ingestion. Home visits are valuable in assessing the environment of the child who has elevated blood lead levels in order to determine the source of lead and to rid the child's environment of the lead contamination. Walls and window sills covered by lead paint must be stripped to bare wood; moldings and baseboards must also be stripped or replaced. Consumers Union suggests two home kits that test for lead painted surfaces: Lead-Check Swabs by HybriVet Systems Inc. (800-262-LEAD), and Frandon Lead Alert by Frandon Enterprises, Inc. (800-359-9000). Only qualified contractors should remove lead from a home. Children should be sent away until the work is completed, or the rooms should be sealed off during renovation. Drinking water may also be a source of lead. Water should be tested if it is from a well or travels through pipes with lead solder. The EPA's safe-drinking-water hot line can help answer questions (800-426-4791). EPA-certified laboratories will test local drinking water for between $15 and $35.

### Evaluating Nursing Care

An increased awareness and understanding regarding the serious consequences of lead poisoning is a major evaluation factor. Communities as well as educators, civil rights activists, and environmental lobbyists should become in-

volved in addressing this hazard. Parents should understand the sources of lead and take actions to test for lead and remove it from the environment. Individuals should realize that only qualified contractors should undertake large removal or renovation projects. Increased awareness and education should increase concern regarding lead in drinking water.

## Neurocutaneous Syndromes

Neurocutaneous syndromes are called phakomatoses and are characterized by tumor formation in the central nervous system, skin, and various organ systems. The disorders are generally inherited, with varying degrees of neurological impairment. These diseases are rare, and only neurofibromatosis and tuberous sclerosis are discussed here.

### Pathophysiology

The pathological mechanism of neurofibromatosis and tuberous sclerosis is unknown. The two diseases are inherited as an autosomal dominant trait.

### Medical Diagnosis and Management

These diseases vary widely in age of onset, severity, and progression.

The classic form of neurofibromatosis is characterized by café-au-lait (light brown) spots on the skin, multiple neurofibromas, and clinical findings of the skeletal, endocrine, and vascular systems. The neurofibromas may be peripheral cutaneous or central neurological tumors. Lesion involvement is extremely variable. Tumors usually involve all layers of underlying soft tissue. They are vascular and nonencapsulated and can grow to enormous size. (Neurofibromatosis received widespread attention with the Broadway play and movie *The Elephant Man,* the story of a Victorian Englishman who was grotesquely deformed with the disease. A more recent portrayal of the disease was in the movie *Mask.*) Central nervous system involvement may result in increased ICP. In some cases the diagnosis of neurofibromatosis may not be made until adolescence.

Tuberous sclerosis is often initially marked by seizures, and is characterized by adenoma sebaceum, a red papular rash covering the nose, cheeks, and chin. Tumor growths in this disease are called "tubers." Children with tuberous sclerosis are often mentally retarded.

Diagnosis is made by tissue sample of a lesion or tumor. Treatment is basically palliative and supportive; there is no cure for these diseases. Surgical removal of tumors is possible for cosmetic effects, but other tumors may continue to appear in the dermal tissue. Careful monitoring to determine malignant changes in lesions is most important.

### Nursing Assessment and Diagnosis

Assessments are typically on an ongoing basis in these children to help identify abnormalities. Nurses should assess developmental parameters, vision and hearing, skeletal function, and blood pressure. Evaluation of neurological function is also important. Nursing diagnoses related to the child with neurocutaneous syndromes might include the following:

- Potential for injury, related to uncontrolled seizures
- Ineffective family coping, related to diagnosis of an incurable disease, long-term hospitalization
- Body image disturbance, related to appearance of tumors
- Impaired social interaction, related to physical appearance
- Sensory/perceptual alterations: visual, auditory, related to tumor growth

### Planning and Implementing Nursing Care

The care of the child with neurofibromatosis is an interdisciplinary endeavor, with the nurse functioning in a primary role. An in-depth physical and psychosocial assessment is imperative. External tumors may be severely disfiguring, and the nurse must assist the family to cope with the stigmata of these external tumors. Internal lesions may cause severe compromise to the child's life. Central nervous system tumors can result in severe and life-threatening increased ICP. Patient/family education is most important to aid in the management of associated symptoms: chronic headaches, constipation due to GI lesions, and pruritus associated with skin lesions.

Genetic counseling should be made available and the family encouraged to use these services. The family should also be encouraged to use local and national support groups. The National Neurofibromatosis Foundation is an excellent source of information on neurofibromatosis.

### Evaluating Nursing Care

Evaluation is based on parental knowledge and adjustment to the child's condition. Genetic counseling and referrals are important keys in assisting the family to cope with the various stresses.

## Neurological Problems of Preschool Children

### Meningitis

Meningitis is an infectious process of the meninges caused most frequently by bacterial invasion (bacterial meningitis) and less frequently by viral (aseptic meningitis)

agents. The majority of bacterial meningitis in children occurs between the ages of 1 month and 5 years; infants between the ages of 6 and 12 months are most susceptible (Krugman, 1985). A variety of causative agents have been identified in meningitis, but *Haemophilus influenzae* type B (H. flu meningitis), *Neisseria meningitis* (meningococcal meningitis), and *Diplococcus pneumonia* (pneumococcal meningitis) are the three most common causative pathogens. Bacterial meningitis is a potentially fatal disease if not treated quickly and vigorously with antimicrobials.

Viral meningitis is caused by a variety of viruses, most commonly enteroviruses. Coxsackievirus, echovirus, and mumps virus are also known to cause the disease. This is a benign, self-limiting disease, with complete recovery in 7 to 10 days.

### Pathophysiology

The bacteria enter the meninges through the bloodstream and spread through the cerebral spinal fluid. The infection may also result from direct invasion caused by injury or neurosurgical procedures. The invading pathogen acts as a toxin, creating a meningeal inflammatory response and a resultant release of purulent exudate. The inflammation spreads quickly via this exudate. The exudate covers the choroid plexus and can obstruct the arachnoid villi, causing hydrocephalus. Vascular congestion and inflammation leads to cerebral edema, which may produce increased ICP. Continued necrosis of brain cortex cells can result in permanent damage and death.

### Medical Diagnosis and Management

Generally, the clinical manifestations of meningitis are similar regardless of the causative organisms. Infants and toddlers (3 months to 2 years) do not necessarily display the classic signs and symptoms of meningitis and may initially present with poor feeding, irritability, and lethargy. Infants may have a high-pitched cry, a bulging fontanel, and a resistance to being held. Posturing may also include opisthotonos, a hyperextension of the neck and spine. In the child over 2 years, onset of symptoms may be preceded by several days of respiratory or gastrointestinal symptoms. Nuchal rigidity (stiff neck) and headache are significant symptoms. Posturing may include a positive Kernig sign (in the supine position with knees and hips flexed, there is pain and resistance to knee extension) and a positive Brudzinski sign (in supine position as the neck is flexed, there is flexion of the hips and knees). A petechial rash on the abdomen and legs may also be present.

Diagnosis and treatment is based on clinical manifestations and the examination of CSF. The child is placed in isolation, and respiratory precautions are instituted for 24 to 48 hours after antibiotic therapy is started. Lumbar puncture is done to identify the causative organism, and appropriate antibiotic therapy is initiated. Lumbar punc-

*Alterations in Neurol...*

*Health ...*

662

episode
dysfu...
ti...

tures are not performed in children with increased ICP, as the procedure can precipitate brain herniation. In meningitis the CSF pressure may be elevated and CSF cloudy. The white blood cell count is elevated, as are protein and lactic acid levels. CSF glucose level is usually decreased. CT scans may be indicated to rule out hydrocephalus and subdural effusions.

Bacterial meningitis requires accurate diagnosis, antibiotic treatment (initially intravenously), and supportive treatment. Supportive treatment involves managing fluid and electrolyte balance, monitoring and treating hydrocephalus or increased ICP, controlling fever, and treatment of secondary infections that may be the sources of the meningitis. Prognosis is dependent on the causative agent, age of the child, and response to therapy. Complications following meningitis are greater in neonates. The younger the child, the greater the risk of permanent damage to the brain, including hydrocephalus.

### Nursing Assessment and Diagnosis

Assessment of the child's neurological function and vital signs is important. Frequent reassessment is needed to monitor changes and treatment response. Level of consciousness is a critical factor in assessing the child's neurological status. Nurses must also watch for signs of increased ICP and any signs of respiratory problems.

Nursing diagnoses related to the child with meningitis may include the following:

- Potential for injury, related to infection and increased ICP
- Potential fluid volume deficit, related to anorexia, lethargy
- Hyperthermia, related to meningeal inflammation
- Pain: headache, related to inflammation of meninges; nuchal rigidity
- Sensory/perceptual deficit, related to neurological sequelae
- Ineffective family coping, related to diagnosis of incurable disease

### Planning and Implementing Nursing Care

Continual monitoring and assessment by the nurse is most important. Nurses must monitor for changes in ICP. In infants the anterior fontanel should be palpated and the head circumference measured daily. Most children are irritable and photophobic. A quiet atmosphere is important; stressful stimuli or manipulations should be kept to a minimum. The child is placed on bed rest, and the head of the bed should be slightly elevated to help decrease cerebral edema.

Temperature elevations are treated with antipyretics and tepid sponge baths or hypothermia mattress. Hyperthermia increases metabolic and oxygen demands of the

body. Nursing management inv... scribed intravenous fluid and antib... otics may be administered intraven... to 14 days; therefore, maintenance... important. The IV site should be care... ing for signs of infiltration or phleb...

Because the onset of meningitis... the family and patient will need em... information about the disease process ...the treatments administered (description of IV therapy, LP, and isolation precautions). Additional long-term rehabilitative care may be necessary if residual deficits continue after the acute recovery period.

### Evaluating Nursing Care

Evaluation is based on the parents' understanding of the condition and diagnostic and treatment regimens. If the child continues on anticonvulsant medication, parents should be able to manage possible seizures. The family should understand the importance of follow-up appointments.

## Encephalitis

Encephalitis is an inflammatory process of the brain. The most common cause is a virus, but encephalitis can also be associated with fungal or bacterial agents. Viral invasion may occur directly into the central nervous system or secondarily through postinfection sequelae. Encephalitis used to be a common complication of measles, mumps, and rubella before immunization against these diseases was available. The disease may still occur following chicken pox, herpes simplex, and Coxsackie virus A and B infections. The most common causative viruses of encephalitis are enteroviruses and arboviruses. Often it is not possible to identify the causative virus.

### Pathophysiology

Infection of the central nervous system often occurs secondary to another infectious process. The infection is carried through the blood to the CNS.

### Medical Diagnosis and Management

The symptoms associated with viral encephalitis are varied. They depend on the severity of the disease and the area of the brain or spinal cord involved. Initial symptoms are similar to those of any viral illness: headache, vomiting, fever, and/or lethargy. Neurological signs then develop, including stiff neck, change in level of consciousness, agitation, restlessness, seizures, focal neurological signs, and cerebral edema. The clinical course may last for days or extend into weeks. Prognosis depends on the severity, type, and neurological involvement. Complete recovery usually occurs in mild cases of encephalitis, but a severe

*...* of the disease can cause permanent neurological *...* *...*ction. Diagnosis is based on the clinical manifesta-*...*ns, examination of CSF to rule out bacterial invasion, and an elevated WBC. In viral encephalitis, the glucose level of CSF is normal with small amounts of protein.

Treatment for viral encephalitis is primarily supportive. The child is usually placed in isolation until the causative organism is identified. Prescribed medications may include steroids to control cerebral edema, antipyretics (acetaminophen) to control fever, analgesics to treat headaches, and anticonvulsants to treat or prevent seizures.

### Nursing Assessment and Diagnosis

Assessment of neurological function to evaluate change in status (development of cerebral edema, change in level of consciousness) is of primary importance. Assessment of the respiratory and cardiovascular systems is also important. Nursing diagnoses related to the child with encephalitis might include the following:

- Altered thought processes, related to neurophysiological pathology
- Pain: headache, related to meningeal inflammation; nuchal rigidity
- Potential altered parenting, related to diagnosis of disease affecting brain function
- Powerlessness, related to untreatable disease

### Planning and Implementing Nursing Care

Nursing care is similar to that for the child with bacterial meningitis. Frequent monitoring of vital signs and neurological status is critical, because children with encephalitis commonly experience seizures. Nurses must observe for changes in behavior, increased lethargy or irritability, changes in feeding pattern, and response to pain. Close monitoring of cardiovascular and respiratory status is important, since rapid changes involving these systems can occur. Vital signs should include noting irregularities in heart rate and respiratory pattern. Supportive nursing care to minimize symptoms is instituted.

Families should be educated regarding the reasons for isolation, and isolation techniques must be taught. Families need a great deal of support to cope with feelings of frustration as the disease runs its course with no specific treatment. If neurological dysfunction results, nurses should work with the family and other health care team members to establish a rehabilitative plan.

### Evaluating Nursing Care

Ideally, the child should recover with no neurological sequelae. The family should be able to deal with their feelings of frustration and powerlessness. If sequelae result, the family is able to accept the child, and future plans are based on reality.

## Neurological Problems of School-Age Children

### Reye Syndrome

Reye syndrome is an acute, multisystem disorder first described in 1963 (Reye, Morgan, & Baral, 1963). The disorder follows a mild viral infection, most frequently influenza or varicella. The syndrome is characterized by encephalopathy and fatty degeneration of the liver. Reye syndrome occurs primarily in children between 5 and 15 years of age. The exact cause is unknown, but a relationship between aspirin administration during viral illness and the disease has been shown (Hurwitz, 1985).

### Pathophysiology

The cell mitochondria are injured and become abnormally large and swollen. This causes cerebral edema, and fatty infiltration of the liver, kidneys, and heart. Hyperammonemia (increased ammonia levels in the blood) results from a reduction in the enzyme that converts ammonia to urea.

### Medical Diagnosis and Management

Onset of the disease is usually preceded by a viral infection. The child appears to be recovering and develops nausea and vomiting, which may be accompanied by lethargy, irritability, or confusion. Deterioration of neurological function can occur in 24 to 48 hours.

Reye syndrome is staged according to level of consciousness, reflexes, and cardiorespiratory status, as outlined by Table 26-5. Identification of the stage at diagnosis aids in determining therapy and predicting prognosis. Prognosis depends on early detection and intervention. Accurate diagnosis is imperative. Brain dysfunction and death can occur if diagnosis and treatment are delayed. Diagnosis is based on history, neurological symptoms, and laboratory data. Lab data show elevated levels of serum glutamic-oxaloacetic transaminase (SGOT), serum glutamic-pyruvic transaminase (SGPT), and lactic dehydrogenase (LDH). Elevated ammonia levels and prolonged prothrombin time also aid in the diagnosis. Some children develop hypoglycemia. There is a disturbance in acid–base balance, with a combined respiratory alkalosis and metabolic acidosis.

Therapy includes management of ICP within normal limits, and maintenance of fluid and electrolyte balance. These children are treated in an intensive care setting. An arterial line and a central venous line are usually inserted to monitor hemodynamics. Intracranial monitoring devices may also be used to continuously measure ICP. Fluids are usually restricted, and intake and output is carefully monitored. A Foley catheter is usually inserted. Mechanical ventilation is often necessary, as hyperventilation helps decrease ICP. The child may be placed in a comatose state

*Table 26–5. Staging of Reye Syndrome*

| Stage | Signs and Symptoms |
|-------|--------------------|
| I | Vomiting, lethargy, and confusion |
| | Rhythmic slowing of EEG |
| | Liver dysfunction |
| II | Disorientation, combativeness, hyperventilation, hallucinations |
| | No abnormal posturing |
| | Appropriate responses to painful stimuli |
| | Evidence of liver dysfunction |
| III | Coma |
| | Decorticate rigidity |
| | Hyperventilation |
| | Preservation of pupillary light and ocular reflexes |
| IV | Deepened coma |
| | Decerebrate rigidity |
| | Loss of oculocephalic reflexes |
| | Large, fixed pupils |
| | Evidence of brain stem dysfunction |
| V | Seizures |
| | Flaccidity |
| | Respiratory arrest |
| | Loss of deep tendon reflexes |

by using drugs such as phenobarbital. Pavulon may also be used to paralyze the skeletal muscles.

Hypoglycemia is controlled by using intravenous hypertonic glucose and NaCl. Young children do not tolerate low blood glucose levels, which can lead to seizures and permanent brain damage. Vitamin K may also be administered to correct abnormal blood clotting, which results from liver dysfunction.

### Nursing Assessment and Diagnosis

Assessment involves specialized nursing skills used in the intensive care setting, including monitoring arterial and central venous pressure, blood gases, and ICP. Nursing diagnoses related to the child with Reye syndrome might include the following:

- Potential for injury: cerebral, related to ICP
- Altered breathing patterns, related to neurological impairment
- Sensory/perceptual alterations, related to cerebral edema
- Ineffective family coping, related to life-threatening disease; care of child in intensive care setting

### Planning and Implementing Nursing Care

Children with Reye syndrome are cared for in the intensive care unit. Priorities in nursing management include assessment to aid in the early identification of the syn-drome; maintenance of the child's airway, breathing, circulation, and ICP; and seizure control. Additional nursing care considerations include fluid restriction and electrolyte balance, controlling hyperthermia, and monitoring vital signs. Detailed discussion of this specialized nursing care is beyond the scope of this text.

Because Reye syndrome occurs rapidly and unexpectedly, parents and the pediatric patient need careful explanations of the disease process and treatment. Nurses should reassure parents about the care being provided and help them cope with various feelings of guilt, anxiety, and fear. Parents often express strong fears related to the intensive care environment.

Prevention of this disease is an important nursing role. The American Academy of Pediatrics recommends that children with symptoms of viral infections (fever, GI upsets, chicken pox) not be given aspirin or aspirin compounds. Changes in the use of aspirin during viral illnesses may be responsible for the lowered incidence of Reye syndrome (Fenichel, 1988).

### Evaluating Nursing Care

Parents should understand the dangers in using aspirin in children and adolescents. *Aspirin should not be given to children or adolescents with viral infections.* Evaluation is based on the child's recovery and the presence of residual effects. The recovering child is supported physically and emotionally.

## Guillain-Barré Syndrome

Guillain-Barré syndrome (GBS), or postinfectious polyneuritis, is an acute neuromuscular disease that is characterized by progressive muscular weakness and paralysis. The exact etiology is unknown, but the disease most often follows a viral infection. In some children, GBS has occurred after immunization, usually involving viral vaccines. The disease most often affects children between the ages of 4 and 10 years. Boys and girls are affected equally. The incidence of the syndrome in children is less than that in adults but appears to be on the rise.

### Pathophysiology

The syndrome is thought to be a cell-mediated autoimmune response to the offending viral agent. An ascending polyneuritis occurs because of diffuse inflammation of peripheral nerves and subsequent segmented demyelination of the nerve fibers.

### Medical Diagnosis and Management

The onset of GBS usually occurs within 2 weeks of a viral illness. There is an abrupt onset of pain and weakness in the lower extremities, which continues in an ascending paralysis that usually peaks at 3 weeks. Cranial nerve paralysis involves nerves VII, IX, and X, resulting in facial weakness and difficulty in swallowing. Respiratory insufficiency may occur due to involvement of the respiratory muscles.

There are no specific diagnostic tests for GBS, but CSF typically reveals an elevated protein level. Diagnosis is based on clinical findings. Prognosis depends on the degree and severity of the polyneuritis. The disease is self-limiting, with about 90% of patients completely recovering. Recovery may take as long as 2 years. Respiratory paralysis is responsible for 10% to 15% of the mortality. Nerve remyelination occurs very slowly in a descending pattern and may take up to 2 years. A small number of patients experience a relapse.

There is no specific treatment for Guillain-Barré syndrome. Initially the child may be placed in the intensive care unit to monitor respiratory status, which may require tracheal intubation and mechanical ventilation. Corticosteroids have been used to treat GBS, but this is controversial.

## Nursing Assessment and Diagnosis

Assessment of the respiratory and circulatory systems is important. Vital signs must be carefully monitored for complications. Neurological assessment should include evaluation of motor strength and cranial nerve impairment. Muscle strength is assessed by having the child squeeze the examiner's hands, and by raising the arms and then the legs as high as possible. Nurses should also test all extremities for deep tendon reflexes. Facial nerve paralysis can be assessed by asking the child to close the eyelids tightly, and then noting the ease of opening. Eye movements and pupillary responses are also observed.

Nursing diagnoses related to the child with Guillain-Barré syndrome might include:

- Impaired physical mobility, related to paralysis
- Impaired gas exchange, related to abdominal and thoracic muscle involvement
- Sensory/perceptual alterations, related to peripheral neuritis; paresthesia
- Impaired swallowing, related to cranial nerve involvement
- Potential impaired skin integrity, related to immobility
- Altered nutrition: less than body requirements, related to difficulty in swallowing
- Pain, related to nerve root involvement

## Planning and Implementing Nursing Care

Nursing care during the acute stage focuses on respiratory and cardiac status. Vital signs must be closely monitored to detect changes in blood pressure, cardiac status, and impending cardiovascular collapse (shock). Respiratory rate, depth, and pattern are noted, and tidal volumes may be measured. Optimal respiratory function is maintained through turning and chest pulmonary therapy. If intuba-

tion or a tracheostomy is performed, appropriate care is instituted.

The child may complain of muscle cramping, and may be hypersensitive to touch. Nurses must be careful in handling the child and limit necessary movement. Joint contractures can be prevented by creating a plan of care that includes regular range of motion exercises, splinting, and supports as necessary to maintain correct anatomic positioning of the child's body.

Maintaining adequate nutrition may include nasogastric tube feedings, due to impaired swallowing. Kidney function and urinary output is managed through adequate hydration, which may include hyperalimentation. Catheterization is employed if urine retention is evident.

Nurses should plan for the recovery period, which can be quite lengthy. Plans should be made for keeping up with school work and developmentally appropriate activities. Nurses can assist in establishing a rehabilitative program and coordinating the various roles of the health care team involved in the child's care.

## Evaluating Nursing Care

Evaluation is based on the recuperative process and the child's return to as normal a life as possible. The child should be able to accept the residual disability with minimal effects on body image. The family is able to accept the child and return to a normal pattern of function.

# Headaches

Headaches occur in children for a variety of reasons. Tension headaches are a common recurring type of headache, but recurring headaches in children may be due to underlying pathology. Underlying causes can include visual disturbances, intracranial masses, and vascular problems.

Migraine headaches are recurring headaches usually occurring in older children and adolescents.

## Pathophysiology

The pathophysiological mechanism of migraine headaches is not completely known. It is believed that the headache is caused by abnormal constriction followed by dilation of the intracranial arteries.

## Medical Diagnosis and Management

Migraine headaches occur in sudden periodic episodes. The child may complain of intense throbbing pain across the temporal area or unilaterally in the frontal regions. Abdominal pains, vomiting, dizziness, and intolerance of light may accompany the headache. Precipitating factors can include stress, fatigue, hunger, or foods and drugs containing tyramine (chocolate, coffee, tea, cola, alcohol, ripened cheeses, nuts, citrus fruits). Attacks in children are usually shorter than in adults. Sleep will sometimes shorten or stop the attack in children. Attacks may last 6 to 12 hours.

Diagnosis is made through medical history and physical examination, as well as CT scan, EEG, and x-rays of the skull. (The scans are usually done to rule out other neurological problems.) Relief may be attained by the use of analgesics (aspirin or acetaminophen). If these analgesics do not relieve the headaches, ergotamine (an α-adrenergic blocking agent) and caffeine may be prescribed. Some children with severe, frequently recurring migraine headaches may be given anticonvulsant medications such as Dilantin.

Supportive therapy, such as rest in a dark, quiet environment or biofeedback, may be used to minimize the associated symptoms. Migraine headaches in children may either disappear at puberty or continue into adulthood. Prognosis is favorable once precipitating factors are known and avoided and an effective medication is determined and prescribed.

### Nursing Assessment and Diagnosis

Assessment includes a detailed family and psychosocial history. A family history of migraines is often present. A description and location of the pain should be explored, as well as any precipitating factors. Classic migraine is seen more often in adolescents and adults and may include a preceding visual aura. The headache is throbbing in nature and unilaterally frontal in location. Abdominal pain, photophobia, and vomiting are also often present. Common migraine is more common in children and usually does not involve an aura.

Nursing diagnoses related to the child with migraine headaches might include the following:

- Pain, related to mechanisms involving intracranial arteries
- Anxiety, related to anticipation of recurring headaches
- Sensory/perceptual alterations, related to pathophysiological mechanisms

### Planning and Implementing Nursing Care

The nursing care plan for children with migraine headaches should include education of the family to eliminate or minimize factors that precipitate the migraine headache, and encouragement of a balanced diet and adequate rest. The family will need assistance in knowing which foods to eliminate from the child's diet. Nurses should reassure families about the benign nature of the headaches.

### Evaluating Nursing Care

Evaluation is based on recognition of precipitating factors and measures instituted to avoid onset of migraine. Evalua-

tion measures also include effectiveness and speed of relief by medication.

## Attention Deficit Disorder

A variety of labels have been used to describe problems of childhood that interfere with socialization, learning, and general development. These labels include learning disabled, minimal brain dysfunction, hyperactivity, cerebral dysfunction, and perceptual deficit syndrome. Attention deficit disorder (ADD) is the accepted term for these problematic behaviors. The syndrome is divided into three subtypes: ADD with hyperactivity, ADD without hyperactivity, and ADD residual type.

### Pathophysiology

The exact etiology of ADD is unknown. There are several theories, including a genetic link, birth trauma causing anoxia, prematurity, neurochemical imbalance, and immune allergic response.

### Medical Diagnosis and Management

Signs and symptoms of ADD vary, but inattention and impulsivity are the prominent symptoms. The disorder is often not diagnosed until the child enters school. The discipline of school makes it difficult for the child to integrate into a classroom setting. The child is easily distracted and unable to follow through on instructions. The child with ADD typically displays temper tantrums, stubbornness, negativism, and low self-esteem. The child is very often characterized as hyperactive. Parents often comment that the child never sits still.

"Soft" neurological signs, such as clumsiness, may be present. EEG may be abnormal. Some children with ADD may have other learning disorders such as dyslexia or visual–motor deficits.

The child usually undergoes physical and psychological testing in an attempt to pinpoint the source of his or her ADD. Therapy includes a combination of counseling, special education programs, and medication. Special diets (Feingold, 1975) are often used and advocated by parents, but these have not been supported by care providers. Counseling includes the entire family. The family needs to know how to minimize the negative behavior of the child and reinforce the child's positive behaviors.

Medications have been used increasingly in children with ADD. Psychoactive drugs such as methylphenidate hydrochloride (Ritalin), dextroamphetamine (Dexedrine), and pemoline (Cylert) have been prescribed for children with hyperactivity, with varying degrees of success in increasing attention span and decreasing impulsiveness. These medications are CNS stimulants, but through "paradoxical response" they act to calm the child. The child needs to be evaluated before and during the course of medication therapy to ensure that the drug is having the desired effect with minimal side effects, which can include anorexia and insomnia. Close follow-up allows the dosage to be adjusted so that the lowest effective dose is used. The medication should be discontinued in children who do not show improvement in their behavior after 2 months of therapy.

### Nursing Assessment and Diagnosis

Family history often reveals learning difficulty or childhood hyperactivity in one of the parents. Prenatal history should be reviewed for alcohol abuse, and birth history should include questions about prematurity or birth apnea, as these children have an increased risk for ADD. Assessment should include questions regarding enuresis and encopresis, since these problems are also associated with ADD. History should also explore how parents and the family deal with the child. In addition to parental descriptions of the child, assessment may also include information from the child's school teachers.

Nursing diagnoses related to the child with attention deficit disorder might include the following:

- Impaired social interaction, related to inability to interact with peers
- Self-esteem disturbance, related to behavior
- Ineffective family coping: compromised, related to inability to deal with the child

### Planning and Implementing Nursing Care

It is important for the nurse to assess the family situation before developing a plan of care. The nurse can help the family with concrete suggestions that can help control the child's behavior (Table 26-6). Nurses may also assist the family by working with counselors to initiate a behavior modification program for the child. Parental involvement is necessary for successful treatment. The management of attention deficit disorders in children is best accomplished by a team approach. Team members include physicians, nurses, counselors, speech therapists, and special education teachers.

Nurses can also help parents deal with various feelings of frustration, anger, and guilt. Parents may need referral to mental health professionals. The family also needs information on national and local organizations that can provide support and information for families of children with ADD. The Association for Children and Adults with Learning Disabilities (4156 Library Rd., Pittsburgh, PA 15234) is one such organization.

### Evaluating Nursing Care

Effectiveness of medication therapy with minimal side effects is an important evaluation factor. Parents should recognize and accept their normal feelings toward the child. Families should function in a normal pattern. The

### Table 26–6. Suggestions for Managing Children with Attention Deficit Disorders

1. Decrease the child's activity level.
   a. Decrease noise level.
   b. Avoid situations that increase excitement.
   c. Decrease distractions.
2. Monitor behaviors, control environment.
   a. Set limitations.
   b. Limit external stimuli.
   c. Enforce rules.
   d. Make sure the child knows the consequences of breaking rules.
   e. Establish regular routines for eating, sleeping, and homework.
   f. Give one direction at a time.
   g. Give the child simple tasks to complete.
   h. Divide tasks into small parts.
3. Increase self-esteem.
   a. Be generous with praise for positive behavior—e.g., completed tasks, homework.
   b. Encourage patience through simple games.
4. Monitor the child's school performance.
   a. Take advantage of special education teachers and other school resources.
   b. Don't assume that the school system will have the resources to provide the appropriate educational environment.
5. Maintain medical therapy.
   a. Give medication at prescribed dosages and times.
   b. Report any adverse effects to the physician.
   c. Follow elimination diets precisely.

child should reach optimal learning capabilities, have a positive self-concept, and be involved in normal peer relationships.

## Brain Tumors

Brain tumors are the most common childhood solid tumor and the second most common childhood cancer after leukemia (Finlay, 1987). They are most commonly seen in the 5- to 10-year age group. Brain tumors are classified by histology and location into two groups. Approximately two thirds of childhood brain tumors are infratentorial (below the tentorium), which includes the cerebellum, fourth ventricle, and the brain stem. Supratentorial brain tumors involve all structures above the tentorium cerebri. The majority of childhood brain tumors are gliomas, originating in the glial cells, the supporting structural cells of the central nervous system.

### Pathophysiology

Brain tumors enlarge and obstruct circulation of the CSF, resulting in increased ICP. As the tumor grows, it also exerts pressure on nervous system components.

## Medical Diagnosis and Management

Symptoms are usually related to the location of the tumor. The most common symptom in children with brain tumors is headache. The headaches are usually intermittent and most commonly occur in the morning after the child wakes up; they also occur with coughing, sneezing, and straining during a bowel movement. When vomiting is present, it occurs more frequently in the morning after awakening. The vomiting usually occurs without nausea and may be projectile. Ataxia (lack of muscle coordination) is most commonly found with cerebellar tumors, as are hypotonia and decreased reflexes.

Cerebral tumors are manifested by behavioral changes in mentality and affect. Changes in dexterity, weakness in the lower extremities, spasticity, paralysis, and slurred speech are indications of cerebral involvement. Seizures may also be present. Increased ICP and brain stem tumors can present with disturbances in vital signs (decreased respirations, decreased pulse rate, or increased blood pressure with a widening pulse pressure). Visual problems (diplopia, strabismus, papilledema, or nystagmus) may also be indicative of a brain tumor.

Diagnosis is based on the child's history, presenting symptoms, and a careful and complete neurological examination. Brain tumors can be classified according to the histology of the malignant cell, whether the tumor is benign or malignant, and the degree of differentiation between the tumor and surrounding tissue. Diagnostic testing includes CT and MRI. Angiography may be performed to detail the tumor's blood supply. Myelogram and electroencephalogram may also be used. Lumbar puncture is *not* done if increased ICP is suspected, because this could precipitate brain herniation, a life-threatening complication.

Surgery is the therapy of choice in children with brain tumors. Prognosis is greatly improved if total excision of the tumor is possible. Some tumors cannot be excised; others can be only partially excised, depending on location, size, and whether they are diffuse or well differentiated. Radiation therapy is used when the tumor is not surgically accessible or when the tumor cannot be completely resected. Radiation therapy is commonly used to treat medulloblastomas and brain stem gliomas. A positive response to radiation therapy depends on the location of the tumor and the child's toleration of the treatments.

Chemotherapy is also used in the treatment of malignant brain tumors. The type of medication used depends on the type of tumor, its location, and the child's tolerance of the medication. Chemotherapy has not been as effective with brain tumors as with other malignancies because many of the chemotherapeutic agents do not readily cross the blood–brain barrier, which is necessary if they are to destroy brain tumor cells. One or multiple drugs may be used as part of the chemotherapy protocol. Drugs most frequently used include vincristine, cisplatin, arabinoside cytosine (Ara-C), carmustine (BiCNU or BCNU), lomustine (CCNU), and intrathecal methotrexate. Corticosteroids may be used initially to reduce cerebral edema.

## Nursing Assessment and Diagnosis

The role of the nurse in caring for a child with a brain tumor involves careful assessment of the child, observing for signs and symptoms of the tumor, preparing the child and family for the diagnostic tests and surgery, supporting the family, caring for the child postoperatively, and preparation and execution of a discharge plan. Discharge planning may include provisions for radiation and/or chemotherapy. Nursing diagnoses related to the child with a brain tumor might include the following:

- Body image disturbance, related to symptoms or shaving of the child's head for surgery
- Potential for injury: physiological, related to symptoms of the brain tumor (ataxia, diplopia), seizures, bone marrow depression
- Altered tissue perfusion, cerebral: increased ICP
- Pain, related to surgical incision, headache
- Potential for infection: postoperative, related to surgical intervention, bone marrow depression with chemotherapy and/or radiation therapy
- Ineffective family coping, related to symptoms and diagnosis

## Planning and Implementing Nursing Care

*Preoperative.*  Nursing care centers on preparing the child and family for the diagnostic procedures. The child and family should be told what to expect pre- and postoperatively. Because of the anxiety preoperatively, information should be simple and based on appropriate level of understanding. A drawing of the brain can be used to clarify explanations. Nurses should repeat information during the postoperative period.

The child's head will be shaved, and nurses can help in preparing the child for this procedure to make it less traumatic. Showing the child how other children have used scarves or wigs may be helpful. The child should be assured that the hair will grow back.

Nurses should discuss postoperative appearance with the child and parents. The child should understand that the head will be bandaged when he or she awakens after surgery. There may be considerable facial edema, and the child may have a headache. If care in the intensive care unit is planned, the family should be oriented to the unit before the surgery.

*Postoperative.*  Vital signs and neurological status are monitored frequently during the first 24 to 48 hours after surgery. The child is positioned to prevent pressure on the operative site. The child's head may be elevated without pillows to aid in reducing facial edema and promoting venous drainage from the cranial vault. Eye care helps prevent corneal ulceration and drying. Nurses must watch for signs of cerebral edema and increased ICP. Usual postoperative nursing care involves monitoring respiratory function, observing for and preventing infection, monitoring intake and output, and maintaining fluid and electrolyte balance.

Headaches are usually managed with analgesics. Sedatives and hypnotics are avoided because they mask the child's neurological status. The child should be observed for the onset of seizure activity. Anticonvulsants may be used. The child's surgical dressing is closely monitored. If drainage is noted on the dressing when the child enters the ICU, the dressing is marked and monitored for any new bleeding or drainage. New or continued drainage should be reported immediately.

If radiation or chemotherapy is to be initiated after surgery, the child and his family must be prepared for these treatment modalities. Radiation therapy will not be started until the surgical site is healed.

Although the prognosis for children with brain tumors continues to improve, significant numbers of children die each year because of CNS tumors. The family needs support in dealing with the uncertainty of the prognosis and the possibility that the child will not survive. Family support groups are helpful in dealing with the problems of radiation therapy, chemotherapy, and the uncertain prognosis.

If the child continues to have neurological deficits postoperatively, the family will need to be taught to care for the child. This may include managing severe sensory, motor, and cognitive deficits, and possibly a seizure disorder. In spite of the child's deficits, the family should encourage independence and self care appropriate to the child's capabilities.

### Evaluating Nursing Care

The child's recovery and degree of impairment are important evaluation points. The family should demonstrate an understanding of the treatment, consequences, and probable side effects. The family should accept the child and allow the child to resume normal activities as much as possible. The family should understand the long-term prognosis for their child and seek appropriate support as needed.

## Seizure Disorders (Epilepsy)

A seizure can be defined as a disturbance in normal brain function resulting from abnormal electrical discharge in the brain. This uncontrolled electrical brain activity can cause loss of consciousness, uncontrolled movement of the body, and changes in sensation, behavior, and the autonomic system. The numerous underlying causes of seizures in childhood are outlined in Table 26-7. The term "epilepsy" refers to a condition in which the child experi-

*Table 26–7.  Underlying Causes of Seizures by Age*

| Age | Cause |
| --- | --- |
| Infancy | Prenatal or perinatal trauma or hypoxia |
| | Infections |
| | Congenital malformations |
| | Metabolic imbalances, hematomas |
| Childhood | Central nervous system infections |
| | Lead poisoning |
| | Head injuries |
| Adolescence | Drug abuse |
| | Alcohol misuse |
| | Intracranial tumors |
| | Medications |
| | Toxins |

ences chronic, recurrent seizures. Many seizure disorders in children are classified as idiopathic epilepsy because underlying pathology cannot be determined.

Approximately 2.5 million Americans (1% of the population) are affected with recurrent seizures. Of the population under 20 years of age, 2% have recurring seizures. The incidence for developing epilepsy is highest in the first year of life, and there appears to be a genetic predisposition.

### Pathophysiology

Seizures result from overly active and hypersensitive abnormal neurons in the brain. These nerve cells can produce abnormal, excessive electrical discharges, causing a seizure. Location of these abnormal cells and the pattern of abnormal discharges determines the clinical manifestations of the seizure. During a seizure there is an increased need for oxygen and glucose. A seizure also results in increased $P_{CO_2}$ levels, increase in lactic acid, and increased cerebral blood flow.

### Medical Diagnosis and Management

Seizures are classified into two major categories: generalized and partial. Generalized seizures involve both hemispheres of the brain. These seizures are bilateral and symmetrical and may or may not involve prodromal syndromes. Partial or focal seizures involve only a limited area of the cerebral cortex. These seizures may be simple or complex. The International League Against Epilepsy has developed a classification schema for seizures that is widely recognized (Bancaud, Henriksen, Rubena-Donnadieu, Seino, & Dreifuss, 1981). Table 26-8 outlines the classifications and clinical manifestations of epileptic seizures.

Diagnosis of a seizure disorder is made by observation or detailed history of seizure activity, the use of an

*Table 26–8. Classification and Clinical Manifestations of Seizures*

| Class | Clinical Manifestations |
|---|---|
| I. Generalized. All generalized seizures are accompanied by loss of consciousness. | |
|   A. Tonic/clonic seizure (grand mal); major motor | *Tonic phase*—rigidity, extension of extremities, jaw fixed. Cessation of respiration, pupils dilated, nonreactive.<br>*Clonic phase*—rhythmic jerking of all extremities, autonomic symptoms. Child may be incontinent.<br>*Postictal phase*—flaccid muscles, amnesia relating to seizure. Child will usually sleep following the seizure. |
|   B. Tonic seizure | *Tonic phase*—with loss of consciousness, autonomic system involvement may last a few seconds to several minutes. |
|   C. Clonic seizure | *Clonic phase*—lasting several minutes. |
|   D. Minor motor; Atonic | Sudden loss of muscle tone followed by postictal confusion, loss of consciousness. |
|   E. Minor motor; Myoclonic | Generalized short, abrupt muscle contractions lasting only a few seconds. Brief period of unconsciousness. Seizures may be clustered (several occurring together). The child may have many myoclonic seizures in one day. Each child will have characteristic movements particular for him or her. |
|   F. Infantile spasm; Jack-knife seizure | Brief flexion of the neck, trunk and/or legs lasting only seconds. The child may experience hundreds each day. Infantile spasms usually subside in late infancy but may convert to generalized tonic/clonic seizures in later childhood. |
|   G. Absence seizure (petit mal) Variations include:<br>    a. With a tonic phase<br>    b. With an atonic phase<br>    c. With automatisms | Brief period of unconsciousness (lasting seconds), which may be accompanied by atonia or clonus. The child may display only a transient staring episode.<br>Automatisms may occur, such as lip smacking or eye blinking. The child may have hundreds of petit mal seizures a day. Absence seizures can be mistaken for learning disabilities or inattention. |
| II. Partial seizure (focal seizure) | Begins in a localized area of the brain. Consciousness is usually maintained during the seizure. |
|   A. Simple partial (focal motor or focal sensory seizures) variations include:<br>    1. With a focal motor component<br>    2. With a sensory component<br>    3. With focal somatosensory signs<br>    4. With autonomic signs<br>    5. With psychic signs | Consciousness is usually maintained in simple partial seizures.<br>*Motor*—abnormal movement of an arm or leg or both (Jacksonian march). May be on one side of the face, followed by additional muscles on the body.<br>*Somatosensory*—tingling, seeing flashing lights, olfactory or auditory sensations, metallic taste.<br>*Autonomic signs*—tachycardia, sweating, flushing, pallor, nausea.<br>*Psychic*—déjà vu, anger, fear, or hallucinations may be experienced. |
|   B. Complex partial seizure | One type begins as a simple partial seizure and progresses to unconsciousness (brief).<br>The child may have motor sensory, psychic, somatosensory, or automatism signs.<br>In another type the child loses consciousness at the outset and may have no other symptom or may have motor, sensory, psychic, or somatosensory symptoms or automatisms.<br>The period of unconsciousness may be recognized by observers or may be so brief that only the child is aware of it. |
|   C. Partial seizure evolving into generalized seizures | Simple or complex partial seizures can progress to generalized seizures. |
| III. Unclassified seizures | Seizures are usually labeled as unclassified when there are insufficient data to label the seizure. Neonatal seizures are very often labeled as unclassified. |

electroencephalogram (EEG) to document changes in the brain's electrical activity, and a careful physical examination to determine presence of pathology. CT or MRI may be performed to detect the presence of lesions in the brain. Generalized or grand mal seizures are relatively easy to identify and document. Absence or petit mal and focal seizures are more difficult to document both by history and EEG findings.

Each type of seizure progresses through a series of phases. The most common phases include tonic, clonic, atonic, and postictal. Not all types of seizures will include all of the phases.

*Aura.* Some children with generalized and psycho-motor seizures may experience a warning just prior to the seizure (aura). The aura may consist of a visual or auditory sensation, nausea, vomiting, or weakness. It is difficult to determine if young children experience auras because they are not always able to associate the sensation with the impending seizure and may not have any recollection of the aura after the seizure.

*Tonic Phase.* In this phase, the child loses consciousness, the muscles are contracted, the jaw is locked, breathing ceases, and the bowel and bladder may empty. The child's back may arch, elbows, wrists and hands flex, and the legs hyperextend. The activity of the autonomic system increases during the tonic phase of a seizure and is manifested by increased perspiration, dilating pupils, increased salivation, and an increase in pulse rate and blood pressure. The tonic phase of a seizure can last from 10 to 30 seconds.

*Clonic Phase.* This phase may involve mild trembling of the child's body to bilateral violent jerking movements. The clonic phase will gradually subside and may last from 30 seconds to one minute.

*Atonic Phase.* The atonic phase during a seizure is manifested by a sudden loss of muscle tone. The child's arm or head will drop or the child will suddenly fall to the ground.

*Postictal Phase.* This occurs at the end of a seizure, primarily after generalized or grand mal seizures. As the tonic/clonic phases subside, the child will take deep breaths. The increased autonomic function ceases. The child will move in and out of a semiconscious or unconscious state. If left alone the child will sleep for several hours. Upon awakening he may have no memory of the seizure. Headache and mental confusion may also be present.

*Status Epilepticus.* In most childhood seizure disorders, a seizure will occur that is singular and self-limiting, lasting only a few minutes. In contrast, status epilepticus involves recurrent, continuous, generalized seizure activity. The seizures recur so frequently that there is no recovery between seizures. The child does not regain consciousness, and the seizures occur in rapid succession. There is a danger of circulatory and respiratory arrest. Status epilepticus is considered a medical emergency. A child in status epilepticus can suffer brain damage and may die if untreated.

The child will need aggressive management with anti-convulsive agents, airway maintenance, and acceptable oxygen saturation levels. The child may require oxygen administration, suctioning, and the establishment of an intravenous line for administering anticonvulsants. Drugs of choice for status epilepticus include Valium, Dilantin, phenobarbital, and dexamethasone (Decadron).

Management of seizures by anticonvulsant medications remains the treatment of choice. The regulation of a child's seizure disorder takes time in order to determine the correct drug or combination of drugs and the correct dosage. The child is started on one drug, and the dosage is adjusted based on seizure control and minimization of side effects. If the first drug does not maintain the child completely without seizure activity even after the maximum tolerated dose is reached, another drug may be used or a second drug may be added until the child, ideally, is seizure free. The child's medications may have to be changed or adjusted as he grows or if tolerance or drug toxicity to the medication develops. Drug levels in the blood are closely monitored. Table 26-9 describes the indications, side effects, and nursing implications of the most commonly used anticonvulsant drugs for children with seizure disorders.

There are a small number of children with epilepsy in whom anticonvulsant drugs do not control seizures. These patients may be candidates for surgery. The purpose of the surgery is to locate the epileptogenic area (area of the brain causing the seizures) and to excise that area without causing further neurological deficits. The surgery may involve the excision of a small area, a lobe of the brain, or a hemispherectomy in children with hemiplegia or an atrophied cerebral hemisphere. The procedure is still relatively rare, and only a small number of children meet the criteria for surgical intervention. One study (Brewer & Sperling, 1988) found that temporal lobectomy—focal resective surgery done for uncontrolled partial epilepsy—resulted in improvement or cure in as many as 90% of treated individuals.

Diet therapy is also used to control recurrent seizures. A ketogenic diet is used to induce a state of ketosis by the use of a high-fat, low-carbohydrate, low-protein diet. The mechanism by which this state of ketosis reduces seizure activity is not known. The diet is not very palatable and is relatively difficult to maintain. It is used most often in young children with absence (petit mal) or myoclonic seizures that have not responded to medications.

## Nursing Assessment and Diagnosis

A thorough history is often the most important factor in assessment of the child with a seizure disorder. Nurses should question about any birth-related problems, such as infection, trauma, or metabolic problems. History of seizures in other family members is important. Information should also be obtained about the child's seizure activity and any possible causes of seizure episodes. Nursing diagnoses related to the child with seizures might include the following:

• Potential for injury, related to seizure activity
• Ineffective individual coping, related to loss of control, fear of injury

## Table 26–9. Antiepileptic/Anticonvulsive Therapy Agents

| Drug | Indication | Side Effects | Nursing Implications |
|---|---|---|---|
| Carbamazepine (Tegretal) | Generalized grand mal, complex partial, focal motor seizures, mixed seizures | Drowsiness, dry mouth, vomiting, double vision, leukopenia, GI upset, thrombocytopenia | See general considerations, below. There may be dizziness and drowsiness with initial doses. This should subside within 3–14 days. |
| Ethosuximide (Zarontin) | Absence seizures (petit mal) | Dry mouth, anorexia, dizziness, headache, nausea, vomiting, GI upset, lethargy, bone marrow depression | See general considerations, below. Use with caution in hepatic or renal disease. |
| Clonazepam (Klonopin) | Absence seizures, myoclonic (petit mal) | Double vision, drowsiness, increased salivation, changes in behavior, bone marrow depression | See general considerations, below. Obtain periodic liver function tests and CBC. Monitor for over-sedation. |
| Paraldehyde | Refractory generalized tonic–clonic seizures (grand mal), status epilepticus | Possible pulmonary edema or hemorrhage, skin rash. Respiratory depression | Use cautiously in children with asthma. Inject IM in deep muscle mass to prevent tissue sloughing. When giving orally, give with juice or milk to mask the taste and smell. Physical dependency may result when used for extended periods of time. Urine testing may be false positive for ketones. |
| Phensuximide (Milcontin) | Absence seizures (petit mal) | Pancytopenia, muscle weakness, headache, nausea, vomiting, anorexia, ataxia, renal damage, hematuria | See general considerations, below. Obtain urine and liver function tests every 4–6 months. May increase incidence of generalized tonic/clonic seizures if used alone to treat children with mixed seizures. |
| Paramethadione (Paradione) | Refractory absence seizures (petit mal) | Bone marrow depression, drowsiness, exfoliative dermatitis, weight loss, bleeding gums | See general considerations, below. Dilute oral solution with water (65% alcohol). Monthly liver function and urine tests should be done. |
| Phenobarbital (Luminol) | Tonic–clonic, generalized | Drowsiness, alteration in sleep patterns, irritability, respiratory and cardiac depression, restlessness, headache | See general considerations, below. Alcohol can enhance the effects of phenobarbital. Blood studies and liver tests are necessary with prolonged use. |
| Phenytoin (Dilantin) | Tonic–clonic generalized, complex and simple partial | Double vision, blurred vision, slurred speech, nystagmus, ataxia, gingival hyperplasia, hirsutism, cardiac arrhythmias, bone marrow depression | See general considerations, below. Alcohol, antacids, and folic acid decrease the effect of Dilantin. Instruct the patient or the parents to notify the dentist that he or she is taking Dilantin in order to monitor hyperplasia of the gums. Inform the patient or parents that the drug may color the urine pink to red–brown. |

*(continued)*

*Table 26–9. Antiepileptic/Anticonvulsive Therapy Agents (Continued)*

| Drug | Indication | Side Effects | Nursing Implications |
|---|---|---|---|
| Primidone (Mysoline) | Tonic/clonic generalized, complex and simple partial seizures | Behavior changes, drowsiness, hyperactivity, ataxia. Bone marrow depression | See general considerations, below. Adverse effects are the same as for phenobarbital. Sedation and dizziness may be severe during initial therapy—dosage may need to be adjusted by the physician. Mysoline partially converts to phenobarbital and should be used cautiously with phenobarbital. |
| Valproic acid (Depakene) | Tonic/clonic, myoclonic absence seizures, mixed seizures | Nausea, vomiting or increased appetite, tremors, elevated liver enzymes, constipation, headaches, depression, lymphocytosis, leukopenia, increased prothrombin time | See general considerations, below. Physical dependency may result when used for prolonged period. Tablets and capsules should be taken whole. Elixir should be taken alone, not mixed with carbonated beverages. Increased toxicity may occur with administration of salicylates (aspirin). |
| Corticotropin hormone (ACTH) | Infantile spasms | Gastric irritation, immunosuppression, hypertension, sodium and fluid retention, impaired wound healing | See general considerations, below. Treatment should be preceded by tests of hypersensitivity and adrenal responsiveness. If administering gel, warm to room temperature. Give slowly, deep IM. Injection is painful. Parents must be taught to give the injections. Diet high in protein to counteract nitrogen loss is necessary. |

**General Nursing Considerations With Anticonvulsant Therapy**

General nursing considerations with anticonvulsant therapy that apply to all or most of drugs given to children include:

1. Warn the patient and family that patients should avoid activities that require alertness and complex psychomotor coordination (heavy equipment, power lawn mowers, climbing).
2. Medication can be given with meals to minimize gastric irritation.
3. The anticonvulsant medications should not be discontinued abruptly as this can precipitate status epilepticus.
4. Anticonvulsant medications generally have a cumulative effect, both therapeutically and adversely.
5. Alcohol ingestion increases the effects of anticonvulsant drugs, exaggerating the CNS depression.
6. Many of the drugs can cause bone marrow depression (leukopenia, thrombocytopenia, neutropenia, megaloblastic anemia). Regular CBCs are necessary to evaluate bone marrow production.
7. The child receives periodic blood tests to determine drug levels in order to monitor therapeutic levels as opposed to toxic blood levels.

- Altered family processes, related to guilt, overprotection of child, concerns regarding medications, inability to meet child's developmental needs
- Noncompliance: treatment program, related to adolescent's struggle for independence

## Planning and Implementing Nursing Care

The nurse plays a major role in maintaining the safety and well-being of a child during a seizure. Precautions to avoid injury during seizure may include having the child wear a helmet when out of bed and providing padded siderails. The child should not be restrained during a seizure. Furniture and other objects should be moved away from the seizing patient. Nothing should be placed in the child's mouth; serious damage can be done by trying to force a padded tongue blade into the mouth during the tonic phase of a seizure. The child's airway can be maintained by placing him in a supine position or a sidelying position, hyperextending his neck, and performing a jaw thrust to open the airway. The sidelying position will also allow secretions to drain from the child's mouth. Loosen clothing that is tight around the neck and place a soft pad under the child's head. Oxygen may be given during a seizure if the child's skin color changes or there is difficulty in breathing. Observation and documentation of the child's seizure is a major responsibility of the nurse. Table 26-10 outlines the important areas of observation and documentation involving a seizure.

During the process of diagnosis and regulation of the

*Table 26–10. Responsibilities in Observing and Documenting Seizures*

Observe and document:
1. Events that occurred immediately before the onset of the seizure
   _____ Presence of an aura
   _____ Flashing light, unusual smell or taste
2. Cardiorespiratory status
   _____ Irregular respirations
   _____ Apnea
   _____ Pallor
   _____ Cyanosis
3. Progression of the seizure through the body
   _____ Body part first affected by the seizure
   _____ Areas of the body affected by the seizure (one or both sides of the body)
4. Type and character of abnormal body activity
   _____ Jerking movements of the trunk and extremities (note which extremities involved)
   _____ Stiffening of the body (tonic)
   _____ Eye movements—deviation right or left
   _____ Head deviation
5. Change in sensorium
   _____ Change in or loss of consciousness
   _____ Point during the seizure when level of consciousness changed
   _____ Degree of orientation during and after the seizure
   _____ Presence of drowsiness or fatigue post-seizure
6. Bowel and bladder function
   _____ Presence of incontinence during or after seizure
7. Duration of the seizure
8. Presence of any abnormal neurological symptoms post-seizure
   _____ Headache
   _____ Behavior changes
   _____ Drowsiness, lethargy
   _____ Aphasia
   _____ Muscle weakness, hemiplegia (usually temporary)

child's seizures, the family needs explanations of diagnostic procedures and treatment, especially regarding anticonvulsant drug therapy. Most important in the teaching plan is assessing the family's knowledge about seizures and epilepsy. A teaching plan can then be devised that will help to dispel the misinformation and myths the family may have about epilepsy. The family is taught about what happens during a seizure and what they must do to protect their child. The family should be instructed to maintain a record of the child's seizures.

Another important aspect of the teaching plan is teaching the family about the anticonvulsant medications, making sure they know the correct dosages. If suspensions are used with young children, the nurse should make sure the parents are drawing up the correct amounts of the liquid. It is important that the medication be given at the same time each day and the prescribed number of times per day. The nurse should stress to the parents that the child's anticonvulsant medications should not be stopped abruptly, as this may precipitate status epilepticus. Regulation of seizures is not possible unless the child receives his medication as prescribed. Parents need to adhere to the prescribed therapy. If the child experiences nausea and vomiting and is unable to take the medicine, his physician should be notified.

The family's verbal and nonverbal behavior should be assessed to determine the degree of anxiety. The family should be encouraged to ask questions. The nurse can assist the family in identifying activities that reduce stress and increase their coping abilities. Research has found that parents with positive attitudes about their child's epilepsy have better coping behaviors (Austin & McDermott, 1988).

The family must understand any lifestyle adjustments required by the condition, as well as any limitations on the child's activity. Parents need to be encouraged not to overprotect the child. The child with a medically controlled seizure disorder can engage in most normal childhood activities. Independence should be encouraged, along with safety precautions as appropriate during such activities as swimming or climbing. Siblings must also be included when working with the family. Parents need to understand some of the feelings siblings may experience and try to keep their lives as normal as possible.

Support groups often help families cope with the anxiety that accompanies a seizure disorder. The child or adolescent with a seizure disorder may have the added stress of poor self-concept and the feeling of being different. These feelings are reinforced after a seizure, especially if it occurs in a peer group. The child may feel inferior and insecure. Encouraging the child and family to talk about such occurrences helps to reduce the negative feelings.

Adolescents may encounter additional stress with peer pressure to experiment with alcohol and drugs and with restrictions in obtaining a driver's license. Concern about future employment and anxieties involving dating place additional stress on the adolescent with a seizure disorder. These adolescents may rebel by stopping medication, denying the condition, and ignoring established restrictions. Nurses can assist adolescents to identify peer support groups to deal with these frustrations and concerns.

### Evaluating Nursing Care

Control of the child's seizure activity is a major evaluation point. The family and child should understand the importance of taking medications as directed and display compliance. The family should accept the child's disorder, and encourage the child to resume as normal a life as possible. Parents should demonstrate care of the child during a seizure. The child should accept the disorder and display a positive approach.

# Neurological Problems of Adolescents

## Head Injuries

Head injury is one of the most common causes of disability and death in children. Over one million children suffer closed head injuries in the United States each year. The term "head injury" encompasses a wide range of injuries, on a continuum of severity from a mild bump to a severely brain-damaging injury.

Head injuries in children are most often caused by motor vehicle accidents, falls, physical abuse, or birth trauma. The etiology of the injury is closely related to the age of the child. Falls are the most common cause of head injury in children under 2 years of age. Child abuse is a major cause of severe head injury in the infant and young child. In the older child and adolescent the most common causes of head injury are accidents involving bicycles or motor vehicles.

### Pathophysiology

Trauma results from physical force impacting on the skull and its contents. Head injuries are classified as scalp injuries, skull (cranial vault) injuries, and brain injuries. Brain injury is the most serious type of head injury, one that can leave permanent motor, sensory, and cognitive deficits. Scalp and skull injuries very often accompany brain injury, although it is possible for a child to have a serious brain injury with little or no evidence of scalp or skull injury.

Scalp injuries may involve a significant blood loss with seemingly minor lacerations due to the scalp's increased vascularity. Scalp injuries are caused by tension to and tearing of the scalp. The severity of the injury is dependent on the type of object causing the injury and the speed and force with which the object contacts the scalp.

Skull injuries result from acceleration–deceleration trauma. In skull injuries the amount of deformation will depend on the characteristics of the skull at the point of impact, the weight of the object, and the velocity and force of the impact (Hickey, 1986). A high-velocity blow most often results in a depressed or perforating skull fracture, with injury to the underlying brain. A low-velocity blow usually results in linear fractures.

Brain injury is due to acceleration–deceleration and rotational forces of the brain within the skull. Because the brain is a semi-solid within the cranial vault, the impact upon a freely moving head causes the brain tissue to accelerate, decelerate, and rotate within the skull. These forces can cause tearing and shearing of brain tissue and rupture of blood vessels within the brain and surrounding meninges. The contusion may occur directly under the site of impact (coup) and/or at the opposite side of the skull (contrecoup) (Fig. 26-6). The contrecoup phenomenon occurs when the impact causes the brain to rebound against the opposite side of the skull.

Head injury can also affect blood vessels, cranial nerves, and other cranial structures. Complications such as obstruction of CSF pathways may cause hydrocephalus and increased ICP. Hemorrhage, cerebral edema, and increased ICP are the three most serious pathophysiological processes that can occur with severe head injury. Hemorrhage and hematomas can result from the tearing and shearing forces that occur as the brain continues to shift and rotate inside the cranial vault at the time of injury. Epidural and subdural hematomas may result in increased ICP.

### Medical Diagnosis and Management

#### Scalp Injuries.    Hemorrhage is the most significant clinical feature of a laceration of the scalp. Scalp lacerations, when present with open head injury, can cause meningitis or brain abscess. Scalp lacerations are treated by aseptic suturing of the lacerations. The wound is cleaned and debrided before suturing. The procedure is

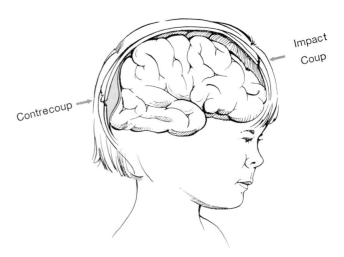

*Figure 26–6.   Coup/contracoup injury in craniocerebral trauma.*

generally done under local anesthesia, but extensive scalp lacerations may be closed under general anesthesia.

*Skull Fractures.* The type, extent, and accompanying symptoms of a skull fracture depend on the velocity, force and mass of the object, the area of the skull involved and the age of the child. Skull fractures may be classified as follows:

1. *Linear fracture.* This is the simplest form of skull fracture, resembling a thin line or crack in the skull without displacement of bone. Most linear fractures do not present any signs other than confirmation by x-ray. The child is observed for any signs of neurological deficits (changes in vital signs, level of consciousness, or motor/sensory deficits), and simple linear fractures are allowed to heal without any additional intervention.
2. *Comminuted fracture.* A cracked eggshell configuration results, with the cracks radiating outward from the site of impact. This type of fracture may also be classified as a depressed skull fracture.
3. *Depressed fracture.* The skull is indented at the point of impact, which may cause compression or shifting of brain tissue and result in significant damage to intracranial contents. The symptoms depend on the area of the brain affected. Because of the increased elasticity of the infant's skull, infants can experience a "ping pong ball" type depressed fracture.
4. *Basal fracture.* Basal skull fractures occur frequently in children and involve a linear fracture through the base of the skull. The two classic signs of basal skull fractures are "raccoon eyes," caused by blood leaking into the frontal sinuses resulting in edema and ecchymosis of the periorbital areas, and "battle sign," manifested by bruising behind the ear caused by bleeding into the mastoid sinus. CSF leakage from the nose or ears may also be present.

*Brain Injury.* Signs and symptoms of brain injury depend on the location and extent of the injury. Trauma to the brain can include lacerations, contusions, concussions, and hematomas. Post-traumatic syndromes and metabolic complications can also occur as a result of brain injury. Post-traumatic syndrome sequelae may include seizures, hydrocephalus, and focal neurological deficits. The symptoms can occur as long as 2 years after injury. Seizures may be generalized or focal and are most likely due to cerebral scarring. Most post-traumatic seizures can be controlled by anticonvulsant therapy. Metabolic complications that can result from head injury include diabetes insipidus, hypo- or hypernatremia, and hyperglycemic hyperosmolar states.

*Concussion.* There may be temporary brief loss of consciousness with transient impairment of neurological function and retrograde amnesia (loss of memory for events that immediately preceded the injury). Antegrade amnesia (loss of memory for events immediately following the injury) may also be present. The initial period is followed by a period of lethargy, irritability, headache, confusion, and vomiting, lasting for less than 24 to 48 hours. Post-concussion syndrome, including personality and behavioral changes, shortened attention span, and continued headaches, may last for 6 months or longer following concussion.

*Contusions and Laceration.* Contusions and lacerations can occur anywhere in the brain. Most result from blunt head trauma. Lesions of the motor cortex can cause motor and speech problems that may be either transient or permanent. Frontal lobe lesions can result in changes in behavior. Large areas of contused brain tissue can act as a space-occupying mass and cause cerebral edema and increased ICP.

*Diffuse Axonal Injury (DAI).* This is also known as a shearing injury, which is characterized by widespread neurological dysfunction. The child may suffer immediate and prolonged loss of consciousness. Cerebral edema is present with accompanying increased ICP. The child's prognosis depends on the severity of the injury. DAI is a serious life-threatening head injury that requires intensive care. The child may have vascular, metabolic, respiratory, and musculoskeletal complications along with DAI and prolonged coma.

*Hematomas.* Epidural hematoma (bleeding between the skull and the dura) and subdural hematoma (bleeding between the dura and the arachnoid layer) are the two most common types of hematomas. Subdural hematomas are more common in infants and young children. They can be classified as acute or chronic. Subdural bleeding is usually venous in origin. Acute subdural hematomas, which occur within 48 hours of a head injury, are characterized by increasing severity of symptoms. Symptoms include headache, agitation, confusion or drowsiness, decreasing level of consciousness, and increasing ICP.

Chronic subdural hematomas may occur days to several months after injury. Signs and symptoms are those of a space-occupying mass, but may be non-specific in nature. The child may experience a shortened attention span, difficulty in concentration in school, and increasing frequency of headaches.

Epidural hematomas are most often attributed to arterial bleeding of the middle meningeal artery. Epidural hematomas are rare in children under 2 years. Epidural hematomas have a rapid onset and can be life-threatening. Symptoms include an initial lucid period lasting minutes to hours followed by rapid deterioration, with headache, seizures, coma, and brain herniation with compression of the brain stem. In some children the period between the injury and the onset of symptoms can be as long as several days.

The diagnosis of skull fractures is usually made on the basis of skull x-rays. Basal skull fractures are not usually visible on x-ray, and diagnosis is based on accompanying symptoms. Skull fractures usually do not require specific treatment. Depressed fractures may have to be elevated surgically to relieve compression. In comminuted fractures bone fragments may need to be debrided from cerebral tissue.

All patients are observed closely for the signs of underlying brain injury. Brain injury is most often confirmed by CT scanning and MRI. Medical management depends on the patient's signs and symptoms. Vigorous management must be instituted to control ICP. Surgical intervention may be needed in patients with mass contusions. Children with progressive signs of subdural hematomas require surgical evacuation. Emergency burr hole evacuation may be necessary for acute subdural hematomas. Epidural hematomas may require evacuation and ligation of the ruptured vessel as well as relief of ICP by burr holes.

### Nursing Assessment and Diagnosis

Continual assessment of neurological status is critical, because the child's condition can quickly change. Nurses must monitor the child's alertness, motor and sensory function, and pupillary response. Assessment for signs of additional injuries is also important, and nurses must always assume that cervical or spinal injuries are present until ruled out. Nursing diagnoses related to the child with a head injury might include the following:

- Ineffective airway clearance related to decreased loss of consciousness
- Altered tissue perfusion: cerebral, related to increasing ICP
- Potential for infection, related to skull fractures/scalp laceration or penetrating wounds
- Sensory/perceptual alteration: level of consciousness, related to injury, secondary cerebral edema
- Ineffective family coping, related to stress of hospitalization, unknown outcome

### Planning and Implementing Nursing Care

The child with a head injury can rapidly develop serious complications. Nurses must consistently and frequently assess, monitor, and document any signs of neurological dysfunction. This includes monitoring vital signs and neurological status frequently. Measures are instituted to minimize or prevent increased ICP.

Motor function assessment should be appropriate for the child's developmental age. Seizure precautions should be instituted. The nurse should assess and note any drainage from the ears and nose, especially if a basilar skull fracture is suspected, in order to monitor for CSF leakage. Nurses can determine if the drainage coming from a child's nose is normal secretions or CSF by testing for the presence of glucose. CSF will test positive for glucose, whereas normal secretions will not. Leakage of CSF indicates a direct open pathway to the brain, and there is a danger of meningitis developing.

Family support during the acute and recovery periods will include knowledge about the child's condition and explanation of medical and nursing management. Parents need support to deal with guilt or anger about the accident. They should be encouraged to spend time with the child, to bring familiar toys from home, and to participate in the child's care as much as possible.

The discharge plan will depend on the degree of recovery. The child may require extensive rehabilitative care. Parents must be taught about post-traumatic syndrome and how to identify signs of hydrocephalus and seizures. They also need to know the importance of regular periodic evaluations in any child who has sustained a head injury. Referring parents for counseling is an important nursing function.

### Evaluating Nursing Care

Evaluation is based on the child's degree of recovery. The family should have realistic expectations for the brain-injured child. The family should seek appropriate counseling to work through feelings of grief, maintain family and marital relationships, and accept the child.

## Spinal Cord Injury

Spinal cord injury (SCI) that results in paraplegia or quadriplegia occurs less frequently in children than in adults because of the greater resilience of the vertebrae in young children. Adolescents and young adults account for the majority of spinal cord injuries in people under 25 years of age. Severe trauma due to motor vehicle accidents accounts for the majority of injuries in adolescents. Sporting accidents such as diving and contact sports also account for spinal cord injuries in the older child and adolescent.

### Pathophysiology

Spinal cord injury results from direct damage to the cord, either from severance of the cord by vertebrae or compression of the cord with or without obvious vertebral involvement. The trauma results in inflammation, edema, and hemorrhage, which can cause additional damage through compression of the blood supply. Spinal cord injuries can be classified according to level of injury, degree of functional impairment, mechanism, and type of injury (Table 26-11).

Cervical injuries in children usually involve vertebrae C-3 through C-5. The injury occurs because of sudden

*Table 26–11.  Classification of Spinal Cord Injuries*

**Level of injury**

Cervical injuries are most common, thoracic injuries are least common.

**Degree of functional impairment**

1. *Complete*—sensory, motor, and autonomic disruption below the level of trauma, usually with irreversible spinal cord damage.
   Quadriplegia—as a result of cervical injury—loss of lower extremity function, with varying degrees of use of upper extremities
   Paraplegia—occurs with thoracic or high lumbar vertebral injury
2. *Incomplete*—results in partial loss of motor and sensory function and can include:
   Anterior cord syndrome—complete motor paralysis with some sensory function
   Brown-Séquard syndrome—ipsilateral motor loss and contralateral loss of sensation (touch and pain)
   Central cord syndrome—motor impairment in upper extremities greater than in lower extremities, some sensory loss

**Mechanism of injury**

1. Flexion/dislocation—head hyperflexes to chest
2. Hyperextension "whiplash" occurs when hit forcefully anteriorly (rear-ended in an automobile accident)
3. Vertical compression—occurs most frequently in diving accidents, causing compression fractures of the vertebrae
4. Rotation may be present with any of the other three mechanisms of injury.*

**Type of injury**

1. Concussion—rare condition causing temporary loss of function. No identifiable neuropathological changes noted on cord exam.
2. Contusion—bruising of the cord causing bleeding into the cord, followed by edema and necrosis. Extent of damage depends on severity of the contusion.
3. Laceration—an actual tear in the cord. Results in permanent injury to the cord.
4. Transection—severing of the cord, completely or partially.
5. Hemorrhage—bleeding into or around the cord. Results in changes in neurochemical components, edema, and neurodeficits.
6. Damage to vessels supplying cord results in ischemia and possible necrosis. Prolonged ischemia will cause permanent deficits.†

Adapted from Fewer (1976).
†Adapted from Hickey, J. (1986). *The clinical practice of neurological and nonsurgical nursing* (2nd ed.). Philadelphia: J. B. Lippincott.

hyperflexion, hyperextension of the neck, or vertical compression of the spine. As the vertebrae are contorted and the intervertebral disks are dislocated, the cord becomes compressed between the vertebrae.

## Medical Diagnosis and Management

Signs and symptoms of SCI vary depending on the severity of cord trauma and the level of the trauma along the spine. Clinical manifestations of SCI are described as occurring in phases.

Phase one is referred to as spinal shock syndrome and involves immediate loss of motor, sensory, autonomic, and reflex function. The child experiences flaccid paralysis, loss of spinal reflexes, and loss of pain, touch, temperature, and pressure sensation below the level of injury. In cervical injury there is usually loss of respiratory function due to flaccidity of the diaphragm. In spinal shock syndrome the child cannot shiver or sweat in response to changes in temperature below the level of injury. With the loss of autonomic nerve response, vasoconstrictive powers are lost, and blood tends to pool in the lower portion of the body, resulting in hypotension. With cervical injury the child can experience bradycardia due to loss of the cardiac acceleration reflex. The symptoms of hypotension, bradycardia, and loss of temperature regulation are referred to as neurogenic shock. Spinal shock may last from a few days to months. The child with an SCI may also experience a loss of bowel and bladder tone.

The second phase is referred to as the early recovery phase. At this time, if the injury is high in the spinal tract, the paralysis changes from flaccid to spastic. The reflex

arcs contract the muscles. The muscles are held in a continual state of contraction because of the loss of upper motor
neuron function. Spasticity of the bowel and bladder also
occurs, resulting in periodic forceful emptying of the
contents of the bowel and bladder. If the injury is low in
the spinal tract, the child will continue to display flaccidity.

The third phase, long-term recovery phase, reflects
the final outcome of motor and/or sensory function. It may
be many months before the degree of residual dysfunction is known. If the initial symptoms of SCI were due to
compression caused by edema, the child may not experience any long-term motor or sensory loss. If complete or
incomplete transection occurred, there will be varying
degrees of spinal cord dysfunction.

Therapy begins at the scene of the injury with immobilization and safe transport to the hospital, the goal of
which is to prevent or minimize further trauma to the
spinal cord. Along with stabilization of the spine, cardiovascular and respiratory function must be assessed and
maintained. A corticosteroid drug may be given intravenously to reduce inflammation and edema of the spinal
cord.

In the hospital the child's spine is stabilized by traction
or surgery (spinal fusion). Traction may also be applied
prior to surgery. Management goals of SCI are stabilization, realignment, and decompression of the cord. Selection of traction or surgery as a treatment modality depends
on the location of the injury, progression of neurological
deficit, presence of penetrating wounds, and the overall
condition of the child. Associated injuries such as head
injuries and increased ICP, chest injuries that severely
compromise the respiratory system, or internal hemorrhage may make successful surgical intervention impossible.

Many SCIs can be managed by traction. The spine is
stabilized by skeletal traction (halo traction, cervical
tongs) and the use of turning frames such as the Stryker
frame. The choice of surgical fusion as opposed to halo
fixation alone in the management of cervical spine injury
is still very controversial. Bucholz and Cheung (1989)
studied the results of patients undergoing one or the other
of these two treatments, and concluded that the halo vest
can be used to treat most patients with cervical spine
injuries. They also concluded that under certain circumstances surgery may be indicated.

### Nursing Assessment and Diagnosis

Frequent assessment of the neurological system helps
determine the scope of injury and any improvement that
may occur. Close evaluation of the child's motor and sensory functions is necessary. Assessment of movement and
sensation can pinpoint the level of the cord injury. Nurses
must also monitor respiratory function, noting adequacy
of ventilation. Nursing diagnoses related to the child with a
spinal cord might include the following:

- Impaired physical mobility, related to loss of
  motor function
- Altered skin integrity, related to immobility,
  skeletal traction
- Altered elimination: bowel and bladder, related to
  bladder and bowel flaccidity or spasticity
- Potential for infection: respiratory or urinary,
  related to decreased chest wall movement, stasis of
  urine in the bladder
- Potential for ineffective coping, related to lengthy
  hospitalization, results of injury and long-term
  outcome

### Planning and Implementing Nursing Care

*Mobility Interference.* *Early Recovery Phase.* If
the child is placed in spinal traction using Crutchfield
tongs, mobility is severely curtailed, and the complications of immobility (thromboembolic problems, respiratory compromise, renal calculi, skin breakdown) are increased. Halo traction with a body vest allows the child to
be up and actively involved in the rehabilitative process.
The degree of mobility depends on the degree of motor or
sensory impairment present. If no paralysis exists, the
child is able to be out of bed and walking, thus preventing
many of the complications of immobilization.

*Late Recovery Phase.* The rehabilitative process begun
in the early phase becomes a comprehensive effort to
assist the child to regain optimal function in the late
recovery phase. Continual assessment of neurological
function with attention to complications as they occur is
important. As the flaccidity that was present in the early
phase of injury evolves into spasticity, exercises must be
initiated that will reduce the spasticity (stretching exercises, physiotherapy, range-of-motion exercises, frequent
repositioning). Passive range of motion exercises are instituted early and continued as long as the paralysis lasts to
control muscle atrophy, osteoporosis, and formation of
contractures. Active exercises of functional muscles help
to strengthen functioning muscle groups and to decrease
the cardiac and respiratory complications of long-term
immobilization.

The child should be encouraged to begin doing as
much for himself as possible. If the child is quadriplegic,
assistive devices may include a portable ventilator and
motorized wheelchair. In addition, because of the tracheostomy needed for assisted ventilation, the child will
need an alternative method of communication. There
are many electronic and computerized communication
devices available to meet this need. The child with paraplegia in the lower extremities may need the assistance
of a wheelchair or leg braces and walking devices
(crutches, walkers). Bowel and bladder training and
assistive devices will be needed by most of these children. Once the child returns home, adaptation must be

made in the home to accommodate the assistive devices needed by the child.

*Airway Clearance.* *Early Recovery Phase.* Children with cervical cord injuries very often require ventilation assistance. The child's respiratory system must be assessed for adequate ventilation and increased secretions. The child should be suctioned at least every 2 hours to maintain an open airway, and deep breathing exercises should be done hourly. Nurses should auscultate the child's chest frequently to assess rate, rhythm, and character of respiration. Intermittent positive-pressure breathing treatments are administered at least once every 8 hours.

*Late Recovery Phase.* If the child has residual sensory and motor loss, continued attention to maintaining optimal respiratory function must be sustained. This includes encouraging deep breathing exercises as well as routine chest physiotherapy. Children with cord injury at C-4 or lower are usually able to be weaned from mechanical ventilation.

*Skin Integrity.* *Early Recovery Phase.* If the child is in the type of traction where bedrest is to be maintained, nurses must assess the skin frequently for reddened areas or breakdown. A Stryker frame or other turning device facilitates maintenance of good skin care. Without these turning frames the child is turned every 2 hours using triple log rolling. Alternating pressure mattresses, pressure pads, sheepskin, and joint protectors can be used to prevent skin breakdown. A high-calorie, high-protein diet is important in maintaining the child's skin. In the child with skeletal traction, the pin sites must be kept meticulously clean to prevent infection. Protocols for cleaning and dressing the pin sites depend on the surgeon and institution, but usually involve cleaning with povidone-iodine solution or applying an antibiotic ointment and a dry sterile dressing over the pin site.

*Late Recovery Phase.* Continued attention to early signs of skin breakdown in the child with motor and sensory dysfunction is important to prevent decubiti formation. The use of braces in the child should alert nurses to assess areas under the braces that may be a focal point for skin breakdown.

In both the early and late phases of recovery, the child with SCI loses much of his temperature regulation ability distal to the level of injury. This makes the child susceptible to changes in environmental temperature. The affected area of the body tends to assume the ambient temperature of the environment, most often tending toward hypothermia. Nurses should assess the child's rectal temperature as well as the color and temperature of the lower extremities. Nursing care consists of preventing excessive loss of body heat and maintaining an environmental temperature that will maintain a normal body temperature. The child and family must be aware of this phenomenon and guard against hypothermia, especially in cold weather.

*Autonomic Hyperreflexia (Dysreflexia).* This phenomenon, which occurs most frequently in children with lesions above T-6, is a sympathetic response that is characterized by paroxysmal hypertension causing headache, flushing, profuse sweating, and bradycardia. The hyperreflexia occurs in response to visceral stimulation such as bowel impaction, distended bladder or abdomen, decubiti, or urinary tract infection. The nurse must immediately reduce or eliminate the stimulus to prevent cerebrovascular involvement. Nursing interventions involve alleviating urinary retention, reducing abdominal distortion, and removing other noxious stimuli that may be precipitating the hyperreflexia. If these initial interventions do not decrease the paroxysmal hypertension, antihypertensive agents (beta blockers) may be given to reduce extreme elevations in blood pressure.

*Altered Elimination Patterns.* *Early Recovery Phase.* A Foley catheter is inserted soon after the injury occurs until the extent of injury and paralysis is determined. This prevents urinary retention and allows nurses to monitor fluid balance and renal function. During this early phase of recovery intermittent catheterization is instituted to encourage reflex bladder emptying. Nurses must pay attention to asepsis and proper technique. A program of intermittent catheterization, which involves decreasing the number of catheterizations and recording the amount of residual urine, is begun.

In the early stage of recovery, paralytic ileus may decrease bowel function. Assessment of bowel function through palpation and auscultation should be done regularly. A bowel program should be initiated that includes stool softeners, suppositories, and digital stimulation. It is important to prevent constipation and fecal impaction, as they can cause autonomic hyperreflexia and stimulate spasticity.

*Late Recovery Phase.* The parents and the child over 9 years of age should be taught intermittent catheterization. Bowel elimination can be regulated by suppositories. Once a pattern is established, stool softeners can usually be discontinued and bowel movements can be controlled through diet. Bowel training is individualized for each patient. Both the child and the parents must be actively involved in the training program. Nurses must be optimistic and a source of support during the process.

*Potential For Infection.* *Early Recovery Phase.* The child in skeletal cervical traction is at risk for infection at the pin sites. The immobilized child is at risk for respiratory and urinary tract infections. The nursing actions relevant to each of these body systems are described above.

*Late Recovery Phase.* The child requiring ventilatory assistance is always at risk for respiratory infections. Urinary tract infections can occur if there is retention of urine or improper technique in intermittent catheterization.

*Ineffective Coping: Family.* *Early Recovery Phase.* The child and parents are usually in a state of shock during this period. The child's condition may be critical, and the parents' only concern may be that the child lives. Parents will need continual and repeated explanation of the child's care and the status of his condition. It is important to remember that persons under stress remember very little of the information given to them. Nurses should repeat information given to parents at regular intervals.

Once the child is stabilized, the parents may begin a grief reaction. Nurses should be supportive, with the goal that this reaction will progress to the parents' acceptance of the child's disabilities. Once the parents begin to accept the child's condition they can begin to actively participate

in his rehabilitation, and the child can draw strength from them as well as from the professional staff.

*Late Recovery Phase.* During this period the child and his family may vacillate in their coping abilities. Once the child begins active rehabilitation the family may be elated with the progress. The initial use of braces or a wheelchair may also result in a realization of the permanence of the child's disability and a reactivation of the grieving process. Table 26-12 summarizes function and dysfunction according to the level of SCI.

The parents and child must be active participants in the rehabilitative process. The parents may need to be reminded to allow the child to assume age-appropriate responsibility for his or her own care. Fostering indepen-

*Table 26–12.  Dysfunction and Rehabilitative Potential After Spinal Cord Injury According to Level of Injury*

| Site | Functional Disability | Rehabilitative Potential |
|---|---|---|
| C1 to C3 | Quadriplegia, loss of respiratory function, loss of sensory function below the chin, loss of bowel and bladder control | Ventilatory assistance needed; tracheostomy; will need skilled nursing care; can use mouthstick or tongue to control computers and electronic devices and electronic wheelchair |
| C2 to C4 | Quadriplegia; potential for hypotension, hypothermia, atonic bladder and ileus; sensory loss below the clavicles, some arm sensation | Possibility of diaphragmatic breathing, may need intermittent ventilatory assistance; may be some bowel/bladder control due to reflex emptying |
| C5 | Quadriplegia; loss of most function below upper shoulders. Intercostal muscles non-functioning, no active bowel or bladder control. Loss of sensation below the clavicles | Control of head, can use adaptive tools for computer assisted devices. There may be some slight sensation of upper extremities. Intact sternomastoid, cervical, and trapezius muscles |
| C6 | Quadriplegia. Loss of function below the shoulders and upper arms. General loss of sensory function below the clavicles, with some arm and thumb sensation | Intact deltoid biceps and external rotators. Some use of upper extremities for self care and transferring, assistive devices needed to use arms |
| C7 | Quadriplegia, incomplete motor dysfunction to parts of arms and hands. General loss of sensation below the clavicles. Loss of bowel and bladder control | Triceps function, some voluntary function of two upper extremities. Greater participation in ADLs. Some patients may assist with dressing. Potential that the adolescent may be able to drive with assistive devices. Intact sensory function of parts of arms and hands |
| C8 | Quadriplegia, incomplete. Loss of motor function to parts of upper extremities. Loss of sensation below the chest, includes parts of arms and hands, loss of bowel and bladder control | Some control of thumb and finger motor function. Can participate, use hands voluntarily with some fine motor control. Can assist in many aspects of ADLS that need hand and arm functional ability |
| T1 to T12 | Paraplegia. Loss of motor control below the waist. T1 to T6, loss of motor function below midchest. Sensory loss below midchest (T1–T6) and below the waist (T6–T12) | Intact motor function of shoulders, arms, hands; varying degrees of chest and torso control between T1 and T12. T6–T12—respiratory function and accompanying respiratory muscles intact. Full control of upper extremities. Maintenance of ADLs requiring upper extremity function. Capable of managing bowel and bladder care |
| Below L1 | Paraplegia. L1–L2—motor dysfunction in legs and pelvis. L3–L4—partial loss of motor control in lower legs and feet. L1–S2—varying degree of sensory loss to abdomen and legs depending on level of injury | L1–L2. Intact hip rotation with some flexion of the legs. Varying ability to walk with braces from L1 to L4. Varying degrees of bowel and bladder control. Child can be relatively independent in ADLs. L5–L1 able to walk without aids. S4 control of bladder and bowel function. Capable of penile erection and ejaculation |

(Adapted from Raimond, J., & Taylor, J. [1986]. *Neurological emergencies: Effective nursing care.* Rockville, MD: Aspen; Hickey, J. [1986]. *The clinical practice of neurological and nonsurgical nursing* [2nd ed.]. Philadelphia: J. B. Lippincott)

dence in these children is most important. Parents may tend to shelter the child, but this only encourages dependence and lowers the child's self-esteem.

*Disturbances in Self-Concept.* The child's self-concept is closely tied to his ability to cope with his disability and his feelings of dependence/independence. The child will undergo changes in self-image as he develops and matures. These changes will parallel and often exaggerate the standard self-image problems of each developmental stage. The child will need the rehabilitation team's support during these times of developmental changes. With each new experience (school, recreational, social) the child may encounter situations that will test his self-confidence and sometimes undermine his self-concept. A strong social support network is most important to build self-confidence and independence.

As the child matures sexually, sexual adjustment should be an integral part of rehabilitation. This basic need has been a grossly neglected part of patient management (Hickey, 1986). The child and adolescent will have not only the normal questions about sexuality, but also questions concerning his or her own disability and sexual function. The parent and health care professional should listen for clues that the child is ready to discuss concerns about sexuality. Specially trained counselors and rehabilitation clinical nurse specialists may be the best persons for the child to discuss his questions and fears with. Many quadriplegic and paraplegic males are capable of achieving an erection through psychic or physical stimulation. Ejaculation may be reflexive but erratic. Sensation will be absent. Woman with quadriplegia or paraplegia will be able to conceive, become pregnant, and have healthy babies, usually by cesarean section. The woman will not be able to experience orgasm.

### Evaluating Nursing Care

Evaluation is based on the various parameters and outcomes as discussed above. Family adjustment should be continually evaluated.

### Summary

The neurological system is a complex communication system that controls body function. Disturbances in this intricate system create alterations in the process by which it receives, integrates, and responds to stimuli. These alterations result in a variety of clinical manifestations. Nurses play an active role in assessing, planning, implementing, and evaluating nursing care provided to children and adolescents with alterations of the neurological system. Nurses must have a thorough understanding of the principles of neurological function. Recognizing how various alterations can affect the brain at different stages of a

child's development is critical to providing nursing care and anticipating potential problems. Nursing care for children with alterations of the neurological system is also based on age-related differences and overall status of neurological maturation. Nurses play a vital role in supporting the child and family affected by these conditions. The fear and anxiety related to these life-threatening and uncertain conditions is an important consideration in the delivery of nursing care. Nurses must be careful to provide some degree of hope, balanced with realistic expectations for the child, as they communicate with the family. Nurses must be prepared to meet the numerous challenges and provide specialized care to children and adolescents with neurological disturbances.

## References

Aucain, P., Kotilainen, A., Gantz, N., Davidson. R., Kellogg, P., & Stone, B. (1986). ICP monitors—epidemiologic study of risk factors and infections. *American Journal of Medicine, 80,* 369–376.

Austin, J., & McDermott, N. (1988). Parental attitude and coping behaviors in families of children with epilepsy. *Journal of Neuroscience Nursing, 20,* 174–179.

Bancaud, J., Henriksen, O., Rubena-Donnadieu, F., Seino, M., & Dreifuss, F. (1981). From the Commission on Classification and Terminology of the International League Against Epilepsy: Proposal for revised clinical and electroencephalographic classification of epileptic seizures. *Epilepsia, 72,* 489–501.

Barlow, P., Mendelow, A., & Lawrence, A. (1985). Clinical evaluation of two methods of subdural pressure monitoring. *Journal of Neurosurgery, 63,* 578–582.

Brewer, K., & Sperling, M. (1988). Neurosurgical treatment of intractable epilepsy. *Journal of Neuroscience Nursing, 20,* 366–372.

Bruya, M. (1981). Planned periods of rest in the intensive care unit: Nursing care activities and ICP. *Journal of Neurosurgical Nursing, 13,* 184–194.

Bucholz, R., & Cheung, K. (1989). Halo vest versus spinal fusions for cervical injury: Evidence from an outcome study. *Journal of Neurosurgery, 70,* 884–892.

Cohen, F. (1984). *Clinical genetics in nursing practice.* Philadelphia: J. B. Lippincott Co.

Dunn, D. W. (1987). Neurofibromatosis in childhood. *Current Problems in Pediatrics, 17*(8), 451–497.

Feingold, B. F. (1975). Hyperkinesis and learning disabilities linked to artificial food flavors and colors. *American Journal of Nursing, 75*(5), 797–803.

Fenichel, G. (1988). *Clinical pediatric neurology: A signs and symptoms approach.* Philadelphia: W. B. Saunders.

Finlay, J., et al. (1987). Progress in the management of childhood brain tumors. *Hematology/Oncology Clinics of North America, 1,* 753–776.

Franges, E. Z., & Beideman, M. (1988). Infections related to intracranial pressure monitoring. *Journal of Neuroscience Nursing, 20,* 94–103.

Gaddy, D. (1980). Meningitis in the pediatric population. *Nursing Clinics of North America, 15*(1), 83–97.

Harper, J. (1989). Use of steroids in cerebral edema: Therapeutic implications. *Heart and Lung, 17,* 70–73.

Hickey, J. (1986). *The clinical practice of neurological and nonsurgical nursing* (2nd ed.). Philadelphia: J. B. Lippincott.

Hurwitz, E. S. (1985). Public health service study on Reye's syndrome and medications. *New England Journal of Medicine, 313,* 849–857.

Ingersoll, G., & Leyden, D. (1986). The Glasgow Coma Scale for patients with head injuries. *Critical Care Nurse, 7,* 26–32.

Jennet, B., & Teasdale, G. (1981). *Management of head injuries.* Philadelphia: F. A. Davis.

Jones, C. Glasgow Coma Scale. (1979). *American Journal of Nursing, 79,* 1551–1553.

Kranstuber, S. (1984). *Know the eight warning signals of possible childhood cancer.* Columbus, OH: American Cancer Society, Franklin County Unit.

Krugman, S., Katz, S., Gershon, A., & Wilfert, C. (1985). *Infectious diseases of children* (8th ed.). St. Louis: C.V. Mosby, pp. 167–191.

Leventhal, B. (1987). Neoplasm and neoplasm-like structures. In Behrman, R., & Vaughan, V. (Eds.). *Nelson's textbook of pediatrics* (13th ed.). Philadelphia: W. B. Saunders, pp. 1079–1109.

Martin, K. (1987). Predicting short-term outcome in comatose head-injured children. *Journal of Neuroscience Nursing, 19,* 9–13.

Mendelow, A., Rowan, J., & Murray, L. (1983). A clinical comparison of subdural screw pressure measurements with ventricular pressure. *Journal of Neurosurgery, 58,* 45–50.

Mitchell, P., & Mauss, N. (1978). Relationships of patient/nurse activity to intracranial pressure variations: A pilot study. *Nursing Research, 27,* 4–10.

Morray, J., Tyler, D., Jones, T., Stuntz, J., & Lemire, R. (1984). Coma scale for use in brain-injured children. *Critical Care Medicine, 12,* 1018–1020.

Neatherlin, J., & Brillhart, B. (1988). Glasgow coma scale scores in the patient post cardiopulmonary resuscitation. *Journal of Neuroscience Nursing, 20,* 104–109.

Parsons, L., Pearce, A., & Page, M. (1985). The effects of hygiene interventions on the cerebrovascular status of severe closed head injured persons. *Research in Nursing and Health, 8,* 173–181.

Pratt, C. (1985). Some aspects of childhood cancer epidemiology. *Pediatric Clinics of North America, 32,* 541–556.

Reye, R., Morgan, G., & Baral, J. (1963). Encephalopathy and fatty degeneration of the viscera. *Lancet, 2,* 749–752.

Snyder, M. (1983). Relationship of nursing activities to increase intracranial pressure. *Journal of Advances in Nursing, 8,* 273–279.

Teasdale, G., & Jennett, B. (1979). Assessment of coma and impaired consciousness: A practical scale. *Lancet, 18,* 81–83.

Walker, R., & Allen, J. (1983). Pediatric brain tumors. *Pediatric Annals, 12,* 383–391.

Waskewitz, M., & Leonard, M. (1986). Early detection of malignancy: From birth to twenty years. *Oncology Nursing Forum, 13,* 50–57.

Wilson, S., Amlins, J., Floyd, S., & McNair, N. (1988). Determining interrater reliability of nurses' assessment of pupillary size and reaction. *Journal of Neuroscience Nursing, 20,* 189–192.

Zeidelman, C. (1980). Increase of intracranial pressure in children: Nursing assessment and intervention. *Journal of Neurosurgical Nursing, 12,* 7–11.

Zimmerman, S. S., & Gildea, J. H. (1985). *Critical care pediatrics.* Philadelphia: W.B. Saunders, Chapter 12.

## Bibliography

Adelstein, W. (1989). C1–C2 fractures and dislocations. *Journal of Neuroscience Nursing, 21,* 149–159.

Ainsworth, H. (1989). The nursing care of children undergoing craniotomy. *Nursing (Lond), 3*(33), 5–8.

Allan, D. (1989). Intracranial pressure monitoring: A study of nursing practice. *Journal of Advanced Nursing, 14*(2), 127–131.

Bare, M. A. (1989). Hemispherectomy for seizures. *Journal of Neuroscience Nursing, 21*(1), 18–23.

Baron, M. C. (1991). Advances in the care of children with brain tumors. *Journal of Neuroscience Nursing, 23*(1), 39–43.

Berkshire, J., & Watson-Evans, H. (1989). Meningioma: A nursing perspective. *Journal of Neuroscience Nursing, 21,* 96–103.

Borkowski, C. (1989). A comparison of pulmonary complications in spinal cord–injured patients with two modes of spinal immobilization. *Journal of Neuroscience Nursing, 21,* 79–85.

Browner, C., Hadley, M., Sonntag, V. & Mattingly, L. (1987). Halo immobilization brace care: An innovative approach. *Journal of Neuroscience Nursing, 19,* 24–29.

Callanan, M. (1988). Epilepsy: Putting the patient back in control. *RN, 51,* 48–55.

Cohen, F. (1987). Neural tube defects: Epidemiology, detection and prevention. *Journal of Obstetric, Gynecologic, and Neonatal Nursing, 2,* 105–115.

Derechin, M. (1987). Pediatric head injury. *Critical Care Nursing Quarterly, 10,* 12–24.

Ferry, P. (1986). *Seizure disorders in children.* Philadelphia: J. B. Lippincott.

Flannery, J. (1991). FAMLI-RESCUE: A family assessment tool for use by neuroscience nurses in the acute care setting. *Journal of Neuroscience Nursing, 23*(2), 111–118.

Fry, S. (1987). The ethical dimension of policy for prenatal diagnostic technologies: The case of maternal serum alpha-fetoprotein screening. *Advances in Nursing Science, 9,* 44–45.

Graham, O., Naveauer, I., & Cummings, C. (1989). A model of ambulatory care of patients with epilepsy and other neurological disorders. *Journal of Neuroscience Nursing, 21,* 108–112.

Grief, L., & Miller, C. (1991). Shunt lengthening: A descriptive review. *Journal of Neuroscience Nursing, 23*(2), 120–126.

Hartshorn, J., & Hartshorn, E. (1986). Nursing interventions for anticonvulsant drug interactions. *Journal of Neuroscience Nursing, 18,* 250–255.

Hinkle, J. (1988). Nursing care of patients with minor head injury. *Journal of Neuroscience Nursing, 20,* 8–16.

Hobdell, E. F., Adamo, F., Caruson, J., Dihoff, R., Neveling, E., & Roncoli, M. (1989). The effect of nursing activities on the intracranial pressure of children. *Critical Care Nurse, 9*(6), 75–79.

Hodges, K., & Root, L. (1991). Surgical management of intractable seizure disorders. *Journal of Neuroscience Nursing, 23*(2), 93–101.

Hugo, M. (1987). Alleviating the effects of care on the intracranial pressure (ICP) of head injured patients by manipulating nursing care activities. *Intensive Care Nursing, 3,* 78–82.

Kaufman, J. (1990). Nurse's guide to assessing the 12 cranial nerves. *Nursing, 20*(6), 56–58.

Kelley, S. (1988). *Pediatric emergency nursing.* Norwalk, CT: Appleton & Lange.

Macedo, A., & Posel, L. (1987). Nursing the family after the birth of a child with spina bifida. *Issues in Comprehensive Pediatric Nursing, 10,* 55–65.

Mahon-Darby, J. (1988). Powerlessness in cervical spinal cord injury patients. *Dimensions of Critical Care Nursing, 1,* 346–355.

Messner, R., & Smith, M. (1986). Neurofibromatoses: Relinquishing the masks: A quest for quality of life. *Journal of Advanced Nursing, 11,* 459–464.

Metcalf, J. (1986). Acute phase management of persons with spinal cord injury: A nursing diagnosis perspective. *Nursing Clinics of North America, 21,* 589–598.

Miller, E., & Williams, S. (1987). Alteration in cerebral perfusion: Clinical concept of nursing diagnosis? *Journal of Neuroscience Nursing, 19,* 183–190.

Mitchell, P. (1986). Decreased adaptive capacity, intracranial: A proposal for a nursing diagnosis. *Journal of Neurosurgical Nursing, 18,* 170–175.

Moore, P. (1988). When you have to think small for a neurological exam. *RN,* 38–44.

Morgan, S. P. (1990). A comparison of three methods of managing fever in the neurological patient. *Journal of Neurosurgical Nursing, 22*(1), 19–24.

Morrison, C. (1987). Brain herniation syndromes. *Critical Care Nurse, 7,* 34, 36–38.

Moskowitz, C. B. (1991). The primary dystonias of childhood. *Journal of Neuroscience Nursing, 23*(3), 175–182.

Nativio, D. G., & Belz, C. (1990). Childhood neurofibromatosis. *Pediatric Nursing, 16*(6), 575–580.

O'Callaghan, T., Dunham, C., & Belzberg, H. (1990). Intracranial hypertension. *Critical Care Report, 1,* 389–394.

Palmer, M., & Wyness, M. (1988). Positioning and handling: Important considerations in the care of the severely head-injured patient. *Journal of Neuroscience Nursing, 20,* 42–49.

Pollack-Latham, C. (1987). Intracranial pressure monitoring: Patient care. *Critical Care Nurse, 7,* 53–56, 58–62, 64–73.

Raimond, J., & Taylor, J. (1986). *Neurological emergencies: Effective nursing care.* Rockville, MD: Aspen Systems Corp.

Reeves, K. (1989). Assessment of pediatric head injury: The basics. *Journal of Emergency Nursing, 15*(4), 329–332.

Romeo, J. H. (1988). The critical care minute after spinal cord injury. *RN,* 61–67.

Stewart-Amidi, C. (1990). An ounce of prevention . . . head and spinal cord injury prevention programs. *Journal of Neuroscience Nursing, 22*(5), 273.

Zegler, L. (1989). Aculocephalic and vestibuli-ocular responses: Significance for nursing care. *Journal of Neuroscience Nursing, 21,* 46–55.

# Alterations in Immune System Function

Mary Ann Ludwig and Thomas Beam

27

*Anatomy*

*Physiology*

*Assessment*

*Nursing Diagnosis*

*Planning Nursing Care*

*Nursing Interventions*

*Evaluation*

*Immune Health Problems of Children*

*General Allergic Reactions*

*Local Allergic Reactions*

*Autoimmune Disorders*

*Summary*

*Nursing Care Plan*

*Photograph by David Finn*

## Learning Objectives

*Upon completion of this chapter the reader will be able to:*

1. *Define the immune system.*

2. *Describe the anatomy and physiology of the immune system.*

3. *Describe assessment procedures related to immune function.*

4. *Explain the pathophysiology of a variety of immune related problems in children.*

5. *Describe the medical management of a variety of immune related problems in children.*

6. *Develop nursing diagnoses for major immune system problems.*

7. *Plan nursing care using the nursing process for children with a variety of immune system problems.*

## Key Terms

*allergy*

*anaphylaxis*

*antibody*

*antigen*

*autoimmunity*

*B-cell*

*basophil*

*cell*

*cell-mediated immunity*

*eosinophil*

*epitope*

*human immunodeficiency virus (HIV)*

*humoral immunity*

*hyposensitization*

*immunogen*

*inflammation*

*killer cell*

*leukocyte*

*lymphocyte*

*macrophage*

*mast cell*

*monocyte*

*mononuclear leukocyte*

*neutrophil*

*nurse cell*

*polymorphonuclear leukocyte*

*T cell*

The immune system is the network of defenses that keeps the body intact and protected from disease. Its main functions are to protect against invasion by infectious agents such as viruses, bacteria, parasites, and fungi, and to provide protection against abnormal cell proliferation (e.g., cancer). Although alterations in the immune system can occur at any point in the life cycle, immunodeficiencies are most often identified in children.

Disorders of immunity are complex and may affect a variety of other body systems. The body systems that are involved in the immune system are shown in Figure 27-1. The manifestations of immune dysfunction can be acute, chronic, and sometimes life threatening. Immune system disorders can be classified into categories including immune deficiencies, autoimmune disorders, allergic or adverse reactions, and abnormal cell proliferation.

## Anatomy

### Cells

The cells of the immune system are called white blood cells. The name is derived from the laboratory observation that three layers form when whole blood is allowed to

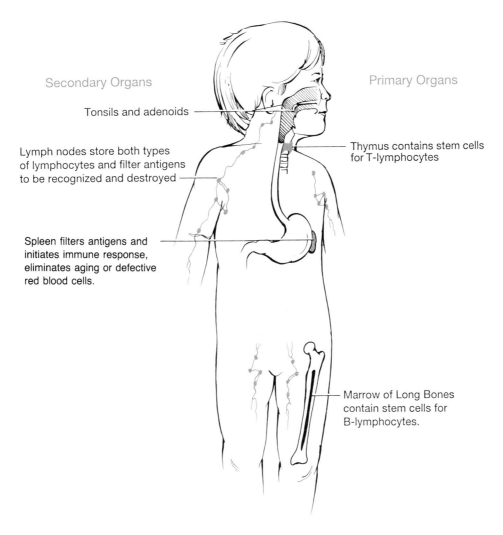

Secondary Organs

Primary Organs

Tonsils and adenoids —

Lymph nodes store both types
of lymphocytes and filter antigens
to be recognized and destroyed —

Spleen filters antigens and
initiates immune response,
eliminates aging or defective
red blood cells.

— Thymus contains stem cells
for T-lymphocytes

— Marrow of Long Bones
contain stem cells for
B-lymphocytes.

*Figure 27–1.   Body systems involved with the immune system.*

stand. The densest layer at the bottom is red and contains mostly erythrocytes (red blood cells) and a few platelets. The uppermost layer is usually clear and contains no cells (plasma). A thin white layer forms between the two and contains the many cells that compose the immune system (white blood cells).

Circulating white blood cells may be divided by their morphology and staining characteristics into five major types: polymorphonuclear leukocytes, including neutrophils, eosinophils and basophils; and mononuclear leukocytes, including lymphocytes and monocytes. The mononuclear cells are usually round and appear either small (lymphocytes) or large (monocytes) under the microscope. The monocytes are also called circulating macrophages, in contrast to similar cells that may be found within certain lymphatic organs such as the liver, spleen, and lymph nodes. In these organs they are called fixed tissue macrophages or histiocytes (Fig. 27-2).

### Polymorphonuclear Leukocytes

Neutrophils constitute about 50% to 70% of the circulating white blood cells in a normal individual. They are short-lived, particularly in the presence of foreign material or invading microorganisms. About one half of the neutrophils are free in the circulation at any given time, and an equal amount—the so-called marginated pool—may be found lining blood vessel walls. In the presence of infection the circulating neutrophils migrate rapidly to the source of invasion. Within 10 to 15 minutes marginated cells enter the vascular pool and then migrate to the infection site. A bacterial infection generally results in a larger than normal proportion of neutrophils in the circulation. Under continued stimulation by invasion of microbial pathogens, the bone marrow produces more neutrophils and also releases less mature neutrophils. This change in proportion and maturity of circulating neutrophilic cells is called a left shift.

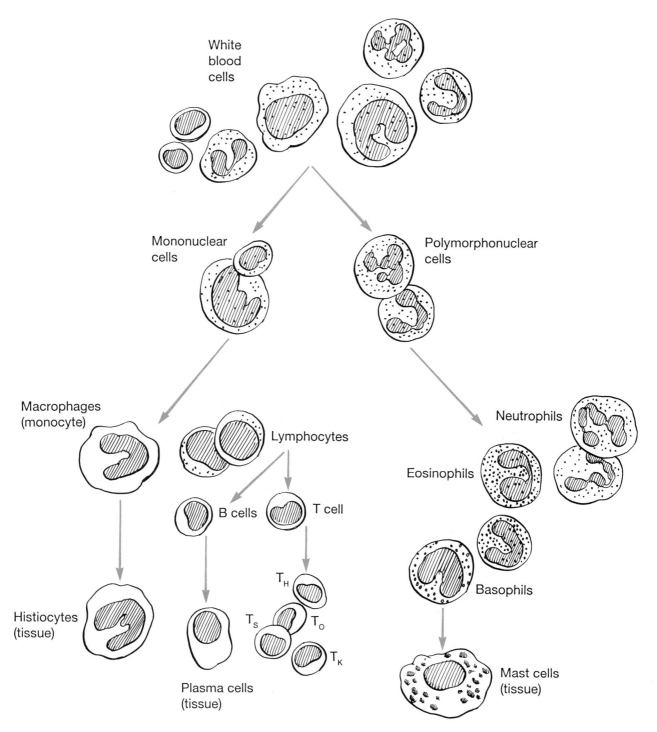

*Figure 27–2.   White blood cells.*

Neutrophils are the first line of cellular defense by the host. These cells attempt to surround invading material (ingestion) and destroy it through release of toxic enzymes and superoxide radicals (digestion). In doing this, the neutrophils self-destruct.

Eosinophils (1% to 3% of the white blood cells) are specifically involved in containing and eradicating parasites and in responding to allergens (i.e., materials that

cause allergy). In the latter circumstance, although the response is appropriate and the allergen is removed, the outcome (allergy) is harmful to the host. Interestingly, primitive human populations (such as remote tribes in Brazil) are routinely infected with parasites but do not show manifestations of allergy. Advanced societies (such as the United States) that are generally free of parasite infestation are most prone to allergies.

Basophils generally compose less than 1% of the circulating polymorphonuclear leukocyte pool. Basophils are more commonly found in tissue, where they are called mast cells. Circulating basophils and fixed tissue mast cells are the chemical storehouse for mounting an inflammatory response. Basophils contain histamine, serotonin, heparin, and a variety of enzymes within their cytoplasmic granules. Fixed basophilic mast cells are generally located in close proximity to a blood vessel wall. Stimulation of the mast cell causes release of its chemicals and enzymes which, in turn, increases vascular permeability and attracts neutrophils and monocytes. This process is called inflammation, or an inflammatory reaction.

### Mononuclear Leukocytes

The second group of cells is mononuclear, and is comprised of lymphocytes and monocytes (see Fig. 27-1). Lymphocytes are more common than monocytes in the circulation pool. Lymphocytes account for approximately 30% of the circulating white cells, whereas monocytes generally account for 5% or less. Lymphocytes are small and round and are composed almost entirely of a nucleus, with a thin rim of cytoplasm. Some lymphocytes are thought to survive for the entire life of the individual. The functional roles of lymphocytes include antigen recognition and memory. Lymphocytes are divided into three major types:

> *T cells* are formed in the bone marrow and migrate to the thymus, where they are processed and released back into the circulation. These mature T cells then localize in various lymphoid organs. Certain T cells encourage antibody production (helper cells, T4 cells, CD4 cells); others inhibit or turn off the immune response (suppressor cells, T8 cells, or CD8 cells). Null cells, delayed hypersensitivity cells, and contrasuppressor cells are other types of T lymphocytes.
>
> *B cells* are formed in the bone marrow and migrate to the human counterpart of the bursa of Fabricius (an unknown site that is discussed below), where they are processed and released back into the circulation. Mature B cells wait for antigenic stimulation, then proliferate and produce antibodies, at which time they are called plasma cells. Plasma cells produce one, and only one, type of antibody.
>
> *Killer cells* (also called cytotoxic T cells) are lymphocytes that can kill other cells chemically without need for support from other components of the immune system.

Monocytes are large cells whose major function is clearance of foreign or damaged material. Monocytes (or macrophages) are phagocytic cells like neutrophils, but they are capable of ingesting and digesting larger-sized material. Circulating monocytes respond well after the polymorphonuclear leukocytes have initiated the inflammatory response. Fixed tissue macrophages (histiocytes) initially do not recognize foreign material but rather process the material and present it to T lymphocytes for recognition. This presentation occurs on the macrophage cell surface, adjacent to markers of self (major histocompatibility complex II markers). Deposition of foreign antigen allows the lymphocyte to compare self and non-self and distinguish between the two. Macrophages also release a variety of chemical mediators of inflammation that perpetuate the inflammatory process.

### Vessels

During the passage of blood from the arteries and arterioles to the venules and veins, both serum and cells may migrate through the vessel walls. The body needs a way to recover these materials; it does so with lymphatics. The lymphatic vessels retrieve these materials and return them via the thoracic duct or right lymphatic duct to the systemic circulation.

Lymphatics drain almost all of the organs of the body, with certain notable exceptions (the brain and the eyes and ears). The peripheral lymphatic system contains unidirectional valves that rely on gravity or muscular contraction to propel lymph back into the circulation. Lymph is a mixture of fluid and electrolytes, proteins, and cells. If lymphatic flow is obstructed, the lymph persists in tissue and is clinically recognized as edema.

### Development of Lymphoid Organs

Precursor cells for all lymphoid cells and organs originate in bone marrow. Lymphocytes, the functional component of lymphoid organs, migrate to the fetal liver and spleen and establish hematopoiesis. How these cells differentiate to become the source of red blood cells, white blood cells, or platelets is not clear. Populations of white cells migrate to the thymus (T cells) to acquire immune competence, then move to the bone marrow or lymphoid organs. These lymphocytes are primarily responsible for cell-mediated immunity. A separate group of lymphocytes migrates to an unknown location called a bursa analogue, named for the bursa of Fabricius, an organ in chickens that facilitates maturation of B-lymphocytes. The discovery of this organ led to the recognition that there are distinctions between T cells and B-cells, and that not all lymphocytes are the same.

### Central Lymphoid Organs

A lymphoid organ is a collection of lymphocytes and macrophages (phagocytic cells). It has an arterial blood supply and venous drainage. Some lymphoid organs have afferent and efferent lymphatics (lymph nodes), whereas others have only efferent lymphatics (the thymus). The spleen has no lymphatics. Lymphoid organs are divided into four types: central, peripheral, gastrointestinal-associated, and bronchus-associated.

The central lymphoid organs include the bone marrow, liver, and thymus. Once hematopoiesis has ceased in the liver and spleen during fetal development, the marrow serves as the only source of blood cells. (However, if there is severe damage to the marrow, the liver and spleen retain some capability to again form blood cells.) The bone marrow contains a mixture of immature and progressively more mature cells. The white blood cell series (phagocytes) accounts for 60% of these cells, the red cell series approximately 20% to 30%, and lymphocytes, monocytes, platelets and plasma cells only 10% to 20%. The proportion of lymphocytes in the marrow declines with aging.

The second central lymphoid organ is the liver. The fetal liver contains both hepatocytes and the same hematopoietic cells found in the marrow. The third central lymphoid organ is the thymus. Lymphocytes found in the cortex of the thymus have been called nurse cells because they are presumed to influence thymocyte differentiation into T-helper, T-suppressor, killer cells, and other types of lymphocytes.

### Peripheral Lymphoid Organs

There are five major types of peripheral lymphoid organs: lymph nodes, the spleen, lymphoid tissue lining the gastrointestinal tract, lymphoid tissue lining the respiratory tract, and the lactating breast. Lymph nodes, which are widely distributed throughout the body, function as filters for lymph fluid derived from various body tissues. Lymphocytes clustered in the deep cortex and surrounding area are thymus-derived (T-lymphocytes). Follicles around the periphery of the lymph nodes contain bursa-derived cells (B-lymphocytes). Macrophages are found throughout the lymph node.

The spleen also has many sinusoids, characterized by large numbers of lymphocytes (white pulp), which surround afferent arterioles. A second area of the spleen is known as red pulp because it contains large numbers of erythrocytes. There are neither afferent nor efferent lymphatics; blood enters through the arteries and arterioles, penetrates through the sinusoids, and drains out through the splenic vein. The sinusoids of the spleen serve as filters for foreign material such as bacteria.

Another cluster of lymphatic tissue is found beneath the mucosal layer of the gastrointestinal tract and respiratory tract. Examples of well-organized collections of lymphatic tissue may be found in the tonsils and the appendix. As thymic involution (regression) occurs with aging, it has been proposed that lymphatics along the GI tract may serve as an alternative source of lymphocytes.

Mucosal cells lining the GI tract can transport foreign material (*antigens*) or viable microorganisms to the lymphatics underneath. Lymphatic vessels serve a similar function. Because of the massive amount and type of foreign material passing through the GI tract, this lymphatic submucosal tissue is believed to play a major role in the development of immunity. Sensitized cells may then be delivered by efferent lymphatics to other lymphoid centers throughout the body. Both B and T lymphocytes are sensitized and distributed from the GI tract.

The lactating breast also functions as a lymphoid organ. During periods of milk production, prolactin stimulates B cells to migrate to the breast and proliferate locally. B cell products (antibodies) are then incorporated into breast milk in high concentrations, providing passive immunity to the infant from the mother.

The lymphoid organs should be perceived as dynamic tissues, constantly interacting with environmental stimuli and subject to migration of T and B cells through their substance. Their interaction with the environmental stimuli starts with ingestion of antigenic material by macrophages and is rapidly followed by activation of T cells. These activated lymphocytes send chemical signals to B cells, causing their proliferation and the secretion of antibody. The process is recognized anatomically by formation of new follicles (germinal centers). When the stimulus is withdrawn, the germinal center is involuted but the experience is preserved through memory B cells. In contrast, when the host response does not include antibody production but, rather, includes delayed hypersensitivity, the follicles remain dormant.

## Physiology

### Basic Pathology

The functional role of the immune system is to distinguish "self" from "non-self" by successfully addressing invading microorganisms and surveillance against tumors. The process may be divided into a series of six steps: encounter, recognition, activation, deployment, discrimination, and regulation.

1. *Encounter.* The process of encounter requires foreign material, known as an antigen, to reach a site in the body that is capable of interacting with the material, breaking it down into its component parts (epitopes), and presenting these parts to cells capable of recognizing the material as foreign. The first cells in this encounter are known as accessory cells. They include monocytes found free in the circulation and macrophages found in a variety of organs and in lymph nodes.

2. *Recognition.* Once the host has successfully encountered the foreign material, immune recognition must occur. The antigen or its component epitopes must stimulate an antibody response.

Antibodies are protein molecules produced by lymphocytes and found in serum. They react with antigens in a lock and key mechanism. There are five different classes of antibodies: IgM, IgG, IgA, IgD, and IgE (Fig. 27-3). Each antibody has a mixture of light chains and heavy chains (small and large protein components). Each chain has a "handle" that is common to that class and a "recognition" part that varies in its size and structure. The antibody recognition site is formed when the epitope and antibody come together.

Antigens may be complete or incomplete. A complete antigen is capable of stimulating an immune response; it is therefore an immunogen. An incomplete antigen is a low molecular weight substance that can serve as an immunogen only if linked to a larger molecule. An incomplete antigen is thus an antigen but not an immunogen.

3. *Activation.* Activation of the system requires interaction of the antigen on the accessory cell surface (monocyte or macrophage) with the T4 helper cell. To assist the process, the accessory cell may secrete interleukin-1 (IL-1), a molecule that prompts cell growth. Once the interaction occurs, the T4 cell enlarges, secretes its own hormonal products (known as lymphokines), and divides repeatedly into a clone of cells. The T4 secretions encourage further T-cell and B-cell growth.

4. *Deployment.* The immunologic message of activity is deployed by secretory products of T-lymphocytes. These products include colony-stimulating factors for marrow-derived cells, interferons, interleukins, and others.

5. *Discrimination.* As mentioned at the outset, the immune system must be able to distinguish self from non-self, i.e., discriminate. This is done by lymphocytes at the macrophage cell surface.

6. *Regulation.* Regulation is the ability to turn the immune system on and off. Tolerance may be perceived as one form of immune regulation. In tolerance, the immune system does not respond to an immune stimulant. This is beneficial when host cells die and need to be cleansed from the system.

T-lymphocytes also play a central regulatory role. T-helper cells activate the system and stimulate its continued proliferation; T-suppressor cells down-regulate the system. Lymphokines play a similar role in turning the system on or off.

## Functional Physiology

### Antibody-Mediated Immunity (B-cell Mediated)

Immunity is generally divided into two categories: antibody-mediated (also called humoral) and cell-mediated. Antibody-mediated immunity is directed against polysaccharide antigens. The following example explains how this system responds to challenge by foreign material: A potential bacterial pathogen, *Haemophilus influenzae,* first encounters the host at mucosal surfaces of the respiratory tract. This organism must adhere to the surface in order to penetrate into deeper tissues. IgA is the main component of mucus that prevents this attachment. The host may also respond with polymorphonuclear leukocytes and macrophages, but the bacterium uses its polysaccharide capsule as a coat of "slime" to evade these phagocytic defenders. If there has been previous exposure to this organism, specific IgG antibodies could be recruited

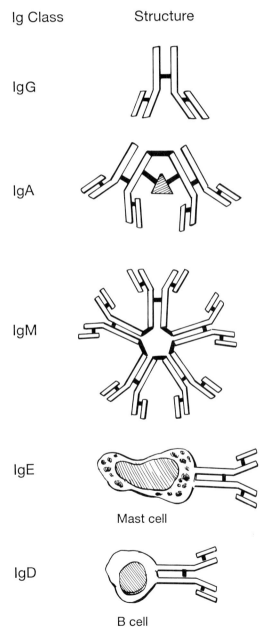

*Figure 27–3. Classes of antibodies.*

as part of the defense (secondary response). However, the person vulnerable to disease has no such antibody. The organism attaches and begins to proliferate at the mucosal surface.

The initial antibody generated in response to the invasion is IgM. It may act in two different ways, either by coating the surface of the bacteria (opsonization) or by precipitating complement on the bacterial surface and producing a bactericidal (lethal) effect. Complement is a series of nine enzymatic proteins circulating in the serum in an inactive form until a challenge by foreign material is recognized.

However, certain individuals are not protected by opsonic or bactericidal antibody. They may be vulnerable to infection because of an overwhelming inoculum of organisms, because of immaturity of their immune response, or because of underlying disease. In these individuals bacteria reach the bloodstream, continue to proliferate, and disseminate to other organs and systems. Targets may include sites such as the central nervous system (meningitis) or joints (septic arthritis). After a brief delay, generally of 3 to 5 days, the host then responds by producing a much more specific immunoglobulin, IgG. Thus, IgM is the first line of humoral defense. It has high sensitivity (responds promptly) but low specificity (discriminates poorly). IgG is the second line of humoral defense. It is generated with some delay (low sensitivity) but is directed very precisely against the specific antigen responsible for disease (high specificity). The cells producing this immunoglobulin protection protect the individual for the rest of his or her life (memory cells).

## Cell-Mediated Immunity (T-cell Immunity)

Most pathogens (including all viruses, fungi, parasites, and certain bacteria, such as salmonella and mycobacteria), and essentially all tumors stimulate a T-cell mediated, B-cell host response. For example, in tuberculosis, organisms are inhaled by a vulnerable host (i.e., a person not previously exposed to tuberculosis). These organisms are captured and processed by pulmonary alveolar macrophages. They are then presented to T-helper cells, which stimulate B cells to make antibodies, but these antibodies are neither opsonic nor mycobactericidal. Therefore, the host is not protected, and the humoral immune system (B-cell mediated immunity) is of no value.

The proliferating organisms migrate to a draining lymph node, and are disseminated throughout the body. If the host is to mount a successful defense, it must occur at this time; otherwise, disease will result. Since antibodies are ineffective in controlling the invasion, cell-mediated immunity must be employed. T-lymphocytes must stimulate macrophages to migrate to the sites of infection. Layers of macrophages and lymphocytes eventually encircle the clusters of growing and dividing organisms, forming granulomas.

In a successful defense, the host remains asymptomatic during this entire process. However, because the defense is one of containment rather than eradication, the host remains vulnerable to reactivation of infection throughout its life. Certain changes such as aging, other systemic disease, or use of medications (especially corticosteroids) may reduce the effectiveness of host defenses and allow reactivation.

For tumor surveillance, both macrophages and lymphocytes protect the host. A special kind of lymphocytes, T killer cells, may be recruited by T helper cells to the site of abnormal cells. The T killer cells are directly cytotoxic. It is suspected that each individual may develop several malignancies during the course of a lifetime. Most are successfully eradicated by the lymphocyte–macrophage system. The ones that escape this defense become clinically apparent as tumors.

## Aberrant Immune Responses

### Autoimmunity

If the host fails to discriminate between self and non-self, an autoimmune process develops. This process may be separated into autoimmunity (having minor and potentially reversible pathologic implications) and autoimmune disease. Autoimmunity often results from exposure to drugs or infectious agents. If the drug is withdrawn or the infectious agent is eradicated, the autoimmune phenomenon may disappear.

Autoimmune disease occurs when the self-directed immune process causes pathologic destruction and functional impairment of host tissues. A wide spectrum of autoimmune diseases have been identified, and some of these are listed in Table 27-1.

### Immune Deficiency

Immune deficiency may be primary (inherited) or acquired (secondary). Primary immunodeficiency syndromes (e.g., X-linked agammaglobulinemia) have been associated with virtually every part of the immune system. In the past, the missing host defense factors were discovered by observing unique clinical syndromes and then trying to identify the element of the immune system that was missing. Spe-

*Table 27–1. Autoimmune Diseases*

Myasthenia gravis
Thyrotoxicosis (Graves disease)
Diabetes mellitus (type I)
Rhinitis and asthma
Systemic lupus erythematosus
Rheumatoid arthritis
Sjögren syndrome
Dermatomyositis, polymyositis
Wegener granulomatosis

cific examples of primary immunodeficiencies are reviewed later in this chapter. A list of disorders as established by the World Health Organization (WHO) and a brief description of the abnormality are presented in Table 27-2.

### Allergic Responses

Allergens (antigens that produce allergy) differ from bacteria by stimulating an immune response mediated by IgE immunoglobulins. Parasites such as amoebae, nematodes, and cestodes also stimulate an IgE response. The first exposure to an allergen yields no clinically apparent response. The allergen may be inhaled—for example, ragweed pollen. Alternatively, it may come in contact with the host via the skin or mucous membranes such as the conjunctivae or nose. If inhaled, the allergen encounters pulmonary alveolar macrophages in the lungs. These cells present the antigen to T-helper lymphocytes, which, in turn, stimulate B lymphocytes to make IgE antibody. The antibody circulates, but also binds to certain cells located at the primary site of exposure. In the case of ragweed pollen these cells include both mast cells and pulmonary alveolar macrophages. Mast cells (fixed tissue basophils) produce a variety of substances that increase vascular permeability and attract inflammatory cells.

On second or subsequent exposures the allergen attaches to the IgE receptor sites on mast cells and macrophages. The response is accelerated. The clinical manifestations are mucus production resulting from increased vascular permeability, plus pus produced by the phagocytic cells. Cough, bronchospasm and sputum production, impaired oxygen exchange caused by the fluid accumulation in the lungs, and systemic manifestations of fever, leukocytosis, and malaise all may result from this exposure.

## Assessment

### History

The medical history of an individual suspected to have a primary or acquired immune disorder is important. Infectious diseases are common in children, and identifiable immune deficiency disorders are very rare. Concern should be raised when a child has recurrent infections of the same organ or system in a brief period of time. The health history includes documenting the number of times the child has had an infection, as well as the number of hospitalizations, the treatments, and the outcomes. The medical history is also important for determining the number and type of laboratory tests needed.

A thorough review of systems must be performed. Otitis and sinusitis are common among children; however, pneumonia occurs infrequently. One or two recurrences of pneumonia caused by respiratory syncytial virus (RSV) over a period of several years is not abnormal. However, if staphylococcal pneumonia recurs, the immune system should be evaluated. Investigation of possible immune system deficiencies should depend on the pathogen responsible for disease.

The review of systems should be very thorough, because clinical manifestations of immune deficiency disorders are often diverse and seemingly unrelated. For example, the Wiskott-Aldrich syndrome takes years to evolve. The initial manifestation is bleeding. Months or years later the affected child sustains recurrent viral infections. However, viral infections are common in childhood, so suspicion of an immune defect may not be aroused. Only when recurrent fungal infections develop may the diagnosis be considered.

In addition to the child's medical history, histories of other family members should be obtained as well to determine any possibly hereditary susceptibility to infection or vulnerability to malignancy. Genetic disorders may already have been diagnosed in older family members.

### Physical Examination

In many cases no physical findings are specifically indicative of immune deficiency disorders. Because height and weight are negatively affected by recurrent infections, they should be carefully monitored at each visit for health care.

*Table 27–2.  WHO Classification of Primary Immunodeficiency Syndromes*

| Syndrome | Cell Line Affected |
| --- | --- |
| Severe combined immunodeficiency | T and B |
| Thymic hypoplasia | T |
| Purine nucleoside phosphorylase deficiency | T |
| Ataxia telangiectasia | T and plasma cells |
| Thymoma | B and T |
| X-linked agammaglobulinemia | B |
| Transcobalamin II | Plasma cells |
| Selective IgA | Plasma and B and T |
| Selective Ig or subclass | Plasma and T |
| Secretory price deficiency | IgA cells |
| Ig with increased IgM | Plasma cells and B |
| Ig with IgM production and without γ and α cells | Selected B cells |
| Transient hypogammaglobulinemia | Plasma cells |
| Antibody but normal or increased globulins | B |
| Kappa chain | B |
| Wiskott-Aldrich syndrome | T and B |
| Varied immunodeficiencies | T and B |

(Adapted from Bluestein, H. G. [1987]. Immunodeficiency diseases. In J. H. Stein [Ed.]. *Internal medicine* [2nd ed., pp. 1226–1227]. Boston: Little, Brown and Company)

Children who fail to reach normal growth milestones and who suffer from recurrent infections warrant diagnostic evaluation.

Each component of the physical examination has potential implications for establishing a diagnosis of an immune deficiency disorder. Red hair, abnormal eyes, unusual ears, imperfect closure of the palate, rales in the chest, hepatomegaly, splenomegaly, skin rashes, and many other findings may indicate immune dysfunction.

## Diagnostic Procedures

The key elements in establishing the medical diagnosis of immune system disorders are laboratory findings. Evaluation should progress from routine screening tests to sophisticated, quantitative measurements of the various components of the immune system and functional assays of various cells and serum factors.

The first test usually ordered is a complete blood count (CBC) with differential to determine the number and type of white blood cells, as well as the number and morphology of red blood cells. A second screening test is the serum protein electrophoresis (SPEP), which may be combined with an immunoelectrophoresis (IEP). The SPEP provides general information about serum proteins, including albumin and alpha and gamma globulins. The IEP provides quantitative information about the amounts of IgM, IgG, and other immunoglobulins in the serum.

A third screening test is determination of total hemolytic complement. Each of the complement components may be analyzed. If any results of screening tests are abnormal, additional diagnostic studies may be required, including bone marrow evaluation, liver–spleen scan, or functional assays for components of the immune system suspected to be deficient.

For suspected allergic disorders, screening tests may also include a CBC with differential. Some allergies produce an abnormally high number of eosinophils in the circulation. Immunoelectrophoresis may identify an excess of IgE in the serum. The most important diagnostic tests for allergies are skin tests. Unfortunately, allergens are not standardized. Most are made of mixtures of substances known to provoke allergic symptoms in large numbers of individuals, such as dog hair, ragweed pollen, and mite dust. The allergens are emulsified and applied topically to the skin into a scratch, or are given intradermally like a PPD test. The evaluation period is 10 to 15 minutes. A wheal and flare response (hive) correlates well with allergy to that substance.

## Nursing Diagnosis

The diagnoses approved by the North American Nursing Diagnosis Association (NANDA) are used when immune system problems are discussed. The most common diagnoses include the following:

*Pattern 1: Exchanging*
- Altered Nutrition: Less than body requirements
- Altered (Specify Type) Tissue Perfusion (Renal, cerebral, cardiopulmonary, gastrointestinal, peripheral)
- Decreased Cardiac Output
- Diarrhea
- Fluid Volume Deficit
- High Risk for Fluid Volume Deficit
- High Risk for Impaired Skin Integrity
- High Risk for Infection
- High Risk for Injury
- Impaired Gas Exchange
- Impaired Skin Integrity
- Ineffective Airway Clearance
- Ineffective Breathing Pattern

*Pattern 3: Relating*
- Altered Family Processes
- Social Isolation

*Pattern 5: Choosing*
- Ineffective Family Coping: Compromised

*Pattern 6: Moving*
- Activity Intolerance
- Altered Growth and Development
- Bathing/Hygiene Self-Care Deficit
- Diversional Activity Deficit
- Dressing/Grooming Self-Care Deficit
- Feeding Self-Care Deficit
- Impaired Physical Mobility
- Sleep Pattern Disturbance
- Toileting Self-Care Deficit

*Pattern 7: Perceiving*
- Body Image Disturbance

*Pattern 9: Feeling*
- Pain

## Planning Nursing Care

Planning nursing care for children with immune problems presents a challenge to nurses because immune system disorders are characterized by a wide range of etiologies and symptoms that affect various body systems. These disorders include immune deficiency diseases, hypersensitivity, autoimmune diseases, and cancer. Nursing care of children with immune disorders focuses on a variety of common concerns, including development of both child and family, acute care, preparation for home care, and chronic care.

## Developmental Considerations

Supporting parents in promoting their child's normal growth and development is one of the primary concerns of nurses who work with children who have immune system disorders. The impact on a child's growth and development varies based on whether the disorder is self-limiting and requires short-term hospitalization (e.g., rheumatic fever or Kawasaki disease), a chronic problem resulting in repeated hospitalizations (e.g., asthma, systemic lupus erythematosus, juvenile rheumatoid arthritis, or immune deficiencies), or is life-threatening, as in the case of acquired immunodeficiency syndrome (AIDS).

When planning nursing care the nurse must take into account that short-term hospitalization often results in developmental regression, which usually resolves once the disease process subsides and the child returns to the home environment. Children with long-term chronic problems that require repeated hospitalizations often experience developmental delays or problems related to the interruption in normal routine and separation from family and peers. (See Chapter 14 for further discussion of the effects of hospitalization on children and families.) Every attempt must be made to foster normal growth and development even in children with life-threatening illnesses such as AIDS, since it is felt that a cure will be found for AIDS. Efforts to prevent growth retardation and developmental delays ensure that children who benefit from advances in AIDS treatment will have the capacity to lead normal lives.

Infants and toddlers diagnosed with immune system disorders should receive regular well child maintenance checkups. Their height and weight should be assessed and plotted regularly. Achievement of developmental milestones should be recorded, and delays should be reported to the primary care provider.

In situations when chronic diarrhea, frequent vomiting, or other adverse reactions to food interfere with the normal growth processes, care must be taken to ensure adequate nutrition. This may be in the form of nutritional supplements, enteral feedings, special diets, or avoidance of foods containing offending allergens.

A program of appropriate infant stimulation activities should be planned and taught to the parents in order to encourage achievement of developmental milestones. Frequent infections that result in a lack of energy also affect achievement of tasks. The nurse can discuss the child's level of development with the family and work with them to plan ways to help the child master tasks despite the effects of the illness.

Older children should be encouraged to make their own decisions and to participate in their own care in order to reinforce their independence and their ability to manage their own health problems. Often children with chronic conditions are sheltered and over-protected, which usually results in frustration and stress for both parents and children. Nurses can intervene by encouraging the parents to treat children as normally as possible. School-age children should attend class and engage in school activities with peers whenever possible. If this is not possible, arrangements should be made for a home school program. Children should be encouraged to participate in age-appropriate activities including sports, hobbies, and stays away from home.

As children approach adolescence it is important to encourage autonomy and self-management. Issues related to burgeoning sexuality must be addressed. Although interactions with peers of both sexes should be encouraged, the adolescent must be aware of the effect of sexual relations on the disease process. Adolescents with AIDS must be supplied with information regarding how to protect friends from the disease. This includes using a condom and diaphragm during sexual activities. Adolescent drug users must be taught to avoid sharing syringes with friends. Female adolescents with AIDS or systemic lupus erythematosus (SLE) must be cautioned regarding the effects of pregnancy on both themselves and the children they conceive. (See specific discussions of AIDS and SLE later in this chapter.)

## Acute Care Considerations

Children with immune system disorders may experience exacerbations leading to frequent hospitalizations. The nurse planning care for children in the acute care setting focuses on a variety of concerns determined by the type of disorder and the body system involved. Some general concerns include protection from infection, relief of pain, immobility, potential for impaired skin integrity, developmental needs, and assessing individual and family coping mechanisms.

### Protection from Infection

Certain immune system disorders result in overwhelming infections. Therefore, protection from infection is a primary responsibility of nurses caring for children in the acute care setting. Children with suppressed immune systems resulting from Wiskott-Aldrich syndrome, DiGeorge syndrome, agammaglobulinemia, and AIDS need protective or reverse isolation while in the hospital setting. The procedures vary, depending on hospital policy and the environmental arrangements available. Generally the child is placed in a private room with corridor doors closed at all times. A clean anteroom may be provided to allow for dressing in sterile clothing, handwashing, and management of food, medication, supplies, equipment, and toys. Some institutions provide germ-free arrangements for children through the use of a laminar airflow system. This system filters dust particles and extremely small contaminants, resulting in almost sterile air within a room or a series of rooms. An anteroom is provided to manage entry of all incoming personnel and visitors, food, medications, toys, and supplies. The nurse caring for the child in protective isolation must be certain to meet not only the physical needs of the child but the social and emotional needs as well.

### Relief of Pain

Certain immune system disorders such as juvenile rheumatoid arthritis (JRA) and SLE involve inflammation, pain, and limitation in joint movement. Therefore, pain management is a nursing priority. Nurses planning care in the acute care setting are generally responsible for assessing pain and providing medical and non-medical pain relief measures. Prescribed medications generally include the salicylates, nonsteroidal anti-inflammatory drugs such as ibuprofen or tolmetin sodium, and corticosteroids. Non-medicinal measures include exercise, application of heat, and diversionary activities. If a physical therapy program is established, the nurse should be sure to communicate with the therapist in order to ensure coordination of activities. These activities might include preparing the child for or transporting the child to treatments such as whirlpool or heat application, carrying out planned exercise between treatments, and performing range-of-motion exercises on both affected and non-affected joints. The nurse, in conjunction with the play therapist (if such services are available in the hospital), should plan appropriate activities to provide diversional activity, including physical activity, play, and social contact with other children. (See Chapter 17 for age-specific activities.)

### Immobility

Treatment of certain immune system disorders may include bedrest in order to prevent complications to the heart and kidneys. Complete bedrest or strictly limited activity may lead to alterations in respiratory, bladder, and bowel status. The nurse planning care for the immobilized child must encourage the child to breathe deeply. Percussion and postural drainage may be necessary. Increased fluid and fiber should be included in the child's diet. Age-appropriate diversional activities that do not tax the child's energy level should be planned. (See Chapter 17 for nursing interventions specific to the immobilized child.)

### Impairment of Skin Integrity

Children with immune system disorders may manifest a variety of skin problems, ranging from the eczematous rash associated with an allergic response to the severely compromised skin of the child with AIDS. During periods of immobility the nurse must be diligent to prevent skin breakdown. Specific skin care depends on the type of lesion involved. (See Chapter 34 for nursing interventions specific to alterations in the integumentary system.)

### Individual/Family Coping

Nurses working with children with immune disorders in the acute care setting must focus on supporting both the child and family during the acute and usually frightening phase of illness. Certain immune disorders are self-limiting, and the family must be given assurance that although the child seems very ill, with treatment he or she may recover with no ill effects. Children with immune system disorders may be in a life-threatening situation, and the

child and family need encouragement to maintain a positive attitude for living and, in some instances, help in adjusting to the possibility of death.

Both the child and the family can become anxious and experience stress related to the severity, duration, and prognosis of the disease. Nursing interventions must focus on helping them recognize and cope with their feelings. The child and family must be supported in expressing their fears and emotions. The nurse may assist them by teaching them about the disease process, treatment, and possible outcomes. Referrals to appropriate community and social services should be made. The family should be encouraged to become involved in support groups and to take time off for themselves and for other children in the family.

## Home Care Considerations

Many immune disorders are long-term chronic conditions requiring home care. Preparation for home care must begin as soon as the child is diagnosed. A careful assessment of the parents' ability to care for the child must be carried out. This assessment must take into consideration physical and intellectual ability, family support systems, and financial considerations.

The nurse preparing a family for home care must focus on the goal of making the child and family as independent as possible. The nurse teaches the family about:

- The disease process and prognosis
- Carrying out all treatments
- Administering medications properly and the side effects that may occur
- Assessing the child for changes in condition, and when to notify the primary health care provider

For further discussion of caring for a child with an acute or chronic condition in the home see Chapter 18 and discussions of specific disease conditions in this chapter.

## Nursing Interventions

### Desensitization

Hyposensitization or immunotherapy alters the immune response or mechanism. The goal of this therapy is to depress the immune response to specific allergens that lead to adverse reactions. This therapy is used when removal or avoidance of the allergen is either not possible or not effective. This treatment can help control symptoms, but does not cure the allergy. Desensitization was introduced in 1912 as a treatment for "hay fever" induced by grass pollen, and is often used today to reduce the signs and symptoms associated with seasonal pollen allergies. Immunotherapy is prescribed for children suffering from allergic rhinitis, IgE mediated asthma, or allergy to stinging insects. It is felt that it is not effective for food allergy.

The treatment consists of identifying the offending allergen and then administering it subcutaneously at frequent intervals, in the form of a dilute extract. The strength is gradually increased in succeeding doses until the child develops a tolerance to the allergen. The child is then maintained at this dose on a regular basis. The therapy may be given just before the time of year when the offending allergen is present in quantity (preseasonally) or throughout the year (perennially). This therapy takes advantage of challenging the host by a different route of administration, which increases IgG antibodies that block the IgE mediated allergic response.

The nurse prepares the child for the procedure by giving a careful explanation to both the child and family and assisting in the procedure. The nurse in the physician's office or clinic may be responsible for having the necessary equipment and supplies ready. These supplies include emergency equipment such as oxygen, epinephrine, intubation supplies, and a tracheostomy set. The child is monitored carefully during the injection and for 20 minutes after the injection for signs of anaphylaxis. (See the section on anaphylaxis under General Allergic Reactions later in this chapter for a discussion of signs, symptoms, and treatment for anaphylaxis.) The child may also experience local reactions, including erythema or edema at the site of injection. These reactions are treated with cold compresses and antihistamines. The child and family should also be taught to observe for delayed symptoms, such as an exacerbation of asthma (wheezing). These symptoms should be reported to the primary health care provider.

## Environmental Control

The preferred method of management of allergic disorders is avoidance of allergens or irritants that elicit the adverse reaction. Once the offending allergens are identified by a careful history or use of allergy skin tests, elimination or avoidance may be all that is needed in many cases of IgE-mediated disease. For example, if there is a reaction to house dust or molds, or dog or cat dander, these allergens must be removed. However, it may be difficult to persuade parents to find another home for the family pet, particularly when there are other children in the family. The parents are usually more willing to do this if the disorder is serious, such as asthma, and the child has a positive skin test to the dander of the pet.

The nurse should provide the family with instructions for maintaining an allergy-free indoor environment, particularly emphasizing the child's bedroom. Table 27-3 provides an example of these instructions. The nurse should review these instructions with the parents and child, provide answers to their questions, and suggest ways that the

*Table 27–3. Environmental Control of Allergens for the Child with Allergies*

Use washable curtains in contrast to draperies. Wash curtains once a month.

Use washable rugs in contrast to wall-to-wall carpeting. Wash rugs once a month.

Dust catchers (banners, shelves with books, trophies, pictures) should be removed from the child's bedroom.

Washable dolls and animals stuffed with foam are acceptable.

Remove feather pillows from bedroom and from adjoining rooms or closets and replace with foam pillows.

Use washable blankets. Remove comforters and quilts (dust collectors).

Closets should contain only clothes to be worn during that particular season. If removal is impossible, then clothing not in use should be put in a zippered plastic clothes bag.

Keep down the amount of dust in the rest of the house as much as possible. Vacuum about twice a week. The patient should be out of the house during thorough cleanings. The child should not be in the area where cleaning will be done and should avoid doing dusty work such as dusting or sweeping (or use a mask over the mouth).

There should be no stuffed furniture in the child's bedroom. Use wooden, metal, or sponge rubber filled furniture if possible. The child's room should contain the minimum amount of furniture.

Keep pets and birds out of the bedroom at *all* times, and try to prohibit them from the house if possible.

Change filters in hot air heating systems frequently. Registers may be covered with layers of fine muslin or cheesecloth, which should also be changed frequently.

Extremely sensitive children should have a cotton mattress replaced by a rubber mattress if possible; or a regular mattress should be covered with allergen-proof cases (available at major department stores). Vacuuming the mattress and box springs at regular intervals is helpful.

Doors and windows in the child's bedroom should be closed whenever possible.

The child's room should be cleaned with a damp cloth *daily.* Thorough overall cleaning should be done *weekly.*

Avoid exposing the child to cigarette smoke or strong odors (for example, aerosol sprays).

Remember, the more you can do for your child
The better off your child will be!!!

(Printed by permission of The Children's Hospital of Buffalo, Allergy/Immunology Division, 219 Bryant Street, Buffalo, New York 14222, [716] 878-7258)

instructions can be carried out. The nurse must emphasize avoiding smoking in the home.

## Drug Therapy

Much of the management of allergic diseases centers on the use of drugs. The drugs used may modulate the antigen-induced release of mediators such as histamines.

Drug therapy may also affect the dilation of airways and smooth muscle relaxation. Specific drugs used for allergic reactions include beta-adrenergic agonists, theophylline, cromolyn sodium, and corticosteroids.

The child with an immune deficiency may receive periodic intravenous administration of immune globulin. Antibiotics are generally prescribed to treat infections, or occasionally as a prophylactic measure. The child with an autoimmune disorder such as JRA or SLE may be treated with nonsteroidal anti-inflammatory drugs, oral gold salts, and corticosteroids.

The role of the nurse in the use of drugs includes their proper administration in the acute care setting and the preparation of the family to administer the medications independently at home. Teaching should include instruction about the action and side effects of the drug; proper administration, including the dose and schedule; and when to report adverse reactions to the primary health care provider. (The use of medications in treatment of specific immune disorders is discussed with the individual disorders.)

## Nutrition

Nutrition plays three roles in the care of the child with immune system disorders:

1. Inadequate nutrition can contribute to the disorder.
2. Adequate nutrition is essential to promote normal growth and development.
3. Avoidance of specific foods is essential when planning care for the child with food allergies.

Children with immune disorders have frequent infections. Inadequate nutrition, particularly insufficient protein, can decrease the body's ability to resist infection. Infection and inflammation leads to an increase in body temperature (fever), which leads to an increased metabolic rate and calorie consumption. Children with gastrointestinal disorders such as diarrhea and vomiting related to AIDS are at risk for inadequate nutrition and dehydration. Therefore, strict attention must be focused on providing adequate caloric intake and fluid balance. Normal growth and development depends on a well-balanced diet with an adequate number of calories to compensate for the presence of infection and increased metabolic and fluid needs.

Preparing nutritious meals for the child with a variety of food allergies is a challenge for parents, and they need support in planning and preparing meals. The parents of children with food allergies must be taught the importance of adequate nutrition while avoiding foods that contain the offending allergens. They must be taught to read labels when shopping and to ask questions related to food preparation when dining away from home. (See the section on food allergy for more specific information.)

The pregnant woman with a food allergy or a strong family history of allergies must avoid foods that contain allergens during pregnancy and while breast-feeding. Food allergens can cross the placenta and are secreted in breast milk, so the child may become sensitized. Mothers should be encouraged to breast-feed their children for the first 6 months before introducing solid foods or milk products. If the mother chooses not to breast-feed, formulas such as Nutramigen or Pregestimil are recommended. Soy-based formulas are no longer recommended because it has been found that many children who are sensitive to milk are also sensitive to soy.

## Evaluation of Nursing Care

Evaluation is a measure of the effectiveness of nursing intervention. Evaluation of nursing care must be based on patient centered goals and expected outcomes. The goals and expected outcomes must be determined by the severity of the illness, the body systems involved, and the ability and willingness of the family to carry out the interventions while caring for the child at home. It is essential to include the child and family in planning care and in determining goals and expected outcomes. Based on evaluation, the goals and expected outcomes should be adjusted to reflect a realistic intervention plan as an ongoing process throughout the course of the illness. Factors to be considered when adjusting the goals and expected outcomes should include changes in the child's condition related to response to treatment, exacerbation of symptoms, and progress related to growth and development.

## Immune Health Problems of Children

### Acquired Immunodeficiency Syndrome

#### Pathophysiology

The causative agent of the acquired immunodeficiency syndrome (AIDS) is the human immunodeficiency virus (HIV). The main population affected by this virus has been young adults, aged 20 to 40 years; however, newborns and children have been infected by transmission of the virus in utero, at the time of delivery from infected mothers, or by transfusion of blood or blood products contaminated with HIV. Older children (teenagers) may acquire the infection through sexual activity or intravenous drug abuse. Finally, sexual abuse of children by infected adults may also result in transmission of the virus.

HIV is a retrovirus, an RNA virus, and currently consists of two families (HIV-1 and HIV-2). HIV-1 has recently emerged as a significant worldwide human pathogen. HIV-2 has been identified only in Western Africa.

HIV consists of a helical ribonucleoprotein, an icosahedral capsid, and a lipoprotein envelope. Several viral genes and their functions have been identified; other viral genes have been localized and characterized, but their functions remain unknown. Identification and understanding of the role of each of the component parts of the virus may make it possible for treatment regimens or vaccines to be developed.

Once the virus is internalized, it uncoats (removes its outer membrane shell) and makes a DNA copy of its genetic material using the enzyme reverse transcriptase. The DNA then becomes randomly incorporated into the host genome. Viral RNA and DNA copy also remain free in the host cell cytoplasm, and the virus may desist from further replication. The absence of further replication is believed to correlate with an asymptomatic infection. Alternatively, lymphocyte activity may be stimulated yielding formation of new virions, viral budding from the host cell, and cell death. Viral infection of circulating monocytes and fixed tissue macrophages occurs, but does not result in a lethal effect on these host cells.

The brain always becomes infected with HIV. Two theories of how virus reaches the central nervous system have evolved. Either a freely circulating virus directly penetrates the blood–brain barrier and infects neuroglial cells, or infected monocytes deliver the virus to the central nervous system where it infects vulnerable cells. Infection of these cells in neonates, infants, and children results in impaired development, encephalopathy, and dementia.

Viral core protein and other component parts of the virus stimulate antibody production. This is an almost universal response to infection, except among newborns, who lack the ability to react to protein antigens.

Progressive infection in adults produces lymphopenia and an inversion of the normal ratio of helper to suppressor lymphocytes ($T_4/T_8$ ratio). The degree of lymphopenia and the absolute number of T helper cells inversely correlate with prognosis. Insufficient information is currently available to reach similar prognostic conclusions about children.

HIV infection also provokes a B cell activation that yields hyperglobulinemia. However, as the T helper cell population declines there is lost ability to respond to new infections or tumor cell antigens. The ability to respond to vaccines also progressively wanes. A small group of newborns follows a different course. These individuals are often premature, lack immunoglobulin, and have intracranial calcification.

With either the hyper- or the hypogammaglobulinemia presentation there is increased vulnerability to infectious agents. These infections stimulate "normal" host defense mechanisms. As T cells proliferate in response to the challenge, dormant viral replication may be activated and the host lymphocytes will die. This makes the host vulnerable to persistent or new infection, which then stimulates further T cell activation and death, resulting in a vicious cycle (Pahwa, 1988).

## Medical Diagnosis and Management

Diagnosis of HIV infection in children up to the age of 15 months is particularly difficult. Infection occurs in utero or at the time of delivery in approximately 50% of newborns whose mothers are infected. Risk of infection does not correlate with degree of illness in the mother, and no reliable predictors have been identified for determining which children might be infected. All newborns of infected mothers have passively transmitted IgG antibodies against HIV, and newborns are normally unable to synthesize IgM antibodies in response to any infecting agent. Antibodies provided by the mother are lost by 6 to 7 months in most infants but may persist up to the age of 15 months. Therefore, false-positive test results for HIV may also persist up to this age.

Alternative methods of diagnosis are being evaluated. The virus can be grown in vitro by culturing circulating lymphocytes from infected infants. A new method of in situ hybridization may demonstrate the virus in tissue sections or monocytes. However, both are still research techniques and are limited to a few laboratories. Other approaches have included detection of viral antigen in serum and improved sensitivity for measuring IgM antibody concentrations. Attempts are also being made to distinguish maternal from infant IgG (Pahwa, 1988).

The diagnosis of HIV infection in children older than 15 months is less complicated. Serum is analyzed for anti-HIV antibody by enzyme-linked immunosorbent assay (ELISA). A positive test is confirmed by a repeat assay using the same methodology. Positive results are then further confirmed by Western blot. All three tests must be positive before establishing the diagnosis of an HIV infection.

Clinical manifestations of illness may be used to assist or replace serologic testing to establish the diagnosis, particularly in neonates and infants. The latest classification for HIV infection in children younger than 13 years is shown in Table 27-4.

Non-specific features of HIV infection include lymphadenopathy, hepatosplenomegaly, unexplained fever, diarrhea, failure to thrive, parotitis, and significant weight loss. The weight loss is involuntary, not related to poor nutritional intake, and must be 10% or more of baseline weight. Progressive neurological disease includes features such as failure to achieve developmental milestones, progressive symmetrical motor deficits, impaired brain growth or actual brain atrophy, and frank dementia.

Lymphoid interstitial pneumonitis (LIP) can be an AIDS-defining illness and represents peribronchial or interstitial infiltration of the lung by T-suppressor cells. HIV has also been identified in tissue sections of the lungs from children with LIP. The chest x-ray shows a bilateral

*Table 27–4.  Classification of Children Under 13 Years of Age with HIV Infection*

**Infection Status**

Class P-0: Indeterminate infection
Class P-1: Asymptomatic infection
Class P-2: Symptomatic infection

**Asymptomatic infection documented (P-1)**

Subclass A: Normal immune function
Subclass B: Abnormal immune function
Subclass C: Immune function not tested

**Symptomatic infection documented (P-2)**

Subclass A: Nonspecific findings
Subclass B: Progressive neurologic disease
Subclass C: Lymphoid interstitial pneumonitis (LIP)
Subclass D: Secondary infectious disease
Subclass E: Secondary cancers
Subclass F: Other diseases possibly HIV-related

(Modified from Centers for Disease Control. [1987]. Classification system for human immunodeficiency virus [HIV] infection in children under 13 years of age. *Morbidity and Mortality Weekly Report, 36,* 225–236)

reticulonodular interstitial pattern (somewhat like a honeycomb), and may suffice to establish the diagnosis without a biopsy. Auscultation of the chest often demonstrates no adventitious sounds. Clubbing of the fingers and respiratory distress may be clinically apparent, and hypoxemia should be confirmed by measuring arterial blood gas.

Once HIV infection has occurred, additional infections characterize the illness. These may be divided into opportunistic and recurrent bacterial infections. Opportunistic pathogens mimic some, but not all, of the diseases seen in adults with AIDS. *Pneumocystis carinii,* cytomegalovirus (CMV), candida, and atypical mycobacteria are commonly identified. The infections are characterized by their severity and failure to respond to conventional therapy. For example, *Candida albicans* may infect the gastrointestinal and respiratory tracts causing ulcerative lesions and profound dysphagia or respiratory distress. *Cryptosporidium,* which may be found as part of the normal gastrointestinal flora, frequently causes severe and untreatable diarrhea in children with HIV infection.

Due to the inability to mount an antibody response to infection or vaccines, many infants and children with AIDS sustain recurrent bacterial infections caused by common pathogens of childhood, including *Haemophilus influenzae* and *Streptococcus pneumoniae.* In contrast to opportunistic pathogens, these organisms can be eradicated by antimicrobial therapy. Therefore, prompt recognition of sepsis, meningitis, pneumonia, osteomyelitis, septic arthritis, and abscesses, as well as identification of the responsible bacterial pathogens and institution of appropri-

ate antimicrobial therapy are critically important to patient survival (Albano & Pizzo, 1988).

B-cell non-Hodgkin lymphomas are the most common malignancies identified in infants and children infected with HIV. A wide variety of other noninfectious and nonmalignant illnesses may be associated with HIV infection. These illnesses are currently being studied.

Treatment of HIV infection in neonates, infants, and children is experimental at present. Only one chemotherapeutic agent, zidovudine (AZT), has been shown to be effective in adults. This drug is now approved for use in children. In a single, prospective, randomized, double-blind clinical trial the number of serious events (*Pneumocystis carinii* pneumonia, malignancy, or death) was significantly reduced by administration of this drug. Further analysis and experience have shown that AZT inhibits viral replication but does not cure the infection. Clinical trials are in progress to determine if there is greater clinical efficacy when treatment is instituted early in the course of the disease, and also whether it may prevent infection following documented exposure to HIV-contaminated blood or body fluids. D dideoxyinosine (DDI) has also recently been approved for treatment of HIV infection in children. It may be used instead of AZT for children who are intolerant of that drug.

Intravenous immune globulin (IVIG) has been used as passive immunotherapy for children with AIDS. Information about efficacy and safety is limited. IVIG does not seem to work for treatment of thrombocytopenia, but it may be of some value in lymphoid interstitial pneumonia (LIP). If corticosteroids are used to treat LIP, coadministration of IVIG is recommended to lessen the risk of bacterial or viral infections secondary to the immunosuppressive effect of the steroids. Immunoglobulin therapy may also be of some value when administered simultaneously with antibiotics for treatment of bacterial infections.

### Nursing Assessment and Diagnosis

Nursing assessment centers on a careful and complete history of the onset of illness, signs and symptoms of the disease, growth and development history, and psychosocial concerns. The assessment varies depending on the developmental level of the child. Parents must be carefully assessed to determine their level of anxiety; knowledge of the disease process including prognosis, treatment, and transmission; and awareness of resources, including financial concerns, support systems, coping strategies, and perception of the child's needs.

Careful consideration must be given to the child's respiratory status because pulmonary disease, particularly pneumocystis carinii, is the primary cause of morbidity and mortality in children with AIDS (Thompson & Gietz, 1985). Careful assessment of skin and mucous membranes is essential since AIDS increases the risk of skin lesions caused by herpes or candidiasis, and overall debilitation associated with AIDS predisposes children to skin breakdown.

Nursing diagnoses for AIDS might include the following:

- High Risk for Infection related to cellular and humoral immunodeficiency
- Ineffective Airway Clearance, Ineffective Breathing Pattern, and Impaired Gas Exchange related to respiratory infections
- Altered Nutrition: Less than body requirements related to diarrhea, nausea, vomiting, anorexia, and dehydration
- High Risk for Injury related to impaired cognitive function, disorders of gait and balance, seizures, and/or paralysis
- Impaired Skin Integrity related to viral infection
- Pain related to viral infection, therapy, side effects of medications
- Activity Intolerance related to debilitated condition, fatigue, weakness, general malaise
- Altered Growth and Development related to chronic debilitating illness
- Ineffective Family Coping: Compromised related to powerlessness, depression, and grieving for anticipated loss of child
- Social Isolation related to fear of transmission of the disease to others

### Planning and Implementing Nursing Care

Nursing interventions for children with AIDS focus on three areas: caring for the child with AIDS, preventing the spread of the virus, and educating the public regarding the disease.

The approach to the care of the child with AIDS varies according to the developmental level of the child and the child's symptoms. Protecting infants and children with AIDS from opportunistic infection is the primary goal of nursing care (Fig. 27-4). The body organs most often affected are the lungs and the skin.

Universal precautions must be used whenever caring for children in acute care settings. All caretakers must engage in good handwashing techniques in order to avoid exposing the child to pathogens. All situations in which there may be contact with blood or body fluids require the use of gloves. Gowns, face shields or goggles, and masks are indicated if an aerosol is likely to be generated, as in surgery or dentistry. The child is at a higher risk of contracting infections from caretakers than caretakers are of contracting AIDS from the child. Infection control procedures are shown in Table 27-5.

Children with AIDS must be monitored closely for changes in respiratory status including fever, increased respirations and heart rate, adventitious lung sounds,

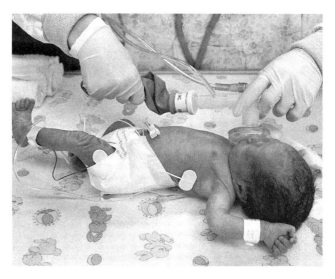

*Figure 27–4. Infant with AIDS. Note use of gloves by caregiver and use of respiratory assist device.*

coughing, and retractions. For children who are active and able to play, running and jumping stimulate deep breathing and encourage lung expansion. Children who are weakened and unable to engage in normal activities must be turned frequently, encouraged to breathe deeply, and suctioned if they are unable to expectorate secretions. Fluid intake should be increased to help liquefy secretions. Oxygen is usually administered, and arterial blood gases should be checked to monitor respiratory status. Antibiotics are administered.

Infants and young children (particularly those not toilet trained) are susceptible to diaper rash from *Candida albicans* and the oral lesions (thrush) associated with this condition. It is the nurse's responsibility to administer medication for the oral lesions and to provide good skin care following diarrhea. Treatment includes gentle cleansing of the area, application of nystatin ointment, and exposure to air. Adolescents with AIDS are often affected by Kaposi's sarcoma, which is characterized by small purple lesions that are not painful but are disfiguring and are of concern to the adolescent's body image. The child should be checked daily for signs of rashes, bruises, blisters, or abrasions, and any of these conditions should be treated immediately to prevent infection.

Even though the prognosis for children with AIDS is poor, enhancement of normal growth and development should be encouraged with the hope that eventually a cure will be found. Children with AIDS generally first present with failure to thrive or weight loss; therefore, careful attention must be paid to nutritional considerations to promote normal growth. Interventions may range from nutritional supplements to intravenous feedings or hyperalimentation.

The achievement of developmental tasks may be delayed due to lack of energy related to frequent infections.

*Table 27–5. Infection Control Procedures for Health Care Workers and Families Caring for Infants or Children Diagnosed or at Risk for AIDS*

| Item | Procedure |
| --- | --- |
| Handwashing | Handwashing is the basic infection control measure and should be practiced diligently before and after the care of all infants and children and immediately after exposure to any body fluid or blood. |
| Gowns | Long-sleeved gowns are recommended for all bedside care that involves direct contact with patients. Many hospitals have this policy for all newborns and infants. |
| Gloves | Gloves are indicated when touching blood or body fluids and should be worn in the delivery room for handling the newborn until the newborn has been bathed. Many delivery rooms and nurseries have instituted this practice for all deliveries. Gloves should also be worn when changing diapers, testing urine and stool specimens, and taking rectal temperatures. |
| Goggles | Goggles are to be worn when at risk for airborne, potentially infected material coming in contact with eyes. Neonatal nurses attending deliveries who will manage the newborn should wear goggles. Goggles should also be worn during surgical procedures. |
| Body fluid spills | Promptly clean patient care areas with standard germicidal agent used in the hospital. Household bleach diluted 1:10 with water can also be used. |
| Disposal of utensils | All needles and syringes should be carefully discarded in labeled, approved containers. Needles should not be recapped. Other articles, such as equipment and linen, should be disposed of according to the hospital policy for "blood and body fluid precautions." |
| Specimens | Specimens should be double-bagged and labeled according to hospital policy for "blood and body fluid precautions." |

(Adapted with permission from Inglis, A. D., & Lozano, M. [1986]. AIDS and the neonatal ICU. *Neonatal Network, 5*[3], 41)

Frequent hospitalizations separate the child from the family and the normal routines of daily life, contributing to both delay in achieving developmental tasks and manifestations of regressive behavior. Nursing interventions should include age-appropriate activities that assist the child in achieving developmental tasks. Care must be taken to avoid isolation and the accompanying loneliness and lack of sensory stimulation. Parents should be encouraged to visit, hold their child, and help with care.

According to Thompson and Gietz (1985), children with AIDS are classified into three groups: "(a) infants whose mothers either had AIDS, were among those groups at high risk for AIDS (such as intravenous drug abusers and Haitian immigrants), or were sexual partners of [members] of high risk groups; (b) infants and children who in the neonatal period received blood transfusions from a donor with AIDS; or (c) children with hemophilia" (p. 278).

All families of children diagnosed with AIDS must deal

with feelings of grief and anger related to the prognosis of a terminal illness. Families of children in category "a" must also deal with guilt and are more apt to have multiple stresses. The mother of the infant who contracted AIDS in utero, as well as other family members, may be seropositive for AIDS. The mother may be debilitated or unable to care for her child or may succumb to the illness. Thus, many of these children become candidates for foster care. AIDS is most prevalent in intravenous drug users, prostitutes, and homosexual or bisexual men. Adolescents with AIDS are likely to be intravenous drug users, homosexual males, or have bisexual sexual partners. Many problems confront their families, and it is important that referrals be made to social services and AIDS support groups within the community.

Families of children who are able to leave the hospital must be carefully prepared before discharge. Parent education must include information about measures to prevent infection (see Table 27-5), principles of skin care, and the importance of proper nutrition. Parents must be taught how to administer all treatments, which might include suctioning, administering oxygen, and enteral feeding or hyperalimentation. The dosage, route of administration, and possible adverse reactions of all medications should be explained. The family must know what changes in the child's condition need to be reported.

All efforts should be made to achieve as normal a lifestyle for the child as possible. The child should be seen regularly by health care providers. Attendance at school or day care is not contraindicated unless the child engages in mouthing behaviors or biting or has frequent nosebleeds, bowel or urinary incontinence, or oozing skin lesions. Every effort should be made to continue the child's education either at home or at school. Adolescents should be informed of the implications of intravenous drug use, alcohol use, and sexual relations.

HIV has been isolated from blood, saliva, semen, breast milk, vaginal secretions, cerebrospinal amniotic fluid, and urine. The disease is known to be transmitted sexually, perinatally, and by direct inoculation as in use of shared needles or accidental punctures of the skin while handling needles of infected patients. The Centers for Disease Control (1987) recommends that health care workers consider "*all* patients as potentially infected with HIV and/or other blood borne pathogens and to adhere rigorously to infection and control precautions for minimizing the risk of exposure to blood and body fluids of all patients" (p. 35). This approach is referred to as "universal blood and body fluid precautions."

Family members need to understand that HIV transmission occurs through intimate contact with body fluids and that non-intimate contact is thought to be safe. They should be taught to wash their hands carefully and to wear latex gloves when coming in contact with body secretions such as blood, stool, and urine. Sharing personal items such as pacifiers, bottles, eating utensils, toothbrushes, and razors should be avoided. Soiled diapers and other articles should be disposed of in tightly secured plastic bags. The child's bedding and clothing should be washed separately in hot soapy water. Eating utensils and toys should be washed in hot soapy water or the dishwasher. All soiled surfaces should be cleaned with a solution of one part bleach to nine parts water. Water used for cleaning should be discarded in the toilet. All babysitters, extended family members, neighbors, and friends who frequently come in contact with the child should also be made aware of the diagnosis and necessary precautions.

If the child attends day care or school, school personnel must be taught universal precautions to protect themselves and other children. Adolescents must be taught to protect their friends. Sexually active adolescents must be taught to use condoms and diaphragms and to avoid genital–oral sex. The importance of birth control should also

be stressed because of the danger of transmitting HIV perinatally. The danger of sharing needles with other drug users should also be explained.

Since AIDS was first identified in 1980, it has engendered fear and anxiety in the public. AIDS is a complex medical problem with no identified cure at this time. Despite efforts to educate the public about altering behaviors to lessen the spread of the disease, its incidence has escalated each year, affecting an increasing number of children, particularly infants born to seropositive mothers.

Nurses play a major role in educating the public regarding the disease process, its prognosis, its mode of transmission, and preventive measures. Preventive education should begin with the very young. Most school health programs include information on AIDS, including mode of transmission, cause of the illness, and sexuality issues. Nurses in schools can contribute to the success of these programs. Nurses working in communities are in a position to become leaders in the development of support groups and committees to address the needs of AIDS patients. They also have an important role in educating the community regarding these needs. Nurses in all settings can engage in research related to management of their clients with AIDS and attitudes of the health care workers caring for them. Table 27-6 is a guide to resources that provide current information about the disease and resources available to children and families with AIDS.

### Evaluating Nursing Care

Evaluation of nursing care is based on patient outcomes. The child should remain free from infections and respiratory complications. In addition, the child should achieve normal nutrition and hydration, and should remain free from injury. The child (if appropriate) and family should demonstrate their understanding of the disease, its prognosis, the treatment regimen, and home care, as well as adaptive coping mechanisms and use of resources. The child and family should also demonstrate the necessary precautions to prevent spread of the disease.

## X-Linked Agammaglobulinemia

### Pathophysiology

X-linked agammaglobulinemia (X-LA) is one of many immunoglobulin deficiency disorders. X-LA is characterized by four features: (1) male sex; (2) onset in infancy or early childhood; (3) serum IgG less than 200 mg/dL with diminished IgA and IgM concentrations for age; and (4) normal cell-mediated immunity. There are both familial and nonfamilial forms of the disease.

Most patients with X-LA have B-cell precursors but

*Table 27–6. AIDS Resource Guide*

| | |
|---|---|
| AIDS Action Council<br>Federation of AIDS-Related Organizations<br>1115½ Independence Avenue, S.E.<br>Washington, DC 20003<br>(202) 547-3101 | Gay Men's Health Crisis, Inc.<br>132 West 24th Street<br>Box 274<br>New York, NY 10011<br>(212) 807-6655 |
| AIDS Institute<br>New York State Department of Health<br>Empire State Plaza<br>Corning Tower, Room 1931<br>Albany, NY 12247<br>1-800-462-1884<br>(pamphlets, posters, flyers) | Haitian Coalition on AIDS<br>255 Eastern Parkway<br>Brooklyn, NY<br>(212) 783-2676<br><br>Modern Talking Picture Service, Inc.<br>5000 Park Street North<br>St. Petersburg, FL 33709-9989<br>"Beyond Fear," a free loan documentary (also available<br>from your local Red Cross chapter) |
| AIDS Medical Foundation<br>230 Park Avenue<br>Suite 1266<br>New York, NY 10169<br>(212) 949-7410 | National AIDS Hotline<br>1-800-342-AIDS |
| Beth Israel Medical Center<br>IV Substance Abuse/AIDS Information<br>First Avenue and 16th Street<br>New York, NY 10003<br>AIDS Hotline<br>1-800-342-AIDS | Nurses Coalition on AIDS (NCOA)<br>584 Castro, Box 498<br>San Francisco, CA 94114<br>(415) 861-6182<br><br>Pediatric AIDS Hotline<br>Albert Einstein College of Medicine<br>Montefiore Medical Center<br>(212) 430-3333 |
| Department of Health and Human Services<br>Centers for Disease Control<br>1600 Clifton Road, NE<br>Atlanta, GA 30333<br>AIDS Hotline<br>1-800-342-AIDS | PWA (People with AIDS) Coalition<br>NEWSLINE<br>P.O. Box 197<br>Murray Hill Station<br>New York, NY 10156 |

lack mature B cells or plasma cells, suggesting a developmental arrest. The current hypothesis is that the derangement causing this disease is lack of gene expression. Carrier females have normal quantities and functions of their immunoglobulin pool (Lederman & Winkelstein, 1985).

## Medical Diagnosis and Management

The usual age of diagnosis is 2.5 years. Upper and lower respiratory tract and gastrointestinal infections are the most common features. Septic arthritis also often occurs. Common childhood bacterial pathogens (*H. influenzae* and *S. pneumoniae*) are the usual etiologic agents, although *Pseudomonas* species are also seen. The recurrence of infection or a family history of other affected individuals prompts diagnostic evaluation by serum protein immunoelectrophoresis (Lederman & Winkelstein, 1985).

The child is treated with intramuscular injection of immune serum globulin (ISG) at a dose calculated to produce a serum level of 300 mg/dL. This is a painful injection. The pain is controlled by mixing a small amount of local anesthetic with the immune serum globulin in the syringe. The child is maintained on this treatment regimen indefinitely. If there is difficulty maintaining the 300 mg/dL

blood level, intravenous plasma from known donors (preferably family members) may be used to transfuse the gamma globulin.

Children are normally infected with a wide variety of viral agents, and the prevailing assumption had been that T-cell–mediated immunity was the critically important defense against these organisms. However, children with X-LA are prone to severe and chronic enterovirus infection, while all tests of T-cell function are normal. The susceptibility to viral infection most often becomes clinically manifest with vaccine-associated paralytic poliomyelitis or chronic enteroviral meningoencephalitis (CEM).

From currently available information it is clear that our understanding of this disease process is incomplete. Immunoglobulin replacement therapy should correct the anomaly but, in some instances, does not. Chronic enteroviral infection does not occur in a normal host, but an immunoglobulin-replaced child with X-LA is still unable to eradicate enterovirus from his system.

## Nursing Assessment and Diagnosis

Nursing assessment of children with X-LA focuses on monitoring for signs of infection and obtaining a complete history of previous infections, including the number and types. Since respiratory infections occur frequently, a complete respiratory assessment should be obtained.

Nursing diagnoses for X-linked agammaglobulinemia might include the following:

- High Risk for infection related to immunosuppression
- Pain related to repeated intramuscular infections of ISG
- Ineffective Breathing Pattern and Impaired Gas Exchange related to repeated respiratory infections
- Altered Family Processes related to caring for a child with life-threatening illness

### *Planning and Implementing Nursing Care*

The child with X-LA and the family need continuous support and education about the permanence of this disorder and the need for continuous vigilance against infection. The family should be taught to report the earliest signs of infection. Parents should also be taught prophylactic chest physical therapy to prevent pneumonia, because children with X-LA are prone to recurrent upper respiratory infections.

### *Evaluating Nursing Care*

A successful outcome for children with X-LA includes remaining free from infection. The child and parents should understand the need to avoid possible causes of infection, as well as the need for repeated injections of ISG.

## *DiGeorge Syndrome*

### *Pathophysiology*

DiGeorge first correlated thymic dysgenesis with impaired cellular immunity. The syndrome that now bears his name is actually quite variable and has also been called the "third and fourth pharyngeal pouch syndrome" (Harvey, Dungan, Elders, & Hughes, 1970; Freedom, Rosen, & Nadas, 1972).

Although there have been several families with more than one case of the syndrome, the racial and sexual patterns of the disorder suggest a sporadic event in morphogenesis rather than a heritable anomaly. Cases have clustered unevenly during certain years and certain times of the year, suggesting that environmental influences such as drugs may play a role. This theory remains unproved (Conley, Beckwith, Mancer, & Tenckhoff, 1979).

DiGeorge syndrome is postulated to result from embryologic damage to the epithelial cells of the third pharyngeal pouch, which forms the thymus, at about 4 weeks gestation. The normal thymus is a bilobate gland located inferiorly to the thyroid. Single accessory thymic nodules may be found on either side of the neck. Variants of the DiGeorge syndrome result from complete absence of all thymic tissue to varying presence of small parts of thymic gland with or without accessory nodules (Harvey, Dungan, Elder, & Hughes, 1970; Conley, Beckwith, Mancer, & Tenckhoff, 1979).

### *Medical Diagnosis and Management*

DiGeorge syndrome most often presents as congenital heart disease. Interrupted aortic arch type B, right aortic arch, and persistent truncus arteriosus are the most common anomalies, and they are frequently fatal within 48 hours after birth. Immediate surgical intervention is often necessary and can be life-saving once the anomaly is recognized (Freedom, Rosen, & Nadas, 1972).

Survivors often have seizures as a result of hypoparathyroidism. This may be corrected with supplemental calcium and often corrects spontaneously if the child reaches 3 years of age. Presumably, small quantities of ectopic parathyroid tissue begin to produce parathyroid hormone.

Immune deficiencies do not become apparent until the child is 1 month of age or older. *Candida* infections, rhinitis, diarrhea, and rashes characterize the early manifestations of immune deficiency. Laboratory testing of these infants shows reduced number of T cells, impaired in vitro response to mitogens (substances that stimulate lymphocyte proliferation), and normal serum immunoglobulin concentrations (IgE may be elevated in some patients).

Patients have a high risk for graft-versus-host disease (GVHD). GVHD occurs when tissue that possesses immune function capabilities, such as bone marrow or blood cells, is given to a patient. The donor tissue (graft) may attack the recipient (host). This is the opposite of normal immune rejection in which the host rejects transfused or transplanted tissue. Therefore, transfusions should be avoided or, if they cannot be avoided, all blood products should be irradiated before transfusion to avoid receipt of donor lymphocytes that might provoke the GVHD (Conley, Beckwith, Mancer, & Tenckhoff, 1979).

Physical examination also demonstrates abnormalities characteristic of the DiGeorge syndrome. Micrognathia, "fish-mouth" appearance, hypertelorism, notched auricular pinnae, anteverted nostrils, and low-set, rotated ears have all been described. Thus the diagnosis is most often based on recognition of congenital cardiac anomalies, hypocalcemia, and abnormal facies. Immune deficiency is a late finding.

Treatment of the immune deficiency is difficult. Thymosin, a thymic hormone, does not seem to reconstitute T cell numbers or function. Intraperitoneal or intramuscular transplantation of cultured thymic epithelial cells has been successful in some cases. Bone marrow transplantation has also been successfully employed. Because thymic tissue often undergoes hyperplasia with time, many survivors of early potentially fatal events do not require transplant therapy (Berger & Sorensen, 1989).

### Nursing Assessment and Diagnosis

Nursing assessment of children with DiGeorge syndrome includes observation for signs and symptoms of cardiac complications, as well as for viral and fungal infections. The parents' understanding of methods used to control the spread of infections (i.e., proper handwashing technique, avoidance of known sources of infection, etc.) should be assessed. The parents' knowledge of measures to prevent injury during seizures should also be assessed.

Nursing diagnoses for DiGeorge syndrome might include the following:

- Decreased Cardiac Output related to heart malfunction
- Fluid Volume Deficit related to decreased cardiac output
- Impaired Gas Exchange related to pulmonary congestion
- Altered Nutrition: Less than body requirements related to fatigue
- High Risk for Injury related to seizure activity
- High Risk for Infection related to immunosuppression
- Altered Family Processes related to caring for a child with a life-threatening illness

### Planning and Implementing Nursing Care

Nursing care of the child with DiGeorge syndrome focuses on three major areas of concern: monitoring cardiac and neurological status, preventing injury from seizures, and avoiding infection. Appropriate nursing interventions must be carried out for the infant undergoing cardiac surgery (see Chap. 24). Seizure precautions should be instituted (see Chap. 26). Children with DiGeorge syndrome need to be monitored carefully while receiving intravenous calcium supplementation. Vital signs should be measured frequently, and the child should be placed on apnea and cardiac monitors. Any arrhythmias should be reported to the physician to avoid tetany of the heart muscle due to transiently high concentrations of serum calcium during intravenous administration.

Because children with DiGeorge syndrome are prone to infection, they are usually placed in isolation. Visitors with respiratory infections are not allowed. The family should be taught isolation technique and good handwashing measures. If the child is to go home, discharge teaching should include methods of preventing infection, seizure precautions, signs and symptoms to be reported to the physician, and appropriate referrals for follow-up care

and support services within the community. Parents need to be supported in the care of their child. They should be taught about the disease process and prognosis and encouraged to verbalize their feelings and concerns.

### Evaluating Nursing Care

Effective nursing care for children with DiGeorge syndrome is measured by an uneventful recovery from cardiac surgery, if surgery was performed. In addition, the child should be free from injuries resulting from seizures, and should experience no complications from calcium administration. The child should experience normal growth and development, and the family should demonstrate their understanding of the disorder and its treatment, as well as adaptive coping mechanisms.

## Wiskott-Aldrich Syndrome

### Pathophysiology

The molecular basis of the Wiskott-Aldrich syndrome is unknown. Most cases are inherited by X-linked transmission, although spontaneous mutation is also believed to occur. No tests are available yet to screen for the defect using amniotic fluid cells or parental cells (Peacocke & Siminovitch, 1987).

Platelets are reduced in number and size from birth. Both reduction in platelet survival and impaired thrombocytopoiesis occur. Functionally, platelet aggregation is reduced, and sudden drops in platelet counts may be attributed to circulating anti-platelet antibodies (Lum, Tubergen, Corash, & Blaese, 1980).

Both cell-mediated and humoral immunity are abnormal. Both synthesis and catabolism of all immunoglobulin classes are increased, with undercompensation of IgM production and overcompensation of IgA and IgE. This worsens progressively as the child ages. The major functional B cell defect is an inability to recognize or respond to bacterial polysaccharide antigens.

Impaired T-cell immunity is manifested by anergy (lack of response) to skin tests, decline in absolute T-cell numbers, production of monocyte inhibitors by T cells, and failure of lymphocyte transformation in response to specific mitogens. (In the test tube, lymphocytes normally increase in number and produce chemicals in response to challenge by mitogens.) The combined T- and B-cell defects result in increased susceptibility to viruses, fungi, parasites and bacteria, as well as certain malignancies (Steele & Burks, 1986).

### Medical Diagnosis and Management

Wiskott-Aldrich syndrome usually becomes apparent during the first few days to weeks of life. Bleeding tendencies, especially at the time of circumcision, are often the first clues. Platelet counts are 5000 to 100,000 (normal is more than 200,000), and platelet transfusion is generally not helpful in correcting the bleeding. Common bleeding sites include skin, gastrointestinal tract, and central nervous system (Berger & Sorensen, 1989). Splenectomy, performed at the age of 1 year or older, restores platelet counts to normal, and functional capacity is markedly improved (Lum, Tubergen, Corash, & Blaese, 1980).

Susceptibility to infections is usually the second clinical manifestation. Otitis media, pneumonia, and meningitis are common. Frequency of infections accelerates as the child ages. Affected children generally do not respond to vaccines against these organisms. Therefore, a combination of prophylaxis with an oral antimicrobial agent such as amoxicillin plus intravenous immunoglobulin infusions offers the best available therapy (Steele & Burks, 1986).

T-cell defects are shown by severe and recurrent infections with herpes simplex, measles, and cytomegalovirus. Infections with *Pneumocystis carinii* and *Candida albicans* develop later as T cell function declines. Late manifestations include vulnerability to certain malignancies, particularly non-Hodgkin lymphoma of the B cell type presenting as an intracranial mass. Early T cell deficiency can be improved with transfer factor therapy. However, nephrotoxicity is a common adverse reaction to this treatment (Steele & Burks, 1986).

The final clinical manifestation is eczema, which may not be apparent until months or years into the disease course. Eczema is treated by conventional methods (see Chap. 34); however, it may worsen if transfusions are administered, and use of systemic corticosteroids to treat the skin disease is limited by the adverse effect of increasing vulnerability to infection (Omerand, 1985).

Cures have been achieved by bone marrow transplantation using a histocompatible sibling donor. Methotrexate prophylaxis has avoided graft-versus-host disease. Following successful transplantation the long-term infectious sequelae of the disease have been eliminated and the eczema has resolved. The latter suggests that the T-cell defect of the host is important to the pathogenesis of eczema, since donor T cells restore the skin to normal. Long-term complications of marrow transplantation and methotrexate suppression in this population are currently unknown (Parkman, Rappeport, Geha, et al., 1978).

For the affected child with no compatible donor, several experimental therapies have been tried, but so far these have been unsuccessful. Survival to the age of 5 to 15 years is becoming commonplace, but severe progressive disabilities characterize the natural history of the disease. Chronic herpes keratitis, bronchiectasis, Coombs positive hemolytic anemia, arteritis, arthritis, nephritis, and food allergies are all commonplace among older children.

### Nursing Assessment and Diagnosis

As with other immune disorders, nurses should carefully assess for signs of infection including otitis media, pneu-

monia, and meningitis. Because Wiskott-Aldrich syndrome often results in eczema, the skin should be thoroughly assessed.

Nursing diagnoses for Wiskott Aldrich syndrome might include the following:

- High Risk for Infection related to immunosuppression
- Pain related to invasive procedures
- Altered Family Processes related to caring for a child with a life threatening illness
- High Risk for Impaired Skin Integrity related to eczema
- Impaired Gas Exchange related to thrombocytopenia/hemorrhage
- Ineffective Breathing Pattern related to respiratory infection

### Planning and Implementing Nursing Care

Care of the child with Wiskott-Aldrich syndrome includes both the acute care setting during exacerbation of the illness and long-term management. The main nursing focus is supporting the family in care of a child with a life-threatening illness by teaching them about the disease process, explaining all the procedures that will be used, and encouraging the family to express their feelings and concerns. In the acute care setting the nurse is responsible for caring for the child during transfusion and biopsy and for preparing the child for surgical procedures such as a splenectomy or bone marrow transplants. The nurse also provides postoperative care and preparation for discharge. Long-term management concentrates on prevention and control of infection, safety measures to protect from injuries that initiate hemorrhage, and skin care to reduce the effects of eczema (see Chap. 34).

### Evaluating Nursing Care

Nursing care is evaluated based on the child's remaining free from infection. The child should show signs of improved skin condition and reduced pain. Parents should demonstrate their understanding of the disorder and should freely express their feelings and concerns.

## General Allergic Reactions

### Anaphylaxis

#### Pathophysiology

Anaphylaxis is a response to non-self that represents an aberrant form of immune reaction. If immunization is perceived as an example of protection against non-self, then anaphylaxis represents a pharmacologic response directed against protection. The events associated with anaphylaxis transpire so rapidly and the manifestations are so profound that is has proved difficult, if not impossible, to adequately study this phenomenon. For further discussion of anaphylaxis, see Chapter 19.

Anaphylaxis is the most severe form of allergy. Although this is an oversimplification, allergic reactions involving the immune system have generally been divided into four types. Anaphylaxis (Type I) is often characterized by a response at a remote site (e.g., food may produce hives). In an anaphylactic reaction, exposure to an allergen may provoke generalized systemic vascular collapse, with diffuse edema, hypotension, tachycardia, respiratory distress, etc. However, the clinical manifestations of the allergic reaction do *not* depend on the amount of exposure to the allergen.

The other forms of allergy include: Type II, or cytotoxic allergy, mediated by IgM, IgG, as seen in transfusion reactions; Type III allergy, immune complex disease, again mediated by IgM, IgG, as seen in post-streptococcal glomerulonephritis; and Type IV, delayed hypersensitivity reactions, which do not involve antibodies or complement, but are mediated through T lymphocytes and macrophages. The classic Type IV hypersensitivity reaction is the positive PPD (tuberculin reaction) (Levy, Roizen, & Morris, 1986).

## Medical Diagnosis and Management

Anaphylaxis occurs more often in women than men and more often among persons who have a history of allergic, atopic, or asthmatic reactions. Most anaphylactic reactions occur extremely rapidly, but are somewhat dependent upon the route of administration of the allergen. Up to 97% of patients who receive an allergen intravenously show clinical manifestation of allergy within 3 minutes. Of patients who die from allergic reactions, one half to three quarters do so within 60 minutes of exposure to the allergen. Some patients who have had previous experience with anaphylactic reactions can recognize an aura; this is important for self-medication to control symptoms.

Substances likely to provoke anaphylactic reactions include antibiotics (with penicillin and ampicillin the most common), radiographic contrast reagents, anesthetics, protamine, and chymopapain. Nonpharmacological causes include foods, insect stings or bites, reptile bites, exercise, environmental stimuli, and even endogenous "natural" substances such as one's own hormones.

For the most part the diagnosis depends on accurate historical information. There is no reliable laboratory test, and provocative tests (i.e., attempts to stimulate the allergic response) should be used only when emergency resuscitative equipment is immediately available. Prick (scratch) testing is often used to detect environmental allergens; intradermal testing is used for drugs, particularly anesthetic agents and penicillins. The most commonly employed in vitro test is the radioallergosorbent

assay test (RAST). It has been standardized for penicillins, anesthetics, muscle relaxants, and trimethoprim. However, it has a high rate of false-negative results.

Once a presumptive clinical diagnosis of an anaphylactic reaction is established, therapy should be instituted immediately. The allergen should be withdrawn if possible. Supplemental oxygen and vascular access by IV catheter are imperative. Intravenous fluids should be infused to maintain blood pressure. Epinephrine should be given intravenously, first as a bolus, then by infusion. Methylprednisolone is commonly used. Aminophylline may be administered if bronchospasm is a significant component of the anaphylactic reaction. Isoproterenol, because of its tendency to cause arrhythmias secondary to excess myocardial oxygen consumption, should be avoided (Levy, Roizen, & Morris, 1986; Fisher, 1987).

## Nursing Assessment and Diagnosis

Nursing assessment for anaphylactic shock centers on identifying children at risk. This includes children with a history of food allergies and allergies to antibiotics, particularly penicillin and ampicillin. Anaphylaxis most commonly occurs in children following penicillin administration or insect stings. Nurses in all settings should be aware of the initial symptoms of the onset of anaphylaxis, which often begin with a tingling sensation around the mouth or face, followed by a feeling of warmth, difficulty in swallowing, and tightness in throat and chest. These are succeeded by flushing, generalized urticaria, angioedema, varying degrees of hoarseness, respiratory stridor, dysphagia, nasal congestion, sneezing, and wheezing. Contractions of smooth muscle occur; the child may lose consciousness and may have feeble heart sounds and bradycardia. Cardiorespiratory arrest may follow (Behrman & Vaughan, 1987). Nurses administering medications to children in the acute care setting or monitoring children following allergy desensitization injections must be aware of the initial symptoms and closely observe the child for adverse reactions. Nurses in schools, camps, or emergency rooms need to closely observe children who have been bitten or stung by insects.

Nursing diagnoses for anaphylactic shock might include the following:

- Altered Cerebral, Cardiopulmonary, and Renal Tissue Perfusion related to systemic effects of shock
- Ineffective Breathing Pattern related to respiratory compromise
- High Risk for Fluid Volume Deficit related to effects of shock

## Planning and Implementing Nursing Care

The nurse's responsibility in caring for children with anaphylactic reactions is to identify children likely to develop allergic reactions, recognize the early signs and symptoms, and provide supportive therapy immediately. If impending shock is suspected, help should be summoned and the child should be kept warm and in a supine or Trendelenburg position. If the reaction is brought on by an insect sting or a desensitizing injection, a tourniquet should be applied just proximal to the site, if possible. Aqueous epinephrine should be administered subcutaneously immediately and then at prescribed intervals. An intravenous infusion must be started to administer aminophylline if bronchoconstriction occurs. Fluids and plasma are given if signs of circulatory collapse are evident. Oxygen should be administered, and a laryngoscope and tracheostomy set-up should be available (Behrman & Vaughan, 1987). Blood pressure and respiratory status must be monitored every 15 minutes, and urine output is measured at regular intervals. Medications are given as ordered, and infusions are monitored following hospital policy.

All treatments must be explained to the child and parents, who must be reassured that everything that can be done is being done. The parents should be kept informed of the child's progress, and every reasonable effort must be made to comfort the parents and allow them to express their fears and feelings.

Once the crisis has passed the causative factor must be identified and documented. Either the parents and child are taught to avoid the offending allergen or, if appropriate, immunotherapy is initiated. It is advisable for the child to wear a medical alert bracelet or tag at all times to ensure appropriate treatment, if needed. If an insect sting caused the reaction, the child and family should be taught measures to reduce exposure to insects. When outdoors, the child should wear shoes or sneakers. When hiking or camping in woods or fields, children should wear long pants and long sleeves. They should avoid brightly colored clothing and perfumes or cosmetics to avoid attracting insects. The family should be instructed to purchase an emergency kit to be kept with the child at all times. These kits, which are commercially available, contain a tourniquet and injectable epinephrine. The family and the child (if old enough) should be taught how to use the equipment.

## *Hypersensitivity Pneumonitis*

### *Pathophysiology*

Asthma is often mediated by IgE (reaginic) antibodies to inhaled allergens; hypersensitivity pneumonitis is not. Lymphocyte–macrophage activation is currently proposed as the major reason for this form of hypersensitivity.

Particles less than 1 μm in diameter are inhaled and exhaled without precipitating on respiratory mucosal surfaces because they are too small. Particles larger than 10 μm adhere to the upper respiratory tract lining and are removed by mucociliary action. However, any particle between 1 and 10 μm in size can reach the terminal

airways, settle, and provoke an immune response. In some individuals this response is manifested as asthma, in others as hypersensitivity pneumonitis.

A wide variety of antigens cause hypersensitivity pneumonitis. In general, these substances may be divided into vegetable, animal, fungal, and chemical compounds as well as products of contaminated stagnant water. In addition to inhaled chemical toxins, certain chemical entities (drugs) mediate a similar immune response when ingested.

IgE, IgM, and IgG antibodies do not appear to play a role in the pathogenesis of hypersensitivity pneumonitis. Instead, the prevailing opinion is that the pathogenesis of hypersensitivity pneumonitis is attributable to T lymphocyte and macrophage activation. Among patients with this disease, the number of both suppressor T cells and macrophages is significantly increased in fluid obtained by washing saline through the lungs using a bronchoscope (bronchoalveolar lavage).

How orally ingested drugs provoke this reaction in the lung is less clear, but the end results are the same: granuloma formation and interstitial fibrosis. Therefore, the prevailing opinion is that the pathogenesis must be similar. Drugs that provoke hypersensitivity pneumonitis include cancer chemotherapeutic agents (e.g., bleomycin, methotrexate, Procarbazine), antibiotics (nitrofurantoin, penicillin, ampicillin, isoniazid), anti-epileptics (Diphenylhydantoin, carbamazepine), anti-asthmatics (cromolyn), and nonsteroidal anti-inflammatory agents (Naproxen). This list is not comprehensive, but it includes most of the drugs associated with hypersensitivity pneumonitis that are used to treat childhood diseases (Cooper & Matthay, 1987).

### *Medical Diagnosis and Management*

Acute hypersensitivity pneumonitis is diagnosed clinically by history and physical exam. Chills, fever, dry cough, shortness of breath, and a general sense of malaise, accompanied by arthralgias and myalgias, characterize the patient's symptoms. The onset generally occurs 4 to 8 hours after exposure to the antigen.

Examination of the chest reveals diffuse rales. The patient is tachypneic and often uses accessory neck muscles to enhance respiratory effort. Intercostal retractions may also be seen. There generally is no evidence of parenchymal consolidation. Rectal temperature is elevated.

Chest x-rays show diffuse interstitial disease and no lobar consolidation. If spirometry is available, it usually shows evidence of restrictive (the capacity of breathing cannot be increased) rather than obstructive (air cannot be exhaled) airflow dynamics.

What usually distinguishes hypersensitivity pneumonitis from infectious causes of interstitial pneumonia is its rapid resolution, particularly if re-exposure to the antigen is avoided. Resolution may occur within several hours.

The chronic form of the disease is more subtle, more difficult to diagnose, and may show clinical signs only after significant pulmonary fibrosis has occurred. This is particularly true for drug-induced hypersensitivity pneumonitis. Skin testing is generally not helpful. Preparation of allergens is unstandardized, and immediate cutaneous wheal and flare reaction often represents a toxic rather than an allergic response. Pulmonary function tests may be performed using the proposed allergen to provoke a hypersensitivity response, but this is a dangerous confirmatory test and should only be performed by a highly qualified pulmonary specialist. Invasive tests such as bronchoalveolar lavage and lung biopsy can provide supportive, but not conclusive, evidence for diagnosis. Justification for these studies is very limited.

Two therapies are available: avoidance of the provocative agent and parenteral or oral corticosteroid therapy. If avoidance of the allergen is not possible or if respiratory distress is severe, corticosteroids should be used. Treatment generally lasts for 1 to 4 weeks, and steroids should be withdrawn gradually. Supplemental oxygen is indicated for patients found to be hypoxic by arterial blood gas analysis.

### Nursing Assessment and Diagnosis

Nursing assessment includes a complete history, with specific attention to possible exposure to allergens. A thorough physical examination is conducted.

Nursing diagnosis for hypersensitivity pneumonitis might include the following:

- Ineffective Airway Clearance, Ineffective Breathing Pattern, and Impaired Gas Exchange related to inflammation and obstruction of the lower respiratory tract
- Fluid Volume Deficit related to tachypnea and fever
- Pain related to fever and dyspnea

### Planning, Implementing, and Evaluating Nursing Care

Nursing care of the child with hypersensitivity pneumonitis centers on assisting the child and parents in identifying and avoiding the offending allergens, and caring for a child with a respiratory illness. Nursing care for children with various pneumonias is discussed in Chapter 23.

## Allergic Rhinitis

### Pathophysiology

Allergic rhinitis is one of the most common allergic reactions. It affects an estimated 17 million people in the United States, 10% to 20% of whom are children. Approximately 5% to 10% of children "outgrow" their sensitivity. Symptoms include nasal edema, vasodilation, mucorrhea, and infiltration of the upper respiratory tract with eosinophils. Upon initial exposure to inhalant antigens the sensitive individual produces IgE antibodies that attach to both mast cells found in conjunctival and nasal tissues and the circulating basophils. On reexposure, a series of enzymatic reactions occurs that causes the disintegration of the mast cells and the release of chemical mediators. Reactions may be either immediate or late responses (from 3 to 12 hours after exposure) (Bailet, 1988). Inhalant allergens commonly associated with this condition include dust, molds, mildew, animal dander, pollen, ragweed, grasses, and trees.

Allergic rhinitis begins in the first two years of life and may be classified as either perennial or seasonal. Perennial allergic rhinitis occurs all year long but is usually most severe in the winter. It is thought that when heating systems are turned on exposure to house dust increases, causing nasal stuffiness, frequent sniffing, and instant rhinorrhea. This is accompanied by mild to moderate itching leading to frequent nose rubbing (the allergic salute). The child also may experience poor appetite, fatigue, and pharyngeal irritation from postnasal drainage. The increased dryness of heated air and greater exposure to pets in the winter also compound the problem.

Seasonal allergic rhinitis, or hay fever, occurs seasonally and is related to inhalation of pollens from trees in late winter and early spring, grasses in spring to late summer, and weeds in late summer and early fall. Seasonal allergy rhinitis usually occurs after 2 years of age and gradually increases in severity over a period of several years.

### Medical Diagnosis and Management

Diagnosis is based on presenting signs and symptoms, a careful history, and the presence of nasal eosinophilia. Table 27-7 shows guidelines for history taking. The child presents with sneezing, rhinorrhea (which is often watery and profuse), bilateral nasal obstruction, and itching of the nose, palate, pharynx, and ears. There may also be redness, tearing, and itching of the eyes. The nasal mucous membranes are bluish and pale, and a clear mucoid nasal discharge occurs. The child often displays characteristic mannerisms related to the relief of nasal itching or attempts to increase the airway. The child may wrinkle the nose and may rub it in a characteristic way (allergic salute). The upward rubbing may lead to a horizontal crease on the dorsum of the upper nose near the tip. Venous stasis resulting from interference with blood flow through edematous nasal mucous membranes results in dark circles under the eyes (allergic shiners). The child usually breathes through the mouth. The diagnosis is supported by the finding of eosinophils in a smear made from nasal secretions. Skin testing with suspected allergens may yield a wheal-and-flare response. Serologic evaluation may identify IgE antibodies to offending allergens.

Once the diagnosis has been confirmed, treatment is directed toward identification of the offending inhalants,

*Table 27–7. Assessment of the Child with Allergies:
Guidelines for Health History*

I. Family history
   A. What allergic conditions do family members have? (asthma, eczema, hay fever, hives, rhinitis, allergies to food or drugs)
   B. Infancy
      1. Were there any specific problems during infancy that might suggest allergy? (milk intolerance, colic, eczema, diarrhea, rashes, recurrent illnesses)
      2. Was the child breast-fed or bottle-fed? What type of formula?
II. Systems review
   A. Eyes—irritation, excessive watering, rubbing eyes, swelling, recurrent infections, allergic shiners
   B. Ears—frequent ear infections, itching, drainage
   C. Nose—rhinorrhea, postnasal drip, sneezing, allergic salute
   D. Mouth—swelling of lips and mouth
   E. Chest—cough, frequent colds, history of croup or pneumonia, wheezing, shortness of breath
   F. GI—food intolerances, colic, diarrhea, vomiting, constipation
   G. Skin—irritation, rashes, hives, dry skin
   H. Behavior—fatigue, irritability, disruptive behavior in school
   I. Other—headaches, failure to gain weight
III. Contributing factors
   Do any of the following provoke allergic symptoms?
   A. Seasonal patterns and potential causative agents
      1. Winter—molds, house dust, upper respiratory infections
      2. Spring—pollen of trees and grasses
      3. Summer—air pollution and insect bites
      4. Summer to fall—weeds
   B. Animals
      1. Pets
      2. Clothing of animal origin
   C. Perfumes, cosmetics, paints
   D. Medications—aspirin, penicillin, sulfa drugs, others
   E. Emotional or social stresses
   F. Home environment
   G. Foods
      1. Severity of symptoms related to specific foods
      2. Temporal relationships—onset of symptoms after eating, duration of symptoms
      3. State of food (processed, cooked, fresh, uncooked)
      4. Potential contamination of food by toxins or additives.
   H. Exercise
   I. Exposure to cold

avoidance of exposure, and use of symptomatic medication or immunotherapy when indicated.

Offending inhalants may be determined by careful history and confirmed by skin or serologic testing. The offending allergens then must be avoided by careful control of the child's environment. Hyposensitization (repeated injections of the allergen in increasing doses) may be considered when symptoms are severe and symptomatic medications have failed or when complications such as chronic recurrent sinusitis, recurrent serous otitis media, and hearing loss are present.

Antihistamines that inhibit the release of mediators of allergy are the medications of choice. Oral and nasal decongestants may be beneficial. Corticosteroid (topical or systemic) therapy can be used for short periods for severe nasal symptoms not controlled by other medications. Sodium cromolyn nasal spray may also be used before the beginning of the pollen season.

### Nursing Assessment and Diagnosis

Nursing assessment includes a careful child and family history to assist in identifying offending inhalant allergens (see Table 27-7 for guidelines for history taking). The physical examination should focus on the child's respiratory status.

Nursing diagnoses for allergic rhinitis might include the following:

- Ineffective Airway Clearance and Ineffective Breathing Pattern related to nasal congestion and discharge

### *Planning and Implementing Nursing Care*

Nursing care focuses on three areas: identifying children at risk, assisting in diagnostic testing, and preparing the family and child for home management.

Nurses in school and ambulatory settings must be aware of the typical signs and symptoms of allergic rhinitis and make appropriate referrals. If the child is to undergo skin testing to identify specific allergens or immunotherapy the nurse must explain the procedure to the child and family. The nurse may assist by carefully observing the child for 20 minutes after the procedure for the early signs of adverse reactions, which include flushing, increased warmth, itching, dyspnea, and wheezing. Necessary equipment for treatment includes tourniquets, needles, syringes, arm board, intravenous tubing, parenteral fluids, oxygen, ambu bags, and oral airways. Epinephrine (adrenalin), diphenhydramine (Benadryl), and a bronchodilator (Bronkosol or Alupent) should be available.

Teaching for home management should include control of the environment and administration of medications. The parents and child must understand the importance of avoiding the offending allergens. Parents should be given detailed instructions for environmental control to avoid allergens, particularly in the child's bedroom (see Table 27-3 for suggestions for removing allergens from the child's environment). Aerosol sprays, tobacco smoke, and woodburning stoves or fireplaces should be eliminated. Using a humidifier in the winter and air conditioning in the summer may help.

The child and parents should be taught the proper dosage, schedule, and mode of administration of all medications. Side effects of medications should be explained. Common side effects of antihistamines include fatigue, insomnia, and anorexia, as well as nausea and vomiting. Parents must be taught which symptoms should be reported to their health care provider. Parents should also be aware that tolerance to medications may develop, and the primary health care provider may have to prescribe alternatives.

Parents must know the signs and symptoms of the allergy and be alert to changes in the child's environment that may cause reactions. The goal of home management should be self-management as soon as children are old enough to control their activities.

### *Evaluating Nursing Care*

Evaluation of nursing care for allergic rhinitis focuses on the child and family's success in controlling the symptoms of the problem. With proper environmental controls and medication the child should experience minimal symptoms. The child and parents should demonstrate their understanding of the condition, preventive measures, and therapeutic regimens.

## Food Allergies

### *Pathophysiology*

Although the existence of food allergies has been questioned by many, from double-blind, randomized, controlled clinical trials it is apparent that foods or their constituents can provoke an allergic response. Pearson and McKee (1985) proposed a classification system that helps to categorize adverse effects of foodstuffs. The first distinction is between usual and unusual reactions. Among the unusual reactions some may be psychogenic, but others are organic and represent a true hypersensitivity response. Toxins, bacterial, or fungal contamination or intolerance of generally benign substances may be responsible. Hypersensitivity reactions are divided into allergic (IgE- and IgG-related), idiosyncratic (metabolic, pharmacological, or autonomic), and idiopathic. True food allergy is believed to represent an IgE-mediated allergic response.

Among individuals with food allergies, a genetic predisposition to allergies, characterized by immediate skin reactivity to inoculation of environmental substances, is commonplace. Other typical findings are asthma, allergic rhinitis, urticaria, and eczema. In fact, food allergy may be clinically manifested by one of these other conditions. Anaphylactic reactions rarely occur in response to food allergy.

IgE antibodies formed subsequent to exposure to foods bind to mast cells along the gastrointestinal tract or at remote sites. Local consequences of mast cell degranulation include vasodilatation, edema of the bowel wall, and mucus secretion. Colonic contractions increase in force and frequency, probably as a result of increased concentrations of prostaglandins E and F. As previously noted, patients with a food allergy often show immediate hypersensitivity at skin test sites. This hypersensitivity can be transferred by intradermal injection of serum from an allergic individual into a normal volunteer. Ingestion of the offending food by the vulnerable volunteer then causes a wheal-and-flare response (Saavedra-Delgado & Metcalfe, 1985).

Non-IgE antibody mediated mechanisms of food allergy have also been proposed, although they are not universally accepted. The mediator of this response is IgG short-term sensitizing antibody (STS). The antibody is heat-stable and belongs to the $IgG_4$ subclass. Milk proteins, especially beta-lactoglobulin, stimulate development of these antibodies. $IgG_4$ is more concentrated along the gastrointestinal tract compared to quantities found in serum. It has been proposed that this subclass of antibodies is responsible for delayed (2 to 4 hour) allergic response to foods (Halpern & Scott, 1987).

## Medical Diagnosis and Management

A number of conditions have been attributed to food allergy but proof of their pathogenesis is lacking. These include recurrent pneumonia, Crohn's disease, ulcerative colitis, celiac disease, infantile colic, hyperactivity, sudden infant death syndrome, arthritis, and personality disorders. However, there is evidence that certain other conditions may be related to food allergy. These include migraines, eosinophilic gastroenteritis, and rhinitis (Cant, 1985).

Placebo-controlled, double-blind food provocation represents the best test available to diagnose food allergy. However, provocative tests should be avoided for patients who have a history of immediate hypersensitivity reaction. Skin testing of food allergens may be helpful. However, most patients with food allergy show cutaneous hypersensitivity to many foods but clinical allergy to only a few. In addition, a negative skin test does not exclude the diagnosis of food allergy.

Multisystem clinical manifestations of food allergy are common. Manifestations generally resolve spontaneously; therefore it is essentially impossible to determine the incidence of this disease. The widely accepted prevalence is 1% to 3% of the population, with higher numbers in childhood. Up to 7.5% of babies demonstrate allergy to cows' milk, with one third of these children losing the clinical manifestations by 1 year of age (Pearson & Mckee, 1985).

The earliest clinical manifestations of food allergy include lip swelling, rhinorrhea, and vomiting, which occur within 30 minutes of ingestion of the allergen. These are followed by urticaria and asthma and finally by diarrhea and eczema. The most likely foods to induce these reactions are cows' milk, eggs, legumes, and fish or shellfish; less common provocative foods are wheat or other cereals, nuts, meats, fruits, tomatoes, cheese, and chocolate. The time at which these foods are introduced into the diet may play a role in their allergenicity. Breast-feeding may play a protective role, particularly if infants receive nothing but breast milk for the first 2 months of life.

A number of pharmacologically active chemicals in foods can produce anaphylactic reactions. These include salicylates, benzoates, azo dyes, sulfur dioxide, metabisulfites, natural histamines, and alcohol.

The only effective treatment for food allergy is avoidance of the offending agent(s). Care must be taken to maintain a nutritionally sound, balanced diet so that the therapy does not become worse than the disease. Therefore, a positive diagnosis should be established by history, double-blind food testing, and repeat challenge over time before withholding suspected foods.

## Nursing Assessment and Diagnosis

Nursing assessment focuses on two distinct areas: identifying children at risk for allergy and assisting in the identification of allergens affecting the child diagnosed with a food allergy.

Nurses must be sensitive to signs and symptoms related to food allergy in infants and young children. When an infant fails to gain weight or has diarrhea, vomiting, and colic-like symptoms, allergic sensitivity to milk or lactose intolerance must be considered. Table 27-8 compares lactose intolerance and milk allergy/sensitivity. Young children may be fussy eaters because they cannot express their feelings regarding pain or discomfort; therefore, they instinctively avoid foods that affect them. Once children have been introduced to solid foods, they may have symptoms that include vomiting, diarrhea, abdominal pain, rhinitis, allergic skin reactions, and behavioral symptoms including lethargy, irritability, restlessness, and moodiness. All children who have these symptoms must be carefully assessed for food allergy. Nurses working in schools or camps should be aware of all children with food allergies, the foods they are allergic to, and the signs and symptoms of an allergic reaction. The most important diagnostic aid is a thorough history (see Table 27-7 for guidelines for history taking).

Another method that may be used to identify offending foods is a food diary. A daily record is kept of everything a child eats and the days on which symptoms appear. The record is than analyzed to identify foods commonly appearing on days when symptoms are present.

Nursing diagnoses for food allergies might include the following:

- Altered Nutrition: Less than body requirements related to the need to restrict certain foods from the child's diet
- Diarrhea related to ingestion of foods causing allergies

## Planning and Implementing Nursing Care

Once it has been determined that a child is having an adverse reaction to food the nurse works with the child and family to identify specific foods or additives causing the reaction. Elimination diets may be used to help identify specific foods. The child is usually placed on an elimination diet containing none of the foods that commonly cause allergic reactions. These foods are then added to the diet gradually, with a new food introduced every 6 to 7

*Table 27–8.  Comparison of Milk Sensitivity/Allergy and Lactose Intolerance*

| Milk Sensitivity | Lactose Intolerance |
| --- | --- |
| **Definition** | |
| Milk protein allergy. Proteins include whey proteins (lactalbumin and lactoglobulin) and casein. | Inability to digest lactose contained in milk and other foods due to a deficiency of lactase in the small intestine. Lactase is an enzyme that hydrolyzes lactose into glucose and galactose so that it can be absorbed. |
| **Incidence** | |
| Occurs in 1%–2% of all children. May be tolerant of milk when older. | Rare in traditional milk-drinking and dairying countries. Low in West Europeans and white Americans. High in Asians, Africans, and Eastern Europeans. Primary deficiency—rare, congenital; symptoms appear soon after birth. Secondary deficiency—common in non-whites and less prevalent in children. |
| **Symptoms** | |
| Frequent loose stools, vomiting, colic. Other symptoms of allergic diseases. | Watery diarrhea, flatulence, abdominal distention, vomiting. Can lead to dehydration, failure to thrive, electrolyte imbalance, metabolic acidosis, lethargy, irritability. |
| **Diagnostic Tests** | |
| Skin tests may be positive to milk. | 1. Test for reducing substances—positive. 2. Stool pH less than 6.0. 3. Disaccharide tolerance test—glucose level rise of less than 20 mg/100 mL. 4. Small bowel biopsy—lactase deficiency. |
| **Treatment** | |
| Eliminate milk and all milk products from diet. | Lactose-free diet should be employed. |

days. If symptoms reappear the food is removed from the diet again.

While the child is on the elimination diet, the nurse helps the family plan nutritious meals while avoiding the foods that cause adverse reactions. The family must be taught to read labels and shop carefully to ensure that the offending foods are avoided. If the child eats in places other than the home, everyone (including babysitters and day care personnel) must be aware of his or her dietary restrictions. The importance of adhering to the diet should be stressed to older children who eat meals at school, at playmates' homes, or in restaurants.

Formula-fed infants who are allergic or sensitive to milk are usually placed on a soy-based formula (e.g., Prosobee or Isomil). All foods containing milk are removed from the child's diet (Table 27-9). Parents and older children must be taught to shop carefully, reading labels to be sure that they do not buy foods that contain the offending allergens. As the number of allergens the child is sensitive to increases, it becomes more and more challenging to identify offending foods. This is particularly true if the child is allergic to milk, wheat, and eggs since these items are found in many foods. Table 27-10 shows common

sources of milk, wheat, and eggs. Parents and children should also be aware of foods in the same food group that can produce allergic symptoms. See Table 27-11 for a list of cross-reacting food groups.

The child must be particularly careful when eating away from home, because he or she may not be aware of all the ingredients used in cooking. This is particularly dangerous if the child has strong reactions and is in danger of severe anaphylactic reactions. The child and parents must understand that when they are in doubt about a food, it should be avoided (Matloff, 1988).

According to Matloff (1988), the parents of all children having documented food-induced anaphylaxis should carry an antihistamine and self-injectable epinephrine for use in the event of accidental ingestions.

A medical alert bracelet should be worn by the child with severe allergies to ensure immediate recognition and treatment of a reaction. Because a food allergy that presents at a young age is more likely to spontaneously remit than a food allergy that begins in late childhood or adulthood, young children with food allergies should be reevaluated every 6 to 12 months by an allergist (Matloff, 1988).

*Table 27—9. Milk-Free Diet*

| Foods Allowed | Foods Not Allowed |
|---|---|
| Milk substitutes: soy milk formulas (Neomull-Soy, Prosobee, Somil, Soyalac), Coffee Rich, Mocha Mix | Milk—fresh, dry, evaporated |
| Unprocessed mature cheese such as cheddar and parmesan | Yogurt, cream cheese, cottage cheese, processed cheese |
| Eggs | Butter, cream, most margarine, foods fried in butter and margarine |
| Oils, lard, chicken and bacon fat, pure vegetable margarine | Meat with milk sauces, gravies, processed or packaged meats, sausages, frankfurters |
| Meats and fish | Instant mashed potatoes |
| All vegetables, fruits, and fruit juices | Bread containing milk. Check commercial and baby cereals and teething biscuits. |
| Breads and cereals without milk (Hillbilly by Colonial, Longhorn and Dark Hollywood by Wonder, water bagels) | All pastries, puddings, cakes, custards, biscuits, ice cream, sherbet, "milk chocolate," muffins, sweet rolls, pancakes, cookies |
| Fruit jellies, gelatin, pastry made with water | All soups containing milk |
| Jam, honey, syrup, sugar, water ices, peanut butter, nuts | Some chocolate and caramel flavorings |
| Meat and vegetable soups | Check commercial dressings and mayonnaise |
| Tea, coffee, carbonated beverages, cocoa powder | |
| Herbs and seasonings | |

(Chow, M. P., Durand, B. A., Feldman, M. N., & Mills, M. A. [1984]. *Handbook of primary pediatric care,* p. 835. Albany, N.Y.: Delmar)

## Local Allergic Reactions

### Asthma

There are two major shortcomings to our current knowledge of asthma: lack of a clear-cut explanation for why asthma occurs and the lack of consensus in the definition of this disease. For purposes of this discussion, asthma is defined as reversible airway obstruction occurring in the presence of non-specific airway hyperreactivity. Both large and small airways are affected (Sheller, 1987).

Three major hypotheses for the etiology of asthma have been proposed: (1) abnormal humoral control of airways, (2) abnormal bronchial smooth muscle, and (3)

*Table 27—10. Common Food Sources of Milk, Wheat, and Eggs*

| Milk | Wheat | Eggs |
|---|---|---|
| Au gratin food | Baked goods | Albumin |
| Baked foods | Biscuits | Bavarian creams |
| Butter | Breads | Bread crumbs (at times) |
| Candy | Bread crumbs | Candy |
| Casein or caseinate | Breakfast cereals | Coffee |
| Cheese | Candy | Creamed foods |
| Chocolate | Coffee substitute | Croquettes |
| Creamed or scalloped foods | Crackers | Custards |
| Curds | Cracker meal | Egg white or powdered |
| Gravy | Dumplings | dry egg |
| Ice cream | Gravy | French ice cream |
| Malted milk | Macaroni | French toast |
| Margarine | Malt | Fritters |
| Milk sherbet | Noodles (spaghetti) | Frostings |
| Pudding | Salad dressing | Meringue |
| Salad dressing | Sauces for vegetables or | Noodles |
| Soups | meats | Pie filling |
| Waffles and biscuits | Soup (bisques or chow- | Root beer |
| Whey | ders) | Salad dressing |
| White sauces | Stuffing | Sauces (hollandaise) |
| Wieners or bologna | Swiss steak | Sausage |
| | Wieners or bologna | Soups |

(Rapp, D. J. [1980]. *Allergies and your family.* New York: Sterling Publishing Company)

*Table 27–11.  Cross-Reacting Food Groups\**

**Dairy Products**

Milk
Butter
Cheese
Yogurt
Ice cream

**Legumes**

Peanuts
Peas
Soybeans
Lentils
Licorice
Beans

**Cashew Family**

Cashews
Mangos
Pistachio

**Plum Family**

Plums
Prunes
Almonds
Apricots
Peaches
Nectarines

**Nightshade Family**

Peppers
Eggplant
Tomatoes
Potatoes

**Parsley Family**

Caraway
Carrots
Celery
Dill

**Walnut Family**

Walnuts
Pecans
Hickory nuts
Butternuts

\* Patients should be given a list of all foods that are in the same food group, since they can all potentially cross-react, producing allergic symptoms of greater or lesser severity. The degree of cross-reactivity in a particular patient is variable.
(Adapted from U.S. Department of Health and Human Services. [1984]. *Adverse reactions to foods. AAAI and NIAID Report.* [Publication No. 84-2442] Bethesda, MD: National Institutes of Health, pp. 21–25)

cellular dysfunction with increased release of chemical mediators. None of these provides a satisfactory, comprehensive explanation of the disease process.

Abnormal humoral control could also be expressed by decreased concentrations of circulating catecholamines; partial beta-adrenergic blockade; increased alpha-adrenergic activity, causing increased airway tone; or abnormalities of the non-adrenergic, non-cholinergic components of the nervous system. However, each of these proposed mechanisms is flawed. First, low levels of catecholamines might allow asthma to occur but do not cause asthma. Second, normal subjects treated with beta blockers do not develop asthma, and patients with asthma are very sensitive to beta-adrenergic agents. Third, alpha agonists produce variable effects on airways, whereas alpha blockade produces no consistent effect. Finally, the neurotransmitters of the non-adrenergic, non-cholinergic system have not been identified.

Abnormality of the smooth muscles does not explain the excess secretions, inflammatory cells, and edema that are characteristic of asthma. Finally, no single mediator can reproduce the spectrum of abnormalities characteristic

of asthma (Hargreave, Dolovich, O'Byrne, Ramsdale, & Daniel, 1986; Tattersfield, 1987).

Asthma may be induced by immunological (IgE-mediated) and non-immunological stimuli. Immunological stimuli are discussed in the section on anaphylaxis. Non-allergic stimuli include exercise, cold, ozone, and viral respiratory tract infections. Inflammation is a consequence of these stimuli, but how or why inflammation develops is not clear. The proposed sequel to this event is increased local production, decreased metabolism, or enhanced sensitivity to cholinergic and alpha-adrenergic mediators of bronchoconstriction, producing increased smooth muscle tone and bronchoconstriction (Owens, 1986).

Because asthma primarily affects the respiratory system, see Chapter 23 for further discussions of pathophysiology, as well as medical diagnosis and management, and the nursing process for care of children with asthma.

## Autoimmune Disorders

### Juvenile Rheumatoid Arthritis

#### Pathophysiology

The etiology and pathogenesis of juvenile rheumatoid arthritis (JRA) are unknown. Animal models exist in nature, and infectious agents are incriminated as causative. Mycoplasma species other than those that infect humans are responsible for arthritides in pigs, mice, and turkeys. *Erysipelothrix rhusiopathiae* causes a chronic arthritis in pigs that mimics human rheumatoid arthritis.

It is suggested that an external stimulant provokes the immune response in humans that results in rheumatoid arthritis. In adults, the prevailing hypothesis is that some antigenic stimulus in a genetically predisposed individual prompts both T-cell– and B-cell–mediated immunity to localize an inflammatory reaction in joints. The inflammatory response in synovial fluid is mediated primarily by polymorphonuclear leukocytes. Continued inflammatory reaction leads to involvement of the synovial membrane and pannus formation (a layer of inflammatory cells overlying the synovium). The pannus destroys cartilage and establishes a chronic and progressive inflammatory reaction (Harris, 1985).

Juvenile rheumatoid arthritis may actually be several diseases. There is no known biochemical abnormality, no identified infectious agent, no specific antigen provoking autoimmunity, and no hereditary predisposition that unifies the various clinical syndromes identified as JRA. Various immune deficiencies have been identified in individual patients (IgA deficiency, complement component deficiency, and agammaglobulinemia), but none of these characterizes most patients with the disease. JRA has also been reported to follow trauma and psychologic stress in some cases. However, the etiology and pathogenesis remain undefined for most patients (Cassidy, 1985).

### Medical Diagnosis and Management

Many conditions may simulate or cause arthritis in childhood. These include infectious diseases (septic arthritis, osteomyelitis, viral-related arthritides), childhood malignancies, noninflammatory conditions of bones and joints ("growing pains," trauma, orthopedic conditions), and other rheumatic diseases (psoriasis, rheumatic fever, dermatomyositis, SLE).

Furthermore, JRA probably is not a single entity but should be divided into three distinct syndromes: systemic onset, polyarticular (affecting many joints), and pauciarticular (affecting few joints). Characteristics of each are summarized in Table 27-12. JRA is not a variant of adult rheumatoid arthritis. Fever, rash, lymphadenopathy, splenomegaly, iridocyclitis, and leukocytosis are more common in children than in adults. Rheumatoid factor and subcutaneous nodules are more frequently identified among adults.

Arthritis is manifested by swelling of a joint or limitation of joint motion accompanied by heat, pain, or tenderness (Fig. 27-5). These manifestations must persist for 6 months or more to establish a diagnosis of arthritis. The affected child must be 16 years of age or younger.

In systemic onset JRA, fever and rash are diagnostically important. The fever is intermittent and usually does not exceed 39°C. Rashes occurs in 90% of children; they may be discrete or confluent, macular or maculopapular, and generally are non-pruritic. Rashes often migrate and vary in association with fever spikes. Koebner's phenomenon is often present: after the skin of an affected child has been rubbed or scratched, macules appear in the location of the stimulus and persist for days. Polyserositis and lymphadenopathy are usually easily discernible on physical examination but are not associated with serious organ dysfunction.

Most patients with polyarticular JRA appear ill at the time of presentation. Large joints are affected more commonly than small, and a subgroup of affected individuals has rheumatoid nodules or IgM rheumatoid factor. In these children arthritis is often progressive and requires intensive therapy. These children also are vulnerable to dryness of the conjunctiva due to decreased lacrimal function.

### Table 27–12. Characteristics of Three Juvenile Arthritis Syndromes

| Finding | Systemic Onset | Polyarticular | Pauciarticular |
|---|---|---|---|
| Fever | Common | Rare | Rare |
| Rash | 80%–90% | Rare | Uncommon |
| Joint findings | Minimal or none | Arthritis in more than 4 joints | Arthritis in up to 4 joints |
| **Organomegaly** | | | |
| Hepatomegaly | Occasional | Uncommon | Rare |
| Splenomegaly | Frequent | Uncommon | Rare |
| **Serositis** | | | |
| Pericarditis | Common | Rare | Rare |
| Pleuritis | Common | Uncommon | Rare |
| **Laboratory Tests** | | | |
| Elevated ESR* | Frequent | Frequent | Uncommon |
| Anemia | Frequent | Frequent | Uncommon |
| Leukocytosis | Frequent | Uncommon | Rare |
| Rheumatoid factor | Rare | Uncommon | Rare |
| ANA† | Rare | Variable | Variable |

* ESR, erythrocyte sedimentation rate; † ANA, antinuclear antibody.
(Data from Calabro, J. J., Eyvazzadeh, C., & Weber, C. A. [1986]. Juvenile rheumatoid arthritis: Early diagnosis, management and long-term prognosis. *Advances in Therapy, 3,* 97; Hollister, J. R. [1988]. Rheumatic disease in childhood. *Pediatrician, 15,* 65; Taranta, A. [1988]. JRA and red herrings. *Hospital Practice, 23,* 129)

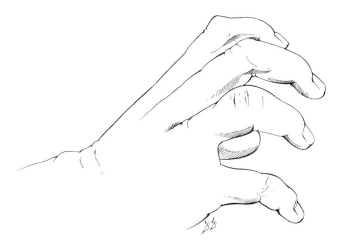

*Figure 27–5. Swelling of joints seen in juvenile rheumatoid arthritis.*

Pauciarticular JRA is manifested by arthritis of one to four joints. Children under the age of 5 may have fever, but older children usually show no systemic manifestations. The major complication of this form of the disease is chronic inflammation of the iris and ciliary body (iridocyclitis), characterized by periods of inflammation and remission; it may lead to blindness if unrecognized.

Laboratory findings for each of the three presentations are summarized in Table 27-12. There is no specific diagnostic test for any form of the disease. Similarly, x-ray changes early in the disease course are subtle and nonspecific. Therefore, they do not help in making the diagnosis. A radionuclide bone and joint scan may provide supportive evidence of JRA (Brewer, 1986).

The diagnosis of polyarticular JRA is supported by findings on arthrocentesis. In the affected joint there is leukocytosis with a predominance of polymorphonuclear cells. Synovial fluid glucose is normal, complement concentration is reduced, and the culture and examination for crystals yields negative results.

The prognosis for most patients with JRA is favorable; at least 50% have a remission, and only a few of these relapse. At the opposite extreme, about 2% of patients with JRA die from the disease or its complications. The most serious complication of systemic disease is myocarditis with congestive heart failure. This often is responsive to treatment with corticosteroids. The worst complication of polyarticular disease is progressive arthritis. The progress can be slowed with appropriate medical therapy. The worst sequela of pauciarticular arthritis is blindness from iridocyclitis. Patients should be evaluated every 3 to 4 months via slit-lamp exam by an ophthalmologist. Early detection and therapy of iridocyclitis are helpful. Topical steroids and mydriatics are effective early in the disease course; systemic corticosteroids and immunosuppressives may be required later.

The mainstay of therapy for JRA is aspirin. Although a variety of other agents may be employed for treatment, tolmetin is the only other drug approved by the FDA for treatment of JRA. Prednisone use should be limited because of its negative effects on growth and development. However, it is life-saving for the treatment of myocarditis in systemic onset disease.

Adjunctive measures include rest and exercise programs, splinting and casting, and use of support groups for psychosocial therapy. Of 100 patients diagnosed with JRA and followed for 25 years, 3 died, 2 of 9 with iridocyclitis became blind, and 15 had limited ability to care for themselves or were dependent on others for care. Nine still had active disease. The largest number were well and no longer had evidence of illness (Calabro, Eyvazzadeh, & Weber, 1986).

### Nursing Assessment and Diagnosis

Nurses should be aware of the signs and symptoms of JRA and should refer children for evaluation when they have joint swelling and pain that lasts longer than 6 weeks or a history of fevers with persistent daily or twice daily spikes of 104°F to 106°F (Page-Goertz, 1989).

Nursing diagnoses for juvenile rheumatoid arthritis might include the following:

- Pain related to joint swelling and stiffness
- Impaired Physical Mobility related to joint swelling and stiffness
- Diversional Activity Deficit related to immobility
- High Risk for Sleep Pattern Disturbance related to pain, discomfort
- Bathing/hygiene, Dressing/grooming, Feeding, Toileting Self-care deficit related to neuromuscular impairment
- Body Image Disturbance related to chronic disease
- Altered Family Processes related to caring for a child with a chronic illness

### Planning and Implementing Nursing Care

The primary goals of treatment for JRA are suppression of the inflammatory process, maintenance of joint function, promotion of normal growth and development, and support of child and family in coping with a chronic illness. Meeting these goals presents a challenge for nurses working with children with JRA and their families. Except for periods of severe exacerbation, children with JRA are cared for at home. Therefore, the nursing role centers on educating parents and children, coordinating activities of the health team, and counseling. Through patient education the child and family learn about the disease and become active, responsible participants in assessment and management of the disease (Rennebohen & Correll, 1984).

Education for the parent and child must begin with a

clear presentation of the nature of the disease process, its unpredictable nature, and the possible outcome. The medication regimen must be carefully explained, emphasizing the need for compliance and the side effects and signs of toxicity. Parents of children taking salicylates should be advised to discontinue them if the child acquires chickenpox or influenza because of the relationship of viral infection to Reye syndrome. Signs and symptoms of gastroenteritis should be reported to the physician. As children grow older they need to become more responsible for compliance with the medication and treatment regimens. Children with JRA are usually put on individualized exercise programs developed by occupational or physical therapists. These programs include joint promotion techniques, as well as range-of-motion and strengthening exercises. Parents and children must be taught how to carry out the exercise program and how to adjust it for periods when the symptoms are exacerbated.

### Suppression of the Inflammatory Process.
Children with JRA experience high fevers either daily or intermittently for varied periods of time. Joint inflammation accompanied by pain or tenderness is also present. Management of these manifestations rests on compliance to the medication regimen including use of anti-inflammatory and antipyretic drugs. Tepid baths and sponging are also effective in reducing fever. Application of heat (using hot water bottles, heating pads, or heat packs) may help eliminate pain in joints. Use of joint supports or splints may also provide relief from pain. The child should avoid activities that stress the joints, such as jogging, jumping, or lifting, and should avoid overexertion when feeling well.

### Maintenance of Joint Function.
Joint stiffness, particularly in the morning and after periods of inactivity, is a major source of discomfort and immobility for children with JRA. Toddlers may be irritable and may cry upon awakening. There are a number of measures that may prevent morning stiffness. Some children report reduction of morning stiffness when sleeping in a sleeping bag or on a water bed or when using an electric blanket. Sleepers or pajamas with feet or thermal underwear or leg warmers can be used. Anti-inflammatory medication, along with a snack, should be taken upon awakening. This should be followed by a warm bath or shower and limbering exercises (Page-Goertz, 1989).

Loss of mobility in specific joints may lead to problems in performing activities of daily living. Decreased mobility in the lower extremities may interfere with walking, and a wheelchair or motorized scooter may be needed. Loss of mobility in the fingers, arms, and shoulders may lead to difficulty in feeding and dressing, including adjusting clothing before and after toileting. School-age children may have difficulty writing, raising their hands to answer questions, and writing on the blackboard.

### Promotion of Normal Growth and Development.
Joint pain and loss of joint function may interfere with achievement and progression of gross and fine motor skills. Older infants may have difficulty learning to crawl, stand, and walk. Alternative ways to explore their environment must be found in order to expand their experiences and allow them to become independent. As children grow older, they may have difficulty keeping up with their peers in normal motor activities and become passive. As children enter the school-age period, many specific problems may occur that lead to embarrassment, anger, and frustration. (It is important for the school nurse and the child's teachers to be aware of the child's condition and any limitations or specific needs.) These problems may carry over into adolescence and interfere with the development of independence, relationships with the same- and opposite-sex peers, and normal physical activities of this age group. These problems can lead to anger, depression, and noncompliance in the adolescent.

### Support of Child and Family.
Nurses in all settings serve as advocates for the child and family to meet the demands of chronic illness. Initially the nurse reinforces the explanation of the disease process and its treatment to the child and family. At this time the parents and child should be encouraged to explore and express their feelings about the limitations of the disease and its effect on the child in terms of being different, having difficulty competing in school and socially, and developing normal relationships with peers. The family will need help in planning a schedule of activities including exercise and rest, compliance to the day regimen, and regular attendance at school. Activities that increase isolation from others should be discouraged, as should overprotective behavior by the parents. Parents should be encouraged to allow the child to assume self-care activities and to become involved in activities and interaction with peers. Parents should be referred to parent support groups within the community and to agencies that provide special services, such as the Arthritis Foundation. (For further discussion of support measures for the family and child see Chaps. 18 and 20.)

## Systemic Lupus Erythematosus

### Pathophysiology

Despite the identification of numerous human autoantigens, characterization of the immune response, and description of the multisystem nature of systemic lupus erythematosus (SLE), the exact cause of immune dysfunction in this disease remains unknown. Viruses have been implicated as etiologic agents, but no virus has been consistently isolated from humans with SLE. Provirus (incomplete virus) has recently been found in the synovium of patients with rheumatoid arthritis, and experimental infection of mice with certain retroviruses can cause a lupus-like illness. It remains possible but unproved that viruses play a role in causing SLE.

However, it appears that genetics influence susceptibility to SLE. Because of the diversity of clinical abnormalities in SLE, genetic factors may be involved in antigen formation, autoantibody production, and manifestations of clinical features. Therefore, it has been preposed that an individual could acquire asymptomatic antigenemia, or antigen/antibody formation without clinical manifestations, or full-blown clinical and immune dysfunction syndrome.

Sex hormones clearly affect disease expression, since 90% of human cases occur among girls and women. Experiments conducted in mice confirm that castration of males or estrogen supplementation of males or females accelerates the clinical disease course. It also has been shown that androgens improve the clearance of immune complexes and increase T suppressor cell numbers and function (such as production of interleukin-2). These are all secondary effects, however; abnormal structure or function of sex hormones has not been identified as causative.

Finally, there is significant immunoregulatory dysfunction in SLE. Stem cells are abnormal, T cells have a diminished proliferative response to mitogens, and delayed hypersensitivity is impaired. B cells are hyperactive and spontaneously produce excess immunoglobulin in vitro compared to normal cells. Natural killer cells are reduced in number and exhibit poor functional capacity. Lymphocyte products such as interleukins and interferons also demonstrate significant abnormalities. All these changes, however, are believed to represent secondary manifestations of disease (Manolis & Schrieber, 1986).

## Medical Diagnosis and Management

The prevalence of SLE in children in the United States is estimated at 0.6 per 100,000, and it occurs four times more often among blacks than whites. Before puberty the ratio of cases between girls and boys is 3:1; after puberty and up to the age of 21 it is 5:1.

Cases are rare before the age of 5 years, but neonatal SLE does occur. Lupus dermatitis, photosensitivity, and occasionally systemic manifestations such as hepatitis or carditis characterize the disease. Diagnosis may be established by skin biopsy and characteristic serology test results (Ro-antibody positive, antinuclear antibody [ANA] positive or negative). Mothers of these infants are more likely to be asymptomatic (60%) than symptomatic; they also are Ro-antibody positive. (Ro is a class of RNA protein complexes not related to messenger, nucleolar, or transfer RNA.) The clinical and serologic features most often resolve spontaneously, but the carditis may be associated with complete heart block and sudden death or with cardiomyopathy and congestive heart failure. Rarely have

cases progressed to persistent rheumatologic disorders (Watson, Lane, Barnett, Bias, & Arnett, 1984).

Most children with SLE have a severe, multisystem disorder. There are 11 criteria for diagnosis of SLE; four or more must be present serially or simultaneously (Table 27-13). In general, affected children have weight loss, anorexia, fatigue, and malaise. They often have fever and sometimes have generalized lymphadenopathy.

The only specific cutaneous manifestation is the butterfly rash on the face (Fig. 27-6). Ulcers may be present on mucous membranes, and patchy alopecia may also develop. The joints may be so severely affected that the initial diagnostic consideration is juvenile rheumatoid arthritis.

Pericarditis or myocarditis characterize the cardiac involvement. Pleuritis, nephritis, cerebritis, and hepatitis all occur in a minority of patients. Children with SLE may develop a syndrome that mimics a ruptured appendix, volvulus, or intussusception. The actual cause of illness is inflammation of an abdominal organ, and unnecessary surgery is associated with high rates of morbidity and mortality (Emery, 1986).

Laboratory evaluation of the child with suspected SLE supports but does not establish the diagnosis. Routine tests should include antinuclear antibody (ANA), renal function studies (urinalysis, BUN, creatinine, 24-hour creatinine clearance, and urine protein quantitation), pulmonary function studies and chest x-ray, EKG and 2D echo-

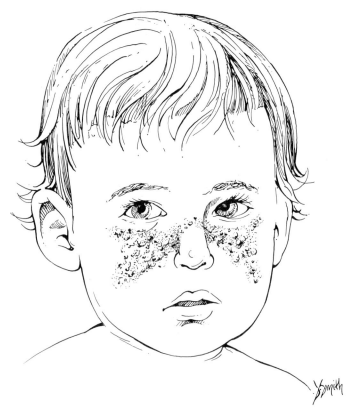

*Figure 27–6.   Facial butterfly rash on a child with systemic lupus erythematosus.*

*Table 27–13. Classification of SLE*

| Criterion | Description |
| --- | --- |
| Malar rash | Fixed erythema, flat or raised, over the malar eminences |
| Discoid rash | Erythematous raised patches with adherent keratotic scaling and follicular plugging |
| Photosensitivity | Skin rash from sunlight |
| Oral ulcers | Painless oral or nasopharyngeal ulcers |
| Arthritis | Tenderness, swelling, or effusion of two or more peripheral joints |
| Serositis | Pleuritis (pain or friction rub) or Pericarditis (EKG changes, rub, or effusion) |
| Renal disorder | Proteinuria greater than 500 mg/day or Cellular casts (red cells, granular, tubular or mixed) |
| Neurologic disorder | Seizures or psychosis |
| Hematologic disorder | Hemolytic anemia with reticulocytosis or Leukopenia (<4000 WBC/mm$^3$) on two or more occasions or Lymphopenia (<1500/mm$^3$) on two or more occasions |
| Immunologic disorder | Positive anti-DNA or False positive RPR or VDRL (serologic tests for syphilis) |
| Antinuclear antibody (ANA) | Abnormal positive titer in absence of drugs known to produce positive test |

cardiogram, liver function studies, creatine phosphokinase (CPK), and hematological evaluation (CBC and differential, PT and PTT, stool for occult blood). Identified abnormalities may be pursued with further testing, if warranted. Every child with SLE should have a kidney biopsy. Prognosis can be correlated with microscopic pathology findings, and therapy is also guided by the results (Ballou, 1987; Emery, 1986).

Treatment for this multisystem disorder is complex and must be tempered by the desire to achieve normal growth and development. Dietary discretion and a good exercise program are basic components of all therapeutic plans. Joint manifestations may be treated with aspirin, nonsteroidal anti-inflammatory agents, and physical therapy. Cutaneous lesions may be suppressed with hydrox-

ychloroquine or topical steroids. However, topical steroids can be systemically absorbed and can also produce depigmentation of the skin at sites where chronically applied. Photosensitivity may be minimized by using sunscreens or may require avoidance of prolonged exposure to the sun.

Systemic disease, particularly hard-to-control systemic illness, requires use of nonspecific anti-inflammatory agents such as corticosteroids and cytotoxic agents. However, these drugs pose serious risk/benefit issues. Careful explanation of the medical aspects of this therapy, plus psychological support from the Lupus Society, Arthritis Foundation, or a similar group, may be the optimal approach (Ballou, 1987; Emery 1986).

### Nursing Assessment and Diagnosis

In suspected cases of SLE nurses should assess for signs of fever, lesions, weight loss, fatigue, joint tenderness, and possibly alopecia. Integumentary examination may reveal a "butterfly" rash across both cheeks and the bridge of the nose. However, nonspecific symptoms may persist for months or years before diagnosis.

Nursing diagnoses for systemic lupus erythematosus might include the following:

- Impaired Skin Integrity related to mouth lesions, urticaria, alopecia, and erythematous rash
- High Risk for Infection related to immune disorder
- Altered Nutrition: Less than body requirements related to anorexia
- Pain related to swollen, edematous joints
- Body Image Disturbance related to effects of the disease including lesions and alopecia
- Altered Family Processes related to caring for a child with a chronic illness

### Planning and Implementing Nursing Care

The focus of long-term management of SLE centers on reversing the autoimmune and inflammatory processes and preventing exacerbations and complications. The nurses' role includes assisting the child and family in adjusting to the disease and its treatment. Because SLE affects adolescents in particular, knowledge of developmental needs of this age group must be considered in providing education and counseling. Education should include basic knowledge about the disease process and prognosis, signs and symptoms, preventive measures, and drug therapy. Management of problems encountered in the school setting is shown in Table 27-14.

Adolescents who have reached the cognitive level of formal operations (and even some preadolescents) may have the capacity to reason logically if information is presented in a simple, straightforward manner. Adolescents should be made aware of the signs and symptoms of SLE so

*Table 27–14.  Management of Problems Specific to the School Setting and the Child with SLE*

| Problem | Intervention Strategies |
|---|---|
| Difficulty climbing stairs/ walking distance | • Elevator permit<br>• Schedule classes to minimize walking and climbing<br>• Two sets of books. Keep 1 in appropriate classroom, other at home to eliminate need for trips to locker<br>• Wheelchair if needed |
| Inactivity stiffness due to prolonged sitting | • Wiggle! Change position every 20 minutes<br>• Sit at side or back of room so can walk around without disturbing others<br>• Ask to be assigned jobs that permit walking (e.g., pass/ collect papers) |
| Difficulty carrying books/ cafeteria tray | • Backpack/shoulderbag for books<br>• 2 sets of books<br>• Determine cafeteria assistance plan (e.g., helper, reserved seat, wheeled cart) |
| Handwriting problems (slow/messy/painful) | • Use "fat" pen/pencil crayons<br>• Felt tip pen<br>• Stretch hands every 10 minutes<br>• Use tape recorder for note taking<br>• Use electric typewriter for reports<br>• Alternatives for timed tests (oral test, extra time)<br>• Educate teacher: messy writing may be unavoidable at time |
| Difficulty with shoulder movement<br>  Dressing<br>  Reaching locker<br>  Raising hand<br>  Writing at blackboard | • Loose-fitting clothing<br>• Velcro closures<br>• O.T. can provide adaptive equipment<br>• Locker modification/alternative place for storage<br>• Devise alternative signaling method<br>• Use large paper that can be raised up |
| Medication administration | • Self medication with prompt from teacher/nurse is ideal. Check with district for their rules. |
| Fatigue | • Rest after lunch<br>• Avoid excess activity at recess<br>• Wheelchair for field trips if needed |
| Tardiness due to morning stiffness | • Plan class schedule with least demanding subjects in morning |

that they may take preventive measures to avoid exacerbations and, when appropriate, contact their health care provider. Warning signs of an exacerbation might include fever, fatigue, anorexia, or chills. Precipitating factors for an exacerbation might include exposure to the sun, insufficient rest, physical or emotional stress, or sudden cessation of steroid therapy (Hartley, 1978).

Exposure to sun should be avoided because it produces visible skin manifestations and also activates more severe organ involvement (Ascheim, 1981). Because adolescents normally participate in outdoor activities, they should be taught to use sunscreens as a daily routine.

Alopecia is temporary in many cases but can be embarrassing to young females. They should be taught to use mild shampoos to control hair loss and to wear scarves or, when necessary, wigs to improve appearance.

The adolescent should be encouraged to engage in activities that maintain range of motion and allow for social interaction with peers. Although jogging should be avoided, swimming and bicycling are good choices. Joint pain can be prevented by allowing for 8 to 10 hours of sleep each night and frequent rest periods during activities.

Family members should be aware of possible central nervous system involvement. These symptoms might include decreased attention span, personality changes, confusion, and inappropriate laughter or crying, as well as psychotic episodes or seizure activity (Ascheim, 1981). Any indication of these symptoms should be reported to the physician.

Fever should always be reported to the health care provider. The use of medications, including dosage, schedules, and side effects, should be covered in detail. Special attention should be given to the side effects of steroids, the danger of sudden withdrawal, and the danger of adrenal crisis and exacerbation of the disease (Ascheim, 1981).

Sexually active adolescents must be warned that pregnancy is a risk for individuals with SLE, especially if the cardiac or renal system is affected. Use of birth control measures must be discussed. Clients who become pregnant should be monitored closely. There is a high incidence of premature births and stillbirths during the third trimester due to exacerbation of the disease (Ascheim, 1981).

Counseling for female adolescents must take into account the changes caused by the disease as they relate to development of body image. According to Ascheim (1981), factors such as distorted body image, dependence, loss of control over their illness, and an uncertain prognosis all affect adolescents' ability to develop life goals and complete developmental tasks.

It is difficult for the nurse dealing with adolescents with SLE to foster normal growth and development. Emphasis should always be placed on what they can do, and provision should be made for some decision-making regarding social activities, scheduling of rest periods and medications, and dietary restrictions. It is essential that adolescents be viewed as individuals and allowed to verbalize their concerns as unique people and sexual beings.

Family concerns must also be addressed. Families often face struggles for independence, feelings of guilt, jealousy, and resentment on the part of the client, siblings and parents (Kellerman, Zelter, Ellenberg, Dash, & Rigles, 1981). Families must be taught to foster self-care in adolescents and to maintain and support all family members. Family members, including siblings, should be included in education and counseling regarding adolescents with SLE.

## Summary

The immune system is a network of defenses that keeps the body intact and free from disease. Immune system disorders may affect a variety of body systems and include deficiencies, autoimmune disorders, allergic reactions, and abnormal cell proliferation. Nursing care for children with immune problems is challenging because immune system disorders are characterized by a wide range of causes and a variety of signs and symptoms that affect various body systems. Nursing care of children with immune disorders focuses on common concerns, including development of the child and family, acute care, preparation for home care, and long-term care. In addition to providing physical care, nurses must also serve as educators and counselors when working with children with immune disorders and their families.

### Standard Care Plan for the Acutely Ill Child with Acquired Immunodeficiency Syndrome

| Nursing Diagnosis | Intervention | Expected Outcome |
|---|---|---|
| Increased susceptibility to infection due to alteration in immune system related to: | Instruct/review infection control measures with family members. | Control or eradication of infection |
| Cellular immunodeficiency (major defense against viral growth, certain bacterial infections, mycobacteria, fungi and parasites) | Instruct family members about preventing transmission of infectious agents. | |
| Humoral immunodeficiency (effective against certain bacterial infections) | Monitor for signs and symptoms of infection. | |
| | Monitor for side effects of antimicrobial agent. | |
| | Review medication dosage, administration schedule, and duration of therapy regularly. | |

*(continued)*

## *Standard Care Plan for the Acutely Ill Child with Acquired Immunodeficiency Syndrome (Continued)*

| Nursing Diagnosis | Intervention | Expected Outcome |
|---|---|---|
| Fever due to:<br>　Opportunistic or bacterial<br>　infection | Monitor temperature.<br>Develop a management plan with medical care provider, including:<br>　Degree of fever and when to report<br>　Use of antipyretics<br>　Use of tepid baths<br>　Fluid intake | Maintain the child's level of comfort. |
| Alteration in comfort/pain related to:<br>　Side effects of treatment<br>　Malignancy<br><br>　Opportunistic infection | Monitor and report alterations in comfort. Assess C/O and level of pain.<br>Assess response to pain medication and consult with medical care providers related to dosage adjustment.<br>Assess for sleep deprivation.<br>Avoid tissue irritation/reduce external stimuli that aggravate discomfort, such as rough clothing, furry stuffed toys, etc.<br>Prevent or minimize scratching—cut nails, apply mittens or elbow restraints when indicated. | Level of comfort will increase. Pain will be controlled. |
| Alteration in Gas Exchange Related to:<br><br>　Opportunistic infection (PCP, etc.)<br><br>　Lymphoid interstitial pneumonitis (LIP) | Assess lung sounds, color, activity tolerance, and rate, rhythm, and character of respirations.<br>Allow child to assume position of comfort. Elevate head of bed.<br>Note frequency, type (productive, non-productive) and effectiveness of cough. Determine if cough interferes with sleep, feeding.<br>Institute chest PT to loosen secretions.<br>Plan for scheduled rest periods to promote energy conservation.<br>Monitor response to and utilization of supplemental oxygen, if appropriate.<br>Monitor response to medications (bronochodilators, steroids, etc.). | Adequate ventilation and oxygenation |
| Alteration in Cognitive and Motor Function Related to:<br><br>　Opportunistic infection<br><br>　HIV encephalopathy | Assist caretakers to deal with the child on a level appropriate to cognitive (and not chronological) age.<br>Encourage participation in daily activities of the family as appropriate.<br>Consultation for occupational, physical and speech therapy as indicated | Maintain level of functioning.<br><br>Minimize loss of function. |

*(continued)*

### Standard Care Plan for the Acutely Ill Child with Acquired Immunodeficiency Syndrome *(Continued)*

| Nursing Diagnosis | Intervention | Expected Outcome |
|---|---|---|
| Malignancy | Instruct/review with parents positioning, skin care, and exercise. | |
| | Assess ability to chew, swallow, and handle secretions. | |
| | Identify need for and obtain equipment such as wheelchairs, etc. | |
| Alteration in Nutrition Related to: | Nutritional assessment and referral if indicated | Child should maintain an adequate nutritional status. |
| Decreased intake of required nutrients | Reassess nutritional status on a regular basis and report increase/decrease in weight. | |
| Malabsorption | | |
| Increased need for nutrients due to chronic infection and increased respiratory needs | Assess the child to determine the causative factors of inadequate intake:<br>Pain<br>Difficulty in swallowing<br>Mouth lesions<br>Dislikes food<br>Coughing spells<br>Nausea/vomiting<br>Diarrhea<br>Fever | |
| | Implement measures to improve nutritional state. | |
| | Nutritional education for family and child | |
| Potential for Bleeding related to: | Assess child and report signs of unusual bleeding. | Nurse will assess for signs of bleeding and intervene appropriately. |
| Thrombocytopenia | Petechiae<br>Multiple ecchymotic areas<br>Bleeding gums<br>Nosebleeds | |
| Platelet dysfunction | Rectal bleeding<br>Unusual joint pain or swelling | |
| Medication | Abdominal pain, distention | |
| | Observe for blood in urine, stool, and emesis. | |
| | Implement measures to prevent bleeding. | |
| | Use small-guage needles for any injection<br>Avoid overinflating of B/P cuffs<br>Soft toothbrush (mouth care)<br>No rectal temps<br>Instruct parent in safety measures | |
| | Notify medical care provider of unusual or prolonged bleeding episodes. | |

*(continued)*

## Standard Care Plan for the Acutely Ill Child with Acquired Immunodeficiency Syndrome (Continued)

| Nursing Diagnosis | Intervention | Expected Outcome |
|---|---|---|
| Alteration in Fluid/Electrolyte Balance related to:<br>Decreased intake of fluid and food<br><br>Vomiting<br><br><br>Diarrhea<br><br><br>Sodium and potassium imbalance due to HIV endocrinopathy and nephropathy | Identify factors that put child at risk for f/e imbalance, e.g., diarrhea, poor nutritional intake, infection, fever, etc.<br><br>Assess child at each visit:<br>Skin turgor<br>Weight loss/gain<br>Change in activity level<br>Seizures<br>Urinary pattern | Maintain fluid/electrolyte imbalance |
| Potential Impairment of Skin Integrity related to:<br>Immobility<br><br><br><br><br><br><br>Diarrhea<br><br>Kaposi's sarcoma | Instruct parent in:<br>ROM to all extremities<br>Position changes<br>Utilize air mattress, etc.<br>Encourage activity as tolerated/permitted.<br>Skin integrity will be maintained. Skin breakdown will be prevented.<br><br>Instruct parents in skin care:<br>Change diapers after each soiling<br>Clean buttocks and genital area<br>Use soap and water<br>Apply protective emollients<br>Expose reddened area to air when feasible<br>Encourage small, frequent feedings | Skin integrity will be maintained. Skin breakdown will be prevented. |
| Open wound and skin lesions | Describe skin lesions accurately; obtain history of onset and course of development.<br><br>Maintain and teach child and family hygienic care and aseptic techniques. | Further spread of infection will be limited. |
| Potential fatigue and exhaustion of care providers | Ongoing assessment of the family's ability to cope with care<br><br>Identify available volunteer and respite services.<br><br>When possible, involve extended family members in care.<br><br>Encourage utilization of support services such as homemaker, etc. Parent will be able to continue caring for child. | |

(Nursing care plan—Pediatric AIDS patient, AIDS Update 1988, Women/Children/Minorities; presented at the New York State Nurses Association Annual Convention, 1988)

# References

Albano, E. A., & Pizzo, P. A. (1988). The evolving population of immunocompromised children. *Journal of Pediatric Infectious Disease, 7,* S79–S86.

Ascheim, J. H. (1981). The adolescent and systemic lupus erythematosus: A developmental and educational approach. *Issues in Comprehensive Pediatric Nursing, 5,* 293–307.

Bailet, I. W. (1988). Allergic rhinitis. In R. A. Dershewitz (Ed.). *Ambulatory pediatric care* (pp. 211–213). Philadelphia:
J. B. Lippincott Company.

Ballou, S. P. (1987). Systemic lupus erythematosus. Controversies in management. *Postgraduate Medicine, 81,* 157–164.

Behrman, R. E., & Vaughan, V. C. (1987). The immunologic system. In R. E. Behrman & V. C. Vaughan (Eds.). *Nelson textbook of pediatrics* (13th ed., pp. 455–544). Philadelphia: W. B. Saunders.

Behrman, R. E., & Vaughan, V. C. (1987). Respiratory allergy. In R. E. Behrman & V. C. Vaugham (Eds.). *Nelson textbook of pediatrics* (13th ed., pp. 494–495). Philadelphia: W. B. Saunders.

Berger, M., & Sorensen, R. U. (1989). Immune defects associated with recurrent infections. *Advances in Pediatric Infectious Disease, 4,* 111–138.

Brewer, E. J., Jr. (1986). Pitfalls in the diagnosis of juvenile rheumatoid arthritis. *Pediatric Rheumatology, 33,* 1015.

Calabro, J. J., Eyvazzadeh, C., & Weber, C. A. (1986). Juvenile rheumatoid arthritis: Early diagnosis, management and long-term prognosis. *Advances in Therapy, 3,* 97.

Cant, A. J. (1985). Food allergy in childhood. *Human nutrition: Applied nutrition, 39A,* 277–293.

Cassidy, J. T. (1985). Rheumatic diseases of childhood. In W. N. Kelley, E. D. Harris, Jr., S. Ruddy, & C. B. Sledge (Eds.). *Textbook of Rheumatology* (2nd ed., pp. 1247–1276). Philadelphia: W. B. Saunders.

Centers for Disease Control. (1987). Recommendations for prevention of HIV transmission in health care settings. *Morbidity and Mortality Weekly Report, 36*(25), 3–18.

Conley, M. E., Beckwith, J. B., Mancer, J. F. K., & Tenckhoff, L. (1979). The spectrum of the DiGeorge syndrome. *Journal of Pediatrics, 94,* 883–890.

Cooper, J. A. D., Jr., & Matthay, R. A. (1987). Drug-induced pulmonary disease. *Disease-a-Month, 33,* 61.

Emery, H. (1986). Clinical aspects of systemic lupus erythematosus in childhood. *Pediatric Clinics of North America, 33,* 1177–1202.

Fisher, M. (1987). Anaphylaxis. *Disease-a-Month, 33,* 433.

Freedom, R. M., Rosen, F. S., & Nadas, A. S. (1972). Congenital cardiovascular disease and anomalies of the third and fourth pharyngeal pouch. *Circulation, 46,* 165–172.

Halpern, G. M., & Scott, J. R., Jr. (1987). Non-IgE antibody mediated mechanisms in food allergy. *Annals of Allergy, 58,* 14–27.

Hargreave, F. E., Dolovich, J., O'Byrne, P. M., Ramsdale, E. H., & Daniel, E. E. (1986). The origin of airway hyper-responsiveness. *Journal of Allergy and Clinical Immunology, 78,* 825–832.

Harris, E. D. (1985). Pathogenesis of rheumatoid arthritis. In

W. N. Kelley, E. D. Harris, Jr., S. Ruddy, & C. B. Sledge (Eds.). *Textbook of rheumatology* (2nd ed., pp. 886–914.). Philadelphia: W. B. Saunders.

Hartley, B. (1978). Systemic lupus: A patient perspective. *Canadian Nurse, 74*(2), 16–20.

Harvey, J. C., Dungan, W. T., Elders, M. J., & Hughes, E. R. (1970). Third and fourth pharyngeal pouch syndrome, associated vascular anomalies and hypocalcemic seizures. *Clinical Pediatrics, 9,* 496–499.

Kellerman, J., Zelter, L., Ellenberg, L., Dash, J., & Rigles, D. (1981). Import of illness in adolescents—crucial issues and coping styles. *Journal of Pediatrics, 97,* 132–138.

Lederman, H. M., & Winkelstein, J. A. (1985). X-linked agammaglobulinemia: An analysis of 96 patients. *Medicine, 643,* 145–156.

Levy, J. H., Roizen, M. F., & Morris, J. M. (1986). Anaphylactic and anaphylactoid reactions. *Spine, 11,* 282–291.

Lum, L. G., Tubergen, D. G., Corash, L., & Blaese, R. M. (1980). Splenectomy in the management of the thrombocytopenia of the Wiskott-Aldrich syndrome. *New England Journal of Medicine, 302,* 892–896.

Manolis, N., & Schrieber, L. (1986). Current concepts in the etiopathogenesis and treatment of systemic lupus erythematosus (SLE). *Australian and New Zealand Journal of Medicine, 16,* 729–743.

Matloff, S. (1988). Adverse reactions to foods. In R. A. Dershewitz (Ed.). *Ambulatory pediatric care* (pp. 226–230). Philadelphia: J. B. Lippincott.

Omerand, A. D. (1985). The Wiskott-Aldrich syndrome. *International Journal of Dermatology, 24,* 77–81.

Owens, G. R. (1986). New concepts in bronchodilator therapy. *American Family Practitioner, 33,* 218–229.

Page-Goertz, S. S. (1989). Even children have arthritis. *Pediatric Nursing, 15*(1), 11–16.

Pahwa, S. (1988). Human immunodeficiency virus infection in children: Nature of immune-deficiency, clinical spectrum and management. *Pediatric Infectious Disease Journal, 7,* 561–571.

Parkman, R., Rappeport, J., Geha, R., Belli, J., Cassady, R., Levey, R., Nathan, D. G., & Rosen, F. S. (1978). Complete correction of the Wiskott-Aldrich syndrome by allogenic bone marrow transplantation. *New England Journal of Medicine, 298,* 921–927.

Peacocke, M., & Siminovitch, K. A. (1987). Linkage of the Wiskott-Aldrich syndrome with polymorphic DNA sequences from the human X chromosome. *Proceedings of the National Academy of Science USA, 84,* 3430–3433.

Pearson, D. J, & McKee, A. (1985). Food allergy. *Advances in Nutritional Research, 7,* 1–37.

Rennebohen, R., & Correll, J. K. (1984. Comprehensive management of juvenile rheumatoid arthritis. *Nursing Clinics of North America, 19,* 647–662.

Saavedra-Delgado, A. M., & Metcalfe, D. D. (1985). Interactions between food antigens and the immune system in the pathogenesis of gastrointestinal diseases. *Annals of Allergy, 55,* 694.

Sheller, J. R. (1987). Review: Asthma: Emerging concepts and potential therapies. *The American Journal of the Medical Sciences, 293,* 298–308.

Steele, R. W., & Burks, A. W., Jr. (1986). Wiskott-Aldrich syn-

drome with fever of unknown origin. *Annals of Allergy,*
*56,* 293–294, 321–323.

Tattersfield, A. E. (1987). The site of the defect in asthma.
*Chest, 91* [Suppl. 6], 184S–189S.

Thompson, S. W., & Gietz, K. R. (1985, July/August). Acquired
immune deficiency syndrome in infants and children. *Pe-*
*diatric Nursing, 11*(4), 278.

Watson, R. M., Lane, A. T., Barnett, N. K., Bias, W. B., Arnett, F.
C., Provost, T. T. (1984). Neonatal lupus erythematosus.
*Medicine, 63,* 362–378.

## Bibliography

Amman, A. J. (1987). Pediatric acquired immunodeficiency
syndrome. In R. D. Feigin & J. D. Cherry (Eds.). *Text-*
*book of pediatric infectious diseases* (2nd ed., pp. 1044–
1049). Philadelphia: W. B. Saunders.

Bock, S. A. (1987). Prospective appraisal of complaints of adverse reactions to foods in children during the first 3
years of life. *Pediatrics, 79,* 683–688.

Brewer, E. (1975). Reduction of morning stiffness and/or pain
using a sleeping bag. *Pediatrics, 56,* 62.

Calhoun, W. J., Fink, J. N., & Novey, H. S. (1989). Hypersensitivity pneumonitis. *Patient Care, 23,* 71.

Daniel, W. A., Jr. (1977). *Adolescents in health and disease*
(pp. 43–46, 60–80.). St. Louis: C. V. Mosby.

Hart, E. M., Karu, J. H., & Fonger, P. A. (1987). Nursing care
of the child with severe combined immune deficiency.
*Journal of Pediatric Nursing, 2,* 373–380.

Hollister, J. R. (1988). Rheumatic disease in childhood. *Pedi-*
*atrician, 15,* 65–72.

Iafrate, R. P., Massey, K. L., & Hendeles, L. (1985). Current
concepts in clinical therapeutics: Asthma. *Clinical Phar-*
*macology, 5,* 206–227.

Ippolito, C., & Gibes, R. M. (1988). AIDS and the newborn.
*Journal of Perinatal Neonatal Nursing, 1*(4), 78–86.

McKinney, R. E., Jr., Katz, S. L., & Wilfert, C. M. (1987).
Chronic enteroviral meningoenecphalitis in agam-
maglobulinemic patients. *Reviews of Infectious Disease, 9,*
334–356.

Miller, M. L., Magivay, D. B., & Warren, R. W. (1986). The immunologic basis of lupus. *Pediatric Clinics of North*
*America, 33,* 1191–1198.

Remold-O'Donnell, E., Zimmerman, C., Kenney, D., & Rosen,
F. S. (1987). Expression on blood cells of sialophorin,
the surface glycoprotein that is defective in Wiskott-Aldrich syndrome. *Blood, 70,* 104–109.

Symposium proceedings on adverse reactions to foods and
food additives. (1986, July). *Journal of Allergy and Clini-*
*cal Immunology, 78*(10).

Taranta, A. (1988). JRA and red herrings. *Hospital Practice,*
*23,* 129–150.

Traver, G. A., & Martinez, M. (1988). Asthma update. Part I:
Mechanisms, pathophysiology, and diagnosis. *Journal of*
*Pediatric Health Care, 2*(5), 221–226.

White, J. E., & Owsley, V. B. (1983). Helping families cope
with milk, wheat and soy allergies. *Maternal-Child Nurs-*
*ing Journal, 8,*(6) 423–428.

# Alterations in Fluid and Electrolyte Balance

Carolyn M. Orlowski and Richard E. Harbin

28

*Fluid Compartments*

*Fluid Balance*

*Factors Affecting Water Movement and Balance*

*Electrolytes*

*Acid–Base Balance*

*Fluid and Electrolyte Requirements*

*Assessment*

*Nursing Diagnosis*

*Planning Nursing Care*

*Nursing Interventions*

*Evaluating Nursing Care*

*Alterations in Acid–Base Balance*

*Alterations in Electrolyte Balance*

*Alterations in Fluid Volume*

*Summary*

*Photograph by David Finn*

## Learning Objectives

*Upon completion of this chapter the reader will be able to:*

1. *Discuss five reasons why fluid balance is more critical in infants and young children than in adults.*

2. *Explain four regulatory mechanisms that maintain fluid and electrolyte balance.*

3. *State the normal range of blood pH and three regulatory mechanisms that interact to maintain it.*

4. *Identify the renal compensatory mechanisms involved in restoring acid–base balance.*

5. *Identify potential changes in vital signs related to fluid and electrolyte imbalance.*

6. *Discuss the causes and signs and symptoms of respiratory acidosis, respiratory alkalosis, metabolic acidosis, and metabolic alkalosis.*

7. *Compare and contrast the causes and signs and symptoms of alterations in the following electrolytes: sodium, potassium, calcium, and magnesium.*

8. *Discuss the causes and signs and symptoms of fluid volume deficit and fluid volume excess.*


## Key Terms

*acid–base balance*

*acidosis*

*active transport*

*alkalosis*

*buffers*

*chronic diarrhea*

*dehydration*

*diffusion*

*electrolytes*

*hydrostatic pressure*

*hypertonic solution*

*hypotonic solution*

*isotonic solution*

*osmolality*

*osmosis*

*osmotic pressure*

*parenteral nutrition*

*pH*

*solute*

*total body water*

The human body's essential fluid is water. Water provides the ions and nutrients needed by body cells, tissues, and organs to sustain normal function and life. Within cells, water provides the internal environment needed for chemical reactions, energy production, and maintenance of homeostasis. It is a transport medium for carrying blood cells and substances to tissues and organs and waste products from these cells. The nurse caring for children must understand the basic principles of fluid dynamics and acid–base balance in order to comprehend how disturbances in these areas affect the child's course of illness.


## Fluid Compartments

Water is the major component of body tissues, and *total body water* is the total amount of water in the body. Total body water varies with age, sex, and body fat content. The full-term newborn's body is composed of 70% to 80% fluid by weight, with this percentage decreasing rapidly during the first 6 months. By 2 years of age, the total body water approaches the adult level of 60%.

Total body water is either *intracellular* or *extracellular*. The intracellular fluid (ICF) contains large amounts of potassium, phosphate, sulfate, and protein. The extracellular fluid (ECF) is made up of *intravascular fluid* (plasma) and *interstitial fluid* (tissue fluid) and contains large amounts of sodium, chloride, and bicarbonate. Although fluid volume and composition vary in different body compartments, the function of total body water as a solvent for electrolytes, proteins, and nutrients is of primary importance.

## Fluid Balance

Infants and young children are particularly vulnerable to fluid volume and concentration imbalances. Infants may ingest and excrete half of their extracellular fluid daily. This daily fluid exchange is related to their high metabolic rate, which is two times higher per unit of weight than that of adults, who may exchange only one sixth of their extracellular fluid each day. The high metabolic rate in infants results in a large amount of metabolic waste, which is removed or excreted through the kidneys. Fluid loss in the form of large urine output accompanies this metabolic waste daily. Neonates lose additional fluid volume because their immature kidneys do not concentrate urine effectively. The temperature-regulating function of body water is heightened in infants and children because of their greater body surface area in proportion to their weight. Infants and young children have two to three times as much body surface area in relation to weight as adults, and premature infants have as much as five times that of the older child or adult.

## Factors Affecting Water Movement and Balance

### Water Transport Mechanisms

Normal physiological function depends on a balance between the water content of the ICF and ECF. Several important processes are involved in the movement of water and solutes between these two fluid spaces. Water provides the medium for transport of cellular nutrients and waste products that maintain the physiological environment. This movement of body water is essential to support cellular functions and occurs relative to specific transport mechanisms, including diffusion, osmosis, hydrostatic pressure, and active and passive transport.

*Diffusion* is the natural, random movement of solutes or particles through a solution, generally from an area of higher concentration to an area of lower concentration, distributing the particles evenly. The rate of solute diffusion is affected by differences in concentration, the size of the particles, and the distance the solutes must travel. Diffusion rate is increased when metabolic rate or temperature is high and when the difference in electrical charge or potential exists between the ions or particles. Many different substances diffuse through semipermeable

cell membranes in both directions, with varying degrees of ease. Some electrolytes move by diffusion; however, positively charged ions such as sodium and potassium do not move readily across cell membranes because membrane pores are lined with similar (positively charged) ions. Other nonelectrolyte substances that play a key role in fluid balance, such as glucose, urea, creatinine, and plasma proteins, are large molecules that must move by a process of *facilitated diffusion,* whereby a specific carrier substance within the membrane aids their movement. Glucose, for example, crosses the cell membrane using the carrier hormone insulin.

*Osmosis* is the transfer of water across a semipermeable cell membrane in response to a concentration difference of solutes. The water moves from an area of low solute concentration to one of high solute concentration, equalizing the concentration of solutes in both areas. This movement results from *osmotic pressure* that develops when two solutions with different concentrations are separated by a semipermeable membrane. The pressure is dependent on the number of particles present in the solution. A more concentrated solution exerts greater pressure, and is termed *hypertonic.* A less concentrated solution, which exerts less osmotic pressure, is termed *hypotonic.* A solution that exerts identical pressure is termed *isotonic.* For example, an isotonic saline solution has the same amount of salt in both intra- and extracellular fluid.

Osmotic pressure is measured in milliosmoles per liter (mOsm/L), which refers to the total number of osmotically active particles in a designated volume of solution. It is generally accepted that the normal osmolality or tonicity of body fluids is 285 to 295 mOsm/L (Behrman & Vaughan, 1987). Water transport mechanisms maintain osmotic equilibrium between intracellular and extracellular fluids. Imbalances in this osmolality related to fluid volume losses or extracellular electrolyte changes have a rapid impact on the intracellular composition. The osmolality or tonicity of a solution introduced into body fluids directly changes the extracellular volume and osmolality of these fluids, resulting in an intracellular response. Water moves into cells when a hypotonic solution is introduced, and water moves out of cells when a hypertonic solution is introduced. Sodium, the principal extracellular cation, determines the osmolality and volume of the extracellular fluid. For example, since isotonic solutions such as 0.9 sodium chloride (NaCl) and 5% D5W have the same tonicity as body fluids, no movement of water occurs. However, when a hypotonic solution such as 0.45 NaCl is introduced, which contains less solute concentration than plasma, water moves into cells. When a hypertonic solution such as 3.0 NaCl or 10% D10W is introduced, which contains higher solute concentrations than plasma, water moves out of cells.

Movement of both water and solutes through a semipermeable membrane from a high-pressure area to a low-pressure area is caused by *hydrostatic pressure.* Hydrostatic pressure forces fluid from the vascular space of the glomerular capillaries into the renal tubules and from the body's capillary network into the interstitial spaces. It is influenced by blood pressure, venous pressure, and capillary flow rate. Plasma proteins maintain a balance in intravascular volume by exerting enough osmotic pressure to retain sufficient circulating volume.

*Active transport* is the energy process of moving solutes and electrolytes across the cell membrane against concentration and electrical gradients. This means moving substances from an area of lesser concentration to an area of greater concentration. The removal of excess sodium from ICF by the "sodium pump" is an example of active transport. When an electrical or pressure difference exists, these molecules are transported with the assistance of energy in the form of adenosine triphosphate (ATP), which is produced in the mitochondria of cells. Sodium, potassium, calcium, chloride, urea, iron, hydrogen, several different sugars, and amino acids are some of the molecules transported with the assistance of a carrier substance. This mechanism is needed to maintain different normal quantities of electrolytes, such as sodium and potassium, in intracellular and extracellular compartments.

*Passive transport* is the movement of water and solutes to areas of lower concentration from areas of greater concentration. Water moves into and out of cells by passive transport.

## Regulatory Mechanisms

The amount of water in the body and plasma is precisely regulated regardless of daily fluctuations in intake. Water is retained or excreted in response to changes in plasma volume and plasma osmolality. Several homeostatic mechanisms are responsible for this critical balance of fluids and electrolytes and include functions of volume receptors and osmoreceptors, hypothalamus, posterior pituitary, and renal tubules. To achieve this balance, the volume of water derived from intake and oxidation of nutrients must equal the volume of fluid lost from the kidneys, gastrointestinal tract, skin, and lungs.

Fluid intake is generally stimulated by a sensation of thirst, which protects against fluid depletion and hypertonicity by maintaining extracellular fluid volume. Thirst is regulated by a center in the mid hypothalamus where osmoreceptors respond to an increase of 1% to 2% in the plasma osmolality, or when *baroreceptors,* sensors for changes in volume, detect fluid volume depletion.

Ingested water is absorbed in the gastrointestinal tract by passive diffusion and active transport mechanisms. Water is lost from the gastrointestinal tract and, through insensible water loss, from the skin and lungs. Additional contributing factors to water loss include body and environmental temperature, rate of respirations, and humidity. Water excretion, regulated by varying rates of urine flow, responds to plasma osmolality. Low plasma osmolality related to an excess amount of water is corrected by excreting a large volume of dilute urine, and high plasma osmolality inhibits fluid loss in the kidneys.

Extracellular fluid volume is further maintained by several hormonal mechanisms, such as antidiuretic hormone (ADH) and aldosterone. ADH is formed in the hypothalamus, stored in the posterior pituitary gland, and released into surrounding capillaries. ADH is released in response to increased extracellular fluid osmolality or concentration and decreased blood volume that results in hypotension and osmoreceptor stimulation. The kidneys play a major role in maintaining normal serum electrolyte levels and regulation of water balance. The presence of ADH increases the permeability of the nephron's collecting ducts and distal tubules, allowing increased water reabsorption into the extracellular fluid. The nephrons either excrete or retain appropriate amounts of electrolytes by altering the composition of urine. This also assists in regulating body pH.

Aldosterone, the principal adrenocortical hormone secreted by the adrenal cortex, increases sodium reabsorption in the renal tubules. As sodium is reabsorbed, so is water, resulting in expansion of the circulating intravascular volume.

## Electrolytes

An *electrolyte* is a substance that develops an electrical charge when dissolved in water. Electrolytes that develop a positive charge are called *cations,* and include potassium, calcium, sodium, and magnesium. Chloride, bicarbonate, sulfate, and phosphate are electrolytes that develop a negative charge, and these are called *anions.* The body is in *electroneutrality* when there are equal numbers of cations and anions.

The electrolyte content of ICF varies from the content of ECF. Table 28-1 compares the electrolyte content of ICF with that of ECF. Potassium and phosphate are the major electrolytes in ICF. The major electrolytes in ECF are sodium and chloride. The sodium concentration accounts

*Table 28–1. Approximate Major Electrolyte Content of Intracellular Fluid and Extracellular Fluid*

| Electrolyte | Intracellular Fluid | Extracellular Fluid |
|---|---|---|
| Sodium ($Na^+$) | 10 mEq/L | 142 mEq/L |
| Potassium ($K^+$) | 150 mEq/L | 5 mEq/L |
| Magnesium ($Mg^{2+}$) | 40 mEq/L | 2 mEq/L |
| Calcium ($Ca^{2+}$) | 1 mEq/L | 5 mEq/L |
| Chloride ($Cl^-$) | 4 mEq/L | 103 mEq/L |
| Bicarbonate ($MCO_3^-$) | 10 mEq/L | 26 mEq/L |

for about 90% of ECF. ECF is also called the *saline compartment,* and ICF may be termed the *water compartment.*

The electrolytes essential to maintaining adequate fluid and electrolyte balance are sodium, potassium, chloride, calcium, and magnesium. Table 28-2 describes the functions and regulation of these important electrolytes.

## Acid–Base Balance

Comprehensive nursing care of infants and children necessitates a thorough understanding of the physiology involved in maintaining acid–base balance. *Acid–base* balance involves mechanisms by which the acidity and alka-

*Table 28–2. Electrolyte Functions and Regulation*

| Electrolyte | Function | Regulation |
|---|---|---|
| Sodium | Major cation of extracellular fluid<br>Principal osmotically active solute responsible for maintaining water volume and distribution<br>Maintains intravascular circulating volume<br>Controls muscle contractility, including cardiac strength<br>Contributes to cell membrane potential and increases permeability essential for nerve impulse conduction<br>Component of the buffer sodium bicarbonate contributing to acid–base balance | Amount of sodium regulated by the balance between intake and output<br>Mechanism that regulates intake is poorly developed; large deficit may result in salt-craving<br>Excess triggers thirst mechanism<br>Absorption from gastrointestinal tract primarily in jejunum<br>Excreted in feces, sweat, urine<br>Kidney is principal organ of sodium regulation, with glomerular and tubular filtration maintaining balance |
| Potassium | Predominant cation of intracellular fluid<br>Establishes cell membrane potential required for nerve impulse conduction and myocardial and skeletal muscle action<br>Important in regulation of intracellular osmolarity and electroneutrality, contributing to maintenance of normal fluid and electrolyte balance, and acid–base equilibrium | Ingested potassium absorbed in the upper gastrointestinal tract; may be exchanged for sodium in the lower gastrointestinal tract<br>Small amounts excreted in feces and sweat; almost 90% excreted by kidneys<br>Filtered out of blood at the glomerulus; reabsorbed by proximal tubules<br>Excreted by distal tubules in exchange for sodium |
| Chloride | Extracellular anion essential to production of hydrochloric acid in the stomach<br>Important in the regulation of pH | Combines with sodium to form sodium chloride before excretion by the kidneys<br>Excess or deficit generally observed in conjunction with sodium balance |
| Calcium and phosphate | Found primarily in bones and teeth; small amounts in tissues and extracellular fluid<br>Positive inotropic agent that increases strength of myocardial contraction<br>Essential for transmission of nerve impulses<br>Component of cell membranes that determines cell strength and permeability<br>Normal blood coagulation maintained as calcium is needed to convert prothrombin to thrombin<br>Facilitates metabolism and absorption of vitamin $B_{12}$ | Vitamin D promotes calcium absorption from duodenum and jejunum along with renal excretion of phosphate<br>Parahormone facilitates absorption of calcium from intestines and kidneys<br>Calcitonin, a thyroid hormone, assists excess calcium excretion by the kidneys<br>Regulation of serum-ionized calcium influenced by parathyroid hormone, calcitonin secretion, thyroid function, glucocorticoid, sex hormone, and growth hormone<br>Regulatory process less precise in infants than in older children or adults |
| Magnesium | Found in bone, specialized cardiac cells, liver, skeletal muscles, and extracellular fluid<br>Role in transmission of nerve impulses and in muscle function | Regulated by the parathyroid gland<br>Absorption occurs in upper gastrointestinal tract, assisted by vitamin D and sodium absorption<br>Absorption decreased by calcium, phosphorous, and increased intestinal mobility<br>Almost two thirds of magnesium is excreted in feces<br>Magnesium balance dependent on urinary excretion and reabsorption in proximal tubule and Henle's loop<br>As blood levels decrease in magnesium, excretion occurs |

linity of body fluids are maintained in a state of equilibrium. The *pH* of a solution is a value that depicts the degree of acidity and represents the hydrogen ion concentration. Blood pH is maintained within a narrow, normal range of 7.35 to 7.45, which facilitates metabolic functioning of body cells. When the hydrogen ion concentration increases, arterial pH decreases below 7.35, and acidosis occurs. A decrease in hydrogen ion concentration causes an absence of acid, which causes the pH to increase above 7.45, and alkalosis occurs. Both acidosis and alkalosis disrupt the balance needed for optimum cellular functioning, and the body reacts by initiating mechanisms to return the pH to a normal range. This is done by means of the chemical buffering systems of the lungs and the kidneys.

## Regulation of Acid–Base Balance

### Chemical Buffering Mechanisms

*Buffers* are metabolic compounds that reduce the free hydrogen ion concentration of body fluids. They maintain the balance between acids and bases by acting instantaneously to either absorb or release hydrogen ions. Principal buffers in the body consist of pairs of compounds and are referred to as buffer systems. The major buffer system is the bicarbonate ($HCO_3$)–carbonic acid ($H_2CO_3$) buffer system. Other minor buffer systems include the phosphate buffer system and the plasma protein buffer system. The normal ratio is 20 parts of bicarbonate to 1 part of carbonic acid. If this ratio is altered, the pH changes. The critical factor in maintaining pH is this ratio, as opposed to absolute values. Acid–base imbalance occurs when either bicarbonate or carbonic acid is increased or decreased to affect this 20 : 1 ratio.

### Respiratory Buffering Mechanisms

The amount of carbon dioxide (and thus carbonic acid) in ECF is controlled by the lungs adjusting ventilation in response to the partial pressure of carbon dioxide ($PaCO_2$) in the blood. In metabolic acidosis, there is an increased hydrogen ion concentration, causing a decrease in the blood pH, and an increased $PaCO_2$, which causes an increase in respiratory rate. Increased respirations allow the lungs to eliminate excess carbon dioxide.

In metabolic alkalosis, there is a decreased hydrogen ion concentration, an increased blood pH, and a decreased $PaCO_2$. The respiratory system decreases the respiratory rate, allowing for retention of carbon dioxide. The respiratory buffering mechanism responds to pH changes within minutes.

### Renal Buffering System

The kidneys regulate the hydrogen ion concentration in extracellular fluid through the excretion or retention of hydrogen and bicarbonate. With an increased hydrogen ion concentration, an increased $PaCO_2$, and a corresponding decrease in pH, the kidneys excrete hydrogen and reabsorb bicarbonate. With a decreased hydrogen ion concentration and an increased pH, the kidneys retain hydrogen and excrete bicarbonate to compensate for the decreased $PaCO_2$ and correct the acid–base imbalance. The renal buffering mechanism responds slowly (taking hours or days) to imbalances in pH.

Normally, hydrogen ion concentrations in the body are controlled with the help of buffers, but buffers are ineffective in maintaining pH in acute disease states or when hydrogen ion production is altered. Compensatory and corrective physiological changes in the lungs and kidneys are needed in addition to the buffer system. This process of compensation is slower than buffering, yet very effective. If the primary problem is a metabolic disorder, the respiratory system responds with a compensatory mechanism. If the primary problem is a respiratory disorder, the kidneys compensate. The actions of the chemical, respiratory, and renal buffering systems are interrelated and work together to correct acid–base imbalances.

## Fluid and Electrolyte Requirements

Body surface area, body weight, and metabolic rate are critical factors that must be accurately calculated when determining fluid and electrolyte requirements. Infants and children are particularly susceptible to the fluid imbalances that result from illness. Daily fluid and electrolyte requirements in children are greater per kg of body weight than the adult as a direct result of greater insensible water losses and larger evaporative body surface area in proportion to circulating fluid volume. The child's higher metabolic rate also requires more water per unit of body weight.

The goal of calculating normal maintenance requirements is to provide adequate amounts of water and electrolytes to sustain a healthy balance or equilibrium. Daily maintenance of fluid and electrolyte requirements are most accurately calculated according to caloric expenditure. This is done by using the relationship of body weight to average calories expended in a 24-hour period. One calorie expended requires 1 mL of water.

## Metabolic Rate

Children have a higher *basal metabolic rate* than adults due to rapid growth. Therefore, fluid and electrolyte requirements must be carefully monitored. This increased metabolic rate necessitates increased water for metabolic waste excretion. The metabolic rate requirements are not fixed and may be increased or decreased under certain conditions. For example, a burn trauma increases the metabolic rate, and hypothermia decreases the rate. Changes in the metabolic rate also influence the caloric expenditure.

## Body Surface Area

Calculation of fluid and electrolyte requirements is made, in part, by determining the child's body surface area in square meters. This is done by comparing the child's height and weight on a Dubois or a West surface area nomogram, depicted in Figure 28-1. A line is drawn from the corresponding height to the weight, which intersects at the square meter value. Adjustments to these standard computations are made in specific disease states, such as dehydration and renal disease, as well as during functional shifts in fluid within the body. The infant's relatively greater body surface area and proportionately larger gastrointestinal tract allow a larger amount of fluid loss through the skin and secretions than occurs in older children and adults. Calculation of fluid requirements using the body surface area formula alone should provide an accurate estimation in all but infants and young children. In infants and young children, fluid requirements can be computed by using formulas based on body weight or total body surface area. These requirements may need modification based on assessment data. The markedly increased proportion of body surface area to total body weight in infants and young children increases the risk for insensible water loss through the skin. The range of average water requirements are shown in Table 28-3.

## Body Weight

Fluid and electrolyte requirements may also be calculated based on body weight alone. This is a standardized estimate and less specific than a calculation based on body surface area. Until a child with an acute imbalance is fully evaluated, this calculation may provide a baseline and guide to fluid and electrolyte maintenance. Use of the body weight alone in determining fluid maintenance does not account for variations in size, shifts in excess fluid stored in the body, or other variables such as metabolic rate, tem-

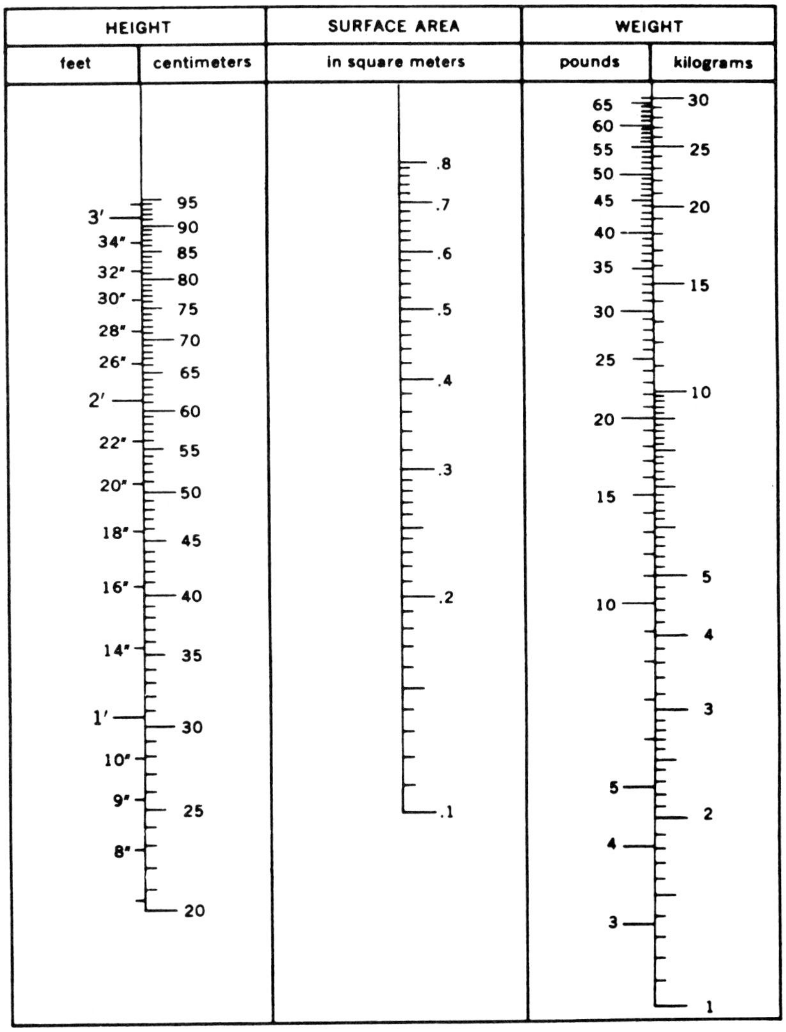

*Figure 28–1. West nomogram for estimating surface area of infants and young children. To determine the body surface area, draw a straight line between the point representing the child's height on the left scale to the child's weight on the right scale. The point at which this line intersects the middle scale is the child's body surface area in square meters. (Courtesy of Abbott Laboratories)*

*Table 28–3.  Range of Average Water Requirements of Children at Different Ages Under Ordinary Conditions*

| Age | Average Body Weight in kg | Total Water in 24 Hours, mL | Water per kg Body wt in 24 Hours, mL |
|---|---|---|---|
| 3 days | 3.0 | 250–300 | 80–100 |
| 10 days | 3.2 | 400–500 | 125–150 |
| 3 mo | 5.4 | 750–850 | 140–160 |
| 6 mo | 7.3 | 950–1100 | 130–155 |
| 9 mo | 8.6 | 1100–1250 | 125–145 |
| 1 yr | 9.5 | 1150–1300 | 120–135 |
| 2 yr | 11.8 | 1350–1500 | 115–125 |
| 4 yr | 16.2 | 1600–1800 | 100–110 |
| 6 yr | 20.0 | 1800–2000 | 90–100 |
| 10 yr | 28.7 | 2000–2500 | 70–85 |
| 14 yr | 45.0 | 2200–2700 | 50–60 |
| 18 yr | 54.0 | 2200–2700 | 40–50 |

(Behrman, R. E., & Vaughan, V. C. [1987]. *Nelson textbook of pediatrics* [13th ed.]. Philadelphia: W. B. Saunders, p. 115)

perature, and imbalances during specific disease states. Use of body weight alone in calculating fluid and electrolyte maintenance is only recommended in basically healthy children who are undergoing minor procedures or treatment.

## Assessment

Nursing assessment of suspected or potential fluid and electrolyte imbalance begins with observation of general appearance. The infant or child should be observed for age-appropriate behavior, making particular note of either lethargy or irritability. As the child moves, overall coordination should be assessed, and the presence of any tremors should be noted. The parents or care-giver should be present throughout the examination when feasible because they may report subtle changes that may either be overlooked or determined to be an individual variation for the child.

Nurses should be familiar with the initial signs and behaviors of ill children. Monitoring for fluid balance disturbances is based on an understanding of normal physiological mechanisms and indicators of disrupted fluid balance.

## History

Parents usually provide specific information regarding the child's behavior. A detailed history complements observation in carrying out the assessment. During the health history, several areas should be explored related to poten-

tial or actual fluid and electrolyte alterations in pediatric patients. Nurses should ask about the child's normal patterns of eating, drinking, and elimination. Subtle changes are often not readily apparent, yet when reviewing specific details with parents, pertinent information can be identified and a baseline established. A pattern of recent intake and output should be compared with the child's normal routines. Questioning about increased thirst may help identify a fluid deficit. Frequency and volume of urinary excretion is important to note. Decreasing frequency, voiding small amounts, and dark-colored urine may indicate the degree or extent of fluid deprivation.

If the infant or child has experienced vomiting or diarrhea, it is important to determine the frequency, duration, and appearance of the vomitus or stool. When possible, ask the parents or care-giver to estimate the volume of fluid lost. If the diarrhea or vomiting follows a pattern or may be related to change in diet, identification of the problem can be facilitated.

Nurses should elicit information about the child's food preferences, amounts typically eaten, and patterns of fluid intake and elimination. Nurses should be alert to various cultural and ethnic customs and beliefs regarding food and fluid intake during illness. The history should also include information about any medications currently being taken.

If possible, a recent healthy weight should be determined and compared with the child's present weight. A pattern of weight loss or lack of normal growth and development may indicate a long-term or chronic nutritional deficit or fluid and electrolyte loss. Conversely, recent weight gain may indicate fluid excess, which is confirmed by physical examination. It is important to determine if a disease process, diet, or medication has contributed to a fluid and electrolyte deficit or excess.

## Physical Examination

Assessment of the child's fluid and electrolyte status includes both qualitative and quantitative evaluation. This systematic examination provides critical information on the current clinical status as well as documentation of a presenting baseline from which clinical trends can be observed and response to treatment evaluated. Comprehensive fluid and electrolyte assessment can be invaluable in diagnosing problems that result from dysfunction of numerous body systems. Table 28-4 identifies the systems and structures that the nurse should examine when assessing children for alterations in fluid and electrolyte balance.

### Vital Signs

Assessing fluid and electrolyte imbalance based on vital signs necessitates obtaining accurate baseline data with the child at rest or at least during a quiet or nonstressed time. The range of normal vital signs (highs and lows) is greater than in adults, and such wide variations that are

*Table 28–4. Physical Assessment for Fluid and Electrolyte Balance*

| Observation | Method of Assessment |
| --- | --- |
| General appearance | Observe for age-appropriate behavior |
| | Note any lethargy or irritability |
| | Assess overall coordination; observe any tremors |
| Skin | Observe color and turgor for altered perfusion or poor hydration |
| | Skin that is taut and shiny or loose and "tented" when pinched represents a fluid excess or deficit of at least 5% |
| Edema | In the presence of fluid overload or hypernatremia, dependent edema may be observed as a late sign in severely ill children |
| | Periorbital edema may be observed as an early sign of fluid excess |
| | Sunken orbits and lack of tears may be seen with a fluid deficit of 10% |
| Capillary refill | Observe the time it takes for nail beds to turn from pale to pink after digital pressure; brisk refill is normal |
| | Venous filling of neck veins is difficult to assess in infants and young children |
| Mucosa | Mucous membranes and conjunctiva are normally pink and moist |
| | Pallor, decreased salivation, and excessive thirst may indicate dehydration |
| Fontanelles | Generally flat and firm |
| | Note depression of anterior fontanelle with fluid deficit; bulging or tense fontanelle with fluid excess |
| | Suture lines are more prominent in presence of fluid deficit; may widen or separate with marked fluid excess |

activity- or stress-induced may mask trends and changes in the data.

Infants and children have faster heart rates and respirations and lower blood pressures than adults. Small quantitative changes in hemodynamics may quickly produce dramatic changes in vital sign parameters. Age-specific vital sign norms are shown in Appendix B; however, clinical changes or trends in an individual child's vital signs may be a more significant indicator of fluid and electrolyte balance. Additionally, clinical judgment should always be used in evaluating vital sign data for the child's health status.

Nurses must be aware that emotional upset and pain can change vital signs in children. When these changes are observed, the causes (either anxiety and fear or the health problem) must be clearly differentiated.

*Temperature.* In the presence of fluid loss, peripheral skin feels cool since blood is shunted to vital organs. Temperature elevation may occur initially in response to mild dehydration and results in increased energy production in the infant and young child. This excess heat cannot be lost through the skin because of decreased blood flow. The temperature returns to normal as energy production decreases. If dehydration becomes worse, the temperature may fall below normal.

*Pulse.* As fluid volume and blood pressure decrease, heart rate increases to compensate for decreased cardiac stroke volume in an effort to maintain adequate circulating volume. Irregularities in the cardiac rhythm may occur in relation to electrolyte imbalances and should be evaluated. Fluid retention may cause a bounding pulse. The apical pulse should be monitored for a full minute and electrocardiogram (ECG) monitoring should be initiated for comprehensive assessment.

*Respirations.* Nurses should observe for irregularities in respiratory rate, pattern, and depth since these may indicate an acid–base imbalance. For example, changes in respirations occur within minutes to compensate for metabolic acidosis, and Kussmaul respirations may be observed as excess acid (in the form of carbon dioxide) is lost. If the child's respiratory rate or depth is increased as a result of a respiratory problem, such as pneumonia or respiratory failure, the nurse should assess for increased insensible water loss and calculate the loss when measuring fluid loss and replacement.

*Blood Pressure.* In adults, blood pressure falls as circulating fluid volume decreases. In children, however, blood pressure is well-maintained initially due to the elasticity of the vessels. Vasoconstriction that occurs with dehydration helps to maintain circulating pressure. A decrease in blood pressure is, therefore, a very late sign of fluid deficit in children and is not usually seen until as much as 10% to 20% of the normal circulating volume is lost. At this point, blood pressure drops rapidly. Blood pressure increases as fluid volume increases.

## Integument

Assessment of the skin's color, temperature, moistness, and elasticity (or turgor) are important in determining the child's state of hydration. A well-hydrated child's skin is warm and dry. Normal skin color is determined by racial and ethnic background, and is discussed in detail in Chapter 34. To assess elasticity, gently pinch a small area of tissue on the abdomen or thigh and observe as it returns to its normal state. If the skin remains raised for several seconds, or "tented," a fluid deficit is probable. Nurses should remember that tenting alone is not always a reliable sign. Edema indicates fluid volume excess. In the older child, edema may be noted in the extremities and abdominal area. Edema is assessed by applying finger pressure to the area and noting how long the indentation remains. The indentation disappears immediately if no edema is present. In fluid volume excess, the indentation lasts only momentarily (mild edema) to several seconds (severe edema).

In the presence of fluid overload and hypernatremia, excess water observed as dependent edema in infants and children is a late sign and is seen only in the severely ill child. Periorbital edema, however, may be seen as one of the first indications of a fluid excess. It is typically most evident in the morning. In severe instances, periorbital edema may cause the child's eyes to be puffy enough to cause vision problems.

## Mucous Membranes

Mucous membranes and conjunctiva are normally pink, moist, and intact. Dry membranes are one of the initial signs of fluid volume deficit. Longitudinal wrinkles on the tongue indicate dehydration. A late sign of dehydration is a tearless cry.

## Head and Neck

The fontanelles are generally flat and firm. Any depression or bulging of the anterior fontanelle or prominence in the suture lines should be noted. Fontanelles are sunken when there is fluid volume deficit and bulging in the presence of a fluid volume excess. Suture lines, which can only be assessed until the fontanelles close, may separate with marked fluid excess and are more evident in the presence of fluid deficit. Venous filling of neck veins is difficult to assess accurately in children and is generally reserved for adolescent and adult assessments.

## Monitoring Weight

Weight is an important indicator of fluid loss or gain. Accuracy of weight measurement is vital. The child should be weighed daily at the same time or twice a day at equal time intervals to consistently compare any weight gain or loss. Infants should be weighed nude; toddlers should be weighed immediately after diapers have been changed or when they have an empty bladder.

## Monitoring Intake and Output

Monitoring intake and output is one of the most important nursing roles related to assessment of alterations in fluid and electrolyte balance. Accurate measurement and recording of intake and output is necessary to fully evaluate hydration status and response to treatment. Measurement of the child's fluid intake should include all sources of fluid when fluid or electrolyte imbalances are suspected.

Urine output in children should average 1 to 2 mL/kg/h with adequate fluid intake. An indwelling urethral catheter is the most accurate way to monitor the rate of urine output in severely ill or unstable children. Accurate measurement of urine output may also be obtained using a 24-hour urine collection bag. For infants and toddlers, the nurse should weigh diapers on a gram scale before and after voiding (dry and wet). One gram of weight equals 1 mL of urine. Diapers that are placed under the infant or child should also be weighed, even if an indwelling catheter is in place or a urine bag is used, in the event that urine leaks or the bag loosens.

Additional fluid losses in diarrhea, vomiting, gastric drainage, and wound drainage should also be measured and recorded as output. Blood losses from wounds or lost blood volume from laboratory tests should be measured when their relative volume is large in comparison with the size of the child.

Comparison of the total fluid intake with the total of all the output measurements should be made at regular intervals, usually every 8 to 12 hours, or more frequently if necessary, to evaluate clinical trends. Daily fluid requirements of infants or children are larger per kilogram of body weight than in adults because of their proportionately larger surface area and resulting evaporative and insensible losses. The child's higher metabolic rate also demands more water per kilogram. Temperature elevation, diaphoresis, and the use of radiant warming beds can increase fluid loss and may contribute to potential imbalance. These factors should be considered in evaluating changes in fluid status.

# Diagnostic Procedures

## Laboratory Tests

Laboratory data that measure changes in the composition of blood and urine provide objective information about

*Table 28–5. Laboratory Tests for Evaluating Fluid Status*

| Test | Normal Range | Clinical Significance |
| --- | --- | --- |
| *Blood urea nitrogen:* Reflects difference between rate of urea synthesis and excretion by the kidneys | 5–15 mg/100 mL in children up to 2 years of age; 10–20 mg/100 mL in older children | Increases with decreased renal function or urine production and with dehydration; decreases with fluid overload and malnutrition |
| *Serum osmolality:* Measures solutes exerting osmotic pressure and reflects total body hydration | 280–294 mOsm/kg | Increases with fluid deficit; decreases with overhydration or fluid excess |
| *Urine osmolality:* Measures the concentration of solute particles per unit of water in urine | 50–1200 mOsm/L | Depends on prior state of hydration; normal is one to one and one half times that of serum |
| *Serum hematocrit:* Measures red blood cell percentage of blood | Newborn: 46%–68%; child: 35%–38%; adolescent: 38%–40% | Increases with isotonic dehydration and hemoconcentration; decreases with fluid overload, anemia, and blood loss |
| *Serum creatinine:* Measures products of muscle metabolism | 0.2–0.5 mg/100 mL in children up to 2 years of age; 0.5–1.5 mg/100 mL in older children | Increases with decreased glomerular filtration rate or when kidney nephrons are destroyed; reflects renal failure status |
| *Urine specific-gravity* | 1.010–1.030 | Decreases with fluid volume excess, high fluid intake, diabetes insipidus, renal failure (unable to concentrate); increases with fluid volume deficit, dehydration |
| *Urine pH* | 4.6–8 (mean = 6) | Increases with metabolic and respiratory alkalosis and with *Pseudomonas, Proteus,* and *Escherichia coli* infections; decreases with metabolic and respiratory acidosis |

the child's fluid and electrolyte status. The laboratory tests most commonly used to evaluate fluid changes and their clinical significance are listed in Table 28-5. Specific electrolyte disturbances are detailed later in this chapter.

## Nursing Diagnosis

Fluid and electrolyte imbalances can result from alterations in any body system. The diagnoses approved by the North American Nursing Diagnosis Association (NANDA) are used when fluid and electrolyte alterations are discussed. The diagnoses used might include the following:

*Pattern 1: Exchanging*
- Altered nutrition: less than body requirements
- Altered nutrition: more than body requirements
- Altered oral mucous membrane
- Altered patterns of urinary elimination
- Altered renal tissue perfusion
- Constipation
- Decreased cardiac output
- Diarrhea
- Fluid volume deficit
- Fluid volume excess
- High risk for fluid volume deficit
- High risk for injury

- Hyperthermia
- Hypothermia
- Impaired gas exchange
- Ineffective airway clearance
- Ineffective breathing pattern

*Pattern 6: Moving*
- Activity intolerance
- Fatigue
- Impaired physical mobility
- Impaired swallowing

*Pattern 7: Perceiving*
- Sensory/perceptual alteration

*Pattern 8: Knowing*
- Altered thought processes

*Pattern 9: Feeling*
- Pain

## Planning Nursing Care

Specific planning and implementation of nursing care is included in the discussion of each problem covered later in this chapter. Providing individualized care to children is facilitated through the application of developmental concepts. These concepts include physiological differences, physical and motor abilities, and psychosocial needs that vary with age and ability. Nurses need to modify assessments and interventions according to the appropriate developmental level of the child. Fluid and electrolyte imbalances and weight changes can occur quickly in children. Accuracy in assessing status and trends is critical. Table 28-6 provides a system-by-system evaluation of fluid and electrolyte imbalances, nursing interventions, and expected outcomes.

Infants and young children depend on adults to provide fluids and nutritional support. The type and quantity of intake and output must be carefully monitored; however, these measurements may be difficult to obtain in the uncooperative child. Nurses must be aware of problems that children experience in maintaining adequate fluid and electrolyte balance that are related to developmental abilities. For example, toddlers learning to feed themselves frequently spill fluids. As a result, nurses need to

*Table 28–6.  Assessment and Management of Electrolyte Imbalances*

| System | Clinical Features | Nursing Management | Expected Outcome |
|---|---|---|---|
| Cardiovascular | Arrhythmias | Monitor ECG changes | Normal ECG |
| | Weak, rapid pulse | Evaluate blood chemistry | Regular pulse |
| | Hypotension | Monitor fluid and electrolyte intake; observe for hyperkalemia, as evidenced by tall, peaked T wave and flat P wave | Normal blood pressure |
| | Generalized edema | | Absence of edema |
| | Decreased peripheral perfusion | Observe for hypokalemia, as evidenced by flat T waves, prolonged S-T segment; observe for ventricular fibrillation | Periphery warm and dry |
| | Pale, cool extremities | | Good capillary return |
| Eyes, ears, nose, and throat | Sunken eyeballs | Monitor blood chemistry and urine specific-gravity value | Return to normal |
| | Absence of tears | Administer saline eye drops | Adequate tears |
| | Darkened periorbital area | Identify probable cause of fluid loss | Absence of orbital discoloration |
| | Dry mucosa, dry tongue | Rehydrate and replace losses; perform meticulous oral care | Moist mucosa |
| | Periorbital edema | Identify probable cause of fluid gain or retention; monitor intake and output for excess intake or decreased output | Decreased periorbital edema; absence of edema |
| Gastrointestinal | Vomiting | Monitor amount of losses, particularly fluid losses | Retention of oral fluids |
| | Liquid, loose stools | | Tolerance of diet |
| | Hard, dry stools | Replace gastric fluid and electrolytes with oral, nasogastric, or intravenous solutions | Normal stools |
| | Elevated temperature | Administer antipyretics as ordered; bathe in tepid water | Temperature returns to normal |
| Genitourinary | Decreased voiding (oliguria) | Monitor urine specific-gravity value, blood chemistry; assess for accurate intake and output; restrict potassium intake | Output of 1–2 cc/kg/h; urine specific-gravity value of 1.010 |
| | Increased voiding (polyuria) | Monitor blood chemistry and urine specific-gravity value | Output proportional to intake |
| Head | Depressed fontanelle | Monitor for signs of fluid loss or decreased intake | Fontanelle level with skull and sutures |
| | Tense, bulging fontanelle | Monitor for signs of increased intracranial pressure; assess adequacy of intake and output | Fontanelle level with skull and sutures |

*(continued)*

*Table 28–6. Assessment and Management of Electrolyte Imbalances (Continued)*

| System | Clinical Features | Nursing Management | Expected Outcome |
|---|---|---|---|
| Integumentary | Skin cool, clammy | Identify signs of fluid loss | Skin warm, dry |
| | Pale periphery | | Pink periphery |
| | "Tenting" of skin | Replace fluid and electrolyte losses orally, nasogastrically, or intravenously, as tolerated | Elastic recoil, good turgor |
| Neuromuscular | Muscle weakness | Assess for electrolyte imbalance | Absence of pain |
| | Confusion, stupor | Evaluate intake and output | Alert, oriented |
| | Muscle cramps | Determine neurological insult, injury, or signs of increased intracranial pressure | Absence of discomfort |
| | Tremors, numbness | Check neurological signs; monitor vital signs | Neurological and vital signs normal |
| Respiratory | Hyperventilation | Assess acid–base balance | Adequate ventilation of all lobes of lungs |
| | Hypoventilation | Evaluate electrolytes, arterial blood gases | |
| | Dyspnea, stridor | Facilitate respirations | Normal respiratory rate, depth |
| | Retractions | Place in Fowler's position | Blood pH is 7.35–7.45 |
| | Nasal flaring | Replace fluid and electrolyte losses; assess for overhydration; provide oxygen respiratory support as indicated | Adequate oxygenation; absence of infection |
| Skeletal | Pathological fractures | Provide comfort | Increased comfort |
| | Osteoporosis | Protect from injury | Adequate calcium intake |
| | Skeletal changes | Complete nutritional assessment | Evidence of normal growth and weight gain |

carefully assess the actual amount of fluids ingested by toddlers in order to be aware of their correct intake. The care plan should include details and specific interventions that work well with the child. Working with the child to learn preferences and fears, likes and dislikes, and terminology related to eating and toileting habits is supportive to the child and facilitates meeting input and output goals.

Diapers can be weighed to calculate output in infants. School-aged children and adolescents understand directions and can be instructed to void "in a cup" so that output can be measured. Toddlers or preschool-aged children are between these two stages since diapers often are unacceptable to them; however, they may have trouble voiding in a cup, and errors or mistakes may occur unless urine bag strappings are used. Toddlers or preschool children with urethral catheters are often anxious because of the physical urge to void, or they may have difficulty with the concept of voiding in bed even though a urine bag or bedpan is in place because they have been taught to use bathroom facilities. Children who have recently been toilet-trained may regress during hospitalization or illness.

Nurses must also consider the family in planning and implementing care. Family structure, environment, and culture must be examined. Financial constraints that may pose a problem should not be overlooked. Education of the family and child that involves often complex conditions

of fluid and electrolyte imbalance is an important nursing function. The family must be included in all planning for successful implementation of the care plan.

## Nursing Interventions

### Oral Fluid and Electrolyte Replacement Therapy

Water and electrolytes are required to replace obligatory losses as well as abnormal losses. Oral fluid and electrolyte therapy is generally the preferred route, if tolerated. Oral therapy may be used alone or in combination with gastric tube or parenteral administration of fluids, electrolytes, and nutrients. Normally, maintaining an adequate oral intake in children who can respond to the thirst mechanism is not a problem. Problems occur when children fail to respond to thirst or when they are too tired or uncomfortable to adequately swallow fluids. Protein and calories are also ultimately needed, but complete oral nutrition is restricted until the child can tolerate fluids.

Electrolyte depletion is of particular concern with gastrointestinal losses and may need to be replaced with oral or intravenous electrolyte solutions. Oral rehydration therapy can be effective in treating dehydration related to diarrhea in a wide range of ages. A simple glucose-electrolyte solution such as Pedialyte given orally may be prescribed, or other clear fluids such as decarbonated cola or ginger ale or Popsicles may be introduced gradually. In oral rehydration due to mild dehydration, 50 mL/kg should be given within 4 hours, and 100 mL/kg should be given over 6 hours when moderate dehydration exists (Behrman & Vaughan, 1987). These volumes are usually increased if diarrhea losses continue or decreased if signs of adequate rehydration exist. If vomiting occurs during the initial 2 hours, small amounts of fluid may still be offered slowly at the discretion of the physician. Once the deficit is replaced, maintenance therapy of 100 mL/kg/24 h can be given until losses, such as diarrhea, stop. As a general rule, the volume of the oral electrolyte solution should equal the volume of fluid loss. If stool or diarrhea losses cannot be measured, an estimate of 10 to 15 mL/kg/h is appropriate.

Nurses should determine if parents understand the meaning of clear liquids. Broth is not used in dehydration because of the high sodium content. Nurses also need to emphasize that milk is inappropriate for rehydration since it causes formation of curds on contact with renin in the stomach. In children with mild dehydration who are able to tolerate oral glucose-electrolyte solutions without exacerbating the losses (vomiting or diarrhea), caloric intake may gradually be increased to full liquids, including protein and fat intake, until the usual diet is tolerated. Administering large amounts of calories prematurely, including milk, may exacerbate vomiting or diarrhea.

Infants or children who are unable or not permitted to take fluids by mouth (NPO status) offer special nursing challenges. Nurses should place a sign over the bed indicating that the child is not to receive fluids. Nurses should remove fluids from the bedside, as well as any other temptations that might remind the child. Oral hygiene is an important factor for the child on NPO status. Older children can brush their teeth and rinse their mouths. For younger children, the mouth can be moistened with moist gauze. Petroleum jelly or a lip moisturizer can be used to keep the lips soft. Ice chips are soothing if allowed by the physician.

## Gastric Feeding

In the cases of infants and children who are tired and lethargic due to lack of rest during acute illnesses or whose respiratory rates are high because of a respiratory infection, offering small amounts of fluid frequently by mouth may be contraindicated. Administration of gastric feedings, whether by duodenal or nasogastric tube, provides these children with the necessary fluids and electrolytes without disturbing their rest and helps them to conserve their energy for breathing. A gastrostomy tube may be inserted for long-term access (see Chap. 29).

Neonates tolerate oral placement of gastric tubes more easily than nasal placement of these tubes. Infants with more than 60 respirations per minute are generally candidates for gastric feeding since the combined efforts of breathing and sucking to eat may prove too tiring. Energy should be expended to compensate breathing alone, and feedings should be provided by means of a nasogastric tube. Young infants are obligatory nasal breathers, so nasogastric feeding tubes should have sufficient room around them to allow some air movement (Fig. 28-2). Large tubes may also place excess pressure on the nares and contribute to tissue breakdown. Insertion of a nasogastric tube provides some advantages for children who cannot drink fluids or who do not like the taste of the electrolyte solution. Techniques for determining the cor-

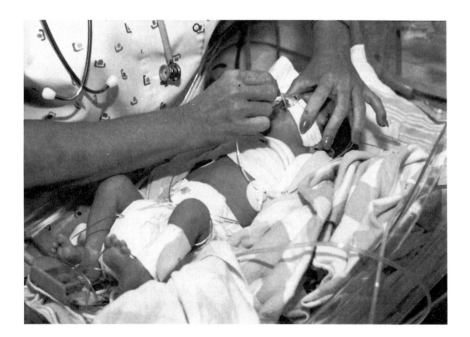

*Figure 28–2. Infant with nasogastric tube.*

rect tube length, as well as for insertion of the tube, are discussed in Chapter 29.

## Parenteral Administration of Fluids and Electrolytes

Since most conditions involving serious disturbance of fluid and electrolyte balance require the parenteral administration of fluids and electrolytes, monitoring intravenous fluid replacement is an important nursing role. *Total parenteral nutrition* (TPN), or *hyperalimentation,* involves the delivery of all necessary fluid and nutritional components directly into the vascular system (Fig. 28-3). It may be indicated in infants or children who are unable to ingest nutrients orally or who are unable to absorb or tolerate nutrients in the gastrointestinal tract. Common conditions for which parenteral nutrition is indicated are sustained vomiting, severe dehydration, chronic intestinal obstruction related to peritoneal sepsis or adhesions, gastrointestinal fistulas, chronic malabsorption syndromes and diarrhea, short bowel syndrome, malignancies, excessive nutritional demands (as in severe burns), and low birth weight in infants whose clinical course is complicated by nutritional deficits and congenital defects.

Either a peripheral or a central venous access can be used to administer parenteral nutrition. Solutions for peripheral delivery are less calorically dense to allow for peripheral vein tolerance. Such solutions contain no more than 12.5% glucose. Direct surgical catheterization of the subclavian or other large vein allows the infusion of concentrated (20%) glucose solutions and amino acids into a rapidly flowing venous system, thereby decreasing the likelihood of thrombophlebitis and sclerosis and providing a secure, long-term route. Central venous access allows delivery of increased calories and protein in a decreased fluid volume.

Nursing care for central venous lines includes observing the site for tenderness, drainage, and signs of inflammation. Meticulous care of the infusion site is essential and includes covering the site with a sterile occlusive dressing, which is changed at specific intervals, depending on institutional policy. Alcohol swabs are used to clean the skin, followed by povidine-iodine solution and an application of povidine-iodine ointment to the site, which is then covered with a sterile dressing. Any redness or purulent drainage must be reported to the physician, and a culture must be obtained. The child's temperature should be monitored, and blood cultures should be ordered after any temperature rise or fall that might indicate sepsis (neonates' temperatures may decrease).

For children receiving parenteral nutrition therapy, nurses should verify the prescribed fluid and glucose content as well the necessary nutrients that are prescribed for each child by the physician. The solutions are usually mixed aseptically in a central pharmacy and often result in complex products that include as many as 25 ingredients. Nurses should monitor children who receive parenteral nutrition therapy for potential complications and imbalances, such as infection, hepatic dysfunction, hyperglycemia, hypoglycemia, acidosis, imbalances and deficiencies of various trace elements and electrolytes, cardiac arrhythmias, and venous thrombosis. Potential complications of lipid therapy include eosinophilia, bilirubin displacement, and ventilation–perfusion abnormalities.

The high concentration of glucose provides an optimum medium for bacterial growth. Strict aseptic technique is critical when changing tubing or caring for infusion sites. The inclusion of a micropore filter on the infusion system helps decrease both potential contaminants and particulate matter.

Nurses should monitor serum glucose levels when initiating parenteral hyperalimentation, when the glucose concentration is changed, or when the infusion rate is altered. Since it takes time for the child's insulin production to respond to changing blood sugar levels, hyperglycemia or hypoglycemia may result. It is necessary to slowly increase or decrease the infusion while closely monitoring the child's response to the change. Glucose checks (using finger sticks for children and heel sticks for infants) together with urine glucose monitoring (often taken hourly as infusion rates are changed) measure sugar and ketones as infusion rates are changed.

## Evaluating Nursing Care

Nursing management of infants and children with acute fluid and electrolyte imbalance problems is aimed at correcting the fluid or electrolyte imbalance. Restoration of

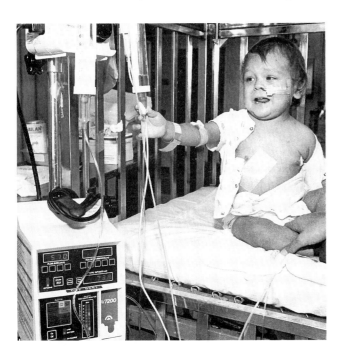

*Figure 28–3. Child receiving total parenteral nutrition.*

normal balance involves careful observation and continuous evaluation of the child's response to fluid replacement or rehydration therapy.

## Alterations in Acid–Base Balance

### Metabolic Acidosis

#### Pathophysiology

Excessive production or retention of hydrogen ions results in the accumulation of acid, or *metabolic acidosis. Primary bicarbonate deficit* is often related to losses in urine and stool. In metabolic acidosis, the arterial pH is below 7.35. Infants and young children have a higher metabolic rate than adults, which can cause an increased rate of acid formation and the potential for acidosis. Neonates are particularly at risk because of their immature buffer mechanisms. The renal system attempts to compensate by excreting excess hydrogen ions and conserving bicarbonate in an effort to raise the pH and reinstate the 20 : 1 proportion. Respiratory compensation includes hyperventilation in an attempt to rid the body of carbon dioxide and the accompanying carbonic acid.

Common causes of metabolic acidosis include incomplete oxidation of fatty acids seen in diabetic ketoacidosis, clinical malnutrition from prolonged illness, and lack of enteral nutrition. Lactic acid also results from abnormal carbohydrate metabolism in hypoxic states, shock, and severe infections. Children with acute or chronic renal failure are at increased risk of metabolic acidosis because of renal insufficiency and accumulation of urea nitrogen, uric acid, and creatinine in the blood. The ingestion of acids, such as salicylates, can also be a contributing factor. Severe diarrhea can result in excessive excretion of bicarbonate, leading to acidosis.

#### Medical Diagnosis and Management

In metabolic acidosis, the arterial pH and bicarbonate level is decreased. Sodium chloride levels are also low, and potassium is increased. The pH of urine falls below 6.0 as the renal system excretes hydrogen ions and reabsorbs bicarbonate. Treatment involves correction of the metabolic defect. Sodium bicarbonate is often used intravenously to raise the arterial pH. Potassium levels must be closely monitored because of potential cardiac dysfunction, particularly ventricular tachycardia and flutter.

#### Nursing Assessment and Diagnosis

The neurological signs and symptoms of metabolic acidosis include initial weakness, headache, and lethargy, which progresses to stupor and coma. Gastrointestinal assessment should include an evaluation of diarrheal fluid loss and gastric loss by means of emesis or nasogastric drainage. A "fruity" breath smell is common due to the excess acetone. Hyperventilation is a common respiratory response in an attempt to compensate for the metabolic dysfunction. The increased depth and rate of respirations are termed *Kussmaul respirations.* Nurses should be alert for signs of fatigue in the child who is unable to maintain the energy level to continue this rapid breathing pattern.

Nursing diagnoses for metabolic acidosis might include the following:

- Fluid volume deficit related to excessive renal or intestinal excretion
- High risk for injury related to neurological status
- Diarrhea related to increased gastrointestinal motility
- Decreased cardiac output related to ventricular tachycardia
- Impaired gas exchange related to respiratory insufficiency
- Activity intolerance related to fatigue and muscle weakness

#### Planning and Implementing Nursing Care

Nursing care includes monitoring intravenous bicarbonate infusion and administering other intravenous solutions, such as glucose, insulin, and potassium. The nurse also should monitor rate of flow and changes in arterial blood gases. If correction of serum pH by administration of intravenous bicarbonate is too rapid, it may result in cerebral edema and neurological complications. Nurses must check vital signs frequently. The respiratory quality and patterns should be noted. The heart rate usually increases as the body systems attempt to compensate. Blood pressure may be lowered because of excessive urine output. Nurses must be alert for signs of potassium imbalance during treatment, such as blood pressure changes, bradycardia, or dysrhythmias. Nurses should accurately monitor and record intake and output, note the patient's state of hydration, and take frequent weight measurements.

#### Evaluating Nursing Care

Evaluation of respiratory rate should provide evidence regarding respiratory compensation. Improvements are also monitored by laboratory values indicating increased pH, serum bicarbonate, and $PaCO_2$. Hydration status should improve if fluid replacement is adequate and if ongoing losses do not complicate the deficit. Evaluation of fluid balance assists in early detection of clinical improvement or status change.

### Metabolic Alkalosis

#### Pathophysiology

*Metabolic alkalosis* can be produced by a gain of bicarbonate or a loss of hydrogen ions. The condition is marked by a pH above 7.45 (decreased hydrogen concentration) and a high bicarbonate concentration. Initial response to metabolic alkalosis is a buffer reaction to correct either the acid deficit or the base excess. As serum pH rises, stimulation of the respiratory center decreases, resulting in carbon dioxide retention (increased $PaCO_2$) and an increased hydrogen ion concentration.

One of the more common causes of metabolic alkalosis is vomiting or gastric suctioning. Other factors that cause the condition include diuretic therapy, in which there is a loss of potassium, and the presence of excessive adrenocortical hormones. Metabolic alkalosis may also result from overtreatment of acute acidosis, in which intravenous bicarbonate is rapidly absorbed. Excessive ingestion of alkali through use of bicarbonate-containing antacids (e.g., Alka-Seltzer) may also cause metabolic alkalosis. Hypokalemia also produces alkalosis by the kidneys conserving potassium, which results in increased hydrogen ion excretion, and by the movement of cellular potassium out into extracellular fluid in an attempt to maintain near-normal serum levels (Metheny, 1987).

## Medical Diagnosis and Management

Laboratory findings reveal increased urine pH (over 7), elevated plasma pH (over 7.45), and elevated serum bicarbonate (greater than 29 mEq/L). Total carbon dioxide above 32 mEq/L is also present. $PaCO_2$ increases as the respiratory system compensates to counteract the increased bicarbonate. Medical treatment is directed at replacing current fluid and electrolyte losses and preventing further losses. Correction of the pH is the major focus and typically involves intravenous or oral fluid and electrolyte replacement.

## Nursing Assessment and Diagnosis

Nursing assessment should focus on the child's overall fluid balance and overall electrolyte balance. Nurses should observe for any clinical evidence of dehydration, including increased heart rate, low urine output, poor skin turgor, and sunken fontanelles or eyes. A decreased respiratory rate may be evidence of attempts to conserve carbonic acid by raising the $PaCO_2$. Nurses should assess the resting respiratory rate and consistently monitor trends while the child is quiet. Attention should be paid to any signs of muscle hypertonicity, twitching, or tremor.

Nursing diagnoses for metabolic alkalosis might include the following:

- Fluid volume deficit related to vomiting or increased renal output
- Decreased cardiac output related to circulatory congestion
- Fatigue related to muscle weakness
- Activity intolerance related to leg cramps, paresthesias
- High risk for injury related to generalized weakness

## Planning and Implementing Nursing Care

Nursing interventions include monitoring vital signs and neurological status. Seizure and airway safety precautions should be implemented because of possible seizures or tetany. The ECG should be monitored for evidence of any potassium-induced arrhythmia. Urine output is monitored to observe for increased excretion of bicarbonate (pH greater than 7.0). Nurses should evaluate for signs of adequate rehydration while monitoring for evidence of fluid volume excess and congestive cardiac failure. Nurses must also measure and record intake and output, administer and monitor intravenous fluid and electrolyte replacements, administer medications, and monitor lab values. Decreased respiratory rate may occur if the pH remains elevated. Sedatives should be given with caution because of further respiratory depression or masked signs of neurological dysfunction.

## Evaluating Nursing Care

After replacement therapy, plasma pH should gradually decrease to within normal range, and electrolytes should become stable. Urine output should stabilize at 1 to 2 mL/kg/h and then gradually increase to normal output. Nurses should identify and monitor changes and trends in pulse, respirations, and blood pressure to detect patterns of improvement in hydration status while observing for fluid volume excess.

# Respiratory Acidosis

## Pathophysiology

*Respiratory acidosis* results from inadequate or decreased pulmonary ventilation. This results in high concentrations of $PaCO_2$, causing elevated carbonic acid levels and elevated hydrogen ion concentration. The pH decreases, and acidosis occurs. The increased production of carbon dioxide stimulates increased respiratory effort and renal excretion to help maintain a normal $PaCO_2$ level. Increases in $PaCO_2$ are initially buffered as the kidneys compensate by increasing hydrogen ion excretion and reabsorption of bicarbonate. This renal compensation takes from several hours to several days (Metheny, 1987).

Common causes of inadequate or decreased pulmonary ventilation that result in respiratory acidosis include airway obstruction (i.e., foreign body obstruction), bronchospasm, laryngeal edema, and central depression of the respiratory center related to drugs or head trauma. Respiratory acidosis can also result from vascular diseases such as pulmonary embolism; problems secondary to congenital cardiac defects; and conditions that cause respiratory muscle weakness such as pneumonia, pulmonary edema, or other chronic obstructive lung diseases.

## Medical Diagnosis and Management

Arterial blood gases provide the most accurate diagnosis. The arterial blood pH is less than 7.35, and the $PaCO_2$ is elevated above 42 mmHg. Bicarbonate levels remain normal (21–28 mEq/L) or slightly elevated because there has been little time for renal compensation. Serum potassium may be elevated, and urine pH is below 6.0. The signs and symptoms of respiratory acidosis include restlessness, rapid and irregular pulse, and ineffective breathing patterns (dyspnea or decreased ventilation). Mild elevation of $PaCO_2$ produces signs of clinical hypoxia and restlessness and high elevation causes increasing listlessness and weakness that, if uncorrected, lead to stupor and coma.

The goal of treatment is to correct the physiological problem and improve ventilation. Treatment may include intubation and assisted ventilation, postural drainage, and administration of antibiotics to treat respiratory infections. During critical episodes, buffering agents such as bicarbonate are administered intravenously.

## Nursing Assessment and Diagnosis

Assessment of respiratory status is essential and includes observation, percussion, and auscultation. Respiratory pattern and quality should be noted as well as any abnormal breath sounds. Cyanosis is a late sign in acidosis and a poor indicator of carbon dioxide levels. Nurses must also assess the child's neurological status and observe for restlessness, which may be an initial sign of poor ventilation.

Nursing diagnoses for respiratory acidosis might include the following:

- Impaired gas exchange related to decreased respiratory rate
- Ineffective airway clearance related to obstruction, increased airway resistance
- Ineffective breathing pattern related to laryngeal edema, depression of the respiratory center, or bronchospasms

## Planning and Implementing Nursing Care

The goals of nursing interventions are to increase ventilation and decrease unnecessary metabolic activity. Nurses can assist the child's breathing efforts by placing the child in a semi-Fowler's position, by encouraging the child to cough and breathe deeply, and by frequently repositioning the child to facilitate gas exchange. Nursing care also includes providing adequate hydration to ease secretion movement and removal. The nurse should help limit activity to conserve energy for breathing efforts. When there is ineffective airway clearance, assisted tracheal suction and chest physiotherapy may be indicated, if tolerated by the child. Other nursing responsibilities include monitoring arterial oxygen levels and administering oxygen as needed, administering antibiotics as prescribed, and implementing pain relief measures as needed.

## Evaluating Nursing Care

The success of interventions can be evaluated by monitoring the trends in the first 24 to 48 hours. Successful interventions should result in a decrease in the rapid heart rate to a normal range, and improved respirations should be seen. In the critically ill child, assessing changes in sensorium may be a good indicator of increased or decreased acidosis. Regular arterial blood gas monitoring provides accurate objective data. Overall evaluation should include signs of improvement in the child's response to the dysfunction and in the child's tolerance of specific interventions.

# Respiratory Alkalosis

## Pathophysiology

*Respiratory alkalosis* results from an excessive loss of carbon dioxide from the body. A primary increase in the rate and depth of respiration causes large amounts of carbon dioxide to be exhaled or "blown off." This reduces the plasma $PaCO_2$, carbonic acid, and hydrogen concentration and leaves an excess of bicarbonate. If the imbalance extends beyond 6 to 8 hours, the pH rises, and the kidneys try to compensate for this excess by rapid buffering to conserve hydrogen ions and by excreting bicarbonate along with sodium and potassium ions. This renal excretion of bicarbonate slowly increases over 24 to 48 hours. The imbalance cannot be completely controlled until the primary problem is corrected.

Several factors or conditions can precipitate the rapid respiration rate or hyperventilation that results in respiratory alkalosis. These include stimulation of the central nervous system by crying, fear, or apprehension; cerebral injury, trauma, or pain; encephalitis or meningitis; drug reactions such as salicylate intoxication, which may irritate or stimulate the central nervous system; elevated body temperature; various cardiac conditions that may result in hyperventilation due to hypoxemia; and overventilation as a result of assisted ventilation.

## Medical Diagnosis and Management

The signs and symptoms of respiratory alkalosis include hyperventilation (deep and rapid breathing above 40 rpm in older children or 60 rpm in infants), headaches, vertigo and syncope, numbness of the face and hands, irritability, and confusion. Physical examination may reveal hyperactive reflexes (Chvostek sign). Laboratory results show a rise in blood pH and a decrease in $PaCO_2$ (less than 35 mmHg). Laboratory tests in healthy children may show the same results if the child has been crying for a long time before the blood specimens are obtained for analysis.

Early in the development of the condition, bicarbonate levels generally remain within the normal range but may later decrease after 12 to 24 hours with attempted compensation. The potassium level gradually decreases as hydrogen ions are conserved, and the urine pH eventually increases above 7.0 to become alkaline. Medical management of respiratory alkalosis involves treating the underlying cause and decreasing respirations. A rebreathing mask is often helpful, and sedation is necessary in overly anxious patients.

### Nursing Assessment and Diagnosis

Assessment of respiratory and neurological status is an important nursing role. Respiratory pattern and quality should be noted. Signs of restlessness or apprehension are noted as are changes in reflexes or neuromuscular function.

Nursing diagnoses for respiratory alkalosis might include the following:

- Impaired gas exchange related to ineffective respiratory efforts
- Ineffective breathing pattern related to increased respiratory rate
- Anxiety related to difficulty in breathing
- Fear related to perceived loss of control
- High risk for injury related to confusion and neuromuscular dysfunction

### Planning and Implementing Nursing Care

Nursing care includes monitoring both the acid–base status and the respiratory status of the patient, giving sedation as ordered, and helping the patient to rebreathe carbon dioxide using the rebreathing mask or other techniques as ordered by the physician. Care can also include administering intravenous chloride if ordered by the physician to neutralize the bicarbonate. Neurological status is monitored, including reflexes, signs of tetany, and complaints of tingling, headache, or vertigo.

Serum potassium levels should be closely monitored since the kidneys, in compensation, excrete large amounts of potassium and sodium along with the bicarbonate. Because of the dizziness and syncope that is often experienced with respiratory alkalosis, the nurse should protect the child from potential falls or injury.

### Evaluating Nursing Care

Ongoing assessment of the child's ventilatory status and frequent sampling of blood gas values help evaluate treatment and interventions directed at increasing $PaCO_2$, decreasing respirations, and correcting acid–base imbalance. Frequent monitoring of the child's response to interventions is crucial, and results should be compared to the baseline acid–base data to evaluate clinical status and validate clinical assessment.

## Alterations in Electrolyte Balance

### Hypercalcemia

#### Pathophysiology

Ionized calcium in the blood is kept in balance primarily by the deposition and mobilization of calcium in bone. Excess serum calcium, or *hypercalcemia,* is usually associated with metabolic changes that increase the mobilization of calcium or impair renal excretion of calcium.

Common causes of hypercalcemia include hyperthyroidism, increased presence of vitamin D, prolonged immobilization, bone malignancies, and prolonged use of thiazide diuretics. Infantile or *congenital hypercalcemia* is caused by excessive vitamin D intake by the mother during pregnancy and is characterized by elflike facial features, failure to thrive, slow development, and hypotonia. Pulmonary and aortic stenosis are characteristic cardiovascular findings associated with congenital hypercalcemia.

#### Medical Diagnosis and Management

The signs of hypercalcemia are generally related to the serum calcium level. Some patients display symptoms with serum levels as low as 12 mg/dL (Goldberger, 1985). Phosphate levels are decreased. The signs and symptoms of hypercalcemia include neuromuscular changes, muscular hypotonicity, lethargy, anorexia, nausea and vomiting, and diarrhea or constipation related to decreased muscle tone. Severe hypercalcemia often produces bone and flank pain related to calcium reabsorption, high calcium excretion, and stone formation in the renal parenchyma. Polyuria may occur. The ECG is not a helpful tool in diagnosing hypercalcemia (Ellman, Demblin, & Seriff, 1982).

Treatment is aimed at decreasing the serum calcium level and increasing urinary calcium excretion. Isotonic saline infusions and intravenous furosemide are often used. Furosemide causes diuresis and increases calcium excretion. Calcitonin may be used to lower the serum calcium level.

#### Nursing Assessment and Diagnosis

One of the major assessment components includes observation for signs of hypotonicity. Nurses should note any muscular weakness or incoordination. Anorexia and constipation can result from decreased tone in smooth and striated muscle. Nurses should assess the child's level of pain. *Hypercalcemia crisis* occurs with an acute rise in the serum calcium level to 17 mg/dL or higher. Severe thirst and polyuria are classical signs of this dangerous condition, which must be rapidly treated to avoid cardiac arrest.

Nursing diagnoses for hypercalcemia might include the following:

- Altered patterns of urinary elimination related to impaired renal tubular function
- Altered nutrition: more than body requirements related to dietary increase of foods high in calcium and vitamin D
- Altered thought processes related to neurologic effects of serum calcium
- Impaired physical mobility related to lethargy and bone or flank pain
- Fatigue related to neuromuscular changes
- Pain related to reduced calcium reabsorption in the bones and renal stones
- Activity intolerance related to muscle weakness
- Constipation related to decreased smooth and striated muscle tone

### Planning and Implementing Nursing Care

The immediate concern is to rehydrate the child and decrease the acute problem so that long-term interventions can be implemented. Nursing care is focused on enhancing excess calcium excretion by administering 0.45% or 0.9% NaCl solutions intravenously. Nurses must be alert for signs of fluid overload, and breath sounds should be monitored at regular intervals. Nurses must also monitor body weight and maintain accurate, hourly intake and output records. During treatment, hourly urine output is typically 200 mL or greater.

The nurse should assist the child with passive range-of-motion exercises since mobilization helps retain calcium in the bone. The child may be given oral phosphate to help lower serum calcium by promoting deposition of calcium in the bone and decreasing gastrointestinal absorption of calcium. Corticosteroids may be prescribed for children who experience hypercalcemia secondary to nonparathyroid tumors. Because of muscle weakness and fragile bones, the nurse should take precautions to protect the child from falls and fractures.

### Evaluating Nursing Care

Accurate intake and output levels are important in evaluating fluid balance since dehydration and polyuria are clinical signs of hypercalcemia. Treatment, including rehydration and diuretics, necessitates careful monitoring of the child's response. It is critical to evaluate adequate renal function. Laboratory tests should show decreased renal calcium excretion in the urine and a stable to decreasing serum calcium level. See Chapter 30 for further information.

## Hypocalcemia

### Pathophysiology

Preservation of adequate calcium levels is regulated by dietary intake, gastrointestinal function and absorption, and renal excretion. Ninety-nine percent of the total body calcium is stored in bone and is unavailable to help replace low intravascular, interstitial, or intracellular calcium. There is an unclear reciprocal relationship between phosphorous increases and serum calcium decreases.

Diarrhea, extensive subcutaneous tissue infection, and stress may result in hypocalcemia. Lack of exposure to the sun or inadequate consumption of vitamin D can also lead to the condition, as can abnormally increased dietary intake of protein. Hypocalcemia can also be seen in patients with hypoparathyroidism, hyperphosphatemia, and acute pancreatitis. Hypocalcemia is also associated with *magnesium deficiency,* which involves suppression of parathyroid hormone, a regulator of serum calcium. Emergency medical treatment consists of giving calcium both orally and intravenously and giving vitamin D supplements.

### Medical Diagnosis and Management

*Tetany* (intermittent tonic spasms) is characteristically associated with hypocalcemia and is manifested by a wide variety of symptoms induced by increased neural excitability. Spontaneous discharges of sensory and motor fibers in peripheral nerves cause these manifestations (Maxwell, Kleeman, & Narins, 1986), which may begin with tingling in the fingers and around the mouth and gradually increase and spread proximally along the limbs. Numbness may also occur, as well as muscular spasms of the extremities and face. *Trousseau sign* (carpal spasm of hand) can be seen with use of blood pressure cuff on the upper arm inflated to about 20 mmHg above systolic pressure. *Chvostek sign* (twitching of facial muscles when the facial nerve is tapped just below the temple) is also an early sign of tetany.

A decreased serum calcium level causes cardiac muscle dilatation, which can result in dysrhythmia and potential cardiac arrest. Acute hypocalcemia causes laryngospasm, airway obstruction, and respiratory arrest. Seizures may also occur in hypocalcemia due to irritability of the central nervous system.

Treatment focuses on correcting the cause of excessive calcium loss and on increasing serum calcium orally or intravenously. Oral calcium supplements are much safer than intravenous administration.

### Nursing Assessment and Diagnosis

Assessment of neuromuscular status is the major nursing role. Nurses should watch for signs of tingling and numbness in extremities. Cardiac and respiratory function and blood pressure must also be closely monitored.

Nursing diagnoses for hypocalcemia might include the following:

- Decreased cardiac output related to dilatation of cardiac muscle
- Ineffective breathing pattern related to laryngospasms
- High risk for injury related to increased irritability of the central nervous system
- Altered nutrition: less than body requirements related to inadequate intake of calcium and/or vitamin D or an abnormally high protein intake

### Planning and Implementing Nursing Care

Nursing care includes observing for signs of respiratory failure, seizure, and tetany, which constitute medical emergencies. Seizure precautions should be instituted. Safety precautions should be used if the child is confused. It may be necessary to establish an artificial airway or infuse calcium gluconate intravenously; thus, vascular access should be maintained to safely manage the acute hypocalcemic state. Calcium chloride should only be given intravenously. Tissue irritation and sloughing can also occur with intramuscular or subcutaneous injection of calcium gluconate. Too rapid infusion of calcium can cause cardiac arrest.

Nurses must also monitor the 24-hour serum calcium content as the serum calcium level normalizes. Hypercalcemia can occur, which is noted by greater than 300 mg of calcium in a 24-hour urine collection. Supplements of vitamin D may be needed to facilitate calcium absorption. The child should be encouraged to eat a nutritious diet that includes good sources of calcium, including dairy products, green leafy vegetables, beans, and peas.

### Evaluating Nursing Care

Continuous assessment of the child's neuromuscular status and blood pressure should indicate whether interventions have been successful. Laboratory results are the most objective measure to evaluate the response to treatment after administration of calcium gluconate.

## Hypermagnesemia

### Pathophysiology

Because the kidneys normally prevent elevation of serum magnesium to dangerous levels, *hypermagnesemia* rarely occurs unless renal function is impaired. Hypermagnesemia is induced with excessive intake of magnesium in the form of antacids, enemas, or milk of magnesia—all of which are most commonly used in adults rather than children.

### Medical Diagnosis and Management

This condition is commonly seen in infants born to mothers treated with intramuscular injections of magnesium sulfate for hypertension due to preeclampsia. It is characterized by cyanosis during feedings, lethargy, hypotonia, and poor feeding. Neonates born prematurely with asphyxia or hypertonia are particularly vulnerable because of underdeveloped renal function. Imbalances in the newborn usually return to normal within 72 hours, and intervention is not indicated unless the levels are critically elevated or there is renal dysfunction. Intravenous administration of calcium helps to reduce the effects of hypermagnesemia. Coma and death may occur when the serum magnesium levels rise above 15 mg/dL.

### Nursing Assessment and Diagnosis

Assessment should include monitoring for low blood pressure and shallow respirations. Nurses must assess for possible central nervous system manifestations including drowsiness and lethargy, neuromuscular weakness, and flaccidity with diminished patellar reflexes. Cardiovascular assessment should include monitoring for sinus bradycardia and heart block.

Nursing diagnoses for hypermagnesemia might include the following:

- Impaired gas exchange related to shallow respirations
- Altered cardiac output related to decreased blood pressure due to peripheral vasodilation
- Altered nutrition: more than body requirements related to excessive intake of magnesium

### Planning and Implementing Nursing Care

Nursing interventions are directed primarily toward monitoring for adequate renal functioning and supportive care if cardiorespiratory failure occurs. Planning includes bedside preparation of artificial airway equipment and ECG monitoring to help in early detection of bradycardia. The nurse should plan for securing vascular access in preparation for any potential emergencies that may arise.

### Evaluating Nursing Care

Clinical improvement can be evaluated through daily serum magnesium levels. Evaluation is also based on hydration and improving renal function.

## Hypomagnesemia

### Pathophysiology

Magnesium deficiency, or *hypomagnesemia,* occurs in response to impaired absorption or too rapid excretion of magnesium in the gastrointestinal tract. It is more common in children than hypermagnesemia.

Common causes include malabsorption syndrome or chronic diarrhea. Bowel resections or short bowel syndromes also pose a potential risk, as does prolonged nasogastric suction. Any infant or child receiving prolonged parenteral fluid therapy will require magnesium supplements. The child receiving diuretic therapy is also at risk. Primary aldosteronism and various renal defects may also result in magnesium loss.

### Medical Diagnosis and Management

Signs and symptoms include neuromuscular irritability manifested by increased reflexes, tetany, tremors, or convulsions. Cardiac manifestations include tachyarrhythmia. Clinical signs and symptoms of hypomagnesemia may be undetected unless specifically assessed. Treatment includes intramuscular or intravascular supplementation as long as the depletion continues. Magnesium sulfate is the most commonly used parenteral solution. Mild hypomagnesemia can be corrected by diet alone.

### Nursing Assessment and Diagnosis

Nurses must closely assess neuromuscular status, observing for signs of muscular weakness or tremors. Assessment for positive Chvostek's and Trousseau's signs are important.

Nursing diagnoses for hypomagnesemia might include the following:

- Altered nutrition: less than body requirements related to impaired absorption or accelerated excretion of magnesium
- Decreased cardiac output related to altered cardiac function
- Impaired swallowing related to tremors
- High risk for injury related to neuromuscular hyperexcitability

### Planning and Implementing Nursing Care

Nurses should be aware that tetany may cause the child to experience difficulty swallowing, thus affecting the child's ability to swallow oral medications. Seizure precautions should be instituted. Nurses should be aware that magnesium replacement solutions can produce flushing and sweating due to peripheral vasodilation. During administration of intravenous magnesium, urine output should be monitored at regular intervals, and the knee-jerk reflex

should be checked periodically. Additional magnesium should not be given if the reflex is absent since this may indicate impending hypermagnesemia. Blood pressure, pulse, and respirations should be checked every 15 minutes. A sharp fall in blood pressure or respiratory distress indicates excessive magnesium.

### Evaluating Nursing Care

Evaluating effectiveness of nursing care includes monitoring serum magnesium levels and assessing improvement in renal or gastric losses of magnesium. Reflexes, vital signs, and cardiac function should be normal.

## Hyperkalemia

### Pathophysiology

*Hyperkalemia,* increased serum potassium, occurs from relatively small increases in total body potassium. Transcellular shifts in response to acidosis may result in high serum potassium even though total body potassium is normal. Movement of potassium out of cells occurs in response to negative nitrogen balance, cellular injury from burns, or trauma. Acute renal failure with accompanying oliguria may impair distal tubular potassium excretion and result in life-threatening hyperkalemia. Decreased excretion of potassium also occurs in adrenal insufficiency, metabolic acidosis, and the use of potassium-sparing diuretics. Too rapid administration of intravenous potassium chloride is a common cause of the condition in children.

### Medical Diagnosis and Management

The most significant signs include cardiac effects seen on ECG. Early changes are peaked narrow T waves and a shortened Q-T interval (Metheny, 1987). These early signs occur when the serum potassium level is 8 mEq/L or greater. Increased serum potassium levels can cause ventricular arrhythmia and bradycardia leading to cardiac arrest. Hyperkalemia also affects the neuromuscular system, causing initial muscle weakness and progressing to muscle paralysis, which is first noticed in the legs. Numbness of the face, tongue, feet, and hands may also be present. Gastrointestinal symptoms include nausea, intermittent intestinal colic, and diarrhea.

Medical interventions include rapid intravenous administration of hypertonic glucose and insulin, which help to pull extracellular potassium into the cells. Administration of sodium polystyrene sulfane (Kayexalate) absorbs excess potassium and increases its excretion. Kayexalate is an ion-exchange resin and may be given orally or as a high-colonic enema during acute elevations. Intravenous calcium may be used to facilitate cardiac contractility. Peritoneal dialysis and hemodialysis are medical options for removal of potassium. Intravenous sodium bicarbonate may be used to temporarily correct the acidosis by shifting potassium into the cells.

### Nursing Assessment and Diagnosis

Monitoring for signs of cardiac changes is a critical nursing function. ECG changes may be the only cardiovascular warning. Observing for signs of muscle weakness or paralysis is important, and particular attention should be given to the child's legs.

Nursing diagnoses for hyperkalemia might include the following:

- Decreased cardiac output related to altered cardiac function and decreased heart rate
- Altered patterns of urinary elimination related to impaired renal function
- Diarrhea related to increased gastrointestinal motility
- Impaired physical mobility related to muscle weakness

### Planning and Implementing Nursing Care

Serum potassium levels should be monitored frequently in patients with renal insufficiency or failure. Changes in intravenous solution to remove potassium additives may be indicated to prevent further elevations of potassium. Cardiac monitoring is usually indicated to detect early signs. The nurse should anticipate medical interventions to alter or lower excess serum potassium levels such as the administration of intravenous hypertonic glucose and insulin. Interventions to monitor, maintain, or improve renal function are also important aspects of nursing care.

### Evaluating Nursing Care

Monitoring the child's response to treatment and interventions is focused on the serum potassium levels after acute administration of Kayexalate or hypertonic glucose and insulin. With intravenous medications, rapid shifts of extracellular potassium back into the cells may cause the serum potassium levels to drop dramatically. Gastrointestinal administration of Kayexalate can take a few hours to effect a change in serum potassium, and the effect varies related to the gastric function of the particular patient.

## Hypokalemia

### Pathophysiology

*Hypokalemia,* decreased serum potassium, results when potassium moves from the extracellular space into the cells in response to alkalosis or when potassium moves out of cells in response to acidosis. Potassium control at the renal level involves filtration at the glomerulus and reabsorption in the proximal tubule. Any condition that increases sodium delivery to the distal tubule also contrib-

utes to potassium excretion. Extra renal losses, such as gastrointestinal losses, also contribute to hypokalemia. Hypokalemia affects cardiac, striated, and smooth muscles.

### Medical Diagnosis and Management

Early signs of hypokalemia include muscle weakness or pain, fatigue, and hyporeflexive states. Cardiovascular changes are reflected in ECG changes, with a peaked P wave, flat T wave, and depressed S-T segment, and by ventricular arrhythmia. Treatment is aimed at increasing potassium intake. If adequate amounts cannot be gained in the diet, or if oral supplements are not feasible, intravenous solutions are used. Metabolic alkalosis creates a shift of potassium into the cells; thus, treating the cause of the alkalosis is preferred to administering potassium supplements.

### Nursing Assessment and Diagnosis

Hypokalemia may be related to the combined effects of digitalis and diuretics, and children receiving these medications must be carefully assessed for signs of hypokalemia. A late sign of hypokalemia in children is decreased cardiac stroke volume and hypertension. The muscular weakness associated with hypokalemia puts the child at risk for potential respiratory insufficiency and insufficient oxygenation. Continuous assessment of gastrointestinal fluid losses is essential.

Nursing diagnoses for hypokalemia might include the following:

- Altered nutrition: less than body requirements related to inadequate intake of potassium
- Fatigue related to muscle weakness
- Decreased cardiac output related to impaired contraction of cardiac muscle
- Diarrhea related to weakness of smooth intestinal muscles
- High risk for fluid volume deficit related to excessive urine output due to inability to concentrate urine

### Planning and Implementing Nursing Care

The nurse should be alert to the fact that oral potassium can be irritating to the gastrointestinal tract and should be diluted with fluids. Nurses must follow the rules for safe administration of intravenous potassium. Intravenous potassium should be well mixed, diluted, and infused slowly. The intravenous site should be carefully assessed for signs of infiltration and tissue damage. Careful monitoring of the intravenous infusion is critical since rapid infusions affect cardiac contractility and may result in fibrillation or cardiac arrest. The nurse should monitor the intake and output, with attention to potential for losses of potassium by nasogastric drainage, by vomiting and diarrhea, or from diuretic therapy. Frequent measures of serum potassium levels may be needed to assess the status of the imbalance.

### Evaluating Nursing Care

As the serum potassium level rises, alkalotic clinical acid–base imbalances should also improve. As serum potassium rises in response to replacement, the nurse should evaluate the adequacy of the urine output and renal function since renal dysfunction contributes to a rapid rise in serum potassium. Chronic hypokalemia, lasting for 10 to 20 days, may alter renal concentrating ability and result in a subsequent loss of ability to conserve potassium. This can be anticipated when there is polyuria and when potassium additives fail to raise the serum levels.

## Hypernatremia

### Pathophysiology

*Hypernatremia* is an increased serum sodium level (greater than 145 mEq/L). It is caused by excessive sodium intake or by dehydration. The excess of sodium increases the osmotic pressure of the blood and causes fluid to shift from the intracellular to extracellular spaces. Dehydration may be due to diarrhea, vomiting, diabetes insipidus, insensible water loss from prolonged fever, and rapid respiratory rates. Hypernatremia may be present in diabetic ketoacidosis and inappropriate antidiuretic hormone syndrome due to diabetes insipidus, in which large amounts of "pure" water are lost and sodium levels are increased.

### Medical Diagnosis and Management

A thorough history should reveal a cause for the dehydration, and clinical laboratory testing that reveals an elevated serum sodium concentration, often exceeding 150 mEq/L, confirms the diagnosis. Treatment is directed at gradual lowering of the serum sodium level by intravenous rehydration over 48 to 72 hours. Too rapid rehydration can result in cerebral edema and seizures.

### Nursing Assessment and Diagnosis

Nurses should monitor for early signs of dehydration, including increased heart rate, elevated temperature and flushed skin, dry mucosa, thirst, and restlessness. Skin turgor can be normal or poor. Assessment of the neurological system includes noting for irritability, lethargy, and decreased responsiveness.

Nursing diagnoses for hypernatremia might include the following:

- High risk for fluid volume deficit related to diarrhea, vomiting
- Altered nutrition: more than body requirements related to sodium excess

- Altered thought processes related to shrinkage of brain cells
- Altered oral mucous membrane related to dehydration
- Hyperthermia related to excessive water loss
- Altered cerebral tissue perfusion related to cerebral edema caused by inability of the blood–brain barrier to keep water from entering brain tissue

### Planning and Implementing Nursing Care

Nursing care includes monitoring intravenous fluid and electrolyte replacement. A central venous line may be needed to monitor central venous pressure. The nurse should obtain accurate weight measurements at regular intervals and document excess weight. Weight change of 50 g/24 h in an infant, 200 g/24 h in a child, or 500 g/24 h in an adolescent should be reported.

Acute monitoring of fluid intake and output is critical. The output goal is a minimum of 1 mL/kg/h with rehydration. Intravenous potassium may be needed, but this should only be administered with sufficient renal function and output. Hemodynamics should be monitored, including heart rate, blood pressure, and respirations. Hourly neurological assessment is critical to note any early symptoms of too rapid rehydration, such as lethargy or irritability.

### Evaluating Nursing Care

Subtle trends in clinical status are critically important to detect. Fluid and electrolyte replacement should improve systemic perfusion. Vital signs should stabilize. Heart rate and temperature should decrease to within a normal range, and blood pressure should stabilize. Pulse pressure may increase, indicating improved circulating volume. Capillary refill should return as peripheral circulation improves. Urine output should increase above 1 mL/kg/h, and urine specific-gravity value should drop below 1.015. Evaluation should also include assessment of neurological status.

## Hyponatremia

### Pathophysiology

*Hyponatremia* is a serum sodium level below normal that occurs in conjunction with water excess or extracellular solute depletion. A serum sodium level of 135 mEq/L indicates a relative deficit of sodium to water. Sodium determines extracellular fluid volume as water moves freely throughout all compartments to restore osmotic imbalances. Hyponatremia may result from osmotic fluid shift due to a gain of water or loss of sodium. Serum sodium deficit is uncommon since the kidney's ability to conserve sodium is excellent. This imbalance can result from normal or excessive fluid intake coupled with a decreased ability to excrete, which occurs in renal disease, congestive heart failure, and fluid overload. Acutely ill children with intracranial disorders demonstrate the syndrome of inappropriate secretion of antidiuretic hormone, which affects intracranial osmoreceptors and causes excess water to be retained. True hyponatremia can also result from extra renal sodium losses related to burns, prolonged diarrhea and vomiting, diuretic therapy, and various renal disorders.

## Medical Diagnosis and Management

When both sodium and water are lost, the signs and symptoms include weakness and confusion, anorexia, oliguria, elevated temperature, flushed skin, varying signs of dehydration, and shock. If sodium is lost but water is not, the clinical presentation is similar to that for fluid volume excess, including mental confusion, convulsions, weakness, and potential for neurological dysfunction related to increased intracranial pressure. Weight may remain stable or increase depending on the severity; urine output may decrease to an oliguric state. A decrease in serum sodium indicates a water excess. Urinary sodium is less than 10 mEq/L, and urine specific-gravity value is low, between 1.002 to 1.004. Medical treatment is sodium administration, either orally, by nasogastric tube, or parenterally. Lactated Ringer's solution or isotonic saline is often used. Restricting water is the preferred treatment if water retention is the primary problem.

## Nursing Assessment and Diagnosis

Nurses should identify patients at risk for hyponatremia. The gastrointestinal system should be assessed for symptoms such as anorexia, nausea, vomiting, or abdominal cramping. The central nervous system is monitored for changes such as lethargy, confusion, or muscle twitches. Nurses should monitor serum sodium for below-normal levels. The specific-gravity value of urine should be checked. The specific-gravity value will be low when sodium is lost through the gastrointestinal tract or through sweating. Nurses must also assess the circulatory status on a regular basis.

Nursing diagnoses for hyponatremia might include the following:

- Altered nutrition: less than body requirements related to inadequate intake or excessive loss of sodium
- High risk for injury related to increased intracranial pressure
- Sensory/perceptual alterations related to neurological changes
- Decreased cardiac output related to fluid accumulation
- Fluid volume deficit related to vomiting

## Planning and Implementing Nursing Care

Fluid losses and gains must be closely monitored, with attention to loss of sodium-containing fluids. Presence of gastrointestinal symptoms, such as anorexia, nausea, vomiting, and abdominal cramping, must be evaluated. Nurses must be aware of central nervous system changes related to water overloading. Serum sodium levels and specific gravity must be closely monitored. Food and fluids with a high sodium content should be encouraged in children able to consume a general diet. Nurses need to be knowledgeable of the sodium content in foods and commonly used parenteral fluids. Nurses must be aware of the precautions and dangers involving intravenous hypertonic saline solutions (3% or 5% NaCl). Too rapid infusion of these solutions can cause death.

## Evaluating Nursing Care

The child should respond to fluid treatment by increased blood pressure, decreased tachycardia, and adequate urine output once hydrated. Urine output should be 0.5 to 1 mL/kg/h, and output should be greater than intake. Since an infants' normal urine output is low, even small reductions in volume can indicate a significant change in renal perfusion and function.

# Alterations in Fluid Volume

## Fluid Volume Excess

### Pathophysiology

*Fluid volume excess* results from the abnormal retention of water and sodium in about the same proportions as their normal existence in extracellular fluid (Metheny, 1987). The condition is secondary to an increase in total body sodium content, which results in an increase in total body water. Fluid volume excess may be caused by simple fluid overload or by a variety of compromised regulatory mechanisms, such as impaired kidney function, congestive heart failure, and excess steroid administration. Excessive administration of isotonic fluids can cause the rate of intake to exceed renal output and lead to fluid volume excess. The condition may also result from ingestion of abnormal amounts of sodium chloride or other sodium salts in the diet.

## Medical Diagnosis and Management

The typical clinical presentation includes peripheral edema, polyuria, and pulmonary edema. Rales are often present in the lungs. The laboratory analysis of serum sodium is normal, but hematocrit and blood urea nitrogen values are decreased due to hemodilution. There is typically a weight gain over a short period of time. Medical treatment is to restrict fluids and to administer diuretics while investigating the primary cause of the child's inability to adequately excrete excess fluids. Dietary sodium restriction is a common treatment mode.

### Nursing Assessment and Diagnosis

The nurse should observe the child for signs of congestive heart failure, prolonged increase in heart rate, any evidence of respiratory distress, rales, dyspnea, or coughing. Polyuria is a normal response to excess fluid in a healthy child, but the child who has congestive heart failure may demonstrate decreased renal output because of decreased renal blood flow. The nurse should assess for any acute weight gain due to retention of fluids.

Nursing diagnoses for fluid volume excess might include the following:

- Decreased cardiac output related to prolonged increase in heart rate
- Altered patterns of urinary elimination related to renal failure
- Impaired gas exchange related to pulmonary edema
- Altered nutrition: more than body requirements related to excessive dietary intake of sodium

### Planning and Implementing Nursing Care

Nursing care includes accurate assessment of the child's fluid intake and output, with special attention to any signs of significant weight changes. Peripheral edema must be monitored and the presence of pitting edema evaluated. Laboratory values also should be checked. During the course of treatment, fluid intake should be adjusted as the fluid balance fluctuates. Vital signs should be obtained at regular intervals, with specific focus on respiratory rate, depth, and aeration. Breath sounds should be assessed for the presence, or worsening, of rales. Nurses should anticipate any acute changes in respiratory status and plan to provide oxygen and respiratory support as indicated.

Because of the threat of neurological complications, neurological assessment should be done every hour. Nurses should also monitor the child's response to diuretics and the rate of parenteral fluid administration. Nurses should be alert to the fact that potassium deficit can also occur as a result of the diuresis and restricted intake of fluids, and should observe for any signs of potassium deficiency. The head of the bed may be elevated to decrease venous return and to aid ventilation. The child should be turned and positioned frequently to avoid skin breakdown.

### Evaluating Nursing Care

The nurse can evaluate the success of interventions by monitoring the physical status of the patient. As fluid excess returns to normal, the heart rate should return to normal for the child's age, and normal breathing patterns should be restored. The need for ventilatory support and oxygen should consequently decrease. Other signs of return to proper fluid balance are weight loss proportional to the imbalance and decreasing peripheral edema. The neurological sequelae should no longer be evident.

## Fluid Volume Deficit

### Pathophysiology

*Fluid volume deficit* occurs when water and sodium losses are proportional. Fluid volume deficit is not dehydration, which involves loss of water alone, and a resulting sodium excess. In fluid volume deficit fluid osmolarity remains unchanged, and water does not shift between the intracellular and extracellular compartments. It may occur alone or in combination with other imbalances. Common causes of fluid volume deficit include vomiting, diarrhea, hemorrhage, infections, diet, gastrointestinal obstructions, and other metabolic dysfunctions. This condition is also related to loss of blood volume, as seen in hemorrhaging.

### Medical Diagnosis and Management

Fluid volume deficit is manifested by weight loss over a short period of time, decreased urinary output, dry mucous membranes, decreased skin and tongue turgor, increased body temperature, increased pulse, and postural hypotension. Blood urea nitrogen, urine specific-gravity value, and hematocrit are all elevated.

In mild deficit, treatment involves oral replacement. In acute fluid loss, the intravenous route is required, and isotonic electrolyte solutions (lactated Ringer's or 0.9% NaCl) are commonly used in the hypotensive child. A hypotonic solution (0.45% NaCl) may be used once normal blood pressure is achieved. Fluid volume deficit must be promptly treated to avoid renal damage.

### Nursing Assessment and Diagnosis

Assessment of vital signs is a major nursing responsibility, as is watching for subnormal body temperature, increased pulse rate, and declining blood pressure. Nurses must also assess neurological status and be alert to changes in sensorium. Assessment also includes measurement and evaluation of intake and output and testing skin turgor.

Nursing diagnoses for fluid volume deficit might include the following:

- Decreased cardiac output related to loss of blood volume
- Impaired skin integrity related to decreased interstitial fluid volume
- Sensory/perceptual alterations related to decreased cerebral perfusion
- Hyperthermia related to increased metabolic rate
- Altered patterns of urinary elimination related to increased or decreased urine output

- Altered oral mucous membrane related to poor hydration and mouth breathing

### *Planning and Implementing Nursing Care*

Intake and output must be carefully measured and evaluated, sometimes on an hourly basis. Accurate daily body weights are critical. If indicated, oral fluids are given. Nurses should consider the child's preferences in fluids and offer nonirritating fluids if oral discomfort is present. If the child has impaired swallowing, the nurse should use an upright position with the head tilted forward for feeding. Thick fluids or semi-solid foods are more easily swallowed than are thin liquids. Frequent oral care is an important nursing intervention. Safety precautions should be instituted in the child with altered sensorium. Skin breakdown can be avoided by frequent turning and the use of moisturizing lotions.

### *Evaluating Nursing Care*

The success of rehydration efforts can be observed through improved intravascular volume evidenced by stable blood pressure, good pulse, and peripheral perfusion. Urine output of a minimum of 1 to 2 mL/kg/h should occur as fluid volume and renal perfusion are restored. An improved level of consciousness should be observed, and weight gain should be slow and steady.

## *Summary*

Infants and children with fluid or electrolyte imbalances demonstrate a wide range of signs and symptoms that are often secondary to the primary diagnosis. The interrelationships among the various body compartments, solutes, and physiological processes that maintain normal fluid and electrolyte balance involve all body systems. Differences in total body water, percentage of extracellular fluid, and the high metabolic rates in infants and young children contribute to their vulnerability to fluid and electrolyte dysfunction. These imbalances occur quickly in most acute illnesses. Detecting subtle, early alterations and trends in fluid and electrolyte balance in infants and young children and evaluating the affect these dysfunctions have on pediatric patients presents a challenge to the most knowledgeable and clinically proficient nurse and should be a major focus of the nursing process in care delivery.

## References

Behrman, R. E., & Vaughan, V. C. (1987). *Nelson textbook of pediatrics* (13th ed.). Philadelphia: W. B. Saunders.

Ellman, H., Demblin, H., & Seriff, N. (1982). The rarity of shortening of the Q-T interval in patients with hypercalcemia. *Critical Care Medicine, 10,* 320.

Goldberger, E. (1986). *A primer of water, electrolyte and acid-base syndromes* (7th ed.). Philadelphia: Lea & Febiger.

Maxwell, M. H., Kleeman, C. R., & Narins, R. G. (1986). *Clinical disorders of fluid and electrolyte metabolism* (4th ed.). New York: McGraw-Hill.

Metheny, N. M. (1987). *Fluid and electrolyte balance.* Philadelphia: J. B. Lippincott.

## Bibliography

Avery, G. B. (1987). *Neonatology: Pathophysiology and management of the newborn* (3rd ed.). Philadelphia: J. B. Lippincott.

Baer, C. E. (1988). Regulation and assessment of fluid and electrolyte balance. In Kinney, M. R., Packa, D. R., & Dunbar, S. B. (Eds.). *AACN's clinical reference for critical care nursing* (2nd ed.). New York: McGraw-Hill.

Carpenito, L. J. (1991). *Nursing diagnosis: Application to clinical practice* (4th ed.). Philadelphia: J. B. Lippincott.

Chenevey, B. (1987, December). Overview of fluids and electrolytes. *Nursing Clinics of North America, 22*(4), 749–759.

Hazinski, M. F. (1991). *Nursing care of the critically ill child* (2nd ed.). St. Louis: C. V. Mosby.

Poyss, A. S. (1987, December). Assessment and nursing diagnosis in fluid and electrolyte disorders. *Nursing Clinics of North America, 22*(4), 773–783.

# Alterations in Gastrointestinal Function

Susan N. Peck and Marianne Buzby

Photograph by David Finn

29

*Embryology*

*Anatomy*

*Digestive Physiology*

*Assessment*

*Nursing Diagnosis*

*Planning Nursing Care*

*Nursing Interventions*

*Evaluating Nursing Care*

*Common Gastrointestinal Problems*

*Congenital Problems of Ingestion*

*Ingestion Problems of Infants and Children*

*Congenital Problems of Digestion*

*Digestion Problems of Infants and Children*

*Congenital Problems of Absorption*

*Absorption Problems of Infants and Children*

*Congenital Problems of Elimination*

*Excretion and Elimination Problems of Infants and Children*

*Other Gastrointestinal Problems*

*Summary*

*Nursing Care Plan*

## Learning Objectives

*Upon completion of this chapter the reader will be able to:*

1. Describe the embryonic development of the gastro-intestinal system.

2. Discuss the anatomy and physiology of the gastro-intestinal system.

3. Identify important data that should be collected during assessment of gastrointestinal function.

4. State nursing diagnoses that apply to most gastro-intestinal problems.

5. Identify nursing interventions that are common to most gastrointestinal problems.

6. Develop a plan for evaluating nursing interventions for gastrointestinal problems.

7. Demonstrate an understanding of the following problems of ingestion: cleft lip and palate; tracheoesophageal fistula; diaphragmatic hernia; gastroesophageal reflux; herpes stomatitis; ingestion of foreign bodies, corrosive substances, and acetaminophen.

8. Demonstrate an understanding of the following problems of digestion: neonatal liver disease; biliary atresia; intestinal atresia; colic; pyloric stenosis; and Wilson disease.

9. Demonstrate an understanding of the following problems of absorption: gastroschisis; omphalocele; necrotizing enterocolitis; malabsorption; celiac disease; Meckel diverticulum; and inflammatory bowel disease.

10. Demonstrate an understanding of the following problems of elimination: Hirschsprung disease; imperforate anus; malrotation; meconium ileus; intussusception; hernias; anal fissures; encopresis; and intestinal polyps.

11. Demonstrate an understanding of the following acute and chronic gastrointestinal problems: omphalitis; appendicitis; hepatitis; cholecystitis; pancreatitis; and peptic ulcer disease.

## Key Terms

absorption

barium enema

colonoscopy

decompression

defecation

digestion

endoscopy

esophagus

excretion

gallbladder

growth failure

hematemesis

hepatocyte

ingestion

intestines

liver

nasogastric tube

ostomy

pancreas

steatorrhea

stoma

stomach

total parenteral nutrition

upper gastrointestinal series

villi

Alterations in gastrointestinal (GI) function are common complaints in children. Viral gastroenteritis and constipation are the most common problems seen by pediatricians. However, GI disorders may be life-threatening, complex disorders that require sophisticated nursing interventions. Nurses should be familiar with the more common GI disorders and related medical diagnoses, management, and nursing interventions in order to promote health and normal functioning in children with these problems and their families.

## Embryology

The primitive gut begins to evolve from the yolk sac during the 4th week of fetal development. Division into the foregut, midgut, and hindgut occurs, and blood flow is supplied to each by a branch of the dorsal aorta. The endoderm of the primitive gut develops into the parenchyma of the liver and pancreas.

The pharynx, lower respiratory tract, esophagus, stomach, duodenum, and entrance of the common bile duct all evolve from the foregut. The esophagus is initially a short tube that rapidly increases in length. During the 5th week of gestation, the stomach develops as a dilation of the foregut. The dorsal border enlarges to become the greater curvature of the stomach. The distal foregut and proximal midgut evolve to become the duodenum.

The hepatic diverticulum evolves from the distal end of the foregut, eventually forming the liver, pancreas, and biliary tree, which includes the gallbladder, cystic duct, and common bile duct.

The midgut evolves into the jejunum, ileum, cecum, appendix, ascending colon, and proximal transverse colon. The elongation of the midgut is rapid, occurring at a faster rate than fetal growth. Elongation of the midgut begins during the 6th week of gestation with the formation of an umbilical loop of gut that projects into the umbilical cord. During this process, many congenital malformations of the GI tract may occur, such as gastroschisis, omphalocele, and malrotation.

The hindgut extends from the midgut to the cloacal (anal) membrane. The distal half of the transverse colon, the descending colon, the sigmoid colon, and the rectum evolve from the hindgut.

## Anatomy

The GI tract, or alimentary canal, extends from the mouth to the anus (Fig. 29-1). The organs that constitute the upper GI system include the mouth, with the sublingual and submaxillary salivary glands; the esophagus; and the stomach. The *esophagus* is a hollow, cylindrical, pliable, and distensible tube that extends from the pharynx to the

stomach. Portions of the esophagus lie in the neck, in the posterior mediastinum, and in the abdomen. The wall of the esophagus consists of three major layers: the mucosa, the submucosa, and the muscularis propria. Two sphincters regulate the entrance and exit of the esophagus: the upper esophageal sphincter (UES) and the lower esophageal sphincter (LES). The esophagus is innervated primarily by the autonomic nervous system. The vagus is the motor nerve of the esophagus. Sympathetic function in the esophagus is poorly understood.

The *stomach* is the large reservoir of the digestive tract. It serves as a mixing and digestive organ and consists of the cardia, the body, and the antrum. The stomach is covered with the peritoneum and is free to move about the abdominal cavity.

The liver, gallbladder, and pancreas are also integral parts of the GI system. The *liver* is the largest gland in the body, serving many complex and integrated functions. Without the liver, life is not possible. The liver has a unique blood circulation. With 30% of the blood coming from the hepatic artery and 70% coming from the portal veins, virtually all the blood that leaves the gut and spleen passes through the liver. The *hepatocyte* is the functional cell of the liver. Plates of hepatocytes provide many functions, including metabolic regulation, detoxification of drugs and gut toxins, synthesis of proteins and hormones, degradation of hormones, transamination and synthesis of urea, removal of ammonia from blood, regulation of blood glucose, and storage site of body glucose.

Deamination of amino acids is an important hepatic function. *Deamination* is the process by which accumulated amino acids are used for energy or stored as fat. This process must occur before an amino acid can be used as an energy source. Twenty amino acids are necessary to meet the body's requirements. The hepatic cells are capable of synthesizing ten amino acids, known as nonessential amino acids. The remaining ten, or the essential amino acids, are supplied through the diet.

*Bilirubin* is another substance excreted by the liver. This pigment is formed from the breakdown of hemoglobin by the reticuloendothelial system located in the spleen, liver, and bone marrow. Free (unconjugated) bilirubin is released into the circulatory system, where it combines with a plasma protein (albumin). Unconjugated albumin-bound bilirubin is absorbed by the hepatic cell membrane and conjugates with glucuronic acid to form conjugated bilirubin glucuronide. Conjugated bilirubin is secreted by active transport through the bile ductules of the liver into the intestines to be excreted in feces (Guyton, 1986).

The *gallbladder* lies behind the liver in the right upper quadrant of the abdomen. The gallbladder's major function is storage of bile until it is needed by the duodenum as food passes through. The sphincter of Oddi relaxes, and the gallbladder contracts, forcing bile through the common duct.

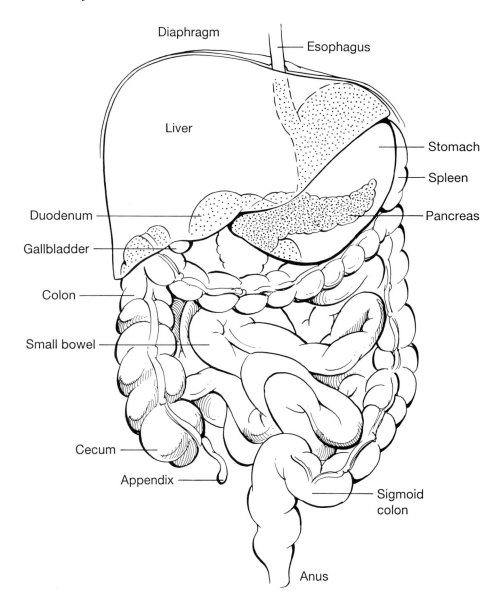

*Figure 29–1.   Anatomy of the gastrointestinal system.*

The *pancreas* lies parallel to and beneath the stomach. This large gland secretes digestive enzymes and two important hormones, insulin and glucagon. The digestive enzymes are combined with a sodium bicarbonate solution and flow through the pancreatic duct to the duodenum.

The *intestines* complete the GI system. The small intestine or bowel includes the duodenum, jejunum, and ileum. The small intestine is about 12 feet long, or over twice the height of an average adult. The cecum and the appendix begin the large intestine, followed by the ascending colon, the transverse colon, the descending colon, the sigmoid colon, and the rectum. The colon is a hollow muscular organ that joins the small intestine at the ileocecal valve. It is about 4.5 feet long. The large intestine is supplied with a rich network of lymphatics in the sub-

mucosa and subserous layers. Innervation is supplied by the autonomic nervous system (Clemente, 1989).

## Digestive Physiology

The GI tract's primary functions are to transport and metabolize the nutrients necessary for the promotion and maintenance of all cells in the body. The breakdown and absorption of nutrients, fluids, electrolytes, and other vital elements occur in the GI tract.

### Ingestion

*Ingestion* begins with the intake of food into the mouth. The pharynx and esophagus are primarily responsible for swallowing. The oropharynx is innervated by the cranial nerves. The primary purpose is to separate the functions of respiration and swallowing. With swallowing, the sphincter relaxes and then contracts, allowing the food bolus to enter the esophagus. The peristaltic wave continues after closure of the UES, propelling the food toward the stomach. The approaching peristaltic waves signal the LES that a food bolus is approaching. The LES maintains closure of the distal esophagus through tonic contractions that relax with swallowing or with esophageal distention to permit movement of contents to the stomach. The LES also prevents reflux (regurgitation of gastric contents into the esophagus). The pyloric sphincter (pylorus) controls the movement of food from the stomach into the duodenum.

## Digestion

The process that converts food into an absorbable substance is called *digestion.* The process is initiated by the salivary glands through the reduction of complex carbohydrates into simpler molecules. Digestion continues in the stomach, where the food bolus mixes with gastric juices composed of water, pepsin, hydrochloric acid, renin, lipase, and mucin. Each has a specific function in the process of digestion. Pepsin (protease), hydrochloric acid, and renin all digest protein, while lipase digests fat. Mucin is a buffer that forms a protective barrier between the gastric acid and the gastric lining. Digestion is completed in the small intestine.

Pancreatic secretions (water, bicarbonate, and pancreatic enzymes) and secretions from the liver (bile) enter the second portion of the duodenum to complete the digestive process. Pancreatic enzymes are important in digestion. Trypsin facilitates the conversion of proteins into amino acids; lipase catalyzes the breakdown of fats into fatty acids and glycerol; and amylase hydrolyses starches and carbohydrates into disaccharides (maltose, sucrose, and lactose). Bile consists primarily of cholesterol, phospholipids, bile salts, and bilirubin. Bile salts play an important role in the absorption of fatty acids, monoglycerides, cholesterol, and other lipids. Without bile salts, about 40% of all ingested fats would be lost in the stool, resulting in *steatorrhea* (fatty stools), and the absorption of fat-soluble vitamins A, D, E, and K would decrease.

## Absorption

The major site for *absorption* is the small intestine. The many folds of the small intestine triple the absorptive capacity of the intestinal mucosa. Finger-like projections, called *villi,* cover the inner surface of the small intestines and increase the absorptive capacity by another 10%. The absorptive surface is further increased by *microvilli,* the epithelial cells that cover each villi. Villi do not line the stomach and large intestine.

Absorption occurs through diffusion and active transport. *Diffusion* is the movement of substances from an area of higher concentration to one of lower concentration. *Active transport* requires energy to move substances across an opposing pressure gradient or against an electric potential, thus allowing cells to select or exclude material from their substances. Small intestine absorption occurs in the epithelial lining by diffusion or active transport.

The end products of carbohydrate and protein digestion are used by the liver. Fatty acids and glycerol are absorbed by the epithelial cells of the villi and eventually enter the circulation by way of the lymphatics. Vitamins are absorbed in the small intestine. Vitamin $B_{12}$ is absorbed only in the terminal ileum. Water and electrolytes are absorbed primarily in the small intestine.

## Excretion

The intestinal contents that remain after digestion and absorption pass through the ileocecal valve into the colon, or large intestine. The colon is responsible for preparing the nondigestible residues for excretion as *feces.*

When the rectum becomes distended with feces, the process of *defecation* begins. Defecation comprises both reflex and voluntary components. Peristaltic waves propel the feces through the colon toward the anus. As the feces approaches the anus, the internal sphincter relaxes, followed by external sphincter relaxation and successful defecation.

## Assessment

The nursing process provides a framework for caring for children with GI problems. Through careful assessment, diagnosis or problem identification, planning, implementation, and evaluation, a comprehensive nursing care plan is developed, and quality nursing care is delivered to the child and family.

## History

The signs and symptoms of GI disorders often reflect systemic processes. Establishing a history of recent weight loss or gain is important. If a child presents with a history of diarrhea but continues to gain weight, in most instances the underlying cause is not severe. *Growth failure* (the failure to gain weight and maintain linear growth) is a symptom that may go unnoticed for a prolonged period of time. Previous growth data is necessary to make the diagnosis of growth failure. GI disorders can contribute to growth failure. A dietary or nutritional assessment determines whether or not the child's nutritional needs are being met. Caloric need and the amount of calories the child is actually receiving must be determined.

An accurate description of any emesis and its relationship to eating is necessary. The forcefulness of the vomiting needs to be determined, along with the consistency, amount, and color of emesis and the presence or absence of blood. *Hematemesis* (blood in the emesis) usually indicates a bleeding lesion in the upper GI tract. The darker the color of the blood, the lower the level of the lesion.

Defecation patterns also need to be identified. Information about the number of stools per day, consistency, color, odor, and presence of blood are important aspects of a GI evaluation. Rectal bleeding also needs to be evaluated. The color of the blood indicates the level of bleeding, with darker red indicating bleeding from higher in the intestine. Differentiating between grossly bloody diarrhea, blood-coated stools, blood-streaked stools, and blood on the toilet paper is important. The description of stools determines the direction of the evaluation.

Children often complain of abdominal pain. Determining the exact location and type of pain is helpful in the diagnostic process. Determining the pain's relationship to meals, activities (e.g., school, play), and defecation also assists in the diagnostic process. Determining whether the pain disturbs the child's sleep is essential. Careful observation of the child's facial expressions during palpation of the abdomen may be the most useful source of information.

Other areas that warrant exploration include a history of fever, past medications, especially antibiotics, and assessment of the skin. A history of changes in skin color (such as jaundice) and turgor is key in the diagnosis of liver disease. Determining if the child has experienced any pruritus, rashes, or unexplained bruising is also useful information.

## Physical Examination

The physical assessment begins with the general appearance of the child. Determination of height, weight, head circumference, and triceps skin folds are necessary to document failure to thrive or growth failure associated with malnutrition. The assessment should include the oral cavity, noting the condition and development of the teeth, and the integrity of the oral mucosa. The abdominal examination includes inspection of the skin, noting skin integrity, color, vasculature, and scars. Abdominal distention should be noted and differentiated from the normal pot belly of a young child. Palpation of the abdomen is important in assessing liver and spleen size as well as the presence of palpable fecal masses. Auscultation of the abdomen is important to determine the presence or absence of bowel sounds.

## Diagnostic Procedures

Evaluation of GI disorders includes laboratory tests, radiographic studies, and invasive procedures. The initial evaluation may include screening studies consisting of a complete blood count (CBC), chemistry panel, and abdominal radiographs. The need for more specific radiographic studies and invasive procedures is determined by the history, physical findings, and results of the screening studies. The most common studies are shown in Table 29-1 and are discussed in this section.

*Table 29–1. Common Diagnostic Procedures*

| Study | Indications | Findings |
|---|---|---|
| Complete blood count with differential | Chronic illness; infection/inflammation; anemia/bleeding; medication reactions | < Hemoglobin<br>↑ White blood cells<br>↓ White blood cells |
| Chemistry Panel | | |
| Electrolytes | Vomiting | Abnormal electrolytes |
| Blood urea nitrogen, creatinine | Diarrhea | (Na, K, CO₂) |
| Total bilirubin | Liver disease | ↑ Blood urea nitrogen, creatinine |
| Direct bilirubin | Malabsorption | ↑ Total bilirubin |
| ALT | Inflammatory bowel disease | ↑ Direct bilirubin |
| AST | Acetaminophen ingestion | ↑ ALT |
| GGT | Wilson disease | ↑ AST |
| Alkaline phosphate | Hepatitis | ↑ GGT |
| Total protein | Cholecystitis | ↑ Alkaline phosphate |
| Albumin | Appendicitis; pancreatitis | ↓ Total protein<br>↓ Albumin |
| Bile acids (serum) | Liver disease | ↑ Serum bile acids |
| Erythrocyte sedimentation rate | Inflammatory bowel disease | ↑ Erythrocyte sedimentation rate |
| (PT/PTT) | Liver disease; malabsorption; Acetaminophen ingestion prior to procedure; disseminated intravascular coagulation | > PT/PTT normal; PT/PTT normal;<br>> PT/PTT if liver dysfunction; PT/PTT normal;<br>> PT/PTT |

*(continued)*

*Table 29–1.  Common Diagnostic Procedures (Continued)*

| Study | Indications | Findings |
|---|---|---|
| Stool specimens cultures | | |
| *Salmonella* | Diarrhea | |
| *Shigella* | Rectal bleeding | |
| *Yersinia* | | |
| *Campylobacter* | | |
| *Clostridium difficile* toxin | Diarrhea; rectal bleeding | |
| Ova and parasite (*Guiardia lamblia*) | Diarrhea; abdominal pain; vomiting | |
| Radiographic studies | | |
| Abdominal radiograph (flat-plate kidney, ureter, and bladder) | R/O constipation<br>Hirschsprung disease, encopresis; imperforate anus<br>R/O obstruction<br>Inflammatory bowel disease; congenital atresia; malrotation; diaphragmatic hernia | |
| Chest radiograph | R/O aspiration<br>Tracheoesophageal fistula; gastroesophageal reflux; foreign body; ingestion; diaphragmatic hernia | |
| Upper gastrointestinal examination with barium; with small bowel follow-through (barium swallow) | Vomiting; gastroesophageal reflux; pyloric stenosis; inflammatory bowel disease; malrotation; peptic ulcer disease | |
| Barium enema (unprepped or prepped) | Meconium ileus; Hirschsprung disease; intussusception; diaphragmatic hernia; inflammatory bowel disease; polyps; appendicitis | |
| Ultrasound | Liver disease; pyloric stenosis; inflammatory bowel disease; appendicitis; cholecystitis; pancreatitis | |
| Nuclear medicine | | |
| Milk scan/gastric-emptying scan | Tracheoesophageal fistula; gastroesophageal reflux; pyloric stenosis | |
| Disida scan | Liver disease; cholecystitis | |
| Meckel scan | Meckel diverticulum | |
| Endoscopic procedures | | |
| Upper endoscopy (esophagus, gastric, duodenum) | Vomiting; gastroesophageal reflux; esophagitis; foreign body; ingestion of corrosive substance; esophageal variceal hemorrhage; celiac disease; malabsorption syndrome; inflammatory bowel disease; peptic ulcer disease | |
| Flexible sigmoidoscopy/colonoscopy | Diarrhea; necrotizing enterocolitis; inflammatory bowel disease; anal fissure; polyps | |
| Biopsies | | |
| Liver—percutaneous liver biopsy | Neonatal liver disease; Wilson disease; hepatitis; acetaminophen poisoning | |
| Small bowel—suction capsule biopsy | Diarrhea; malabsorption syndrome; celiac disease | |
| Rectal biopsy—suction (Rubin's tube) | Hirschsprung disease | |
| pH Probe and manometry | Gastroesophageal reflux | |
| Lactose breath test | Lactose intolerance; malabsorption; celiac disease; inflammatory bowel disease | |

*Biochemical parameters* (e.g., CBC with differential, chemistry panel, erythrocyte sedimentation rate) provide information about the general health of the child and determine the direction of the evaluation. Other biochemical parameters frequently used in the diagnosis of GI disorders include prothrombin time, partial thromboplastin time, serum carotene, folate levels, serum bile acids, gamma glutamyltransferase, alanine aminotransferase, aspartate aminotransferase, and alkaline phosphatase. The *hydrogen breath test* is a diagnostic study for lactose intolerance and is also used in the evaluation of malabsorption to determine small bowel mucosal integrity. The *D-xylose* absorption study is also done to evaluate small bowel mucosal integrity. *Stool cultures* are routinely done in the evaluation of GI dysfunction. Stool cultures look for the presence of *Salmonella, Shigella, Yersinia,* and *Campylobacter* organisms in the stool. Stool cultures for ova and parasites primarily look for *Giardia lamblia,* a parasite that is now endemic in many parts of the United States and Canada. *Clostridium difficile* is a frequent cause of bloody diarrhea in children, especially following antibiotic use. A fresh or frozen specimen must be cultured to obtain accurate results.

Radiographic studies provide important information, aiding in the diagnosis of GI disorders. *Abdominal radiographs* outline the intestines, documenting the presence and location of feces. *Ultrasound* documents the location of abdominal organs, the presence of abdominal masses, and the patency of the abdominal vasculature. This noninvasive study is useful in the evaluation of hepatobiliary and pancreatic diseases.

*Barium studies* are frequently used in the diagnosis of GI disorders. The *upper gastrointestinal series (UGI)* uses barium to visualize the structure and motility of the esophagus, stomach, and duodenum. With the addition of a small bowel follow-through to the UGI, it is possible to evaluate the jejunum and ileum as well. An air-contrast UGI (in which air is forced into the upper GI tract) enables assessment of the mucosal integrity. A *barium enema* provides similar assessments of the colon. Patient preparation is important to the success of a barium enema. The colon is cleansed through a combination of dietary restrictions, enemas, and cathartics. A barium enema without prior cleansing is performed when the diagnosis of Hirschsprung disease or intussusception is suspected.

*Endoscopy* allows direct visualization of both the upper and lower GI tract and is useful in diagnosing mucosal injury, structural abnormalities, and bleeding lesions through a flexible fiberoptic "scope." It consists of bundles of thin, flexible, transparent fibers that transmit light through the GI tract. Endoscopy can be performed using a video system. This allows the physician to view the procedure on a monitor and to tape the procedure for future reference. Biopsies can be performed through endoscopy, allowing tissue diagnosis. An *upper endoscopy* (*esophagoscopy* or *gastroscopy*) permits direct visualization of the esophagus, stomach, and duodenum and also is performed as a means of foreign body retrieval. A *lower endoscopy* permits visualization of the large intestine. A *sigmoidoscopy* is the inspection of the rectum and sigmoid colon with a rigid or flexible sigmoidoscope. *Colonoscopy* provides visualization of the entire colon to the ileocecal valve. Mucosal integrity, ulceration, and inflammation are easily seen with endoscopy and confirmed by tissue obtained by biopsy.

Patient preparation varies with the extent of examination. Depending on their age, patients undergoing an upper endoscopy need only be NPO for 4 to 6 hours preceding the procedure. Children scheduled for a lower endoscopy are on a clear liquid diet for 48 to 72 hours before the procedure. A cathartic is given orally 36 hours and 12 hours before the procedure. Enemas may also be required the night before or the morning of the procedure, or at both times. Older children may be given the option of using hyperosmolar polyethylene glycol-electrolyte solutions as a cleansing preparation, avoiding the clear liquid diet, cathartic, and enemas. These solutions are very salty, and drinking an 8-ounce glass every 15 minutes for a total of 3 to 4 liters is required. Only very determined children are successful with this form of preparation.

After the endoscopy, vital signs are monitored frequently. The physician needs to be notified of changes in vital signs, pain, vomiting, or bleeding. The child may resume a regular diet after tolerating clear liquids.

A *small bowel biopsy* is done when there is a possibility of a mucosal abnormality of the small bowel. It can be done by means of an upper endoscopy or with a Watson-Crosby capsule. A capsule biopsy is done using fluoroscopy. The child swallows the capsule, which is attached to a rubber tube. The capsule and tubing is then guided to the small bowel, and a tissue sample is taken by using suction on the end of the tubing. *Rectal biopsies* are obtained in a similar manner using a Rubin tube inserted in the rectum. Rectal biopsies are indicated when Hirschsprung disease is suspected. *Percutaneous needle liver biopsy* is a safe method of obtaining tissue for histological examination and culture. Indications for the procedure are unexplained hepatomegaly, persistent elevations of liver functions, and suspected metabolic or structural disease.

Gastrointestinal disorders may require surgery and result in an ostomy. The ostomies may be temporary or permanent.

## Nursing Diagnosis

Establishing nursing diagnoses for the child and family with a GI problem is an important part of the nursing process. Listed below are the more common nursing diagnoses associated with GI dysfunction. Children with chronic GI disorders may have several nursing diagnoses based on the ongoing assessments and interventions provided by the nurses coordinating the child's and family's care.

*Pattern 1: Exchanging*
- Altered nutrition: less than body requirements
- Altered nutrition: potential for more than body requirements
- Altered oral mucous membrane
- Altered GI tissue perfusion

- Bowel incontinence
- Constipation
- Decreased cardiac output
- Diarrhea
- Fluid volume deficit (1)
- High risk for altered body temperature
- High risk for aspiration
- High risk for fluid volume deficit
- High risk for impaired skin integrity
- High risk for infection
- High risk for poisoning
- Impaired skin integrity
- Impaired tissue integrity
- Ineffective airway clearance
- Ineffective breathing pattern

*Pattern 3: Relating*
- Altered family processes
- High risk for altered parenting
- Impaired social interaction

*Pattern 5: Choosing*
- Ineffective family coping: compromised

*Pattern 6: Moving*
- Activity intolerance
- Altered growth and development
- Impaired swallowing
- Toileting self-care deficit

*Pattern 7: Perceiving*
- Self-esteem disturbance
- Sensory/perceptual alterations

*Pattern 9: Feeling*
- Anxiety
- Fear
- High risk for violence: self-directed or directed at others
- Pain

## Planning Nursing Care

Gastrointestinal disorders in children range from benign, self-limiting disorders, such as viral gastroenteritis, to life-threatening disorders, such as liver failure. Planning and implementing nursing care for the child with a GI disorder may be complex. GI disorders often involve many systems, and nursing assessments need to reflect the systems involved.

## Developmental Considerations

Upon admission to the hospital, it is important to assess the child and family's level of understanding regarding the diagnosis and the need for hospitalization. Most children with significant GI disorders are chronically ill and require repeated hospitalizations. However, the child and family's level of acceptance of the diagnosis varies according to the child's developmental level, the length of time since the diagnosis, the their ability to function as a family, the child's ability to attend school and play, and their understanding of the prognosis. Determining both the child and parents' cognitive level and learning styles is important. Do the child or parents have a learning disability? Are they able to read? Does the child learn best through games? These assessments allow the nurse to plan successful interventions. The impact of hospitalization on children and families is discussed in Chapter 17.

## Acute Care Considerations

Gastrointestinal disorders may be acute and life-threatening. Hospitalization is often necessary. It is imperative that the nursing care delivered to the patient and family reflect the skilled assessment made on admission and throughout the hospitalization. Chronically ill children also experience acute exacerbations of their disease that require interventions similar to those who suddenly become ill.

## Chronic Care Considerations

Chronically ill children require support of their routine health care and their emotional well-being. Growth and development must be assessed and appropriate interventions implemented. Attention must also be paid to the child's ability to function within the existing environment. It is important that developmental milestones continue to be met. Parents are an integral part of the planning, implementation, and follow-up of interventions designed for the chronically ill child.

## Home Care Considerations

Children with GI problems require many levels of home care. Intravenous antibiotic therapy, home hyperalimentation, and enteral feedings are the most common home care interventions. The primary concern with all home care is that the family be well prepared, willing, and able to provide the needed care. The child must be stable, and the medical and nursing plans must be implemented before discharge. The family's lifestyle must be considered in developing a home care plan. Arrangements must be made for the equipment, supplies, and nursing needs required by the child and family.

## Nursing Interventions

The nursing interventions used to treat GI problems are usually supportive. The interventions for specific disorders are discussed later in this chapter. Interventions that apply to most disorders are discussed in this section.

## Nutrition

Due to the underlying illness, it is common for children with GI disorders to be anorexic, losing calories through vomiting or diarrhea; or they may be unable to tolerate eating. Providing adequate calories is important and may be accomplished through a variety of methods. Attention should be paid to developmentally appropriate foods, tolerance of caloric supplements, and tolerance of alternative feeding options, such as nasogastric (NG) or gastrostomy feedings. The most common diets used for children are shown in Table 29-2.

*Total parenteral nutrition* (TPN) is an alternative method of supplying adequate calories, protein, and fat for a child that cannot be fed orally or by NG tube. TPN delivers high concentrations of protein (amino acids), glucose, and electrolytes by way of a central venous catheter. TPN can also be infused through a peripheral intravenous catheter in lower concentrations of protein and glucose. Intravenous fat emulsion (lipids) provides additional calories and fats (essential fatty acids). It is delivered simultaneously with the TPN. Children receiving central TPN and lipids are at risk for septicemia. Nurses must use sterile technique in caring for the catheter and must maintain a clean environment to minimize the risk of infection.

*Nasogastric* and *gastrostomy feedings* are effective methods of delivering calories to children who are unable to meet maintenance requirements orally. The NG tube is inserted through the nares and passed down the esophagus into the stomach. Accurate insertion length is determined by measuring from the nose to the earlobe and then to a point midway between the xiphoid process and the umbilicus (Weibley et al., 1987). This point is marked on the tube with a piece of tape. The lubricated (using water-soluble lubricant) tip of the tube is inserted into the nares to the predetermined mark. This is best accomplished with the child's head in a neutral or hyperflexed position. The NG tube is passed quickly, and the child is encouraged to swallow on command. Sucking on a pacifier is helpful for infants. Placement is validated by auscultating the stomach during injection of an air bolus by means of a syringe attached to the end of the feeding tube. Aspiration of stomach contents confirms proper placement. The NG tube is then taped securely to the child's nose or cheek. Placement should be rechecked before each use of the NG tube.

The indications for a gastrostomy tube include the need for prolonged supplemental feedings; inability to take food orally; and intolerance to passage of an NG tube. A gastrostomy tube is initially placed surgically or endoscopically. Once the stoma and gastrostomy tract are well developed, the gastrostomy tube may be changed as needed. The responsibility for replacing gastrostomy tubes varies with institutions. Nursing interventions are directed toward maintenance of the stoma, skin integrity, and feeding tolerance. Transpyloric feeding (jejunal feedings) may be necessary if a child is unable to tolerate gastric feedings or is at risk for aspiration as a result of *gastroesophageal reflux* (GER). Parent and child education is important to the success of this intervention.

## Decompression

Many children with GI disorders require decompression of the GI tract. The decision to begin this intervention is made by the physician; however, it is a nursing responsibility to maintain and care for the child once the decision is made. In some instances, the nurse places the tube. This is accomplished using an NG tube, gastrostomy tube, jejunal tube, or rectal tube. Suction is often applied to the tube to eliminate the buildup of gastric secretions. Nursing care of gastric decompression tubes is the same as that for feeding tubes.

## Elimination

Children with GI disorders may have difficulty with elimination. Whether the child has constipation or diarrhea, nursing interventions are aimed at providing comfort and maintaining skin integrity. Dietary manipulations may help alleviate symptoms. High-fiber diets are used to manage constipation. High-fat diets and fluid restrictions may help to manage diarrhea. The BRAT diet (bananas, rice, applesauce, and tea or toast) is recommended for children with diarrhea.

An *ostomy* is a surgical opening in the abdominal wall that allows passage of intestinal contents through a *stoma* rather than through the rectum. Nursing interventions are directed toward successful adaptation of the child and family to the ostomy. Preoperative preparation requires interdisciplinary collaboration and focuses on appropriate placement of the stoma (so it does not interfere with clothing), lifestyle issues, and peer acceptance. If possible, the child should meet a child of similar age with an ostomy before the surgery. Postoperative adaptation is enhanced

*Table 29-2.    Commonly Used Diets*

| Diet | Indications |
| --- | --- |
| High fiber | Constipation; irritable bowel syndrome; encopresis; abdominal pain; anal fissures |
| Lactose free | Lactose intolerance; inflammatory bowel disease; malabsorption; celiac disease; diarrhea |
| Low residue | Inflammatory bowel disease; abdominal pain |
| Gluten free | Celiac disease |
| High fat | Diarrhea—chronic; malabsorption; failure to thrive |
| High protein/ high calorie | Inflammatory bowel disease; malabsorption; failure to thrive |

with well-fitting appliances and education focused on care and maintenance of the ostomy.

## Drug Therapy

Numerous pharmacological agents are used in the treatment and management of GI disorders and are discussed in the context of specific disease processes later in this chapter. Those frequently prescribed include vitamin supplements, antiinflammatory agents, $H_2$-antagonists, antidiarrheal agents, laxatives, lubricants, and immunosuppressive agents. Nursing interventions include educating the child and family in the administration, side effects, and systemic effects of the medication to ensure an effective response to the pharmacological therapy.

## Preoperative and Postoperative Nursing Care

The nursing care of infants and children requiring surgery follows a few basic principles. Preoperative nursing care focuses on preparing the child for the surgery. The nurse should obtain accurate weight and height measurements. The nurse must assess the child's vital signs for indicators of discomfort and dehydration, such as increased heart rate and blood pressure. The child's skin integrity should be evaluated for signs of infection, dehydration, and breakdown. The nurse should evaluate the child's level of discomfort using verbal description by the child and observing the child's behavior. Preoperative education of the child and parents includes familiarizing them with the procedure, the anticipated results of the surgery, and what to expect after surgery.

The child is made NPO 4 to 6 hours before surgery to decrease the risk of aspirating stomach contents during intubation. The oral, sucking needs of infants should not be overlooked and may be met with a pacifier.

Postoperative care of the child addresses hydration status, tolerance of diet advancement, signs of infection, tolerance of increasing activity levels, and understanding of education. Hydration status is evaluated by obtaining an accurate record of the child's intake (IV and PO) and output (urine, stool, drainage). Observing the child's skin turgor is also useful in determining adequate hydration. An accurate daily weight is necessary to assess the child's response to altered nutrition and diet intake. When active bowel sounds have returned to normal, the child should begin oral fluid intake. The nurse's assessment of how the child tolerates fluids influences how the child's diet is advanced. The child's wound should be observed for signs of infection, including drainage (volume, color), redness of the skin, and site tenderness. The child's level of discomfort and the effectiveness of pain therapy should be assessed by observing the child's behavior, vital signs, and level of activity. The nurse should administer analgesics as

directed by the physician. Discharge teaching should be evaluated. This includes returning to a normal diet, specific wound care as directed by the physician, increasing activity, and returning to school.

Nursing care of the child who requires surgery is evaluated through continued reassessment of the child's condition and monitoring of expected outcomes, which include the following: the operative site should be well healed and free of infection; the child should be well nourished and able to tolerate oral feedings; the family should demonstrate care of NG tube, gastrotomy tube, or ostomy, as indicated, as well as administration of medications; resources needed for home care should be established; the parents and family should verbalize concerns and feelings regarding the child's problem and interventions; and the child and family should demonstrate coping mechanisms.

## Evaluating Nursing Care

The goal of nursing care delivered to children with GI disorders is to promote health and function in the context of acute or chronic illness. Most children with GI disorders experience remission, and a small percentage die. Evaluation of the nursing care provided must include evaluation of the child and family's response—and that of the health care team as well. Evaluation criteria for specific disorders is discussed at the end of each problem that follows.

## Common Gastrointestinal Disorders

### Acute and Infectious Diarrhea

Acute diarrhea is one of the most common disorders in childhood. In the United States, children average 1 to 2 episodes of diarrhea per year before 5 years of age (Bishop & Ulshen, 1988). *Diarrhea* is defined as an increase in the normal frequency, water content, or volume of stools. It is important to understand that a normal stooling pattern is variable, and diarrhea should be considered as a change in a person's usual pattern.

#### Pathophysiology

Four principal pathophysiological processes produce diarrhea: secretory, cytotoxic, osmotic, and dysenteric. *Secretory diarrhea* occurs when bacteria, parasites, or toxins stimulate secretion of fluid and electrolytes from the principal secretory cells in the small intestines. As a result, there is an excess of fluid in the gut, and large, watery stools occur.

*Cytotoxic diarrhea* is caused by the destruction of

mucosal cells of the villi in the small intestines. This process causes a decreased surface area of the small intestines, which results in a decreased capacity to absorb fluid and electrolytes.

*Osmotic diarrhea* occurs when high concentrations of substances such as sorbitol, which is malabsorbed, move through the gut. These substances cause fluid to be pulled into the intestine, leading to liquid stools.

*Dysenteric diarrhea* occurs when bacteria invade the mucosa and submucosa of the small intestines, causing inflammation. Edema, bleeding, and leukocyte infiltration occur. As a result, the fluid absorption capacity of the large intestines is diminished. The irritated bowel has increased motility, leading to frequent, liquid stools. The stools are often bloody and occasionally contain pus and white blood cells.

Bacteria that are known to cause diarrhea include *Escherichia coli, Salmonella, Shigella, Campylobacter jejuni, Yersina enterocolitica,* and *Clostridium difficile.* Viruses that cause diarrhea include *Normalk-like* viruses and *rotavirus.*

The most common intestinal parasite in the United States is *Giardia lamblia,* with a high occurrence rate in day care centers. Symptoms include explosive, foul-smelling, watery stools; abdominal pain, flatulence, and bloating. The symptoms may be acute, self-limiting, or chronic. Symptomatic children are treated with quinacrine hydrochloride (Atabrine), furazolidone (Furoxone), or metronidazole (Flagyl). Since it is possible for children to be asymptomatic carriers, identifying and treating these children in the day care setting is a preventive strategy.

## Medical Diagnosis and Management

Medical diagnosis and management begins with a history, physical examination, and the appropriate laboratory studies, focused on evaluating the child's hydration status and the causative agent for the illness.

Laboratory studies are obtained based on the history and physical examination in order to further evaluate hydration status and the cause of the illness. Appropriate studies include urinalysis, blood urea nitrogen, and electrolytes, which help determine hydration status. Stool cultures should be obtained to rule out bacterial pathogens, *Campylobacter, Salmonella,* and *Shigella* infection. A fresh stool specimen is obtained to rule out *Giardia* infection. Stool pH and glucose are obtained to rule out a malabsorptive process. If these studies are normal, a viral diarrheal process is suspected.

Initial management of acute diarrhea focuses on rehydration of the child. Most children with acute diarrhea are successfully managed as outpatients; however, children who are more than 10% dehydrated or who are hypernatremic should be admitted to the hospital for intravenous rehydration (DeWitt, 1989).

Children who are not vomiting may drink the rehydration solution until they are satisfied. Children who are vomiting should be offered 15 to 30 mL every 15 to 30 minutes. Despite the vomiting, the net retention of the solution is generally enough to rehydrate the child. If the child shows no improvement in 4 to 6 hours, hospitalization should be considered. Children who tolerate the rehydration solution for at least 24 hours may begin to advance their diets.

After diarrheal illnesses, 20% of infants have a temporary lactose intolerance (Book, 1984). As a result, a lactose-free formula may be used for several weeks. Formula should be introduced at half strength and gradually advanced as tolerated, assessing for recurrent vomiting or increased stooling. For toddlers and older children, foods that are high in carbohydrates and lactose-free sugars should be introduced first. If these are tolerated well, the diet should be advanced to normal.

In acute diarrhea, the use of antiemetics, absorbent agents, and gut antimotility agents is generally not recommended. The diarrhea and vomiting in the acute illness should be viewed as the body's attempt to rid itself of the infectious agent. Although none of these pharmacological agents are overtly dangerous to children, they can decrease the speed at which the body can clear the illness. If pharmacological agents are administered, the symptoms of diarrhea may resolve, but the infection may persist.

## Nursing Assessment and Diagnosis

The nursing assessment begins with an overall assessment of the child. Evaluation of the mucous membranes and skin for hydration status is useful for determining the degree of dehydration. The child's vital signs also provide valuable information when assessing hydration status. If the skin is doughy and does not return to its usual shape, the child is probably severely dehydrated. In infants, the anterior fontanelle, as well as the eyes, should be assessed for a sunken appearance, indicating dehydration. An elevated temperature increases insensible water loss. A decreased blood pressure and increased pulse indicate moderate to severe dehydration. The child's current weight, when compared with previous weights, is useful for assessing the degree of dehydration. The current weight serves as a baseline for assessing the child's progress through the illness.

The remainder of the physical examination should focus on identifying evidence of any concurrent or chronic illness. The nurse should assess the child's diet and stooling pattern. Information about the parents' response to the child's illness and their comfort and understanding of the plan of care is essential.

Nursing diagnoses for diarrhea might include the following:

- Diarrhea related to the infectious process
- Fluid volume deficit related to diarrhea

- Altered nutrition: less than body requirement related to diarrhea
- High risk for impaired skin integrity related to dehydration

### *Planning and Implementing Nursing Care*

The goals of nursing care for children with acute or infectious diarrhea include maintaining adequate hydration and caloric intake to promote recovery; maintaining skin integrity; and educating the family about the infection, its treatment, and prevention. When a child is hospitalized for rehydration as a result of acute diarrhea, the nurse is the primary person responsible for monitoring the intravenous fluid therapy that has been ordered. The nurse must maintain an accurate record of the child's intake (both oral and intravenous) and output. This information, in addition to an accurate daily weight and the child's vital signs, is necessary to assess the child's hydration status and response to therapy. Assessing the skin for signs of irritation and providing good skin care are essential.

The stooling pattern is monitored for changes in frequency and volume. Alterations in the child's stooling pattern may indicate the child's response to therapy. The nurse should assess the child's tolerance of feedings and advance them as directed.

Observing the child's behavior provides helpful assessment information. For example, a child who is crying with the legs drawn toward the abdomen may be experiencing discomfort. The child who is active and playful is probably feeling well and needs age-appropriate toys for distraction and play during recovery.

Patient and parent education focuses on management of the illness. Explanations of treatment plans and procedures in advance allows parents to prepare and support their child. When the child is ready to be discharged, the parents should be told what to expect if the diarrhea recurs and when to call the doctor. Advancing the child's diet further may be necessary at home. Parents should be given guidelines for advancing the diet and determining how the child is tolerating it. Anticipatory guidance focused on preventing future recurrences is a primary component of nursing care. Explanations about how these infections occur and discussions about good handwashing to prevent the spread of the infection are helpful.

### *Evaluating Nursing Care*

Nursing care of the child with diarrhea may be evaluated by the child's response to the interventions. When the child exhibits adequate nutritional intake and growth, nursing interventions have been successful and appropriate. The child should recover from the illness with good skin integrity. The parents should verbalize and demonstrate an understanding of the necessary care and should understand prevention strategies.

## *Constipation*

### *Pathophysiology*

*Constipation,* the passage of infrequent, hard stools, occurs in up to 10% of children. Since the meaning of "infrequent" is variable, it is necessary to obtain a clear history from the parents about how the current stooling pattern differs from normal. A history of constipation usually includes episodes of stools that are painful or difficult to pass. Normal stool formation was discussed earlier in this chapter.

*Functional* constipation is an acquired problem (as opposed to a congenital problem). Ninety-eight percent of all constipated children have functional constipation. In infancy, constipation frequently occurs when there is a change in the diet, for example, when low-fiber foods, such as rice, cereal, or cheese are introduced. In late infancy, an excessive amount of whole cow's milk contributes to constipation. In toddlers, functional constipation is often associated with voluntary stool withholding, which is learned during toilet training. As a result of stool withholding, the rectosigmoid colon becomes increasingly distended and requires a larger amount of stool to produce the impulse to defecate. As the rectum becomes more distended, it becomes less sensitive; over a period of months, the child may lose the sensation to defecate. In addition, the large stools that the child passes may cause rectal fissures and pain, causing the child to associate defecation with pain.

### *Medical Diagnosis and Management*

Management of functional constipation begins with a complete history and physical examination. The diet history is evaluated for foods that may contribute to this problem, including excessive milk or low fiber. The child's stooling pattern before the onset of the constipation and the current pattern should be discussed. Determining whether the child has begun toilet training and if the parents are able to identify withholding behaviors, such as hiding or squeezing the legs together, provides valuable information for the treatment plan. If the parents have seen red blood wrapped around the stool or if the child describes the stools as painful, intermittent rectal fissures may be compounding the problem.

The physical examination frequently reveals a distended abdomen with a palpable round mass in the lower left quadrant. The anus should be inspected for placement, innervation, and evident fissures. The child with functional constipation generally has normal anal sphincter tone and a large rectal vault. Local anatomical abnormalities that may cause constipation, such as congenital anal stenosis, rectoperineal fistula, compression of the rectum by neoplasm, or abscesses, may be identified during this portion of the examination (Altschuler, 1987).

An internal rectal examination is used to determine

the presence of an impaction and to evaluate the tone and capacity of the rectum. A tightly constricted, empty rectum may indicate Hirschsprung disease. Other causes of constipation may include metabolic diseases, medication (e.g., opiates), and spinal injuries.

Treatment of constipation begins with evacuation of the stool stored in the colon. This is most effectively accomplished with enemas. A mineral oil enema is administered first to lubricate the stool. This is followed by two to three consecutive Fleet enemas, at least one per day, to help the child evacuate most of the stored stool. Additional enemas may be necessary in some cases. After the rectum has been sufficiently evacuated, the child is maintained on a laxative so that the stools may be passed easily and not withheld. A nonstimulating laxative, such as Kondremul, may be used in high enough doses to enable the child to pass a moderate-sized stool regularly, while causing the child to be unable to withhold the stool. Kondremul is a combination of mineral oil and Irish moss. It acts as a lubricant and a bulk-forming agent, which allows the child to pass soft, formed stools. Because it is oil-based, there is the possibility of a decrease in the absorption of fat-soluble vitamins. It is recommended that children on this medication take a multivitamin at a time other than when they take the Kondremul.

Bowel retraining is an essential part of managing functional constipation. Parents are instructed to establish two times a day when the child is to sit on the toilet. The most effective times are usually early in the morning and after dinner. This pattern establishes stooling as part of the daily routine. With the use of a laxative and supportive encouragement, the child should be able to pass some stool once a day. Sitting on the toilet should last from 5 to 15 minutes, depending on the age of the child. Obviously, this behavior modification is inappropriate for infants and young toddlers; however, school-age children should be encouraged to sit for 15 minutes. There is no need for negative reinforcement if the child does not produce a stool. The child should be shown that cooperating with sitting is good and producing a stool is even better. Having the parents and the child maintain a calendar of the stools passed (by marking the day with a sticker) is one means of providing positive reinforcement for the child. It is also useful during office visits as an accurate record of the child's progress.

A high-fiber diet is recommended to add bulk to the stools, thereby increasing peristalsis. This may be a challenge in some cases, since toddlers and preschoolers are notoriously picky eaters. Fiber supplements such as Citrucel or Fiber-all crackers may also be used. Other dietary changes include increasing fruit juices and fluids in general, while decreasing consumption of milk.

Once the child has regular, daily stools for at least 1 month, the laxative therapy may be gradually reduced. If the child has recurrent episodes of constipation, the laxative is increased again, and weaning should not occur until a regular stooling pattern is reestablished. For many children, this management plan takes 3 to 6 months for total recovery. With support and persistence, constipation is a manageable disorder.

### Nursing Assessment and Diagnosis

Nursing assessment of the child with constipation is directed toward the child's current stooling pattern and identifying any contributing factors to the problem. The child's diet must be evaluated. The nurse should investigate the child's experience with toilet training and address the parents' views on this developmental milestone. The child and the parents' understanding of the treatment plan and their commitment to successfully managing the constipation need to be assessed.

Nursing diagnoses for constipation might include the following:

- Constipation related to withholding stools
- Pain related to difficulty defecating
- Anxiety related to fear of painful defecation
- Altered nutrition: potential for more than the body requirements related to dietary changes
- Altered parenting related to toilet training

### Planning and Implementing Nursing Care

The role of the nurse working with families who have a child with constipation focuses on support and education. Although the initial response to the therapy described is usually excellent, the total process must span several months. It may be difficult for parents and children to remain committed to the treatment regimen until the problem is completely resolved. The nurse is a valuable support person for parents and children since there are many education opportunities.

### Evaluating Nursing Care

The effectiveness of nursing care is evaluated by the resolution of the child's constipation. The parents' and the child's ability, when appropriate, to verbalize an understanding of constipation, the contributing factors, and the treatment plan are all valuable indicators for evaluating the effectiveness of nursing care.

## Encopresis

### Pathophysiology

*Encopresis* is defined as regular fecal incontinence of formed or liquid stool by a child older than 4 years of age with no organic cause (Younger & Hughes, 1983). Encopresis occurs in about 2% to 3% of preschool- and school-aged children. There is a greater incidence in boys than girls.

The primary cause of this problem is constipation. For reasons that may be unclear, the child begins to withhold stool, which forms a fecal impaction, leading to a distended lower colon (Granger, 1987). The loose stool higher in the colon leaks around the fecal impaction, resulting in soiling. There may be decreased rectal sensation, due to chronic distention, that signals the urge to stool, and most children are unaware that the soiling episodes occur.

Rarely is encopresis caused by an organic illness; however, the possibilities include lead poisoning, cystic fibrosis, hyperthyroidism, and inadequate nutrition (Younger & Hughes, 1983). It is important to differentiate encopresis from Hirschsprung disease.

Encopresis is not strictly a physiological problem, but in most cases, there is an associated behavioral factor (Younger & Hughes, 1983). The child may appear to be unaware and unaffected by the recurrent soiling. This causes a great deal of frustration and anxiety for the parents. Conversely, the child may be anxious about the lack of control of bodily functions. The impact on the development of peer relationships may be influenced by the child's soiling.

## Medical Diagnosis and Management

The diagnosis of encopresis is based on the child's medical history and a physical examination. The child should have a complete physical examination to rule out organic causes for the encopresis. Abdominal and rectal examinations are essential. Loops of stool-filled intestines may be palpable on abdominal examination. The rectal examination may reveal decreased anal tone, a large distended rectal vault, and hard formed or soft liquid stool. On occasion, an abdominal radiograph may be used to assess the volume of impacted stool and the colonic distension.

Medical management is the same as for constipation. There is controversy over whether encopresis should be considered a behavioral problem and whether psychotherapy should be used in the management of encopresis. It is felt that in some cases, the child psychologist is helpful and essential to the success of the treatment plan.

## Nursing Assessment and Diagnosis

Encopresis is a chronic problem that requires frequent follow-up care and support from health care professionals. Nursing assessment is the same as for constipation but should also focus on how the child and parents are coping with this frustrating problem. In addition, the nurse may need to determine the implications of this problem in the school setting and the need for intervention. Finally, the nurse should assess the child and parents for their level of frustration and ability to cope with and manage this problem. Parental frustration and an angry or withdrawn child may force this problem to persist.

Additional nursing diagnoses for encopresis might include the following:

- Bowel incontinence related to fecal impaction and leakage
- Self-esteem disturbance related to soiling
- Impaired social interaction related to soiling
- High risk for altered parenting related to frustration

## Planning and Implementing Nursing Care

In addition to the planning and implementation discussed for constipation, the nurse should work with parents to provide positive reinforcement for the child's desire to use the toilet. Negative reinforcement may place undue pressure on the child and cause stool withholding.

School-aged children with encopresis frequently have problems during school hours. The nurse should work with the school nurse and the teacher to help avoid any problems that may arise in school and to plan for managing the soiling episodes if they occur. When appropriate, the nurse should work with the physician and the family to determine the usefulness of working with a child psychologist to manage any associated behavioral problems.

## Evaluating Nursing Care

Evaluation of nursing care should focus on the resolution of soiling episodes and the family's response to therapy. This evaluation should occur frequently and continually until the problem resolves since this is a chronic problem with a relatively high incidence of recurrence.

# Acute Vomiting

## Pathophysiology

Vomiting is the forceful ejection of stomach contents through the nose and mouth. It occurs as the result of contraction of the abdominal muscles against a relaxed stomach (Andorsky, 1987d). Vomiting is controlled by the "vomiting center" located in the medulla. Acute infections, central nervous system pathology (head trauma), metabolic disease, toxic ingestion, mechanical obstruction, food intolerance, and functional disorders (anorexia, GER) all cause vomiting.

## Medical Diagnosis and Management

Medical diagnosis is based on determining the cause of the vomiting. A careful history and physical examination are essential. The history should include the age of the infant, the onset of vomiting, and the frequency of episodes. The relationship to feedings may help differentiate acute vomiting from a more chronic problem, such as reflux or ulcers. The ingestion of potentially toxic substances should be investigated. The color and volume of the vomitus should be evaluated. Green bilious vomitus is indicative of an anatomical small bowel obstruction (Andorsky, 1987d). Red or dark brown emesis may be blood; however, the dietary intake should be reviewed for foods and dyes that may discolor the vomitus. Associated symptoms such as fever and diarrhea may indicate an infectious etiology, while localized abdominal pain is more consistent with diagnoses such as appendicitis, pancreatitis, and cholecystitis. Children with metabolic or central nervous system causes of vomiting may have a change in level of consciousness.

Physical examination of the child with vomiting helps determine the management. An overall assessment of the child's hydration status is necessary. An abdominal examination that reveals tenderness or masses helps in identifying and treating the cause of the vomiting. A rectal examination is used to evaluate the child for referred abdominal tenderness and lower abdominal masses. A detailed neurological examination may be indicated for central nervous system causes of vomiting.

Usually, vomiting begins with an acute onset and lasts 24 to 48 hours. If the vomiting does not resolve within 1 to 2 days or if the child develops moderate to severe dehydration, additional serological, urine, and radiographic studies may be necessary to plan further management.

Medical management for acute vomiting begins with making the child NPO for 2 to 4 hours to allow the vomiting to subside. Offering 15 to 30 cc of clear liquids every 15 to 20 minutes helps to maintain the child's hydration status. If these small volumes are tolerated, the volume may be increased over the next 24 hours. The child may then be placed back on an age-appropriate diet.

### Nursing Assessment and Diagnosis

Nursing assessment begins with a complete history. The history should include onset, duration, and frequency of vomiting. The color and volume of the emesis, in addition to the relationship to feeding, should be determined. The nurse should investigate exposure to possible toxic substances and any associated symptoms.

Physical assessment of the child with vomiting begins with an overall assessment of hydration status (see the discussion of diarrhea for more specific information). Examination of the abdomen may provide additional information for identifying the cause of the vomiting if it is not simply an acute viral process.

Nursing diagnoses for acute vomiting might include the following:

- High risk for fluid volume deficit related to vomiting
- High risk for altered nutrition: less than body requirements related to vomiting

### Planning and Implementing Nursing Care

Nursing care for the child with acute vomiting is focused on assessment of the child for causes that are other than viral. This is accomplished by careful history-taking and physical examination. After this, rehydration takes priority. The nurse should review with parents the plan for oral rehydration and signs of intolerance of oral fluids since these are generally managed at home. Parents should be advised when to call their primary care provider if the problem continues and when to return for a follow-up visit.

### Evaluating Nursing Care

The effectiveness of nursing care is evaluated by cessation of the vomiting and maintenance of adequate hydration. The parents should understand the oral rehydration process and be able to implement it.

## Congenital Problems of Ingestion

Children with problems of ingestion are unable to ingest nutrients normally or cannot process oral feedings. The most common causes are congenital abnormalities.

### Cleft Lip and Palate

#### Pathophysiology

A cleft lip and palate result from incomplete embryonic development. The *cleft lip* is the result of an incomplete fusion of the oral cavity. It may occur alone or in conjunction with a cleft palate. The severity of the defect is variable; it may be unilateral or bilateral, with an indentation in the lip under one nostril to a wide, deep fissure involving the lip and nostril (Fig. 29-2). Generally, the development of the external nose, nasal cartilages, nasal septum, and maxillary alveolar ridges are involved. Dental abnormalities, including missing, malformed, and misplaced teeth are common on the side of the cleft, especially in severe cases.

The *cleft palate* occurs with an incomplete fusion of the primary and secondary palatine plates. As with cleft lips, cleft palates vary in severity. The soft palate may be involved, or the defect may extend through the hard palate, as far forward as the incisive foramen. Wide central palatal clefts are often associated with partial or complete absence of nasal septal development. This results in an extensive communication between the nasal and oral cavity. Occasionally, small clefts occur in the soft palate that are difficult to distinguish from the uvula; small clefts also can occur in the soft palate musculature with an intact mucosa. These lesions may not be recognized until the child is older (Wetmore, 1987).

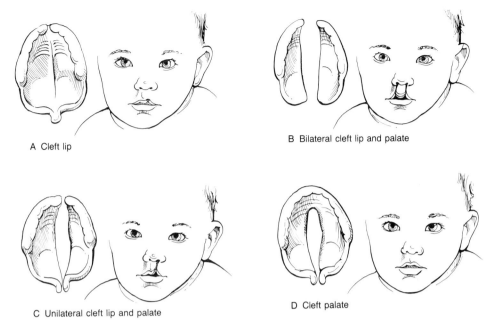

A Cleft lip

B Bilateral cleft lip and palate

C Unilateral cleft lip and palate

D Cleft palate

*Figure 29–2.   Cleft lip and cleft palate.*

## Medical Diagnosis and Management

A cleft lip and most cleft palates are obvious at birth. The appearance of the child is an immediate concern of the parents. Feeding the child with a severe cleft in the lip and palate may be difficult, resulting in leakage of secretions and formula into the nasal cavity. The infant gags and chokes while feeding and frequently develops nasal sinus infections. Speech may be delayed and hypernasal and may involve poor articulation. Eustachian tube function may be impaired, with frequent occurrences of otitis media and chronic otitis media (Wetmore, 1987).

Surgical correction of the cleft lip is usually completed between the ages of 2 to 3 months. A bilateral cleft lip requires a two-stage procedure due to technical difficulties in correcting both clefts at one time. Correction of the cleft palate is delayed until about 18 months. Delay past 18 months of age may result in delayed speech and increased difficulty in attaining a good repair. Repair of the cleft palate may also require a staged procedure. After the repair, many children require speech therapy (Wetmore, 1987).

## Nursing Assessment and Diagnosis

The presence of a cleft lip is evident at birth. The initial assessment documents the location and extent of the defect. The visualization of the cleft palate occurs during crying, and the extent of the lesion is an estimation. If there is no evidence of a cleft lip, then the palate lesion is detected during the newborn assessment by palpating the palate with a finger. The nursing assessment must include the emotional reaction of the parents and family to the child and the defect.

Nursing diagnoses for a cleft lip or palate might include the following:

- Altered nutrition: less than body requirement, related to ineffective sucking
- High risk for aspiration related to cleft palate
- Altered oral mucous membrane related to cleft lip or palate
- Impaired skin integrity related to cleft lip or palate
- High risk for altered parenting related to impaired parent–infant bonding
- Altered family process related to hospitalization of the child

## Planning and Implementing Nursing Care

In planning nursing care for the newborn with cleft lip or palate, it is necessary to determine the goals for preoperative care, postoperative care, and home management. The initial goals are to determine and implement a feeding method and to prepare the infant and family for surgery. It is also important to deal with the parental reaction to the defect. A cleft lip can be severely disfiguring and can produce a strong negative reaction in people. It is important for the nurse to address the concerns of the family regarding the defect and the potential for optimal surgical correction. It is also important for the nurse to emphasize the positive aspects of the infant's appearance.

A cleft lip or palate interferes with the newborn's

ability to suck and to compress the areola of the breast, thus making feeding a challenge to parents and nurses. Early consultation with cleft palate specialists may prevent some of the frustration and defeat of trying to establish a feeding method. With the involvement of the palate, oral feedings often escape through the nose. Feedings are best tolerated in an upright position. Special nipples and feeding devices are often necessary since these babies are unable to generate enough suction to use a normal nipple. A variety of special nipples have been developed and used with varying success. Nipple feeding has the advantage of meeting the infant's need to suck and encourages the use of the sucking muscles, which is important later in speech development. Infants with a cleft lip or palate require careful monitoring during feeding because of a tendency to cough and choke. Frequent burping is advised to alleviate the tendency to swallow large amounts of air with feedings.

Many infants have difficulty using a nipple and require alternative means of feeding. The Breck feeder, a rubber-tipped medicine dropper, and the Asepto syringe provide efficient and safe ways of feeding. All have rubber tubes that extend into the mouth and reduce the reflux of formula through the nose. The formula is delivered to the back of the tongue. The rate of flow of the formula is determined by the nurse or parent in response to the infant's ability to handle the feeding. Occasional spoon-feeding with formula thickened with cereal is necessary. It is important to include the parents in determining the best feeding method for their baby.

Preoperatively, it is important to familiarize the family with the procedure and expectations for multiple future operations. Other aspects of preoperative care are addressed earlier in this chapter.

During the initial postoperative period, the operative site must be protected. Following a cleft lip repair, it may be necessary to protect the suture line from tension caused by facial movements and crying. This is accomplished by taping or using an appliance taped to the infant's cheeks to relax the operative site. The infant's arms should be restrained to prevent rubbing the site. The most effective and humane method is by using elbow restraints that prevent use of the lower arm without restraining total movement. Infants should be placed on their sides with back and abdomen supports to prevent them from rolling onto their abdomen and rubbing the suture line on the linens. The infant's position should be changed frequently, and the family should be encouraged to hold, cuddle, and comfort the child. Arm restraints need to be removed periodically to provide relief and allow for assessment of the underlying skin. Feedings are resumed as soon as they are tolerated. Nipple feeding is avoided until the suture line is well healed. The mouth and suture line must be cleansed after feedings. Meticulous care of the suture line is an important nursing responsibility since optimal healing and an excellent cosmetic repair is the goal.

After the repair of a cleft palate, it is important to avoid using suction or placing foreign objects in the mouth, including thermometers, tongue depressors, or straws. Infants may lie on their abdomen; however, elbow restraints are recommended to keep the hands away from the mouth. Pacifiers are avoided until the suture line is well healed. Diet is advanced as tolerated, with fluids given using a cup. A soft diet is provided until the operative site is well healed to prevent damage to the newly repaired palate.

Home management is initially concentrated on feedings and wound care. As the child grows, the family is faced with many different issues that require the expertise and coordination of many services. It is important that the parents be included in all decisions concerning the care of their child and understand the purpose of consultations and interventions. The ultimate goal for the child and family is health, optimal surgical repair, and normal self-esteem.

### Evaluating Nursing Care

Nursing care is evaluated by assessing the effectiveness of the interventions during the hospitalization and by monitoring the expected outcomes. The child with a cleft lip or palate should be discharged with the following outcomes: the operative site should show evidence of normal healing, with no signs of infection; the child should be adequately nourished, with no signs of aspiration; the infant's skin should remain intact with no evidence of irritation; and the parents and family should demonstrate the ability to care for child and should verbalize their concerns and feelings regarding the child's health problem and health care needs.

## Tracheoesophageal Fistula and Esophageal Atresia

### Pathophysiology

*Esophageal atresia* with or without a *tracheoesophageal fistula* (TEF) occurs in about 1 in 4000 live births, with an increased incidence in mothers with polyhydramnios. The most common anatomical finding is that of a proximal sac with a TEF distal to the end of the esophageal pouch (Dudgeon, 1987d). As with other congenital anomalies, esophageal atresia and TEF are the result of incomplete embryonic development. Many variations of esophageal atresia and TEF are depicted in Figure 29-3.

### Medical Diagnosis and Management

Infants commonly present during the newborn period with coughing, choking, and cyanosis. These symptoms may be followed by increased gastric distention and GER of gastric contents into the distal airway. Some infants do not exhibit respiratory symptoms but have increased salivation and require frequent suctioning. The diagnosis of esophageal atresia is made by attempting to pass an NG or

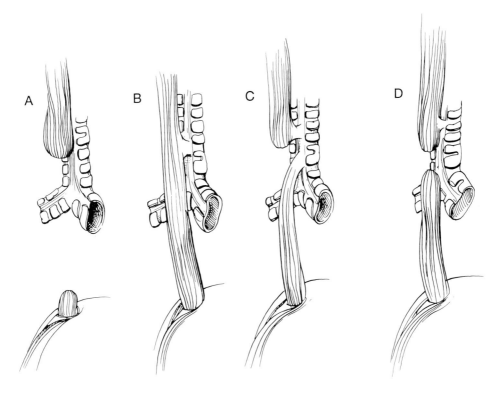

*Figure 29–3.* (A) *Esophageal atresia without tracheoesophageal fistula.* (B) *Tracheoesophageal fistula without atresia.* (C) *Atresia with proximal and distal fistulas.* (D) *Atresia with proximal tracheoesophageal fistula.*

orogastric tube. If an obstruction is met at about 7 to 10 cm, the tube is taped in place, and radiographic confirmation is obtained (Dudgeon, 1987d; Schwartz, 1988). TEF without esophageal atresia may be misdiagnosed in early infancy due to the size and location of the fistula. The frequent respiratory complications are then attributed to other disorders. Continued investigation leads to the diagnosis between 3 months and 2 years of age (Dudgeon, 1987d).

After the diagnosis of esophageal atresia and TEF, medical management focuses on protecting the respiratory system. Continuous aspiration of the esophageal pouch is required, using a soft, sump catheter. The infant's head is elevated to a 30- to 45-degree angle to reduce tracheal contamination. The infant remains NPO and receives intravenous nutrition.

Definitive surgical repair varies depending on the severity of the defect and the age of the child. If the infant is premature, the procedure is often staged, with a gastrostomy tube being placed for decompression soon after diagnosis, followed by a definitive repair. In full-term infants, the surgical repair may be accomplished in one operation.

### Nursing Assessment and Diagnosis

Nursing assessment of the infant with esophageal atresia or TEF begins in the delivery room immediately after birth. The diagnosis is suspected in any infant who has

difficulty managing secretions, who has copious mucus, or who has unexplained episodes of cyanosis. Most infants with TEF have difficulty with the initial feeding. After swallowing normally, the infant coughs and struggles, often returning the fluid through the nose and mouth. Cyanosis results from laryngospasm, which is caused by saliva flowing into the larynx from the proximal esophageal pouch. Any finding leading the nurse to suspect TEF or esophageal atresia must be reported to the physician immediately.

Nursing diagnoses for esophageal atresia and TEF might include the following:

* Altered nutrition: less than body requirements related to obstruction
* High risk for infection related to aspiration
* High risk for fluid volume deficit related to NPO status
* High risk for aspiration related to TEF
* High risk for impaired skin integrity related to surgery
* Altered oral mucous membrane related to NPO status
* High risk for altered parenting related to impaired parent–infant bonding
* Altered family processes related to hospitalization of the child
* Pain related to surgery

### Planning and Implementing Nursing Care

When planning nursing care for infants with TEF, it is important to include the concerns of the parents. Infants with TEF are immediately transferred to the intensive care unit or to another institution that is able to provide the care the child needs. Consequently, the parents are separated from their baby, and bonding is altered. Visitation and communication must be encouraged and facilitated.

Preoperatively, infants with TEF or esophageal atresia have difficulty managing secretions and are at risk for aspiration. Placing the infant in a supine position, with the head of the bed elevated at least 30 degrees minimizes this risk. Frequent suctioning is also imperative. Other aspects of preoperative care were addressed earlier in this chapter.

Care of infants after surgical repair of a TEF is similar to care for any high-risk newborn. Most infants with TEF require insertion of a gastrostomy tube to control air entering the stomach through the fistula and to decrease the risk of GER. After surgery, the gastrostomy tube is placed to straight drainage. The infant remains NPO, and intravenous nutrition is maintained until gastrostomy feeding is tolerated, usually by the 2nd or 3rd day after surgery. Gastrostomy feedings continue until the anastomotic site is healed, generally 7 days later. A barium swallow is done to evaluate the repair for leaks. At this time, oral feedings are restarted with care. Oral needs of the infant who is NPO can be met with a pacifier. Infants who require a staged repair are discharged on gastrostomy feedings. Many infants with esophageal atresia require a cervical esophagoscopy to drain the upper esophageal pouch until the surgical repair is completed. This may result in secretions irritating the skin surrounding the stoma. Careful maintenance of the site alleviates the problem.

It is not uncommon for the child with TEF and esophageal atresia to have difficulty swallowing and eating, especially if the child was unable to eat for prolonged periods of time. It often becomes necessary to teach the child to eat at a later age. Referral to a feeding specialist may be advised.

### Evaluating Nursing Care

Nursing care is evaluated through continual reassessment and monitoring of expected outcomes. Evaluation criteria for the infant who has undergone surgery were discussed earlier in the chapter.

## Diaphragmatic Hernia

### Pathophysiology

A *diaphragmatic hernia* results when the fetal diaphragm fails to develop, allowing abdominal organs to enter the thorax and interfere with the normal growth of the lungs. This defect occurs in about 1 in 2000 live births. The mortality associated with a diaphragmatic hernia is about 50% because of the pulmonary hypoplasia (Wesson, 1991c; Gregory & Kitterman, 1987).

### Medical Diagnosis and Management

The most common symptom of a diaphragmatic hernia in a newborn is acute respiratory failure. Older infants and children may present with dyspnea, intermittent abdominal pain, or vomiting related to a bowel obstruction (Wesson, 1991c).

On physical examination, the infant with a diaphragmatic hernia has decreased breath sounds on the side of the hernia. On percussion, the affected area may produce a dull sound rather than the resonance that is heard when a healthy lung field is percussed. The diagnosis of diaphragmatic hernia is made by chest and abdominal radiographs, which reveal abdominal organs in the chest cavity. A UGI or barium enema may be used to confirm the diagnosis (Gregory & Kitterman, 1987; Wesson, 1991c).

On diagnosis, the infant with a diaphragmatic hernia is stabilized before surgical repair. Extracorporeal membrane oxygenation helps to decrease lung damage. All infants require ventilatory support after surgical repair of a diaphragmatic hernia (Nugent, 1986).

### Nursing Assessment and Diagnosis

Nursing assessment of the infant with a diaphragmatic hernia begins in the delivery room. An infant with respiratory distress or respiratory failure should be carefully evaluated. Infants who develop dyspnea, tachypnea, cyanosis, and acidosis are also at risk.

Nursing diagnoses for diaphragmatic hernia might include the following:

- Ineffective breathing pattern related to decreased lung volume
- Altered nutrition: potential for less than body requirements related to surgery and decreased pulmonary function
- High risk for infection related to surgery
- Altered GI tissue perfusion related to diaphragmatic hernia
- High risk for altered parenting related to interruption of the bonding/attachment process
- Altered family process related to hospitalization
- Pain related to surgery

### Planning and Implementing Nursing Care

Preoperative nursing care of the infant with a diaphragmatic hernia follows the guidelines discussed earlier in the chapter. Special attention should be paid to minimizing decompensation of the infant's respiratory status by consoling the infant to minimize crying. A pacifier should be offered frequently. The infant should be placed in a semi-Fowler position to decrease intrathorax pressure. Suction and oxygen should be readily available. Postoperative care was addressed earlier in the chapter.

### Evaluating Nursing Care

The success of nursing interventions is evaluated by the infant's stable respiratory function, freedom from infection, and ability to eat sufficiently to sustain growth. The parents should be able to demonstrate their understanding of the diagnosis, therapy, surgical procedure, and anticipated outcomes. They should be able to verbalize concerns about the infant's health problem and identify and use appropriate resources.

# Ingestion Problems of Infants and Children

## Gastroesophageal Reflux

### Pathophysiology

*Gastroesophageal reflux* is the return of stomach contents into the esophagus. It is the result of a neuromuscular failure of the lower esophageal sphincter. The major features of the syndrome are effortless vomiting, failure to gain weight, and aspiration pneumonia. GER may exist without obvious vomiting and may produce such complications as protein-losing enteropathy, neuropsychiatric syndromes, and apnea.

It is estimated that GER occurs in 1 in 500 live births. Most children present by 6 weeks of age, with symptoms of vomiting or failure to thrive, and outgrow the syndrome by about 18 months of age. The greatest improvement occurs at about 8 to 10 months of age when the child sits upright. Fifty percent of children with GER require medical evaluation and therapy of some kind.

None of the symptoms of GER are classical, making diagnosis difficult. The primary symptom associated with GER includes unexplained vomiting or regurgitation. This is seen in 90% of infants diagnosed with GER and varies in degree of severity. If GER is not diagnosed shortly after onset, weight loss, failure to thrive, and anemia may also become evident.

*Esophagitis* is not a symptom but a complication of GER. Older children who are able to describe their symptoms often complain of substernal burning and upper abdominal discomfort, both of which are related to esophagitis. Esophagitis results from the recurrent irritation of the esophageal mucosa by acidic gastric juices. Irritability during feedings or the refusal to eat are indications of GER, especially if there is a previous history of unexplained vomiting. The probable cause of this difficulty is an esophageal stricture, which is a late symptom of GER. This is the result of esophageal scarring and is seen most frequently in neurologically impaired children. If bleeding esopha-

gitis has developed, there may be sufficient blood loss to cause anemia and occult blood in the stools. Occasionally, blood-tinged vomitus may be observed.

Pulmonary symptoms or complications have been linked to GER. Aspiration pneumonitis, bronchitis, or pneumonia is seen in 15% to 30% of infants later diagnosed as having GER. Persistent pulmonary disorders, such as asthma in older children, have been linked with GER, as have apnea and sudden infant death syndrome (Hillemeier, 1991).

### Medical Diagnosis and Management

The diagnostic evaluation of a child with suspected GER begins with a thorough history. Inspection of the child may reveal a torticollis. It is felt that infants with GER position themselves in this manner to relieve the pain accompanying the esophagitis. The child's growth pattern must be established and evidence of malnutrition evaluated. The respiratory examination may reveal wheezing, rales, or congestion. A rectal examination is done to check for guaiac-positive stools. Laboratory data of CBC and chemistry panel are necessary to determine the presence and degree of anemia as well as any biochemical abnormalities that accompany recurrent vomiting, dehydration, and malnutrition. Diagnostic procedures follow in a systematic order in most instances. A UGI series may be done on a child suspected of having GER. A chest radiograph may document pulmonary infiltrates resulting from aspiration, which may lead to suspicion of GER, especially in infants.

A variety of other diagnostic tests are used, including a milk/gastric *scintiscan* to evaluate gastric emptying; *esophageal manometry* to document esophageal motility; and prolonged pH monitoring to document the presence of acidic gastric contents in the esophagus. The normal pH of the esophagus is 6 to 7. A diagnosis of GER is confirmed if the pH in the esophagus is less than 4 for an extended period of time. Upper endoscopy is also used to visualize and document mucosal changes due to esophagitis.

In a child with uncomplicated GER, the self-limiting factor of the disease may preclude the need for medical therapy. Most babies have some degree of GER, and good anticipatory guidance is all the parents require to allow them to manage successfully without significant medical intervention. Traditional noninvasive therapy consists of upright positioning, thickened feedings, and small, frequent feedings. Positioning the infant at a 45- to 60-degree angle in an infant seat or car seat has been standard procedure for many years. It has recently been shown, however, that placing a child supine with the head of the infant's crib elevated 45 degrees is more beneficial than upright positioning (Orenstein & Whittingham, 1983). To prevent the baby from sliding, rolls of blankets or sandbags may be propped against their bottom, or a sling can be used (Fig. 29-4). Commercial wedges and slings are also available.

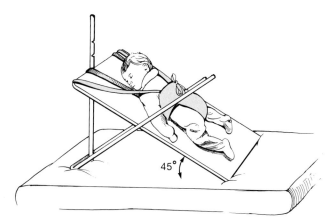

*Figure 29–4.  Child in a sling with the head of the crib elevated 45 degrees.*

Thickened feedings are effective since it is more difficult to regurgitate a heavier mass. Small, frequent feedings allow for adequate gastric emptying and decrease the chance of vomiting.

Many infants require medications to promote recovery. Bethanechol, a cholinergic agent, is used to treat GER since it elevates the LES pressure. Metoclopramide is also used to treat GER since it promotes gastric emptying. Antacids, cimetidine, and ranitidine are used to neutralize the gastric contents, thus decreasing esophageal irritation.

Overnight continuous NG feedings are also used to treat GER in selected infants. This has proved effective in infants with poor weight gain and delayed gastric emptying. It provides for optimal caloric intake and has a soothing effect on an irritated esophagus.

Failure to respond to medical therapy or the delayed diagnosis of GER may require surgical intervention. Children with severe neurological damage often require surgical therapy, known as a *fundoplication.*

### Nursing Assessment and Diagnosis

Assessment of the child with GER begins with observation of the child's general appearance and behavior. It is important to obtain height, weight, and head circumference measurements to determine if the child is failing to thrive. It is also important to obtain an accurate feeding history to determine what methods have been attempted to eliminate or alleviate the vomiting.

Nursing diagnoses for GER might include the following:

- Pain related to esophageal irritation from acidic gastric juices
- High risk for aspiration related to vomiting
- Ineffective airway clearance related to positioning
- Altered family process related to parental anxiety
- High risk for fluid volume deficit related to vomiting

- Altered nutrition: less than body requirements related to vomiting

### Planning and Implementing Nursing Care

Parental reassurance is central to planning and implementing nursing care for children with GER. As stated previously, the traditional therapy for GER is positioning, thickened feedings, and small frequent feedings. Reassuring the parents that children do outgrow this problem is often the most useful information they will receive. If surgery is required, then the nursing care must reflect the pre- and postoperative management discussed earlier in this chapter. Discharge instructions must be clear and fully understood by the parents.

### Evaluating Nursing Care

The effectiveness of the nursing interventions is evaluated by a decrease in the frequency of vomiting. Improvement in growth and development is also easily measured. Most important is the parents' comfort with the diagnosis and their confidence in being able to care for the child at home.

## Herpes Stomatitis

### Pathophysiology

Herpes simplex is a virus that is spread by person-to-person contact. Once infected, the person becomes a carrier and may spread the virus from obvious lesions or through virus in the mucous membranes (Scott, 1987). *Herpes stomatitis* is caused by type 1 herpes simplex virus. It typically occurs in young children between 2 and 4 years of age (Wetmore, 1987). The child may have a high fever for 1 to 2 days before the oral lesions appear. The oral vesicles erupt, leaving small, shallow ulcerations and red, swollen gingiva. The oral lesions are painful, and the child may begin to drool, causing the development of lesions around the mouth. The pain usually subsides by 5 days after onset. Submandibular lymphadenopathy may also be present (Scott, 1987).

### Medical Diagnosis and Management

Diagnosis is based on the child's clinical presentation. Herpes simplex antibody titers may be measured in the serum to differentiate between a primary and recurrent infection (Scott, 1987).

Poor oral intake and dehydration are common disorders due to the painful oral lesions. Analgesic mouthwashes used before eating may provide some relief. Antiviral agents, such as acyclovir, may be used topically, orally, or intravenously.

### Nursing Assessment and Diagnosis

Assessment of oral intake and hydration are important to ensure that the painful lesions are not significantly interfering with the child's nutritional status. The child's level of discomfort should be assessed as well as the effectiveness of the analgesic mouthwash, if used. The family's understanding of the diagnosis, the child's infectious status, and the plan of care should also be assessed.

Nursing diagnoses for herpes stomatitis might include the following:

- Pain related to lesions
- Altered nutrition: less than body requirements related to decreased intake
- Altered oral mucous membrane related to lesions

### Planning and Implementing Nursing Care

Children with herpes stomatitis are managed as outpatients in most cases. The nurse should discuss the use of analgesic mouthwash immediately before eating to promote better intake. Reviewing signs and symptoms of dehydration with parents is important so that parents know when to call for follow-up care. Parents should also be educated about the spread of the virus, proper handwashing techniques, and the need not to share eating utensils.

### Evaluating Nursing Care

The effectiveness of the nursing care may be evaluated by relief of pain, nutritional maintenance, and prevention of spread of infection. The family should demonstrate an understanding of the plan of care and their comfort with following the plan.

## Ingestion of Foreign Bodies

### Pathophysiology

Foreign body ingestion is a common pediatric problem. Although toddlers and preschoolers are notorious for placing foreign objects in their mouths, this problem is reported in all age groups. Buttons, coins, batteries, small toys, and pen caps are often ingested. Fortunately, most ingested foreign objects pass into the stomach and through the intestines without causing problems. Signs and symptoms of respiratory distress, bowel obstruction, or bowel perforation are indications for immediate action and removal of the object.

### Medical Diagnosis and Management

Foreign body ingestion is generally diagnosed by the history. Frequently, the parents tell the nurse or physician that the child has swallowed the object. The management of the problem varies depending on the object ingested and the child's symptoms.

After a complete history and physical examination, the child should have an abdominal radiograph and a possibly a chest radiograph to locate the position of the foreign body. Objects found in the esophagus should be removed immediately with an endoscope. Blunt objects, such as buttons and coins, that are located in the stomach may be allowed to pass through the intestines as long as there are no associated symptoms, such as abdominal pain, vomiting, or fever. Progression of the object through the intestines should be followed with monthly abdominal radiographs. There is no evidence that the use of laxatives or special diets promotes the passage of the foreign body (Wesson, 1991d). If the child complains of any associated symptoms that might indicate an intestinal obstruction or perforation, the object should be surgically removed as quickly as possible. Sharp objects, such as pins, may also be followed with weekly radiographs, unless signs or symptoms of complications develop (Wesson, 1991d).

There has been much concern about the appropriate management of the ingestion of the small batteries used in cameras, hearing aids, and watches. These batteries contain caustic chemicals that may irritate and damage the GI mucosa. Litovitz (1985) reported that 90% of the batteries ingested passed uneventfully through the intestines in less than 2 weeks. Progress of the batteries should be followed with weekly abdominal radiographs and should only be surgically removed if complications develop.

### Nursing Assessment and Diagnosis

Most children who ingest foreign bodies are taken to the emergency room or a pediatrician's office. Nursing assessment should focus on identifying the object that was ingested as well as evaluating the child for respiratory distress and signs or symptoms or GI complications. Vomiting may indicate an obstruction or perforation of the bowel. The temperature should be measured to assess for fever resulting from peritonitis. The nurse should examine the child's chest and observe respirations for signs of distress or increased respiratory effort. The abdominal examination should focus on localizing any pain that may be present and observing the child for signs of a bowel obstruction or peritonitis, including change in bowel sounds and distended abdomen. In most cases, this problem is followed on an outpatient basis, so it is imperative that the nurse assess the parents' level of anxiety and their understanding of the treatment and follow-up plan.

Nursing diagnoses for ingestion of foreign bodies might include the following:

- Ineffective airway clearance related to ingestion of foreign body
- High risk for infection related to bowel perforation

- Anxiety (parental) related to child's condition and possible guilt
- Fear (child) related to procedures

### Planning and Implementing Nursing Care

Once the child has been evaluated for complications that require immediate medical or surgical intervention, the nurse should review the treatment plan with the parents and the child. The parents may require reassurance that their child is likely to pass this foreign body without any complications. The plan for following the progress of the object should be explained to the parents. Family education addressing the need to observe the stools for the object should be discussed. Parents should be taught the signs and symptoms of the complications that may occur and how to manage them. Should endoscopic or surgical removal of the object become necessary, the parents and child will need support and education to prepare them for the procedure. The nurse must also address the issue of preventing this problem from recurring.

### Evaluating Nursing Care

Nursing care may be evaluated by the child's passing the ingested object without complications and the parents' demonstrated understanding of the information provided to them. Whether or not the child has multiple episodes of foreign body ingestion may be valuable information about the effectiveness of the prevention education and the anticipatory guidance provided.

## Ingestion of Corrosive Substances

In the early 1970s, there was an epidemic of household ingestions of liquid lye cleaners (Leape, Ashcraft, Scrapilli, & Holder, 1971). The incidence has decreased due to child-resistant packaging, but drain cleaners continue to have alkali concentrations high enough to cause significant injury if ingested. Home pregnancy tests also contain a high concentration of alkali (Grenga, 1983). Alkali ingestions result primarily in oral and esophageal injuries.

Acid ingestions occur less often, and esophageal injury is typically less severe. Stronger acids cause ulceration and perforation to the stomach and duodenum.

### Pathophysiology

Alkali substances cause rapid liquefying necrosis in the skin, mouth, and esophagus and result in second- and third-degree burns. During the first 48 hours after ingestion, the body's inflammatory response causes edema. Two to four days later, the necrotic tissue at the burn sites begins to slough, and the edema recedes. Over the next 2 weeks, as the esophagus heals, there is a proliferation of fibrotic tissue, followed by collagen deposits (Moore,

1986). This process leads to stricture formation. Mediastinitis and peritonitis may be associated with second- and third-degree burns of the esophagus, as is perforation. Ulcerations may take several months to heal.

### Medical Diagnosis and Management

Children who ingest caustic substances have immediate symptoms. Oropharyngeal burns may be evident. There is no correlation between the severity of oropharyngeal burns and esophageal burns. Children with third-degree esophageal burns or perforation become acutely ill and typically have a fever, tachycardia, and possibly shock. Additional symptoms may include drooling, chest pain, and dysphagia. Respiratory symptoms such as stridor may present at any time depending on the degree of injury to the glottis and trachea. Aspiration of a caustic substance may be confirmed by radiograph.

Vomiting should not be induced. There is a risk of increasing the esophageal injury with regurgitation of the alkali solution, in addition to the risk of aspiration. The child who has ingested caustic substances should be admitted to the hospital for immediate aspiration of the stomach, followed by cool-water lavage. Intravenous fluids are started, and the child remains NPO until after the endoscopy. Endoscopy is performed to evaluate the degree of esophageal injury and assess for signs of fibrotic tissue and stricture formation. If there is no evidence of esophageal burns, the child may be discharged.

Children with first-degree burns are generally observed in the hospital for 1 to 2 days. Usually, fluids are tolerated by the 2nd day, and the diet may be advanced as tolerated. Treatment with antibiotics and steroids for several weeks is used for all children with severe oropharyngeal burns or esophageal burns. Both steroids and antibiotics help to reduce stricture formation (Postlethwait, 1983).

### Nursing Assessment and Diagnosis

Assessment begins with physical examination of the child. The face and hands are checked for burns, but the chest and lower extremities should also be examined for splash burns from the substance. The child's respiratory status should be assessed repeatedly for stridor and difficulty breathing. The child's inability to swallow or manage oral secretions may indicate potential trauma to the esophagus. Signs and symptoms of perforation include acute onset of chest pain, fever, and tachycardia, so the child's vital signs are essential information.

After the child's immediate condition has stabilized, nursing assessment focuses on the child's ability to tolerate oral fluids and the family's understanding of the plan for endoscopy, medication, and medical follow-up treatment.

Nursing diagnosis for ingestion of a caustic substance might include the following:

- Impaired tissue integrity related to burns
- Pain related to burns
- Impaired swallowing related to pain
- Altered nutrition: less than body requirements related to difficulty swallowing
- Altered family processes related to the need for immediate care

### Planning and Implementing Nursing Care

Once the assessment of the child has been completed, the nurse implements direct care. The child's skin should be cleansed to prevent spread of the substance to other areas of the body. Gastric aspiration of the corrosive substance is necessary. This is followed by cool-water lavage of the stomach. The nurse should monitor the child's vital signs during this procedure to assess for signs of shock. After this acute care, the child's hydration status should be evaluated and intravenous fluids administered as directed by the physician. The child and the parents need education to prepare them for the endoscopy.

As the child is offered oral fluids, an accurate intake and output record is necessary to assess hydration status and feeding tolerance. Difficulty swallowing and vomiting may be signs of stricture formation. Before discharge, the child and parents need education about signs and symptoms of stricture formation, diet advancement, medications (if discharged on oral antibiotics), and the follow-up plan. Finally, information about how to prevent caustic ingestion and poisonings in the future is necessary.

### Evaluating Nursing Care

Nursing care may be evaluated by determining patient outcomes and the child and parent's understanding of prevention measures. Patient outcomes include adequate nutrition and hydration and relief from pain. The child and family should demonstrate an understanding of prevention, home care, and follow-up care.

## Acetaminophen Ingestion

### Pathophysiology

Acetaminophen is commonly used as an analgesic and antipyretic and is rapidly absorbed after oral ingestion. The peak plasma level occurs between 30 and 60 minutes after ingestion. With overdose ingestion, however, the peak level may be delayed an additional 3 hours. Acetaminophen is metabolized by the liver, most which becomes an inert metabolite. A small percentage (about 4%) is conjugated to a metabolite that is toxic to the liver (Rumack, 1987). In an overdose, these toxic metabolites build up and cause hepatic necrosis by interfering with hepatocyte function (Black, 1980).

### Medical Diagnosis and Management

According to Rumack (1987), there are four stages in the course of acetaminophen poisoning. During the first 24 hours, the child presents with general malaise, nausea, vomiting, and diaphoresis. In stage 2, the child's plasma level may exceed toxic levels by 6 to 14 hours after ingestion. In stage 3, other biochemical parameters, such as liver function, peak during the 2nd to 4th day after ingestion. A liver biopsy at this time would show centrilobular necrosis. During stage 4, about 1 week after the ingestion, the toxicity resolves. Long-term follow-up examination (3 months to 1 year) shows no sequelae.

Management of the child with acetaminophen toxicity is based on a plasma level drawn at the peak of toxicity, about 4 to 6 hours after ingestion. If hepatotoxicity is suspected, the child should be treated with N-acetylcysteine (Mucomyst), which should be given within the first 16 hours of ingestion to be most effective. The child is given 1 loading dose, followed by a dose every 4 hours for a total of 8 doses.

Emetic or absorptive agents may be used when the child is initially seen. These interventions decrease the available acetaminophen for absorption and can be used as long as they do not interfere with the initiation of Mucomyst therapy. The child is also assessed for changes in cardiorespiratory function.

### Nursing Assessment and Diagnosis

Assessment of the child with acetaminophen poisoning begins with a complete history and physical examination. The nurse should determine the strength of the acetaminophen that was ingested, the volume ingested, and time of ingestion as well as any antidote therapy given before hospitalization. An overall assessment of the child may reveal physical signs of toxicity, such as general malaise or diaphoresis. Initial vital signs provide important baseline information about systemic manifestations of toxicity.

Nursing diagnoses for acetaminophen poisoning might include the following:

- High risk for poisoning related to acetaminophen ingestion
- Fluid volume deficit related to nausea and vomiting
- Pain related to nausea and vomiting
- High risk for aspiration related to vomiting
- High risk for violence: self-directed related to possible suicide attempt

### Planning and Implementing Nursing Care

The goals of nursing care are removal of the poison; observation of latent toxic effects; implementation of medical therapy for complications; and prevention of recurrent poisoning. Syrup of ipecac may be given to the child with acetaminophen poisoning. Reassurance for the child and family about the effects of ipecac may be helpful during this uncomfortable phase of therapy. Monitoring the child's intake and output are important to ensure that adequate hydration is maintained. Late toxic effects of acetaminophen poisoning are monitored biochemically; however, frequent vital signs and evaluation of level of consciousness may provide cues about systemic effects.

Prevention of recurrent poisoning is essential. Determination of whether this poisoning was accidental or purposeful is necessary so that appropriate education and referrals can be made.

### Evaluating Nursing Care

Positive outcomes of nursing care for the child with acetaminophen poisoning include the following: emetic and adsorbent agents are administered in a timely manner; the child does not aspirate emesis; signs and symptoms of toxicity are anticipated in observations and documented; the child and family demonstrate an understanding of prevention strategies; and appropriate supportive referrals are initiated.

## Congenital Problems of Digestion

### Biliary Atresia

*Biliary atresia* is the absence of the extrahepatic biliary system between the hilus of the liver and the duodenum. The extent of involvement varies; however, there is complete obstruction of bile flow, resulting in biliary cirrhosis. Biliary atresia also occurs in infants with situs inversus (abdominal organs reversed) and polysplenia syndrome (multiple small spleens). The term *intrahepatic biliary atresia* applies to intrahepatic bile duct paucity (Alagille's syndrome) and should not be confused with biliary atresia.

### Pathophysiology

Biliary atresia is generally not a failure of embryological development. It is an acquired lesion that probably begins late in fetal or early in neonatal life. It may be associated with congenital malformations and anomalies, suggesting more than one etiology that leads to a final common outcome. Many etiologies have been explored, but no definitive cause has been identified. Biliary atresia rarely occurs in siblings within a family (Piccoli & Witzleban, 1991b).

Infants with biliary atresia are generally full-term and appear healthy, despite being jaundiced. The gestational history is unremarkable. Appetite and weight gain are initially normal, but stools become progressively pale during the first weeks of life. The infant initially may have

physiological jaundice, which develops into hyperbilirubinemia. This is generally recognized between 2 and 6 weeks of age when the urine becomes dark and the stools become pale. The total serum bilirubin is between 6 and 12 mg/dL, with a conjugated fraction of 50% to 80% of the total (Piccoli & Witzleban, 1991b). Serum aminotransferases (ALT, AST) are mildly elevated, while the alkaline phosphatase and gamma glutamyltransferase are markedly elevated. Physical examination reveals hepatomegaly; and often, splenomegaly is seen as well.

### Medical Diagnosis and Management

No one test confirms the diagnosis of biliary atresia. An abdominal ultrasound excludes other causes of obstructive jaundice, such as choledochal cyst. The patency of the extrahepatic biliary system is demonstrated by a nuclear scintiscan. A percutaneous liver biopsy is performed. The histological finding of intrahepatic bile duct proliferation suggests a mechanical obstruction, indicating the need for laparotomy and operative cholangiogram. If the extrahepatic system cannot be demonstrated by cholangiogram, then surgical intervention is necessary.

The most common surgical procedure performed to establish bile flow is the Kasai hepatoportoenterostomy. The residual biliary system is removed. The surface of the liver is dissected, an area through which bile can drain is exposed, and a limb of jejunum is attached in a Roux-en-Y fashion to maintain the patency of the intestine and allow bile drainage into the intestine (Fig. 29-5). Success of the procedure varies depending on the age of the child at the time of surgery, with best results occurring in infants 90 days of age or younger.

Long-term prognosis is guarded in infants with biliary atresia. Establishment of bile flow and resolution of the jaundice appears to be correlated to the best outcome. Patients who remain jaundiced require liver transplantation by the age of 8 years, while those with established bile flow and resolution of jaundice have a 90% chance of surviving past age 10 years without further intervention. Survival to the third decade with a high quality of life has been reported (Piccoli & Witzleban, 1991b).

Cholangitis is the most common complication of the Kasai procedure. It is most frequent during the first 2 years after surgery. It must be considered with any febrile illness after surgical intervention for biliary atresia. Aggressive intravenous antibiotic therapy is indicated. Chronic prophylaxis with oral antibiotics is also recommended.

### Neonatal Liver Disease

*Neonatal liver disease* is a group of obstructive or metabolic diseases that result in liver dysfunction in the newborn. Although it does not occur during the neonatal period, Wilson disease is included here since medical and nursing management for Wilson disease are similar to

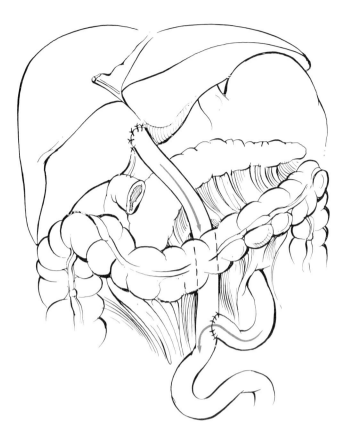

*Figure 29–5. Kasai procedure.*

those for other liver diseases of childhood and adolescence.

A *choledochal cyst* is a congenital cystic dilatation of the common bile duct. It causes obstructive jaundice, resulting in dilatation of the extrahepatic and intrahepatic bile ducts. It is more common in females and has a much higher incidence in the Far East (Piccoli & Witzleban, 1991b). The etiology of the choledochal cyst remains unclear.

*Arteriohepatic dysplasia* (Alagille syndrome) is characterized by a marked reduction of intrahepatic bile ducts and cholestasis. It occurs in association with cardiac, vertebral, ocular, facial, renal, and neurodevelopmental abnormalities. It is a familial disease that has a wide variation in clinical symptoms in affected individuals. The incidence of Alagille syndrome is 1 in 100,000 births, with an equal sex distribution (Mueller, 1987). It is believed that Alagille syndrome is an inherited disorder; however, sporadic cases may occur. The exact genetic marker and autosomal penetration have not been determined (Piccoli & Witzleban, 1991a).

$\alpha_1$-*Antitrypsin deficiency* is the most common metabolic disease for children who undergo liver transplantation. It is an autosomal recessive disorder that results in low serum concentrations of $\alpha_1$-antitrypsin. The consequences include premature pulmonary emphysema and

chronic liver disease in infants and children. In the United States, the prevalence has been described as 1 in 2000 people. It is more common among whites of Northern European ancestry (Perlmutter, 1991). The mechanism by which $\alpha_1$-antitrypsin deficiency causes liver disease is not understood.

### Medical Management

The medical management of neonatal liver disease requires careful monitoring of liver function. This is accomplished through routine follow-up examination, with review of biochemical parameters. The goals of therapy are aimed at minimizing systemic consequences while maximizing growth and development. Vitamin supplementation with water-soluble vitamins and nutritional interventions are initiated at the time of diagnosis (Table 29-3).

In children with chronic liver disease, portal hypertension results from impaired blood flow to or through the liver. Portal hypertension is caused by cirrhotic changes (intrahepatic scarring) that collapse and distort the hepatic vasculature. Portal hypertension can occur at any stage of liver disease. Splenomegaly is generally the first sign in children. Hematemesis, melena, nosebleeds, or an unexplained decrease in hemoglobin level may also indicate portal hypertension; massive hematemesis is usually the first symptom in children.

Orthotopic liver transplantation is now considered a therapeutic modality for end-stage liver disease and intractable variceal hemorrhage in pediatrics.

## Wilson Disease

### Pathophysiology

Wilson disease is an autosomal recessive disorder of copper metabolism, in which excessive copper accumulates in the liver, brain, kidneys, cornea, and skeletal systems with inadequate excretion (Frommer, 1974). Hepatic disease

*Table 29–3. Vitamin Supplementation for Chronic Liver Disease*

| Medication | Dosage | Indications |
|---|---|---|
| Vitamin A | 5000 IU/day | Neuropathy; retinopathy |
| Vitamin D | 4000 IU/day | Rickets |
| Vitamin E Succinate | 400 IU/day | Neuropathy |
| TPGS | 25 mg/kg/day | Abnormal extraocular movement |
| Vitamin K | 5 mg/week unless PT/PTT abnormal | Coagulopathy |

Levels are monitored and doses changed accordingly.

occurs when the copper overload leads to the destruction of liver tissue. It occurs in 1 in 30,000 people. Presentation is usually in childhood; however, the diagnosis may not be confirmed until adulthood.

### Medical Diagnosis and Management

The clinical symptoms of Wilson disease rarely present before the age of 5 and are usually seen during adolescence. Hepatic dysfunction is the most common presentation in children; however, the diagnosis must be considered in older children and adolescents with neurological abnormalities. Symptoms may include malaise, anorexia, and lethargy. Signs of progressive liver disease, such as jaundice, petechiae, hematemesis, and ascites, may also be seen. Neurological symptoms include gradual onset of clumsiness, dysarthria, drooling, tremors, loss of fine motor skills, and psychological disturbances.

Most children with Wilson disease have a low serum level of the copper-binding protein, so urinary copper excretion is usually elevated. A liver biopsy may be necessary to determine the amount of actual copper in the liver. Asymptomatic siblings should also be screened for Wilson disease.

Treatment of Wilson disease is aimed at improving the excretion of copper and decreasing dietary intake of copper-containing foods. Penicillamine is a sulfa-containing amino acid that chelates the copper, which is then excreted in the urine. There is usually dramatic improvement in symptoms with the initiation of therapy. Dietary restriction of copper-containing foods, including liver, shellfish, nuts, cocoa, chocolate, and mushrooms, is recommended.

### Nursing Assessment and Diagnosis

Nursing assessment of the infant or child with chronic liver disease requires a careful history and physical examination. The nurse should obtain information regarding dietary intake and stooling pattern, including consistency, frequency, volume, color, and presence of blood. It is also important to determine changes in the child's personality or behavior, including sleeping patterns. The nurse should assess for the signs and symptoms of infection and systemic consequences, including fever, jaundice, pruritus, xanthomas, petechiae, edema, ascites, hematemesis, and melanotic stools. Delays in growth and development are an anticipated consequence of chronic liver dysfunction. The child should be assessed for progressive accomplishment of developmental milestones.

Physical examination provides key information about the child's nutritional status and overall well-being. Accurate length, weight, and head circumference measurements should be obtained and plotted on the growth chart and compared with previous growth data. Vital signs provide important baseline information about systemic function. Examination of the skin may reveal jaundice, xanthomas, lesions resulting from scratching, petechiae, and

prominent subcutaneous vessels. Sclera and mucous membranes may also be icteric. A cardiac murmur may be associated with some types of chronic liver disease. Examination of the abdomen frequently reveals hepatosplenomegaly. Ascites may also be evident. There may be decreased strength and muscle tone as a systemic consequence. Muscle wasting may occur as a result of malnutrition.

Nursing diagnoses for chronic liver disease might include the following:

- Altered nutrition: less than body requirements related to malabsorption and anorexia
- High risk for infection related to altered immune status and surgery
- High risk for fluid volume deficit related to decreased intake
- Decreased cardiac output related to altered blood flow
- Altered GI tissue perfusion related to altered vasculature
- High risk for impaired skin integrity related to malabsorption
- Sensory/perceptual alteration related to neuropathies resulting from vitamin E deficiency
- Altered family processes related to having a child with chronic illness

### Planning and Implementing Nursing Care

Nursing care of infants with chronic liver disease is primarily supportive. Vital signs are taken routinely, with the frequency determined by the child's status. In some instances, intravenous hydration may be necessary. In most cases, infants are able to tolerate oral nutrition. Supplementation of vitamins in water-soluble preparations is essential (see Table 29-3). Medications may be prescribed to control and minimize pruritus. These include phenobarbital, cholestyramine, ursodeoxycholic acid, and rifampin. Careful attention to skin integrity is important in preventing infection. Application of lubricating lotions and trimming the child's fingernails may help in preventing self-inflicted lesions.

The concerns and educational needs of the parents and family must be addressed. Education should include discussion of the diagnosis, disease process, and the medical and surgical plan of care. Nutritional requirements and interventions, medications, growth and development, and evidence of progressive disease must also be discussed. The schedule for routine health maintenance should be outlined for the family. Information regarding supportive services, including community resources, also should be made available to the family.

### Evaluating Nursing Care

Nursing care is evaluated through continual reassessment and monitoring of expected outcomes. The outcomes for the child and family with chronic liver disease include the following: the surgical incision or biopsy site should be healing normally and remain free from infection; the child's growth and development should be maximized; the family should demonstrate an understanding of nutritional interventions and medication administration, including vitamin supplementation; skin integrity should be maintained; and self-inflicted lesions should be minimized. The parents and family should be able to verbalize their concern and feelings regarding the child's problem, and they should demonstrate their understanding of procedures, the diagnosis, and expected outcomes. The family should also be able to identify and use appropriate resources.

## Intestinal Atresia

*Intestinal atresia* is the complete obstruction of the lumen of the bowel. There are several types of intestinal atresia, which can involve the duodenum, jejunum, ileum, and colon. Duodenal atresia occurs in 1 in 30,000 live births, with a high incidence in children with Down syndrome. Duodenal atresia is also associated with other congenital anomalies, including esophageal atresia, malrotation, imperforate anus, and congenital heart disease (Wesson, 1991b). Jejunal atresia and ileal atresia are more common than duodenal atresia, with the reported incidence varying from 1 in 332 to 1 in 5000 births (Grosfeld, 1986). Associated anomalies are less common than with duodenal atresia. Colonic atresia occurs in about 1 in 40,000 live births (Grosfeld, 1986).

### Pathophysiology

Intestinal atresia is thought to be the result of an intrauterine event, such as arterial occlusion, volvulus, or intussusception. The cause leads to necrosis of the intestine, which is then reabsorbed, leaving blind proximal and distal ends, often accompanied by a gap in the mesentery. Peristalsis causes increased dilation at the end farthest from the obstruction. After the repair, the dilated segment may have ineffective peristalsis, leading to a functional obstruction and poorly coordinated muscle activity (Wesson, 1991b).

### Medical Diagnosis and Management

Neonatal intestinal atresia is associated with polyhydramnios in half of all cases. The diagnosis of intestinal atresia can be made in utero by sonogram; however, it should be confirmed at birth. Infants with an intestinal obstruction present with bilious vomiting and abdominal distention and fail to pass meconium. The abdomen may be grossly distended, with visible and palpable loops of bowel. The infant may also be jaundiced. Diagnosis is made by radiographic studies.

The initial treatment is aimed at stabilizing the infant with intravenous fluids, NG suction, and correction of fluid

and electrolyte imbalances. Once this is accomplished, surgical repair of the atretic segment or segments is undertaken. It is always preferable to have an end-to-end anastomosis of the resected bowel. A gastrostomy tube may be placed to provide gastric decompression and access for feeding after surgery. Occasionally, long segments of bowel must be removed, and an ostomy is placed. An adequate length of bowel, at least 30 cm of jejunum and ileum with an ileocecal valve, must be left after surgery for an optimal recovery. Short bowel syndrome is a complication of surgical resection of intestinal atresia. If too much bowel is removed, the infant requires prolonged TPN. Most infants with intestinal atresia who do not have complicating factors survive. The prognosis for infants with multiple atresia depends on the amount of bowel present after resection.

### Nursing Assessment and Diagnosis

The nursing assessment of the infant with intestinal atresia begins immediately after birth. The infant with abdominal distention, bilious vomiting, and failure to pass meconium is at risk.

Nursing diagnoses for intestinal atresia might include the following:

- Altered nutrition: less than body requirements related to obstruction
- High risk for infection related to surgery
- Constipation related to bowel dysfunction
- Altered GI tissue perfusion related to surgery
- High risk for fluid volume deficit related to vomiting
- High risk for aspiration related to vomiting
- High risk for impaired skin integrity related to malnutrition and surgery
- High risk for altered parenting related to decreased parental bonding
- Altered family process related to hospitalization
- Pain related to surgery

### Planning and Implementing Nursing Care

As with any infant born with a significant problem, it is important to include the concerns of the parents when planning nursing care. Infants with intestinal atresia are frequently transferred to another institution for management and surgery, thus separating the parents from their baby and interrupting the bonding process. It is important to facilitate communication, encourage visitation, and allow the parents to participate in the care of their child.

Before surgery, the infant is stabilized with gastric decompression using an NG tube and low, intermittent suction. The infant is NPO, and intravenous nutrition is initiated. After surgery, the infant is placed on TPN, which is continued until oral feedings have been established. NG suction is maintained until bowel function is established and oral feedings are introduced. It is important to maintain skin integrity around the ostomy and to instruct the parents in care of the ostomy (Wesson, 1991b).

Home management initially concentrates on maintaining adequate nutrition and promoting growth. For most infants who undergo surgical resection for an intestinal atresia, oral feedings with NG supplementation provide their caloric needs. Some may require continuous NG feedings or gastrostomy feedings at night to supplement their daytime oral intake. Those who are left with a limited amount of small bowel and develop short bowel syndrome may require TPN at home. These children and their families are faced with long-term home care needs that require the expertise and coordination of many services. Nurses can assist these families by making appropriate referrals.

### Evaluating Nursing Care

The expected outcomes for the infant with intestinal atresia and the family include the following: the operative site should be well healed and free of infection; the child should be able to tolerate oral feeding; and the child should be well nourished. Depending on the surgical interventions used, the family should be able to demonstrate care of the NG tube or gastrostomy tube or, if appropriate, care of an ostomy. Home care should be established, as needed. The parents and family should be able to verbalize their concerns and feelings regarding the child's disorder and interventions and should identify and use appropriate resources.

## Digestion Problems of Infants and Children

### Colic

*Colic* is one of the most frustrating disorders confronting parents and health care providers. Colic affects 10% to 20% of all infants (Forsyth, 1989), and its incidence is not related to the infant's sex, birth order, or race, nor is it less prevalent in breast-fed versus bottle-fed infants (Gillies, 1987). Colic is generally described as a complex of symptoms, which include excessive crying (greater than 3 hours per day) of unknown cause in an infant between the ages of 3 weeks and 3 months (Gillies, 1987; Taubman, 1988). Infants are described as inconsolable during these episodes, and their behavior suggests abdominal pain. Frequently, these infants are observed pulling their legs up toward the abdomen, which may be distended; clenching their fists; and struggling to expel flatus (Carey, 1984; Taubman, 1988). The diagnosis of colic is made when there is no organic cause for the crying (Pinyerd & Zipf, 1989; Taubman, 1988).

### Pathophysiology

The exact cause of colic is unclear. Intrinsic causes might include milk allergy, an immature GI tract, or an immature central nervous system. Extrinsic causes might include maternal anxiety, inappropriate responses to the infant's cues, or inappropriate feeding techniques. Despite extensive research focused on identifying the causes of colic, a great deal of controversy persists. Carey (1984) suggested that a combination of intrinsic and extrinsic factors may interact to cause the excessive crying in the colicky infant.

### Medical Diagnosis and Management

The first step in managing an infant with colic is to rule out an organic cause for the excessive crying. This is accomplished with a complete history and physical examination. If organic causes for crying, such as GER, constipation, rectal fissures, urinary tract infections, upper respiratory tract infections, or otitis media, are evident, the crying should resolve when the appropriate therapy is administered.

A detailed feeding history should be obtained. This should include the type of formula, frequency and volume of feedings, and family history of allergies. Both overfeeding and underfeeding have been associated with colic, as have early and late introduction of infant cereals. Frequently, nutritional management results in many formula changes, with minimal improvement in the crying. As a result, the parents and health care providers become increasingly frustrated. Forsyth (1989) demonstrated that while there was some improvement in the colic when infants were switched from a cow's milk formula to a casein hydrolysate formula, the improvement was diminished over time and was inconsistent among infants. Other recent literature suggests using soy formulas for managing colic, despite the opposition of the American Academy of Pediatrics Committee on Nutrition (Pinyerd & Zipf, 1989). If the excessive crying is related to a milk protein allergy, the symptoms should resolve when that protein is removed from the diet.

Colic has also been associated with increased intestinal gas in infants. It is still unclear whether colicky infants have different intestinal gas patterns from noncolicky infants (Geertsma & Hyams, 1989). Management therapies include changing the nipple used by the infant to decrease the amount of air swallowed and positioning the infant vertically to enhance burping. Similar therapies focus on helping the infant to expel the intestinal gas by using rectal stimulation with a thermometer or a glycerin suppository. None of these approaches have proved effective in managing colic (Pinyerd & Zipf, 1989).

A variety of medications have been used to treat colic. These include sedatives, antispasmodics, and antiflatulents. These agents have not been shown to be effective in managing colic.

Parental response to the crying caused by colic has also been investigated. Parents may describe colicky infants as difficult to care for if they appear inconsolable. Parents may feel frustrated, angry, and inadequate if their infant cries excessively. Taubman (1988) demonstrated that when parents were counseled to respond to their infant's crying as communication (ie, hungry, wet, tired), there was a greater decrease in the infant's crying than when the infant was left to cry. Hunsicker and Barr (1986) demonstrated that increased carrying of the infant led to a decrease in the crying time. Holding or cuddling the infant is also often effective (Fig. 29-6). Most recently, management of colic using infant stimulation with vibration has shown some effective decrease in infant crying.

### Nursing Assessment and Diagnosis

It is evident that the etiology of colic is as obscure as the most effective management plan. It is well known, however, that colic is a common and frustrating problem for parents. There are many implications in the management of colic for nurses. The "patient" in the management of colic is both the infant and the parents. Nurses must assess the infant's overall state of health using objective growth data and the physical examination. Nurses should assess the parents' knowledge about, and comfort with, normal infant behavior. They should observe parent–infant interactions and assess the parents' responses to the infant's behavior. The parents' level of frustration with this problem and their infant's behavior must also be assessed.

Nursing diagnoses for colic might include the following:

- Pain related to gas
- Ineffective family coping: compromised related to the infant's crying
- Alteration in parenting related to crying and altered parental bonding

*Figure 29–6. Father holding a colicky baby.*

### Planning and Implementing Nursing Care

Nurses must reassure parents that their infant is healthy based on objective growth data, which includes an accurate height, weight, and head circumference. The nurse should review appropriate nutrition and feeding routines with the parents, educate parents about normal infant behavior, and help them understand that the infant's crying is a means of communicating a need or want. Helping the parents to interpret this crying so that they may respond quickly and appropriately may be accomplished using role-modeling.

Nurses can help parents acknowledge that colic is a frustrating disorder and reassure parents that feelings of frustration are normal. Identifying ways that parents may cope with their frustration may be useful. Encouraging parents to place the infant in a safe place (crib, playpen) and walk away for 5 or 10 minutes is one of the best ways to relieve the frustration.

### Evaluating Nursing Care

The effectiveness of the nursing care implemented may be evaluated by the parents' comfort with the fact that their infant is healthy. The parents' ease and comfort in responding to their infant's needs may also be an indicator for evaluating the nursing interventions.

## Pyloric Stenosis

### Pathophysiology

The cause of pyloric stenosis is unknown. The problem is not always present at birth, but develops in the first few weeks of life. It is more common in first-born male whites by a factor of 1 : 5. Infant males born to mothers who had pyloric stenosis have the highest risk of developing the disorder. In pyloric stenosis, the circular muscle of the pyloric sphincter, the opening between the stomach and the duodenum, hypertrophies, resulting in an obstructive process.

### Medical Diagnosis and Management

Infants with pyloric stenosis present with projectile vomiting, which does not contain bile. The vomiting usually starts in the 3rd week of life. There is a history of initially feeding well, with the infant becoming fretful and anxious as the feeding progresses. The infant is irritable and hungry but, as the process continues, becomes increasingly lethargic and malnourished. Gastric peristalsis is visible on physical examination, and a pyloric olive-shaped mass is usually palpable in the epigastric area, thus confirming the diagnosis. If a pyloric olive-shaped mass is not present, the diagnosis is made using ultrasound studies, which confirm the presence of the mass, or by barium swallow, which shows a long, narrow pyloric channel. Infants with pyloric stenosis are at risk for dehydration and metabolic alkalosis as a result of the persistent vomiting.

*Pyloromyotomy* is the treatment of choice in most instances of pyloric stenosis. It is a simple procedure, in which the pyloric muscle is released, allowing the mucosa of the pyloric canal to expand, relieving the gastric outlet obstruction. Before surgery, gastric evacuation and decompression are accomplished using an NG tube. Fluid and electrolyte alterations are corrected intravenously. After surgery, the infant is NPO for 8 to 24 hours, then is slowly progressed to the previous formula. The infant is usually discharged from the hospital in 3 days.

### Nursing Assessment and Diagnosis

Pyloric stenosis needs to be considered in an infant with persistent, projectile vomiting and failure to thrive. The nursing assessment begins with a thorough history of the infant's feeding patterns, the relationship of the vomiting to feedings, and a description of the emesis. It is also important to document the infant's length and weight, noting growth patterns. The presence of a distended abdomen, visible gastric peristalsis, and signs of dehydration are key assessment findings.

Nursing diagnoses for pyloric stenosis might include the following:

- High risk for fluid volume deficit related to vomiting
- Altered nutrition: less than body requirements related to vomiting
- High risk for impaired skin integrity related to malnutrition and surgery
- High risk for altered parenting related to hospitalization
- Pain related to altered peristalsis and surgery

### Planning and Implementing Nursing Care

Planning and implementing nursing care for infants with pyloric stenosis are discussed under pre- and postoperative nursing care, covered earlier in this chapter.

### Evaluating Nursing Care

Nursing care is evaluated through the monitoring of expected outcomes, which include the following: the infant should be able to tolerate normal feeding without vomiting; the infant should recover from the surgery without complications; and the parents and family should be able to demonstrate their ability to care for the infant at home.

# Congenital Problems of Absorption

## Gastroschisis and Omphalocele

*Gastroschisis* or *omphalocele* are abdominal wall defects seen at birth. Together, these defects occur in 1 per 6000 to 10,000 live births. Both defects are associated with other congenital abnormalities that may result in intestinal obstruction, such as malrotation, volvulus, and intestinal atresia.

### Pathophysiology

*Omphalocele* occurs when the abdominal contents herniate through the umbilical ring, usually with an intact peritoneal sac. *Gastroschisis* is the herniation of abdominal contents laterally and usually to the right of the umbilical ring, without an intact peritoneal sac.

### Medical Diagnosis and Management

Both gastroschisis and omphalocele are visible defects; thus, the diagnosis is made in the delivery room. Initial medical management is directed to stabilizing the infant before surgical intervention. Intravenous fluid management is necessary due to the increased fluid losses the infant sustains as a result of the exposed bowel. Hypothermia must be avoided. Sterility of the defect must be maintained, and broad-spectrum antibiotics are used prophylactically to prevent infection.

Medical and surgical management depends on the size of the defect, the presence or absence of a peritoneal sac, the gestational age and size of the infant, and the presence of other associated disorders. Nonoperative management of omphalocele with topical agents has been tried with limited success (Dudgeon, Colombani, & Beaver, 1987a). Surgical closure is attempted in either a primary repair or a staged procedure. The repair should be accomplished without an increase in abdominal pressure since this can result in a diminished blood flow to the intestines, resulting in ischemia. Increased abdominal pressure can also influence respiratory and cardiac function. After surgery, GI function returns slowly, requiring TPN. Many infants with gastroschisis or omphalocele experience complications such as intestinal obstruction related to adhesions, malrotation, and midgut volvulus, and they require further surgery.

### Nursing Assessment and Diagnosis

Nursing assessment of the infant with gastroschisis and omphalocele begins in the delivery room. It is important to monitor vital signs, being aware that the infant is at risk for fluid fluctuations and hypothermia as a result of the exposed bowel. It is also important to assess for signs of infection.

Nursing diagnoses for an abdominal wall defect might include the following:

- Altered nutrition: less than body requirements related to increased metabolic needs
- High risk for infection related to exposed intestines
- High risk for altered body temperature related to exposed intestines
- Altered GI tissue perfusion related to exposed bowel
- Decreased cardiac output related to intra-abdominal pressure
- Impaired skin integrity related to abdominal wall defect
- Altered family processes related to hospitalization
- Pain related to surgery

### Planning and Implementing Nursing Care

Before surgery, the infant is stabilized with gastric decompression using an NG tube and low suction. Fluid and electrolyte fluctuations are managed by intravenous fluids. It is important to prevent hypothermia by placing the infant under a warmer and monitoring the infant's temperature frequently. Surgical repair of the defect depends on the age and size of the infant and on the size of the defect. Complete repair may require several operations, leaving an exposed segment of bowel until the repair is completed. Care must be taken to keep the area clean and covered with a moist sterile drape. Signs of infection should be monitored carefully.

After surgery, the infant is placed on TPN until GI function returns and the infant tolerates oral feedings. After surgery, vital signs must be monitored closely for any change in cardiac and respiratory status. Diminished blood flow to the intestine results in ischemia, necessitating further surgical resections and potentially resulting in short bowel syndrome. Skin integrity must be maintained around the site of the defect. Wound care is important to facilitate adequate closure.

It is important to include concerns of the parents when planning the nursing care for an infant born with a significant problem. Parents should be kept informed of the planned treatment and possible outcomes and should be instructed in home care.

### Evaluating Nursing Care

The nursing care of the infant with an abdominal wall defect is evaluated through continual reassessment of the infant's condition and monitoring of expected outcomes. The expected outcomes include the following: the opera-

tive site should be well healed and free of infection; the child should be well nourished and tolerate oral feeding and other necessary nutritional interventions; the family should be able to demonstrate care for the infant; home care should be established as needed; and appropriate resources should be identified and used. The parents and family should be able to verbalize concerns and feelings regarding the infant's disorder and intervention.

## Absorption Problems of Infants and Children

### Necrotizing Enterocolitis

#### Pathophysiology

*Necrotizing enterocolitis* (NEC) is an acquired ulcerative and necrotic process that primarily affects the distal small bowel and colon. Most cases are seen in preterm infants, but 10% to 20% of full-term infants develop NEC (Brown & Sweet, 1982). The incidence of NEC is increasing as the signs and symptoms are more readily identified and as more aggressive therapy for low-birth-weight preterm infants is available.

The etiology of NEC is unknown; however, there is general agreement that precipitating factors include enteral feeding, infection, and ischemia. Enteral feedings provide a substrate in the gut for bacteria, which potentiates the bacterial activity in an immature gut (Israel, 1991). The primary bacteria are normal bowel flora that cross into the peritoneum and circulate through the injured bowel. Ischemia may precede the development of NEC (Touloukian, 1986). Risk factors for ischemia are umbilical lines and systemic disorders that result in altered gut perfusion.

#### Medical Diagnosis and Management

The diagnosis of NEC is based on clinical presentation and can be confirmed by radiographic studies. In the early stage, the infant may present with poor feeding, vomiting, increasing residuals with NG feedings, mild abdominal distention, and occult blood in the stools. Systemic manifestations may include temperature instability, lethargy, apnea, and bradycardia.

Initial therapy is supportive and anticipatory. In the early stage of NEC, enteral feedings are withheld, and an NG tube is connected to suction to decompress the bowel. Nutritional, fluid, and electrolyte needs are met with intravenous fluids. Because bacteria have been implicated in causing NEC, and the infant typically appears septic, blood, stool, and urine cultures are taken and broad-spectrum antibiotics are given intravenously. Repeated abdominal radiographs are obtained to assess progression of the disease. The infant must be monitored closely for systemic complications (apnea, disseminated intravascular coagulation, metabolic acidosis, "third-spacing" fluids). If the symptoms resolve, oral elemental feedings may be introduced in small, dilute amounts and slowly advanced as tolerated.

Surgical intervention is necessary when symptoms progress. Symptoms include abdominal wall cellulitis, abdominal mass, or fixed dilated loop of bowel visible on radiograph. All necrotic and perforated bowel is resected. This generally results in a temporary ileostomy. Depending on the amount of bowel resected, short bowel syndrome may be a life-long sequela of NEC. Touloukian (1986) reports that a complete recovery is possible in up to 80% of infants with NEC if diagnosis is made and interventions are initiated early.

### Nursing Assessment and Diagnosis

Nursing assessment of the infant with NEC is focused on hydration status, signs of progressive NEC, and systemic sequelae. An overall physical assessment of the infant, including weight and vital signs, with particular attention to the abdomen and abdominal girth, is important. The infant's stooling pattern and feeding tolerance also provide information about the infant's status. If surgical intervention is necessary, the wound should be assessed, as should the infant's level of comfort. Assessment of the infant's tolerance of gradual advancement of oral intake and intravenous nutrition is necessary.

Nursing diagnoses for NEC might include the following:

- Fluid volume deficit related to increased metabolic needs
- Altered nutrition: less than body requirements related to NPO status
- High risk for infection related to NEC
- Impaired skin integrity related to NEC and surgery
- Diarrhea related to NEC
- Altered GI tissue perfusion related to NEC and surgery
- High risk for altered parenting related to compromised parent–infant bonding and hospitalization
- Pain related to surgery

### Planning and Implementing Nursing Care

When planning and implementing nursing care, the determination of physiological status is accomplished with accurate vital signs, weight, and intake and output records. Examination of the abdomen may provide information about the progression of NEC. Maintaining nutrition and hydration status with oral and intravenous nutritional supplements is essential to promote recovery. Evaluating the infant's level of comfort by observing activity and vital signs is important. If surgery is required, the wound must be examined for signs of infection (erythema, discharge, warm to touch), and function of the ostomy should be assessed.

Parent–infant interaction should be encouraged. Parents should be provided with opportunities to cuddle the infant and participate in routine care. Parents should be educated about care of the ostomy if it is not reanastomosed before discharge.

### Evaluating Nursing Care

Nursing care should be evaluated continually. Positive outcomes of care for the infant with NEC include the following: maintenance of adequate nutritional and hydration status; early detection of signs and symptoms of progressive NEC; prevention of infection; and positive parent–infant interaction.

## Malabsorption

*Malabsorption* syndromes are characterized by chronic diarrhea, abdominal distension, and failure to thrive. It is now possible to differentiate between congenital and acquired conditions that affect the transport or use of nutrients. Malabsorption also applies to diseases that result from pancreatic insufficiency (cystic fibrosis), biliary tract disease (biliary atresia), villous atrophy (celiac disease), and specific hydrolysis or transport defects. Anatomical defects may also result in malabsorption, such as the short bowel syndrome following intestinal resections in the newborn.

### Pathophysiology

The pathophysiology of these defects vary and are discussed with the specific disorders. In cystic fibrosis, pancreatic insufficiency results from a mechanical obstruction of the pancreatic ducts by the thickened mucous gland secretions. This obstruction prevents essential pancreatic enzymes from reaching the duodenum, thus impairing digestion and resulting in malabsorption of nutrients and vitamins. The most obvious consequence of malabsorption is lack of growth. Malabsorption slows weight gain before it affects height. Subcutaneous fat may disappear, muscle may waste, and the skin sags. Growth stops, and development is compromised. With nutritional intervention, these symptoms resolve; however, continued growth failure may result in stunting of growth and delayed puberty.

Severe and rapid progression of malabsorption affects other physiological functions besides growth. Vitamin K malabsorption results in decreased synthesis of blood-clotting factors. Long-term calcium and vitamin D malabsorption results in osteoporosis, spontaneous bone fractures, and rickets. Protein-losing enteropathy states (celiac disease, Crohn disease, bacterial overgrowth) result in hypoalbuminemia and edema. Other disorders include microcytic anemia related to iron malabsorption, low serum folate, low vitamin A levels, and low vitamin E levels, leading to loss of tendon reflexes and ataxia with prolonged deficiency states.

## Medical Diagnosis and Management

The common presenting symptom of malabsorptive illnesses is chronic diarrhea. The history and physical examination include the overall well-being of the child. It is important to determine length of illness, characteristics of the stools, and relationship of diarrhea to diet and timing of meals. Activity level and psychomotor development are also assessed. Physical examination focuses on the presence of abdominal distension and signs of systemic consequences, such as clubbing of fingers, muscle wasting, and growth delay.

Medical management is aimed at providing sufficient calories to facilitate growth and other physiological functions. The initial step is to alter the diet of the infant or child. Dietary manipulation, including removal of the offending agent (eg, gluten in celiac disease) is all that is necessary. Supplementation of the missing agent (eg, pancreatic enzymes, or vitamins in liver disease) also helps. In severe villous atrophy or short bowel syndrome, it is often necessary to feed infants and children by NG tube or gastrostomy tube, often with slow continuous feedings over 12 to 24 hours per day. TPN is often necessary in children with malabsorptive syndromes.

## Nursing Assessment and Diagnosis

Nursing assessment of the infant or child with malabsorption requires a careful history and physical examination. It is important to obtain information regarding dietary intake, introduction of solids, and stooling pattern, including frequency, consistency, and color. Changes in personality and overall behavior should be noted. It is important to determine the signs and symptoms of systemic consequences, which include fever, bruising, petechiae, edema, and bone fractures. Determination of achievement of developmental milestones is necessary.

Physical examination provides confirming information regarding the child's nutritional status and overall well-being. Accurate length, weight, head circumference, and anthropometric data should be obtained and plotted on the growth chart. This data must be assessed in relation to previous growth points. Vital signs provide important baseline information about systemic function. The infant may appear thin and wasted, with a lack of subcutaneous fat and sagging skin. Examination of the skin may reveal bruising or petechia. Excoriation of the diaper area may

accompany diarrhea. Edema of the extremities is common. The abdominal examination is unremarkable.

Nursing diagnoses for malabsorption might include the following:

- Altered nutrition: less than body requirements related to malabsorption
- High risk for infection related to malnutrition
- Diarrhea related to malabsorption
- High risk for fluid volume deficit related to diarrhea
- High risk for impaired skin integrity related to malnutrition and diarrhea
- High risk for altered parenting related to chronic illness
- Pain related to abdominal distension and altered skin integrity

## Planning and Implementing Nursing Care

The nursing care of children with malabsorption is aimed at providing adequate nutrition to promote growth and development. Vital signs are monitored routinely. Oral nutrition is initiated using formulas designed to promote growth. The caloric concentration may be altered to maximize the child's oral intake. It is often necessary to supplement additional calories with medium-chain triglyceride oil, microlipids (fats), or polycose. When oral nutrition is insufficient to promote growth, NG or gastrostomy feedings may be instituted. Often, NG feedings follow oral feedings or may be administered continuously through the night while the infant sleeps. TPN may be necessary in severe cases of malabsorption. Careful attention to skin integrity, especially in the diaper area, is important to prevent infection.

The concerns and emotional needs of the parents and family must be addressed. Education should include diagnosis, disease process, medical plan of care, and nutritional interventions. Discussions regarding nutritional needs should include the importance of nutrition in growth and development. The family must be well prepared in administering NG or gastrostomy feedings before discharge. The decision to discharge a child on TPN must be a team decision, with the parents active participants.

## Evaluating Nursing Care

The expected outcomes of nursing care include the following: the child's nutritional status should be improved; the child's skin integrity should be maintained; the family should demonstrate their understanding of and ability to provide nutritional interventions; and the family should be able to verbalize feelings and concerns regarding the child's disorder. The family also should identify and use appropriate resources.

## Celiac Disease

### Pathophysiology

Celiac disease and cystic fibrosis are the most common causes of malabsorption in infants and children. *Celiac disease,* or gluten-sensitive enteropathy, is the result of small bowel mucosal injury following the ingestion of foods that contain gluten, such as breads and cereals. The importance of hereditary and environmental factors in celiac disease remain unknown, as do the relationship of infant feeding practices and the introduction of solid foods, especially foods that contain gluten.

Diarrhea is the most common symptom, and it varies in severity. It may initially be intermittent and progressively become chronic. In about half of patients, the diarrhea is pale, foul-smelling, greasy, and bulky. A few infants have profuse, life-threatening diarrhea. Constipation has also been reported with celiac disease.

Behavioral abnormalities are common. These children are fretful, irritable, uncooperative, difficult to handle, and apathetic. A dramatic personality change is seen with the removal of gluten from the diet.

Anorexia is seen in all patients with celiac disease. A decreased caloric intake, compounded by stool losses, results in failure to thrive. Weight is more severely affected than height; however, in older children, short stature may be the only presenting clinical feature.

Abdominal distension is the result of poor abdominal musculature accompanied by decreased intestinal motility and increased accumulation of gas and secretions. Dilated loops of bowel are easily identified through a thin abdominal wall. Muscle wasting is seen in the arms, legs, and buttocks.

Anemia caused by iron deficiency is usually present. Deficiencies in fat-soluble vitamins are also common. Vitamin K deficiencies may result in epistaxis, ecchymoses, and, rarely, intestinal hemorrhage. Malabsorption of vitamin D may result in osteomalacia and occasionally rickets (Andorsky, 1987c).

### Medical Diagnosis and Management

The diagnostic evaluation of a child with suspected celiac disease begins with a thorough history of growth parameters, diet, and feeding patterns, including the age when cereal (gluten) was introduced. It is also important to ask about the child's behavior and stools. On physical examination, classical findings include a small, malnourished-appearing child, with abdominal distension and muscle wasting, as well as some of the more subtle findings of clubbing of the fingers, smooth tongue, long eyelashes, and peripheral edema.

Screening studies include the d-xylose absorption test, one of the most sensitive screening tests for celiac disease (see Table 29-1). Since lactose malabsorption frequently occurs with the damaged small bowel mucosa, a lactose breath test is helpful in diagnosing malabsorption. Other parameters of malabsorption are folate level, carotene, and antigliadin antibody. A CBC documents the presence of anemia.

A definitive diagnosis of celiac disease is made by a small bowel biopsy. The tissue biopsy shows a flattening of the villi, a flat villus lesion, or, in severe cases, a complete absence of intestinal villi.

The therapy for celiac disease is complete withdrawal of gluten from the diet. This includes wheat, rye, barley, and oats. The clinical response to the withdrawal of gluten from the diet is dramatic. Within days, the child's appearance and disposition changes. Stools become more formed and less frequent. The appetite improves, and weight returns to normal, with a slower progression of catch-up growth for height. Normal mucosal architecture returns within 6 months. Reintroduction of gluten or a gluten challenge is recommended after 2 years of dietary management. This is done to determine the permanence of the gluten intolerance.

Compliance with a gluten-free diet is important for initial catch-up growth, continued good health, and avoidance of nutritional deficiencies. Failure to comply with the diet results in lower stature and weight in young adults. There is also an increased incidence of malignancy in untreated individuals.

### Nursing Assessment and Diagnosis

Nursing assessment of the child with celiac disease begins with the child's general appearance and behavior. It is important to determine the child's nutritional status, growth status with parameters of height, weight, and head circumference, and developmental level. A diet history, with likes and dislikes, is also important.

Nursing diagnoses for celiac disease might include the following:

* Diarrhea related to malabsorption
* Altered nutrition: less than body requirements
* High risk for fluid volume deficit related to diarrhea
* Altered growth and development related to malnutrition
* Pain related to abdominal distention

### Planning and Implementing Nursing Care

Nursing care is aimed at educating the child and parents. Children should be prepared for procedures, as appropriate for their developmental level. Parents should understand the procedures and should be informed of potential complications. Once a diagnosis has been made, the nursing care is directed toward helping the child and parents understand and adhere to a gluten-free diet. It is important to enlist the help of a nutritionist since a gluten-free diet involves reading labels and avoiding thickeners and stabilizers found in processed foods. Maintaining a gluten-free diet becomes increasingly difficult as children enter school and become adolescents. It is recommended that patients with celiac disease avoid gluten throughout their lives. Although it is difficult to maintain this diet when symptoms are not present, support groups are often helpful.

### Evaluating Nursing Care

Nursing care is evaluated by the child and parents' comfort and understanding of the diagnostic process and final diagnosis. The family's understanding of a gluten-free diet and the child's response to the dietary regimen are valuable indicators of successful nursing interventions.

## Meckel Diverticulum

### Pathophysiology

*Meckel diverticulum,* a sac that protrudes from the wall of the ileum near the ileocecal sphincter, results from an incomplete closure of the yolk stalk. It occurs in 2% to 4% of the population and is one of the more common causes of rectal bleeding in children. Bleeding may occur as a result of gastric acid secretion and ulceration.

### Medical Diagnosis and Management

The most common symptom of Meckel diverticulum is rectal bleeding. Diagnosis is made by a nuclear scintiscan specific to gastric mucosa. Surgical resection of the Meckel diverticulum is performed.

### Nursing Assessment and Diagnosis

Nursing assessment begins with monitoring vital signs. Shock is a potential complication because of the massive rectal bleeding. It is important to keep accurate intake and output records, especially noting the amount of bleeding. The coping mechanisms of the family must also be assessed, along with the comfort status of the child. Postoperative nursing assessments are the same as for other abdominal surgeries, discussed earlier in the chapter.

Nursing diagnoses for Meckel diverticulum might include the following:

- High risk for infection related to surgery
- High risk for fluid volume deficit related to diarrhea
- Altered family processes related to the child's hospitalization

### Planning and Implementing Nursing Care

Nursing care provided to a child with Meckel diverticulum is supportive and is aimed at promoting recovery after abdominal surgery. The child's comfort must be maintained with appropriate analgesics. Hydration status is assessed along with diet progression. The child must remain free of infection, and skin integrity of the wound must be maintained with sterile dressing changes. The parents need to be instructed in home care and must feel secure in their ability to care for the child at home.

### Evaluating Nursing Care

Patient and parent understanding of the diagnosis and therapies, as well as their response to the hospitalization, are criteria for evaluating nursing care. Outcome criteria that must be monitored include the following: the child should be free of infection and pain; the parents should be able to demonstrate their understanding of the condition and its treatment as well as the ability to care for their child at home; and the family should also be able to identify and use appropriate resources.

## Inflammatory Bowel Disease

The term *inflammatory bowel disease* (IBD) is used to denote two disease processes, ulcerative colitis and Crohn disease. IBD is an inflammation of the small intestine, large intestine, or both. It is seen in school-aged children, adolescents, and young adults. Most patients are diagnosed between the ages of 10 and 30 years; however, children are being diagnosed at younger ages as well. IBD occurs in 60 to 100 per 100,000 people, and its etiology is unknown.

### Pathophysiology

*Crohn disease* involves all five layers of the bowel wall. The most common site of inflammation is the terminal ileum, with areas of inflammation found throughout the GI tract. *Ulcerative colitis* is an inflammatory process of the colonic mucosa, with diffuse ulcerations of the epithelial lining. The inflammation is continuous, often extending from the rectum to the cecum.

### Medical Diagnosis and Management

The symptoms of ulcerative colitis and Crohn disease are similar; diarrhea is common in both disorders. It is accompanied by gross rectal bleeding, lower abdominal pain, mild anorexia, and weight loss in ulcerative colitis. In Crohn disease, gross rectal bleeding is rare, but occult blood may be present. Other signs are anorexia, abdominal pain, weight loss, and growth failure.

The diagnosis of IBD is based on clinical presentation, biochemical parameters, radiographic findings, endoscopic findings, and biopsy information. Documentation of previous growth is important in determining if there is growth failure. Many children with IBD appear chronically ill at the time of diagnosis. Abdominal examination may reveal right lower quadrant tenderness or fullness along with diffuse tenderness in other quadrants. Rectal examination may reveal evidence of perianal disease, skin tags, fissures, or fistulas (commonly seen with Crohn disease).

Initial diagnostic tests include a CBC, chemistry panel, and erythrocyte sedimentation rate (see Table 29-1). The CBC documents anemia states and elevated platelet counts, which are often seen in IBD. A chemistry panel is done to evaluate liver function, albumin, and total protein to determine the degree of mucosal damage and malnutrition. An elevated erythrocyte sedimentation rate is an indicator of inflammation. Stool cultures are also obtained to rule out an infectious process. Colonoscopy is performed to document mucosal injury and the extent of the disease. The UGI documents the presence or absence of small bowel disease. A barium enema evaluates colonic disease and is not routinely done if a colonoscopy is performed.

Medical management is aimed at alleviating the acute symptoms as quickly as possible and preventing relapse of the inflammation with maintenance therapy. Sulfasalazine, a combination of salicylate and sulfa antibiotic, is the initial therapy of choice. Olsalazine is an alternative for patients who are allergic to sulfa medications. Steroids may be necessary to induce a remission but are used with caution because of their side effects.

Surgical intervention may be necessary in some cases. Surgery cures patients with ulcerative colitis since removal of the colon eliminates the disease. In Crohn disease, however, the inflammation may recur at another site after resection.

### Nursing Assessment and Diagnosis

The nurse's assessment begins with the general appearance and behavior of the child. It is important to assess the nutritional status, growth status with height and weight, and developmental level of the child. The history must include information regarding elimination, including number of stools per day, consistency, presence of blood, and pain with defecation. A dietary history is necessary to elicit information about anorexia, food likes and dislikes, and the relationship of food to pain and defecation. Comfort status is also important since abdominal cramping can be severe with IBD.

Nursing diagnoses for inflammatory bowel disease might include the following:

- Activity intolerance related to malnutrition
- Diarrhea related to inflammation
- Pain related to inflammation
- Altered nutrition: less than body requirements related to diarrhea and malnutrition
- High risk for impaired skin integrity related to malnutrition and diarrhea

### Planning and Implementing Nursing Care

Nursing interventions for IBD are directed at supportive care and education of the child and family. Since IBD is a life-long disease, it is imperative that the child and family learn about the disease process, the dietary implications, the medication regimen and possible side effects, as well as the role stress may play in the disease.

Patient and family preparation is also a goal of nursing care. Patients being evaluated for IBD undergo many invasive procedures and require preprocedure education.

### Evaluating Nursing Care

Nursing care is evaluated by the child and parents' understanding of the diagnosis, therapy, chronicity of the disease, and nutritional interventions. The child's activity level should return to normal, and there should be no evidence of diarrhea or pain. The child and parents should be able to demonstrate their understanding of the diagnosis, prognosis, and therapy and should verbalize their concerns and feelings regarding the child's health problem and needs. The child and family should also be able to identify and use appropriate resources.

## Congenital Problems of Elimination

### Hirschsprung Disease

#### Pathophysiology

*Hirschsprung disease* (aganglionic megacolon) is a congenital disorder of the large bowel motility that results in chronic constipation and obstruction in infants and children. Hirschsprung disease is caused by the absence of ganglion cells from the myenteric plexus. The aganglionic segment of bowel, the internal sphincter, and the anal canal remain contracted, causing a functional obstruction with dilatation and hypertrophy of the proximal bowel. Hirschsprung disease occurs in 1 in 500 births. It is more common in males than females (4:1) and is more frequent in relatives of identified patients (Kirschner, 1991; Andorsky, 1987a). Hirschsprung disease generally occurs in full-term infants. The age at diagnosis depends on the length of the aganglionic segment and the severity of symptoms.

#### Medical Diagnosis and Management

Infants with Hirschsprung disease present with constipation, abdominal distention, vomiting, and poor feeding. They often fail to pass meconium in the first 24 hours after birth. Enterocolitis (severe, watery diarrhea) may occur at about 6 weeks of age. It can be life-threatening and occasionally is diagnosed as a viral illness. Older children present with intractable constipation without fecal soiling or encopresis (see section on encopresis). They often have a poor appetite and may have poor growth as well.

Diagnosis of Hirschsprung disease is based on the history and physical examination findings. Abdominal distention is common. Rectal examination reveals an empty rectal vault of normal size. A rectal biopsy, documenting the absence of ganglion cells in the myenteric plexus, is the standard method for diagnosing Hirschsprung disease.

The management of Hirschsprung disease is aimed at relieving the intestinal obstruction, restoring peristalsis, and preserving the external anal sphincter function. Infants require a colostomy proximal to the aganglionic segment of bowel. Definitive surgery is delayed until the infant weighs about 20 pounds. Older children may not require a preliminary decompression colostomy. Several procedures are used to correct Hirschsprung disease, all of which remove the aganglionic segment of intestine and are followed by a primary reanastomosis of the intestine, or the normal proximal intestine is pulled through the muscular sleeve of the rectum. The prognosis after surgery is favorable, with fecal continence being the goal.

### Nursing Assessment and Diagnosis

Nursing assessment of the infant or child with Hirschsprung disease requires a careful history and physical examination. Stooling history, including frequency, consistency, when the infant passed meconium, and the need for intervention, is important. Dietary intake and achievement of developmental milestones should be explored. Physical examination includes accurate weight, length, and head circumference plotted on the growth curve and compared with previous measurements. Examination of the abdomen reveals abdominal distension with palpable stool masses. Rectal examination reveals an empty rectal vault.

Nursing diagnoses for Hirschsprung disease might include the following:

- High risk for infection related to intestinal obstruction
- Constipation related to the disease process
- High risk for fluid volume deficit related to the ostomy
- High risk for impaired skin integrity related to the ostomy
- High risk for altered parenting related to hospitalization
- Altered growth and development related to malnutrition and hospitalization
- Toileting self-care deficit related to the ostomy and constipation
- Pain related to surgery and constipation

### Planning and Implementing Nursing Care

The nursing care of the child with Hirschsprung disease varies with the age at which the child is diagnosed and the child's overall clinical status.

Before surgery, the infant with Hirschsprung disease may require gastric decompression with an NG tube and intravenous hydration until surgery. Older children with chronic, intractable constipation require cathartics and enemas to decompress the bowel before surgery. After surgery, an NG tube remains in place until bowel function returns. A colostomy is generally necessary initially. It is important to maintain the skin integrity around the ostomy and to familiarize the parents and child with colostomy care.

The concerns and educational needs of the parents and family must be addressed. Education should include the diagnosis, disease process, medical and surgical plan of care, and long-term needs.

### Evaluating Nursing Care

Nursing care of the infant or child with Hirschsprung disease is evaluated thorough continuing assessment and the monitoring of expected outcomes. Expected outcomes include the following: the operative site should be well healed and free of infection; the child should be well nourished and able to tolerate oral feedings; and skin integrity should be maintained. The child and family should demonstrate their understanding of the condition and its treatment and should be able to care for the ostomy in the home. The parents should also verbalize their feelings and concerns regarding the child's health problem.

## Anorectal Malformations

### Pathophysiology

Anorectal malformations occur in 1 in 5000 live births. They are usually obvious at birth and are generally manifested by a lack of an anal opening. They range in severity from a mild stenosis of the anus to a complex syndrome with other associated disorders. An imperforate anus is the result of abnormal development that occurs during the first trimester of pregnancy. The most common syndrome associated with anorectal malformations is the VATER/VACTERL syndrome. This includes vertebral abnormalities (V), anal atresia (A), tracheoesophageal fistula (TE), radial and renal disorders (R), and cardiac (C) and limb (L) abnormalities.

Anorectal defects are classified according to the level of rectum descent (stops) and the relationship to the puborectalis sling of the levator ani musculature complex (the primary muscle of continence). A *low defect* is seen when the rectum has descended through the puborectalis sling. The internal and external anal sphincters are present and functional, but there is no patent connection to the perineum. In an *intermediate defect,* the rectum is at the level or below the puborectalis sling, with a correctly positioned anal dimple and external anal sphincter. In a *high defect* the rectum ends above the puborectalis sling. In these cases, there is an absence of internal and external anal sphincters, and there is usually an associated genitourinary fistula. The higher the defect, the greater the incidence of other associated anomalies.

### Medical Diagnosis and Management

Anorectal malformations result in a distal form of intestinal obstruction. Even infants with a partial anal opening or fistula may be partially obstructed. Consequently, an NG tube is necessary to avoid gastric distension, vomiting, and aspiration. The infant is NPO, and intravenous fluids are administered. Urinalysis is done to detect the presence of meconium or fecal material. This documents the presence of a rectourethral fistula, a sign of a high lesion. A decompressive colostomy is necessary if the anal opening is too small or absent. In low or intermediate lesions, the caliber of the fistula, the adequacy of the opening, and the position of the anal opening are assessed before surgical intervention. If the opening is adequate for defecation, repeated dilatations are initiated and an anoplasty is performed at 3 to 5 months of age. If the opening is inadequate, an anoplasty is done earlier. Complications after surgery include recurrent rectourinary fistula, constipation, and incontinence. Infants with low and intermediate lesions are generally able to achieve normal continence, whereas infants with high lesions have more difficulty achieving acceptable continence until 10 to 12 years of age.

### Nursing Care

Nursing care of the infant with an anorectal malformation is the same as the nursing care for infants with congenital intestinal obstruction (intestinal atresia, Hirschsprung disease). The same nursing diagnoses also apply.

## Malrotation

*Malrotation* is the failure of the bowel to rotate and become normally fixed at the duodenum as it returns from its extracolonic position at about 10 weeks' gestation. It is frequently associated with other anomalies.

Infants and children with malrotation present with symptoms of obstruction, anorexia, and bilious vomiting. The diagnosis is confirmed by barium enema, which shows the cecum in the right upper quadrant of the abdomen. The medical therapy for malrotation is surgical correction, returning the bowel to its normal position.

### Nursing Care

The nursing care of the infant with abdominal malformations (gastroschisis, intestinal atresia) also applies to the infant with malrotation.

## Meconium Ileus

A meconium ileus is the obstruction of the small bowel and colon caused by abnormal meconium. This condition occurs in 15% to 20% of infants with cystic fibrosis.

The cause of meconium ileus is not known but is believed to be related to pancreatic insufficiency and abnormal intestinal secretions (Wesson, 1991a; Dudgeon, Colombani, & Beaver, 1987c). Clinically, the infant with a meconium ileus presents with bilious vomiting and abdominal distension during the first day or two of life. Other causes for intestinal obstruction must be considered. A family history of cystic fibrosis is highly suggestive of the diagnosis. Abdominal radiographs may aid in the diagnosis by showing the presence of trapped air in the meconium. A contrast enema aids in the diagnosis and has a therapeutic effect as well. The hyperosmotic contrast medium (Gastrografin) tends to soften and loosen the meconium and facilitates its passage into the colon and finally defecation. If this is unsuccessful, surgical intervention may be required.

After the evacuation of meconium, the diagnosis of cystic fibrosis must be confirmed by sweat test when the infant is several months of age. Further therapy depends on this diagnosis.

### Nursing Care

The nursing assessment of the infant with meconium ileus begins in the newborn period with the documentation of the passage of meconium. It is important to note abdominal distention and the subsequent findings of intestinal obstruction, such as bilious vomiting. It is also important to assess the infant's hydration status and have intravenous access available. Nursing diagnoses, planning, interventions, and evaluation are the same as for Hirschsprung disease or intestinal atresia.

# Excretion and Elimination Problems of Infants and Children

## Intussusception

### Pathophysiology

*Intussusception* occurs when a segment of the bowel telescopes into another segment distal to it, typically at the ileocecal valve, with the ileum going into the cecum and colon (Fig. 29-7). One of the most common causes of

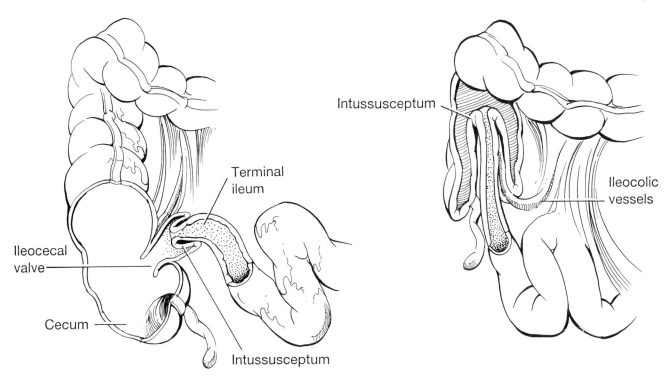

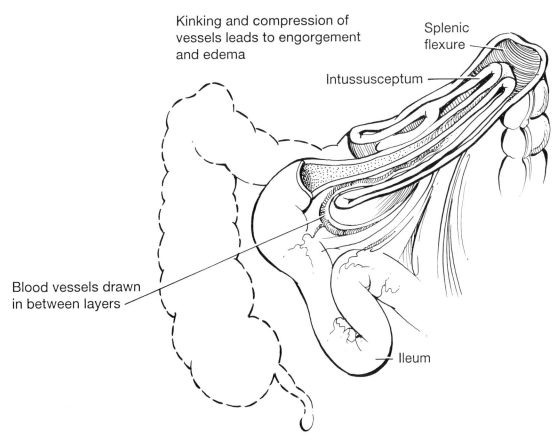

*Figure 29–7. Development of an intussusception.*

intestinal obstruction in infants, it is generally seen between 3 and 12 months of age and occurs more frequently in males than females. The cause is unknown; however, it has been associated with viral enteritis (Wesson, 1991a).

## Medical Diagnosis and Management

Infants with intussusception typically have a sudden onset of vomiting and severe, crampy abdominal pain. The pain resolves but reoccurs with increasing frequency. Diarrhea is a less common symptom. The child progressively becomes more irritable and lethargic. Physical examination of the abdomen may reveal a palpable, sausage-shaped mass that crosses the right upper and middle abdomen. The symptoms warrant a barium enema, which is not only diagnostic but therapeutic. The continuous pressure of the enema reduces or pushes back the invaginated ileum. If hydrostatic reduction is not possible, then a surgical laparotomy is performed, and any ischemic bowel is removed.

## Nursing Assessment and Diagnosis

Nursing assessment requires a careful history and physical examination. It is important to determine the general health of the child and to establish a pain history that includes onset, frequency, and perceived intensity. Dietary intake, presence of vomiting, and stooling pattern, frequency, consistency, and color are important. Activity, behavior, and sleeping patterns need to be determined.

Nursing diagnoses for intussusception might include the following:

- High risk for infection related to surgery
- High risk for fluid volume deficit related to vomiting and bleeding
- Altered GI tissue perfusion related to intussusception
- Altered family process related to hospitalization
- Pain related to surgery

## Nursing Care

Vital signs are monitored frequently to document clinical status. The concerns of the family must be addressed as they relate to diagnosis, hydrostatic reduction of the intussusception, and potential surgical reduction. After a successful reduction by barium enema, oral feedings are initiated and advanced as tolerated. The child is observed overnight and discharged to home when full diet is tolerated. Pre- and postoperative care was discussed earlier in the chapter. Evaluation of nursing care is the same as for other GI surgical procedures.

## Umbilical Hernias

### Pathophysiology

The most common hernia in infancy is an *umbilical hernia,* which occurs when there is incomplete closure of the abdominal wall where the umbilical vessels exit the abdomen (Dudgeon, Colombani, & Beaver, 1987a; Fig. 29-8). When the peritoneal sac bulges through this fascial defect, the hernia becomes evident (Ziegler, 1987). Strangulation of abdominal contents is rare, and the defect usually resolves without intervention by 3 to 4 years of age. Umbilical hernias are more frequently seen in low-birth-weight infants. There is also a greater incidence in premature infants versus full-term infants and in black infants versus white infants.

### Medical Diagnosis and Management

An umbilical hernia appears as a soft bulge at the umbilicus. Since the incidence of umbilical hernia strangulation is rare, and the hernia generally resolves on its own, the medical intervention is to wait until the child is 3 to 4 years old before considering surgical intervention. Surgical correction is usually performed on an outpatient basis. Many parents believe that applying pressure to the hernia helps to minimize the size and promote the resolution of the hernia. There are no data to support this belief; in fact, applying pressure to the hernia with a coin, abdominal binder, or tape may result in skin disorders and infection.

### Nursing Assessment and Diagnosis

Nursing care of the child with an umbilical hernia is primarily focused on educating the parents. An umbilical hernia is generally a benign problem that resolves on its own; however, many parents are concerned about the

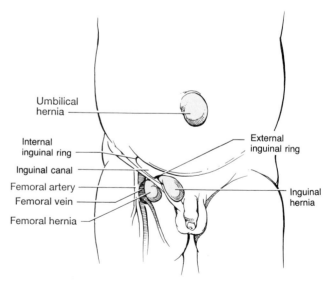

*Figure 29–8. Locations of hernias.*

mass on their child's abdomen. In addition to allaying the parents' fears, the nurse should assess the skin integrity of the hernia for signs of infection and strangulation, including purple discoloration and pain. If the hernia does not resolve by 3 to 4 years of age, the nurse needs to educate the parents and the child about the pre- and postoperative care for surgical correction of the hernia.

Nursing diagnoses for an umbilical hernia might include the following:

- High risk for impaired skin integrity related to home remedies and surgery
- High risk for alteration in parenting related to anxiety and surgery
- Altered GI tissue perfusion related to strangulation

### Planning and Implementing Nursing Care

Patient and parent education must address the facts that an umbilical hernia is, in most cases, benign; the hernia spontaneously resolves with time; and pressure applied to the area does not promote healing and may cause skin breakdown and infection. In addition, the nurse should allow the family time to verbalize their concerns about the child. In order for the nurse to plan the appropriate education, the family's cultural and belief system must be understood.

Pre- and postoperative care of the child requiring surgical repair of an umbilical hernia was discussed earlier in this chapter. This surgery is generally elective.

### Evaluating Nursing Care

The evaluation of nursing care is based primarily on the parent's understanding of the care and management of the umbilical hernia. In the rare instance when the child requires surgical repair of the hernia, evaluation of nursing care should encompass the child's and parents' understanding of the preoperative and postoperative teaching and the child's response to the care.

## Inguinal Hernia

### Pathophysiology

An *inguinal hernia* is the protrusion of abdominal contents into the inguinal or scrotal area. Fluid passing into this area results in the formation of a *hydrocele*. When abdominal structures move past the external inguinal ring, a bulge develops in the groin. This bulge is usually above and lateral to the pubis but may extend down into the scrotum (Nakayama & Rowe, 1989) (see Fig. 29-8). Although there is only a 5% to 10% chance of strangulation of an inguinal hernia, surgical correction is recommended (Ziegler, 1987). Inguinal hernias are eight times more common in boys (Campbell, 1989).

### Medical Diagnosis and Management

Diagnosis of an incarcerated hernia is made by history and physical examination. The physical examination generally reveals a mass in the pubic area. On occasion, the hernia is not present at the time of the office visit, but the parents describe a history of a mass in the groin that comes and goes. Asking the child to bear down, or restraining the child's arms and legs, may produce the hernia as the child struggles. Crying and increasing abdominal pressure may cause the hernia to swell. Inguinal hernias do not spontaneously resolve; however, they may be reduced manually. With the child lying in a supine position, gentle pressure at the base of the hernia may reduce it.

Surgical correction of an inguinal hernia is usually elective and is done on an outpatient basis. If the hernia is red, hard, or painful at the time of the examination, emergency surgery should be done to reduce the hernia and minimize the risk of complications.

### Nursing Assessment and Diagnosis

Nursing assessment is immediately focused on the condition of the hernia and the resulting urgency of the surgical correction. The physical examination should include a detailed assessment of the groin in addition to a complete physical examination to screen the child for any obvious problems that would increase the risk of surgery.

Postoperative assessment of the child includes the level of comfort and hydration status and evaluating the incision site for drainage and infection.

Educating the patient and parents regarding the surgery is integral to preparing them for the preoperative and postoperative process.

Nursing diagnoses for an inguinal hernia might include the following:

- Pain related to surgery
- Altered GI tissue perfusion related to strangulation of the hernia

### Planning and Implementing Nursing Care

Preoperative care of the child with an inguinal hernia includes assessing the site of the hernia for signs of incarceration (color, tenderness, warmth) and assessing the child for signs of infection that would increase the risk of surgery. In addition, the nurse should allow the parents and child to ask any questions and to discuss their concerns or fears.

Postoperative care was discussed earlier in this chapter. Since this procedure is generally done on an outpatient basis, the nurse must teach the parents to observe the child for signs of discomfort and the response to the analgesic administered. In addition, the parents need to care for the child's incision at home, and the nurse should review signs of infection with them.

### Evaluating Nursing Care

Nursing care may be evaluated by determining the parents' understanding of the preoperative and postoperative processes. The child's response to the pain management and diet advancement are also valuable indicators for evaluating the related nursing care.

## Anal Fissures

The most common cause of bright-red rectal bleeding in infancy and childhood is anal fissures. A fissure is a superficial tear in the anal tissue and is most commonly found posteriorly (Dudgeon, Colombani, & Beaver, 1987b). The tears are frequently the result of local trauma to the anal canal caused by hard stools, or they may result from sexual abuse. Chronic anal fissures or skin tags may be indicators of a more serious illness, such as inflammatory bowel disease, and further investigation is necessary. Surgical correction of recurrent anal fissures is rare. Anal fissures are diagnosed by direct inspection of the anus.

## Intestinal Polyps

### Pathophysiology

A polyp is a protrusion from the mucosal surface of the GI tract (Winter, 1991). Polyps may occur as single or multiple lesions. Juvenile polyps account for about 90% of polyps in childhood (Mestre, 1986). *Juvenile polyps* are the most common cause of painless rectal bleeding in children 2 to 5 years old. These polyps are primarily benign rectal and colonic lesions. Acute bleeding may occur from autoamputation of the polyp. Chronic bleeding occurs when the polyp becomes ulcerated or partially amputated. Associated symptoms may include abdominal cramps, prolapse of the polyp through the rectum with stooling, diarrhea, and urgency. There is a low incidence of recurrence of juvenile polyps.

### Medical Diagnosis and Management

Diagnosis is based on a history and physical examination. The child has intermittent, painless, bright-red rectal bleeding. The bleeding may occur over several months. On physical examination, juvenile polyps are frequently palpable since they are usually located in the rectal area. A CBC may be ordered to evaluate for anemia depending on the volume of blood lost. Juvenile polyps are removed by colonoscopy in a procedure called a *polypectomy*.

### Nursing Assessment and Diagnosis

Nursing assessment begins with a careful history and physical examination to determine the degree and fre-

quency of bleeding and stability of the child's condition. In general, children with polyps appear healthy, but the bleeding is traumatic for the family. Once the diagnosis is confirmed, the nurse should assess the child's and parents' understanding of the colonoscopy.

Nursing diagnoses for juvenile polyps might include the following:

- Impaired tissue integrity related to polypectomy
- Altered GI tissue perfusion related to bleeding
- Fear related to bleeding and colonoscopy

### Planning and Implementing Nursing Care

Nursing care focuses on assessing the child's stability and the family's understanding of teaching. The nurse should obtain vital signs and a stool test for blood. Once the diagnosis is confirmed, the nurse should prepare the child and parents for the colonoscopy by discussing the bowel preparation regimen, sedation for the procedure, and what the procedure entails.

After the polypectomy, the nurse should discuss follow-up care and when to call the office. Small amounts of bleeding may be expected, but if the bleeding persists, a return visit should be scheduled.

### Evaluating Nursing Care

Nursing care is evaluated in terms of the child's and family's preparation for the procedure and follow-up care. The child should show minimal signs of complications after the procedure.

## Other Gastrointestinal Problems

## Omphalitis

### Pathophysiology

*Omphalitis* is a serious infection of the umbilicus. The umbilical cord usually dries up and falls off between the 2nd and 3rd week of life. During this time period, a small degree of erythema around the stump is normal, but if the newborn develops a severe bacterial infection, omphalitis results. Omphalitis may result in peritonitis or necrotizing fasciitis by spreading through the umbilical vein (Charlton & Phibbs, 1987). These are potentially life-threatening complications for a newborn.

### Medical Diagnosis and Management

Diagnosis is based on physical examination. The umbilicus appears erythematous, and there may be edema. If secondary peritonitis has resulted, abdominal tenderness may be evident, and the infant is febrile (Shandling, 1991b).

Medical management of omphalitis consists of intravenous antibiotics. If peritonitis develops, a peritoneal tap may be necessary for a bacterial culture. Depending on the culture results, a laparotomy may be required (Shandling, 1991b). Before surgery, the newborn must be treated with antibiotics and hydration fluids to minimize the risk of complications.

### Nursing Assessment and Diagnosis

Nursing assessment begins with examination of the newborn's umbilicus. Typically, the umbilical stump becomes black and hard and falls off. The skin at the base of the umbilical stump is pink and moist and is a good medium for bacterial growth. Inspecting the site for drainage indicative of infection is important. If an infection is evident, the newborn should be assessed for signs of a systemic infection. A clear discharge may signify a connection between the umbilicus and the bladder, a patent urachus (De-Angelis, 1984).

The primary nursing diagnosis for omphalitis is high risk for impaired skin integrity related to infection.

### Planning and Implementing Nursing Care

Nurses should educate parents about the care of the umbilicus. Daily cleansing of the stump with mild soap and water once or twice a day is sufficient to minimize the risk of infection. A small amount of alcohol may be used to help dry the stump. The umbilical stump should be kept dry and not tucked in the diaper. Parents should be told that a small amount of clear or pink odorless discharge is normal up to 2 days after the stump falls off. If parents notice any other discharge, the infant should be seen by their primary care provider.

### Evaluating Nursing Care

The effectiveness of nursing care may be determined by the prevention of infection and the parents' knowledge about and comfort with caring for the umbilical stump.

## Appendicitis

### Pathophysiology

The most common cause for emergency laparotomy in children is acute appendicitis (Shandling, 1991a). The greatest incidence occurs between 15 and 24 years of age. Appendicitis rarely occurs in infants, toddlers, and preschoolers. There is a slightly higher incidence in males than females.

Appendicitis usually results from an obstruction of the appendix by fecal material or a foreign body, which causes stasis in the appendix. Bacteria distal to the obstruction proliferates, and mucus production increases, causing the appendix to become distended and inflamed (Dudgeon, Colombani, & Beaver, 1987b). The appendix becomes gangrenous due to the distention and inflammation and may rupture, allowing the bacterial infection to enter the peritoneal cavity (Shandling, 1991a).

### Medical Diagnosis and Management

Appendicitis is diagnosed by history and physical examination. The child describes a periumbilical, colicky pain that becomes more constant and localized over 1 to 2 days (Shandling, 1991a). This intense pain localizes in the right lower quadrant, and the child may develop a low-grade fever (38.5°C) and decreased appetite. Nausea and vomiting may also occur. If the appendix ruptures, the child may report less pain. As the infection spreads through the abdominal cavity, the child has diffuse abdominal pain and tenderness, vomiting, and malaise (Dudgeon, Colombani, & Beaver, 1987b). The resulting peritonitis causes many complications, leading to a prolonged hospital stay.

The child is hesitant to move and guards the right side by flexing the right hip or walking stooped over. Palpation of the abdomen may reveal severe tenderness in the right lower quadrant, and a mass may be palpable in the lower quadrants if the appendix has ruptured and an abscess has developed (Dudgeon, 1987b). Examination of the child's external genitalia helps to rule out incarcerated hernia and pelvic inflammatory disease. The child should be assessed for signs of dehydration (skin turgor, mucous membranes, urine output).

A CBC is done to determine if the child has an infection, which is evident by an elevated white blood cell count; however, the degree of elevation is variable depending on the degree of inflammation. Radiography or ultrasound provide little useful information.

The therapy for appendicitis is surgical removal of the inflamed appendix. If a ruptured appendix is suspected, the child is given antibiotics intravenously before surgery and for about 10 days after surgery. Clear fluids are given initially, and the diet is advanced as tolerated. The child whose appendix was not ruptured may be discharged by the 3rd postoperative day. In the case of a ruptured appendix, hospitalization usually lasts about 10 days.

### Nursing Assessment and Diagnosis

Nursing assessment of the child with appendicitis is focused on the pre- and postoperative needs of the child and the parents as discussed earlier in this chapter.

Nursing diagnoses for appendicitis might include the following:

- High risk for infection related to possible rupture of the appendix
- Altered nutrition: less than body requirements related to diet manipulation
- Pain related to appendicitis and surgery
- Altered parenting related to hospitalization

## Planning and Implementing Nursing Care

Pre- and postoperative nursing care for the child with appendicitis was discussed earlier in this chapter.

## Evaluating Nursing Care

Evaluation of nursing care is determined by the child's uneventful recovery from the surgery and hospitalization.

# Hepatitis

Hepatitis may occur due to drugs, toxins, and viral agents. The viral agents may be classified as *hepatotropic viruses,* which affect the liver primarily, and *systemic viruses,* which may affect the liver in addition to other body systems. Systemic viral infections include cytomegalovirus, Epstein-Barr virus, herpes simplex virus, herpes zoster virus, varicella, rubella, and human immunodeficiency virus, in addition to many others. Hepatotropic viruses are hepatitis A virus (HAV), hepatitis B virus (HBV), hepatitis C virus (HCV), hepatitis D virus (HDV), and non-A, non-B virus. This section discusses hepatotropic viral hepatitis.

## Pathophysiology

*Hepatitis A virus* is the most common form of viral hepatitis in the pediatric population (Balistreri, 1988). HAV is a simple RNA-containing enterovirus that replicates in the liver. The active virus is secreted from the liver through the biliary system into the small intestine and, as a result, is highly infectious in the stool. HAV is spread predominately through the fecal–oral route but is also found in contaminated shellfish and other foods that have been handled under poor sanitary conditions.

The incubation period of HAV is 2 to 6 weeks after exposure. The highest concentration of virus in the stool is usually about 2 weeks before the onset of jaundice, which makes this a highly infectious virus (Centers for Disease Control, 1990). Day care centers and institutions account for about 30% of the cases of HAV (Smith, 1986). Children typically have mild cases.

*Hepatitis B virus* is a DNA virus of the hepadnavirus family. The virus has a shell that contains antigen. As the virus replicates in the liver, large amounts of hepatitis B surface antigen ($HB_sA_g$) may be identified. The primary route of transmission is sexual or parenteral contact with an infected person. HBV infection is much more complex than HAV. About 90% of all neonates exposed to HBV at birth become chronic carriers if appropriate prophylaxis is not administered (Balistreri, 1988). American children infected with HBV usually are exposed to high-risk situations; infants of mothers who are chronic carriers; hemophiliacs or children receiving blood transfusions; children involved with intravenous drug abuse; or institutionalized children. The incubation period for HBV is about 50 to 180 days. Early signs of infection include urticaria, arthralgia, and arthritis. Other clinical signs and symptoms include anorexia, malaise, nausea, vomiting, and abdominal pain.

*Hepatitis D virus* is a defective RNA virus that requires the presence of HBV to replicate and cause disease. HDV occurs as a coinfection (simultaneous infection with HBV) or as a superinfection of HBV. Coinfection usually resolves (Centers for Disease Control, 1990). Superinfection, however, is usually chronic and may exacerbate the HBV infection.

*Hepatitis C virus* is the first of the non-A, non-B viruses. HCV has been associated with transfusion-acquired hepatitis. The incubation period is 2 to 26 weeks, with a peak incidence at about 7 weeks. Most patients do not develop jaundice, but serological studies show wide fluctuations in aminotransferases.

*Hepatitis E virus,* or endemic non-A, non-B virus, is rarely seen in the United States.

## Medical Diagnosis and Management

Elevations of aminotransferases suggest hepatitis. Careful interpretation of serological screening studies that include markers for viral hepatitis and titers for infections such as Epstein-Barr virus and cytomegalovirus is essential.

Treatment of the child with viral hepatitis is primarily supportive care guided by symptoms. Bed rest may be necessary in the early acute phase. Adequate nutritional intake is essential. School-aged children may return to school as soon as they feel well. Infants and young children should not return to day care settings for 2 weeks after the onset of symptoms (Balistreri, 1988). Hospitalization is necessary if the child has signs of liver failure, such as encephalopathy or coagulopathy. Regular follow-up examination important so that the child may be assessed for indicators of chronic hepatitis.

Prevention of the spread of viral hepatitis is essential. There is no vaccine available for HAV; however, extensive studies have proved that prophylactic immunoglobulin and postexposure immunoglobulin in the early incubation period are 80% to 90% effective in preventing HAV infection (Centers for Disease Control, 1990).

Hepatitis B prevention is more complex. Three types of vaccines are available for HBV prophylaxis, and the current recommendation is for high-risk groups to be vaccinated before exposure. The high-risk groups include health care professionals, clients and staff in institutions for the developmentally disabled, staff of day care centers where children who have HBV attend, hemodialysis patients, sexually active homosexual men, drug users, people receiving frequent blood transfusion products, household and sexual contacts of HBV carriers, and children originally from endemic areas who are $HB_sA_g$-negative.

Special guidelines have been developed for infants of mothers who are HBV carriers. These infants should receive HBV immunoglobulin, 0.5 mL IM, within 12 hours of birth. An initial dose of HBV vaccine should be given simultaneously, and the series of doses should be completed. Research indicates that this schedule provides at least 5 to 7 years of adequate titers for immunity. The issue of boosters is still undecided.

At this time, there are no prophylactic medications for HCV, HDV, and HEV.

### *Nursing Assessment and Diagnosis*

In most instances, children with viral hepatotropic hepatitis are cared for at home. In addition to an assessment of the child's physical status, the family's understanding of the disease, infectious risks, therapy, and follow-up care must be evaluated. Changes in the child's behavior may be a symptom of liver failure and should be assessed. The history should identify who has been in contact with the child, and appropriate prophylaxis measures should be determined.

Nursing diagnoses for viral hepatitis might include the following:

- High risk for infection transmission related to viral hepatitis
- Altered nutrition: less than body requirements related to anorexia
- Activity intolerance related to fatigue
- Impaired social interaction related to fear of viral transmission

### *Planning and Implementing Nursing Care*

Nursing care is primarily supportive for the child with viral hepatitis. Small, frequent, high-calorie meals may provide the child with adequate nutritional intake despite anorexia. Rest periods should be provided throughout the day; strict bed rest is rarely imposed on children. Changes in personality and alterations in the wake/sleep cycle should be recorded by parents. Asking older children to write their name or copy a basic object may demonstrate subtle changes in mental status that require immediate medical evaluation. The child's physical examination should focus on the skin, eyes (jaundice), and abdomen (tenderness, hepatosplenomegaly).

Education about the infection, its prognosis, and management should be provided. Counseling regarding preventing spread of the virus is essential. Appropriate referrals for immunoglobulin and vaccination should be provided for family and community members.

### *Evaluating Nursing Care*

Evaluation of nursing care includes determining that the child's nutritional and energy needs have been met and that complications of hepatitis have been avoided. The parents should demonstrate their understanding of the

education provided and should be referred for therapy and prophylaxis to prevent spread of the infection.

## *Cholecystitis*

Acute cholecystitis results from an obstruction of the cystic duct followed by an inflammatory response. In most cases, acute cholecystitis is idiopathic in childhood. Gallstones are rare in children under 21 years old, but within that age group, they most often occur in obese adolescent girls (Thaler, 1987). Cholecystitis has been associated with common acute viral illnesses.

Care for children and adolescents with colecystitis is the same as for adults. Readers are referred to a medical-surgical nursing text for further information.

## *Pancreatitis*

*Pancreatitis,* an inflammation of the pancreas, may be classified as acute or chronic. Acute pancreatitis may be seen in a single episode or repeatedly. Chronic pancreatitis is rare in children, and care is similar to that for adults. Readers are referred to a medical-surgical nursing text for further information.

## *Peptic Ulcer Disease*

### *Pathophysiology*

A *peptic ulcer* is an erosion of the mucosal wall of the stomach, pylorus, or duodenum. Primary ulcers occur in otherwise heathy people with no history of medication use. They are insidious in onset, and the prognosis is excellent with proper therapy. Secondary ulcers are associated with underlying systemic disorders or occur as consequences of medical therapy with various medications. The etiology of peptic ulcer disease remains unclear.

### *Medical Diagnosis and Management*

Abdominal pain is the most common symptoms of peptic ulcers. Younger children describe the pain as periumbilical, while older children and adolescents describe it as epigastric. The pain may occur episodically throughout the day and night. The pain may or may not be relieved with food. Vomiting is common and may be the only symptom in young children. Other symptoms include nausea, dyspepsia (heartburn), and flatulence. GI bleeding is an uncommon presentation in primary ulcers but does occur in 80% of secondary ulcers (Byrne, 1987).

Diagnosis may be made with documentation of a lesion. An upper endoscopy is performed to confirm the diagnosis. Therapy is aimed at neutralizing the gastric sections to facilitate healing. Numerous agents are available, ranging from antacids (Maalox, Mylanta) to $H_2$-receptor blockers (cimetidine, ranitidine). Sucralfate, a coating agent, is effective in treating duodenal ulcers (Byrne, 1987). Dietary manipulation is not indicated in children. Surgical intervention is indicated when perforation, obstruction, uncontrollable bleeding, or intractability is present.

### Nursing Assessment and Diagnosis

Nursing assessment begins with a history and physical examination. Dietary intake and medication use must be established. A history of the pain, including location, frequency, intensity, and duration, is important. The effect of food on the pain, as well as a history of vomiting, are also assessed. The physical examination may be unremarkable. Stools are often positive for blood.

Nursing diagnoses for peptic ulcer disease might include the following:

- Impaired tissue integrity related to the lesion
- Pain related to the lesion

### Planning and Implementing Nursing Care

The nursing care of children with peptic ulcer disease includes monitoring vital signs to determine changes in clinical status in preparation for diagnostic procedures. The child is made NPO, and an intravenous line is established before the endoscopic evaluation. Educational preparation includes a description of the equipment, sedation procedures, and interventions after the procedure. Administration of medications must take into account the interactions between $H_2$-receptor blockers and coating agents. These medications should not be administered together since sucralfate inhibits the action of the $H_2$-receptor blocker. Antacids are administered 1 hour before and 2 hours after meals. Parents should understand how to administer the medication, its mechanism of action, and the administration schedule. The family should also understand the diagnosis, the disease process, and the medical plan of care.

### Evaluating Nursing Care

The nursing care of children with peptic ulcer disease is evaluated by monitoring of expected outcomes. The child should be free from pain, well nourished, and able to tolerate oral feedings. The child and family should demonstrate their understanding of the medication regimen.

### Summary

Since proper nutrition is essential for normal growth and development, GI function must be maintained. GI problems are among the most numerous and common disorders of infancy and childhood, and they vary in severity from a mild case of diarrhea to complex, life-threatening illness. Alterations in GI function can be caused by structural defects, obstructions, inflammations, or malabsorption, and they can affect the processes of ingestion, digestion, absorption, and elimination. Nurses interact with children and their families in assessing and identifying problems and in providing direct care as well as information, education, and support.

# Nursing Care Plan

### Assessment

Peter Billingsworth is a 2½-month-old boy brought to the pediatrician's office for well-baby check-up.

### Chief Complaint

Peter's mother is concerned about Peter's vomiting after every bottle. The emesis is ruining the carpet.

### Subjective Assessment

*Past History:* Uncomplicated pregnancy and delivery. Full-term healthy infant with no illnesses or hospitalizations.

*Present History:* Effortless vomiting throughout the day. Mother notes change in effect—becoming more fussy. Due for first immunizations. No history of fever or change in stools. Diet of standard cow's milk infant formula.

*(continued)*

# Nursing Care Plan *(Continued)*

***Family History:*** Mother is 28 years old; father is 30 years old. Both are healthy and employed. Older sister, Sarah, is 18 months old and healthy. Maternal and paternal grandparents are alive and well. No family history of gastrointestinal illnesses.

## Objective Assessment

***Physical Examination:*** T. 37°C (98.6°F) (rectal); P. 130; R. 32; B.P. 90/50 (R arm); weight 6.4 kg (14 lb) (50% [NCHS percentile]); height 61.8 cm (24.5 in) (50% [NCHS percentile]).

| | |
|---|---|
| Integument: | Pink, warm, good turgor, no rashes |
| Head: | Normocephalic, anterior fontanel open, flat, and soft |
| Eyes: | Red reflex, sclera white |
| Ears: | Tympanic membrane pearly gray, clear visualization of landmarks |
| Nose: | Patent nares |
| Throat: | Pharynx without erythema |
| Neck: | Supple, no lymphadenopathy |
| Thorax and Lungs: | Clear to auscultation, no rales, no wheezing |
| Heart: | Normal rhythm, no murmur |
| Abdomen: | Round, soft, nontender, no palpable masses, no organomegaly |
| Genitalia: | Normal |
| Musculoskeletal: | No hip click |
| Neurological: | Moro and startle reflexes present |

## Medical Diagnosis

Gastroesophageal reflux

## Nursing Care Plan for an Infant with Gastroesophageal Reflux

| Goals | Nursing Interventions | Evaluation Criteria |
|---|---|---|
| **NURSING DIAGNOSIS #1:** *Alteration in nutrition: less than body requirements related to vomiting* | | |
| (S) Infant will receive appropriate caloric intake to promote growth and development | Thicken feedings with rice cereal<br><br>Small frequent feedings<br><br>Position infant supine HOB elevated 30° following feedings | Infant's vomiting is decreased<br><br>Infant's growth continues at 50% |
| **NURSING DIAGNOSIS #2:** *Potential for aspiration related to ineffective airway clearance secondary to vomiting and positioning* | | |
| (S) Infant will not aspirate | Position infant supine HOB elevated 30° following feedings<br><br>Quiet activity following feedings<br><br>Do not elevate legs over abdomen (diaper change) | Infant will have no signs or symptoms of respiratory distress |

*(continued)*

# Nursing Care Plan *(Continued)*

*NURSING DIAGNOSIS #3: Alteration in family process related to parental anxiety*

(S) Parents will be comfortable with diagnosis and care of infant

Parental education:

1. Diagnosis
2. Thickened feedings
3. Small, frequent feedings
4. Positioning
5. Quiet activities
6. Diaper changing

Parents display decreased anxiety, over vomiting episodes

Parents verbalize care of child

# References

Altschuler, S. M. (1987). Constipation. In Schwartz, M. W., Charley, E. G., Curry, T. A., & Ludwig, S. (Eds.). *Principles and practice of clinical pediatrics.* Chicago: Year Book Medical Publishers, 160–193.

Andorsky, M. B. (1987a). Aganglionic megacolon (Hirschsprung's disease). In Rudolph, A. M. (Ed.). *Pediatrics.* Norwalk, CT: Appleton & Lange, 946–947.

Andorsky, M. B. (1987b). Constipation. In Rudolph, A. M. (Ed.). *Pediatrics.* Norwalk, CT: Appleton & Lange, 900–901.

Andorsky, M. B. (1987c). Gluten-sensitive enteropathy. In Rudolph, A. M. (Ed.). *Pediatrics.* Norwalk, CT: Appleton & Lange, 925–927.

Andorsky, M. B. (1987d). Vomiting. In Rudolph, A. M. (Ed.). *Pediatrics.* Norwalk, CT: Appleton & Lange, 902–903.

Balistreri, W. F. (1983). Viral hepatitis. *Pediatric Clinics of North America, 35*(2), 375–407.

Bishop, W. P., & Ulshen, M. H. (1987). Bacterial gastroenteritis. *Pediatric Clinics of North America, 35*(1), 69–88.

Black, M. (1980). Acetaminophen toxicity. *Gastroenterology, 78,* 382–392.

Book, L. S. (1984). Vomiting and diarrhea. *Pediatrics, 74,* 950–951.

Brown, E. G., & Sweet, A. Y. (1982). Neonatal necrotizing enterocolitis. *Pediatric Clinics of North America, 29,* 1149–1170.

Byrne, W. J. (1987). Peptic disease in children. In Rudolph, A. M. (Ed.). *Pediatrics.* Norwalk, CT: Appleton & Lange, 916–917.

Campbell, J. R. (1989). Inguinal and scrotal problems in infants and children. *Pediatric Annals, 18*(3), 189–191.

Carey, W. B. (1984). "Colic"—primary excessive crying as an infant-environment interaction. *Pediatric Clinics of North America, 31*(5), 993–1004.

Centers for Disease Control. (1990). Protection against viral hepatitis: Recommendations of the Immunization Practices Advisory Committee (IPAC). *MMWR, 39*(S-2), 1–26.

Charlton, V. E., & Phibbs, R. H. (1987). Examination of the newborn. In Rudolph, A. M. (Ed.). *Pediatrics.* Norwalk, CT: Appleton & Lange, 112–122.

Clemente, C. D. (Ed.). (1985) *Gray's anatomy of the human body* (30th American ed.). Philadelphia: Lea & Febiger.

DeAngelis, C. (1984). *Pediatric primary care* (3rd ed.). Boston: Little, Brown & Company.

DeWitt, T. G. (1989). Acute diarrhea in children. *Pediatrics in Review, 11*(1), 6–13.

Dudgeon, D. L., Colombani, P. M., & Beaver, B. L. (1987a). Abdominal wall defects. In Rudolph, A. M. (Ed.). *Pediatrics.* Norwalk, CT: Appleton & Lange, 952–955.

Dudgeon, D. L., Colombani, P. M., & Beaver, B. L. (1987b). Colonic and anorectal lesions: Surgical considerations. In Rudolph, A. M. (Ed.). *Pediatrics.* Norwalk, CT: Appleton & Lange, 947–951.

Dudgeon, D. L., Colombani, P. M., & Beaver, B. L. (1987c). Jejunoileal lesions: Surgical considerations. In Rudolph, A. M. (Ed.). *Pediatrics.* Norwalk, CT: Appleton & Lange, 941–946.

Dudgeon, D. L., Colombani, P. M., & Beaver, B. L. (1987d). Tracheoesophageal fistula and esophageal atresia. In Rudolph, A. M. (Ed.). *Pediatrics.* Norwalk, CT: Appleton & Lange, 909–911.

Frommer, D. J. (1974). Defective biliary excretion of copper in Wilson's disease. *Gut, 15,* 125–129.

Forsyth, B. W. (1989). Colic and the effect of changing formulas: A double-blind, multiple crossover study. *Journal of Pediatrics, 115*(4), 521–526.

Geertsma, M. A., & Hyams, J. S. (1989). Colic—a pain syndrome in infancy? *Pediatric Clinics of North America, 36*(4), 905–919.

Gillies, C. (1987). Infant colic: Is there anything new? *Journal of Pediatric Health Care, 1*(6), 305–312.

Granger, R. H. (1987). Bladder and bowel control disorders. In Rudolph, A. M. (Ed.). *Pediatrics.* Norwalk, CT: Appleton & Lange, 58–60.

Gregory, G. A., & Kitterman, J. A. (1987). Lesions of the diaphragm. In Rudolph, A. M. (Ed). *Pediatrics.* Norwalk, CT: Appleton & Lange, 1374–1375.

Grenga, T. E. (1983). A new risk of lye ingestion by children. *New England Journal of Medicine, 308,* 156–157.

Grosfeld, J. L. (1986). Jejunoileal atresia and stenosis. In Welch, K. J., Randolph, J. G., Ravitch, M. M., O'Neill, J. A., & Rowe, M. I. (Eds.). *Pediatric surgery.* Chicago: Year Book Medical Publishers, 808–810.

Guyton, A. C. (1986). *Textbook of medical physiology* (7th ed.). Philadelphia: W.B. Saunders.

Hillemeier, A. C. (1991). Reflux and esophagitis. In Walker, W. A., Durie, P. R., Hamilton, J. R., Walker-Smith, J. A., & Watkins, J. B. (Eds.). *Pediatric gastrointestinal disease: Pathophysiology, diagnosis, management.* Philadelphia: B. C. Decker, 417–422.

Hunsicker, U. A., & Barr, R. G. (1986). Increased carrying reduces infant crying: A randomized controlled study. *Pediatrics, 77,* 641–648.

Israel, E. J. (1991). Necrotizing enterocolitis. In Walker, W. A., Durie, P. R., Hamilton, J. R., Walker-Smith, J. A., & Watkins, J. B. (Eds.). *Pediatric gastrointestinal disease: Pathophysiology, diagnosis, management.* Philadelphia: B. C. Decker, 639–646.

Kirschner, B. S. (1991). Hirschsprung's disease. In Walker, W. A., Durie, P. R., Hamilton, J. R., Walker-Smith, J. A., & Watkins, J. B. (Eds). *Pediatric Gastrointestinal Disease: Pathophysiology, diagnosis, management.* Philadelphia: B. C. Decker, 829–832.

Leape, L., Ashcraft, K. W., Scrapilli, D. G., & Holder, T. M. (1971). Hazard to health—liquid lye. *New England Journal of Medicine, 284,* 478–480.

Litovitz, T. L. (1985). Battery ingestions: Product accessibility and clinical course. *Pediatrics, 75,* 469–476.

Mestre, J. R. (1986). The changing pattern of juvenile polyps. *American Journal of Gastroenterology, 81,* 312–314.

Moore, W. R. (1986). Caustic ingestions: Pathophysiology, diagnosis and treatment. *Clinical Pediatrics, 25,* 196.

Mueller, R. F. (1987). The Alagille syndrome (arteriohepatic dysplasia). *Journal of Medical Genetics, 24,* 621–626.

Nakayama, D., & Rowe, M. I. (1989). Inguinal hernia and the acute scrotum in infants and children. *Pediatrics in Review, 11*(3), 87–93.

Nugent, J. (1986). Extracorporeal membrane oxygenation in the neonate. *Neonatal Network, 4*(4), 27–38.

Orenstein, D. R., & Whittingham, P. R. (1983). Positioning for prevention of infant gastroesophageal reflux. *Journal of Pediatrics, 103,* 534–537.

Perlmutter, D. H. (1991). α1-Antitrypsin deficiency. In Walker, W. A., Durie, P. R., Hamilton, J. R., Walker-Smith, J. A., & Watkins, J. B. (Eds.). *Pediatric gastrointestinal disease: Pathophysiology, diagnosis, management.* Philadelphia, PA: B. C. Decker, 976–991.

Piccoli, D. A., & Witzleban, C. L. (1991a). Disorders of the intrahepatic bile ducts. In Walker, W. A., Durie, P. R., Hamilton, J. R., Walker-Smith, J. A., & Watkins, J. B. (Eds.). *Pediatric gastrointestinal disease: Pathophysiology, diagnosis, management.* Philadelphia, PA: B. C. Decker, 1124–1140.

Piccoli, D. A., & Witzleban, C. L. (1991b). Disorders of the extrahepatic bile ducts. In Walker, W. A., Durie, P. R., Ham-

ilton, J. R., Walker-Smith, J. A., & Watkins, J. B. (Eds.). *Pediatric gastrointestinal disease: Pathophysiology, diagnosis, management.* Philadelphia, PA: B. C. Decker, 1140–1151.

Pinyerd, B. J., & Zipf, W. B. (1989). Colic: Idiopathic, excessive, infant crying. *Journal of Pediatric Nursing, 4*(3), 147–161.

Postlethwait, R. W. (1983). Chemical burns of the esophagus. *Surgical Clinics of North America, 63,* 915–924.

Rumack, B. H. (1987). Acetaminophen poisoning. In Rudolph, A. M. (Ed.). *Pediatrics.* Norwalk, CT: Appleton & Lange, 722–723.

Schwartz, D. L. (1988). Congenital malformations and surgical intestinal emergencies of infancy. In Silverberg, M., & Daum F. *Textbook of pediatric gastroenterology.* Chicago: Year Book Medical Publishers, 194–240.

Scott, T. F. (1987). Infectious diseases. In Schwartz, M. W., Charney, E. B., Curray, T. A., & Ludwig, S. (Eds.). *Principles and practice of clinical pediatrics.* Chicago: Year Book Medical Publishers, 416–430.

Shandling, B. (1991a). Appendicitis. In Walker, W. A., Durie, P. R., Hamilton, J. R., Walker-Smith, J. A., & Watkins, J. B. (Eds.). *Pediatric gastrointestinal disease: Pathophysiology, diagnosis, management.* Philadelphia: B. C. Decker, 754–757.

Shandling, B. (1991b). Peritonitis. In Walker, W. A., Durie, P. R., Hamilton, J. R., Walker-Smith, J. A., & Watkins, J. B. (Eds.). *Pediatric gastrointestinal disease: Pathophysiology, diagnosis, management.* Philadelphia: B. C. Decker, 496–499.

Smith, D. P. (1986). Common day-care disease: Patterns and prevention. *Pediatric Nursing, 12*(3), 175–179.

Swenson, O., Sherman, J., Fisher, J. (1973). Diagnosis of congenital megacolon. An analysis of 501 patients. *Journal of Pediatric Surgery, 8,* 587.

Taubman, B. (1988). Parental counselling compared with elimination of cow's milk or soy mild protein for the treatment of infant colic syndrome: A randomized trial. *Pediatrics, 81*(6), 756–761.

Thaler, M. M. (1987). The liver and bile ducts. In Rudolph, A. M. (Ed.) *Pediatrics.* Norwalk, CT: Appleton & Lange, 991–993.

Touloukian, R. J. (1986). Necrotizing enterocolitis. *Pediatric Case Reports in Gastrointestinal Diseases, 6*(1), 1–7.

Weibley, T. T., Adamson, M., Clinkscales, N., Curran, J., & Bramson, R. (1987). Gavage tube insertion in the premature infant. *American Journal of Maternal Child Nursing, 12,* 24–27.

Wesson, D. (1991a). Acute intestinal obstruction. In Walker, W. A., Durie, P. R., Hamilton, J. R., Walker-Smith, J. A., & Watkins, J. B. (Eds.). *Pediatric gastrointestinal disease: Pathophysiology, diagnosis, management.* Philadelphia: B. C. Decker, 486–493.

Wesson, D. (1991b). Congenital anomalies. In Walker, W. A., Durie, P. R., Hamilton, J. R., Walker-Smith, J. A., & Watkins, J. B. (Eds.). *Pediatric gastrointestinal disease: Pathophysiology, diagnosis, management.* Philadelphia: B. C. Decker, 477–484.

Wesson, D. (1991c). Hernia. In Walker, W. A., Durie, P. R., Hamilton, J. R., Walker-Smith, J. A., & Watkins, J. B. (Eds.). *Pediatric gastrointestinal disease: Pathophysiology, diagnosis, management.* Philadelphia: B. C. Decker, 494–496.

Wesson, D. (1991d). Trauma and foreign bodies. In Walker, W. A., Durie, P. R., Hamilton, J. R., Walker-Smith, J. A., & Watkins, J. B. (Eds.). *Pediatric gastrointestinal disease: Pathophysiology, diagnosis, management.* Philadelphia: B. C. Decker, 484–486.

Wetmore, R. F. (1987). The oral cavity. In Rudolph, A. M. (Ed.). *Pediatrics.* Norwalk, CT: Appleton & Lange, 889–989.

Winter, H. S. (1991). Intestinal polyps. In Walker, W. A., Durie, P. R., Hamilton, J. R., Walker-Smith, J. A., & Watkins, J. B. (Eds.). *Pediatric gastrointestinal disease: Pathophysiology, diagnosis, management.* Philadelphia: B. C. Decker, 739–753.

Younger, J. B., & Hughes, L. S. (1983). No-fault management of encopresis. *Pediatric Nursing,* 185–187.

Ziegler, M. M. (1987). Lumps and bumps. In Schwartz, M. W., Charney, E. B., Curry, T. A., & Ludwig, S. (Eds.). *Principles and practices in clinical pediatrics.* Chicago: Year Book Medical Publishers, 493–499.

## Bibliography

Boatwright, D. M., & Crummete, B. D. (1991, Winter). Preparing children for endoscopy and manometry. *Gastroenterology nursing,* 142–145.

Buzby, M. (1989). Chronic diarrhea: Management in pediatrics. *Journal of Pediatric Health Care, 3*(3), 163–165.

Castiglia, P. T. (1987). Encopresis. *Journal of Pediatric Health Care, 1*(6), 335–337.

Castiglia, P. T. (1988). Failure to thrive. *Journal of Pediatric Health Care, 2*(1), 50–51.

Eastham, E. J. (1991). Peptic ulcer. In Walker, W. A., Durie, P. R., Hamilton, J. R., Walker-Smith, J. A., & Watkins, J. B. (Eds.). *Pediatric gastrointestinal disease: Pathophysiology, diagnosis, management.* Philadelphia: B. C. Decker, 438–457.

Ellett, M. L. (1990). Constipation/encopresis: A nursing perspective. *Journal of Pediatric Health Care, 4*(3), 141–146.

Ellett, M. L. (1991, Winter). General anesthesia: An alternative to sedation for endoscopic procedures. *Gastroenterology Nursing,* 166–168.

Gans, S. L. (1990). Managing children with hernia or undescended testicles. *Pediatric Consult, 8*(2), 1–8.

Huddleston, K. C., & Ferraro, A. R. (1991). Preparing families of children with gastrostomy feedings. *Pediatric Nursing, 17*(2), 153–158.

Jackson, W. D., & Grand, R. J. (1991). Crohn's disease. In Walker, W. A., Durie, P. R., Hamilton, J. R., Walker-Smith, J. A., & Watkins, J. B. (Eds.). *Pediatric gastrointestinal disease: Pathophysiology, diagnosis, management.* Philadelphia: B. C. Decker, 592–608.

Jackson, W. D., & Grand, R. J. (1991). Ulcerative colitis. In Walker, W. A., Durie, P. R., Hamilton, J. R., Walker-Smith, J. A., & Watkins, J. B. (Eds.). *Pediatric gastrointestinal disease: Pathophysiology, diagnosis, management.* Philadelphia: B. C. Decker, 608–618.

Kenna, M. A., & Bluestone, C. D. (1988). Foreign bodies in the air and food passages. *Pediatrics in Review, 10*(1), 25–31.

McGee, Linda. (1987). Feeding gastrostomy. *Journal of Enterostomal Therapy, 14,* 74–8.

Moore, K. L. (1988). *Essentials of human embryology.* Toronto: B. C. Decker.

Paarlberg, J., & Balint, J. P. (1985). Gastrostomy tubes: Practical guidelines for home care. *Pediatric Nursing, 11*(2), 99–102.

Peck, S. M., & Griffith, D. J. (1988). Reducing portal hypertension and variceal bleeding. *Dimensions of Critical Care Nursing, 7*(5), 269–279.

Perez, R. C., Beckom, K., & Jebaraa, L. (1984). Care of the child with a gastrostomy tube: Common practical concerns. *Issues in Comprehensive Pediatric Nursing, 7*(2/3), 107–119.

Silverman, R., & Roy, C. (1986). *Pediatric clinical gastroenterology* (3rd ed.). St. Louis: C. V. Mosby.

Stadtler, A. C. (1989). Preventing encopresis. *Pediatric Nursing, 15*(3), 282–284.

Starkey, J. F., Jefferson, P. A., & Kirby, D. A. (1988, January). Taking care of percutaneous endoscopic gastrostomy. *American Journal of Nursing,* 42–45.

# Alterations in Renal Function

Richard E. Harbin and Michael W. Neft

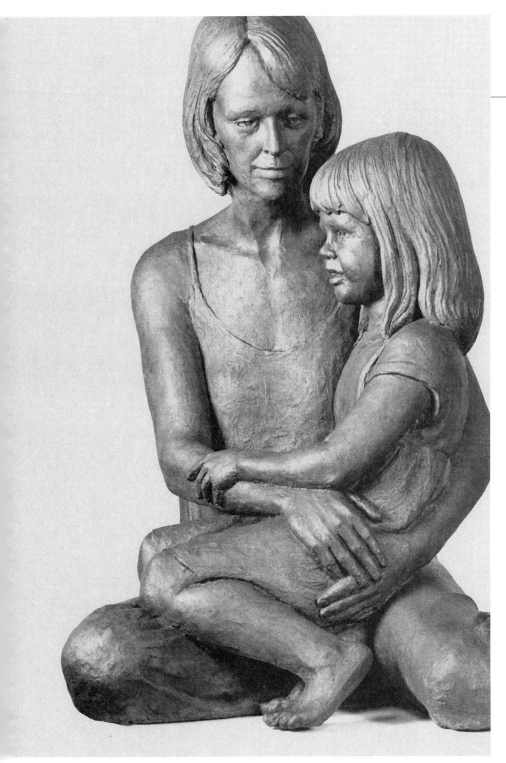

*Sculpture by Charles Parks*

*30*

*Embryology*

*Anatomy and Physiology*

*Assessment*

*Nursing Diagnosis*

*Planning and Implementing Nursing Care*

*Nursing Interventions*

*Evaluating Nursing Care*

*Congenital Renal Problems*

*Renal Problems of Neonates*

*Renal Problems of Infants*

*Renal Problems of Toddlers and Preschoolers*

*Acute Renal Problems*

*Chronic Renal Problems*

*Dialysis*

*Renal Transplantation*

*Summary*

*Nursing Care Plan*

## Learning Objectives

*Upon completion of this chapter the reader will be able to:*

1. *Demonstrate an understanding of embryological development of the renal system.*

2. *Discuss the structure and function of the renal system.*

3. *Discuss the principles involving glomerular filtration, and tubular reabsorption and secretion.*

4. *Review the assessment of the renal system.*

5. *Discuss the diagnostic procedures used to evaluate the function of the renal system.*

6. *Formulate nursing diagnoses for the child with a renal system disorder.*

7. *Identify nursing interventions applicable to the child with a renal system disorder.*

8. *Discuss the treatment modalities and nursing interventions used for the child with problems related to congenital anomalies, obstruction, infection, and alteration of renal filtration.*

9. *Discuss the indications, principles, and nursing interventions for the child undergoing kidney dialysis.*

10. *Discuss the psychosocial aspects involved in the planning and implementation of nursing care for the child with a renal problem.*

## Key Terms

*azotemia*

*bladder*

*blood urea nitrogen (BUN)*

*Bowman's capsule*

*calyx*

*catheterization*

*chordee*

*dialysis*

*epispadias*

*glomerulus*

*hematuria*

*hemodialysis*

*hypospadias*

*intravenous pyelogram*

*kidney*

*loop of Henle*

*nephron*

*oliguria*

*peritoneal dialysis*

*pyuria*

*reflux*

*renal corpuscle*

*renal pelvis*

*renal tubule*

*serum creatinine*

*uremia*

*ureter*

*urethra*

*urethroplasty*

*voiding cystourethrogram*

Alterations in renal function affect the child's overall good health and homeostasis. The organs of the renal system interact with and affect many of the other body systems to maintain composition and volume of body fluids. In addition to fluid regulation and waste elimination, the renal system also affects the endocrine, circulatory, and reproductive systems. Disease states that have an impact on the renal system and interfere with its normal function result in numerous sequelae to a variety of the body's systems and processes. Chronic illness involving renal dysfunction can have a serious impact on the child's growth and development, as well as on the function of the child's family.

## Embryology

Development of the renal or urinary system is similar to the development of the reproductive system. The renal and reproductive systems share components in their normal function.

### The Kidney and Ureter

The embryo develops three successive sets of renal organs. The first is the pronephros, or "forekidney," which appears early in the fourth week and is a nonfunctional structure. The mesonephros, or "midkidney," replaces the first organ as it degenerates late in the fourth week and may function during the development of the permanent kidney. The mesonephros degenerates by the end of the embryonic period, and generally disappears except for its ducts, which become genital ducts in males or form vestigial remnants in females. The third kidney is the metanephros, or "hindkidney," which appears in the fifth week and becomes the permanent kidney. This final kidney initiates function at about eight weeks and actively forms urine throughout the fetal period. This urine mixes with amniotic fluid which is swallowed by the fetus. The kidneys are first located in the pelvis but gradually ascend to the abdomen during the fetal period.

### The Bladder and Urethra

The cloaca, the expanded terminal part of the hindgut of the digestive system, divides into a dorsal rectum and a ventral urogenital sinus during the sixth week. The urogenital sinus and adjacent connective tissue, mesenchyme, form the bladder and urethra. The bladder enlarges, absorbing the mesonephric ducts and developing the opening for the ureters. The female urethra and much of the male urethra have the same origin as the bladder.

### The Adrenal Glands

The adrenal glands develop from different origins. The adrenal cortex develops from mesoderm and the medulla from neuroectoderm. The medulla of the adrenal gland develops from the neural crest. Adrenal gland development begins during the fifth week of pregnancy. Differentiation of the adrenal cortex begins late in the fetal period, and is completed at 4 years of age.

## Anatomy and Physiology

The renal system comprises the kidneys, ureters, bladder, and urethra (Fig. 30-1). The kidneys are two bean-shaped organs located retroperitoneally on each side of the vertebral column. The left kidney is slightly higher than the right kidney, which is displaced by the liver. The kidneys are slightly lower in children than in adults. Urine is produced in the kidneys and transported to the bladder via the ureters, long tube-like structures composed of mucosal, muscle, and fibrous layers through which urine is transported by peristalsis. The ureters join the posterior bladder at an oblique angle that serves to prevent reflux, or urine backflow.

The bladder is a muscular pouch located in the anterior inferior portion of the pelvic cavity that collects urine. The capacity of the bladder at birth is approximately 15 to 20 mL, increasing to the adult capacity of 700 mL. The urethra is a hollow tube that carries urine from the bladder. The urethral sphincter relaxes when the bladder reaches a certain volume. The male urethra is approximately five times longer than the female urethra. The urethra is shorter in children than in adults.

### Renal Function

The central functional unit of the kidney is the nephron, which regulates and maintains volume and composition of body fluids and excretes soluble wastes. Each kidney contains between 1 million and 1.5 million nephrons. A nephron is composed of a renal tubule and a renal corpuscle. The renal corpuscle consists of the glomerulus, a network of capillaries between the afferent and efferent arterioles that is encased by Bowman's capsule. This capsule filters materials in and out of the glomerulus and acts as the beginning point for the renal tubule, which passes through the nephron. As it progresses, the tubule changes names—it begins as the proximal convoluted tubule, then becomes the loop of Henle, the distal convoluted tubule, and the collecting duct, and finally ends at the collecting tubule. These collecting tubules join other collecting tubules or ducts that open into a calyx. The calyces converge into the renal pelvis, a section of the kidney that is attached to the ureter. Urine drains from the renal calyces into the ureters and is transported to the bladder.

The kidneys maintain the body's acid–base and fluid electrolyte balance and remove waste products through urine production. Urine formation involves the processes of glomerular filtration and tubular reabsorption and secretion.

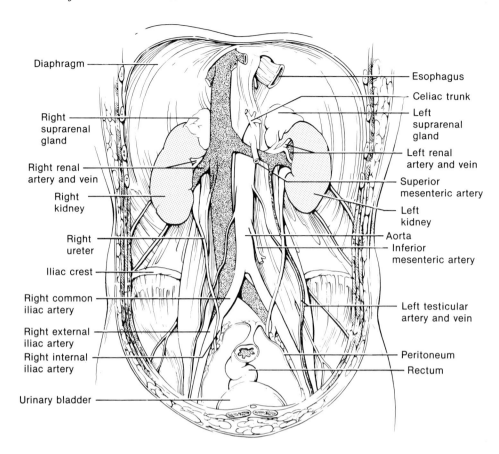

*Figure 30–1. Anatomy of the renal system. (Patrick, M.L., et al. [1991].* Medical-surgical nursing *[2nd ed.]. Philadelphia: J.B. Lippincott, p. 991)*

## Glomerular Filtration

Urine is initially produced at the glomerulus through the process of filtration of plasma. Blood enters the glomerulus at a high pressure, which forces plasma fluid and solutes through the glomerular membrane into Bowman's capsule. Filtration occurs when the pressure within the glomerular capillaries is greater than the colloidal osmotic pressure (COP) of the plasma proteins. Glomerular filtration rate (GFR) is a measurement of the glomerular filtrate produced per minute, and is determined by blood pressure, effective filtration pressure, and the permeability of the glomerular capillaries. If any of these factors are altered, the GFR will be affected. The normal glomerular filtration rate is 125 mL/minute.

## Tubular Reabsorption and Secretion

The glomerular filtrate then passes through the renal tubules, where about 99% is reabsorbed and returned to the plasma. Tubular cells reabsorb the substances essential for homeostasis, such as water and electrolytes. Tubular cells also function to secrete out nonessential substances such as ammonia, potassium, and uric acid. The substances are secreted into the lumen of the renal tubule,

aiding in their elimination. Tubular reabsorption and secretion can occur either as an active or as a passive process. Active transport requires energy and involves the reabsorption of sodium, potassium, glucose, calcium, phosphate, and amino acids. Passive transport involves osmosis or diffusion. Urea, water, chloride, bicarbonates, and phosphates are reabsorbed through passive transport.

Children do not obtain adult glomerular filtration and absorption values until after 1 year of age. This delay is related to higher pressures in the blood vessel component that supplies each nephron. The newborn is thus less efficient and slower in disposing of excess water and solute. The newborn is also unable to concentrate urine until the third month of life (de Wardener, 1985), due to the shortness of the loop of Henle where sodium and water are reabsorbed.

## Assessment

A systematic approach is necessary in the nursing assessment of a child with a suspected renal system problem. The kidneys play a central role in the child's general health and homeostasis, and a problem involving the renal system can affect numerous body systems. The renal system also affects circulation, reproductive function, and hormonal regulation. In addition to the possibility of multiple systems involvement, nurses must also consider a broad range of signs and symptoms in the nursing assessment of the renal system.

## History

Review of urinary function should be included in every history. Nursing assessment should involve a detailed history, because many renal problems can have subtle manifestations initially and result in complications if undetected. The child's sex and age are important factors in the assessment. The presenting complaints, and the incidence or likelihood of various disorders, vary with age. The young child may present with symptoms that fail to focus on the urinary system.

Nursing assessment includes the history, physical examination, and observation of symptoms. As in all children, the parents are crucial in obtaining valid information and may assist in gaining the child's cooperation. One part of the history that can be very important is information about the terms the child uses for bodily functions. Table 30-1 outlines important subjective data to be obtained from a detailed nursing history.

*Table 30–1. Subjective Data and Nursing History of Renal System*

I. Family history
   A. Kidney disease
   B. Diabetes
   C. Hypospadias
   D. Enuresis

II. Prenatal history
   A. Maternal injury
   B. Medications; exposure to toxins, alcohol, drugs, or cigarettes
   C. Parental contact with a sexually transmitted disease and treatment
   D. Presence of polyhydramnios (excessive amniotic fluid) or oligohydramnios (sparse amniotic fluid); other complications
   E. Number of umbilical cord vessels
   F. Neonatal voiding problems

III. Developmental history
   A. Information on toilet training and normal urinary habits
   B. Any regression after urinary control achieved
   C. Terms used by child and family for urinary functions and organs

IV. Past history
   A. Kidney disease
   B. Urinary tract infection
   C. History of back trauma
   D. Venereal disease; vaginitis
   E. Hospitalizations for renal system disease

V. Review of urinary system
   A. Voiding pattern
   B. Polyuria
   C. Dysuria
   D. Oliguria
   E. Edema
   F. Color and odor of urine

VI. Present illness
   A. Presenting problem
   B. Precipitating factors
   C. Duration, location, severity
   D. Changes in feeding or fluid intake
   E. Change in appetite
   F. Alteration in sleeping pattern
   G. Behavior changes: irritability, easily fatigued
   H. Vaginal or penile discharge; itching
   I. Gastrointestinal complaints
   J. Sexual contacts if STD suspected

## Physical Examination

A complete physical examination should be performed as described in Chapter 5. As in any procedure, the nurse should alter the approach to the examination based on the child's age and developmental stage. The child may be very anxious because the exam involves a thorough examination of the genitals. Using appropriate drapes and respecting the child's modesty are key aspects in maintaining his or her privacy. It is best to defer the most threatening aspects of the examination until last.

## Diagnostic Procedures

### Urine Collection

Older children are usually cooperative in providing urine specimens. Special techniques or collection devices are necessary when urine specimens are needed from infants and young children who do not have bladder control. Nurses may want to encourage fluids for an hour preceding specimen collection to assist in easier voiding for the child.

*Clean Catch.* Most samples for urinalysis should be obtained using the clean-catch midstream method. The specimen can be collected from toilet-trained children after proper cleaning of the perineum or the penis. Girls should be instructed to spread the labia apart and clean the vulva and meatus with the cleaning solution using sterile cotton balls. Cleansing strokes proceed from front to back, using a separate cotton ball for each stroke. This procedure is then repeated with water to remove the cleaning agent. The labia should remain separated, and the child is encouraged to begin voiding. After the stream has started and during the stream flow, the urine is caught in a sterile container. In boys, the tip of the penis is cleaned and rinsed appropriately prior to specimen collection. The foreskin should be retracted for cleansing and remain retracted during urine collection.

Plastic collection bags with adhesive around the openings are used in infants and children who are unable to control urination. The proper cleaning procedure is done before the collection bag is applied. A diaper can be placed over the collector to help prevent it from becoming dislodged. Nurses should check the child frequently to see if voiding has occurred. The most accurate result is obtained when the urine is fresh, and there is also less chance of skin breakdown due to urine contact. The collection bag should be gently removed to avoid skin injury, and the skin should be cleaned before the child is rediapered.

*Catheterization.* Catheterization is a threatening and anxiety-producing nursing intervention for children. This is particularly true for preschool children due to the conflicts they encounter during Freud's phallic

stage. Careful preparation and education are extremely important for children who are old enough to understand explanations. The use of a doll can often assist in explaining the procedure. The child should be allowed to handle and play with the equipment; this can assist in overcoming his or her fears and may result in increased cooperation.

The nurse should be familiar with the institution's bladder catheterization procedure. Strict attention to aseptic technique is necessary to prevent introduction of infection. (Techniques for catheterization are discussed later in this chapter.)

*Bladder Tap.* A bladder tap may be used to obtain a sterile urine specimen in infants. This procedure involves needle puncture of the skin and underlying bladder. The abdomen is scrubbed with a betadine solution prior to insertion of a 22-gauge needle just above the symphysis pubis into the bladder. Infants are restrained to prevent accidental trauma. This procedure involves very few complications. It must be explained to parents, as it may otherwise cause unnecessary concern.

### Urine Tests

Examination of urine is the easiest and fastest method for assessment of the child with a possible renal system disorder. A routine urinalysis measures pH and specific gravity and determines the presence of glucose, protein, blood, or ketones. Microscopic examination checks for cells, casts, bacteria, and crystals. Normal urine values and the clinical significance of alterations are listed in Table 30-2. The color, odor, and appearance of the urine should be described and the method of collection documented.

### Radiographic Studies of Renal Function

*Intravenous Pyelogram.* An intravenous pyelogram (IVP), or excretory urogram, is used to study the upper urinary tract. A radiopaque contrast medium is injected intravenously, and x-rays are taken at intervals to allow visualization of calyces, renal pelvis, ureters, and bladder. Preprocedural care usually involves restriction of food and fluids and administration of cathartics or enemas for bowel emptying. Nurses must avoid using the word "dye" when explaining the contrast medium; this word may confuse and frighten younger children. The child should be told that there will be a general feeling of warmth while the contrast material is injected, as well as burning at the injection site and nausea. An important nursing responsibility when radiographic studies are being performed involves checking for past allergic reactions. Nurses should be alert for signs of sensitivity reaction to the contrast medium (itching, sneezing, wheezing, flushed skin), which usually occurs within minutes after injection.

*Table 30–2. Urine Values*

| Test | Normal Values | Clinical Significance of Alterations |
|---|---|---|
| **Physical Tests** | | |
| Color | Pale amber to gold | Cloudy: sediment, may be bacteria |
| | | Reddish pink or brown: blood |
| | | Yellow, brown, or green: bile pigments |
| Specific gravity | 1.010–1.030 | Related to kidney's ability to concentrate dilute urine |
| | | Increased: dehydration, nephrosis |
| | | Decreased: overhydration, glomerulonephritis, severe renal disease |
| **Chemical Tests** | | |
| pH | 4.5–8.0 | Affected by medications and diet; alkalinity beyond 8.0 suggests infection by a urea |
| | Average: 6.0 | splitting bacteria (*Proteus*) |
| Protein | Negative | Increased: most kidney disease, infections |
| Glucose | Negative | Increased: diabetes mellitus, impaired tubular reabsorption |
| Ketones | Negative | Increased: acidosis (diabetes mellitus, fever, starvation) |
| **Microscopic Tests** | | |
| Red blood cells | 1–2 | Increased: Menstrual flow, trauma, infection, glomerulonephritis, pyelonephritis, neoplasms |
| White blood cells | | Increased: urinary tract infection |
| Casts | Negative | Increased: renal disorders, renal damage |
| Crystals | Negative | Increased: calculi |

*Voiding Cystourethrogram.* A voiding cystourethrogram (VCUG) helps visualize the lower urinary tract and demonstrates structural defects and vesicoureteral reflux. The procedure involves catheterizing and filling the bladder with contrast medium, with films taken before, during, and after voiding. Nurses need to prepare the child carefully for catheterization and must explain the importance of voiding after catheterization. The child may be embarrassed to urinate on the examining table, and parents are often helpful in reassuring the child that this is part of the test.

A variety of other radiographic studies may be used to provide information about renal system function and structure. A KUB is a flat plate radiograph of the *k*idneys, *u*reters, and *b*ladder that helps evaluate anatomical conditions. A renal scan, which enhances kidney visualization and provides a detailed picture of excretory performance, can reveal congenital anomalies and intrarenal masses. In renal angiography contrast medium is injected directly into the renal artery and the renal vascular system is visualized to identify abnormalities in renal circulation. Children are usually sedated prior to this procedure.

## Cystoscopy

Cystoscopic examination involves direct visualization of the bladder, ureters, and urethra by means of a lighted tubular lens. General anesthesia is used in infants and children. Before the procedure nurses must prepare the child in deep breathing and coughing techniques. The child must also be prepared for post-procedural pain and burning with urination. Drinking extra fluids after the procedure may help alleviate this discomfort by decreasing urinary concentration. Nurses should observe for urinary retention and hematuria following cystoscopy.

## Renal Biopsy

This procedure involves the removal of a small piece of kidney tissue via a biopsy needle. The tissue then undergoes special staining and microscopic examination. Various studies help to determine the type and severity of kidney disease and also determine appropriate therapy and its value. The child is usually premedicated, and the biopsy site is injected with a solution of 1% lidocaine (Xylocaine) to numb the area. Although the child is awake during the procedure, nurses should reassure the child that no pain, but only a deep pushing, will be felt. Supplemental anesthesia may be used in extremely anxious children. Usual hospital policy stipulates strict bed rest for at least 12 hours following renal biopsy. Nurses should monitor the child's pulse and blood pressure as ordered and check the biopsy site at regular intervals for bleeding. Hypotension, severe pain, and gross hematuria are all signs of active bleeding and must be reported immediately. All voided urine during the first 12 hours is checked with reagent dipsticks for bleeding. The child may experience mild flank tenderness for a day or so following the procedure.

### Renal Ultrasound

Renal ultrasound is a noninvasive visualization procedure that involves bouncing high-frequency sound waves off the kidneys to form an electronic image. Renal ultrasound is useful in visualizing major congenital anomalies, reflux, tumors, masses, calculi, and renal trauma. Nurses should explain to the child undergoing this procedure that a lubricant or gel is applied to the abdomen and flank and a transducer that sends and receives sound waves is passed over the area. Reassure the child that the procedure is painless. The child should be told that it is important to remain still during the procedure.

### Blood Urea Nitrogen and Serum Creatinine

Blood urea nitrogen (BUN) and serum creatinine tests are used to measure the concentration of nitrogenous wastes in blood. Concentrations of these wastes are elevated with impaired kidney function. Creatinine concentration in normal plasma is age-related and increases with increasing muscle mass. Creatinine levels are also increased with impaired renal function.

BUN is influenced by a number of variables other than renal perfusion, and therefore is not as specific a measure of changes in renal function as is the serum creatinine. The BUN value is increased with renal disease, and generally the amount of BUN elevation relates to disease severity. Values may be decreased in overhydration, liver failure, or low-protein diet.

## Nursing Diagnosis

The diagnoses approved by the North American Nursing Diagnosis Association are used when renal system problems are discussed. The most common diagnoses used for renal problems include:

*Pattern 1: Exchanging*
- Altered Nutrition: Less than body requirements
- Altered Nutrition: More than body requirements
- Altered patterns of urinary elimination
- Altered tissue perfusion, renal
- Constipation
- Diarrhea
- Fluid volume deficit
- Fluid volume excess
- Functional incontinence
- High risk for fluid volume deficit
- High risk for impaired skin integrity
- High risk for infection
- High risk for injury
- Impaired skin integrity
- Total incontinence
- Urinary retention

*Pattern 2: Communicating*
- Impaired verbal communication

*Pattern 3: Relating*
- Altered family processes
- High risk for altered parenting
- Impaired social interaction

*Pattern 5: Choosing*
- Ineffective individual coping

*Pattern 6: Moving*
- Activity intolerance
- Altered growth and development
- Diversional activity deficit
- Fatigue
- High risk for activity intolerance
- Impaired physical mobility
- Toileting self-care deficit

*Pattern 7: Perceiving*
- Body image disturbance

*Pattern 9: Feeling*
- Anxiety
- Fear
- Pain

## Planning and Implementing Nursing Care

Planning and implementation of nursing care is discussed in relation to each problem presented in this chapter. The child's developmental stage must be assessed; nurses should not rely completely on chronological age in evaluating communication, personal–social assessment, or appropriate treatment modalities. It is important to have peers visit the school-age child during hospitalization. Nurses should encourage self-care and independence.

Problems involving the renal system often involve numerous procedures. Nurses should patiently explain the procedure if the child is old enough to understand. Dolls are often helpful for demonstration of the procedure, and the child should be encouraged to handle the equipment that will be used. Nurses can help to promote the child's sense of control by talking about how he or she can assist in the procedure. Such teaching might include explaining the need to remain still during a procedure, instructing the child in the use of self-distracting techniques, and showing the position that will be used for the procedure.

Before a planned surgical procedure, nurses can help to alleviate associated anxiety and fear by a thorough explanation to the child and family of planned events. A tour and short orientation of the various hospital units where tests and procedures will be done is helpful. Nurses should be mindful of the preschool child's fears of castration or mutilation, and clearly show the child the location of the incision. Dolls are very helpful in teaching about location of tubes, dressings, and catheters. It is important to describe any immobilizing devices that might be necessary and to reassure the child that normal activities will be allowed following the specified restriction. After surgery, it is important to reassure the child that the genitals are intact. A mirror can be helpful in allowing children to visualize their genitals.

Teaching for home care is an important nursing role. Home catheterization is often required in renal system problems. Procedures for home catheterization should be taught early in the hospitalization in order to ensure that all the participants in care have had adequate learning opportunities. Older children and adolescents should be taught self-catheterization. Home care for renal system problems usually involves maintaining appropriate follow-up procedures, administering medications, working with the child's school to provide an effective educational environment, and working with the child to develop self-esteem.

## Nursing Interventions

In addition to planning appropriate educational approaches for child and family, nurses may be responsible for direct care. Nursing interventions include performing catheterization and caring for a patient with an indwelling catheter, keeping a record of intake and output, evaluating hydration status, and administering medications.

## Catheterization

Nurses should be familiar with their institution's procedure guidelines for bladder catheterization (Fig. 30-2). The equipment for catheterization in children is the same as that for adults, except for catheter size. A size 8 or 10 French catheter is typically used in infants and children. Nurses should always wash their hands before and after catheter care. The perineal area is cleansed according to procedure.

Catheterization of the infant can sometimes be a problem because the bladder is higher and more anterior than in the adult, and the urethra lies under and around the symphysis. Good lighting is critical in catheterizing the infant female because of the difficulty in locating the meatus. Once the catheter has been introduced, it should be directed downward. In the male, the penis should be held on both sides in an erect position while the catheter is gently inserted. Once the urine begins to flow, the catheter should be inserted slightly further. A sterile cup or other container is used to collect the urine. After the urine flow has stopped, the catheter should be removed slowly, with the tip kept up following withdrawal to avoid spillage. Adolescents require a larger catheter, usually No. 10 or higher.

It is important to note the child's position and avoid any looping or kinking of the tubing. Infants may require restraints to keep them from pulling at the tubing. The urine collection bag should be kept at a level lower than the child's bladder; this facilitates urine drainage. Nurses must make sure that the collection bag is not fastened to the bedrails and that it is placed in such a position that it does not become caught when siderails are raised or lowered.

Care of the child with an indwelling catheter includes observation for signs of obstruction. Such signs include no urine output for over 1 hour, bladder distention, or large blood clots in the urine. If there are no kinks in the tubing, irrigation with sterile normal saline may remove the obstruction.

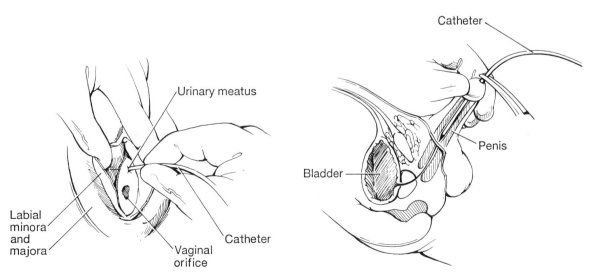

*Figure 30–2. Bladder catheterization (female and male).*

## Intake and Output

The child who is hospitalized due to a renal system disorder usually requires accurate record keeping of intake and output. Nurses must use precise measurement techniques in recording fluid intake and urine output. Diapers must be weighed before and after voiding. The weight in grams equals the milliliters voided. Potty chairs are often useful in collecting urine for the toilet-trained child. Parents can be extremely helpful in the accuracy of intake and output records, and nurses should teach them about the importance of accurate measurement and recording.

## Maintaining Hydration

Body weight is a sensitive indicator of a child's hydration status. Hospitalized children with renal disorders are usually weighed daily. It is vital to weigh the child at the same time each day, using the same scale.

Skin turgor is another method nurses use to assess hydration. Skin turgor decreases in states of dehydration. Skin temperature and color should be noted. The skin may be cool when there is fluid loss, and may also be gray in color. Decreased skin temperature and gray color are caused by decreased peripheral circulation.

Hydration level can also be monitored by determining mucous membrane moisture and observing for the presence of tears. In addition to an absence of tears in fluid deficit, the child's cry may be weak and high-pitched. In infants, the fontanelles may become depressed with dehydration.

## Drug Therapy

Nurses must carefully monitor any intravenous therapy in the child with a disorder of the renal system. The nurses should be familiar with possible drug side effects. Rate of flow should be checked frequently and recorded accurately on the flow sheet. If an infusion pump is used, the nurse should be familiar with how the pump functions and check that it is functioning correctly. Nurses must also check the intravenous site for possible infiltration. If the area is taped, careful inspection is needed. Depending on the institution's policy, intravenous tubing needs to be completely changed every 24 to 48 hours. Accurate recording of IV fluid and medication is necessary.

## Evaluating Nursing Care

Evaluation of compliance with prescribed treatments and nursing interventions may include increased knowledge of the condition by parents and the child; decreased instances of infection; maintaining fluid restrictions; improved urinary output; or ability to perform a home self-catheterization. The child's acceptance of alternative physical activities,

such as swimming and tennis rather than football, may protect the fragile renal system. It is important not to interrupt the child's education and to maintain as normal a routine as possible.

## Congenital Renal Problems

### Exstrophy of the Bladder

#### Pathophysiology

Exstrophy of the bladder is the most common major anomaly of the lower urinary and genital tracts, occurring in approximately one out of 30,000 births (Fig. 30-3). It is present more frequently in males than in females and is not familial. Exstrophy of the bladder is a result of the failure of the mesoderm to invade the cephalad extension of the dorsal membrane; the extent of this failure determines the degree of the anomaly. In this condition the anterior surface of the bladder is actually on the abdominal wall instead of being enclosed within the abdomen. Males experience epispadias accompanied by a wide and shal-

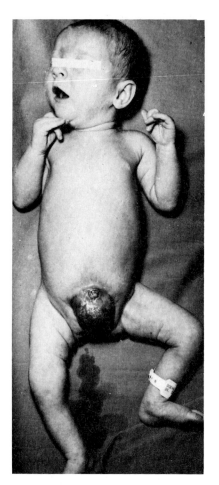

*Figure 30–3. Exstrophy of the bladder. (Crowley, L.V. [1974]. **An introduction to clinical embryology. *Chicago: Year Book Medical Publishers*)**

low scrotum. Other anomalies that are frequently seen with exstrophy of the bladder are cleft scrotum, shortened penis, and undescended testes. Females also have epispadias, with duplication of the clitoris and wide separation of the labia. Other problems that may occur in both sexes include hip malformations, rectal prolapse with the anus displaced forward, and inguinal hernias due to musculoskeletal malformation in the pelvic region.

### Medical Diagnosis and Management

Treatment begins at birth by covering the bladder with a sterile plastic dressing that prevents drying of the bladder but allows for urine flow. Petroleum gauze should be avoided because the petroleum jelly is absorbed by the gauze and clothing, causing the gauze to adhere to the mucosa and to strip off superficial layers when removed (Jeffs, 1987). The dressing should be changed every 2 hours to minimize irritation.

Surgical closure is the preferred method of treatment, and the surgery is usually done within the first 48 hours of life. When the surgical process begins at the newborn stage of life, children have a better chance for having a functional bladder.

### Nursing Assessment and Diagnosis

Nursing assessment involves examination of the child, as well as assessment of parental adaptation and understanding of the anomaly, treatment options, prognosis, and available resources.

Nursing diagnoses for exstrophy of the bladder might include the following:

- High risk for infection related to a break in the skin integrity
- Altered patterns of urinary elimination related to anatomical deficit
- High risk for altered parenting related to the birth of a child with a defect
- Impaired skin integrity, related to the structural defect
- Impaired physical mobility, related to required physical restraint
- Pain, related to the anomaly and surgery

### Planning and Implementing Nursing Care

Children with exstrophy of the bladder present a challenge to nursing care from birth. The bladder must be appropriately covered to prevent drying. Meticulous skin care is important since the skin surrounding the bladder is continually bathed in urine. These infants are typically fussy. Attempts should be made to calm the infant so that the chance of the hernia being aggravated and the possibility of rectal prolapse are lessened.

Frequent diaper changes are essential; after each stool the skin must be cleansed carefully and thoroughly to decrease the likelihood of infection and skin breakdown. Protective skin creams serve as barriers to irritation.

Nursing care also includes providing emotional support for the parents. Nurses must instruct parents regarding the anomaly, the repair procedures, and proper nursing care and techniques. Parents need support since their desire for the "perfect child" has been shattered. Nurses should encourage parents to assume as much care as possible for the child.

Postoperative care is similar to that for any surgical patient. The operative site is checked for redness, swelling, and exudate that might indicate infection. Elastic bandages and dressings over the bladder must be changed frequently. Circulation in the distal extremities should be monitored. Urine flow should be evaluated and antibiotics administered as ordered.

### Evaluating Nursing Care

Evaluation of the care given to these children should reveal no increase in skin breakdown or infection. Bonding between the child and parents should be facilitated and progress noted. Parental understanding of the disorder should increase, and the parents should assist with and assume responsibility for some of the child's care.

## Hypospadias

### Pathophysiology

Hypospadias is the most common congenital anomaly of the penis, occurring in one of 350 births (Sadove, 1988). Hypospadias results from incomplete fusion of the urethral folds along the midline; the urinary meatus is located on the ventral side of the penis (Fig. 30-4). The anomaly varies in severity and is classified based on the position of the urethral opening. Commonly the urinary meatus is located on the shaft or near the glans; in more severe forms, the opening is located on the perineum. These cases usually result in urinary incontinence. *Chordee*, a ventral curvature of the penis caused by a fibrous band of tissue that extends behind the urethra to the glans, is associated with hypospadias.

### Medical Diagnosis and Management

The goal of surgical treatment is to straighten the penis and restore normal appearance and function. Surgery may be done during either infancy or the preschool period. There may be fewer psychological problems if the repair is performed in the child's first year of life (Belman, 1984). Circumcision is postponed due to the likelihood that the foreskin will be used in the repair process.

### Nursing Assessment and Diagnosis

Assessment includes examining the perineum and locating the meatus. Alterations in the urinary stream often aid

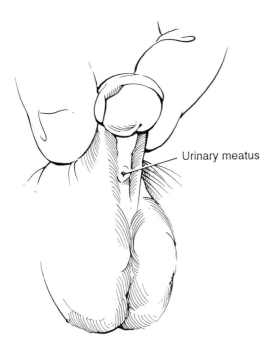

*Figure 30–4.   Hypospadias.*

in the diagnosis. Nurses must assess parental understanding of the anomaly and the treatment plans.

Nursing diagnoses for hypospadias might include the following:

- Altered patterns of urinary elimination, related to the physiologic condition
- Anxiety, related to fear of mutilation
- Body image disturbance, related to the child's perception of the condition

### Planning and Implementing Nursing Care

Careful preparation of the parents and child is important. Early childhood fear of mutilation is prevalent, and the child may focus on genital mutilation and castration anxiety (Buckholz, 1988). Parents may express concern about reproductive function. Both parents and child need to be educated about cosmetic results following repair, since the penis may not appear perfect following corrective surgery (urethroplasty).

Dressing changes are usually kept to a minimum to facilitate skin graft healing after surgery. Extremity restraints are used, and sedation may be needed in the excessively fussy child. Providing diversionary activities for these children is a nursing challenge. Nurses should let the child see his penis as soon as possible after the surgery. Parents are taught about the care of stents or catheters and irrigation techniques. Nurses should educate parents regarding the use of prescribed medications. Increasing fluid intake should be encouraged.

### Evaluation of Nursing Care

The parents and child should understand the results and future implications of the surgery. Parents should be able to demonstrate their understanding of home care.

## Epispadias

### Pathophysiology

Epispadias is a condition in which the urethral meatus is located on the dorsal side of the penis (Fig. 30-5). The condition is rare and is usually a component of exstrophy of the bladder. Epispadias is classified according to the position of the urethral meatus on the penis. In its mildest form the meatus is located in the dorsum of the glans. If the meatus is located along the dorsal aspect of the penile shaft, and the penis is curved dorsally, is flattened, and is smaller than usual, the anomaly is more severe. In the worst form of this anomaly, the meatus is located at the penopubic junction; the penis is short and blunt. The symphysis pubis is widened and the client is usually incontinent, with the prepuce hanging from the ventral surface.

### Medical Diagnosis and Management

Surgical repair of this condition usually occurs between 2 and 3 years of age. In the mildest form of epispadias the reconstructive procedure consists of restructuring the penis and urethra. Children with more severe forms require reconstructive procedures such as those performed for exstrophy of the bladder. Circumcision should not be

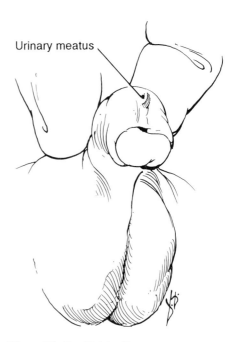

*Figure 30–5.   Epispadias.*

performed on these children because the foreskin may be needed for the reconstruction.

### Nursing Assessment and Diagnosis

Nursing assessment involves documenting the location of the meatus. Assessment also includes documenting flow, strength, and direction of the urine stream. Nurses should also assess the parents' understanding of the condition and the procedures for correction.

Nursing diagnoses for epispadias might include the following:

- Total incontinence, related to position of the urethral meatus
- Anxiety, related to possible altered sex role identification
- Pain, related to the operative procedure
- High risk for impaired skin integrity, related to incontinence

### Planning and Implementing Nursing Care

The child's skin must be assessed continually because of the incontinence that is experienced with more severe forms of this anomaly. Frequent diaper changes and the use of barrier creams, as well as thorough cleansing of the area, are important to prevent skin breakdown. Postoperative care involves monitoring for wound infection and urinary tract infection.

Nurses should thoroughly explain all procedures to the parents. Parents may be concerned about the physical appearance of the child's penis and may have questions about sexual function. Careful explanation in simple terms must also be provided to the child. The child needs reassurance that his penis will remain intact.

### Evaluating Nursing Care

Evaluating care of children with epispadias includes the degree of skin breakdown, the acceptance of the anomaly and the repair procedure, and the prevention of negative postoperative sequelae.

## Renal Problems of Neonates

### Wilms Tumor

#### Pathophysiology

Wilms tumor (nephroblastoma) is a malignant neoplasm of the kidney. It occurs most often in young children, most of whom are 2 to 3 years of age when diagnosed, but it may also occur in adolescents. Wilms tumor is usually found in only one kidney, where it replaces normal renal tissue. This form of cancer is frequently associated with congenital anomalies such as aniridia (absent iris) and with renal or genitourinary anomalies.

### Medical Diagnosis and Management

The National Wilms Tumor Study has developed a classification system that divides the disease into 5 stages. Stage I tumors are limited to the kidney and can be removed completely. Stage II tumors extend beyond the kidney but can be completely removed. Stage III tumors are confined to the abdomen and have no metastatic spread. Stage IV tumors have metastatic involvement, commonly involving the lung. Stage V involves bilateral renal tumors.

The signs and symptoms of this type of neoplasm include a firm, nontender upper quadrant mass; hematuria; hypertension; fever; abdominal pain; anorexia; malaise; or vomiting. The hypertension results from renal ischemia brought about by pressure from the tumor on the renal artery. Some of the diagnostic tests employed are intravenous pyelogram (IVP), computed tomography (CT) scan, and abdominal and chest x-rays, as well as a complete blood count (CBC), urinalysis, renal function tests, and coagulation studies. Treatment usually consists of immediate surgical excision of the tumor or the entire kidney. Combination chemotherapy with vincristine and actinomycin may be started in patients with localized disease; doxorubicin may be added for patients with more advanced disease. Radiation treatment may be added for patients with disease more severe than Stage I. Three factors influence the prognosis in Wilms tumor: favorable or unfavorable histology, hematogenous metastases, and lymph node involvement (Gellis & Kagan, 1986). The long-term survival rate for adequately treated patients is about 90% (Belasco, Chatten, & D'Angio, 1984).

### Nursing Assessment and Diagnosis

Abdominal palpation should be avoided to prevent trauma and the possibility of metastases due to rupture of the renal capsule. Educational needs of the patient and family are very important. The patient and family must be prepared for the initiation of chemotherapy, since treatment is instituted rapidly.

Postoperative assessment focuses on prevention of complications. Vital signs, fluid, and electrolytes are carefully monitored. The surgical dressing is checked for drainage. Nurses should note any change in abdominal girth; an increase indicates internal hemorrhage or distention. Chemotherapy and radiation treatment side effects must be included in postoperative care considerations; these side effects include nausea, vomiting, and fatigue.

The patient's and family's emotional states must be continually assessed. Because the child is acutely ill and is hospitalized, feelings of isolation may be experienced due to decreased social interaction and powerlessness. Owing to the nature of this illness, these children are usually chronic patients and must be given some type of control of their situation. They should be encouraged to interact with peers and attend school so that development can be as normal as possible.

Nursing diagnoses for Wilms tumor might include the following:

- High risk for injury, physiological, related to rupture of the tumor and seeding of tumor cells
- Impaired skin integrity, related to the surgical procedure
- Impaired social interaction, related to illness and hospitalization
- Altered family processes, related to care needs of the sick or hospitalized child
- Ineffective family coping, related to the child's illness and hospitalization
- Body image disturbance, related to surgery and side effects of chemotherapy

### Planning and Implementing Nursing Care

Prior to surgery the potential for metastases can be decreased by limiting abdominal palpation. A sign should be placed above the patient's bed so that palpation is not done. Abdominal girth should be measured every day to check the growth of the tumor.

Vital signs help to monitor for the hypertension that accompanies a Wilms' tumor and the hypotension that occurs following excision of the tumor. Hypertension may produce headaches with photophobia, vomiting, and shortness of breath.

Bilateral breath sounds should be auscultated postoperatively at least once every shift to check for signs and symptoms of atelectasis. Educating the child and encouraging deep breathing and coughing preoperatively will prepare the child for the postoperative period. Early ambulation must be encouraged postoperatively to further decrease the likelihood of pulmonary complications.

Assessment of the operative site should include checking for redness, swelling, purulent drainage, and bleeding. An oral temperature greater than 101°F (38.4°C) should be reported. Any signs and symptoms of bleeding, such as decreased blood pressure with increased heart rate, pallor, diaphoresis, lightheadedness, lethargy, frank bleeding from the wound site, or abdominal pain or swelling, should be reported.

Side effects of chemotherapy and radiation treatment—i.e., hair loss, anorexia, peripheral neuropathy, and nausea and vomiting—must be assessed. Hats or hairpieces may be used to cover the head during hair loss. Anorexia may be handled with a dietary consultation and attempts to provide the patient with appetizing meals. The administration of antiemetics before chemotherapy may alleviate the symptoms of nausea and vomiting.

Patient and family teaching must be initiated as soon as possible. These children frequently undergo surgery within 48 to 72 hours following diagnosis, and the family may feel overwhelmed. Teaching should be repeated frequently to help strengthen the parents' understanding of the disease. Issues such as powerlessness, hopelessness, disturbance in body image, and fear must be addressed by allowing the child and family to express their feelings openly. Comprehensive patient and family teaching and the involvement of the family in the child's care can help decrease emotional negative reactions.

Impaired social interaction can be minimized by allowing liberal visitation by the child's friends and siblings who can serve as a support system. Encouraging the child to interact with other children on the pediatrics unit is also helpful.

### Evaluating Nursing Care

Evaluation of nursing care is directed toward assessment of vital sign changes after removal of the tumor, monitoring infection status, and evaluating response to chemotherapy and radiation treatment. The family should assume some of the patient's care and verbalize their feelings about the disease and treatment.

# Renal Problems of Infants

## Hemolytic-Uremic Syndrome

### Pathophysiology

Hemolytic-uremic syndrome (HUS) is an acute renal disease distinguished by a triad of manifestations: acute renal failure, hemolytic anemia, and thrombocytopenia. It is the most common cause of acute renal failure in children, and occurs mainly in children between the ages of 2 months and 8 years. Although many theories exist, the cause of hemolytic-uremic syndrome is unknown. Both infectious agents and immunological responses have been proposed as possible causes. The site of damage is the endothelial lining of the glomerular arterioles. The capillary walls in the glomeruli thicken and clotting occurs locally. Red blood cells are fractured as they pass through the occluded portion of the vessels, and are quickly destroyed by the liver and spleen. This results in hemolytic anemia. Thrombocytopenia occurs because of intrarenal platelet adhesion.

### Medical Diagnosis and Management

The disease is marked by two stages—a prodromal stage and an acute stage. The prodromal stage is characterized by an episode of abdominal pain with diarrhea and vomiting. Other signs and symptoms may include fever, malaise, nausea, lymphadenopathy, and edema. The acute phase follows, with symptoms that include severe gastroenteritis with bloody diarrhea as well as bleeding from gums, nose, vagina, and urinary tract. The child is typically weak and anemic due to this bleeding. Renal failure occurs with either reduced (anuria) or increased (oliguria) urinary output and accompanying hypertension. The neurological system may also be involved, with symptoms ranging from irritability to convulsions or coma.

Laboratory studies in the child with HUS reveal a decreased hemoglobin and hematocrit, elevated BUN, increased reticulocyte count, white blood cell count increased to as much as 30,000/mm$^3$, and platelet count decreased to 20,000 to 100,000/mm$^3$. Microscopic hematuria and proteinuria are found in urinalysis. Additional findings include guaiac-positive stools.

The medical treatment of these children centers on correcting hematological alterations, improving the renal status, and controlling complications. Initial measures include those used in treating acute renal failure—correcting electrolyte imbalances, controlling hypertension, and replacing fluids. Peritoneal dialysis and hemodialysis have proved to be effective. The use of heparin or fibrinolytic agents is controversial and has not been effective as a treatment option. Prognosis is greatly improved by early diagnosis and aggressive treatment. Approximately 90% of children with HUS recover completely, with the remainder experiencing various degrees of residual renal problems or hypertension (Bergstein & Michael, 1987).

### Nursing Assessment and Diagnosis

Assessment of children with HUS is aimed at identifying the signs and symptoms of the disease and being cognizant of the many complications that can arise both from both the disease entity and the treatment.

Nursing diagnoses for hemolytic-uremic syndrome might include the following:

- High risk for fluid volume deficit, related to the use of anticoagulants and thrombolytic treatment
- Altered nutrition: Less than body requirements, related to nausea, vomiting, diarrhea, and anorexia
- Diarrhea, related to disease processes
- Fluid volume excess, related to renal failure
- Fatigue, related to anemia and fluid volume alterations
- Altered family processes, related to the child's illness and hospitalization

### Planning and Implementing Nursing Care

Nursing care includes frequent assessment for signs and symptoms of bleeding. Vomitus, stools, and urine must be tested for the presence of blood. The child should be protected from injury that could produce internal or external bleeding. Direct pressure must be applied to all venipuncture sites. Vital signs must be monitored frequently due to the hypertension experienced by these children with renal involvement and their potential for systemic sequelae.

Signs and symptoms of fluid volume overload due to renal failure or fluid volume deficit due to nausea, vomiting and diarrhea, must be assessed. In fluid volume overload, hypertension is noted, along with respiratory difficulty, edema (external or pulmonary), and bulging fontanelles in infants. In fluid volume deficit, dry, cracked, and possibly bleeding mucous membranes are noted, as well as poor skin turgor, sunken eyes, and sunken fontanelles in infants.

Any childhood illness has an impact on the entire family. The family's response to illness must be considered. The nurse must be alert for signs of despair, fear, and anxiety. The family must be permitted to express frustrations and anxieties. Social service and psychiatric consultations should be used as needed.

The family's lack of familiarity with the signs, symptoms, and complications of hemolytic-uremic syndrome must be addressed. Frequent, patient, and understandable explanations are the cornerstone of discharge planning. The family must be educated and supported in order to enable them to cope with caring for the child at home.

### Evaluating Nursing Care

Evaluation of nursing care is aimed at limiting the amount of bleeding the patient experiences. Adequate fluid balance with stable vital signs is an additional goal. Family coping mechanisms must be evaluated in relation to their applicability to the current situation and the implications for future interactions. The family should understand the disease process and the plan of care.

## Renal Problems of Toddlers and Preschoolers

### Acute Glomerulonephritis (Poststreptococcal)

#### Pathophysiology

Acute postinfectious glomerulonephritis (AGN) is an immune complex disease that occurs due to immunological injury. It was once thought to occur only secondary to group A beta-hemolytic streptococci, but the current theory is that a variety of microorganisms are involved (Glassock, Cohen, Adler, & Ward, 1986). Antibodies interact with foreign antigens that remain in the glomerulus, which leads to immune complex formation and glomerular injury (Jordan & Lemire, 1982). Once the glomeruli are injured, filtration decreases. When this occurs, less sodium and water are excreted; hypertension, edema, and

**824** *Health Problems of Children and Adolescents*

heart failure result. This disease is generally seen in children over 2 years of age, more often in males than in females (Glassock et al., 1986). Recovery is complete in 95% of these children. On occasion, acute renal insufficiency may occur after the acute episode.

## Medical Diagnosis and Management

Among the symptoms and complications associated with acute glomerulonephritis are hypertension, fluid overload, edema, electrolyte imbalances, oliguria, and hematuria. Diagnosis may be based on the results of blood chemistries and a urinalysis. The urinalysis reveals red blood cells, white blood cells, red blood casts, and protein. Blood chemistry reveals an elevated BUN and creatinine. The erythrocyte sedimentation rate (ESR) and antistreptolycin titer (ASO) is elevated due to exposure to streptococcal infection.

Treatment usually requires hospitalization. Development of acute hypertension that is resistant to typical antihypertensive agents may be managed with IV sodium nitroprusside (Nipride). If hypertensive encephalopathy develops, the symptoms will usually subside after the blood pressure is brought under control. Fluid overload and edema are usually treated with furosemide (Lasix) or hydrochlorothyazide in conjunction with sodium and fluid restrictions. Peritoneal dialysis or hemodialysis may be initiated if the fluid overload is severe enough to cause pulmonary edema or congestive heart failure in conjunction with oliguria.

The child may be placed on an increased calorie diet to decrease protein breakdown. Sodium and protein are usually limited. After 2 to 4 days of treatment, diuresis begins. Diuresis indicates resolving disease, and the majority of children completely recover over a period of 2 weeks.

## Nursing Assessment and Diagnosis

Pertinent physical assessment factors include vital signs, particularly the presence or absence of hypertension, edema, proteinuria or hematuria; intake and output patterns; the child's growth; and complaints of fatigue, malaise, headaches, and GI disturbances such as anorexia and vomiting. Psychosocial assessment factors include patient and family coping and their level of understanding of the disease process and its treatment. The effects of the illness and its complications on the child are also considered, especially the child's school attendance, interaction with family and peers, and outlook on the illness.

Nursing diagnoses for acute glomerulonephritis may include the following:

- Fluid volume excess
- Anxiety, related to illness and hospitalization
- Altered patterns of urinary elimination
- High risk for infection
- Altered family processes, related to care needs of the sick or hospitalized child
- Ineffective individual coping, related to the effects of the illness on the child
- High risk for activity intolerance, related to fatigue, malaise, headache, and GI disturbances

## Planning and Implementing Nursing Care

Vital signs, particularly heart rate and blood pressure, must be carefully monitored. Hypertension and its resolution after initiation of drug therapy must be noted. Hypotension and tachycardia, which are side effects of antihypertensive agents, must be assessed. Edema must be monitored throughout the body. Fluid and electrolyte imbalances due to poor renal filtration occur, with resultant edema. Electrolyte imbalance symptoms include cramping, paresthesias, cardiac rhythm disturbances, and disorientation. Fluid balance is monitored via intake and output. Daily weights in the same clothes, at the same time of day, and on the same scale are essential. Activity levels are usually determined by the child.

Patient and family teaching should be based on their current knowledge. The reasons for lab work and diagnostic tests, as well as medicines and their side effects, should be explained. Including the child and family in the plan of care is essential. Normal activity should be encouraged, when balanced with adequate rest. Children should be told that rest periods will help them feel better and that these breaks are not a punishment. A sodium-restricted diet may be ordered due to hypertension and edema. Nurses should teach parents the importance of preventing infections during the recovery period.

## Evaluating Nursing Care

Effectiveness of care is evaluated by an acceptable blood pressure, fluid and electrolyte balance without significant derangement, an adequate nutritional intake, and an increase in the patient's and family's knowledge level accompanied by a display of adequate coping mechanisms. The child will also be free of infection.

## Alport Syndrome

### Pathophysiology

Alport syndrome is the most common form of hereditary nephritis. The etiology is essentially unknown; however, it appears to be hereditary. Most theories suggest a lack of basement membrane antigen and/or a defect in the biochemical components (Glassock et al., 1986). Initially the renal biopsy is negative; after the first decade of life, biopsy reveals glomerular sclerosis, tubular atrophy, interstitial swelling, and fibrosis.

### Medical Diagnosis and Management

Diagnosis is based on patient symptoms and the results of the biopsy. Initially the patient will have asymptomatic microscopic or gross hematuria. Biopsy is done when the patient with microscopic hematuria also has proteinuria. Hearing and sight problems occur in a small number of clients. Hypertension may occur late in the disease process.

Management of clients with this syndrome is largely supportive. Males fare worse than females, generally developing end-stage renal failure in their second or third decade, occasionally with hearing loss. Because this form of nephritis is genetically mediated, the services of a genetic counselor should be offered to the family.

### Nursing Assessment and Diagnosis

Assessment includes monitoring the results of the urinalysis for hematuria and proteinuria. Pertinent physical assessment factors include vital signs: the presence or absence of hypertension; edema; proteinuria or hematuria; intake and output patterns; the child's height and weight in relation to age; complaints of fatigue, malaise, and headaches; and GI disturbances such as anorexia or vomiting. The child's vision and hearing should be screened. Psychosocial assessment factors include child and family coping and knowledge regarding disease process and its treatment, the child's school attendance, interaction with family and peers, and outlook on the illness.

Nursing diagnoses for Alport Syndrome might include the following:

- Altered nutrition: Less than body requirements related to anorexia or vomiting
- Altered patterns of urinary elimination related to decreased fluid intake
- Altered family processes, related to illness and hospitalization
- Ineffective individual coping, related to the child's illness and prognosis
- High risk for activity intolerance, related to fatigue, malaise, headache, and GI disturbances
- High risk for injury related to visual and auditory deficits
- Impaired verbal communication related to auditory deficits

### Planning and Implementing Nursing Care

Nursing plans, interventions, and evaluation of nursing care are similar to those for acute glomerulonephritis. The sequelae of visual and auditory disturbances may be seen in some children. Their inability to understand sensory stimuli may cause them to become noncommunicative, withdrawn, or uncooperative; this must be kept in mind when planning nursing care. Patience and understanding must be conveyed to the family and client. The child should have regular auditory and ophthalmic evaluations. Alternate communication forms should be taught by the appropriate professionals as needed.

## Nephrotic Syndrome (Nephrosis)

### Pathophysiology

Nephrotic syndrome is characterized by proteinuria, hypoalbuminemia, edema, and hyperlipidemia. It occurs in 16 out of 100,000 children (Gellis & Kagan, 1986). The condition is idiopathic in 95% of children. In the remaining 5%, the syndrome is the result of some form of glomerulonephritis. Nephrosis is not hereditary.

Proteinuria is the result of increased capillary wall permeability. The cause is unknown. The protein loss is quite significant, exceeding 2 g per day. Once the albumin is lost, colloidal osmotic pressure decreases, permitting fluid to escape from the intravascular space to the interstitial space. The resulting decrease in the intravascular volume also stimulates the release of antidiuretic hormone (ADH), which encourages the reabsorption of water. The low colloidal osmotic pressure results in the loss of the reabsorbed sodium and water into the interstitial space. This mechanism is the reason for the edema seen in these children.

### Medical Diagnosis and Management

Idiopathic nephrotic syndrome usually follows an apparent viral illness. Periorbital, pedal, and pretibial edema are seen initially, with eventual generalized edema. Weight increase, ascites, or pleural effusions, as well as decreasing urine output, may occur. The child is typically pale, fatigued, and anorexic; abdominal pain and diarrhea are common. Hypertension is not usually noted in these patients. Significant lab data include urinalysis with +3 to +4 proteinuria, with occasional microscopic hematuria and an elevated specific gravity.

Edema is managed with diuretics and sodium restriction. Mild to moderate edema is usually handled with chlorothiazide. If hypokalemia develops, spironolactone may be used. Fluid restriction is not needed. Severe edema, characterized by respiratory distress, ascites, or scrotal edema, necessitates hospitalization. Corticosteroids are used to resolve the edema, and thiazide diuretics may also be employed in this edematous stage.

### Nursing Assessment and Diagnosis

Nursing assessment is aimed at noting the patient's signs and symptoms and their severity. Close observation of intake, output, and weight helps determine the pattern of fluid retention. Measurement of abdominal girth assists in monitoring edema. The urine must be checked frequently for protein.

Nursing diagnoses for nephrotic syndrome might include the following:

- High risk for fluid volume deficit, related to use of diuretics
- Fluid volume excess, related to water and sodium retention
- Altered nutrition: Less than body requirements, related to anorexia
- Activity intolerance, related to fatigue
- Altered nutrition: Less than body requirements for protein
- Altered nutrition: More than body requirements for salt
- Impaired skin integrity related to edema
- High risk for infection related to decreased defense mechanisms
- Impaired social interaction, related to frequent illness
- Altered family processes, related to a chronically ill family member
- Anxiety, related to illness and hospitalization
- Body image disturbance, related to sequelae of the illness and side effects of drug treatment

### Planning and Implementing Nursing Care

Fluid balance must be carefully monitored. Meticulous intake and output measurements and daily weights are essential. The child should be weighed at the same time and wearing the same attire each day, using the same scale. Signs and symptoms of electrolyte imbalance must be assessed. These may include cramping, paresthesias, cardiac rhythm disturbances, and disorientation.

Appropriate nutritional intake is essential for growth and development. This can present a challenge, because these children are usually anorexic. Small, frequent meals are generally best. Dietary consultation may be helpful to evaluate nutritional needs.

Careful monitoring for the side effects of drug therapy is important. Steroids may cause alteration in glucose metabolism, fluid retention, psychosis, and hypertension. Albumin may cause fluid overload, with hypertension and congestive heart failure. Measures must be taken to keep the patient away from those who might cause infection, but without totally isolating the child. Alopecia (if it occurs) must be handled very delicately, since this is very upsetting to children and their body image.

Maintaining skin integrity is also important. Edematous areas suffer from increased skin breakdown and the possibility of infection. Diapers should be changed frequently to prevent skin irritation due to urine acidity. If severe scrotal edema is present, a scrotal support may be used.

Skin breakdown can be prevented by thorough cleaning and drying of the skin around the scrotum. The child should be reassured that the scrotal size will return to normal with treatment.

The family's coping mechanisms and dynamics must be carefully evaluated. Because of the nature of this syndrome, with its exacerbations and remissions, the coping mechanisms of both parents and child must be assessed and adequate support given. The family must have an understanding of the nature of the disease as well as of signs and symptoms, possible complications, and treatment regimens. Teaching about the prevention of infection is essential. Parents should understand that steroid therapy can mask infection, and they should be alert for signs of a fever or any changes in their child. Nurses should encourage normal activities for the child to promote growth and development.

### Evaluating Nursing Care

Evaluation focuses on fluid balance patterns and their sequelae, as well as the effectiveness of treatment and any resultant adverse effects. The patient's and family's coping and knowledge level must also be evaluated.

## Urinary Tract Infections

### Pathophysiology

Urinary tract infection (UTI) results from bacterial growth in the normally sterile urinary system. Infection may involve the lower urinary tract (urethra and bladder), or the upper urinary tract (ureters, renal pelvis, calyces, and renal parenchyma). The term UTI is applied to all sites of infection anywhere within the urinary tract. The major causative organism in urinary tract infections is *Escherichia coli*. Other responsible organisms are *Klebsiella* and *Enterobacter*. These three organisms account for the majority of all UTIs. Viral infections occur on occasion. During the neonatal period the urinary tract may be infected by bacteria received from the bloodstream. Thereafter, infection is caused by bacteria ascending into the urinary tract. After 4 months of age, urinary tract infections occur predominantly in females (Durbin & Peter, 1984). Various factors allow bacteria to enter the urinary system. Major factors contributing to UTIs include vesicoureteral reflux, renal calculi, urinary stasis, and obstruction.

In uncomplicated infection, inflammation is usually limited to the bladder (cystitis). Repeated infections may produce changes in the bladder wall, particularly where the ureters enter the bladder (vesicoureteral valves). Damage to these valves may permit reflux of urine during voiding, which allows bacteria access to the kidneys. This can result in kidney infections (pyelonephritis), which affect the normal concentrating and filtering mechanisms of the kidney. Chronic infection leads to scarring and loss of renal tissue. Scarring associated with reflux appears to occur mainly in children under 5 years of age.

## Medical Diagnosis and Management

Clinical manifestations vary with age. In infancy symptoms include fever, weight loss, failure to thrive, nausea, vomiting, diarrhea, and jaundice. Later in childhood, pain with voiding, frequency, incontinence associated with urgency, bedwetting of new onset, abdominal pain, and foul-smelling urine are noted. Hematuria may be seen as a result of hemorrhagic cystitis caused by *E. coli.* Pyelonephritis is evidenced by fever, chills, and flank or abdominal pain. Forty percent of UTIs in children are asymptomatic, and many children have complaints unrelated to the urinary system (Hellerstein, Wald, Winberg, Nelson, & McCracken, 1984).

Diagnosis is confirmed by urine culture. Bacteria greater than 100,000/mL is diagnostic of UTI. When urine cultures are between 10,000/mL and 100,000/mL a repeat culture is indicated. Routine urinalysis may reveal hematuria (blood in the urine), or pyuria (pus or white blood cells in the urine). Additional, more specific tests may include ultrasonography, intravenous pyelogram (IVP), and a voiding cystourethrography (VCUG).

Treatment involves the use of oral or intravenous antibiotics. Sulfamethoxazole-trimethoprim (Bactrim or Septra) and the sulfonamides (Gantrisin) are commonly used antibiotics. A 3-day course of antibiotics is often adequate to treat an uncomplicated lower urinary tract infection. If symptoms of kidney involvement, such as flank pain or vomiting, are apparent, the child will usually be admitted to the hospital and started on IV antibiotics. After the antibiotics are completed, follow-up urine cultures are usually done at intervals—sometimes up to 6 months after infection—to ensure the urine's sterility.

## Nursing Assessment and Diagnosis

Assessment is aimed at noting the child's voiding pattern and the characteristics of the urine. It is also wise to note the manner in which the female child is cleaned after urinating, to determine whether or not there is any fecal contamination. The child should be questioned about stinging during or just after urination. Children may also experience urgency to void but complain of being unable to urinate. Complaints of flank or lower abdominal pain must be carefully evaluated.

Nursing diagnoses for urinary tract infections might include the following:

- Altered patterns of urinary elimination, related to the infection
- Total incontinence, related to the infection
- Pain, related to the infection
- Fluid volume deficit, related to nausea, vomiting, and diarrhea

## Planning and Implementing Nursing Care

The child should be encouraged to drink fluids frequently to dilute the urine and flush the bladder. Nurses should instruct the child to urinate frequently and to empty the bladder completely to prevent urine retention. Young children may need to be reminded about the importance of frequent voiding. Catheterization at home may be required to prevent urine retention, and nurses should carefully educate parents about home catheterization and home urine cultures.

Nurses should educate the child and parents regarding radiological procedures that are ordered. Nurses play an essential role in teaching parents about possible causes and prevention of urinary tract infections. Proper wiping of the female perineal area from front to back to prevent fecal contamination is a critical teaching point. Wearing cotton underwear and avoiding chemical irritants such as bubble baths are additional preventive measures. Girls are often instructed to take showers instead of baths to avoid contamination from sitting in irritating substances.

The child and family should be educated regarding the importance of taking the correct amount of prescribed antibiotic at the designated intervals. It is often helpful to write out these medication instructions for families. Nurses should stress the importance of completing the full course of medication and may need to contact the school nurse to ensure proper medication administration at school. Nurses should stress the importance of follow-up care and repeat urine cultures to rule out kidney disease.

## Evaluating Nursing Care

Evaluation is focused on the resolution of the infection and lack of recurrence. Child and parental knowledge and practice of prevention measures are positive outcomes.

# Vesicoureteral Reflux (VUR)

## Pathophysiology

Vesicoureteral reflux (VUR) is an abnormal condition involving the backward flow of urine in the urinary tract. Vesicoureteral reflux is the most common reflux abnormality, and occurs when urine flows from the bladder back into the ureters and the renal pelvis. It generally results from an incompetence of the valvular mechanism at the ureterovesical junction. The condition involves problems with the muscular layer in the ureter or abnormal insertion of the ureter into the bladder. Problems with the kidney itself may result from an increase in pressure on the renal pelvis during micturition, and the ease with which bacteria can pass from the bladder to the kidney due to the reflux.

There are five different classifications of vesicoureteral reflux, from grade I (the least complicated form) to grade V (the most complex form) (Fig. 30-6). Spontaneous resolution occurs in approximately 80% of cases of grades I and II. The risk of renal scarring or nephropathy increases with the complexity of the disorder.

## *Medical Diagnosis and Management*

VUR is usually discovered when investigating a UTI. The diagnostic tools utilized may include excretory venogram, voiding cystourethrogram, and cystoscopy. The goal of management is to prevent renal scarring, maintain renal function, and keep the client free of UTIs. Treatment for the child with grade I or II VUR is antibiotic prophylaxis with sulfamethoxazole and trimethroprim (Bactrim) or nitrofurantoin (Furadantin).

Follow-up involves urine cultures every 4 to 8 weeks, and CBCs every 3 to 8 months. In addition to assisting with assessment of infection, the CBC is helpful in monitoring bone marrow depression, which is a rare side effect of Bactrim. Voiding cystourethrograms and urograms are done yearly to monitor renal growth and the persistence or absence of VUR. The more complex grades of VUR, III through V, usually require surgical management. The surgical procedures employed involve reimplantation of the

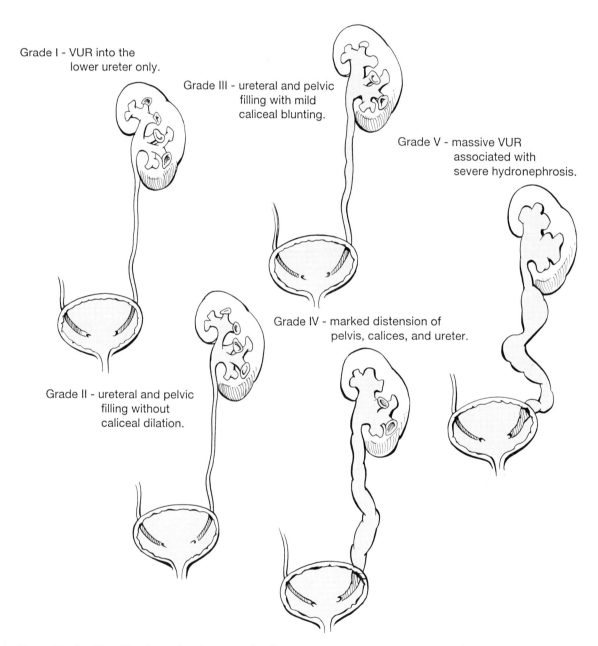

Grade I - VUR into the lower ureter only.

Grade III - ureteral and pelvic filling with mild caliceal blunting.

Grade V - massive VUR associated with severe hydronephrosis.

Grade II - ureteral and pelvic filling without caliceal dilation.

Grade IV - marked distension of pelvis, calices, and ureter.

*Figure 30–6.   Classifications of vesicoureteral reflux.*

ureters and creation of an adequate submucosal tunnel (Woodward & Rushton, 1987). The success rate of these procedures is high.

### Nursing Assessment and Diagnosis

Nursing assessment is aimed at noting the child's voiding pattern and the characteristics of the urine. Foul-smelling, concentrated, or cloudy urine indicate infection and should signal the need for further investigation. Voiding small amounts frequently, as well as experiencing a sense of urgency or pain, also indicate the need for assessment.

Nursing diagnoses for vesicoureteral reflux might include the following:

- High risk for infection, related to retention of urine
- Altered patterns of urinary elimination, related to structural defect
- Pain, related to the infection
- Altered family process, related to illness and hospitalization

### Planning and Implementing Nursing Care

The urine is checked for color, concentration (specific gravity), and odor. Accurate intake and output measurement is essential to note frequency and amount of urine output. Appropriate teaching must be done with the patient and family to explain the disorder and the treatment. The patient and family must be allowed to vent their feelings about the illness and hospitalization and any frustrations they are experiencing.

Postoperative care includes assessment of the operative site for redness, swelling, purulent drainage and bleeding. Ureteral reimplantation procedures usually involve ureteral catheters, or stents. A suprapubic or straight catheter is also present postoperatively. The stents are covered by sterile dressings. The initial gross hematuria gradually clears. The catheters are usually removed before discharge.

Teaching should include the importance of proper hygiene, regular voiding, and increased fluids to prevent infection. Instruction in taking prescribed medication and recognizing signs of UTI is also an important nursing measure.

### Evaluating Nursing Care

Management of UTIs can be evaluated by a decrease or absence of UTIs and reports of adequate urine output without discomfort, frequency or urgency. The family's coping strategies should be effective, and family members should demonstrate an understanding of the disorder and its treatment.

## Acute Renal Problems

### Acute Renal Failure

#### Pathophysiology

Acute renal failure (ARF) results from impaired kidney function caused by damage to the renal tissue. The kidneys are unable to excrete wastes, concentrate urine, or conserve electrolytes. *Azotemia*, an accumulation of nitrogenous wastes in the blood, and *oliguria*, reduction of urine output to less than 0.5 mL/kg/hour (Maxwell, 1987), are the principal clinical manifestations of acute renal failure. *Uremia*, which is another term used in renal failure, indicates an advanced state in which retention of nitrogenous wastes results in toxic symptoms and may involve other body systems. Acute renal failure is usually reversible, but there are varying degrees of long-term impaired function, and pediatric mortality rates are still significant.

Prerenal, intrarenal, and postrenal causative factors are used to classify acute renal failure. Prerenal causes are due to decreased perfusion of the kidney, which, if left unchecked, produces renal parenchymal damage. Prerenal causes of renal failure in small children may include massive fluid losses (vomiting, diarrhea) or the shift of fluid into third spaces as seen in burns or nephrotic syndrome. Hypovolemia, hypotension, and hypoxemia are three prerenal causes of acute renal failure.

Intrarenal causes are disease processes that affect the kidney itself. Glomerulonephritis, intravascular coagulation, and the hemolytic uremic syndrome are three types of intrarenal causes of acute renal failure. Other examples may include acute tubular necrosis (ATN) and interstitial nephritis. In acute tubular necrosis, the tubular cells die, causing acute renal failure. The cause of this necrosis is not fully understood. Acute interstitial nephritis is usually the result of a hypersensitivity reaction to a drug.

Postrenal ARF is due to obstruction of the urinary tract below the kidneys. This obstruction may take the form of a calculus, clot, tumor, or obstructive uropathies. Both ureters must be blocked for renal failure to occur secondary to urethral obstruction.

### Medical Diagnosis and Management

The symptoms seen in children with ARF may be the result of either the disorder itself or the disease process that produced it. The principal manifestation of ARF is oliguria. Other common symptoms include edema, pallor, tachypnea, vomiting, lethargy, and abnormal laboratory values. Urine testing is not diagnostic for ATN, but a low specific gravity indicates decreased urine concentrating ability. Significant lab results include anemia, altered platelets, and fluid and electrolyte abnormalities.

Treatment is generally supportive until the kidneys recover. Management involves restoring and maintaining fluid and electrolyte and acid–base balance, managing hypertension, and treating infection. Prevention of permanent renal damage is the ultimate goal.

Hyperkalemia is a problem frequently noted in ARF clients. Potassium cannot be excreted at normal levels by the damaged renal system. Potassium also shifts from within cells to the vascular system due to metabolic acidosis. Hyperkalemia is a life-threatening imbalance because of the associated cardiac conduction abnormalities. One of the first treatment steps is restriction of dietary potassium. Sodium is usually also restricted to prevent additional fluid being drawn into the vascular component.

If serum potassium levels are greater than 5.5 mEq/L but less than 7.0 mEq/L, sodium polystyrene sulfonate (Kayexalate), a resin that exchanges sodium ions for potassium ions in the gastrointestinal tract, may be used; it is given either orally or rectally. The objective is an osmotic diarrhea that causes the patient to lose potassium in the stool. If the potassium level is greater than 7 mEq/L, sequential intravenous infusion of calcium gluconate, sodium bicarbonate, and glucose with regular insulin is instituted. The calcium decreases the myocardial irritability created by the hyperkalemia, the sodium bicarbonate decreases the potassium, and the glucose-and-insulin combination causes potassium to shift from the extracellular into the intracellular space. These measures do not last more than a few hours, so many of these patients may require dialysis (Levinsky, 1987).

Acidosis, if severe, is treated with just enough sodium bicarbonate to raise the pH to 7.20. A certain amount of acidosis is not unusual with ARF. More sodium bicarbonate is not given because rapid IV infusion of this electrolyte may precipitate tetany. Hypertension is initially treated with sodium and water restriction. In severe hypertension, diazoxide is the drug of choice for children. For less severe hypertension, diuretics, beta-blockers, and vasodilators may be used. If seizure activity occurs, treatment is aimed at the precipitating cause. Anticonvulsants are of limited value in patients with renal failure. Anemia is generally not treated unless it is the result of an active hemorrhage or the hemoglobin is less than 7 g. The diet of these clients is initially restricted to carbohydrates and fats.

Reversible ARF involves three distinct phases. The oliguric phase may last for several days or weeks. In this phase, urine output is markedly decreased, with fluid and electrolyte imbalance. The child is at risk for hypovolemia, congestive heart failure, hyperkalemia, metabolic acidosis, uremia, and infection. The second phase, the diuretic phase, involves a gradual increase in urine output and then a high volume output. BUN levels continue to rise and then level off. Major patient risks involve the loss of potassium and sodium, and resulting electrolyte imbalance. This phase may last for several weeks. The recovery phase lasts from several months to a year, during which time renal function and laboratory values return to normal. Some children experience residual kidney damage.

### Nursing Assessment and Diagnosis

Pertinent physical assessment factors include vital signs, particularly the presence or absence of hypertension, edema, proteinuria or hematuria; intake and output patterns; the child's growth pattern; complaints of fatigue, malaise, and headache; and GI disturbances such as anorexia or vomiting.

Psychosocial assessment factors include patient and family coping, their educational level regarding the disease process and its treatment, the child's school attendance, interaction with family and peers, and outlook on the illness. Finally, the nurse must consider how to prepare the family and child for what may be a poor prognosis. How much of a "normal" child's life the patient will be able to experience should be noted and discussed with the family as well.

Nursing diagnoses for acute renal failure might include the following:

- Fluid volume excess, related to impaired regulatory mechanisms
- High risk for infection, related to decreased body defenses and fluid overload
- Altered family processes, related to hospitalization of the child
- Ineffective individual coping, related to the effects of hospitalization
- High risk for activity intolerance, related to fatigue, malaise, headache, and GI disturbances
- Altered nutrition: Less than body requirements, related to anorexia or vomiting

### Planning and Implementing Nursing Care

Nursing interventions focus on evaluating responses to treatments and managing the numerous medications, fluids, and monitoring devices. These children are usually treated in an intensive care unit. Cardiac and respiratory status is closely monitored. Family teaching is important in helping the parents understand the disease and cope with the critically ill child. The reasons for lab tests, other diagnostic tests, and medications and their side effects should be explained. The child and family should actively participate in the plan of care.

### Evaluation of Nursing Care

Effectiveness of nursing care is evaluated by: the absence of signs of infection, an acceptable blood pressure, fluid and electrolyte balance without significant derangement, an adequate nutritional intake, and a demonstrated understanding of the disorder and its treatment by the child and the family.

## Renal Trauma

### Pathophysiology

Blunt trauma from an automobile accident is the most common cause of renal trauma in young children. Blunt trauma involves sudden deceleration of the human body in which ribs or upper lumbar vertebral processes may contuse or lacerate the kidney. Adolescents often suffer renal trauma from sports injuries or motorcycle accidents.

### Medical Diagnosis and Management

Diagnosis is based on the triad of history, physical examination, and diagnostic testing. Kidney damage is typically indicated by flank pain and the presence of hematuria. Costovertebral pain, upper abdominal tenderness, contusion or palpable mass, and crepitance over the low rib cage or lumbar vertebrae may also be present. Urinalysis may show gross or microscopic hematuria. The amount of blood present in the urine bears no correlation with the degree of injury. An intravenous pyelogram (IVP) is used to evaluate renal injury as well as function. If the IVP is normal and the child has mild hematuria, a mild renal contusion is probable. A poorly visualized kidney on IVP suggests major renal trauma, and arteriography may be employed to pinpoint the location and severity of the injury. CT scanning may assist in making or confirming the diagnosis of renal trauma. Surgical exploration is the mode of treatment for all penetrating injuries because of the associated high incidence of intra-abdominal injury.

Moderate renal injury is treated at home with bed rest and observation. Children with abnormal findings are hospitalized to monitor renal status. Approximately 10% of blunt renal trauma patients require surgery to stop hemorrhage or to salvage a kidney.

### Nursing Assessment and Diagnosis

Nursing assessment includes investigating complaints of pain, observing for overt physical signs of trauma, and noting hematuria. Vital signs, intake and output, serum electrolytes, and hemoglobin/hematocrit are closely monitored.

Nursing diagnoses for renal trauma might include the following:

- Pain, related to traumatic injury
- High risk for infection, related to injury complications
- High risk for altered patterns of urinary elimination, related to injury
- Impaired social interaction, related to illness and hospitalization
- Anxiety, related to injury and hospitalization

### Planning and Implementing Nursing Care

Nursing care is based on close observation of the child with renal injury. Renal status must be closely monitored by intake and output, vital signs, lab tests, and the presence of hematuria. In the postoperative child, pain must be assessed for location, quality, duration, intensity, and the factors that relieve it. Care of nephrostomy or ureterostomy tubes must be meticulous to ensure free flow of urine and to prevent infection, as well as leakage and resultant skin breakdown.

Patient and family teaching should be initiated as soon as possible. The suddenness of the injury and hospitalization of the child may overwhelm the family. Teaching should be repeated as frequently as needed. The child and family should be encouraged to express their feelings verbally. Information about signs of hemorrhage or renal damage are important in discharge planning. Periodic follow-up also includes blood pressure measurements to detect renal damage.

### Evaluating Nursing Care

Evaluation of nursing care is aimed at noting the patterns of hematuria, pain, and urinary elimination. The patient should show no signs or symptoms of infection or hypertension. Parents should understand the signs of hemorrhage or renal damage.

## Chronic Renal Problems

## Chronic Glomerulonephritis

### Pathophysiology

Chronic glomerulonephritis (CGN) is a progressive form of renal disease involving the glomeruli. The disease is broken down into three histological types based on changes in the capillary walls and other tissue changes in the kidney. Persistent glomerulonephritis lacks a specific histological picture, and recovery is delayed. Chronic glomerulonephritis involves advanced glomerular disease. Rapidly progressive glomerulonephritis involves an acute illness that results in rapid decrease in renal function over a period of 6 to 12 months.

CGN includes a variety of various disease processes. Most cases involve immunological mechanisms that directly affect either the kidney or the glomeruli. This leads to increased glomerular damage and eventual chronic disease. The condition may occur without any history of acute glomerular disease or any other disease, resulting in significant renal destruction before symptoms appear. Ultimately renal insufficiency results.

## Medical Diagnosis and Management

Elevated BUN, creatinine, and uric acid levels indicate poor renal function. Signs and symptoms of CGN vary from hematuria or proteinuria, to nephrotic syndrome and uremia. Hypertension is seen with most cases of CGN. Diuretic therapy and sodium restriction are used to manage hypertension. Antihypertensive therapy is used for marked hypertension. Serum electrolytes are monitored due to the possibility of severe potassium depletion secondary to some diuretics and increased calcium due to the use of the thiazides. Corticosteroids combined with the use of cytotoxic drugs may also be used to decrease the incidence of some bone marrow depression from immunosuppressive agents. The results of these medicines are generally disappointing; either the immune reaction cannot be suppressed or the cause of the disorder and its progression is not immune-related. The prognosis for these patients is generally poor. Treatment is aimed at supportive care as opposed to definitive treatment.

## Nursing Assessment and Diagnosis

Assessment includes vital signs, particularly the presence or absence of hypertension; edema; proteinuria or hematuria; intake and output patterns; and complaints of fatigue, malaise, headache and GI disturbances such as anorexia and vomiting. Nurses should play a role in evaluating the impact of the condition on the child's physical, emotional, psychological, and social development, especially school attendance, and interaction with family and peers.

Nursing diagnoses for chronic glomerulonephritis might include the following:

- Fluid volume excess, related to renal failure
- High risk for infection, related to depressed immune status
- Altered nutrition: Less than body requirements for protein
- Altered nutrition: More than body requirements for salt
- Social isolation, related to illness and hospitalization
- Altered family processes, related to illness and hospitalization of the child
- Fatigue, related to chronic disease
- Ineffective individual coping, related to hospitalization
- Altered growth and development, related to the prognosis of the illness

## Planning and Implementing Nursing Care

Vital signs, particularly heart rate and blood pressure, must be monitored. Hypertension and its resolution after initiation of drug therapy should be noted. Nurses should also be alert for signs of hypotension and tachycardia, which are side effects of antihypertensive agents. It is also important to check for edema, including the face and sacrum.

Fluid and electrolyte imbalances due to poor renal filtration occur with resultant edema. Due to this decreased filtration, meticulous measurement of intake and output is necessary. Daily weights in the same clothes, at the same time of day, and on the same scale are essential. Nurses should watch for symptoms of electrolyte imbalance, such as cramping, paresthesias, and disorientation. The likelihood of electrolyte imbalance increases as renal disease progresses. Patient and family teaching is based on their current knowledge base. Reasons for lab work, diagnostic tests, and medications and their side effects should be explained. Including the child and family in the plan of care is essential. Normal activities such as school attendance and extracurricular activities should be encouraged. The child's adjustment to a prescribed diet should be noted. Consultation with the dietitian may assist the child to maintain adequate nutritional intake. Rest periods should be encouraged if needed due to fatigue. The child should understand that taking rest periods is part of the treatment and not a punishment.

## Evaluating Nursing Care

Effectiveness of care is evaluated by an acceptable blood pressure, fluid and electrolyte balance without significant derangement, an adequate nutritional intake, and an increase in the patient's and family's understanding of the disease and the treatment. Because the care of these patients is largely supportive, evaluation focuses on an improvement in their status.

# Chronic Renal Failure

## Pathophysiology

Chronic renal failure (CRF) is a result of progressive reduction in renal function due to irreversible damage to the nephrons. The causes of chronic renal failure in children seem to run parallel with their age. At less than 5 years of age, the etiology of chronic renal failure is anatomical in nature. At greater than 5 years of age, the etiology involves a glomerular disease state or a hereditary problem. There are numerous causes of CRF, but infection and congenital anomalies are the most common.

Chronic renal failure progresses in four diagnostic stages. In the first stage, decreased renal reserve, the child

process is used in end-stage renal disease. Hemodialysis requires placement of an arteriovenous shunt for permanent access to the child's bloodstream; the shunt may be either external or subcutaneous. The hemodialysis procedure is carried out approximately three times per week for a period of 3 to 6 hours.

## Peritoneal Dialysis

Peritoneal dialysis uses the abdominal cavity to act as the semipermeable membrane through which water and solutes move by osmosis and diffusion. A permanent catheter is surgically placed in the peritoneal cavity for access. The process of intermittent peritoneal dialysis (IPD) involves the attachment of the child's catheter to an automated peritoneal dialysis machine for up to 12 hours three to four times a week. This is usually done at night. The machine instills and withdraws the dialysate automatically. A frequently used procedure is continuous ambulatory peritoneal dialysis (CAPD). In this process, the child or parents instill the dialysate via a sterile plastic bag, which is then rolled up and secured to the abdomen or placed in the child's pocket. After a specified "dwell" time (usually 4 to 6 hours), the bag is reattached and refills by gravity with the solute-laden dialysate. This procedure is repeated three to five times daily.

CAPD is rapidly becoming the preferred treatment in children because it offers improved control of uremia. It also allows for a more continuous control of sodium and water balance, which permits the child a more liberal diet and less fluid restriction. An even more apparent benefit is the freedom afforded the child and family by not having to rely on a machine.

The third type of peritoneal dialysis, continuous cycling peritoneal dialysis (CCPD), is a combination of IPD and CAPD. Dialysis is done at night via machine, and during the day a small amount of dialysate solution remains in the abdomen. This solution is removed in the first machine cycle at night.

The most serious complication of peritoneal dialysis is peritonitis due to unsterile technique. Additional problems are outlined in Table 30-4. Nurses should note that the efficiency of the peritoneum as a dialyzer decreases over time. Extended periods of dialysis therapy result in growth retardation.

### Nursing Assessment and Diagnosis

The patient's fluid balance, weight, and vital signs should be monitored. Children undergoing peritoneal dialysis run the risk of fluid volume deficit and overload due to the fluid shifts caused during the procedure. Temperature is monitored to check for signs and symptoms of peritonitis. The dialysate returning from the patient's abdomen is checked for fluid color and character. It should appear clear or straw-colored. Small doses of heparin may be

*Table 30–4.  Problems Associated With Peritoneal Dialysis*

**Cardiovascular**

Arrhythmias
Cardiac arrest
Pulmonary edema
Hypertension
Hypotension
Fluid volume excess

**Infections**

Bacterial or fungal peritonitis
Diverticulitis
Incisional infection
Pancreatitis

**Metabolic**

Hyperglycemia, hypoglycemia
Hyperkalemia, hypokalemia
Metabolic alkalosis
Protein depletion
Obesity

**Neurological**

Seizures

**Pulmonary**

Pneumonia
Aspiration
Respiratory arrest
Decreased lung capacity

**Treatment-Related**

Bleeding
Pain
Leakage
Scrotal edema
Decreased drainage
Hernia at incision site
Intestinal perforation

added to each bottle of dialysate to prevent the abdominal catheter from becoming plugged with small clots. Potassium may also be added to prevent hypokalemia. The abdominal dressing should be checked for dampness, which indicates leakage around the catheter.

Nursing diagnoses for the child undergoing dialysis might include the following:

- High risk for infection, related to catheter insertion site
- Diversional activity deficit, related to length of time needed for dialysis
- Altered family processes, related to the child's illness

# Nursing Care Plan

## Assessment

Kimberly is an 8-year-old female seen in the outpatient clinic.

### Chief Complaint

Pain on urination; urinary urgency and frequency for 1 day.

### Subjective Assessment

*Past History:* No previous history of urinary tract infections. Kimberly has been essentially healthy except for 3 instances of otitis media, during her first year of life. Her immunization status is current.

*Present History:* Kimberly's mother states that she has been complaining of burning and pain on urination. Kimberly feels the urge to urinate frequently, but very little urine is passed. There are no complaints of lower abdominal pain. Kimberly has been afebrile and shows no other symptoms.

*Family History:* Mother is 32 years old and father is 34 years old; there is one older sibling, an 11-year-old brother, and a younger sister, age 7 years. All family members are well. The paternal and maternal grandparents are alive and well except for hypertension in the maternal grandfather, which is controlled by medication.

### Objective Assessment

*Physical Examination:* T. 37°C (98.6°F) otic; P. 90; radial; R. 22; B.P. 105/60 R arm sitting; weight: 26.3 kg (58 lb); height 129.5 cm (51 in)

| | |
|---|---|
| Integument: | Clear with normal turgor |
| Head: | Normal |
| Eyes: | PERRLA, fundoscopic exam normal |
| Ears: | TMs pearly grey with good light reflex and mobility |
| Nose: | Mucous membranes pink and moist |
| Throat: | Clear, normal tonsils |
| Neck | Supple without lymph-adenopathy |
| Thorax and Lungs: | Clear lung fields |
| Heart: | Regular rate and rhythm without murmur |
| Abdomen: | Soft without masses or organomegaly; slight tenderness over left flank |
| Genitalia: | Normal female |
| Musculoskeletal: | Full ROM; no deformities |
| Neurological: | Alert reflexes: DTR's 2+, symmetrical |

### Diagnostic Tests and Results

Laboratory findings: Urine specific gravity 1.015, pH 7, protein 1+
Micro examination reveals bacteria
WBC 10–12/HPF
Urine sent for culture and sensitivity

### Medical Diagnosis

Urinary Tract Infection

### Medical Plan

Antibiotic therapy

## Nursing Care Plan for a Child with a Urinary Tract Infection

| Goals | Nursing Interventions | Evaluation Criteria |
|---|---|---|
| *NURSING DIAGNOSIS #1: Altered patterns of urinary elimination: Incontinence due to UTI* | | |
| (S) Continence will be regained | Medications will be administered as prescribed | Child will be continent |
| (S) The child and parents will understand the symptoms and treatment of UTIs | Instruct child and parents on signs, symptoms, and treatment of UTIs | |

*(continued)*

# Nursing Care Plan *(Continued)*

| Goals | Nursing Interventions | Evaluation Criteria |
|---|---|---|
| (L) Proper cleansing technique of the child after toileting will be demonstrated by parents to decrease the likelihood of recurrence of UTIs | Instruct child/parents on the proper techniques for post toileting hygiene | |
| (L) Skin breakdown secondary to incontinence will be avoided | Inspect skin meticulously for any signs and symptoms of breakdown and report findings; provide skin care after each elimination | |

| Goals | Nursing Interventions | Evaluation Criteria |
|---|---|---|

*NURSING DIAGNOSIS #2: Alteration in comfort due to pain, urinary urgency, and increased temperature secondary to infection*

| Goals | Nursing Interventions | Evaluation Criteria |
|---|---|---|
| (S) Alteration in comfort will be relieved | Give analgesics as ordered and assess effectiveness | Child will be pain free |
| (L) The child will be infection free | Maintain light clothing/covering if child is experiencing discomfort from fever | |
| | Encourage child to change underwear as frequently as needed | |
| | Assist with diversionary activities to help decrease perception of pain | |

| Goals | Nursing Interventions | Evaluation Criteria |
|---|---|---|

*NURSING DIAGNOSIS #3: High Risk for alteration in fluid balance secondary to nausea, vomiting and diarrhea*

| Goals | Nursing Interventions | Evaluation Criteria |
|---|---|---|
| (S) Alteration in comfort will be relieved | Assess for signs and symptoms of hypovolemia: sunken fontanelles; dry, cracked mucous membranes; excessive tachycardia; hypotension in the older child; dark, concentrated urine | Child will take fluids normally |
| | Encourage oral fluids as tolerated | |
| | Maintain meticulous intake and output | |
| | Daily weights | |
| | Maintain viligence over I.V. therapy to assure correct intake and decrease potential for fluid overload | |

- Ineffective individual coping, related to the illness and the need for dialysis
- Anxiety, related to the prognosis
- Constipation, related to dialysis

### Planning and Implementing Nursing Care

The child must be monitored for any signs of infection. The dialysate outflow is checked for change in color or evidence of bleeding. The catheter site should be checked for leakage. Inflow and outflow must be accurately monitored. Catheter position may need to be altered if there is leakage or slowed inflow. Kinked tubing or the tubing position may result in altered outflow of solution; repositioning may be helpful. Internal hemodialysis shunts also must be checked for patency when not in use. Vital signs must be checked frequently to assess for changes secondary to fluid shifts. As the disease progresses, patients with renal failure become sensitive to the fluid shifts that occur during dialysis, with resultant hypotension.

Nutritional status must be monitored. Oral intake should be encouraged within the child's dietary constraints. Small, frequent meals during dialysis may lessen abdominal distention and discomfort. Constipation is a complication of dialysis. Nurses should monitor bowel sounds, abdominal distention, type and frequency of stools, and abdominal pain. Laxatives should be provided as needed when dietary modification is insufficient. Nurses must also promote activity for the child by helping the child find a position that is comfortable during dialysis and that facilitates play activities.

### Evaluating Nursing Care

The objective of dialysis is to remove waste products from the body. Evaluation includes improvement in electrolyte, BUN, and creatinine values; decreased edema; and improved vital signs. The child and family should understand the need for dialysis and appear comfortable with the procedures.

## Renal Transplantation

The treatment of choice for chronic renal failure is renal transplantation. Numerous factors influence the survival rate of both the recipient and the graft, including age of recipient, closeness of the tissue type, pre-transplant blood transfusions, prior history of transplant, and immunosuppressive therapy.

Transplant outcome is improved if the new kidney is obtained from a live, related donor as opposed to a cadaver. Immunologically, a related donor ensures a higher survival rate. Additionally, the older the child is at the time of transplantation, the more favorable the postoperative course. Active malignancy is usually a criterion for exclusion from renal transplant. Transplantation is usually postponed for 1 year after treatment for Wilms' tumor; recurrence is not a significant factor after that time. If the patient has an infection, it must be resolved before surgery due to the immunosuppressive therapy that follows transplantation (Fine & Ehrlich, 1985).

Corticosteroids (prednisone) are used in the immunosuppressant therapy. Cyclosporine and antilymphocyte globulin may also be used. This therapy suppresses not only the immune response of the recipient but also the body's capacity to fight infections, placing the child at risk for overwhelming infections. The first 3 months after transplant, these patients are particularly at risk for infection by the herpes viruses. Corticosteroids have numerous side effects that create problems for transplant recipients. Adolescents often have problems dealing with side effects such as obesity, acne, and hirsutism. Long-term effects include retarded growth, Cushing syndrome, cataracts, and gastric ulcers.

Cyclosporine A has shown promise as an anti-rejection agent for pediatric renal transplantation patients. Its use decreases the amount of steroids needed by decreasing production of T-cells. One disadvantage is that doses may occasionally be increased in children in order to maintain blood levels. A transient nephrotoxicity may occur, but this usually resolves with a decreased dosage. A moderate decrease in the glomerular filtration rate may also occur and is significant because of associated growth retardation. Other negative side effects of cyclosporine A in children include recurrence of hemolytic uremic syndrome, neurotoxic side effects, facial hirsutism, and a worsening cushingoid appearance (Chapman & Morris, 1986).

Bilateral nephrectomy is no longer a prerequisite for transplantation. The kidneys are removed only if they are harmful to the child. Erythropoietin production, vitamin D metabolism, and residual renal tissue indicate the importance of preserving even minimally functioning renal tissue.

### Nursing Assessment and Diagnosis

The goal of nursing assessment is to monitor these children preoperatively for the various sequelae discussed under renal failure. Postoperatively, the child is assessed for signs and symptoms of infection. Infection is a much more formidable problem in the transplant patient due to immunosuppression, rejection corticosteroid toxicity, hepatic dysfunction, and hypertension. Nursing diagnosis for renal transplantation might include the following:

- Fluid volume excess
- High risk for injury, related to hypertension

- Anxiety, related to illness and hospitalization
- Pain, related to the disease process and surgery
- High risk for infection, related to surgery and immunosuppression
- Impaired social interaction, related to illness and hospitalization
- Social isolation, related to illness and hospitalization
- Ineffective family coping, related to child's illness and hospitalization

### Planning and Implementing Nursing Care

Nursing care goals following transplant involve preventing and treating kidney rejection and infection. Rejection can occur immediately or over a time span of 1 to 2 years after transplantation. Signs of rejection include fever, abdominal pain, hypertension, and decreased urine output. As renal function deteriorates, BUN and serum creatinine levels rise. There are many potential complications related to a transplant procedure. Assessment of the operative site should include checking for redness, swelling, perineal drainage, and bleeding. A temperature greater than 101°F (38.4°C) should be reported. Any signs and symptoms of bleeding such as decreased blood pressure with increased heart rate, pallor, diaphoresis, lethargy, frank bleeding from the wound site, abdominal pain, or swelling should be reported. These patients are usually hospitalized for 2 to 4 weeks. Nurses should be aware of the numerous emotional and psychological conflicts involving transplantation. Kidney transplantation offers an end to the limitations and trials of dialysis and the child's diet restrictions. Families and the child can display various concerns regarding the procedure, including ethical conflicts involving the transplant organ and donor selection. Nurses often play a critical role as a case manager for these children, coordinating care from various members of the health care team. Nurses must also be prepared to provide support if the kidney is rejected. Community resources can provide family support.

The side effects of corticosteroid therapy often lead to noncompliance, and are related to emotional and social problems in adolescents. Adolescent girls are particularly sensitive to the cosmetic side effects, and often discontinue the drugs. They need to be helped to understand the temporary nature of these physical changes and the reasons why they must take the medication.

### Evaluating Nursing Care

Evaluation is based on change in renal function postoperatively. Most children and families respond well to transplantation and resume normal life activities within a year of the surgery. Adolescents should understand the implications of corticosteroid therapy and have methods for dealing with the emotional stress.

## Summary

Renal diseases can create numerous emotional and financial strains on children and their families and can produce a great deal of fear involving a wide variety of concerns. The nursing care of children and adolescents with alterations in renal function offers a unique opportunity for nurses to interact with children and their family members. Many of the diseases and disorders affecting the renal system can be devastating for children and their families. Nurses are challenged by the numerous health problems facing children with chronic illness, as well as by the disease complications. Disturbances in body image are a common complication. Complex renal problems not only lead to a state of chronic illness but seriously affect growth and development.

Caring for the family, providing support and education, and preparing members for home care become critical nursing interventions. Many renal problems also involve emotional and psychological implications related to impaired genital appearance or function. Care of the child with renal alteration requires competent nursing skills to deal with a wide variety of procedures, specimen collection, accurate observation, and recording of intake and output, and numerous mechanical devices. Nurses caring for children with renal problems may also be involved in the complex area of organ transplantation.

## References

Belasco, J. B., Chatten, J., D'Angio, G. J. (1984). Wilms' tumor. In W. W. Sutow, D. J. Fernbach, & T. J. Vietti (Eds.). *Clinical pediatric oncology* (3rd ed.). St. Louis: C. V. Mosby.

Belman, A. B. (1984, March). Early surgery for hypospadias. *Hospital Practice, 19*(3), 192–198.

Bergstein, J. M., & Michael, A. F. (1987). The urinary system. In R. E. Behrman & V. C. Vaughan (Eds.). *Nelson textbook of pediatrics* (13th ed.). Philadelphia: W. B. Saunders, pp. 1143–1147.

Buckholz, V. W. (1988). Perioperative nursing care of the pediatric hypospadias patient. *Clinics in Plastic Surgery, 15*, 399–404.

Chapman, J. R., & Morris, P. J. (1986). Long-term effects of short-term cyclosporine. *Transplantation Proceedings, 16*, 185–191.

deWardener, H. E. (1985). *The kidney* (5th ed.). New York: Churchill Livingstone.

Durbin, W. A., & Peter, G. (1984). Management of urinary tract infections in infants and children. *Pediatric Infectious Diseases, 3*, 564–574.

Fine, R. N., & Ehrlich, R. M. (1985). Renal transplantation in children. In P. P. Kelalis, L. K. King, & A. B. Belman

(Eds). *Clinical pediatric urology* (2nd ed.). Philadelphia: W. B. Saunders.

Gellis, S. S., & Kagan, B. M. (Eds). (1990). *Current pediatric therapy* (13th ed.). Philadelphia: W. B. Saunders.

Glassock, R. J., Cohen, A. H., Adler, S., & Ward, H. (1991). Secondary glomerular diseases. In B. M. Brenner & F. C. Rector (Eds.). *The kidney* (4th ed.). Philadelphia: W. B. Saunders.

Hellerstein, S., Wald, E. R., Winberg, J., Nelson, J. D., & McCracken, G. H. (1984). Consensus: Roentgenographic evaluation of children with urinary tract infection. *Pediatric Infectious Diseases, 3,* 291–293.

Jeffs, R. D. (1987). Exstrophy, epispadias and cloacal and urogenital sinus abnormalities. *Pediatric Clinics of North America, 34,* 1233–1253.

Jordan, S. C., & Lemire, J. M. (1982). Acute glomerulonephritis. *Pediatric Clinics of North America, 29,* 857–873.

Levinsky, N. (1991). Fluids and electolytes. In Wilson, J., et al. (Eds.). *Harrison's principles of internal medicine* (12th ed.). New York: McGraw-Hill, pp. 278–289.

Maxwell, L. G. et al. (1987). Renal failure. In M. Rogers (Ed.). *Textbook of pediatric intensive care.* Baltimore: Williams & Wilkins.

Sadove, R. C., Horton, C. E., & McRoberts, J. W. The new era of hypospadias surgery. *Clinics in Plastic Surgery, 15,* 341–354.

Woodward, J. R., & Rushton, H. G. (1987). Reflux uropathy. *Pediatric Clinics of North America, 34,* 1349–1364.

## Bibliography

Doleys, D. M., & Dolce, J. J. (1982). Toilet training and enuresis. *Pediatric Clinics of North America, 29,* 297–313.

Chambers, J. K. (1987). Fluid and electrolyte problems in renal and urologic disorders. *Issues in Comprehensive Pediatric Nursing, 10,* 815–826

Ganick, D. J. (1987). Wilms' tumor. *Hematology and Oncology Clinics of North America, 1,* 695–719.

MacGeorge, L. (1986). Nursing assessment with cyclosporine A. *Oncology Nursing Forum, 13,*(1) 9.

Neff, E. J. A. (1987). Nursing the child undergoing dialysis. *Issues in Comprehensive Pediatric Nursing, 10,* 173–185.

Richard, C. J. (1986). *Comprehensive nephrology nursing.* Philadelphia: J. B. Lippincott.

Rimar, J. M. (1985). Cyclosporine for organ transplantation. *American Journal of Maternal Child Nursing, 10,* 237.

Rivers, R. (1987, August). Nursing the kidney transplant patient. *RN, 50*(8), 46–53.

Sheldon, C. A., & Duckett, J. W. (1987). Hypospadias. *Pediatric Clinics of North America, 34,* 1259–1265.

Sheldon, C. A., McLorie, G. A., & Churchill, B. M. (1987). Renal transplantation in children. *Pediatric Clinics of North America, 34,* 1209–1227.

Stark, J. L. (1988). A quick guide to urinary tract assessment. *Nursing 88, 18*(7), 57–58.

# Alterations in Reproductive Function

Richard E. Harbin

*Photograph by David Finn*

**31**

*Embryology*

*Anatomy and Physiology*

*Female Reproductive Development*

*Male Reproductive Development*

*Assessment*

*Nursing Diagnosis*

*Planning and Implementing Nursing Care*

*Evaluating Nursing Care*

*Reproductive Problems of Neonates and Infants*

*Reproductive Problems of Toddlers and Preschoolers*

*Reproductive Problems of School-Aged Children*

*Reproductive Problems of Adolescents*

*Menstrual Problems of Adolescents*

*Vulvovaginitis*

*Breast Problems*

*Reproductive Problems of Male Adolescents*

*Sexual Abuse*

*Sexually Transmitted Diseases*

*Summary*

*Nursing Care Plan*

## Learning Objectives

*Upon completion of this chapter the reader will be able to:*

1. *Demonstrate an understanding of the embryonic development of the reproductive system, including the concept of sex differentiation.*

2. *Discuss anatomy and physiology of the reproductive system.*

3. *Identify the important subjective and objective data that should be collected during assessment of the reproductive system.*

4. *Formulate nursing diagnoses for alterations in reproductive function.*

5. *Plan and implement appropriate nursing interventions applicable to the child or adolescent with a reproductive system disorder.*

6. *Analyze the effectiveness of nursing interventions, including therapy, education, and prevention measures.*

7. *Synthesize knowledge about reproductive disorders with aspects of total care of the client, family, and community.*

## Key Terms

**ambiguous genitalia**

**androgens**

**clitoris**

**estrogen**

**fallopian tubes**

**gonad**

**hypogonadism**

**incest**

**labia**

**leukorrhea**

**menarche**

*menstrual cycle*

*menstruation*

*ovaries*

*penis*

*precocious puberty*

*prepuce*

*rape*

*scrotum*

*sex differentiation*

*testes*

*thelarche*

*uterus*

*vulva*

The female and male reproductive systems include both internal and external structures. These systems are essential not only to proliferation of the human species but to human sexuality as well. The primary organs of the reproductive system are the *gonads,* which are the *ovaries* in the female and the *testes* in the male. Reproduction is possible due to the gonads and their internal and external accessory structures.

## Embryology

The genetic sex of an embryo is established at the time of fertilization, but the primitive gonad of both sexes is identical until the 7th week of embryonic life. This period is called the *indifferent stage* of reproductive development. Initially, the normal human embryo is potentially bisexual. The development of specific organs or structures in the embryonic period is called *sex differentiation*.

The sex chromosome complex determines gonadal sex, or the type of gonad that develops from the indifferent gonad. At 7 weeks, testicular development begins under control of the Y chromosome. Absence of the Y chromosome results in ovarian differentiation, which is slow to develop and is not identifiable until the 10th week.

Two pairs of genital ducts, *wolffian* and *müllerian* ducts, develop early in fetal life, and both are present for a time in the embryo. Normal development includes differentiation of one pair and regression of the other. In the female, the müllerian ducts differentiate into the fallopian tubes, the uterus, and the upper portion of the vagina, and the wolffian ducts regress. In the male, the wolffian ducts form the vas deferens, seminal vesicles, and epididymis, while the müllerian ducts regress. Differentiation of male sexual structures is dependent on fetal testicular hormones, while female differentiation occurs when these hormones are absent.

The external genitalia develop from the urogenital sinus and appear similar until the end of the 9th week. In the female, the genital tubercle becomes the *clitoris,* developing like the penis except that urogenital folds do not fuse. These unfused urogenital folds form the labia minora, and the labioscrotal folds form the labia majora. In the male, the genital tubercle elongates to become the penis, and the urogenital folds fuse along the ventral penile surface to form the urethra. The labioscrotal folds fuse in the midline, forming the scrotum. Fusion of the urethral and labioscrotal folds is completed by the 12th week, but phallic enlargement continues throughout the embryonic period under influence of androgenic hormones. The external genitalia of the fetus are recognizably male or female by the 12th week of embryonic life.

Abnormalities of sexual differentiation interfere with embryonic development, resulting in a condition termed *intersexuality* or *hermaphroditism.* A hermaphrodite is a person with *ambiguous genitalia.* This condition is relatively rare. Histological appearance of the gonads is used to classify intersexual conditions. *True hermaphrodites* have both ovarian and testicular tissue. Most have an ambiguous phallus, with hypospadias or fairly normal-appearing male genitalia. It is rare to see completely normal female external genitalia. Male *pseudohermaphrodites* have testes, and female pseudohermaphrodites have ovaries.

## Anatomy and Physiology

### Female

The female internal reproductive organs consist of the uterus, fallopian tubes, ovaries, and vagina. The uterus is located behind the urinary bladder and consists of the fundus, the body, and the cervix. The fallopian tubes extend laterally and downward on each side of the uterus.

The fallopian tubes transport the egg to the uterus. The ovaries, which produce ova, are behind the fallopian tubes. The vagina extends from the cervix to its opening on the perineum. The anatomy of the female reproductive system is shown in Figure 31-1.

The female external reproductive structures (Fig. 31-2) are termed the *vulva,* and include the mons pubis, labia, clitoris, Skene's and Bartholin's glands, and vaginal orifice. The *mons pubis* is a fat pad above the symphysis pubis. The labia include the *labia majora,* which are two prominent longitudinal folds beginning at the mons pubis and extending almost to the anus, and the *labia minora,* which border the vaginal orifice and unite anteriorly in the hood or prepuce of the clitoris. The *clitoris* is located anterior to the urinary meatus and is homologous to the male penis. Skene's glands, posterior to the urethral orifice, and Bartholin's glands, located on each side of the vaginal orifice, have a moistening function.

### Male

The male internal reproductive organs are the seminal vesicles, the prostate, Cowper's glands, and a portion of the vas deferens. The anatomy of the male reproductive system is shown in Figure 31-3. The seminal vesicles are two membranous pouches lying behind the urinary bladder. The seminal vesicle ducts join with the vas deferens in forming the ejaculatory duct. Secretions from the seminal vesicles increase the amount of seminal fluid. The prostate gland is located inferior to the bladder and the internal urethral orifice. The prostate secretes a fluid that acts to increase sperm motility. The Cowper's glands are on each of the urethra just below the prostate gland. These glands produce a preejaculation secretion that serves to protect the sperm and facilitate its movement.

The penis, testes, and scrotum are the external male reproductive organs. The penis, the male organ of copulation, consists of a shaft that ends in a slight enlargement, the *glans penis.* The glans is covered by the *prepuce* or *foreskin,* which is attached to the body of the penis. The testes are enclosed in a pouch called the *scrotum,* which is divided by a septum. The testes are suspended by the spermatic cords, which contain the *vas deferens.* Posterior to each testis is the *epididymis,* a reservoir for sperm.

## Female Reproductive Development

The female reproductive system is also controlled by a complex, interacting hormone system. Follicle-stimulating hormone (FSH), luteinizing hormone (LH), and luteotropic hormone (LTH) are the female gonadotropic hormones involved. These hormones stimulate the ovaries to produce the hormones *estrogen* and *progesterone.* Estrogen regulates development and function of the reproduc-

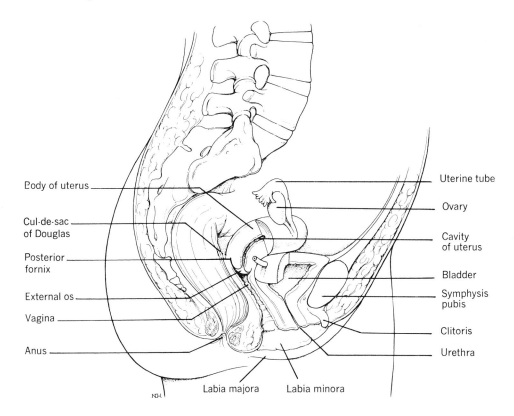

*Figure 31–1. Anatomy of the female reproductive system. (Chaffee, E.E., & Greisheimer, E.M. [1974].* Basic physiology and anatomy *[3rd ed.]. Philadelphia: J.B. Lippincott)*

tive organs. Progesterone plays a major role in preparing the endometrium for implantation of the fertilized egg.

## The Menstrual Cycle

Beginning at puberty, and normally continuing throughout the reproductive years, females experience a rhythmic cycle that prepares the reproductive system for pregnancy. This cycle is repeated on an average of every 28 days, although this time frame may vary widely and still be considered normal. The menstrual cycle comprises two additional cycles, the ovarian and endometrial cycles.

The ovarian cycle involves gonadotropin stimulation

of the ovaries and results in the maturation and release of a single ovum from the ovary. Ovulation, the release of this ovum, typically occurs 2 weeks before the next expected menstrual period.

The endometrial cycle controls the preparation of the endometrium or lining of the uterus for implantation of a fertilized ovum. At ovulation, progesterone is secreted, resulting in a thickening of the uterine endometrium. If the ovum is fertilized, implantation may occur. If the ovum is not fertilized, there is a rapid decrease of estrogens and progesterone, which causes an eventual sloughing of the endometrial layer. This results in *menstruation,* which lasts for 3 to 7 days.

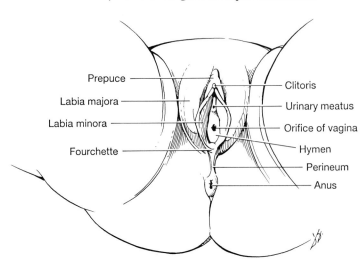

*Figure 31–2.    External female anatomy.*

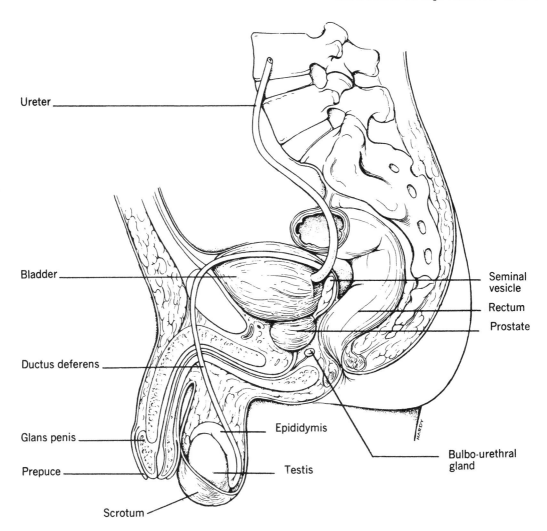

*Figure 31–3. Anatomy of the male reproductive system. (Chaffee, E.E., & Greisheimer, E.M. [1974].* Basic physiology and anatomy *[3rd ed.]. Philadelphia: J.B. Lippincott)*

## Male Reproductive Development

While the external genitalia are progressing through the Tanner stages (see Chap. 16), the pubertal male begins producing sperm. The process of producing sperm is called *spermatogenesis* and is triggered by FSH. LH is essential for the development of the seminal vesicles and the prostate and for the functions of semen production and ejaculation. Male sex hormones are called *androgens,* with *testosterone* identified as the primary androgen since it is secreted in much greater quantity than other androgens.

## Assessment

Because of the embarrassment children and adolescents associate with their sexual maturation, assessment of the reproductive system requires a special degree of sensitivity by the examiner. It is critical to establish an objective, nonthreatening atmosphere. It is important to phrase questions appropriately and to project a feeling of being comfortable in discussing any concerns or answering questions. Parents relate most of the history during evalua-

tion of a younger child, but the child should be included as much as possible. Including the child before the physical examination helps in establishing a rapport. It also helps to have the parent hold the younger child during portions of the examination. Examination of the genitalia is usually the last section of physical assessment. This helps to facilitate the development of a trusting relationship with the child.

The approach and specific questions for assessment of adolescents are discussed in Chapter 16. The nurse must remember the importance of confidentiality when the adolescent is involved. Nurses need to reassure adolescents that information will not be discussed with parents or anyone without their specific permission.

## History

Patient history provides important data for evaluation of the reproductive system. Obtaining an accurate genetic history is particularly important, as is a complete prenatal history. The nurse should question the mother regarding medications taken during the pregnancy. Data collected may assist in the need for further evaluation for possible intersex abnormalities in a newborn.

Family history of sterility, menstrual disorders, inguinal hernias, and other reproductive conditions should be thoroughly reviewed. A reproductive history for the adolescent female should include: age at onset of menarche, frequency and cycle of periods, amount of flow, incidence of dysmenorrhea, and date of the most recent normal period. Adolescents should be asked about concerns regarding their breasts, including sensitivity and changes in size or asymmetry.

Specific, concrete questions should be used to ascertain sexual activity, knowledge of contraception, and exposure to sexually transmitted diseases. Sexually active females should be questioned regarding pregnancies, miscarriages, and abortions. Gynecological review should include questions regarding vaginal discharge or bleeding, pain with intercourse, and amenorrhea.

The adolescent male reproductive history includes information concerning the penis and testicles. Questions should be asked about genital pain, swelling, discoloration, and discharge. As with females, specific questions should be used to determine sexual activity, contraceptive use, and exposure to sexually transmitted diseases.

## Physical Examination

Physical examination of the reproductive system includes inspection and palpation of the external genitalia. This can be an anxiety-producing procedure for both the child and parents. Nurses must also resolve any fears or anxieties they might have regarding examination of the genitalia because these feelings will be communicated to the patient and increase any anxiety already present. Older school-aged children and adolescents are usually particularly apprehensive, and time should be taken to allow them to voice concerns and ask questions. At any age, a direct, matter-of-fact approach usually is the most effective. Nurses should attempt to gain an awareness of the family's attitudes toward sex and the genitalia and adjust the approach accordingly.

Inspection and palpation of the breasts, abdominal examination, and pelvic examination as indicated in females is also part of the physical examination of the reproductive system. The breasts in both sexes should be inspected for enlargement, symmetry, or discharge and palpated for masses or tenderness. It is not uncommon to see asymmetry of the breasts in the female school-aged child or adolescent. Nurses should be aware that one breast normally develops at a faster rate than the other. Nurses should reassure adolescent girls about this asymmetry and use this time to teach or stress the need for breast self-examination. The Tanner breast stage of development should be documented. Gynecomastia in the male should be noted.

Examination of the female external genitalia begins with identifying the structures through inspection and palpation, noting size and location. The infant is easily examined when lying supine and with good lighting directed toward the genitalia. The older child can be examined in a frog-leg position while seated in the mother's lap or while reclined on the examining table. The examiner, child, or parent can then spread the labia to allow inspection of the external genitalia. The vaginal orifice is exposed by gentle upward traction on the labia majora. An otoscope provides a good light source and uses an instrument with which the child is already familiar. The nurse should reassure the child that the otoscope will not touch or enter her body. If symptoms suggest the need for further visualization of the vagina, the knee-chest position is usually employed.

The labia majora should be smooth, symmetrical, and without fusion or masses. A mass might suggest gonads. The inguinal regions should also be inspected for masses, the presence of which might suggest gonads, lymph nodes, or hernia. The labia minora can be completely separated. The vaginal orifice is easily inspected and normally appears reddened. The nurse should observe for any bruising of the genitalia, which may be due to accidental trauma or may be associated with sexual abuse. The newborn may have a mucoid, bloody vaginal discharge, resulting from withdrawal from maternal estrogen stimulation. This normal finding is present during the first week of life and requires no treatment. The prepubertal child should have no vaginal discharge or odor. The adolescent may normally have a clear mucoid discharge, known as *physiological leukorrhea.*

A pelvic examination is indicated in any female child with vaginal bleeding or signs of a serious condition. Pelvic examination in the adolescent is indicated by irregular menstruation, severe dysmenorrhea, vaginal discharge, unexplained abdominal pain, or a history of sexual activity. Routine pelvic examination should be initiated at age 17 to 18, regardless of sexual activity (Braverman, 1989). The initial pelvic examination is a source of much apprehension and distress for the adolescent girl. Nurses should be sensitive to these feelings and anxieties, since this first pelvic examination can significantly affect how the female views her own health care. Time must be allowed for a complete explanation of what will be done and why it is necessary. It is helpful to show the adolescent the equipment beforehand and to use pictures or a model of female anatomy to describe the procedure. Often, allowing the adolescent to hold a hand mirror during the examination assists in explaining anatomy and providing reassurance.

Assessment of the male external reproductive system includes inspection and palpation of the penis, scrotal sac, and the testes. Penis size is noted, remembering that individual size and circumference have wide variations. A very short penis (less than 2 cm length in the newborn) should alert the nurse to the possibility of intersex anomalies, and further assessment is needed.

The foreskin of the uncircumcised penis should be retracted and reduced. The foreskin in infants is usually not retractable, except to allow for urination. The foreskin should never be forced back; it slowly retracts with time, and by 2 years of age it is usually fully retractable. Any penile masses or lesions should be noted. The opening of the urethra should be midline at the end of the penis. In the adolescent, pubic hair is described, and the genitalia are rated according to the appropriate Tanner stage.

The scrotum should be inspected and palpated for edema or masses. The scrotum normally appears relatively large in infants. It may also be enlarged due to delivery trauma or hormones transferred from the placenta, or enlargement may indicate a hydrocele, hernia, or hematocele. In the older child, scrotal enlargement may indicate *orchitis,* an inflammation of the testicle, which is usually accompanied by the scrotal skin appearing red and shiny. The testes are palpated for size and consistency. The spermatic cords should be traced from the testes upward and examined for any swelling or masses. Nurses should remember that the right spermatic cord is shorter than the left, and thus the right testicle is higher in the scrotal sac than the left. Evaluation for undescended testes is an important component of the examination. If the testes are not palpable in the newborn scrotum, they may descend when the infant is placed sitting in a basin of warm water. The older boy can be asked to sit on a chair with his knees against his chest, which may force the testes into the scrotum. The testes may also be "milked" down by palpating downward along the inguinal canal into the scrotum. If the testes cannot be located in the inguinal canal or scrotum by 2 years of age, the boy should be referred for consultation.

Nurses should access for scrotal enlargement or discoloration caused by trauma or testicular torsion. Nurses must be alert to signs of sexual abuse, such as bruises or lesions of the penis, scrotum, or perineal area. Suspicious findings also include any tear or swelling near or on the vaginal opening or anus; recurrent urinary tract infections; and pain on urination or penile discharge in young boys. Any venereal disease in a younger child or chronic vaginitis should also alert the nurse to the possibility of sexual abuse.

## Nursing Diagnosis

The diagnoses approved by the North American Nursing Diagnosis Association are used when reproductive system disorders are discussed. The most common diagnoses used for reproductive disorders include:

*Pattern 1: Exchanging*
- Altered nutrition: less than body requirements
- Altered patterns of urinary elimination
- High risk for infection
- High risk for impaired skin integrity
- Impaired skin integrity
- Impaired tissue integrity

*Pattern 3: Relating*
- Altered family processes
- Altered parenting
- Altered sexuality patterns
- High risk for altered parenting
- Impaired social interaction
- Sexual dysfunction
- Social isolation

*Pattern 5: Choosing*
- Ineffective family coping
- Ineffective individual coping
- Noncompliance (specify)

*Pattern 6: Moving*
- Activity intolerance
- Altered growth and development
- Fatigue

*Pattern 7: Perceiving*
- Body image disturbance
- Self-esteem disturbance
- Situational low self-esteem

*Pattern 9: Feeling*
- Anxiety
- Fear
- Pain
- Rape-trauma syndrome

## Planning and Implementing Nursing Care

Planning and implementing nursing care is discussed in relation to each problem presented in this chapter. Education of parents and children is an important nursing function, beginning with teaching parents proper hygiene of the newborn genital area. The area should be carefully washed after urination or defecation, including separation of the labia in girls and retraction of the foreskin in boys for cleansing. The child and parents should be taught hygienic measures involving toilet training.

Adolescent girls and boys should be instructed about the physiology of menstruation. Girls should receive information about sanitary napkins, tampons, hygiene, activity, and relief of menstrual cramps. Adolescent boys should understand about nocturnal emissions and be assured that they are normal occurrences.

Careful and thoughtful explanation of conditions related to the reproductive system and the treatment is essential for parents and the child. If the child is hospitalized, the nurse must remember that responses are related to the child's age and developmental stage. If a surgical procedure is required, nurses should be mindful of the preschool child's fears of castration or mutilation. Anxiety and fear may be alleviated by a thorough explanation of planned events. The child should be reassured that the procedure is not a punishment. The school-aged child may exhibit fears concerning genital inadequacy and loss of body control or mastery. Planning for appropriate play in this age group is important; this is facilitated by placing the child in a room with children of the same age and sex. Adolescents are particularly aware of their developing sexuality, and they typically express great anxiety about any illness or surgery involving the reproductive system. Nurses must be aware of these feelings and explain each procedure in detail. Adolescents have a strong need for privacy, and careful draping during examinations is important. Examination findings should be reviewed with the adolescent to alleviate anxieties and fears.

Most parents find it almost impossible to view their child as a sexual being, with sexual desires and needs. Nurses may be involved in helping parents understand their adolescents. To assist parents in understanding these sexual concerns and in exploring their own feelings about sex, nurses must first examine their own attitudes and values.

## Evaluation of Nursing Care

Evaluation of patient compliance with prescribed treatments and of effectiveness of nursing interventions may include determining whether the child's and parents' knowledge of the condition is sufficient. The child should have decreased instances of infection, the disease should be contained, and the patient should comply with medication schedules. If the nurse becomes involved in community and school prevention programs, evaluation should also include assessing the results of education about the disease and the success in reaching and treating contacts.

## Reproductive Problems of Neonates and Infants

### Ambiguous Genitalia

The birth of a baby with ambiguous genitalia is a psychosocial and diagnostic emergency, and evaluation needs to be rapidly accomplished so that the parents can decide whether to raise the child as a male or a female. The external genitalia may be described as ambiguous if there is (1) a phallic structure (clitoris or penis), with the urogenital opening at the base; (2) partial fusion of the labia; and (3) absence of gonads or a single gonad in an incompletely formed scrotum (Mazur, 1984).

## Hydrocele

### Pathophysiology

A *hydrocele* is a collection of fluid in the scrotum (Fig. 31-4). This condition may be associated with inguinal hernia and can be classified as communicating or noncommunicating. *Noncommunicating* hydroceles are usually noted at birth and present as mild scrotal swelling caused by fluid trapped in the portion (tunica vaginalis) within the scrotum. The fluid is usually absorbed, and no treatment is necessary. This type of hydrocele is not reducible and is easily transilluminated.

In a *communicating* hydrocele, the processus vaginalis remains open from the scrotum to the abdominal cavity. This hydrocele varies in size during the day, dependent on position and activity. A communicating hydrocele may be present at birth or appear later in life. An underlying hernia is often associated with this type of hydrocele, and surgery is usually required.

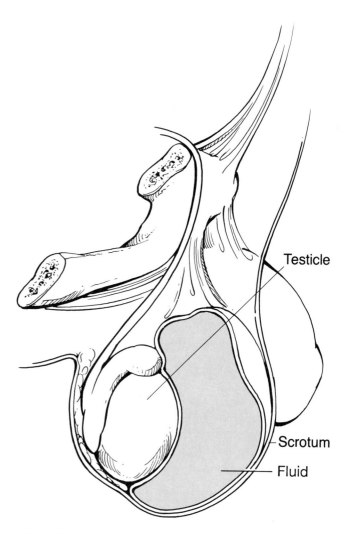

*Figure 31–4.   Hydrocele.*

## Medical Diagnosis and Management

The defect is diagnosed by observation and palpation. Most hydroceles resolve spontaneously. Surgery is usually done if the defect is large or does not resolve after the first year. Surgery is performed to close the processus vaginalis. Most hydrocele repairs are done on an outpatient basis.

## Nursing Assessment and Diagnosis

Nursing assessment includes inspecting the neonate's scrotum for signs of swelling. Assessment for possibility of inguinal hernia is also important. Parents can be asked about varying size of the scrotum. In a communicating hydrocele, the scrotal sac increases with crying or straining and is larger in the evening and smaller in the morning. This change in size is due to varying intraabdominal pressure and position. Unlike a hernia, a hydrocele cannot be reduced. If a light is held to the scrotum (*transillumination*), a hydrocele is translucent compared with a hernia, which usually appears opaque with this procedure.

Nursing diagnoses for a hydrocele might include the following:

- Pain related to strangulation of the intestines
- High risk for altered parenting related to stress of having an ill child

## Planning and Implementing Nursing Care

Parents should be reassured that the child's scrotum will return to normal size as the fluid is absorbed. There is no danger to the child's future reproductive capacity. Nursing care for the child undergoing surgical repair for a hydrocele is similar to that for inguinal hernia (see Chap. 29).

## Evaluating Nursing Care

Evaluation includes observing normal resolution of the hydrocele and assessing parental understanding of the condition.

## Phimosis

### Pathophysiology

*Phimosis* is a tightening or narrowing of the preputial opening of the foreskin that prevents retraction over the glans penis. It is a normal condition in infants and usually disappears by the age of 2 years. Treatment is not required unless the urinary meatus is occluded.

## Medical Diagnosis and Management

The initial clinical sign is a decreased urinary stream. Mild cases are treated by manual retraction of the foreskin and proper cleansing of the area. Severe phimosis is treated by circumcision, an excision of the foreskin to release the glans.

## Nursing Assessment and Diagnosis

Nurses should observe the neonate's urinary stream for quantity and force. The meatal opening should be examined for size and position. A small, pinpoint meatal opening may cause urinary obstruction. In the uncircumcised child, the foreskin should not forcibly be retracted for inspection of the glans since this may cause inflammation leading to phimosis.

Nursing diagnoses for phimosis might include the following:

- Altered patterns of urinary elimination related to occlusion of the meatus
- Body image disturbance related to abnormal appearance of penis

## Planning and Implementing Nursing Care

The parents should be taught the proper method for cleaning an uncircumcised penis. The foreskin does not need to be forcibly retracted for effective cleaning. For the child undergoing circumcision, routine preoperative and postoperative care is planned. The older child should receive careful explanation of the procedure, including thoughtful reassurance that penis function will not be altered. Care of the circumcision depends on the procedure, which involves using a scalpel, Hollister Plastibell, or Gomco clamp (see Chap. 11 for circumcision procedures). Parents should be instructed regarding signs of infection, unusual swelling, or excessive bleeding.

## Evaluating Nursing Care

Evaluation is based on determining that uneventful healing of the circumcision has occurred or that the condition resolves itself as the child grows older.

## Testicular Torsion

### Pathophysiology

Torsion of the testicle is a condition in which the testicle hangs free from its vascular structures. The testis can twist around the structures and occlude the blood supply.

### Medical Diagnosis and Management

Torsion in neonates is usually asymptomatic except for a scrotal mass. In the older child, the onset of torsion is usually acute and follows trauma or strenuous activity. There is intense pain and tenderness, with lower abdominal pain and a red, swollen scrotum. Treatment is surgical correction in which the testicle is attached to the scrotal tissue.

### Nursing Assessment and Diagnosis

Assessment includes observation of the child's scrotum and obtaining a history concerning recent trauma or intense activity. Nurses need to be alert to the possibility of testicular torsion in children who present with scrotal pain.

Nursing diagnoses for torsion of the testes might include the following:

- Pain related to occluded blood supply to the testes
- Body image disturbance related to abnormal appearance of swollen scrotum

### Planning and Implementing Nursing Care

The focus of nursing care is on relief of pain and distracting the child from his pain. To provide effective care, the nurse should learn the child's terminology for his scrotum and penis. Teaching should be geared to the child's level of understanding.

Scrotal support may be helpful preoperatively, and postoperatively, ice bags may be used to reduce the swelling. The child may ambulate and be as active as desired after surgery. Nursing care also involves care of the surgical incision and surrounding area to prevent infection.

### Evaluating Nursing Care

Evaluation is based on determining that the child resumed normal activity as soon as possible. The child's discomfort should be reduced, and any body image disturbance should be resolved.

## Reproductive Problems of Toddlers and Preschoolers

### Cryptorchism

#### Pathophysiology

Failure of one or both testes to descend into the scrotum is *cryptorchidism*. The testes normally descend into the scrotum during the 7th to 9th month of fetal life. The descent of the testes can be interrupted at any point. Failure to descend may result from hormonal deficiency, mechanical obstruction, or testicular failure. Failure of the right testicle to descend is the most common presentation of this defect. This condition is seen in 3% of full-term males and in 20% of preterm males.

#### Medical Diagnosis and Management

Diagnosis is not made on the findings of one examination because the cremasteric reflex may cause retractile testes.

A pediatric urologist is usually consulted to affirm the diagnosis. There is a wide spectrum of treatment options, from no treatment to a trial of human chorionic gonadotropin. Generally, no therapeutic intervention is considered before the first birthday, since many cryptorchid testes descend in the first year of life. Hormonal therapy may be started at any time after the first year and is usually not delayed past age 5. If therapy with human chorionic gonadotropin fails, surgical placement of the testes in the scrotum (orchiopexy) is the treatment of choice. The surgery is usually performed by the time the child is 2 to 3 years old to avoid degenerative changes in the testicular germinal epithelium.

Various tension devices may be employed to keep the testicle in the scrotal sac, or it may be attached to the inner wall of the scrotum. The surgery is usually a same-day procedure. If the testicle is absent, a prosthetic implant is used for cosmetic and psychological reasons. The testes' remaining in the abdomen after puberty results in sterility because of expended exposure to normal body temperature. There is also an increased risk of malignancy when the testes remain in the abdomen.

### Nursing Assessment and Diagnosis

Careful assessment is important in differentiating cryptorchidism from normal retracted testes due to the cremasteric reflex, which involves temporary retraction of the testes by the cremasteric muscles. Nurses should remember that the cremasteric reflex is stimulated by cold or touch. This reflex is particularly active after 6 months of age. The method for "milking" a retracted testicle down into the scrotum was reviewed previously. The child may also be asked to assume a squatting position to force the retracted testicle down into the scrotal sac. This position also acts to diminish the cremasteric reflex. An undescended testicle cannot be pushed into the scrotum.

Nursing diagnoses for cryptorchidism might include the following:

- High risk for injury related to decreased function and atrophy
- Anxiety related to surgical procedure involving genitals
- Body image disturbance related to abnormal size and shape shape of scrotum

### Planning and Implementing Nursing Care

This condition creates a great deal of anxiety for both the child and parents. Nurses need to provide support and detailed explanations regarding the surgical procedure. Preoperative teaching includes a description of the surgical traction devices that may be used. The child may be aware of the empty scrotum and express anxiety regarding its smaller shape and size. Parents may be concerned about the future fertility of their child, and nurses should intervene by educating the parents about reduced fertility rates and the long-term risk of malignant testicular tumor associated with the condition if it is left untreated. Nurses can play an important role in teaching parents and older boys the procedure for testicular self-examination. Testicular self-examination is stressed since the risk of testicular tumor development is not significant until 30 to 40 years of age.

Postoperative nursing care includes prevention of infection by careful cleaning of the operative site. If a traction device is used, it should be checked for proper tautness. Use of traction devices require the child to be on bed rest until the tension suture is removed, which is usually in 5 to 7 days. Ice packs to the scrotum and analgesics may be used to relieve pain.

### Evaluating Nursing Care

Evaluation is centered assessing whether the anxieties and fears of the child and his parents are relieved. Appropriate teaching should prepare the child and parents for the surgical procedure and postoperative care at home. Long-term evaluation is based on the child maintaining periodic follow-up care.

## Reproductive Problems of School-Aged Children

### Precocious Puberty

The syndrome of precocious puberty involves development of secondary sexual characteristics before normal onset. Breast development before age 7.25 years or initiation of menses before 9.25 years is considered precocious in girls. In boys, pubic hair growth before age 9.5 years is considered precocious. It is important to distinguish between true or idiopathic precocious puberty and pseudoprecocious puberty.

### Pathophysiology

In true precocious puberty, normal hypothalamic-pituitary-gonadal function is activated at an abnormally early age, producing maturation and development of the gonads. In most cases, no cause is found for premature activation. A dysfunction of the central nervous system results in menstruation in girls and testicular maturation and spermatogenesis in boys. True precocious puberty is more commonly classified as *idiopathic* or *constitutional precocity,* in that no cause can be found. It is nine times more common in girls than in boys.

In *pseudoprecocious puberty,* secondary sexual characteristics occur due to abnormal production of estrogens or androgens without maturation of the gonads. No ova or sperm are formed because the disorder occurs without pituitary gonadotropic stimulation. Most cases are caused by early overproduction of sex hormone. This is usually due to a tumor of the ovary or testes, or it may result from exogenous sources of androgens or estrogens.

### Medical Diagnosis and Management

Laboratory findings in true precocious puberty show increased levels of FSH, LH, and estrogen or testosterone. A bone-age film is done to evaluate bone maturation. These children have accelerated growth during childhood but are often below average as adults because of early epiphyseal closure of the long bones caused by the growth spurt. They frequently have histories of excessive mood changes and emotional lability.

Treatment for idiopathic true precocious puberty is seldom helpful. Medroxyprogesterone acetate (Depo-Provera) has been used with limited success. This drug has no effect on growth or skeletal maturation; side effects include hypertension and glucose intolerance. Treatment of precocious pseudopuberty focuses on the specific cause, if it is known.

### Nursing Assessment and Diagnosis

Nurses should obtain a detailed history from parents to determine how long signs of early puberty have been present. Obtaining information about sudden linear growth is important. Parents should also be asked about the child's access to hormones (oral contraceptives, hand creams with estrogen) because these may be factors in the disorder. The nurse should observe for signs of pubertal development during physical examination and compare these with age norms.

Nurses should also be aware of two similar deviations that may occur in the school-aged child: premature thelarche and premature adrenarche (pubarche). *Premature thelarche* is breast tissue development before puberty without any other signs of precocious puberty. The breast tissue around the nipple area increases, but the nipple and areola pigmentation do not change. The development of pubic hair before puberty, without any signs of precocious puberty, is termed *premature adrenarche.* Neither of these conditions require any treatment, and nurses should reassure parents and the child.

Nursing diagnoses for precocious puberty might include the following:

- Altered growth and development related to early development of secondary sexual characteristics
- Body image or self-esteem disturbance related to premature sexual development and short stature due to early epiphyseal closure
- Ineffective family coping related to parents' concerns regarding sexuality

## *Planning and Implementing Nursing Care*

Nursing interventions center on psychological support and education of the child and family. Nurses need to help the child and parents understand and deal with the changes in physical appearance. These children often withdraw because they feel different from their peers. Peers should be told about the reasons for the physical changes and instructed that everyone experiences these changes, just at an older age.

Nurses need to be acutely aware that there may be many fears or concerns that the family is unable to express. Parents may be uncomfortable discussing the process of puberty due to feelings about their own sexuality. Parents should understand that this disorder does not accelerate the child's sexual interests. The child's dress and social activities should be age-appropriate. Parents may also need guidance in dealing with the child regarding unrealistic expectations. Nurses should reassure the child with idiopathic sexual precocity and the parents that this is a normal process occurring at an early age.

### *Evaluating Nursing Care*

Evaluation includes determining the child's and family's level of understanding of the physical changes taking place and their ability to openly verbalize their feelings. The child should be able to deal with peer reactions and should achieve age-appropriate developmental tasks at a normal rate. Family communication patterns, as well as those in the school setting, should also be evaluated.

## *Reproductive Problems of Adolescents*

### *Delayed Maturation*

If no signs of puberty are evident in a girl by age 13 years or in a boy by age 14 years, evaluation for pubertal delay is necessary.

### *Pathophysiology*

One of the more common causes is *constitutional delay of puberty*. This is a variant of normal growth, seen more frequently in boys than in girls. These children appear physically younger than their age and typically lag 2 to 4 years behind average in height, bone age, and pubertal development. Similar delays in pubertal maturation can also result from low weight, prolonged but temporary malnutrition, intensive athletic training, chronic system disease, or hormonal deficiencies. Delayed puberty may be caused by primary or secondary hypogonadism. Primary hypogonadism is a dysfunction of the gonads.

## *Medical Diagnosis and Management*

In constitutional delay of puberty, there is often a family history of delayed puberty. No additional evaluation of these children is needed if the growth rate is normal, height is at or slightly below the third percentile, and bone age is delayed by 2 to 4 years (Plotnick, 1990). No treatment is necessary for mild to moderate constitutional delay.

Diagnostic studies for delayed puberty include bone age, buccal smear for sex chromatin pattern and a chromosomal analysis, and measurement of gonadotropins.

Ovarian dysfunction, or primary hypogonadism, is most commonly caused by *Turner syndrome*, a disorder of the sex chromosomes. Females with this disorder have 45 X chromosomes and no Y chromosome, and they fail to develop sexually at puberty. Turner syndrome may be present in as many as 4% of all human conceptions (Shapiro, 1990). This syndrome can be diagnosed at birth and is characterized by a webbed neck, a low hair line, a high, arched palate, and edema of the hands and feet. Coarctation of the aorta and pulmonary stenosis are associated with this disorder. Turner syndrome is more frequently diagnosed in early adolescence when the girl fails to increase in height or secondary sexual characteristics do not appear. No specific treatment is recommended until the growth rate slows, and then growth hormone is used to promote linear growth. Estrogen therapy may be used to develop secondary sex characteristics, but this therapy must be short-term because of the associated risks and possible early closure of the epiphyses. Females with Turner syndrome are sterile. Secondary hypogonadism in females is a failure to secrete normal levels of gonadotropin and is treated with estrogens.

Primary hypogonadism in males results in decreased androgen production. *Klinefelter syndrome* is the most common type of primary hypogonadism, indicated by one or more additional X chromosomes, most commonly genotype 47,XXY. Occasionally mental retardation is present, but affected boys are usually normal at birth. They are marked in childhood by tall stature with slim builds and long limbs. The condition is typically discovered in adolescence due to concerns about gynecomastia and small testes. It is often not diagnosed in adult men until they seek treatment for infertility. Diagnosis is confirmed by chromosomal analysis. Treatment is administration of testosterone. Secondary hypogonadism in males is a failure of the testes to develop due to nonstimulation by gonadotropic hormones. Treatment is administration of androgen.

## *Nursing Assessment and Diagnosis*

Physical examination is the major assessment tool for delayed puberty. Special attention to body proportions and use of the Tanner scales should be included. A careful family history is important in evaluating constitutional delay. Close observation for early signs of sexual maturation is critical.

Nursing diagnoses for delayed maturation might include the following:

- Altered growth and development related to the disease process
- Body image disturbance related to nonappearance of secondary sexual characteristics
- Impaired social interaction related to embarrassment
- Self-esteem disturbance related to not appearing like peers

## Planning and Implementing Nursing Care

Nurses need to offer support to adolescents with delayed maturation. These young people need to be educated about various diagnostic studies to determine the cause of delay. Adolescents have concerns about body image since they look different than their peers. Nurses should also be aware of self-esteem problems. If the diagnosis includes sex chromosome disorders, a careful explanation should be provided as well as descriptions of the treatment and its affects on physical appearance. Affected adolescents and their families need counseling about sterility and possible alternative methods for parenthood. Nurses should assure these adolescents that sexual function is not diminished. Some may need referral for counseling to help them deal with peer relationships and self-esteem.

## Evaluating Nursing Care

Evaluation includes determining the client's understanding of the diagnosis. If sex steroid therapy is indicated, the purpose and results should be clearly understood. Attainment of normal peer relationships is an important evaluation goal.

# Menstrual Problems of Adolescents

## Amenorrhea

### Pathophysiology

The absence of menses, or amenorrhea, may be either primary or secondary. There are a wide variety of causes for both primary and secondary amenorrhea. Any disorder that affects function of the hypothalamus, pituitary, ovaries, or the uterus and vagina may result in amenorrhea. When menarche is delayed past 17 years of age, it is considered *primary amenorrhea*. This condition has also been termed *delayed menarche*. Constitutional delay in

puberty is a common reason for primary amenorrhea. *Secondary amenorrhea* is a cessation of more than six menstrual cycles after menstruation has become established. Amenorrhea can occur in females who engage in strenuous physical activity and is believed to be related to a low body-fat ratio. Amenorrhea may also be seen in chronic illness, psychological disturbances, and nutritional deficiencies, and its presence should be considered in the diagnosis of anorexia nervosa.

## Medical Diagnosis and Management

Medical management focuses on discovery of the cause and appropriate treatment. A careful history and physical examination may prevent unnecessary diagnostic tests. Many females with amenorrhea spontaneously begin menses. The initial work-up for primary amenorrhea focuses on attention to growth parameters to evaluate differential diagnoses. In the female whose uterus and vaginal canal are normal but who has experienced no pubertal development, blood levels of FSH are measured. Normal or low levels indicate hypothalamic or pituitary disorders, and high levels indicate problems with the ovary. In the female for whom puberty has initiated but menses has not appeared because of anatomical factors of the uterus or vagina, a karyotype is indicated. A progesterone challenge test is indicated in the female with normal development and normal anatomy. The first step in evaluating secondary amenorrhea is a pregnancy test. If this is negative, diagnostic options are similar to those for primary amenorrhea.

## Nursing Assessment and Diagnosis

Nursing assessment includes a detailed history and physical examination. Family history involving onset or delayed menstruation in mother or sisters is a critical component, since genetic factors influence menses.

Nursing diagnoses for amenorrhea might include the following:

- Anxiety related to the absence of menses
- Body image disturbance related to feelings of being different from peers

## Planning and Implementing Nursing Care

Nurses should provide sensitive reassurance to adolescents experiencing delayed menarche due to a delay in normal maturation. Nurses can offer psychological support to the anxious adolescent and help in explaining various diagnostic tests or procedures.

## Evaluating Nursing Care

The adolescent should understand the reason for the delay of menstruation and display decreased anxiety. Evaluation procedures for females with organic causes vary.

# Dysmenorrhea

## Pathophysiology

*Dysmenorrhea* refers to a symptom complex that results in painful menstruation. The causes for dysmenorrhea are divided into two types: primary or functional dysmenorrhea and secondary or organic dysmenorrhea. Most cases of dysmenorrhea in adolescents are of the primary type, which is associated with ovulatory menstrual cycles.

*Primary dysmenorrhea* is caused by the increased production of prostaglandins, which act on the myometrium to produce increased resting muscle tone, excessive uterine contractions, and ischemia resulting in pain. There is a strong hereditary pattern in primary dysmenorrhea. Organic causes of *secondary dysmenorrhea* include anomalies such as genital atresia, imperforate hymen, and cervical canal stenosis. Endometriosis is often a cause in the older adolescent with a chronic history of increasingly painful menstruation. Pelvic inflammatory disease is also frequently associated with dysmenorrhea in adolescents.

## Medical Diagnosis and Management

Dysmenorrhea is marked by lower abdominal or back pain, and it may or may not include nausea, diarrhea, or headache. There is a high incidence of dysmenorrhea in adolescent females. The condition is usually characterized as mild, moderate, or severe, based on the severity of the symptoms. Most adolescents have mild dysmenorrhea, in which discomfort is not severe and does not interfere with their daily routines. Moderate dysmenorrhea involves 2 to 3 days of pain and is often accompanied by other symptoms. This discomfort is mildly incapacitating. Severe dysmenorrhea is uncommon but is often the primary complaint in the ambulatory setting. This type of dysmenorrhea is manifested by intense, incapacitating cramps, with pain that lasts more than 2 days. Gastrointestinal symptoms, such as nausea, vomiting, and diarrhea, frequently accompany severe dysmenorrhea.

Nonsteroidal antiinflammatory drugs are the treatment of choice. These drugs decrease the production of prostaglandins. Acetylsalicylic acid is a relatively weak drug in this class and has generally been replaced by ibuprofen (Motrin, Advil), naproxen sodium (Anaprox), and mefenamic acid (Ponstel). Low-dose combination oral contraceptives are also effective but usually are used only in sexually active females desiring contraception.

## Nursing Assessment and Diagnosis

A complete menstrual history is taken, including questions about pain with menses. It is important to obtain information about when the painful periods began (at menarche or later), where in the menstrual cycle the pain begins, the duration and location of the pain, and any associated symptoms. A complete pelvic examination is not required for every female with dysmenorrhea. Questions regarding sexual activity are also necessary to differentiate virginal and nonvirginal girls. If the girl is virginal and symptoms of primary dysmenorrhea are mild, treatment can be initiated on a trial basis without a pelvic examination. Virginal adolescents experiencing moderate or severe types of primary dysmenorrhea need an assessment of internal pelvic structures before treatment. This can be accomplished by means of inspection of the vulva and vaginal introitus and bimanual rectoabdominal examination. Dysmenorrhea in nonvirginal females requires a complete pelvic examination, including cultures for sexually transmitted organisms. Symptoms indicative of secondary dysmenorrhea also necessitate a complete pelvic examination.

Nursing diagnoses for dysmenorrhea might include the following:

- Activity intolerance related to menstrual discomfort
- Pain related to uterine contractions

## Planning and Implementing Nursing Care

Nurses are often the first people approached by young adolescents with questions regarding menstrual disorders. It is important for nurses to listen carefully to their concerns since these exchanges provide an excellent opportunity for health teaching regarding menstruation. Nurses can also be instrumental in dispelling myths about menstruation and act to promote healthy sexuality.

Nurses can provide adolescents with a variety of measures to decrease the discomfort. Sometimes simple exercise, such as pelvic rocking, or a heating pad placed on the abdomen or lower back brings relief. If nonsteroidal antiinflammatory drugs are used, nurses should educate adolescents about possible side effects, such as gastrointestinal symptoms or central nervous system complaints. Nurses should inform adolescents who are beginning to take oral contraceptives to relieve the pain of primary dysmenorrhea that it often takes 2 or 3 months for the effect to be realized.

## Evaluating Nursing Care

Evaluation is based on determining the successful resolution of discomfort with medication and supportive measures. The adolescent should have a normal activity level throughout the menstrual cycle, with minimal discomfort.

# Premenstrual Syndrome

*Premenstrual syndrome* (PMS) is a condition involving congestive dysmenorrhea that appears 7 to 10 days before the onset of menses. It disappears with the onset of menses. The etiology of PMS is unknown, and investigation as to its cause is under way. The retention of water and sodium resulting from the production of progesterone after ovulation is thought to be a significant factor. There are numerous symptoms associated with PMS; the most common include irritability, headache, backache, bloating of the abdomen and breasts, and crying spells. These symptoms vary in individual patients and in individual menstrual cycles. PMS does not usually occur before late adolescence.

Treatment includes supportive measures and the administration of mild analgesics. Diuretics and tranquilizers are sometimes used for fluid retention and irritability. Dietary salt restriction has proved helpful to some patients. Nursing management includes education regarding the menstrual cycle, counseling, and referral as needed.

## Dysfunctional Uterine Bleeding

### Pathophysiology

*Dysfunctional uterine bleeding* (DUB) describes a clinical syndrome of irregular, sometimes excessive bleeding that lacks a specific etiology. Adolescents often experience irregular menstrual bleeding during the first few years after menarche. This is usually the result of anovulatory cycles, which are considered normal.

Bleeding occurs because of hormonal imbalances in the menstrual cycle. In the anovulatory cycle, there is no ovulation or production of progesterone. The endometrium is stimulated only by estrogen, which eventually leads to continuing endometrial shedding and breakthrough bleeding.

### Medical Diagnosis and Management

Abnormal menstrual bleeding is defined as bleeding that lasts beyond 8 days, begins more frequently than every 21 days, and requires more than ten tampons or eight sanitary pads daily (Wilson, 1990). Dysfunctional uterine bleeding can be a gynecological emergency, and timely medical evaluation is important. In the adolescent, DUB may result from immaturity, variation of normal function, or abnormality of hypothalamic, pituitary, or ovarian hormones. The most common cause is chronic anovulation. A wide scope of causes must be considered, including hypothyroidism, polycystic ovary syndrome, adrenal insufficiency, bleeding disorders, diabetes mellitus, and tumors of the reproductive tract. Other more obvious causes of abnormal menses include complications of pregnancy, trauma, and infectious processes.

Medical management is determined by the cause and severity of the bleeding. Dilatation and curettage are seldom required. Iron supplementation is usually indicated for all patients. Reassurance and follow-up is indicated for heavy or irregular periods without anemia or other abnormal features. Laboratory tests may be done to measure LH, FSH, estradiol, progesterone, or androgen levels. Both moderate and severe cases are treated with hormonal therapy. Oral contraceptives containing estrogen and synthetic progesterone are frequently used. This hormonal therapy continues for a minimum of 3 months to build up the endometrial lining.

### Nursing Assessment and Diagnosis

A history of the menstrual cycle to determine the severity of blood loss is the first step. Age of menarche and usual pattern of menses should be noted. Blood loss should be quantified in terms of length, frequency, and number of tampons or sanitary pads used each day. The adolescent should be questioned about sexual activity, trauma, and use of oral contraceptives. Physical examination should include a pelvic examination. Cultures for gonorrhea and chlamydia should be obtained, and a spun hematocrit helps to diagnose anemia.

Nursing diagnoses for dysfunctional uterine bleeding might include the following:

- Altered sexuality patterns related to excessive bleeding
- Fatigue related to anemia
- Body image disturbance related to feeling different from peers
- Altered nutrition: Less than body requirements, related to nausea from oral progestins

### Planning and Implementing Nursing Care

Nursing care for adolescents with DUB should focus on health teaching. Nurses should educate adolescents about the normal menstrual cycle, the factors affecting this cycle, and the importance of keeping an accurate record of the menstrual cycle. Adolescents should be instructed concerning common side effects of hormone use, such as nausea and breast tenderness, breakthrough bleeding, or spotting. Nurses can assume an important role in explaining to parents and adolescents how oral contraceptives help alleviate abnormal bleeding. Parents with children in early stages of adolescence may have strong concerns and fears about oral contraceptives. Parents may also believe that contraceptive use will initiate sexual activity. Nurses should use the term "hormonal medication" in such instances and avoid mention of the contraceptive function.

### Evaluating Nursing Care

The adolescent should demonstrate appropriate knowledge regarding the menstrual cycle, including the recording of her menstrual cycles. The adolescent on hormone therapy should understand the purpose of the therapy and the importance of reporting side effects.

## Endometriosis

### Pathophysiology

*Endometriosis* is the growth of tissue resembling the endometrium outside the uterus in various sites throughout the pelvis. The etiology of endometriosis is not fully understood, but the most accepted theory proposes that it is caused by the backward flow of menstrual fluid and tissue through the fallopian tubes. The symptoms of endometriosis are variable, but it is generally characterized by pelvic pain or pressure and increasing dysmenorrhea. If the bowel or urinary tract are involved, there may be intestinal or urinary tract symptoms. Coitus can intensify the pain.

### Medical Diagnosis and Management

Diagnosis cannot be made without histological confirmation by means of laparoscopy. Treatment in the adolescent differs because at this age the disorder may be associated with a congenital anomaly. Any anatomical lesion responsible for reflux of menstrual fluid must be surgically corrected. In adolescents with minimal disease, treatment consists of observation, analgesics, nonsteroidal anti-inflammatory drugs, or hormonal therapy. Endometriosis often becomes chronic and requires management by a gynecologist.

### Nursing Assessment and Diagnosis

Nursing assessment and diagnosis guidelines are similar to those used for dysmenorrhea. Assessment is aimed at ruling out other possible causes of pelvic pain.

### Planning, Implementing, and Evaluating Nursing Care

Nursing interventions and evaluation measures are similar to those used in caring for primary dysmenorrhea.

## Vulvovaginitis

*Vulvovaginitis* refers to infection involving the vulva and vagina. This is one of the most common gynecological concerns of adolescence, but complaints related to the vulva and vagina are common through the entire female life cycle. *Leukorrhea* is a term implying a vaginal discharge containing mucous and cellular elements of the endometrium. The first step in diagnosis is to determine whether this condition is physiological or pathological.

Physiological leukorrhea is a normal vaginal discharge and is not indicative of vaginitis. This discharge increases in volume with estrogen stimulation and is seen in the newborn as well as during early adolescence. An increase in circulating gonadotropins in the female occurs at about 8 years of age. About 2 years thereafter, significant levels of circulating estrogens can be measured. The vagina undergoes significant changes as a result of these estrogens. The vaginal mucosa increases from a prepubertal thickness of 2 to 4 layers up to a thickness of some 30 to 40 cell layers, which causes an increased production and shedding of the vaginal epithelial cells. The pH of the vagina changes from neutral to slightly acidic, resulting in changes of the normal bacterial flora. Finally, the cervical mucous glands begin producing a thin, watery mucoid discharge in significant amounts.

The initial appearance of this discharge is particularly annoying to some young females, and it is frequently unduly alarming to their parents. In the ambulatory setting, premenarchal girls frequently report a vaginal discharge. Often, the complaint is initiated by the mother, who notices staining of her daughter's panties. This staining is due to the discharge consisting primarily of protein, which leaves a yellow stain when heated during washing. The nurse can play an important role in educating the adolescent about these normal physiological changes involving the reproductive system, as well as in instructing parents to avoid undue concern. The nurse should explain that this is a normal discharge resulting from chemical, bacterial, and mucosal changes that are a part of normal development. The nurse can reassure the adolescent that the quantity of the discharge will decrease as a more mature hormonal balance is reached.

If an adolescent girl of any age presents with vaginal discharge with accompanying signs and symptoms, an infectious process should be suspected, and appropriate diagnostic studies are needed. Symptoms may include dysuria, pruritus, and abnormal vaginal discharge. Evaluation should include questions about quantity, color, odor, and amount of discharge. The patient should also be questioned about associated pruritus and any related symptoms. If the patient is sexually active, a sexual history, including contraceptive use and information about the last menstrual period, is vital. A complete pelvic examination is usually necessary for an accurate assessment. Essentially, only four categories of infectious processes involve the vagina: candidiasis, trichomoniasis, bacterial vaginosis, and venereal diseases.

## Candidiasis

### Pathophysiology

*Candidiasis* is caused by the fungus *Candida albicans*. Other species of fungi exist in the vagina but seldom cause disease. The prevalence of vulvovaginal candidiasis in the United States is estimated at 30% to 40% of vulva infections (Connell & Tatum, 1985). The infection is often referred to as *moniliasis*, but this term is no longer correct; the term *Monilia* is now used only for certain classes of plant pathogens.

Genital yeast infections are generally not sexually acquired. Numerous environmental and biological factors are related to the epidemiology of candidiasis, but many of the mechanisms are unclear. Menstruation alters the vaginal pH and creates a favorable medium for yeast growth. Tight nylon panties increase heat and moisture, which can cause candidiasis, as can the use of broad-spectrum antibiotics. Other predisposing factors include oral contraceptives, diabetes, obesity, corticosteroids, and pregnancy.

### Medical Diagnosis and Management

Typically, the infection is manifested by pruritic vaginovulvar erythema and a whitish, cottage cheese–like discharge. Dysuria, frequency, and dyspareunia (painful intercourse) may also be present. Diagnosis is made by potassium hydroxide microscopic evaluation of the vaginal secretion. Current treatment of choice includes miconazole nitrate vaginal cream or suppository, clotrimazole cream or vaginal tablet, or butoconazole cream. Male sexual partners are not routinely treated. Treatment should also include sexual abstinence to allow healing of the vaginal epithelium and to avoid chronic recolonization of the male partner.

## Trichomoniasis

### Pathophysiology

*Trichomonas vaginalis* is a protozoa and is the only pathogenic species of trichomonads that commonly involves the urogenital area. *Trichomoniasis* is one of the most frequent sexually acquired conditions, with prevalence related to sexual activity and number of sex partners.

### Medical Diagnosis and Management

Vaginal discharge is present in 50% to 75% of females infected and tends to be foul-smelling, yellow-green, and frothy. Vaginal and vulvar itching is common and is often intense. Symptoms often initiate or worsen at the onset or termination of menses. Males usually remain asymptomatic, although urethral discharge, dysuria, and mild irritation may occur. Diagnosis is confirmed by microscopic evaluation with a saline-drop wet mount.

The treatment of choice is metronidazole for 10 days. It is not used during pregnancy owing to its teratogenic potential. Asymptomatic male partners must also be treated since they can continue to be a reservoir of the disease. Metronidazole has many side effects and, like disulfiram (Antabuse), blocks the metabolism of ethanol. Consequently, alcohol should not be consumed during treatment.

## Bacterial Vaginosis

### Pathophysiology

*Bacterial vaginosis* is the most common cause of abnormal vaginal discharge (Paavonen & Stamm, 1987). It is sexually transmitted, with the male often being the asymptomatic carrier. This condition was originally termed nonspecific vaginitis because a variety of organisms were believed responsible. Later it was called *Gardnerella* vaginitis, but it is now recognized to be caused by multiple organisms, including *Gardnerella vaginalis*. The term *bacterial vaginosis* is favored since vaginal inflammation is not a prominent feature.

### Medical Diagnosis and Management

Vaginal discharge in bacterial vaginosis is slightly increased, thin, grayish-white (flour paste–like), nonirritating, and has a "fishy" odor. This odor is often stronger during menstruation and after intercourse. It is usually the offensive odor that causes patients to seek care. It is rarely pruritic. A saline wet mount reveals "clue cells," epithelial cells covered with gram-negative bacilli.

The treatment of choice is metronidazole. Ampicillin is used in the pregnant patient. Male sex partners are not usually treated.

## Foreign Bodies

Abnormal vaginal discharge can also be caused by foreign bodies in the vagina. The most common causative object in adolescents is a forgotten tampon. A variety of other objects commonly found in the vagina include diaphragms, condoms, and various items used for masturbation. Various physical, chemical, and allergenic substances are responsible for contact vulvovaginitis.

Discharge caused by a foreign body is profuse and extremely malodorous, although vaginal inflammation is usually mild. Once the object is removed, the discharge usually resolves spontaneously. The longer the object is left in the vagina, the more other problems present. Vaginal irrigation with warm saline is helpful in removing soft objects such as paper or cloth. Antibiotic therapy is sometimes necessary if an object has been in the vagina a long time. Removal of the irritant is indicated in contact vulvovaginitis. Sitz baths and cold compresses are also helpful.

### Nursing Assessment and Diagnosis

Inspection and examination of the genitalia is an important nursing role. Signs of discharge, irritation, swelling, or itching are noted and reported to the physician. An accurate sexual history is vital. Nurses should assess for infections when younger children rub and scratch their genitals or cry while urinating. Children may need to be questioned about masturbation or the insertion of objects into the vagina. Nurses should not forget the possibility that sexual abuse can cause vulvovaginitis.

Nursing diagnoses for vulvovaginitis might include the following:

- Impaired skin integrity related to inflammation of the vaginal mucosa

- Situational low self-esteem related to having a sexually transmitted disease
- Pain related to urethral irritation

### Planning and Implementing Nursing Care

Health education is an important nursing intervention. Education about anatomy is often needed because the adolescent may not know the location of the vaginal opening or how to insert medication. A review of hygiene practices, such as wiping from front to back after toileting, is valuable. Adolescents should be educated about the cause and treatment of their condition. Nurses should stress the importance of following the treatment regimen. Compliance may need to be overly stressed in adolescents using vaginal medications because the process can be messy due to leakage and may cause an uncomfortable feeling. Sexually active adolescents need to understand the need for abstinence during treatment for some problems, as well as the possible need to identify, assess, and treat sex partners. Nurses should educate adolescents about safe-sex practices, including the use of condoms to prevent vulvovaginitis.

### Evaluating Nursing Care

Evaluation is based on determining the adolescent's understanding of the condition, its treatment, and prevention. Sex partners should be evaluated, if indicated, and appropriately treated. The correct use and removal of condoms should be explained.

## Breast Problems

### Polythelia

*Polythelia,* or extra nipples, is found in 2% of the general population. These nipples can develop anywhere along the embryonic "milk line." A rarely seen anomaly is *polymastia,* or supernumerary breasts, which also occur along the milk line. Usual locations are below the breast on the chest or upper abdomen. Problems with these two conditions are rare. Two similarly rare conditions are *amastia* (absence of a breast) and *athelia* (absence of a nipple).

A nipple that fails to extend beyond the breast surface is termed an *inverted nipple.* This condition can be noted from birth, and careful hygiene is necessary to prevent infection. Adolescents may express concern about the cosmetic appearance. Surgical correction is possible but prevents any future breast-feeding.

### Idiopathic Breast Hypertrophy

This condition is termed *juvenile hypertrophy* when it occurs in adolescents. It can involve one or both breasts and may be familial. The usual history relates a rapid growth of the breasts, shortly after thelarche. The cause of juvenile hypertrophy is unknown, although theories include pubertal hormones and increased tissue sensitivity.

The condition can cause extreme embarrassment and psychological and physical problems. Problems may include poor posture, headaches (caused by neck strain), neck or back pain, and dermatitis. Hypertrophy of one breast can be confused with a breast tumor, usually a giant fibroadenoma. Reduction mammoplasty is usually delayed until late adolescence.

### Nursing Management

Nurses can help the adolescent consider and understand the choice of surgical intervention. Potential outcomes and complications need to be clearly explained. Nurses should explain that scarring can occur but is usually confined to the underside of the breasts. Nurses should also explain that a mammogram is needed 1 year after surgery to establish a baseline and to avoid future confusion caused by scarring.

## Benign Breast Disease

The term *benign breast disease* can create confusion that is often intensified by care providers who use various terms for normal breast changes and disease. Fibrocystic change is the most common cause of breast masses in adolescents. The term *fibrocystic breast disease* is losing favor but remains prevalent in literature. These masses are generally diffuse, cordlike nodules in both breasts that often enlarge and become tender before and during menses. The incidence in adolescence is unclear.

### Nursing Management

Nurses should explain normal physiological breast changes to adolescents and emphasize the importance of breast self-examinations. Any changes in masses should be noted and reported. Treatment includes firm brassiere support, reassurance that the masses are not cancer, and use of mild analgesics. The use of oral contraceptives in improving benign breast disease is controversial.

## Traumatic Breast Lesions

Increased adolescent female participation in contact sports has resulted in a higher incidence of chest and breast trauma. Breast abnormalities may occur as a result of trauma. Contusions, hematomas, and small lacerations resulting from trauma seldom require special care. Contusions are generally poorly defined, tender masses that resolve in about 2 weeks. Breast infections in nonlactating adolescents are rare. Trauma from a human bite can cause infection and may require antibiotic therapy to prevent mastitis.

# Reproductive Problems of Male Adolescents

## Gynecomastia

### Pathophysiology

*Gynecomastia* is the growth of breast tissue that frequently occurs in boys during puberty. Growth of breast tissue may be found in one or both breasts. Gynecomastia can be divided into type I (benign adolescent hypertrophy) and type II (physiological, with or without evidence of underlying organic disease) (Greydanus & Shearin, 1990). Type I is thought to be caused by a transient imbalance of pubertal hormones and appears in about two thirds of all teenage boys. Type II may result from various organic causes, including familial inheritance, and a wide variety of drugs. Gynecomastia is also seen in Klinefelter's syndrome.

### Medical Diagnosis and Management

Clinical examination establishes the diagnosis. Benign adolescent hypertrophy lasts from several months to a year and gradually resolves. Chromosome studies may be done if Klinefelter's syndrome is suspected. If the condition does not resolve, a subcutaneous mastectomy for cosmetic purposes may be performed.

### Nursing Assessment and Diagnosis

A thorough history is important in assessing gynecomastia. Growth rate, onset of breast growth and rapidity of change, and familial incidence are key points. During physical examination, the Tanner stage is noted, as are breast size and contour and unilateral or bilateral involvement. Nurses should distinguish gynecomastia from fat padding seen in obese adolescents.

Nursing diagnoses for gynecomastia might include the following:

- Body image disturbance related to increased breast tissue
- Anxiety related to being different from peers
- Impaired social interaction related to embarrassment at having to remove shirt during sports, physical education class, and other situations

### Planning and Implementing Nursing Care

Gynecomastia can be an extremely distressing condition to young males. Adolescents are concerned about their appearance, and these boys may think they are transforming into girls. Nurses can educate adolescents about the normalcy of gynecomastia and provide emotional support. Reassurance that this condition resolves over a period of time is important. Nurses should point out that this resolution time may be extended, lasting more than a year.

### Evaluating Nursing Care

Evaluation is based on assessing the adolescent's understanding of the common occurrence of this condition. The adolescent should feel less embarrassment about removing his shirt.

# Sexual Abuse

Sexual abuse is a problem of enormous proportions. The true incidence of child sexual abuse is undocumented, but it is believed to be one of the most common crimes against children. A variety of factors come into play that prevent sexual abuse from being accurately reported, but it is estimated that 6% of children in the United States are sexually abused each year (Finkelhor & Hotaling, 1984).

There is no universal definition for sexual abuse, but it is generally defined as the exploitation of children and adolescents in sexual activities without their consent and in violation of accepted family roles and society norms. It is a crime involving exploitation of a child's vulnerability. The children eventually feel helpless and powerless to stop the assaults and may attribute the blame to themselves.

Sexual abuse may occur in a variety of forms. *Incest* refers to sexual relations between family members, including stepparents, grandparents, uncles, aunts, and nonrelated siblings. *Rape* is attempted or successful sexual intercourse through force or by intimidation or deception. *Molestation* includes various forms of sexual contact, including fondling and caressing the genitals, penetration of body orifices with fingers or objects, masturbation, or fellatio. Abuse involving sexual *exploitation* may include child pornography and child prostitution.

### Medical Diagnosis and Management

There is no typical profile of the sexually abused child. Table 31-1 lists potential signs of sexual abuse involving children. Few sexually abused children present with physical trauma. Discovery of sexual abuse is usually through disclosure, which may occur in a variety of ways. Disclosure may include observation of the act and subsequent report or confrontation, or findings on physical examination may arouse suspicion in the clinician and lead to questioning the child. The child or adolescent may report the relationship or experience to a teacher, a trusted adult, or a friend. Suspicions may also be heightened by clues such as excessive gifts or money. It is important that the child be believed when disclosure occurs. Reports of sexual abuse are not childhood fantasies and should be accepted as the truth until proved otherwise.

All health care workers are required by the Federal Child Abuse Prevention and Treatment Act of 1974 to report suspected and actual cases of child abuse and neglect. Nurses who fail to report suspected child abuse face pun-

## Table 31–1.   Signs of Sexual Abuse

**Physical Signs**

Difficulty walking or sitting

Bruises, bleeding, or lacerations of the external genitalia or anal areas

Pain on urination

Pain, swelling, or itching of the genital area

Vaginal or penile discharge

Enlarged vaginal or rectal orifice

Sexually transmitted disease

Recurrent urinary tract infections

**Behavioral Signs**

Regressive behavior, such as bed-wetting or thumb-sucking

Sleep disturbances

Sudden onset of new fears

Withdrawal

Personality changes (depression, hostility, anger, aggression)

Change in school performance

Running away from home

Suicidal attempts or thoughts

Substance abuse

Advanced sexual behavior or knowledge

---

ishment according to individual state laws. Information regarding abuse is not considered to be confidential and must be reported. Nurses reporting suspected child abuse are protected from civil action.

Investigation is multifaceted owing to the various legal, health, and social factors. The initial interview of the child is an important event. It is generally agreed that the use of tape recorders or, increasingly more common, video recorders to document this initial interview is appropriate. This minimizes repeated questioning, which is often emotionally traumatic and increasingly stressful.

Treatment is aimed at protecting the child, providing therapy to family members, and reestablishing the family as a functional unit. Treatment is complex and involves numerous services. A detailed discussion of treatment is beyond the scope of this chapter, but indicators for family success in treatment include the offender's admitting guilt and accepting full responsibility for the act, the nonoffending parent's believing and not blaming the child as well as acknowledging failure to protect the child, and the victim's understanding and forgiving the offender and nonoffending parent. Many families are not salvageable, and disintegration takes place through divorce or the child's decision not to live with either parent.

### Nursing Assessment and Diagnosis

A complete history and physical examination is necessary. The examination should begin with nongenital components. If possible, it is best to reassure the child that an "internal" examination is not required. Sedation may be indicated if a pelvic examination is needed in a prepubertal child. The first step in examining the female genitalia is inspection for any bruises, lacerations, irritation, or bleeding. Nurses should also be alert for signs of herpes infection or any venereal warts. The anterior vagina and hymen are examined using a good light source. The labia minora are retracted to view the hymen. Important observations include presence of the hymen, size of the opening, and any signs of bleeding or scarring.

Examination of the male genitalia should note any penile bruising, erythema, or discharge. Observation for any signs of sexually transmitted diseases, such as ulcers or papules, is important. Examination of the child's rectum should not be neglected. The perirectal area should be examined for scars, bruising, warts, and small skin tags. Hemorrhoids in children are rare, and their presence should be considered as suspicious of abuse. Digital examination of the rectum is not required.

Nursing diagnoses for sexual abuse might include the following:

- Ineffective individual coping related to emotional trauma
- Ineffective family coping related to awareness of the assault
- Pain related to genital injury
- Altered family processes related denial of the problem
- Social isolation related to feelings of guilt or shame
- Self-esteem disturbance related to physical assault

### Planning and Implementing Nursing Care

The primary goal of nursing care involves intervention to protect the child from further abuse. Nurses need to interact with a variety of disciplines concerned with child protection and family therapy. Nursing care for victims of incest varies according to the child's age and developmental level. The child may display behaviors ranging from fearful and withdrawn to clinging. Nursing care is adjusted to deal with these behaviors, but consistency, appropriate teaching, and involvement of the child are always indicated. Nurses can help the child or adolescent deal with feelings of shame or guilt. These children need reassurance that they are not responsible for what has happened to them.

Nurses must deal with personal feelings related to the abused child and the family. Typically, initial feelings are of anger and disgust toward the family. Bringing such feelings under control and employing a nonjudgmental approach is a difficult task. Nurses must remember that the parents are essential components in providing family-centered care and must not be excluded. Working with the parents and keeping them informed are important nursing interventions.

Nurses must be informed about resources within the local community. Discharge planning for the hospitalized child must include the community health nurse. Nurses can play a vital role in initiating the coordination of community services needed for the child and family. Local self-help groups that may be available include Parents United and Daughters and Sons United.

Prevention of sexual abuse is an important nursing role. There has been an increased focus in many communities and schools on teaching children how to prevent sexual abuse. Resource materials on prevention programs are available from the National Committee for the Prevention of Child Abuse (332 S. Michigan Ave., Suite 950, Chicago, IL 60604). Education is also aimed at adults to help them protect their children from possible abuse. Nurses can play active roles in these educational efforts.

Nurses can also assist in early identification of potential problems and refer these families to appropriate community resources. A number of predictive measures and tools can be used to identify families at risk. One of the most widely used screening instruments is the Child Abuse Potential Inventory (Milner & Wimberley, 1979). It is important for nurses to recognize that these various screening instruments are limited in use and that their reliability and validity have not been established. Many educational programs address risk factors and attempt to identify forces that cause dysfunctional parenting. Nurses' participation in these programs provide excellent opportunities to identify problems that may lead to sexual abuse.

### Evaluating Nursing Care

Evaluation in some instances can be based on determining the progress of the family's return to a functional state. Participation in family and individual counseling is a key factor. Periodic evaluation of change in family behavior patterns and family growth is essential. The child should resume a normal life and appropriate relationships with others. In instances in which the child is removed from the home or chooses to live apart from the parents, evaluation may be based on the child's adjustment to such life changes and attainment of a normal emotional well-being.

## Incest

*Incest* accounts for 80% of all reported child sexual abuse and is the most damaging to the child. Incest results in serious, long-term consequences. Most cases involve the father or stepfather and daughter. Mother–son, mother–daughter, and sibling incest account for most of the remaining cases. Incestuous relationships between father and daughter are usually prolonged, lasting several years. The usual age of the female victim at initiation of the incestuous relationship is between 10 and 14 years. Boys

are also victims of sexual abuse, although the incidence of such abuse is highly underreported. The child is usually afraid to report the relationship because of fear of retaliation, of being disbelieved, or of causing family disruption.

Incest usually indicates severe family problems that may include dysfunctional marriage, sexual estrangement, alcoholism, violence, physical abuse, and various psychological factors. Often, the mother is passive and essentially gives up her role to the daughter. Other family members may be aware of the incest but allow it to occur, believing that it will hold the family together. The child is thus a double victim, abused by one adult and unprotected by the other.

## Rape

*Rape* is a legal term that describes penetration (genital, anal, or oral) of a person without consent and with the use of force, fear, or fraud. Rape is an act to express power over others or anger at others. *Statutory rape* refers to sexual intercourse with a female below the age of consent, which varies from state to state. *Date rape,* a situation in which the victim knows the rapist, is also an increasing crime in the United States. An estimated half of rape victims are between the ages of 10 and 19, and half of this group are under age 16. Many of these adolescents are physically assaulted in addition to the sexual assault. Vaginal lacerations and male genital injuries are common.

The person who has been sexually assaulted should be thoroughly evaluated to determine the extent of physical and emotional injury. Physical examination and specimen collection should be done without delay. Most institutions have a specific protocol for these procedures, including testing for sexually transmitted diseases. This protocol should be strictly followed because of the importance of evidence for future legal proceedings. As in questioning the sexually abused child, interview of the rape victim is critical. Assessment should be conducted by an experienced person, and the interview may be video recorded.

Nurses can offer support during this time, helping to explain procedures and tests. Rape is an extremely traumatic experience, with potentially devastating psychological effects. The victim's reaction to the assault is termed *rape trauma syndrome* and usually occurs in two phases. The first phase is called the *acute phase of disorganization* and includes disbelief, shock, or dismay. Many victims are so disorganized that they delay seeking medical care for hours and even for several days. Many victims never seek attention. Some experience feelings of guilt, blaming themselves for the assault.

The second phase is called *reorganization* and defines the recovery period in which the victim adjusts to the incident. This phase can be lengthy and often includes chronic depression, anxiety reactions, and various sexual dysfunctions. Counseling may be needed by a wide variety of professionals to deal with the emotional aftermath of the rape.

Many of the nursing interventions used for the sexually abused child are applicable to the victim of rape. Nurses must focus on the goal of reducing the stress on the victim. The interrogation and follow-up questioning by law enforcement officers and other health professionals can often be extremely stressful. Nurses should not neglect the need to provide support to the victim's family. Parents may express many reactions, from guilt to blame, and they often experience the same disorganization as their child. Long-term follow-up care is necessary, and appropriate referrals should be made as soon as possible. Many communities have a rape crisis center, which serves as an essential resource.

## Sexually Transmitted Diseases

The highest age-specific rates of sexually transmitted diseases involve sexually active adolescents. This rate is still considered less than the true number because of underreporting and missed diagnoses. Adolescents are at high risk because of increasingly early exposure to sexual intercourse and an increase in sexual partners. This risk factor is also affected by the fact that adolescents often delay seeking medical intervention.

### Pelvic Inflammatory Disease

#### Pathophysiology

*Pelvic inflammatory disease (PID)* is an acute or chronic infection involving the upper reproductive system. Gonococcus was previously considered the principal causative agent in PID, but recent studies reveal a variety of organisms responsible for the infection, including *Neisseria gonorrhoeae* (25% to 50%), *Chlamydia trachomatis* (25%–43%), and nongonococcal, nonchlamydial causes (25%–84%) (Sweet, 1987). Introduced to the vagina during sexual intercourse, the infecting agent spreads in an ascending fashion from the lower to the upper genital tract, ultimately reaching the fallopian tubes. An inflammatory reaction occurs that causes scarring and possible occlusion of the fallopian tubes.

Pelvic inflammatory disease is a major consequence of sexually transmitted diseases. The incidence of PID in adolescent females continues to rise, occurring in nonwhite adolescents at a rate more than twice that of white adolescents (Washington, Sweet, & Shafer, 1985).

#### Medical Diagnosis and Management

Pelvic inflammatory disease has a variety of clinical signs and symptoms, including fever, lower abdominal pain, increased vaginal discharge, and irregular vaginal bleeding. Clinical presentation may vary depending on causative organism, affected structures, and severity of the disease. There is usually a generalized tenderness of the lower abdomen without palpable masses, and pelvic examination reveals a purulent cervical discharge. Bimanual examination elicits extreme tenderness of the cervix and uterus (Chandelier's sign). Treatment goals are aimed at preserving fertility and preventing ectopic pregnancy. Treatment includes administration of broad-spectrum antibiotic therapy since it is often impossible to determine the exact microbial agents in each patient. Hospitalization of adolescents with acute PID should be strongly considered to ensure completion of the antibiotic regimen. These patients are placed on intravenous antibiotics. Adolescents with PID who are treated as outpatients must be evaluated within 48 hours to determine the effectiveness of therapy.

Early diagnosis with aggressive treatment reduces the many potential sequelae of PID. Tuboovarian abscess and perihepatitis are among the short-term consequences of acute PID. Long-term sequelae include infertility, ectopic pregnancy, chronic pelvic pain, and pelvic adhesions.

### Nursing Assessment and Diagnosis

A detailed and accurate history of sexual activity is important. Obtaining such a history means gaining the adolescent's trust and involves issues of confidentiality. Nurses need to assess the adolescent's knowledge of PID as well as of its treatment and prevention.

Nursing diagnoses for pelvic inflammatory disease might include the following:

- High risk for infection related to the disease process
- Impaired tissue integrity related to inflammation of the fallopian tubes
- Pain related to the infection
- Social isolation related to shame
- Situational low self-esteem related to having a sexually transmitted disease
- Sexual dysfunction related to painful intercourse

### Planning and Implementing Nursing Care

Nursing interventions should focus on education concerning the causes and characteristics of PID as well as its treatment and prevention. Education must also include the importance of strict adherence to the treatment regimen and treatment of sex partners. Education for prevention of PID should include facts about safe-sex practices, with particular emphasis on the correct use of condoms and proper condom removal.

Nurses should be aware that PID can intensify conflict between the adolescent and her parents. It may mark the parents' discovery that their daughter is sexually active. Nurses can play a key role in helping both parties explore their feelings and approach solutions to this dilemma. The adolescent may also display emotional problems related to infertility and sexual functioning and should be encouraged to verbalize her feelings. Nurses can encourage the family and peers to offer support.

### Evaluating Nursing Care

Evaluation is based on assessing the adolescent's understanding of PID, its treatment, and methods for prevention. Adolescents should demonstrate an understanding of proper use of condoms.

## Chlamydia Trachomatis

Chlamydial infection is the most prevalent sexually transmitted disease in adolescents and is likely the most devastating. About 3 to 5 million Americans are affected by chlamydial infection each year. As many as half of all cases of nongonococcal urethritis in men are believed to be caused by *C. trachomatis* infection. The recent substantial increases in tubal infertility are believed to be related to chlamydial infection.

### Pathophysiology

Chlamydiae are a group of obligatory intracellular parasites, containing both DNA and RNA, that infect squamocolumnar cells. *C. trachomatis* is a major sexually transmitted disease pathogen and is the organism responsible for this disease. The cervix serves as an important reservoir, and a carrier state can last for several months. Chlamydia is responsible for a number of medical disorders, including pneumonia, urethritis, cervicitis, and neonatal conjunctivitis. Studies note that 15% to 37% of pregnant adolescents are infected with chlamydia, and half of their newborns develop inclusion conjunctivitis (Hammerschlag, 1989).

### Medical Diagnosis and Management

Infection can occur at several sites and can cause a variety of distinct disease syndromes; however, chlamydia does not always produce clinically apparent infections. Often, symptoms are so mild that they are ignored. Cervicitis is usually asymptomatic, with up to 70% of genital infections in women being asymptomatic. When present, symptoms are nonspecific and may include dysuria, vaginal discharge, or vaginal pruritus. Examination reveals a mucopurulent cervical discharge. One of the most serious complications of chlamydial infection in adolescent females is pelvic inflammatory disease. In men, the most common genital infection resulting from chlamydia is urethritis. Symptoms include urethral discharge, dysuria, or urethral itching.

Diagnosis is made from cervical tissue cultures. Adequate samples of cervical epithelial cells are required for this culture, since vaginal discharge alone often yields negative results. Numerous tests are being marketed, including the Microtrak Immunofluorescent Test and the Chlamydiazyme test. Among serological tests available is the 4-hour enzyme-linked immunosorbent assay (*ELISA*).

Treatment for uncomplicated cases includes tetracycline or doxycycline. Erythromycin can be used in pregnant adolescents or if drug allergy exists. Antibiotics are usually administered for 7 days. Sulfisoxazole, administered for 10 days, is an alternative antibiotic. Therapy also includes treating all sex partners.

### Nursing Assessment and Diagnosis

Nursing assessment includes patient history regarding vaginal discharge, irritation, or other genital complaints. Males should be questioned regarding dysuria, frequency, urethral itching, and urethral discharge. Sexually active adolescents should be carefully questioned about sex partners whose past sexual history is unknown.

Nursing diagnoses for chlamydial infections might include the following:

- Altered patterns of urinary elimination related to genital discomfort
- Sexual dysfunction related to complications of the disease
- Noncompliance related to treatment regimen and failure to engage in safe-sex practices
- Ineffective individual coping related to possible complications
- Self-esteem disturbance related to having a sexually transmitted disease

### Planning and Implementing Nursing Care

Nursing interventions include planning to ensure optimal compliance with the treatment regimen by helping clients establish a method for remembering to take the medication. Written information on the causative organism and treatment is helpful for adolescents. Nurses must stress the importance of all sex partners being examined and treated. Instructions should reinforce the need to abstain from sexual activity until treatment is completed and all sex partners have been evaluated. Nurses can play an important role in educating adolescents in prevention of reinfection by discussing the consistent use of condoms and safe-sex practices.

### Evaluating Nursing Care

Evaluation includes assessing patient compliance with medications, containment of the disease, patient knowledge of the disease process and preventive measures, and involvement by the nurse in community and school prevention programs.

## Gonorrhea

Incidence rates of gonorrhea among adolescents continue to rise. It is estimated that there are two unreported cases for every reported case of gonorrhea, affecting over 500,000 adolescents each year. Gonorrhea rates are higher in males and in minority and low socioeconomic populations. Estimated transmission from one sexual exposure is 50% to 60% from an infected male to uninfected female and 35% from an infected female to an uninfected male (Morse, Moreland, & Thompson, 1990).

### Pathophysiology

Gonorrhea is caused by *Neisseria gonorrhoeae,* a gram-positive diplococcus that infects columnar and transitional epithelium. The organisms progressively invade the mucosa and submucosa and, upon death, produce an inflammatory response that results in the distinctive purulent exudate. Squamous epithelium is not affected, but the prepubertal vaginal epithelium is susceptible since it has not been keratinized by estrogen influence.

### Medical Diagnosis and Management

Symptomatic males typically have dysuria and a profuse yellow discharge. These signs may appear from 1 day to 2 weeks after sexual contact. Diagnosis is established by a gram stain of the urethral discharge. Recent data reveal a significant percentage of asymptomatic infected males; these infected males are typically frequent transmitters of gonorrhea.

Half of all infected women are asymptomatic (Morse, Moreland, & Thompson, 1990). Mild dysuria or non-specific cystitis are often initial signs. Untreated cervical infection may lead to PID and disseminated gonococcal infection, which is a result of gonococcal bacteremia. Other complications may include abscesses in Bartholin's and Skene's glands. *Dermatitis–arthritis syndrome* is the most common form of disseminated gonococcal infection and includes symptoms of fever, chills, skin lesions, and arthralgia, usually involving the hands, feet, and elbows. When cultures are taken from the female, specimens of exudate from the urethra or cervix should be placed on selective media (Martin-Lewis, modified Thayer-Martin, or New York City media). Menses is not a contraindication for obtaining a specimen.

Treatment is complicated by resistant strains of gonococci, including penicillinase-producing *N. gonorrhoeae* (PPNG), which inactivates penicillins. PPNG strains became endemic in the United States in 1981, and since 1984 they have increased dramatically. There is a variety of treatment regimens, but the current drug of choice is ceftriaxone. The Centers for Disease Control (1989) recommend treatment involving antibiotic regimens that are effective against resistant strains. For clients with an allergy to β-lactam drugs, intramuscular spectinomycin is recom-

mended. Drug therapy using the penicillins is no longer employed unless the patient was infected in a geographic area that is nonendemic for PPNG or the organism is known to be penicillin-sensitive.

### Nursing Assessment and Diagnosis

Nursing assessment includes observation and reporting of vaginal discharges, redness and irritation of the external genitalia, and any associated symptoms. Males should be questioned regarding urethral discharge and dysuria. Nurses must suspect the possibility of child abuse in the young child infected with gonorrhea. Sexually active adolescents should be carefully questioned about sex partners whose past sexual history is unknown.

Nursing diagnoses for gonorrhea might include the following:

- Altered patterns of urinary elimination related to genital discomfort
- Sexual dysfunction related to complications of the disease
- Social isolation related to communicability of the disease
- Ineffective individual coping related to effects on family interactions
- Self-esteem disturbance related to having a sexually transmitted disease

### Planning and Implementing Nursing Care

Nursing planning and interventions include education regarding disease transmission and preventive measures. Adolescents should be taught the correct use of condoms and instructed about safe-sex practices. All sexual partners must be notified and treated. Education to prevent reinfection includes instruction on the use of condoms until negative cultures are obtained. The patient must return 4 to 7 days after treatment for follow-up cultures. Screening for secondary and tertiary complications, such as pelvic inflammatory disease, prostatitis, and sterility, must be included in individual care plans.

### Evaluating Nursing Care

Evaluation of nursing care measures includes assessing the containment of the disease and the patient's knowledge of the disease process and preventive measures. The nurse may become involved in community and school prevention programs.

## Syphilis

### Pathophysiology

Syphilis is caused by the spirochete *Treponema pallidum.* Syphilis is transmitted by sexual intercourse or from a pregnant women to her fetus in utero. Outside the human body, the organism is rapidly killed. Untreated, syphilis becomes a chronic disease that spreads throughout the body and can produce manifestations in every organ system. The disease is viewed in four stages.

The first stage, *primary syphilis,* develops an average of 3 weeks after exposure. The clinical manifestation, a chancre, is a red, indurated, painless sore that appears at the site of exposure, usually on or near the genitals. Chancres may also occur on the cervix, pharynx, or rectum. Single lesions are typical, but multiple primary chancres are not uncommon. These primary lesions heal spontaneously, usually within 6 weeks.

*Secondary syphilis,* the next stage of the disease, appears from 6 weeks to 6 months after infection. The primary chancre may still be present; however, it is typically healed when generalized, nonspecific symptoms appear. These symptoms include fever, malaise, headache, anorexia, and arthralgia. Over half of infected clients have a generalized lymphadenopathy. This stage is also manifested by a rash, sometimes called a *syphilid.* This rash varies in appearance and occurs in about 75% of patients. The rash frequently covers the palms of the hands and soles of the feet, which helps distinguish it from other dermatoses. The signs and symptoms of this secondary stage last only a few weeks and resolve without treatment. Syphilis is most readily transmitted during the first year of infection.

*Latent syphilis* is the period when the signs and symptoms of secondary syphilis have disappeared. Clients have no clinical manifestations but may be infectious for years. Latent syphilis progresses to *late syphilis,* a condition that may occur from 2 to 30 years after the original infection.

### Medical Diagnosis and Management

Diagnosis is confirmed by serological tests. Nonspecific tests include the Venereal Disease Research Laboratory test, unheated serum reagin test, rapid plasma reagin test, and reagin screen test. Specific antibody tests include the fluorescent treponemal antibody absorption test and hemaglutination treponemal test. The treatment choice is benzathine penicillin. Tetracycline or erythromycin is administered for 15 days to clients who are allergic to penicillin.

### Nursing Assessment and Diagnosis

Nursing assessment should include a history of all sexual contacts for the preceding 3 months. All symptoms should be noted.

Nursing diagnoses vary depending on the stage of the disease. The following diagnoses may be applicable:

- Potential for infection related to multisystem involvement
- Impaired tissue integrity related to the disease process

- Impaired social interaction related to the mechanism of disease spread
- Ineffective individual coping related to fears about complications
- Self-esteem disturbance related to society and family belief systems
- Anxiety related to having a sexually transmitted disease

### Planning and Implementing Nursing Care

Nursing interventions are designed to inform the client about the treatment and its possible side effects. People with secondary syphilis commonly experience Jarisch-Herxheimer reaction a few hours after penicillin treatment. The symptoms include nausea, fever, chills, malaise, arthralgia, and headache. Nurses can assure clients that these symptoms typically subside within 24 hours. Bed rest and analgesics should be encouraged. Nurses should be alert for this reaction so that it is not confused with a penicillin allergy. Nurses should educate clients about oral medications, stress the importance of medical evaluation of all sex partners, and encourage the use of condoms. Follow-up appointments should be planned. If the patient is hospitalized, blood and body fluid, as well as drainage and secretion precautions, should be monitored.

### Evaluating Nursing Care

Evaluation includes follow-up serology studies, assessing results of disease education, and success in identifying and contacting sex contacts.

## Human Papillomavirus

Infection of the genital tract with the *human papillomavirus* (HPV) is the second most common sexually transmitted disease (Story, 1987). Genital warts, *condylomata acuminatum*, are the most recognizable manifestation of HPV infections, but these infections have been proved to be associated with squamous atypia and invasive carcinoma of the anogenital tract.

### Pathophysiology

Human papillomavirus infects the skin and mucous membranes. The virus replicates in the nuclei of infected epithelial cells. There are more than 40 serotypes of HPV viruses, but 6 types are responsible for genital warts, which are transmitted through sexual contact. People are believed to be the most contagious during the first 3 months of infection.

### Medical Diagnosis and Management

There is a wide spectrum of HPV-associated conditions, ranging from the typical genital warts to clinically inapparent infection. Condyloma acuminata are flesh-colored papules that can be found on any part of the genitals (including the vagina, urethra, bladder, or anal canal). These papules typically have finger-like projections that cause them to have a rough surface. Condyloma can become so large that they cause deformity of normal structures. Obstruction of the urethral meatus in males is not uncommon. Flat genital warts, *condylomata plana,* may appear as flesh-colored or hypopigmented. Diagnosis is made on the basis of clinical appearance, aided by application of acetic acid and use of magnifying lenses. Treatment includes the use of podophyllin, laser surgery, and cryotherapy. Research is investigating the use of 5-fluorouracil cream to suppress recurrences of genital warts after eradication.

### Nursing Assessment and Diagnosis

Nursing assessment includes careful gloved inspection of the genital area for any signs of the disease. Females should be questioned about other sexually transmitted diseases, such as trichomonal vaginitis, monilial vaginitis, and gonococcal cervicitis, since condyloma acuminatum is often associated with these diseases. It is also important to ask about the presence of genital warts in sex partners.

Nursing diagnoses for HPV might include the following:

- Body-image disturbance related to a feeling of embarrassment, shame, or betrayal
- Sexual dysfunction related to complications of the disease and discomfort resulting from treatment
- Altered patterns of urinary elimination related to disease process
- Ineffective individual coping related to fears about complications
- Self-esteem disturbance related to having a sexually transmitted disease

### Planning and Implementing Nursing Care

Nurses must assess the client's reaction to the diagnosis and understanding regarding transmission, treatment, and health implications. Nurses should ensure that the relationship between HPV infection and cancer is understood. Clients need to be educated regarding the various treatments. Nurses should teach clients about the importance of protecting normal tissue from podophyllin. Most techniques require that podophyllin be washed off in 4 to 6 hours to avoid blistering. Nurses should stress the importance of keeping appointments for clients who need weekly applications.

Female clients should be educated regarding the relationship of cervical HPV infection and the presence of penile warts in sex partners. Adolescents should be instructed that the incidence of infection increases with frequent, casual sexual intercourse. Clients should understand the difficulty in totally eradicating the virus; a minimum of 6 months should pass before the client should feel lesion-free. Women with cytological evidence of HPV should be educated regarding the importance of routine screening with Pap smears.

### Evaluating Nursing Care

Evaluation is based on assessing the client's understanding of the infection, its transmission, and possible complications. Clients should be compliant in seeking routine Pap smears and appropriate follow-up. Evaluation is also needed regarding the client's body image and self-concept.

## Genital Herpes

Genital herpes virus infections have increased dramatically in the United States. Among sexually active youth, 3% to 12% have positive cultures for herpes simplex. The greatest increase is among middle- and upper-class individuals (Morse, Moreland, & Thompson, 1990).

### Pathophysiology

Genital herpes infections are caused by the *herpes simplex virus* (HSV). The infection is transmitted during sexual intercourse or by oral–genital sexual activity. Two types of herpes simplex viruses exist; both types cause genital herpes infections. Type 2 HSV is responsible for about 90% of genital herpes cases. Recurrent infection is characteristic of this virus. The consequences of maternal genital herpes infection on the fetus can be quite severe, and neonatal HSV infection is a serious disorder.

### Medical Diagnosis and Management

Primary genital infection occurs after sexual contact with an infected person and an incubation period of 2 to 12 days. A small group of vesicles appear, which develop into painful ulcers that last 15 to 20 days and then heal. Typical lesions in men occur on the glans penis, urethra, penile shaft, or perianal region. In women, lesions are characteristically located around the introitus, urethral meatus, or the labia. In both sexes, the lesions may spread to the thighs, buttocks, and surrounding regions. Recurrent genital herpes varies from person to person, but generally the symptoms and signs are milder and of shorter duration than the primary infection. Diagnosis is made by microscopic examination of scraping from lesions treated with Wright-Giemsa stain (Tzanck test). A Pap smear may also be used to confirm the diagnosis. Specific viral cultures may be used to make a definitive diagnosis. There is no specific cure for genital herpes, but acyclovir has proved successful in reducing some of the symptoms and the duration of the disease occurrences. Topical acyclovir is ineffective in recurrent cases, and oral

# Nursing Care Plan

## Assessment

Juan Rodriguez is a 15-month-old male seen in the ambulatory pediatric clinic for his periodic well baby exam.

### Chief Complaint

Juan has been followed periodically in the well baby clinic for an undescended right testicle.

### Subjective Assessment

*Past History:* Juan's undescended testicle was initially noted at his 2-week exam. The left testicle is in the scrotum and is easily palpated. The right testicle has been intermittently palpated in the abdomen, but all attempts to "milk down" the testicle have been unsuccessful. Other than the undescended testicle, his growth and development have been normal.

*Present History:* Juan is switching from breastfeeding to using a cup. He is eating baby foods and some table foods. He is walking and uses several words.

*Family History:* Mother is 22 years old and father is 23 years old; Juan is the only child; the paternal and maternal grandparents are alive and well.

### Objective Assessment

*Physical Examination:* Temperature: 37°C (98.6°F), otic; pulse: 120, radial; R. 26; B.P. 90/56, R arm; weight: 11.3 kg, 25 lb; height: 81 cm, 32 in

| | |
|---|---|
| Integument: | Clear with normal turgor |
| Head: | Normal; anterior fontanelle 1 cm x 1 cm |
| Eyes: | PERRLA |
| Ears: | TMs pearly grey with good light reflex and mobility; moderate cerumen in canals |
| Nose: | Patent; mucous membranes moist |
| Throat: | Clear without exudates |
| Neck: | Supple without lymphadenopathy |
| Thorax and Lungs: | Clear fields |
| Heart: | Regular rate and rhythm without murmur |
| Abdomen: | Soft without masses or organomegaly |
| Genitalia: | Normal uncircumcised male; left testicle palpated in scrotum. Right testicle palpated in lower abdomen. Cannot be manually drawn into scrotum. |
| Musculoskeletal: | Full ROM; leg lengths equal |
| Neurological: | Alert; grossly intact |

### Medical Diagnosis

Undescended Testes

### Medical Plan

Surgical evaluation

## Nursing Care Plan for a Child with an Undescended Testicle

| Goals | Nursing Interventions | Evaluation Criteria |
|---|---|---|
| **NURSING DIAGNOSIS #1: High Risk for Injury (Infertility, malignancy)** | | |
| (L) The child will experience minimal complications from the disorder<br><br>(L) The child will resume normal play activities | Explain the disorder, any interim treatment, and the surgical repair<br><br>Encourage parents to express concerns especially related to issues of sterility and future sexual function | The parents and child will demonstrate an understanding of cryptorchidism by verbally describing the condition, the pathophysiology, and associated complications |

*(continued)*

# Nursing Care Plan *(Continued)*

| Goals | Nursing Interventions | Evaluation Criteria |
|---|---|---|
| (S) The child will experience minimal problems related to surgical repair<br><br>(S) The parents will be supportive of the child throughout hospitalization and the recovery period | Prepare the child and family for hospitalization and surgery<br>Provide parents with information and support<br><br>Following surgery, monitor vital signs and observe for signs of vascular obstruction to testicles or skin breakdown of the scrotal sac | The parents and the child will demonstrate knowledge about the treatments and surgical repair by verbal explanation |

| Goals | Nursing Interventions | Evaluation Criteria |
|---|---|---|

**NURSING DIAGNOSIS #2: Anxiety, related to surgical procedure**

| Goals | Nursing Interventions | Evaluation Criteria |
|---|---|---|
| (L) The child will have a normal body image and suffer no psychological sequelae<br><br>(S) The child and parents will understand the purpose of the surgical repair<br><br>(S) The child will express concerns about the surgical procedure | Encourage parents to verbalize fears and concerns<br>Clarify parental misconceptions<br>Describe and explain the procedure<br>Prepare toddler-age child as close to time of the procedure as possible | The child will express his fears and concerns about hospitalization and the surgical procedure<br><br>The parents will express their fears related to surgery and the child's sexual function and future fertility |

| Goals | Nursing Interventions | Evaluation Criteria |
|---|---|---|

**NURSING DIAGNOSIS #3: Pain, related to surgical procedure**

| Goals | Nursing Interventions | Evaluation Criteria |
|---|---|---|
| (S) The child will report no pain | Assess child for signs of pain<br>Focus on preventing pain rather than allowing the child to become uncomfortable<br>Administer analgesics as prescribed<br>Provide comfort through appropriate positioning; avoid elevation or pressure on scrotum<br>Assess and provide care to the surgical wound | The child will be free from pain |

acyclovir is used in most instances, including severe, frequently recurrent HSV disease. Chronic suppressive oral acyclovir is safe and effective for at least a year at a time. After a year, the drug is stopped for a short period to reevaluate the natural recurrence frequency. If the recurrence frequency has diminished enough, chronic prophylaxis is discontinued. Use of intravenous acyclovir is under evaluation. This drug should not be used during pregnancy or lactation.

### Nursing Assessment and Diagnosis

Assessment includes obtaining an accurate history of the illness and a description of the symptoms and lesions. A thorough sexual history regarding possible exposure is important.

Nursing diagnosis for genital herpes might include the following:

- Altered sexuality patterns related to discomfort or abstinence from intercourse
- Impaired tissue integrity related to the lesions
- Altered tissue integrity related to oral lesions
- Pain related to genital ulcers
- Anxiety related to the long-term nature of the disease

### Planning and Implementing Care

The involved area should be kept clean and dry. A hair dryer may be useful in drying the lesions. A variety of measures, such as Sitz baths, loose-fitting clothing, and underwear with a cotton crotch, may provide symptomatic relief. Abstinence from intercourse should be encouraged while symptomatic. Nurses should educate clients regarding the use of condoms to protect sex partners. Clients who become pregnant must inform their obstetricians that they have genital herpes. If active lesions are present before delivery, caesarean delivery is indicated to prevent direct exposure of the infant to the maternal virus. Women with genital herpes should receive semiannual Pap smears.

### Evaluating Nursing Care

Evaluation of nursing care is based on assessing the client's understanding of the disease, its transmission, and preventing others from becoming infected. Clients should abstain from intercourse when lesions are present and should always use condoms.

## Acquired Immune Deficiency Syndrome

Sexual contact is responsible for transmission of over three quarters of all acquired immune deficiency syndrome cases. For further discussion of this disease, see Chapter 27.

## Summary

Providing nursing care to children and adolescents with alterations of the reproductive system can be extremely challenging. The disorders and diseases of this body system involve anatomy about which most clients are sensitive and anxious. Reproductive diseases can produce a great deal of fear, involving a wide variety of concerns. Body image disturbances are common complications with disorders of reproductive function.

A critical component of nursing care includes an accurate, detailed, and focused history. Physical assessment includes inspection and examination of the genitals and the surrounding areas. Nurses must be comfortable with their own sexuality in order to function in an objective and honest manner. They must establish a sense of trust to obtain reliable and complete answers to sensitive and personal questions. Nurses can play a major role in assisting adolescents in their development as sexual beings. Nurses must first be familiar with adolescent sexuality and then develop guidelines for approaching adolescents.

Nurses can play a vital role in educating adolescents in the prevention of sexually transmitted diseases. These education efforts may be the only chance of checking a potentially devastating outbreak of acquired immune deficiency syndrome in the adolescent population. Education about sexually transmitted diseases may also be the single most effective method of preventing disease-related infertility in many of today's sexually active young people. Prevention of sexually transmitted diseases should be addressed in all health care facilities as well as in school and community settings.

## References

Braverman, P. K., & Strasburger, V. C. (1989). Why adolescent gynecology? *Pediatric Clinics of North America, 36*(6), 481.

Centers for Disease Control. (1989, September 1). Sexually transmitted diseases treatment guidelines. *Morbidity and Mortality Weekly Report* (Suppl. 38), 1–43.

Connell, E. B., & Tatum, H. J. (1985). *Sexually transmitted diseases: Diagnosis and treatment.* Durant, OK: Creative Informatics.

Finkelhor, D., & Hotaling, G. T. (1984). Sexual abuse in the national incidence study of child abuse and neglect. *Child Abuse and Neglect, 8,* 23–28.

Greydanus, D. E., & Shearin, R. B. (1990). *Adolescent sexuality and gynecology.* Philadelphia: Lea & Febiger.

Hammerschlag, M. R. (1989). Chlamydial infections. *Journal of Pediatrics, 114,* 727–734.

Mazur, T. (1984). Ambiguous genitalia: Detection and counseling. *Pediatric Nursing, 9*(6), 417–421.

Milner, J. S., & Wimberley, R. C. (1979). An inventory for the identification of child abusers. *Journal of Clinical Psychology, 35,* 95–100.

Morse, S. A., Moreland, A. A., & Thompson, S. E. (1990). *Sexually transmitted diseases.* Philadelphia: J. B. Lippincott.

Paavonen, J., & Stamm, W. E. (1987). Lower genital tract infections in women. *Infectious Disease Clinics of North America, 1,* 179–198.

Plotnick, L. P. (1990). Growth, growth hormone, and pituitary disorders. In Oski, F. A., De Angelis, C. D., Feigin, R. D., & Warshaw, J. B. (Eds.). *Principles and practice of pediatrics.* Philadelphia: J. B. Lippincott, pp. 1803–1811.

Shapiro, L. J. (1990). Signs and symptoms of inborn errors of metabolism. In Oski, F. A., De Angelis, C. D., Feigin, R. D., & Warshaw, J. B. (Eds.). *Principles and practice of pediatrics.* Philadelphia: J. B. Lippincott, pp. 1981–1986.

Story, B. (1987, December). Condylomata acuminata: An epidemic with malignant potential. *Physician Assistant, 11*(12), 13–23.

Sweet, R. L. (1987). Pelvic inflammatory disease and infertility in women. *Infectious Disease Clinics of North America, 1,* 199–215.

Washington, A. E., Sweet, R. L., & Shafer, M. B. (1985). Pelvic inflammatory disease and its sequelae in adolescents. *Journal of Adolescent Health Care, 6,* 298–310.

Wilson, D. W. (1990). Menstrual disorders. In Oski, F. A., De Angelis, C. D., Feigin, R. D., & Warshaw, J. B. (Eds.). *Principles and practice of pediatrics.* Philadelphia: J. B. Lippincott, pp. 721–726.

## Bibliography

Emans, S. J., Woods, E. R., Flagg, N. T., & Freeman, A. (1987). Genital findings in sexually abused, symptomatic, and asymptomatic girls. *Pediatrics, 79,* 778.

Enterline, J. A., & Leonardo, J. P. (1989). Condylomata acuminata (venereal warts). *Nurse Practitioner, 14*(4), 8–13.

Fisher, M., Swenson, P. D., Risucci, D., & Kaplan, M. H. (1987). Chlamydia trachomatis in suburban adolescents. *Journal of Pediatrics, 111,* 617–620.

Khoiny, F. E. (1989). Pelvic inflammatory disease in the adolescent. *Journal of Pediatric Health Care, 3*(5), 230–236.

Ott, M. J., & Jackson, P. L. (1989). Precocious puberty: Identifying early sexual development. *Nurse Practitioner, 14*(4), 21–30.

Pietsch, J. (1985). Breast disorders. In Lavery, J. P., & Sanfilippo, J. S. (Eds.). *Pediatric and adolescent obstetrics and gynecology.* New York: Springer-Verlag, pp. 96–104.

Treybig, M. (1989). Primary dysmenorrhea or endometriosis? *Nurse Practitioner, 14*(5), 8–18.

# Alterations in Endocrine Function

Patricia T. Castiglia, Deborah Kramer, Carolyn Fong, and Terri H. Lipman

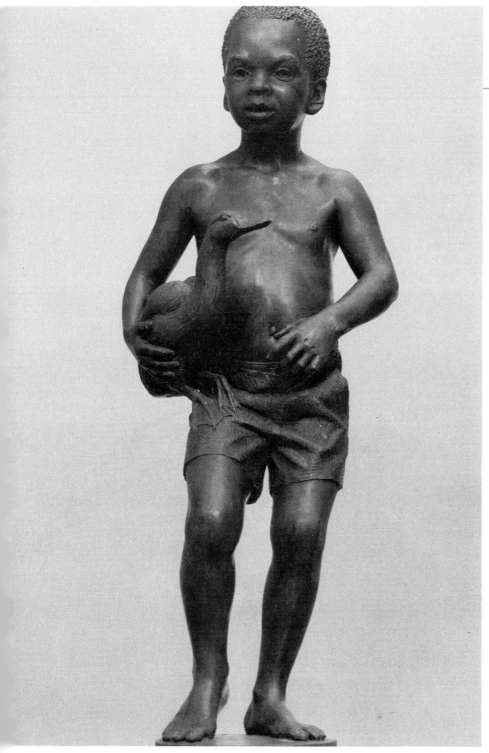

*32*

*Embryology*

*Anatomy and Physiology*

*Assessment*

*Nursing Diagnosis*

*Planning Nursing Care*

*Nursing Interventions*

*Endocrine Problems of Infancy and Early Childhood*

*Endocrine Problems of School-Aged Children and Adolescents*

*Chronic Endocrine Problems*

*Summary*

*Nursing Care Plan*

*Sculpture by Charles Parks*

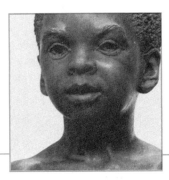

The endocrine system is made up of a small group of glands that work with the nervous system to coordinate and regulate the major body systems. Controlled by a series of feedback mechanisms, the endocrine glands release hormones with highly specific functions into the bloodstream, where they are carried to "target" tissues and organs. In health, the components of this system maintain homeostasis in a complex network of interactions. Dysfunction of any one part of the system, however, as when a gland either overproduces, underproduces, or fails to secrete hormones, can have wide-ranging effects not only on the target body organs but on other body systems as well. The nursing role is vital in helping children with endocrine disorders and their families adjust to the acute and long-term effects of such disorders.

## Embryology

Each of the organs of the endocrine system develops in utero at different stages and within different body systems.

The *pituitary gland,* which is divided into two parts, develops from two different sources. The adenohypophysis, or anterior pituitary, develops from the oral ectoderm of the roof of the primitive mouth. The neurohypophysis, or neural portion of the pituitary, develops at about the 21st day of gestation from the neuroectoderm of the floor of the diencephalon.

The *thyroid gland* develops in the 3rd week of gestation from a down-growth of the floor of the pharynx known as the thyroid diverticulum. By the 7th week, the thyroid has reached its final placement in front of the trachea. By the end of the 3rd month, thyroid hormones are evident in the fetal bloodstream.

Originating from the third and fourth pharyngeal pouches, development of the *thymus* and the two *parathyroid glands* appears closely linked. After the 4th or 5th week of gestation, the third pharyngeal pouch gives rise to the parathyroid glands, which fuse and form the thymus. Later, the parathyroid glands separate from the thymus and go to the dorsal surface of the thyroid gland.

The *pancreas* develops from the dorsal and ventral pancreatic buds of the endodermal cells arising from the primitive gut. As the duodenum grows, it shifts the ventral bud dorsally and the dorsal, and ventral bud fuse to form the pancreas.

The two *adrenal glands* are each divided into two distinct parts that originate in different sites. The *adrenal cortex* develops from the mesoderm beginning at about the 5th week of gestation and continuing autonomously until the 5th month, at which point it depends on adrenocorticotropic hormone for its development. The *adrenal medulla* forms from the neuroectoderm as cells derived from the neural tube beginning at about the 45th day. Adrenal development is not complete until 18 to 24 months after birth.

The genital glands, or *gonads,* of both sexes originate from the primordia. Gonadal development begins in the 5th week of gestation when the germinal epithelium develops on the medial aspect of the urogenital ridge. At about the 7th week, the embryo with a Y chromosome develops testes, producing masculinizing hormones that stimulate the further development of the penis and scrotum and suppress the development of the paramesonephric ducts. In the absence of Y chromosome, the mesonephric ducts regress, and the paramesonephric ducts develop into the uterus. The ovaries are identifiable by the 10th week of gestation.

## Anatomy and Physiology

The endocrine system consists of seven ductless glands that function solely in the endocrine system. In addition, associated glands and structures, such as the thymus, function in other systems as well. The primary endocrine glands are the pituitary, the thyroid, the parathyroids, the adrenal glands, the islets of Langerhans within the pancreas, and the ovaries and testes (the gonads). These glands work independently, interdependently, and together with the nervous system to secrete chemical messengers called *hormones* that regulate body functions (Fig. 32-1). Hormones literally set in motion necessary body processes, affecting energy production, metabolism of nu-

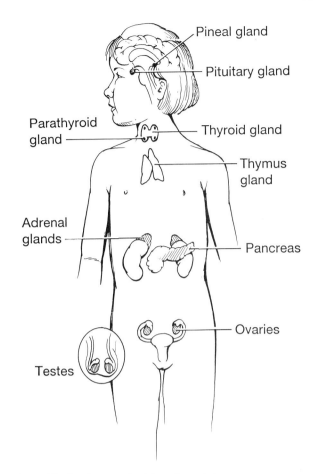

*Figure 32–1. Anatomical location of the endocrine glands.*

trients, fluid and electrolyte balance, growth and development, and reproduction (Bullock & Rosendahl, 1988).

Although each gland in the endocrine system has its own functions, the release of hormones from one organ is often dependent on stimulation by release of hormones from another. The pituitary, in particular, is essential to the functioning of the thyroid, adrenal cortex, and the gonads. Hormones released by the pituitary with this function are called the *tropic hormones* (from the Greek *tropos,* "to turn toward"), and the glands they influence are referred to as *target glands.*

The hormones maintain homeostasis by stimulating changes in a target organ. The target organ then releases a different hormone, which elevates blood levels that inhibit the release of the first (tropic) hormone. When the blood level falls to a certain level, the gland once again secretes a tropic hormone that in turn stimulates the target organ. This action to maintain homeostasis is called *negative feedback* (Fig. 32-2).

## The Pituitary Gland

The pituitary gland, or *hypophysis,* is a small, round structure located in the sella turcica of the sphenoid bone and attached to the hypothalamus through the infundibular

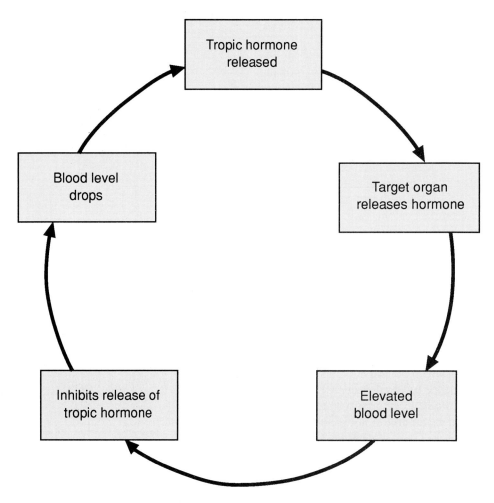

*Figure 32–2.   Negative feedback mechanism in regulating homeostasis by the endocrine glands.*

stalk. The pituitary is divided into the anterior and posterior lobes. The anterior lobe (adenohypophysis) contains the glandular part of the pituitary, and the posterior lobe (neurohypophysis) contains the neural part of the pituitary.

### The Adenohypophysis

The *adenohypophysis* is regulated by stimulation or inhibition of hormone secretions that come from the hypothalamus. In response to these chemical messages, the anterior lobe secretes the appropriate hormone. The tropic hormones (those that regulate functions of other endocrine glands) released by the pituitary are thyroid stimulating hormone (TSH), adrenocorticotropic hormone (ACTH), follicle-stimulating hormone (FSH), and luteinizing hormone (LH). Two other hormones released by the adenohypophysis are growth hormone, or somatotropin (GH or STH), and prolactin (PRL). Although these two hormones do not regulate the functions of other glands, they do play important roles in overall body growth and development (Fig. 32-3).

Adrenocorticotropic hormone controls the production and secretion of the adrenal cortex hormones. ACTH acts directly on the body cells by stimulating the liver to remove glucose from the blood and store it in the form of glycogen, which increases the catabolism of fats by the body's cells.

Follicle-stimulating hormone and LH are also referred to as *gonadotropic hormones* because they specifically affect the gonads. The secretion of FSH and LH follow a cyclic pattern in females. FSH activates cells in the ovaries to secrete estrogen and stimulates the development of an egg each month. FSH also stimulates the secretion of progesterone. LH stimulates the release of the developed egg and prepares the uterus for implantation of a fertilized egg. In males, FSH stimulates the testes to secrete testosterone and produce sperm. LH in the male is called *interstitial cell stimulating hormone* (ICSH). ICSH stimulates the secretion of testosterone through the Leydig's cells of the testes.

Prolactin is activated by stimulation of the nipples and is released in the absence of dopamine and a hypo-

Hypothalamus
Production

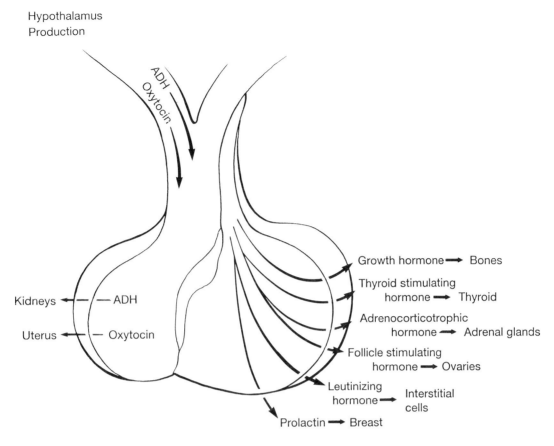

*Figure 32–3.* *The pituitary gland: hormones released and target organs.*

thalamic PRL-inhibitory factor. PRL secretion increases during pregnancy, reaching a peak at childbirth.

Growth hormone, which, like PRL, has no specific target organ, affects the hard and soft tissues of the body to maintain and increase growth. Action of GH is influenced by other hormones and by nutritional status, exercise, stress, diurnal variations, and sleep (Bullock & Rosendahl, 1988). GH directly affects the growth of bone and cartilage, facilitates protein metabolism as well as decreased protein breakdown, and has a strong effect on fat and glucose metabolism. GH requires the presence of carbohydrate for its work and, although its main function seems to be the promotion of healthy growth in the child, it clearly plays a role in the functioning of the body throughout adulthood as well. It also promotes fat catabolism and the breakdown of increased glycogen (which is stored in the liver) into glucose. These later two mechanisms are called the *diabetogenic effect* because they lead to hypoglycemia.

The secretion of GH is stimulated by hypoglycemia, which activates secretion of somatotropin releasing factor (SRF) by the hypothalamus. Once the blood sugar level returns to normal, the SRF is no longer secreted, and the pituitary stops secreting GH.

## The Neurohypophysis

The *neurohypophysis* does not function as an endocrine gland. Instead, it is composed of pituicytes, which are similar to nerve tissue. Pituicytes run from the hypothalamus, down the infundibular stalk. The hypothalamus sends the hormones oxytocin and antidiuretic hormone (ADH; also called vasopressin) along these neurons to the neurohypophysis where they are stored. When stimulated, the hypothalamus sends impulses through these pituicytes, instructing the anterior lobe to release the stored hormones into the blood. Oxytocin is released before giving birth and is responsible for stimulating the contraction of smooth muscle cells of the pregnant uterus. In addition, an infant's sucking on the mother's breast sends nerve impulses to the hypothalamus, which in turn stimulates the neurohypophysis to release the stored oxytocin. Oxytocin stimulates the cells around the ducts of the mammary gland to contract. ADH helps regulate circulation by causing constriction of the arterioles, thus elevating blood pressure. It also effects water loss through the kidneys. It is produced when receptors in the hypothalamus detect low water concentration in the blood. ADH is released from the neurohypophysis into the bloodstream and brought to the kidney, where urine output is decreased. When the hypothalamic receptors detect a high water concentration level, the secretion of the hormone is stopped, and urine output is again increased.

Hyposecretion or hypersecretion of a pituitary hormone can produce systemic and complicated disorders. One such disorder is growth hormone deficiency, which occurs if GH is undersecreted during the growth years, causing the slowing of bone and organ growth and the epiphyseal plates to close before normal height is reached. Treatment for pituitary dwarfism includes administering human GH before the closure of the epiphyseal plates. Hypersecretion of GH during childhood causes the growth of long bones to accelerate, a condition called *gigantism*. Hypersecretion of gonadotropin hormones leads to precocious puberty, which is discussed in Chapter 31.

## The Thyroid

The thyroid is located just below the trachea, with two lobes connected by the isthmus flanking either side of the windpipe. The thyroid's primary function is to regulate the rate of metabolism.

The thyroid synthesizes the hormones thyroxine ($T_3$) and triiodothyronine ($T_4$) with the help of iodine. Thyroid tissue traps iodine and concentrates it in the follicular lumen for synthesis of thyroid hormones. Evidence indicates that $T_3$ is the metabolically active hormone at the cellular level. Only 20% of circulating $T_3$ is secreted by the thyroid; the remainder is produced in peripheral tissues by deiodination of $T_4$. Thyroid hormones are transported in the blood, bound to protein-binding proteins, of which the major one is thyroxine-binding globulin (TBG). The functions of $T_4$ and $T_3$ are to increase oxygen consumption, stimulate protein synthesis, affect carbohydrate and lipid metabolism, and promote growth and development. Thyroid hormone synthesis is regulated by thyroid-stimulating hormone (TSH), which is secreted by the anterior pituitary. The secretion of TSH is controlled by thyrotropin-releasing hormone (TRH), which is synthesized in the hypothalamus. A decrease in thyroid hormone production causes a compensatory increase in levels of TRH and TSH (Fig. 32-4).

The thyroid also contains a group of cells called parafollicular (or C) cells. These cells secrete a hormone called calcitonin, which helps to maintain blood calcium levels, inhibits skeletal demineralization, and promotes calcium deposition in bone.

Hyposecretion of thyroid hormones during the

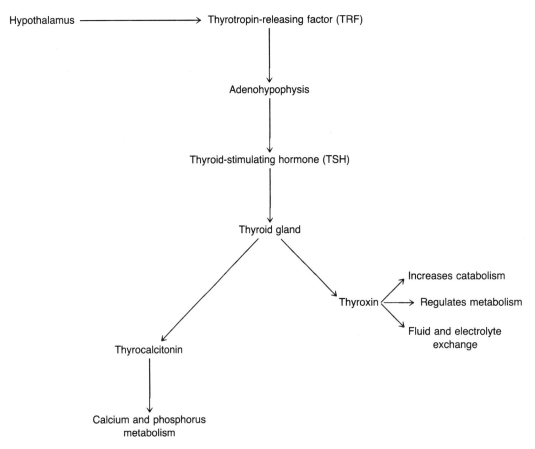

*Figure 32–4.  Thyroid gland: hormone secretion and action.*

growth years results in hypothyroidism; hypersecretion can result in hyperthyroidism.

## The Parathyroids

The four tiny parathyroid glands are located on the dorsal surface of the lateral lobes of the thyroid. They secrete parathyroid hormone (PTH), which regulates calcium by promoting bone resorption, thereby releasing calcium and phosphate ions into the blood. PTH increases reabsorption of the calcium from the intestine into the blood and increases the rate at which the kidney reabsorbs calcium from the urine into the blood. It also promotes excretion of phosphate in the renal tubules. PTH increases blood calcium and decreases blood phosphate. When the calcium ion level in the blood is low, more PTH is released, causing calcium to move from the bone, urine, and intestines to the blood. Calcium blood level rises, and less PTH is released. The low calcium ion level stimulates the thyroid gland to release more thyrocalcitonin, which causes the calcium to be reabsorbed by the bone, resulting in a low calcium ion level (Fig. 32-5). Hyposecretion of the parathyroids causes hypocalcemia, and hypersecretion results in hypercalcemia and hypophosphatemia.

## The Thymus

Although it is not always classified as an endocrine gland, the thymus plays an important role in the endocrine system and appears to be regulated by the pituitary. It is located behind the sternum and between the lungs. It is the primary central gland of the lymphatic system. The thymus secretes the hormone thymosin, which stimulates maturation of the thymic lymphocytes, or T-lymphocytes, necessary to the immune response in infants and young children. After puberty, the thymus begins to atrophy, although it does not completely disappear.

## The Islets of Langerhans

The islets of Langerhans are clusters of cells located in the pancreas. They are divided into two types of cells: $\alpha$ cells, which produce glucagon, and $\beta$ cells, which produce insulin for regulation of blood glucose.

Glucagon increases the blood glucose level by accelerating the conversion of liver glycogen into glucose. The blood sugar rises, and the islets no longer stimulate the cells to secrete glucagon. When the blood level drops again, chemical sensors in the $\alpha$ cells once again stimulate the secretion of glucagon (Fig. 32-6). Hypersecretion of glucagon can result in hyperglycemia.

Insulin increases the buildup of protein in cells by transporting glucose from the blood to the cells for energy. Insulin also decreases blood sugar by accelerating the conversion of glucose into glycogen. When blood sugar levels are high, insulin is secreted by the $\beta$ cells. When blood sugar levels are low, secretion stops.

The hyposecretion of insulin results in diabetes mellitus, with the excretion of glucose in the urine. Glucose is unable to enter the cells without insulin, so fats and proteins must be broken down into glucose, causing weight loss and the release of ketones. Increased ketone production causes a form of acidosis called *ketosis*. As lipids are transported to hungry cells from storage, lipid particles are deposited on the walls of blood vessels, causing hardening of the arteries and circulatory disorders. Dehydration, loss of sodium, and increased urine production result.

Hyperinsulinism may be due to hyperplasia of the islet cells. This condition causes a decreased blood glucose level; the secretion of GH, epinephrine, and glucagon; and the symptoms of anxiety, sweating, tremors, increased heart rate, and weakness. The lack of glucose available to the brain cells causes mental disorientation, convulsions, unconsciousness, shock, and death.

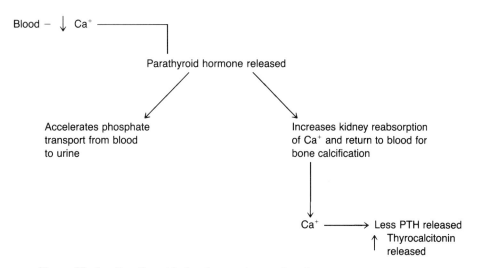

*Figure 32–5. Parathyroid gland: secretion and action.*

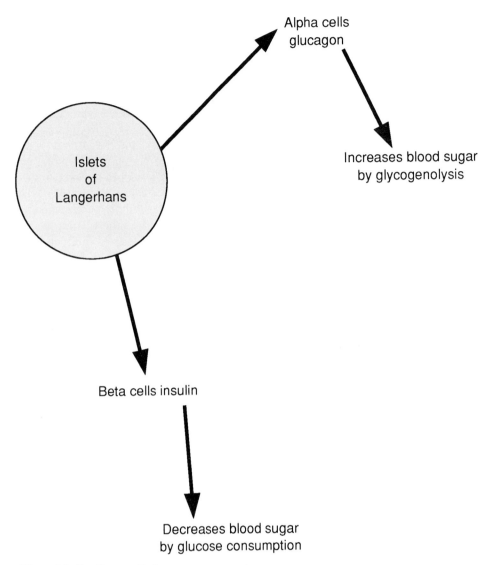

*Figure 32–6.    Pancreatic hormones.*

## The Adrenal Glands

The adrenal glands are located on the top of each kidney. Each gland has two distinct parts, the cortex and the medulla, with two separate functions.

### The Adrenal Cortex

The *adrenal cortex* is responsible for secreting three major steroid groups: the mineralocorticoids, the glucocorticoids, and the sex steroids. The ability of the adrenal gland to synthesize steroid hormones is dependent on the pituitary gland's ability to secrete the peptide hormone ACTH.

The most important mineralocorticoid is aldosterone, which regulates the reabsorption of sodium and the excretion of potassium by the kidneys. Aldosterone maintains blood pressure and extracellular fluid volume by causing the tubule of the kidneys to increase the reabsorption of sodium. This sodium reabsorption also causes water retention and the reabsorption of chloride and bicarbonate. At the same time that aldosterone removes sodium from the urine and retains it in the blood, it also takes potassium from the blood and moves it into the urine, thereby decreasing the reabsorption of potassium. It is believed that aldosterone, along with angiotensin and renin, is related to the development of hypertension (Fig. 32-7). Direct blood levels of decreased sodium or increased potassium stimulate the adrenal cortex to increase aldosterone secretion.

Aldosterone is secreted when the body is dehydrated. Receptors in the hypothalamus detect the low blood pressure caused by the small blood volume and secrete a neurohumor to the adrenal cortex that stimulates kidney cells to secrete the enzyme renin. Renin converts angiotensinogen to angiotensin I and then angiotensin II. In

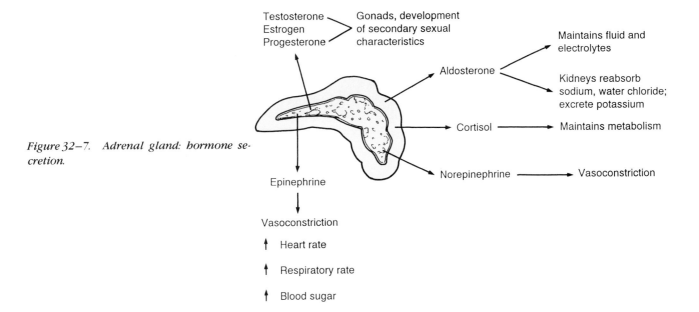

*Figure 32–7. Adrenal gland: hormone secretion.*

the adrenal cortex, the neurohumor stimulates the secretion of aldosterone, and angiotensin II stimulates aldosterone secretion. This, in turn, causes increased fluid retention and increased blood pressure.

The *glucocorticoids,* notably cortisol, are a group of hormones involved in stress reduction and glucose, protein, and fat metabolism as well as the inhibition of the inflammatory processes. The glucocorticoids ensure that sufficient energy is provided by promoting the breakdown of carbohydrates to glucose and increasing the rate at which amino acids are removed from cells to the liver. The amino acids may be converted to glucose when glycogen and fat levels are low or have been used for the synthesis of enzymes. Glucocorticoids also aid the movement of fats from cells, which enables them to be broken down for energy. These actions increase blood sugar levels.

This hyperglycemic effect makes the body respond more energetically in an effort to combat stress. Stress and low blood levels of glucocorticoids stimulate cortisol secretion. Glucocorticoids also increase the sensitivity of blood vessels to constricting chemicals that may increase blood pressure. They also are anti-inflammatory in that they decrease blood vessel dilation and edema. The hypothalamus is stimulated by glucocorticoids and secretes a neurohumor called corticotropin-releasing factor (CRF), which initiates the release of ACTH from the anterior lobe of the pituitary. ACTH is carried through the blood to the adrenal cortex, which stimulates glucocorticoid secretion.

Adrenocorticotropic hormone is released into the circulation in a pulsatile manner. It has a relatively short plasma half-life. The binding of ACTH to specific receptors in the adrenal cortex results in cortisol synthesis. The release of ACTH is affected by stress and diurnal variations. Low cortisol levels increase the rate and intensity of ACTH secretion. Chronic elevation of ACTH leads to overstimula-

tion and resultant hyperplasia of the adrenal cortex (New, del Balzo, Crawford, & Speiser, 1990).

*Gonadocorticoids,* the androgens, affect the development of secondary sexual characteristics.

Disorders of the adrenals are caused by hyposecretion or hypersecretion of a hormone. Hypersecretion of aldosterone results in decreased potassium concentration, leading to muscular paralysis (due to the neurons being unable to depolarize). It also leads to high blood pressure and edema caused by increased blood volume.

Hyposecretion of glucocorticoids results in Addison disease; hypersecretion results in Cushing syndrome. Both these conditions are discussed in this chapter.

Hypersecretion of androgens in male infants and young children causes an enlarged penis. In young men, it causes premature development of secondary sexual characteristics, advanced bone maturation, and early closure of growth plates. In full-grown men, it causes increased body hair, sexual drive, and penile size. Hypersecretion in females in utero causes masculinization and ambiguity of the genitalia. Hypersecretion in young girls causes premature sexual development, advanced bone maturation, and early closure of growth plates. In all females, it causes increased body hair, deepening of the voice, small breasts, an enlarged clitoris, and increased muscularity. Hyposecretion results in the delayed development of pubic and axillary hair for both sexes.

### The Adrenal Medulla

The *adrenal medulla* synthesizes epinephrine and norepinephrine. Epinephrine increases blood pressure by constricting blood vessels and increasing the heart rate. It also increases the respiratory rate and blood sugar level, stimulates cellular metabolism, and dilates the respiratory passageways. With stress, the hypothalamus sends nerve impulses to the sympathetic nerves, which stimulate secretion of epinephrine from the medulla.

Hypersecretion of the medullary hormones causes high blood pressure, elevated blood and urine sugar levels, increased basal metabolic rate, and sweating.

## The Gonads

The gonads in females produce estrogen and progesterone. The action of estrogens include the development and maintenance of reproductive organs; the development of breasts and secondary sex characteristics; the reabsorption of sodium and water; the increase of protein anabolism and promotion of epiphyseal closure; and the acceleration of the sex drive. Progesterone prepares the endometrium for a fertilized ovum, maintains pregnancy, and prepares breasts to secrete milk.

Follicle-stimulating hormone released by the anterior pituitary stimulates the development of the ovarian follicle and the subsequent secretion of estrogen. LH, also secreted by the anterior pituitary, stimulates the ovarian follicles to initiate ovulation and the production of progesterone. This action initiates menstruation. An elevated estrogen level inhibits the secretion of FSH.

In the male, the gonads are oval-shaped glands located in the scrotum called *testes*. They produce testosterone, which initiates and maintains secondary sexual characteristics and the development of male sex organs. Testosterone also maintains bone growth, protein anabolism, and the stimulation of the testes to produce spermatozoa. This action effects epiphyseal closure and stimulates sexual function.

Secreted at the onset of puberty, ICSH stimulates the interstitial Leydig cells to produce testosterone. High testosterone blood levels inhibit the anterior pituitary release of ICSH. When testosterone is not produced, the low blood level of testosterone stimulates the anterior pituitary to secrete ICSH. Disorders of the gonads include delayed or lack of sexual development due to hyposecretion or precocious puberty and early epiphyseal closure due to hypersecretion.

## Assessment

### History

Obtaining a detailed genetic, prenatal, birth, developmental, and nutritional history is very important in assessing endocrine function. The nurse must be sensitive to the particular concerns of each family, listen carefully, and phrase questions in a manner that will elicit complete and accurate histories (Table 32-1).

### Table 32–1. Guidelines for Assessment of Endocrine Disorders

**Prenatal History**

During the pregnancy, did the mother have any medical problems such as high blood pressure, bleeding, infections, diabetes, or endocrine disorders?
Did the mother take any medications?
Did the mother take any street drugs?
How much alcohol did the mother drink?
Does the mother smoke?
Was the mother on a special diet or hospitalized during the pregnancy?
Did the pregnancy last the full 9 months?

**Birth History**

How long was the labor and what type of delivery was it?
Were there any complications during the labor and delivery?
Was anesthesia used?
Were forceps used?
Was the baby born head first?
What were the baby's gestational age, height, and weight at birth?
What were the baby's Apgar scroes at birth?
Did the baby cry?
Was the baby blue?
Was the baby given oxygen?
How did the baby look at birth?
Did the baby look different than the mother had expected?
How many days did the baby stay in the nursery?
Did the baby have any infections or jaundice?
Was the baby breast or bottle fed?
How did the baby feed; were there any problems?

**Past Medical History**

Has the child had any infections? How were they treated, at what age, and for how long?
Has the child been hospitalized or had any operations?
Does the child have any allergies?
Has the child grown steadily?
What has the child's weight gain been?
Has the child had any immunizations? Which ones and when?
When did the child begin to walk?
How did the child's development compare with that of other children of the same age?
When did the child begin sexual development?
How did the child do in school?

**Family History**

What are the mother's and father's ages and state of health?
What are the siblings' ages, sexes, and state of health?
Are the grandparents alive? What is their state of health?
Does anyone in the family have diabetes, thyroid problems, or any endocrine disorder?

*(continued)*

*TABLE 32–1. Guidelines for Assessment of Endocrine Disorders (Continued)*

**Present History–Nutrition History**

How is the child's appetite?

What did the child eat yesterday? (24-hr. recall)

Was that a typical day's diet?

How much does the child drink?

Does the child use a lot of salt or sugar on food?

How often does the child urinate?

What are the child's bowel patterns?

What is the child's sleep pattern?

How does the child's development compare with that of other children of the same age

Does the child like school?

How has the child's progress been in school?

Does the child have friends?

What does the child like to play?

Does the child engage in much physical activity?

Does the child get tired more easily than other children of the same age?

Has there been a recent change in the child's activity level?

How does the child deal with stress?

Does the child get along with others?

How does the child's sexual development compare with that of others of the same age?

Do the parents have any questions or concerns?

Does the child have headaches, dizziness, or a general feeling of weakness?

Has the child ever had any seizures?

Does the child have any bone or joint pain?

Has the child experienced any visual or hearing change?

Does the child develop any type of rash?

Have there been any recent changes or problems?

## Physical Examination

Physical assessment of endocrine function should focus on bone development, facial characteristics, and secondary sex characteristics. The physical examination begins with assessment of general appearance and body proportions. The nurse observes whether body proportions are appropriate for chronological and maturational age. Growth failure or excessive growth can be identified when height and weight are plotted regularly on standardized growth charts. The nurse also observes the child's facial features. A round face, flattened nasal bridge, large protruding tongue, low anterior hairline, and delayed dentition can be signs of an endocrine dysfunction. A careful eye examination is performed in assessing for bulging eyes, a condition called *exophthalmos.*

The genitalia and secondary sex characteristics are assessed at each well-child visit. Newborn genitalia are assessed at birth to determine if ambiguous genitalia or hypospadias exist. In addition, male external genitalia are assessed for descended testes and length, diameter, and pigmentation of the penile tissue. Female external genitalia are assessed for fusion of the labia and abnormal size of the clitoris.

Secondary sexual characteristics are assessed using the Tanner staging scale (see Chap. 16). Breast development and pubic and axillary hair are assessed in the female. Pubic and scrotum hair, as well as growth of the penis, are assessed in the male.

Since endocrine disorders affect skin texture, the nurse must assess the skin for thickness, dryness, coarseness, hyperpigmentation, flushing, abdominal striae, maculopapular skin rashes, jaundice, and mottling or sweating. The nurse also observes the nails for brittleness and cracking.

In addition, blood pressure, respiratory rate, and apical pulse rates must be obtained. The nurse performs a complete neurological examination, testing all cranial nerves and deep tendon reflexes. Endocrine disorders often manifest themselves in alterations in the neurological system. The breath odor is assessed for a fruity smell that is associated with diabetes mellitus.

## Diagnostic Procedures

The results of blood, urine, and radiographic studies are used in the diagnosis of specific endocrine disorders. These tests are discussed with each condition in this chapter.

## Nursing Diagnosis

The following nursing diagnoses may apply to endocrine disorders. Planning, implementation, and evaluation of nursing care for each of the diagnoses is included in the discussions of specific disorders when the diagnoses apply.

*Pattern 1: Exchanging*
- Altered nutrition: less than body requirements
- Altered patterns of urinary elimination
- Altered renal or cardiopulmonary tissue perfusion
- Constipation
- Decreased cardiac output
- Diarrhea
- Fluid volume deficit
- High risk for fluid volume excess
- High risk for fluid volume deficit
- High risk for impaired skin integrity
- High risk for infection
- High risk for injury
- Impaired skin integrity

- Impaired tissue integrity
- Ineffective airway clearance
- Ineffective breathing pattern

*Pattern 3: Relating*
- Altered family processes
- High risk for altered parenting
- Impaired social interaction
- High risk for social isolation

*Pattern 5: Choosing*
- Ineffective family coping: compromised
- Ineffective individual coping

*Pattern 6: Moving*
- High risk for activity intolerance
- Altered growth and development
- Diversional activity deficit
- Fatigue
- Impaired physical mobility
- Impaired swallowing
- Sleep pattern disturbance

*Pattern 7: Perceiving*
- Body image disturbance
- Hopelessness
- High risk for self-esteem disturbance
- Visual sensory alterations

*Pattern 8: Knowing*
- Altered thought processes

*Pattern 9: Feeling*
- Anxiety
- Fear
- Pain

## Planning Nursing Care

A primary goal for the family of a child with an endocrine disorder is to maintain or reestablish functioning at a prediagnosis level. The nurse should ascertain how the family perceives the change and what they have done in the past when change occurred. It is important to identify the family's support systems and to determine how they have coped in the past. With this information, the nurse can help the family to develop alternative ways of dealing with the situation and help them to expand their coping mechanisms.

The nurse can build on the parents' strengths by providing information about the endocrine disorder. In this way, the parents become active contributors to the development of the care plan for their child.

Siblings are also affected by the illness of a brother or sister. They may resent the additional chores they must now assume or the attention and special care the sick child receives. The sibling may feel unloved or frightened by a sudden lack of limit-setting while their parents are preoccupied. The healthy siblings may also feel embarrassed by having a "sick" sibling or by changes in their sibling's physical appearance, which is a common feature of endocrine dysfunction.

Nurses can help siblings verbalize their feelings and concerns and can also help the parents discuss these feelings with their children. Parents should be encouraged to spend time alone with other children, offering positive feedback and letting them know they are loved and important.

## Developmental Considerations

Some endocrine disorders require hospitalization or long-term home management. The child's response to the disorder or treatment regimen varies depending on age and developmental level.

Hospitalization may be damaging to the infant's development of a sense of trust, unless steps are taken to ensure consistent provision of care and time for relaxed parent–infant interactions. It is important for the nurse to encourage family members to hold and cuddle the infant and to provide alternate types of stimulation.

Since toddlers are developing motor and verbal skills and are struggling for autonomy, hospitalization can prove especially limiting to their developmental progress. An endocrine disorder may lead the parents to become more involved in the child's care or make them less willing to allow the child choices in daily activities. The nurse can help the child and family by providing the toddler with choices, when possible, to give the child some sense of control. It is also important to encourage the toddlers to feed, dress, and toilet themselves to the degree possible. This not only lets children know that they are in control but also helps prevent overprotection by the parents.

Preschool-aged children are focused on developing peer relationships and taking pride in their accomplishments. They seek approval of peers, teachers, and parents. The nurse should teach parents how to continue to foster the child's motor and social skills through a self-paced, goal-directed program that sets realistic goals and encourages a sense of enthusiasm in achieving them.

The school-aged child's self-concept is greatly influenced by the level of peer acceptance the child experiences. Children with endocrine disorders may be classified as different because of changes in physical appearance or lifestyle, and they may not gain peer acceptance, leading to feelings of inferiority. Nurses can help families by openly discussing the difficulties that these children are experiencing. Children wish to be like their peers, but they may have less energy, a different diet, or a different physical appearance. A primary goal is to help the child recognize differences and strengths and foster those strengths in relation to peers (such as in computers, art, or humor). Nurses should encourage children to use the telephone during hospitalization or home care to maintain contact with their peers. Helping the parents understand the needs of children in this age group should prevent conflict and parental overprotection.

Adolescents are striving for their own identity apart from their parents and seek peer approval. An endocrine disorder may increase parental involvement in the adolescent's life, a situation that often meets with much resentment and conflict. Mother–daughter relationships in diabetic adolescents have the potential for serious conflict. The daughter may resist plans of care and diet and insulin schedules in response to her own feeling of not wanting to be different. The situation may spiral when the mother becomes more involved and the child increases her resistance. Parents need to understand their own emotional difficulty in "letting go" to permit the adolescent to manage the disorder. Adolescents may be ambivalent about their care because they do not want to be different from their peers. They may resist adhering to schedules and resent being checked up on. A clear-cut "role contract" can be set up to help prevent conflict, overdependence, and overprotectiveness.

## Acute Care Considerations

The hospitalization of a child presents a crisis for the child and family. This can occur at the time of diagnosis, surgery, or when a major, life-threatening alteration in functioning occurs. Hospitalization also presents the family with a different, unfamiliar routine that is coupled with pain and child–parent separations.

The nurse can help the family by keeping the child and the family informed as much as possible about the endocrine disorder and the child's progress. The nurse should explain, in understandable terms, what will be done and how it will done.

The health care team should share with the parents their own experiences of the child's strengths and special characteristics. Parents should be encouraged to stay with the child to keep separation at a minimum. Explaining to the parent and child that this disorder is not a result of anything they did helps to diminish guilt felt by the parents and fosters acceptance of the situation by the parents and the child.

Play can help children act out their feelings of separation, anger, and resistance to the new routine. Through play, children regain control over the environment and can begin to participate in the plan of care.

## Chronic Care Considerations

Endocrine disorders are often chronic illnesses that have lifelong implications and that also may carry genetic implications for the future.

At the time of the diagnosis, the child and family may react with shock and denial. It is important to help the family refrain from blaming one another or themselves, especially if the disorder is genetic. Some parents live with the constant grief and fear of having a child who may not develop fully or who may die. It is important to help the family to deal with their concerns so that they can work toward maintaining a sense of normalcy. The child's self-esteem can be enhanced by fostering realistic life goals, developing strengths and autonomy, and encouraging social activities.

## Home Care Considerations

Most children with endocrine disorders are managed at home. Parents and children may have fears related to their ability to manage the illness effectively; and education and follow-up are the keys to success in home care. Teaching parents and children to manage their care also gives them back the control and individuality that they had before the disorder. Frequent health maintenance follow-up focuses on normalcy, which, together with knowledge of emergency access, helps keep the family and health care team in partnership.

It is important to help the family define their support systems. This provides the parents with a support network that can help provide the occasional, much-needed respite care. In addition, support groups for children and families can make families realize they are not alone. Families feeling socially isolated can share their concerns with a group and have their feelings and concerns validated.

The parent's role in caring for the chronically ill child cannot be overemphasized. Parental acceptance of the disorder allows the child to reach the heights of his or her potential.

## Nursing Interventions

### Client and Parent Education

The functioning of the endocrine glands and their relationship to each other, and the actions of hormones and their various diagnostic and therapeutic regimes, may seem almost incomprehensible to the child and parents. Therefore, effective educational strategies are of the greatest importance.

If the child is experiencing fatigue, the nurse can help the child and the parents to understand that this is expected with the particular condition the child has, and that they can mutually plan rest periods during the day. The nurse should teach them that the environment should be quiet, with minimal external stimuli. If frequent urination is a problem, the child should be encouraged to void before the rest period.

When body image, self-esteem, or self-confidence present problems, the nurse can assist parents in communicating with the school nurse and teachers. Information about the child's high energy levels or easy fatigability should be shared with those who will be frequently relating to the child. Rest periods during the school day can be planned. In the case of very young children, parents need to be advised to provide appropriate stimulation (play time) during the child's periods of high energy. The older child should learn how to maximize high energy periods by balancing them with rest periods.

Nurses must be familiar with diagnostic and therapeutic procedures associated with endocrine dysfunction so that they can reassure parents by explaining the reason for and steps of procedures. Nurses must cooperate with physicians in determining the appropriate educational approach. Questions must be answered honestly. Sometimes, role-playing is a useful anticipatory teaching tool as well as a means for emotional ventilation of fears and anxieties.

When pain is a factor, the nurse must discuss methods of pain management, including pharmacological management. If family coping is compromised, the nurse must assess the family's typical coping strategies and their current strategies and work with them to develop positive coping mechanisms. Coping strategies may be compromised by interpersonal conflicts, inadequate parenting, a lack of family involvement, too much involvement, or financial strain. It is important that the family develop confidence in their ability to cope. This requires an ongoing assessment because the variables may fluctuate during the course of the disease.

Interrelationships with siblings may be altered. Parents need to be taught not only how to relate to the affected child in a manner that is not overprotective but also how to schedule time and attention to meet the needs of other children in the family. Parents need to recognize that the siblings may develop feelings of guilt or jealousy and that these feelings may be expressed in play or drawings.

When nutrition is a problem, a 24-hour dietary history is obtained and discussed with the parents and child. Diet modifications can be mutually planned once everyone understands the rationale.

Generally, teaching sessions for children should not last longer than 15 minutes; parental sessions should last about 45 minutes. It is best to plan a teaching sequence, with each session building on the earlier sessions.

## Drug Therapy

A variety of drug therapies are used in the treatment of endocrine dysfunctions. Each is discussed in relation to the disorders presented in this chapter. In general, nursing interventions involving drug therapy include the safe administration of medications and instructing the child and parents on the expected drug actions and techniques of administration of the prescribed medication.

## Nutrition

In addition to basic good nutrition, there are specifically designed nutritional programs that are especially effective for certain endocrine dysfunctions. Nutritional programs used in the therapeutic management of specific endocrine disorders are discussed with the disorders. Often, a registered dietitian works with other members of the health care team and the client and family to design a program aimed at optimal growth and development of the client.

## Endocrine Problems of Infancy and Early Childhood

### Hypopituitarism

#### Pathophysiology

*Hypopituitarism* (also called *dwarfism*) can result in a deficiency of the anterior pituitary growth hormone (GH or STH), which is known as growth hormone deficiency. There are several known causes for this deficiency (Table 32-2). Hypopituitarism has been found to occur in association with midline facial and central nervous system developmental defects, such as cleft lip and palate and septooptic dysplasia (Dean & Winter, 1989). The child with hypopituitarism has a normal height and weight at birth, but the growth rate diminishes in the first 2 years of life. Although the child is short in stature, body proportions are appropriate. Sexual development is usually delayed. If the condition is accompanied by a lack of adequate gonadotropins, sexual maturation will never occur.

#### Medical Diagnosis and Management

Because GH is secreted in a pulsatile manner, a random GH level is of little significance. A single low GH level may indicate GH deficiency or may be normal in a child who is not experiencing one of the few GH peaks that occur throughout the day. Therefore, in order to assess GH secretion, pharmacological agents must be given to stimulate the pituitary to secrete growth hormone. The usual provocative agents are L-dopa, insulin-induced hypoglycemia, arginine, and Glucagon. Serial blood levels are drawn after the administration of the drugs to determine the peak levels of GH secretion. Levels below 10 ng/mL after two provocative tests establish the diagnosis of growth hormone deficiency. Medical treatment includes hormone replacement with biosynthetic hormone injections. During the first year of treatment, the child usually grows 7.5 to 10 cm; growth in the subsequent years is usually 5 to 7.5 cm per year. If the cause of the hormone deficiency is a tumor, it must be surgically removed.

## Table 32–2.  Causes of Hypopituitarism

Genetic disorders (GH gene is located on the long arm of chromosome 17)

Trauma

Infection

Removal of the pituitary gland (hypophysectomy)

Nonsecreting pituitary tumors

Tumors that impinge on the pituitary because of their proximity

Idiopathic—no organic lesion can be found

Vascular lesions

### Nursing Assessment and Diagnosis

Children with growth hormone deficiency may have a particular facies: frontal bossing, depression of the nasal bridge, and a "doll-like" appearance. Height and weight curves plotted over time are important indicators of growth problems. Nurses should be alert for signs that these measurements are decreasing in velocity in the first 2 years of life. Children with cleft palate and cleft lip must be observed carefully. Male newborns with micropenis and cryptorchidism should also be assessed regularly. The early identification of this disorder is a nursing responsibility.

Because there is a possible genetic component to this disorder, the nurse should take a careful family history. Parental concerns and observations of the child should also be elicited.

Nursing diagnoses for the child with hypopituitarism might include the following:

- Altered growth and development related to a deficiency in GH
- Body image disturbance related to altered growth and associated feelings of being different
- Ineffective individual coping related to lack of family support
- Ineffective family coping: compromised related to difficulty adjusting to child's prognosis

### Planning and Implementing Nursing Care

The nurse must reinforce the importance of long-term management of the disorder. Hormonal levels must be monitored during periods of growth and illness so that replacement therapy dosages can be regulated. Height and weight measurements must be recorded precisely on a growth chart. The child should grow at least 5 cm per year. If this level of growth is not achieved, the child must be reevaluated and radiographs taken to determine if premature epiphyseal closure of long bones has occurred.

Children may develop problems with self-concept because their short stature makes them appear younger than their chronological ages, and so they may be treated as if they are younger. Parents, teachers, and care-givers must be encouraged to treat these children in a manner appropriate for chronological age. Parents should encourage children to develop interests and friendships with children of their age.

### Evaluating Nursing Care

With appropriate intervention and consistent compliance with the medication regimen, it is usually expected that the child will be able to achieve an appropriate height. The child should be able to develop a positive self-image, to progress in school, and to have age-appropriate interests. The parents may need continued support over the long period of childhood to help alleviate their anxiety and make positive family adjustments to their child's illness.

## Hypothyroidism

Hypothyroidism is caused by a deficiency in thyroid hormone, which results in a hypometabolic state. The clinical features of hypothyroidism vary depending on the cause and degree of deficiency. Two major types of hypothyroidism affect children: congenital and acquired. One of the most severe forms of congenital hypothyroidism is *cretinism,* which is manifested by dwarfism, mental deficiency, puffy facial features, a large tongue, muscular incoordination, umbilical hernia, and dry skin. Because neonatal screening for congenital hypothyroidism is mandated in the newborn nursery, these severe symptoms are rare.

*Acquired hypothyroidism* is hypothyroidism that occurs in a child who was previously euthyroid. It can occur as the result of medical treatment for other disorders. Children receiving radiation for cancer of the head, neck, and spine, for instance, may have the side effect of primary thyroid insufficiency and a deficiency in thyroid-releasing hormone.

## Congenital Hypothyroidism
### Pathophysiology

Congenital hypothyroidism results from an inadequate fetal production of thyroid hormone. About midway in gestation, the fetal hypothalamic–pituitary–thyroid axis begins to function independently of the mother, and the thyroid gland is able to trap iodine from ingested food to produce $T_4$, the primary thyroid hormone. Any malfunction in the fetus's ability to manufacture its own $T_4$ can prove damaging to fetal development. This condition occurs twice as often as phenylketonuria.

Congenital hypothyroidism occurs in about 1 in 4000 newborns and at a 2.5–3:1 female/male ratio (Coody, 1984). Defective or abnormal formation of the thyroid is the primary cause. Neonates can experience transient congenital hypothyroidism when mothers with hyperthyroidism receive antithyroid medication, such as propylthiouracil, which crosses the placenta and blocks fetal thyroid synthesis. Transient congenital hypothyroidism can also occur if the mother ingests excessive amounts of iodine.

In some children with congenital hypothyroidism, limited production of thyroid hormone may prevent the clinical features of the disease from appearing until the child is much older, up to age 5 years.

## Medical Diagnosis and Management

Most children with congenital hypothyroidism are identified early because of state-wide mandatory newborn screening tests, which evaluate blood levels of thyroid hormones obtained with a heel stick puncture. A thyroid scan may also be performed using a radioactive iodine ($^{123}$I) uptake measurement. Knee radiographs are done to determine if the normal ossification of the epiphyses of the distal femur and proximal tibia has occurred. Delayed bone maturation occurs when low levels of $T_4$ were present during fetal life.

Medical treatment should be initiated as quickly as possible. If untreated, congenital hypothyroidism causes intellectual impairment and neurological dysfunction. Levothyroxine is the drug of choice. Although linear and skeletal growth respond well to this treatment, ultimate intellectual ability is related to the age when treatment is begun. If treatment is delayed beyond the age of 3 to 6 months, the prognosis for normal intelligence is poor (Bacon, Spencer, Hopwood, & Kelch, 1990). Pharmacological treatment continues throughout the child's lifetime, with dosages adjusted as the child grows.

Follow-up examination is important, and the child should be reexamined after 4 weeks, then every 3 months in the first year. Developmental assessments, such as the Bayley Scale of Infant Development and the Vineland Social Maturity Scale, should be performed periodically.

## Nursing Assessment and Diagnosis

A careful history, with particular attention to feeding, stooling, and behavior patterns is very important. The nurse should be alert for the history of an unusually quiet, good baby who sleeps a great deal. A developmental assessment and weight and height measurements should be performed. On physical examination, a protuberant abdomen (a possible indicator of an umbilical hernia), a thick tongue, or dry skin may be found. The fontanelles (anterior and posterior) may be larger than expected. In particular, a posterior fontanelle of greater than 0.5 cm should be interpreted as an important sign (Bacon, Spencer, Hopwood, & Kelch, 1990).

Nursing diagnoses for hypothyroidism might include the following:

- Constipation related to decreased gastrointestinal motility

- Altered growth and development related to deficient thyroid hormone
- High risk for altered parenting related to fears regarding the potential outcome of the condition and the long-term treatment
- Altered nutrition: less than body requirements related to a lack of appetite

## Planning and Implementing Nursing Care

The nurse must prepare the child and family for diagnostic procedures early in the care period. This includes clarifying and expanding the child's and parents' understanding of the medical diagnosis as well as teaching them about the plan for care. Parents may need assistance with the techniques of administering the medication. Levothyroxine, a tablet, can be crushed and mixed with a teaspoon of water or formula and administered with an eye dropper. The medication should be given 20 to 30 minutes before feeding to reduce the possibility of the infant vomiting it up after feeding. When the child is older, the crushed medication can be added to a spoonful of cereal or fruit. Parents must be instructed about the importance of administering the medication every day. If a dose is missed, a double dose should be given the following day (Coody, 1984). As children grow, they must also understand the necessity for taking the medication daily for their entire lives.

The child's appetite and activity should improve with treatment. With a balanced diet, including sufficient fiber, constipation should be minimized. Parents may need to readjust to a child who may be more active and cry more than before treatment began. They may need help in relating to an active child rather than the docile child to whom they had become accustomed.

Parents are concerned about hereditary aspects of the condition. They should be informed that inheritance is dependent on the cause. For example, inborn errors of thyroid hormone synthesis are autosomal recessive, and siblings have a one in four chance of being affected. Thyroid dysgenesis has only a 1 in 4000 chance, and hypothalamic–pituitary hypothyroidism is sporadic (Coody, 1984).

## Evaluating Nursing Care

A positive outcome would be the child's attainment of maximum physical and mental ability. Compliance with the treatment plan and consistent follow-up by the caregivers are also positive outcomes. Another evaluation measure might be that the parents receive genetic counseling, if indicated. Long-term follow-up includes monitoring blood thyroid hormone levels and assessing physical and mental development throughout the child's life.

## Acquired Hypothyroidism

### Pathophysiology

The most frequent cause of acquired hypothyroidism in children and adolescents is chronic lymphocytic thyroiditis (Hashimoto thyroiditis), which usually occurs after the age of 6 years. Acquired hypothyroidism may be due to a congenitally defective thyroid that furnishes sufficient amounts of hormone early in life but produces inadequate amounts later in childhood. Another cause is iodine deficiency. *Endemic goiter* is the most common thyroid disease worldwide, but it is now only rarely seen in the United States because of the addition of iodine to salt and other foods (Coody, 1984). A *goiter* is a hypertrophic thyroid gland, usually seen as a pronounced swelling in the neck.

The onset of acquired hypothyroidism is insidious. Sometimes, the only sign is short stature. Signs of acquired hypothyroidism are found in Table 32-3. Even though the delayed Achilles tendon reflex is not always reliable, it is one of the most useful diagnostic findings (Bacon, Spencer, Hopwood, & Kelch, 1990).

### Medical Diagnosis and Management

Medical diagnosis is confirmed by laboratory studies, including $T_4$ and $T_3$ (radioimmunoassay) and TSH. Measurement of triiodothyronine ($T_3$) resin uptake helps to rule out the possibility of a deficiency of thyroid-binding globulin as a cause of decreased $T_4$. Other studies may be done to evaluate pituitary–adrenal function or GH deficiency. Bone radiographs of the hand reveal significant delays in bony maturation. Many young hypothyroid girls have multiple small pelvic cysts, which are detected by ultrasound (Bacon, Spencer, Hopwood, & Kelch, 1990).

Administration of synthetic L-thyroxine is the medical

### Table 32–3. Signs of Acquired Hypothyroidism in Childhood

Short stature
Lethargy
Tendency to gain weight
Intolerance to cold
Increased need for sleep
Poor school performance
Slow growth of nails and scalp hair
Face appears dull and puffy
Hair is coarse and brittle
Skin may be dry and cool
Complexion is sallow
Delayed Achilles tendon reflex
Precocious puberty

treatment of choice. Periodic $T_4$ and TSH tests are administered biannually once the maintenance dose has been established. Normal height is usually achieved within 1 to 2 years of treatment.

### Nursing Assessment and Diagnosis

Nursing assessment should include a thorough history and physical examination. The history should include information regarding appetite, sleep habits, sensitivity to cold, and school performance. A history of medications and food should be used to ascertain iodine intake. A familial history should include whether there are any family members who have had thyroid or pituitary disorders.

Physical examination includes assessment of height and weight, with measurements plotted at regular intervals on growth grids. The nurse should examine the neck for a palpable thyroid and observe for neck swelling. General assessment includes facial features, for color and puffiness; hair texture, for coarseness or brittleness; and skin, for dryness. The nurse should observe for signs of secondary sex characteristics at an inappropriately early age and should check tendon reflexes.

Nursing diagnoses for acquired hypothyroidism might include the following:

- Fatigue related to lack of thyroid hormone
- Sleep pattern disturbance related to increased sleep needs with thyroid deficiency
- Altered growth and development related to decreased thyroid hormone production
- Body image disturbance related to changing facial and body appearance
- High risk for altered parenting related to child's altered physical appearance and activity level

### Planning and Implementing Nursing Care

The child and parents need to be instructed regarding the treatment regimen and expected outcomes. Parents need to know that an increase in growth and reversal of other symptoms usually occur a few months after treatment. They need to be reassured that permanent brain damage does not occur after 2 or 3 years of age. With proper treatment, the child should achieve normal intellectual functioning. Parents should also be informed, and encouraged to inform teachers and others, that as the child becomes less lethargic and more active, a reduced attention span and an increased activity level may be noted in school.

### Evaluating Nursing Care

With treatment, physical changes can appear to be quite dramatic. Compliance with the treatment program must be carefully monitored. Parental and child interactions are expected to change over time as the child increases activity and also progresses through expected developmental stages.

## Hypoparathyroidism

### Pathophysiology

*Hypoparathyroidism* may cause a deficiency of PTH. The PTH deficiency results in low serum calcium and high serum phosphorus levels, which cause seizures and *tetany* (muscle spasms), especially in the face, hands, feet, and larynx. Hypoparathyroidism may develop from (1) parathyroidectomy or thyroidectomy; (2) hypoplasia or aplasia (DiGeorge syndrome) of the parathyroid glands; (3) transient PTH deficiency in the infant born to a mother with hyperparathyroidism or diabetes mellitus; (4) transient PTH deficiency in infants with immature parathyroid glands who are fed milk formulas with a high phosphate/calcium ratio; (5) autoimmune phenomena; or (6) an inherited X-linked recessive trait (seen in males). *Pseudohypoparathyroidism* is an X-linked dominant trait in which there is an increased production of PTH, but the tissues do not respond to it. This also results in low serum calcium and high serum phosphorus levels, despite the high serum PTH.

### Medical Diagnosis and Management

The classical neuromuscular signs and symptoms of hypoparathyroidism are tetany, muscle pain and cramps, numbness and tingling of the hands and feet, laryngeal or carpopedal spasms, and seizures. The teeth are soft, erupt late, and have irregular enamel formation. The skin is dry and coarse, the hair brittle, and the nails thinned with transverse grooves. Cataracts, keratoconjunctivitis, photophobia, and blepharospasm may be present. Nausea, vomiting, diarrhea, and constipation may appear due to gastrointestinal system irritation. Mental retardation develops if the condition is not diagnosed and treated early.

Children with pseudohypoparathyroidism have the same signs and symptoms but have a higher incidence of mental retardation. They are short in stature, with round faces, short necks, and short, stubby fingers.

Laboratory findings show decreased serum calcium (5 to 7 mg/dL) and increased serum phosphorus (6 mg/dL). Levels of plasma PTH are low, except in pseudohypoparathyroidism, where they are high. Bone radiograph findings are usually normal, although some areas may have increased bone density.

For management of tetany or convulsions, intravenous calcium gluconate, with concurrent administration of vitamin D or dihydrotachysterol, is given to increase calcium levels. Long-term maintenance includes oral calcium supplements and dihydrotachysterol or large doses of vitamin D. A high-calcium and low-phosphorus diet is recommended. The levels of serum calcium, phosphorus, and vitamin D are monitored frequently to determine the therapeutic efficacy and to avoid renal damage. Vitamin D toxicity is a potential complication; therefore, any complaints of abdominal cramps, nausea and vomiting, increased urination, dizziness, headache, photophobia, or tinnitus should be noted.

### Nursing Assessment and Diagnosis

A major nursing responsibility in the care of the child with hypoparathyroidism is the recognition of hypocalcemia. Assessment for unexplained tetany or convulsions, irritability, numbness and tingling of the hands and feet, and gastrointestinal symptoms indicates the need for laboratory assessment of serum calcium. The physical examination may show positive Chvostek and/or Trousseau signs. Frequent assessment of serum calcium and vitamin D levels can prevent potential hypercalcemia and vitamin D toxicity during therapeutic management.

Nursing diagnoses for hypoparathyroidism might include the following:

- Altered growth and development related to lack of serum calcium
- High risk for injury related to seizures
- Ineffective airway clearance related to laryngeal spasms
- Ineffective family coping: compromised, related to an unanticipated illness in family member

### Planning, Implementing, and Evaluating Nursing Care

Much of the planning and implementation of nursing care for the child with hypoparathyroidism is related to the physical manifestations of hypocalcemia. Nursing care for altered growth and development includes frequent assessment of the infant or child for signs and symptoms of hypocalcemia; intravenous infusion of calcium gluconate (this must be done carefully, since extravasation causes tissue sloughing; closely monitoring the heart rate (if the heart rate falls below 100 bpm, the infusion of calcium gluconate is discontinued); recording the success of a high calcium diet, if ordered; and noting the signs and symptoms of altered growth and development. The evaluation criteria for this diagnosis include the following: the child is alert and shows signs of normal growth and development; and there are no signs of hypocalcemia.

Planning and implementating nursing care for the child who is at high risk for injury includes practicing seizure and safety precautions at all times; reducing environmental stimuli; avoiding unnecessary handling of the infant; and discussing with the parents reasons for minimal holding of infant during the acute phase of illness. The evaluation criteria for this nursing diagnosis are that the child is resting quietly and that seizure and safety precautions are in effect.

Nursing care for the nursing diagnosis of ineffective airway clearance includes: assessing for laryngospasm, such as tightness in the throat, hoarseness, and stridor; noting signs of possible respiratory distress; and placing a tracheotomy set and injectable calcium gluconate at the bedside for emergency use. The evaluation criteria for this nursing diagnosis include the following: the child is in no respiratory distress; and a tracheotomy set and calcium gluconate are at the bedside.

The nursing care for ineffective family coping includes encouraging the parents, after the acute phase, to hold and feed the infant in order to reestablish parent–infant attachment; providing emotional support to parents and encouraging expressions of anxiety or fears; and facilitating parent–infant bonding by encouraging frequent visits and telephone progress reports. The evaluation criteria for this nursing diagnosis include the following: the family openly expresses their feelings about the illness; and they telephone frequently, visit, and ask for nursing reports on the infant's progress.

## Diabetes Insipidus

### Pathophysiology

*Neurogenic diabetes insipidus* (DI) is a disorder of the posterior pituitary gland that results from a deficient secretion of ADH (vasopressin). Many cases are idiopathic, but others can be attributed to tumors (especially craniopharyngiomas), infections (meningitis or encephalitis), trauma (accidental or surgical), or vascular anomalies (aneurysms). When ADH secretion is deficient, the kidneys fail to reabsorb water, causing fluid loss. *Nephrogenic* DI, a rare, sex-linked hereditary disorder, is caused by the unresponsiveness of the renal tubules of the kidneys to normal secretions of ADH. Fluid is lost in large amounts.

The major symptoms of DI are *polyuria* (excessive urine output) and *polydipsia* (excessive thirst). Other symptoms might include dehydration with fever and weight loss, increased irritability, vomiting, constipation, or even hypovolemic shock. The 24-hour intake and output is increased, and the urine is usually pale with a specific-gravity value no greater than 1.005. Clinically, this entity may be confused with diabetes mellitus, but in DI there is no glycosuria.

### Medical Diagnosis and Management

For diagnostic purposes, a 6-hour water deprivation test is performed in the hospital. Clients with DI, even with fluid deprivation, have a high volume of urine and low osmolarity; the specific-gravity value fails to rise in spite of rising serum osmolarity. When Pitressin, the commercial form of ADH, is given, both the specific-gravity value and osmolarity of the urine rise quickly. These positive responses to

Pitressin may be used to help establish the diagnosis. Unresponsiveness to Pitressin usually indicates nephrogenic DI.

As always, the purpose and procedure of each test must be carefully explained to the parents. The health team must monitor the client's pulse, blood pressure, weight, urine output, urine specific-gravity value, serum sodium, potassium, blood urea nitrogen (BUN), calcium, and creatinine. Rising serum osmolality is a danger sign in the dehydrated child and requires termination of the fluid restriction.

During hospitalization, the child should be given free access to water to prevent dehydration and shock. In neurogenic DI, a common drug therapy is intramuscular injections of ADH (e.g., Pitressin Tannate) every 2 to 3 days. This medication must be warmed to body temperature and shaken in the ampule. The oil must be injected deeply into the muscle with a 1-inch, 20- to 22-gauge needle, followed by vigorous massage of the area. The injection sites should be systematically rotated. Another effective alternative is a simple, painless form of synthetic vasopressin, desmopressin (DDAVP), which can be given by intranasal spray twice a day.

In contrast, children with nephrogenic DI do not benefit from ADH therapy. Management includes dietary restriction of salt and protein, use of thiazide diuretics, and provision of adequate water to maintain normal osmolarity of body fluids.

### Nursing Assessment and Diagnosis

A careful nursing history can alert the nurse to the presence of DI. Inquiry about any signs of increased irritability relieved by water feedings, or increased frequency of diaper changes, can help document the illness. During hospitalization, the nurse should assess the child carefully for signs of dehydration, including poor skin turgor, fever, thirst, and polyuria; and rising serum sodium, BUN, hematocrit, and urine specific-gravity levels. The child's weight should be assessed daily before breakfast to determine weight loss that is greater than 3% to 5%. By providing only measured amounts of fluids at the bedside, an accurate intake assessment can be recorded. Hourly assessment of urinary output must also be accurately recorded.

Nursing diagnoses for DI might include the following:

- High risk for fluid volume deficit related to excessive urine output
- Altered family processes related to a child's chronic illness

### Planning and Implementing Nursing Care

The nursing care plan should focus on the potential for dehydration in the child. Nursing care for high risk for fluid volume deficit includes closely monitoring for dehydration (checking for poor skin turgor, dry mucous membranes, sunken fontanelles, weight loss, absence of tears, tachycardia, and low urine specific-gravity; administration of Pitressin or DDAVP, as ordered; and monitoring for adverse effects of Pitressin (hypertension, hyponatremia, or water intoxication) or DDAVP (pallor, abdominal cramps, and nausea).

Nursing care for altered family processes includes encouraging the parents to talk about their potential feelings of anger, guilt, or fear; and helping the parents to realize that the treatment is lifelong.

### Evaluating Nursing Care

Evaluation of nursing care for the child with DI focuses on the level of success achieved in resolving the specific nursing diagnoses. The child should appear well hydrated, with urinary output, urine specific-gravity values, serum electrolyte levels, and skin turgor within age-appropriate limits.

The parents should be able to give correct information about DI and to correctly demonstrate how to prepare and administer vasopressin. They should be able to identify the signs of underdosage and overdosage of vasopressin. Older children and their parents should realize that thirst is a protective mechanism and should allow the child to drink as much as desired because limiting intake does not decrease the urinary output. If nasal spray is prescribed, the parents should have extra nasal spray available and use it when urinary output increases.

The family members should be able to openly discuss their feelings about the illness.

## Hypoglycemia

### Pathophysiology

*Hypoglycemia,* or low blood sugar, is a frequent complication of diabetes mellitus (discussed later in this chapter), but it is also a disorder that affects some newborns, especially those born to diabetic mothers. It is a serious disorder because the brain uses glucose for metabolism and normal functioning. Prolonged hypoglycemia may cause irreparable brain damage.

### Medical Diagnosis and Management

Diagnosis of hypoglycemia is confirmed by two independent laboratory analyses of blood glucose concentration. In the newborn, hypoglycemia is confirmed with plasma glucose levels less than 25 mg/dL for low-birth-weight infants and less than 35 mg/dL for term infants in the first 72 hours, and 45 mg/dL thereafter. Cerebral signs may include jitteriness or tremors, lethargy, seizures, apneic spells, cyanosis, or coma. Tachypnea, tachycardia, sweating, pallor, and irritability may occur in response to the release of excess epinephrine.

Medical management of hypoglycemia includes frequent monitoring of blood glucose levels and feedings as early as 2 hours after birth, when tolerated. Continuous intravenous glucose, in amounts sufficient to maintain the infant's glucose within normal limits, may be necessary. Complications from this treatment include fluid overload and thrombosis of the vein. Concentrated glucose solutions over 10 mg/dL may be administered by means of an umbilical artery catheter because of the faster blood flow, but not an umbilical vein catheter because of the risk of thrombosis. After the infant has stabilized, gradual tapering of glucose infusion for 24 hours prevents a rebound hypoglycemic incident. When the cause of the hypoglycemia is hyperinsulinism, surgical removal of the adenoma, or total or near-total pancreatectomy in non-tumor cases, is often necessary. Medical treatment with the use of diazoxide has been successful in some non-tumor cases.

### Nursing Assessment and Diagnosis

Early assessment of potential hypoglycemia through careful observation of all newborns is a major nursing responsibility. Identifying high-risk infants and periodically screening blood glucose levels is important. Some infants with hypoglycemia have no symptoms at all, while others may have a variety of symptoms. In the infant exhibiting signs of possible hypoglycemia, a simple and quick test using Dextrostix or a Glucometer can be performed by the nurse on a heelstick sample of blood. For the Dextrostix, the nurse must allow the blood to remain on the reagent strip for exactly 1 minute before comparing it to the color chart. Color changes indicating glucose levels under 45 mg/dL should be confirmed by immediate laboratory testing of plasma glucose concentrations. Careful and proper handling of laboratory blood specimens is essential, especially since storage at room temperature increases glycolysis.

Nursing diagnoses for hypoglycemia might include the following:

- Altered nutrition: less than body requirements related to poor intake and lethargy
- High risk for fluid volume excess related to intravenous dextrose administration
- Ineffective family coping: compromised related to child's unanticipated illness

### Planning, Implementing, and Evaluating Nursing Care

The planning and implementation of nursing care for altered nutrition includes giving infants at risk for hypoglycemia an early feeding of sterile water to assess the integrity of the gastrointestinal tract, then giving 5% to 10% glucose feedings; breast-feeding or bottle-feeding the infant as soon as possible after delivery; giving intra-

venous dextrose to infants with significant hypoglycemia, especially when feedings are poorly tolerated; and frequently monitoring the blood glucose level using Dextrostix, Glucometer, or laboratory analysis for prompt management of hypoglycemia. The procedure should be repeated every 1 to 2 hours for the first 8 hours, then every 4 hours for 2 days. Evaluation of this nursing diagnosis includes determining that the infant has no signs of hypoglycemia, such as jitteriness, apathy, seizures, apneic spells, pallor, tachycardia, sweating, or irritability. Although these are classic signs of hypoglycemia, infants may exhibit only lethargy and poor feeding.

Nursing care for high risk for fluid volume excess includes recognizing potential dangers of concentrated dextrose infusion (i.e., rapid infusion causing circulatory overload, hyperglycemia, and intracellular dehydration); maintaining the ordered flow rate to decrease chances of fluid overload (the rate of intravenous administration should never be accelerated to "catch-up" on intravenous infusion); decreasing the administration of intravenous glucose gradually to avoid hypoglycemia; and close observation of the intravenous site because extravasation of the concentrated solution can cause sloughing of tissue. The evaluation criteria for this nursing diagnosis include the following: the intravenous infusion of dextrose is at the rate ordered; there are no signs of extravasation or infection at the intravenous site; and there are no signs of circulatory overload, hyperglycemia, or intracellular dehydration.

Nursing care for ineffective family coping includes providing emotional support to parents, encouraging expression of anxiety or fears; and facilitating frequent visitations and giving frequent telephone progress reports to promote parent–infant bonding, especially since these infants may not feed well or behave responsively toward parents. The evaluation criteria include the following: the family freely expresses feelings about the illness; and they receive frequent progress reports on the condition of the infant and visit as often as possible.

## Adrenal Crisis (Acute Adrenocortical Insufficiency)

### Pathophysiology

*Acute adrenocortical insufficiency*, a relatively rare disease in childhood, may result from a number of causes, including infection or trauma, that result in hemorrhage into the adrenal gland. Sometimes, however, there is no identifiable cause (Bacon, Spencer, Hopwood, & Kelch, 1990). Early symptoms include weakness, fever, abdominal pain, hypotension, dehydration, and shock (New, del Balzo, Crawford, & Speiser, 1990). Other signs may include hypoglycemia, hyponatremia, and hyperkalemia. If not quickly treated, the disease can be life-threatening.

### Medical Diagnosis and Management

Medical treatment includes intravenous infusion of cortisol and fluid replacement to restore electrolyte balance and fluid volume (Bacon, Spencer, Hopwood, & Kelch, 1990). If an infection was the predisposing factor, antibiotic therapy is begun. If the child is in shock, plasma or normal saline should be infused in the first hour (New, del Balzo, Crawford, & Speiser, 1990). As the child improves, dosages are decreased, with a maintenance dose obtained within 5 days.

### Nursing Assessment and Diagnosis

Acute adrenal crisis usually constitutes a medical emergency, and early identification of the disorder is vital. Nurses functioning as triage officers in emergency rooms, office nurses, and school nurses are likely to be the first to examine a child brought in with this disorder. A history must be quickly ascertained, particularly regarding recent illnesses or injury. Signs of shock must be quickly assessed, including cold, clammy skin, tachycardia, hypotension, restlessness, pallor, circulatory insufficiency, reduced cardiac output, and diminished urinary output.

Nursing diagnoses for adrenal crisis might include the following:

- Anxiety related to restlessness
- Ineffective breathing patterns related to circulatory insufficiency
- Decreased cardiac output related to circulation insufficiency
- Fluid volume deficit related to fluid loss
- Altered patterns of urinary elimination related to fluid deficit
- Fear (child and parental) related to the acute symptoms

### Planning and Implementing Nursing Care

Nursing care focuses on administering fluids and medications as prescribed; treating for shock, if required, by elevating the lower extremities; and monitoring heart rate, pulse, and blood pressure. The child and parents must be alerted to the risk for future acute episodes. They should be advised to obtain a Medic Alert tag. Children placed on replacement glucocorticoid treatment should be given an emergency kit of hydrocortisone injection to be used in case of an accident or any severe stress (New, del Balzo, Crawford, & Speiser, 1990).

### Evaluating Nursing Care

Reversing the symptoms of shock is the primary evaluation. Subsequent evaluation considers the child and parents' knowledge of the condition and their ability to adhere to the medical regimen prescribed. The prevention of further acute episodes is a major evaluation measure.

## Congenital Adrenal Hyperplasia

### Pathophysiology

*Congenital adrenal hyperplasia* (CAH) is an autosomal recessive genetic disorder caused by a deficiency of any of the five enzymes needed to synthesize cortisol. As a result of decreased cortisol synthesis, the pituitary sends a message to increase cortisol production, causing a rise in ACTH and adrenal hyperplasia. Elevated levels of ACTH excessively activate steroid hormone production, particularly adrenal androgens (testosterone). Excessive production of testosterone results in virilization, which is usually undetected in males but may be manifested in childhood by precocious puberty. In females, the virilization is evident at birth in the form of ambiguous genitalia, which consist of an enlarged clitoris, some degree of labial fusion, and hyperpigmentation of the labia.

Mineralocorticoid production may be either excessive or insufficient. In the more severe salt-losing forms of the disorder, fluid and electrolyte imbalances may occur.

If untreated, CAH can result in an increased rate of bone growth with early epiphyseal closure and resulting short stature. Precocious puberty also occurs and is manifested by early development of secondary sexual characteristics (discussed in Chapter 16).

### Medical Diagnosis and Management

Diagnostic studies are usually done when physical abnormalities such as ambiguous genitalia lead to suspicion of CAH. These studies include determination of 17-hydroxy-progesterone levels, a plasma renin activity to detect sodium depletion, and sonography to determine the presence of internal reproductive organs. As in all cases of ambiguous genitalia, chromosome typing is done to determine sex identification.

Medical management of CAH includes administration of corticosteroids to decrease the levels of ACTH and the process of virilization. Depending on the level of severity, surgical correction of the external female genitalia may be required. In cases where salt depletion is a problem, mineralocorticoids may be given. In general, when pharmacological therapy is initiated early, the effects of CAH are reduced.

### Nursing Assessment and Diagnosis

As in all cases of ambiguous genitalia, nurses must assess parent–infant attachment behaviors as well as the parents' adaptive abilities. Because CAH can cause water and sodium depletion, children must be closely monitored for signs of dehydration. Nurses must also assess for CAH in cases of precocious puberty.

Nursing diagnoses for CAH might include the following:

- High risk for altered parenting related to having a child with ambiguous genitalia
- High risk for fluid volume deficit related to sodium and water losses
- Altered growth and development related to precocious puberty or other effects of virilization

### Planning and Implementing Nursing Care

Nurses can assist parents in coping with the diagnosis by explaining the nature of the problem. Parent–infant attachment should be facilitated, and parental coping mechanisms should be carefully monitored. Nurses can help parents understand the surgical interventions that will be used to correct the problem and can give parents information regarding the pharmacological management. Parents should also be taught to monitor for signs of dehydration. When signs of precocious puberty appear, nurses should make appropriate referrals.

### Evaluating Nursing Care

Evaluation of nursing care is based on parental demonstration of an understanding of the disorder and its treatment. Effects of the problem should be minimal, and the child should demonstrate normal growth and development.

## Cushing Syndrome (Hypercortisolism)

### Pathophysiology

*Cushing syndrome* is the name given to the metabolic effects of a marked increase of circulating glucocorticoids. Up to age 7 years, adrenal tumors, adenomas, or carcinomas are the most the common causes of the disorder. After age 7 years, an increased secretion of ACTH with secondary hyperplasia is the usual cause. In addition to the increase in glucocorticoids, an increase in androgen production may also occur.

The disease affects many organ systems. Alterations in the distribution of body fat are evident. "Buffalo obesity," in which the thorax and abdomen exhibit greater obesity than the extremities, is a classic sign. Other signs include a moon face, slender extremities, thin skin, striae, hirsutism, acne, and short stature. Although diabetes and hypertension may also be present, they are not specific to the diagnosis.

### Medical Diagnosis and Management

Medical diagnosis of Cushing syndrome requires a variety of tests. Osteoporosis and retarded skeletal maturation may be found on radiological examination. Sometimes, a differential white blood cell count reveals leukocytosis and lymphopenia (Bacon, Spencer, Hopwood, & Kelch, 1991).

Serum cortisol levels are usually high, and the expected diurnal variation does not occur. Ultrasound and adrenal scanning may be useful in identifying adrenal tumors, which cause about 20% of all cases (Sheeler, 1989). The best screening test is a 24-hour urine assay for free cortisol. If urinary 17-hydroxysteroids are high, a dexamethasone suppression test is indicated. The dexamethasone suppression test, in which plasma cortisol is measured at 8:00 a.m. after dexamethasone is given at 11:00 p.m., is known to have a high false-positive rate, so tests may have to be repeated several times (Sheeler, 1989).

Medical treatment depends on the underlying cause. If the cause is increased corticotropin secretion by the pituitary, microsurgery may be performed. Adrenal adenoma and adrenocortical nodular dysplasia are also treated surgically. Drugs that inhibit adrenal function, such as metyrapone, or those that interfere with neurotransmitters, such as cyproheptadine, may be unpredictable and may also cause undesirable side effects, such as weight gain.

### Nursing Assessment and Diagnosis

Children are examined and assessed for the physical signs listed previously. Blood pressure readings establish the presence of hypertension. Weight should be accurately recorded, and the distribution of body fat also should be noted. Skin should be assessed for hirsutism or acne. Height should be measured and compared with previous height measurements. Cushing syndrome is seldom seen in children who are growing normally.

Assessment also should include the child and parents' concerns about the child's physical appearance, the length of time the symptoms have been present, and whether or not muscle weakness has been noted. Behavior changes should also be assessed because psychiatric disturbances are common and may range from mild irritability or excitability to frank steroidal psychosis.

Nursing diagnoses for Cushing syndrome might include the following:

- Impaired physical mobility related to muscle weakness
- High risk for impaired skin integrity related to poor wound healing secondary to excessive glucocorticoids
- Altered growth and development related to diminished skeletal growth
- Body image disturbance related to fat distribution, moon face, hirsutism, or acne
- Self-esteem disturbance related to altered self-perception and reactions of others to changed physical appearance
- Hopelessness related to fears regarding the child's prognosis if metastasis has occurred

### Planning and Implementing Nursing Care

The child and parents need support and information about the illness, diagnostic tests, and treatment. It is important to treat the child in an age-appropriate manner, with sensitivity to the child's feelings of vulnerability about appearance. Prevention of wounds should be emphasized. The child should be assisted with movements if muscle weakness is present. Since many adrenal carcinomas have metastasized by the time medical assistance is sought, nursing care is supportive in terms of comfort for the child and grief resolution for the parents.

### Evaluating Nursing Care

The child and the parents should be able to demonstrate appropriate knowledge about the condition, the diagnostic tests, and the prescribed treatment, including the medication regimen and the importance of compliance to the child's recovery. If surgery is performed, the postoperative recovery should be uneventful.

## Endocrine Problems of School-Aged Children and Adolescents

### Anterior Pituitary Dysfunction

#### Pathophysiology

Excess secretion of GH by the anterior pituitary causes gigantism in children and acromegaly in adults. Eosinophil or mixed-cell adenomas of the anterior pituitary gland are often responsible for this excessive production of GH, although in some cases hypersecretion may be related to a decreased feedback signal from a target gland, which makes the pituitary increase hormone production (Bullock & Rosendahl, 1988).

*Gigantism* occurs when the hypersecretion of GH begins in infancy or childhood, before closure of the epiphyseal shafts, resulting in growth of the long bones until the person reaches heights of 8 to 9 feet. Because GH stimulates growth in all body tissues, however, body proportions are usually normal. Bone age determinations are normal or advanced. Children may attain as much as three times the normal height for their age.

With *acromegaly,* hypersecretion of GH occurs after puberty and epiphyseal closure so that tissues thicken and growth occurs primarily in the hands, feet, and face.

#### Medical Diagnosis and Management

If GH hypersecretion is prolonged, the child may develop a bulking appearance. The ears, supraorbital ridge, and nose may thicken. The fingers thicken, and radiograph reveals an arrow-shaped appearance of the distal phalanges. The tongue may thicken, and the paranasal sinuses may enlarge. The voice may deepen, and chewing may become difficult. Additional physical changes may include a barrel chest, bowed legs, osteoporosis, and arteriosclerosis.

The glucose suppression test is specific for hyperpituitarism. Glucose is expected to suppress GH secretion. If a glucose infusion does not suppress the hormone level to below the accepted normal value of 5 mg, the test is positive and suggests hyperpituitarism. Computed tomography scans, skull radiographs, arteriography, and pneumoencephalography are additional assessments that help to identify the presence and size of a pituitary lesion. If a tumor is found, surgery or radiation is indicated.

### Nursing Assessment and Diagnosis

The importance of growth curve measurement as a tool for early detection of hyperpituitarism cannot be overemphasized. Excessive growth should be referred for medical evaluation.

Physical changes in appearance should be noted. Muscles should be assessed for signs of weakness. Vision should be assessed because the tumor might cause visual disorders. A history of behavioral and emotional changes should be obtained.

The nurse should assess parental and child knowledge about the condition, especially before surgery. After surgery, care involves monitoring vital signs and neurological status. Signs of intracranial hemorrhage include a falling pulse rate, increased blood pressure, pupil inequality, or alteration in consciousness.

Nursing diagnoses for gigantism might include the following:

- Altered growth and development related to excessive GH
- High risk for social isolation related to altered physical appearance
- Altered family processes related to concerns over the child's condition
- Impaired swallowing related to physical changes in the throat and tongue
- Self-esteem disturbance related to changes in physical appearance
- Visual alterations related to effects of a tumor
- Anxiety, child and parent, related to surgery and prognosis
- Impaired physical mobility related to stiffness of joints

### Planning and Implementing Nursing Care

The nurse must be able to provide emotional support to the child and family who may feel stress and anxiety related to the body changes. Arthritis can be painful, and

the nurse should instruct the child and parents about the administration of medications and range-of-motion exercises. If the child is having visual problems, the nurse should maximize visual ability by making sure the child can see the care-giver and by using visual aids.

One of the nurse's primary responsibilities before surgery is to provide information and support. The parents need to understand that bone changes cannot be corrected but that soft tissue deformities can be prevented. Postoperatively, vital signs and neurological status must be evaluated frequently. Blood sugar must also be monitored frequently because falling GH levels may precipitate hypoglycemia. GH has an insulin-antagonist effect; therefore, intake and output must be carefully monitored because transient diabetes can cause polyuria. Nasal packing is used if the surgery involves a trans-sphenoidal procedure. The dressing must be checked for drainage (cerebrospinal fluid leaks may occur).

Hormones are prescribed after surgery, and the importance of hormonal replacement therapy should be emphasized. Regular follow-up examination is necessary. There is a slight chance that the tumor might reappear. Because the hormone schedule is so important, the child should have the replacement schedule accessible at school or day care and should also wear a Medic Alert tag. Hormones should not be stopped suddenly.

### Evaluating Nursing Care

Compliance with the medication regimen and follow-up care and a successful postoperative course are important evaluation measures. The child and family should demonstrate an understanding of the condition. The resolution of the child's emotional problems will undoubtedly take an extended period of time. Success in school adjustment and in making friends and other evidence of positive self-esteem are additional desired outcomes.

## Hyperthyroidism (Graves Disease, Thyrotoxicosis)

### Pathophysiology

*Hyperthyroidism* is caused by excessive secretion of thyroid hormone, specifically $T_3$ and $T_4$, which results in increased circulation of thyroid hormone to the cells and acceleration of all metabolic activities, including basal metabolic rate, energy expenditure, and heat production (Bullock & Rosendahl, 1988). The most common form of hyperthyroidism is *Graves disease,* also termed *diffuse toxic goiter* or *primary hyperthyroidism.* Although the etiology of this disease is still not fully understood, it is believed that there is an autoimmune component. Genetic factors are also accepted contributors to the disease; more than one person in the same family is often affected.

Severe stress has also been implicated as triggering the disease.

## Medical Diagnosis and Management

The incidence of Graves disease increases steadily in the first 10 years of life, with the peak incidence in adolescence. Girls are affected three to six times more often than boys (Bacon, Spencer, Hopwood, & Kelch, 1990). Graves disease is a multisystem disorder, but clinical manifestations are subtle and vary greatly. Excessive motion, weight loss in spite of an increasing appetite, and exophthalmos are often seen in children. Diagnosis is made on the presence of diffuse thyroid hyperplasia. Severe infiltrative ophthalmopathy is seldom seen in children, and pretibial myxedema has never been reported (Bacon, Spencer, Hopwood, & Kelch, 1990).

The onset is usually insidious. The most common complaints are found in Table 32-4. These signs and symptoms suggest the medical diagnosis, which is confirmed by radioimmunoassay showing increased levels of serum $T_3$ and $T_4$ and decreased levels of TSH. A thyroid scan reveals an increased iodine-131 ($^{131}I$) uptake. Increased serum protein-bound iodine and decreased serum cholesterol and lipids may also be found. Ultrasonography may be used as a means of confirming subclinical ophthalmopathy.

Treatment of hyperthyroidism is directed toward controlling the rate of thyroid hormone secretion. Long-term treatment with thioamides, such as propylthiouracil (PTU) or methimazole, which block the formation of $T_3$ and $T_4$, is the treatment of choice. PTU also blocks the formation of $T_4$ to $T_3$ (Bacon, Spencer, Hopwood, & Kelch, 1990). Almost complete thyroidectomies may be done in children if

## Table 32–4. Signs and Symptoms of Hyperthyroidism

**Complaints**

Nervousness, excessive sweating, anorexia
Increased appetite with or without weight loss
Dyspnea, fatigue, weakness, heat intolerance
Diarrhea, tremor, palpitations
Amenorrhea or oligomenorrhea
Decreased school performance, difficulty concentrating

**Signs on Physical Examination**

Enlarged thyroid (goiter)
Persistent tachycardia
Systolic hypertension (with widened pulse pressure)
Mild exophthalmos
Smooth, moist, warm skin
Eyelid retraction and stare
Tremulousness of outstretched hands

other treatment measures fail. High-energy β-rays may be used to destroy thyroid tissue.

Radioactive iodine ($^{131}I$) was formerly used to treat adults only, but it has been used increasingly with people of all ages in rare instances. Ionizing radiation has also been found to be an acceptable approach for children (Hamburger, 1985).

## Nursing Assessment and Diagnosis

Early detection of hyperthyroidism can be facilitated by school and office nurses who are alert to the signs and symptoms. One of the first clues may be school problems in a child who has previously done well in school. Teachers may comment that the child seems unable to concentrate. Children may exhibit signs of nervousness, such as difficulty sleeping, rapid speech, easy fatigability, and intolerance to heat.

Vital signs and weight must be assessed. Sometimes, sedation is ordered for nervousness. Intake and output must be assessed to ensure adequate hydration and fluid balance. The nurse, the child, and the parents must be alert for the signs and symptoms of an acute episode, called a *thyroid storm*. Signs of a thyroid storm include tachycardia, hyperkinesis, fever, vomiting, and hypertension.

Compliance with the prescribed medication regimen should be assessed. The child should also be assessed for effects of medications, such as signs of hypertension or agranulocytosis.

Hypothyroidism and hypoparathyroidism may occur after surgery. The pulse rate and character (i.e., a slow, faint pulse) may be indicative. The child may become lethargic, and the skin may be cool and dry. If the child becomes increasingly nervous, anxious, or depressed, or complains of sensory disturbances or tingling of the fingers and hands, the nurse should suspect hypoparathyroidism with hypocalcemia. The nurse should assess for Chvostek sign (tap over the parotid gland and observe for facial muscle spasm). Muscle spasms in the hands and wrists should be noted and reported to the physician.

Nursing diagnoses for Graves disease might include the following:

- Altered nutrition: less than body requirements related to excessive metabolic rate
- Fatigue related to excessive activity
- Sleep pattern disturbance related to excessive metabolic rate
- Diarrhea related to excessive metabolic rate
- Altered thought processes related to inability to concentrate
- High risk for altered parenting related to child's chronic illness
- Anxiety (child and parental) related to behavior

changes caused by illness, treatment, and prognosis

## Planning and Implementing Nursing Care

Children must be carefully observed and monitored to prevent acute episodes and complications. The disease process and the significance of behavioral changes must be explained to the child, parents, and teachers. Irritable children should be encouraged to rest in a cool, quiet room. If weight loss is a problem, frequent feedings (6 meals a day) are indicated. A diet that is high in calories, carbohydrates, and protein is recommended. Vitamin supplements are frequently indicated. If edema is present, a low-sodium diet is indicated. If iodine is a pharmacological treatment, it should be taken through a straw to prevent tooth discoloration. Iodides should be given with milk to prevent gastrointestinal distress.

Postoperative nursing care is focused on preventing complications. The child must be checked for bleeding, respiratory distress (a tracheotomy tray should be at the bedside), hoarseness, or signs of hypoparathyroidism (tetany, numbness). Postoperatively, the child can be placed in a semi-Fowler's position, with the head and neck supported by sandbags to relieve pressure on the incision.

Children taking propranolol should be observed for signs of hypotension, such as dizziness and decreased urinary output. Those taking PTU and methimazole must have their CBCs monitored to check for leukopenia, thrombocytopenia, and agranulocytosis. These medications should be taken with meals to minimize gastrointestinal distress. Over-the-counter cough medicines should be avoided since they may contain iodine. Children who have received [131]I therapy should be instructed not to expectorate or cough freely for 24 hours since the sputum is radioactive for this time.

All treatments and procedures must be explained to the child and parents. Parents should also be encouraged to express their feelings about the child's behavior, the disease, treatments, and prognosis. The nurse should communicate or help parents to communicate with the school nurse and teachers to develop a consistent approach in relating to the child.

## Evaluating Nursing Care

Nursing care can be evaluated on the basis of success in preoperative monitoring of the child during diagnostic procedures; a positive, complication-free postoperative recovery; and long-term effectiveness of the nursing care plan. Two important evaluation criteria are the child's and family's adjustment to the condition and treatment plan; and the school nurse's and teachers' ability to recognize symptoms that indicate hypersensitivity to medications.

# Thyroiditis (Hashimoto Disease)

## Pathophysiology

The chronic, autoimmune form of thyroiditis, often called *Hashimoto disease,* occurs primarily in women between the ages of 30 and 50 but can occur at any age. The two most common findings with Hashimoto disease are a palpable goiter and high levels of circulating autoantibodies. Defects of hormone synthesis in the thyroid result in overproduction of TSH by the pituitary, leading to gradual, asymptomatic enlargement of the thyroid gland (Bullock & Rosendahl, 1988). The gland is not tender when palpated. About 55% to 65% of children seen in pediatric endocrine clinics have Hashimoto's thyroiditis (Bacon, Spencer, Hopwood, & Kelch, 1990).

Thyroiditis may also present in a subacute form associated with the sequelae of mumps, influenza, or coxsackievirus or adenovirus infection. Bacterial infection of the thyroid can result in inflammation of the thyroid gland. Tuberculosis, actinomycosis, or syphilis may cause a chronic infection.

## Medical Diagnosis and Management

Medical diagnosis is based on history and laboratory data. Laboratory tests include serum $T_3$, $T_4$, TSH, antithyroglobulin, and microsomal complement fixation antibody tests. A thyroid scan is also done but is not as useful as other tests. Children with thyroiditis have a high incidence of positive antibodies. The thyroid microsomal complement fixation test may be positive when antithyroglobulin has not been detected. Elevated TSH suggest thyroiditis.

The recommended therapy for thyroiditis is lifelong replacement therapy with synthetic L-thyroxine for children with increased TSH values or large or locally symptomatic goiters (Bacon, Spencer, Hopwood, & Kelch, 1990). Even with treatment, however, these children may eventually develop hypothyroidism. If replacement therapy does not decrease the goiter, further studies should be done.

The presence of a solitary, firm, and irregular nodule on the thyroid is occasionally indicative of carcinoma. The usual treatment for papillary carcinoma of the thyroid is subtotal thyroidectomy and suppressive doses of thyroid hormone. With surgery, the prognosis is usually good.

## Nursing Assessment and Diagnosis

Because thyroiditis is usually asymptomatic, a comprehensive history is important. If there is a family history of thyroiditis or other autoimmune diseases, or if there is a history of tuberculosis or a recent viral illness, the medical diagnosis of thyroiditis should be suspected.

The neck should be examined for edema or redness, and the size of the thyroid noted. The awareness of the child and parents regarding the nature of the illness should be explored.

Nursing diagnoses for thyroiditis might include the following:

- Impaired swallowing related to surgical procedure
- High risk for altered nutrition: less than body requirements related to difficulty in swallowing after surgery
- Ineffective airway clearance related to pressure on the trachea

### *Planning and Implementing Nursing Care*

If the child is experiencing difficulty in swallowing, a liquid diet should be offered. Daily measurement of the neck establishes the rate of enlargement. Hypothyroidism is a complication of Hashimoto disease; therefore, parents need to observe for lethargy, constipation, and cold intolerance.

If a thyroidectomy is performed, postoperative care includes assessing vital signs, observing for signs of tetany, checking dressings for bleeding, and watching for respiratory difficulties. As mentioned previously, a tracheotomy tray and calcium gluconate should be readily available.

The nurse should reinforce the need for lifelong hormone replacement therapy. The parents should understand the philosophy, the treatment, and the possible side effects.

### *Evaluating Nursing Care*

The child and parents should be knowledgeable about thyroiditis and the medication regimen and should comply with the medication and follow-up visit schedules. A routine postoperative recovery and the child's return to home and school activities are also important evaluation measures. If postsurgical complications occur, nursing care is evaluated on the prompt and effective assessment and interventions by the nurse.

## *Hyperparathyroidism*

### *Pathophysiology*

*Hyperparathyroidism* is caused by overactivity of one or more of the four parathyroid glands. *Primary hyperparathyroidism* is usually caused by a benign adenoma of one or more of the parathyroid glands, which causes failure of the normal feedback mechanism to decrease PTH secretion. Both PTH and serum calcium levels increase. Although primary hyperparathyroidism usually occurs in people between the ages of 30 and 50 years, children can be affected. *Secondary hyperparathyroidism* occurs as a compensatory mechanism: parathyroid activ-

ity increases in an attempt to combat hypocalcemia caused by some other disorder. Possible causes of hypocalcemia include vitamin D deficiency, rickets, chronic renal failure, or osteomalacia (softening of the bone [related to laxative abuse or phenytoin]).

### *Medical Diagnosis and Management*

Primary hyperparathyroidism with associated hypercalcemia can affect many body tissues and organs. Osseous changes may occur and are usually reported as vague bone pains. Gastrointestinal symptoms may include nausea, vomiting, constipation, and abdominal discomfort. Neuromuscular symptoms include muscle atrophy, weakness, easy fatigability, twitching of the tongue, and paresthesia in the extremities (Mimouni & Tsang, 1990). Renal disturbances include polydipsia, polyuria, and hypertension. Symptoms of central nervous system involvement include confusion, depression, impaired memory, and hallucinations. Skin necrosis and cataracts may also be present. In the neonate, respiratory distress (poorly developed rib cage), hypotonia, poor feeding, anemia, weight loss, and dehydration may occur. Hypercalcemia is more pronounced and renal lithiasis is less common in infants than in older children (Mimouni & Tsang, 1990).

Medical diagnosis of primary hyperparathyroidism is confirmed by the radioimmunoassay finding of a high serum PTH with accompanying hypercalcemia. Over 90% of all cases of confirmed hypercalcemia are caused by hyperparathyroidism and malignancy (Potts, 1990). In the past, there were problems with the reliability of PTH immunoassays in relation to distinguishing between hyperparathyroidism and hypercalcemia of malignancy. The new PTH assays are based on double antibody techniques and are now the method of choice for this distinction (Potts, 1990). Radiographs show defuse demineralization of bones, bone cysts, outer cortical absorption, and bone erosion of the radial aspect of middle fingers. Cortical bone, not trabecular bone, is lost (Potts, 1990). Cortical bone loss is usually measured by single photon absorptiometry in the forearm. Trabecular bone of the spine can be assessed by quantitative computerized tomography. Laboratory tests include urine and serum analysis for calcium, chloride, and alkaline phosphatase levels. These are all elevated in hyperparathyroidism. Serum phosphorous is decreased.

Primary hyperparathyroidism is treated by surgical removal of the adenoma. One half of one gland must be left to maintain normal PTH levels. If all the parathyroids must be removed, an autotransplant of some parathyroid tissue into the forearm may be done. Bone pain can be relieved in about 3 days, but renal damage may be irreversible.

Secondary hyperparathyroidism may be caused by hypocalcemia of maternal origin, vitamin D deficiency, rickets, or disordered vitamin D metabolism. Laboratory findings may show normal or slightly decreased serum calcium levels and variable serum phosphorus levels. The underlying cause must be treated. A medical goal is to restore calcium balance. Drugs ordered may include vitamin D, which is used to promote calcium absorption, aluminum hydroxide, which is used to reduce phosphate absorption, and calcium salts. Even after normal calcium levels are reached, the parathyroid glands may not return to normal size.

### Nursing Assessment and Diagnosis

The nurse should assess the lungs for signs of pulmonary edema and check the heart rate and heart sounds to ascertain cardiac status. Blood pressure should be monitored regularly to assess for hypertension. Urine should be strained to check for stones. Physical mobility should be assessed, as should all complaints of pain or discomfort.

After surgery, the child should be monitored frequently for signs of respiratory distress. A tracheotomy tray should be kept at the bedside. Swelling at the operative site should be assessed. The child should also be observed for mild signs of tetany, including tingling of the hands and around the mouth. Mental status must be assessed and changes noted.

Nursing diagnoses for hyperparathyroidism might include the following:

- High risk for injury related to neuromuscular pain or weakness
- Altered renal tissue perfusion related to hypercalcemia
- Altered cardiopulmonary tissue perfusion related to hypercalcemia
- Altered patterns of urinary elimination related to renal calculi
- Pain related to bone pain or renal involvement
- High risk for activity intolerance related to pain or fatigue
- High risk for injury related to bone demineralization
- Altered thought processes related to disease process

### Planning and Implementing Nursing Care

The primary nursing goal is the early identification and treatment of hyperparathyroidism. Children often complain of pain in the legs, which many people call "growing pains." Nurses must be aware that bone pain is a common symptom of hyperparathyroidism. Fractures also occur frequently. Affected children may need assistance with movement. Measures need to be taken to prevent fractures, such as using bed rails and removing scatter rugs. Parents need to be cautioned to use care when lifting the

child. Radiographs identify the weak areas, and these areas should receive special care. The child experiencing muscle weakness should be encouraged to get as much rest as possible.

Chronic renal failure is the most common cause of secondary hyperparathyroidism. All urine should be strained for calculi. To prevent calculi, children should be encouraged to increase their fluid intake (sometimes by as much as 100%). Cranberry and apple juice, which are high in acid, help to maintain a low pH of the urine. Less acid in the urine results in decreased solubility of calcium salts. When the child is being hydrated to reduce the serum calcium level, it is important to accurately assess intake and output. Children who receive intravenous solutions should have their lungs auscultated often to detect signs of pulmonary edema.

The nurse must also be alert to signs of gastrointestinal disturbance, which may indicate peptic ulcers. These symptoms include increasing pain in the epigastrium. Antacids and small bland meals may be prescribed; however, care must exercised because many antacids contain calcium. It is important that the physician specify the antacid to be used. In addition, signs of confusion, impaired memory, lack of interest, or depression should be brought to the physician's attention.

If a parathyroidectomy is done, the child must be checked frequently for signs of respiratory distress. This may be caused by edema of the trachea. A tracheotomy tray should be readily available. The operative site must be observed for edema. The child is placed in a semi-Fowler's position with support (by sandbags) to the head and neck to decrease edema. Complaints of tingling in the hands or around the mouth may indicate mild tetany. Intravenous calcium gluconate must be available in the event that the condition progresses to tetany. Usually, the child is ambulated as soon as possible, not only to improve general circulation and respiratory status but also to accelerate bone recalcification, which is stimulated by bone pressure.

### Evaluating Nursing Care

Upon discharge, the child and family must understand the purpose, expected results, and possible side effects of prescribed medications. Their understanding and compliance with the prescribed treatment are important evaluation measures.

Follow-up care is important, and the need for periodic laboratory tests must also be emphasized. Again, compliance in keeping these appointments is a good evaluation criterion. The most important indicator of the success of nursing interventions is the ability of the child to continue to grow and develop along normal parameters. The child who can recuperate in a timely fashion from surgery, resume childhood activities, and understand, at an appropriate time, the disease and the implications in maintaining health, is a child with a positive outcome.

## Chronic or Primary Adrenocortical Insufficiency (Addison Disease)

### Pathophysiology

*Chronic adrenocortical insufficiency*, or Addison disease, is rarely seen in children. It occurs with destruction of adrenocortical tissue, which may be caused by a variety of conditions, including tuberculosis, trauma, fulminating infections, the effects of certain drugs, or leukemia.

A common clinical feature of this disorder is hyperpigmentation of the skin due to the excessive secretion of ACTH and melanocyte-stimulating hormone (MSH). Other symptoms include anorexia, loss of weight, generalized weakness, nausea and vomiting, diarrhea, and perhaps dehydration, especially during periods of physical stress. Hyperkalemia, hypoglycemia, and hyponatremia may also be present.

Associated cardiovascular abnormalities include postural hypotension, decreased cardiac size, decreased cardiac output, and a weak, irregular pulse. Alopecia and mucocutaneous candidiasis may also appear. Many patients have accompanying psychiatric symptoms, such as depression, apathy, negativism, or confusion (Johnstone, Rundell, & Esposito, 1990).

Females have less pubic hair due to decreased androgen secretion. They may also have diminished menses or amenorrhea. Males are not as affected because the testicular androgens continue to be produced.

### Medical Diagnosis and Management

The medical diagnosis is verified by an elicited response to a synthetic ACTH preparation, Cortrosyn. Plasma cortisol levels are low to absent, and the ACTH level is high. Urinary 17-ketosteroids and 17-hydroxycorticosteroid are low. Serum potassium and blood urea nitrogen are high. Fasting blood sugar is low. Frequently, there is a low white blood cell count, and the hematocrit and eosinophils are elevated. Radiographs may reveal calcification in the adrenal area, pulmonary or renal tuberculosis, or a small heart.

The medical treatment for children with Addison disease requires the administration of both glucocorticoids (Cortisol) and mineralocorticoids (Aldosterone). Corticosteroid replacement with cortisone or hydrocortisone is the usual treatment. This supplementation is required for life and must be increased when infections, surgery, or other forms of stress are present. Fluid and electrolyte balance is achieved through daily oral doses of fludrocortisone, a synthetic mineralocorticoid, a steroid that retains fluid. This is always titrated to the lowest effective dose and is gradually reduced for long-term therapy. Children with this disorder should be able to live normal lives except that they and their parents must be alert for signs of adrenal crisis (as described earlier in this chapter).

### Nursing Assessment and Diagnosis

The child's weight and intake and output must be carefully assessed to determine if volume depletion has occurred. The diet history is useful in determining if the child is anorexic and if the child has a craving for salt. Urine should be checked for glucose and acid–base balance. The child must also be assessed for signs of infection or stress.

Nursing diagnoses for Addison disease might include the following:

- High risk for altered peripheral, vascular, and renal tissue perfusion related to electrolyte disturbance and hypotension
- Decreased cardiac output related to decreased cardiac size and hypotension
- Sensory/perceptual alterations related to depression, confusion, apathy
- Body image disturbance related to skin discoloration and, in girls, changes in secondary sex characteristics
- Impaired social interaction related to physical and mental changes, such as weakness, depression
- Altered family processes related to the stress of a chronic illness

### Planning and Implementing Nursing Care

Nurses must monitor vital signs carefully and observe for signs of shock. Hormone replacement therapy is administered as ordered, and parents are instructed about the purpose, correct dosage, and adverse effects of such therapy. They must also be taught to observe for signs of infection or stress and to report these because drug dosages may need to be adjusted.

The child's weight and intake and output must be observed for signs of volume depletion. Until the mineralocorticoids take effect, increased fluid intake is advised. Diabetes may occur with chronic adrenocortical insufficiency, and blood sugars need to be monitored because steroids may alter insulin requirements. Diet should be monitored to ensure that sodium and potassium balances are maintained. If the child is anorexic, small, frequent feedings may help to maintain nutritional status by increasing caloric intake. Usually, a high-protein, high-carbohydrate diet is prescribed.

The child should be observed for signs of fluid retention, such as fluid around the eyes and face (cushingoid signs). Steroids given in the late afternoon may cause insomnia. Signs of bruising (petechiae) should be noted.

The child and parents should be taught that this condition requires steroid therapy for life. They must be alert for signs of infection, stress, injury, or extreme variations in temperature exposure because dosage adjustments may be necessary to prevent an adrenal crisis. The child should wear a Medic Alert bracelet, and the name and dosage of the medication should be available at school and any place where the child spends considerable time. If a crisis occurs, the nurse is responsible for administering medications, monitoring intravenous therapy, monitoring vital signs, and measuring intake and output (hourly urine). Signs of shock and deviations from the expected outcomes must be reported immediately.

### Evaluating Nursing Care

Maintenance with steroid replacement therapy is the primary evaluation measure. The child and parents should comply with the prescribed regimen and demonstrate an awareness of the etiology of the disorder, the factors that should be brought to the physician's attention, and the factors that precipitate a crisis. The child's progress in school, social interactions, and positive self-image are indicators of psychosocial adjustment.

## Pheochromocytomas

### Pathophysiology

*Pheochromocytomas* are rare tumors of the adrenal medulla that cause increased output of the medulla hormones, often resulting in hypertension (Bullock & Rosendahl, 1988).

Since this is primarily an adult disorder, readers are referred to a medical-surgical nursing text for additional information.

## Chronic Endocrine Problems

## Diabetes Mellitus

*Diabetes mellitus* is a disorder characterized by the relative or absolute lack of insulin production by the β-cells of the pancreas, resulting in an impairment of glucose metabolism. The two major forms of diabetes are *insulin-dependent diabetes mellitus* (IDDM; type I) and *non−insulin-dependent diabetes* (NIDDM; type II). In IDDM, the body is completely or almost completely unable to to make insulin. In the absence of insulin replacement therapy, fat and protein catabolism result in the development of ketosis. In NIDDM, the body still makes insulin, but either produce an inadequate supply or cannot use the insulin properly.

An estimated 150,000 people under 20 years of age have diabetes mellitus. About 1 in 600 school-age children develops the disease (Siminerio, 1986). The vast majority of children or adolescents with diabetes mellitus have the insulin-dependent type, and the remainder of the discussion will focus on this form.

IDDM is an autoimmune disease. Although inheritable, diabetes mellitus is not transferred according to simple genetic laws. Research has shown that certain gene combinations seem to make some people especially prone to the disease; however, other events, such as viral infections or an autoimmune attack, must occur to make diabetes emerge. In addition, tumors of the pancreas, pancreatitis, and steroid use may contribute to development of the disease. Although viruses seem to be involved in IDDM, diabetes is not transmitted from one person to another.

### Pathophysiology

The lack of insulin causes metabolic and physiological changes in almost all parts of the body. Without adequate insulin, glucose does not leave the blood to enter the muscle and fat cells; therefore, the blood glucose level increases (hyperglycemia). When the serum glucose level nears 200 mg/dL, the kidneys are unable to completely reabsorb all the glucose in the glomerular filtrate, and by obligatory osmotic diuresis, the glucose appears in the urine (glycosuria). Large amounts of electrolytes (e.g., sodium, potassium, calcium, phosphate, and magnesium) are also excreted by the kidneys. This diuretic action causes excessive urination (polyuria) and dehydration. In turn, excessive thirst (polydipsia) occurs in an attempt to relieve the dehydration.

Since glucose is unavailable for cellular metabolism when insulin is inadequate, the tissues turn to fat for fuel. Large amounts of fats break down into fatty acids and flow to the liver and other tissues, where they are oxidized for energy. The liver also converts some fatty acids into ketones. Excessive ketone bodies accumulate and are excreted in the urine (ketonuria). Additional sodium and potassium are lost as ketone bodies are transported out of the nephron tubules. The ketone bodies readily produce excessive quantities of free hydrogen ions, causing metabolic acidosis. The body is not able to compensate, and an elevated carbonic acid level dissociates into water and carbon dioxide, further lowering the blood pH. Kussmaul respirations, the deep hyperventilation characteristic of metabolic acidosis, is a respiratory buffering system that attempts to eliminate the excess carbon dioxide. In addition, the excess ketones are excreted by the lungs, resulting in an acetone (or fruity) odor on the breath.

Without glucose entering the cells, protein is also metabolized to provide energy for cell activity. When body protein breaks down, gluconeogenesis increases, and further hyperglycemia develops. As the lethargic body attempts to meet its energy needs, the hunger mechanism is triggered, but excess food intake (polyphagia) simply elevates the blood glucose level further. With unchecked ketoacidosis, dehydration, electrolyte imbalance, coma, and eventually death occur.

## Medical Diagnosis and Management

The three cardinal signs of diabetes mellitus are polyuria, polydipsia, and polyphagia. Other initial clinical manifestations of the disease include lethargy, weight loss, bedwetting, and glucosuria without ketonuria. The child with ketoacidosis presents with Kussmaul respirations and acetone breath along with abdominal discomfort, nausea, and vomiting. Other symptoms include blurred vision, dry skin, and slow-healing sores.

Diagnosis is possible based on the above conditions. Further testing to confirm diabetes mellitus may include a fasting blood sugar test (usually greater than 130 mg/dL) and a glucose tolerance test (elevated blood glucose greater than 200 mg/dL 2 hours after glucose administration). During ketoacidosis, arterial pH, serum carbon dioxide, and electrolyte panels are obtained.

A reliable index of long-term glucose control is the measurement of hemoglobin $A_{1C}$ (glycosylated hemoglobin). This blood test determines the amount of excess glucose available to each red cell over its 120-day life span. The measurement reflects how often the blood sugars have been high for the past 2 to 3 months. The test does not vary with diet, exercise, stress, or time of day.

The child or adolescent with IDDM is treated with a combination of insulin therapy, a meal plan, and an exercise plan. The treatment is most successful when it is flexible and accommodates the child's individual concerns, stress level, activity patterns, food and beverage habits, and lifestyle. The treatment plan attempts to balance insulin, food, and exercise to achieve normal blood sugar levels (euglycemia). Acceptable blood glucose readings are between 80 to 150 mg/dL before eating and between 80 to 180 mg/dL 2 hours after eating.

## Nursing Assessment and Diagnosis

Nursing assessment of the diabetic child includes monitoring the child's emotional condition, physical condition, level of consciousness, fluid intake and urinary output, meal plans, vital signs, blood sugar levels, urine ketone levels, and urine specific-gravity values. Cardiac monitoring, serum electrolytes, and arterial blood gases are monitored closely during periods of crises. Cardiac changes due to hypokalemia (a U wave after the T wave) or increasing hyperkalemia (elevated and spreading T wave) must be assessed. When ordered, the nurse must administer and monitor intravenous infusions of insulin, sodium, potassium, and sodium bicarbonate.

Nursing diagnoses for diabetes mellitus might include the following:

- Fluid volume deficit related to vomiting and polyuria secondary to ketoacidosis
- Impaired tissue integrity related to hyperglycemia and ketoacidosis
- Impaired tissue integrity related to metabolic imbalance secondary to hypoglycemia
- High risk for infection related to high glucose levels and malnutrition
- Impaired skin integrity related to decreased circulation and increased blood glucose
- Altered nutrition: less than body requirements related to defect in glucose metabolism
- Altered family processes related to situational crisis
- High risk for self-esteem disturbance related to insulin dependency
- Diversional activity deficit related to hospitalization

## Planning, Implementing, and Evaluating Nursing Care

The planning and implementation of nursing care for fluid volume deficit includes checking for poor skin turgor, sunken fontanelles, absence of tears, and dry mucous membranes every 4 hours; monitoring glucose serum electrolytes, hemoglobin, hematocrit, serum osmolality, BUN, and creatine, as ordered; maintaining strict intake and output records; weighing the patient on admission and every day at the same time on the same scale; providing fluid replacement with intravenous fluids, as ordered, until urine is negative for glucose and ketones; and monitoring vital signs, including blood pressure and level of consciousness, as ordered. The evaluation criterion for this nursing diagnosis would be that the child demonstrates no signs of dehydration.

Planning and implementing nursing care for impaired tissue perfusion includes observing for precipitating factors to ketoacidosis (infection, stress, omission of insulin); observing for signs of ketoacidosis (cerebral edema, dehydration, hyperkalemia, or hypokalemia); administering safe care if the child is in a coma; monitoring blood glucose levels, as ordered, recording findings and reporting significant changes; testing urine for ketones and specific-gravity values; monitoring baseline and serial blood gases for evidence of metabolic acidosis; administering and monitoring insulin drip and electrolytes, as ordered, and recording appropriately; administering dextrose-free intravenous fluids, as ordered, to replace fluid losses (this is usually ordered until blood glucose falls to 200–300 mg/dL or until urine acetone clears); monitoring closely for impending signs of hypoglycemia (anxiety, tremors, diaphoresis, tachycardia, seizures, headache, impaired vision) and reporting symptoms promptly; and discontinuing the insulin drip gradually and beginning subcutaneous insulin, as ordered. The evaluation criterion for impaired tissue integrity is that the child remains free of injury from hyperglycemia and ketoacidosis.

Nursing care for impaired tissue integrity includes observing for signs of hypoglycemia (irritability, seizures, complaints of headache, hunger, and impaired vision);

monitoring blood glucose levels, as ordered; testing for glucose if the child complains of a "funny" feeling; and offering simple carbohydrates (half cup of orange juice, 5 small gum drops, 2–4 lifesavers, or 1–2 tbsp honey) if the child is awake; or injecting with Glucagon, as ordered. The evaluation criterion is that the child receives simple carbohydrates when needed and lacks signs of hypoglycemia.

Nursing care for high risk for infection includes monitoring and reporting signs and symptoms of infection (high temperature, chills, increased heart rate, redness at injury site); using aseptic hand-washing technique; teaching aseptic handwashing technique to the family and patient; instructing the child on good oral hygiene; and instructing the child on signs and symptoms of urinary tract infections (frequency and burning on urination). Nursing interventions have been successful if the child remains free of infection and can state infection prevention measures.

Nursing care for impaired skin integrity includes inspecting the skin for areas of redness or breakdown, especially the skin folds, spaces between toes, lower legs, pressure points, and injection sites; maintaining optimal nutritional status; and reporting any skin breakdown. Nursing interventions have been successful if the child is free of redness and irritation of skin.

Planning and implementing nursing care for altered nutrition includes assessing for signs and symptoms of malnutrition (weight loss greater than ideal weight, weakness, fatigue); checking blood sugar levels, as ordered; increasing diet as ordered, after NPO status; monitoring the percentage of the meal that is eaten; assisting with selection of appropriate foods; collaborating with a registered dietitian and family members; and providing meals and snacks on time. Nursing interventions have been successful if the child's weight remains stable or increases.

Nursing care for altered family processes includes keeping the family informed of the child's status and progress; assessing interpersonal relationships within the family; assisting the family with problem solving; arranging for a spiritual or social service consult, as needed; referring the family to the American Diabetes Association for contacts with other families in similar situations; answering all questions and involving the family in the child's care, whenever possible; and allowing the family to freely express fears and feelings of guilt. Nursing measures have been successful if the family copes with situational crises with minimal family disruption; and the family expresses feelings and concerns.

Planning and implementing nursing care for high risk for self-esteem disturbance includes encouraging the child to freely express feelings; assisting the child in solving problems associated with diabetes; encouraging the child to continue normal activities; and suggesting involvement with special groups and facilities for children with diabetes. Nursing measures have been successful if the child verbalizes feelings, maintains activities and relationships from prediagnosis days, and is involved with special diabetes groups.

The planning and implementation of nursing care for diversional activity deficit includes providing activities in the hospital that are similar to the child's level of activity at home; arranging physical activity through the occupational therapy program; and adjusting insulin and food intake to reflect the normal level of activity and diet projected for the child at home. The effectiveness of nursing interventions is determined by the child's participation in regularly scheduled exercise similar to the activity level expected when discharged.

*Insulin Therapy.* Insulin therapy is the cornerstone of diabetes treatment. Insulin binds to insulin receptors on cell surfaces, allowing glucose to enter the cell. It is manufactured in 100 units of insulin per milliliter (U-100). Insulin can be rapid, intermediate, or long-acting (Table 32-5). The amount and type prescribed depends on the child's height, weight, metabolic rate, physical maturity, blood glucose level, usual diet, and regular exercise. It is not a reflection of the severity of the diabetes.

Combinations of insulin are given to ensure that peak action occurs at the time the child's blood glucose level would be highest. Usually, two thirds to three fourths of the total daily dose is given in the morning before breakfast to cover the daytime meals, and the remainder of the daily dose is given before dinner to obtain nocturnal coverage. Most children take a combination of rapid-acting insulin to prevent a sharp rise in blood sugar after a meal and intermediate-acting insulin for longer coverage. Injections should be given at fairly consistent times each day to avoid overlaps between doses and gaps in insulin coverage. The insulin is given subcutaneously except in acidosis, when the intravenous or intramuscular route may be used.

Various types of insulin are available, including pork/beef, purified pork, purified beef, and laboratory-manufactured human insulin. The highly purified products have been demonstrated to cause fewer allergic reactions (such as redness and swelling at the injection site), less insulin insensitivity, and a decreased incidence of tissue hypertrophy or atrophy. Beef insulin is more immunogenic than pork insulin. The insulin can be kept at room temperature, but it should not be exposed to temperature extremes or direct sunlight. Airline x-ray machines do not hurt insulin.

The physician may change the overall dosage of insulin for any number of reasons. For instance, some endogenous insulin secretion may return after 2 or 3 weeks of insulin treatment. This "honeymoon period" is the result of the secretion of insulin from the remaining functional β-cells. Insulin therapy may be adjusted but should not be discontinued. Adolescence is another time when dosages may be adjusted upward to handle hormonal changes and

*Table 32–5.  Examples of Types of Insulin and Their Action Times*

| Product | Manufacturer | Form | Onset | Peak | Duration |
|---|---|---|---|---|---|
| **Rapid-Acting** | | | | | |
| Regular | Novo Nordisk | Pork | 30 min | 2.5–5 h | 8 h |
| Semilente | Novo Nordisk | Beef | 1–2 h | 5–10 h | 16 h |
| Humulin R | Lilly | Human | 15–30 min | 2–4 h | 6–8 h |
| Purified Pork R | Novo Nordisk | Pork | 30 min | 2.5–5 h | 8 h |
| **Intermediate-Acting** | | | | | |
| Humulin L | Lilly | Human | 1–3 h | 6–12 h | 18–24 h |
| Purified Pork L | Lilly | Pork | 2–3 h | 7–15 h | 22 h |
| NPH | Novo Nordisk | Beef | 1–2 h | 4–12 h | 24 h |
| Iletin II | Lilly | | | | |
| Lente | Lilly | Beef/pork | 1–3 h | 6–12 h | 18–26 h |
| **Long-Acting** | | | | | |
| Ultralente | Novo Nordisk | Beef | 4 h | 10–30 h | 36 h |
| Humulin | Lilly | Human | 4–6 h | 8–20 h | 24–28 h |

growth spurts. In addition, insulin dosages often need adjustments when a child's activity patterns change, such as during the winter when the child needs more insulin because of less activity, or during the summer when the child's insulin dosage may be decreased to accommodate for increased activities. Stressful times such as during surgery, illness, or emotional upsets can also increase insulin requirements.

Insulin injections may be difficult and frightening for a child and family members. Accepting the fact that insulin is a necessary element of the child's daily life is a major hurdle. Children often ask why they need insulin and hope that eventually they will not need injections. The basic injection technique (pinch with injection with a 90-degree angle of the needle) should be practiced initially on an orange, then on a mannequin or doll, next on the parents or the nurse, and finally on the child. As little time as possible should elapse between the initial instruction and the actual injection to allay anxiety (Fig. 32-8).

The child and family must go home with all the information they need about insulin administration. A home health nurse referral for outpatient diabetic teaching may help, but diabetic teaching should begin in the hospital. The child and family must know the insulin prescribed, its onset, peak action time, and the effective duration. They need to know the various types of insulin, the proper mixing, and the drawing up of insulin into a syringe (i.e., drawing up the short-acting insulin before the long-acting insulin, then using within 5 minutes of mixing).

A rotation pattern for injection sites, based on whether the parent or child administers the insulin, is important (Fig. 32-9). The upper arms, thighs, and outer area of the abdomen are common sites for self-injection because of easy access for the child. The buttocks can be used by

*Figure 32–8.  A child giving himself insulin. (Courtesy of the Nursing Department, Thomason Hospital, El Paso, Texas)*

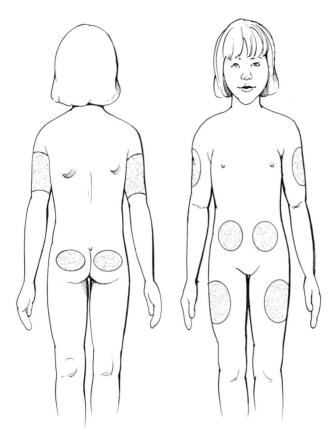

*Figure 32–9.   Subcutaneous injection sites.*

family members for injection. Rotation of sites is important to prevent atrophy of the subcutaneous fat or fibrous swelling from repeated usage of the same spot. Each site should be scored in rows, leaving 1 inch between injection sites. Giving four to six injections in one area, then moving to another area, will minimize variation in absorption rates, especially since different areas of the body have different absorption rates. Vigorous exercise also enhances absorption in the exercised muscle. The recording of glucose monitoring, insulin injection, time, dose, site, and the child's reactions should also be emphasized.

Insulin syringes should be compared for accuracy, strength, and comfort, then selected by the family. A 28-gauge, 1/2-inch needle is generally used, unless the child is obese. Use of the same type of syringe at all times is recommended to prevent errors in dosage. Parents should be cautioned not to substitute types of insulin or insulin syringes to save money; however, disposable needles and syringes can be reused at home for up to 7 days without risk of infection, provided that the child and parents are taught the proper procedures for storage and cleanliness of the equipment (Poteet, Reinert, & Ptak, 1987).

Some people who are motivated to maintain tight control of their diabetes have found the continuous, portable insulin pump helpful. The pump, worn on a belt, delivers a steady, 24-hour, low dose of insulin through a needle inserted under the skin of the abdomen, flank, or thigh. The wearer can deliver extra insulin to cover meals. The pump can be removed and the catheter capped for bathing, swimming, or other exercise. The child and parents must know how to operate the device (the mechanics, the battery changes, and the alarm systems), prepare the insulin, load the syringe, insert the catheter, adjust the insulin flow for routine needs and for illnesses, and connect and disconnect the catheter. Since the pump does not sense the blood glucose level and then change insulin delivery, the use of a home glucose monitoring device is essential with a pump to modify insulin flow as needed.

*Nutritional Plan.* The nutritional program is usually ordered by the physician, planned with the family by a registered dietitian, and reinforced and supported by the nurse. Meal planning should consider two major goals: (1) keeping blood sugar near normal levels by avoiding insulin reaction and hyperglycemia, and (2) providing the calories and nutrients needed to maintain normal growth and weight. Decisions about the meal plan should include the child's individual characteristics, needs, food preferences, cultural patterns, and lifestyle. The meal plan must cover food choices, timing of meals, and portion sizes. Calorie recommendations take into account the child's age, sex, weight, height, and activity level.

Most meal plans include a balanced intake of nutrients from all four food groups to ensure adequate energy intake and good health. The American Diabetes Association (1986) recommends 50% to 60% of the calories from carbohydrate, about 12% to 20% from protein, and the rest from fat.

The last decade has brought a tremendous reversal in nutritional recommendations for diabetes treatment, from low-carbohydrate, high-fat diets to high-carbohydrate, high-fiber, low-fat diets. Most dietitians recommend complex carbohydrates, such as starchy vegetables, whole grain products, and beans, which cause less of a blood-sugar rise than refined sugars, sweeteners, and processed starches. Concentrated sugars, such as candy and soda pop, are generally discouraged. Meal plans should also restrict high saturated fat and cholesterol (i.e., animal products including butter, lard, whole milk, and fatty meats) to prevent atherosclerosis in later life. Some evidence suggests that substituting high-fiber foods (beans, raw vegetables, fresh fruit, and bran) for low-fiber foods (white bread and refined flour) may reduce cholesterol levels in the blood. Fiber may also help keep blood sugar down after a meal, lowering insulin requirements.

It is important that meals be timed to complement the timing and action of injected insulin, which has a predictable onset, peak effect, duration of action, and absorption rate. Eating specified amounts of foods at generally fixed times can help control diabetes. Meal plans generally include three meals and two or three snacks eaten at set times each day. Without the snacks, the constant release of insulin makes the child prone to hypoglycemia between meals. For example, most children eat meals at standard meal times and then have snacks at midmorning (to cover the morning rapid-acting insulin), midafternoon (to cover the peak of the intermediate-acting insulin), and before bed (to prevent low blood sugar during the night). If the child has more exercise than usual, added snacks may be needed. Conversely, if the child has more food than usual, extra activity may be needed (see additional safety rules for nutrition and exercise in Table 32-6).

To simplify meal planning, the food intake can follow an exchange-type meal program based on the Exchange Lists for Meal Planning by the American Diabetes Association and the American Dietetic Association. Foods are divided into six categories (starch/bread, meat, vegetable, fruit, milk, and fat), and any food and its portion on a list can be exchanged for any other food on the same list. The meal plan specifies how many exchanges, or portions, can be chosen from each category at each meal.

For the exchange program, scales and other measures are used for about 3 months; later, the family members and client can estimate the portions. In general, families that have everyone eating the same foods at meals, instead of providing a separate meal for the child with diabetes, minimize the child's feelings of being different. When possible, allowing the child to buy lunch at school has the same effect. Many schools distribute lunch menus a week early, which allows the child and parents to discuss meal choices in advance. The nutritional value of foods is em-

phasized by teaching families to read food labels. A list of the nutritional value of popular fast-food items served at major chains can be obtained from the American Diabetes Association.

Adolescents with diabetes needs to know that the ingestion of alcohol or drugs (such as cocaine or amphetamines) can potentially result in hypoglycemia. The alcohol augments the glucose-lowering effects of insulin, and the stimulants increase metabolism while decreasing a person's appetite. Any substance that alters judgment affects the person's ability to balance food, insulin, and exercise requirements.

After the acute phase, the adjustment of insulin dosage to diet and exercise begins. The major responsibility of the nurse in this instance is the education or reeducation of the client and family. As soon as possible, the child or family should assume major responsibility for diabetic management and care under the supervision of the nurse. This includes the same meticulous recording of intake and output, blood or urine glucose, urine acetone levels, and insulin administration. It also involves careful planning and timing of the daily diet and daily activities. Client education is an ongoing, long-term nursing activity based on the changing needs of the diabetic child and family.

Children can check their own urine and blood glucose and administer their own insulin at about 9 or 10 years of age. To do this they must understand the pathophysiology of diabetes, general hygiene for foot care, vision and dental check-ups, and care of minor abrasions and illnesses. Children and their families need to understand that the child is not an invalid. Exercise can lower blood sugar levels. It also strengthens the lungs, heart, and circulatory system, builds muscles, reduces stress, and builds self-confidence. The child can compensate for a decrease in blood sugar by having a snack before the activity. If a hypoglycemic reaction occurs, the child can eat or drink something sugary, which should always be kept available. If ketones are present in the urine, the child should not exercise, since insulin is already breaking down fats.

*Testing.* Testing of both blood sugar and urine ketone levels can help determine if the child's management plan is controlling diabetes effectively. Test results should be monitored and recorded over a period of time, then used as a guide for making adjustments in the diet, insulin dose, or activity level. Persuading a child to self-test can be a challenge. Motivating strategies, such as praise, extra privileges, or earning points toward a gift, may help. Compromises, such as testing twice a day instead of three or four times a day, may also help. Stressing accuracy and regularity is most important. A high reading may seem "bad" to a child, so try to respond in a nonjudgmental manner. Concentrate on helping the child keep the blood sugar in line.

Self-testing of blood or urine sugar levels two to four

**Table 32-6. Safety Rules for Diabetic Children**

**Nutrition**

Maintain total calorie intake
Develop a daily well-balanced meal plan using the four food groups
Eat extra food for extra activity
Plan extra activity for extra food
Keep consistent meal times
Avoid pure sugar foods (candy, soda)
Increase intake of fiber
Decrease cholesterol and saturated fat intake

**Exercise**

Exercise with a buddy
Test blood sugar before exercise
If ketones are in urine, restore control first
Have a snack before exercise that is not covered by the meal plan
Carry some form of sugar at all times to treat hypoglycemia
Wear an ID bracelet or necklace
Try to inject the insulin into a non-exercising muscle
Drink plenty of fluids, especially in hot weather

times a day is usually recommended, most often before each meal and the bedtime snack. Occasional testing 2 hours after a meal provides valuable information regarding peak blood sugar levels. A test should not be done unless 2 hours have passed since food was eaten. Testing for ketones may be done every morning. The health team should help the family decide which test to use and how often it should be done, based on the child's age and willingness to perform the test. Although children may prefer urine testing over blood testing, the results obtained from blood tests provide more precise information.

Home blood glucose monitoring is done by putting a drop of blood, obtained by a finger-stick instrument (Penlet or Autolet), on a test strip. Finger punctures are most effective on the outer edge of the fingers. The fingers do not need to be cleansed with alcohol because it toughens the skin, making future punctures difficult; it is recommended that soap and warm water be used for cleansing. Readings are obtained by analyzing the Chemstrip bG or Dextrostix (i.e., the color change of the strip based on the amount of sugar in the blood) or by obtaining a numerical reading using a Glucometer or Dextrometer. The accuracy of test results using a glucose monitoring strip can be affected by the size and placement of the blood sample on the strip, the timing of the test, and the patient's hematocrit level.

Urine tests for sugar or ketones involve dipping a test strip in a urine sample. The color change of the strip indicates the level of sugar or ketones in the urine. Usually, a +1 urine glucose level is acceptable because it reflects a slight spillage of sugar, ruling out hypoglycemia, yet insufficient glucose to produce hyperglycemic reactions.

Urine ketone monitoring indicates ketones in the urine resulting from fatty acid breakdown. Ketones appear in the urine at the following times: when there is inadequate insulin dosage; when there is an illness; when there is inadequate food intake due to starvation; and when the drop in blood sugar, after an insulin reaction, has prompted the body to turn to fat for energy. Urine ketones must always be checked when the blood sugar is above 240 mg/dL, when urine sugar is above 2%, or when the person feels sick. Ketones are measured as small/trace, moderate, or large. Positive ketone results in the morning may be a sign of low blood sugar during the night followed by a rebound effect.

There are many advantages to blood glucose monitoring over urine testing. Sometimes, there is a poor correlation between a blood glucose reading and a simultaneous urine glucose testing. If the test urine has been in the bladder several hours, it reflects sugar levels of several hours ago, whereas the blood test gives a direct reading of the blood sugar level at the time of testing. Blood testing can give a very low numerical reading (telling the child when the blood sugar is dangerously low), whereas urine testing only reveals when the blood sugar is high enough to cause the kidneys to filter excess sugar into the urine. The specific renal threshold of the child affects the negative reading of urine testing. Therefore, a child with a high threshold for sugar will not spill sugar until the blood sugar is as high as 220 mg/dL, far above the normal level of 180 mg/dL. Compared with blood tests, urine tests have more false readings. High doses of aspirin or vitamin C produce an incorrect urine test reading.

*Complications of Ketoacidosis.* Ketoacidosis, the most complete state of insulin deficiency, is a life-threatening condition that requires immediate attention. It occurs when the body cannot use carbohydrates for energy. The body turns to fat breakdown for nourishment, producing ketone bodies as a byproduct. Some common causes of ketoacidosis are inadequate insulin, acute illness, growth spurts, emotional upset, undiagnosed or newly diagnosed diabetes, overeating, insufficient exercise, and poor diabetes management. Stress (illness, surgery, or emotional upset) can cause ketoacidosis because the body increases its production of hormones (such as adrenaline) that block the action of insulin. After the initial symptoms of hyperglycemia occur (glycosuria, polyuria, polydipsia), the more severe symptoms of ketoacidosis occur. To avoid ketoacidosis, the family must treat the hyperglycemia promptly.

The physician should be notified immediately if urine ketones are moderate or large; if ketones are present after more than one test; if the child appears dehydrated; if the child's breath smells fruity; if ketones are accompanied by high blood sugar or persistent vomiting; if the child's level of alertness changes; or if the child has difficulty breathing.

During hospitalization, management with adequate intravenous regular insulin, fluids and electrolytes, and plasma expanders establishes renal blood flow and can reverse the diabetic ketoacidosis. Vital signs, level of consciousness, urine specific-gravity values, and volume, as well as hourly blood sugar testing, urine ketone testing, and cardiac monitoring, should be assessed and recorded. Cardiac changes due to hypokalemia or hyperkalemia should be reported. When serum glucose levels reach 250 mg/dL, dextrose infusion is generally restarted to prevent hypoglycemia.

After acute stages of the ketoacidosis, regular subcutaneous insulin is administered, and oral feedings, as tolerated, are initiated in a pattern of three meals and three snacks. Blood glucose testing is done before meals and at bedtime. If blood glucose monitoring is not possible, the physician may order double-voided urine specimens. The double-voided specimen is obtained by first having the child void one half hour before the test is done. This specimen is measured and discarded. One half hour later, a second specimen is collected and measured for glucose and acetone. Insulin dosages are usually adjusted according to the previous day's tests. The total amount of regular insulin is slowly decreased when the child is stabilized. A split-dose insulin schedule of short-acting and intermediate-acting insulin is then prescribed.

*Complications of Hypoglycemia.* The most common medical emergency for a diabetic child is hypoglycemia, often called *insulin shock*. The episode must be treated promptly because, if allowed to progress, low blood sugar can lead to seizures and possibly brain damage or death. Neurological signs and symptoms generally appear when the blood glucose drops below about 30 mg/dL. The most common causes of hypoglycemia are too much insulin, too little food (or food eaten too late), or too much unplanned exercise. Many of the early symptoms, such as hunger, increased pulse rate, hyperactivity, increased respiratory rate, and weakness, are caused by epinephrine, which tries to raise blood sugar. Other symptoms, however, such as headaches, incoherent speech, seizures, and coma, are signs that the brain is being deprived of energy.

Children with diabetes should be taught to notify an adult when they feel "strange" or "not like themselves" in any way. All diabetic children should have an identification bracelet explaining their condition so that emergency measures can be initiated promptly. Adults who spot irritability or sudden changes in personality in the child should consider the possibility of a reaction. Blood glucose testing is the best way to determine whether or not blood sugar is low. When in doubt, treat. Give the child about 10 to 15 g of glucose, such as 5 lifesavers, 10 small gumdrops, 1 to 2 tbsp of honey, 4 oz of nondiet soda, 2 tbsp of cake icing, or a half cup of orange juice. The simpler the sugar, the more rapidly it is absorbed. If there is not a positive response, the same treatment may be repeated in 15 minutes. If the child is having difficulty swallowing or is too listless to drink, cake frosting squirted under the tongue can be absorbed by the buccal membrane. Aspiration is much less likely with a paste or gel than a liquid.

Insulin reactions can be prevented by following recommended meal plans, planning snacks before vigorous exercise, and making sure the insulin dose is correct. If the child continues to have insulin reactions, despite following the rules, the insulin dose must be decreased or the food plan adjusted with the help of the physician. Infrequent, mild reactions are sometimes unavoidable, are not harmful, and may be a good indicator of tight control.

Everyone treated with insulin should carry some form of sugar at all times in case of emergency. Some examples are glucose tablets, sugar cubes, Lifesavers, Cake Mate tube cake icing, or small gumdrops. If a snack or mealtime is approaching when the reaction occurs, the child should be treated and then should eat the scheduled snack or meal. If a snack or meal is not planned soon, however, the child should follow the sugar with a snack containing a complex carbohydrate and protein (2 to 4 soda crackers and 1 oz of cheese or 1 tbsp of peanut butter) to avoid another reaction. This food is not subtracted from the day's food plan. The complex carbohydrate and protein, which generally have a longer and less dramatic effect on blood sugar, prevent the blood sugar from dropping again after the reaction is initially treated.

If the child has a convulsion or is unconscious, the adult should treat the child immediately with Glucagon. Glucagon, a hormone normally produced in the pancreas, is prescribed for immediate home treatment of hypoglycemia. The commercial powder is mixed with the accompanying diluent and injected intramuscularly or subcutaneously into the child. The dosage can be repeated after 20 minutes. It requires about 10 to 15 minutes to elevate the blood glucose level by causing the liver to release stored glucose into the bloodstream. If the child regains consciousness, the Glucagon should be followed by oral administration of simple sugars. However, Glucagon may cause nausea and vomiting. If the child does not respond to Glucagon, then the parents must seek prompt emergency care. The child needs an intravenous infusion of glucose to avoid brain damage. It is important that all who care for the child know how to use Glucagon, including baby-sitters and teachers.

It is not always easy to distinguish between insulin shock (hypoglycemia) and diabetic coma (hyperglycemia); however, diabetic coma is very rare in children. Laboratory studies reveal low blood sugar and lack of sugar and ketones in the urine of the child in insulin shock; they reveal high blood sugar, glycosuria, and ketonuria in the child in diabetic coma. In most cases, treating the child for shock with glucagon will do no significant harm; however, a child already in insulin shock must never be given more insulin.

The *Somogyi reaction* is an abnormal increase in blood sugar that occurs after an episode of hypoglycemia. Stress hormones, particularly epinephrine and glucagon, respond when blood sugar levels fall below normal. As a result, glycogen is converted into glucose and released into the blood. Sometimes, the body does not adequately slow the release of these stress hormones after the blood sugar levels have returned to normal. Therefore, high blood sugar can result hours after an insulin reaction. Also, small amounts of ketones can appear in the urine because the hormones cause the body to break down fats. Rebounds are difficult to spot and should be suspected if there is a pattern of blood sugar readings of low, high, low, high, accompanied by small amounts of ketones in the urine.

*Complications of Illness.* On days when the child is ill, plans should include guidelines for adjusting insulin, advice about when to test for glucose and ketones, how to make dietary adjustments, and having the physician's telephone number available at all times. Insulin should never be omitted, even if the child is not eating well. Always check urine ketones at least twice a day during any illness, especially when vomiting is involved, since ketones can cause vomiting. Stress causes the body to use insulin more rapidly. The doctor should be called if the child has vomited more than once. Some doctors have children add periodic doses of rapid-acting insulin, perhaps every 2 to 4 hours, based on test results on the day that they are ill. If the child cannot tolerate solid food, then calories and carbohydrates should be provided with high-calorie drinks. If the child is vomiting, give a teaspoon of liquid every 10 minutes. Give liquids such as fruit juice, Popsicles, or chicken broth. Parents must encourage fluid intake to prevent dehydration. Also, blood sugar and urine ketones should be monitored frequently, especially before meals and at bedtime, until blood sugar levels and insulin dosages return to normal.

In summary, balancing insulin, diet, and exercise is the dynamic challenge of diabetes management for the child and family. The nurse has a major role in educating the family based on the developmental needs of the child. Effective self-management of the diabetes should be the ultimate goal for a diabetic child. A child or adolescent with well-managed diabetes will demonstrate enhanced self-esteem and optimal physical and emotional growth and development.

## Summary

Endocrine system disorders in children are related primarily to oversecretion or undersecretion of hormones and the associated effects on body growth and functioning. Medical treatments seek to modify hormonal secretions by administration of hormones if undersecretion is the problem, or by altering or removing the source of hypersecretion through surgical intervention and drug therapy if oversecretion is the problem. Because many endocrine disorders are long-term problems and involve changes in physical appearance, children are at risk for developing self-image problems. Nursing care emphasizes the establishment of feelings of control and self-esteem for the child and the demonstration of knowledge about the disease and development of healthy coping mechanisms for the child and family.

# Nursing Care Plan

### Assessment

Susan Lee is a 7-year-old girl brought to the pediatrician's office at 2:00 P.M. by her mother.

#### Chief Complaint

Susan complains of abdominal pain, nausea, and vomiting. Susan's mother reports a fruity odor on Susan's breath.

#### Subjective Assessment

**Past History:** Regular visits to a pediatrician for routine well-child care. No prior illnesses or hospitalization; all immunizations up-to-date.

**Present History:** Complaints of recent weight loss, tiredness, frequent bedwetting, frequent urination, thirst for fluids, and constant hunger in past month. Abdominal complaints in past 48 hours.

**Family History:** Mother is 28 and divorced from father, who is 30. No siblings. Maternal and paternal grandparents are alive and well. No family history of asthma, allergies, seizures, or heart disease. Maternal sister has diabetes mellitus.

#### Objective Assessment

**Physical Examination:** T. 37°C (98.6°F) (oral route); P. 90 (radial); R. 20; B.P. 105/65 (R. arm); weight 20.5 kg (45 lb) (10%); height 114 cm (46 in) (10%).

| | |
|---|---|
| Integument: | Clear and intact, dry mucous membranes and skin; poor skin turgor |
| Head: | Normalcephalic |
| Eyes: | PERRLA, EOM's intact, fundoscopic exam WNL |
| Ears: | Otoscopic exam WNL |
| Nose: | No drainage, no erythema |

*(continued)*

# Nursing Care Plan *(Continued)*

| | |
|---|---|
| Throat: | No erythema or exudate |
| Neck: | Supple, nodes non-palpable |
| Thorax and Lungs: | Kussmaul respirations, no retractions, breath sounds clear |
| Heart: | Normal $S_1$, $S_2$; no murmur |
| Abdomen: | Active bowel sounds in all quadrants, tenderness in all quadrants on palpation, no masses |
| Genitalia: | WNL |
| Musculoskeletal | Full ROM |
| Neurological: | Lethargic, reflexes normal and symmetrical, irritable and restless |

### Diagnostic Test and Results:

Blood sugar = 350 mg/dl

### Medical Diagnosis:

Insulin-dependent diabetes mellitus

### Medical Plan:

Admit to hospital, monitor blood glucose concentration, begin insulin therapy, prevent complications.

## Nursing Care Plan for a Child with Diabetes Mellitus

| Goals | Nursing Interventions | Evaluation Criteria |
|---|---|---|
| **NURSING DIAGNOSIS #1:** *Fluid volume deficit related to vomiting and polyuria secondary to ketoacidosis* | | |
| (S) Child will regain adequate hydration within 24 hours<br><br>(L) Child will continue to maintain adequate hydration during hospitalization | Assess hydration status q 4 hours<br>  Skin turgor<br>  Dry mucous membranes<br>Monitor serum electrolytes<br>  Hemoglobin<br>  Hematocrit<br>  Serum osmolarity<br>  BUN and CR<br>Monitor I & O q 4 hours<br>Weigh child on admission and qd, on same scale<br>Monitor vital signs, including blood pressure and level of consciousness, as ordered<br>Encourage p. o. fluid as ordered (child may be NPO initially until glucose is stabilized)<br>Provide IV replacement for urine output, as ordered | Child is well hydrated with good skin turgor and moist mucous membranes. |

*(continued)*

# Nursing Care Plan *(Continued)*

*NURSING DIAGNOSIS #2: Impaired tissue perfusion related to hyperglycemia and ketoacidosis*

| Goals | Nursing Interventions | Evaluation Criteria |
|-------|----------------------|---------------------|
| (S) Child will be euglycemic during hospitalization | Recognize signs of ketoacidosis and hyperglycemia: <br> Abdominal pain, vomiting <br> Kussmaul respirations <br> Signs of dehydration <br> Acetone/fruity breath <br> Somnolence or coma <br><br> Observe for precipitating factors to ketoacidosis (infection, stress, omission of insulin) <br><br> Observe for complications of ketoacidosis (cerebral edema, dehydration, hyperkalemia, hypokalemia) <br><br> Monitor blood glucose levels, as ordered, then record findings and report significant changes <br><br> Administer insulin drip and electrolytes, as ordered, monitor rate q 30–60 minutes, record carefully <br><br> Monitor, record, and report signs of hypoglycemia: <br> Diaphoresis <br> Anxiety <br> Tremors <br> Tachycardia <br> Seizures <br> Irritability and headache <br> Impaired vision <br><br> Monitor blood gases for signs of metabolic acidosis <br><br> Test urine for ketones and specific gravity; record and report significant findings | Child is free of injury from hyperglycemia and ketoacidosis. |

*(continued)*

# Nursing Care Plan *(Continued)*

*NURSING DIAGNOSIS #3: Altered Nutrition: Less than body requirements related to defect in glucose metabolism*

| Goals | Nursing Interventions | Evaluation Criteria |
|---|---|---|
| (S) Child maintains weight during hospitalization<br><br>(L) Child increases weight in next 2 months | Assess for signs and symptoms of malnutrition (weight loss greater than ideal weight, weakness, fatigue)<br><br>Check blood sugar levels, as ordered<br><br>Increase diet as ordered, after NPO status<br><br>Monitor and record percentage of meal eaten<br><br>Collaborate with registered dietician and family members on menu plan<br><br>Provide meal and snacks that child likes on time | Child consumes sufficient amount of nutrients and gains weight |

*NURSING DIAGNOSIS #4: Altered family process related to situational crisis*

| Goals | Nursing Interventions | Evaluation Criteria |
|---|---|---|
| Family will cope with situational crises with minimal family disruption during hospitalization | Keep family informed of child's progress and involve them in child's care<br><br>Assess interpersonal relationships within family<br><br>Assist family with problem solving<br><br>Arrange for spiritual/social service consult, as needed<br><br>Refer family to American Diabetes Association for networking with other families in similar situations<br><br>Allow family to freely express fears or guilt | Family copes well with child's new diagnosis; family expresses concerns |

*(continued)*

# Nursing Care Plan *(Continued)*

*NURSING DIAGNOSIS #5: Knowledge deficit related to newly diagnosed diabetic*

| *Goals* | *Nursing Interventions* | *Evaluation Criteria* |
|---|---|---|
| (S) Child and family will state and demonstrate the requisite diabetic management knowledge before discharge from hospital | Educate parents and child regarding diabetic management: Provide information on the nature of diabetes mellitus Provide information on daily snack and meal planning Provide information on insulin and the injection procedure Teach urine and blood glucose testing skills Provide information regarding personal hygiene and exercise Teach signs of hypoglycemia and hyperglycemia Teach how to treat hypoglycemia (with food or simple sugars) and action plan for hyperglycemia Teach importance of careful record keeping | Child and family demonstrates an understanding of requisite diabetic management information and skills. |

## References

American Diabetes Association. (1986). Nutrition recommendations and principles for individuals with diabetes mellitus. *Diabetes Care, 10,* 126–132.

Bacon, G. E., Spencer, M. L., Hopwood, N. J., & Kelch, R. P. (1990). *A practical approach to pediatric endocrinology.* Chicago: Year Book Medical Publishers.

Bullock, B. L., & Rosendahl, P. P. (1988). *Pathophysiology: Adaptations and alterations in function* (2nd ed.). Glenview, IL: Scott, Foresman.

Coody, D. (1984). Congenital hypothyroidism. *Pediatric Nursing, 10*(5), 342–346.

Dean, H. J., & Winter, J. S. (1989). Abnormalities of pubertal development. In Collu, R., Ducharme, J. R., & Guyda, H. J. *Pediatric endocrinology* (2nd ed.). New York: Raven Press, 331–336.

Hamburger, J. I. (1985). Management of hyperthyroidism in children and adolescents. *Journal of Clinical Endocrinology Metabolism, 60*(1019), 46–50.

Johnstone, P. A. S., Rundell, J. R., & Esposito, M. (1990). Mental status changes of Addison's disease. *Psychosomatics, 31*(1), 103–107.

Mimouni, F., & Tsang, R. D. (1990). Parathyroid and vitamin D related disorders. In Kaplan, S. A. *Clinical pediatric endocrinology,* Chap. 11. Philadelphia: W. B. Saunders, 427–453.

New, M. I., del Balzo, P., Crawford, C., & Speiser, P. W. (1990). The adrenal cortex. In Kaplan, S. A. (Ed.). *Clinical pediatric endocrinology.* Philadelphia: W. B. Saunders.

Poteet, G., Reinert, B., & Ptak, H. (1987). Outcome of multiple usage of disposable syringes in the insulin-requiring diabetic. *Nursing Research, 35,* 350–352.

Potts, J. T., Jr. (1990). Clinical review 9: Management of asymptomatic hyperparathyroidism. *Journal of Clinical Endocrinology and Metabolism, 70*(6), 1489–1493.

Sheeler, L. R. (1989). Cushing's syndrome. *Urologic Clinics of North America, 16*(3), 447–455.

Siminerio, L. (1986). *Children with diabetes.* Alexandria, VA: American Diabetes Association.

# Bibliography

Anderson, J. W. (1989). Recent advances in carbohydrate nutrition and metabolism in diabetes mellitus. *Journal of the American College of Nutrition, 8*(S), 61S–67S.

Bertorelli, A. M. (1990). Nutrition counseling: Meeting the needs of ethnic clients with diabetes. *Diabetes Educator, 16*(4), 295–299.

Clark, L. M., & Plotnick, L. P. (1990). Insulin pumps in children with diabetes. *Journal of Pediatric Health Care, 4*(1), 3–10.

Collins, C., & Lipman, T. H. (1985). The endocrine system. In Hayman, L. L., & Sporing, E. M. *Handbook of pediatric nursing.* New York: John Wiley & Sons, pp. 478–520.

Daly, M., & Michael, S. R. (1989). Treating hypoglycemia. *Diabetes Educator, 15*(4), 320–321.

Felicetta, J. V. (1989). Cushing's syndrome: How to pinpoint and treat the underlying cause. *Postgraduate Medicine, 86*(8), 79–90.

Fisher, D. A. (1990). The thyroid. In Kaplan, S. *Clinical pediatric endocrinology.* Philadelphia: W. B. Saunders.

Harris, A. S. (1989). Clinical experience with desmopressin: Efficacy and safety in central diabetes insipidus and other conditions. *Journal of Pediatrics, 114*(4), 711–718.

Kulkarni, K., Miller, P. F., & Dew, N. (1989). What every diabetes educator needs to know about hypoglycemia. *Diabetes Educator, 15*(1), 28–29.

Lipman, T. H. (1989). Assessing family strengths to guide plan of care using Hymovich's framework. *Journal of Pediatric Nursing, 4*(3), 186–196.

Lipman, T. H., Difazio, D. A., Meers, R. A., & Thompson, R. L. (1989). A developmental approach to diabetes in children: Birth through preschool. *American Journal of Maternal Child Nursing, 14*(5), 330–332.

Lipman, T. H., Difazio, D. A., Meers, R. A., & Thompson, R. L. (1989). A developmental approach to diabetes in children: Birth through preschool. *American Journal of Maternal Child Nursing, 14*(4), 255–259.

Lumley, W. A. (1989). Recognizing and reversing insulin shock. *Nursing 89, 19*(9), 34–41.

Moossa, A. R., Baker, L., & Lavelle-Jones, M. (1987). Hypoglycemic syndrome in infancy and childhood. *Western Journal of Medicine, 146*(5), 585–588.

Oldham, J., & Campbell, R. K. (1987). Treatment of the hospitalized hypoglycemic patient. *Diabetes Educator, 13*(3), 310–311.

Ryan, C., Atchison, J., Puczynski, S., Puczynski, M., Arslanian, S., & Becker, D. (1990). Mild hypoglycemia associated with deterioration of mental efficiency in children with insulin-dependent diabetes mellitus. *The Journal of Pediatrics, 117*(1), 32–38.

Samanta, A., Denham, J., Jowett, N. I., & Burden, A. C. (1986). Management of the acutely ill diabetic patient. *Intensive Care Nursing, 1,* 194–203.

Solomon, B. L. (1980). The hypothalamus and the pituitary gland: An overview. *Nursing Clinics of North America, 15*(3), 435–451.

Steinburg, C. (1990). Teaching the teacher. *Diabetes Forecast,*

Solomon, B. L. (1980). The hypothalamus and the pituitary gland: An overview. *Nursing Clinics of North America, 15*(3), 435–451.

Walfish, P. G., & Tseng, K. H. (1989). Thyroid physiology and pathology. In Collu, R., Ducharme, J. R., & Guyda, H. J. *Pediatric endocrinology* (2nd ed.). New York: Raven Press, pp. 367–416.

# Alterations in Musculoskeletal Function

Sallie S. Page-Goertz

*Sculpture by Charles Parks*

33

*Embryology*

*Anatomy*

*Physiology*

*Assessment*

*Nursing Diagnosis*

*Planning Nursing Care*

*Nursing Interventions*

*Evaluating Nursing Care*

*Common Musculoskeletal Problems in Children*

*Congenital Musculoskeletal Problems*

*Musculoskeletal Problems of Infants, Toddlers, and Preschoolers*

*Musculoskeletal Problems of School-Age Children and Adolescents*

*Summary*

*Nursing Care Plan*

*Upon completion of this chapter the reader will be able to:*

1. *Discuss the anatomy and physiology of the musculoskeletal system.*

2. *Describe bone healing and remodeling.*

3. *Identify key components in the nursing assessment of musculoskeletal function.*

4. *Formulate nursing diagnoses for musculoskeletal problems.*

5. *Discuss the developmental considerations necessary in planning nursing care for children with musculoskeletal problems.*

6. *Differentiate the types of fractures seen in childhood.*

7. *Discuss the nursing care for children in casts, traction, or braces.*

8. *Plan and implement appropriate nursing care measures for specific musculoskeletal problems.*

9. *Analyze the outcomes of nursing interventions for musculoskeletal problems including prevention, education, therapeutic, and supportive measures.*

*Key Terms*

cartilage

compound fracture

countertraction

diaphysis

disuse atrophy

endosteum

ephiphyseal plate

ephiphysis

fracture

joint

joint capsule

ligament

medullary cavity

myoblast

ossification

osteoblast

periosteum

synovial joint

synovial membrane

tendon

The musculoskeletal system (MS) provides both form and function for the human body. Structural elements of this system include bones, muscles, joints, tendons, and ligaments. These structures perform various functions, including support, protection, movement, and hematopoiesis. Both genetic influences and mechanical forces control the growth and development of the MS system. While genetic influences are determined at the time of conception, mechanical forces are determined by the environment and include physical activity, gravity, weight-bearing, and tension from muscle movement.

## Embryology

The elements of the musculoskeletal system are derived from mesenchymal tissue that appears in the second embryonic week. By the end of the third week, the mesoderm and the notochord begin dividing into paired cuboidal bodies called somites. Eventually 43 pairs of these blocks of tissue develop. The axial skeleton, associated musculature, and dermal structures arise from these blocks of tissue.

Bones of the upper extremities develop before those

of the lower extremities, and proximal bones develop before distal bones. In early fetal life, the midportion of bones is cartilaginous. Mesodermal tissue surrounds the area to form hyaline cartilage models, which become ossified by endochondral ossification, a process that involves destruction of the cartilage in the models and the deposition of bone in the center (diaphysis) of a long bone. Endochondral ossification occurs in the axial skeleton (vertebral column and ribs) and the appendicular skeleton (shoulder and pelvic girdles and the limb bones). A second process, intramembranous ossification, forms the thin, flat bones of the skull. In this process, mesodermal cells form a membrane which later serves as a foundation for deposition of bonelike tissue.

These ossification processes begin around the eighth week of fetal life and, by 12 weeks, primary ossification centers appear in nearly all bones of the extremities. Secondary centers of ossification involving the ends of the long bones appear after birth.

The muscular system develops from mesodermal cells called myoblasts, embryonic cells that develop into muscle fiber cells.

## Anatomy

### Bones

The adult skeleton has 206 bones. Other pieces are in the skeleton at birth, but these pieces are joined by the processes of union and ossification, as in the bones of the skull.

Figure 33-1 illustrates the anatomical features of long bones, which include the following:

*Diaphysis.* The main shaftlike portion of a long bone, which is hollow. The hollow is initially filled with red bone marrow, then later with yellow bone marrow. The diaphysis is made of compact bone. The ephiphyses, which are the end portions of long bones, are formed of spongy bone.

*Ephiphyseal plate.* The growth center between the diaphysis and epiphysis. Cellular proliferation at these centers is responsible for longitudinal growth. Calcification of the ephiphyseal plate signals the end of growth.

*Articular cartilage.* The thin layer of cartilage covering the articular surface of epiphyses that serves as a cushion between the bones.

*Medullary cavity.* A hollow area in the diaphysis that is filled with marrow.

*Endosteum.* A membrane that lines the medullary cavity.

*Periosteum.* A dense fibrous membrane that covers the bone.

*Subperiosteal space.* The space between the periosteum and the bone.

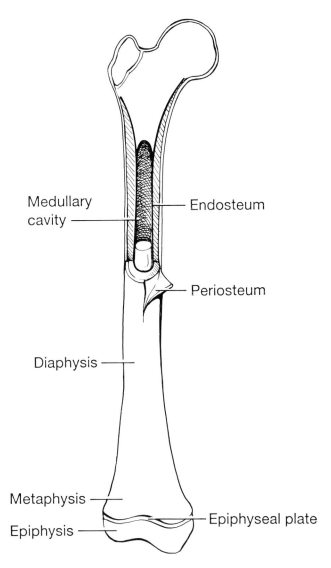

*Figure 33–1.* *Anatomical features of long bones.*

### Bone Growth and Ossification

Bone growth involves an increase in diameter as well as an increase in length (Fig. 33-2). Growth in diameter occurs on the bone's external surface as new bone is laid down to increase the bone's diameter; growth in length occurs at the epiphyseal plates, which are located near the ends of the long bones. Growth continues until these plates calcify during puberty. Bony fusion of the epiphysis with the diaphysis marks the end of skeletal growth. The epipyseal plate produces new bone cells in ossification centers.

Normal bone growth requires an intact epiphyseal plate, a normal blood supply, and intermittent pressure from physical activity and weight bearing. Ossification, or bone formation, involves two complex processes: synthesis of organic matrix by osteoblasts (bone-forming cells) and calcification of the matrix. The status of the epiphyseal plate is of critical importance, particularly in children who have alterations in musculoskeletal function.

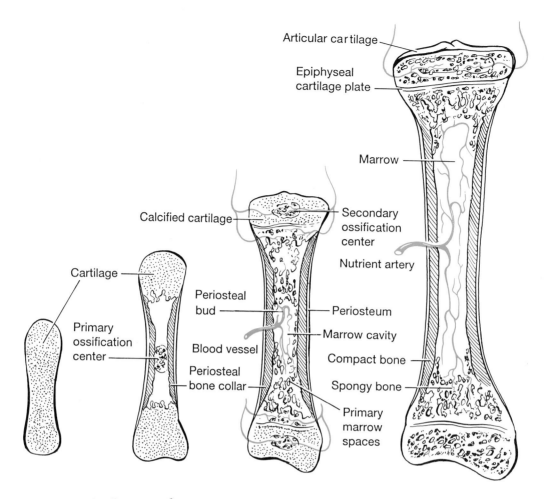

*Figure 33–2.  Bone growth.*

Abnormal conditions can affect future growth of the MS system. Complete growth and development of the skeletal system takes from 20 to 23 years.

## Joints

A joint is a connection between bones that makes movement of body parts possible. There are three types of joints: fibrous joints (synarthroses) that do not allow movement, such as the skull; cartilaginous joints (amphiarthroses) that allow slight movement, such as the costal joints between ribs and sternum; and synovial joints (diarthroses) that allow free movement, such as knees or elbows.

Synovial joints are the most common and complex joints and are frequently involved in traumatic injuries or disease states. Figure 33-3 identifies the structural features of synovial joints, including the following:

*Joint capsule.* An extension of the periosteum of the bones. The capsule binds the articulating bones to one another.

*Synovial membrane.* Lines the inner surface of the joint capsule. It secretes synovial fluid, which lubricates the joints and provides nutrients to the articular cartilage.

*Articular cartilage.* Covers and cushions the ends of the bones.

*Joint cavity.* The small space between the articulating bones that allows the bones to move.

*Ligament.* Fibrous tissue that connects the articular ends of bones, forming a strong binding.

*Tendon.* Connect muscle to bone at a joint.

## Skeletal Muscles

Skeletal muscle is composed of bundles of muscle fibers. Each individual's total number of muscle cells is established at birth, and this number never increases. Muscle enlargement results from hypertrophy of existing cells. This hypertrophy is only temporary unless it is maintained by regular exercise. Dead muscle cells are replaced by fibrous tissue.

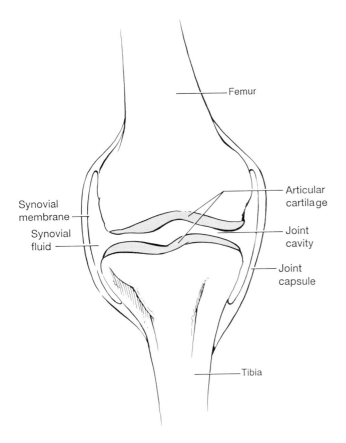

*Figure 33–3. Synovial joint.*

## *Physiology*

### *Functions of Bones, Joints, and Muscles*

Bone functions as both a structure and an organ. In its function as a structure, bone provides a framework for the body, acts as a lever for skeletal muscles, and protects vital organs. As an organ, bone facilitates erythrocyte production and stores minerals such as calcium and phosphorus.

Joints serve to segment the skeleton, allow motion between segments, and permit growth between the segments. Bones and joints cannot move themselves. Skeletal muscles work with bones and joints to provide active movement. The skeletal muscles also produce a large portion of body heat and allow maintenance of body position.

The molecular structure of muscles, and their response to calcium, allow for contraction and relaxation of the individual muscle fibers as well as the whole muscle body. The breakdown of adenosine triphosphate (ATP) creates energy for muscle action. Each muscle fiber functions under the all-or-none law: the fiber contracts maximally or not at all. The force of the muscle's contraction is determined by the number of individual muscle fibers contracting at one time.

Skeletal muscles produce movement by pulling on bones. Contraction of skeletal muscles causes tendons to exert force on the joints, resulting in movement of the bone. This movement is either involuntary (reflex) or voluntary. Disuse atrophy, which is a weakness or a decrease in muscle size, results from a lack of normal use. Contracture, or the shortening of a muscle, occurs when a muscle is maintained in a shortened position for a prolonged period.

### *Hematopoiesis*

Hematopoiesis, the formation and production of red and white blood cells and platelets by bone marrow, begins during fetal life. In children younger than 5 years, all bones produce blood cells and platelets. After 5 years of age, red marrow is gradually replaced by yellow marrow or fat in all but the membranous bones (pelvis, sternum, ribs, and vertebrae). By age 20, blood cells and platelets are produced only by marrow in these few sites.

### *Bone Healing and Remodeling*

Fractures in children heal more rapidly than in adults due to the increased osteogenic activity of the periosteum and endosteum. For example, in an infant a fractured femur heals in about 3 weeks, whereas in an adult it can take as long as 18 weeks. Non-union of fractures is rare in normal children.

The process of bone healing takes place in five stages. Hematoma formation begins the process when blood from torn vessels and the fractured bone collects around the fracture. Clotting factors in the blood form a fibrin mesh that provides a framework for the growth of fibroblasts and new capillary buds. Granulation tissue forms and replaces the clot. During the cellular proliferation stage osteoblasts (bone-forming cells) multiply at both ends of the fracture, forming cartilage and connective tissue, which eventually provides a link between the surfaces of the fracture.

During callus formation osteoblasts continue to proliferate and form a more solid bridge between the bone fragments. Blood supplies the area with the necessary nutrients to form the callus. Ossification occurs next, when the bone fragments are united and the callus is replaced by bone.

The final stage is remodeling, when the excess callus is absorbed in the marrow space and around the outside of the fracture. The absorption of the excess callus makes the site of the fracture thicker, and thus stronger, than it was before the fracture. The entire process of bone healing can take up to 9 months, depending on the child's age, the severity of the fracture, the amount of bone loss, and the degree of immobilization that is achieved.

## Assessment

### History

The format for the history for children with alterations of musculoskeletal function varies with the nature of the complaint and the age of the child. The nursing history for acute and chronic musculoskeletal problems focuses on information that is outlined in Table 33-1. Complaints of a more chronic nature demand a careful review of systems and past medical history, as well as family history, in order to identify potential causes, patient problems, and nursing diagnoses. These also are outlined in Table 33-1. Integrity of the neurologic system must also be assessed.

One part of the nursing assessment is to ascertain the effects of the condition on the child's activities. It is helpful if the child or care givers can describe in detail the child's approach to usual daily activities. The following history of a 12-month-old infant provided by her mother is an example: "Amy wakes up at 7. She used to stand in her crib and call to us, but the last few days she has not been able to stand up—so she sits and cries out to us. She's crawling much more now and has stopped trying to walk up the stairs." Subtle changes in activity or approach to an activity may be important diagnostic clues, as well as early signs of exacerbation of certain chronic musculoskeletal diseases such as muscular dystrophy or juvenile rheumatoid arthritis.

### Physical Examination

Appraisal of the musculoskeletal system involves inspection and palpation. General inspection should begin with observation when the child enters the examination room. Critical sites for inspection are the hips, legs, and feet, because these areas are most commonly affected by musculoskeletal abnormalities. Stance or posture, symmetry of movement, gait, joint motion, spinal curvature, muscle bulk, and strength are assessed. A measuring tape is used to assess symmetry and limb length. These observations should not be hindered by clothing. An accurate measurement of height or length is important. This measurement reflects bone growth. It is important to graph the height-to-weight ratio, using standardized growth charts (see Appendix B).

A neurological evaluation is also part of the assess-

### Table 33–1. Nursing History for Musculoskeletal Problems

**Acute Problems**

| | |
|---|---|
| Description of the injury | How, where, when |
| Musculoskeletal symptoms | Pop, snap, tear |
| | Changes in sensation |
| | Changes in movement |
| Pain | Location, intensity, duration |
| Other symptoms | Dizziness, fever, malaise |
| First aid treatment | |
| Other health problems | Allergies, chronic problems |
| Medications | Currently taking, allergies |
| Immunization (tetanus) status | |

**Congenital or Chronic Problems**

| | |
|---|---|
| History | Family, perinatal, past injuries, exposure to infection, developmental milestones |
| Effect of problem on activities of daily living | Changes required in routines for self-care, play, school, etc. |
| Dietary history | Food allergies, vitamin D supplement if breastfed, vitamin D–fortified milk |
| Musculoskeletal system review | |
|     Joints | Swelling, redness, warmth; refusal to move, stiffness, pain |
|     Bones | Fractures, deformity, pain |
|     Muscles | Weakness, swelling, pain |
|     Movement | Limited asymmetry, pain |
| Neurologic systems review | |
| Treatment to date | Medication, therapy, splints, braces, casts |
| Response to treatment | |

ment (see Chapter 26). Various portions of the physical examination are age-specific. These examination specifics are outlined in Table 33-2 and the display.

Because the musculoskeletal system depends on certain vitamins and minerals for normal growth, it is essential that children receive enough of these nutrients. A complete dietary history should be taken to ensure that children are receiving sufficient quantities of vitamins A, $B_1$, C, and D, as well as calcium, magnesium, phosphorus, potassium, and sodium.

## Diagnostic Procedures

Various imaging techniques assist in the diagnosis of musculoskeletal problems. Radiographs are used to formulate diagnoses and evaluate the effectiveness of treatment. In addition to x-rays, several special radiographic techniques may be used. These tests include radionuclide scans, magnetic resonance imaging (MRI), computed tomography (CT), ultrasonography, and Doppler imaging. In addition, tests to evaluate neurologic integrity may be done. An

*Table 33–2. Age-Appropriate Physical Assessment of the Musculoskeletal System*

**Newborn/Infant**

| | |
|---|---|
| General | Position of comfort |
| | Spontaneous/symmetrical movement of extremities |
| | Tone |
| | Gross motor skills |
| | Reflexes |
| | Palpate along extremities checking for masses |
| Neck | Note presence of mass or limited neck motion—seen in torticollis |
| Clavicle | Palpate clavicle |
| Upper extremities | Assess shoulder range of motion |
| | Check hands for extra digits, webbing |
| Hips | Limited abduction, asymmetrical gluteal folds (see Fig. 33–7) |
| | Ortolani maneuver |
| | Barlow maneuver |
| | Galeazzi sign |
| Lower extremities | Bowlegged is normal |
| | Note inturning toes/forefoot or abnormally turning ankle |
| Spine | C-shaped curve in sitting position |
| | Note dimple, hair tufts, cysts on lower back |

**Toddler**

| | |
|---|---|
| General | Stance and gait—lordosis, "pot belly," bowlegged until about age 2, broad-based stance to maintain balance |
| | Gross motor skills—walk, run |
| | Palpate extremities, checking for masses |
| Neck | Range of motion |
| Upper extremities | Range of motion, symmetry |
| Lower extremities | Hip range of motion |
| | Assess for tibial torsion: with child seated, medial malleolus should be anterior to the lateral malleolus; with child prone and knees flexed, foot should be in neutral position |

**Preschooler**

| | |
|---|---|
| General | Stance and gait—lordosis, knock-kneed, some in-toeing |
| | Gross motor skills—walk, run, hop, jump, skip |
| Remainder same as for toddler | |

**School-Age and Adolescent Sports Evaluation**

| | |
|---|---|
| General | Stance and gait—as for adult, with progressively less in-toeing |
| Extremities | Palpate extremities for masses |

## Fourteen-Step Evaluation of Musculoskeletal Function

1. Arms at side, face examiner
   *Observation*: head tilt, shoulder asymmetry, enlarged, acromioclavicular joint, waist asymmetry, swollen knee or ankle
2. Tighten quadriceps
   *Observation*: atrophy of vastus medialis
3. Neck motion—look at floor, at ceiling; over left shoulder, right shoulder; put right ear on right shoulder, left ear on left shoulder
   *Observation*: limited or asymmetric motion
4. Raise arms from sides, touch hands above head with elbows extended
   *Observation*: asymmetrical elevation of shoulder, inability to raise arms to the vertical
5. Hold arms horizontal in front of body, hand pushed down by examiner
   *Observation*: atrophy of anterior deltoid muscle, pain
6. Hold arms horizontal, elbow bent 90 degrees, forearms pointed toward ceiling
   *Observation*: asymmetrical forearm position
7. Extend and flex elbows in above position
   *Observation*: asymmetrical elbow extension or flexion
8. Arms at side, elbows flexed 90 degrees, pronate and supinate forearms
   *Observation*: loss of motion
9. Spread fingers, then make fist
   *Observation*: lack of finger flexion, swollen joints, finger deformity
10. Scoliosis screen (see Fig. 33-12)
11. Stand on tiptoes
    *Observation*: asymmetry in heel elevation, atrophy of calf muscles
12. Rise on heels
    *Observation*: Achilles tendon asymmetry, asymmetry of forefoot elevation
13. Assume squatting position
    *Observation*: asymmetry of heel elevation, knee flexion
14. Arise from squatting
    *Observation*: asymmetry in rising

(Adapted from: Garrick, J. G. [1988]. Orthopedic screening exam for children and adolescents. Presentation at the American Academy of Pediatrics. San Francisco, October, 1988)

electromyelogram may be performed to assess nerve conduction when changes in muscle strength are observed.

Closed or open biopsies of soft tissue or bone are used to evaluate infection or malignancy. These biopsies may be done under either local or general anesthesia, depending on the site, the extent of the biopsy, and accompanying procedures.

Arthroscopy allows direct visualization of a joint by means of insertion of an endoscope into the joint. This procedure is most commonly used on the knee, and permits cartilage removal, ligament repair, and other minor surgical procedures without the need for general anesthesia.

Laboratory evaluation includes tests for electrolytes such as sodium, potassium, calcium, and phosphorus that affect muscle contraction and bone mineralization. Muscle enzyme levels may also be assessed. Tests to evaluate possible autoimmune problems include immunoglobulins, antinuclear antibody, rheumatoid factor, and others. Blood and joint fluid may be evaluated for infection.

## Nursing Diagnosis

Nursing diagnoses approved by the North American Nursing Diagnosis Association are used when musculoskeletal problems are discussed. The most common diagnoses for alterations in musculoskeletal function include the following:

*Pattern 1: Exchanging*
- Altered nutrition: less than body requirements
- Altered nutrition: more than body requirements
- Altered peripheral tissue perfusion
- Constipation
- Fluid volume deficit
- High risk for impaired skin integrity
- High risk for infection
- High risk for injury
- Hyperthermia

*Pattern 3: Relating*
- Altered family processes
- Altered parenting
- Impaired social interaction

*Pattern 5: Choosing*
- Noncompliance

*Pattern 6: Moving*
- Activity intolerance
- Altered growth and development
- Self-care deficit
- Fatigue
- Impaired physical mobility

*Pattern 7: Perceiving*
- Body image disturbance
- Self-esteem disturbance

*Pattern 9: Feeling*
- Fear
- Pain

## Planning Nursing Care

Children undergoing procedures need support, information, comfort, and opportunities for play therapy. Cognitive rehearsal, self-talk, distraction, and relaxation techniques may enhance coping abilities of older preschoolers, school-age children, and adolescents. Parents should always be allowed to be with their children during procedures; however, they also may need assistance in developing coping strategies to effectively support their children during frightening or painful procedures. Use of pre-medication with anti-anxiety agents may be appropriate. If the procedure requires that the child be absolutely immobile for a prolonged period of time, sedation may be required.

## Developmental Considerations

Most musculoskeletal conditions involve alterations in mobility, either temporary or permanent. Impairment of mobility can interfere with the child's development beyond the obvious effects on gross or fine motor skills. Impaired mobility can result in potential social isolation, an altered body image, and continued dependence on others for self-care activities. These effects may hinder psychosocial as well as cognitive development in children. Nursing care plans must include measures to minimize the negative developmental effects of impaired mobility.

For infants or toddlers, limited locomotion interferes with opportunities for exploration of the environment that normally occur with crawling and walking. The use of scooter boards can replace crawling as a means of facilitating exploration.

Preschoolers are in the process of acquiring self-care and other skills. Impaired fine or gross motor function can inhibit development in this area. Thoughtful choices regarding clothing and utensils can diminish the effects of these limitations. Opportunities for social interaction must be provided for preschoolers. Youngsters can be taught simple responses to questions from peers regarding any visible physical differences. Childhood games can be adapted to accommodate children with impaired motor function.

School-age children are continuing to advance in physical, cognitive, and social skills. As peer groups become more important to them, simple musculoskeletal problems such as sprains or minor fractures can make them the center of attention, but serious problems can cause them to avoid peer relationships for fear of ridicule.

School-age children may require Individual Educational Plans (IEP) to identify strengths and weaknesses that affect academic performance so that the best approach to care is provided. Under Public Laws 94-142 and 99-457, all children from birth through adolescence have the right to equal education; special services such as transportation, physical and occupational therapy, or intermittent home-bound teaching must be provided.

Adolescents with acute or chronic musculoskeletal problems face heightened concerns regarding altered body image, sexuality, and plans for the future. Guiding them in an assessment of skills and interests related to career goals is important. Vocational/rehabilitation referrals may help adolescents with chronic impairment. Parents need ongoing encouragement to work with their children toward the goal of developing realistic plans for independent living.

For adolescents, acute problems are just as devastating as chronic problems. Injured athletes may experience depression related to loss of peer interaction, loss of activity, and possible interruption of their future athletic careers. Ideally, injury rehabilitation occurs with the team so that peer contact is maintained.

## Acute Care Considerations

Acute care is provided at the time of musculoskeletal trauma or orthopedic surgery. Nursing care focuses on prevention of common physiologic complications of injury or surgery, including neurovascular impairment, bleeding, pain, and the effects of immobilization. Psychosocial concerns such as development, social isolation, school, and family must also be considered in planning care.

## Chronic Care Considerations

Families with children who have chronic musculoskeletal conditions need ongoing support to meet the needs both of their ill child and of other family members as well. Providing information regarding the effect that the illness will have on the child's future development, as well as day-to-day living, is very important. Nurses often serve as service coordinators for children with chronic musculoskeletal problems. Since these children often receive services from a variety of health care disciplines, the service coordinator works with children and their families to develop a coordinated plan of care that is suited to the needs of these children and their families.

## Home Care Considerations

With the increased availability of home nursing services and durable medical equipment, many children who need long-term therapy for musculoskeletal problems are treated at home. Children undergoing traction or IV therapy may be candidates for home care referral, rather than prolonged hospital stays. Children in terminal phases of conditions such as muscular dystrophy may choose to be at home as well. If home care is feasible, providing families with precise, written information about the child's management reduces the likelihood of complications of therapy. Arrangements for homebound teaching also must be made for the school-age child.

## Nursing Interventions

### Pre- and Postoperative Care

Musculoskeletal surgical procedures have many purposes. They can be performed to realign fractured bones, to correct congenital deformities, to release joint and soft tissue contractures, and to improve function. Procedures may either be "closed" (requiring no incision), as in certain fracture or dislocation reductions, or "open" (requiring a surgical incision), as with pinning or nailing a slipped epiphysis or performing a biopsy.

The focus of preoperative care is to minimize fear and anxiety in the child and parents, and to provide information regarding the usual pre- and postoperative routines to be expected. Young children are more receptive to this information through play activities such as using gowns, masks, and other equipment. If they will have a cast after surgery, they can apply a cast to a doll or stuffed toy. Older children may prefer to read about their procedure. They can practice activities that will be new to them in the postoperative period, such as log-rolling, eating supine, or voiding in the bed pan. If they will be in the intensive care unit (ICU), a preoperative tour may help decrease their anxiety.

The focus of postoperative care includes preventing complications related to the surgical procedure and immobilization, as well as providing pain relief for the child. The most urgent musculoskeletal complication is neurovascular impairment due to constrictive edema to a body part. Extremities are elevated to reduce postoperative swelling. Frequent neurovascular assessment of affected extremities is required in the first hours after surgery (usually every 15 to 30 minutes). See the discussion of cast care below for additional information.

If a bandage or cast is in place, stains are noted to monitor bleeding or drainage. Notes should include the time size, and color of the stain. The cast is handled carefully to avoid altering the shape.

### Care of a Child in a Cast

Casts are used to immobilize joints above and below a fracture, operative site, or diseased site in order to prevent movement that would interfere with alignment and heal-

ing at the site. Casting may also be used to aid in correction of congenital deformities. Figure 33-4 shows a variety of casts that are commonly used for children. Materials used for casts include plaster of Paris, fiberglass, and polyurethane resins. The latter two materials are lighter in weight and water resistant, and they dry rapidly. While the cast is drying it should be handled with the flat part of the hands, not the fingers, to avoid making indentations that can cause pressure sores. Additional suggestions for nursing care of a child in a cast are shown in Table 33-3.

*Table 33–3. Nursing Care for the Child in a Cast*

Prevent neurovascular impairment
   Frequent assessment (see Table 33-4)
   Elevate extremity to reduce swelling
Check cast for tightness
Promote cast integrity
Promote even drying
   Turn child every two hours
   Keep cast uncovered
   Avoid heater fans as cast will dry on outside while remaining wet on inside; may risk thermal injury to underlying tissue
Protect cast from deformity during drying
   Use flat of hands to move cast (identations from fingers will cause skin breakdown)
   Do not use abductor bars for turning the cast
Maintain cleanliness of cast
   Perineal protection
   Wrap plastic around perineal window to protect from soiling
   Use plastic-back diapers or sanitary pads for infants/toddlers
   Keep shoulders higher than buttocks during toileting to prevent urine from flowing beneath cast
   Soiled areas can be cleansed with low-abrasive cleanser
Prevent skin breakdown
   Keep items/cast particles from getting between skin and cast
   Inspect skin for evidence of pressure areas
   Keep exposed area clean
   Apply rubbing alcohol to skin at edges of cast
   Avoid lotions and powders
   Petal edges of cast with adhesive tape to prevent crumbling
Prevent impaired respiratory function
   Turn, encourage coughing and deep breathing
   Observe respiratory rate/effort; secretions
   Monitor temperature
Prevent infection under cast
   Promote skin integrity
   Note any complaint of pain
   Check for foul odor or discharge under cast
   Monitor vital signs
Promote optimum development
   Avoid isolating child in room
   Move bed to play area; use wagon or scooter boards to aid mobility
   Provide opportunities for appropriate cognitive, social, and fine motor activities

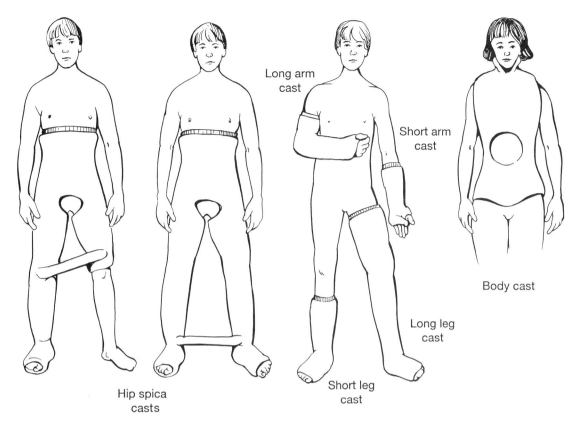

*Figure 33–4.   Casts used for pediatric musculoskeletal problems.*

Integrity of neurovascular supply to the affected extremity must be assessed frequently when the child is in traction or a cast (Table 33-4). During cast drying, hourly checks of neurovascular integrity are required. If any of the assessment parameters are abnormal, the physician should be consulted immediately and measures should be taken to relieve the constriction. Unrelieved neurovascular impingement can lead to permanent damage of the extremity within minutes to hours. Any signs of pallor, coolness, edema, or decreased pulse should be reported immediately.

The cast is removed with a cast saw, which cannot

*Table 33–4.   Assessing Neurovascular Integrity of an Extremity in Cast or Traction*

|  | Normal | Abnormal |
| --- | --- | --- |
| **Circulation Assessment** | | |
| Pulse | Present | Absent |
| Color | Pink | White, blue, red |
| Warmth | Warm | Cool, hot |
| Swelling | None | Present |
| Capillary refill | < 3 secs | > 3 secs |
|  | Press toe/finger to blanch; observe return of blood flow. | |
| **Neurological Assessment** | | |
| Movement | Able to move | Unable to actively move |
| Sensation | Feels touch normally | Numbness, tingling, no sensation |
| Pain | Minimal | Extreme |

injure the child. The saw is very noisy, causing children to be anxious about their fate. Prior to cast removal, play therapy involving a cast saw and casts on dolls may help alleviate the child's fears.

After cast removal, the affected extremity may appear wasted due to disuse muscle atrophy. The child is likely to exhibit some weakness as well. Usually, normal childhood activity resolves these problems. However, if the child is reluctant to use the injured part or if atrophy or weakness persist, a planned exercise program should be instituted with follow-up to ensure return to normal musculoskeletal function.

## Care of a Child in Traction

Traction is used for a variety of reasons: to provide alignment of a fracture; to immobilize a specific body part; to rest an extremity; to treat soft tissue contractures; to treat a dislocation or deformity; and rarely (in children) to relieve muscle spasms. Traction is an extended pulling force placed on the body; countertraction is a force that counteracts the direct pull. Weights and pulleys are used to determine the magnitude and direction of the traction forces. The child's position in bed—flat, upright, or Trendelenburg—determines the magnitude of countertraction. The interaction of these forces serves to maintain alignment of fracture sites as well as to minimize muscle spasms.

Traction equipment is used for suspension as well. In this case, body parts are suspended, but pulling forces are not used. Suspension is prescribed to elevate or rest body parts.

There are two types of traction: skin and skeletal. In skin traction, traction is applied indirectly by pulling on the skin surface. Either adhesive or nonadhesive traction may be used. Adhesive traction is used for continuous skin traction; nonadhesive traction is used for intermittent traction that facilitates care of the child. Intermittent traction is periodically released and then reapplied as ordered.

Skeletal traction is applied directly to the bone with the use of pins or wires directly into or through the bone. Usually this type of traction is continuous, and is released only by the physician. Figure 33-5 shows different types of traction/suspension encountered in the pediatric setting.

The child in traction may have significant discomfort related to muscle spasms due to traction pull. Adequate pain relief is provided through the use of muscle relaxants and analgesics. Assisting the child to cope with the confinement and immobilization of traction presents the nurse with the most challenging aspect of the child's care. Every effort must be made to provide the child with opportunities for peer interaction and play. Table 33-5 provides information on caring for a child in traction and prevention of complications of traction.

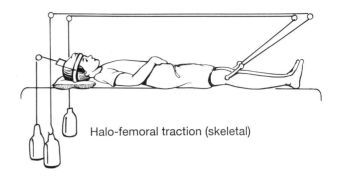

Halo-femoral traction (skeletal)

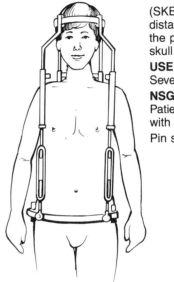

(SKELETAL)—Pins applied to distal femur or iliac wings of the pelvis halo attached to skull
**USE:**
Severe scoliosis
**NSG IMP:**
Patient can be ambulatory with halo–pelvic traction
Pin site care

Halo-pelvic traction (skeletal)

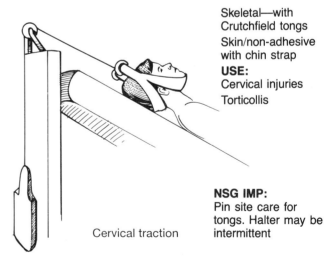

Skeletal—with Crutchfield tongs
Skin/non-adhesive with chin strap
**USE:**
Cervical injuries
Torticollis

**NSG IMP:**
Pin site care for tongs. Halter may be intermittent

Cervical traction

*Figure 33–5. Types of traction used for pediatric musculoskeletal problems.*

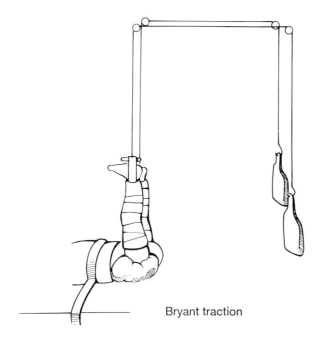

Skin, adhesive or non-adhesive
**USE:**
Congenital hip dysplasias
Fractured femur
Child under 12–14 kg (26–30 lbs)
**NSG IMP:**
Foot should be able to move freely
Buttocks slightly elevated
May need restraint to prevent rotation of trunk
Neurovascular assessment critical

Bryant traction

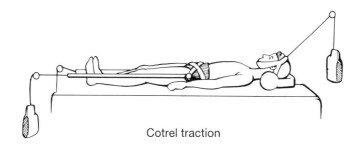

Intermittent, uses special chin strap and pelvic girdle
**USE:**
Preoperative scoliosis—for partial correction and flexibility
**NSG IMP:**
Patient is taught to use this system

Cotrel traction

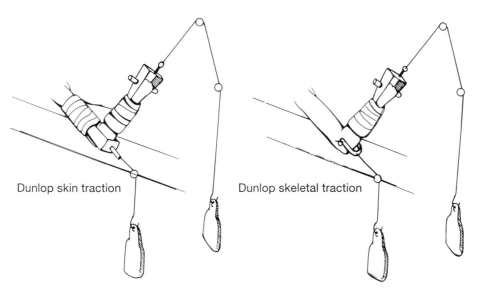

Skin or skeletal
**USE:**
Supracondylar fractures
**NSG IMP:**
Neurovascular assessment critical

Dunlop skin traction        Dunlop skeletal traction

*Figure 33–5.   (continued)*

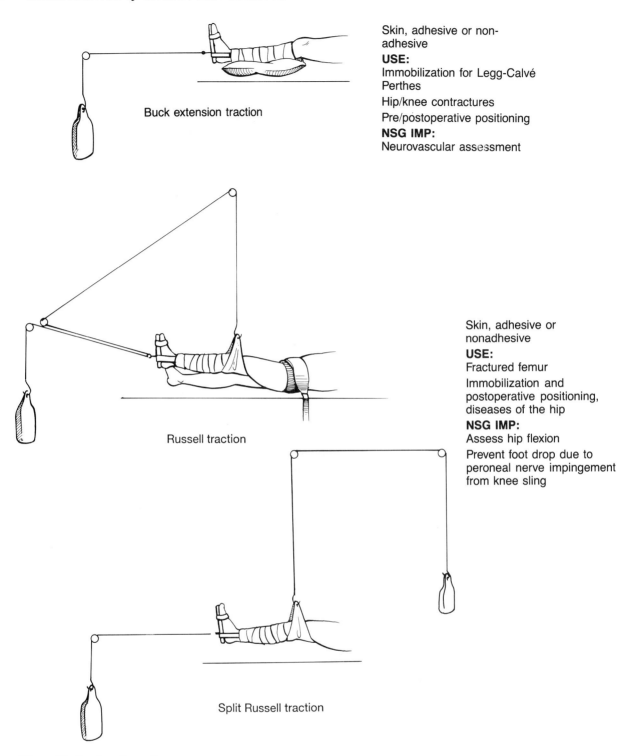

Buck extension traction

Skin, adhesive or non-
adhesive
**USE:**
Immobilization for Legg-Calvé
Perthes
Hip/knee contractures
Pre/postoperative positioning
**NSG IMP:**
Neurovascular assessment

Russell traction

Skin, adhesive or
nonadhesive
**USE:**
Fractured femur
Immobilization and
postoperative positioning,
diseases of the hip
**NSG IMP:**
Assess hip flexion
Prevent foot drop due to
peroneal nerve impingement
from knee sling

Split Russell traction

*Figure 33–5.    (continued)*

## Care of a Child with an Ilizarov External Fixator

The Ilizarov External Fixator (IEF) was developed in the Soviet Union over 30 years ago but has only recently been used in the United States. The device is used to immobilize fractures, lengthen bones, or correct angular or rotational defects. A system of wires, rings, and telescoping rods is used to lengthen limbs by manual distraction of two opposing bone ends and filling of this gap by bone regeneration (Newschwander & Dunst, 1989). *Distraction* is a process that results in bone regeneration by separating the opposing bones. The IEF is used with great success to treat leg length discrepancies and can result in up to 15-cm

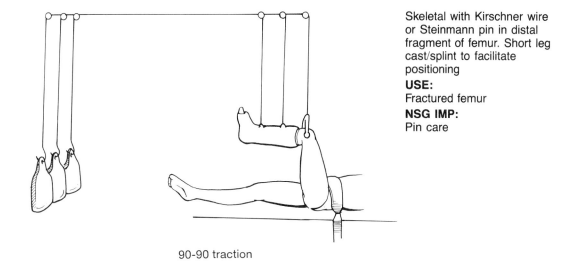

Skeletal with Kirschner wire
or Steinmann pin in distal
fragment of femur. Short leg
cast/splint to facilitate
positioning
**USE:**
Fractured femur
**NSG IMP:**
Pin care

90-90 traction

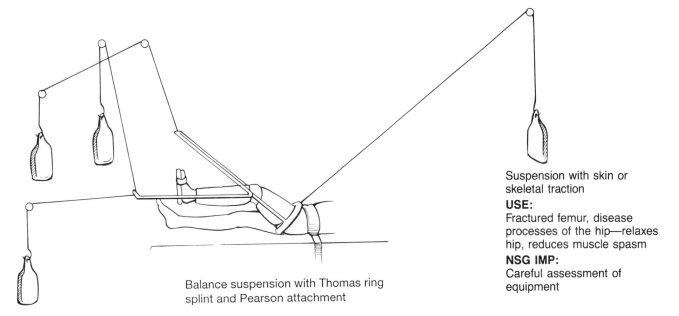

Suspension with skin or
skeletal traction
**USE:**
Fractured femur, disease
processes of the hip—relaxes
hip, reduces muscle spasm
**NSG IMP:**
Careful assessment of
equipment

Balance suspension with Thomas ring
splint and Pearson attachment

*Figure 33–5.  (continued)*

gains in limb length. Bone lengthening occurs at the rate of 1 cm per month. The device is used most often in school-age children or adolescents.

The child and family should be prepared for the procedure, the use of the device, and its appearance before surgery. Children also need help in coping with the reaction from others, including staring and questions (Carlino, 1991).

The IEF may utilize either a threaded rod or a graduated telescoping rod to accomplish the distraction procedure. The rods are turned or advanced and marked to note the starting point and subsequent advancement. Children should be familiar with how to turn the device; this allows them a sense of control. Children who understand

how to turn the device themselves report less discomfort (Carlino, 1991).

Postoperative care is similar to other operative procedures. In the initial postoperative period, patient-controlled analgesia is often used. Partial weight bearing and distraction may help to decrease discomfort. Physical therapy should begin as soon as possible, and partial weight bearing with crutches is started on the fourth day after surgery. Full weight bearing is not allowed until distraction is completed and bone consolidation has occurred. Discharge planning includes education on pin care, physical therapy exercises, and advancing the distraction rods; planning for return to school and resuming normal activities is also a part of planning. Follow-up care includes

*Table 33–5.  Nursing Care for the Child in Traction*

Maintain integrity of traction
    Check function of each component
    *Weights:* hanging freely; correct amount
    *Ropes:* center track of pully; taut; tied securely; no fraying
    *Pulleys:* should remain in same site
    *Frames:* stable
Prevent neurovascular complications
    Frequent assessment (see Table 33-4)
    Assess wraps for tightness
    Report altered neurovascular status immediately to physician
Prevent skin breakdown
    Change position frequently
    Observe for evidence of pressure—redness or skin breakdown
    Massage pressure points to increase circulation
    Use special mattresses to reduce risk of skin breakdown (eggcrate, sheepskin, alternating pressure mattress)
    Alcohol to skin; avoid lotion or powder
Prevent complications of skeletal traction
    Check pin sites for infection or inflammation
    Leave crusts at pin sites
    Note signs of pin slippage—notify physician
    Apply topical antibiotic as ordered
    Check pin screws—should be tight
    If end of pin exposed, place cork over end
Prevent complications of skin traction
    Carefully wrap/rewrap, checking for constriction
    Note signs of constrictive edema (swelling, altered neurovascular assessment)
    Inspect skin every 2–4 hours
    Alcohol to skin
    Notify physician of altered skin integrity

device maintenance, periodic radiographs, and physical therapy evaluations. After the desired limb lengthening and bone consolidation, the device is removed. The child is placed on crutches and may wear a cast for 1 month.

## Drug Therapy

Because inflammation occurs with many musculoskeletal disorders, anti-inflammatory agents are often prescribed. Some of these drugs may also help with pain control, which is common to many orthopedic problems. Pain control in children is a challenging aspect of nursing care. Nonverbal clues that may indicate discomfort include increased pulse and respiratory rates, rigid posture, drawn facial expressions, and refusal to play or participate in care. Often the child does not request medication or denies having pain because of fear of injections. Children who still have an IV in place can be reassured that an injection will not be necessary if they request medication for pain since it can be administered through the IV, without causing any pain. Whenever possible, oral medications should be given for pain. Analgesics are effective in treating severe pain only when adequate blood levels of the analgesics are maintained by regular administration (Eland, 1988). Medications that are ordered on a PRN basis may be administered on a regular schedule at the nurse's discretion for moderate to severe pain following an operation or injury. A child cannot and should not be expected to request a PRN medication. Table 33-6 lists common analgesics for musculoskeletal problems.

## Nutrition

Adequate nutrition is always a concern for immobilized or chronically ill children. Sufficient protein and calories to meet needs for healing and growth are required. Healing is delayed in children with a negative nitrogen balance. Lack of weight bearing leads to osteoporosis, hypercalcemia, and, occasionally, hypercalciuria.

Since constipation is a concern for immobilized youngsters, a diet high in fiber and fluid is encouraged. Use of these dietary measures reduces the need for stool softeners, laxatives, or enemas. Management of constipation should be preventive.

## Child/Parent Education

With the exception of acute trauma, most musculoskeletal diseases require management over long periods of time, from weeks to years. Thus, children and their families will be responsible for day-to-day management of the problem.

Nurses are in a key position to assist these families in learning care management skills. Table 33-7 lists content areas to be included in the process of family teaching. Written information should accompany verbal or audiovisual teaching. To enhance the learning and retention of information by the child and family, teaching should take place over several short sessions. If specific activities or exercises are part of the therapeutic regimen, families must be given a chance to do a return demonstration of the activity so that competence can be assessed.

## Evaluating Nursing Care

Effectiveness of nursing care can be assessed by patient outcomes. General outcomes for children with musculoskeletal injuries or conditions include the following:

Children have maintained normal development within physical limitations.

Children are free of complications of immobility.

Children have no permanent damage related to therapeutic techniques.

Children and their families verbalize understanding of the condition, its treatment, and prevention of potential complications.

*Table 33–6. Anti-Inflammatory and Analgesic Agents Used for Musculoskeletal Problems*

| Drug | Route(s) | | | | Advantages ( + )/Disadvantages ( − ) |
|------|------|------|------|------|------|
| **Nonsteroidal anti-inflammatory drugs (NSAIDs)** | | | | | |
| **Salicylates** | PO | PR | | | − Contraindicated for children with hematologic disorders |
| | | | | | − Association with Reye syndrome |
| | | | | | − GI irritation |
| | | | | | + Inexpensive (ASA) |
| | | | | | + Potent anti-inflammatory |
| **Naproxen** | PO | | | | − GI irritation |
| | | | | | − Potential nephrotoxicity |
| | | | | | − Expensive |
| | | | | | + BID dosing |
| | | | | | + Liquid form available |
| | | | | | + Potent anti-inflammatory |
| **Ibuprofen** | PO | | | | − GI irritation |
| | | | | | − Potential nephrotoxicity |
| | | | | | + Potent anti-inflammatory |
| | | | | | * No FDA approval for children under 12 |
| **Aspirin** | PO | PR | | | − GI irritation |
| | | | | | − Associated with Reye syndrome. Not recommended for children under 13 |
| | | | | | + Better anti-inflammatory than acetaminophen |
| **Acetaminophen** | PO | PR | | | − No anti-inflammatory properties |
| | | | | | + Very effective in combination with narcotics |
| **NSAIDS in general** | PO | | | | − GI irritation |
| | | | | | + Superior anti-inflammatory properties to aspirin or acetaminophen |
| **Morphine** | PO | PR | IV | IM | |
|   **Oral Liquid** | PO | | | | − Tastes terrible |
| | | | | | + Inexpensive |
|   **Slow-release tablet** | PO | | | | + Small, easy to swallow |
|   **Quick-release tablet** | PO | | | | + Tiny tablet, immediately available |
| | | | | | − Expensive |
| **Codeine** | PO | | | | − Nauseating, tastes bad |
| | | | | | + Small pill |
| | | | | | + Effective analgesia |
| | | | | | + Increased effectiveness with Tylenol |
| **Meperedine** | PO | | | IM | − Short duration |
| | | | | | − IM—painful lumps |
| | | | | | − PO—tastes bitter |
| | | | | | − Metabolite occupies opiate receptor sites, preventing active drug from providing pain relief |
| | | | | | − Metabolite build-up increases irritability, tremors, CNS excitation |
| | | | | | + Tiny tablet |
| | | | | | Recommend only for single-dose situations |

*(continued)*

*Table 33–6. Anti-Inflammatory and Analgesic Agents Used for Musculoskeletal Problems (Continued)*

| Drug | Route(s) | Advantages (+)/Disadvantages (−) |
|---|---|---|
| **Narcotics in general** | | − Constipation<br>+ Effective<br>Increased effectiveness with acetaminophen<br>Minimal risk of respiratory depression |

(Adapted from Eland, J. M. [1988]. Pharmacologic management of acute and chronic pediatric pain. *Issues in Comprehensive Pediatrics, 11,*93–112)

## Common Musculoskeletal Problems in Children

### Sprains, Strains, Avulsions, and Contusions

#### Pathophysiology

A sprain is a partial or complete tear of a ligament. A strain is partial or complete tear of a muscle or tendon caused by overuse or stretching. An avulsion is the pulling of tendons away from their bone insertion sites. A contusion, or bruise, is a skin and soft tissue injury. Disruption of blood vessels with these injuries results in bleeding into the tissue with hematoma formation. Sprains are graded mild (first degree), moderate (second degree), or severe (third degree). Mild sprains are caused by stretching of a ligament, and result in local tenderness, slight swelling, and impaired joint function. Moderate sprains are caused by partial tearing of a ligament, and result in joint pain, more severe loss of function, rapid swelling, and discoloration. Severe sprains are caused by complete tearing of the ligament and are usually not painful after the initial injury because the ligament is not stretched. However, there is usually hemorrhage, swelling, and loss of joint function.

### Medical Diagnosis and Management

The diagnosis of strains, sprains, avulsions, and contusions is usually confirmed by a history of the injury and the presenting symptoms. Emergency management of these injuries follows the RICE format: rest, ice, compression, and elevation. This treatment reduces swelling, bleeding, and pain. The amount of rest required depends on the classification and extent of the injury. Crutches may be used to limit weight bearing and facilitate rest. Ice is applied for 15 to 20 minutes repeatedly during the first 48 to 72 hours following injury. Ice should not be applied directly or continuously to the skin, because this may cause thermal injury and reflex vasodilation. The injured part is compressed with an elastic bandage and elevated.

Third degree sprains and strains may require surgery or casting. Following these injuries, a rehabilitation exercise program should be initiated to enable return to preinjury activity level and to avoid future sprain injuries.

### Nursing Assessment and Diagnosis

Nurses assess sprains, strains, avulsions, and contusions by obtaining a history of the activity that was being performed at the time of the injury and by assessing the amount of pain, swelling, and discoloration, as well as mobility of the affected area.

Nursing diagnoses for strains, sprains, avulsions, and contusions might include the following:

- Pain related to the trauma
- Impaired physical mobility related to pain

*Table 33–7. Child and Family Education for Musculoskeletal Problems*

Expected course of disease or disorder
Signs of potential complications of disease or its treatment
Techniques for preventing complications of disease or its treatment
Therapeutic regimen
  Medications: schedule, potential side effects
  Use of orthotic devices or traction
  Exercise program: specific activities, schedule, limitations on activities
  Dietary concerns
When to contact the health care provider
  Disease complications
  Complications from orthotics/cast/traction
  Persistent side effect of medication
How to contact health care provider
Enhancing developmental progress in face of impaired mobility
  Plan for school
  Peer relationships
  Maximize opportunities for utilizing fine motor, visual/auditory, and cognitive skills

## Planning and Implementing Nursing Care

Nursing care for strains, sprains, avulsions, and contusions consists primarily of relieving the pain and preventing further swelling. Acetaminophen can be administered for pain. The affected area should be wrapped in an elastic bandage. Ice should be applied as soon as possible, since this helps relieve the pain and reduces further swelling. The affected area should be elevated above the level of the heart to prevent fluid accumulation and further swelling. The child should limit use of the affected area as much as possible for several days. The child and parents should be taught methods for preventing these types of injuries. An exercise program for strengthening injured extremities and appropriate joint supports may prevent reinjury.

## Evaluating Nursing Care

Evaluation of nursing care focuses on relief of pain and reduction of swelling. The child and parents should also demonstrate an understanding of preventive measures that can be used to avoid these types of injuries in the future.

# Dislocations

## Pathophysiology

A dislocation is the movement of a bone from its normal position in the joint, usually as a result of trauma. Any joint can be dislocated, but the most common are the elbow, shoulder, hip, and wrist. Depending on the severity of the trauma, damage may also be done to the ligaments.

## Medical Diagnosis and Management

Most dislocations are obvious, because the displacement of the bone from the joint results in an abnormal contour. The extent of the dislocation can be confirmed by radiographic examination. Pain is severe, particularly on movement of the joint. The joint is reduced, either manually or surgically, as soon as possible since swelling can complicate reduction. After reduction, the joint is immobilized until it has had time to heal.

## Nursing Assessment and Diagnosis

Nursing assessment should include a history of the trauma and physical examination. Tenderness, swelling, and movement of the joint should be noted.

Nursing diagnoses for dislocations might include the following:

• Pain related to the injury
• Impaired physical mobility related to the dislocation and pain

• Anxiety related to the surgical procedure, if warranted

## Planning and Implementing Nursing Care

Nursing care depends on the method of reduction. If surgery is indicated nurses need to provide pre- and postoperative care, as discussed earlier in the chapter. Following reduction, the nurse should provide the child and parents with information on the immobilization procedures to be used (sling, splint, etc.), activity restrictions, and administration of analgesics. The parents should be instructed to monitor for complications such as swelling, numbness, tingling, or color changes. If indicated, the need for follow-up care should be emphasized.

## Evaluating Nursing Care

Evaluation of nursing care for dislocations focuses on alleviating the child's pain, minimizing complications, and restoring full range of motion to the joint.

# Fractures

## Pathophysiology

There are several types of fractures, as demonstrated by Figure 33-6. Fractures may be simple, in which case there is no break in the skin over the fracture site, or compound, in which a bone fragment pierces the skin. A *bend* occurs when the bone bends to the breaking point and will not straighten completely without intervention. Bends occur most frequently in the ulna and fibula. A *buckle* results from compression failure of the bone, with the bone telescoping on itself. Buckles tend to occur near the metaphyses. A *greenstick fracture* occurs when the bone does not fracture completely through after the break, and elastic recoil of soft tissue may realign the pieces. Without appropriate intervention in greenstick fractures, a muscle pull can reopen the break, resulting in bone growth deformities. A *complete fracture* occurs when the bone is completely broken and neither fragment is attached to the other. Complete fractures are rare in children.

Fractures in long bones may result in increased longitudinal growth. This factor places the child at risk for arm and leg length discrepancies. Leg length discrepancies are more serious due to long-term effects on stance and gait.

The most common sites of fractures during childhood include the following:

*Clavicle.* These fractures are most often related to birth injury.

*Humerus.* Supracondylar fractures of the humerus occur when the child falls forward on the hands with the elbows straight. This injury has a high incidence of neurovascular complications due to the

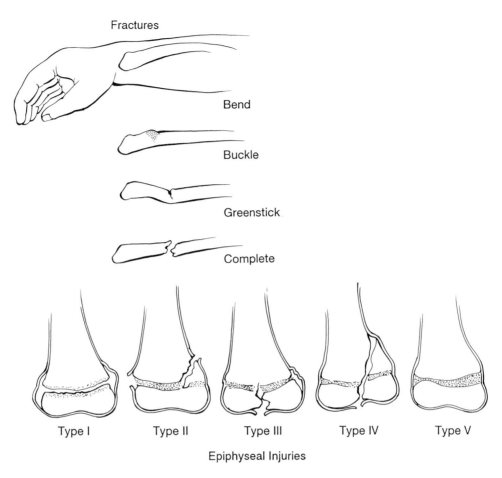

Fractures

Bend

Buckle

Greenstick

Complete

Type I    Type II    Type III    Type IV    Type V

Epiphyseal Injuries

*Figure 33–6.    Fractures seen in children. (*Top*) Types of bone fractures: bend, buckle, green-stick, and complete. (*Bottom*) Epiphyseal fractures: Type I, through the physis; Type II, through the physis and out through the metaphysis; Type III, along the physis and transgresses the epiphysis; Type IV, transgresses the metaphysis and the epiphysis; and Type V, compression resulting from a crushing injury (on left).*

anatomical relationships of the brachial artery and nerves to the fracture site.

*Radius and ulna.* Fractures of the forearm occur when the child falls on the hands with the elbows flexed.

*Femur.* Fractures are usually of the middle third of the femur. This injury is often associated with child abuse.

*Epiphyseal plate fractures.* The epiphyseal plate is weaker than associated ligaments or the joint capsule in children. Injuries that would cause torn ligaments or joint dislocation in adults result in epiphyseal plate fractures in children. Any fracture of the epiphyseal plate has the potential for growth deformity. Permanent damage results in cessation of growth or asymmetrical growth of the injured bone.

### Medical Diagnosis and Management

The diagnosis of a fracture is confirmed by radiograph. Fractured bone must be aligned and immobilized for healing to occur. The type and location of the fracture dictates the method of realignment or reduction. Closed reduction is accomplished by realigning the bone through manipulation. Open reduction requires surgical intervention, and often the fracture is corrected by using screws, plates, or rods to keep the bone in proper alignment. The bone is then immobilized using traction, a cast, or a combination of both to maintain the alignment until the bone heals. Treatment complications are related to excessive local pressure, excessive traction, and infection.

### Nursing Assessment and Diagnosis

Nurses should assess the child's level of pain, swelling, and degree of mobilization. It is also important to obtain a history of the injury; however, this is often difficult. Children may be reluctant to provide details if they were doing something forbidden (e.g., climbing a tree or riding on a skateboard).

Nurses should be aware that fractures in infants and young children may result from abuse. When the injury history does not correspond to physical findings, further evaluation is necessary. The law requires that suspicion of child neglect or physical abuse be reported. Radiographic examination of the injury often reveals old fracture sites in various stages of healing. These children should be admitted to the hospital or placed in fost r care during treatment and investigation. See Chapter 14 for further discussion of child abuse.

Nursing diagnoses for a fracture might include the following:

- Pain related to the fracture or to surgery
- High risk for impaired skin integrity related to use of a cast or traction
- Impaired physical mobility related to pain
- High risk for infection related to surgery or skeletal traction
- Self-care deficit related to pain or immobilization from traction or a cast

### Planning and Implementing Nursing Care

Nursing interventions for fractures include administration of analgesics, as ordered; instructing the parents on warning signs of neurological or vascular impairment; instructing the child and family on care of the cast; and teaching alternate methods of ambulation, such as using crutches, if appropriate. Nurses should also provide guidelines for restrictions on activities while the child is in a cast or traction.

Parents should be warned that signs of neurological or vascular impairment should be reported immediately. These signs might include tingling or numbness in the extremity, severe pain, pallor or redness, or cool skin. Care for the child in a cast or in traction is discussed earlier in this chapter.

### Evaluating Nursing Care

Evaluation of nursing care includes the child's reported decrease in pain, and maintenance of as normal a daily routine as possible. No signs of neurological or vascular complications will be reported, and skin integrity will be maintained.

## Congenital Musculoskeletal Problems

A variety of musculoskeletal problems may be immediately apparent at birth due to the child's physical appearance. These problems cause great distress for parents who are anticipating the birth of a healthy, normal child. Although parental reactions may vary, the experience of grief over the loss of their idealized "perfect" child is of concern. Nurses can facilitate parents' coping mechanisms by providing access to appropriate information about the particular problem: its cause; the treatment plans for the problem; and the implications for the child's future development. Nurses must remember that no deviation from "normal" is trivial or minor in the eyes of a newborn's parents. They need ongoing support as they begin the parent–infant acquaintance process.

When children are born with congenital musculoskeletal problems, nurses should make every attempt to facilitate normal parent–infant attachment. Whenever possible, parents should be encouraged to hold, examine, cuddle, and talk to the infant. If parents are hesitant to interact with the child or express anxiety over the infant's condition, nurses need to evaluate parents' concerns and assist them in working through their concerns.

Additionally, assistance in meeting the costs of ongoing medical care may be needed. Most states have programs that provide financial assistance to qualified families. Nurses should be aware of these resources in the community so referral can be made as soon as possible.

## Congenital Hip Dysplasias

Congenital hip dysplasias (CHD) are abnormalities of the hip joint including subluxations and dislocations.

### Pathophysiology

The precise etiology of CHD is unknown. Theories of causation include the possible effect of maternal estrogen on the fetus causing unusual ligamentous laxity; prolonged knee hyperextension with breech positioning; and genetic factors (Herring, 1990). Infants born in the breech position have an increased incidence of CHD, whether delivered vaginally or by cesarean section. Subsequent siblings have a tenfold increase in risk of being born with CHD. One in 60 newborns has hip instability and one in 1000 has hip dislocation (Scoles, 1988).

### Medical Diagnosis and Management

The unstable hip can easily be subluxed or dislocated with manipulation. The subluxed femoral head rides on the edge of the acetabulum. In the dislocated hip, the femoral head is outside the acetabulum. If a hip is subluxed or dislocated, the acetabulum cannot develop normally. Untreated, the abnormality is progressive, resulting in muscular contraction of the affected hip and major gait abnormalities. If diagnosis and treatment do not occur until after the age of 1 year, this condition can lead to development of osteoarthritis early during the usual life span, even if normal gait is achieved.

Clinical evidence of CHD changes with age. In the newborn, hip instability is noted on clinical exam. Tests for CHD are shown in Figure 33-7. When the Ortolani maneuver is performed, the examiner feels the femur sliding into the acetabulum with a "click" or "thunk" if the hip is abnormal. The Barlow test causes an abnormal hip to dislocate. Other signs seen in the newborn with CHD include asymmetry of the gluteal fold and of hip abduction; limited abduction of thighs; and relative

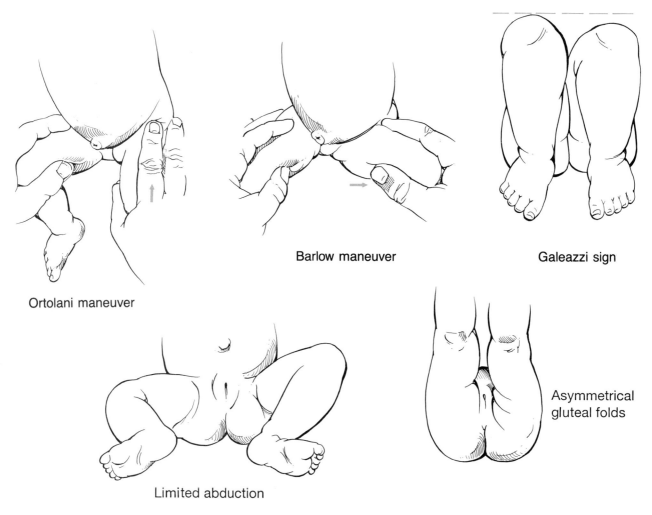

Ortolani maneuver

Barlow maneuver

Galeazzi sign

Limited abduction

Asymmetrical gluteal folds

*Figure 33–7. Assessment of congenital hip dysplasia.*

femoral foreshortening (Galeazzi sign). The child of walking age has a noticeable limp (Trendelenburg gait) (Fig. 33-8).

Radiographs are often normal, or show very subtle changes in newborns, but are more reliable after 3 months of age (Staheli, 1989). Ultrasound examination of the hip is a very helpful diagnostic tool in the newborn period (MacEwen & Zembo, 1987). The severe consequences of late treatment of CHD make assessment of the infant's hips at each "well child" visit essential.

The goal of treatment is to restore alignment of the hip joint and to maintain pain-free function. The infant's hip must be positioned in flexion and abduction so that the femoral head is directed toward the acetabulum. Many devices are used to maintain this position. Most commonly used is the Pavlik harness (Fig. 33-9). The prescribed abduction/flexion device is worn continuously for 2 to 4 months, and is usually not removed at all during the initial weeks of treatment. In the later phases of treatment, the device may be removed briefly for bathing. If the infant does not respond to this treatment, or is older than 6

months, traction and closed reduction of the dislocation are performed under general anesthesia. A spica cast (a cast that contains the lower torso and extends to either one or both extremities) is applied to maintain the reduction.

If diagnosis is delayed or the infant does not respond to bracing, treatment is complicated by the development of soft tissue contractures around the hip. These tissues must be gently stretched prior to closed or open reduction of the hip dislocation and application of a spica cast. Traction for 10 days to 3 weeks may be needed to stretch soft-tissue contractures. Bryant traction (see Fig. 33-5) is used for children who weigh less than 35 pounds. Skin traction is preferred to skeletal traction, in order to avoid complications associated with use of the skeletal pin (MacEwen & Zembo, 1987).

After treatment of soft tissue contractures, closed or open reduction is accomplished with the child under anesthesia. A hip spica cast or rigid brace is applied and worn for approximately 6 months. Revisions in the cast or brace are required to allow for growth. Treatment of the older child is difficult and often involves reconstructive

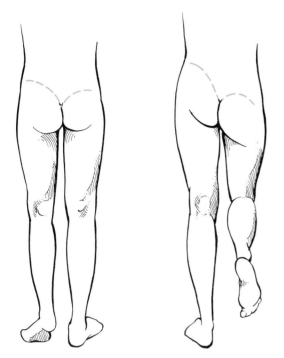

*Figure 33–8. Trendelenburg gait.*

surgery. In this case, recovery from CHD is usually not complete, and early osteoarthritis may result.

### Nursing Assessment and Diagnosis

Nurses working with newborns and infants should be aware of the signs of CHD. Careful assessment of children for CHD is critical.

Nursing diagnoses for CHD might include the following:

- Impaired physical mobility, related to congenital instability or incorrect placement of the femur head within the acetabulum
- High risk for injury (neurovascular impairment) related to the cast being too tight; postoperative edema within a cast; or improper positioning of traction apparatus
- Altered parenting related to lack of knowledge of how to care for the child

### Planning and Implementing Nursing Care

When educating parents regarding abduction/flexion devices, specific, written instructions are required. According to Corbett (1988), parents of infants using a Pavlik harness reported problems related to harness application, bathing, clothing, and transportation of the infant. Seventy-five percent of the parents removed the harness for bathing, without physician permission.

Parents often experience such a high level of stress upon learning that their infant has health problems that they are unable to listen effectively. Parents should be involved as early as possible in the care of their child. Return demonstrations are vital in assessing parental understanding of the treatment regimen. The physician should give specific instructions as to when and for how long the infant may be without the device. If the device has straps, such as the Pavlik harness, they should be marked so that the device can be replaced properly. The nurse can guide the parents in developing plans for meeting the infant's physical and developmental needs. Because of the immobility necessitated by a cast, diversional activities such as mobiles should be placed near the child. For the child requiring a hip spica cast, parents require cast care instructions as well. Parents should be instructed to monitor for signs of neurovascular impairment (discussed earlier) and to report any signs immediately. Care should be take to turn the child frequently to avoid development of pressure sores. The cast should be kept clean and dry and protected from urine and stool.

### Evaluating Nursing Care

Evaluation of nursing care for infants with CHD includes evidence that the child is maintaining current developmental status in all areas except gross motor. Parents should be able to demonstrate proper use of abduction or flexion devices. If home traction is used, parents should be able to demonstrate care of their infant and equipment. Home health referrals are made as indicated. For the child in a spica cast, parents demonstrate their ability to meet the child's altered physical and developmental needs. Parents should be able to verbalize their understanding of follow-up plans.

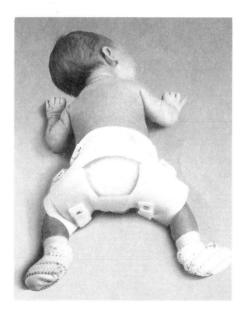

*Figure 33–9. Pavlik harness. (Courtesy of CAMP International, Inc., Jackson, MI)*

## Talipes Equinovarus (Clubfoot)

### Pathophysiology

Talipes equinovarus, or clubfoot, is a complex deformity that involves all bones of the foot, resulting in forefoot adduction combined with inversion and supination along with varus inversion and equinus of the hind part of the foot (Fig. 33-10). The disorder can be either unilateral or bilateral. Incidence is 1 per 1000 births, with males more commonly affected (Sponseller & Tolo, 1990). Although the precise cause is not known, evidence suggests a combination of genetic and environmental factors. Once this defect occurs, the risk in future children is between 3% and 5%. Children of parents who are also affected have a 25% chance of having children with the disorder (Carroll, 1990). Developmental problems that occur at 9 to 10 weeks gestation lead to a rigid deformity, whereas those occurring later in gestation due to positional problems are likely to cause a more flexible deformity. Children with myelomeningocele often have associated equinovarus deformities. If treatment is not instituted, these deformities progress with development of severe contractures and rigidity.

### Medical Diagnosis and Management

Diagnosis is made by examination, manipulation, and x-ray. Ideally, management begins during the first week of life. The foot is manipulated into the desired position and a plaster cast is applied. Casts are changed weekly, to allow for growth and ongoing manipulation into the normal position. Casts are used for 6 to 8 weeks, followed by bracing with splints or corrective shoes for several more months. If this type of management is not effective, surgery is required.

### Nursing Assessment and Diagnosis

This condition is usually apparent at birth. Nursing diagnoses for clubfoot might include the following:

- Impaired physical mobility, related to congenital foot position

- High risk for altered peripheral tissue perfusion, related to decreased circulation and pressure from cast
- Potential altered parenting, related to fear and concerns about the condition, and problems in holding infant with casts

### Planning and Implementing Nursing Care

Parents need careful instruction regarding care of the child who is in a cast, corrective shoes, or splints. Parents are taught to observe the child's toes for signs of neurovascular impairment. Measures to maintain skin integrity are demonstrated for the child using splints or special shoes. Any evidence of skin irritation must be evaluated, as this may indicate the need for adjustment of fit of casts, shoes, or splints. Parental understanding of the follow-up plan is crucial for successful treatment.

### Evaluating Nursing Care

Evaluation is based on the child's maintenance of normal growth and developmental activities. The parents should demonstrate an understanding of the condition and the rationale for treatment. Parents should demonstrate comfort in holding and interacting with the infant, as well as proficiency in checking neurovascular status.

## Metatarsus Adductus

### Pathophysiology

In metatarsus adductus, the forefoot is adducted and supinated, and the hindfoot is in a neutral position. Tibial torsion often accompanies this foot deformity. It is thought to be caused by intrauterine positioning.

### Medical Diagnosis and Management

Diagnosis of metatarsus adductus is made based on the examination of the deformity at birth. Corrective action is begun immediately after birth. If the deformity is minimal, gentle stretching exercises may be sufficient to correct the

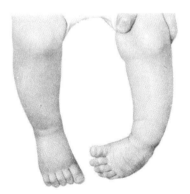 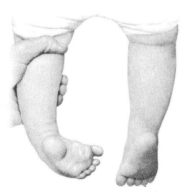

*Figure 33-10. Talipes equinovirus, a common foot deformity seen in infants. (From Clinical Education Aid. No. 15 [1965]. Columbus, OH: Ross Laboratories)*

problem. If the deformity is significant, casts are applied and changed every 1 to 2 weeks until the defect is corrected. Following correction, a holding cast or Denis-Browne splint may be used during the night. Corrective shoes are used during the day.

### Nursing Care

Careful observation of newborns contributes to identification of this deformity for timely referral and treatment. Nursing diagnoses for metatarsus adductus are similar to those for talipes equinovirus.

Parents should be encouraged to hold the infant and to provide additional sensory and motor experiences. Nursing interventions and evaluation are similar to those for talipes equinovarus.

## Congenital Torticollis

### Pathophysiology

Torticollis is a congenital or acquired disorder resulting from a shortening of the sternocleidomastoid muscle. The precise cause is unknown.

### Medical Diagnosis and Management

Diagnosis is made by examination. The neck is flexed, causing head tilt toward the affected side. At birth, the head tilt is obvious. Radiographs of the cervical spine are done to rule out other congenital anomalies. During the first month of life, a palpable mass is noted over the muscle. The abnormal head position may cause deformities of the face and skull.

Treatment begins as soon as possible with passive stretching exercises. If there is sufficient normal muscle, the sternocleidomastoid muscle will stretch with growth. If exercises are not successful, operative intervention is required for contracture release.

### Nursing Assessment and Diagnosis

Newborns are examined at birth for normal range of motion of the neck. Nurses should observe infants for limited head movement.

Nursing diagnoses for torticollis might include the following:

- Impaired physical mobility related to decreased ability to move neck
- Altered family processes related to fear about the outcome of the condition

### Planning and Implementing Nursing Care

Parents are taught to perform the following exercise with their infant: lateral stretching, touching the ear to the shoulder on the normal side, while rotating the head so that the chin touches the shoulder of the affected side. Activities that encourage the infant to turn the head toward the normal side are demonstrated to parents. These include positioning the infant so that turning is necessary to hear or see toys or activity in the room. Nurses can also suggest ways that feeding and play can be used to encourage desired head turning.

### Evaluating Nursing Care

Evaluation is based on parental demonstration of the stretching exercises, and strict adherence to the exercise schedule. The child should show progressive improvement in neck movement and control.

## Osteogenesis Imperfecta

### Pathophysiology

Osteogenesis imperfecta (OI) or "brittle bones" comprises a genetically acquired group of syndromes, each with somewhat different characteristics, including skeletal fragility, short stature, scoliosis, abnormal dentition, blue sclera and tympanic membranes, and ligamentous laxity. In most instances, the inheritance pattern is autosomal dominant (Table 33-8). Individuals with this disorder appear to have an underlying disorder of collagen synthesis (Zaleske, Doppelt, & Mankin, 1990). Consequently, bone is

### Table 33–8. Classifications of Osteogenesis Imperfecta

**Type I**

Autosomal dominant
Bone fragility
Blue sclerae
Onset of fractures after birth

**Type II**

Autosomal recessive
Lethal in perinatal period

**Type III**

Autosomal recessive
Fractures at birth
Progressively deforming
Normal sclerae
Normal hearing

**Type IV**

Autosomal dominant
Bone fragility
Normal sclerae and hearing

(Adapted from Zaleski, D. J., Dopeltl, S. H., & Mankin, H. J. [1986]. Metabolic and endocrine abnormalities of the immature skeleton. In Morissey, R. T. [ed.]. *Lovell and Winter's pediatric orthopedics* [3rd ed.] Philadelphia: J. B. Lippincott, p. 230)

abnormally formed. These brittle bones are broken with minimal trauma.

## Medical Diagnosis and Management

Diagnosis is based on physical assessment, family history, and chromosome analysis. Radiographs reveal generalized osteopenia, or diminished amount of bone tissue. Complications of OI are frequent fractures, particularly of the lower extremities, skeletal deformities, scoliosis, and dental problems. Although fractures usually heal quickly, the callus is abnormal and is easily deformed by forces associated with weight bearing or movement. This abnormality results in skeletal deformities, which are difficult if not impossible to prevent. Multiple fractures and deformities in the lower extremities interfere with ambulation. Treatment of scoliosis in children with OI is particularly difficult since the poor quality of their bones impedes the use of internal fixation devices (see discussion of scoliosis later in this chapter) (Zaleske, Doppelt, & Mankin, 1990).

No treatment has been developed for the underlying disorder of collagen synthesis. Care focuses on treatment of acute fractures, long-term rehabilitation to maintain ambulation, and education of family and child as well as genetic counseling.

## Nursing Assessment and Diagnosis

Nurses should be aware of the various manifestations of this condition. Blue sclera, caused by thinness of the sclera, are a classic sign. In its milder form, medical attention is sometimes sought because of delayed walking or a fracture. Children with multiple fractures may be mistakenly thought to be victims of physical abuse. Pain from these fractures is mild or absent due to lack of soft-tissue trauma.

Nursing diagnoses for osteogenesis imperfecta might include the following:

- High risk for injury related to brittle bones
- Impaired social interaction related to need to take precautions against injury
- Impaired physical mobility related to musculoskeletal impairment and fractures
- Altered growth and development related to need for protection against the possibility of fractures and from acquired deformities

## Planning and Implementing Nursing Care

Nurses must handle these children gently to avoid fractures. Routine care activities may need modification for the severely affected child. For diapering, infants should be lifted underneath their buttocks rather than by the ankles.

Families and older children are taught the importance of trauma avoidance, recognition of fractures, and emergency splinting techniques. Children with OI should be encouraged to develop interests that involve fine motor

and intellectual abilities rather than those involving gross motor skills. The Osteogenesis Imperfecta Foundation, Inc. (P.O. Box 838, Manchester, NH 03105) and the American Brittle Bone Society (1256 Merrill Drive, Marshallton, West Chester, PA 19380) provide vital information about this condition to families.

## Evaluating Nursing Care

Evaluation of nursing care for children with OI includes determining that the child is achieving growth and development that are as normal as possible, given the limitations of the disorder. The child will engage in activities that lessen the likelihood of injury. The child and family will demonstrate measures to prevent injury as well as first aid measures to be implemented if an injury occurs.

# Musculoskeletal Problems of Infants, Toddlers, and Preschoolers

## Torsional Deformities

### Pathophysiology

Torsional (or rotation) deformities of the femur or tibia are some of the most common orthopedic problems. Internal tibial torsion (or toeing in) is common in infants due to intrauterine positioning, and is frequently seen in toddlers and preschool-age children. Femoral anteversion is the internal rotation of the femur that causes the entire extremity to rotate inward. Femoral anteversion is caused by intrauterine positioning or, in some cases, by hereditary factors.

### Medical Diagnosis and Management

Diagnosis of internal tibial torsion or femoral anteversion is established by physical examination. The degree of tibial rotation is determined by measurement of the thigh–foot angle. If the condition does not improve by 18 months of age, corrective night splints such as the Denis Browne splint may be used. These splints maintain the leg in relative external rotation. The deformity is typically corrected after a year of treatment. Occasionally surgery may be required to correct the problem. Femoral anteversion is generally mild and decreases with growth, requiring no intervention.

### Nursing Assessment and Diagnosis

Nurses assist in identification of children who may need referral for evaluation of torsional problems. Assessment includes observation of intoeing gait.

Nursing diagnoses for torsional deformities might include the following:

- High risk for injury related to noncompliance with treatment plan

- Fear related to application of splints at night
- Impaired physical mobility related to foot position

### Planning and Implementing Nursing Care

Education about the pathophysiology and rationale for treatment or lack of treatment of torsional problems is an important nursing role. For infants or children who need orthotic devices, education regarding appropriate use is coordinated with physicians and therapists. Parents should understand the importance of using splints to treat torsional problems and may need support in being firm about their use when the child is resistant. Parents are taught to assess skin integrity as a routine step in use of splints. The parents should also be taught to encourage the child to sit cross-legged, rather than in a squat position (kneeling with buttocks between the legs and feet turned inward). The child should not sleep prone with the buttocks up and feet turned inward.

### Evaluating Nursing Care

Parents should demonstrate understanding of how to apply and use a splint, and voice the importance of strict compliance with the treatment plan. Children should demonstrate an ability to comply with the treatment plan by wearing splints or braces as prescribed, and should remain free from injury related to the torsional problems.

## Genu Varum and Genu Valgum

*Genu varum* (bowlegs) and *genu valgum* (knock knees) are also common and usually benign problems. Genu varum and femoral anteversion often appear together. Extreme conditions of varus (nonphysiologic varus) may be congenital or familial. The etiology may also involve Blount's disease (abnormal growth of the proximal tibia with extreme internal tibial torsion) or rickets. Nonphysiologic or extreme valgus may also be congenital or familial. The condition may also be related to rickets, polio, obesity, or trauma.

Genu varum and valgum are normally present in infants and toddlers. If bowlegs persist beyond 3 years of age further investigation is warranted. Knock knees that persist beyond about the age of 7, particularly if accompanied by conditions such as leg or hip asymmetry, should be investigated.

## Septic Arthritis
### Pathophysiology

Joint infections are often secondary to osteomyelitis, but they may also result from bacterial invasion causing an inflammatory response with pus formation. The cause of infectious arthritis is usually staphylococcal or streptococcal organisms that spread hematogenously from distant primary sources such as impetigo, otitis media, or other infection. Debris and enzymes produced by the organisms can destroy the articular cartilage, causing permanent joint destruction. Joint infections can extend beyond the joint into adjacent bone. Joints affected include the hip, ankle, elbow, knee, or shoulder, with the hip most frequently involved. Toddlers are most often affected.

### Medical Diagnosis and Management

Symptoms are both local and systemic. Localized symptoms include extreme pain with movement, decreased range of motion, or refusal to move a joint. Often the child assumes a flexed position of comfort. In superficial joints, swelling, warmth and redness are present. Systemic symptoms include fever, sweating, chills, and malaise.

Joint fluid is aspirated for bacterial and viral cultures. Cultures may be negative, because pus can inhibit bacterial growth. Increased white blood cell count and erythrocyte sedimentation rate are seen. Bone scans may aid in the diagnosis.

Treatment is instituted immediately with antibiotics, both parenterally and with intra-articular irrigations. Intravenous antibiotics are usually administered initially, followed by several weeks of oral therapy. The determination of which route to use is made based on the duration and extent of the infection. At the time of diagnosis, arthrotomy (surgical exploration of the joint) is performed to remove pus and irrigate the joint with antibiotics. However, joint irrigation is not recommended by all orthopedists (Chung, 1986). Complications of inadequate or delayed treatment of this disorder are joint destruction, shortening of the limb, and joint stiffness.

### Nursing Assessment and Diagnosis

Nursing assessment is similar to that for osteomyelitis.

Nursing diagnoses for septic arthritis might include the following:

- Pain related to the infectious process
- Impaired physical mobility related to pain
- High risk for injury related to neurovascular impairment
- Hyperthermia related to the infectious process

### Planning and Implementing Nursing Care

Care of children with septic arthritis is similar to care of those with osteomyelitis. Adequate pain relief is very important. Casts, splints, or traction may be used to immobilize the joint as a comfort measure and to reduce risk of spread of infection. Monitoring for neurovascular impairment related to these techniques is required. The child needs frequent monitoring of vital signs due to the potential complications of septic shock.

Normally, the child feels better after 2 to 3 days of

effective treatment. At this time, focus of care is on assisting the child and family to cope with prolonged immobilization. Developmentally appropriate activities are provided.

### Evaluating Nursing Care

Evaluation of effective care includes the child's verbalization of decreased pain and increased comfort level. The child's developmental level is maintained. Complications of the disease and treatment are prevented, and the parents and child should understand treatment plans and the need for follow-up care (Coffman, 1986).

# Musculoskeletal Problems of School-Age Children and Adolescents

## Osteomyelitis

### Pathophysiology

Osteomyelitis, infection of the bone, is seen most often in children between the ages of 5 and 14 years. Although any bone may be affected, osteomyelitis occurs most commonly in the long bones. If not treated promptly and appropriately, the infection spreads to the subperiosteal space and ruptures the periosteum with leakage of pus into the surrounding soft tissue or joint. Chronic osteomyelitis may result.

In 80% to 90% of the cases, infection is caused by staphylococcus aureus spread from another primary site such as skin trauma, skin, ear, or throat infection. In a growing child, the metaphyseal area is highly vascular with fine capillary loops where bacteria may lodge and multiply. Furthermore, phagocytosis seems to be less active in the metaphysis (Green & Edwards, 1987). Thus, osteomyelitis usually occurs in the metaphyseal area, near the epiphyseal plate.

### Medical Diagnosis and Management

Diagnosis is based on clinical assessment and confirming laboratory and radiologic studies. Initial symptoms are related to cellulitis (tissue inflammation), including redness, swelling, and tenderness at the site. Systemic symptoms follow and include fever, malaise, chills, and vomiting. If sepsis has progressed, symptoms of septic shock will be present, including fever, chills, and increased heart and respiratory rates. The child often refuses to use the involved limb due to pain.

Bony changes are not evident on radiograph until several days after onset of infection. Technetium bone scan may assist in confirming the clinical diagnosis. Many orthopedists strongly recommend bone aspiration or open biopsy to establish the diagnosis as well as to plan treatment (Chung, 1986; Green & Edwards, 1987). Laboratory studies usually reveal increased white blood cell count and increased erythrocyte sedimentation rate. Cultures of material obtained by bone aspiration or biopsy are helpful in ascertaining the diagnosis and planning drug therapy.

Management includes prompt initiation of parenteral antibiotics. Treatment formerly required 6 weeks of intravenous (IV) drug administration of antibiotics. Research findings have shown, however, that shorter term (5–10 days) IV therapy followed by long-term oral antibiotics for a total of 6 weeks of antibiotics is effective. However, the child and family must be able to comply with the therapeutic regimen as well as weekly outpatient laboratory and clinical evaluations in order to be a candidate for prolonged oral therapy rather than IV therapy. If there is no improvement within 24 to 48 hours with drug treatment, surgical removal of the necrosed bone is required.

### Nursing Assessment and Diagnosis

Nurses play an important role in early detection. Fever or complaints of a painful, swollen joint should direct the nurse to suspect acute osteomyelitis. Nurses should observe for a child guarding a joint against movement.

Nursing diagnoses for osteomyelitis might include the following:

- Pain related to infectious process
- Impaired physical mobility related to infection
- High risk for injury related to neurovascular impairment and reinfection
- Hyperthermia related to the infectious process

### Planning and Implementing Nursing Care

Nursing care goals include monitoring for sepsis and management of fever and pain. Antibiotics are administered as ordered. Teaching the child and family about the disease and its treatment is also an important nursing function. Medications as well as physical measures are used to reduce pain. The involved limb is often splinted or put in traction to reduce movement. Immobility helps relieve pain as well as reduce the spread of infection. In the acute phase of this condition, the child usually has a poor appetite and may vomit. Children should be encouraged to drink small amounts of clear liquids until vomiting stops. If treatment involves an open wound, isolation precautions are followed. If surgical debridement of the bone is required, nurses should provide normal postoperative care for the child.

As the child begins to recover, play activities and stimulation are important components of nursing care. Nurses should involve the parents and siblings in the child's care. Nurses can help siblings understand that their brother or sister may have to limit their activities and household responsibilities for a period after returning to the home.

If home IV therapy is considered, parent and child education and home nurse referral is vital. A heparin lock is usually used for home antibiotic therapy, and parents should be instructed on its maintenance. Homebound educational services are also important. With prompt diagnosis and treatment, the child should have no residual problems.

### Evaluating Nursing Care

Prevention of sepsis by careful monitoring of vital signs, as well as prompt reporting of deviations from normal, is an expected outcome. The child's pain should be well controlled with analgesia and positioning. Evaluation should be based on the child's and parents' understanding of the disease and the treatment regimen. Parents should demonstrate how to administer antibiotics and maintain a heparin lock.

## Abnormal Spinal Curves

Three types of abnormal curvatures of the spine may occur. *Kyphosis* is excessive posterior curvature of the mid-thoracic spine. Causes of this disorder include abnormal posture as well as a variety of underlying diseases including Scheuermann disease (vertebral osteochondrosis) and, more rarely, other congenital or acquired neuromuscular diseases. Progressive back pain and deteriorating posture are reasons for seeking health care. Management includes exercises to strengthen thoracic muscles (Chung, 1986), use of the modified Milwaukee brace, and surgery if the curve is progressive despite conservative treatment.

*Lordosis* is excessive anterior curvature of the lumbar spine due most often to other underlying neuromuscular diseases or spinal deformity. Children usually are asymptomatic. Treatment consists of postural exercises and weight loss, if indicated.

*Scoliosis* is a lateral spinal curvature. Curves may be non-structural when caused by leg length discrepancy, hip or knee flexion contractures, or pain. Structural curves may be idiopathic or due to neuromuscular diseases or congenital malformations. Complications from untreated scoliosis include curve progression with cardiorespiratory compromise, progressive back pain, and degenerative arthritis of the spine.

## Idiopathic Scoliosis

### Pathophysiology

Seventy percent of scoliosis is found to be idiopathic. The exact cause is unknown, although there seems to be some genetic influence. Progression of idiopathic scoliosis (IS) depends on the age of onset. Infantile IS (birth to 3 years) resolves without treatment in 90% of those affected. In juvenile scoliosis (age 4 to 9 years), curves remain small

and flexible. Adolescent scoliosis (age 10 to cessation of growth) may or may not progress depending on the sex and age of the child. Although incidence of IS in girls is the same as that in boys, girls are more likely to have curves greater than 10 degrees and are five to ten times more likely to have curves that become worse. The most common scoliosis involves a right thoracic curve.

### Medical Diagnosis and Management

Scoliosis is often unrecognized until there is some degree of deformity visible. Diagnosis is established by examination (Fig. 33-11) and radiographs. Prognosis is related to the age of the child at onset and to type and severity of curvature. Children with curvatures less than 20 degrees are observed periodically during growth (every 3–6 months) to evaluate progression. Curves of 25 to 40 degrees require bracing or electrical stimulation; curves greater than 50 degrees generally require spinal fusion. Exercises are helpful only in cases of postural rather than structural scoliosis.

The purpose of spinal fusion procedures is to straighten the spine as much as possible. There are several different approaches to operative management, including Harrington rods, Luque wires, Dwyer instrumentation, and Cotrel-Dubousset instrumentation, among others. Each technique has advantages and disadvantages. Most procedures require the use of a cast or brace for a period after surgery. The Cotrel-Dubousset approach allows for earlier ambulation (on average, by day 5) and return to school at 1 month postoperatively (Cotrel, Dubousset, & Guillaumat, 1988; Jacobs-Zacny & Horn, 1988). Postoperative casting is not required, but a brace may be used for several months.

### Nursing Assessment and Diagnosis

Detection of scoliosis is an important nursing role. Many states require scoliosis screening by school nurses. Girls should be screened in grades 6, 7, and 8 and boys in grades 7, 8, and 9 (Scoles, 1988). Boys should remove their shirts; girls may be screened while wearing a brassiere or a halter top. Screening examination consists of observing the child from the front, side, back, and forward bend positions (Fig. 33-12). The nurse checks for presence of asymmetry of shoulder height, scapular asymmetry, unequal distance between arms and waist, uneven pelvis, and rib hump. From the front, breasts may appear unequal in size due to vertebral rotation. A scoliometer might be used for more accurate determination of vertebral rotation. Any positive findings indicate possible scoliosis. Between 5% and 10% of children have positive findings on screening examinations (Scoles, 1988).

Nursing diagnoses for idiopathic scoliosis might include the following:

• High risk for noncompliance related to wearing a brace

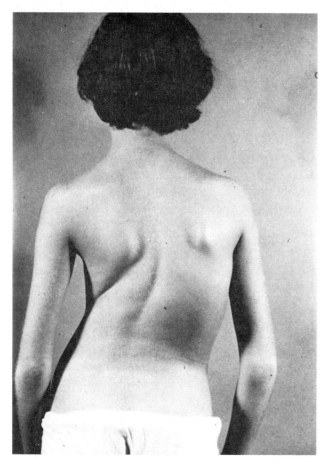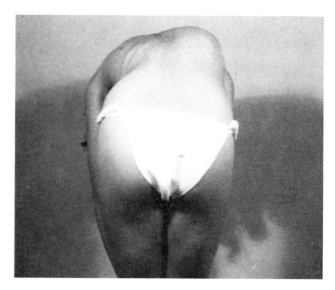

*Figure 33–11.    Scoliosis. (O'Connor, B.J. [1976]. Scoliosis: Classfication and diagnosis in pediatric othopedics.* ONAJ, *3, 84)*

- Impaired physical mobility related to postoperative management
- Pain related to surgical intervention
- Body image disturbance related to the physical deformity or need for a brace
- Potential impaired skin integrity, related to impairment of neurovascular integrity to lower extremities and use of a brace, cast, and electrical stimulators
- Constipation related to immobility

### Planning and Implementing Nursing Care

*Care of the Child Requiring Electrical Stimulation.* Lateral electrospinal stimulation of the paraspinal muscles on the convex side of the curve may halt progression in 70% to 75% of children with curves between 20 degrees and 40 degrees (Herbert & Bobechko, 1987). Treatment is done for at least 8 hours each night with either an implantable or a surface electrode system. Stimulation continues until skeletal maturity. This method avoids the problems involving body image and noncompliance that occur with bracing. Herbert (1987) reports that only 2 of 250 patients did not use stimulators as directed.

Patients using these systems are instructed in use of the equipment and lead placement for the skin surface system. Skin must be checked for signs of irritation. All routine activities can continue without interruption. Outpatient follow-up at intervals of 3 to 4 months is required to ensure correct lead placement and evaluate treatment efficacy.

*Care of the Child With a Milwaukee Brace.*
A Milwaukee brace serves to prevent progression of curves (Fig. 33-13). The brace is worn 23 of 24 hours per day and removed only for bathing or swimming. Family and client are instructed to observe the skin daily for evidence of irritation from the brace. Use of a smooth undershirt under the brace is helpful for protection of the skin. Lotions and powders are not used, as they may increase irritation. If irritation persists, the family should contact the health provider to make adjustments in the

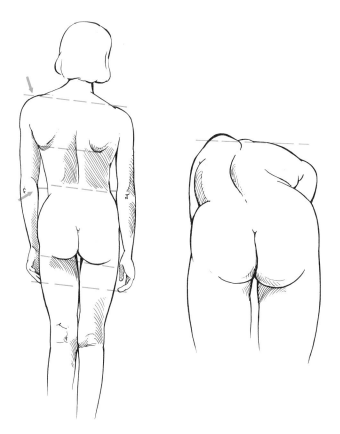

*Figure 33–12.   Scoliosis screening.*

brace. Loose-fitting clothing is worn outside the brace. Most daily activities may be continued without limitation. Exceptions include contact sports and activities such as horseback riding and trampolining.

Wearing the brace may be very stressful for the adolescent because of concerns over peer reaction, body image, and activity restriction. The nurse can assist the child and family in developing strategies to cope with the necessity of long-term bracing treatment. Bracing is often required until growth ends. The time spent in the brace is then gradually reduced from 23 hours per day to none over a period of 6 to 12 months. Occasionally bracing treatment is not effective and operative intervention becomes necessary.

*Care of the Child Requiring Operative Intervention.* Preoperative teaching prepares the child and family for both the preoperative period and the immediate and long-term postoperative period. Specific details will change depending on the procedure performed. Before surgery the child should practice log-rolling and respiratory therapy routines as well as toileting and eating while supine. Planning a preoperative tour of the intensive care unit and meeting the nursing staff is helpful for both child and parents. Talking to someone who has had a

successful operative course provides the child facing surgery with an ideal chance to talk about his or her concerns.

After this type of surgical procedure, patients are admitted to the ICU for nursing care. The spinal incision is normally covered with a pressure dressing. If the procedure requires a cast, this is applied 7 to 10 days after surgery. The focus of nursing care is prevention/observation of potential complications. The child must remain flat, turning as a unit (log-rolling) every 2 hours to prevent skin breakdown and respiratory complications. Signs should be posted on the bed to warn persons caring for the patient that only log-rolling is allowed. Flexion/rotation of the back may disrupt the bone grafting of the fusion or the instrumentation.

Vital signs, intake and output, neurovascular integrity, gastrointestinal function, and incision site are monitored frequently to detect complications. Pain is a major concern requiring aggressive nursing management. Use of a patient-controlled analgesia pump allows the child to administer frequent, small doses of analgesia such as morphine, which is very effective for the first few days. Subsequently, acetaminophen with codeine or other medications should be given on a scheduled basis. Regular medication administration provides more effective relief (Eland, 1988).

The adolescent who requires a cast postoperatively needs assistance with learning altered self-care routines and planning for clothing. Nurses should assure girls that the cast does not interfere with breast development or menses.

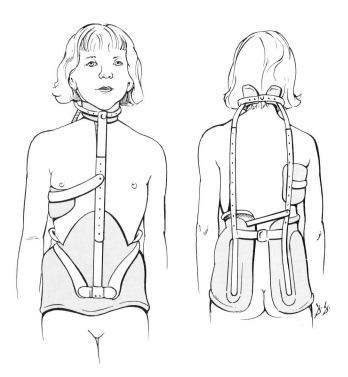

*Figure 33–13.   Milwaukee brace.*

## Evaluating Nursing Care

Effective nursing care may be evaluated on the following outcome criteria:

Patient has maintained skin integrity.

Patient/family is able to verbalize pre- and post-operative expectations.

Patient/family is able to demonstrate use of orthotic devices (brace, cast, electrical stimulator).

Patient/family demonstrates ability to perform self-care within constraints of restricted activity.

Patient/family is able to list signs/symptoms that should prompt them to seek medical advice.

Patient/family is able to verbalize home care instructions, including follow-up appointments.

Patient's home environment is adapted as needed (Coffman, 1986).

## Osteosarcoma

### Pathophysiology

Osteosarcoma is a rapidly growing malignant tumor of the bone arising from osteoblasts. This tumor comprises 20% of skeletal malignancies. It is found primarily in adolescents and young adults ages 10 to 25, with equal incidence in males and females (Springfield, 1990). Primary lesions typically are found in areas of active skeletal growth: the distal femur, proximal tibia, or proximal humerus. Metastases commonly involve the lungs.

### Medical Diagnosis and Management

The primary symptom is progressive pain at the site, unrelated to physical activity and often worse at night (Conrad, 1989). Bony tenderness at the tumor site is common. Radiographs are often diagnostic. Bone biopsy confirms the diagnosis.

On hospital admission for diagnostic evaluation, skeletal radiographs, total body technetium bone scan, and computed tomography are done to identify metastatic lesions and plan the approach to treatment. Laboratory evaluation includes complete blood count, platelet count, and liver function studies.

Because these tumors grow rapidly, many children have pulmonary metastases at the time of diagnosis; thus, osteosarcoma tends to have a poor prognosis. The five-year survival rate is about 50% (Springfield, 1990). Treatment includes limb amputation or limb salvage procedures, depending on the site and size of the lesion. The use of pre- and postoperative chemotherapy regimens has increased survival rates dramatically (Rosen, 1985). Preoperative chemotherapeutic agents shrink the tumor and kill the peripheral metastatic cells. This treatment reduces the size of the mass requiring excision and may prevent pathologic fractures (Schubiner & Simon, 1987). Drugs that may be employed include doxorubicin (Adriamycin) cyclophosphamide, actinomycin-D, vincristine, and cisplatin. Radiation therapy is not usually helpful.

## Ewing's Sarcoma

### Pathophysiology

This skeletal tumor is markedly different from osteosarcoma. It originates in myelogenic cells of the bone marrow. This tumor affects people between 10 and 30 years of age, with the highest incidence in the second decade of life. Males are affected about twice as often as females. Bones most commonly affected are the pelvis, humerus, and femur. There are often early metastases to the lungs, other bones, and lymph nodes.

### Medical Diagnosis and Management

Symptoms include local pain and swelling at the site. Associated systemic symptoms include fever, fatigue, anorexia, weight loss, and malaise. Pathologic fractures may be the presenting sign. Diagnosis is based on radiograph and biopsy results. Further diagnostic work-up is similar to that done for osteosarcoma, with the addition of bone marrow aspiration and 24-hour urine collections for vanillylmandelic acid and catecholamines to rule out neuroblastoma (malignant hemorrhagic tumor composed of cells that resemble neuroblasts).

The tumor is very sensitive to radiation. Treatment combines radiotherapy and chemotherapy in a variety of different protocols. Drugs used include vincristine, actinomycin-D, cyclophosphamide, dactinomycin, and adriamycin. Five year survival is greater than 75% (Chung, 1986). In selected cases, tumor resection or amputation is done.

### Nursing Assessment and Diagnosis

Nursing assessment includes monitoring for signs of increasing pain in limbs, inflammation, or the presence of a mass. The child may complain of pain or may avoid using the limb. Other signs include limping or frequent infections. Early detection and referral are essential, since the prognosis is improved with early intervention.

Nursing diagnoses for skeletal neoplasms might include the following:

- Pain related to presence of the tumor, diagnostic procedures, and surgery
- High risk for injury related to tumor growth and metastases
- Impaired physical mobility related to loss of a limb
- Fear related to the diagnosis and the need for surgery or chemotherapy
- Self-esteem disturbance related to peer reaction to

loss of a limb or loss of hair caused by chemotherapy

## Planning and Implementing Nursing Care

The initial focus of nursing care is providing support for the child and family faced with a diagnosis that implies potential loss of life and major change in body image. Chapter 25 discusses nursing care concerns related to chemotherapy administration.

If amputation or limb salvage procedures are planned, preoperative teaching is conducted. The child and family members may have many questions regarding the effects of surgery and chemotherapy on function in the immediate and more distant future. Children must be informed about what is to happen to them. Often parents are reluctant to be open with their child regarding the diagnosis and treatment. Nurses can work with other team members in assisting parents to cope with this difficult task. The child and the parents need time to receive information and understand the implications of the diagnosis and treatment. They may be verbal about their concerns or they may be silent. The nurse should be sensitive to their needs for information and emotional support.

Postoperative care of the child who has had an amputation includes prevention of bleeding, providing pain relief, and reducing swelling. Usually a compression dressing is applied to prevent bleeding. Although the extremity can be elevated to reduce edema, elevation should not be continuous or for prolonged periods as flexion contractures may result. The child and family are encouraged to assist with stump care. Strengthening exercises and gait retraining begin soon after the procedure.

Discharge planning should include teaching about care of the prosthesis and stump, parameters for contacting the physician, and understanding of required follow-up care for chemotherapy, monitoring, and rehabilitation. For the child who has had an amputation or has experienced hair loss with chemotherapy, discharge planning should also include role playing as preparation for dealing with peer reactions to the change in appearance. The use of humor is often very effective and therapeutic for the child.

Candlelighters Childhood Cancer Foundation can provide information regarding special programs for children with amputations. The child and family may need ongoing support as they adjust to living with cancer.

## Evaluating Nursing Care

Evaluation of nursing care focuses on the child's and family's adaptation to the diagnosis, as well as compliance with treatment regimens. The child and family should demonstrate an understanding of the disorder, the treatment, possible outcomes, and the need for follow-up care. If amputation was required they should be able to demonstrate proper care for the stump and use of a prosthesis. They should also show increasing signs of adaptive behaviors, and the child should participate in developmentally appropriate activities within his or her physical limitations.

## Slipped Capital Femoral Epiphysis

### Pathophysiology

Slipped capital femoral epiphysis (SCFE) is displacement of the femoral head both downward and backward relative to the neck of the femur due to disruption of the epiphyseal plate (Busch & Morrissy, 1987). The etiology is unknown. Males are more commonly affected than females, and occurrence usually takes place at the onset of puberty, with girls affected approximately two years earlier than boys (Morrissy, 1990). The disorder is most common in overweight or tall, thin adolescents. SCFE is associated with a variety of endocrine and other systemic disorders.

### Medical Diagnosis and Management

The child may be relatively asymptomatic or have pain localized to the groin, buttock, lateral hip, or knee. Hip motion is limited. Radiographs reveal widening of the epiphyseal plate and displacement of the femoral head. Inflammation in the hip joint also occurs, leading to complaints of pain and limp. Laboratory studies reveal abnormal immunoglobulins and complement levels in some cases.

Treatment is surgical. The epiphysis is pinned to prevent further slippage. With early diagnosis and treatment, prognosis is good for normal hip function. Delayed intervention increases the child's risks for degenerative arthritis of the joint.

### Nursing Assessment and Diagnosis

If this condition is suspected, the child or adolescent should be immediately referred to a physician and instructed to avoid unnecessary weight bearing. Nurses should suspect this problem if the child complains of fatigue after walking or standing, or experiences mild hip pain.

Nursing diagnoses for slipped capital femoral epiphysis might include the following:

- Pain related to displacement of the femoral head and surgery
- Impaired physical mobility related to pain, traction, and crutches
- Altered nutrition: More than body requirements, related to obesity
- High risk for impaired skin integrity related to prolonged bed rest
- Constipation related to poor diet or immobility

## Planning and Implementing Nursing Care

Nursing care involves pre- and postoperative pain management. After the pinning procedures, the child may require traction for 7 to 10 days, followed by non–weight-bearing ambulation with crutches until the epiphysis closes (Bloom & Crawford, 1985). Coordination of care with the physical therapist and home health care personnel is important. Nurses should be aware of concerns related to prolonged immobilization and altered self-care abilities. If the client is obese, a weight-reduction diet should be initiated. Dietary planning should also include measures to relieve the child's constipation. Nurses should involve both the parents and the child in the planning for this diet. Nurses must clarify that the child and parents understand the imposed mobility limits.

## Evaluating Nursing Care

Evaluation is based on the child's and parents' understanding of the treatment plan. Parents should have a plan for revising daily activities and school attendance if weight bearing is prohibited. Follow-up also includes monitoring for involvement of the opposite hip. Parents should display an understanding of the condition's early symptoms.

# Legg-Calvé-Perthes Disease

## Pathophysiology

Legg-Calvé-Perthes Disease, also called coxa plana, is an avascular necrosis or osteonecrosis of the femoral head. The cause is unknown. It occurs between four and five times more often in boys than in girls. Peak age at diagnosis is 7 years, with a range of 2 to 12 years. Caucasians are affected more frequently than children of other races. In addition, there is an association between this condition and low birth weight. Twenty percent of the cases are bilateral. A positive family history occurs in 20% of the cases. Bone growth of affected children may be delayed by 1 to 3 years (Thompson & Salter, 1987).

In Phase I of this condition the blood supply to the capital femoral head is interrupted and the femoral head becomes partially or totally necrotic. This phase can last up to 1 year. In Phase II gradual revascularization takes place and the necrotic bone is absorbed and replaced with connective tissue. In Phase III the connective tissue ossifies, resulting in healing.

## Medical Diagnosis and Management

The child does not become symptomatic until Phase II. A limp, often associated with pain in the groin, lateral hip, or knee, may persist up to a year before treatment is sought. The child may complain of fatigue and stiffness in the hip joint. Physical assessment reveals limited range of motion of the hip and decreased thigh circumference as evidence of muscle atrophy.

The treatment is to reduce distortion of the femoral head during the healing process and to restore and maintain hip range of motion. Initial treatment involves 1 to 2 weeks of bed rest. Balanced suspension may be used to reduce pain from hip irritability and associated muscle spasm. Physical therapy and occasionally gentle abduction traction may be required to restore hip motion.

Two approaches for preventing deformity of the femoral head during healing are used: nonoperative and operative. Both approaches allow the acetabulum to function as a mold for the femoral head. Children younger than 6 with minimal involvement may be observed closely every 2 to 4 months. Nonoperative methods use abduction casts or orthoses to redirect the femoral head into the acetabulum. These devices are required for 12 to 17 months after clinical onset of the disease.

Surgical treatment consists of various types of osteotomies, which nail the femoral head to the trochanter. The advantage of operative treatment is that the child has only 2 months of restricted activity, versus a year or more of restrictions with nonoperative treatment.

## Nursing Assessment and Diagnosis

Nurses play an important role in the initial identification of this disease and the appropriate referral of affected children for medical evaluation. Signs include limited range of motion or movement in the affected hip or hips, which may be seen as a limp. The child may also complain of chronic pain in the affected hip.

Nursing diagnoses for Legg-Calvé-Perthes disease might include the following:

- Impaired physical mobility related to pain
- Noncompliance related to unwillingness to wear a brace
- High risk for infection related to surgical procedure
- Impaired social interaction related to restricted activities
- High risk for injury related to microfractures caused by activity
- Pain related to the disease process and surgery

## Planning and Implementing Nursing Care

Nursing care during Phase II includes pain management and assisting the child to cope with immobilization during bed rest/traction therapy. If the therapy is conducted at home, visiting nurse and homebound teacher referral may be indicated. Children treated with abduction casts or orthoses need to be taught how to carry out activities of daily living within the movement limitations imposed by these devices.

Nurses must be creative in helping the child who feels well and is normally active to cope with the idea of now being essentially inactive. It is helpful if the child has a hobby or is interested in starting a hobby such as model building, crafts, or painting.

### Evaluating Nursing Care

Evaluation of nursing care for children with Legg-Calvé-Perthes disease focuses on maintaining as normal growth and development as possible during the course of the disease. If surgery is indicated, the child will have a normal postoperative recovery without infection. If nonsurgical interventions are used the child and family will demonstrate an understanding of the treatment regimen and the need for use of the brace.

## Duchenne Muscular Dystrophy

### Pathophysiology

*Muscular dystrophy* is the term used for a group of inherited disorders that cause progressive degeneration and weakness of skeletal muscles. Duchenne muscular dystrophy is the most common form of muscular dystrophy in children. Half of the cases are X-linked, whereas the remainder occur sporadically. Genetic counseling should be provided, as it is likely that all subsequent male offspring of the parents will be affected. Maternal aunts, their female offspring, and female siblings may be carriers. Males are almost exclusively affected; the incidence is 1 in 3000 live births (Drennan, 1990). Muscle wasting is progressive and leads to death, usually in late adolescence due to infection or cardiopulmonary failure.

### Medical Diagnosis and Management

Diagnosis is based on clinical findings of muscle weakness, presence of increased muscle enzyme creatinine phosphokinase (CPK), and muscle biopsy. Electromyelogram and nerve conduction studies are usually performed to rule out other causes of weakness. Electrocardiogram and pulmonary function studies establish the degree of cardiovascular and pulmonary involvement. Symptoms begin between 18 and 36 months of age, starting with weakness in muscles of the pelvic girdle. This weakness is noted clinically by Gower sign, in which the child "climbs up his legs" using the hands in order to get from a sitting to standing position. Pseudohypertrophy of the calf muscles is a classic sign of the disease, caused by excess fibrous tissue and fat replacing muscle fibers. Cardiac muscle involvement is universal. Some children have delayed or impaired cognitive development.

Management is supportive. Various techniques and equipment are used to minimize deformity, prolong ambulation, and assist with activities of daily living. Knee-ankle-foot orthoses may prolong ambulation for several years (Drennan, 1990). Shoulder girdle weakness prevents use of crutches for assistance.

### Nursing Assessment and Diagnosis

Nurses should be alert to the initial manifestations of this disease. A thorough history may reveal early difficulties with gross motor skills such as jumping, running, and climbing. These children also typically have difficulty arising from a sitting or lying position. Physical examination may reveal muscle weakness in spite of muscle hypertrophy, particularly in the calves.

Nursing diagnoses for muscular dystrophy might include the following:

- Impaired physical mobility related to muscle weakness
- High risk for injury related to weakness and unsteady gait
- Self-esteem disturbance related to inability to achieve normal developmental tasks
- Activity intolerance related to fatigue
- Altered nutrition: More than body requirements, related to decreased calorie expenditure
- Altered family processes related to the progressive nature of the disease and the need for increasing care

### Planning and Implementing Nursing Care

Nurses should facilitate coordination of care with physicians and physical and occupational therapists for these families. The child and parents must be taught how to manage activities of daily living in the face of progressive reduction of strength. As muscular strength decreases, the child becomes more susceptible to injury from falls or other accidents, so the child and parents should be provided with suggestions on how to make the child's environment safe. The child and parents also need to be taught how to balance the need for normal activity with the fatigue that accompanies muscular dystrophy. An important nursing goal is the prevention of obesity. Nurses can assist the family in adjusting caloric intake to match decreased activity. With the progression of the disease the child needs greater care, which can put a strain on the family. Nurses can help identify resources for the parents, and can help them obtain ongoing assistance in coping with the eventual disease outcome should be offered to the family. The Muscular Dystrophy Association of America, Inc. (810 7th Avenue, New York, NY 10019), is very active in supporting research and care for these children.

## Evaluating Nursing Care

Evaluation of nursing care for children with muscular dystrophy includes determining that the child is achieving growth and development as normal as possible, while remaining free from injury. To the greatest extent possible the child should continue to engage in normal activities. The child and parents should demonstrate an understanding of the nature of the disease, its progression, and ways to adapt to the symptoms. The child and family should avail themselves of available resources.

# Patellofemoral Stress Syndrome

## Pathophysiology

Patellofemoral stress syndrome (PSS) is one of several overuse syndromes seen in adolescents and young adults. Overuse syndromes are common problems that result from repetitive trauma to bones, joints, tendons, ligaments, or muscles. PSS results from improper alignment of the patella within the femoral groove, causing chronic retropatellar irritation with knee flexion. The exact etiology is unknown. Repeated trauma and body build may predispose the young athlete to these problems. Onset often corresponds with the adolescent growth spurt. The terms "patellofemoral stress syndrome" or "retropatellar pain syndrome" are preferred over "chondromalacia patella," which is a pathologic condition in which there is actual softening or erosion of the cartilage behind the patella.

## Medical Diagnosis and Management

Symptoms of PSS include diffuse pain of the anterior knee. Occasionally, the pain is identified as retropatellar, but usually the child is unable to localize the pain. Typically the child with this condition is involved in an activity that demands frequent and repetitive knee flexion such as running or jumping. Stair climbing and sitting aggravate the pain. A change in frequency, intensity, and duration of exercise, or of the playing surface (dirt to artificial turf) may lead to this condition or other overuse syndromes (Garrick, 1988).

On physical examination, the child is unable to hyperflex the knee. A knee effusion as well as thigh atrophy may be observed. Treatment involves rest and avoidance of aggravating activities until symptoms subside. Knee orthoses (elastic support or light weight brace) may help minimize pain (Scoles, 1988). Nonsteroidal anti-inflammatory drugs (e.g., salicylate or ibuprofen) may be prescribed. Ice applied to the knee after exercise provides anti-inflammatory and analgesic effects. Quadricep strengthening with an exercise program of progressive resistive straight-leg raises is recommended (Busch, 1990). If initial rest, medications, and physical therapy do not provide relief, operative treatment may be required.

# Osgood-Schlatter Disease

## Pathophysiology

Osgood-Schlatter disease is another overuse syndrome affecting the tibial tubercle, just under the knee. This condition is seen in boys and girls typically at the time of the adolescent growth spurt. Hyperflexion activities with intense running (e.g., basketball, soccer, sprinting) cause inflammation of the tibial tubercle.

## Medical Diagnosis and Management

The main complaint involves pain in the anterior aspect of the knee. Pain usually diminishes with rest. Examination reveals enlargement, tenderness, and occasionally erythema of the tibial tuberosity.

Treatment includes initial rest, ice and ice massage, nonsteroidal anti-inflammatory drugs, and an exercise program. Crutches may be required initially to relieve stress. Prevention of recurrence includes continued exercises for quadriceps strengthening/flexibility and the use of a horseshoe pad around the knee to protect the tibial tuberosity from injury. If the youngster complains of knee pain or limps, athletic participation must be postponed. If the child plays regardless of the pain, there is the risk of developing progressive tendinitis, quadricep weakening, and patellar dislocation (Garrick, 1988).

## Nursing Assessment and Diagnosis

Nursing assessment for overuse syndromes includes a complete history and physical examination. The history may reveal that pain occurs following exertion, repeated knee flexion, stair climbing, or jumping. Physical examination usually reveals considerable local tenderness.

Nursing diagnoses for overuse syndromes might include the following:

- Pain related to the injury
- High risk for injury related to continued repetition of activities that cause pain

## Planning and Implementing Nursing Care

Nurses most often see adolescents with these two overuse syndromes in the outpatient setting. Nurses need to be familiar with the treatment rationales involving each syndrome and the consequences if treatment protocols are not followed. Sports participation is not known to cause rapid worsening of patellofemoral stress syndrome. Continued participation in activities that cause knee pain, however, means that the knee will probably be chronically painful. The young athlete must then decide whether or not ongoing participation is worth the pain. Many decide that they would prefer to participate and learn how to cope with the pain. The nurse can assist the child and

# Nursing Care Plan

## Assessment

Jill, a 7-month-old girl, has been brought in for application of a hip spica cast. She appears well nourished and is content in her father's arms.

### Chief Complaint

Congenital hip dysplasia

### Subjective Assessment

*Past History:* Congenital hip dysplasia was diagnosed somewhat late, at 4 months of age. Pavlik harness was used for 8 weeks in an effort to reduce hip dislocation. This was unsuccessful. Soft-tissue contractures developed as a consequence of the limited hip abduction. Home traction was undertaken to stretch the soft tissue prior to closed reduction of the hip and spica cast application under anesthesia.

*Present History:* Parents express concern regarding caring for their daughter with a cumbersome cast.

*Family History:* Mother is 24 years old, father is 27 years old; both are in good health. She has one sister, age 3, who is also in good health.

### Objective Assessment

*Physical Examination:* T. 37.5°C (99.6°F); P. 115; R. 25; B.P. 80/60; weight 7.7 kg (17 lb) (50% [NCHS percentile]); height 68 cm (26¾ in) (50% [NCHS percentile]).

| | |
|---|---|
| Integument: | Clear, warm, moist, good turgor |
| Head: | Normal |
| Eyes: | Fundoscopic exam normal |
| Ears: | Otoscopic exam normal |
| Nose: | Normal |
| Throat: | Tonsils normal, no exudate |
| Neck: | Supple, without lymph-adenopathy |
| Thorax and Lungs: | Symmetrical shape, clear lung fields |
| Heart: | Normal rhythm, no murmur |
| Abdomen: | Active bowel sounds in all quadrants, no pain, tenderness or masses |
| Genitalia: | Normal |
| Musculoskeletal: | Limited abduction of the left hip, and asymmetrical gluteal folds and femoral foreshortening (Galeazi sign). (Ortolani maneuver does not elicit a "thunk" or "click," as the hip is not relocatable due to the soft tissue contractures.) |
| Neurological: | Reflexes normal and symmetrical, anxious, irritable, restless |

### Medical Diagnosis

Congenital hip dysplasia

## Nursing Care Plan for a Child with Congenital Hip Dysplasia

| Goals | Nursing Interventions | Evaluation Criteria |
|---|---|---|
| *NURSING DIAGNOSIS #1: Knowledge deficit regarding hospital procedures* | | |
| (S) Family will be able to verbalize understanding of routines | Explain usual routines, protocols related to anesthesia, recovery room, post-casting care | Family verbalizes understanding of routines |

*(continued)*

# Nursing Care Plan *(Continued)*

| Goals | Nursing Interventions | Evaluation Criteria |
|---|---|---|
| (L) Family will know how to utilize equipment and access services | Orient family to environment and services | Family is able to utilize equipment and access services |

*NURSING DIAGNOSIS #2: High Risk for impairment of skin integrity due to cast/incontinence*

| Goals | Nursing Interventions | Evaluation Criteria |
|---|---|---|
| (S) Skin will be free of areas of damage | Assessment of skin integrity every 4 hours<br><br>Instruct parents in proper cast care | Skin is damage free |

*NURSING DIAGNOSIS #3: Impaired mobility due to cast*

| Goals | Nursing Interventions | Evaluation Criteria |
|---|---|---|
| (S) Parents will verbalize ways to meet mobility needs | Demonstrate ways to provide mobility and facilitate care giving | Parents verbalize and implement methods to meet mobility needs |

*NURSING DIAGNOSIS #4: High Risk for altered growth and development due to impaired mobility and decreased tacile stimulation*

| Goals | Nursing Interventions | Evaluation Criteria |
|---|---|---|
| (L) Infant will demonstrate normal development in all areas except gross motor | Demonstrate ways to provide mobility and facilitate care giving<br><br>Discuss infant's continued needs for touch and demonstrate how to provide for them—child will still enjoy cuddling<br><br>Utilize wagon/stroller to put infant in upright position in front of flat surface with toys she can reach for and enjoy<br><br>Utilize brightly colored toys and mirrors | Infant demonstrates normal development in all areas except gross motor |

*NURSING DIAGNOSIS #5: Potential alteration in bowel elimination—constipation*

| Goals | Nursing Interventions | Evaluation Criteria |
|---|---|---|
| (S) Infant will have normal stools | Encourage intake of fluids, fruits, and vegetables in infant's diet | Infant experiences normal bowel elimination, does not suffer from constipation |

*NURSING DIAGNOSIS #6: Potential sleep pattern disturbance due to disruption of routine and discomfort of cast*

| Goals | Nursing Interventions | Evaluation Criteria |
|---|---|---|
| (S) Child will sleep comfortably for 4–6-hour periods | Position in crib using foam wedge to elevate upper body<br><br>Alternatively, assess comfort level in prone position, assess need for support of lower extremities so toes are not pressing into mattress<br><br>Provide brief comforting if infant awakens | Child's sleep pattern remains undisturbed |

952

family in this decision. Education of the child regarding use of orthoses, medications, and the exercise program is part of nursing care, in coordination with the physician and physical therapist.

Working with the adolescent with Osgood-Schlatter disease presents the challenge of helping the child understand the importance of decreasing physical activity. In the athlete or active adolescent, any period of time seems to be a long time. Nurses can help the child to understand the benefits of treatment by pointing out that one of its goals is to assist the child in achieving future maximum athletic potential. Ideally, rehabilitation for all sports-related conditions can be undertaken at the same time and place as team practice. This facilitates the child's peer interaction and may reduce the depression noted in the injured young athlete.

### Evaluating Nursing Care

Nursing care for overuse syndromes is evaluated by the child or adolescent's reports of decreased pain. While remaining active, the child should comply with the treatment program.

## Sports-Related Injuries

More than 30 million children participate in organized sports activities outside the school setting. Potential for injury in these children is dependent upon their ability, health, and physical maturity, the sport in which they participate, and adherence to the rules. The sport with the highest injury risk is football. Mechanisms of sports injuries include repetitive microtrauma as seen with overuse syndromes, and acute overload injuries causing sudden stress to bone or, more commonly, soft tissues as seen with contusions, sprains, strains, and dislocations. Injuries may include damage to the epiphyseal plate, stress fractures, and avulsions.

The knee is one of the most common athletic injury sites. A blow to the side of the knee can result in medial collateral and lateral collateral ligament injury. Severe hyperextension of the knee results in anterior cruciate ligament injury.

Stress fractures often result from a rapid increase in a specific activity. These fractures may result in a progressive loss of bone at a specific site and can eventually result in a complete fracture. Treatment involves rest and may include immobilization.

Injury prevention is an important role for nurses working with young athletes. Aspiring athletes should be counselled regarding individual suitability for particular sports. This counselling involves assessment of the child's size, physical maturity, and level of conditioning. Nurses can also help educate young athletes concerning conditioning and the use of weight training. Conditioning should be a progressive process, involving appropriate increase in activity and periods of rest. Weight training should always be supervised, and young athletes should be encouraged to use lighter weights while performing more repetitions of exercises.

## Summary

The nursing care of children with musculoskeletal problems presents a unique opportunity to interact with many other health professionals as well as with children and members of their families. The overall goals of nursing intervention are to: minimize complications associated with a particular injury or disease while maximizing the child's development and capabilities for adaptation to any temporary or permanent changes in musculoskeletal function.

## References

Bloom, M. L., & Crawford, A. H. (1985). Slipped capital femoral epiphysis: An assessment of treatment modalities. *Orthopedics, 8,* 36.

Busch, M. T. (1990). Sports medicine in children and adolescents. In R. T. Morrissy (Ed.). *Lovell and Winter's pediatric orthopaedics* (2nd ed.). Philadelphia: J. B. Lippincott pp. 1091–1128.

Busch, M. T., & Morrissy, R. T. (1987). Slipped capital femoral epiphysis. *Orthopedic Clinics of North America, 18,* 637–647.

Carlino, H. Y. (1991). The child with an Ilizarov external fixator. *Pediatric Nursing, 17*(4), 355–358.

Carroll, N. (1990). Clubfoot. In R. T. Morrissy (Ed.). *Lovell and Winter's pediatric orthopaedics* (2nd ed.). Philadelphia: J. B. Lippincott pp. 927–956.

Chung, S. M. K. (1986). *Handbook of pediatric orthopedics.* New York: Van Nostrand Reinhold.

Coffman, S. P. (1986). The musculoskeletal system. In G. M. Scipien, M. U. Barnard, M. A. Chard, J. Howe, & P. Phillips (Eds.). *Comprehensive pediatric nursing.* New York: McGraw-Hill, 1247–1306.

Conrad, E. U. (1989). Pitfalls in diagnosis: pediatric musculoskeletal tumors. *Pediatric Annals, 18*(1), 45–47, 50–52.

Corbett, D. (1988). Information needs of parents of a child in a Pavlik harness. *Orthopedic Nursing, 7*(2), 20–22.

Cotrel, Y., Dubousset, J., & Guillaumat, M. (1988). New universal instrumentation in spinal surgery. *Clinical Orthopedics, 227,* 10–23.

Drennan, J.C. (1990). Neuromuscular disorders. In R. T. Morrissy (Ed.). *Lovell and Winter's pediatric orthopaedics* (2nd ed.). Philadelphia: J. B. Lippincott, pp. 381–463.

Eland, J. M. (1988). Pharmacologic management of acute and chronic pediatric pain. *Issues in Comprehensive Pediatric Nursing, 11*(2-3), 93–111.

Garrick, J. G. (1988). Academy of Pediatrics postgraduate course. San Diego.

Green, N. E., & Edwards, K. (1987). Bone and joint infections in children. *Orthopedic Clinics of North America, 18(4),* 555–576.

Herbert, M. A., & Bobechko, W. P. (1987). Paraspinal muscle stimulation for the treatment of idiopathic scoliosis. *Orthopedics, 10(8),* 1125–1132.

Herring, J. A. (1990). Congenital dislocation of the hip. In R. T. Morrissy (Ed.). *Lovell and Winter's pediatric orthopaedics* (2nd ed.). Philadelphia: J. B. Lippincott, pp. 815–850.

Jacobs-Zacny, J. M., & Horn, M. J. (1988). Nursing care of adolescents having posterior spinal fusion with Cotrel-Dubousset instrumentation. *Orthopedic Nursing, 7(1),* 17–21.

MacEwen, G. D., & Zembo, M. M. (1987). Current trends in the treatment of congenital dislocation of the hip. *Orthopedics, 10,* 1663.

Morrissy, R. T. (1990). Slipped capital femoral epiphysis. In R. T. Morrissy (Ed.). *Lovell and Winter's pediatric orthopaedics* (2nd ed.). Philadelphia: J. B. Lippincott, pp. 885–904.

Newschwander, G., & Dunst, R. (1989). Limb lengthening with an Ilizarov external fixator. *Orthopaedic Nursing, 8(3),* 15–21.

Rosen, G. (1985). Preoperative (neoadjuvant) chemotherapy for osteogenic sarcoma: A ten year experience. *Orthopedics, 8,* 659.

Schubiner, J. M., & Simon, M. A. (1987). Primary bone tumors in children. *Orthopedic Clinics of North America, 18,* 577–595.

Scoles, P. V. (1988). *Pediatric orthopedics in clinical practice.* Chicago: Year Book Medical Publishers.

Sponseller, P. D., & Tolo, V. T. (1990). Bone, joint, and muscle problems. In F. A. Oski, C. D. DeAngelis, R. D. Feigin, & J. B. Warshaw (Eds.). *Principles and practice of pediatrics.* Philadelphia: J. B. Lippincott, pp. 939–969.

Springfield, D. S. (1990). Bone and soft tissue tumors. In R. T. Morrissy (Ed.). *Lovell and Winter's pediatric orthopaedics* (2nd ed.). Philadelphia: J. B. Lippincott, pp. 325–363.

Staheli, L. (1989). Management of congenital hip dysplasia. *Pediatric Annals, 18*(1), 4, 26–27, 29–32.

Thompson, G. H., & Salter, R. B. (1987). Legg-Calvé-Perthes disease: Current concepts and controversies. *Orthopedic Clinics of North America, 18,* 617–635.

Zaleske, D. J., Doppelt, S. H., & Mankin, H. J. (1990). Metabolic and endocrine abnormalities of the immature skeleton. In R. T. Morrissy (Ed.). *Lovell and Winter's pediatric orthopaedics* (2nd ed.). Philadelphia: J. B. Lippincott, pp. 229–233.

## Bibliography

Asher, M. A. (1988). Scoliosis evaluation. *Orthopedic Clinics of North America, 19,* 805.

Dyment, P. G. (1986). Management of soft tissue trauma in adolescent athletes. *Journal of Adolescent Health Care, 7*(6 Suppl), 1335–1353.

Feller, N., Gunnip, A., Stout, J., Bull, M., Stroup, K.B., & Stephanadis, J. (1986). A multidisciplinary approach to developing safe transportation for children with special needs. *Orthopedic Nursing, 5,* 25.

Fixsen, J., & Lloyd-Roberts, G. (1988). *The foot in childhood.* London: Churchill Livingstone.

Hansell, M. J. (1988). Fractures and the healing process. *Orthopedic Nursing, 7*(1), 43.

Hensinger, R. N. (1987). Congenital dislocation of the hip. *Orthopedic Clinics of North America, 18,* 597.

Hensinger, R. N., & Fielding, J. W. (1990). The cervical spine. In R. T. Morrissy (Ed.). *Lovell and Winter's pediatric orthopaedics* (2nd ed.). Philadelphia: J. B. Lippincott, pp. 703–739.

Morrissy, R. T. (1990). *Lovell and Winter's pediatric orthopaedics* (2nd ed.). Philadelphia: J. B. Lippincott.

O'Neill, D. B., & Micheli, L. J. (1988). Overuse injuries in the young athlete. *Sports Medicine, 7,* 591.

Page-Goertz, S. (1987). Patterns of impairment: Juvenile rheumatoid arthritis. In M. H. Rose, & R. B. Thomas (Eds.) *Children with chronic conditions.* Orlando, FL: Grune & Stratton.

Renshaw, T. (1986). *Pediatric orthopedics.* Philadelphia: W. B. Saunders.

# Alterations in Integumentary Function

Mary Ann McClellan and Maribeth Moran

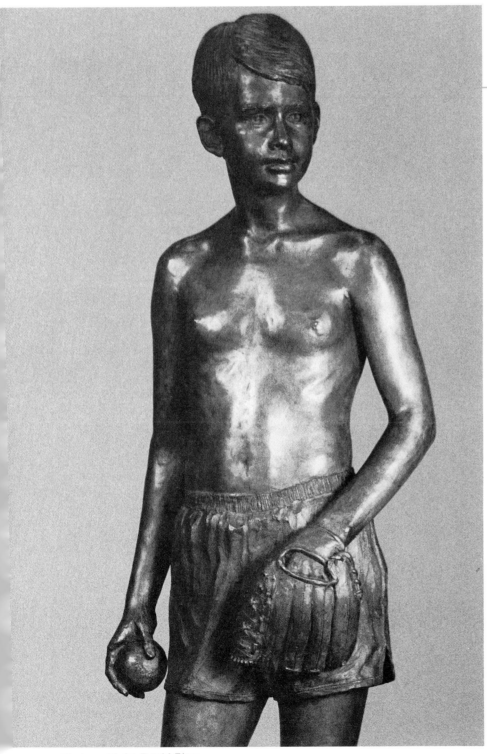

*34*

*Anatomy and Physiology*

*Assessment*

*Nursing Diagnosis*

*Planning Nursing Care*

*Evaluating Nursing Care*

*Integumentary Problems of Infants*

*Integumentary Problems of Children*

*Integumentary Problems of Adolescents*

*Infestations*

*Viral Infections*

*Fungal Infections*

*Bacterial Infections*

*Drug Reactions*

*Acute Integumentary Problems*

*Summary*

*Photograph by David Finn*

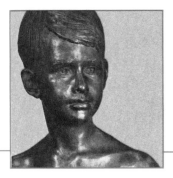

## Learning Objectives

*Upon completion of this chapter the reader will be able to:*

1. *State the major components of the integumentary system.*

2. *Discuss the physiological functions of the integumentary system.*

3. *Identify dermatological conditions seen in infants, children, and adolescents.*

4. *Describe the pathophysiology, medical diagnosis, and management of common pediatric integumentary problems.*

5. *Implement all steps of the nursing process in caring for children with integumentary problems.*

6. *Explain the pathophysiological effects of burns on the various body systems.*

7. *Identify the three phases of burns and describe the medical and nursing management during each phase.*

## Key Terms

*acute stage in burn care*

*alopecia*

*autograft*

*contracture*

*dermatitis*

*dermis*

*ectoderm*

*endoderm*

*epidermis*

*eschar*

*excoriation*

*hemangioma*

*heterograft*

*homograft*

*hypodermis*

*mesoderm*

*rehabilitative stage in burn care*

*resuscitative stage in burn care*

The major components of the integumentary system are the skin, the hair, and the nails. These components not only reflect a person's general health status, they also serve as indicators of more general disturbances.

Because the components of the integumentary system are so visible, parents and children may become upset over disturbances that they perceive as affecting the child's appearance and functional ability. Burns are of special concern because they are always emergencies, are possibly life-threatening, and can result in permanent disfigurement as well as loss of some functions.

Many infectious diseases (e.g., varicella, rubeola, Rocky Mountain spotted fever, and Lyme disease) primarily have integumentary manifestations. These problems are discussed in Chapter 19.

To effectively apply the nursing process, the nurse should understand the structure and functions of the integumentary system; measures that can be taken to prevent problems, and how these can be taught to parents and children; principles of nursing management; and the nurse's role as a member of the health care team.

## Anatomy and Physiology

All body organs develop from the three germ layers: the *endoderm* (innermost layer), the *mesoderm* (middle layer), and the *ectoderm* (outermost layer). The skin, hair, and nails all arise from the ectoderm. These three layers develop from the embryonic disk by the 17th day of gestation. Consequently, any abnormality during the prenatal period may have either direct or related effects on the developing organs.

## *Skin*

The skin is the largest body organ, weighing about 9 pounds in the average adult. It varies in thickness from about 1 to 4 mm and consists of three major layers: the *epidermis,* the *dermis,* and the *hypodermis* or subcutaneous layer. The layers of the skin are shown in Figure 34-1. The subcutaneous layer includes fat deposits and serves to support the two outer layers.

The dermis is a rich complex of blood vessels, nerves, and glands, including the *eccrine* and *apocrine* sweat glands. The eccrine sweat glands, which serve to regulate body heat, are present from birth but become increasingly active with maturity, reaching peak activity at puberty. Apocrine sweat glands are found primarily in the axillae and pubic regions and do not become active until puberty. The secretions of the apocrine glands, when combined with bacteria, produce the characteristic odor of perspiration. Other glands found in the dermis include the sebaceous glands, which usually contain a hair follicle and secrete sebum, an oily substance that helps the skin retain water. The dermis nourishes the cells of the epidermis as they develop and migrate upward to form the outermost protective layer of flat sheets of dead skin cells.

The skin cells of infants are loosely attached to each other; this causes easy blistering in response to trauma. Infants' skin also contains more water than that of adults. As children grow, the skin toughens and becomes less well hydrated.

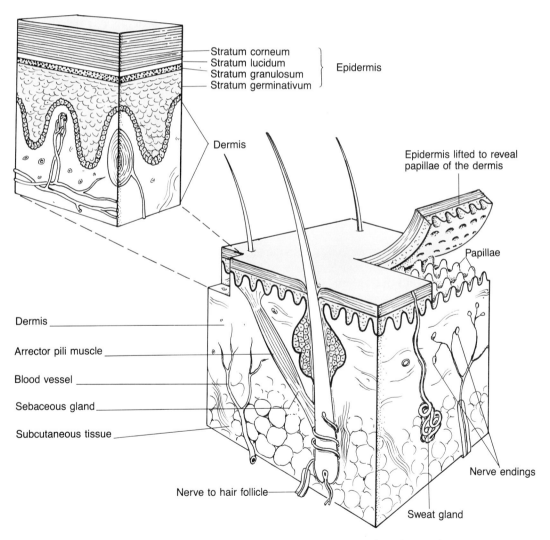

*Figure 34–1. Layers of the skin. (Chaffee, E.E., & Lytle, I.M. (1980).* Basic physiology and anatomy. *Philadelphia: J.B. Lippincott, p. 72)*

## Hair

Hair follicles are present over the entire body, with the exception of the palms of the hands and soles of the feet. The hair follicles produce either fine, short vellus body hair or the darker, longer terminal hair that is found on the scalp, eyebrows, beard, axilla, and genital areas Melanocytes produce pigment in the hair shaft matrix, as they do in the skin, to create various hair colors.

Scalp hair follicles may number as many as 300 in each square centimeter, with an average total of 100,000. Scalp hair continues to grow for from 2 to 6 years; other body hair grows for about 6 months and, as a result, is much shorter. As with the visible outer skin layer, the visible part of the hair is dead.

Hair loss, or *alopecia,* can result from infections such as tinea capitis, endocrine disorders, drug reactions, chemotherapy, various hairstyles or preparations, or from unexplained causes. Although the hair grows back in many cases, children with alopecia require considerable emotional support.

## Nails

Hornlike nail plates are formed from the epidermis at the tips of the digits. The lunula is the part of the nail that grows about 0.5 mm each week. Underlying blood vessels cause the pink color of the nails. A normal variation in clients with pigmented skin is a dark, lengthwise, melanin band. In white children, this finding may mean a melanoma and requires medical evaluation.

## Assessment

Assessment of the integumentary system must include information about the child's developmental level, general health status, ethnic background, and cultural factors. Assessment of the child's health status takes place during an initial or periodic visit of the well child, during a problem-specific visit, or during an emergency visit. In addition to the history, inspection and, when appropriate, palpation are performed.

## History

The history should include information about childhood diseases, immunizations, allergies, diet, and environmental hazards as well as the use of alcohol and drugs. General considerations to be included in the history are identified in Table 34-1. This information provides a starting point for the physical assessment.

The history for the routine visit or the present integumentary disturbance should include information about the skin, hair, and nails as outlined in Table 34-1. The past

history is necessary to ascertain previous problems, treatments, and the resolutions of integumentary problems. The family history is important for understanding genetic patterns or predispositions for integumentary problems. There may be a history of familial allergic diseases or familial hair loss.

The nurse should inquire about any changes in the child's integumentary system since the last contact as well as about the child's and family's activities. Specific questions depend on the child's developmental stage, past history, season of the year, and child or parent concerns. For infants, the nurse should ascertain the child's feeding history, including whether the child is breast-fed or bottle-fed, what type of formula is used, and what and when solid foods were introduced. The nurse should also assess the types of clothing the child wears, including the amount of clothing and the laundering practices. It is also important to note the type of diapers worn, how cloth diapers are laundered, whether the child wears plastic pants, and what routines are used to cleanse the diaper area.

For older children, the nurse should assess eating habits, history of allergies or skin disorders, and possible exposure to infectious diseases. This is particularly important for children who attend day care centers. Additional considerations include whether the child has any habits that could exacerbate a problem, such as constant pulling of the hair, scratching, or nail-biting.

Additional questions may arise during or after the physical assessment. For example, some dermatologists recommend asking about drug use since some drugs can cause rashes (Lookingbill & Marks, 1986).

In the case of severe injury or other life-threatening situations, such as burns, assessment is focused on priorities for maintaining life and minimizing serious effects of any pathology. Consequently, the history is generally limited to events immediately preceding the emergency and to major significant data. If the child is not conscious or is very young, others present may be able to supply the information. Physical assessment of the integumentary system may supply more information in this situation than the history. For example, the cool, pale, clammy skin of a client in shock is essential data. The cherry-pink color of an unconscious client may indicate carbon dioxide poisoning.

## Physical Examination

The two techniques used in physical examination of the integumentary system are inspection and palpation. Inspection of the hair, skin, and nails begins during the general survey and is continued as part of the regional assessment or as assessment of the entire integumentary system. It is important to remember that mucous membranes are part of the integumentary system when examining the head and neck. An infant with a monilial diaper rash (skin) may also have oral candidiasis (mucous mem-

*Table 34–1. Guidelines for a History of the Integumentary System*

| Component | Information to Be Sought |
|---|---|
| **General Considerations** | |
| Skin care habits | Cleansing routine: soaps, oils, lotions, or other topical applications used |
| | Home remedies applied |
| | Sunscreen agents used |
| | Recent changes in skin care habits |
| Hair care habits | Cleansing routine: shampoo and rinses used |
| | Color preparations or permanents used |
| | Recent changes in hair care habits |
| Nail care habits | Any difficulty in clipping or trimming nails |
| | Instruments used for nail care |
| Other considerations | Medications: topical or systemic; prescribed or over-the-counter |
| | Exposure to environmental hazards: dyes, chemicals, plants, toxic substances, frequent immersion of hands in water, frequent sun exposure |
| | Recent physiological or psychological stress |
| **History of the Present Illness** | |
| Skin | Changes in skin: dryness, pruritus, sores, rashes, lumps, color, texture, odor, amount of perspiration; changes in a wart or mole; lesion that does not heal or is chronically irritated |
| | Occurrence: date of initial onset, time sequence of occurrence and development, sudden or gradual onset, date of recurrence, if any |
| | Symptoms: itching, pain, exudate, bleeding, color changes, seasonal or climate variations |
| | Location: skin folds, extensor or flexor surfaces, localized or generalized |
| | Associated symptoms: presence of systemic disease or high fever, relationship to stress or leisure activities |
| | Recent exposure to drugs, environmental toxins, or chemicals; exposure to people with similar conditions |
| | Apparent cause: client perception of cause |
| | Travel history: where, when, length of stay, exposure to diseases, contact with travelers |
| | What the client has been doing for the problem: medications or preparations used (prescribed or over-the-counter), response to treatment, what makes the condition worse or better |
| | How the child and family are adjusting to the problem |
| Hair | Changes in hair: loss or growth, distribution, texture, color |
| | Occurrence: sudden or gradual onset, symmetrical or asymmetrical pattern, recurrence |
| | Associated symptoms: pain, itching, lesions, presence of systemic disease or high fever, recent psychological or physical stress |
| | Exposure to drugs, environmental toxins, or chemicals, including commercial hair care chemicals |
| | Nutrition: dietary changes, dieting, malnutrition |
| | What the client has been doing for the problem: medications or preparations used (prescribed or over-the-counter), response to treatment, what makes the condition worse or better |
| | How the child and family are adjusting to the problem |
| Nails | Changes in nails: splitting, breaking, discoloration, ridging, thickening, markings, separation from nail bed |
| | Associated symptoms: pain, swelling, exudate, presence of systemic disease or high fever, recent psychological or physical stress |
| | Occurrence: sudden or gradual onset, relationship to injury of nail or finger |
| | Recent exposure to drugs, environmental toxins, or chemicals; frequent immersion of hands in water |
| | What the client has been doing for the problem: medications or preparations used (prescribed or over-the-counter), response to treatment, what makes the condition worse or better |
| | How the child and family are adjusting to the problem |

branes). Mucous membranes can also be useful in assessing cyanosis or jaundice in clients with darkly pigmented skin.

It is essential for nurses to assess the entire integumentary system, even during problem-specific visits. There may be other lesions that are related to the chief complaint, and a significant, previously unidentified lesion may be found. The skin may also provide clues to other underlying conditions (e.g., pallor may indicate anemia).

In the absence of natural light, overhead fluorescent lighting is used for accurate assessment. The room should be sufficiently warm so that the child does not become chilled (which can cause mild cyanosis) but not so warm that the child becomes flushed. A penlight is helpful for inspecting the mouth, and a ruler is needed to accurately measure lesions. Palpation is generally done with the pads or tips of the fingers. Physical assessment includes noting the color, temperature, and texture of the skin, hair, and nails, as well as skin turgor and the presence of primary or secondary lesions. Common lesions are shown in Figure 34-2. Physical assessment techniques for the skin, hair, and nails are the same for infants and children as for adults. Refer to texts on physical assessment for additional information.

### Skin Color

Although variations in color depend on race, color changes in the skin may be significant findings. Generalized areas of darkly pigmented brown skin may be caused by the sun or may indicate pituitary tumors, Addison's disease, or liver disease. Areas of black skin indicate tissue death; these areas may be localized in the case of gangrene or generalized due to burns. Blue skin can be caused by anxiety or a cold environment, whereas circumoral pallor may indicate cardiovascular or pulmonary disease. Reddish-blue skin may be caused by increased amounts of hemoglobin, reduced hemoglobin (containing decreased amounts of oxygen), or capillary stasis and may indicate polycythemia. Red skin is caused by the increased visibility of physiological oxyhemoglobin and results from dilation of blood vessels or increased blood flow as seen in fever, alcohol intake, viral exanthems, hives, local inflammation, or blushing. Yellowing of the skin can be caused by accumulation of hardened tissue as seen in calluses on the palms of the hands or soles of the feet. It can also be caused by an increase in bile pigment (jaundice) as seen in physiological jaundice, breast-milk jaundice, or other serious infections (e.g., sepsis). Yellow skin is also caused by increased levels of carotene (often from carrots or other yellow/orange vegetables) or by retention of yellow pigments, as in chronic renal disease. Localized areas of white skin may result from a decrease or absence of melanin, as seen in vitiligo or some rashes. Generalized white skin results from albinism or decreased oxygenated red blood cells, as seen in anemia.

### Ethnic Variations

The integumentary systems of different ethnic groups vary in many ways. Nurses must be aware of these variations or they may miss significant signs or become concerned over normal findings. For example, pallor in black-skinned people may be manifested by an ashen appearance. The assessment of cyanosis in dark-skinned people is best accomplished by observing the color of the lips and oral mucosa rather than the nail beds. Jaundice in dark-skinned people is detected by examining the hard palate, and flushing is best noted at the tips of the ears. Table 34-2 gives the general characteristics, normal variations, and common dermatological conditions for Asians, blacks, Hispanics, Native Americans, and whites.

### Diagnostic Tests

A variety of diagnostic tests are used to determine the exact causes of integumentary problems. The most common diagnostic tests include the following:

**Potassium hydroxide (KOH) test** is used to determine the presence of fungal infection on the skin or hair.

**Tzanck smear** is used to distinguish viral diseases from nonviral diseases (e.g., herpes simplex, varicella, or herpes zoster).

**Wood's light** (ultraviolet light) is used to diagnose selected fungal and bacterial infections.

(*text continues on page 968*)

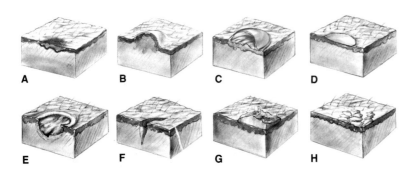

*Figure 34–2. Basic types of skin lesions. (A–C) Primary lesions (may arise from previously normal skin): (A) macule; (B) papule; (C) vesicle. (D–H) Secondary lesions (result from changes in primary lesions): (D) erosion; (E) ulcer; (F) fissure; (G) crust; (H) scale. (From Bates, B. [1991]. A guide to physical examination and history taking [5th ed.]. Philadelphia: J.B. Lippincott, p. 147)*

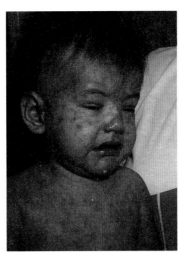

*Color Plate 19–1.   Rubeola. (Oski, F.A., DeAngelis, C.D., Feigin, R.D., & Warshaw, J.B. [1990].* Principles and practice of pediatrics. *Philadelphia: J.B. Lippincott)*

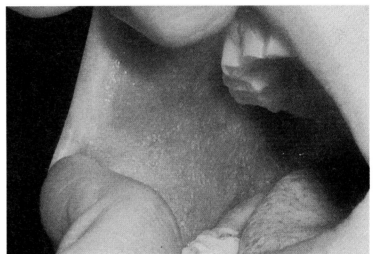

*Color Plate 19–2.   Koplik's spots. (Booth, I.W., & Wozniak, E.R. [1984].* Pediatrics. *London: Gower Medical Publishing)*

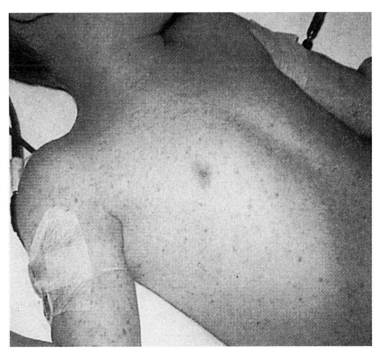

*Color Plate 19–3.   Rocky Mountain spotted fever. (Farrar, W.E., & Lambert, H.P. [1984].* Infectious diseases. *London: Gower Medical Publishing)*

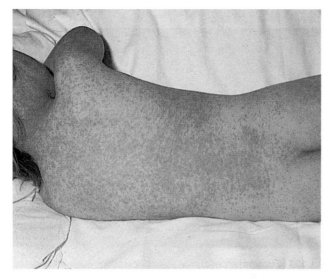

*Color Plate 19—4. Roseola. (Booth, I.W., & Wozniak, E.R. [1984].* Pediatrics. *London: Gower Medical Publishing)*

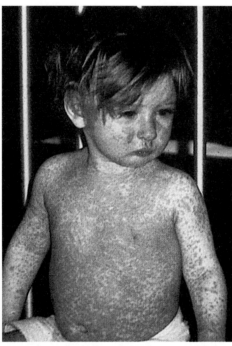

*Color Plate 19—5. Rubella (German measles). (Farrar, W.E., & Lambert, H.P. [1984].* Infectious diseases. *London: Gower Medical Publishing)*

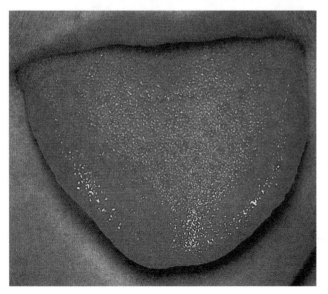

*Color Plate 19—6. Strawberry tongue. (Farrar, W.E., & Lambert, H.P. [1984].* Infectious diseases. *London: Gower Medical Publishing)*

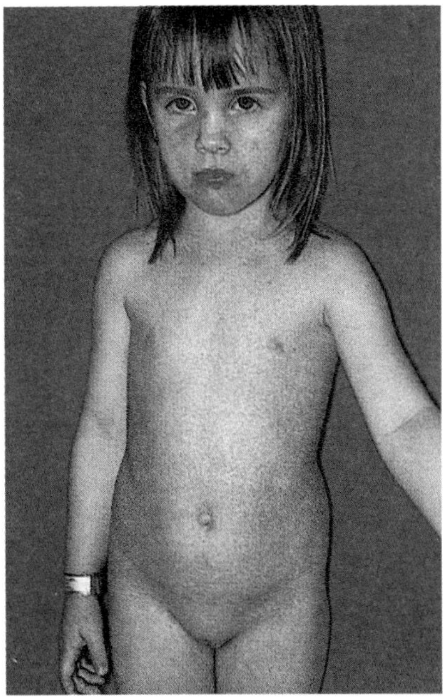

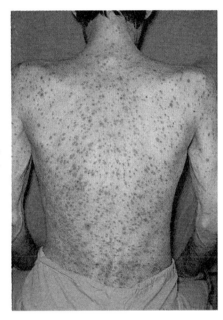

*Color Plate 19–7.   Scarlet fever (scarlatina). (Farrar, W.E., & Lambert, H.P. [1984].* Infectious diseases. *London: Gower Medical Publishing)*

*Color Plate 19–8.   Varicella (chickenpox). (Farrar, W.E., & Lambert, H.P. [1984].* Infectious diseases. *London: Gower Medical Publishing)*

*Color Plate 19–9.   Gray membrane on the tonsils and uvula in diphtheria. (Farrar, W.E., & Lambert, H.P. [1984].* Infectious diseases. *London: Gower Medical Publishing)*

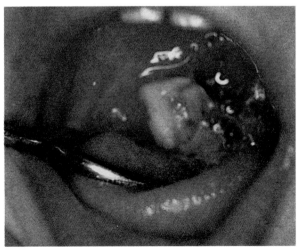

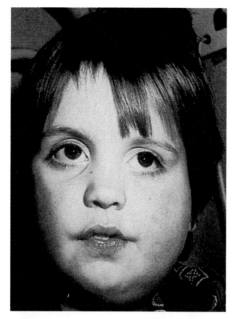

*Color Plate 19–10. Mumps. (Farrar, W.E., & Lambert, H.P. [1984].* Infectious diseases. *London: Gower Medical Publishing)*

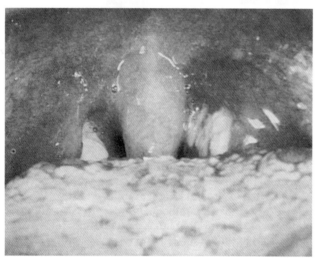

*Color Plate 19–11. Infectious mononucleosis. (Farrar, W.E., & Lambert, H.P. [1984].* Infectious diseases. *London: Gower Medical Publishing)*

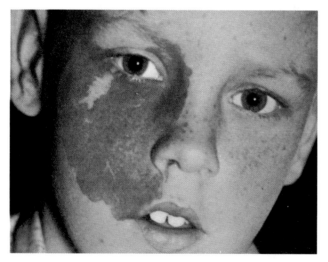

*Color Plate 34–1. Hemangioma. (Sauer, G.C. [1991].* Manual of skin diseases *[6th ed.]. Philadelphia: J.B. Lippincott)*

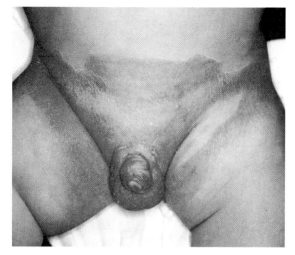

*Color Plate 34–2.    Diaper dermatitis. (Sauer, G.C. [1991].* Manual of skin diseases *[6th ed.]. Philadelphia: J.B. Lippincott)*

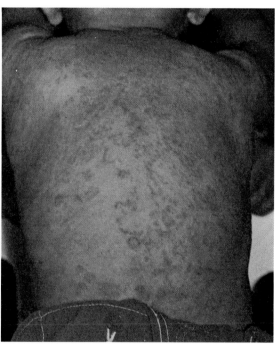

*Color Plate 34–3.    Atopic dermatitis (eczema). (Sauer, G.C. [1991].* Manual of skin diseases *[6th ed.]. Philadelphia: J.B. Lippincott)*

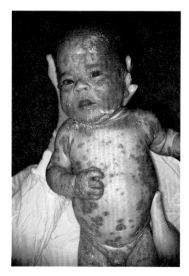

*Color Plate 34–4.    Psoriasis. (Oski, F.A., et al. [1990].* Principles and practice of pediatrics. *Philadelphia: J.B. Lippincott)*

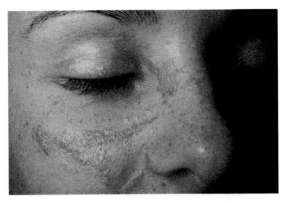

*Color Plate 34–5.   Poison ivy. (Sauer, G.C. [1991].* Manual of skin diseases *[6th ed.]. Philadelphia: J.B. Lippincott)*

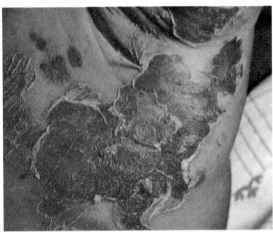

*Color Plate 34–6.   Impetigo. (Sauer, G.C. [1991].* Manual of skin diseases *[6th ed.]. Philadelphia: J.B. Lippincott)*

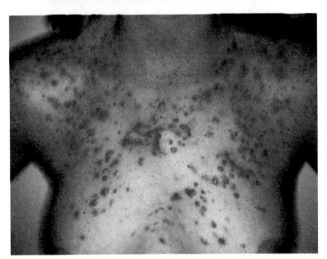

*Color Plate 34–7.   Acne vulgaris. (Sauer, G.C. [1991].* Manual of skin diseases *[6th ed.]. Philadelphia: J.B. Lippincott)*

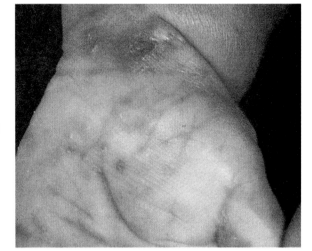

*Color Plate 34–8. Scabies. (Farrar, W.E., & Lambert, H.P. [1984].* Infectious diseases. *London: Gower Medical Publishing)*

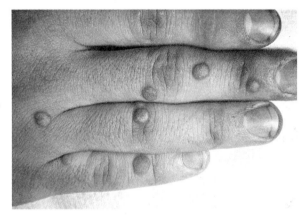

*Color Plate 34–9. Common warts. (Sauer, G.C. [1991].* Manual of skin diseases *[6th ed.]. Philadelphia: J.B. Lippincott)*

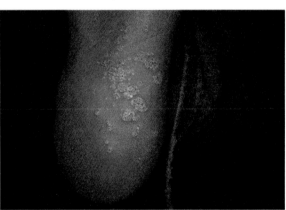

*Color Plate 34–10. Plantar warts. (Sauer, G.C. [1991].* Manual of skin diseases *[6th ed.]. Philadelphia: J.B. Lippincott)*

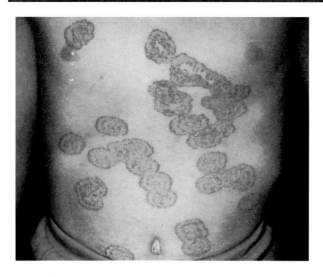

Color Plate 34–11. Tinea capitis. (Sauer, G.C. [1991]. Manual of skin diseases [6th ed.]. Philadelphia: J.B. Lippincott)

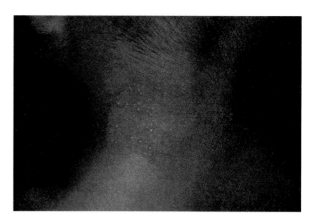

Color Plate 34–12. Tinea corporis. (Sauer, G.C. [1991]. Manual of skin diseases [6th ed.]. Philadelphia: J.B. Lippincott)

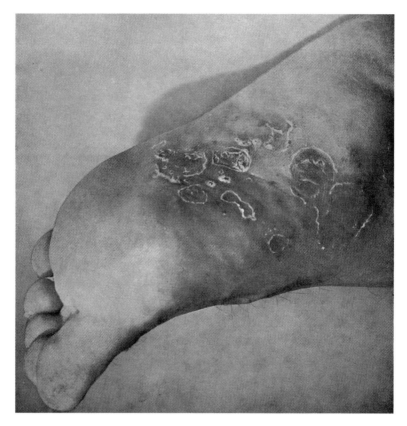

Color Plate 34–13. Tinea pedis. (Sauer, G.C. [1991]. Manual of skin diseases [6th ed.]. Philadelphia: J.B. Lippincott)

*Table 34–2. Ethnic Variations in the Integumentary System*

| | Characteristic or Condition | Nursing Implications |
|---|---|---|
| **ASIANS** | | |
| Skin | Fewer apocrine sweat glands than in whites and blacks | Mild to absent body odor |
| | Ear wax tends to be dry | Do not confuse flaky appearance of dry cerumen with a dry eczematous lesion. |
| | Pigmentation varies from brown to pale white with yellowish tinge | Infants are lightly pigmented at birth; skin becomes darker with age, until pigmentation peaks at 6 to 8 weeks. |
| | | Pallor is best detected in nail beds, conjunctivae, oral mucosa, or tongue, which are normally reddish-pink. |
| | | May need to palpate rashes that are difficult to see |
| | | Japanese skin types vary in response to ultraviolet light and tanning (Kawada, 1986). |
| | | Some fair-skinned Asians may look down on darker-skinned countrymen. Pigmentation increases resistance to skin cancer. |
| Hair | Sparse body hair | Chest hair may be entirely absent in males. |
| | Hair may be straight, curly, or wavy; fine to coarse | Male pattern baldness is rare among Vietnamese. |
| | Hair color may vary from reddish brown to black | |
| ***Normal Variations and Findings*** | | |
| | Mongolian spots | Important to document since they may be misdiagnosed as bruises and evidence of child abuse |
| | | Do not assume that parents know what these are. |
| | | No positive correlation between degree of general pigmentation and presence or extensiveness of mongolian spots. Considered related to blue nevus, nevus of Ota, and nevus of Ito; do not become malignant |
| | | Mongolian spots tend to fade as skin becomes thicker with age. |
| | Blue nevus | Common on face in darker races. Pigmentation persists throughout life. May become malignant |
| | Futcher's line or Voigt's line | Abrupt transition line at junction of darker posterolateral and lighter anteromedial skin on upper arm |
| | | Has been reported in Japanese clients |
| | | No differences in amount of distribution of melanin in skin on each side of line |
| | Nail pigmentation | Nail beds may appear diffusely darker than those of whites. |
| ***Common Dermatological Conditions*** | | |
| | Cleft lip, cleft palate | Highest case rate in Japanese (2.13 per 1000 live births) |
| | Nevus of Ota and Nevus of Ito | Most common in Orientals |
| | |   Nevus of Ota: Patchy discoloration of face, usually bluish |
| | |   Nevus of Ito: Same features except involves shoulder and sides of neck rather than face |
| | | These nevi darken during menses; pigment more intense after age 11 |
| | | May progress to malignant melanoma. Sensorineural deafness may be associated with nevus of Ota. Cosmetic coverage of lesions is usually helpful in improving child's self-concept. |
| | | Considered related to blue nevus and mongolian spots |
| | Erythema toxicum neonatorum | Nearly as common in a series of Japanese newborns as among white newborns (Hidano, Purwoko, & Jitsukawa, 1986) |

*(continued)*

*Table 34–2. Ethnic Variations in the Integumentary System (Continued)*

|  | Characteristic or Condition | Nursing Implications |
|---|---|---|
| **ASIANS** (cont.) | Malignant melanomas | Most occur on palmar and plantar areas. |
|  |  | Dysplastic nevus (precursor lesion) not well identified in Japanese skin |
|  | Scabies and impetigo | Most common skin diseases in Vietnamese children |
|  | Eczema | Clinical observation that this condition is common among Chinese infants in America |
|  | Epicanthic folds | May cause children to seem as if they have strabismus even if eye muscles are balanced |
| ***Common Dermatological Responses*** |  |  |
|  | Hypopigmentation | Response to inflammatory process. Usually transitory, with skin returning to normal color in a few weeks |
|  | Hyperpigmentation | May occur in scar tissue, especially in darker-skinned Asians |
| **BLACKS** |  |  |
| Skin | Increased cutaneous melanin: melanin granules are larger, placed singly in epidermal cells, and do not break down easily | Protective effects against solar radiation. |
|  |  | Melasma more common in dark-skinned clients; may never fade if triggered by oral contraceptives. |
|  | Outermost layer of skin is more compact and has more cell layers than whites' skin. | Resists irritation better; more effective barrier against external insults. |
|  | More apocrine sweat glands than Native Americans and Asians | Strong body odor. |
|  | Ear wax tends to be wet. | May need to irrigate external auditory canals to see tympanic membranes. |
|  | Varying degrees of pigmentation | Infants are lightly pigmented at birth; they become darker until pigmentation peaks at 6 to 8 weeks. |
|  |  | Pallor best detected in nail beds, conjunctivae, oral mucosa, or tongue, which are normally reddish-pink. |
|  |  | Palpate rashes that are difficult to see. |
|  |  | In dark-skinned black children, erythema is dusky-red or violet; cyanosis can appear black |
| Hair | Cross-section shows hair flattened and elliptical. Black hair may spontaneously knot. | Rubbing or minor trauma of picking at hair can lead to so-called wooling effect. |
|  | May have 60%–70% more sebaceous secretion on hair than whites. Oily material excreted onto growing hair fiber may be thicker in black clients. | Important consideration for nurses assisting with grooming; nurses should be nonjudgmental about normal physiology when teaching about hygiene |
|  |  | Both male and female black children may have hair plaited until 1 or 2 years of age. |
|  | Variety of textures |  |
| ***Normal Variations and Findings*** |  |  |
|  | Lip pits and preauricular pits | May occur together or separately. More common in blacks than in whites and Asians. Lip pits may vary from slight dimpling to 4 mm in commissure of lips. |
|  | Mongolian spots | Important to document this normal finding since these have been misdiagnosed as bruises and evidence of child abuse |
|  |  | Do not assume that parents know what mongolian spots are |
|  |  | No positive correlation between degree of pigmentation and presence or extensiveness of mongolian spots |
|  |  | Considered to be related to nevus of Ota, nevus of Ito, and the blue nevus. Mongolian spots, however, do not become malignant. |

*(continued)*

*Table 34–2. Ethnic Variations in the Integumentary System (Continued)*

| | Characteristic or Condition | Nursing Implications |
|---|---|---|
| **BLACKS** (cont.) | | Tend to fade as skin becomes thicker with age |
| | | May see freckling effect of pigmented lesions over mongolian spots in black children |
| | Blue nevus | Blue nevi of face common in darker races. Pigmentation persists throughout life. |
| | | Common blue nevus more common in blacks; may be present at birth; does not become malignant |
| | | Cellular blue nevus is larger, multiple, and less common; may become malignant |
| | Pigmented marks; sharply demarcated macules, light tan to dark brown | More common in blacks than in whites, Native Americans, or Hispanics |
| | | Color of these marks varies with skin color. |
| | Voigt's line or Futcher's line | Abrupt transition line between darker posterolateral and lighter anteromedial skin of upper arms |
| | | Similar lines may occur on the chest and abdomen. |
| | | No clinical or histopathological differences between skin on either side of lines |
| | Pigmentation of oral tissues | Varies with degree of cutaneous pigmentation |
| | | May be light brown patches or macules or diffuse, deep purplish-blue or brown |
| | | Most commonly seen on gums or hard palate; may also occur on tongue or mucous membranes |
| | | Difficult to use "lead line" of gums in plumbism to aid in diagnosis in black child with gum pigmentation. May confuse pigmentation with petechiae in child with sore throat (possible streptococcus or mononucleosis infections) |
| | | Pigmentation of oral tissues may be present in newborns as early as 3 hours after birth. |
| | Nail pigmentation | Usually bands, i.e., pigmented longitudinal stripes |
| | | May be diffuse pigmentation of nail, especially in darker clients |
| | | Pigmentation of toenails tends to be similar to that of fingernails in same person. |
| | | Not usually present at birth |
| | | Cyanosis of nail beds especially difficult to identify in child with pigmented nails |
| | Pearly penile papules | Small, whitish, benign papules in linear rows on corona and coronal sulcus of glans |
| | | May be more related to uncircumcised status |
| | | Increase in frequency with puberty; decrease with older age |
| ***Common Dermatological Conditions*** | | |
| | Neonatal jaundice (ABO incompatible) | ABO incompatibility twice as likely in black infants as in white infants |
| | | All mothers and infants should be ABO-typed at delivery. |
| | | Neonatal jaundice more difficult to detect in black infants |
| | | Jaundice best assessed in sclerae or oral mucous membranes in daylight |
| | Polydactyly | High incidence in blacks |
| | | Management depends on presence of bone, position, and number of extra digits. |
| | Supernumerary nipples | Most common in black females |
| | | May appear as pits, dimples, or "moles" in milk line in prepubertal child |

*(continued)*

*Table 34–2.  Ethnic Variations in the Integumentary System (Continued)*

| | Characteristic or Condition | Nursing Implications |
|---|---|---|
| **BLACKS** (cont.) | Transient neonatal pustular melanosis | Most common in black newborns; usually present at birth |
| | | Benign disorder with no treatment |
| | | Vesiculopustular lesions disappear in 24 to 48 hours; hyperpigmented pinhead macules generally regress in 3 weeks to 3 months |
| | Acropustulosis of infancy | Most common in black infants aged 2 to 12 months; persists up to 2 years |
| | | Crops of pruritic papulopustules or vesiculopustules appear for 7 to 10 days; remiss; and then recur in 2 or 3 weeks, especially on palms and soles |
| | | Child restless and irritable |
| | | Usual treatment is soporific dose of antihistamine (e.g., dapsone) |
| | | Resolves spontaneously |
| | Nevus of Ota and Nevus of Ito | Bluish-gray speckled macules |
| | | May be present at birth or shortly thereafter |
| | | Nevus of Ota located on face along 5th cranial nerve. |
| | | Sclera and conjunctiva may be involved. |
| | | Nevus of Ito located on shoulder, side of neck, or upper arm. |
| | | Nevi persist throughout life; may become malignant |
| | Pseudofolliculitis barbae | Nearly unique to black males |
| | | Shaving causes hair from curved follicle to reenter the skin, resulting in 1- to 3-mm papules, or papulopustles. |
| | | Not shaving and growing a beard may cure condition. |
| | | Use of depilatory may help. |
| ***Common Dermatological Responses*** | | |
| | Lability of pigmentation | Hyperpigmentation or hypopigmentation in response to inflammation |
| | | Can lead to more anxiety than the original lesions |
| | | Usually improves over time |
| | | Skin bleaches with hydroxyquinoline have been known to cause hyperpigmentation. |
| | | Hypopigmentation usually improves more rapidly since only epidermis is involved. |
| | | The pigmentary changes follow the shape and size of the original lesion. |
| | Accentuation of follicles | Atopic dermatitis is often follicular in black clients. Examples of other conditions with exaggerated follicular response include pityriasis rosea, tinea versicolor, and pomade acne. |
| | Mesenchymal response | Fibroelastic tissue abnormalities from excessive repair after an injury include keloids, hypertrophic scars, and lichenification. |
| | | Keloids usually appear between the ages of 10 and 30 years. |
| | | Ear-piercing should be done in infancy to avoid keloid formation. |
| | | Most common sites for keloids are ear lobes, upper back, shoulders, and anterior chest. |
| | | May have clawlike extensions beyond edges of traumatized areas; hypertrophic scars do not |
| | | Keloids are pruritic; may be tender or painful; rarely ulcerate |
| | | Laser treatment probably most successful |
| **HISPANICS** | | |
| Skin | Varying degrees of pigmentation | Infants are lightly pigmented when born; grow darker with age, until pigmentation peaks about 6 to 8 weeks. Pallor best |

*(continued)*

*Table 34–2. Ethnic Variations in the Integumentary System (Continued)*

|  | Characteristic or Condition | Nursing Implications |
| --- | --- | --- |
| **HISPANICS** (cont.) | Largest percentage have tan to dark brown skin | detected in nail beds, conjunctivae, oral mucosa, or tongue, which are normally reddish-pink. May need to palpate rashes that are hard to see |
|  |  | Ashen color may result from vasoconstriction or anemia. |
|  |  | Protection against solar and other irritation |
|  |  | Less susceptible to skin cancer than are whites |
| Hair | Varying textures: wavy, curly, straight; mostly black or dark brown | Important to be aware of varying inheritance of Hispanic clients |
| ***Normal Variations and Findings*** |  |  |
|  | Mongolian spots | Important to document these since they may be misdiagnosed and evidence of child abuse |
|  |  | Do not assume parents know what mongolian spots are. |
|  |  | No positive correlation between degree of general pigmentation and presence or extensiveness of mongolian spots |
|  |  | Considered closely related to nevus of Ota, nevus of Ito, and blue nevus; do not become malignant |
|  |  | Tend to fade as skin becomes thicker with age |
| ***Common Dermatological Conditions*** |  |  |
|  | Lead lines in mouth | Young children living in poor housing conditions are at risk. |
|  | Rat bites | In children in old, rat-infested housing |
|  | Dermatitis from chemicals | Migrant workers' families at risk; children may be taken to field, even if too young to work |
|  | Fungal infections, infestations (lice and scabies), insect bites | Children of migrant workers at special risk for these conditions |
| ***Common Dermatological Responses*** |  |  |
|  | Hypopigmentation | In response to inflammatory process; usually is transitory, and normal skin color returns in a few weeks |
|  | Increased risk of keloid formation | In Hispanics with black ancestry |
| **NATIVE AMERICANS** |  |  |
| Skin | Eskimos perspire less than whites on trunks and extremities but more than whites on their faces. | Allows temperature control after excess dampening of clothes, which could be life-threatening |
|  | Fewer apocrine sweat glands in Native Americans than in blacks and whites | Mild to absent body odor |
|  | Native Americans tend to have dry ear wax. | Do not confuse flaky appearance of ear with a dry, eczematous lesion. |
|  | Varying degrees of pigmentation | Infants are lightly pigmented at birth; they grow darker with age, until peak of pigmentation at 6 to 8 weeks. |
|  |  | Pallor best assessed in nail beds, conjunctivae, oral mucosa, or tongue, which are normally reddish-pink |
|  |  | May need to palpate rashes that are hard to see |
|  |  | May have less blistering (e.g., with diaper rash) |
|  |  | Decreased skin cancer among Native Americans; as little as 25% of the number of cases seen in whites |
| Hair | Variations; texture may be coarse to fine; hair may be straight, wavy, or curly | Important to be aware of client's self-identification as Native American |
|  |  | May use tribal traditional care methods |
| Nails | Generally diffusely darker | Bands rare; need to consider melanoma of nail if any are found |

*(continued)*

*Table 34–2. Ethnic Variations in the Integumentary System (Continued)*

| | Characteristic or Condition | Nursing Implications |
|---|---|---|
| **NATIVE AMERICANS** (cont.) | | |
| ***Normal Variations and Findings*** | | |
| | Mongolian spots | Important to document these since they may be misdiagnosed as bruises and evidence of child abuse |
| | | May be referred to by some Native Americans as "the mark of the Indian" |
| | | Do not assume that parents know what mongolian spots are. |
| | | No positive correlation between degree of general pigmentation and presence or extensiveness of mongolian spots |
| | | Tend to fade with age as skin becomes thicker |
| | | Considered to be related to blue nevus, nevus of Ota, and nevus of Ito; do not become malignant |
| | Epicanthic folds | Can make child appear to have strabismus even when eye muscle balance is normal |
| | Ashen skin | Due to dryness and pigmentation. Especially evident on extremities. Mothers often manage this with lotion or other lubricant. |
| ***Common Dermatological Conditions*** | | |
| | Albinism | Varies with tribe: rate of 1 per 200 in Hopi, Zuni, and Jemez (Southwestern Native American tribes). Increased risk for solar damage |
| | Hereditary polymorphic light eruption | Affects members of many Northern and Southern Native American tribes. Results from exposure to sunlight. Symptoms appear in 75% of affected children by age 16. |
| | | Lesions often become secondarily infected, including impetigo. |
| | | Skin improves during winter. Sunscreens may be ineffective since these children are sensitive to sun's long ultraviolet rays. This condition has not been found in Eskimos or in Indians of the Pacific Northwest. |
| | | Many variations in lesions, but one type usually dominates in any one person. |
| | | Scarring may result from these lesions. |
| | | Lesions may appear within $\frac{1}{2}$ hour of sun exposure in 2 or more days. |
| | | Lesions may be pruritic, leading to slow healing from trauma of scratching. |
| | | Native American culture defines sun as necessary to health. |
| | | Topical medications used in treatment, including corticosteroid creams, can burn and sting, decreasing compliance. |
| | Cleft lip, cleft palate | Second highest case rate in Native Americans (1.38 per 1000 live births), after Japanese |
| | | Genetic component has been shown to exist for this anomaly in Native Americans. |
| | Congenital dislocated hip with unequal gluteal or thigh folds | Most common in Native Americans. Important to be alert for unequal gluteal and thigh folds and consequent assessment of hip function |
| | Hyperbilirubinemia | Native American infants tend to have higher bilirubin levels than whites. Bilirubin levels in Eskimo infants tend to peak on days 4 and 5 and remain elevated for a longer period. Do not discontinue breast-feeding routinely when infant's bilirubin level is 10 mg/100 mL. |
| ***Common Dermatological Responses*** | | |
| | Hypopigmentation | Occurs with inflammatory reactions (e.g., diaper rash) |
| | | Usually transitory, and normal pigmentation returns in a few weeks |

*(continued)*

*Table 34–2. Ethnic Variations in the Integumentary System (Continued)*

| | Characteristic or Condition | Nursing Implications |
|---|---|---|
| **WHITES** | | |
| Skin | Variations in skin tone (e.g., sallow, pink) and in pigmentation. Greatest sebaceous production not clearly established in literature. | Important to be aware of appearance of client's skin when healthy to assist in assessment of illness |
| | More apocrine sweat glands than Asians and Native Americans | Strong body odor |
| | Ear wax tends to be wet. | External auditory canals may need to be irrigated to see the tympanic membranes. |
| Hair | Variation in hair: straight, wavy, or curly; very fine to thick; blonde to black | Important to be aware of significance of hair and appearance to client |
| ***Normal Variations and Findings*** | | |
| | Cutis marmorata | Reticulated, bluish mottling of skin on trunk and extremities of infants and young children |
| | | May be persistent in children with Down syndrome, trisomy 18 |
| | Café-au-lait spots | Common finding; significant if multiple, larger than 1 cm, located in axilla or inguinal areas |
| | Freckles | Increase with age; especially in school-aged children as deep pigmented cells surface and with repeated exposure to sunlight. |
| | Nevus flammeus | "Stork-bite" marks more obvious in white infants; may seem to persist longer than in darker-skinned infants |
| ***Common Dermatological Conditions*** | | |
| | Pilonidal dimples | Most common in white males. Any associated sinus tract may extend into spinal column, with possibility of meningitis. May have associated cyst |
| | Psoriasis | Inherited disorder, most common in whites; affects 1% to 3% of population. Erythematous, scaly papules, especially of elbows, knees, extensor surfaces of limbs, genitalia, lumbosacral area. Oral drugs not usually prescribed for children due to side effects |
| | Cystic acne | Most common in white males; may have serious psychological outcomes. Goals of treatment include prevention of follicular hyperkeritinization, reduction of the fatty acids and causative bacteria, and elimination of comedones, cysts, and nodules. |
| | Malignant melanomas | Most commonly affect those with fair skin, blue eyes, and red or blonde hair. May be a genetic basis in some patients. Congenital pigmented nevus (1% to 2.5% of newborns) have much more malignant potential than those appearing later in life. May occur as brown or black discoloration of nail, with development of pigmented band |
| | Hemagiomas | Strawberrylike, cavernous, mixed types. Generally grow rapidly first 8 to 10 months, then spontaneously resolve. May need to be treated with prednisone or surgery |
| ***Common Dermatological Responses*** | | |
| | Solar damage | Increased risk for sunburn. Severe sunburn five times (or more) in life-time increases risk of skin cancer significantly. Greatest risk in fair-skinned, blue-eyed blondes or redheads. Use hats, clothing, and SPF 15 or higher sunscreens to protect children's skin. |
| | Increased likelihood of blistering, papular response | With traumatic, solar, chemical, bacterial or viral insult Erythema more obvious with lighter skin |

**Cultures** are used to confirm and characterize pathogens but are usually limited to fungi and bacteria since viral cultures are less available.

**Patch tests** are used to identify causes of delayed responses to contact allergens.

**Skin biopsies** are used to establish diagnoses in skin nodules that could be malignant, plaques with unusual shapes and colors, primary blistering disorders, and lupus erythematosus.

**Tuberculin tests** (PPD, Mantoux, Tine, and Mono-Vac) are used to determine whether infection with the tubercle bacillus has taken place.

Refer to a diagnostic test reference book for further information.

## Nursing Diagnosis

The following nursing diagnoses are frequently used for children with integumentary system problems:

*Pattern 1: Exchanging*
- Altered nutrition: less than body requirements
- Fluid volume excess
- High risk for infection
- High risk for injury
- Impaired skin integrity

*Pattern 3: Relating*
- Social isolation

*Pattern 6: Moving*
- Activity intolerance
- Bathing/hygiene self-care deficit
- Impaired physical mobility

*Pattern 7: Perceiving*
- Body image disturbance
- Self-esteem disturbance
- Sensory/perceptual alterations, visual, auditory

*Pattern 9: Feeling*
- Anxiety
- Fear
- Pain

## Planning Nursing Care

When planning care for a child with integumentary disorders, nurses should consider the child's developmental stage, racial and genetic background, ethnic practices, acute or chronic care needs, and home care considerations.

To prevent integumentary problems in children, nurses should keep the following principles in mind:

- Maintain cleanliness to reduce potential pathogens and irritating or abrasive substances.

- Avoid sun (ultraviolet) damage to decrease the risk of skin cancer.
- Avoid low temperature and low humidity to prevent chapping and cracking of skin and freezing of exposed areas.
- Avoid excess moisture and occlusion to reduce the likelihood of bacterial and fungal infections.
- Adapt skin care for racial or ethnic variations (e.g., black children tend to have dry skin).
- Prevent skin trauma, abrasions, and burns.
- Promote healing of skin lesions.
- Avoid contact irritants (e.g., soaps, wool, etc.).

Nursing interventions for integumentary problems frequently include the application of topical medications for dermatological problems as well as teaching children and parents the proper way to apply the medication. Topical preparations are shown in Table 34-3.

## Developmental, Racial, and Ethnic Considerations

Consideration of the developmental stage assists in determining the normal characteristics of the skin and appendages and in recognizing alterations that are likely to occur at a particular age or stage. For example, infants' skin (especially premature infants') is very thin, which causes decreased thermoregulation and can cause increased absorption of harmful topical products (e.g., hexachlorophene). In addition, infants' low levels of oil on the skin provide less of a protective barrier. In adolescents, increased eccrine and apocrine sweat gland activity can lead to body odor, whereas increased sebaceous gland activity can lead to acne.

Racial and genetic considerations and ethnic practices are also important when assessing the child. Black children tend to have drier skin than whites. Preauricular skin pits, extra nipples in females, and keloid scar formation (hyperplastic scar tissue) are much more common in black children. "Corn-rowing" hair or using a hair pick may cause areas of baldness that can become permanent if these practices continue. Some conditions involving the integumentary system are genetically transmitted. For example, neurofibromatosis is an autosomal dominant disorder in which café-au-lait spots are seen, and soft tissue and bone tumors develop at the onset of puberty.

## Acute Care Considerations

Nurses frequently assess and treat acute integumentary system problems in a variety of settings, including offices, health clinics, schools, emergency rooms, inpatient units, and accident sites as well as in homes. Acute problems vary from skin infections of different degrees, bites, and stings to major integumentary trauma, such as severe lacerations or burns.

*Table 34-3. Topical Preparations for Treatment of Dermatological Conditions*

| Preparation | Characteristics | Purposes | Nursing Implications |
|---|---|---|---|
| Creams (water-based) | Oil in 20% to 50% water; white; nongreasy; disappears when rubbed in; many ingredients, including preservatives | Lubricating effect | Sometimes contact dermatitis results from preservatives or from fragrances. May need to use fragrance-free lubricant. More appropriate than ointments when humidity is increased or in occluded body areas |
| Ointments (oil-based) | Solids with little or no water; greasy; clear; no preservatives | Used for increasing moisture, maximizing penetration of active ingredient, and occlusion; lubricating effect | May cause too much heat retention for comfort; do not rub into skin |
| Lotions | Powder suspended in water. Example: Calamine lotion | Evaporation of water is cooling; powder layer stays on skin as protection | May need to be shaken before application |
| Solutions, sprays, aerosols, tinctures | Ingredients mixed in alcohol | Alcohol evaporates and leaves ingredients on skin | Especially helpful in hairy areas of body |
| Gels | Transparent, colorless, semi-solid emulsions that become liquid when rubbed on skin; alcohol base | Effective penetration of steroids and in drugs applied to scalp and for acne | Burn or sting due to alcohol |
| Baths | Tar emulsions; colloidal oatmeal; cornstarch or bath oils | Decrease pruritus; cleanse acute eruptions; hydrate lesions when moisturizer is applied after bath | Bathe once or twice each day, for no longer than 30 minutes since maceration may result. Pat, do not rub, dry. |

One of the most common integumentary problems is sunburn. It can range from mild to very severe. Nurses should advise parents to carefully apply topical sunscreens to prevent or minimize the effects of ultraviolet rays. Parents should be advised that the higher the sun protection factor (SPF), the greater the protection. The most effective sunscreens have paraaminobenzoic acid (PABA), and a minimum rating of 15 is recommended for most children.

In all acute care situations, nurses need to be aware of compounding factors, such as children's anxieties about the unknown, including places, people, and procedures; their need for parental support; and their right to be informed in ways they can understand about what will happen to them during assessment and treatment. Safety, including appropriate restraint to avoid injury, when necessary, is also important. Comforting children during and after painful procedures and encouraging mastery of their fears through play activities are helpful.

## Chronic Care Considerations

Chronic care for integumentary system problems is usually provided by nurses on an outpatient basis, although some acute episodes may require hospitalization. Chronic integumentary health problems are disorders that persist for 6 months or longer. Caring for a child who has a

condition like psoriasis (with periods of remission and exacerbation) or hemangiomas (which may worsen over a period of time before improvement) can be frustrating for children, parents, and nurses. A condition such as atopic dermatitis may require environmental changes that are disruptive for the entire family. When conditions are genetically transmitted, such as neurofibromatosis, parents may have to cope with their own feelings about giving the disease to their children.

Some skin problems may involve other body systems. For example, epidermolysis bullosa, a genetic blistering disease, may also include anemia, constipation, lactose intolerance, contractures, muscle atrophy, fusion of toes or fingers, and damaged corneas and conjunctivae. Priorities in nursing care change depending on the status of the involved body systems.

## Home Care Considerations

Home care of integumentary system problems can range from first aid for insect stings to posthospitalization care for burns or other trauma. Parents should have a first aid kit and know how to treat minor lacerations and abrasions as well as nontoxic bites and stings. They should understand the need for medical care for bites from dogs or other animals. They should also know which burns require medical attention and which can be treated at home.

Home care of children after hospitalization for serious problems such as burns can be demanding for parents. Nurses must be certain that parents understand the purpose of the treatments and can carry them out. Parents should know how to prevent complications and which signs and symptoms require medical evaluation. They should be aware of the expected outcomes of home care, including the time frame for improvements in the child's condition. Nurses can be an important source of information by providing referrals to support groups and respite care.

## Evaluating Nursing Care

Evaluating nursing care of children with integumentary problems depends on the type of problem and its severity. Evaluation includes observing the child's and parent's responses to nursing care, determining their progress in achieving realistic goals, and revising care plans based on the evaluation of outcomes. Compliance with treatment regimens is an indication that the child and parents are adapting to the problem. Measurable outcomes include understanding of the problem and its treatment as well as monitoring for possible complications. Evaluation of long-term care in the home, as for burns, may require visits by home care nurses and other health care personnel to assist the parents and the child to achieve a better quality of life.

## Integumentary Problems of Infants

### Hemangiomas

#### Pathophysiology

Hemangiomas are developmental defects of the skin. The lesions are circumscribed and are derived from vascular components. Vascularity creates a red, blue, or purple color in the lesions (see Color Fig. 34-1).

There are two types of hemangiomas. *Capillary hemangiomas* (nevus flammeus, port wine stains, strawberry hemangiomas, and cherry hemangiomas) are composed of small, superficial vessels. *Cavernous hemangiomas* are composed of primarily dilated, well-differentiated vessels or sinusoidal blood spaces, but they may have a superficial capillary component. They are dome-shaped, deep, soft, bluish nodules. Complications of cavernous hemangiomas include obstruction of a vital orifice, visual obstruction, platelet trapping syndrome, and cardiac decompensation.

#### Medical Diagnosis and Management

Diagnosis of hemangiomas in children is based on inspection of the lesions. Biopsies rarely are performed on raised hemangiomas.

Usually, no treatment is required; most hemangiomas resolve spontaneously. Port wine stains may be covered with cosmetics if the parent or child wishes to do so. Argon laser treatment may be used in older children. Prednisone may be prescribed to help resolution of cavernous and mixed hemangiomas. Topical antibiotics are used to treat secondary infections in ulcerated hemangiomas.

#### Nursing Assessment and Diagnosis

Assessment includes determining the child's developmental level; level of activity; the number, size, and location of the lesions; what supervision is done by the caretaker; and the amount of time spent with other children. The type and location of lesions, hygiene practices, and the amount of "weeping" from the lesions should be noted. The parents' and child's understanding of the cause (lesions may be part of a syndrome), the treatment or lack of it, their responses to comments or questions by others, and their knowledge of expected outcomes and complications should be assessed. The nurse should also assess the parents' practices in caring for the lesions, their understanding of the signs and symptoms of problems, and their general care of the child. The nurse also should determine the parents' and child's responses to the appearance of the lesions and to others' reactions. Parent–child interaction should be noted. The location of lesions, any encroachment of the eye or ear, the rate at which the lesions are growing or shrinking, and the parents' understanding of potential problems are important to ascertain.

Nursing diagnoses for hemangiomas might include the following:

- High risk for injury related to abrasion of the lesions
- High risk for infection related to impaired skin integrity
- Body image disturbance related to appearance of the lesions
- Sensory alteration related to obstruction of eyes or ears

#### Planning and Implementing Nursing Care

Parents may need to keep the lesions covered with protective clothing to reduce the occurrence of abrasions. There is a chance of serious bleeding if a massive cavernous hemangioma is damaged. Although vigilance about avoiding trauma to hemangiomas is essential, parents should avoid overprotecting the child. Nurses should encourage and promote good general hygiene, appropriate nutrition, reduction of trauma to lesions, and reporting of signs of early infection to the physician. Parents and children should be taught the cause of the lesions, the expected outcome, treatment options and their rationales, and possible complications. If the parents can read, written instructions can be given to them. If the parents cannot read, instructions can be provided for them on audio tapes. Parents and children must be encouraged to express their feelings, concerns, and frustration about the appearance of the lesions and the treatment. Parents should be informed of possible impairment of vision or hearing, depending on the location of the lesion. Parents should be encouraged to keep medical appointments so that potential problems can be monitored.

### Evaluating Nursing Care

There should be no severe scarring or trauma to the lesion if protective measures are successful. The lesion should show no signs or symptoms of infection; if infection develops, it should be recognized and treated within 2 days. The parents and child should demonstrate an understanding of the causes and treatment of the lesions. As a result of expressing their feelings, the parents and child should report decreased anxiety. Careful monitoring by health professionals should assist in preventing damage by the lesions to developing sensory structures; vision and hearing should be normal.

## Diaper Dermatitis
### Pathophysiology

*Diaper dermatitis* is an irritant reaction from prolonged exposure to constant moisture, irritating chemicals, intestinal enzymes, stool, and high environmental heat. Shiny erythema is evident over the gluteus, genitalia, lower abdomen, and upper thighs. Vesicles and erosions, erythematous papules, oozing, and ulceration may also be present (see Color Fig. 34-2). Diaper dermatitis may become complicated by *Candida albicans* fungal infections or by streptococcal or staphylococcal infections.

### Medical Diagnosis and Management

Medical diagnosis is made on the basis of the distribution of areas of erythema, the color of the rash and lesions, and the history of its onset, duration, and treatment. Management includes giving parents instructions about frequent diaper changes, cleansing the diaper area with warm water, using a bland, protective ointment, and avoiding excess heat and humidity. Local bacterial infections may be treated with a topical antibiotic (e.g., Neosporin or Polysporin). A topical corticosteroid may be used for mild inflammations. Infections with *C. albicans* need to be treated with topical nystatin, clortrimazole, or miconazole. Clioquinol and iodoquinol should not be used for diaper dermatitis because they are neurotoxic, and even greater absorption occurs through inflamed skin than through normal skin (American Academy of Pediatrics, 1990).

### Nursing Assessment and Diagnosis

Nursing assessment includes evaluating the type and extent of the lesions and a history of discomfort in the infant.

Assessment should also include information regarding the parents' knowledge of the cause, treatment, and prevention of diaper rash as well as of possible outcomes if the dermatitis is not treated. Observation of the skin should include noting whether the skin is intact or broken. The general hygiene status of the infant and the hygienic practices of the parents should also be assessed, including the type of diapers used, laundering practices and detergents, and types of soaps and lotions.

Nursing diagnoses for diaper dermatitis might include the following:

* Pain related to skin sensitivity
* Impaired skin integrity related to the lesions
* High risk for infection related to the infectious process

### Planning and Implementing Nursing Care

Medical evaluation and treatment are indicated if there is evidence of a bacterial or yeast infection. When a monilial diaper rash is determined, the mouth should also be assessed for thrush. Parents should be instructed about the need to change soiled diapers immediately, proper cleansing of the diaper area, and the importance of not using occlusive plastic pants; they should be encouraged to expose the area to the air each day. The appropriate use of topical medications should also be reviewed with the parents. The signs of yeast and bacterial infections should be discussed with the parents as well as the consequences if these infections are not treated. Review the function of the skin as a barrier to infection.

### Evaluating Nursing Care

If there is evidence of a bacterial or yeast infection, the infant should be evaluated by a physician for a medical diagnosis. The parents should be able to express their understanding of the importance of changing diapers immediately, keeping the diaper area clean, and using topical medications appropriately. The parents also should be able to recall the signs and consequences of yeast and bacterial infections. They should demonstrate their understanding of the importance of intact skin for a healthy infant.

## Atopic Dermatitis (Eczema)
### Pathophysiology

The cause of atopic dermatitis is unknown. Family history is usually positive for atopic dermatitis or asthma. The infantile phase occurs in children 2 months to 2 years of age. The chest, face, scalp, neck, and extensor surfaces of the arms and legs are involved, primarily with erythematous papulovesicles and oozing (see Color Fig. 34-3). Infants may have very dry skin that leads to scratching and inflammation.

The childhood phase occurs in children 4 to 10 years old. Lesions are usually more scattered, on the flexor surfaces of the extremities and neck. Lichenification, excoriations, and dry papules are common.

### Medical Diagnosis and Management

No single diagnostic criterion exists. Clinical features of eczema include itching, a characteristic pattern of the lesions, a personal and family history of asthma or allergic rhinitis, dry skin with itching during periods of sweating, and paradoxical vasoconstrictive cutaneous responses.

Medical management includes use of medications such as topical corticosteroids, antihistamines, and tar compounds for the chronic phase. Hydration of the skin is also an important management concern. Irritants such as wool, changes in environmental temperature, and occlusive clothing should be avoided.

### Nursing Assessment and Diagnosis

Assessment includes documenting the extent and severity of lesions; noting the child's irritability, restlessness, complaints of pain, or pruritus; identifying how the parents handle and dress the child; and ascertaining the parents' and child's knowledge of the cause, factors that exacerbate the condition, the treatment, medications, and possible complications. In assessing older children, the nurse should note responses to the appearance of lesions and perceptions of how others treat the child as well as knowledge and practices related to cleanliness and hygiene. For example, the nurse should determine whether the child knows that fingernails should be kept short and clean to reduce the occurrence of infection from scratching or touching the area.

Nursing diagnoses for atopic dermatitis might include the following:

- Pain related to pruritus
- High risk for infection related to scratching
- Impaired skin integrity related to lesions
- Self-concept disturbance related to appearance

### Planning and Implementing Nursing Care

The child and family should be instructed about the chronicity of the disease but should be reassured that eczema can be managed. The importance of skin hydration, the proper use of topical medications as recommended or prescribed, and the avoidance of sensitizing or irritating substances should be included in the teaching plan. Parents should be taught how to assess discomfort, especially for infants and toddlers. Parents and children should be counseled about identifying allergens in the child's environment. Ways of promoting self-care should be discussed for older children as well as ways of promoting the child's positive self-concept. The significance of open lesions as sites of possible infection must be emphasized. Parents and children should be counseled about appropriate hygiene methods and application of topical medications.

### Evaluating Nursing Care

Parents and older children should be able to voice understanding of recommended skin care and knowledge about the use of medications. Parents should be able to state behaviors in infants and toddlers that indicate discomfort. Parents should be able to use a checklist or other systematic method to identify allergens in the home. Older children should assume responsibility for their own topical medication use. Parents should voice an understanding of ways of preventing negative self-concept. Parents and older children should demonstrate an understanding of the meaning of the loss of an intact skin barrier. Parents should identify appropriate methods for preventing skin infections.

## Integumentary Problems of Children

### Psoriasis

#### Pathophysiology

*Psoriasis* is an inflammatory rash that results from an accelerated number of dividing cells. Transit time from the basal layer to the top of the stratum corneum is reduced from 28 days to 3 or 4 days, too fast for cells to shed. Consequently, sharply demarcated, erythematous papules and plaques with characteristic silvery scales develop (see Color Fig. 34-4). These may occur anywhere. Although the disease usually starts in adulthood, it may begin in infancy. There is a genetic predisposition to psoriasis, but the etiology is unknown. Pruritus may be mild to severe.

#### Medical Diagnosis and Management

Diagnosis is usually made clinically. A potassium hydroxide slide of scale scrapings can help rule out a fungal infection, if necessary. A biopsy of a lesion may be done.

The most recommended medical treatments for children are topical coal tar preparations with or without ultraviolet light. Topical fluorinated glucocorticoids may be used, but not systemic steroids, due to the severe reaction that may follow withdrawal. Methotrexate may be used for the most severe, disabling forms. Psoralen with ultraviolet light (PUVA therapy) is not recommended for children.

#### Nursing Assessment and Diagnosis

Assessment includes a history of itching; observation of the child scratching; the appearance of excoriations from scratching; and signs of irritability in infants. The nurse should note the location and severity of lesions; the child's developmental and activity level; and parental supervision. The presence of abrasions, excoriations, open lesions, and the child's general hygiene should also be noted. The nurse should assess the parents' and child's understanding of the condition, the treatment and rationale, expected outcomes, complications, and ways to reduce the likelihood of new lesions (e.g., trauma). It is also important to ascertain the parents' and child's practices in caring for lesions, the child's general health status, and the child's emotional health.

Nursing diagnoses for psoriasis might include the following:

- Impaired skin integrity related to lesions
- High risk for infection related to loss of protective skin covering
- Body image disturbance related to appearance of rash

### Planning and Implementing Nursing Care

The nurse should encourage appropriate use of prescribed medications. The mechanical removal of scales from the scalp may be needed. Forceful removal of scales is discouraged. Lesions, especially on knees and elbows, may have to be protected with clothing. Parents should also be encouraged to maintain good general hygiene by keeping the child's nails cut, reducing pruritus as much as possible, and covering lesions with clean clothing. Parents and children should be instructed about the condition, the signs and symptoms, treatment and rationale, expected outcomes, and chronicity of the condition. Cooperation with the treatment plan, including the appropriate use of medications and protection of areas likely to be traumatized, should be encouraged. The consequences of the loss of skin integrity should be explained. The nurse should encourage appropriate care by parents and self-care by children, when possible. This may require adaptation to the family's abilities and the home situation. Parents should be encouraged to avoid overprotecting the child.

### Evaluating Nursing Care

The child should report that the treatments have resulted in a decrease in the itching sensation. The parents should report less irritability in the infant or child. The number of excoriations (from scratching) should be reduced. Major trauma or chronic, exacerbating trauma to lesions should be avoided. No signs of infection should develop in the lesions. Parents and children should be able to demonstrate an understanding of psoriasis, the care methods, and how to use them. The parents and, when possible, the child should voice an understanding of the problem and ways to minimize its effects.

## Poison Ivy, Oak, and Sumac Dermatitis

### Pathophysiology

*Poison ivy, oak,* and *sumac dermatitis* are forms of contact dermatitis, an inflammation in the epidermis and superficial dermis caused by external chemical agents. Reactions to the sensitizing agent urushiol may occur from a few hours to a few days after exposure and last about 3 weeks. The pruritic lesions are characteristically red papules, vesicles, and bullae (see Color Fig. 34-5).

Children under the age of 3 years are less likely to be sensitized than are older children; however, even infants can be exposed to sensitizing agents from contact with their parents' clothes. Severe cutaneous involvement can result in acute nephritis (hematuria, edema, hypertension, and headache). Respiratory symptoms also may occur.

### Medical Diagnosis and Management

Poison ivy, oak, and sumac dermatitis are usually diagnosed based on the presenting symptoms and a history of exposure. Topical steroids and systemic antihistamines are used to treat mild cases. Acute, severe, generalized dermatitis is treated with systemic steroids and wet soaks.

### Nursing Assessment and Diagnosis

Assessment includes a history of itching or of irritability in infants and observations of the child scratching and excoriations of the lesions from scratching. The physical examination reveals the presence of blisters, bullae, and vesicles; regional edema; and possible respiratory distress caused by edema. The nurse must also assess the child's and parents' understanding of the cause of the lesions, treatment, outcomes, possible complications, and future responses on exposure. It is also important to assess the child's and parents' practices in caring for the lesions and in preventing exposures to poisonous plants. The nurse should note open lesions, excoriations, the length and condition of the child's nails, any infection source already present in the body, and immune system status.

Nursing diagnoses for poison ivy, oak, and sumac dermatitis might include the following:

- Impaired skin integrity related to lesions
- Pain related to pruritus
- Fluid volume excess related to the inflammatory process
- High risk for infection related to the lesions

### Planning and Implementing Nursing Care

Supportive and educative measures include the proper administration of prescribed medications; avoidance of excessive sunlight; wearing of cool, nonirritating clothing;

and avoidance of reexposure to poisonous plants. Open lesions should be kept clean and dry, and the parents and child should be instructed about signs of infection. If an infection exists, they should be taught how to avoid transmission (e.g., a dressing over the infected area, good handwashing). It is particularly important that the child and parents be taught about the management, complications, and prevention of poison plant dermatitis as well as the appropriate care for lesions and how to prevent recurrence. In endemic areas parents should be taught how to recognize the plants and that after contact with the plant, the area should be washed immediately with cool water and soap. The resolution of lesions that have had additional damage can usually be accomplished by maintaining good skin hygiene, reducing trauma to the area, and allowing bullae to resolve. Scratching of excoriations can be minimized by keeping nails trimmed and by wearing cool, loose, soft clothing.

### Evaluating Nursing Care

Evaluation of nursing care entails assessing that symptoms are alleviated and infection is prevented. The parents and child should demonstrate knowledge about the condition and its treatment. The child should have decreased pruritus, and the infant should be less irritable. As a result of medication, existing blisters, bullae, and vesicles should resolve, with no new ones developing. No signs of infection should be seen in the lesions. The child and parents should voice an understanding of management, complications, prevention, and methods of care, and they should follow the treatment recommendations. There should be no extension of abraded, excoriated, denuded skin in the area of lesions nor any additional damage.

## Impetigo

### Pathophysiology

*Impetigo* is a bacterial infection of the superficial skin layers. It is caused by group A, β-hemolytic *Streptococcus* species, *Staphylococcus aureus,* or a combination of both. Impetigo begins as small vesicles that progress to erosions with moist, honey-colored crusts (see Color Fig. 34-6). They may occur on any part of the body, but they appear most commonly on the face. The crusts and the drainage are contagious. The child may either autoinoculate other parts of the body or transmit the infection to other people. An important clinical manifestation is that the lesions are pruritic.

### Medical Diagnosis and Management

The clinical features of impetigo are usually sufficient for a medical diagnosis to be made. Gram-staining of the moist drainage or performing a culture can verify the causative organism.

Medical management includes administration of systemic antibiotics (oral penicillin or erythromycin) for 7 to 10 days. The child with only a few, small, nonbullous lesions may be treated with topical bacitracin or neomycin. Other recommendations include washing or soaking off the crusts three to four times a day, with or without application of iodine ointment or a bland emollient. The major concern in patients with impetigo is poststreptococcal glomerulonephritis, which may lead to renal failure.

### Nursing Assessment and Diagnosis

Nursing assessment includes noting the extent and character of the lesions, the amount of drainage and crusting, and the degree of discomfort from pruritus. It is important to ascertain the parents' and child's knowledge of the condition, its communicability, its treatment, and the expected outcomes. It is also important to ascertain treatments that have been used and the parents' ability to carry out care instructions. The child's feeling of self-comfort with the appearance of the lesions (especially on the face) and with the responses of other people should be assessed. What kinds of contacts does the child have? Does the child attend a day care center or school? Do any other family members have lesions? What is the general hygiene of the child and parents? The nurse should note the extent and depth of lesions and any edema resulting from the renal failure of glomerulonephritis. Other signs of glomerulonephritis include oliguria, anuria, and cola-colored urine.

Nursing diagnoses for impetigo might include the following:

- Pain related to pruritus
- Bathing/hygiene self-care deficit related to painful lesions
- Self-esteem disturbance related to appearance of the lesions
- Impaired skin integrity related to excoriation
- Fluid volume excess related to possible associated kidney malfunction

### Planning and Implementing Nursing Care

Parents should be encouraged to wash off the crusts and drainage two or three times per day and to give antihistamines as prescribed. The parents, child, and other caretakers should be instructed about the cause, autoinoculation, treatment and side effects, expected outcomes, and complications of the disease. The child and parents should be counseled concerning hygiene measures, including cutting the nails every day, and about the use of topical or oral medications. The child should be encouraged to express concerns about appearance and the possible responses of other children and adults. Both the child and parents should be instructed about ways to control the spread of impetigo to others (e.g., by not sharing towels). The nurse should instruct the parents and child about the possibility of extended infection, including signs and symptoms, and when to contact the physician. The parents should be told about the possibility of glomerulonephritis and should be alerted to those signs and symptoms.

### Evaluating Nursing Care

There should be a decrease in sensations of pruritus, and the parents should report that there is a decrease in the number of times that the child scratches the lesions (usually half as often). The child and parents should express an understanding of the causes, treatment, complications, and care of the condition. The child should express feelings of increased self-comfort with his or her appearance. Both the child and parents should demonstrate their understanding of ways to prevent transmission of the infection as well as their understanding of the possibility of extended infection. The parents also should understand the possibility of developing glomerulonephritis and be able to recognize signs and symptoms of this complication (see Chap. 30).

## Seborrheic Dermatitis

### Pathophysiology

*Seborrheic dermatitis* is a chronic, superficial, inflammatory process of hairy body regions, especially the scalp, eyebrows, and face. It results from the accumulation of excessive sebum, although the exact mechanism is unknown. It occurs most frequently in infants under 6 months of age and in adolescents.

Seborrheic dermatitis is characterized by erythema; dry, greasy scales; and cycles of remissions and exacerbations. The accompanying pruritus may be mild or absent. There appears to be a genetic predisposition, and the condition can be precipitated or exacerbated by emotional distress. It is known as *Leiner's disease* if the entire body of the infant is involved.

### Medical Diagnosis and Management

Seborrheic dermatitis can easily be confused with atopic dermatitis, psoriasis, histiocytosis X, and other conditions. No laboratory tests are useful in the diagnosis, which is established by history and by examination of the skin.

Medical management usually consists of using an antiseborrheic shampoo with selenium. Other treatments include salicylic acid or tar shampoos, and topical steroids (except on the face). In the most severe cases, systemic antibiotics may be used. Mechanical removal (e.g., with a comb or brush) of the scales from the scalp is helpful. Leiner's disease requires hospitalization and supportive care (e.g., intravenous therapy).

### Nursing Assessment and Diagnosis

Nursing assessment includes ascertaining the parents' and child's understanding of the condition, cause, treatment, and the length of time the condition will probably last. The parents' and child's ability to provide care for the condition, including removal of scales and use of prescribed medication or shampoo, should be assessed. Other areas of particular concern for adolescents include ascertaining how the adolescent's self-concept is affected by the condition, including withdrawal or isolation. The extent and severity of the lesions, compliance with care regimens, and general hygiene practices should be investigated.

Nursing diagnoses for seborrheic dermatitis might include the following:

- Bathing/hygiene self-care deficit related to the inability to care for the lesions alone
- Self-esteem disturbance related to the appearance of the lesions
- Impaired skin integrity related to the lesions

### Planning and Implementing Nursing Care

The parents and child should be taught about the condition and the factors that may cause improvement or worsening of the lesions. The nurse should demonstrate or instruct the parents and child about the removal of scales, the use of selenium shampoo, and the application of topical medications. Adolescents should be encouraged to express concerns about their appearance, and the nurse should validate positive self-perceptions.

### Evaluating Nursing Care

An important part of evaluation of nursing care is the ability of the parents and child to demonstrate their understanding of the condition and the methods to control spreading of the lesions. There should be no signs of infection of seborrheic lesions.

## Integumentary Problems of Adolescents

### Acne Vulgaris

#### Pathophysiology

*Acne vulgaris* affects the pilosebaceous units of the skin and is found mainly on the face and upper trunk. The cause is multifactorial and consists of the following: (1) increased sebum production when sebaceous glands are stimulated by androgens, (2) outlet obstruction of the pilosebaceous canal caused by keratin impaction, (3) accumulation of sebaceous and keratinous debris behind the

*Table 34–4.  Grading Scale for Acne*

Grade I (mild): Comedones, occasional papules

Grade II (moderate): Comedones, papules, occasional pustules

Grade III (severe): Comedones, papules, pustules, abscesses

Grade IV (congloblate): Comedones, papules, pustules, abscesses, widespread scarring

---

obstruction, and (4) growth of anaerobic bacteria, which contribute in an unknown way to inflammatory acne lesions (see Color Fig. 34-7). Specific foods or types of food do not appear to be related to the incidence of acne. The severity of acne is graded according to the criteria presented in Table 34-4.

## Medical Diagnosis and Management

The medical diagnosis of acne is determined by the presenting lesions. Bacterial culture may be needed to rule out infection. Medical management includes: (1) topical comedolytic agents, usually benzyl peroxide and tretinoin (vitamin A); (2) antibiotics, either topical (erythromycin, clindamycin, tetracycline) or systemic (tetracycline, erythromycin, minocycline); (3) systemic retinoids in patients with the most severe cases; and (4) patient education about the chronicity of the condition and about friction increasing its severity.

## Nursing Assessment and Diagnosis

Nursing assessment includes documentation of pain, especially of acutely inflamed pustules and cysts. The nurse must also determine the adolescent's understanding of the development and treatment of acne, how to use medications, the possible side effects, and the length of time acne outbreaks may be expected to last. During the physical examination, the nurse should note any increased inflammation or purulent drainage. The adolescent's general hygiene should also be noted. The nurse should also inquire about the adolescent's practices in treating the acne and about nutrition and general hygiene. It is also important to assess the adolescent's self-perception and how others respond to the acne. The nurse should carefully note the extent and depth of any ruptured lesions and whether the adolescent has a habit of picking or squeezing the lesions.

Nursing diagnoses for acne might include the following:

- Pain related to inflammation of the skin
- Impaired skin integrity related to eruptions
- High risk for infection related to loss of skin integrity
- Self-esteem disturbance related to the appearance of the lesions

## Planning and Implementing Nursing Care

Warm soaks can help alleviate discomfort, and pressure should be avoided over the affected area. The adolescent and the parents should be taught about the development of acne, the treatment, hygiene measures, the use of appropriate medications, the importance of avoiding occlusive materials, and basic nutrition. The adolescent should be instructed about the risk for infection, the signs and symptoms of superimposed infection, and ways to avoid infection. Adolescents should be encouraged to express their feelings about their appearance.

## Evaluating Nursing Care

The adolescent should report decreased discomfort from the pain of lesions. Both the adolescent and the parents should be able to express an understanding of the development and treatment of acne. The adolescent should demonstrate an understanding of the risk of infection and the proper methods of caring for acne. Long-term goals for the adolescent include increased self-esteem, a positive self-image, and good hygiene habits.

# Infestations

## Pediculosis

### Pathophysiology

*Pediculosis* (lice infestation) may be caused by three types of lice. *Pediculus humanus capitis* (head louse) inhabits the hair of the head and the eyelashes. *P. humanus corporis* (body louse) lives in the seams of clothing or in bedding. *Phthirus pubis* (pubic or crab louse) mainly inhabits the hairs of the genital area but may extend to other hairy areas of the body (e.g., axillae, beard).

All lice suck blood from human hosts. They are transmitted directly or indirectly to others but rarely cause serious diseases in industrialized countries. Head lice are the most common type. Pubic lice are found in sexually active adolescents.

## Medical Diagnosis and Management

Diagnosis is made clinically. Itching of the scalp—especially of the occipital and postauricular area—and oval translucent nits attached to the hair shafts indicate head lice infestation. Pubic lice can be found attached to the skin. Body lice can be seen in the seams of clothing.

Medical management consists of two topical applications of lindane (shampoo or lotion) either on 2 consecutive days or 1 week apart. Eurax (10% N-ethyl-o-crotonotoluide) is used for pregnant women because of potential damage to the fetus from lindane. Infants and pregnant women may also use 5% to 10% sulfur in petrolatum. The mechanical removal of lice and nits (e.g., by combing the hair, washing or dry-cleaning clothes) is also important.

### Nursing Assessment and Diagnosis

Nursing assessment includes direct or reported observation of the child scratching, excoriations of infested areas, and reports of pruritus. The skin should be inspected for signs of bites by lice, pustules, and excoriations from scratching. During the history, the nurse should assess for behaviors that promote the transmission of lice, such as sharing combs, hats, pillows, or the same bed. In addition, the nurse should assess the parents' and child's understanding of the condition and its causes; the child's general hygiene, excoriations, and nail length; the child's and parents' practice in treating and preventing infestation; and the child's and parents' responses to the diagnosis and to others' reactions. When one or two children in a day care center are found to have lice, nurses usually assess all children in the class or school. Parents are given information on the signs, symptoms, and home treatment.

Sexual abuse should be considered when young children are found to have pubic lice. When sexually active adolescents have pubic lice, the nurse should also assess for sexually transmitted diseases (STDs) and for contraceptive knowledge and use, as well as for knowledge of methods to prevent the spread of STDs.

Nursing diagnoses for pediculosis might include the following:

- Pain related to pruritus
- High risk for impaired skin integrity related to excoriation
- High risk for infection related to loss of protective skin through excoriation
- High risk for infection related to multiple sexual partners
- Self-esteem disturbance related to the infestation

### Planning and Implementing Nursing Care

The nurse should encourage the appropriate use of the prescribed pediculicide. The child and parents should be taught about the characteristics of lice as well as the signs, symptoms, treatment, side effects, and expected outcomes. They should also be taught about the need to maintain hygiene, reduce scratching, and keep hands and nails clean. Demonstrations of how to use the pediculicide, comb the hair, and maintain hygiene should be given. The child and parents should be encouraged to express their feelings about the diagnosis and to discuss possible reactions of others. The parents, child, and other caretakers should be taught methods for controlling transmission. If sexual abuse is suspected, the child should be referred to the physician and appropriate mandated re-

porting should be done. If needed, the sexually active adolescent should be referred for sexually transmitted disease evaluation and for instruction about contraceptives.

### Evaluating Nursing Care

The parents and child should voice their understanding of the use of the pediculicide; the characteristics of lice, the treatment, and side effects; and the need for careful hygienic measures. They should demonstrate this by practicing recommendations. The child and parents should demonstrate self-care ability to treat and prevent further infestations. As a result of expressing their feelings, the child and parents should state feelings of increased self-comfort. The sexually abused child and sexually active adolescent should receive other needed health care.

## Scabies

### Pathophysiology

Scabies infestations are caused by the mite *Sarcoptes scabiei.* Canine scabies is known as sarcoptic mange and may cause infestations and even epidemics in humans. The mites burrow in the stratum corneum and travel as much as 5 mm every day for 1 or 2 months before they die (see Color Fig. 34-8). Severe pruritus results about 1 month after initial infestation as a humoral-mediated allergic response. Scabies is highly contagious through direct or indirect contact and is most common in groups of school-aged children.

### Medical Diagnosis and Management

The diagnosis of scabies is usually made after finding mites or eggs in scrapings. Simultaneous treatment of other members of the household and close contacts (e.g., baby-sitter) is necessary. Lindane, sulfur, or crotamiton is applied to all skin surfaces from the neck down (see discussion of pediculosis). Itching may persist for several weeks after treatment.

### Nursing Assessment and Diagnosis

Assessment includes the parents' report of infant or toddler irritability; observation of the child scratching and excoriations from scratching; the length and cleanliness of the child's nails; hygienic practices; and the presence of open lesions. The nurse should assess the child's and parents' understanding of the cause of the condition, treatment and side effects, expected outcomes, and complications, along with their practices regarding the management of the condition. The nurse also should assess the child's and parents' responses to the diagnosis, including any feelings of diminished self-esteem, and their responses to peer reactions. The extent and location of open lesions, denuded areas, and excoriations on skin should be noted. The transmission control measures of the parents and child should be assessed. Is the child in a day care or school setting? Are there pets in the household that might be a source of infestation?

Nursing diagnoses for scabies might include the following:

- Pain related to pruritus
- High risk for impaired skin integrity related to excoriation
- High risk for infection related to loss of protective skin covering through excoriation
- Self-esteem disturbance related to the infestation

### Planning and Implementing Nursing Care

The nurse should encourage the appropriate use of a scabicide. The skin should be kept as cool as possible. Antihistamines may be used to diminish the symptoms; irritating materials should not be worn next to the skin. General hygiene measures include cleanliness of the skin and hands and short nails. Children and parents should be taught about the cause of scabies, the characteristics of the mite, transmissibility, treatment and side effects, expected outcomes, and complications. Treatment should include the prevention of reinfestation of the child and others. The child and parents should be encouraged to express their feelings and concerns about the diagnosis and the possible reactions of others.

### Evaluating Nursing Care

There should be a reduced itching sensation within several weeks after treatment. The child and parents should be able to demonstrate their understanding of the condition and should agree to follow the plan of care. No signs of secondary infection should develop. No new lesions or open or denuded areas should appear on the skin. The child and parents should express feelings of increased self-comfort.

## Insect Bites and Stings

### Pathophysiology

Insect bites and stings result in local inflammatory reactions due to injected foreign protein and chemicals. *Hives* (wheals) occur as acute skin reactions; inflammatory papules are signs of more chronic reactions. Stinging insects include bees, wasps, and fire ants; mosquitoes, fleas, flies, and bedbugs are biting insects. Humans can also be bitten by spiders and ticks. Not all people are sensitive to these insects.

### Medical Diagnosis and Management

Diagnosis is usually made clinically on the basis of signs and symptoms. The long-term treatment goal is avoidance

of contact with the insect to prevent recurrence. Treatment of the symptoms is aimed at decreasing pruritus and pain and can include the use of steroids and antihistamines. Recluse spider bites, which can result in skin necrosis, may require skin grafts. Some people are so allergic to insect stings (especially wasps, bees, or fire ants) that they have life-threatening anaphylactic reactions and must be treated with adrenaline or antihistamines. Some desensitization procedures are followed in individuals with known allergies to certain types of insect stings.

### Nursing Assessment and Diagnosis

Nursing assessment includes identifying the quality and location of pain; edema at the site of the bite or sting; and respiratory difficulty in the event of anaphylactic reaction. The nurses should assess the child's and parents' understanding of the effects of the bite or sting, the treatment, and possible complications. Damage or destruction of the skin and any apparent opening into the skin from the sting or bite should be carefully recorded.

Nursing diagnoses for insect bites or stings might include the following:

- Pain related to the sting or bite
- Fluid volume excess related to edema
- Impaired skin integrity related to the sting or bite

### Planning and Implementing Nursing Care

Ice should be applied to the site of the bite or sting to reduce edema and pain. The area should be elevated to deter the spread of the toxin, and pressure should not be applied to the area. Emergency treatment for anaphylaxis may be required. If the child is known to be allergic, adrenaline should be available for subcutaneous injection. Parents should be instructed to check the expiration date of the adrenaline at frequent intervals. The amount of adrenaline needed must be recalculated each year as the child grows. Information about the type of toxin, reaction, treatment and outcome, complications, and when to call the physician should be given to the child and caretakers, including teachers. The area of the bite should be kept clean, and the child's hands and nails should also be kept clean to reduce the possibility of infection.

### Evaluating Nursing Care

The child should report decreased pain sensations with treatment. Anaphylactic reactions should be prevented or reversed. The parents and child should demonstrate their understanding about the toxin, reactions, treatment, and prevention. The child and parents should cooperate with plans to reduce infection and will follow the course of desensitization treatment, if recommended.

## Viral Infections
### Warts (Verruca)
#### Pathophysiology

Warts (verruca) are benign tumors, an overgrowth of epidermal cells resulting from infection by one or more of the human papilloma viruses identified as causative agents. These lesions may occur anywhere on the body. They occur most often in children between the ages of 12 to 16 years. There are four types of warts: *common* (see Color Fig. 34-9); *plantar*, which occur on the soles of the feet (see Color Fig. 34-10); *flat*; and *anogenital* (venereal warts; condyloma acuminatum).

#### Medical Diagnosis and Management

The diagnosis of warts is usually made clinically. A biopsy may be done to exclude verrucous carcinoma. Any suspicion of syphilis or the occurrence of anogenital warts in children or in sexually active adolescents requires diagnostic evaluation for sexually transmitted diseases or child abuse.

Warts usually disappear eventually, even if untreated; however, the appearance and possible discomfort from large warts (especially plantar warts) can make removal by excision, cryosurgery, or salicylic acid desirable. Condylomata in moist areas are usually treated with 20% podophyllin; often, several topical treatments are required.

#### Nursing Assessment and Diagnosis

Assessment includes a history of pain (especially with periungual or plantar warts or warts that are repeatedly traumatized), the location of the warts, their size, and any evidence of trauma. The child and parents' understanding of the condition, cause, treatment, probability of recurrence, and possibility of scarring should be assessed. Repeated trauma, self-treatment in attempting to remove the warts, and general hygiene should also be included in the assessment. The nurse should assess the child's and parents' practices in caring for lesions before and after medical treatment. The child's feelings about how his or her appearance is affected by the lesions should be assessed, especially if the warts are on the face or hands. In children with venereal warts, the nurse should assess for other evidence of sexual abuse, other sexually transmitted diseases, and warts on other parts of the body.

Nursing diagnoses for warts might include the following:

- Pain related to pressure on the wart
- High risk for injury related to location of the wart
- High risk for infection related to trauma to the wart
- Self-esteem disturbance related to appearance of the wart

#### Planning and Implementing Nursing Care

Medical evaluation and treatment of the warts should be recommended. The child and parents should be taught about the cause, problems, treatment, results, and possible recurrence of the warts. The child and parents should be taught about the need to reduce trauma to the lesion, the need to maintain hygiene, how to recognize signs of infection, and when to call the physician. The nurse should instruct the child and parents in the appropriate care of lesions, with demonstrations as appropriate. Children should be encouraged to express their feelings about their appearance. Medical treatment should be recommended for children with venereal warts. If sexual abuse is suspected, the child may need to be referred to a child protective unit. Sexually active adolescents may need referral for sex education.

#### Evaluating Nursing Care

The child should experience decreased pain if the warts are in sensitive areas. The child and parents should be able to demonstrate their understanding of hygienic practices, of the causes and treatment of the condition, and of the signs of infection. They should also demonstrate an understanding of appropriate care of the lesions, and should be able to provide return demonstrations. The child with venereal warts should receive medical care.

## Fungal Infections
### Candidiasis
#### Pathophysiology

*Candidiasis* is an inflammatory reaction in the skin or mucous membranes that results from an epidermal infection by *Candida albicans*. The skin infection presents as a "beefy," red erythematous area with surrounding satellite papules and pustules, usually at sites of increased moisture and warmth. Oral infection, or *thrush*, appears as white plaques attached to mucous membranes, which may bleed when plaques are scraped off. *Vulvovaginitis* may have a white, cheesy discharge; the severity of discomfort increases with the degree of erythema and edema.

*C. albicans* is not pathogenic and normally colonizes in the skin and bowel, particularly the colon. The resulting inflammatory response causes dermatitis and prevents invasion of deeper tissues. Predisposing factors include the use of systemic antibiotics, diabetes mellitus, and the use of oral contraceptives.

#### Medical Diagnosis and Management

Medical diagnosis of candidiasis is usually confirmed when a potassium hydroxide examination of affected tissue is positive for hyphae and pseudohyphae. Medical treatment usually includes topical application of an antifungal agent (nystatin, miconazole, clortrimazole). Keeping the affected skin dry is important in diaper candidiasis and when the infection is present in skin folds. Nystatin oral suspension is often used for thrush. Clortrimazole or miconazole are usually used for vulvovaginitis. For severe symptoms in paronychia, vulvovaginitis, or candidiasis of the skin, a topical corticosteroid is useful. A follow-up visit 5 to 7 days after starting treatment is needed to determine effectiveness of the treatment.

### Nursing Assessment and Diagnosis

Nursing assessment includes noting signs of pain or discomfort at the site of the yeast infection and signs of irritability in infants. Areas of skin subjected to trauma and areas of denuded skin should be noted. The nurse should assess the child's and parents' understanding of the yeast infection, the signs and symptoms, treatment, medications and side effects, expected outcomes, associated problems, and recognition of superimposed infections. General hygiene used in caring for an infant and possible exposure to bacteria should be determined.

Nursing diagnoses for candidiasis might include the following:

- Pain related to dermal eruptions
- Impaired skin integrity related to lesions

### Planning and Implementing Nursing Care

Parents should be instructed to keep the area clean, dry, and covered with antifungal cream. The child should wear nonirritating materials such as cotton. Parents should be educated about the need to protect infected skin from excoriations, even mild trauma. The child and parents should be taught about the disease, its cause, treatment, medications and side effects, and expected outcomes. Parents should be taught to monitor the skin for signs of superimposed infection as well as how to maintain skin hygiene and proper handwashing techniques.

### Evaluating Nursing Care

The child should feel more comfortable, and the parents should report that the child is less irritable. Parents should express an understanding of the need to protect the infected skin and to monitor for signs of superimposed infection. The child and parents should demonstrate an understanding of the disease, its cause, and its treatment. No additional denuded areas should occur in the infected site.

## Tinea

### Pathophysiology

*Tinea* is a superficial fungal infection of soft keratin (the outer skin layer) or of hard keratin (the hair and nails) by a fungal parasite. The infection causes a variety of lesions, but the most common are usually pruritic, scaling, erythematous papules, plaques, and patches, often with a serpiginous (snakelike) border. Common examples of tinea in children include tinea capitis, tinea corporis, tinea faciali, tinea cruris, tinea manuum, and tinea pedis.

*Tinea capitis,* or ringworm of the scalp, is caused by *Microsporum canis* (from dogs), *M. audouinii,* and *Trichophyton tonsurans. T. tonsurans* is the most common cause. Infective organisms may be transmitted directly or through infected combs, hats, barber scissors, and so forth. Prepubertal children are the most susceptible to infection. Ringworm of the scalp usually presents as a round, scaling area of alopecia. It may progress to a red, boggy, swollen, pustular area (kerion; see Color Fig. 34-11).

*Tinea corporis,* or ringworm of the body, occurs most commonly in children. Usually, there is a history of exposure to a dog or cat. The infecting organisms are usually *M. canis* or *Trichophyton mentagrophytes.* The infection may present with one or several annular lesions that have an elevated, scaling border and central clearing (see Color Fig. 34-12). The lesions are usually only mildly pruritic and are found on most exposed areas of the body, including the arms, face, and shoulders.

*Tinea faciali,* or ringworm of the face, is also commonly seen in children. The lesions are usually erythematous and scaly and may have a butterfly-like pattern of distribution. Pustules may be present.

*Tinea cruris* is an erythematous, scaly eruption on the inner thighs and inguinal creases. The scrotum is seldom involved. The infection is unusual before adolescence. Athlete's foot may also be present. Tinea cruris is more common in athletes and other physically active adolescents because of increased moisture from perspiration.

*Tinea manuum,* or ringworm of the hand, occurs without the child originally having tinea of the feet. Tinea manuum usually affects only one hand. It is more common in the postpubertal adolescent.

*Tinea pedis,* or ringworm of the feet, is caused by *Trichophyton mentagrophytes* or *T. rubrum.* Tinea pedis appears in three clinical forms: fissures between the toes, with the surrounding skin erythematous and scaling; vesicles and erosions on the instep, usually of one foot; or diffuse scaling of one or both feet, with increased scaling in the skin creases (see Color Fig. 34-13). Tinea pedis is more common in the postpubertal adolescent.

### Medical Diagnosis and Management

Tinea infections are usually diagnosed after potassium hydroxide examination of scale (skin tinea) or of hair and follicles (scalp tinea). The most common organism causing tinea capitis (*T. tonsurans*) does not fluoresce under a Wood's light. Identifying and treating the human or animal source is also recommended.

Tinea capitis must be treated by a 1- to 3-month course of oral griseofulvin. Ketoconazole may be given orally in resistant cases. Topical antifungal agents are not recommended. Selenium shampoo (e.g., Selsun) can reduce the number of fungal organisms on the hair.

Tinea corporis may be treated with clotrimazole, miconazole, haloprogin, and tolnaftate cream or solution twice a day to all lesions. With this treatment, the lesions usually clear in 2 to 3 weeks. A follow-up visit in 2 weeks can be helpful.

Tinea faciali may be treated topically with clotrimazole, miconazole, or haloprogin creams. Lesions usually clear in 2 to 3 weeks.

Tinea cruris must be distinguished from candidiasis and intertrigo. It may be treated with clotrimazole, miconazole, or haloprogin creams until the lesions clear. It is also important to keep the affected area dry.

Tinea manuum and tinea pedis are usually diagnosed clinically. Examining scrapings of the lesions in potassium hydroxide solution on a slide is diagnostic if the differential is questionable. For mild interdigital lesions of the feet, effective treatment consists of using an antifungal powder, such as tolnaftate, and keeping the area dry. Otherwise, creams of clotrimazole, miconazole, or haloprogin should be applied two to three times a day. Domeboro soaks, two to four times a day, are recommended for acute lesions that are blistered and oozing.

### Nursing Assessment and Diagnosis

Nursing assessment includes noting the characteristics, distribution, and extent of the lesions; excoriations from scratching; and the child's complaints of itching. The skin should be observed for signs of secondary bacterial infection. All skin areas should be examined for tinea infections. The child's and parents' understanding of the disease, treatment, appropriate use of drugs, and prevention of transmission should be evaluated. Their practices in caring for the condition and their general hygiene should be assessed. The nurse should also assess the child's and parents' feelings of comfort with the diagnosis, and their perceptions of others' responses to the disease.

Nursing diagnoses for tinea might include the following:

- Pain related to pruritus
- High risk for infection related to skin breakdown
- Impaired skin integrity related to excoriation
- Body image disturbance related to appearance

### Planning and Implementing Nursing Care

The child and parents should be instructed in consistent use of the prescribed medication, whether topical or systemic. They should understand that an antihistamine may help reduce kerion. The lesions should be kept clean and should be washed to reduce spores. The parents and child should be taught how to prevent possible secondary infections; the cause of the disease; its treatment; its transmission to other areas of the body and to other people; and

the need for continued treatment, including the use of medications and treatment of the source. The nurse should encourage the expression of feelings about the diagnosis, the appearance, and the possible responses of others.

### Evaluating Nursing Care

The child should report reduced feelings of itching. The parents and child should be able to demonstrate their understanding of the cause of the disease, its treatment, and its transmission. The child and parents should express increased comfort with their feelings about tinea and should report using methods recommended to prevent transmission of the disease.

## Bacterial Infections
### Pathophysiology

Bacterial infections include abscesses, cellulitis, folliculitis, and furuncles. Most bacterial skin infections are caused by *Staphylococcus aureus* or group A, β-hemolytic streptococci. *S. aureus* can colonize the skin and may enter through traumatized stratum corneum or a hair follicle. Group A streptococci usually is inoculated in damaged skin (e.g., scratches, insect bites), and a subsequent infection is established.

*Abscesses* and *furuncles* are pus-filled nodules in the dermis. They are usually caused by *S. aureus.* The nodules are red, tender, and fluctuant. *Cellulitis* is a deep skin infection that causes localized erythematous areas. It is usually caused by group A streptococci or *S. aureus. Folliculitis* is an inflammation of a hair follicle or follicles and is usually caused by staphylococci.

### Medical Diagnosis and Management

The diagnosis of bacterial infections is made on the basis of clinical findings. Gram-positive cocci will be found in staphylococcal folliculitis. A culture may be done. Abscesses and furuncles may be incised, and a culture may be done on the purulent material obtained.

For mild cases of folliculitis, an antiseptic cleanser should be used every day for several weeks. More severe cases should be treated with a systemic antibiotic (e.g., erythromycin) for 7 to 10 days. The primary treatment of abscesses and furuncles is incision and drainage, followed by systemic erythromycin or penicillinase-resistant penicillin. Cellulitis is treated with a systemic antibiotic. For mild cases or infection located on an extremity, treatment consists of a systemic antibiotic, warm soaks, and bed rest. For severe infections or those located on the face, the child is hospitalized and given intravenous antibiotics.

### Nursing Assessment and Diagnosis

Nursing assessment includes the identification of localized pain and its intensity as well as behavioral indicators (crying and irritability). The parents' and child's understanding of the cause of the lesions, treatment, expected outcomes, and complications should be assessed. Signs or symptoms of infection, on any skin area, including fevers and systemic infection, should be noted. In addition, the parents' and child's practices in treating the condition, the general hygiene of the skin, and handwashing practices should be assessed.

Nursing diagnoses for bacterial infections might include the following:

- Pain related to pruritus
- High risk for infection related to loss of skin integrity

### Planning and Implementing Nursing Care

Warm soaks can be applied to areas of infection. Pressure on the area (such as from tight clothing) should be prevented. The parents and child should be informed that using a systemic antibiotic will improve localized symptoms. The child and parents should be educated about the cause, signs and symptoms, and treatment of the infection as well as about the appropriate use of prescribed medications and their side effects and complications. The child may require hospitalization in severe cases.

### Evaluating Nursing Care

The child should experience decreased pain in the affected area, and parents should report less irritability. The child and parents should be able to demonstrate an understanding of the cause and treatment of bacterial infections. They should also be able to express their understanding of the possibility of the spread of the infection.

## Drug Reactions

### Pathophysiology

Drug reactions may occur in response to systemic or topical drugs. The reactions vary but may include exanthema, urticaria, bullae, or purpura. Immediate allergic reactions occur within 1 hour and include manifestations of anaphylaxis.

Accelerated reactions occur in 1 to 72 hours and usually consist of itching and hives. Late reactions may occur more than 3 days after initiation of drug therapy and may be manifested by urticaria, serum sickness, or exanthematous eruptions (the most common reaction).

In hives, immunoglobulin E is the most common immunological mechanism, resulting in histamine release from mast cells. Other drugs can cause direct release of histamine from mast cells. The mechanism for the exanthematous (morbilliform) eruption is not clear.

### Medical Diagnosis and Management

The expression, "for any rash, think drug," shows the variety of lesions that can result from drug reactions. Medical diagnosis is made on the basis of a complete history and the clinical appearance of the rash. No laboratory tests can diagnose a drug eruption or indicate a specific drug. Skin tests are available only for penicillin and only for symptoms of hives and anaphylaxis.

Treatment for less serious reactions generally consists of withdrawal of the drug. More serious reactions may require oral antihistamines, soothing tepid water baths, drying antipruritic lotions, topical steroids, or systemic corticosteroids by mouth. Treatment protocols for anaphylaxis include adrenaline, antihistamines, and systemic steroids.

### Nursing Assessment and Diagnosis

Nursing assessment includes noting the extent and character of the lesions; irritability or fussiness in infants; complaints of itching in older children; observed scratching; and edema. Observation of signs of anaphylactic shock and respiratory distress should be noted immediately. The nurse should ascertain the child's and parents' understanding of the cause, treatment, and expected outcomes of the lesions. The nurse should assess the child's general hygiene measures. The extent of the lesions, any breaks in the skin, and whether blisters are intact or broken should be noted.

Nursing diagnoses for drug reactions might include the following:

- Pain related to pruritus
- Fluid volume excess related to edema
- Impaired skin integrity related to excoriation

### Planning and Implementing Nursing Care

The nurse should encourage the appropriate use of antihistamines. The child should be kept as cool as possible, and nonirritating materials should be worn. The child should be monitored for anaphylactic reactions, and the nurse must be prepared to institute emergency protocols. The nursing care plan should include education of the child and parents about the cause of the drug reaction, the child's response, the treatment, and expected outcomes. The need to prevent trauma and abrasions to affected skin should be emphasized. In particular, parents should be warned not to rupture the bullae. Keeping the child's nails trimmed daily helps reduce excoriations. Parents must be able to provide the drug name and the child's reaction in future health care situations in order to avoid future reactions. A "Medic-Alert" bracelet may be recommended for severe allergies.

Alterations in Integumentary Function 983

## Evaluating Nursing Care

The child should experience decreased sensations of itching. Parents should observe that the infant is less irritable. If the child has an anaphylactic reaction, emergency treatment is necessary. The child and parents should demonstrate understanding of the cause of the reaction, treatment, and expected outcomes, as well as the need to advise future health care providers. In addition, there should be no increased damage to the skin from external forces or trauma.

# Acute Integumentary Problems

## Burns

Burn injuries, especially in children, are among the most critical and frightening situations nurses encounter. Each year, two million people receive medical attention for burns; 7800 die; and 30% of these deaths occur in children under the age of 15 (Behrman & Vaughan, 1987). Fires and burns cause the greatest number of accidental deaths at home of 1- to 14-year-old children (East, 1988).

Most burns result from accidents at home caused by carelessness or ignorance. Most could have been prevented. Typically, infants and toddlers are burned by scalding, either in the bath or when they pull hot liquids from a stove. The curiosity of preschool and school-aged children may lead them to play with matches or experiment with fire. Most burns in adolescents come from flames, either from combustible fuels or other solvents. Although hot liquid and flame burns are the most common, chemicals and electricity also cause burns. Prevention is an important aspect of burn care of children.

### Pathophysiology

Since the skin is the largest organ of the body and has numerous functions, destruction of the skin from a major burn causes many serious physiological consequences. No organ system is left untouched. Since various body systems are maturing during infancy and childhood, children have an especially difficult time maintaining homeostasis after a serious burn. For example, infants are at higher risk for complications from burn injuries because of their immature fluid and electrolyte regulatory mechanisms and the decreased ability of their immune systems to fight off secondary infections.

The pathophysiology and patient care of burn injuries are organized into three stages: the resuscitative stage, the acute stage, and the rehabilitative stage. The *resuscitative stage* occurs during the first 72 hours after the burn. The hypovolemic and diuretic phases are substages used to describe fluid shifts that occur during the first 72 hours. The *acute stage* may last from several weeks to months.

The *rehabilitative stage* occurs from several months to years after the initial trauma.

*Fluids and Electrolytes.* Major burns cause changes in fluid and electrolyte balance that are even more critical in children than in adults. (For a discussion of fluid and electrolytes, see Chap. 28.) Shifts in fluids and electrolytes are caused by tissue damage, increased capillary permeability, and changes in hydrostatic pressure within the capillaries.

Immediately after the burn, tissue damage results in loss of large amounts of fluid and protein through the burn wound. Even in areas that are not burned, fluid and protein are lost from increased capillary permeability, or "holes" in the capillaries. This fluid accumulates in interstitial spaces, resulting in edema. In addition, loss of protein results in changes in hydrostatic pressure, which causes more fluid to ooze into interstitial spaces.

Stress results in the secretion of aldosterone, which helps the body retain sodium. Despite this mechanism, serum sodium levels are decreased since sodium is lost in burn exudate and edema. Serum potassium is elevated because damaged cells release it into the bloodstream, and sluggish kidneys are slow to excrete it. Because of massive fluid loss, this initial stage is described as the *hypovolemic phase.* Shock is a major problem during the first 24 to 48 hours after the injury.

The *diuretic phase* usually begins 48 to 72 hours after the burn, when rapidly healing capillaries can again contain fluid and proteins within the bloodstream. Fluid in interstitial spaces is drawn back into blood vessels. Diuresis occurs as extra volume in the circulatory system is excreted by the kidneys that are now functioning more effectively. Sodium continues to be lost in burn exudate and through diuresis. Also, serum potassium levels fall during this stage.

*The Circulatory System.* During the hypovolemic stage, shock is a major problem. The body attempts to maintain blood flow to vital organs such as the brain and heart at the expense of other organs such as the kidneys and intestines. Acute renal failure and formation of Curling's or stress ulcers are complications of hypovolemia.

Circulation to the periphery may also be compromised. If burns of the digits are circumferential, constriction by burn tissue may further diminish circulation and can result in loss of fingers and toes.

Heat destroys red blood cells; however, anemia is not evident initially because of hemoconcentration from fluid losses. Anemia usually develops within 4 to 7 days after the injury (Behrman & Vaughan, 1987).

*The Respiratory System.* The leading cause of complications and death in burn patients is not the burn itself but inhalation injury (Lybarger, 1987). The respiratory system of a burned child must be assessed carefully, especially if there are burns on the face and neck. These conditions, as well as a history of burns sustained within an enclosed space, suggest inhalation injury, as does black, sooty sputum (Gaston, 1980).

Heat and toxic substances released during fires cause inflammation and damage to the mucosal lining of the respiratory tract, stimulating mucus production and swelling that can result in obstruction and pulmonary edema (Desai, 1984). Carbon monoxide poisoning causes systemic problems such as tissue hypoxia from reduced oxygen-carrying capacity of hemoglobin (Desai, 1984). Chemical injury to the lower airway can result in pneumonia and adult respiratory distress syndrome (Lybarger, 1987). Circumferential chest wounds cause constriction that limits pulmonary expansion. The end result is decreased air exchange and tissue hypoxia.

*Acid–Base Balance.* Metabolic acidosis usually occurs in the burned patient. Decreased blood flow to tissues from hypovolemia results in tissue hypoxia. The tissues begin anaerobic metabolism, which results in accumulation of acidic by-products. Acidosis is compensated by respiratory alkalosis.

*The Immune System.* One of the major functions of the skin is to prevent invasion by microorganisms that cause infections. With the protective layer burned away, germs invade the body because dead skin is an excellent medium for their growth. The child's immature immune system, coupled with decreased protein levels, diminishes the ability to fight infection and creates an atmosphere that is favorable to sepsis.

*The Gastrointestinal System.* Metabolism increases dramatically in the child who has sustained a large burn. The body requires large amounts of various nutrients, especially calories, proteins, vitamins, and minerals, to rebuild and replace burned tissue and to fight infection.

Also, since burned skin can no longer maintain temperature balance, hyperthermia and hypothermia frequently occur. Body temperature fluctuations impose further nutritional demands since calories must be expended to maintain normothermia.

Decreased gastrointestinal motility, as well as Curling or stress ulcers, are frequent complications of burn trauma. All these factors, coupled with the sick child's diminished appetite, create serious nutritional problems.

*The Neurological System.* Neurological dysfunctions develop in some children with burns and seem to be the result of cerebral edema. Just as fluid shifts in other parts of the body cause edema, extracellular fluid also increases in the brain. Clinical features may include coma, disorientation, irritability, and seizures (Kaye, 1988).

*The Musculoskeletal System.* The musculoskeletal effects of burns become evident during the acute and rehabilitative stages of burn care. Contracture and scar formation occur in healing of all wounds but are especially troublesome in the pediatric burn patient.

As healing progresses, new cells exert a centripetal pull on surrounding tissues, resulting in a decrease in size of skin coverage of the wound. When the wound is over a joint, this process produces a *contracture* (Fig. 34-3).

As scar tissue matures, increasing amounts of inelastic collagen form, producing more contractures and hypertrophic scarring. This process peaks 3 to 6 months after the burn and continues until skin growth is complete (Wagner, 1981).

*Assessment of Size and Burn Depth.* Because a child's body parts are proportionately different from those of an adult, the "rule of nines" method for determining size or percentage of the body burned in adults is not accurate for children. Figure 34-4 shows an adaptation of the rule of nines to body surface area of various ages. Using the adapted charts, the percentage of body surface burned is determined by estimating what percentages of limbs, trunk, and head are burned, and adding the percentages. These assessments aid in directing medical treatment and in anticipating scarring and healing time. The extent of the burn must also be determined. Classifications and descriptions of burn depth are shown in Table 34-5.

### Medical Management

At the scene of the injury, the primary goal of treatment is to stop the burning process. If clean, cold water is available, the wound should be soaked. Ice water should not be used because the ice can cause further tissue damage (Zuker, 1988). Airway patency, breathing effectiveness, and circulatory status must be assessed. If inhalation injury is expected, humidified 100% oxygen should be provided (Lybarger, 1987).

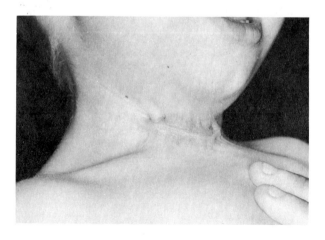

*Figure 34–3. Contracture following a burn injury. (Pillitteri, A. [1987]. Child health nursing. Philadelphia: J.B. Lippincott, p. 1319)*

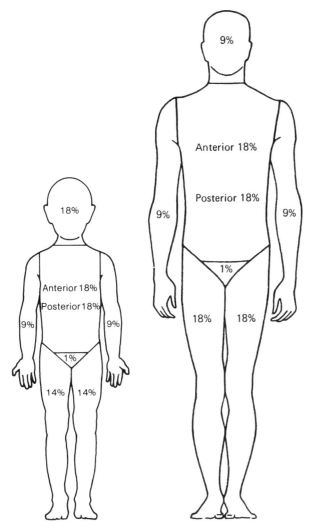

*Figure 34–4. Adaptation of the "rule of nines" for estimation of body surface area in burned children. (Adapted from Scherer, J.C. [1986].* Introductory medical-surgical nursing *[4th ed.]. Philadelphia: J.B. Lippincott, p. 687)*

***Resuscitative Stage.*** During the *resuscitative stage,* the burned child is assessed and treated for airway and breathing problems, especially if there is evidence of smoke inhalation or airway burns. Cardiopulmonary function is determined, followed by a quick inspection of burn wounds and other injuries (Behrman & Vaughan, 1987).

An intravenous infusion of lactated Ringer's solution, isotonic saline, or plasma is begun using a large-bore catheter to replace lost fluids and maintain blood volume. The use of colloids, such as albumin, is controversial. Intravenous fluids are given during the first 24 hours to restore hydration, correct acid–base imbalances, and maintain perfusion of vital organs. Various formulas are used to calculate fluid requirements based on body surface and percentage of the body burned (Behrman & Vaughan, 1987). Fluid replacement is usually considered sufficient if urine output is at least 1 mL/kg/h.

Burn wounds are cleansed, then covered with topical antimicrobial agents and dressings. A tetanus booster is given for tetanus prophylaxis, and sometimes parenteral antibiotics are ordered (Mikhail, 1988). Sedatives and analgesics may also be administered, but the child must be observed carefully for respiratory depression caused by these drugs (Behrman & Vaughan, 1987; Carvajal, 1988).

Often, a nasogastric tube is inserted to prevent vomiting, and a urinary catheter is placed to measure urine output. The child is usually NPO for at least 24 hours.

***Acute Stage.*** During the *acute stage,* after the first 24 hours, fluid requirements are usually about three fourths of the first day's allowance. Albumin and packed red blood cells can be given during this stage to replace losses because the healed capillaries keep blood proteins within the intravascular space (Behrman & Vaughan, 1987). Also, potassium replacements may be given 36 to 48 hours after the injury to maintain electrolyte balance and prevent cardiac arrhythmia (Freeman, 1984).

*Table 34–5. Classification of Burn Depth*

| Traditional Classification | Description | Descriptive Classification |
|---|---|---|
| First degree | Injury only to outer layer of skin; painful, red; heals completely in a few days (e.g., sunburn) | Superficial burns |
| Second degree | Injury to epidermis; blister formation; weeping of fluid; painful; heals in 14–17 days | Superficial burns |
| | | Partial-thickness burns |
| | Partial injury to dermis; may heal in 3–4 weeks; may become deeper from ischemia and infection | Deep burns |
| Third degree | Epidermis and dermis is destroyed; hair follicles and nerve endings are destroyed; no pain; can heal only with graft | Full-thickness burns |
| Fourth degree | Total destruction of skin with injury to fat, muscle, or bone; needs grafting | |

Milk feedings may be started by mouth, if tolerated, and the diet progresses to soft foods on the second or third day. Providing food helps the stomach prevent the formation of Curling ulcers. If drainage from the nasogastric tube contains blood, cimetidine (Tagamet) or antacids, or both, may be given.

The child's body requires large amounts of various nutrients to rebuild and replace burned tissue while maintaining normal growth. Energy needs may increase 200% above normal requirements; this extra need may continue for weeks or even months after the burn (Robinson, Lawler, Chenoweth, & Garwick, 1986). The following formula (Robinson, Lawler, Chenoweth, & Garwick, 1986) is one of many used to calculate caloric needs of children:

$$40 - 60 \text{ kcal/kg (preburn body weight)} + 40 \text{ kcal (percent burn)} = \text{caloric need}$$

For example, a 10-kg baby with a 40% burn needs 2200 kcal/day. Normal caloric needs for a healthy 10-kg infant would be about 1000 kcal/day.

The use of total parenteral nutrition to deliver amino acids, glucose, fats, vitamins, and minerals intravenously to children eliminates the need to ingest such large quantities of food. Before the advent of total parenteral nutrition, many burned children died because they were unable to consume adequate nutrients.

When the gastrointestinal system can tolerate feedings, the child is encouraged to take high-quality protein foods by mouth. Since such large amounts of nutrients are required, continuous or intermittent nasogastric tube feedings, consisting of high-calorie formulas, may be used to supplement the ill child's often meager appetite.

During the acute stage, medical management also focuses on prevention of infection. Sepsis is the most dangerous threat to the burned child at this time since it is impossible to keep a burn wound sterile (Behrman & Vaughan, 1987). Therefore, it is essential to protect tissue and promote healing.

Wounds must be inspected and cultures obtained as indicated so that infections can be diagnosed quickly. Antibiotic therapy is initiated if there are any signs of infection.

Burn wounds are cleansed and debrided on a regular basis, often twice a day. The wounds are soaked and washed in the Hubbard tank or shower where, with the aid of whirlpool hydrotherapy, *eschar* (dead tissue) is removed (Fig. 34-5). Eschar provides an excellent medium for bacterial growth and prevents the regeneration of healthy tissue; it must be eliminated as soon as it forms. This procedure is a painful, frightening experience for the child, so expert nursing care and physical therapy must be provided. In some cases, eschar is so thick it must be surgically excised. This procedure is called an *escharotomy*.

After the burn wound is cleansed, various methods of treatment are used, including topical medications and dressings. Table 34-6 shows an overview of the various

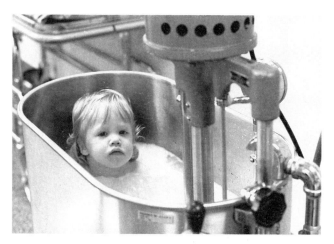

*Figure 34–5. Child receiving hydrotherapy in a Hubbard tank.*

types of topical medications used on burn wounds. Table 34-7 shows a comparison of different techniques of burn dressing.

Full-thickness burns must be grafted to heal. *Autografts,* in which skin is transferred from one part of the patient's body to another, are used. Almost any unburned area can be used as a donor site (Freeman, 1984). A *dermatome* (an instrument that cuts thin slices of skin) is used to harvest the skin, which is then meshed and stretched to provide as much coverage as possible. Dressings are placed over grafts and are left undisturbed for at least 72 hours. The graft should attach to underlying tissue and function like normal skin. Many grafts may be needed to cover the burn.

*Homografts* (skin from another human) or *heterografts* (skin from another species, usually a pig) are also used but are only temporary coverings to decrease pain, the possibility of infection, and fluid and heat loss. These types of grafts do not adhere to the wound (Wagner, 1981).

Two other important goals of medical management during the acute and rehabilitative stages are preserving joint function and minimizing scar formation. Even though musculoskeletal effects of burns become more evident during the rehabilitative stage of burn care, treatment must begin early in the acute stage. A team approach that involves physical therapists, occupational therapists, nurses, and physicians is necessary to meet these goals.

Prevention of contractures and scarring is accomplished through the use of positioning, splinting, exercise, and pressure (Wagner, 1981; Fader, 1988). Positioning is used primarily with patients confined to bed to promote functional use of joints. Children tend to assume a comfortable position, so they should be helped and checked frequently to maintain proper positioning.

Splinting is another form of positioning that is used to immobilize a body part (Fig. 34-6). Full-thickness burns should be splinted within 24 hours, but splinting can be delayed for other types of burns until problems arise (Fader, 1988).

*Table 34–6. Topical Medications Used in Burn Care*

| Medication | Action | Additional Information and Nursing Implications |
|---|---|---|
| Silver sulfadiazine (Silvadene) | Antimicrobial; damages bacterial cell wall; impairs DNA replication; broad-spectrum, including some fungi | Should be applied to a thickness of $1/16$ inch; does not sting; can cause transient leukopenia; used with open and closed techniques |
| Mafenide acetate (Sulfamylon) | Sulfonamide; broad-spectrum antimicrobial | Penetrates eschar rapidly and deeply; may cause metabolic acidosis; causes pain; readily absorbed from wound; usually used with open technique |
| Povidone-iodine | Broad-spectrum antiseptic | Used with open and semi-closed techniques; does not cause pain |
| Silver nitrate solution | Antimicrobial; inhibits bacterial growth | Leaves black stains; may cause electrolyte imbalances; minimal systemic absorption |
| Scarlet Red | Antimicrobial; provides low pH so bacteria will not grow | Used on donor sites and partial-thickness burn wounds; does not cause pain; promotes skin growth; stains red |
| Sutilains (Travase) | Proteolytic enzyme; dissolves nonviable protein and exudate | Used to debride wounds; may cause pain; no systemic toxicity |

Exercise programs are planned and initiated by physical therapists on the first day of admission. Passive and active range-of-motion exercises, as well as other types, are used both in and outside the whirlpool.

Pressure garments are also used to minimize scar formation (Fig. 34-7). Mechanical pressure is applied continuously to scars for 12 to 18 months after healing. Pressure garments are worn 23 hours per day and are removed only for bathing (Fader, 1988).

*Rehabilitation Stage.* The goals of care for the patient and family during the rehabilitation stage focus on preserving and promoting function, developing methods for coping with disfigurement, and promoting normal

*Table 34–7. Comparison of Open and Closed Methods of Burn Treatment*

| Method | Advantages | Disadvantages |
|---|---|---|
| Open: No dressings are used; burns are covered with topical antimicrobial | Allows for continual observation. Allows for easier movement of limbs. Less expensive. Exposure to air reduces risk of *Pseudomonas* infection | Frequent reapplication of topical antimicrobial is necessary. More painful. Burns are visible |
| Closed: Topical antimicrobial and dressings are used to cover wounds | Covering wounds reduces evaporation, heat loss, and pain. Burns are covered and thus are not so frightening to see. Less topical agent is used | More expensive in terms of materials and nursing care hours. Increased risk of *Pseudomonas* infection |

Both methods require cleansing of wounds in hydrotherapy and reapplication of topical antimicrobial, usually two or three times a day.

*Figure 34–6.  Splinting of a burn injury.*

growth and development. As these goals are met, children can again resume their normal place within their families and society. Care must be provided in a multidisciplinary team effort that includes nurses, physicians, physical and occupational therapists, psychologists, and social workers. This stage is most important for recovery and may continue for years after the injury.

## Nursing Diagnoses

Nursing diagnoses for burns might include the following:

- Pain related to tissue damage
- High risk for infection related to loss of protective covering of the skin

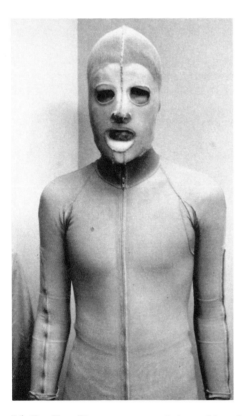

*Figure 34–7.  Use of pressure garments to avoid contractures and scar formation.*

- Altered nutrition: less than body requirements related to increased caloric needs and anorexia
- Fluid volume deficit related to dehydration caused by thermal injury
- Impaired physical mobility related to pain
- Activity intolerance related to pain
- Anxiety related to painful procedures, possible outcomes
- Fear related to painful procedures
- Social isolation related to need for infection control

## Planning and Implementing Nursing Care

Nursing care plans and interventions must consider the severity of the burns, the areas involved, and the treatment plan as well as education and psychological support for the child and family.

Immediately after a severe burn, the child must be observed for signs of shock. Electrolyte balance should be carefully monitored and imbalances treated as quickly as possible, usually by means of intravenous therapy, which replaces lost fluids and maintains blood volume. Usually a catheter is inserted to monitor urine output.

Analgesics and sedatives should be administered as prescribed. If the child is sedated, the nurse should carefully monitor the child's respiratory status.

The burn areas should be carefully cleansed and covered with topical antimicrobial dressings to prevent infection. The prevention of secondary infections is a primary consideration in caring for children with burns. Careful cleansing to remove dead tissue is often a nursing responsibility. The application of medications and sterile dressings is also a nursing responsibility.

When skin grafts are done, postsurgical care is employed. Dressings are usually changed by the physician, but not for at least 72 hours.

Greater nutritional demands after a burn necessitate increased caloric intake to maintain normal body temperature and promote wound healing. High-calorie, small feedings are usually well tolerated, even though the child has little appetite. If a nasogastric tube is inserted, the nurse must carefully observe and record any drainage, since blood may indicate the presence of Curling ulcers.

The child and family should be encouraged to express their feelings and discuss their concerns. The child may experience psychological problems related to the disfigurement of the burn or movement limitations. The child and family may need the support of psychologists or psychiatrists to cope with problems related to self-esteem and body image. Parents may need support if they feel guilt over the cause of the burn. The child and parents should be taught strategies for preventing burn injury in the future.

All nursing plans must include referrals to other appropriate health care specialists. Since severe burns require long-term planning and interventions, a team approach facilitates recovery.

### *Evaluating Nursing Care*

The most positive outcome for children who have been burned is recovery with minimal sequelae. For children with extensive burns, successful evaluation of nursing care includes the absence of infection, maintenance of hydration and nutrition, and minimal impairment of physical mobility. The child and family should demonstrate positive coping abilities and compliance with treatment regimens.

## *Summary*

The integumentary system is of critical importance to the overall health of children. Integumentary health problems may be limited to the skin, as in pigmented nevi; or they may be genetic and related to defects in other systems. Still other problems may result from immune responses, as in atopic dermatitis. Integumentary problems that alter children's appearance can significantly affect their body image and self-esteem, as may occur in adolescents with acne. In addition, health practices established in childhood can influence the health of the integumentary system later in life, as can be seen in the relationship between a sun tan and the development of skin cancer.

Burn injuries in children are one of the most frightening and complicated challenges nurses face; however, nurses who work with burned children and their families have many unique opportunities. Since burn injuries heal slowly, nurses maintain close contact with these patients over a long period of time and can observe a variety of health processes, coping skills, and family dynamics.

Nurses can offer much-needed care to children with integumentary problems and their families. Since integumentary problems affect all age groups, nurses have an opportunity to interact with children at various stages of growth and development and to provide holistic care for children and their families.

## References

American Academy of Pediatrics, Committee on Drugs. (1990). Clioquinol (Iodochlorhydroxyquin, Vioform) and iodoquinol (Diiodohydroxyquin): Blindness and neuropathy. *Pediatrics, 86*(5), 797–798.

Behrman, R. E., & Vaughan, V. C. (1987). *Nelson textbook of pediatrics* (13th ed.). Philadelphia: W. B. Saunders.

Carvajal, H. F. (1988). Resuscitation of the burned child. In Carvajal, H. F., & Parks, D. H. (Eds.). *Burns in children: Pediatric burn management.* Chicago: Year Book Medical Publishers.

Desai, M. H. (1984). Inhalation injuries in burn victims. *Critical Care Quarterly, 77*(3), 1–6.

East, M. K. (1988). Epidemiology of burns in children. In Carvajal, H. F., & Parks, D. H. (Eds.). *Burns in children: Pediatric burn management.* Chicago: Year Book Medical Publishers.

Fader, P. (1988). Preserving function and minimizing deformity: The role of the occupational therapist. In Carvajal, H. F., & Parks, D. H. (Eds.). *Burns in children: Pediatric burn management.* Chicago: Year Book Medical Publishers.

Freeman, J. W. (1984). Nursing care of the patient with a burn injury. *Critical Care Nurse, 4*(6), 52–67.

Gaston, S. F. (1980). Inhalation injury: Smoke inhalation. *American Journal of Nursing, 80*(1), 94–100.

Hidano, A., Purwoko, R., & Jitsukawa, K. (1986). Statistical survey of skin changes in Japanese neonates. *Pediatric Dermatology, 3*(2), 140–144.

Kawada, A. (1986). UVB-induced erythema, delayed tanning, and UVA-induced immediate tanning in Japanese skin. *Photodermatology, 3*(6), 327–333.

Kaye, E. M., & Butler, I. J. (1988). Neurologic complications of burns in childhood. In Carvajal, H. F., & Parks, D. H. (Eds.). *Burns in children: Pediatric burn management.* Chicago: Year Book Medical Publishers.

Lookingbill, D. P., & Marks, J. G. (1986). *Principles of dermatology.* Philadelphia: W. B. Saunders.

Lybarger, P. M. (1987). Inhalation injury in children: Nursing care. *Issues in Comprehensive Pediatric Nursing, 10*(1), 33–50.

Mikhail, J. N. (1988). Acute burn care: An update. *Journal of Emergency Nursing, 14*(1), 9–18.

Robinson, C. H., Lawler, M. R., Chenoweth, W. L., & Garwick, A. E. (1986). *Normal and therapeutic nutrition* (17th ed.). New York: Macmillan.

Wagner, M. M. (1981). *Care of the burn-injured patient.* Littleton, MA: PSG Publishing Company.

Zuker, R. M. (1988). Initial management of the burn wound. In Carvajal, H. F., & Parks, D. H. (Eds.). *Burns in children: Pediatric burn management.* Chicago: Year Book Medical Publishers.

## Bibliography

Atchison, N., Guercio, P., & Monaco, C. (1986). Pain in the pediatric burn patient: Nursing assessment and perception. *Issues in Comprehensive Pediatric Nursing, 9*(6) 399–409.

Bayley, E. W., & Smith, G. A. (1987). The three degrees of burn care. *Nursing 87, 17*(3), 34–41.

Clore, E. R. (1989). Dispelling common myths about pediculoses. *Journal of Pediatric Health Care, 3*(1), 28–33.

Coody, D. (1987). There is no such thing as a good tan. *Journal of Pediatric Health Care, 1*(3), 125–132.

Esterly, N. B. (1987). Cutaneous hemangiomas, vascular strains, and associated syndromes. *Current Problems in Pediatrics, 17*(1), 7–69.

Fisher, A. A. (1986). *Contact dermatitis* (3rd ed.). Philadelphia: Lea & Febiger.

Guzzo, C., Honig, P. J., & Rabinowitz, L. G. (1987). Fungal infections from head to toe. *Patient Care, 21*(9), 62–66.

Hildreth, M., & Carvajal, H. F. (1982). Caloric requirements in burned children: A simple formula to estimate daily caloric requirements. *Journal of Burn Care Rehabilitation, 3*(2), 78–80.

Joyner, M. (1988). Hair care in the black patient. *Journal of Pediatric Health Care, 2*(6), 281–287.

Longmire, A. W., & Broom, L. A. (1987). Vietnamese coin rubbing. *Annals of Emergency Medicine, 16*(5), 602.

Lookingbill, D. P., & Marks, J. G. (1986). *Principles of dermatology.* Philadelphia: W. B. Saunders.

McDonald, C. J. (1988). Structure and function of the skin: Are there differences between black and white skin? *Dermatologic Clinics, 6*(3), 343–347.

McLaurin, C. I. (1988). Cutaneous reaction patterns in blacks. *Dermatologic Clinics, 6*(3), 353–362.

McLaurin, C. I. (1988). Pediatric dermatology in black patients. *Dermatologic Clinics, 6*(3), 457–473.

Mosley, S. (1988). Inhalation injury: A review of the literature. *Heart & Lung, 17*(1), 3–9.

Nicol, N. H. (1987). Atopic dermatitis: The (wet) wrap-up. *American Journal of Nursing, 87*(12), 1560–1563.

Overfield, T. (1985). *Biologic variation in health and illness: Race, age, and sex differences.* Menlo Park, CA: Addison-Wesley.

Parks, B. R. (1988). Use of topical steroids in children. *Pediatric Nursing, 14*(4), 337–340.

Philbin, P., & Marvin, J. A. (1982). Management of the pediatric patient with a major burn. *Journal of Burn Care Rehabilitation, 3*(2), 118–125.

Primeaux, M. H. (1977). American Indian health care practices. *Nursing Clinics of North America, 12*(1), 55–65.

Primeaux, M. H. (1977). Caring for the American Indian patient. *American Journal of Nursing, 77*(1), 91–94.

Quan, M., & Strick, R. A. (1988). Management of acne vulgaris. *American Family Physician, 38*(2), 207–218.

Rook, A., Wilkinson, D. S., Ebling, F. J. G., Champion, R. H., & Burton, J. L. (Eds.). (1986). *Textbook of dermatology* (4th ed.), Vol. 1. Boston: Blackwell Scientific Publications.

Rosen, T., & Martin, S. (1981). *Atlas of Black dermatology.* Boston: Little, Brown & Company.

Sauer, G. C. (1991). *Manual of skin diseases* (6th ed.). Philadelphia: J. B. Lippincott.

Weston, W. L. (1986). *Practical pediatric dermatology* (2nd ed.). Boston: Little, Brown & Company.

# Alterations in Sensory Function

Patricia T. Castiglia

Photograph by David Finn

35

*Embryology*

*Anatomy and Physiology*

*Assessment*

*Nursing Diagnosis*

*Planning Nursing Care*

*Nursing Interventions*

*Evaluating Nursing Care*

*Congenital Vision Problems*

*Vision Problems of Infants
and Toddlers*

*Vision Problems of Preschool- and
School-Aged Children*

*Visual Problems of Adolescents*

*Acute Vision Problems*

*Chronic Vision Problems*

*Hearing Problems of Infants and
Toddlers*

*Hearing Problems of Children and
Adolescents*

*Nasal Problems of Infants, Toddlers,
and Adolescents*

*Summary*

*Nursing Care Plan*

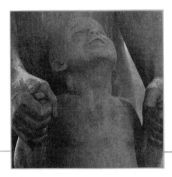

### Learning Objectives

*Upon completion of this chapter the reader will be able to:*

1. *Discuss the anatomy and physiology of the eye, the ear, the nose, and the taste buds.*

2. *Describe assessment techniques for vision, hearing, smell, and taste.*

3. *Identify appropriate nursing diagnoses for sensory disorders.*

4. *Develop nursing care plans and identify appropriate nursing interventions for sensory function disorders.*

5. *Develop an evaluation plan for the identified nursing interventions.*

6. *Describe the following disorders that can affect vision: congenital cataracts, congenital and juvenile glaucoma, dacryostenosis, retinopathy of prematurity, ophthalmia neonatorum, trachoma inclusion conjunctivitis, strabismus, retinoblastoma, rhabdomyosarcoma, myopia, hyperopia, astigmatism, styes, retinal detachment, and trauma.*

7. *Discuss the concept of legal blindness and identify nursing responsibilities for the affected child and family.*

8. *Describe the following disorders that affect hearing: acute otitis media, chronic middle-ear effusion, mastoiditis, and otitis externa.*

9. *Discuss the impact of noise on hearing.*

10. *Describe the following nasal disorders: acute nasopharyngitis, acute pharyngitis, sinusitis, and allergic rhinitis.*

### Key Terms

*accommodation*

*aqueous humor*

*cerumen*

*conjunctiva*

*cornea*

*eustachian tube*

*lacrimal gland*

*nystagmus*

*refraction*

*retina*

*tympanic membrane*

*vitreous humor*

Although alterations and problems in sensory function are seldom life-threatening, they can have a serious impact on a child's ability to achieve normal growth and development. Through the senses of sight, hearing, smell, taste, and touch, children discover themselves, their families and other people, and the world around them. Although sensory disorders can be as transient and minor as a common cold, they can also be as permanent and devastating as blindness or deafness. Each of the chapters in Unit III discusses ways in which the sensory system can enhance normal growth and development. This chapter explores ways in which nurses can provide anticipatory guidance to prevent sensory problems, help children and families recover from alterations in sensory function, and assist children and families in adapting to sensory loss.

## Embryology

The eye begins to develop in the first 4 weeks of gestation. It begins as an evagination of the lateral aspect of the forebrain. The embryonic optic stalk becomes the optic nerve, and the larger distal portion becomes the optic cup. The optic cup has two layers, which form the retina. Most of the development of the eye is completed by the first trimester of gestation. It is known, for example, that if a mother contracts rubella during this point in gestation, the lenses of the eyes may be affected, and the child may develop cataracts. Rod and cone cells and ganglionic cells develop by the 6th month. The cornea and sclera are formed from the outer layer surrounding the optic and lens vesicles. The sclera becomes continuous with the dura mater of the brain. The upper and lower eyelids are present by the 12th week of gestation, but they are fused. The conjunctival sac is in the fused space. By the 24th week, the eyelashes and eyebrows are more defined.

The ear is fairly well developed by the 3rd month of pregnancy. The pinna of the outer ear is well defined by the 7th week of gestation. By 11 weeks it resembles the adult ear. The eustachian tube and the tympanic cavity form from the same embryonic pharyngeal pouch. As the tympanic cavity expands, the auditory ossicles (incus, stapes, and malleus) become suspended.

The nose develops from the palate, which is formed in the 7th week of gestation. From the palate, the turbinate cartilage eventually forms into turbinate bones. The foundation of olfactory development occurs during the 4th week of gestation.

## Anatomy and Physiology

### The Eye

The eye is composed of an external and an internal eye. The *external eye* is composed of the eyelids, tear duct apparatus (lacrimal glands), conjunctiva, and cornea. The *internal eye* is composed of the sclera, iris, pupil, lens, ciliary body, retina, and vitreous chamber. Figure 35-1 shows the internal and external structures of the eye.

The eyelids and eyelashes act to protect the eyes. The eyelids also provide lubrication to the eye, and blinking the eyelids distributes the lubricant. The conjunctiva lines the lids and is continuous with the anterior portion of the

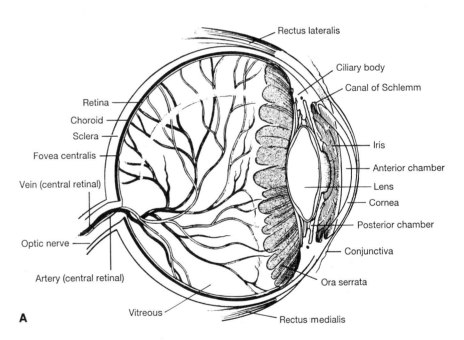

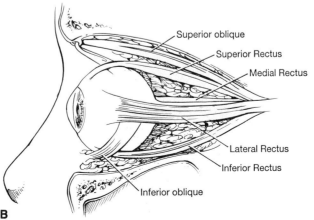

*Figure 35–1. Internal (A) and external (B) structure of the eye.*

eye globe. It is thin and transparent and contains many small blood vessels. The lacrimal gland is located superior and slightly lateral to the globe and functions to produce tears. Tears serve to lubricate the eye. The cornea is a clear, curved, smooth, fine-layered cover protecting the iris and the pupil. It is relatively large in newborns (about 10 mm) and achieves adult size (12 mm) by age 2 (Behrman & Vaughan, 1987).

The sclera is the white, fibrous outer covering of the globe. It is the location of the insertion of the extraocular muscles (see Fig. 35-1). An iris that is light blue in newborns may change color as the child matures. The newborn's pupils tend to be small. When a light is shined in one pupil, both pupils constrict; this is called the *pupillary reflex.* The purpose of the lens, which is transparent, is to focus light on the retina. The ciliary muscles control the size of the lens. When contracted, these muscles allow the lens to *accommodate* (adjust for near and far vision); when the muscles relax, accommodation ceases. The ciliary body is located in a circle behind the iris. The secretory component of the ciliary body assists in the circulation of fluids in the eye.

The *aqueous humor*, the fluid produced in the eye, is clear and is located between the iris and the cornea. The *vitreous humor,* a transparent, avascular gel, is located behind the lens and in front of the retina. The *retina* is the innermost layer of the eye and contains the *optic disc,* the *macula,* and the *retinal vessels.* The retina is composed of *rods,* which are necessary for night vision and visual field movement, and *cones,* which register color and daylight. Light impulses are transmitted from the retina to the optic nerve, through the optic tract, then to the midbrain and the visual cortex of the occipital region of the brain.

Light rays must pass to the retina by passing through the cornea, the aqueous humor, the lens, and the vitreous humor. Defects in these structures may block or distort the image. Most vision defects are caused by *refractive errors.*

Ordinarily, light rays bend as they pass through the lens and fall on the retina. The light rays may focus in front of the retina, resulting in *myopia* (nearsightedness), or behind the retina, resulting in *hyperopia* (farsightedness).

## The Ear

The ear is usually divided into three compartments (Fig. 35-2). The *external ear* is composed of the auricle, the external auditory canal, and the lateral surface of the *tympanic membrane* (eardrum). The tympanic membrane vibrates when struck by sound waves and transmits these sound waves to the middle ear. The *middle ear* lies between the tympanic membrane and the inner ear. The middle ear is filled with air and the *ossicles* (malleus, incus, and stapes), which bridge the gap to the inner ear. The function of the ossicles is to transmit sound waves to the inner ear.

The *eustachian tube* connects the middle ear and the nasopharynx and acts to clear secretions and to equalize pressure between the middle ear and the atmosphere. Since it tends to be wider and shorter in children than in adults, the eustachian tube does not have the advantage of a downward curve that facilitates drainage. The shape of the eustachian tube is thought to be a contributing factor to the greater incidence of middle-ear infections in children. The eustachian tube can be obstructed by infection, allergy, enlarged adenoids, or functional conditions, such as the anatomical position of the tube in infants or a cleft palate.

The inner ear contains the *cochlea* and the *vestibular apparatus*—the *semicircular canal.* The semicircular canal responds to movement of the head and, along with visual orientation, helps to maintain balance and to regulate body position. *Corti's organ,* the sense organ of hearing, is located in the cochlea. When the sensory cells in Corti's organ are bent by vibrations, a transmission occurs

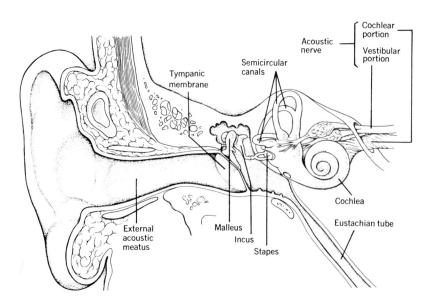

*Figure 35–2. Anatomy of the ear.*

along the auditory pathway to the cerebral cortex. Coding of the pitch and intensity of sound occurs in the auditory pathway.

## The Nose

The nose comprises both external and internal structures (Fig. 35-3). The external nose consists of the nasal bones, part of the maxilla, and cartilage (composing the lower two thirds of the nose). The internal nose is composed of two cavities separated by the nasal septum. Three turbinates (conchae) project from the lateral wall and open to the paranasal sinuses.

The olfactory region for the nose is located between the nasal septum and the superior turbinate. The olfactory nerve is the first cranial nerve; it innervates the olfactory epithelium. There are four pairs of paranasal sinuses: the maxillary, the ethmoid, the frontal, and the sphenoid. The ethmoid and maxillary sinuses are developed in infancy; the frontal sinuses develop at 7 or 8 years of age, and the sphenoid sinuses develop after puberty. There are no known functions for the paranasal sinuses. They are non-collapsible, nonexpandable, bony cavities that are usually filled with air. An infection (sinusitis) can result from retained thick mucus, polyps, tumors, or trauma; symptoms of sinusitis include edema, pain, tenderness, and fever. If untreated (usually with antibiotics), these infections can result in destruction of the sinus walls.

The main functions of the nose are to provide and maintain an airway, to filter inspired air, to humidify the air by its passage through mucus, to serve as a warming duct for inspired air, and to smell. Infants are able to smell about 2 hours after birth. They appear to be able to identify the smell of breast milk very early, and it is thought that they can identify the smell of their mothers, whether or not they are breast fed. The eustachian tube serves as an airway, providing an anatomical communication between the nasopharynx and the middle ear (Fig. 35-4).

## The Taste Buds

The taste buds are bundles of slender cells with hairlike branches that form the projections on the tongue, which are known as papillae. Taste buds must be stimulated by liquids (a function of saliva).

There are four basic tastes: sweet, salt, sour, and bitter. All other tastes are combinations of these. Taste is perceived from the anterior two thirds of the tongue. The center of the tongue has very few taste buds. A sweet taste is discerned at the tip of the tongue; a salty taste is at the lateral margins of the tongue; sourness and bitterness are perceived at the posterior portion. Other senses, such as smell and touch, also influence taste perception. Infants can distinguish between sweet and bitter tastes. This is documented by their active sucking for sweet tastes and turning away from bitter tastes.

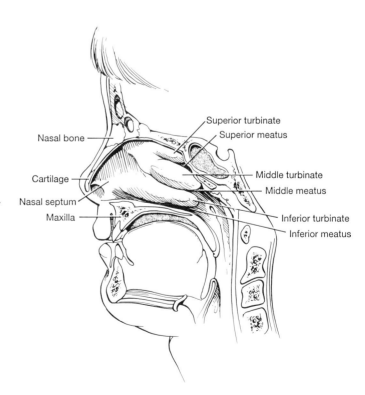

*Figure 35-3. Anatomy of the nose.*

Nasal bone

Cartilage

Nasal septum

Maxilla

Superior turbinate
Superior meatus

Middle turbinate
Middle meatus

Inferior turbinate
Inferior meatus

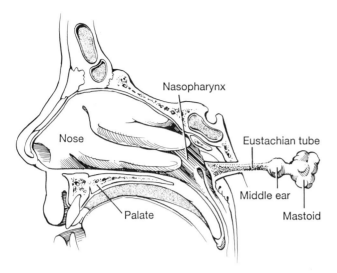

*Figure 35–4.  The eustachian tube and the nasopharynx.*

## Assessment

### History

A complete, detailed history is important in the assessment of sensory function. The prenatal history elicits information relative to the mother's health during the pregnancy. Of particular relevance are the following questions:

- Did you have an infection during pregnancy?
- If so, at what point in the gestation did it occur?
- How long did the illness last?
- How severe were the symptoms?
- Did you take any medications?
- If so, what type and for how long?

The birth history should elicit the type and length of delivery and whether or not any problems occurred. Relevant questions may include the following:

- After the baby was born, were there any problems?
- Has the child had a history of accidents, illnesses, operations, or hospitalizations?
- Do either parent or other members of the family have a history of sensory function problems?

The review of systems for sensory function should include the type of questions listed in Table 35-1. A history of habits is obtained by questions regarding eating behaviors, sleeping patterns, play activities, and interpersonal relationships.

The following questions should be asked regarding the present illness:

- How long has the child been ill?
- What signs and symptoms are present?
- Have the child's usual activities changed?
- Are there any habits accompanying this condition, such as rubbing the nose or pulling on the ears?
- Has the child been exposed to any illnesses?
- What treatment, if any, has been done so far?

### Physical Examination

#### The Eye

Inspection is the primary method of eye examination, but the eyelids are also palpated. *Ptosis,* or drooping of the lid, may be observed. The globe should be examined for *exophthalmos* (protrusion), and the lids should be long enough to cover the eye. If the upper lid does not cover the eye, the nurse should be aware of possible causes, such as exophthalmos or facial nerve paralysis. If the eye is not covered, extreme dryness of the eye and susceptibility to abrasion may result. The nurse should look for signs of Down syndrome (upward slanting of the eyes) or Treacher-Collins syndrome (downward slanting). The "setting sun" expression, with the sclera exposed above the iris, is seen in advanced hydrocephalus or in brainstem lesions; however, it may also be elicited in some normal, full-term infants and in many preterm infants when they are rapidly lowered from a sitting to a supine position.

*Styes* or *hordeolums* are inflammations of the sebaceous glands near the lashes and are usually caused by staphylococci. They appear as painful, red, swollen, tender areas near the eyelashes. The inner aspect of the upper lid is examined for the possibility of internal hordeolums. Sometimes, *chalazions* (swellings that are firm, discrete, and nontender) are found on the lids. Nits or lice may also be found on the eyelids. The eyelids may be observed to roll out (ectropion) or roll in (entropion). *Epicanthic folds,* vertical folds of skin covering the inner canthus, are more prevalent in Asians and in children with Down syndrome (trisomy 21). Edema or erythema of the conjunctiva is usually a sign of infection.

The muscles of the eye should be assessed. A *tropia* is an overt strabismus (a turning or deviation of the eye). A *phoria* is a tendency for the eye to wander, which may occur when the child is sick or tired. The Hirschberg test for strabismus can be performed on children over 6 months of age. In a darkened room a light is shined in the child's eyes. The light reflection should be located in the same position on each pupil. The cover test can also be performed on children older than 6 months. An object is held 12 inches from the eyes. One eye is covered with a card or the examiner's hand, which is then quickly removed. The covered eye should be in the same position as the uncovered eye.

*Anisocoria,* a difference in pupil size, may be noted on

*Table 35–1.  Review of Systems for Sensory Function:*
*Sample Questions*

| Function to Be Assessed | Relevant Questions |
| --- | --- |
| Eye function | Do the child's eyes ever cross? |
| | Does the child squint? |
| | Do the eyes tear excessively? Are they red? |
| | How is the child doing in school? |
| | Does the child bring objects up close to the eyes or sit close to the television to see? |
| | What kind of activities does the child like? |
| | Is there a history of ptosis (drooping eyelids)? |
| | Does the child blink often? |
| Ear function | Does the child have frequent colds? |
| | Does the child have frequent earaches? |
| | Does the child appear to hear? |
| | Are there times when the child appears not to hear? When? How often? |
| | What is the child's speech pattern? |
| | How is the child doing in school? |
| | Does the child pull on his or her ears? |
| | Does the child respond to questions? |
| | Is there a discharge other than cerumen (wax)? |
| Nose function | Does the child have persistent nosebleeds? |
| | Does the child have frequent colds? |
| | Is the child a mouth-breather? |
| | Does the child complain of pain? |
| | Can the child report various smells? |
| Taste bud function | Is the child's appetite good? |
| | Does the child report taste sensations different from those reported by others? |

physical examination. Although this can be normal, it might also be a sign of central nervous system damage. Dilatation of the pupil might be a sign of poisoning, glaucoma, retinoblastoma, or intracranial insult. Constriction of the pupil might be a sign of intracranial damage or morphine poisoning.

Other physical findings might include Brushfield spots, coloboma, or nystagmus. *Brushfield spots* are white speckles on the iris usually seen in children with Down syndrome or other syndromes associated with mental retardation. A *coloboma* is a notch that can occur in the eyelid or in the iris. If it involves only the iris and not the choroid or retina, there is usually no problem (Fig. 35-5). *Nystagmus* is the term for rapid, jerky movements of the eye. Infants who do not yet focus may have short periods of nystagmus; however, continuous nystagmus at any age should be referred since it could result from neurological or ocular disorders such as cataracts, muscle weakness, or astigmatism.

Use of the ophthalmoscope allows visualization of the internal structures of the eye, including the red reflex, the optic disc, the macula, the fundus and vessels, and the vitreous and aqueous humors (Fig. 35-6). The *red reflex* is observed as an orange-red glow. The color should be relatively uniform, with no dark or opaque spots. The most prominent landmark of the retina is the *optic disc,* which should be round with sharp borders. It is pink in light-skinned people and yellow-orange in dark-skinned people. The *macula* is about two disc diameters temporal to the disc. It is a light-sensitive area. The pinpoint area of gleaming light of the macula is the *fovea centralis.* The *fundus* is usually orange-red, but some variation in color exists. It is examined for lesions (red lesions are hemorrhages), color, shape, and the presence of arteries and veins. Arteries are about one fourth narrower than veins and reflect a light reflex from the retina. Veins are larger and have no light reflex. Vessels should be inspected for notches, hemorrhages, tortuousness, exudates, and vein pulsation. Diagnostic (assessment) procedures for vision are found in Table 35-2.

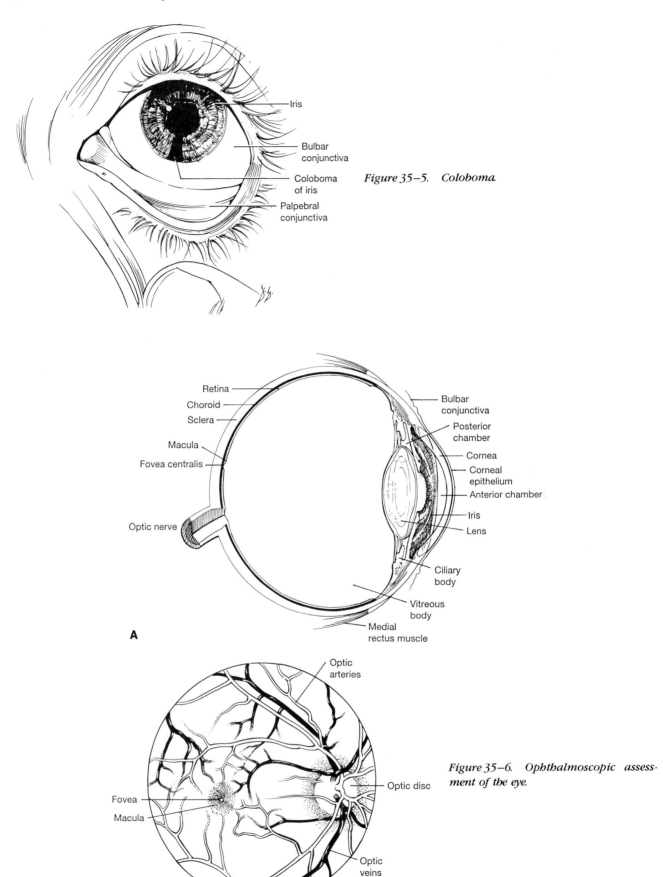

Figure 35–5.   Coloboma.

Figure 35–6.   Ophthalmoscopic assessment of the eye.

*Table 35—2.  Diagnostic Procedures for Vision*

| Test | Procedure |
|---|---|
| Acuity | Snellen's E chart or alphabet chart is useful for children at or above the third grade level. It is placed 20 feet from the child. The passing score is the line at which most letters or symbols are correctly identified. Children from 4 to 8 years old can usually read the 20/30 line with both eyes. That is, they can read at 20 feet what will later be read, if vision is normal, at a distance of 30 feet. The score of 20/20 is usually obtained by the fourth grade. The titmus machine is designed to alleviate the need to establish the distance of 20 feet. It is designed to measure visual acuity in the same manner. There are home vision tests that use the letter E. The Denver Developmental Screening Test includes a vision test that uses cards with pictures to be identified (see Appendix A). |
| Color | Color blindness occurs more frequently in males than females. Assessment of color discrimination is important because early learning activities rely heavily on color identification, as do certain occupations that the child might select. Color perception is tested with Ishihara's plates for older children. Ishihara's plates are a series of colored plates with figures composed of dots imbedded in a background of similar-colored dots. A person who is color blind cannot distinguish the hidden figure. Younger children can be tested for color discrimination with colored balls, yarn, crayons, or other objects. |
| Visual fields | An object—a small toy, a finger, or a light—can be moved systematically in all four quadrants to ascertain the range of motion of the eyes. The cover test is useful in determining if the eyes are straight. With one eye covered, the position of the uncovered eye is observed. When the covered eye is uncovered, it is observed for consensus. |

### The Ear

Inspection of the external ear includes assessment of ear alignment with the eye–occiput line. Low-set ears are associated with chromosomal disorders, such as trisomy 13. Examination with the otoscope reveals the tympanic membrane, which is normally a light, translucent, pearly-gray color. The *light reflex* is seen as a sharply demarcated triangular shape. The *umbo,* the end of the malleus, appears as a small white spot at the top of the light reflex. The long arm of the malleus is seen anterior and superior to the umbo. It looks like a whitish line from the umbo to the edge of the tympanic membrane.

The tympanic membrane must always be tested for mobility. The usual test for mobility can be performed by a nurse or a physician. Using an otoscope with pneumatic tubing, air is puffed against the tympanic membrane; this should cause the membrane to move. Failure to move or bulging of the membrane indicates the presence of fluid in the middle ear. Sometimes *cerumen* (wax) may block visualization of the membrane; it is removed when an infection is suspected. Diagnostic (assessment) procedures for testing hearing are presented in Table 35-3.

### The Nose

The examination of the nose includes the exterior nose and sinus areas and as much of the internal nose as can be visualized using a nasal speculum or otoscope. Are the nasal cavities clear? Is the nose red and inflamed? Are there bumps on the nose? The nose should be palpated along the ridge to feel for abnormalities. The frontal sinus is palpated by placing two fingers below the eyebrows and pressing upward. The frontal and maxillary sinuses can be percussed to ascertain if there is pain. Pressure on the sinuses by percussion may elicit pain or discomfort responses. With the otoscope, the nasal septum and mucosa are examined. There may be septal perforations, polyps, or tumors. To check for perforation, the nurse should shine the light in one nostril and see if it can be seen on the other side. The color of the nasal mucosa should be noted. Erythematous mucosa is indicative of infection; pale, boggy mucosa is a sign of allergy; gray, swollen mucosa results from chronic rhinitis.

**Smell.** The child should be asked to identify odors that are usually familiar to young children. Each nostril is tested while the other nostril is blocked. Vials containing substances such as peanut butter and orange extract are used. Conditions such as colds and allergies may interfere with smell, as can defects in the olfactory receptors in the nasal mucosa, the olfactory bulb, or olfactory tract.

### The Tongue

The color and movement of the tongue should be observed and the size of the papillae and frenulum noted. A

*Table 35–3.  Diagnostic Procedures for Testing Hearing\**

| Test | Procedure |
| --- | --- |
| Audiometric testing | Skill is required to use the audiometer. The child wears ear phones, and sounds are transmitted to one ear at a time. The most important speech frequencies of 500, 1000, 2000, 3000, 4000, and 6000 Hz are usually tested. The sounds are given at varying degrees of loudness or intensity (decibels). Young children may be especially difficult to evaluate because of inability to communicate responses or to understand directions. |
| Rinne test | This test compares air conduction with bone conduction. A tuning fork (512 Hz) is struck to begin vibration and then placed on the handle of the mastoid. The child is asked if he or she hears the sound. If the answer is "yes," the child is told to indicate when the sound is no longer heard. At that point, the tuning fork is placed outside the meatus of the same ear. The child is asked if he or she can hear it at that point. The child should be able to hear it at that time because air conduction is better than bone conduction. Children with a conductive hearing loss will have a negative Rinne test, that is, bone conduction will be better than air conduction. |
| Weber's test | A vibrating tuning fork (512 Hz) is placed firmly against the center of the child's head. The child is asked where the sound is greater or if it is the same in both ears. Normally, it is the same in both ears. This test compares bone conduction in both ears. If the sound is less on one side or the other, the conductive hearing loss is on the affected side. |

\*Hearing tests for neonates and infants are discussed in Chapters 11 and 12, respectively.

child is said to be *tongue-tied* if the tip of the tongue cannot reach the lips. Usually, no treatment is required; however, if sucking or articulation is impaired, the physician may decide to nick the edge of the frenum with blunt-pointed scissors and then separate the membrane. A *geographic tongue* is the term given to a tongue that has irregular areas of differently textured papillae. A white coating of the tongue can be caused by thrush (see Chap. 11). *Macroglossia,* a large tongue, is a sign of several syndromes, including Down syndrome and Hurler syndrome (gargoylism). A white strawberry tongue is a sign of scarlet fever; after several days it appears as a raspberry tongue. Deviation of the tongue to one side may indicate injury to the 12th cranial nerve. The taste buds per se cannot be examined but are tested using diagnostic procedures.

*Taste.* The assessment of taste is frequently conducted by asking children to close their eyes as the examiner places substances on their tongues. It is thought that closing the eyes diminishes the possible influence of vision on taste discrimination. Sweet (sugar), sour (lemon juice or vinegar), and salt are used to assess taste; usually, the bitter taste is not tested. The substance is placed on the child's extended tongue. It is helpful to dissolve substances in water before application to the tongue with a swab. Sips of water may be taken between the application of each substance—especially salt and sugar. To accurately

test taste perception, the child must be old enough to understand the test and follow directions.

*Speech.* *Speech screening* can be performed using the Denver Articulation Screening Test. This test is easy, fast, and inexpensive to administer (see Appendix A). The child repeats words while the examiner listens carefully for the sounds being evaluated. Twenty-two words are used and 30 sounds are evaluated. Many articulation errors tend to decrease, often by the third grade, without any therapy. Other speech problems, such as lateral lisps, require therapy.

Lexicon or vocabulary is also routinely screened. Between 8 months and 2 years of age, most children can say about 100 words. This increases to 900 words by 3 years of age and to 1500 words by age 4 (Alexander & Brown, 1979). Spoken vocabulary is usually thought to be less than recognition vocabulary—that is, children can recognize many words before they can say them.

## Nursing Diagnosis

The diagnoses approved by the North American Nursing Diagnosis Association (NANDA, 1990) are used when sensory problems are discussed. The most common diagnoses used for sensory problems include the following:

*Pattern 1: Exchanging*
- Altered tissue perfusion
- High risk for infection
- High risk for injury
- Impaired tissue integrity
- Ineffective airway clearance

*Pattern 3: Relating*
- Altered family processes
- Altered parenting
- High risk for altered parenting
- Social isolation

*Pattern 5: Choosing*
- Ineffective family coping: Compromised
- Ineffective individual coping
- Noncompliance

*Pattern 6: Moving*
- Diversional activity deficit
- High risk for activity intolerance
- Impaired swallowing

*Pattern 7: Perceiving*
- Body image disturbance
- Sensory alterations (visual, auditory)

*Pattern 9: Feeling*
- Anxiety
- Fear
- Pain

## Planning Nursing Care

Planning and implementation of nursing care is discussed in relation to each problem presented in this chapter. To develop nursing care plans and nursing interventions, a careful assessment must be conducted. The responses to the assessment should direct the nursing care plan. Nurses should be careful not to rely completely on chronological age for evaluation of communication, for personal and social assessment, or for the determination of appropriate treatment modalities. Nursing care plans should be directed by questions such as the following:

- What is the status of the family unit?
- What is the child's environment like?
- Do the parents or other family members have similar sensory problems?
- Do financial constraints pose problems that need to be considered in developing the plan?
- Has the child been exposed to a variety of stimuli?

The family must be included in all planning if successful implementation of the care plan is to occur.

Acutely ill children are not usually assessed for sensory acuity. Acute conditions arising from sensory problems are discussed later in the chapter. Chronic illnesses, such as otitis media and rhinitis, may affect sensory function. A thorough history is important to ascertain the effects of the illness on the sensory system. The nursing care plan might include educational interventions for the child and family, instruction regarding the administration of medications (e.g., the instillation of eye drops), planning adjustments needed in the school setting (e.g., sitting in the front of the classroom), maintaining appropriate follow-up measures, and developing strategies to help the child develop self-esteem. Other interventions might include referrals to social services, parenting groups, or other support groups.

## Nursing Interventions

In addition to planning appropriate education approaches for the child and family, the nurse may be responsible for direct care. Nursing interventions include the administration of medications by the nurse or the instruction of caregivers in the techniques of administration.

### Eye Medications

Medications may be instilled into the eye for several reasons. Mydriatics, which dilate the pupil, may be instilled to visualize the inner eye during diagnostic procedures. They do not paralyze the ciliary muscle of accommodation. Phenylephrine, 1% to 2% (Neo-synephrine), and 1% hydroxyamphetamine are often used. Because they increase intraocular pressure, mydriatics are not used when glaucoma or hypertension is present. Photophobia and the blurring of near objects occurs for 1 to 6 hours after administration.

Cycloplegics cause the pupil to dilate and also produce paralysis of accommodation (cycloplegia). The ciliary muscles are paralyzed to allow examination of the eyes. Sometimes, cycloplegics are prescribed for acute inflammations of the iris and for refraction. Atropine sulfate (0.25%–2%), scopolamine hydrobromide (0.2%), and Cyclogyl (1%) are examples of cycloplegics. Topical ophthalmic antibiotics, such as erythromycin and bacitracin, may be prescribed for specific infections.

It is usually easier for two people to instill eye medications in young children. One person secures the head and controls body movement; the other retracts the eyelid to insert the medication into the palpebral conjunctiva.

### Ear Medications

Medications may be prescribed to soften cerumen (Cerumenex, Debrox, or hydrogen peroxide) and to alleviate pain or control infection (antibiotics, Auralgan). The drops should be at room temperature before administration. If the child is not too anxious, one person can instill ear drops; however, the ear canal must be straightened by holding the pinna. For children under 2 years of age, the pinna should be pulled down and back to facilitate the passage of the ear drops into the ear canal. If the child is over 2 years old, the pinna should pulled up and back (see Fig. 5-14 on page 101). The young child should be placed in a side-lying position with the treated ear uppermost and should remain in this position for several minutes to ensure proper instillation.

## Interventions for Epistaxis (Nosebleeds)

Most nosebleeds stop without intervention. When intervention is required, firm pressure should be applied to the lateral side of the nose against the septum for 2 to 10 minutes. If bleeding persists, epinephrine (1 : 1000) may be applied. A silver nitrate stick may be applied by a physician when the bleeding is controlled. When it is difficult to stop the bleeding, the nose may be packed by an otolaryngologist.

## Evaluating Nursing Care

Although conditions affecting the sensory system can be treated and may result in positive outcomes, impairment of sensory function usually involves adaptation. It may be impossible to completely restore a sense to optimal function, but children may be able to use sensory aids. Glasses or hearing aids may be prescribed, or, if these would not be helpful, the child can be instructed in other techniques such as lip reading or braille, which can help the child adjust to the environment. Sensory loss is difficult, if not impossible, to measure, and nursing care for sensory function problems may not significantly improve function in some cases. Indications of compliance with prescribed treatments includes knowledge of the condition by parents and child, school performance, social interactions, and self-esteem. Communication techniques that are appropriate for sensory problems must be developed. Referrals must be initiated to appropriate agencies, support groups, and educational programs for children and parents.

## Congenital Vision Problems

### Congenital Cataracts

A cataract occurs when the crystalline lens loses its transparency. Congenital cataracts may be caused by "any viral, metabolic, hereditary, or unknown process that occurs before birth and results in abnormal development of the lens" (Kovalesky, 1985, p. 198). This condition occurs in one of every 250 live births. One of the most common causes of childhood blindness is *deprivation amblyopia*

(loss of vision resulting from nonuse of the eye) caused by congenital cataracts.

Many times it is difficult to determine whether cataracts are acquired or congenital since they may not be identified until the child is beyond the neonatal period. Acquired cataracts can be caused by trauma, radiation, diabetes, enzyme deficiencies, the long-term use of steroids, or total parenteral nutrition. Monocular cataracts (a cataract in one eye) in children frequently result in amblyopia. Other problems commonly seen in children with congenital cataracts include strabismus, nystagmus, and microphthalmia (abnormal smallness of one or both eyes) (Kovalesky, 1985). High incidence of cataracts is seen in children with Down syndrome, trisomy 13, congenital rubella, hypoglycemia, or hypocalcemia. Although cataracts are also seen in children with galactosemia, dietary treatment can result in their disappearance. Children diagnosed with *Lowe syndrome* (oculocerebrorenal syndrome) usually develop cataracts (Kovalesky, 1985).

The treatment for cataracts is surgical removal as soon as possible after birth. The prognosis declines if cataract removal is delayed until after 6 months of age, a critical period in visual development. Older children (over 8 to 9 years of age) may develop amblyopia. Usually, there is a better outcome for bilateral than unilateral cataracts. Amblyopia occurs more often and is more severe in children with unilateral cataracts. Screening for opacities can successfully be done using an ophthalmoscope. After cataract surgery, the child has no lens (*aphakia*) and therefore is unable to accommodate or focus at close range. After the inflammation from the surgery subsides, the child is fitted for contact lenses or glasses. Usually, by 5 or 6 years of age, the child requires bifocal or reading glasses with contact lenses. Plastic lenses for glasses have proved effective for children since they are lighter and more durable. Until the child is old enough to assume responsibility for contact lens care (cleanliness, insertion, and removal), parents must be instructed in the techniques and assume the responsibility. It is essential to emphasize the need for handwashing before touching the contact lenses. Soft contact lenses are generally prescribed; cleaning, insertion, and removal techniques are taught by the ophthalmologist or optician. There is controversy regarding the use of permanent plastic lenses inserted into the eye after surgery in children.

### The Nursing Process for Cataracts

Nursing assessment for cataracts is conducted by observation and assessment with an ophthalmoscope. Cataracts are identified by the appearance of a "white" pupil (an opacity), ocular or physical problems, or reduced visual acuity. If no red reflex can be visualized or if it is only partially visualized, a referral should be made to an ophthalmologist. Often a slit lamp (a binocular microscope) is used to see opacities anterior to the lens.

Nursing diagnoses for cataracts might include the following:

- High risk for injury related to decreased visual acuity
- Altered family processes related to increased care demands of the visually impaired infant or child
- High risk for altered parenting related to lack of knowledge of procedures for caring for a child with a visual impairment

Planning and implementation of nursing care includes referral to an ophthalmologist; information-sharing and clarification with parents; assisting in pre- and postsurgical care; administering medications; providing information for the child and parents on strategies for adapting to the decreased visual acuity; working with the child and family regarding the care and wearing of glasses or contact lenses; and visual acuity checks.

After surgery, the child's eyes may be covered with patches. Infants may be sedated for the first 24 hours. It is important to prevent vomiting and crying since these activities increase intraocular pressure and may result in injury to the sutures. Parents should be encouraged to remain with the child to keep the child calm. There should not be severe pain after surgery, so extreme discomfort and restlessness should be reported to the physician.

Evaluation of nursing care is accomplished by analysis of the success achieved in resolving the problems identified and specified in the nursing diagnoses. The child should remain free from injury and should show signs of normal growth and development patterns that take into account adaptations necessitated by visual disturbance. Parents should demonstrate appropriate care and normal parenting activities.

## Congenital and Juvenile Glaucoma

*Glaucoma* is the term used to describe increased intraocular pressure. It is generally believed that this condition is inherited through an autosomal recessive gene. A number of syndromes are associated with glaucoma, such as Wilms' tumor, neurofibromatosis (von Recklinghausen's disease), Marfan syndrome, and rubella. Most cases (about 80%) are diagnosed by the first year of life.

Glaucoma that develops after 3 years of age is termed *juvenile glaucoma.* It occurs more often in males than females and is associated with myopia. These children have visual field and acuity losses.

The symptoms of glaucoma include epiphora (excessive tearing), blepharospasm (lid spasm), photophobia, a hazy appearance, and enlargement of the cornea. The child may appear mentally retarded, but this may be a consequence of visual disturbance and decreased visual stimuli. The later the symptoms appear, the better the prognosis.

The usual treatment is surgery because topical anti-glaucoma drugs have been found generally ineffective in children. Surgical procedures usually must be repeated several times in an effort to keep the intraocular pressure within normal limits. The surgical treatment, called *goniotomy,* attempts to reduce the pressure exerted by aqueous humor in the anterior cavity of the eye (posterior to the cornea and anterior to the lens). This surgery attempts to produce an anterior chamber angle wide enough to open the outflow tracts (Schlemm's canal). More than one operation may be needed to accomplish this. Even if the optic nerve becomes completely destroyed by glaucoma, the intraocular pressure can remain elevated and cause severe pain. When medications can no longer relieve the pain, enucleation may be done.

### The Nursing Process for Glaucoma

Nursing assessment is performed through observation and detailed history taking. Because glaucoma is inherited through an autosomal recessive pattern, a thorough family history is important.

Nursing diagnoses for glaucoma might include the following:

- Anxiety related to lack of knowledge of pre- and postoperative routines and procedures and outcome of surgery
- High risk for injury related to environmental hazards
- Altered parenting related to increased demands of caring for a child during repeated hospitalizations
- Altered tissue perfusion related to increased intraocular pressure
- Noncompliance related to prolonged treatment regimen
- Pain related to photophobia
- Diversional activity deficit related to decreased sensory stimulation

Planning and implementing nursing care involves instructing the parents, the child, and family members about the condition, medical interventions, and follow-up procedures to ensure that the child receives the necessary ongoing treatment. Parents should be instructed to remove potential environmental hazards and should be provided with a list of resources or support groups.

Evaluation consists of determining if the child has the best possible visual functioning and if the child and family have an appropriate level of understanding of the treatment regimens for glaucoma. The child should demonstrate normal, age-appropriate growth and development.

## Dacryostenosis

Infants who have recurrent conjunctivitis should be evaluated for *dacryostenosis,* a stricture or narrowing of a lacrimal duct. A common condition in newborns, it involves a membrane covering the distal end of the lacrimal duct. Symptoms include redness, swelling, excessive tearing, pain, fever, and an increased purulent discharge when pressure is applied to the punctum (a small opening at the margin of each eyelid that opens into the lacrimal duct and releases tears). Oral antibiotics may be used after a culture is done. If resolution does not occur by 3 months of age, lacrimal probing is done under general anesthesia. If the child is born with the lacrimal sac filled with secretion, the probing may be done earlier (Crawford & Morin, 1983).

Nursing assessment includes checking for signs of infection by applying pressure on the lacrimal sac, which may release a discharge (pus or mucus) from the punctum (Crawford & Morin, 1983).

Nursing diagnoses for dacryostenosis might include the following:

- High risk for infection related to inadequate primary defenses
- Pain related to pressure from the enlarged lacrimal sac

The physician may order massaging of the lacrimal sac to try to open the punctum. If ordered, the nurse should instruct the parents to gently massage the tear sac once or twice a day in a downward manner from the lower inner orbital rim, pressing toward the corner of the eye. If necessary, probing is done by an ophthalmologist. Nurses may assist in the procedure by restraining the child and by educating the parents about the procedure. Evaluation relates to the successful resolution of the blockage.

## Vision Problems of Infants and Toddlers

### Retinopathy of Prematurity

The term *retinopathy of prematurity* (ROP) is more inclusive than the term commonly used, *retrolental fibroplasia,* which is actually the final stage of ROP. ROP is a potentially blinding condition characterized by "abnormal development of the retinal vasculature of preterm infants" (Luna, Dobson, Carpenter, & Biglan, 1989, p. 580).

Even though the effects of high levels of oxygen on the retina were discovered in the early 1950s, this disease is still a problem with preterm infants. This is undoubtedly due to the facts that an increased number of infants are being born preterm and that more preterm infants are surviving. Generally, ROP affects infants weighing under 1001 g at birth. "The total incidence of ROP in infants weighing 501–750 g is almost 100% with severe ROP developing in about 30%" (Kretzer & Hittner, 1988, p. 1151). As weight increases, the incidence and severity of ROP decreases. Fielder, Ng, and Levene (1986) report that in 143 premature infants studied, the initial ophthalmological examination was normal, but 80% of these infants developed ROP between 32.5 and 38.5 weeks of age.

In the primary phase of ROP, high levels of oxygen cause constriction of the large retinal vessels and destroy smaller retinal capillaries. In utero, the spindle cells of the retina are in a relatively hypoxic environment. After premature birth, these spindle cells are stressed by a hyperoxic environment.

Even after the termination of oxygen therapy, a danger exists; this is called the vasoproliferative phase. New vessels grow, but they continue to shunt blood to the damaged capillaries. In about 20% of these infants, cicatrization (scarring) may occur. Various classification systems are used to rate the severity.

Usually, the diagnosis of ROP is made a few days before discharge, when oxygen administration has been discontinued. The American Academy of Pediatrics directs that at-risk infants be examined by an ophthalmologist before discharge. This usually requires dilatation of the eyes. Infants with identifiable or suspected ROP are examined at 1- to 6-week intervals. If the examination is negative, the child is usually scheduled for a 3- to 6-month recheck. Most cases of ROP resolve spontaneously; however, there is a danger that the vasoproliferative phase may recur, placing the child in the final stage of retrolental fibroplasia.

Possible treatments include vitamin E therapy, which continues to be controversial. Vitamin E is an antioxidant used to suppress the development of severe ROP. Mean plasma concentrations of vitamin E should be maintained at between 1.2 and 3.5 mg % (Kretzer & Hittner, 1988). Kretzer and Hittner report favorable results from the use of tocopherol (vitamin E); however, Phelps, Rosenbaum, Isenberg, Leake, & Dorey (1987) conducted a randomized double-masked trial, and their data did not support the use of vitamin E. Another treatment being investigated is cryotherapy, which entails the application of a destructive cold probe to the scleral surface. For the cryotherapy to be effective, it must be undertaken before the retinopathy progresses too far. By the time cryotherapy must be initiated, however, there is no way to predict whether or not spontaneous resolution might occur (Phelps, 1988). The decision to treat with cryotherapy involves many considerations, including the severity of the disease, whether both eyes should be treated, and the probability of long-term side effects. Phelps and Phelps (1989) recommend that both eyes be treated in severe disease, and when the severity is unequal, that the worst eye be treated.

### The Nursing Process for Retinopathy of Prematurity

The primary goal of nursing management is prevention of ROP. Nurses must carefully and frequently assess preterm infants receiving oxygen to be certain that the concentration is correct.

Nursing diagnoses for ROP might include the following:

- Impaired tissue integrity related to constriction or destruction of retinal vessels
- Ineffective family coping: Compromised related to concerns about the child's potential health problem
- Altered family processes related to the need to care for a sick child
- Diversional activity deficit related to visual impairment
- Sensory/perceptual alteration: Visual related to the inability to see

Nurses plan and intervene by interacting with parents and families, by providing information, and by giving pre- and postoperative surgical care, if required, and follow-up interventions. The pre- and postoperative care depends on the nature of the condition requiring surgical repair. Many premature infants have accompanying problems that may require surgery.

Careful measurement of oxygen levels is essential. Partial pressure of oxygen ($PaO_2$) levels for infants receiving oxygen should be kept between 80 and 100 mmHg; levels of 100 mmHg and over increase the risk for the occurrence of ROP. The best way to measure $PaO_2$ is transcutaneously. All infants receiving oxygen who weighed less than 2000 g at birth, or who were born at less than 36 weeks' gestation, should be examined by an ophthalmologist at discharge and again at 3 to 6 months of age. Arterial blood levels and oxygen levels in the isolette must be measured.

Parents must be instructed to monitor vision as the child grows. Parents may need support in recognizing the fact that in spite of the child's blindness, his or her life can be happy, productive, and satisfying. Evaluation is based on the physical, psychological, and social adjustment of the child and family.

## Ophthalmia Neonatorum

*Ophthalmia neonatorum* is a bilateral conjunctivitis found in infants under 1 month of age. Its origin may be chemical, mechanical, or bacterial. Chemically, it may be caused by the instillation of silver nitrate as a prophylaxis against gonococcal infection. In these cases, the onset is rapid (3–24 hours after birth), and the conjunctivitis disappears spontaneously in 3 to 5 days. The only treatment is to wipe away the discharge with sterile gauze or cotton.

Bacterial conjunctivitis is caused by *Neisseria gonorrhea* incurred during passage through a contaminated birth canal or from the hands of attending staff. Signs of infection appear 2 to 4 days after birth, and the discharge is copious 1 to 2 days later. A smear and culture are performed. If the Gram's stain is positive, the baby should be isolated and started on topical sulfacetamide or tetracycline and parenteral aqueous penicillin. Prompt treatment is necessary to prevent corneal damage.

### The Nursing Process for Ophthalmia Neonatorum

Nursing assessment includes inspection for evidence of purulent discharge from the eyes. If a discharge is observed, the appearance and duration are noted and reported.

Nursing diagnoses for ophthalmia neonatorum might include the following:

- Anxiety (parental) related to the cause of the infection (when caused by a maternal infection)
- Pain related to instillation of medication
- High risk for altered parenting related to infant's inability to see parents and provide appropriate attachment (bonding) behaviors

Nursing planning and interventions are designed to minimize the infective process by clean or sterile technique, as indicated; administer topical and systemic medications as prescribed by the physician; and clarify parental understanding of the condition and the treatment. When the infection is caused by gonorrhea, the parents may need assistance in coping with the guilt they may feel for having caused the infection. Nursing interventions must ensure that the mother has also been referred for treatment.

Since eye contact is an important part of the parent and infant bonding process, interventions should focus on providing every opportunity for the infant to be able to see the parents. It is customary to delay instillation of eye drops until after the first reactivity period.

Newborns who have gonococcal conjunctivitis must be isolated. Eye discharge is copious. Nurses should wear gloves and gowns. The eyes should be irrigated with saline before the drops are instilled with a sterile medicine dropper or a sterile bulb syringe. The sterile solution should be at room temperature, and care must be taken not to splash the irrigating fluid or discharge into the infant's other eye or into the nurse's eyes.

Evaluation of nursing interventions includes determining a decrease in or cessation of the discharge from the eyes, the successful resolution of the infection, and maintenance of the parent and infant bonding process.

## Trachoma

*Trachoma* is a chronic infectious disease of the conjunctiva and cornea caused by a strain of the bacteria *Chlamydia trachomatis*. Although rare in the United States, it is the leading cause of blindness in the world and is endemic in areas of northern Africa, the Middle East, Australia, Central and South America, and the Indian subcontinent.

Trachoma is manifested as a slow, progressive conjunctivitis that causes the lids to thicken; eventually, the cornea is affected. The child experiences inflammation, pain, photophobia, and lacrimation. Follicles form on the upper eyelids until the granulation invades the cornea; eventually, it causes blindness. Treatment is instituted with ophthalmic sulfa or tetracycline ointments. The most effective method of diagnosis is isolation in cell culture, but the most widely used and less sensitive method is the Giemsa stain (Schachter et al., 1988).

Nursing diagnoses for trachoma might include the following:

- Pain related to conjunctivitis, thickening lids, and corneal changes
- Impaired tissue integrity related to the progressive infection
- Body image disturbance for older children related to the inability to see
- Anxiety related to child's decreasing sensory reception
- High risk for injury related to decreasing ability to see
- Visual sensory alterations related to decreasing ability to see

Nursing interventions are developed to increase and clarify knowledge of the condition, to aid in the administration of medications, and to contain the spread of the infection. Nursing care of the child with trachoma includes the administration of ophthalmic medications. Gloves should be worn to prevent the spread of bacterial infection. The child will be fearful and may have eye discomfort. Parents will be anxious about the possibility that their child might be blind. The nurse must provide a climate in which the child and parents can feel free to discuss their concerns. The nurse should provide the parents with the knowledge they need and should devise diversional activities for the child.

Evaluation is measured by parental demonstration of knowledge concerning the necessity for compliance with therapeutic regimens and by the success of treatment.

## Inclusion Conjunctivitis (Blennorrhea)

Inclusion conjunctivitis is caused by chlamydial agents, which are also known as TRIC (*tra*choma and *i*nclusion *c*onjunctivitis) agents. Chlamydial infections are the most prevalent sexually transmitted diseases. Newborns from 5 to 15 days of age may develop this infection after passage through the birth canal of an infected mother. "Approximately half of all infants born to infected mothers are infected with, or colonized by, the organism. Of those infants colonized, 30 to 40 percent will develop conjunctivitis and 10 to 20 percent will develop pneumonia" (Pruessner, Hansel, & Griffiths, 1986, p. 82).

Symptoms include swollen eyelids and infected conjunctiva, followed by copious mucopurulent discharge (with later onset than the gonococcal discharge). No damage to the eyes or vision occurs, and the infection tends to resolve spontaneously within several weeks to several months after onset. Treatment with oral erythromycin syrup can shorten the course of the disease. Erythromycin ophthalmic ointment is effective for the conjunctiva but does not eradicate the organism from the nasopharynx (Pruessner, Hansel, & Griffiths, 1986). Erythromycin ophthalmic ointment (0.5%), applied within 1 hour after birth, is used in many hospitals instead of silver nitrate drops because it is effective against both *N. gonorrhoeae* and *C. trachomatis.*

Chlamydial conjunctivitis can also be acquired by swimming in contaminated water. The discharge appears in 3 to 4 days; infected children have enlarged lymph nodes, and noticeable follicles appear inside the lower eyelids. Follicles are not seen in infants because lymphoid tissue is not well developed. Ophthalmic sulfonamide or tetracycline is the accepted treatment (Kovalesky, 1985).

### The Nursing Process for Inclusion Conjunctivitis

Nurses should assess for the presence of swollen eyelids and infected conjunctiva. Purulent discharge and cobblestone-appearing conjunctiva should be noted.

Nursing diagnoses for inclusion conjunctivitis might include the following:

- Impaired tissue integrity related to the infectious process
- Body image disturbance in older children related to altered appearance
- Anxiety related to the disease process and medication regimens

Nursing plans and interventions focus on the effective transmittal of knowledge regarding the condition, its contagious nature, and the importance of accurate instillation of medications; administration of oral antibiotics; and allaying parental fears.

Evaluation measures are concerned with the success of the interventions selected.

## Strabismus (Squint)

*Strabismus* is the name for the condition in which the eyes do not correctly align. The squinting eye is the abnormal condition in strabismus, whereby the eye cannot be focused with the fixated eye. This means that two separate images, rather than one, are reflected on the retina. This condition usually affects young children; about half of those affected develop it by 1 year of age. In an attempt to cope with *diplopia* (double vision), the child may learn to suppress the vision in one eye. This suppression leads to dimness of the vision in that eye, or functional amblyopia. Organic amblyopia may be caused by positioning of the extraocular muscle or cranial nerve palsy. It is important to note that organic amblyopia is irreversible, whereas functional amblyopia may respond to treatment.

Continual strabismus is called a *tropia.* With *esotropia,* the eye turns inward (crossed eyes); with *exotropia,* the eye turns outward (walleye). The terms *hypertropia* (upward) or *hypotropia* (downward) describe eyes that are higher or lower than the other. A *phoria* is a strabismus that is seen only when the child is examined with a cover test (discussed earlier). A slight jerking movement when the cover is removed indicates that some strabismus is present. After each eye is tested, the child should be told to focus on a distant object, and the test is repeated.

Two other conditions, both examples of pseudo-strabismus, are sometimes confused when an assessment is being made. Newborns often appear to have strabismus, but on examination the corneal light reflex is appropriate and the child is noted to have a flat nose and prominent epicanthic folds. The appearance of strabismus is due to the facial features of the child; strabismus does not actually exist. *Hypertelorism,* or widely spaced eyes, may also give the impression of strabismus.

The ophthalmologist frequently uses a prism, the Krinsky test, to center the reflex and to measure the deviation. To test for near point of convergence, which is necessary for reading and close work, the child stares at an object in the center of vision. The object is then moved toward the child. The distance of the object when the eyes cease to move toward each other usually is less than 6 inches; this is called the "breaking point."

Usually, the earlier the treatment begins, the better the results. Glasses or bifocals are prescribed for children with accommodative esotropia. Occlusion therapy (eye patch) may be done for amblyopia that accompanies strabismus. Sometimes exercises are recommended. Anticholinesterase drugs are used on a short-term basis for some cases. Most children with congenital esotropia require surgery.

The usual surgical treatment for strabismus is the resection or recessing of one or more extraocular muscles. The muscle is shortened in resection and lengthened in recession. Surgery may be done on an outpatient basis or in a same-day surgical unit. Some physicians place a patch over the affected eye after surgery; others cover both eyes to prevent eye movement. After surgery, an antibiotic and steroid eye ointment is instilled as prescribed.

### The Nursing Process for Strabismus

Nursing assessment includes careful observation and use of the appropriate screening tests. One of the basic screening tests for strabismus is the Hirschberg test. This test involves shining a light into the child's eyes in a darkened room and observing where the light reflex falls. The reflex should fall in the center of the eyes or slightly toward the nasal septum; in a child with strabismus, the reflex is not equal and appears off center. The cover test is also useful in assessing for strabismus.

Nursing diagnoses for strabismus might include the following:

- Body image disturbance in older children related to unusual appearance of eyes
- Altered parenting related to lack of knowledge regarding surgical correction
- High risk for injury related to difficulty in focusing and associated visual problems
- Anxiety related to the child and parents' fears about visual ability or appearance

The nursing plan and interventions include a thorough assessment; appropriate referral; information clarification as needed; and instruction on the administration of medications, pre- and postoperative care, and follow-up. Children should be referred to an ophthalmologist if strabismus is suspected. Children should be prepared for surgery for strabismus at a level appropriate to their developmental level. They need to be told that they may have some pain for a short time after surgery. They should be instructed about eye patches if these are to be used. Children should also be told that their arms may be restrained after surgery to prevent them from touching their eyes. Parents should be encouraged to remain with their children after surgery to help allay their fears. Evaluation measures must be continued over a long period since one third of strabismus surgeries must be repeated (Kovalesky, 1985).

### Retinoblastoma

*Retinoblastoma* is a rare, malignant, primary retinal tumor in children. It occurs in about 1 in 20,000 live births. If the disease spreads beyond the eye the mortality rate approaches 100%, but with early diagnosis the survival rate is 92% (Mafee et al., 1987).

Hereditary forms of the disease are caused by autosomal dominance. One type of retinoblastoma is associated with the deletion of band 14 of the long arm of chromosome 13. It is generally accepted that all bilateral cases are genetic and most unilateral cases are nongenetic (Parkin, Stiller, Draper, & Bieber, 1988). One eye was affected in 66% to 75% of the cases reported (Mafee et al., 1987). The child may develop strabismus as the eye becomes nonfunctional. Unfortunately, it can spread quickly along the optic nerve to involve the other eye.

The most common sign of the disease is leukokoria (white, pink-white, or yellow-white pupillary reflex). This is a reflection of light from a white or light-colored intraocular mass, membrane, or retinal detachment. An ophthalmologist must perform a complete fundus examination to further assess the presence of a tumor. Accurate diagnosis and prompt treatment are extremely important because of the tendency of the tumor to spread locally. Visual acuity tests, ultrasonography, computed tomography, and magnetic resonance imaging are excellent assessment tools. A complete oncology examination should be conducted.

Small tumors may regress by laser therapy or cryotherapy, depending on the location of the tumor. Cryotherapy uses cold to destroy the tumor. Photocoagulation may be used to destroy the blood vessels supplying the tumor. Enucleation may be done for larger tumors—especially for unilateral tumors that have destroyed vision. Chemotherapy is used when metastasis has occurred or has a high probability of occurring.

### The Nursing Process for Retinoblastoma

Nursing assessment of children with signs and symptoms of retinoblastoma includes obtaining a thorough family history since retinoblastoma may be inherited. When retinoblastoma is suspected, the child and family should be referred to an ophthalmologist immediately for further evaluation.

Nursing diagnoses for retinoblastoma might include the following:

- Visual sensory alteration related to decreased or absent sensory transmission
- Pain related to possible pressure from a tumor
- Anxiety related to the threat of a change in health status and the need for genetic counseling
- Altered family processes related to the child's illness
- High risk for injury related to sensory deficit

Nursing plans and interventions are designed to meet the identified needs. In particular, most parents become extremely fearful when they hear that their child has a tumor. If the symptoms have been present for a period of time, the parents may feel guilty that they did not seek help earlier. All treatment modalities require careful explanations. Enucleation, in particular, can be very frightening.

After surgery for enucleation, a large pressure dressing is placed over the eye socket. The dressing must be checked for signs of bleeding. Usually, after 48 hours the physician removes the dressing and replaces it with an eye patch. Irrigation of the socket and the application of topical antibiotics may be prescribed. Arm restraints may be necessary. About 3 weeks after surgery, a prosthesis may be prescribed.

Parents and the child may be fearful about the spread of the tumor and the prognosis. Older children and their parents may be concerned about appearance. Nurses can provide knowledge and emotional support as well as physical care.

Wherever possible, group exchanges offer opportunities for sharing and support.

Evaluation of all nursing plans and interventions addresses the levels of success in achieving the desired outcomes.

### Rhabdomyosarcoma

*Rhabdomyosarcomas,* the most common form of malignancy of the orbit, are soft tissue tumors. No hereditary or familial cause has been identified. Although rhabdomyosarcomas occur most frequently in the head and neck, other sites include the genitourinary tract, the extremities, and the retroperitoneum. The peak occurrence is between 2 and 6 years of age, with a second peak occurrence during puberty.

Clinical signs develop rapidly and include exophthalmus, often associated with ptosis of the upper eyelid. Symptoms may include poorly localized pain, headache, and loss of visual acuity. If the tumor extends into the nasal cavity, nosebleeds may occur.

The computed tomography scan is considered the best means of determining the size and location of orbital masses. Early biopsy is necessary because rhabdomyosarcoma grows so rapidly. Treatment consists of radiotherapy combined with systemic chemotherapy. Chemotherapeutic drugs used for rhabdomyosarcomas include vincristine, cyclophosphamide, and dactinomycin, among others.

### The Nursing Process for Rhabdomyosarcoma

Nurses must carefully observe children in whom rhabdomyosarcoma is suspected. The occurrence of ptosis should be carefully noted, and any indications of visual deficiency, headache, or pain should be reported immediately to an ophthalmologist.

Nursing diagnoses for rhabdomyosarcomas might include the following:

- Anxiety related to a threatened change in health status of the child
- Fear (parental and child) related to diagnostic procedures, the treatment regimen, and the possible outcome
- Pain related to headaches, diagnostic procedures, and treatment
- Ineffective family coping: Compromised related to severity of disease

Nursing plans and interventions should be designed to clarify knowledge, to provide emotional support, to assist with the administration of medications, and to provide follow-up care.

Evaluation includes determining the success of treatments and adjustment to the situation.

## Vision Problems of Preschool- and School-Aged Children

### Refractive Errors

When light rays are bent as they pass through the eyeball to the retina, they may not focus properly on the retina. The term used for the bending of light rays is *refraction*; when the rays do not focus on the retina, it is known as a *refractive error*. Refractive errors include myopia and hyperopia, with or without astigmatism.

### Myopia

Most cases of *myopia* (nearsightedness) are of the simple type, which are inherited through a recessive gene. Simple myopia is caused by a mismatch between the corneal curvature and eye length. In myopia, the length of the eyeball causes light rays to focus in front of the retina. Concave lenses are used to correct vision. Pathological myopia may occur in children with Down syndrome, Marfan syndrome, or retrolental fibroplasia. This type of myopia can lead to degeneration of the retina and can result in retinal detachment with a subsequent loss of vision.

Most cases of myopia are detected during the school years when the child complains of headaches, fatigue, and an inability to see the blackboard from a distance. Frequently, the child is observed squinting. Children with myopia tend to avoid sports or activities requiring distance vision and may prefer activities such as reading. As myopia progresses, children may hold reading material closer and closer to their eyes. Usually, night blindness is associated with myopia, although Khouri et al. (1988) discuss a family whose members have hyperopia (farsightedness) with night blindness. A number of studies have examined intelligence scores in relation to myopia; some have found these children to have higher scores in reading, arithmetic, and general abilities, but this association is not clear. Williams et al. (1988) report the strongest association between background characteristics (i.e., both genetic and environmental factors) and refractive error to be maternal mental ability rather than environmental influences.

Myopia is treated with prescription lenses, either glasses or contact lenses. Radical keratotomy, a treatment developed in the Soviet Union, is a painless procedure performed under local anesthesia that attempts to decrease the curvature of the eye. The procedure takes only about 15 minutes but is still considered experimental.

### The Nursing Process for Myopia

School nurses continually assess children for myopia. Children with myopia may complain of headaches or may have difficulty seeing the blackboard. Teachers may refer students to the school nurse because of poor schoolwork or because they notice the child squinting while looking at the blackboard. Parents may also note these problems and bring them to the teacher's attention. School nurses should be able to screen children for this problem and make appropriate referrals.

Nursing diagnoses for myopia might include the following:

- Pain related to headaches
- Visual sensory alterations related to decreased ability to see, as manifested by squinting, inability to see the blackboard, and poor grades
- Body image disturbance related to need to wear corrective lenses
- High risk for injury related to decreased ability to see
- Noncompliance related to refusal to wear corrective lenses

Nurses, especially those working in schools, need to plan and intervene in ways that facilitate the child's acquiring the best visual correction possible while establishing a favorable self-image. Children with myopia need to be examined every 6 to 12 months because growth spurts occur in the eye as well as in the rest of the body. They need to be encouraged to wear their glasses as prescribed and to be made to feel that they look good with glasses. The frames must fit comfortably and be appropriately sized.

Evaluation measures deal with immediate and long-term adjustment to myopia and treatment with glasses or contact lenses.

### Hyperopia

*Hyperopia* (farsightedness) is a common condition in young children and is considered normal. It may be caused by a short globe diameter or a cornea that is too flat; either condition causes the light rays to focus behind the retina. Older children may complain of headaches, blurred vision, nausea, or fatigue. Parents or teachers may note that these children hold books at a distance or that they are not interested in activities requiring close attention.

Lenses are prescribed; if the condition is mild, they may be worn for close work only. More severe cases require that lenses be worn at all times. Observation and vision screening are important assessment tools.

Nursing diagnoses for hyperopia might include the following:

- Pain related to headaches, nausea, blurred vision, or fatigue
- Visual sensory alteration related to blurred vision and headaches
- Noncompliance related to failure to wear corrective lenses

Nurses need to be able to explain the condition and to encourage the child to wear glasses or contact lenses as prescribed.

## Astigmatism

*Astigmatism* is caused by an irregular or uneven curve of the cornea. It can occur by itself or with myopia or hyperopia, and is thought to be inherited. Children may complain of blurred vision, burning eyes, or headaches, and they may be observed to squint. Treatment involves wearing corrective lenses.

Nurses are responsible for the assessment, referral, and follow-up care of children with astigmatism. They should know that children may complain of blurred vision during the adjustment period when they first get the lenses. Children should be encouraged to wear their lenses, and the adaptive process should be explained. They may eventually need to wear lenses only for tasks that strain their eyes.

Nursing diagnoses for astigmatism might include the following:

- Pain related to headaches or burning eyes
- Visual sensory alteration related to altered sensory reception
- Noncompliance related to failure to wear corrective lenses

Children need to be evaluated regularly because the astigmatism may change as they grow.

## Visual Problems of Adolescents

The conditions discussed under adolescence are not entirely unique to this age group; however, since they more frequently occur during adolescence, they have been placed in this section.

## External Hordeolum (Stye)

Styes are purulent inflammations of a sebaceous gland or hair follicle near the eyelashes. They usually appear red, and they are painful and swollen. After a few days, pus is discharged and the swelling subsides. Treatment consists of the application of warm compresses and topical antibiotics.

Nursing assessment includes simple visual observation of the eyelids for redness and swelling.

Nursing diagnoses for styes might include the following:

- Pain related to inflammation
- High risk for infection related to inadequate personal hygiene

Children and parents should be taught good hand-washing technique and should be advised about the potential for further spread of the infection. Instruction may also be needed regarding the application of warm compresses and topical antibiotics.

## Retinal Detachment

*Retinal detachment* is a separation of one layer of the retina from another layer. The detachment can be caused by a spontaneous degenerative process, trauma, or infection. When the retina is separated from the choroid in the back of the eye, a hole usually results in the retina. The hole allows the vitreous humor to leak between the choroid and the retina.

Not all children complain of a problem; some relate no problems until a serious loss of vision occurs. Complaints may include light flashes, shadows, or blurred vision. Pain is not usually associated with retinal detachment. Vision is affected in varying degrees depending on the site of detachment. Examination of the fundus reveals grayish areas at the site. There may be a loss of vision on the opposite side of the detachment. The prognosis varies depending on the site and extent of the tear. If uncorrected, the child will perceive a shadow that slowly grows in size. If the center of the retina is unaffected, vision is normal when the child looks straight ahead. If the detachment is not treated, total blindness can result.

Photocoagulation (laser) sealing of the tear is performed as quickly as possible. Surgery may be done, or if the cause is inflammatory, steroids may be used (Kovalesky, 1985). If the hole is small, it can be closed by scarring the area by heat, lasers, electrical current, or cold. The scar is held against the retina by local pressure, which is accomplished by a variety of surgical techniques.

Preoperative care varies with the physician's orders and can range from complete bed rest to unrestricted activity. Preoperative medications may include mydriatics and cycloplegics to dilate the eye in preparation for surgery and antibiotics to prevent infection.

The degree of postoperative pain varies; analgesics are usually prescribed. The eye is kept dilated by administering mydriatics and cycloplegics for 2 to 6 weeks after surgery. Occasionally, antibiotics and steroid eye preparations are prescribed. A pressure dressing may be applied for the first 12 to 24 hours after surgery, after which an eye dressing is used. If edema or discomfort persists, cold compresses may be ordered. Activities that might increase intraocular pressure, such as bending or lifting heavy objects, should be avoided.

### The Nursing Process for Retinal Detachment

Nurses need to be alert to symptoms of retinal detachment and the need to refer the child to an ophthalmologist immediately if a detachment is suspected. Nursing assessment includes obtaining a detailed history of the symptoms. The ophthalmic examination may reveal a gray retina with dark and tortuous vessels. A hole or tear may be observed in the retina.

Nursing diagnoses for retinal detachment might include the following:

- Anxiety related to decreasing sensory reception and possible light flashes, shadows, or blurred vision
- Fear related to diagnostic procedures and corrective treatments
- Visual sensory alteration related to decreasing ability to see

Nursing interventions include assessing the child in relation to the symptoms of visual disturbance. By taking a through history, the nurse should determine if there has been a recent injury or trauma and should assess the duration and progression of the symptoms. Prompt referral to an ophthalmologist is essential. The child and parents may need reinforcement of the explanation given by the ophthalmologist, and the nurse should encourage them to express their feelings. It is also essential that children and parents be educated about the prescribed treatment regimen and the need for follow-up care.

## Acute Vision Problems

### Eye Trauma

Trauma to the eye may be an isolated event or it may be associated with multiple injuries, such as those resulting from automobile accidents. Fortunately, the anatomical structure of the orbit provides some protection for the eye. The eye should be examined directly, sometimes under general anesthesia, to determine the possibility or extent of injury.

Trauma injuries may result from birth and may include orbital hemorrhage, orbital fracture, or injuries to the optic nerve or the extraocular muscles (Crawford & Morin, 1983). Other instances of trauma include lid lacerations, trauma from forceful blows, and lacerations caused by foreign bodies in the eye. A hemorrhage into the *anterior* chamber of the eye, usually caused by trauma, is called *hyphema*. Young children may be burned by walking into hot objects such as cigarettes. Cleansing agents, including aerosol sprays, also can be irritating to the eyes. Trauma injuries must be assessed by an ophthalmologist. Treatment may involve surgery, medications, and application of eye patches.

### The Nursing Process for Eye Trauma

Because trauma to the eye usually requires assessment and diagnosis by an ophthalmologist, the nurse should obtain as accurate a history of the accident as possible. In addition, the external condition of the eye should be noted as well as the child's level of pain.

Nursing diagnoses for eye trauma might include the following:

- Pain related to trauma
- High risk for infection related to compromised integrity of the protective covering of the eye
- Anxiety related to threatened ability to see
- Fear related to diagnostic procedures and corrective treatments

Nursing interventions should be preventive. Nurses should teach parents and children how to protect their eyes from trauma; for example, young children should not use pointed objects or scissors, and older children should be taught proper techniques for insertion and removal of contact lenses.

The child or adolescent may be anxious if patches are placed on one or both eyes. Dim light is more comfortable and facilitates rest. The child should be observed for signs of infection, inflammation, or hemorrhage in the affected eye and for inflammation in the unaffected eye. Ocular pain may persist for a period of time, and the nurse may help by instilling medications as ordered. The child and parents may feel anxious or guilty about the circumstances causing the trauma. The nurse should encourage the child and parents to express their concerns and feelings.

## Chronic Vision Problems

### Impaired Vision

Legally, people with low vision have central visual acuity (in the better eye) between 20/60 and 20/200. Legally blind people have a central visual acuity of 20 degrees or less, or vision in the better eye of 20/200 or less (Kovalesky, 1985). Many people who are legally blind have some residual vision. One in 2500 school children in the United States is legally blind; in most of these children, blindness occurred before their first birthday (Kovalesky, 1985).

Parents may notice that the child does not respond to them or to objects presented to him or her. If the child is very young, there may be some disturbance in the attachment process. Older children and their families have to learn to cope with the shock of lost vision and with the reactions of denial, anger, and grief. Usually, the pediatrician refers the child and family to an ophthalmologist. Some conditions, such as cataracts and glaucoma, can be treated. Other conditions may remain stable, deteriorate, or improve. Support groups such as the National Association for Parents of the Visually Impaired can be helpful. The American Foundation for the Blind has pamphlets that provide useful information. Special educational and social programs can maximize the child's development.

## The Nursing Process for Impaired Vision

Nursing assessment of children with chronic visual problems includes careful observation and assessment of visual ability through screening tests. It is important for nurses to assess how children perceive themselves and their relationships with their families and their peers.

Nursing diagnoses for impaired vision might include the following:

- High risk for injury related to decreased visual acuity
- Visual sensory alteration related to decreased ability to see
- Self-care deficit related to decreased ability to see
- Social isolation related to inability to cope with visual loss
- Self-esteem disturbance related to visual loss

Children with chronic vision problems require long-term nursing care. They and their families must be encouraged to maintain follow-up care and visits to the physician. Educational planning must be coordinated by the health team in the school. The child may need special seating, large-print books, audio tapes of class materials, or special educational facilities. If the impaired vision is progressive, some children and parents experience chronic grief. In these cases, the development of effective coping mechanisms is important. Evaluation is concerned with effective adaptation to the impaired vision.

## Hearing Problems of Infants and Toddlers

Electrophysiological data suggest that whereas the middle and inner ears are anatomically mature in full-term infants, maturation of auditory processes occurs during the first 18 months of life. During this period, one of the most common problems for children is otitis media.

### Acute Otitis Media

*Acute otitis media* (AOM) is an inflammation of the middle-ear space. The incidence of AOM substantially increases after 6 months of age; about one of every three children experiences AOM by the second birthday. It is much less common after 6 or 7 years of age. Causes of middle-ear dysfunction include eustachian tube dysfunction, nasal allergy, diseased adenoid tissue, or diseased sinuses.

In infants, the eustachian tube is shorter, more horizontal, and wider than it is in older children and adults. It is also more distensible. These anatomical factors facilitate the passage of foreign matter up the eustachian tube. Another factor that contributes to fluid pooling in the eustachian tube in infants and young children is that they frequently lie in the supine position, which inhibits drainage of fluid from the eustachian tube.

It is thought that bottle feeding of an infant in a supine position may contribute to the incidence of AOM. It has also been suggested that formula-fed infants may be more susceptible to pooling of fluids in the middle ear than breast-fed infants because of the position in which they are held during feedings.

Acute otitis media is more prevalent in boys, whites, Alaskan natives, and American Indians. The rising incidence of AOM may be related to the increased numbers of children attending day care. This may be due to the greater spread of upper respiratory infections in a somewhat confined environment (Stoll, 1989). Children from large families also appear to have a greater incidence of AOM. The most important and best-documented risk factor is that of bacterial infection. In addition, increased pressure behind the eardrum (tympanic membrane) may result in its perforation or rupture.

The two organisms usually implicated in AOM are *Streptococcus pneumoniae* and *Haemophilus influenzae.* AOM usually begins a few days after a cold or upper respiratory infection. Symptoms may include earache, loss of hearing, fever, and a feeling of fullness or pressure in the ear. AOM is of recent onset and may last 2 to 6 weeks. If the child is treated with antibiotics, the symptoms usually subside in 24 to 48 hours after therapy is initiated. The young, nonverbal child may be irritable or may pull on the affected ear. The child may cry or scream. Frequently, children have an associated infectious or allergic rhinitis. In the northern hemisphere, the incidence is highest in the winter or early spring.

Acute otitis media is usually treated with antibiotics. Amoxicillin is usually employed for a period of 10 days. For persistent cases, a broad-spectrum antibiotic, such as cefaclor, may be prescribed. Amoxicillin and clavulanate potassium (Augmentin) may be prescribed if AOM is not cleared with amoxicillin (Chan et al., 1988). Prednisone, in conjunction with sulfamethoxazole and trimethoprim, has also been used with success (Berman, Grose, & Zerbe, 1987). Antihistamines and decongestants are usually considered to be ineffective. For fever, acetaminophen may be prescribed. Symptoms of AOM subside rapidly with antibacterial treatment, but cases with effusion respond less rapidly.

In a number of cases, an episode of acute otitis media is followed by effusion. It is difficult to determine whether or not the effusion is infected without tympanocentesis, which is not recommended at the time of initial diagnosis. The effusion may last from 6 weeks to 3 months. If the tympanic membrane is discolored and bulging, with impaired mobility, an infection is likely. With effusion, the tympanic membrane appears lusterless, opacified, hyperemic, and has poor mobility, but no bulging is seen. An increased incidence of parental smoking is associated with middle-ear effusions (Hinton & Buckley, 1988).

# Chronic Middle-Ear Effusion

*Chronic middle-ear effusion* is the most frequent cause of hearing loss in young children and the most frequent cause for operative procedures. An inflammation is chronic if it lasts more than 3 months. Other terms for chronic middle-ear effusion include *chronic secretory otitis media, nonsuppurative otitis media,* and *glue ear.* Effusion usually results in a moderate conductive hearing loss. It is almost always associated with perforation of the eardrum. Drainage from the ear, tinnitus (ringing in the ear), and loss of hearing may be the presenting symptoms.

Myringotomy, an incision made in the anteroinferior aspect of the tympanic membrane, may be performed for children with recurrent otitis media or chronic serous otitis media. Usually, this is followed by the insertion of tympanostomy tubes. These tubes remain in place for a period from 2 months to 6 years, when they fall out (Hughes & Wight, 1988). The procedure is usually performed under general anesthesia, as 1-day surgery, and the child is usually discharged as soon as fluids can be taken. There is usually a slight serous or mucoid drainage after the insertion of the tubes. Sometimes, steroid otic drops are prescribed to reduce inflammation of the external ear canal. Adenoidectomy for chronic middle-ear effusion is less frequently used today because it is a difficult procedure that may be complicated by hemorrhage (Gates, Avery, Prihoda, & Cooper, 1987).

## The Nursing Process for Chronic Ear Problems

Nursing assessment includes a thorough history and physical examination. The following questions may assist in the assessment: Are there any predisposing factors, such as a family history of recurrent or chronic otitis media with effusion, recent upper respiratory infection, or nasal allergy? Does the child attend day care?

The physical examination must include visualization of the tympanic membrane using an otoscope. The pneumatic otoscope is a most valuable tool in testing for mobility of the tympanic membranes. The usefulness of pneumatic otoscopy, however, is influenced by the skill of the examiner. Another useful tool, the acoustic otoscope, measures the ability of the tympanic membrane to reflect sound. Fluid or thickening of the eardrum increases the reflection of sound (Jehle & Cottington, 1989). Tympanometry is also a useful assessment measure when diagnosis is difficult. An electroacoustic impedance bridge is placed in the ear, and tympanic membrane compliance is measured by exerting varying pressures. Compliance indicates middle-ear pressure. Maximum compliance occurs when the pressure in the ear canal equals the air pressure in the middle-ear space. A flat curve on the tympanogram indicates that effusion is present (Castiglia, Aquilina, & Kemsley, 1983). Additional assessment may be

done by Weber's test, in which a tuning fork is used to indicate where the affected ear hears the sound. The Rinne test also uses a tuning fork but seeks to determine air and bone conduction. Usually, air conduction is greater than bone conduction; however, when chronic otitis media is present, bone conduction is greater than air conduction. Obviously, Weber's and Rinne tests are not usually helpful for preschool-aged children because younger children are unable to participate in the tests in an appropriate manner; they have short attention spans and, therefore, may not be able to understand the directions.

Speech assessment should also be conducted as another means of attempting to discern if the child hears all sounds. The Denver Articulation Screening Examination may be used for a general speech assessment (see Appendix A).

Nursing diagnoses for chronic ear problems might include the following:

- Auditory sensory alteration related to impaired sensory reception and transmission
- Anxiety related to diagnostic procedures and treatment measures
- Pain related to chronic infections or surgical procedures
- Altered family processes related to child's inability to receive auditory stimulation

The nursing care plan should include actions to assist in the medical management, including administering medications and assisting with procedures.

The nurse is frequently asked by patients and parents to explain procedures. Parents need to be instructed about how to instill ear drops if they are ordered (Fig. 35-7). Parents may ask whether the child can get water in the ears with the tubes in place. This is controversial among physicians; some recommend the use of custom-made ear molds or ear plugs, whereas others do not feel they are necessary. Diving is not permitted because the pressure change may rupture the oval or round window, causing permanent deafness. Chlorine in water may cause inflammation.

Parents should be informed that the tubes usually fall out spontaneously. When this happens, they should inform the physician, who will check to be certain that reinsertion is not needed. An emphasis of teaching includes the need for compliance with treatment regimens.

Nurses assess hearing, language development, and developmental progress. Frequently, they are the first to speak to the parents about any discrepancies in sensory and general development. As a result, nursing plans include referrals to physicians or other health care professionals. If the parents have not recognized any signs of sensory discrepancy, they may not understand the severity of the condition. Later, they may blame themselves for not recognizing signs of speech delay or hearing impairment.

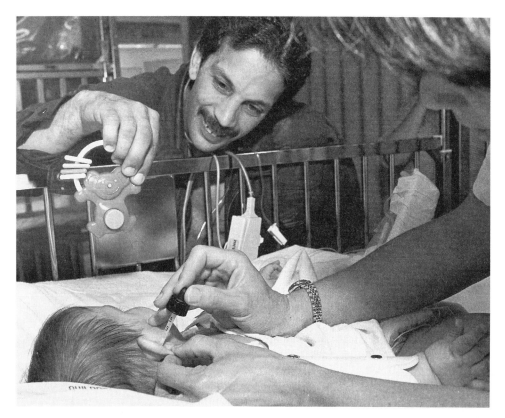

*Figure 35–7. Instilling ear drops. (Source: Kathy Sloane)*

Follow-up care and support for the family are important nursing activities, as is continued monitoring of the child's status.

## Mastoiditis

*Mastoiditis,* an inflammation of one of the mastoid bones, may appear as a complication of acute or chronic otitis media. Acute mastoiditis following acute otitis media has become rare because of early antimicrobial therapy for acute otitis media. Radiograph of the mastoid reveals cloudiness. Chronic suppurative otitis media with mastoiditis may be associated with perforation of the tympanic membrane or *cholesteatoma* (a cystlike mass). There may be episodic or continuous purulent discharge. The most common organisms involved are gram-negative bacilli (e.g., *Bacillus proteus*).

Mastoiditis may follow sore throat and respiratory infection, diphtheria, measles, and scarlet fever. Symptoms usually include earache and tinnitus. The mastoid process (located in the postauricular area) may become painful and swollen. The pinna may be displaced inferiorly and anteriorly. Mastoiditis without postauricular swelling may occur (Ibekwe & Okoye, 1988). Treatment may involve tympanocentesis, myringotomy, and administration of systemic ampicillin. If left untreated, the infection may progress to form a subperiosteal abscess, break through the

mastoid tip into the neck, or fistulize into the external ear canal (Behrman & Vaughan, 1987). If osteitis occurs, mastoidectomy is required.

If surgery is required, an incision is made behind the pinna, and the mastoid area is scraped clean. Drains are inserted to prevent the formation of hematomas. The drains are usually removed 3 to 4 days after surgery. A pressure dressing is usually applied after surgery, and antibiotics are prescribed.

### The Nursing Process for Mastoiditis

During the nursing assessment, the physical examination usually reveals postauricular swelling and tenderness. There may be a discharge from the ear. The nursing history reveals that the child has been treated for chronic otitis media; otoscopic examination may reveal a tear in the tympanic membrane.

Nursing diagnoses for mastoiditis might include the following:

* Auditory sensory alteration related to tinnitus, congestion
* Pain related to swelling, tinnitus

Nurses must be able to explain the condition and the prescribed regimen; instruct regarding proper medication regimens; administer pre- and postoperative care; and instruct the child and family about the condition and treatment. Nurses must monitor children after surgery for signs of edema or hemorrhage. The child may complain of pain, nausea, or dizziness. Oral fluids must be given gradually until the nausea disappears. The child should be positioned on the side, with the bed flat or slightly elevated and the affected ear uppermost.

Parents need to be instructed about the administration of antibiotics and how to change the dressing at home. The child should not be allowed to take showers until the physician recommends it.

Evaluation of nursing care should demonstrate that postsurgical recovery is uneventful, pain is managed as needed, and the surgical incision heals without complication.

## Otitis Externa (Swimmer's Ear)

*Otitis externa* (swimmer's ear) results from the loss of cerumen, which has a protective function, and the chronic irritation or maceration of the ear canal. This situation results from excessive moisture in the ear canal in which bacteria (e.g., *Pseudomonas aeruginosa*), streptococci, or fungi grow.

Pain in the ear that is aggravated by movement of the pinna is the predominant symptom. The pain may be preceded by itching. Swelling of the ear canal and severe pain may make otoscopic examination impossible. Topical neomycin otic ointments and corticosteroids have been found to be effective treatments. Children with recurrent bouts of otitis externa may be advised by the physician to instill dilute alcohol or acetic acid immediately after swimming or bathing (Behrman & Vaughan, 1987).

Nursing diagnoses may include the following:

- Pain and pruritus related to swelling in the external ear canal
- Auditory sensory alteration related to decreased sensory reception

The nurse must plan to discuss the condition with the child and parents, instill otic medications, and teach the procedure for instilling ear medications. Follow-up care, especially in relation to identifying chronicity, is important.

## Hearing Problems of Children and Adolescents

### Hearing Loss Induced by Noise

Noise (undesired sound) of all types is accepted, tolerated, and expected in modern society. Control of noise is often difficult to implement. Sound is measured in terms of frequency, intensity, and exposure time. Most people are sensitive to sounds in the 500 to 3000 Hz range.

It has long been known that exposure to loud noises for long periods of time can affect hearing. This type of hearing loss—a sensorineural loss—is irreversible. The most important action, therefore, is prevention.

The specific mechanism for hearing loss caused by noise is not known. A degeneration of the sensory hair cells of the cochlea has been noted. These hair cells cannot be repaired or replaced (Dobie, 1987). In cases of severe noise, the eardrum may rupture.

Tinnitus frequently accompanies noise-induced hearing loss. Other signs may include the muffling of sound or a discomfort in the ears.

Even short-term exposure to high-intensity sound may affect hearing. The risk to the ears of children compared with adults is not known. If the intense noise is heard for only a short period of time, there may be a temporary hearing loss with recovery after a few hours.

Noise is too great when people have trouble trying to talk over it, when tinnitus is reported, and when temporary hearing loss occurs. The following are examples of causes of high noise levels to which most children are exposed: firecrackers, power mowers and trimmers, snow blowers, motorcycles, snowmobiles, model airplane engines, and firearms (Bordley, Brookhauser, & Tucker, 1986). Premature and ill infants are continually exposed to the noise of incubators and other life-saving equipment. Of increasing concern in recent years has been the exposure of adolescents to high-intensity rock music. Many adolescents like to have as many speakers as possible and also like to wear earphones for extended periods (Fig. 35-8).

### The Nursing Process for Hearing Loss Induced by Noise

Nursing assessment is conducted by obtaining a detailed history designed to elicit signs and symptoms relevant to hearing. Audiometric evaluation should be included initially, and repeat testing should be planned.

Nursing diagnoses for hearing loss induced by noise might include the following:

- Auditory sensory alteration related to extreme exposure to noise over an extended period of time
- Anxiety related to hearing loss
- Ineffective individual coping related to sensory deprivation

Nursing care plans should emphasize the prevention of primary and subsequent hearing loss through the education of parents and children. Adolescents consider loud music a part of their lifestyle. Since adolescents have an impact on the type of music played and the equipment purchased in our society, they seem able to dictate increas-

*Figure 35–8.    Adolescent with earphones.*

ingly louder music. Their absorption in loud music may be viewed as an escape from the constraints of daily living and typifies the adolescent developmental stage. Parents may need to set limits on the amount of time a child can wear earphones or listen to loud music. In addition, an audiometric analysis of hearing should be performed periodically. One problem in identifying hearing loss is that children may not actually realize that they have a hearing loss. Unfortunately, hearing aids offer only limited help. Advocates for children must seek to minimize noise exposure for children in much the same way that OSHA attempts to protect workers.

Evaluation of nursing plans should focus on the early recognition of hearing loss, the prevention of further loss, and the establishment of noise control regulations for children.

## Nasal Problems of Infants, Toddlers, and Adolescents

### Acute Nasopharyngitis (Common Cold)

*Acute nasopharyngitis* is the most infectious process of childhood. It is caused by many different viruses, but the rhinoviruses are thought to be the primary agents. Other causative agents include the parainfluenza virus, the respiratory syncytial virus, the adenovirus, the coronavirus, and the enterovirus. Most children experience three to six infections per year; these infections are more severe in younger children. The greatest incidence appears to occur in the fall, but more complications appear to occur in midwinter.

Younger children are usually afebrile, whereas older

children may have low-grade fevers. Infants frequently present with fever, restlessness, sneezing, and irritability, accompanied by nasal discharge; they may also have vomiting or diarrhea. Older children may experience chills, sneezing, headache, general malaise, and low-grade fevers. The acute phase of acute nasopharyngitis may last from 4 to 10 days.

Treatment for acute nasopharyngitis is symptomatic and includes comfort measures, prevention of complications, and measures to relieve local irritations. Nasal preparations such as ephedrine may be ordered to relieve nasal congestion. Normal saline nose drops and suction with a bulb syringe may be ordered for infants in an attempt to relieve nasal congestion. Vaporizers and humidifiers are also used to facilitate nasal breathing. The use of antihistamines and decongestants is debatable. Acetaminophen should be used for relief of fever. Aspirin should be avoided because of the association between its use and Reye's syndrome.

### Acute Pharyngitis

*Acute pharyngitis* includes all acute infections of the pharynx, such as pharyngotonsillitis and tonsillitis. It is generally caused by viruses but may be caused by group A β-hemolytic streptococcus. Viral pharyngitis has a gradual onset with fever, malaise, anorexia, and moderate throat pain. Streptococcal pharyngitis usually develops suddenly in children over 3 years old. Initially, there may be only fever and general malaise. Throat symptoms are frequently absent for the first 12 to 24 hours (Castiglia & Aquilina, 1982). Sore throat, hoarseness, and a nonproductive cough may appear about the third or fourth day. The pharyngitis is usually of viral origin when two or more of the following symptoms are present: conjunctivitis, cough, hoarseness, and rhinitis. Viral pharyngitis is infectious for several days.

Throat cultures should be done to identify the causative organisms. The use of antibiotics should be deferred until the results of the throat culture are available. Streptococcal pharyngitis is treated with penicillin or with erythromycin for children who are allergic to penicillin. Bed rest, various saline gargles, and cool, bland liquids are palliative measures that may make the child more comfortable. Once penicillin therapy has begun, the child with streptococcal pharyngitis is no longer infectious to others (usually 24 to 48 hours). It is important to treat streptococcal pharyngitis in order to prevent additional infections such as scarlet fever, rheumatic heart disease, and acute glomerulonephritis. Children who should be protected from streptococcal infections (e.g., postrheumatic fever) should receive prophylactic antibiotics.

Repeat throat cultures are ordered for streptococcal infections. If the repeat culture is positive for group A β-hemolytic streptococci, either the child did not complete the 14-day antibiotic therapy, an organism that is resistant to that antibiotic is present, or a new infection has been acquired. It is also possible that the child may be a carrier if, after continued treatment, a third culture is positive (Castiglia & Aquilina, 1982).

### The Nursing Process for Acute Pharyngitis

Nursing assessment includes a comprehensive history of the illness, a review of the symptoms, and a physical assessment. Laboratory results of throat cultures confirm the causative agent.

Nursing diagnoses for acute pharyngitis might include the following:

- Hyperthermia related to the infective process
- Fatigue related to the infective process
- Impaired swallowing related to swelling in the throat
- Pain related to inflammation in throat, cough

Nursing intervention measures include administering medications and instructing the parents and child about the illness (Behrman & Vaughan, 1987). The parents and child must be informed of the necessity to take all the antibiotics as ordered to ensure that the infective process is halted. In addition, the nurse should instruct the parents about comfort measures, such as rest and warmth, as well as about fever-reduction measures, including administration of acetaminophen and fluids. Throat discomfort can be reduced by giving the child cool liquids, lozenges, or warm normal saline gargles. Parents should be instructed to adhere to follow-up measures prescribed by the physician.

### Chronic Tonsillitis

It is believed that the tonsils serve to protect children against upper respiratory infections. When the tonsils become inflamed, they swell and block the passage of air and food. The adenoids usually become swollen as well and block the nasal passages. The child must breathe through the mouth and becomes uncomfortable.

In chronic tonsillitis, the tonsils are chronically infected and hypertrophic. Surgical treatment for chronic tonsillitis is controversial. Usually, but not always, a tonsillectomy and adenoidectomy are performed at the same time. The usual indicators for a tonsillectomy include four or more episodes of β-hemolytic streptococcal pharyngitis (diagnosed by cultures) within 1 year as well as airway obstruction resulting from hypertrophied tonsils or peritonsillar abscess. The child should be between 2 and 3 years of age.

Nursing diagnoses for chronic tonsillitis might include the following:

- Pain related to the infectious process and the surgical procedure
- Impaired swallowing related to tonsillar edema
- Anxiety related to surgical procedures

Nursing care includes preparation of the child for surgery and for the postoperative pain the child will feel. Many hospitals have programs that help prepare children for surgery. After surgery, nursing interventions include maintaining the airway, observing for signs of hemorrhage, and comfort measures. The child is positioned either on the abdomen or side to facilitate drainage of secretions. Symptoms of hemorrhage include frequent swallowing (of blood), restlessness, tachycardia, pallor, or vomiting bright red blood. Analgesics and ice collars can be used for comfort. Clear, cool fluids should be offered, followed by soft foods such as ice cream.

### Sinusitis

Sinusitis may be either acute or chronic. Symptoms of acute sinusitis include fever, headache, localized pain or a sense of fullness, localized tenderness to pressure, and edema over the affected sinus. Radiographs of the affected sinus appear opaque. Treatment is directed toward shrinking the nasal mucous membranes to facilitate sinus drainage. Phenylephrine nose drops or spray, can be used four times per day for 5 days. Systemic decongestants may also be employed.

When sinusitis is chronic, obstructive causes, such as nasal polyps, infected teeth, or infected adenoids, should be evaluated. Symptoms of chronic sinusitis may include low-grade fever, general malaise, anorexia, headaches, localized pain, or sneezing attacks. Treatment includes decongestants and antibiotics. Surgery is done only if all other measures fail.

### The Nursing Process for Sinusitis

Nursing assessment includes a comprehensive history of the illness, a review of the symptoms, and a physical assessment.

Nursing diagnoses for sinusitis might include the following:

- Ineffective airway clearance related to edema of the sinuses
- Pain related to edema and tenderness of the mucous membranes

Nursing care for sinusitis includes providing the child and parents with information regarding administration of prescribed medications and other prescribed treatments. Nurses should stress the need for follow-up assessment.

### Allergic Rhinitis

*Allergic rhinitis* may be related to a seasonal incidence. Age also appears to be a factor in the incidence since children under 5 years old seldom have allergic rhinitis. Hay fever is an example of an acute type of allergic rhinitis. Some cases, however, occur year-round.

Although not generally considered a serious condition, allergic rhinitis symptoms range from mild to severe and debilitating. Nasal discharge may be profuse, and the mucous membranes of the nose usually become swollen. Sneezing (sometimes paroxysmal); itching of the nose, palate, pharynx, and ears; and runny, itchy eyes may add to the general discomfort. Nasal discharge that becomes thick, greenish, or purulent indicates the presence of a bacterial infection.

A smear of nasal secretions is generally ordered and reveals a predominance of eosinophils in allergic rhinitis. The first treatment is to try to avoid exposure to suspected irritating substances. The allergist may further assess the causative agents by skin testing (in vivo) or by in vitro (radioallergosorbent test—RAST) criteria.

Skin-testing usually confirms allergies to substances identified in the history. A small area (usually on the back) is scratched with a needle or lancet, and an allergen extract is applied to the site. Sites are arranged in rows. An alternate form of skin testing is the prick method, which involves putting a drop of allergen extract on the skin and then pricking the skin. With either method of testing, a positive reaction occurs when erythema and wheals form at the site of offending agents. The severity of the allergy, however, cannot be assessed by the reaction to the skin test.

Intradermal or intracutaneous testing can also be done. The volar surface of the arm is used for the administration of an allergen extract (1 : 1000) in a dose of 0.02 mL. Children should never be left alone during skin testing. The radioallergosorbent test measures the immunoglobulin E present in blood serum and can also identify the antibodies produced in response to a specific allergen.

Immunotherapy (hyposensitization) is often successful when the allergic response is mediated by IgE antibody–antigen interaction, which involves allergens that cannot be avoided. If this is not successful, drug therapy may be employed; this may include the use of antihistamines or decongestants. If nasal obstruction is a problem, pseudoephedrine or phenylpropanolamine (sympathomimetics) may be used. Topical corticosteroids are often effective in patients who do not respond to antihistamine or decongestant therapy. Cromylin sodium nasal solution is sometimes used for patients with persistent, perennial rhinitis.

### The Nursing Process for Allergic Rhinitis

Nursing assessment includes taking a complete history and carefully observing for indicators of allergic rhinitis. Bilateral nasal obstruction usually occurs. The mucous membranes of the nose may have a bluish tinge, and they are pale when visualized with a nasal light. The nasal discharge is usually pale. The child may be observed wrinkling or rubbing the nose. Upward rubbing of the nose is a typical action that is called the "allergic salute" (Fig. 35-9).

Dark circles under the eyes may be observed. These

*Figure 35–9. A child doing the "allergic salute." Note dark circles under the eyes.*

are due to venous stasis resulting from the decreased blood flow through the edematous nasal passages. Mouth breathing is frequently seen or reported.

Nursing diagnoses for allergic rhinitis might include the following:

- Ineffective airway clearance related to edema of the nasal passages
- High risk for activity intolerance related to infection

Nursing plans should include referral to an allergist for evaluation and treatment. Nurses can provide anticipatory guidance by advising parents on how to remove suspected allergens from the child's environment. In addition, nurses should provide information on prescribed medication administration and other treatments. The need for adequate rest should be stressed so that the child maintains normal activities to the greatest extent possible.

Evaluation of the therapy relates to the child's comfort and ability to function.

### Summary

Development of sensory function begins in the embryonic stage. At birth, the infant can perceive tactile stimulation, can respond to light, has poor visual acuity, and can react to sudden, loud noises. Children over 4 years of age have both primary sensory sensation and secondary (cortical) sensation. Primary sensory sensations include touch, pain, pressure, temperature, vibration and motion, and position change. Secondary sensory sensations include point localization, two-point discrimination, graphesthesia, and stereognosis (Chow, Durand, Feldman, & Mills, 1984).

The primary role of the nurse is the assessment of alterations in sensory function. The nurse is frequently the first person to identify deviations, to discuss findings and recommendations with the child and family, and to make appropriate referrals. An interdisciplinary approach to sensory problems is the most effective plan. Physicians, therapists (e.g., speech therapists), social workers, and educators should work with nurses to plan for the maxi-

mum quality of life possible for the child, the parents, and the family. Evaluation of treatment includes the evaluation of social and educational factors. Long-term planning must be implemented for many conditions, and the child and family must be supported throughout the diagnostic, treatment, and follow-up periods.

# Nursing Care Plan

## *Assessment*

Brian Kane is a 4-year-old who was brought to the outpatient clinic by his mother at the request of his teacher.

### *Chief Complaint*

Inattention in class and reports by Brian of intermittent earaches and popping in his ears for about 1 week.

### *Subjective Assessment*

*Past History:* Brian's mother stated that Brian had not had a fever but that he had had an ear infection 2 months ago that was discovered during a routine physical examination. He was given amoxicillin for 10 days, but the recheck after 2 weeks revealed that the infection had not cleared. His mother stated that another antibiotic was then ordered. She did not remember the name of the medication, nor did she return for a subsequent check-up. She said that Brian finished the medication and acted well. She also said that Brian had had three or four earaches every year since he was born but that he never really complained or got sick with them.

*Present History:* Brian had a slight cold about 1 week ago. He did not have a fever and continued to attend nursery school. His teacher told his mother that he occasionally held his ears during the past week but that he participated in all activities. She expressed some concern because Brian sometimes acts as though either he does not hear the teacher or else is inattentive.

*Family History:* Brian's mother is 30 years old, and his father is 32 years old. There is one older sibling, a 6-year-old sister. All are well. The pater-

nal and maternal grandparents are alive and well. The paternal grandfather has had a hearing loss since he was very young.

### *Objective Assessment*

*Physical Examination:* T. 37°C (oral); P. 120 (radial); R 22; B.P. 100/55 (R. arm); weight 18 kg (50%); height 106 cm (60%).

| | |
|---|---|
| Integument: | Clear with good turgor |
| Head: | Normal |
| Eyes: | PERRLA and EOM intact |
| | Fundoscopic examination normal |
| | Dark circles under eyes |
| Ears: | TM retracted, translucent, and dull |
| | Light reflex distorted bilaterally and yellowish in color |
| | No mobility evidenced |
| | Tympanometry indicates increased pressure as evidenced by an almost flat curve (type B) |
| | Rinne test indicates bone conduction is greater than air conduction |
| | Weber test (250 Hz) goes to left ear |
| Nose: | Mucous membranes dull and boggy |
| Throat: | Enlarged palatine tonsils (3×) |
| | No exudate, no erythema |
| Neck: | Posterior cervical nodes palpable without tenderness |
| | Full range of motion |

*(continued)*

# Nursing Care Plan *(Continued)*

| | | | |
|---|---|---|---|
| Thorax and Lungs: | All lung fields clear | Speech: | Clear |
| Heart: | Heart rate regular; N1. $S_1 S_2$; no murmur | | Appears to have difficulty with "th" and "v" sounds |
| Abdomen: | Active bowel sounds in all quadrants | | Appropriate responses to questions |
| | No pain, tenderness, or masses | | |
| Genitalia: | Normal circumcised, testes palpated in scrotum | | |
| Musculoskeletal: | Full range of motion | | |
| | Leg lengths equal | | |
| Neurological: | Alert reflexes: DTRs 2+ and symmetrical | | |

A full-threshold audiogram revealed the following:

| Right | Left |
|---|---|
| 25 dB at 250 Hz | 30 dB at 250 Hz |
| 20 dB at 500 Hz | 25 dB at 500 Hz |
| 15 dB at 1000 Hz | 20 dB at 1000 Hz |
| 5 dB at 2000 Hz | 10 dB at 2000 Hz |
| 15 dB at 4000 Hz | 20 dB at 4000 Hz |
| 25 dB at 8000 Hz | 35 dB at 8000 Hz |

## *Nursing Care Plan for a Child With Hearing Loss*

| *Goals* | *Nursing Interventions* | *Evaluation Criteria* |
|---|---|---|
| **NURSING DIAGNOSIS #1: Auditory sensory alteration related to impaired sensory reception and transmission** | | |
| (S) The child will continue in nursery school <br><br> (L) The long-term effects of hearing loss will be minimized | Stress importance of complying with referral to ear, nose, and throat specialist <br><br> Refer to audiologist for evaluation <br><br> Refer to speech therapist for evaluation <br><br> Encourage parents to share information with the nursery school teacher <br><br> Encourage parents to explore the possibility of having the child seated toward the front of the room for story time and other activities that require careful listening | The child has been evaluated by an ear, nose, and throat specialist, an audiologist, and a speech therapist <br><br> The child should be reported to be paying more attention in school |
| **NURSING DIAGNOSIS #2: Anxiety related to diagnostic procedures and treatment measures** | | |
| (S) The child and parents will understand the purpose of tympanocentesis and tympanostomy tubes | Encourage verbalization of concerns and feelings | An interdisciplinary plan of care is designed that includes the teacher |

*(continued)*

# Nursing Care Plan *(Continued)*

| Goals | Nursing Interventions | Evaluation Criteria |
|---|---|---|
| (S) The child and parents will understand the action of the prescribed medications and the dosage regimens<br><br>(L) The child and parents will understand the etiology and treatment of chronic middle-ear effusion, and the need for follow-up evaluation | Assist in formulating questions for the physician, the audiologist, and the speech therapist<br><br>Clarify misconceptions<br><br>Describe and explain diagnostic procedures<br><br>Explain the purpose of the tympanocentesis procedure and tympanostomy tubes<br><br>Teach appropriate regimen for prescribed medications<br><br>Stress importance of follow-up evaluation and care | The parents and the child demonstrate an understanding of chronic middle-ear effusion by verbally describing the condition, the cause the physiological mechanisms, treatment, and follow-up |

*NURSING DIAGNOSIS #3: Pain related to chronic infections or surgical procedures*

| Goals | Nursing Interventions | Evaluation Criteria |
|---|---|---|
| (S) The child will report no pain | Encourage child to describe pain to either the nurse or the parents<br><br>Attempt to prevent the pain rather than letting child become uncomfortable<br><br>Administer medications as prescribed<br><br>Educate parents regarding pain management and administration of medications | The child is free from pain |

*NURSING DIAGNOSIS #4: Altered family processes related to child's inability to receive auditory stimulation*

| Goals | Nursing Interventions | Evaluation Criteria |
|---|---|---|
| (S) The child and parents will comply with the treatment plan<br><br>(S) The child and parents will be able to explain the etiology of chronic middle-ear effusion | Encourage the child and parents to verbalize feelings and concerns<br><br>Encourage parents to participate in the child's care<br><br>Assist in identification and use of external resources (e.g., audiologist, speech therapist, etc.) | The parents and the child demonstrate knowledge about the treatment by explanation and compliance |

# References

Alexander, M. M., & Brown, M. S. (1979). *Pediatric physical diagnosis for nurses.* New York: McGraw-Hill.

Behrman, R. E., & Vaughan, V. C. (1987). *Nelson textbook of pediatrics* (13th ed.). Philadelphia: W. B. Saunders.

Berman, S., Grose, K., & Zerbe, G. O. (1987). Medical management of chronic middle-ear effusion. *American Journal of Diseases of Children, 141,* 690–694.

Bordley, J. E., Brookhauser, P. E., & Tucker, G. F. (1986). *Ear, nose and throat disorders in children.* New York: Raven Press.

Castiglia, P. T., & Aquilina, S. (1982). Streptococcal pharyngitis: A persistent challenge. *Pediatric Nursing, 8*(6), 377–382.

Castiglia, P. T., Aquilina, S., & Kemsley, M. (1983). Focus: Nonsuppurative otitis media. *Pediatric Nursing, 9*(6), 427–430.

Chan, K. H., Mandel, E. M., Aakette, H. E., Bluestone, C. D., Bass, L. W., Blatte, M. M., Breck, J. M., Reisinger, K. S., Wolfson, J. H., Wucher, F. P., Fall, P., & Kim, H. K. (1988). A comparative study of amoxicillin-clavulanate and amoxicillin. *Archives of Otolaryngology—Head and Neck Surgery, 114,* 142–146.

Chow, M. P., Durand, B. A., Feldman, M. N., & Mills, M. A. (1984). *Handbook of pediatric primary care* (2nd ed.). New York: John Wiley & Sons.

Crawford, J. S., & Morin, J. D. (1983). *The eye in childhood.* New York: Grune & Stratton.

Dobie, R. A. (1987). Noise-induced hearing loss: The family physician's role. *American Family Physician, 35*(12), 141–148.

Fielder, A. R., Ng, Y. K., & Levene, M. I. (1986). Retinopathy of prematurity: Age at onset. *Archives of Disease in Childhood, 61,* 774–758.

Gates, G. A., Avery, C. A., Prihoda, T. J., & Cooper, J. C. (1987). Effectiveness of adenoidectomy and tympanostomy tubes in the treatment of chronic otitis media with effusion. *New England Journal of Medicine, 317*(23), 1444–1451.

Hinton, A. E., & Buckley, G. (1988). Parental smoking and middle ear effusions in children. *The Journal of Laryngology and Otology, 102,* 992–996.

Hughes, L. A., & Wight, I. D. (1988). Tympanostomy tubes: Long-term effects. *Annals of Family Practice, 38*(5), 186–190.

Ibekwe, A. O., & Okoye, B. C. (1988). Subperiosteal mastoid abscesses in chronic suppurative otitis media. *Annals of Otology, Rhinology and Laryngology, 97,* 373–375.

Jehle, D., & Cottington, E. (1989). Acoustic otoscopy in the diagnosis of otitis mediae. *Annals of Emergency Medicine, 18*(4), 396–400.

Khouri, G., Mets, M. B., Smith, V. C., Wendell, M., & Pass, A. S. (1988). X-Linked congenital stationary night blindness. *Archives of Ophthalmology, 106*(10), 1417–1422.

Kovalesky, A. (1985). *Nurses' guide to children's eyes.* New York: Grune & Stratton.

Kretzer, F. L., & Hittner, H. M. (1988). Retinopathy of prematurity: Clinical implications of retinal development. *Archives of Diseases in Childhood, 63,* 1151–1167.

Luna, B., Dobson, V., Carpenter, N. A., & Biglan, A. W. (1989). Visual field development in infants with stage 3 retinopathy of prematurity. *Investigative Ophthalmology and Visual Science, 30*(3), 580–582.

Mafee, M. F., Goldberg, M. F., Greenwald, M. J., Schulman, J., Malmed, A., & Flanders, A. E. (1987). Retinoblastoma and stimulating lesions: Role of CT and MR imaging. *Radiologic Clinics of North America, 25*(4), 667–682.

Parkin, D. M., Stiller, C. A., Draper, G. J., & Bieber, C. A. (1988). The international incidence of childhood cancer. *International Journal of Cancer, 42,* 511–520.

Phelps, D. L. What does the cryotherapy preliminary report mean? *Pediatrics, 81*(6), 884–886.

Phelps, D. L., & Phelps, C. E. (1989). Cryotherapy in infants with retinopathy of prematurity. *Journal of the American Medical Association, 261*(12), 1751–1756.

Phelps, D. L., Rosenbaum, A. L., Isenberg, S. J., Leake, R. D., & Dorey, F. J. (1987). Tocopherol efficacy and safety for preventing retinopathy of prematurity: A randomized, controlled, double-masked trial. *Pediatrics, 79*(4), 489–500.

Pruessner, H. T., Hansel, N. K., & Griffiths, M. (1986). Diagnosis and treatment of chlamydial infections. *Annals of Family Practice, 34*(1), 81–92.

Schachter, J., Moncada, J., Dawson, C. R., Sheppard, J., Courtright, P., Said, M. E., Zaki, S., Hafez, S. F., & Lorinez, A. (1988). Nonculture methods for diagnosing chlamydial infection in patients with trachoma: A clue to the pathogenesis of the disease? *The Journal of Infectious Diseases, 158*(6), 1347–1352.

Stoll, S. (1989). Otitis media: Update on a common, frustrating problem. *Postgraduate Medicine, 85*(1), 40–53.

Williams, S. M., Sanderson, G. F., Share, D. L., & Silva, P. A. (1988). Refractive error, IQ and reading ability: A longitudinal study from age 7 to 11. *Developmental Medicine and Child Neurology, 30,* 735–742.

# Bibliography

Balkany, T. J., & Pashley, N. R. T. (1986). *Clinical pediatric otolaryngology.* St. Louis: C. V. Mosby.

Becker, G. D., Eckberg, T. J., & Goldware, R. R. (1987). Swimming and tympanostomy tubes: A prospective study. *Laryngoscope, 97,* 740–741.

Bluestone, C. D. (1982). Otitis media in children: To treat or not to treat? *New England Journal of Medicine, 306*(23), 1399–1418.

Callahan, C. W., & Lazority, S. (1988). Otitis media and language development. *Annals of Family Practice, 37*(5), 186–190.

Fireman, P. (1988). Otitis media and its relationship to allergy. *Pediatric Clinics of North America, 35*(5), 1075–1090.

Ghory, J. (1982). OME: Leading causes of preventable hearing loss. *The Journal of Respiratory Diseases, 3*(10), 127–142.

Jahn, A. F., & Santos-Sacchi, J. (1988). *Physiology of the ear.* New York: Raven Press.

Ogle, J. W., & Lauer, B. A. (1986, November) Acute mastoiditis. *American Journal of Diseases in Children, 140,* 1178–1182.

Paradise, J. L. (1980). Otitis media in infants and children. *Pediatrics, 65*(5), 917–943.

Ruttum, M. S., Nelson, D. B., Wamser, M. J., & Balliff, M. (1987). Detection of congenital cataracts and other ocular media opacities. *Pediatrics, 79*(5), 815–817.

Vade, A., & Armstrong, D. (1987). Orbital rhabdomyosarcoma in childhood. *Radiologic Clinics of North America, 25*(4), 701–714.

Wald, E. R., Dashefsky, B., Byers, C., Guerre, N., & Taylor, F. (1988). Frequency and severity of infections in day care. *The Journal of Pediatrics, 112*(4), 540–546.

# Appendices

**Appendix A: Assessment Tools    1027**

Denver Articulation Screening Exam    1028

Denver II    1030

Home Inventory for Families of Infants and Toddlers, Birth to 3    1032

HOME Inventory for Families of Preschoolers, 3 to 6    1034

**Appendix B: Physiological Measurements    1036**

Growth Chart for Girls—Birth to age 36 months    1037

Growth Chart for Boys—Birth to age 36 months    1038

Growth Chart for Girls—Ages 2 to 18 years    1039

Growth Chart for Boys—Ages 2 to 18 years    1040

Head Circumference Chart for Girls    1041

Head Circumference Chart for Boys    1042

Pulse, Respiration, and Blood Pressure Values for Children    1043

**Appendix C: Normal Laboratory Values    1044**

Blood    1044

Urine    1047

Sweat    1048

Cerebrospinal Fluid    1049

Bone Marrow    1049

Stool    1049

**Appendix D: Calculating Pediatric Drug Dosages    1050**

Rules Based on Age    1050

Rules Based on Weight    1051

Rule Based on Body Surface Area    1052

**Appendix E: Temperature and Weight Conversion    1053**

Temperature Conversion Table    1053

Weight Conversion Table    1054

**Appendix F: Vaccines Commonly Used in the United States    1055**

# Appendix A:
# Assessment Tools

# DENVER ARTICULATION SCREENING EXAM
### for children 2½ to 6 years of age

Instructions: Have child repeat each word after you. Circle the underlined sounds that he pronounces correctly. Total correct sounds is the Raw Score. Use charts on reverse side to score results.

Name:

Hosp. No.:

Address: _____

_____

---

Date: _____ Child's age: _____ Examiner: _____ Raw score: __

Percentile: _____ Intelligibility: _____ Result: _____

| | | | | |
|---|---|---|---|---|
| 1. table | 6. zipper | 11. sock | 16. wagon | 21. leaf |
| 2. shirt | 7. grapes | 12. vacuum | 17. gum | 22. carrot |
| 3. door | 8. flag | 13. yarn | 18. house | |
| 4. trunk | 9. thumb | 14. mother | 19. pencil | |
| 5. jumping | 10. toothbrush | 15. twinkle | 20. fish | |

Intelligibility: (circle one)
1. Easy to understand
2. Understandable ½ the time
3. Not understandable
4. Can't evaluate

Comments:

---

**A**

Date: _____ Child's age: _____ Examiner: _____ Raw score: __

Percentile: _____ Intelligibility: _____ Result: _____

| | | | | |
|---|---|---|---|---|
| 1. table | 6. zipper | 11. sock | 16. wagon | 21. leaf |
| 2. shirt | 7. grapes | 12. vacuum | 17. gum | 22. carrot |
| 3. door | 8. flag | 13. yarn | 18. house | |
| 4. trunk | 9. thumb | 14. mother | 19. pencil | |
| 5. jumping | 10. toothbrush | 15. twinkle | 20. fish | |

Intelligibility: (circle one)
1. Easy to understand
2. Understandable ½ the time
3. Not understandable
4. Can't evaluate

Comments:

---

Date: _____ Child's age: _____ Examiner: _____ Raw score: __

Percentile: _____ Intelligibility: _____ Result: _____

| | | | | |
|---|---|---|---|---|
| 1. table | 6. zipper | 11. sock | 16. wagon | 21. leaf |
| 2. shirt | 7. grapes | 12. vacuum | 17. gum | 22. carrot |
| 3. door | 8. flag | 13. yarn | 18. house | |
| 4. trunk | 9. thumb | 14. mother | 19. pencil | |
| 5. jumping | 10. toothbrush | 15. twinkle | 20. fish | |

Intelligibility: (circle one)
1. Easy to understand
2. Understandable ½ the time
3. Not understandable
4. Can't evaluate

Comments:

---

*(A) Denver Articulation Screening Examination (DASE) for children 2½ to 6 years of age. (B) Percentile rank. (From A.F. Drumwright, University of Colorado Medical Center, 1971)*

**To score DASE words:** Note raw score for child's performance. Match raw score line (extreme left of chart) with column representing child's age (to the closest previous age group). Where raw score line and age column meet number in that square denotes percentile rank of child's performance when compared to other children that age. Percentiles above heavy line are ABNORMAL percentiles, below heavy line are NORMAL.

## PERCENTILE RANK

| Raw Score | 2.5 yr. | 3.0 | 3.5 | 4.0 | 4.5 | 5.0 | 5.5 | 6 years |
|-----------|---------|-----|-----|-----|-----|-----|-----|---------|
| 2 | 1 | | | | | | | |
| 3 | 2 | | | | | | | |
| 4 | 5 | | | | | | | |
| 5 | 9 | | | | | | | |
| 6 | 16 | | | | | | | |
| 7 | 23 | | | | | | | |
| 8 | 31 | 2 | | | | | | |
| 9 | 37 | 4 | 1 | | | | | |
| 10 | 42 | 6 | 2 | | | | | |
| 11 | 48 | 7 | 4 | | | | | |
| 12 | 54 | 9 | 6 | 1 | 1 | | | |
| 13 | 58 | 12 | 9 | 2 | 3 | 1 | 1 | |
| 14 | 62 | 17 | 11 | 5 | 4 | 2 | 2 | |
| 15 | 68 | 23 | 15 | 9 | 5 | 3 | 2 | |
| 16 | 75 | 31 | 19 | 12 | 5 | 4 | 3 | |
| 17 | 79 | 38 | 25 | 15 | 6 | 6 | 4 | |
| 18 | 83 | 46 | 31 | 19 | 8 | 7 | 4 | |
| 19 | 86 | 51 | 38 | 24 | 10 | 9 | 5 | 1 |
| 20 | 89 | 58 | 45 | 30 | 12 | 11 | 7 | 3 |
| 21 | 92 | 65 | 52 | 36 | 15 | 15 | 9 | 4 |
| 22 | 94 | 72 | 58 | 43 | 18 | 19 | 12 | 5 |
| 23 | 96 | 77 | 63 | 50 | 22 | 24 | 15 | 7 |
| 24 | 97 | 82 | 70 | 58 | 29 | 29 | 20 | 15 |
| 25 | 99 | 87 | 78 | 66 | 36 | 34 | 26 | 17 |
| 26 | 99 | 91 | 84 | 75 | 46 | 43 | 34 | 24 |
| 27 | | 94 | 89 | 82 | 57 | 54 | 44 | 34 |
| 28 | | 96 | 94 | 88 | 70 | 68 | 59 | 47 |
| 29 | | 98 | 98 | 94 | 84 | 84 | 77 | 68 |
| 30 | | 100 | 100 | 100 | 100 | 100 | 100 | 100 |

B

To score intelligibility:

| | **NORMAL** | **ABNORMAL** |
|---|-----------|-------------|
| 2 ½ years | Understandable ½ the time, or, "easy" | Not understandable |
| 3 years and older | Easy to understand | Understandable ½ time Not understandable |

Test result:  1. NORMAL on Dase and Intelligibility = NORMAL
2. ABNORMAL on Dase and/or Intelligibility = ABNORMAL

*If abnormal on initial screening rescreen within 2 weeks.
If abnormal again child should be referred for complete speech evaluation.

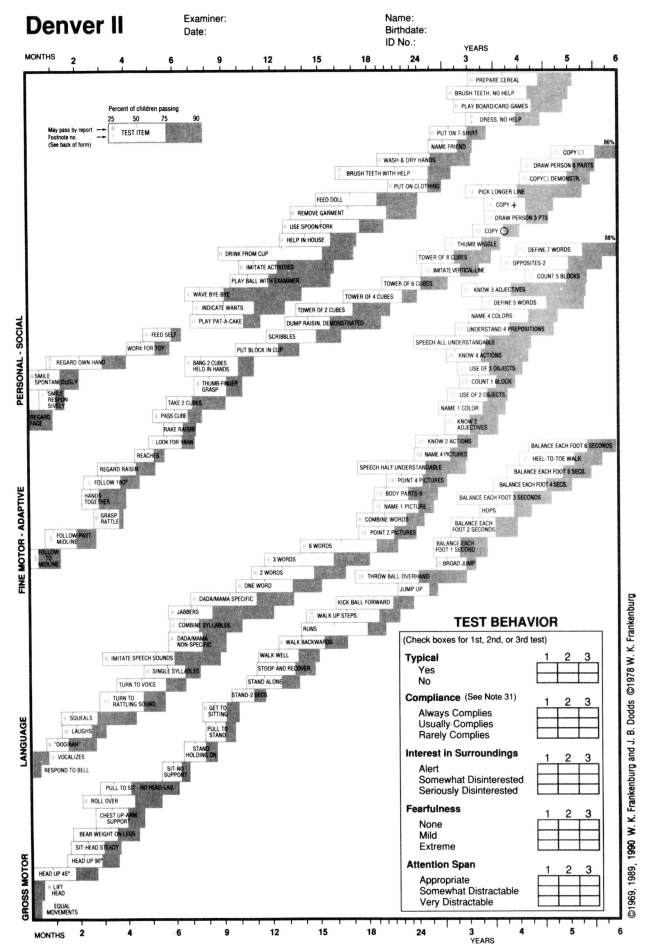

Denver II. (Copyright 1969, 1989, 1990 by W.K. Frankenburg and J.B. Dodds. Copyright 1978 W.K. Frankenburg)

# DIRECTIONS FOR ADMINISTRATION

1. Try to get child to smile by smiling, talking or waving. Do not touch him/her.
2. Child must stare at hand several seconds.
3. Parent may help guide toothbrush and put toothpaste on brush.
4. Child does not have to be able to tie shoes or button/zip in the back.
5. Move yarn slowly in an arc from one side to the other, about 8" above child's face.
6. Pass if child grasps rattle when it is touched to the backs or tips of fingers.
7. Pass if child tries to see where yarn went. Yarn should be dropped quickly from sight from tester's hand without arm movement.
8. Child must transfer cube from hand to hand without help of body, mouth, or table.
9. Pass if child picks up raisin with any part of thumb and finger.
10. Line can vary only 30 degrees or less from tester's line.
11. Make a fist with thumb pointing upward and wiggle only the thumb. Pass if child imitates and does not move any fingers other than the thumb.

12. Pass any enclosed form. Fail continuous round motions.

13. Which line is longer? (Not bigger.) Turn paper upside down and repeat. (pass 3 of 3 or 5 of 6)

14. Pass any lines crossing near midpoint.

15. Have child copy first. If failed, demonstrate.

When giving items 12, 14, and 15, do not name the forms. Do not demonstrate 12 and 14.

16. When scoring, each pair (2 arms, 2 legs, etc.) counts as one part.
17. Place one cube in cup and shake gently near child's ear, but out of sight. Repeat for other ear.
18. Point to picture and have child name it. (No credit is given for sounds only.)
    If less than 4 pictures are named correctly, have child point to picture as each is named by tester.

19. Using doll, tell child: Show me the nose, eyes, ears, mouth, hands, feet, tummy, hair. Pass 6 of 8.
20. Using pictures, ask child: Which one flies?... says meow?... talks?... barks?... gallops? Pass 2 of 5, 4 of 5.
21. Ask child: What do you do when you are cold?... tired?... hungry? Pass 2 of 3, 3 of 3.
22. Ask child: What do you do with a cup? What is a chair used for? What is a pencil used for?
    Action words must be included in answers.
23. Pass if child correctly places <u>and</u> says how many blocks are on paper. (1, 5).
24. Tell child: Put block **on** table; **under** table; **in front of** me, **behind** me. Pass 4 of 4.
    (Do not help child by pointing, moving head or eyes.)
25. Ask child: What is a ball?... lake?... desk?... house?... banana?... curtain?... fence?... ceiling? Pass if defined in terms of use, shape, what it is made of, or general category (such as banana is fruit, not just yellow). Pass 5 of 8, 7 of 8.
26. Ask child: If a horse is big, a mouse is __? If fire is hot, ice is __? If the sun shines during the day, the moon shines during the __? Pass 2 of 3.
27. Child may use wall or rail only, not person. May not crawl.
28. Child must throw ball overhand 3 feet to within arm's reach of tester.
29. Child must perform standing broad jump over width of test sheet (8 1/2 inches).
30. Tell child to walk forward, ⚬⚬⚬⚬➤ heel within 1 inch of toe. Tester may demonstrate.
    Child must walk 4 consecutive steps.
31. In the second year, half of normal children are non-compliant.

**OBSERVATIONS:**

# *HOME Inventory for Families of Infants and Toddlers, Birth to Three.*

Family Name _____ Date _____ Visitor _____

Child's Name _____ Birthdate _____ Age _____ Sex _____

Caregiver for visit _____ Relationship to child _____

Family Composition _____

(Persons living in household, including sex and age of children)

Family                    Language                 Maternal                  Paternal
Ethnicity _____ Spoken _____ Education _____ Education _____

Is Mother                 Type of work             Is Father                 Type of work
Employed? _____ when employed _____ Employed? _____ when employed _____

Address _____ Phone _____

Current child care arrangements _____

Summarize past
year's arrangements _____

Caregiver for visit _____ Other persons present _____

Comments _____

_____

## SUMMARY

| Subscale | | Score | Percentile Range | | |
|---|---|---|---|---|---|
| | | | Lowest Middle | Middle Half | Upper Fourth |
| I. | Emotional and Verbal RESPONSIVITY of Parent | | 0–6 | 7–9 | 10–11 |
| II. | ACCEPTANCE of Child's Behavior | | 0–4 | 5–6 | 7–8 |
| III. | ORGANIZATION of Physical and Temporal Environments | | 0–3 | 4–5 | 6 |
| IV. | Provision of Appropriate PLAY MATERIALS | | 0–4 | 5–7 | 8–9 |
| V. | Parent INVOLVEMENT with Child | | 0–2 | 3–4 | 5–6 |
| VI. | Opportunity for VARIETY in Daily Stimulation | | 0–1 | 2–3 | 4–5 |
| | TOTAL SCORE | | 0–25 | 26–36 | 34–45 |

For rapid profiling of a family, place an X in the space that corresponds to the raw score on each subscale and the total score.

## HOME Inventory* (Birth to Three)

Place a plus (+) or minus (−) in the space next to each item if the behavior is oberved during the visit or if the parent reports that the conditions or events are characteristic of the home environment. Enter the subtotals and the total on the front side of the Record Sheet.

I. EMOTIONAL and Verbal RESPONSIVITY

1. Parent spontaneously vocalized to child twice. _____
2. Parent responds verbally to child's verbalizations. _____
3. Parent tells child name of object or person during visit. _____
4. Parents speech is distinct and audible. _____
5. Parent initiates verbal exchanges with visitor. _____
6. Parent converses freely and easily. _____
7. Parent permits child to engage in "messy" play. _____
8. Parent spontaneously praises child at least twice. _____
9. Parent's voice conveys positive feelings toward child. _____
10. Parent caresses or kisses child at least once. _____
11. Parent responds positively to praise of child offered by visitor _____

Subtotal: _____

*For complete wording of items, please refer to the Administration Manual.

*(continued on next page)*

II. ACCEPTANCE of Child's Behavior

12. Parent does not shout at child. _____
13. Parent does not express annoyance with or hostility to child. _____
14. Parent neither slaps nor spanks child during visit. _____
15. No more than one instance of physical punishment during past week. _____
16. Parent does not scold or criticize child during visit. _____
17. Parent does not interfere or restrict child more than three times. _____
18. At least ten books are present and visible. _____
19. Family has a pet. _____
    Subtotal: _____

III. ORGANIZATION of Environment

20. Substitute care is provided by one of three regular substitutes. _____
21. Child is taken to grocery store at least once/week. _____
22. Child gets out of house at least four times/week. _____
23. Child is taken regularly to doctor's office or clinic. _____
24. Child has special place for toys and treasures. _____
25. Child's play environment is safe. _____
    Subtotal: _____

IV. Provision of PLAY MATERIALS

26. Muscle activity toys or equipment. _____
27. Push or pull toy. _____
28. Stroller or walker, kiddie car, scooter, or tricycle. _____
29. Parent provides toys for child during visit. _____
30. Learning equipment appropriate to age—cuddly toys or role-playing toys. _____

31. Learning facilitators—mobile, table and chairs, high chair, play pen. _____
32. Simple eye-hand coordination toys. _____
33. Complex eye-hand coordination toys. (those permitting combination). _____
34. Toys for literature and music. _____
    Subtotal: _____

V. Parental INVOLVEMENT with Child

35. Parent keeps child in visual range, looks at often. _____
36. Parent talks to child while doing housework. _____
37. Parent consciously encourages developmental advance. _____
38. Parent invests maturing toys with value via personal attention. _____
39. Parent structures child's play periods. _____
40. Parent provides toys that challenge child to develop new skills. _____
    Subtotal: _____

VI. Opportunities for VARIETY

41. Father provides some care daily. _____
42. Parent reads stories to child at least three times weekly. _____
43. Child eats at least one meal per day with mother and father. _____
44. Family visits relatives or receives visits once a month or so. _____
45. Child has three or more books of his/her town. _____
    Subtotal: _____

TOTAL SCORE

*(From Caldwell, B.M., & Bradley, R.H. [1984]. Home observation for measurement of the environment [revised edition]. Little Rock, AR: Center for Child Development)*

# HOME Inventory for Families of Preschoolers, Three to Six.

Family Name _____ Date _____ Visitor _____

Child's Name _____ Birthdate _____ Age _____ Sex _____

Caregiver for visit _____ Relationship to child _____

Family Composition _____

(Persons living in household, including sex and age of children)

| | | | |
|---|---|---|---|
| Family Ethnicity _____ | Language Spoken _____ | Maternal Education _____ | Paternal Education _____ |
| Is Mother Employed? _____ | Type of work when employed _____ | Is Father Employed? _____ | Type of work when employed _____ |

Address _____ Phone _____

Current child care arrangements _____

Summarize past

year's arrangements _____

Caregiver for visit _____ Other persons present _____

Comments _____

## SUMMARY

| Subscale | Score | Percentile Range | | |
|---|---|---|---|---|
| | | Lowest Middle | Middle Half | Upper Fourth |
| I. LEARNING STIMULATION | | 0–2 | 3–9 | 10–11 |
| II. LANGUAGE STIMULATION | | 0–4 | 5–6 | 7 |
| III. PHYSICAL ENVIRONMENT | | 0–3 | 4–6 | 7 |
| IV. WARMTH AND AFFECTION | | 0–3 | 4–5 | 6–7 |
| V. ACADEMIC STIMULATION | | 0–2 | 3–4 | 5 |
| VI. MODELING | | 0–1 | 2–3 | 4–5 |
| VII. VARIETY IN EXPERIENCE | | 0–4 | 5–7 | 8–9 |
| VIII. ACCEPTANCE | | 0–2 | 3–3 | 4 |
| TOTAL SCORE | | 0–29 | 30–45 | 46–55 |

For rapid profiling of a family, place an X in the space that corresponds to the raw score.

## HOME Inventory* (Three to Six)

Place a plus (+) or minus (−) in the space next to each item if the behavior is oberved during the visit or if the parent reports that the conditions or events are characteristic of the home environment. Enter the subtotals and the total on the front side of the Record Sheet.

I. LEARNING STIMULATION

1. Child has toys which teach color, size, shape. _____
2. Child has three or more puzzles. _____
3. Child has record player and at least five children's records. _____
4. Child has toys permitting free expression. _____
5. Child has toys or games requiring refined movements. _____
6. Child has toys or games which help teach numbers. _____
7. Child has at least ten children's books. _____
8. At least ten books are visible in the apartment. _____
9. Family buys and reads a daily newspaper. _____
10. Family subscribes to at least one magazine. _____
11. Child is encouraged to learn shapes. _____

Subtotal: _____

*For complete wording of items, please refer to the Administration Manual.

(continued on next page)

II. LANGUAGE STIMULATION

    12. Child has toys that help teach the names of animals. \_\_\_\_

    13. Child is encouraged to learn the alphabet. \_\_\_\_

    14. Parent teaches child simple verbal manners (please, thank you) \_\_\_\_

    15. Mother uses correct grammar and pronunciation. \_\_\_\_

    16. Parent encourages child to talk and takes time to listen. \_\_\_\_

    17. Parent's voice conveys positive feeling to child. \_\_\_\_

    18. Child is permitted choice in breakfast or lunch menu. \_\_\_\_

                Subtotal: \_\_\_\_

III. PHYSICAL ENVIRONMENT

    19. Building appears safe. \_\_\_\_

    20. Outside play environment appears safe. \_\_\_\_

    21. Interior of apartment not dark or perceptually monotonous. \_\_\_\_

    22. Neighborhood is esthetically pleasing. \_\_\_\_

    23. House has 100 square feet of living space per person. \_\_\_\_

    24. Rooms are not overcrowded with furniture. \_\_\_\_

    25. House is reasonably clean and minimally cluttered. \_\_\_\_

                Subtotal: \_\_\_\_

IV. WARMTH AND ACCEPTANCE

    26. Parent holds child close 10-15 minutes per day. \_\_\_\_

    27. Parent converses with child at least twice during visit. \_\_\_\_

    28. Parent answers child's questions or requests verbally. \_\_\_\_

    29. Parent usually responds verbally to child's speech. \_\_\_\_

    30. Parent praises child's qualities twice during visit. \_\_\_\_

    31. Parent caresses, kisses, or cuddles child during visit. \_\_\_\_

    32. Parent helps child demonstrate some achievement during visit. \_\_\_\_

                Subtotal: \_\_\_\_

V. ACADEMIC STIMULATION

    33. Child is encouraged to learn colors. \_\_\_\_

    34. Child is encouraged to learn patterned speech (songs, etc.). \_\_\_\_

    35. Child is encouraged to learn spatial relationships. \_\_\_\_

    36. Child is encouraged to learn numbers. \_\_\_\_

    37. Child is encouraged to learn to read a few words. \_\_\_\_

                Subtotal: \_\_\_\_

VI. MODELING

    38. Some delay of food gratification is expected. \_\_\_\_

    39. TV is used judiciously. \_\_\_\_

    40. Parent introduces visitor to child. \_\_\_\_

    41. Child can express negative feelings without reprisal. \_\_\_\_

    42. Child can hit parent without harsh reprisal. \_\_\_\_

                Subtotal: \_\_\_\_

VII. VARIETY IN EXPERIENCE

    43. Child has real or toy musical instrument. \_\_\_\_

    44. Child is taken on outing by family member at least every other week. \_\_\_\_

    45. Child has been on trip more than fifty miles during last year. \_\_\_\_

    46. Child has been taken to a museum during past year. \_\_\_\_

    47. Parent encourages child to put away toys without help. \_\_\_\_

    48. Parent uses complex sentence structure and vocabulary. \_\_\_\_

    49. Child's art work is displayed some place in house. \_\_\_\_

    50. Child eats at least one meal per day with mother and father. \_\_\_\_

    51. Parent lets child choose some foods or brands at grocery store. \_\_\_\_

                Subtotal: \_\_\_\_

VIII. ACCEPTANCE

    52. Parent does not scold or derogate child more than once. \_\_\_\_

    53. Parent does not use physical restraint during visit. \_\_\_\_

    54. Parent neither slaps nor spanks child during visit. \_\_\_\_

    55. No more than one instance of physical punishment during past week. \_\_\_\_

                Subtotal: \_\_\_\_

*(From Caldwell, B.M., & Bradley, R.H. [1984].* Home observation for measurement of the environment *[revised edition]. Little Rock, AR: Center for Child Development)*

# Appendix B:
# Physiological Measurements

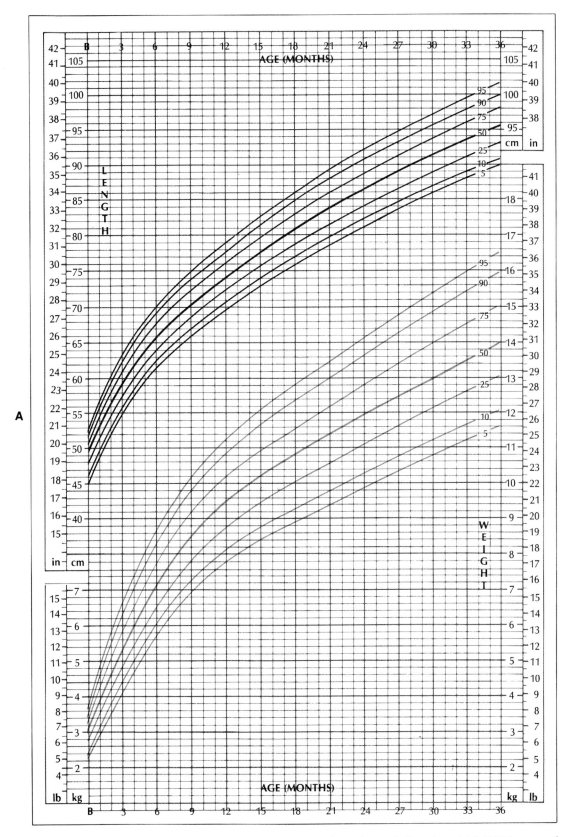

*Growth charts for girls* (A) *and boys* (B) *birth to age 36 months—physical growth (length, weight), NCHS percentiles. (Adapted from Hamill, P.V.V., et al. [1979]. Physical growth: National Center for Health Statistics percentiles. Am. J. Clin. Nutr., 32, 607–629. Data from the Fels Research Institute, Wright State University School of Medicine, Yellow Springs, Ohio. Courtesy of Ross Laboratories, 1980)*

*(Continued on next page)*

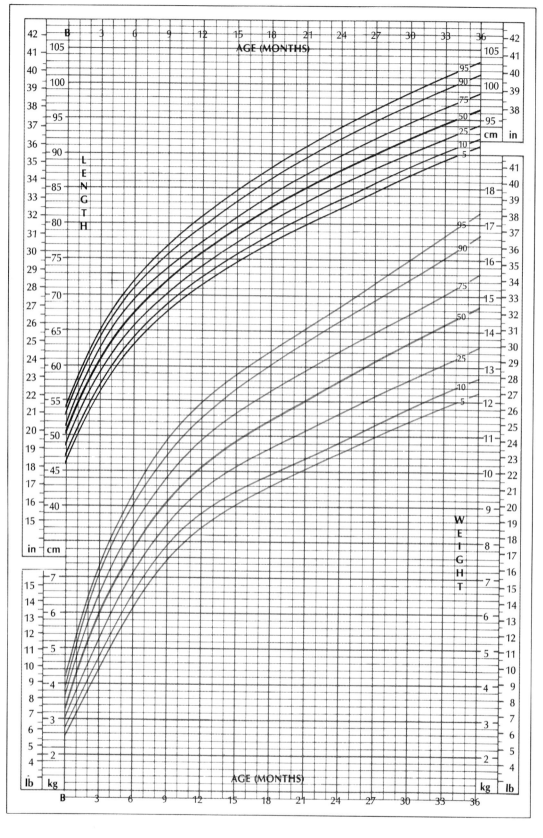

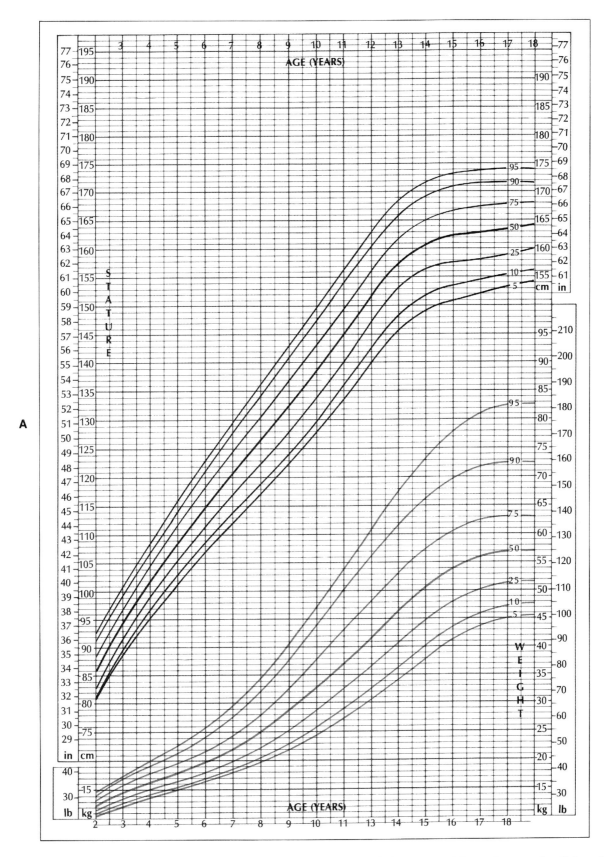

*Growth charts for girls* (A) *and boys* (B) *ages 2 to 18 years—physical growth (stature, weight), NCHS percentiles. (Adapted from Hamill, P.V.V., et al. [1979]. Physical growth: National Center for Health Statistics percentiles. Am. J. Clin. Nutr., 32, 607–629. Data from the National Center for Health Statistics, Hyattsville, MD. Courtesy of Ross Laboratories, 1980)*

*(Continued on next page)*

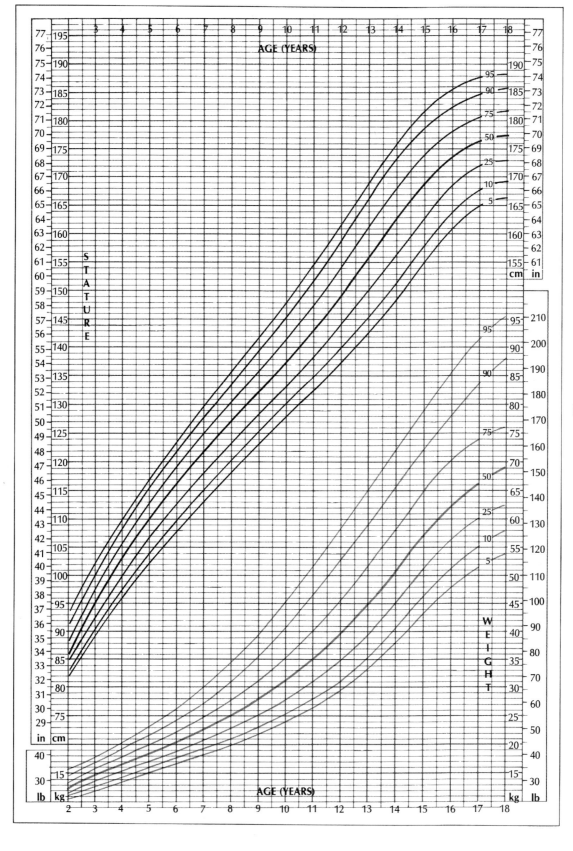

B

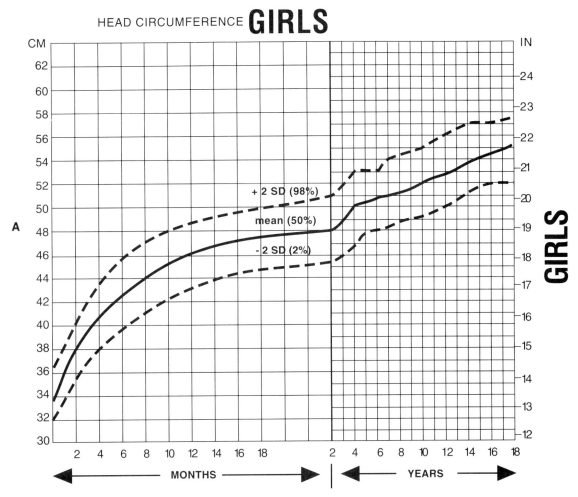

*Head circumference charts for girls* (A) *and boys* (B). *(Nelhaus, G. [1968]. Composite international and interracial graphs.* Pediatrics, 41, *106. Copyright American Academy of Pediatrics, 1968)*

*(Continued on next page)*

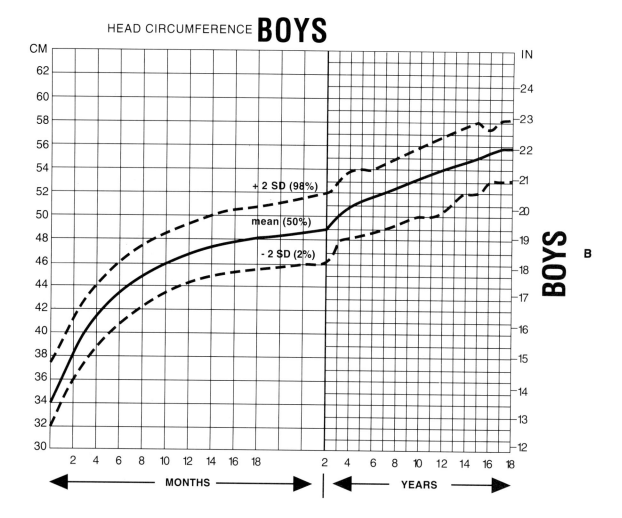

HEAD CIRCUMFERENCE **BOYS**

## Pulse, Respiration, and Blood Pressure Values for Children

### Table B-1. Pulse Rate at Various Ages

| Age | Range | Average |
|---|---|---|
| Newborn | 70–170 | 120 |
| 1–11 months | 80–160 | 120 |
| 2 years | 80–130 | 110 |
| 4 years | 80–120 | 100 |
| 6 years | 75–115 | 100 |
| 8 years | 70–110 | 90 |
| 10 years | 70–110 | 90 |

| | Girls | | Boys | |
|---|---|---|---|---|
| | Range | Average | Range | Average |
| 12 years | 70–110 | 90 | 65–105 | 85 |
| 14 years | 65–105 | 85 | 60–100 | 80 |
| 16 years | 60–100 | 80 | 55–95 | 75 |
| 18 years | 55–95 | 75 | 50–90 | 70 |

(Vaughan, V.C., III, & McKay, R. J. Jr. [Eds.]. [1975]. *Textbook of pediatrics* [10th ed.]. Philadelphia: W. B. Saunders.)

### Table B-2. Variations in Respirations with Age

| Age | Rate per Minute |
|---|---|
| Newborn | 40–90 |
| 1 year | 20–40 |
| 2 years | 20–30 |
| 3 years | 20–30 |
| 5 years | 20–25 |
| 10 years | 17–22 |
| 15 years | 15–20 |
| 20 years | 15–20 |

(Lowrey, G. H., [1973]. *Growth and development of children* [6th ed.]. Copyright © 1973 by Year Book Medical Publishers, Inc., Chicago. Used by permission.)

### Table B-3. Normal Blood Pressure for Various Ages

| Age | Systolic (Mean ± 2 SD) | Diastolic (Mean ± 2 SD) |
|---|---|---|
| Newborn | 80 ± 16 | 46 ± 16 |
| 6 months– 1 year | 89 ± 29 | 60 ± 10* |
| 1 year | 96 ± 30 | 66 ± 25* |
| 2 years | 99 ± 25 | 64 ± 25* |
| 3 years | 100 ± 25 | 67 ± 23* |
| 4 years | 99 ± 20 | 65 ± 20* |
| 5–6 years | 94 ± 14 | 55 ± 9 |
| 6–7 years | 100 ± 15 | 56 ± 8 |
| 8–9 years | 105 ± 16 | 57 ± 9 |
| 9–10 years | 107 ± 16 | 57 ± 9 |
| 10–11 years | 111 ± 17 | 58 ± 10 |
| 11–12 years | 113 ± 18 | 59 ± 10 |
| 12–13 years | 115 ± 19 | 59 ± 10 |
| 13–14 years | 118 ± 19 | 60 ± 10 |

*The point of muffling is shown as the diastolic pressure.
(Haggerty, R. J., Maroney, M. W., & Nadas, A. S. [1956]. Essential hypertension in infancy and childhood. *J. Dis. Child., 92,* 536. Copyright © 1956, American Medical Association.)

### Table B-4. Mean Blood Pressure at Wrist and Ankle in Infants (Flush Technique)

| Age | Blood Pressure at Wrist | | Blood Pressure at Wrist | |
|---|---|---|---|---|
| | Mean | Range | Mean | Range |
| 1–7 days | 41 | 22–66 | 37 | 20–58 |
| 1–3 months | 67 | 48–90 | 61 | 38–96 |
| 4–6 months | 73 | 42–100 | 68 | 40–104 |
| 7–9 months | 76 | 52–96 | 74 | 50–96 |
| 10–12 months | 57 | 62–94 | 56 | 102 |

(Moss, A. J., Indirect methods of blood pressure measurement. *Pediatr. Clin. North Am., 25,* 3. Data from Moss, A. J., & Adams, F. H. [1962]. *Problems of blood pressure in childhood.* Springfield, Ill.: Thomas.)

# Appendix C:
# Normal Laboratory Values

## Blood

### Acetone

1–6 mg/100 mL

### Acid–Base Measurements

|       | Neonate        | Child          |
|-------|----------------|----------------|
| pH    | 7.32–7.42      | 7.35–7.45      |
| $pCO_2$ | 30–40 mm Hg  | 35–45 mm Hg    |
| $pO_2$  | 60–80 mm Hg  | 80–100 mm Hg   |
| $HCO_3$ | 20–26 mEq/L  | 22–28 mEq/L    |

### Alkaline Phosphatase

30–205 IU/L

### Ammonia

| Premature | 100–200 $\mu$g/100 mL |
| Newborn   | 90–150 $\mu$g/100 mL  |
| Child     | 45–80 $\mu$g/100 mL   |

### Amylase

28–108 IU/L at 37°C (98.6°F)

### Bilirubin

| Total    | Less than 1.5 mg/dL |
| Direct   | 0.2–0.4 mg/dL       |
| Indirect | 0.4–0.8 mg/dL       |

### Bleeding Time

1–3 minutes

### BUN

4–8 mg/100 mL

### Calcium

9–11 mg/100 mL

### Chloride

97–104 mEq/L

## Cholesterol

| | |
|---|---|
| Full-term newborn | 45–167 mg/100 mL |
| Infant | 70–190 mg/100 mL |
| Child | 135–175 mg/100 mL |
| Adolescent | 120–210 mg/100 mL |

## Complete Blood Count (CBC)

| | Hb (gm/dL) | Hct (%) | WBC (per UL) | RBC (millions/μL) | Retic (%) | Plat (μL) |
|---|---|---|---|---|---|---|
| Newborn | 14–24 | 54 + 10 | 8–38,000 | 4.1–7.5 | 2–8 | 350,000 |
| 1 month | 11–17 | 35–50 | 5–1,500 | 4.2–5.2 | 0–0.5 | 300,000 |
| 1 year | 11–15 | 36 | 1–15,000 | 4.1–5.1 | 0.4–1.8 | 260,000 |
| 8–12 years | 13–15.5 | 40 | 5–12,000 | 4.5–5.4 | 0.4–1.8 | 260,000 |

| | Lymphocytes (%) | Eosinophils (μL) | Monocytes (%) |
|---|---|---|---|
| Newborn | 20 | 20–1000 | 10 |
| 1 month | 56 | 150–1150 | 7 |
| 1 year | 53 | 70–550 | 6 |
| 8–12 years | 31 | 100–400 | 7 |

| | MCV (mean corpuscular volume) (cu) |
|---|---|
| Newborn | 85–125 |
| 1 month | 90 |
| 1 year | 78 |
| 8–12 years | 82 |

| | MCHC (mean corpuscular hemoglobin concentration) (%) |
|---|---|
| Newborn | 36 |
| 1 month | 34 |
| 1 year | 33 |
| 8–12 years | 34 |

## Copper

| | |
|---|---|
| 0–6 months | <70 μg/100 mL |
| 6 months–5 years | 27–153 μg/100 mL |
| 5–17 years | 94–234 μg/100 mL |

## CPK

0–70 IU/L

## Creatinine (mg/dL)

| Age | Female | Male |
|---|---|---|
| Newborn | 0.2–1.0 | 0.2–1.0 |
| 1 year | 0.2–0.5 | 0.2–0.6 |
| 2–3 years | 0.3–0.6 | 0.2–0.7 |
| 4–7 years | 0.2–0.7 | 0.2–0.8 |
| 8–10 years | 0.3–0.8 | 0.3-0.9 |
| 11–12 years | 0.3–0.9 | 0.3–1.0 |
| 13–17 years | 0.3–1.1 | 0.3–1.2 |

## Fibrinogen

200–400 mg/dL

## Glucose

| | |
|---|---|
| Newborn | 20–80 mg/dL |
| Child | 60–110 mg/dL |

## *Immunoglobulin Levels*

| | IgG (mg/dL) | IgM (mg/dL) | IgA (mg/dL) |
|---|---|---|---|
| Newborn | 831–1231 | 6–16 | 0–5 |
| 1–3 months | 310–549 | 20–40 | 8–34 |
| 4–6 months | 240–613 | 26–60 | 10–46 |
| 7–12 months | 442–880 | 31–77 | 19–55 |
| 13–25 months | 553–970 | 27–73 | 26–74 |
| 26–36 months | 710–1075 | 40–80 | 35–108 |
| 3–5 years | 700–1257 | 38–74 | 66–120 |
| 6–8 years | 667–1180 | 40–90 | 80–170 |
| 9–11 years | 890–1359 | 45–112 | 70–190 |
| 12–16 years | 822–1563 | 70–126 | 85–210 |

## *Iron—total (µg/dL)*

| | |
|---|---|
| Newborn | 20–157 |
| 6 weeks–3 years | 20–115 |
| 3–9 years | 20–141 |
| 9–14 years | 21–151 |
| 14–16 years | 20–181 |

## *Iron Binding Capacity (µg/dL)*

| | |
|---|---|
| Newborn | 59–175 |
| Children/Adolescents | 250–400 |

## *Lead*

<10 µg/dL whole blood

## *LDH*

| | |
|---|---|
| Birth | 290–501 IU/L |
| 1 day | 185–404 IU/L |
| 1 month–2 years | 110–244 IU/L |
| 3–17 years | 80–165 IU/L |

## *Magnesium*

1.2–1.8 mEq/L

## *Osmolality*

275–295 mOsm/L

## *Phenylalanine (mg/100 mL)*

| | | |
|---|---|---|
| Premature | 0–5 days | 1–6 |
| | 5–21 days | 3–27 |
| | >21 days | 2–7 |
| Newborn | 0–1 days | <6 |
| | 2–10 days | 1–7 |
| Children | | 0.7–3.5 |
| Adolescent | | <4 |

## *Phosphorus*

| | | |
|---|---|---|
| Premature— | Birth | 5.6–8.0 mg/dL |
| | 6–10 days | 6.1–11.7 mg/dL |
| | 20–25 days | 6.6–9.4 mg/dL |
| Full term— | Birth | 5.0–7.8 mg/dL |
| | 3 days | 5.8–9.0 mg/dL |
| | 6–12 days | 4.9–8.9 mg/dL |
| Children— | 1 year | 3.8–6.2 mg/dL |
| | 10 years | 3.6–5.6 mg/dL |

## Potassium (mEq/L)

| | |
|---|---|
| Premature | 4.5–7.2 |
| Full term | 3.7–5.2 |
| Child | 3.5–5.8 |
| Adolescent | 3.5–5.8 |

## Proteins

| | Premature | Full-Term | Infant | Child |
|---|---|---|---|---|
| Total | 4.3–7.6 g/100 mL | 4.6–7.4 | 4.8–7.7 | 6.0–8.0 |
| Albumin | 2.8–3.9 g/100 mL | 2.3–5.1 | — | 3.2–5.5 |

## PT

13 + 2 seconds

## PTT

| | |
|---|---|
| Premature | <120 seconds |
| Newborn | <90 seconds |
| Thereafter | 24–40 seconds |

## SGOT (Alt) (IU/L)

| | |
|---|---|
| 1-5 days | 5–120 |
| Infant | 8–40 |
| Preschool–Adolescent | 8–40 |

## SGPT (AST) (IU/L)

| | |
|---|---|
| 1-5 days | 5–90 |
| Infant | 5–35 |
| Preschool–Adolescent | 5–35 |

## Sodium

135–144 mEq/L

## Triglycerides (mg/dL)—(blood collected after 12–16 hour fast, except cord blood)

| | |
|---|---|
| Cord | 14–61 |
| Children | 10–175 |
| Adolescent | 30–135 |

## Uric Acid

2.6 mg/dL

## Zinc

| | |
|---|---|
| Newborn | 25% adult value |
| 1 year | 50% adult value |
| Adult | 80–165 ug/100 mL |

# Urine

## Urinalysis

| | | |
|---|---|---|
| pH | Newborn | 5.0–7.0 |
| | Thereafter | 4.8–7.8 |
| SG | Newborn | 1.001–1.020 |
| | Thereafter | 1.001–1.030 |
| Sugar | Negative | |
| Protein | Newborn | 240 mg/day |
| (Quantitative) | Child | 30–50 mg/day |
| | Adolescent | 25–70 mg/day |
| (Qualitative) | Negative | |

| Leukocytes | 0.4 |
|---|---|
| Casts | rare |
| Erythrocytes | rare |

### Addis Count (12-hour specimen)

| Red cells | <1 million |
|---|---|
| White cells | <2 million |
| Casts | <10,000 |
| Protein | <55 mg |

### Catecholamines

0.4–2.0 µg/kg/day

### Chloride

170–254 mEq/day

### Creatinine

| Newborn | 7–10 mg/kg/day |
|---|---|
| Child | 20–30 mg/kg/day |

### Lead

<400 µg/day; sample collected for 24 hrs.

### Osmolality

| Infant | 50–600 mOsm/L |
|---|---|
| Child | 50–1400 mOsm/L |

### Potassium

25–123 mEq/day

### Sodium

| Infant | 0.3–3.5 mEq/day |
|---|---|
| Child | 5.6–17 mEq/day |

### Urobilinogen

<3 mg/day

### VMA (vanillymandelic acid)

| 1st day | Full term | 606 ÷ 429 µg/day |
|---|---|---|
| | Premature | 187 ÷ 111 µg/day |
| 15th day | Full term | 471 ÷ 196 µg/day |
| | Premature | 2506 ÷ 1319 µg/day |
| <2 years | 0.1–8.6 mg/L | |
| 2–14 years | 0–10.2 mg/L | |

## Sweat

### Sodium

| 5 weeks–11 months | 5–24 mEq/L |
|---|---|
| 1–9 years | 3–36 mEq/L |
| 10–16 years | 6–52 mEq/L |

### Chloride

<45 mEq/L
Fibrocystic disease >50 mEq/L

## *Cerebrospinal Fluid*

| | |
|---|---|
| Pressure | 40–200 mm $H_2O$ |
| Appearance | Clear |
| WBC | Neonates—8–9; >6 months–0 |
| Glucose | Neonates—50–52; >6 months–>40 (40–60% of blood glucose level) |
| Protein | Neonates—90–115; >6 months–<40 |
| Chloride | 110–128 mEq/L |
| Sodium | 138–150 mmol/L |
| SG | 1.007–1009 |

## *Bone Marrow*

| | |
|---|---|
| Myeblasts | 0–4% |
| Promyelocytes | 0–6% |
| Myelocytes | 7–25% |
| Metamyelocytes | 7–30% |
| Polymorphonuclear neutrophils | 5–30% |
| Eosinophils | 1–10% |
| Lymphocytes | 5–45% |
| Monocytes | 0–7% |
| Pronormoblasts | 0–8% |
| Normoblasts | 4–35% |

## *Stool*

| | | |
|---|---|---|
| Fecal fat | 0–6 years | <2 g/day |
| | Thereafter | 2–6 g/day |
| Fecal urobilinogen | 2–12 months | 0.03–14 mg |
| | 5–10 years | 2.7–39 mg |
| | 10–14 years | 7.3–99 mg |

(Normal values may differ, depending on the laboratory method used in processing the specimen.)

# Appendix D:
# Calculating Pediatric Drug Dosages
# (Age, Weight, Body Surface Area)*

## Rules Based on Age

### Fried's Rule: For Newborns to 2-Year-Olds

- Determine the child's age in months.
- Divide the age in months by 150.
- Multiply by the adult dose.
- Use $\dfrac{\text{Age (in months)}}{150} \times$ normal adult dose.
- If necessary, use $\dfrac{\text{desired amount}}{\text{on-hand}} \times$ quantity
  = amount to give.

**Example:** The physician prescribed Dolanex elixir for a 15-month-old. The normal adult dose is 325 mg every 4 to 6 hours. Dolanex elixir is available as 325 mg/5 mL. Use Fried's Rule:

$$\text{Pediatric dose} = \frac{\text{age in months}}{150}$$
$$\times \text{ normal adult dose}$$

$$\text{Pediatric dose} = \frac{15 \text{ months}}{150}$$

$$= \frac{1}{10} \times 325 \text{ mg} = 32.5 \text{ mg}$$

Because Dolanex is available as 325 mg/5 mL, additional computation is necessary to determine the amount of milliliters to give. Use:

$$\frac{\text{Desired amount}}{\text{On-hand}} \times \text{ quantity}$$
$$= \text{ amount to give}$$

$$\frac{32.5 \text{ mg}}{325 \text{ mg}} = \frac{1}{10}$$

$$\frac{1}{10} \times 5.0 \text{ mL} = 0.5 \text{ mL}$$

Answer = 0.5 mL

### Young's Rule: For Children Ages 1 to 12

- Determine the child's age in years.
- Divide the age in years by the age in years + 12.
- Multiply by the adult dose.
- Use $\dfrac{\text{Age (in years)}}{\text{age (in years)} + 12} \times$ normal adult dose.
- If necessary, use $\dfrac{\text{desired amount}}{\text{on-hand}} \times$ quantity
  = amount to give.

**Example:** The physician prescribed Milk of Magnesia for an 8-year-old patient. The normal adult dose is 30 mL. Use Young's Rule:

$$\text{Pediatric dose} = \frac{\text{age (in years)}}{\text{age} + 12}$$
$$\times \text{ normal adult dose}$$

$$\text{Pediatric dose} = \frac{8}{8 + 12}$$

$$= \frac{8}{20} = \frac{2}{5} \times \overset{6}{\cancel{30}} \text{ mL} = 12 \text{ mL}$$

Answer = 12 mL

**Example:** A physician prescribed Dolanex elixir for a 4-year-old. The normal adult dose is 325 mg every 4 to 6 hours. Dolanex elixir is available as 325 mg/5 mL. Use Young's Rule:

$$\text{Pediatric dose} = \frac{\text{age (in years)}}{\text{age (in years)} + 12}$$
$$\times \text{ normal adult dose.}$$

$$\text{Pediatric dose} = \frac{4}{4 + 12} = \frac{4}{16}$$

$$= \frac{1}{4} \times 325 \text{ mg} = 81 \text{ mg}$$

*From Boyer, M.J. (1991). *Math for nurses* (2nd ed.). Philadelphia: J.B. Lippincott.

Use:

$$\frac{\text{Desired amount}}{\text{on-hand}} \times \text{quantity}$$
$$= \text{amount to give}$$

$$\frac{81 \text{ mg}}{325 \text{ mg}} = \frac{1}{4}(\text{approximate})$$

$$\frac{1}{4} \times 5.0 \text{ mL} = 1.25 \text{ mL}$$

Answer = 1.25 mL

## *Rules Based on Weight*

### *Clark's Rule: For 2-Year-Olds and Older Children*

- Determine the child's weight in pounds.
- Divide the weight by 150.
- Multiply by the normal adult dose.
- Use $\frac{\text{weight in pounds}}{150} \times$ normal adult dose.
- If necessary, use $\frac{\text{desired amount}}{\text{on-hand}} \times$ quantity = amount to give.

***Example:*** The physician prescribed Dolanex elixir for a 4-year-old who weighs 30 pounds. The normal adult dose is 325 mg every 4 to 6 hours. Dolanex elixir is available as 325 mg/5 mL. Use Clark's Rule:

$$\text{Pediatric dose} = \frac{\text{weight in pounds}}{150}$$
$$\times \text{normal adult dose.}$$

$$\text{Pediatric dose} = \frac{30}{150} = \frac{1}{5}$$

$$\frac{1}{5} \times 325 \text{ mg} = 65 \text{ mg}$$

Use:

$$\frac{\text{Desired amount}}{\text{on-hand}} \times \text{quantity}$$
$$= \text{amount to give}$$

$$\frac{65 \text{ mg}}{325 \text{ mg}} = \frac{1}{5}$$

$$\frac{1}{5} \times 5 \text{ mL} = 1.0 \text{ mL}$$

Answer = 1.0 mL

Sometimes medications are prescribed in milligrams/kilogram of body weight. Since there are 2.2 pounds in a kilogram, you must convert the child's weight in pounds to kilograms before you can calculate the drug dosage. The rule below tells you how to calculate drug dosages when the drug is ordered according to kilograms of body weight.

## *Rule: To Change Pounds to Kilograms, Follow These Steps:*

- Determine the patient's body weight in pounds.
- Divide by 2.2.
- Solve the problem using the appropriate rule.

***Example:*** The physician prescribed 20 mg of amoxicillin/kg of body weight to be administered q 8 hours in equally divided doses. The patient weighed 44 pounds and was 5 years old. Divided by 2.2 to determine body weight in kilograms.

$2.2\overline{\smash{)}44.0.}$ Move the decimal point in the divisor and the dividend the same number of places. Put the decimal point directly above the line for the quotient.

$22\overline{\smash{)}440}$ = 20. (quotient)

Answer = 20 kg

Use: Use a proportion to solve for $x$.

$$20 \text{ mg}{:}1 \text{ kg}{::}x \text{ mg}{:}20 \text{ kg}$$
$$1x = 20 \times 20$$
$$1x = 400$$
$$x = 400 \text{ mg}$$

400 mg will be divided into three equal doses. 400 mg ÷ 3 = 133 mg to be given every 8 hours.

Answer = 133 mg

## Rule Based on Body Surface Area

Basing a pediatric dosage on body surface area is the most accurate way of determining the amount of drug to give.

## Rule: To Determine a Pediatric Dosage Based on Body Surface Area, Follow These Steps:

- Estimate the child's body surface area in square meters ($m^2$). Refer to a nomogram (Chapter 8, Fig. 8-1).*
- Use:

$$\frac{\text{Child's surface area in square meters}}{1.73 \; m^2 \; (\text{surface area of an average adult})}$$

$\times$ adult dose

*The nomogram is used to determine body surface area. To use the nomograms in Figure 8-1, you need to draw a straight line from the patient's height to his weight. You will intersect the body surface column at a number that indicates the patient's body surface area in square meters ($m^2$).

- If necessary, use a proportion to solve for *x*.

***Example:*** The physician prescribed Benadryl 150 mg/$m^2$/day, for an 8-year-old child who weighs 75 pounds and is 50 inches tall (4 feet, 2 inches). The normal adult dose is 25 mg, q.i.d. The nurse would give ___ mg q.i.d. Use Body Surface Area Rule:

$$\text{Child's surface area in } \frac{\text{square meters } (m^2)}{1.73 \; m^2}$$

$\times$ adult dose

$$\frac{1.05 \; m^2}{1.73 \; m^2} = 0.60 \times 25 \; mg = 15.17 \; mg$$

To prepare Benadryl for administration it would be best to drop the .17 and prepare 15 mg.

Answer = 15 mg, q.i.d.

# Appendix E:
# Temperature and Weight Conversion

**Table E-1.   Temperature Conversion Table (Centigrade to Fahrenheit)**

| Celsius (C°) | Fahrenheit (F°) | Celsius (C°) | Fahrenheit (F°) |
|---|---|---|---|
| 34.0 | 93.2 | 38.6 | 101.4 |
| 34.2 | 93.6 | 38.8 | 101.8 |
| 34.4 | 93.9 | 39.0 | 102.2 |
| 34.6 | 94.3 | 39.2 | 102.5 |
| 34.8 | 94.6 | 39.4 | 102.9 |
| 35.0 | 95.0 | 39.6 | 103.2 |
| 35.2 | 95.4 | 39.8 | 103.6 |
| 35.4 | 95.7 | 40.0 | 104.0 |
| 35.6 | 96.1 | 40.2 | 104.3 |
| 35.8 | 96.4 | 40.4 | 104.7 |
| 36.0 | 96.8 | 40.6 | 105.1 |
| 36.2 | 97.1 | 40.8 | 105.4 |
| 36.4 | 97.5 | 41.0 | 105.8 |
| 36.6 | 97.8 | 41.2 | 106.1 |
| 36.8 | 98.2 | 41.4 | 106.5 |
| 37.0 | 98.6 | 41.6 | 106.8 |
| 37.2 | 98.9 | 41.8 | 107.2 |
| 37.4 | 99.3 | 42.0 | 107.6 |
| 37.5 | 99.6 | 42.2 | 108.0 |
| 37.8 | 100.0 | 42.4 | 108.3 |
| 38.0 | 100.4 | 42.6 | 108.7 |
| 38.2 | 100.7 | 42.8 | 109.0 |
| 38.4 | 101.0 | 43.0 | 109.4 |

Conversion of Celsius (Centigrade) to Fahrenheit: $(9/5 \times \text{temperature}) + 32$.
Conversion of Fahrenheit to Celsius (Centigrade): $(\text{Temperature} - 32) \times 5/9$.

*Table E-2. Weight Conversion Table (Pounds and Ounces to Grams)*

| Lbs. | Ounces | | | | | | | | | | | | | | | |
|---|---|---|---|---|---|---|---|---|---|---|---|---|---|---|---|---|
| | 0 | 1 | 2 | 3 | 4 | 5 | 6 | 7 | 8 | 9 | 10 | 11 | 12 | 13 | 14 | 15 |
| 0 | — | 28 | 57 | 85 | 113 | 142 | 170 | 198 | 227 | 255 | 283 | 312 | 340 | 369 | 397 | 425 |
| 1 | 454 | 482 | 510 | 539 | 567 | 595 | 624 | 652 | 680 | 709 | 737 | 765 | 794 | 822 | 850 | 879 |
| 2 | 907 | 936 | 964 | 992 | 1021 | 1049 | 1077 | 1106 | 1134 | 1162 | 1191 | 1219 | 1247 | 1276 | 1304 | 1332 |
| 3 | 1361 | 1389 | 1417 | 1446 | 1474 | 1503 | 1531 | 1559 | 1588 | 1616 | 1644 | 1673 | 1701 | 1729 | 1758 | 1786 |
| 4 | 1814 | 1843 | 1871 | 1899 | 1928 | 1956 | 1984 | 2013 | 2041 | 2070 | 2098 | 2126 | 2155 | 2183 | 2211 | 2240 |
| 5 | 2268 | 2296 | 2325 | 2353 | 2381 | 2410 | 2438 | 2466 | 2495 | 2523 | 2551 | 2580 | 2608 | 2637 | 2665 | 2693 |
| 6 | 2722 | 2750 | 2778 | 2807 | 2835 | 2863 | 2892 | 2920 | 2948 | 2977 | 3005 | 3033 | 3062 | 3090 | 3118 | 3147 |
| 7 | 3175 | 3203 | 3232 | 3260 | 3289 | 3317 | 3345 | 3374 | 3402 | 3430 | 3459 | 3487 | 3515 | 3544 | 3572 | 3600 |
| 8 | 3629 | 3657 | 3685 | 3714 | 3742 | 3770 | 3799 | 3827 | 3856 | 3884 | 3912 | 3941 | 3969 | 3997 | 4026 | 4054 |
| 9 | 4082 | 4111 | 4139 | 4167 | 4196 | 4224 | 4252 | 4281 | 4309 | 4337 | 4363 | 4394 | 4423 | 4451 | 4479 | 4508 |
| 10 | 4536 | 4564 | 4593 | 4621 | 4649 | 4678 | 4706 | 4734 | 4763 | 4791 | 4819 | 4848 | 4876 | 4904 | 4933 | 4961 |
| 11 | 4990 | 5018 | 5046 | 5075 | 5103 | 5131 | 5160 | 5188 | 5216 | 5245 | 5273 | 5301 | 5330 | 5358 | 5386 | 5414 |
| 12 | 5443 | 5471 | 5500 | 5528 | 5557 | 5585 | 5613 | 5642 | 5670 | 5698 | 5727 | 5755 | 5783 | 5812 | 5840 | 5868 |
| 13 | 5897 | 5925 | 5953 | 5982 | 6010 | 6038 | 6067 | 6095 | 6123 | 6152 | 6180 | 6209 | 6237 | 6265 | 6294 | 6322 |
| 14 | 6350 | 6379 | 6407 | 6435 | 6464 | 6492 | 6520 | 6549 | 6577 | 6605 | 6634 | 6662 | 6690 | 6719 | 6747 | 6776 |
| 15 | 6804 | 6832 | 6860 | 6889 | 6917 | 6945 | 6973 | 7002 | 7030 | 7059 | 7087 | 7115 | 7144 | 7172 | 7201 | 7228 |
| 16 | 7257 | 7286 | 7313 | 7342 | 7371 | 7399 | 7427 | 7456 | 7484 | 7512 | 7541 | 7569 | 7597 | 7626 | 7654 | 7682 |
| 17 | 7711 | 7739 | 7768 | 7796 | 7824 | 7853 | 7881 | 7909 | 7938 | 7966 | 7994 | 8023 | 8051 | 8079 | 8108 | 8136 |
| 18 | 8165 | 8192 | 8221 | 8249 | 8278 | 8306 | 8335 | 8363 | 8391 | 8420 | 8448 | 8476 | 8504 | 8533 | 8561 | 8590 |
| 19 | 8618 | 8646 | 8675 | 8703 | 8731 | 8760 | 8788 | 8816 | 8845 | 8873 | 8902 | 8930 | 8958 | 8987 | 9015 | 9043 |
| 20 | 9072 | 9100 | 9128 | 9157 | 9185 | 9213 | 9242 | 9270 | 9298 | 9327 | 9355 | 9383 | 9412 | 9940 | 9469 | 9497 |
| 21 | 9525 | 9554 | 9582 | 9610 | 9639 | 9667 | 9695 | 9724 | 9752 | 9780 | 9809 | 9837 | 9865 | 9894 | 9922 | 9950 |
| 22 | 9979 | 10007 | 10036 | 10064 | 10092 | 10120 | 10149 | 10177 | 10206 | 10234 | 10262 | 10291 | 10319 | 10347 | 10376 | 10404 |

# Appendix F: Vaccines Commonly Used in the United States

| Name of Vaccine | Dose | Route of Administration | Primary Immunization Schedule | Booster Schedule | Contraindications | Side Effects |
|---|---|---|---|---|---|---|
| DPT* Diphtheria/pertussis/tetanus | 0.5 mL | IM | 2 months, 4 months, 6 months | 18 months | CNS disease, Hx of screening, high fever, or seizures after previous DPT | Tenderness, redness, or swelling at injection sites |
| TOPV* Trivalent oral polio virus vaccine (Sabin vaccine) | 0.5 mL | PO | 2 months, 4 months | 18 months and 4–5 years | Pregnancy immuno-deficiency (can use IPV if necessary) | Rarely paralytic disease in recipients or contacts |
| IPV Inactivated polio virus vaccine (Salk vaccine) | 0.5 mL | IM | 2 months, 4 months, 6 months | | | Local irritation |
| MMR* Measles/mumps/rubella | 0.5 mL | SC | 15 months | Either school entry (4–6 years) as recommended by the Immunization Practices (AICP) or at junior high school (11–12 years) as recommended by the American Association of Pediatrics (AAP)† | Pregnancy febrile illness recently received immune serum globulin (ISG) Immunodeficiency disease | Irritation at injection site; generalized rash 10–14 days after injection |
| *Haemophilus influenzae* | 0.5 mL | SC | 18 months | None | | Local irritation at injection site |
| Hepatitis B Plasma derived (HBIG) Or Recombinant DNA | 10 µg (0.5 mL) under 10 yrs; 20 µg (1.0 mL) over 10 yrs 5 µg (0.5 mL) under 10 yrs | IM | Babies born to HBsAg-positive mothers should receive HBIG at birth | Series of 3 doses; Protection for 5 yrs; 1 month and 6 months<br><br>1 month and 6 months after first injection | Only plasma-derived vaccine should be used for immuno-suppressed patients | Arthralgia, neurological reactions |

* May be administered simultaneously.
† In high-risk areas, children can receive the first dose at 12 months. In epidemics, children 6 months and older should be immunized. In these cases, the school doses are given as described.

# Index

Page numbers in *italics* indicate illustrations; those followed by *t* indicate tables.

## A

Abandonment, standards of care and, 45
Abdomen
  assessment of, 104
  auscultation of, 90–91
  palpation of, 92–93, 104
  percussion of, 91–92, 92t, 104
Abdominal pain
  in appendicitis, 801
  assessment of, 762
  in peptic ulcer disease, 803
Abdominal thrust, 546, *546*
ABO incompatibility, 200, 616–617
  in blacks, 963t
Abortion, adolescent's legal right to, 47
Abscess
  brain, in tricuspid atresia, 594
  cutaneous, 981–982
  retropharyngeal, 545–546
Absence seizures, 669t. *See also* Seizures
Abuse. *See* Child abuse and neglect
Accident prevention, 16, 17t. *See also* Traumatic injuries
  in adolescent, 347
  in infants, 245–248
    in hospital, 370
  in preschoolers, 299–300
  in school-age children, 320–322
  in toddlers, 269t, 269–270
Accommodation, 64
Acetabular dysplasia, 190–191
Acetaminophen
  for musculoskeletal disorders, 931t
  poisoning by, 781–782
Acetone, normal values for, 1044t
Achondroplasia, 204t
Acid-base balance, 733–734
  alterations in, 744–747
  assessment of, 526, 526t
  in burns, 984
  normal values for, 1044t
Acidosis
  assessment of, 526, 526t
  metabolic, 734, 744
    in acute renal failure, 830
    assessment of, 526, 526t
    in burns, 984
  respiratory, 745–746
Acne, 335, 349, 975–976
  cystic, 967t
  infantile, 243
Acoustic otoscopy, 1013
Acoustic stimulation test, for fetal well-being, 174
Acquired immunodeficiency syndrome, 698–703
  assessment in, 700
  clinical manifestations of, 699–700
  educational and support services for, 704
  infection precautions in, 702t
  medical diagnosis and management of, 699–700
  nursing care for, 701–703
  nursing diagnoses for, 701
  pathophysiology of, 698–699
  transmission of, prevention of, 702t, 703
  vaccine for, 421
Acrocyanosis, 185, 189
Acromegaly, 893–894
Acropustulosis of infancy, 964t
ACTH, 874, 879
  hypersecretion of
    in congenital adrenal hyperplasia, 892
    in Cushing syndrome, 892–893
Active transport, 732
Actual nursing diagnosis, 113–114
Aculturation, 33–34
Acute adrenocortical insufficiency, 891–892
Acute glomerulonephritis, 823–824
Acute nasopharyngitis, 1016
Acute pharyngitis, 1016–1017
Acute renal failure, 829–831
Acute tubular necrosis, 829
Adaptation, 63–64
Adaptive aids, in cerebral palsy, 444, *445, 449*
Adaptive behavior, 451
Addiction. *See also* Substance abuse
  definition of, 473

Addiction (*continued*)
  multiple, 473
Addis count, 1048t
Addison disease, 899–900
Adenohypophysis
  anatomy and physiology of, 874
  dysfunction of, 893–894
  embryology of, 872
Adenoids, 517
Adenoma
  anterior pituitary, 893–894
  parathyroid, 897
Admission
  for day hospital stay, 382
  emergency, 383
  to intensive care unit, 383–384
  interview for, 385
  parents' and children's responses to, 384
Adolescence
  morbidity and mortality in, 333–334
  stages of, 331t–332t, 332–333
Adolescent
  accident prevention for, 347
  androgenic-anabolic steroid use by, 357–358
  assessment for, 343–346
  common concerns of, 347–360
  communication with, 343
  dental care for, 346–347
  depression in, 358, 359t
  developmental tasks of, 68t, 346
  eating disorders in, 353–355
    national organizations for, 360
  as emancipated minor, 47, 346
  emotional concerns of, 342–343
  growth and development of, 330–360
    cognitive, 331t, 340–341
    physical, 334–339
    psychosexual, 340
    psychosocial, 331t–332t, 341–343
  health promotion for, 346–347
  history taking for, 344t, 344–345
  Hodgkin disease in, 629–631
  hospitalization of, 376–377. *See also* Hospitalization
  immunizations for, 344–345
  informed consent for, 47
  interpersonal relationships of, 331t, 339, 341
  interviewing of, 82, 84t, 343–344
  medical rights of, 346
  moral development in, 340–341
  nutrition in, 338–339, 339t, 345–346
  peer relationships of, 331t, 339, 341, 342–343
  physical appearance of, 339
  physical examination of, 345
  pregnancy in, 334, 350, 352–353
    prevention of, 350–352, 351t
  puberty in, 335–337, 337–338, 338t, 348
  sex role identification in, 341–342
  sexuality of, 341–343, 344, 349–350, 350t
  sleep needs of, 339
  substance abuse by, 478. *See also* Substance abuse
  suicide in, 334, 358–360, 359t
    substance abuse and, 473
  violent behavior in, 334
Adolescent fathers, 352
Adolescent-parent family, 27
Adoptive family, 9
Adrenal crisis, 891–892

Adrenal glands, 878–880
  congenital hyperplasia of, 892
  embryology of, 811
  tumors of, Cushing syndrome and, 892–893
Adrenarche, premature, 851
Adrenergic sympathomimetics, bronchodilator, 531
Adrenocortical insufficiency, 899–900
  acute, 891–892
Adrenocorticotropic hormone (ACTH), 874, 879
  hypersecretion of
    in congenital adrenal hyperplasia, 892
    in Cushing syndrome, 892–893
Adrenocorticotropin, 222
Adventitious breath sounds, 524
Advocacy, for disabled, 463–464
Aerosol therapy, 528, *530*
  for asthma, 555–558, 556t–557t
African-Americans
  cultural beliefs of, 37
  integumentary system in, 962t–964t
Agammaglobulinemia, X-linked, 703–705
Aganglionic megacolon, 794–795
Age, gestational
  determination of, 191–192, *192, 193*
  fetal growth and development estimation by, 164, *164*
Agranulocytes, 608
AIDS. *See* Acquired immunodeficiency syndrome
Air encephalography, 641t
Airway maintenance
  endotracheal intubation for, 534
  in hypoparathyroidism, 889
  in neonate, 194
  in neurological disorders, 647
  in spinal cord injury, 679
  tracheostomy for, 534–535, *535*
    home care for, 407, *407, 535*
    nursing care plan for, 559–561
Alagille syndrome, 782, 783
Al-Anon, 485
Alateen, 485
Albinism, 204t
Albright's hereditary osteodystrophy, 205t
Albumin, for neonatal hyperbilirubinemia, 615
Albuterol sulfate (Proventil, Ventolin), for asthma, 556t
Alcohol, fetal/neonatal effects of, 207, *207,* 475
Alcoholics Anonymous, 485
Alcoholism. *See also* Substance abuse
  definition of, 473
  screening for, 478, 479t
Aldosterone, 732, 878–879
Alkali burns, oral/esophageal, 780–781
Alkaline phosphatase, normal values for, 1044t
Alkalosis
  assessment of, 526, 526t
  metabolic, 525, 526t, 734, 744–745
  respiratory, 746–747
Allergens, 693
Allergic rhinitis, 710–712, 1017–1018
Allergic salute, 710, 1018, *1018*
Allergic shiners, 710, 1018
Allergies, 693
  anaphylaxis in, 418, 707–709
    epinephrine for, 418t, 709
  assessment in, 711t
  to contrast media, 814
  desensitization for, 696–697
  to drugs, 707–709

cutaneous manifestations of, 982–983
drug therapy for, 697–698
environmental control for, 697, 697t
eosinophils in, 688
food, 698, 712–714, 714t, 715t
history in, 711t
hypersensitivity pneumonitis and, 709–710
inhalational, 709–712
to insect bites and stings, 978
local, 715–716
rhinitis and, 709–712
seasonal, 710–712
skin tests for, 694, 968
systemic, 707–715
testing for, 1018
transfusion, 612–613
to vaccines, 418, 418t
Alopecia, 958
Alpha₁-antitrypsin deficiency, 783
Alpha-fetoprotein screening, prenatal, 171
for Down syndrome, 455
for neural tube disorders, 651
Alport syndrome, 824–825
Alternative birthing centers, 169
Alveolar pneumocytes, 518
Alveolar sacs, 518
Amastia, 858
Ambiguous genitalia, 843, 848
Amblyopia
deprivation, 1002
in strabismus, 1006–1007
Ambulation, in toddler, 258, 268–269
Amenorrhea, 853
American Indians
cultural beliefs of, 37
integumentary system in, 965t–966t
American Nurses Association Code of Ethics, 44
American Nurses Association Standards of Maternal and Child Health Nursing Practice, 20, 46
American Nurses Association Standards of the Perinatal Nurse Specialist, 46
Amino acid deamination, 759
Aminophylline (Theophylline), for asthma, 556t
Ammonia, normal values for, 1044t
Amnesia, 675
Amniocentesis, 171–172
for Down syndrome diagnosis, 455
indications for, 166–167, 172
in Rh incompatibility, 609
Amnion, 161
Amniotic fluid, 161
analysis of, 171–172
for Down syndrome diagnosis, 455
indications for, 166–167, 172
in Rh incompatibility, 609
Amphiarthroses, 918
Amputation, 947
Amylase, normal values for, 1044t
Anabolic steroids, 357–358
Anal fissures, 800
Analgesics. *See also* Pain
for hospitalized children, 379
for immune disorders, 695–696
for musculoskeletal disorders, 931t
Anal period, 61–62
Anal stage, 263
Anaphylaxis, 707–709

epinephrine for, 418t, 709
vaccine-induced, 418, 418t
Androgenic-anabolic steroids, 357–358
Androgens, 845
hypersecretion of, 879
Anemia
aplastic, 626–627
Cooley, *621,* 621–622
hemolytic, in hemolytic-uremic syndrome, 822–823
in infant, 222, 619–622
iron-deficiency, 319, 620–621
in neonate, 618–619
in premature infant, 210
sickle cell, 624–626
Anencephaly, 649
Aneurysm, coronary artery, in Kawasaki disease, 422
Angiography
cardiac catheterization and, 576
cerebral, 639t
renal, 815
Animal bites
rabies and, 435–436
treatment of, 435
Anion, 732
Anisocoria, 99, 646, 996–997
Anogenital warts, 865–866, 979
Anorectal malformations, 795–796
Anorexia nervosa, 354, 360
Antacids, for peptic ulcer disease, 804
Antegrade amnesia, 675
Anterior fontanel, 98, *98,* 187, *187*
Anterior pituitary gland
anatomy and physiology of, 874
disorders of, 893–894
embryology of, 872
Anthropometric measurements, 345
in obesity diagnosis, 353
Antibiotics
for osteomyelitis, 942
for respiratory infections, 531
for urinary tract infections, 827
Antibodies, *691,* 691–692
Antibody-mediated immunity, 691–692
Anticholinergics, bronchodilator, 531
Anticipatory grief, 500
Anticipatory imagery, 311
Anticonvulsants, 670, 671t–672t, 673
for febrile seizures, 648–649
for increased intracranial pressure, 648
Antidiuretic hormone, 732, 875
deficiency of, in diabetes insipidus, 889–890
Antigens, 689, 691–692
blood group, 608
in ABO incompatibility, 200, 616–617
in Rh incompatibility, 199, 609, 616
Antihistamines, for respiratory disorders, 534
Anti-inflammatory agents, for musculoskeletal disorders, 931t
Antitussives, 534
Anus
imperforate, 191
malformations of, 795–796
neonatal assessment of, 191
Anxiety
castration, 287
separation, 8–9
vs. grief, 491

Anxiety, separation (*continued*)
    hospitalization and, 370, 372, 373
        in infant, 230, 233
        in toddler, 263–264, 268
    stranger, 230, 233
Aorta
    coarctation of, *587,* 587–588, *588*
    stenosis of, 588–589, *589*
    in tetralogy of Fallot, 592–593, *593*
    transposition of, *590,* 590–591
Apgar test, 185–186, 186t
    for families, 31, 32t, 87
Aphakia, 1002
Apical pulse, 572
Aplastic anemia, 626–627
Aplastic crisis, in sickle cell disease, 625
Apnea, 522
    home monitoring for, *406,* 406–407
    of prematurity, 542
Apneustic respiratory center, 520
Apocrine sweat glands, 957
Appendicitis, 801–802
Aqueduct of Sylvius stenosis, 654
Aqueous humor, *993, 994*
Argininosuccinic-aciduria, 204t
Arm. *See* Extremities
Arnold-Chiari malformation, 654
Arousal-seeking theory, 69
Arrhythmias
    in hyperkalemia, 750
    in hypokalemia, 750
Arterial blood gas values, 525–526, 526t
    in cardiovascular disorders, 576–577
    in neonate, 179t, 180
    in respiratory acidosis, 746
Arterial switch procedure, for transposition of great
        arteries, 591
Arteriohepatic dysplasia, 783
Arthralgia
    in arthritis. *See* Arthritis
    in rheumatic fever, 597–598
Arthritis
    juvenile rheumatoid, 716–719
    septic, 941–942
    in systemic lupus erythematosus, 720, 721t
Arthroscopy, 922
Articular cartilage, 917, 918, *919*
Artificial ventilation, 534–535, *535. See also* Intubation;
        Mechanical ventilation; Tracheostomy
Ascariasis, 432
Aseptic meningitis, 660–661
Asians
    cultural beliefs of, 34–35
    integumentary system in, 961t–962t
Asphyxia neonatorum, 538–539
Aspiration
    of bone marrow, 610
    of foreign objects, 546–547
    of hydrocarbons, 551
    of meconium, 537–538
Aspiration pneumonia, 551–552
Aspirin
    for juvenile rheumatoid arthritis, 718, 719
    for Kawasaki disease, 422–423
    for musculoskeletal disorders, 931t
    Reye syndrome and, 435, 662, 663
Assessment. *See* Nursing assessment

Assessment of Premature Infants Behavior, 187
Assimilation, 34, 64
Asthma, 555–558, 556t–557t, 715–716
Astigmatism, 1010
Ataxia, in cerebral palsy, 445
Athelia, 858
Athetosis, in cerebral palsy, 445
Athlete's foot, 980–981
Atlanto-axial subluxation, in Down syndrome, 456, 457
Atonic seizures, 669t. *See also* Seizures
Atopic dermatitis, 521, 971–972
Atopy, 521
Atraumatic care, 379
Atresia
    biliary, 782
    esophageal, 774–776, *775*
    intestinal, 785–786
Atrial septal defect, *583,* 583–584
Atrioventricular canal defect, 585–586
Atrioventricular node, 569–570
Atrioventricular septal defect, 585–586
Attachment, infant-parent, 69–72, 184–185, 194, *195, 196,*
        233–234
    assessment of, *106,* 194, *195*
Attention deficit disorder, 665–666, 666t
Audiological testing, 101, 200, 241, 292, 318–319, 1000t, 1013.
        *See also* Hearing assessment
Aura, seizure, 670
Auscultation, 90–91
    of bowel sounds, 103
    of breath sounds, 90–91, 524–525
    of chest, 524
    of heart, 103, 572, 573t
Autism, 458–461, 459t–460t. *See also* Disabled
Autoimmune disorders, 716–723
Autoimmunity, 692
Automobile accidents, 245–246, 320, 347
    preschoolers and, 299
    substance abuse and, 473
    toddlers and, 269t, 269–270
Autonomic hyperreflexia (dysreflexia), in spinal
        cord injury, 679
Autonomic nervous system, 636
Autonomy, in toddler, 262, 263t, 267
Avulsions, 932–933
Axillary temperature, 96
Azotemia, in acute renal failure, 829
AZT (zidovudine), 700

**B**
Babinski reflex, 108, 190t
Baby Doe regulations, 49–50
Baby food, 225–226, 226t
Bacille Calmette-Guérin vaccine, 437
Back, neonatal assessment of, 189
Bacteria, 417t
Bacterial conjunctivitis, 188, 196–197
Bacterial endocarditis, 595–596
Bacterial meningitis, 660–661
    neonatal, 656–657
Bacterial pneumonia, 549–550
Bacterial skin infections, 981–982
Bacterial vaginosis, 857
Bacteriuria, in urinary tract infections, 827
Balloon pump, intraaortic, 577
Barbiturates, for increased intracranial pressure, 648t

Barium studies, 763t, 764
Barlow maneuver, 935, *936*
    for congenital hip disorders, 190–191
Baroreceptors, 732
Barrel chest, 521–522
Bartholin's glands, 843, *844*
Basophils, 608, 689
Bathing, of infant, 243
Batteries, button, ingestion of, 779
B cell, 689, *691*
B-cell mediated immunity, 691–692
BCG vaccine, 437
Bed rest, in immune disorders, 696
Bedtime guidelines
    for preschoolers, 283–284
    for toddlers, 271
Bed-wetting, 298–299
Behavioral assessment, 89
    for infant, 241
Behavioral controls, 379
Behavioral rehearsal, 379–380
Behaviorism, 66–67
Behavior modification, 68
    disciplinary, 39
Benign breast disease, 858
Benign breast hypertrophy, male, 859
Benign breast hypertrophy, male, 859
Bereavement, 491. *See also* Death and dying
Bicarbonate
    in metabolic acidosis, 744
    in metabolic alkalosis, 744
    in respiratory acidosis, 746
    in respiratory alkalosis, 746–747
Bicarbonate-carbonic acid buffer system, 734
Biliary atresia, 782
    malabsorption in, 790–791
Bilirubin, 759
    conjugated, 609–6101, 759
    neonatal analysis of, 609–610
    normal values for, 1044t
    unconjugated, 609, 759
Binge eating, in bulimia, 355
Biopsy
    of bone marrow, 610
    of kidney, 815
    of liver, 764
    of rectum, 764
    of small intestine, 764
Biot respirations, 523
Birth control, 350–352, 351t
Birth control pills, 351t
    for dysfunctional uterine bleeding, 855
Birth defects. *See* Congenital defects
Birthing centers, 169
Birthmarks, 189, 967t, 970–971
Bites
    animal
        rabies and, 435–436
        treatment of, 435
    insect, 978
    stork, 189, 967t
    tick
        Lyme disease and, 423–424
        Rocky Mountain spotted fever and, 425–426
Biting, in infant, 232–233
Black Africans
    cultural beliefs of, 37

integumentary system in, 962t–964t
Bladder
    anatomy of, 811
    capacity of, 811
    catheterization of, 814
        at home, 817
        in neural tube defects, 653
        in spinal cord injury, 679
        technique for, 817
    embryology of, 811
    exstrophy of, *818,* 818–819
Bladder control
    for bedwetters, 298–299
    in neural tube defects, 653
    in toilet training, 271–272
Bladder tap, 814
Blalock-Taussig shunt
    for tetralogy of Fallot, 592
    for tricuspid atresia, 594
Blastocyst, 161
Bleeding. *See also* Hemorrhage
    in aplastic anemia, 626, 627
    in hemophilia, 622–623
    in idiopathic thrombocytopenic purpura, 627
    nasal, management of, 1002
    in neonate, 198–199
    rectal
        anal fissures and, 800
        assessment of, 762
        intestinal polyps and, 800
        in Meckel diverticulum, 793
    uterine, dysfunctional, 855
    in Wiskott-Aldrich syndrome, 706
Bleeding time, 610
    normal values for, 1044t
Blended family, 9, 27–28
Blenorrhea, 1006
Blood. *See also* Hematological disorders; Hematological
        system
    constituents of, 606–609
    oxygenation of, 571
    pH of, 734
    production of, 606–607
    Rh typing of, 608
Blood-brain barrier, 637
Blood cholesterol test, for preschoolers, 292
Blood clotting. *See* Coagulation
Blood count
    in cardiovascular disorders, 576–577
    in immune disorders, 694
    normal values for, 1045t
    in school-age child, 319, 319t
Blood gas monitoring, 525–526, 526t
    in cardiovascular disorders, 576–577
    in neonate, 179t, 180
    in respiratory acidosis, 746
Blood glucose monitoring, in diabetes, 906
Blood group antigens, 608
Blood group incompatibility
    ABO, 200, 609, 616
    Rh, 199, 616–617
Blood pressure
    in hypertension, 600
    in infant, 222
    measurement of, 96–97, *97,* 572–574, 573t
    normal values for, 1043t
    in preschooler, 292

Blood pressure (*continued*)
  in school-age child, 319
Blood sampling, fetal
  from scalp, 174–175
  from umbilical cord, 172
Blood tests, 609–610
  in cardiovascular disorders, 576–577
  in immunological disorders, 694
  normal values for, 1045t
Blood transfusion
  exchange, 613
  in hematological disorders, 612–613
  in hydrops fetalis, 200
  in neonatal hyperbilirubinemia, 615
  reaction to, 612–613
  twin-to-twin, 173
Blood types, 608
Blood urea nitrogen (BUN), 739t, 816
  normal values for, 1044t
Blue nevus, 961t, 963t
Body lice, 976–977
Body measurements, 93–95
  in adolescent, 334–335
  growth charts for, 235, 1037–1040
  in infant, 235–236, 1037t
  in preschooler, 290, 1039t
  in school-age child, 316
  in toddler, 265, 1039t–1041t
Body surface area
  calculation of, 735, *735*
    for burn estimation, 984, *985,* 985t
    for drug dosage, 133, *133,* 1052
  fluid and electrolyte requirements and, 735
Body temperature. *See* Temperature
Body weight. *See* Weight
Bonding, 69–72, 184–185, 233–234
  assessment of, *106,* 194, *195, 196*
Bone
  anatomy of, 917, *917*
  bend of, 933, *934*
  brittle, in osteogenesis imperfecta, 939–940
  buckle of, 933, *934*
  cancer of, 946–947
  embryology of, 916–917
  fractures of. *See* Fracture(s)
  growth and ossification of, 917–918, *918*
  healing and remodeling of, 919
  infection of, 942–943
Bone marrow, 606–607
  aspiration and biopsy of, 610
  hematopoiesis in, 919
  in immune system, 223
  as lymphoid organ, 689–690
  normal values for, 1049t
Bone marrow transplantation
  in aplastic anemia, 626, 627
  in leukemia, 628
  in Wiskott-Aldrich syndrome, 707
Bottle feeding, 201, 202t, 244
  in colic, 786
  for premature infant, 209
  weaning from, 248
Bowel. *See also under* Intestinal
Bowel control
  in neural tube defects, 653
  in spinal cord injury, 679
Bowel sounds, 104

auscultation of, 90–91
Bowlegs, 941
Bowman's capsule, 811
Brace, Milwaukee, 944–945, *945*
Bradypnea, 522
Brain. *See also* Nervous system; Neurological disorders
  abscess of, in tricuspid atresia, 594
  anatomy and physiology of, *635,* 635–636
  computed tomography of, 639t
  embryology of, 634–635
  growth of, 217–218
  herniation of, 647
  injury of, in head trauma, *674,* 674–676
  tumors of, 666–668
Brain stem auditory evoked responses, 641t
Brain stem evoked potentials, 641t
Brazleton Neonatal Behavioral Assessment Scale, 87, 187
Breast(s)
  benign disease of, 858
  development of, 335, 337, *337,* 338t, 348
    premature, 851
  examination of, 846
  fibrocystic disease of, 858
  hypertrophy of
    idiopathic, 858
    in males, 349
  male, hypertrophy of, 859
  self-examination of, 348
  supernumerary, 858
  traumatic injuries of, 858
Breast-feeding, 200–201, 243–244
  jaundice and, 181
  for premature infant, 209
  weaning from, 24850
Breast milk
  vs. cow's milk, 201t
  vs. formula, 224t, 224–225, 225t
  nutrient content of, 224t, 224–225, 225t
Breathing. *See also under* Respiratory
  assessment of, 102, 522–525, 523t
  Biot, 523
  Cheyne-Stokes, 523
  control of, 519–520
  in infant, 222
  Kussmaul, 523
    in metabolic acidosis, 774
  mechanics of, 518–519
  obstructive, 523
  periodic, 522
  rate of
    assessment of, 96, 522–523, 523t
      in neonate, 186
    normal values for, 1043t
Breath sounds, 524–525
  auscultation of, 90–91
Bronchi, 518
Bronchial breath sounds, 524
Bronchioles, 518
Bronchiolitis, 544–545
Bronchodilators, 531
  for asthma, 555, 556t–557t, 558
Bronchopulmonary dysplasia, 539–540
Bronchoscopy, 526, 526–527
Bronchovesicular breath sounds, 524
Brown fat, 181–182
Brushfield spots, 99, 997
Bryant traction, *927*

Buckle, bone, 933, *934*
Buck's extension traction, *928*
Buffers, 734
Bulimia, 354–355
BUN (blood urea nitrogen), 739t, 816
    normal values for, 1044t
Bundle branches, 569–570
Bundle of His, 569–570
Burns, 983–989
    alkali, oral/esophageal, 780–781
    contractures in, 984, *984*
        management of, 987, *988*
    debridement of, 986
    estimation of size and depth of, 984, *985,* 985t
    first degree, 985t
    fourth degree, 985t
    full-thickness, 485t
    grafting of, 986, 987t
    in infants, 247–248
    inhalation injury and, 983–984
    medical management of, 984–988
        acute stage of, 985–987
        open vs. closed, 986, 987t
        rehabilitation stage of, 987–988
        resuscitative stage of, 985
    nursing care for, 988–989
    nursing diagnoses for, 988
    partial-thickness, 485t
    pathophysiology of, 983–984
    prevention of, in preschoolers, 299
    scarring of, management of, 987, *988*
    second degree, 985t
    systemic effects of, 983–984
    third degree, 985t
    topical medications for, 986, 987t
Butterfly rash, in systemic lupus erythematosus, *720,* 721t
Button batteries, ingestion of, 779


C
Calcium
    function of, 733t
    imbalance of, 747–750
        in hypoparathyroidism, 888
    metabolism of, 733t
        parathyroid glands and, 876, *877*
    normal values for, 1044t
Calcium disodium edetate (CaEDTA), for lead
            poisoning, 658–659
Cambodians
    cultural beliefs of, 34–35
    integumentary system of, 961t–962t
Camp, for disabled, 463
Cancer
    of bone, 946–947
    of brain, 666–668
    chemotherapy for, 628, 629, 667
    of eye, 1007–1008
    hematological, 628–629
    of kidney, 821–822
    staging of, 630
Candidiasis, 979–980
    in diaper dermatitis, 243, 980
    oral, 102, 188–189
        in neonate, 198
    vaginal, 856–857
Cao gio, 35

Capillary hemangioma, 967t, 970–971
Caput succadaneum, 188, *188*
Car accidents, 245–246, 320, 347
    preschoolers and, 299
    substance abuse and, 473
    toddlers and, 269t, 269–270
Carbamazepine (Tegretal), 671t
Carbohydrates, in breast milk, 224t, 225, 225t
Carbon dioxide
    in acid-base balance, 734
    partial pressure of, 520
        in metabolic acidosis, 744
        in metabolic alkalosis, 744–745
        in respiratory acidosis, 745–746
        in respiratory alkalosis, 746–747
    in pulmonary gas exchange, 520
Carbonic acid bicarbonate buffer system, 734
Carbon monoxide poisoning, 984
Cardiac arrhythmias
    in hyperkalemia, 750
    in hypokalemia, 750
Cardiac catheterization, 576
Cardiac circulation, 569, *570*
Cardiac conduction system, 569–570
Cardiac disease. *See* Heart disease
Cardiac output, 570
Cardiac pacemaker
    permanent implanted, 581–582
    postoperative, 580–581
Cardiac surgery, 580–582
Cardiac tamponade, 581
Cardiopulmonary resuscitation, 579–580
Cardiovascular disorders, 567–602
    acquired, 595, 595–601
    assessment of, 571–577, 594–595
    congenital, 583–595
        acyanotic, 583t, 583–590
        cyanotic, 583t, 590–595
        nursing care for, 594–595
    diagnostic procedures in, 576–577
    drug therapy for, 582
    finger clubbing in, 575, *575*
    general assessment in, 574
    growth and development in, 574
    hepatic assessment in, 575
    history in, 571–572
    integument in, 574–575
    nursing care in
        acute care considerations in, 578
        chronic care considerations in, 578–579
        developmental considerations in, 578
        evaluation of, 583, 595
        home care considerations in, 579, 579t
        planning of, 578–579, 595
        postoperative, 580–582, 595
    nursing diagnoses in, 577–578, 594–595
    nursing interventions in, 579–583, 595
    nutrition in, 574, 582–583
    physical examination in, 572–576
    renal assessment in, 575–576
    surgery for, 580–582, 595
Cardiovascular system
    in adolescent, 335
    anatomy of, 568–570, *568–570*
    embryology of, 567–568
    in fetus, 567, *568*
    in infant, 222

Cardiovascular system (*continued*)
    in neonate, 567–568, *569*
    physiology of, 570–571
    in toddler, 257
Carditis, in rheumatic fever, 597, 598
Care contract, for home care, 394, *395*
Carotenemia, 245
Car seats
    for infants, 245–246
    for toddlers, 269–270, *270*
Cartilage, articular, 917, 918, *919*
Cartilaginous joints, 918
Case management
    for disabled, 442
    for home care, 392–393
Castration anxiety, 287
Casts, 924t, 924–926, *925,* 925t
Cataracts, congenital, 1002–1003
Cathecholamines, urinary, normal values for, 1048t
Catheterization
    bladder, 814
        at home, 817
        in neural tube defects, 653
        in spinal cord injuries, 679
        technique for, 817
    cardiac, 576
Cation, 732
Caucasians, integumentary system in, 967t
Caustics, ingestion of, 780–781
Cavernous hemangioma, 189, 967t, 970–971
C cells, 876
Celiac disease, 790, 791
Cell-mediated immunity, 691–692
Cellulitis, 981–982
Celsius-Fahrenheit conversion chart, 1053t
Central nervous system. *See* Brain; Nervous system
Centration, in preoperational thought, 285
Cephalocaudal development, 59, 162
Cephalohematoma, 188
Cerebellar function, assessment of, 106
Cerebellum, 635, *635*
Cerebral angiography, 639t
Cerebral blood flow, 637
Cerebral dysfunction, attention deficit disorder and, 665–666
Cerebral edema, 643–644. *See also* Intracranial
        pressure, increased
Cerebral function, assessment of, 105–106
Cerebral palsy, 443–451. *See also* Disabled
    associated disorders in, 443
    ataxic, 445
    classification of, 443t, 443–444, 444t
    clinical manifestations in, 443t, 444t, 444–445, *446*
    diagnosis of, 445, *446, 447*
    dyskinetic, 444–445
    education in, 450
    etiology of, 443
    incidence of, 443
    limb involvement in, 443t, 443–444, 444t
    mixed type, 445
    nursing care for, 450–451
    nutrition in, 446–447, *447, 449*
    physical therapy for, 447
    play in, 450
    positioning and handling in, 447–449
    spastic, 444
    Strauss syndrome in, 444t
    support groups for, 450, 468–469

    treatment of, 446
Cerebral perfusion pressure, 637
Cerebral vascular resistance, 637
Cerebrospinal fluid, 635–636, *636*
    accumulation of, in hydrocephalus, 654–656, *655*
    in increased intracranial pressure, 636–637
    leakage of, 676
    normal values for, 1049t
    shunt for, 654–656, *655*
Cerebrum, 635, *635*
Certified pediatric nurse practitioner, 21
Cerumen, 999
    ethnic variations in, 962t, 965t
    softeners for, 1001–1002
Cervical traction, *926*
Chalazion, 996
Checkups. *See* Health maintenance visits
Chelation therapy, for lead poisoning, 301, 658–659
Chemical conjunctivitis, 196–197
Chemistry panel
    in gastrointestinal disorders, 761t
    normal values for, 1046t–1048t
Chemotherapy
    for brain tumors, 667
    for leukemia, 628, 629
Cherry hemangiomas, 967t, 970–971
Chest
    assessment of, 102, 521–524, *522, 523*
    barrel, 521–522
    deformities of, 102
    expansion of, assessment of, 523–524
    funnel, 522, *523*
    measurement of, 95
        in neonate, 186
    percussion of, 91–92, *92,* 92t, *93*
    pigeon, 522, *523*
    radiography of
        in cardiovascular disorders, 576
        in respiratory disorders, 527
Chest physiotherapy, 530
Chest tubes, *541,* 541–542
    in cardiac surgery, 580, 581
Chewing tobacco, 355–356
Cheyne-Stokes respirations, 523
Chickenpox, 427–428
    vaccine for, 420
Child(ren). *See also* Adolescent; Infant; Neonate; Preschooler;
        School-age child; Toddler
    burden of illness on, 11t
    discipline of, 38–39
    historical concepts of, 8–9
    hospitalized. *See* Hospitalization
    interviewing of, 82–84, 84t
    legal rights of, 12–14, 43
    mortality trends in, 9–11, 10t–12t
    parenting of. *See* Parenting
    withholding or withdrawing treatment from, 47–50
Child abuse and neglect, 294–295, 295t, 934–935
    disability and, 450–451
    reporting of, 15, 859–860
    risk factors for, 317
    sexual, 859–862
        pubic lice and, 977
    substance abuse and, 480
Childbirth. *See also* Labor
    at home, 169
    setting for, 169

Child health assessment. *See* Nursing assessment
Child health care
  comprehensive, 143–147
  consultation in, 143
  continuity of, 143–147
  for disabled, at school, 52–54
  government spending for, *10,* 14–15
  increased costs of, 17–18
  referral in, 143
  teaching in, 139–143
Child health nursing
  challenges and rewards of, 6–7
  contemporary concepts in, 7–8
  current problems and future directions in, 16–17
  evaluation of, 151–155
  expanded roles in, 21–22
  health care system changes affecting, 17–18
  integrating knowledge in, 21
  legislation affecting, 14–17
  nursing process in, 18, *19*
  professional organizations for, 21–22
  publications for, 21–22
  quality assurance in, 155
  systems approach to, 21
Child Life Department, 381–382
Chinese
  cultural beliefs of, 34–35
  integumentary system of, 961t–962t
Chlamydiae, 417t
Chlamydial conjunctivitis, 196–197, 1005–1006
Chlamydial infection
  pelvic inflammatory disease and, 862
  sexually transmitted, 863
Chlamydial pneumonia, 549–550
Chloride
  function and regulation of, 733t
  serum, normal values for, 1044t
  sweat
    in cystic fibrosis, 1048
    normal values for, 1048t
  urinary, normal values for, 1048t
Choanal atresia, 536–537
Choking, in infants, 248
Cholecystitis, 803
Choledochal cyst, 783
Cholesteatoma, 1014
Cholesterol levels
  normal values for, 1045t
  in preschoolers, 292
Chondromalacia patella, 950
Chordee, 819
Chorea, in cerebral palsy, 445
Chorion, 161
Chorionic villus sampling, 172
  indications for, 166–167
Christmas disease, 205t, 622–624
Chromosomal defects, 165, 203t, 203–206. *See also*
          Congenital defects
  in Down syndrome, 456
  prenatal diagnosis of, 171–173
    indications for, 166–167
Chromosomes, 164, *165*
  sex, 164
Chronic adrenocortical insufficiency, 899–900
Chronic glomerulonephritis, 831–832
Chronic illness. *See also* Disabled
  family adaptation to, 402, 403t

home care for. *See* Home care
Chronic middle ear effusion, 1013–1014
  nursing care plan for, 1019–1021
Chronic renal failure, 832–833.834t
  hyperparathyroidism in, 898
Chumship, 341
Chvostek's sign, 748
Cigarette smoking, 355
Cilia, *993,* 994
Ciliary muscles, *993, 994*
Circulation
  cardiac, 569, *570*
  cerebral, 637
  fetal, 567, *568*
  infant, 222
  neonatal, 179, 567–568, *569*
  pulmonary, 518
Circumcision, 191, 197–198, *198*
  in phimosis, 849
Claiming, 69–71
Clark's rule, for pediatric drug dosages, 1051
Classification of Newborns—Based on Maturity and
          Intrauterine Growth, 192, *193*
Clavicle, fracture of, 933–935
Clean catch urine specimen, 814
Cleft lip and palate, 772–774, *773*
  ethnic factors in, 961t, 966t
  hypopituitarism and, 884–885
Client teaching. *See* Health teaching
Clitoris, 843, *844*
Clonazepam (Klonopin), 671t
Clonic seizures, 669t. *See also* Seizures
Closed heart surgery, 580–582
Closed questions, 84–85
Clothing, for infant, 243
Clotting. *See* Coagulation
Clubbing, of fingers, in cardiovascular disorders, 575, *575*
Clubfoot, 191, 938, *938*
Coagulation, 608–609
  tests of, 610
    normal values for, 1047t
Coagulation factors, 609
  deficiencies of, 622–624
Coarctation of aorta, *587,* 587–588, *588*
Cocaine. *See also* Substance abuse
  fetal/neonatal effects of, 475
Cochlea, 994, *994*
Codeine, for musculoskeletal disorders, 931t
Codependency, 473
CoDependents Anonymous (CODA), 485
Cognitive assessment, 106
Cognitive controls, 379
Cognitive development
  in adolescent, 331t, 340–341
  concepts of death and, 491–492, 497
  in infant, 228–231, 229t
  in neonate, 184
  Piaget's theory of, 63–64, 65t, *66,* 228–230, 229t
  preoperational stage of, 64, 261–262, 284–285
  in preschooler, 284–287
  in school-age child, 311, 312t
  in toddler, 261–262, 262–265
Cognitive rehearsal, 379–380
Cognitive styles, 313
Cold, common, 1016
Cold stress, in premature infant, 209
Colic, 786–787

Colitis, ulcerative, 793–794
Collective monologue, 285
Coloboma, 997, *998*
Colon. *See also under* Bowel; Intestinal
    anatomy of, 760, *760*
    polyps o800
Colonoscopy, 763t, 764
Color blindness, 205t
    assessment for, 999t
Colostomy, 766–767
Colostrum, 200
    for eye infection prophylaxis, 197
Coma
    diabetic, 907
    level of, Glasgow Coma Scale for, 644–646, 645t
Common atrioventricular orifice, 585
Common cold, 1016
Common warts, 979
Communal family, 28
Communication
    with adolescent, 343
    family, 33
    in health assessment interview, 81–83
    in infant, *234,* 234–235
    nonverbal, 82
    techniques of, 84–85, 85t
    verbal, 82
Comparative negligence, 46
Complement system, 223
Complete blood count, 610
    in cardiovascular disorders, 576–577
    in immune disorders, 694
    normal values for, 1045t
    in school-age child, 319, 319t
Computed tomography, of brain, 639t
Computerized care plan, 123, *124–125*
Computers, for disabled, 450
Concrete operational thought, 64, 311
Concussion, 675
Conditioning, 67
Condoms, 351t
Conduction system, cardiac, 569–570
Condylomata acuminata, 865–866
Condylomata plana, 866
Cones, retinal, *993,* 994
Confidentiality, 52
Congenital adrenal hyperplasia, 892
Congenital cataracts, 1002–1003
Congenital defects. *See also specific defects*
    cardiovascular, 583–595
    chromosomal, *165,* 165–166
    genetic, 203t–205t, 203–206
    maternal infections and, 206–207
    polygenic and multifactorial, 166, 206t
    prenatal diagnosis of, 171–172, 455
        indications for, 166–167, 172
    risk factors for, 202–207
    rubella and, 166–167, 286, 426
    teratogenic, 166–168, 167t
    withholding treatment for, 48–50
Congenital glaucoma, 1003
Congenital hip dysplasia, 105, 935–937, *936, 937*
    in Native Americans, 966t
    neonatal assessment for, 189–191
    nursing care plan for, 952–953
Congenital hypercalcemia, 747
Congestive heart failure, 598–600

    in aortic coarctation, 588
    nursing care plan for, 601–602
Conjunctiva, 993, *993*
    assessment of, 99
Conjunctivitis
    bacterial, 196–197
    chemical, 196–197, 1005
    chlamydial, 196–197, 207, 1005–1006
    gonococcal, 207
    gonorrheal, 188, 196–197, 1005
    inclusion, 1006
    neonatal, 1005–1006
Consciousness, level of, evaluation of, 644–647, 645t
Consent, informed, 46–47
    for immunizations, 418
Conservation, cognitive, 261, 311, 312t
Conspiracy of silence, 499
Constipation, 769–770
    encopresis and, 770–771
    in Hirschsprung disease, 794–795
Constitutional delay of puberty, 852
Consultation, 143
Continuity of care, 143–146
Contraception, sterilization for, of mentally retarded, 52
Contraceptives, 350–352, 351t
    adolescent's legal right to, 47
    oral, 351t
        for dysfunctional uterine bleeding, 855
Contracoup injury, 674, *674*
Contractures, burn, 984, *984*
    management of, 987, *988*
Contrast media, allergy to, 814
Contributory negligence, 46
Contusion, 932–933
    of brain, 674, 675
    of kidney, 831
Convulsions. *See* Seizures
Cooley anemia, *621,* 621–622
Cooperative play, 312–313
Coping
    by children of substance-abusing parents, 479
    individual/family, in immune disorders, 696
    ineffective family, in spinal cord injury, 680–681
Copper, serum, normal values for, 1045t
Copper overload, in Wilson disease, 783–785
Cornea, *993,* 994
    curvature of, refractive errors and, 1009–1010
Coronary artery aneurysm, in Kawasaki disease, 422
Coronary vessels, 569, *570*
Corporal punishment, 38–39
Corrosives, ingestion of, 780–781
Cortical motor integration, 106
Cortical sensory interpretation, 106
Corticosteroids. *See* Steroids
Corticotropin hormone, for seizures, 672t
Corticotropin-releasing hormone, 879
Cortisol, 879
    hypersecretion of
        in congenital adrenal hyperplasia, 892
        Cushing syndrome and, 892–893
Corti's organ, 994, *994*
Cost containment measures, 18
Cotrel traction, *927*
Cough(ing)
    assessment of, 521
    in newborn, 190t
    in pertussis, 429

in postural drainage, 530
whooping, 429
Cough suppressants, 534
Coup/contracoup injury, 674, *674*
Couvade syndrome, 168
Cowper's glands, 843, *845*
Cow's milk
vs. breast milk, 201t
sensitivity to, vs. lactoase intolerance, 714t
Coxa plana, 948–949
CPK (creatine phosphokinase), normal values for, 1045t
Crack. *See* Cocaine
Crackles, 524
Cradle cap, 243
Cranial nerves, 636
assessment of, 106
Cranial sutures, 187, *187*
premature closure of, 218
Craniostosis, 218
Craniosynostosis, 656
Craniotabes, 188
Creatinine, serum, 816
in fluid and electrolytes imbalances, 739t
normal values for, 1045t
Creatinine phosphakinase (CPK), normal values for, 1045t
Crepitation, 524
Cretinism, 885–886
Crib death, 543–544
Cri-du-chat, 189
Critical period, 61, 67
Crohn disease, 793–794
malabsorption in, 791
Cromolyn sodium (Intal), for asthma, 557t
Croup, 542–543
nursing care plan for
assessment in, 107
diagnosis in, 117–118
evaluation in, 152–154
implementation in, 144–146
planning in, 127–128
Crust, *960*
Cry, of neonate, 189
Crying
infant, 248–249, 370
in colic, 786
trained night, 227
Cryotherapy, for retinopathy of prematurity, 1004
Cryptorchidism, 850–851
nursing care plan for, 868–869
Cuandero, 36
Culture, 31–33
death and dying and, 497–498
infant growth and development and, 235
Cushing syndrome, 892–893
Cutis marmorata, 967t
Cyanosis
in cardiovascular disease, 574–575, 583
with congenital defects, 592–595
in tetralogy of Fallot, 592
Cycloplegics, 1001
Cyclosporine A, in kidney transplantation, 836
Cyst, choledochal, 783
Cystic acne, 967t, 975–976
Cystic fibrosis, 204t, 542–555
malabsorption in, 790–791
sweat test for, 1048
Cystitis, 826–827

nursing care plan for, 838–839
Cystoscopy, 815
Cystourethrography, voiding, 815
Cytomegalovirus infection
fetal effects of, 167, 206
vaccine for, 420
Cytotoxic diarrhea, 767–768
Cytotoxic T cells, 689

**D**

Dacryostenosis, 1003–1004
Dactylitis, in sickle cell disease, 624
Dance reflex, 190t
Dandy-Walker syndrome, 654
Date rape, 861
Dating, 342
Day care, 289
government support for, 15–16
Day hospital stays, 382–383
Deamination, amino acid, 759
Death and dying, 490–509
children's concepts of, 491–492, 497
communication in
with child, 504–506
with family, 506
cultural aspects of, 497–498
cure vs. care goals in, 502, 502t
effects of
on nurses, 507–508
on parents and families, 507
family themes and, 498–500
fears in, 497t, 504
grief therapy for, 503, 506, 506t
hope in, 503–504
nursing care in, planning of, 502–503
nursing diagnoses in, 500–502
nursing interventions in, 503–507
nursing process in, 492–507, 493t–496t
assessment in, 492–500
evaluation in, 506–507
setting for, 502–503t
with short vs. long preparation time, 491
social support in, 498
socioeconomic issues in, 498
spiritual issues in, 497–498
stages of, 491
support groups for, 503, 509
unfinished business in, 500
Deceleration, heart rate, in labor, 174
Decerebration, 646, *646*
Decidua basales, 161
Decidua capsularis, 161
Decidua vera, 161
Decongestants, side effects of, 531–534
Decortication, 646, *646*
Deductive reasoning, 284
Deep tendon reflexes, assessment of, 108. *See also* Reflex(es)
Deer tick bites, Lyme disease and, 423–424
Degree of Bother Inventory, 194, *196*
Dehydration. *See also* Fluid and electrolyte imbalances
clinical manifestations of, 736–738, 737t
in diabetes insipidus, 889–890
in diarrhea, 768–769
fluid replacement for, 741–743, 768–769
vs. fluid volume deficit, 754
hypernatremia and, 752

Delayed menarche, 853
Delta optical density analysis, in Rh incompatibility, 609
Deltoid muscle, injection into, 135, *137*
Dental care
    for adolescent, 346–347
    for disabled, 465
    for preschooler, 293
    for school-age child, 320
    for toddler, 266–267
Dentition, 227t, 227–228
Denver Articulation Screening Test, 1000, 1028–1029
Denver Developmental Screening Test, 87, 237, 290,
        1030–1031
    for toddler, 265
Denver Prescreening Developmental Questionnaire, 87–88
Dependent nursing interventions, 132
Depression, 358, 359t
Deprivation amblyopia, 1002
Dermatitis
    atopic, 971–972
    bacterial, 981–982
    diaper, 243, 971, 980
    fungal, 243, 856–857, 979–981
    seborrheic, 975
Dermatitis-arthritis syndrome, gonococcal, 864
Dermis, 957
Desensitization
    allergic, 696–697
    systematic, for hospitalized children, 379
Desferoxamine, for thalassemia, 621–622
Desmopressin, for diabetes insipidus, 889–890
Detachment, 499
Development, definition of, 59. *See also* Growth
        and development
Developmental assessment, 87–88
    Denver Developmental Screening Test for, 1028–1031
    in infant, 236–238, 241
    in preschooler, 290
    in toddler, 265
Developmental delay
    in Down syndrome, 456
    mental retardation and, 451, 453
Developmental disability. *See also* Disabled
    definition of, 441
    legal definition of, 441
Developmental milestones, 70t–71t
Developmental tasks, 61, 67–68
    of adolescent, 346
    of infant, 26567t
    of preschooler, 293–294
    of school-age child, 320, 323t
    of toddler, 267
Dexamethasone suppression test, 893
Dextrose, for hypoglycemia, 890, 891
Dextrostix, for hypoglycemia diagnosis, 890, 891
Diabetes insipidus, 889–890
Diabetes mellitus, 900–912
    assessment in, 901
    diet in, 904–905, 905t
    glucose testing in, 905–906
    hypoglycemia in, 900, 906–907
    illness in, 907–908
    insulin-dependent, 900–912
    insulin shock in, 907
    insulin therapy for, 902–904, *903,* 903t, *904*
    ketoacidosis in, 906–907
    medical diagnosis and management of, 901

    non–insulin-dependent, 900
    nursing care for, 901–908
    nursing care plan for, 908–912
    nursing diagnoses for, 901
    pathophysiology of, 876–877, 900
    safety rules for, 905t
Diabetic coma, 907
Diabetogenic effect, 875
Diagnoses, nursing. *See* Nursing diagnoses
Diagnosis related groups, 128–129
Dialysis, 833–836
Diaper dermatitis, 243, 971, 980
Diaphragm, contraceptive, 351t
Diaphragmatic hernia, 776–777
Diaphysis, 917, *917*
Diarrhea, 767–769
    in celiac disease, 791, 792
    in giardiasis, 433
    in malabsorption, 791
    in shigella, 433
Diarthroses, 918
Diencephalon, 635, *635*
Diet. *See also* Feeding; Food; Nutrition
    for adolescent, 338–339, 339t
    in chronic renal failure, 833
    diabetic, 904–905, 905t
    elimination, 713–714
    gluten free, 766t, 792–793
    high-calcium, in hypoparathyroidism, 888
    high fat, 766t
    high fiber, 766t
    high protein/high calorie, 766t
    for infant, 224t–226t, 224–226, 243–245
    ketogenic, 670
    lactose-free, 766t
    low residue, 766t
    in malabsorption, 791
    milk-free, 714, 715t
    in pregnancy, 170
    for preschooler, 280–283
    for school-age child, 309–311, 310t
    for toddler, 260, 260t
    vegetarian, 226, 226t
Dietary history, 345–346
Diffuse axonal injury, 675
Diffuse toxic goiter, 894–896
Diffusion, 731
DiGeorge syndrome, 705–706, 888
Digestion
    in infant, 221
    physiology of, 760–761
Digitalis, for congestive heart failure, 600
Diphtheria, 428–429
    immunization for, 241–242, 242t, 267t, 318t, 417–420,
        419t, 1055
Diplegia, in cerebral palsy, 444
Diplopia, 1006–1007
Disability
    family adaptation to, 402, 403t
    home care for. *See* Home care
Disabled, 441–469
    case managed coordinated care for, 442
    early intervention/stimulation programs for, 441–442
    education of, 16, 441, 450, 454–457
    family adaptation to, 461–462
    legislation affecting, 441
    long-term planning for, 464

mainstreaming of, 52–54, 323, 442
medical treatment of
 right to, 51–52
 withdrawing or withholding of, 47–50
normalization for, 404
parenting of, 461
recreation and play needs of, 462–463
rights of, 16
school nursing care for, 52–54
sex education for, 464
siblings of, 461–462
support groups for, 461, 462t
Discharge, for day hospital stay, 382–383
Discharge planning, 126, 382, 386
for home care, 397, 400–401
Discipline, 38–39
of disabled, 463
of preschooler, 302
of toddlers, 272, 273
Disease. *See also* Illness
Disease transmission, modes of, 417, 417t, 418t
Dislocation, 933
congenital hip, 105, 189–191, 935–937, *936, 937*
 in Native Americans, 966t
 nursing care plan for, 952–953
Displacement, 499
Distraction, bone, 928
Diuretics
for congestive heart failure, 600
for increased intracranial pressure, 648t
Diverticulum, Meckel, 793
Dizygotic twins, 173
Doctors Ought to Care (DOC), 474
Documentation, of client health care evaluation, 151
Dosage, calculation of, 133, *133,* 1050–1052
Down syndrome, 455–458. *See also* Disabled
Drainage
of cerebrospinal fluid, 654–656, *655*
chest, in pneumothorax, *541,* 541–542
postural, 530, *532–532*
Drain cleaners, ingestion of, 780–781
Drawing, by preschooler, *279,* 279–280
Drowning and near-drowning, 246–247, 270, 320
Drug(s)
accidental ingestion of, 270–271, 271t, 300
action of, age-related variables in, 530–531
administration of
 developmental guidelines for, 136t
 intramuscular, 135, *137l*
 intravenous, 135
 oral, 133–135, *134*
 rectal, 135
allergic reaction to, 707–709
 cutaneous manifestations of, 982–983
dosage calculation for, 133, *133,* 1050–1052
for ear disorders, 1001–1002
for eye disorders, 1001
hypersensitivity pneumonitis and, 709
pupillary function and, 646
teratogenic, 167t
Drug abuse. *See* Substance abuse
Duchenne muscular dystrophy, 205t, 949–950
Ductus arteriosus, 567, *568, 569*
closure of, 179t
patent, *586,* 586–587
Dullness, on percussion, 92, 92t
Dunlop traction, *927*

Duodenal atresia, 785–786
Duodenal ulcers, 803–804
hyperparathyroidism and, 898
Duong, 35
Dwarfism, pituitary, 876, 884–885
D-xylose absorption test, 764, 792
Dying. *See* Death and dying
Dysenteric diarrhea, 768
Dyskinesia, in cerebral palsy, 444–445
Dysmenorrhea, 854
Dyspnea, 522

**E**
Ear. *See also* Hearing assessment; Hearing impairment
anatomy and physiology of, 994, *994*
assessment of, 101, *101*
 in neonate, 188
disorders of, 1012–1016
 assessment in, 999, 1000t
 nursing care in, 1001–1002
 nursing diagnoses in, 1000–1001
embryology of, 993
glue, 1013
inflammation of, 1012–1015
position of, 98, *99*
swimmer's, 1015
in toddler, 259
Ear drops, 1001–1002
instillation of, 1013, *1014*
Eardrum, 994, *994*
examination of, 999
incision of, in otitis media, 1013
Earwax, 999
Eating. *See also* Feeding
Eating disorders, 353–355
national organizations for, 360
Eccrine sweat glands, 957
Echocardiography, 576
fetal, 171
Economic factors, in home care, 391
Ectoderm, 161, 161t, 956
Eczema, 971–972
in Wiskott-Aldrich syndrome, 707
Edema. *See also* Fluid and electrolyte imbalances
cerebral, 643–644. *See also* Intracranial pressure, increased
in fluid volume excess, 754
in neonate, 189
in nephrotic syndrome, 825, 826
signs of, 737t, 738
Education. *See also* Health teaching; Learning
for disabled, 16, 52–54, 441, 441–442
 with cerebral palsy, 450
 legal requirements for, 441
for Down syndrome children, 456–457
for mentally retarded, 454–455
sex, for disabled, 464
for substance abuse prevention, 481–484
Education of All Handicapped Children Act, 16, 441
Edwards syndrome, 203t
Eggs, food sources of, 715t
Ego, 61
Egocentrism, 261, 284–285
in adolescent, 340
Ego diffusion, 341
Ego identity, 341

Eisenmenger syndrome, 585
Electra complex, 62
Electrocardiography, 576
    in hyperkalemia, 750, 751
    in hypokalemia, 750, 751
Electroencephalography, 640t
Electrolytes, 732–734. *See also* Fluid and electrolyte
        imbalances
    in extracellular fluid, 732t
    functions and regulation of, 733t
    in intracellular fluid, 732t
    requirements for, 734–736
    transport of, 731–732
Electromyoneurography, 640t
Electroneutrality, 732
Electronic fetal heart rate monitoring, 174, *174*
Electrophoresis, serum protein, in immune disorders, 694
Electrospinal stimulation, for scoliosis, 944
Elimination diet, 713–714
Emancipated minor, 47, 346
Embryonic development, 161, 161t
Emergency department, admission to, 383
Emotional illness, treatment of, legal issues in, 51
Employee Assistance Program, for substance abusers, 485
Empowerment, family, for home care, 402–405
Enanthem, 425
Encephalitis, 661–662
Encephalocele, 649–654, *650*
Encephalography, air, 641t
Encephalopathy, neonatal hypoxic-ischemic, 538
Encopresis, 770–771
Enculturation, 31
Endemic disease, 417t
Endemic goiter, 887
Endocardial cushion defects, 585–586
Endocarditis, bacterial, 595–596
Endocrine disorders
    assessment in, 880–881
    chronic, 900–908
    client and parent education in, 883–884
    drug therapy in, 884
    history in, 880, 880t–881t
    in infancy and early childhood, 889–893
    nursing care in, planning of, 882–883
    nursing diagnoses in, 881–882
    nursing interventions in, 883–884
    nutrition in, 884
    physical examination in, 881
    in school-age children and adolescents, 893–900
Endocrine system
    in adolescent, 335
    anatomy and physiology of, *873,* 873–880
    embryology of, 872–873
    in infant, 222
    negative feedback in, 873, *874*
    in reproductive development, 843–845
    target glands in, 873
Endoderm, 161, 161t, 956
Endometrial cycle, 844
Endometriosis, 856
Endoscopy, 763t, 764
Endosteum cavity, 917, *917*
Endotracheal intubation, 534
End-stage renal disease, 833
Enema
    barium, 763t, 764
    for constipation, 770

*En face* position, 184, *185*
Engrossment, 185
Enteral feeding, 743, *743,* 766
    necrotizing enterocolitis and, 789
    for premature infant, 209
Enterobiasis, 432–433
Enterocolitis, necrotizing, 789–790
Enucleation, 1008
Enuresis
    nocturnal, 298–299
    primary, 298
    secondary, 298
Environment, culture and, 33
Eosinophils, 608, 688
    normal values for, 1045t
Epicanthal fold, 99, *101,* 962t, 996
Epidemic, 417t
Epidemiology
    definition of, 417t
    principles of, 416–417
Epidermis, 957
Epididymis, 843, *845*
Epidural hematoma, 675–676
Epigenetic principle, 287
Epiglottis, 517
Epiglottitis, 547–548
Epilepsy, 668–674. *See also* Seizures
Epiloia, 204t
Epinephrine, 879–880
    for anaphylaxis, 418t, 709
    for asthma, 556t
Epiphyseal plate, 917, *917*
    fractures involving, 934
Epispadias, 105, 191, *820,* 820–821
Epistaxis, management of, 1002
Epstein's pearls, 188
Equilibration, 63
Equipment vendors, home care, selection of, 398, *399*
Erection, penile, 348
Erikson's psychosocial theory, 62–63, *63, 66*
    adolescent and, 341
    infant and, 231–233
    preschooler and, 287
    school-age child and, 313–314, 314t
    toddler and, 262, 263t
Erosion, *960*
Erythema infectiosum, 421
Erythematous rash, 421
Erythema toxicum neonatorum, 189, 961t
Erythroblastosis fetalis, 199, 616
Erythrocyte porphyrin count, in lead poisoning, 301
Erythrocytes, 571, *607,* 607–608
    antigenic properties of, 608
    assessment of, 610
    formation and destruction of, 607
    in neonate, 179–181, *180*
    normal values for, 1045t
    sickled, 624, *624*
Erythrocytosis, 609
Erythromycin ointment, for ophthalmia neonatorum, 197
Erythropoiesis, 607–608
Eschar, burn, 986
Escharotomy, 986
Esophagitis, 777
Esophagoscopy, 763t, 764
Esophagus
    anatomy of, 759

atresia of, 774–776, *775*
corrosive burns of, 780–781
Esophoria, 100
Esotropia, 1007
Espiritistas, 36
Estimation of Gestational Age by Maturity Rating, 192, *192*
Estrogen, 843–844, 880
Ethical decision making, 43–44, *45*
Ethical issues, in home care, 410–411, 443
Ethics, code of, 44
Ethnic family organization, 33–34
Ethnicity, 33
Ethosuximide (Zarontin), 671t
Eustachian tube, 994, *994, 995*
Evaluation
documentation and communication of, 151
methods of, 150–151
of nursing care, 151–155
in nursing care plan, 152–154
in nursing process, 18, *19,* 150–155
self-evaluation and, 155
Ewing's sarcoma, 946–947
Exanthem, 421
Exanthem subitum, 426
Exchange transfusion, 613
for hydrops fetalis, 200
for neonatal hyperbilrubinemia, 615
Excretory urography, 814
Exercise
in cerebral palsy, 450, 469
in mental retardation, 453, 469
Exophoria, 100
Exophthalmos, 881, 996
Exotropia, 1007
Expiration, 519
Expiratory reserve volume, 525
Expressive milestones, 234*234*
Extended family, 9, 26
External ear, 994, *994*
inflammation of, 1015
External fixator, Ilizarov, 928–930
Extracellular fluid, 731
electrolyte content of, 732t
Extremities
assessment of, 105
in neonate, 189–191
in cerebral palsy, 443t, 443–444, 444t
Eye. *See also* Vision assessment; Vision impairment
anatomy and physiology of, *993,* 993–994
assessment of, 99–101, *101*
disorders of
in adolescents, 1010–1012
assessment in, 996–1000, 999t
congenital, 1002–1004
in infants and toddlers, 1004–1008
nursing care for, 1001–1002
nursing diagnoses in, 1000–1001
in preschool and school-age children, 1010–1012
embryology of, 992–993
examination of, 996–997
injuries of, 1011
medications for, 1001
neonatal assessment of, 188
in toddler, 259
Eye drops, 1001
Eyelid, drooping, 99

**F**
Fabry disease, 205t
Facilitated diffusion, 731
Fade factor, 288
Fahrenheit-Celsius conversion chart, 1053t
Fallopian tubes, 843, *844*
Falls, prevention of, in infants, 246
Familial dysautonomia, 204t
Familial hypercholesterolemia, 204t
Familial hypophosphatemia, 205t
Family
adolescent-parent, 27
Asian, 34–35
black-American, 37
blended, 27–28
care-giving by. *See* Home care
communal, 28
current trends in, 25
developmental stages and tasks of, 28–30, 29t–30t
ethnic, 33–34
extended, 26
gay/lesbian, 27
Hispanic, 36–37
historical concepts of, 25
homeless, 28
Native American, 37
nuclear, 26
older-parent, 28
one-child, 28
single-parent, 26–27
assessment of, 238
step, 27–28
structure and functions of, 23, 25t
substance-abusing, 476–477
types of, 9
Family Adaptability, Parternship, Growth, Affection, and Resolve (APGAR) Test, 31, 32t, 87
Family assessment, 85–87, *86. See also* Nursing assessment
for infant, 238
for preschooler, 290–291
for school-age child, 317
for toddler, 266
Family empowerment, for home care, 402–405
Family function assessment, 30–31, 31t–32t
Family Functioning Index (FFI), 31, 31t
Family/nurse relationship, stages in, 402, 403t
Family themes, in death and dying, 499–500
Family tree, 85, *86*
Farsightedness, 1009–1010
Fasting blood sugar test, for diabetes mellitus, 901
Fat, brown, 181–182
Fathering
by adolescent, 352
of infant, 233–234
of neonate, 71–72, 184–185, 194. *See also* Parenting
Fears, in preschooler, 296–297
Febrile seizures, 647–648
Fecal impaction, 769–770
Fecal incontinence, 770–771
Feces. *See* Stool
Feeding. *See also* Diet; Nutrition
in autism, 459t–460t
bottle, 201, 202t, 244
in colic, 786
of premature infant, 209
weaning from, 248
breast, 200–201, 243–244

Feeding, breast (*continued*)
  jaundice and, 181
  for premature infant, 209
  weaning from, 248
 in cardiovascular disorders, 582–583, 600
 in cerebral palsy, 446–447, *447, 449*
 in cleft lip and palate, 773–774
 in colic, 786
 in congestive heart failure, 600
 enteral, 743, *743,* 766
  necrotizing enterocolitis and, 789
  of premature infant, 209
 gastric, 742–743
 in gastroesophageal reflux, 778
 of infant, 200–201, 202t, 243–245
  gastrointestinal development and, 221
  in hospital, 370
 in intestinal atresia, 786
 introduction of solid foods in, 244–245
 in myelomeningocele, 652
 of preschooler, 280–283
 of school-age child, 309–311, 310t
 of toddler, 260
 total parenteral, 743, *743*
  at home, 410
  necrotizing enterocolitis and, 789–790
  for premature infant, 209
 tube, 742, 766
  after esophageal atresia/tracheoesophageal
   fistula repair, 776
  at home, 409–410
Feeding pump, 409
Feeding tube, 409–410, 742, 766
Feet. *See* Foot
Feetham Family Functioning Scale, 32t, 87
Femoral anteversion, 940–941
Femoral epiphysis, slipped, 947–948
Femoral fracture, 934
Femoral head, avascular necrosis of, 948–949
Fetal alcohol effect, 475
Fetal alcohol syndrome, 207, *207,* 475
Fetal circulation, 567, *568*
Fetal distress, in labor, 174, *174*
Fetal hemoglobin, 222
Fetal monitoring, in labor, 174, *174*
Fetography, 171
Fetoscopy, 172
Fetus
 alpha-fetoprotein screening for, 171
 blood sampling from
  from scalp, 174–175
  from umbilical cord, 172
 cardiovascular system in, 567–568
 echocardiography for, 171
 endocrine system in, 872–873
 gastrointestinal system in, 759
 growth and development of, 161–173
  assessment of, 170–175
  environmental influences on, 167–168
  estimation of by gestational age, 163, 164t
  genetic influences on, 164–167
  in multiple pregnancy, 173
  nutrition and, 170
  patterns of, 172–173
  timetable of, *163,* 164t
 growth retardation in, 172, 206
 heart rate monitoring in, 174, *174*

 hematological system in, 606–607
 kidneys in, 811
 magnetic resonance imaging of, 171
 musculoskeletal system in, 916–917
 nervous system in, 634–635
 reproductive system in, 842–843
 respiratory system in, 517
 substance abuse effects of, 207, *207,* 475–476
 ultrasonography of, 171, 173
 urinary tract in, 811
Fever
 in juvenile rheumatoid arthritis, 719
 seizures in, 647–648
Fibrinogen, normal values for, 1045t
Fibrocystic breast disease, 858
Fibrous joints, 918
Field dependence/field independence, cognitive, 313
Fifth disease, 422
Financial factors, in home care, 391
Fine motor development, in infant, *219,* 219–220, *220,*
  220t
Finger clubbing, in cardiovascular disorders, 575, *575*
Fingernails. *See* Nails
Fissures, *960*
 anal, 800
Fistula, tracheoesophageal, 774–776, *775*
Flammeus nevi, superficial, 189
Flatness, on percussion, 92, 92t
Flat warts, 979
Flow, circulatory, 567
Flu. *See* Influenza
Fluid
 diffusion of, 731
 extracellular, 731
  electrolyte content of, 732t
 interstitial, 730
 intracellular, 730–731
  electrolyte content of, 732t
 intravascular, 730
Fluid administration
 in hematological disorders, 612
 in rehydration therapy, 741–743
  in diarrhea, 768–769
 in renal disorders, 818
Fluid and electrolyte balance, 731
 in burns, 983
 factors affecting, 731–732
 in neonate, 182–183
 regulation of, 732
Fluid and electrolyte imbalances
 acid-base alterations in, 744–747
 assessment in, 736–738, 740t–741t
 diagnostic procedures in, 738–739, 739t
 history in, 736
 nursing care in
  evaluation of, 743–744
  planning of, 739–741
 nursing diagnoses in, 739
 nursing interventions in, 740t–741t, 741–743
 physical examination in, 736–738, 737t
 replacement therapy for, 741–743, 768–769
Fluid compartments, 730–731
Fluid intake
 monitoring of, 738, 818
 regulation of, 732
Fluid loss
 in burns, 983

mechanisms of, 732
Fluid output, monitoring of, 738
Fluid requirements, 734–736, 736t
Fluid transport, 731–732
Fluid volume deficit, 754–755
Fluid volume excess, 753–754
  high risk for, 891
Fluoride, supplemental, 225, 228
Foam, contraceptive, 351t
Focal seizures, 669t. *See also* Seizures
Folk remedies, 35–37
Follicle stimulating hormone, 874, 880
Folliculitis, 981–982
Fontanels, 98, *98,* 187, *187*
  in fluid imbalance, 738
Fontan procedure, for tricuspid atresia, 594
Food. *See also* Diet; Feeding; Nutrition
  allergies to, 698, 712–714, 714t, 715t
  aspiration of, 546–547
  egg-containing, 715t
  for infants, 225–226, 226t
  milk-containing, 715t
  oral medication administration via, 134
  solid, introduction of, 244–245
  wheat-containing, 715t
Food allergies. *See also* Allergies
Food groups, cross-reacting, 716t
Foot
  athlete's, 980–981
  club, 191
  congenital deformities of, *938,* 938–939
  ringworm of, 980–981
Foramen ovale, 567, *568, 569*
  closure of, 179t
Forced expiratory flow, 525
Forced vital capacity, 525
Foreign bodies
  aspiration of, 546–547
  ingestion of, 779–780
  vaginal, 857–858
Foreign language speakers, 33
Foreign travel, immunizations for, 420, 420t
Foreskin, 843, *845*
  assessment of, 105, 847
  in phimosis, 849
Formal operational stage, 64, 340
Formula, vs. breast milk, 224t, 224–225, 225t
Formula feeding, 201, 202t, 244
  in colic, 786
  for premature infant, 209
  weaning from, 248
Fovea centralis, 997, *998*
Fracture(s), 933–935, *934. See also* Musculoskeletal disorders
  casts for, 924t, 924–926, *925,* 925t
  external fixation of, 928–930
  healing of, 919
  in osteogenesis imperfecta, 939t, 939–940
  of skull, 675, 676
  stress, 951
  traction for, 925t, 926, *926–929,* 930t
  types of, 933, *934*
Fremitus, 524
Freudian theory, 61–62
  adolescent and, 340
  infant and, 233
  preschooler and, 287
  school-age child and, 313

toddler and, 262–263
Friction rub, in pericarditis, 597
Fried's rule, for neonatal drug dosages, 1050
Friendships, 314–315
  of adolescent, 331t, 339, 341, 342–343
  of school-age child, 314–315
Functional residual capacity, 525
Fundus, 997, *998*
Fungal infections. *See also* Candidiasis
  of skin, 243, 856–857, 979–981
Fungi, 417t
Funnel chest, 522, *523*
Furuncle, 981–982
Futcher's lines, 961t, 963t

**G**

Gagging reflex, 190t
Gallbladder, anatomy of, 759, *760*
Galleazzi sign, 936, *936*
Gallstones, 803
Gamma globulin
  immunization with, 417–418, 431
  for Kawasaki disease, 423
*Gardnerella* vaginosis, 857
Gas, intestinal, in colic, 786
Gas exchange, pulmonary, 520
Gastric feeding, 742–743
Gastric ulcers, 803–804
  hyperparathyroidism and, 898
Gastroesophageal reflux, 777–778
  in infant, 221
  nursing care plan for, 804–806
Gastrointestinal disorders
  assessment in, 761–764
  decompression in, 766
  diagnostic procedures in, 762t–763t, 762–764
  drug therapy for, 767
  elimination in, 766–767
  history in, 761–762
  infectious, 432–434
  nursing care in
    evaluation of, 767
    planning of, 765
  nursing diagnoses in, 764–765
  nursing interventions in, 765–767
  nutrition in, 766
  physical examination in, 762
  surgery for, 767
Gastrointestinal system
  absorption in, 761
  anatomy of, 759–760, *760*
  in burns, 984
  digestion in, 761
  embryology of, 759
  excretion in, 761
  in infant, 221–222
  ingestion in, 760–761
  physiology of, 760–761
  in toddler, 257
Gastroschisis, 788–789
Gastroscopy, 763t, 764
Gastrostomy tube feeding, 766
  after esophageal atresia/tracheoesophageal fistula repair, 776
  at home, 409–410
Gay/lesbian family, 27

Gene, 164
Genetic disorders, 165, 165–167, 203t–205t, 203–206. *See also* Congenital defects
  prenatal diagnosis of, 171–173
    indications for, 166–167
Genetic influences, on fetal growth and development, 164–167
Genetic inheritance, laws of, 165–166
Genital herpes, 866–867
Genital phase, 62
Genitals. *See also* Reproductive disorders; Reproductive system
  ambiguous, 843, 848
  anatomy and physiology of, 843, *844, 845*
  embryology of, 843
  in endocrine disorders, 881
  examination of, 846–847
    in neonate, 191
    in suspected sexual abuse, 860
Genital warts, 865–866, 979
Genital yeast infections, 856–857, 980
Genogram, 85, *86*
Genotype, 167t
Genu varum, 105, 941
Geographic tongue, 102, 1000
German measles, 426–427
  congenital, 166–167, 206, 426
  immunization for, 241–242, 242t, 267t, 318t, 417–420, 429t, 1055
  postnatal, 427
Gesell's maturation theory, 68
Gestational age
  determination of, *191,* 191–192, *192*
  fetal growth and development estimation by, 164, *164*
  neonatal classification by, 192–193
Giac, 35
Giardiasis, 433, 768
Gigantism, 876, 893–894
Gingiva, assessment of, 102
Glans penis, 843, *845*
Glasgow coma scale, 644–646, 645t
Glaucoma, 1003
Glomerular filtration, 812
Glomerulonephritis
  acute (poststreptococcal), 823–824
  chronic, 831–832
Glucagon, 876, 907
Glucocorticoids, 879
  hypersecretion of, Cushing syndrome and, 892–893
Glucose
  for hypoglycemia, 890–891
  metabolism of, in diabetes mellitus, 900
  serum, normal values for, 1045t
  sources of, for diabetics, 907
  testing for, in diabetes, 901, 905–906
  urine, normal values for, 1047t
Glucose-6-phosphate dehydrogenase deficiency, 618
Glucose tolerance test, for diabetes mellitus, 901
Glue ear, 1013
Glue sniffing, 324t
Glutamic oxaloacetic transaminase, serum (SGOT), normal values for, 1047t
Glutamic pyruvate transaminase, serum (SGOT), normal values for, 1047t
Gluten-free diet, 766t, 792
Gluten-sensitive enteropathy, 792
Gluteus medius muscle, injection into, 135, *137*
Goiter, 887

diffuse toxic, 894–896
Gonadocorticoids, 879
Gonadotropic hormones, 874
Gonads, 880
Goniotomy, 1003
Gonococcal conjunctivitis, 207
Gonorrhea, 864
  conjunctivitis and, 188, 196–197, 207, 1005
  pelvic inflammatory disease and, 862
Government programs, child health, *10,* 14–15
G6PD deficiency, 205t
Grafts, for burns, 987, 987t
Graft-versus-host disease, in DiGeorge syndrome, 705
Grams–pounds and ounces conversion chart, 1054
Grand mal seizures, 669, 669t. *See also* Seizures
Granulocytes, 608
Graphesthesia, 106
Grasp, development of, 219, *220,* 220t
Grasping, in infant, 232–233
Grasp reflex, 190t
Graves disease, 894–896
Great arteries, transposition of, *590,* 590–591
Greenstick fracture, 933, *934*
Grief. *See also* Death and dying
  anticipatory, 500
  definition of, 491
  resolution of, 507
  with short vs. long preparation time for death, 491
  survivor, 500
  symptoms of, 500, 501t
Grief therapy, 503, 506, 506t
Grippe. *See* Influenza
Gross motor development, in infant, *218,* 218–219, 219t
Growing pains, 309
Growth, definition of, 59
Growth and development, 59–73
  of adolescent, 330–360. *See also* Adolescent, growth and development of
  assessment of, 89, 93–95. *See also* Nursing assessment
  in cardiovascular disease, 574
  cephalocaudal, 59, 162, 217
  determinants of, 217
  developmental task theory of, 67t, 67–68, 68t
  of embryo, 161, 161t
  Erikson's theory of, 62–63, *63, 66*
  of fetus, 161–173. *See also* Fetus, growth and development of
  Freud's theory of, 61–62
  genetic influences on, 164–167
  Gesell's maturation theory of, 68
  of infant, 217–235. *See also* Infant, growth and development of
  Kohlberg's theory of, 65–66
  language and, 66, 69
  learning theories of, 66–68
  Maslow's hierarchy of needs and, 60, *60*
  of neonate, 178–211. *See also* Neonate
  nursing implications of, 72–73
  of parents, 72
  patterns of, 59, 217
  Piaget's theory of, 63–64, 65t, *66*
  play theories of, 68–69
  of preschooler, 276–303. *See also* Preschooler, growth and development of
  proximodistal, 59, 217
  of school-age child, 308–325. *See also* School-age child, growth and development of
  social learning theory of, 67

stage theories of, 60–66
of toddler, 255–273. *See also* Toddler, growth and
  development of
Growth charts, 235, 1037–1040
Growth hormone, 875
  deficiency of, 876, 884–885
  hypersecretion of, 893–894
Growth hormones, 222
Growth measurements. *See* Body measurements
Growth retardation
  in gastrointestinal disorders, 761
  intrauterine, 172, 206
Guillain-Barré syndrome, 663–664
Guilt, in death and dying, 499
Guilt movie, 500
Gynecomastia, 349, 859

**H**
*Haemophilus influenzae* infection, 434–435
  epiglottitis and, 547
  immunization for, 417–420, 419t, 435, 1055
Hair
  anatomy and physiology of, 958
  disorders of
    diagnostic tests for, 960–968
    history in, 958, 959t
    nursing care for, 968–970
    nursing diagnoses for, 968
    physical examination in, 958–960, 961t–967t
  ethnic variations in, 961t–967t, 968
  loss of, 958
  pubic, 335, *335, 336,* 338, 338t
Hair follicles, 958
Halo traction, 678, *926*
Hand
  control of, development of, *219,* 219t, 219–220, *220*
  ringworm of, 980–981
Handedness, 280
Hand-foot syndrome, in sickle cell disease, 624
Handicap, definition of, 441
Handicapped. *See* Disability; Disabled
Handicappism, definition of, 441
Harlequin color change, 189
Hashimoto thyroiditis, 887, 896–897
Havighurst's developmental task theory, 61. *See also*
  Developmental tasks, 67t, 67–68, 68t
Hay fever, 710–712, 1017–1018
Head, of neonate, assessment of, *187,* 187–188, *188*
Headache, 664–665
  in brain tumor, 667, 668
Head circumference
  chart for, 1041–1042
  measurement of, 95, *95,* 236
    in hydrocephalus, 655
    in infant, 217–218
    in neonate, 186
Head growth, in infant, 217–218
Head injuries, 674–676
Head lag, 188
Head lice, 976–977
Head Start, 15, 289
Health
  concepts of, 11–12, *12*
  ethnic beliefs about, 33–34
  hot/cold theory of, 34
Health assessment. *See* Nursing assessment
Health care. *See* Child health care

Health history, 88–89
Health insurance
  diagnosis related groups and, 128–129
  home care and, 391
Health maintenance organizations, 18
Health maintenance visits
  for infant, 239–250
  for preschooler, 291–293
  for school-age child, 318t, 318–320
  for toddler, 266, 267t
Health promotion
  for adolescent, 346–347
  for infant, 239–250
  for preschooler, 291–303
  for school-age child, 318–324
  for toddler, 266–273
Health teaching, 139–143
  determination of needs for, 140
  discharge, 385–386
  for home care, 397–398, 404–405, 397–398
  learning contract for, 141, 142t
  methods for, 141t, 140141
  settings for, 139–140
  tools for, 142–143
Hearing assessment, 101, 1000t
  in infant, 220, 241
  in neonate, 183
  in preschooler, 292
  in school-age child, 318–319
  in toddler, 259
Hearing impairment
  in acute otitis media, 1012
  in Alport syndrome, 824–825
  assessment in, 996–1000
  in chronic middle ear effusion, 1012–1013
  noise-induced, 1015–1016
Heart. *See also under* Cardiac; Cardiovascular
  anatomy of, 102, *104,* 568–569, *570*
  assessment of, 102–103, *104*
  auscultation of, 572, 573t
  blood flow through, 569, *570*
  catheterization of, diagnostic, 576
  conduction system of, 569–570
  congenital anomalies of, 583–595
  fetal, 567, *568*
  in infant, 222
  in neonate, 567–568, *569*
  in toddler, 257
Heart disease. *See also* Cardiovascular disorders
  in Down syndrome, 456
  in Kawasaki disease, 423
Heart failure, congestive, 598–601
  in aortic coarctation, 588
  nursing care plan for, 601–602
Heart murmurs, 103
  in atrial septal defects, 584
  in endocardial cushion defects, 586
  grading of, 572, 573t
  in pulmonic stenosis, 590
  in tricuspid atresia, 593
  in truncus arteriosus, 592
  in ventricular septal defects, 585
Heart rate
  fetal, monitoring of, 174, *174*
  in infant, 222, 572t
  measurement of, 572, 572t
    in neonate, 186, 572t
  normal values for, 1043t

Heart sounds, 103
  auscultation of, 90–91, 572, 572t, 573t
Heart surgery, 580–582
Heat loss, in neonate, 181t, 181–183, *182*
Height
  in adolescent, 334–335, 348
  growth charts for, 235, 1037–1040
  in infant, 236
  measurement of, 94, *94*
  in preschooler, 280
  in school-age child, 309, 316
  in toddler, 257, 257t
Heimlich maneuver, 546, *546*
Helper cells, 223
Hemangiomas, 189, 967t, 970–971
Hemarthrosis, in hemophilia, 622
Hematemesis, 762
Hematocrit
  in fluid and electrolyte imbalances, 739t
  normal values for, 1045t
  in school-age child, 319, 319t
Hematological disorders
  in adolescents, 629–631
  assessment of, 609–610
  blood product administration in, 612–613
  bone marrow transplantation in, 613
  diagnostic procedures in, 609–610
  drug therapy in, 612
  history in, 609
  hydration in, 612
  in infants, 619–622
  in neonates, 614–619
  nursing care for
    acute care considerations in, 611
    chronic care considerations in, 611
    developmental considerations in, 611
    evaluation of, 613–614
    home care considerations in, 612
    planning of, 611–612
  nursing diagnoses in, 610–611
  nursing interventions in, 612–613
  nutrition in, 612
  physical examination in, 609
  in preschool and school-aged children, 626–629
  in systemic lupus erythematosus, 721t
  in toddlers, 622–626
Hematological system
  embryology of, 606–607
  physiology of, 607–609
Hematological tests, 609–610
  in cardiovascular disorders, 576–577
  normal values for, 1045t
Hematoma, intracranial, 675–676
Hematopoiesis
  in bone marrow, 919
  in neonate, 179–181, *180*
Hemodialysis, 833–836
Hemodynamic parameters, 570–571
Hemoglobin, 571
  assessment of, 610
  in cardiovascular disorders, 576–577
  in infant, 222, 242
  in neonate, *180*, 181
  normal values for, 1045t
  in school-age child, 319, 319t
Hemolytic anemia
  in hemolytic-uremic syndrome, 822–823

in premature infant, 210
Hemolytic disease of newborn, 199, 615–617
Hemolytic reaction, to blood transfusion, 612–613
Hemolytic-uremic syndrome, 822–823
Hemophilia, 205t, 622–624
Hemoptysis, in cystic fibrosis, 553
Hemorrhage. *See also* Bleeding
  intracranial, in premature infant, 209
  ocular, 1011
Hemorrhagic disorders, neonatal, 616, 617
Hepatitis A, 431, 802–803
Hepatitis B, 431–432, 802–803
  fetal effects of, 206
  immunization for, 417–420, 419t, 802–803, 1055
Hepatitis C, 802
Hepatitis D, 802
Hepatitis non-A, non-B, 432, 802
Hepatocyte, 759
Hepatoportoenterostomy, Kasai, 782, *783*
Hepatotoxicity, acetaminophen, 781–782
Hereditary osteodystrophy, 205t
Hereditary polymorphic light eruption, 966t
Hereditary spherocytosis, 204t
Hering-Breuer reflex, 520
Heritage consistency theory, 33–34
Hermaphroditism, 843
Hernia
  diaphragmatic, 776–777
  inguinal, 104, 799–800
    hydrocele and, 848–849
  umbilical, 104, *798,* 798–799
Herniation, of brain, 647
Heroin. *See also* Substance abuse
  fetal/neonatal effects of, 476
Herpes simplex infection
  fetal/neonatal effects of, 206
  genital, 866–867
  vaccine for, 420–421
Herpes stomatitis, 778–779
Herpes zoster, vaccine for, 420
High fat diet, 766t
High fiber diet, 766t
High protein/high calorie diet, 766t
High risk nursing diagnosis, 114
Hip
  assessment of, 105
  avascular necrosis of, 948–949
  congenital dysplasia of, 105, 189–191, 935–937, *936, 937*
    in Native Americans, 966t
    nursing care plan for, 952–953
  neonatal assessment of, 189–191
  slipped capital femoral epiphysis in, 947–948
Hip spica cast, *925*
  for congenital hip dysplasia, 936
Hirschberg test, for strabismus, 996, 1007
Hirschsprung disease, 794–795
Hispanics
  cultural beliefs of, 36–37
  integumentary system in, 964t–965t
Histiocytes, 689
Hives, 421
  drug-induced, 982
Hodgkin disease, 629–631
Home and family assessment
  for infant, 238, 1032–1033
  for preschooler, 290–291, 1034–1035
  for school-age child, 317

for toddler, 266, 1032–1033
Home birth, 169
Home care, 390–411
    advantages of, 392
    advocacy and, 463–464
    in AIDS, 702–703
    apnea monitoring in, *406,* 406–407
    art of, 401–405
    assessment for, 393–396, *395*
        of client factors, 394
        of community factors, 395–396
        of economic factors, 396
        of environmental factors, 394–395
        of family factors, 394
    cardiopulmonary resuscitation in, 579–580
    in cardiovascular disorders, 579, 579t
    care contract for, 394, *395*
    case management for, 392–393
    changing child health care needs and, 391
    changing health care delivery and, 391–392
    changing view of family and, 392
    child and family readiness for, 394–396
    client and family education for, 397–398
    community support network for, 399–400, 401
    cost containment initiatives and, 391
    costs of, 396
    definition of, 390–391
    development of, factors affecting, 391–392
    disadvantages of, 392
    discharge planning for, 397, 400–401
    discipline and, 463
    early education/stimulation programs for, 441–442
    in endocrine disorders, 883
    environmental modifications for, 405
    equipment vendors for, selection of, 398, *399*
    evaluation in, 410
    family-centered, 442
    family empowerment in, 402–405
    funding for, 391
    in gastrointestinal disorders, 765
    in hematological disorders, 612
    in hemophilia, 622–623
    historical background of, 391
    in immune disorders, 696
    implementation of, 401–410
    in integumentary disorders, 969–970
    interdisciplinary team for, 393
    interpersonal relationships and, 401–405
    legal and ethical issues in, 410–411, 443
    long-term planning for, 464
    in musculoskeletal disorders, 923–924
    in neural tube defects, 653
    normalization in, 404, 578
    nurse/family relationship and, 402–405, 403t
    nurse's role in, 442–443
    nursing diagnoses for, 396–397
    oxygen administration in, 407–409, *408*
    parenteral nutrition in, 410
    parent teaching for, 404–405
    planning for, 397–401
    program selection for, 398, 398t
    providers for, identification of, 398, 398t
    record keeping in, 405, 464
    recreation and play and, 462
    in renal disorders, 817
    for respiratory disorders, 528
    respite care for, 400, 465
    science of, 405–410
    sibling adaptation to, 404
    support groups for, 400, 401, 461–462
    technological aspects of, 405–410
    in terminal illness, 503
    tracheostomy management in, 407, *407,* 535, 559–561
    tube feeding in, 409–410
Homeless family, 28
Home Observation and Measurement of the Environment
        (HOME), 87, 266, 290–291, 317, 1032–1035
Home Screening Questionnaire, 266
Homosexual family, 27
Homosexuality, 341–342
Hope, in death and dying, 503–504
Hordeolum, 996, 1010
Hormones, 873. *See also* Endocrine system
    gonadotropic, 874
    tropic, 873
Hospice care, 503
Hospital-acquired infections, 416
Hospitalization, 368–387
    admission in
        interview for, 385
        parents' and children's responses to, 384
        types of, 382–384
    of adolescents, 376–377
    atraumtic care in, 379
    in autism, 460–461
    behavioral and cognitive rehearsal in, 379–380
    children's responses to, 377
    day stays in, 382–383
    developmental stages and, 369–377
    discharge planning in, 382, 386
    early discharge in, 18
    emergency, 383
    factors affecting, 369
    of infants, 369–371
    infection transmission in, 416
    isolation in, 384
    of mentally retarded, 455
    minimizing effects of, 378–379
    modeling in, 380
    orientation in, 385
    parental responses to, 378
    parent teaching for, 385–386
    in pediatric intensive care unit, 383–384
    play in, 380–382
    preadmission visits for, 377
    preparation for, 377–378, 379
    of preschoolers, 373–374
    of school-age children, 374–376
    stress immunization in, 379
    substance abuse withdrawal in, 479t
    systematic desensitization in, 379
    in terminal illness, 502–503
    of toddlers, 371–373
Hot/cold health model, 34
Huffing, 530
Human immunodeficiency virus infection, 698–703. *See also*
        Acquired immunodeficiency syndrome
    classification of, 700t
    medical diagnosis and management of, 699–700
    pathophysiology of, 698–699
    prevention of, 702t, 703
    vaccine for, 421
Human papillomavirus infection, 865–866
Human response patterns, 117t

Humerus, fracture of, 933–935
Humidification, for oxygen and drug administration, 408, 529
Hunter syndrome, 205t
Huntington disease, 204t
Hurler syndrome, 204t
Hyaline membrane disease, 540–541
Hydration. *See also* Fluid administration
   assessment of, 818
   in hematological disorders, 612
Hydrocarbons, aspiration of, 551
Hydrocele, 191, 799, *848,* 848–849
Hydrocephalus
   in neural tube defects, 651
   in premature infant, 210
Hydrogen breath test, 763
Hydrogen ion concentration
   increased, in metabolic acidosis, 744
   reduced, in metabolic alkalosis, 744–745
   regulation of, 734
Hydrophobia, in rabies, 435
Hydrops fetalis, 189
   in ABO incompatibility, 2009199
   in Rh incompatibility, 199
Hydrostatic pressure, 732
Hyperactivity, 665–666
Hyperalimentation, 743, *743,* 766
   at home, 409–410
   necrotizing enterocolitis and, 789–790
   for premature infant, 209
Hyperbilirubinemia, neonatal, *180,* 180–181, 614–615
   in ABO incompatibility, 200
   in blacks, 963t
   breast-feeding and, 181
   in Native Americans, 964t
Hypercalcemia, 747–748
Hypercholesterolemia, familial, 204t
Hypercortisolism, 892–893
Hyperendemic disease, 417t
Hyperglycemia, in diabetes mellitus, 900, 907
Hyperinsulinism, 877
   hypoglycemia and, 890
Hyperkalemia, 750–751
   in acute renal failure, 830
Hypermagnesemia, 749
Hypernatremia, 752
Hyperopia, 1009–1010
Hyperparathyroidism, 897–898
Hyperpituitarism, 893–894
Hyperpnea, 522
Hyper-resonance, 92, 92t
Hypersensitivity. *See also* Allergies
Hypersensitivity pneumonitis, 709–710
Hypertelorism, 1007
Hypertension, 600–601
   intracranial, 643–647
   portal, 783
   in pregnancy, magnesium sulfate for, neonatal hypermagnesemia and, 749
Hyperthyroidism, 894–896
Hypertonic solution, 731
Hypertropia, 1007
Hyperventilation, 522
   controlled, for increased intracranial pressure, 648t
   respiratory alkalosis and, 746
Hyphema, 1011
Hypocalcemia, 748–479
   in hyperparathyroidism, 888

Hypodermis, 957
Hypoglycemia, 890–891
   in diabetes, 907
Hypogonadism, primary, 852
Hypokalemia, 751–752
Hypomagnesemia, 750
   hypocalcemia and, 748
Hyponatremia, 752–753
Hypoparathyroidism, 888–889
Hypophosphatemia, familial, 205t
Hypopituitarism, 884–885
Hyposensitization, allergic, 696–697
Hypospadias, 105, 191, 819–820, *820*
Hypothalamus, 635, *635,* 875
Hypothermia
   for increased intracranial pressure, 648t
   in spinal cord injury, 679
Hypothyroidism, 885–888
   acquired, 886–888
   congenital, 885–886
   thyroiditis and, 896–897
Hypotonia, in cerebral palsy, 445
Hypotonic solution, 731
Hypotropia, 1007
Hypoventilation, 523
Hypoxemia, oxygen therapy for, 528, *529*
Hypoxia, 571
Hypoxic-ischemic encephalopathy, neonatal, 538
Hypoxic spells, in tetralogy of Fallot, 592

**I**

Ibuprofen, for musculoskeletal disorders, 931t
Ice, for sprains, strains, and contusions, 932–933
Ichthyosis, X-linked, 205t
Id, 61
Idealism, in adolescent, 340
Identity vs. identity diffusion, 341
Idiopathic breast hypertrophy, 858
Idiopathic thrombocytopenic purpura, 627
IgA, 223, 223t
   normal values for, 1046t
IgG, 223, 223t
   normal values for, 1046t
IgM, 223, 223t
   normal values for, 1046t
Ileal atresia, 785–786
Ileostomy, 766–767
Ileus, meconium, 796
Ilizarov external fixator, 928–930
Illness
   chronic. *See also* Disability; Disabled
      home care for. *See* Home care
   concepts of, 11–12, *12*
   in diabetes, 907–908
   terminal. *See* Death and dying
Immune deficiency, 692–693, 693t
Immune disorders. *See also* Allergies
   assessment in, 693–694
   diagnostic procedures in, 694
   drug therapy for, 697–698
   history in, 693
   infection prevention in, 695
   nursing care for
      evaluation of, 698
      planning of, 694–696
   nursing diagnoses in, 694

nutrition in, 698
pain relief in, 695–696
physical examination in, 693–694
Immune globulin
in AIDS, 700
for hepatitis, 417–418, 431, 802–803
for X-linked agammaglobulinemia, 704
Immune system
'aberrant responses in, 692–693
activation of, 691
allergic responses and, 693
anatomy of, 686–690, *689*
autoimmunity and, 692
deployment of, 691
discrimination in, 691
encounter in, 691
immune deficiency and, 692–693, 693t
in infant, 223, 223t
lymphoid organs of, *687,* 689–690
physiology of, 690–692
recognition in, 691–692
regulation of, 691
Immunity
antibody-mediated (B-cell mediated), 691–692
cell-mediated (T-cell mediated), 692
Immunization(s), 417–421, 425
for adolescent, 344–345
anaphylactic reaction to, 418, 418t
for foreign travel, 420, 420t
gamma globulin, 417–418
for hepatitis B, 802
for infant, 241–242, 242t
legal aspects of, 418–420
passive, 417
for preschooler, 291–293
for school-age child, 318, 318t
side effects of, 420
stress, for hospitalized children, 379
for toddler, 266, 267t
vaccines for, 417–418, 419t, 1055
for viral infections, 420, 802
Immunoglobulins, 223, 223t
normal values for, 1046t
Immunosuppression, in kidney transplantation, 836
Imperforate anus, 191
Impetigo, 973–974
neonatal, 198
Implementation
consultation in, 143
continuity of care in, 143–147
developmental considerations in, 132–139
health teaching in, 139–143
in nursing care plan, 144–146
in nursing process, 18, *19,* 132–147
referral in, 143
Imprinting, 69
Incest, 861
Inclusion conjunctivitis, 1006
Incontinence
fecal, 770–771
urinary, 298–299
Incubator, 182, *182*
heat regulation in, 209
noise levels in, 210, 1015
Independent nursing interventions, 132
Individual Family Service Plan, 397
Individual monologue, 285

Inductive reasoning, 284
Industry vs. inferiority, 313–314, 314t
Infant
accidents in, 245–248, 370
anemia in, 619–622
attachment in, 233–234
bathing of, 243
behavioral assessment for, 241
body measurements in, 235–236, 1037
bonding with, 69–72, 184–185, 194, *195, 196,* 233–234
bronchiolitis in, 544–545
cardiovascular system in, 222
clothing for, 243
croup in, 542–543
crying in, 248–249
dentition in, 227t, 227–228
developmental assessment for, 236–238, 241
developmental tasks of, 67t
diaper dermatitis in, 243, 971, 980
endocrine system in, 222–223
family and home assessment for, 238
feeding of. *See* Feeding
gastrointestinal system in, 221–222
growth and development of
assessment of, 235–239
body system, 221–224
of brain, 217–218
cognitive, 228–231, 229t
communicative, *234,* 234–235
cultural influences on, 235
determinants of, 217
deviations in, 236
general characteristics of, 217
of head, 217–218
motor, 218–220, *218–220,* 221t
normal variations in, 220
patterns of, 217
psychosocial, 231–235
sensory, 220–221
health history for, 239, 241t
health promotion for, 239–250
hearing assessment for, 220, 241
hemoglobin count in, 242, 1045
hospitalization of, 369–370, 370–371. *See also* Hospitalization
immune system in, 223, 223t
immunization for, 241–242, 242t. *See also* Immunization
language development in, *234,* 234–235
large-for-gestational age, 210–211
liver in, 222
musculoskeletal system in, 224
neurological disorders in, 647–657
newborn. *See* Neonate
nursing care for, goals of, 216–217
nutrition in, 224t–226t, 224–226
play in, 230–231
postmature, 210–211
premature, 168
anemia in, 210
apnea in, 542
behavioral assessment for, 187
definition of, 193
feeding of, 209
hemorrhage in, 209–210
hypoglycemia in, 208
lung immaturity in, 208
retinopathy in, 210, 1004–1005

Infant (*continued*)
  retrolental fibroplasia in, 210
  risk factors for, 202–207, 203t
  sensory needs of, 210
  thermoregulation in, 209
 renal system in, 223–224
 reproductive disorders in, 848–850
 respiratory disorders in, 542–546
 respiratory system in, 222
 retropharyngeal abscess in, 545–546
 safety precautions for, 245–248
 sexuality of, 238–239
 skin care for, 243
 sleep in, 226–227, 249
 small-for-gestational age, 194, 210
 spitting up in, 221
 stool in, 221–222
 sudden death of, 543–544
 teething in, 228
 temperament in, 233–234
  assessment of, 237t, 237–238
 thumb sucking in, 249–250
 urinalysis in, 242–243
 vision in, assessment of, 220, 239
 weaning of, 248
Infant Care Review Committees, 50
Infantile acne, 243
Infantile paralysis, 430
 immunization for, 241–242, 242t, 417–420, 419t
Infant mortality rate, 9–10, 10t
Infant-parent attachment, 69–72, 184–185, 233–234
 assessment of, 194, *195, 196*
Infant states, assessment of, 187
Infections, 416–437. *See also specific infections*
 bone, 942–943
 in Down syndrome, 457
 fungal. *See* Fungal infections
 gastrointestinal, 432–434
 immunization for. *See* Immunization(s)
 isolation techniques for, 384, 421, 421t, 701, 702t
 joint, 941–942
 neonatal, prevention of, 194–199
 nosocomial, 416
 opportunistic
  in AIDS, 699–700
  in Wiskott-Aldrich syndrome, 707
  in X-linked agammaglobulinemia, 704
 parasitic, 432–434
  cutaneous, 976–878
 prevention of, in immune disorders, 695
 rash-causing, 421–428
 reporting of, 416
 skin, 979–982
 in spinal cord injury, 679–680
 streptococcal, in neonate, 199
 teratogenic, 167t
 TORCH, 206–207
 transmission of, 416–417, 417t
 urinary tract, 826–827
  nursing care plan for, 838–839
 without rash, 428–437
Infectious mononucleosis, 434
Inflammation, 689
Inflammatory bowel disease, 793–794
Influenza, 434–435
 immunization for, 417–420, 419t, 1055
Informed consent, 46–47

 for immunizations, 418
Infusion pump, feeding, 409
Inguinal hernia, 104, 799–800
 hydrocele and, 848–849
Inhalation injury, 983–984
Initiative vs. guilt, 287
Injection
 insulin, *903,* 903–904, *904*
 intramuscular, 135, *137*
 technique for, 292–293, *293*
Injuries. *See* Accident prevention; Traumatic injuries
Inner ear, 994, *994*
Insect bites and stings, 978
 Lyme disease and, 423–424
 Rocky Mountain spotted fever and, 425
Inspection, in physical examination, 90
Inspiration, 519
Inspiratory capacity, 525
Inspiratory reserve volume, 525
Institutional review boards, 54–55
Insulin, 876, *878*
Insulin pump, 904
Insulin shock, 907
Insulin therapy, for diabetes mellitus, 902–904, *903,*
  903t, *904*
Insurance
 diagnosis related groups and, 128–129
 home care and, 391
Integration of lust, 341
Integumentary disorders
 acute, 983–989
 in adolescents, 975–976
 diagnostic tests for, 960–968
 drug-induced, 982–983
 in infants, 970–972
 infectious, 978–982
 nursing care for, 968–970
 nursing diagnoses for, 968
 parasitic, 976–978
 in school-age children, 972–975
Integumentary system. *See also* Hair; Nails; Skin
 anatomy and physiology of, *957,* 957–958
 in cardiovascular disorders, 574–575
 disorders of, assessment in, 958–968
 embryology of, 956–957
 ethnic variations in, 961t–967t
 neonatal assessment of, 189
Intelligence. *See* Cognitive development
Intensive care unit, admission to, 383–384
Intercourse, sexual, in adolescence, 349–350, 350t
Interdependent nursing interventions, 132
Interdisciplinary health care team, for home care, 393
Interpersonal relationships
 of adolescent, 331t, 339, 341, 342–343
 in autism, 459t–460t
 home care and, 401–405
 of school-age child, 314–315
Intersexuality, 843
Intershift report, 151t
Interstitial cell stimulating hormone, 874, 880
Interstitial fluid, 730
Intervention, in nursing process, 18, *19*
Interview
 admission, 385
 with adolescent, 343–344
 in nursing assessment, 81t, 81–85, 84t, 85t
Intestinal atresia, 785–786

Intestinal gas, in colic, 786
Intestinal malabsorption, 790–791
Intestinal malrotation, 796
Intestinal obstruction
    anorectal malformations and, 795–796
    in Hirschsprung disease, 794–795
    intussusception and, 796–798, 797
    malrotation and, 796
Intestinal polyps, 800
Intestines. *See* Bowel; Colon; Small intestine
Intimacy, 341
Intra-aortic balloon pump, 577
Intracellular fluid, 730–731
    electrolyte content of, 732t
Intracranial hemorrhage, in premature infant, 209
Intracranial pressure
    increased, 643–647
        clinical manifestations of, 644–647
        medical therapy for, 647
        nursing management of, 647, 648t
        pathophysiology of, 636–637, 643–644
        in Reye syndrome, 662–663
    monitoring of, 644
    regulation of, 636–637
Intradermal test, for allergens, 694, 968, 1018
Intrahepatic biliary atresia, 782
Intramuscular drug administration, 135, 136t, 137
Intrauterine growth retardation, 172, 206
Intravascular fluid, 730
Intravenous drug administration, 135, 136t
Intravenous fluid therapy. *See* Fluid administration
Intravenous immune globulin, in AIDS, 700
Intravenous pyelography, 814
Intraventricular hemorrhage, in premature infant, 210
Intubation
    chest, 541, 541–542
        in cardiac surgery, 580, 581
    endotracheal, 534
    for feeding, 742, 766
        after esophageal atresia/tracheoesophageal fistula
            repair, 776
        at home, 409–410
    for gastrointestinal decompression, 766
Intuitive thought, 311
Intussusception, 796–798, 797
Inverted nipple, 858
Ipecac syrup, 247, 271, 300
Iridocyclitis, in juvenile rheumatoid arthritis, 718
Iris, 993, 994
    assessment of, 99
Iron
    dietary, for infants, 245
    normal values for, 1046t
    supplemental, 225, 620
Iron-deficiency anemia, 319, 620–621
Islets of Langerhans, 876, 878
Isoetharine (Bronkosol, Bronkometer), for asthma, 556t
Isolation techniques, 384, 421, 421t, 701, 702t
Isolette. *See* Incubator
Isotonic solution, 731

**J**
Jack-knife seizures, 669t. *See also* Seizures
Japanese
    cultural beliefs of, 34–35
    integumentary system of, 961t–962t

Jarisch-Herxheimer reaction, 865
Jatene switch procedure, for transposition
            of great arteries, 591
Jaundice
    in blacks, 963t
    neonatal, 180, 180–181, 614–615
        in ABO incompatibility, 200
        breast-feeding, 181
        in Native Americans, 964t
Jejunal atresia, 785–786
Joint(s)
    anatomy of, 918, 918
    bleeding into, in hemophilia, 622–623
    dislocations of, 933. *See also* Hip dysplasia, congenital
    infections of, 941–942
    in juvenile rheumatoid arthritis, 718, 719
    painful, in rheumatic fever, 597–598
Joint capsule, 918, 919
Joint cavity, 918, 919
Journals, child health nursing, 22
J receptors, 520
Juvenile breast hypertrophy, 858
    male, 859
Juvenile glaucoma, 1003
Juvenile polyps, intestinal, 800
Juvenile rheumatoid arthritis, 716–719

**K**
Karyotype, 164, 165
Kasai hepatoportoenterostomy, 782, 783
Kawasaki disease, 422t, 422–423, 598
Kernicterus, 200, 614
Ketoacidosis, in diabetes, 906–907
Ketones, in diabetes, 900
    monitoring of, 906
Ketosis, 876
Kidney. *See also under* Renal
    in acid-base balance, 734
    anatomy and physiology of, 811–812
    biopsy of, 815
    in cardiovascular disorders, 575–576
    embryology of, 811
    in infant, 223–224
    injuries of, 831
    polycystic, 204t
    in toddler, 258
    transplantation of, 836–837
    ultrasonography of, 816
    Wilms' tumor of, 821–822
Killer cells, 223, 689
Kilograms-pounds conversion, 1051
King's theory of goal attainment, 21
Klinefelter syndrome, 203t, 852
Knee
    knock, 941
    overuse syndromes and, 950–951
    painful
        in Osgood-Schlatter disease, 950–951
        in patellofemoral stress syndrome, 950–951
    sports injuries of, 951
Knock knees, 941
Kohlberg's moral development theory, 63–64, 286–287, 316,
            340–341
Koplik's spots, 425
Krinksy test, for strabismus, 1007
KUB film, 815

Kussmaul respirations, 523
  in metabolic acidosis, 744

**L**

Labia majora, 105, 843, *844*
Labia minora, 105, 843, *844*
Labor. *See also* Childbirth
  fetal monitoring in, *174,* 174–175
  premature, 168
Laboratory values, normal, 1044t–1049t
Laceration
  of brain, 675
  of kidney, 831
  of scalp, 674–675
Lacrimal duct, obstruction of, 1003–1004
Lacrimal gland, *993,* 994
Lactate dehydrogenase, normal values for, 1046t
Lacto-ovovegetarian diet, 226, 226t
Lactose breath test, 763t
Lactose-free diet, 766t
  post-diarrheal, 768
Lactose intolerance
  colic and, 786
  vs. milk sensitivity, 714t
  post-diarrheal, 768
Lactovegetarian diet, 226, 226t
Landau reflex, 190t
Language development, 66, 69, 70t–71t
  in autism, 459t–460t
  Denver Articulation Screening Examination for, 1000, 1028–1029
  in infant, *234,* 234–235
  in preschooler, 287, 291t
  in toddler, 264, 264t
Lanugo, 189
Laotians
  cultural beliefs of, 34–35
  integumentary system in, 961t–962t
Large-for-gestational age infant, 210
Large intestine. *See* Bowel; Colon; Intestinal
Laryngeal stridor, 536
  in croup, 543
Laryngeal webbing, 536
Laryngomalacia, 536
Laryngotracheobronchitis, nursing care plan for, 107
Larynx, 517–518
Latchkey children, 322
Latency period, 62, 313
LDH (lactate dehydrogenase), normal values for, 1046t
Lead
  poisoning by, 300–302, 657–659, 658t
    in infants, 247
  serum, normal values for, 1046t
  urinary, normal values for, 1048t
Learning. *See also* Cognitive development
Learning contract, 141, 142t
  for home care, 394, *395*
Learning disability, 665–666
Learning theories, 66–68
Left bundle branch, 569–570
Left-sided heart failure, 599
Leg. *See* Extremities
Legal issues
  in child abuse and neglect, 15, 859–860
  for disabled, 441
  in home care, 410–411

  in immunization, 418–420
  in substance abuse in pregnancy, 480
Legal rights of children, 12–15, 42–55, 346
  with disabilities, 52–54
  to education, 52–54
  emancipated minor, 47, 346
  to medical treatment, 47–50
  with mental illness, 50–52
  to privacy and confidentiality, 52
  reproductive, 47, 52
  in research protocols, 54–55
Legg-Calvé-Perthes disease, 948–949
Legislation, affecting child welfare, 14–17
Leiner disease, 975
Length, body, measurement of, 94, *94,* 186
Lens, ocular, *993, 994*
Lesbian family, 27
Lesch-Nyhan syndrome, 205t
Leukemia, acute, 628–629
Leukocytes, 608
  assessment of, 610
  mononuclear, 689
  in neonate, 181
  normal values for, 1045t
  polymorphonuclear, 687–688
  types of, 687–689, *688*
Leukodystrophy, metachromatic, 205t
Leukorrhea, 856
  physiological, 846, 856
Level of consciousness, evaluation of, 644–647, 645t
Levothyroxine, for hypothyroidism, 886
Lexicon, assessment of, 1000
Lice infestations, 976–977
Ligaments, 918
  tears of, 932–933
Light reflex, otoscopic, 999
Limbs. *See* Extremities
Lip
  cleft, 772–774, *773*
    ethnic factors in, 961t, 966t
    hypopituitarism and, 884–885
  pitting of, 962t
Lipids, in breast milk, 224–225
Lipoid pneumonia, 551–552
Liver
  anatomy of, 759, *760*
  biopsy of, 764
  in cardiovascular disorders, 575
  in infant, 222
  as lymphoid organ, 689–690
  palpation of, 104
Liver disease/dysfunction
  acetaminophen poisoning and, 781–782
  chronic, nursing care in, 784–785
  neonatal, 782–783
  portal hypertension in, 783
  vitamin supplementation in, 783, 783t
  in Wilson disease, 783–785
Lock Clamshell Septal Occluder, for atrial septal defects, 584
Lockjaw. *See* Tetanus
Loop of Henle, 811
Low-birth-weight infant, definition of, 193
Lower endoscopy, 763t, 764
Lower extremity. *See* Extremities
Lowe syndrome, 1002
Low-residue diet, 766t
Lumbar puncture, 639t

Lungs. *See also under* Pulmonary; Respiratory
  anatomy of, 518
  assessment of, 102
  auscultation of, 90–91
  fetal, 517
Lupus erythematosus, systemic, 719t, 719–723, *720, 720t*
Lust, integration of, 341
Luteinizing hormone, 874, 880
Lyme disease, 423–424
Lymphatics, 689
Lymph nodes, 690
  in cancer staging, 630
  palpation of, 99, *100*
Lymphocytes, 608, *687,* 689
  normal values for, 1045t
Lymphoid interstitial pneumonitis, in AIDS, 699–700
Lymphoid organs, development of, *687,* 689–690

**M**
Macrobiotic diet, 226, 226t
Macrocephaly, 218
Macroglossia, 1000
Macrophages, 689
Macula, 997, *998*
Macular rash, 421
Macule, *960*
Mafenidine (Sulfamylon), for burns, 987t
Magical thinking, 373
Magnesium
  function and regulation of, 733t
  imbalance of, 749–750
    hypocalcemia and, 748
    neonatal, 749
  normal values for, 1046t
Magnesium sulfate, for hypertension of pregnancy, neonatal
    hypermagnesemia and, 749
Magnetic resonance imaging
  fetal, 171
  in neurological disorders, 640t
Mainstreaming, 52–54, 323, 442
Malabsorption, 790–791
Malignant melanoma, 962t, 967t
Malpractice, 44–46
Manonegro, 36
Mantoux test, 242, 436, 968
Marijuana. *See also* Substance abuse
  fetal effects of, 475
Marrow, 606–607
Masks, oxygen, 528, *529*
Maslow's hierarchy of needs, 60, *60*
Mass-to-specific growth, 217
Mast cells, 689, *691*
Mastoiditis, 1014–1015
Masturbation, 302, 344, 349, 374
Maternal attachment. *See* Bonding
Maturation theory, 68
Mature minor doctrine, 346
Mean corpuscular hemoglobin concentration, normal values
    for, 1045t
Mean corpuscular volume
  normal values for, 1045t
  in school-age child, 319t
Measles, 424–425
  immunization for, 241–242, 242t, 318, 318t, 417–420, 419t,
    425, 1055
Mechanical ventilation, 534–535, *535*

  in neonate, 194
    bronchopulmonary dysplasia and, 539–540
Meckel diverticulum, 793
Meconium, 191t
Meconium aspiration, 537–538
Meconium ileus, 796
Medicaid, 14
  diagnosis related groups and, 128–129
Medical diagnoses, vs. nursing diagnoses, 113t
Medical treatment
  preparation for and implementation of, 137–139
  withholding or withdrawing of, 47–50
Medicare, diagnosis related groups and, 128–129
Medication. *See* Drug(s)
Medicine cups, 134
Medullary cavity, 917, *917*
Medullary respiratory center, 520
Megacolon, aganglionic, 794–795
Melanoma, 962t, 967t
Memory, assessment of, 106
Menarche, 337
  delayed, 853
Mendelian disorders, 165–166
Meningitis, 660–661
  neonatal, 656–657
Meningocele, 649–654, *650*
Menkes disease, 205t
Menstrual cycle, 844–845
Menstruation, 347–348
  abnormal bleeding in, 855
  delayed or absent, 853
  disorders of, 853–855
  onset of, 337
  painful, 854
  premenstrual syndrome and, 854–855
Mental development. *See* Cognitive development
Mental illness, treatment of, legal issues in, 51
Mental retardation, 451–458. *See also* Disabled
  adaptive behavior and, 451
  in autism, 458
  classification of, 451t, 451–452
  clinical, 452
  definition of, 451
  vs. developmental delay, 451
  in Down syndrome, 455–458
  early identification of, 453
  education and training in, 454–455
  etiology of, 451, 452t
  exercise in, 453, 469
  incidence of, 451
  lead poisoning and, 658t
  microcephaly and, 656
  mild, 451t, 452
  moderate, 451t, 452
  neurological signs of, 453
  nursing care in, 454–455
  prevention of, 451
  profound, 451t, 452
  severe, 451t, 452
  sociocultural, 452–453
  sterilization in, 52
  support groups for, 454, 468–469
  treatment of, 453
  withholding or withdrawing treatment in, 48–50
Mental symbolism, 284
Meperidine, for musculoskeletal disorders, 931t
Mesoderm, 161, 161t, 956
Metabolic acidosis, 734, 744

Metabolic acidosis (*continued*)
  in acute renal failure, 830
  assessment of, 526, 526t
  in burns, 984
Metabolic alkalosis, 734, 744–745
  assessment of, 526, 526t
Metabolic rate, fluid and electrolyte requirements
      and, 734–745
Metachromatic leukodystrophy, 205t
Metaproterenol (Alupent, Metaprel), for asthma, 556t
Metatarsus adductus, 938–939
Methadone, fetal/neonatal effects of, 476
Methimazole, for hyperthyroidism, 895, 896
Methylxanthines, bronchodilator, 531
Mexican-Americans
  cultural beliefs of, 36–37
  integumentary system in, 964t–965t
Microcephaly, 218
Microencephaly, 656
Middle ear, 994, *994*
  chronic effusion in, 1013–1014
Middle ear effusion, chronic, nursing care plan
      for, 1019–1021
Migraine, 664–665
Milia, 189
Milk
  breast
    vs. cow's milk, 201t
    vs. formula, 224t, 225t
    nutrient content of, 224t, 224–225, 225t
  cow's
    vs. breast milk, 201t
    sensitivity to, vs. lactose intolerance, 714t
  food sources of, 715t
Milk-free diet, 715t
Milwaukee brace, for scoliosis, 944–945, *945*
Mineralocorticoids, 878–879
Minerals, in breast milk, 224t, 225t, 225–226
Minimal brain dysfunction, 665–666
Minor
  emancipated, 47, 346
  legal rights of, 47, 346
Minor treatment statutes, 47, 346
Mist tent, 528, *530*
Modeling, 39, 380
Mongolian spots, 189, 961t, 962t, 966t
Moniliasis, 979–980
  in diaper dermatitis, 243, 970
  oral, 102, 188–189
    in neonate, 198
  vaginal, 856–857
Monocytes, 608, *687,* 689
  normal values for, 1045t
Monologue
  collective, 285
  individual, 285
Mononuclear leukocytes, 689
Mononucleosis, infectious, 434
Monosomy, 165
Monozygotic twins, 173
Monro-Kellie hypothesis, for increased intracranial
      pressure, 636–637
Mons pubis, 843, *844*
Moral development
  in adolescent, 340–341
  conventional, 287, 316, 340–341
  Kohlberg's theory of, 63–64, 286–287, 316, 340–341

  postconventional, 341
  preconventional, 287, 316
  in preschooler, 286–287
  in school-age child, 315–316
Morality of constraint, 315
Morality of cooperation, 315
Moral realism, 65
Moral relativism, 65
Moro reflex, 183, 190t
Morot function, assessment of, 106
Morphine, for musculoskeletal disorders, 931t
Mortality trends, 9–11, 10t–12t
Mosaicism, 165, 456
Mothering, of neonate, 184. *See also* Bonding; Parenting
Mothers Against Drunk Driving (MADD), 482–485
Motorcycle accidents, 347
Motor development, 70t–71t
  in autism, 459t–460t
  in infant, 218–220, *218–220,* 221t
  in preschooler, 279–280
  in school-age child, 309, 316, 316t
  in toddler, 258–259, 268–269
Motor function, increased intracranial pressure and, 646–647
Motor seizures, 669t. *See also* Seizures
Motor vehicle accidents, 245–246, 320, 347
  preschoolers and, 299
  substance abuse and, 473
  toddlers and, 269t, 269–270
Mourning, 491. *See also* Death and dying
Mouth
  examination of, 102, *103*
    in neonate, 188–189
  moniliasis of, 102, 188–189, 198
Mucocutaneous lymph node syndrome, 422t, 422–423
Mucokinetic agents, 534
Müllerian ducts, 843
Multiple addiction, 473
Multiple classification, 311
Mumps, 429
  immunization for, 241–242, 242t, 267t, 318t, 417–420, 419t, 1055
Murmurs. *See* Heart murmurs
Muscles, ocular, *993,* 994
Muscular development, in adolescent males, 349
Muscular dystrophy, 205t, 949–950
Musculoskeletal disorders
  assessment in, 105, 920t–922t, 920–922
  casts in, 924t, 924–926, *925,* 925t
  child/parent education in, 930, 932t
  congenital, 935–942
  diagnostic procedures in, 921–922
  drug therapy for, 930, 931t–932t
  history in, 920, 920t
  in infants, toddlers, and preschoolers, 940–942
  nursing care in
    evaluation of, 930
    planning of, 922–924
  nursing diagnoses for, 922–923
  nursing interventions for, 924–930
  nutrition in, 930
  physical examination in, 920–921, 921t
  in school-age children and adolescents, 942–951
  surgery for, 924
  traction in, 925t, 926, *926–928,* 930t
Musculoskeletal system
  anatomy of, 917–918, *917–919*
  embryology of, 916–917

in infant, 224
physiology of, 919
in toddler, 258
Mustard procedure, for transposition of great arteries, 591
Mutual regulation, 23
Mydriatics, 1001
Myelination, 258
Myelodysplasia. *See* Spina bifida
Myelography, 641t
Myelomeningocele, 649–654, *650*
Myoclonic seizures, 669t. *See also* Seizures
Myopia, 1009
Myringotomy, 1013

**N**
Nail-patella syndrome, 204t
Nails
    anatomy of, 958
    disorders of
        diagnostic tests for, 960–968
        history in, 958, 959t
        nursing care for, 968–970
        nursing diagnoses for, 968
        physical examination in, 958–960, 961t–967t
    ethnic variations in, 961t–967t
Naproxen, for musculoskeletal disorders, 931t
Nar-Anon, 485
Narcotics. *See also* Substance abuse
    for musculoskeletal disorders, 931t–932t
Narcotics Anonymous, 485
Nasal aspiration, 546–547
Nasogastric feeding, 409–410, 742, 766
    at home, 409–410
Nasopharyngitis, acute, 1016
Nasopharynx, 517, 995, *996*
Native Americans
    cultural beliefs of, 37
    integumentary system in, 965t–966t
Near-drowning, 246–247, 270, 320g
Nearsightedness, 1009
Nebulizers, 528, *530*
Neck
    assessment of, 98–99
    in congenital torticollis, 939
Necrotizing enterocolitis, 789–790
Neglect, 294–295
Negligence, 44–46
    comparative, 46
    contributory, 46
Neonatal Behavioral Assessment Scale, 187
Neonatal care, regionalization of, 203t
Neonatal Individualized Developmental Care and Assessment
        Plan, 187
Neonatal Perception Inventory, 194, *195*
Neonatal period, definition of, 178
Neonatal withdrawal syndrome, maternal opiate abuse
        and, 476
Neonate. *See also* Infant
    ABO incompatibility in, 200
    anemia in, 618–619
    Apgar score for, 185–186, 186t
    apnea of prematurity in, 542
    assessment in, 185–194
        of anus, 191
        of back, 189
        behavioral, 187

body measurements in, 186
        of cry, 189
        of ears, 188
        of extremities, 189–190
        of eyes, 188
        of genitals, 191
        of gestational age, 191–192, *192, 193*
        of head, 187
        of infant states, 187
        of integument, 189
        of mouth, 188–189
        of nose, 188
        of parent-child attachment, 194, *195, 196*
        for risk factors, 202–211
        vital signs in, 186
    bilirubin in, 609–610
    bonding with, 184–185
    bottle feeding of, 201, 202t, 209, 244
        in colic, 786
    breast-feeding of, 200–201, 209, 243–244
        jaundice and, 181
    bronchopulmonary dysplasia in, 539–540
    circulatory changes in, 179, 567–568, *569*
    circumcision of, 191, 197–198, *198*
    classification of, by gestational age, 193–194
    cognitive development in, 184
    congenital defects in. *See* Congenital defects
    conjunctivitis in, 188, 196–197, 207, 1005–1006
    drug dosage calculation for, 1050
    fluid and electrolyte adaptations in, 182–183
    glucose-6-phosphate dehydrogenase deficiency in, 618
    growth and development of, 178–211
    health promotion for, 194–201
    hematological disorders in, 614–619
    hematopoietic adaptations in, 179–181.*180*
    hemolytic disease of, 199, 615–617
    hemorrhage in, 198–199
    hemorrhaghic disorders in, 198–199, 617
    high-risk
        postnatal assessment for, 207–211
        prenatal assessment for, 202–207
    hydrops fetalis and, 199, 200
    hypermagnesemia in, 749
    hypoxic-ischemic encephalopathy in, 538–539
    infection in, prevention of, 194–199
    jaundice in, *180*, 180–181, 614–615
        in ABO incompatibility, 200
        in blacks, 963t
        breast-feeding and, 181
        in Native Americans, 964t
    large-for-gestational age, 210–211
    liver disease in, 782–783
    low-birth-weight, 193
    meconium aspiration in, 537–538
    meningitis in, 656–657
    microcephaly in, 656
    mortality rates for, 9–10, 10t
    neural tube defects in, 654–656, *655*
    neurological disorders in, 651–657
    nutrition in, 200–201
    omphalitis in, 800–801
    parenting of, 211
    physiological adaptation in, 178–184
    pneumothorax in, 541–542
    polycythemia in, 617–618
    postmature, 193, 210–211
    premature. *See* Infant, premature

Neonate (*continued*)
  psychosocial adaptations in, 184
  reproductive disorders in, 848–850
  respiratory adaptations in, 179, 179t
  respiratory disorders in, 537–542
  respiratory distress syndrome in, 540–541
  resuscitation of, 194
  Rh incompatibility and, 199, 616
  risk factors for, 202–211
  sensory development in, 183–184
  septicemia in, 199
  skin in
    assessment of, 189
    care of, 198
  small-for-gestational age, 193, 210
  substance abuse effects on, 207, *207,* 475–476
  term, 193
  thermoregulation in, 181t, 181–182, *182*
  thrush in, 102, 198
  umbilical cord care in, 194–196, *196*
  vitamin K supplementation for, 181, 198–199
  witholding treatment for, 48–50
Nephritis, hereditary, 824–825
Nephroblastoma, 821–822
Nephrogenic diabetes insipidus, 889
Nephron, 811
Nephrosis, 825–826
Nephrotic syndrome, 825–826
Nerves
  cranial, 636
    assessment of, 106
  spinal, 636
Nervous system
  anatomy of, 635, *635*
  assessment of, 105–106, 638, 639t–641t
  in burns, 984
  central, 635–636
  disorders of. *See* Neurological disorders
  embryology of, 634–635
  peripheral, 636
  physiology of, 635–636
  in toddler, 258
Neuman's health care system model, 21
Neural tube defects, 649–654, *650*
  hydrocephalus in, 651, 654–656, *655*
Neurocutaneous syndromes, 659–660
Neurofibromatosis, 204t, 659–660
Neurogenic diabetes insipidus, 889–890
Neurohypophysis
  anatomy and physiology of, 872, 875–876
  disorders of, 889–890
  embryology of, 872
Neurological assessment, 105–106, 638, 639t–641t
Neurological disorders
  in adolescents, 674–681
  assessment of, 637–638
  diagnostic procedures for, 638, 639t–641t
  history in, 637–638
  hypocalcemia and, 748–749
  hypomagnesemia and, 750
  increased intracranial pressure in, 636–637, 643–647
  level of consciousness in, 644–647, 645t
  in neonates and infants, 647–657, 651–657
  nursing care for
    evaluation of, 643
    implementation of, 642–643
    planning of, 642

  nursing diagnoses for, 638–642
  physical examination in, 638
  in preschool children, 660–662
  pupillary function in, 646
  in school-age children, 662–674
  in toddlers, 657–660
Neutrophils, 608, 687–688
Nevus, 189
Nevus flammeus, 967t, 970–971
Nevus of Ito, 961t, 964t
Nevus of Ota, 961t, 964t
Newborn. *See* Neonate
Nightingale, Florence, 19–20
Nightmares, 283
Night terrors, 283
Night waking, in infants, 249
90–90 traction, *929*
Nipples
  inverted, 858
  supernumerary, 858, 963t
Nocturnal enuresis, 298–299
Noise, in incubators, 210, 1015
Noise-induced hearing loss, 1015–1016
Non-A, non-B hepatitis, 432, 802
Nondisjunction, chromosomal, 165
Non–rapid eye movement (REM) sleep, 226–227
Nonrebreathing mask, 528, *529*
Nonverbal communication, 82
Normalization, 578
  for chronically ill/disabled child, 404
North American Nursing Diagnosis Association, nursing diagnoses, classification of, 115, 117t, 118t
Nose
  anatomy and physiology of, 995, *995*
  assessment of, 101–102
    in neonate, 188
  disorders of, 1016–1018
  embryology of, 993
  examination of, 999
  foreign bodies in, 546–547
Nosebleeds, 1002
Nuclear family, 9, 26
Nuclear magnetic resonance, in neurological disorders, 640t
Nurse
  effect of death on, 507–508
  legal responsibilities of, 44–46
Nurse advocacy, legal and ethical aspects of, 43
Nurse/family relationship, home care and, 402–405, 403t
Nursery school, 289
Nursing
  child health. *See* Child health nursing
  standards of care for, 44–45, 46
Nursing assessment, 18, *19,* 81–108
  developmental assessment in, 87–88
  family assessment in, 85–87, *86*
  health history in, 88–89
  in home care, 393–396, *395*
  interview in, 81t, 81–85, 84t, 85t
  in nursing care plan, 107
  in nursing process, 18, *19*
  physical examination in, 93–106. *See also* Physical examination
    skills for, 90–93, *92,* 92t, *93*
  review of systems in, 90, 90t–91t
Nursing care. *See* Child health care; Child health nursing
Nursing care plan, 122–129
  assessment in, 107

clients' and families' roles in, 123–124
computerized, 123, *124–125*
for congenital hip dysplasia, 952–953
for congestive heart failure, 601–602
for croup, 107, 117–118, 127–128, 144–146, 152–154
developing goals for, 123–124
for diabetes mellitus, 908–912
evaluation in, 152–154
for gastroesophageal reflux, 804–806
implementation in, 144–146
individualized, 123
interventions in, 124–125, 127–128
nursing diagnoses in, 117–118
planning in, 127–128
priorities for, 123
standardized, 123
for tracheostomy, 559–561
for undescended testis, 868–869
for urinary tract infection, 838–839
for ventricular septal defect, 602
Nursing diagnoses, 18, *19,* 111–129, 231–233
actual, 113–114
for cardiovascular disorders, 577–578
components of, 114
data collection and interpretation for, 114
for death and dying, 500–502
defining characteristics of, 113, 114
definition of, 113
for endocrine disorders, 881–882, 901
evolution of, 112
for gastrointestinal disorders, 764–765
health problem in, 114
for hematological disorders, 610–611
high risk, 114
for home care, 396–397
hypothetical, 115114–115
for immune disorders, 694
vs. medical diagnoses, 113t
for mental retardation, 454
for neurological disorders, 638–642t–641t
North American Nursing Diagnosis Association
    classification of, 115, 117t, 118t
in nursing care plan, 116–117
in nursing process, 114–115
pediatric, 115
related factors in, 113, 114
for renal disorders, 816
for reproductive disorders, 847
for respiratory disorders, 527
for sensory disorders, 1000–1001
statement of, 115
for substance abuse, 479–480
types of, 113–114
validation of, 115
wellness, 114
Nursing implementation
definition of, 132
developmental considerations in, 132–139
Nursing interventions
dependent, 132
implementation of, 18, *19,* 132–147
independent, 132
interdependent, 132
in nursing care plan, 124–125, 127–128, 144–146
Nursing process, 18, *19*
assessment in, 18, *19,* 81–108, 114. *See also*
    Nursing assessment

data collection and interpretation in, 114
diagnosis in, 18, *19,* 112–119. *See also* Nursing diagnoses
evaluation in, 18, *19,* 150–155. *See also* Evaluation
hypothesis generation and testing in, 114–115
implementation in, 18, *19,* 132–147. *See also*
    Implementation
planning in, 18, *19,* 122–129
validation of findings in, 115
Nursing roles, 6–7
Nursing theory, 18–21
Nutrients, in breast milk, 224–226
Nutrition, 139. *See also* Diet; Feeding; Food; Nutrtition
in adolescent, 338–339, 339t, 345–346
in burns, 986, 988
in cardiovascular disease, 574
in cystic fibrosis, 553, 554
in diabetes mellitus, 904–905, 905t
in gastrointestinal disorders, 766
government programs for, 15
in hematological disorders, 612
in home care, 409–410
in immune disorders, 698
in infant, 224t–226t, 224–226
in malabsorption, 791
in musculoskeletal disorders, 930
in neonate, 200–201
in pregnancy, 170
in premature infant, 209, 789–790
in preschooler, 280–283
in respiratory disorders, 535
in school-age child, 309–311, 310t
in toddler, 260, 260t
total parenteral, 743, *743,* 766
    at home, 410
    necrotizing enterocolitis and, 789–790
Nystagmus, 100, 997
Nystatin (Mycostatin), for thrush, 198

## O

Obesity, 310, 355–356
    in Cushing syndrome, 892, 893
    in Down syndrome, 456
Objective thought, 311
Object permanence, 230, 261
Obstructive breathing, 523
Ocular muscles, *993,* 994
Oedipal conflict, 62, 287
Olfactory nerve, 995
Oliguria, in acute renal failure, 829
Omphalitis, 800–801
Omphalocele, 788–789
Open-ended questions, 84–85
Open heart surgery, 580–582
Operant conditioning, 67
Ophthalmia neonatorum, 188, 196–197, 207, 1005
Ophthalmoscopic examination, 100, 997, *998*
Opiates. *See also* Substance abuse
    fetal/neonatal effects of, 476
Optic disc, *993,* 994, 997, *998*
Oral cavity
    candidiasis of, 188–189
        in neonate, 198
    examination of, 102, *103*
        in neonate, 188–189
Oral contraceptives, 351t
    for dysfunctional uterine bleeding, 855

Oral medications, administration of, 133–135, *134*
Oral period, 61, 232–233
Oral rehydration therapy, 741–742
Oral stage, 263
Oral temperature, 95–96, *96*
Orbital rhabdomyosarcoma, 1008
Orchitis, 847
    in mumps, 429
Orem's self-care theory, 20–21
Organic solvents, abuse of, 324t
Organization, biological, 63
Orientals
    cultural beliefs of, 34–35
    integumentary system in, 961t–962t
Orientation, in hospitalization, 385
Orofaciodigital syndrome, 205t
Oropharynx, 517
Orthopnea, 522
Ortolani test, 935, *936*
    for congenital hip disorders, 190–191
Osgood-Schlatter disease, 950–951
Osmolality
    serum, 739t
        normal values for, 1046t
    urine, 739t
        normal values for, 1048t
Osmosis, 731
Osmotic diarrhea, 768
Osmotic pressure, 731
Ossicles, auditory, 994, *994*
Ossification, 917–918, *918*
Osteogenesis imperfecta, 204t, 939t, 939–940
Osteomyelitis, 942–943
Osteosarcoma, 946
Ostium primum defects, 583, 585–586
Ostium secundum defects, 583
Ostomy, 766–767
Otitis externa, 1015
Otitis media
    acute, 1012
    chronic nonsuppuratory, 1013
    chronic secretory, 1013
        nursing care plan for, 1019–1021
    mastoiditis and, 1014–1015
Otoscopy, 101, 1013
Ounces and pounds–grams conversion chart, 1054
Outbreak, disease, 417t
Ovarian cycle, 844
Ovaries, 843, *844*
Overhydration. *See also* Edema; Fluid and electrolyte
        imbalances
Overuse syndromes, 950
Overweight, 310, 355–356
    in Cushing syndrome, 892, 893
    in Down syndrome, 456
Ovovegetarian diet, 226, 226t
Oxygen
    partial pressure of, 520
    in pulmonary gas exchange, 520
Oxygen administration, 528, *529, 530*
    for asthma, 555–558
    with concentrated oxygen, 408
    with cylinder oxygen, 408
    equipment for, 408–409
    at home, 407–409, *408*
    with humidification, 408
    with liquid oxygen, 408

    masks for, 528, *529*
    mist tent for, 528, *530*
    retinopathy and, 1004–1005
Oxygenation
    monitoring of, 525–526, 577
    physiology of, 571
Oxygen monitoring, transcutaneous, 526
Oxygen saturation, transcutaneous, 577
Oxytocin, 875

**P**
Pacemaker
    permanent implanted, 581–582
    postoperative, 580–581
Pacifiers, 249–250
PaCO$_2$
    in metabolic acidosis, 744
    in metabolic alkalosis, 745
    in respiratory acidosis, 745–746
    in respiratory alkalosis, 746–747
Pain
    abdominal
        in appendicitis, 801
        assessment of, 762
        in peptic ulcer disease, 803
    growing, 309
    in hospitalized children, 379
    in immune disorders, 695–696
    joint
        in juvenile rheumatoid arthritis, 716–719
        in rheumatic fever, 597–598
    menstrual, 854
    in musculoskeletal disorders, drugs for, 930, 931t–932t
    perception of, assessment of, 106
    postoperative, in cardiovascular surgery, 581
    in respiratory disorders, 521
    sensation of, in neonate, 183
    in sickle cell crisis, 625–626
    in teething, 228
Palate, cleft, 772–774, *773*
    ethnic factors in, 961t, 966t
    hypopituitarism and, 884–885
Palmar crease, in Down syndrome, *455*
Palpation, 92–93
    of abdomen, 104
    of pulse, 92–93, 96, 572
Pancreas
    anatomy of, 760, *760*
    in diabetes mellitus, 876–877, 900
Pancreatitis, 803
Pancuronium (Pavulon), for increased intracranial
        pressure, 648t
Papilledema, 646
Papules, 421, *960*
Parafollicular cells, 876
Paraldehyde, 671t
Parallel play, 262
Paralysis
    in Guillain-Barré syndrome, 663–664
    in neural tube defects, 649–654
    in spinal cord injury, 676–681, 680t. *See also* Spinal cord
        injury
Paramethidione (Paradione), 671t
Paranasal sinuses, 995, *995*
Paraphrasing, 85
Paraplegia. *See* Paralysis

Parasitic infections, 432–434
  cutaneous, 976–978
Parathyroid glands, 876, *877*
  disorders of, 888–889, 897–898
Parathyroid hormone, 876
  deficiency of, 888–889
Parent(s)
  growth and development of, 72
  interviewing of, 82
  support groups for. *See* Support groups
  withholding or withdrawing of treatment by, 47–48
Parenteral nutrition
  at home, 410
  total, 743, *743*
    necrotizing enterocolitis and, 789–790
Parent-infant attachment, 69–72, 184–185, 233–234
  assessment of, 194, *195, 196*
Parenting, 37–38
  of disabled child, 461
  of infant, 233–234, 250–251
  of neonate, 184–185, 211
  preparation for, 168–169
  of preschooler, 302–303
  of school-age child, 324–325
  of spinal cord injured child, 680–681
  of toddler, 273
Parenting Profile Assessment, 317
Parents Anonymous, 295
Parent teaching
  for home care, 392, *393,* 397–398, 404–405
  for parents of hospitalized child, 385–386
Parietal fontanel, 187*187*
Parietal pleura, 518
Parotitis. *See* Mumps
Partial rebreathing mask, 528, *529*
Partial seizures, 669t. *See also* Seizures
Partial thromboplastin time, 610
  normal values for, 1047t
Passive transport, 732
Patau syndrome, 203t
Patch tests, for allergens, 968
Patellofemoral stress syndrome, 950–951
Patent ductus arteriosus, *586,* 586–587
Paternal attachment, 71–72, 184–185, 233–234. *See also* Bonding
Patient teaching. *See* Health teaching
Pavlik harness, 936, *937*
Pearly penile papules, 963t
Pectus carinatum, 102, 522, *523*
Pectus excavatum, 102, 522, *523*
Pectus profundus, 521–522
Pediatric home care. *See* Home care
Pediatric intensive care unit, admission to, 383–384
Pediatric nurse practitioner, 21
Pediatric nursing. *See* Child health nursing
Pediculosis, 976–977
Peer relationships
  of adolescent, 331t, 339, 341, 342–343
  of school-age child, 314–315
Pelvic examination, 846
Pelvic inflammatory disease, 862–863
Penicillin
  allergy to, 707–709
  Jarisch-Herxheimer reaction and, 865
Penis, 843, *845*
  assessment of, 104–105
  circumcision of, 191, 197–198, *198*

congenital anomalies of, 191, 819–821, *820*
  in epispadias, *820,* 820–821
  examination of, 847
  in hypospadias, 819–820, *820*
  neonatal assessment of, 191
  pearly papules of, 963t
  pubertal changes in, *336,* 337–338, 338t, 348
Peptic ulcer disease, 803–804
  hyperparathyroidism and, 898
Perceptual deficit syndrome, 665–666
Percussion, 91–92, *92,* 92t, *93*
  of abdomen, 104
  of chest, 524, 530
Percutaneous umbilical blood sampling, 172
Pericarditis, 596–597
Pericardium, 568, *570*
Perinatal nurse specialist, American Nurses' Association Standards for, 46
Periodic breathing, 522
Periosteum, 917, *917*
Peripheral nervous system, 636
Peripheral perfusion assessment, 570–571, 571t
Peritoneal dialysis, 835t, 835–836
Personality, assessment of, 89
Pertussis, 429–430
  immunization for, 241–242, 242t, 267t, 318t, 417–420, 419t, 1055
Petit mal seizures, 669, 669t. *See also* Seizures
pH, 734
  esophageal, in gastroesophageal reflux, 777
  in metabolic acidosis, 744
  in metabolic alkalosis, 744–745
  in respiratory acidosis, 746
  in respiratory alkalosis, 746–747
  urine, 739t, 815t
    normal values for, 1047t
Phagocytosis, 223, 607
Phakomatoses, 659–660
Phallic stage, 62, 287
Pharyngitis, 547
  acute, 1016–1017
  streptococcal, 549, 1016–1017
    glomerulonephritis after, 823–824
    rheumatic fever and, 597
Pharynx, 517
Phenobarbital (Luminol), 671t
Phensuximide (Milcontin), 671t
Phenylalanine, normal values for, 1046t
Phenylketonuria, 201
Phenytoin (Dilantin), 671t
Pheochromocytoma, 900
Phimosis, 105, 849
Phobia, school, 318
Phoria, 996, 1007
Phosphate, function and regulation of, 733t
Phosphorus, normal values for, 1046t
Phototherapy
  for neonatal hyperbilirubinemia, 615
  for physiological jaundice, 181
Physical examination, 93–106
  of abdomen, 104
  developmental approaches to, 93
  of ears, 101, *101*
  of eyes, 99–101, *101*
  general survey in, 97
  of genitalia, 104–105
  growth measurements in, 93–95

Physical examination (*continued*)
  of head and neck, 98–99.*98, 99*
  of heart, 102–103, *104*
  of mouth and throat, 102, *103*
  of musculoskeletal system, 105
  of nose, 101–102
  of reflexes, 108
  of sensory function, 106–108
  of skin, 97–98
  of thorax and lungs, 102
  vital signs in, 95–97, 572t, 572–574, *573,* 573t
Physical therapy, in cerebral palsy, 447
Physiological anemia, of infancy, 222, 619–622
Physiological jaundice, *180,* 180–181, 614–615
  in blacks, 963t
  breast-feeding and, 181
  in Native Americans, 964t
Physiological leukorrhea, 846
Piaget's cognitive theory, 63–64, 65t, *66*
  adolescent and, 340
  infant and, 228–230, 229t
  preschooler and, 284–285
  school-age child and, 311, 312t
  toddler and, 261–262
Piaget's moral theory, school-age child and, 315
Pica, 301, 657
Pigeon chest, 102, 522, *523*
Pigmentation, ethnic variations in, 961t–967t
Pilonidal dimple, 967t
Pincer grasp, 219, *220,* 220t
  in toddler, 258–259
Pinworms, 432–433
Pitressin, for diabetes insipidus, 889–890
Pituicytes, 875
Pituitary
  anatomy and physiology of, *873,* 873–876, *875*
  anterior
    anatomy and physiology of, 874–875, *875*
    disorders of, 893–894
    embryology of, 872
    in infant, 222–223
  posterior
    anatomy and physiology of, *875,* 875–876
    disorders of, 889–890
Pituitary dwarfism, 876, 884–885
Placenta, 161–162, *162*
Placing reflex, 190t
Planning
  in nursing care plan, 127–128
  in nursing process, 18, *19,* 122–129
Plantar warts, 979
Plasma, 609
  fresh frozen, for hemophilia, 622–623
Plasma thrombin time, 610
Platelets, 608–609
  deficiency of
    in aplastic anemia, 626
    in idiopathic thrombocytopenic purpura, 627
    in Wiskott-Aldrich syndrome
    normal values for, 610t, 1045t
Play
  in cerebral palsy, 450
  cooperative, 312–313
  development of, 70t–71t
  for disabled, 462–463, 469
  in early school years, 312–313
  during hospitalization, 371t, 374, 375–376
  in infancy, 230–231, 232t
  in mental retardation, 453
  parallel, 262
  in preschool years, 285–286, 287
  purposes of, 381–382
  symbolic, 262
  theories of, 68–69, 72t, 380–381
  therapeutic, 68–69
  in toddler period, 262, 263
  types of, 381
Pleura, 518
Pleural friction rub, 524
Plumbism, 300–302, 657–659, 658t
Pluripotent stem cells, 607
Pneumatic otoscopy, 1013
Pneumocytes, 518
Pneumonia, 549–552
  bacterial, 549–550
  in cystic fibrosis, 552–553
  lipoid, 551–552
  viral, 550
Pneumonitis
  hypersensitivity, 709–710
  lymphoid interstitial, in AIDS, 699–700
Pneumotaxic respiratory center, 520
Pneumothorax
  in cystic fibrosis, 553
  neonatal, 541–542
Point of maximum impulse, in heart rate measurement, 572
Poisoning
  acetaminophen, 781–782
  carbon monoxide, 984
  corrosive, 780–781
  in infants, 247
  lead, 247, 300–302, 657–659, 658t
  in preschoolers, 299–300
  in toddlers, 270–271, 271t
Poison ivy, 973–974
Poison oak, 973–974
Poison sumac, 973–974
Poliomyelitis, 430
  immunization for, 241–242, 242t, 417–420, 419t, 1055
Polycystic renal disease, 204t
Polycythemia, 571
  neonatal, 617–618
Polydactyly, 204t, 963t
Polydipsia, in diabetes insipidus, 889
Polymastia, 858
Polymorphonuclear leukocytes, 608, 687–688
Polyps, intestinal, 800
Polysubstance abuse, 473. *See also* Substance abuse
Polythelia, 858
Polyuria, in diabetes insipidus, 889
Portal hypertension, 783
Port wine stain, 189, 967t, 970–971
Positioning, in cerebral palsy, 447–449, *450*
Posterior fontanel, 98, *98,* 187, *187*
Posterior pituitary gland
  anatomy and physiology of, 875–876
  disorders of, 889–890
  prenatal development of, 872
Postmaturity, 193, 210–211
Poststreptococcal glomerulonephritis, 823–824
Postural drainage, 520, *532–533*
Posturing
  decerebrate, 646, *646*
  decorticate, 646, *646*

Potassium
  function and regulation of, 733t
  imbalance of, 750–752
  normal values for, 1047t
  urinary, normal values for, 1048t
Potassium hydroxide test, 960
Pounds and ounces–grams conversion chart, 1054
Pounds-kilograms conversion, 1051
Poverty, government programs for, 14–17
Povidone-iodine, for burns, 987t
PPD test, 242
Preauricular pits, 962t
Precocious puberty, 851–852
Preconventional stage, 65–66
Prednisone, for asthma, 557t
Pregnancy
  adolescent, 334, 350, 352–353
    prevention of, 350–352, 351t
  assessment in, for high-risk neonate, 202–207
  cytogenetic testing in, 171–172, 455
    indications for, 166–167, 172
  fetal/neonatal risk factors in, 202–211
  hypertension in, magnesium sulfate for, neonatal
      hypermagnesemia and, 749
  infections in, fetal/neonatal effects of, 206–207
  multiple, 173
  nutrition in, 170
  preparation for, 168–169
  psychosocial impact of, 168–170
  risk factors in, 203t, 203–207
  sibling preparation in, 169–170
  substance abuse in
    fetal/neonatal effects of, 207, *207*, 475–476
    prevention of, 482
    reporting of, 480
  in systemic lupus erythematosus, 723
  weight gain in, 170
Preluxation, of hip, 190–191
Premature adrenarche, 851
Premature infant. *See* Infant, premature
Premature thelarche, 851
Premenstrual syndrome, 854–855
Prenatal care, 353
Preoperational stage, of cognitive development, 64, 261–262,
    284–285
Prepuce, 843, *845*
Preschooler
  accidents in, 299–300
  assessment for, 290–291
  body measurements in, 290, 1039t
  day care and nursery school for, 288–289
  developmental screening of, 290
  developmental tasks of, 67t, 293–294
  discipline of, 302
  fears in, 296–297
  growth and development of, 276–303
    moral, 286–287
    motor, 278–2804
    physical, 278–284
    psychosocial, 287–289
  home and family assessment for, 290–291
  hospitalization of, 373–374. *See also* Hospitalization
  immunizations for, 291–293
  language development in, 287, 291t
  nutrition in, 280–283
  parenting of, 302
  play in, 285–286

  respiratory disorders in, 546–548
  sex education for, 302
  sex role identification in, 288
  sibling rivalry in, 295–296
  sleep in, 283–284
  temper tantrums in, 297–298
  typical characteristics of, 277t
Pressure, circulatory, 567
Pressure garments, for burns, 986, *988*
Preterm infant. *See* Infant, premature
Preventive health care. *See also* Health promotion
  recommendations for, 239, 240t
Primidone (Mysoline), 672t
Prism test, for strabismus, 1007
Privacy rights, 52
Professional standards of care, 44–45, 46
Progesterone, 844
Projectile vomiting, in pyloric stenosis, 787–788
Projection, 499
Prolactin, 222, 874
Propylthiouracil, for hyperthyroidism, 895, 896
Prostate, 843, *845*
Protein(s)
  in breast milk, 224t, 225, 225t
  normal values for, 1047t
Proteinuria, 825
  normal values for, 1047t
Prothrombin time, 610
  normal values for, 1047t
Protozoa, 417t
Proximal-distal development, 59, 217
Pseudofolliculitis barbae, 964t
Pseudohermaphroditism, 843
Pseudohyperparathyroidism, 205t
Pseudohypoparathyroidism, 888
Pseudoprecocious puberty, 851
Pseudostrabismus, 1007
Psoriasis, 967t, 972–973
Psychiatric illness, treatment of, legal issues in, 51
Psychoanalytic theory, 61–62, 233
Psychological intervention, disciplinary, 39
Psychosexual beliefs, hospitalization and, 374
Psychosexual development, in adolescent, 340
Psychosocial adaptation, in neonate, 184
Psychosocial development
  in adolescent, 331t–332t, 341–343
  in preschooler, 287–289
  in school-age child, 313–315, 314t
  in toddler, 262–265
Psychosocial theory, Erikson's, 62–63, *63, 66*
Ptosis, 99, 996
Puberty, 843–845
  in boys, *335, 336,* 337–338, 338t, 348
  delayed, 852–853
  in Down syndrome, 457
  in girls, *336,* 337, *337,* 338t, 348
  onset of, 337
  precocious, 851–852
  pseudoprecocious, 851
  rating scales for, 335, *335–337*
Pubic hair, 335, *335, 336,* 338, 338t
Pubic lice, 976–977
Publications, child health nursing, 22
Public health, principles of, 416–421
Puerto Rican–Americans
  cultural beliefs of, 36–37
  integumentary system in, 964t–965t

Pulmonary artery, transposition of, *590, 590–591*
Pulmonary circulation, 518, 571
Pulmonary compromise, postoperative, in cardiovascular surgery, 581
Pulmonary function tests, 525
Pulmonary gas exchange, 520
Pulmonary ventilation, deficient, respiratory acidosis and, 745–746
Pulmonic stenosis, 589–590
    in tetralogy of Fallot, 592–593, *593*
Pulse
    measurement of, 96, 572, 572t
        in neonate, 186
    normal values for, 1043t
    palpation of, 92–93
Pulse oximetry, 525–526, 577
Punishment, 38–39. *See* Discipline
Pupil, *993,* 994
    assessment of, 99–100
    in increased intracranial pressure, 646
Pupillary reflex, 994
Purkinje fibers, 569–570
Purpura, idiopathic thrombocytopenic, 627
Pustular melanosis, transient neonatal, 964t
Pyelography, intravenous, 814
Pyelonephritis, 826–827
Pyloric stenosis, 787–788
Pyloromyotomy, 788

**Q**

Quadriplegia. *See* Paralysis
Quality assurance, 155
Questions
    closed, 84
    open-ended, 84–85

**R**

Rabies, 435–436
Radiant warmer, for neonate, 182, *182*
Radiation therapy
    for brain tumors, 667
    for Hodgkin disease, 630, 631
Radiography
    abdominal, 763t, 764
    chest
        in cardiovascular disorders, 576
        in respiratory disorders, 527
    renal, 814–815
    skeletal, 921
Radius, fracture of, 934
Rales, 524
Rape, 861–862
Rapid eye movement (REM) sleep, 226–227
Rash. *See also* Dermatitis
    definition of, 421
    diaper, 243, 971, 980
    drug-induced, 982–983
    erythematous, 421
    in fifth disease, 422
    in juvenile rheumatoid arthritis, 717
    in Kawasaki disease, 422
    in Lyme disease, 424
    macular, 421
    in measles, 425
    papular, 421, *960*

    in Rocky Mountain spotted fever, 425
    in roseola, 426
    in rubella, 427
    in scarlet fever, 427
    in syphilis, 865
    in systemic lupus erythematosus, *720,* 721t
    in varicella, 428
Rastelli procedure, for transposition of great arteries, 591
Reasoning
    deductive, 284
    inductive, 284
Receptive milestones, 234, *234*
Record keeping, in home care, 405, 464
Recreation. *See* Exercise; Play; Sports
Rectal abnormalities, congenital, 795–796
Rectal biopsy, 764
Rectal bleeding
    anal fissures and, 800
    assessment of, 762
    intestinal polyps and, 800
    in Meckel diverticulum, 793
Rectal drug administration, 135, 136t
Rectal temperature, 95, *96*
Rectus femoris muscle, injection into, 135, *137*
Red blood cells. *See* Erythrocytes
Red reflex, 997
    in vision testing, 221
Referral, 143
Reflecting, 85
Reflection/impulsivity, cognitive, 313
Reflex(es)
    assessment of, 108
    Babinski, 108, 190t
    in cerebral palsy, 444, 444t, 445
    dance, 190t
    grasp, 190t
    Hering-Breuer, 520
    Landau, 190t
    light, otoscopic, 999
    Moro, 183, 190t
    neonatal assessment of, 190t, 191–192
    placing, 190t
    pupillary, 994
    red, 997
        in vision testing, 221
    respiratory, 520
    rooting, 183, 189, 190t
    sucking, 189
    tonic neck, 190t
    wallowing, 190t
Reflux
    gastroesophageal
        in infant, 221
        nursing care plan for, 804–806
    vesicoureteral, 827–829, *828*
Refractive errors, 1009–1010
Regression, in toddler, 268
Rehabilitation, in spinal cord injury, 678–679
Rehydration therapy. *See also* Fluid administration
    in diarrhea, 768–769
    oral, 741–742
    parenteral, 743
Relativism, 311
Relaxation training, 380
Religious beliefs, 33
    death and dying and, 497–498
    withholding or withdrawing treatment and, 48

Renal angiography, 815
Renal biopsy, 815
Renal buffering system, 734
Renal corpuscle, 811
Renal disorders
    assessment in, 812–814, 813t
    diagnostic procedures in, 814–816
    dialysis in, 833–836
    drug therapy for, 818
    history in, 813, 813t
    in infants, 822–823
    in neonates, 821–822
    nursing care in
        evaluation of, 818
        planning and implementation of, 816–817
    nursing diagnoses in, 816
    nursing interventions in, 817–818
    physical examination in, 814
    in toddler and preschoolers, 823–829
Renal failure
    acute, 829–831
    chronic, 832–833, 834t
        hyperparathyroidism in, 898
    end-stage, 833
Renal function, 811–812
Renal scan, 815
Renal system
    anatomy and physiology of, 811–812, *812*
    embryology of, 811
    radiography of, 814–815
Renal transplantation, 836–837
Renal trauma, 831
Renal tubules
    acute necrosis of, 829
    anatomy of, 811, *812*
    in urine formation and transport, 812
Renal ultrasound, 816
Reporting
    of child abuse and neglect, 15, 859–860
    of substance abuse in pregnancy, 480
Reproductive disorders
    in adolescents, 852–867
    assessment in, 845–847
    history in, 845–846
    in neonates and infants, 848–850
    nursing care in
        evaluation of, 848
        planning and implementation of, 847–848
    nursing diagnoses in, 847
    physical examination in, 846–847
    in school-age children, 851–852
    sexually transmitted, 862–867
    in toddlers and preschoolers, 850–851
Reproductive rights, of minors, 47, 52
Reproductive system
    anatomy and physiology of, 843, *844, 845*
    development of. *See also* Puberty; Sexual maturation
        indifferent stage of, 842
        sex differentiation stage of, 842
    embryology of, 842–843
Research protocols, children's involvement in, 54–55
Residual volume, 525
Res ipsa loquitor, 46
Resistance to flow, circulatory, 567
Resonance, 92, 92t
Respiration
    assessment of, 102, 522–525, 523t

Biot, 523
Cheyne-Stokes, 523
control of, 519–520
in infant, 222
Kussmaul, 523
    in metabolic acidosis, 744
mechanics of, 518–519
obstructive, 523
periodic, 522
rate of
    assessment of, 96, 522–523, 523t
        in neonate, 186
    normal values for, 1043t
Respiratory acidosis, 745–746
    assessment of, 526, 526t
Respiratory alkalosis, 746–747
    assessment of, 526, 526t
Respiratory control, 519–520
Respiratory disorders
    aerosol therapy for, 528–529, *530*
    arterial blood gas values in, 525–526, 526t
    assessment of, 520–527
    bronchoscopy in, 526
    chest physiotherapy for, 530
    congenital, 536–537
    diagnostic procedures for, 525–527
    drug therapy for, 530–534
    history in, 520–521
    humidification for, 529
    in infant, 542–546
    inhalation therapy for, 528–529
    in neonate, 194, 537–542
    nursing care in
        evaluation of, 535–536
        planning of, 527–528
    nursing diagnoses for, 527
    nursing interventions in, 528–535
    nutritional needs in, 535
    oxygen therapy for, 528, *529*
    physical examination in, 521–525
    postural drainage for, 530, *532–533*
    pulmonary function tests in, 525
    radiological evaluation of, 527
    in toddler and preschooler, 546–548
Respiratory distress syndrome, 540–541
Respiratory failure, neonatal, 538–539
Respiratory insufficiency
    diaphragmatic hernia and, 776
    respiratory acidosis and, 745–746
Respiratory mechanics, 518–519
Respiratory patterns, assessment of, 522–525
Respiratory rate
    assessment of, 96, 522–523, 523t
        in neonate, 186
    normal values for, 1043t
Respiratory reflexes, 520
Respiratory system, 517–561
    in acid-base balance, 734
    anatomy of, 517–518
    in burns, 983–984
    embryology of, 517
    in infant, 222
    in neonate, 179
    physiology of, 518–520
    in toddler, 257
Respite care, 400
Respondeat superior, 45–46

Restating, 85
Restraint
    for injection, 292–293, *293*
    methods of, 135, *138*
Resuscitation
    cardiopulmonary, 579–580
    of neonate, 194
Retardation
    growth
        in gastrointestinal disorders, 761
        intrauterine, 172, 206
        mental. *See* Mental retardation
    sociocultural, 452–453
Reticulocytes, normal values for, 1045t
Reticuloendothelial system, 606–607
Retina, *993, 994*
    detached, 1010–1011
Retinoblastoma, 1007–1008
Retinopathy of prematurity, 210, 1004–1005
Retrolental fibroplasia, 210, 1004–1005
Retropatellar pain syndrome, 950–951
Retropharyngeal abscess, 545–546
Review of systems, 90, 90t–91t
Reye syndrome, 435, 662–663
Rhabdomyosarcoma, orbital, 1008
Rheumatic fever, 597–598
Rheumatoid arthritis, juvenile, 716–719
Rh incompatibility, 199, 616
    blood typing for, 608
    prenatal diagnosis of, 609
Rhinitis, allergic, 710–712, 1017–1018
RhoGAM, 199, 616
Rhonchi, 524
Rh typing, 608
Ribavirin, for bronchiolitis, 544
Rickets, vitamin-D–resistant, 205t
Rickettsiae, 417t
Right bundle branch, 569–570
Right-sided heart failure, 599
Right to life cases, 49–50
Right ventricular hypertrophy, in tetralogy
        of Fallot, 592–593, *593*
Riley-Day syndrome, 204t
Ringworm, 980–981
Rinne test, 1000t, 1013
Rocky Mountain spotted fever, 425–426
Rods, retinal, *993, 994*
Rooting reflex, 183, 189, 190t
Roseola, 426
Roundworms, 432
Roy's adaptation theory, 21
Rubella, 426–427
    congenital, 166–167, 206, 426
    immunization for, 241–242, 242t, 267t, 318t, 417–420,
        419t, 1055
    postnatal, 427
Rubeola, 424–425
    immunization for, 241–242, 242t, 267t, 318, 318t, 417–420,
        419t, 425, 1055
Rugae, 337
Rule of nines, for burn estimation, 984, *985,* 985t
Russell traction, *928*


**S**
Sabine vaccine, 242t, 419t, 1055
Safety precautions
    for adolescent, 347

for infant, 245–248
    in hospital, 370
    for preschooler, 299–300
    for school-age child, 320–322
    for toddler, 269t, 269–270
Sagittal fontanel, 187, *187*
Salicylates, for musculoskeletal disorders, 931t
Saline compartment, 733
Salk vaccine, 242t, 419t, 1055
Same-day surgery, 382
Sarcoma
    Ewing's, 946–947
    osteogenic, 946
Scabies, 977
Scale, *960*
Scalp
    injuries of, 674–675
    lice infestation of, 976–977
    ringworm of, 980–981
    seborrheic dermatitis of, 975
Scapegoating, 499
Scarlatina, 427
Scarlet fever, 427
Scarlet Red, for burns, 987t
Scars, burn, 984, *984*
    management of, 987, *988*
Schema, 64
School. *See also* Education
    adjustment to, 313, 317–318
School-age child
    abuse and neglect of, 316
    accidents in, 320–322
    assessment for, 316–318
    body measurements in, 316–317, 1039t
    developmental tasks of, 67t, 320, 321t
    growth and development of, 308–325
        cognitive, 311, 312t
        moral, 315–316
        motor, 309, 316, 316t
        physical, 309–311
        psychosocial, 313–315, 314t
        sensory, 309
    handicapped, mainstreaming of, 323
    home and family assessment for, 317
    hospitalization of, 374–376. *See also* Hospitalization
    latchkey, 322
    nutritional needs of, 309–310, 310t
    parenting of, 324–325
    peer relationships of, 314–315
    play in, 312–313
    school adjustment in, 313, 317–318
    sex education for, 323
    sleep in, 310–311
    substance abuse by, 323, 324t, 477–478. *See also* Substance
        abuse
    television viewing by, 323–324, 325t
School Lunch Program, 15
School phobia, 318
Sclera, *993, 994*
Scoliosis
    idiopathic, 943–946
    screening for, 319–320
Scrotum, 843, *845*
    assessment of, 104–105, 847
Seasonal allergic rhinitis, 710–712
Seat belts, 320
Seborrheic dermatitis, 975
Secretory diarrhea, 767

Seizures, 668–674
  in brain tumors, 667, 668
  causes of, 668t
  classification of, 668–669, 669t
  clinical manifestations of, 669t, 669–670
  in DiGeorge syndrome, 705, 706
  drugs for, 670, 671t–672t, 673
  febrile, 647–648
  hypocalcemia and, 748–749
  hypomagnesemia and, 750
  medical diagnosis and management of, 668–670, 669t, 671t
  nursing care for, 642, 672–674
  observation and documentation of, 673t
  pathophysiology of, 668
  tonic-clonic, 669t
Self-concept disturbance, in spinal cord injury, 681
Self-evaluation, 155
Semicircular canal, 994, *994*
Seminal vesicles, 843, *845*
Semiotic function, 284
Senning procedure, for transposition of great arteries, 591
Sense of intimacy, 341
Sensorimotor stage, 64
Sensory deprivation, in hospitalized infants, 370–371, 371t
Sensory development
  in infant, 220–221
  in preschooler, 280
  in school-age child, 309
  in toddler, 259–260
Sensory disorders. *See also* Hearing impairment;
      Vision impairment
  assessment in, 996–1000
  history in, 996
  nursing care for, 1001–1002
  nursing diagnoses in, 1000–1001
  physical examination in, 996
Sensory overload, in hospitalized infants, 370–371
Sensory system. *See also* Ear; Eye; Hearing; Nose; Smell;
      Taste; Vision
  anatomy and physiology of, 993–995, *993–995*
  assessment of. *See* Hearing assessment; Vision assessment
  embryology of, 992–993
  in neonate, 183
Senu valgum, 941
Separation anxiety, 8–9
  vs. grief, 491
  hospitalization and, 370, 372, 373
  in infant, 230, 233
  in toddler, 263–264, 268
Septic arthritis, 941–942
Septicemia, neonatal, 199
Seriation, 311
Serum consituents. *See also* specific constituents, e.g.,
      Creatinine
Serum constituents, normal values for, 1044t–1048t
Serum osmolality, 739t
  normal values for, 1046t
Serum protein electrophoresis, in immune disorders, 694
Setting sun sign, 996
Sex chromosomes, 164, *165*
  disorders of, 203t
Sex education
  for disabled, 464
  for preschooler, 302
  for school-age child, 323
Sex role identification
  in adolescent, 341–342

in preschooler, 288
in school-age child, 315
in toddler, 264–265
Sexual abuse, 294–295, 859–862
  pubic lice and, 977
  reporting of, 15, 859–860
  risk factors for, 317
  substance abuse and, 480
Sexual assault, 861–862
Sexuality
  of adolescent, 341–343, 344, 349–350, 350t
  of infant, 233, 238–239
  of preschooler, 287, 288, 302
  of school-age child, 313, 315, 323
  after spinal cord injury, 681
  of toddler, 262–263, 264–265
Sexually transmitted diseases, 862–867
  fetal/neonatal effects of, 207
Sexual maturation. *See also* Puberty
  assessment of, in endocrine disorders, 881
  delayed, 852–853
  in Down syndrome, 457
  premature, 851–852
  rating systems for, 335, *335–337*
SGOT (serum glutamic oxaloacetic transaminase), normal
      values for, 1047t
SGPT (serum glutamic pyruvate transaminase), normal values
      for, 1047t
Shaman, 35
Shigella, 433–434
Shingles, vaccine for, 420
Shock
  in acute adrenocortical insufficiency, 891–892
  anaphylactic, 707–709
    epinephrine for, 709, 718t
    vaccines and, 718, 718t
  in burns, 983
  insulin, 907
  spinal, 677
Short bowel syndrome, 785, 786
Short stature, 348. *See also* Height
  in hypopituitarism, 876, 884–885
Shunt
  left-to-right
    in acyanotic congenital heart disease, 583
    in atrial septal defects, 584
    in ventricular septal defects, 584
  right-to-left, in cyanotic congenital heart disease, 583
  surgical
    cerebrospinal fluid, 210, 654–656, *655*
    for tetralogy of Fallot, 592
    for tricuspid atresia, 594
Sibling adaptation
  to home care, 404
  to neonate, 169–170, 185
Sibling rivalry
  in preschooler, 295–296
  in toddler, 268
Sickle cell disease, 204t, 624–626
Sickle cell trait, 624
Sight. *See* Vision assessment; Vision impairment
Sigmoidoscopy, 763t, 764
Silence, as communication technique, 85
Silver nitrate drops, for gonococcal conjunctivitis, 196
  ophthalmia neonatorum and, 1005
Silver nitrate solution, for burns, 987t
Silver sulfadiazine (Silvadene), for burns, 987t
Simian crease, in Down syndrome, *455*

Single parent family, 9, 26–27
  assessment of, 238
Sinoatrial node, 569
Sinuses, paranasal, 995, *995*
Sinusitis, 1017
Sinus venosus defects, 583
Sixth disease, 426
Skateboarding accidents, 347
Skeletal traction, 926, *927–929, 930t*
  in spinal cord injury, 678
Skene's glands, 843, *844*
Skin
  anatomy and physiology of, 957, *957*
  assessment of, 97–98, 958–969
    in endocrine disorders, 881
  bacterial infections of, 981–982
  biopsy of, 968
  in cardiovascular disorders, 574–575
  color of, 960
  in dehydration, 738
  disorders of
    assessment in, 97–98, 958–968
    diagnostic tests for, 960–968
    history in, 958, 959t
    nursing care for, 968–970
    nursing diagnoses for, 968
    physical examination in, 958–960, 961t–967t
  in edema, 738
  ethnic variations in, 961t–967t, 968
  fungal infections of, 243, 856–857, 979–981
  infestations of, 976–978
  lesions of, types of, *960*
  in neonate
    assessment of, 189
    care of, 198
  thermal injuries of. *See* Burns
  viral infections of, 979
Skin care
  in immune disorders, 696
  in infant, 243
  in neonate, 198
  in spinal cord injury, 679
Skinfold measurement, 345
  in obesity diagnosis, 353
Skin tests, for allergens, 694, 968, 1018
Skin traction, 926
Skin turgor
  assessment of, 98
  hydration and, 818
Skull, fractures of, 675, 676
Sleep
  in adolescent, 339
  in hospitalized child, 370, 374
  in infant, 226–227, 249
  in neonate, 187
  in preschooler, 283–284
  in school-age child, 310–311
  in toddler, 261, 271
Sleepwalking, 283
Slipped capital femoral epiphysis, 947–948
Small-for-gestational age infant, 210
  definition of, 194
Small intestine. *See also under* Bowel; Intestinal
  anatomy of, 760, *760*
  biopsy of, 764
  endoscopy of, 763t, 764
Smell
  assessment of, 999

  in infant, 221
  in toddler, 259
Smiling, in neonate, 183
Smoke inhalation, 983–984
Smokeless tobacco, 355–356
Smoking, 355
Sneezing, in newborn, 190t
Snuff, 355–356
Social relationships
  of adolescent, 331t, 339, 341, 342–343
  in autism, 459t–460t
  of school-age children, 314–315
Sociocultural retardation, 452–453
Socioeconomic issues, in death and dying, 498
Sodium
  function and regulation of, 733t
  imbalance of, 752–753
  sweat
    in cystic fibrosis
      normal values for, 1048t
  urinary, normal values for, 1048t
Sodium bicarbonate. *See also* Bicarbonate
  for metabolic acidosis, 744
Sodium chloride, for hypercalcemia, 748
Sodium polystyrene sulfonate (Kayexalate)
  for hyperkalemia, 830
  for hypermagnesemia, 750, 751
Sodium pump, 732
Solid food, for infants, 225–226, 226t
Solution
  hypertonic, 731
  hypotonic, 731
  isotonic, 731
  osmolality of, 731
  pH of, 734
Solvents, abuse of, 324t
Somatomedin, 222
Somatosensory evoked potentials, 641t
Somatotropin, 875
  deficiency of, 876, 884–885
  hypersecretion of, 893–894
Somogyi reaction, in diabetes, 907
Spanking, 38–39
Spasticity, in cerebral palsy, 444
Special Olympics, 453, 469
Special Supplemental Food Program for Women, Infants, and Children (WIC), 15
Speech. *See also* Language development
Spermatogenesis, 845
Spermicides, 351t
Spherocytosis, hereditary, 204t
Spica cast, *925*
  for congenital hip dysplasia, 936
Spina bifida, 649–654, *650*
Spinal assessment, 105
  in neonate, 189
Spinal cord injury, 676–681
  classification of, 677t
  level of, prognosis and, 680t
  medical management and diagnosis of, 677–678
  nursing assessment and diagnosis in, 678
  nursing care for, 678–681
  pathophysiology of, 676–677
  phases of, 677–678
Spinal curvature, abnormalities of, 943–946
Spinal fusion, 678
  in scoliosis, 943, 945–946
Spinal nerves, 636

Spinal shock, 677
Spiritual issues, in death and dying, 497–498
Spirochetes, 417t
Spitting up, in infant, 221
Spleen, 690
    palpation of, 104
Splenic sequestration crisis, in sickle cell disease, 624–625
Splints
    for burn contracture prevention, 986, *988*
    for torsional deformities, 940, 941
Split Russell traction, *928*
Sports, 320–322, 322t
    androgenic-anabolic steroid use in, 357–358
    for disabled, 453, 469
    injuries in, 951
Sprains, 932–933
Sputum, assessment of, 521
Squint, 1006–1007
Stage theories, of growth and development, 60–66
Staging, cancer, 630
Standardized care plans, 123
Standards of care, 44–45, 46
Staphylococcal infections, skin, 981–982
    in neonate, 198
Staphylococcal pneumonia, 549–550
Stature. *See* Height
Status asthmaticus, 555
Status epilepticus, 670
Statutory rape, 861
Stem cells, 607
Stenosis
    aortic, 588–589, *589*
    aqueduct of Sylvius, 654
    pulmonic, *589,* 589–590
        in tetralogy of Fallot, 592–593, *593*
    pyloric, 787–788
Stepfamily, 27–28
Stereogenesis, 106
Sterilization
    bottle, 202t
    surgical, of mentally retarded, 52
Steroids
    for Addison disease, 899–900
    androgenic-anabolic, 357–358
    for asthma, 557t
    for idiopathic thrombocytopenic purpura, 627
    for increased intracranial pressure, 648t
    in kidney transplantation, 836
    for respiratory disorders, 531–534
Stimulation. *See also* Play
    for disabled, 441–442
    for hospitalized children, 370, 371t
Stings, insect, 978
Stomach, anatomy of, 759, *760*
Stomatitis, herpes, 778–779
Stool
    assessment of, 762
    impacted, 769–770
    in infant, 221–222
    in neonate, 191t
    normal values for, 1049t
Stool cultures, 764
Stork bites, 189, 967t
Strabismus, 100, 1006–1007
    Hirschberg test for, 996
Strains, 932–933
Stranger anxiety, 230, 233
Strauss syndrome, in cerebral palsy, 444t

Strawberry hemangioma, 189, 967t, 970–971
Strawberry tongue, in scarlet fever, 427
Streptococcal infection
    glomerulonephritis after, 823–824
    neonatal, 199
Streptococcal pharyngitis, 549, 1016–1017
    rheumatic fever and, 597
Streptococcal pneumonia, 549–550
Stress fractures, 951
Stress immunization, for hospitalized children, 379
Stricture, esophageal, corrosive ingestion and, 780–781
Stridor, 525
    laryngeal, 536
    in croup, 543
Stroke volume, 570
Students Against Driving Drunk (SADD), 481–482
Stye, 996, 1010
Subdural hematoma, 675–676
Subdural hemorrhage, in premature infant, 209
Subluxation
    atlanto-axial, in Down syndrome, 456, 457
    congenital hip, 105, 189–191, 935–937, *936, 937*
        in Native Americans, 966t
        neonatal assessment for, 189–191
        nursing care plan for, 952–953
Subperiosteal space, 917, *917*
Substance abuse, 355–357, 471–486
    by adolescent, 478
        history for, 344
        signs of, 478–479
    assessment in, 478–479
    causes of, 474–475
    co-dependency and, 473
    definition of, 473
    effects of, on fetus and neonate, 475–476
    expectancy effect in, 474
    extent of, 473, 477
    nursing care for, 478–481
    nursing process in, 478–481
    by parents, effects of on children and
        adolescents, 476–477, 478
    in pregnancy, 207, *207,* 475–476
        fetal and neonatal effects of, 207, *207*
        prevention of, 482
        reporting of, 480
    prevention of, 481–482
    by school-age child, 323, 324t, 477–478
    scope of, 473–474
    screening for, 478, 479t
    signs and symptoms of, 357
    societal costs of, 473–474
    stages of, 357t
    suicide and, 473
    treatment planning and implementation for, 480–481
    withdrawal in, signs and symptoms of, 479t
Subvalvular aortic stenosis, 589
Sucking needs, in infant, 249–250
Sucking reflex, 189
Suctioning. *See also* Airway maintenance
    in meconium aspiration, 537–538
    of newborn, 194
    of tracheostomy, 535
Suffocation
    in infants, 246
    in preschoolers, 299
Sugar. *See* Glucose
Suicide, 358–360, 359t
    adolescent, 334

Suicide (*continued*)
　　substance abuse and, 473
Summarizing, 85
Sunburn, 967t, 969
Superego, 61
Superficial reflexes, assessment of, 108. *See also* Reflex(es)
Superficial telangiectasia, 189
Supernumerary breast, 858
Supernumerary nipples, 858, 963t
Support groups
　　for AIDS, 704
　　for autism, 460, 468
　　for bereaved parents, 503
　　for cerebral palsy, 450, 468
　　for death and dying, 509
　　for disabled, 461, 462t, 468–469
　　for home care, 400, 401, 468
　　for mental retardation, 454, 468
　　for subtance abuse, 481, 485–486
Suppressor cells, 223
Surfactant, 179, 518
Surgery
　　for bone cancer, 947
　　for brain tumor, 667–668
　　for cataracts, 1002–1003
　　for cleft lip and palate, 773–774
　　for epilepsy, 670
　　for esophageal atresia/tracheoesophageal fistula, 776
　　for gastrointestinal disorders, 767
　　for Hirschsprung disease, 795
　　hospitalization for. *See* Hospitalization
　　for hydrocephalus, 655–656
　　for intestinal atresia, 785–786
　　for musculoskeletal disorders, 924
　　for neural tube defects, 652
　　for omphalocele, 789
　　for pyloric stenosis, 788
　　same-day, 382
　　for scoliosis, 943, 945–946
　　for seizures, 670
　　for spinal cord injury, 678
　　for Wilms' tumor, 822
Survivor grief, 500
Sutilans (Travase), for burns, 987t
Sutures, cranial, 187, *187*
　　premature closure of, 187, *187*
Sweat
　　chloride in, 1048t
　　sodium in, 1048t
Sweat glands, 957
Sweat test, for cystic fibrosis, 1048t
Swimmer's ear, 1015
Symbolic function, 284
Symbolic play, 262
Synarthroses, 918
Synovial joints, 918, 919, *919*. *See also* Joint(s)
Synovial membrane, 918, *919*
Syphilis, 864–865
　　congenital, 207
Syringe, for medication administration, 134
Syrup of ipecac, 247, 271, 300
Systematic desensitization, for hospitalized children, 379
Systemic lupus erythematosus, 719t, 719–723, *720,* 720t

**T**
Tachypnea, 522
Tactile fremitus, 102

Talipes equinovarus, 191, 938, *938*
Tall stature, 348. *See also* Height
　　abnormal, 893–894
Tanner scales, 335, *335–337*
Target glands, 872
Taste, 995
　　assessment of, 1000
　　in infant, 221
　　in toddlers, 259
Taste buds, 995
Tay-Sachs disease, 204t
T cell, 223, 689
　　cytotoxic, 689
T-cell deficiency
　　in DiGeorge syndrome, 706
　　in Wiskott-Aldrich syndrome, 707
T-cell mediated immunity, 692
Teaching. *See* Health teaching
Teeth
　　care of
　　　　in adolescent, 346–347
　　　　in disabled, 465
　　　　in preschooler, 293
　　　　in school-age child, 320
　　　　in toddler, 266–267
　　development and eruption of, 102, *103,* 227t, 227–228
　　examination of, 102
　　in school-age child, 316–317
　　in toddler, 257–258
Teething, 228
Telangiectasia, superficial, 189
Television, 323, 325t
Temperament, in infant, 233–234
　　assessment of, 237t, 237–238
Temperature
　　measurement of, 95–96, *96*
　　　　in neonate, 186
　　regulation of
　　　　in neonate, 181t, 181–182, *182*
　　　　in premature infant, 209
Temperature conversion chart, 1053t
Temper tantrums, 272–273
　　in preschooler, 297–298
Tendon(s), 918, 919
　　avulsion of, 932–933
　　strains of, 932–933
Tendon reflexes, deep. *See also* Reflex(es)
　　assessment of, 108
Teratogens, 166–168, 167t
Terbutaline (Brethine, Bricanyl), for asthma, 557t
Terminal illness. *See* Death and dying
Term infant, definition of, 193
Testes, 843, *845*
　　assessment of, 105
　　as endocrine glands, 880
　　examination of, 847
　　pubertal changes in, *336,* 337–338, 338t
　　self-examination of, 348
　　torsion of, 849–850
　　undescended, 850–851
　　　　nursing care plan for, 868–869
Testosterone, 845, 880
Tetanus, 430–431
　　immunization for, 241–242, 242t, 318t, 417–420, 419t, 430–431, 1055
Tetany
　　hypocalcemia and, 748
　　hypomagnesemia and, 750

in hypoparathyroidism, 888
Tetralogy of Fallot, 592–593, *593*
Tet spells, in tetralogy of Fallot, 592
Thalamus, 635, *635*
Thalassemia, *621,* 621–622
Thanatology, 491
Thelarche, premature, 851
Therapeutic play, 68–69
Thermoregulation
    in neonate, 181t, 181–182, *182*
    in premature infant, 209
Thirst
    in diabetes insipidus, 889
    regulation of, 732
Thorax. *See* Chest
Thought. *See also* Cognitive development
    intuitive, 311
    magical, 373
    objective, 311
Throat
    examination of, 102, *103*
    sore. *See* Pharyngitis
Thrombin time, 610
Thrombocytes, 608–609
Thrombocytic crisis, in sickle cell disease, 625
Thrombocytopenia, in hemolytic-uremic syndrome, 822–823
Thrush, 102, 188–189
Thumb sucking, in infants, 249–250
Thymosin, 876
Thymus, 876
    dysgenesis of, DiGeorge syndrome and, 705
    as lymphoid organ, 689–690
Thyroid
    anatomy and physiology of, 876
    disorders of, 885–888, 894–897
Thyroid hormone
    deficiency of
        acquired, 886–888
        congenital, 885–886
    hypersecretion of, 894–896
Thyroiditis, 887, 896–897
Thyroid stimulating hormone, 874, 876
    hypersecretion of, in Hashimoto thyroiditis, 896
Thyroid storm, 895
Thyrotoxicosis, 894–896
Thyrotropin, 222
Thyrotropin-releasing hormone, 876
Thyroxine (T₃), 876
    deficiency of
        acquired, 887
        congenital, 886
    hypersecretion of, 894–896
Tibial torsion, 940–941
Tick bites
    Lyme disease and, 423–424
    Rocky Mountain spotted fever and, 425
Tidal volume, 525
Tinea, 980–981
Tine test, 242, 319, 436, 968
Tissue oxygenation, 571
Tobacco use, 355–356
Toddler
    accident prevention for, 269t, 269–270
    assessment in, 265–266
    body measurements in, 265, 1039t–1041t
    developmental screening in, 265
    developmental tasks of, 267
    discipline of, 272, 273t

growth and development of, 255–273
    cognitive, 261–262
    motor, 258–259, 268–269
    physical, 256–261, 257t
    psychosocial, 262–265
    sensory, 259–260
health promotion for, 266–273
home and family assessment for, 266
hospitalization of, 371–373. *See also* Hospitalization
independence in, 267
language development in, 264, 264t
need for routine in, 268
new baby and, 268
parenting of, 273
play of, 262, 263
poisoning of, 270–271, 271t
regression in, 268
respiratory disorders in, 546–548
separation anxiety in, 263–264, 268
sex role identification in, 264–265
sibling rivalry in, 268
sleep in, 261, 271
temper tantrums in, 272–273
toilet training of, 271–272
Toenails. *See* Nails
Toilet training, 271–272
Tomography, computed, of brain, 639t
Tongue
    examination of, 102, 999–1000
    geographic, 102, 1000
    strawberry, in scarlet fever, 427
Tongue-tie, 1000
Tonic-clonic seizures, 669t. *See also* Seizures
Tonic neck reflex, 190t
Tonic seizures, 669t. *See also* Seizures
Tonsillitis, 548–549
    acute, 1016–1017
    chronic, 1017
Tonsils, 517
Tooth. *See* Teeth
TORCH infections, 206–207
Torsional deformities, of femur/tibia, 940–941
Tort, 44
Torticollis, congenital, 939
Total body water, 730
Total hemolytic complement, in immune disorders, 694
Total lung capacity, 525
Total parenteral nutrition, 743, *743,* 766
    at home, 409–410
    necrotizing enterocolitis and, 789–790
Touch
    in infant, 221
    in toddler, 259
Toxoplasmosis, fetal effects of, 206
Toys, 231, 232t. *See also* Play
Trachea, 518
Tracheal breath sounds, 524
Tracheobronchial tree, 518
Tracheoesophageal fistula, 774–776, *775*
Tracheostomy, 534–535, *535*
    home care for, 407, *407,* 535
    nursing care plan for, 559–561
Trachomal conjunctivitis, 1005–1006
Traction, 925t, 926, *926–929,* 930t
    in spinal cord injury, 678
Trained night crying, 227
Transcutaneous oxygen monitoring, 526
Transcutaneous oxygen saturation, 577

Transductive reasoning, 284
Transfusion
    exchange, 613
        in hydrops fetalis, 200
        in neonatal hyperbilirubinemia, 615
    twin-to-twin, 173
Transfusion reaction, 612–613
Transient neonatal pustular melanosis, 964t
Translocation, chromosomal, 165
    in Down syndrome, 456
Transplant
    bone marrow, 613
        in aplastic anemia, 626, 627
        in leukemia, 628
        in Wiskott-Aldrich syndrome, 707
    renal, 836–837
Transposition, of great arteries, *590,* 590–591
Traumatic injuries
    of breast, 858
    of eye, 1011
    of head, 674–676
    prevention of. *See* Accident prevention
    of spinal cord, 676–681
    sports-related, 951
Travel, immunizations for, 241, 420, 420t
Treatment
    preparation for and implementation of, 137–139
    withholding or withrawing of, 47–50
Trichomoniasis, 857
Tricuspid atresia, 593–594, *594*
Triglycerides, normal values for, 1047t
Triiodothyronine (T$_4$), 876
    deficiency of
        acquired, 887
        congenital, 886
    hypersecretion of, 894–896
Triple X syndrome, 203t
Trisomy, 165
Trisomy 13, 203t
Trisomy 18, 203t
Trisomy 21, 203t, 456
Trophoblast, 161, 161t
Tropia, 996, 1007
Tropic hormones, 873
Trousseau's sign, 748
True hermaphrodite, 843
Truncus arteriosus, *591,* 591–592
Trust vs. mistrust, 262, 263t
    in infant, 231–232
Tube feeding, 742, 766
    gastrostomy, after esophageal atresia/tracheoesophageal
        fistula repair, 776
    at home, 409–410
    nasogastric, 409–410, 766
Tuberculin test, 242, 272, 319, 436, 968
Tuberculosis, 436–437
    screening for, 242, 272, 319, 436, 968
Tuberous sclerosis, 204t, 659–660
Tubes. *See* Intubation
Tumor(s)
    anterior pituitary, 893–894
    brain, 666–668
    retinal, 1007–1008
    Wilms', 821–822
Turgor, skin
    assessment of, 98
    hydration and, 818

Turner syndrome, 203t, 852
24-hour dietary recall, 345–346
Twins
    dizygotic, 173
    monozygotic, 173
    pregnancy with, 173
Tympanic membrane, 994, *994*
    examination of, 999
    incision of, in chronic otitis media, 1013
Tympanostomy tubes, 1013
Tympanotomy, 1013
Tympany, 92, 92t
Tzanck smear, 960

**U**
Ulcerative colitis, 793–794
Ulcers, *960*
    peptic, 803–804
        hyperparathyroidism and, 898
Ulna, fracture of, 934
Ultrasonography
    fetal, 171, 173
    renal, 816
Umbilical cord, 162
    blood sampling from, 172
    care of, 194–196, *196*
Umbilical hernia, 104, *798,* 798–799
Umbilicus
    care of, 801
    infection of, 800–801
Umbo, 999
Umbrella occluder
    for atrial septal defects, 584
    for patent ductus arteriosus, 587
Unipotent stem cells, 607
United Nations Declaration of the Rights of the Child, 13–14
Universal precautions, 421t
    in AIDS, 701, 702t
Upper endoscopy, 763t, 764
Upper extremity. *See* Extremities
Upper gastrointestinal series, 763t, 764
Uremia, in acute renal failure, 829
Ureter, 811
Urethra, 811
Urethritis
    chlamydial, 863
    gonococcal, 864
Uric acid, normal values for, 1047t
Urinalysis, 814, 815t
    in diabetes, 906
    in infant, 242–243
    normal values for, 1047t–1048t
    in school-age child, 319
    in urinary tract infection, 827
Urinary catheterization, 814
    at home, 817
    in neural tube defects, 653
    in spinal cord injury, 679
    technique for, 817
Urinary system
    in infant, 233–234
    in toddler, 258
Urinary tract infection, 826–827
    nursing care plan for, 838–839
Urine
    formation of, 811–812

normal values for, 1047t–1048t
  pH of, 739, 739t
    normal values for, 1047t
  specific gravity of, 739t, 815t
Urine osmolality, 739t
Urine output, monitoring of, 738, 741, 818
Urine sample, collection of, 814
Urobilinogen, normal values for, 1048t
Urography, excretory, 814
Urticaria, 421
  drug-induced, 982
Uterine bleeding, dysfunctional, 855
Uterus, 843, *844*

**V**

Vaccine(s), 417–418, 419t, 1055. *See also* Immunization(s)
  anaphylactic reaction to, 418, 418t
  BCG, 437
Vagina, 843, *844*
Vaginal foreign bodies, 857–858
Vaginitis, 856–857, 980
Vaginosis, bacterial, 857
Valproic acid (Depakene), 672t
Valvular aortic stenosis, 589
Vanillymandelic acid, urinary, normal values for, 1048t
Varicella, 427–428
  vaccine for, 420
Vas deferens, 843, *845*
Vasopressin deficiency, in diabetes insipidus, 889–890
Vastus lateralis muscle, injection into, 135, *137*
Vectors, infectious, 417t
Vegetarian diet, 226, 226t
  for preschooler, 281
Vehicle, infectious, 417t
Vehicular accidents. *See* Car accidents
Vendors, home care equipment, selection of, 398, *399*
Venereal warts, 979
Ventilation
  artificial, 534–535, *535*
  deficient, respiratory acidosis and, 745–746
  mechanical, for neonate, 194, 534–535
    bronchopulmonary dysplasia and, 539–540
Ventricular hypertrophy, right-sided, in tetralogy of Fallot, 592–593, *593*
Ventricular septal defect, *584*, 584–585
  in endocardial cushion defect, 586
  nursing care plan for, 602
  in tetralogy of Fallot, 592–593, *593*
Ventriculoatrial shunt, 654–656
Ventriculoperitoneal shunt, 210, 654–656, *655*
Venturi mask, 528, *529*
Verbal communication, 82. *See also* Langauge development
Vernix caseosa, 189, 198
Verucca, 979
Vesicle, *960*
Vesicoureteral reflux, 827–829, *828*
Vesicular breath sounds, 524
Vestibular apparatus, 994, *994*
Vibration
  chest, 530
  perception of, assessment of, 106
Vietnamese
  cultural beliefs of, 34–35
  integumentary system in, 161t–1612t
Viral infections
  of skin, 979

  vaccines for, 420
Viral meningitis, 660
Viral pharyngitis, 547
Viral pneumonia, 550
Viruses, 417t
Visceral pleura, 518
Vision assessment, 100–101, 996–1000, 999t, 1011–1012
  in infant, 220, 239
  in mentally retarded, 454
  in neonate, 183
  in preschooler, 292
  in school-age child, 309, 318–319
  in toddler, 259
Vision impairment
  in Alport syndrome, 824–825
  amblyopia and, 1006–1007
  assessment and management of, 996–1000, 1011–1012
  congenital cataracts and, 1002–1003
  conjunctivitis and, 1005–1006
  glaucoma and, 1003
  juvenile rheumatoid arthritis and, 718
  refractive errors and, 1008–1010
  retinal detachment and, 1010–1011
  retinoblastoma and, 1007–1008
  retinopathy of prematurity and, 1004–1005
Visual evoked potentials, 641t
Visual fields, assessment of, 999t
Vital signs
  measurement of, 95–97, 186, 258t, 572t, 572–574, *573*, 573t
  normal values for, 1043t
Vitamin E, for retinopathy of prematurity, 1004
Vitamin K, in neonate, 181, 198–199
Vitamins, supplemental, 225
  in neonatal liver disease, 783, 783t
Vitreous humor, *993*, 994
Vocabulary. *See also* Language development
  assessment of, 1000
Voiding. *See also* Incontinence
  in neural tube defects, 653
  in spinal cord injury, 679
Voiding cystourethrography, 815
Voigt's lines, 961t, 963t
Volume replacement. *See also* Fluid administration
  in rehydration therapy, 741–743
    in diarrhea, 768–769
Vomiting
  acute, 771–772
  assessment of, 762
  bulimic, 354–355
  in neonate, 190t
  in poisoning, 271
  projectile, in pyloric stenosis, 787–788
Von Recklinghausen's disease, 204t
Von Willebrand's disease, 204t
Vulva, 843, *844*
Vulvovaginitis, 856

**W**

Wallowing reflex, 190t
Warts, 979
  genital, 865–866, 979
Washington Guide to Promoting Development in the Young Child, 265, 290
Water. *See also* Fluid
  total body, 730

Water compartment, 733
Water safety, 246–247, 270, 320
Weaning, 248
Web, laryngeal, 536
Weber's test, 1000t, 1013
Weight
    in adolescent, 334–335
    in drug dosage calculation, 133
    fluid and electrolyte requirements and, 735–736
    growth charts for, 235, 1037–1040
    in infant, 236
    measurement of, 94–95
    in neonate, 186
    in preschooler, 280
    in school-age child, 309, 316
    in toddler, 257, 257t
Weight gain
    in fetus, 172
    in infant, 217
    in pregnancy, 170
Weightlifting, 349
Weight loss, in AIDS, 699
Weight loss programs, 353–354
Well baby checkups, 239–250
Wellness nursing diagnoses, 114
West nomogram, for body surface area, 133, *133*, 735, *735*
Wharton's jelly, 162
Wheat, food sources of, 715t
Wheezes, 524–525
White blood cells, 608. *See* Leukocytes
Whites, integumentary system in, 967t
Whooping cough, 429–430

immunization for, 241–242, 242t, 267t, 318t, 417–420, 419t
WIC program, 15
Wilms' tumor, 821–822
Wilson disease, 783–785
Wiskott-Aldrich syndrome, 706–707
Withdrawal, in substance abuse
    in neonate, 476
    signs and symptoms of, 479t
Wolffian ducts, 843
Wood's light, 960
Wood tick bites, Rocky Mountain spotted fever and, 425
Worm infections, 432–433

**X**
Xeroderma pigmentosa, 205t
X-linked agammaglobulinemia, 703–705
X-linked ichthyosis, 205t

**Y**
Yawning, in newborn, 190t
Yeast infections. *See* Candidiasis
Yin and yang, 35
Young's rule, for pediatric drug dosages, 1050–1051

**Z**
Zen macrobiotic diet, 226, 226t
Zidovudine (AZT), 700
Zinc, normal values for, 1047t